KEY TO MAP PAGES

344-345
Shetland Islands
342-343
Lerwick

Key to Regions

South West England
South East England
London
Wales
West Midlands
East Midlands
East of England
North West England
Yorkshire
North East England
Scotland

Key to this map

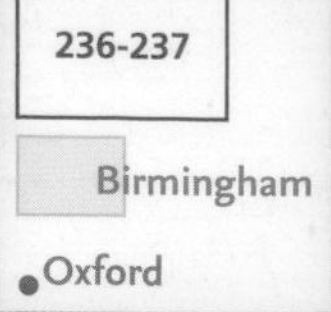

236-237
Birmingham
Oxford

Road maps

Urban area maps

City / Town centre plans

Seasonal symbols

Spring
Summer
Autumn
Winter
Rainy day

For a full list of tourist symbols please refer to page 142

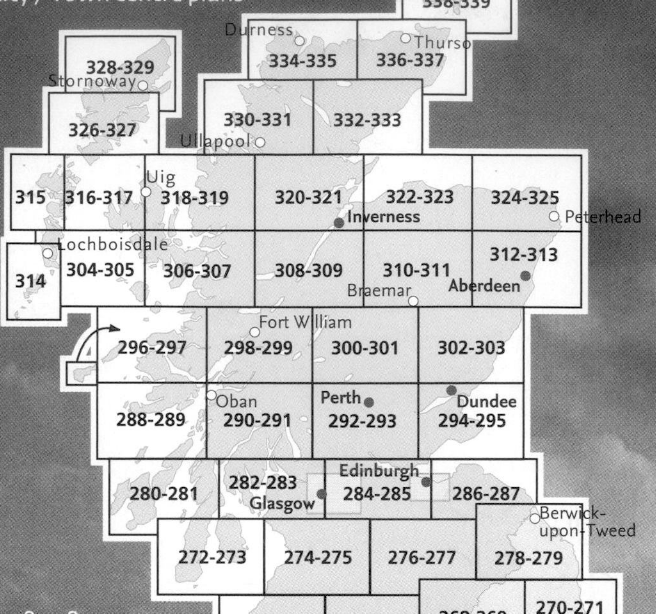

340-341
Orkney Islands
Kirkwall
338-339
Durness
334-335
Thurso
336-337
328-329
Stornoway
326-327
330-331
332-333
Ullapool
Uig
315
316-317
318-319
320-321
322-323
324-325
Inverness
Peterhead
Lochboisdale
314
304-305
306-307
308-309
310-311
312-313
Braemar
Aberdeen
Fort William
296-297
298-299
300-301
302-303
Oban
Perth
Dundee
288-289
290-291
292-293
294-295
Edinburgh
280-281
282-283
284-285
286-287
Glasgow
Berwick-upon-Tweed
272-273
274-275
276-277
278-279

City & town centre plans

Aberdeen	338
Bath	338
Birmingham	378-379
Blackpool	389
Bournemouth	389
Bradford	390
Brighton	390
Bristol	391
Cambridge	391
Canterbury	392
Cardiff	392
Carlisle	393
Cheltenham	393
Chester	394
Coventry	394
Derby	395
Dover	395
Dundee	396
Durham	396
Eastbourne	397
Edinburgh	397
Exeter	398
Folkestone	398
Glasgow	386-387
Gloucester	399
Guildford	399
Harrogate	400
Hastings	400
Hereford	401
Hull	402
Inverness	401
Kingston upon Hull	402
Leeds	384-385
Leicester	402
Lincoln	403
Liverpool	380-381
London	376-377
Manchester	382-383
Middlesbrough	403
Milton Keynes	404
Newcastle upon Tyne	404
Norwich	405
Nottingham	405
Oxford	406
Perth	406
Plymouth	407
Portsmouth	407
Reading	408
Salisbury	408
Sheffield	409
Southampton	409
Stoke-on-Trent	410
Stratford-upon-Avon	410
Sunderland	411
Swansea	411
Swindon	412
Torquay	412
Watford	413
Weston-super-Mare	413
Winchester	414
Windsor	414
Worcester	415
York	415

Urban area maps

Birmingham	358-359
Bournemouth	347
Bradford	370-371
Bristol	352
Cardiff	351
Coventry	360
Derby	362
Edinburgh	373
Glasgow	374-375
Greater Manchester	368-369
Leeds	370-371
Leicester	361
Liverpool	366-367
London	354-357
Manchester	368-369
Merseyside	366-367
Milton Keynes	353
Newcastle upon Tyne	372
Newport	351
Nottingham	363
Plymouth	346
Portsmouth	348-349
Sheffield	365
Southampton	348-349
Stoke-on-Trent	364
Swansea	350
West Midlands	358-359

DISCOVER BRITAIN

Britain is a beguiling group of islands, packed with mountains, moors, rivers, lakes and forests, brimming over with plants and wildlife, and enclosed by miles and miles of beautiful coastline.

This Touring Atlas and Guide identifies, locates and describes many of the best places to visit within Britain and gently reminds us that getting out and about is not exclusively a summer activity.

Britain is open 24 hours a day and 365 days a year and this book can be the inspiration for travel, entertainment and adventures whatever the season.

Gairloch sunset

CONTENTS

Understanding the Landscape	**5-14**
Understanding Natural History	**15-19**
Regenerating the Landscape	**20-21**
Myths and Legends	**22**

Avebury stone

Sarsen Stones
In the dry valleys these boulders litter the landscape; they are the famous 'Sarsen' stones, used by stone age man to build Avebury stone circle and other prehistoric monuments.

Discover Britain by region **23-131**

The country is split into the following regions within which you will find information for over 1300 places to visit. If you know the name of the attraction you are looking for, use the index to find its details. Each description has a map reference for you to locate it and wherever applicable a phone number and website. Where appropriate there are also symbols to advise if an attraction is suited to a rainy day and if it is especially appealing during a particular season.

South West England	23-38
South East England	39-53
London	54-61
West Midlands	62-68
East Midlands	69-75
East of England	76-84
Yorkshire	85-91
North West England	92-100
North East England	101-105
Wales	106-114
Scotland	115-131

Symbols
- Spring
- Summer
- Autumn
- Winter
- Rainy day

For a full list of tourist symbols please refer to page 142.

Portmeirion Village 217 E4
This unique, if eccentric 'village' was created during the mid 20th century by the architect Clough Williams-Ellis in a flamboyant, Mediterranean style on his privately-owned peninsula on the beautiful Tremadoc Bay.
☎ 01766 770000 www.portmeirion-village.com

All attractions are referenced to the largest scale mapping.

Within the attraction descriptions there are 200 'Outstanding' features which are highlighted yellow.

Any description with an empty symbol ☐ can be found as a place or area name on the map.

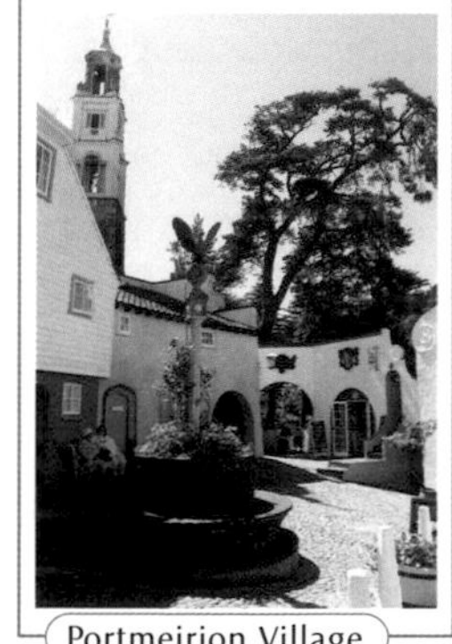

Portmeirion Village

Route planning mapping **132-141**

As well as helping you plan your journey, this mapping also shows the location of 200 'Outstanding' tourist features.

Route planning map

Key to map symbols **142-143**

Road mapping **144-345**

Over 1300 tourist features are highlighted on detailed road mapping.

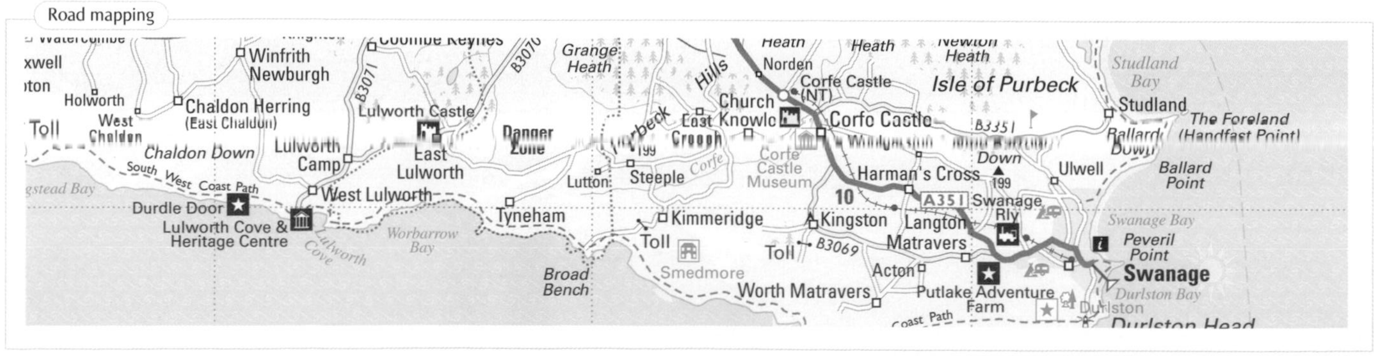

Winfrith Newburgh
Chaldon Herring (East Chaldon)
Lulworth Castle
East Lulworth
Lulworth Camp
West Lulworth
Durdle Door
Lulworth Cove & Heritage Centre
Tyneham
Kimmeridge
Steeple
Smedmore
Broad Bench
Worth Matravers
Corfe Castle
Corfe Castle Museum
Church Knowle
Harman's Cross
Kingston
Langton Matravers
Acton
Putlake Adventure Farm
Swanage
Isle of Purbeck
Studland
Ulwell
Ballard Point
Peveril Point
Durlston
Grange Heath
Norden

Road mapping

Urban area maps 346-375

These maps help you navigate through the suburbs of Britain's major cities.

Plymouth	346
Bournemouth	347
Southampton and Portsmouth	348-349
Swansea	350
Cardiff and Newport	351
Bristol	352
Milton Keynes	353
London	354-357
West Midlands	358-359
Coventry	360
Leicester	361
Derby and Nottingham	362-363
Stoke-on-Trent	364
Sheffield	365
Merseyside	366-367
Greater Manchester	368-369
Leeds and Bradford	370-371
Newcastle	372
Edinburgh	373
Glasgow	374-375

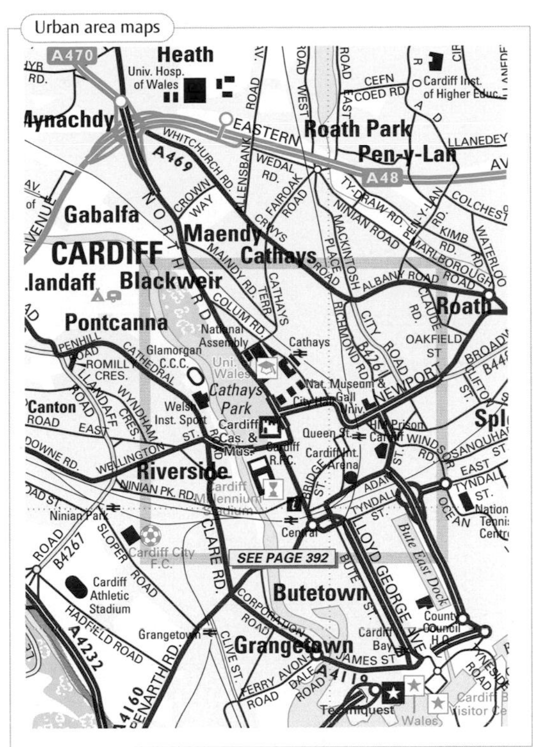

Urban area maps
Heath
Univ. Hosp. of Wales
Roath Park
Pen-y-Lan
A470
A469
A48
Gabalfa
Maendy
CARDIFF
Cathays
Blackweir
Pontcanna
Roath
National Assembly
Cathays Park
Canton
Riverside
SEE PAGE 392
Cardiff Athletic Stadium
Butetown
Grangetown
A4232
A4160
A4119

Central city maps 376-387

Six of Britain's busiest city centres are mapped in great detail to enable you to find your destination with ease.

London	376-377
Birmingham	378-379
Liverpool	380-381
Manchester	382-383
Leeds	384-385
Glasgow	386-387

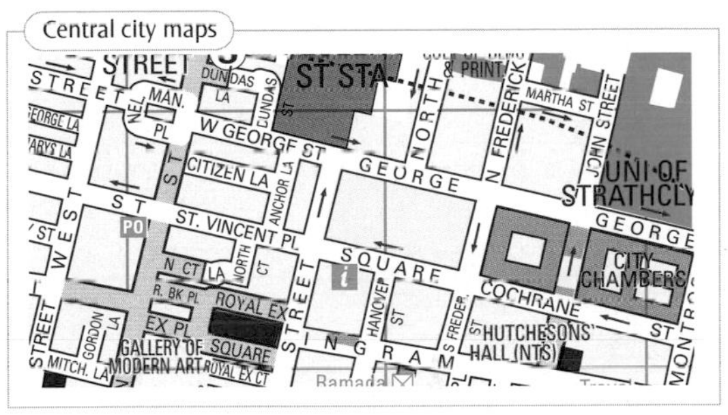

Central city maps
W GEORGE ST
GEORGE
ST. VINCENT PL
SQUARE
UNI OF STRATHCLY
CITY CHAMBERS
COCHRANE
HUTCHESONS' HALL (NTS)
GALLERY OF MODERN ART
ROYAL EX SQUARE
INGRAM

Town and city plans 388-415

Layouts of Britain's diverse towns and cities provide an overview of each location and a brief guide aids exploration.

Aberdeen, Bath	388
Blackpool, Bournemouth	389
Bradford, Brighton	390
Bristol, Cambridge	391
Canterbury, Cardiff	392
Carlisle, Cheltenham	393
Chester, Coventry	394
Derby, Dover	395
Dundee, Durham	396
Eastbourne, Edinburgh	397
Exeter, Folkestone	398
Gloucester, Guildford	399
Harrogate, Hastings	400
Hereford, Inverness	401
Kingston upon Hull, Leicester	402
Lincoln, Middlesbrough	403
Milton Keynes, Newcastle	404
Norwich, Nottingham	405
Oxford, Perth	406
Plymouth, Portsmouth	407
Reading, Salisbury	408
Sheffield, Southampton	409
Stoke-on-Trent, Stratford-upon-Avon	410
Sunderland, Swansea	411
Swindon, Torquay	412
Watford, Weston-super-Mare	413
Winchester, Windsor	414
Worcester, York	415

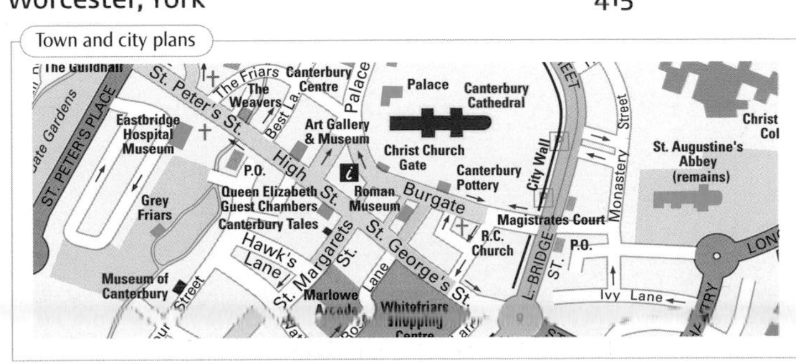

Town and city plans
St. Peter's St.
ST. PETER'S PLACE
Eastbridge Hospital Museum
Grey Friars
The Weavers
Canterbury Centre
Art Gallery & Museum
Palace
Canterbury Cathedral
Christ Church Gate
High St.
Burgate
Canterbury Pottery
Queen Elizabeth Guest Chambers
Roman Museum
Canterbury Tales
Magistrates Court
R.C. Church
St. Augustine's Abbey (remains)
Museum of Canterbury
Marlowe Arcade
Whitefriars Shopping Centre
Ivy Lane
St. George's St.
St. Margarets St.
Hawk's Lane
Monastery Street

Index to place names and places of interest 416-456

Credits

Wast Water

The rich tapestry of Britain's landscape looks permanent and immovable; in fact it is constantly changing and what we see today is just a tiny moment in time. Mountains the size of the Himalayas, vast lava flows, tropical seas, huge ice sheets and animals the size of several London buses have come and gone over the millennia and the legacy of these can be seen in the current landscape. Here in Britain, the earth is quieter now, the changes less dramatic than at times in the past, but they are still going on in the form of weathering and gradual changes in sea level, and every now and again a small tremor is a reminder of the stresses at work beneath the surface.

Since the very end of the last Ice Age, a mere 10,000 years ago, the flora and fauna we know today managed to gain a foothold and have developed over the years. Britain's landscape diversity has led to a wide variety of habitats, from the rocky and sometimes barren Scottish Highlands to the lush wooded valleys of southern England. Man, naturally adaptable, has left many marks on the face of the land, some ephemeral, but some extend back into the mists of time.

The next few pages give a brief insight into the 'hows' and 'whys' of Britain's landscape; its formation, natural history and the changes wrought by the hand of man. Look differently at the view. Take time to appreciate the beauty.

GUIDE TO GEOLOGY

SEDIMENTARY ROCKS Ⓢ

Formed from sediments, of various sizes, deposited and slowly compacted into solid rock.

There are two types:

Transported sediments are bits of existing rocks which fall down hillsides, eventually being washed into streams. They are worn down further by rolling along the stream bed, eventually being carried into lakes or the sea, where the largest and heaviest are dropped first (they can also be blown there or deposited by ice). As further debris accumulates on top of them, they are compacted into solid rock, the size of the original particles defining the type of eventual 'sedimentary rock'. Conglomerates form from pebbles, and mudstones from the tiniest particles.

Non-transported sediments in Britain, are limestone and chalk. These are formed from the shells and skeletons of sea creatures and corals. As the creatures die, they sink to the floor, eventually being compressed into rock.

ROCK AGES

The time period during which a rock was formed is given a name in geology. These names have not been used in the text for the sake of simplicity but as an example, a sedimentary rock formed 300 million years ago would be called a 'Carboniferous sedimentary rock', however, if it had been formed 100 million years ago, it would be a 'Cretaceous sedimentary rock' and so on. Refer to any geology book for the full table.

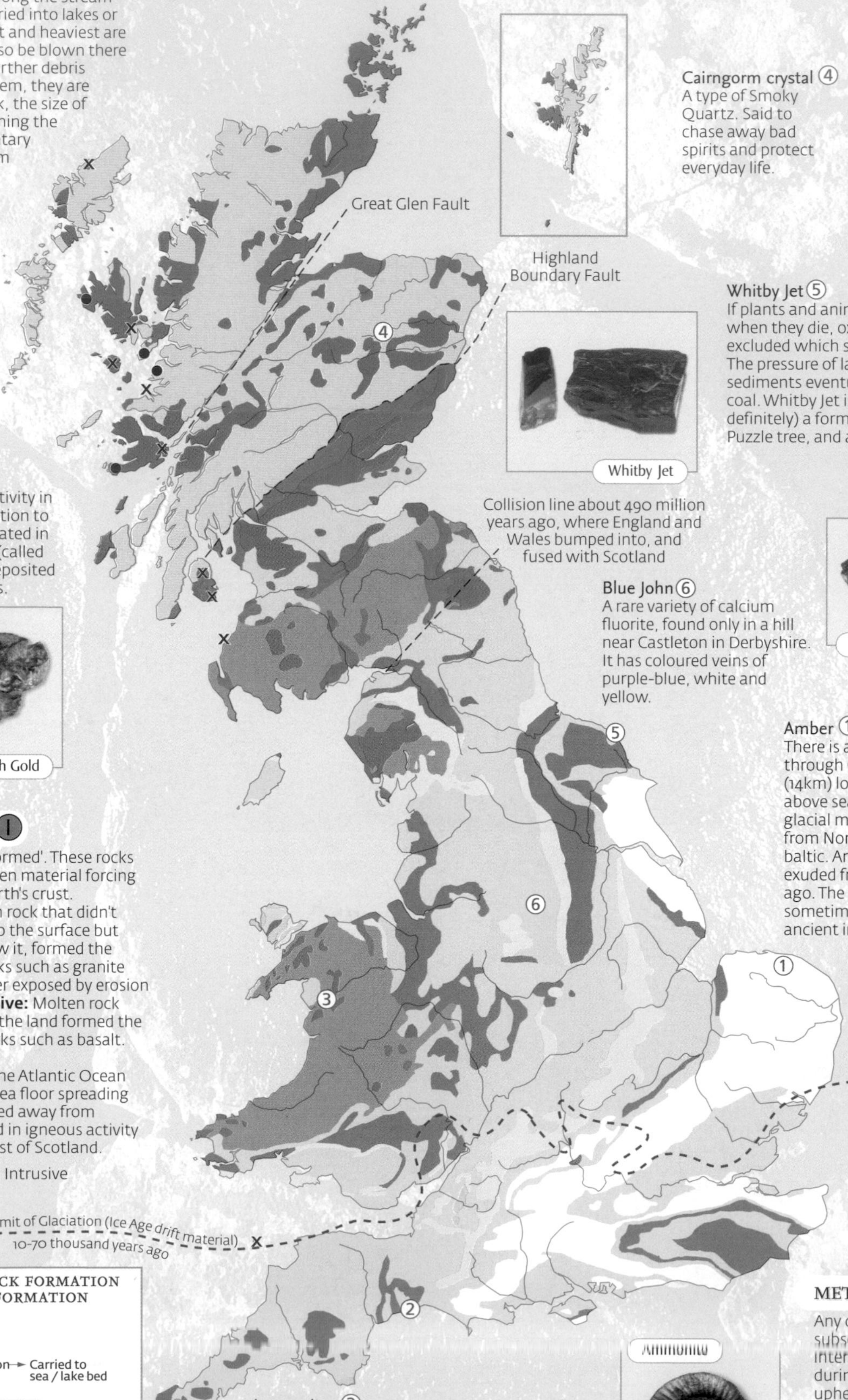

SEDIMENTARY ROCKS
- Unconsolidated Sands & Shell Banks
- Clay
- Chalk
- Limestone
- Sandstone
- Greywacke and Slate (metamorphic)
- Mixed Hard Sediments including sandstone, shale, mudstone, greywacke, slate and limestone

IGNEOUS ROCKS
- Igneous (Extrusive/intrusive)

METAMORPHIC ROCKS
- Gneiss, Schist, Quartzite etc

Great Glen Fault

Highland Boundary Fault

Collision line about 490 million years ago, where England and Wales bumped into, and fused with Scotland

Southern Limit of Glaciation (Ice Age drift material) 10-70 thousand years ago

Cairngorm crystal ④
A type of Smoky Quartz. Said to chase away bad spirits and protect everyday life.

Cairngorm crystal

Whitby Jet ⑤
If plants and animals are covered quickly when they die, oxygen and bacteria are excluded which stops their decomposition. The pressure of layer upon layer of these sediments eventually compresses them into coal. Whitby Jet is probably (but not definitely) a form of fossilised Monkey Puzzle tree, and a form of coal.

Whitby Jet

Welsh Gold ③
Very basically, volcanic activity in Wales caused gold in solution to be forced into fissures created in earlier, solidified magma (called Greenstone). Gold was deposited along with quartz in veins.

Welsh Gold

Blue John ⑥
A rare variety of calcium fluorite, found only in a hill near Castleton in Derbyshire. It has coloured veins of purple-blue, white and yellow.

Blue John

Amber ①
There is a gigantic ridge running through Cromer in Norfolk, 8.7 miles (14km) long and up to 290 feet (90m) above sea level. It is the remains of a glacial moraine and contains rock from Norway and amber from the baltic. Amber started life as resin exuded from trees millions of years ago. The final hard, translucent stone sometimes contains remains of ancient insect species.

Amber

IGNEOUS ROCKS Ⓘ

Igneous means 'fire-formed'. These rocks were made from molten material forcing its way up into the Earth's crust. **Intrusive:** The molten rock that didn't quite break through to the surface but cooled in a mass below it, formed the 'intrusive' igneous rocks such as granite and gabbro, often later exposed by erosion at the surface. **Extrusive:** Molten rock that poured out onto the land formed the 'extrusive' volcanic rocks such as basalt.

60 million years ago the Atlantic Ocean was born, caused by sea floor spreading when Greenland moved away from Scotland. This resulted in igneous activity all along the west coast of Scotland.

● Volcanic x Intrusive

METAMORPHIC ROCKS Ⓜ

Any of the three rock groups, subsequently altered by intense heat and/or pressure, during periods of major upheaval, into another rock type. Limestone can become marble, mudstones can turn into slate and gemstones can be formed.

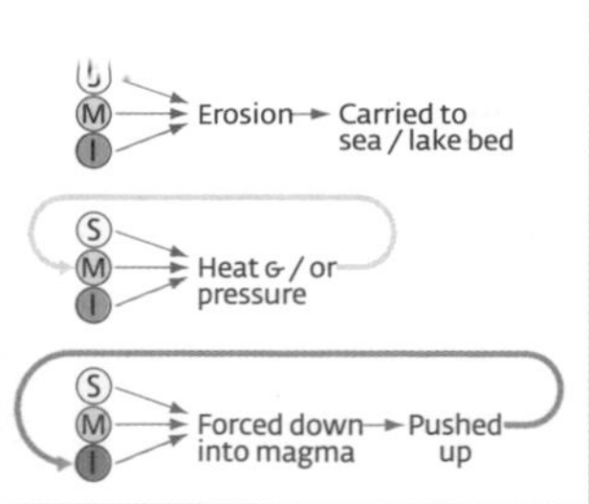

Ammonites ②
The rocks in Lyme Regis were laid down in a fairly deep tropical sea. Large ammonites, up to 24 inches (60cm) across, are scattered all over Monmouth beach and small ones can often be found where they have been washed out of the cliffs. Have a look in the wonderful fossil shop. Note: Do not dig in the cliffs.

CYCLE OF ROCK FORMATION AND RE-FORMATION

- S, M, I → Erosion → Carried to sea / lake bed
- S, M, I → Heat & / or pressure
- S, M, I → Forced down into magma → Pushed up

UNDERSTANDING THE LANDSCAPE

GUIDE TO THE PROTECTED AREAS OF BRITAIN

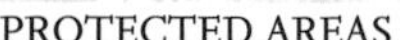

PROTECTED AREAS

Areas of England, Wales and Scotland are recognised as being Nationally or even Internationally important for the habitats and flora and fauna they support. Certain areas of the countryside have therefore been given designations affording them some protection against inappropriate development and destruction.

NATIONAL PARKS

Landscapes managed to conserve and enhance the wildlife, natural beauty and cultural heritage of an area, and to inform and involve the public in this process. Most of the land is privately owned, with the various National Park Authorities working with the owners to conserve these special areas.
For more information see: www.anpa.gov.uk

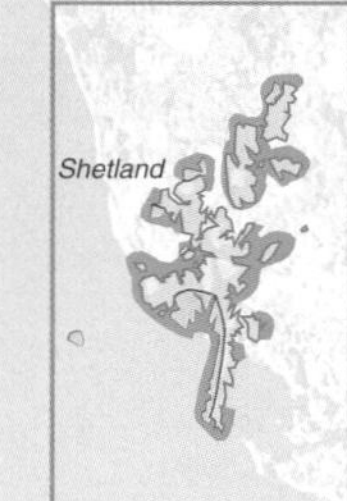

Shetland

GEOLOGICAL SITES

In England, there are 1200 'Geological Sites'. These have been chosen by English Nature to represent key places to understand the geology of England.
For more information see:
www.english-nature.org.uk

AREAS OF OUTSTANDING NATURAL BEAUTY (AONB)

There are over 40 'Areas of Outstanding Natural Beauty' in England and Wales. In Scotland there are around 40 'National Scenic Areas' (NSA). The principle is to conserve the natural beauty of these areas.
For more information see:
www.aonb.org.uk and www.snh.org.uk

NATIONAL NATURE RESERVES (NNR)

There are well over 200 National Nature Reserves in England, and around 73 in Scotland. Many are designated as 'Spotlight' reserves and are the best places to appreciate some of the most important examples of habitats and wildlife in the country. Although these areas have been set up primarily to protect the flora and fauna, the public are encouraged to visit them and observe wildlife, taking care not to disturb their environment. There are also Local Nature Reserves, and Marine Nature Reserves.
For further information see:
www.english-nature.org.uk and www.snh.org.uk

Key to symbols

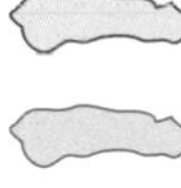

- National Parks
- Areas of Outstanding Natural Beauty (AONB) and National Scenic Areas (NSA)
- Heritage coast
- (2) Places mentioned in pages 8 - 14

The New Forest and South Downs are currently being considered for designation as National Parks.

RAMSAR SITES

Wetlands of International Importance (particularly waterfowl habitat).

OTHER PROTECTED SITES

There are also: RSPB Nature Reserves, Special Areas of Conservation (SAC) (non-bird), Special Protection Areas (SPA) (wild birds), Wildlife Trust reserves, Wildfowl and Wetland centres, World Heritage sites and Biosphere reserves.

ENVIRONMENTALLY SENSITIVE AREAS (ESA)

In England and Wales, over 25 areas have been chosen where farmers are offered incentives to farm in a sustainable and environmentally friendly way.

For more information see:
www.defra.gov.uk

SITES OF SPECIAL SCIENTIFIC INTEREST (SSSI)

Often sites of rare habitat (such as lowland heath or raised bogs), or endangered and fragile flora, fauna or geology. There are over 5,000 sites in England and Wales and around 1,450 in Scotland. For further information see:
www.english-nature.org.uk and www.snh.org.uk

HERITAGE COAST

Around the coast of Britain, there are informally designated stretches of coastline, managed to control inappropriate development that would detract from their natural beauty. So far, there are in the region of 46 along the coasts of England and Wales and many under consideration in Scotland. Here they are called 'Preferred Conservation Zones' - (PCZ) For further information see:
www.countryside.gov.uk and www.ccw.gov.uk and www.snh.org.uk

EAST ANGLIA

Grimes Graves (2)

Hundreds of saucer shaped hollows on the surface are evidence of Neolithic flint mining. Around 2300 BC, early man excavated flint and made axes with which to chop down trees and cultivate the land. The poor soils were soon spent, so the people moved on. An early example of 'slash and burn'.

Map ref. 213 G4

Grimes Graves

Norfolk Broads

Photo: Mike Page

(1) **Norfolk Broads**

This peaceful landscape of meandering waterways looks timeless. In fact, the retreating glaciers left a huge reed swamp over East Anglia, which gradually became woodland. By the early middle ages several inundations by the sea had left a patchwork of marsh, fen, woodland and swamp, the latter covering what is now the Broads. Centuries of vegetation had grown and died, creating thick layers of peat. After the Norman conquest, Norwich was developing quickly and needed fuel; peat was perfect and over the next 350 years this valuable resource was dug out by hand, until Mother Nature caused the sea level to rise once more, flooding the peat workings to create the tranquil waterways of the Broads.

Map ref. 229 E4

Flint is:

Liquid silica, fused with limestone or other sediments. This forms a hard, brittle, fine-grained rock and can be found as nodules within limestones and shales.

Flint building detail

Flint wall

Flint was used as a building material where little else was available.

CHALK DOWNS

Marlborough Downs

The smooth rounded Marlborough Hills are typical of a chalk landscape. They are divided by 'dry' valleys, probably formed when water in the chalk was frozen and glacial surface streams eroded the rock. Sometimes, steep scarps have formed, demonstrating the varying hardness of the chalk layers. Most of the downlands are waterless due to the very porous nature of chalk and spring lines are common where the water meets the impermeable clays beneath. Lower down the slopes the soil is richer, here you will find woodlands, meadows and orchards.

Marlborough Downs (3)

Map ref. 182 D5

Chalk is:

The purest and whitest form of limestone. It contains a large proportion of tiny plates called Coccoliths. Chalk is very porous and relatively soft, forming rounded ridges. Water seeps down and accumulates as large underground reservoirs.

COTSWOLDS

Cotswolds

The rolling Cotswold Hills are the result of an event that took place 180 million years ago. A bulge formed under the North Sea and as a consequence, a shallow warm sea formed over an area from Somerset to The Midlands. In the Cotswolds, Oolites (see 'Limestone is:' below for description) settled on the bottom forming the characteristic limestone of the area. This sedimentary rock has been gently folded and eroded into the hills and valleys we see today. Sheep have always been the mainstay of this rural landscape; the Saxon meaning of 'Cotswolds' actually means 'Hills of the Sheepfolds'.

(4) **Roof tiles**

Harder blocks of limestone were quarried underground, and then left on the surface. The action of frost shattered them into thin sheets, which were used for roof tiles.

Map ref. 197 D5

Lower Slaughter – Roof tiles

Limestone is:

Bits of shells and sea creatures, which fall to the bottom in areas of shallow warm water, eventually compressing into rock. 'Oolitic' Limestone is a special type and comprises tiny round pellets formed by the particles being rolled around on the watery bed first, building up layers of calcium, then being cemented together. Stand on the Cotswold Hills and you're on what was once the bed of a tropical sea or lake.

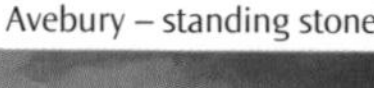

Avebury – standing stone

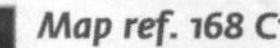

Map ref. 168 C1

(3) **Sarsen Stones**

The chalk layers were overlaid with sandstone, most of which has weathered away. However, in places, the sandstone was cemented together with silica to form hard blocks. In the dry valleys these boulders litter the landscape; they are the famous 'Sarsen' stones, used by stone age man to build Avebury Ring and other prehistoric monuments.

Cotswold Water Park

Map ref. 182 C3

(5) **Cotswold Water Park**

A beautiful area of over 114 lakes and ponds form the water park, the result of gravel extraction dating from the 1920s. Cotswold Oolitic Limestone underlies the park, covered in a layer of clay. On top of this, repeated glaciations dumped up to eight metres of sand and gravel. The high water table soon causes the newly dug gravel pits to fill with water. As it filters up through the limestone it becomes crystal clear, pure and alkaline; ideal for wildlife and water sports. The Thames starts just to the west of the area, water flowing into it through the lakes.

FIELDS

Fields - Ridge & Furrow

Ancient Field Systems

Ever since man first picked up a seed and planted it in the earth, there have been fields of a sort. In the Bronze Age, low banks of stone in narrow parallel lines with short cross divisions ran for miles across Dartmoor; the Dartmoor 'reaves'. Fields of the Iron Age were nothing more than small pastures separated by large stony banks, clustered around a settlement. The Romans probably had fields in the Fens and the Anglo-Saxons invented large 'open' field systems. The commonest patterns we see in the fields today are post-Norman Conquest; rows of 'humped' strips, around 11 yards (10m) wide, formed by the method of ploughing used; this was the 'ridge and furrow' field system which reached its peak in the mid 1300s. It is most typically found in The Midlands, North-East England and Central Scotland, and is distinguished by having no formal divisions of hedges or walls. Hedges used to enclose fields are a relatively modern invention.

Hedges were gradually planted between the 13th and 17th centuries. Then between the early 1700s and mid 1800s, the infamous 'Enclosure Acts' replaced Medieval ridge and furrow fields with new areas bounded by hedges. Similar reorganisation produced straight stone walls in Scotland. With mechanisation and the internal combustion engine, came bigger agricultural machinery which resulted in the removal of many hedgerows from the mid 20th century.

Portable, woven wooden hurdles were used to enclose stock before permanent settlements came into being.

Between 1750 and 1850 Oliver Rackham estimated that over 200,000 miles (320,000km) of hedges were planted.

HEDGEROWS

Ancient Hedgerows

Medieval England was full of hedges but not often around 'fields'. There are hedges described in the Anglo-Saxon 'perambulations', as boundary markers. So how do you know if you are looking at an ancient hedge? Look for clues: if a hedgerow crosses rows of wide ridge and furrow it's probably post-1700; if it follows a parish boundary it could be Saxon. If it has woodland flora underneath, it was possibly part of a woodland edge, and if it is on top of an earth bank, again it could be ancient. There is no exact science to tell the age of a hedge, although some can be identified on old maps. A rough estimation can be made by counting the number of species of shrubs and trees in any 90 foot (27.5m) length and multiplying it by 100 to give the number of years. For example, if a 90 foot (27.5m) stretch contains several Dog Rose, some Hawthorn and Elder, then three multiplied by 100 will give an age of 300 years. This only works south of Derbyshire and has many other pitfalls but it is fun and might amuse the children for a while.

The New Agricultural Landscape

Farming is entering a new age. There have always been farmers helping wildlife but now they are being encouraged to do so as the emphasis is shifting from intensive production to environmentally friendly schemes. In arable areas you may well see a large, bushy hedgerow with a permanent 6½ foot (2m) wide strip of tussocky grass next to it. This is a 'Field Margin' left unploughed and unsprayed to provide habitat for over-wintering wildlife. Next to this there might well be a wide strip of temporarily uncropped ground, this is 'Set Aside' land, again good for wildlife. In some areas, the first few metres of the crop might look rather weedy, this area is a 'Conservation Headland' and has been left free from herbicides to encourage some of our rare arable flowers to flourish. Don't be surprised to see wooden boxes put up for owls, bats, birds and even dormice.

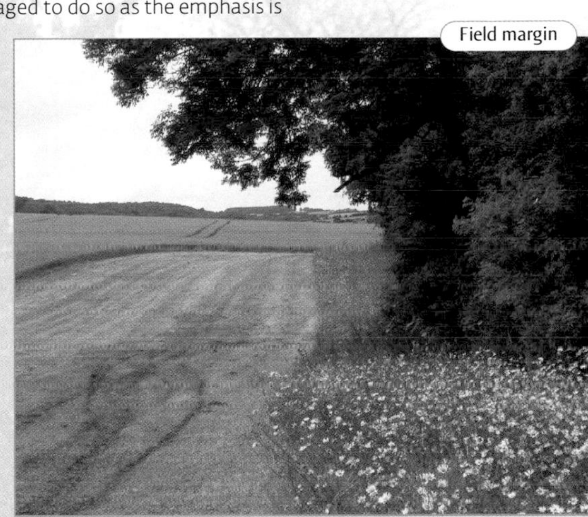

Field margin

PREHISTORY

Glastonbury Tor

Map ref. 166 C4

(7)

Glastonbury Tor

Hard sandstone caps the Tor, protecting the softer layers of limestones and clays underneath from erosion. However, the terracing on its slopes is still a cause for controversy. Are they the result of natural differential erosion of the rock layers, medieval strip farming for grain or vines, or a Neolithic maze pattern carved into the hill to form a ritual pathway to the top?

Maiden Castle

This chalk hilltop was inhabited from the late Stone Age through to Roman times. The original village can no longer be seen on the surface.

Maiden Castle

Map ref. 154 C4

Dartmoor – Bowerman's Nose

Dartmoor

280 million years ago, a mass of molten rock was pushed up underneath the sedimentary rocks covering Dartmoor, during a period of intense folding. The magma cooled slowly deep within the Earth, forming granite, which was exposed by weathering millions of years later. Around the edges, the intense heat and pressure metamorphosed surrounding material into slate and produced deposits of tin and copper ores. The impermeable granite supports a large mire and bog; the source of many Devon rivers and local legends. Above this mire the bare rock has been shaped into dramatic tors by wind, water and ice. These rocky landmarks have names like 'Bowerman's Nose'.

Map ref. 152 A4

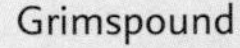

Grimspound

Beneath Hookney Tor you can make out a walled enclosure of about 4 acres (1.6 ha). It dates from the Bronze Age and contains circles of granite boulders or 'hut circles'. The wall was probably once topped with a wooden palisade.

WOODLAND

Ancient woodland

When the ice retreated and the climate started to get warmer, about 10,000 years ago, plants began to colonise the land. By the time the sea level rose to cut Britain off from mainland Europe, around 6,000 years ago, thirty or so types of trees and shrubs had established themselves here; these we call our 'native' species. Since that time, many other species have arrived, most deliberately introduced by man. Some of these reproduce quite happily and are called 'naturalised' species; others are still classed as 'exotic'. Of the original 'wildwood' nothing now remains, and most of our woodlands are a complex mix of old and new, natural and planted. There are pockets of 'Ancient Semi-Natural Woodland', the most precious of which are those descended from woodlands known to have been in existence from at least AD1600, having been managed in some way by man. It is difficult to date a woodland, but ancient woodland will probably have a large, wide ditch and bank or large stone wall exactly following a sinuous woodland edge. Other signs include 'indicator' species such as Herb Paris.

Coppiced Woodland

Management of deciduous woodland

In the past, a woodland 'stayed if it paid'; this is how many have survived. Where trees were **coppiced**, the stem was cut off at ground level to produce multiple stems for fencing and charcoal, some trees were left to develop into tall 'standards' between the coppice, and then felled for timber. This cycle allows light into the woodland, allowing flowers and shrubs to flourish, so that butterflies, dormice and birds are encouraged. Trees in some woods were **pollarded**; the same as coppicing but the stem is cut off above the browsing line so that animals could graze underneath but not eat the new wood shoots. Today, these methods are being reintroduced; new markets are opening up for woodland products with environmental schemes helping to fund them.

Pollarded tree

Veteran trees

Britain has many very old individual trees, unlike the rest of Europe. They are sometimes mentioned as boundary markers in the Anglo Saxon perambulations and support precious wildlife, such as the endangered Stag Beetle. In a veteran tree, the growth rate has slowed, but this does not mean it is dying. Some veterans are even hollow but still perfectly healthy. There is a register of over 126,000 ancient and rare trees growing in the British Isles today. Have a look at the Tortworth Chestnut in Gloucestershire, The Silver Fir at Strone, Argyll or the Holker Hall Great Lime, Cumbria.

Veteran tree

Stag Beetle

Holker Hall Great Lime

(9) ***Map ref.* 249 E5**

(10) Sherwood Forest

Not an area of dense forest but open heathland with pockets of woodland. A 'forest' was simply an unfenced area where someone powerful could keep deer.

***Map ref.* 224 B1**

Native pine woodland

Caledonian Pines are a subspecies unique to Scotland and form several ancient semi-natural woodlands there. Their management has to be entirely different to that for deciduous woodland, as they do not coppice. To allow natural regeneration, the main requirement is for deer, stock and rabbit proof fencing. Occasionally, it might be necessary to clear the ground in some way, as the trees are natural colonisers of disturbed ground. Otherwise, they can be left to themselves. These precious woods are a vital habitat for many of Scotland's endangered species.

Upper Loch Torridon – Caledonian Pines

***Map ref.* 319 E4**

Hatfield Forest

(11) Hatfield Forest

A rare example of a Royal Forest as it was in Medieval England. It includes areas of coppice and old pollards.

***Map ref.* 187 E1**

BRITAIN'S COASTLINE

Britain's coastline

Britain has approximately 12,100 miles (19,500km) of coastline, including all the islands, and one of the most extreme tidal ranges in the world. (In spring, the tidal range at Chepstow can be 40 feet (12.2m)). This, along with constant pounding from the Atlantic and North Sea and scouring by wind, rain and the ice age, has left a coastline of great diversity and character.

(12) Mortehoe coastline

***Map ref.* 163 E1**

Winchelsea Beach

(13) ***Map ref.* 161 E2**

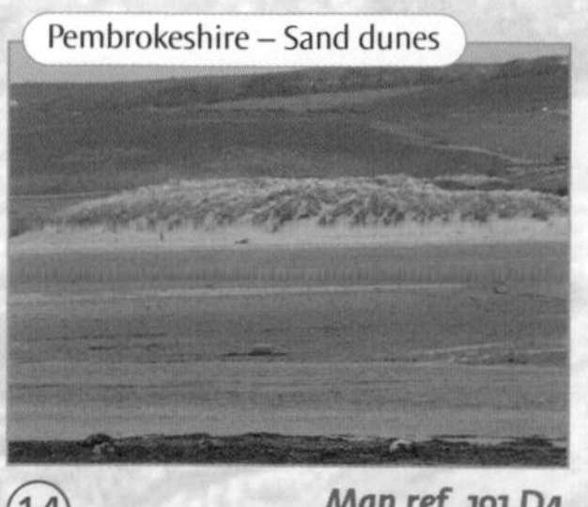

Pembrokeshire – Sand dunes

(14) ***Map ref.* 191 D4**

Pembrokeshire Coastal Path

Charmouth

(15) ***Map ref.* 153 G3**

YORKSHIRE DALES

Ingleborough

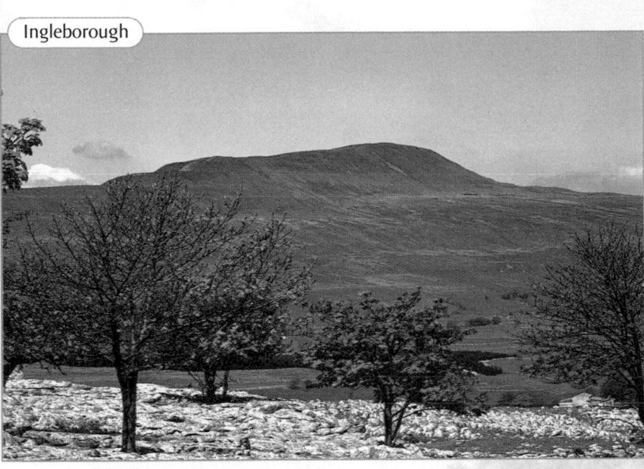

Yorkshire Dales & Hills

Sandwiches of shales, hard sandstones and limestones topped with Millstone Grit overlie almost horizontal layers of very old limestone. Differential erosion of these layers gives the characteristic 'stepped' appearance of the hills of Pen-y-Ghent and Ingleborough. Evidence of glaciation is everywhere, many valleys show the classic 'U' shape and around Ribblehead is an amazing landscape of rounded hummocks, 'drumlins'; material dumped and moulded by glaciers. Villages tend to be restricted to the valleys, with their rivers and walled fields. The slopes and moors are mostly grazed by sheep, arable farming never having been very successful here. The whole area has a feeling of timelessness and peace. Sit back and listen to the song of the skylark.

Limestone pavement

Rainwater seeps into the natural vertical cracks (joint planes) of this rock, gradually dissolving it and widening the joints (grykes) leaving large blocks (clints) between them; hence 'limestone pavements' are formed. Good examples can be seen around Ingleborough and Malham. The grykes can be several feet wide and deep and harbour some rare native alpine plants.

Limestone pavement

16

Malham Cove

Map ref. 243 E1

Malham Cove

A river once cascaded into the valley from the top of the cliff, but it has long since found a way through the porous rock further upstream and now appears at the base.

Gaping Ghyll

Water runs off the moors and tops, over the harder layers, then disappears underground through the porous limestone rock into 'swallow holes'. Gaping Ghyll is such a hole, 350 feet (91.5m) deep with the highest known waterfall in England.

17

Austwick – Norber Stones

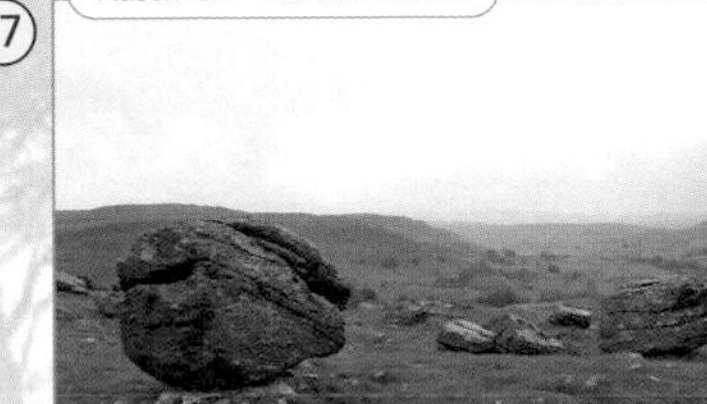

Norber stones

Sandstone blocks were carried here by glaciers and abandoned on the limestone plateau when the ice melted. Limestone erodes more quickly than sandstone; the result is a bizarre landscape of dark, hard sandstone boulders perched precariously on small pedestals of white limestone.

NORTH PENNINES

19 Great Whin Sill, North Pennines

Under the sedimentary rocks is an almost horizontal layer of dolerite, an igneous rock forced up and between the beds of sandstone. In places, millions of years of erosion by weather and ice have exposed it at the surface. This is the Great Whin Sill, which, on average, is 100 feet (30.5m) thick. It extends for 100 miles (160km) from Upper Teesdale to the Northumberland coast. On the Pennine escarpment and in Teesdale, the outcrops of dolerite appear as craggy, dark, vertical columns of rock; High Cup Nick and Cronkley Fell are good examples. Where the hot molten rock came into contact with surrounding limestone, the latter changed into a coarse grained marble called 'sugar limestone', which is home to many rare Teesdale plants.

North Pennines

21

Hadrian's Wall

The Romans took advantage of the northern escarpment of the hard Great Whin Sill, using it as a base on which to build Hadrian's Wall.

Hadrian's Wall

Teesdale – High Force

High Force waterfall

The River Tees tumbles over the exposed hard dolerite, gradually quarrying away the softer rock beneath. Eventually, the overhang becomes too heavy and crashes down. Over time therefore, the waterfall is slowly retreating upstream.

Map ref. 261 E5

22

Lindisfarne – Holy Island

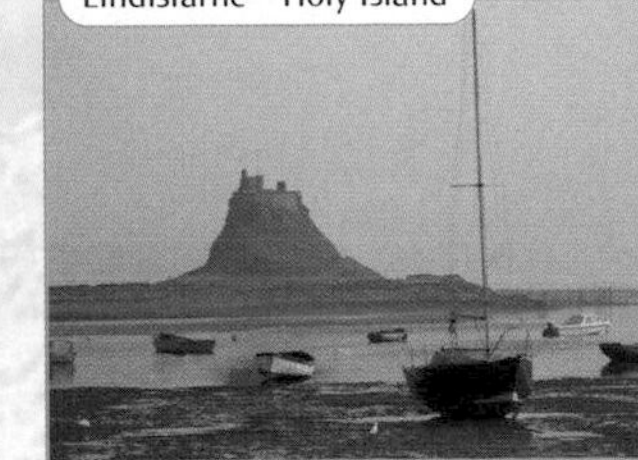

23

Farne Islands

The pounding action of the North Sea waves wore away the sandstone protecting the dolerite here on the coast. The hard igneous rocks were left as isolated, craggy islands in the sea.

Map ref. 279 F2

LAKE DISTRICT

Lake District

A landscape full of variety, from precipitous, craggy fells to gently wooded valleys and lakes. The underlying geology is complex but basically volcanic, changed by heaving, folding, heat, pressure and glaciation. In places the mountains are the remains of lavas and ashes metamorphosed to varying degrees; the softer ones and overlying sedimentary rocks having been eroded away. The main volcanic area is in the centre, with the high craggy peaks of Sca Fell, Helvellyn and the Langdale Pikes. Underneath these volcanic rocks lies a large mass of granite, pushed up in the distant past, and exposed by erosion in areas such as Ennerdale and Shap. In the north, Skiddaw is made from the oldest rocks of the Lake District, originally fine sedimentary material, altered by heat and pressure into the 'Skiddaw Slates', then eroded into smooth but steep mountains. The lakes themselves owe their existence to the glaciers. The ice over-deepened the valleys, which slowly filled with water, giving the final touch to this beautiful landscape.

Lake District – Wast Water

18 *Map ref.* 248 C2

Mardale – Blea Tarn

20

Blea Tarn

Blea Tarn was formed in the hollow left by a small glacier.

Map ref. 249 D2

Wales

A land of spectacular and varied scenery, resulting from a highly complex geological past and several inundations by the sea. The coastline has everything from wide sandy bays to spectacular cliffs. Inland, there are mountain peaks, rolling hills, valleys and lakes.

(31) Great Orme

Once an island of hard limestone; sand and alluvial deposits built up to join it to the mainland. Llandudno sits on these deposits.

Gwaun Valley

Formed by meltwater flowing beneath a glacier under extreme pressure, this beautiful sheltered wooded valley is a valuable habitat with SSSI (Site of Special Scientific Interest) status.

Cambrian Mountains

(25)

Central Wales

Smooth, flat-topped hills characterise this area, although the uniformity of the plateau is somewhat of a mystery. The rocks consist of much folded and faulted sandstones, mudstones and slates, so why are the tops flat? One theory suggests that having been inundated by the sea several times after the folding process, the peaks were eroded flat by strong currents carrying sand and stones.

(29)

Gwaun Valley

Map ref. 190 D4

(24) Sarn Badrig

A shallow subtidal reef, (one of several) which extends for about 15 miles (24km) from Mochras Island into Cardigan Bay. It was formed from the detritus of a glacial terminal moraine when sea levels were much lower and this was dry land; some of it can still be seen at a very low tide and you can walk out along it (check tide tables). Legends of a 'lost land' are associated with it.

(26) ***Map ref. 217 F2***

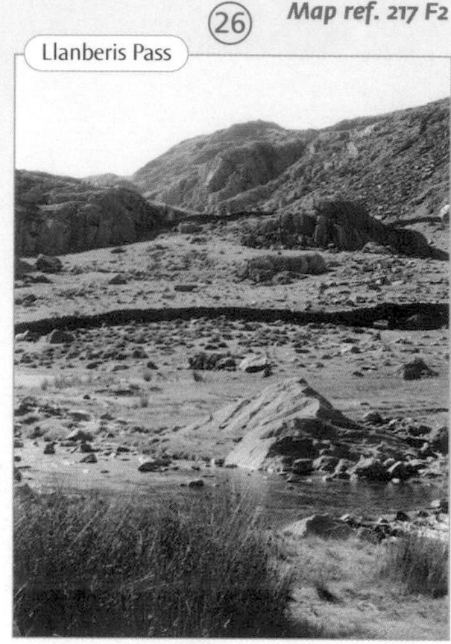

Llanberis Pass

Llanberis Pass

A classic glaciated valley, carved from volcanic rocks. Along it, older mudstones have been turned into high quality slate by heat and pressure. These are famous for their ability to cleave into thin, strong sheets, as a result, vast slate quarries scar the landscape.

(27)

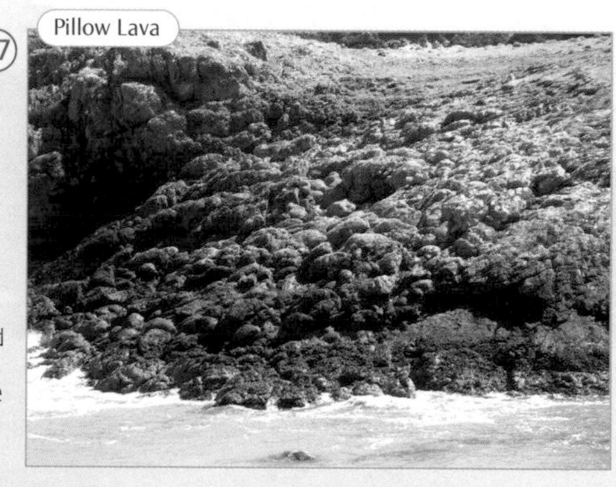

Pillow Lava

Strumble Head

Another volcanic area but of a different sort. Here the lava erupted under the sea and cooled very quickly into typically rounded 'pillow' shapes. This happened several times before the sea level fell leaving these strange shapes exposed on the headland.

Snowdonia

(26) Snowdon

Snowdon is actually made up of volcanic material which erupted on the floor of an ancient sea. It was later uplifted to become dry land, and this is why you will find fossilised shells on the top.

Map ref. 217 F2

Brecon Beacons

(28) Brecon Beacons

These mountains have been carved from a massive block of Old Red Sandstone, glaciers having scooped out the northern slopes.

Map ref. 193 G1

(30)

Gower – Rhossili Beach

Gower

A quiet and lovely peninsula, the whole area has been designated as an 'Area of outstanding Natural Beauty' (AONB). The high ridge of Cefn Bryn, which runs across the middle of the plateau, is made of hard Old Red Sandstone, uplifted and folded. The Rhossili Downs are made from the same rock and give rise to the spectacular 200 foot (61m) high cliffs of Rhossili Bay. The southern part is tough limestone, forming cliffs with beautiful bays where the sea has exploited weaknesses in the rock.

Map ref. 178 A4

Teifi Valley

Today, the river Teifi between Llechryd and Cardigan has an uneven bed of slate debris. This is due to 19th century slate extraction in the gorge. Tons of slate waste was dumped in the river, almost choking it. Eventually, the waste had to be disposed of on Rosehill Marsh, as large boats could no longer travel upriver. This slate debris now forms one of the many habitats in the Welsh Wildlife Centre. It is thought that the original Teifi followed a more westerly course but during the last ice age, material dumped around the Welsh coast by the glacier that formed over Ireland, blocked it, forcing the river to carve a new, deeper gorge.

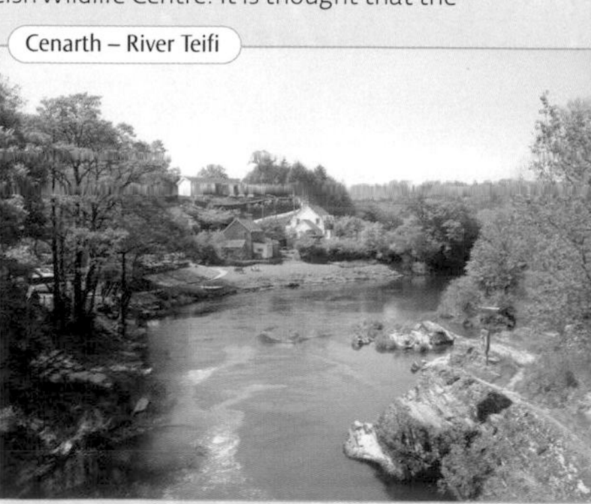

Cenarth – River Teifi

SCOTLAND

THE BIRTHPLACE OF GEOLOGY

Edinburgh Castle

Map ref. 397 E1

32

Edinburgh Castle and the Royal Mile

Somewhere around 380 million years ago, the volcano underneath what is now Edinburgh Castle stopped pouring out lava. It cooled into a basalt 'plug'. Time passed, the surrounding sedimentary rocks were slowly worn away. Then less than two million years ago, ice sheets moved past the remains of the volcano, plucking off the rest of the softer rock and dumping it in a long tail to the east of the plug. On this ridge was built the 'Royal Mile'. To the north of the tail, the glacier carved out a gorge now occupied by Princess Street gardens and to the south, a similar hollow is the location for Grassmarket.

The Royal Mile

32

Map ref. 397 E2

Rannoch Moor

Robert Louis Stevenson picked out this landscape for his novel 'Kidnapped'. Some call it desolate: blanket bog formed on impermeable rock, treacherous to cross on foot. The underlying rock is granite, usually associated with mountains, so why is the moor flat? It was once a granite mountain, but the rock is coarse and crumbles. Erosion plus several passes of ice have plucked and scraped the surface flat, leaving the surrounding mountains (which are made of even harder metamorphic rocks) resembling an amphitheatre. It is a true wilderness, one of the few left in Britain.

33

Rannoch Moor

Map ref. 299 F4

Loch Lomond

If you look at the pattern of Scottish Lochs to the north of Loch Lomond, you will see that they form a radial pattern. The loch was bulldozed out only ten and a half thousand years ago by a glacier, which was based somewhere in the centre of this pattern. The ice followed the line of a major crack in the land called the 'Highland Boundary Fault' plucking out the already loose rocks along the fault line and gouging out a trough with the rocks it carried. When the ice melted, the empty chasm filled with water. Today, the sea is kept at bay by debris dumped at the side of the ancient glacier. To the south of the Loch, the line of the fault can be seen clearly, running along the islands and Conic Hill.

35

Loch Lomond

Map ref. 283 E1

Loch Ness

36

Loch Ness lies in the Great Glen Fault, the dividing line that runs from Fort William to Inverness. In the distant past, the land to the north of this fault moved south-west, then back again, the total displacement being around 80 miles (130km). Along this classic 'wrench' fault, travelled ice, plucking out the rock debris to such a depth that the Loch holds around three times the volume of water as Loch Lomond, although its surface area is much less. Significant earth tremors associated with continuing movement of the Great Glen Fault, normally occur three times a century; the last one was in 1901!

Loch Ness

Map ref. 309 E2

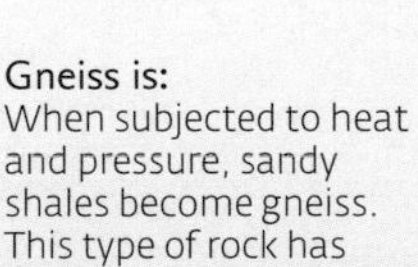

Gneiss is:
When subjected to heat and pressure, sandy shales become gneiss. This type of rock has distinctive bands of light and dark minerals.

Suilven

Sutherland boasts some of the most spectacular and ancient, if not highest, mountain landscape in Scotland. Suilven is a monolith of almost horizontally banded hard Torridonian sandstone in a flat expanse of ancient Lewisian gneiss, itself around 2,900 million years old. Roughly 4.5 miles (7km) of sediments from the rivers of Greenland (to which Scotland was joined) were laid on top of the already eroded Lewisian gneiss about 900 million years ago, when the whole area was basking in the sun at around 15 degrees north. Earth movements and sea level changes eventually allowed the area to become dry land and millions of years of erosion have subsequently left the 'hard cores' of the sedimentary layers standing proud.

Suilven

Map ref. 331 D3

34

Loch Lomond is the largest freshwater loch in Scotland at 27.5 sq miles (71.1 sq km)

Staffa – Fingal's Cave

Map ref. 288 C1

Staffa, Fingal's Cave

Off the west coast of Mull, the tiny island of Staffa exhibits some of the most amazing geological scenery in the world. For centuries man thought the regular basalt columns of 'Fingal's Cave' could not possibly be natural. Sixty million years ago, Greenland and North America were torn away from Scotland by the birth of the Atlantic Ocean, and lava poured out along this tear. The top slaggy crust on Staffa is the result of lots of bubbles, holes and minerals in the lava. The central part cooled to produce columns which have a polygonal structure. The base cooled more slowly, producing a denser texture and solid base.

Regular Basalt columns

Map ref. 326 C3

The Atlantic Ocean is named after the giant Atlas, who held up the sky on his shoulders. His father was the Titan Iapetus - after which the Iapetus Ocean was named.

When they were first uplifted, around 400 million years ago, the Caledonian Mountains were taller than the Himalayas are now.

Isle of Jura – Raised Beach

40

Scotland has 790 islands but only about 1/6th are inhabited.

40

Isle of Jura – Isolated sea eroded arch

Isle of Jura

Another phenomenon of the west coast can be seen on the western beaches of Jura. When the land was covered in ice, sea level fell (as it was locked in solid form). When it melted, not only did sea level rise once more, but so did the land, having been physically pushed down by the weight of ice. The land mass is still rising today; this is called 'isostatic uplift'. To further complicate matters, the whole of Britain is tilting down in the southeast and up in the northwest. As a consequence, the beaches formed at the end of the glaciation have been raised in stages, forming 'raised beaches'.

Taransay – Machair

39 Taransay, Machair

The Outer Hebrides face the full force of the Atlantic. This position, combined with the geology, has produced a unique landscape called 'Machair'. The beach is mainly wave pounded shells and sand, blown inland onto the low-lying marshes to produce a rich, alkaline soil. Easily damaged, modern farming techniques would destroy it, so it is treated gently and as a consequence, the grassland contains many rare flowers.

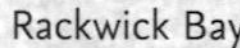

Rackwick Bay

Once a continuous plateau of sandstone, the sea level rose after the last ice age and created this archipelago of over 70 individual islands, collectively known as the Orkney Islands. Around 500 million years ago, a huge igneous mass pushed up under the sea from the depths of the Earth. Over the years, this was covered by layers and layers of sediments, the youngest of which were eroded away during periods of uplift and glaciation. On Hoy, the banding in the cliffs shows strata of tough, pebbly sandstones, unique in the Orkneys. Rackwick Bay is an excellent example, with massive sea-smoothed boulders up to 10 feet (3m) across littering the beach.

The longest river in Scotland is the River Tay at 120 miles (193km).

Cairngorms & Loch Morlich

38

Cairngorms

Until 420 million years ago, Scotland and England were on different continents, separated by the Iapetus Ocean. Both were in the southern hemisphere and moving north (Scotland much more slowly). At the Tropic of Capricorn, they collided, fusing into one landmass in a seamless join roughly along the line of Hadrian's Wall. Over millions of years, the force of the collision buckled the surface rocks, forming the Central Highlands. Deep below, granite was pushing its way up underneath the folding mountains, forming the infant Cairngorms. The rose-coloured granite, deeply buried for so long, is now exposed at the surface.

Map ref. 310 B4

41

Orkney Islands – Rackwick Bay

Map ref. 338 B3

UNDERSTANDING NATURAL HISTORY

The following habitats are home to many species of the flora and fauna found in Britain today.

DECIDUOUS WOODLAND

Use Collins Gems, Wild Guides and Nature Guides for good general information. Field Guides for detail or Complete British Wildlife for everything you need in one book.

Common Dormouse

Look for gnawed hazelnuts, smooth on the inside, teeth marks on surface. Has fluffy tail and ginger colour. Purrs and snores.

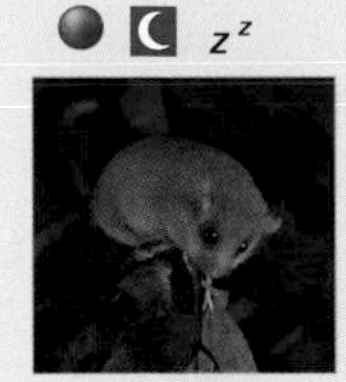

(Muscardinus avellanarius)

Royal Society for the Protection of Birds
www.rspb.org.uk

Hazlenut

Radial teeth marks
Smooth inner surface

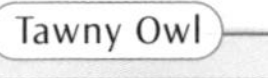

Tawny Owl

Small owl the size of a pigeon. Likes large trees with nesting holes. Call is "Hoo hoo hoo hoooo". Pellets under trees will contain bones of small mammals.

(Strix aluco)

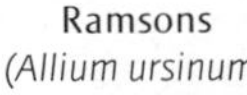

Ramsons

(Allium ursinum)
Smells of garlic.

Tree creeper

Climbs up tree trunks, often in a spiral pattern. Has a long, thin, downcurved bill.

(Certhia familiaris)

Great Spotted Woodpecker

Drums on tree trunks in spring. Distinctive black and white markings. The male has a red nape. Likes large mature trees with holes for nesting.

(Dendrocopos major)

Blue tit

Particularly likes oak trees which provide it with hundreds of caterpillars for babies in spring. Often hangs upside down on the ends of branches to reach food.

(Parus caeruleus)

Badger

Extensive system of large holes with freshly dug earth outside. Distinctive footprints (front and back different).

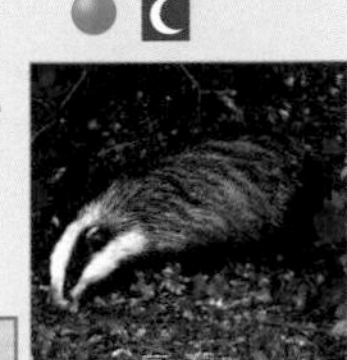

(Meles meles)

Ragged robin

(Lychnis flos-cuculi)

Wood anemone

(Anemone nemorosa)
In the sun, will raise their heads and open petals.

Silver-washed fritillary

Silver sheen on underside of hind wings. Likes Bramble flowers. Caterpillars feed exclusively on violets.

(Argynnis paphia)

Herb paris

(Paris quadrifolia)
Indicator of old woodland.

MOUNTAIN

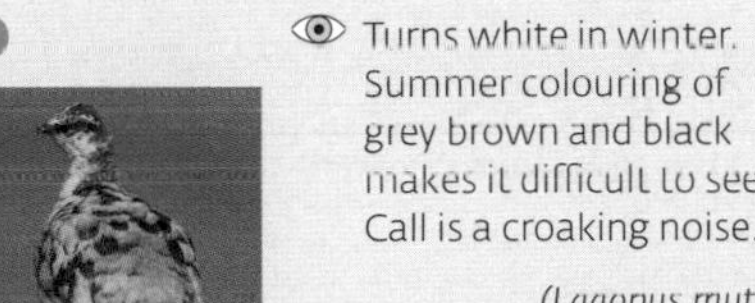

Ptarmigan

Turns white in winter. Summer colouring of grey brown and black makes it difficult to see. Call is a croaking noise.

(Lagopus mutus)

Don't be surprised to see wallabies hopping about in the Peak District, wild boar roaming Kent woodlands or even black panthers in the Forest of Dean.

Crowberry

(Empetrum nigrum)
Winter food for moorland and mountain birds.

Golden eagle

Second largest bird in the UK. Tends not to like forests, preferring open areas.

(Aquila chrysaetos)

Mountain hare

Black tipped ears. Often turns white in winter. Small tracks going directly up slopes, doesn't zig-zag.

(Lepus timidus)

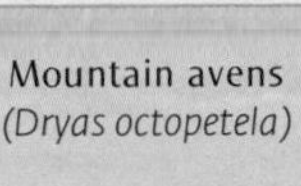

Mountain avens

(Dryas octopetela)

HEDGEROWS

Natural History Museum
www.nhm.ac.uk

Wren

Tiny bird with tail held almost vertically. Loud ringing song and loud, persistent 'tik tik tik' when alarmed.

(Troglodytes troglodytes)

Bird song varies according to geographical region.

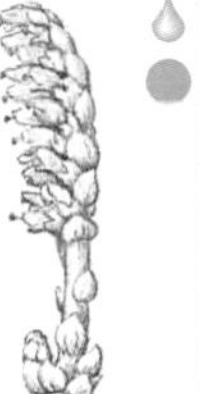

Toothwort

(Lathraea squamaria)
Parasitic plant, especially on hazel.

Common shrew

High pitched 'twitters' coming from the grass, especially in March/April.

(Sorex aranaeus)

The pygmy shrew is Britain's smallest mammal. It weighs less than a 10p coin and must eat this weight of food every day to survive.

Lords-and-Ladies

(Arum maculatum)

Holly blue

Flies higher than other blues. Found near Holly in spring and Ivy in late summer.

(Celastrina argiolus)

Pignut

(Conopodium majus)
Pigs love the roots, hence the name.

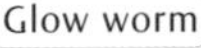

Glow worm

Green glow at night from the wingless female. Snails are a large part of the larvae's diet and the snails preferred are found in chalk and limestone areas.

(Lampyris noctiluca)

Song thrush

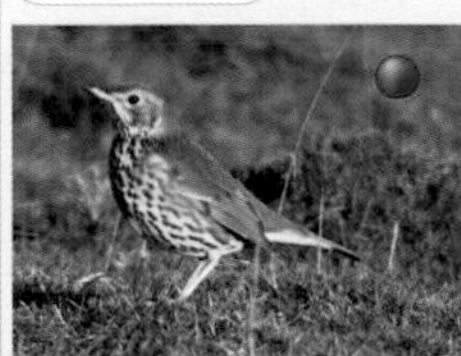

Dark brown spots underneath. Repeats phrases when singing. Uses a stone to smash open snail shells.

(Turdus philomelos)

Symbols

Status (fauna) - This has been generalised to give an indication of sensitivity and rarity. Where this cannot be definitely established, no symbol is given. For more information, see www.jncc.gov.uk

Not endangered | Of concern | Endangered | Identification clues | Nocturnal | z^z Hibernates

Soil (flora) - Symbols are only shown for plants that will only grow in specific conditions.

Acid (peaty) soil | Alkaline (chalky) soil | Damp soil | Dry soil

GRASSLAND

Eyebright
(Euphrasia officinalis)
Pretty but parasitic plant.

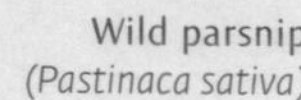

Wild parsnip
(Pastinaca sativa)

Common blue

Males are bright blue. Likes Fleabane. Usually seen in groups. Rests head down on stems.

(Polyommatus icarus)

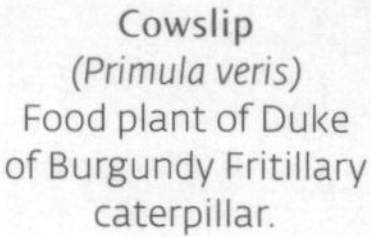

Cowslip
(Primula veris)
Food plant of Duke of Burgundy Fritillary caterpillar.

Orange tip

Only males have orange tips. Prefers damp areas.

(Anthocharis cardamines)

Common field grasshopper

Listen for 6 to 10 half-second chirps, evenly spread over 12 seconds.

(Chorthippus brunneus)

The stoat has a black tip to its tail. The weasel, with no 't' in its name, doesn't.

The Mammal Society
www.abdn.ac.uk

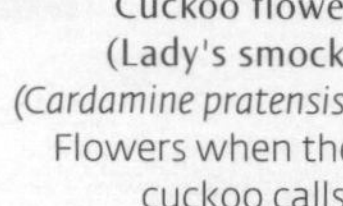

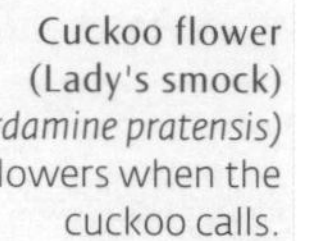

Cuckoo flower
(Lady's smock)
(Cardamine pratensis)
Flowers when the cuckoo calls.

Stoat

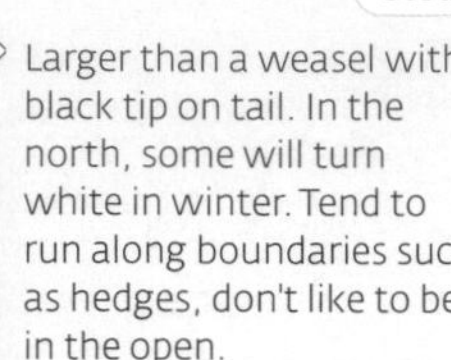

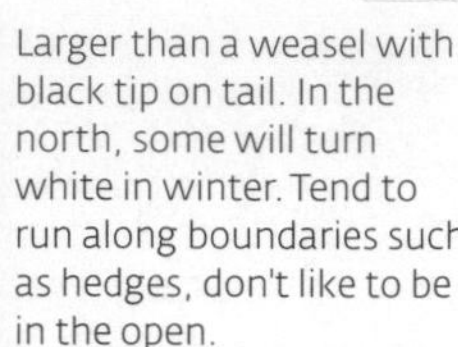

Larger than a weasel with black tip on tail. In the north, some will turn white in winter. Tend to run along boundaries such as hedges, don't like to be in the open.

(Mustela erminia)

Cinnabar moth

Caterpillars eat Ragwort, which makes them poisonous.

(Tyria jacobaeae)

Harebell
(Campanula rotundifolia)
Called Bluebells in Scotland.

Lapwing

Black crest. Call 'kee-ee-wit'. Breeds on farmland, usually in short spring sown crops and pasture.

(Vanellus vanellus)

Quaking grass
(Briza media)
Makes a lovely rattling sound in the wind.

LOWLAND HEATH

Adder

z z

Black or brown zig-zag marking down back – but colours and pattern can vary. Poisonous but not usually deadly. Basks in sun.

(Vipera berus)

Bell heather
(Erica cinerea)

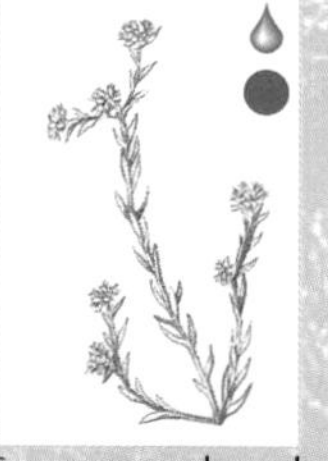

Common cudweed
(Filago vulgaris)
Once given to cows as medicine.

Stonechat

Male has black head, red chest, white on side of neck. Song sounds like pebbles being knocked together 'wee tak tak'.

(Saxicola torquata)

Gorse
(Ulex europaeus)

Hobby

Under parts have dark streaks. Has a white neck. Wings are swept back in flight. Takes prey on the wing. Migrates in winter.

(Falco subbuteo)

Heath spotted orchid
(Dactylorhiza maculata)

Clouded Buff Moth

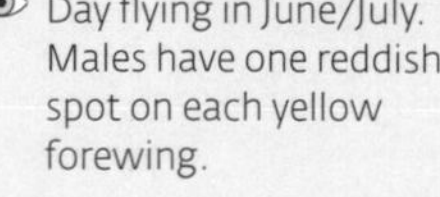

Day flying in June/July. Males have one reddish spot on each yellow forewing.

(Diacrisia sannio)

MOORLAND & BOG

Red deer

Russet coloured coat with no white spots on adults. Largest of the British deer with branching antlers which are shed in late winter.

(Cervus elaphus)

Exmoor pony

Usually dark brown, with a broad face and back and short legs.

(Equus caballus)

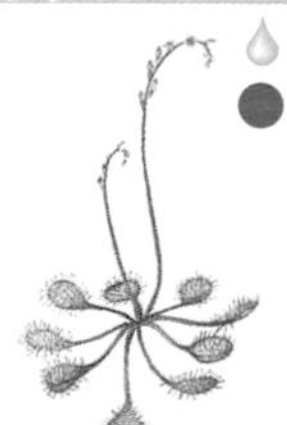

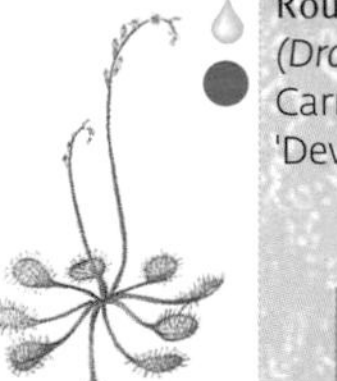

Round leaved sundew
(Drosera rotundifolia)
Carnivorous plant. 'Dew' is really 'glue'.

Bog asphodel
(Narthecium ossifragum)

Mountain ringlet

Usually found above 1600 feet (500m). Likes to feed on Tormentil flowers.

(Erebia epiphron)

Merlin

Smallest bird of prey. Long, square-ended tail.

(Falco columbarius)

Cranberry
(Vaccinium oxycoccus)

Golden plover

The male is gold and brown above, black underneath with a white dividing line in summer. Typically stands still, feeds, runs a bit, stops, feeds and so on.

(Pluvialis apricaria)

URBAN

Hedgehog

The only spiny British mammal. Listen for noisy grunting sounds at dusk in spring. Often hibernates in piles of wood meant for bonfires, check before lighting.

(Erinaceus europaeus)

An adult hedgehog has around 5000 spines.

Butterfly Bush
(Buddleia davidii)
Garden escapee. Loved by butterflies and bees.

Mason bee

Little piles of mortar at the base of walls are a clue to the nest of this solitary bee.

(Osmia rufa)

The tiny pipistrelle bat can eat up to 3000 insects in one night.

Rosebay willowherb
(Epilobium angustifolium)
Also called 'fireweed' as it grows where fire has been.

Peacock butterfly

The 'eyespots' on this butterfly supposedly confuse birds and deter other predators. Loves Buddleia.

(Inachis io)

House cricket

Native of warmer climes, found in warm buildings. Sometimes mistaken for a cockroach.It has a lovely song.

(Acheta domesticus)

House martin

White rump and a forked tail. Mud nest below house eaves. Summer migrant. Attractive, twittering song.

(Delichon urbica)

Fox

Reddish brown, tail bushier in winter. Footprints fall in one line. Mainly seen at dawn and dusk.

(Vulpes vulpes)

Habitat

The place where a species lives. The species shown here often move from one habitat to another for different parts of their life cycle. For example toads can breed in ponds, forage in long vegetation and hibernate in stone walls.

The Bat Conservation Trust
www.bats.org.uk

CONIFEROUS WOODLAND

Crested tit

Distinctive black and white crest. Often hangs upside down on thin branches looking for seeds and insects.

(Parus cristatus)

Yellow birds nest
(Monotropa hypopitys)
No green parts.

A flock of goldfinches is called a 'charm'.

Wild cat

(mainly)

Looks like a large tabby with a thicker, blunt tail. Needs areas of varied habitat. Solitary and shy. Only found in Scotland.

(Felis sylvestris)

Pinewood mushroom
(Agaricus silvaticus)

Injured creatures
If you find an injured creature, phone the RSPCA 0870 55 55 999 or SSPCA (Scotland) 0870 73 77 722

Capercaillie

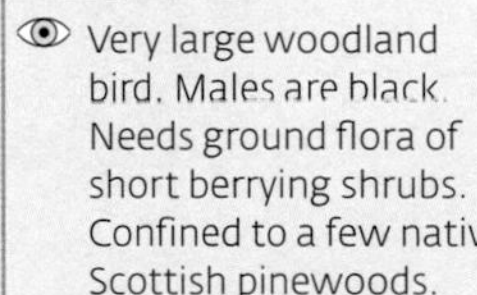

Very large woodland bird. Males are black. Needs ground flora of short berrying shrubs. Confined to a few native Scottish pinewoods.

(Tetrao urogallus)

Giant wood wasp

HARMLESS! Flies May to August.

(Urocerus gigas)

Ling
(Calluna vulgaris)

Pine marten

(mainly)

Dark brown/reddish coat with orange/yellow throat/chest. Might be seen chasing red squirrels in trees.

(Martes martes)

Red squirrel

Thick bushy tail, large ear tufts in winter. Usually orange to red/chestnut fur. Nests high in trees using twigs and a lining of moss and grass.

(Sciurus vulgaris)

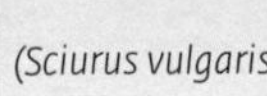

Biodiversity
The number of different species on Earth.

ARABLE FARMLAND

Yellowhammer

Yellow with black streaks and red/orange rump. Song 'a little bit of bread and no cheese'. Likes open areas with bushy hedgerows.

(Emberiza citrinella)

Harvest mouse

Makes nest of woven shredded grass (still attached to the stalk) within the stalks of grasses and reeds.

(Micromys minutus)

Ivy-leaved speedwell
(Veronica hederifolia)

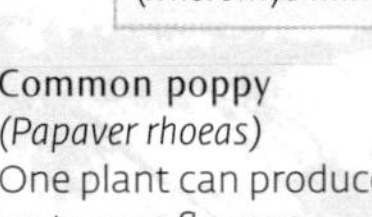

Common poppy
(Papaver rhoeas)
One plant can produce up to 500 flowers.

Skylark

Males ascend and sing a beautiful warbling song in spring and summer. Has a small crest. Prefers open areas with low hedges and no trees.

(Alauda arvensis)

Brown hare

Long black tipped ears. Rests in a scrape in the ground (doesn't burrow). Boxing hares are a male and a female.

(Lepus europaeus)

Field forget-me-not
(Myosotis arvensis)

Wild pansy
(Viola tricolor)

The common dormouse can spend up to 3/4 of its life asleep.

Grey Partridge

Plump bird with orange face. Look particularly along hedgerows where there is a wide grassy margin.

(Perdix perdix)

Barn owl

White heart shaped face and pure white underneath. Completely silent in flight. Call is a loud shriek. Owl pellets on ground will contain bones of small mammals.

(Tyto alba)

Common fleabane
(Pulicaria dysenterica)
Once burnt to get rid of fleas.

Swallowtail

Likes thistles and ragged robin. Caterpillars only feed on milk parsley. Only in East Anglia.

(Papilio machaon)

FEN & MARSH

Raft spider

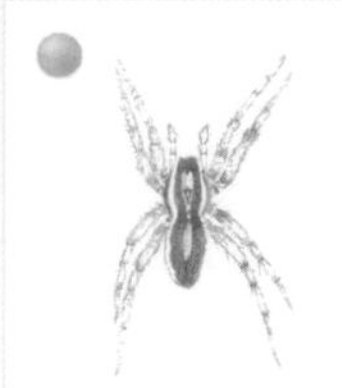

Britain's largest spider. Female's body can be almost an inch (22mm) long. Sits at boggy pool edges with legs on water.

(Dolomedes fimbriatus)

Yellow wagtail

Tail has white edges which it wags up and down. Black legs. Runs a lot. Summer visitor.

(Motacilla flava)

Marsh Harrier

Long tail. Wings held in a 'V' shape. Spring courtship involves aerial acrobatics.

(Circus aeruginosus)

Devil's-bit scabious
(Succisa pratensis)

Butterfly Conservation
www.butterfly-conservation.org

Marsh fritillary

Sheen to underside of wings. Likes devil's-bit scabious the caterpillars spinning a fine web in its leaves.

(Euphydryas aurinia)

Redshank

Long red legs and orange base to bill. Male yodels in flight "tu-udle".

(Tringa totanus)

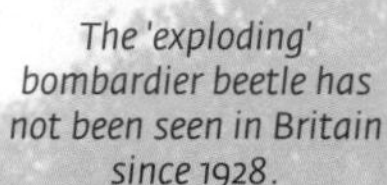

The 'exploding' bombardier beetle has not been seen in Britain since 1928.

Pintail

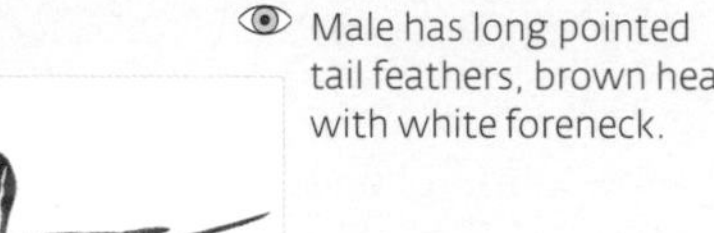

Male has long pointed tail feathers, brown head with white foreneck.

(Anas acuta)

Marsh marigold
(Caltha palustris)

STILL WATER & REEDBEDS

Water vole

Rat-sized but longer fur, blunt nose and tiny ears. Creates a 'lawn' of shorter grass around banks. Shiny black droppings. 'Ratty' of 'Wind in the Willows' fame.

(Arvicolla terrestris)

Emperor dragonfly

Largest wingspan of any British dragonfly. Dark line runs full length of back. Male sky blue, female greenish.

(Anax imperator)

Reed bunting

Male in summer has black head and throat with distinctive white stripe between the two. Tail feathers are white and deeply forked.

(Emberiza schoeniclus)

Common reed
(Phragmites australis)
Stems used for thatching.

Common newt

Only seen in ponds in spring when breeding. At this time, male has an undulating crest with spotted flanks. The underside is often bright orange with spots.

(Triturus vulgaris)

Bittern

Rare. Try RSPB reserves in spring, where there are reedbeds. May hear its booming call, almost like a foghorn.

(Botaurus stellaris)

A toad can live for 40 years.

Yellow water lily
(Nuphar lutea)
Pods shaped like brandy bottles.

Common toad

Dry warty skin. Prefers to walk rather than hop. Only seen in ponds in spring when breeding. Lays long strings of spawn rather than clumps.

(Bufo bufo)

English Nature
www.english-nature.org.uk

Great crested grebe

Black crest. Courtship display facing each other and moving heads quickly from side to side, usually with a bill full of water plants. Strange grating bark call.

(Podiceps cristatus)

General advice
Do not disturb wildlife or damage their habitats.

RIVERS & STREAMS

Atlantic Salmon

Best seen when travelling upstream to spawn, jumps out of the water to traverse waterfalls.

(Salmo salar)

Banded demoiselle

Male has distinctive 'thumbprint' on wings and a wingspan of 2.5 inches (60mm).

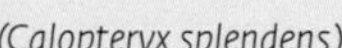

(Calopteryx splendens)

Watercress
(Nasturtium officinale)
Don't eat - may have liver fluke eggs on.

Kingfisher

Brilliant colouring. Makes tunnel in river bank. Often perches on branch over water.

(Alcedo atthis)

Water crowfoot
(Ranunculus aquatilis)

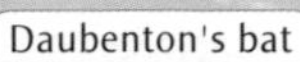

Daubenton's bat

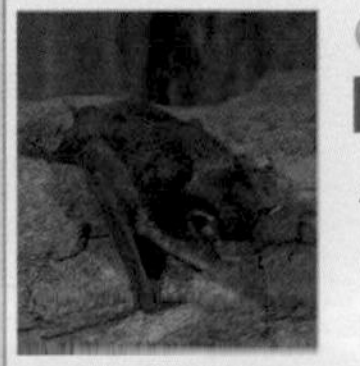

Flies very low over water to catch prey. If you have a bat detector, listen at 35-85kHz.

(Myotis daubentonii)

Otter

Brown fur, large whiskers and white chest. Can be 36 inches (90cm) long. Five-toed, webbed feet.

(Lutra lutra)

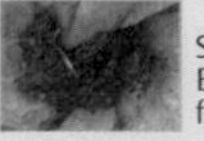

Spraint (Otter poo). Black, full of tiny fish bones.

SEA CLIFFS & BEACH

Sanderling

Runs backwards and forwards with the waves. Winter visitor and passage migrant in autumn and spring.

(Calidris alba)

Puffin

Unmistakable markings. Prefers high sea cliffs and offshore islands. Occasionally nest in old rabbit burrows.

(Fratercula arctica)

Green shore crab

Usually greenish but can have considerable patterning. Up to 2.5 inches (60mm) long. Tolerant of low salinity so can be found far up in estuaries.

(Carcinus maenas)

Thrift
(Armeria maritima)

Sea gooseberry

Lights run along body. Gets trapped in rock pools.

(Pleurobrachia pileus)

Common brittlestar

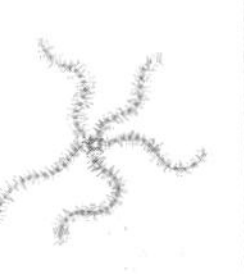

Five thin spiny arms around a disc of about 0.75 inches (20mm). Has five jaws.

(Ophiothrix fragilis)

Sea campion
(Silene maritima)

Fulmar

Yellow/blue bill. Skims waves with stiff wings. If disturbed when nesting they spit a greenish oil.

(Fulmarus glacialis)

Gem anemone

Rock pools. Up to 3 inches (80mm) tall. Up to 48 green 'tentacles'.

(Bunodactis verrucosa)

Chough

Looks like a crow but has red bill and legs. Only on west coasts.

(Pyrrhocorax pyrrhocorax)

Sheep's-bit scabious
(Jasione montana)
Often eaten by sheep.

SAND DUNES

Common lizard

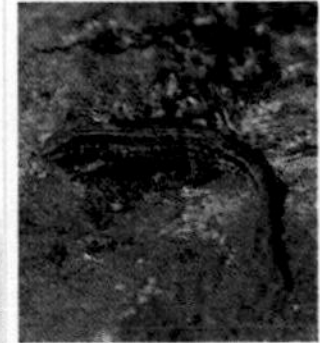

Black stripe along back. Basks in sun in spring. Can shed its tail if caught, then grow a new one.

(Lacerta vivipara)

Sea holly
(Eryngium maritimum)

Green tiger beetle

Green with two creamy yellow spots, one on each wing case. 0.625 inch (16mm) long.

(Cicindela campestris)

Yellow horned poppy
(Glaucium flavum)
Pods can grow up to 30cm long.

Sandwich Tern

Black cap with short crest and long black bill with yellow tip. Call is a rasping "kirrick". Summer visitor.

(Sterna sandvicensis)

Common milkwort
(Polygala vulgaris)
Was once thought to increase milk production in cows.

ESTUARY & SALT MARSH

Curlew

Long down curved bill. Distinctive, haunting call, 'cooor-li'.

(Numenius arquata)

Sea aster
(Aster tripolium)

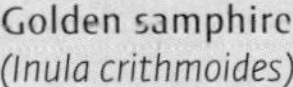

Golden samphire
(Inula crithmoides)

Oystercatcher

Long orange bill, long pink legs. Black and white plumage. Eats cockles.

(Haematopus ostralegus)

Common sea lavender
(Limonium vulgare)

Sea wormwood
(Artemisia maritima)
Aromatic leaves.

Research has shown that some birds dream the song they are going to sing in the morning.

Shelduck

Large red bill with bump on the top. Chestnut/orange band around chest in the breeding season.

(Tadorna tadorna)

COASTAL WATERS

Thornback Ray

Diamond-shaped flat fish with spines along its long tail. Egg cases found on the beach called 'Mermaid's purses'.

(Raja clavata) Egg case

Grey seal

Flat head and 'Roman' nose, unlike round head of Common seal. Also longer than Common. Pups born on shore late summer and autumn.

(Halichoerus grypus)

Bottle nosed dolphin

Very social, usually in groups. Has short 'snout'. Worth going on a boat trip to see, will often swim in front or at the side of the boat.

(Tursiops truncatus)

TRANSPORT

Canals

Canal building in Britain goes back thousands of years - short stretches were excavated to link rivers. Car Dyke, which stretched 56 miles (89km) across the Fens, was built by the Romans and can still be seen today. However, canals as we know them came into being because of the Industrial Revolution. Before the mid 1700s, goods were transported slowly and in small quantities by horse and cart on poor roads, or by sea, at great expense. With the discovery that coke could be used to smelt iron ore, huge quantities of coal were needed for this and associated industries. The first canal to be built was commissioned by the 3rd Earl of Bridgewater to transport coal from his mines to Manchester. The Bridgewater Canal opened in 1761 and was a huge success; 30 tons could be carried in a single load. By the 1830s there were over 4000 miles (7000km) of canals. However, the developing railways sounded the death knell for canal haulage. Even when wages were cut so far that boatmen had to house their families on board, railways were still more profitable and much faster. Other European countries had modernised and widened their canals, so that loads of 2,000 tons could be carried, but investment for canals here was not forthcoming. Many were abandoned and by the 1960s their numbers had halved. Luckily, at about this time, working people were taking more holidays and had more disposable income; the 'boating holiday' era had begun. Today, many miles have been restored, their narrow width making them almost unique in Europe and an historical treasure. Towpaths are being upgraded for cycling, walking and fibre-optic cableways. There is even a small revival for goods haulage due to congestion on the roads. Full circle, we might say.

Shropshire Union Canal

www.visitheartofengland.com

Burnley – Weavers Triangle

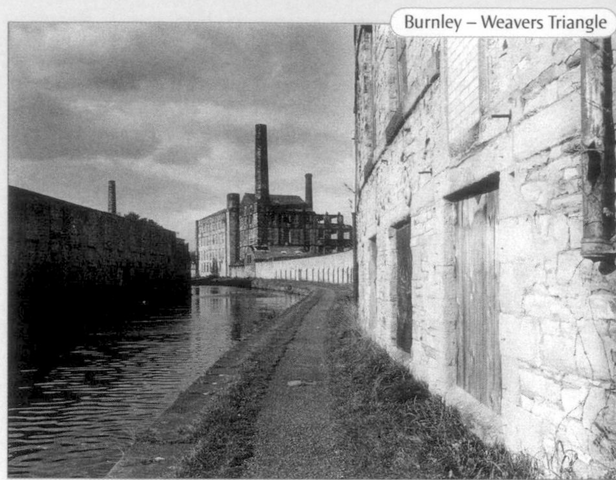

Map ref. 243 E4

Railways

The world's first steam locomotive was built by Richard Trevithick in 1803. After that, several engineers built steam engines and in 1830 the Liverpool to Manchester line became the world's first main line railway to carry passengers and freight on a double track line of metal rails, using steam locomotives built by George and Robert Stephenson. Over the next 20 years, over 6000 miles (9650 km) of public railways were built in Britain. When World War I broke out in 1914, there were 20,053 miles (32,265km) of track and 23,000 locomotives. However, their heyday was over and by the 1960s, for various organisational and political reasons, the railways were in financial trouble and the inevitable hatchet fell. Over 2,000 stations were closed and railway lines were ripped up. It has taken many years but the value of these disused tracks is at last being realised. Many footpaths and cycleways are being created enabling us to enjoy the flora and fauna along these corridors, which escaped the chemical persecution of their arable and pastoral cousins; without the railways, we might have lost many of them.

Tyseley – railway track

Brampton Valley Way

Map ref. 210 C4

ENERGY

Coal

It was coal that fired the Industrial Revolution. Wherever coal could be transported, industry would spring up. Iron foundries, glass works, potteries and brickworks. However, as with any finite resource, supply eventually became a problem and cheaper foreign coal made it uneconomic to dig the deeper pits needed to access our own. Worries about global warming prompted the 1992 Earth Summit in Rio de Janeiro, where the search for alternative energy supplies started in earnest.

Rhondda Valley – colliery

Map ref. 179 F3

Short Rotation Coppice (SRC)

Look for fields of 'shrubs' or unfamiliar tall grasses; 'biofuels' grown to be burnt in pollution free, high-tech converters, producing heat, or power, or both. Around 100 acres (40ha) of 'short rotation willow coppice' (willow cut every two or three years), could keep a village of about 50 houses warm *ad infinitum*. This growing system is excellent for wildlife, soaks up pollutants and is resistant to most pests and diseases. Classed as 'carbon neutral' it only releases carbon taken up by the plant during its short growing cycle.

Field of short rotation Willow coppice

Wind farms

Evidence of alternative energy sources are appearing all over the landscape of Britain. Wind farms are probably the best known, taking pure energy from the air. They already supply enough power for around 400,000 households.

Map ref. 204 D4

Llywernog – wind farm

Other

In the future we may see solar panels lining motorways to power lights and signs, barrages in estuaries collecting energy from the tides and small, privately owned water mills capturing the energy of streams once more, this time to drive turbines instead of grinding stones. You may even fill your car with methane from landfill sites.

TEXTILES

Until the mid 1700s, spinning and weaving was a domestic industry, but various inventions speeded up the process. In 1771, Richard Arkwright established the world's first successful water-powered cotton spinning mill at Cromford in Derbyshire, and became known as the 'father of the factory system'. Cotton production became centred in Lancashire and the west of Scotland, wool in West Yorkshire and south-west England, silk and linen in northern England. In 1912, cotton manufacture peaked at 8 billion yards (7.25 billion metres). All was well until World War I. It was no longer possible to export cloth, so countries such as Japan set up their own factories and never looked back. Between the two world wars, 800 mills closed. Although there was a slight revival in the 1950s, by the 1980s textile production in the north-west had all but ceased. Hundreds of mills lay derelict and many were pulled down. Today, the potential of the remaining fine buildings has been recognised; several are now World Heritage Sites. At Saltaire, West Yorkshire, the old mill buildings house galleries, a restaurant, antiques and other ventures. New Lanark on the banks of the Clyde has been restored to a working community and is a huge tourist attraction. Other less famous mills have found new uses - Ebley Mill in Stroud, Gloucestershire has been given a new lease of life as the District Council building.

Stroud – Ebley Mill

Map ref. 182 A2

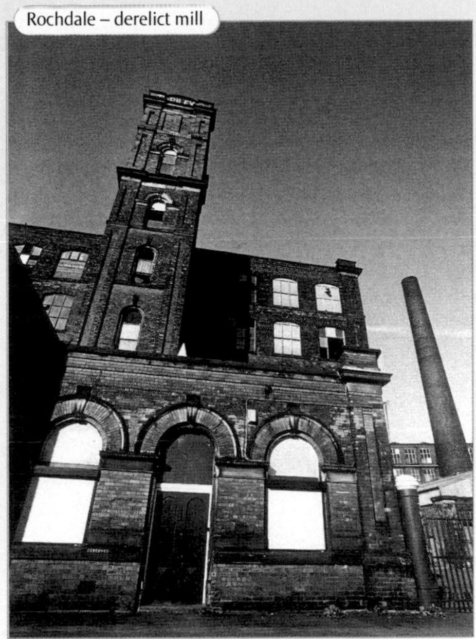

Rochdale – derelict mill

Map ref. 234 C1

SHIPBUILDING

Britain has always been a seafaring nation and with the developments in sail and the invention of the compass. Ships were built for trade and exploration from as early as the 14th century. During the 18th century, the Navigation Acts (requiring all British trade to be carried by British ships), and the growth of the British Empire stimulated shipbuilding further; by the 19th century the British shipbuilding industry was the largest in the world. Eventually iron replaced wood and steam replaced sail. In 1914, the tonnage from British shipyards was more than the rest of the world put together; employment reached around 300,000. However, for various economic reasons, shipbuilding here started to decline. In the 1970s South Korea moved into shipbuilding, assisted by the World Bank, this was the final straw. British construction methods were outdated and none of the 'rescue packages' instigated by the government worked. 1977 saw nationalisation of the industry; 1983 saw privatisation. Warship yards survived but those producing merchant shipping all but disappeared. All is not doom and gloom however. British shipyards still produce around 27 ships a year (although we have the capacity to produce twice that number) and Britain is a world leader in ship repairs, building warships and small specialist ships, marine equipment manufacture and ship conversions. Derelict dockyards, like those at Hartlepool, have been revived with the building of a huge new marina and some of the old buildings house new industries and tourist attractions. A similar story is told of Cardiff Docks, hit in particular by the decline in the coal and steel industries, the whole area has seen a remarkable regeneration (the second largest in Europe) with a visitor centre and various tourist attractions. Many new media and IT based industries have been attracted to the revamped and new business parks.

Cardiff Bay

Map ref. 180 A5

Cranes in disused docks

FORESTRY

Trees are a significant part of the landscape, they give it character. They can be used for screening unsightly developments, as sound barriers, for stabilising banks and spoil heaps, but mostly we see them as woodlands. After World War II, the government instigated mass planting of conifers to ensure reserves for the future. At that time, issues of wildlife and aesthetics were unheard of. Blocks and lines of conifers were planted in mostly upland areas all over the country; Kielder Forest is a prime example. Those forests are now reaching maturity but instead of chopping them all down and replanting in the same way, different methods are being used, to enhance conservation and amenity value. Landscaping and conservation now work hand in hand with commercial timber production. Trees are being removed in groups over a longer time scale so that stream sides are cleared or archaelogical features enhanced, hill contours are followed and biodiversity increased. Some upland moorland is being allowed to revert to woodland (its natural state) by fencing out livestock. Within the woodlands themselves, rides are widened to let more light in, benefiting flora and fauna. This also helps access for forestry equipment, as the ground is drier.

Scotland – block conifer plantation

Glades and rides within a woodland provide a microclimate for wildlife - and somewhere to stack timber. When planting today, valuable habitats such as lowland heath are left alone, straight lines are avoided, trees are planted to blend in with the surrounding landscape character and contours of the land and a mix of broadleaved and coniferous trees are used. This has led to forests being areas for recreation as well as timber production, for example there are sculpture trails in the Forest of Dean. The new National Forest is being planted in the English midlands, it covers three counties and 200 square miles (518 sq km). The aim is to make one third of the area woodland (commercial and conservation), incorporating learning and recreational facilities. Over four million trees have been planted to date.

Open ride in modern woodland

Forest of Dean – Sculpture Trail

Map ref. 181 F1

MYTHS AND LEGENDS

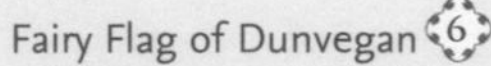

GIANTS

Where did giant tales come from? One story says they were descendents of Ham, the 'bad' son of Noah. Another, that they were the result of a union between the banished daughters of a King of Greece and demon spirits. In practice, people probably believed that the easiest explanation for monuments such as Stonehenge was that huge giants must have built them.

Callanish giants (9)

Callanish Stones

Thirteen giant people were reputedly turned to stone when they refused to let St Kieran build a church here or be baptised by him. The Gaelic name for Callanish is "na Fir Bhreign", meaning 'the false men'.

SAINTS

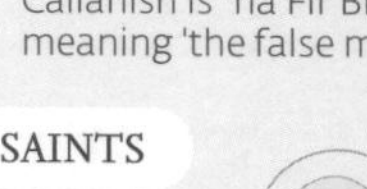

Many legends surround the making of Saints, often involving birds and animals or miraculous events.

St. Brynach (7)

St. Brynach journeyed to Nevern, where an angel appeared and told him to look for a white sow. The sow showed him where to build a church and this he did. In the churchyard stands a Celtic cross. On the seventh day of April, the Saint's day, a cuckoo is said to perch here and sing for the first time in the year.

Nevern churchyard

Cuckoo

In order to be allowed to live in this world and the Land of Eternal Youth, the cuckoo had to promise never to build a nest in either world and so never bring up or know her own children.

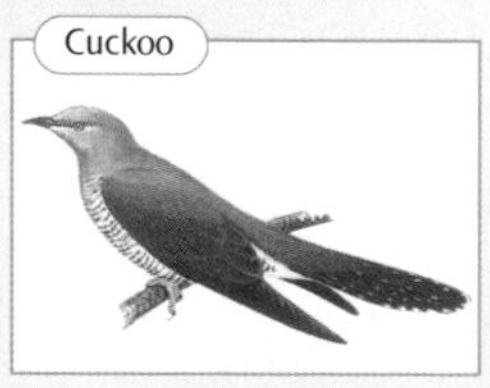
Cuckoo

Cantre'r Gwaelod (4)

There was a land in Cardigan Bay, rich and fertile with 16 cities, protected from the sea by great sea walls. One night, the guardian of the sluice gates, Seithennin, got drunk and forgot to close the gates. The sea swept in, drowning everybody except a few survivors who escaped onto Snowdon (see Sarn Badrig, Understanding the Landscape).

LOST LANDS

The legend of Cantre'r Gwaelod and others relating to submerged lands could stem from actual inundations by the sea, when Neolithic man was around to witness them.

Severn Bore

WATER

Water, the giver of life, has always been associated with spirits and deities. Holy wells are often places previously used for pagan worship.

Sabrina (1)

The river Severn is, according to legend, inhabited by an ancient British river spirit 'Sabrina'. One story relates that when the Roman army attempted to cross the river and attack the British leader Caractacus, and the Druids, the priests called on Sabrina and she drove the bore up the river, drowning the whole Roman army.

Fairy Flag of Dunvegan (6)

Still kept in Dunvegan Castle is a fragile scrap of cloth. Legend says it is part of a flag given to a previous chief by his fairy wife. When unfurled, it gives victory to the MacLeod Clan in battle, makes their marriages fruitful and magically charms the herrings in the loch into the nets.

Dunvegan Castle

Stornoway
Dunvegan
Inverness
Dundee
Glasgow
Edinburgh
Newcastle upon Tyne
Carlisle
Middlesbrough
Isle of Man
Blackpool
Bradford
Leeds
Kingston upon Hull
Manchester
Liverpool
Chester
Sheffield
Porthmadog
Stoke-on-Trent
Nottingham
Norwich
Leicester
Wolverhampton
Birmingham
Ipswich
Cardigan
Gloucester
Oxford
LONDON
Swansea
Bristol
Cardiff
Guildford
Brighton
Portsmouth
Dorchester
Plymouth

FAIRIES

Stories of folk existing in 'another dimension' to our own occur all over the world. In Britain they are best known as 'fairies'. They can be good (like the 'Brownies' who will do your housework for you), seem to be friendly towards farmers wives and always pay for anything they take. They can be spiteful, taking human babies and putting strange 'changelings' in their place. Mostly, they are seen as mischievous. The origins of these tales in Scotland seem to relate to the ancient Pictish people and in England and Wales, perhaps to the Bronze Age people, superseded by Iron Age (fairies are said to have a deep loathing of iron).

St. Winifred's Well (5)

This well appeared on the spot where Winifred's head fell after being cut off by an unwelcome suitor called Caradog, son of a local chieftan. St. Bueno, her uncle, laid her head next to her neck, where it miraculously rejoined. Caradog was swallowed by the earth and Winifred lived out her days as a nun.

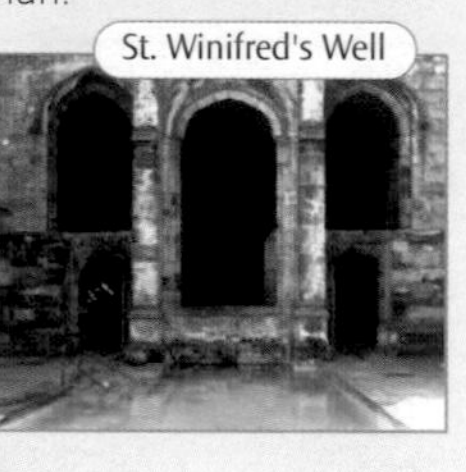
St. Winifred's Well

The Sockburn Worm

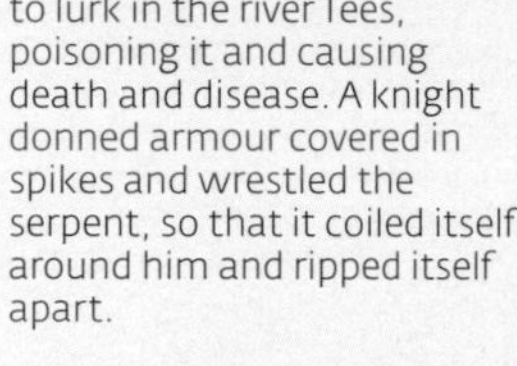

The Sockburn Worm (8)

A venomous serpent was said to lurk in the river Tees, poisoning it and causing death and disease. A knight donned armour covered in spikes and wrestled the serpent, so that it coiled itself around him and ripped itself apart.

Cowslip

St. Peter was said to have dropped the keys to Heaven and the first Cowslip sprang up from where they fell.

Cowslip

MOVING CHURCHES

In an attempt to Christianise pagan sites of worship, many churches were built on them, sometimes in what seemed like strange places, outside of a village. There are many legends to explain these locations, often involving the devil or the building stones themselves moving.

Cerne Abbas giant (1)

A Danish giant was terrorising the people of Dorset. One day, he ate too many sheep and became sleepy, so he lay down. While he slept, the villagers crept up on him and cut off his head. As a warning to other giants, they carved his outline into the chalk.

Cerne Abbas giant

Dunsfold church (3)

According to legend, this church is half a mile from the village because the stones to build it kept moving to this site when they were left overnight.

Dunsfold church

SOUTH WEST ENGLAND

The long, tapering finger of land that forms the far south west is favoured with a temperate climate and endowed with soft, timeless beauty. The pretty coastline, sometimes rugged, other times gentle, and the green, upland expanses of Dartmoor, Exmoor and the Cotswolds, together with an abundance of charming chocolate-box villages, all merit exploration. Echoes of bygone times lie scattered through the region, adding a hint of legend and mysticism in contrast to today's more up-to-the-minute attractions.

Mevagissey Harbour

A La Ronde (NT) — 152 D4

A remarkable 16-sided house built in the late 18th century on the instructions of two cousins, Jane and Mary Parminter, on their return from a Grand Tour of Europe. Many items on show were collected by the ladies during their tour and amongst the more unusual features of internal decoration are a feather frieze and a gallery encrusted by shells.

☎ 01395 265514 www.nationaltrust.org.uk

Abbotsbury Swannery & Sub-Tropical Gardens — 154 B4

A sheltered coastal location behind Chesil Beach provides a distinctive microclimate which has allowed this 20 acre (8ha) woodland garden to flourish. There are magnificent spring displays of camellias, magnolias and rhododendrons, exotic species such as bamboos, palms and bananas, and themed areas like the Mediterranean, Himalayan and New Zealand gardens.

Down on the shore, in the lee of Chesil Beach, there has been a swannery for over 600 years, established by Benedictine monks in the 14th century. Up to 1000 swans may be in residence at any one time, and between late May and late June it is possible to walk amongst the swans and observe newborn cygnets close up.

☎ 01305 871387 (Gardens) www.abbotsbury-tourism.co.uk
☎ 01305 871858 (Swannery)

Alice in Wonderland Family Park — 347 C2

A 7 acre (2.5ha) theme park based on the books of Lewis Carroll, the focal point being one of Europe's largest hedge mazes with over 5000 bushes trained to form shapes of characters from the Alice books. Other attractions include rides, particularly for younger children, indoor and outdoor play areas and a theatre giving short shows based on the Alice characters.

☎ 01202 483444 www.aliceinwonderlandpark.co.uk

American Museum — 167 E1

An early 19th century manor house which, since the late 1950s, has been home to a museum illustrating American history, culture and way of life. 18 rooms have been decorated and furnished to depict the evolution of American homes and their fashions from the 17th to 19th centuries and there are also collections of quilts and textiles, Folk Art and Native American Art. The attractive grounds contain a re-created piece of George Washington's garden at Mount Vernon.

☎ 01225 460503 www.americanmuseum.org

Antony House (NT) — 150 A2

On the Lynher River estuary, north-west of Torpoint, this fine example of an 18th century manor house contains collections of paintings, textiles and furniture. The grounds, landscaped by Humphrey Repton, contain the National Collection of Hemerocallis.

☎ 01752 812191

Avebury Ring

Arlington Court (NT) — 163 G1

An early 19th century house on the site of two previous buildings. The 3000 acre (1200ha) estate was home to the Chichester family for over 500 years, and the house contains many of the diverse and exotic acquisitions of the last owner, Miss Rosalie Chichester. There are extensive formal and informal gardens, delightful woodland walks, a small carriage museum and a bat cave where a large colony of lesser horseshoe bats can be observed by closed-circuit television.

☎ 01271 850296 www.nationaltrust.org.uk

Ashton Court Estate — 352 A3

A magnificent estate of 850 acres (340ha) designed by Humphrey Repton and comprising woods and parkland, red and fallow deer herds, and outstanding views over Bristol and beyond. A diversity of natural habitats makes this an important wildlife site, of great interest to naturalists, while for the more physically active there are mountain bike, orienteering and horse riding trails, and golf courses. The site is also host to a range of events, notably the Bristol International Balloon Festival held every year in August.

The 19th century mansion houses a visitor centre and café but is not otherwise open to the public.

☎ 0117 963 9174 www.bristol-city.gov.uk

At-Bristol — 391 C1

Three separate attractions housed in a new complex close to the waterfront in the centre of Bristol, providing a fascinating range of educational entertainment.

'Wildwalk' is a stroll through plant and animal evolution using displays and interactive exhibits.

'Explore' is an imaginative, interactive science exhibition divided into four themes related to the brain, engineering and technology, global communications, and the Curiosity Zone which explores the oddities of the physical environment.

The IMAX theatre is a four-storey high screen with surround sound, making the viewer feel part of the action. A range of short films can be seen each day, with the emphasis on science and wildlife.

☎ 0845 345 1235 www.at-bristol.org.uk

Athelhampton — 155 D3

A splendid 15th century manor house with impressive Grade I gardens. The central feature of the house is the Great Hall, built in 1493 by Sir Robert Martyn, a former Lord Mayor of London.

The 20 acre (8ha) garden was designed by Inigo Thomas in the late 19th century and, in addition to the world famous topiary pyramids, there are eight walled gardens inspired by the Renaissance, fountains, pavilions and a 16th century dovecote.

☎ 01305 848363 www.athelhampton.co.uk

Auk Walk — 147 E1

A clifftop walk near Trevalga which, between April and July, overlooks the nesting sites of puffins, guillemots and razorbills.

Avebury Ring & Alexander Keiller Museum (NT) — 168 C1

Around 4500 years old, this is possibly the largest stone circle in Europe, the surviving sarsen stones being enclosed by a substantial earthwork almost 1 mile (1.6km) in circumference. Within this there were two smaller stone circles, though little remains of the more northerly.

Information about Avebury Ring can be found in the Alexander Keiller Museum (for which there is a charge), named after the former owner of the site who endeavoured to restore the area following the plunder and removal of stones which took place, particularly in medieval times. The museum gives an excellent overview of the site, explains the known history and displays artefacts uncovered during archaeological excavations.

☎ 01672 539250 www.nationaltrust.org.uk
www.english-heritage.org.uk

Babbacombe Model Village — 151 F1

An ingenious miniature English landscape set in 4 acres (1.5ha) of beautiful gardens with over 400 models built on a scale of 1:12. Originally intended to represent the archetypal English village and its rural surroundings, the project has expanded to incorporate a comprehensive range of buildings, with particular emphasis on domestic architecture. The setting is enhanced by the many attractive water features flowing through the gardens, and is particularly enchanting in summer when illuminated at dusk.

☎ 01803 315315 www.babbacombemodelvillage.co.uk

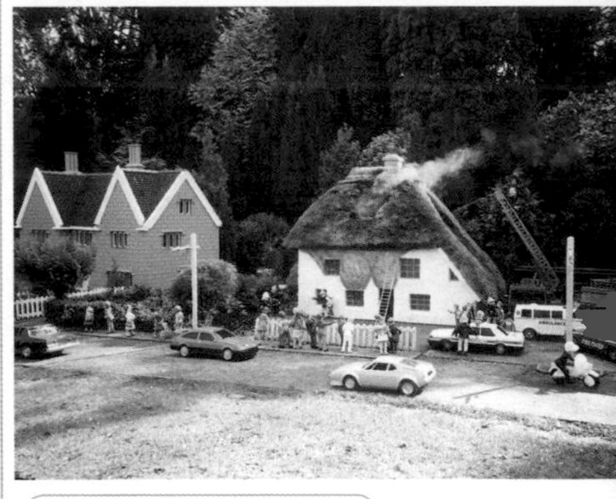

Babbacombe Model Village

Barrington Court (NT) — 153 G1

A lovely Elizabethan manor house owned by the National Trust but let as showrooms for antique furniture. The gardens, influenced by Gertrude Jekyll, are a notable feature, consisting of a series of walled, themed 'rooms' such as the White Garden, Lily Garden and Kitchen Garden.

☎ 01460 241938 www.nationaltrust.org.uk

Bath — 167 E1

The only hot springs in the country are the source of Bath's name and of its importance as a fashionable resort and tourist attraction. This in turn generated the wealth which enabled the construction of the wonderful Georgian buildings which have helped to give Bath its World Heritage Site status.

Even before the Romans arrived and built the amazing baths complex, the hot springs were a site of veneration for local Celtic tribes. However, following the Romans' departure, interest was lost in the springs and it was not until the early 18th century that it attained its position as the epitome of fashionable society. This was due largely to the efforts of Richard 'Beau' Nash, who transformed Bath from provincial town to unrivalled centre of fashion. Sea bathing eventually superseded spas as the fashionable cure, but Bath was left with a splendid architectural heritage with masterpieces such as the Circus, Royal Crescent, Assembly Rooms and Pulteney Bridge.

www.visitbath.co.uk

Bath Abbey
388 E2

Built between 1499 – 1616, this is one of England's last great medieval churches, known by the Elizabethans as the 'Lantern of the West' because of the abundance of stained glass. The most impressive example is the great East Window, illustrating 56 scenes from the life of Christ.

Externally, the most remarkable feature is the west front, carved angels commemorating a dream of the founder, Bishop Oliver King. A small but informative museum in the vaults traces the abbey's history.

☎ 01225 422462

Batsford Arboretum
197 D4

Overlooking the Evenlode Valley, at 55 acres (22 ha) this is one of the largest collections of trees and shrubs in the country with over 1500 species. The park dates back to the 17th century when the original gardens were more formal than those seen today. This transition took place in two stages – towards the end of the 19th century by Algernon Freeman-Mitford who created the wild garden, and after World War II when the wild garden had fallen into neglect and the 2nd Lord Dulverton set about creating the arboretum. Some of the features of the original wild garden are still present – the Japanese Rest House and Buddha, Rockeries and the Hermits Cave.

☎ 01386 701441 www.batsarb.co.uk

Bennetts Water Garden
154 C4

An 8 acre (3ha) area of landscaped lakes, formerly clay pits from the local brickworks. With 150 varieties of waterlily flowering in summer, this is one of the best displays in the country, and there are connections with Monet's Garden at Giverny. There is also a small museum devoted to local village life and the history of the site.

☎ 01305 785150 www.waterlily.co.uk

Berkeley Castle & Gardens
181 F3

Completed in 1153 by Lord Maurice de Berkeley for Henry II in order to guard the Severn Estuary, the layout of the castle has changed little since the end of the 14th century. It is England's oldest inhabited castle and is still home to the Berkeley family after 25 generations. The cell where King Edward II was held captive for 18 months before his murder in 1327 can be seen, as can the 30ft (9m) deep dungeon. The extensive grounds feature a butterfly house, lily pond and the bowling alley where Elizabeth I played bowls with her courtiers.

☎ 01453 810332 www.berkeley-castle.com

Bath – Royal Crescent

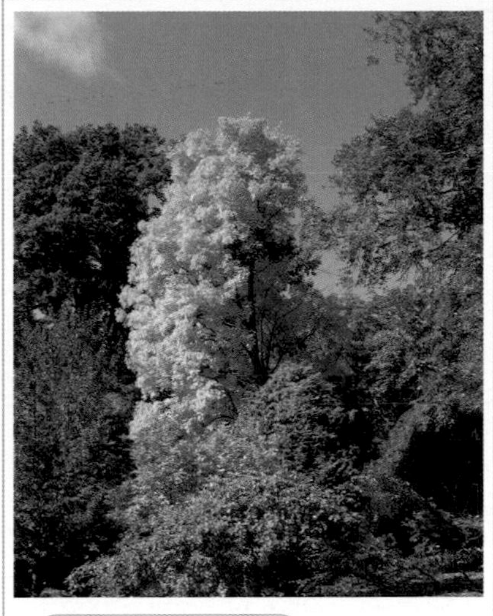

Batsford Arboretum

Berry Pomeroy Castle
151 E1

With a reputation as one of the most haunted castles in England, this decidedly atmospheric ruin is splendidly located on a crag above a wooded valley. The oldest part is thought to date from the 14th century, but the main building, a large mansion, was built between 1548 – 1613 and was subsequently abandoned later in the 17th century.

☎ 01803 866618 www.english-heritage.org.uk

Bicton Park Gardens
153 D4

Delightful gardens and parkland covering 63 acres (25ha) featuring an amazing 19th century domed Palm House, arguably one of the world's most beautiful garden buildings. Other highlights include the Italian Garden and Pinetum. For the less horticulturally inclined, there is a rural life museum, a 1.5 mile (2.5km) narrow-gauge railway and adventure playground.

☎ 01395 568465 www.bictongardens.co.uk

Big Sheep, The
163 E3

Innovative attraction combining traditional sheep-related activities such as shearing, lambing, feeding and sheepdog trials, with more unusual enterprises such as Ewetopia, an adventure play area, sheep racing, complete with knitted jockeys, and duck trials.

☎ 01237 478800 www.thebigsheep.co.uk

Birdland
197 D5

Birdland opened in 1957 and moved to its present 7 acre (3ha) natural setting in 1989. There are over 500 birds with more than 50 aviaries for parrots, hornbills and toucans, amongst many other species. The River Windrush winds through the park creating a natural habitat for flamingos, pelicans and storks. The penguins are always popular, especially at feeding time.

☎ 01451 820480 www.birdland.co.uk

Blaise Castle House Museum
352 A1

A late 18th century castle folly in beautiful grounds designed by Humphrey Repton. The museum has a fine social history collection including an excellent range of domestic equipment, a Victorian toy room including model trains, period costumes and paintings.

☎ 0117 903 9818 www.bristol-city.gov.uk

Bodmin & Wenford Railway
147 E3

Operating from Bodmin General station, this is Cornwall's only standard-gauge steam railway. It consists of two lines, one interchanging with the main line at Bodmin Parkway. Most trains are steam-hauled over 6.5 miles (10km) of track.

☎ 0845 125 9678 www.bodminandwenfordrailway.co.uk

Bodmin Moor
147 F2

A large expanse of granite moorland dotted with tors in the north and many Bronze Age and Neolithic sites, particularly in the south. Brown Willy, Cornwall's highest point at 1377ft (420m), is located here in the bleaker northern part of the moor. Daphne du Maurier's famous novel 'Jamaica Inn' is set on the moor around Altarnun and Bolventor.

Bowood House & Gardens
167 G1

Built in the early 18th century, but partly demolished in 1955, Bowood is an elegant Georgian mansion. Its most notable features are Robert Adam's magnificent library, the laboratory where Joseph Priestley discovered oxygen, the Orangery, now a picture gallery, and the Sculpture Gallery. The 2000 acre (800ha) grounds, however, are arguably Bowood's chief attraction. Landscaped by Lancelot 'Capability' Brown, complete with elegant parkland, Cascade Waterfall, Hermit's Cave and a Doric temple by the tranquil lake, they make a splendid backdrop to the house. For six weeks in spring the magnificent rhododendron gardens are open, with thousands of flowering bulbs elsewhere in the grounds. For children there is an excellent adventure playground and soft play area.

☎ 01249 812102 www.bowood.org

Bradley Manor
152 B5

A small 15th century manor house in a tranquil setting of woodland and open fields. The Great Hall is a particularly interesting feature.

☎ 01626 354513 www.nationaltrust.org.uk

Brewers Quay
154 C5

A converted harbourside brewery housing a range of shops, activities and attractions.

'The Timewalk' depicts 600 years of Weymouth's history as seen through the eyes of the brewery cat and her predecessors. 'Brewery Days' looks at the area's brewing heritage through interactive displays and audiovisual presentations. 'Discovery' is a hands-on science centre with over 60 interactive items.

☎ 01305 777622 www.brewers-quay.co.uk

Bristol City Museum & Art Gallery
352 B2

One of the largest museums in the south west, housed in an impressive Edwardian Baroque building. There are detailed displays relating to local geology, archaeology and natural history, interesting temporary exhibitions and some unusual art exhibits.

☎ 0117 922 3571 www.bristol-city.gov.uk

Bristol Industrial Museum
391 C1

Located in the Floating Harbour in a converted goods transit shed, the museum is home to a wide range of exhibits relating to Bristol's industrial heritage. The port's history is told through models, paintings and memorabilia, and there are exhibitions on the printing and packaging industry, and Bristol's part in the infamous slave trade triangle.

☎ 0117 925 1470 www.bristol-city.gov.uk

Bristol Zoo
352 B2

For a generation brought up on safari parks, Bristol Zoo might seem a rather modest establishment, but there is plenty to see. It comprises a 12 acre (5ha) site with delightful gardens providing a colourful backdrop to over 300 fascinating species with a particular emphasis on conservation of wildlife and its natural habitats. There are zoo trails and a good adventure playground for children.

☎ 0117 973 8951 www.bristolzoo.org.uk

British Empire & Commonwealth Museum
391 C3

A fascinating museum detailing the history of the British Empire and subsequent development of the Commonwealth, from the voyage of John Cabot in 1497 to the present day. There are 20 themed galleries devoted to exploration, trade and conquest, illustrated by a wide selection of artefacts, costumes, photographs and film clips, with an imaginative variety of interactive exhibits.

☎ 0117 925 4980 www.empiremuseum.co.uk

Brownsea Island
155 G4

Located in the sheltered waters of Poole harbour, this 500 acre (200ha) island boasts a wide range of natural habitats such as saline lagoon, heathland and freshwater lakes. This haven for wildlife is home to such rarities as red squirrels, glow worms, water voles, dragonflies and over 20 species of butterfly. There are hides to observe both breeding colonies and migrant birds, and a boardwalk through reed beds passes near the heronry.

Historically, the island is chiefly famous as the site of Lord Baden-Powell's first camp in 1907 which led to the formation of the Scout movement.

Access is by pedestrian ferry from the mainland, and away from the reserve there are woodland walks with delightful views.

☎ 01202 707744 www.nationaltrust.org.uk

Buckfast Abbey
150 D1

This was originally founded in 1018, but was abandoned after the Dissolution of the Monasteries until 1882 when Benedictine monks took over the site and rebuilt the abbey in a traditional Anglo-Norman style with some particularly striking stained glass work. There is an informative exhibition on the site and shops selling a variety of produce from Benedictine monasteries across Europe. Physic, Sensory and Lavender gardens have been re-created in the grounds.

☎ 01364 645500 www.buckfast.org.uk

Buckland Abbey (NT)
150 A1

Originally a 13th century monastery overlooking the Tavy valley, this was subsequently converted to a family home, initially owned by the sea-faring Grenville family. In 1581 the property was bought by Sir Francis Drake and it remained in his family until 1942. Features include the fine, oak-panelled Great Hall, exhibitions on Drake's achievements and adventures, Elizabethan gardens and craft workshops.

☎ 01822 853607 www.nationaltrust.org.uk

Cadhay
153 D3

An attractive Tudor manor house approached through an avenue of lime trees. The fine 15th century timbered roof of a previous dwelling has been incorporated into the Great Hall.

☎ 01404 812432 www.eastdevon.net

Caen Hill Locks
168 A1

An impressive flight of 29 locks on the Kennet and Avon Canal at Devizes, raising the water level 240ft (73m) in 2.5 miles (4km)

Canonteign Falls
152 B4

Located in a natural hillside gorge landscaped 160 years ago, this claims to be England's highest waterfall at almost 220ft (66m). After being neglected for years, the site has been restored to reveal striking rock formations, lakes and waterfalls. Additional features include a Victorian fern garden, wetland nature reserve, children's play areas and adventure playground.

☎ 01647 252434 www.canonteignfalls.com

Carnewas & Bedruthan Steps
146 C3

Spectacular coastal scenery of cliffs and rocky beach. Access to the beach is via a stairway from the clifftop at Carnewas, where a National Trust shop is housed in a former mine office. The Steps are a series of rock stacks along the beach, produced as a consequence of marine erosion.

☎ 01637 860563 www.nationaltrust.org.uk

Castle Drogo (NT)
152 A3

Contrary to appearances, this is an early 20th century building designed by Sir Edwin Lutyens and built in an outstanding position above the Teign valley. Constructed of specially quarried granite, the foundations were cut into the hillside, and in some rooms the exposed rock can be seen. Overall, it presents a striking combination of medieval style with modern comfort.

Outside, established formal gardens provide a colourful setting in spring and summer, and there are lovely woodland walks, some providing magnificent views over the Teign valley.

☎ 01647 433306 www.nationaltrust.org.uk

Chambercombe Manor
163 F1

Located in a tranquil valley, Chambercombe was mentioned in the Domesday Book, though the present house dates from the 12th century. Eight rooms are on display, with period furniture from Elizabethan to Victorian times. Very atmospheric, and rumoured to be haunted.

☎ 01271 862624 www.chambercombemanor.co.uk

Cheddar Gorge & Caves
166 B2

Cheddar Gorge is the most dramatic natural feature of the Mendip area, a mile (1.6km) long chasm with cliffs, almost vertical in places, around 400ft (120m) high. A drive through the gorge, for which access is free, is a breathtaking experience, more so when taken out of season as, not surprisingly, this is a popular attraction and can be crowded in summer. For walkers, there is a 3 mile (5km) clifftop circular walk which provides fine views, and which can be accessed by Jacob's Ladder, 274 steps up the side of the gorge.

The lower end of the gorge in Cheddar village has succumbed to commercial tourist pressure, but the caves offer visitors the chance to see some amazing stalactite and stalagmite formations in the dramatic Gough's Cave. Cox's Cave nearby is smaller, with narrow passages and some striking coloured formations. There is also an exhibition on the life of a cave dwelling man, based on remains discovered in the caves dating from Palaeolithic times.

☎ 01934 742343 www.cheddarcaves.co.uk

Chedworth Roman Villa (NT)
182 C1

Discovered in 1864 and now owned by the National Trust, the Villa sits at the head of a small valley overlooking the River Colne. It would have been one of the grandest houses in the Cotswolds at the time it was built, with evidence of 32 rooms, and there are still substantial remains including two Roman baths and some extremely well-preserved mosaic flooring. There are audiovisual demonstrations and a museum within the grounds.

☎ 01242 890256 www.nationaltrust.org.uk

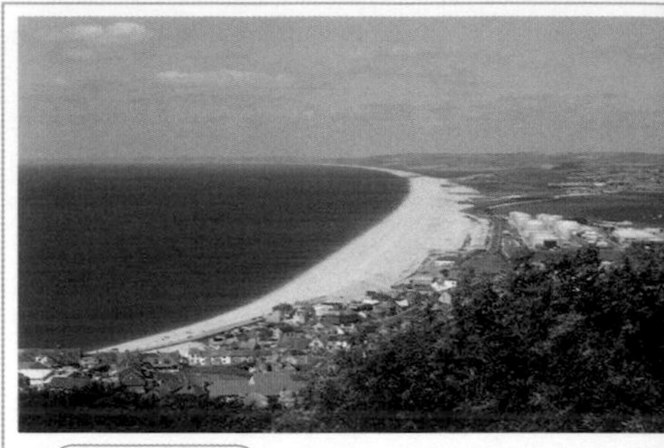

Chesil Beach

Chesil Beach
154 B4

An 18 mile (29km) shingle ridge running from Burton Bradstock to Portland, effectively tying the island to the mainland. South of Abbotsbury the ridge is detached from the coast, enclosing The Fleet, a brackish lagoon and setting for J. Meade Faulkner's definitive smuggling story 'Moonfleet'.

An interesting feature of the beach is the increase in size of its component flint and quartzite stones, from pea size in the west to fist size at Portland, where the ridge can be up to 45ft (14m) high. This is a popular site with sea anglers, but powerful offshore currents, probably a factor in the feature's formation, make it very dangerous for bathers.

Chettle House
155 F1

A delightful Queen Anne manor house providing an excellent example of English Baroque architecture. Complemented by 5 acres (2ha) of attractive gardens. Limited opening.

☎ 01258 830858

Christchurch Priory
347 D3

Considered to be the longest parish church in Britain at over 300ft (90m), this splendid medieval monastic building is noted for its exceptional interior carvings. Access to the tower, via 120 steps up a spiral staircase, is sometimes available for a small charge, and is worth it for the splendid views.

☎ 01202 485804 www.christchurchpriory.org

Chysauster Ancient Village
144 B3

A late Iron Age courtyard village believed to have been inhabited at least up until the Roman occupation. The settlement consisted of eight or more oval stone houses, each surrounding a courtyard, and a stone wall enclosed the whole complex. Within the houses some rooms were for human occupation, others for animals or food storage.

☎ 01831 757934 www.english-heritage.org.uk

Cleeve Abbey
164 D3

A late 12th/early 13th century Cistercian abbey particularly noted for its well preserved cloisters, considered amongst the finest in England. Other distinctive features include the remarkable timber roof in the refectory and medieval wall paintings.

☎ 01984 640377 www.english-heritage.org.uk

Cleeve Common
196 B5

Cleeve Common is the high spot of the Cotswold Hills, rising to 1083ft (330 m) above sea level, with, on a clear day, far-reaching views across to the Malvern Hills and the Brecon Beacons in South Wales. The Common is protected by the Wildlife and Countryside Act and is a Site of Special Scientific Interest. The area was cleared of forest over 10,000 years ago and has been used for livestock grazing ever since. Rock climbing is popular on Cleeve Cloud and the public golf course is a test on the exposed hilltop.

☎ 01242 522878 www.cleevecommon.freeserve.co.uk

Clevedon Court (NT)
180 D5

Surviving virtually intact from its construction in 1320, the house incorporates parts of older buildings including a 12th century tower and 13th century hall. The contents include fine collections of glass, Eltonware and furniture, and there are sketches by William Makepeace Thackeray who wrote much of 'Vanity Fair' here. There are attractive terraced gardens giving good sea views.

☎ 01275 872257 www.nationaltrust.org.uk

Clouds Hill (NT)
155 E3

A tiny, rather isolated cottage which formed a retreat for T.E. Lawrence (Lawrence of Arabia) following his desert achievements. The four rooms on display contain memorabilia and an exhibition on his life. Open only part of each week.

☎ 01929 405616 www.nationaltrust.org.uk

Clovelly
162 D3

Cars are prohibited from this unique village where a steep cobbled street lined with delightful, flower-covered, whitewashed houses runs down to a tiny harbour. As the streets are too steep for motor transport, donkeys were formerly used for conveying heavy loads and, although now superseded by hauled sledges, are still on hand for children's rides in summer.

The harbour and distinctive quay are the most memorable features and, although fishing is no longer of major importance, it is still a feature of village life. This, together with sympathetic management, ensures the village retains its character whilst proving a popular attraction.

☎ 01237 431781 www.clovelly.co.uk

Coleridge Cottage (NT)
165 E3

For three years from 1797, this was home to the poet Samuel Taylor Coleridge where he wrote, amongst other works, 'The Rime of the Ancient Mariner'. Part of the cottage containing his memorabilia is open to the public.

☎ 01278 732662 www.nationaltrust.org.uk

Coleton Fishacre (NT)
151 F2

Built in the Arts and Crafts style of the late 19th century for the D'Oyly Carte family, this house is distinguished for its internal decoration influenced by the Art Deco movement.

The garden is particularly noted for its range of tender and exotic plants which thrive in the sheltered, moist environment. The terrace gardens are delightful with their range of colour and diversity in summer, whilst woodland pathways through the less formal stream-fed valley lead to coastal walks with panoramic views.

☎ 01803 752466 www.nationaltrust.org.uk

Combe Martin Wildlife & Dinosaur Park
163 G1

A 25 acre (10ha) parkland, ideal for children, with a range of animals and birds including falconry displays, butterfly house, otter pool, sea lions, snow leopards, wolves and a large meerkat enclosure. The dinosaur museum houses not only fossils but also models animated by computer technology, the star being a full-size Tyrannosaurus Rex. There are also botanical gardens containing subtropical plants, and a range of indoor activities.

☎ 01271 882486 www.dinosaur-park.com

Compton Acres
347 B3

The attractive 10 acre (4ha) gardens were devised around 1920 by Thomas Simpson who wanted to create a series of separate garden 'rooms', each illustrating a specific national garden style. National styles include Japanese, Egyptian, Italian, Indian, Canadian, Spanish and Scottish, each with appropriate plants and statuary. The result is a series of delightful gardens in a location giving stunning views over Poole Harbour and surrounding hills.

☎ 01202 700778 www.comptonacres.co.uk

Compton Castle (NT)
151 E1

Built between the 14th and 16th centuries, this fortified manor house has been the Gilbert family home almost continuously for the last 600 years. The original buildings, dating from 1350 and fortified in Henry VIII's reign, have remained unaltered since.

☎ 01803 875740 www.nationaltrust.org.uk

Cookworthy Museum
150 D3

Opened in 1971, this fascinating museum, housed in the Old Grammar School, displays items associated with rural life and social history in the Kingsbridge area, particularly in the 19th and early 20th centuries.

☎ 01548 853235 www.devonmuseums.net

Corfe Castle (NT)
155 F4

A hilltop ruin which dominates the surrounding countryside. Built by the Normans in the late 11th century to replace an earlier Saxon structure which had been the site of the murder of King Edward the Martyr in AD978, the castle controlled the route through the Purbeck Hills. It was used as a prison, and subsequently as a treasury and hunting lodge by King John in the early 12th century, whilst Henry III added further walls, towers and gatehouses.

The last owners were the Bankes family, Lady Mary Bankes holding the castle against Parliamentary attack for a long period during the Civil War. The steep hillside and thick walls made the castle almost impregnable, and it required the treachery of one of the besieged officers for it to be taken. Subsequently, the destruction of the castle was ordered, and it is a credit to the soundness of the original construction that it took several months to reduce it to the ruin that can be seen today. The rubble was not wasted; much of it was used to build Corfe Castle village.

☎ 01929 481294 www.nationaltrust.org.uk

Cornish Cyder Farm, The
146 B4

Guided tours round probably the largest Cornish cider maker in Cornwall. The farm also produces liqueurs and other fruit products. Admission to the farm is free.

☎ 01872 573356 www.thecornishcyderfarm.co.uk

Cornish Engines (NT)
145 D2

Local engineer Richard Trevithick developed the high pressure steam system which originally powered these two impressive beam engines. Their purpose was to operate the winding gear to transport men and ore through the mineshafts and to pump out water from depths of around 1800ft (550m). The Industrial Discovery Centre on the same site provides an absorbing perspective on Cornwall's industrial heritage.

☎ 01209 315027

Cornish Seal Sanctuary
145 E4

On the Helford Estuary, just east of Gweek. One of Europe's leading marine animal rescue centres, comprising a hospital and rehabilitation pools, and caring for around 50 abandoned or injured seals and otters. Feeding demonstrations take place throughout the day.

☎ 01326 221361

Cotehele (NT)
150 A1

On the River Tamar just west of Calstock. Originally a medieval manor house, improved and enlarged by Sir Richard Edgcumbe and his son between 1490 and 1520. Subsequent alterations have not substantially affected their work, making this one of the least altered medieval houses in the country. The gardens provide all year round colour and are crossed by a network of woodland and riverside walks.

☎ 01579 351346

Cotswold Farm Park
196 D5

The park has a wide variety of animals including rare breeds, pets and working animals such as oxen and sheepdogs. The tractor school gives 3 to 12 year olds the chance to learn to drive battery and pedal powered tractors, and the Touch Barn enables visitors to get close to the smaller animals. There are daily and seasonal demonstrations such as milking, lambing and shearing.

☎ 01451 850307 www.cotswoldfarmpark.co.uk

Corfe Castle

Cotswold Hills — 182 A3

The Cotswolds, an Area of Outstanding Natural Beauty, run for 60 miles (96km) from Bath north eastwards to the Warwickshire border and eastwards towards Oxford. The hills are not particularly high – the high point of 1083ft (330m) is on Cleeve Common near Cheltenham – but the landscape is rich and varied, from rolling hills to steep sided valleys. The picturesque towns and villages are frequently busy, especially in the north, but there are many quiet and peaceful areas to be found. The 100 mile (160km) Cotswold Way winds its way from Chipping Campden in the north, southwards to Bath. Passing such places of interest as Hailes Abbey, Woodchester Mansion, the Tyndale Monument and the Stone Age long barrows of Belas Knap and Hetty Pegler's Tump, the walk is always interesting and takes in some of the country's finest countryside. The belt of limestone that stretches across central England gives the Cotswolds much of their character in the buildings and drystone walls that help to blend the towns and villages seamlessly with the open countryside.

☎ 01242 522878 www.cotswoldsaonb.com

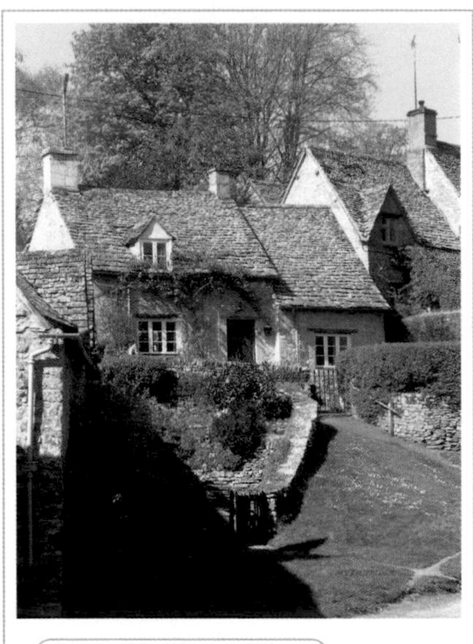

Cotswold village – Bibury

Cotswold Water Park — 182 C3

With 133 lakes formed as the result of gravel extraction and covering over 2000 acres (809ha), this is considered Britain's largest water park. The lakes provide a variety of associated watersports including angling, sailing, canoeing, water-skiing and windsurfing, but there are also land-based activities on offer. There are several nature reserves with public access within the country park areas, the bird life being of special interest. Opportunities abound for walking, cycling and adventure activities, and a bathing beach is open in summer. Access is free, but there is a charge for activities.

☎ 01285 862962 www.waterpark.org

Crealy Adventure Park — 152 D3

A good day out for families with children, having activities suitable for all ages and interests. These include adventure playgrounds, farm animals, a variety of rides and lakeside walks.

☎ 01395 233200 www.crealy.co.uk

Dartington Crystal — 151 D1

Guided tours of the factory enable visitors to learn about glass production, from the initial stage of blowing the molten glass through to the finishing process of completed items. A visitor centre traces the history of glass production and holds live demonstrations of glass-making skills, whilst the activity centre provides hands-on family entertainment. There is a large factory shop on site.

☎ 01805 626242 www.dartington.co.uk

Dartmoor — 149 F2

A National Park, perhaps the last untouched wilderness of southern England, this is an extensive, bare upland area of granite with clusters of rocky summits or tors of between 1000-2000ft (300-600m). Scenery ranges from almost featureless tracts of open moorland in the north, to the wooded valleys of the Teign and Dart in the south.

The more remote areas of high moorland have a rather forbidding reputation, enhanced in part by its use as an atmospheric setting for Sir Arthur Conan Doyle's story 'The Hound of the Baskervilles'. In good weather the area is outstanding walking country, with a mixture of old rail tracks (a legacy of former mineral extraction) and ancient footpaths. Possibly due to a more favourable past climate, there are around 2000 prehistoric sites on the moor, the Bronze Age village of Grimspound being perhaps the best example, and the area is considered one of the most significant locations for Bronze Age relics in Europe. The more wooded and hospitable moorland fringes are home to the many fast flowing streams tumbling down from the uplands, particularly attractive spots being Lydford Gorge and Becky Falls.

Dartmouth Castle — 151 E2

The first to be designed with specific respect to artillery use, this 15th century castle has a superb location on the narrow entrance to the Dart estuary. A contributor to the coastal defence system over the last 500 years, the building is still in good repair. Informative displays recount the castle's history.

☎ 01803 833588 www.english-heritage.org.uk

Dean Heritage Centre — 181 F1

Set around a restored corn mill and millpond, the centre looks at various aspects of the Forest of Dean – geology, hunting, crafts, the industrial heritage including iron and coal mining.

☎ 01594 822170 www.deanheritagemuseum.com

Dinosaur Museum — 154 C3

Devoted entirely to dinosaurs and their world, this museum has a range of imaginative and interactive exhibits. It is possible to handle some of the actual fossil bones and life-size reconstructions, and there is a wealth of factual information for visitors. There is a well-stocked shop.

☎ 01305 269880 www.dinosaur-museum.co.uk

Dobwalls Family Adventure Park — 147 G3

A theme park based on the miniature railway hobby of John Southern, a local farmer. Around 10 steam and diesel trains based on the American style railroads travel along 2 miles (3km) of track. Additional attractions include an impressive adventure playground, children's driving school and wildlife art gallery.

☎ 01579 320325

Dunster Castle & Gardens (NT) — 164 C3

Dating from at least Norman, and possibly Saxon times, the castle has a magnificent site on a wooded hill above the village of Dunster. The chief medieval relic is the 13th century gatehouse, while the main building, dating from 1617, was substantially remodelled for domestic use in Victorian times.

The 28 acre (11ha) gardens are equally interesting with unusual and subtropical plants, including the National Collection of Arbutus (strawberry trees), probably England's oldest lemon tree, camellias, magnolias and a fine display of spring bulbs. There are extensive views across Exmoor, the Quantock Hills and the Bristol Channel.

☎ 01643 821314 www.nationaltrust.org.uk

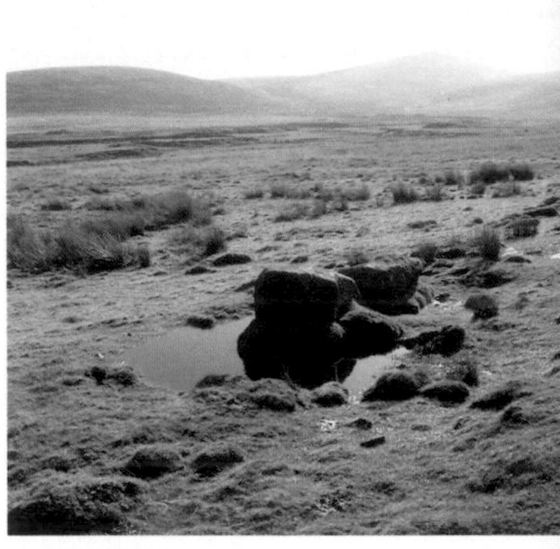

Dartmoor

Dunster Watermill — 164 C3

There was mention of a mill on this site in the Domesday Book, but the current building dates from the 18th century and has been restored. Visitors can watch the milling process and there is a collection of old-fashioned agricultural machinery, and a tearoom.

☎ 01643 821759 www.nationaltrust.org.uk

Durdle Door — 155 E4

This is a natural sea arch composed of Portland limestone formed where marine erosion has exploited an area of weakness in the rock. A short but energetic and breathtaking hike of just over 1 mile (1.6km) west along the cliffs from Lulworth Cove brings the walker to this fascinating feature. Cheats can park at the nearby holiday park for a small fee and stroll to the coast.

Dyrham Park (NT) — 181 G5

Impressive and little altered late 17th century house set in 268 acres (105ha) of deer park, built for William Blathwayt, a minister in William III's government. It contains some fine furnishings, paintings and a collection of Delftware, popular at the time in deference to the king's Dutch origins. Park and ride access is arranged to preserve the original setting.

☎ 0117 937 2501 www.nationaltrust.org.uk

East Lambrook Manor — 154 A1

Delightful Grade I cottage style garden created in the mid 20th century by Margery Fish and portrayed in her popular book 'We Made a Garden'. Established with the conservation of endangered species in mind, the garden was neglected in the 1970s but has since been sympathetically restored to provide a wealth of colour and scent, including the National Collection of Geraniums. The house is not open to the public, but the 17th century malthouse is used for art exhibitions.

☎ 01460 240328 www.eastlambrook.com

East Somerset Railway
167 D3

Also known as the Strawberry Line, steam trains run along the 2.5 mile (4km) track which includes a 1 in 56 gradient, one of the steepest for an English preserved railway. It was founded by the wildlife artist David Shepherd and the station complex includes an art gallery, as well as an engine shed and workshops. It is advisable to phone in advance for train times.

☎ 01749 880417 www.eastsomersetrailway.org

Eden Project
147 E4

This has been described as 'the world's largest greenhouse' but that is a gross oversimplification of the botanical diversity contained within.

Opened in 2001 and still undergoing further development, the Eden Project was devised by Tim Smit (who also redeveloped the Lost Gardens of Heligan). Its purpose is to illustrate how the human race depends on plants, and aims to provide levels of interest appropriate to all ages and scientific abilities.

The site was originally a vast clay pit 200ft (60m) deep and 35 acres (14ha) in area. It comprises two biomes constructed from transparent hexagonal plastic on a galvanized steel tubing framework. Each of these has its own controlled environment designed to replicate conditions in one of the world's major climatic regions. Outside can be found plants from temperate climates such as the prairies, Himalayas and western Europe. Displays in each area show how man interacts with these environments and the uses to which the plants are put.

A deservedly popular attraction, which at peak times may be closed to prevent overcrowding.

☎ 01726 811911 www.edenproject.com

Eden Project

Edmondsham House

155 G1

Delightful Tudor manor house with later Georgian additions set in an attractive 6 acre (2ha) garden with lovely spring bulbs, unusual trees and an organic walled garden. There is also an interesting octagonal Victorian dairy and the remains of a medieval cock fighting pit. Limited opening.

☎ 01725 517207

Escot
153 D3

220 acres (88ha) of parkland designed by Lancelot 'Capability' Brown and containing a wide range of animals and related activities including falconry displays, bear enclosures, otters, an extensive collection of tropical and freshwater fish, maze and wetland conservation area. There are also children's activities and pleasant walks through the colourful gardens and parkland. Access to the aquatic centre and wetlands area is free.

☎ 01404 822188 www.escot-devon.co.uk

Exeter Cathedral
398 B2

Miraculously escaping major structural damage during the World War II bombing of Exeter, the cathedral and its close provide an historic retreat amidst the post-war rebuilding of the city centre. Evidence of Christian worship on this site dates from the 5th century, but the oldest features of the current building are the twin Norman towers dating from the early 12th century. Much of the cathedral was rebuilt during the late 13th and 14th centuries, building materials being local stone from Beer and Purbeck limestone, and this provides perhaps England's finest example of Decorated Gothic architecture. Other notable aspects are the 14th century minstrels' gallery, the bishop's throne which dates from 1312 and is one of the finest examples of wood carving surviving from this period, the elaborate choir stalls with 13th century misericords and the 500 year old astronomical clock. Of more recent interest are the Exeter Rondels, delightfully embroidered cushions on the north and south walls of the nave depicting, in around 14 million stitches, scenes of local and national history.

☎ 01392 255573 www.exeter-cathedral.org.uk

Exmoor
164 A3

Unlike the other moorlands of the south-west peninsula, Exmoor is composed of sandstone rather than granite, a feature reflected in its scenery which is less bleak than its neighbours. Acidic soils give rise to a typical high moorland flora of heathers interspersed with bilberry, though on the fringes are pleasant wooded river valleys which provide a greater diversity of wildlife than the upland plateau.

There are many attractive places to visit, including the area around Oare and Badgworthy Water (setting for the novel 'Lorna Doone'), Tarr Steps, and the little towns of Dulverton, Dunster, Porlock and Washford. Dunkery Beacon, the highest point at 1703ft (519m), provides views as far as the Brecon Beacons to the north and the Mendips to the east. The moor ends abruptly at the coast with a series of headlands and cliffs, the latter being amongst the highest in England. Minehead is the chief coastal resort, but Watchet, Blue Anchor and Porlock Weir are well worth a visit. Over 600 miles (960km) of foot and bridlepath cross the moor, making it a popular area for walking and riding.

Farleigh Hungerford Castle
167 E2

Extensive ruins of a 14th century castle built by Sir Thomas Hungerford. The chapel has undergone major conservation work and contains particularly fine wall paintings, stained glass and tombs of the Hungerford family.

☎ 01225 754026 www.english-heritage.org.uk

Finch Foundry (NT)
149 G1

Opened in 1814, this water-powered forge produced hand tools for the agricultural and mining industries until 1960. Regular demonstrations show the three waterwheels driving the massive tilt hammers and grindstone.

☎ 01837 840046 www.nationaltrust.org.uk

Flambards Village Theme Park
145 D4

A theme park combining historical re-creations with the more characteristic adventure rides such as roller coaster and log flume.

The Victorian Village comprises shops and houses furnished and equipped with original items, while 'Britain in the Blitz' is an authentic representation of a street blitzed in World War II.

☎ 01326 573404

Fleet Air Arm Museum
166 C5

A museum dedicated to the history of maritime aviation and in particular the Royal Naval Air Service. There are around 40 historic aircraft on display, together with a range of exhibits – a particular highlight is the Carrier Hall which contains a representation of a 1970s aircraft carrier. The Restoration Hangar has a viewing window for visitors to observe ongoing projects. For younger visitors there is an adventure playground and a flight simulator.

☎ 01935 840565 www.fleetairarm.com

Forde Abbey
153 G2

In a superb location on the banks of the River Axe, this former Cistercian monastery, founded in 1140, became a private home in 1649. The beautifully furnished rooms have splendid plaster ceilings, and a particular treasure is the set of Mortlake Tapestries of designs originally drawn for the Sistine Chapel.

The 30 acre (12ha) gardens are considered amongst the best in England, with borders displaying vivid colour, an impressive rockery, wonderful bog garden with drifts of Asiatic primulas and a background of sweeping lawns and mature specimen trees.

☎ 01460 221900 www.fordeabbey.co.uk

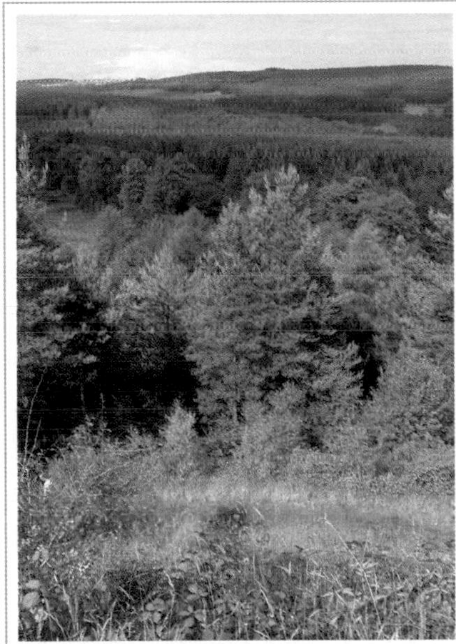

Forest of Dean

Forest of Dean
181 F1

Lying between the Rivers Wye and Severn, this former royal hunting forest has the largest area of 150 year old oak trees in Britain. Ponds, streams, an arboretum and nature reserve make this an area where peace and tranquilty can be enjoyed along with a rich cultural and industrial heritage which can be investigated through several themed trails. Speech House is now a hotel and conference centre but was built in 1676 as a hunting lodge for Charles II. It later becoming a meeting place for the locals and is still a focal point for the entire forest. Amongst the diverse flora and fauna are rare birds, wild boar and even an occasional polecat. There is ample opportunity for outdoor pursuits – canoeing, caving, climbing, cycling and horse riding or just a leisurely stroll around one of the many lakes and ponds.

☎ 01594 812388 www.forestofdean.gov.uk

Geevor Tin Mine 144 A3

A working tin mine until 1990, this is one of the largest mining history sites in the country. The mine's surface buildings have been restored and visitors can look round the processing plants where the ore was crushed. A highlight is an underground tour of an adit, or horizontal passage, which gives the merest hint of the former working conditions. A small museum has a model of the site plan and describes the method of tin production.

☎ 01736 788662 www.geevor.com

Glastonbury Abbey 166 B4

Magnificent ruins of an historic abbey whose foundation by Saxon kings in the 7th century probably predates the town. The repeated target of Viking attacks in the 8th and 9th centuries, the abbey's fortunes were revitalised by St Dunstan's appointment as abbot in AD940, and the building was considerably enlarged. A devastating fire in 1184, and the subsequent need for rebuilding funds, led to the Arthurian legend when the monks fortuitously 'discovered' the bodies of Arthur and Guinevere buried in the graveyard.

The abbey did not survive the Dissolution of the Monasteries, but the remains, together with an interpretation area, clearly indicate its wealth and importance in medieval times. The Glastonbury Thorn, legendary off-shoot of Joseph of Arimathea's staff, still grows in the grounds.

☎ 01458 832267 www.glastonburyabbey.com

Glastonbury Tor 166 C4

This solitary mound of Triassic rock rises 518ft (158m) above the southern edge of the Somerset Levels in an area subject to tidal inundations as recently as the early 17th century. The tor was settled in Neolithic times with a lake village at its base. The summit tower has been re-opened after structural repairs and the tor can be reached by a park and ride bus from the abbey, for which there is a small charge.

Goonhilly Satellite Earth Station

Glendurgan (NT) 145 E4

Located at the mouth of the Helford Estuary, this splendid 40 acre (16ha) valley garden was created in 1820. It contains many fine specimen trees, including a poplar which grew 79ft (24m) in 14 years, and an interesting laurel maze. In spring there is an outstanding display of magnolias, camellias and wild flowers.

☎ 01326 862090 www.nationaltrust.org.uk

Gloucester Cathedral 399 B2

Christian worship has taken place on this site since AD679 though the present building was started in 1089 and consecrated in 1100. King Henry III was crowned here, the only monarch to have been crowned outside Westminster since the Norman conquest. The 14th century fan vaulted cloisters are amongst the earliest and finest in the world. There are frequent exhibitions and guided tours to the top of the tower (for which there is a charge), reached by climbing 269 steps.

☎ 01452 528095 www.gloucestercathedral.org.uk

Gloucestershire & Warwickshire Railway 196 C5

Originally part of the Great Western main line from Cheltenham to Birmingham which closed in 1960, this steam and diesel railway passes through picturesque Cotswold scenery during a 20 mile (32km) round trip from Toddington to Cheltenham Racecourse. There is a static display of locomotives and rolling stock at Toddington station.

☎ 01242 621405 www.gwsr.plc.uk

Godolphin House 144 C3

Dating from around 1475, this delightful Tudor/Stuart mansion was for generations home to the Godolphin family whose fortune was founded on tin. The house contains some fine 16th and 17th century English oak furniture and paintings, and there are interesting formal medieval gardens and a wagon collection in the Elizabethan stables.

☎ 01736 763194 www.godolphinhouse.com

Golden Cap 154 A3

This sea cliff, the highest on the south coast at 626ft (191m), is named and formed from a sandstone outcrop weathered to a golden brown. There are spectacular views from the summit, particularly the panorama from Start Point in the west to Portland in the east.

www.nationaltrust.org.uk

Goonhilly Satellite Earth Station 145 E4

Located on the barren uplands of the Lizard peninsula, this is one of the world's largest satellite communications centres, with a site comprising more than 60 satellite dishes. The main dish, measuring 108ft (33m), has listed building status. The station deals with huge numbers of television broadcasts, international telephone calls and e-mails via satellite equipment and fibre optic cables.

The informative visitor centre is host to a range of activities including its interactive exhibition area with high speed internet access and virtual imaging. A guided tour of the site, which is a National Nature Reserve, is also available.

☎ 0800 679593 www.goonhilly.bt.com

Great Chalfield Manor (NT) 167 F1

Built in the late 15th century and sensitively restored in Edwardian times, this delightful moated manor house has beautiful oriel windows and the original Great Hall, complete with minstrels' gallery.

☎ 01225 782239 www.nationaltrust.org.uk

Hailes Abbey (NT) 196 C4

This Cistercian abbey was founded in 1246 and in 1270 was gifted a phial containing what was said to be the blood of Christ. After the 1539 Dissolution, parts of the site survived as a mansion house but fell into disuse in the 18th century. Excavation of the heavily overgrown site took place in the late 19th century. Little is left of the buildings apart from the remains of the cloister arches.

☎ 01242 602398 www.nationaltrust.org.uk

Hardy Monument 154 C4

Standing 770ft (240m) above sea level on the highest point of Black Down Hill, this 70ft (21m) monument was erected in memory of Thomas Masterman Hardy, captain of the *Victory* at the Battle of Trafalgar. 121 stone steps lead to the top from where there are magnificent views.

Hardy's Cottage 154 D3

A small cob and thatch cottage with delightful garden, birthplace of the novelist Thomas Hardy in 1840 and built by his great grandfather. Two of Hardy's books were written here and set in the local area.

☎ 01305 262366 www.nationaltrust.org.uk

Hartland Quay 162 C3

An isolated hamlet at the end of a toll road (charge in summer only), dwarfed by dramatic cliffs whose contorted structure provides evidence of former massive earth movements. Reduced now to a few cottages and tourist facilities, including a museum depicting the area's history, Hartland Quay was once a thriving little port supplying this remote area. Walks on the surrounding cliffs provide breathtaking views of this austere coastline.

www.elmscott.freeservers.com

Hay Tor Granite Tramway 152 A5

A relic of the former granite quarrying industry, these tracks, constructed of the stone they were built to carry, run from the flanks of Hay Tor to Stover Canal some 10 miles (16km) away.

Hestercombe 165 F5

Three centuries of garden history are contained in this 50 acre (20ha) Grade I garden.

The Georgian landscape garden, designed in the late 1750s by Coplestone Warre Bampfylde whose family owned the estate from 1391 – 1872, comprises lakes, pleasant woodland walks and temples set in 40 acres (16ha). The Victorian garden was created for Viscount Portman in the late 19th century, and in summer the formal bedding provides an exuberance of colour. However, Hestercombe is best known for its Edwardian garden, designed by Sir Edwin Lutyens and planted by Gertrude Jekyll in what is considered to be their finest collaboration.

☎ 01823 413923 www.hestercombegardens.com

Hestercombe

Hidcote Manor Gardens (NT) 197 D3

The Hidcote estate was bought by a wealthy American widow in 1907. The garden was created by her son, Lawrence Johnston, who took a keen interest in gardening which grew to a point where his designs were to have influences on many other gardens, for example Sissinghurst. The garden is arranged as a series of outdoor 'rooms', creating many different moods as a journey through the garden is taken. The garden is now in the ownership of the National Trust.

☎ 01386 438333

Hidcote Manor Gardens

Holnicote Estate (NT) — 164 C3

Given to the National Trust in 1944 by Sir Richard Acland, the estate consists of more than 12,000 acres (5042ha) of varied scenery, ranging from moors and woodlands, to cliffs and beaches. It includes the high points of Exmoor at Dunkery and Selworthy Beacons, with their sensational views, and a 5 mile (8km) stretch of coastline. The village of Selworthy, one of the prettiest on the moor, was built by the Acland family for their estate workers.

☎ 01643 862452 www.nationaltrust.org.uk

Horton Court (NT) — 181 G4

The remains of a 12th century rectory, probably the oldest in England, consisting of a Norman hall and a particularly good example of an ambulatory.

☎ 0117 937 2501 www.nationaltrust.org.uk

Iford Manor — 167 E2

Delightful Grade I early 20th century garden in a hillside setting by the River Frome, formerly owned by the architect and landscape gardener Harold Peto. It was designed in an Italianate style, complete with terraces, colonnade, cloisters, statuary and fountains, but there is also a lovely meadow of naturalised bulbs, notably martagon lilies. There are magnificent views of the local countryside.

☎ 01225 863146 www.ifordmanor.co.uk

Jurassic Coast — 153

This stretch of East Devon and Dorset coastline, between Exmouth in the west and Studland in the east, has been designated a World Heritage Site. Its outstanding geological and palaeontological locations, coupled with stunning and varied coastal scenery, make a visit almost compulsory to appreciate this fine example of the natural landscape.

www.jurassiccoast.com

Kennack Sands — 145 E5

Two sheltered, sandy beaches, considered amongst the cleanest in Britain, located in an Area of Outstanding Natural Beauty.

Killerton (NT) — 152 C2

A hillside garden of around 20 acres (8ha) landscaped by John Veitch. The garden is particularly lovely in spring, although attractive throughout the year. The 18th century house contains period furniture and is home to a significant costume collection which changes annually. The extensive surrounding parkland provides delightful walks.

☎ 01392 881345 www.nationaltrust.org.uk

Kingston Lacy (NT) — 155 F2

Designed in the 17th century for the Bankes family following the slighting of Corfe Castle, and later restyled by Sir Charles Barry, this mansion is home to a wealth of treasures. These include paintings by Titian, Rubens and Raphael, an impressive marble staircase from Italy and a striking Spanish room decorated in gilded leather.

The formal garden is surrounded by 250 acres (100ha) of wooded parkland with waymarked walks, or there are longer walks along ancient trackways that can be taken through the 8795 acre (3520ha) estate.

☎ 01202 883402 www.nationaltrust.org.uk

Kingston Maurward Park — 154 C3

Gardens and parkland of 35 acres (14ha) surrounding a delightful Georgian mansion which is now an agricultural college. The restored Edwardian Garden is divided into a series of outdoor 'rooms' and there is an attractive rose garden, colourful herbaceous borders and drifts of spring bulbs, while the National Collections of Penstemons and Salvias are also kept here. A small farm park provides interest for children.

☎ 01305 215000 www.kmc.ac.uk

Knightshayes Court (NT) — 152 C1

Designed by William Burges, this elaborate Victorian Gothic house features ornate interior decoration including painted ceilings and a minstrels' gallery.

The 50 acre (20ha) gardens, amongst the finest in the county, are of interest throughout the year and contain both formal and informal plantings.

☎ 01884 254665 www.nationaltrust.org.uk

Knoll Gardens — 347 B1

A garden of 6 acres (2.5ha) with interesting water features and over 6000 well-labelled plants from around the world in colourful themed gardens. It includes the National Collection of Mahonias and a developing retail nursery.

☎ 01202 873931 www.knollgardens.co.uk

Lacock Abbey (NT) — 168 A1

Founded in 1232, but converted to a country house around 1540 following the Dissolution of the Monasteries. The cloisters, chapter house, sacristy and monastic rooms have been preserved, while an octagonal tower was built in the Tudor period, and further work in the 18th century included a fine Gothic entrance hall. The grounds have lovely displays of spring flowers, a Victorian woodland garden and restored botanic garden. A converted 16th century barn houses the Fox Talbot Museum of Photography, which commemorates the work of the pioneering photographer who lived here.

☎ 01249 730277 www.nationaltrust.org.uk

Land's End — 144 A4

Traditionally considered the south west extremity of the British mainland, this is a granite headland with spectacular cliff scenery. Although commercialisation with a theme park is considered by some to have spoiled the area, a short walk along the cliffs provides an escape from the crowds to a more natural environment.

Lanhydrock (NT) — 147 E3

This imposing residence originally dates from the 17th century but was largely rebuilt following a devastating fire in 1881. 50 rooms are open to the public, including state rooms and nurseries, sculleries and kitchens, containing state-of-the-art Victorian furniture and equipment, and the house provides a fascinating insight into the 'Upstairs, Downstairs' way of life. However, the centrepiece is the impressive 96ft (30m) Long Gallery, chief relic of the 17th century building, with its splendid plasterwork ceiling depicting scenes from the Old Testament.

The 900 acre (364ha) estate, extending down to the banks of the River Fowey, includes both formal and woodland areas as well as parkland, and contains some exceptional specimen trees from a collection started in the early 17th century. Magnificent spring displays of magnolias, camellias and rhododendrons give way in summer to colourful herbaceous borders and annual bedding in the formal garden.

☎ 01208 265950 www.nationaltrust.org.uk

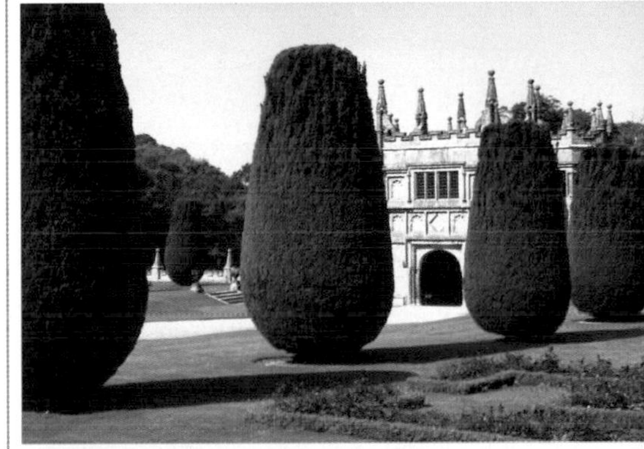

Lanhydrock

Lappa Valley Railway — 146 C4

This 15 inch (38cm) narrow-gauge railway was originally a mineral line running between Newquay and East Wheal Rose. A short section, passing through a scenic valley, has been restored. The surrounding parkland includes woodland walks and play areas.

☎ 01872 510317 www.lappavalley.co.uk

Launceston Castle — 148 D2

Located in a commanding position above the town where it formerly controlled the main route into Cornwall, this is now a medieval castle ruin built on the motte of the original Norman stronghold.

Launceston Steam Railway — 147 G1

This narrow-gauge steam railway links Launceston with the little village of New Mills, a distance of 2.5 miles (4km). The carriages are hauled by Victorian steam locomotives through scenic countryside and there are a range of walks that can be taken from both stations. The railway workshops in Launceston are open to visitors.

☎ 01566 775665

Lizard Peninsula — 145 E4

The coastal scenery of the Lizard peninsula is a striking combination of headlands, coves, cliffs and stacks cut out of the distinctive red and green serpentine rock which is typical of this area. Particularly attractive are Mullion Cove, Kynance Cove and Cadgwith village, while more dramatic

locations include the west coast cliffs and the collapsed cavern which forms the Devil's Frying Pan. The peninsula culminates in Lizard Point, a headland forming the southerly tip of the British mainland.

Longleat House — 167 F3

A magnificent Elizabethan mansion set in 900 acres (360ha) of rolling park landscaped by Lancelot 'Capability' Brown.

The house, built for Sir John Thynne, and still belonging to his descendants, was completed in 1580. Inside, it has been sumptuously decorated with gilded, painted Italianate ceilings designed by John Dibblee Crace in the 1870s and 1880s. Furniture ranges from 16th century English pieces to splendid French work of the 17th and 18th centuries, together with some unusual Italian examples. Many other treasures have been accumulated by the family over the centuries, including a fine collection of paintings by English, Dutch and Italian masters, 16th and 17th century Flemish tapestries and 40,000 books housed in seven libraries.

The grounds, bordered by woodland, include formal gardens, plantings of rhododendrons and a handsome lake.

☎ 01985 844400 www.longleat.co.uk

Longleat House

Longleat Safari Park — 167 F3

Set in the magnificent grounds of Longleat House, the Park was opened in 1966, the first of its kind in the country. Since then, an amazing range of attractions has been added, though lions, tigers, elephants, giraffes and many other animals can still be seen in the drive-through Safari Park. The grounds boast several mazes and labyrinths, including arguably the world's largest yew hedge maze, further animal attractions, a permanent Dr Who exhibition, narrow-gauge railway, boat trips, simulator rides and children's play areas. A passport ticket is available for the attractions package.

☎ 01985 844400 www.longleat.co.uk

Lost Gardens of Heligan — 145 G2

This is one of Europe's largest garden restoration projects. Originally developed by the Tremayne family in the late 18th century, the 57 acres (23ha) of gardens gradually descended into an apparent wilderness when the house was taken over as a military hospital in World War I and most of the workforce of 22 gardeners enlisted. Little was done to remedy the situation until the early 1990s, when the structure of the original magnificent garden was uncovered, largely at the instigation of Tim Smit who inspired the Eden Project.

The estate, including gardens and parkland, totals about 200 acres (80ha), with palm trees, tree ferns and bamboos giving it a subtropical atmosphere. Extensive flower and vegetable gardens are now back in production. Visitors can bear witness to the estate's return to productivity by sampling the results in the garden's restaurant.

☎ 01726 845100 www.heligan.com

Lulworth Castle — 155 E4

A 17th century hunting lodge badly damaged by fire in 1929 and subsequently restored. Features include a reconstructed kitchen, dairy, cellar and laundry. The adjacent Roman Catholic chapel was the first to be built after the Reformation, its design reflecting George III's stipulation that its identity should be disguised before he gave permission.

☎ 01929 400352 www.lulworth.com

Lulworth Cove & Heritage Centre — 155 E4

An accident of geology, where the sea has breached resistant coastal limestone rocks to erode the softer clay and sand deposits inland, has led to the development of this striking, circular cove. Elsewhere in the area exposed rocks bear witness to massive earth movements millions of years ago, a particularly memorable example being at Stair Hole just west of the cove's mouth.

The focal point of the Heritage Centre is a rock display tracing the geological history of the area. A video shows how the power of the sea has directly influenced the development of this amazing natural scenery.

☎ 01929 400587 www.lulworth.com

Lundy Island — 162 B1

A granite island, 3 miles (5km) north to south and 0.5 miles (1km) east to west, located at the entrance to the Bristol Channel 11 miles (17km) north-north-west of Hartland Point. Noted particularly for its scenery and wildlife, most of the island has been designated a Site of Special Scientific Interest, while the surrounding sea area is currently England's only Marine Nature Reserve.

The island rises to a height of 400ft (120m), the exposed west coast having the more dramatic scenery, whilst exposure to salt spray ensures a maritime flora including thrift and sea campion. Trees are restricted to the more sheltered east coast which is home to the Lundy Cabbage, found only on the island. 35 different breeding species of bird nest here, notably the puffin; Lundy means 'puffin island' in Norse. The surrounding coastal waters are home to sea anemones, sponges and corals, some brightly coloured, and also to seals and basking sharks. Access is by the *Oldenburg*, the island's own boat which sails from Bideford three times a week in summer and twice weekly in winter.

☎ 01271 863636 www.lundyisland.co.uk

Lost Gardens of Heligan

Lydford Gorge (NT) — 149 E2

Dramatic and awe-inspiring gorge carved into slate from the Upper Devonian period, a less durable rock than the granite traditionally associated with Dartmoor. The force of the water carried along rocks and boulders which have carved out sizeable potholes in the river bed, the most striking of these being the Devil's Cauldron which forms a breathtaking whirlpool.

The gorge is 1.5 miles (2.5km) long, up to 200ft (70m) deep and includes the 100ft (35m) White Lady Waterfall. A circular walk descends through woodland to the White Lady then follows a delightful route through the gorge itself and is particularly attractive in Autumn. In places the path can be narrow and slippery.

☎ 01822 820320 www.nationaltrust.org.uk

Lydiard Mansion — 182 C4

A beautifully restored Georgian mansion now under council ownership, former home of the Bolingbroke family and still containing their furniture and paintings. The surrounding parkland with its lawns, lakes and woodland offers pleasant walks, and there are children's play areas. Access to the grounds is free.

☎ 01793 770401 www.swindon.gov.uk

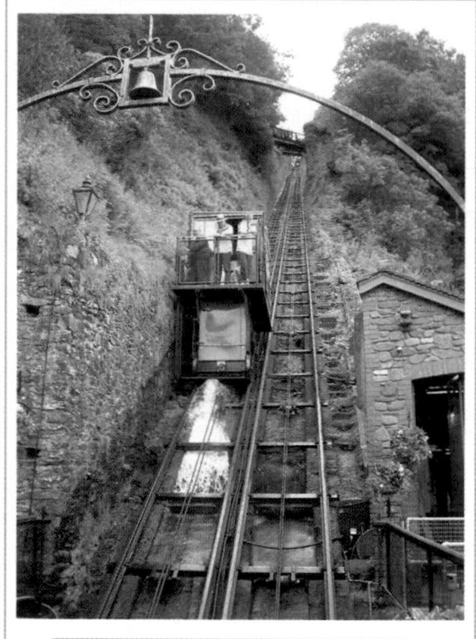

Lynton & Lynmouth Cliff Railway

Lynton & Lynmouth Cliff Railway — 164 A3

Funded by Sir George Newnes (the wealthy London publisher of 'Tit Bits' and 'The Strand') and completed in 1890, the cliff railway is a magnificent example of Victorian engineering and ingenuity. At the time, it greatly enhanced the tourist potential of this picturesque area, by giving visitors easy access from Lynmouth, where the boats docked, to Lynton, at the top of the 500ft (152m) cliff.

Open to the public at specific times; a trip on this 'green' listed monument is a must.

Lytes Cary Manor (NT) — 166 C5

Delightful manor house, with 14th century chapel, dating mainly from the 15th century when the Great Hall was built, but extended in the 16th century. The house was restored in the 20th century and furnished in period style, while the garden was also replanted in a series of 'rooms' with topiary and colourful, well-stocked herbaceous borders.

☎ 01458 224471 www.nationaltrust.org.uk

Lydford Gorge

Maiden Castle
154 C4

The name deriving from the Celtic 'Mai Dun', or Great Hill, this is one of the largest Iron Age hillforts in Europe, first developed in Stone Age times around 3000BC. Bronze Age burials have been discovered in one area, but the site was increased to its current size of 47 acres (19ha) in the Iron Age, around 450 – 300BC. Around AD43 the fort was taken by the Romans. The foundations of a Roman temple built in the 4th century can still be seen. The fort was later abandoned, but even today remains a hugely impressive site.

www.english-heritage.org.uk

Mapperton
154 B3

A delightful terraced garden around a 17th century manor house (limited opening). The upper garden is Italianate, with topiary and formal borders, and steps leading down to fish ponds.

☎ 01308 862645 www.mapperton.com

Marwood Hill
163 F2

A privately owned, colourful 20 acre (8ha) garden including three small lakes. The extensive collection of plants comprises, amongst others, alpines, clematis, camellias, rhododendrons and fine tree species such as eucalyptus.

☎ 01271 342528

Mendips
166 B2

A ridge of Carboniferous limestone stretching some 25-30 miles (40-48km) roughly between Weston-super-Mare and Shepton Mallet. Although the landscape consists mainly of rounded summits, with a high point of 1068ft (325m) at Black Down, the hills rise quite sharply from the surrounding lowlands, particularly in the north west, and provide extensive views across Exmoor, the Bristol Channel, Somerset and Wiltshire.

The most dramatic scenery can be seen in the famous Cheddar Gorge, a mile (1.6km) long ravine exposing steep cliffs (see page 26). A smaller, unspoilt version can be found at Ebbor Gorge near Wookey Hole. Evidence of prehistoric settlement is common in the area, with Neolithic, Bronze Age and Iron Age remains. From Roman times until the 19th century, lead mining was important, and abandoned mine workings can still be seen on the plateau.

Milton Lodge
166 C3

Attractive Grade II terraced gardens on a hillside overlooking Wells, providing magnificent views of the cathedral. Highlights include naturalised spring bulbs, a variety of climbers, old fashioned and shrub roses and a 7 acre (3ha) arboretum.

☎ 01749 672168

Minack Theatre
144 A4

The location on the granite cliffs above Porthcurno beach gives this open-air theatre a spectacular and atmospheric setting. A 17-week summer season includes a wide range of productions which are cancelled only in extreme weather conditions. The visitor centre explains the theatre's history and evolution.

☎ 01736 810181 www.minack.com

Minterne
154 C2

Formality has not been a consideration in these 20 acres (8ha) of lovely gardens landscaped in the 18th century. A chain of small lakes and streams provides a home for moisture-loving and water plants, whilst major collections of rhododendrons, cherries and acers provide magnificent spring colour and splendid autumn foliage.

☎ 01300 341370

Monkey World
155 E4

A spacious rescue and rehabilitation centre for primates, set in a delightful area of Dorset heath and woodland. The unspoilt 65 acre (26ha) site is home to more than 150 animals of 15 different species, including over 50 chimpanzees, probably the largest group outside Africa.

☎ 0800 456600
☎ 01929 462537 www.monkeyworld.co.uk

Moors Valley Country Park
156 A2

A 750 acre (300ha) park providing a range of leisure and recreational facilities in a pleasant countryside setting of lakes and woodland. Attractions include an adventure playground, steam railway, golf course, cycle hire and high ropes course. There is an extensive network of foot and cycle paths, and nature trails.

☎ 01425 470721 www.moors-valley.co.uk

Morwellham Quay Museum
149 E3

Important since the 12th century as the nearest river port to Tavistock, Morwellham became particularly significant following the discovery of rich copper veins in the locality in the 1840s. The mines closed in the late 19th century and Morwellham was abandoned until 1970 when work was started on an open-air museum. This museum has carefully and accurately re-created the port and associated industrial and domestic buildings to provide a fascinating insight into the life of what was once one of Europe's major copper ports.

☎ 01822 832766 www.morwellham-quay.co.uk

Mount Edgcumbe

346 A3

Superbly located on a hill overlooking Plymouth Sound, this was the family home of the Edgcumbes, built in the 16th century to replace the residence at Cotehele. Following bomb damage in World War II the house was restored by Adrian Gilbert Scott and is furnished with the family's possessions, including Regency furniture, paintings and 16th century tapestries.

☎ 01752 822236 www.gardensincornwall.co.uk

Mount Edgcumbe Country Park
346 A3

The grounds of Mount Edgcumbe House were developed in the late 18th century to create Cornwall's first landscaped park. The site covers 865 acres (346ha), and as well as the parkland there is a formal area comprising English, French and Italian gardens with the addition of two new gardens to celebrate the family's past links with Australia and America. The park also holds the National Collection of Camellias. There are attractive pathways through the grounds with fine sea views.

☎ 01752 822236 www.gardensincornwall.co.uk

Museum of Costume

388 D1

A sumptuous display, arguably one of the best in the world, of more than 150 figures in original costumes and accessories, from the 16th century to the present day. Housed in the grandly decorated Assembly Rooms (to which entry is free), there is an excellent audio guide to the museum.

☎ 01225 428126 www.museumofcostume.co.uk

National Marine Aquarium
407 C3

Displayed on three floors, the visitor is taken through a range of reconstructed habitats, from the start of a moorland stream through estuarine and coastal environments to the ocean depths. An engrossing array of aquatic species can be seen, from the bizarre to the beautiful, and there are displays, talks and presentations providing information on the species themselves and the environments, sometimes threatened, that they inhabit.

A new venture has been the sinking of the ex-Royal Navy frigate, *HMS Scylla*, in Whitsand Bay to form an offshore reef. The aim is to study its colonisation by marine life and this can be viewed via underwater camera technology from the aquarium.

This is an exceptionally well-thought-out attraction designed to inform the public about marine habitats.

☎ 01752 600301 www.national-aquarium.co.uk

National Marine Aquarium

National Maritime Museum Cornwall 145 F3

In a striking building which dominates the quayside, this museum is devoted to the sea, boats and their importance in people's lives, with particular emphasis on Cornwall.

☎ 01326 313388 www.nmmc.co.uk

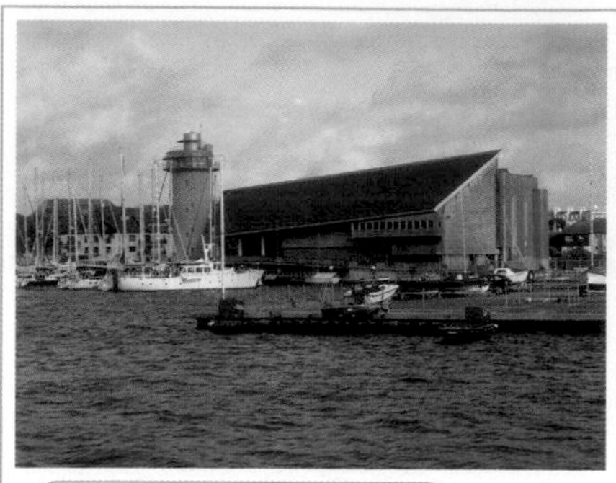

National Maritime Museum

National Waterways Museum 399 B1

200 years of Britain's waterway heritage is exhibited over 3 floors of this historic listed warehouse built in 1873. There are many interesting displays, as well as trips along the canal. The entrance to the museum is in the form of a replica lock chamber complete with dripping water.

☎ 01452 318200 www.nwm.org.uk

Newark Park (NT) 181 G3

A Tudor hunting lodge originally built in around 1550 which was converted into a castellated house by James Wyatt at the end of the 18th century. Limited opening from April to October, but also open weekends in February for an impressive display of snowdrops.

☎ 01453 842644 www.nationaltrust.org.uk

Newquay Zoo 146 C3

The chance to see a wide range of exotic species, housed where possible in natural enclosures. Traditional zoo activities such as feeding displays and children's farm are combined with a special emphasis on wildlife conservation and the associated breeding programme for endangered species.

☎ 01637 873342 www.newquayzoo.co.uk

No. 1 Royal Crescent 167 E1

The first to be built in Royal Crescent in 1768, this imposing Palladian town house has been meticulously restored complete with authentic furnishings and pictures.

☎ 01225 428126 www.bath-preservation-trust.org.uk

Owlpen Manor 182 A3

Bought by the Mander family in 1974, since when the 16th century manor house and estate have been revived and restored. The formal gardens comprise seven hanging terraces dating back to the 16th and 17th centuries and the estate has walks through beech and bluebell woods. The house contains wall paintings, family portraits and Cotswold arts and crafts. There is also a resident ghost, Queen Margaret of Anjou, wife of Henry VI, who stayed here prior to his defeat at Tewkesbury.

☎ 01453 860261 www.owlpen.com

Paignton & Dartmouth Steam Railway 151 E2

A delightful 7 mile (11km) trip from Paignton to Kingswear which gives breathtaking views of Lyme Bay and the Devon coast before passing through woodland along the Dart estuary. It is possible to turn this into a day excursion by taking the passenger ferry from Kingswear to Dartmouth followed by a river trip to Totnes and bus back to Paignton. A 'Round Robin' ticket is available for this.

☎ 01803 555872 www.paignton-steamrailway.co.uk

Paignton Zoo 151 E2

Set in 75 acres (30ha) of attractive surroundings with the emphasis on natural habitats and endangered species conservation, this well organised zoo is home to over 1300 animals and birds. A range of feeding activities and other events takes place every day and in addition there is a miniature railway, playground and animal education centre.

☎ 01803 697500 www.paigntonzoo.org.uk

Painswick Rococo Garden 182 A1

Restoration of the heavily overgrown garden in the 1980s was inspired by a painting by local artist Thomas Robins which showed the 6 acre (2.5ha) site in its original 18th century layout. February sees a spectacular display of snowdrops.

☎ 01452 813204 www.rococogarden.co.uk

Pencarrow  147 E2

A grand, family-owned Georgian mansion with splendid collections of furniture, porcelain and pictures. The 50 acre (20ha) grounds comprise fine formal and woodland gardens with waymarked walks and over 700 varieties of rhododendron giving a spectacular display in spring. The woodland contains a large number of Monkey Puzzle trees – the name is said to have originated here after a guest scraped his hand on one and commented: 'It would puzzle a monkey.'

☎ 01208 841369 www.pencarrow.co.uk

Pendennis Castle 145 F3

This formed part of the coastal defences set up by Henry VIII in response to the threat of war from France and Spain following his divorce from Catherine of Aragon. Occupying a superb site on a headland overlooking the entrance to Carrick Roads, the castle consists of a round tower and gate surrounded by a lower curtain wall. A further outer defence was added by Elizabeth I, but the castle was only attacked during the Civil War when it was besieged by Parliamentarians for five months. A Discovery Centre incorporates interactive displays on the castle's history.

☎ 01326 316594 www.english-heritage.org.uk

Plymouth Dome 407 C2

A visitor centre using multimedia technology to trace the city's history and maritime connections, with breathtaking views of Plymouth Sound from the observation galleries.

☎ 01752 603300 www.plymouthdome.info

Porthcurno Sands 144 A4

A beautiful stretch of clean, silvery sand makes this amongst the best of Cornwall's beaches. Exhilarating walks along the coastal path to the east lead to Treryn Dinas, one of the most spectacular of the Cornish headlands, crowned by the precarious Logan Stone.

Portland Castle 154 C5

A well preserved example of Henry VIII's coastal fortresses overlooking Portland Harbour. Although not seeing action until the 17th century, when it was seized by both Parliamentarians and Royalists, the castle has always had a significant role in coastal defence, being a seaplane station in World War I and heavily involved in D-Day preparations in World War II.

☎ 01305 820539 www.english-heritage.org.uk

Powderham Castle 152 C4

Home to the Courtenay family since 1390, the castle lies in a beautiful setting in a 4000 acre (1600ha) estate on the River Exe estuary. The state rooms are richly decorated and furnished and the marble hall is also of interest, containing a 13ft (4.5m) long case clock.

The grounds provide a variety of activities, including woodland walks, working blacksmith and wheelwright, and children's secret garden.

☎ 01626 890243 www.powderham.co.uk

Prinknash Abbey & Park 182 A1

Around 30 monks live at the abbey which was not completed until 1972. The abbey buildings extend to over 300 acres (120ha) and include the workshops and the old abbey of St Peter's Grange. The surrounding Bird and Deer Park has a children's castle, a Tudor wendy house, aviaries, ponds and lakes, and an abundance of deer, geese, cranes and peacocks.

☎ 01452 812066 www.prinknash-bird-and-deerpark.com

Prior Park (NT) 167 E1

A magnificent location on a hillside to the south of Bath provides the 18th century mansion of Prior Park with splendid panoramic views of the city and surrounding countryside. The delightful landscape garden was created by local businessman Ralph Allen, with input from the poet Alexander Pope and Lancelot 'Capability' Brown. The house is now a school and not open to the public. There is no parking, but a frequent bus service runs from the city centre.

☎ 01225 833422 www.nationaltrust.org.uk

Putlake Adventure Farm 155 F5

An unpretentious farm attraction particularly suitable for younger children, hosting a whole range of activities.

☎ 01929 422917 www.putlakefarm.co.uk

Quince Honey Farm 164 A5

One of the largest honey farms in Britain, with over 1500 hives spread across Devon and Exmoor. In the exhibition area honey bees can be observed at close range, nesting in a variety of man-made and natural habitats as well as in state-of-the-art observation hives.

A wide range of honey-based products is available at the centre's shop.

☎ 01769 572401 www.quincehoney.co.uk

Red Lodge 391 B1

Elizabethan house dating from 1590, substantially modernised around 1730 and now furnished to represent both periods. The highlight is the Great Oak Room with its magnificent oak panels and splendid carved stone chimneypiece.

☎ 0117 921 1360 www.bristol-city.gov.uk

Ridgeway, The

This ancient trackway, formerly used by drovers, traders and occasionally invaders, has been in use for at least 5000 years. There is much evidence of prehistoric occupation in the surrounding area in the form of burial mounds and hill forts, and there is a particularly memorable stretch taking in Wayland's Smithy, Uffington Castle and the adjacent White Horse. The track runs from Overton Hill near Avebury along the north edge of the Marlborough and Berkshire Downs, crosses the Thames at Goring and continues along the west edge of the Chiltern Hills to Ivinghoe Beacon. The plant life is of special interest as, in some areas, the characteristic, and increasingly rare chalk grassland can still be seen. The bird and insect life is also worthy of note.

Roche Chapel 147 D3

Remains of a 14th century chapel perched on a rocky outcrop on the site of what is thought to be an early Christian hermit's cell.

Roman Baths & Pump Room 388 E2

One of the outstanding Roman sites in Britain, founded in the first century AD for pilgrims visiting the sacred hot springs of the temple to Sulis Minerva. After the Romans left, the site fell into disrepair although the town continued to grow, but by the early 17th century the springs were again attracting interest. A visit in 1702 by Queen Anne further encouraged this interest and by 1720 the town was becoming a highly fashionable spa. Further development in the 19th century led to the uncovering and preservation of the Roman site.

As far back as 10,000 years ago the hot springs had generated human attention as a source of healing. The magnificent Roman complex used lead pipes to conduct the water to a series of bathing rooms which have now been excavated and can be visited, together with the temple remains, hypocausts and cold plunges, aided by an audio guide.

The elegant Pump Room (free entry) was the headquarters of fashionable 18th century society and the visitor can emulate this by taking the waters, or less adventurously, morning coffee or afternoon tea.

☎ 01225 477785 www.romanbaths.co.uk

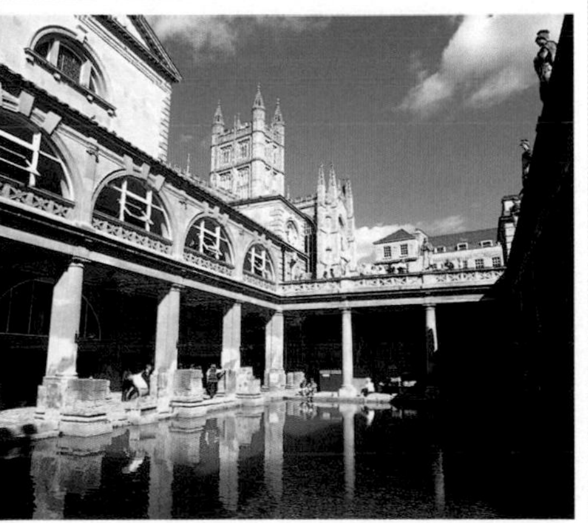

Roman Baths & Pump Room – Bath

Rosemoor 163 F4

A regional centre for the Royal Horticultural Society (RHS), second only to the gardens at Wisley in importance. Originally 8 acres (3ha), the garden was given to the RHS and a further 32 acres (13ha) was added. The surrounding woodland has been purchased to provide an attractive natural backdrop.

Many rare and interesting plants flourish here, and the woodland garden is considered to be particularly lovely. Other areas of interest include the Rose Garden with 2000 roses in around 200 varieties, stream and bog gardens, colour theme gardens and a kitchen garden.

☎ 01805 624067 www.rhs.org.uk

Russell-Cotes Art Gallery & Museum 389 F2

This museum houses a combination of the exotic and eclectic in a rather extravagant Italianate villa, built as a testament to the worldly success of Sir Merton Russell-Cotes, who gave it to the town of Bournemouth in 1922, complete with artworks and a notable collection of late 19th century furniture.

☎ 01202 451858 www.russell-cotes.bournemouth.gov.uk

S.S. Great Britain 352 B3

Built in Bristol by Isambard Kingdom Brunel in 1843, this is the world's first (and only surviving) ocean-going, iron hulled steam ship driven by a screw propellor. Designed as a passenger vessel for the North Atlantic crossing, she subsequently carried 15,000 migrants to Australia, 40,000 troops to the Crimea, and coal to California, but ended up abandoned in the Falkland Islands. In 1970 she was returned to Bristol, to the same dry dock where she was built. The dockside museum tells the history of this remarkable ship.

☎ 0117 926 0680 www.ss-great-britain.com

St Just in Roseland 145 F3

Although architecturally the church is not of special interest, it has an enchanting waterside setting and a steeply sloping graveyard described by John Betjeman as 'Perhaps the most beautiful churchyard on Earth' with its profusion of palms and subtropical shrubs.

St Mawes Castle 145 F3

Located on a headland on the east side of the Carrick Roads, this castle was built to defend against a possible French and Spanish invasion following Henry VIII's divorce from Catherine of Aragon and is an excellent example of Tudor military architecture. Captured by Parliamentarians in 1646, with far less trouble than its neighbour Pendennis, it was not re-fortified until the early 20th century, when it formed part of the coastal defences for World Wars I and II.

☎ 01326 270526 www.english-heritage.org.uk

St Michael's Mount (NT) 144 C3

Dramatic granite island accessible on foot via a causeway at low tide and by ferry at other times. Although generally accepted as a place of spiritual significance, the original settlement on the island may have been a late Iron Age port. The 5th century saw the start of the mount's importance as a place of pilgrimage, when legend has it that a group of fishermen had a vision of St Michael. A Benedictine monastery was founded on the summit in 1135, and following the Dissolution of the Monasteries by Henry VIII the ruins of the building were incorporated into a castle.

The steep slopes of the mount are clothed in subtropical vegetation, and a unique maritime garden of some 20 acres (8ha) has been developed on terraces. The 200ft (60m) ascent to the castle via the cobbled Pilgrims' Steps is quite steep in places, but is well worth it for the spectacular views. The castle itself contains displays of weaponry and other militaria, period furniture, paintings and miniatures.

☎ 01736 710507 www.nationaltrust.org.uk

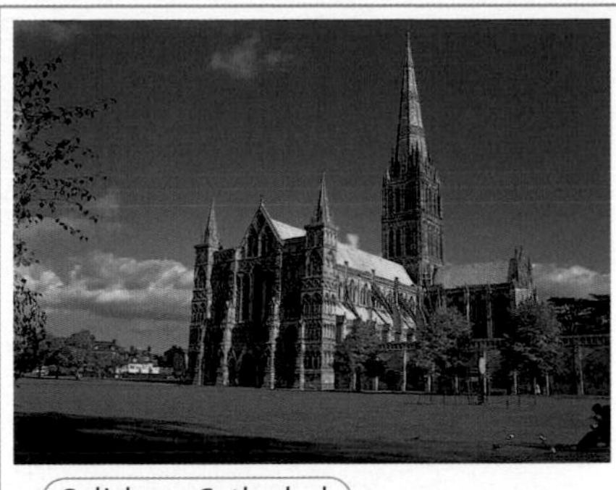

Salisbury Cathedral

Salisbury Cathedral 408 F2

At Salisbury, one of the world's most celebrated spires soars above an Early English masterpiece of a cathedral, the whole comprising a singularly beautiful medieval building which inspired the famous painting by John Constable. Raised between 1220 – 1258, and with the spire added between 1285 – 1315, this comparatively rapid construction led to a remarkable conformity of style, characterised by slender Purbeck marble pillars, narrow pointed arches and high vaulting.

Inside, the cathedral is relatively austere following a sprucing up by James Wyatt in the 18th century. Treasures include one of the world's oldest working clocks dating from the 14th century, and the largest cloisters in England lead to the beautiful octagonal chapter house which contains one of the four surviving original versions of Magna Carta, considered the best preserved.

The exceptional spire, at 404ft (123m) the tallest in Britain, rests on foundations only 6ft (2m) deep. Guided tours take visitors 332 steps up the tower to the base of the spire and give splendid views over the city.

The cathedral is set in a delightful, large Close which itself contains some memorable buildings, many dating from the 18th century.

☎ 01722 555120 www.salisburycathedral.org.uk

Saltram House (NT) 346 B2

A former Tudor house redeveloped as a splendid Georgian mansion set in a landscaped park overlooking the Plym estuary. Many of the original contents remain and there are significant pieces by Chippendale and Wedgwood as well as several portraits by Sir Joshua Reynolds, who lived locally. There is some notable work by Robert Adam, and a magnificent 18th century Axminster carpet. There is also an interesting period kitchen, formal gardens and woodland walks.

☎ 01752 333500 www.nationaltrust.org.uk

Sherborne Castle 154 C1

A splendid Tudor mansion built by Sir Walter Raleigh in 1594 and subsequently extended in the 17th and 18th centuries by the Digby family who have owned it since 1617. The state rooms show a range of decorative styles from the 16th to 19th centuries and there are excellent collections of furniture and fine arts.

The grounds are considered to be amongst the finest to be created by Lancelot 'Capability' Brown, with a 50 acre (20ha) lake and magnificent specimen trees. The 20 acre (8ha) garden has delightful drifts of spring bulbs, colourful summer borders and striking autumn colour. Within the grounds are the remnants of a Norman castle destroyed in the Civil War.

☎ 01935 813182 www.sherbornecastle.com

Silbury Hill 168 B1

Constructed around 2500BC, probably using some of the chalk rubble excavated from Avebury, this is thought to be the highest man-made mound in Europe at 130ft (40m). It is estimated that it would have taken 1000 men 10 years to build. No archaeological excavations have ever discovered anything of significance in the mound and its purpose has never been satisfactorily explained.

Unfortunately, continuous wear and tear by people climbing the mound has meant that access is now prohibited.

Slimbridge Wildfowl & Wetlands Trust 181 G2

Originated in 1946 by Sir Peter Scott, Slimbridge is the centre of the Wildfowl and Wetlands Trust (WWT) and has become one of the most important wildfowl and wetland conservation centres in the world. 800 acres (320ha) contain species from all over the world, including the rare Hawaiian Goose (Ne Ne) which has been returned to its native habitat because of the success of the breeding project at Slimbridge. The informative visitor centre gives an insight into the birds that make Slimbridge their home, including the largest collection of ducks, geese and swans in the world. There are also sculpture trails, an art gallery and events throughout the year. Winter sees thousands of wild geese feeding in the Severn Estuary which can be viewed from the observation tower.

☎ 01453 890333 www.wwt.org.uk

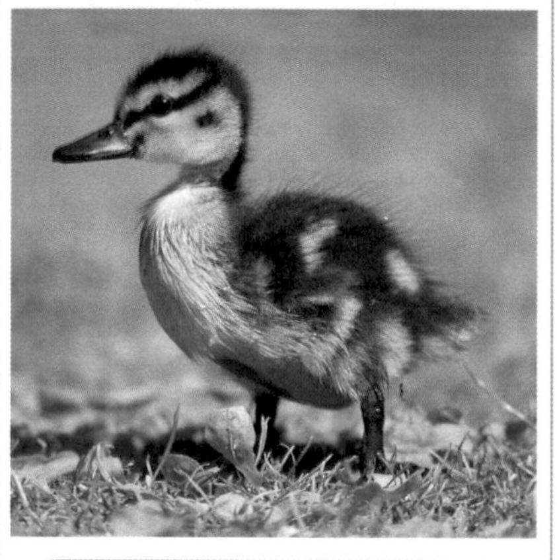

Slimbridge Wildfowl & Wetlands Trust

Snowshill Manor (NT) 196 C4

In 1919 Charles Wade bought the ruined manor with its 14 acres (5.5ha) of land which he set about restoring using traditional skills. The renovated manor was used as a storage area for the enormous variety of artefacts collected from all over the world. Wade actually lived in the small cottage in the grounds. The tranquil organic gardens give lovely views across the surrounding Cotswold countryside.

☎ 01386 852410 www.nationaltrust.org.uk

South Devon Railway 151 D1

This scenic steam railway winds its way along 7 miles (10.5km) of the Dart valley between Buckfastleigh and Totnes on a former Great Western Railway branch line. On site at Buckfastleigh there is a small museum and the chance to see the restoration of some of the rolling stock. There are also model railway exhibits, a children's play area and riverside walks.

☎ 01364 643338 www.southdevonrailway.org

Stapehill Abbey Crafts & Garden 347 B1

A 19th century Cistercian abbey, now used for a variety of craft workshops. The attractive 30 acre (12ha) gardens are home to many rare and unusual species and include a striking Japanese Garden.

The Countryside Museum has exhibits on social and agricultural history and an assortment of village shops, and Home Farm has a selection of farm animals to be viewed.

☎ 01202 861686

STEAM Museum of the Great Western Railway  412 A1

A fascinating museum on the restored site of the former Swindon Railway Works, as much concerned with the lives of the thousands of employees and passengers of the Great Western Railway (GWR) as with the locomotives themselves. Hands-on exhibits and ingenious displays trace the history of the GWR and give an insight into the skills and dedication of the railway workers in every aspect of the enterprise, from Isambard Kingdom Brunel's initial inspiration onwards.

☎ 01793 466646 www.steam-museum.org.uk

Stembridge Tower Mill (NT) 166 B4

Located in a prominent position overlooking the Somerset Levels, this is the last remaining thatched windmill in England. It was built in 1822 and remained in operation until 1910.

☎ 01458 250818 www.nationaltrust.org.uk

Stoke sub Hamdon Priory (NT) 154 A1

A group of buildings, the remains of a chantry built for a provost and four chaplains in the 14th century by the Beauchamp family. The complex consists of a Great Hall, the only part open to the public, private rooms and a range of outbuildings.

☎ 01985 843600 www.nationaltrust.org.uk

Stonehenge 168 C3

An awe-inspiring prehistoric monument constructed in stages between about 5000 and 3000 years ago, now designated a World Heritage Site. The original purpose is uncertain, but suggestions include an astronomical observatory, temple or other sacred site.

Stonehenge was originally a simple bank and ditch excavated by tools made of antler, wood and bone. Some centuries later an inner stone circle was added, though not completed, using bluestones from the Prescelly Mountains in Pembrokeshire. Subsequent modification led to the central altar stone being surrounded by an inner horseshoe of rearranged bluestones and an outer sarsen horseshoe. The final, and major building phase around 1500BC brought massive sarsen stones of up to 50 tons (56 tonnes) from the Marlborough Downs 20 miles (32km) away. These were erected and capped by stone lintels to make a continuous outer ring. The central axis aligns with the point of sunrise on Midsummer Day, giving credence, without supporting evidence, to the idea of Stonehenge as an astronomical calendar.

Today, Stonehenge is effectively an impressive ruin, stones having fallen or been used in the past as a surreptitious resource for other local building projects. Visitors cannot generally walk among the stones, but the site is very atmospheric and views of the stones, particularly near dawn or dusk, are breathtaking.

☎ 01980 624715 www.english-heritage.org.uk

Stourhead (NT) 167 E4

Unlike most estates, where the house takes pride of place, here the 2600 acres (1052ha) of grounds are by far the superior draw, providing an exceptional example of the English landscape garden.

The house, built in 1721 by Colen Campbell for the banker Henry Hoare, is an elegant example of Palladian architecture and contains some good early Chippendale furniture and choice paintings.

Henry Hoare's son, also Henry, designed the garden after returning from a Grand Tour in 1741, his purpose being to emulate scenes from paintings by Poussin and other European landscape artists. The centrepiece, a magnificent lake, was formed by damming the River Stour. The rhododendrons, for which the garden is famed in spring, were a later addition.

King Alfred's Tower, the 150ft (46m) red brick folly at the far end of the estate, provides magnificent views across the grounds and surrounding countryside (open summer afternoons only).

☎ 01747 841152 www.nationaltrust.org.uk

Stuart Line Cruises 152 D4

A family run firm based in Exmouth offering a variety of cruises either in the sheltered Exe estuary or along the coast to Sidmouth, Teignmouth or Torbay. A great opportunity to view the unique south Devon coastal scenery from the sea.

☎ 01395 222144 www.stuartlinecruises.co.uk

Studland Heath (NT) 155 G4

This National Nature Reserve on the Isle of Purbeck covers around 1500 acres (631ha) and supports a variety of habitats including heathland, bog and sand dunes. A central feature is the Little Sea, an acidic freshwater lake around which are four hides to observe wintering wildfowl. Another significant area to the west of the reserve is Godlingston Heath, a large tract of lowland heath with populations of all six British species of reptile and the rare Dartford Warbler. Wading birds can be seen on coastal sites and the area is notable for its insect population, particularly dragonflies and butterflies. Footpaths, nature trails, birdwatching hides and leaflets provide access and information for the visitor. There is a parking charge.

☎ 01929 450259 www.nationaltrust.org.uk

Sudeley Castle 196 C5

Once owned by Ethelred the Unready, and more famously home to Katherine Parr, the sixth wife of Henry VIII, Sudeley was a victim of Cromwell's destruction and lay derelict for over 200 years until the ambitious restoration project was started in 1837. There are themed exhibitions, impressive furniture and paintings from such artists as Rubens, Van Dyck and Turner. Ten distinct gardens covering 14 acres (5.5ha) surround the castle and feature a ruined 15th century Tithe Barn. The tomb of Katherine Parr lies in the 15th century St Mary's Church.

☎ 01242 602308 www.sudeleycastle.co.uk

Stonehenge

Swanage Railway
155 G5

A 6 mile (10km) stretch of standard-gauge steam railway running between Swanage and Norden on a trip lasting 25 minutes. The route passes through lovely countryside, including the spectacular ruins of Corfe Castle. A variety of special events takes place throughout the year.

☎ 01929 425800 www.swanagerailway.co.uk

Tank Museum
155 E4

With exhibits ranging from 'Little Willie', the first tank ever built in 1915, to the British Army's most recent 'Challenger 2', this museum contains one of the world's most impressive collections of armoured fighting vehicles. In school holidays, 'Tanks in Action!' displays take place.

☎ 01929 405096 www.tankmuseum.co.uk

Tate St Ives
144 C2

In a splendid location above Porthmeor beach, this art gallery displays work by modern British artists in both permanent and temporary exhibitions. The building itself is quite distinctive and has received several awards for its architecture.

☎ 01736 796226 www.tate.org.uk

Tintagel Castle
148 A2

A dramatic clifftop location gives this extensive, ruined medieval castle spectacular views along the north Cornish coast. Situated on a promontory approached via a narrow neck of land, such an excellent defensive site is likely to have been in use from much earlier times, and Iron Age, Celtic and Roman occupations have been suggested. This lengthy history of occupancy, coupled with the windswept, romantic atmosphere, has helped enhance the idea of Tintagel as the legendary castle of King Arthur.

☎ 01840 770328 www.english-heritage.org.uk

Tintagel Old Post Office
147 E1

Delightful 14th century manor house in the village centre, one room of which was used as a post office in the 19th century.

☎ 01840 770024 www.nationaltrust.org.uk

Tintinhull House (NT)
154 B1

Lovely, colourful formal garden of 1.5 acres (0.5 ha) developed around a 17th century manor house by Phyllis Reiss between 1933 – 61. The planting scheme, influenced by the style of Hidcote, is divided into seven 'rooms', each with its own theme but integrating sympathetically with the others. The house is not open to the public.

☎ 01935 822545 www.nationaltrust.org.uk

Tiverton Castle
152 C1

Although Norman in origin, only the tower and gatehouse remain; the remainder has been much altered, depicting a range of architectural styles. There are attractive gardens and an especially good collection of Civil War arms and armour. Limited opening outside July and August.

☎ 01884 253200 www.tivertoncastle.com

Tiverton Museum
152 C1

A mid 19th century school houses what is probably the largest social history collection in the south west.

☎ 01884 256295 www.tivertonmuseum.org.uk

Torre Abbey
412 E1

Founded in 1196, but partly destroyed during the Dissolution of the Monasteries in 1539, only fragments of the original buildings remain, including the medieval barn and gatehouse. It was converted to a country house and then substantially remodelled in the 19th century and now belongs to the local council, serving in part as a museum and art gallery. There are collections of silver, glass, maritime paintings, Pre-Raphaelite and 20th century art and a room devoted to Agatha Christie memorabilia. Access is free to the grounds which include palm and cactus houses.

☎ 01803 293593 www.torre-abbey.org.uk

Trebah Garden
145 E4

A subtropical garden of 25 acres (10ha) developed in a steep, wooded ravine which conjures up a jungle atmosphere. It is particularly noted for its tree ferns and palms, blue and white hydrangeas and 100 year old rhododendrons. The gardens descend over 200ft (60m) to a private beach on the Helford River estuary.

☎ 01326 250448 www.trebah-gardens.co.uk

Trelissick (NT)
 145 F3

A lovely woodland park of around 370 acres (148ha) with magnificent views across the Fal estuary. As with many Cornish coastal gardens, tender and exotic plants flourish, but Trelissick is especially noted for its magnolias, camellias and hydrangeas. The house is not open to the public.

☎ 01872 862090 www.nationaltrust.org.uk

Trengwainton (NT)
 144 B3

A garden of interest throughout the year, but especially in spring and early summer, with splendid displays of magnolias, camellias and rhododendrons. Many of the plants found here were brought back from Frank Kingdom Ward's plant hunting expedition in the 1920s. A series of walled gardens contain unusual species particularly suited to the mild climate, and the stream garden in particular is a feast of colour with its primulas, lysichitums and lilies. Superb coastal views can be seen from the restored terrace over Mounts Bay and the Lizard.

☎ 01736 363148 www.nationaltrust.org.uk

Trerice (NT)
146 C4

An attractive Elizabethan manor house considered to be something of an architectural gem with its detailed plaster ceilings, splendid fireplaces and distinctive gabling following the Dutch style. Furnishings include a range of oak and walnut furniture, unusual clocks, embroideries and paintings. The pleasant grounds are planted with an eye for colour and foliage, and the former stables house a small museum tracing the development and history of the lawnmower.

☎ 01637 875404 www.nationaltrust.org.uk

Tresco Abbey Gardens
146 A1

From acacias to agaves, and palms to proteas, these marvellous subtropical gardens, located on the site of a former abbey founded in AD964, contain an amazing variety of plants. The garden was developed between 1843 – 72 by Augustus Smith, who enhanced the naturally mild climate by building tall windbreaks to shelter the site from the worst of the weather.

The site also incorporates the Valhalla Museum of ships' figureheads.

☎ 01720 424105 www.tresco.co.uk

Trewithen
146 D5

Outstanding woodland garden created by George Johnstone in the first half of the 20th century. Covering around 30 acres (12ha), the gardens are particularly famous for their splendid collections of magnolias, camellias and rhododendrons. The attractive, early Georgian house is open to the public for a limited period in summer.

☎ 01726 883647 www.trewithengardens.co.uk

Truro Cathedral
 146 C5

The first cathedral in Britain to be consecrated since the Reformation, this beautiful neogothic building was designed by John Loughborough Pearson and completed in 1910. It was built on the site of St Mary's Parish Church (consecrated in 1259), and part of the old building was incorporated into the new cathedral which has a commanding central location in the city. The Victorian stained glass windows are considered amongst the finest in the world, and other notable features include the Father Willis organ and an excellent collection of Victorian embroidery.

☎ 01872 276782 www.trurocathedral.org.uk

Tyntesfield (NT)
181 E5

A splendid Victorian house built in the Gothic Revival style, with lots of towers and turrets. The interior has been little altered, and there is an extensive collection of Victorian decorative arts plus a range of domestic offices and a family chapel. The unspoilt 500 acre (200ha) estate comprises parkland, lovely formal gardens with superb views from the terrace, and a delightful kitchen garden. This is a recent acquisition by the National Trust, and is undergoing extensive renovation. Admission is by pre-booked guided tour. It will be some years before the house is fully open. Access is by a park and ride service from Nailsea.

☎ 0870 458 4500 www.nationaltrust.org.uk

Ugbrooke
152 B5

Home to the Clifford family for the past 300 years, this former Tudor mansion was substantially rebuilt by Robert Adam in 1750, the chapel and library wing being particularly characteristic of Adam's style. The house fell into some disrepair in the mid 20th century but has been handsomely and meticulously restored and contains fine displays of furniture, paintings, embroideries and a rare military collection.

The parkland was landscaped by Lancelot 'Capability' Brown and contains many fine specimen trees, while the formal gardens include a box parterre, Spanish garden and lakeside walks.

☎ 01626 852179

Watermouth Castle
163 F1

Built in 1825, this castellated mansion is now a popular family destination with a great range of attractions including mechanical music demonstrations, a maze, cider making and dairy exhibits, and a wide selection of children's rides and play activities.

☎ 01271 863879 www.watermouthcastle.com

Watersmeet House (NT)
164 A3

Former fishing lodge built in 1832 in a beautiful wooded valley at the confluence of Hoar Oak Water and the East Lyn River. It now houses a National Trust information centre and shop, serving as a focus for the many delightful walks in the area.

☎ 01271 850887 www.nationaltrust.org.uk

Wells Cathedral
166 C3

Dominating the centre of Wells, England's smallest city, this has been the site of a religious building since the 8th century. The present cathedral was founded in 1180, but was built in phases over the following 400 years, thus incorporating several different architectural styles. However, the original Saxon font was retained and is still used for baptisms.

The splendid west front, one of the most outstanding façades in the country, was completed in 1250 and accommodates nearly 300 pieces of statuary. Within the magnificent Gothic interior are unusual scissor-shaped arches, constructed as additional support when the combined weight of tower and spire proved too much for the lower stage of the tower. The upper tower and spire were subsequently destroyed by fire and not rebuilt; the lower tower was rebuilt to a height of 182ft (55m), the highest in the county.

Other highlights include the 14th century clock, amongst the oldest in the world, mid 20th century colourful embroideries in the choir, medieval stained glass, and probably the longest medieval library building (168ft, 51m) in England, containing documents which date from the 10th century.

☎ 01749 674483

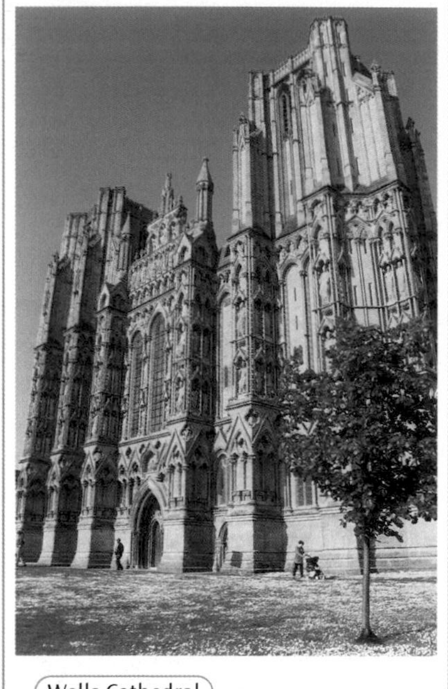

Wells Cathedral

West Kennet Long Barrow
168 C1

Possibly England's finest burial mound, this Neolithic chambered tomb was the site of around 50 burials. Measuring 343ft (105m) by 76ft (23m), the mound's entrance is protected by massive sarsen stones and it is possible to walk into the stone burial chamber a short way into the mound.

www.english-heritage.org.uk

West Somerset Railway
165 E4

At 20 miles (32km), this is one of the longest stretches of preserved steam railway in Britain. It runs along the north Somerset coast from Minehead to Watchet, then continues inland via several small stations to Bishop's Lydeard. The original line continued to Taunton, and there is a bus link for those wishing to complete the journey.

☎ 01643 704996 www.west-somerset-railway.co.uk

Westbury Court (NT)
181 G1

This water garden originated between 1696 and 1705 and was the National Trust's first garden restoration. It is the earliest Dutch water garden remaining in the country and has been planted with species dating back to before 1700. A restored pavilion sits at the head of a long canal bordered by yew hedges, and in the grounds are a walled garden and a Holm oak, said to be the oldest in the country.

☎ 01452 760461 www.nationaltrust.org.uk

Westbury White Horse
167 F2

The chalk downs of central Wiltshire are ideal for these massive hill carvings which are not, as generally assumed, particularly ancient. The Westbury horse is considered the oldest in the county and is perhaps the best sited. It is thought to date from the late 17th century, replacing an earlier one, possibly of Saxon origin. Above the horse is a large Iron Age fort with excellent views.

www.wiltshirewhitehorses.org.uk

Westonbirt – The National Arboretum

182 A3

The Arboretum is now in the care of the Forestry Commission but originates from 1829 when Robert Holford decided to extend his father's estate at Westonbirt. There are 18,000 trees and shrubs from all over the world, many of them rare or endangered, and some of which date back to the original planting, making this one of the finest tree collections in the world. Covering 600 acres (240 ha), it is not only the trees that make Westonbirt special but also the wild flowers, fungi, birds and animals that can be enjoyed along 17 miles (27km) of paths and trails. The displays of rhododendrons, azaleas, magnolias and the wild flowers in the Silk Wood are at their best in May, while autumn sees a spectacular change of colour throughout the gardens. The International Festival of Gardens takes place from June to September.

☎ 01666 880220

Wheal Martyn
147 E4

A fascinating look at the history of the china clay industry on a 26 acre (10ha) site dating from the 1870s and restored in the 1970s. Some areas of the site are still in active production and can be seen from a viewing platform. The visitor centre has displays and exhibits on both the raw materials and finished products of the industry and a trail takes the visitor round the old clay works. The site also contains a nature trail and adventure play area.

☎ 01726 850362 www.wheal-martyn.com

Wilton House
168 B4

Following the Dissolution of the Monasteries, the Benedictine site and land at Wilton were granted by Henry VIII to William Herbert, who incorporated the abbey ruins into a Tudor mansion. After a fire in 1647, Inigo Jones and John Webb redesigned and rebuilt the house in the Palladian style. The chief features of this rebuilding are the state rooms, particularly the Single and Double Cube rooms, so-called because of their precise dimensions, and renowned for their outstanding painted ceilings and elaborate plasterwork. The Double Cube room, arguably the foremost surviving example of a 17th century state room in England, was designed for the exhibition of family portraits by Van Dyck, and these can still be seen in their original setting. Elsewhere in the house there are paintings by Reynolds, Rembrandt, Brueghel, Rubens and Poussin, amongst others, making a collection which is considered one of the finest in Europe.

The 21 acre (8.5ha) grounds, bounded by the Rivers Nadder and Wylye, contain both formal gardens and landscaped parkland. Fine specimen trees can be seen on the woodland walks and there are architectural features such as the well-known Palladian Bridge. Other additions include the Millennium Water Feature and, for younger visitors, an adventure playground.

☎ 01722 746729 www.wiltonhouse.com

Woodchester Mansion
182 A2

A highly unusual place to visit, the mansion was abandoned before completion in 1870 and is in virtually the same state now. Much of the impressive craftsmanship of the time can be seen, something that would not have been possible if the mansion had been finished. Endangered lesser and greater horseshoe bats live in the roof spaces which can be observed by closed-circuit cameras. The mansion is open at weekends during the summer months.

☎ 01453 750455 www.woodchestermansion.org.uk

Westonbirt – The National Arboretum

Woodlands Leisure Park
151 E2

One of the biggest indoor activity complexes in the country, including the three-floor Ice Palace, specifically designed for the under sevens. Outdoors comprises 60 acres (24ha) of rides and activities in a wooded valley.

☎ 01803 712598 www.woodlandspark.com

Wookey Hole Caves & Papermill

166 C3

Spectacular caves carved out where underground streams have percolated through carboniferous limestone, gradually dissolving the rock over millions of years. Later precipitation of this dissolved limestone has resulted in striking formations of stalactites and stalagmites, some of which resemble human figures, most notably the Witch of Wookey. The dramatic nature of the caves is emphasised by skilful lighting.

Excavations have demonstrated that the caves were inhabited as long as 30,000 years ago, and tools have been discovered together with bones from species such as woolly rhinoceros, cave lions, mammoths and hyenas. Occupation is thought to have continued until Roman times.

The emerging underground River Axe at Wookey Hole has, in the past, been harnessed to provide water power, initially for woollen mills and subsequently for paper making. Visitors can see this traditional paper making process at the restored paper mill.

☎ 01749 672243 www.wookey.co.uk

SOUTH EAST ENGLAND

This appealing corner of England is alive with attractive market towns, quaint villages, historical stately homes, beautiful gardens and huge, strategically sited castles. Here, the wooded Weald and the green sward of the South Downs lead down to the Channel coast with its small traditional harbours and large bustling shipping ports. From Europe this is often the gateway to England, giving visitors the opportunity to acquaint themselves with the foibles and idiosyncrasies of Britain in one of its most pleasant and verdant regions.

Bodiam Castle

Alfriston Clergy House (NT) — 160 A3

A thatched, half-timbered 14th century Wealden Hall House with a pretty cottage garden. It was the first historic building acquired by the National Trust in 1896, purchased for a nominal £10. The house is oak framed and infilled with wattle and daub. One of the beams has a carving of an oak leaf which some believe gave rise to the adoption of the National Trust's famous logo.

☎ 01323 870001 www.nationaltrust.org.uk

Amberley Museum — 158 C2

This 36 acre (14.5ha) open-air museum, occupying a former chalk quarry, is dedicated to south east England's industrial past, also featuring various craftspeople demonstrating their skills. Visitors can travel around the site by vintage bus and narrow-gauge railway.

☎ 01798 831370 www.amberleymuseum.co.uk

Arundel Castle — 158 C3

Situated on a hill with views over the River Arun and out to sea, this castle is an impressive sight, dominating the nearby town with its towers and battlements. The castle began life at the end of the 11th century with the building of the motte. The gatehouse dates from 1070, but most of the rest is 19th century.

Arundel Castle is the ancestral home of the Dukes of Norfolk, who have played an important role in English history, the third duke being the uncle of both Anne Boleyn and Catherine Howard, wives of Henry VIII.

Within the castle there are fine collections of paintings by Van Dyck, Gainsborough, as well as 16th century furniture, tapestries, clocks and armour. The magnificent grounds include a Victorian kitchen and flower gardens. The Fitzalan Chapel is worth a visit.

☎ 01903 882173 www.arundelcastle.org

Arundel Castle

Ascott (NT) — 199 D5

This was formerly a half-timbered 17th century farmhouse but was much altered and enlarged when it came into the ownership of the de Rothschild family in 1876. The outstanding art collection contains paintings by Gainsborough, Rubens, Hogarth and some of the Dutch masters, whilst there is also some notable Chinese porcelain and Chippendale furniture. Outside the grounds extend to some 260 acres (104ha) with fine specimen trees, herbaceous borders, a Dutch garden and an unusual topiary sundial.

☎ 01296 688242 www.nationaltrust.org.uk

Ashdown House (NT) — 183 E4

Built in the 1660s in an isolated location high up on the Berkshire Downs, this is an unusual Dutch style house constructed from local dressed chalk blocks. It was probably designed by William Winde who spent his formative years in Holland with Royalist exiles, and who may well have been influenced by the French architect Francois Mansart who built a strikingly similar chateau in Normandy.

Public access is restricted to the hall, the impressive staircase and the cupola leading on to the roof, from where there are wonderful views. There are attractive woodland walks on the estate.

☎ 01793 762209 www.nationaltrust.org.uk

Ashmolean Museum — 406 B2

Claiming to be Britain's first museum, the Ashmolean opened in 1683, displaying a collection of natural history specimens assembled by the Tradescant family. Although chiefly famed for their horticultural expertise, the Tradescants were wide-ranging and idiosyncratic collectors, their acquisitions including not only natural history items but, amongst many others, a picture made from feathers, the Passion of Christ carved on a plum stone and a hat band of snake bones. The collection was transferred to the ownership of Elias Ashmole who presented it to Oxford University. In the late 19th century, it was rehoused in the magnificent neoclassical building which is its present home. It was subsequently merged with the university's art collection.

☎ 01865 278000 www.ashmol.ox.ac.uk

Basildon Park (NT) — 184 B5

Handsome late 18th century Palladian mansion with impressive classical façade, built of Bath stone and salvaged from neglect in the mid 20th century. The richly decorated interior contains some fine plasterwork, the Shell Room, with its unusual collection of sea shells, and a striking Octagon Room. Waymarked walks can be taken through the 400 acres (160ha) of attractive parkland and there are small but colourful formal gardens.

☎ 0118 984 3040 www.nationaltrust.org.uk

Bateman's (NT) — 160 B1

This attractive 17th century stone-built house was home to Rudyard Kipling from 1902 to 1936, with many of the rooms kept as Kipling left them. The delightful gardens contain a water mill.

☎ 01435 882302 www.nationaltrust.org.uk

Battle Abbey — 160 C2

Partially ruined abbey on the site of the Battle of Hastings, traditionally said to have been founded by William the Conqueror in 1070 to atone for the terrible loss of life incurred during the conquest of England. The gatehouse, built circa 1338, is the best preserved part of the abbey. Supposedly, the altar was located on the very spot where Harold II died.

☎ 01424 773792 www.english-heritage.org.uk

Bayham Abbey — 173 F5

Now an impressive ruin, located in a pretty wooded valley. Bayham Abbey was founded around the turn of the 13th century, and built from local golden sandstone. During the 18th century the site was landscaped to create the effect of a 'romantic' ruin.

☎ 01892 890381

Beachy Head — 160 A4

Forming an abrupt termination of the South Downs, the 535ft (163m) high chalk cliffs at Beachy Head are an awe-inspiring sight, dwarfing the lighthouse on the rocks below. Spectacular panoramic views are on offer.

Beale Park — 184 B5

Gilbert Beale had a passion for birds, to the extent that his favourite peahen would accompany him round the estate in his Rolls Royce. Now, nearly 50 years later, this superb collection of birds has grown considerably and the park has an impressive record with rare species, both with breeding and returning them to the wild.

The site, on the banks of the River Thames, covers around 400 acres (160ha) of parkland and ancient watermeadow, and boasts a remarkable array of aviaries. There are also rare breeds of farm animals, adventure play areas, a deer park, meerkat enclosure, maze and narrow-gauge railway. Boat trips can be taken on the river, and special events take place in school holidays.

☎ 0118 984 5172 www.bealepark.co.uk

Beaulieu Abbey — 348 A4

The name 'Beaulieu' is thought to derive from the Saxon 'beo ley' or bee meadow, subsequently interpreted as 'beau lieu' or beautiful place by the Norman scribes of the Domesday Book. The Cistercian abbey was founded here by King John in 1204 and built with stone brought in from the Isle of Wight and Caen in Normandy. The estate of 10,000 acres (4000ha) was a wealthy one and consequently a magnificent abbey was built. This was subsequently ruined during the Dissolution of the Monasteries, the monks' refectory being converted to form the parish church. The cloister is the best preserved part of the abbey, while the Domus, or lay brothers' dwelling, remained entire and now houses an excellent exhibition on life in the medieval abbey. The remaining stone was removed to build coastal defences at Southsea Castle.

☎ 01590 614604 www.beaulieu.co.uk

Beaulieu Palace House — 348 A4

Following the Dissolution of the Monasteries, Beaulieu Abbey estate was sold to the Earl of Southampton, an ancestor of the current owner, Lord Montagu. The Palace House was built in the 19th century around the abbey gatehouse, producing a curious combination of 14th century Gothic, as seen in the fan vaulted ceilings, and Baronial style Victorian architecture. Inside can be seen family portraits and other treasures of the Montagu family.

☎ 01590 614604 www.beaulieu.co.uk

Bedgebury National Pinetum — 173 G5

Covering 320 acres (129.5ha) in an attractive landscaped valley setting, the pinetum has over 6000 trees including vulnerable and endangered species. The pinetum was first established as the National Conifer Collection in 1925.

☎ 01580 211044 www.bedgeburypinetum.org.uk

Bekonscot Model Village — 185 E3

This is a 1930s re-creation of Britain in miniature. A pleasantly landscaped site of more than 40,000 sq ft (3716 sq m) boasts scaled down models of villages, farms, churches, castles, and even a zoo and a racecourse, together with a working coal mine, fishing port and steam fair. There is also a model railway with 7000ft (2100m) of track.

☎ 01494 672919 www.bekonscot.com

Bembridge Windmill (NT) 157 F4

Built around 1700 and in use until 1913, this is the only surviving windmill on the Isle of Wight. It contains a complete set of restored wooden machinery, most of it original.

☎ 01983 873945 www.nationaltrust.org.uk

Bentley Wildfowl & Motor Museum 159 G2

The Bentley estate is centred on a Palladian style mansion containing some fine furnishings and paintings. Surrounding the house are formal gardens using yew hedging to create 'outside rooms', and a large waterfowl collection including ducks, geese, swans and flamingos in an attractive natural setting of trees, lakes and ponds. The motor museum has over 100 exhibits including veteran, vintage and classic cars, and motorcycles.

☎ 01825 840573 www.bentley.org.uk

Birdworld 170 D3

Sufficient birds of all shapes, sizes, colours and habits for even the most demanding of ornithologists, displayed in 26 acres (10ha) of carefully designed grounds. There is an established breeding programme, particularly with the Humboldt penguins, making the peak of the breeding season in May and June a good time to visit, but there is plenty to see at other times, including Underwater World with aquarium and alligator swamp.

☎ 01420 22140 www.birdworld.co.uk

Bishop's Palace 157 E1

The impressive ruins of the medieval seat of the Bishops of Winchester, set in wooded grounds. The palace was built in 1136 by Henry de Blois, brother of King Stephen, and was subsequently enlarged in the 14th century by William of Wykeham before being reduced to its present state by Parliamentary forces in 1644. The remains of the Great Hall can be seen, together with the three-storey tower. The ground floor of the Dower House has been restored as a 19th century farmhouse.

☎ 01489 892460 www.english-heritage.org.uk

Blackgang Chine 157 D5

Originally developed in the 1840s as a scenic garden for Victorian tourists, this clifftop site of around 40 acres (16ha) has gradually evolved into a family leisure park.

The park endeavours to provide a mix of entertainment and education, the former catered for by a variety of attractions such as the water chute, roller coaster, gentler rides for younger children and nursery rhyme scenes. More informative displays can be seen in the maritime museum on the restored quayside and at the replica Victorian saw mill, complete with working engines.

☎ 01983 730330 www.blackgangchine.com

Blenheim Palace 183 G1

A stunning example of English Baroque architecture, Blenheim Palace was built for John Churchill, 1st Duke of Marlborough, following his victory at the Battle of Blenheim.

The palace was designed by Sir John Vanbrugh and built between 1705 – 22. The building itself covers 14 acres (5.5ha), whilst the grounds, landscaped by Lancelot 'Capability' Brown in the 1760s, extend to over 2000 acres (800ha).

Internally, the palace is sumptuously and elaborately decorated and furnished; there are gold leaf ceilings by Nicholas Hawksmoor, marble and stone carvings by Grinling Gibbons, frescoes by Louis Laguerre and portraits by Reynolds, Romney and Van Dyck. The ceiling of the Great Hall, 67ft (20m) high, has a painting depicting Marlborough's victory at Blenheim and the Long Library, a particularly impressive 183ft (56m), has a magnificent stucco ceiling.

The palace was also the birthplace of Sir Winston Churchill. Five rooms, including his birth room, are devoted to the Churchill Exhibition, with memorabilia tracing his life and work.

The grounds were originally designed by Henry Wise, Queen Anne's gardener, but now only the walled garden remains, and much of the later work, including the splendid lake, was by Lancelot 'Capability' Brown, while the Italian Garden and Water Terraces were designed by Achille Duchene in the early 20th century. The parkland provides hours of pleasant walking, and there is also a maze, adventure playground and butterfly house.

☎ 01993 811091 www.blenheimpalace.com

Bletchley Park Museum 353 C3

A Victorian mansion, formerly Britain's World War II code breaking headquarters, now housing a fascinating museum devoted to cryptography and computing. During the war, around 12,000 people worked here, their greatest success was to crack the German Enigma code. Guided tours are included in the entry fee.

☎ 01908 640404 www.bletchley park.org.uk

Bluebell Railway 159 F1

The Bluebell Railway, named after the profusion of bluebells seen beside the line in spring, is the only all-steam, standard-gauge, preserved railway in the country. It extends for 9 miles (14.5km) from Sheffield Park in the south, via Horsted Keynes, to Kingscote in the north.

British Railways closed the line in March 1958 as a cost cutting exercise; two years later 4 miles (6.5km) to the north of Sheffield Park were reopened by a group of enthusiasts. Since then, a further 5 miles (8km) have been added. There are plans to extend the track as far as East Grinstead where it will connect with the main line.

The railway's headquarters and locomotive department are situated at Sheffield Park station where an impressive selection of engines can be found. Some older locos date from the 1870s, with the newest built as late as the 1950s. There is also a museum of small exhibits, a model railway, a shop, a restaurant and a real ale bar at this station. The restoration and maintenance of carriages and wagons takes place at Horsted Keynes where work in progress can be seen from a viewing gallery.

☎ 01825 720800 www.bluebell-railway.co.uk

Bocketts Farm Park 171 G2

This is a working farm with a variety of farm animals and crops, set in scenic downland countryside. Features include tractor rides, children's play areas, pig races, plus seasonal events such as lambing and harvesting.

☎ 01372 363764 www.bockettsfarm.co.uk

Bodiam Castle

Bodiam Castle (NT) 160 C1

Everyone's favourite; a picture book castle with massive sandstone walls and towers rising from a broad moat, spiral staircases, battlement walks and hidey-holes to explore. Today, only a small part of the interior survives.

Bodiam was built in the late 14th century by Sir Edward Dalyngrigge, who had amassed considerable wealth in the wars against France, as a defensive stronghold protecting the Rother Valley from the French. It was intended to be a comfortable home as well as a defensible castle and symbolized the movement from traditional castle to comfortable manor house.

The castle was left partially ruined after attack in 1645 during the Civil War. Repairs to the building commenced in the 19th century, and during the early 20th century the castle was sympathetically restored by its then owner Lord Curzon who bequeathed it to the National Trust in 1926.

In addition to the castle, visitor attractions include a museum containing objects found during the restoration by Lord Curzon, plus a restaurant.

☎ 01580 830436 www.nationaltrust.org.uk

Borde Hill 159 F1

A large, mainly informal garden, created at the turn of the 19th century, set in 200 acres (80ha) of Grade II* parkland. The formal gardens, situated by

Blenheim Palace

the house (not open to the public) include walled, rose and herbaceous gardens; and restored Victorian greenhouses. Many of the rare trees and shrubs were introduced from the Himalayas as seed by plant hunters. Seasonal interest includes rhododrendrons and magnolias in the spring, roses and herbaceous plants in the summer, and impressive autumn colours.

☎ 01444 450326 www.bordehill.co.uk

Box Hill Country Park (NT) 171 G2

One of the best known summits of the North Downs; an area of natural beauty comprising woodland, with abundant box trees, and chalk downland with impressive views to the south. Near the summit there is an information centre, shop and a fort dating from the 1890s.

☎ 01306 885502 www.nationaltrust.org.uk

Breamore 156 A1

A red brick Elizabethan manor house, constructed in the characteristic E-shape of the period, set in beautiful parkland in the Avon valley. It is still a family home, and contains fine collections of furniture, porcelain and tapestries, whilst the wood-panelled Great Hall displays 16th and 17th century portraits. A carriage museum in a converted stable block contains the last operational stage coach in England, and there is an informative countryside museum in the old farmyard. An adventure playground and maze provide additional entertainment for children.

☎ 01725 512468 www.breamorehouse.com

Broadlands 169 E5

Originally a 16th century house, remodelled in the 18th century to create a handsome Palladian mansion, Broadlands is beautifully set in sweeping lawns bordered by the River Test and in grounds landscaped by Lancelot 'Capability' Brown.

A particular feature of the house is the magnificent Saloon with its white and gold plaster ceiling. Many of the fine furnishings, paintings and sculptures were originally acquired by the family of Lord Palmerston, noted Victorian prime minister whose birthplace this was and whose life is remembered in an exhibition here. A more recent resident was Lord Mountbatten of Burma, and an interesting and informative exhibition on his life and times has been staged by his grandson, Lord Romsey, the present owner.

Open from mid June to late August.

☎ 01794 505010 www.broadlands.net

Brooklands Museum 171 F1

This motoring and aviation museum is situated on the site of the world's first motor racing circuit. Not only is it steeped in motor racing history, but it was also the site of the first powered flight by a Briton in a British aeroplane in 1908. Today the museum contains over 30 aircraft and part of the steeply banked, original racing circuit.

☎ 01932 857381 www.brooklandsmuseum.com

Broughton Castle 197 G4

A medieval manor house built around 1300 and set on an island surrounded by a 3 acre (1ha) moat. Much of the original building remains, but it was greatly enlarged in the late 16th century, adding splendid decorative plasterwork, panelling and fireplaces. The castle was a secret meeting place for Parliamentarians during the Civil War, and at one stage it was besieged and captured by Royalists. There is an interesting display of arms and armour from this period in the Great Hall. The grounds contain colourful herbaceous borders, roses, climbers and a formal walled garden. Not open every day; it is advisable to telephone in advance.

☎ 01295 276070 www.broughtoncastle.demon.co.uk

Buckinghamshire County Museum 184 D1

An interesting collection which uses interactive displays to recount the cultural, social and natural history of the county. Exhibits include information on woodlands, farming, fossils, Celts and Romans, and there is also a programme of temporary exhibitions and an art gallery.

The museum building is also home to the Roald Dahl Children's Gallery, a hands-on exhibition where characters from Roald Dahl's books bring to life aspects of history, natural history, science and technology. Entry is by timed ticket. There is a charge for the Dahl Gallery but the museum is free.

☎ 01296 331441 www.visitbuckinghamshire.org

Buckinghamshire Railway Centre 184 C1

This is a working steam museum boasting one of the biggest collections of locomotives, wagons and carriages in the country. As well as the opportunity to ride on steam-hauled trains, there is a good-sized miniature railway and the chance to see restoration work in progress.

☎ 01296 655450 www.bucksrailcentre.org.uk

Buckler's Hard Maritime Museum 348 A4

Buckler's Hard is a delightful, unspoilt 18th century village located on the Beaulieu River. Proximity to timber from the New Forest and a depth of water sufficient to launch substantial warships combined to create a shipbuilding industry here during the 18th century. Two rows of terraced Georgian cottages housed the workforce, and some have been reconstructed to depict the lives of the workers and their families. The Maritime Museum traces the story of this local industry. River trips are available in the summer.

☎ 01590 616203 www.bucklershard.co.uk

Burnham Beeches 185 E4

A splendid Chilterns beech wood of around 574 acres (232ha) which has been a protected public open space since 1880. The woods are home to a diversity of wildlife, including rare plants, insects and fungi, and are known for their striking autumn colour.

Buscot Park (NT) 183 E3

An 18th century Palladian mansion with a remarkable collection of paintings and furniture belonging to the Faringdon Collection Trust. Paintings include works by Rembrandt, Rubens, Murillo and Reynolds, some particularly notable Pre-Raphaelite pieces and contemporary items, and there is furniture designed by Thomas Hope and Robert Adam.

The landscaped park features an Italianate water garden created by Harold Peto in the early 20th century.

☎ 08453 453387
☎ 01367 240786 www.buscot-park.com

Canterbury Cathedral 392 B2

The cathedral was founded in AD597 by St Augustine, a missionary from Rome, and has been the centre of the English church ever since. Today, the impressive cathedral, along with nearby St Martin's Church and St Augustine's Abbey, is a World Heritage Site.

The architectural styles of the cathedral range from Norman to Perpendicular. The large crypt is the oldest part of the present building and dates from the 11th century. Rebuilt after a fire, the 12th century Quire features beautiful stained glass windows depicting miracles and stories associated with Thomas Becket. Famously murdered here in 1170, he is one of the cathedral's most notable archbishops. Two years later he was made a saint. As a result of his martyrdom the cathedral became one of the world's most important centres of pilgrimage.

The magnificent nave, comprising tall columns and vaulted arches, was built in the 14th century and took 28 years to complete. Visitors can see medieval tombs within the cathedral including those of King Henry IV and Edward, the Black Prince.

To get the most out of a visit to this remarkable building, guided and audio tours are available.

☎ 01227 762862 www.canterbury-cathedral.org

Canterbury Cathedral

Canterbury Tales, The 392 B2

A series of superb reconstructions of medieval streets and Thomas Becket's shrine set inside the historic St Margaret's Church. It tells of Chaucer's famous characters on their journey from the Tabard Inn in London to Canterbury Cathedral, bringing them all very much to life.

☎ 01227 479227 www.canterburytales.org.uk

Carisbrooke Castle & Museum 157 D4

Such an obvious defensive site almost demanded the construction of a castle, and there is evidence that people complied, certainly from Saxon times and probably before. The present castle dates from around 1100, and still retains the typical motte and bailey outline, but was considerably enlarged in the late medieval period. Following the Armada in 1588 it was further fortified, and the wellhouse and its tread wheel were added so that water could be drawn more easily from the 161ft (49m) well in the event of siege.

Carisbrooke's chief claim to fame is as the place of imprisonment of Charles I prior to his trial and execution.

The museum is housed in the Great Hall of the Constable's Lodgings and contains memorabilia on Charles I, as well as general information on the Isle of Wight's history.

☎ 01983 522107 www.english-heritage.org.uk

Chartwell (NT) 173 D3

The family home of Winston Churchill for over 40 years, he purchased it in 1924 because he fell in love with the impressive views over the Weald. The large brick built house is still full of many of his personal possessions. Churchill also left his mark on the attractive gardens, creating lakes, garden walls and rockeries.

☎ 01732 868381 www.nationaltrust.org.uk

Chastleton House (NT) 197 E5

One of the most outstanding Jacobean properties in England, Chastleton has been continuously occupied by one family since its construction in the early 17th century. Particular treasures include elaborate plasterwork, Florentine tapestries and delightful glassware. Entry is by timed ticket and it is advisable to book in advance.

☎ 01608 674355 www.nationaltrust.org.uk

Chatham Historic Dockyard & World Naval Base 173 G2

The history of the dockyards extends back over 400 years. Nelson's famous flagship the *Victory* was built here in 1765. Today, on an 80 acre (32.5ha) site, visitors can see vessels including a World War II destroyer *H.M.S. Cavalier*, the modern submarine *Ocelot*, and *H.M.S. Gannet* which is the last surviving Victorian navy sloop. The site also contains a museum and an exhibition on the Royal National Lifeboat Institution.

☎ 01634 823807 www.chdt.org.uk

Chenies Manor House 185 F3

Queen Elizabeth slept in this 15th century manor house on several occasions, and the building still contains reminders of this period in its furniture and tapestries. Additionally, there is an interesting collection of antique dolls, while the restored 16th century pavilion in the grounds houses various exhibitions.

The delightful gardens are well known for their tulip display, and there are themed areas including a Tudor sunken garden, white garden, herbaceous borders, physic garden and kitchen garden.

☎ 01494 762888 www.visitbuckinghamshire.org

Chichester District Museum 158 A3

Local history museum housed in an 18th century corn store. Includes artefacts excavated from around Chichester.

☎ 01243 784683 www.chichester.gov.uk/museum/

Chiltern Open Air Museum 185 F3

Over 30 historic buildings have been constructed on this attractive 45 acre (18ha) park and woodland site. Most of the buildings were rescued from destruction and have been carefully dismantled and moved from their original locations to create this museum. The diverse display includes re-creations of a Victorian farmyard, complete with animals, a 1940s fully furnished 'prefab' and an Iron Age enclosure. There is even an Edwardian Public Convenience.

There are also demonstrations of traditional skills and information on the methods and materials used to make the buildings. There are plenty of hands-on activities and, throughout the year, there are various special events.

☎ 01494 871117 www.coam.org.uk

Chilterns 184 C4

The chalk downland which makes up the Chilterns extends from Luton in the north-east and runs south-west through Buckinghamshire and Oxfordshire to the southern edge at the River Thames. The open nature of the countryside, dotted with beech hangers and attractive villages, makes this delightful walking country, and part of the Ridgeway, a prehistoric track, runs through the area. Splendid views can be seen from vantage points such as Coombe Hill, with a height of 853ft (260m), Ivinghoe Beacon, and the windmill above Turville village.

Clandon Park (NT) 171 F2

Impressive Palladian mansion built circa 1731 for the 2nd Lord Onslow. Notable for its imposing two-storey marble entrance hall with magnificent Italian plasterwork ceiling. The house contains the Gubbay collection of furniture and porcelain, along with tapestries and the Ivo Forde Meissen collection of Italian comedy figures. The gardens, designed by Lancelot 'Capability' Brown in 1781, include a grotto, Maori house and parterre.

☎ 01483 222482 www.nationaltrust.org.uk

Claremont Landscape Garden (NT) 171 G1

One of the earliest examples surviving today of a 'landscape' garden. Dating from circa 1715, many of the great names in landscape gardening played a part including Charles Bridgeman, Sir John Vanbrugh, William Kent and Lancelot 'Capability' Brown. Extending to 49 acres (20ha) the garden includes a lake, impressive grass amphitheatre and grotto.

☎ 01372 467806 www.nationaltrust.org.uk

Claydon (NT) 198 C5

A charming, mainly 18th century house belonging to the Verney family until the mid 20th century. The unassuming exterior hides a wealth of extravagance in interior decoration. This was carved in the rococo style by Luke Lightfoot and the house contains some of the most remarkable decorative carving in the country, seen at its most outstanding in the Chinese Room. The saloon, library and stairwell boast some beautiful plasterwork, whilst the stairs are decorated with mahogany, ebony and ivory parquetry.

Florence Nightingale was a frequent visitor after her sister's marriage to Sir Henry Verney, and there is a display of memorabilia relating to her life and work.

☎ 01296 730349 www.nationaltrust.org.uk

Chiltern Open Air Museum

Cliveden (NT) 185 E4

A splendid 400 acre (160ha) estate in a magnificent location 200ft (60m) above the River Thames. The impressive house, designed by Sir Charles Barry and former home to the Astor family, is now an hotel with limited public access (telephone for opening times), but the principal attractions are the gardens and views. Planting has been designed to give colour and interest throughout the year.

☎ 01628 605069 www.nationaltrust.org.uk

Cobham Hall 173 F2

Large, attractive red brick mansion dating from 1584, set in 150 acres (61ha) of parkland landscaped by Humphrey Repton. The interior features a notable hall by James Wyatt in the Gothic style and a granite staircase dating from 1602. The house is currently an independent school and opening times are therefore restricted to the Easter and summer holidays.

☎ 01474 824319

Coombe Hill 185 D2

At 853ft (260m), this is one of the highest points on the Chiltern Hills, with magnificent views over the surrounding countryside. The monument on the summit is dedicated to the men of Buckinghamshire who were killed during the Boer War.

Cotswold Wildlife Park 183 E2

Set in 140 acres (56ha) of attractive gardens and parkland surrounding a 19th century mansion, the Wildlife Park is home to a wide range of animals. As well as the usual large animal attractions there are also endangered species such as the giant tortoise, red panda, and Asiatic lion.

There is a children's farmyard with domestic animals and a good adventure playground. A regular programme of events and talks takes place, particularly in summer.

☎ 01993 823006 www.cotswoldwildlifepark.co.uk

Cowper & Newton Museum 199 D2

Orchard Side, one of a pair of Georgian houses which now make up the museum, was the former home of the poet and hymn-writer William Cowper. Visitors can see his manuscripts and memorabilia, together with some belonging to his friend, the local curate John Newton who composed 'Amazing Grace'. There are also local history displays and an interesting textile exhibition.

☎ 01234 711516 www.mkheritage.co.uk

Danebury Ring 169 E4

An Iron Age hill fort, dating from about 500BC, with substantial defensive earthworks enclosing a 13 acre (5ha) site. Its name comes from 'dun', meaning hill, and 'bury', meaning fort.

The earliest evidence for occupation is Neolithic artefacts but the hill fort itself was not built until around 475BC and was abandoned around 100BC.

The site has been extensively excavated to reveal evidence for 75 roundhouses and many more rectangular storage buildings, and many of the finds can be seen at the Museum of the Iron Age in Andover. The isolated site has magnificent views over the surrounding downland.

www.hants.gov.uk

Deal Castle 175 F3

Coastal defensive fort built in 1539 during the reign of Henry VIII to protect England from France and Spain. Constructed in the shape of a Tudor Rose, the walls were deliberately built low and rounded to avoid enemy fire from the sea. Visitors can explore the underground passages and see the 53 gunports.

☎ 01304 372762 www.english-heritage.org.uk

Denbies Wine Estate 171 G2

Extending to 265 acres (107ha) on the slopes of the North Downs, this is the largest vineyard in Britain. Visitors can tour the working winery, experience guided wine tasting, and take the vineyard train up to the North Downs Way where there are excellent views.

☎ 01306 876616 www.denbiesvineyard.co.uk

Denmans — 158 B3

Richly and artistically planted, Denmans extends to approximately 4 acres (1.5ha) and is owned by garden writer and designer John Brookes. Highlights include an attractive walled garden and a glass area for the more tender species.

☎ 01243 542808 www.denmans-garden.co.uk

Dickens House Museum — 175 F2

The museum commemorates Charles Dickens' association with Broadstairs. It is said that Mary Pearson Strong, who once lived here, was the inspiration for the character of Betsey Trotwood, in Dickens' famous book 'David Copperfield'. Memorabilia and personal items such as the author's own letters are on display.

☎ 01843 861232 www.dickenshouse.co.uk

Dorney Court — 185 E5

A timber-framed, brick infilled 15th century building with a magnificent great hall and gallery, considered to be one of the finest examples of a Tudor manor house in England. Home to the Palmer family for over four centuries, the house contains many family portraits, fine furniture and heirlooms. The pleasant gardens have a particular claim to fame – here was grown the first pineapple to be cultivated in England. Opening is limited so it is advisable to telephone in advance.

☎ 01628 604638 www.dorneycourt.co.uk

Dover Castle — 395 E2

Well preserved Norman castle, on the site of a Roman fortress which in turn occupied that of an Iron Age Fort. Situated 375 feet (114m) above sea level, the castle has played a key role in the defence of the realm: William the Conqueror saw its importance and strengthened the castle shortly after the Battle of Hastings. However, much of the castle as we see it today dates from the reign of Henry II when the impressive four-storey keep, the distinctive inner bailey and part of the outer walls were built, creating a concentric fortress. Just prior to the death of King John the castle was damaged by a French siege and his son, Henry III, was quick to carry out strengthening work completing the outer bailey. The castle maintained its defensive role right up to and including World War II, when the tunnels under the castle became the headquarters from which the evacuation of Dunkirk was directed. Exhibitions and displays highlight key events in the castle's chequered and well documented history. A walk along the battlements gives the visitor a commanding view over the harbour.

☎ 01304 201628 www.english-heritage.org.uk

Dover Castle

Druidstone Park — 174 D2

In 12 acres (5ha) of attractive gardens and woodland, visitors can see a variety of animals including owls, deer, wallabies and various wildfowl. The open-air art park features sculptures in a variety of media, some by well-known artists. Children can also explore the farmyard with its pigs, llamas, donkeys and ponies.

☎ 01227 765168 www.druidstone.net/

Drusillas Park — 160 A3

Ideal for children, this small zoo primarily features the smaller species of animal housed in naturalistic environments. Over 100 species can be seen, such as meerkats, monkeys and penguins. There is also a walk-through bat enclosure and a wide range of play and hands-on activities.

☎ 01323 874100 www.drusillas.co.uk

Eastbourne Pier — 397 B3

Built in the 1870s, this 1000 ft (305m) long pier was designed by Eugenius Birch, using an ingenious method whereby the legs that support the pier sit on special cups allowing it to move from side to side in bad weather. Attractions include a restored Victorian Camera Obscura, bars, restaurant, café, amusement arcades and night club.

☎ 01323 410466 www.eastbournepier.com

Emmetts (NT) — 173 D3

Bequeathed to the National Trust in 1965, this mainly informal hillside garden dates from 1860 - 70. In about 1900, it was extended to 5 acres (2ha). Emmetts is particularly attractive in the spring with a profusion of daffodils and, later on, bluebells.

☎ 01732 751509 www.nationaltrust.org.uk

Exbury Gardens — 348 A4

A magnificent 250 acre (100ha) woodland garden set on the east side of the Beaulieu River. It is particularly famed for its rhododendron collection, started in the 1920s by the banker Lionel de Rothschild, who imported more than 1000 varieties and bred from these to produce 400 more, providing sensational colour from April to June. There are also good collections of magnolias and camellias, while the daffodil meadow, rock garden, rose garden and herbaceous borders greatly extend the garden's period of interest. Pleasant walks can be taken in the woodlands, and a 12.5 inch (30cm) narrow-gauge railway runs through part of the grounds.

☎ 023 8089 9422 www.exbury.co.uk

Finkley Down Farm Park — 169 E3

A great variety of farm animals, domestic pets and poultry can be seen on this working farm. Adventure playground and informative countryside museum.

☎ 01264 324141 www.finkleydownfarm.co.uk

Firle Place — 159 G3

A Tudor house remodelled in the 18th century, in an attractive setting at the foot of the South Downs. It has been home to the Gage family for over 500 years and houses collections of Old Master paintings such as Reynolds and Gainsborough, fine furniture and porcelain.

☎ 01273 858335 www.firleplace.co.uk

Fishbourne Roman Palace — 158 A3

Discovered in 1960, the remains of the north wing of this 1st century palace are enclosed by a modern building. The largest collection of in-situ Roman mosaics in Britain can be seen, along with remains of a bath suite, courtyards, corridors and hypocausts. A museum displays artefacts from excavations on and around the site and there is a Roman garden that has been replanted to its original plan.

☎ 01243 785859 www.sussexpast.co.uk

Fisher's Farm Park — 171 F5

Family attraction with farmyard animals including ducks, sheep, goats, shire horses and Shetland ponies. There are also adventure play areas which include a 25ft (7.5m) climbing wall, merry-go-round and trampolines.

☎ 01403 700063 www.fishersfarmpark.co.uk

Fort Brockhurst — 157 F2

A 19th century fort, one of several in the area built for the protection of Portsmouth. It has remained essentially unaltered, particular features being the moated keep, parade ground and gun ramps. Opening is limited so it is advisable to telephone in advance.

☎ 023 9258 1059 www.english-heritage.org.uk

Fort Victoria Country Park — 156 C4

The remains of Fort Victoria, which was built to protect the western entry to the Solent, now house a variety of attractions. These include a fascinating aquarium concentrating on local marine life, one of the largest model railway layouts in the country, a marine heritage exhibition and planetarium. The surrounding 50 acres (20ha) of grounds provide woodland and seashore walks. There is a cost for attractions but entry to the park is free.

☎ 01983 823893 www.fortvictoria.co.uk

Godstone Farm — 172 C3

This popular farm park features indoor and outdoor play areas as well as farm animals, chipmunks and llamas.

☎ 01883 742546 www.godstonefarm.co.uk

Great Coxwell Barn (NT) — 183 E3

A substantial medieval barn built in the 13th century as part of a Cistercian cell under the control of Beaulieu Abbey. It is constructed chiefly from Cotswold stone, with the original doors still in place on the east and west walls. Internally the roof is supported by the original oak posts and trusses, though most of the rafters have been replaced.

☎ 01793 762209 www.nationaltrust.org.uk

Great Dixter — 160 D1

A beautiful Tudor house built circa 1460 and restored in 1910 by Edwin Lutyens. It has one of the largest timber framed halls in the country and is home to gardening writer Christopher Lloyd. The 5 acre (2ha) garden, also designed by Lutyens, has been developed by Lloyd, producing a combination of historical design and contemporary and adventurous planting. The garden contains clipped topiary, wild meadow flowers, mixed borders including the famous 'long border' which is some 200ft (60m) long, ponds, walls, stone steps and paths.

☎ 01797 252878 www.greatdixter.co.uk

Great Tew — 197 F5

This could be described as a quintessential English village, with terraces of Cotswold stone cottages, most built in the 1630s for Lord Falkland's estate workers. The cottages are a mixture of thatched and stone-roofed, and a pub and village green complete the picture.

Grey's Court (NT) — 184 C4

An unusual 14th century house, rebuilt in the 16th century and subsequently modified but still retaining one of the original towers. A distinctive feature is the Tudor wheelhouse where donkeys turned the wheel which brought water up from a 200ft (61m) well.

The 8 acre (3ha) gardens are a particularly attractive aspect, set among the ruins of the 14th century building. Telephone in advance to check for opening times.

☎ 01494 755564 www.nationaltrust.org.uk

Groombridge Place Gardens — 173 E5

The walled, formal gardens were designed in the 17th century by John Evelyn and are set against a delightful moated manor house (not open to the public) of the same age. The grounds extend to 200 acres (80ha) and feature herbaceous borders, pools, woodland and rose garden. There is also the 'enchanted forest' to explore.

☎ 01892 863999 www.groombridge.co.uk

H.M.S. Victory — 407 D1

Now lying in dry dock, the *Victory* is the oldest commissioned warship in the world and the flagship of the Second Sea Lord, though she is of course best known as Lord Nelson's flagship at the Battle of Trafalgar in 1805. Commissioned in 1778, her excellent sailing qualities caused several admirals to choose her as their flagship, and although her active career ended in 1812 it was agreed that she should be preserved as a memorial to Nelson and this distinguished period of the Royal Navy's history. Tours are not available from July to the end of school summer holidays due to pressure of numbers, but guides are on hand to answer visitors' questions.

☎ 023 9272 2562 www.hms-victory.com

H.M.S. Warrior — 407 E1

Launched in 1860, *H.M.S. Warrior* was the world's first iron-hulled, armoured battleship and was then considered the most formidable ever seen. She was powered both by sail and steam, and has now been restored to her original launch condition. Visitors are able to explore the four large decks which illustrate life in the Victorian navy.

☎ 023 9272 2562 www.hmswarrior.org

Hammerwood Park — 172 D5

This neoclassical house was built in 1792 by Benjamin Latrobe who was later responsible for the Capitol, and the porticos of the White House in Washington D.C. It was converted into flats after World War II and owned by the pop group Led Zeppelin in the 1970s. It gradually fell into disrepair until rescued in 1982 by the present owners who give guided tours and tell of the continuing process of restoration.

☎ 01342 850594 www.hammerwoodpark.com

Haslemere Educational Museum — 171 E4

This family museum was founded in 1888 and opened to the public in 1895. Permanent galleries include: geology, natural history and human history. There are interactive displays, interesting collections and even a real Egyptian mummy.

☎ 01428 642112 www.haslemeremuseum.co.uk

Hastings Castle (Ruins) — 400 F2

Originally built by William the Conqueror in 1066 as a wooden fort on an earth motte, it was rebuilt in stone in 1070 as the first permanent Norman castle in the country. It is now a ruin commanding panoramic views of Hastings. Visitors to the castle can see an audiovisual show 'The 1066 Story' about the Battle of Hastings and the history of the castle.

☎ 01424 781111

Hatchlands (NT) — 171 F2

An 18th century brick built mansion set in a 430 acre (174ha) park designed by Humphrey Repton. The interior contains early examples of work by Robert Adam as well as a fine collection of keyboard instruments once owned, or played by famous composers including J.C. Bach, Beethoven, Chopin, Mozart and Purcell.

☎ 01483 222482 www.nationaltrust.org.uk

Herstmonceux Castle — 160 B2

Beautiful parkland, woodland and well kept Elizabethan gardens extending to 550 acres (220ha) are centred on a brick built 15th century moated castle (not open to the public). There is a children's woodland play area and nature trail. The estate is also the site of the Observatory Science Centre, former home of the Royal Greenwich Observatory (separate entry fee).

☎ 01323 833816 www.herstmonceux-castle.com

Hever Castle — 173 D4

This romantic, double-moated, 13th century castle was the childhood home of Anne Boleyn, and later owned by Anne of Cleves. The castle contains prayer books inscribed and signed by Anne Boleyn. There are also Tudor portraits, furniture, tapestries and a collection of miniature houses with period decoration and furnishings.

The spectacular gardens were constructed between 1904 and 1908. Features include a 35 acre (14ha) lake, Italian gardens with statuary and sculptures, a 360ft (110m) herbaceous border and herb garden. There are two mazes: a traditional yew hedge maze and an unusual water maze.

☎ 01732 865224 www.hevercastle.co.uk

High Beeches — 172 B5

20 acres (8ha) of Grade II* listed woodland, water and wild flower garden dating from the early 20th century. It contains a varied and extensive collection of plants and is particularly colourful in spring and autumn.

☎ 01444 400589 www.highbeeches.com

Highclere Castle — 169 F2

This former Georgian mansion, set in magnificent parkland landscaped by Lancelot 'Capability' Brown, was extravagantly refurbished both internally and externally by Sir Charles Barry in the 1840s. The lavishly decorated rooms embrace a variety of styles including Gothic, Moorish and rococo, which somehow combine to form a splendid example of High Victorian architecture.

The castle is the ancestral home of the Earls of Carnarvon, and there is an exhibition of Egyptian artefacts brought back by the 5th Earl following the Tutankhamen excavations in the 1920s.

The 7th Earl was the Queen's racing manager, and there is an exhibition on horse racing history.

Opening times are limited.

☎ 01635 253210 www.highclerecastle.co.uk

Hinton Ampner (NT) — 169 G5

Considered to be one of the great gardens of the 20th century, designed on the basis of a Victorian garden by Ralph Dutton, the 8th Lord Sherborne. The house stands on a ridge with magnificent views over downland scenery. The terraced gardens are a transformation of a Victorian remnant into a masterpiece of formal and informal plantings using predominantly pastel shades. Only open on certain days of the week in summer.

☎ 01962 771305 www.nationaltrust.org.uk

Hop Farm Country Park — 173 F4

Once a working hop farm, this large group of Victorian oast houses forms the setting for this family attraction. Amongst the entertainments are shire horse displays, an animal farm, children's play areas, a military vehicle display as well as a visit to the 'Hop Story' museum.

☎ 01622 872068 www.thehopfarm.co.uk

Horton Park Farm — 171 G1

Situated within the Horton Country Park, this popular attraction features a wide range of farm animals to feed and cuddle. There are also rare breeds, an adventure playground, indoor play area, a maze and tractor rides.

☎ 01372 743984 www.hortonpark.co.uk

Howletts Wild Animal Park — 175 D3

Founded by the late John Aspinall, this wild animal park is set in mature parkland and has the largest breeding colony of gorillas in captivity. It is notable for encouraging bonding between the keepers and their animals as Aspinall believed that this improved the emotional wellbeing of the animals and has led to successful breeding programmes. Other animals include the largest herd of African elephants in the UK, tigers, leopards, deer and rare monkeys.

☎ 01303 264647 www.howletts.net

Hughenden Manor (NT) — 185 D3

The home of former prime minister, Benjamin Disraeli, from 1847 – 71, and extensively restyled during this period by the Victorian Gothic architect E.B. Lamb. The interior has been left much as Disraeli would remember it, with his books, furniture, pictures and other memorabilia of his life. The 5 acre (2ha) gardens were designed by Disraeli's wife, Mary Anne. There are colourful herbaceous borders and formal annual bedding, woodland walks and an orchard with old varieties of apples and pears. Limited opening so it is advisable to telephone in advance.

☎ 01494 755573 www.nationaltrust.org.uk

Ightham Mote (NT) — 173 E3

A very attractive moated manor house dating from 1330 surrounded by a lovely garden with lakes and woodland. The interior of the house has a rich history, with the Great Hall dating from the 1340s, a 14th century crypt, a Tudor chapel and a Jacobean fireplace.

☎ 01732 810378 www.nationaltrust.org.uk

Isle of Wight Pearl — 156 D4

An extensive collection of all types of pearl jewellery. Visitors can learn how pearls are cultivated, see a replica of the world's largest pearl and learn how the jewellery is made.

☎ 01983 740352 www.isle-of-wight-pearl.com

Isle of Wight Zoo — 157 F4

Specialising in big cats, the zoo is home to around 20 tigers, many actually born here, and there is plenty of opportunity to observe the animals and learn more about them and their conservation. Other big cats are represented: lions, leopards,

jaguars and panthers, and there is also a fascinating lemur enclosure, snakes, insects and a good display of tarantulas. There is a regular programme of informative talks about the animals.

☎ 01983 403833 www.isleofwightzoo.com

Jane Austen's House 170 C4

An unpretentious 17th century red brick house where Jane Austen lived from 1809 – 17 and where she wrote or revised her six famous novels. The house is furnished in period style and contains many items associated with the author and her family, including letters and papers, furniture and first editions of the novels.

☎ 01420 83262 www.janeaustenmuseum.org.uk

Kent & East Sussex Railway 160 D1

Preserved steam and diesel engines run along this attractive standard-gauge line which runs for 10.5 miles (17km) from Tenterden to Bodiam (a short distance from the medieval castle). The line was built as the first light railway in Britain. At Tenterden, the headquarters, there is a museum plus the carriage and wagon workshop.

☎ 01580 765155 www.kesr.org.uk

Knole (NT) 173 E3

This enormous Tudor mansion, made of Kentish ragstone and set in a 1000 acre (405ha) deer park with 26 acre (10.5ha) landscaped grounds, was built in the mid 15th century for the Archbishop of Canterbury, Thomas Bourchier. It later passed to Henry VIII and then in 1603 it was gifted by Elizabeth I to her cousin Thomas Sackville, 1st Earl of Dorset. Extensive alterations and additions were made by the 1st Earl up to 1608 which transformed the house dramatically, particularly the interior. Today the house is notable for its 365 rooms – one for each day of the year, 52 staircases – one for each week of the year, and its 7 courtyards – one for each day of the week.

Knole contains an impressive collection of 17th century furniture started by the 1st Earl and continued by his descendents, most notably the 6th Earl who was Lord Chamberlain to William III. Later, the 3rd Duke, great-grandson of the 6th Earl, continued the collection by adding many valuable paintings.

☎ 01732 462100 www.nationaltrust.org.uk

Knole

Lamb House (NT) 161 E1

This brick fronted house, set in a one acre (0.5ha) walled garden in the centre of Rye, was built by James Lamb in 1723, the year he became mayor of Rye. George I stayed here in 1726 and acted as godfather to Lamb's son. The American novelist Henry James lived at Lamb House from 1898 to 1916 and the house is primarily devoted to mementoes of his time here.

☎ 01372 453401 www.nationaltrust.org.uk

Leeds Castle & Gardens 174 A3

Set on two islands in the middle of a large artificial lake, this beautiful castle was constructed in the 12th century as an impregnable stronghold, the barbican being built during the reign of Edward I. Six of the medieval queens of England have occupied the castle including Eleanor and Margaret, the wives of Edward I. Converted into a royal palace by Henry VIII, it has been restored and now contains a magnificent collection of medieval furnishings, French and English furniture and fabrics, tapestries and paintings by Degas, Pissarro, and Vuillard. Inside are also the Queen's Gallery, Banqueting Hall and Chapel. There are 500 acres (202ha) of parkland and gardens to explore, within which are an aviary, a maze and a grotto. The Woodland Garden provides a display of narcissi and daffodils in spring.

☎ 01622 765400 www.leeds-castle.com

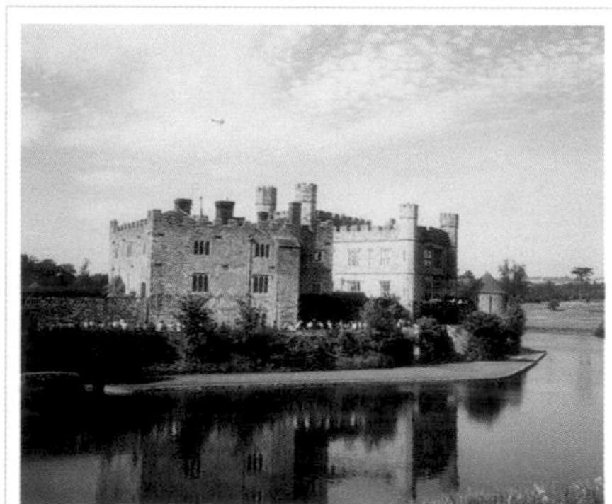

Leeds Castle

Legoland 185 E5

Every small child's dream come true, Legoland is aimed at the 4-12 age group, with a mixture of incredible models, toned down theme park rides and special activities.

Particular highlights include the Rat Trap, an intricate arrangement of slides, climbing nets and walkways, The Dragon roller coaster, the water chute at Pirate Falls, and for the younger children, Duplo Land. The Mindstorms workshops will appeal more to older children, with the chance to construct robots, while visitors of all ages should appreciate Miniland, where 50 million Lego bricks have been used to re-create miniature versions of Europe's capital cities.

☎ 08705 040404 www.legoland.co.uk

Leonardslee Gardens 159 E1

This spectacular 240 acre (97ha) woodland garden is a riot of colour in May and June when the rhododendrons and azaleas are in flower. Located in a valley with seven lakes (originally used in iron smelting to provide power) this garden was acquired in 1889 by Sir Edmund Loder who set about an ambitious planting programme. Other attractions include an alpine house, bonsai exhibition, Victorian motor car collection and a herd of semi-wild wallabies that were first introduced over 100 years ago.

☎ 01403 891212 www.leonardslee.com

Lewes Castle 159 G2

This ruined castle dates from [illegible] and is unusual in having two mottes. The shell keep dates from the early 12th century and two semi-octagonal towers were built in the 13th century along with a range of buildings inside the shell wall. The impressive barbican, one of the best preserved castle barbicans in England, was added in the 14th century. There are magnificent views from the towers of the town of Lewes and the surrounding countryside.

☎ 01273 486290 www.sussexpast.co.uk

Living Rainforest 184 A5

This unique rainforest conservation project, with its thousands of weird, wonderful and, in some cases, endangered species, has been constructed under 20,000sq ft (1836sq m) of glass deep in rural Berkshire. There are two distinct regions represented, Amazonia and Lowland Tropical, each with its characteristic climate and flora. Of particular note is the splendid collection of orchids and the 8ft (2.5m) lily pads on view between June and October.

☎ 01635 202444 www.livingrainforest.org

Look Out Discovery Park 171 D1

Very much a hands-on attraction, this interactive science and nature exhibition will have a particular appeal to children. Themed zones look at topics such as light and colour, body and perception, and woodland and wildlife.

The centre is set in 2600 acres (1040ha) of Crown Estate woodland and there are plenty of nature trails and walks, and a 70ft (22m) tower providing views over the surrounding countryside.The Coral Reef swimming pool with its Wild West Rapids is also across the way.

☎ 01344 354400 www.bracknellforest.gov.uk

Loseley House 171 E3

Beautiful Elizabethan mansion set in the 1400 acre (566ha) Loseley Park. The house, dating from 1562, was built with stone from the ruins of Waverley Abbey and contains many fine works of art and panelling from Henry VIII's Nonsuch Palace. The estate comprises a formal 2.5 acre (1ha) walled garden (which is subdivided into five themed components), managed woodland and agricultural land. The well known Loseley ice cream and other dairy products are produced from the estate's herd of Jersey cows.

☎ 01483 304440 www.loseleypark.com

Legoland

Lullingstone Castle 173 E2

Situated in the lovely Darenth valley, this historic family mansion, first built in the late 15th century, was extensively altered during the reign of Queen Anne who was a frequent visitor to Lullingstone. The Tudor gatehouse was one of the earliest in England to be built entirely of bricks. There are fine state rooms, the impressive Great Hall, the grand staircase and library. Outside is the church of St Botolph containing a fine Tudor rood screen.

☎ 01322 862114

Lullingstone Roman Villa 173 E2

Discovered in 1939, the site has been preserved within a modern building. The villa is thought to have been built during the 1st and 2nd centuries, although much of what can be seen today dates from the 4th century and includes well preserved floor mosaics, frescoes and a bathing complex. There is also the remains of one of the earliest Christian chapels.

☎ 01322 863467 www.english-heritage.org.uk

Mapledurham House & Mill 184 B5

An attractive H-shaped red brick house built in the late 16th century and set in pleasant parkland on the banks of the River Thames. Within the house are fine plasterwork ceilings and an impressive oak staircase, while a private family chapel designed in 'Strawberry Hill' Gothic with original elaborate plasterwork was added in 1797. There are literary connections with Alexander Pope, John Galsworthy and Kenneth Grahame.

An interesting feature in the grounds is a 15th century water mill restored to full working order and producing flour and bran.

Opening mainly restricted to weekends in the summer season.

☎ 0118 972 3350 www.mapledurham.co.uk

Marwell Zoo 169 G5

A well designed and carefully laid out zoo specialising in the conservation of endangered species but also with plenty of established favourites. Animals are housed in large, open enclosures and can be viewed via special walkways or road and rail trains. For children there is the Encounters Village where animals can be handled. There are regular special events during school holidays.

☎ 01962 777407 www.marwell.org.uk

Mary Rose 407 D1

Built around 1510, the *Mary Rose* was quite innovative for her time in that she could fire a broadside using heavy cannon. Prior to this, ships engaged at close quarters for hand-to-hand fighting.

A favourite ship of Henry VIII, the *Mary Rose* sank in 1545; the king was watching from Southsea Castle as he took part in a skirmish with the French. She was not seen again above water until 1982 and is now on display in the Ship Hall.

A short walk away, the *Mary Rose* Museum displays over 1200 artefacts retrieved from the wreck and surrounding sea bed. In addition there is information on how the wreck was raised.

☎ 023 9272 2562 www.maryrose.org

Michelham Priory 160 A3

Sitting on an island surrounded by the longest water-filled medieval moat in England, the building dates from 1229. Originally an Augustinian Priory until the Dissolution in 1537, it then became a country house. Exhibits include furniture, tapestries and artefacts. The gardens are in a variety of historic and contemporary styles and include a physic garden, cloister garden and orchard. There is also a working water mill.

☎ 01323 844224 www.sussexpast.co.uk

Mid Hants Railway 170 B4

Delightful steam railway nicknamed 'The Watercress Line' as it was formerly used to transport fresh watercress to market. Ten miles (16km) of track have been restored between Alresford and Alton, passing through lovely countryside – including watercress beds. The stations are restored to give a pre-war atmosphere and there is a visitor centre at Alresford. A programme of special events runs throughout the year.

☎ 01962 733810 www.watercressline.co.uk

Milton's Cottage 185 E3

Timber-framed 16th century cottage where the poet John Milton brought his family in 1665 to escape the Great Plague in London. Here he completed 'Paradise Lost' and commenced 'Paradise Regained'. The building houses first editions and other memorabilia, and has delightful cottage gardens.

☎ 01494 572313 www.miltonscottage.org

Modern Art Oxford 406 C2

This was established in 1965 and is arguably one of the foremost displays of contemporary art outside London, with exhibits from around the world including works by Ed Ruscha, Yoko Ono, Louise Bourgeois, Tracey Emin, David Goldblatt and Marina Abramovic. Work on display encompasses a variety of art forms; painting, sculpture, photography, design, film, video and architecture. Housed in a refurbished Victorian brewery, the museum also has a wide ranging programme of regular talks, events and children's workshops.

☎ 01865 722733 www.modernartoxford.co.uk

Monk's House (NT) 159 G3

Small country home of novelist Virginia Woolf and her husband Leonard, purchased by them in 1919. The rooms contain mementoes of the life and times of the famous 'Bloomsbury Group' of which they were key players. Extracts of Virginia's diaries and a display of her photographs can be seen in the garden room where she used to write.

☎ 01372 453401 www.nationaltrust.org.uk

Mottisfont Abbey Gardens (NT) 169 E5

The 12th century priory at the centre of this 20,000 acre (800ha) estate became a private house after the Dissolution of the Monasteries. However, the site's chief claim to fame, its walled rose garden designed by Graham Stuart Thomas, was only created in 1972, and is home to the National Collection of Old Fashioned Roses. Although these only have a short flowering period in June, elsewhere the gardens have been planted for interest throughout the season. The 'font' or spring, from which the place name is derived, is in the grounds.

☎ 01794 340757 www.nationaltrust.org.uk

Museum of Canterbury 392 B1

Part of the museum is housed in what was once a hospital for poor priests dating from the 13th century. There are a wide range of exhibits, including archaeological finds and historical collections dating from pre-Roman to the present day.

☎ 01227 452747 www.canterbury-museums.co.uk

Museum of Oxford 406 B2

Housed in the historic Town Hall, this museum traces the history of Oxford and the university. There is a particularly fine medieval collection, fascinating reconstructed interiors of city buildings from the 16th century onwards, paintings, furniture and many other items connected with the city and university.

☎ 01865 815559 www.oxford.co.uk

National Motor Museum 348 A4

In 1952 Lord Montagu of Beaulieu inherited five historic vehicles and started the museum as a tribute to his father who had been a pioneer of motoring in Britain. The initially small display proved so popular that, in 1972, a purpose-built museum was developed in the park surrounding Lord Montagu's home at Beaulieu. This now houses over 250 historically important vehicles, a magnificent collection of motoring memorabilia including film, books, photographs and permanent displays. Highlights of the collection include some of the world's oldest cars such as Fiats and Renaults, record breakers such as Golden Arrow and Bluebird, a motorsport gallery celebrating Grand Prix racing and rallying, and a James Bond experience with cars and boats from the films. Visitors can travel round the grounds by monorail or open-topped replica 1912 London bus.

☎ 01590 612345 www.beaulieu.co.uk

Needles Pleasure Park

Needles Pleasure Park 156 C4

A spectacular chairlift ride provides unique views of the striking coloured sands of the Alum Bay cliffs and across to The Needles and lighthouse. There are also boat trips, children's rides and games, tours round the Isle of Wight Sweet Factory and glass blowing demonstrations at Alum Bay Glass.

A short walk along the cliffs is a 19th century fort, Needles Old Battery. As well as an exhibition on the site's history, a 200ft (60m) tunnel leads to a viewpoint with unrivalled views across to the Needles, three distinctive jagged, eroded remnants of the former chalk cliffs.

☎ 0870 458 0022 www.theneedles.co.uk

New Forest 156 B1

Contrary to expectation, much of this 150 square mile (388sq km) Area of Outstanding Natural Beauty is not actually still forested; rather it is a mixture of woodland and heath, poor sandy soils giving little incentive for cultivation. The Forest was designated a royal hunting preserve by William the Conqueror in 1079 and, at this time, punishment for trespass included mutilation and even death; now around 8 million people visit the area each year.

Although close to large centres of population, once away from the main roads there is a distinct feeling of having 'got away from it all'. The Forest itself is relatively sparsely settled, with only Lyndhurst and Brockenhurst of any significant size. However, the high visitor numbers in recent years have called for practical measures, such as the 40mph (64kph) speed limit throughout the Forest, to protect the environment, the wildlife, the ponies and other grazing animals.

The harsh penalties meted out in the 11th century were later rescinded and the local owner-

occupiers, or Commoners, were granted certain rights, such as the freedom to graze livestock or more obscurely, turbary (peat cutting). These rights are administered by the Verderers, and the Verderers Court, which is held every two months, is considered to be the oldest court of law in England. The distinctive Forest landscape, with its free-grazing ponies, cattle and sheep, is a consequence of these ancient laws.

The remoter parts of the Forest, particularly the wetland areas, are home to some of Britain's rarest plant, animal and insect species, whilst the open heathland is of particular interest to birdlovers. The scenery, although not dramatic in terms of relief, makes for pleasant walking and cycling country.

New Forest

New Forest Museum & Information Centre — 156 C2

The place to visit for all the background information on the Forest and its inhabitants. There are interactive displays on the area's geology, and specific exhibits on wildlife, history and culture. The famous New Forest Embroidery is on display and there is a regular programme of temporary exhibitions.

☎ 023 8028 2269 www.newforestmuseum.org

Nymans (NT) — 159 E1

This beautiful 30 acre (12ha) garden set on the side of a sheltered valley was created by three generations of the Messel family dating from 1890. The garden originally surrounded a 14th century manor house which was largely destroyed by fire in 1947, and the ruins give an atmospheric backdrop to the planting. The garden is designed as a series of 'rooms' with hedges, walls and trees providing shelter for rare and exotic plants.

☎ 01444 400321 www.nationaltrust.org.uk

Osborne House — 157 E3

This was the rural retreat for Queen Victoria and her family, away from the pressures of ceremonial life. The house was designed by Prince Albert with technical input from Thomas Cubitt. The Prince was an admirer of Italian art and architecture and his design was based on the style of an Italian villa, complete with towers and terraces. As a widow, Victoria was a frequent visitor until her death in 1901, and many of the apartments have been preserved with little change since then, in keeping with her wishes.

The interior design of Osborne House is equally lavish. The Grand Corridor is lined by marble sculptures, and there are portraits and frescoes which underline the family's links with Europe and the Empire. Particularly sumptuous is the Durbar Room, built in the early 1890s to celebrate the Queen's role as Empress of India.

Within the grounds, 'Swiss Cottage', the royal equivalent of a Wendy House, was built with Prince Albert's intention of providing his children with the basics of housekeeping and cookery. There is also the ultimate boys' toy, Victoria Fort, which the royal princes helped to construct.

The pleasant gardens were laid out by Prince Albert in Italianate terraces, with beautiful views across the Solent, and there is a restored walled garden.

☎ 01983 200022 www.english-heritage.org.uk

Owl House, The — 173 F5

This 16th century timber-framed house (not open to the public) was purchased by Lady Dufferin in 1952. The gardens, extending to 16 acres (6.5ha), were created during her time here and include expansive lawns, woodland walks and sunken water gardens.

☎ 01892 890230 www.owlhouse.com

Oxford — 406

Originally an important Saxon town, thanks to its strategic position where the Rivers Thames and Cherwell meet, the key date in Oxford's development as a major university town was 1167 when all Anglo-Norman students were expelled from the Sorbonne and selected Oxford as a suitable alternative. The first three colleges, Balliol, Merton and University, were built in the 13th century and others followed slowly over time so that now the university has around 15,000 students and 39 colleges. The city centre is dominated by the attractive college buildings, many of which are open to the public. Of particular interest are Christ Church, with its splendid Great Hall, Magdalen, with its riverside gardens, and Merton. Some of the colleges charge admission and access may be limited in term time. Other impressive buildings are the Bodleian Library, Ashmolean Museum and Sheldonian Theatre, an early design by Sir Christopher Wren. The city's cathedral, the smallest in England, is in Christ Church College, where it doubles as the college chapel. Famous literary, scientific and theological associations abound, and the museums contain major historical, natural history and scientific collections. Oxford is essentially a medieval city, and is best visited by public transport. The centre is compact and there is an excellent park and ride system.

www.visitoxford.org

Oxford Story — 406 B2

A time car ride through the history of Oxford University in carriages designed as desks. The associated audiovisual presentation provides information both on the development of the university and the many influential people who have passed through its doors.

☎ 01865 790055 www.oxfordstory.co.uk

Osborne House

Oxfordshire Museum, The — 183 G1

Located in a fine town house in Woodstock, this illuminating museum has plenty of information on the social history of the county, permanent displays tracing the story of the inhabitants, landscapes, buildings and industries from earliest times to the present day. There is also a special gallery for children and a purpose-built gallery for temporary exhibits.

☎ 01993 811456 www.oxfordshire.gov.uk

Palace Pier — 390 F3

Opened on 20th May 1899, this 1722ft (525m) long pier (Grade II* listed) features filigree ironwork arches and some of the original kiosks. Over the years, these basic attractions have been joined by a huge array of modern-day amusements such as a funfair, arcades, night club, bars and restaurants.

☎ 01273 609361 www.brightonpier.co.uk

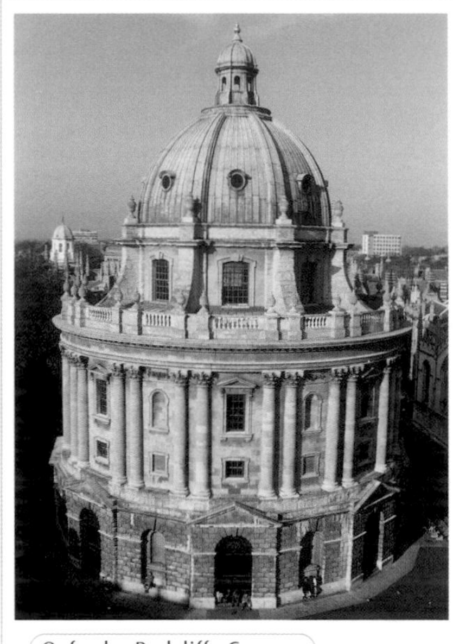

Oxford – Radcliffe Camera

Paradise Park — 159 G3

This varied attraction, set in colourful themed gardens, is ideal for children. It focuses on the local area's history and includes life-size moving dinosaurs, a model village featuring Sussex landmarks, a collection of fossils, crazy golf and a miniature railway.

☎ 01273 512123 www.paradisepark.co.uk

Parham House — 158 C2

This 'E' shaped Elizabethan house, built in 1577 with later additions, has panelled rooms hung with portraits and 17th century furniture, some of which is still covered with the original needlework. Parham is surrounded by extensive grounds including a deer park and an attractive 11 acre (4.5ha) garden featuring a brick and turf maze and a 4 acre (1.5ha) walled garden, the flowers from which are used to adorn the house.

☎ 01903 744888 www.parhaminsussex.co.uk

Paulton's Park — 156 C1

A leisure park of 140 acres (56ha) particularly suitable for families, with over 50 rides and activities, including a log flume and roller coaster. In addition there is a good collection of exotic birds and wildfowl in aviaries and ponds, a 19th century working waterwheel, 10 acre (4ha) lake and Romany Museum providing insight into traditional gipsy life.

☎ 023 8081 4455 www.paultonspark.co.uk

Penshurst Place 173 E4

Built of local sandstone, this impressive castellated manor house dates from the 14th century and has been occupied by the Sidney family since 1552. The house is notable for its outstanding medieval Barons Hall built in 1341 with its 60ft (18m) high chestnut-beamed roof. The State Rooms contain a collection of paintings from the 15th to 17th centuries, furniture, tapestries and armour. The vast 10 acre (4ha) walled garden, created between 1570 and 1666, is formed into a series of garden rooms divided by a mile of yew hedging. The variety of planting gives all year round interest. Also of interest is the deer park and toy museum.

☎ 01892 870307 www.penshurstplace.com

Petworth House (NT) 171 E5

Situated on the edge of a 700 acre (283ha) landscaped deer park and adjacent to the town of Petworth, this magnificent 17th century mansion was built around an older manor house owned by the Earls of Northumberland. The park, landscaped in the mid 18th century, is considered to be one of Lancelot 'Capability' Brown's finest and is home to Europe's largest herd of fallow deer.

The house contains the National Trust's largest and finest collection of pictures, the foundations of which were laid by Charles Seymour, 6th Duke of Somerset, when he acquired the house in 1690 on his marriage to the Earl of Northumberland's daughter. On the Duke's death the house passed by marriage to the Wyndham family. Charles Wyndham, the 2nd Earl of Egremont, added to the existing collection of Italian, French and Dutch Old Masters and acquired ancient sculpture from Rome and Greece. The 3rd Earl of Egremont continued the tradition. He collected contemporary British paintings. Interestingly, he was a patron of Turner, providing a studio for him at Petworth and many of Turner's paintings can be seen in the house. The 3rd Earl also acquired work from Gainsborough and Reynolds.

Following alterations to the house in the 1870s only two of the original 17th century interiors remain: a baroque chapel and a marble hall with black and white checked floor.

☎ 01798 343929 www.nationaltrust.org.uk

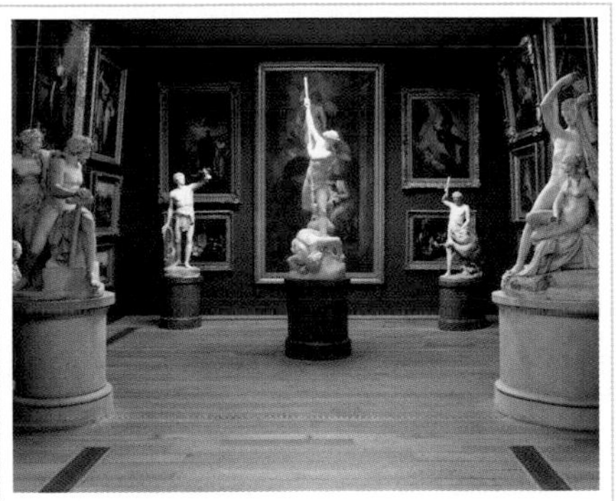

Petworth House

Pevensey Castle 160 B3

Dating from Roman times, and occupied by the Normans in 1066, the castle's location as a possible invasion point led to several sieges during its history. It eventually became uninhabited by the 16th century and fell into ruin. A gun emplacement was built there during the Spanish Armada and the castle was again used during World War II. Pillboxes from that time can still be seen. There are towers, battlements and dungeons to explore.

☎ 01323 762604 www.english-heritage.org.uk

Pitt Rivers Museum 406 A2

A unique collection of objects from all over the world, with something of interest for everyone.

The museum was founded in 1884 when Lt-Gen Pitt-Rivers, a prominent figure in the world of anthropology and archaeology, donated his collection of over 18,000 items to Oxford University. This collection has now been considerably enlarged to comprise over half a million objects, displayed according to function.

☎ 01865 270927 www.prm.ox.ac.uk

Polesden Lacey (NT) 171 G2

Attractive Regency house in a beautiful setting on the North Downs. It was the home for many years of society hostess, Mrs Ronald Greville, who was a friend of Edward VII. It contains sumptuous interiors and is especially renowned for its paintings. The future George VI and Queen Elizabeth spent part of their honeymoon here in 1923. The gardens have lovely views and extend to 30 acres (12ha), including lawns, walled garden and herbaceous borders.

☎ 01372 452048 www.nationaltrust.org.uk

Port Lympne Wild Animal Park 174 D5

The park was created in 1973 when John Aspinall bought the Port Lympne estate. It comprises a 350 acre (140ha) reserve where the animals can roam in relatively unconstrained conditions. Aspinall supported an ethos of bonding between keepers and animals that has resulted in successful breeding programmes. At the park visitors can see a large group of black rhinos, Asian elephants, tigers and lions, amongst others. Also open to the public is the house, built during World War I, with its 15 acre (6ha) formal garden.

☎ 01303 264647 www.howletts.net

Portchester Castle 349 E3

One of England's oldest fortifications, Portchester was originally built in the 3rd century AD by the Romans as part of a chain of fortresses known as the Saxon Shore forts, built in response to Saxon raids. The massive walls, 20ft (6m) high and 10ft (3m) thick, are amongst the finest surviving examples of this period in northern Europe. Subsequently occupied almost continuously until the 19th century, the site was initially a walled settlement with an impressive Norman keep, part of which still stands, then respectively a castle, royal palace, military hospital and a gaol for French prisoners during the Napoleonic Wars.

☎ 023 9237 8291 www.english-heritage.org.uk

Portsmouth Cathedral 407 F1

Formerly the parish church of Portsmouth, cathedral status was granted in 1927 when the diocese of Portsmouth was created. The original building dates from the 12th century, and the transept and sanctuary still remain, combined with a 17th century nave and tower, rebuilt following Civil War damage. A cupola was added in 1703 and the modern nave and aisles in the mid 20th century, producing an unusual fusion of style with a central tower. Internally, there are several interesting features including the Navy Aisle, with its maritime connections, the remains of a 13th century wall painting, a fine 16th century Florentine majolica plaque and a 20th century bronze statue of John the Baptist.

☎ 023 9282 3300 www.portsmouthcathedral.org.uk

Portsmouth Historic Dockyard 407 E1

The development of the dockyard at Portsmouth was initiated by Richard I in the 1190s and evolved over succeeding centuries. It became the construction centre for Henry VIII's fleet and received Royal Dockyard status in 1670 when Charles II founded the Royal Navy. By 1800 the navy had nearly 700 ships and the dockyard was considered the largest industrial complex in the world. Apart from a blip at the end of the Napoleonic Wars, expansion was almost continuous throughout the 19th century. In the 20th century the dockyard was vital to Britain's successes in both World Wars, but since then has been in decline due to defence cuts and streamlining of the armed services. The Naval Base remains the premier home port for the Royal Navy, but the title of Royal Dockyard has gone.

The historic Georgian part of the dockyard is now open to the public and this provides a unique opportunity to experience 500 years of the Royal Navy's history, from the remains of the 16th century ship *Mary Rose*, to Action Stations, which uses interactive technology to illustrate the role of the modern navy. In between, a visit to *H.M.S. Victory* reveals the privations suffered by sailors in Nelson's fleet, the scrupulously restored *H.M.S. Warrior* displays a state of the art mid-19th century warship, the Royal Naval Museum gives a detailed history of the service from the 18th century onwards, while Warships by Water harbour tours give a glimpse of the modern operational fleet.

☎ 023 9272 2562 www.flagship.org

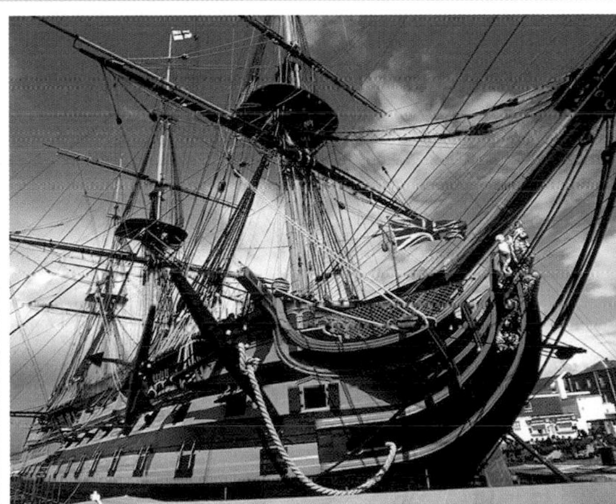

H.M.S. Victory – Portsmouth Historic Dockyard

Pulborough Brooks RSPB Nature Reserve 158 C2

Created in 1989, this 420 acre (170ha) reserve primarily consists of an area of wet grassy meadows which flood in winter. Thousands of water birds such as swans, ducks, geese and wading birds visit the site, especially as winter migrants. There is a visitor centre housed in a converted barn and a 2 mile (3.2km) circular trail.

☎ 01798 875851 www.rspb.org.uk

Quebec House (NT) 173 D3

General James Wolfe, who led the British to victory over the French in the Battle of Quebec in 1759, lived here as a boy. Named after the battle, this gabled red brick house dating from the 16th century, contains an exhibition paying tribute to his life and the victory that made his name.

☎ 01732 868381 www.nationaltrust.org.uk

Richborough Castle — 175 F2

Now a ruin, this fort is thought to date from the Roman invasion in AD43 and, with Watling Street starting at its east gate, became their main entry point into Britain en route to London. Today, flint walls rising to 25ft (7.5m) high can be seen and the foundations of a triumphal arch that was originally over 80ft (24m) high. There is a museum containing artefacts found on site and an exhibition on Roman life.

☎ 01304 612013 www.english-heritage.org.uk

River & Rowing Museum — 184 C4

A museum dedicated to rowing and the River Thames, and to Henley, the town where they are inextricably linked.

There are three themed galleries – the Rowing Gallery, the Thames Gallery and the Henley Gallery.

An additional walk-through attraction, particularly aimed at children, re-creates the characters and settings of Kenneth Grahame's 'Wind in the Willows'.

☎ 01491 415600 www.rrm.co.uk

Robin Hill Country Park — 157 E4

The 88 acres (35ha) of this country park combine nature trails and woodland walks with theme park rides and adventure playgrounds.

☎ 01983 527352 www.robin-hill.com

Rockbourne Roman Villa — 156 A1

Discovered in 1942 by a farmer digging out a ferret, this extensive villa was occupied from the 2nd century AD until the end of Roman rule in Britain in the 5th century AD. Although much of the area has been excavated, part has been backfilled for protection since the site is not under cover. However, the outlines are marked out, and mosaic floors and underfloor heating systems can be viewed. A museum displays artefacts found on the site, including pottery, jewellery and a large hoard of coins.

☎ 01725 518541 www.hants.gov.uk

Romney Marsh — 174 C5

This fertile, flat landscape (once under the sea) was reclaimed from marshland in medieval times, and is protected from flooding by a shingle bank. Running along the landward side of the marsh is the 23 mile (37km) long Royal Military Canal, which was built during the Napoleonic wars. The Marsh, as well as being home to the longwool Romney sheep, is also rich in flora and fauna, and is a favourite spot for birdwatchers.

Romney, Hythe & Dymchurch Railway — 174 D5

Originally opened in July 1927 to transport the public, this 15 inch narrow-gauge railway now covers a distance of 13.5 miles (22km) from the Cinque Port of Hythe to Dungeness. The line travels through the seaside resort of Dymchurch, and also New Romney where there is a Toy and Model Railway museum.

☎ 01797 362353 www.rhdr.org.uk

Rousham House — 197 G5

An unspoilt 17th century house, later extended and remodelled by William Kent in the style of a Gothic Tudor mansion. However, the original staircase and some 17th century panelling still remain, together with Kent's painted parlour containing some of his furniture and painted ceiling.

The landscape garden at Rousham, started by the royal gardener Charles Bridgeman, was further developed and elaborated on by Kent. It remains almost as he left it, with many 18th century water features and temples still in existence. There is also an attractive walled garden with colourful herbaceous border, parterre and pigeon house.

The house opens two days a week in summer, but the garden is open all year. No children under 15.

☎ 01869 347110 www.rousham.org

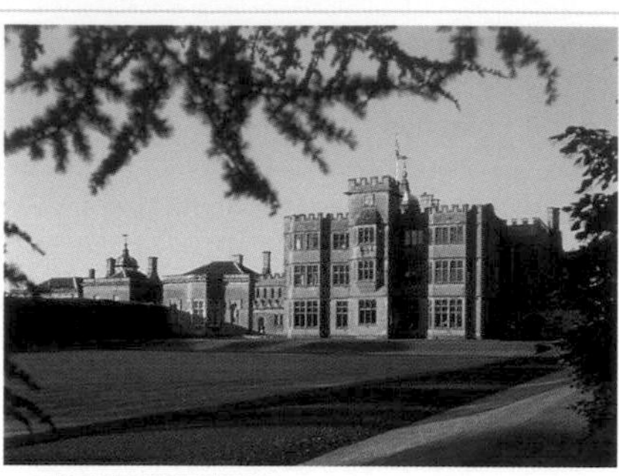

Rousham House

Royal Navy Submarine Museum — 349 E4

A fascinating museum tracing the history and explaining the principles of submarine technology and warfare. Visitors can see *Holland I*, the Royal Navy's first submarine, recovered from the sea bed almost 70 years after sinking on her way to the breakers yard and now fully restored. This can be compared to *H.M.S. Alliance*, preserved fully equipped from when she ended service in 1973 and now in dry dock.

☎ 023 9252 9217 www.rnsubmus.co.uk

Royal Pavilion — 390 F2

With its 'Hindu Style' domes and minarets, this Regency Palace is one of the most distinctive and unusual buildings in Britain. Originally a farmhouse, it was transformed for the notoriously profligate Prince Regent (later George IV). In 1787 Henry Holland was commissioned to enlarge the property; further alterations and additions were made by John Nash between 1815 and 1822 . The result was the extravagant Indian and Chinese influenced palace that we see today. The Pavilion has undergone a substantial programme to restore it to its former glory, and stands in restored Regency gardens which have been replanted to Nash's original 1820s design.

The lavish interior features impressive and unusual rooms; notably the Entrance Hall with its Chinese motif wall decorations and the 162ft (49m) Long Gallery, also with a distinctly Chinese décor. The Banqueting Room is stunning with a 45ft (14m) high painted ceiling, with the huge one ton crystal chandelier suspended from a carved dragon. In 1820, the King's Apartments were finally finished, coinciding with George IV's accession and today contain much of the original furniture. After the death of George IV in 1830, the palace was used by William IV and then Queen Victoria who sold it on to the town council in 1850.

☎ 01273 290900 www.royalpavilion.org.uk

Royal Victoria Country Park — 348 B3

Located on the site of a former military hospital, the park covers over 100 acres (40ha) of landscaped grounds, woodlands, marsh and beach, and there are nature trails, walks, a narrow-gauge railway and, in summer, a programme of events. A Sensory Garden has also been developed here, designed for scent, sound, colour and texture. The only remaining feature of the hospital is the chapel, which houses a museum of the hospital's history.

☎ 023 8045 5157 www.hants.gov.uk

Rycote Chapel — 184 B2

A 15th century chapel retaining the original furniture, with outstanding carved and painted woodwork, two roofed pews and a musicians' gallery.

☎ 023 9258 1059 www.english-heritage.org.uk

St Mary's House — 159 D3

Originally built as a pilgrims' inn, this timber-framed house dates from 1470. Features of the house include an Elizabethan staircase, Gothic fireplaces along with 16th century marquetry and furniture. The gardens have unusual animal topiary, herbaceous borders and a rose garden.

☎ 01903 816205

Sandham Memorial Chapel (NT) — 169 F1

A red brick chapel built in the 1920s as a memorial to Lieutenant H.W. Sandham, who died following the Macedonia campaign. Inside, the chapel walls are lined with a dramatic series of murals by Stanley Spencer who had been an orderly on the campaign.

☎ 01635 278394 www.nationaltrust.org.uk

Royal Pavilion – Brighton

Savill Garden — 185 E5

Beautiful 35 acre (14ha) garden set within Windsor Great Park comprising woodland, a formal rose garden and herbaceous borders. Named after Eric Savill (deputy surveyor of Windsor Park and Woods) who began work on it for George V in 1932. The garden has a magnificent display of rhododendrons and azaleas giving it superb colour in the spring, although it is worth a visit at any time of year.

☎ 01753 847518 www.savillgarden.co.uk

Scotney Castle Garden (NT) — 173 F5

Surrounding the ruins of a 14th century moated castle are picturesque 19th century gardens created by Edward Hussey. The rich planting includes rhododendrons and azaleas giving superb spring colour, plus many Japanese maples, tulip trees and liquidambers which give a splendid display in autumn.

☎ 01892 891081 www.nationaltrust.org.uk

Sea Life Centre — 390 F3

Aquarium in a Victorian building with superb ocean tunnel display where visitors can walk through the ocean amongst sharks, rays and giant turtles. There is also a giant Pacific octopus and touch tanks where visitors can hold crabs and feed rays.

☎ 01273 604234 www.sealifeeurope.com

Seven Sisters Country Park 160 A4

The country park lies within an Area of Outstanding Natural Beauty and is a designated Site of Special Scientific Interest. It was established in 1971 and encompasses 700 acres (283ha) either side of the River Cuckmere. The site comprises a wide range of habitats including the beautiful chalk downland with its unique flora and fauna, wetland, coastal and marine environments. The park takes its name from the famous Seven Sisters white cliffs formed where the chalk of the South Downs meets the sea.

There are a number of 18th century flint barns within the park, one of those in Exceat has been converted into a visitor centre. As well as enjoying the area on foot, visitors can also hire bicycles and canoes.

☎ 01323 870280 www.sevensisters.org.uk

Seven Sisters Country Park

Sheffield Park (NT) 159 G1

With their wide range of rare and unusual trees and shrubs, these beautiful gardens have the character of a landscaped arboretum. They were created for the first Earl of Sheffield in the late 18th century by Lancelot 'Capability' Brown and Humphrey Repton, and extend to 120 acres (48.5ha). In 1909 the estate was acquired by Arthur G. Soames who, over the next 25 years, was responsible for refining the overall design and introduced much of the varied and exotic planting we see today.

Four large lakes form the centrepiece of the garden. Waterfalls and a 25ft (7.5m) cascade connect the lakes together and are spanned by attractive ornamental bridges. In the spring there are magnificent displays of bluebells and daffodils, then later on, rhododendrons and azaleas make an impressive splash of vibrant colour. In summer, red, white and pink water lily flowers add colour to the lakes.

☎ 01825 790231 www.nationaltrust.org.uk

Sir Harold Hillier Gardens & Arboretum 169 E5

A unique collection of shrubs and trees which is one of the largest of its kind in the world. The gardens were established by Sir Harold Hillier in 1953, and extend to over 180 acres (70ha). The collection comprises over 42,000 plants from the world's temperate regions, grown in themed gardens which are designed so that there is colour and interest throughout the year. The Visitor and Education Pavilion describes the purpose and background history of the gardens.

☎ 01794 368787 www.hilliergardens.org.uk

Sissinghurst Castle (NT) 174 A5

These world famous gardens created in the 1930s by writer and poet Vita Sackville-West and her husband, diplomat and writer Sir Harold Nicolson, were first opened to the public in 1938. He was the designer who liked formality and clean lines, and she was the romantic plantswoman who liked profusion and surprise; two gifted people whose talents blended perfectly. Much of the garden's charm is due to the backdrop provided by the Elizabethan buildings, the focal point of which is a four-storey red brick tower, to one side of which is a moat.

The garden extends to 6 acres (2.5ha) and is comprised of a series of 10 'outdoor rooms' divided by hedges of rose, hornbeam and yew, as well as walls. This stunning garden has had an important influence on garden design and planting in the late 20th century.

☎ 01580 710700 www.nationaltrust.org.uk

Smallhythe Place (NT) 174 A5

Early 16th century half-timbered farmhouse, once home to Victorian actress Dame Ellen Terry who lived here from 1899 until her death in 1928. The house contains various mementoes from Terry and her theatrical contemporaries, including a letter from Oscar Wilde.

☎ 01580 762334 www.nationaltrust.org.uk

Southampton Maritime Museum 409 F2

Housed in a 14th century warehouse with impressive timber roof, built for the wool trade, the museum recounts the story of the Port of Southampton. There are models of the great passenger liners, a panoramic layout of the docks, and interactive exhibits showing how the ships and docks function.

☎ 023 8022 3941 www.southampton.gov.uk

Southsea Castle & Museum 157 F3

Built in 1544 as part of Henry VIII's coastal defences, and said to have been designed by the king himself. Its initial purpose was to protect the large fleet of warships based in Portsmouth Harbour, including the flagship *Mary Rose* which sank in front of the castle in 1545.

The building remained an active military base until 1960. During the preceding 400 years it was captured by Parliamentarians in 1642, suffered major damage from an explosion in 1759, was renovated and enlarged in the early 19th century and used as a military prison in Victorian times.

☎ 023 9282 7261 www.southseacastle.co.uk

Spitfire & Hurricane Memorial, R.A.F. Manston 175 F2

The permanent home of two original examples of World War II fighter aircraft along with associated memorabilia. Visitors can see a prototype of the 'Dambusters' bouncing bomb plus a display telling the story of combat over Kent during the war.

☎ 01843 821940 www.spitfire-museum.com

Sissinghurst Castle

Squerryes Court 172 D3

An attractive brick-built 17th century manor house, home to the Warde family since 1731. The interior of the house contains tapestries dating from 1720, 17th century paintings, as well as furniture and porcelain. The 20 acre (8ha) garden includes a lake, herbaceous borders, and a formal garden which has been restored using the original plans.

☎ 01959 562345 www.squerryes.co.uk

Standen (NT) 172 C5

Built between 1892 and 1894, the house was designed by Philip Webb, a lifelong friend and colleague of William Morris, and is a fine showpiece of the Arts and Crafts movement. It contains furniture, tapestries and paintings of the period, along with Morris textiles and wallpapers. There are lovely views from the beautiful 10 acre (4ha) hillside garden.

☎ 01342 323029 www.nationaltrust.org.uk

Staunton Country Park 157 G1

Extending to over 1000 acres (400ha), this was created by Sir George Staunton in the early 18th century as a Regency Pleasure Garden, and is now one of the few remaining Regency parks in the country. Sir George was a noted botanist and authority on China, and the park was inspired by his travels in the Far East.

The tropical glasshouses, rebuilt to Sir George's original designs, contain unusual plants from rainforest environments. There is also a yew maze, puzzle garden, play area, ornamental lake and range of unusual follies.

☎ 023 9245 3405 www.hants.gov.uk

Stoneacre (NT) 173 G3

An attractive half-timbered house dating from 1480 and restored in the 1920s. It features a Great Hall spanned by impressive timberwork. Outside is a 20th century cottage garden.

☎ 01622 862157 www.nationaltrust.org.uk

Stonor Park 184 C4

The red brick Tudor façade disguises a building dating originally from the 12th century and extended in the 14th century, set in a lovely wooded valley on the slopes of the Chilterns. Internally, the rooms are decorated in 18th century Gothic style and there are some interesting paintings and Mortlake tapestries. There is also an exhibition on the life and work of St Edmund Campion, who sought refuge here at the time of the Reformation.

The attractive hillside gardens have displays of daffodils, narcissi, irises and roses, and there are good views over the surrounding deer park.

☎ 01491 638587 www.stonor.com

Stowe School 198 B4

One of the finest Georgian landscape gardens (NT) in the country, covering 350 acres (140ha) of parkland, valleys, views, lakes and rivers, laid out between 1713 – 25. There are over 30 temples dotted around the grounds, designed by well-known architects of the day such as William Kent and Sir John Vanbrugh, and many of these have been restored. The Temple family, who owned Stowe at this time, were fortunate to have the successive services of three of the great landscape gardeners of the time, Charles Bridgeman, William Kent and Lancelot 'Capability' Brown.

The magnificent house at the centre of the park is

now a public school, with access limited mainly to school holidays, but the park is open on a more regular basis.

☎ 01280 822850 (Garden) www.nationaltrust.org.uk
☎ 01280 818282 (House) www.stowe.co.uk

Tangmere Military Aviation Museum — 158 B3

Tangmere, one of Britain's earliest airfields, was operational between 1917 – 1970, and the museum, which started in 1982, traces the history of flight-based warfare, emphasising Tangmere's links with the Royal Air Force and Battle of Britain.

☎ 01243 775223 www.tangmere-museum.org.uk

Thorpe Park — 171 F1

This popular theme park covers over 500 acres (200ha) and is located on the site of former gravel pits which have been landscaped into a series of lakes. This watery location has been used to set the main theme of the park, that of water rides.

The park is divided into a number of areas. These include, amongst others, 'Ranger Country', 'Lost City', 'Neptune's Kingdom', 'Canada Creek' and 'Octopus Garden'. Elsewhere in the park is Nemesis Inferno, a feet-free roller coaster – a real 'white knuckle' experience.

In addition to all the rides there is also a traditional 1930s farm where children can stroke the sheep, pigs and cows.

☎ 01932 562633 www.thorpepark.co.uk

Thorpe Park

Tonbridge Castle (Ruins) — 173 E4

Remains of a Norman motte and bailey castle set in 14 acres (5.5ha) of grounds. Within the impressive 13th century gatehouse visitors can experience castle life through interactive displays and an audio tour.

☎ 01732 770929 www.tonbridgecastle.org

Tunbridge Wells Museum & Art Gallery — 173 E5

Museum of local and natural history, plus an art gallery, which has frequently changing art and craft exhibitions.

☎ 01892 554171 www.tunbridgewells.gov.uk/museum

Uffington Castle & White Horse (NT) — 183 E4

Belying its name, Uffington Castle has no connection with medieval fortifications but is an imposing Iron Age hill fort covering 8 acres (3ha) close to the Ridgeway, an ancient track.

The White Horse, cut into the chalk of the hillside to the east of the castle, is 374ft (114m) long and rather stylised in appearance. Tests indicate a Bronze Age origin, and the figure is thought to represent Epona, a horse goddess, though it will come as no surprise that many legends have developed around this feature.

www.english-heritage.org.uk

Uppark (NT) — 157 G1

A late 17th century house in an attractive setting high on the South Downs. The estate, extending to 50 acres (20ha), was designed by Humphrey Repton. The interior is Georgian and includes paintings, furniture, textiles and ceramics, and an 18th century dolls' house with its original contents. The servants' quarters can also been seen.

☎ 01730 825857 www.nationaltrust.org.uk

Valley Gardens  — 171 E1

These beautiful gardens with their impressive displays of rhododendrons, azaleas, magnolias, camellias and carpeting of daffodils cover an area of 200 acres (80ha) within Windsor Great Park. As well as the amazing spring colour, they are very attractive in the autumn.

☎ 01753 847518 www.crownestate.co.uk

Ventnor Botanic Gardens — 157 E5

One of the youngest botanical gardens in the country, started in 1970 on the site of a former hospital. The potential of the location, with its mild climate, was recognised by the late Sir Harold Hillier, the famous plantsman, and the 22 acre (9ha) garden was designed and planted with help from his nurseries, tender plants flourishing in the sheltered environment. Unfortunately a combination of harsh winters and stormy weather in the 1980s destroyed a large number of species, and the replacements have only recently become established.

☎ 01983 855397 www.botanic.co.uk

Vyne, The (NT) — 170 B2

A splendid red brick Tudor mansion built for Henry VIII's Lord Chamberlain, Lord Sandys. Subsequent modifications in the 17th century include the first classical portico of its kind in the country, and there were some further 18th century alterations. Notable features include the Long Gallery, a sweeping Palladian staircase, and the Tudor chapel. The garden has some good herbaceous border displays, and the estate consists of a further 500 acres (200ha) of park and woodland, providing attractive walks.

☎ 01256 881337 www.nationaltrust.org.uk

Waddesdon Manor (NT) — 184 C1

The external appearance of this late Victorian building owes more to the style of a 16th century French chateau than a conventional English country house. It was built for Baron Ferdinand de Rothschild, its primary purpose being to display his splendid collection of French decorative arts. There are also paintings by Gainsborough, Reynolds, Romney, and Dutch and Flemish masters. The wine cellars contain a collection of over 15,000 bottles, some dating back to 1868.

The late 19th century formal gardens surrounding the house are amongst the finest Victorian gardens in Britain, and include a magnificent, colourful parterre, carpet bedding, rose garden, specimen trees, fountains and an extensive collection of French, Dutch and Italian statuary. The centrepiece is the ornate, cast iron rococo aviary which has an interesting collection of exotic birds.

☎ 01296 653226 www.waddesdon.org.uk

Wakehurst Place (NT) — 172 C5

The setting of Wakehurst Place is superb, with fine views across the Sussex Weald. The gardens, which comprise a mixture of walled gardens, woodland, water gardens and lakes, a Himalayan glade, plus more formal planting, surround a 16th century sandstone mansion (not owned by the Trust) and extend to 170 acres (70ha). Much of the impressive collection of trees and shrubs were originally planted by Gerald Loder, 1st Lord Wakehurst, between 1903 and 1936 and then by Sir Henry Price who bequeathed the garden to the National Trust in 1963. Two years later the Royal Botanic Gardens leased the gardens from the Trust to complement their work at Kew.

The wide variety of native and exotic trees give rise to impressive autumn colours when the maples, American beech and larch come into their own. In spring the woodland floors are scattered with bluebells, and later on, rhododendrons create a superb sight.

Wakehurst Place is also home to the Millennium Seed Bank, an ambitious project to safeguard over 24,000 plant species from around the world. An exhibition allows visitors to see the ongoing seed preservation and research in progress.

☎ 01444 894066 www.nationaltrust.org.uk

Walmer Castle & Garden — 175 F4

Tudor castle built 1539 – 40 as a coastal artillery fortress for Henry VIII. In 1708 the castle became the residence of the Lords Warden of the Cinque Ports, some of the most famous encumbents being the Duke of Wellington, Sir Winston Churchill and the Queen Mother. Visitors can enjoy the attractive gardens and see the room where Wellington died.

☎ 01304 364288 www.english-heritage.org.uk

Waterperry — 184 B2

An 80 year old garden with a fine collection of alpines, herbaceous plants, shrubs and trees.

The herbaceous borders are a particularly attractive feature, carefully planted to ensure that colour is continuous from May through to October. There are also delightful formal rose gardens, raised beds of alpines, a knot garden and riverside walks.

A fascinating collection of agricultural and horticultural tools is housed in an 18th century granary in the grounds.

☎ 01844 339226 www.waterperrygardens.co.uk

Weald & Downland Open Air Museum — 158 A2

Almost 50 historic buildings dating from the 13th to the 19th century have been rebuilt on this attractive 50 acre (20ha) parkland site in the lovely South Downs countryside. The buildings were rescued from destruction and have been carefully dismantled and moved from their original locations to create this museum. The site illustrates traditional rural life in an inspiring way.

☎ 01243 811363 www.wealddown.co.uk

Wellington Country Park — 170 C1

A good range of activities in this 350 acres (140ha) of woodland, parkland and lakes. For younger children there is an adventure playground, small breeds farm and miniature railway, while other options include fishing on the lake, nature trails, and camping and caravanning facilities. There are events taking place throughout the year.

☎ 0118 932 6444 www.wellington-country-park.co.uk

Wakehurst Place

West Berkshire Museum 169 F1

Two of Newbury's most historic buildings, the 17th century Cloth Hall and 18th century Granary, are now home to an absorbing museum of local history. There are specific galleries devoted to the Kennet and Avon Canal, traditional local industries, costume and local history. The Civil War is also a major theme, two battles of the period having taken place locally. There is a programme of special exhibitions.

☎ 01635 30511 www.westberks.gov.uk

West Dean Gardens 158 A2

In an attractive setting at the foot of the South Downs, this 35 acre (14ha) garden contains specimen trees, herbaceous planting and a Victorian walled kitchen garden with 16 restored glasshouses and frames. A notable feature of the garden is a 300ft (100m) pergola by Harold Peto dating from 1911. Over recent years extensive planting of bulbs has taken place resulting in spectacular spring displays. The garden holds two National Collections, that of the Tulip Tree and Horse Chestnut.

☎ 01243 818210 www.westdean.org.uk/site/gardens/

West Wycombe Park (NT) 184 D3

Extravagant 18th century Italianate mansion with the external appearance of a classical temple. Inspired by Grand Tours, there are splendid painted ceilings, and furniture, paintings and sculpture dating from the mid 18th century ownership of Sir Francis Dashwood, who founded the notorious Hell Fire Club. Club members were drawn from the upper echelons of society, and local mythology had them indulging in Satanic rites, though reality was probably wine, women and a spot of free thinking. Sir Francis also created the beautiful rococo landscape garden in the 300 acres (150ha) of parkland surrounding the house.

An unusual addition to the grounds are the Hell Fire Caves. Again the inspiration of Sir Francis, the existing caves were greatly extended in the 1750s by a remarkable feat of engineering. Although providing a suitably atmospheric meeting place for the Hell Fire Club, Sir Francis's motives were partly altruistic in that the work provided employment for local villagers following a series of failed harvests. The caves are privately owned and there is an additional entry fee.

☎ 01494 533739 www.nationaltrust.org.uk

Winchester Cathedral 414 B2

One of the great cathedrals of England, and perhaps one of the best examples of Gothic Perpendicular architecture to be found.

The original minster was built by King Cenwalh of Wessex in AD643 and was the royal Saxon cathedral, burial place of kings. The foundations can still be seen adjacent to the West Door but this building was replaced by Bishop Walkelin, the first Norman bishop, who laid the foundations of the present cathedral in 1079, building materials including stone from the Isle of Wight and local timber. The cathedral was completed within 14 years, but over the following centuries underwent much modification, particularly between 1350 – 1450 when the original Romanesque nave was transformed to the English Gothic style, mainly due to the efforts of Bishop William of Wykeham. The nave measures 556ft (170m), making Winchester the longest medieval church in Europe. The whole building is an ecclesiastical and architectural treasure house.

Within the cathedral is a statue to William Walker, a deep sea diver who could be said to have single-handedly saved the cathedral from collapse at the beginning of the 20th century. He spent five years working underwater in complete darkness replacing the decaying timber of the ancient foundations.

☎ 01962 857200 www.winchester-cathedral.org.uk

Windsor Castle 414 D3

Strategically placed above the River Thames and a day's march from London, William the Conqueror selected Windsor as the site for a fort to protect the western approach to the capital. Since then it has become the largest and oldest occupied castle in the world.

William's original building was a wooden motte and bailey fort constructed in 1079. Henry II replacing this with stone outer walls and a round tower in 1165. In the succeeding centuries monarchs have enlarged and modified the castle, militarily if necessary, or decoratively in more peaceful times, and the building today occupies a site of 12 acres (5ha).

The magnificent State Rooms contain outstanding pictures from the Royal Collection including works by Holbein, Rembrandt and Canaletto, fine furniture, painted ceilings and carvings by Grinling Gibbons. These rooms are used for ceremonial and state occasions and may be closed when the Queen is in residence. In the winter months the richly decorated Semi State Rooms can also be viewed. The Drawings Gallery houses changing exhibitions of material drawn from the Royal Library and other treasures.

Within the precincts is St George's Chapel, built in the late 15th century and one of Britain's finest examples of Gothic architecture. It contains the tombs of 10 monarchs and the great battle sword of Edward III hangs on one of the walls.

Outside the castle, one of the best known of British ceremonies, the Changing of the Guard, takes place throughout the year. It is advisable to telephone in advance to check days and times.

It is important to note that this is a working palace, and that some areas may be closed off at short notice.

☎ 01753 869898 www.the-royal-collection.org.uk

Wisley R.H.S. Gardens 171 F2

Home to the Royal Horticultural Society since its donation by Sir Thomas Hanbury in 1903, this garden was first established by George Wilson in 1878, a scientist and keen gardener, with the aim of growing difficult plants successfully.

The gardens extend to 204 acres (97ha) along the banks of the River Wey and are of interest to both keen horticulturalists and those who are just after a visual treat. Visitors can wander amongst the model gardens which give ideas that can be easily applied at home. The gardens also feature glasshouses, sweeping lawns, 420ft (128m) long herbaceous borders, an impressive rock garden and the Jubilee arboretum.

In front of the half-timbered Tudor-style building, which is used as a laboratory and offices, is a formal canal which is an impressive sight when the water lilies are in flower. The gardens look spectacular all through the year; in spring the Alpine meadow is stunning, with its carpet of yellow daffodils, the rose gardens and herbaceous borders are a riot of colour in the summer, the large number of trees provide autumn colour and in winter the heated glasshouses come into their own with their colourful exotics.

☎ 01483 224234 www.rhs.org.uk/gardens/wisley/

Witley Common Information Centre (NT) 171 E3

Located on Witley Common, an area of lowland heath and woodland with a wide variety of plant and animal life, this purpose-built education and information centre houses a countryside exhibition explaining the area's importance and management.

☎ 01428 683207 www.nationaltrust.org.uk

Worthing Museum & Art Gallery 158 D3

The museum has an emphasis on local history and is housed in an Edwardian building. It contains collections of ceramics, toys, textiles, geology, a variety of temporary exhibitions and a sculpture garden.

☎ 01903 239999 ext 1140 www.worthing.gov.uk/leisure/museumartgallery/
☎ 01903 221150 (Saturdays)

Yarmouth Castle 156 C4

Completed in 1547, this was the final castle to be built in Henry VIII's coastal defence system, following a French invasion of the Isle of Wight in 1545. It is of a fairly simple design, consisting of a basic square with no central tower. Bounded by the sea to the north and east, the south and west walls were protected by a moat, filled in at the end of the 17th century. Around 1600 a large gun battery was built in the north part of the courtyard, while domestic buildings filled the south side. The gun platform now provides splendid views across the harbour and Solent.

☎ 01983 760678 www.english-heritage.org.uk

Wisley R.H.S. Gardens

LONDON

England's multi-cultural capital vibrates with round-the-clock reminders of its long and prestigious history. 'Old Father Thames' washes through a panorama of imposing buildings old and new, offering tastes of English tradition, cultural opportunities, avant-garde events and shopping galore. London is the definitive twenty-four hour city where the leisure facilities, entertainment, sporting venues and diversity of events are amongst the best in the world.

Houses of Parliament

Bank of England Museum 356 B3

An interesting insight into the role of finance, from the foundation of the bank in 1694 by Royal Charter to the high-tech world of modern banking. Besides displays of gold and banknotes, there is also a Roman mosaic floor (uncovered during rebuilding work in the 1930s) plus a variety of interactive displays.

☎ 020 7601 5491 www.bankofengland.co.uk/museum

Britain At War 356 B3

A re-creation of what life was like for the ordinary people of London during the Blitz. There are realistic reconstructions, including an underground air-raid shelter, an Anderson shelter and a BBC studio. Through the use of sights, sounds and special effects, visitors can get a real feel for the atmosphere of war-torn London.

☎ 020 7403 3171 www.britainatwar.co.uk

British Museum 376 J3

This is the oldest public museum in the world and was founded in 1753 when Sir Hans Sloane bequeathed his considerable collection of artefacts, along with his library and herbarium, to the nation in return for paying his heirs £20,000. George II and the Parliament of the time, led by the Speaker, Arthur Onslow, were persuaded to accept the gift and a public lottery was held to raise the necessary funds. The next year Montagu House was acquired in order to house the collection which has since increased to over six million objects. Over the years the building has had to expand to accommodate this huge collection, and the bulk of the neoclassical building which visitors see today, including the impressive south front, dates from 1852.

The museum houses the world's greatest collection of antiquities including the national collections of archaeology and ethnography, with treasures from all over the globe. Highlights include the Rosetta Stone, the Elgin Marbles and the Sutton Hoo treasure. There are also Egyptian mummies, which include not only humans but cats, baboons and even crocodiles, and the 2000 year old peat-preserved Lindow Man. The exhibits are so rich and varied that to attempt to see them all in a single visit would be impossible.

☎ 020 7323 8299 www.thebritishmuseum.ac.uk

British Museum

Buckingham Palace 376 D11

Built in 1705, and originally called Buckingham House, it was purchased by George III for his wife Queen Charlotte in 1761. Over the years it has been remodelled and extended a number of times, firstly by George IV with the assistance of his architect John Nash. A new suite of rooms was added and the north and south wings were rebuilt, with the Marble Arch as a centrepiece to the courtyard. The arch was later removed and now stands near the north east corner of Hyde Park. Queen Victoria made further alterations and additions, most notably the East Front which was designed by architect Edward Blore in 1847. Due to the deterioration of the stone, this was subsequently refaced in 1913 creating the familiar façade that we see today. Soon after Queen Victoria's accession in 1837, it became the monarch's official London residence.

The palace is open during August and September with visitors able to see 19 of the state rooms. These include the Throne Room, the Blue Drawing Room, the impressive White Drawing Room and the 150ft (46m) Picture Gallery. The huge Ballroom can also be seen; at 122ft (37m) long and 60ft (18m) wide, it is used for State banquets and can accommodate 150 guests. Treasures that can be seen within the palace include paintings by artists such as Rembrandt and superb examples of English and French furniture.

☎ 020 7766 7300 www.royal.gov.uk/output/page555.asp

Buckingham Palace

Cabinet War Rooms 376 H10

An intriguing underground suite of rooms used by Winston Churchill and his war cabinet as a meeting, planning and information centre during World War II. On display are the soundproofed Cabinet War Room, a Map Room, the original hot-line and scrambler used by Churchill when communicating with President Roosevelt, Churchill's private quarters and the desk from which he made some of his famous wartime broadcasts.

☎ 020 7930 6961 www.iwm.org.uk/cabinet/

Chessington World of Adventures 171 G1

This popular attraction, covering 65 acres (27ha), combines the original zoo with a modern theme park. The zoo has a wide range of animals including a family group of West Lowland gorillas, sea lions, penguins and a variety of big cats such as lions, tigers and leopards. A gentle monorail allows visitors to travel over the animal enclosures for a superb bird's eye view.

The theme park is divided into a number of areas and has all the usual thrill rides, along with those more suitable for younger children. 'The Forbidden Kingdom' has the white-knuckle ride Rameses' Revenge which revolves riders through a full 360° and blasts them with water; 'Transylvania' features The Vampire, Britain's first hanging roller coaster which also swings riders from side to side; 'Toytown' is ideal for the little ones as they can wear themselves out on Toadie's Crazy Cars and Berry Bouncers; 'Mystic East' features Dragon Falls, a traditional log flume, which has the usual plunge at the end, and Samurai where riders are spun round – not for those with delicate stomachs! Visitors can also enjoy 'Beanoland', where foam-filled balls can be catapulted, and 'Pirates Cove' where the Black Buccaneer pirate ship rocks riders from side to side. The sheer variety of attractions means that there is something for everyone.

☎ 01372 729 560 www.chessington.co.uk

Chiswick House 355 C4

This fine 18th century domed villa, designed by Lord Burlington in 1728, was modelled on Palladio's Villa Rotonda at Vicenza. The William Kent interiors, particularly the reception rooms which include a domed saloon and velvet room, are sumptuous. Many have painted ceilings and gilded decorations, and feature period furnishings. Kent, alongside royal gardener Charles Bridgeman, was also responsible for the design of the gardens where he continued the Italianate theme with Doric columns, statues and obelisks, plus a cascade.

☎ 020 8995 0508 www.english-heritage.org.uk

Covent Garden 377 K6

Once the site of the famous fruit and flower market, this area is now a fashionable pedestrianised piazza. The arcades are lined with small specialist shops and there are plenty of places to eat and drink. The atmosphere is lively, with street entertainers a real highlight. The Jubilee Hall plays host to a variety of markets, including antiques, arts and crafts. Surrounding the piazza, visitors can also see St Paul's church, built by Inigo Jones and completed in 1633, London's Transport Museum, the Theatre Museum and the Royal Opera House.

Cutty Sark 357 C4

This famous tea clipper, built in 1869, was the fastest in the tea race from China and subsequently, when used in the Australian wool trade, she consistently set new speed records. Visitors can explore the ship and see where the sailors ate, slept and worked, and there is also an impressive collection of carved figureheads to be seen.

☎ 020 8858 3445 www.cuttysark.co.uk

Dulwich Picture Gallery 357 B5

Much of the collection was put together by French art dealer Noël Desenfans and Sir Francis Bourgeois between 1790 and 1795, for the king of Poland. Due to the king's abdication they took over responsibility for the collection and it was left in Sir Francis's will to Dulwich College in 1811, with the stipulation that the paintings should go on public display. A purpose built gallery designed by Sir John Soane houses the pictures, which include works by Claude, Cuyp, Rembrandt, Rubens, Van Dyck, Gainsborough and Canaletto.

☎ 020 8693 5254 www.dulwichpicturegallery.org.uk

Eltham Palace 186 D5

A 1930s mansion constructed around a Great Hall, built for Edward IV in the 1470s. The house was commissioned by Stephen Courtauld, millionaire patron of the arts, and his wife Virginia. It had all the latest electrical gadgets including a centralised vacuum cleaner and sound system. The interior exhibits superb examples of Art Deco styling, for example, the dining room has black and silver doors, an aluminium ceiling and maple walls. The bathroom features onyx and gold mosaic. The gardens extend to 19 acres (7.5ha) and include a moat, rose garden and pergola.

☎ 020 8294 2548 www.english-heritage.org.uk

Fenton House (NT) 354 D2

A late 17th century house containing collections of fine porcelain, early keyboard instruments and Georgian furniture. Outside is a walled garden with roses, orchard and a kitchen garden.

☎ 020 7435 3471 www.nationaltrust.org.uk

Geffrye Museum 356 B3

The museum is housed in several 18th century almshouses, with attractive gardens. Through a series of period rooms, the changing style of domestic interiors and furniture of the English middle classes from 1600 to the present day are shown.

☎ 020 7739 9893 www.geffrye-museum.org.uk

Greenwich – Old Royal Observatory

Greenwich 357 C4

Situated on the River Thames and a designated World Heritage Site, Greenwich is of international significance. It has a long and interesting history with strong royal and maritime links. Greenwich Park, which affords superb views, is the oldest royal park in London. The 17th century Royal Naval College, designed by Sir Christopher Wren, is built on the site of the Royal Palace of Greenwich. As the primary royal residence from the 15th to 17th centuries, it was the birthplace of Henry VIII and Elizabeth I. Alongside the river are the *Cutty Sark*, the fastest tea clipper of her time, and *Gipsy Moth IV*, on which Sir Francis Chichester was the first person to circumnavigate the globe single-handedly in 1967. The National Maritime Museum, which includes the Palladian style Queen's House designed by Inigo Jones, can also be visited.

The Old Royal Observatory, built by Wren in 1675, is the home of Greenwich Mean Time and the world's Prime Meridian – Longitude 0°, where the eastern and western hemispheres meet. The brass meridian line can be seen set into the ground, and you can stand with a foot in each hemisphere. The building contains a collection of time keeping, astronomical and navigational objects. Also of interest are the 19th century Ranger's House and St Alfege Church.

☎ 0870 608 2000 www.greenwichwhs.org.uk

H.M.S. Belfast 356 B3

Launched in 1938, this was the Royal Navy's largest cruiser of World War II. It participated in the sinking of the German battle cruiser *Scharnhorst* in 1943 and remained in Navy service until 1965. Most of the ship can be visited, including the engine room, boiler room and the bridge. There are displays depicting life on board during the war.

☎ 020 7940 6300 www.iwm.org.uk/belfast

Ham House (NT) 186 A5

An outstanding 17th century house, built in 1610 and enlarged in the 1670s, containing an impressive collection of paintings, furniture and textiles. The formal 17th century gardens have been restored to their original form.

☎ 020 8940 1950 www.nationaltrust.org.uk

Hampton Court Palace & Garden 355 A6

Located on the banks of the River Thames, this impressive building, covering approximately 6 acres (2.5ha), was originally built by Cardinal Thomas Wolsey, and dates from the early 16th century. He presented it to Henry VIII in 1528 to try and regain favour after he failed to annul the king's marriage to Catherine of Aragon. After becoming a royal palace, it was rebuilt and extended a number of times. Henry was responsible for the construction of the magnificent hammerbeamed hall and the vast kitchens. In the 1690s William and Mary commissioned Sir Christopher Wren to rebuild the palace, but due to a lack of time and money much of the Tudor palace survived. The two differing architectural styles can be seen clearly today. At this time the interior was decorated by some of the best artists and craftsmen of the day – Tijou, Grinling Gibbons, Laguerre and Verrio.

Visitors can enjoy the magnificent state apartments which contain furniture, tapestries and paintings from the Royal Collection. Other attractions include a rare 'real tennis' court on which Henry VIII once played. The grounds include 60 acres (25ha) of beautiful gardens. There is a 1 mile (1.6km) - long canal, extensive radiating avenues of limes and clipped yews, an orangery, and the famous maze. The privy garden, an attractive parterre, to the south of the palace, dates from William and Mary's reign and, after many years of neglect, was restored to its former glory during the 1990s.

☎ 0870 752 7777 www.hrp.org.uk

Horniman Museum 357 B5

An eccentric and eclectic international collection of arts, crafts and artefacts housed in a purpose-built museum set in 16 acre (6ha) grounds. Originally collected by tea merchant and world traveller Frederick J Horniman, the exhibits cover a remarkable range, from torture devices, Egyptian mummy cases and masks, musical instruments to an enormous stuffed walrus. An ideal family attraction.

☎ 020 8699 1872 www.horniman.ac.uk

Houses of Parliament 377 K11

Also known as the Palace of Westminster and home to the main seat of Government. The original palace was built in the first half of the 11th century by Edward the Confessor and remained the main residence of the monarch until the first half of the 16th century when it moved to Whitehall. The Lords, however, continued to meet at Westminster. In 1834 the building was badly damaged by fire and all but the crypt, Jewel Tower and Westminster Hall survived. The hall, which is 240ft (73m) by 60ft (18m) has a magnificent hammerbeam oak roof. Most of the present building was constructed in Gothic Revival style between 1840 and 1888 by Charles Barry and Augustus Pugin and contains 1100 rooms, 100 staircases and over 2 miles (3km) of passages.

Situated on the River Thames, the building is an impressive sight with its two towers, one at each end. The Victoria Tower on the south west corner, on which the Union Jack flies when parliament is sitting, rises to a height of 336ft (102m). St Stephens clock tower (commonly known as Big Ben), to the north, is 316ft (96m) high and is famous the world over. It has four clock faces, each 23ft (7m) in diameter and contains the 13 ton bell, 'Big Ben', cast in 1858.

The Houses of Parliament are worth a visit, just to see the exterior, but visitors can also take a guided tour of the palace during the summer recess and see the impressive interiors.

☎ 020 7219 4272 www.parliament.uk

Imperial War Museum 377 P13

The museum has displays covering warfare from World War I to the present day and majors on Britain and the Commonwealth. Natural light from the domed atrium illuminates an impressive collection of tanks and weapons including a V2 rocket and also a Spitfire. Not only does it include conventional hardware of war but also interesting exhibits relating to war's impact on the population at large. For example there are displays on rationing, morale-boosting, censorship and there is also an exhibition on the Holocaust. The arts associated with wartime can also be seen, such as photographs, letters, paintings and poetry, and there are also old newsreels and period music.

☎ 020 7416 5320 www.iwm.org.uk

Houses of Parliament

Kensington Palace

354 D3

Built by Sir Christopher Wren and bought by William III in 1689. Queen Victoria was born here in 1819 and on her 70th birthday the State Apartments were opened to the public. It was home to Diana, Princess of Wales, and is currently the residence of several members of the Royal Family. The Royal Ceremonial Dress Collection, dating from the 18th century, is on display, including some of Diana's dresses.

☎ 0870 751 5170 www.hrp.org.uk

Kenwood House

354 D2

This impressive neoclassical mansion, adjacent to Hampstead Heath, was remodelled by Robert Adam between 1764 and 1773. The house contains an outstanding collection of paintings with works by Turner, Gainsborough, Rembrandt, Vermeer, Van Dyck and Reynolds. The landscaped grounds, laid out by Humphrey Repton, are often the venue for lakeside open air concerts in the summer.

☎ 020 8348 1286 www.english-heritage.org.uk

London Aquarium

377 L10

Located in the cellars of County Hall (previously home to the now defunct Greater London Council) on the banks of the River Thames, this is one of the largest aquaria in Europe. At the centre of the aquarium there are two huge tanks extending over two floors, one displaying the sealife of the Pacific and one of the Atlantic. Visitors can see large 6ft (2m) long sharks, conger eels, stingrays and also the daily feeding of the fish by divers. Elsewhere there are slightly smaller tanks with themed areas displaying varying aquatic habitats, such as coral reefs and tropical rivers with piranha fish. There is a display of unusual and beautiful sea horses and also touch tanks where children are encouraged to touch the rays, crabs and starfish.

☎ 020 7967 8000 www.londonaquarium.co.uk

AQUARIUM

London Aquarium

London Dungeon

356 B3

In the vaults under London Bridge Station, this horror museum houses a gruesomely realistic exhibition of sacrifices, tortures, plagues, murders and executions. It is not recommended for the nervous or squeamish as the reconstructions and atmosphere of the place make for quite a scary experience.

☎ 020 7403 7221 www.dungeons.co.uk

London Eye

377 L10

Opened in 2000 as part of the millennium celebrations, at 450ft (135m) this observation wheel is the world's highest. It has become one of London's most recognisable landmarks comprising 32 capsules, each holding up to 25 people. The slow, gentle ride takes 30 minutes and gives visitors plenty of time to take in the splendid views.

Conceived and designed by architects David Marks and Julia Barfield, it is positioned in a prime location on the south bank of the River Thames and overlooks many of London's famous and impressive landmarks such as the Houses of Parliament, Westminster Abbey, St Paul's Cathedral and Buckingham Palace. On a clear day views of up to 25 miles (40km) can be seen.

To get the most from the experience it is worthwhile studying a map and the photoguide to help pick out key landmarks. These can be purchased at the London Eye shop.

☎ 0870 500 0600 www.londoneye.com

London Eye

London Zoo

356 A3

Founded in 1828, this was the world's first scientific zoo. In many ways the zoo was pioneering; in 1849 it introduced a reptile house – the first in the world, then the first public aquarium and the first insect house were built in 1853 and 1881 respectively.

Covering an area of 36 acres (14.5ha), it houses over 650 species of animals and participates in breeding programmes for over 140 of them. Visitors can follow a recommended route to ensure that they do not miss anything; this is marked by use of green footprints on the ground.

All the usual zoo animals, and more, are present, such as lions, apes, elephants and a variety of birdlife. Ever popular, the giraffes live in style within a neoclassical residence designed by Decimus Burton. Within the same hoofed animal area, extravagantly marked okapi, tapir and bongoes can be found. The children's zoo is in a farmyard setting and contains domesticated animals from around the world. These include camels, llamas and reindeer, as well as the more familiar sheep, cows, pigs, hens and ducks. Other attractions include the huge walk-through aviary, designed by Lord Snowdon, and Moonlight World, where nocturnal creatures can be seen. The Millennium Conservation Centre, with its advanced low-energy design, houses the Web of Life Exhibition; this is well worth a visit. Biodiversity is the focus, the extraordinary range of life on earth is explored, showing adaptation to different environments.

☎ 020 7722 3333 www.londonzoo.co.uk

London Zoo - Rhino Iguana

London's Transport Museum

377 K6

Telling the story of the world's largest urban passenger transport system, the museum contains gleamingly preserved survivors from the first cabs to trolleybuses and modern day tube trains. There are lots of hands-on exhibits where visitors can try out the controls. The museum, which was opened in 1980, is housed in the attractive old Covent Garden flower market building.

☎ 020 7379 6344 www.ltmuseum.co.uk

Lord's Cricket Ground & Museum

354 D3

The ground at Lord's is the headquarters of English cricket and the official home of the Marylebone Cricket Club (MCC). Guided tours are available, and include visits to the grounds, the futuristic-looking media centre, the players' dressing room, and, when not in use, the Long Room with its portraits of famous cricketers. The tour also includes a visit to the world's oldest sporting museum, the MCC Museum, where, among other exhibits, the famous Ashes urn is on show.

☎ 020 7616 8656 www.lords.org

Madame Tussaud's & the Planetarium

376 A1

This famous waxwork collection started out as a small touring exhibition in 1802, brought from France by Madame Tussaud. Over the years the collection has grown and diversified enormously, and in recent years topical interactive activities have been introduced. Today, visitors can see amazingly life-like and life-sized waxwork figures of villains and heroes, politicians and royalty, popstars and film stars, from the past and present; mingle with sporting and media stars, sing and dance with celebrities and learn football tips from England team members.

'The Chamber of Horrors' is probably the best known and most notorious part of the exhibition: Dr Crippen stares out from behind bars; grim and bloodthirsty punishments and a reconstruction of Jack the Ripper's London, with its eerie atmosphere,

Madame Tussaud"s

can be seen. In the 'Grand Hall', many world leaders and royalty, from past and present, are gathered together. 'Premiere Night' brings together stars of the silver screen from 1914 to the present day. To finish, a ride on the 'Spirit of London' is a must, where visitors travel on small black cabs through London's turbulent history.

The Planetarium is next door and can also be visited on the same ticket. There are interactive exhibits and scale models as well as a fascinating show that takes visitors on a voyage of discovery into the solar system and beyond. Both educational and entertaining, it gives a great feel for the vastness and beauty of the universe.

☎ 0870 400 3000 www.madame-tussauds.co.uk

Monument, The 356 B3

Designed by Sir Christopher Wren and his colleague Dr Robert Hook, it was built between 1671 and 1677 to commemorate the Great Fire of London and to celebrate the subsequent rebuilding of the city. Made from Portland stone and standing 202ft (61.5m) tall, it is the tallest free-standing stone column in the world. Its height is significant as it is exactly 202ft away from the site of the baker's shop in Pudding Lane where the fire started in 1666. It has a spiralled, cantilevered staircase with 311 steps. The climb is worthwhile as the view from the top is superb.

☎ 020 7626 2717

Morden Hall Park (NT) 355 D6

The parkland, with the River Wandle flowing through it, extends to over 125 acres (50ha) and was once a deer park. It comprises meadows, wetlands and a superb rose garden planted in a random design with over 2000 plants. Other attractions include independently-run craft workshops, a city farm and garden centre.

☎ 020 8545 6850 www.nationaltrust.org.uk

Museum in Docklands 356 C3

Located in a converted Georgian warehouse on West India Quay, the museum traces the history of London's docks and river from Roman times, through its heyday, its post-war decline, and on to its recent regeneration. There are 12 galleries over five floors, and the exhibits include artefacts, paintings and photographs, accompanied by interactive displays.

☎ 0870 444 3856 www.museumindocklands.org.uk

Museum of Childhood 356 B3

Housing the children's section of the Victoria and Albert Museum, this museum contains an impressive collection of toys and childhood artefacts, the national collection of children's costume, plus a gallery telling the story of childhood in London's East End.

☎ 020 8980 2415 www.museumofchildhood.org.uk

Museum of Garden History 377 L13

The museum is housed in the former church of St Mary-at-Lambeth in whose churchyard are the graves of the two John Tradescants, father and son, who were royal gardeners during the reigns of Charles I and II. The museum tells the story of gardening through the ages. Part of the churchyard has been laid out as a garden in the style characteristic of the Tradescants' time, including a replica of a 17th century knot garden, along with some of the well-known plants they brought back from their travels, such as the Tulip Tree.

☎ 020 7401 8865 www.cix.co.uk/~museumgh

Museum of London 377 S3

Over 2000 years of London's history are on display, divided into seven permanent and well laid out galleries. These range from the Iron Age 'London before London', through Roman, Tudor and Stuart times, to 'World City' (1789 to 1914) when London became the world's first metropolis. Exhibits include over 1.1 million objects and there are attractive reconstructions of streets and interiors. The River Thames is shown to have a key role in the development and life of the city through the ages.

☎ 0870 444 3852 www.museumoflondon.org.uk

National Army Museum 355 D4

Tells the story of the British Army over the last 500 years, from Agincourt to the present day. It chronicles all the major British campaigns and has a large 400 sq ft (37 sq m) model of the battle of Waterloo, containing over 70,000 model soldiers. Other exhibits include the skeleton of Napoleon's horse, a reproduction of a World War I trench and a lamp used by Florence Nightingale.

☎ 020 7730 0717 www.national-army-museum.ac.uk

National Gallery 376 H7

In a commanding position on the north side of Trafalgar Square, the gallery is where the nation's major collection of historical paintings is housed. Founded in 1824, the collection has grown over the years, often due to the generosity of wealthy benefactors, and now numbers over 2300 Western European paintings, mostly dating from 1260 to 1900.

The gallery is divided into four wings. The Sainsbury Wing, opened in 1990, contains some of the earlier Renaissance paintings, including those by Van Eyck, Botticelli, Leonardo da Vinci and Raphael; the West Wing takes us from 1500 to 1600 with works by, amongst others, Titian, Holbein and Michelangelo. In the North Wing, works by Rubens, Van Dyck, Rembrandt and Vermeer are on show, taking us from 1600 to 1700; and finally the East Wing exhibits paintings dating from 1700 to 1900 and features works by Gainsborough, Constable, Monet, Cezanne and Van Gogh. To do justice to the collection it is best not to try and see everything in one visit.

☎ 020 7747 2885 www.nationalgallery.org.uk

National Maritime Museum 357 C4

Housed in architecturally important buildings including The Queen's House by Inigo Jones, the museum tells the story of Britain and the sea; its navy, merchants and explorers. A nautical enthusiast's paradise, there are some 20 galleries with exhibits including models of ships, clocks and watches, contemporary and historic paintings, carved figureheads, weapons and fine silver collections. There are also plenty of hands-on activities.

☎ 020 8858 4422 www.nmm.ac.uk

National Portrait Gallery

National Portrait Gallery 376 H7

Founded in 1856 by historian Philip Stanhope as a gallery of original portraits to commemorate British history. Today, visitors can see over 1000 works which are arranged chronologically within the gallery, from medieval times to the present day. The focus of the collection is the subjects of the paintings rather than the painters themselves. The full portrait collection, the largest in the world, contains over 10,000 pictures in a variety of media: oils, watercolours, sculptures, caricatures, miniatures, photographs and also silhouettes. Paintings of kings, queens, politicians, musicians, artists and poets, ranging from the likes of Shakespeare to Madonna are on display. In addition to the permanent galleries there is a varied programme of temporary exhibitions throughout the year.

The well stocked shop and rooftop restaurant offering excellent views of London are worth a visit.

☎ 020 7306 0055 www.npg.org.uk

National Gallery

Natural History Museum

355 D4

In 1856 Professor Richard Owen, the Superintendent of the Natural History section of the British Museum, campaigned for more space to display the exhibits. A site in South Kensington was purchased and a new, purpose-built museum was constructed, opening to the public in 1881. Lavishly decorated with plants and animals, the resulting 4 acre (1.5ha) museum building is a masterpiece. The main entrance consists of a dramatic series of recessed arches on decorated columns leading to the imposing Central Hall, which contains a huge 85ft (26m) skeleton of a dinosaur – Diplodocus.

The collection is vast and varied, covering all aspects of the natural world, both as traditional exhibits and interactive displays. The Darwin Centre allows visitors to take a look behind the scenes and see scientists working on the collection. A real favourite, especially with the children, is the Dinosaur Exhibition, where there is an animatronic Tyrannosaurus Rex, skeletons and plenty of touch screens. The Earth Galleries, entered through a giant globe, feature displays on the origins of the universe and there is an earthquake simulator where visitors can experience this phenomenon. Other exhibits worth a visit are the huge, life-sized model of a blue whale and the creepy crawlies. The museum is enormously enjoyable as well as educational and there really is too much to see in one visit.

☎ 020 7942 5000 www.nhm.ac.uk

Natural History Museum

Osterley Park & House (NT)

355 A4

Set in extensive parkland, the original Tudor mansion was transformed in the 18th century into a neoclassical villa by Robert Adam. Considered by many to be some of his finest work, it features superb plasterwork, carpets and furniture.

☎ 020 8232 5050 www.nationaltrust.org.uk

Royal Academy of Arts

376 E7

Founded in 1768, the Royal Academy holds major temporary public exhibitions throughout the year. Sir Joshua Reynolds – who was the first president – Gainsborough, Turner and Constable all studied and have exhibited here. Located in Burlington House, a superb early 18th century mansion, one of the few surviving in the West End, the academy is probably most famous for its inspirational annual Summer Exhibition, which displays thousands of works by living artists for view and sale. In addition to the wide range of temporary exhibitions, a suite of rooms, restored to their former 18th century grandeur, houses highlights from the permanent collection. Entry to this is free. The full collection comprises mainly British art from the last 200 years and includes at least one work by all past and present members of the academy.

☎ 020 7300 8000 www.royalacademy.org.uk

Royal Air Force Museum

354 C1

Located on the former airfield at RAF Hendon, and opened in 1972, the museum, housed in five huge buildings, contains a collection of over 100 full-sized aircraft, along with artefacts and other memorabilia. 'Milestones of Flight' covers the history of flight, from the earliest attempts to modern day supersonic jet fighters. For younger visitors the Aeronauts Gallery has plenty of interactive exhibits where they can test their piloting skills.

☎ 020 8205 2266 www.rafmuseum.org.uk

Royal Botanic Gardens, Kew

355 B4

This superb 300 acre (121.5ha) botanic garden was founded by Princess Augusta (mother of George III) in 1759, and in July 2003 it was afforded World Heritage Site status. Kew's reputation as the foremost botanical institution in the world was originally developed by its first two directors, Sir William Hooker (appointed in 1841) and his son Sir Joseph (who succeeded his father in 1865).

The gardens have one of the largest and most diverse collections of plant species in the world; over 60,000 species of plant are displayed in both formal and informal settings, and in the many greenhouses, which themselves cover an area of 4 acres (1.5ha). Within the grounds are the Queen's Garden, which has been laid out in 17th century style, the grass garden and the herbaceous garden. The lake, aquatic garden and ten-storey pagoda were designed by Sir William Chambers in 1760. Major features of Kew are the magnificent curved glass Palm House (built in 1848) and the Temperate House (completed in 1868), designed by Decimus Burton and Richard Turner. In more recent years the Princess of Wales Conservatory was constructed and has a variety of climatic areas, from the humid tropics through to desert conditions. There is plenty of interest to keep everyone happy, both botanical experts and those just wanting to absorb the beauty of the grounds.

☎ 020 8332 5655 www.rbgkew.org.uk

Royal Mews, Buckingham Palace

376 D12

Built in 1825 to a design by John Nash, the Mews give an insight into the work of the Royal Household department that provides transport for the Royal Family, both horse-drawn and motor. The Royal Mews are home, for most of the year, to 30 or so horses used in official and ceremonial duties. Visitors can also see the remarkable state carriages, most notably the Gold State Coach made in 1761 and the Irish State Coach bought by Queen Victoria in 1852 and used for the state opening of parliament.

☎ 020 7766 7302 www.royal.gov.uk/output/page556.asp

St Martin-in-the Fields Church

376 J7

Overlooking Trafalgar Square, this church was designed by James Gibbs and was consecrated in 1726. With its attractive spire and portico, its design has been much copied throughout the world, especially in the United States. Among the notable events to have taken place here are the christening of Charles II in 1630 and the burials of Nell Gwynne, William Hogarth, Sir Joshua Reynolds and Thomas Chippendale.

The church hosts lunchtime and evening concerts and has a brass rubbing centre. It also has a long history of work with the homeless.

☎ 020 7766 1100 www.stmartin-in-the-fields.org

St Paul's Cathedral

St Paul's Cathedral

377 S5

Designed by Sir Christopher Wren, the current St Paul's rises to a height of 365ft (111m) and is the fifth cathedral to stand on the site. It was built between 1675 and 1710, the previous cathedral having been destroyed during the Great Fire of London. Its design was revolutionary and Wren

Royal Botanic Gardens, Kew

encountered opposition from the Dean and Chapter who wanted a more traditional church. Fortunately, Wren's vision and determination won through, resulting in the masterpiece of design and engineering that we see today; the magnificent dome providing one of the best known London landmarks.

After St Peter's in Rome, St Paul's dome is the second largest in the world and has three viewing galleries. The Whispering Gallery runs around the interior and has unusual acoustics – a whisper against its walls is audible on the opposite side. Encircling the outside at 173ft (53.5m) is the Stone Gallery, and at 280ft (85.5m) is the Golden Gallery which runs around the highest point of the dome, from which the views across the city are superb. To reach here, visitors need to climb 530 steps.

The enormous scale and grandeur of the interior is breathtaking, with massive arches and lofty ceilings. The decoration is extravagant, richly gilded throughout and with brightly coloured mosaics in the Quire, which were originally planned by Wren, but not installed until 1891 – 1904. The interior also features carving by Grinling Gibbons, decorative metal work by Jean Tijou, sculpture by Henry Moore and the magnificent organ, which has been played by both Handel and Mendelssohn. Among the cathedral's 300 memorials is one to the Duke of Wellington whose body lies in the crypt, alongside the tombs of Admiral Nelson and Sir Christopher Wren.

☎ 020 7236 4128 www.stpauls.co.uk

Science Museum 355 D4

Opened in 1857, on land purchased with the profits from the Great Exhibition of 1851, the museum comprises over 40 galleries spread over seven floors. The huge collection, with over 10,000 items on show, focuses on science and scientific advances over the last 300 years, not only from Britain but also from around the world. The exhibits range from steam power, where visitors can see Stephenson's *Rocket*, to space exploration with the surprisingly small *Apollo 10* command module on display. There are a diverse range of galleries, with topics spanning computing, printing, nuclear power, flight, marine engineering and food, seen in a social as well as purely scientific light. The Wellcome Wing concentrates on contemporary science, medicine and technology and has an IMAX 3D cinema (for which there is a charge). Throughout the museum there are a vast number of interactive and hands-on displays, which really help to illustrate scientific principles, not only for the children, but for the adults too.

☎ 0870 870 4868 www.sciencemuseum.org.uk

Science Museum – Space Auditorium

Shakespeare's Globe Theatre 377 S7

The current Globe Theatre, officially opened in 1997, is a careful reconstruction of the original, which was built nearby in 1599, and for which Shakespeare wrote some of his greatest plays. The reconstruction was the dream of American actor-director Sam Wanamaker, who, sadly, never lived to see its completion. In its construction, techniques and materials as close to the original as possible have been used. It is open to the elements in the centre and has a thatched roof; as a consequence, when it rains, the 'groundlings' (the audience standing in front of the stage) get wet, just as they did in Shakespeare's day. During performances, which take place between May and September, the whole atmosphere is designed to be just as it was 500 years ago; there is no hi-tech lighting or wizardry and the crowd is encouraged to participate by shouting, cheering and jeering.

In a space beneath the theatre is the UnderGlobe where there is an exhibition of Shakespeare's life and times, with displays on the original as well as the current Globe. The exhibition includes a range of live demonstrations and interactive displays. There are also interesting tours of the whole site when there are no plays in progress.

☎ 020 7902 1500 www.shakespeares-globe.org

Somerset House 377 L6

The building, dating from the 1770s, now houses three major art collections (for which there is a charge). The Courtauld Gallery features a collection of paintings by artists such as Michelangelo, Monet and Van Gogh. The Gilbert Collection contains mainly decorative arts including jewel-encrusted gold snuffboxes. The Hermitage Rooms provide a splendid setting for varied exhibitions often featuring collections loaned from the State Hermitage Museum in St Petersburg. Areas on free public view include the Nelson Staircase, the Seamen's Waiting Hall and the King's Barge House with multimedia presentations telling the building's story. Outside a central courtyard features an impressive 55 jet fountain which is converted to an ice rink during the winter.

☎ 020 7845 4600 www.somerset-house.org.uk

Syon House 355 B4

This 16th century house, standing in 40 acre (16ha) grounds landscaped by Lancelot 'Capability' Brown, has been home to the Dukes of Northumberland since 1594. Catherine Howard, Henry VIII's fifth wife, was imprisoned here before her execution in 1542 and Lady Jane Grey began her 9-day reign here after Edward VI's death. Robert Adam made many alterations from 1762 – 1769, creating imaginative and elegant interiors – the variety of each room is exceptional.

☎ 020 8560 0881 www.syonpark.co.uk

Tate Britain 357 A4

Overlooking the River Thames, the gallery dates from 1897 and was built on the site of the Millbank Penitentiary, a former prison, to house the collection of 19th century art given to the nation by the sugar magnate, Sir Henry Tate. The permanent collection has grown enormously over the years, and today the gallery holds the largest collection of British art in the world, with works dating from 1500 to the present day. Temporary shows include the controversial Turner Prize Exhibition.

Visitors can see work by artists such as

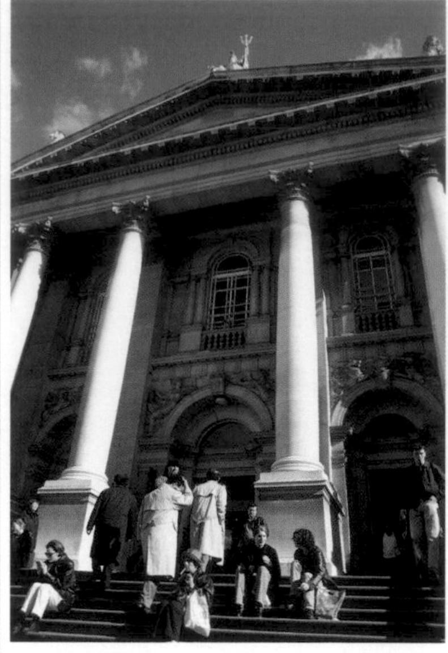

Tate Britain

Gainsborough, Stubbs, Blake, Constable, Bacon, Hirst, Hockney and Hepworth. The adjoining Clore Gallery houses the Turner bequest, comprising thousands of paintings and studies, left to the nation by Turner on condition that they remained together.

☎ 020 7887 8000 www.tate.org.uk/britain

Tate Modern 377 R8

The gallery, situated on the south bank of the River Thames opposite St Paul's Cathedral, was opened in May 2000 and features international modern art from 1900 to the present day. It is housed in the vast, former Bankside Power Station, designed by Sir Giles Gilbert Scott (designer of the red telephone box) in 1947. The sheer scale of the building creates a superb setting in which to exhibit. The vast hall, once occupied by the power station turbines, allows huge works of art to be displayed.

The permanent exhibits are arranged thematically into four main areas: Still life/Object/Real Life; Nude/Action/Body; History/Memory/Society; and Landscape/Matter/Environment. Works by Picasso, Matisse, Dali, Warhol, Monet and Bacon, amongst many others, can be seen. Throughout the year there are also a series of temporary exhibitions including three major loan exhibitions.

☎ 020 7887 8000 www.tate.org.uk/modern

Tate Modern

Thames Barrier Visitor Centre 357 D4

The visitor centre has multimedia presentations, models and displays describing the construction and operation of this movable flood barrier, which, at 1700ft (520m) long, is the world's largest. It was officially opened in 1984.

☎ 020 8305 4188

Theatre Museum 377 K6

Located in specially converted premises in Covent Garden, this museum is dedicated to artefacts associated with the performing arts, ranging from theatre to puppetry. The collection includes over a million theatre programmes and playbills (not all on display).

☎ 020 7943 4700 www.theatremuseum.vam.ac.uk

Tower Bridge Experience 356 B3

Tower Bridge has been a distinctive London landmark since 1894. Its fascinating history and the story of how it was built is told in the Tower Bridge Experience through the use of interactive displays. Visitors can see the engine rooms and climb up to the 140ft (42.5m) high walkways from which there are superb views of London.

☎ 020 7403 3761 www.towerbridge.org.uk

Tower of London 356 B3

Dating back to the 11th century, the Tower has been part of London's history for over 900 years. During this time it has had many roles, serving as a royal palace, an arsenal, royal mint, jewel house, royal menagerie (the ravens are now the only survivors) and, most notoriously, as a jail and place of execution. There are many different things for the visitor to see, either independently, or with the help of the distinctively dressed Yeoman warders (Beefeaters), who are happy to combine their traditional ceremonial role with that of tourist guide.

The oldest part is the massive rectangular 90ft (27.5m) high White Tower. Originally built as a fortress and residence providing accommodation for the king, today visitors can see a wide range of arms and armour. The Bloody Tower is associated with the deaths of the two princes in 1483. Sir Walter Raleigh was also imprisoned here for 13 years. The scaffold site on Tower Green is where seven famous prisoners were executed including Anne Boleyn, Catherine Howard and Lady Jane Grey, their bodies being buried in the adjacent Chapel of St Peter ad Vincula. Prisoners often entered the Tower from the Thames through Traitor's Gate. Be sure not to miss the Crown Jewels, a glittering and well laid out array which mainly date from the Restoration in 1660, when Charles II ascended the throne. Also worth a visit is the Medieval Palace which comprises a series of rooms shown as they may have looked during the reign of Edward I. All in all, there is a vast range of things to see, with Britain's rich and turbulent royal history evident at every turn.

☎ 020 7709 0765 www.tower-of-london.org.uk

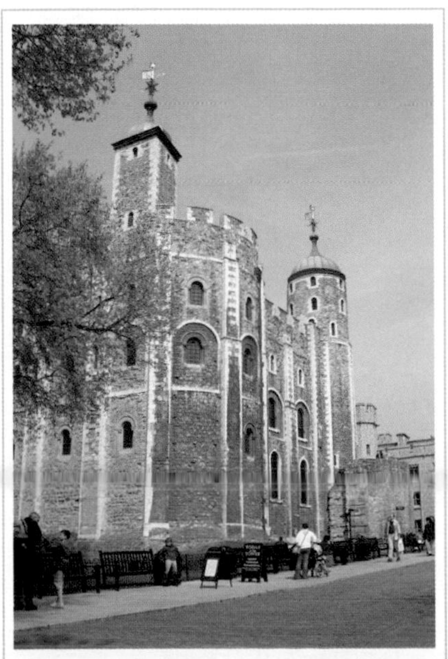

Tower of London

Victoria & Albert Museum

Victoria & Albert Museum 355 D4

Established in 1852 with profits from the Great Exhibition, and originally called the Museum of Manufactures, then the South Kensington Museum, it was finally renamed the V&A in 1899. This national museum of art and design has exhibits from all over the world, spanning over 2000 years. It is vast and labyrinthine, with four floors and over 145 galleries covering an area of 10 acres (4ha).

The collection is immense and wide-ranging with over 4 million objects as diverse as the carved oak Great Bed of Ware, made in 1590, which measures 12ft (3.6m) square, and the tiny Indian miniature paintings. Other exhibits include Oriental ceramics, Chippendale and Art Nouveau furniture, Italian Renaissance sculpture, and a significant collection of paintings by John Constable. The museum also contains Indian film posters, photographs and around 500,000 watercolours, engravings and etchings. The British Galleries are a popular destination with exhibits dating from the 16th to 20th centuries, encompassing works by famous designers such as William Morris, Charles Rennie Mackintosh and Robert Adam.

With 7 miles (11km) of galleries to explore it is impossible to see everything in one visit.

☎ 020 7942 2000 www.vam.ac.uk

Westminster Abbey 376 J12

Steeped in history, the abbey is the coronation church of all the crowned sovereigns since William the Conqueror, whose coronation took place in the original Norman building in 1066. Very little of the Norman structure remains; most of the magnificent Gothic building seen today was built by Henry III between 1245 and his death in 1272. After his death, progress was slow and the nave, which at 102ft (31m) is the highest in England, was not completed until 1517. The famous west towers, which rise to a height of 225ft (69m) were a much later addition and were completed in 1745.

Both architecturally and historically, the abbey is an absolute feast with an impressive array of tombs and memorials to some of Britain's most important figures. Within the chapel of St Edward the Confessor is his great shrine along with the tombs of Henry III, Edward I, Edward III, Richard II and Henry V. Nearby is the Coronation Chair, upon which all England's monarchs (except Edward V and Edward VIII) have been crowned since 1308. Henry VII's Chapel is magnificent, with an intricately detailed fan vaulted ceiling. It is the final resting place of Henry VII, Mary I and Elizabeth I. Within the nave can be seen the tomb of the unknown warrior whose body was laid here as a memorial to the thousands who died in World War I. The octagonal Chapter House, which between 1253 and 1547 was one of the regular meeting places of Parliament, still contains its original coloured tile floor and medieval wall paintings. Visitors can also see the Cloisters and the museum which is situated in the Norman undercroft.

☎ 020 7222 5152 www.westminster-abbey.org

Westminster Abbey

Westminster Cathedral 376 E13

Completed in 1903, this is the principal Roman Catholic church in England. The neo-Byzantine style, with its distinctive red brickwork and horizontal white stone stripes, is eyecatching. The spacious interior has the broadest nave in England and is richly decorated with multicoloured mosaics and marble.

☎ 020 7798 9055 www.westminstercathedral.org.uk

WEST MIDLANDS

Famous as the traditional 'Black Country', for so long the powerhouse of British manufacturing and forever associated with the famous makes of motor vehicles that it designed and built. Yet, outside of this cluster of throbbing industrial towns and cities, with their lively culture and retail attractions, the surrounding counties seem to have deliberately distanced themselves from this influence. Here quaint historic charm and rural calm appear to continue unchallenged.

New Place Garden, Stratford-upon-Avon

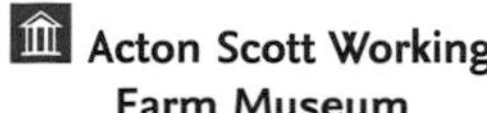

Acton Scott Working Farm Museum 207 D4

This museum re-creates the working practices of early 20th century farming. The land is worked using horses and machinery in use at the time and there are traditional demonstrations of the skills of the blacksmith, carpenter, wheelwright and farrier along with butter making, milking by hand, lambing, shearing and cider making. Amongst the wide variety of animals are Tamworth pigs, Longhorn cattle and Shropshire sheep.

☎ 01694 781306

Alton Towers Leisure Park 222 B3

A family day out, or maybe two days as there is so much to fit into one day. Set around the historic 19th century Gothic mansion and its landscaped gardens which date back to 1860, the theme park features exotically named rides such as Nemesis, Oblivion, the Flume and Spinball Whizzer. The famous Corkscrew is situated in UG Land which has a prehistoric theme and features virtual reality games. There are themed areas for younger children such as Cred Street, Old MacDonald's Farmyard and Adventure Land. Unfortunately it is necessary to queue for most of the rides though some have a time slot booking system. There is disabled access to most of the rides though some enforce height restrictions for safety reasons.

☎ 08705 204060 www.alton-towers.co.uk

Ancient High House 221 G5

Built in 1595 by John Dorrington, this Tudor building is the largest timber-framed town house in England. King Charles and his nephew Prince Rupert stayed here in 1642 at the beginning of the Civil War and, when overrun by the Parliamentarians the following year, it became a prison for Royalist prisoners. Extensive renovations by the Borough Council has enabled the building to be opened to the public, and exhibits of period furniture, wallpapers and costumes can be enjoyed. It is also home to the Staffordshire Yeomanry Museum.

☎ 01785 619131

Anne Hathaway's Cottage 197 D2

The pre-marital home of the wife of William Shakespeare, and of her descendants until the late 19th century. It is a Tudor 12-roomed thatched farmhouse, parts of which date back to the 15th century. Recent additions to the lovely garden are the Shakespeare Tree Garden, which has many of the trees mentioned in his plays, and a maze, the design of which dates from the Elizabethan era.

☎ 01789 292100

Arbury Hall 209 F4

The original house is Elizabethan but it was transformed in the 18th century into one of the finest examples of Gothic Revival architecture in the country. Home to the Newdegate family since the 16th century, many of the superb rooms are open to the public. There are superb vaulted ceilings and displays of art, glass, porcelain and antique furniture. The house is surrounded by fine landscaped gardens with lakes and woodland walks.

☎ 024 7638 2804

Ash End House Children's Farm 359 F1

A small, family run farm where the visitor can get close to the animals, many of which are under cover in case of bad weather. There is wheelchair access throughout the farm.

☎ 0121 329 3240 www.ashendhouse.fsnet.co.uk

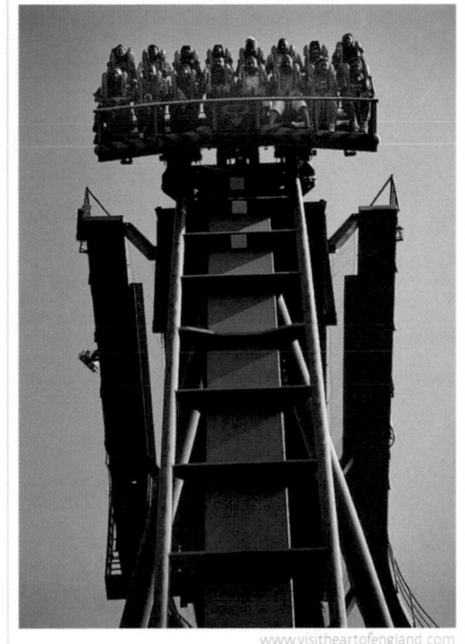

www.visitheartofengland.com

Alton Towers Leisure Park

Attingham Park (NT) 207 E1

A late 18th century mansion with magnificent interiors, built originally for the 1st Earl of Berwick, now owned by the National Trust. Guided tours are available which give an insight into life up and downstairs, as the kitchens and servants quarters are open to the public. The picture gallery was designed by John Nash who constructed the curved ceiling out of iron and glass. Surrounding the house are mature gardens, deer park, woodland and riverside walks, and in the walled garden is a children's adventure playground.

☎ 01743 708162 www.nationaltrust.org.uk

Avoncroft Museum of Historic Buildings 196 B1

An unusual museum which has over 25 historical buildings from the last 700 years, painstakingly dismantled and rebuilt on a site of 25 acres (10ha). Originally the aim was to rescue and restore only timber-framed buildings, but such has been the success of the venture that all manner of buildings are now on show, including a 1946 prefab, a working windmill, church and gaol.

☎ 01527 831363 www.avoncroft.org.uk

Baddesley Clinton (NT) 209 D5

This moated house sits in grounds of 120 acres (48ha) and has been largely unchanged for almost 400 years. The original building dates from the 15th century and stayed in the family of its owner, the Under Treasurer of England, John Broome, until it was acquired by the National Trust in 1981. The house has three priest's holes which were installed in the late 16th century by Henry Ferrers, a staunch Roman Catholic. The gardens include ponds and lakeside walks, a walled garden and nature trail.

☎ 01564 783294 www.nationaltrust.org.uk

Baggeridge Country Park 358 A1

This was largely developed by the District Council after the closure of the mineworks in 1968. It is the northern part of the park that was once one of the largest and most modern coal mines in the world. Trees have been planted to augment those that have developed naturally since the closure of the mine, and meadows have been created which now include a visitor centre and caravan park. The southern part of the park features ponds and streams, and was designed by Lancelot 'Capability' Brown for the Earl of Dudley.

☎ 01902 882605

Benthall Hall (NT) 207 F2

A 16th century sandstone house which was given a more Gothic look in the 18th century. The magnificent interior has fine oak panelling and a carved oak staircase, while the plasterwork is equally stunning. The 3 acre (1.2ha) grounds include a restored plantsman's garden as well as a rock garden, rose garden and terraces. There is also a 17th century Restoration church which holds services on alternate Sundays.

☎ 01952 882159 www.nationaltrust.org.uk

Berrington Hall (NT) 195 E1

This elegant house was designed and built in the late 18th century by Henry Holland while the parkland was designed by his father-in-law, Lancelot 'Capability' Brown. The main feature is a 14 acre (5.6ha) lake, which has sweeping views down the valley to the Brecon Beacons. The exterior sandstone walls from which the house is built give it a severe first impression, but the interior is delicate with beautifully detailed ceilings and a spectacular staircase hall.

☎ 01568 615721 www.nationaltrust.org.uk

Biddulph Grange Garden (NT) 221 F2

These 15 acre (9ha) gardens were the conception of James Bateman in the mid 19th century in order to display his wide ranging and extensive plant collection from all over the world – a common practice for Victorian gardens. The gardens are laid out as a series of smaller themed gardens, including Egyptian and Chinese gardens, pinetum and rock garden, all connected by pathways, steps and tunnels (making access difficult for wheelchairs and pushchairs). The gardens fell into disuse during World War I when the Grange was used as a hospital, and since its acquisition by the National Trust has been, and continues to be, extensively restored. There is a quiz and trail for children.

☎ 01782 517999 www.nationaltrust.org.uk

Birmingham Botanical Gardens 378 C14

Founded in 1832, these 15 acres (6ha) of beautiful gardens have a variety of interest including exotic flora, play areas and aviaries. Many different types of habitat are on display – an alpine yard, winter garden, wetlands, pinetum and cottage garden to name but a few.

There are four glasshouses with themes of tropical, subtropical, Mediterranean and arid. It is also home to the National Bonsai Collection.

☎ 0121 454 1860 www.birminghambotanicalgardens.org.uk

Biddulph Grange Garden

Black Country Living Museum — 358 B2

A faithful reproduction of a village dating from the turn of the 20th century is the centrepiece of this museum which focuses on the industrial heritage of the West Midlands. There are even caverns and an underground coal mine. Guides in period costume are on hand to demonstrate traditional skills – there is a forge, foundry, colliery, cobbler – and there is plenty to occupy the children. Most of the museum is set outdoors but there is also an interactive exhibition hall, gift shop and tearoom.

☎ 0121 557 9643 www.bclm.co.uk

Bredon Tithe Barn (NT) — 196 B4

This 14th century Tithe Barn is built of local Cotswold stone and was lovingly restored after a fire in 1980. It is around 140ft (44m) in length with an aisled interior giving it a distinctly ecclesiastical feel. It also features a remarkable stone chimney cowling.

☎ 01684 855300 www.nationaltrust.org.uk

Buildwas Abbey — 207 F2

Founded by the Savignacs in 1135 and merged with the Cistercian Order soon after, the abbey changed little until the Dissolution and is unusual in that the cloister is situated north of the main church. Parts of the original tiled floor of the Chapter House still exist and, apart from the roof, the building is still virtually intact. Research has uncovered evidence of water channels and fishponds, most probably used as a source of food by the monks.

☎ 01952 433274 www.english-heritage.org.uk

Burford House Gardens — 195 E1

7 acres (3ha) of beautiful gardens on the banks of the River Teme, originally designed by John Treasure in 1952 to complement the Georgian Burford House. Home to the National Clematis Collection, of which there are over 300 varieties, there is also a clematis maze. Wisteria Burford cascades down the rear wall of the house and is a beautiful sight when it flowers in May. The house has a contemporary art gallery which is open during the summer months and there is a garden centre, gift shop and licensed café.

☎ 01584 810777 www.burford.co.uk

Cadbury World — 359 D4

A visitor centre devoted entirely to chocolate and designed to be of particular interest to children, but with plenty to interest all. Learn the process of chocolate manufacture, experience imaginative rides through a world of chocolate. There are also television adverts from the last 40 years and a 1930s sweet shop. It is advisable to book tickets in advance, especially during the summer holidays.

☎ 0121 451 4159 www.cadburyworld.co.uk

Cannock Chase Country Park — 208 B1

One of the largest country parks in Britain, covering 4000 acres (1600ha) which lies within one of the smallest Areas of Outstanding Natural Beauty, Cannock Chase. There are many designated Sites of Special Scientific Interest and the visitor centre is the starting point for many of the well-signposted walks running through the park.

☎ 01543 876741

Cannon Hill Park — 359 D3

One of the most popular parks in Birmingham, with a variety of landscapes including flowerbeds, lakes, a wild flower meadow and woodland, which is part of a conservation area. There are plenty of facilities – canoeing, tennis courts, bowling and putting greens and a tearoom which is housed inside the Midland Arts Centre.

☎ 0121 442 4226

Black Country Living Museum

Carding Mill Valley & Long Mynd (NT) — 206 D3

Stretching across an area 10 miles (16km) long and 2 to 4 miles (3.5 to 6.5km) wide south of Shrewsbury, the Long Mynd holds much of interest, including several prehistoric barrows and earthworks, and is ideal walking country. Carding Mill Valley is a steep-sided valley offering a good, though strenuous route onto the ridge. There is a National Trust information centre and tearoom next to the car park.

☎ 01694 723068 www.nationaltrust.org.uk

Charlecote Park (NT) — 197 E2

A 16th century house visited by both Queen Victoria and Elizabeth I – the entrance porch still has the coat of arms of Elizabeth I to commemorate her stay of two nights in 1572. All of the rooms are luxuriously furnished, the dining room and library having particularly exquisite ceilings in the Elizabethan Revival style. The formal gardens open out onto 250 acres (100ha) of parkland designed by Lancelot 'Capability' Brown where, allegedly, Shakespeare was once caught poaching deer.

☎ 01789 470277 www.nationaltrust.org.uk

Commandery, The — 415 C2

An historic timber-framed building which was the headquarters of Charles II during the Civil War, though its origins date back much further than that, possibly to the 11th century. Most of the current building dates from the 15th century and has undergone many changes to reflect the style of the period.

☎ 01905 361821 www.worcestercitymuseums.org.uk

Coors Visitor Centre — 222 D5

Formerly the Bass Museum, the Coors Visitor Centre tells the story of the long and distinguished history of brewing in Burton and also in Britain in general. There is a visitor centre, frequently changing exhibitions and a computerised journey around Burton in 1881 which will be of interest to children, as will the magnificent shire horses.

☎ 0845 600 0598 www.coorsvisitorcentre.co.uk

Coughton Court (NT) — 196 C1

The house has been in the Throckmorton family since 1409 and has remained relatively unchanged since the Tudor gatehouse was built in 1530. There are exhibits relating to Mary, Queen of Scots, including the chemise she was wearing when she was executed, and also a Gunpowder Plot exhibition – at the time the house was rented out to one of the plotters, Sir Everard Digby. The grounds include one of the country's finest walled gardens and also a lake, riverside walk, bog garden and orchard.

☎ 01789 400777 www.coughtoncourt.co.uk

Coventry Cathedral — 394 E2

The old Cathedral was famously bombed in November 1940 during the devastation of Coventry and the remains have been incorporated into the new Cathedral which was consecrated in 1962. A new chapel was added to celebrate the millennium, and the visitor centre has many displays showing the history of the Cathedral and the city of Coventry.

☎ 01203 227597 www.coventrycathedral.org.uk

Coventry Transport Museum — 394 D2

The largest collection of British vehicles in the world, at the birthplace of the British motor industry. The collection includes cars, vans, trucks, bicycles and motorbikes from the present day back to 1896 when the first factory was established. Famous marques such as Daimler, Maudsley, Triumph, Jaguar, Riley and Humber are represented.

☎ 024 7683 2425 www.transport-museum.com

Croft Castle (NT) — 194 D1

This impressive country manor house has fine Georgian interiors and furniture while the curtain wall and round towers at each corner date from the 14th and 15th centuries. Apart from a break of 177 years in the 18th and 19th centuries, the Croft family have lived on this site since the Norman conquest though the castle is now maintained by the National Trust. The grounds include an avenue of 350 year old Spanish chestnuts, and adjacent to the castle are the remains of the earthworks of the original fort.

☎ 01568 781246 www.nationaltrust.org.uk

Dorothy Clive Garden, The
221 E4

Set amongst lovely hilly countryside, the garden has a variety of landscapes in its 8 acres (3ha) – woodland, alpine, a water garden and summer borders. The garden has been extended into an old quarry which is now the rhododendron garden, shaded with trees and also featuring a waterfall.

☎ 01630 647237 www.dorothyclivegarden.co.uk

Drayton Manor Park
209 D2

A 250 acre (96ha) theme park with such evocatively named rides as Pandemonium, Excalibur and Apocalypse. Gentler rides can be taken in Splash Canyon, or on Excalibur where fire-breathing dragons are encountered on a journey through medieval England. Height restrictions are enforced for safety on some rides. As well as the rides there is a zoo covering 15 acres (6ha) with over 100 species, a rare breeds farm, exotic animal reserves and a museum showing the history of Drayton Manor.

☎ 08708 725252 www.draytonmanor.co.uk

Dudley Zoo & Castle
358 B2

A magnificent location for a zoo, being set in the grounds of the ruins of Dudley Castle – the route through the zoo has cleverly been designed to take in the old castle walls. The 40 acres (16ha) is home to more than 200 species, many endangered. There is a visitor centre which also concentrates on the archaeological excavations which have been carried out locally.

☎ 01384 215313 www.dudleyzoo.co.uk

Drayton Manor Park – Pandemonium Ride

Dudmaston (NT)
207 G4

This 17th century house has exhibits of the flower paintings of Francis Derby dating from the same time, as well as modern and botanical art. The grounds include rock, rose and bog gardens and are especially impressive in the spring with collections of rhododendrons and azaleas. There are also woodland and lakeside walks in the 300 acre (120ha) parkland.

☎ 01746 780866 www.nationaltrust.org.uk

Eastnor Castle
195 G4

Built by the 1st Earl Somers in 1820, and extensively restored after 1949, the castle is still privately owned by his descendants – the Hervey-Bathurst family. Much of the original work of the interior, designed by Robert Smirke, is still in evidence, particularly in the Staircase Hall, Dining Room and Red Hall, which has a magnificent collection of armour moved here in 1989 from the Great Hall. The grounds are magnificent, comprising an arboretum, lake and deer park in which there are mazes and nature trails.

☎ 01531 633160 www.eastnorcastle.com

Fleece Inn, The (NT)
196 C3

Owned by the National Trust, this half-timbered, medieval house has been used as an inn since 1848. It has remained largely unchanged since then, but was originally in use as a farmhouse and animal shelter.

☎ 01386 831173 www.nationaltrust.org.uk

Goodrich Castle
195 E5

Guarding an ancient crossing point of the River Wye, this well-preserved 12th century ruin is constructed out of the red sandstone on which it sits. Despite seeing action during the Civil War, much of the castle is complete, including the three-storey keep as well as archways, pillars and passageways, giving a good idea of the castle as it was. There are outstanding views across the Wye Valley and the surrounding countryside.

☎ 01600 890538 www.english-heritage.org.uk

Greyfriars, The (NT)
415 C2

Built in 1480 by Thomas Greene, this timber-framed merchant's house was added to in the 17th and 18th centuries, and was rescued from demolition during World War II. None of the original 15th century furnishings survive but there is Georgian wallpaper and 16th and 17th century tapestries and furniture. The large double doors open out to a cobbled passageway and a small walled garden.

☎ 01905 23571 www.nationaltrust.org.uk

Hagley Hall
358 A4

The home of Lord and Lady Cobham was originally built between 1756 and 1760 by the 1st Lord of Lyttelton at a cost of £25,000, twice the original estimate. In 1925 a fire destroyed parts of the house, including the library and some of the extensive art collection, though it was subsequently restored to its former glory. There is fine plasterwork by Francesco Vassali, Chippendale furniture, and family portraits amongst the art collection which includes works by Van Dyck, Reynolds and Lely. The Hall is surrounded by a 350 acre (135ha) deer park.

☎ 01562 882408 www.hagleyhall.info

Hall's Croft
410 F2

Once the home of John Hall, a physician, who married Shakespeare's eldest daughter, Susanna, in 1607. The hall and parlour are the oldest parts of this timber-framed house, which dates from the early seventeenth century, and is furnished as it would have been at the time. The grounds include a herb garden containing herbs that Hall would have used in his practice.

☎ 01789 204016 www.shakespeare.org.uk

Hanbury Hall (NT)
196 B1

A William and Mary style country house built in 1701 which features splendid painted ceilings and an impressive staircase. There is a collection of porcelain on display as well as exhibitions on the family and local history. The grounds include a 20 acre (8ha) garden which is surrounded by parkland covering 400 acres (160ha). Amongst the many interesting features are an orangery, mushroom house, ice house and an 18th century bowling green.

☎ 01527 821214 www.nationaltrust.org.uk

Harvard House
197 E2

This impressive timber-framed building was built in 1596 by Thomas Rogers and has remained unchanged since then. His grandson, John Harvard, emigrated to America in 1647 and died only a year later. It was a bequest in his will that helped to establish Harvard University in Cambridge, Massachusetts. The Museum of British Pewter is housed within the building.

☎ 01789 204507 www.shakespeare.org.uk

Harvington Hall 208 A5

The largest number of priest's holes in Britain are to be found in this Elizabethan manor house which was originally built in 1580 and is now owned by the Roman Catholic Archdiocese of Birmingham. Many of the original wall paintings still adorn the walls, having been discovered beneath a layer of whitewash in 1936. Large numbers of birds are attracted by the moat and the two lakes in the gardens, which also include a Georgian chapel and a malt house.

☎ 01562 777846 www.harvingtonhall.com

Hatton Country World 197 E1

Comprises two separate attractions – Hatton Shopping Village and Hatton Farm Village. The shopping village comprises arts and craft shops, alongside antique outlets and larger retailers, set amongst converted Victorian farm buildings.

The Farm Village is set in open countryside and has plenty for children – sheep racing, a guinea pig village, play areas, a maze along with demonstrations and exhibitions of farm craft. There is a charge to pay for entry.

☎ 01926 843411 www.hattonworld.com

Haughmond Abbey 207 E1

Once part of a thriving and prosperous community, this ruined Augustinian Abbey is now in the care of English Heritage. The medieval beamed ceiling in the Chapter House is impressive, as is its 12th century entrance. Work on the surrounding fields has revealed that the abbey ruins were incorporated into the grounds of the now demolished 18th century Sundome House.

☎ 01743 709661 www.english-heritage.org.uk

Hawkstone Park 220 C5

Restored after years of neglect, this 18th century parkland covers an area in excess of 100 acres (40ha) and is now a Grade 1 listed landscape. Intricate archways, a ruined medieval castle, winding pathways, tunnels, passageways and an underground grotto give the visitor a fascinating, though at times strenuous, 3 to 4 hour round trip of the grounds.

☎ 01939 200611 www.hawkstone.co.uk

Hereford Cathedral 401 B2

Standing on the banks of the River Wye, much of the original 12th century cathedral still survives today although extensive restoraton took place in the 18th and 19th centuries. It is probably most famous for the Chained Library and Mappa Mundi exhibitions housed in the New Library building. Mappa Mundi dates from around 1300 and is the most complete and largest medieval world map still in existence. There is also an interactive exhibition which makes use of both original artefacts and the latest computer technology. Entry to the Cathedral is free but there is a charge for the exhibitions.

☎ 01432 359880 www.herefordcathedral.org

Hergest Croft Gardens 194 B2

The estate dates back to 1267 but this garden of wooded valleys and glades, flower beds and open grassland was created in 1912 when the estate was bought by the Banks family. There are over 4000 shrubs and trees in four distinct areas of the garden covering over 50 acres (20ha) – the Kitchen Garden, Park Wood, the Azalea Garden and the Edwardian House which has an old rockery and croquet lawn.

☎ 01544 230160 www.hergest.co.uk

Hodnet Hall Gardens 220 D5

60 acres (24ha) of magnificent gardens in the ownership of the Heber-Parcy family. The design has changed over hundreds of years to match the three different sites of the homes of the family and their ancestors. There is a variety of shrubs and plants designed to give colour to the gardens throughout the summer, as well as woodland walks and a chain of ornamental pools. The 17th century tearoom is well worth a visit.

☎ 01630 685786

Ironbridge Gorge 207 F2

The Iron Bridge, the first bridge in the world to be constructed completely of iron, is the focal point of the 'Valley of Invention' which was at the centre of the industrial revolution in Britain. Now a World Heritage Site, ten museums tell the story of the industrial revolution and the part this area played in it. The Blists Hill Victorian Town is an open-air re-creation of a late 19th century working community where even old money can be bought at the bank and used in the local shops and pubs. On some Saturdays there are re-enactments of a Victorian wedding ceremony. The Museum of the Gorge looks at the effects of the revolution on the beautiful gorge itself, and the Broseley Pipeworks, which closed in 1957, is presented as if it were still a working factory. There is also a Museum of Iron, China Museum and Tile Museum, as well as the Bridge and Tollhouse where there is an exhibition and souvenir shop. A passport ticket can be bought to give access to all ten museums and, as they cover an area of around 6 square miles (15 sq km), a shuttle bus runs between them at weekends and on bank holidays.

☎ 01952 884391 www.ironbridge.co.uk

Kenilworth Castle 360 A3

An impressive 11th century ruined castle which has been radically altered and extended since then. John Dudley acquired the castle in the 16th century but was executed for his part in the plot to place Lady Jane Grey on the throne. His son, Robert Dudley, created formal gardens where he entertained Queen Elizabeth I on several occasions. Now in the care of English Heritage, some of the 12th century buildings in the inner courtyard survive, as does the Tudor gatehouse.

☎ 01926 852078 www.english-heritage.org.uk

Letocetum Roman Baths & Museum (NT) 208 D2

The remains of a Roman bathhouse and an inn have been excavated at this site which was an overnight halt on Watling Street, the main road from London to North Wales. A museum exhibits many of the artefacts that have been discovered on the site and gives the historical background to the site.

☎ 01543 480768 www.nationaltrust.org.uk

Lichfield Cathedral 208 D1

Situated in a peaceful close surrounded by half-timbered buildings, this Gothic cathedral dates from the 14th century. With three spires, known as the 'Ladies of the Vale', it is unique amongst medieval cathedrals. The Lichfield Gospels, an 8th century manuscript, is on display in the Chapter House, which dates from 1249 and is one of the most beautiful parts of the cathedral. There is a visitor centre and a licensed restaurant situated in an elegant 18th century house next to the cathedral.

☎ 01543 306240

Little Malvern Court 195 G3

Home to the Berington family since the Dissolution of the Monasteries in 1539 and comprising the 14th century Prior's Hall and the Victorian Manor House. The interior features paintings by the family along with many examples from Europe, and there is a fine collection of 18th and 19th century needlework. Lovely views can be taken from the gardens covering 10 acres (4ha) which once belonged to the 12th century priory that stood on the site.

☎ 01684 892988

Ludlow 207 E5

A 12th century market town, with 500 listed buildings, which retains its original grid-like layout. Amongst the listed buildings are the 17th century Feathers Hotel, the Broadgate, which is the only surviving gate from the old city walls, and the medieval Reader's House with its three-storey Jacobean porch. The Church of St Lawrence has the grandeur of a cathedral and shows, in one of its stained glass windows, the life of St Lawrence, Ludlow's patron saint. The geology of the area and the town's local history are the main themes of the museum in the Assembly Rooms.

☎ 01584 875053 www.ludlow.org.uk

www.visitheartofengland.com

Ironbridge Gorge

Ludlow Castle 207 E5

Built in the late 11th century to repel Welsh marauders, the castle has much that is original, including the keep, chapel and some of the doorways. It became a royal palace under Edward IV, and home of the Council of the Marches, responsible for the government of Wales and the borders. There are many exhibitions, displays and events throughout the year.

☎ 01584 873355 www.ludlowcastle.com

Malvern Hills 195 G3

Stretching for 9 miles (15km) with a high point of 1380ft (425m) at Worcestershire Beacon, the Malvern Hills divide the counties of Herefordshire and Worcestershire. Easily accessible either from the towns on the flanks of the hills or from the numerous car parks that are dotted around the entire length. This is a designated Area of Outstanding Natural Beauty which can be extremely busy in good weather though quieter spots can be found even during the busiest periods.

☎ 01684 560616 www.malvernhillsaonb.org.uk

Mary Arden's House 197 D2

Glebe Farm is the home of William Shakespeare's mother, Mary Arden – for years it was thought that the adjacent timber-framed Palmer's Farm was her home but it has only recently been discovered not to be so.

The Shakespeare Countryside Museum is housed in the outbuildings which include a dovecote, smithy, cider press and workshop containing a variety of Elizabethan farm implements. There are frequent displays of falconry.

☎ 01789 204016 www.shakespeare.org.uk

National Sea Life Centre 378 G8

Set in the rejuvenated canalside area of Birmingham, one of the many highlights is the completely transparent tunnel giving the impression that the visitor is completely surrounded by all manner of sea creatures, including sharks and rays. Conservation is an important part of the centre's activities and is part of the SOS (Save Our Seas) scheme which works with many worldwide conservation groups. The seahorse breeding and conservation centre allows visitors to see work normally carried on behind the scenes.

☎ 0121 643 6777 www.sealifeeurope.com

Packwood House (NT) 209 D5

This 16th century house was extensively restored between the two World Wars by Graham Baron Ash and donated to the National Trust in 1941. It played host to Henry Ireton, Cromwell's general, before the Battle of Edgehill in 1642, and also to Charles II after his defeat at Worcester in 1651. There is a large number of sundials and clocks adorning the walls while the impressive gardens include yew trees with a theme of the 'Sermon on the Mount'.

☎ 01564 783294 www.nationaltrust.org.uk

Potteries Museum & Art Gallery 410 A2

A local history museum examining all aspects of the area, from the world famous pottery industry through to community, wildlife and geology. The centrepiece of the wartime section of the museum is a Spitfire designed by Reginald Mitchell who was educated in Hanley and served his apprenticeship in Fenton before going on to design the Spitfire. He died in 1937 before he saw it enter full service.

☎ 01782 232323

RAF Museum 207 G2

Formerly the Aerospace Museum, the RAF Museum has a collection of over 70 aircraft from Britain, Germany, Argentina, America and Japan. There are also air force vehicles, missiles and engines, and ever-changing exhibitions. The aircraft are mainly housed in three hangars with themes of transport and training, warplanes, research and development. The restoration work which is ongoing at the museum can be observed from the viewing gallery, and the annual air show is always popular.

☎ 01902 376200 www.rafmuseum.org.uk

Ragley Hall 196 C2

The family home of the Marquess and Marchioness of Hertford, this magnificent Palladian house was built in 1680 and stands in grounds of over 400 acres (160ha) designed by Lancelot 'Capability' Brown. The Great Hall has superb baroque plasterwork by James Gibbs and included in the fine art collection is the mural 'The Temptation' by Graham Rust. The grounds include woodland walks, a maze, adventure playground and rose garden.

☎ 01789 762090 www.ragleyhall.com

Ryton Organic Gardens 360 C3

10 acres (4ha) of totally organic gardens covering all aspects of organic gardening – composting, pest control, flower, fruit and vegetable production amongst many others. A natural area includes trees, wild flower meadow and lake. The Paradise Garden is dedicated to the late Geoff Hamilton, the popular presenter of 'Gardeners World'. It is also home to the headquarters of the Henry Doubleday Research Association which promotes organic gardening and farming.

☎ 024 7630 3517 www.hdra.org.uk

Severn Valley Railway 207 G3

This standard-gauge steam railway runs for a distance of 16 miles (26km) from Bridgnorth to Kidderminster and passes through beautiful Severn Valley countryside, including a trip across a 200ft (60m) single span bridge. The station at Bewdley has a model railway and workshops where restoration work on one of the largest collections of locomotives and rolling stock in the country can be viewed.

☎ 01299 403816 www.svr.co.uk

Shakespeare's Birthplace 410 D2

A half-timbered house bought by the Bard's father, John Shakespeare, in the mid 16th century, a few years before Shakespeare's birth in 1564, and which remained in the family until 1806. 16th and 17th century furniture adorn the interior and, of particular interest, are the signatures of famous visitors engraved into a window in the Birth Room. The visitor centre has a multitude of original exhibits and displays, and there is a lovely traditional English garden.

☎ 01789 204016 www.shakespeare.org.uk

Shugborough Estate (NT) 222 A5

This Georgian mansion is the ancestral home of Lord Lichfield and has exhibitions of period silver, furniture, paintings and china. Amongst the many events throughout the summer are craft, weaving and gardening weekends and also a fully working water mill where milling demonstrations take place. The 900 acres (360ha) of gardens and parkland include a yew tree which is thought to be the widest tree in the country.

☎ 01889 881 388 www.nationaltrust.org.uk

Spetchley Park 196 A2

Surrounding the 19th century mansion (not open to the public) these gardens have been owned by the Berkeley family since 1605. Formal clipped hedges, fountain gardens, herbaceous borders and winding paths offer so much of interest in this 30 acre (19ha) garden (not open to the public on Saturdays). The 110 acre (70ha) Deer Park is not open during June.

☎ 01453 810303 www.spetchleygardens.co.uk

Stafford Castle 221 G5

There is plenty to see and do at this 900 year old castle originally built by William the Conqueror but largely destroyed during the Civil War. The visitor centre has displays of finds made in archaeological excavations. Historical re-enactments and Shakespeare theatrical productions are a feature of the summer months, for which there is an admission charge. There is also a herb garden which was originally planted for medicinal purposes.

☎ 01785 257698

Stokesay Castle 206 D4

This 13th century fortified manor house, now in the care of English Heritage, is one of England's finest and is set in beautiful countryside amongst the Shropshire Hills, not far from the Welsh border. Many parts of the castle are original, including the Great Hall in which the roof timbers are soot blackened from the open hearth. The solar chamber has a magnificent Jacobean fireplace and the delightful 17th century gatehouse is probably more ornamental than strategic.

☎ 01588 672544 www.english-heritage.org.uk

Symonds Yat 181 E1

A large loop in the River Wye has Symonds Yat Rock at its narrowest point. This impressive wooded gorge is a nesting place for the rare peregrine falcon which can be observed from the RSPB information area at the top of the rock during the summer months. A steep descent from the large car park, for which there is a charge, leads to Symonds Yat East where there is a popular inn and café, while an unusual hand pulled ferry crosses the Wye to Symonds Yat West, where there is a visitor and heritage centre.

☎ 01600 713899

Tamworth Castle 209 E2

A Norman motte and bailey castle dating from the 12th century, with numerous additions since then, including the medieval Banqueting Hall. 15 rooms are open to the public with displays from throughout the castle's history. There are many events including ghost vigils and tours in search of the many ghosts allegedly seen in the castle. There are also frequent Shakespearian plays. Beneath the castle are the pleasure grounds with floral terraces, play areas, tennis courts, crazy golf and a café.

☎ 01827 709629 www.tamworthcastle.freeserve.co.uk

Thinktank 379 Q7

One of the largest millennium projects, with a wide range of different things to do and see for all the family. Science and nature are brought to life by displays, many of which are interactive, in ten different galleries. Local history is featured, as is nature, medicine, a vision of the future and the oldest working steam engine in the world, designed by James Watt.

☎ 0121 202 2222 www.thinktank.ac

Warwick Castle

Tutbury Castle 222 D5

This 11th century castle has played host to many royal guests including giving safe harbour to Charles I and his nephew Prince Rupert during the Civil War. Because of this, Cromwell ordered the castle to be dismantled though it was rebuilt in 1662. Mary, Queen of Scots was imprisoned here and, of all the places she was imprisoned, it is said that she had a special loathing for Tutbury. There is also a secret staircase, privy garden and herbery.

☎ 01283 812129 www.tutburycastle.com

Upton House (NT) 197 F3

This 17th century house has wonderful collections of 18th century furniture, tapestries, art and porcelain. The house was bought by Walter Samuel, the Chairman of Shell, in 1927. He carried out extensive modifications to both interior and exterior and gave the house and his collections to the National Trust in 1948. This included his splendid art collection of works by El Greco, Canaletto, Stubbs and Hogarth. There are 31 acres (12.5ha) of terraced garden containing herbaceous borders, fruit and vegetable gardens.

☎ 01295 670266 www.nationaltrust.org.uk

Viroconium Roman Town 207 E2

With a population of over 6000, Viroconium (Wroxeter) was once the fourth largest city in Roman Britain. The remains are extensive and include city walls and the fully excavated public baths. Beneath these are timber buildings dating from the early part of the first century when a garrison was stationed here before it was moved to Chester and Viroconium became an important trading centre. A visitor centre explains the history of the town as well as exhibiting many of the artefacts discovered on the site.

☎ 01743 761330

Warwick Castle 197 E1

Set on the banks of the River Avon, this is one of the finest examples of 14th century fortifications in Britain. Real-life characters help to bring the castle to life and life-sized waxworks add detail to many of the displays, which include an accurate re-creation of the visit of the Prince of Wales, later to become Edward VII, in 1898. The macabre dungeon and torture chamber are reached down a narrow flight of stairs – the writings of a Royalist held during the Civil War can still be seen on the wall. The Great Hall is amongst the luxuriously decorated state rooms which has Oliver Cromwell's death mask on display and also paintings by masters such as Van Dyck and Rubens.

The grounds were designed by Lancelot 'Capability' Brown and include walks along the Avon, an 18th century conservatory and Victorian Rose Garden. There is also a restored mill and engine house which was used to produce the electricity of the household at the turn of the 20th century. There are many events throughout the year including fireworks concerts, medieval festivals and birds of prey displays. A good day out for all the family.

☎ 0870 442 2000 www.warwick-castle.co.uk

Wedgwood Story Visitor Centre 364 C3

Wedgwood Pottery was founded in 1759 by Josiah Wedgwood and his legacy can be seen during a tour of the state-of-the-art factory that includes hands-on demonstrations. Film and interactive displays are used to tell the story of the company and exhibits from all periods of its history are on display. The shop sells exclusive designs as well as seconds and discontinued lines.

☎ 01782 282986 www.thewedgwoodstory.com

West Midland Safari Park 208 A5

A 4 mile (6km) drive through the 150 acre (94ha) park gives access to all manner of exotic animals including elephants, lions, tigers, rhinoceros, bison, llama, antelope. Home to the country's only pride of white lion, of which there are only around 70 remaining worldwide, and white tigers, of which there are only around [illegible]. There are also shows planned out at different times of the day – sea lion shows and hippo feeding, and chances to get close to animals such as snakes and crocodiles.

☎ 01299 400700 www.wmsp.co.uk

Weston Park 208 A2

Mentioned in the 11th century Domesday Book, though the present house was built in 1671. There are nine elegant rooms, including a library with over 3000 books, and the magnificent dining room which has a large collection of art by Van Dyck. The expansive grounds, designed by Lancelot 'Capability' Brown, are formal around the house and include a restored terrace garden as well as parkland including lakes, pools and the deer park. There is plenty for children with a miniature railway, animal centre and adventure playground.

☎ 01952 852100 www.weston-park.com

Wightwick Manor (NT) 208 A3

Built by the Mander family at the end of the 19th century to designs influenced by the Arts and Crafts movement, and decorated with original William Morris materials, Kempe glass and Pre-Raphaelite art. Descendants of the family still live in part of the manor. The 17 acre (7ha) garden is a delight with topiaries, terraces and ponds.

☎ 01902 761108 www.nationaltrust.org.uk

Wilderhope Manor (NT) 207 E3

On the edge of Wenlock Edge stands this Elizabethan manor house. It is now in use as a youth hostel and, as such, it is largely unfurnished which allows the skill of the craftsmen who created the oak spiral staircase, timber-framed walls and plaster ceilings to be appreciated to its full extent. Limited opening.

☎ 01694 771363

Worcester Art Gallery & Museum 415 A2

In an historic Victorian building which also houses the city library, this local museum focuses on the history, geology and natural history of the area. A fully stocked 19th century chemist shop is amongst the exhibits of interest, as is the section of the museum devoted to the Worcestershire Regiment and Yeoman Cavalry. The art gallery has frequently changing contemporary art exhibitions from local and national artists.

☎ 01905 25371 www.worcestercitymuseums.org.uk

Worcester Cathedral 415 C2

The Cathedral stands on the site of an ancient Saxon monastery which was largely destroyed in 1041. Rebuilding started in 1064 and, after a series of problems including a fire and collapse of the tower, was all but complete by the time of its dedication in 1218. Time took its toll on the cathedral and it was not until the Victorians undertook a massive restoration programme that it took on the form that we see today. The richly decorated tombs of Prince Arthur and King John can be found near the High Altar.

☎ 01905 28854 www.cofe-worcester.org.uk/cathedral

Wyre Forest 207 G5

Once a popular hunting ground with an area of 4200 acres (1680ha) but which used to cover most of the West Midlands. Forest clearance for agriculture started during Neolithic times and continued through to the 16th century when the demand for both timber products and also charcoal was at its height. The visitor centre is southwest of Bewdley at Callow Hill and is the starting point for many trails. It also has a restaurant, gift shop and information on all aspects of the forest.

☎ 01299 266944 www.wyreforest.net

EAST MIDLANDS

In the south lie the misty, fertile fens, with their regimented rows of salads and brassicas. Then to the north are the rolling chalky wolds, shimmering with acres of gently whispering cereal crops. This region is truly Britain's kitchen garden. Further east the restless waves of the North Sea pound the chalky coastline and here, for generations, the windswept sandy beaches have played host to the skilled workers and families of the large midland cities in an ageless seaside tradition.

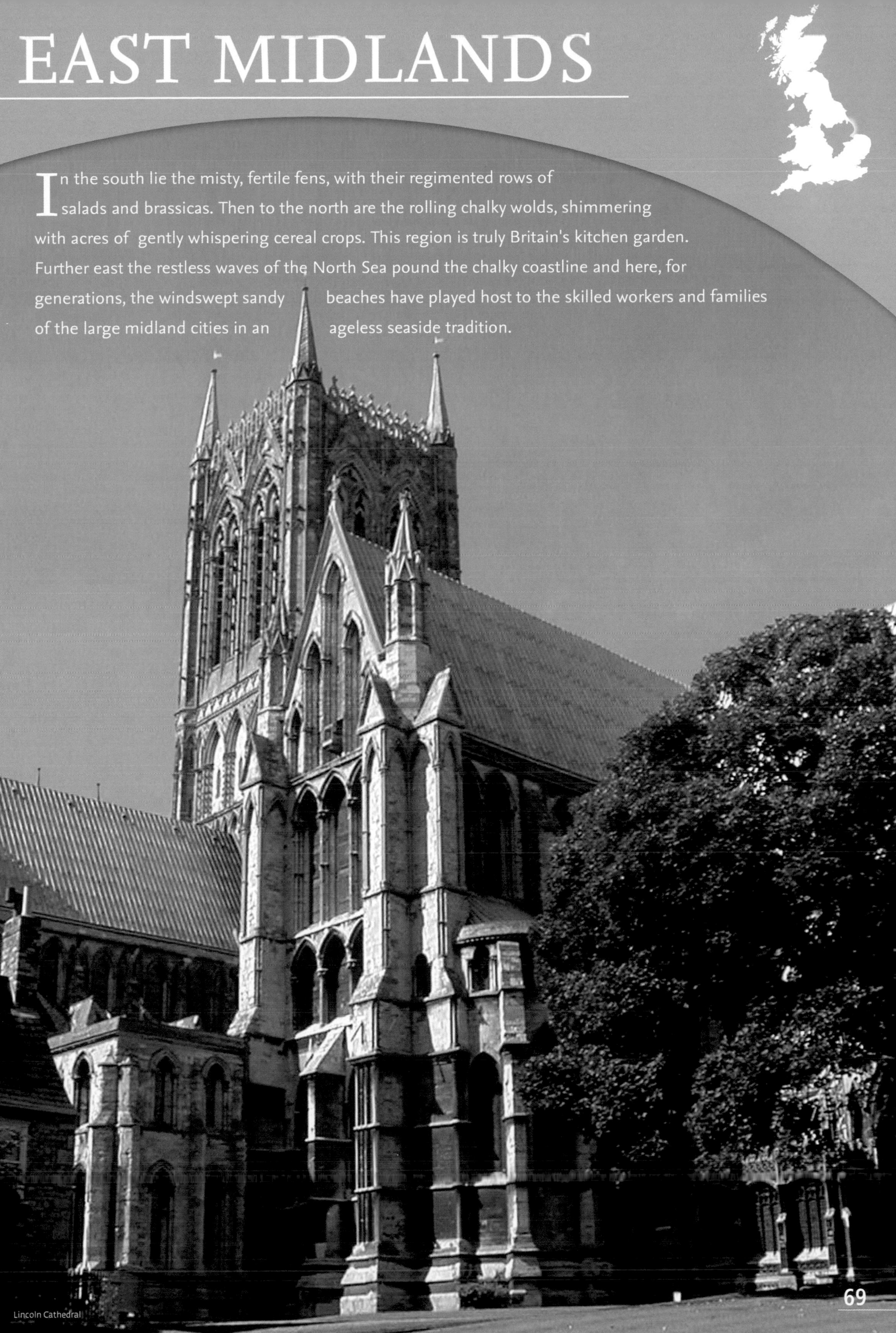

Lincoln Cathedral

Althorp House 198 B1

Since 1508, Althorp House has been home to the Spencer family. The classically-styled house in its typically English parkland was thrust into the limelight by the tragic death in 1997 of Diana, Princess of Wales, herself a member of the family. She now rests in peace on an island in the centre of the lake. Although there is no public access to the island, there is an excellent exhibition about Diana housed in the former stable block. Audiovisual displays relate to her life and work, with poignant memorabilia such as school reports and her beautiful wedding dress. Diana's involvement with various charities is well known and the Diana, Princess of Wales Memorial Fund, set up to continue this work, gets a high profile; all proceeds from the entrance fees go to this fund.

The house itself contains many treasures, which can be viewed by the public. In particular, there is an exceptional collection of portraits by artists such as Gainsborough, Van Dyck and Rubens.

Open July to September only.

☎ 0870 167 9000 www.althorp.com

Althorp House

American Adventure Theme Park 362 C1

Right on the edge of the glorious Derbyshire Peak District and set around a 32 acre (13ha) lake (once an opencast mine), this exciting theme park includes the tallest Skycoaster in Europe, a 200ft (61m) high face-first, free-fall, white-knuckle experience. Try the Motion Master, which synchronises a seat with what is happening in an action packed film. Then there is Nightmare Niagara, a triple drop log flume, and The Missile, a roller coaster with six completely circular loops. Tiny tots and the faint-hearted are also catered for, and the management promise that with over 100 rides, there will be 'no unacceptably long queues'.

☎ 0845 330 2929 www.americanadventure.co.uk

American Adventure Theme Park

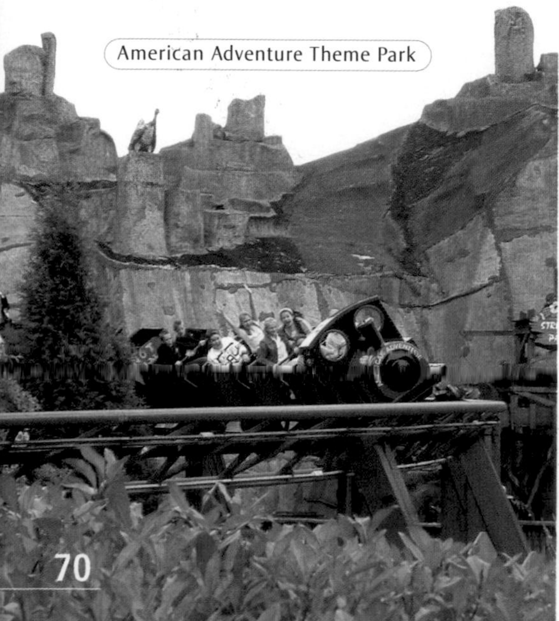

Barnsdale Gardens 211 E1

Built over several years by gardener Geoff Hamilton, all the 35-plus model gardens from the various TV series can be seen here. Plant nursery and excellent coffee shop.

☎ 01572 813200 www.barnsdalegardens.co.uk

Battle of Britain Memorial Flight Visitor Centre 226 A2

Exhibition and guided tours of the maintenance hangar containing the Memorial Flight aircraft, including an Avro Lancaster, Chipmunks, Dakota, Hurricanes and Spitfires.

☎ 01526 344041 www.lincolnshire.gov.uk

Beacon Hill Country Park 361 A1

Part of Charnwood Forest, and now included as part of the new National Forest, the network of paths running through the 335 acres (135ha) of grassland, mixed woodland and heath, make the park ideal for walking and picnics. Beacon Hill itself (at 802ft (245m) the second highest point in Leicestershire) was once home to Bronze Age people and remains of their Hill Fort can still be seen. It now sports a toposcope, pointing out interesting features in the surrounding landscape.

☎ 01509 890048 www.leics.gov.uk

Belton House (NT) 225 E4

Built in the Restoration style for Sir John Brownlow in the late 1600s, this sumptuous country house is well worth a visit for the wealth of elaborate woodcarving and plasterwork, not to mention the fine furniture, silverware and tapestries. A magnificent Orangery graces the formal gardens and the substantial landscaped parkland includes a lake; perfect for a leisurely stroll. If the children get bored, head for the Adventure Playground and Wildlife Discovery Centre. The Stables Restaurant also includes a children's menu.

☎ 01476 566116 www.nationaltrust.org.uk

Belvoir Castle 224 D4

For 1000 years Belvoir has been home to the Dukes of Rutland. Meaning 'beautiful view', the name is actually pronounced 'beaver' and the view is right across the glorious Vale of Belvoir. The present castle was built in the early 1800s after a fire destroyed the previous one, and it contains many fine paintings and sculptures along with French furniture, tapestries and porcelain. There is also a fascinating museum dedicated to the history of the Queens Royal Lancers. Outside, the sloping lawns lead to the terraced formal gardens and the secluded Duchess' Spring Gardens.

☎ 01476 871000 www.belvoircastle.com

Bestwood Lodge Country Park 363 E1

Just four miles (6km) north of Nottingham, this 650 acre (263ha) park was once part of the ancient Sherwood Forest. 20 miles (32km) of footpaths now wind through a remarkable range of habitats, from reedbeds to woodland and heath. Over 150 species of birds inhabit the park.

☎ 0115 927 3674 www.nottinghamshire.gov.uk

Bolsover Castle 236 B5

Looking like a 'proper' castle, this 'Little Castle' is really a 17th century mansion house built to represent the romantic ideal of chivalry and elegance. Walking around, an imaginative audiovisual presentation re-creates the atmosphere of the time. The huge Riding House, originally built by William Cavendish to train horses in the art of manege, has been converted into a Discovery Centre and the restored garden boasts a fountain with 23 new statues. There is a visitor centre, café, and picnics are allowed in the grounds.

☎ 01246 822844 www.english-heritage.org.uk

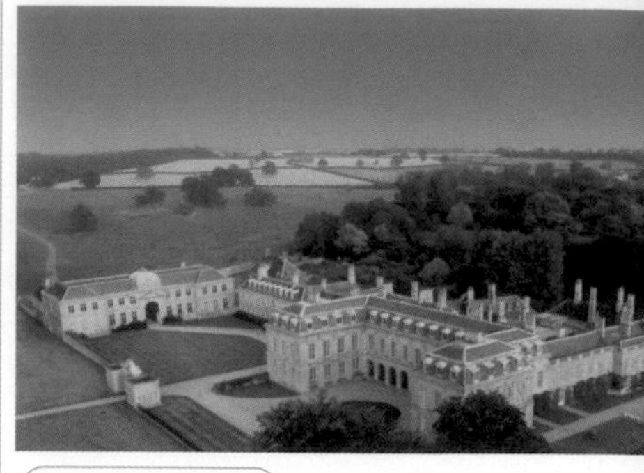

Boughton House

Boughton House 211 E4

The 'English Versailles', so called because of the French-style changes made to the original 1500s Tudor monastic building. Home to the Dukes of Buccleuch, the interior is richly furnished and the ceilings are decorated with delightful mythical scenes. The Buccleuch collection of fine art is world renowned, including works by Van Dyck and Caracci. There is a superb armoury and ceremonial coach, and the grounds house a tearoom, play area and walled garden with plant centre. House open August only. Grounds open May to August.

☎ 01536 515731 www.boughtonhouse.org.uk

Bradgate Park 361 A2

Leicestershire's largest country park is famous for its large deer herd and Lady Jane Grey (queen of England for nine days). The ruins of Bradgate house, her birthplace, lie amongst the granite outcrops. However, the chapel has survived and houses a small museum. The tower folly 'Old John' stands on the ridge and is a famous local landmark. Excellent for walking.

☎ 0116 236 2713 www.leics.gov.uk

Buxton Museum & Art Gallery 235 E5

Follow the time line of the Peak District through seven rooms of geology, archaeology and history. Exhibitions feature work by local artists.

☎ 01298 24658 www.derbyshire.gov.uk

Calke Abbey (NT) 223 E5

An interesting example of a baroque country house captured in its state of decline. The last baronet died here in 1924 and left splendidly decorated rooms, where the family had lived, along with deserted, run-down areas, abandoned due to lack of servants. Little restoration work has been done, in order to preserve the remarkable social history it portrays. There is an extensive natural history collection, wonderful parkland, café and shop, and a walled garden with Auricula theatre.

☎ 01332 863822 www.nationaltrust.org.uk

Canons Ashby 198 A2

The house takes its name from an Augustinian Priory, the church surviving on a hilltop in the grounds. Home to the Dryden family since it was built in the mid 1500s, it has remained virtually the same since 1710. The Jacobean plasterwork is exceptional and the Elizabethan wall paintings have been superbly restored. The formal gardens have been brought back to their 18th century glory.

☎ 01327 861900 www.nationaltrust.org.uk

Carsington Water 223 D1

This 741 acre (300ha) reservoir was originally designed to collect water at times of high rainfall and release it back into the River Derwent in times of drought. It has also proved to be an excellent centre for water sports, fishing, walking, cycling and picnicking. The extensive modern visitor centre has an interactive display explaining how the reservoir was constructed, as well as shops, restaurant and a café. Half a million trees and shrubs were planted to landscape the area and provide habitat for wildlife and there are two hides from which to observe the many birds in the Wildlife Centre. The Watersports Centre will hire out canoes, dinghies and windsurfers, and provide instruction on how to use them, or you can take your own craft. A network of waymarked footpaths and bridleways allow for walking, horse riding and cycling (bikes can be hired). For younger children, there is a large adventure playground and families can cook their own food in the designated barbeque areas. Facilities for the less able are particularly good.

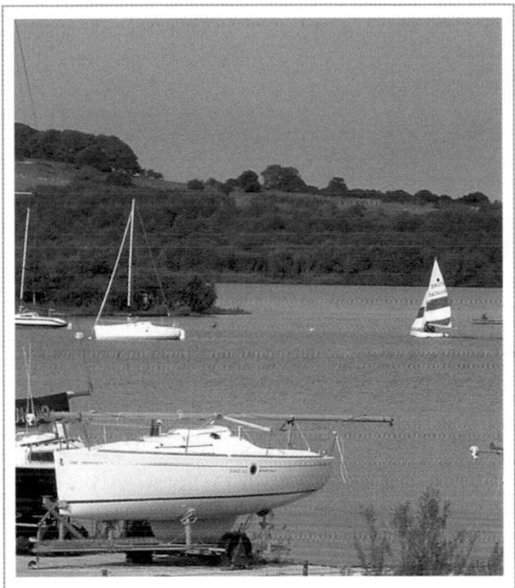

Carsington Water

Chatsworth House 235 G5

In the heart of the Derbyshire Peak District stands one of Britain's best loved stately homes, the residence of the Duke and Duchess of Devonshire. The magnificent house has over 25 beautifully decorated and furnished rooms, containing some of the finest treasures to be found in a private collection.

There are over 100 miles (161km) of walks through the 1000 acres (405ha) of Lancelot 'Capability' Brown designed parkland, which includes a lovely 100 acre (41ha) garden and the famous gravity fed waterworks, which power spectacular fountains and a waterfall cascading down a long flight of stone steps. Chatsworth has never rested on its laurels; the estate has been developed to provide a first-class adventure playground, with 'commando' style rope walks down to safe water and sand play areas for tiny tots. A working farmyard allows children to get really close to the animals and a 28-seat trailer provides tours of the woods and parkland. The maze is a challenge, and for shopaholics there is a farm shop selling Estate and local produce as well as one selling everything from furniture to porcelain. There are brass band concerts on a Sunday and events throughout the year. Truly a top-class family day out.

☎ 01246 565300 www.chatsworth-house.co.uk

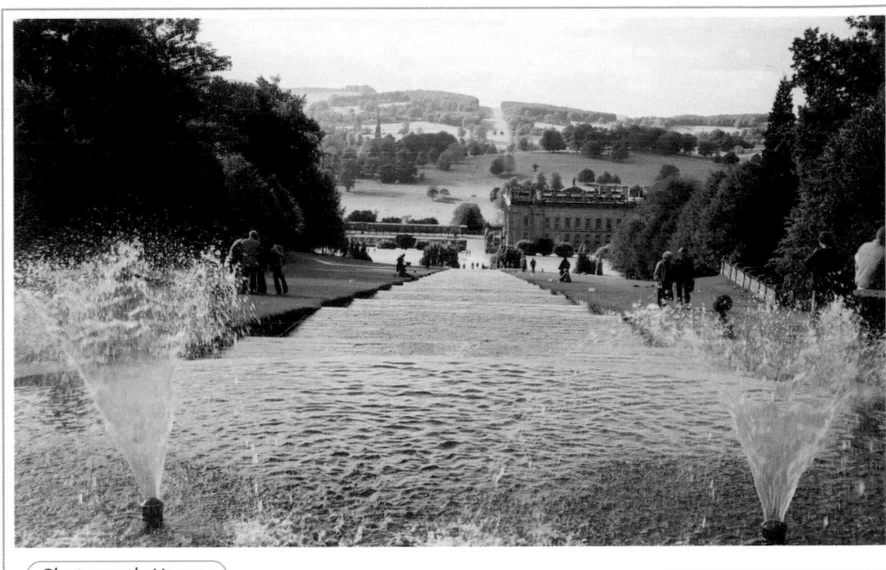

Chatsworth House

Church Farm Museum 227 D1

Just outside Skegness town centre is a restored farmyard, showing life as it was in rural Lincolnshire around the turn of the 20th century. Besides the farmhouse, there is a 'mud and stud' thatched cottage and various farm buildings, all with period exhibitions. Outside, the orchard has old apple tree varieties and a herd of Lincolnshire Longwool sheep graze the paddock. There are always things going on, such as baking and threshing, and refreshments are available.

☎ 01754 766658 www.lincolnshire.gov.uk

Clumber Country Park (NT) 236 D5

Lovely country park of over 3800 acres (1537ha) with heath, woods and farmland. There is a serpentine lake and an avenue of lime trees (reputedly the longest in Europe) as well as a superb chapel in the Gothic Revival style, temples, a classical bridge and a walled kitchen garden with magnificent glasshouses. Excellent for walking and cycling (bikes can be hired) with refreshments in the stable block.

☎ 01909 476592 www.nationaltrust.org.uk

Coton Manor Wildlife Garden 210 B5

Ten acre (4ha) garden with a wide range of interesting and unusual plants. Five acre (2ha) bluebell wood, which is a real picture in spring, as well as an orchard and wild flower meadow. Plant nursery and excellent tearoom.

☎ 01604 740219 www.cotonmanor.co.uk

Denby Pottery 223 E3

Get messy and have a go at making a plate or a frog. Daily tours, excellent factory shop, cookery demonstrations, museum, garden, Dartington Crystal and gift shops, restaurant and children's play area.

☎ 01773 740799 www.denbyvisitorcentre.co.uk

Derby Industrial Museum 395 A2

The site of the world's oldest factory (the silk mills, built in the early 1700s) is appropriately the location for this museum. It tells the story of Derby's industrial heritage; mining, pottery, foundry work, railway engineering and a major exhibition of Rolls Royce aero-engines form the backbone of the museum. There are regularly changing displays and events.

☎ 01332 255308 www.derby.gov.uk

Doddington Hall 237 F5

This beautiful Elizabethan mansion, gatehouse and family church were completed in 1600 and the exterior has remained unchanged. However, the interior is a surprise, having been completely redecorated and furnished in the Georgian style in the mid-1700s. The wonderful array of textiles, paintings and artefacts collected since give it a very 'lived in' air.

Outside, the lovely gardens occupy 6 acres (2.4ha), most of which are walled, with formal topiary and herbaceous planting. There is also a wild garden and intriguing turf maze. Refreshments are served in the Gatehouse.

☎ 01522 694308 www.doddingtonhall.com

Donington Grand Prix Collection 223 F5

Five halls contain the world's largest collection of Grand Prix cars (over 130), from the oldest to the newest. Also helmets, veteran and vintage cars and much more. Gift shop selling models, videos, books and other merchandise.

☎ 01332 811027 www.doningtoncollection.com

Dove Dale 222 C2

The River Dove flows along a limestone gorge, giving its name to the area of Dovedale, arguably the most beautiful of the Derbyshire Dales. The river itself is excellent for trout fishing and has been immortalised by Isaac Walton in his book 'The Compleat Angler'. Classified as an Area of Outstanding Natural Beauty, the valley runs for over two miles (3.2km) and there are beautiful walks both along it and in the surrounding hills, which are the remains of ancient coral reefs.

Dove Dale

Elvaston Castle Country Park 362 B3

The first country park in Britain, Elvaston includes 200 acres (81ha) of grounds containing formal gardens, woodland, nature trails, an ornamental lake and estate museum. Refreshments and shop.

☎ 01332 571342 www.derbyshire.gov.uk

Eyam Museum 235 G5

The rat weather vane gives a clue to the theme of this museum; the 1665 outbreak of the Bubonic Plague. The story of this community is told from its beginnings in prehistory, through the tragedy of the plague (the villagers isolated themselves so as not to spread the disease), to its recovery and regrowth through the Industrial Revolution and beyond.

☎ 01433 631371 www.eyammuseum.demon.co.uk

Fantasy Island 227 D1

Rides are classified as 'Extreme Thrill' (with names such as 'Absolutely Insane' and 'The Beast') and 'Family Fun' (Europe's largest ferris wheel, for example, and a train ride through the world of the Jellikins for the little ones). Most of the rides are inside and with over 15 places to eat, a huge market and over 30 shops in the Mall, the weather is largely irrelevant.

☎ 01754 874668 www.fantasyisland.co.uk

Foxton Locks

Foxton Locks 210 C4

Located on the Grand Union Canal, Foxton Locks were built to solve the problem of raising boats the 75ft (22.5m) between Market Harborough and the hill summit a few miles north. Ten locks were constructed between 1810 and 1814 to form the 'Foxton Staircase' and it takes 45 minutes and 25,000 gallons (113,650l) of water for one boat to negotiate all ten; the water passing into side ponds, where it is stored. At the start of the 20th century, in order to speed up the passage of boats in an attempt to compete with the railways, the famous 'Inclined Plane' was built. Considered one of the 'Seven Wonders of the Waterways', the structure was designed by Gordon Cale Thomas and built by Gwynne of London. It consisted of two tanks, each filled with water, large enough to carry two narrow boats or a barge. A 25 horsepower engine enabled the tanks to travel up and down the slope in 12 minutes, also saving many thousands of gallons of water. However, due to lack of improvements on the rest of the canal and the success of the railways, the Inclined Plane lift was uneconomic and only operated for about ten years before being abandoned and eventually sold for scrap in 1928. The museum on the site tells the story and shows the plans for rebuilding it.

The towpaths and surrounding area are lovely for walks and there is a pub and café at the locks.

☎ 01162 792657 www.fipt.org.uk

Gainsborough Old Hall 237 F4

Over 500 years old, this timber framed medieval manor house has a superb Great Hall, medieval kitchen and interesting furniture. Audio tours available.

☎ 01427 612669 www.english-heritage.org.uk

Gibraltar Point 227 D2

An internationally important National Nature Reserve, this 1000 acre (430ha) site contains many constantly changing coastal habitats, namely sand dunes, saltmarsh, freshwater marsh, sandbanks and mudbanks. Stretching from Skegness to the Wash, this is a haven for overwintering and breeding birds, and footpaths and hides have been constructed to enable visitors to observe but not disturb them.

☎ 01754 762677 www.lincstrust.org.uk

Great Central Railway 361 B3

Britain's only main line double track steam railway offers rides from Loughborough to Leicester stations. Dine in style, drive an engine, enjoy a 'themed' ride (such as a 'who dunnit') or try a Santa Special. Museum, engine sheds and shop at the Loughborough end.

☎ 01509 230726 www.gcrailway.co.uk

Grimsthorpe Castle 225 F5

Dating from the 13th century, this castle with its impressive baroque frontage has an interesting collection of tapestries, paintings and fine furniture, including thrones from the House of Lords. Surrounded by 3000 acres (1213ha) of parkland, there is a family cycle trail, a Woodland Adventure Playground, a tour with the Park Ranger (who will point out the wealth of wildlife), a shop and a café.

☎ 01778 591205 www.grimsthorpe.co.uk

Gunby Hall (NT) 226 C1

Lovely red brick 18th century house with fine oak panelling and period furnishings. Nine acres (3.6ha) of beautiful gardens with traditional flowers, fruit and vegetables.

☎ 01909 486411 www.nationaltrust.org.uk

Haddon Hall 222 D1

Parts of the hall date back to 1170, when the illegitimate son of William the Conqueror held it. However, it was not until 200 years later that the building was completed. Remarkably well preserved, it has featured in many period dramas and films.

Home of the Manners family since 1567, areas of interest include the Medieval Banqueting Hall, with Minstrels Gallery, the Great Chamber, which has many fine tapestries, and the Long Gallery, of early 17th century lineage, where the Elizabethan gentry and their ladies could take gentle walking exercise in inclement weather.

The beautiful gardens were brought back from a derelict state by the 9th Duchess of Rutland, who created a romantic garden with herbaceous borders and terraced rose gardens. The 17th century stable block houses a licensed restaurant and there is a gift shop.

☎ 01629 812855 www.haddonhall.co.uk

Haddon Hall

Harborough Museum 210 C4

The history of this planned medieval market town (many medieval yards still exist) is told through displays in this museum. The story of Market Harborough's famous corset making industry is explained with old photographs and models, including a steam former used to shape the corsets. There is a reconstruction of a bootmaker's workshop, many photographs and texts from the town as it was, and archaeological finds, including artefacts from the nearby Drayton Roman Villa and Naseby battlefield.

☎ 01858 821085 www.leics.gov.uk

Hardwick Hall (NT) 223 F1

Designed by Robert Smythson for the wealthy Bess of Hardwick, no expense was spared to build this magnificent example of Elizabethan grandeur. Imposing symmetrical towers and acres of glittering glass windows give a stunning first impression. Hardwick Hall displays the National Trust's most important collection of textiles in the country, including the Gideon Tapestries, which hang in the Long Gallery and cover the 167ft (50m) long wall. Other items of interest include period furniture, portraits and armour.

Before living here, Bess lived in Hardwick 'Old' Hall (now managed by English Heritage), the remains of which can be seen on the hilltop next to the 'New' Hall. It was the wealth accumulated from her four husbands that enabled her to move!

Outside, a herb garden, orchard and formal flower beds are enclosed by courtyards, and surrounding this is a country park containing rare breeds of sheep and cattle. There is also a stonemasons centre, which can be visited.

☎ 01246 850430 www.nationaltrust.org.uk

Hardwick Hall

Heights of Abraham
223 E2

The journey of discovery starts with a spectacular ride in a cable car over the River Derwent and Matlock Bath village, to the summit. At the top there is an old lead mine, the Great Rutland Cavern Nestus Mine, and the Great Masson Cavern to explore, the latter including a film presentation on how it was formed. Climb the Prospect Tower for magnificent views. There are two adventure playgrounds, woodland walks, the 'Who, Why, What' story of the Estate, excellent gift shops, and refreshments in The Terrace café, Woodlanders restaurant and the Tavern.

☎ 01629 582365 www.heights-of-abraham.co.uk

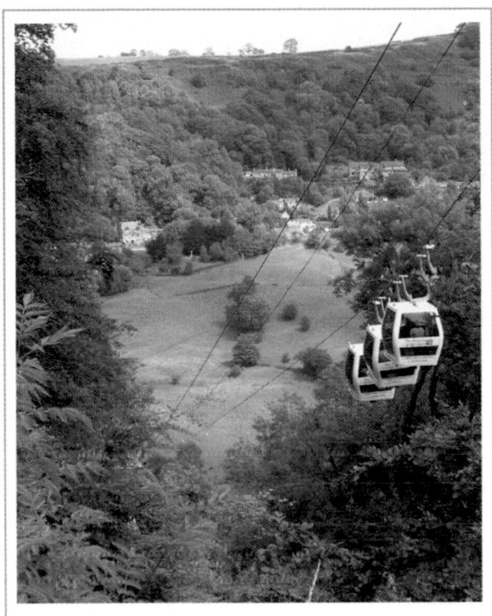

Heights of Abraham

Kedleston Hall (NT)
362 A2

A mansion in the neoclassical style with a remarkable array of Robert Adam interiors. The state rooms still have their original furniture, and an amazing display of Indian artefacts (collected by Lord Curzon, Viceroy of India in the early 1900s) can be seen in the Eastern Museum. The mansion is surrounded by parkland, which includes a restored 18th century garden. There is a shop and restaurant.

☎ 01332 842191 www.nationaltrust.org.uk

Lincoln Castle
403 B2

Built in 1068, this impressive and massive early Norman castle on its hilltop houses one of the four surviving copies of the Magna Carta, sealed by King John in 1215. There are still many original features to see, and a walk along the walls outside provides superb views across the surrounding countryside.

☎ 01522 511068 www.lincolnshire.gov.uk

Lincoln Cathedral
403 B2

Sharing the central hill with Lincoln Castle, this magnificent cathedral is one of the finest medieval buildings in Europe. Originally built in 1072 from local limestone, it was consecrated in 1092 and has been a place of worship ever since. It was damaged by fire in 1141 and an earthquake in 1185 caused considerable collapse. Rebuilt by the Bishop of Lincoln (St Hugh), he incorporated huge flying buttresses on the outside so that fewer supporting structures were needed on the inside. This allowed large windows to be installed and gave the inside an open and airy feel. In 1237 the central tower collapsed, which was not replaced for several years. By 1549 there were three towers, each with a spire; the central one blew down and the others were eventually removed, being considered unsafe!

The cathedral library contains many important manuscripts, including one written by the Venerable Bede in the late tenth century. The medieval library often exhibits books and manuscripts and there are guided roof and floor tours daily (except Sundays).

☎ 01522 544544 www.lincolncathedral.com

Lyddington Bede House
211 D3

Originally built as a wing of a medieval palace, owned by the Bishops of Lincoln, it was seized by the Crown in 1547 and given to Lord Burghley. He converted it into small rooms, almshouses, for the poor, with the condition that they learn a craft and attend church. Audio tour of the rooms.

☎ 01572 822438 www.english-heritage.org.uk

Lyveden New Bield (NT)
211 E4

Designed in the shape of a cross, Sir Thomas Tresham built (but did not complete) this Elizabethan 'Lodge' to show his religious convictions. It has remained almost unchanged since 1605. The layout of the water garden is also original, containing terraces and fascinating spiral mounds.

☎ 01832 205358 www.nationaltrust.org.uk

Mam Tor
235 F4

Known locally as 'shivering mountain', the summit of Mam Tor stands high above Hope and Edale. Popular with walkers, several well-maintained paths reach the top and along its ridgeway, where there are impressive views. Traces of an Iron Age fort can be found on the summit.

Melbourne Hall & Gardens
223 E5

Two Prime Ministers and Lady Caroline Lamb (the mistress of Lord Byron) have lived here. Originally built in the 12th century, most of the building was demolished and rebuilt in the 17th century. It now contains a fine collection of furniture and paintings and is the home of Lord and Lady Kerr. The formal gardens are beautifully laid out in the French style, with delightful fountains and an intriguing yew tunnel. House open in August only.

☎ 01332 862502

Melton Carnegie Museum
210 C1

Through displays of local archaeology, art, industry and rural pursuits, the museum tells the story of the market town of Melton Mowbray and the surrounding area.

☎ 01664 569946 www.leics.gov.uk

Museum of Lincolnshire Life
403 A1

Two centuries of social history are explored in this museum, which occupies the old barracks of the Loyal North Lincoln Militia; interactive displays tell the story of the Regiment. The fascinating history of local crafts is told and there are impressive collections representing agricultural and industrial heritage.

☎ 01522 528448 www.lincolnshire.gov.uk

National Space Centre
361 B3

Follow the brown signs with the rocket logo to this amazing centre covering all aspects of space research. For the over 5s, the Space Theatre shows amazing films about different worlds, how the universe was born and the edge of the known universe; under 5s can be treated to a 'Sunshine Show'. There are lots of buttons to push on hands-on displays in the five galleries. The first gallery looks at astronauts, the second is about our exploration of the universe to date, the third investigates our own solar system and the fourth examines how the huge advances in technology, due to space research, affect our lives on Earth. The final gallery takes a peek into the possible future. The silver 135ft (41m) rocket-shaped building contains a glass lift, which enables observation of the huge Blue Streak and Thor Able rockets. A truly inspiring and exciting day out.

☎ 0116 261 0261 www.nssc.co.uk

National Tramway Museum

223 E2

Set in a restored period village, including shops, cafés, a pub and a museum (which holds the largest national collection of electric trams). One ticket allows all day rides up and down the street on trams from all over the world. A workshop enables observation of 'work in progress' on trams being restored.

☎ 0870 758 7267 www.tramway.co.uk

Lincoln Cathedral

Newstead Abbey
223 G2

A 'must see' for Byron devotees, Newstead houses mementoes of one of England's most notorious poets. Originally built as an Augustinian priory, it was converted into a country house by the Byron family in the mid 1500s. Although much of the Abbey is now a ruin, there are beautifully furnished period rooms – although look out for the 'White Lady' ghost!

The walled garden, lake and exquisite Japanese gardens are set within the 300 acre (121.5ha) estate.

☎ 01623 793557 www.newsteadabbey.org.uk

Nine Ladies Stone Circle
222 D1

On Stanton Moor, a circle of nine evenly-spaced stones stand in a 33ft (10m) diameter circle in a large, open woodland glade. The tallest stone stands at 2.3ft (0.7m) and there is one outlier, the King Stone. An atmospheric reminder of the mysterious past.

☎ 01629 816200 www.english-heritage.org.uk

Northampton Central Museum
198 C1

Fascinating museum concentrating on Northampton's boot and shoe industry. The collection of footwear is one of the largest in the world, featuring every aspect of shoe design and manufacture. There are also impressive displays of oriental and British ceramics, and Italian paintings.

In another section of the museum, the history of the county of Northamptonshire is explained with exhibits from the surrounding area.

☎ 01604 838111 www.northampton.gov.uk

Nottingham Castle Museum & Art Gallery
405 F1

The original Nottingham Castle was built in the early 1100s but was completely demolished in 1651. A new one was built on the same site by the Duke of Newcastle, which was gutted by fire in 1831. The shell was restored in 1878 to house a museum, which now displays a superb collection of fine art, ceramics, metalwork and glass. With children in mind, there are hands-on exhibitions and the 'Look Out' playground includes watch towers and a medieval barn. Tours of the city caves are available from the museum, and there is a café and shop.

☎ 0115 915 3700 www.nottinghamcity.gov.uk

Oakham Castle
211 D2

The superb Great Hall remains from the original 12th century castle. It contains fine sculptures and an amazing collection of horseshoes, mounted on the walls, the oldest of which probably dates from 1470. The custom was that every visiting peer of the realm had to give a horseshoe to the Lord of the Manor on his or her first visit. HRH The Princess Royal gave one of the latest in 1999.

☎ 01572 758440 www.rutnet.co.uk

Peak Cavern
235 F4

This huge cavern has the largest natural cave mouth in Britain. A complete village once existed here, making ropes for the local lead mining industry. The guided tour passes various awe inspiring features, including the Great Cave which measures 150ft (45m) by 90ft (27m).

☎ 01433 620285 www.peakcavern.co.uk

Peak District
235 F3

Essentially separated into the rugged sandstone Dark Peak and gentler limestone White Peak areas, the Peak District is very much a product of man, through farming, mining and quarrying. It has been inhabited since the end of the last Ice Age.

Peak District – Monsal Head

The first National Park, the Peak District displays an amazing variety of habitats on its uplands and in its sheltered Dales, making it very pleasant walking country. The villages are picturesque and welcoming. Look out for the floral art of 'Well Dressing' in many villages, a custom largely confined to this area, and try the famous 'Bakewell Puddings' (not tarts) in the town of Bakewell. Visit the many caverns (with a guide) or relax in one of the many teashops or traditional pubs.

☎ 01629 816200 www.peakdistrict.org

Peveril Castle
235 F4

Built in the 11th century to guard the King's Manor, this castle, on its high vantage point, offers superb views across the Peak District of Derbyshire.

☎ 01433 620613 www.english-heritage.org.uk

Pickfords House Museum
395 B1

The former home of Joseph Pickford (architect), this Grade 1 listed Georgian town house is furnished in period style; even down to the housekeeper's cupboard. It shows vividly how an ordinary professional gentleman and his servants would have lived at the time. There are also displays of toys and toy theatres, textiles and costumes. Outside, the garden has been re-created in the style of the period.

☎ 01332 255363 www.derby.gov.uk

Poole's Cavern
235 E5

The subterranean Wye Brook has dissolved the limestone rock here over millennia to form this magnificent cavern. Neolithic man sheltered here, Celts and Romans worshipped here, a robber called Poole is said to have hidden here in the 15th century, and people have visited it to marvel at its wonders since the 1600s. There are some fantastic formations fashioned from the slowly dripping limestone rich water; stalactites, stalagmites, rimstone pools, flowstones and curtain features, some of which have been coloured by minerals leaching out from the hills above. The entrance was once quite restricted, so in the late 1800s, the owner used dynamite to enlarge it (destroying some large features in the process). In this era, the cavern held a bandstand, museum and monkey house and was illuminated by large candelabra. Luckily, the caves are now appreciated solely for their natural beauty and today's guides will not threaten abandonment at the end of the passage without further pay!

Research has shown that the cave system stretches for around one and a half miles (2.4km) beyond the boulder rubble at the current end. The visitor centre at the entrance has information on the so far unseen caves, tells the history of the cavern and has an exhibition of artefacts found in it.

☎ 01298 26978 www.poolescavern.co.uk

Renishaw Hall & Gardens
236 B5

The grounds of Renishaw Hall contain lakeside walks, a sculpture trail, yuccary, a host of traditional and exotic plants and a café. The stable houses art galleries and a museum, which includes an exhibition of clothing from the last 150 years. Guided tours available.

☎ 01246 432310 www.sitwell.co.uk

Rutland County Museum
211 D2

The rural history of England's smallest county is told in a building originally designed as an indoor riding school for the Rutland Fencible Cavalry. Further buildings house galleries, local crafts, a café and shop.

☎ 01572 758440 www.rutnet.co.uk

Poole's Cavern

Sherwood Forest Country Park 224 B1

Natural sandy heathland and ancient oaks have produced a fascinating ecosystem, represented in this 450 acre (182ha) country park, part of the former Royal Hunting Forest. The famous hollow 'Major Oak', where the legendary Robin Hood supposedly hid, can be found here and there are many waymarked woodland trails to explore. The excellent visitor centre illustrates the legends and natural history of the Forest, with displays and videos; it also houses two shops and a café.

☎ 01623 824490 www.nottinghamshiretourism.co.uk

Sherwood Pines Forest Park 224 B1

With over 2960 acres (1200ha) of heath and woodland, this is an excellent area for safe cycling (cycles can be hired), walking, horse riding and picnics. For young children, there is an adventure playground.

☎ 01623 822447 www.forestry.gov.uk

Shipley Country Park 362 C1

This 600 acre (243ha) country park includes woodlands, lakes and two large, flat, open areas popular for kite flying. There are many walks and cycle tracks, a sculpture trail, bird hide, adventure playground, visitor centre, shop, picnic site and coffee shop.

☎ 01773 719961 www.derby.gov.uk

Snibston Discovery Park 209 G1

This former 100 acre (40.5ha) colliery site has been transformed into a unique museum and discovery centre for science and technology. Ride on the colliery railway and have a go on over 90 experiments to discover the wonders of science. Ex-miners give guided tours of the old colliery and, by contrast, the Science Alive gallery is full of state of the art interactive games illustrating scientific principles in fun ways. There is a separate gallery for under 8s and under 5s. Good restaurant and excellent access for the less able.

☎ 01530 278444 www.leics.gov.uk

Speedwell Cavern 235 F4

This is a former lead mine incorporating several naturally formed chambers and an amazing underground canal. 105 steps lead down to the waterway, where a boat will take visitors on a guided tour of this atmospheric 200 year old mine. At the end is an awesome, massive cavern, with a 65.5ft (20m) waterfall. The roof disappears into blackness, too high to be seen and the water is so deep it was believed to be bottomless.

☎ 01433 620512 www.speedwellcavern.co.uk

Springfields Outlet Shopping Village & Festival Gardens 226 A5

25 acres (10ha) of beautiful plants to delight gardeners and florists alike. Bulbs plus trees, shrubs, herbaceous plants, a semi-tropical greenhouse and display gardens. For shopaholics, there is a factory outlet shopping village.

☎ 01775 724843

Stainsby Mill 236 A5

On the Hardwick Estate is a water-powered mill. Producing flour as far back as the 13th century, the machinery was replaced in the mid 1800s. Now restored, flour is ground regularly and can be purchased here.

☎ 01246 850430 www.nationaltrust.org.uk

Stanford Hall 210 A5

Lovely 17th century house in grounds alongside the River Avon. Beautifully furnished with a fine collection of Tudor and Stuart paintings and a magnificent library. The former stables house a motorcycle museum with racing and vintage machines, and there is a full scale replica of the early 'Hawk' flying machine. The grounds include a rose garden, nature trail and, of course, tearooms.

☎ 01788 860250 www.stanfordhall.co.uk

Stoke Bruerne Waterways Museum 198 C2

A former cornmill in the lovely village of Stoke Bruerne was chosen to house this fascinating museum, which recalls 200 years of the inland waterways. The busy Grand Union Canal is immediately outside, with boat trips available along it. Refreshments can be found in the village.

☎ 01604 862229 www.thewaterwaystrust.org

Sudbury Hall (NT) 222 C4

Richly decorated late 17th century house with a very elaborate Great Staircase. Interesting mythological decorative paintings, Grinling Gibbons woodcarvings and magnificent plasterwork. Shop, tearoom and picnic site.

☎ 01283 585337 www.nationaltrust.org.uk

Sudbury Hall Museum (NT) 222 C4

The National Trust Museum of Childhood is housed in a service wing of the main Hall. Everything about children from the 1700s to the present day. Toys and games along with a re-created Victorian schoolroom and examples of child employment. There is a treasure hunt to play and, at Christmas, tea with Santa.

☎ 01283 585337 www.nationaltrust.org.uk

Sulgrave Manor 198 A3

Beautiful Tudor House where George Washington's ancestors lived. Guided tours are given around the furnished rooms, gardens and George Washington Exhibition. Café and shop.

☎ 01295 760205 www.stratford.co.uk

Tales of Robin Hood 405 E1

Travel back to Sherwood Forest in the time of Robin Hood. Experience the sights, sounds and smells of the age from a guided carriage. Opportunities to try archery and brass rubbing or listen to a storyteller. Falconry demonstrations at weekends.

☎ 0115 948 3284 www.robinhood.uk.com

Tattershall Castle (NT) 226 A2

Imposing and impressive 15th century tower, one of the first to be built of red brick. Fortified and moated, it was restored in the early 1900s and has four storeys of huge rooms with massive Gothic fireplaces, stained glass windows and brick vaulting.

☎ 01526 342543 www.nationaltrust.org.uk

Treak Cliff Cavern 235 F4

One of the first 'Blue John' mines, where the beautifully coloured mineral was extracted. Amazing stalactites and stalagmites can be seen on the guided tour.

☎ 01433 620571 www.bluejohnstone.com

Twycross Zoo 209 F2

Twycross covers 40 acres (16ha) of countryside and is famous for its collection of primates. These include man's closest relative, the bonobo, along with the smallest pygmy marmosets, through orang-utans, chimpanzees, gibbons and mountain gorillas. Baby animals are always arriving and are a popular attraction, as is feeding time in the sealion pen. Other animals include lions, giraffes, flamingos, the rare Mhorr gazelle, penguins, seals, snakes, crocodiles and elephants, to name but a few. For younger children there is 'Pets Corner' and an adventure playground. Three quarters of the 1000-plus animals here are classified as endangered and one of the main functions of the zoo is as a captive breeding centre to help in their conservation; information on this and other aspects of the zoo are available through the various exhibitions and information boards.

☎ 01827 880250 www.twycrosszoo.com

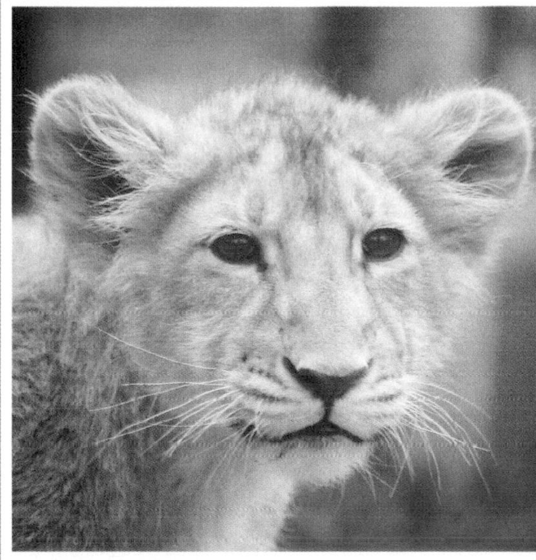

Twycross Zoo – Lion Cub

Wicksteed Park 211 D5

Opened in the 1920s, Wicksteed was one of the first big amusement parks; it still has a less 'frantic' air than some others. The large boating lake, gardens, pitch and putt and quite magical miniature railway are a welcome breath of quieter days, whereas the roller coaster, twin pirate ship and twin-seat racing cars cater for those seeking thrills. There is a huge, free playground for younger children and plenty of places to shop and eat. A very pleasant day out catering for all.

☎ 01536 512475 www.wicksteedpark.co.uk

Woolsthorpe Manor (NT) 225 E5

Birthplace and home of Sir Isaac Newton, this small, 17th century manor house contains a 'Young Newton' exhibition and an early edition of his 'Principia' work. In the barn is a Science Discovery Centre and café, and a descendant of the apple tree, under which Newton is said to have discovered the principles of gravity, grows in the orchard.

☎ 01476 860338 www.nationaltrust.org.uk

Ye Olde Pork Pie Shoppe 210 C1

Still made to the original recipe, pork pies have been baked by Dickinson & Morris in this shop since 1851. Next door they have opened a sausage shop, and both shops offer demonstrations.

☎ 01664 562341 www.porkpie.co.uk

EAST OF ENGLAND

Wide, pastel-hued skies, reedy flat fens, secluded nature reserves, river estuaries and delightful coastal towns characterise this area. East of Norwich, the interconnecting waterways of the Broads offer a unique area for leisure and recreation. Few hills rise to interrupt the distant views of cathedral cities and timeless villages, with their rich historic stories. This is the home of artists and musicians and also one much favoured by boatlovers, birdwatchers, equestrians and antiquarians.

Wicken Fen National Nature Reserve

Alby Crafts & Gardens — 228 D2

Working craft centre in converted brick and flint farm buildings surrounded by 4 acres (1.5ha) of attractive gardens.

☎ 01263 761590 www.albycrafts.co.uk

Aldenham Reservoir Country Park — 186 A3

Comprising 175 acres (70ha) of woodland and parkland with a 65 acre (26ha) reservoir. There are plenty of things to do and see including fishing, sailing, a rare breeds farm, children's adventure play area, nature trails and a re-creation of Winnie the Pooh's 100 Aker Wood. There is a charge for parking.

☎ 020 8953 9602 www.hertsdirect.org/aldenham

Anglesey Abbey (NT) — 200 D1

This attractive Jacobean house was built on the site of an earlier Augustinian priory. Much of what visitors see today is the legacy of Huttleston Broughton, 1st Lord Fairhaven, who bought the house in 1926 and, over the next thirty years, accumulated a large collection of paintings, books, furniture, tapestries and clocks. He also landscaped the superb gardens which extend to 98 acres (40ha), and comprise both formal and informal designs. The lawns and avenues of trees combine with more structured planting to provide colour all year round and are enhanced by Lord Fairhaven's fine collection of statuary. Within the grounds is Lode Mill, an 18th century working water mill.

☎ 01223 810080 www.nationaltrust.org.uk

Audley End

Audley End — 200 D4

This magnificent Jacobean mansion was built between 1603 and 1614 by Thomas Howard, the 1st Earl of Suffolk, on the site of a former abbey. At the time, it was the largest house in England. In 1668, it briefly became a royal palace when it was purchased by Charles II for £50,000, for his use when visiting the races at Newmarket. Between 1708 and 1753 a large part of the house was demolished; the building we see today is just a small part of the original.

In the 1760s much of the interior was remodelled by Robert Adam and, today, visitors can see over thirty rooms containing attractive period furnishings. Adam's work can also be seen in the extensive grounds where he created ornamental garden buildings to enhance the superb landscape park laid out by Lancelot 'Capability' Brown in 1762. There are fine Victorian gardens featuring a parterre, originally laid out in 1830 and re-created in 1993, a rose garden, as well as a walled garden of approximately 10 acres (4ha) within which is an impressive 170ft (52m) long vine house.

☎ 01799 522399 www.english-heritage.org.uk

Banham Zoo — 214 B3

Opened in 1968 and set in 35 acres (14ha) of beautiful parkland and gardens, this attractive zoo features over 1000 animals, including big cats, reptiles, penguins and kangaroos. Visitors can tour the site on the Safari Roadtrain, which gives an excellent overview of the animals.

☎ 01953 887771 www.banhamzoo.co.uk

Bedford Museum — 199 F3

Housed in the former Higgins & Sons Brewery, the collection of this local museum focuses on Bedfordshire's social and natural history, geology and archaeology.

☎ 01234 353323 www.bedfordmuseum.org

Beth Chatto Gardens, The — 202 B5

In 1960 Beth and Andrew Chatto took 4 acres (1.5ha) of inhospitable wasteland and decided to create a garden. It seemed like an impossible task, with its sunbaked, sandy slopes and boggy areas, but the colourful gardens visitors can see today are a testament to their horticultural skill. On the site are four main areas: the scree, gravel, woodland and water gardens, each with their own gardening challenges.

☎ 01206 822007 www.bethchatto.co.uk

Blickling Hall (NT) — 228 C3

An impressive sight, Blickling Hall is an early 17th century Jacobean mansion built mainly of red brick and limestone. Highlights within the house include the spectacular 125ft (38m) Long Gallery with its superb plaster ceiling, a library, an oak staircase and fine collections of paintings, furniture and tapestries. The parkland surrounding the house was landscaped in the 18th century and includes an artificial lake and 600 acres (243ha) of woodland. Unusually, within the grounds there is a burial pyramid.

☎ 01263 738030 www.nationaltrust.org.uk

Bourne Mill (NT) — 202 B5

Originally built as a fishing lodge in 1591, this Grade I listed building, with attractive 'Dutch' gables, was converted to a mill in the 19th century. It has a 4 acre (1.5ha) mill pond and much of the machinery, including the waterwheel, is in working order.

☎ 01206 572422 www.nationaltrust.org.uk

Bressingham Steam Museum & Gardens — 214 B3

Created by horticulturalist Alan Bloom, visitors can see main line locomotives, traction engines and an elaborate Victorian steam roundabout against a lovely backdrop of colourful landscaped gardens. Not to be missed are rides on the working narrow gauge railways that run for more than 5 miles (8km) around the gardens, lake and woods. For garden lovers, the 6 acre (2.5ha) Dell Garden, featuring 47 island beds of perennials, provides a superb show of colour in the summer. There is also a 'Dad's Army' exhibition.

☎ 01379 686900 www.bressingham.co.uk

Burghley House — 211 F2

This superb Tudor mansion was built between 1565 and 1587 by William Cecil (later Lord Burghley), who was Elizabeth I's Lord Treasurer and principal advisor. It is set in a 300 acre (120ha) deer park landscaped in 1756 by Lancelot 'Capability' Brown. Externally, the mansion remains virtually unchanged and is considered by many to be one of the finest examples of late Elizabethan architecture. The interior was extensively remodelled in the late 17th century and contains the work of Antonio Verrio, Grinling Gibbons and Louis Laguerre. The beautiful interiors are a marvellous showcase for the house's impressive collection of art, which was amassed largely by the 5th and 9th Earls of Exeter (Lord Burghley's descendants) who were both avid collectors.

☎ 01780 752451 www.burghley.co.uk

Cambridge — 200 C2

Situated on the banks of the River Cam, Cambridge is a combination of narrow medieval streets and magnificent buildings. Flanking the river are The Backs, a picturesque mixture of lawns, formal gardens and open spaces.

The fairly compact city centre is dominated architecturally by the historic University, the hi-tech industries that have developed in recent years tending to be confined to the outskirts. There are 31 colleges, rich both historically and architecturally. The first college, Peterhouse, was founded in 1284 by the Bishop of Ely. Queens' College is notable for its unusual wooden Mathematical Bridge – built originally without the use of nails. Perhaps the most famous of the colleges is the 15th century King's College whose chapel has an outstanding fan vaulted ceiling and exceptional stained glass windows. Other colleges include Magdalene College, where the fellows still dine by candlelight, and the most recent, Robinson College, which was founded in 1974 by a local millionaire. Many of the good and great studied at the University – luminaries include Sir Isaac Newton, Samuel Pepys, Archbishop Thomas Cranmer, Oliver Cromwell, William Wordsworth and, more recently, the likes of Stephen Hawking and the 'Pythons' John Cleese, Eric Idle and Graham Chapman. Guided walks around the city and colleges leave from the Tourist Information Centre daily throughout the year and, especially if time is short, they are a good way to get a feel for what there is to see.

Cambridge also offers a fine range of museums to visit: the Fitzwilliam Museum has an eclectic collection of art and artefacts, the Sedgwick Museum of Geology has a lovely gem collection, and the Cambridge University's Museum of Zoology has a fascinating collection of animals; visitors can see a giant ground sloth, now extinct, that was collected in Victorian times.

☎ 0906 586 2526 (60p/min) www.visitcambridge.org

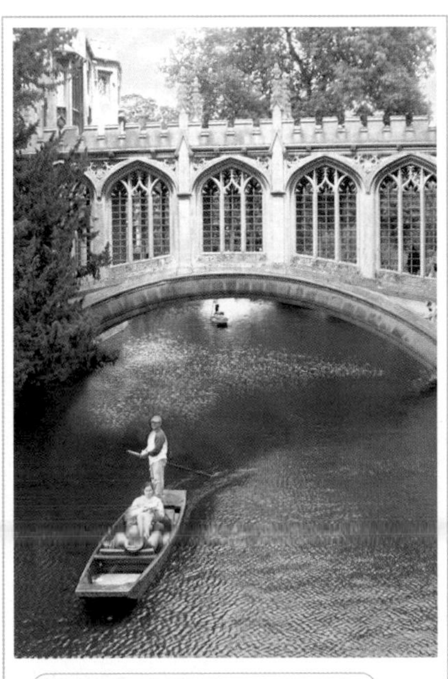

Cambridge – The Bridge of Sighs

Cambridge American Military Cemetery & Memorial
200 B2

A beautiful and moving tribute to the American servicemen and women who lost their lives in World War II. The peaceful site, with over 3800 headstones, extends to 30.5 acres (12ha) and is framed on two sides by woodland. There is a memorial building made of Portland stone within which the museum room contains a superb 30ft by 18ft (9m x 5.5m) map: 'The Mastery of the Atlantic – The Great Air Assault'.

☎ 01954 210350 www.abmc.gov

Cambridge University Botanic Gardens
391 F2

This attractive 40 acre (16ha) garden was founded by Professor John Stevens Henslow (who was Charles Darwin's teacher) in 1831. It was opened to the public in 1846 and today contains thousands of plant species in lovely landscaped settings, including nine National Collections.

☎ 01223 336265 www.botanic.cam.ac.uk

Castle House (Sir Alfred Munnings Art Museum)
202 B4

From 1919 to 1959 Castle House was home to Sir Alfred Munnings, artist and past president of the Royal Academy, famous for his equestrian paintings. The house, a mixture of Tudor and Georgian architecture, and surrounded by 40 acres (16ha) of land, is presented much as it was when Munnings lived in it and includes his furniture and many of his paintings.

☎ 01206 322127 www.siralfredmunnings.co.uk

Cecil Higgins Art Gallery
199 F3

Originally home to the Higgins family, who were wealthy Bedford brewers, this Victorian mansion is furnished as it would have been in the late 19th century. An adjoining gallery was added in 1976, which has changing exhibitions of paintings, prints and drawings. Artists include Gainsborough, Constable, Turner, Rembrandt and Picasso. Also on display are collections of silver, glass, ceramics and the Thomas Lester lace collection.

☎ 01234 211222 www.cecilhigginsartgallery.org

Clacton Pier
189 E1

The pier, which dates from 1871, was a catalyst for the development of Clacton as a seaside resort. Originally it was a landing pier, but soon became popular with day-trippers from London and for promenading. The first pier was quite a humble affair; only 160 yards (146m) long and 4 yards (3.5m) wide. The pier now covers an area of 6.5 acres (2.5ha) and is packed with fairground rides, a Seaquarium and all the usual pubs, restaurants and side stalls.

☎ 01255 421115 www.clactonpier.co.uk

Colchester Castle Museum
202 A5

Housed in the largest Norman keep in Britain, the museum has a wide range of exhibits spanning 2000 years of British History. There is a superb display on the siege of Colchester during the English Civil War, and various Roman relics. Visitors can also take a tour of the Roman vaults which still lie under the present castle – it was built on the foundations of the Roman Temple of Claudius.

☎ 01206 282 939 www.colchestermuseums.org.uk

Colchester Zoo
202 A5

This superb zoo, which has over 200 rare and endangered species, is set in 60 acres (24ha) of attractive parkland. The enclosures have been designed to replicate the natural environments of the animals as closely as possible. The rich animal life of Africa has several enclosures including the 'Kingdom of the Wild', which houses many of the grazing animals of the African savannah such as zebras, ostriches, pygmy hippos and white rhinos. 'Elephant Kingdom' features the zoo's breeding herd of African elephants, and 'Chimp World' is always popular. 'Playa Patagonia' is well worth seeing; an impressive 26 yard (24m) long tunnel allows visitors to view sea lions swimming above their heads. The zoo is also home to one of the best large cat collections in Europe, including the rare white tiger.

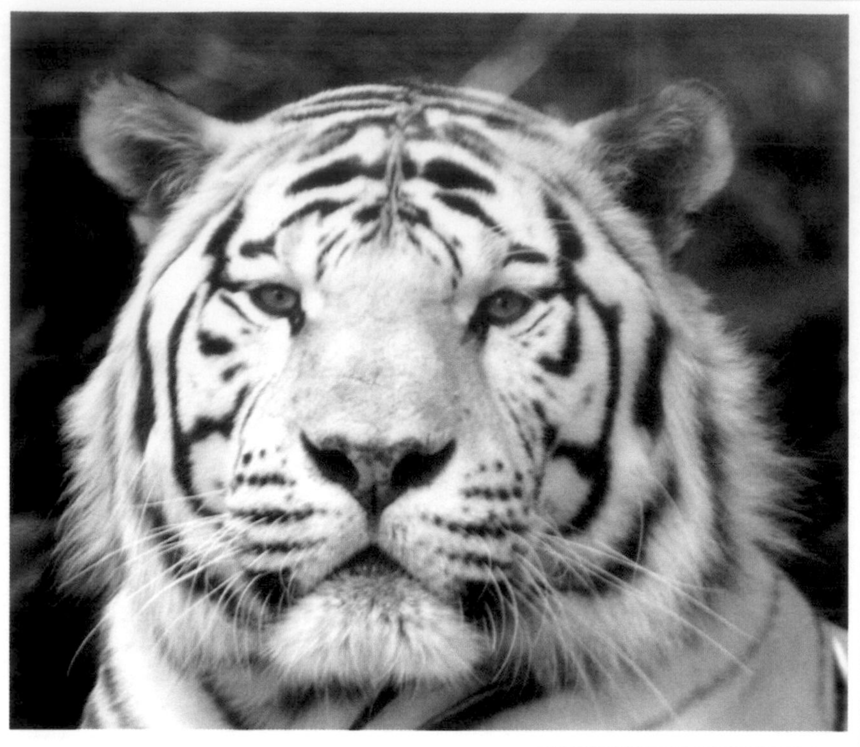

Colchester Zoo – White Tiger

Daily displays allow visitors to get closer to the animals; the penguin parade is always a favourite and visitors even get a chance to feed the elephants and giraffes.

☎ 01206 331292 www.colchester-zoo.com

Cressing Temple Barns
201 F5

There are two timber-framed barns on the site: the Barley Barn built in the early 13th century and the Wheat Barn built in the mid to late 13th century. Both barns have been rebuilt over the years but some of the original constructions remain. Also to be seen are a blacksmith's shop, a bakehouse and a reconstructed Tudor garden.

☎ 01376 584903

Cromwell Museum
212 A5

Following the execution of Charles I in 1649, Oliver Cromwell came to power and ruled the country until his death in 1658. This museum, situated in the old Huntingdon Grammar School where he was a pupil, houses memorabilia and possessions relating to his life.

☎ 01480 375830 edweb.camcnty.gov.uk/cromwell

Denny Abbey & Farmland Museum
200 C1

Originally founded in 1159, this Benedictine abbey features superb Norman interiors and displays telling the story of the abbey through the centuries. Over the years it has housed the Knights Templars and the Poor Clares (nuns of the Franciscan order), eventually becoming a farmhouse.

The Farmland Museum looks at the rural history of the local area and farming over the years. Attractions include a village shop, a traditional farmer's cottage and a 17th century stone barn.

☎ 01223 860988 www.dennyfarmlandmuseum.org.uk

Docwra's Manor Gardens
200 B3

An attractive series of enclosed gardens, designed to display differing characteristics. The gardens are divided by walls, hedging and farm buildings surrounding a Queen Anne farmhouse.

☎ 01763 261473

Dunstable Downs (NT)
199 F5

This popular location for kite-flying comprises 510 acres (206ha) of beautiful chalk grassland and farmland with superb views over the Vale of Aylesbury. There are circular walks, a picnic area and a countryside centre with interpretive displays and a shop.

☎ 01582 608489 www.nationaltrust.org.uk

Dunwich Heath (NT)

203 F1

A beautiful area of lowland heath on the Suffolk coast. The terrain, which covers 215 acres (87ha), includes large tracts of purple heather, as well as gorse, woodland, sandy cliffs and a mile (1.6km) long sandy beach. The heath is rich in insect and birdlife and is home to the now rare ant-lion and nightjar. An information centre is housed in converted coastguard cottages.

☎ 01728 648501 www.nationaltrust.org.uk

East Anglia Transport Museum
215 F2

A reconstructed 1930s style street and attractive woodland area are the perfect setting for visitors to enjoy a trip on beautifully preserved vehicles from the first half of the 20th century. These include trams, buses, trolleybuses, cars, steamrollers and a variety of other light commercial vehicles.

☎ 01502 518459 www.eatm.org.uk

Easton Farm Park
203 D2

Set in 35 acres (14ha) of lovely countryside, this farm park has lots of things for children to see and do. There are plenty of farm animals including Suffolk Punch horses, goats, sheep, rabbits, hens and cows. Children can also ride the Shetland ponies and will be fascinated by watching chicks hatch in the Chick Nursery and by Mildred, a wooden cow who moos and can also be milked. There is also an adventure play area, and the River Deben provides lovely river walks.

☎ 01728 746475 www.eastonfarmpark.co.uk

Elton Hall
211 F3

Dating from Tudor times, this romantic house is a combination of medieval, Gothic and classical architectural styles and has been home to the Proby family for over 350 years. The house has superb furniture, porcelain and some outstanding paintings by Constable, Gainsborough and Reynolds. The Library has over 12,000 books including Henry VIII's prayer book, complete with his writing. The beautiful gardens are especially good in the summer; the herbaceous borders are a riot of colour and the rose garden, which includes highly scented old fashioned roses, is stunning. There is also a sunken garden, a knot garden and a Gothic orangery, as well as an arboretum.

☎ 01832 280468

Ely Cathedral
212 D5

This magnificent cathedral dates from the late 11th century and was originally built as a monastic church, gaining cathedral status in 1109. It still retains several monastic outbuildings. After the Dissolution it continued to exist as a cathedral except for a brief period in the 17th century when Oliver Cromwell used it as a stable for his cavalry horses. The architecture is unusual with a 248ft (75.5m) long Norman nave and a remarkable 14th century Octagon Tower.

☎ 01353 667735 www.cathedral.ely.anglican.org

Epping Forest
186 D3

This 6000 acre (1800ha) remnant of a vast medieval forest has large tracts that are recognised as Sites of Special Scientific Interest. It is part open space, part woodland and has been owned by the Corporation of London since 1878. There are some lovely walks including part of the long distance footpath, the Forest Way. In Tudor times the forest was used for hunting, and Elizabeth I's timber-framed hunting lodge can still be seen. An information centre has interesting displays on the forest.

☎ 020 8532 0188

Fairhaven Gardens

229 E4

Delightful woodland and water garden covering an area of 180 acres (73ha) which includes South Walsham Inner Broad. There are 3 miles (5km) of lovely walks, and boat trips are available on the broad at an extra cost. There are superb displays of primroses and candelabra primulas in the spring, and marvellous autumn colours afforded by the numerous mature trees.

☎ 01603 270449 www.norfolkbroads.com/fairhaven

Fairlands Valley Park
200 A5

The park extends to 120 acres (48.5ha) and includes an 11 acre (4.5ha) lake where watersports are available. It is also home to a variety of wildlife.

☎ 01438 353241 www.stevenage-leisure.co.uk/fairlands

Felbrigg Hall (NT)
228 C2

This magnificent 17th century house is set in an estate of over 1700 acres (690ha). The house contains superb 18th century furniture and paintings collected by William Windham II (who inherited the house in 1749) when on his Grand Tour. The parkland has lovely waymarked walks taking visitors past some very ancient trees. There is also a 500 acre (200ha) wood and a walled garden which includes a combination of decorative planting and a traditional kitchen garden.

☎ 01263 837444 www.nationaltrust.org.uk

Fitzwilliam Museum
391 F2

The museum owes its foundation to the bequest of Richard, the 7th Viscount Fitzwilliam of Merrion in 1816, who left his collection along with funds to house them, to the University of Cambridge. The current collection, which has grown considerably over the years, is superb, including paintings by Titian, Rubens, Canaletto, Gainsborough, Monet and Picasso, antiquities from Ancient Egypt, Rome, China and Greece, medieval manuscripts, sculpture, furniture, coins and medals.

☎ 01223 332900 www.fitzmuseum.cam.ac.uk

Flag Fen Bronze Age Centre
212 A3

Flag Fen is one of the most important Bronze Age sites in Europe. Visitors can see 3000 year old timber that was once part of a wooden structure that crossed a shallow lake, and is contained within a purpose built preservation hall. Reconstructed Iron Age and Bronze Age round houses can be seen and, within the visitor centre, there is a museum containing artefacts found on the site. During the summer archaeologists can often be seen at work.

☎ 01733 313414 www.flagfen.com

Flatford Mill & Bridge Cottage (NT)
202 B4

The 18th century mill, made famous by landscape artist John Constable (1776 – 1837) and once owned by his father, is itself not open to the public but there are organised walks (at a charge) during the summer months pointing out the locations illustrated in his work. Just upstream from the mill is the 16th century thatched Bridge Cottage which features a Constable exhibition.

☎ 01206 298260 www.nationaltrust.org.uk

Framlingham Castle
203 D1

This 12th century castle, surrounded by grass-covered earthworks, has crenellated towers topped with Tudor chimneys linked by impressive 43ft (13m) high curtain walls. The wall walk along the top is open to visitors and commands excellent views. Within the walls, the visitor centre now occupies what was once a poor house dating from 1729. This is one of a number of uses the castle has been put to over the years; it has also served its time as a prison and a school.

☎ 01728 724189 www.english-heritage.org.uk

Fritton Lake Countryworld
229 F5

Many activities are available, all centred around a 150 acre (61ha) lake. Attractions include a children's farm, heavy horse stables, formal Victorian gardens, falconry centre, adventure playground, 9 hole golf course and 18 hole putting green, a miniature railway, fishing and boating on the lake, cycle trails and lovely woodland walks.

☎ 0871 2224244 www.frittonlake.co.uk

Gainsborough's House
201 G3

This 16th century townhouse, with 18th century brick façade, is the birthplace of the artist Thomas Gainsborough (1727 - 88). The house contains a large collection of his paintings, drawings and prints along with 18th century furniture and objects. There is also a changing programme of contemporary exhibitions throughout the year.

☎ 01787 372958 www.gainsborough.org

Grafham Water
199 G1

This large water park, extending to 1500 acres (600ha), has a variety of activities including sailing, fishing, cycling, and a nature reserve with trails and hides. There is a charge for car parking.

☎ 01480 812154

Grime's Graves
213 G4

These fascinating Neolithic flint mines date from 4000 to 5000 years ago. Visitors can descend 30ft (10m) by ladder into one of the shafts and see the radiating galleries where ancient man worked the high quality flint with antler picks.

☎ 01842 810656 www.english-heritage.org.uk

Hamerton Zoo Park
211 G5

Established as a wildlife conservation sanctuary in 1990 and set in 15 acres (6ha) of parkland, the zoo specialises in rare, endangered and unusual animals with species totalling over 100. Animals that can be seen include wolves, porcupines, snakes, giant millipedes and African land snails, as well as monkeys, sloths and an array of colourful birds.

☎ 01832 293362 www.hamertonzoopark.com

Harrold-Odell Country Park
199 E2

This attractive 144 acre (58ha) park, situated beside the River Great Ouse, with its lakes, water meadows, woodland and nature reserve, is a haven for wildlife. It is worth taking binoculars as the site attracts large numbers of wildfowl, especially in winter. There is a hide, and an information centre with café.

☎ 01234 720016 www.ivelvalley.co.uk

Hatfield Forest (NT)
187 E1

There are some delightful walks and nature trails around this rare surviving example of a medieval royal hunting forest. Extending to over 1000 acres (400ha) of ancient woodland and pasture, it supports a wide variety of flora and fauna including 400 year old pollarded oaks and hornbeams, fallow deer, and, in the summer, cattle can be seen grazing. There are also two ornamental lakes and a grotto called the Shell House, both dating from the 18th century.

☎ 01279 874040 www.nationaltrust.org.uk

Hatfield House
186 B2

This superb Jacobean house, set in 4000 acres (1600ha) of parkland, was built in 1611 by Robert Cecil, 1st Earl of Salisbury, who was Chief Minister to James I. It has remained in the Cecil family ever since. The luxurious interior exhibits superb examples of Jacobean craftsmanship, such as the magnificent carved oak staircase and long gallery. There are also impressive paintings by Reynolds, Hilliard and Mytens, an armoury and fine 16th, 17th and 18th century furniture and tapestries.

The house was built on the site of an earlier 15th century palace which was home to Elizabeth I for much of her childhood. Most of the old Tudor red bricked palace was destroyed to build the new house but one wing, including the great

banqueting hall, where Elizabeth held her first Council of State on her accession in 1558, still survives in the grounds of the current mansion.

The beautiful 42 acre (17ha) gardens situated adjacent to the house were originally laid out by John Tradescant the Elder, who was employed by the 1st Earl. Tradescant was a great plant hunter and he brought huge quantities of plants from Europe. Over the years the layout of the gardens has changed many times, most notably in the 18th century when the fashion for landscape gardening resulted in much of the earlier Jacobean formality being swept away. Today, the gardens are totally organic and have been restored to display much of their varied history, with a knot garden, lime walk, privy garden with yew hedges and a wilderness garden.

☎ 01707 287010 www.hatfield-house.co.uk

Hatfield House – Long Gallery

★ Henry Moore Foundation 186 D1

Seventy acre (28ha) estate, gifted to the foundation by Henry Moore, with sculpture gardens and fields. There is an ever changing display of his work. Visits by appointment only.

☎ 01279 843333 www.henry-moore-fdn.co.uk

Holkham Hall 227 G3

This impressive Palladian mansion was built on the site of an earlier manor house between 1734 and 1764 for the 1st Earl of Leicester, Thomas Coke, and is based on designs by William Kent. During his Grand Tour of Europe the 1st Earl had amassed a vast collection of valuable art and artefacts and he wanted a suitably grand house in which to display them. The resulting mansion, built of sand-coloured local brick, with its pedimented portico, square corner towers and side wings, has been little altered over the years, but unfortunately the 1st Earl never saw the finished building as he died in 1759, five years before it was completed.

The interior of the house is superb, the pink marble and alabaster entrance hall, designed by the 1st Earl in collaboration with Lord Burlington, being particularly impressive. Stairs from the hall lead to the elaborate state rooms on the first floor with their superb collections of statuary, furniture, tapestries and splendid paintings by Gainsborough, Van Dyck, Rubens, Claude Lorraine and Poussin.

The 3000 acre (1200ha) landscaped grounds surrounding the house were set out by Lancelot 'Capability' Brown and include a mile-long lake and thousands of trees. Today the park is home to a large herd of fallow deer and the lake has many species of wildfowl. There is no charge to enter the grounds and there are lovely walks around the lake and, in the summer, boat trips.

Other attractions include the Holkham Bygones Collection, the nursery garden, the Holkham Pottery and a history of farming exhibition.

☎ 01328 710227 www.holkham.co.uk

★ Horsey Windpump (NT) 229 F3

Restored five-storey windpump built in 1912. From the top there are marvellous views across Horsey Mere.

☎ 01493 393904 www.nationaltrust.org.uk

Houghton Hall 227 F5

This superb Palladian house, surrounded by 350 acres (142ha) of parkland and gardens, was built between 1722 and 1735 for Britain's first Prime Minister, Sir Robert Walpole. Designed by James Gibbs, and later refined by Colen Campbell, the whole house was built to impress; the main block features magnificent corner towers topped by domes, and is connected to service blocks by curved colonnades.

The extravagant interiors were designed and furnished by William Kent and include the highly ornamented Stone Hall, which features a bust of Sir Robert and lavish ornamentation and sculptures by Rysbrack. The Great Staircase is made of carved mahogany and rises to the full height of the house. The rooms are a magnificent showcase for the impressive collection of pictures, sculptures, china and tapestries. Visitors can also see the huge Model Soldier Collection, amassed during the lifetime of the 6th Marquess of Cholmondeley, the current owner's father.

The beautiful grounds include extensive parkland, home to a large herd of white fallow deer, and a 5 acre (2ha) walled garden which is divided into areas devoted to fruit and vegetables, a 400ft (120m) long herbaceous border, a formal rose garden with over 150 varieties, glass houses and a croquet lawn.

☎ 01485 528569 www.houghtonhall.com

Holkham Hall – Marble Hall

★ Houghton Mill (NT) 212 A5

Set in a picturesque spot on an island in the Great Ouse, this weather-boarded working water mill dates from the 18th century. There are milling demonstrations on Sunday afternoons (water levels permitting), working models, interactive displays, an art gallery and lovely riverside walks.

☎ 01480 301494 www.nationaltrust.org.uk

Hyde Hall 187 G3

A lovely 24 acre (9.75ha) hilltop garden acquired by the Royal Horticultural Society in 1993. There is year round colour: highlights include lovely herbaceous borders, ornamental ponds, a large collection of roses, the National Collection of Viburnum and the acclaimed Dry Garden.

☎ 01245 400256 www.rhs.org.uk

Houghton Hall

Ickworth (NT) 201 G1

This unusual house dates from 1795 and was built to display the collection of art accumulated by Frederick Hervey, Bishop of Derry and later 4th Earl of Bristol, during his Grand Tour. The Italianate house is dominated by a massive oval 98ft (30m) high rotunda, with curved corridors leading to two wings. Many of the descendants of the 4th Earl were also great collectors and today the house has a superb array of paintings, including works by Gainsborough, Titian and Velàzquez. The Hall is set in a 1800 acre (73ha) Lancelot 'Capability' Brown landscaped park which features some magnificent ancient specimen trees. There are lovely gardens laid out in formal Italianate style dating from the 19th century, situated to the south of the house.

☎ 01284 735270 www.nationaltrust.org.uk

Imperial War Museum (Duxford) 200 C3

Built during World War I, the aerodrome at Duxford was one of the earliest RAF stations in the country and saw action during World War II. It is now home to one of the world's largest collections of preserved civil and military aircraft and is Europe's premier aviation museum. The 7 acres (2.8ha) of exhibition space include some two hundred planes. A free road train runs at regular intervals to take visitors around the site.

Original World War I hangars contrast with the award-winning American Air Museum building designed by Lord Foster. Housed within this superb roof structure is an impressive collection of American combat aircraft.

In the Land Warfare Hall is a huge collection of tanks, military vehicles and artillery. Other hangars contain naval helicopters and midget submarines, a Battle of Britain exhibition and a British aircraft collection.

Duxford is one of the largest centres for aircraft restoration in the world and visitors can view the work in progress. Most weekends during the summer there is an opportunity to experience a flight over Duxford in a 1930s passenger bi-plane and several air shows take place during the year.

☎ 01223 835000 www.iwm.org.uk/duxford

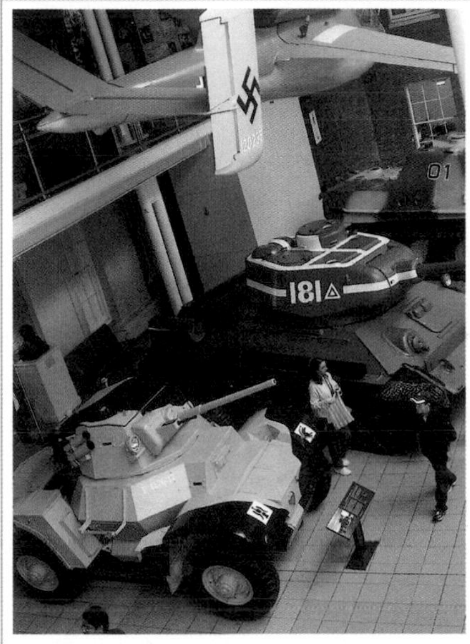

Imperial War Museum

Kentwell Hall 201 G3

This beautiful red brick moated Tudor mansion, dating from the mid 16th century, is approached by a three-quarter mile (1.2km) long lime-tree avenue. The interior of the house was remodelled in 1825 and contains a large collection of 16th century artefacts. On selected weekends visitors can enjoy re-creations of everyday Tudor life. In the courtyard there is a superb brickwork maze in the shape of a Tudor rose, and the grounds contain clipped yews, a fine walled garden with original 17th century layout, and a rare breeds animal farm.

☎ 01787 310207 www.kentwellhall.co.uk

Knebworth House 200 A5

Home to the Lytton family since 1490, the original red brick Tudor manor house underwent extensive remodelling in the 19th century. This resulted in the rather eccentric Gothic appearance we see today with its extravagant façade of turrets, domes and gargoyles.

Within the house visitors can see the superb Jacobean Banqueting Hall with early 17th century oak screen and minstrels' gallery, the Victorian-Gothic state drawing room and the armoury.

The house is situated within 250 acre (101ha) grounds which include a deer park and lovely woodland areas. There are 25 acres (10ha) of gardens designed by Sir Edwin Lutyens who married Lady Emily Lytton, sister of the 2nd Earl of Lytton, in 1897. Features of the garden include an attractive formal rose garden, twin pleached lime avenues, herbaceous borders and a maze. Other attractions include a giant children's adventure playground, a three-quarter mile (1.2km) miniature railway and a dinosaur trail with 72 life-size fibreglass dinosaurs. Knebworth is also famous for its rock concerts and as a film location.

☎ 01438 812661 www.knebworthhouse.com

Lavenham Guildhall (NT)  202 A3

This early 16th century timber-framed building overlooks Lavenham's market place and was built by one of the Guilds who regulated the local wool trade. Over the years it has been used for many different purposes: prison, town hall, workhouse and for housing evacuees during World War II. Inside there are exhibitions on the medieval woollen cloth trade, local history, farming, industry and a replica of the Guildhall at the time it was built.

☎ 01787 247646 www.nationaltrust.org.uk

Layer Marney Tower 188 C1

This 16th century Tudor gatehouse is the tallest in Britain at some 80ft (24m) tall. It was originally planned as a large palace by Henry, 1st Lord Marney, Henry VIII's keeper of the Privy Seal, but he died in 1523, followed two years later by his son, leaving no male heirs and an unfinished building.

The gatehouse has superb Italianate terracotta decoration and fine brickwork, and is set in formal gardens. There are exhibitions within the tower including a model of the palace as it may have looked had it been completed. Other attractions include a rare breeds farm and a medieval barn.

☎ 01206 330784 www.layermarneytower.co.uk

Leighton Buzzard Light Railway 199 E5

Originally built in 1919 to connect the many sand quarries in the area, this 2ft (610mm) narrow-gauge railway now runs for 3 miles (4.8km) giving a 70-minute round trip. It houses one of the largest collections of steam and diesel narrow-gauge locomotives in the United Kingdom.

☎ 01525 373888 www.buzzrail.co.uk

Linton Zoo 201 D3

Set in 16 acres (6.5ha) of gardens, a visit to this zoo provides an enjoyable day out. There is a focus on conservation, education and breeding programmes, with the animals being housed in enclosures resembling their natural habitats as closely as possible. Big cats, giant tortoises and tarantula spiders are among the animals to be seen.

☎ 01223 891308 www.lintonzoo.com

Knebworth House

Lodge RSPB Nature Reserve, The 199 G3

The gardens surrounding this 19th century Tudor-style house (the house is the RSPB's UK headquarters and is not open to the public) are run by organic methods and include formal gardens, a wildlife area, herbaceous border and large specimen trees. There is also a nature reserve which is a mixture of sandy heath and woodland. When the bluebells are in flower in the spring, the woods are a lovely sight. In the reserve there are over 3 miles (5km) of paths to explore and a variety of birds such as woodpeckers, warblers, woodlarks and hobby may be seen.

☎ 01767 680541 www.rspb.org.uk/reserves/guide/t/thelodge/index.asp

Mangapps Railway Museum 188 C3

A standard-gauge working museum giving a three-quarter mile (1.2km) ride through pleasant countryside. Restored stations and signal boxes from various sites around East Anglia can be seen, as well as 10 locomotives and over 80 carriages and wagons. There are also impressive collections of railway signalling equipment and railway relics.

☎ 01621 784898 www.mangapps.co.uk

Melford Hall (NT) 201 G3

Queen Elizabeth I was entertained in this red brick Tudor mansion in 1578. The exterior has changed little since then and is notable for its six octagonal towers with pepper-pot roofs and tall chimneys.

The interior features a panelled banqueting hall, Regency library, an 18th century drawing room and a display of watercolours by Beatrix Potter. Outside is an attractive garden with lawns and trees.

☎ 01787 880286 www.nationaltrust.org.uk

Mole Hall Wildlife Park 201 D4

Twenty acres (8ha) of gardens and grounds surrounding a moated manor house (closed to the public). A variety of animals can be seen including otters, chimps, deer, owls and wildfowl. There is also a tropical butterfly pavilion, pets corner and a water maze.

☎ 01799 540400 www.molehall.com

Mountfitchet Castle 200 D5

A Norman castle destroyed in 1215 with only fragments of masonry remaining. In the early 1980s an earth and timber castle was constructed along with a village of thatched buildings, including a smithy, a brew house and a dovecote, where visitors can learn about life in Norman England. The scene is completed with animals such as chickens and sheep wandering about.

☎ 01279 813237 www.mountfitchetcastle.com

Muckleburgh Collection, The 228 C1

Set on the site of an anti-aircraft artillery range from World War II, the museum, located in the old NAAFI building, has Britain's largest working military collection, with over 120 vehicles including 16 working tanks and 3000 other exhibits. On Sundays visitors can usually see a tank in action and take a ride on a US armoured personnel carrier, the Gama Goat.

☎ 01263 588210 www.muckleburgh.co.uk

Museum of East Anglian Life 202 B2

This 70 acre (28ha) open-air museum has a variety of historic buildings including the 13th century Abbot's Hall tithe barn. Many of the other buildings have been moved from their original settings and reconstructed on the site, such as the attractive working Alton Water Mill, Edgar's Farmhouse and Eastridge Windpump. There are also various rare breed farm animals to see including Suffolk Punch horses, Suffolk sheep and Red Poll Cattle, as well as working steam engines.

☎ 01449 612229 www.eastanglianlife.org.uk

National Horseracing Museum
201 E1

The museum is full of interest even to the novice, with displays on horses and courses, famous jockeys and trainers. There are trophies, portraits and paintings as well as films of classic races.

☎ 01638 667331 www.nhrm.co.uk

Nene Valley Railway
211 G3

A standard-gauge 7.5 mile (12km) railway which runs between Yarwell and Peterborough. It is home to a fine collection of steam locomotives, both British and continental, as well as rolling stock. There is also a small museum and, for children, Thomas the Tank Engine has his own little branch line.

☎ 01780 784444 www.nvr.org.uk

Norfolk Broads
229 E4

Made up of rivers, lakes and fens, this nationally important wetland provides a unique, but delicate environment for a wide range of wildlife. Three principal rivers: the Thurne, Yare and Waveney, flow through the area, occasionally opening out into wide lakes called 'broads'. These were created by peat cutting dating back to about the 9th century. In the 13th to 14th centuries the sea level rose, flooding the peat pits.

This rare wetland habitat is a haven for a wide range of flora and fauna, including some endangered insects such as the beautiful Swallowtail butterfly and the Norfolk Hawker dragonfly which are unique to the area. The tranquil waterways are alive with ducks, swans, coots, moorhens, herons, kingfishers and the exotic-looking Great Crested Grebe who can be seen carrying their humbug-striped young on their backs in the spring. There are over 190 miles (300km) of footpaths, and bicycles can be hired to explore the peaceful country lanes, but, without a doubt, the best way to get around is by boat. Take a leisurely journey along the 125 miles (200km) of navigable lock-free waterways and Broads, and the stress of civilisation feels like it is a million miles away.

☎ 01603 610734 www.broads-authority.gov.uk

Norfolk Broads

Norwich Castle Museum & Art Gallery
405 B2

The museum and art gallery is housed within a magnificent Norman keep, originally part of a royal palace, situated on a mound overlooking the city. Visitors can see collections of fine art, natural history, archaeology, silverware and ceramics. In addition to the permanent displays there are also regular temporary exhibitions.

☎ 01603 493625 www.museums.norfolk.gov.uk

Norwich Cathedral
405 B2

Founded in the 11th century, with many later changes and additions, the present cathedral has a tall elegant spire, and, at 315ft (96m), it is second only in height to Salisbury. The 180ft (55m) square monastic cloisters, which feature intricate fan vaulting, date from the 14th and 15th centuries and are the largest in England. The cathedral is also notable for the large number of attractive, brightly painted, roof bosses in the nave and cloisters.

☎ 01603 218321 www.cathedral.org.uk

Orford Castle
203 F3

This unusual 90ft (27m) high multi-sided keep was built in the mid to late 12th century by Henry II and was once part of a larger castle. Spiral stairs lead to a maze of rooms. A climb to the top is rewarded by views over the surrounding countryside.

☎ 01394 450472 www.english-heritage.org.uk

Orford Ness
203 F3

This is the largest vegetated shingle spit in Europe. It was taken over by the military in 1913 and was a secret test site until the mid-1980s. It is now a National Nature Reserve and its variety of habitats, including mudflat, shingle, salt marsh and brackish lagoons, make it an important site for flora and fauna, in particular breeding and overwintering birds. Access is by ferry and visitors can follow a fascinating 5.5 mile (8.8km) route, that can be walked in total or in part.

☎ 01394 450900 www.nationaltrust.org.uk

Oxburgh Hall (NT)
213 F2

This magnificent red brick moated manor house was built by the Bedingfeld family and dates from 1482. It has an unusual appearance with its ornate stepped gables and tall, twisted chimney stacks. Although remodelled extensively during the mid 19th century, the Gatehouse, with its octagonal turrets rising to 80ft (24m), remains relatively unaltered. Within the hall can be seen finely carved oak furniture, some original Victorian wallpapers and fine textiles, including needlework by Mary, Queen of Scots and Bess of Hardwick. Outside there are walled and kitchen gardens, a Victorian French parterre and woodland walks.

☎ 01366 328258 www.nationaltrust.org.uk

Paradise Wildlife Park
186 C2

Ideal for children with a variety of animals including pandas, large cats, tapirs, meerkats, camels and zebra, as well as the more familiar farmyard animals. There is also a funfair, amusements, crazy golf and a woodland railway.

☎ 01992 470490 www.pwpark.com

Paycocke's (NT)
201 G5

Dating from around 1500, this timber-framed house was built for cloth merchant John Paycocke as a wedding present for his son Thomas. It contains fine wood panelling and carving as well as a display of Coggeshall lace. Outside there is an attractive cottage garden leading to a small river.

☎ 01376 561305 www.nationaltrust.org.uk

Peckover House & Garden (NT)
212 C2

This Georgian brick-built town house dates from about 1722 and has some fine rococo decoration in plaster and wood. It is the former home of Quaker banker Jonathon Peckover. Within the house there is a restored Victorian library and collections of decorative and applied art. The house sits within a lovely 2 acre (0.8ha) walled Victorian garden with mature trees, croquet lawn, herbaceous borders and an orangery.

☎ 01945 583463 www.nationaltrust.org.uk

Peterborough Cathedral
211 G3

This magnificent Norman cathedral dates from 1118 and has a dramatic 13th century west front with three enormous arches. The interior is equally impressive with a rare 13th century painted wooden nave ceiling and exquisite fan vaulting in the retro-choir dating from about 1500. The cathedral is the burial place of Henry VIII's first wife, Catherine of Aragon.

☎ 01733 343342 www.peterborough-cathedral.org.uk

Peterborough Museum & Art Gallery
211 G3

This impressive town house dating from 1816 became the home of the museum and art gallery in the 1930s. It has displays of local history and archaeology including many Roman relics. There are also bone models and straw marquetry made by Napoleonic prisoners of war.

The art collection contains works dating from the 1600s to the present day including paintings by Van Huysum, Sickert and Turner.

☎ 01733 343329 www.peterboroughheritage.org.uk

Pleasure Beach
229 G5

Set on the seafront at Great Yarmouth, this amusement park has all the familiar rides, such as roller coasters, dodgems and carousels. All ages are catered for, with the thrill factor ranging from extreme white knuckle to gentle children's merry-go-rounds. Rides can be paid for individually by tokens, or wristbands can be purchased.

☎ 01493 844585 www.pleasure-beach.co.uk

St Albans Cathedral
186 A2

The cathedral, which dates from the 11th century, has had numerous additions over the years including the opening of a new Chapter House in 1982. It has a long low appearance, extending 550 ft (168m) east to west with a squat sturdy looking tower. The Norman part of the building was begun in 1077 using Roman bricks and tiles salvaged from the ruins of the nearby Roman town of Verulamium. These can be seen today in the walls of the tower.

The cathedral is well known as a site of national pilgrimage as it contains the shrine of St Alban, the first British Christian martyr, who was executed on this site in AD209. Also to be seen are medieval wall paintings and decorated ceilings.

☎ 01727 860780 www.stalbanscathedral.org.uk

St George's Guildhall (NT)
227 E5

Constructed between 1410 and 1420, this is the largest surviving English medieval guildhall. The impressive Great Hall, situated on the upper floor, with its original open timber roof, is 101ft by 29ft

(30m x 8m). Other 15th century features which survive intact are the five large buttresses supporting the north wall. The building has now been converted into an arts centre and is generally closed on performance days.

☎ 01553 765565 www.nationaltrust.org.uk

Sandringham House 227 E5

The current house dates from 1870 and was built for the Prince of Wales (later Edward VII) in Neo-Elizabethan style from red brick with pale stone dressings. It has been passed down through the generations as a private royal residence and is used by the present Queen as her country retreat. The main ground floor rooms, which are still used regularly by the royal family, can be seen. Many objects collected by Queen Alexandra and Queen Mary are on show, and in the Ballroom there is an exhibition of the Duke of Edinburgh's collection of wildlife art. Outside in the coach and stable block there is a museum displaying many family possessions as well as some of the gifts given to the royal family over the years.

The house sits in beautiful 60 acre (24ha) gardens with lakes, glades and an abundance of trees. The acid soil allows the growth of stunning rhododendrons and azaleas, making it particularly attractive in the spring. There is also a 600 acre (243ha) country park, which is free, and which has some lovely woodland and heath areas with nature trails and a visitor centre.

☎ 01553 772675 www.sandringhamestate.co.uk

Shaw's Corner (NT) 186 A1

This red brick Edwardian house was the home of the Irish playwright George Bernard Shaw from 1902 until his death in 1950. The rooms are still set out as he left them, with his personal effects providing a fascinating insight into his life. The 3.5 acre (1.4ha) richly planted gardens have lovely views over the local countryside and contain the revolving hut where Shaw used to write.

☎ 01438 820307 www.nationaltrust.org.uk

Shepreth Wildlife Park 200 B3

Situated in a lovely countryside setting with three lakes, the centre started out as a wildlife sanctuary, and one of the park's aims is to raise money for its rescued and unwanted animals and its hospital. There are plenty of animals to see: terrapins live in Combat Lake, whilst meerkats and squirrel monkeys live on Combat Island. Mountain lions, tigers and lynx can be seen in the Big Cat House, and Waterworld and Bug City provide a home to insects and invertebrates. Just as popular are the horses, goats, ducks and geese which can be hand fed.

☎ 09066 800031 (25p/min) www.sheprethwildlifepark.co.uk

Shrine of Our Lady of Walsingham 228 A2

This has been a centre for pilgrimage since 1061, when Richeldis de Faverches, a local noblewoman, had a vision in which she was told by the Virgin Mary to build a replica of the Holy House in Nazareth. Today, a 20th century red brick church sits on the site of the shrine.

☎ 01328 820239 www.walsingham.org.uk

Somerleyton Hall & Gardens 215 F2

This extravagant Victorian mansion was built between 1844 and 1851 for the railway entrepreneur Sir Morton Peto. No expense was spared; lavish carving is evident throughout, both in wood and stone, there are sumptuous state rooms and an impressive entrance hall. The clock on the stable block is of particular interest as it was originally designed by Vulliamy for the Houses of Parliament.

The superb gardens extend to 12 acres (4.8ha) and include a yew hedge maze planted in 1846, a walled garden and glasshouses by Sir Joseph Paxton (designer of the Crystal Palace).

☎ 0871 2224244 www.somerleyton.co.uk

Sandringham House

Southend Pier 188 B4

The present iron pier first opened in 1889 and was extended to its current length in 1929. At 2360 yards (2158m) it is the longest pleasure pier in the world. A train service runs the length of the pier. At the shore end is a museum (admission charge) with exhibits giving an insight into the pier's history. At the pier head sea fishing is popular; there are also pleasure boat trips, a lifeboat station and information centre to visit.

☎ 01702 215620 www.southendpier.co.uk

Standalone Farm 200 A4

This 170 acre (68ha) model farm provides visitors with an opportunity to learn about rural life and farming. There are daily milking demonstrations, exhibits of farm machinery and natural history. Animals that can be seen include sheep, cows, donkeys, shire horses, rabbits and guinea pigs. There is also an arboretum containing 35 species of newly planted trees.

☎ 01462 686775 www.letchworthgardencity.net/standalone

Suffolk Wildlife Park 215 G3

Set in 80 acres (32ha) of coastal parkland, visitors can see a wide variety of mainly African animals, including big cats, giraffes, zebras, white rhinos, buffalo and snakes. There is a safari road train to take visitors around the site.

☎ 01502 740291 www.suffolkwildlifepark.co.uk

Swiss Garden 199 G3

Created in the early 19th century by Lord Ongley, this is a lovely 10 acre (4ha) example of a Swiss picturesque garden centred around a pretty thatched cottage. There are walks and vistas, a grotto, networks of ponds and islands with ironwork bridges, some fine conifers, shrubs and woodland glades.

☎ 01767 626236

Thetford Forest Park 213 F3

This working forest is the largest lowland pine forest in Britain. The varied habitat, which also includes broadleaf woodland and areas of heathland, supports a rich variety of wildlife; there is a chance of seeing crossbills and nightjars and red deer might even be spotted.

Scattered around the forest there are a number of picnic sites where visitors can relax and explore, and at its heart is the High Lodge Forest Centre which provides a variety of activities. Bikes are available for hire and there are a number of cycle trails: gentle ones suitable for families and a black route for the more experienced and adventurous riders. For those aged 10 and over there is an exciting rope course in the tree tops high above the forest floor and an adventure playground suitable for the smaller children. Other attractions include a large maze and a giant sculpture trail which includes a huge red squirrel. There is also a shop and restaurant.

☎ 01842 810271 www.forestry.gov.uk

Tilbury Fort 187 F5

Situated in a strategic position on the north bank of the River Thames, this late 17th century fort was designed to withstand heavy artillery fire; low lying, with double moats and brick-fronted earth embankments. There are exhibitions showing how the fort protected London from seaborne attack. Nearby, Elizabeth I gave a speech rallying her forces on the eve of their battle against the Spanish Armada.

☎ 01375 858489 www.english-heritage.org.uk

Titchwell Marsh 227 F3

This wetland nature reserve on the Norfolk coast, with reed bed and shallow lagoon habitats, is managed especially for birds by the RSPB. It is an important site for breeding avocets and, in the summer, marsh harriers can be seen. The cold weather sees the arrival of migrant and overwintering birds in the lagoons including large numbers of ducks and geese. There are three easily accessible hides for the use of visitors.

☎ 01485 210779 www.rspb.org.uk/reserve/guide/t/titchwell/

Verulamium Museum 186 A2

This museum contains re-creations of Roman scenes, showing everyday Roman life. There are also displays of interesting local finds including wall paintings, jewellery and some superb mosaics. During excavations nearby in 1989, a coffin and the remains of a Roman man were found. The museum has called him 'Postumus' and a video tells the fascinating story of the associated excavation and conservation work.

☎ 01727 751810 www.stalbansmuseums.org.uk/verulamium_museum.htm

Thetford Forest Park

Verulamium Roman Town
186 A2

At the height of the Roman occupation, Verulamium, now St Albans, was the third largest town in Britain. Set within a park are sections of the boundary wall, hypocaust and the remains of a theatre built about AD140. This is the only known example in Britain of a Roman theatre with a stage, rather than an amphitheatre. The remains of some of the Roman buildings were used in the construction of St Albans Cathedral.

☎ 01754 768837 www.verulamium.co.uk

Waltham Abbey
186 C2

It is said that King Harold II left from here to face William of Normandy at the Battle of Hastings in 1066, his body being returned to the abbey for burial. Outside the present abbey church are two inscribed stones marking the spot where King Harold's body is believed to lie. Following the Dissolution, the abbey was partly demolished and the remains that can be seen today include a late 14th century gatehouse that was once part of the cloisters, and part of the Norman abbey nave which was incorporated into the present Waltham Abbey Church. Within the nave can be seen striking spiral and zig-zag patterned columns and a superb painted ceiling.

☎ 01992 767897 www.english-heritage.org.uk www.walthamabbeychurch.co.uk

West Stow Country Park
213 F5

Set on the southern edge of the Breckland in the Lark Valley, this 125 acre (50ha) country park comprises heath, lake and woodland. Nature trails and bird hides enable visitors to enjoy the wide variety of flora and fauna that thrive in the park as a result of this habitat diversity.

An added attraction within the park is a reconstruction of an Anglo-Saxon village, built using original tools and techniques. This is located on the site of an original settlement and finds from the site are displayed in an interpretation centre.

☎ 01284 728718 www.stedmunds.co.uk/west_stow.html

Whipsnade Wild Animal Park
185 F1

Opened to the public in 1931, this is now one of Europe's largest wildlife conservation parks. It is set in nearly 600 acres (242ha) with over 3000 animals including hippos, rhinos, giraffe, vultures, cheetahs, bison, bears, tigers and much, much more. Visitors can travel around the large site using the free safari tour bus or on the narrow-gauge Great Whipsnade Railway. There is an impressive 17 acre (6.8ha) elephant paddock, the Splashzone where visitors can see the sea lions being fed, a children's farm and adventure playground, and a discovery centre where there is almost everything from seahorses to giant centipedes.

☎ 01582 872171 www.whipsnade.co.uk

Wicken Fen National Nature Reserve (NT)
212 D5

A haven for wildlife, and almost the last remnant of the extensive fen landscape that once covered eastern England. There are numerous paths enabling visitors to explore this fascinating area, as well as several hides, a restored Fenman's cottage and the last working windpump in the fens. The William Thorpe Visitor Centre has displays telling the story of the fen and its wildlife.

☎ 01353 720274 www.nationaltrust.org.uk

Wimpole Hall (NT)
200 B2

This magnificent 18th century house, the largest in Cambridgeshire, has a striking domed yellow drawing room by Sir John Soane and a library and chapel by James Gibbs; the chapel features a trompe l'oeil painting by Sir James Thornhill.

The landscaped grounds, with lakes and Gothic folly, are equally impressive: they extend to 360 acres (145ha) and were landscaped by the foremost practitioners of the time, namely Charles Bridgeman, Lancelot 'Capability' Brown and Humphrey Repton. The formal gardens around the house include parterres, a rose garden and a walled vegetable garden. The estate was purchased by Rudyard Kipling's daughter, Elsie Bambridge, who left it to the National Trust in 1976.

☎ 01223 207257 www.nationaltrust.org.uk www.wimpole.org

Wimpole Home Farm (NT)
200 B3

This 'model' farm, built in 1794 by Sir John Soane, an agricultural and farming enthusiast, features thatched farm buildings and the Great Barn which is now home to a museum of farming methods and equipment. A variety of animals including many rare breeds of cattle, sheep, pigs and poultry can be seen, as well as a Victorian dairy.

☎ 01223 207257 www.nationaltrust.org.uk www.wimpole.org

Woburn Abbey
199 E4

Woburn has been home to the Earls and Dukes of Bedford for nearly 400 years. The current Palladian style mansion, built on the site of a 12th century Cistercian monastery, is set in a 3000 acre (1200ha) deer park. In the 17th century the 4th Earl built a new wing on the site of the old abbey church. This contains an intriguing grotto with elaborately carved stonework resembling stalactites and seaweed, as well as 18th century furniture carved in the shape of sea shells with dolphins supporting the seats and table tops. The 4th Duke commissioned the west wing in 1747 which includes the grand series of state rooms.

Within the house there are over 250 paintings dating from as early as the 16th century, including works by Van Dyck, Gainsborough, Reynolds and Velázquez. The Venetian Room has 21 views of Venice by Canaletto, commissioned by the 4th Duke during his Grand Tour. There is also some excellent 18th century furniture, silver pieces by renowned Huguenot silversmiths, and some superb porcelain, including the Sèvres dinner service presented to the 4th Duchess by Louis XV in 1763.

The grounds were landscaped by Humphrey Repton at the beginning of the 19th century and are home to ten species of deer, including the rare Père David Chinese deer. Repton's Red Book, showing his plans for the grounds, can be seen in the Library. There is a hornbeam maze, masses of rhododendrons and a lake.

Within the estate is the famous Safari Park where visitors can enjoy seeing the animals wandering freely (additional charge).

☎ 01525 290666 www.woburnabbey.co.uk

Wood Green Animal Shelter
200 A1

The shelter at Godmanchester is one of three, the first of which was founded in Wood Green, London in 1924. At 50 acres (20ha), this is the largest and welcomes visitors who are interested in rehousing or learning about the animals, or who just want to look around. In addition to the animals there are charity, gift and pet accessory shops, water gardens, a wind turbine and a playground.

☎ 08701 904090 www.woodgreen.org.uk

Woodbridge Tide Mill
203 D3

A restored, Grade I listed working tide mill driven by the water held in a pond that is filled twice daily by the incoming tide. There are demonstrations at low tide.

☎ 01473 626618 www.tidemill.org.uk

Woodside Farm
185 F1

There are hundreds of animals to see here: monkeys, llamas, flamingos and giant tortoises, as well as the usual farm animals, all within a 7 acre (2.8ha) site. Children are encouraged to help feed and handle the animals. Other attractions include an adventure play area and an 18 hole crazy golf course.

☎ 01582 841044 www.woodsidefarm.co.uk

Wrest Park
199 F4

The magnificent gardens, which extend to some 90 acres (36ha), were originally laid out in the early 18th century, and are the main attraction here. There are woodland walks, avenues, a canal, a formal parterre, marble fountains, an orangery and a fine pavilion by Thomas Archer. The 19th century house, built in the style of an 18th century French chateau, has a few ornately plastered rooms open to visitors.

☎ 01525 860152 www.english-heritage.org.uk

Wroxham Barns
229 E3

Traditional and contemporary craftsmen and women can be seen at work in this rural craft centre located in 18th century restored farm buildings. There is also a children's farm in a farmyard setting and a funfair.

☎ 01603 783762 www.wroxham-barns.co.uk

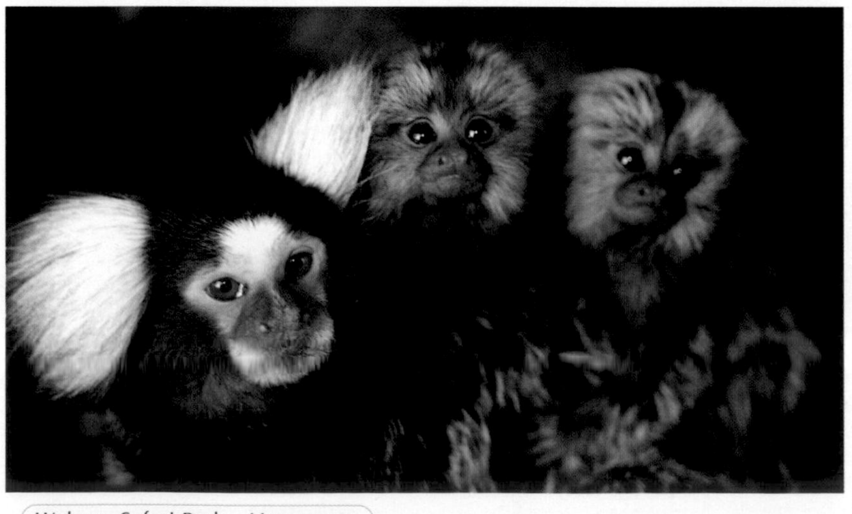

Woburn Safari Park – Marmosets

YORKSHIRE

This vast historic area encompasses all that is best within Britain. From the south the huge, bustling conurbations gradually surrender to the individual barren moors intermingled with the beautiful dales. Then, north east, over the mighty A1(M), passing through dozens of picturesque towns and villages, are the wild, scenic moors and forests of North Yorkshire. These end abruptly at the east coast where the traditional seaside resorts with their faded gentility still provide the quintessential English holiday experience.

View from hillside, Yorkshire

YORKSHIRE

1853 Gallery
244 A4

The 1853 Gallery is housed in a Grade II listed textile mill that was built in 1853. Featured within its three art galleries are hundreds of works by Bradford-born artist David Hockney. The gallery exhibits his lithographs, etchings, home made prints, photo collages and oil paintings, along with his early drawings. Displays of historical old mill items and objets d'art can also be viewed amongst the pictures.

☎ 01274 531163 www.saltsmill.org.uk

Aysgarth Falls & National Park Centre
251 F4

The River Ure forms this magnificent triple flight of waterfalls as it descends over limestone rock ledges through Wensleydale. The Upper Fall featured in the film 'Robin Hood, Prince of Thieves'. Enjoy a riverside walk linking the Upper, Middle and Lower Falls, for stunning views and scenery, and discover how the Aysgarth Falls were created, by visiting the Aysgarth Falls National Park Centre.

☎ 01969 663424

Bagshaw Museum
371 E3

Step back in time at Bagshaw Museum, housed within this enchanting Gothic mansion, complete with imposing copper tower. As well as admiring the interior Gothic décor, find out about the social and local history of Batley and what it was like to live in the area in the 19th century. Additionally, gain a fascinating insight into Ancient Egyptian life, view the Oriental decorative arts and encounter the enchanting world of the tropical rainforest.

☎ 01924 326155

Bempton Cliffs
255 E5

The chalk cliffs from Flamborough Head to Bempton provide a sanctuary for over 200,000 nesting birds. An RSPB reserve, this is the largest seabird colony in England. From the specially provided viewing areas, puffins, gannets, kittiwakes, guillemots, razorbills, fulmars and herring gulls can be seen. Most rewarding if visited during the breeding season between April and August.

☎ 01262 851179 www.rspb.co.uk

Beningbrough Hall (NT)
245 E2

This grand Georgian mansion was built in 1716. It now houses numerous 18th century treasures, including over 100 portraits loaned from the National Portrait Gallery. Its impressive Baroque interior boasts outstanding woodcarving and plasterwork, an unusual central corridor spanning the entire length of the house, and a fully equipped Victorian laundry. Outside is a wonderful walled garden, interesting wood sculptures, potting shed, wilderness play area and 7 acres (3ha) of parkland to be enjoyed.

☎ 01904 470666 www.nationaltrust.org.uk

Bolling Hall
370 C2

Much of this splendid period house dates back to the 1600s and was once home to the Bolling family. The Hall displays a variety of period furnishings and oak furniture, together with stained-glass windows depicting Coats of Arms in the central hall. The house also contains a medieval tower to the 18th century wing.

☎ 01274 723057

Bolton Abbey Estate
243 G2

Belonging to the Duke and Duchess of Devonshire since the 1750s, this Yorkshire country estate encompasses 30,000 acres (12,200ha) of parkland beside the River Wharfe. Central to the estate, and near to the village of Bolton Abbey, is the 12th century Bolton Priory. Explore the medieval buildings and enjoy some of the 80 miles (130km) of moorland, woodland and riverside paths, including Strid Wood, the largest remaining acidic woodland in Yorkshire.

☎ 01756 718009 www.boltonabbey.com

Bolton Castle
251 F3

Bolton Castle is an enormous 14th century fortress, with walls 9ft (3m) thick and towers rising 100ft (30m). In 1568, Mary, Queen of Scots, was imprisoned within its walls and Royalists were besieged here during the Civil War. Within the castle, tableaux portray life here during the 15th century. Outside, there is a medieval garden and walled herb garden, together with a vineyard, rose gardens, a maze and an orchard.

☎ 01969 623981 www.boltoncastle.co.uk

Bradford Industrial Museum
371 D1

Originally a 19th century spinning mill, this museum depicts industrial life as it was back then. The complex is complete with the mill owner's house, back-to-back cottages, working shire horses, stables, and mill machinery.

☎ 01274 435900

Bramham Park
244 D3

This French-inspired garden was created in the early 18th century. Its water gardens, cascades and geometric avenues, designed by Robert Benson, First Lord Bingley, remain virtually unaltered since their formation. There are 66 acres (27ha) of impressive vistas, long pathways lined with tall beech hedges leading to surprising views, temples, ornamental ponds, cascades, and a fine rose garden. The fine Queen Anne house is open to the public by appointment only.

☎ 01937 846000 www.bramhampark.co.uk

Brontë Parsonage Museum
243 G4

Formerly home to the famous Brontë family, this Parsonage has been carefully preserved into a museum. On show are eleven rooms furnished as they were in the mid 1850s, including the dining room, the kitchen, Mr Brontë's study, Charlotte's room and the children's study. Throughout are displays of the siblings' books and manuscripts, letters to friends and their personal possessions.

☎ 01535 642323 www.bronte.info

Burton Constable Hall
247 D4

On show inside this stately Elizabethan mansion are 30 wonderfully preserved rooms in 18th and 19th century fashion. They are styled with fine furniture, paintings and sculptures. There is a 'Cabinet of Curiosities' containing an intriguing collection of fossils, natural history and scientific instruments and a library containing 5000 books. Within the stable block is a riding centre, and there are 200 acres (80ha) of parkland, landscaped by Lancelot 'Capability' Brown.

☎ 01964 562400 www.burtonconstable.com

Cannon Hall Country Park
235 G2

Meander around over 70 acres (30ha) of parkland and formal gardens, first landscaped in the 1760s. The historic walled garden contains over 40 varieties of pear trees, first grown in the 18th century, along with peaches and nectarines. In one of the greenhouses is the Cannon Hall vine, grown from a seed brought back from the continent in 1802. The Hall contains a museum displaying fine paintings, glassware, pottery, furniture and a collection of military items set in period rooms.

☎ 01226 790270

Captain Cook Memorial Museum
254 C1

From 1746, James Cook lodged in the attic of this 17th century harbourside house, whilst an apprentice to Captain John Walker. In commemoration of the great explorer, the museum recounts Cook's Whitby years and his later achievements. There are models, maps and manuscripts, letters, ship plans, original paintings and drawings, as well as artefacts from his voyages.

☎ 01947 601900 www.cookmuseumwhitby.co.uk

Castle Howard
253 G5

A magnificent stately home, built in 1699 by the architect Sir John Vanbrugh. Castle Howard, with its famous dome, can be found in the Howardian Hills, between Malton and Thirsk. The castle continues to be home to the Howard family, where they have resided since it was built. Inside are exceptional collections of art, including paintings by Canaletto, Holbein, Gainsborough and Reynolds, and furniture by Chippendale and Sheraton. There are also impressive antique sculptures and a splendid collection of porcelain and china. Furthermore, costumed characters take on the role of historic personalities to re-enact life as it used to be in this stately home.

More can be seen outside, in over 1000 acres (400ha) of gardens and parklands. There are also exceptional temples, lead statues and monuments, lakes, waterways and fountains. All of which makes a trip to Castle Howard a wonderful day out.

☎ 01653 648333 www.castlehoward.co.uk

Castle Howard

Colour Museum 390 B1

Interactive galleries look at the history, development and technology aspects of colour. The perceptions, use and effects of light and colour, as well as the progress of dying techniques and textile printing, can all be explored.

☎ 01274 390955

Dalby Forest Drive 254 B4

Dalby Forest Drive extends for 9 scenic miles (15km) across hills, through valleys, past lakes and over streams. Stop along the way to enjoy one of the many walks to access stunning views and scenery. Encounter the northern edge of the plateau and dales, ancient earthworks created before the Dark Ages, Jurassic rock formations, ravines and the valley lake. Much of the extensive woodlands comprise spruces and pines, although along the valleys there are oak, ash and alder trees, some of which are descendants of the ancient forest. In addition to the diverse plant life and outstanding landscape, wildlife, such as roe deer, crossbills and nightjars, can also be found in abundance.

The visitor centre is located 1 mile (1.5km) along the drive from the Thornton Dale entrance. Here, information about Dalby, together with maps and booklets relating to the various trails, can be obtained.

☎ 01751 472771 www.forestry.gov.uk/dalbyforest

Duncombe Park 253 F4

Duncombe Park provides a classic example of an 18th century landscaped garden, surrounding a Baroque mansion, now home to Lord and Lady Feversham. There are 35 acres (15ha) of fine terraces, lawns, trees, temples and a scented 'secret garden'. Wonderful views extend over the valley and distant moors. Beyond the gardens are over 400 acres (160ha) of parkland. Half is now a National Nature Reserve with enjoyable waymarked walks.

The house, containing 18th century portraits and period furniture, can be accessed by guided tour only.

☎ 01439 770213 www.duncombepark.com

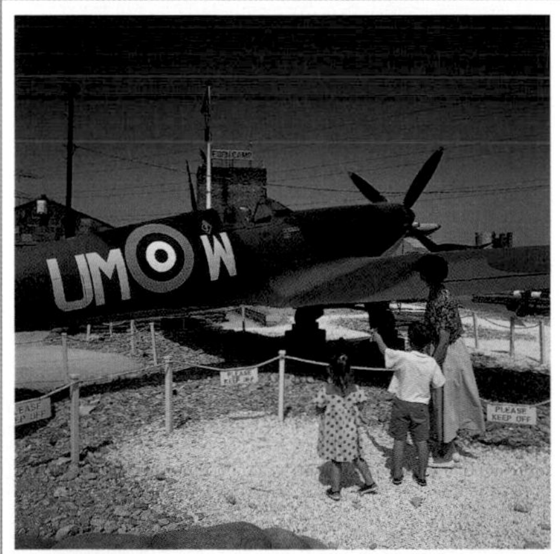
UM W

Eden Camp

Eden Camp 253 G5

Wartime Britain is magnificently brought to life at this award winning museum. Constructed within a former prisoner of war camp, the huts re-enact life during World War II. The sights, sounds and smells of everyday life during the war can be truly experienced.

Each hut conveys a different aspect of the war, including the rise of the Nazi Party, the outbreak of war, rationing, evacuees, propaganda, women at war, the Blitz, animals at war, the munitions factories, the rescue services and much more. Additional huts depict military and political events of World War II from a worldwide perspective, including scenes such as the Dambusters and The Great Escape. Another covers conflicts experienced by British forces since 1945 and yet another looks at World War I, incorporating a re-created trench.

The Eden Camp music hall is of particular interest to children, where puppets, representing some of the great entertainers of the time, perform well-known wartime songs. There is also an assault course, a number of military vehicles and a large collection of artillery.

☎ 01653 697777 www.edencamp.co.uk

Elsham Hall Country & Wildlife Park 238 A1

In the grounds of Elsham Hall is a unique venture, a combination of wildlife, arts and crafts. There is a theatre, craft centre, exhibition gallery, carp feeding jetty, butterfly garden walkway, adventure playground, arboretum, falconry centre and much more.

☎ 01652 688698 www.elshamhall.co.uk

Eureka! Museum for Children 370 B3

This is an interactive museum, designed especially for children aged 3-12 years. Over 400 hands-on exhibits can be explored, touched, listened to and smelt, based around 4 main themes: Me and My Body; Invent, Create, Communicate; Living and Working Together; and Our Global Garden. Everything has been developed to inspire.

☎ 01422 330069 www.eureka.org.uk

Flamingo Land Theme Park 253 G4

Set in 375 acres (152ha), this theme park is packed full of fun for all the family. Eight white-knuckle roller coasters and six other thrilling rides are key attractions. Ride on Wall's Magnum Force, Europe's only triple looping coaster, Cliff Hanger, Europe's tallest tower ride, or Terroriser, The Bullet, Corkscrew and Top Gun.

Another attraction is the large zoo with over 1000 animals, from around the world, including Siberian tigers, meerkats, Humboldt penguins, exotic birds and the UK's largest flock of pink flamingos. There is a water ride that travels through the Lost Kingdom – a themed area that incorporates part of the zoo, past the hippos, rhinos and giraffes. There are plenty of rides for younger children and a children's zoo. A number of family shows, too, are performed throughout the day.

☎ 01653 668287 www.flamingoland.co.uk

Fountains Abbey & Studley Royal Water Garden (NT) 244 B1

This amazing 800 acres (325ha) World Heritage Site, situated in the valley of the River Skell, shelters the ruins of over 10 historic buildings. One of these ruins is the imposing remains of a 12th century Cistercian Abbey, with its 15th century tower rising 170ft (52m). There is also an Elizabethan mansion, with two rooms open for viewing and a Victorian church, with fine stained-glass windows and ornate interior. Three floors of the 12th century monastic water mill, once used to produce flour for the monks, can be explored, too.

The wonderful landscaped gardens contain an 18th century water garden, ornamental lakes with temples, statues and cascades, all of which can be enjoyed and admired. Additionally, hundreds of red, sika and fallow deer roam in the medieval deer park.

☎ 01969 640382 www.fountainsabbey.org.uk

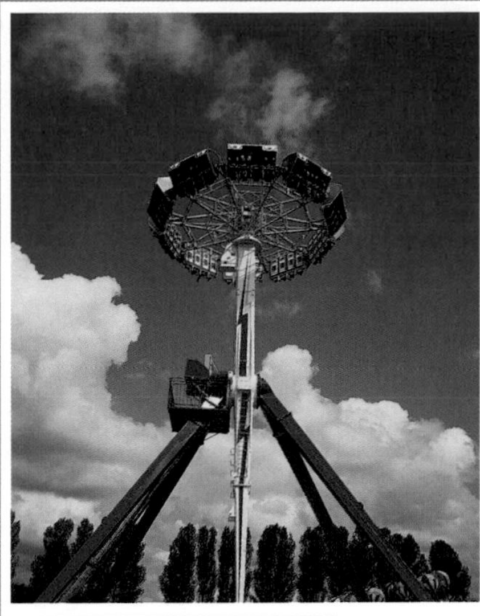

Flamingo Land Theme Park

Harewood House 244 C3

Renowned for its wonderful architecture and interiors by Robert Adam, this exceptional stately home belongs to the Earl of Harewood. Collections include exquisite Chippendale furniture, fine porcelain, and 18th century and Italian renaissance works of art. There are also royal photographs and memorabilia, from the 1930s to 1960s, when HRH Princess Mary lived here.

The impressive grounds, landscaped by Lancelot 'Capability' Brown, include lakeside and woodland walks. Alternatively, take a boat trip across the lake.

A visit to the Bird Garden is a must, with over 100 rare and exotic birds from around the world, including threatened species from Africa, America and Australia. There is also an excellent adventure playground.

☎ 0113 218 1010 www.harewood.org

Harlow Carr 244 B2

These botanical gardens, owned by the Royal Horticultural Society, cover 68 acres (30ha) in which the suitability of growing plants in the northern climate is assessed. Of particular interest are the scented garden, the streamside garden, flower and vegetable trial gardens, the rock garden, herbs and ornamental grasses, to name just a few. There is also an arboretum, model village and plant centre.

☎ 01423 565418 www.rhs.org.uk

Fountains Abbey

Helmsley Castle (Ruins)

253 F4

The dramatic ruins of Helmsley Castle include the 12th century keep and Tudor mansion. Two deep ditches cut down into the solid rock around the castle to form impressive earthworks.

☎ 01439 770442

Huddersfield Narrow Canal & Standedge Experience

235 E2

The Huddersfield Narrow Canal, which runs for 23 miles (40km), is split in two by Standedge Tunnel. At 3.25 miles (5km) long and 645ft (200m) above sea level, it is Britain's highest, longest and deepest canal tunnel. The Standedge Visitor Centre, with its interactive exhibition and guided boat trip through part of the tunnel, provides a remarkable account of how it was engineered in the 18th century.

☎ 01484 844298 www.standedge.co.uk

Jorvik

415 E2

Viking history is re-created using the well-preserved remains discovered on the site on which the museum now stands. Journey back over 1000 years to AD975 and experience the Viking way of life through the reconstructed streets, complete with sights, sounds and smells. Visitors travel in 'time-capsule' viewing cars to be taken past and through two-storey dwellings and over backyards and rooftops. From the archaeological finds, the houses and shops are laid out exactly as they were, and even the faces of the people on exhibition have been reconstructed from actual Viking skulls.

Also on display are over 800 items found during the archaeological dig, including a wonderfully preserved 8th century Anglo Saxon helmet. Special exhibitions throughout the year feature hands-on activities, artefacts and new academic research based around themes such as seafaring, craft skills, bones and warfare.

☎ 01904 543403 www.jorvik-viking-centre.co.uk

Jorvik

Jorvik Glass

245 G1

Located within the splendid grounds of Castle Howard, Jorvik Glass Centre provides workshop demonstrations of glass-blowing. A variety of glassware is available in the gift shop.

☎ 01653 648555

Kirklees Light Railway

235 G1

Take a 50 minute return trip on this steam train, admiring the beautiful scenery whilst travelling through two of the South Pennine valleys. This fifteen inch gauge railway runs 4 miles (6km) from Clayton West and into the longest tunnel on this gauge of line. There is also a visitor centre, children's play area, and steam models on display.

☎ 01484 865727

Kirkstall Abbey

244 B4

Situated on the River Aire in attractive parkland, Kirkstall Abbey is one of the UK's best preserved Cistercian monasteries. The Abbey was built between 1152 and 1182 and much of it has survived up to eaves level including the church, part of the 16th century tower, the transept, cloisters and the Chapter House.

☎ 0113 230 5492 www.kirkstall.org.uk/abbey

Leeds City Art Gallery & Museum

384 J5

This excellent art gallery displays a variety of fine art collections from the 19th and 20th centuries. Find outstanding English watercolours, traditional prints, Pre-Raphaelite paintings and Henry Moore sculptures, along with contemporary works. Entry is free.

☎ 0113 247 8248 www.leeds.gov.uk/artgallery

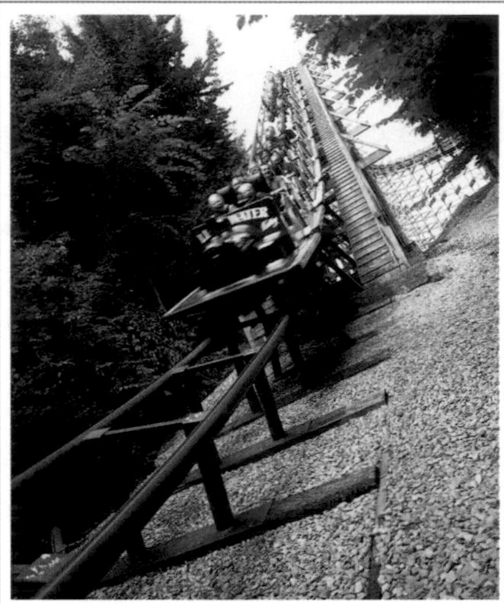

Lightwater Valley Park

Lightwater Valley Park

252 B5

Thrills, excitement and pleasurable family entertainment can all be found at this fun-packed theme park, set in 175 acres (71ha) of parkland. For the adventurous, there are several white-knuckle rides, including the Ultimate Beast, Europe's longest coaster at 1.5 miles (2.5km), and the Sewer Rat built 40ft (12m) underground. There is also the Black Widow's Web giant ferris wheel, the Beaver Rapids log flume and the Wave giant swing boat. Younger children, too, are well catered for, with specially designed mini amusements, including the Ladybird roller coaster and Spinning Teacups.

Recover at a gentler pace with a number of more leisurely attractions. Tour the park on the Lightwater Express steam train or enjoy the boating lake. Additional amusements include go-karting and a children's farm.

☎ 0870 458 0040 www.lightwatervalley.co.uk

Lotherton Hall

245 D4

An Edwardian country home, formerly owned by the Gascoigne family. On display are fine collections of pottery, paintings, sculpture, furniture, jewellery, ceramics, silver, oriental art and British costume. The surrounding grounds and parkland boast a re-created Edwardian garden, a medieval deer park and a 12th century chapel. The Bird Garden houses over 200 species, many of which are rare and endangered, including flamingos, snowy owls and hornbills.

☎ 0113 281 3259 www.leeds.gov.uk/lothertonhall

Magna Centre

365 B1

This Science Adventure Centre is set in a splendidly converted former steelworks. Inside are hands-on, interactive experiences based around the four main elements used to make steel. The Fire Pavilion examines the advantages of fire and its explosive possibilities, while the Air Pavilion is in an airship structure, hovering above the floor. Be prepared to get wet in the Water Pavilion, by shooting water cannons, launching a water-powered rocket or creating a hot geyser. In the Earth zone, manoeuvre a JCB or explode a rock face.

☎ 01709 720002 www.visitmagna.co.uk

Malham Cove

243 E1

This huge, curved rock face, rising up around 260ft (80m), is formed of natural limestone. The top of the cove provides an excellent example of limestone pavement, pitted with deep cracks and crevices as a result of the weathering of such terrain.

Manor House

244 A3

This Elizabethan manor house is built on the site of a former Roman fort. The museum recounts Ilkley's local history with exhibits from Roman through to Victorian times, when the area became a spa town. In the gallery are displays of works from local artists and craftspeople.

☎ 01943 600066

Merchant Adventurers Hall

415 E2

Built in the mid 14th century, this Guildhall is York's largest timber-framed building and is believed to be one of the finest medieval halls in Europe. In addition to the Great Hall, where merchants conducted their business, there is the Undercroft, or hospital, and the Chapel. On display are fine collections of furniture, portraits, silver and jewellery, together with information about the lives of the merchants during medieval times.

☎ 01904 654818 www.theyorkcompany.co.uk

Middleton Railway

244 C5

Of great historical importance, this is the oldest working railway in the world, having been established by an Act of Parliament in 1758. It was also the first to succeed commercially with steam locomotives in 1812, as well as being the first standard gauge railway to be operated by volunteers in 1960. View the collection of industrial steam and diesel engines or travel on the railway for a family day out at Middleton Park, with woodland, nature trails, picnic area and lake.

☎ 0113 271 0320 www.middletonrailway.org.uk

National Museum of Photography, Film & TV

National Railway Museum

Millennium Galleries & Winter Gardens
409 B3

Housed within a modern and stylish complex are four galleries, showcasing visual arts, crafts and design by contemporary designers and past masters. The Metalwork Gallery exhibits decorative metalwork and silverware, and recounts the history of the city's metalworking trade. John Ruskin's collection of paintings, manuscripts, papers, books and architectural plastering are also on display and there are special collections from places including the Victoria and Albert Museum and the Tate. Adjacent are the Winter Gardens, in a stunning temperate glasshouse, containing 2500 plants and 150 different species.

Admission into the galleries and Winter Gardens is free; charges apply for the special exhibitions.

☎ 0114 278 2600

Mount Grace Priory (NT)
252 D3

Built in the late 14th century, these ruins are better preserved than any of the other ten Carthusian monasteries in England. The Carthusian monks lived a hermit's life in small two-storey cells with a garden. One of these has been reconstructed to replicate how the monks lived and worked. In spring, the grounds are awash with daffodils, making it a particularly attractive place to visit. Adjacent is a 17th century manor house, built on the site of the monastery guesthouse, housing an exhibition and arts and crafts.

☎ 01609 883494 www.nationaltrust.org.uk

National Museum of Photography, Film & TV
390 C2

The museum's interactive galleries provide a fascinating insight into the world of photography, film and television, both past and present. Among over three million items on display are the world's first negative, the earliest television footage, and Louis Le Prince's 1888 film of Leeds Bridge, regarded as the first example of moving pictures. Explore the history of popular photography and discover the digital age of computers, special effects and virtual reality. Learn how television cameras work, discover how animation is created, read the news, see the cameras used on 'James Bond' films, or find the toys from 'Play School'.

Alongside these galleries is the five-storeys-high IMAX screen, which regularly features 3D and other films, as well as two other conventional cinemas, which show films from around the world.

The permanent galleries are free to visit, whilst there are admission charges for the cinemas and some special exhibitions.

☎ 0870 701 0200 www.nmpft.org.uk

National Railway Museum
415 E1

Over 200 years of railway history is celebrated in style, providing a terrific family day out – for free. Complete with sounds and smells, the atmosphere of steam and rail travel is wonderfully re-created. A splendid collection of locomotives can be found on display in the Great Hall, recounting the story of the railway from Rocket to Eurostar. Inspect the Mallard, the world's fastest steam locomotive, explore Queen Victoria's luxurious royal carriage and examine the Japanese Bullet Train, in conjunction with a short video presentation. There are millions of railway artefacts, too, including models, silver and crockery, nameplates, clocks and watches, tickets, photographs, workshop tools, posters, engineering drawings, and even a lock of Robert Stephenson's hair.

The Working Railway demonstrates how signals work, the technology behind them and their development over time. Children will enjoy the Interactive Learning Centre where hands-on exhibits explain the workings of trains and the railway. Engineers and craftspeople can be watched in the Works Wing while they carry out conservation work, and children can also build their own model train here.

Rides on the miniature railway are available most weekends and school holidays, and on the steam train during school holidays.

☎ 01904 6212621 www.nrm.org.uk
☎ 01904 686286 (24hr info line)

Normanby Hall Country Park & Farming Museum
237 G1

A mansion built in the Regency style, with a rural museum, Victorian walled garden, beautiful grounds with woodland, deer park and nature trails. For children there is an adventure playground and miniature railway. Tearoom and plant nursery.

☎ 01724 720588 www.northlincs.gov.uk

North Bay Miniature Railway
254 D4

Two trains operate on this miniature railway, which runs from Peasholm Gap in North Bay. Each train can carry up to 100 people, travelling almost a mile (1.6km), complete with a tunnel, bridges, signals, stations and gradient boards all reproduced to scale.

☎ 01723 373333

North York Moors
253 F2

The vast, heather-clad moorlands, breathtaking open landscape, extensive woodlands and serenity are what make the North York Moors National Park special. Extending east of the A19, from the A170 in the south to the A171 in the north, the Moors are bounded on the eastern side by ragged cliffs and untouched coastline, overlooking the North Sea. There are over 1400 miles (2253km) of paths and tracks to follow, including the Cleveland Way National Trail.

A journey through Dalby Forest, or a steam train trip on the North Yorkshire Moors Railway, provides a wonderful way to explore the stunning and varied countryside. The area's historic heritage includes magnificent ruined abbeys, besieged castles, period buildings and gardens, and informative museums. Rievaulx Abbey, Whitby Abbey, Captain Cook Memorial Museum, Duncombe Park and Mount Grace Priory all warrant a visit. The coastal fishing villages and ancient towns of Whitby and Scarborough are popular places, whilst Robin Hood's Bay offers fossil hunting.

Many television and film makers have valued the area, having featured some of the unspoilt villages and stations of the North York Moors in 'Heartbeat', 'Harry Potter and the Philosopher's Stone', 'Brideshead Revisited', 'Poirot' and 'Sherlock Holmes', to name just a few.

www.moors.uk.net

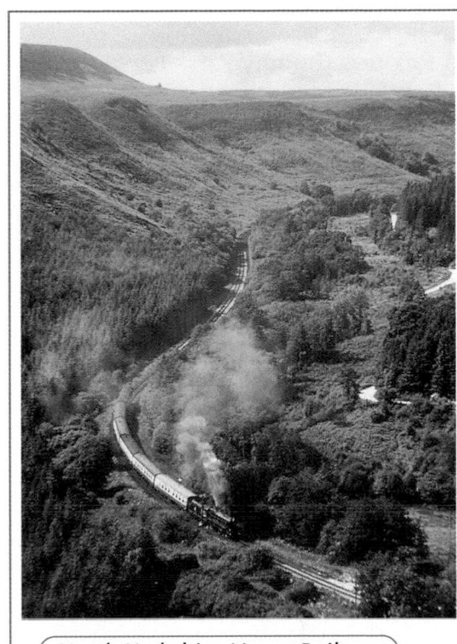

North Yorkshire Moors Railway

North Yorkshire Moors Railway
254 B4

Travel on a steam train across the North Yorkshire Moors National Park on one of the earliest and most historic lines in the North of England. Stretching 18 miles (29km) from Pickering to Grosmont, the journey passes through beautiful countryside, charming villages and authentically restored stations. George Stephenson originally built the railway line, which includes one of the steepest rail gradients in the country between Goathland and Grosmont.

The railway and its stations have regularly featured in a variety of television programmes and films, including 'Heartbeat', 'Harry Potter and the Philosopher's Stone', 'Brideshead Revisited', 'Poirot', 'Sherlock Holmes' and 'All Creatures Great and Small'. Stop off along the way to enjoy the attractions and pleasant walks in the area. The Locomotive Shop and engine sheds can be accessed at Grosmont.

☎ 01751 472508 www.northyorkshiremoorsrailway.com
☎ 01751 473535 (Talking Timetable)

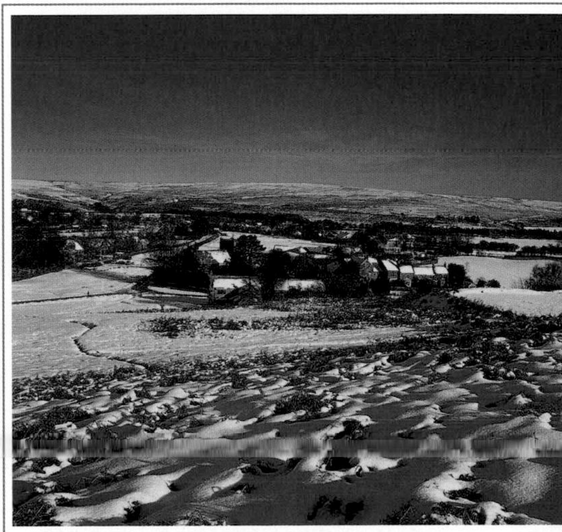

North York Moors – Goathland

Pleasure Island Theme Park — 238 D2

Six white-knuckle terror rides, lots of family rides, fun rides for the little ones, and superb classic rides on restored machines, including a 1920s 'Flying Chair' and a 1905 Carousel. Entertainment galore and lots of places to eat.

☎ 01472 211511 — www.pleasure-island.co.uk

Pugneys Country Park — 371 F4

One of the two lakes in this country park caters for non-powered watersports, including fishing, canoeing, windsurfing and sailing. Equipment is available for hire if required. The other smaller lake is a nature reserve with two bird hides.

☎ 01924 302360

Richmond Castle — 252 A2

High on the cliffs above the River Swale stands the imposing Richmond Castle. Built by William the Conqueror to control the north, some of its original 11th century walls remain. The rectangular keep, rising 100ft (30m) with walls 11ft thick (3.5m), was built in the 12th century and remains almost intact. There is also an exhibition centre displaying some of the artefacts excavated from the site, where the castle's history can be explored.

☎ 01748 822493 — www.english-heritage.org.uk

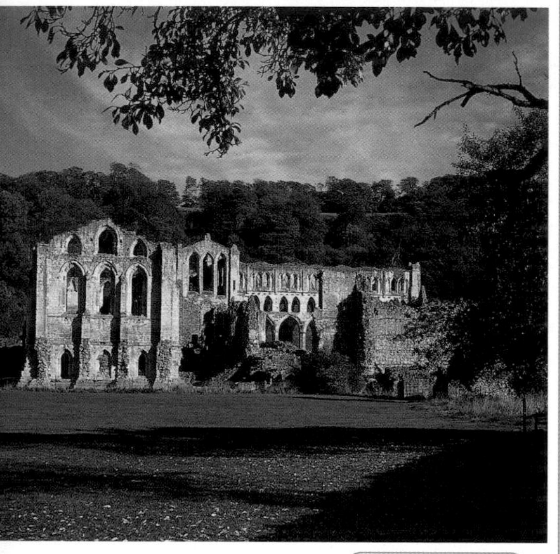

Rievaulx Abbey

Rievaulx Abbey — 253 E4

Set amongst the wooded hills of Rye Dale are the majestic ruins of this once powerful Cistercian monastery. Founded in 1132, this impressive abbey was built unconventionally, being hampered by the terrain, with its central aisle laid north to south, rather than the usual east to west direction.

The nave dates from 1135, whilst the towering presbytery, which is virtually intact, was rebuilt in the 13th century. Several outbuildings can also be identified, some standing to a good height. The monks' refectory is clearly evident with its wonderful arched lancet windows, along with the spectacular remains of the 13th century choir.

There is a visitor centre and a fascinating museum with interactive exhibits exploring the site's history.

☎ 01439 798228 — www.english-heritage.org.uk

Ripley Castle — 244 B1

Home to the Ingilby family since the early 1300s, discover 700 years of political, military, religious and social history. Most of the current building dates from the 16th century, including the three-storey, fortified tower complete with a priest's secret hiding hole. On display are fine paintings, furniture, books and china, and the tower houses a collection of Royalist armour. The delightful gardens include a walled garden, which contains the National Hyacinth Collection, the kitchen garden, with rare vegetables, and the hot houses are filled with tropical plants. There is also a deer park and lakeside walks.

☎ 01423 770152 — www.ripleycastle.co.uk

Royal Armouries Museum — 385 N9

Housing a fascinating collection of arms and armour, the museum covers 3000 years of history with over 8000 exhibits. The five galleries spectacularly explore the themes of war, tournaments, hunting, self-defence and oriental warfare. Complementing the exhibits are many interactive touch-screen demonstrations, enjoyable films, costumed demonstrations and dramatised interpretations. More fun can be discovered outside, weather permitting, including jousting, falconry and horsemanship. The craft of gun making and leather working can also be observed, along with the falcons, hunting dogs and other animals in the Menagerie. Entrance for the main museum collection is free; charges apply for special themed events such as the shooting galleries.

☎ 0113 220 1999 — www.armouries.org.uk

Scarborough Art Gallery — 254 D4

Displayed within this Italianate villa are fine art collections by local artists and by those who painted in Scarborough, such as Grimshaw, H.B. Carter and Lord Leighton. The paintings feature Scarborough's wonderful seascapes and views. The gallery is particularly appealing to a family audience. There are hands-on displays, pictures and paintings depicting Scarborough's history from fishing village to popular seaside resort. Children can also dress up in costumes and masks as one of the characters from the paintings.

☎ 01723 374753

Scarborough Castle — 255 D4

Towering above the town and harbour, Scarborough Castle stands on a headland 300ft (91m) above sea level. The castle was built in the 12th century and has endured numerous Civil War sieges and bombardment during World War I. Explore the remains of the imposing, three-storey keep, built in the 12th century, medieval chapels, the curtain walls, and 13th century barbican. The site also provides evidence of earlier Iron Age settlements and remains of a Roman signal station.

☎ 01723 372451 — www.english-heritage.org.uk

Sewerby Hall & Gardens — 247 E1

Sewerby Hall is set in 50 acres (20ha) of parkland with fabulous coastal views over Bridlington Bay. This stylish Georgian house contains the East Yorkshire Museum featuring local history, archaeology, photography, and contemporary arts and crafts. One of the rooms is dedicated to the record-breaking aviator, Amy Johnson, displaying her souvenirs and mementoes. The gardens offer woodland walks, a delightful Old English Garden, pleasure gardens, children's zoo, adventure playground, 19th century Orangery, pitch and putt golf and putting green.

☎ 01262 673769 — www.sewerby-hall.co.uk

Shandy Hall — 253 E5

This authentically restored house belonged to the amusing parson, Laurence Sterne. It is where he completed his two novels, 'Tristram Shandy' and 'A Sentimental Journey', in the 1760s. Two acres (1ha) of lovely gardens surround the house, complete with old fashioned roses and unusual cottage garden plants. The shop sells Sterne's books and unusual plants.

☎ 01347 868465

Shibden Hall — 370 B3

Shibden Hall is an impressive, half-timbered manor house, dating back to 1420. Different rooms portray varying styles of architecture and furnishings associated with a particular era. Explore the 15th century kitchen, the 17th century dining room or the 16th century housebody. Its 17th century barn houses a folk museum with a notable collection of horse-drawn vehicles, while its reconstructed workshops display 19th century craft tools. The surrounding 90 acres (36ha) of parkland provide woodland walks, miniature railway, boating lake and play area.

☎ 01422 352246

Skipton Castle — 243 F2

A wonderfully preserved, fully roofed, medieval castle, having survived a three-year siege during the Civil War. Inspect the banqueting hall, the kitchen, bedchamber and privy, climb to the top of the Watch Tower and back down to the dungeons below. Furthermore, unwind in the Chapel Terrace overlooking the town and surrounding woodland, or in the cobbled Tudor courtyard complete with a yew tree planted in the 17th century.

☎ 01756 792442 — www.skiptoncastle.co.uk

Spurn Head — 239 E1

Spurn Head, curling at the mouth of the Humber Estuary, marks the southernmost point of the Yorkshire Coast. The sandy peninsula extends for about 3.5 miles (5.5km) with a rough track passable by cars almost to its end (best to check the tide times). A rather uninhabited place, but its mudflats and saltmarsh attract thousands of birds and migrating species, including rare varieties such as yellow-browed warblers and wrynecks.

Temple Newsam — 244 C4

Displayed within their original room settings in this wonderful Tudor-Jacobean mansion are extensive collections of fine paintings, furniture, silver, porcelain and Leeds pottery. Amongst the furniture collection are some excellent Chippendale masterpieces. The surrounding parkland, and gardens designed by Lancelot 'Capability' Brown, extend 2 sq miles (518ha) and incorporate a woodland garden, an Italian garden and a walled garden. Additionally, there is a Rare Breeds Centre, with over 400 animals.

☎ 0113 264 7321 — www.leeds.gov.uk/templenewsam

Thorp Perrow Arboretum — 252 B4

The 85 acres (35ha) of woodland contain one of the largest and finest collections of trees and shrubs in the north of England. There are four national collections of ash, lime, walnut and laburnum, as well as oaks, ornamental cherries, willows and hazels. The arboretum is attractive throughout the year with thousands of daffodils in spring, tree blossom, bluebells and wild flowers in summer, and spectacular colours in autumn. Enjoy woodland walks, tree trails, nature trails, children's trail, lake and 16th century Spring Wood. The falconry centre provides demonstrations and hands-on experience of birds of prey.

☎ 01677 425323 — www.thorpperrow.com

Tropical World

244 C4

This attraction houses the largest tropical plant collection outside Kew Gardens. The Amazon rainforest, the African and American deserts and the North Sea waters are all captivatingly re-created. Discover over 30 varieties of butterflies, along with nocturnal owl monkeys, Egyptian fruit bats and bush babies, tropical fish and birds, terrapins and reptiles, all living amongst the tropical environments.

☎ 0113 266 1850

Wakefield Cathedral

244 C5

First built in the 14th century and much restored in the 19th century, Wakefield Cathedral boasts the tallest spire in Yorkshire. Inside, it also features a 17th century font, 15th century masonry and carvings, and excellent Victorian stained-glass windows by Kempe.

☎ 01924 373923 www.wakefield-cathedral.org.uk

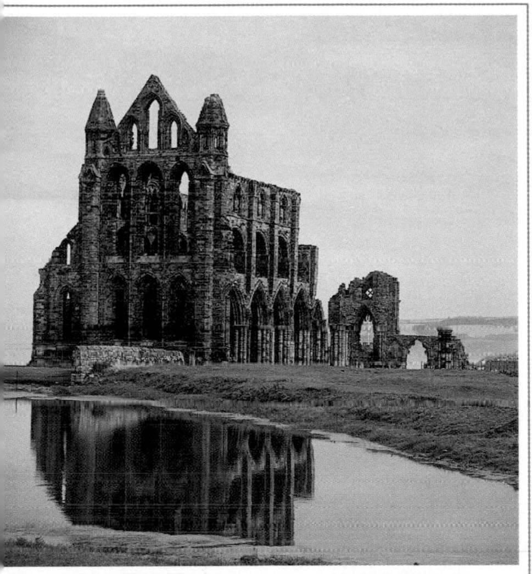

Whitby Abbey

Whitby Abbey

254 C1

High on the cliff above the harbour stand the dramatic ruins of Whitby Abbey. Founded by Abbess St Hilda in AD657, the abbey was destroyed by the Vikings and rebuilt by the Normans in the 13th century. Amongst the ruins is the Benedictine Church, dating from the 13th and 14th centuries, complete with an impressive three-tiered choir and north transept. The abbey's 2000 year history is interactively re-created with computer-generated images, audiovisual displays and activities in the visitor centre, housed in the remains of a 17th century house. There are also displays of archaeological artefacts from the site and a restored 17th century stone garden.

This is a wonderful place to visit and has been an inspirational site for many, from saints to writers, including Bram Stoker, author of 'Dracula'.

☎ 01904 603568 www.english-heritage.org.uk

White Scar Cave

250 C5

The guided tour of White Scar Cave, one of the longest and most spectacular natural caves in Britain, covers 1 mile (1.6km) and takes about 80 minutes. Underground streams, waterfalls, stalactites, stalagmites, and other natural limestone formations can all be seen. There is also a massive cavern formed during the Ice Age containing thousands of stalactites and several prehistoric mud pools.

☎ 01524 241244 www.whitescarcave.co.uk

York

415

The city of York is rich in history, splendour and variety. The Romans, who founded the city in AD71, the Vikings, the Normans, and the Georgians have all left their mark. The medieval walls, which include remnants of the Roman fortress walls, still surround the city, within which are narrow medieval streets and alleyways, including the infamous 'Shambles'. Visit the many museums that recount the site's changing times and display various archaeological finds, including York Castle Museum, Jorvik Viking Centre, the Yorkshire Museum and the more chilling York Dungeon.

York Minster is England's largest medieval Gothic church and the Merchants Adventurers' Hall is evidence of York's prospering times, during the Middle Ages, as a trading city operating under Guilds. With the Victorian Age came an economic revival for York through the railways, and the National Railway Museum celebrates over 200 years of railway history.

There are also interesting shops, wonderful parks and gardens, river and bus trips, bars, cafés and guided walks, including an evening 'Ghost Walk'.

www.york-tourism.co.uk

York Castle Museum

415 E2

Over 400 years of social history are revealed within the walls of what was once the city's old prison. The museum displays a remarkable collection of over 100,000 everyday items including period costumes, jewellery, arms, armour and toys. Encounter prison life 200 years ago by peering into cells, one of which housed the notorious highwayman, Dick Turpin, and read the graffiti still on the walls. The re-created cobbled streets, lined with replica shops, and reconstructed living rooms, provide a fascinating insight into how the Victorians lived.

☎ 01904 687687 www.yorkcastlemuseum.org.uk

York Dungeon

415 E2

Encounter the more gruesome side of York's history to discover the chilling aspects of superstition, torture, death and pain experienced over the last 2000 years. Tour round York's 14th century plague-ridden streets, meet Guy Fawkes as he is tortured to unveil the gunpowder plot and its conspirators, hear the infamous highwayman, Dick Turpin, recount his tales before being hanged. Then there are the Witchcraft trials, the ferocious Viking invaders, and the local woman crushed to death by stones – all have a story to tell.

☎ 01904 632599 www.thedungeons.com

York Minster

415 E2

York Minster is a stunning medieval Gothic cathedral and the largest in northern Europe. Building began in the 13th century, but it took until the 15th century to be completed. The numerous, beautiful stained-glass windows are a key feature. Admire the Norman stained-glass windows in the nave, the Five Sisters Window in the north transept containing 100,000 pieces of glass, and the Great East Window with 27 panels. The Chapter House reveals fine carvings and the north transept is styled with polished stone columns.

In the Undercroft, Treasury and Crypt there is a museum that relates the cathedral's varied history over the last 2000 years. A climb to the top of the central tower is well worth the effort for magnificent views.

☎ 01904 557216 www.yorkminster.org

Yorkshire Dales

250 D4

Outstanding beauty, spectacular natural landscapes, diverse habitats and a tranquil environment can all be used to describe the Yorkshire Dales, 1700 sq miles (4400 sq km) of which make up the Yorkshire Dales National Park.

The dramatic limestone and gritstone landscape, particularly in the southern dales (including Malhamdale and Airedale), provides stunning scenery with the rocky limestone cliffs and pavements, dramatic waterfalls and many caves. Bolton Abbey, White Scar Cave and Malham Cove are popular attractions, while the towering Three Peaks (Pen-y-Ghent, Ingleborough and Whernside) provide fabulous viewpoints.

Less rugged countryside and valleys depict the more northern and eastern dales, with wild flower and hay meadows, heather topped moors, woodland and picturesque villages. There are also many castles, abbeys, museums and gardens to explore including Constable Burton Hall, Bolton Castle, Thorp Perrow Arboretum, Fountains Abbey, and Aysgarth Falls.

The Pennine Way, Dales Way footpath, Coast to Coast Walk and the Settle to Carlisle Railway all pass through the Dales. The area, with its striking surroundings and picturesque rural villages, has also provided the backdrop to many television programmes and films, including 'Emmerdale', 'Robin Hood: Prince of Thieves', 'All Creatures Great and Small' and 'Calendar Girls'.

www.yorkshiredales.org.uk

Yorkshire Dales – Conistone

Yorkshire Museum

415 D1

Packed full of archaeological, Roman, Viking, Anglo-Saxon and medieval finds, the museum reveals a host of historic treasures. Amongst the collections are ancient fossils, medieval jewellery, including the spectacular Middleham Jewel, fine pottery and decorative arts. Outside, 10 acres (4ha) of botanical gardens can be explored, where there are also some interesting buildings including the ruins of the Benedictine St Mary's Abbey, a 14th century hospitium, a preserved section of a Roman fortress and a working observatory.

☎ 01904 687687 www.yorkshiremuseum.org.uk

Yorkshire Sculpture Park

235 G1

Artistically arranged within 500 acres (202ha) of pleasant 18th century landscaped parkland are major modern and contemporary sculptures. Exhibits from well-known names include those by Henry Moore, Elizabeth Frink and Barbara Hepworth. There are also two indoor galleries, a regularly changing programme of exhibitions and a visitor centre.

☎ 01924 830302 www.ysp.co.uk

NORTH WEST ENGLAND

Today the dark industrial images of the past are consigned to history and the busy urban sprawl of Manchester and Liverpool offer some of the very best in city design and culture. But nowhere in the country is the stark contrast between urban and rural life more apparent than in this region. Just a short distance up the M6 is the misty, dreamy Lake District, England's most popular national park. Here sixteen major lakes and England's highest mountains are packed into an area approximately thirty miles long and thirty miles across.

Jetty on Derwent Water

Abbot Hall Art Gallery & Museum of Lakeland Life

249 G3

Within the Georgian house of Abbot Hall there is a fine collection of British art from the 18th century onwards, including works by Ruskin, Constable and Romney. Exhibitions of national interest are held here and sculpture, arts, crafts and 18th century objets d'art also feature.

The Museum of Lakeland Life illustrates 250 years of Cumbrian history and has re-created period rooms, workshops and shops. There are personal effects and exhibits relating to 'Swallows and Amazons' author Arthur Ransome, and collections of Victoriana and costume.

☎ 01539 722464 www.abbothall.org.uk www.lakelandmuseum.org.uk

Acorn Bank (NT)

260 C5

A walled garden with a large collection of culinary herbs, medicinal plants, shrubs, roses, herbaceous borders and orchards of old English fruit trees. A path through the ancient oak woodland leads to a restored water mill on Crowdundle Beck. Lovely displays of daffodils and wood anemones in spring.

☎ 017683 61893 www.nationaltrust.org.uk

Adlington Hall

234 D4

Originally built as a hunting lodge in 1040 by the Legh family, the present structure incorporates parts of the original building as well as Tudor, Elizabethan and more modern additions. The Hall is home to the largest 17th century organ in the country. The gardens were landscaped in the 18th century in the style of Lancelot 'Capability' Brown and now also include a maze and rose garden. Only open on selected days during the summer.

☎ 01625 820875 www.adlingtonhall.com

Adrian Sankey Glass Makers

249 E2

Visitors may view unique contemporary glass being made by craftspeople using the traditional methods of glass-blowing and hand finishing.

☎ 015394 33039 www.glassmakers.co.uk

Aira Force (NT)

260 A5

70ft (21m) waterfall set amongst woodland on the west side of Ullswater, spanned by a small arched stone bridge.

www.nationaltrust.org.uk

Anderton Boat Lift

234 A5

The boat lift is the only one of its kind in the UK, and when it was built in 1875 it was the first anywhere in the world. Boats enter one of two counterbalanced water-filled tanks which then pass each other mostly by the process of gravity. The rise is 50ft (15m) between two sections of the Trent and Mersey Canal. A visitor centre explains the processes fully and there are trips up and down the lift on a specially built glass-bottomed boat.

☎ 01606 786777 www.andertonboatlift.co.uk

Aquarium of the Lakes

249 E4

An award winning aquarium with more than 30 habitat exhibits of the creatures living in and around the streams, rivers and lakes of the Lake District. These include otters, ducks, trout, eels, pike, perch, and also the giant crabs, sharks and rays of Morecambe Bay. Imaginatively themed to follow the journey of a Lakeland river from its source to the sea, with interactive displays and a cinema presentation of life above and below the surface of Lake Windermere.

☎ 015395 30153 www.aquariumofthelakes.co.uk

Arley Hall

234 A4

The hall is set in superb gardens which are considered by many to be among the best in Europe. There are fine double herbaceous borders, two walled gardens, a shrub rose garden and yew topiary. The present day hall dates from between 1832 and 1845, although parts of the original Tudor building remain. The hall has fine wood panelling, plasterwork, porcelain and a wonderful library.

☎ 01565 777353 www.arleyhallandgardens.com

Astley Hall Museum & Gardens

233 G1

Dating back to Elizabethan times, this country house has textile, art, glassware and ceramic collections and a unique display of furniture. The house is set in extensive woodland and gardens.

☎ 01257 515555 www.astleyhall.co.uk

Beacon Fell Country Park

242 B3

The Fell lies within the Forest of Bowland Area of Outstanding Natural Beauty and the majority of its 185 acres (75ha) are covered by coniferous forest. There are panoramic views from the top of Beacon Fell where a triangulation pillar marks the site of the original warning beacon. A number of walks and cycle paths are clearly marked and a visitor centre is open during the summer.

☎ 01995 640557 www.lancashire.gov.uk/environment/countryside/sites/beaconf.asp

Beatles Story

380 D10

Charting the history of the rise to fame of the four boys from Liverpool. There is a replica of The Cavern Club, a walk-through Yellow Submarine, and displays of Beatles memorabilia.

☎ 0151 709 1963 www.beatlesstory.com

Beeston Castle (Ruins)

220 C2

There are stunning views to be seen from this 13th century ruined castle which stands tall on sandstone crags overlooking the Cheshire Plains – it is well worth the steep climb to the top. The Castle of the Rock exhibition outlines the history of the site, from prehistoric times to the Civil War when the castle was eventually destroyed by the Parliamentarians in 1646.

☎ 01829 260464 www.english-heritage.org.uk

Birdoswald (Banna)

260 C1

In a commanding position overlooking the River Irthing, this well-preserved Roman fort was one of 16 along Hadrian's Wall. Parts of the walls and gateways remain and the fort is linked to Harrow's Scar Milecastle by an impressive section of the Wall. Excavations have revealed a basilica and granaries, and the site has an interactive visitor centre and self-guided trail. Birdoswald continued to be used after the Roman departure up until the 17th century and a farmhouse dating to that period remains.

☎ 016977 47602 www.birdoswaldromanfort.org.uk

Blackpool Piers

241 G4

Blackpool has three piers, each with its own style of entertainment. The North Pier is the oldest, built in 1863 and now a listed building, and is the quietest of the piers with the more genteel attractions. Central Pier is great for the children with a traditional funfair including a Big Wheel which gives superb views along the coastline. The South Pier is the place for adrenaline junkies to head to with various opportunities to jump, be thrown, tossed or swung out over the sea. Entrance to all the piers is free although there is a charge for amusements.

☎ 01253 343097 www.blackpoollive.com

Blackpool Pleasure Beach

241 G4

There are over 140 rides and attractions at this hugely popular amusement park on Blackpool's Promenade, founded in 1896. As well as a large selection of modern white-knuckle rides like The Big One, Europe's tallest (235ft, 72m) and fastest (85mph) roller coaster, and the Avalanche, based on a bobsleigh run, there are a selection of much older wooden roller coasters; the Big Dipper dates from 1923 and the twin track Grand National (two cars racing against each other on parallel tracks) from 1935. Valhalla is a truly spectacular ride in the dark with fire and lots of water. For younger children there is Beaver Creek, a theme park within a theme park, with its own selection of rides and amusements. There are a number of musical and dance shows performed daily and there are over 50 places to eat and drink as well as all the usual gift shops and traditional seaside entertainments. The rides vary in price, usually based on their 'scare' value, and tickets can be bought individually, in books or the cheaper option of a wristband if a whole day's visit is planned.

☎ 0870 444 5566 www.bpbltd.com

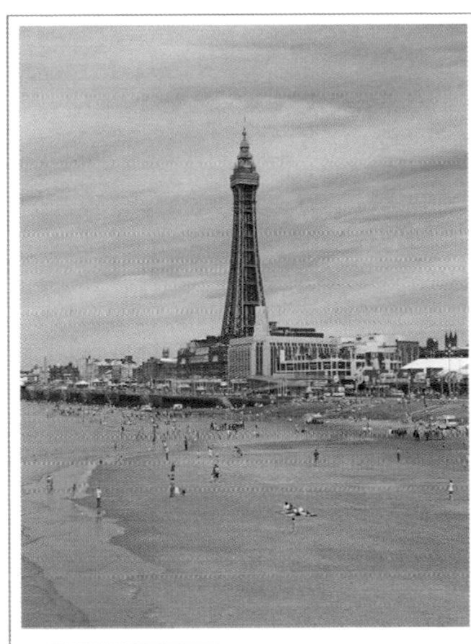

Blackpool Tower

Blackpool Tower

389 C1

The tower was opened in 1894 as the town's very own version of the Eiffel Tower in Paris, and was originally to be called the Blackpool Eiffel Tower. Just 30 years later it was considered for demolition as the steel used in its construction had become corroded, but instead, over a period of three years, the entire structure was replaced and the tower is now one of the town's most well-known attractions. It stands 518ft (158m) tall and is a spot of elegance on Blackpool's crowded seafront. An all-inclusive entry fee gives access to the Tower Circus, the Ballroom, the Aquarium, Jungle Jim's adventure playground and, of course, a trip to the top of the tower. There has been a circus here, between the legs of the tower, since the early days although the shows are now always entirely animal free. The Edwardian Ballroom is home to a mighty Wurlitzer organ on which Latin and old-time dance music is played. Visitors can take to the dance floor themselves or simply participate in high tea whilst others twirl past them. At the top of the tower the Walk of Faith is not for the faint-hearted, as a glass floor allows visitors the chance to look straight down onto the promenade far below.

☎ 01253 622242 www.blackpooltower.co.uk

Blackpool Zoo
241 G4

This 32 acre (13ha) zoo has a collection of over 400 animals including gorillas, lions, tigers and elephants. Gorilla Mountain allows visitors to get up close to the inhabitants and the Swimulator gives the opportunity for visitors to experience the thrill of riding with dolphins without getting wet! There are also keeper talks, animal feeding times, a miniature railway and a Children's Zoo where young children can feed and stroke many domestic animals.

☎ 01253 830830 www.blackpoolzoo.org.uk

Blackwell The Arts & Crafts House
249 F3

In a beautiful position overlooking Lake Windermere, Blackwell was designed by M.H. Baillie Scott between 1897 and 1900 as a holiday home for a wealthy Manchester brewer. It is a wonderful example of the architecture of the Arts and Crafts Movement. Much of the original interior decoration, including stained glass and carved panelling, remains intact and is complemented with furniture, paintings, arts and crafts. Changing exhibitions of historic and contemporary applied arts and crafts are held in upstairs galleries.

☎ 015394 46139 www.blackwell.org.uk

Blue Planet Aquarium
233 F5

Britain's largest aquarium attraction has two floors of exhibits, interactive displays and, for those with diving experience, a chance to swim with sharks. There is sealife on display from all over the world in imaginative displays which re-create varying water environments. Krakatoa has deadly species from the Indo-Pacific swimming amongst submerged temples and statues. The Underwater Safari conveys visitors through the longest (233ft, 71m) underwater viewing tunnel in the world where they are surrounded by sharks and other temperate fish from around the world, as well as 16,000 tons of water! Piranhas, stingrays and electric eels can be seen in the Amazonia display, and children can get their hands on starfish, rays, urchins and sea anemones in the touch pools. The knowledgeable staff are on hand to answer questions and give talks throughout the day. There is a large Caribbean-themed restaurant and a gift shop.

☎ 0151 357 8800 www.blueplanetaquarium.com

Bolton Museum, Art Gallery & Aquarium
234 B2

A good local museum with displays on Egyptology, natural and local history, geology and archaeology. The art gallery has some fine 20th century sculpture and there is a small aquarium with some rare fish species.

☎ 01204 332211 www.boltonmuseums.org.uk

Blue Planet Aquarium

Brantwood
249 E3

Standing on the east side of Coniston Water, with fine views of the lake and mountains beyond, Brantwood was the home of thinker, writer and artist John Ruskin from 1872 – 1900. Originally built in 1797, some rooms are much as Ruskin left them, and contain his art collection, own paintings, furniture, books and personal items. Extensive woodland and themed gardens created by Ruskin surround the house.

☎ 015394 41396 www.brantwood.org.uk

Bridgemere Garden World
221 E3

This huge garden nursery reputedly grows more plants, in more varieties, than anywhere else in Britain, and has over 5000 species on site at any time. 7 acres (3ha) of the nursery have been developed into a series of gardens designed to inspire customers. Many of the gardens are reconstructions of Chelsea Flower Show gold medal winners and range in style from country cottage to modern day patio gardens.

☎ 01270 520381 www.bridgemere.co.uk

Brookside Garden Centre & Miniature Railway
234 D4

This half-mile (1km) circuit makes its way around the garden with authentic signals, signal box and a replica of a West Country station. There are five locomotives in all, three steam and two diesel. The addition of a high level bridge and 65ft (20m) tunnel add to the interest. Passengers sit astride the train in the open and therefore the running of the train is weather dependent.

☎ 01625 872919 www.brookside-miniature-railway.co.uk

Camelot Theme Park
233 G1

The five magical lands at this Arthurian themed park are filled with rides, shows and other attractions which means that there is something here for all the family. The scariest rides are to be found in Land of the Brave, with the spinning roller coaster Whirlwind a popular attraction. King's Realm is filled with rides for all the family and for smaller members there is Merlin's Playland. Young children will also love Squire Bumpkin's Friendly Farm where there are plenty of animals to pat and stroke. Finally, Knight's Valley is the land of the shows – the half-hour jousting tournament is well worth a look.

☎ 01257 453044 www.camelotthemepark.co.uk

Carlisle Castle
393 B2

An imposing Norman fortress with a fascinating and eventful history due in no small part to its proximity to the English and Scottish border. Mary, Queen of Scots was imprisoned here in 1568 after her abdication from the Scottish throne, and the castle also featured in the Wars of the Roses and the Jacobite Rising.

The impressive 12th century keep still stands, as does the inner gatehouse with portcullis known as the Captain's Tower. 'Licking stones' found in a room used as a dungeon are grim testimony to the conditions of those imprisoned here. The King's Own Royal Border Regiment Museum is located within the castle.

☎ 01228 591922 www.english-heritage.org.uk

Carlisle Cathedral
393 B2

Originally founded in 1122, the cathedral today is notable for the large east window which contains some 14th century stained glass, the choir with distinctive 14th century barrel-vaulted blue starry ceiling, a 16th century carved Flemish altarpiece (Brougham Triptych) and medieval carving and paintings. Cathedral and diocesan silver is displayed in the Treasury.

☎ 01228 548151 www.carlislecathedral.org.uk

Cartmel Priory
249 E5

This fine Augustinian priory church, founded in 1188, reflects many periods of ecclesiastical architecture and is still in use today. It contains notable stained glass and carved choir stalls. Also remaining is the original priory gatehouse (National Trust) which is used as the Cartmel Heritage Centre.

☎ 015395 36874 www.nationaltrust.org.uk

Castlerigg Stone Circle
259 F4

Megalithic circle of 38 stones in a beautiful setting surrounded by Lakeland fells. Dating from about 3000 years ago, the circle is 100ft (30m) in diameter and encloses a smaller rectangle of ten stones. The site is thought to have been used as a tribal gathering place, although the precise use is unknown.

www.english-heritage.org.uk

Chester – Eastgate Clock

Chester
394

Chester has a rich history that covers nearly 2000 years. In AD79 the Romans built their largest known fortress here, named Deva after the river Dee. The Dewa Roman Experience and the Grosvenor Museum both have good insights into life in Chester during Roman times. There are various relics of Roman structures scattered around the town, including a partially excavated amphitheatre which would once have held 7000 spectators. Chester has the most complete city walls of anywhere in Britain and it is possible to walk the whole way around, a distance of about 2 miles (3km), although in a number of places the walls are not much higher than the current street height. The centre of Chester has a Tudor look to it with lots of black and white architecture. The four main streets are lined with the Rows, two-storey open galleried half-timbered arcades, some of which are thought to be 700 years old. The most picturesque of these are along Eastgate Street which is also home to the Eastgate Clock, erected to celebrate Queen Victoria's Diamond Jubilee. It is reputedly the most photographed timepiece after Big Ben. Alongside the River Dee are the Groves, a great place for riverside walks, and there are lovely views from one of the many boat trips.

Chester Cathedral 394 B2

There has been Christian worship on the site of the cathedral since the 10th century, when a Benedictine monastery dedicated to St Werburgh was founded. During the 13th century work began on a new church on the site, built in the Gothic style. It was constructed around the original Norman church which was then taken down from the inside. Parts of this Norman building are still in evidence, for example in the refectory which now houses the cafeteria. The Gothic style church took around 250 years to complete and this long history of worship has led to all architectural styles being represented in the building. In 1541, following the dissolution of the monasteries, the church was dedicated as the Cathedral Church of Christ and the Blessed Virgin Mary. Over many years the church became neglected until, in the late 19th century, Sir George Gilbert Scott masterminded a major restoration project. Of particular note are the intricate medieval carvings above the choir stalls featuring dragons, angels and monsters. It was here that Handel first rehearsed 'The Messiah' and a copy of his annotated score is on display. Digital audio tours are available using hands-free equipment. Admission charges have now been introduced.

☎ 01244 324756 www.chestercathedral.org.uk

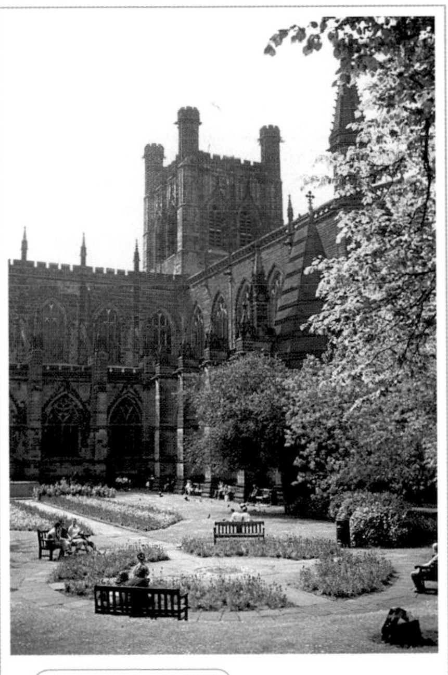
Chester Cathedral

Chester Zoo 233 F5

Without doubt one of the best zoos in Europe, with a well-respected history of conservation work, Chester Zoo is the largest garden zoo in Britain, covering over 110 acres (50ha). Over 7000 animals can be seen, from around 500 different species, at least half of which are rare or endangered and many of which are part of successful breeding programmes. When the zoo was founded by George Mottershead in 1934 he wanted it to be a zoo without bars and he achieved this by creating large enclosures with natural barriers. The 11 miles (17km) of footpath wind their way around the award winning gardens and, if this seems too much to do on foot, hop on the Zoofari overhead railway or the waterbus. The Monkey Islands exhibit is home to the largest colony of chimpanzees in the country and the Twilight Zone bat cave has free-flying bats. There are over 60 species of mammals from tiny harvest mice to the giant Asian elephants, as well as reptiles, birds, fish and amphibians. A series of short, fun and informative talks take place at various enclosures throughout the day and there is a full programme of feeding sessions. Refreshments are readily available and there is a gift shop.

☎ 01244 380280 www.chesterzoo.org.uk

Chester Zoo

Cholmondeley Castle Gardens 220 C2

Romantically landscaped gardens, pretty in any season, are set in the grounds of the Gothic style Cholmondeley Castle (not open to the public). The parkland has an ancient private chapel, rare breeds of animals, including llamas, and lakeside and woodland walks.

☎ 01829 720838

Dalton Castle (NT) 248 C4

A rectangular 14th century tower which houses a local history exhibition.

☎ 01524 701178 www.nationaltrust.org.uk

Dock Museum 241 E1

The museum illustrates Barrow's history from the earliest times with particular emphasis on the 19th century industrial development through iron and steel, then shipbuilding and engineering. There is a collection of ships' models and computer access to the Vickers Photographic Archive of the workings of the Barrow Shipyard. There are also displays of archaeology, geology, natural history, and an art gallery. The museum is in a modern building over a Victorian dry dock.

☎ 01229 894444 www.dockmuseum.org.uk

Dove Cottage 249 E2

Home of the poet William Wordsworth from 1799 – 1808, where he wrote much of his greatest poetry. Home, too, of his sister Dorothy, his wife Mary (whom he married in 1802) and three eldest children. Originally built in the 17th century as an inn, the small two-storey house has oak panelling and Westmoreland slate floors, and is little changed from Wordsworth's day. It also has a delightful cottage garden and orchard.

The adjoining Wordsworth Museum illustrates the life of the poet and his circle with rare books, personal memorabilia, portraits, paintings of Grasmere, and a unique collection of original manuscripts (including a selection of Wordsworth's poems and Dorothy Wordsworth's 'Grasmere Journals').

☎ 015394 35544 www.wordsworthlakes.co.uk

Dunham Massey Hall, Park & Gardens (NT) 368 B4

An early Georgian manor house that was extensively remodelled in the early 20th century, resulting in sumptuous Edwardian interiors. Over 30 rooms are open to the public, including the refurbished kitchen, laundry and servants' quarters. Of particular note is the 18th century walnut furniture, the silver collection of the 2nd Earl of Warrington, and some fine paintings. The house is set in 250 acres (101ha) of wooded deer park with formal avenues of trees, an orangery and a working 17th century mill.

☎ 0161 941 1025 www.nationaltrust.org.uk

Ellesmere Port Boat Museum 233 F5

The canal basin and historic dock where the Shropshire Union Canal meets the River Mersey is home to what claims to be the world's largest collection of traditional canal craft. The museum owns over 5000 items, ranging from large boats to canal company buttons, although not all are on display. Indoors there are exhibits of industrial heritage, waterways objects, working steam machinery and a series of dock workers' cottages re-creating scenes from domestic life between the 1840s and 1950s. Most of the boats on display can be stepped onto to give an insight into life aboard a small narrowboat. There are daily canal boat cruises with live commentary around this once busy port, now redeveloped with craft workshops.

☎ 0151 355 5017 www.boatmuseum.org.uk

Fell Foot Park (NT) 249 E4

Restored 18 acre (8ha) Victorian park on the south shore of Windermere with trails, picnic sites and rowing boats for hire. Well suited to families with children. Lovely displays of daffodils in spring, followed by rhododendrons.

☎ 01539 531273 www.nationaltrust.org.uk

Formby Red Squirrel Reserve (NT) 233 D1

The reserve at Formby is an unspoilt stretch of coastline with miles of walks through pine woods and sand dunes. It is one of the only places left in this country where it is possible to see red squirrels. There is a charge for car parking.

☎ 01704 878591 www.nationaltrust.org.uk

Furness Abbey 248 D5

The extensive red sandstone ruins of this medieval abbey are found in a peaceful setting in a wooded valley. Founded in 1123 by Stephen, later King of England, Furness became one of the richest Cistercian abbeys in England. The visitor centre has some interesting stone carvings from the abbey and an exhibition about the life of the monks.

☎ 01229 823420 www.english-heritage.org.uk

Gawthorpe Hall (NT) 243 E4

Gawthorpe was the home of the Shuttleworth family and there is a fine display of needlework, lace and costume collected by the last family member to live here. Built in 1600, this imposing house was restored in the middle of the 19th century, creating the opulent interiors on display today. There are a number of society portraits, on loan from the National Portrait Gallery, hanging in the long gallery. In summer, there are pleasant walks in the riverside grounds.

☎ 01282 771084 www.nationaltrust.org.uk

Grizedale Forest Park

249 E3

This extensive area of mixed woodland between Coniston Water and Windermere is a centre for recreational activities, including walking and cycling, with picnic areas and around 100 sculptures set within the forest. The visitor centre has a forest exhibition and keeps guide maps for all the waymarked trails. Bike hire is available and there is a high-ropes aerial adventure course.

☎ 01229 860010 www.grizedaleforestpark.co.uk

H.M. Customs & Excise National Museum

380 D9

The museum, located on the ground floor of the Merseyside Maritime Museum, tells the exciting story of the continual battle between smugglers and duty men from 1700 to the present day. See displays of some of the strange seizures made by customs, such as a guitar made from turtle, and learn about the techniques used to combat current day smugglers.

☎ 0151 478 4499 www.customsandexcisemuseum.org.uk

Holker Hall

Hare Hill (NT)

234 C5

This garden is particularly impressive in spring when the rhododendrons and azaleas are in flower. At the heart of the woodland garden is a walled garden with a pergola and wire sculptures.

☎ 01625 584412 www.nationaltrust.org.uk

Harris Museum & Art Gallery

242 B5

Large collections of British paintings, ceramics, glass and costume are displayed in this impressive Greek revival building. The history of the town is brought to life in the Story of Preston Gallery and there is a lively series of contemporary art and social history exhibitions.

☎ 01772 258248 www.visitpreston.com/whats_on/museums/harris/htm

Heaton Hall

369 D1

Heaton Hall is a fine neoclassical country house set in [illegible] acres ([illegible]) of public parkland. Many of the building's original features have been retained, such as the ornate scrolling plasterwork, the classically inspired paintings and the unusual Pompeiian Cupola room. The principal rooms in the house have been restored and furnished to reflect life here as it was in the late 18th and early 19th centuries.

☎ 0161 773 1231 www.manchestergalleries.org.uk

High Cup Nick

260 D5

A dramatic curved rocky basalt cliff at the head of a well-defined V-shaped valley in the North Pennines – an inspiring panorama for the determined walker.

Hill Top (NT)

249 E3

This 17th century farmhouse owned by Beatrix Potter remains virtually unchanged, with furniture and china ornaments just as she left them. Beatrix Potter bought Hill Top in 1905 from the proceeds of the sale of her first books, which included 'The Tale of Peter Rabbit'. Although she did not live here all the time, the house was her inspiration and appears in the pictures and stories in many of her later books. Usually very busy in summer when entrance numbers are controlled.

☎ 015394 36239 www.nationaltrust.org.uk

Holker Hall

249 E5

The Cavendish family stately home originally dates from the 17th century but has many later additions and alterations. The pink sandstone Victorian west wing, open to the public, was rebuilt in Elizabethan style after a fire in 1871. The interior is richly furnished and decorated with ornate plaster ceilings, linenfold panelling, silk wall hangings, marble fire surrounds and a carved oak staircase. Paintings grace the walls and there is a collection of Wedgwood Jasper Ware.

Holker Hall is surrounded by a deer park and 25 acres (10ha) of award-winning formal and woodland gardens, with ornamental ponds and fountains and also a wild flower meadow. Rhododendrons, magnolias and azaleas are spectacular in spring and there is a National Collection of Styracaceae. The Great Holker Lime, probably planted in the early 17th century, has an enormous fluted trunk measuring 26ft (8m) across.

The Lakeland Motor Museum, housed in the former stables, has an extensive collection of transport and motoring memorabilia, and includes a display illustrating the record-breaking speed exploits of the Campbell family. There is a full size replica of Bluebird. A number of special events are held at Holker including an annual garden festival.

☎ 015395 58328 www.holker-hall.co.uk

Hutton-in-the-Forest

260 A4

Home of Lord Inglewood's family since 1605, this 17th century house is built around a medieval pele tower. Altered in the 18th and 19th centuries, Hutton-in-the-Forest now reflects a wide variety of architectural and decorative styles but retains its classical façade. The house contains fine furnishings, paintings and ceramics while the grounds include a walled garden dating from 1730, topiary terraces and a woodland walk.

☎ 017684 84449 www.hutton-in-the-forest.co.uk

Jodrell Bank Observatory & Arboretum

234 B5

Jodrell Bank is a leading radioastronomy facility and the huge attraction is the 200ft (76m) Lovell Radio telescope, the second largest in the world. An observational footpath allows visitors to get up close to the telescope and view it from all angles. There is a small exhibition about the work of the observatory, and a state-of-the-art visitor centre is under construction. The 35 acre (14ha) arboretum has over 2000 species of tree and shrub and there are a number of nature trails to help explore this colourful area.

☎ 01477 57133 www.jb.man.ac.uk

Knowsley Safari Park

367 D1

When the park opened in 1971 it was the first to have drive-through animal enclosures. There are now 5 miles (8km) of roads to drive, which allow visitors to view the wild animals, including lions, elephants, giraffes and buffalo, in natural settings. There is a bypass route for those too wary to take their cars into the baboon enclosure, where the animals can be viewed from a safe distance. The entrance fee also includes admission to Lake Farm, a children's farm, the Reptile House, the information centre and a chance to view the sealion show. There is a small amusement park, for which an additional charge is made.

☎ 0151 430 9009 www.knowsley.com/safari

Lady Lever Art Gallery

366 A3

Set in the garden village created by William Hesketh Lever for the workers at his soap factory, this gallery was founded in 1922 and dedicated to his wife. It has a superb collection of Victorian paintings including Turner and the pre-Raphaelite Rossetti, a large collection of Wedgwood, and a host of memorabilia relating to Lord Leverhulme's fascination with Napoleon.

☎ 0151 478 4136 www.ladyleverartgallery.org.uk

Lake District

248 D2

An inspiration to writers and painters, and a mecca for walkers and climbers, the Lake District is one of the most beautiful parts of Britain. It was glacial action that led to the development of the distinctive landscape of rounded mountain summits with ribbon lakes. The area is designated as a National Park, covering 885 square miles (2292 sq km) and containing over 1800 miles (2897 km) of footpaths. It encompasses England's longest and deepest lakes – Windermere and Wast Water respectively – and England's highest mountain, Scafell Pike.

The variety of scenery is breathtaking. Each of the lakes has an individual character and the mountains are broken up by crags, ridges, tarns and streams. Sheep farming has long been the agricultural heritage of the area and the fells are sheep cropped and dotted with small farms and dry stone walls. Picturesque villages and vibrant market towns complete the picture.

With unprecedented access to the countryside, walking and climbing are the most popular leisure activities but there are countless opportunities and facilities for cycling, boating, angling and other outdoor pursuits. Museums, heritage centres, historic houses and gardens, family attractions and the many literary associations of the area, most notably with Wordsworth, are also a draw to visitors. The Lake District can be very busy in the summer, Windermere in particular being a hive of activity, but the National Park and other organisations work hard to maintain the balance between preserving the unique natural beauty of the area and catering for the many visitors.

Lake District Visitor Centre at Brockhole

249 E2

Interactive exhibitions and special events are designed to give visitors of all ages an insight into the Lake District National Park and how the unique landscape is cared for. The centre is housed in a late 19th country house set within 30 acres (12ha) of landscaped gardens on the shores of Windermere.

Visitors are encouraged to enjoy the grounds and there are lakeside walks, an adventure playground and cruises on the lake.

☎ 015394 46601 www.lake-district.gov.uk

Lakeside & Haverthwaite Railway 249 E4

Three and a half miles (6km) of track with steep gradients running through the scenic Leven Valley from Haverthwaite to Lakeside at the south end of Windermere. Both steam and diesel locomotives are in service with a daily timetable operating between April and October.

☎ 01539 31594

Lancaster City Museum 242 A1

Based in a grand Georgian former town hall built in 1873, this museum illustrates the city's history, from Neolithic times to the present day.

☎ 01524 64637 www.lancaster.gov.uk/council/museums

Leighton Hall 249 F5

This neogothic mansion is home to the furniture-making Gillow family, and is set in 1550 acres (627ha) of landscaped parkland. The hall has early and rare examples of Gillow furniture, fine paintings, a 19th century walled garden, and a small collection of birds of prey which fly daily. The hall is open to the public from May to September.

☎ 01524 734474 www.leightonhall.co.uk

Levens Hall 249 F4

An imposing grey stone Elizabethan mansion built round a large square medieval pele tower which has been lived in by the Bagot family for centuries and is still a family home. The house has fine ceiling plasterwork, oak panelling, carved oak chimney pieces, embossed leather wall coverings and notably contains a collection of Jacobean furniture and some early English patchwork.

It is for the yew topiary gardens, however, that Levens is world-renowned. The gardens were designed around 1694 by a Frenchman, Guillaume Beaumont, who had previously laid out the gardens at Hampton Court. Beaumont's original design at Levens remains unchanged today. A huge number and variety of shapes have been clipped out of the common and golden yew and there are also impressive box and beech hedges. Each year it takes from August to December for all the hedges to be clipped. The hedging provides a wonderful backdrop to seasonal bedding and herbaceous borders. Levens also has parkland with a herd of fallow deer, and a working steam engine collection.

☎ 015395 60321 www.levenshall.co.uk

Levens Hall – Topiary Gardens

Little Moreton Hall (NT) 221 F2

Arguably Britain's finest timber-framed manor house, which has an exterior virtually unchanged since it was built in 1580. The interior is unfurnished but the wainscotted long gallery, cobbled courtyard and 17th century knot garden are well worth a look.

☎ 01260 272018 www.nationaltrust.org.uk

Liverpool Cathedral  380 J11

Nothing about this cathedral has been done on a small scale. It is the largest Anglican cathedral in Europe and the fifth largest cathedral in the world. It has the largest working organ with over 9700 pipes, the highest and heaviest church bells, and the highest Gothic arches ever built. This neogothic structure looks much older than it really is – it was only completed in 1978, 74 years after it was designed by Giles Gilbert Scott. It is well worth a climb up the tower, two consecutive lifts followed by 108 steps, as there are panoramic views over Liverpool and towards the Welsh Hills. Part of the way up the tower is the Elizabeth Hoare Embroidery Gallery where there is a sumptuous display of Victorian and Edwardian ecclesiastical embroidery. The gallery also gives fine views over the interior of the cathedral from some 100ft (30m) above the floor level. Although entrance to the cathedral is free, visitors are requested to make a donation towards the running costs of this beautiful building. There is a charge for climbing the tower, and for viewing the embroidery display.

☎ 0151 702 7217 www.liverpoolcathedral.org.uk

Liverpool Museum  380 G5

This museum has hugely varied collections of exhibits covering just about every imaginable topic – from Egyptian tombs, to the night sky, via the Amazonian rainforests. There are fascinating exhibits on dinosaurs, the natural and physical sciences, an award winning hands-on Natural History exhibition, a Space and Time gallery. The Planetarium (there is a small fee) has half-hour shows including the solar system, space exploration and stunning images from the Hubble telescope. Besides the permanent displays, there is an ever-changing programme of special events and attractions.

☎ 0151 478 4399 www.liverpoolmuseum.org.uk

Lake District – Tarn Hows

Lowry, The 368 C2

This shimmering building of metal and glass at the redeveloped Salford Quays houses the largest public collection of works by L.S. Lowry. There are some 350 paintings and drawings on display, including many of his well-known industrial scenes with their stylised matchstick men, as well as his lesser-known mountain and seascapes. There are changing exhibitions, combining works from the collection with those borrowed from other institutions, and private collections as well as paintings, sculptures and photographs by other local artists. ArtWorks is an interactive exhibition designed to encourage the creativity of visitors. There are also two theatres which offer a variety of performances including ballet, drama, opera and comedy. On a warm day it is possible to sit on the quayside with refreshments from one of the cafés or bars.

☎ 0161 876 2000
☎ 0870 787 5780 www.thelowry.com

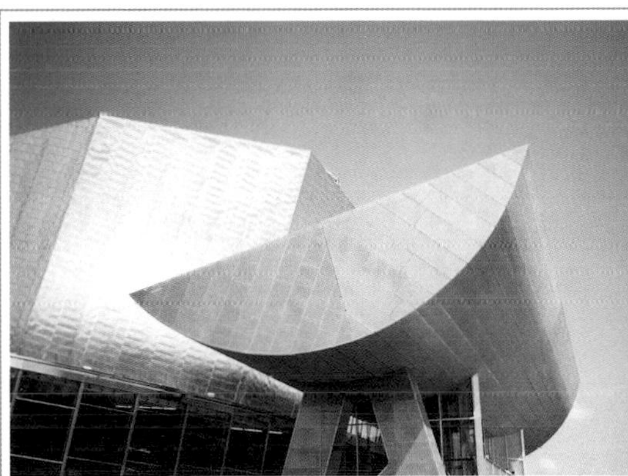

The Lowry

Lyme Park (NT) 235 D4

This country estate covers nearly 1400 acres (567ha) of wild moorland and parkland which are home to red and fallow deer. The property at its centre combines Elizabethan, Georgian and Regency architecture, together with an Italianate interior. The state rooms have Mortlake tapestries, Grinling Gibbons wood carvings and a fine collection of English clocks. Back outside, the hall is surrounded by 17 acres (7ha) of Victorian gardens boasting a flowering sunken garden, Jekyll-style herbaceous borders and a reflection lake. The house featured as Pemberley in the BBC's adaptation of Jane Austen's 'Pride and Prejudice'.

☎ 01663 762023 www.nationaltrust.org.uk

Manchester Art Gallery  383 K7

There are over 2000 items on display in this city centre gallery. The collection is particularly known for its 19th century British paintings and includes works by some of the great pre-Raphaelites. There is also an exceptional collection of decorative art and craft work, from ancient Greek pottery to contemporary furniture. The Manchester Gallery houses work from local artists, including Lowry, and the Interactive Gallery aims to open children's minds to art. Audio tours of the collection are available.

☎ 0161 235 8888 www.manchestergalleries.org.uk

Martin Mere 233 F1

This Wildfowl and Wetland Trust site teems with wild geese, swans, ducks and flamingos, and is a year-round attraction. In the landscaped waterfowl gardens it is possible to feed some of the world's rarest and most endangered species of bird by hand. The visitor centre is excellent and explains the need for conserving the wetlands as well as hosting exhibitions and special events.

☎ 01704 895181 www.wwt.org.uk

Mersey Ferries 380 B8

One of the best ways to see Liverpool's landmark Liver building is from the equally famous Mersey Ferry. As well as the regular commuter ferry for Birkenhead and Wallasey, there is a 50-minute river explorer cruise which incorporates a lively commentary on the history of Liverpool and Europe's oldest ferry.

☎ 0151 330 1444 www.merseyferries.co.uk

Merseyside Maritime Museum 380 D9

This huge museum in Liverpool's Albert Dock is the second largest of its kind in the country and tells the story of one of the world's greatest ports. There are a number of fascinating exhibitions including one that explores the role of Liverpool in the transatlantic slave trade and another, the Emigrant Gallery, that allows the visitor to share in the experiences of those who left Liverpool for the New World. There are numerous objects associated with nautical archaeology, maritime paintings, ships' models, and galleries about the Titanic and the Lusitania. During the summer it may be possible to board one of the preserved ships in the dock outside.

☎ 0151 478 4499 www.merseysidemaritimemuseum.org.uk

Mirehouse 259 F4

In a wonderful setting near to Bassenthwaite Lake and beneath Skiddaw, this 17th century house is still used as a family home. Wordsworth, Tennyson, Carlyle and Southey all visited Mirehouse and some of their letters are on display, together with a collection of Francis Bacon manuscripts. In front of the house is a wild flower meadow, there are adventure playgrounds in the woods, an orchard with regional fruit varieties, a bee garden and lakeside walk. The house has limited opening but the grounds are open daily from April to October.

☎ 017687 72287 www.mirehouse.com

Muncaster Castle 248 C3

Situated in a remote part of Cumbria, Muncaster is a 19th century castle incorporating parts of earlier buildings including the medieval pele tower. It has been in the same family since the 13th century and is said to be haunted. The elegant rooms, including the Great Hall and Octagonal Library, display a great number of treasures collected over the centuries.

There are 77 acres (31ha) of gardens and woodland to explore with walks overlooking Eskdale. In late spring there are carpets of bluebells and many species of rhododendrons in flower. An Owl Centre in the grounds houses owls, buzzards, kestrels and red kites, and is the headquarters of the World Owl Trust. The centre has flying displays and video footage from cameras placed in nesting boxes.

☎ 01229 717614 www.muncaster.co.uk

Museum of Liverpool Life 380 C9

This museum celebrates Liverpool's people, their culture, achievements and contribution to life in this country over the last century. A varied range of displays looks at all aspects of Liverpool life. The City Soldiers gallery tells the story of the King's Regiment, the River Room concentrates on life around the Mersey, and the Mersey Culture section looks at popular music, home-grown soap operas, football and the Grand National.

☎ 0151 478 4080 www.museumofliverpoollife.org.uk

Museum of Science & Industry 382 F8

An impressive museum that provides enough entertainment for a whole day out. It is based in the buildings of the world's oldest passenger railway station. George Stephenson's Rocket arrived here in 1830 on its inaugural journey from Liverpool. There are 13 galleries in all; there is a reconstruction of a Victorian sewer with all the appropriate smells, a Power Hall which has huge working engines and locomotives, and a hands-on science centre called Xperiment, all of which help to bring the industrial and scientific past to life. The newest gallery looks at the contribution that Manchester scientists past and present have made to the modern world, as well as featuring some recent developments such as odourless socks!

☎ 0161 832 2244 www.msim.org.uk

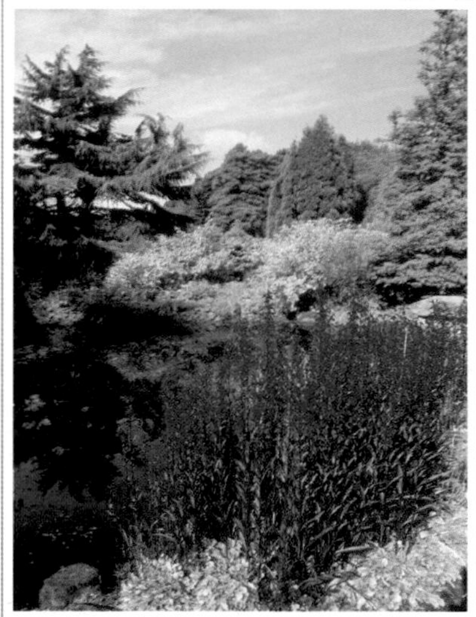

Ness Botanic Gardens

Ness Botanic Gardens 233 E5

Ness Botanic Gardens were founded by the Liverpool cotton merchant Arthur Kilpin Bulley in 1898. Bulley was interested in introducing new plant species from abroad, and in particular he believed that Himalayan and Chinese mountain plants would grow well in this country. When Bulley died the garden was gifted to the University of Liverpool who has since maintained and developed the gardens with an emphasis on research, conservation and education. There are now 62 acres (25ha) of gardens, greenhouses and experimental grounds, with an extensive collection of specimen trees and shrubs which include many rhododendrons and azaleas. There are also renowned rock, rose, heather and water gardens. The gardens have a number of interest trails, a visitor centre, gift shop, tearoom and children's play areas.

☎ 0151 353 0123 www.nessgardens.org.uk

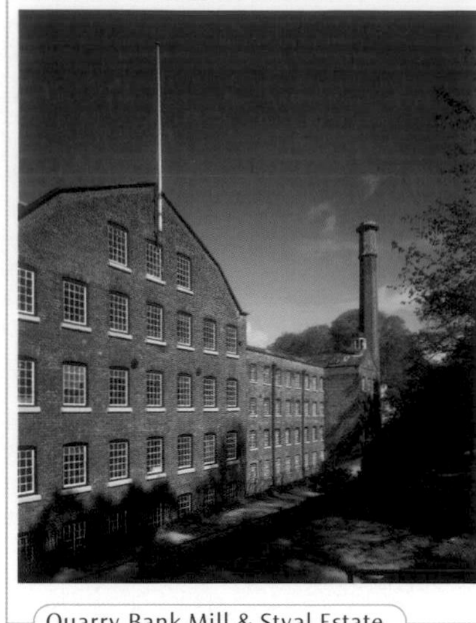

Quarry Bank Mill & Styal Estate

Nether Alderley Mill (NT) 234 C5

This restored 15th century water mill has working Victorian machinery and is powered by overshot (the water flows over the wheel rather than under it) tandem wheels. Flour grinding demonstrations occasionally take place, water supplies permitting.

☎ 01625 584412 www.nationaltrust.org.uk

Ordsall Hall 369 D2

A fine black and white half-timbered manor house in the incongruous surroundings of Salford city centre. There is a fully restored and furnished Great Hall, a bedroom and Tudor kitchen to be explored, as well as a chance of spotting The White Lady, Ordsall Hall's ghost. Closed on Saturdays.

☎ 0161 872 0251 www.salford.gov.uk/ordsallhall

Pleasureland Amusement Park 233 E1

Originally opened in 1920 with just a helter skelter and a roller coaster, Pleasureland has now expanded to have over 100 rides and attractions. There are a few big white-knuckle rides such as the Traumatizer, a suspended coaster, and Space Shot which launches riders 120ft (37m) into the air, as well as more traditional roller coasters, a log-flume and ghost train. There is also an area with rides especially for young children. Admission to the park is free although the rides themselves are not. Visitors can purchase a wristband which will give unlimited rides all day.

☎ 08702 200204 www.pleasureland.uk.com

Quarry Bank Mill & Styal Estate (NT) 234 C4

Situated in 384 acres (155ha) of the beautiful countryside of Styal Country Estate, this museum is a fantastic place to learn about the social and industrial history of this country. Quarry Bank Mill is a fully preserved and working example of a Georgian cotton mill powered by the largest working water wheel in Europe. Cotton is still spun and woven here and is available for sale in the shop. Inside the mill there are hands-on displays, demonstrations from hand spinning to large-scale factory weaving, and an 1840s steam-powered beam engine which is worked daily. The Apprentice House was built in 1790 to house pauper children who worked at the mill. The conditions in which these children lived and worked is now brought to life with the aid of enthusiastic guides in period costume who engage visitors in conversation and discussion. Visitors are encouraged to ask questions, test the straw filled beds, touch all the objects in the house and pump water from the well in the yard. Styal village was a tiny hamlet before the mill arrived but by 1840 it was a thriving village with most of its inhabitants working at the mill. It claims to be the least altered factory colony in this country with well-preserved workers' cottages, chapel, school and shop, and the whole village has an idyllic rural atmosphere. The estate land around the village and mill has some wonderful riverside and woodland walks.

☎ 01625 527468 www.quarrybankmill.org.uk

Railway Age, The — 221 E2

A wide range of electric, steam and miniature locomotives, a model railway and an impressive collection of signalling equipment.

☎ 01270 212130 www.therailwayage.co.uk

Ravenglass & Eskdale Railway — 248 B3

A narrow-gauge railway running 7 miles (11km) from the coast at Ravenglass to Dalegarth Station near Boot in Eskdale, with a journey time of around 40 minutes. Small steam locomotives pull passengers through spectacular scenery with the Scafell range of mountains in view for much of the time. There is a choice of open and covered carriages, and the service is often used by walkers and cyclists to get into the heart of Lakeland. 'La'al Ratty', the water vole mascot for the railway, keeps children amused, sometimes acting as guard, train driver or stationmaster. The railway was first opened in 1875 to transport iron ore, and at Ravenglass Station there are displays of memorabilia and photographs illustrating the line's history.

☎ 01229 717171 www.ravenglass-railway.co.uk

Ravenglass & Eskdale Railway

Rheged – the Village in the Hill — 260 A5

A vast purpose-built family attraction named after Cumbria's Celtic Kingdom of Rheged and designed to blend in with the landscape. It is built into a disused limestone quarry and has a grass covered roof, the largest in Europe. Although the building covers 85,000 square feet (719 sq m) on five different levels, the glass atriums and windows provide ample light and spectacular views. A stream runs through the building and there are small lakes outside.

Apart from the unique construction, the main draw is a giant cinema screen the size of six double-decker buses. Spectacular epic films are shown each day including features on Cumbrian myths and legends, the Lakeland landscape, the underwater world, and the ascent of Everest.

Rheged is also home to the National Mountaineering Exhibition which celebrates Britain's mountaineering heritage. Exhibits include clothing, equipment, photographs and film. Additionally, there is a children's indoor play area, local food, craft and gift shops, restaurant, art exhibitions and a full programme of special events. Free car parking and entry to the building.

☎ 01768 868000 www.rheged.com

Ribchester Roman Fort & Museum — 242 C4

This museum is built on the site of a Roman fort occupied from AD78 and is dedicated to the history of Bremetenacum Veteranorum, the Roman name for Ribchester. There are some interactive exhibits, Roman replicas like the Ribchester Parade Helmet, and collections of weaponry, jewellery, coins and pottery. The external remains of the Roman granary can also be seen by visitors.

☎ 01254 878261 www.ribchestermuseum.org

Rydal Mount — 249 E2

Little has changed at Rydal Mount since William Wordsworth lived here with his family from 1813 until his death in 1850. The house was originally a 16th century farm cottage but was made much larger in the 18th century. Furnished as it would have been in Wordsworth's day, the house has some of his poetry, personal possessions and family portraits on display.

The extensive picturesque terraced gardens were designed by Wordsworth and there are wonderful views of Rydal Water, Windermere and the surrounding fells. Rydal Mount was beloved by all Wordsworth's family and was a source of inspiration to the poet.

☎ 015394 33002 www.wordsworthlakes.co.uk

Salford Museum & Art Gallery — 382 B4

Lark Hill Place is a re-created Victorian shopping street with original shop fronts and authentic period rooms. LifeTimes focuses on real people and events to tell the story of Salford over the last 200 years. The Victorian Gallery has a permanent collection of paintings and sculpture, and hosts temporary exhibitions of work by local and national artists.

☎ 0161 736 2649 www.salford.gov.uk/leisure/museums/salfordmuseum.htm

Salt Museum — 234 A5

Cheshire has been a large producer of salt for over 2000 years. It is the only place in Britain where it is still produced on a large scale, and this interesting museum at Northwich explains the vital importance of salt to human life, as well as describing the production process.

☎ 01606 41331 www.saltmuseum.org.uk

Silk Museum & Paradise Mill — 234 D5

Macclesfield was one of Britain's main silk spinning and weaving centres during the late 18th and early 19th centuries. Paradise Mill is now an award winning museum where knowledgeable guides, many of them former silk workers, take visitors around the restored jacquard handlooms and demonstrate the intricate processes involved in silk work. The Silk Museum, housed in what was once the Macclesfield School of Art, has displays on the properties of silk, the textile industry and the social history of the area.

☎ 01625 612045 www.silk-macclesfield.org

Sizergh Castle & Gardens (NT) — 249 F4

Originally built in the 14th century by the Strickland family, who still live here, the massive fortified tower developed into a manor house with the addition of a Great Hall in the 15th century and two long wings during the Elizabethan period. There are some remarkable oak-panelled rooms, most notably the bedroom known as the Inlaid Chamber, and fine Elizabethan carved wooden chimneypieces. The house contents include period oak furniture, family portraits, china and Jacobite relics.

Sizergh has an impressive limestone rock garden with a large collection of hardy ferns, a Dutch garden with flowering cherries and a rose garden underplanted with bulbs. Specimen trees and shrubs provide wonderful autumn colour. Extensive walks with views of the Lakeland fells and Morecambe Bay are to be enjoyed in the 1600 acre (638ha) estate.

☎ 015395 60070 www.nationaltrust.org.uk

South Lakes Wild Animal Park — 248 D5

Opened in 1994, this is now a major conservation zoo park. Animals from many parts of the world are kept in mixed groups in natural surroundings, and others are free to roam the park. Among around 100 species of animals are kangaroos, bears, rhinos, giraffes, antelope, lemurs, cheetahs, lions, primates and rare Amur and Sumatran tigers. Animal hands-on sessions are held with the zoo keepers providing a wealth of information. Feeding sessions include the spectacle of the tigers climbing tall poles for their meat, a device designed to exercise their muscles. A miniature railway operates in summer.

The park takes part in coordinated breeding programmes and works to conserve natural habitats all over the world to save endangered species. It is also home of the Sumatran Tiger Trust which works in Sumatra to protect the remaining wild tigers.

☎ 01229 466086 www.wildanimalpark.co.uk

South Tynedale Railway — 260 D3

This is England's highest narrow-gauge railway. Restored steam and diesel locomotives run for over two miles (3km) from the station at Alston through the beautiful South Tyne valley to Kirkhaugh in the North Pennines. The return journey takes 50 minutes but passengers may spend time at Kirkhaugh and return on a later train.

☎ 01434 381696 www.strps.org.uk

Stagshaw Garden (NT) — 249 E2

A hillside woodland garden overlooking Windermere with rhododendrons, azaleas and camellias. A beck runs through the garden with several small waterfalls. Open April to June only, at other times by appointment

☎ 015394 46027 www.nationaltrust.org.uk

Stapeley Water Gardens & Palms Tropical Oasis — 221 D2

Stapeley is the country's largest and best regarded water garden centre, with hundreds of water plants displayed, and for sale, in pools. The water lilies are particularly impressive between June and September. The Palms Tropical Oasis, for which there is a fee, has palm trees, parrots, reptiles, monkeys and creepy-crawlies in heated glasshouses.

☎ 01270 623868 www.stapeleywatergardens.com

Tabley House 234 B5

This is the only 18th century Palladian house in the north west. The son of the original owner was the first patron of British art and built up quite a collection of paintings, including works by Turner and Reynolds, many of which are still on display in the locations they were originally intended for. The house is also home to a collection of fine furniture, including pieces by Gillow and Chippendale.

☎ 01565 750151 www.tableyhouse.co.uk

Tate Liverpool 380 C9

Home to the national collection of modern art in the north of England, Tate Liverpool has four floors of contemporary art. There are exhibitions of art from the Tate Collection and special exhibitions of work from other public and private collections, including some from overseas. There are free talks and guided tours daily. There is a charge for some special exhibitions.

☎ 0151 702 7400 www.tate.org.uk

Tatton Park (NT) 234 B4

This is one of the most complete historic estates open to visitors, and there is plenty here to occupy for a whole day. There are two historic houses, 1000 acres (400ha) of parkland containing some magnificent gardens, and a working farm. The opulent mansion was built at the end of the 18th century and gives a wonderful glimpse into how the original owners, the Egerton family, lived. The state and family rooms still contain many of the original furnishings, contents and paintings, including two Canalettos. The fully restored servants' quarters are a stark contrast. The second house is the Tudor Old Hall – downstairs paints a realistic picture of medieval life, whilst upstairs the rooms are styled as they would have been in the early 1600s. The final room of the tour is a re-creation of an estate worker's cottage from 1958. The gardens, perhaps the best feature of the estate, are extensive and incorporate many different styles. There is a walled garden, a beech maze, a fernery, an Italianate garden and one of the finest examples of a Japanese garden in Europe. Home Farm is always popular with children, especially when the piglets are just being born, and the adjacent fields have sheep, cattle and chickens. The farm works as it did during the 1930s, with vintage farm implements and rare breeds of animal. All of this is set in open parkland where herds of fallow deer roam freely.

☎ 01625 534400 www.tattonpark.org.uk

Tegg's Nose Country Park 234 D5

Tegg's Nose is a distinctive hill with open heather moorland, meadows and woodland. A series of well-marked footpaths take visitors to some tremendous views over the Cheshire countryside towards North Wales. There is an excellent visitor centre.

☎ 01625 914279 www.cheshire.gov.uk/countryside/outandabout/teggs_nose_country_park

Tullie House 393 B2

With collections of archaeology, history, wildlife, geology and fine and decorative arts, this modern museum has many hands-on and audiovisual exhibits, and provides interest and entertainment for all ages. The troubled history of the Borders area, from prehistory through to medieval times and beyond, is illustrated with the use of sight, sound and smell in the 'Border Galleries'. The growth of Carlisle as a main railway centre is featured and there are changing contemporary art exhibitions. Tullie House, the Jacobean House which gave the museum its name, stands within the grounds.

☎ 01228 534781 www.tulliehouse.co.uk

Ullswater Steamers 259 G5

Three traditional Victorian vessels cruise the eight miles (13km) of Ullswater all year round. Steamer services started on the lake in 1859 and a passenger service has continued ever since, although the ships are now oil powered. Ullswater is unspoilt, and from the lake there are dramatic views of Helvellyn, England's second highest mountain. Passengers may travel between any of the piers at Glenridding, Howtown and Pooley Bridge or buy a round trip ticket.

☎ 017684 82229 www.ullswater-steamers.co.uk

Walker, The 380 G5

This gallery houses one of the country's finest collections of artwork outside London. There is European art from the 14th century right up to the present day, including works by Rembrandt, Poussin and Degas. The speciality of this gallery however is British art, including a major collection of Victorian paintings and pre-Raphaelite work. 20th century art is represented by Cezanne, Monet, Lucien Freud and David Hockney, whilst two temporary exhibition galleries show contemporary work.

☎ 0151 478 4199 www.thewalker.org.uk

Walton Hall Gardens 367 F3

A heritage centre in the gardens tells the story of the Walton Estate, of Lewis Carroll and his connections with Walton Hall (not open to the public) and the local natural history. There are ornamental gardens, spacious lawns, picnic areas, a children's zoo and woodland trails, as well as a number of waymarked trails from the gardens leading out into the surrounding countryside.

☎ 01925 601617 www.warrington.gov.uk/entertainment/parks/walton

Whinlatter Forest 259 E4

An upland forest park with waymarked trails through the forest, routes to the top of the surrounding fells, a permanent orienteering course, adventure playground and picnic areas. The first trees were planted here in 1919 and the Forestry Commission Visitor Centre at the top of Whinlatter Pass has displays about the forest. From May to September there are CCTV pictures at the visitor centre of osprey chicks being reared in local nests. Viewpoints throughout the park afford spectacular vistas of the Lake District and across to Scotland.

☎ 017689 78469 www.whinlatterforestpark.co.uk

Whitworth Art Gallery 369 D2

The Whitworth is home to a collection of British watercolours, including paintings by Turner, modern art and sculpture, and the largest collection of textiles and wallpapers outside of the Victoria and Albert Museum in London. The works are grouped and displayed in themes which change once or twice a year.

☎ 0161 275 7450 www.whitworth.man.ac.uk

Windermere Lake Cruises 249 E3

Traditional and modern launches carry over a million passengers each year between Waterhead (Ambleside), Bowness and Lakeside on Windermere. The oldest boat in the fleet is *The Tern*, a railway steamer built in 1891. Daily services operate all year and circular cruises of the lake, the longest in England, or shorter sightseeing trips are available. Traditional rowing boats and self-drive motor boats may also be hired.

☎ 015395 31188 www.windermere-lakecruises.co.uk

Windermere Steamboat Museum 249 F3

A fascinating collection of historic steam and motor boats moored in a covered wet dock, with launch trips if the weather is fair. Among the vintage boats is the steam launch *Dolly*, reputedly the oldest mechanically powered boat in the world, built around 1850 and restored to her former glory after spending 67 years on the bed of Ullswater. Among other attractions at the museum are model boats and a model boats pond, 'Swallows and Amazons' exhibition, Beatrix Potter's rowing boat, and displays about how Windermere has been used for transport since Roman times.

☎ 015394 45565 www.steamboat.co.uk

World of Beatrix Potter Attraction 249 F3

The 'Tales of Beatrix Potter' are brought to life in an amazingly detailed re-creation of the scenes inhabited by her characters using sounds, music, lighting effects and even smells. Of great appeal to children and all lovers of Beatrix Potter's books.

☎ 015394 88444 www.hop-skip-jump.com

Tatton Park

NORTH EAST ENGLAND

The evocative ruin of Hadrian's Wall stretches like a ribbon across this remotely beautiful border country. Yet, in stark contrast to the armed conflicts of the past the industrial revolution brought a different type of struggle to the area. Coal, steel, railways and shipbuilding helped create dozens of 'boom' settlements. Over the years these have mellowed into towns and cities of real character bustling with residents who are genuinely proud of their heritage and unrivalled in their hospitality.

Hadrian's Wall

Alnwick Castle & Garden 279 F5

Just to the north of Alnwick town centre and rising impressively above the River Aln, the castle has been home to the Percys, ancestral family of the Duke of Northumberland, since 1309. It is the second largest lived-in castle in England (after Windsor).

The exterior view of this austere and striking medieval fortress, with its life-size stone figures standing guard on the battlements, is in stark contrast to the sumptuous state rooms furnished in Italian Renaissance style. Adam ceilings and fireplaces are the legacy of restoration by the first Duke of Northumberland in the 18th century and there are fine paintings and porcelain.

The Regimental Museum of the Northumberland Fusiliers is housed in the Abbots Tower. Archaeological exhibits, the Percy coach, dungeon, gun terrace and landscaped grounds by Capability Brown are among other attractions. Often used as a film location, scenes from the 'Harry Potter' films have been filmed at the castle.

The Alnwick Garden (separate charge) is a project underway to transform the former 18th century sloping walled garden into a modern, innovative garden and notably features The Grand Cascade.

☎ 01665 511350 www.alnwickcastle.com www.alnwickgarden.co.uk

Alnwick Castle & Gardens

Arbeia Roman Fort & Museum 372 D1

In a commanding position at the mouth of the River Tyne, the Roman stone fort of Arbeia was the supply base for Hadrian's Wall. Reconstructed buildings, including the impressive West Gate, and a varied display of archaeological finds from weapons to jewellery, present a picture of life on the northern frontier of Roman Britain. Archaeologists may be seen at work on excavations and children will enjoy Time Quest, for which there is a charge, an opportunity to find out what it is like to be an archaeologist.

☎ 0191 456 1369

Auckland Castle 262 B4

The official residence of the Bishop of Durham, dating back over 800 years, with state rooms and the magnificent 12th century St Peter's Chapel. Limited opening. Unusual 18th century Deer House in adjoining parkland.

☎ 01388 601627 www.auckland-castle.co.uk

BALTIC The Centre for Contemporary Art 404 F3

Opened in 2002, the Baltic is housed in the former grain warehouse of a 1950s flour mill. It is a vast and imposing building close to the Tyne Bridge on the south bank of the river. There is no permanent collection but a changing programme of exhibitions displayed in five galleries with facilities to cater for all art media. Envisaged as an 'Art Factory', there are artists' studios and work is created through commissions and by the work of artists-in-residence. The centre has a rooftop restaurant with excellent views of Tyneside.

☎ 0191 478 1810 www.balticmill.com

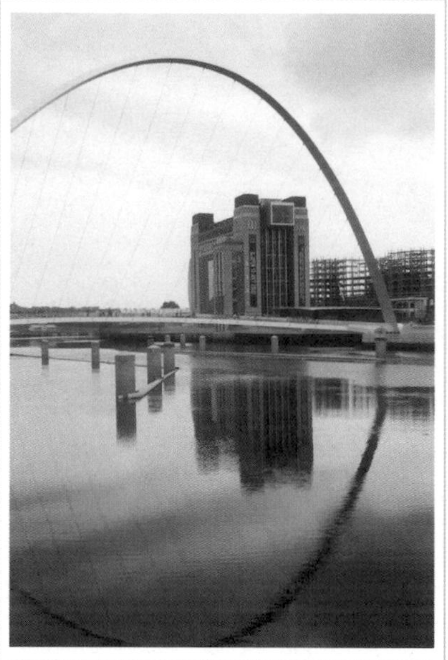

BALTIC The Centre for Contemporary Art

Bamburgh Castle 279 F3

Formidable Norman castle dominating the seaside village of Bamburgh, much restored in the 18th and 19th centuries but still retaining the original large square keep. The castle is stunningly situated on a rocky outcrop above a long white sandy beach with views seawards of the Farne Islands and Holy Island.

Bamburgh withstood many sieges but fell into disrepair after sustaining severe damage during the Wars of the Roses in 1464. The first Lord Armstrong, inventor, engineer and industrialist, carried out major restoration and refurbishment in the 19th century, and Bamburgh is still the home of the Armstrong family today.

Paintings, furniture, tapestries, china and glassware are displayed in the fine King's Hall and Cross Hall. The old laundry building houses an Aviation Artefact Museum with many parts from crashed World War II aircraft, while the Armstrong Museum portrays the life of the first Lord Armstrong through his work as an engineer. There is an impressive collection of armour and a dungeon.

☎ 01668 214515 www.bamburghcastle.com

Beamish, North of England Open Air Museum 262 B2

Celebrating the industrial, rural and social heritage of the north-east, Beamish shows how people lived and worked in the 1800s and early 1900s. A town, colliery village and railway station have been re-created with many authentic buildings being dismantled elsewhere and brought to the site. Staff in period costume are a wealth of information.

Visitors may go shopping in the town shops, and there is also a bank, dentist and newspaper office in the main street. Guided tours of the drift mine take visitors underground. The colliery village includes tiny pit cottages, a chapel and a school where playing with traditional toys in the playground is a popular activity. Cheese is made on a working farm, nearby is a manor house and, by way of contrast, there is a Victorian fairground.

Trams link the various areas, and replica buses and horse-drawn vehicles provide other means of transport. Covering over 300 acres (120ha), Beamish provides a full day out for all the family. Winner of both British and European Museum of the Year awards.

☎ 0191 370 4000 www.beamish.org.uk

Bede's World 372 C2

Dedicated to the 8th century monk, the Venerable Bede, who chronicled the ecclesiastical history of the time, this is an absorbing day out for all the family. Bede's World incorporates the monastic site of St Paul's, a museum, an Anglo-Saxon demonstration farm and herb garden. Many fascinating archaeological finds are displayed in the interactive exhibition which explores early medieval life and Christian heritage.

☎ 0191 489 2106 www.bedesworld.co.uk

Belsay Hall, Castle & Gardens 270 C4

30 acres (12ha) of picturesque landscaped gardens surround 19th century neo-classical Belsay Hall and a ruined Jacobean manor house with 14th century tower house. All were owned by the Middleton family for 600 years. Notable for a quarry garden, rhododendrons and many exotic species of plants. A winter garden ensures Belsay is worth a visit in any season.

☎ 01661 881636 www.english-heritage.org.uk

Bamburgh Castle

Beamish, North of England Open Air Museum

Brinkburn Priory
270 D2

The Augustinian priory of Brinkburn, founded around 1135, is set amongst woodland beside the River Coquet. On a fine day the priory grounds are a lovely place for a picnic. Restored in the 19th century, the church of the original monastery survives intact and contains some striking wooden contemporary sculptures by Fenwick Lawson. Venue for the Brinkburn Music Summer Festival. Standing nearby is a Gothic style manor house.

☎ 01665 570628 www.english-heritage.org.uk

Captain Cook Birthplace Museum
253 E1

Learn about the life of Captain James Cook and his voyages of exploration in this interesting hands-on museum that will appeal to adults and children alike. Located in the landscaped grounds of Stewart Park, close to where Cook was born.

☎ 01642 311211

Cragside (NT)
270 C1

Aptly named, the Victorian home of the first Lord Armstrong is built on a crag surrounded by rock gardens. Contains many original contents and fascinating gadgets invented by Armstrong. In the 1880s Cragside enjoyed central heating, hot and cold running water and, most remarkably, was lit by hydro-electricity using the man-made lakes in the grounds. Well-known for rhododendrons in late spring, the extensive and varied landscaped woodland estate can be explored by car or on foot.

☎ 01669 620333 www.nationaltrust.org.uk

Dunstanburgh Castle (NT)
279 G4

Extensive and dramatic ruins of a 14th century castle on headland cliffs. Reached by coastal footpath from Craster or Embleton.

☎ 01665 576231 www.english-heritage.org.uk/ www.nationaltrust.org.uk

Durham Cathedral

Durham Cathedral
396 E2

Dominating the Durham city skyline, this awe-inspiring cathedral, with three massive towers, stands high above and in an almost complete loop of the River Wear. The present cathedral was largely built between 1093 and 1133 and is considered to be the greatest piece of Romanesque architecture in Britain. The nave, however, has pointed arches which makes it unique for this period.

The cathedral contains the tomb of Cuthbert, 7th century Bishop of Lindisfarne, and of the Venerable Bede who wrote about the life of St Cuthbert. Exhibitions tell the story of the cathedral and how it was built and 'The Treasures' in the 13th century undercroft displays St Cuthbert's cross and fragments of his coffin. The medieval Monk's Dormitory has a wonderful hammer-beam oak roof and houses part of the cathedral library. Visitors may climb the 325 steps of the tower.

Together with Durham Castle (built 1072), which is now part of the university, the cathedral is designated a World Heritage Site.

☎ 0191 386 4266 www.durhamcathedral.co.uk

George Stephenson's Birthplace (NT)
262 A1

A small 18th century stone tenement where railway engineer George Stephenson was born in 1781. Typical of those built for mining families at that time, with whole families living in just one room, it is furnished as it may have been in Stephenson's day.

☎ 01661 843276 www.nationaltrust.org.uk

Hadrian's Wall 261 G1

The wall is a well preserved and impressive Roman frontier fortification, built between AD122-128 on the orders of Emperor Hadrian at the height of the Roman Empire. It extends 73 miles (118km) from Bowness-on-Solway to Wallsend. No doubt intended as a symbol of Roman power, it was used to control trade and the movement of people in the region. It is now a designated World Heritage Site.

The original height of the wall was around 15ft (5m) and was bounded on the north by a defensive ditch and on the south by a ditch between turf ramparts. It included turret watch towers, milecastles and forts. The wall is all the more dramatic for much of it being built on ridges and crags and set amidst beautiful countryside. Numerous car parks on the B6318 give walkers access to the paths alongside the wall.

At the east end of the wall is Segedunum, the remains of a fort once holding a garrison of 600 soldiers, and now an award-winning museum. It includes a reconstructed section of wall and Roman baths, while nearby is 88yds (80m) of original wall.

www.hadrians-wall.org www.english-heritage.org.uk

Hamsterley Forest 261 G5

A beautiful area of mixed woodland between Weardale and Teesdale, extending over 5000 acres (2000ha) with waymarked walks, horse riding trails and cycle routes. The Visitor Centre is the starting point of a 4 mile (6.5km) forest drive (toll charge).

☎ 01434 220242

Hancock Museum 404 D2

A small natural history museum with a wealth of exhibits, live animals and interactive displays showing how the planet and the animal and plant kingdoms evolved. A great place for children to visit, the Hancock also features the 'Land of the Pharaohs' gallery with two Egyptian mummies and a varied programme of touring exhibitions.

☎ 0191 222 6765

Hartlepool Historic Ships 263 E4

The lively Historic Quay is a reproduction of an 18th century seaport complete with shops, houses and a quayside littered with barrels, carts, anchors and ropes. Exhibitions in the quayside buildings give visitors a taste of seafaring at the time of Nelson, and there is an interactive children's maritime adventure centre. Staff in period costume add to the atmosphere.

Afloat in the dock is the restored *HMS Trincomalee*, a frigate built in 1817 by the East India Dock Company at Bombay (separate entry fee). Moored outside the nearby Museum of Hartlepool (free) is the paddle steamer *PSS Wingfield*, a former Humber ferry.

☎ 01429 860077

High Force 261 E5

Spectacular 70ft (21m) waterfall, said to be England's largest, in upper Teesdale. Reached by a pretty woodland walk.

Holy Island 279 F2

Holy Island is accessible by a causeway passable at low tide and is set within the Lindisfarne National Nature Reserve. Founded in the 7th century by St Aidan, the monastery at Lindisfarne became an important centre of Christian learning and the beautiful illuminated Lindisfarne Gospels were written here.

The ruined 12th century Benedictine priory has a rainbow arch still standing over the nave, and the museum contains notable Anglo-Saxon carvings and illustrates how the monks lived.

With stones taken from the priory, the formidable looking Lindisfarne Castle was built in the 16th century to protect the island from the Scots. Converted into a private home in 1903 by architect Edwin Lutyens, the castle contains a fine collection of early 17th century oak furniture and has a small walled garden designed by Gertrude Jekyll. Also on the island is a Heritage Centre and St Aidan's Winery, where Lindisfarne Mead is made. Entry to the island is free but there are charges for the attractions.

☎ Priory: 01289 389200 www.english-heritage.org.uk
☎ Castle: 01289 389244 www.nationaltrust.org.uk
☎ Heritage Centre: 01289 389044 www.lindisfarne-heritage-centre.org

Housesteads (Vercovicium) (NT) 261 D1

The best-preserved Roman fort in Britain, Housesteads was one of sixteen bases along Hadrian's Wall. Built around AD124 to house 800 infantry soldiers, it was in use until the end of the Roman occupation of Britain in the early 5th century. The fort contains the headquarters building, commander's house, barracks, hospital, latrines and granaries. There is a site museum.

☎ 01434 344363 www.english-heritage.org.uk www.nationaltrust.org.uk

Howick Hall Gardens 279 G5

This was once the home of British Prime Minister Earl Grey, for whom the tea was blended to suit the water at Howick. Surrounding the 18th century house (not open) there are terraces, herbaceous borders and notably a woodland garden planted with rhododendrons, azaleas, camellias and magnolias. Lovely displays of snowdrops in February are followed by other spring bulbs. From the garden a path leads to a sandy cove at Howick Haven.

☎ 01665 577285 www.howickgarden.org.uk

Hadrian's Wall, Housesteads

Kielder Forest — 269 E2

In the remotest part of the Northumberland National Park, close to the Scottish border, Kielder Forest covers an area of 153,000 acres (62,000ha) with mainly Sitka spruce. There is estimated to be 150 million trees in the forest. Timber production is ongoing and an increasing diversity of trees is being planted. The forest is home to deer, red squirrels and many birds of prey, and surrounds Kielder Water, the largest man-made lake in Europe. Ideal for walking, cycling, boating and fishing, the area has three visitor centres and numerous tourist facilities. Sculpture trails and public art are also among the attractions in the Kielder area.

☎ 01434 220643 www.kielder.org

Laing Art Gallery — 404 E2

Internationally renowned watercolours hang in a dedicated gallery and the extensive collection of oil paintings include works by John Martin, Joshua Reynolds, Thomas Gainsborough, Holman Hunt, Burne Jones and a growing number of contemporary paintings. With the emphasis on locally produced decorative art, the Laing also has collections of silver, glass and ceramics. 'Art on Tyneside' illustrates the history of the region's art and craft traditions and there is a gallery specifically aimed at young children.

☎ 0191 232 7734

Life Science Centre — 404 F1

Interactive and entertaining educational centre which illustrates some of the mysteries of life. In innovative ways, such as a motion simulator ride and a sound and light show in a theatre modelled as a brain, the centre takes a look at evolution, the basics of DNA, what all living things have in common and what goes on in the human mind. Housed in a striking modern building next to Newcastle main line rail station.

☎ 0191 243 8223 www.lifesciencecentre.org.uk

National Glass Centre — 411 A3

An innovative metal and glass building on the north bank of the River Wear, dedicated to the use of glass in the fields of design and technology, and as contemporary art. Exhibitions and interactive galleries look at the centuries-old tradition of glassmaking in Sunderland, and illustrate the many and surprising ways in which glass is used today. Visitors may walk along the glass roof and watch students from the University of Sunderland in the glass factory. Master craftspeople also give regular demonstrations of glassmaking.

☎ 0191 515 5555 www.nationalglasscentre.com

Ormesby Hall (NT) — 253 E1

Set in an attractive garden, this 18th century Palladian mansion has some notable interior plasterwork and carved wood decoration. There is an impressive stable block still in use and a restored Victorian laundry and kitchen with scullery and game larder. Also of interest is a model railway exhibition.

☎ 01642 324188 www.nationaltrust.org.uk

Queen Elizabeth II Country Park — 271 E3

Once the site of one of the largest colliery spoil heaps in Europe, this landscaped country park features maturing woodland, a 40 acre (16ha) lake and a variety of wildlife. Ideal for picnics and walks. A cycle path runs around the lake where canoeing, windsurfing and fishing are popular. The Woodhorn Colliery Museum, on the edge of the park, is housed in former colliery buildings, and a narrow gauge railway runs for 0.6 miles (1km) linking the museum to the lakeside.

☎ 01670 856968

Raby Castle — 262 A5

An impressive medieval castle set in a 200 acre (80ha) deer park, Raby was built by the Nevills and has been home to Lord Barnard's family for over 350 years. The interior chambers provide many historical insights and range from the Barons' Hall, where 700 knights gathered to plot the 'Rising of the North', to the medieval kitchen which was used until 1954. Many of the rooms date from the 18th and 19th centuries and contain works of art and fine furniture. Visitors can also enjoy the grounds which include a large walled garden, rose garden and old yew hedges.

☎ 01833 660202 www.rabycastle.com

Seaton Delaval Hall — 271 F4

A splendid Palladian mansion designed by Sir John Vanbrugh in 1718, after he had already completed Blenheim Palace and Castle Howard. The central turreted block has a grand portico and is flanked by two substantial wings which creates a vast forecourt. A fine parterre, pond and fountain created in the 20th century complements the house and there are impressive stables in the east wing. Limited opening.

☎ 0191 237 1493

Shipley Art Gallery — 372 A2

An arts and crafts museum with a renowned collection of contemporary furniture, textiles, metalwork, ceramics, glass and jewellery. By way of contrast, there are some old masters paintings and an exhibition illustrating the history of Gateshead.

☎ 0191 477 1495

South Shields Museum & Art Gallery — 372 D1

This museum brings to life the 20th century social history of South Tyneside and illustrates the dramatic changes which have taken place during that time. Also features the story of popular novelist Catherine Cookson who was born locally in 1906 and whose writing reflects the life and times of the area. Alongside the museum's art collection, the interactive art gallery gives visitors the opportunity to explore the techniques and materials used by artists.

☎ 0191 456 8740

Teesdale Hay Meadows, Forest-in-Teesdale — 261 E5

The rich grasslands of the North Pennines provide a wonderful display in summer when the hay meadows are awash with a striking variety and abundance of tall grasses. Additionally, a vast assortment of wild flowers, including wood anemone, frog orchid, adder's tongue fern and ragged robin will be found blossoming amongst the grasses. The area also attracts nesting farmland birds such as redshank, skylark and meadow pipit.

Vindolanda (Chesterholm) Roman Fort — 261 D1

The remains of a Roman fort (AD127) and surrounding civilian settlement about 2 miles (3km) south of Hadrian's Wall. There are ongoing excavations and archaeologists have revealed a succession of forts on the site. The well-preserved artefacts in the museum include armour, boots, shoes, jewellery and coins. Among the most significant finds have been letters and documents written in ink on wood; photographs of these tablets are on display. A section of Hadrian's Wall has been reconstructed in timber and stone to its original height and there are full-scale replicas of a Roman temple, shop, house and a Northumbrian croft.

☎ 01434 344277 www.vindolanda.com

Wallington (NT) — 270 C3

Built in 1688, Wallington was for generations home to the Blackett and Trevelyan families. The house contains fine rococo plasterwork and the central hall is decorated in Pre-Raphaelite style with pictures reflecting Northumbrian history. There are paintings and porcelain as well as a collection of dolls' houses. The extensive grounds include a beautiful walled garden and Edwardian conservatory, woodland and a path along the banks of the River Wansbeck.

☎ 01670 773600 www.nationaltrust.org.uk

Warkworth Castle — 271 E1

Standing on a hill above the River Coquet, the well-preserved ruins dominate the town of Warkworth. The castle was once home to the powerful Percy family and was the setting for several scenes in Shakespeare's 'Henry IV'. Dating mainly from the 12th to the 14th centuries, the remains include a magnificent eight-towered keep, chapel, great hall and decorated lion tower. Special events for visitors are regularly staged here.

☎ 01665 711423 www.english-heritage.org.uk

Wildfowl & Wetlands Trust Washington — 372 C3

Many species of waterbirds can be enjoyed in any season in this area of ponds and woodland. It provides a stopping place and wintering habitat for migratory birds after their flight across the North Sea. Large numbers of curlew and redshank roost here and there is a breeding colony of heron. The site is easily accessible with well laid out paths. It has hides and an excellent visitor centre.

☎ 0191 416 5454

Yeavering Bell — 278 D4

This hill at the edge of the Cheviots is crowned by the largest Iron Age hillfort in Northumbria covering 14 acres (6ha) with a stone rampart enclosing much of the summit. A steep path leads to the top, from where there are spectacular views over the surrounding landscape.

WALES

Dwelling in the "Land of Song", the Welsh nation treasures a proud culture based on Europe's oldest language which is still very much alive today. Three sides of the predominantly rural principality are fringed with beckoning shorelines. Sparkling water tumbles down the rugged mountainsides into beautiful lakes which act as mirrors for the stunning scenery and ever changing sky. Experience the grandeur and wildness of three national parks with all their varied natural glory and absorb the Welsh history glimpsed in her castles, crafts and Celtic heritage.

Llynnau Mymbyr and Snowdon

Aberconwy House (NT) 231 F5

A 14th century merchant's house within the town of Conwy containing furnished rooms and an audiovisual presentation. Displays depict scenes of daily life from nearly six centuries.

☎ 01492 592246 www.nationaltrust.org.uk

Aberdulais Falls (NT) 350 D1

Natural waterfalls in the Vale of Neath provide the energy for a fascinating industrial site with a unique hydroelectric scheme. Over four centuries, a waterwheel provided the power for the production of copper and tin goods. Today the Turbine House contains an interactive computer, fish pass, display panels and an observation window with good views of the falls.

☎ 01639 636674 www.nationaltrust.org.uk

Aberglasney Gardens 192 B5

Restored in recent years to reveal Jacobean origins, the 10 acres (4ha) of colourful gardens lie in a valley east of Carmarthen. Known as 'The Garden Lost in Time', the area features pools, a yew tunnel, walled gardens, an ancient cloister garden and woodland, as well as collections of rare plants.

☎ 01558 668998 www.aberglasney.org.uk

Abergwesyn Pass 193 E2

A scenic, remote 14 mile (22km) drive crosses the Cambrian Mountains following an old drovers' route. The lower forests give way to high, deserted moorland providing a taste of wild Wales.

Afan Argoed Country Park 179 E3

Deep in the Afan valley, inland from Port Talbot, the Forest Park covers 25 tranquil square miles (10 ha) with trails for walking and cycling, orienteering, picnic areas, camping, pony trekking and educational visits. The visitor centre features the history and wildlife of the area, including historical remains from early settlements and the South Wales Miners' Museum created by ex-colliers. Charge for car parking in summer.

☎ 01639 850564 www.neath-porttalbot.gov.uk

Anglesey Sea Zoo 217 D1

A varied collection of local marine life is housed in Wales' largest marine aquarium, on the shores of the Menai Strait. The Sea Zoo has a walk-through shipwreck, lobster hatchery and discovery pools, as well as a shark pool and fish forest. Tropical displays are also included and conservation is an important aspect of the work of the zoo. Outside is an adventure playground, boating lake and seasonal crab fishing.

☎ 01248 430411 www.angleseyseazoo.co.uk

Barry Island Pleasure Park 165 E1

Occupying a promontory south of Cardiff, the Park has over 50 rides and attractions including the popular Log Flume, Viper Rollercoaster, Sea Ray Pirate Ship and Galloping Horses. The Park is surrounded by shops and catering facilities.

☎ 01446 732844 www.barryisland.com

Beaumaris Castle 231 E5

The castle sits in the town of Beaumaris, on the shores of the Menai Strait, and offers fine views across to the mountains of Snowdonia. This was the last and largest of King Edward's edifices, erected to establish his authority over the Welsh. Beaumaris Castle was started in 1295 and, although never fully completed, it remains remarkably intact and is a designated UNESCO World Heritage Site.

Here is an impressive example of military architecture, having an outer moat and perfectly symmetrical double concentric walls within. The fortified dock has moorings for ships of considerable size. The high walls, gatehouses and strong towers were intended as stout defences, but the castle never came under attack. The inner buildings accommodated a Great Hall, luxurious rooms, kitchens, stables and a chapel. Visitors can also explore the fascinating interior passageways found inside the walls of the inner ward.

☎ 01248 810361 www.cadw.wales.gov.uk

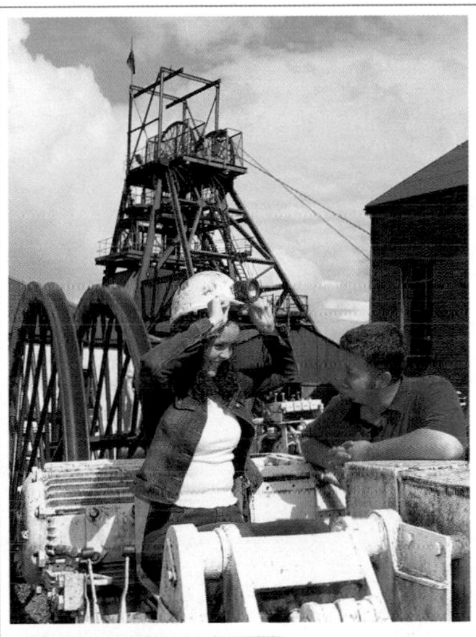

Big Pit Mining Museum

Big Pit Mining Museum 180 B2

Overlooking a traditional mining valley at Blaenavon, Big Pit had been a working coal mine for over 200 years until its closure in 1980. The present tour guides are all former miners. On the surface are colliery workings, reconstructed buildings and the old pit-head baths to explore, but the main attraction is the 300ft (90m) descent in the pit cage; hard hat and lamp are provided. The hour-long guided tour recalls life at the coal face and leads through underground roadways, air doors and stables to the shafts and coal faces. Warm clothing and appropriate footwear are advised and restrictions apply to young children going underground. The whole experience merits two to three hours and catering is supplied by the original miners' canteen. Education packs are available and special events are arranged throughout the season.

☎ 01495 790311 www.nmgw.ac.uk/bigpit

Beaumaris Castle

Bodnant Gardens (NT) 231 G5

Renowned for the dazzling springtime and early summer blooms, these 80 acres (32.5ha) of magnificent gardens overlook the river Conwy and distant Snowdonia. An array of colours is provided, especially by the collections of rhododendrons, camellias and magnolias and a vibrant laburnum arch. The garden has been developed over its hundred year history by generations of the Aberconway family and includes a succession of terraces featuring a water lily pond, roses, a croquet lawn, a canal and magnolias. A woodland valley garden, known as The Dell, provides an attractive contrast to the formal plantings of the Italianate terraces.

At the end of the formal garden sits the Pin Mill, an early 18th century lodge which became a pin factory, then a tannery, before being transported from the west of England to its present site.

The botanical collections nurtured at Bodnant are world famous, but beauties also abound which require little knowledge of plants. The gardens are planted on a hillside and run right down to the river.

☎ 01492 650460 www.nationaltrust.org.uk

Bodnant Gardens

Brecon Beacons 193 G5

Four distinct upland ranges lie within the beautiful national park which extends over 520 sq m (837 sq km) in the heart of southern Wales. The picturesque landscape is characterised not only by gentle, grassy hillsides and light woodlands, but also by steep craggy mountains. Central are the prominent Beacons themselves, rising to 2906ft (886m) at the summit of Pen-y-Fan. In the west are the rolling hills of Fforest Fawr with their deep valleys and ancient hunting forest and also the solitary, wild Black Mountain. The range known as the Black Mountains lies at the eastern edge of the park towards the English border. The most southerly region offers a landscape of caves and waterfalls amongst the limestone pavements.

Prehistoric sites have been identified within the park and later structures follow the progress of history through the ambitious days of castle building after the Norman conquest.

Within its five visitor centres, the park authorities promote a large variety of attractions for all ages, including museums, theatres and family activity centres. In the open air are a wealth of opportunities for walking, cycling, horse-riding, caving, gliding, watersports, golf and fishing. Expert tuition is available for trying new skills and there are facilities for hiring and purchasing appropriate equipment.

☎ 01874 624437 www.breconbeacons.org

Brecon Beacons

Brecon Beacons Visitor Centre 193 F5

At an altitude of 1100ft (335m), amidst the grandeur of the Brecon Beacon mountains, the purpose-built centre houses resource material, souvenirs, a model and displays of the area, as well as a café. The centre is surrounded by open hillside, giving wide views across the valley to the distinctive summit of Pen y Fan, the highest peak in South Wales. Informative staff and printed guides describe local points of interest and suggest a fine variety of walks, graded from easy to moderate.

☎ 01874 623366 www.breconbeacons.org

Brecon Mountain Railway 179 G1

This narrow-gauge railway, starting at Pant Station just north of Merthyr Tydfil, follows a scenic 3.5 mile (5km) track into the Brecon Beacon mountains. The all-weather observation coaches are hauled by a vintage steam locomotive; the return journey takes just over an hour. Panoramic views abound from the end station where there are many opportunities for walks and a picnic site. Special events are organised at certain times of year and the train can be hired for parties.

☎ 01685 722988 www.breconmountainrailway.co.uk

Cadair Idris 204 C1

Steeped in Celtic legends, the beautiful 11 mile (17km) ridge of Cadair Idris, on the southern flank of the Snowdonia National Park, comprises five peaks, with the highest point, Penygadair, at almost 3000ft (900m). A variety of tracks, varying in difficulty, lead to the ridge, and all give breathtaking views of the surrounding countryside and the distant coast.

Caerleon Roman Fortress, Baths & Amphitheatre 351 D1

North of Newport stand the substantial remains of a Roman fortress, including the baths, barrack blocks, fortress wall and 5000-seater amphitheatre, together with an imaginative Roman legionary museum. This is the site of the significant 50 acre (20ha) Roman fortress of Isca, encompassing a complete town dating from AD75, with much still on view. The museum shows how the Romans lived and fought, with interactive displays and special events suitable for all ages, sufficient for several hours' visit.

☎ 01633 423134 www.nmgw.ac.uk

Caernarfon Castle 217 D1

Built on a promontory projecting out into the Menai Strait, this UNESCO World Heritage Site castle dominates the town of Caernarfon and has survived in fine condition. Construction was started by Edward I in 1283 as part of his ring of castles intended to control Welsh uprisings, and it was planned as a royal residence and seat of government. The building was completed by Edward II in 1322. Massive walls run between the 11 great polygonal towers, topped by battlemented wall walks, giving the castle formidable defences. Also incorporated into the scheme were drawbridges, heavy doors and six portcullises. Each of the towers is different and one included a water gate enabling supplies to be brought by sea.

The Queen's Tower houses the regimental museum of the Royal Welch Fusiliers. An audiovisual presentation explains the history and customs associated with the castle. Continuing a tradition established by Edward I, the castle is the venue for the investiture of the Prince of Wales, as was the scene in 1969 when Prince Charles was presented to the people here.

☎ 01286 677617 www.cadw.wales.gov.uk

Caernarfon Castle

Caerphilly Castle 351 A1

Right in the town centre, Caerphilly is the largest castle in Wales, but was never a royal residence. It was built by Red Gilbert de Clare to defend the territory of Henry III against Welsh Prince Llywelyn the Last. The medieval fortress, started in 1268, occupies a strategically important 30 acre (12ha) site, having a complex design of massive gatehouses, water defences and stout concentric walls. The most unusual feature of the castle is one of the towers which leans outwards at an angle ten degrees from vertical – the result of subsidence.

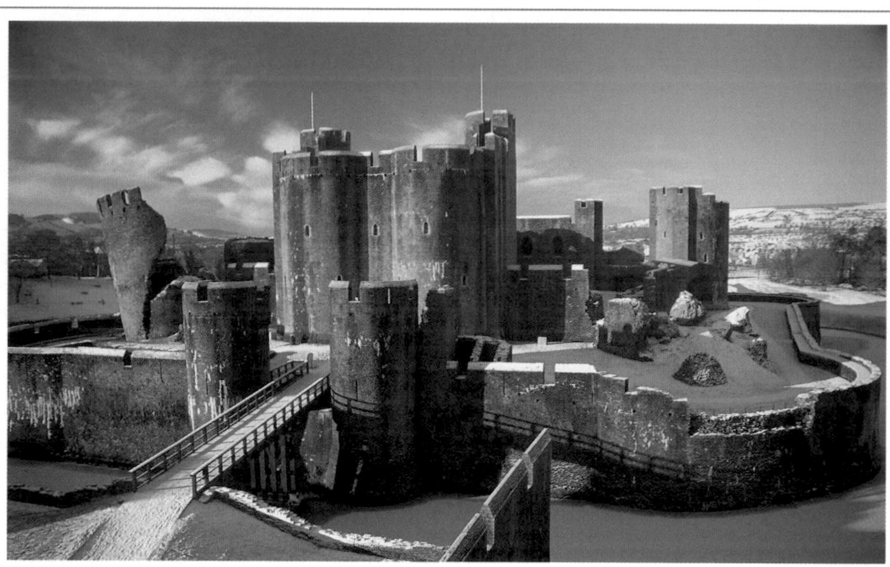

Caerphilly Castle

An extensive water system provided the first point of defence around the castle, followed by a rectangular enclosure with robust outer and inner walls. The latter contain two great gatehouses and the remains of the hall. In the heart of the castle are the living areas, together with kitchens, a chapel and domestic quarters.

Over the past 200 years the complex has undergone much restoration. Visitors can watch an audiovisual display and see replica siege engines in the visitor centre.

☎ 029 2088 3143 www.cadw.wales.gov.uk

Cardiff Castle & Museum 392 E2

The castle is situated in the heart of the city and was commissioned in Victorian times by the 3rd

Marquess of Bute in an elaborate neogothic style. Highly decorative, fantasy adornments abound, particularly in the clock tower, fountains and lavish interiors. The Welsh Regiment Museum is situated within the castle grounds.

☎ 029 2087 8100 www.cardiffcastle.com

Carew Castle 176 D2

The substantial ruins of Carew Castle stand on river meadows between the village and an ancient tidal mill. The castle was built between the 13th and 16th centuries and was the site of the Great Tournament of 1507. Firstly a Norman stronghold, then an elegant royal Elizabethan residence, it displays many fine architectural features. A circular walk links the castle, mill, causeway, millpond, 11th century Celtic cross and medieval bridge.

☎ 01646 651782 www.carewcastle.com

Carreg Cennen Castle 178 C1

These old ruins, high on a crag near Trapp in the Black Mountains, were rebuilt in the 13th and 19th centuries. Visitors can explore prehistoric caves, battlements and vaulted passageways, and enjoy the outlook from the grassy hilltop.

☎ 01558 822291 www.cadw.wales.gov.uk

Castell Dinas Bran (Ruins) 219 F3

Both a hillfort and medieval castle, the ruins stand high above Llangollen. It is reputedly the final hiding place of the Holy Grail, a treasured Christian relic. Access is by public footpath taking some 20 minutes each way.

☎ 01938 553670

Celtica 204 D3

This multimedia presentation focusing on the Celts is housed in Y Plas, a 17th century mansion just outside Machynlleth. The lively experience provides information on the heritage and culture of the Celts by way of an hour-long audio tour through eight themed galleries. Topics range from culture and beliefs to life as a tribe member, and are located within areas described, for example, as the Vortex, the Foundry, the Roundhouse and The Forest.

☎ 01654 702702 www.celticawales.com

Centre For Alternative Technology 205 D2

Situated in the hills north of Machynlleth, the Centre for Alternative Technology has been operating for over 25 years by a charity raising awareness of environmental concerns in daily living. The gardens and visitor centre provide information on renewable energy, environmental building, energy efficiency and organic cultivation in a captivating and educational way. Seven acres (3ha) of the site are on public display and can be accessed in summer by a water-balanced cliff railway. Attractions and resources are suitable for all ages.

☎ 01654 702400 www.cat.org.uk

Ceredigion Museum 204 B4

A restored Edwardian theatre is home to this museum of local history from the Stone Age to modern times. Displays include items of archaeology, folk life, agriculture, crafts, industry and art.

☎ 01970 633088 www.ceredigion.gov.uk

Chepstow Castle 181 E3

Strategically set overlooking a Wye Valley gorge, Chepstow was one of the first stone castles to be built in Britain. Construction was commenced in 1068 as a stronghold for the Norman conquest of south-east Wales and is unusual in having no early timber base. Over successive centuries the defences were enlarged and in the 12th century the impressive edifice was divided into four separate, connecting sections. Towering over the present-day entrance is the gatehouse containing a prison in one of its round towers. Further additions included a second hall, tower, gatehouse and comfortable living quarters with well-equipped kitchens and storerooms.

The castle came under siege twice during the Civil War and now visitors can see exhibitions on the history of its construction. Life-sized models of the medieval lords who occupied the castle, and a dramatic Civil War battle scene illustrate the changing role of Chepstow Castle through the Middle Ages. Outdoor evening theatre is often performed here in summer.

☎ 01291 624065 www.cadw.wales.gov.uk

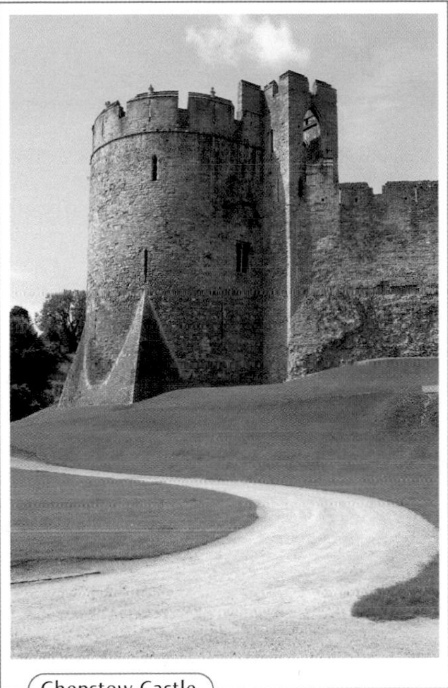

Chepstow Castle

Chepstow Museum 181 E3

An elegant town house has been transformed into a museum describing the town's colourful history in imaginative settings. Displays and artistic interpretations show the development of Chepstow as a fortified stronghold and busy port.

☎ 01291 625981 www.chepstow.co.uk

Chirk Castle (NT) 219 F4

The castle, to the west of Chirk, still has the original 14th century high walls and drum towers and has been continuously occupied for over 400 years. The state rooms contain fine items of furniture, tapestries and portraits. The formal gardens adjoining the castle contain superb yews, roses and climbing plants, whilst further away lie a hawk house, rock garden and shrub garden with pool. Parkland surrounds the estate and particularly noteworthy are the wrought iron entrance gates.

☎ 01691 777701 www.nationaltrust.org.uk

Colby Woodland Garden (NT) 177 E2

The garden is set in 8 acres (3ha) of beautiful woodland in a sheltered valley leading to the south Pembrokeshire coast at Amroth. The colourful bluebells, rhododendrons and azaleas are at their best in late spring, but at other times plants also feature around a themed sculpture trail, a walled kitchen garden and a Gothic-style gazebo.

☎ 01834 811885 www.nationaltrust.org.uk

Conwy Castle 231 F5

Occupying an imposing location over the river in the centre of Conwy town, the castle is one of the most important examples of military architecture in Europe. It was built for Edward I in 1283-9 by 1500 craftsmen, with supplies brought in by sea. Eight huge drum towers with pinnacled battlements dominate the two wards of the castle. The large outer ward was accessed from the town, whereas the inner ward, with the royal apartments, was approached only by water. The Middle Gate connected the two sections. The building remains in an excellent state of preservation, despite having suffered attacks during the Civil War and later.

An exhibition portrays Edward I and his campaign of castle building. The panoramic views from the top of the turrets stretch to the distant mountains and out across the sea, but the castle itself is best viewed from the far side of the estuary.

☎ 01492 592358 www.cadw.wales.gov.uk

Cosmeston Country Park 165 E1

Old quarries just west of Cardiff have been transformed into a 200 acre (81ha) landscaped park, featuring two lakes with watersports, facilities for children, orienteering courses, a forest school, bridleways, a sculpture trail and a maths trail. Woodland, grassland and wetlands support conservation areas. Within the park lies a 14th century reconstructed medieval village which hosts special events throughout the year and which can be toured on payment of an entrance charge.

☎ 029 2070 1678 www.valeofglamorgan.gov.uk

Criccieth Castle 217 E4

Overlooking Tremadog Bay, the ruins include the inner wall, impressive gatehouse and original wall walk dating from the 13th century. A cartoon video shows the story of Gerald of Wales and other Welsh princes.

☎ 01766 52227 www.cadw.wales.gov.uk

Conwy Castle

Denbigh Castle
219 D1

The ruins of this Norman fortification overlook Denbigh town. It retains a large gatehouse, three towers, a steep barbican and an ancient, weathered statue, probably of Edward I.

☎ 01745 813385 www.cadw.wales.gov.uk

Erddig

Dinefwr Park (NT)
192 C5

Pleasant walks cross this wooded parkland just outside Llandeilo. Deer have been a feature of the estate for over one thousand years and Lancelot 'Capability' Brown designed the landscape around a medieval castle and Newton House.

☎ 01558 823902 www.nationaltrust.org.uk

Dolaucothi Gold Mine (NT)
192 C3

At Pumsaint, in deepest Wales, the Romans discovered gold deposits in the river Cothi and evidence remains of their sophisticated and ingenious tunnels, aqueducts and caverns. A second gold rush followed in the late nineteenth century and now visitors, equipped with miners' lamps and helmets, can tour the workings, hear the history and try gold panning for themselves. Waymarked paths lead through the surrounding wooded hillsides.

☎ 01558 825146 www.nationaltrust.org.uk

Elan Valley Visitor Centre
 192 F1

Four artificial lakes were created in the valley in the early 20th century to provide water for Birmingham. The Visitor Centre is approached from Rhayader and contains an exhibition and interactive resources on the history and nature of the area, renowned for its birdlife. Walks lead around the reservoirs in the peaceful Cambrian mountains, giving good vantage points of the dams and drowned valleys. The area is particularly attractive in autumn.

☎ 01597 810880 www.elanvalley.org.uk

Electric Mountain
217 E1

A fascinating view inside the Dinorwig hydroelectric station near Llanberis includes interactive exhibitions and art galleries. Visitors can book an underground minibus tour deep inside the mountain to see the enormous turbines in action. The natural science theatre offers a presentation on the natural history of the Snowdonia area.

☎ 01286 870636 www.electricmountain.co.uk

Erddig (NT)
220 A3

Dating from the 18th century, this impressive estate near Wrexham was the home of the Yorke family, whose generosity towards their staff can be appreciated by viewing the large house. The grand 'upstairs' state rooms boast fine collections of furniture and original artefacts, whilst 'below stairs' the servants' quarters give fascinating glimpses into the lives of the workers. An extensive range of outbuildings are also of considerable interest and include a display of vintage vehicles in the stable yard. There is much to attract all ages, and regular event days are planned throughout the season, including horse-drawn carriage rides.

Walks lead through the garden areas into a large park with woodland. The gardens feature an array of speciality fruit trees, the national collection of ivies, a Victorian parterre and yew walks.

As most rooms have no electric lighting, it is advisable to visit on bright days to fully appreciate the pictures and textiles.

☎ 01978 315151 www.nationaltrust.org.uk

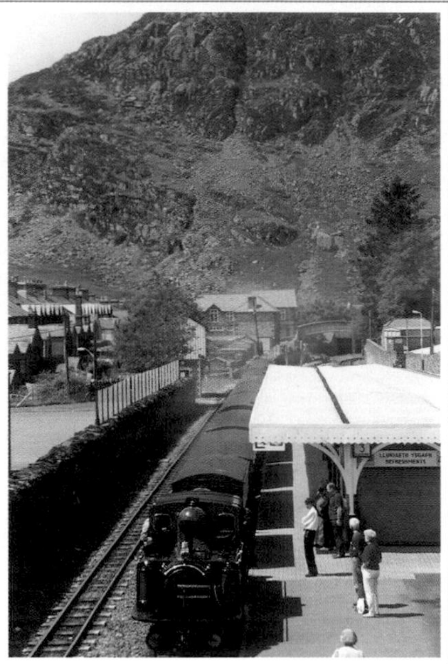

Ffestiniog Railway

Ffestiniog Railway
217 F3

The 13.5 mile (20km) narrow-gauge railway links Blaenau Ffestiniog with the harbour at Porthmadog. Now it is a quaint passenger ride, but it was first opened in 1836 as a means of carrying slate from the quarries. The high demand for slate brought steam power to the line, which is one of its main attractions. Interesting feats of engineering can be observed on the journey, including the Cob, a substantial embankment across the river estuary, and, higher up near Tanygrisiau, the only spiral on a public railway in Britain.

Not only is the railway, with its original rolling stock, appealing to enthusiasts, but the location amidst the glorious scenery of Snowdonia makes the route highly popular with all visitors. It is possible to leave the train at a number of stations en route and the situation of Tan-y-Bwlch station makes it an ideal starting point for beautiful walks. Blaenau Ffestiniog station is now linked with the standard gauge line from Llandudno Junction. Shops can be found at three of the stations, with displays and stocks of railway memorabilia and souvenirs. The railway runs to a set timetable and offers special 'Guest Driving' days.

☎ 01766 516024 www.festrail.co.uk

Glynn Vivian Art Gallery & Museum
411 E2

The gallery contains examples of fine art, decorative and applied art, costume, textiles and archives. Of special interest is the collection of porcelain and Swansea china, in addition to the contributions from contemporary Welsh artists.

☎ 01792 516900 www.swansea.gov.uk

Gower
178 A4

The peninsula of Gower, west of Swansea, is 15 miles (24km) long and about 6 miles (10km) wide with many historical features. Gower is also an Area of Outstanding Natural Beauty thanks to both its coastal and inland environments. The shoreline follows cliffs, dunes, beaches, marshes and river estuaries, whilst the interior comprises pleasant hills, valleys, woods, heaths, caves and commons. Gower Heritage Centre at Parkmill contains a crafts and rural life museum based around a working medieval water mill.

www.swansea.gov.uk

Great Aberystwyth Camera Obscura
204 B4

High on Constitution Hill at the north end of town, and accessed by a cliff railway, this is the world's biggest Camera Obscura. The huge 14 inch (35cm) lens focuses on over 1000 square miles (400 ha) of land and seascape, all reflected onto a circular screen in the viewing gallery below.

☎ 01970 617642 www.cardiganshirecoastandcountry.com

Great Orme Country Park
231 F4

The imposing headland to the west of Llandudno is 2 miles (3km) long and can be accessed by footpaths, road, bus, Victorian Tramway or cabin lift. Of interest are the geology, rich wildlife, archaeology and landscape of the peninsula, in addition to a visitor centre, gardens, a copper mine, and leisure facilities such as a ski slope and a programme of events on land and water.

☎ 01492 874151 www.conwy.gov.uk

Harlech Castle
217 E4

This rugged castle was built on the rocks above Cardigan Bay, once lapped by waves, but now overlooking sand dunes where the sea has retreated. Construction began during Edward I's second campaign in Wales from 1283, and its protected position, walls and artillery platforms made the castle stoutly defensible. It was taken by Owain Glyndwr in the siege of 1404, in the last great uprising of the Welsh against the occupying English, and was held by him for four years.

The castle is concentric, with strong outer walls. The inner walls contained the main living quarters, and the imposing twin-towered gatehouse, with its residential apartments, is one of the main features of the castle. The massive eastern façade, the guardroom and the castle's wide round towers, designed to intimidate attackers, are all impressive. The entrance is at the position of a second drawbridge which

Harlech Castle

used to lower onto towers, of which only the foundations remain. The mighty structure commands superb views out to sea and to the mountains of Snowdonia.

☎ 01766 780552 www.cadw.wales.gov.uk

Kidwelly Castle 178 A2

The substantial and well preserved remains of Kidwelly Castle, south of Carmarthen, are set within the site of an earlier earth and timber ringwork. The massive, concentric castle was started in the mid 13th century and developed impressively over three centuries, eventually becoming a judicial court. The entrance is guarded by a large gatehouse and visitors can climb the round towers, walk on the extensive walls and explore the dungeons.

☎ 01554 890104 www.cadw.wales.gov.uk

Lamphey Palace 176 D2

Just east of Pembroke, the ruins of this medieval bishop's palace remain an impressive sight, surrounded by fishponds, orchards and parkland. Of particular note are the shell of the Great Hall and the chapel.

☎ 01646 672224 www.pembroke-wales.uk.com

Llanberis Lake Railway 217 E1

This scenic narrow-gauge railway skirts Lake Padarn, near Llanberis, with great views of Snowdon. Steam locomotives haul the tourist carriages and the return trip of 5 miles (8km) takes about an hour, including stops.

☎ 01286 870549 www.lake-railway.freeserve.co.uk

Llanerchaeron (NT) 192 A2

This little-changed 1790s gentleman's estate comprises a carefully restored, Nash-designed house with outbuildings, now operating as an organic farm. Produce is on sale and walks lead through the wooded valleys.

☎ 01558 825147 www.nationaltrust.org.uk

Llansteffan Castle (ruins) 177 G1

The castle ruins sit on a steep ridge overlooking Carmarthen Bay and are witness to its expansion since its Norman origins. Visible now are two baileys surrounded by thick walls and a Tudor gatehouse.

☎ 01267 241756 www.cadw.wales.gov.uk

Llanthony Priory (ruins) 194 B5

Hidden in a remote valley in the Black Mountains, the substantial ruins of this ancient Cistercian priory form a striking picture against the green surrounding hillsides. The priory was built in the 12th century and includes examples of both Gothic and Norman architecture. The monastic foundation was soon abandoned and the buildings fell into disuse. However, today there is a small inn and hotel built into the part of the priory where the abbot would once have lived.

☎ 029 2082 6185 www.cadw.wales.gov.uk

Llechwedd Slate Caverns  218 A3

Tours of the massive slate caverns in Blaenau Ffestiniog include underground rides, sound and light shows, and a hard hat walk bringing to life the days of the Victorian miners. The Deep Mine tour descends steeply by railway car and the Miners' Tramway focuses on the historical details of the industry. On the surface stands the original Llechwedd village with facilities for visitors.

☎ 01766 830306 www.llechwedd-slate-caverns.co.uk

Manorbier Castle 177 D3

Accessed by a delightful narrow lane, Manorbier Castle overlooks a sandy bay in south Pembrokeshire. Once a Norman stronghold, today's structure dates from the 12th century and is in remarkably good condition. The castle has many interesting features, including a baronial hall, stout gatehouse, state apartments, gardens and a chapel. The family of the current owners have lived here for over 300 years and it was the birthplace, in 1146, of Giraldus Cambrensis who wrote extensively of his travels around Wales.

☎ 01834 871394

Museum of Welsh Life 180 A5

A fascinating open-air museum covering 100 acres (40ha) near Cardiff illustrates the rich heritage of Wales, showing lifestyles, buildings and traditions through five hundred years of folk history. Original buildings have been transported here from many parts of Wales and painstakingly reconstructed, including craftsmen's workshops, a school, cottages, shops, a mill, farmhouse and a chapel. Demonstrations of many crafts enliven a visit and hands-on opportunities are available for visitors to try their skills. Produce from the farm, mill and other sources on the site are often on sale.

The museum is situated in the grounds of the impressive St Fagans castle which is also open, as are the surrounding gardens. Purpose-built, large indoor galleries house exhibits of costume, daily life and farming implements. Traditional festivals, music and dance events are staged regularly throughout the year. To do justice to the whole enterprise, which has no entrance charge, and to allow time to explore the extensive grounds, at least a half day visit is recommended.

☎ 029 2057 3500 www.nmgw.ac.uk

National Botanic Garden of Wales 178 B1

The Millennium showpiece Garden of Wales lies in the Tywi Valley, upstream from Carmarthen in a peaceful 18th century park of 568 acres (230ha). With the aim of raising awareness of the natural and manmade world, it focuses on conservation, horticulture, science, the arts, leisure and education.

The centrepiece of the garden is the impressive Great Glasshouse, designed by Norman Foster to hold 1000 panes and containing plants from the world over in their natural climates. Outside, the landscape has been built with a deep ravine, rock terraces, waterfalls and lakes to display a multitude of different plantings. Separate sections include a genetic garden and a physic garden. Visitors are encouraged to enjoy the sights, taste the country, experience the sounds, and smell the seasonal scents.

The Gallery in the Garden has a changing schedule of exhibitions on themes such as arts and science, botanical illustration, photography, traditional and contemporary art. Educational programmes are geared to all ages using state-of-the-art technology, and the Garden has become an internationally renowned centre for botanical science.

☎ 01558 668768 www.gardenofwales.org.uk

National Museum & Gallery  392 E2

Found in the heart of Cardiff, this lively museum covers the fascinating 4600 million year history of Wales up to the present day. It is well known for its art treasures, particularly the fine collection of French Impressionist works, but also covers science and natural history through interactive hands-on exhibits. Special events are staged for families, and temporary exhibitions merit further enquiry.

☎ 029 2039 7951 www.nmgw.ac.uk

National Showcaves Centre for Wales  178 B1

An awesome series of natural caves under the Brecon Beacons at Dan yr Ogof offers a variety of attractions suitable for the whole family. Self-guided tours lead through the skilfully illuminated chambers of the huge Cathedral showcave and the Bronze Age Bone cave, accompanied by commentaries. It is advisable to wear warm clothing and stout shoes. Other areas are devoted to an Iron Age farm, dinosaur park, museum, shire horse centre and farmyard.

☎ 01639 730801 www.showcaves.co.uk

National Woollen Museum 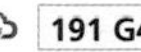 191 G4

A former, busy woollen mill in northern Carmarthenshire has been transformed into a

National Botanic Garden of Wales

museum on the history of the industry. Working exhibitions demonstrate the technical process of 19th century production from the fleece to the fabric. Within the grounds are craft workshops and also Melin Teifi, a fully working mill.

☎ 01559 370929 www.nmgw.ac.uk

Newborough Warren 216 D1

This long stretch of dunes to the south-west of Anglesey is part of a nature reserve, giving distant views to Snowdonia. Natural life abounds and footpaths also give access to a pine forest.

Oakwood Leisure Park 177 D1

Well signposted in south Pembrokeshire, Oakwood is a major theme park with some of the fastest, tallest and wettest rides in the country. Children are catered for with age-appropriate attractions, including the KidzWorld play area. In summer holidays the park stays open until 10pm for a spectacular fireworks and waterscreen light show.

☎ 01834 891373 www.oakwood-leisure.com

Oystermouth Castle (ruins) 350 A3

Although ruined, Oystermouth Castle, on its mound at the west of Swansea Bay, is well preserved. Of note are its late 13th century decorated windows, gatehouse, chapel and Great Hall.

☎ 01792 368732 www.cadw.wales.gov.uk

Pembrey Country Park 178 A2

A 500 acre (202ha) wooded park, Pembrey lies on a sandy stretch of coast south of Carmarthen. The 8 mile (13 km) long Cefn Sidan beach is noted for its swimming and fishing. Other facilities provided (some with entrance charges) are crazy golf, dry ski slope, forest walks, nature trails, horse riding and a small railway.

☎ 01554 833913 www.carmarthenshire.gov.uk

Pembroke Castle 176 C2

Its defensive situation above the river in Pembroke enhances the grandeur of this largely intact castle. The birthplace of Henry VII, the first Tudor king, it has a remarkable history dating back 800 years. The stronghold survived ferocious attacks during the Civil War, but still much remains, including the enormous 80ft (24m) high round keep, thick ramparts, a gatehouse, barbican, Great Hall and dungeon tower. There is an interpretive centre, brass rubbing and special living history days in summer.

☎ 01646 681510 www.pembrokeshirecoast.org

Pembrokeshire Coast National Park 176 B3

Britain's only truly coastal national park covers 240 sq m (620 sq km) of spectacular landscape around Wales' south-western shore. It is renowned for its beautiful scenery, prolific variety of wildlife and historic significance.

The 200 mile (320km) coastal path can be strenuous in parts, but many stretches provide gentler walks. Nowhere in the park is further than 10 miles (16km) distant from the sea. The landscape ranges from steep cliffs to expansive beaches, wooded slopes and inland hills, all supporting special habitats for many rare and endangered plants, birds and animals. Grey seals, porpoises and dolphins may be glimpsed off shore, and some of the maritime islands are home to huge, protected colonies of seabirds. Inland areas are also worth exploring to discover rare plants and insects in the woodlands, heath and marsh areas.

Signs of human activity across the centuries are found in the shape of tombs, burial cairns, castles, crosses, cottages, quarries and quays. The many Iron Age forts, Norman castles and monuments are reminders of the people who lived here over the centuries and of the area's place in history.

☎ 01437 764636 www.pembrokeshirecoast.org

Pembrokeshire Coast

Penhow Castle 180 D3

This is reputedly Wales' oldest lived-in castle, spanning 860 years. Once the home of medieval knights, it is now the ancestral home of the Seymour family. Tours lead from the drawbridge through the historic periods, visiting the battlements, Norman keep and bedchamber, Great Hall with a minstrels' gallery, the Victorian housekeeper's room and kitchens. The entrance fee includes a choice of themed audio tours, such as musical, domestic history, cooks, young adventurer or, in the evening, a candlelight tour.

☎ 01633 400800 www.penhowcastle.com

Penmon Priory (ruins) 231 E4

The ruins of the 12th century priory lie at the eastern edge of Anglesey, alongside the old St Seiriol's Well, church and ancient dovecot. The rocky coastline provides views of the Puffin Island seabird colonies.

Penrhyn Castle (NT)  231 E5

This imposing 19th century castle outside Bangor was built in Norman style and contains remarkably luxurious furnishings, artworks and decor. The kitchen and service rooms have been restored to their 1894 state, ready prepared for a banquet for the Prince of Wales. Outbuildings house a railway museum and a doll museum. The 45 acres (18ha) of grounds include a walled garden, special plant collections and parkland overlooking the Menai Strait.

☎ 01248 371337 www.nationaltrust.org.uk

Pistyll Rhaeadr 219 D4

The highest waterfall in England and Wales cascades down 240ft (74m) and is known as the 'Hidden Pearl of Wales', located in the heart of the principality. It is a spectacular sight, especially after rainfall.

☎ 01691 780392 www.pistyllrhaeadr.co.uk

Plantasia  411 E3

This giant hothouse garden pyramid is found in Swansea's Parc Tawe and houses rare and exotic plants from around the world. Butterflies, insects, reptiles, fish, monkeys and birds also inhabit the three climate zones, providing visitors with a colourful and authentic atmosphere.

☎ 01792 474555 www.swansea.gov.uk

Plas Newydd, Llangollen 219 F3

Renowned as the home of the two 'Ladies of Llangollen' from 1780 to 1831, Plas Newydd is an impressive Gothic black and white house. It is noted not only as the Regency home of the independent, eccentric spinsters, but also for its interior furnishings and fittings and newly-restored, peaceful gardens.

☎ 01824 708250 www.denbighshire.gov.uk www.llangollen.com/plas/html

Plas Newydd, Anglesey (NT)  217 E1

Splendidly set on the Anglesey coast of the Menai Strait, this 18th century stately mansion, enjoying spectacular views to Snowdonia, was the former home of the Marquess of Anglesey. The house combines classical and Gothic architecture and featured inside are paintings by Rex Whistler, including his largest work. The cavalry museum in the servants' quarters commemorates the Battle of Waterloo and displays various campaign relics.

Expansive gardens offer informal walks among fine collections of flowering trees and shrubs, with many exotic plants thriving in the mild climate. In addition to the spring garden, there is a summer terrace, Australasian arboretum, a formal Italianate garden, a woodland area and an

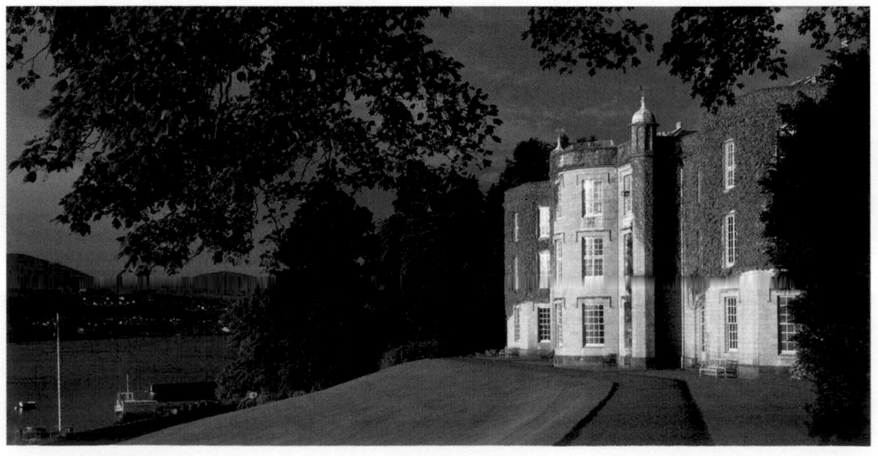

Plas Newydd

adventure play trail. The rhododendron garden, situated some way from the house, is only open from April to early June during flowering time. Autumn, too, brings its own seasonal colours to the grounds.

A marine walk leads along the shore, and historical boat trips are available from the jetty in good weather.

☎ 01248 715272 www.nationaltrust.org.uk

Plas-yn-Rhiw (NT) 216 B5

Originating in the 16th century, this small manor house is situated towards the end of the Lleyn Peninsula, affording breathtaking sea views. Once fallen into disrepair, the attractive house has been restored and 50 acres (20ha) of gardens reclaimed, reaching down to the shoreline. The house contains much of the original furniture and utensils. Subtropical shrubs, box hedges and grass paths divide the ornamental gardens; a stream and waterfall cascade down to the sea, and snowdrop woods provide a backdrop to the house.

☎ 01758 780219 www.nationaltrust.org.uk

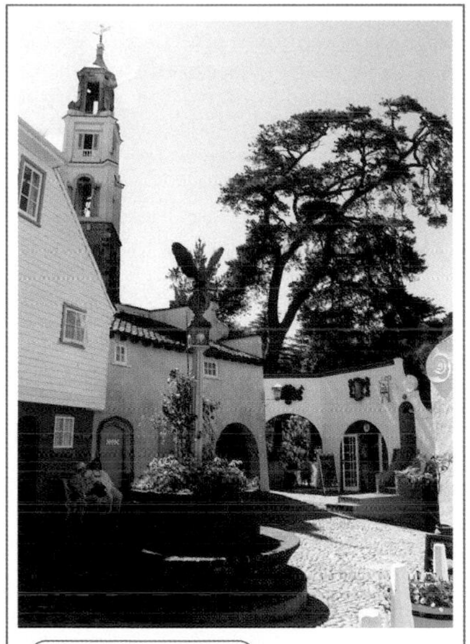

Portmeirion Village

Portmeirion Village 217 E4

This unique, if eccentric 'village' was created during the mid 20th century by the architect Clough Williams-Ellis in a flamboyant, Mediterranean style on his privately-owned peninsula on the beautiful Tremadog Bay. The 175 acres (70 ha) were transformed from a neglected wilderness into a fantasy of pastel-washed cottages, classical towers and lodges, piazzas and archways, façades and fountains, stairways and shops, grottoes and colonnades. Restaurants and hotels form an integral part of the village, as do a range of shops, including the popular Portmeirion Pottery. Here Noel Coward wrote 'Blithe Spirit', and it has been the haunt of many artists, writers and composers of world renown; the village is also well known as the location for the TV series 'The Prisoner'.

The surrounding gardens benefit from the warm influence of the Gulf Stream, enabling many subtropical plants to flourish, in addition to substantial groves of rhododendrons, azaleas and hydrangeas, and a variety of impressive evergreen trees. The woodlands enclose two lakes and reach down to sandy areas of beach and an elegant quayside. Portmeirion has a charm of its own which can only be fully experienced by allowing generous time for a visit.

☎ 01766 770000 www.portmeirion-village.com

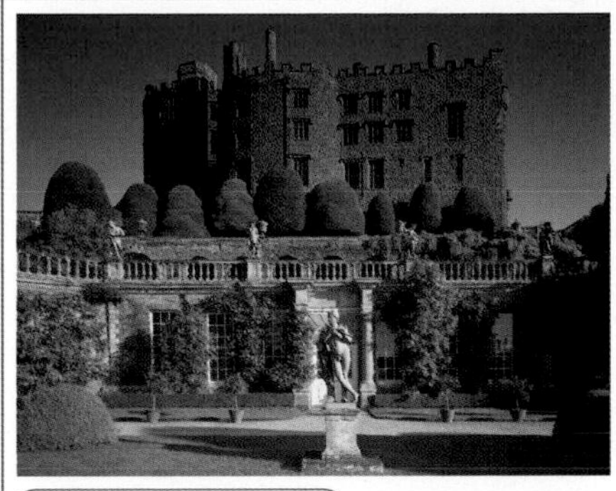

Powis Castle & Garden

Powis Castle & Garden (NT) 206 B2

Both the house and gardens of this property near Welshpool are of particular interest. The medieval castle was built on a prominent rock by Welsh princes, and over the course of later centuries was endowed with fine collections of artwork and furniture by the Herbert and Clive families. Of special note are the Clive Museum with beautiful treasures from India, and the 19th century state coach and livery in the coach house.

The castle overlooks 55 acres (22ha) of world-famous terraced gardens designed in Italian and French styles with sumptuous plantings, statues, an orangery and an aviary. Rare and tender plants are sheltered by large yew hedging; the terrace walls and herbaceous beds exude colour, and containers display imaginative arrangements of plantings. In the lower gardens can be found pyramidal apple trees, a vine tunnel and roses. An informal area of woodland was laid out in the 18th century on the ridge opposite the formal gardens and specimen trees are planted on the grassland slopes.

☎ 01938 551944 www.nationaltrust.org.uk

Raglan Castle 180 D2

Situated in central Monmouthshire, Raglan Castle is a fine example of a medieval fortress palace. Building commenced in 1435 and it developed more as a luxurious Tudor residence than a military base, although it was subjected to siege during the Civil War and was greatly damaged by Cromwell's troops. Raglan was further ransacked after the Restoration and by the 19th century had become very much a ruin. The oldest remaining structure is known as the Yellow Tower of Gwent, named after the colour of the stone from which it was built. The tower was surrounded by more walls and a moat. Later additions included the Pitched Stone Court, the Great Gatehouse and Fountain Court, the rather grand living quarters. The Great Hall is positioned between two courtyards and dates mainly from Elizabethan times.

Today's ruins give an insight into the lavish way of life of its former occupants, and hints of a French influence in elements of the architecture. The changing history of the castle is explained by displays in the closet tower and two rooms of the gatehouse.

☎ 01291 690228 www.cadw.wales.gov.uk

Rhuddlan Castle & Twt Hill 232 B5

Just south of Rhyl stand the stone remains of Edward I's 13th century stronghold. Today the most prominent structures are the gatehouse, walls and towers, as well as the decorative fireplaces of the drawing room. The grounds contain formal gardens, woodlands and ponds. Limited opening in summer only.

☎ 01745 590777 www.cadw.wales.gov.uk

St David's Cathedral & Bishop's Palace 190 A5

Situated in the heart of the charming, small city of St David's, the Cathedral has been a dominant presence since the 12th century. It was built in Norman transitional style and has undergone many transformations under successive bishops. The nearby ruins of the Bishop's Palace date from the 14th century. Many notable features adorn the cathedral, and the surrounding gardens are an additional attraction. There is a bookshop and guided tours; an annual classical music festival takes place in late spring.

☎ 01437 720517 www.stdavidscathedral.org.uk

St David's Head 190 A5

A dramatically beautiful coastline within easy walking distance from Whitesands also provides access to a ruined ancient fort. Offshore lie the islands known as The Bishops and Clerks, best viewed by boat.

Segontium Roman Museum 217 D1

The museum depicts the significant Roman occupation of the area, dating back to AD77. Excavated finds from the nearby Roman fort are displayed, plus records of this remote Roman regiment.

☎ 01286 675625 www.nmgw.ac.uk

Raglan Castle

WALES

Snowdon Mountain Railway — 217 E2

Starting from Llanberis, the dramatic 4.5 mile (7km) ride to the summit of Snowdon on this Victorian rack and pinion railway takes two and a half hours return and ascends 3200ft (980m). The narrow-gauge line affords breathtaking views of Snowdonia and beyond, traversing woodlands, a viaduct and then the open mountainside with an average gradient of 1 in 8. Three of the four coal-fired steam locomotives date from the late 19th century. The trip allows half an hour at the summit station.

☎ 0870 458 0033 www.snowdonrailway.co.uk

Snowdonia National Park — 217 F1

Named after the highest mountain in Wales, the national park covers 827 sq m (2142 sq km) in the counties of Gwynedd and Conwy. It is primarily a wild area of great natural beauty – a landscape of majestic mountains, lush valleys and glittering lakes, surrounded by unspoilt coastlines. The rivers of Snowdonia tumble down the mountains as rushing streams, and arrive at the sea in wide estuaries, providing, along their way, ideal habitats for a huge diversity of plants and wildlife. The area holds much appeal for the naturalist, the mountaineer, the rambler, the artist and the water lover, as well as to those who simply appreciate its stunning scenery.

The Park's study centre is located at Plas Tan y Bwlch near Maentwrog and a Welcome Centre is situated in Betws-y-Coed at one of the park gateways. The main industry of Snowdonia is still hill farming, but tourism is also a major contributor to the economy. Walking and climbing are the most popular pursuits for visitors who have over 2000 miles (3400km) of delightful footpaths to explore. The great majority of the local population regard Welsh as their first language and signs of Welsh history and culture abound, from castles to cottages and from song to sheepdog trials.

☎ 01766 770274 www.snowdonia-npa.gov.uk

South Stack Cliffs — 230 A4

Bird watching and lighthouse viewing make the journey to this far tip of Holy Island well worthwhile. The spectacularly located lighthouse sits on a rocky promontory, but it is accessible only on foot via a steep descent of over 400 steps. Spring and early summer are the best times to observe the multitude of seabirds, including shearwaters, skuas, guillemots, razorbills and puffins, wheeling around the dramatic cliffsides. The visitor centre contains exhibitions on the bird life and the natural environment, plus the history of the lighthouse.

☎ 01407 762181

Strata Florida Abbey — 193 D1

Cistercian monks built the abbey in the 12th century on the banks of the river Teifi in mid Wales, but only the ruined church and cloister survive from this once-important centre of learning.

☎ 02920 500200 www.cadw.wales.gov.uk

Swallow Falls — 218 A2

The Welsh name Rhaeadr Ewynnol (foamy rapids) aptly describes these rushing torrents above Betws-y-Coed. A pedestrian walkway overlooks the wild river, as it carries the waters of Snowdonia towards the sea. A spectacular sight, especially after rain.

Talyllyn Railway — 204 C2

The historic, narrow-gauge Talyllyn steam railway dates from 1865 and runs 7 miles (11.5km) from Tywyn on the west coast, inland to Nant Gwernol. The authentically restored rolling stock chugs through beautiful wooded countryside, with stops en route to admire dramatic waterfalls, particularly from Dolgoch station. The round trip takes just over two hours, but there are also opportunities to explore extensive forest walks in the unspoilt Fathew Valley. For real enthusiasts, Footplate Experience Courses and special events can be arranged.

☎ 01654 710472 www.talyllyn.co.uk

Techniquest — 180 A5

Located in the Cardiff Bay redevelopment area, this educational and fun discovery centre is suitable for the whole family. Techniquest aims to promote understanding and appreciation of science. On offer are 160 stimulating hands-on exhibits, puzzles and challenges in the shape of a Planetarium, a laboratory, a discovery room, a hi-tech science theatre and other enjoyable and accessible environments. Facilities are also available for groups and school tours. Allow at least two hours for a visit.

☎ 029 2047 5475 www.techniquest.org

Tintern Abbey (Ruin) — 181 E3

Once a favoured site for artists and poets including William Wordsworth, the graceful ruins of the 13th century Cistercian Abbey overlook the beautiful Wye valley north of Chepstow. Much of the Abbey is preserved and it offers a fascinating glimpse into the life and times of the medieval monks.

☎ 01291 689251 www.tintern.org.uk

Tredegar House — 351 C2

For more than five centuries this imposing mansion near Newport was home to the powerful Morgan family. Some 30 rooms are open to the public and the interior is furnished sumptuously with original pieces. Costumed guides lead tours describing life 'upstairs' and 'below stairs'. Outside are 90 acres (37ha) of landscaped gardens and parkland with lakes, carriage rides and craft workshops.

☎ 01633 815880 www.newport.gov.uk

Tretower Castle & Court — 194 A5

The stone keep of this castle in the Brecon Beacons was built as a fortification in the 13th century. The nearby Court was added in the following century to serve as a comfortable residence. Various stages in the development of both buildings can be seen, including the detailed craftsmanship of the Court. The re-created 15th century garden is at its best in early summer.

☎ 01874 730279 www.cadw.wales.gov.uk

Tudor Merchant's House (NT) — 177 E3

A late 15th century prosperous merchant's house near Tenby harbour has been furnished to depict lifestyles from Tudor days onwards. Interesting features include original frescoes, a Flemish chimney and small herb garden.

☎ 01834 842279 www.nationaltrust.org.uk

Tŷ Mawr Wybrnant (NT) — 218 A2

Tucked away in a beautiful, peaceful valley, this small stone house holds a special significance in the history of the Welsh language. Here in the 16th century the entire Bible was first translated into Welsh by Bishop William Morgan. Restoration work has returned the house to its probable original state and it now contains a display of Welsh bibles and related exhibits.

☎ 01690 760213 www.nationaltrust.org.uk

Upton Gardens — 176 D2

Overlooking the waters of Milford Haven, the landscaped gardens cover 35 acres (14ha) and offer secluded, inclined woodland walks. The main planting contains over 250 species of trees and shrubs, including some exotic varieties.

☎ 01646 651782 www.pembrokeshirecoast.org.uk

Vale of Rheidol Railway — 204 C5

Starting from Aberystwyth main line station, this narrow-gauge steam train climbs steeply upwards along a spectacular 12 mile (19km) track and requires 3 hours for the round trip (allowing an hour at the beauty spot of Devil's Bridge). The original engines and carriages, built in 1902 to transport passengers and lead, are still in use. Highlights of the trip are three historic bridges at the summit spanning the Devil's Punchbowl whirlpool. Walks abound amid the rugged, wooded landscape.

☎ 01970 625819 www.rheidolrailway.co.uk

Welsh Slate Museum — 217 E2

The vast, old Dinorwig slate quarry in the Padarn Country Park near Llanberis has been transformed into an imaginative museum of the bygone industry. Exhibitions, demonstrations, multimedia presentations, restored buildings, children's activities and tours bring to life the work of the quarrymen. The museum offers a fascinating, free day out for the whole family.

☎ 01286 870630 www.nmgw.ac.uk

Snowdonia

SCOTLAND

From the grassy hills of the Borders to the desolate Cuillin Ridge of Skye, the landscape of Scotland is breathtaking in its variety. Lonely glens, sparkling lochs and ever-changing skies give the land a challenging character, which is reflected in the qualities of the Scottish people. Tough and self-reliant, they have produced some of Britain's finest soldiers, its boldest explorers and most astute industrialists.

Kilchurn Castle, Loch Awe

Abbot House — 285 F1

This restored 15th century house was originally the residence of the Abbot of Dunfermline. It is steeped in history and even survived the great fire of 1624. Exhibits and audiovisual displays trace Scotland's story from Pictish to modern times and recount details about King Robert the Bruce, St Margaret and other figures who played a role in the history of Scotland's most ancient capital.

☎ 01383 733266 www.abbothouse.co.uk

Abbotsford House — 277 G2

Sir Walter Scott, the novelist, bought a farmhouse here in 1811, replacing it with a castellated and turreted mansion in the Scottish Baronial style and naming it Abbotsford in memory of the Melrose Abbey monks who forded the River Tweed here. He gleaned architectural ideas from many sources, including Melrose Abbey, Linlithgow Palace and Rosslyn Chapel. Internally the house is little altered and visitors can see the author's personal possessions, 9000 volume library and eclectic collection of historic relics such as a lock of Bonnie Prince Charlie's hair and Mary, Queen of Scots' crucifix. The armoury bristles with historic weapons and the entrance hall is festooned with the skulls of elk and wild cattle.

☎ 01896 752043

Aberdeen Art Gallery — 388 B2

An elegant building opened in 1885 that houses one of the finest art collections in the UK. It includes 18th century portraits, paintings by many well known Impressionists and important works by modern British artists such as Nash, Nicholson and Bacon. The gallery also has a collection of Aberdeen silver and other arts and crafts.

☎ 01224 523700 www.aagm.co.uk

Aberdour Castle — 285 F1

Overlooking the harbour is a 13th century fortified residence. There are also the ruins of the 14th century keep along with other buildings built and extended in later centuries. One of these is still roofed and contains a gallery on the first floor, complete with painted ceiling, illustrating how it was furnished in 1650. There is also a restored walled garden with a fine circular dovecot and terraced garden.

☎ 01383 860519 www.historic-scotland.gov.uk

Angus Folk Museum (NTS) — 302 B5

The museum is within Kirkwynd Cottages, a row of six reconstructed early 18th century cottages with stone-slabbed roofs. The interiors display one of the finest folk collections of domestic relics in Scotland. There is also an agricultural collection in the farm steading opposite, including a restored 19th century horse-drawn hearse, providing an insight into rural livelihoods over the last 200 years.

☎ 01307 840288 www.nts.org.uk

Antonine Wall — 284 C2

This Roman fortification stretched 38 miles (61km) from Bo'ness on the Forth to Old Kilpatrick on the Clyde. Built circa AD142 – 3, it consisted of a turf rampart on stone foundation behind a ditch 12ft (3.7m) deep and 40ft (12m) wide. Forts were positioned approximately every 2 miles (3km) and linked by a cobbled road. It was probably abandoned around AD163. Remains are best preserved in the Falkirk/Bonnybridge area.

☎ 0131 668 8800 www.historic-scotland.gov.uk

Aonach Mòr Mountain Gondola & Nevis Range Ski Centre — 299 D2

Britain's only mountain gondolas take passengers up Aonach Mòr, beside Ben Nevis, to 2150ft (655m). Enjoy spectacular views of the Highlands and Islands and walks through forest tracks. The gondola also provides access to Britain's largest downhill mountain bike track. During the winter season, the Nevis Range provides Scotland's highest winter ski and snowboard area, with ski school and ski hire. There is a mountain restaurant, bar and shop at 2150ft (655m).

☎ 01397 705825 www.nevisrange.co.uk

Arbroath Abbey — 303 E5

The substantial ruins of a Tironesian monastery founded by William the Lion in 1178. The Abbey is most notably associated with the signing of the Declaration of Arbroath in 1320, which asserted Scotland's independence from England. There is also a herb garden, exhibits about life in the Abbey and the Declaration, and a visitor centre.

☎ 01241 878756 www.historic-scotland.gov.uk

Ardkinglas Woodland Garden — 291 D3

Overlooking Loch Fyne is one of the finest collections of conifers in Britain. Within the woodland garden is one of Europe's mightiest conifers, a 250 year old silver fir with a girth of 31ft (9.6m), and one of Britain's tallest trees, a grand fir over 200ft (61m) tall. There is also a spectacular display of rhododendrons and a gazebo containing a 'scriptorium' themed around a collection of literary quotes.

☎ 01499 600261 www.ardkinglas.com

Arduaine Gardens (NTS) — 289 G4

A 20 acre (8ha) garden on a promontory with fine views overlooking Loch Melfort. Noted particularly for rhododendrons, azaleas, magnolias and other interesting trees and shrubs, which flourish in the warm sheltered climate created by the North Atlantic Drift.

☎ 01852 200366 www.nts.org.uk

Auchindrain Township Open Air Museum — 290 C4

Auchindrain is an original West Highland township of great antiquity and the only communal tenancy township in Scotland to have survived on its centuries-old site. The conserved township buildings are furnished and equipped as they would have been at the end of the 19th century and provide a fascinating glimpse of Highland life.

☎ 01499 500235 www.auchindrainmuseum.org.uk

Bachelors' Club (NTS) — 274 C3

A 17th century thatched house with period furnishings where Robert Burns and his friends formed a debating club in 1780. Burns also attended dancing classes and was initiated as a Freemason here.

☎ 01292 541940 www.nts.org.uk

Balmacara Estate & Lochalsh Woodland Garden (NTS) — 307 E2

Traditional crofting is still carried out on this beautiful Highland estate. There are wonderful views of Skye and Applecross, and the woodland garden provides sheltered lochside walks among pines, ferns, fuchsias, hydrangeas and rhododendrons. Amongst the villages on the estate is Plockton, an outstanding conservation area and location for the television series 'Hamish Macbeth'. A small visitor centre is located at Balmacara Square. Charges apply for the garden.

☎ 01599 566325 www.nts.org.uk

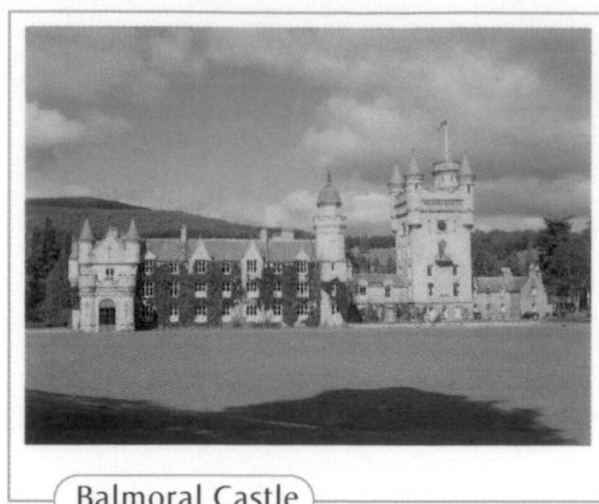

Balmoral Castle

Balmoral Castle — 311 E5

Situated on the south side of the River Dee, Balmoral has been the Highland holiday home of the Royal Family since 1852. The present castle was designed by Aberdeen City architect William Smith under the keen eye of Queen Victoria's husband, Prince Albert, who considered the castle they previously leased on the site too small. The pale colour of the granite stone used in the building is quite distinctive and was quarried from nearby Glen Gelder.

The only part of the castle open to the public is the ballroom which has items from within the castle on display; paintings, porcelain and the Balmoral Tartans and Tweeds collection. In the stables there are carriages on view, while in the carriage hall there is a display of commemorative china and an exhibition about the Balmoral Estate.

Three acres (1ha) of formal gardens include a conservatory and Victorian glasshouses, kitchen garden and water garden, and there are waymarked walks along the river and through the woods. Guided ranger walks, land rover safaris and pony trekking are also available. Balmoral is only open to the public between April and July.

☎ 013397 42534 www.balmoralcastle.com

Bannockburn 1314 — 292 D5

This is the site of the famous battle in 1314 when Robert the Bruce, King of Scots, defeated the English Army of Edward II. The Heritage Centre stages a colourful exhibition, with life-size figures of Bruce and William Wallace, heraldic flags and an audiovisual presentation on the Battle of Bannockburn.

☎ 01786 812664 www.nts.org.uk

Barry Mill (NTS) — 294 D1

A working 19th century meal mill. There are full demonstrations on weekend afternoons, and displays outline the history of the mill.

☎ 01241 856761 www.nts.org.uk

Baxters Highland Village — 323 F3

The story of Baxters, the Scottish food company, began in 1868 when George Baxter opened a small grocery store in Fochabers. At the Highland Village there is a presentation of the Baxters story, cookery demonstrations and the re-creation of George Baxter's original shop.

☎ 01343 820393 www.baxters.com/village

Bealach na Ba — 319 D5

Scotland's highest road, between Loch Kishorn and Applecross, provides a spectacular drive, climbing to the summit at 2056ft (625m). Bealach na Ba translates to 'Pass of the Cattle', denoting its original purpose. The challenging drive is well rewarded and there are parking areas to enjoy the fabulous views. Beyond the summit, the road descends to Applecross, a peaceful fishing village.

Beecraigs Country Park
285 D2

Nestled high in the Bathgate Hills, Beecraigs covers an area of 915 acres (370ha) and offers a wide range of leisure and recreational pursuits. There are various walks and trails as well as a well-stocked fishery, a deer farm which sells its own venison, and the opportunity to participate in archery, orienteering, abseiling and skiing. There is a charge for some of these activities.

☎ 01506 844516 www.beecraigs.com

Ben Lawers National Nature Reserve (NTS)
292 B1

Located north-east of Killin is Perthshire's highest mountain, Ben Lawers, rising 3984ft (1214m). It is noted for its rich variety of mountain plants and bird population, including raven, ring-ouzel, ptarmigan, dipper and curlew. There is a nature trail and ranger-guided walks in summer.

☎ 01567 820397 www.nts.org.uk

Ben Nevis
299 D2

At 4406ft (1344m), this is Britain's highest mountain and is popular for both rock climbing and hill walking. Ben Nevis is best seen from the north approach to Fort William, or from the Gairlochy Road, across the Caledonian Canal. At the top are the ruins of the Mountain Top Observatory, where Victorian scientists collected data, whatever the weather.

To the south, the Water of Nevis plummets through a steep wooded gorge. Glen Nevis offers wonderful gorge walks and the visitor centre provides information on the fascinating history, geology, flora and fauna of Ben Nevis and Glen Nevis. There are ranger guided walks during June, July and August.

Ben Nevis

Blackhouse
329 E3

A traditional Hebridean thatched and chimneyless house dating from the 1870s with byre, attached barn and stackyard. It is fully furnished and a peat fire burns in the hearth. Opposite is a furnished 1920s crofthouse, or whitehouse, which replaced the blackhouse dwellings. The visitor centre provides informative displays.

☎ 01851 710395 www.historic-scotland.gov.uk

Blackness Castle
285 E1

A 15th century stronghold, once one of the most important fortresses in Scotland and one of four castles the Articles of Union left fortified. Shaped like a ship with three sides surrounded by water, it has served as a royal castle, a state prison in Covenanting times and a powder magazine in the 1870s. More recently, it has been a film location for the BBC production of 'Hamlet'. Visitors can explore inside, walk the walls and climb the central tower.

www.historic-scotland.gov.uk

Blacksmith's Shop
268 B5

Built around 1712, this became a world famous centre for runaway marriages when Scottish law permitted marriage at 16 without parental consent, while English law did not. Gretna Green was the closest place to the border for eloping couples and an exhibition traces the history of these runaway weddings which took place in the Blacksmith's Shop, the nearest building to the stagecoach stop.

☎ 01461 338441 www.gretnagreen.com

Blair Castle
301 D3

This white turreted baronial castle, set within magnificent grounds, was the traditional seat of the Dukes and Earls of Atholl. The oldest part, Cumming's Tower, dates back to 1269. Over 30 rooms convey more than 700 years of history. Discover fine collections of furniture, portraits, lace, china, costumes, arms, armour, Jacobite relics and Masonic regalia. Explore the deer park, restored 18th century walled garden, woodland, riverside and mountain walks.

☎ 01796 481207 www.blair-castle.co.uk

Bonawe Iron Furnace
290 C1

The restored remains of this charcoal-fuelled furnace, once used for iron smelting, is the most complete example of its type. Established in 1753, it functioned until 1876. Displays illustrate the iron-making process. Open from end of April to September only.

☎ 01866 822432 www.historic-scotland.gov.uk

Bo'ness & Kinneil Railway
285 D1

Savour the nostalgia of the railway age and travel by steam train from Bo'ness to visit Birkhill Fireclay Mine. The scenic 7 mile (11km) round trip passes via the south shore of the Firth of Forth, through woodlands, and crosses the Antonine Wall. Regular timetable during the summer, plus special events.

☎ 01506 822298 www.srps.org.uk

Bothwell Castle
375 E3

Regarded as the finest 13th century stronghold in the country, Bothwell Castle was much fought over by the Scots and English during the Wars of Independence. Substantial ruins of this red sandstone castle remain today in a picturesque setting alongside the River Clyde.

☎ 01698 816894 www.historic-scotland.gov.uk

Bowhill House
277 F3

A splendid Georgian mansion in impressive woodland setting, containing a remarkable collection of French furniture designed by Andre Boulle, paintings by Canaletto, Gainsborough, Reynolds and Van Dyck, tapestries and fine porcelain. There are some interesting historical exhibits including letters from Queen Victoria and proof copies of Sir Walter Scott's books.

There are walks and an adventure playground in the grounds. The house is only open in July; check in advance for opening times of grounds.

☎ 01750 22204

Branklyn Gardens (NTS)
293 G2

Started in 1922 on the site of a former orchard, Branklyn is an outstanding 2 acre (0.8ha) garden with rhododendrons, alpines, herbaceous and peat garden plants. These are predominantly from China, Tibet, Bhutan and the Himalayas, and include the blue Himalayan poppy.

☎ 01738 625535 www.nts.org.uk

Britannia
373 C1

Launched in 1953 onto the Clyde, the Royal Yacht served the Queen and royal family for state visits, diplomatic functions and royal holidays for 44 years. Today *Britannia* is moored in Leith Docks alongside the Ocean Terminal shopping centre. The tour begins in the visitor centre where the history of the yacht and its royal connections are explained. Five decks of the ship are then open for exploration including the bridge, admiral's quarters, the officers' mess, the state rooms, the engine room and some of the living quarters used privately by the Queen and Prince Philip.

☎ 0131 555 5566 www.royalyachtbritannia.co.uk

Britannia

British Golf Museum
294 C3

Touch screen and audiovisual displays, together with a fascinating collection of memorabilia, trace the history of golf from the Middle Ages through to the present day.

☎ 01334 460046 www.britishgolfmuseum.co.uk

Brodick Castle (NTS)
 273 F2

An imposing, originally 13th century red sandstone castle on a site occupied initially by Irish and later by Vikings. Extended in the 17th and 19th centuries, the pleasant interior belies the somewhat forbidding exterior.

Brodick's greatest treasures are its gardens; the woodland garden, started in 1923, is home to one of Europe's finest rhododendron collections, magnificent in spring, whilst the walled garden contains tender and exotic plants encouraged by the mild climate.

Set at the foot of Goat Fell, the estate provides scenic trails, abundant wildlife and an adventure playground.

☎ 01770 302202 www.nts.org.uk

Brodie Castle (NTS)
 322 B4

The oldest parts of Brodie Castle are 16th century, although the Brodie family owned land here as early as the 12th century. The well-furnished castle interior contains fine French furniture, porcelain, and a major art collection of modern British and French paintings. There are some impressive ornate plasterwork ceilings, a large library and fully equipped Victorian kitchen.

The grounds are famous for the spring display of daffodils, many of them specialist varieties, and there are woodland walks and a four acre (2ha) pond with wildlife observation hides. The park also contains a notable carved Pictish stone.

☎ 01309 641371 www.nts.org.uk

Broughton House (NTS) 266 A5

Delightful 18th century town house, home between 1901 – 33 to the artist Edward Hornel, who helped establish an artists' colony in Kirkcudbright. Some of his paintings hang in the gallery here, later ones influenced by visits to Japan.

The 2 acre (1ha) garden consists of distinct compartments including Hornel's Japanese-style garden. Check in advance for opening times.

☎ 01577 330437 www.nts.org.uk

Burg (NTS) 288 D2

Covering an area of 1405 acres (569ha), this is a spectacular and remote part of Mull. The high, volcanic cliffs are known as 'The Wilderness', denoting the area's wild terrain. MacCulloch's Fossil Tree, engulfed by lava 50 million years ago, can be reached by a steep iron ladder down to the beach at low tide. There is no vehicular access to Berg; it is reached by a 6 mile (10km) walk from Kilfinichen Bay.

www.nts.org.uk

Burns National Heritage Park 274 B4

Set up in 1995, this embraces several sites in the Alloway area closely connected with Robert Burns, considered Scotland's national poet.

The whitewashed Burns Cottage is the poet's birthplace, a small, dark, gloomy building giving a good impression of impoverished 18th century rural existence. Adjacent is the Museum, tracing Burns' life and displaying his manuscripts and memorabilia. A short distance away is the modern Tam O' Shanter Experience with entertaining audiovisual presentations on the poet's life and a re-enactment of his famous poem, 'Tam O' Shanter'. The ruined Alloway Kirk across the road is the burial place of Burns' father and one of the settings for 'Tam O' Shanter', as is the nearby stone arch Brig O' Doon. The neoclassical Burns Monument, decorated with characters from the poems, has pleasant, well-tended gardens.

☎ 01292 443700 www.burnsheritagepark.com

Burns National Heritage Park

Burrell Collection 374 B3

This award winning purpose-built museum houses a magnificent collection gifted to the city of Glasgow in 1944 By Sir William Burrell, a shipping magnate, and his wife, Constance. Visitors can see ancient artworks from China, Egypt, Greece and Rome including Egyptian alabaster and Chinese jade. There are remarkable collections of tapestries, oriental rugs, medieval metalwork, stained glass and paintings by Manet, Degas and Rembrandt, as well as modern sculpture including works by Rodin and Epstein. A number of rooms from Burrell's home, the 16th century Hutton Castle, have been perfectly re-created. The building itself is light and airy and its woodland setting within Pollok Country Park ensures all the objects on display are shown at their very best. Free guided tours are available and there is a good tearoom and restaurant on the lower floor.

☎ 0141 287 2550 www.glasgowmuseums.com

Caerlaverock Castle 267 E4

A splendid moated, triangular 13th century castle, with a substantial keep gatehouse at the northern apex, entered by a footbridge. Its impregnable appearance is reinforced by the desolate surroundings of the Solway coast, though the castle was captured on several occasions. Capture invariably resulted in damage, and the castle is consequently a mixture of building styles, both externally and internally. It was finally abandoned in 1640 when it was wrecked by the Covenanters.

☎ 01387 770244 www.historic-scotland.gov.uk

Caerlaverock Wildfowl & Wetlands Trust 267 E4

A splendid 1350 acres (546ha) of protected saltmarsh and mudflat bordering the Solway Firth. Well designed observation towers and hides provide visitors with exceptional views of migratory wildfowl, notably the Barnacle Geese of Svalbard, most of whom overwinter here. There is still plenty of bird life in summer, and there are nature trails through the meadows and knowledgeable to staff to answer the inevitable questions.

☎ 01387 770200 www.wwt.org.uk

Cairn Gorm Mountain 310 B4

This granite mountain mass of rounded summits includes some of Scotland's highest peaks. It is a popular area for hill walkers, climbers and skiers. The Cairngorms are Britain's only example of Arctic tundra vegetation and the area provides a habitat for populations of red deer, mountain hare, snow buntings and ptarmigans. Cairn Gorm summit, at 4086ft (1245m), provides fantastic views of the lochs, forests and surrounding mountains.

www.cairngormmountain.com

Cairngorms National Park 310 B5

The Cairngorms National Park stretches 1400 sq miles (3800 sq km), making it Britain's largest national park area. Aviemore is the commercial centre for the area. In winter, the village is a mecca for skiers and snowboarders and in summer there are facilities for pony trekking, mountain biking, fishing, sailing, windsurfing and canoeing. Whilst the peaks are popular with climbers, there are also forest and river treks to follow, as well as walks around and through the villages, including Newtonmore and Boat of Garten.

The funicular railway, Scotland's only mountain railway, takes visitors on a spectacular and comfortable journey to Ptarmigan Station on Cairn Gorm, 490ft (150m) below the summit. The Ski Centre can be found 9 miles (14km) south-east of Aviemore. Other attractions include the Cairngorm Reindeer Centre and Cairngorm Sled-dog Adventure Centre.

☎ 01479 861261 www.cairngorms.co.uk

Burrell Collection

Calderglen Country Park 284 A4

The park covers an area of 440 acres (180ha) and is made up of grassland, wooded gorge and several fine waterfalls. There are over 8 miles (13km) of nature trails through the woods and alongside the River Calder. The visitor centre has information about the park. There is also an ornamental garden, children's zoo, play area, shop and café.

☎ 01355 236644

Caledonian Railway 303 E4

From the unique Victorian terminus at Brechin, board a steam train and journey back in time as you travel the falling grade to Bridge of Dun, where the Royal Trains used to stop. From here, enjoy a scenic walk along the River South Esk and visit the bird sanctuary, Montrose Basin. Back at Brechin, there is a static display of model trains. Steam hauled trains run at weekends from the end of May to beginning of September.

☎ 01356 622992 www.caledonianrailway.co.uk

Callanish Standing Stones 328 D4

A unique cruciform setting of megaliths, second in importance only to Stonehenge, which were erected about 3000BC. An avenue of 19 monoliths leads north from a circle of 13 stones, with rows of more stones fanning out to the south, east and west. Inside the circle is a small, chambered tomb. There is a visitor centre, including an audiovisual presentation about the stones (for which there is a small charge).

☎ 01851 621422 www.historic-scotland.gov.uk

Callendar House 284 C2

Callendar House encapsulates 600 years of Scotland's history, from medieval times to the 20th century. Great historical visitors of the house include Mary, Queen of Scots, Cromwell and Bonnie Prince Charlie. Permanent attractions include displays on the story of Callendar House, and on the Falkirk area during the great social revolution of 1750 – 1850.

☎ 01324 503770 www.falkirkmuseums.demon.co.uk

Cardoness Castle 265 G5

An excellent example of a fortified tower house, this late 15th century stronghold is now a well preserved ruin. The four-storey building still retains the original staircase, vaulted basement and elaborate fireplaces, and has views over the Water of Fleet to Fleet Bay.

☎ 01557 814427 www.historic-scotland.gov.uk

Carlyle's Birthplace (NTS) 267 F3

Thomas Carlyle, the author, historian and social reformer, was born in 1795 in the unpretentious, whitewashed Arched House built by his father and uncle. It is now a tiny museum featuring his personal memorabilia. True to his roots, Carlyle refused burial in Westminster Abbey and his grave can be found in the churchyard behind the cottage.

☎ 01576 300666 www.nts.org.uk

Castle Campbell 293 E5

Once known as Castle Gloom, the castle is set high on a promontory above Dollar Glen. Built towards the end of the 15th century by the 1st Earl of Argyll, it was burned by Cromwell in the 1650s. The original tower, however, is well preserved along with its courtyard and Great Hall. The 60 acres (24ha) of woodland in the glen make an attractive walk to the castle.

☎ 01259 742408 www.historic-scotland.gov.uk

Castle Fraser (NTS) 312 C3

A magnificent castle completed in 1636 and one of the most sophisticated Scottish buildings of the period. It has a notable Great Hall with tall windows and a high ceiling, striking in its simplicity. Castle Fraser also contains a wealth of historic portraits, curtains, carpets and bedhangings. There is a formal walled garden in the grounds.

☎ 01330 833463 www.nts.org.uk

Castle Menzies 300 D4

This imposing 16th century castle presents a fine example of the transition between a Z-plan clan stronghold and a later mansion house. Seat of the clan chiefs for over 400 years, Castle Menzies was involved in a number of historic occurrences, which are recounted in the museum.

☎ 01887 820982

Castle of Mey 337 E1

Originally the seat of the earls of Caithness, 16th century Mey Castle became the Scottish summer holiday retreat of Her late Majesty Queen Elizabeth, The Queen Mother, between 1952 and 2002. It was built to a Z-plan, characteristic of its era, with towers and corbelled turrets. The Great Wall of Mey, standing 12ft (3.7m) high, protects the attractive walled garden from the strong winds and salt spray.

☎ 01847 851473 www.castleofmey.org.uk

Cawdor Castle 322 A4

Cawdor Castle is the name romantically associated with Shakespeare's Macbeth, and dates originally from the 14th century. The medieval tower and drawbridge are still intact and generations of art lovers and scholars are responsible for the eclectic collection of paintings, books, tapestries and porcelain found in the castle. There are three beautiful gardens, five nature trails, a nine-hole golf course, putting green, and gift shop.

☎ 01667 404615 www.cawdorcastle.com

Corrieshalloch Gorge (NTS) 320 A2

Here is one of the finest examples of a box canyon in Britain, forming a spectacular 200ft (61m) deep, mile-long (1.6km) gorge. A viewing platform stretched across the gorge looks up towards the magnificent Falls of Measach.

☎ 01445 781200 www.nts.org.uk

Craigievar Castle (NTS) 312 A4

Completed in 1626, Craigievar is an excellent example of Scottish baronial architecture although it was built for a merchant, William Forbes. It is like the castles of fairytales with the seven storeys topped with turrets, gables and corbels. The interior has original ornate plasterwork ceilings and a fine collection of 17th and 18th century furniture. The grounds have woodland walks.

☎ 013398 83635 www.nts.org.uk

Craigmillar Castle 373 C2

The oldest part of the castle is the L-shaped tower built in the early 1400s which was later surrounded by an embattled double curtain wall. By the end of the 16th century it was a comfortable residence and today, partially ruined, the castle still retains a strong sense of the mighty fortress it once was. Mary, Queen of Scots, has close links with the castle. She fled here following the murder of Rizzio, and the murder of her second husband was plotted here.

☎ 0131 661 4445 www.historic-scotland.gov.uk

Cruachan Power Station Visitor Centre 290 C2

A guided tour takes visitors 0.5 miles (1km) inside Ben Cruachan to a huge cavern to see a reversible pumped storage scheme where water power is converted into electricity. The visitor centre houses touch screen and computer video technology to explain how electricity is produced.

☎ 01866 822618 www.visitcruachan.co.uk

Cuillin Hills 306 A2

The Cuillin Hills form a major sight on the Isle of Skye, their jagged summits of volcanic rock and granite evident from most parts of the island. Several peaks reach over 3000ft (914m), suitable for only the experienced climber. The mountains, however, can still be enjoyed on many walks, particularly from Elgol, Sligachan and the Glenbrittle road near Carbost.

Cuillin Hills

Crathes Castle (NTS) 312 C5

An impressive 16th century tower house with remarkable original painted ceilings and a collection of Scottish furniture and family portraits. It was the home of the Burnett family for more than 350 years until it was given to the National Trust in 1951. The walled garden, originally the kitchen garden, was divided in the 20th century into eight separate themed gardens with many herbaceous plants. Several waymarked trails lead through the mixed woodland of the Crathes Estate.

☎ 01330 844525 www.nts.org.uk

Crichton Castle 286 A3

A large castle built around a medieval tower house to create an elegant interior courtyard. The arcaded range erected by the Earl of Bothwell between 1581 and 1591 has a façade of faceted stonework in an Italian Renaissance style.

☎ 01875 320017 www.historic-scotland.gov.uk

Crossraguel Abbey 274 A5

The substantial remains of a 13th century Cluniac monastery founded by the Earl of Carrick. The chapter house and gatehouse are amongst the best preserved and visitors can view the abbey precincts and surroundings from the top of the latter. The abbey was abandoned during the Reformation in the late 16th century.

☎ 01655 883113 www.historic-scotland.gov.uk

Culloden (NTS) 321 G5

Site of the fierce battle on 16 April 1746, when the Hanoverian Army defeated the forces of Bonnie Prince Charlie, thereby ending the Jacobite uprising. Turf and stone dykes have been reconstructed on their original spot. The Graves of the Clans, the Well of the Dead, the Memorial Cairn, the Cumberland Stone and the Field of the English can also be seen. The visitor centre houses a Jacobite exhibition.

☎ 01463 790607 www.nts.org.uk

Culross Palace (NTS) 285 D1

Built in 1597 – 1611 for local entrepreneur Sir George Bruce, the palace features its original decorative interiors and period 17th and 18th century furnishings. The restored 17th century garden contains rare herbs and perennials of the period. Elsewhere in Culross village, discover the remains of a Cistercian Abbey founded in 1217, the eastern part of which forms the present parish church. The Town House provides an exhibition of the area's history.

☎ 01383 880359 www.nts.org.uk

Culzean Castle (NTS) 274 A4

A dramatic clifftop location and splendid design by Robert Adam in the late 18th century makes Culzean (pronounced Cullane) one of the most impressive of Scotland's stately homes. Replacing the original 15th century structure, the exterior, with arrow slits and battlements, evokes the medieval period, but the elegant interior exemplifies the classical designs favoured by Adam. The spectacular Oval Staircase is considered one of his finest achievements, while the sumptuous Circular Saloon makes a striking contrast to the surrounding natural scenery.

The 565 acre (233ha) estate, now a country park, provides woodland, clifftop and seashore walks, deer park, aviary and swan pond. The 30 acre (12ha) gardens include a large, colourful walled garden.

☎ 01655 884455 www.nts.org.uk

Dallas Dhu Distillery — 322 C4

A picturesque small distillery established in 1899. Although no longer in production, Dallas Dhu is maintained in working order to enable visitors to take a close look at every part of the traditional distilling process and see exactly how whisky is made.

☎ 01309 676548 www.historic-scotland.gov.uk

David Livingstone Centre (NTS) — 375 E4

Scotland's famous explorer and missionary was born here in 1813. He spent his childhood in a one-room tenement, which remains much as it was in Livingstone's day. The rest of the tenement block now houses a museum on the life of the great explorer, with many of his personal belongings on display.

☎ 01698 823140 www.nts.org.uk

Dean Castle — 274 C2

A splendid collection of restored buildings comprising a 14th century fortified keep with a 15th century palace, dungeon, battlements, banqueting hall, kitchens and minstrels' gallery. The museum contains a significant collection of arms and armour, medieval musical instruments, tapestries and some Robert Burns manuscripts. Entry to the castle is by guided tour only.

The surrounding 200 acre (80ha) country park provides a variety of attractions including formal gardens, nature trails and a ranger service offering guided walks. There is a varied programme of events in summer.

☎ 01563 522702 www.deancastle.com

Dean Gallery — 373 B1

This impressive neoclassical building was originally an orphanage but now houses a huge collection of work by the distinguished Scottish sculptor Eduardo Paolozzi. The gallery is also home to the Dada and Surrealist collections from the Gallery of Modern Art across the road.

☎ 0131 624 6200 www.natgalscot.ac.uk

Deep Sea World — 285 F1

Enjoy a spectacular diver's eye view of the marine environment by travelling along a moving walkway through a long transparent viewing tunnel. Come face to face with sand tiger sharks and watch divers hand feed them. Touch the live exhibits in the large rock pools. Visit the stunning Amazonian Experience, which features ferocious piranhas, poisonous golden dart frogs, electrifying eels and the deadly stonefish.

☎ 01383 411880 www.deepseaworld.co.uk

Dirleton Castle & Gardens — 286 C1

The oldest part of this romantic castle dates from the 13th century and, although the castle was destroyed in 1650, there are still large parts of the original masonry in evidence. The gardens dating from the 16th century are well worth a look.

☎ 01620 850330 www.historic-scotland.gov.uk

Discovery Point & R.R.S. Discovery — 396 C2

Centred on the Royal Research Ship *Discovery*, Captain Scott's famous polar exploration ship, this visitor centre vividly re-creates her historic voyages. Spectacular exhibits, interactive displays and special effects bring to life the story of the ship and a short dramatic film re-enacts the Antarctic expedition and its rescue.

Combine a visit with nearby Verdant Works, a restored 19th century jute works surrounding a cobbled courtyard.

☎ 01382 201245 www.rrsdiscovery.com

R.R.S. *Discovery*

Dornoch Cathedral — 332 C5

This small, well maintained cathedral was founded in 1224 by Gilbert, Archdeacon of Moray and Bishop of Caithness. Partially destroyed by fire in 1570 and restored in 1835 – 37, and again in 1924, the fine 13th century stonework is still visible. There are 27 magnificent stained glass windows and impressive woodwork.

☎ 01862 810357

Drum Castle (NTS) — 312 C4

The 13th century tower of Drum is one of the three oldest tower houses in Scotland. Jacobean and Victorian extensions made the house into a fine mansion and it contains notable portraits and furniture, much from the 18th century. Drum was the home of the Irvine family for more than 650 years and a room displays family memorabilia. The extensive grounds include a collection of historic roses established by the National Trust in 1991, an arboretum and the ancient oak woodland of the 'Old Wood of Drum'.

☎ 01330 811204 www.drum-castle.org.uk www.nts.org.uk

Drumlanrig Castle — 266 C1

A sweeping drive through a wooded avenue leads to an imposing late 17th century castle built of local pink sandstone. Originally a 15th century castle, it was converted, complete with turrets, towers and cupolas, for the 1st Duke of Queensberry. The state rooms have splendid oak panelling, Louis XIV furniture and paintings by Holbein, Murillo, Rembrandt and Brueghel.

The 40 acres (16ha) of formal and informal gardens are being restored according to the original plans, and new rhododendron areas are being created using seed collected from the wild. The adjacent Drumlanrig Country Park has waymarked trails, wildlife including red squirrels and otters, and some magnificent specimen trees. There is a visitor centre and a ranger service offers a programme of guided walks.

☎ 01848 330248 www.buccleuch.com

Drummond Castle Gardens — 293 D3

This is one of Scotland's largest formal gardens with magnificent early Victorian parterre, fountains, terracing and topiary. It is laid out in the form of a St Andrew's cross, centred around a multi-faceted 17th century sundial, carved by John Milne, master mason to Charles I.

☎ 01764 681257 www.drummondcastlegardens.co.uk

Drummond Castle Gardens

Drumpellier Country Park — 375 E2

The park covers an area of 500 acres (202ha) of open grassland, mixed woodland, lowland heath and two natural lochs, one of which is a Site of Special Scientific Interest. A diverse range of wildlife can be seen by visitors and a network of paths makes all areas of the park accessible. There is a visitor centre and café, a road train, play area, and boat hire and fishing on the lochs.

☎ 01236 422257 www.northlan.gov.uk/leisure+and+tourism

Dryburgh Abbey — 277 G2

Founded in the 12th century in a delightful location on the banks of the River Tweed, the pink sandstone abbey remains demonstrate several architectural styles as the buildings were frequently assailed by the English, until 1545 when they were abandoned. Even so, Dryburgh is the most complete of the Border abbeys, the barrel vaulted chapter house being particularly impressive. Sir Walter Scott is buried here, as is Field Marshal Earl Haig, the World War I leader.

☎ 01835 822381 www.historic-scotland.gov.uk

Duart Castle — 289 G1

This is one of Scotland's oldest inhabited castles and home to the 28th Chief of Clan Maclean. The keep, built in 1360, adjoins the original courtyard. Used as a garrison for Government troops after the 1745 Rising, it then fell into ruin but was restored by Sir Fitzroy Maclean in 1911.

☎ 01680 812309 www.duartcastle.com

Duff House — 324 B3

Designed by William Adam for the first Earl of Fife in 1735, Duff House is one of the best examples of Georgian baroque architecture in Britain, and houses paintings, furniture and tapestries from the collections of the National Galleries of Scotland.

Duff House is surrounded by parkland and there are woodland walks by the River Deveron. The grounds are free and open all year.

☎ 01261 818181 www.duffhouse.org.uk

Duncansby Head — [illegible]

Duncansby Head is located at the north-eastern edge of the Scottish mainland, beyond John o' Groats. Its lighthouse commands a fine view of Orkney, the Pentland Skerries and the east coast headlands.

Slightly to the south are the Duncansby Stacks, three huge stone needles in the sea, along with the sandstone cliffs, severed with deep crevices (geos), one of which is bridged by a natural rocky arch.

Dundee Contemporary Arts 396 C1

Centre for contemporary art and film with five floors containing two galleries, cinema, print studio, craft shop, visual research centre and activity room. Admission to the galleries and exhibitions is free, with a charge for the cinema.

☎ 01382 606220 www.dca.org.uk

Dunfermline Abbey & Palace 285 E1

The remains of the great Benedictine abbey founded by Queen Margaret in the 11th century. The foundations of her church are under the present 12th century Romanesque style nave. Robert the Bruce is buried in the choir, now the site of the present parish church. Of the monastic buildings, the ruins of the refectory, pend and guesthouse remain.

☎ 01383 739026 www.historic-scotland.gov.uk

Dunnottar Castle 303 G1

A spectacular ruin 160ft (48.5m) above the North Sea, recognisable to many film buffs as the setting of Franco Zeffirelli's film 'Hamlet' which starred Mel Gibson. Situated on a flat-topped promontory with sheer cliffs on three sides, and linked to the mainland by a narrow neck of land, Dunnottar's dramatic defensive position ensured a rich and colourful history.

Between the 9th and 17th centuries the castle was fought over many times and for over three hundred years was held by the Keiths, who were Earls Marischal of Scotland, the most powerful family in Scotland. In 1297 William Wallace attacked the English garrison and burnt the wooden castle here, and Mary, Queen of Scots was a visitor in 1562 and 1564. Most famously, in 1652 the Scottish crown jewels, the Honours of Scotland, were hidden here safely for eight months during a siege by Cromwell's army.

Today several buildings from different periods remain, including the 14th century tower house. Access is by means of a steep path and steps.

☎ 01569 762173 www.dunechtestates.co.uk

Dunrobin Castle 333 D4

Overlooking the sea and set within magnificent formal gardens, Dunrobin Castle has belonged to the Earls and Dukes of Sutherland for centuries. It was originally a square keep, built in the 13th

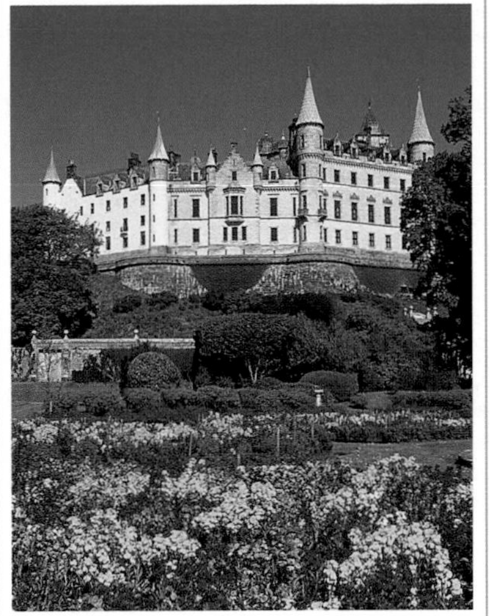

Dunrobin Castle

century by Robert, Earl of Sutherland, after whom it was named Dun Robin. Its turreted, chateau style appearance resulted after extensive modifications by Sir Charles Barry during the 1840s, after he had completed the new Houses of Parliament. As Scotland's most northerly great house, the castle is also its largest, with 189 rooms, and its oldest continuously-inhabited home.

Period rooms display fine paintings, furniture, family memorabilia and even a steam-powered fire engine.

The sheltered gardens, with their formal parterres, were first laid in 1850 and were inspired by those of Versailles. There are falconry demonstrations and a Victorian museum includes an exceptional collection of Pictish stones.

☎ 01408 633177

Duthie Park & David Welch Winter Gardens 313 E4

This popular 50 acre (20ha) park with boating lake and Winter Gardens was first laid out in the late 19th century. It is just a short walk from Aberdeen city centre, next to the River Dee. The world-renowned David Welch Winter Gardens, renamed in recognition of the work of a former Aberdeen Parks Director, covers two acres (1ha) and is one of the largest covered gardens in Europe.

Eas a' Chual Aluinn 331 E2

This is Britain's tallest waterfall, dropping 658ft (200m) at the head of Loch Glencoul. Seals and the occasional elusive otter may be seen on the loch.

Easdale Island Folk Museum 289 G3

The Island of Easdale was once the centre of the slate industry. This museum, set amongst former quarriers' cottages, provides a fascinating account of industrial and domestic life on the island during the 18th and 19th centuries.

☎ 01852 300370 www.slate.org.uk

Edinburgh 285 G2

Edinburgh is a superb city for visitors and with most of the interesting features so close together it is great for exploring on foot. The city grew up around the castle and it still dominates the skyline today. The Royal Mile, consisting of mostly medieval buildings, runs east from the castle to the

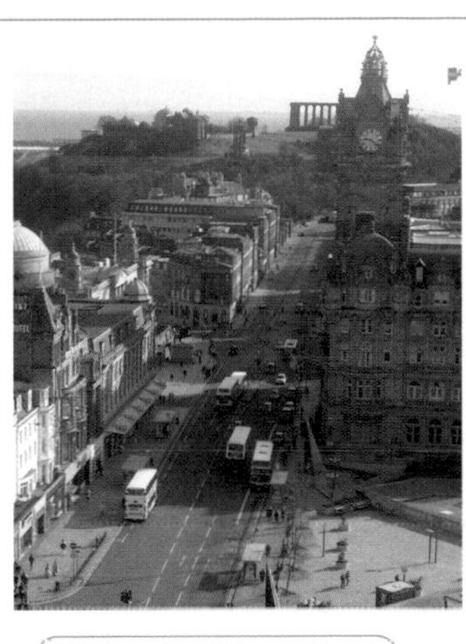

Edinburgh – Princes Street

Palace of Holyroodhouse, through the heart of the Old Town. Numerous narrow street and alleys lead off it, many with fascinating architecture to explore. The New Town is immediately to the north, separated only by the beautiful Princes Street Gardens. In stark contrast to the Old Town, it is full of spacious terraces and crescents that are some of the finest examples of Georgian town planning in Europe. The Water of Leith walkway takes visitors to the unspoilt Dean Village. To the east of the main city centre is Holyrood Park, a 650 acre (263ha) oasis of peace with hills, crags, moorlands, marshes and lochs. Arthur's Seat, within the park, is the core of an extinct volcano (822ft, 251m high) and it is worth a walk to the top for superb views over the entire city and the Firth of Forth. Each August the city really comes to life as, over a period of three weeks, the Festival takes place. It is a combination of theatre, dance, music and comedy with performances at all hours of the day and night.

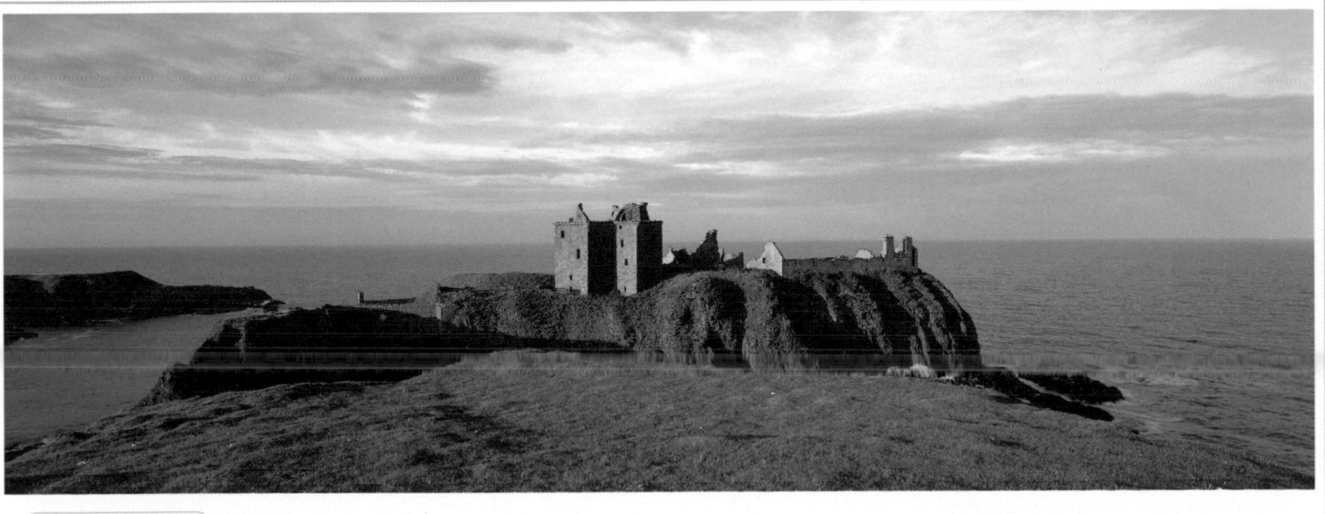

Dunnottar Castle

Edinburgh Castle

397 E1

The castle rises from an extinct volcanic outcrop and dominates the city that has grown up around it. There has been some kind of fortress up on the hill since the 7th century although the oldest part of the present castle, St Margaret's Chapel, was built during the 12th century. In its early years the castle was a royal residence but has assumed an increasingly military role over time, and today still houses an important garrison for the Scottish regiments. The Scottish crown jewels are on display alongside the Stone of Destiny. In the castle vaults, once used as cells for military prisoners, is Mons Meg cannon, a 15th century siege gun which could fire a 500 pound stone a distance of 2 miles (3km). The Royal Apartments inside the palace have been sensitively restored to their 16th century splendour and the chamber where Mary, Queen of Scots gave birth to James VI (James I of England) are especially worth a look. Each day at one o'clock a gun is fired from the castle, originally for the benefit of ships in the Firth of Forth, a tradition that has continued unbroken since the 17th century. Knowledgeable guides lead frequent tours of the castle although it is also possible to wander freely. Each August the grounds play host to the Military Tattoo with massed bands, pipes, drums and display teams from around the world.

☎ 0131 225 9846 www.historic-scotland.gov.uk

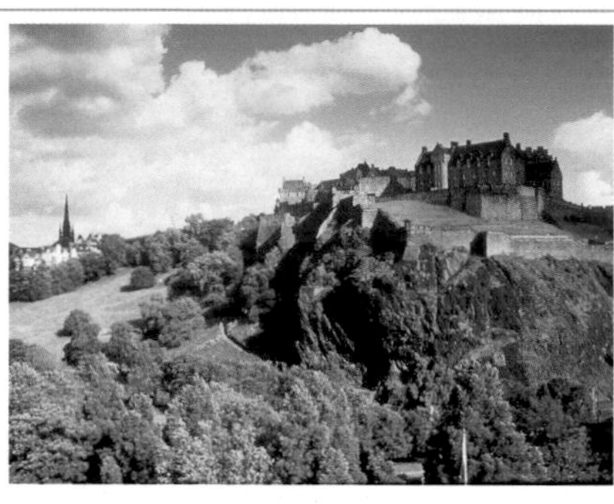

Edinburgh Castle

Edinburgh Zoo

373 A2

Established in 1913 by the Royal Zoological Society of Scotland, and set in 80 acres (32ha) of beautiful parkland on the side of Corstorphine Hill. The zoo has over 1000 animals, many of them rare or threatened in the wild, ranging in size from the tiny blue poison arrow frogs to the giant white rhinos. The zoo is best known for its penguins, which swim in the world's largest penguin pool and participate in the Penguin Parade, to the delight of children of all ages.

☎ 0131 314 0300 www.edinburghzoo.org.uk

Edinburgh Zoo

Edzell Castle & Garden

303 D3

The castle is a late medieval, red stoned tower house incorporated into a 16th century courtyard mansion. There is a splendid walled garden, laid out by Sir David Lindsay in 1604. Its walls incorporate a wonderful display of heraldic and symbolic sculptures, alternating with recesses filled with flowers and bird's nests. At its far corners, find a well preserved, two-storey summerhouse and the remains of a bathhouse.

☎ 01356 648631 www.historic-scotland.gov.uk

Eilean Donan Castle

307 E2

Situated on an islet in Loch Duich, this picturesque and inhabited castle dates back to 1214. It passed into the hands of the Mackenzies of Kintail, who became the Earls of Seaforth, was garrisoned by Spanish Jacobite troops in 1715 and blown up by the English. During the 20th century, the castle was fully restored.

☎ 01599 555202 www.eileandonancastle.com

Elgin Cathedral (Ruins)

323 E3

The magnificent and substantial ruin of the 13th century cathedral known as the 'Lantern of the North' and regarded by many as the most beautiful in Scotland. Interesting features include the 15th century octagonal chapter house with vaulted ceiling and a Pictish cross-slab in the choir. Spectacular views of the cathedral and surrounding area are possible from a platform at the top of one of the massive towers.

☎ 01343 547171 www.historic-scotland.gov.uk

Elgin Museum

323 E3

Internationally renowned for its fossils and Pictish stones, the museum houses unique collections of natural history, geology, archaeology, art, ethnography and the social history of the Moray area.

☎ 01343 543675 www.elginmuseum.org.uk

Fair Isle

342 A5

Situated between Orkney and Shetland, Fair Isle is one of Britain's most isolated inhabited islands. Most famous for the intricately patterned knitwear which bears its name, this craft continues today. It is important, too, for its birdlife and there are many opportunities for ornithological studies, including the Bird Observatory. The island's archaeology provides much interest and traditional crofting is also still in evidence.

www.fairisle.org.uk
www.nts.org.uk

Falkirk Wheel

284 C1

A spectacular wheel reconnects the Union Canal up 82ft (25m) to the Forth and Clyde Canal. Weighing 1300 tonnes (2205 pounds), it is equivalent in height to a nine-storey block of flats and is the world's only rotating boat lift. The visitor centre provides information about the construction of the wheel and the restoration of the canal.

☎ 01324 619888 www.thefalkirkwheel.co.uk

Falkland Palace (NTS)

294 A4

Built in the 1500s, Falkland Palace formed the country residence of the Stewart Kings and Queens. Restored period rooms on view include the Chapel Royal, the King's Bedchamber and the Queen's Room. The fine gardens contain the original royal tennis court, built in 1539 and the oldest still in use in Britain today.

☎ 01337 857397 www.nts.org.uk

Falls of Clyde Wildlife Reserve & Visitor Centre

284 C5

The reserve covers almost 150 acres (59ha) of ancient woodland along both sides of the gorge alongside the River Clyde. The Clyde flows over four waterfalls within the reserve, the largest of which, Corra Linn, features an 84ft (26m) drop. The reserve, run by the Scottish Wildlife Trust, has recorded sightings of over 100 species of bird and in spring and summer it is possible to catch sight of breeding peregrine falcons. The visitor centre, housed in the old Dye House at New Lanark, has information on all the wildlife that make the reserve their home.

☎ 01555 665262 www.swt.org.uk

Fife Folk Museum

294 B3

The local museum is housed in a 17th century tollbooth and 18th century weavers' cottages overlooking the Ceres Burn. The collection illustrates the social, economic and cultural history of rural Fife.

☎ 01334 828180 www.fifefolkmuseum.co.uk

Finlaystone House Gardens

283 E2

140 acres (57ha) of woodland, waterfalls and gardens surround the 14th century Finlaystone House (not open to the public). The family-run estate overlooks the River Clyde and there are spectacular views across the Firth. The extensive gardens were originally laid out in 1900 and are considered to be among the finest in Scotland. The whole estate can be explored via a number of trails leading to picnic sites and adventure play areas. There is also a visitor centre.

☎ 01475 540505 www.finlaystone.co.uk

Floors Castle

278 B3

Thought to be Scotland's largest inhabited castle, this magnificent, castellated Georgian mansion was designed by William Adam although the more flamboyant turrets and cupolas were added in Victorian times. The public apartments display an outstanding collection of 17th and 18th century French furniture, together with magnificent Brussels tapestries, paintings by Matisse and Augustus John, and European and Chinese porcelain.

The herbaceous borders in the walled garden are splendidly colourful in summer, while the extensive parkland which overlooks the River Tweed offers a range of woodland walks.

☎ 01573 223333 www.floorscastle.com

Floors Castle

Fort George 321 G4

A vast site of one of the most outstanding artillery fortifications in Europe, having been planned in 1747 as a base for George II's army and completed in 1769. It continues to serve as a barracks and remains virtually unaltered. There is much to see, including the Queen's Own Highlanders Regimental Museum.

☎ 01667 462777 www.historic-scotland.gov.uk

Fyvie Castle (NTS) 312 C1

Adorned with turrets, gables and towers, Fyvie is one of the finest examples of Scottish baronial architecture. The five towers were reputedly built by, and named after, each of the families who owned the castle in succession – Preston, Meldrum, Seton, Gordon and Leith. The oldest part dates from the 13th century and there are ghosts and legends associated with the castle. The interior has some original 17th century plaster ceilings, an impressive decorated wheel staircase and collections of portraits, arms and armour, and 17th century tapestries. In the landscaped parkland visitors can enjoy a variety of scenic lochside walks. Traditional Scottish fruits and vegetables are grown in the old walled garden.

☎ 01651 891266 www.nts.org.uk

Gallery of Modern Art 387 M7

Opened in 1996 and housed in an elegant neo-classical city centre building, this popular gallery shows contemporary artwork by British artists. There is also a wide range of temporary exhibitions and a programme of events including music, drama and dance.

☎ 0141 229 1996 www.glasgowmuseums.com

Georgian House (NTS) 397 E1

The north side of Charlotte Square has been referred to as Robert Adam's masterpiece and is perhaps the finest example of neoclassical architecture in the country. The Georgian House at number 7 has had three floors elegantly restored to reflect the way the house would have looked during its ownership by the Lamont Family who bought the house in 1796.

☎ 0131 226 3318 www.nts.org.uk

Gladstone Court Museum  276 B2

A reconstructed Victorian street which brings to life small town life as it was during the second half of the 19th century. The town of Biggar has more museums per head of population than anywhere else in Scotland – others are Greenhill Covenanters' House, the Gasworks Museum, the Puppet Theatre and Moat Park Heritage Centre.

☎ 01899 221573 www.biggar-net.co.uk/museums

Gladstones Land (NTS)  397 E2

A superb example of a 17th century tenement house, this six-storey mansion has been wonderfully restored to indicate what life was like here in the 1600s. Particularly impressive are the decorated ceilings and wall friezes of the Painted Chamber.

☎ 0131 226 5856 www.nts.org.uk

Glamis Castle 302 B5

Originally a 14th century, three-storey keep, the present turreted castle was modified in the 17th century. One of the oldest parts is Duncan's Hall, legendary setting for Shakespeare's 'Macbeth'. Family home to the Earls of Strathmore, it was the late Queen Mother's childhood home and birthplace of Princess Margaret. On display are fine collections of china, paintings, tapestries and furniture.

☎ 01307 840394 www.glamis-castle.co.uk

Glasgow Botanic Garden 374 B2

Since 1842 these gardens have been a tranquil oasis in Glasgow's bustling West End. The gardens have long been known for their glasshouses and the largest is the huge Kibble Palace erected in 1873 and home to tree ferns from Australia and New Zealand, and plants from Africa, the Far East and the Americas. Other specialist plant collections include cacti, orchids and begonias.

☎ 0141 334 2422

Glasgow School of Art  386 J5

The work of Charles Rennie Mackintosh (1868 – 1928) has become synonymous with Glasgow. He blends organic forms with linear and geometric designs to create fabulous architecture, furniture and art work. Mackintosh was a student at the Glasgow School of Art before winning a competition to design a new building to house the school. Built between 1897 and 1907, the building is today considered to be his finest example of work and is the earliest example of a complete art nouveau building in the country. The only way to see the interior of the building is on a student-led guided tour.

☎ 0141 353 4526 www.gsa.ac.uk

Glasgow Science Centre  386 A8

A stunning titanium-clad building alongside the Clyde. The site is made up of three attractions – the IMAX theatre, the three-storey Science Mall and the Glasgow Tower. The IMAX has a cinema screen larger than a five-a-side football pitch and shows 2D and 3D films. The Science Mall has hundreds of hands-on exhibits, workshops and a planetarium. The Glasgow Tower, which at 328ft (100m) is the highest free-standing structure in Scotland and the only 360 degree rotating structure in the world, has information on past and future developments in Glasgow as well as superb views from the top. Tickets can be purchased for single attractions or there is a double ticket allowing entrance to two attractions.

☎ 0141 420 5000 www.gsc.org.uk

Glencoe 298 D4

This is a highly dramatic and historic glen. It has been the scene of numerous feudal clashes, particularly between the MacDonald and Campbell clans, and is probably best known for the 1692 massacre of part of the MacDonald clan by soldiers of King William. In fact, its name translates as 'Valley of Weeping'.

Its steep-sided mountains offer superb walking and climbing. Geologically, they also provide an example of a collapsed volcano. Red deer, wildcats, golden eagles and rare arctic plants can be seen among the breathtaking peaks and spectacular waterfalls. There are many walks, some more challenging than others.

☎ 01854 811307 www.nts.org.uk

Glencoe Visitor Centre (NTS) 298 D4

The visitor centre buildings have been laid out as a 'clachan' or small settlement and have fascinating interactive displays and exhibits about the history, geology and conservation of the area. A video recording recounts the massacre of part of the MacDonald clan by soldiers of King William in 1692. The Glencoe Lookout Station shows web cam images and the 'Living on the Edge' exhibition includes information about the history of mountaineering.

☎ 01855 811307 www.nts.org.uk

Glenfiddich Distillery 323 F5

Situated close to the river Fiddich, the distillery produces the only Highland single malt whisky that is distilled, aged and bottled at the same site. Glenfiddich is the world's biggest selling single malt and visitors can tour the distillery where production first started on Christmas Day 1887. Although the tour is free, there is a charge for a much longer connoisseur's tour and tasting.

☎ 01340 820373 www.glenfiddich.com

Glenfinnan Monument (NTS) 298 B1

Set amid superb Highland scenery at the head of Loch Shiel, Glenfinnan monument was erected in 1815 in tribute to the clansmen who died for the Jacobite cause. It is sited where Bonnie Prince Charlie raised his standard in 1745. The information centre recounts the Prince's campaign with displays and an audiovisual programme. Nearby is the Glenfinnan Viaduct, a spectacular railway viaduct with 21 arches, built in 1901.

☎ 01397 722250 www.nts.org.uk

Glenluce Abbey (NTS) 264 C5

Founded in 1192, the Cistercian monks' diligence in draining the surrounding marshes to create productive land ensured the abbey's survival. The chapter house, built around 1500, has endured almost intact with unusual decorative carvings and a ribbed vault ceiling providing splendid acoustics. More prosaic, but equally interesting are the well preserved clay drains and waterpipes laid by the monks. A small museum displays artefacts relating to the abbey, which was finally abandoned in 1560.

☎ 01581 300541 www.historic-scotland.gov.uk

Glencoe

Glenturret Distillery 293 D2

Whisky is still produced in the traditional manner at Scotland's oldest Highland malt distillery (established in 1775). Set in a picturesque location, enjoy free tasting as well as the Famous Grouse Experience in the interactive visitor centre.

☎ 01764 656565 www.glenturret.com

Gordon Highlanders Regimental Museum — 313 E4

Striking exhibits from a unique collection, recalling 200 years of service of the regiment which largely recruited soldiers from north east Scotland. The medal display includes 12 Victoria crosses. Interactive screens and an audiovisual theatre serve to dramatise the history of this famous regiment which was amalgamated to form The Highlanders (Seaforth, Gordons and Camerons) in 1994.

☎ 01224 311200 www.gordonhighlanders.com

Grampian Transport Museum — 312 A3

An extensive collection of historic road vehicles, many of them rare and unusual, which illustrates the history of road travel and transport in north-east Scotland. Among the items is the Craigievar Express, a steam powered tricycle built in 1895. With working exhibits, video presentations and the opportunity to climb aboard many vehicles, including a snow plough, it is a lively museum with lots to do.

☎ 019755 62292 www.gtm.org.uk

Greenhill Covenanters' House — 276 B2

A 17th century farmhouse, rescued from 10 miles down the road and rebuilt here piece by piece. The museum returns the visitor to troubled times when James VI, Charles I and II, and James VII tried to rule against the wishes of the majority of the population and the Kirk of Scotland. The tale is simply, but comprehensively, told through the life of Lady Greenhill, the then owner of the farmhouse.

☎ 01899 221752 www.biggar-net.co.uk/museums

Grey Mare's Tail (NTS) — 276 C4

Spectacular 200ft (61m) waterfall tumbling from the corrie containing Loch Skene down a rocky gorge into Moffat Water. Reached by a path that is precipitous in places.

☎ 01556 502575 www.nts.org.uk

Haddo House (NTS) & Country Park — 313 D1

Haddo House is an elegant Georgian mansion designed by William Adam in 1732 for the 2nd Earl of Aberdeen, while much of the splendid interior decoration is Adam Revival style dating from the 1880s. Haddo has a beautiful library and contains some fine furniture and an extensive art collection. The formal garden includes terracing with rose beds.

Adjacent is Haddo Country Park, open all year, with waymarked trails, 3 miles (5km) of surfaced paths and wildlife hides.

☎ 01651 851440 www.nts.org.uk

Hermitage Castle — 268 C2

A vast, eerie ruin of a forbidding fortress in a bleak moorland setting, dating from the 14th and 15th centuries and consisting of four towers and connecting walls. The imposing medieval exterior is deceptive as certain features resulted from a Victorian restoration, and inside the structure is little more than a ruin.

☎ 01387 376222 www.historic-scotland.gov.uk

Hermitage, The (NTS) — 301 E5

Interesting walks in mixed woodland, containing one of Britain's tallest Douglas fir trees. The focus is a delightful 18th century folly, Ossian's Hall, set above a wooded gorge of the River Braan.

☎ 01796 473233 www.nts.org.uk

Highland Folk Museum — 309 G4

An open-air museum, partly housed in an 18th century shooting lodge, illustrating the social history of people in the Highlands. There is another site at Newtonmore.

☎ 01540 661307 www.higlandfolk.com

Highland Wildlife Park — 310 A4

Discover Scottish wildlife, from native species to creatures long extinct, in 180 acres (73ha) of parkland. Encounter enormous bison, ancient breeds of sheep and one of the world's rarest mammals, the Przewalski's Horse, by driving through the main reserve (staff will drive those without a car). Special themed events are held at weekends.

☎ 01540 651270 www.highlandwildlifepark.org

Hill House (NTS) — 283 D1

Charles Rennie Mackintosh designed this house for the publisher Walter Blackie in 1904. A masterpiece of domestic architecture synthesizing traditional Scottish style with avant-garde innovation, this extraordinary building still looks modern today. Mackintosh, with his wife Margaret, also designed the interiors and most of the furniture.

☎ 01436 67900 www.nts.org.uk

Hill of Tarvit Mansion House & Garden (NTS) — 294 B3

Sir Robert Lorimer designed this fine Edwardian house to provide a setting for his important collection of French, Chippendale style and vernacular furniture. Superb paintings, Flemish tapestries and Chinese porcelain and bronzes adorn the interiors. Lorimer also designed the formal gardens.

☎ 01334 653127 www.nts.org.uk

Hopetoun House

Hopetoun House — 285 E2

Set in 100 acres (40ha) of magnificent parkland on the shores of the Firth of Forth, this house is one of Scotland's finest stately homes. It is the work of William Bruce, the architect who designed Holyroodhouse, and was later extended by William Adam. The magnificent state rooms feature the original 18th century furniture, remarkable paintings including works by Gainsborough, Raeburn and Canaletto, rococo ceilings, 17th century Aubusson tapestries, Meissen porcelain and some spectacular chandeliers in the Ballroom. The extensive parkland has woodland and riverside walks, a deer park and a walled garden.

☎ 0131 331 2451 www.hopetounhouse.com

House of Dun (NTS) — 303 E4

Overlooking the Montrose Basin is this beautiful Georgian house, designed in 1730 by William Adam and containing superb contemporary plasterwork. Home during the 19th century to Lady Augusta Kennedy-Erskine, daughter of William IV, many of her belongings remain, as well as her wool work and embroidery.

☎ 01674 810264 www.nts.org.uk

House of the Binns (NTS) — 285 E2

Built between 1612 and 1630 by Thomas Dalyell, the house reflects the change in style of Scottish homes during the 17th century, from fortified stronghold to spacious mansion. Four of the main rooms have elaborate plasterwork ceilings and there is some fine furniture dating mostly from the late 18th and early 19th centuries. Outside there are woodland walks to a panoramic viewpoint over the Firth of Forth. The house is only open from June to September.

☎ 01506 834225 www.nts.org.uk

Hugh Miller's Cottage (NTS) — 321 G3

The famous stonemason, geologist, writer and church reformer, Hugh Miller (1802 – 56), was born in this furnished thatched cottage, built around 1698. His life and work can be explored through exhibits of his belongings, including his fine fossil collection, his writings and video footage.

☎ 01381 600245 www.nts.org.uk

Huntingtower Castle — 293 F2

Known as Ruthven Castle until 1600, Huntingtower Castle is a 15th century castellated mansion. A 17th century range links its two fine and complete towers. A key feature is the outstanding painted ceiling. Noteworthy historic events include a visit by Mary, Queen of Scots, the capture of King James the VI, and the birth of the Jacobite commander, Lord George Murray.

☎ 01738 627231 www.historic-scotland.gov.uk

Hutchesons' Hall (NTS) — 387 N7

Built between 1802 and 1805, this elegant building replaced a 17th century hospice, and statues of George and Thomas Hutcheson, taken from the original building, have been incorporated into the frontage. A major rebuild in 1876 heightened the hall and made the way for an impressive staircase. The hall now houses a National Trust for Scotland shop and visitor centre and an exhibition entitled Glasgow Style displaying works by young Glasgow designers.

☎ 0141 552 8391 www.nts.org.uk

Inveraray Castle — 290 C4

The Duke of Argyll's family, the senior branch of the Campbell Clan, moved here in the early 15th century. The present building, in the style of a castle, was erected between 1745 and 1790, replacing a previous fortified keep. Explore the grand staterooms, and some of the former bedrooms, and view the famous collections of armour, French tapestries, paintings, and fine Scottish and European furniture. The Clan Room contains a genealogical display. Gardens are open by appointment only.

☎ 01499 302203 www.inveraray-castle.com

Inveraray Jail — 290 C4

This award winning attraction re-creates prison life in the 1800s. There are fascinating exhibitions, such as 'Torture, Death and Damnation' where the crank machine, whipping table and hammocks can all be tested first-hand, along with the sounds and smells of everyday life locked in the cells.

☎ 01499 302381 www.inverarayjail.co.uk

Inverewe Gardens (NTS) 319 E1

A world-famous garden created from a once barren peninsula on the shore of Loch Ewe by Victorian gardener Osgood Mackenzie. Exotic plants from many countries flourish here in the mild climate created by the warm currents of the North Atlantic Drift. Find Himalayan rhododendrons, Tasmanian eucalypts, and other subtropical plants from New Zealand, Chile and South Africa.

Much of the garden's structure is original, with work having been started in 1863 and continued by Mackenzie's daughter, until she handed over the estate to the Trust. There is also a visitor centre and access to the wider estate.

☎ 01445 781200 www.nts.org.uk

Iona (NTS) 288 B2

St Columba began to spread the gospel here in AD563, from where Christianity spread throughout Scotland and beyond. Explore the abbey, home to the Iona Community, with a beautiful interior and carvings, the 13th century priory, the oldest cemetery in Scotland, containing the graves of many kings and chiefs, the restored St Oran's Chapel, and the 10th century St Martin's Cross. There are also superb long sandy beaches, turquoise seas and unrivalled views.

☎ 01631 570000 (National Trust Office) www.nts.org.uk

Italian Chapel 339 D2

Italian prisoners of war, whilst constructing the Churchill Barriers in World War II, transformed two corrugated iron Nissen huts into this ornate chapel. Its beautiful interior is the result of their ingenuity and craftsmanship. The painting of Madonna and Child is by Domenico Chiocchetti.

☎ 01865 781279

J.M. Barrie's Birthplace & Camera Obscura (NTS) 302 B4

J.M. Barrie, creator of 'Peter Pan', was born in this two-storey weaver's cottage in 1860. The upper floors have been furnished to reflect the era and an exhibition about Barrie's literary and theatrical work is housed next door. Camera Obscura, found within the cricket pavilion on Kirrie Hill, was presented to Kirriemuir by the author.

☎ 01575 572646 www.nts.org.uk

Jarlshof Prehistoric & Norse Settlement 343 G5

A complex of ancient settlements within 3 acres (1.2ha) can be found on this extraordinarily important site. The oldest is a Bronze Age village of oval stone huts. Above this is an Iron Age broch and wheelhouses, and even higher still is an entire Viking settlement. A house, built around 1600, sits on the crest of the mount. Displays in the visitor centre explain Iron Age life and the history of the site.

☎ 01950 460112 www.historic-scotland.gov.uk

Inveraray Jail

Inverewe Gardens

Jedburgh Abbey 278 A5

Dominating the skyline in Jedburgh's centre, this red sandstone abbey was founded by David I in the 12th century, probably on the site of a 9th century church. The remarkably complete abbey church is mostly Romanesque and early Gothic in design, with a fine rose window and richly carved Norman doorway. Cloister remnants have been uncovered and artefacts found are on display at the visitor centre, together with an excellent exhibition on life in the monastery.

Jedburgh suffered various assaults during border warfare and was abandoned in 1560, though the church was used for another three centuries.

☎ 01835 863925 www.historic-scotland.gov.uk

Kelburn Castle & Country Centre 282 D4

Family home of the Earls of Glasgow, comprising a Norman keep within a 16th century castle with later additions, all surrounded by spectacular natural scenery. Activities include assault and adventure courses, horse riding, soft play and, for the less energetic, pets corner, delightful gardens and woodland walks through the Secret Forest. Ranger service and special weekend events.

☎ 01475 568685 www.kelburncountrycentre.com

Kellie Castle (NTS) 294 D4

The oldest part of Kellie Castle dates from 1360, but most of the present building was completed around 1606. It was sympathetically restored by the Lorimer family, who lived here in the 1870s. Inside, there are splendid painted ceilings and panelling, as well as excellent furniture designed by Sir Robert Lorimer. The extensive grounds include a lovely organic Victorian walled garden.

☎ 01333 720271 www.nts.org.uk

Kelso Abbey 278 B3

The largest of the Border abbeys founded by David I in 1128, Kelso was a fine example of Romanesque architecture. Little now remains of this once wealthy and powerful establishment; English raids in the first half of the 16th century focused on the abbey and destruction was completed in 1545 when 100 defenders were slaughtered. All that remains is part of the north-west transept, tower and a fragment of the nave.

☎ 0131 668 8800 www.historic-scotland.gov.uk

Kilchurn Castle 290 D2

A substantial ruin based on a square tower built by Colin Campbell of Glenorchy, circa 1550. It was much enlarged in 1693 by Ian, Earl of Breadalbane, whose arms are over the gateway with those of his wife. The castle incorporates the first purpose-built barracks in Scotland and commands spectacular views down Loch Awe. Open during summer only.

☎ 0131 668 8800 www.historic-scotland.gov.uk

Kildalton Church & Crosses 280 C5

The Old Church at Kildalton is the site of the finest intact High Cross in Scotland. Carved in the late 8th century, the Celtic cross stands 9ft (2.7m) high. There are also several other fine carved gravestones in the churchyard.

☎ 0131 668 8800 www.historic-scotland.gov.uk

Killiecrankie 301 E3

Just north of Pitlochry is the site of the battle of Killiecrankie in 1689, won by the Highland Jacobites under Bonnie Dundee. On the edge of the wooded gorge is the Pass of Killiecrankie Visitor Centre, which relates the fierce encounter. From here, a path leads to 'Soldiers Leap', where a fleeing government soldier made a spectacular jump over the River Garry during the battle.

☎ 01796 473233 www.nts.org.uk

Kilmartin House Museum 290 A5

Within a six-mile (10km) radius of Kilmartin Valley, over 350 ancient monuments can be found, including 150 that are prehistoric. This award-winning archaeological museum examines the relationship between Scotland's richest prehistoric landscape and its people. Artefacts from ancient monuments, reconstructions and interactive audiovisual displays make a fascinating exhibition.

☎ 01546 510278 www.kilmartin.org

Kintail Estate & Morvich (NTS) 307 G3

This west Highland estate is home to the Falls of Glomach, an impressive 370ft (113m) high waterfall, and the Five Sisters of Kintail, four of which are over 3000ft (915m). The site of the Battle of Glen Shiel, which took place in 1719, is also within this area, 5 miles (8km) from Morvich. The best access to the mountains is from the Countryside Centre at Morvich.

☎ 01599 511231 www.nts.org.uk

Kirkcaldy Museum & Art Gallery 294 A5

Located in the attractive War Memorial Gardens, the gallery contains fine and decorative arts of local and national importance. There is an outstanding collection of 18th to 20th century Scottish paintings, and probably the largest public collection of works by William McTaggart and the Scottish colourist, S.J. Peploe, outside the National Galleries of Scotland.

☎ 01592 412860

Lennoxlove  286 C2

Lennoxlove House is the seat of the Duke of Hamilton and there are fine collections of furniture and family portraits belonging to the Hamilton family. The earliest part of the house, the rectangular keep, was built well before 1400 and there have been extensions and additions during every century since. The various owners of the house have associations with the Stewarts and there are a number of mementoes belonging to Mary, Queen of Scots, including her death mask.

☎ 01620 823720 www.lennoxlove.org

Lighthouse, The  387 L8

Scotland's Centre for Architecture, Design and the City is the long-term legacy of Glasgow being the UK City of Architecture and Design in 1999. This Charles Rennie Mackintosh-designed building, once owned by the Herald newspaper, has a distinctive tower at one corner which gives it the name the Lighthouse. It houses the Mackintosh Interpretation Centre which features plans, photos and models of his work, and there are great views over the city skyline from the top of the tower.

☎ 0141 221 6362 www.thelighthouse.co.uk

Linlithgow Palace 285 E2

The ruin of a great 15th century Palace on the edge of Linlithgow Loch which is associated with many of Scotland's best known historical figures; James V and Mary, Queen of Scots, were both born here. The palace was damaged by fire in 1746 and it has been a roofless ruin ever since. The chapel is worth a look and the galleried Great Hall is magnificent. The quadrangle courtyard has a richly-carved 16th century fountain.

☎ 01506 842896 www.historic-scotland.gov.uk

Linn of Tummel (NTS) 301 E3

Follow a riverside nature trail, from Garry Bridge, through mixed woodland to the meeting place of the Rivers Garry and Tummel. The Linn of Tummel, which translates as 'pool of the tumbling stream', comprises a series of rocky rapids in a beautiful setting.

☎ 01796 473233 www.nts.org.uk

Loch an Eilein Visitor Centre & Forest Trail 310 A4

An island in Loch an Eilein harbours the remains of a 15th century castle. An ancient pine forest surrounds the loch, with some species dating back to the era of Bonnie Prince Charlie. There is a waymarked forest trail and a visitor centre.

Loch Lomond & The Trossachs National Park 291 F4

In 2002, Loch Lomond and the Trossachs were inaugurated as Scotland's first National Park. The park stretches from Arrochar to Callander, west to east, and from Balloch to Crianlarich, south to north. It is an area of contrasts, depicted by the lochs, wooded hills and lowlands in the south to the rugged and dramatic Highland mountains in the north. Ben Lomond towers over Loch Lomond, Britain's largest expanse of fresh water, and visitors can enjoy the wild glens and unspoilt lochs of the Trossachs. The Breadalbane area boasts numerous mountains over 3000ft (915m), including Ben More, Ben Lui, Ben Challum and Ben Vorlich, whilst the Argyll Forest in the west is overlooked by the Arrochar Alps and bounded by sea lochs.

Loch Lomond Shores visitor centre in Balloch provides the main gateway into the National Park.

☎ 01389 722600 www.lochlomond-trossachs.org

Loch Ness Monster Exhibition Centre 309 E2

The story of Loch Ness, the monster and other mysteries of the area are presented in a wide-screen cinema. Find out about the sightings of 'Nessie' and the various search expeditions, view the account of John Cobb's world water speed record attempt in 1953 on Loch Ness and hear about the 18th century mysterious 'footprints'.

☎ 01456 450342 www.lochness-centre.com

Lochore Meadows Country Park 293 G5

Green and pleasant countryside reclaimed from coal mining wasteland in the 1960s, set around a large lake. Find a variety of activities within the 1200 acres (486ha), including golf, fishing, sailing, windsurfing, walking and horse riding. There is also a nature reserve with a bird-watching hide and ancient historical remains, such as Lochore Castle. Admission to the park is free, with charges for the activities.

☎ 01592 414300 www.lochore-meadows.co.uk

Logan Botanic Garden 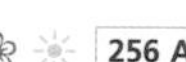 256 A2

The exceptionally mild climate, courtesy of the Gulf Stream, makes this one of Scotland's most exotic gardens, allowing a colourful array of tender plants to thrive. Many specimens are of wild origin, particularly representing the temperate regions of the Southern Hemisphere. The peat garden comprises a delightful collection of meconopsis, primulas, trilliums and dwarf rhododendrons. The walled garden has spring interest with magnolis, camellias, rhododendrons and a splendid collection of half-hardy perennials for summer colour. The woodland garden boasts mature eucalyptus and unusual, colourful southern hemisphere shrubs. Recent introductions are a result of plant hunting trips to Chile. There is also a Discovery Centre informing visitors of the work of the National Botanic Gardens of Scotland.

☎ 01776 860231 www.rbge.org.uk

Maes Howe 340 B5

This chambered cairn is the finest megalithic (Neolithic) tomb in the British Isles. It consists of a large mound 115ft (35m) in diameter covering a stone-built passage and a large burial chamber with cells in the walls. Vikings and Norse crusaders carved the runic inscriptions in the walls. Admission, shop and tearoom are at the nearby 19th century Tormiston Mill.

☎ 01856 761606 www.historic-scotland.gov.uk

Manderston  287 F4

Manderston could well be described as a celebration of opulence; a relatively modest 18th century house transformed by architect James Kinross into an extravagant, neoclassical Edwardian mansion.

Luxurious rooms boast intricate plasterwork, silk and velvet wall hangings, panelling and fine furniture. Marble abounds, from inlaid floors to the magnificent, probably unique staircase with its silver-plated balustrade. For contrast, the 'below stairs' element is also on view, together with a large collection of Blue John pieces and a biscuit tin museum.

Similarly, no expense was spared on the 56 acre (22ha) grounds. There are four splendid formal Edwardian terraces overlooking a lake and informal woodland gardens, while the walled gardens combine colourful plantings with fountains and statuary.

☎ 01361 883450 www.manderston.co.uk

McManus Galleries  396 B2

Contained within this Victorian Gothic building, designed by Sir George Gilbert Scott, are some remarkable collections of national importance. The galleries feature local history, costume, natural history, archaeology, decorative arts and a superb Scottish Victorian art collection. Do not miss the magnificent Albert Hall with its fine stained glass window and vaulted roof.

☎ 01382 432350 www.dundeecity.gov.uk/mcmanus

Meigle Sculptured Stones 302 A5

This is one of the most notable collections of Dark Age sculpture in Western Europe. There are 26 carved stones, the largest over 8ft (2m) tall.

☎ 01828 640612 www.historic-scotland.gov.uk

Loch Lomond

Mellerstain

Mellerstain 278 A3

A superb Georgian mansion representing some of the best architectural work of William Adam, who began the building in 1725, and his son, Robert, who completed it some 50 years later, giving a wonderful opportunity to compare their styles. The Robert Adam interior decoration is an outstanding feature of Mellerstain, the exquisite ceilings preserved in the original colours being particularly remarkable. Interior decoration is matched by the furnishings; pieces by Chippendale, Hepplewhite and Sheraton, and paintings by Van Dyck, Gainsborough and Aikman.

The gardens are formal, comprising Italianate terraces with magnificent views of the Cheviot Hills whilst the grounds, designed by William Adam in the style of Lancelot 'Capability' Brown, make a splendid backdrop to the house.

☎ 01573 410225 www.mellerstain.com

Melrose Abbey 277 G2

A Cistercian abbey founded in 1136 by David I, noted for its elegant and elaborate masonry. Largely demolished by the English in 1385, it was rebuilt in the Gothic style but was finally destroyed in 1545. It is considered the most beautiful of the great Border abbeys, delicately carved stonework giving an intimation of its former splendour. The outer shell of the abbey church is still extant, with its magnificent east window.

An embalmed heart, thought to be that of Robert the Bruce, was found here. On his express wish it was taken for burial in the Holy Land, but the courier was killed in Spain and the heart returned to Scotland.

☎ 01896 822562 www.historic-scotland.gov.uk

Mount Stuart 282 C4

A spectacular Victorian Gothic house, Mount Stuart is the ancestral home of the Marquess of Bute. Its splendid interiors and architecture include a mix of astrological designs, stained glass and marble. In the 300 acres (121ha) of grounds and gardens there is a mature Victorian pinetum, arboretum and exotic gardens.

☎ 01700 503877 www.mountstuart.com

Mousa Broch 343 D5

This is the finest surviving Iron Age broch tower, standing over 40ft (12m) high. The stairs can be climbed to the parapet.

☎ 01466 793191 www.historic-scotland.gov.uk

Museum of Childhood 397 E3

Devoted to the history of childhood, this is an enchanting, colourful and extremely noisy place! Children love this museum for the sheer quantity of dolls, trains, models, games and books from all over the world, and adults love it for its nostalgia factor.

☎ 0131 529 4142 www.cac.org.uk

Museum of Flight 286 C2

There are around 50 complete aircraft, 80 engines and 5000 items of aircraft related equipment on display at Scotland's national aviation museum. The planes range from the oldest, the Hawk glider of 1896, to modern passenger airlines, supersonic jet fighters and Concorde. There are special exhibitions on space flight, early aviation and air traffic control. An annual airshow gives visitors the chance to see many planes in flight.

☎ 01620 880308 www.nms.ac.uk/flight

Museum of Scotland 397 E2

Scotland's national museum is housed in a striking, modern sandstone building completed in 1998. The museum traces the history and achievements of Scotland and its people, from the country's geological beginnings right up to the present day. The lower floors cover the period up to about 1700 with displays of rocks and fossils, Roman, Pictish and Gaelic artefacts. Two floors are devoted to Industry and Empire and tell of how the Scots pioneered many aspects of heavy engineering. The top floor covers the 20th century and is based around items that Scottish people thought best represented their country, which has resulted in displays on Irn-Bru and football strips, amongst others. There are free themed tours at regular intervals throughout the day and audio guides are available.

☎ 0131 247 4422 www.nms.ac.uk

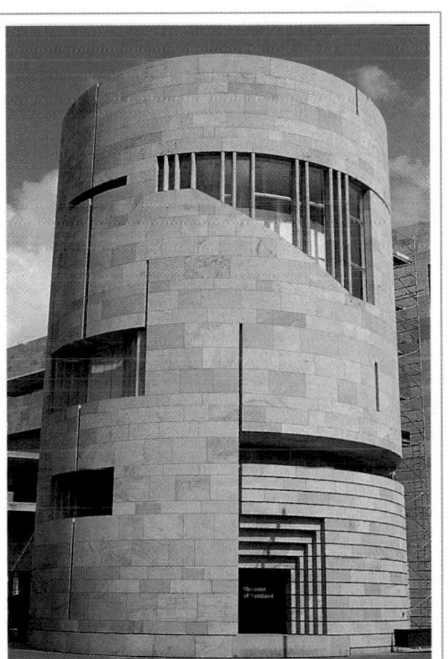
Museum of Scotland

Museum of Scottish Lead Mining 275 G4

Set in Wanlockhead, Scotland's highest village in the dramatic Lowther Hills, the museum traces 300 years of local lead mining history. A walk-through exhibition in the excellent visitor centre explains mining and extraction processes, and there is a good display of local minerals, including galena, chalcopyrite and sphalerite. A village trail includes a guided tour round Lochgell Lead Mine, together with restored miners' cottages.

☎ 01659 74387 www.leadminingmuseum.co.uk

National Gallery of Scotland 397 E2

This fine Greek temple style building was designed by William Henry Playfair and opened to the public in 1859. It houses Scotland's greatest collections of European paintings and sculpture from the Renaissance to post-impressionist periods. There are works by Raphael, Titian, El Greco, Turner, Degas and Van Gogh as well as a superb collection of Scottish art featuring important works by Wilkie, Raeburn and Ramsay.

☎ 0131 624 6200 www.natgalscot.ac.uk

National Wallace Monument 292 D5

The National Wallace Monument takes visitors back 700 years to the days of Scotland's first struggle for independence. The story of William Wallace, freedom fighter and national hero, is told along with events that shaped this period of history. Climb the 246 steps to the top of the 220ft (67m) high tower for superb views.

☎ 01786 472140 www.stirling.co.uk/attractions/wallace.htm

Neidpath Castle 276 D2

A rare example of a 14th century castle converted to a 17th century tower house, in a spectacular setting above the River Tweed. Massive walls, some 12ft (3.5m) thick in places, withstood Civil War bombardment longer than any other castle in the area, while inside is a pit prison cut out of the rock. The Great Hall hosts an exhibition of beautiful batik wall hangings depicting the life of Mary, Queen of Scots. Check in advance for opening times.

☎ 01721 720333

New Lanark World Heritage Site 284 C5

New Lanark is a superb example of a restored industrial village with plenty to keep a family busy for most of the day. Founded in 1785 by David Dale and Richard Arkwright as a centre for cotton spinning, the elegant sandstone buildings sit alongside the River Clyde in a remarkable rural setting. Dale's son-in-law, Robert Owen, took over the management of the site in 1798 and his belief in looking out for the welfare of his workers led to him setting up a cooperative store, a nursery to allow mothers with young children to work, adult education facilities, decent housing and a social centre for the community of 2500 people. Owen's 'social experiment' was viewed with scorn by all of his competitors but his beliefs soon proved fruitful and the business was greatly improved. The Institute for the Formation of Character now houses the award winning visitor centre and the Millennium Experience, an innovative ride which explains Owen's aspirations and ideas for a better future. Visitors can also look around the village store, Owen's house and mill workers' cottages. A passport ticket gives access to all of these attractions.

☎ 01555 661345 www.newlanark.org

New Lanark World Heritage Site

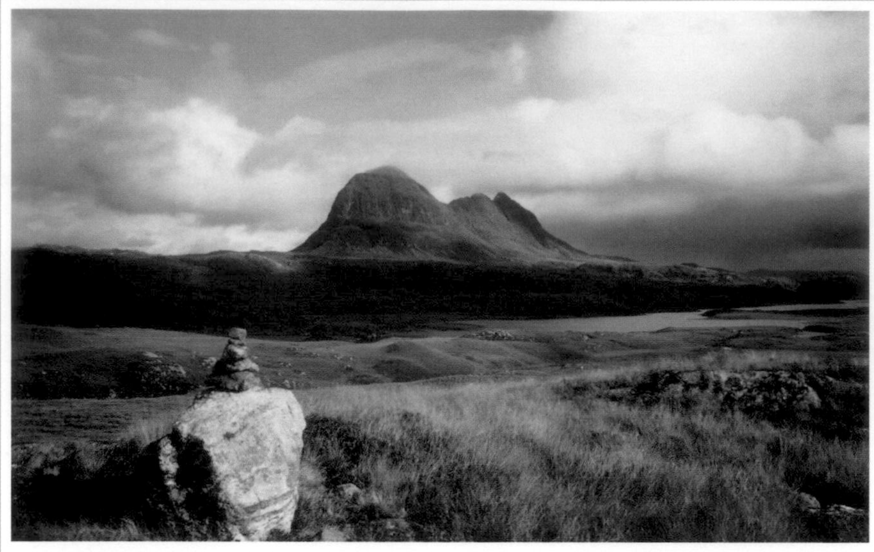
North West Highlands – Suilven

North West Highlands 320 A5

The North West Highlands provides a stunning and dramatic landscape of rugged mountains, hidden glens, moorlands, pine forests, secluded sandy beaches and sea lochs.

In Torridon, find mountain peaks towering over 3000ft (914m), whilst Ullapool is a thriving fishing village. Other remote villages along the north-west coast include Lochinver and Kinlochbervie. In Poolewe, find Inverewe Gardens, formed from a once barren peninsula on the shore of Loch Ewe, where exotic plants flourish in the warm climate created by the North Atlantic Drift. Alternatively, drive on Scotland's highest road, Bealach na Ba, climbing to the summit at 2056ft (625m) for spectacular views.

There are many natural features to look out for, too. Eas a' Chual Aluinn is Britain's tallest waterfall, and Corrieshalloch Gorge is one of Britain's finest examples of a box canyon. From here, a viewing platform stretched across the gorge looks up towards the magnificent Falls of Measach. Smoo Cave, in Durness, is an impressive limestone cave which has formed at the head of a narrow coastal inlet. The wild surroundings are also home to a variety of wildlife including red deer, eagles, otters and seals.

Old Man of Hoy 338 A2

Standing off the magnificent cliffs of north-west Hoy is this prominent, isolated sea stack. Comprised of red sandstone, it stands at 450ft (137m) high. The Old Man of Hoy can also be seen from the Scrabster to Stromness ferry.

Our Dynamic Earth 397 E3

This is a great family attraction based in a tented futuristic looking dome. Ten themed areas make use of dramatic special effects, stunning imagery and state-of-the-art interactive displays to take the visitor on a journey of discovery from the very beginning of time to our unknown future. Visitors begin their journey in the time machine elevator which takes them back to the creation of the universe before moving through a series of galleries that explain how the earth and continents were formed, how life has developed on earth and all about the seas and oceans.

☎ 0131 550 7800 www.dynamicearth.co.uk

Paisley Museum & Art Galleries 374 A3

The Paisley Pattern is a well-known fabric design of swirling teardrops or pine cones. Paisley Museum has the world's largest collection of Paisley shawls, as well as the looms on which these intricately patterned garments were created. There is also a nationally important collection of ceramics and many fine 19th century Scottish paintings.

☎ 0141 889 3151 www.renfrewshire.gov.uk

Palace of Holyroodhouse 397 E3

Largely a 17th century building, the north-west tower was built in 1501 for James IV. Holyroodhouse is the Queen's official residence in Scotland and it is used for state ceremonies. The Great Gallery occupies the whole of the first floor of the north wing, and in it hang 89 portraits of real and legendary kings of Scotland. The state apartments reflect the changing tastes of successive monarchs and are renowned for their fine stucco ceilings. Mary, Queen of Scots' chambers can be viewed in the west corner tower. The Queen's Gallery, for which there is a separate charge, hosts a programme of changing exhibitions from the Royal Collection, focusing primarily on works from the Royal Library at Windsor Castle.

☎ 0131 556 5100 www.royal.gov.uk

Our Dynamic Earth

Paxton House 287 G4

Superb 18th century Palladian mansion, designed by John and James Adam and further embellished by brother Robert, providing an interesting contrast in styles. As well as the notable interior decoration, this is essential viewing for furniture enthusiasts, with one of the greatest Chippendale collections in Scotland and fine Regency furniture by William Trotter of Edinburgh. The large art gallery, an out-station for the National Galleries for Scotland, has a programme of temporary exhibitions.

The 80 acres (32ha) of parkland surrounding the house offer walks along the banks of the River Tweed and an adventure playground.

☎ 01289 386291 www.paxtonhouse.com

People's Story Museum  397 E3

A lively museum, in the picturesque Canongate Tolbooth which was built in 1591. It uses oral history, reminiscence and written sources to tell the story of the lives, work and leisure of the ordinary people of Edinburgh, from the late 18th century to the present day.

☎ 0131 529 4057 www.cac.org.uk

Pitmedden Garden (NTS) 313 D2

A 17th century walled garden, notable for the Great Garden which is made up of four parterres of elaborate designs in boxwood hedging. These are filled with colourful annual bedding in summer. Interest is also provided by large herbaceous borders, roses, espalier fruit trees, roses and an herb garden. On the surrounding 100 acre (40ha) estate there is the Museum of Farming Life.

☎ 01651 842352 www.nts.org.uk

Pollok House (NTS)  374 B3

The Pollok Estate has been the home of the Maxwell family since the 13th century and the current house, an impressive Edwardian country mansion, was built in 1740. Sir William Stirling Maxwell (1818 – 1878) was an authority on the art and history of Spain and his collection of works by Goya and El Greco is superb. There is also a fine collection of the work of English poet and artist William Blake, as well as silverware and furnishings from the Edwardian period. The gardens are also worth a look with a collection of over 1000 species of rhododendron. Entrance is free from November to March.

☎ 0141 616 6410 www.nts.org.uk

Preston Mill & Phantassie Dovecot (NTS) 286 C2

A picturesque 18th century grain mill that was used commercially up until 1959. Today the mill no longer produces grain but visitors can see and hear the machinery and water wheel in action. There is an exhibition on milling and a display on the history of Preston Mill. It is a short scenic walk to the Phantassie Dovecot which once held 500 birds.

☎ 01620 860426 www.nts.org.uk

Priorwood (NTS) 277 G2

A specialist garden with varied and colourful herbaceous borders, plants being especially selected for drying qualities. This takes place on the premises where visitors can learn about the art of dried flower arranging.The garden also has an organic orchard growing historic apple varieties.

☎ 01896 822493 www.nts.org.uk

Queensferry Museum
285 F2

Traces the history of the people of Queensferry, the historic ferry crossing to Fife, the building of the Forth road and rail bridges, and the wildlife in the Forth estuary.

☎ 0131 331 5545 www.cac.org.uk

Rannoch Moor
299 F4

A wild, remote and fairly level area of around 50 sq miles (130 sq km), at an altitude of 1000ft (305m) surrounded by mountains. It is predominantly covered in a mixture of heather, peat bogs, rocks, and numerous lochs and streams. From the moor, enjoy fine views of Black Mount, Glencoe and the Grampians.

Rannoch Station can be found at the end of the B846, from where the only way to cross east to west is by foot. The main roads travel along its outer edges, while the West Highland Railway crosses it from south to north. Both the north and the south shores of the 10 mile (16km) long Loch Rannoch can be travelled along, with the south being the more scenic. The Blackwood of Rannoch, situated on the southern shore, is one of the last remaining examples of ancient Caledonian Forest and an important source of Scots Pine seed. An ancient burial ground of St Michael's can also be found. Loch Ericht lies to the north, accessed via a tunnel aqueduct.

There are plenty of scenic walks to enjoy on the moor. The lochs are also popular for trout fishing, while their sandy shores and islands attract many birds such as black-throated divers and goosander.

Ring of Brogar
340 A5

The Ring of Brodgar (also known as the Ring of Brogar) is a magnificent circle of upright stones, dating back to the Neolithic period. A ditch encloses the stones and is spanned by entrance causeways.

☎ 01855 841815 www.historic-scotland.gov.uk

Rosslyn Chapel
285 G3

A mysterious 15th century chapel that is thought to be just part of a much larger once-planned collegiate church whose foundations have been excavated. The carvings on the exterior and inside are outstanding; there are botanically accurate plants and leaves as well as biblical, pagan and masonic symbology.

☎ 0131 440 2159 www.rosslynchapel.org.uk

Royal Botanic Garden

Rannoch Moor

Royal Botanic Garden
373 B1

The Botanics are acknowledged to be some of the finest gardens in the world and the beautifully landscaped gardens cover an area of over 70 acres (28ha). The amazing Glasshouse Experience, a series of ten themed glasshouses with five different climatic zones to suit plants from all over the world, is home to giant water lilies and amazing orchids. There is an elegant 1850s glass topped Palm House, which is Britain's tallest and houses a 200 year old palm tree. Other spectacular areas are the Chinese Hillside, the renowned Rock Garden, the Scottish Heath Garden and an arboretum with over 200 species of tree. Guided tours are available between April and September for a fee.

☎ 0131 552 7171 www.rbge.org.uk

Royal Museum of Scotland
 397 E2

Thirty-six galleries of varying sizes present artefacts from around the globe, natural history specimens, and engines and other industrial machinery. The Main Hall, with its elegant Victorian bird-cage design, is flooded with natural light and provides a great sense of space and tranquility with fountains and fish ponds.

☎ 0131 247 4219 www.nms.ac.uk

Royal Scots Regimental Museum, The
397 E1

Housed in a 1900 Drill Hall, this museum contains paintings, artefacts, silver and medals illustrating the Regiment's illustrious history from its formation in 1633.

☎ 0131 310 5016 www.theroyalscots.co.uk/museum

St Abb's Head (NTS)
 287 G3

A 200 acre (80ha) National Nature Reserve on a dramatic, isolated promontory of black volcanic rock. Between April and August sheer 300ft (91m) cliffs provide nest sites for seabird colonies including kittiwakes, guillemots, razorbills and fulmars, while puffins tunnel into the clifftop. The visitor centre's remote camera link allows observation of the birds during the nesting season (entry fee). The headland provides splendid coastal views while the offshore waters are part of Scotland's first voluntary marine nature reserve.

☎ 01890 771443 www.nts.org.uk

St Andrews Cathedral
294 D3

The remains of one of the largest cathedrals in Scotland and the associated domestic ranges of the priory. The museum houses an outstanding collection of early Christian and medieval monuments, and other objets trouvés. St Rules Tower, in the precinct, is part of the first church of the Augustinian canons at St Andrews, built early in the 12th century. A climb up 150 steps is rewarded with fabulous views at the top. Combine a visit with St Andrews Castle.

☎ 01334 472563 www.historic-scotland.gov.uk

St Bride's Church
275 G2

The oldest structure in the village of Douglas, this church was built during the late 14th century. Originally the parish church of Douglas, it later became the mausoleum of the Black Douglas family. The restored choir, which contains three canopied monuments to the Douglas family, and the south side of the nave remain. Access to the church can be arranged by contacting the key keeper, details of which are on the church gate.

☎ 01555 851657 www.historic-scotland.gov.uk

St Giles Cathedral
 397 E2

Not strictly a cathedral, as it was only the seat of a bishop on two brief occasions in the 17th century, but the historical title seems to have stuck. The basic structure of the church is late 15th century, although parts of the early 12th century Norman chapel still remain. The cathedral is renowned for its Victorian and 20th century stained glass, Reiger organ and beautiful Thistle Chapel.

☎ 0131 225 9442 www.stgiles.net

St Magnus Cathedral
 338 D2

The cathedral was founded by Jarl Rognvald and dedicated to his uncle, St Magnus. The remains of both men are in the massive east choir piers. The original building dates from 1137 – 1200, but sporadic additional work went on until the late 14th century. It contains some of the finest examples of Norman architecture in Scotland, with small additions in transitional styles and some early Gothic work. A charge applies to tour the tower and upper areas, and should be booked in advance.

☎ 01856 874894

SCOTLAND

Scone Palace
293 G2

A castellated palace, enlarged and embellished in 1803, incorporating the 16th century and earlier palaces. Notable for its grounds and pinetum, and its magnificent collection of porcelain, furniture, ivories, 18th century clocks and 16th century needlework. From the 9th century, Moot Hill at Scone was the site of the famous Coronation Stone of Scone (the Stone of Destiny), and crowning place of Scottish Kings. In 1296 the English seized the Stone and took it to Westminster Abbey. Returned to Scotland's Edinburgh Castle in 1997, a replica now stands on Moot Hill.

☎ 01738 552300 www.scone-palace.co.uk

Scottish Crannog Centre
300 C5

A unique re-creation of an Iron Age loch dwelling, or crannog, this timbered and thatched house, standing on stilts within Loch Tay, has been authentically built using evidence obtained from underwater archaeological excavations of crannogs preserved in the loch.

☎ 01887 830583 www.crannog.co.uk

Scottish Fisheries Museum
295 D4

Housed in 16th to 19th century buildings, the museum describes the history of fishing in Scotland up to the present day.

☎ 01333 310628 www.scottish-fisheries-museum.org

Scottish Maritime Museum
274 B2

An informative museum on the harbourside at Irvine, with sailing and working boats, lifeboats and a collection of documents, photographs and artefacts interpreting Scotland's maritime history.

Indoor exhibits are based in the huge Linthouse Engine Shop which was dismantled and relocated from the Linthouse Shipyard in Govan in 1992. Nearby is a restored tenement flat, typical home to a 1920s shipyard worker. The floating exhibits are moored by the quay. In addition, there is ongoing restoration work on a variety of vessels.

☎ 01294 278283 www.scottishmaritimemuseum.org

Scottish National Gallery of Modern Art
373 B1

Set in beautiful parkland, the gallery has a superb collection of 20th century paintings, graphic art and sculpture amounting to almost 4000 pieces. There are fine examples of work by Lichtenstein, Matisse and Picasso and an unrivalled collection of Scottish art including works by Charles Rennie Mackintosh. The sculpture garden in the grounds has work by Barbara Hepworth, Eduardo Paolazzi and Henry Moore.

☎ 0131 624 6200 www.natgalscot.ac.uk

Scottish National Portrait Gallery
397 D2

Provides a unique visual history of Scotland, told through portraits of the figures who shaped it: royals and rebels, poets and philosophers, heroes and villains. The portraits are all of Scots although not all are by Scots; there is work by Rodin, Van Dyck and Gainsborough. The gallery is also home to the Scottish National Photographic Collection.

☎ 0131 624 6200 www.natgalscot.ac.uk

Scottish Seabird Centre
286 C1

Visitors can watch live pictures, via remote cameras, of the sea birds that make the islands in the Firth of Forth their home. Amongst the estimated 150,000 sea birds are gannets, thought to be the largest colony in the world, terns, guillemots and puffins, as well as seals and dolphins. There is also a cinema showing films on the wildlife, interactive displays and boat trips out to the islands themselves. There are superb views of Bass Rock and the other islands in the Firth of Forth from the roof terrace.

☎ 01620 890202 www.seabird.org

Seton Collegiate Church
286 B2

The chancel and apse of a lovely 15th century church with a transept and steeple added in 1513. Much of the church is in good condition and is full of interesting detail. The grounds of the church have the remains of a number of buildings thought to be priests' houses and there is a display of stonework from Seton Palace, destroyed in 1715.

☎ 01875 813334 www.historic-scotland.gov.uk

Skara Brae
340 A5

This site contains the best preserved group of Stone Age houses in Western Europe. A storm in 1850 lifted the sand covering the area to reveal the remains of this former fishing village. Ten one-roomed houses can be found, joined by covered passages, and contain their original stone furniture, hearths and drains. They provide a remarkable illustration of life in Neolithic times.

☎ 01856 841815 www.historic-scotland.gov.uk

Smith Art Gallery & Museum
292 C5

Displays and exhibitions encapsulate the history of Stirling through a wonderful collection of fine art and natural history. Some unusual pieces on view include the world's oldest dated curling stone, ancient tartans, prehistoric whalebones and the world's oldest football.

☎ 01786 471917 www.smithartgallery.demon.co.uk

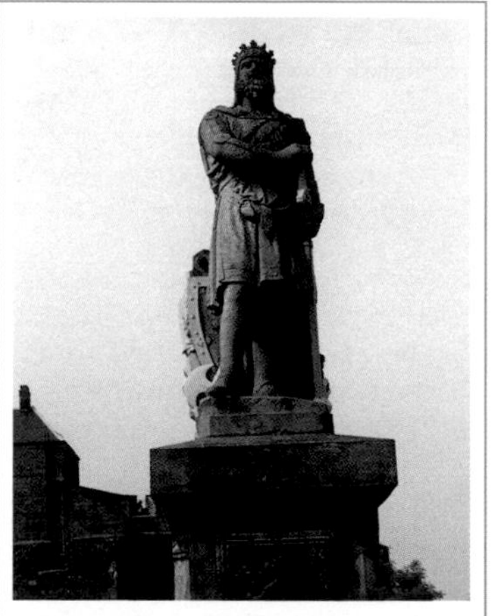

Stirling Castle – Robert the Bruce statue

Smoo Cave
334 D2

This impressive limestone cave has formed at the head of a narrow coastal inlet. An easy and safe access path leads into the cave from the road above. At 100ft (30m) wide and 50ft (15m) high, this is arguably one of the largest cave entrances in Britain. A wooden pathway extends into the second inner chamber, where Allt Smoo falls from an opening in the roof. A small boat provides access to the third chamber. The outer cave contains an ancient midden, indicating that Stone Age man once lived there. The cave is free to enter on foot, whilst a charge applies to enter by boat.

☎ 01971 511259 www.smoocave.org

Souter Johnnie's Cottage (NTS)
274 A5

A thatched cottage, home to souter (cobbler) John Davidson, a drinking companion of Robert Burns, and inspiration for Souter Johnnie in Burns' poem 'Tam O' Shanter'. The cottage contains Burns memorabilia and a reconstructed cobbler's workshop.

☎ 01655 760603 www.nts.org.uk

Staffa (Fingal's Cave) (NTS)
288 C1

This romantic, uninhabited island is famed for its extraordinary basaltic column formations. The best known of these is Fingal's Cave, 227ft (69m) deep and 66ft (20m) high. This cathedral-like structure, constantly pounded by the sea, was the inspiration for Mendelssohn's Hebrides overture. The cave can be viewed from a boat, which lands on the island if weather conditions permit. A colony of puffins can also be found nesting during spring and summer.

☎ 01631 570000 www.nts.org.uk

Stewartry Museum

266 A5

A purpose-built Victorian building opened in 1893 providing a home for a fascinating and quirky range of exhibits depicting the social and natural history of the Solway coast. There are also works by local artists, temporary exhibitions and a family and local history information service.

☎ 01557 331643

Stirling Castle
292 C5

Considered by many as Scotland's grandest castle, it is certainly one of the most important. Most of the building dates from the 15th and 16th centuries, when it became a popular Royal residence. The castle architecture is outstanding. The Great Hall and the Gatehouse, built by James IV, the magnificent Renaissance palace, built by James V, and the Chapel Royal, rebuilt by James VI, are amongst the key highlights. Mary, Queen of Scots was crowned here in 1543 and narrowly escaped death by fire in 1561. The medieval kitchens have been re-created, complete with models of cooks preparing a banquet in the 16th century.

Stirling Castle is set high on a volcanic outcrop, and commands stunning views, including the battlefields of Stirling Bridge and Bannockburn, Ben Lomond and the Trossachs.

☎ 01786 450000 www.historic-scotland.gov.uk

Storybook Glen
313 D5

A delight for children of all ages, this 20 acre (8ha) unusual theme park has over 100 models of fairytale and nursery rhyme characters set in beautiful landscaped gardens.

☎ 01224 732941 www.storybookglenaberdeen.co.uk

Strathclyde Country Park
375 F4

1000 acres (404ha) of woodland, rough wetlands, wildlife refuges and neat open parkland surround the 200 acre (80ha) man-made Strathclyde Loch. The park offers a huge variety of recreational activities (many of which have a fee) including watersports, horse riding, fishing, orienteering and cycling as well as numerous way-marked trails, sports pitches, sandy beaches and picnic areas. The visitor centre has information on the natural history and wildlife of the park. Within the park are the remains of Bothwellhaugh Roman Fort and Bathhouse. The park is also home to Scotland's largest theme park, M & D's, which has more than 40 rides and a large indoor entertainment complex.

☎ 01698 266155 www.northlan.gov.uk/leisure+and+tourism

Strathisla Distillery 323 G4

The oldest working distillery in the Highlands, established in 1786, and home to Chivas Regal blended Scotch whisky in which Strathisla single malt is predominant. The distillery takes water from the Broomhill Spring which Dominican monks used to make beer in the 13th century. There is a comprehensive self-guided tour of the distillery and whisky tasting.

☎ 01542 783044 www.chivas.com

Strathnaver Museum 335 G2

The former parish church of Farr was converted into this local museum and shows the story of the Strathnaver Clearances and the Clan Mackay.

☎ 01641 521418

Strathspey Railway 310 B3

A trip on this steam railway, reopened in 1978, runs 5 miles (8km) from Aviemore to Boat of Garten. The line now extends to Broomhill, also known as Glenbogle in the BBC TV series 'Monarch of the Glen'.

It operates mainly throughout the summer, but also on other occasions, so it is advisable to check the timetable.

☎ 01479 810725 www.strathspeyrailway.co.uk
☎ 01479 812220 (talking timetable)

Summerlee Heritage Park 375 F2

Said to be Scotland's noisiest museum, Summerlee Heritage Park preserves and interprets the history of the steel and engineering industries that were once dominant in the surrounding area. Spread over 25 acres (10ha), there is plenty to see including a reconstructed Miners Row where the living conditions of the miners from the 1840s to the 1960s can be experienced, and a re-created mine where their working conditions can be examined.

☎ 01236 431261 www.northlan.gov.uk/leisure+and+tourism

Sweetheart Abbey 267 D4

Splendid late 13th/early 14th century ruin founded by Devorgilla, Lady of Galloway, in memory of her husband John Balliol, and named because she was buried with her husband's embalmed heart which she carried with her in a casket after his death.

The 30 acre (12ha) site is dominated by the shell of the abbey church with its substantial central tower and lofty arched nave, but the most interesting feature is the great precinct wall. While not perhaps a professional defensive work, it was sufficiently formidable to deter raiding gangs.

☎ 01387 850397 www.historic-scotland.gov.uk

Strathclyde Country Park

Tantallon Castle 286 C1

This formidable castle has a majestic setting on cliffs overlooking the Firth of Forth and Bass Rock. A stronghold of the Douglas family, it was built at the end of the 14th century but after a number of sieges it was finally destroyed by Cromwell in 1651. The massive 50ft (15m) high curtain wall is all that remains intact.

☎ 01620 892727 www.historic-scotland.gov.uk

Thirlestane Castle 286 C5

Originally a 14th century fortress converted to a home by William Maitland, Secretary of State to Mary, Queen of Scots. Further restyling in the 17th century by Sir William Bruce created state rooms with arguably some of the finest plasterwork ceilings in Britain. Paintings include works by Gainsborough, Romney and Hopper, whilst the nursery wing contains a large collection of historic toys. The Border Country Life Museum is located here, and there are woodland walks and an adventure playground in the grounds.

☎ 01578 722430 www.thirlestanecastle.co.uk

Threave Castle 266 B4

Set on an island in the River Dee, access is by ferry following a 0.5 mile (1km) walk across fields.

Though probably settled here as far back as AD500, the present structure, a massive 5-storey keep, was built by Archibald the Grim in the 1370s. The castle had a turbulent history as home of the 'Black' Douglas clan, and was extended in the 15th century with substantial artillery fortification during a significant disagreement with James II. Besieged by the Covenanters, it was slighted and abandoned in 1640, but was briefly used to house Napoleonic prisoners of war.

☎ 0131 668 8800 www.historic-scotland.gov.uk

Threave Gardens (NTS) 266 B4

Gardens of around 60 acres (24ha), developed as a horticultural training centre by the National Trust for Scotland and maintained by students. Well worth visiting at almost any time, with spectacular springtime displays of nearly 200 varieties of daffodil, complemented by rhododendrons and other early flowering shrubs, extensive herbaceous colour in summer, striking trees and heathers in autumn, and rock, peat, walled and formal gardens.

☎ 01556 502575 www.nts.org.uk

Torosay Castle 289 G1

This Victorian family home contains furniture, pictures, china, family albums and scrapbooks dating from Edwardian times. The surrounding 12 acres (5ha) of gardens include formal terraces and a statue walk set amidst fuchsia hedges. There are also woodland and water gardens, a eucalyptus walk, oriental garden and rockery. Extensive views past Duart Castle and the Sound of Mull to the mountains of Arran and Lorne.

☎ 01680 812421 www.holidaymull.org/members/torosay.html

Torridon (NTS) 319 F4

Around 16,000 acres (6475ha) of some of Scotland's finest mountain scenery whose peaks rise over 3000ft (914m). Of major geological interest, Liathach and Beinn Alligin are formed of red sandstone, some 750 million years old, and their summits of white quartzite, some 600 million years old. The visitor centre, at the junction of the A896 and Diabaig road, has an audiovisual presentation on the local wildlife. There is also a deer museum and deer park, and ranger-led walks in season.

☎ 01445 791221 www.nts.org.uk

Traquair House 277 E2

Dating from the 12th century, and originally a royal hunting lodge, this is considered the oldest continuously inhabited house in Scotland, visited by 27 Scottish and English monarchs. Presenting a striking, whitewashed façade, internally many original features remain, including vaulted cellars, a medieval staircase and priest's hole. Furniture, fittings and memorabilia bear a fascinating testimony to the vagaries of Scottish political and domestic life over the centuries. There is also an 18th century working brewery with tastings in summer, maze, trails and adventure playground.

☎ 01896 830323 www.traquair.co.uk

Urquhart Castle 309 E2

The ruins of one of the largest castles in Scotland are found on the shores of Loch Ness. First built in the 1230s on the site of a vitrified fort, the castle fell into decay after 1689 and was blown up in 1692 to prevent it being occupied by Jacobites. Many of the remains are 14th century and the Grant Tower is 16th century.

☎ 01456 450551 www.historic-scotland.gov.uk

Vikingar! Experience, The 282 D3

A multimedia display on local Viking history, from the earliest raids to their defeat at the Battle of Largs in 1263. The adjacent leisure complex houses a swimming pool, cinema and play area.

☎ 01475 689777 www.vikingar.co.uk

Weaver's Cottage (NTS) 283 F3

The village of Kilbarchan was, in 1830, home to over 800 weavers' looms. Today, the last remaining hand loom can be seen in this typical 18th century weaver's cottage. There are displays of local and historical weaving interest, an attractive cottage garden where plants are grown to make natural dyes and a presentation explaining the village's links with the famous Paisley patterned shawls.

☎ 01505 705588 www.nts.org.uk

West Highland Line 298 D2

Travel from Fort William to Mallaig on the West Highland Line, either on Scotrail or on the Jacobite Steam Train, which leaves in the morning and returns late afternoon. The round trip covers 84 miles (135km) and tours through magnificent Highland scenery.

Cross the 100ft (30m) high Glenfinnan Viaduct, and go past Loch Shiel and the monument commemorating where Bonnie Prince Charlie raised his standard. Travel through Arisaig, the UK's most westerly main line railway station, then via Loch Morar, which, at 1077ft (328m), is Britain's deepest loch. Enjoy great views en route of the Isles of Rum, Eigg, Muck and Canna, and the southern tip of Skye.

The journey stops at Glenfinnan and there is plenty of time to explore Mallaig and its harbour before returning.

☎ 01463 239026 www.steamtrain.info
www.scotrail.co.uk

Whithorn Priory 257 E2

St Ninian founded a church here around AD400, and this site is considered the cradle of Christianity in Scotland. The ruined priory, once the cathedral church of Galloway, was built in the 12th century as his tomb had become a place of pilgrimage. The ecclesiastical history of the site is complex, and finds from the ongoing archaeological work, including some fine Celtic crosses, are on display in the museum.

☎ 01988 500508 www.historic-scotland.gov.uk

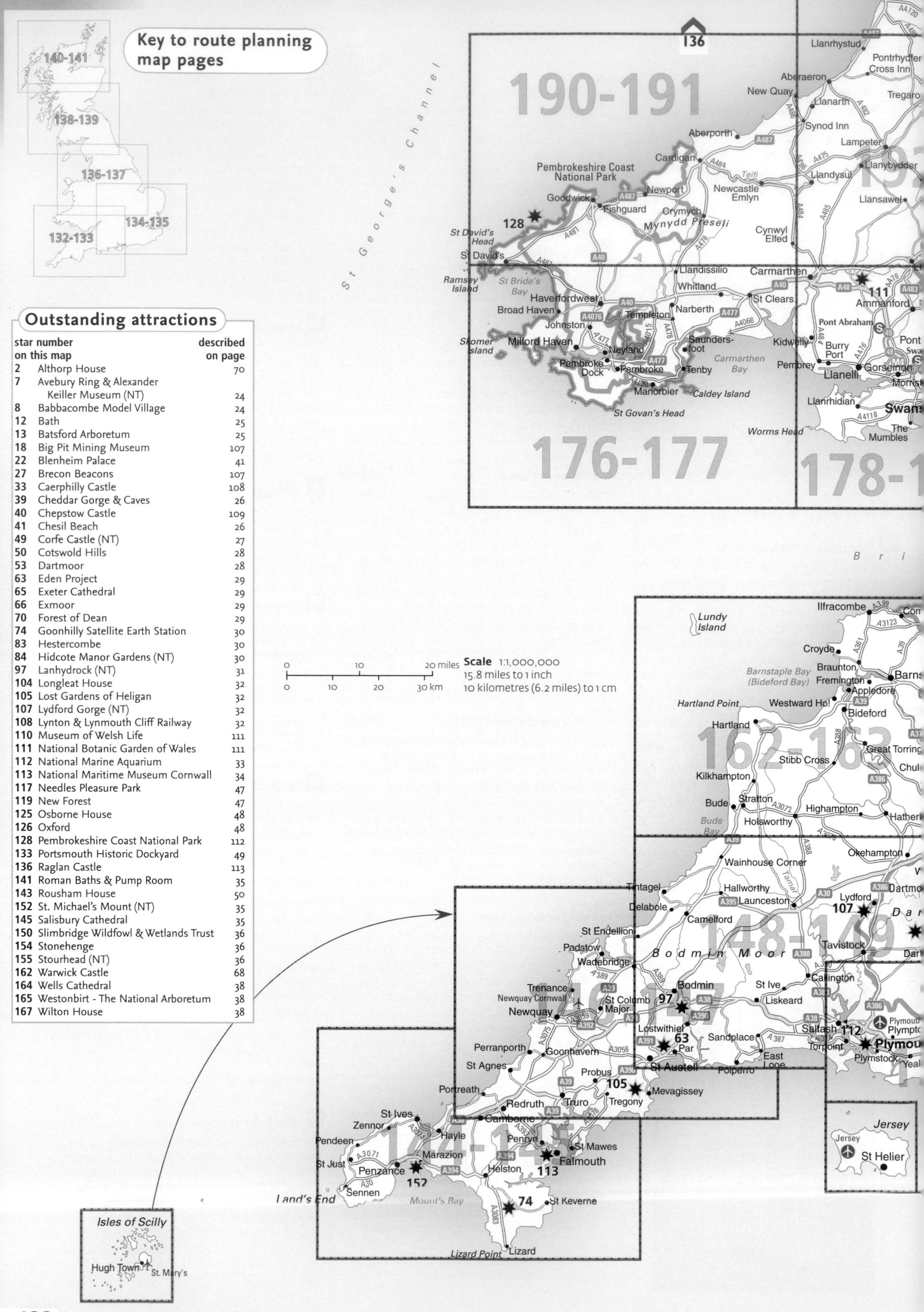
140-141
138-139
136-137
134-135
132-133
Key to route planning map pages
St George's Channel
136
190-191
176-177
178-1
162-163
148-149
146-147
144-145
Llanrhystud
Pontrhydfer
Cross Inn
Aberaeron
New Quay
Llanarth
Tregaro
Synod Inn
Aberporth
Lampeter
Cardigan
Llanybydder
Pembrokeshire Coast National Park
Newport
Newcastle Emlyn
Llandysul
Goodwick
Fishguard
Crymych
Llansawel
Mynydd Preseli
128
St David's Head
St David's
Cynwyl Elfed
Llandissilio
Carmarthen
Ramsey Island
St Bride's Bay
Whitland
111
Haverfordwest
St Clears
Ammanford
Broad Haven
Narberth
Templeton
Johnston
Pont Abraham
Skomer Island
Milford Haven
Neyland
Saundersfoot
Kidwelly
Burry Port
Pembroke Dock
Pembroke
Tenby
Carmarthen Bay
Pembrey
Llanelli
Gorseinon
Manorbier
Caldey Island
Llanrhidian
St Govan's Head
Worms Head
The Mumbles
Bri
Lundy Island
Ilfracombe
Croyde
Braunton
Barnstaple Bay (Bideford Bay)
Fremington
Appledore
Hartland Point
Westward Ho!
Bideford
Hartland
Great Torring
Stibb Cross
Kilkhampton
Bude
Stratton
Highampton
Bude Bay
Holsworthy
Okehampton
Wainhouse Corner
Tintagel
Hallworthy
Lydford
Launceston
Delabole
107
Camelford
St Endellion
Padstow
Wadebridge
Bodmin Moor
Tavistock
Trenance
Newquay Cornwall
Bodmin
St Ive
Callington
Newquay
St Columb Major
97
Liskeard
Lostwithiel
63
Par
Sandplace
Saltash
112
Plymouth
Perranporth
Goonhavern
Torpoint
Plymstock
St Agnes
St Austell
East Looe
Polperro
Probus
105
Mevagissey
Portreath
Truro
Tregony
Redruth
St Ives
Camborne
Zennor
Hayle
Pendeen
Penryn
St Mawes
Marazion
St Just
Penzance
Falmouth
Helston
113
152
Sennen
Land's End
Mount's Bay
74
St Keverne
Lizard Point
Lizard
Jersey
St Helier
Isles of Scilly
Hugh Town
St. Mary's
0
10
20 miles
0
10
20
30 km
Scale 1:1,000,000
15.8 miles to 1 inch
10 kilometres (6.2 miles) to 1 cm

Key to route planning map pages

Outstanding attractions

star number on this map		described on page
2	Althorp House	70
7	Avebury Ring & Alexander Keiller Museum (NT)	24
8	Babbacombe Model Village	24
12	Bath	25
13	Batsford Arboretum	25
18	Big Pit Mining Museum	107
22	Blenheim Palace	41
27	Brecon Beacons	107
33	Caerphilly Castle	108
39	Cheddar Gorge & Caves	26
40	Chepstow Castle	109
41	Chesil Beach	26
49	Corfe Castle (NT)	27
50	Cotswold Hills	28
53	Dartmoor	28
63	Eden Project	29
65	Exeter Cathedral	29
66	Exmoor	29
70	Forest of Dean	29
74	Goonhilly Satellite Earth Station	30
83	Hestercombe	30
84	Hidcote Manor Gardens (NT)	30
97	Lanhydrock (NT)	31
104	Longleat House	32
105	Lost Gardens of Heligan	32
107	Lydford Gorge (NT)	32
108	Lynton & Lynmouth Cliff Railway	32
110	Museum of Welsh Life	111
111	National Botanic Garden of Wales	111
112	National Marine Aquarium	33
113	National Maritime Museum Cornwall	34
117	Needles Pleasure Park	47
119	New Forest	47
125	Osborne House	48
126	Oxford	48
128	Pembrokeshire Coast National Park	112
133	Portsmouth Historic Dockyard	49
136	Raglan Castle	113
141	Roman Baths & Pump Room	35
143	Rousham House	50
152	St. Michael's Mount (NT)	35
145	Salisbury Cathedral	35
150	Slimbridge Wildfowl & Wetlands Trust	36
154	Stonehenge	36
155	Stourhead (NT)	36
162	Warwick Castle	68
164	Wells Cathedral	38
165	Westonbirt - The National Arboretum	38
167	Wilton House	38

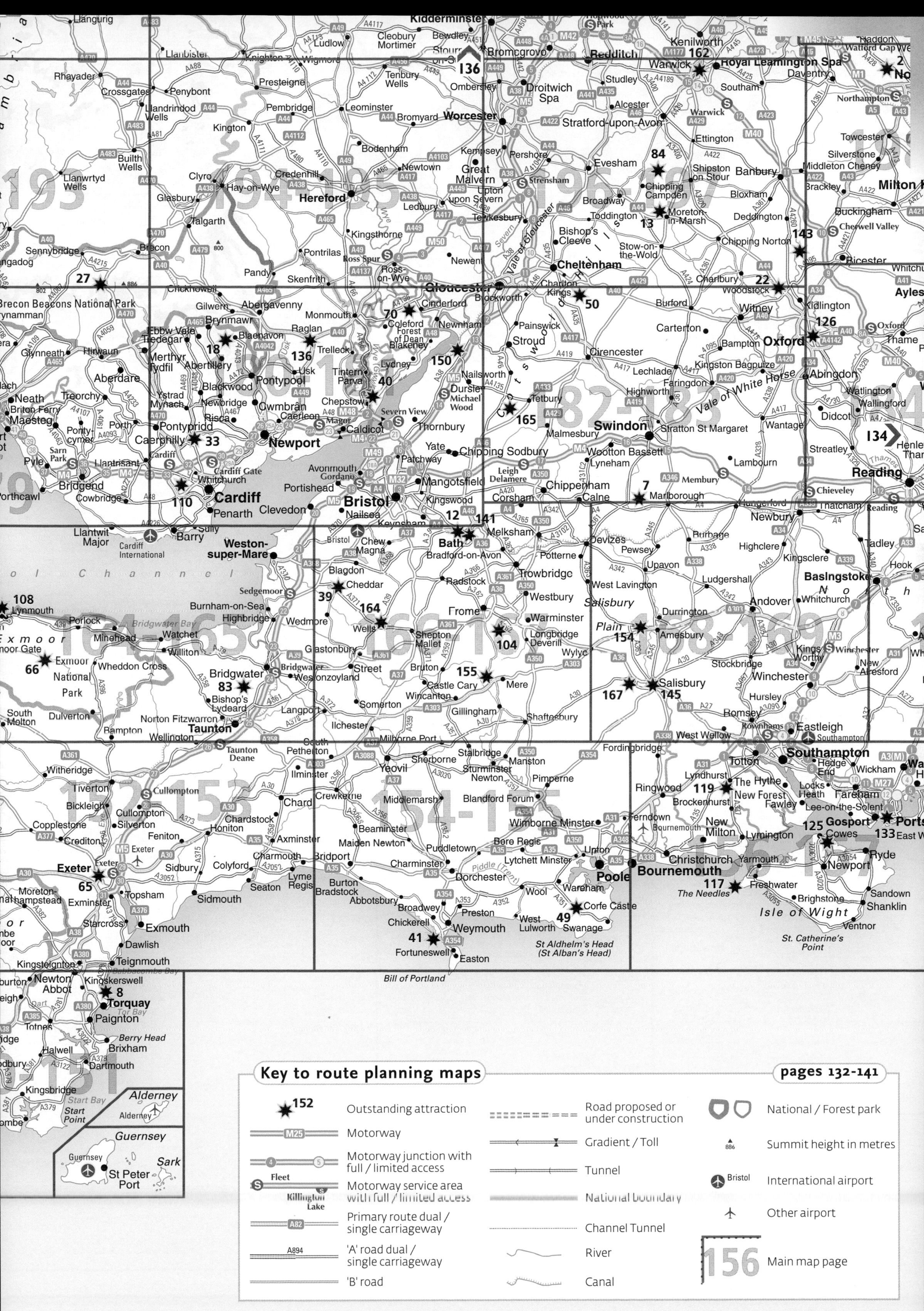

Kidderminster
Kenilworth
Warwick
Royal Leamington Spa
Daventry
Ludlow
Cleobury Mortimer
Bewdley
Bromsgrove
Redditch
Llanidloes
Llangurig
Knighton
Wigmore
Tenbury Wells
Ombersley
Droitwich Spa
Studley
Southam
Rhayader
Crossgates
Penybont
Presteigne
Llandrindod Wells
Pembridge
Leominster
Bromyard
Worcester
Stratford-upon-Avon
Alcester
Northampton
Kington
Bodenham
Kempsey
Pershore
Evesham
Ettington
Towcester
Silverstone
Builth Wells
Llanwrtyd Wells
Clyro
Hay-on-Wye
Glasbury
Credenhill
Hereford
Newtown
Great Malvern
Upton upon Severn
Ledbury
Tewkesbury
Broadway
Chipping Campden
Shipston on Stour
Banbury
Middleton Cheney
Brackley
Milton Keynes
Talgarth
Kingsthorne
Toddington
Moreton-in-Marsh
Bloxham
Deddington
Buckingham
Bishop's Cleeve
Stow-on-the-Wold
Chipping Norton
Brecon
Pontrilas
Ross Spur
Ross-on-Wye
Newent
Cheltenham
Sennybridge
Pandy
Skenfrith
Gloucester
Brockworth
Charlton Kings
Charlbury
Woodstock
Aylesbury
Brecon Beacons National Park
Abergavenny
Cinderford
Gilwern
Brynmawr
Monmouth
Coleford
Forest of Dean
Blakeney
Newnham
Painswick
Burford
Witney
Kidlington
Ebbw Vale
Tredegar
Blaenavon
Raglan
Stroud
Carterton
Oxford
Thame
Glynneath
Hirwaun
Merthyr Tydfil
Abertillery
Usk
Trelleck
Tintern Parva
Lydney
Dursley
Cirencester
Lechlade
Bampton
Kingston Bagpuize
Abingdon
Aberdare
Pontypool
Blackwood
Michael Wood
Nailsworth
Faringdon
Highworth
Vale of White Horse
Watlington
Wallingford
Neath
Treorchy
Ystrad Mynach
Newbridge
Cwmbran
Chepstow
Tetbury
Briton Ferry
Maesteg
Risca
Caerleon
Severn View
Didcot
Pontypridd
Magor
Caldicot
Thornbury
Malmesbury
Swindon
Stratton St Margaret
Wantage
Caerphilly
Newport
Yate
Chipping Sodbury
Wootton Bassett
Streatley
Henley-on-Thames
Pyle
Llantrisant
Cardiff Gate
Patchway
Avonmouth
Lyneham
Lambourn
Bridgend
Whitchurch
Gordano
Leigh Delamere
Chippenham
Membury
Reading
Porthcawl
Cowbridge
Cardiff
Portishead
Mangotsfield
Kingswood
Bristol
Corsham
Calne
Marlborough
Chieveley
Penarth
Clevedon
Nailsea
Keynsham
Hungerford
Newbury
Thatcham
Llantwit Major
Cardiff International
Barry
Sully
Weston-super-Mare
Chew Magna
Bath
Melksham
Devizes
Pewsey
Burbage
Highclere
Kingsclere
Tadley
Bradford-on-Avon
Potterne
Upavon
Blagdon
Trowbridge
West Lavington
Ludgershall
Basingstoke
Radstock
Sedgemoor
Cheddar
Westbury
Salisbury Plain
Andover
Whitchurch
Burnham-on-Sea
Highbridge
Lynmouth
Porlock
Bridgwater Bay
Wedmore
Wells
Frome
Warminster
Durrington
Minehead
Watchet
Williton
Exmoor
Glastonbury
Shepton Mallet
Longbridge Deverill
Amesbury
Kings Worthy
Winchester
Exmoor National Park
Wheddon Cross
Bridgwater
Westonzoyland
Street
Bruton
Wylye
Stockbridge
New Alresford
Castle Cary
Mere
Salisbury
Bishop's Lydeard
Wincanton
Hursley
Somerton
Gillingham
South Molton
Dulverton
Norton Fitzwarren
Langport
Romsey
Eastleigh
Bampton
Taunton
Ilchester
Shaftesbury
Wellington
Taunton Deane
South Petherton
Milborne Port
West Wellow
Southampton
Stalbridge
Fordingbridge
Totton
Hedge End
Wickham
Witheridge
Yeovil
Sherborne
Sturminster Newton
Marnhull
Ilminster
Lyndhurst
The Hythe
Tiverton
Cullompton
Crewkerne
Chard
Middlemarsh
Blandford Forum
Pimperne
Ringwood
Brockenhurst
New Forest
Fawley
Locks Heath
Fareham
Lee-on-the-Solent
Bickleigh
Chardstock
Wimborne Minster
Ferndown
Bournemouth
New Milton
Gosport
Portsmouth
Copplestone
Silverton
Honiton
Beaminster
Lymington
Cowes
Crediton
Feniton
Axminster
Maiden Newton
Puddletown
Bere Regis
Lytchett Minster
Upton
Christchurch
Yarmouth
Ryde
Exeter
Sidbury
Colyford
Charmouth
Bridport
Charminster
Poole
Bournemouth
Newport
Dorchester
Seaton
Lyme Regis
Burton Bradstock
Wareham
Freshwater
Moretonhampstead
Exminster
Topsham
Sidmouth
Abbotsbury
Wool
The Needles
Brighstone
Sandown
Shanklin
Broadwey
Preston
Corfe Castle
Isle of Wight
Starcross
Exmouth
Chickerell
Weymouth
West Lulworth
Swanage
Ventnor
Dawlish
Fortuneswell
St Aldhelm's Head (St Alban's Head)
St. Catherine's Point
Kingsteignton
Teignmouth
Easton
Newton Abbot
Kingskerswell
Bill of Portland
Torquay
Paignton
Totnes
Berry Head
Brixham
Halwell
Dartmouth
Kingsbridge
Start Bay
Start Point
Alderney
Guernsey
St Peter Port
Sark

Key to route planning maps

pages 132-141

152	Outstanding attraction
M25	Motorway
	Motorway junction with full / limited access
Fleet / Killington Lake	Motorway service area with full / limited access
A82	Primary route dual / single carriageway
A894	'A' road dual / single carriageway
	'B' road
	Road proposed or under construction
	Gradient / Toll
	Tunnel
	National boundary
	Channel Tunnel
	River
	Canal
	National / Forest park
886	Summit height in metres
Bristol	International airport
	Other airport
156	Main map page

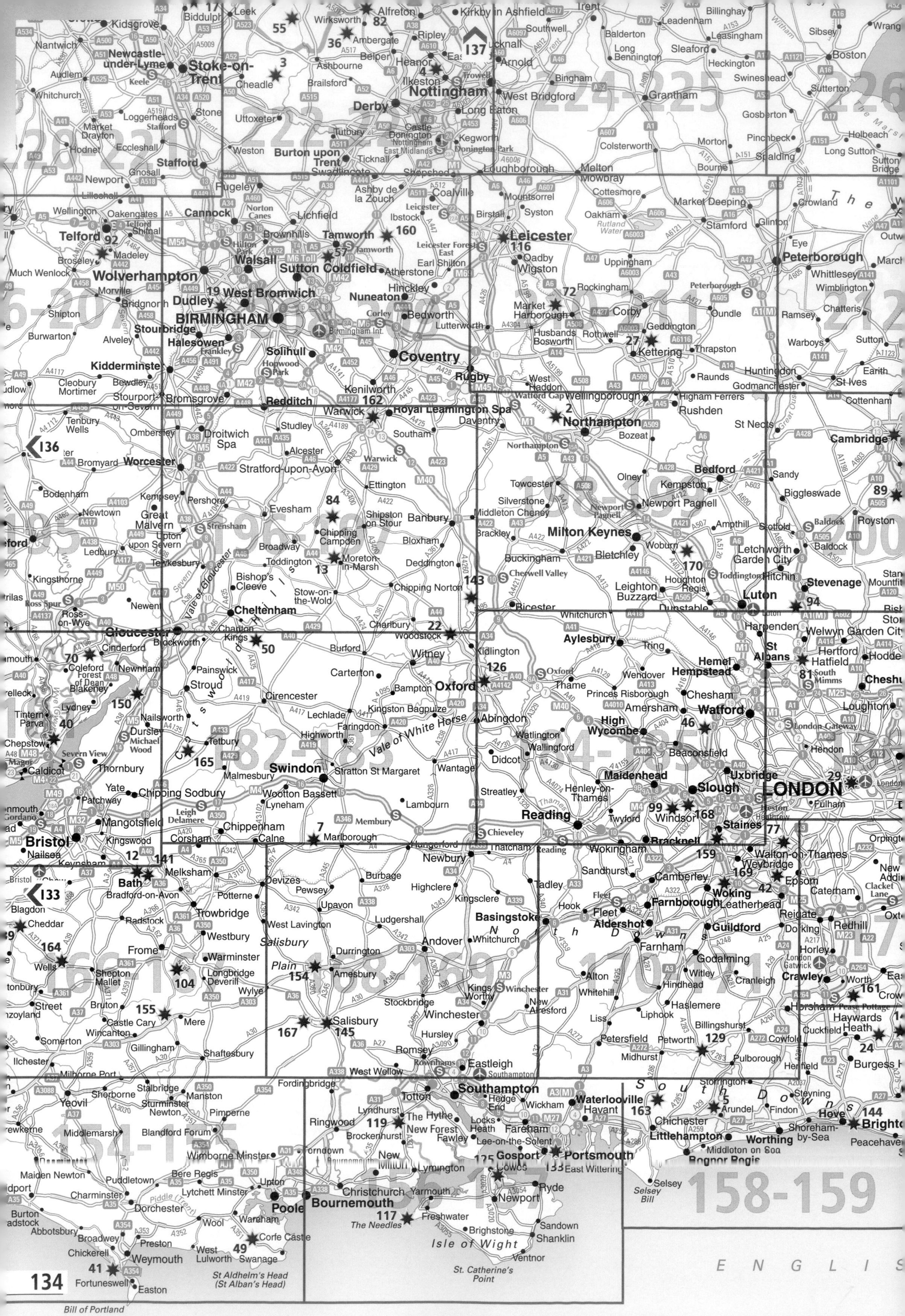

137
136
133
220-221
222-223
224-225
226
206-207
208-209
210-211
212
195
196-197
198-199
200
181
182-183
184-185
166-167
168-169
170-171
154-155
156-157
158-159
Kidsgrove
Biddulph
Leek
Wirksworth
Alfreton
Kirkby in Ashfield
Billinghay
Nantwich
Newcastle-under-Lyme
Stoke-on-Trent
Ashbourne
Ambergate
Ripley
Heanor
Hucknall
Southwell
Arnold
Leadenham
Sleaford
Boston
Audlem
Keele
Cheadle
Brailsford
Belper
Ilkeston
Nottingham
West Bridgford
Bingham
Grantham
Swineshead
Whitchurch
Stone
Derby
Long Eaton
Sutterton
Market Drayton
Loggerheads
Stafford
Uttoxeter
Tutbury
Castle Donington
Kegworth
Colsterworth
Gosberton
Hodnet
Eccleshall
Weston
Burton upon Trent
Ticknall
East Midlands
Morton
Pinchbeck
Holbeach
Long Sutton
Spalding
Sutton Bridge
Newport
Gnosall
Swadlincote
Shepshed
Loughborough
Melton Mowbray
Bourne
Fugeley
Ashby de la Zouch
Coalville
Mountsorrel
Cottesmore
Market Deeping
Crowland
Wellington
Oakengates
Cannock
Norton Canes
Lichfield
Ibstock
Birstall
Syston
Oakham
Rutland Water
Stamford
Telford
Shifnal
Brownhills
Tamworth
Leicester
Peterborough
Broseley
Madeley
Walsall
Sutton Coldfield
Atherstone
Earl Shilton
Oadby
Wigston
Uppingham
Much Wenlock
Wolverhampton
Whittlesey
March
Morville
Bridgnorth
Dudley
West Bromwich
Hinckley
Nuneaton
Rockingham
Wimblington
Shipton
BIRMINGHAM
Corley
Bedworth
Market Harborough
Corby
Oundle
Chatteris
Ramsey
Burwarton
Alveley
Stourbridge
Halesowen
Frankley
Birmingham Int.
Lutterworth
Husbands Bosworth
Rothwell
Geddington
Kettering
Thrapston
Warboys
Kidderminster
Solihull
Hopwood Park
Coventry
Rugby
Sutton
Cleobury Mortimer
Bewdley
Stourport-on-Severn
Bromsgrove
Kenilworth
West Haddon
Raunds
Huntingdon
Godmanchester
Earith
St Ives
Tenbury Wells
Redditch
Warwick
Royal Leamington Spa
Watford Gap
Wellingborough
Higham Ferrers
Rushden
Cottenham
Droitwich Spa
Studley
Southam
Daventry
Northampton
St Neots
Cambridge
Ombersley
Bromyard
Worcester
Alcester
Stratford-upon-Avon
Bozeat
Olney
Bedford
Sandy
Biggleswade
Bodenham
Kempsey
Pershore
Ettington
Towcester
Silverstone
Kempston
Newport Pagnell
Great Malvern
Newtown
Strensham
Evesham
Shipston on Stour
Banbury
Middleton Cheney
Ampthill
Stotfold
Baldock
Royston
Upton upon Severn
Ledbury
Broadway
Chipping Campden
Bloxham
Brackley
Milton Keynes
Woburn
Letchworth Garden City
Tewkesbury
Toddington
Moreton-in-Marsh
Deddington
Buckingham
Bletchley
Kingsthorne
Bishop's Cleeve
Stow-on-the-Wold
Chipping Norton
Cherwell Valley
Houghton Regis
Hitchin
Stevenage
Ross Spur
Newent
Cheltenham
Leighton Buzzard
Dunstable
Luton
Ross-on-Wye
Vale of Gloucester
Bicester
Whitchurch
Charlbury
Woodstock
Harpenden
Welwyn Garden City
Gloucester
Brockworth
Charlton Kings
Aylesbury
Tring
Kidlington
St Albans
Hertford
Hatfield
Cinderford
Coleford
Forest of Dean
Newnham
Burford
Witney
Hemel Hempstead
South Mimms
Painswick
Stroud
Carterton
Oxford
Thame
Wendover
Blakeney
Bampton
Princes Risborough
Chesham
Lydney
Cirencester
Lechlade
Kingston Bagpuize
Abingdon
Amersham
Watford
Loughton
Tintern Parva
Nailsworth
Faringdon
Vale of White Horse
High Wycombe
London Gateway
Chepstow
Dursley
Michael Wood
Tetbury
Highworth
Watlington
Wallingford
Beaconsfield
Hendon
Severn View
Magor
Caldicot
Thornbury
Malmesbury
Swindon
Stratton St Margaret
Wantage
Didcot
Maidenhead
Uxbridge
LONDON
Yate
Chipping Sodbury
Wootton Bassett
Lyneham
Lambourn
Streatley
Henley-on-Thames
Slough
Patchway
Leigh Delamere
Membury
Reading
Twyford
Windsor
Heston
Heathrow
Fulham
Mangotsfield
Chippenham
Calne
Marlborough
Hungerford
Chieveley
Staines
Bristol
Kingswood
Corsham
Newbury
Thatcham
Wokingham
Bracknell
Walton-on-Thames
Orpington
Nailsea
Keynsham
Melksham
Devizes
Burbage
Pewsey
Sandhurst
Camberley
Weybridge
Epsom
New Addington
Bath
Bradford-on-Avon
Highclere
Kingsclere
Tadley
Woking
Leatherhead
Caterham
Clacket Lane
Blagdon
Potterne
Upavon
Basingstoke
Hook
Fleet
Farnborough
Reigate
Redhill
Oxted
Cheddar
Radstock
Trowbridge
West Lavington
Ludgershall
Aldershot
Guildford
Dorking
Westbury
Salisbury Plain
Durrington
Andover
North Downs
Farnham
Horley
London Gatwick
Frome
Warminster
Amesbury
Godalming
Crawley
Worth
Wells
Shepton Mallet
Longbridge Deverill
Witley
Cranleigh
Crowborough
Glastonbury
Wylye
Kings Worthy
Winchester
New Alresford
Alton
Hindhead
Horsham
Pease Pottage
Street
Bruton
Castle Cary
Mere
Stockbridge
Whitehill
Liphook
Haslemere
Haywards Heath
Langport
Wincanton
Salisbury
Liss
Billingshurst
Cuckfield
Somerton
Gillingham
Shaftesbury
Hursley
Petersfield
Petworth
Cowfold
Ilchester
Romsey
Rownhams
Eastleigh
Midhurst
Pulborough
Henfield
Burgess Hill
Milborne Port
West Wellow
Southampton
Storrington
Steyning
Yeovil
Sherborne
Stalbridge
Manston
Sturminster Newton
Fordingbridge
Totton
Hedge End
Wickham
Waterlooville
Havant
South Downs
Arundel
Findon
Hove
Brighton
Crewkerne
Pimperne
Lyndhurst
The Hythe
Fawley
Locks Heath
Fareham
Chichester
Worthing
Shoreham-by-Sea
Middlemarsh
Blandford Forum
Ringwood
New Forest
Brockenhurst
Lee-on-the-Solent
Littlehampton
Peacehaven
Wimborne Minster
Ferndown
New Milton
Gosport
Portsmouth
Middleton on Sea
Bognor Regis
Maiden Newton
Puddletown
Bere Regis
Lymington
Cowes
East Wittering
Bridport
Charminster
Lytchett Minster
Upton
Christchurch
Yarmouth
Ryde
Selsey
Selsey Bill
Burton Bradstock
Dorchester
Poole
Bournemouth
Newport
Wool
Wareham
The Needles
Freshwater
Sandown
Abbotsbury
Broadwey
Preston
Corfe Castle
Brighstone
Shanklin
Chickerell
Weymouth
West Lulworth
Swanage
Isle of Wight
Ventnor
Fortuneswell
Easton
St Aldhelm's Head (St Alban's Head)
St. Catherine's Point
Bill of Portland
ENGLIS

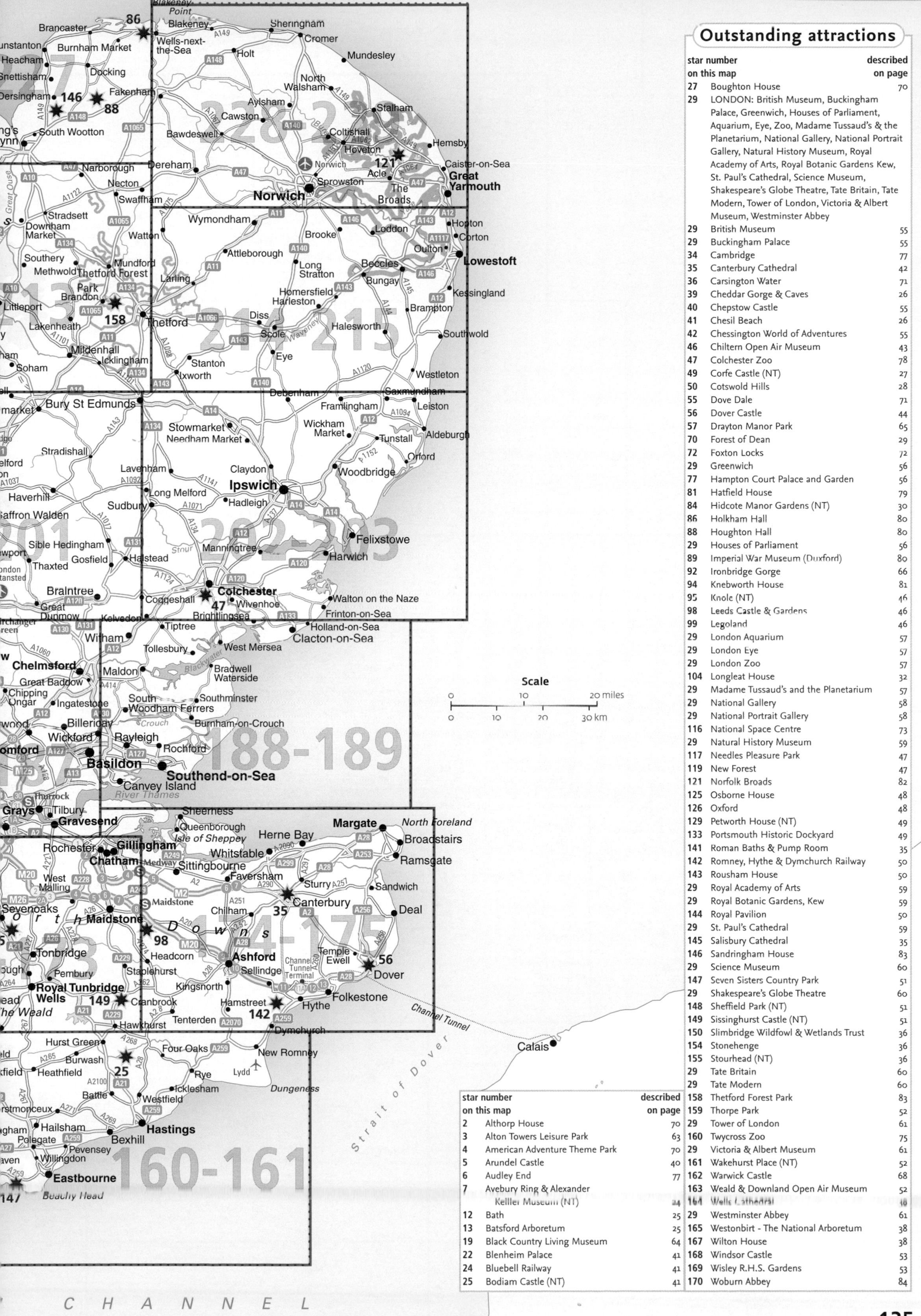

Blakeney Point
Brancaster
86
Blakeney
Sheringham
Cromer
Wells-next-the-Sea
Holt
Mundesley
Burnham Market
Heacham
Docking
North Walsham
Fakenham
146
88
Aylsham
Stalham
Cawston
Coltishall
Hemsby
South Wootton
Bawdeswell
Hoveton
121
Narborough
Dereham
Norwich
Acle
Caister-on-Sea
Great Yarmouth
Necton
Sprowston
The Broads
Swaffham
Norwich
Stradsett
Downham Market
Wymondham
Hopton
Watton
Brooke
Loddon
Corton
Oulton
Attleborough
Lowestoft
Southery
Mundford
Methwold
Thetford Forest
Long Stratton
Beccles
Bungay
Larling
Kessingland
Park
Brandon
Homersfield
Harleston
Littleport
158
Brampton
Diss
Thetford
Lakenheath
Scole
Halesworth
Southwold
Mildenhall
Eye
Icklingham
Stanton
Soham
Ixworth
Westleton
Debenham
Saxmundham
Bury St Edmunds
Framlingham
Leiston
Stowmarket
Wickham Market
Needham Market
Tunstall
Aldeburgh
Stradishall
Orford
Lavenham
Claydon
Woodbridge
Ipswich
Haverhill
Long Melford
Sudbury
Hadleigh
Saffron Walden
Felixstowe
Sible Hedingham
Manningtree
Harwich
Gosfield
Halstead
Thaxted
Braintree
Coggeshall
Colchester
47
Walton on the Naze
Wivenhoe
Great Dunmow
Kelvedon
Brightlingsea
Frinton-on-Sea
Tiptree
Holland-on-Sea
Witham
Clacton-on-Sea
Tollesbury
West Mersea
Chelmsford
Bradwell Waterside
Maldon
Great Baddow
Chipping Ongar
Ingatestone
South Woodham Ferrers
Southminster
Burnham-on-Crouch
Billericay
Wickford
Rayleigh
Rochford
Basildon
Southend-on-Sea
Canvey Island
River Thames
Thurrock
Grays
Tilbury
Gravesend
Sheerness
Queenborough
Isle of Sheppey
Herne Bay
Margate
North Foreland
Broadstairs
Rochester
Gillingham
Chatham
Whitstable
Ramsgate
Sittingbourne
West Malling
Faversham
Sturry
Sandwich
Canterbury
35
Maidstone
Deal
Sevenoaks
Chilham
North Downs
98
Tonbridge
Headcorn
Ashford
Temple Ewell
56
Pembury
Staplehurst
Sellindge
Dover
Royal Tunbridge Wells
Kingsnorth
Folkestone
149
Cranbrook
Hamstreet
142
Hythe
The Weald
Tenterden
Hawkhurst
Dymchurch
Channel Tunnel
Calais
Hurst Green
Four Oaks
New Romney
Burwash
25
Lydd
Heathfield
Rye
Dungeness
Strait of Dover
Battle
Icklesham
Westfield
Hailsham
Hastings
Polegate
Bexhill
Pevensey
Willingdon
Eastbourne
147
Beachy Head
CHANNEL
Scale
0 10 20 miles
0 10 20 30 km
188-189
160-161

Outstanding attractions

star number on this map		described on page
2	Althorp House	70
3	Alton Towers Leisure Park	63
4	American Adventure Theme Park	70
5	Arundel Castle	40
6	Audley End	77
7	Avebury Ring & Alexander Keiller Museum (NT)	34
12	Bath	25
13	Batsford Arboretum	25
19	Black Country Living Museum	64
22	Blenheim Palace	41
24	Bluebell Railway	41
25	Bodiam Castle (NT)	41
27	Boughton House	70
29	LONDON: British Museum, Buckingham Palace, Greenwich, Houses of Parliament, Aquarium, Eye, Zoo, Madame Tussaud's & the Planetarium, National Gallery, National Portrait Gallery, Natural History Museum, Royal Academy of Arts, Royal Botanic Gardens Kew, St. Paul's Cathedral, Science Museum, Shakespeare's Globe Theatre, Tate Britain, Tate Modern, Tower of London, Victoria & Albert Museum, Westminster Abbey	
29	British Museum	55
29	Buckingham Palace	55
34	Cambridge	77
35	Canterbury Cathedral	42
36	Carsington Water	71
39	Cheddar Gorge & Caves	26
40	Chepstow Castle	55
41	Chesil Beach	26
42	Chessington World of Adventures	55
46	Chiltern Open Air Museum	43
47	Colchester Zoo	78
49	Corfe Castle (NT)	27
50	Cotswold Hills	28
55	Dove Dale	71
56	Dover Castle	44
57	Drayton Manor Park	65
70	Forest of Dean	29
72	Foxton Locks	72
29	Greenwich	56
77	Hampton Court Palace and Garden	56
81	Hatfield House	79
84	Hidcote Manor Gardens (NT)	30
86	Holkham Hall	80
88	Houghton Hall	80
29	Houses of Parliament	56
89	Imperial War Museum (Duxford)	80
92	Ironbridge Gorge	66
94	Knebworth House	81
95	Knole (NT)	46
98	Leeds Castle & Gardens	46
99	Legoland	46
29	London Aquarium	57
29	London Eye	57
29	London Zoo	57
104	Longleat House	32
29	Madame Tussaud's and the Planetarium	57
29	National Gallery	58
29	National Portrait Gallery	58
116	National Space Centre	73
29	Natural History Museum	59
117	Needles Pleasure Park	47
119	New Forest	47
121	Norfolk Broads	82
125	Osborne House	48
126	Oxford	48
129	Petworth House (NT)	49
133	Portsmouth Historic Dockyard	49
141	Roman Baths & Pump Room	35
142	Romney, Hythe & Dymchurch Railway	50
143	Rousham House	50
29	Royal Academy of Arts	59
29	Royal Botanic Gardens, Kew	59
144	Royal Pavilion	50
29	St. Paul's Cathedral	59
145	Salisbury Cathedral	35
146	Sandringham House	83
29	Science Museum	60
147	Seven Sisters Country Park	51
29	Shakespeare's Globe Theatre	60
148	Sheffield Park (NT)	51
149	Sissinghurst Castle (NT)	51
150	Slimbridge Wildfowl & Wetlands Trust	36
154	Stonehenge	36
155	Stourhead (NT)	36
29	Tate Britain	60
29	Tate Modern	60
158	Thetford Forest Park	83
159	Thorpe Park	52
29	Tower of London	61
160	Twycross Zoo	75
29	Victoria & Albert Museum	61
161	Wakehurst Place (NT)	52
162	Warwick Castle	68
163	Weald & Downland Open Air Museum	52
164	Wells Cathedral	36
29	Westminster Abbey	61
165	Westonbirt - The National Arboretum	38
167	Wilton House	38
168	Windsor Castle	53
169	Wisley R.H.S. Gardens	53
170	Woburn Abbey	84

256-257
Whithorn
Drummore
Burrow Head
Mull of Galloway
258-259
Maryport
Seaton
Cockermouth
Workington
Distington
Whitehaven
Frizington
Cleator Moor
St Bees Head
St Bees
Egremont
Lake District
National Park
Seascale
Gosforth
138
Keswick
Water
Buttermere
96
Ullswater
Patterdale
Cumbrian Mountains
Grasmere
Ambleside
Troutbeck
Windermere
Coniston
Broughton in Furness
Newby Bridge
Kendal
100
Milnthorpe
85
Burton-in-Kendal
Grange-over-Sands
Millom
Ulverston
Dalton-in-Furness
Barrow-in-Furness
Aldingham
Carnforth
248-249
St John's Chapel
139
Penrith
Temple Sowerby
Middleton-in-Teesdale
Appleby-in-Westmorland
Barnard Castle
Shap
Brough
Bowes
Tebay
Orton
Kirkby Stephen
Muker
250-251
Yorkshire Dales
National Park
Sedbergh
Bainbridge
Hawes
Killington Lake
173
Kirkby Lonsdale
Horton in Ribblesdale
Ingleton
Burton-in-Kendal
Kettlewell
Isle of Man
Point of Ayre
Andreas
Ramsey Bay
Ramsey
Kirk Michael
Peel
Laxey
Laxey Bay
Foxdale
Onchan
Douglas
Dalby
Port Erin
Isle of Man
Port St Mary
Castletown
Calf of Man
240-241
Morecambe Bay
Morecambe
Isle of Walney
Heysham
Lancaster
Cockerham
Fleetwood
Cleveleys
Thornton
Poulton-le-Fylde
Blackpool
21
20
Kirkham
Freckleton
Lytham St Anne's
Preston
Blackburn
242-243
Hornby
Clapham
Settle
Long Preston
Garstang
Newton
Clitheroe
Barnoldswick
Colne
Nelson
Padiham
Burnley
Great Harwood
Accrington
Todmorden
Rawtenstall
Darwen
Leyland
IRISH SEA
230-231
232-233
Southport
Chorley
Burscough Bridge
Charnock Richard
Ramsbottom
Rochdale
Bolton
Bury
Formby
Ormskirk
Skelmersdale
Standish
Wigan
Oldham
Crosby
Kirkby
Hindley
Leigh
Newton-le-Willows
106
Salford
Manchester
Bootle
St Helens
Huyton
Wallasey
Birkenhead
Liverpool
Warrington
Widnes
Sale
Stockport
West Kirby
Bebington
Heswall
Runcorn
157
135
Wilmslow
Alderley Edge
Knutsford
Ellesmere Port
118
23
Frodsham
Weaverham
Northwich
Macclesfield
45
Chester
Amlwch
Moelfre
Llannerch-y-medd
Anglesey
Holyhead
Valley
Holy Island
15
Llangoed
Pentraeth
Llangefni
Beaumaris
Bangor
130
Llanfairpwllgwyngyll
Menai Bridge
Llandudno
Conwy Bay
Conwy
48
Rhôs-on-Sea
Colwyn Bay
Llanfairfechan
Llansanffraid Glan Conwy
26
Abergele
Rhyl
Prestatyn
Rhuddlan
Holywell
St Asaph
Flint
Connah's Quay
Hawarden
Llanfair Talhaiarn
Denbigh
Mold
43 &44
Buckley
Bretton
Tarporley
Winsford
Middlewich
Sandbach
Congleton
17
Biddulph
Crewe
Kidsgrove
Nantwich
Newcastle-under-Lyme
Stoke-on-Trent
Keele
Bethesda
Caernarfon
32
Menai Strait
Llanwnda
Llanberis
Snowdon (Yr Wyddfa)
Capel Curig
Llanrwst
Betws-y-coed
Ruthin
Caernarfon Bay
Penygroes
151
Blaenau Ffestiniog
Pentrefoelas
Rhosllanerchrugog
64
Wrexham
Ruabon
Overton
Farndon
Audlem
Whitchurch
Beddgelert
67
Llanaelhaearn
Nefyn
Lleyn Peninsula (Pen Llŷn)
Tremadog
Criccieth
Porthmadog
132
Ffestiniog
Snowdonia
National Park
Trawsfynydd
Bala
Bala Lake (Llyn Tegid)
Corwen
Llangollen
Llandrillo
Chirk
Gobowen
Oswestry
Ellesmere
Wem
Market Drayton
Hodnet
Loggerheads
Eccleshall
Stone
Stafford
Gnosall
Newport
216-217
218-219
220-221
Tremadog Bay
Pwllheli
Llanbedrog
Abersoch
80
Harlech
Aberdaron
Porth Neigwl (Hell's Mouth)
Bardsey
Llanuwchllyn
Penybontfawr
Llanelltyd
Dolgellau
Barmouth
Barmouth Bay (Bae Bermo)
Mallwyd
Llangadfan
Lake Vyrnwy (Llyn Efyrnwy)
Llanfyllin
Cambrian Mountains
Shrewsbury
Wellington
Oakengates
Telford
92
Shifnal
Madeley
Broseley
Cannock
134
Welshpool
Bayston Hill
Llanfair Caereinion
Minsterley
Corris
Machynlleth
Tywyn
Aberdyfi
Eglwys Fach
Cardigan Bay
(Bae Ceredigion)
204-205
Montgomery
Chirbury
Church Stretton
Much Wenlock
Wolverhampton
Morville
Bridgnorth
Dudley
19
Birmingham
Newtown
Bishop's Castle
Shipton
206-207
Stourbridge
Halesowen
Alveley
Severn (Hafren)
Llanidloes
Craven Arms
Burwarton
Aberystwyth
Llangurig
Clun
Kidderminster
Bewdley
Cleobury Mortimer
Ludlow
Devil's Bridge
Llanbister
Knighton
Wigmore
Stourport-on-Severn
Bromsgrove
Llanrhystud
Pontrhydfendigaid
Cross Inn
Rhayader
Presteigne
Tenbury Wells
Ombersley
Droitwich Spa
Crossgates
Penybont
Aberaeron
New Quay
Tregaron
Llandrindod Wells
Pembridge
Leominster
Bromyard
Worcester
Llanarth
Kington
Synod Inn
Aberporth
Lampeter
Builth Wells
Bodenham
Kempsey
Pershore
190-191
132

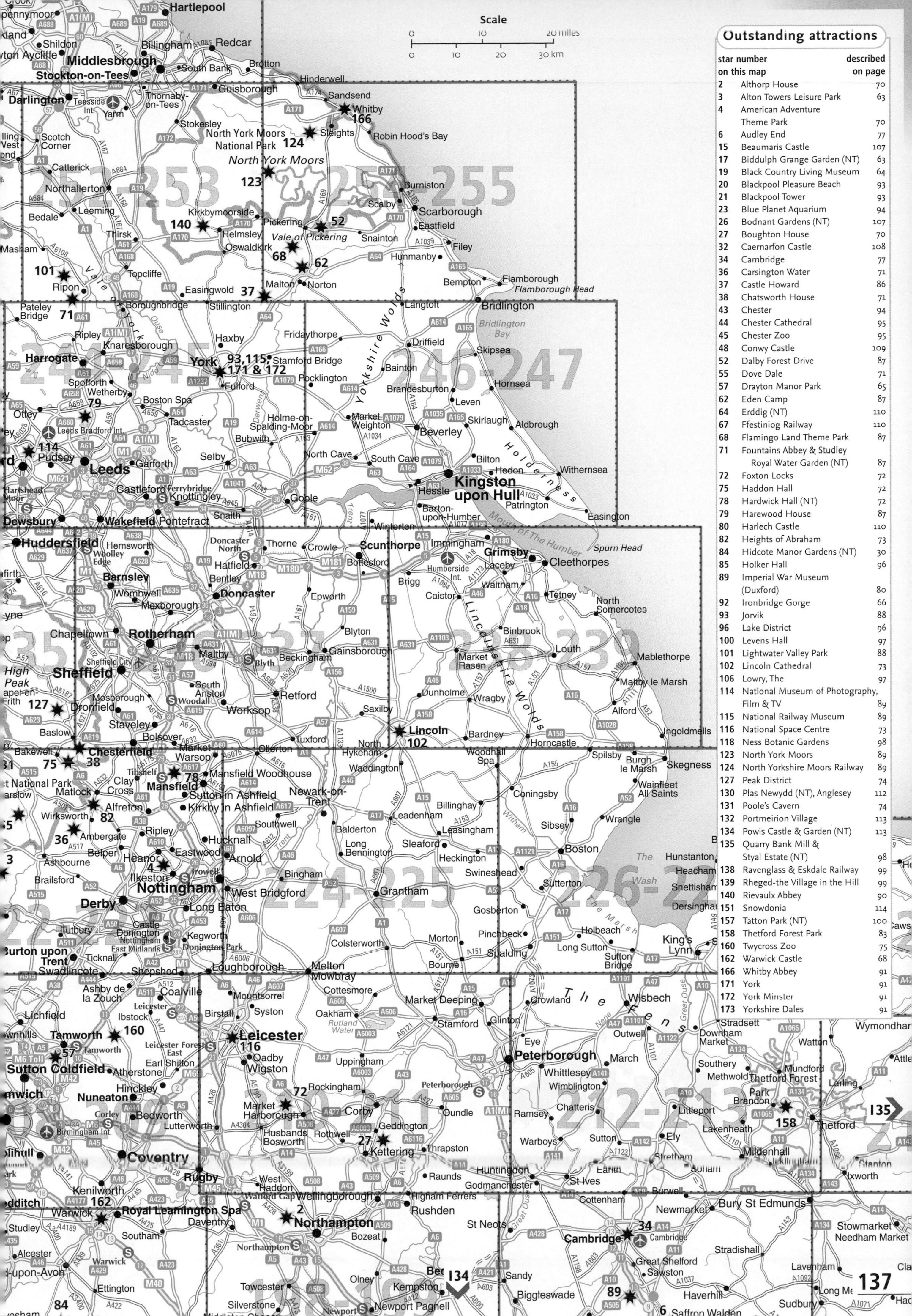

Scale
0 10 20 miles
0 10 20 30 km

Outstanding attractions

star number on this map		described on page
2	Althorp House	70
3	Alton Towers Leisure Park	63
4	American Adventure Theme Park	70
6	Audley End	77
15	Beaumaris Castle	107
17	Biddulph Grange Garden (NT)	63
19	Black Country Living Museum	64
20	Blackpool Pleasure Beach	93
21	Blackpool Tower	93
23	Blue Planet Aquarium	94
26	Bodnant Gardens (NT)	107
27	Boughton House	70
32	Caernarfon Castle	108
34	Cambridge	77
36	Carsington Water	71
37	Castle Howard	86
38	Chatsworth House	71
43	Chester	94
44	Chester Cathedral	95
45	Chester Zoo	95
48	Conwy Castle	109
52	Dalby Forest Drive	87
55	Dove Dale	71
57	Drayton Manor Park	65
62	Eden Camp	87
64	Erddig (NT)	110
67	Ffestiniog Railway	110
68	Flamingo Land Theme Park	87
71	Fountains Abbey & Studley Royal Water Garden (NT)	87
72	Foxton Locks	72
75	Haddon Hall	72
78	Hardwick Hall (NT)	72
79	Harewood House	87
80	Harlech Castle	110
82	Heights of Abraham	73
84	Hidcote Manor Gardens (NT)	30
85	Holker Hall	96
89	Imperial War Museum (Duxford)	80
92	Ironbridge Gorge	66
93	Jorvik	88
96	Lake District	96
100	Levens Hall	97
101	Lightwater Valley Park	88
102	Lincoln Cathedral	73
106	Lowry, The	97
114	National Museum of Photography, Film & TV	89
115	National Railway Museum	89
116	National Space Centre	73
118	Ness Botanic Gardens	98
123	North York Moors	89
124	North Yorkshire Moors Railway	89
127	Peak District	74
130	Plas Newydd (NT), Anglesey	112
131	Poole's Cavern	74
132	Portmeirion Village	113
134	Powis Castle & Garden (NT)	113
135	Quarry Bank Mill & Styal Estate (NT)	98
138	Ravenglass & Eskdale Railway	99
139	Rheged-the Village in the Hill	99
140	Rievaulx Abbey	90
151	Snowdonia	114
157	Tatton Park (NT)	100
158	Thetford Forest Park	83
160	Twycross Zoo	75
162	Warwick Castle	68
166	Whitby Abbey	91
171	York	91
172	York Minster	91
173	Yorkshire Dales	91

135
134

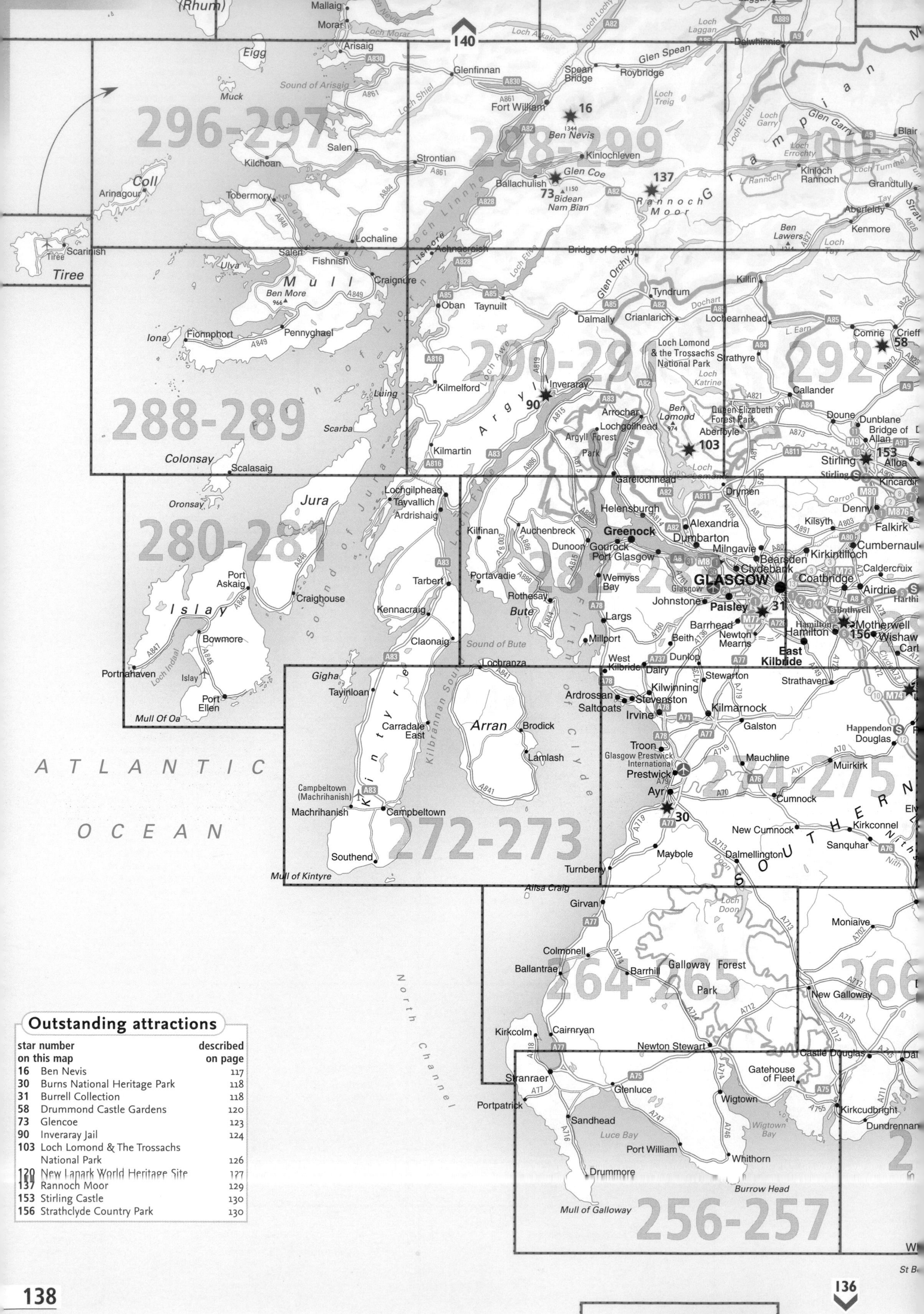
Outstanding attractions
star number on this map
described on page
16 Ben Nevis 117
30 Burns National Heritage Park 118
31 Burrell Collection 118
58 Drummond Castle Gardens 120
73 Glencoe 123
90 Inveraray Jail 124
103 Loch Lomond & The Trossachs National Park 126
120 New Lanark World Heritage Site 127
137 Rannoch Moor 129
153 Stirling Castle 130
156 Strathclyde Country Park 130
140
136
296-297
298-299
300-301
288-289
290-291
292-293
280-281
282-283
272-273
274-275
264-265
266
256-257
ATLANTIC
OCEAN
North Channel
Firth of Clyde
Sound of Jura
Firth of Lorn
Sound of Mull
Sound of Arisaig
Sound of Bute
Kilbrannan Sound
Grampian
SOUTHERN
GLASGOW
Fort William
Ben Nevis
Glen Coe
Rannoch Moor
Oban
Inveraray
Mull
Iona
Tiree
Coll
Eigg
Muck
Jura
Islay
Colonsay
Oronsay
Scarba
Luing
Lismore
Gigha
Kintyre
Arran
Bute
Argyll
Mull of Kintyre
Mull of Oa
Mull of Galloway
Ailsa Craig
Stirling
Greenock
Paisley
Dumbarton
Helensburgh
Ayr
Prestwick
Kilmarnock
Irvine
Largs
Dunoon
Campbeltown
Stranraer
Girvan
Newton Stewart
Galloway Forest Park
Wigtown
Kirkcudbright
Castle Douglas
Luce Bay
Wigtown Bay
Burrow Head
Point of Ayre
Isle of Man

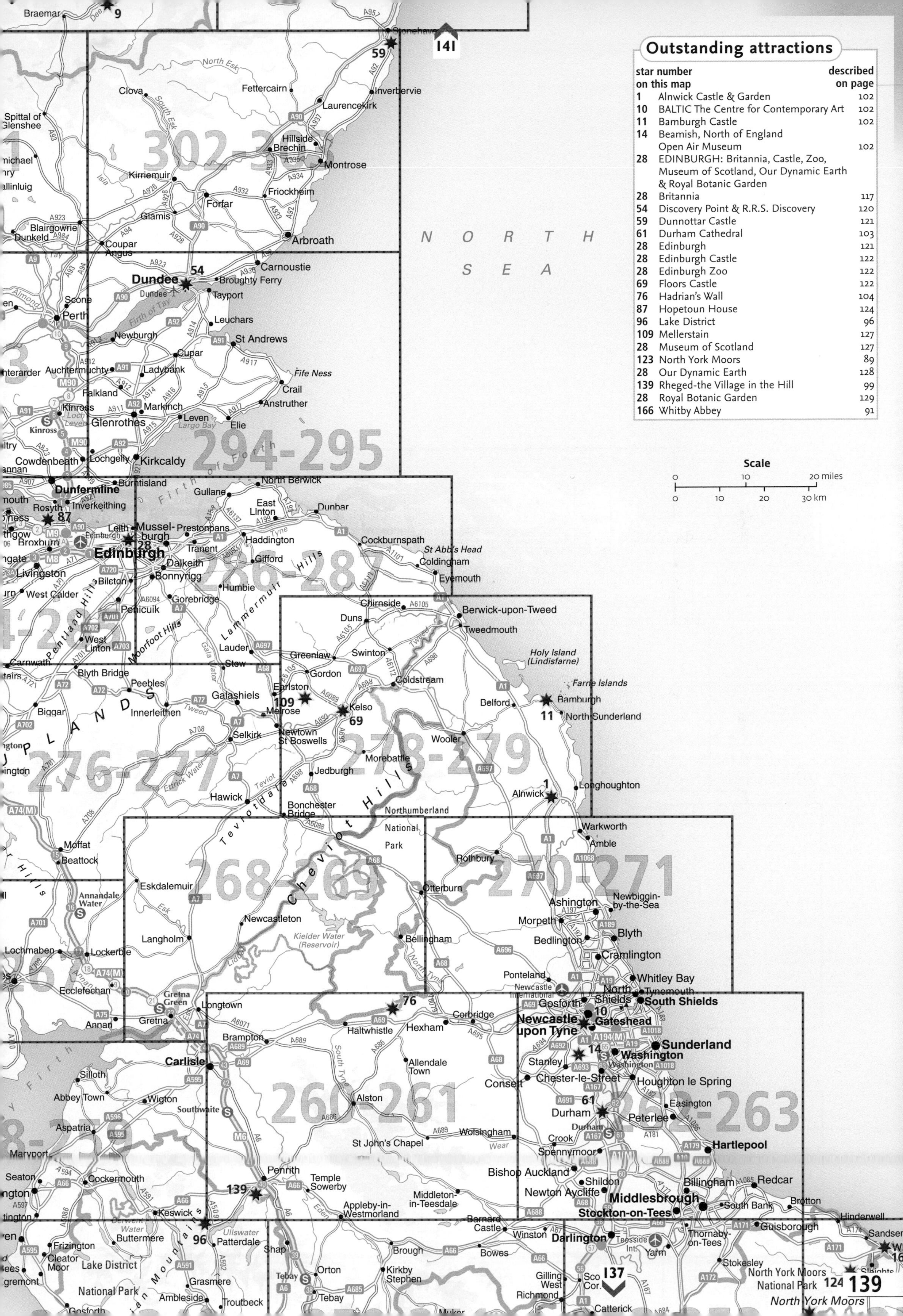

Outstanding attractions
star number on this map | described on page
1 Alnwick Castle & Garden 102
10 BALTIC The Centre for Contemporary Art 102
11 Bamburgh Castle 102
14 Beamish, North of England Open Air Museum 102
28 EDINBURGH: Britannia, Castle, Zoo, Museum of Scotland, Our Dynamic Earth & Royal Botanic Garden
28 Britannia 117
54 Discovery Point & R.R.S. Discovery 120
59 Dunnottar Castle 121
61 Durham Cathedral 103
28 Edinburgh 121
28 Edinburgh Castle 122
28 Edinburgh Zoo 122
69 Floors Castle 122
76 Hadrian's Wall 104
87 Hopetoun House 124
96 Lake District 96
109 Mellerstain 127
28 Museum of Scotland 127
123 North York Moors 89
28 Our Dynamic Earth 128
139 Rheged-the Village in the Hill 99
28 Royal Botanic Garden 129
166 Whitby Abbey 91
Scale
0 10 20 miles
0 10 20 30 km
NORTH SEA
141
302-303
294-295
286-287
284-285
278-279
276-277
268-269
270-271
260-261
262-263
137
124
North York Moors

Outstanding attractions

star number on this map		described on page
9	Balmoral Castle	116
51	Cuillin Hills	119
59	Dunnottar Castle	121
60	Dunrobin Castle	121
91	Inverewe Gardens (NTS)	125
122	North West Highlands	128

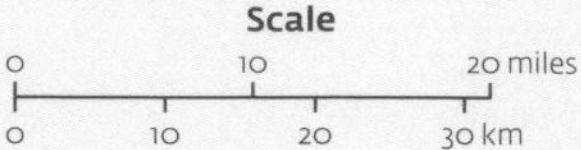
Scale
0 10 20 miles
0 10 20 30 km

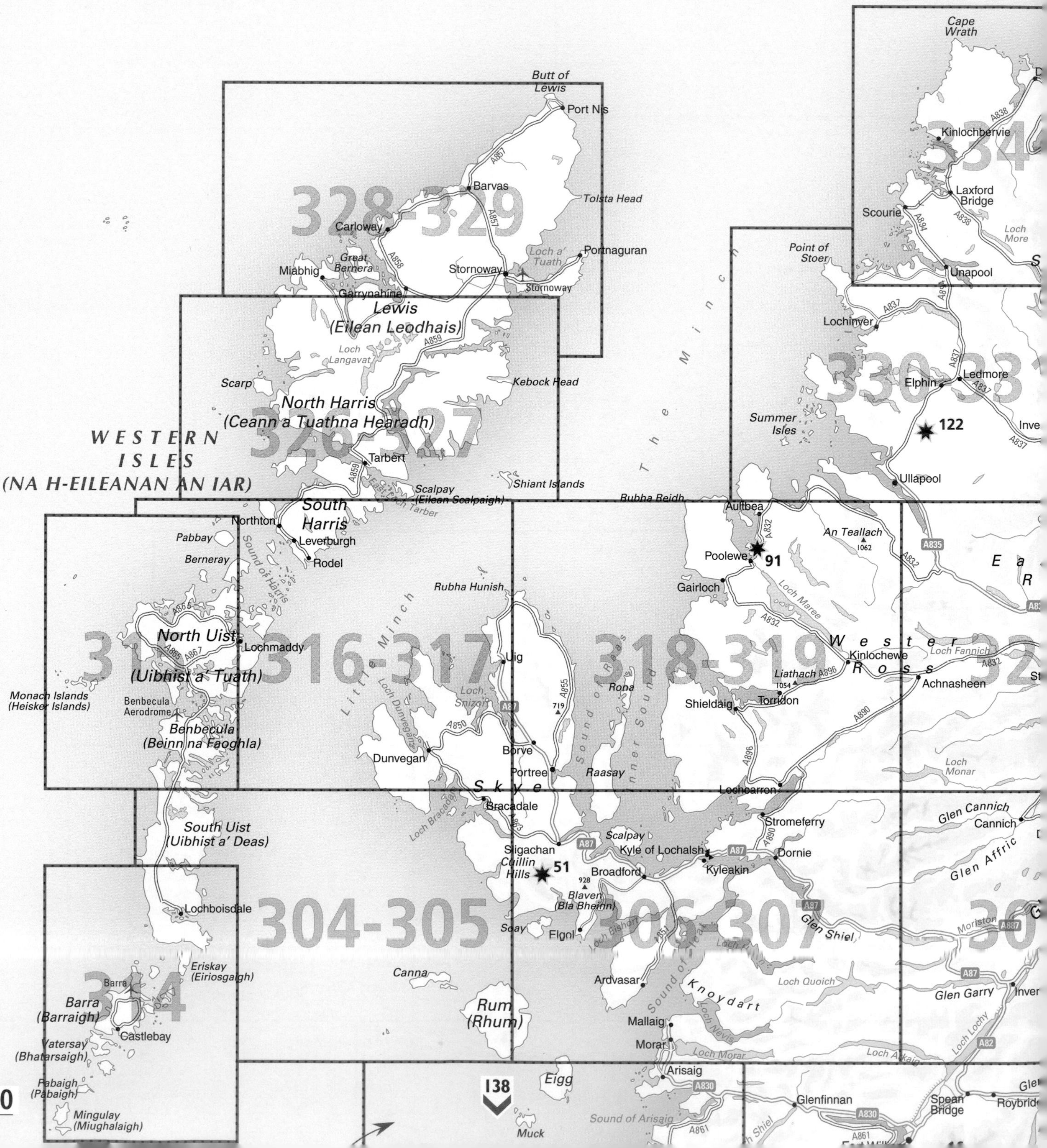

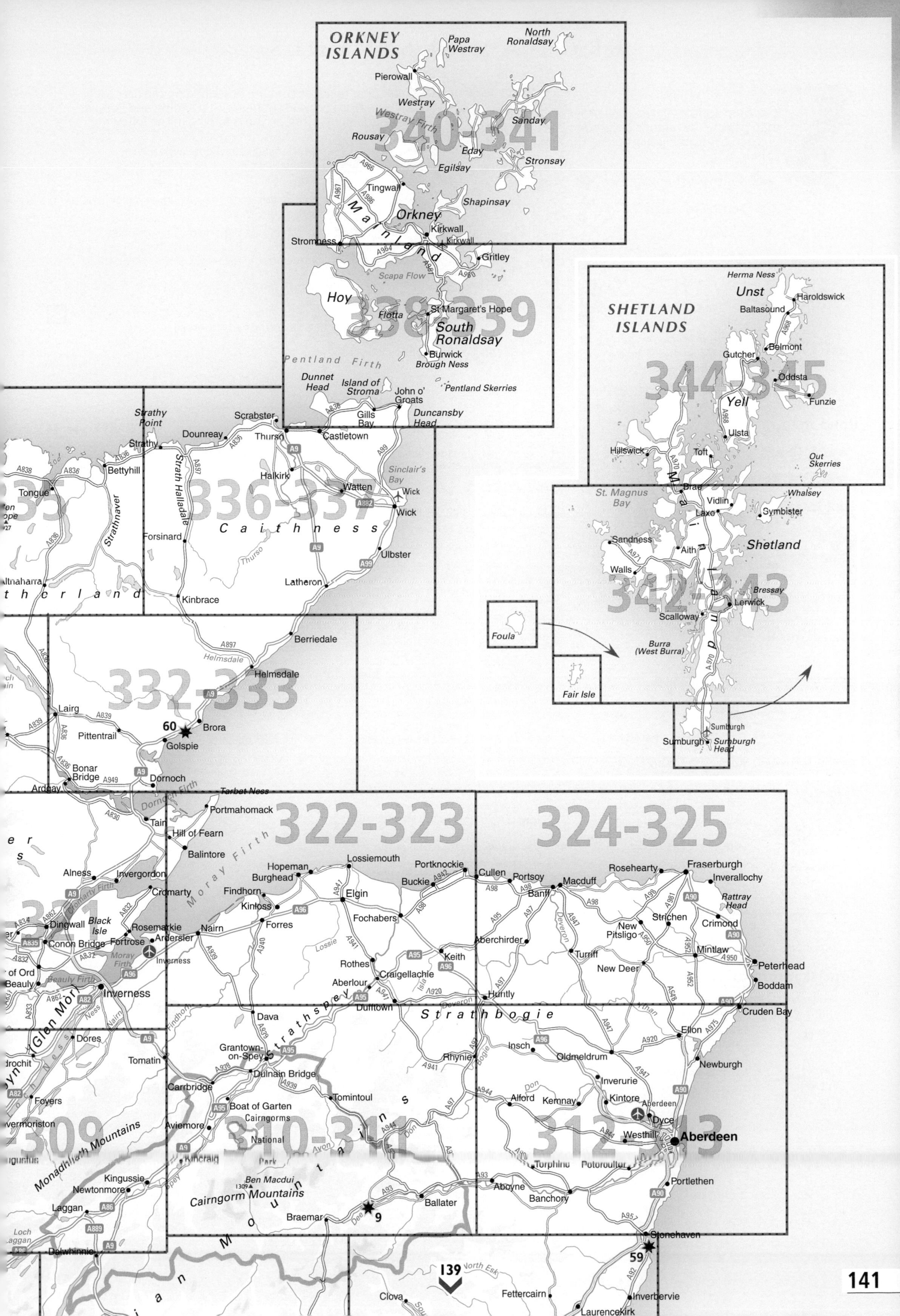
ORKNEY ISLANDS
Papa Westray
North Ronaldsay
Pierowall
Westray
Westray Firth
Sanday
Rousay
340-341
Eday
Stronsay
Egilsay
Tingwall
Shapinsay
Orkney
Mainland
Kirkwall
Stromness
Gritley
Scapa Flow
Hoy
Flotta
St Margaret's Hope
338-339
South Ronaldsay
Burwick
Brough Ness
Pentland Firth
Dunnet Head
Island of Stroma
John o' Groats
Pentland Skerries
Gills Bay
Duncansby Head
SHETLAND ISLANDS
Herma Ness
Unst
Haroldswick
Baltasound
Belmont
Gutcher
344-345
Oddsta
Yell
Funzie
Ulsta
Hillswick
Toft
Out Skerries
St. Magnus Bay
Brae
Whalsey
Vidlin
Laxo
Symbister
Sandness
Aith
Shetland
Walls
342-343
Bressay
Lerwick
Scalloway
Foula
Burra (West Burra)
Fair Isle
Sumburgh
Sumburgh Head
Strathy Point
Scrabster
Strathy
Dounreay
Thurso
Castletown
Bettyhill
Tongue
Strath Halladale
Halkirk
Sinclair's Bay
Watten
Wick
336-337
Strathnaver
Forsinard
Caithness
Ulbster
Altnaharra
Latheron
Sutherland
Kinbrace
Berriedale
Helmsdale
332-333
Lairg
Pittentrail
60
Brora
Golspie
Bonar Bridge
Ardgay
Dornoch
Dornoch Firth
Tarbat Ness
Portmahomack
322-323
324-325
Tain
Hill of Fearn
Balintore
Moray Firth
Lossiemouth
Portknockie
Cullen
Portsoy
Macduff
Rosehearty
Fraserburgh
Inverallochy
Hopeman
Burghead
Buckie
Banff
Rattray Head
Alness
Invergordon
Cromarty
Findhorn
Elgin
Kinloss
Forres
Fochabers
Strichen
Crimond
Black Isle
Dingwall
Rosemarkie
Nairn
New Pitsligo
Aberchirder
Conon Bridge
Fortrose
Ardersier
Inverness
Turriff
Mintlaw
Beauly Firth
Beauly
Keith
New Deer
Peterhead
Rothes
Boddam
Aberlour
Craigellachie
Inverness
Huntly
Dufftown
Strathspey
Strathbogie
Cruden Bay
Glen Mor
Dava
Ellon
Dores
Insch
Oldmeldrum
Newburgh
Tomatin
Grantown-on-Spey
Rhynie
Inverurie
Dulnain Bridge
Carrbridge
Tomintoul
Alford
Kemnay
Kintore
Aberdeen
Foyers
Boat of Garten
Cairngorms
Dyce
Westhill
Aberdeen
Aviemore
National Park
310-311
312-313
Monadhliath Mountains
Kincraig
Torphins
Peterculter
Kingussie
Ben Macdui
Portlethen
Newtonmore
Cairngorm Mountains
Aboyne
Banchory
Laggan
Ballater
Braemar
9
Loch Laggan
Stonehaven
Dalwhinnie
59
139
North Esk
Clova
Fettercairn
Inverbervie
Laurencekirk
141

KEY TO MAP SYMBOLS

This map appears in the top corner of all road map pages. The regions covered by the mapping on each page are highlighted in the appropriate colour.

South West England
South East England
London
West Midlands
East Midlands
East of England
Yorkshire
North West England
North East England
Wales
Scotland

The tourist features that are described on the preceding pages fall into two categories; Outstanding and Popular. These are highlighted on the mapping in the following colours:

- British Museum — Outstanding attractions have a purple symbol and name which are highlighted in yellow.
- Museum of London — Popular attractions have a purple symbol with a purple name.
- Edinburgh Castle / Dean Gallery — On large scale mapping the tourist symbol may be replaced by a building shape. These are depicted in the same colours as the symbols.

For a full list of all the tourist symbols please see panel at the bottom of this page.
Within the attraction descriptions, any feature with an empty symbol ☐ can be found as a place or area name on the road mapping.

A51-*TO CHESTER* Destination boxes surround the mapping to indicate the next key place along major routes.

158 ➤ Page continuation arrow

Road mapping

pages 144-345

M5	Motorway
M6Toll	Toll motorway
8 9	Motorway junction with full / limited access
Maidstone, Birch, Sarn	Motorway service area with off road / full / limited access
A556	Primary route with dual / single carriageway
A30	'A' road dual / single carriageway
B1403	'B' road dual / single carriageway
	Minor road
	Road with restricted access
	Roads with passing places
	Road proposed or under construction
24	Multi-level junction (occasionally with junction number)
	Roundabout
4	Road distance in miles between markers
	Road tunnel
	Steep hill (arrows point downhill)
Toll	Level crossing / Toll
St. Malo 8hrs(10hrs)	Car ferry route with journey times; daytime and (night-time)
	Railway line / station / tunnel
South Downs Way	National Trail / Long Distance Route
	Airport with scheduled services
Ⓗ	Heliport
Ⓟ	Park and Ride site (operates at least 5 days a week)
	Built up area
☐ ▫	Town / Village / Other settlement
Hythe	Seaside destination
	National boundary
KENT	County / Unitary Authority boundary and name
	National Park
	Forest / Regional Park boundary
	Woodland
Danger Zone	Military range
468 ▲941	Spot / Summit height (in metres)
	Lake / Dam / River / Waterfall
	Canal / Dry canal / Canal tunnel
	Lighthouse
	Beach
SEE PAGE 347	Area covered by urban area map

metres	feet
900	2950
700	2295
500	1640
300	985
150	490
0	0
water	water
land below sea level	land below sea level

0 2 4 6 miles
0 2 4 6 8 10 km

Map scale 1:200,000
3.2 miles to 1 inch / 2km to 1 cm

Tourist information

pages 144-375

A selection of tourist detail is shown on the mapping. It is advisable to check with the attraction or local tourist information centre regarding opening times and facilities available. Where a symbol appears purple on the map, its description can be found within pages 23–131.

- Tourist information centre (open all year)
- Tourist information centre (open seasonally)
- Ancient monument
- 1643 Battlefield
- Camp site / Caravan site
- Castle
- Country park
- Ecclesiastical building
- Football club (Major British club)
- Garden
- Golf course
- Historic house
- Major shopping centre / Outlet village
- Major sports venue
- Motor racing circuit
- Museum / Art gallery
- Nature reserve
- Preserved railway
- Racecourse
- Theme park
- University
- Wildlife park or Zoo
- Other interesting feature
- (NT) (NTS) National Trust / National Trust for Scotland property

Urban area maps

pages 346-375

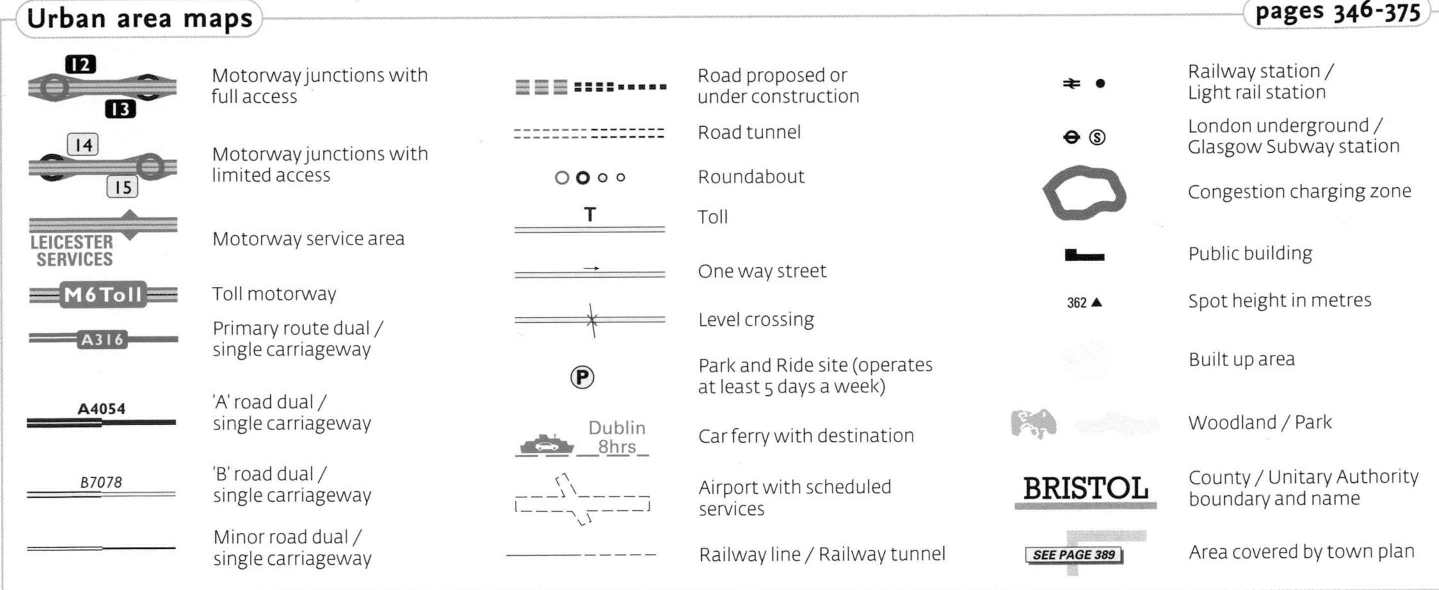
12
13
Motorway junctions with full access
14
15
Motorway junctions with limited access
LEICESTER SERVICES
Motorway service area
M6Toll
Toll motorway
A316
Primary route dual / single carriageway
A4054
'A' road dual / single carriageway
B7078
'B' road dual / single carriageway
Minor road dual / single carriageway
Road proposed or under construction
Road tunnel
Roundabout
T
Toll
One way street
Level crossing
Park and Ride site (operates at least 5 days a week)
Dublin 8hrs
Car ferry with destination
Airport with scheduled services
Railway line / Railway tunnel
Railway station / Light rail station
London underground / Glasgow Subway station
Congestion charging zone
Public building
362
Spot height in metres
Built up area
Woodland / Park
BRISTOL
County / Unitary Authority boundary and name
SEE PAGE 389
Area covered by town plan

Central city maps

pages 376-387

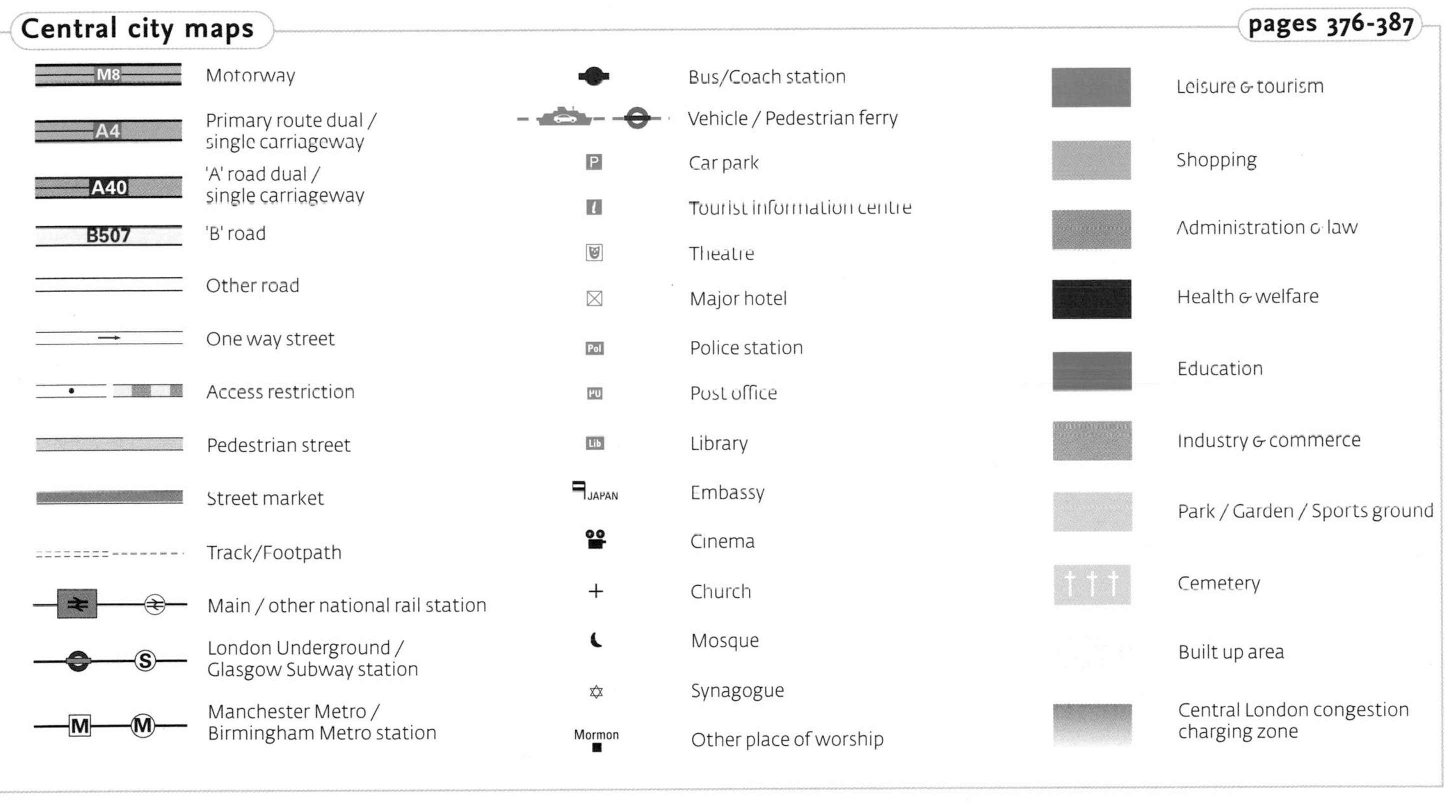
M8
Motorway
A4
Primary route dual / single carriageway
A40
'A' road dual / single carriageway
B507
'B' road
Other road
One way street
Access restriction
Pedestrian street
Street market
Track/Footpath
Main / other national rail station
London Underground / Glasgow Subway station
M
Manchester Metro / Birmingham Metro station
Bus/Coach station
Vehicle / Pedestrian ferry
P
Car park
Tourist information centre
Theatre
Major hotel
Pol
Police station
PO
Post office
Lib
Library
JAPAN
Embassy
Cinema
Church
Mosque
Synagogue
Mormon
Other place of worship
Leisure & tourism
Shopping
Administration & law
Health & welfare
Education
Industry & commerce
Park / Garden / Sports ground
Cemetery
Built up area
Central London congestion charging zone

Town plans

pages 388-415

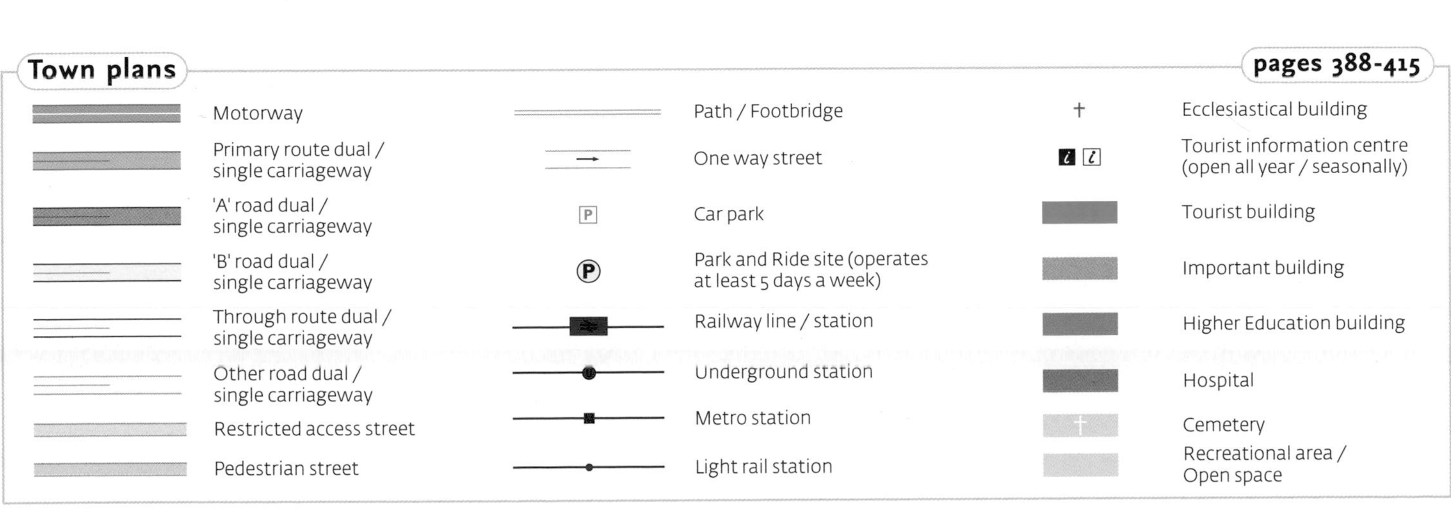
Motorway
Primary route dual / single carriageway
'A' road dual / single carriageway
'B' road dual / single carriageway
Through route dual / single carriageway
Other road dual / single carriageway
Restricted access street
Pedestrian street
Path / Footbridge
One way street
P
Car park
Park and Ride site (operates at least 5 days a week)
Railway line / station
Underground station
Metro station
Light rail station
Ecclesiastical building
Tourist information centre (open all year / seasonally)
Tourist building
Important building
Higher Education building
Hospital
Cemetery
Recreational area / Open space

The sea level at **Newlyn** is the point from which all heights in Britain are measured. For example, Snowdon is calculated to be 3,560 feet (1,085m) above sea level, so it is 3,560 feet (1,085m) higher than the sea level at Newlyn.
Sea level at Newlyn was originally calculated from hourly readings, using an automatic tide gauge, taken between May 1915 and April 1921.
This tide gauge is located in the Ordnance Survey Tidal Observatory on the south pier at Newlyn. ***Map ref. B4***

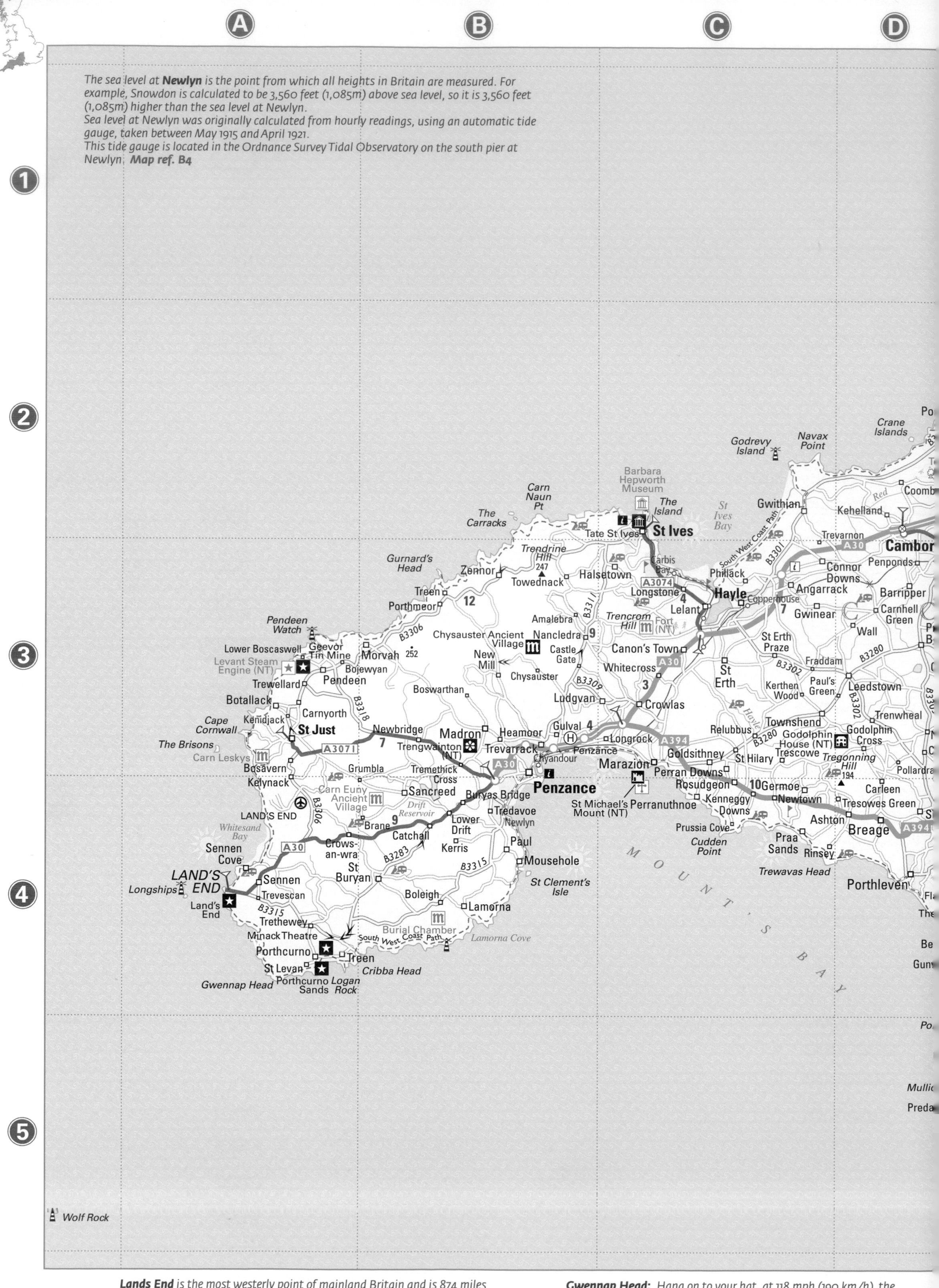

A
B
C
D
1
2
3
4
5
Godrevy Island
Navax Point
Crane Islands
Barbara Hepworth Museum
The Island
St Ives Bay
Gwithian
Kehelland
Carn Naun Pt
The Carracks
Tate St Ives
St Ives
Trevarnon
Trendrine Hill
247
Gurnard's Head
Zennor
Towednack
Halsetown
Carbis Bay
A3074
South West Coast Path
B3301
Phillack
Hayle
Connor Downs
Penponds
Angarrack
Barripper
Treen
Porthmeor
12
Longstone
4
Lelant
Copperhouse
7
Gwinear
Carnhell Green
Amalebra
B3311
Trencrom Hill
Fort (NT)
Pendeen Watch
B3306
Chysauster Ancient Village
Nancledra
9
St Erth Praze
Wall
Lower Boscaswell
Geevor Tin Mine
Morvah
252
Castle Gate
Canon's Town
Fraddam
B3280
Levant Steam Engine (NT)
Bojewyan
New Mill
Chysauster
Whitecross
A30
St Erth
B3302
Paul's Green
Trewellard
Pendeen
Boswarthan
B3309
3
Kerthen Wood
Leedstown
Botallack
B3318
Carnyorth
Ludgvan
Crowlas
Cape Cornwall
Kenidjack
St Just
Newbridge
Madron
Heamoor
Gulval
4
Relubbus
Townshend
Trenwheal
The Brisons
A3071
7
Trengwainton (NT)
Trevarrack
Longrock
A394
Godolphin House (NT)
Godolphin Cross
Carn Leskys
Chyandour
Penzance
Goldsithney
St Hilary
Trescowe
Tregonning Hill
194
Bosavern
Grumbla
Tremethick Cross
A30
Marazion
Perran Downs
Pollardras
Kelynack
Carn Euny Ancient Village
Sancreed
Buryas Bridge
Penzance
Rosudgeon
10
Germoe
Carleen
B3306
Drift Reservoir
Tredavoe
St Michael's Mount (NT)
Perranuthnoe
Kenneggy Downs
Newtown
Tresowes Green
LAND'S END
Whitesand Bay
Brane
9
Lower Drift
Newlyn
Prussia Cove
Ashton
Breage
A394
Sennen Cove
A30
Crows-an-wra
Catchall
Kerris
Paul
Cudden Point
Praa Sands
Rinsey
B3283
B3315
Mousehole
St Clement's Isle
MOUNT'S BAY
Trewavas Head
LAND'S END
Longships
Sennen
St Buryan
Porthleven
Land's End
Trevescan
Boleigh
Lamorna
B3315
Trethewey
Minack Theatre
Burial Chamber
South West Coast Path
Lamorna Cove
Porthcurno
Treen
St Levan
Cribba Head
Gwennap Head
Porthcurno Sands
Logan Rock
Wolf Rock

Lands End is the most westerly point of mainland Britain and is 874 miles (1,407km) by road from John O' Groats. It is the closest point to North America, if you travel due west, for 2,500 miles (4,000km), from here, you will arrive in Newfoundland. ***Map ref. A4*** ***Also on page 31***

Gwennap Head: Hang on to your hat, at 118 mph (190 km/h) the highest ever gust of wind, on a low level site in Britain, was recorded here on the 15th December 1979. ***Map ref. A4***

D
E
146
F
G
A392–TO NEWQUAY
A39–TO WADEBRIDGE
A30–TO BODMIN
A391–TO BODMIN
A390–TO LISKEARD
147
1
2
3
4
5
Crantock
Penhale Point
Carines
Rosecliston
Holywell
Ligger Pt
Holywell Bay Fun Park
Tresean
Cubert
Penhale Sands
Ligger Bay (Perran Bay)
Mount
Rose
Rejerrah
Perranporth
Goonhavern
Bolingey
Bawden Rocks (Man and his Man)
St Agnes Head
Trevellas
St Agnes
St Agnes Leisure Park
Mithian
Penhallow
Perranzabuloe
Zelah
The Cornish Cyder Farm
Goonvrea
Goonbell
Towan Cross
Porthtowan
Mount Hawke
Allet Common
Three Burrows
Tregavethan
Mawla
Blackwater
Chacewater
Threemilestone
Gloweth
Scorrier
Hugus
Baldhu
Mount Ambrose
Redruth
Twelveheads
St Day
Cross Lanes
Bissoe
Pool
Carn Brea Village
Carharrack
Cusgarne
Pennance
Carnkie
Gwennap
Lanner
Four Lanes
Cornish Engines (NT)
Dolenowe
Penhalvean
Ponsanooth
Perranarworthal
Devoran
Stithians
Stithians Reservoir
Burras
Carnkie
Long Downs
Rame
Mabe Burnthouse
Lezerea
Porkellis
Edgcumbe
Crelly
Trenear
Seworgan
Wendron
Treverva
Trebarvah
Trevenen
Brill
Constantine
Trewennack
Helston
Gweek
Cornish Seal Sanctuary
Porth Navas
Mawnan Smith
Glendurgan (NT)
Durgan
Trebah Garden
Mawnan
Helford
Trelowarren
Mawgan
Halliggye Fogou
Garras
Manaccan
St Martin
St Anthony-in-Meneage
Nare Point
Flushing
Roskorwell
Porthallow
Tregidden
Newtown-in-St-Martin
Goonhilly Satellite Earth Station
Tregarne
Tregowris
St Keverne
Porthoustock
Manacle Point
Rosenithon
The Manacles
Cross Lanes
Tumuli
Traboe
Lanarth
Cury
St Winwaloe
LIZARD PENINSULA
Goonhilly Downs
Mullion
Erisey Barton
Trelan
Coverack
Lowland Pt
Penhale
Gwenter
Ponsongath
Gwendreath
Kennack Sands
South West Coast Path
Kuggar
Black Head
Ruan Major
Ruan Minor
Cadgwith
Grade
Toll
Kynance Cove
Landewednack
Lizard
Hot Point
LIZARD POINT
Newquay Pearl
Kestle Mill
Trerice (NT)
Newlyn East
Lappa Valley Rly
Newlyn Downs
Mitchell
Carland Cross
Truthan
St Allen
Trispen
St Erme
Shortlanesend
Idless
Kenwyn
Tresillian
Truro
Cathedral
Merther
St Clement
Royal Cornwall Museum
Malpas
Kea
Playing Place
Old Kea
Lamorran
St Michael Penkevil
Penelewey
Coombe
Carnon Downs
Trelissick (NT)
Penpol
Feock
Angarrick
Stockdale
Mylor Bridge
Penryn
Mylor
Flushing
Falmouth
Budock Water
Penjerrick
Maenporth
National Maritime Mus Cornwall
FALMOUTH BAY
Rosemullion Head
St Just in Roseland
St Mawes
St Mawes Castle
Pendennis Castle
Pendennis Point
Zone Point
St Anthony
Bohortha
Gerrans
Portscatho
Trewithian
Gerrans Bay
Nare Head
Philleigh
Treworthal
Treworga
Treworlas
Veryan
Veryan Green
Ruan Lanihorne
Trewarthenick
Tregony
Portloe
Veryan Bay
White Cross
St Columb Road
Indian Queens
Fraddon
St Dennis
Blue Anchor
St Enoder
Summercourt
Retew
Treviscoe
Chapel Town
Meledor
Scarcewater
Brighton
Trelassick
New Mills
St Stephen
Coombe
Ladock
Tregear
Grampound Road
Probus
Trewithen
Creed
Grampound
Enniscaven
Trezaise
Coldvreath
Bugle
Gothers
Hensbarrow Downs
Roseve
Whitemoor
Stenale
Penwith
Nanpean
Carthew
Ruddlemoor
Foxhole
High Street
Wheal Martyn
ST AUSTELL
Trewoon
St Mewan
Polgooth
Hewas Water
Sticker
London
Lost Gardens of Heligan
St Ewe
Polmassick
Kestle
Mevag
Portme
Trevarrick
St Michael Caerhays
Gorran Churcht
Portholland
Gorran
Boswinger
Ponaro
Dodman Point
Maenea

At 49° 57′ 30″ N **Lizard Point** is the most southerly point of mainland Britain. ***Map ref. D5***

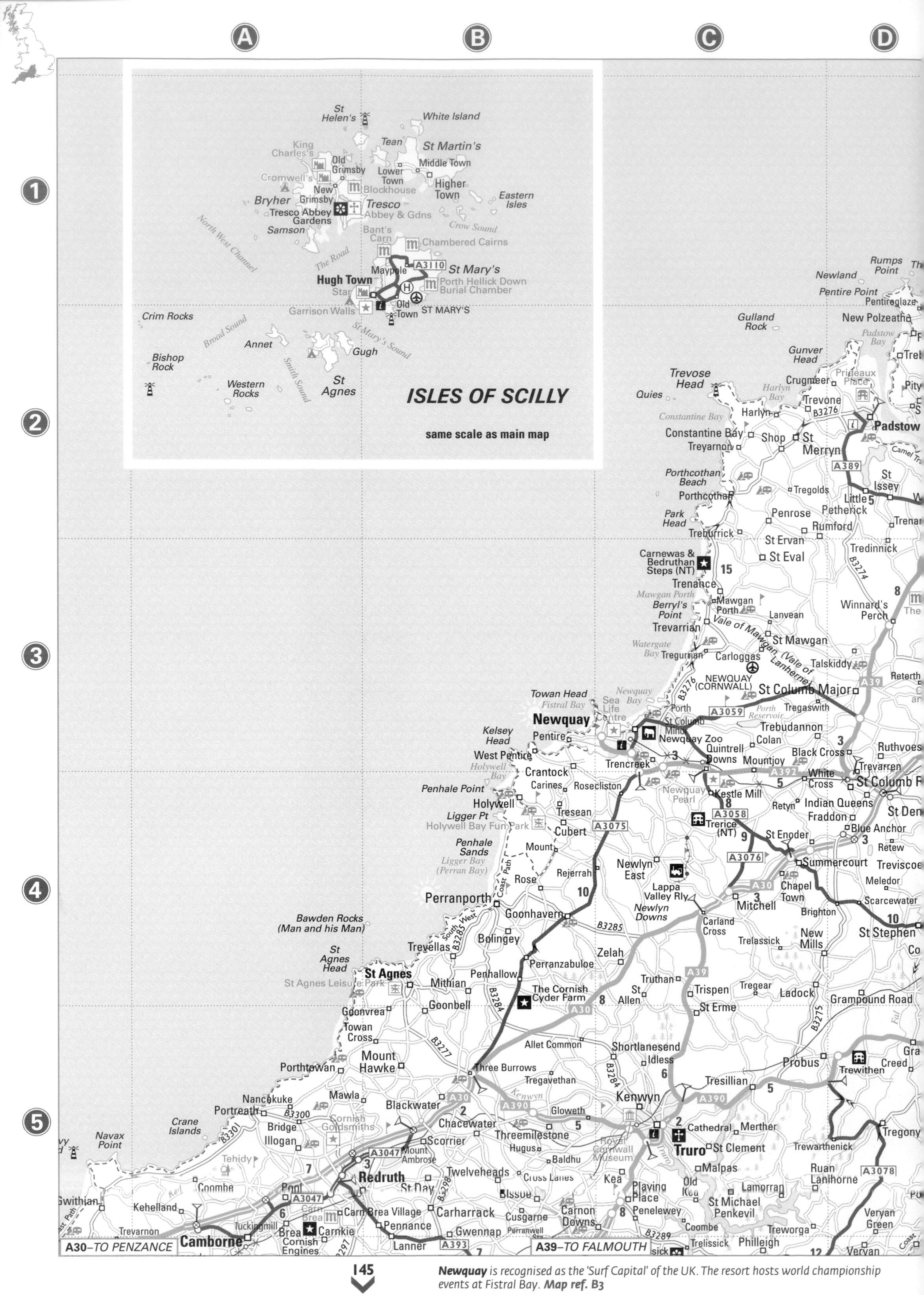

A
B
C
D
1
2
3
4
5
ISLES OF SCILLY
same scale as main map
St Helen's
White Island
Tean
St Martin's
King Charles's
Old Grimsby
Lower Town
Middle Town
Higher Town
Cromwell's
New Grimsby
Blockhouse
Eastern Isles
Bryher
Tresco
Tresco Abbey Gardens
Abbey & Gdns
Crow Sound
Samson
Bant's Carn
Chambered Cairns
North West Channel
The Road
A3110
St Mary's
Maypole
Hugh Town
Porth Hellick Down Burial Chamber
Star
Garrison Walls
Old Town
ST MARY'S
Crim Rocks
Broad Sound
St Mary's Sound
Annet
Gugh
Bishop Rock
Smith Sound
Western Rocks
St Agnes
Rumps Point
Newland
Pentire Point
Pentireglaze
New Polzeath
Padstow Bay
Gulland Rock
Gunver Head
Trevose Head
Crugmeer
Prideaux Place
Harlyn Bay
Quies
Constantine Bay
Harlyn
Trevone
B3276
Padstow
Treyarnon
Shop
St Merryn
A389
Porthcothan Beach
Porthcothan
Tregolds
St Issey
Little Petherick
Park Head
Penrose
Rumford
Treburrick
St Ervan
Tredinnick
Carnewas & Bedruthan Steps (NT)
St Eval
15
B3274
Trenance
Mawgan Porth
Berryl's Point
Mawgan Porth
Lanvean
Winnard's Perch
Trevarrian
Vale of Mawgan (Vale of Lanherne)
Watergate Bay
Tregurrian
St Mawgan
Carloggas
Talskiddy
NEWQUAY (CORNWALL)
St Columb Major
A39
Towan Head
Fistral Bay
Newquay Bay
Sea Life Centre
Newquay
Porth
A3059
Porth Reservoir
Tregaswith
Kelsey Head
Pentire
St Columb Minor
Newquay Zoo
Trebudannon
Colan
Quintrell Downs
West Pentire
Trencreek
Black Cross
Ruthvoes
Holywell Bay
Crantock
Mountjoy
A392
White Cross
Trevarren
Penhale Point
Carines
Rosecliston
Newquay Pearl
Kestle Mill
St Columb Road
Holywell
Tresean
Retyn
Indian Queens
Ligger Pt
Holywell Bay Fun Park
A3058
Fraddon
Cubert
A3075
Trerice (NT)
St Enoder
Blue Anchor
Penhale Sands
Ligger Bay (Perran Bay)
Mount
Newlyn East
A3076
Summercourt
Retew
Rejerrah
Lappa Valley Rly
Chapel Town
Treviscoe
Rose
Coast Path
Meledor
Perranporth
10
Newlyn Downs
Mitchell
Scarcewater
Bawden Rocks (Man and his Man)
Goonhavern
B3285
Carland Cross
Brighton
St Stephen
South West
Trelassick
New Mills
Trevellas
Bolingey
St Agnes Head
Zelah
St Agnes
Perranzabuloe
St Agnes Leisure Park
Penhallow
Truthan
Mithian
B3284
The Cornish Cyder Farm
St Allen
Trispen
Tregear
Ladock
Grampound Road
Goonbell
St Erme
Goonvrea
Towan Cross
B3277
B3275
Allet Common
Shortlanesend
Mount Hawke
Idless
Probus
Trewithen
Creed
Porthtowan
Three Burrows
Tresillian
Tregavethan
A390
Nancekuke
Mawla
Blackwater
Kenwyn
Portreath
B3300
Gloweth
Crane Islands
Bridge
Cornish Goldsmiths
Chacewater
Cathedral
Merther
Navax Point
Illogan
Scorrier
Threemilestone
Truro
Tregony
B3301
A3047
Mount Ambrose
Hugus
Royal Cornwall Museum
St Clement
Trewarthenick
Tehidy
Redruth
Baldhu
Malpas
Ruan Lanihorne
A3078
Coombe
Pool
St Day
Twelveheads
Cross Lanes
Kea
Old Kea
Lamorran
Kehelland
Carn Brea Village
Carharrack
Bissoe
Playing Place
St Michael Penkevil
Trevarnon
Tuckingmill
Carn Brea
Pennance
Cusgarne
Carnon Downs
Penelewey
Veryan Green
Camborne
Brea
Carnkie
Gwennap
B3289
Coombe
Treworga
Cornish Engines
Lanner
A393
Trelissick
Philleigh
Veryan
A30–TO PENZANCE
A39–TO FALMOUTH

145

Newquay *is recognised as the 'Surf Capital' of the UK. The resort hosts world championship events at Fistral Bay.* ***Map ref. B3***

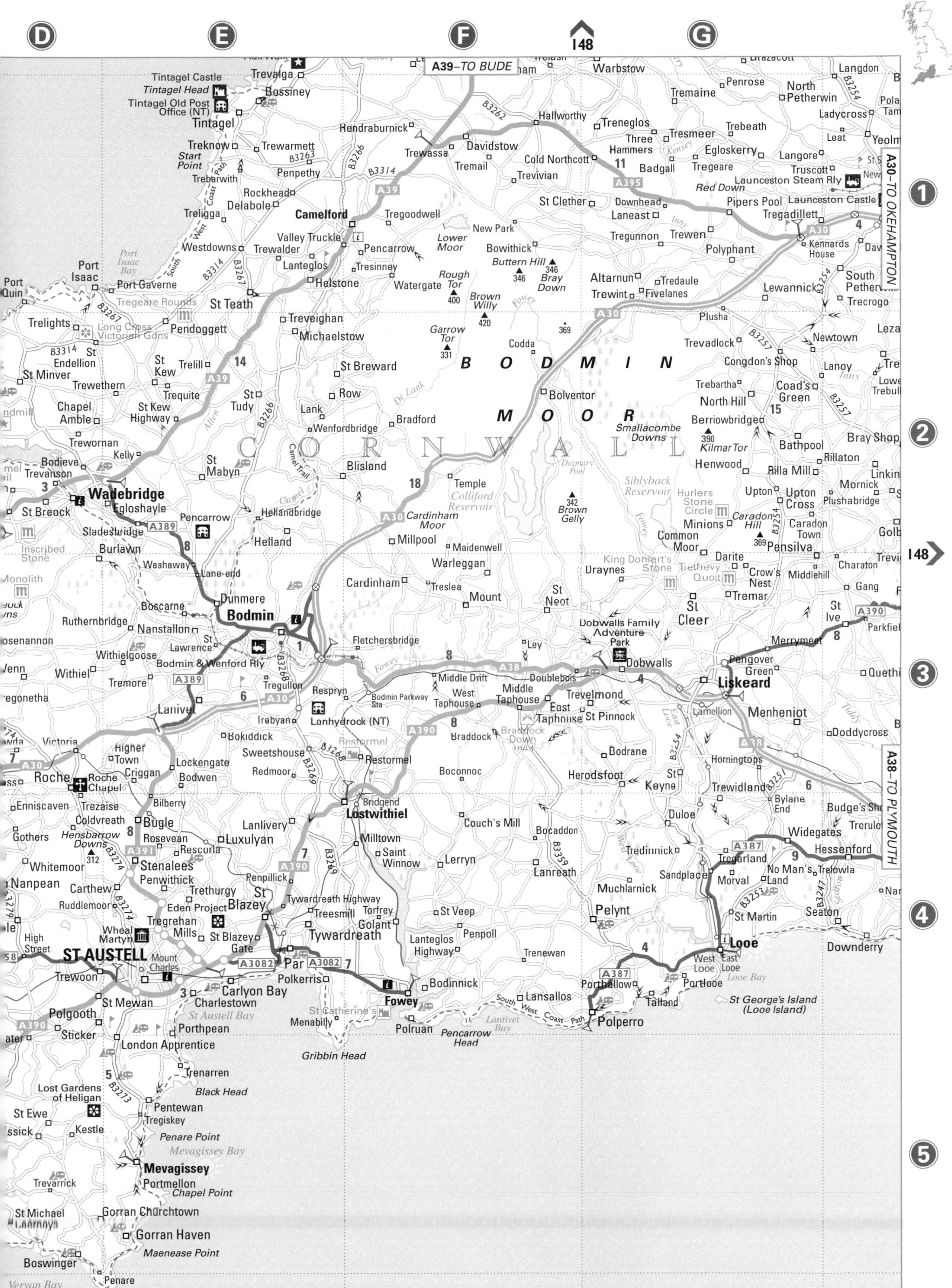
A39–TO BUDE
Warbstow
Langdon
Tintagel Castle
Trevalga
Tintagel Head
Bossiney
Tintagel Old Post Office (NT)
Tintagel
Penrose
Tremaine
North Petherwin
Ladycross
Hallworthy
Treneglos
Hendraburnick
Trebeath
Tresmeer
Three Hammers
Egloskerry
Leat
Yeolm
Treknow
Trewarmett
Start Point
Trewassa
Davidstow
Langore
Tremail
Cold Northcott
Badgall
Tregeare
Truscott
Trebarwith
Penpethy
Trevivian
Launceston Steam Rly
Red Down
A30–TO OKEHAMPTON
Rockhead
Delabole
Downhead
St Clether
Pipers Pool
Launceston Castle
Tregadillett
Treligga
Camelford
Tregoodwell
Laneast
New Park
Lower Moor
Tregunnon
Trewen
Westdowns
Valley Truckle
Trewalder
Pencarrow
Bowithick
Polyphant
Kennards House
Port Isaac Bay
Port Isaac
Lanteglos
Tresinney
Butter Hill
Rough Tor
Bray Down
Altarnun
Tredaule
Port Quin
Port Gaverne
Helstone
Watergate
Brown Willy
Trewint
Fivelanes
Lewannick
South Petherwin
Trecrogo
Tregeare Rounds
St Teath
Treveighan
Plusha
Trelights
Long Cross Victorian Gdns
Pendoggett
Michaelstow
Garrow Tor
Codda
Trevadlock
Newtown
St Endellion
St Breward
Congdon's Shop
Lanoy
St Minver
St Kew
Trelill
B O D M I N
Trebartha
Coad's Green
Trewethern
Trequite
St Tudy
Row
Bolventor
North Hill
Chapel Amble
St Kew Highway
Lank
Bradford
Wenfordbridge
M O O R
Smallacombe Downs
Berriowbridge
Bray Shop
Treworman
C O R N W A L L
Kilmar Tor
Bathpool
Rillaton
Kelly
Bodieve
St Mabyn
Blisland
Dozmary Pool
Henwood
Rilla Mill
Trevanson
Temple
Colliford Reservoir
Siblyback Reservoir
Hurlers Stone Circle
Upton
Upton Cross
Mornick
Wadebridge
Egloshayle
Camel Trail
Brown Gelly
Caradon Hill
Plushabridge
St Breock
Pencarrow
Hellandbridge
Cardinham Moor
Minions
Caradon Town
Sladesbridge
Common Moor
Pensilva
Inscribed Stone
Burlawn
Helland
Millpool
Maidenwell
Darite
Washaway
Warleggan
King Doniert's Stone
Trethevy Quoit
Draynes
Crow's Nest
Charaton
Middlehill
Monolith
Lane-end
Cardinham
Treslea
Tremar
Gang
Dunmere
Mount
St Neot
St Cleer
St Ive
Boscarne
Bodmin
Ruthernbridge
Nanstallon
Dobwalls Family Adventure Park
Parkfield
Merrymeet
Fletchersbridge
Ley
Withielgoose
Lawrence
Bodmin & Wenford Rly
Dobwalls
Pengover Green
Withiel
Tremore
Middle Drift
Doublebois
Quethiock
Tregullon
Liskeard
Respryn
Bodmin Parkway Sta
West Taphouse
Middle Taphouse
Trevelmond
East Taphouse
St Pinnock
Menheniot
Lanivet
Lamellion
Irebyan
Lanhydrock (NT)
Braddock
Doddycross
Bokiddick
Restormel
Victoria
Higher Town
Sweetshouse
Bodrane
Horningtops
A38–TO PLYMOUTH
Lockengate
Restormel
Roche
Roche Chapel
Criggan
Redmoor
Bodwen
Boconnoc
Herodsfoot
St Keyne
Trewidland
Bylane End
Bilberry
Bridgend
Lostwithiel
Duloe
Budge's Shop
Enniscaven
Trezaise
Coldvreath
Bugle
Lanlivery
Couch's Mill
Widegates
Gothers
Hensbarrow Downs
Rosevean
Luxulyan
Milltown
Boduddon
Trerulefoot
Rescorla
Saint Winnow
Tredinnick
Tregarland
Hessenford
Whitemoor
Stenalees
Lerryn
Lanreath
Sandplace
No Man's Land
Trelowla
Nanpean
Penwithick
Penpillick
Morval
Carthew
Trethurgy
St Blazey
Tywardreath Highway
Muchlarnick
Ruddlemoor
Eden Project
Treesmill
Torfrey
St Veep
Pelynt
St Martin
Seaton
High Street
Wheal Martyn
Tregrehan Mills
St Blazey Gate
Golant
Tywardreath
Penpoll
Looe
Downderry
ST AUSTELL
Mount Charles
Par
Polkerris
Lanteglos Highway
Trenewan
West Looe
East Looe
Looe Bay
Trewoon
Carlyon Bay
Bodinnick
Porthallow
Portlooe
St Mewan
Charlestown
St Catherine's
Fowey
South West Coast Path
Lansallos
Talland
St George's Island (Looe Island)
Polgooth
St Austell Bay
Menabilly
Lantivet Bay
Polperro
Sticker
Porthpean
Polruan
Pencarrow Head
London Apprentice
Gribbin Head
Trenarren
Lost Gardens of Heligan
Black Head
St Ewe
Pentewan
Tregiskey
Kestle
Penare Point
Mevagissey Bay
Mevagissey
Trevarrick
Portmellon
Chapel Point
St Michael Caerhays
Gorran Churchtown
Gorran Haven
Maenease Point
Boswinger
Penare
Veryan Bay
1 2 3 4 5
148

In 1584 Sir Francis Drake was voted into the House of Commons as MP for **Bossiney**. *Map ref. E1*

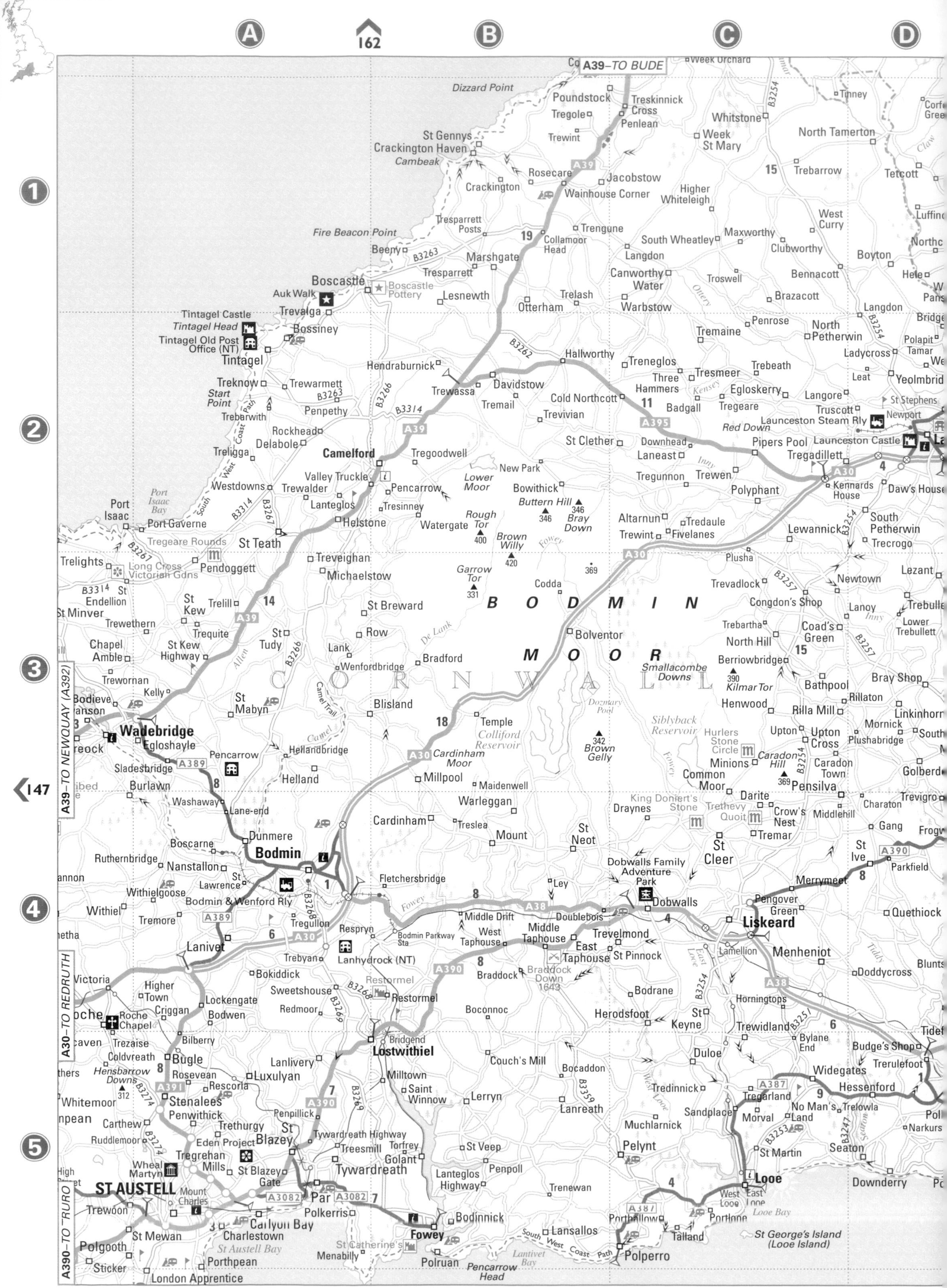
A
162
B
C
D
1
2
3
4
5
147
A39–TO BUDE
A39–TO NEWQUAY (A392)
A30–TO REDRUTH
A390–TO TRURO
Dizzard Point
Poundstock
Treskinnick Cross
Tregole
Penlean
Week Orchard
Tinney
Whitstone
Week St Mary
North Tamerton
St Gennys
Crackington Haven
Cambeak
Trewint
Rosecare
Jacobstow
Crackington
Wainhouse Corner
Higher Whiteleigh
Trebarrow
Tetcott
Fire Beacon Point
Tresparrett Posts
Trengune
South Wheatley
Maxworthy
Clubworthy
West Curry
Boyton
Collamoor Head
Langdon
Beeny
Marshgate
Tresparrett
Canworthy Water
Troswell
Bennacott
Boscastle
Boscastle Pottery
Lesnewth
Trelash
Warbstow
Brazacott
Auk Walk
Otterham
Langdon
Tintagel Castle
Trevalga
Tintagel Head
Bossiney
Tremaine
Penrose
North Petherwin
Tintagel Old Post Office (NT)
Tintagel
Hallworthy
Ladycross
Tamar
Hendraburnick
Treneglos
Trebeath
Treknow
Trewarmett
Trewassa
Davidstow
Three Hammers
Tresmeer
Egloskerry
Langore
Start Point
Penpethy
Tremail
Cold Northcott
Badgall
Tregeare
Leat
Yeolmbridge
St Stephens
Truscott
Treligga
Treknow
Rockhead
Trevivian
Launceston Steam Rly
Newport
Delabole
Camelford
Tregoodwell
St Clether
Downhead
Red Down
Pipers Pool
Launceston Castle
Laneast
Tregadillett
Valley Truckle
New Park
Westdowns
Trewalder
Pencarrow
Lower Moor
Bowithick
Tregunnon
Trewen
Polyphant
Kennards House
Daw's House
Port Isaac
Port Isaac Bay
Lanteglos
Tresinney
Buttern Hill
Rough Tor
Bray Down
Altarnun
Tredaule
South Petherwin
Port Gaverne
Helstone
Watergate
Brown Willy
Trewint
Fivelanes
Lewannick
Trecrogo
Tregeare Rounds
St Teath
Trelights
Long Cross Victorian Gdns
Pendoggett
Treveighan
Michaelstow
Plusha
Lezant
Newtown
St Endellion
Garrow Tor
Codda
Trevadlock
St Minver
St Kew
Trelill
St Breward
B O D M I N
Congdon's Shop
Lanoy
Trebullett
Trewethern
Trequite
Bolventor
Trebartha
North Hill
Coad's Green
Chapel Amble
St Kew Highway
St Tudy
Row
Lank
Bradford
M O O R
Berriowbridge
Wenfordbridge
Smallacombe Downs
Kilmar Tor
Bray Shop
Trewornan
Kelly
C O R N W A L L
Bathpool
Rillaton
Bodieve
Henwood
Rilla Mill
Linkinhorne
Wadebridge
Egloshayle
St Mabyn
Blisland
Temple
Colliford Reservoir
Dozmary Pool
Siblyback Reservoir
Hurlers Stone Circle
Upton
Upton Cross
Mornick
Plushabridge
Pencarrow
Hellandbridge
Cardinham Moor
Brown Gelly
Minions
Caradon Hill
Caradon Town
Sladesbridge
Burlawn
Helland
Millpool
Maidenwell
Common Moor
Pensilva
Golberdon
Washaway
Lane-end
Warleggan
King Doniert's Stone
Trethevy Quoit
Darite
Draynes
Crow's Nest
Middlehill
Charaton
Trevigro
Cardinham
Treslea
Gang
Boscarne
Dunmere
Mount
St Neot
Tremar
St Cleer
St Ive
Bodmin
Ruthernbridge
Nanstallon
Dobwalls Family Adventure Park
Parkfield
St Lawrence
Fletchersbridge
Ley
Merrymeet
Withielgoose
Bodmin & Wenford Rly
Dobwalls
Pengover Green
Withiel
Middle Drift
Doublebois
Liskeard
Quethiock
Tremore
Tregullon
Respryn
West Taphouse
Middle Taphouse
Trevelmond
Bodmin Parkway Sta
East Taphouse
St Pinnock
Lamellion
Menheniot
Lanivet
Trebyan
Lanhydrock (NT)
Braddock
Braddock Down 1643
Blunts
Doddycross
Victoria
Bokiddick
Restormel
Higher Town
Sweetshouse
Lockengate
Bodrane
Horningtops
Roche
Criggan
Redmoor
Boconnoc
Herodsfoot
St Keyne
Roche Chapel
Bodwen
Trewidland
Tideford
Trezaise
Bilberry
Bridgend
Lostwithiel
Duloe
Bylane End
Budge's Shop
Coldvreath
Bugle
Lanlivery
Couch's Mill
Bocaddon
Trerulefoot
Hensbarrow Downs
Rosevean
Rescorla
Luxulyan
Milltown
Widegates
Hessenford
Whitemoor
Stenalees
Saint Winnow
Lerryn
Tredinnick
Trelowla
Tregarland
Penwithick
Lanreath
Sandplace
No Man's Land
Carthew
Penpillick
Trethurgy
St Blazey
Tywardreath Highway
Morval
Narkurs
Ruddlemoor
Eden Project
Treesmill
Torfrey
Muchlarnick
St Veep
Pelynt
St Martin
Seaton
Tregrehan Mills
Golant
Wheal Martyn
St Blazey Gate
Tywardreath
Penpoll
Lanteglos Highway
Trenewan
Looe
Downderry
ST AUSTELL
Mount Charles
Par
West Looe
East Looe
Trewoon
Polkerris
Bodinnick
Porthallow
Portlooe
Looe Bay
Carlyon Bay
Charlestown
St Catherine's
Fowey
Lansallos
Talland
St George's Island (Looe Island)
Polgooth
St Mewan
St Austell Bay
Menabilly
Polruan
Lantivet Bay
Polperro
South West Coast Path
Sticker
Porthpean
Pencarrow Head
London Apprentice

Bodmin Moor: *This is a sweeping expanse of rugged moorland covering over a hundred square miles of central Cornwall. The area is seeped in myth and legend, not least the tales of the 'Beast of Bodmin Moor'. Over the last twenty years there have been more than sixty recorded sighting of the 'Beast', generally thought to be a big cat, like a panther, which preys on other wild animals and farm livestock.* ***Map ref. B3 Also on page 25***

Tavistock: *Crowndale, just south of Tavistock is the birthplace of Sir Francis Drake. Drake is one of Britain's most famous sea captains. He was the first Englishman to sail around the World in 1580 and later became famous for routing the Spanish Armada.* ***Map ref. E3***

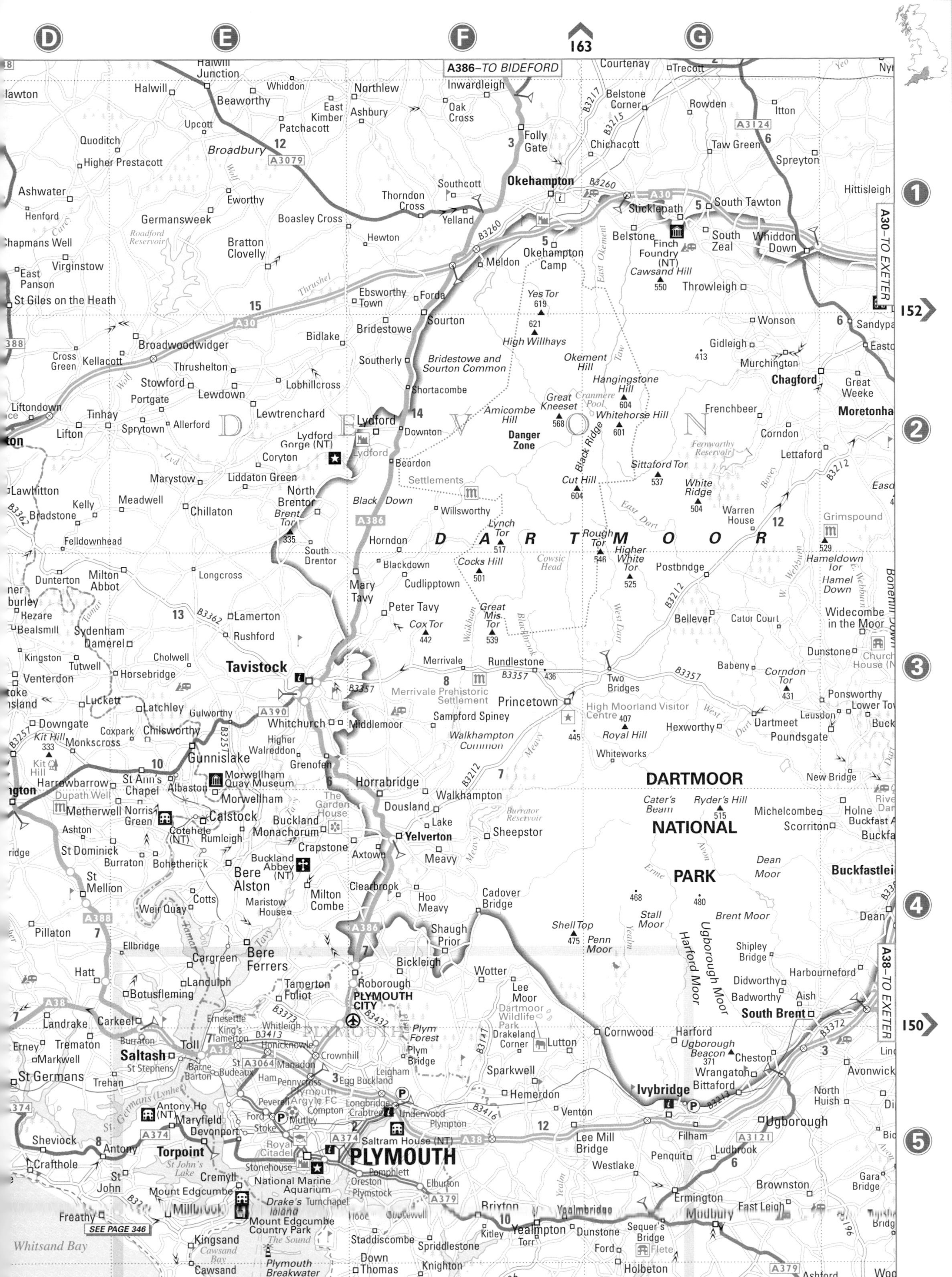

D
E
F
G
163
A386–TO BIDEFORD
Halwill Junction
Halwill
Whiddon
Beaworthy
Northlew
Inwardleigh
Courtenay
Trecott
Belstone Corner
Rowden
Itton
East Kimber
Ashbury
Oak Cross
Patchacott
Upcott
Quoditch
Broadbury
A3079
Higher Prestacott
Folly Gate
Chichacott
Taw Green
A3124
Spreyton
Ashwater
Henford
Eworthy
Germansweek
Southcott
Thorndon Cross
Okehampton
B3260
A30
Sticklepath
South Tawton
Hittisleigh
Yelland
Boasley Cross
Roadford Reservoir
Chapmans Well
Bratton Clovelly
Hewton
Meldon
Okehampton Camp
Belstone
Finch Foundry (NT)
Cawsand Hill
South Zeal
Whiddon Down
A30–TO EXETER
Virginstow
East Panson
St Giles on the Heath
Ebsworthy Town
Forda
Yes Tor
619
550
Throwleigh
Sourton
Wonson
Sandypark
152
Bridestowe
Bidlake
Broadwoodwidger
High Willhays
621
Gidleigh
413
Easton
Cross Green
Kellacott
Thrushelton
Southerly
Bridestowe and Sourton Common
Okement Hill
Murchington
Chagford
Great Weeke
Stowford
Lewdown
Lobhillcross
Shortacombe
Hangingstone Hill
604
Portgate
Great Kneeset
Cranmere Pool
Moretonhampstead
Liftondown
Tinhay
Lifton
Sprytown
Allerford
Lewtrenchard
Lydford
Lydford Gorge (NT)
Downton
Amicombe Hill
568
Whitehorse Hill
601
Frenchbeer
Corndon
Danger Zone
Fernworthy Reservoir
Lettaford
Coryton
Beardon
Sittaford Tor
537
Marystow
Liddaton Green
Settlements
Cut Hill
604
White Ridge
504
Lawhitton
North Brentor
Kelly
Meadwell
Chillaton
Brent Tor
Black Down
Willsworthy
Warren House
Grimspound
Bradstone
Felldownhead
335
South Brentor
A386
Horndon
Lynch Tor
517
DARTMOOR
Rough Tor
546
Higher White Tor
525
Hameldown Tor
529
Dunterton
Milton Abbot
Longcross
Blackdown
Cudlipptown
Cocks Hill
501
Cowsic Head
Postbridge
Hamel Down
Mary Tavy
Peter Tavy
Cox Tor
442
Great Mis Tor
539
Bellever
Widecombe in the Moor
Hezare
Lamerton
Rushford
Sydenham Damerel
Bealsmill
Kingston
Tutwell
Cholwell
Tavistock
Merrivale
Rundlestone
B3357
436
Two Bridges
Babeny
Dunstone
Corndon Tor
431
Church House (NT)
Venterdon
Horsebridge
Merrivale Prehistoric Settlement
Princetown
High Moorland Visitor Centre
407
Ponsworthy
Luckett
Latchley
Gulworthy
A390
Whitchurch
Middlemoor
Sampford Spiney
Royal Hill
Hexworthy
Dartmeet
Poundsgate
Leusdon
Downgate
Coxpark
Chilsworthy
Kit Hill
333
Monkscross
Higher Walreddon
Walkhampton Common
445
Whiteworks
Gunnislake
Grenofen
Harrowbarrow
St Ann's Chapel
Albaston
Morwellham Quay Museum
Horrabridge
DARTMOOR NATIONAL PARK
New Bridge
Dupath Well
Metherwell
Norris Green
Morwellham
Calstock
The Garden House
Dousland
Walkhampton
Burrator Reservoir
Cater's Beam
Ryder's Hill
515
Michelcombe
Holne
Buckfast
Scorriton
Ashton
Cotehele (NT)
Rumleigh
Buckland Monachorum
Lake
Yelverton
Sheepstor
St Dominick
Burraton
Bohetherick
Crapstone
Buckland Abbey (NT)
Axtown
Meavy
Dean Moor
Buckfastleigh
St Mellion
Bere Alston
Clearbrook
Hoo Meavy
Cadover Bridge
468
480
Weir Quay
Cotts
Maristow House
Milton Combe
Stall Moor
Brent Moor
Dean
Pillaton
A388
Ellbridge
Shaugh Prior
Shell Top
475
Penn Moor
Shipley Bridge
Harford Moor
Ugborough Moor
Cargreen
Bere Ferrers
Bickleigh
Wotter
Hatt
Landulph
Tamerton Foliot
Roborough
Lee Moor
Didworthy
Harbourneford
Botusfleming
PLYMOUTH CITY
Dartmoor Wildlife Park
Badworthy
Aish
South Brent
A38–TO EXETER
150
Landrake
Carkeel
Ernesettle
King's Tamerton
Whitleigh
Plym Forest
Drakeland Corner
Lutton
Cornwood
Harford
Ugborough Beacon
371
Erney
Trematon
Burraton
Toll
Honicknowle
Crownhill
Plym Bridge
Cheston
Markwell
Saltash
St Stephens
Barne Barton
Budeaux
Manadon
Leigham
Sparkwell
Wrangaton
Avonwick
St Germans
Trehan
Ham
Pennycross
Egg Buckland
Hemerdon
Ivybridge
Bittaford
North Huish
Antony Ho (NT)
Peverell
Plymouth Argyle FC
Compton
Mutley
Longbridge
Crabtree
Underwood
Plympton
Venton
Maryfield
Ford
Devonport
Stoke
Ugborough
Sheviock
Antony
Torpoint
A374
Royal Citadel
Saltram House (NT)
Lee Mill Bridge
Filham
A3121
Crafthole
St John's Lake
PLYMOUTH
Penquit
Ludbrook
Stonehouse
Pomphlett
Westlake
St John
Cremyll
National Marine Aquarium
Oreston
Plymstock
Elburton
A379
Brownston
Gara Bridge
Mount Edgcumbe
Turnchapel
Ermington
Freathy
Millbrook
Drake's Island
Brixton
Yealmbridge
Modbury
Fast Leigh
SEE PAGE 346
Mount Edgcumbe Country Park
Hooe
Goosewell
Kitley
Yealmpton
Dunstone
Sequer's Bridge
Whitsand Bay
Kingsand
Cawsand Bay
The Sound
Staddiscombe
Spriddlestone
Torr
Ford
Flete
Down Thomas
Knighton
Holbeton
Cawsand
Plymouth Breakwater
Ashford

Dartmoor Prison, Princetown: *Built in 1809 to hold prisoners of war. Almost 1,500 French and American prisoners died here under a very brutal regime and were all buried just outside the prison walls. Dartmoor closed as a prisoner of war establishment in 1815 but was reopened in 1850 for civilian prisoners serving long sentences and those subject to hard labour. It was always regarded as 'the end of the line' for inmates and there have been numerous calls for it to close. However, as a listed building it cannot be demolished, so since 1980 it has been revamped and modernised and continues to be part of the prison system.* ***Map ref. F3***

150

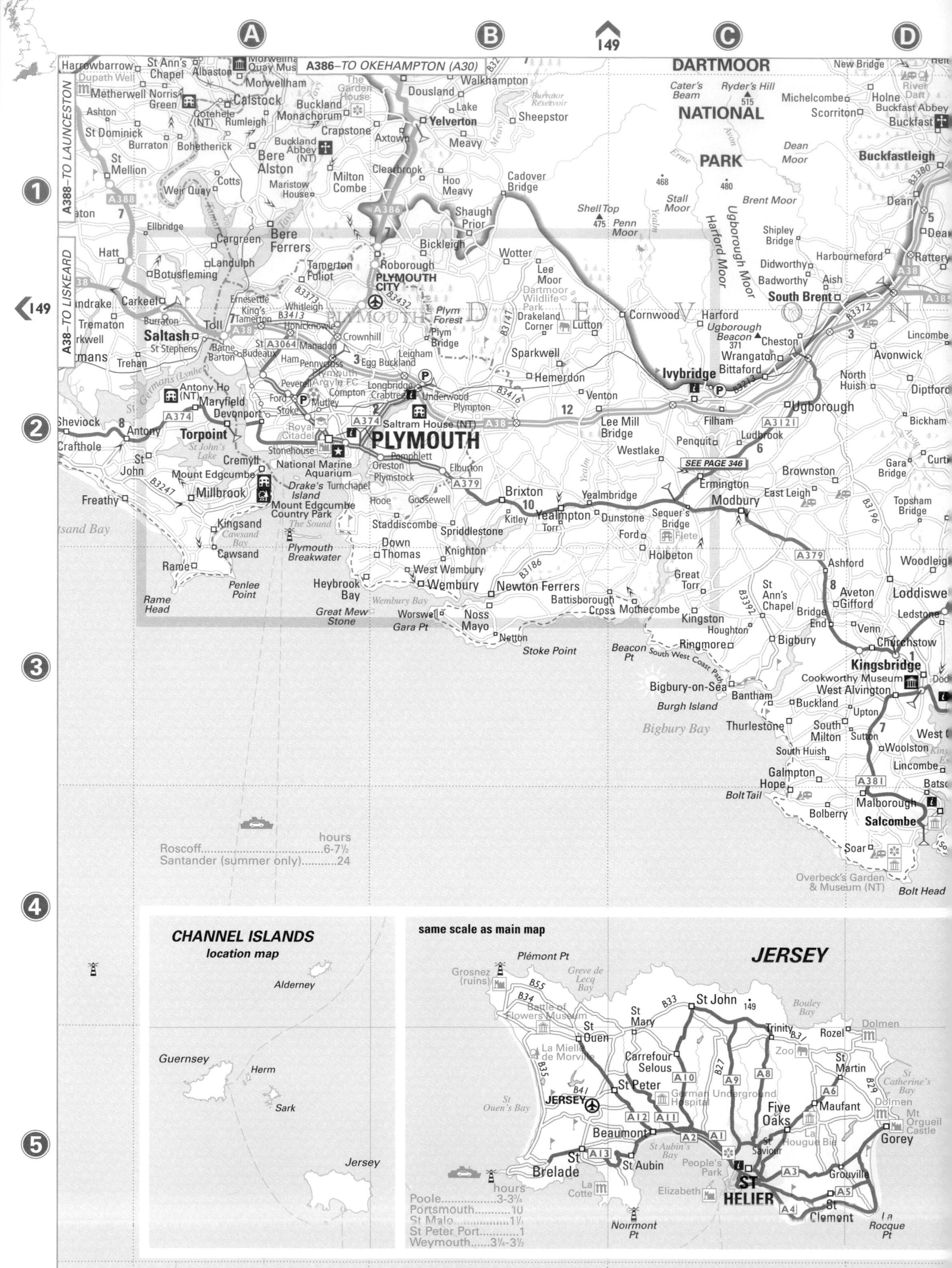

A
B
149
C
D
A386–TO OKEHAMPTON (A30)
A388–TO LAUNCESTON
A38–TO LISKEARD
149
1
2
3
4
5
DARTMOOR
NATIONAL
PARK
Harrowbarrow
St Ann's Chapel
Albaston
Morwellham Quay Mus
Morwellham
Dupath Well
Metherwell
Norris Green
Calstock
Ashton
Cotehele (NT)
Rumleigh
Monachorum
Buckland
The Garden House
Walkhampton
Dousland
Lake
Yelverton
Sheepstor
Burrator Reservoir
St Dominick
Burraton
Bohetherick
Crapstone
Axtown
Meavy
Buckland Abbey (NT)
St Mellion
Bere Alston
Clearbrook
Milton Combe
Maristow House
Hoo Meavy
Cadover Bridge
Weir Quay
Cotts
Shaugh Prior
Ellbridge
Cargreen
Bere Ferrers
Bickleigh
Hatt
Landulph
Botusfleming
Tamerton Foliot
Roborough
PLYMOUTH CITY
Wotter
Lee Moor
Dartmoor Wildlife Park
Drakeland Corner
Lutton
Cornwood
Harford
Ugborough Beacon
371
Cheston
Wrangaton
Bittaford
Ivybridge
Carkeel
Ernesettle
King's Tamerton
Whitleigh
Trematon
Burraton
Toll
Saltash
Honicknowle
Crownhill
Plym Forest
Plym Bridge
Sparkwell
Hemerdon
Venton
St Stephens
Barne Barton
St Budeaux
Manadon
Ham
Pennycross
Egg Buckland
Leigham
Trehan
Antony Ho (NT)
Maryfield
Devonport
Peverell
Ford
Stoke
Mutley
Compton
Longbridge
Crabtree
Underwood
Plympton
Saltram House (NT)
Lee Mill Bridge
Filham
Penquit
Ludbrook
Ugborough
Sheviock
Antony
Torpoint
Royal Citadel
PLYMOUTH
Westlake
Crafthole
St John
St John's Lake
Cremyll
Stonehouse
Pomphlett
Oreston
Plymstock
National Marine Aquarium
Elburton
SEE PAGE 346
Ermington
Modbury
Mount Edgcumbe
Millbrook
Drake's Island
Turnchapel
Mount Edgcumbe Country Park
Hooe
Goosewell
Brixton
Yealmbridge
Yealmpton
Kitley
Torr
Dunstone
Sequer's Bridge
Flete
Ford
Holbeton
Freathy
Kingsand
Cawsand Bay
Cawsand
The Sound
Plymouth Breakwater
Staddiscombe
Spriddlestone
Down Thomas
Knighton
West Wembury
Wembury
Newton Ferrers
Battisborough Cross
Mothecombe
Great Torr
Rame
Rame Head
Penlee Point
Heybrook Bay
Great Mew Stone
Wembury Bay
Worswell
Noss Mayo
Gara Pt
Netton
Stoke Point
Kingston
Houghton
Ringmore
Beacon Pt
South West Coast Path
Bigbury-on-Sea
Burgh Island
Bigbury Bay
Bantham
Thurlestone
Bigbury
St Ann's Chapel
Bridge End
Aveton Gifford
Loddiswell
Venn
Churchstow
Kingsbridge
Cookworthy Museum
West Alvington
Buckland
Upton
South Milton
Sutton
South Huish
Woolston
Galmpton
Hope
Bolt Tail
Malborough
Bolberry
Salcombe
Soar
Overbeck's Garden & Museum (NT)
Bolt Head
Lincombe
Cater's Beam
Ryder's Hill
515
Michelcombe
Holne
Scorriton
Buckfast Abbey
Buckfast
Buckfastleigh
Dean Moor
468
480
Stall Moor
Shell Top
475
Penn Moor
Brent Moor
Shipley Bridge
Harbourneford
Didworthy
Badworthy
Aish
South Brent
Harford Moor
Ugborough Moor
Dean
Rattery
New Bridge
Lincombe
Avonwick
North Huish
Diptford
Bickham
Brownston
East Leigh
Gara Bridge
Topsham Bridge
Ashford
Woodleigh
Ledstone
hours
Roscoff.................................6-7½
Santander (summer only)..........24
CHANNEL ISLANDS
location map
Alderney
Guernsey
Herm
Sark
Jersey
same scale as main map
JERSEY
Plémont Pt
Grosnez (ruins)
Greve de Lecq Bay
Battle of Flowers Museum
St John
Bouley Bay
St Mary
St Ouen
Trinity
Rozel
Dolmen
La Mielle de Morville
Carrefour Selous
Zoo
St Martin
St Catherine's Bay
St Peter
German Underground Hospital
St Ouen's Bay
JERSEY
Five Oaks
Maufant
Dolmen
Mt Orgueil Castle
Gorey
Beaumont
La Hougue Bie
St Aubin's Bay
St Saviour
St Brelade
St Aubin
People's Park
ST HELIER
Grouville
Elizabeth
La Cotte
St Clement
La Rocque Pt
Noirmont Pt
hours
Poole................3-3¾
Portsmouth..........10
St Malo..............1½
St Peter Port...........1
Weymouth......3¼-3½

Plymouth: *On the 15th August 1620 the original group of 'Pilgrim Fathers' left Southampton in two ships, the Speedwell and the Mayflower. But the Speedwell became un-seaworthy before they reached Land's End and both ships returned to Plymouth. There, many of the Speedwell's passengers transferred to the Mayflower and on the 6th September 1620 they set off again in search of their new life in the New World. The Mayflower took 66 days to reach Cape Cod where eventually the settlers created a new settlement which they called Plymouth.* ***Map ref. A2***

Devonport: *Infamous double agent Guy Burgess was born here in 1910. He became a Soviet spy and fled to Russia in 1951. Burgess died in Moscow in 1963.* ***Map ref. A2***

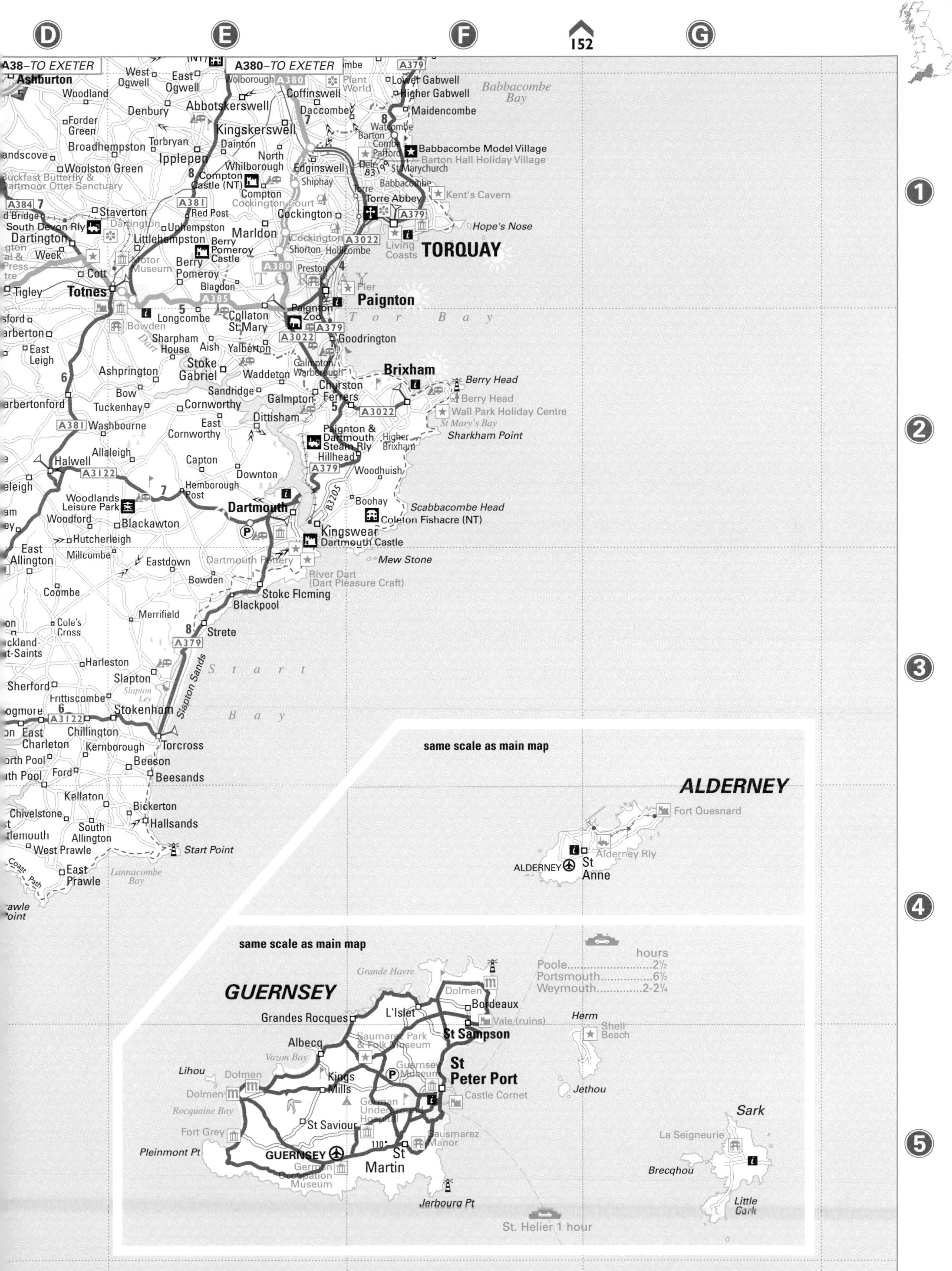

D
E
F
152
G
A38–TO EXETER
A380–TO EXETER
Ashburton
Woodland
West Ogwell
East Ogwell
Denbury
Abbotskerswell
Coffinswell
Plant World
Daccombe
Lower Gabwell
Higher Gabwell
Maidencombe
Babbacombe Bay
Forder Green
Broadhempston
Torbryan
Ipplepen
Kingskerswell
Dainton
North Whilborough
Edginswell
Shiphay
Watcombe
Barton
Babbacombe Model Village
Barton Hall Holiday Village
St Marychurch
Babbacombe
Kent's Cavern
Woolston Green
Buckfast Butterfly & Dartmoor Otter Sanctuary
Compton Castle (NT)
Compton
Cockington Court
Cockington
Torre Abbey
Hope's Nose
Staverton
Red Post
Dartington
South Devon Rly
Dartington
Upper Dippenhall
Littlehempston
Marldon
Berry Pomeroy Castle
Berry Pomeroy
Shorton
Hollicombe
Living Coasts
TORQUAY
Week
Motor Museum
Preston
Cott
Pier
Tigley
Totnes
Blagdon
Paignton
Paignton Zoo
Tor Bay
Bowden
Longcombe
Collaton St Mary
Goodrington
Sharpham House
Aish
Yalberton
East Leigh
Ashprington
Stoke Gabriel
Waddeton
Galmpton Warborough
Brixham
Berry Head
Bow
Tuckenhay
Sandridge
Cornworthy
Galmpton
Churston Ferrers
Wall Park Holiday Centre
St Mary's Bay
Harbertonford
Washbourne
East Cornworthy
Dittisham
Paignton & Dartmouth Steam Rly
Higher Brixham
Sharkham Point
Allaleigh
Halwell
Capton
Hillhead
Downton
Woodhuish
Hemborough Post
Woodlands Leisure Park
Dartmouth
Boohay
Scabbacombe Head
Woodford
Blackawton
Coleton Fishacre (NT)
Kingswear
Dartmouth Castle
Hutcherleigh
Millcombe
East Allington
Eastdown
Dartmouth Pottery
Mew Stone
Bowden
River Dart (Dart Pleasure Craft)
Coombe
Stoke Fleming
Blackpool
Merrifield
Cole's Cross
Strete
Harleston
Start Bay
Slapton
Slapton Ley
Slapton Sands
Sherford
Frittiscombe
Stokenham
Chillington
East Charleton
Kernborough
Torcross
Beeson
Ford
Beesands
Kellaton
Bickerton
Chivelstone
South Allington
Hallsands
West Prawle
Start Point
East Prawle
Lannacombe Bay
Coast Path
same scale as main map
ALDERNEY
Fort Quesnard
Alderney Rly
ALDERNEY
St Anne
same scale as main map
GUERNSEY
hours
Poole 2½
Portsmouth 6½
Weymouth 2-2¼
Grande Havre
Dolmen
Bordeaux
Vale (ruins)
Herm
Shell Beach
Grandes Rocques
L'Islet
St Sampson
Albecq
Saumarez Park & Folk Museum
Vazon Bay
Lihou
Dolmen
Kings Mills
Guernsey Museum
St Peter Port
Castle Cornet
Jethou
Rocquaine Bay
German Underground Hospital
Sark
St Saviour
Fort Grey
Sausmarez Manor
La Seigneurie
Pleinmont Pt
GUERNSEY
St Martin
German Occupation Museum
Brecqhou
Jerbourg Pt
Little Sark
St. Helier 1 hour
1
2
3
4
5

Slapton Sands: *During Exercise Tiger, a training exercise for D Day, German E-Boats intercepted and sank some of the small landing craft, killing over 700 American soldiers. A recovered Sherman Tank, on the beach, is a permanent memorial to this action.* ***Map ref. E3***

Torquay: *The Gleneagles Hotel in Asheldon Road, Wellswood was the original setting for Fawlty Towers the 1970s comedy series which starred John Cleese.* ***Map ref. F1***

Torquay: *Agatha Christie, Britain's greatest 'whodunnit' novelist, was born here in 1896. In all she wrote 78 crime stories and died aged 80 in 1976.* ***Map ref. F1***

164

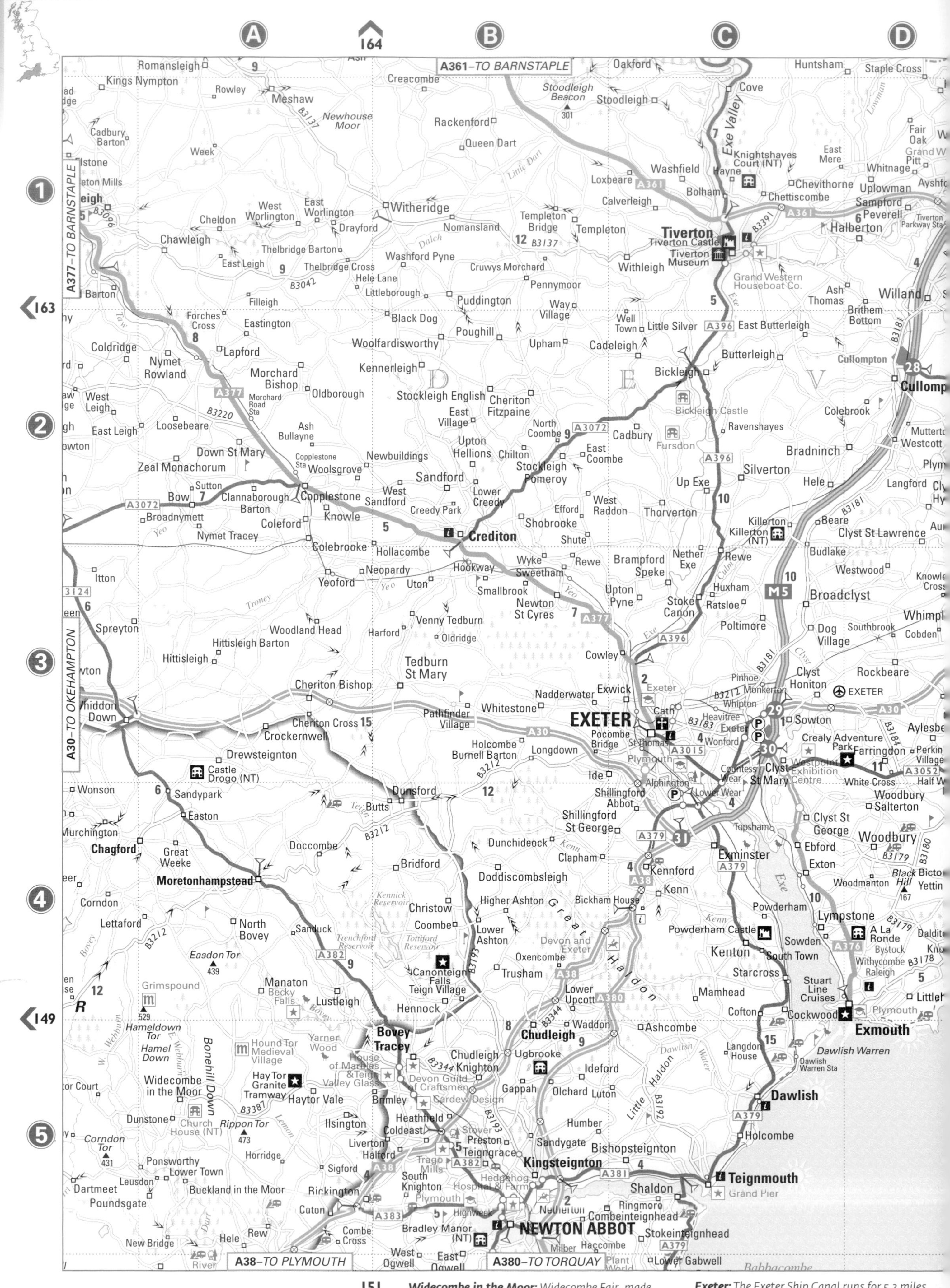

A
B
C
D
1
2
3
4
5
163
149
A361–TO BARNSTAPLE
A377–TO BARNSTAPLE
A30–TO OKEHAMPTON
A38–TO PLYMOUTH
A380–TO TORQUAY
Romansleigh
Kings Nympton
Rowley
Meshaw
Creacombe
Newhouse Moor
Rackenford
Queen Dart
Oakford
Stoodleigh Beacon
Stoodleigh
Cove
Huntsham
Staple Cross
Cadbury Barton
Week
Exe Valley
Knightshayes Court (NT)
Fair Oak
East Mere
Whitnage
Pitt
Washfield
Loxbeare
Calverleigh
Bolham
Hayne
Chevithorne
Uplowman
Chettiscombe
Sampford Peverell
Tiverton Parkway Sta
Halberton
West Worlington
East Worlington
Witheridge
Drayford
Cheldon
Chawleigh
Templeton Bridge
Templeton
Nomansland
Tiverton
Tiverton Castle
Tiverton Museum
Thelbridge Barton
Thelbridge Cross
East Leigh
Washford Pyne
Cruwys Morchard
Withleigh
Grand Western Houseboat Co.
Hele Lane
Littleborough
Pennymoor
Ash Thomas
Willand
Filleigh
Puddington
Way Village
Brithem Bottom
Forches Cross
Eastington
Black Dog
Well Town
Little Silver
East Butterleigh
Poughill
Upham
Cadeleigh
Butterleigh
Coldridge
Lapford
Woolfardisworthy
Cullompton
Nymet Rowland
Morchard Bishop
Kennerleigh
Bickleigh
Oldborough
Stockleigh English
Cheriton Fitzpaine
Bickleigh Castle
Colebrook
West Leigh
Morchard Road Sta
East Village
North Coombe
Cadbury
Ravenshayes
Loosebeare
Ash Bullayne
Fursdon
East Leigh
Upton Hellions
Chilton
East Coombe
Bradninch
Westcott
Down St Mary
Copplestone Sta
Newbuildings
Woolsgrove
Stockleigh Pomeroy
Silverton
Zeal Monachorum
Sandford
Lower Creedy
Up Exe
Hele
Langford
Sutton
Bow
Clannaborough Barton
Copplestone
West Sandford
West Raddon
Creedy Park
Efford
Thorverton
Killerton
Killerton (NT)
Beare
Broadnymett
Nymet Tracey
Coleford
Knowle
Crediton
Shobrooke
Clyst St Lawrence
Shute
Colebrooke
Hollacombe
Budlake
Wyke
Rewe
Brampford Speke
Nether Exe
Rewe
Westwood
Itton
Neopardy
Hookway
Sweetham
Yeoford
Uton
Smallbrook
Huxham
Broadclyst
Upton Pyne
Newton St Cyres
Stoke Canon
Ratsloe
Spreyton
Woodland Head
Venny Tedburn
Harford
Oldridge
Poltimore
Dog Village
Southbrook
Whimple
Cobden
Hittisleigh Barton
Hittisleigh
Tedburn St Mary
Cowley
Rockbeare
Cheriton Bishop
Pinhoe
Monkerton
Honiton Clyst
EXETER
Whiddon Down
Nadderwater
Exwick
Whipton
Whitestone
Pathfinder Village
Cheriton Cross
Crockernwell
EXETER
Cath
Heavitree
Sowton
Aylesbeare
Pocombe Bridge
St Thomas
Wonford
Holcombe Burnell Barton
Longdown
Crealy Adventure Park
Farringdon
Perkins Village
Drewsteignton
Castle Drogo (NT)
Ide
Alphington
Countess Wear
Clyst St Mary
Westpoint Exhibition Centre
White Cross
Wonson
Sandypark
Dunsford
Shillingford Abbot
Lower Wear
Woodbury Salterton
Easton
Butts
Shillingford St George
Topsham
Clyst St George
Murchington
Chagford
Great Weeke
Doccombe
Dunchideock
Ebford
Woodbury
Clapham
Exminster
Exton
Moretonhampstead
Bridford
Doddiscombsleigh
Kennford
Kenn
Woodmanton
Black Hill
Yettington
Corndon
Kennick Reservoir
Christow
Higher Ashton
Bickham House
Powderham
Lympstone
Lettaford
North Bovey
Coombe
Lower Ashton
Devon and Exeter
Powderham Castle
A La Ronde
Sowden
Dalditch
Easdon Tor
Sanduck
Trenchford Reservoir
Tottiford Reservoir
Oxencombe
Kenton
South Town
Bystock
Withycombe Raleigh
Canonteign Falls
Teign Village
Trusham
Starcross
Grimspound
Manaton
Becky Falls
Lustleigh
Lower Upcott
Mamhead
Stuart Line Cruises
Littleham
Hennock
Cofton
Cockwood
Exmouth
Hameldown Tor
Hamel Down
Hound Tor Medieval Village
Yarner Wood
Bovey Tracey
Chudleigh
Waddon
Ashcombe
Dawlish Warren
Dawlish Warren Sta
Langdon House
House of Marbles & Teign Valley Glass
Chudleigh Knighton
Ugbrooke
Ideford
Widecombe in the Moor
Hay Tor Granite Tramway
Haytor Vale
Devon Guild of Craftsmen
Cardew Design
Gappah
Olchard
Luton
Little Haldon
Dawlish
Bonehill Down
Brimley
Dunstone
Church House (NT)
Rippon Tor
Ilsington
Heathfield
Humber
Corndon Tor
Horridge
Coldeast
Stover
Liverton
Preston
Sandygate
Bishopsteignton
Holcombe
Halford
Teigngrace
Ponsworthy
Lower Town
Sigford
Trago Mills
Kingsteignton
Teignmouth
Dartmeet
Leusdon
Poundsgate
Buckland in the Moor
Rickington
South Knighton
Hedgehog Hospital & Farm
Shaldon
Grand Pier
Coton
Ringmore
Netherton
Combeinteignhead
New Bridge
Hele
Rew
Combe Cross
Bradley Manor (NT)
NEWTON ABBOT
Stokeinteignhead
Milber
Haccombe
River
West Ogwell
East Ogwell
Lower Gabwell
Babbacombe

151

Widecombe in the Moor: *Widecombe Fair, made famous in the song concerning the adventures of Old Uncle Tom Cobley and all, is held here. The fair dates back to around the 1850s.* ***Map ref. A5***

Exeter: *The Exeter Ship Canal runs for 5.3 miles (8.5km) and is the oldest post-Roman canal in Britain, dating back to 1563.* ***Map ref. C3***

D
E
F
165
G
M5–TO BRIDGWATER
A358–TO TAUNTON
A303–TO YEOVIL (A3088)
A35–TO DORCHESTER
154
1
2
3
4
5
Holywell
Lake
Rockwell Green
White Ball
Holcombe Rogus
Sampford Arundel
Sampford Moor
Wrangway
Red Ball
Wellington Monument (NT)
Nicholashayne
Blackmoor
Lowton
Ford Street
Wiltown
Luxhay Reservoir
West Buckland
Poundisford Park
Corfe
Pitminster
Blagdon Hill
Staple Fitzpaine
Staple Hill
SOMERSET
Bickenhall
Curland
Hatch Green
Stewley
Kenny
Ashill
Windmill Hill
Hastings
Broadway
Horton
Ilton
Rapps
Isle Abbotts
Walrond's Park
Puckington
Stocklinch
Barrington
Barrington Court (NT)
East Lambrook
West Lambrook
Westport
Shepton Beauchamp
South Petherton
Whitelackington
Hurcott
Horton Cross
Ilminster
Seavington St Michael
Seavington St Mary
Kingstone
Allowenshay
Dinnington
Dowlish Ford
Dowlish Wake
Hinton St George
Black Down Hills
Burnworthy
Clayhidon
Rosemary Lane
Churchstanton
Birch Wood
Blackwater
Appledore
Prescott
Woodgate
Millhayes
Whitehall
Culmstock
Culm Valley
Stapley
Fyfett
Buckland St Mary
Craddock
Hackpen Hill
Hemyock
Willand
Churchingford
Bishopswood
Ham
Crock Street
Donyatt
Sticklepath
Combe St Nicholas
Newtown
Beetham
Northay
Ashill
Smithincott
Bolham Water
Madford
Hole
Smeatharpe
Marsh
Whitestaunton
Wadeford
Chardleigh Green
Knowle St Giles
Chaffcombe
Cudworth
Chillington
Blackborough
Sheldon
Slade
Kentisbeare
Dunkeswell
Newcott
Beacon
Howley
Higher Wambrook
Crimchard
Hornsbury Furnham
Chard
Purtington
Coombe
Roundham
Hewish
Cricket St Thomas
The Wildlife Park at Cricket St Thomas
Luppitt
Upottery
Yarcombe
Crawley
Wambrook
Street
Wayford
Rawridge
Burridge
Forton
Tatworth
Winsham
Clapton
Kerswell
Beacon
South Chard
Forde Abbey
Netherhay
Broadhembury
Stockland
Furley
Chard Junction
Laymore
Chardstock
Thorncombe
Blackdown
Colliton
Luton
Upton
Payhembury
Combe Raleigh
Wick
Monkton
Millhayes
Holmsleigh Green
Membury
Alston
Chilson
Holditch
Hewood
School House
Burstock
Pilsden Pen
Godford Cross
Awliscombe
Cotleigh
Churchill
Lower Tale
Lower Cheriton
Buckerell
Honiton
Ham
Dalwood
Loughwood Meeting House (NT)
Smallridge
Weycroft
Hawkchurch
Northay
Westhay
Birdsmoor Gate
Marshalsea
Colestocks
Higher Cheriton
Weston
Wilmington
Offwell
Widworthy
Marshwood
Bettiscombe
Pilsdon
Feniton
Hamlet
Axminster
Axminster Museum
Millbrook
Fishpond Bottom
Fenny Bridges
Escot
Gittisham
Kilmington
Shave Cross
Marshwood Vale
Alfington
Shute
Hampton
Raymond's Hill
Monkton Wyld
Fairmile
Cadhay
Ottery St Mary
Putts Corner
Church Green
Seaton Junction
Shute Barton
Wootton Fitzpaine
Whitchurch
Ryall
Farway
Northleigh
Woodbridge
Whitford
Maidenhayne
Harcombe Bottom
Catherston Leweston
Fernwood
Wiggaton
West Hill
Broad Down
Southleigh
Colyton
Musbury
Yawl
Morcombelake
Blackbury Camp
Seaton Tramway
Charmouth
Fluxton
Sidbury
Sand
Colyford
Combpyne
Uplyme
Golden Cap
Metcombe
Tipton St John
Coombe
Harcombe
Axmouth
Rousdon
Lyme Regis
Seatown
Newton Poppleford
Harpford
Bowd
Stowford
Sidford
Salcombe Regis
Bulstone
Old Bakery (NT)
Dowlands
Pinhay
South West Coast Path
Weston
Marine House
Seaton
Beer
Street
Branscombe
Seaton Bay
Beer Head
Colaton Raleigh
Pinn
Sidmouth
Donkey Sanctuary
Otterton
Fairlynch Arts Centre & Museum
Budleigh Salterton

Axminster *carpets were first produced here in 1755 and the company is still located here today.* ***Map ref.*** *F3*

Lyme Regis*, and the beach along to Charmouth, is a haven for fossil hunters. Along with the more common ammonites, belemnites and gryphaea, finds also include dinosaur fossils, such as ichthyosaur, plesiosaur and pterosaur, in the Jurassic rocks.* ***Map ref.*** *G3*

A
B
C
D
166
153
1
2
3
4
5
A303, A37–TO SHEPTON MALLET
A303–TO HONITON (A30)
A35–TO HONITON
Martock
Tintinhull House (NT)
Chilthorne Domer
Yeovil Marsh
Mudford
Sandford Orcas
Poyntington
Henstridge
Milborne Port
Stoke sub Hamdon
Montacute House (NT)
Montacute
South Petherton
YEOVIL
Sherborne
Sherborne Castle
Odcombe
Brympton
Barwick
Bradford Abbas
Norton-sub-Hamdon
Chiselborough
West Coker
East Coker
North Coker
Stoford
Thornford
Longburton
Caundle Marsh
Bishop's Caundle
Merriott
Hinton St George
Haselbury Plucknett
Hardington Mandeville
Ryme Intrinseca
Yetminster
Lillington
SOMERSET
Crewkerne
North Perrott
Misterton
Closworth
Halstock
Melbury Osmond
Chetnole
Leigh
Hermitage
Holnest
Cricket St Thomas
The Wildlife Park at Cricket St Thomas
Clapton Court
Winsham
South Perrott
Mosterton
Corscombe
Chedington
Evershot
Melbury Bubb
Hilfield
Batcombe
Minterne Magna
Minterne Parva
Buckland Newton
BLACKMOOR
DORSET
Broadwindsor
Beaminster
Pilsdon Pen
Stoke Abbott
Toller Whelme
Rampisham
Frome St Quintin
Up Cerne
Cerne Abbas
The Giant (NT)
Piddletrenthide
Up Sydling
Cattistock
Sydling St Nicholas
Netherbury
Parnham
Mapperton
Chilfrome
Maiden Newton
Marshwood Vale
Melplash
North Poorton
Toller Porcorum
Godmanstone
Nether Cerne
Piddlehinton
Whitchurch Canonicorum
Powerstock
Wynford Eagle
Frampton
Eggardon Hill
Charmouth
Morcombelake
North Chideock
Symondsbury
Bradpole
Loders
Uploders
West Compton
Grimstone
Stratton
Charminster
Golden Cap
Chideock
Bridport
Walditch
Askerswell
Compton Valence
Bradford Peverell
Wolfeton
Tutankhamun Exhibition
Dorset County Mus
Dinosaur Mus
Stinsford
Kingston Maurward Park
Seatown
Eype
Bothenhampton
Shipton Gorge
Chilcombe
Kingston Russell
Winterbourne Abbas
Dorchester
Poundbury
West Bay
North Hill
Burton Bradstock
Litton Cheney
Long Bredy
Poor Lot Barrows
Nine Stones
Winterbourne Steepleton
Maiden Castle
Winterborne Came
Puncknowle
Littlebredy
Martinstown
Hardy Monument (NT)
Swyre
Kingston Russell Stone Circle
Bronkham Hill
Winterborne Monkton
Winterborne Herringston
West Bexington
White Hill
Black Down
South West Coast Path
Portesham
Abbotsbury
Abbotsbury Swannery & Sub-tropical Gardens
St Catherine's Chapel
Abbey
Upwey
Bincombe
Rodden
Broadwey
Sutton Poyntz
White Horse
Littlemoor
Osmington
Chesil Beach
West Fleet
Langton Herring
Buckland Ripers
Nottington
Jordan Hill Roman Temple
Preston
Overcombe
Radipole
Chickerell
Sea Life Centre
Weymouth Bay
Bennetts Water Garden
Melcombe Regis
WEYMOUTH
Charlestown
Westham
Brewers Quay
Nothe Fort
East Fleet
Wyke Regis
Ferry Bridge
Portland Harbour
Guernsey, Jersey, St Malo (summer only)
Portland Castle
Castletown
Fortuneswell
Grove
Easton
Isle of Portland
Weston
Southwell
Bill of Portland

On the 18th July 1955, ***Martinstown*** recorded almost 11 inches (279mm) of rain in 24 hours. This is the highest to date of anywhere in Britain. ***Map ref. C4***

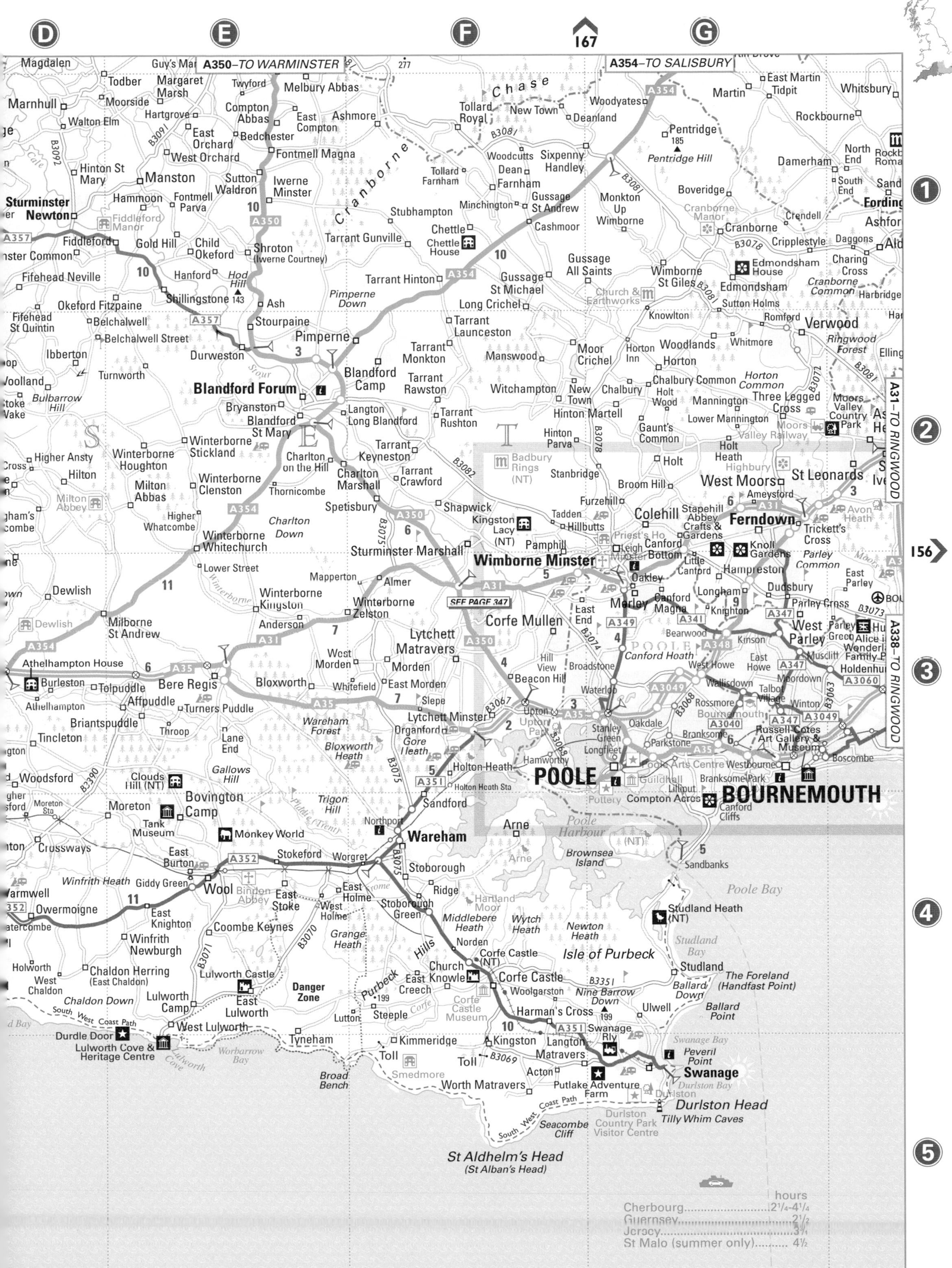

D
E
F
G
167
A350–TO WARMINSTER
A354–TO SALISBURY
Sturminster Newton
Blandford Forum
Pimperne
Cranborne Chase
Wimborne Minster
Ferndown
Verwood
Colehill
West Moors
St Leonards
Corfe Mullen
Lytchett Matravers
Bere Regis
Tolpuddle
Puddletown
Bovington Camp
Wool
Wareham
POOLE
BOURNEMOUTH
Poole Harbour
Brownsea Island
Sandbanks
Poole Bay
Studland
Isle of Purbeck
Corfe Castle
Lulworth Camp
Swanage
Durlston Head
St Aldhelm's Head
(St Alban's Head)
Kingston Lacy (NT)
Clouds Hill (NT)
Monkey World
Tank Museum
Compton Acres
Durdle Door
Lulworth Cove & Heritage Centre
SEE PAGE 347
A31–TO RINGWOOD
A338–TO RINGWOOD
156
1
2
3
4
5
hours
Cherbourg 2¼-4¼
Guernsey 2½
Jersey 3¼
St Malo (summer only) 4½

Tolpuddle: *Six farm labourers were arrested here in 1834 for trade union activity and sentenced to be transported to Australia. They became known as the Tolpuddle Martyrs. Following this a great working class struggle was organised demanding the freedom of the six and they were eventually returned to England.* ***Map ref. D3***

Clouds Hill: *This is the former home of T E Lawrence, commonly known as Lawrence of Arabia. He died in the nearby Bovington Camp Military Hospital on the 19th May 1935 following an accident on his Brough Superior Motorcycle.* ***Map ref. E3 Also on page 27***

A
B
168
C
D
1
2
3
4
5
155
A338–TO SALISBURY
A36–TO SALISBURY
M3–TO WINCHESTER
A31–TO WIMBORNE MINSTER
A35–TO POOLE
Fordingbridge
Ringwood
Ashley Heath
St Leonards
St Ives
Verwood
Alderholt
Ashford
Rockbourne Roman Villa
Damerham
Breamore
Woodfalls
Landford
West Wellow
Nomansland
Cadnam
Totton
North Baddesley
Rownhams
Nursling
Marchwood
Dibden
Hythe
Lyndhurst
New Forest Museum & Information Centre
THE NEW FOREST
Proposed National Park
Bolderwood
Emery Down
Minstead
Ashurst
Burley
Brockenhurst
Beaulieu
National Motor Museum
Beaulieu Abbey
Palace House
Blackfield
Holbury
Exbury
Bucklers Hard
Buckler's Hard Maritime Museum
Sway
Boldre
Lymington
Lymington Pier Sta
New Milton
Hordle
Barton on Sea
Milford on Sea
Keyhaven
Christchurch
Christchurch Priory
Mudeford
Highcliffe
Bransgore
Sopley
Hurn
Alice in Wonderland Family Park
BOURNEMOUTH
West Parley
Christchurch Bay
Hengistbury Head
SEE PAGE 347
Yarmouth
Fort Victoria Country Park
Yarmouth Castle
Totland
Freshwater
Freshwater Bay
Norton Green
The Needles
Needles Pleasure Park
The Needles Old Battery (NT)
Compton Bay
Shalfleet
Newtown
Brighstone
The Undercliff
Atherfield
½hr
Cowes has a sailing history that is second to none and is generally renowned as the home of World Yachting. Throughout the year it hosts some of the greatest international sailing events especially during 'Cowes Week' in August and is home to The Royal Yacht Squadron which was founded in 1815. The world's first hovercraft - the Saunders-Roe SRN1 – flew here in 1959. Map ref. D3

The **New Forest** was created by William the Conqueror in 1079 mainly for the purpose of hunting deer and wild boars. 21 years later, his son, William II, was killed while hunting in the forest by a misdirected arrow near the spot now marked by the Rufus Stone. It is now an important recreational area which retains many original rural practices such as the pasturing of ponies and the rights of local inhabitants known as commoners. It is soon to become Britain's smallest National Park. ***Map ref. B2 Also on page 47***

Parkhurst: *Nearby is Parkhurst Prison which has held some of the most dangerous and notorious prisoners in Britain, including the Great Train Robbers, the Kray twins and the Yorkshire Ripper. The prison was opened in 1838 and the location was chosen because it was close to a deep water anchorage that could be used by ships transporting the convicts to Australia.* ***Map ref. D3***

D
E
169
F
G
A3–TO GUILDFORD
A27–TO CHICHESTER
158
1
2
3
4
5
Crowdhill
Fisher's Pond
Lower Upham
Down
Dean
Corhampton
Meonstoke
Bishopstoke
EASTLEIGH
Fair Oak
Wintershill
Durley Street
Ashton
Dundridge
Droxford
Brockbridge
Upper Swanmore
Newtown
Bishop's Waltham
Bishop's Palace
Swanmore
SOUTHAMPTON
Horton Heath
Itchen Valley
Durley
Hillpound
Soberton
Chidden
Chidden Holt
Clanfield
Queen Elizabeth
Chalton
South Harting
East Harting
Elsted
Uppark (NT)
North Marden
Compton
West Marden
Up Marden
East Marden
H A M P S H I R E
Moorgreen
Long Common
Curdridge
Waltham Chase
Hambledon
Catherington
Horndean
Blendworth
Finchdean
Soberton Heath
Hoe Gate
Worlds End
Anthill Common
Lovedean
Deanlane End
Forestside
Botley
Shedfield
Shirrell Heath
Newtown
Denmead
Ammore
Cowplain
Hedge End
Manor Farm
Curbridge
Burridge
Swanwick
Wickham
Hundred Acres
Forest of Bere
Furzeley Corner
WATERLOOVILLE
A3(M)
Red Hill
Rowland's Castle
Stansted Park
Stoughton
Walderton
SUSSEX
WEST
Bursledon
Old Netley
Lower Swanwick
Whiteley
Crockerhill
North Boarhunt
Southwick
Durrants
Staunton Country Park
Aldsworth
Lordington
Woodend
Hound
Sarisbury
Park Gate
Funtley
Boarhunt
Stakes
Leigh Park
Funtington
Hamble
Locks Heath
Titchfield Abbey
Catisfield
Wallington
Ports Down
Purbrook
HAVANT
Woodmancote
New Brighton
Westbourne
Hamble-le-Rice
Warsash
Hook
Titchfield
FAREHAM
Portchester
Port Solent
Wymering
Cosham
Drayton
Bedhampton
Denvilles
Warblington
Emsworth
Hambrook
Broad
Little Posbrook
Portchester Castle
Horsea Island
Langstone
Hermitage
Southbourne
Nutbourne
Fishbourne
Holy Trinity
Bosham
SEE PAGES 348-49
Northney
Thorney Island
Chidham
Fawley
Ashlett
Meon
Stubbington
Portsmouth Harbour
PORTSMOUTH
Bridgemary
Hilsea
North End
Stoke
North Hayling
West Thorney
Fort Brockhurst
Whale Island
Elson
Gunwharf Quays
Portsea Island
Fleet
Hayling Island
Bosham Hoe
Owers
Calshot
1hr
Hill Head
Hardway
Rowner
Brockhurst
Langstone Harbour
Chichester Harbour
West Itchenor
Shipton Green
Lee-on-the-Solent
Portsmouth Historic Dockyard
Fratton
Portsmouth FC
Milton
GOSPORT
Portsea
West Town
South Hayling
Windmill
West Wittering
Stone Point
SOLENT
Browndown
Alverstoke
Cathedral
Southsea
Eastoke
Hayling Bay
Stokes Bay
Southsea Castle & Museum
PORTSMOUTH
East Wittering
Earnley
Bracklesham
Cowes Roads
Cowes
Gilkicker Point
Gurnard
East Cowes
Osborne Bay
Osborne
Osborne House
½ hr
Bracklesham Bay
Northwood
Whippingham
St Mildred
Ryde Roads
Ryde
Wootton
Fishbourne
Quarr Hill
Spring Vale
Nettlestone Point
Parkhurst
Parkhurst Forest
Wootton Bridge
Wootton Common
Binstead
Swanmore
Brickfields Horse Country
Seaview
Nettlestone
Littletown
Isle of Wight Steam Rly
Flamingo Park
Forest Side
NEWPORT
Havenstreet
St Helens
Bembridge Point
Hunny Hill
Staplers
Gunville
Carisbrooke Castle & Mus
Robin Hill
Downend
East Ashey
Bembridge
Foreland
Clatterford
Shide
Nunwell
Bembridge Windmill (NT)
Brading
Whitecliff Bay
ISLE OF WIGHT
Bowcombe
Blackwater
Arreton
Roman Villa
Hillway
Gatcombe
Merstone
Newchurch
Alverstone
Isle of Wight Zoo
Yaverland
Culver Cliff
Queen's Bower
Geology Museum
Chillerton
Rookley
Winford
Sandown
ISLE OF WIGHT (SANDOWN)
Lake
Sandown Bay
Shorwell
Rookley Green
Apse Heath
Sandy Way
Kingston
All Saints
Godshill
Whiteley Bank
Shanklin Chine
Shanklin
Sandford
Little Atherfield
Roud
Chale Green
Appuldurcombe
Wroxall
Luccombe Village
Stenbury Down
Nettlecombe
Dunnose
Pyle
Bierley
Whitwell
Bonchurch
Chale
Niton
St Lawrence
Ventnor
Blackgang
Blackgang Chine
Ventnor Botanic Gardens
The Undercliff
Rocken End
St Catherine's Point
hours
Bilbao.....35
Caen.....6-(7¼)
Caen (summer only)....3¼
Cherbourg.....2¾-(7)
Guernsey.....6½
Jersey.....10
Le Havre.....2¾-5
St. Malo.....8¾(10½)

Ryde: *The seaside pier is a typical English invention. Ryde Pier, on the Isle of Wight, opened on 26th July 1814 and was the first of the numerous promenade piers which are still major features of English seaside resorts.* ***Map ref. E3***

The Needles: *These are a series of chalk stacks on the western most point of the Isle of Wight. The sea around The Needles is treacherous and the first lighthouse was built here in 1785. The current lighthouse, at the western edge of The Needles was built in 1850.* ***Map ref. B4 Also on page 47***
In all the Isle of Wight has 60 miles (97km) of coastline and there are over 4000 shipwrecks recorded on the Admiralty Charts of the area. ***Map ref. D4 Also on page 47***

Lee-on-the-Solent: *Location of the former Fleet Air Arm base H.M.S. Daedalus. From here in 1931 a Supermarine S6b designed by RJ Mitchell, creator of the Spitfire, set a new world air speed record of 407.5 mph (656km/h)* ***Map ref. E2***

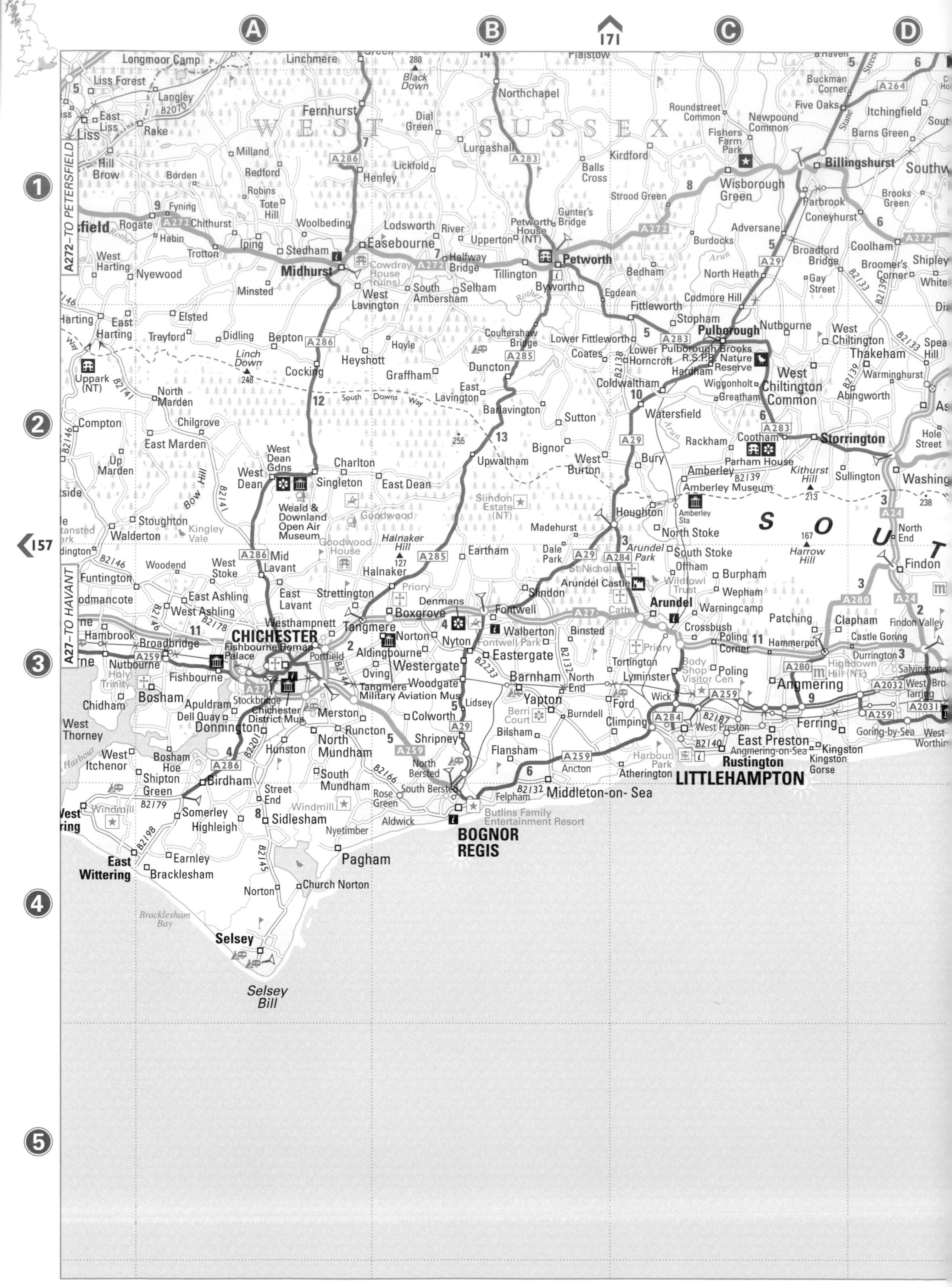

A
B
C
D
171
157
1
2
3
4
5
A272–TO PETERSFIELD
A27–TO HAVANT
WEST SUSSEX
Longmoor Camp
Liss Forest
Langley
Liss
East Liss
Rake
Linchmere
Black Down
Fernhurst
Dial Green
Northchapel
Lurgashall
Milland
Redford
Borden
Robins
Tote Hill
Hill Brow
Fyning
Rogate
Chithurst
Habin
Trotton
Iping
Woolbeding
Stedham
Lickfold
Henley
Lodsworth
River
Easebourne
Midhurst
Cowdray House (ruins)
Halfway Bridge
Upperton
Petworth House (NT)
Petworth
Tillington
Byworth
Gunter's Bridge
Balls Cross
Kirdford
Strood Green
Roundstreet Common
Fishers Farm Park
Newpound Common
Wisborough Green
Buckman Corner
Five Oaks
Itchingfield
Barns Green
Billingshurst
Southwater
Parbrook
Coneyhurst
Brooks Green
Adversane
Burdocks
Coolham
Broomer's Corner
Shipley
Broadford Bridge
Gay Street
North Heath
Bedham
Egdean
Fittleworth
Codmore Hill
Stopham
Pulborough
Nutbourne
West Chiltington
Thakeham
Warminghurst
Abingworth
West Chiltington Common
Storrington
Sullington
Washington
Kithurst Hill
Cootham
Parham House
Rackham
Amberley
Amberley Museum
Watersfield
Wiggonholt
Greatham
Pulborough Brooks R.S.P.B. Nature Reserve
Hardham
Lower Horncroft
Lower Fittleworth
Coates
Coldwaltham
West Harting
Nyewood
Minsted
West Lavington
South Ambersham
Selham
Elsted
East Harting
Harting
Treyford
Didling
Bepton
Linch Down
Cocking
Heyshott
Hoyle
Graffham
Coultershaw Bridge
Duncton
East Lavington
Barlavington
Sutton
Bignor
South Downs Way
Uppark (NT)
North Marden
Compton
Chilgrove
East Marden
Up Marden
West Dean Gdns
West Dean
Charlton
Singleton
East Dean
Upwaltham
West Burton
Bury
Houghton
North Stoke
South Stoke
Offham
Burpham
Wepham
Slindon Estate (NT)
Goodwood
Weald & Downland Open Air Museum
Stoughton
Kingley Vale
Walderton
Bow Hill
Halnaker Hill
Halnaker
Madehurst
Dale Park
Arundel Park
Eartham
Mid Lavant
East Lavant
Woodend
West Stoke
Funtington
East Ashling
West Ashling
Strettington
Priory
Denmans
Boxgrove
Westhampnett
Tangmere
Slindon
Fontwell
Fontwell Park
Walberton
Binsted
Arundel Castle
Arundel
Wildfowl Trust
Warningcamp
Crossbush
Poling Corner
Patching
Clapham
Findon
Findon Valley
North End
Harrow Hill
Castle Goring
Hammerpot
Durrington
Highdown Hill (NT)
Salvington
Angmering
Poling
Body Shop Visitor Cen
Lyminster
Tortington
Priory
CHICHESTER
Fishbourne Roman Palace
Broadbridge
Hambrook
Nutbourne
Holy Trinity
Fishbourne
Bosham
Chidham
West Thorney
Portfield
Aldingbourne
Norton
Nyton
Eastergate
Westergate
Oving
Tangmere Military Aviation Mus
Woodgate
Barnham
Yapton
Burndell
Ford
Climping
Wick
Lidsey
Berri Court
Bilsham
Flansham
Apuldram
Dell Quay
Stockbridge
Chichester District Mus
Donnington
Merston
Colworth
Runcton
North Mundham
Hunston
Shripney
North Bersted
South Bersted
Bosham Hoe
West Itchenor
Shipton Green
Birdham
Street End
South Mundham
Rose Green
Felpham
Middleton-on-Sea
Ancton
Atherington
Harbour Park
LITTLEHAMPTON
Rustington
East Preston
Angmering-on-Sea
West Preston
Ferring
Kingston
Kingston Gorse
Goring-by-Sea
West Worthing
Tarring
Somerley
Highleigh
Sidlesham
Windmill
Aldwick
Nyetimber
BOGNOR REGIS
Butlins Family Entertainment Resort
Pagham
Church Norton
Norton
Earnley
Bracklesham
East Wittering
West Wittering
Bracklesham Bay
Selsey
Selsey Bill
SOUTH
North End
A286
A283
A272
A29
A285
A27
A259
A284
A280
A24
A2032
A2031
B2070
B2138
B2139
B2133
B2146
B2141
B2178
B2179
B2198
B2145
B2201
B2144
B2166
B2132
B2233
B2187
B2140

*The airfield at **Tangmere** played a crucial role in the 1940 Battle of Britain. One of its most famous fighter pilots was Douglas Bader who was stationed there, first as CO of 242 Squadron, flying Hurricanes and later as leader of three Spitfire Squadrons.*
On 9th August 1941 Bader shot down two German ME109s before colliding with a third. He was forced to bale out and was taken POW by the Germans. In all he was credited with destroying 23 enemy aircraft. His exciting association with Tangmere is marked by the nearby Bader Arms Public House. ***Map ref. B3***

Brighton: *The Aquarium roundabout near Brighton Pier is claimed to be Britain's oldest traffic roundabout, dating from 1925.* ***Map ref. F3***

D
E
172
F
G
A24–TO DORKING
A23–TO LONDON GATWICK AIRPORT (M23)
A22–TO EAST GRINSTEAD
A26–TO ROYAL TUNBRIDGE WELLS
A22–TO EASTBOURNE
A27–TO EASTBOURNE
160
1
2
3
4
5
Handcross
Nymans (NT)
Ashfold Crossways
Staplefield
Ardingly
Ardingly Resr
Horsted Keynes
Birch Grove
Chelwood Gate
Chelwood Common
Duddleswell
Poundgate
Stone Cross
Nutley
Cackle Street
Heron's Ghyll
Fairwarp
High Hurstwood
Danehill
Furner's Green
Sheffield Green
Sheffield Park (NT)
Maresfield
Five Ash Down
Pound Green
Hadlow Down
Denne Park
Mannings Heath
Lower Beeding
Monk's Gate
Slaugham
Nuthurst
Leonardslee Gardens
Warninglid
Slough Green
Brook Street
Borde Hill
Whitemans Green
Cuckfield
Lindfield
Paxhill Park
Bluebell Rly
HAYWARDS HEATH
Copsale
Crabtree
The Maplehurst
Bar
Bolney
Ansty
Scayne's Hill
Fletching
Splayne's Green
Buxted
Ringles Cross
Uckfield
New Town
Piltdown
Newick
North Chailey
Sandrocks
Cowfold
Twineham Green
Hickstead
Wivelsfield
Wivelsfield Green
Shortbridge
Beeches Farm
Ridgewood
Framfield
Palehouse Common
West Grinstead
Wineham
Twineham
Goddards Green
Burgess Hill
Ditchling Common
Chailey
South Street
Newick Park
Horsted Place
Little Horsted
Isfield
Spithurst
South Common
Partridge Green
Sayers Common
Albourne Green
High Cross
Bines Green
Blackstone
Albourne
Henfield
Hurstpierpoint
Hurst Wickham
Keymer
Hassocks
Ditchling
Danny
Plumpton Green
Plumpton
Streat
Westmeston
East Chiltington
Mount Pleasant
Barcombe Cross
Barcombe
Rose Hill
Halland
Shortgate
Bentley Wildfowl & Motor Museum
Whitesmith
Laughton
Ashurst
Woodmancote
New Hall
Oreham Common
Small Dole
Muddleswood
Clayton
Pyecombe
Cooksbridge
Hamsey
Norlington
Ringmer
Broyle Side
Holme's
Ditchling Beacon
South Downs Way
Mount Harry
Offham
Rushy Green
Glyndebourne
Glynde Place
Bramber
Fulking
Poynings
Edburton
Steyning
Upper Beeding
St Mary's House
Botolphs
Coombes
Proposed National Park
DOWNS
BRIGHTON & HOVE
Foredown Tower
Stanmer
Sussex
Patcham
Lewes
Lewes 1264
Lewes Castle
South Malling
Cliffe Hill
Mount Caburn
Glynde
Middle Farm & English Farm Cider Centre
Ripe
Chalvington
Mus of Sussex Archaeology
Kingston near Lewes
Coldean
Hollingbury
Withdean
Preston
Falmer
Moulsecoomb
Newmarket Hill
Beddingham
Iford
Rodmell
West Firle
Firle Place
Charleston Farmhouse
Selmes
Alciston
Firle Beacon
Berwick
North Lancing
Lancing
Kingston by Sea
Southwick
Portslade
Fishersgate
Shoreham-by-Sea
SHOREHAM
Marlipins
Portslade-by-Sea
West Blatchington
British Engineerium
Preston Manor
Bevendean
Brighton
Woodingdean
Monk's House (NT)
Southease
Tarring Neville
Royal Pavilion
HOVE
Kemp Town
Ovingdean
Grange Art Gall & Mus
Telscombe
Piddinghoe
South Heighton
Paradise Park
Alfriston
Palace Pier
BRIGHTON
Volks Electric Rly
Rottingdean
Saltdean
Telscombe Cliffs
Peacehaven
Newhaven
Denton
Bishopstone
East Blatchington
Cuckmere
Exceat
Seaford
Worthing Mus & Gallery
WORTHING
South Lancing
Dieppe (summer only) 2hrs
Forest
EAST SUSSEX
Ouse
Adur
A281
A23
A272
A273
A2300
A275
A22
A26
A27
A259
A2037
A2038
A270
B2110
B2115
B2114
B2036
B2028
B2111
B2112
B2113
B2116
B2117
B2118
B2135
B2183
B2102
B2192
B2124
B2123
B2026
248
195
164
217

Bluebell Railway: *Following the swingeing cuts of the 1960s the Bluebell Railway became the first preserved standard gauge passenger railway in the world. It has now been in service for over 40 years. Today, whenever you see an old railway or railway station on a film or TV programme, chances are it is this one.* ***Map ref. F1 Also on page 41***

Battle of Lewes 1264: *Following the rebel barons' victory over King Henry III, Simon de Montfort established England's first parliament before he was killed in battle at Evesham in 1265.* ***Map ref. F2***

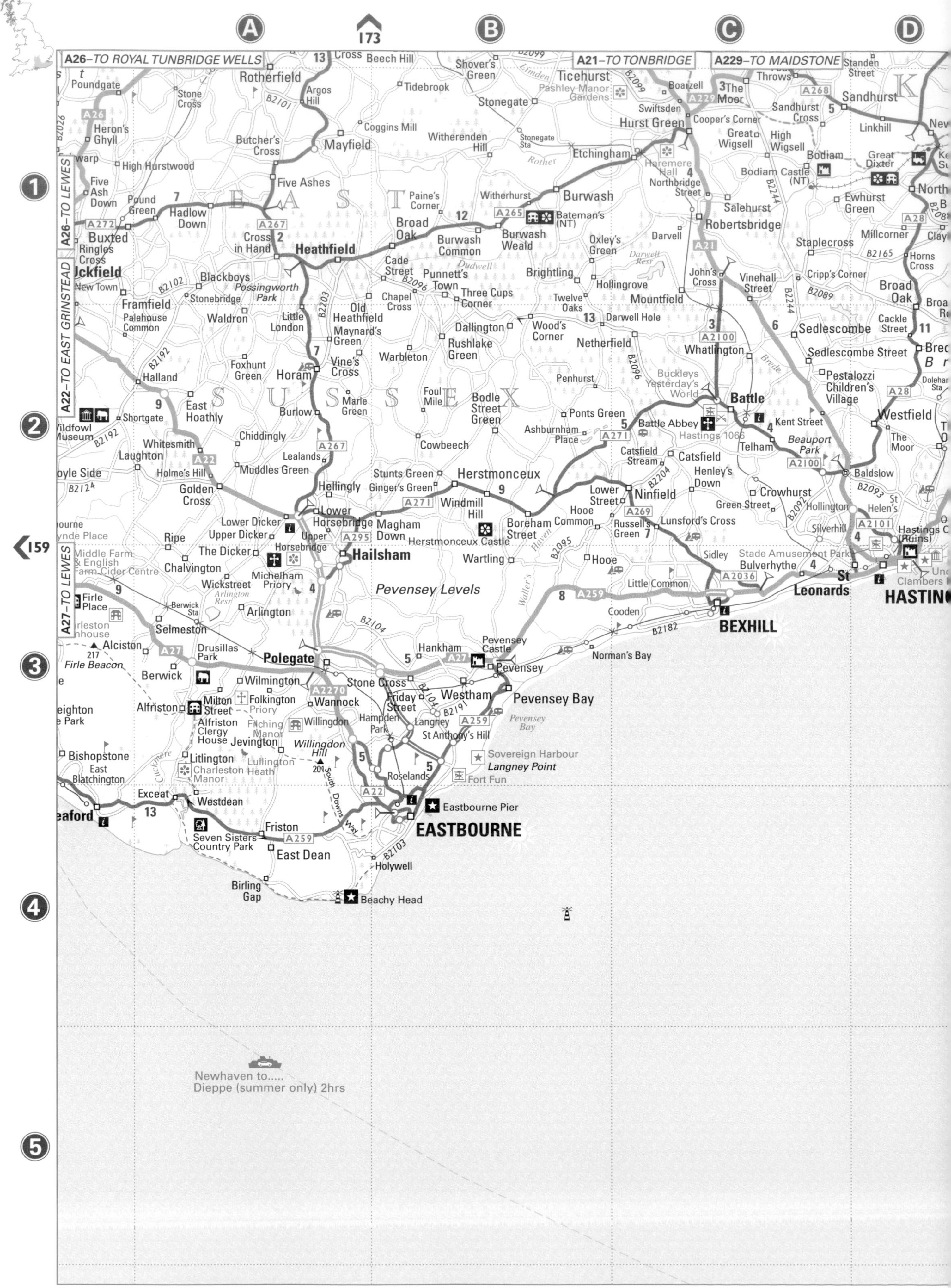

A
B
C
D
173
A26–TO ROYAL TUNBRIDGE WELLS
A21–TO TONBRIDGE
A229–TO MAIDSTONE
A26–TO LEWES
A22–TO EAST GRINSTEAD
A27–TO LEWES
159
1
2
3
4
5
Poundgate
Rotherfield
Argos Hill
Beech Hill
Tidebrook
Shover's Green
Ticehurst
Pashley Manor Gardens
Boarzell
The Moor
Standen Street
Sandhurst
Sandhurst Cross
Swiftsden
Hurst Green
Cooper's Corner
Stonegate
Stone Cross
Heron's Ghyll
Butcher's Cross
Coggins Mill
Mayfield
Witherenden Hill
Stonegate Sta
Etchingham
Great Wigsell
High Wigsell
Linkhill
Bodiam
Great Dixter
High Hurstwood
Five Ashes
Haremere Hall
Northbridge Street
Bodiam Castle (NT)
Five Ash Down
Pound Green
Hadlow Down
E A S T
Paine's Corner
Witherhurst
Burwash
Salehurst
Ewhurst Green
Robertsbridge
Buxted
Cross in Hand
Heathfield
Broad Oak
Burwash Common
Bateman's (NT)
Burwash Weald
Oxley's Green
Darvell
Staplecross
Millcorner
Ringles Cross
Uckfield
New Town
Blackboys
Possingworth Park
Stonebridge
Cade Street
Punnett's Town
Brightling
Hollingrove
John's Cross
Vinehall Street
Cripp's Corner
Horns Cross
Broad Oak
Framfield
Palehouse Common
Waldron
Little London
Old Heathfield
Chapel Cross
Three Cups Corner
Twelve Oaks
Mountfield
Darwell Hole
Sedlescombe
Cackle Street
Maynard's Green
Dallington
Wood's Corner
Netherfield
Whatlington
Sedlescombe Street
Foxhunt Green
Horam
Vine's Cross
Warbleton
Rushlake Green
Penhurst
Buckleys Yesterday's World
Pestalozzi Children's Village
Halland
East Hoathly
Marle Green
Foul Mile
Bodle Street Green
Battle
Westfield
Shortgate
Burlow
S U S S E X
Ponts Green
Ashburnham Place
Battle Abbey
Hastings 1066
Kent Street
The Moor
Beauport Park
Wildfowl Museum
Whitesmith
Chiddingly
Lealands
Cowbeech
Telham
Catsfield Stream
Catsfield
Laughton
Muddles Green
Henley's Down
Baldslow
Holme's Hill
Stunts Green
Herstmonceux
Crowhurst
Golden Cross
Hellingly
Ginger's Green
Lower Street
Ninfield
Hollington
St Helen's
Windmill Hill
Hooe Common
Green Street
Lower Dicker
Lower Horsebridge
Magham Down
Boreham Street
Russell's Green
Lunsford's Cross
Silverhill
Hastings Castle (Ruins)
Upper Dicker
Upper Horsebridge
Herstmonceux Castle
Ripe
Middle Farm & English Farm Cider Centre
The Dicker
Hailsham
Wartling
Hooe
Sidley
Stade Amusement Park
Chalvington
Bulverhythe
Michelham Priory
Wickstreet
Arlington Resr
Pevensey Levels
Little Common
St Leonards
HASTINGS
Clambers
Firle Place
Berwick Sta
Arlington
Cooden
BEXHILL
Selmeston
Alciston
Drusillas Park
Hankham
Pevensey Castle
Norman's Bay
217
Firle Beacon
Polegate
Pevensey
Berwick
Wilmington
Stone Cross
Westham
Pevensey Bay
Milton Street
Folkington
Wannock
Friday Street
Alfriston
Priory
Hampden Park
Langney
Alfriston Clergy House
Filching Manor
Willingdon
St Anthony's Hill
Jevington
Willingdon Hill
Sovereign Harbour
Bishopstone
Litlington
Lullington Heath
Langney Point
East Blatchington
Charleston Manor
Roselands
Fort Fun
South Downs Way
Exceat
Westdean
Eastbourne Pier
Seaford
Cuckmere
Seven Sisters Country Park
Friston
EASTBOURNE
East Dean
Holywell
Birling Gap
Beachy Head
Newhaven to.....
Dieppe (summer only) 2hrs

John 'Mad Jack' Fuller was born in ***Brightling*** *in 1757 and inherited a thriving iron forge which made weapons for the British Navy. Mad Jack later became Squire of Brightling and an MP but is best remembered as a great English eccentric who was obsessed with building follies. The Sussex countryside is dotted with his creations which include towers, a temple, a needle and a pyramid. He gifted a lifeboat station and the first wooden lighthouse at Beachy Head. Mad Jack also bought Bodiam Castle in order to save it from a firm of builders who intended to demolish it. He died in 1834.* ***Map ref. B1***

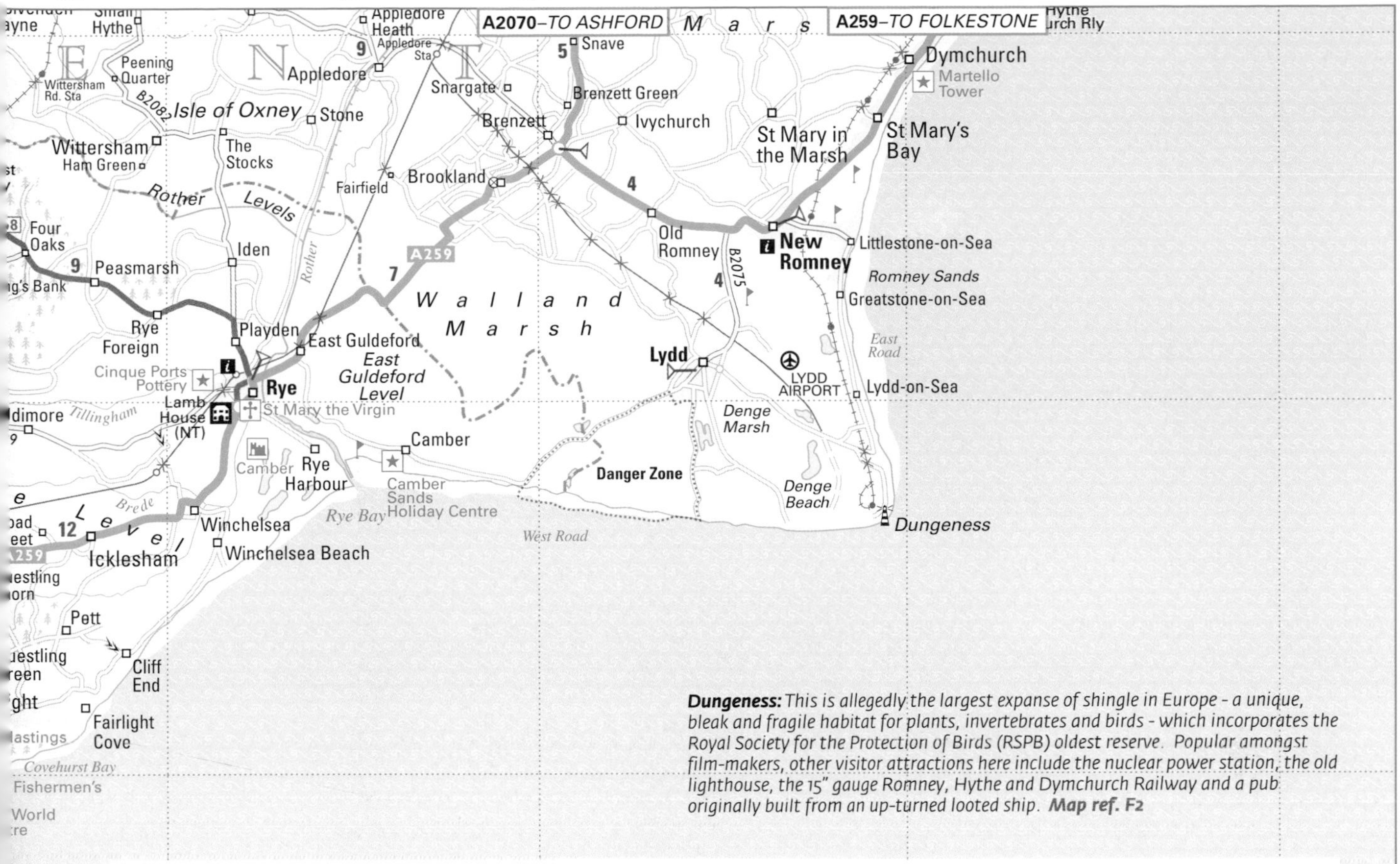

D E F G
174

A2070–TO ASHFORD
A259–TO FOLKESTONE

Appledore Heath
Appledore Sta
Snave
Dymchurch
Martello Tower
Peening Quarter
Wittersham Rd. Sta
Appledore
Snargate
Brenzett Green
Isle of Oxney
Stone
Brenzett
Ivychurch
St Mary in the Marsh
St Mary's Bay
Wittersham
Ham Green
The Stocks
Fairfield
Brookland
Rother Levels
Four Oaks
Peasmarsh
Iden
Old Romney
New Romney
Littlestone-on-Sea
Romney Sands
Greatstone-on-Sea
Walland Marsh
Rye Foreign
Playden
East Guldeford
East Guldeford Level
Lydd
Lydd Airport
Lydd-on-Sea
Cinque Ports Pottery
Rye
Lamb House (NT)
St Mary the Virgin
Denge Marsh
Camber
Camber
Rye Harbour
Camber Sands Holiday Centre
Danger Zone
Denge Beach
Dungeness
Rye Bay
West Road
Winchelsea
Winchelsea Beach
Icklesham
Pett
Cliff End
Fairlight Cove
Covehurst Bay

Dungeness: *This is allegedly the largest expanse of shingle in Europe - a unique, bleak and fragile habitat for plants, invertebrates and birds - which incorporates the Royal Society for the Protection of Birds (RSPB) oldest reserve. Popular amongst film-makers, other visitor attractions here include the nuclear power station, the old lighthouse, the 15" gauge Romney, Hythe and Dymchurch Railway and a pub originally built from an up-turned looted ship.* ***Map ref. F2***

CHANNEL TUNNEL TERMINAL MAPS

Eurotunnel: Access from the UK

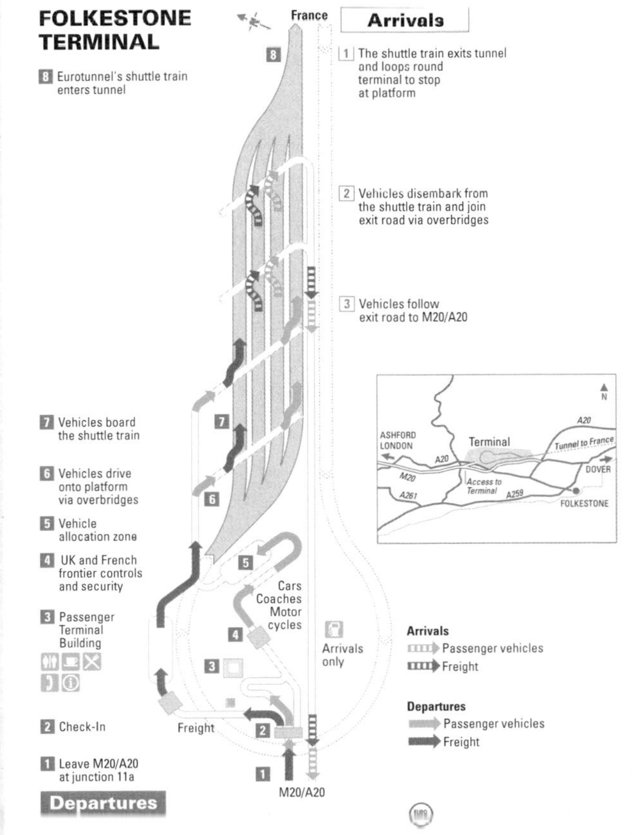

FOLKESTONE TERMINAL

France

Arrivals

1 The shuttle train exits tunnel and loops round terminal to stop at platform

2 Vehicles disembark from the shuttle train and join exit road via overbridges

3 Vehicles follow exit road to M20/A20

ASHFORD LONDON
Terminal
A20
Tunnel to France
DOVER
M20
Access to Terminal
A261
A259
FOLKESTONE

8 Eurotunnel's shuttle train enters tunnel

7 Vehicles board the shuttle train

6 Vehicles drive onto platform via overbridges

5 Vehicle allocation zone

4 UK and French frontier controls and security

3 Passenger Terminal Building

2 Check-In

1 Leave M20/A20 at junction 11a

Cars Coaches Motor cycles

Arrivals only

Freight

M20/A20

Arrivals
Passenger vehicles
Freight

Departures
Passenger vehicles
Freight

Departures

Eurotunnel: Access from France

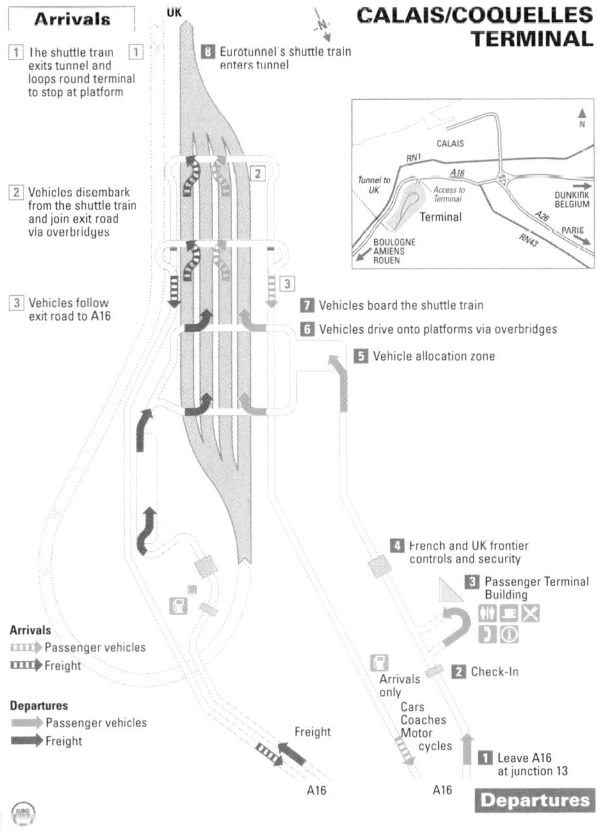

CALAIS/COQUELLES TERMINAL

UK

Arrivals

1 The shuttle train exits tunnel and loops round terminal to stop at platform

2 Vehicles disembark from the shuttle train and join exit road via overbridges

3 Vehicles follow exit road to A16

8 Eurotunnel's shuttle train enters tunnel

CALAIS
RN1
A16
Tunnel to UK
Access to Terminal
Terminal
DUNKIRK BELGIUM
A26
PARIS
RN43
BOULOGNE AMIENS ROUEN

7 Vehicles board the shuttle train

6 Vehicles drive onto platforms via overbridges

5 Vehicle allocation zone

4 French and UK frontier controls and security

3 Passenger Terminal Building

2 Check-In

1 Leave A16 at junction 13

Arrivals only

Cars Coaches Motor cycles

Freight

A16

Arrivals
Passenger vehicles
Freight

Departures
Passenger vehicles
Freight

Departures

Norman's Bay: *The Norman Army sailed from St. Valery across the English Channel on the evening of the 27th September 1066 and landed in England, on the morning of 28th September, at what has since been called Norman's Bay. From there they proceeded inland and two weeks later defeated King Harold at the Battle of Hastings.* ***Map ref. B3***

Rye: *This picturesque Sussex town was one of the entry points for the 'Black Death' which plagued Britain from 1348 to 1353. The Cinque Ports of the south east, which traded with the rest of the world, and the smugglers who haunted the marshes, brought in the fleas which carried the deadly Tersina Pestis bacteria which eventually killed a third of Europe's people. Deadman's Lane, in Rye, is thought to be where they buried their plague victims.* ***Map ref. E1***

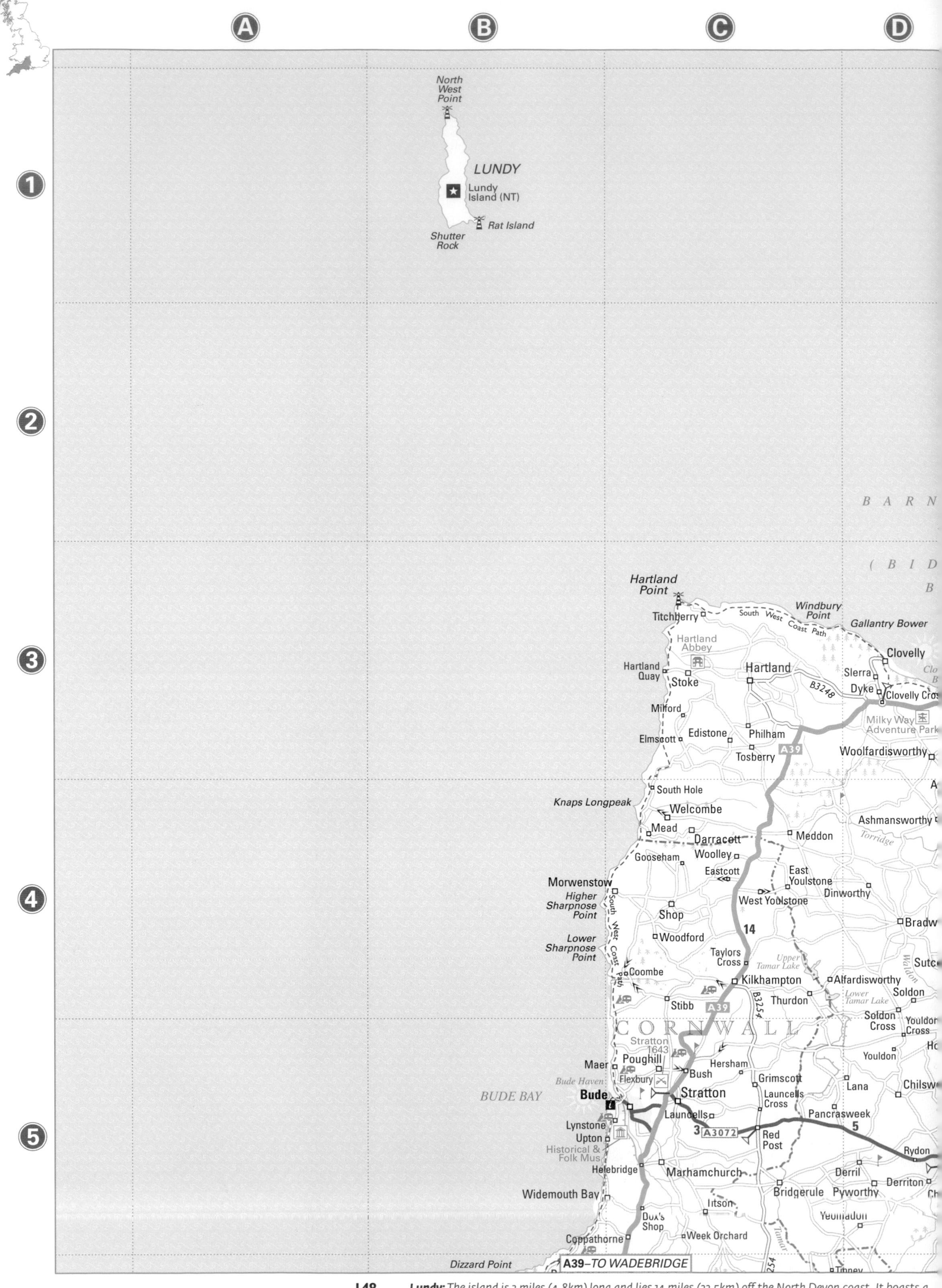
A
B
C
D
1
2
3
4
5
North West Point
LUNDY
Lundy Island (NT)
Rat Island
Shutter Rock
Hartland Point
Titchberry
South West Coast Path
Windbury Point
Gallantry Bower
Hartland Abbey
Clovelly
Hartland Quay
Stoke
Hartland
B3248
Slerra
Dyke
Milford
Edistone
Philham
Elmscott
Tosberry
A39
Milky Way Adventure Park
Woolfardisworthy
South Hole
Knaps Longpeak
Welcombe
Ashmansworthy
Mead
Darracott
Meddon
Torridge
Gooseham
Woolley
Eastcott
East Youlstone
Morwenstow
Dinworthy
Higher Sharpnose Point
West Youlstone
Shop
14
Lower Sharpnose Point
Woodford
Taylors Cross
Upper Tamar Lake
Coombe
Kilkhampton
Alfardisworthy
Lower Tamar Lake
Soldon
Stibb
B3254
Thurdon
Soldon Cross
Youldon Cross
CORNWALL
Stratton 1643
Poughill
Youldon
Maer
Hersham
Bude Haven
Flexbury
Bush
Grimscott
BUDE BAY
Bude
Stratton
Launcells Cross
Lana
Launcells
Pancrasweek
5
Lynstone
3
A3072
Red Post
Upton
Historical & Folk Mus
Rydon
Helebridge
Marhamchurch
Derril
Derriton
Widemouth Bay
Bridgerule
Pyworthy
Titson
Dux's Shop
Week Orchard
Tamar
Coppathorne
Dizzard Point
A39–TO WADEBRIDGE

148

Lundy: *The island is 3 miles (4.8km) long and lies 14 miles (22.5km) off the North Devon coast. It boasts a castle, three lighthouses, an inn and a church and is the first designated Marine Nature Reserve in Britain. Lundy's rugged shores have proved to be a graveyard for over 130 ships which lie wrecked off its coast.*
Map ref. B1 Also on page 32

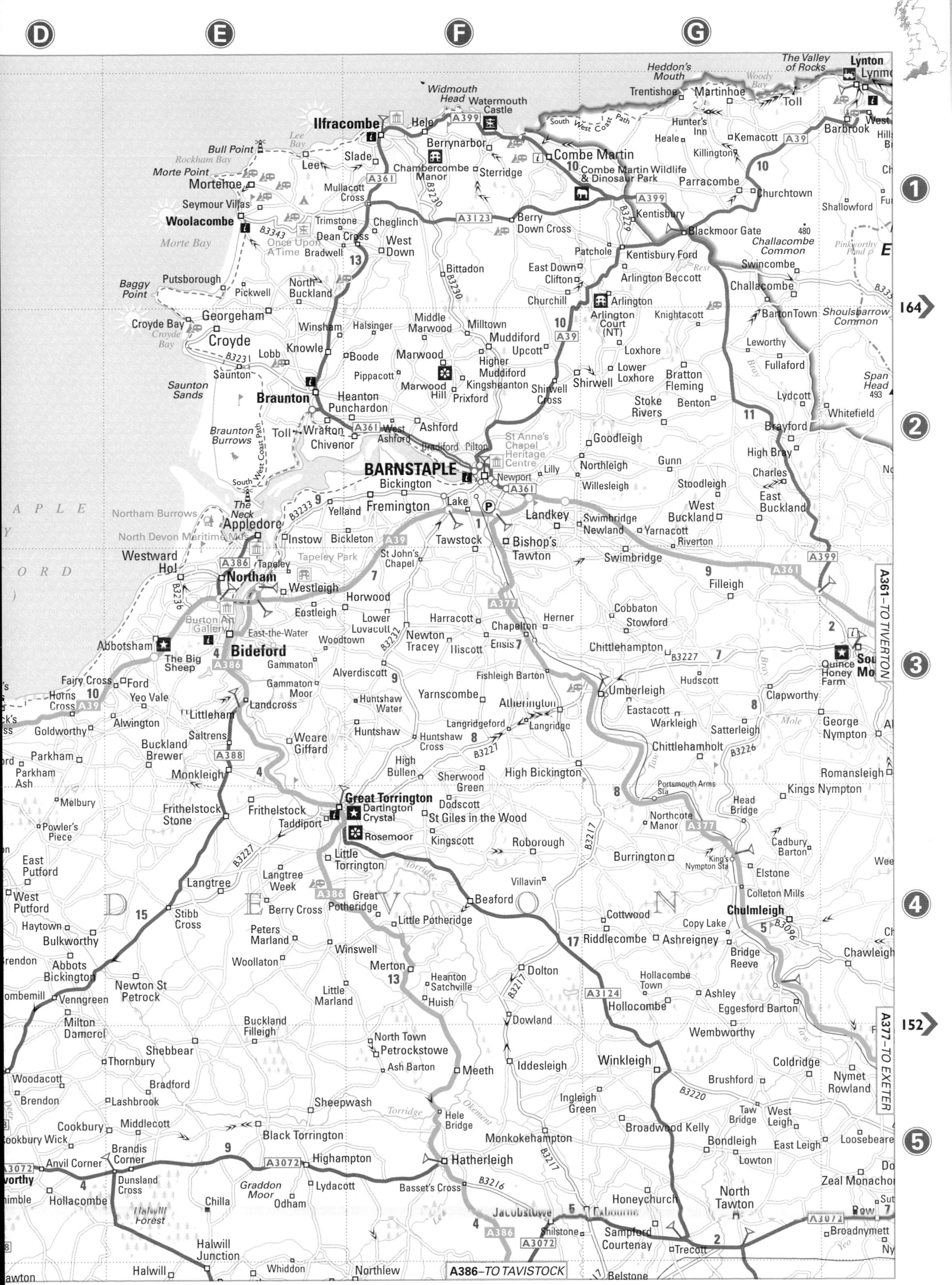

D
E
F
G
Heddon's Mouth
The Valley of Rocks
Lynton
Woody Bay
Widmouth Head
Watermouth Castle
Trentishoe
Martinhoe
Toll
Ilfracombe
Hele
A399
South West Coast Path
Hunter's Inn
Heale
Kemacott
A39
Barbrook
Lee Bay
Bull Point
Berrynarbor
Killington
Rockham Bay
Slade
Lee
Combe Martin
Morte Point
Chambercombe Manor
Sterridge
10
Combe Martin Wildlife & Dinosaur Park
Mortehoe
A361
B3230
Parracombe
Churchtown
Seymour Villas
Mullacott Cross
Woolacombe
Trimstone
Cheglinch
A3123
Berry Down Cross
A399
B3229
Kentisbury
Shallowford
B3343
Dean Cross
West Down
Blackmoor Gate
480
Challacombe Common
Morte Bay
Once Upon A Time
Bradwell
13
Patchole
Kentisbury Ford
Pinkworthy Pond
Bittadon
East Down
Resr
Swincombe
Baggy Point
Putsborough
Pickwell
North Buckland
Clifton
Arlington Beccott
Challacombe
Churchill
Arlington
Croyde Bay
Georgeham
Winsham
Halsinger
Middle Marwood
Milltown
10
Arlington Court (NT)
Knightacott
Barton Town
Shoulsbarrow Common
164
Croyde
Croyde Bay
Knowle
Muddiford
A39
Leworthy
B3231
Lobb
Boode
Marwood
Upcott
Loxhore
Fullaford
Saunton
Pippacott
Higher Muddiford
Lower Loxhore
Bratton Fleming
Span Head
493
Saunton Sands
Marwood Hill
Kingsheanton
Shirwell Cross
Shirwell
Braunton
Heanton Punchardon
Prixford
Stoke Rivers
Benton
Lydcott
Whitefield
Braunton Burrows
Toll
Wrafton
A361
West Ashford
Ashford
11
Brayford
Chivenor
Bradiford
Pilton
St Anne's Chapel Heritage Centre
Goodleigh
West Coast Path
BARNSTAPLE
Lilly
Northleigh
Gunn
High Bray
Charles
South
Bickington
Newport
Willesleigh
Stoodleigh
The Neck
A361
East Buckland
Northam Burrows
B3233
Yelland
Fremington
Lake
West Buckland
Appledore
9
Landkey
Swimbridge Newland
North Devon Maritime Mus
Instow
Bickleton
A39
Tawstock
1
Yarnacott
Bishop's Tawton
Riverton
Westward Ho!
A386
Tapeley
Tapeley Park
St John's Chapel
Swimbridge
A399
B3236
Northam
7
9
A361
Westleigh
Filleigh
A361–TO TIVERTON
Horwood
Eastleigh
A377
Cobbaton
Burton Art Gallery
Lower Lovacott
Harracott
Herner
Stowford
East-the-Water
Newton Tracey
Chapelton
2
Abbotsham
Woodtown
B3232
Ensis
7
Chittlehampton
Bideford
The Big Sheep
4
Iliscott
B3227
7
Quince Honey Farm
A386
Gammaton
Alverdiscott
9
Fishleigh Barton
Hudscott
Fairy Cross
Ford
Gammaton Moor
Horns Cross
10
Yeo Vale
Huntshaw Water
Yarnscombe
Atherington
Umberleigh
Clapworthy
A39
Landcross
Eastacott
8
Littleham
Alwington
Langridgeford
Langridge
Warkleigh
Satterleigh
Mole
George Nympton
Goldworthy
Saltrens
Weare Giffard
Huntshaw
Huntshaw Cross
8
Buckland Brewer
Chittlehamholt
B3227
B3226
Parkham
A388
Parkham Ash
Monkleigh
4
High Bullen
Sherwood Green
High Bickington
Romansleigh
Kings Nympton
Portsmouth Arms Sta
8
Melbury
Great Torrington
Dodscott
Frithelstock Stone
Frithelstock
Dartington Crystal
Head Bridge
Powler's Piece
Taddiport
St Giles in the Wood
Northcote Manor
A377
Rosemoor
Kingscott
Roborough
Cadbury Barton
B3227
B3217
East Putford
Little Torrington
Burrington
King's Nympton Sta
Torridge
Langtree Week
Elstone
Langtree
Villavin
West Putford
A386
Great Potheridge
Colleton Mills
D
E
V
O
N
Beaford
15
Stibb Cross
Berry Cross
Cottwood
Chulmleigh
Little Potheridge
Haytown
Peters Marland
Copy Lake
Bulkworthy
17
Riddlecombe
Ashreigney
5
B3096
Winswell
Bridge Reeve
Chawleigh
Frendon
Abbots Bickington
Woollaton
Merton
13
Dolton
Hollacombe Town
Heanton Satchville
Newton St Petrock
B3217
Combemill
Venngreen
Little Marland
A3124
Ashley
Huish
Hollocombe
Eggesford Barton
Milton Damerel
Dowland
152
A377–TO EXETER
Buckland Filleigh
Wembworthy
North Town
Shebbear
Petrockstowe
Thornbury
Winkleigh
Coldridge
Woodacott
Ash Barton
Meeth
Iddesleigh
Nymet Rowland
Brushford
Bradford
B3220
Brendon
Lashbrook
Ingleigh Green
Sheepwash
Torridge
Okement
Taw Bridge
West Leigh
Cookbury
Middlecott
Hele Bridge
Broadwood Kelly
Cookbury Wick
Bondleigh
East Leigh
Loosebeare
Black Torrington
Monkokehampton
Brandis Corner
9
Lowton
A3072
Anvil Corner
A3072
Highampton
Hatherleigh
4
Dunsland Cross
Graddon Moor
Lydacott
B3217
North Tawton
Zeal Monachorum
Hollacombe
Bassett's Cross
B3216
Chilla
Odham
Honeychurch
Halwill Forest
4
Jacobstowe
5
Exbourne
Row
A3072
A386
Shilstone
Sampford Courtenay
Broadnymett
Halwill Junction
A3072
2
Trecott
Whiddon
Halwill
Northlew
A386–TO TAVISTOCK
Belstone
1
2
3
4
5

149

Braunton Burrows: *Almost 2450 acres (1000ha) of shifting sand dunes make this area so unusual that it has been designated by UNESCO as a 'Biosphere Reserve'. This recognises its status and affords it international protection.* ***Map ref. E2.***

A
B
179
C
D
1
2
3
4
5
Monknash
Monkton
Marcross
Llantwit Major
St Donats
Nash Point
Boverton
B4265
Llanmaes
Eglwys-Brewis
St Athan
Flemings
Llanbethe
Llancadle
Gileston
West Aberthaw
Breaksea Pt
BRISTOL CHA
Foreland Point
Lynton & Lynmouth Cliff Rly
Lynmouth Bay
Countisbury Cove
The Valley of Rocks
Lynton
Lynmouth
Countisbury
Watersmeet House (NT)
Woody Bay
Toll
East Lyn
Wilsham
West Lyn
Barbrook
Hillsford Bridge
Brendon
Malmsmead
Oare
Tippacott
Cheriton
South West Coast Path
Culbone
Culbone Hill
387
413
A39
11
Porlock Weir
Porlock Bay
Toll
West Porlock
Porlock
Bossington
Selworthy Beacon
308
Lynch
Holnicote Estate (NT)
North Hill
Allerford
Selworthy
Holnicote
Horner
Woodcombe
Minehead
Hindon
8
Bratton
Butlins Family Entertainment Resort
Periton
Alcombe
Dunster Sta
Blue Anchor Bay
Marsh Street
Blue Anchor
Dunster
Carhampton
Old Cle
Tivington
Wootton Courtenay
Knowle
Luccombe
Stoke Pero
Huntscott
Ranscombe
Cowbridge
Dunster Castle & Gardens(NT)
Dunster Watermill (NT)
Timberscombe
Withycombe
Bickham
Croydon Hill
365
Burrow
7
Dunkery Hill
Dunkery Beacon
519
Codsend Moors
Quarme
emacott
A39
10
Churchtown
Shallowford
Furzehill
9
B3223
Brendon Common
South Common
Gate
480
Challacombe Common
Hoaroak Hill
473
Pinkworthy Pond
EXMOOR
Dry Hill
444
Swincombe
allacombe
Exe
B3358
9
Dure Down
EXMOOR
Barton Town
Shoulsbarrow Common
Barle
Simonsbath
B3223
10
Edgcott
B3224
Exford
Luckwell Bridge
Cutcombe
Wheddon Cross
A396
Luxborough
Rodhuish
Cleeve Ab
Beggearn
Lower Roadwater
Roadwater
Leworthy
Fullaford
Bray
Span Head
493
Lydcott
Long Holcombe
436
NATIONAL
409
Blacklands
PARK
Exe
Great Nurcot
Triscombe
Lype Hill
423
Kingsbridge
Treborough
BRENDON HILLS
B3224
Leighlan
Chapel
11
Brayford
Whitefield
North Radworthy
Kinsford Water
Withypool Common
Withypool
Winsford Hill
426
Winsford
North Quarme
West Howetown
Gupworthy
Withiel Florey
High Bray
Charles
Worth Hill
Barle
SOMERSET
Exton
North Heasley
South Radworthy
Dane's Brook
Knaplock
B3223
Week
Liscombe
Bridgetown
Brompton Regis
Clatworthy Reservoir
East Buckland
Heasley Mill
Tarr Steps
A396
Molland Common
Woolcotts
A361–TO BARNSTAPLE
Twitchen
Hawkridge
Higher Combe
15
Hartford
317
Wimbleball Lake
B3190
Coom End
A399
North Molton
A361
Molland
Barle
Dulverton
B3222
Haddon Hill
Upton
Huish Champfl
DEVON
Yeo
Battleton
Bury
Chipstab
West Anstey
B3223
Skilgate
Radding
2
4
Bish Mill
Yeo
Yeo Mill
East Anstey
Nightcott
Brushford
Timewell
Wate
South Molton
Quince Honey Farm
B3227
Bishops Nympton
Newtown
12
B3227
Oldways End
Sowerhill
Upcott
Exebridge
Morebath
B3227
12
Petton
Clapworthy
East Knowstone
Highleigh
Shillingford
8
Mole
George Nympton
Crooked Oak
Alswear
Ash Mill
A361
Knowstone
A396
Bampton
Clayhanger
Mariansleigh
Rose Ash
14
Oakfordbridge
Romansleigh
9
Rackenford Moor
Oakford
Huntsham
Staple Cross
Kings Nympton
Rowley
Creacombe
A361–TO TIVERTON
Cove

163

Lynmouth: *Scene of the disastrous floods of the East and West Lyn rivers during the night of 15 August 1952 which resulted in the destruction of much of the village. 34 people were killed and 165 buildings wholly or partially destroyed.* ***Map ref. A3.***

Porlock Hill: *Over the years this notorious stretch of road, with its 25% (1 in 4) incline and tight curves, has caused travellers countless problems. The main coast road was first negotiated by a motor car in 1900 as a bet. If required, the nearby scenic toll road avoids the need to travel along this road.* ***Map ref. B3***

152

Quantock Hills: *Covering an area of 48 square miles and reaching a height of 1260 feet (384m) the Quantock countryside is one of the most delightful areas of Britain. It was the first in England to get AONB (Area of Outstanding Natural Beauty) status back in 1956 and is also designated as a SSSI (Site of Special Scientific Interest) because it contains almost 10% of the world's maritime heathland.* ***Map ref. E3***

180

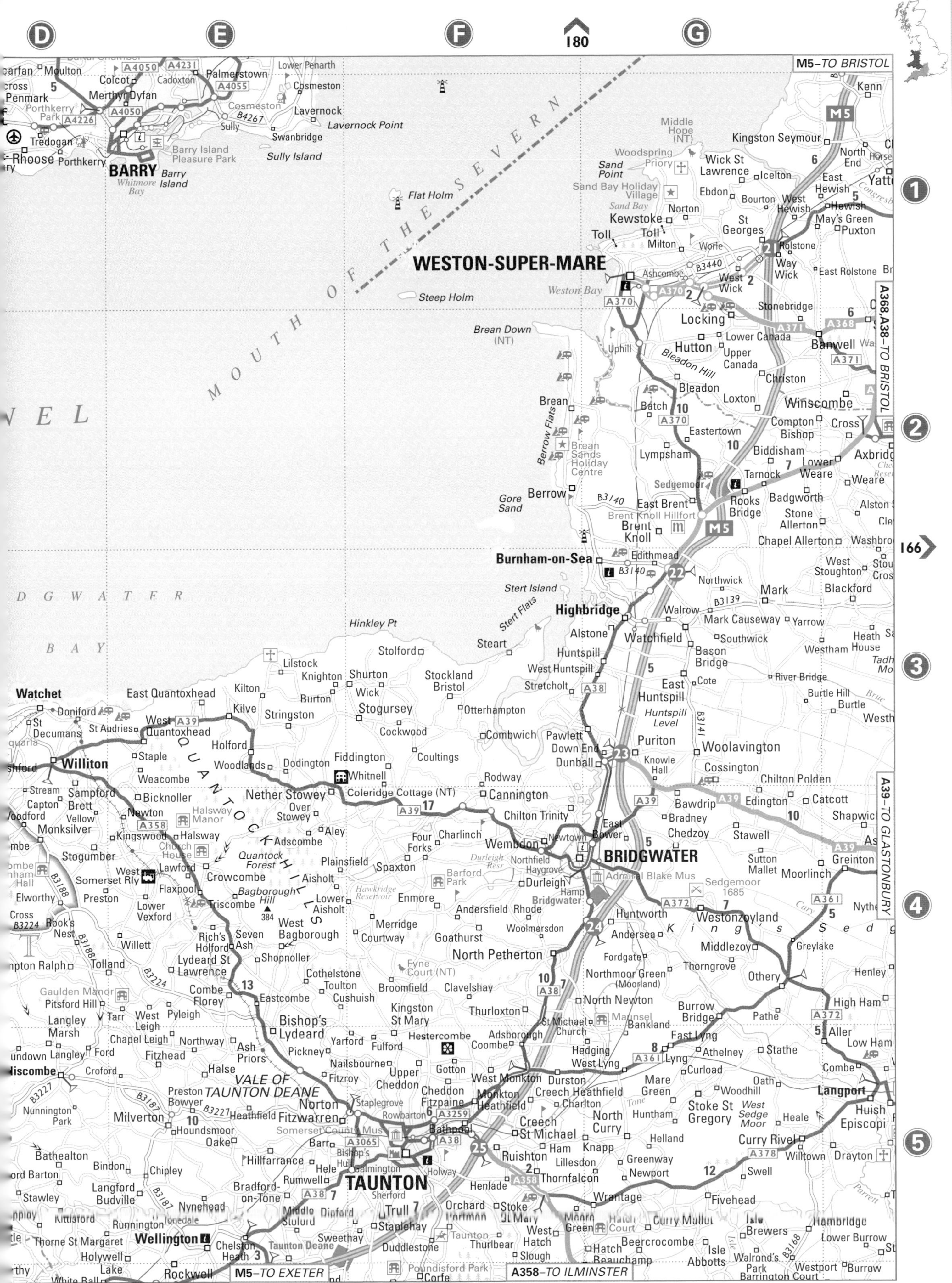
D
E
F
G
1
2
3
4
5
M5–TO BRISTOL
A368,A38–TO BRISTOL
A39–TO GLASTONBURY
M5–TO EXETER
A358–TO ILMINSTER
BARRY
Barry Island
Whitmore Bay
Barry Island Pleasure Park
Rhoose
Porthkerry
Tredogan
Penmark
Porthkerry Park
Merthyr Dyfan
Colcot
Cadoxton
Palmerstown
Lower Penarth
Cosmeston
Lavernock
Lavernock Point
Sully
Swanbridge
Sully Island
Flat Holm
Steep Holm
MOUTH OF THE SEVERN
WESTON-SUPER-MARE
Weston Bay
Kewstoke
Sand Point
Sand Bay Holiday Village
Woodspring Priory
Middle Hope (NT)
Kingston Seymour
Wick St Lawrence
Icelton
Ebdon
Norton
Bourton
West Hewish
St Georges
Worle
Milton
Toll
Ashcombe
West Wick
Locking
Stonebridge
Banwell
Hutton
Lower Canada
Upper Canada
Bleadon Hill
Bleadon
Christon
Loxton
Winscombe
Uphill
Brean Down (NT)
Brean
Berrow Flats
Brean Sands Holiday Centre
Batch
Eastertown
Lympsham
Compton Bishop
Cross
Axbridge
Biddisham
Tarnock
Lower Weare
Weare
Sedgemoor
Rooks Bridge
Badgworth
Stone Allerton
Chapel Allerton
Berrow
Gore Sand
East Brent
Brent Knoll Hillfort
Brent Knoll
Burnham-on-Sea
Edithmead
Northwick
Mark
Blackford
West Stoughton
Stert Island
Highbridge
Walrow
Mark Causeway
Yarrow
Hinkley Pt
Stert Flats
Steart
Alstone
Watchfield
Southwick
Bason Bridge
Westham
Heath House
Stolford
Huntspill
West Huntspill
Stretcholt
East Huntspill
Cote
River Bridge
Burtle Hill
Burtle
Huntspill Level
Puriton
Woolavington
Knowle Hall
Cossington
Chilton Polden
Pawlett
Down End
Dunball
Bawdrip
Edington
Catcott
Bradney
Chedzoy
Stawell
Shapwick
Sutton Mallet
Greinton
Moorlinch
BRIDGWATER
Wembdon
Newtown
East Bower
Durleigh Resr
Northfield
Haygrove
Durleigh
Admiral Blake Mus
Sedgemoor 1685
Bridgwater
Hamp
Westonzoyland
King's Sedgemoor
Huntworth
Andersea
Middlezoy
Greylake
Nythe
Watchet
Doniford
St Decumans
East Quantoxhead
Kilton
Kilve
Lilstock
Knighton
Burton
Shurton
Wick
Stogursey
Stockland Bristol
Otterhampton
Combwich
Stringston
West Quantoxhead
St Audries
Holford
QUANTOCK HILLS
Williton
Staple
Weacombe
Woodlands
Dodington
Fiddington
Whitnell
Coultings
Rodway
Cannington
Coleridge Cottage (NT)
Nether Stowey
Over Stowey
Chilton Trinity
Sampford Brett
Bicknoller
Halsway Manor
Newton
Capton
Vellow
Monksilver
Kingswood
Halsway
Adscombe
Aley
Four Forks
Charlinch
Church House
Quantock Forest
Stogumber
Lawford
Crowcombe
Plainsfield
Spaxton
Barford Park
Somerset Rly
Aisholt
Flaxpool
Bagborough Hill 384
Elworthy
Preston
Triscombe
Lower Aisholt
Hawkridge Reservoir
Enmore
Andersfield
Rhode
Lower Vexford
West Bagborough
Merridge
Courtway
Goathurst
Woolmersdon
Rook's Nest
Willett
Rich's Holford
Seven Ash
Shopnoller
North Petherton
Fordgate
Tolland
Lydeard St Lawrence
Cothelstone
Fyne Court (NT)
Northmoor Green (Moorland)
Thorngrove
Othery
Henley
Gaulden Manor
Combe Florey
Eastcombe
Toulton
Cushuish
Broomfield
Clavelshay
North Newton
Burrow Bridge
High Ham
Pitsford Hill
Tarr
West Leigh
Pyleigh
Bishop's Lydeard
Kingston St Mary
Thurloxton
St Michael Church
Maunsel
Bankland
Pathe
Aller
Langley Marsh
Chapel Leigh
Northway
Ash Priors
Yarford
Hestercombe
Adsborough
Fast Lyng
Athelney
Stathe
Low Ham
Langley
Ford
Fitzhead
Pickney
Fulford
Coombe
Hedging
West Lyng
Lyng
Curload
Combe
Wiscombe
Croford
Halse
Nailsbourne
Gotton
Upper Cheddon
Durston
Mare Green
Oath
VALE OF TAUNTON DEANE
Fitzroy
Cheddon Fitzpaine
West Monkton
Monkton Heathfield
Creech Heathfield
Woodhill
Langport
Preston Bowyer
Norton Fitzwarren
Staplegrove
Rowbarton
Charlton
Stoke St Gregory
West Sedge Moor
Huish Episcopi
Nunnington Park
Milverton
Heathfield
Somerset County Mus
Bathpool
Creech St Michael
North Curry
Huntham
Heale
Houndsmoor
Oake
Barr
Bishop's Hull
Ham
Knapp
Helland
Curry Rivel
Bathealton
Hillfarrance
Hele
Galmington
Holway
Ruishton
Lillesdon
Greenway
Newport
Swell
Willtown
Drayton
Bindon
Chipley
Rumwell
TAUNTON
Sherford
Henlade
Thornfalcon
Langford Budville
Bradford-on-Tone
Nynehead
Orchard Portman
Stoke St Mary
Wrantage
Fivehead
Stawley
Kittisford
Runnington
Middle Stolford
Dipford
Trull
Staplehay
Moorland
Hatch Court
Curry Mallet
Isle Brewers
Hambridge
Lower Burrow
Thorne St Margaret
Wellington
Holywell
Lake
Chelston Heath
Taunton Deane
Sweethay
Duddlestone
Taunton
Thurlbear
West Hatch
Slough
Hatch Beauchamp
Beercrocombe
Isle Abbotts
Walrond's Park
Westport
Burrow
Rockwell
Poundisford Park
Corfe
Barrington Court
Kenn
M5
North End
Yatton
East Hewish
May's Green
Puxton
Rolstone
Way Wick
East Rolstone
Alston
Washbrook
Stoughton Cross
Tadham Moor
Westhay
Sutton
Wisley
Knole
DGWATER BAY

Hatch Beauchamp: *The nearby church is the final resting place of Col. John Rouse Merriot Chard VC Royal Engineers. As Lt. Chard be commanded a small garrison of 140 soldiers which heroically defended Rorke's Drift during the Zulu Wars.* ***Map ref. G5***

153

Weston-super-Mare: *Traditional seaside resort with two piers. The Grand Pier built in 1904 is still open and is listed by the Department of the Environment as a monument of historic importance. The other, Birnbeck Pier, which opened in 1867, is now closed, but is unusual because it is the only pier in the country that links the mainland to an island. This pier is a Grade II listed structure.* ***Map ref. G1***

166

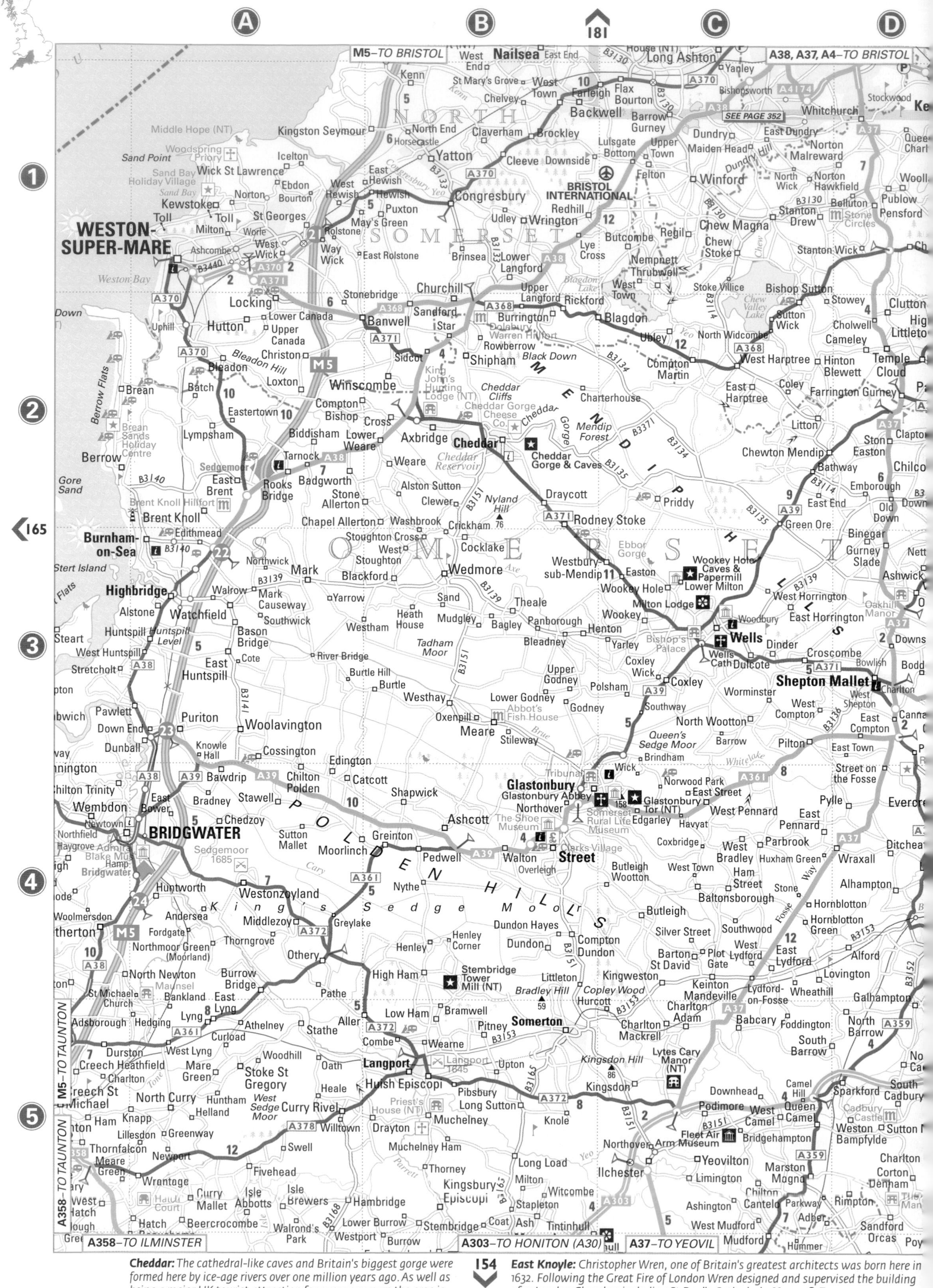

181
165
154
A
B
C
D
1
2
3
4
5
M5–TO BRISTOL
A38, A37, A4–TO BRISTOL
SEE PAGE 352
M5–TO TAUNTON
A358–TO TAUNTON
A358–TO ILMINSTER
A303–TO HONITON (A30)
A37–TO YEOVIL
WESTON-SUPER-MARE
Weston Bay
Middle Hope (NT)
Sand Point
Woodspring Priory
Sand Bay Holiday Village
Kewstoke
Wick St Lawrence
Kingston Seymour
Nailsea
West End
East End
Long Ashton
Yanley
Bishopsworth
Stockwood
Kenn
St Mary's Grove
West Town
Chelvey
Farleigh
Flax Bourton
Backwell
Barrow Gurney
Dundry
Whitchurch
East Dundry
Norton Malreward
Maiden Head
Claverham
Brockley
North End
Horsecastle
Yatton
Cleeve
Downside
Lulsgate Bottom
Upper Town
Felton
Winford
North Wick
Norton Hawkfield
Pensford
Publow
Belluton
Stanton Drew
Stone Circles
Congresbury
BRISTOL INTERNATIONAL
Redhill
Wrington
Udley
Chew Magna
Regil
Butcombe
Chew Stoke
Nempnett Thrubwell
Lye Cross
NORTH SOMERSET
Icelton
Ebdon
Bourton
Norton
Toll
Milton
Worle
St Georges
West Wick
Ashcombe
West Hewish
East Hewish
Puxton
May's Green
Rolstone
East Rolstone
Way Wick
Brinsea
Lower Langford
Upper Langford
Rickford
Blagdon
Blagdon Lake
West Town
Stoke Villice
Bishop Sutton
Stowey
Clutton
Chew Valley Lake
Sutton Wick
North Widcombe
Cholwell
Cameley
Temple Cloud
Hinton Blewett
Locking
Stonebridge
Churchill
Sandford
Star
Banwell
Burrington
Dolebury Warren Hillfort
Rowberrow
Shipham
Black Down
Ubley
Compton Martin
West Harptree
East Harptree
Coley
Farrington Gurney
Hutton
Uphill
Lower Canada
Upper Canada
Christon
Bleadon
Bleadon Hill
Sidcot
Loxton
Winscombe
Batch
Eastertown
Brean
Berrow Flats
Brean Sands Holiday Centre
Berrow
Lympsham
King John's Hunting Lodge (NT)
Cheddar Cliffs
Cheddar Gorge Cheese Co.
Charterhouse
Mendip Forest
MENDIP HILLS
Litton
Compton Bishop
Cross
Biddisham
Lower Weare
Axbridge
Cheddar
Cheddar Gorge & Caves
Cheddar Reservoir
Weare
Tarnock
Badgworth
Rooks Bridge
Stone Allerton
Alston Sutton
Clewer
Nyland Hill
Draycott
Priddy
Chewton Mendip
Ston Easton
Bathway
Emborough
East End
Green Ore
Binegar
Gurney Slade
Gore Sand
Sedgemoor
East Brent
Brent Knoll Hillfort
Brent Knoll
Burnham-on-Sea
Edithmead
Stert Island
Chapel Allerton
Washbrook
Crickham
Stoughton Cross
West Stoughton
Cocklake
Rodney Stoke
Ebbor Gorge
Westbury-sub-Mendip
Easton
Wookey Hole Caves & Papermill
Wookey Hole
Lower Milton
Milton Lodge
Wookey
West Horrington
East Horrington
Oakhill Manor
Ashwick
Highbridge
Northwick
Mark
Blackford
Wedmore
Walrow
Mark Causeway
Yarrow
Sand
Theale
Alstone
Watchfield
Southwick
Westham
Heath House
Mudgley
Bagley
Panborough
Henton
Woodbury
Wells
Dinder
Steart
Huntspill
Huntspill Level
Bason Bridge
Cote
Tadham Moor
Bleadney
Yarley
Bishop's Palace
Wells Cath
Dulcote
Croscombe
West Huntspill
Stretcholt
East Huntspill
River Bridge
Burtle Hill
Burtle
Upper Godney
Coxley Wick
Coxley
Polsham
Worminster
Shepton Mallet
Charlton
Pawlett
Puriton
Westhay
Lower Godney
Abbot's Fish House
Godney
Southway
North Wootton
West Compton
East Compton
West Shepton
Down End
Woolavington
Oxenpill
Meare
Stileway
Queen's Sedge Moor
Barrow
Pilton
East Town
Dunball
Knowle Hall
Cossington
Brindham
Edington
Catcott
Chilton Polden
Bawdrip
Tribunal
Wick
Norwood Park
East Street
Street on the Fosse
Chilton Trinity
Wembdon
Bradney
Stawell
Shapwick
Glastonbury
Glastonbury Abbey
Glastonbury Tor (NT)
West Pennard
Pylle
East Pennard
Evercreech
Newtown
East Bower
Chedzoy
Northover
Somerset Rural Life Museum
Edgarley
Havyat
BRIDGWATER
Northfield
Haygrove
Admiral Blake Museum
Hamp
Sedgemoor 1685
Sutton Mallet
Moorlinch
Greinton
Ashcott
The Shoe Museum
Clarks Village
Walton
Street
Overleigh
Coxbridge
West Bradley
Parbrook
Huxham Green
Wraxall
Ditcheat
Pedwell
Butleigh Wootton
West Town
Ham
Street
Stone
Alhampton
Huntworth
Westonzoyland
Nythe
POLDEN HILLS
King's Sedge Moor
Baltonsborough
Hornblotton
Woolmersdon
Andersea
Middlezoy
Greylake
Dundon Hayes
Butleigh
Hornblotton Green
Fordgate
Northmoor Green (Moorland)
Thorngrove
Henley Corner
Henley
Compton Dundon
Dundon
Silver Street
Southwood
West Lydford
East Lydford
Alford
Othery
Barton St David
Plot Gate
Burrow Bridge
North Newton
Maunsel
High Ham
Stembridge Tower Mill (NT)
Littleton
Kingweston
Keinton Mandeville
Lydford-on-Fosse
Lovington
Wheathill
Galhampton
St Michael's Church
Bankland
East Lyng
Lyng
Pathe
Bradley Hill
Copley Wood
Hurcott
Charlton Adam
Babcary
Foddington
North Barrow
South Barrow
Adsborough
Hedging
Athelney
Curload
Aller
Stathe
Low Ham
Bramwell
Pitney
Somerton
Charlton Mackrell
Lytes Cary Manor (NT)
Durston
West Lyng
Creech Heathfield
Mare Green
Woodhill
Stoke St Gregory
Combe
Wearne
Oath
Langport
Langport 1645
Upton
Kingsdon Hill
Kingsdon
Downhead
Camel Hill
Sparkford
South Cadbury
Charlton
Creech St Michael
North Curry
Huntham
Helland
West Sedge Moor
Curry Rivel
Heale
Huish Episcopi
Pibsbury
Long Sutton
Priest's House (NT)
Knole
Podimore
West Camel
Queen Camel
Cadbury Castle
Weston Bampfylde
Sutton
Ham
Knapp
Lillesdon
Greenway
Willtown
Drayton
Muchelney
Muchelney Ham
Fleet Air Arm Museum
Bridgehampton
Northover
Ilchester
Yeovilton
Limington
Marston Magna
Thornfalcon
Meare Green
Newport
Swell
Fivehead
Thorney
Long Load
Charlton Horethorne
Corton Denham
Wrantage
Curry Mallet
Isle Abbotts
Isle Brewers
Hambridge
Kingsbury Episcopi
Milton
Witcombe
Stapleton
Chilton Cantelo
Ashington
Parkway
Rimpton
Adber
West Hatch
Hatch Court
Hatch
Beercrocombe
Walrond's Park
Westport
Lower Burrow
Burrow
Stembridge
Coat
Ash
Tintinhull
West Mudford
Mudford
Hummer
Sandford Orcas
Poyntington

Cheddar: *The cathedral-like caves and Britain's biggest gorge were formed here by ice-age rivers over one million years ago. As well as being a major UK tourist attraction for over 200 years the area is also an SSSI (Site of Special Scientific Interest).* ***Map ref. B2***

East Knoyle: *Christopher Wren, one of Britain's greatest architects was born here in 1632. Following the Great Fire of London Wren designed and supervised the building of 51 London Churches including St Paul's Cathedral.* ***Map ref. F4***

182

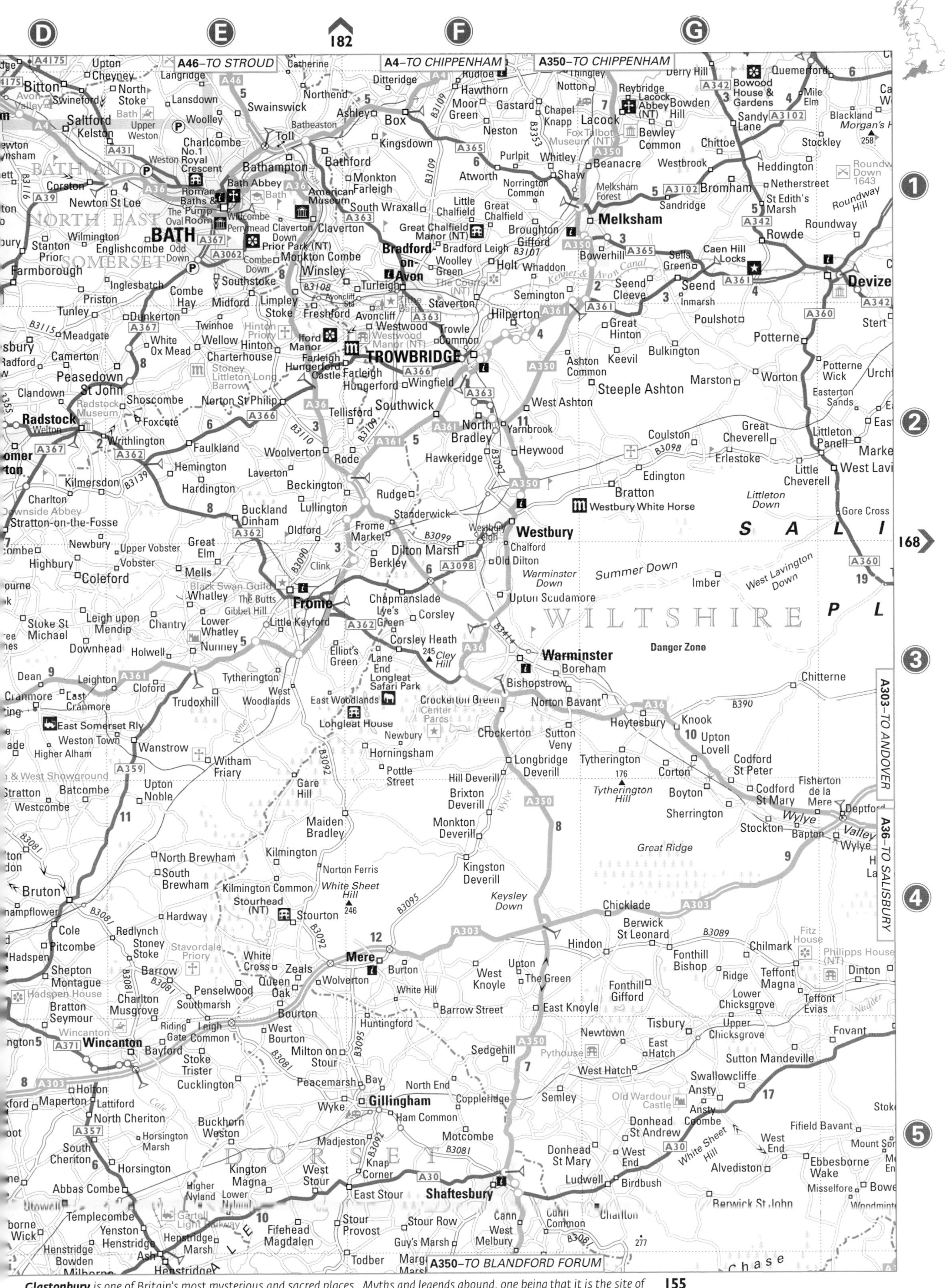
D
E
F
G
A46–TO STROUD
A4–TO CHIPPENHAM
A350–TO CHIPPENHAM
A303–TO ANDOVER
A36–TO SALISBURY
A350–TO BLANDFORD FORUM
Upton Cheyney
Bitton
North Stoke
Langridge
Lansdown
Swainswick
Catherine
Northend
Ditteridge
Rudloe
Hawthorn
Moor Green
Gastard
Chapel Knapp
Notton
Thingley
Reybridge
Lacock Abbey (NT)
Lacock
Bowden Hill
Derry Hill
Bowood House & Gardens
Quemerford
Mile Elm
Sandy Lane
Blackland
Morgan's Hill
Saltford
Kelston
Bath
Upper Weston
Woolley
Batheaston
Ashley
Box
Kingsdown
Neston
Fox Talbot Museum (NT)
Bewley Common
Chittoe
Stockley
Weston
Charlcombe
No.1 Royal Crescent
Toll
Bathford
Purlpit
Whitley
Beanacre
Westbrook
Heddington
Roundway Down 1643
BATH AND NORTH EAST SOMERSET
Corston
Newton St Loe
Roman Baths & Pump Room
Bath Abbey
American Museum
Monkton Farleigh
Atworth
Norrington Common
Shaw
Melksham Forest
Sandridge
Bromham
Netherstreet
St Edith's Marsh
Roundway Hill
BATH
Widcombe
Perrymead
Claverton Down
Claverton
South Wraxall
Little Chalfield
Great Chalfield
Great Chalfield Manor (NT)
Broughton Gifford
Melksham
Rowde
Roundway
Wilmington
Stanton Prior
Englishcombe
Odd Down
Combe Down
Prior Park (NT)
Monkton Combe
Bradford-on-Avon
Bradford Leigh
Woolley Green
Holt
Whaddon
Bowerhill
Sells Green
Caen Hill Locks
Devizes
Farmborough
Inglesbatch
Southstoke
Winsley
Turleigh
The Courts (NT)
Kennet & Avon Canal
Seend Cleeve
Seend
Priston
Combe Hay
Midford
Limpley Stoke
Avoncliff
Staverton
Semington
Inmarsh
Tunley
Dunkerton
Freshford
Hilperton
Poulshot
Stert
Meadgate
Twinhoe
Hinton Priory
Iford Manor
Westwood
Westwood Manor (NT)
Trowle Common
Great Hinton
Potterne
White Ox Mead
Wellow
Hinton Charterhouse
Hungerford
Farleigh Castle
TROWBRIDGE
Ashton Common
Keevil
Bulkington
Potterne Wick
Urchfont
Camerton
Stoney Littleton Long Barrow
Farleigh Hungerford
Wingfield
Steeple Ashton
Marston
Worton
Easterton Sands
Peasedown St John
Clandown
Shoscombe
Norton St Philip
Radstock Museum
Radstock
Welton
Foxcote
Tellisford
Southwick
West Ashton
North Bradley
Yarnbrook
Great Cheverell
Coulston
Littleton Panell
Writhlington
Faulkland
Woolverton
Rode
Heywood
Hawkeridge
Erlestoke
Market Lavington
West Lavington
Hemington
Laverton
Edington
Little Cheverell
Kilmersdon
Hardington
Beckington
Rudge
Bratton
Littleton Down
Charlton
Buckland Dinham
Lullington
Standerwick
Westbury White Horse
Gore Cross
Stratton-on-the-Fosse
Frome Market
Westbury Leigh
Westbury
SALISBURY PLAIN
Oldford
Newbury
Upper Vobster
Great Elm
Dilton Marsh
Chalford
Highbury
Vobster
Clink
Berkley
Old Dilton
Summer Down
West Lavington Down
Coleford
Mells
Warminster Down
Imber
Black Swan Guild
The Butts
Frome
Chapmanslade
Upton Scudamore
Whatley
Gibbet Hill
WILTSHIRE
Stoke St Michael
Leigh upon Mendip
Chantry
Lower Whatley
Little Keyford
Lye's Green
Corsley
Danger Zone
Nunney
Corsley Heath
Downhead
Holwell
Elliot's Green
Lane End
245 Cley Hill
Warminster
Boreham
Dean
Leighton
Cloford
Tytherington
Longleat Safari Park
Bishopstrow
Chitterne
Cranmore
East Cranmore
Trudoxhill
West Woodlands
East Woodlands
Crockerton Green
Center Parcs
Norton Bavant
East Somerset Rly
Longleat House
Heytesbury
Knook
Weston Town
Wanstrow
Newbury
Crockerton
Sutton Veny
Upton Lovell
Higher Alham
Witham Friary
Horningsham
Longbridge Deverill
Tytherington
Codford St Peter
Bath & West Showground
Pottle Street
Corton
Fisherton de la Mere
Stratton
Batcombe
Upton Noble
Gare Hill
Hill Deverill
176 Tytherington Hill
Boyton
Codford St Mary
Westcombe
Brixton Deverill
Deptford
Sherrington
Wylye Valley
Stockton
Bapton
Wylye
Maiden Bradley
Monkton Deverill
Great Ridge
North Brewham
Kilmington
South Brewham
Norton Ferris
Kingston Deverill
Bruton
Kilmington Common
White Sheet Hill 246
Keysley Down
Stourhead (NT)
Stourton
Chicklade
Hardway
Berwick St Leonard
Cole
Redlynch
Fitz House
Pitcombe
Stoney Stoke
Stavordale Priory
Mere
Hindon
Fonthill Bishop
Chilmark
Philipps House (NT)
Hadspen
White Cross
Zeals
Burton
Upton
Ridge
Teffont Magna
Dinton
Shepton Montague
Barrow
Queen Oak
Wolverton
West Knoyle
The Green
Fonthill Gifford
Hadspen House
Charlton Musgrove
Penselwood
White Hill
Lower Chicksgrove
Teffont Evias
Bratton Seymour
Southmarsh
Bourton
Barrow Street
East Knoyle
Tisbury
Upper Chicksgrove
Fovant
Wincanton
Riding Gate
Leigh Common
West Bourton
Huntingford
Newtown
East Hatch
Bayford
Milton on Stour
Sedgehill
Pythouse
Sutton Mandeville
Stoke Trister
West Hatch
Swallowcliffe
Cucklington
Peacemarsh
Bay
North End
Ansty
Holton
Maperton
Gillingham
Coppleridge
Semley
Old Wardour Castle
Latiford
Wyke
Ham Common
Donhead St Andrew
Ansty Coombe
North Cheriton
Buckhorn Weston
Fifield Bavant
Horsington Marsh
Madjeston
Motcombe
West End
South Cheriton
Donhead St Mary
West End
White Sheet Hill
Alvediston
Ebbesborne Wake
Horsington
Kington Magna
West Stour
Knap Corner
DORSET
Higher Nyland
Lower Nyland
Ludwell
Birdbush
Abbas Combe
East Stour
Shaftesbury
Misselfore
Berwick St John
Templecombe
Gartell Light Railway
Stour Provost
Stour Row
Cann
Cann Common
Charlton
Yenston
Fifehead Magdalen
West Melbury
Henstridge
Henstridge Marsh
Guy's Marsh
Henstridge Bowden
Henstridge Ash
Todber
Chase
277

Glastonbury is one of Britain's most mysterious and sacred places. Myths and legends abound, one being that it is the site of the first church in Britain founded by Joseph of Arimathea who landed here with the Holy Grail. Also, as the Isle of Avalon, it is associated with King Arthur. Even today the strangely terraced Tor, with its enigmatic tower, is a magnet for those into nature, mythology, folklore, legend, Christianity and paganism...... Not a bad music festival either. *Map ref. B4*

155
168

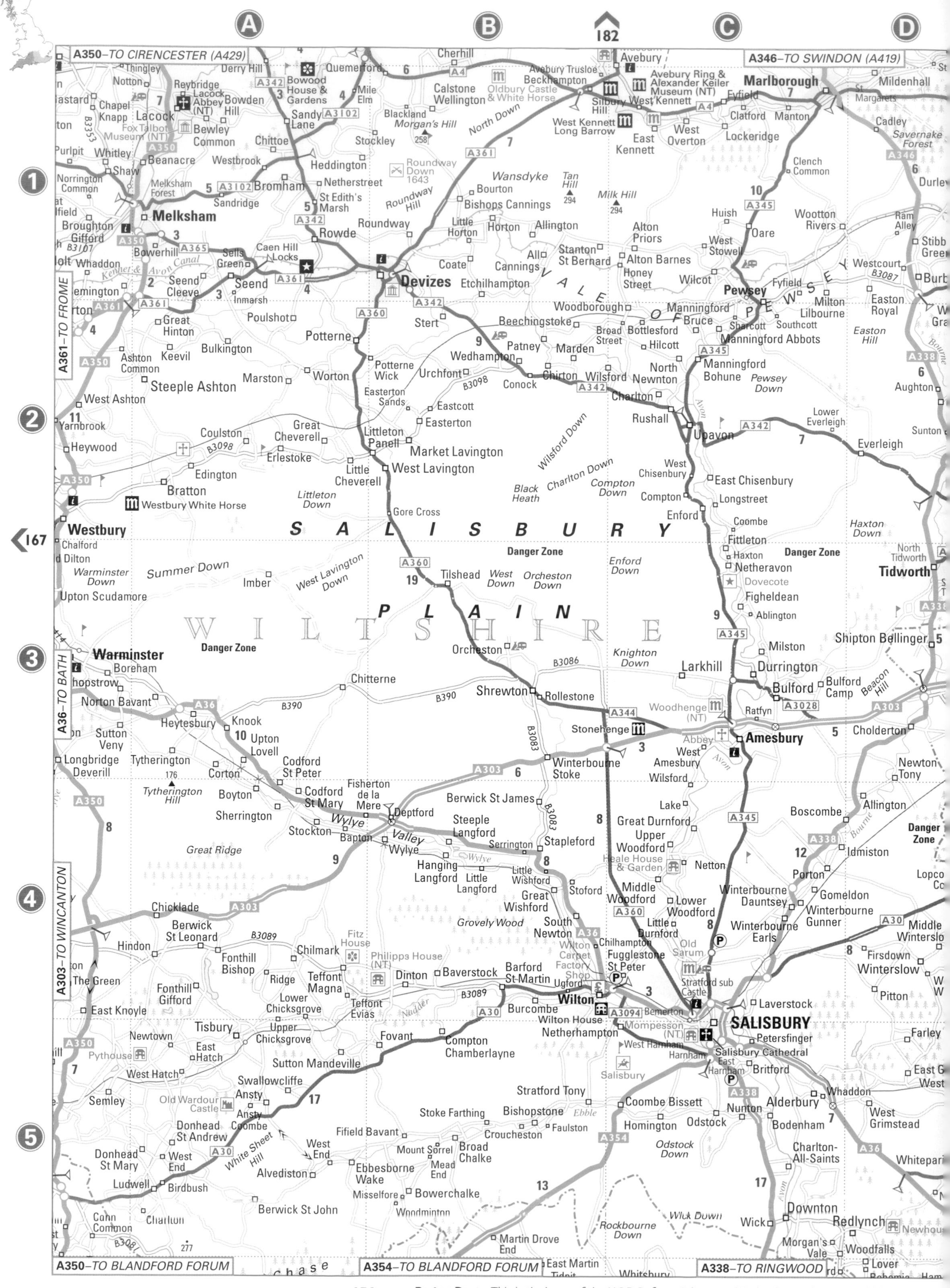
A
B
182
C
D
A350–TO CIRENCESTER (A429)
A346–TO SWINDON (A419)
Cherhill
Avebury
Avebury Trusloe
Beckhampton
Avebury Ring & Alexander Keiller Museum (NT)
Marlborough
Mildenhall
Thingley
Derry Hill
Quemerford
Notton
Reybridge
Lacock Abbey (NT)
Bowood House & Gardens
Mile Elm
Calstone Wellington
Oldbury Castle & White Horse
Silbury Hill
West Kennett
Fyfield
Chapel Knapp
Lacock
Bowden Hill
Fox Talbot Museum (NT)
Bewley Common
Sandy Lane
Blackland
Morgan's Hill
North Down
West Kennett Long Barrow
East Kennett
West Overton
Clatford
Manton
Cadley
Savernake Forest
Lockeridge
Whitley
Beanacre
Chittoe
Stockley
Shaw
Westbrook
Heddington
Roundway Down 1643
Clench Common
Norrington Common
Melksham Forest
Bromham
Netherstreet
Wansdyke
Tan Hill
Bourton
Durley
St Edith's Marsh
Roundway Hill
Bishops Cannings
Milk Hill
Huish
Wootton Rivers
Broughton Gifford
Melksham
Sandridge
Roundway
Little Horton
Horton
Allington
Alton Priors
Oare
Bowerhill
Rowde
Caen Hill Locks
Sells Green
Kennet & Avon Canal
Stanton St Bernard
Alton Barnes
West Stowell
Whaddon
Seend Cleeve
Seend
Coate
All Cannings
Honey Street
Wilcot
Westcourt
Devizes
Etchilhampton
Pewsey
Fyfield
Milton Lilbourne
Easton Royal
Inmarsh
VALE OF PEWSEY
Woodborough
Manningford Bruce
Southcott
Sharcott
Easton Hill
Poulshot
Stert
Beechingstoke
Broad Street
Bottlesford
Manningford Abbots
Great Hinton
Potterne
Patney
Hilcott
Bulkington
Keevil
Ashton Common
Wedhampton
Marden
North Newnton
Manningford Bohune
Pewsey Down
Aughton
Potterne Wick
Worton
Marston
Urchfont
Chirton
Wilsford
Steeple Ashton
Conock
Easterton Sands
Charlton
West Ashton
Eastcott
Easterton
Rushall
Lower Everleigh
Yarnbrook
Great Cheverell
Littleton Panell
Upavon
Sunton
Heywood
Coulston
Erlestoke
Wilsford Down
Everleigh
Market Lavington
Little Cheverell
West Lavington
West Chisenbury
East Chisenbury
Edington
Charlton Down
Bratton
Black Heath
Compton Down
Longstreet
Compton
Littleton Down
Westbury White Horse
Gore Cross
Enford
Westbury
SALISBURY
Coombe
Haxton Down
Chalford
Dilton
Fittleton
Danger Zone
Haxton
Danger Zone
North Tidworth
Warminster Down
Summer Down
Imber
West Lavington Down
Tilshead
West Down
Orcheston Down
Enford Down
Netheravon
Tidworth
Dovecote
Upton Scudamore
Figheldean
PLAIN
Ablington
WILTSHIRE
Shipton Bellinger
Danger Zone
Milston
Knighton Down
Warminster
Orcheston
Durrington
Boreham
Larkhill
Bishopstrow
Chitterne
Bulford
Bulford Camp
Beacon Hill
Norton Bavant
Shrewton
Rollestone
Ratfyn
Woodhenge (NT)
Heytesbury
Knook
Stonehenge
Amesbury
Cholderton
Sutton Veny
Upton Lovell
Abbey
West Amesbury
Longbridge Deverill
Tytherington
Codford St Peter
Winterbourne Stoke
Newton Tony
Corton
Wilsford
Tytherington Hill
Boyton
Codford St Mary
Fisherton de la Mere
Berwick St James
Lake
Allington
Boscombe
Sherrington
Deptford
Steeple Langford
Great Durnford
Danger Zone
Wylye Valley
Upper Woodford
Idmiston
Stockton
Bapton
Wylye
Serrington
Stapleford
Great Ridge
Heale House & Garden
Netton
Hanging Langford
Little Langford
Little Wishford
Porton
Lopcombe Corner
Great Wishford
Stoford
Middle Woodford
Lower Woodford
Winterbourne Dauntsey
Gomeldon
Chicklade
Grovely Wood
Winterbourne Gunner
Berwick St Leonard
South Newton
Little Durnford
Winterbourne Earls
Middle Winterslow
Hindon
Fitz House
Chilmark
Wilton Carpet Factory Shop
Chilhampton
Fugglestone St Peter
Old Sarum
Firsdown
Fonthill Bishop
Philipps House (NT)
Winterslow
The Green
Ridge
Teffont Magna
Dinton
Baverstock
Barford St Martin
Ugford
Stratford sub Castle
Fonthill Gifford
Lower Chicksgrove
Teffont Evias
Burcombe
Wilton
Laverstock
Pitton
East Knoyle
Bemerton
SALISBURY
Newtown
Tisbury
Upper Chicksgrove
Fovant
Compton Chamberlayne
Wilton House
Netherhampton
Mompesson (NT)
Petersfinger
Farley
Pythouse
East Hatch
West Harnham
Salisbury Cathedral
West Hatch
Sutton Mandeville
Harnham
East Harnham
Britford
East Grimstead
Salisbury
Swallowcliffe
Semley
Old Wardour Castle
Ansty
Stratford Tony
Whaddon
Ansty Coombe
Coombe Bissett
Alderbury
Donhead St Andrew
Stoke Farthing
Bishopstone
Faulston
Nunton
Odstock
Homington
West Grimstead
Bodenham
Fifield Bavant
Croucheston
Donhead St Mary
West End
White Sheet Hill
West End
Mount Sorrel
Broad Chalke
Odstock Down
Charlton-All-Saints
Whiteparish
Ebbesborne Wake
Mead End
Alvediston
Ludwell
Birdbush
Bowerchalke
Misselfore
Berwick St John
Woodminton
Downton
Wick Down
Wick
Redlynch
Newhouse
Cann Common
Charlton
Rockbourne Down
Martin Drove End
Morgan's Vale
Woodfalls
A350–TO BLANDFORD FORUM
Chase
A354–TO BLANDFORD FORUM
East Martin
Whitsbury
A338–TO RINGWOOD
Lover
167
A361–TO FROME
A36–TO BATH
A303–TO WINCANTON
1
2
3
4
5
156

Porton Down: *This is the home of the MOD Defence Science and Technology Laboratory which houses one of the largest groups of scientists and engineers employed within Britain's public service. From 1939 up to the 1960s it is alleged that almost 20,000 so called human 'guinea pigs' volunteered to assist in tests carried out here which were supposedly aimed at finding a cure for the common cold.* ***Map ref. C4/D4***

D E 183 F G

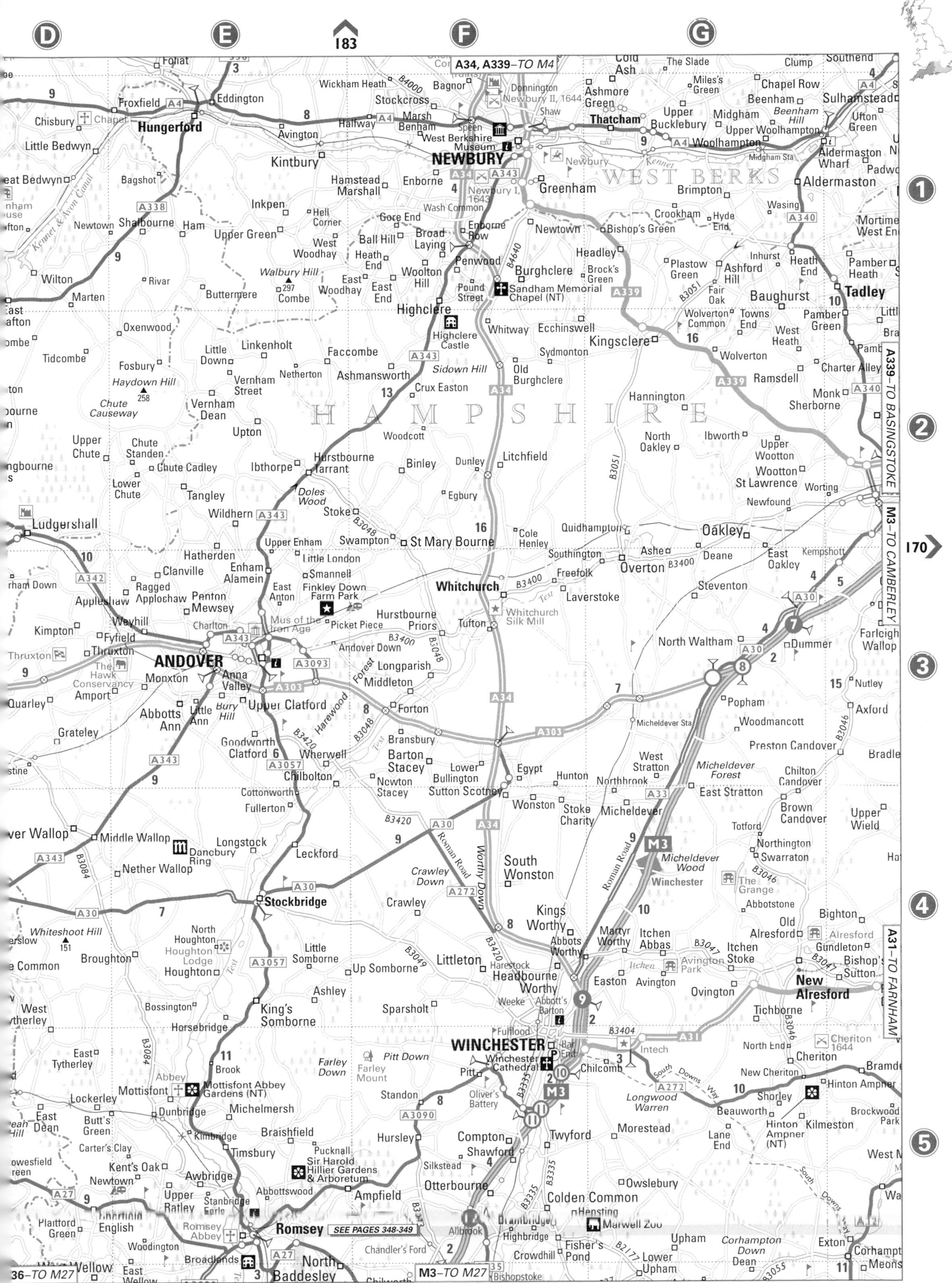
A34, A339–TO M4
Hungerford
Froxfield
Eddington
Chisbury
Little Bedwyn
Kintbury
Avington
Halfway
Marsh Benham
Speen
West Berkshire Museum
NEWBURY
Donnington
Newbury II, 1644
Shaw
Bagnor
Stockcross
Wickham Heath
Cold Ash
Ashmore Green
Thatcham
The Slade
Upper Bucklebury
Miles's Green
Chapel Row
Midgham
Beenham
Beenham Hill
Upper Woolhampton
Woolhampton
Midgham Sta
Southend
Clump
Sulhamstead
Ufton Green
Aldermaston Wharf
Padworth
Aldermaston
WEST BERKS
Brimpton
Greenham
Newbury I, 1643
Wash Common
Enborne
Hamstead Marshall
Bagshot
Shalbourne
Ham
Inkpen
Hell Corner
Gore End
Upper Green
West Woodhay
Ball Hill
Broad Laying
Enborne Row
Newtown
Bishop's Green
Crookham
Hyde End
Wasing
Headley
Heath End
East End
Woolton Hill
Penwood
Burghclere
Brock's Green
Sandham Memorial Chapel (NT)
Pound Street
Plastow Green
Ashford Hill
Inhurst
Heath End
Pamber Heath
Tadley
Baughurst
Fair Oak
Walbury Hill 297
Combe
East Woodhay
Rivar
Marten
Wilton
Buttermere
Highclere
Highclere Castle
Whitway
Ecchinswell
Kingsclere
Wolverton Common
Towns End
West Heath
Pamber Green
Oxenwood
Linkenholt
Little Down
Faccombe
Sydmonton
Wolverton
Tidcombe
Fosbury
Haydown Hill 258
Chute Causeway
Vernham Street
Vernham Dean
Netherton
Ashmansworth
Sidown Hill
Old Burghclere
Crux Easton
Ramsdell
Charter Alley
Monk Sherborne
HAMPSHIRE
Hannington
Upton
Woodcott
North Oakley
Ibworth
Upper Wootton
Wootton St Lawrence
Worting
Newfound
Upper Chute
Chute Standen
Chute Cadley
Lower Chute
Tangley
Ibthorpe
Hurstbourne Tarrant
Binley
Dunley
Litchfield
Doles Wood
Egbury
Ludgershall
Wildhern
Stoke
Cole Henley
Quidhampton
Oakley
Upper Enham
Swampton
St Mary Bourne
Southington
Ashe
Deane
East Oakley
Kempshott
Hatherden
Little London
Smannell
Enham Alamein
Clanville
Ragged Appleshaw
Appleshaw
Penton Mewsey
East Anton
Finkley Down Farm Park
Whitchurch
Freefolk
Overton
Laverstoke
Steventon
Whitchurch Silk Mill
Kimpton
Weyhill
Charlton
Fyfield
Thruxton
Mus of the Iron Age
Picket Piece
Hurstbourne Priors
Tufton
Andover Down
Longparish
North Waltham
Dummer
Farleigh Wallop
ANDOVER
The Hawk Conservancy
Monxton
Anna Valley
Middleton
Forest
Amport
Upper Clatford
Forton
Popham
Nutley
Axford
Quarley
Abbotts Ann
Little Ann
Bury Hill
Harewood
Grateley
Goodworth Clatford
Wherwell
Bransbury
Barton Stacey
Micheldever Sta
Woodmancott
Preston Candover
Bradley
Chilbolton
Cottonworth
Lower Bullington
Newton Stacey
Sutton Scotney
Egypt
Hunton
West Stratton
Northbrook
Micheldever Forest
Chilton Candover
East Stratton
Fullerton
Wonston
Stoke Charity
Micheldever
Brown Candover
Upper Wield
Totford
Middle Wallop
Over Wallop
Danebury Ring
Longstock
Nether Wallop
Leckford
Roman Road
Worthy Down
Crawley Down
South Wonston
Micheldever Wood
Winchester
Northington
Swarraton
The Grange
Abbotstone
Stockbridge
Crawley
Kings Worthy
Bighton
Whiteshoot Hill 151
North Houghton
Houghton Lodge
Broughton
Houghton
Little Somborne
Up Somborne
Littleton
Harestock
Headbourne Worthy
Abbots Worthy
Martyr Worthy
Itchen Abbas
Itchen Stoke
Avington Park
Old Alresford
Alresford
Gundleton
Bishop's Sutton
New Alresford
Easton
Avington
Ovington
Tichborne
West Tytherley
Bossington
Ashley
Sparsholt
King's Somborne
Weeke
Abbott's Barton
Horsebridge
Fulflood
WINCHESTER
Intech
North End
Cheriton 1644
Cheriton
East Tytherley
Brook
Farley Down
Farley Mount
Pitt Down
Pitt
Winchester Cathedral
Chilcomb
South Downs Way
New Cheriton
Bramdean
Hinton Ampner
Mottisfont
Mottisfont Abbey Gardens (NT)
Lockerley
Standon
Oliver's Battery
Longwood Warren
Shorley
Beauworth
Brockwood Park
East Dean
Butt's Green
Dunbridge
Michelmersh
Hinton Ampner (NT)
Kilmeston
Lane End
Twyford
Morestead
Kimbridge
Braishfield
Hursley
Compton
Shawford
Carter's Clay
Timsbury
Pucknall
Sir Harold Hillier Gardens & Arboretum
Kent's Oak
Awbridge
Newtown
Silkstead
Otterbourne
Owslebury
Upper Ratley
Stanbridge Earls
Abbottswood
Ampfield
Colden Common
Hensting
Marwell Zoo
Plaitford Green
English
Romsey Abbey
Romsey
SEE PAGES 348-349
Allbrook
Highbridge
Upham
Corhampton Down
Exton
Corhampton
Meonstoke
Wellow
Woodington
Broadlands
Chandler's Ford
Crowdhill
Fisher's Pond
Lower Upham
Dean
East Wellow
North Baddesley
Bishopstoke
M3–TO M27
A36–TO M27
A339–TO BASINGSTOKE
M3–TO CAMBERLEY
A31–TO FARNHAM

1 2 3 4 5 170

157

Romsey: *Famous as 'Kingsmarkham' in the 1988–1993 TV adaptation of the Ruth Rendell Mysteries starring George Baker.* ***Map ref. E5***

184

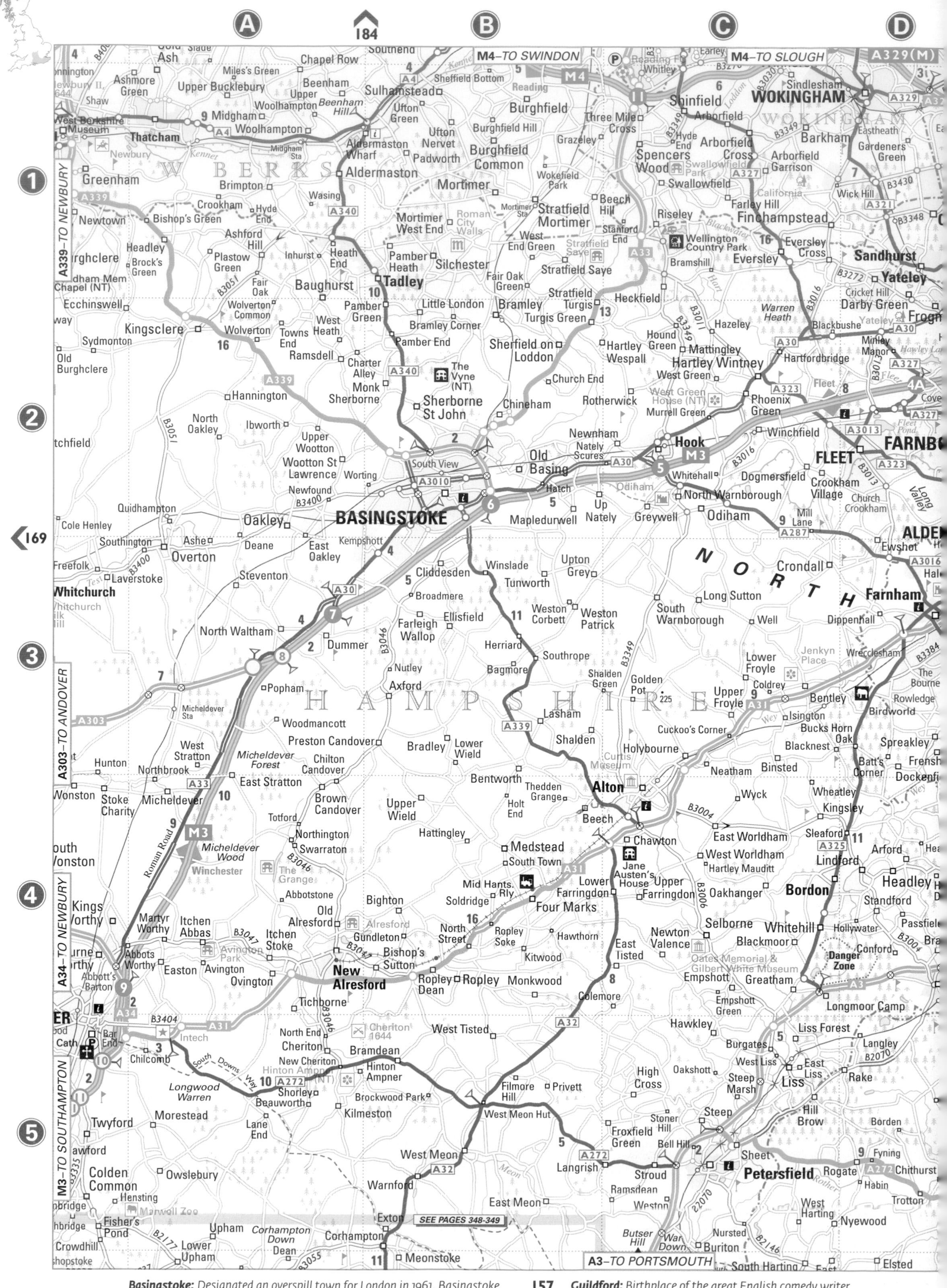

A
B
C
D
1
2
3
4
5
M4–TO SWINDON
M4–TO SLOUGH
A329(M)
A339–TO NEWBURY
A303–TO ANDOVER
A34–TO NEWBURY
M3–TO SOUTHAMPTON
A3–TO PORTSMOUTH
SEE PAGES 348-349
Ash
Chapel Row
Southend
Miles's Green
Ashmore Green
Upper Bucklebury
Beenham
Upper Woolhampton
Beenham Hill
Sulhamstead
Sheffield Bottom
Reading
Burghfield
Three Mile Cross
Shinfield
Arborfield
WOKINGHAM
Sindlesham
Barkham
Eastheath
Gardeners' Green
West Berkshire Museum
Thatcham
Midgham
Woolhampton
Ufton Green
Ufton Nervet
Burghfield Hill
Grazeley
Hyde End
Arborfield Cross
Arborfield Garrison
Newbury
Aldermaston Wharf
Padworth
Burghfield Common
Spencers Wood
Swallowfield Park
Swallowfield
Greenham
Brimpton
Aldermaston
Mortimer
Wokefield Park
Wick Hill
Crookham
Wasing
Stratfield Mortimer
Beech Hill
Riseley
California
Farley Hill
Finchampstead
Newtown
Bishop's Green
Hyde End
Mortimer West End
Roman City Walls
West End Green
Stratfield Saye
Stanford End
Wellington Country Park
Eversley Cross
Eversley
Sandhurst
Ashford Hill
Headley
Plastow Green
Brock's Green
Inhurst
Heath End
Pamber Heath
Silchester
Bramshill
Yateley
Burghclere
Chapel (NT)
Fair Oak
Baughurst
Tadley
Fair Oak Green
Stratfield Saye
Cricket Hill
Darby Green
Ecchinswell
Wolverton Common
Pamber Green
Little London
Bramley
Stratfield Turgis
Heckfield
Warren Heath
Frogmore
Kingsclere
Wolverton
Towns End
West Heath
Bramley Corner
Turgis Green
Hazeley
Blackbushe
Sydmonton
Ramsdell
Pamber End
Sherfield on Loddon
Hartley Wespall
Hound Green
Mattingley
Minley Manor
Old Burghclere
Charter Alley
The Vyne (NT)
Hartley Wintney
Hartfordbridge
Monk Sherborne
Church End
West Green
Hannington
Sherborne St John
Chineham
Rotherwick
West Green House (NT)
Murrell Green
Phoenix Green
Fleet
North Oakley
Ibworth
Upper Wootton
Newnham
Nately Scures
Winchfield
Hook
FARNBOROUGH
Wootton St Lawrence
Worting
South View
Old Basing
FLEET
Dogmersfield
Crookham Village
Church Crookham
Newfound
Hatch
Odiham
Whitehall
North Warnborough
Quidhampton
Oakley
BASINGSTOKE
Mapledurwell
Up Nately
Greywell
Mill Lane
Cole Henley
Southington
Ashe
Deane
East Oakley
Kempshott
Ewshot
Freefolk
Laverstoke
Overton
Steventon
Cliddesden
Winslade
Tunworth
Upton Grey
Crondall
Whitchurch
Broadmere
Long Sutton
Farnham
Farleigh Wallop
Ellisfield
Weston Corbett
Weston Patrick
South Warnborough
Well
Dippenhall
North Waltham
Dummer
Herriard
Southrope
Lower Froyle
Jenkyn Place
Wrecclesham
Nutley
Bagmore
Shalden Green
Golden Pot
Coldrey
Bourne
Popham
Axford
Upper Froyle
Bentley
Rowledge
Micheldever Sta
HAMPSHIRE
Lasham
Isington
Birdworld
Woodmancott
Cuckoo's Corner
Bucks Horn Oak
Spreakley
West Stratton
Preston Candover
Bradley
Lower Wield
Shalden
Holybourne
Blacknest
Hunton
Northbrook
Micheldever Forest
Chilton Candover
Curtis Museum
Neatham
Binsted
Batt's Corner
Frensham
Dockenfield
East Stratton
Bentworth
Thedden Grange
Wonston
Stoke Charity
Micheldever
Brown Candover
Upper Wield
Holt End
Alton
Wyck
Wheatley
Kingsley
Totford
Beech
Roman Road
Hattingley
Chawton
East Worldham
Sleaford
Northington
Swarraton
Medstead
West Worldham
Hartley Mauditt
Arford
South Wonston
Micheldever Wood
South Town
Jane Austen's House
Lindford
Winchester
The Grange
Mid Hants. Rly
Lower Farringdon
Upper Farringdon
Oakhanger
Headley
Abbotstone
Bighton
Soldridge
Four Marks
Bordon
Standford
Kings Worthy
Old Alresford
Alresford
Martyr Worthy
Itchen Abbas
Itchen Stoke
Gundleton
North Street
Ropley Soke
Hawthorn
Newton Valence
Selborne
Whitehill
Hollywater
Passfield
Avington Park
Bishop's Sutton
East Tisted
Blackmoor
Conford
Abbots Worthy
Easton
Avington
Kitwood
Oates Memorial & Gilbert White Museum
Danger Zone
Abbott's Barton
Ovington
New Alresford
Ropley Dean
Ropley
Monkwood
Empshott
Greatham
Tichborne
Colemore
Empshott Green
Longmoor Camp
B3404
Intech
North End
Cheriton 1644
West Tisted
Hawkley
Liss Forest
Bar End
Cheriton
Burgates
Langley
Chilcomb
South Downs Way
New Cheriton
Bramdean
West Liss
East Liss
Liss
Hinton Ampner
High Cross
Oakshott
Steep Marsh
Rake
Longwood Warren
Shorley
Filmore Hill
Privett
Beauworth
Brockwood Park
Hill Brow
Kilmeston
West Meon Hut
Stoner Hill
Steep
Borden
Twyford
Morestead
Lane End
Froxfield Green
Bell Hill
Sheet
Fyning
West Meon
Langrish
Chithurst
Colden Common
Owslebury
Stroud
Petersfield
Rogate
Habin
Warnford
Ramsdean
Trotton
Hensting
Marwell Zoo
East Meon
Weston
West Harting
Nyewood
Fisher's Pond
Upham
Corhampton Down
Exton
Corhampton
Butser Hill
War Down
Nursted
Lower Upham
Dean
Buriton
Crowdhill
Meonstoke
South Harting
Elsted

169

Basingstoke: *Designated an overspill town for London in 1961, Basingstoke was almost totally rebuilt with a new town centre, pedestrian precincts and multi-storey car parks. The population increased from 26,000 in 1960 to 60,000 in 1973 and is today over 100,000.* ***Map ref. B2***

157

Guildford: *Birthplace of the great English comedy writer P G Wodehouse (1881–1975). Pelham Grenville Wodehouse, 'Plum' to his friends, is best remembered for the creation of Bertie Wooster and his faithful and resourceful manservant Jeeves.* ***Map ref. E3***

185

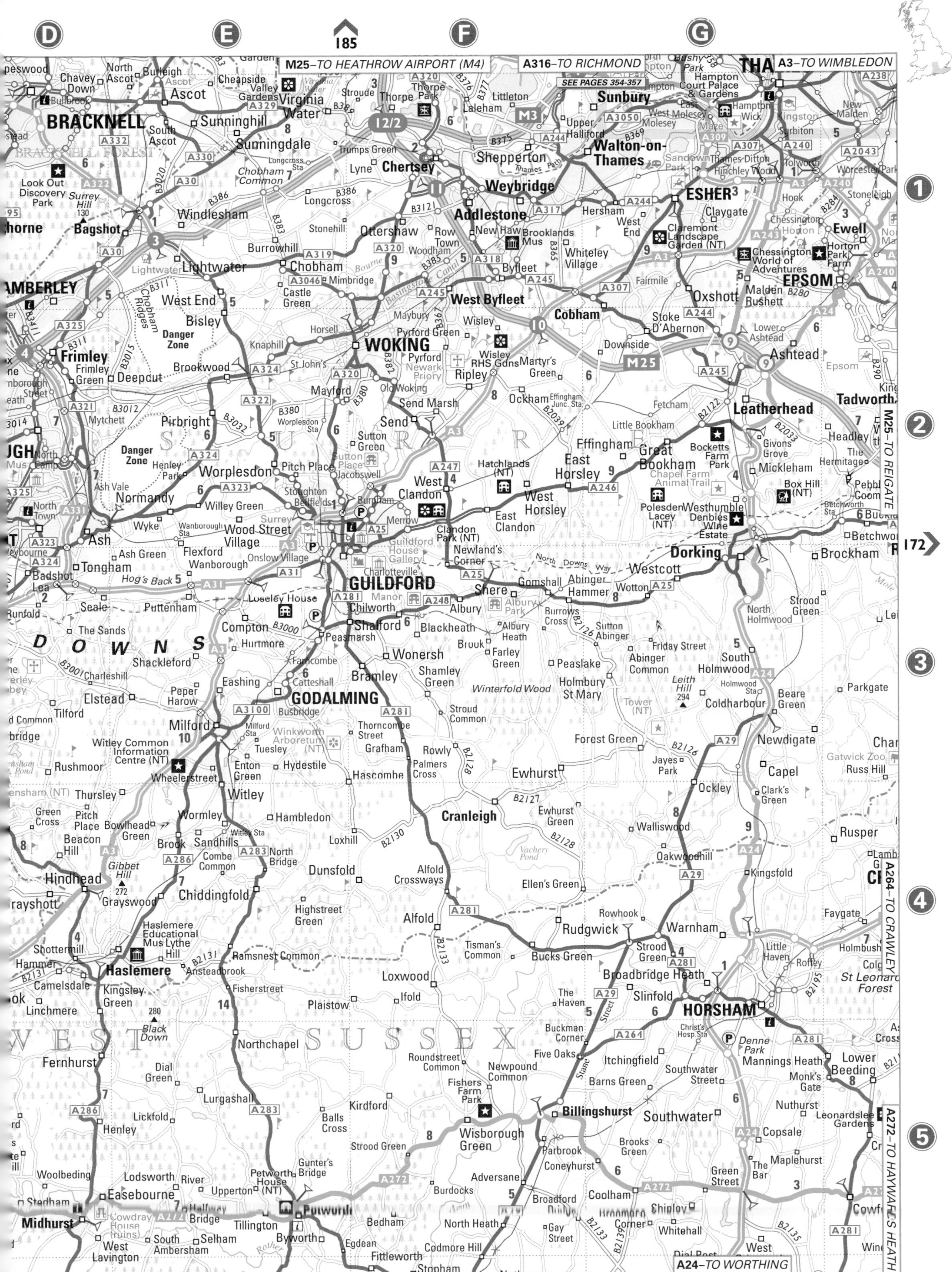

D
E
F
G
M25–TO HEATHROW AIRPORT (M4)
A316–TO RICHMOND
A3–TO WIMBLEDON
SEE PAGES 354-357
M25–TO REIGATE
A264–TO CRAWLEY
A272–TO HAYWARDS HEATH
A24–TO WORTHING
1
2
3
4
5
172
BRACKNELL
Ascot
Sunninghill
Sunningdale
Virginia Water
Chertsey
Shepperton
Sunbury
Walton-on-Thames
Weybridge
Addlestone
ESHER
Ewell
EPSOM
Oxshott
Cobham
Ashtead
Leatherhead
Tadworth
Bagshot
Windlesham
Lightwater
Chobham
West End
Bisley
Frimley
Deepcut
Brookwood
WOKING
West Byfleet
Ripley
Ockham
Send
Pirbright
Worplesdon
Normandy
West Clandon
West Horsley
East Horsley
Effingham
Great Bookham
Dorking
Westcott
GUILDFORD
Shere
Gomshall
Abinger Hammer
Shalford
Wonersh
Bramley
GODALMING
Milford
Witley
Chiddingfold
Haslemere
Hindhead
Cranleigh
Ewhurst
Rudgwick
Warnham
HORSHAM
Slinfold
Billingshurst
Southwater
Wisborough Green
Petworth
Midhurst
Fernhurst
Northchapel
Capel
Newdigate
Ockley
Rusper
Cowfold
Brockham
SURREY
DOWNS
WEST SUSSEX

Horsham: *During a violent hailstorm on 5th September 1958 hailstones of 2–3 inches (70–80mm) diameter were measured. One single hailstone weighed in at 6.7 oz (190 grams) and is the largest recorded hailstone in Britain.* ***Map ref. G4***

158

Brookwood: *From the mid nineteenth century, the amount of bodies in London requiring burial was causing great concern, so 2,000 acres (800ha) of Woking's common land was purchased from Lord Onslow in 1852 in order to establish a single great metropolitan cemetery. By 1854 Brookwood was the largest cemetery in the world and even today it remains the largest in the UK. Since 1854 almost a quarter of a million bodies have been interred here. Since 1917 separate military cemeteries, administered by the Commonwealth War Graves Commission have also been located here.* ***Map ref. E2***

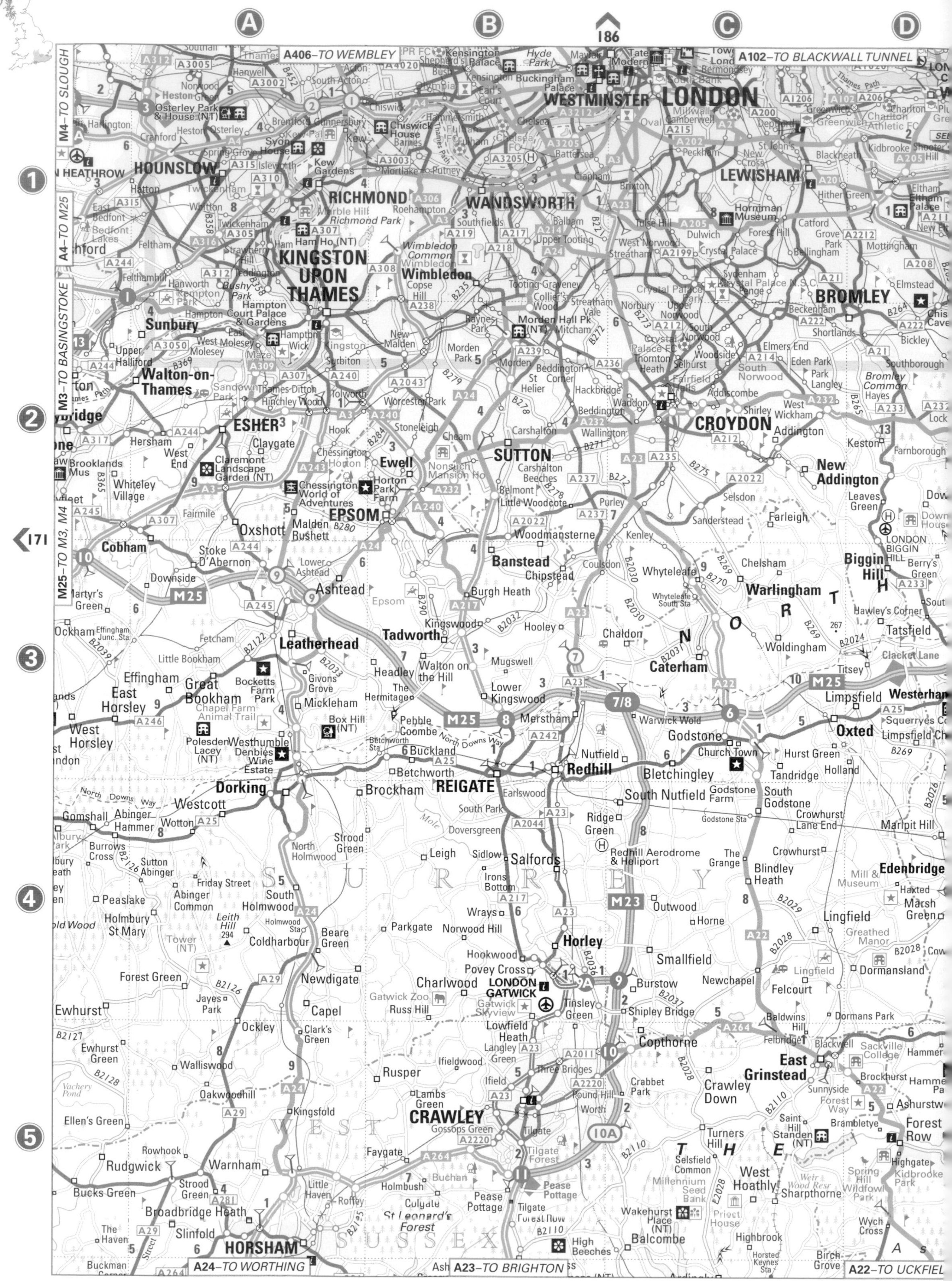

A
B
C
D
186
A406–TO WEMBLEY
A102–TO BLACKWALL TUNNEL
M4–TO SLOUGH
A4–TO M25
M3–TO BASINGSTOKE
M25–TO M3, M4
171
1
2
3
4
5
WESTMINSTER
LONDON
HOUNSLOW
RICHMOND
WANDSWORTH
LEWISHAM
KINGSTON UPON THAMES
Wimbledon
BROMLEY
Sunbury
Walton-on-Thames
ESHER
CROYDON
SUTTON
Ewell
EPSOM
Cobham
Oxshott
Ashtead
Banstead
Leatherhead
Tadworth
Caterham
Warlingham
Biggin Hill
New Addington
Dorking
REIGATE
Redhill
Oxted
Godstone
Horley
LONDON GATWICK
CRAWLEY
East Grinstead
HORSHAM
Edenbridge
Lingfield
Forest Row
SURREY
WEST SUSSEX
NORTH
M25
M23
A24–TO WORTHING
A23–TO BRIGHTON
A22–TO UCKFIELD

Purley: **Purley:** *In February 1898 Henry Lindfield became the first person ever to die in a car crash. He died from injuries he sustained when his car left the road at Purley Corner whilst driving to Brighton.* ***Map ref. C2***

159

Biggin Hill Airport *was first established as a Royal Flying Corps station in 1917, but it is best known as a World War II 'fighter station' from which the RAF fought the crucial 'Battle of Britain' in the summer of 1940.* ***Map ref. D2***

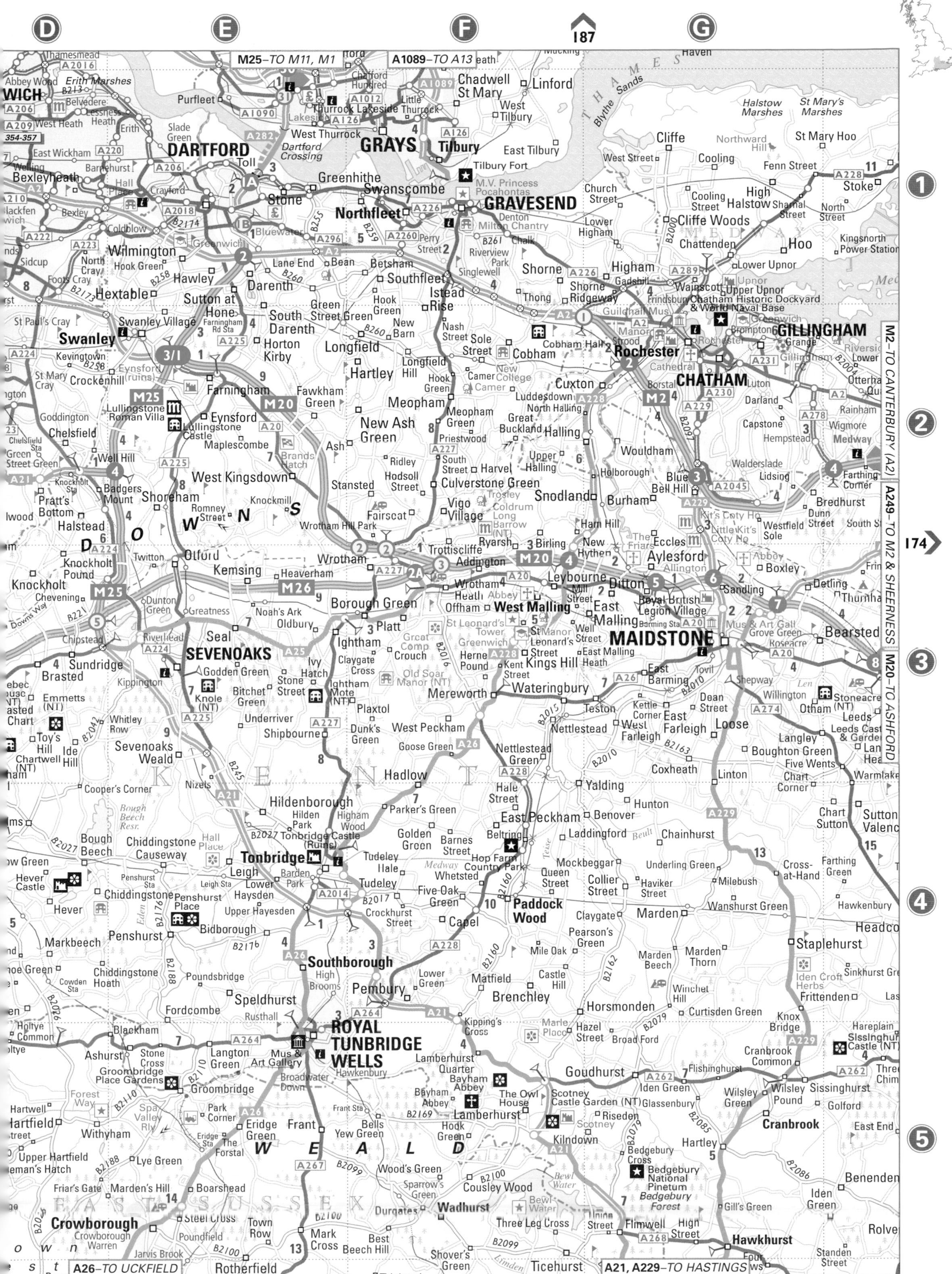
D
E
F
187
G
M25–TO M11, M1
A1089–TO A13
M2–TO CANTERBURY (A2)
A249–TO M2 & SHEERNESS
M20–TO ASHFORD
174
A26–TO UCKFIELD
A21, A229–TO HASTINGS
1
2
3
4
5
DARTFORD
GRAYS
Tilbury
GRAVESEND
Northfleet
Swanscombe
Greenhithe
Stone
Purfleet
West Thurrock
Dartford Crossing
Chadwell St Mary
Linford
West Tilbury
East Tilbury
Tilbury Fort
Cliffe
Cooling
Cliffe Woods
High Halstow
Hoo
Stoke
Kingsnorth Power Station
Halstow Marshes
St Mary's Marshes
St Mary Hoo
Higham
Shorne
Gadshill
Chattenden
Upnor
Chatham Historic Dockyard & World Naval Base
GILLINGHAM
Rochester
Strood
CHATHAM
Borstal
Luton
Darland
Capstone
Hempstead
Rainham
Wigmore
Walderslade
Lidsing
Bredhurst
Blue Bell Hill
Burham
Wouldham
Eccles
Aylesford
Cuxton
Halling
Snodland
Cobham
Meopham
Longfield
Hartley
New Ash Green
Fawkham Green
Ash
Stansted
Vigo Village
Trottiscliffe
Addington
Birling
Ryarsh
Wrotham
Wrotham Heath
Borough Green
Platt
Ightham
Ivy Hatch
Offham
West Malling
East Malling
Leybourne
Ditton
Larkfield
Kings Hill
Mereworth
Wateringbury
Teston
Barming
MAIDSTONE
Bearsted
Detling
Thurnham
Boxley
Sandling
Otham
Langley
Loose
Linton
Coxheath
Boughton Green
East Farleigh
West Farleigh
Nettlestead
Yalding
Hunton
Laddingford
Chainhurst
Marden
Staplehurst
Headcorn
Sutton Valence
Chart Sutton
Swanley
Hextable
Wilmington
Hawley
Sutton at Hone
Darenth
South Darenth
Horton Kirby
Farningham
Eynsford
Lullingstone Castle
Lullingstone Roman Villa
Crockenhill
Shoreham
Otford
Kemsing
Heaverham
Seal
SEVENOAKS
Sevenoaks Weald
Riverhead
Sundridge
Brasted
Chipstead
Chevening
Knockholt
Halstead
Badgers Mount
Pratt's Bottom
West Kingsdown
Plaxtol
Shipbourne
Hadlow
Hildenborough
Tonbridge
Leigh
Penshurst
Chiddingstone
Hever
Bidborough
Southborough
Pembury
Speldhurst
Langton Green
ROYAL TUNBRIDGE WELLS
Groombridge
Crowborough
Rotherfield
Mark Cross
Wadhurst
Lamberhurst
Goudhurst
Kilndown
Bedgebury National Pinetum
Flimwell
Hawkhurst
Cranbrook
Sissinghurst
Benenden
Ticehurst
Brenchley
Horsmonden
Matfield
Paddock Wood
East Peckham
Capel
Five Oak Green
Tudeley
Bexleyheath
Crayford
Bexley
Sidcup
Erith
Belvedere
Bluewater
K E N T
W E A L D
D O W N S
E A S T S U S S E X

Dorking: *Sir Laurence Olivier (1907–1989) was born here. He won an Academy Award for his role as Hamlet in 1948 and went on to become one of Britain's best known actors.* ***Map ref. A4***

160

Hartfield: *In 1925 the Milne family moved into nearby Cotchford Farm where A A Milne wrote his Winnie the Pooh books, including his son Christopher Robin in the stories. Some of the locations from the stories are identifiable in the area, including the recently restored bridge where the Poohsticks game was invented.* ***Map ref. D5***

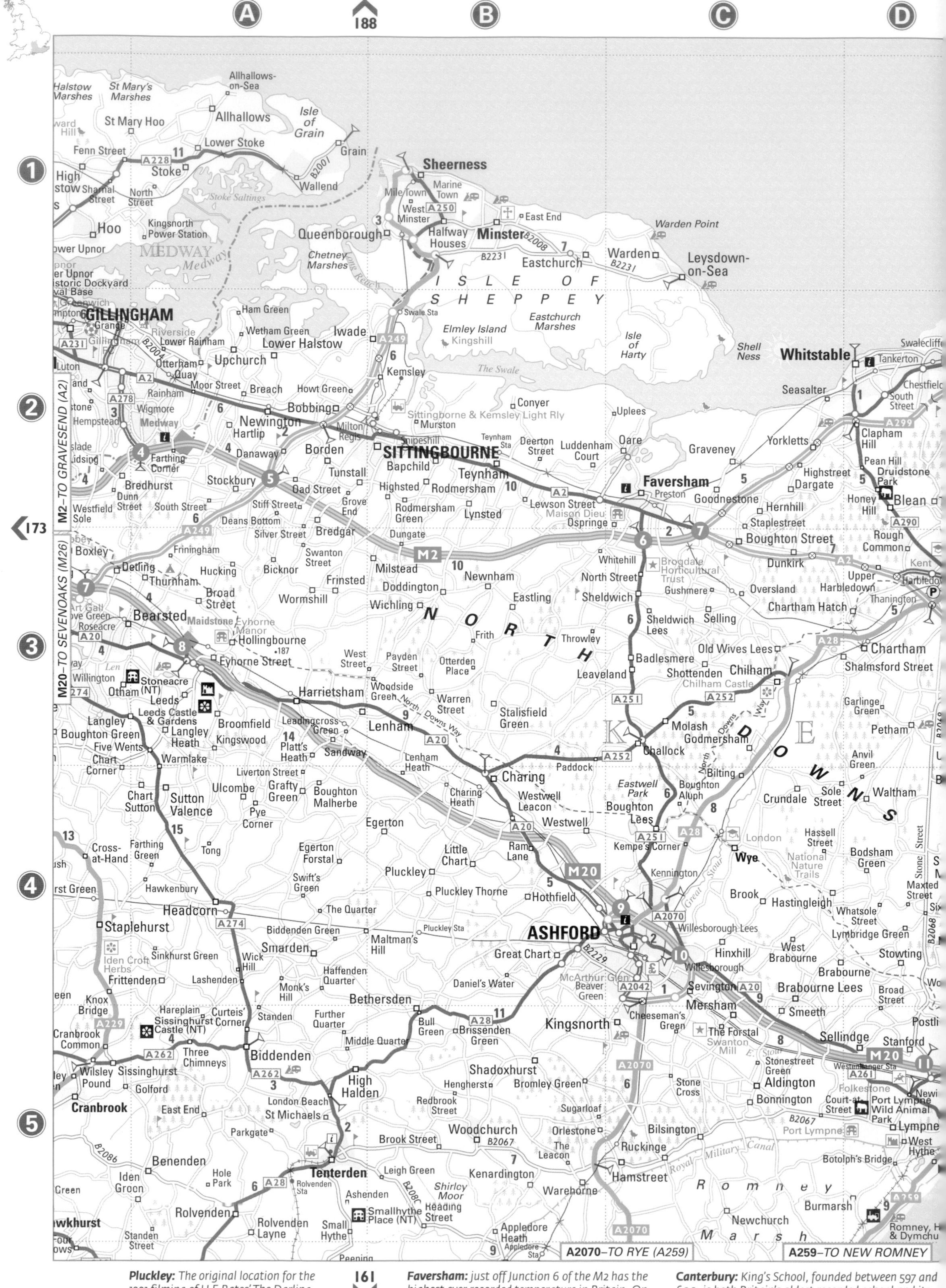

A
B
C
D
188
1
2
3
4
5
173
161
M2–TO GRAVESEND (A2)
M20–TO SEVENOAKS (M26)
A2070–TO RYE (A259)
A259–TO NEW ROMNEY
Halstow Marshes
St Mary's Marshes
Allhallows-on-Sea
Allhallows
Isle of Grain
St Mary Hoo
Fenn Street
Lower Stoke
Grain
A228
Stoke
High Halstow
Shamal Street
North Street
Stoke Saltings
Wallend
B2001
Sheerness
Marine Town
Mile Town
West Minster
A250
East End
Hoo
Kingsnorth Power Station
Queenborough
Halfway Houses
Minster
B2008
Warden Point
Lower Upnor
Upper Upnor
Historic Dockyard
MEDWAY
Medway
Chetney Marshes
Long Reach
B2231
Eastchurch
Warden
Leysdown-on-Sea
ISLE OF SHEPPEY
GILLINGHAM
Grange
Riverside
Ham Green
Swale Sta
Eastchurch Marshes
Wetham Green
Iwade
Elmley Island
Kingshill
Isle of Harty
Shell Ness
Whitstable
Tankerton
Swalecliffe
A231
B2004
Lower Rainham
Lower Halstow
A249
Luton
Otterham Quay
Upchurch
Kemsley
The Swale
Moor Street
Breach
Howt Green
Seasalter
Chestfield
South Street
Rainham
A2
A278
Wigmore
Medway
Hempstead
Newington
Bobbing
Conyer
Uplees
A299
Sittingborne & Kemsley Light Rly
Murston
Hartlip
Milton Regis
Snipeshill
Teynham Sta
Deerton Street
Luddenham Court
Oare
Yorkletts
Clapham Hill
Danaway
Borden
SITTINGBOURNE
Graveney
Farthing Corner
Bapchild
Teynham
Highstreet
Pean Hill
Druidstone Park
Tunstall
Faversham
Dargate
Bredhurst
Stockbury
Oad Street
Highsted
Rodmersham
Preston
Goodnestone
Hernhill
Honey Hill
Blean
Dunn Street
South Street
Grove End
Rodmersham Green
Lynsted
Lewson Street
Maison Dieu
Ospringe
Westfield Sole
Stiff Street
Staplestreet
A290
Deans Bottom
Dungate
Boughton Street
Rough Common
Silver Street
Bredgar
Whitehill
Boxley
Friningham
Swanton Street
M2
Brogdale Horticultural Trust
Dunkirk
Kent
Detling
Hucking
Bicknor
Milstead
Newnham
North Street
Gushmere
Oversland
Harbledown
Thurnham
Frinsted
Doddington
Sheldwich
Thanington
Broad Street
Wormshill
Eastling
Chartham Hatch
Bearsted
Maidstone
Eyhorne Manor
Wichling
Sheldwich Lees
Selling
Roseacre
A20
Hollingbourne
Frith
NORTH DOWNS
Throwley
Old Wives Lees
Chartham
West Street
Payden Street
Otterden Place
Badlesmere
Eyhorne Street
Shottenden
Chilham
Shalmsford Street
Len
Leaveland
Willington
Stoneacre (NT)
Chilham Castle
Otham
Harrietsham
Woodside Green
Warren Street
A251
A252
Leeds
Leeds Castle & Gardens
Stalisfield Green
Garlinge Green
Langley
Broomfield
Leadingcross Green
Lenham
North Downs Way
Molash
Godmersham
Petham
Boughton Green
Langley Heath
Kingswood
Platt's Heath
Challock
Five Wents
Sandway
Lenham Heath
Paddock
Anvil Green
Chart Corner
Warmlake
Liverton Street
Charing
Bilting
Eastwell Park
Boughton Aluph
Chart Sutton
Sutton Valence
Ulcombe
Grafty Green
Boughton Malherbe
Charing Heath
Westwell Leacon
Crundale
Sole Street
Waltham
Pye Corner
Boughton Lees
Egerton
Westwell
London
Hassell Street
Cross-at-Hand
Farthing Green
Tong
Egerton Forstal
Little Chart
Ram Lane
Kempe's Corner
Wye
Bodsham Green
National Nature Trails
Pluckley
M20
Kennington
Hawkenbury
Swift's Green
Pluckley Thorne
Hothfield
Brook
Hastingleigh
Headcorn
The Quarter
Great Stour
Whatsole Street
Staplehurst
A274
Biddenden Green
Maltman's Hill
Pluckley Sta
ASHFORD
A2070
Willesborough Lees
Lymbridge Green
Smarden
Great Chart
B2229
Hinxhill
West Brabourne
Stowting
Iden Croft Herbs
Sinkhurst Green
Wick Hill
Haffenden Quarter
Willesborough
Frittenden
Lashenden
Monk's Hill
Daniel's Water
McArthur Glen
Beaver Green
A2042
Sevington
Brabourne
Brabourne Lees
Broad Street
Knox Bridge
Bethersden
Mersham
Smeeth
Hareplain
Curteis' Corner
Standen
Further Quarter
Bull Green
A28
Brissenden Green
Kingsnorth
Cheeseman's Green
The Forstal
Swanton Mill
Sellindge
Stanford
Sissinghurst Castle (NT)
A229
Cranbrook Common
Middle Quarter
A262
Three Chimneys
Biddenden
Shadoxhurst
Stonestreet Green
Westenhanger Sta
A261
Wilsley Pound
Sissinghurst
Golford
High Halden
Hengherst
Bromley Green
Stone Cross
Aldington
Folkestone
Cranbrook
East End
London Beach
Redbrook Street
Bonnington
Court-at-Street
Port Lympne Wild Animal Park
St Michaels
Sugarloaf
B2067
Port Lympne
Lympne
Parkgate
Woodchurch
Orlestone
Bilsington
Brook Street
West Hythe
B2086
Benenden
Tenterden
The Leacon
Ruckinge
Royal Military Canal
Botolph's Bridge
Leigh Green
Kenardington
Hamstreet
Iden Green
Hole Park
Rolvenden Sta
B2080
Shirley Moor
Romney Marsh
Ashenden
Warehorne
Burmarsh
Rolvenden
Smallhythe Place (NT)
Heading Street
Newchurch
Hawkhurst
Standen Street
Rolvenden Layne
Small Hythe
Appledore Heath
Appledore Sta
Romney, Hythe & Dymchurch
Peening

Pluckley: *The original location for the 1991 filming of H E Bates' The Darling Buds of May which starred David Jason, Pam Ferris, Catherine Zeta Jones and Philip Franks.* ***Map ref. B4***

Faversham: *just off Junction 6 of the M2 has the highest ever recorded temperature in Britain. On the 10th August 2003 it peaked at 38.5°C (101.3°F).* ***Map ref. C2***

Canterbury: *King's School, founded between 597 and 600, is both Britain's oldest recorded school and its oldest recorded charity.* ***Map ref. D3***

Channel Tunnel: *The idea of a cross channel tunnel had been around for years before one eventually opened in 1994. An early scheme was discussed between Britain and France in 1802 but never got off the ground because of the Napoleonic Wars. Between 1880 and 1883 trial tunnels were dug on both sides of the Channel but were abandoned in 1883 amidst fears of a French invasion. In 1973, after Britain joined the Common Market, it was agreed to build a traditional rail tunnel, but construction was abandoned by Harold Wilson's government due to a financial crisis. Work on the current tunnel started in 1987 and it was eventually opened in 1994, two years late and millions of pounds over budget. The tunnel is 31 miles (50km) long and an average of 150 feet (45.5m) below the seabed. It was constructed by 13,000 engineers and workers. Interestingly the size of Britain increased by 90 acres (36.5ha) when spoil from the tunnel was deposited and landscaped at an area now known as Samphire Hoe.* ***Map ref. F4***

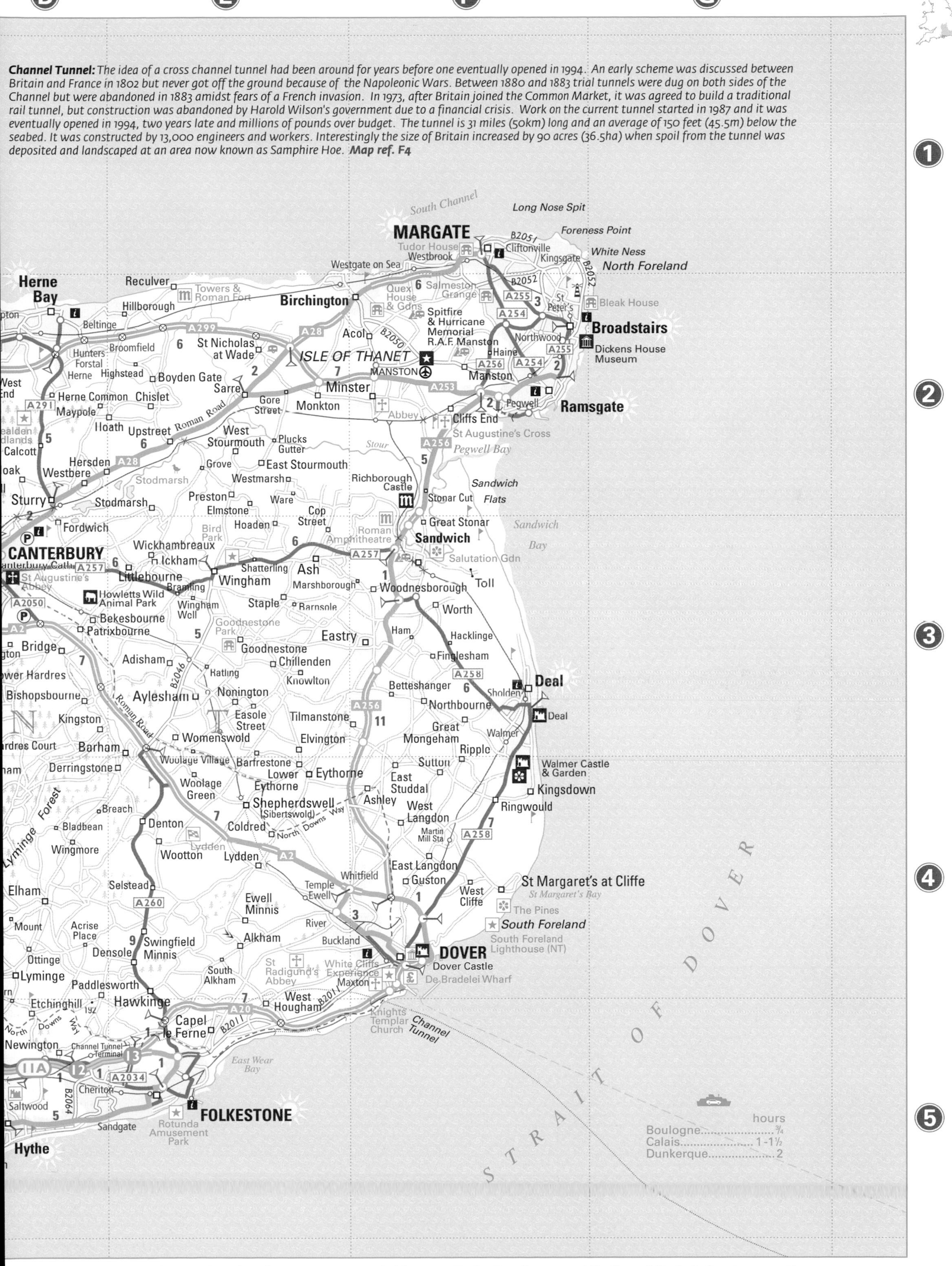
D
E
F
G
1
2
3
4
5
South Channel
Long Nose Spit
MARGATE
Foreness Point
White Ness
North Foreland
Westgate on Sea
Herne Bay
Reculver
Towers & Roman Fort
Birchington
Quex House & Gdns
Salmestone Grange
Hillborough
Beltinge
Broomfield
St Nicholas at Wade
ISLE OF THANET
Spitfire & Hurricane Memorial R.A.F. Manston
Broadstairs
Bleak House
Dickens House Museum
Northwood
Haine
Manston
Minster
Monkton
Ramsgate
Pegwell
Cliffs End
St Augustine's Cross
Pegwell Bay
Sarre
Boyden Gate
Chislet
Herne Common
Maypole
Hoath
Upstreet
West Stourmouth
Plucks Gutter
Gore Street
East Stourmouth
Hersden
Westbere
Stodmarsh
Sturry
Fordwich
Grove
Westmarsh
Preston
Elmstone
Ware
Richborough Castle
Stonar Cut
Sandwich Flats
Great Stonar
Sandwich
Sandwich Bay
Cop Street
Hoaden
Roman Amphitheatre
CANTERBURY
Wickhambreaux
Ickham
Littlebourne
Bramling
Wingham
Shatterling
Ash
Marshborough
Woodnesborough
Toll
Salutation Gdn
Howletts Wild Animal Park
Wingham Well
Staple
Barnsole
Worth
Bekesbourne
Patrixbourne
Goodnestone Park
Goodnestone
Eastry
Ham
Hacklinge
Finglesham
Bridge
Adisham
Chillenden
Knowlton
Hatling
Nonington
Aylesham
Betteshanger
Sholden
Deal
Bishopsbourne
Kingston
Easole Street
Tilmanstone
Northbourne
Great Mongeham
Walmer
Barham
Womenswold
Elvington
Ripple
Walmer Castle & Garden
Derringstone
Woolage Village
Barfrestone
Lower Eythorne
Eythorne
Sutton
East Studdal
Kingsdown
Woolage Green
Shepherdswell (Sibertswold)
Ashley
West Langdon
Ringwould
Breach
Bladbean
Denton
Coldred
North Downs Way
Martin Mill Sta
Wingmore
Wootton
Lydden
Lyminge Forest
Whitfield
East Langdon
Guston
St Margaret's at Cliffe
St Margaret's Bay
Elham
Selstead
Temple Ewell
Ewell Minnis
West Cliffe
The Pines
South Foreland
South Foreland Lighthouse (NT)
Mount
Acrise Place
Swingfield Minnis
Alkham
River
Buckland
DOVER
Dover Castle
Densole
Ottinge
Lyminge
Paddlesworth
South Alkham
St Radigund's Abbey
White Cliffs Experience
Maxton
De Bradelei Wharf
Etchinghill
Hawkinge
West Hougham
Knights Templar Church
Channel Tunnel
Capel le Ferne
Newington
Channel Tunnel Terminal
Cheriton
East Wear Bay
Saltwood
FOLKESTONE
Sandgate
Rotunda Amusement Park
Hythe
STRAIT OF DOVER
hours
Boulogne ¾
Calais 1-1½
Dunkerque 2

Folkestone: *William Harvey (1578–1657) was born here. Harvey studied medicine at Cambridge and is credited with discovering the circulation of the blood.* ***Map ref. E5***

Sandwich, Dover, Hythe, New Romney and Hastings: *Collectively these towns are the original 'Cinque Ports'. In medieval times, Royal Charters granted them special privileges such as freedom from tolls and customs duties, freedom of trade and their own judicial courts. This was in return for the use of their fishing and cargo vessels and crews for military service. This service, which lasted over three hundred years eventually formed into the first British Navy.*

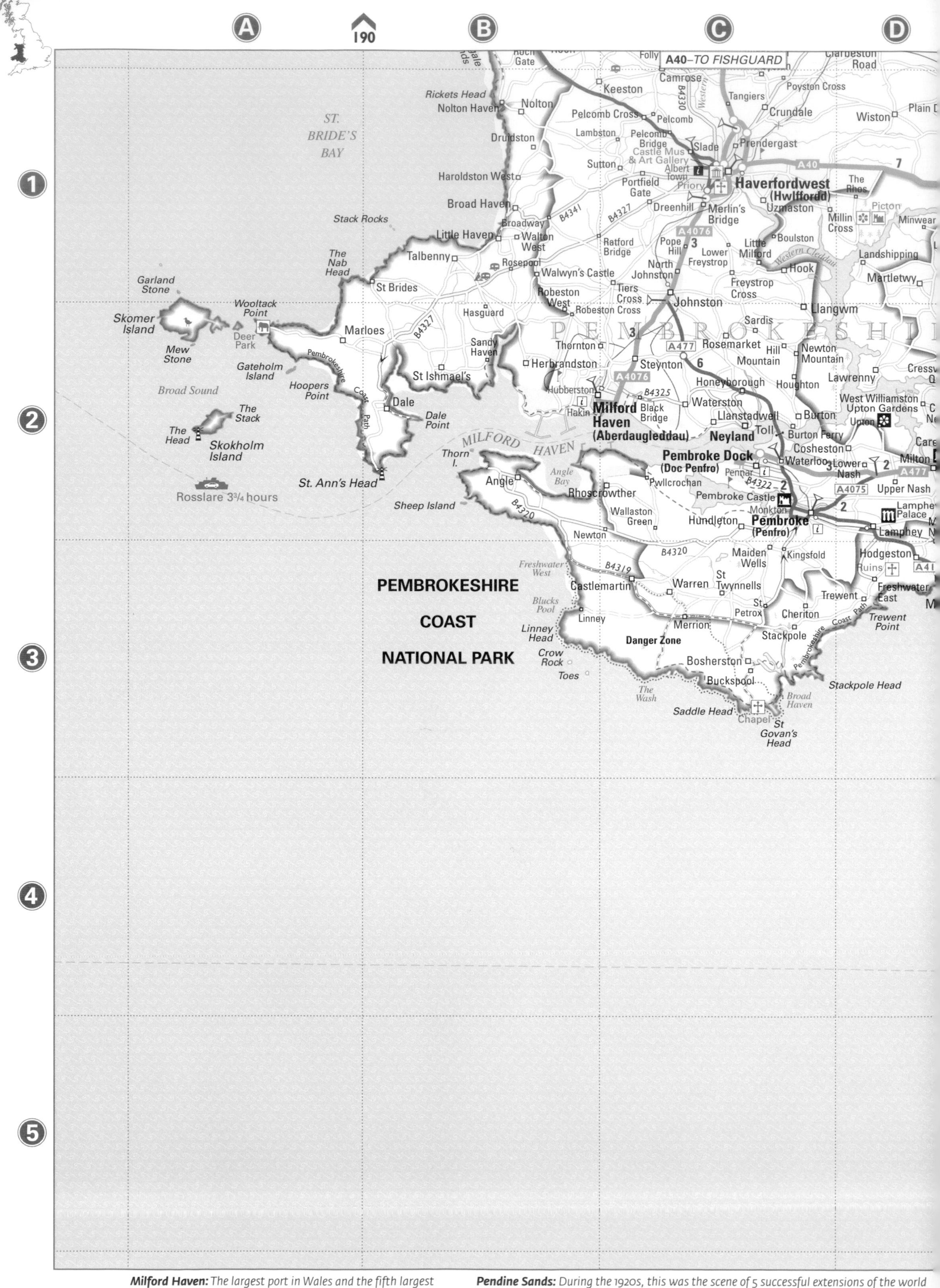

A
190
B
C
D
1
2
3
4
5
A40–TO FISHGUARD
ST. BRIDE'S BAY
Rickets Head
Nolton Haven
Nolton
Druidston
Haroldston West
Broad Haven
Stack Rocks
Little Haven
Broadway
Walton West
Talbenny
The Nab Head
St Brides
Rosepool
Walwyn's Castle
Garland Stone
Skomer Island
Wooltack Point
Deer Park
Mew Stone
Gateholm Island
Marloes
Hasguard
Sandy Haven
St Ishmael's
Herbrandston
Broad Sound
Hoopers Point
Pembrokeshire Coast Path
Dale
Dale Point
The Stack
The Head
Skokholm Island
Rosslare 3¾ hours
St. Ann's Head
Thorn I.
MILFORD HAVEN
Sheep Island
Angle
Angle Bay
Rhoscrowther
Pwllcrochan
Wallaston Green
Newton
Freshwater West
Castlemartin
Blucks Pool
Linney
Linney Head
Crow Rock
Toes
PEMBROKESHIRE COAST NATIONAL PARK
Danger Zone
Warren
St Twynnells
St Petrox
Cheriton
Merrion
Stackpole
Bosherston
Buckspool
The Wash
Saddle Head
Chapel
St Govan's Head
Broad Haven
Stackpole Head
Trewent
Trewent Point
Freshwater East
Hodgeston
Ruins
Lamphey
Lamphey Palace
Upper Nash
Lower Nash
Milton
Kingsfold
Maiden Wells
Hundleton
Pembroke (Penfro)
Monkton
Pembroke Castle
Pembroke Dock (Doc Penfro)
Pennar
Waterloo
Cosheston
Burton Ferry
Burton
Upton
West Williamston Upton Gardens
Neyland
Llanstadwell
Toll
Waterston
Honeyborough
Milford Haven (Aberdaugleddau)
Black Bridge
Hakin
Hubberston
Steynton
Rosemarket
Hill Mountain
Newton Mountain
Houghton
Lawrenny
Sardis
Johnston
Tiers Cross
Robeston West
Robeston Cross
Thornton
North Johnston
Freystrop Cross
Llangwm
Hook
Little Milford
Lower Freystrop
Pope Hill
Ratford Bridge
Boulston
Western Cleddau
Landshipping
Martletwy
Millin Cross
Picton
Minwear
The Rhos
Uzmaston
Merlin's Bridge
Dreenhill
Portfield Gate
Haverfordwest (Hwlffordd)
Albert Town
Priory
Castle Mus & Art Gallery
Pelcomb Bridge
Slade
Prendergast
Sutton
Lambston
Pelcomb Cross
Pelcomb
Keeston
Camrose
Tangiers
Crundale
Poyston Cross
Wiston
Clarbeston Road
Folly
Roch Gate
PEMBROKESHIRE
A40
A477
A4076
A4075
B4327
B4341
B4325
B4322
B4320
B4319
B4330

Milford Haven: *The largest port in Wales and the fifth largest port in the UK.* ***Map ref. B2***

Pendine Sands: *During the 1920s, this was the scene of 5 successful extensions of the world land speed record by the drivers Malcolm Campbell and J G Parry-Thomas. Parry-Thomas was tragically killed here trying to take the record back off Campbell in 1927 – the last attempt at the land speed record made on British 'soil'.* ***Map ref. F2***

191

D
E
F
G
A40–TO LLANDEILO
A48–TO M4
Rhydywrach
Amgoed
Gorfod
Meidrim
Sarnau
Johnstown
Gelly
Clynderwen
Llanfallteg
Llangynin
Bron-y-gaer
Llanllwch
Bethesda
Cwmfelin Boeth
Whitland Abbey
Bancyfelin
Llanddewi Velfrey
Pwll-trap
Croesyceiliog
Llawhaden
Whitland (Hendy-Gwyn)
Llangynog
Ffynnon
Trevaughan
Llwyn-y-brain
Backe
St Clears (Sanclêr)
Llangain
Redstone Bank
Canaston Bridge
Narberth (Arberth)
Crinow
Lampeter Velfrey
CARMARTHENSHIRE
Llan-mill
Brandy Hill
205
Llanddowror
Cwmllyfri
Camp Hill
Cold Blow
Tavernspite
Llandeilo Abercywyn
Llanybri
Princes Gate
Templeton
Cross Hands
Crunwere Farm
Red Roses
Llandawke
Laugharne (Lacharn)
Llansteffan
Ludchurch
Llanteg
Llansadurnen
Plashett
Broadway
Llansteffan Castle
Ferryside (Glanyferi)
Reynalton
Folly Farm
Marros
Brook
Cliff
Wharley Point
Broadway
Thomas Chapel
Loveston
Colby Woodland Garden (NT)
Amroth
Pendine (Pentywyn)
Llanmiloe
East Marsh
Laugharne Burrows
Ginst Point
Broadlay
Llansaint
Begelly
Kilgetty
Jeffreyston
Stepaside
Pendine Sands
Laugharne Sands
St Ishmael
Kidwelly (Cydweli)
Cresselly
Pentlepoir
Broadmoor
East Williamston
Cold Inn
Saundersfoot
Saundersfoot Bay
Llandyry
Redberth
Welsh Motor Sports Centre
Monkstone Point
Great Wedlock Dinosaur Experience
New Hedges
Tenby Roads
Pembrey Forest
Cefn Sidan Sands
Pembrey (Pen-bre)
Tenby (Dinbych-y-pysgod)
Gumfreston
St Catherine's Island
Pembrey Country Park
Norchard
Tudor Merchant's House (NT)
Penally
Lydstep
Giltar Point
Caldey Sound
Monastery
St Margaret's Island
Caldey Island
Priory
Chapel Point
Old Castle Head
CARMARTHEN BAY
Broughton Bay
Burry Holms
Rhossili Bay
Hillend
Rhossili Downs
Rhossili
Worms Head
Middleton
(NT)
Cork to Swansea (Mar-Dec) 10 hours
A40
A477
A4066
A478
A4115
A4075
A484
B4313
B4328
B4314
B4315
B4316
B4318
B4586
B4585
B4299
B4298
B4312

178

Laugharne: *This ancient town is best known for its association with poet and writer Dylan Thomas who lived in the Georgian Boathouse overlooking the River Taf for sixteen years. Dylan Marlais Thomas was born in Swansea on the 27th October 1914 and died in New York on the 9th November 1953. He is buried in Laugharne churchyard.* ***Map ref. G1***

192

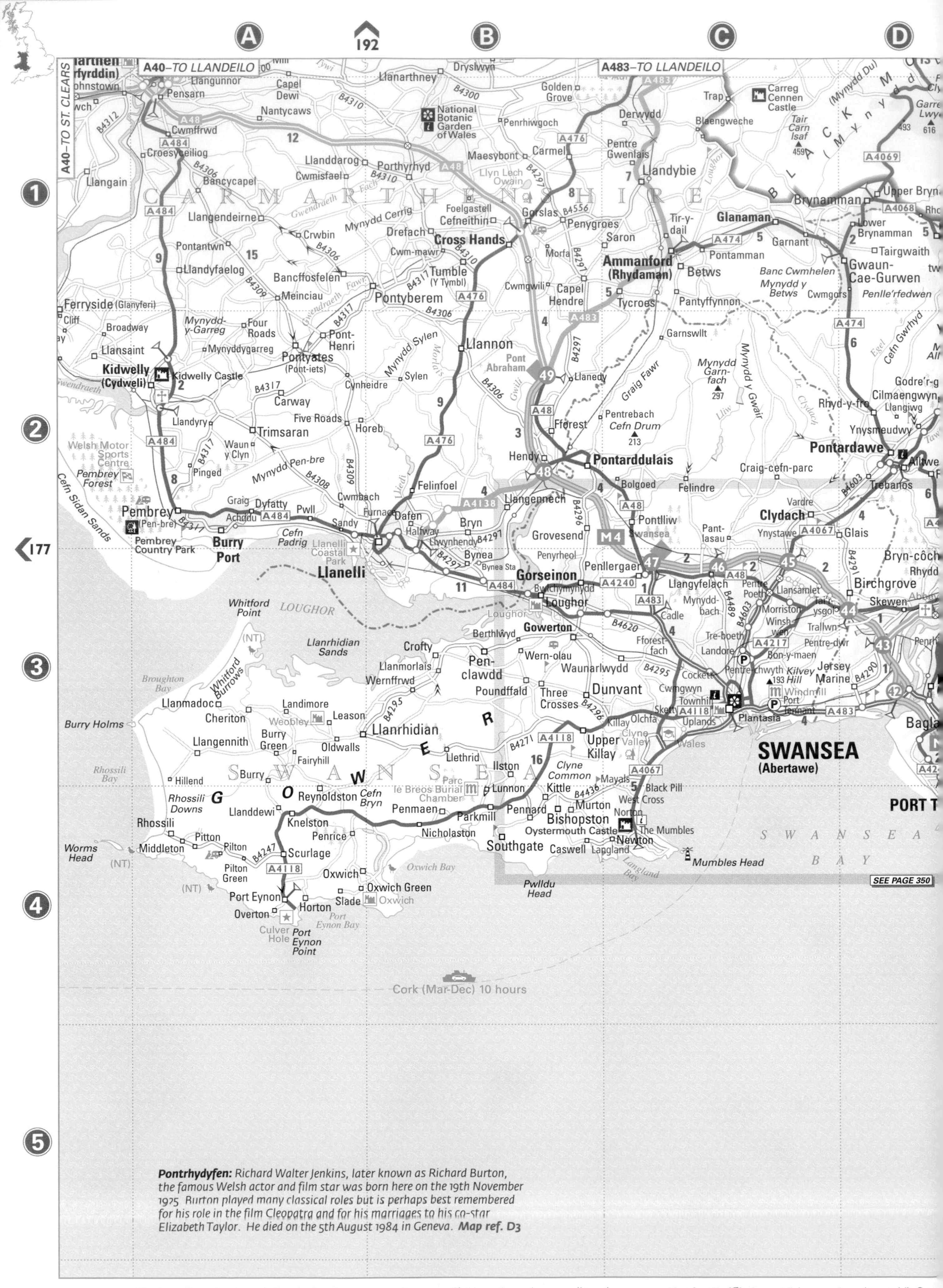
A
B
C
D
1
2
3
4
5
177
A40–TO LLANDEILO
A483–TO LLANDEILO
A40–TO ST. CLEARS
Llangunnor
Pensarn
Cwmffrwd
Croesyceiliog
Llangain
Bancycapel
Capel Dewi
Nantycaws
Llanarthney
Dryslwyn
National Botanic Garden of Wales
Golden Grove
Penrhiwgoch
Llanddarog
Porthyrhyd
Cwmisfael
Maesybont
Carmel
Llyn Lech Owain
Derwydd
Trap
Carreg Cennen Castle
Blaengweche
Tair Carn Isaf
Pentre Gwenlais
Llandybie
CARMARTHENSHIRE
BLACK MOUNTAIN
Brynamman
Upper Brynamman
Lower Brynamman
Llangendeirne
Crwbin
Mynydd Cerrig
Foelgastell
Cefneithin
Gorslas
Penygroes
Tir-y-dail
Glanaman
Garnant
Drefach
Cross Hands
Saron
Pontantwn
Llandyfaelog
Cwm-mawr
Tumble (Y Tymbl)
Morfa
Ammanford (Rhydaman)
Betws
Pontamman
Tairgwaith
Gwaun-Cae-Gurwen
Banc Cwmhelen
Mynydd y Betws
Cwmgors
Penlle'rfedwen
Bancffosfelen
Meinciau
Pontyberem
Cwmgwili
Capel Hendre
Tycroes
Pantyffynnon
Ferryside (Glanyferi)
Cliff
Broadway
Mynydd-y-Garreg
Four Roads
Pont-Henri
Garnswllt
Llansaint
Mynyddygarreg
Pontyates (Pont-iets)
Mynydd Sylen
Llannon
Pont Abraham
Mynydd Garn-fach
Mynydd y Gwair
Cefn Gwrhyd
Kidwelly (Cydweli)
Kidwelly Castle
Cynheidre
Sylen
Llanedy
Graig Fawr
Godre'r-graig
Cilmaengwyn
Llangiwg
Carway
Five Roads
Horeb
Pentrebach
Cefn Drum
Rhyd-y-fro
Ynysmeudwy
Landyry
Trimsaran
Fforest
Welsh Motor Sports Centre
Waun y Clyn
Mynydd Pen-bre
Hendy
Pontarddulais
Pontardawe
Alltwen
Craig-cefn-parc
Trebanos
Pembrey Forest
Pinged
Felinfoel
Bolgoed
Felindre
Vardre
Cefn Sidan Sands
Graig
Dyfatty
Achddu
Pwll
Cwmbach
Llangennech
Clydach
Pembrey (Pen-bre)
Pembrey Country Park
Burry Port
Cefn Padrig
Llanelli Coastal Park
Llanelli
Sandy
Furnace
Dafen
Halfway
Llwynhendy
Bryn
Bynea
Bynea Sta
Grovesend
Pontlliw
Pant-lasau
Ynystawe
Glais
Penyrheol
Penllergaer
Gorseinon
Bwlchymynydd
Loughor
Llangyfelach
Mynydd-bach
Birchgrove
Pentre Poeth
Llansamlet
Tair-ysgol
Skewen
Bryn-côch
Rhydding
Whitford Point
LOUGHOR
Llanrhidian Sands
Berthlwyd
Gowerton
Cadle
Morriston
Winsh-wen
Trallwn
Tre-boeth
Fforest-fach
Landore
Bôn-y-maen
Pentre-dŵr
Crofty
Llanmorlais
Wernffrwd
Pen-clawdd
Wern-olau
Waunarlwydd
Cockett
Pentrechwyth
Kilvey Hill
Jersey Marine
Broughton Bay
Whitford Burrows
Llanmadoc
Cheriton
Landimore
Weobley
Leason
Poundffald
Three Crosses
Dunvant
Cwmgwyn
Townhill
Windmill
Port Tennant
Burry Holms
Llangennith
Burry Green
Oldwalls
Llanrhidian
Killay
Olchfa
Sketty
Uplands
Plantasia
Upper Killay
Clyne Valley
Wales
SWANSEA (Abertawe)
Baglan
Fairyhill
Llethrid
Ilston
Clyne Common
Rhossili Bay
Hillend
Burry
GOWER
SWANSEA
Parc le Breos Burial Chamber
Lunnon
Kittle
Mayals
Black Pill
West Cross
PORT TALBOT
Rhossili Downs
Llanddewi
Reynoldston
Cefn Bryn
Penmaen
Parkmill
Pennard
Murton
Norton
Bishopston
Rhossili
Knelston
Pitton
Penrice
Nicholaston
Southgate
Oystermouth Castle
The Mumbles
Newton
SWANSEA BAY
Worms Head
Middleton
Pilton
Scurlage
Caswell
Langland
Langland Bay
Mumbles Head
Pilton Green
Oxwich
Oxwich Bay
Pwlldu Head
SEE PAGE 350
Port Eynon
Oxwich Green
Slade
Horton
Overton
Port Eynon Bay
Culver Hole
Port Eynon Point
Cork (Mar-Dec) 10 hours
Pontrhydyfen: Richard Walter Jenkins, later known as Richard Burton, the famous Welsh actor and film star was born here on the 19th November 1925. Burton played many classical roles but is perhaps best remembered for his role in the film Cleopatra and for his marriages to his co-star Elizabeth Taylor. He died on the 5th August 1984 in Geneva. **Map ref. D3**

The Mumbles: *On the 25th March 1807 the first ever passenger railway service in the world was opened between here and Swansea. Prior to the opening of The Swansea and Mumbles Railway, the only route between the two places was along the beach.* ***Map ref. C4***

Swansea: *Sir Harry Secombe, comedian, singer, film star and writer was born in the St Thomas area of Swansea on the 8th September 1921. Sir Harry is best remembered as Neddy Seagoon, a member of the 'Goon Show'. He died aged 79 on the 12th April 2001.* ***Map ref. C3***

Merthyr Tydfil: *On 21st February 1804 the world's first steam railway engine, built by Richard Trevithick, successfully hauled 70 passengers and 10 tons of iron on the 9 mile (14km) route from Merthyr to Abercynon.* ***Map ref. G2***

D
E
193
F
G
FFOREST FAWR
A470–TO BRECON
BRECON BEACONS (BANNAU BRYCHEINIOG)
POWYS
A465–TO ABERGAVENNY
180
RHONDDA
NEATH
PORT TALBOT
AFAN FOREST PARK
VALE OF NEATH
CYNON
TAFF
BRIDGEND
MERTHYR
VALE OF GLAMORGAN
CARDIFF
M4–TO NEWPORT
A48–TO CARDIFF
MERTHYR TYDFIL
Aberdare
Mountain Ash (Aberpennar)
Pontypridd
Porth
Ferndale
Treorchy
Tonypandy
Maesteg
Pyle
Porthcawl
BRIDGEND (Pen-y-Bont ar Ogwr)
Pencoed
Llantrisant
Cowbridge
Ystradgynlais
Glynneath (Glyn-Nedd)
Hirwaun
Resolven
Aberdulais
Abercynon
Nelson
Church Village
Beddau
Llanharan
Pontyclun
Tonyrefail
Gilfach Goch
Ogmore Vale
Pontycymer
Aberkenfig
Ogmore-by-Sea
Southerndown
Llantwit Fardre
Ystrad Mynach
1
2
3
4
5
164

Aberfan: *At 9.15 am on Friday 21st October 1966 a coal waste tip, made unstable by heavy rain, slid down a Welsh mountainside engulfing the Pantglas Junior School and almost twenty houses in the small village of Aberfan. The disaster happened so quickly that nobody was rescued after 11am on hat day and 116 school children, half of the entire school, and 5 of their teachers were amongst the dead. After a week of round the clock digging, the final death toll was confirmed as 144.* ***Map ref. G2***

164

Llantrisant: *Famous as the town which houses The Royal Mint. Here they produce all the currency for the UK. The Royal Mint is Britain's oldest surviving business, having been founded in London in 886.* ***Map ref. G4***

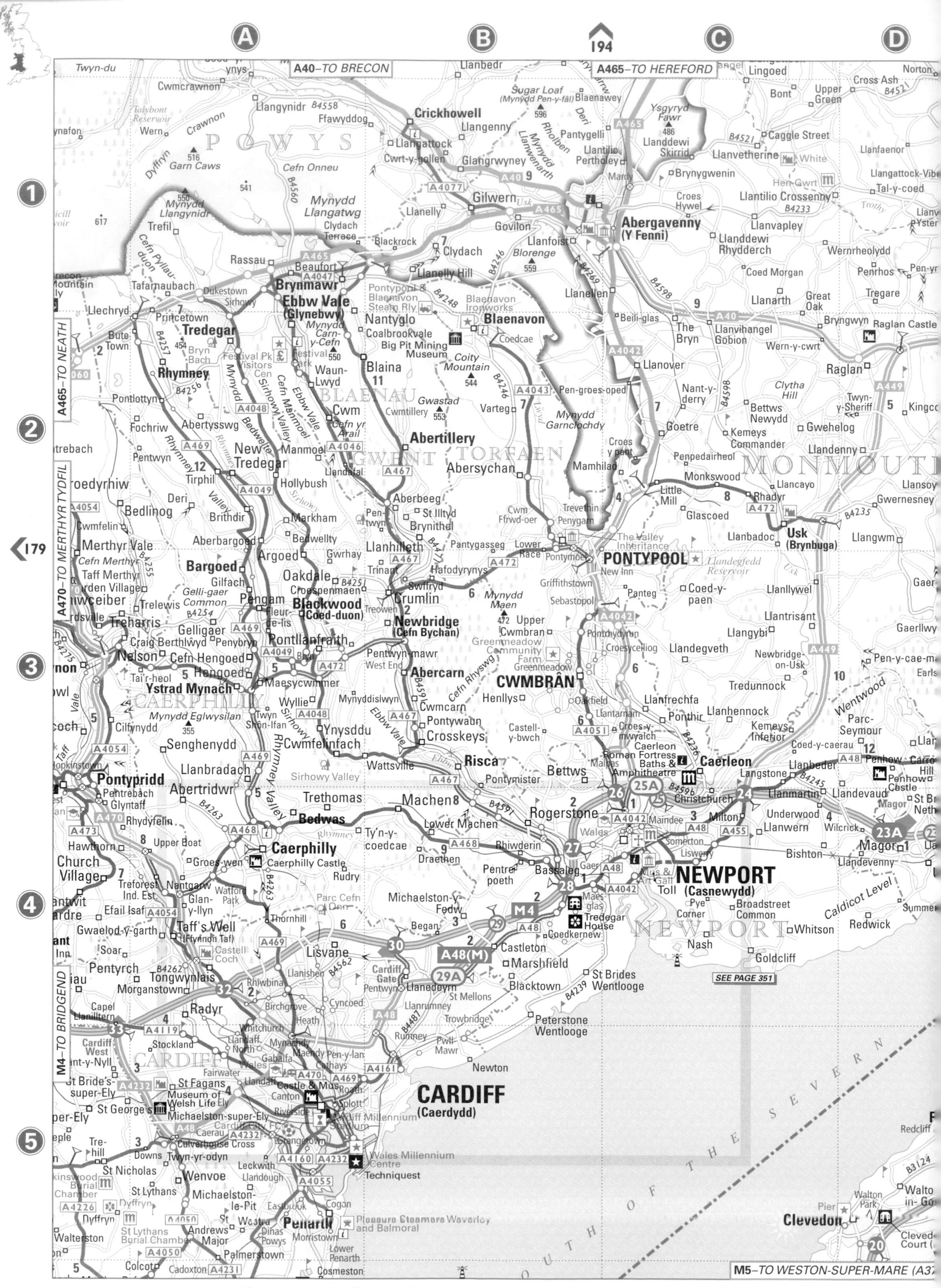

A
B
194
C
D
A40–TO BRECON
A465–TO HEREFORD
Twyn-du
Cwmcrawnon
Llangynidr
Talybont Reservoir
Wern
Crawnon
POWYS
516
Garn Caws
Cefn Onneu
Ffawyddog
Crickhowell
Llangenny
Llangattock
Cwrt-y-gollen
Glangrwyney
Llanbedr
Sugar Loaf (Mynydd Pen-y-fâl)
596
Blaenawey
Pantygelli
Llantilio Pertholey
Mardy
Ysgyryd Fawr
486
Llanddewi Skirrid
Llanvetherine
White
Lingoed
Bont
Upper Green
Cross Ash
Norton
Caggle Street
Llanfaenor
Llangattock-Vibon-Avel
Brynygwenin
Hen Gwrt
Llantilio Crossenny
Tal-y-coed
Croes Hywel
Llanvapley
Abergavenny (Y Fenni)
Llanddewi Rhydderch
Wernrheolydd
Coed Morgan
Penrhos
Tregare
Llanarth
Great Oak
Bryngwyn
Raglan Castle
Raglan
550
Mynydd Llangynidr
541
Mynydd Llangatwg
617
Trefil
Clydach Terrace
Gilwern
Llanelly
Govilon
Llanfoist
Blorenge
559
Blackrock
Clydach
Llanelly Hill
Rassau
Beaufort
Brynmawr
Tafarnaubach
Dukestown
Sirhowy
Ebbw Vale (Glynebwy)
Pontypool & Blaenavon Steam Rly
Blaenavon Ironworks
Blaenavon
Coedcae
Llanellen
Llanover
Beili-glas
The Bryn
Llanvihangel Gobion
Wern-y-cwrt
Llechryd
Princetown
Tredegar
Bute Town
454
Bryn Bach
Festival Pk Visitors Cen
Mynydd Carn-y-Cefn
550
Festival Park
Nantyglo
Coalbrookvale
Big Pit Mining Museum
Coity Mountain
544
Blaina
Waun-Lwyd
Rhymney
Pontlottyn
Fochriw
Abertysswg
BLAENAU GWENT
Cwm
Cefn yr Arail
Gwastad
553
Cwmtillery
Abertillery
Varteg
Pen-groes-oped
Nant-y-derry
Goetre
Clytha Hill
Bettws Newydd
Kemeys Commander
Twyn-y-Sheriff
Gwehelog
Kingcoed
A465–TO NEATH
Pentwyn
New Tredegar
Manmoel
Llandafal
TORFAEN
Abersychan
Mynydd Garnclochdy
Croes y pant
Mamhilad
Penpedairheol
Monkswood
Llandenny
MONMOUTHSHIRE
Tirphil
Deri
Bedlinog
Brithdir
Hollybush
Aberbeeg
St Illtyd
Brynithel
Cwm Ffrwd-oer
Penygarn
Trevethin
Little Mill
Glascoed
Rhadyr
Llancayo
Llansoy
Gwernesney
Usk (Brynbuga)
Llangwm
A470–TO MERTHYR TYDFIL
Merthyr Vale
Cefn Merthyr
Taff Merthyr Garden Village
Aberbargoed
Markham
Bedwellty
Argoed
Gwrhay
Llanhilleth
Pantygasseg
Lower Race
Pontymoel
PONTYPOOL
Llandegfedd Reservoir
New Inn
The Valley Inheritance
Llanbadoc
Bargoed
Gilfach
Gelli-gaer Common
Trelewis
Oakdale
Croespenmaen
Trinant
Hafodyrynys
Swffryd
Crumlin
Mynydd Maen
472
Griffithstown
Sebastopol
Panteg
Coed-y-paen
Llanllywel
Gaer-fawr
Treharris
Gelligaer
Pengam
Fleur-de-lis
Blackwood (Coed-duon)
Treowen
Newbridge (Cefn Bychan)
Upper Cwmbran
Greenmeadow Community Farm
Pontrhydyrun
Croesyceiliog
Llantrisant
Llangybi
Llandegveth
Newbridge-on-Usk
Gaerllwyd
Pen-y-cae-mawr
Earlswood
Craig Berthlwyd
Penybryn
Nelson
Cefn Hengoed
Hengoed
Tai'r-heol
Pontllanfraith
Pentwyn-mawr
West End
Abercarn
Cefn Rhyswg
CWMBRÂN
Henllys
Oakfield
Llantarnam
Llanfrechfa
Tredunnock
Llanhennock
Ponthir
Kemeys Inferior
Parc-Seymour
Wentwood
Ystrad Mynach
Maesycwmmer
CAERPHILLY
Mynydd Eglwysilan
355
Cilfynydd
Senghenydd
Wyllie
Twyn Shôn-Ifan
Ynysddu
Cwmfelinfach
Mynyddislwyn
Cwmcarn
Pontywaun
Crosskeys
Castell-y-bwch
Croes-y-mwyalch
Caerleon
Roman Fortress Baths & Amphitheatre
Coed-y-caerau
Penhow
Penhow Castle
Carrow Hill
Pontypridd
Pentrebach
Glyntaff
Llanbradach
Abertridwr
Sirhowy Valley
Wattsville
Risca
Bettws
Pontymister
Langstone
Llanbeder
Llanmartin
Llandevaud
Christchurch
Caerleon
St Brides Netherwent
Magor
Rhydyfelin
Hawthorn
Upper Boat
Trethomas
Bedwas
Machen
Lower Machen
Rogerstone
Maindee
Milton
Underwood
Llanwern
Wilcrick
Caerphilly
Caerphilly Castle
Groes-wen
Ty'n-y-coedcae
Draethen
Rhiwderin
Bassaleg
Somerton
Liswerry
Bishton
Magor
Llandevenny
Church Village
Treforest Ind. Est.
Nantgarw
Watford Park
Rudry
Parc Cefn Onn
Pentre-poeth
Gaer
NEWPORT (Casnewydd)
Toll
Pye Corner
Broadstreet Common
Caldicot Level
Summerleaze
Redwick
Efail Isaf
Glan-y-llyn
Thornhill
Michaelston-y-Fedw
Maes-glas
Tredegar House
Coedkernew
NEWPORT
Nash
Whitson
Goldcliff
Gwaelod-y-garth
Taff's Well (Ffynnon Taf)
Began
Castleton
Marshfield
Soar
Castell Coch
Lisvane
Llanishen
Cardiff Gate
Pentwyn
Llanedeyrn
St Mellons
Blacktown
St Brides Wentlooge
SEE PAGE 351
Pentyrch
Tongwynlais
Morganstown
Rhiwbina
Birchgrove
Cyncoed
Llanrumney
Trowbridge
Peterstone Wentlooge
M4–TO BRIDGEND
Capel Llanilltern
Radyr
Whitchurch
Heath
Rumney
Pwll-Mawr
Cardiff West
Stockland
Llandaff North
Gabalfa
Roath
Cathays
Newton
CARDIFF
St Bride's-super-Ely
St Fagans
Museum of Welsh Life
Fairwater
Llandaff
Castle & Mus
Canton
Splott
CARDIFF (Caerdydd)
St George's
Michaelston-super-Ely
Cardiff City FC
Caerau
Riverside
Millennium Stadium
Culverhouse Cross
Grangetown
Wales Millennium Centre
Techniquest
Tre-hill
Downs
Twyn-yr-odyn
Leckwith
Llandough
St Nicholas
Tinkinswood Burial Chamber
Wenvoe
St Lythans
Michaelston-le-Pit
Dyffryn
Eastbrook
Cogan
St Andrews Major
Penarth
Pleasure Steamers Waverley and Balmoral
Dinas Powys
Morristown
Walterston
St Lythans Burial Chamber
Palmerstown
Lower Penarth
Colcot
Cadoxton
Cosmeston
SOUTH OF THE SEVERN
Redcliff Bay
Walton Park
Walton-in-Gordano
Pier
Clevedon
Clevedon Court
M5–TO WESTON-SUPER-MARE (A370)
179
1
2
3
4
5

165

River Severn Road Bridges: *The first Severn Road Bridge, which linked the M4 motorway to South Wales, was opened by the Queen on the 8th September 1966. The bridge is in two parts, the first crosses the River Severn and replaced the old Beachley to Aust ferry. The second part spans the River Wye near Chepstow. The main span is 3,240 feet (987m), the tops of the towers reach 445 feet (135.5m) and the structure is built to withstand 100 mph (160km/h) winds. The second Severn Bridge joining England and Wales was opened on the 5th June 1996. It is almost 3.2 miles (5km) long and the pylon heights reach 449 feet (137m). This bridge is reputed to have cost over £300m.* ***Map ref. E4***

D E 195 F G

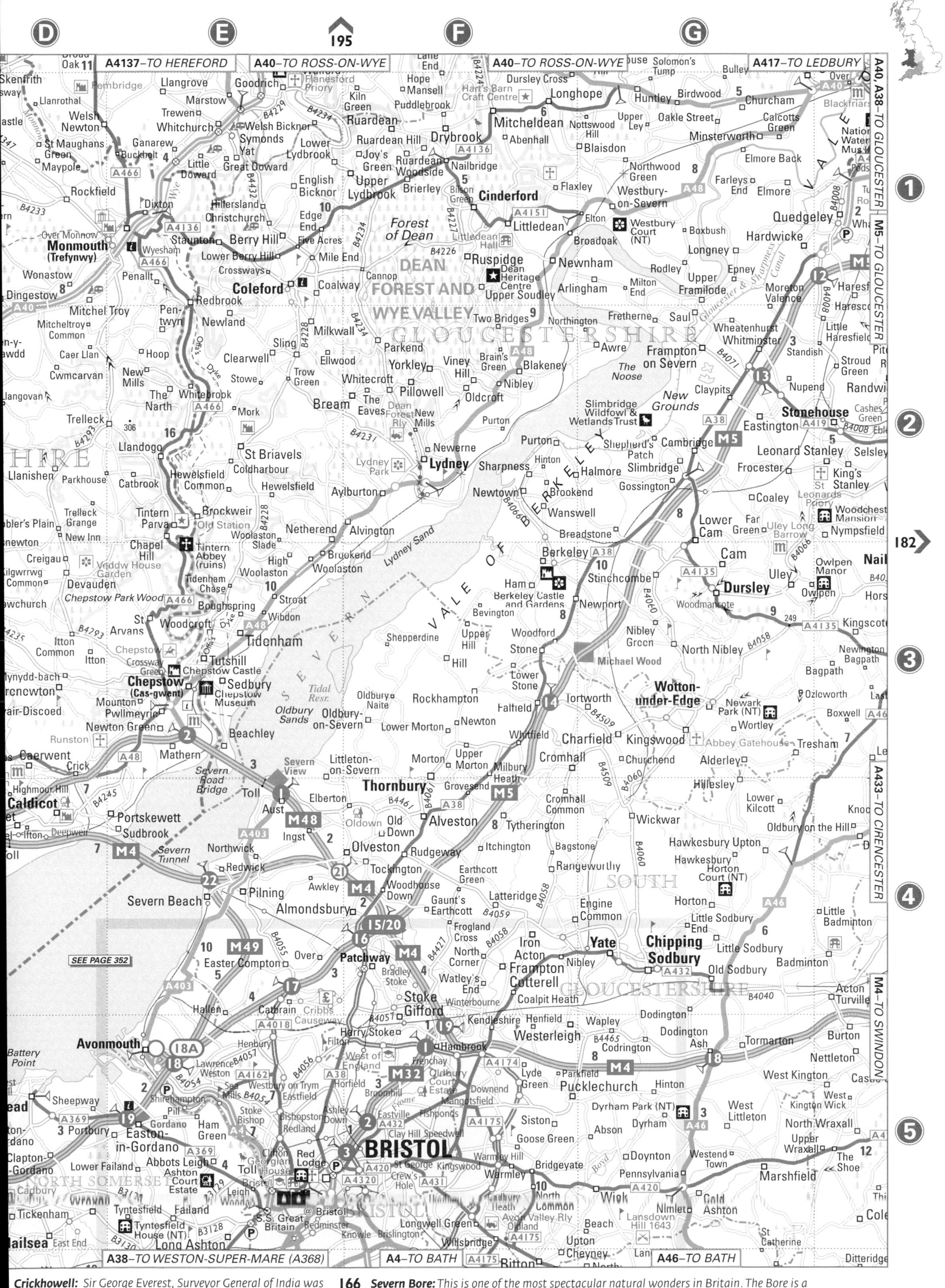
A4137–TO HEREFORD
A40–TO ROSS-ON-WYE
A40–TO ROSS-ON-WYE
A417–TO LEDBURY
A40, A38–TO GLOUCESTER
M5–TO GLOUCESTER
A433–TO CIRENCESTER
M4–TO SWINDON
A38–TO WESTON-SUPER-MARE (A368)
A4–TO BATH
A46–TO BATH
SEE PAGE 352
Monmouth
(Trefynwy)
Coleford
Cinderford
Mitcheldean
Longhope
Newnham
Lydney
Chepstow
(Cas-gwent)
Caldicot
Thornbury
Dursley
Wotton-under-Edge
Chipping Sodbury
Yate
Stonehouse
Avonmouth
BRISTOL
DEAN FOREST AND WYE VALLEY
Forest of Dean
GLOUCESTERSHIRE
SOUTH GLOUCESTERSHIRE
NORTH SOMERSET
VALE OF BERKELEY
SEVERN
Slimbridge Wildfowl & Wetlands Trust
Berkeley Castle and Gardens
Chepstow Castle
Tintern Abbey (ruins)
Severn Road Bridge
Severn Tunnel
Quedgeley
Berkeley
Frampton on Severn
Michael Wood

Crickhowell: *Sir George Everest, Surveyor General of India was born here in 1790. Everest spent over 25 years of his life mapping India and was the first person to survey the Himalayas. He was knighted in 1861 and the highest peak in the Himalayas was officially named after him in 1865.* ***Map ref. B1***

166

Severn Bore: *This is one of the most spectacular natural wonders in Britain. The Bore is a large 'surge wave' caused by the huge tidal range and shape of the river estuary. It can reach up to 10 feet (3m) in height and travel at up to 13 mph (21km/h). The best Bores usually occur ahead of the spring tide and travel up the river for over 20 miles (32km) between Awre and Gloucester. The Severn is also Britain's longest river at 220 miles (354km).* ***Map ref. G2***

182

196

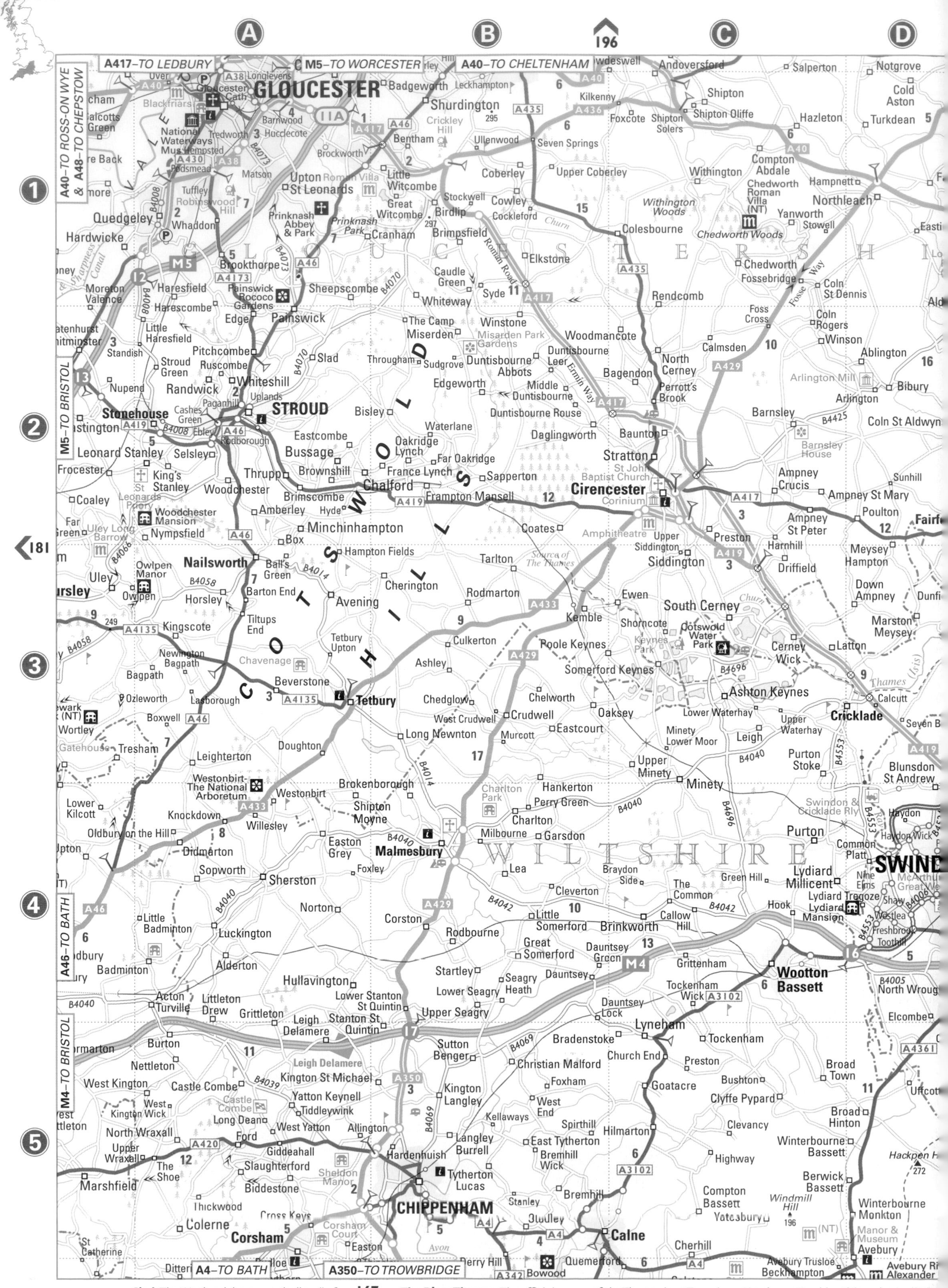

A
B
C
D
1
2
3
4
5
A417–TO LEDBURY
M5–TO WORCESTER
A40–TO CHELTENHAM
A40–TO ROSS-ON WYE & A48–TO CHEPSTOW
M5–TO BRISTOL
A46–TO BATH
M4–TO BRISTOL
A4–TO BATH
A350–TO TROWBRIDGE
GLOUCESTER
STROUD
Stonehouse
Nailsworth
Tetbury
Malmesbury
CHIPPENHAM
Corsham
Calne
Cirencester
Wootton Bassett
Cricklade
Lyneham
C O T S W O L D   H I L L S
W I L T S H I R E
G L O U C E S T E R S H I R E
Andoversford
Shipton
Shipton Oliffe
Salperton
Notgrove
Cold Aston
Hazleton
Turkdean
Badgeworth
Shurdington
Leckhampton
Crickley Hill
Bentham
Brockworth
Ullenwood
Seven Springs
Upper Coberley
Coberley
Cowley
Cockleford
Withington
Withington Woods
Compton Abdale
Chedworth Roman Villa (NT)
Chedworth Woods
Hampnett
Northleach
Yanworth
Stowell
Colesbourne
Little Witcombe
Great Witcombe
Upton St Leonards
Birdlip
Brimpsfield
Cranham
Prinknash Abbey & Park
Prinknash Park
Stockwell
Elkstone
Chedworth
Fossebridge
Coln St Dennis
Quedgeley
Hardwicke
Whaddon
Tuffley
Robinswood Hill
Matson
Barnwood
Hucclecote
Tredworth
National Waterways Museum
Hempsted
Podsmead
Brookthorpe
Haresfield
Harescombe
Painswick
Painswick Rococo Gardens
Edge
Sheepscombe
Caudle Green
Syde
Whiteway
Rendcomb
Foss Cross
Coln Rogers
Winson
Moreton Valence
Little Haresfield
Standish
Pitchcombe
Ruscombe
Stroud Green
Whiteshill
Randwick
Nupend
Slad
The Camp
Miserden
Misarden Park Gardens
Througham
Sudgrove
Winstone
Duntisbourne Abbots
Duntisbourne Leer
Middle Duntisbourne
Duntisbourne Rouse
Woodmancote
North Cerney
Bagendon
Perrott's Brook
Calmsden
Ablington
Arlington Mill
Arlington
Bibury
Edgeworth
Bisley
Waterlane
Daglingworth
Baunton
Stratton
Barnsley
Barnsley House
Coln St Aldwyn
Eastcombe
Bussage
Oakridge Lynch
Far Oakridge
France Lynch
Brownshill
Chalford
Sapperton
Thrupp
Brimscombe
Frampton Mansell
Ampney Crucis
Ampney St Mary
Ampney St Peter
Sunhill
Poulton
Fairford
Leonard Stanley
Selsley
Frocester
King's Stanley
Woodchester
Coaley
Woodchester Mansion
Nympsfield
Uley
Owlpen Manor
Owlpen
Amberley
Minchinhampton
Box
Hampton Fields
Coates
Tarlton
Upper Siddington
Siddington
Preston
Harnhill
Driffield
Meysey Hampton
Down Ampney
Ball's Green
Barton End
Horsley
Avening
Cherington
Rodmarton
Ewen
Kemble
South Cerney
Cerney Wick
Marston Meysey
Kingscote
Tiltups End
Tetbury Upton
Culkerton
Ashley
Shorncote
Cotswold Water Park
Keynes Park
Poole Keynes
Somerford Keynes
Latton
Newington Bagpath
Bagpath
Chavenage
Beverstone
Ozleworth
Lasborough
Boxwell
Tresham
Chedglow
West Crudwell
Crudwell
Chelworth
Oaksey
Eastcourt
Murcott
Long Newton
Ashton Keynes
Lower Waterhay
Upper Waterhay
Minety Lower Moor
Leigh
Calcutt
Seven Bridges
Leighterton
Doughton
Upper Minety
Minety
Purton Stoke
Blunsdon St Andrew
Westonbirt - The National Arboretum
Westonbirt
Brokenborough
Shipton Moyne
Charlton Park
Hankerton
Perry Green
Charlton
Swindon & Cricklade Rly
Lower Kilcott
Knockdown
Willesley
Oldbury on the Hill
Didmarton
Easton Grey
Milbourne
Garsdon
Purton
Common Platt
Haydon
Haydon Wick
SWINDON
Sopworth
Sherston
Foxley
Lea
Braydon Side
The Common
Green Hill
Lydiard Millicent
Lydiard Tregoze
Lydiard Mansion
Cleverton
Little Badminton
Norton
Corston
Little Somerford
Callow Hill
Hook
Brinkworth
Luckington
Rodbourne
Great Somerford
Dauntsey Green
Grittenham
Freshbrook
Toothill
Badminton
Alderton
Startley
Seagry Heath
Dauntsey
Tockenham Wick
North Wroughton
Acton Turville
Littleton Drew
Grittleton
Hullavington
Lower Seagry
Lower Stanton St Quintin
Upper Seagry
Dauntsey Lock
Elcombe
Leigh Delamere
Stanton St Quintin
Burton
Sutton Benger
Bradenstoke
Tockenham
Christian Malford
Church End
Preston
Broad Town
Nettleton
Kington St Michael
Yatton Keynell
Tiddleywink
West Kington
Castle Combe
Kington Langley
Foxham
Goatacre
Bushton
Clyffe Pypard
Uffcott
Kington Wick
West Yatton
Long Dean
Allington
Kellaways
West End
Spirthill
Hilmarton
Clevancy
Broad Hinton
North Wraxall
Ford
Langley Burrell
East Tytherton
Bremhill Wick
Winterbourne Bassett
Upper Wraxall
Giddeahall
Hardenhuish
The Shoe
Slaughterford
Tytherton Lucas
Highway
Hackpen Hill
Marshfield
Sheldon Manor
Biddestone
Bremhill
Berwick Bassett
Compton Bassett
Windmill Hill
Yatesbury
Winterbourne Monkton
Thickwood
Colerne
Cross Keys
Stanley
Studley
Corsham Court
Easton
Manor & Museum
Avebury
Cherhill
Quemerford
Bowood
Avebury Trusloe
Beckhampton
St Catherine
Ditteridge
Derry Hill
Avon
Thames
Churn
Fosse Way
Ermin Way
Roman Road
Source of The Thames
Amphitheatre
Corinium
St John Baptist Church

Slad: The Woolpack here was the 'local' of the writer Laurie Lee. The pub features in his most famous book 'Cider with Rosie'. Laurie Lee died in 1997 and is buried in the churchyard just across the road. ***Map ref.*** ***A2***

The River Thames: The official source of the Thames is at Trewsbury Mead near Kemble. Although very little water is visible at this point, a stone marks the exact spot. From its source the River Thames journeys some 215 miles (346km) to the North Sea, making it England's longest river, with 191 miles (307km), from Lechlade, being navigable waterway. Below Teddington Lock the river is tidal although it remains as fresh water down as far as Battersea. ***Map ref.*** ***B3***

181

167

197

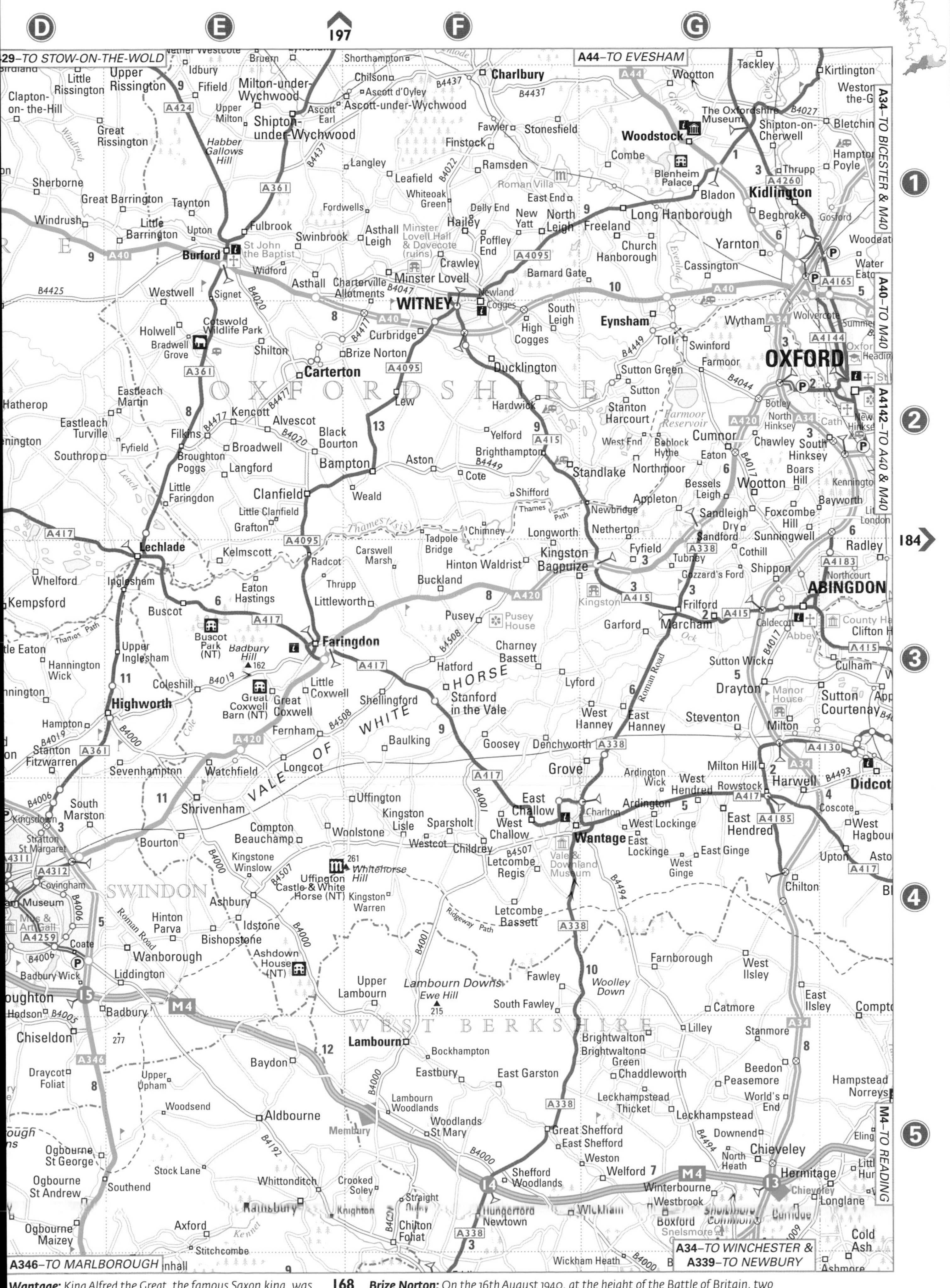
D
E
F
G
A429–TO STOW-ON-THE-WOLD
A44–TO EVESHAM
A34–TO BICESTER & M40
A40–TO M40
A4142–TO A40 & M40
M4–TO READING
A34–TO WINCHESTER &
A339–TO NEWBURY
A346–TO MARLBOROUGH
1
2
3
4
5
Little Rissington
Upper Rissington
Idbury
Bruern
Fifield
Milton-under-Wychwood
Shorthampton
Chilson
Ascott d'Oyley
Ascott-under-Wychwood
Charlbury
Wootton
Tackley
Kirtlington
Weston-on-the-Green
Clapton-on-the-Hill
Upper Milton
Shipton-under-Wychwood
Great Rissington
Habber Gallows Hill
Fawler
Stonesfield
Woodstock
The Oxfordshire Museum
Shipton-on-Cherwell
Bletchingdon
Hampton Poyle
Finstock
Langley
Leafield
Ramsden
Combe
Blenheim Palace
Thrupp
Sherborne
Great Barrington
Taynton
Whiteoak Green
Roman Villa
East End
Bladon
Kidlington
Fordwells
Delly End
New Yatt
North Leigh
Freeland
Long Hanborough
Begbroke
Gosford
Windrush
Little Barrington
Upton
Fulbrook
Swinbrook
Asthall Leigh
Minster Lovell Hall & Dovecote (ruins)
Hailey
Poffley End
Church Hanborough
Yarnton
Woodeaton
Burford
St John the Baptist
Crawley
Cassington
Water Eaton
Widford
Minster Lovell
Barnard Gate
Westwell
Signet
Asthall
Charterville Allotments
WITNEY
Newland
Cogges
South Leigh
Eynsham
Wytham
Wolvercote
Holwell
Cotswold Wildlife Park
Curbridge
High Cogges
Toll
Swinford
Bradwell Grove
Shilton
Brize Norton
Farmoor
OXFORD
Carterton
Ducklington
Sutton Green
Sutton
OXFORDSHIRE
Eastleach Martin
Lew
Hardwick
Stanton Harcourt
Farmoor Reservoir
Botley
North Hinksey
Hatherop
Kencott
Alvescot
Eastleach Turville
Black Bourton
Yelford
Cumnor
Chawley
South Hinksey
Filkins
Broadwell
Fyfield
Brighthampton
West End
Bablock Hythe
Eaton
Southrop
Broughton Poggs
Langford
Bampton
Aston
Cote
Standlake
Northmoor
Boars Hill
Kennington
Little Faringdon
Clanfield
Weald
Shifford
Bessels Leigh
Wootton
Appleton
Bayworth
Little Clanfield
Newbridge
Sandleigh
Foxcombe Hill
Grafton
Thames (Isis)
Chimney
Longworth
Netherton
Dry Sandford
Sunningwell
Radley
Lechlade
Kelmscott
Carswell Marsh
Tadpole Bridge
Kingston Bagpuize
Fyfield
Tubney
Cothill
Radcot
Hinton Waldrist
Gozzard's Ford
Shippon
Northcourt
Whelford
Inglesham
Eaton Hastings
Thrupp
Buckland
Kingston
Frilford
ABINGDON
Kempsford
Buscot
Littleworth
Pusey
Pusey House
Garford
Marcham
Caldecott
County Hall
Buscot Park (NT)
Badbury Hill
Faringdon
Charney Bassett
Ock
Abbey
Clifton Hampden
Upper Inglesham
Hannington Wick
Hatford
Sutton Wick
Culham
Little Coxwell
Lyford
Drayton
Manor House
Sutton Courtenay
Highworth
Coleshill
Great Coxwell Barn (NT)
Great Coxwell
Shellingford
Stanford in the Vale
West Hanney
East Hanney
Steventon
Milton
Hampton
Fernham
WHITE HORSE
Baulking
Goosey
Denchworth
Stanton Fitzwarren
Sevenhampton
Watchfield
Longcot
VALE OF
Grove
Ardington Wick
West Hendred
Milton Hill
Rowstock
Harwell
Didcot
South Marston
Shrivenham
Uffington
East Challow
Ardington
Kingston Lisle
Sparsholt
West Challow
Wantage
Charlton
West Lockinge
East Hendred
Coscote
West Hagbourne
Stratton St Margaret
Compton Beauchamp
Woolstone
Westcot
Childrey
East Lockinge
East Ginge
Bourton
Kingstone Winslow
Letcombe Regis
Vale & Downland Museum
West Ginge
Upton
Aston
SWINDON
Covingham
Uffington Castle & White Horse (NT)
Whitehorse Hill
Kingston Warren
Ashbury
Museum
Chilton
Hinton Parva
Idstone
Letcombe Bassett
Ridgeway Path
Coate
Bishopstone
Wanborough
Ashdown House (NT)
Farnborough
West Ilsley
Badbury Wick
Liddington
Upper Lambourn
Lambourn Downs
Ewe Hill
Fawley
Woolley Down
East Ilsley
Compton
Hodson
Badbury
South Fawley
Catmore
Chiseldon
WEST BERKSHIRE
Lilley
Stanmore
Lambourn
Brightwalton
Brightwalton Green
Bockhampton
Baydon
Beedon
Draycot Foliat
Upper Upham
Eastbury
East Garston
Chaddleworth
Peasemore
Hampstead Norreys
Woodsend
Lambourn Woodlands
Leckhampstead Thicket
World's End
Aldbourne
Membury
Leckhampstead
Woodlands St Mary
Great Shefford
Downend
Ogbourne St George
East Shefford
Chieveley
Weston
North Heath
Stock Lane
Welford
Shefford Woodlands
Hermitage
Ogbourne St Andrew
Southend
Whittonditch
Crooked Soley
Winterbourne
Chieveley
Longlane
Straight Soley
Westbrook
Ramsbury
Knighton
Hungerford Newtown
Wickham
Shalbourne Common
Curridge
Boxford
Ogbourne Maizey
Axford
Chilton Foliat
Snelsmore
Cold Ash
Stitchcombe
Wickham Heath
Ashmore

Wantage: *King Alfred the Great, the famous Saxon king, was born here in AD849. Renowned for defending his kingdom against the Vikings, and for burning the cakes, Alfred died in AD899 at the age of 50 and is buried in Winchester Cathedral.* ***Map ref. F4***

Brize Norton: *On the 16th August 1940, at the height of the Battle of Britain, two maraurdering German Junkers 88 bombers attacked the RAF station at Brize Norton destroying 46 British aircraft which were still in the hangers of the maintenance unit and training school.* ***Map ref. E2***

168

184

A B C D

198

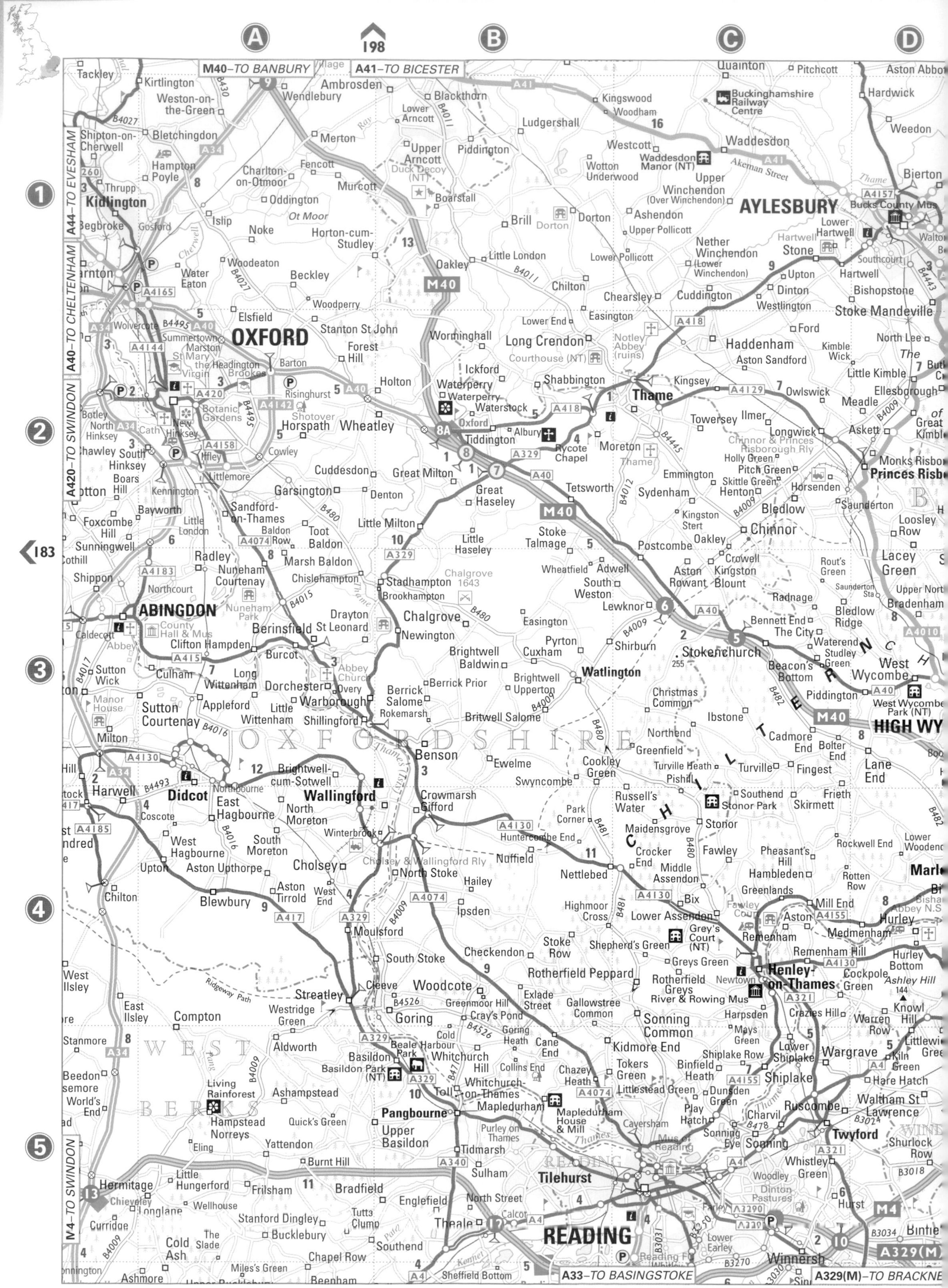

M40–TO BANBURY
A41–TO BICESTER
A44–TO EVESHAM
A40–TO CHELTENHAM
A420–TO SWINDON
M4–TO SWINDON
A33–TO BASINGSTOKE
A329(M)–TO BRACKNE
OXFORD
AYLESBURY
ABINGDON
READING
Kidlington
Thame
Didcot
Wallingford
Henley-on-Thames
Watlington
Chinnor
Princes Risb
West Wycombe
HIGH WY
Twyford
Tilehurst
Pangbourne
Goring
Benson
Chalgrove
Wheatley
Haddenham
Stokenchurch
Waddesdon
Bicester
O X F O R D S H I R E
C H I L T E R N
W E S T B E R K S

1
2
3
4
5

183

170

Oxford University is the oldest English-speaking university in the world, having been founded over 900 years ago. During this time it has provided the world with 40 Nobel prize-winners and the country with 25 Prime Ministers. *Map ref. A2*

Beaconsfield: *Although born in East Dulwich on the 11th August 1897, Enid Blyton, creator of 'Noddy' and 'The Famous Five', lived here, in Penn Road, Beaconsfield from 1938 up to her death in 1968. During her lifetime she wrote over 700 books which were translated into 40 different languages and sold over 400 million copies worldwide.* **Map ref. E3**

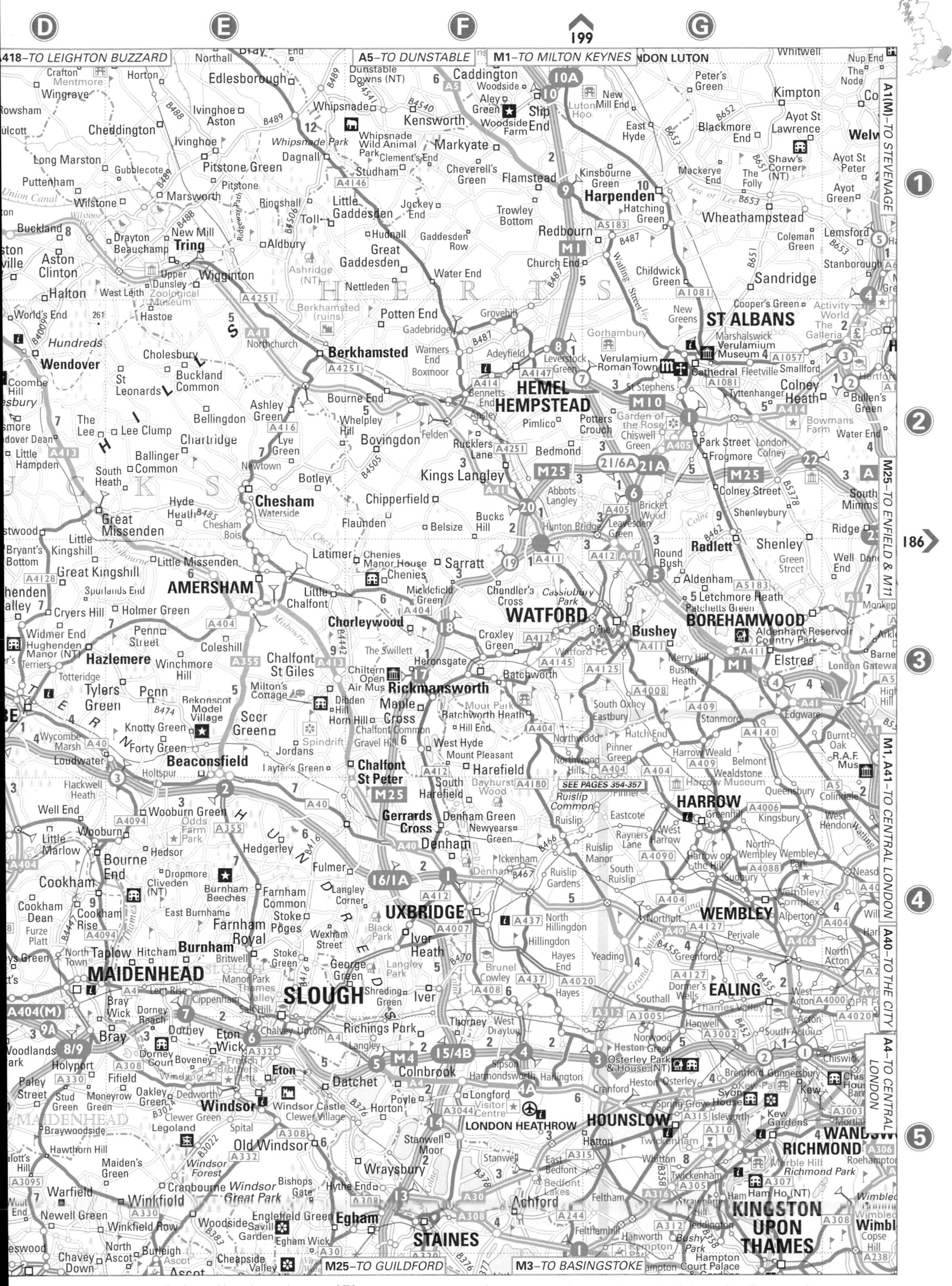

D
E
F
G
199
A418–TO LEIGHTON BUZZARD
A5–TO DUNSTABLE
M1–TO MILTON KEYNES
A1(M)–TO STEVENAGE
M25–TO ENFIELD & M11
186
M1, A41–TO CENTRAL LONDON
A40–TO THE CITY
A4–TO CENTRAL LONDON
M25–TO GUILDFORD
M3–TO BASINGSTOKE
1
2
3
4
5
SEE PAGES 354-357
ST ALBANS
HEMEL HEMPSTEAD
Harpenden
Berkhamsted
Tring
Wendover
Chesham
AMERSHAM
WATFORD
Rickmansworth
BOREHAMWOOD
HARROW
Beaconsfield
Hazlemere
UXBRIDGE
WEMBLEY
EALING
MAIDENHEAD
SLOUGH
Windsor
HOUNSLOW
LONDON HEATHROW
RICHMOND
STAINES
Egham
KINGSTON UPON THAMES

171

Iver Heath: *The Pinewood Studios located here, house the world's largest film stage, used in the production of the James Bond films.* ***Map ref. F4***

London Heathrow Airport: *The world's busiest international airport, handling around 63 million passengers per year. To the west of the airport, the section of the M25 between junctions 13 and 14 is Britain's busiest road.* ***Map ref. F5***

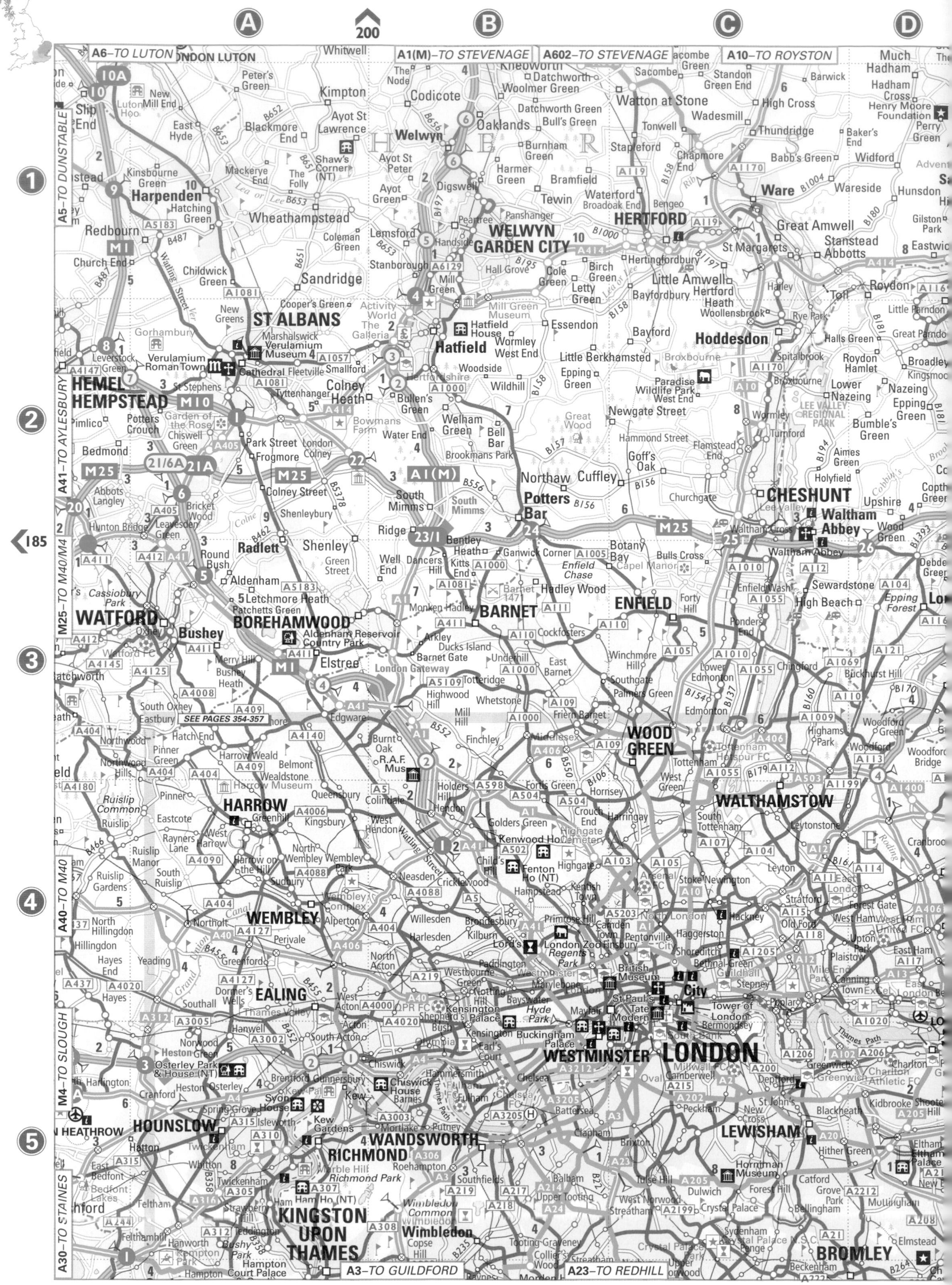

200

A B C D

1 2 3 4 5

A6–TO LUTON
A1(M)–TO STEVENAGE
A602–TO STEVENAGE
A10–TO ROYSTON
A5–TO DUNSTABLE
A41–TO AYLESBURY
M25–TO M40/M4
A40–TO M40
M4–TO SLOUGH
A30–TO STAINES
A3–TO GUILDFORD
A23–TO REDHILL
SEE PAGES 354-357

185

172

London: *The world's first Underground railway was opened by the Metropolitan Railway Company in 1863 between Paddington and Farringdon.* ***Map ref. B4***

Barking: *Bobby Moore, captain of the England football team that won the 1966 World Cup was born here on the 12th April 1941. He began his career at West Ham in 1956 and is acknowledged to be one of the best defenders ever to play in the English league. Bobby died of cancer on the 24th February 1993 at the age of 51.* ***Map ref. D4***

201

D
E
F
G
M11–TO CAMBRIDGE
A130–TO LONDON STANSTED AIRPORT (A120)
A131–TO BRAINTREE
A12–TO COLCHESTER
A127–TO SOUTHEND-ON-SEA
A20–TO SWANLEY
M25–TO REIGATE
M2–TO CANTERBURY (A2)
1
2
3
4
5
188
HARLOW
CHELMSFORD
BRENTWOOD
ROMFORD
BASILDON
DARTFORD
GRAYS
GRAVESEND
Epping
Chipping Ongar
Billericay
Wickford
Ingatestone
Great Waltham
Little Waltham
Boreham
Hatfield Peverel
Sheering
Hatfield Broad Oak
Little Hallingbury
Great Hallingbury
Hatfield Forest (NT)
High Ongar
North Weald Bassett
Kelvedon Hatch
Doddinghurst
Blackmore
Writtle
Danbury
Bicknacre
Woodham Ferrers
South Woodham Ferrers
Rayleigh
Hockley
Thundersley
South Benfleet
Canvey Island
Corringham
Stanford- le- Hope
South Ockendon
Orsett
Chadwell St Mary
Tilbury
Tilbury Fort
Aveley
Purfleet
West Thurrock
Swanscombe
Northfleet
Greenhithe
Stone
Wilmington
Hextable
Darenth
Shorne
Higham
Hoo
Cliffe
Cliffe Woods
Stoke
Upminster
Hornchurch
Dagenham
Rainham
Bexleyheath
Crayford
Bexley
THURROCK
THAMES
MEDWAY
Coryton
Thames Haven
Mucking
Linford
Hyde Hall
Thorndon
Pitsea
Vange
Laindon
Langdon Hills
Ramsden Heath
Stock
Margaretting
Galleywood
Great Baddow
Sandon
Mountnessing
Shenfield
Hutton
Ingrave
Herongate
East Horndon
West Horndon
Bulphan
Harold Wood
Harold Hill
Havering-atte-Bower
Stapleford Abbotts
Abridge
Theydon Mount
Navestock
Stanford Rivers
Fyfield
Willingale
Roxwell
Good Easter
Pleshey
Terling
Little Baddow
Rettendon
Runwell
Battlesbridge
Crays Hill
Great Burstead
Little Burstead
Dartford Crossing

Greensted: *The Saxon church here is known as the oldest wooden church in the world.* ***Map ref. E2***

173

202

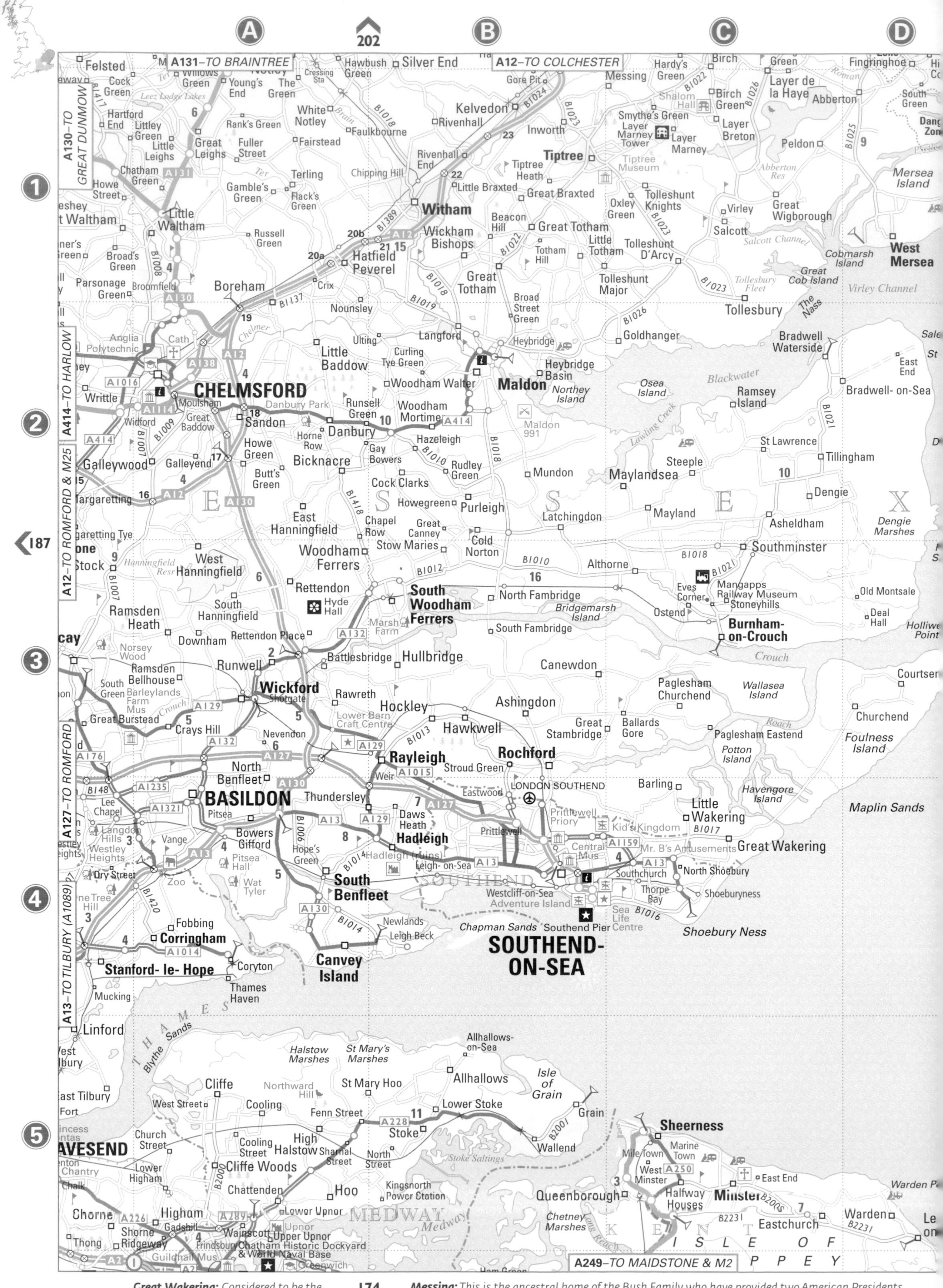
A
B
C
D
1
2
3
4
5
187
A131–TO BRAINTREE
A12–TO COLCHESTER
A130–TO GREAT DUNMOW
A414–TO HARLOW
A12–TO ROMFORD & M25
A127–TO ROMFORD
A13–TO TILBURY (A1089)
A249–TO MAIDSTONE & M2
Felsted
Silver End
Hawbush Green
Kelvedon
Tiptree
Witham
Messing
Birch
Layer de la Haye
Abberton
Fingringhoe
Peldon
Mersea Island
West Mersea
Tollesbury
Goldhanger
Heybridge
Heybridge Basin
Maldon
Northey Island
Osea Island
Blackwater
Bradwell Waterside
Bradwell-on-Sea
Ramsey Island
St Lawrence
Tillingham
Steeple
Maylandsea
Mayland
Dengie
Asheldham
Dengie Marshes
Southminster
Althorne
Latchingdon
Mundon
Purleigh
Cold Norton
North Fambridge
South Fambridge
Bridgemarsh Island
Mangapps Railway Museum
Burnham-on-Crouch
Crouch
Canewdon
Paglesham Churchend
Wallasea Island
Paglesham Eastend
Potton Island
Foulness Island
Churchend
Courtsend
Havengore Island
Maplin Sands
Little Wakering
Great Wakering
North Shoebury
Shoeburyness
Shoebury Ness
Southend Pier
SOUTHEND-ON-SEA
Chapman Sands
Westcliff-on-Sea
Adventure Island
Sea Life Centre
Thorpe Bay
Southchurch
Prittlewell
Rochford
LONDON SOUTHEND
Eastwood
Ashingdon
Hawkwell
Hockley
Hullbridge
Rayleigh
Thundersley
Hadleigh
Leigh-on-Sea
South Benfleet
Canvey Island
BASILDON
Pitsea
Wickford
Runwell
Rettendon
South Woodham Ferrers
Woodham Ferrers
Hyde Hall
Battlesbridge
Rawreth
East Hanningfield
West Hanningfield
South Hanningfield
Downham
Ramsden Heath
Billericay
Crays Hill
Great Burstead
Laindon
Vange
Bowers Gifford
Stanford-le-Hope
Corringham
Fobbing
Coryton
Thames Haven
Mucking
Linford
Danbury
Woodham Walter
Woodham Mortimer
Hazeleigh
Bicknacre
Little Baddow
Langford
Great Totham
Little Totham
Tolleshunt D'Arcy
Tolleshunt Major
Tolleshunt Knights
Great Braxted
Little Braxted
Wickham Bishops
Hatfield Peverel
Boreham
CHELMSFORD
Writtle
Galleywood
Great Baddow
Sandon
Broomfield
Little Waltham
Great Leighs
Terling
Rivenhall
Faulkbourne
White Notley
Cressing
Cliffe
Cooling
High Halstow
St Mary Hoo
Allhallows
Isle of Grain
Grain
Lower Stoke
Stoke
Wallend
Hoo
Cliffe Woods
Higham
Chattenden
Upper Upnor
Chatham Historic Dockyard & World Naval Base
Sheerness
Minster
Queenborough
Eastchurch
Warden
ISLE OF SHEPPEY
MEDWAY
THAMES

Great Wakering: *Considered to be the driest place in Britain with an average rainfall of less than 20 inches (500mm) per year.* ***Map ref. C4***

174

Messing: *This is the ancestral home of the Bush Family who have provided two American Presidents. The Bush family left Essex to settle in America during the 17th Century.* ***Map ref. C1***

203

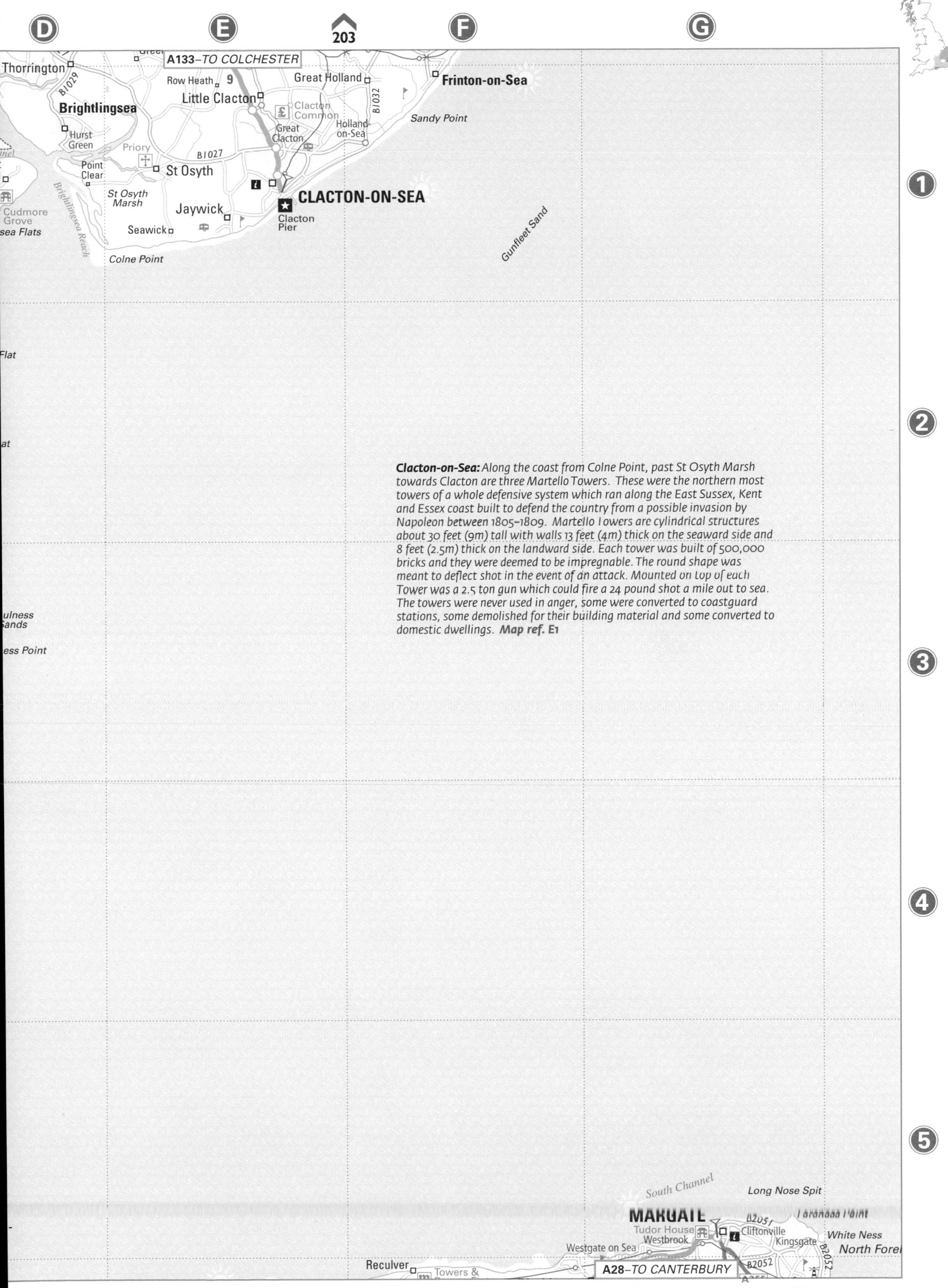

D
E
F
G
1
2
3
4
5
A133–TO COLCHESTER
Thorrington
B1029
Brightlingsea
Hurst Green
Priory
Point Clear
Brightlingsea Reach
St Osyth Marsh
Cudmore Grove
Colne Point
Row Heath
9
Little Clacton
Great Holland
Clacton Common
Great Clacton
Holland-on-Sea
B1032
B1027
St Osyth
Jaywick
Seawick
CLACTON-ON-SEA
Clacton Pier
Frinton-on-Sea
Sandy Point
Gunfleet Sand
Flat
ulness Sands
ess Point
South Channel
Long Nose Spit
MARGATE
Tudor House
Westbrook
Cliftonville
Kingsgate
White Ness
North Fore
Westgate on Sea
Reculver
Towers &
A28–TO CANTERBURY
B2051
B2052

Clacton-on-Sea: *Along the coast from Colne Point, past St Osyth Marsh towards Clacton are three Martello Towers. These were the northern most towers of a whole defensive system which ran along the East Sussex, Kent and Essex coast built to defend the country from a possible invasion by Napoleon between 1805–1809. Martello Towers are cylindrical structures about 30 feet (9m) tall with walls 13 feet (4m) thick on the seaward side and 8 feet (2.5m) thick on the landward side. Each tower was built of 500,000 bricks and they were deemed to be impregnable. The round shape was meant to deflect shot in the event of an attack. Mounted on top of each Tower was a 2.5 ton gun which could fire a 24 pound shot a mile out to sea. The towers were never used in anger, some were converted to coastguard stations, some demolished for their building material and some converted to domestic dwellings.* ***Map ref. E1***

175

Canvey Island: *From 6pm on the 31st January 1953, exceptionally strong winds combined with a higher than average spring tide caused a 'storm surge' which led to devastating flooding all along the east coast of England. Hurricane force winds were recorded at 10pm at Felixstowe and the surge reached Canvey Island just after midnight on the 1st February causing absolute devastation. In all 307 people lost their lives in the flood, over 250,000 acres (100,000ha) of land were immersed and the cost in today's figures would be over five billion pounds. These floods are generally regarded as Britain's worst ever peacetime disaster.* ***Map ref. A4***

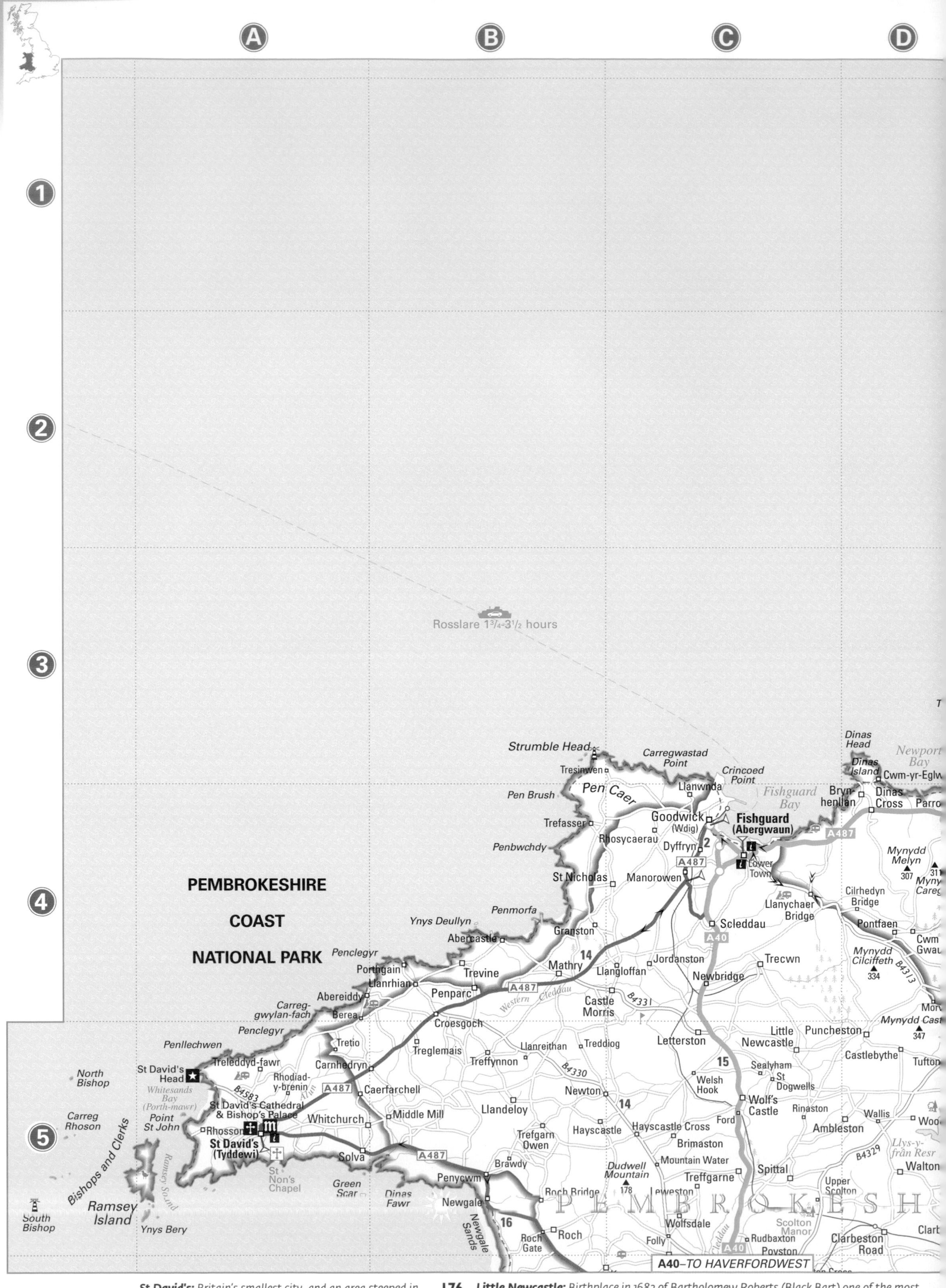
A
B
C
D
1
2
3
4
5
Rosslare 1¾-3½ hours
PEMBROKESHIRE
COAST
NATIONAL PARK
Strumble Head
Carregwastad Point
Crincoed Point
Dinas Head
Dinas Island
Newport Bay
Cwm-yr-Eglw
Tresinwen
Pen Caer
Llanwnda
Fishguard Bay
Bryn-henllan
Dinas Cross
Parro
Pen Brush
Trefasser
Goodwick
(Wdig)
Fishguard
(Abergwaun)
A487
Rhosycaerau
Dyffryn
2
Penbwchdy
A487
Lower Town
Mynydd Melyn
307
Myny Careg
St Nicholas
Manorowen
Cilrhedyn Bridge
Llanychaer Bridge
Penmorfa
Ynys Deullyn
Granston
Scleddau
Pontfaen
Abercastle
A40
Cwm Gwau
14
Mathry
Llangloffan
Jordanston
Trecwn
Mynydd Cilciffeth
334
B4313
Penclegyr
Porthgain
Trevine
Llanrhian
A487
Newbridge
Abereiddy
Penparc
Western Cleddau
Castle Morris
B4331
Carreg-gwylan-fach
Berea
Croesgoch
Mynydd Cast
347
Penclegyr
Letterston
Little Newcastle
Puncheston
Penllechwen
Tretio
Treglemais
Llanreithan
Treddiog
Castlebythe
Treleddyd-fawr
Treffynnon
15
Sealyham
St Dogwells
Tufton
North Bishop
St David's Head
Whitesands Bay
(Porth-mawr)
Rhodiad-y-brenin
Carnhedryn
B4583
A487
Caerfarchell
B4330
Welsh Hook
Newton
14
Wolf's Castle
Rinaston
Carreg Rhoson
Point St John
St David's Cathedral & Bishop's Palace
Whitchurch
Middle Mill
Llandeloy
Wallis
Woo
Ambleston
Rhosson
St David's
(Tyddewi)
Alun
Hayscastle
Hayscastle Cross
Ford
Trefgarn Owen
Brimaston
Llys-y-frân Resr
Bishops and Clerks
Ramsey Sound
Solva
A487
B4329
Brawdy
Mountain Water
Dudwell Mountain
178
Spittal
Walton
St Non's Chapel
Penycwm
Treffgarne
Upper Scolton
Green Scar
Dinas Fawr
Roch Bridge
Leweston
Ramsey Island
Newgale
PEMBROKESH
South Bishop
Ynys Bery
Newgale Sands
16
Wolfsdale
Scolton Manor
Clarb
Roch Gate
Roch
Folly
Rudbaxton
Clarbeston Road
Poyston
A40
A40–TO HAVERFORDWEST

St David's: *Britain's smallest city, and an area steeped in ancient religion, both Christian and pagan. St David's Cathedral, built in AD1180 has been a place of pilgrimage for over 1200 years. It is a Celtic Cathedral and a focal point of Celtic heritage.* ***Map ref. A5***

176

Little Newcastle: *Birthplace in 1682 of Bartholomew Roberts (Black Bart) one of the most notorious Pirates ever. Roberts was the first sea captain to fly the 'Jolly Roger' (the skull and crossbones flag). He was killed by grapeshot aboard his flagship Royal Fortune, during a battle with HMS Swallow, off the coast of Gabon in 1722.* ***Map ref. C5***

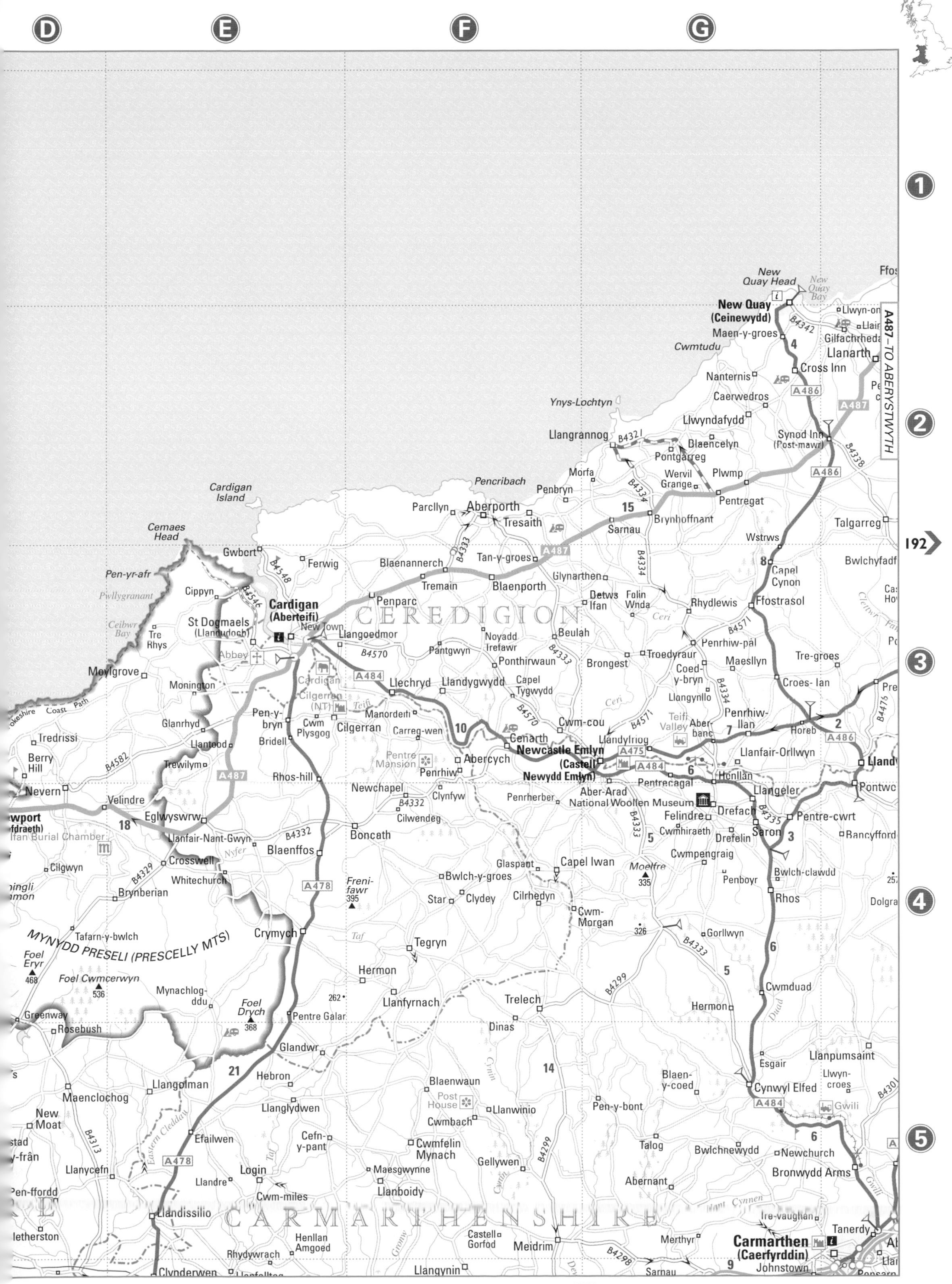
D
E
F
G
1
2
3
4
5
192
177
A487 – TO ABERYSTWYTH
New Quay Head
New Quay Bay
New Quay
(Ceinewydd)
Maen-y-groes
Cwmtudu
Llwyn-on
Llain
Gilfachrheda
Llanarth
Cross Inn
Nanternis
Caerwedros
Ynys-Lochtyn
Llwyndafydd
Llangrannog
Blaencelyn
Pontgarreg
Synod Inn
(Post-mawr)
Morfa
Wervil Grange
Plwmp
Pencribach
Penbryn
Pentregat
Cardigan Island
Parcllyn
Aberporth
Tresaith
Brynhoffnant
Sarnau
Talgarreg
Cemaes Head
Wstrws
Gwbert
Ferwig
Blaenannerch
Tan-y-groes
Capel Cynon
Bwlchyfadfa
Pen-yr-afr
Pwllygranant
Cippyn
Tremain
Blaenporth
Glynarthen
Cardigan
(Aberteifi)
Penparc
Betws Ifan
Folin Wnda
Rhydlewis
Ffostrasol
CEREDIGION
Ceibwr Bay
Tre Rhys
St Dogmaels
(Llandudoch)
New Town
Llangoedmor
Noyadd Trefawr
Beulah
Penrhiw-pâl
Abbey
Pantgwyn
Ponthirwaun
Troedyraur
Tre-groes
Moylgrove
Brongest
Coed-y-bryn
Maesllyn
Monington
Cardigan
Llechryd
Llandygwydd
Capel Tygwydd
Croes-lan
Pembrokeshire Coast Path
Cilgerran (NT)
Teifi
Llangynllo
Glanrhyd
Pen-y-bryn
Manordeifi
Cwm Plysgog
Cilgerran
Carreg-wen
Cwm-cou
Teifi Valley
Aberbanc
Penrhiw-llan
Horeb
Tredrissi
Llantood
Bridell
Cenarth
Llandyfriog
Newcastle Emlyn
(Castell)
Llanfair-Orllwyn
Berry Hill
Trewilym
Pentre Mansion
Abercych
Rhos-hill
Penrhiw
Newydd Emlyn
Henllan
Nevern
Newchapel
Pentrecagal
Llangeler
Pontwelly
Velindre
Clynfyw
Penrherber
Aber-Arad
National Woollen Museum
Drefach
Pentre-cwrt
Newport
(Trefdraeth)
Eglwyswrw
Cilwendeg
Felindre
Cwmhiraeth
Saron
Llanfair-Nant-Gwyn
Boncath
Drefelin
Bancyfford
Crosswell
Blaenffos
Cwmpengraig
Nyfer
Cilgwyn
Glaspant
Capel Iwan
Moelfre
335
Bwlch-clawdd
Whitechurch
Bwlch-y-groes
Penboyr
Brynberian
Freni-fawr
395
Star
Clydey
Cilrhedyn
Rhos
Dolgran
Cwm-Morgan
Tafarn-y-bwlch
326
Gorllwyn
Foel Eryr
468
MYNYDD PRESELI (PRESCELLY MTS)
Crymych
Taf
Tegryn
Foel Cwmcerwyn
536
Hermon
Mynachlog-ddu
Cwmduad
Foel Drych
368
262
Llanfyrnach
Trelech
Hermon
Greenway
Pentre Galar
Rosebush
Dinas
Glandwr
Esgair
Llanpumsaint
Hebron
14
Blaen-y-coed
Llwyn-croes
Llangolman
Blaenwaun
Cynwyl Elfed
Maenclochog
Post House
Llanglydwen
Llanwinio
Pen-y-bont
Gwili
New Moat
Cwmbach
Efailwen
Cefn-y-pant
Cwmfelin Mynach
Talog
Bwlchnewydd
Newchurch
Gellywen
Bronwydd Arms
Llanycefn
Maesgwynne
Login
Llandre
Abernant
Cwm-miles
Llanboidy
Pen-ffordd
Cynnen
Tre-vaughan
Llandissilio
CARMARTHENSHIRE
Tanerdy
Castell Gorfod
Henllan Amgoed
Meidrim
Merthyr
Carmarthen
(Caerfyrddin)
Rhydywrach
Johnstown
Letterston
Clynderwen
Llangynin
Sarnau
Cynin
Eastern Cleddau
A487
A484
A486
A475
A478
A485
B4342
B4321
B4334
B4333
B4548
B4546
B4570
B4571
B4582
B4329
B4332
B4335
B4313
B4299
B4298
B4338
B4476
B4301
B4459

Mynydd Preseli (Prescelly Mountains) : *Up to 80 4-ton 'blue stones' used in the building of Stonehenge in Wiltshire were quarried here. They were probably transported overland from the mountains down to Milford Haven and then taken by raft and finally overland again to their destination, a distance of 135 miles.*
Map ref. D4

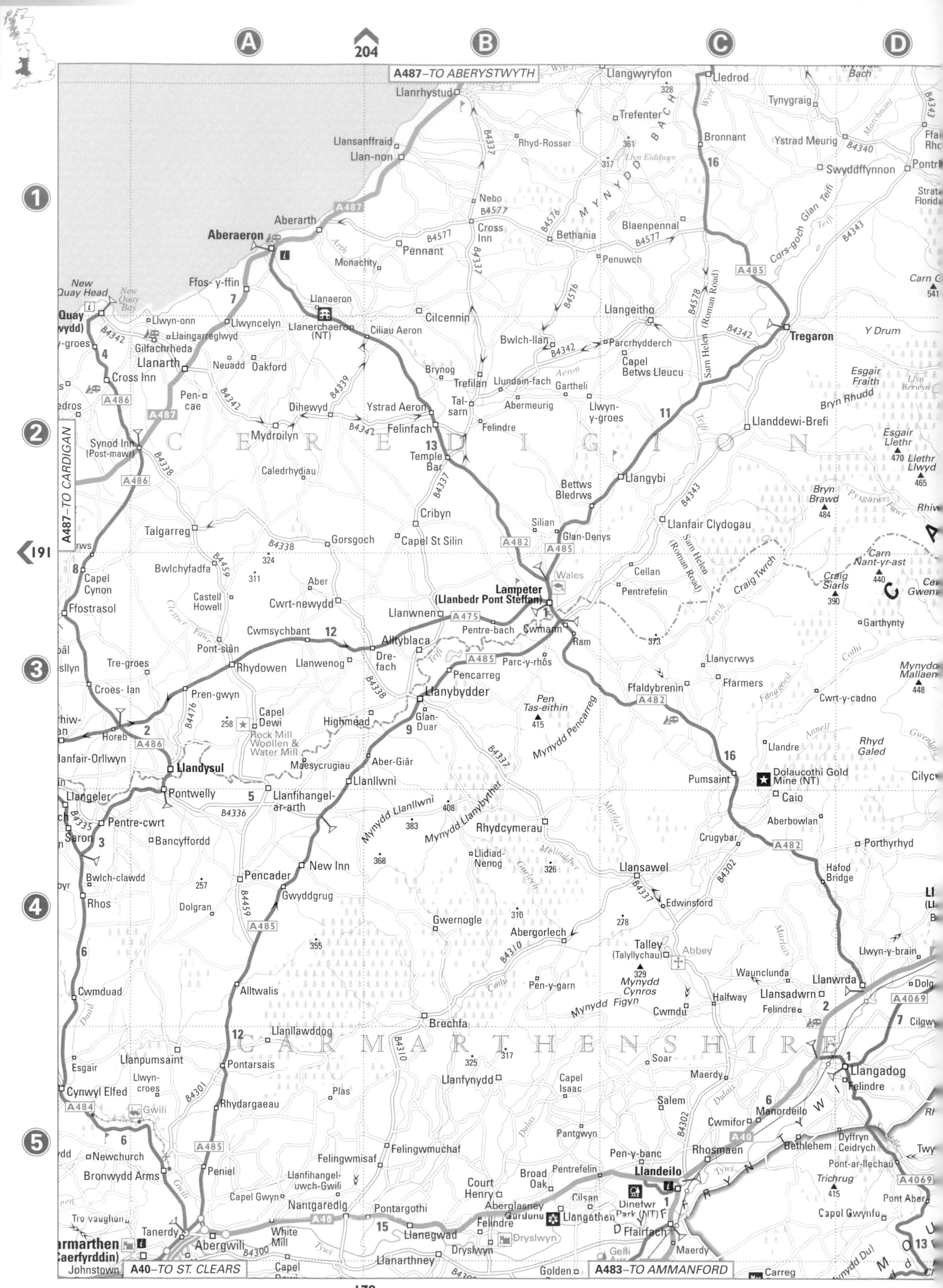
A
B
C
D
204
A487–TO ABERYSTWYTH
1
2
3
4
5
191
A487–TO CARDIGAN
Llangwyryfon
Lledrod
Llanrhystud
Trefenter
Tynygraig
Bronnant
Ystrad Meurig
Llansanffraid
Llan-non
Rhyd-Rosser
Llyn Eiddwen
Swyddffynnon
MYNYDD BACH
Nebo
Aberarth
Aberaeron
Cross Inn
Pennant
Bethania
Blaenpennal
Penuwch
Monachty
Cors-goch Glan Teifi
New Quay Head
New Quay Bay
Ffos-y-ffin
Llanaeron
Cilcennin
Llangeitho
Tregaron
Y Drum
Llwyn-onn
Llwyncelyn
Llanerchaeron (NT)
Ciliau Aeron
Sarn Helen (Roman Road)
Llaingarreglwyd
Gilfachrheda
Bwlch-llan
Parcrhydderch
Llanarth
Neuadd
Oakford
Capel Betws Lleucu
Esgair Fraith
Cross Inn
Brynog
Trefilan
Llundain-fach
Gartheli
Llyn Berwyn
Bryn Rhudd
Pen-cae
Dihewyd
Ystrad Aeron
Tal-sarn
Abermeurig
Llwyn-y-groes
Llanddewi-Brefi
Synod Inn (Post-mawr)
Mydroilyn
Felinfach
Felindre
Temple Bar
CEREDIGION
Esgair Llethr
Llethr Llwyd
Caledrhydiau
Llangybi
Bettws Bledrws
Bryn Brawd
Pysgotwr Fawr
Cribyn
Talgarreg
Silian
Llanfair Clydogau
Gorsgoch
Capel St Silin
Glan-Denys
Bwlchyfadfa
Capel Cynon
Ffostrasol
Castell Howell
Aber
Cwrt-newydd
Lampeter (Llanbedr Pont Steffan)
Wales
Cellan
Pentrefelin
Sarn Helen (Roman Road)
Craig Twrch
Carn Nant-yr-ast
Craig Siarls
Llanwnen
Garthynty
Cwmsychbant
Pentre-bach
Cwmann
Ram
Alltyblaca
Pont-siân
Dre-fach
Parc-y-rhôs
Llanycrwys
Tre-groes
Rhydowen
Llanwenog
Pencarreg
Mynydd Mallaen
Croes-lan
Pren-gwyn
Llanybydder
Pen Tas-eithin
Ffaldybrenin
Ffarmers
Cwrt-y-cadno
Capel Dewi
Rock Mill Woollen & Water Mill
Highmead
Glan-Duar
Horeb
Mynydd Pencarreg
Llandre
Rhyd Galed
Llandysul
Maesycrugiau
Aber-Giâr
Pumsaint
Dolaucothi Gold Mine (NT)
Llangeler
Pontwelly
Llanllwni
Llanfihangel-ar-arth
Caio
Pentre-cwrt
Mynydd Llanllwni
Mynydd Llanybydder
Rhydcymerau
Aberbowlan
Saron
Bancyffordd
Crugybar
Porthyrhyd
Lllidiad-Nenog
Llansawel
Hafod Bridge
New Inn
Bwlch-clawdd
Pencader
Rhos
Gwyddgrug
Dolgran
Edwinsford
Gwernogle
Abergorlech
Talley (Talyllychau)
Abbey
Llwyn-y-brain
Wauncluda
Llanwrda
Mynydd Cynros
Pen-y-garn
Mynydd Figyn
Cwmduad
Alltwalis
Halfway
Llansadwrn
Cwmdu
Felindre
Brechfa
Llanllawddog
CARMARTHENSHIRE
Llanpumsaint
Soar
Esgair
Pontarsais
Llanfynydd
Capel Isaac
Maerdy
Llangadog
Felindre
Llwyn-croes
Cynwyl Elfed
Plas
Salem
Manordeilo
Gwili
Rhydargaeau
Cwmifor
Pantgwyn
Newchurch
Peniel
Felingwmuchaf
Pen-y-banc
Rhosmaen
Bethlehem
Dyffryn Ceidrych
Felingwmisaf
Bronwydd Arms
Llanfihangel-uwch-Gwili
Broad Oak
Pentrefelin
Llandeilo
Pont-ar-llechau
Trichrug
Court Henry
Capel Gwyn
Nantgaredig
Pontargothi
Aberglasney Gardens
Cilsan
Dinefwr Park (NT)
Llangathen
Pont Aber
Capel Gwynfo
Felindre
Ffairfach
Tanerdy
Llanegwad
Dryslwyn
White Mill
Abergwili
Maerdy
Carmarthen (Caerfyrddin)
Llanarthney
Johnstown
A40–TO ST. CLEARS
Golden
A483–TO AMMANFORD
Carreg
178

Llanwrtyd Wells: *Claims to be the smallest town in Wales and is the home of the annual World Bog Snorkelling Championships.* ***Map ref. E3***

Lampeter *has the oldest University in Wales and with less than 2000 students can claim to be the smallest university in Europe. It was founded by Bishop Thomas Burgess in 1822 and admitted its first students on St David's Day 1827.* ***Map ref. B3***

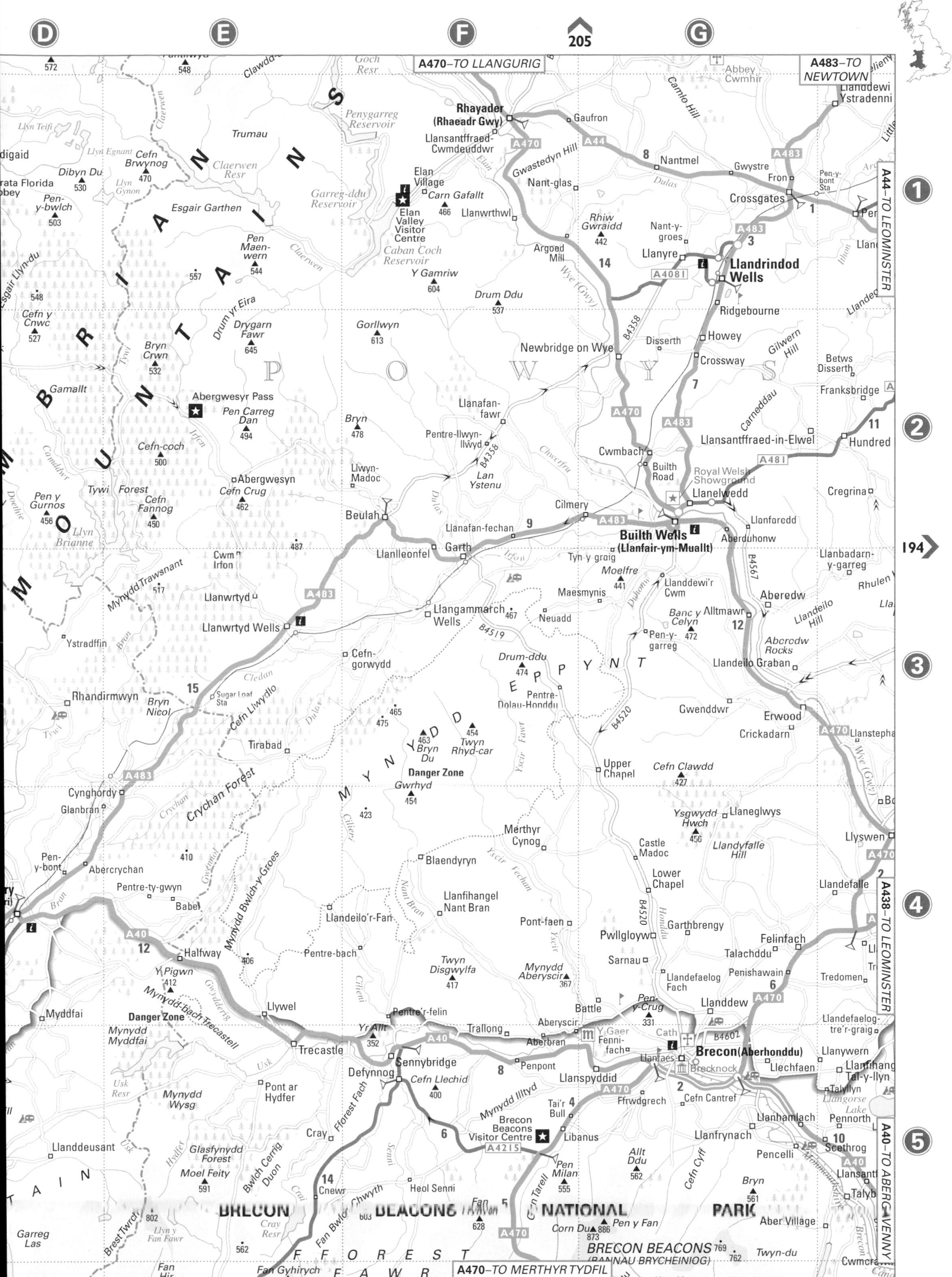

D
E
F
G
205
A470–TO LLANGURIG
A483–TO NEWTOWN
A44–TO LEOMINSTER
A438–TO LEOMINSTER
A40–TO ABERGAVENNY
A470–TO MERTHYR TYDFIL
194
179
1
2
3
4
5
Rhayader (Rhaeadr Gwy)
Elan Village
Elan Valley Visitor Centre
Llandrindod Wells
Newbridge on Wye
Builth Wells (Llanfair-ym-Muallt)
Llanwrtyd Wells
Llangammarch Wells
Beulah
Garth
Sennybridge
Trecastle
Brecon (Aberhonddu)
Brecon Beacons Visitor Centre
Abergwesyn Pass
Royal Welsh Showground
Danger Zone
CAMBRIAN MOUNTAINS
POWYS
MYNYDD EPPYNT
FFOREST FAWR
BRECON BEACONS NATIONAL PARK

Tregaron: *A 19th century 'Drovers' town where Welsh farmers gathered to walk their sheep and cattle all the way to London to sell at the markets. Famous as the birthplace of Twm Sion Cati, an outlaw described as the Welsh Robin Hood on whom the popular TV series Hawkmoor was based. To the north of the town, Tregaron Bog (Cors Caron) is the best remaining example of an active raised bog in Wales.* ***Map ref. C2***

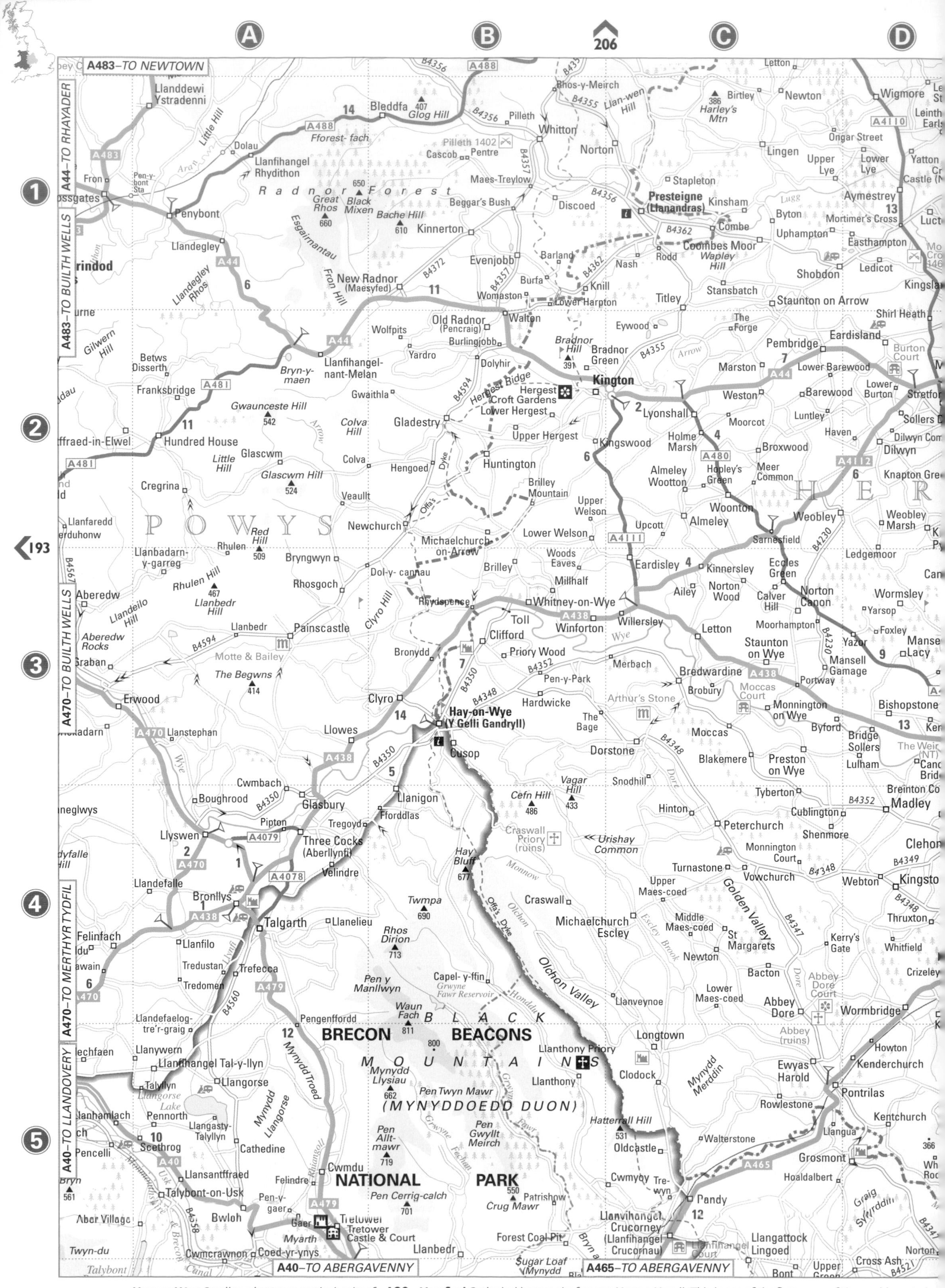

A
B
206
C
D
1
2
193
3
4
5
A483–TO NEWTOWN
A44–TO RHAYADER
A483–TO BUILTH WELLS
A470–TO BUILTH WELLS
A470–TO MERTHYR TYDFIL
A40–TO LLANDOVERY
A40–TO ABERGAVENNY
A465–TO ABERGAVENNY
180
Llanddewi Ystradenni
Bleddfa
407 Glog Hill
Pilleth
Whitton
Rhos-y-Meirch
Llan-wen Hill
386 Harley's Mtn
Birtley
Newton
Wigmore
Leinthall Earls
Little Hill
Dolau
Fforest- fach
Pilleth 1402
Cascob
Pentre
Norton
Lingen
Ongar Street
Upper Lye
Lower Lye
Yatton
Llanfihangel Rhydithon
Fron
Pen-y-bont Sta
Radnor Forest
650 Black Mixen
Great Rhos 660
Bache Hill 610
Maes-Treylow
Beggar's Bush
Stapleton
Presteigne (Llanandras)
Kinsham
Aymestrey
Mortimer's Cross
Penybont
Discoed
Byton
Combe
Uphampton
Llandegley
Esgairmantau
Fron Hill
Kinnerton
Evenjobb
Barland
Nash
Rodd
Coombes Moor
Wapley Hill
Easthampton
Shobdon
Ledicot
Llandrindod
Llandegley Rhos
New Radnor (Maesyfed)
Burfa
Knill
Lower Harpton
Womaston
Titley
Stansbatch
Staunton on Arrow
Kingsland
Gilwern Hill
Old Radnor (Pencraig)
Walton
Eywood
The Forge
Shirl Heath
Wolfpits
Burlingjobb
Bradnor Hill 391
Bradnor Green
Pembridge
Eardisland
Burton Court
Betws Disserth
Yardro
Dolyhir
Llanfihangel-nant-Melan
Bryn-y-maen
Franksbridge
Kington
Marston
Lower Barewood
Gwaithla
Hergest Ridge
Hergest Croft Gardens
Lower Hergest
Weston
Barewood
Lower Burton
Stretford
Gwaunceste Hill 542
Colva Hill
Gladestry
Lyonshall
Moorcot
Luntley
Sollers Dilwyn
Hundred House
Llanfihangel-in-Elwel
Upper Hergest
Holme Marsh
Haven
Dilwyn
Little Hill
Glascwm
Glascwm Hill 524
Colva
Hengoed
Huntington
Kingswood
Broxwood
Almeley Wootton
Hopley's Green
Meer Common
Knapton Green
Cregrina
Veaullt
Brilley Mountain
Upper Welson
POWYS
Llanfaredd
Red Hill 509
Newchurch
Offa's Dyke
Michaelchurch-on-Arrow
Lower Welson
Upcott
Almeley
Wootton
Weobley
Weobley Marsh
Sarnesfield
Llanbadarn-y-garreg
Rhulen
Bryngwyn
Woods Eaves
Brilley
Eardisley
Kinnersley
Eccles Green
Ledgemoor
Aberedw
Rhulen Hill 467
Llanbedr Hill
Llandeilo Hill
Rhosgoch
Dol-y- cannau
Clyro Hill
Millhalf
Ailey
Norton Wood
Calver Hill
Norton Canon
Wormsley
Yarsop
Rhydspence
Whitney-on-Wye
Toll
Willersley
Winforton
Letton
Moorhampton
Foxley
Aberedw Rocks
Llanbedr
Painscastle
Clifford
Wye
Staunton on Wye
Yazor
Mansel Lacy
Craban
Motte & Bailey
The Begwns 414
Bronydd
Priory Wood
Merbach
Mansell Gamage
Pen-y-Park
Bredwardine
Brobury
Moccas Court
Portway
Erwood
Clyro
Hay-on-Wye (Y Gelli Gandryll)
Hardwicke
Arthur's Stone
The Bage
Monnington on Wye
Byford
Bishopstone
Llanstephan
Llowes
Cusop
Dorstone
Moccas
Blakemere
Preston on Wye
Bridge Sollers
Lulham
The Weir (NT)
Cwmbach
Boughrood
Glasbury
Llanigon
Ffordd-las
Cefn Hill 486
Vagar Hill 433
Snodhill
Tyberton
Breinton Common
Madley
Llyswen
Pipton
Tregoyd
Three Cocks (Aberllynfi)
Craswall Priory (ruins)
Urishay Common
Hinton
Peterchurch
Cublington
Shenmore
Velindre
Hay Bluff 677
Monnow
Monnington Court
Turnastone
Vowchurch
Clehonger
Llandefalle
Bronllys
Twmpa 690
Craswall
Upper Maes-coed
Golden Valley
Webton
Kingstone
Talgarth
Llanelieu
Michaelchurch Escley
Middle Maes-coed
St Margarets
Thruxton
Felinfach
Llanfilo
Rhos Dirion 713
Olchon
Escley Brook
Newton
Kerry's Gate
Whitfield
Tredustan
Trefecca
Tredomen
Olchon Valley
Bacton
Abbey Dore Court
Crizeley
Pen y Manllwyn
Capel- y-ffin
Grwyne Fawr Reservoir
Llanveynoe
Lower Maes-coed
Abbey Dore
Wormbridge
Llandefaelog-tre'r-graig
Pengenffordd
Waun Fach 811
BLACK
Longtown
Abbey (ruins)
Howton
Kenderchurch
Llanywern
Llanfihangel Tal-y-llyn
BRECON
800
BEACONS
Llanthony Priory
Clodock
Mynydd Merddin
Ewyas Harold
Talyllyn
Llangorse
Llangorse Lake
Mynydd Troed
MOUNTAINS
Mynydd Llysiau 662
Llanthony
Pontrilas
Llanhamlach
Pennorth
Llangasty-Talyllyn
Mynydd Llangorse
Pen Twyn Mawr
(MYNYDDOEDD DUON)
Rowlestone
Kentchurch
Scethrog
Cathedine
Pen Allt-mawr 719
Pen Gwyllt Meirch
Hatterrall Hill 531
Oldcastle
Walterstone
Llangua
Pencelli
Cwmdu
Grosmont
Llansantffraed
Felindre
NATIONAL
PARK
Cwmyoy
Trewyn
Hoaldalbert
Talybont-on-Usk
Pen-y-gaer
Pen Cerrig-calch 701
550 Patrishow
Crug Mawr
Pandy
Graig Syfyrddin
Aber Village
Bwlch
Gaer
Tretower Castle & Court
Myarth
Llanvihangel Crucorney (Llanfihangel Crucornau)
Llanfihangel Court
Llangattock Lingoed
Twyn-du
Cwmcrawnon
Coed-yr-ynys
Llanbedr
Forest Coal Pit
Sugar Loaf (Mynydd
Bryn
Norton
Cross Ash
Bont
Upper Green
Talybont
Brecon Canal
Usk
HER

Hay-on-Wye: *Small market town on the banks of the River Wye famous for its large concentration of bookshops. With over 30 of these to choose from Hay-on-Wye is the most popular centre in Britain for booklovers.* ***Map ref. B3***

Hereford *Cathedral houses the famous Mappa Mundi. This is one of the first maps of the world created on a single sheet of vellum (calf skin) around AD1300. As well as being a map it also depicts the history of mankind and illustrates the marvels of the natural world, biblical events and mythology.* ***Map ref. E4***

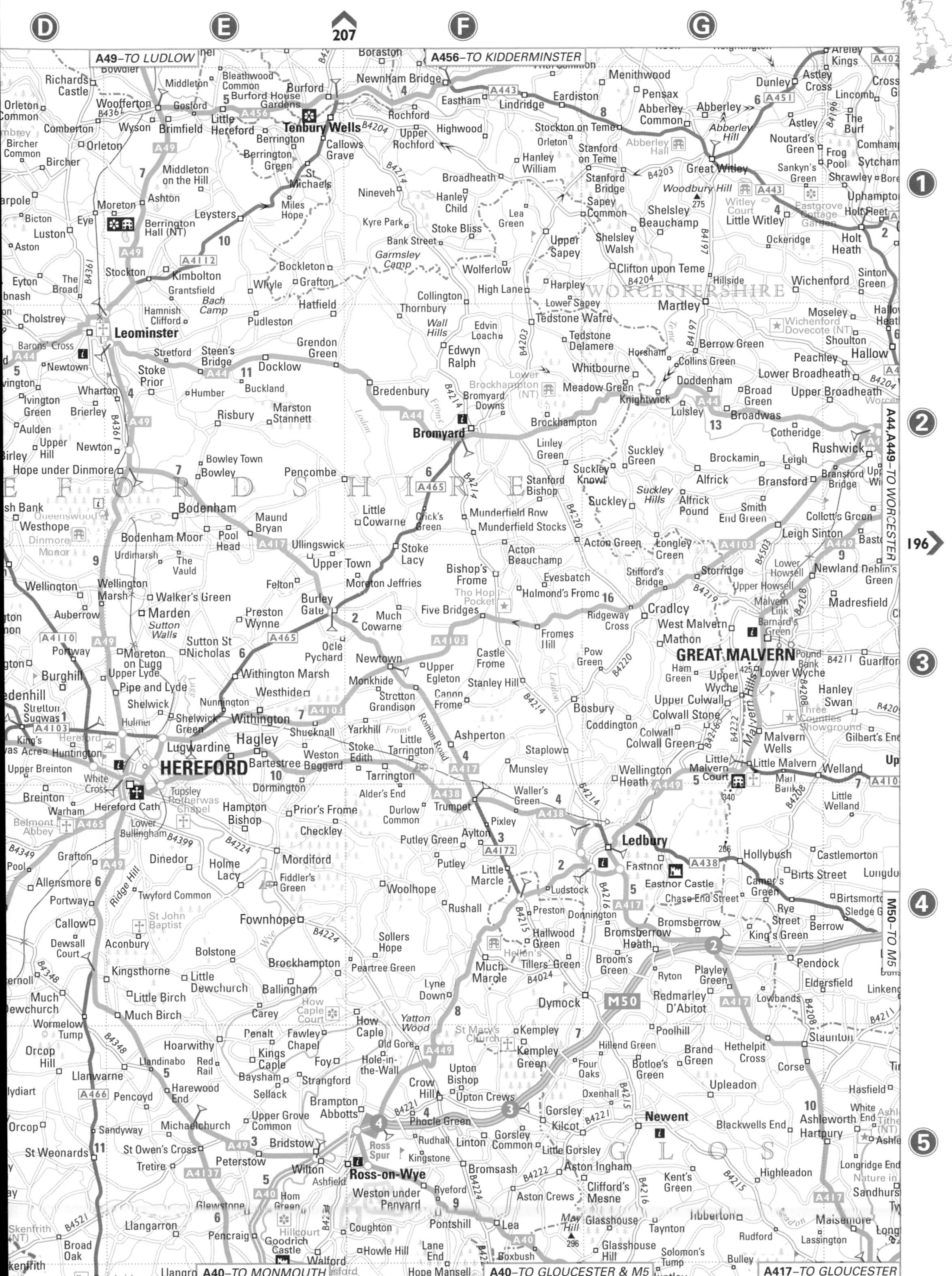
D
E
207
F
G
A49–TO LUDLOW
A456–TO KIDDERMINSTER
A44,A449–TO WORCESTER
196
M50–TO M5
A40–TO MONMOUTH
A40–TO GLOUCESTER & M5
A417–TO GLOUCESTER
Tenbury Wells
Leominster
Bromyard
HEREFORD
GREAT MALVERN
Ledbury
Newent
Ross-on-Wye
WORCESTERSHIRE
HEREFORDSHIRE
GLOS
1
2
3
4
5

Great Malvern: *Famous for its abundance of springs and wells. It is claimed that St Ann's Well was the source of the first bottled water to be sold in Britain in 1850.* ***Map ref. G3***

181

Little Malvern: *Basil Charles Godfrey Place, Royal Navy, was born here on the 19th July 1921. Lieutenant Place was awarded the Victoria Cross for a daring midget submarine attack on the German Battleship Tirpitz. The Tirpitz, sister ship of the Bismark, was 50,000 tons and had a crew of 2,340. The attack at Kaa Fjord, Norway on the 22nd September 1943 involved attaching magnetic mines to the hull which put the battleship out of action for several weeks. Lt. Place VC died in December 1994.* ***Map ref. G3***

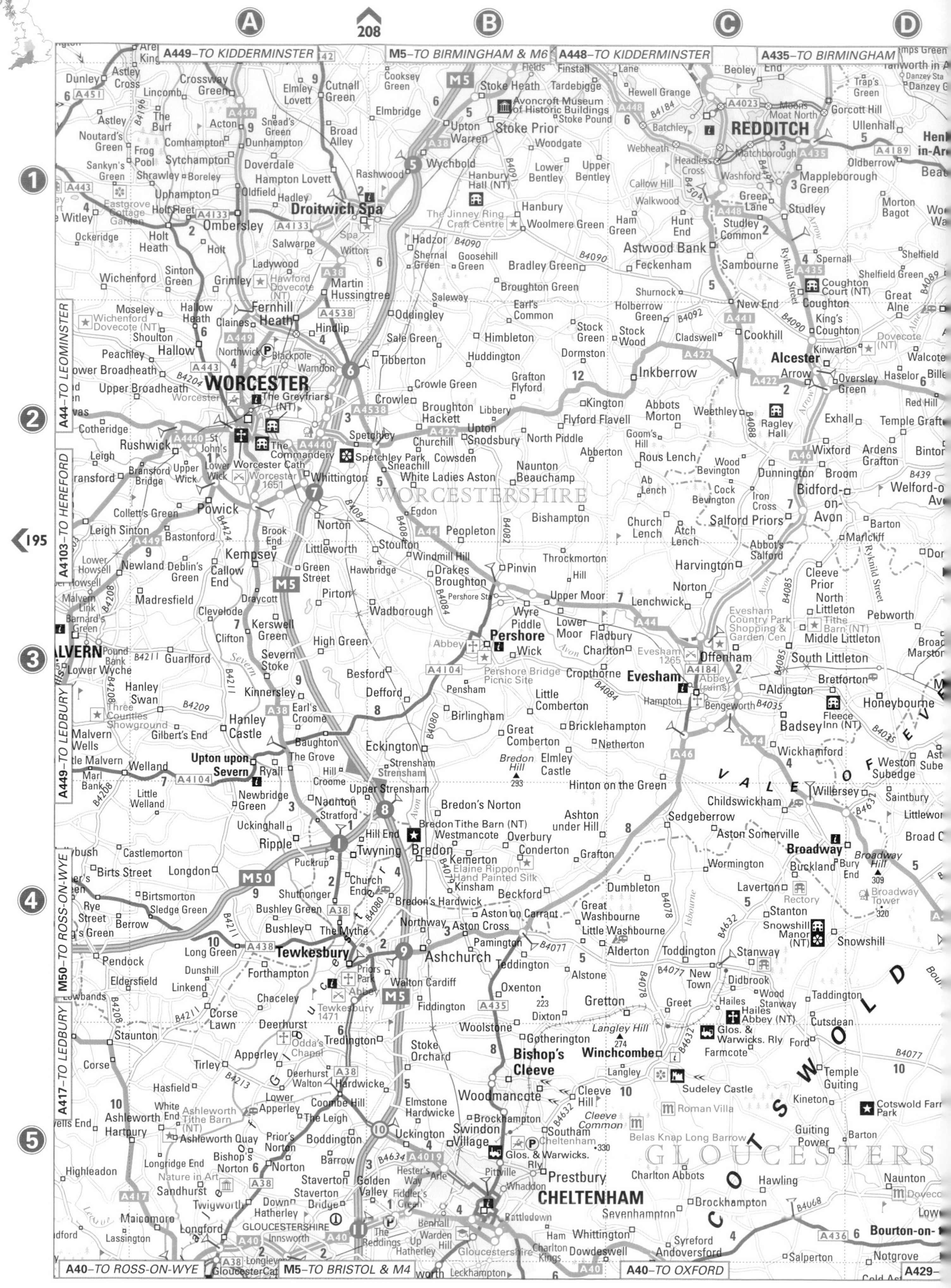

A
B
C
D
208
A449–TO KIDDERMINSTER
M5–TO BIRMINGHAM & M6
A448–TO KIDDERMINSTER
A435–TO BIRMINGHAM
A44–TO LEOMINSTER
A4103–TO HEREFORD
A449–TO LEDBURY
M50–TO ROSS-ON-WYE
A417–TO LEDBURY
A40–TO ROSS-ON-WYE
M5–TO BRISTOL & M4
A40–TO OXFORD
195
1
2
3
4
5
REDDITCH
Droitwich Spa
WORCESTER
Alcester
Inkberrow
Astwood Bank
Feckenham
Ombersley
Hallow
Kempsey
Pershore
Evesham
Bidford-on-Avon
Upton upon Severn
Tewkesbury
Ashchurch
Bredon
Broadway
Winchcombe
Bishop's Cleeve
CHELTENHAM
Prestbury
Woodmancote
WORCESTERSHIRE
GLOUCESTERSHIRE
VALE OF EVESHAM
COTSWOLDS
Avoncroft Museum of Historic Buildings
The Jinney Ring Craft Centre
Hanbury Hall (NT)
Spetchley Park
The Commandery
Worcester Cath
The Greyfriars (NT)
Coughton Court (NT)
Ragley Hall
Middle Littleton Tithe Barn (NT)
Evesham Country Park Shopping & Garden Cen
Bredon Tithe Barn (NT)
Fleece Inn (NT)
Snowshill Manor (NT)
Hailes Abbey (NT)
Sudeley Castle
Belas Knap Long Barrow
Cotswold Farm Park
Glos. & Warwicks. Rly
Tewkesbury 1471
Odda's Chapel
Ashleworth Tithe Barn (NT)
Broadway Tower
M5
M50
Severn
Avon

Tewkesbury: *Scene of a bloody battle of the Wars of the Roses. Many of the defeated Lancastrians sought refuge in Tewkesbury Abbey only to be captured by the Yorkists and executed in the town square. The site of the battle is still known locally as 'Bloody Meadow'.* ***Map ref. A4.***

182

Droitwich: *Famous for its Brine Spa. The natural Droitwich brine contains 2.5 pounds of salt for each gallon of water, that's ten times more than normal sea water and on a par with the Dead Sea. It was possible to float weightlessly in the warm brine of the 1876 Brine Baths. These baths were replaced in 1985 with the first new Spa facility to be built in Britain in the twentieth century.* ***Map ref. A1.***

209

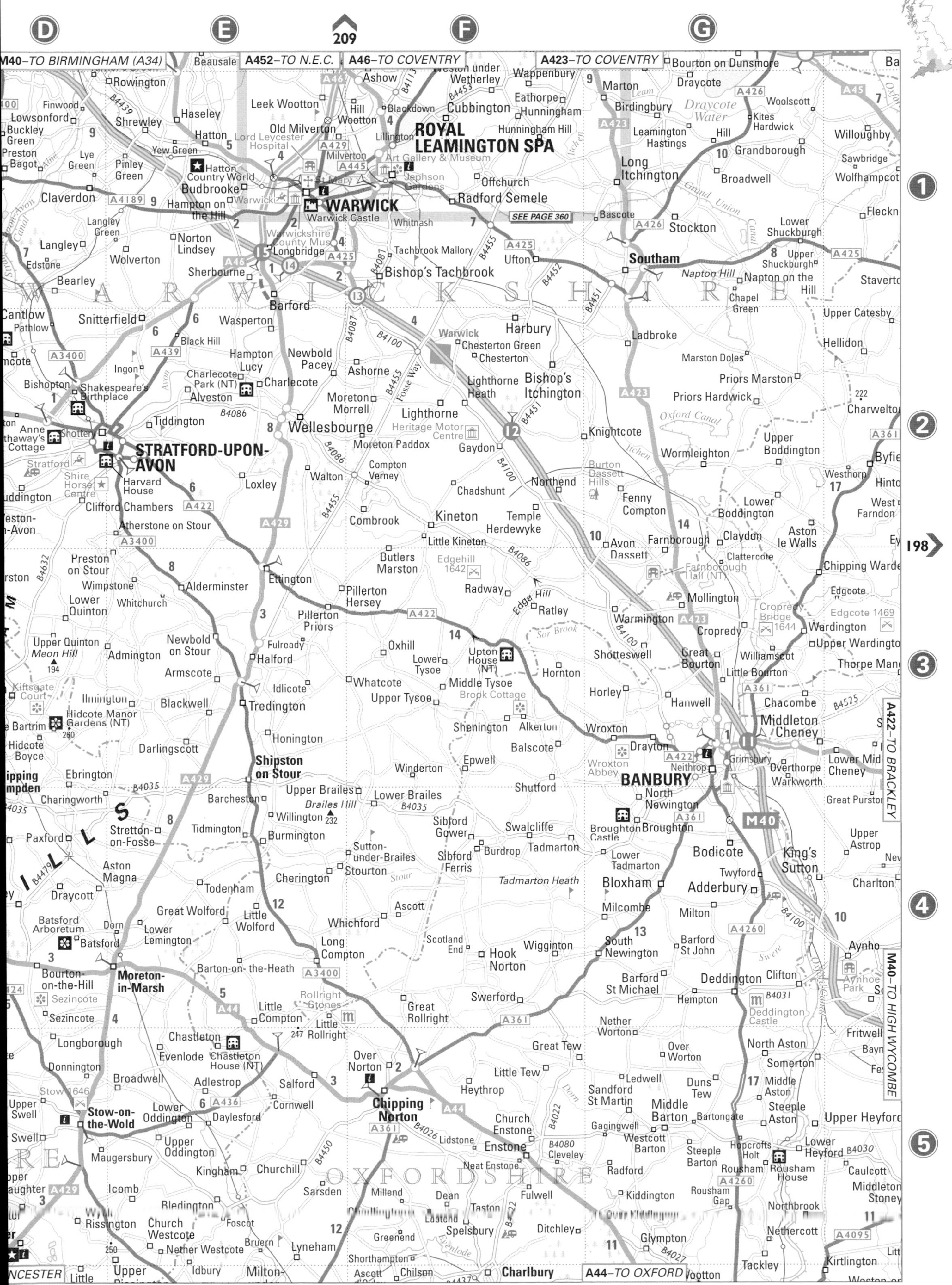

D
E
F
G
M40–TO BIRMINGHAM (A34)
A452–TO N.E.C.
A46–TO COVENTRY
A423–TO COVENTRY
Beausale
Rowington
Ashow
Weston under Wetherley
Wappenbury
Marton
Bourton on Dunsmore
Draycote
Finwood
Lowsonford
Buckley Green
Preston Bagot
Shrewley
Haseley
Hatton
Leek Wootton
Hill
Blackdown
Cubbington
Eathorpe
Hunningham
Birdingbury
Draycote Water
Kites Hardwick
Woolscott
Willoughby
Old Milverton
Wootton
ROYAL LEAMINGTON SPA
Hunningham Hill
Leamington Hastings
Hill
Grandborough
Sawbridge
Wolfhampcote
Lye Green
Pinley Green
Yew Green
Lord Leycester Hospital
Lillington
Milverton
Art Gallery & Museum
Jephson Gardens
Long Itchington
Broadwell
Hatton Country World
Budbrooke
Offchurch
Radford Semele
Claverdon
Hampton on the Hill
Warwick
WARWICK
Warwick Castle
SEE PAGE 360
Bascote
Flecknoe
Langley Green
Whitnash
Stockton
Lower Shuckburgh
Langley
Norton Lindsey
Warwickshire County Museum
Longbridge
Tachbrook Mallory
Ufton
Southam
Upper Shuckburgh
Edstone
Wolverton
Bishop's Tachbrook
Napton Hill
Napton on the Hill
Staverton
Bearley
Sherbourne
Barford
Chapel Green
WARWICKSHIRE
Cantlow
Pathlow
Snitterfield
Wasperton
Harbury
Ladbroke
Upper Catesby
Black Hill
Warwick
Chesterton Green
Chesterton
Hellidon
Hampton Lucy
Newbold Pacey
Ashorne
Marston Doles
Ingon
Charlecote Park (NT)
Charlecote
Lighthorne Heath
Bishop's Itchington
Priors Marston
Alveston
Moreton Morrell
Lighthorne
Priors Hardwick
Charwelton
Bishopton
Shakespeare's Birthplace
Tiddington
Wellesbourne
Heritage Motor Centre
Oxford Canal
Anne Hathaway's Cottage
Shottery
STRATFORD-UPON-AVON
Moreton Paddox
Gaydon
Knightcote
Upper Boddington
Byfield
Wormleighton
Stratford
Shire Horse Centre
Harvard House
Compton Verney
Walton
Loxley
Burton Dassett Hills
Westhorp
Hinton
Chadshunt
Northend
Fenny Compton
Lower Boddington
West Farndon
Clifford Chambers
Combrook
Kineton
Temple Herdewyke
Aston le Walls
Weston-on-Avon
Atherstone on Stour
Little Kineton
Avon Dassett
Farnborough
Claydon
Preston on Stour
Butlers Marston
Edgehill 1642
Clattercote
Farnborough Hall (NT)
Chipping Warden
Wimpstone
Alderminster
Ettington
Pillerton Hersey
Radway
Edge Hill
Ratley
Mollington
Edgcote
Lower Quinton
Whitchurch
Pillerton Priors
Warmington
Cropredy
Cropredy Bridge 1644
Edgcote 1469
Wardington
Upper Wardington
Upper Quinton
Meon Hill
Admington
Newbold on Stour
Fulready
Halford
Oxhill
Lower Tysoe
Upton House (NT)
Sor Brook
Shotteswell
Great Bourton
Williamscot
Thorpe Mandeville
Armscote
Hornton
Little Bourton
Kiftsgate Court
Ilmington
Blackwell
Idlicote
Whatcote
Middle Tysoe
Upper Tysoe
Brook Cottage
Horley
Hanwell
Chacombe
Hidcote Manor Gardens (NT)
Tredington
Shenington
Alkerton
Wroxton
Middleton Cheney
Hidcote Bartrim
Hidcote Boyce
Darlingscott
Honington
Balscote
Drayton
Chipping Campden
Ebrington
Shipston on Stour
Winderton
Epwell
Wroxton Abbey
Neithrop
Grimsbury
Overthorpe
Warkworth
Lower Middleton Cheney
BANBURY
Charingworth
Barcheston
Upper Brailes
Brailes Hill
Lower Brailes
Shutford
North Newington
Great Purston
Willington
Sibford Gower
Swalcliffe
Broughton Castle
Broughton
Upper Astrop
Paxford
Stretton-on-Fosse
Tidmington
Burmington
Sutton-under-Brailes
Sibford Ferris
Burdrop
Tadmarton
Lower Tadmarton
Bodicote
King's Sutton
Aston Magna
Stourton
Cherington
Todenham
Tadmarton Heath
Bloxham
Twyford
Adderbury
Charlton
Draycott
Great Wolford
Little Wolford
Ascott
Milcombe
Milton
Batsford Arboretum
Dorn
Lower Lemington
Whichford
Batsford
Scotland End
Hook Norton
Wigginton
South Newington
Barford St John
Aynho
Long Compton
Barton-on-the-Heath
Bourton-on-the-Hill
Moreton-in-Marsh
Barford St Michael
Deddington
Clifton
Aynho Park
Sezincote
Rollright Stones
Great Rollright
Swerford
Hempton
Deddington Castle
Little Compton
Little Rollright
Nether Worton
Fritwell
Chastleton
Chastleton House (NT)
Evenlode
Longborough
Great Tew
Over Worton
North Aston
Donnington
Over Norton
Little Tew
Ledwell
Somerton
Broadwell
Adlestrop
Salford
Sandford St Martin
Duns Tew
Middle Aston
Stow 1646
Heythrop
Middle Barton
Bartongate
Steeple Aston
Upper Swell
Lower Oddington
Daylesford
Cornwell
Chipping Norton
Church Enstone
Upper Heyford
Stow-on-the-Wold
Swell
Upper Oddington
Lidstone
Enstone
Gagingwell
Westcott Barton
Steeple Barton
Hopcrofts Holt
Lower Heyford
Maugersbury
Cleveley
Neat Enstone
Rousham
Rousham House
Caulcott
Kingham
Churchill
OXFORDSHIRE
Radford
Middleton Stoney
Upper Slaughter
Icomb
Sarsden
Millend
Dean
Fulwell
Kiddington
Rousham Gap
Northbrook
Bledington
Taston
Rissington
Church Westcote
Foscot
Lyneham
Chadlington
Spelsbury
Ditchley
Glympton
Nethercott
Nether Westcote
Bruern
Greenend
Evenlode
Shorthampton
Tackley
Kirtlington
Little Rissington
Upper
Idbury
Milton-
Ascott
Chilson
Charlbury
A44–TO OXFORD
Wootton
A422–TO BRACKLEY
M40–TO HIGH WYCOMBE
CIRENCESTER
1
2
3
4
5

Stow-on-the-Wold: *The Royalist in Digbeth Street is probably the oldest pub building in Britain, containing beams carbon-dated to 947AD.* ***Map ref. D5.***

Banbury: *The place in the nursery rhyme 'Ride a Cock Horse to Banbury Cross'. In fact there have been several Banbury Crosses over the years but the surviving one stands at the junction of four major roads and was built in 1859 to commemorate the marriage of the then Princess Royal to Prince Frederick of Prussia.* ***Map ref. G3.***

198
183

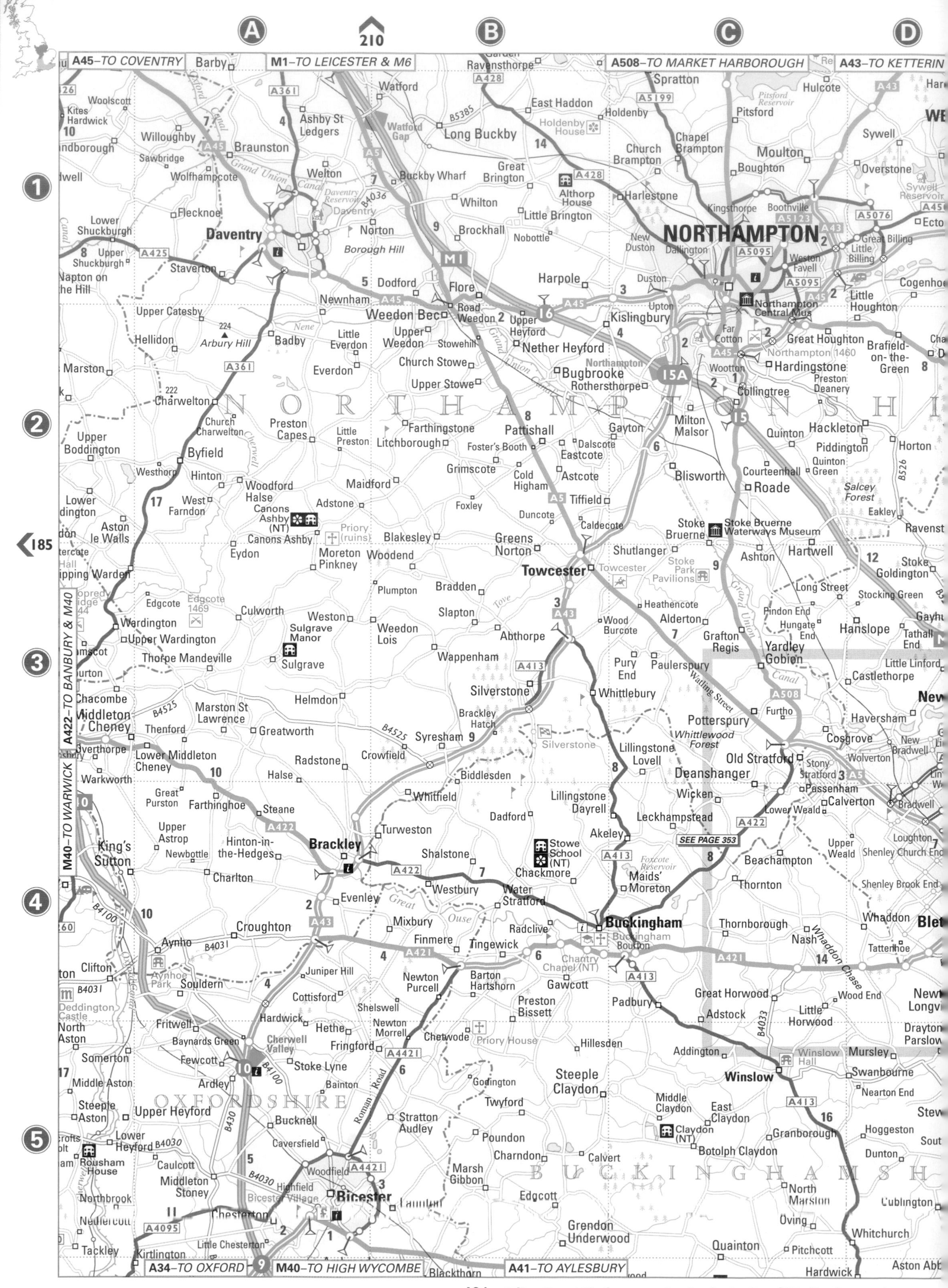
A
B
C
D
210
1
2
3
4
5
185
184
A45–TO COVENTRY
M1–TO LEICESTER & M6
A508–TO MARKET HARBOROUGH
A43–TO KETTERIN
A422–TO BANBURY & M40
M40–TO WARWICK
A34–TO OXFORD
M40–TO HIGH WYCOMBE
A41–TO AYLESBURY
Barby
Ravensthorpe
Spratton
Hulcote
Watford
East Haddon
Holdenby
Pitsford
Pitsford Reservoir
Woolscott
Kites Hardwick
Ashby St Ledgers
Holdenby House
Willoughby
Braunston
Long Buckby
Chapel Brampton
Church Brampton
Sywell
Sawbridge
Moulton
Boughton
Overstone
Wolfhampcote
Welton
Buckby Wharf
Great Brington
Althorp House
Harlestone
Sywell Reservoir
Daventry Reservoir
Daventry
Whilton
Kingsthorpe
Boothville
Flecknoe
Norton
Little Brington
Lower Shuckburgh
Brockhall
Nobottle
New Duston
NORTHAMPTON
Ecton
Borough Hill
Dallington
Great Billing
Little Billing
Upper Shuckburgh
Weston Favell
Napton on the Hill
Staverton
Dodford
Flore
Harpole
Duston
Cogenhoe
Newnham
Weedon Bec
Road Weedon
Upper Heyford
Kislingbury
Upton
Northampton Central Mus
Little Houghton
Upper Catesby
Nene
Little Everdon
Upper Weedon
Stowehill
Nether Heyford
Far Cotton
Great Houghton
Brafield-on-the-Green
Hellidon
Arbury Hill
Badby
Everdon
Church Stowe
Northampton
Bugbrooke
Wootton
Hardingstone
Marston
Upper Stowe
Rothersthorpe
Preston Deanery
Charwelton
Collingtree
NORTHAMPTONSHI
Church Charwelton
Preston Capes
Little Preston
Farthingstone
Pattishall
Gayton
Milton Malsor
Quinton
Hackleton
Upper Boddington
Litchborough
Foster's Booth
Dalscote
Eastcote
Piddington
Horton
Byfield
Blisworth
Courteenhall
Quinton Green
Westhorp
Hinton
Woodford Halse
Maidford
Grimscote
Cold Higham
Astcote
Roade
Salcey Forest
Lower Boddington
West Farndon
Adstone
Foxley
Tiffield
Canons Ashby (NT)
Duncote
Eakley
Aston le Walls
Priory (ruins)
Caldecote
Stoke Bruerne
Stoke Bruerne Waterways Museum
Ravenst
Canons Ashby
Blakesley
Greens Norton
Shutlanger
Hartwell
Eydon
Moreton Pinkney
Woodend
Towcester
Stoke Park Pavilions
Ashton
Stoke Goldington
Chipping Warden
Plumpton
Bradden
Long Street
Stocking Green
Edgcote
Edgcote 1469
Culworth
Heathencote
Pindon End
Gayhu
Slapton
Alderton
Hungate End
Wardington
Weston
Weedon Lois
Wood Burcote
Hanslope
Tathall End
Upper Wardington
Sulgrave Manor
Abthorpe
Grafton Regis
Yardley Gobion
Thorpe Mandeville
Sulgrave
Wappenham
Pury End
Paulerspury
Little Linford
Castlethorpe
Chacombe
Helmdon
Silverstone
Whittlebury
Watling Street
Furtho
Middleton Cheney
Marston St Lawrence
Brackley Hatch
Potterspury
Haversham
Thenford
Greatworth
Syresham
Whittlewood Forest
Cosgrove
New Bradwell
Overthorpe
Lower Middleton Cheney
Radstone
Crowfield
Lillingstone Lovell
Old Stratford
Stony Stratford
Wolverton
Warkworth
Halse
Biddlesden
Deanshanger
Passenham
Great Purston
Farthinghoe
Steane
Whitfield
Lillingstone Dayrell
Wicken
Calverton
Bradwell
Dadford
Leckhampstead
Lower Weald
Upper Astrop
Hinton-in-the-Hedges
Turweston
Akeley
SEE PAGE 353
Loughton
King's Sutton
Newbottle
Brackley
Shalstone
Stowe School (NT)
Upper Weald
Shenley Church End
Charlton
Chackmore
Foxcote Reservoir
Beachampton
Maids' Moreton
Westbury
Water Stratford
Thornton
Shenley Brook End
Evenley
Great Ouse
Mixbury
Radclive
Buckingham
Thornborough
Whaddon
Croughton
Finmere
Tingewick
Buckingham Bourton
Nash
Aynho
Tattenhoe
Whaddon Chase
Clifton
Juniper Hill
Newton Purcell
Barton Hartshorn
Chantry Chapel (NT)
Aynhoe Park
Souldern
Gawcott
Great Horwood
Wood End
Deddington Castle
Cottisford
Preston Bissett
Padbury
Adstock
Little Horwood
North Aston
Shelswell
Fritwell
Hardwick
Hethe
Newton Morrell
Chetwode
Priory House
Hillesden
Drayton Parslow
Baynards Green
Cherwell Valley
Fringford
Addington
Winslow Hall
Mursley
Somerton
Fewcott
Stoke Lyne
Winslow
Swanbourne
Middle Aston
Ardley
Bainton
Godington
Steeple Claydon
Nearton End
Roman Road
OXFORDSHIRE
Twyford
Middle Claydon
East Claydon
Steeple Aston
Upper Heyford
Stratton Audley
Bucknell
Claydon (NT)
Granborough
Hoggeston
Lower Heyford
Rousham House
Poundon
Caversfield
Botolph Claydon
Dunton
Caulcott
Charndon
Calvert
Middleton Stoney
Woodfield
Marsh Gibbon
BUCKINGHAMSH
Northbrook
Highfield
Bicester Village
Bicester
Edgcott
North Marston
Cublington
Chesterton
Oving
Grendon Underwood
Whitchurch
Tackley
Little Chesterton
Quainton
Pitchcott
Kirtlington
Blackthorn
Hardwick
Aston Abb

Stony Stratford: *The Cock and The Bull Inns sit side by side on the main street which was the old coach route from London. Coach drivers would stop over here and exchange gossip; this gave rise to the term Cock and Bull Story.* ***Map ref. C3***

Milton Ernest: *The famous wartime bandleader Glenn Miller flew from nearby Twinwood Airfield, in a single-engine Norseman aircraft on Friday 15th December 1944 and was never seen again. His band were due to play a concert to allied troops stationed in Paris and Miller was flying out ahead of the main band. At 6pm on Christmas Eve 1944 a Press Release announced that Glenn Miller was dead.* ***Map ref. F2***

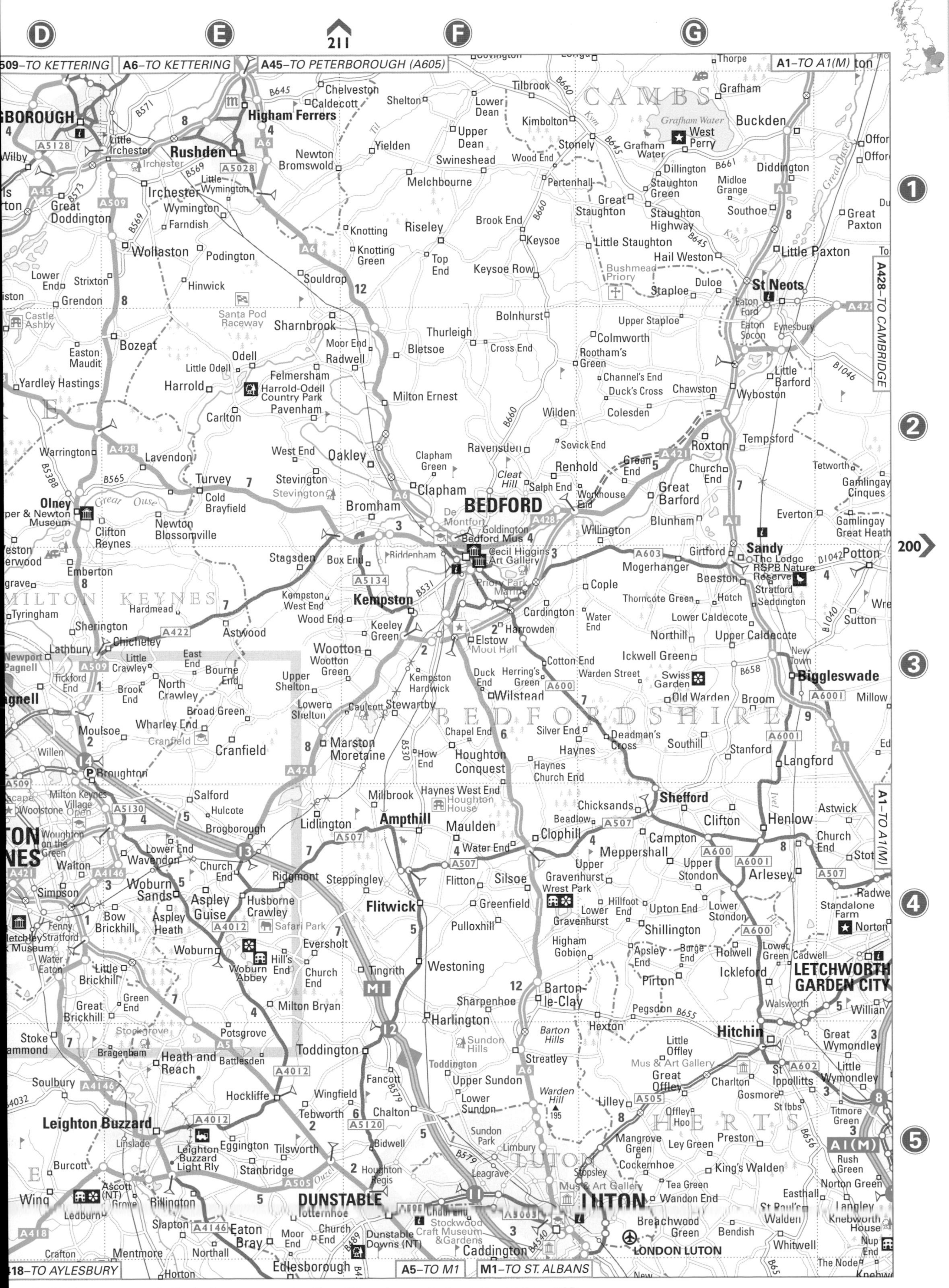
D
E
211
F
G
A509–TO KETTERING
A6–TO KETTERING
A45–TO PETERBOROUGH (A605)
A1–TO A1(M)
Thorpe
Grafham
CAMBS
Grafham Water
West Perry
Buckden
Tilbrook
Kimbolton
Stonely
Chelveston
Caldecott
Shelton
Lower Dean
Upper Dean
Higham Ferrers
Rushden
Little Irchester
Irchester
Newton Bromswold
Yielden
Swineshead
Wood End
Pertenhall
Great Staughton
Dillington
Staughton Green
Midloe Grange
Diddington
Offord
Great Paxton
Southoe
Staughton Highway
Little Paxton
Little Staughton
Hail Weston
St Neots
Little Wymington
Wymington
Farndish
Great Doddington
Wollaston
Podington
Knotting
Knotting Green
Riseley
Top End
Brook End
Keysoe
Keysoe Row
Melchbourne
Bushmead Priory
Staploe
Duloe
Eaton Ford
Eaton Socon
Eynesbury
Lower End
Strixton
Grendon
Hinwick
Souldrop
Castle Ashby
Santa Pod Raceway
Sharnbrook
Bolnhurst
Upper Staploe
Colmworth
Thurleigh
Cross End
Rootham's Green
Channel's End
Duck's Cross
Chawston
Wyboston
Little Barford
Easton Maudit
Bozeat
Odell
Little Odell
Moor End
Radwell
Bletsoe
Felmersham
Harrold
Harrold-Odell Country Park
Pavenham
Milton Ernest
Carlton
Yardley Hastings
Wilden
Colesden
Tempsford
Roxton
Warrington
Lavendon
West End
Oakley
Clapham Green
Clapham
Ravensden
Sovick End
Renhold
Green End
Church End
Great Barford
Tetworth
Gamlingay Cinques
Gamlingay
Gamlingay Great Heath
Olney
Cowper & Newton Museum
Turvey
Stevington
Cold Brayfield
Bromham
Cleat Hill
Salph End
Workhouse End
BEDFORD
De Montfort
Goldington
Bedford Mus
Cecil Higgins Art Gallery
Blunham
Everton
Clifton Reynes
Newton Blossomville
Emberton
Stagsden
Box End
Biddenham
Willington
Girtford
Sandy
The Lodge RSPB Nature Reserve
Potton
200
MILTON KEYNES
Hardmead
Tyringham
Sherington
Chicheley
Kempston
Kempston West End
Wood End
Keeley Green
Priory Park Marina
Cardington
Mogerhanger
Copple
Beeston
Stratford
Seddington
Thorncote Green
Hatch
Water End
Lower Caldecote
Upper Caldecote
Sutton
Astwood
Elstow
Moot Hall
Harrowden
Northill
Ickwell Green
Lathbury
Newport Pagnell
Tickford End
Little Crawley
East End
Bourne End
North Crawley
Brook End
Wootton
Wootton Green
Upper Shelton
Kempston Hardwick
Duck End
Herring's Green
Wilstead
Cotton End
Warden Street
Swiss Garden
Old Warden
Biggleswade
Broom
Lower Shelton
Caulcott
Stewartby
BEDFORDSHIRE
Broad Green
Wharley End
Cranfield
Moulsoe
Willen
Marston Moretaine
How End
Chapel End
Houghton Conquest
Silver End
Haynes
Haynes Church End
Deadman's Cross
Southill
Stanford
Langford
Broughton
Milton Keynes Village
Woolstone
Salford
Hulcote
Brogborough
Millbrook
Haynes West End
Houghton House
Lidlington
Ampthill
Maulden
Chicksands
Beadlow
Shefford
Clifton
Henlow
Astwick
Church End
Campton
Clophill
Meppershall
Upper Stondon
Arlesey
Woughton on the Green
Walton
Lower End
Wavendon
Church End
Woburn Sands
Aspley Guise
Ridgmont
Husborne Crawley
Steppingley
Flitton
Silsoe
Water End
Upper Gravenhurst
Wrest Park
Hillfoot End
Upton End
Lower Stondon
Standalone Farm
Radwell
Norton
Simpson
Bow Brickhill
Aspley Heath
Safari Park
Flitwick
Greenfield
Lower Gravenhurst
Shillington
Fenny Stratford
Bletchley
Woburn
Woburn Abbey
Hill's End
Eversholt
Pulloxhill
Higham Gobion
Apsley End
Burge End
Holwell
Ickleford
Lower Green
Cadwell
LETCHWORTH GARDEN CITY
Water Eaton
Little Brickhill
Church End
Tingrith
Westoning
Pirton
Great Brickhill
Green End
Milton Bryan
Sharpenhoe
Barton-le-Clay
Pegsdon
Walsworth
William
Stoke Hammond
Stockgrove
Potsgrove
Harlington
Barton Hills
Hexton
Hitchin
Great Wymondley
Little Wymondley
Bragenham
Heath and Reach
Battlesden
Toddington
Sundon Hills
Streatley
Little Offley
Mus & Art Gallery
St Ippollitts
Soulbury
Hockliffe
Fancott
Upper Sundon
Warden Hill
Great Offley
Charlton
Gosmore
Wingfield
Lower Sundon
Lilley
Offley Hoo
HERTS
St Ibbs
Titmore Green
Leighton Buzzard
Tebworth
Chalton
Linslade
Leighton Buzzard Light Rly
Eggington
Tilsworth
Bidwell
Sundon Park
Limbury
Mangrove Green
Ley Green
Preston
Rush Green
Burcott
Stanbridge
Houghton Regis
Leagrave
LUTON
Stopsley
Cockernhoe
King's Walden
Norton Green
Ascott (NT)
Wing
Billington
Totternhoe
DUNSTABLE
Mus & Art Gallery
Tea Green
Wandon End
Easthall
St Paul's Walden
Langley
Knebworth House
Ledburn
Slapton
Eaton Bray
Moor End
Church End
Dunstable Downs (NT)
Stockwood Craft Museum & Gardens
Caddington
Breachwood Green
Bendish
Whitwell
Nup End
Crafton
Mentmore
Northall
LONDON LUTON
Edlesborough
The Node
A418–TO AYLESBURY
Horton
A5–TO M1
M1–TO ST. ALBANS
A428–TO CAMBRIDGE
A1–TO A1(M)
1
2
3
4
5

The M1 Motorway: *towards Birmingham was opened on the 2nd November 1959 by Ernest Marples the Minister of Transport. When it was first opened there was no speed limit. The first 72 miles was built in 19 months, employing a 5,000 labour force, at a cost of £17,000,000. One mile was constructed every 8 days. The motorway currently carries 88,000 vehicles per day compared to 13,000 when it was first opened. Traffic is heaviest between junctions 7 and 10, St Albans to Luton.*

185

A B C D

212

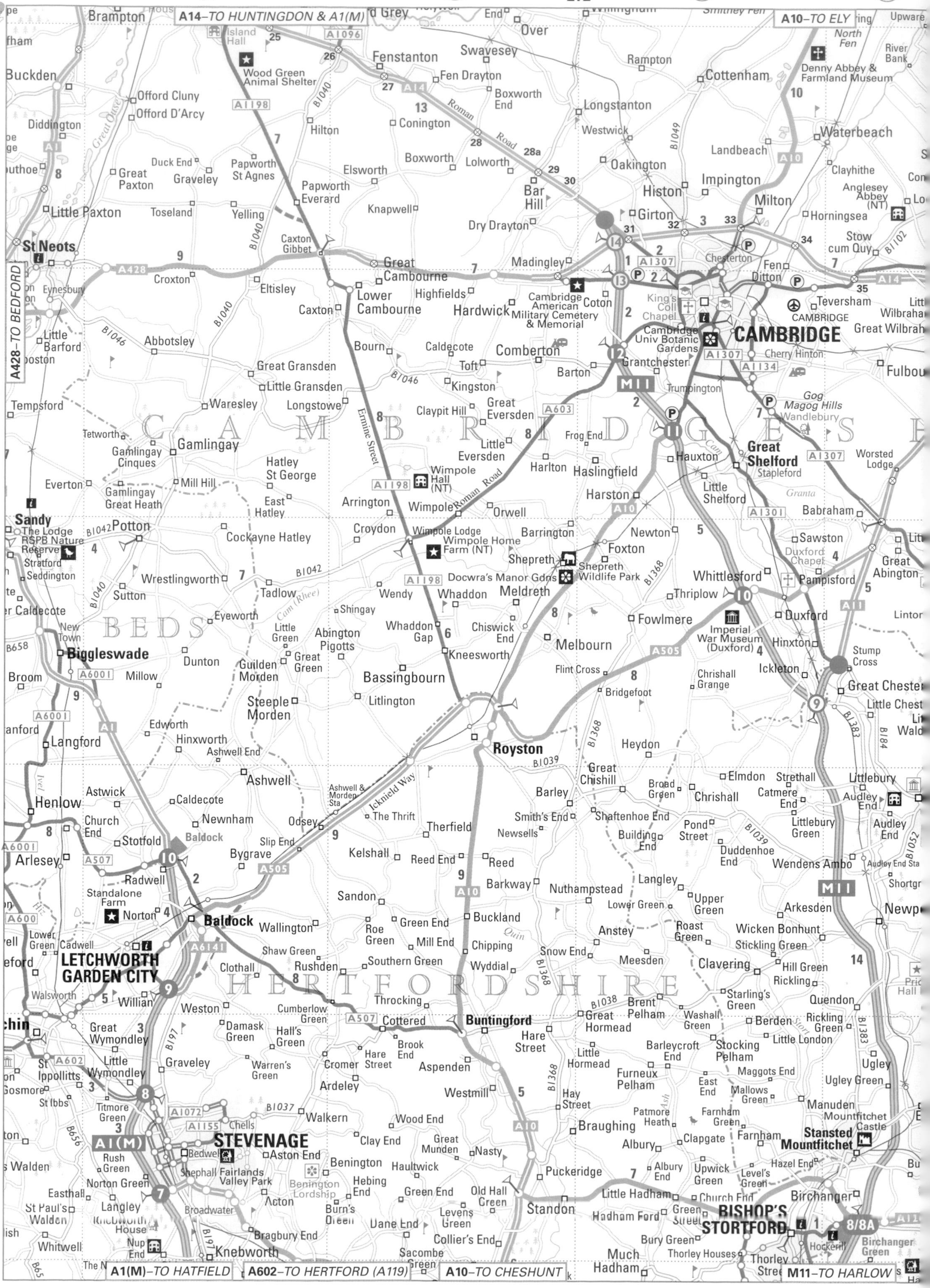

A14–TO HUNTINGDON & A1(M)

A10–TO ELY

A428–TO BEDFORD

199

A1(M)–TO HATFIELD

A602–TO HERTFORD (A119)

A10–TO CHESHUNT

M11–TO HARLOW

1 2 3 4 5

Letchworth Garden City: *This was the first Garden City to be built in Britain. Ebenezer Howard (1850–1928) was the driving force behind its development. He and others formed Garden City Ltd. in 1903 and issued shares to raise the capital needed. They purchased Letchworth Manor and the surrounding land and building work started in 1903.* ***Map ref. A4***

186

Newmarket: *Horse Racing started here with the first recorded race taking place in 1622. A horse belonging to Lord Salisbury beat one owned by the Marquess of Buckingham for a prize of £100.* ***Map ref. E1***

213

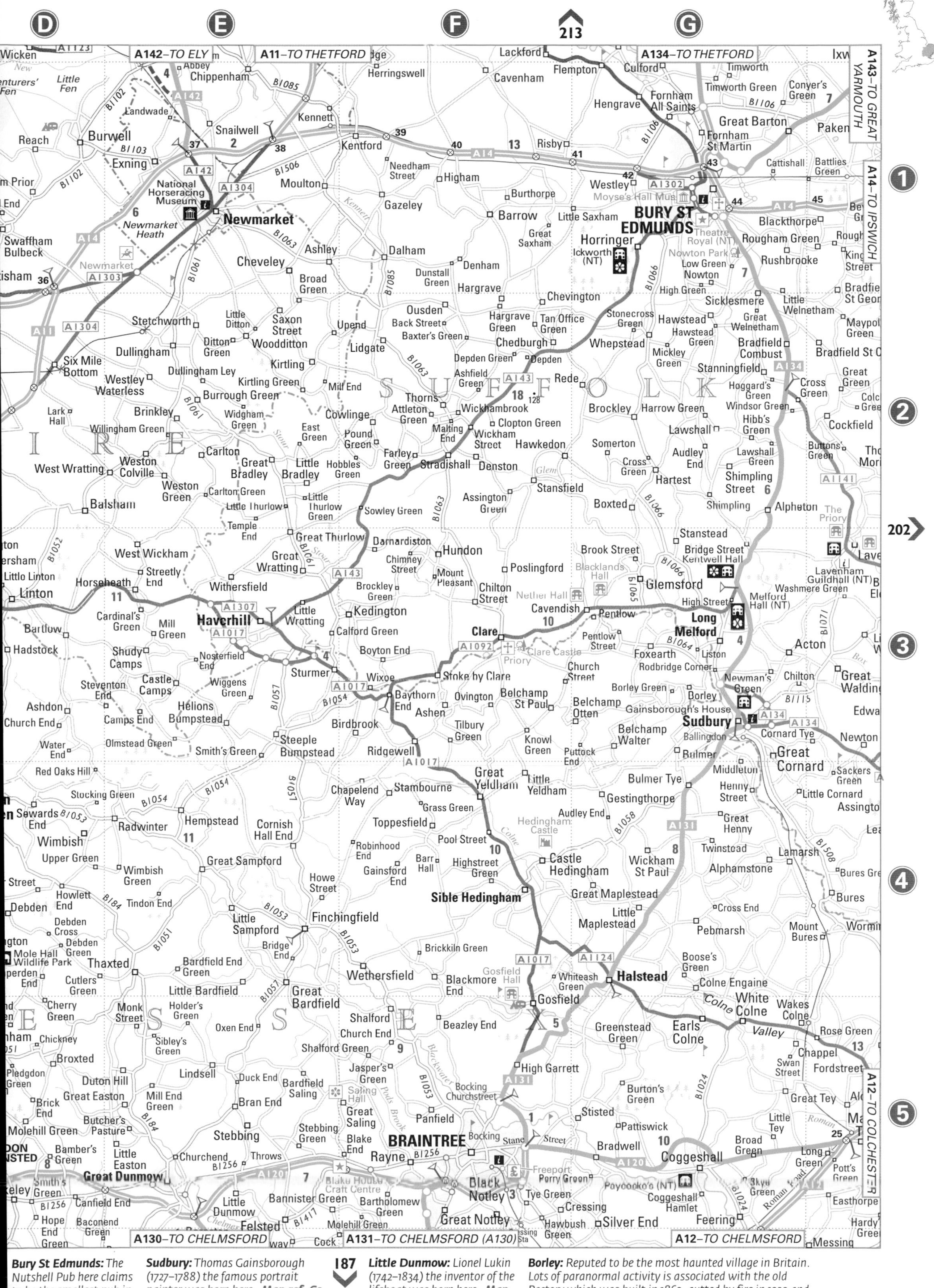
D
E
F
G
A142–TO ELY
A11–TO THETFORD
A134–TO THETFORD
A143–TO GREAT YARMOUTH
A14–TO IPSWICH
A12–TO COLCHESTER
A130–TO CHELMSFORD
A131–TO CHELMSFORD (A130)
A12–TO CHELMSFORD
1
2
3
4
5
Wicken
Chippenham
Herringswell
Lackford
Flempton
Cavenham
Culford
Timworth
Timworth Green
Conyer's Green
Fornham All Saints
Hengrave
Great Barton
Fornham St Martin
Pakenham
Landwade
Kennett
Reach
Burwell
Snailwell
Kentford
Risby
Exning
Needham Street
Higham
Moulton
Gazeley
Burthorpe
Barrow
Little Saxham
Westley
Moyse's Hall Mus.
BURY ST EDMUNDS
Cattishall
Battlies Green
Blackthorpe
Rougham Green
Rushbrooke
National Horseracing Museum
Newmarket
Newmarket Heath
Swaffham Bulbeck
Ashley
Dalham
Great Saxham
Horringer
Ickworth (NT)
Theatre Royal (NT)
Nowton Park
Low Green
Nowton
Cheveley
Broad Green
Dunstall Green
Denham
Hargrave
Chevington
High Green
Sicklesmere
Little Welnetham
Great Welnetham
Stetchworth
Little Ditton
Saxon Street
Upend
Ousden
Back Street
Baxter's Green
Hargrave Green
Tan Office Green
Stonecross Green
Hawstead
Hawstead Green
Bradfield Combust
Ditton Green
Woodditton
Lidgate
Chedburgh
Whepstead
Mickley Green
Dullingham
Kirtling
Depden Green
Depden
Stanningfield
Six Mile Bottom
Westley Waterless
Dullingham Ley
Kirtling Green
Mill End
Ashfield Green
Rede
Hoggard's Green
Cross Green
Burrough Green
Thorns
Wickhambrook
Brockley
Harrow Green
Windsor Green
Lark Hall
Brinkley
Widgham Green
Cowlinge
Attleton Green
Clopton Green
Lawshall
Hibb's Green
Cockfield
Willingham Green
East Green
Pound Green
Malting End
Wickham Street
Hawkedon
Somerton
Audley End
Lawshall Green
Carlton
Weston Colville
West Wratting
Great Bradley
Little Bradley
Hobbles Green
Farley Green
Stradishall
Denston
Cross Green
Hartest
Shimpling Street
Weston Green
Carlton Green
Little Thurlow
Little Thurlow Green
Assington Green
Stansfield
Boxted
Shimpling
Alpheton
The Priory
Balsham
Sowley Green
Temple End
Great Thurlow
Darnardiston
Stanstead
West Wickham
Chimney Street
Hundon
Brook Street
Bridge Street
Kentwell Hall
Streetly End
Great Wratting
Mount Pleasant
Poslingford
Blacklands Hall
Lavenham Guildhall (NT)
Washmere Green
Linton
Horseheath
Withersfield
Brockley Green
Chilton Street
Nether Hall
Glemsford
Melford Hall (NT)
Cardinal's Green
Mill Green
Haverhill
Little Wratting
Kedington
Cavendish
Pentlow
High Street
Long Melford
Bartlow
Calford Green
Clare
Pentlow Street
Liston
Acton
Hadstock
Shudy Camps
Nosterfield End
Boyton End
Clare Castle
Priory
Foxearth
Rodbridge Corner
Church Street
Sturmer
Stoke by Clare
Newman's Green
Chilton
Great Waldingfield
Steventon End
Castle Camps
Wiggens Green
Wixoe
Baythorn End
Ovington
Belchamp St Paul
Borley Green
Borley
Ashdon
Helions Bumpstead
Ashen
Belchamp Otten
Gainsborough's House
Sudbury
Church End
Camps End
Birdbrook
Tilbury Green
Belchamp Walter
Ballingdon
Cornard Tye
Newton
Water End
Olmstead Green
Steeple Bumpstead
Smith's Green
Ridgewell
Knowl Green
Puttock End
Bulmer
Great Cornard
Red Oaks Hill
Great Yeldham
Little Yeldham
Bulmer Tye
Middleton
Sackers Green
Stocking Green
Chapelend Way
Stambourne
Henny Street
Little Cornard
Sewards End
Radwinter
Hempstead
Grass Green
Gestingthorpe
Assington
Wimbish
Cornish Hall End
Toppesfield
Audley End
Great Henny
Hedingham Castle
Upper Green
Pool Street
Twinstead
Lamarsh
Great Sampford
Robinhood End
Barr Hall
Highstreet Green
Castle Hedingham
Wickham St Paul
Alphamstone
Bures Green
Wimbish Green
Gainsford End
Howe Street
Sible Hedingham
Great Maplestead
Bures
Howlett End
Tindon End
Debden
Finchingfield
Little Maplestead
Cross End
Debden Cross
Little Sampford
Pebmarsh
Mount Bures
Wormingford
Debden Green
Mole Hall Wildlife Park
Bridge End
Brickkiln Green
Thaxted
Bardfield End Green
Wethersfield
Gosfield Hall
Boose's Green
Cutlers Green
Little Bardfield
Great Bardfield
Blackmore End
Whiteash Green
Halstead
Colne Engaine
Cherry Green
Monk Street
Holder's Green
Gosfield
White Colne
Wakes Colne
Oxen End
Shalford
Beazley End
Greenstead Green
Earls Colne
Colne Valley
Rose Green
Chickney
Sibley's Green
Shalford Church End
Broxted
Shalford Green
Chappel
Swan Street
Fordstreet
Pledgdon Green
Lindsell
Jasper's Green
High Garrett
Duton Hill
Duck End
Bardfield Saling
Saling Hall
Bocking Churchstreet
Burton's Green
Great Easton
Mill End Green
Brick End
Great Tey
Bran End
Great Saling
Panfield
Stisted
Little Tey
Butcher's Pasture
Molehill Green
Stebbing
Stebbing Green
Blake End
BRAINTREE
Bocking
Stane Street
Pattiswick
Bradwell
Broad Green
Bamber's Green
Little Easton
Churchend
Throws
Rayne
Coggeshall
Long Green
Great Dunmow
Freeport
Perry Green
Paycocke's (NT)
Skye Green
Pott's Green
Smith's Green
Little Dunmow
Blake House Craft Centre
Black Notley
Tye Green
Coggeshall Hamlet
Canfield End
Bannister Green
Bartholomew Green
Cressing
Eastthorpe
Hope End Green
Baconend Green
Felsted
Molehill Green
Great Notley
Hawbush Green
Silver End
Feering
Hardy's Green
Messing
Roman Road
SUFFOLK
ESSEX

Bury St Edmunds: *The Nutshell Pub here claims to be the smallest pub in Britain.* ***Map ref. G1***

Sudbury: *Thomas Gainsborough (1727–1788) the famous portrait painter was born here.* ***Map ref. G3***

187

Little Dunmow: *Lionel Lukin (1742–1834) the inventor of the lifeboat was born here.* ***Map ref. E5***

Borley: *Reputed to be the most haunted village in Britain. Lots of paranormal activity is associated with the old Rectory which was built in 1863, gutted by fire in 1939 and demolished in 1944.* ***Map ref. G3***

202

214

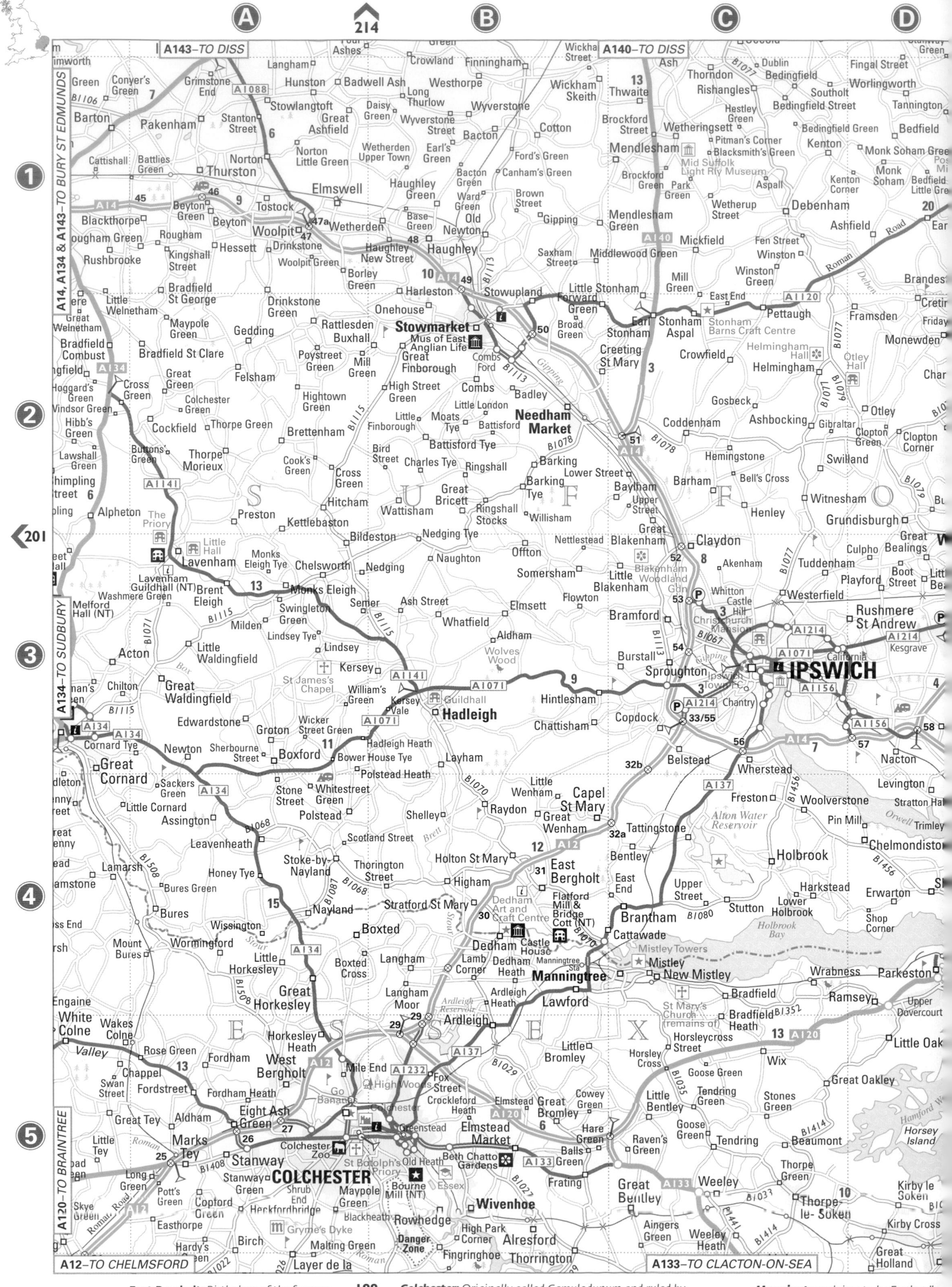
A
B
C
D
A143–TO DISS
A140–TO DISS
A14, A134 & A143–TO BURY ST EDMUNDS
A134–TO SUDBURY
A120–TO BRAINTREE
A12–TO CHELMSFORD
A133–TO CLACTON-ON-SEA
1
2
3
4
5
Langham
Crowland
Finningham
Wickham Street
Thorndon
Dublin
Bedingfield
Fingal Street
Worlingworth
Conyer's Green
Grimstone End
Hunston
Badwell Ash
Westhorpe
Long Thurlow
Wickham Skeith
Thwaite
Rishangles
Southolt
Bedingfield Street
Tannington
Barton
Pakenham
Stanton Street
Stowlangtoft
Daisy Green
Great Ashfield
Wyverstone
Wyverstone Street
Cotton
Brockford Street
Wetheringsett
Hestley Green
Bedingfield Green
Bedfield
Bacton
Norton Little Green
Wetherden Upper Town
Earl's Green
Ford's Green
Mendlesham
Pitman's Corner
Blacksmith's Green
Kenton
Monk Soham Green
Cattishall
Battlies Green
Norton
Thurston
Canham's Green
Mid Suffolk Light Rly Museum
Brockford Green
Park Green
Aspall
Kenton Corner
Monk Soham
Bedfield Little Green
Elmswell
Haughley Green
Bacton Green
Ward Green
Brown Street
Wetherup Street
Debenham
Blackthorpe
Beyton Green
Beyton
Tostock
Wetherden
Base Green
Old Newton
Gipping
Mendlesham Green
Ashfield
Rougham
Rougham Green
Kingshall Street
Hessett
Woolpit
Drinkstone
Haughley
Haughley New Street
Saxham Street
Middlewood Green
Mickfield
Fen Street
Winston
Rushbrooke
Woolpit Green
Borley Green
Winston Green
Bradfield St George
Harleston
Stowupland
Little Stonham
Mill Green
East End
Brandeston
Little Welnetham
Drinkstone Green
Onehouse
Forward Green
Earl Stonham
Stonham Aspal
Pettaugh
Framsden
Great Welnetham
Maypole Green
Gedding
Rattlesden
Buxhall
Stowmarket
Mus of East Anglian Life
Broad Green
Stonham Barns Craft Centre
Bradfield Combust
Bradfield St Clare
Poystreet Green
Mill Green
Great Finborough
Combs Ford
Creeting St Mary
Crowfield
Helmingham Hall
Helmingham
Otley Hall
Monewden
Hoggard's Green
Cross Green
Great Green
Felsham
Hightown Green
High Street Green
Combs
Badley
Windsor Green
Colchester Green
Little London
Needham Market
Gosbeck
Ashbocking
Gibraltar
Otley
Clopton Green
Clopton Corner
Hibb's Green
Cockfield
Thorpe Green
Brettenham
Little Finborough
Moats Tye
Battisford
Coddenham
Battisford Tye
Lawshall Green
Buttons' Green
Thorpe Morieux
Cook's Green
Bird Street
Charles Tye
Ringshall
Barking
Lower Street
Hemingstone
Swilland
Chimpling Street
Cross Green
Great Bricett
Barking Tye
Baylham
Barham
Bell's Cross
Witnesham
Alpheton
Preston
Hitcham
Wattisham
Ringshall Stocks
Willisham
Upper Street
Henley
Grundisburgh
The Priory
Kettlebaston
Bildeston
Nedging Tye
Great Blakenham
Claydon
Great Bealings
Little Hall
Lavenham
Monks Eleigh Tye
Chelsworth
Nedging
Naughton
Offton
Nettlestead
Akenham
Tuddenham
Culpho
Lavenham Guildhall (NT)
Brent Eleigh
Somersham
Little Blakenham
Blakenham Woodland Garden
Playford
Boot Street
Washmere Green
Monks Eleigh
Flowton
Whitton
Westerfield
Melford Hall (NT)
Swingleton Green
Semer
Ash Street
Elmsett
Castle Hill
Rushmere St Andrew
Milden
Whatfield
Bramford
Christchurch Mansion
Lindsey Tye
Aldham
Kesgrave
Acton
Little Waldingfield
Lindsey
Wolves Wood
Burstall
Sproughton
California
Kersey
IPSWICH
St James's Chapel
Ipswich Town FC
Chilton
Great Waldingfield
William's Green
Kersey Vale
Guildhall
Hadleigh
Hintlesham
Chantry
Edwardstone
Groton
Wicker Street Green
Chattisham
Copdock
Cornard Tye
Newton
Sherbourne Street
Boxford
Hadleigh Heath
Bower House Tye
Layham
Belstead
Nacton
Great Cornard
Polstead Heath
Wherstead
Levington
Sackers Green
Stone Street
Whitestreet Green
Little Wenham
Capel St Mary
Freston
Woolverstone
Stratton Hall
Little Cornard
Polstead
Shelley
Raydon
Great Wenham
Alton Water Reservoir
Pin Mill
Trimley
Assington
Tattingstone
Leavenheath
Scotland Street
Chelmondiston
Stoke-by-Nayland
Thorington Street
Holton St Mary
East Bergholt
Bentley
Holbrook
Lamarsh
Honey Tye
Higham
East End
Upper Street
Harkstead
Erwarton
Bures Green
Stratford St Mary
Lower Holbrook
Bures
Nayland
Dedham Art and Craft Centre
Flatford Mill & Bridge Cott (NT)
Brantham
Stutton
Shop Corner
Wissington
Boxted
Holbrook Bay
Mount Bures
Wormingford
Dedham
Castle House
Cattawade
Mistley Towers
Little Horkesley
Boxted Cross
Langham
Lamb Corner
Dedham Heath
Manningtree
Mistley
New Mistley
Wrabness
Parkeston
Great Horkesley
Langham Moor
Ardleigh Reservoir
Ardleigh Heath
Bradfield
Ramsey
White Colne
Wakes Colne
Ardleigh
Lawford
St Mary's Church (remains of)
Bradfield Heath
Upper Dovercourt
Horkesley Heath
Horsleycross Street
Little Oakley
Valley
Rose Green
Fordham
West Bergholt
Little Bromley
Horsley Cross
Wix
Chappel
Mile End
Fox Street
Goose Green
Great Oakley
Swan Street
Fordstreet
Fordham Heath
High Woods
Crockleford Heath
Cowey Green
Little Bentley
Tendring Green
Stones Green
Eight Ash Green
Elmstead Heath
Great Bromley
Great Tey
Aldham
Elmstead Market
Hare Green
Goose Green
Raven's Green
Tendring
Beaumont
Hamford Water
Horsey Island
Little Tey
Marks Tey
Stanway
Colchester Zoo
St Botolph's Priory
Old Heath
Beth Chatto Gardens
Balls Green
Thorpe Green
Long Green
Stanway Green
COLCHESTER
Shrub End
Bourne Mill (NT)
Frating
Great Bentley
Weeley
Kirby le Soken
Skye Green
Pott's Green
Copford Green
Heckfordbridge
Maypole Green
Wivenhoe
Thorpe-le-Soken
Easthorpe
Grymes Dyke
Blackheath
Rowhedge
High Park Corner
Aingers Green
Weeley Heath
Kirby Cross
Hardy's Green
Birch
Malting Green
Danger Zone
Fingringhoe
Alresford
Thorrington
Great Holland
Layer de la
Roman Road
Gipping
Stour
Box
Brett
Orwell
Deben
S
U
F
O
E
S
S
E
X

201

188

East Bergholt: *Birthplace of the famous painter John Constable (1776–1837) who went to school at nearby Dedham. So famous are his works that the surrounding area is known as Constable Country.* ***Map ref. B4***

Colchester: *Originally called Camulodunum and ruled by King Cunobelin, who was Old King Cole in the nursery rhyme. Colchester claims to be the oldest recorded town in Britain. It was a main centre of Roman Britain and its Norman Castle is the biggest in Europe.* ***Map ref. A5 Also on page 78***

Manningtree *claims to be England's smallest market town.* ***Map ref. C4***

D
E
F
G
215
A12–TO LOWESTOFT
Peasenhall
Sibton
Yoxford
Darsham
Westleton
Westleton Heath
Brundish
Goddard's Corner
Badingham
Middleton
Dunwich Heath (NT)
Maypole Green
A1120
Capon's Green
Dennington
Bruisyard
Dorley's Corner
Middleton Moor
Theberton
Vineyard & Winery
Bruisyard Street
Curlew Green
North Green
East Bridge
Saxtead
East Green
Saxtead Green
Cransford
Rendham
Kelsale
Leiston Abbey
Brabling Green
Carlton
Framlingham
Framlingham Castle
Sweffling
Knodishall Green
Leiston
Sizewell
Apsey Green
Cole's Green
North Green
Great Glemham
Saxmundham
B1119
Mill Green
Benhall Street
Sternfield
Knodishall
Coldfair Green
Aldringham
Parham
Silverlace Green
Stratford St Andrew
Benhall Green
Friston
Thorpe Ness
Snape Watering
Knodishall Common
Thorpeness
Kettleburgh
Hacheston
Farnham
The Meare
Hoo
Easton
Glemham Hall
Church Common
Marlesford
Gromford
A1094
Easton Farm Park
Little Glemham
Snape
Moot Hall
Campsea Ashe
Blaxhall
Aldeburgh
Wickham Market
Iken
High Street
Slaughden
Wickham Market Sta
Aldeburgh Bay
Pettistree
Tunstall
A12
Tunstall Forest
Sudbourne
13
Ufford
Rendlesham
Chillesford
A1152
Butley Mills
Melton
Eyke
Friday Street
Butley
B1084
Bromeswell
Orford Castle
Orford
Rendlesham Forest
Butley Low Corner
Butley Abbey
Orford Ness
Sutton Hoo Tumuli
Gedgrave Hall
Orford Ness (NT)
Woodbridge Tide Mill
Capel St Andrew
Orford Beach
Sutton
Boyton
Waldringfield
Shottisham
Hollesley
Newbourne
Hollesley Bay
Shingle Street
Ramsholt
Hemley
Alderton
Bawdsey
Kirton
Falkenham
59
Felixstowe Ferry
Bawdsey Manor
Trimley St Mary
60
Trimley Marshes
Walton
Old Felixstowe
Walton Lower Street
61
Felixstowe
Manning's Amusement Park
62
A154
Harwich Harbour
Landguard Fort
Landguard Point
hours
Esbjerg....................................19
Cuxhaven (Hamburg).............20
Hoek van Holland...................3¾
The Naze
Walton on the Naze
Walton Pier
1
2
3
4
5

Dunwich Heath: *Set within an Area of Outstanding Natural Beauty (AONB), this is a remnant of the original Sandlings Heaths. It is an important conservation area and very popular with birdwatchers as it is home to some rare species such as the Nightjar and Dartford Warbler.*
Map ref.** F1 **Also on page 78

189

Felixstowe: *This is the largest container port in the UK and one of the largest in Europe. Almost 50% of all British deep sea container trade now passes through Felixstowe. The port was first developed as 'The Felixstowe Railway and Pier Company', by Colonel George Tomline in 1875.*
***Map ref.** E4*

A 217 B C D

1 2 3 4 5

A470–TO BETWS-Y-COED

A487–TO ABERAERON

Aberystwyth: *Home of the National Library of Wales the University of Wales, Aberystwyth. The river Rheidol, which feeds into the old harbour is the steepest river in Britain and the Electric Cliff Railway, which climbs Constitution Hill, is the longest cliff railway in the country.* ***Map ref. B4***

192

Trannon: *The moor here is home to the Carno Wind Farm, which at the time of completion in 1996 was the largest in Europe. There are 56 turbines with a combined maximum generating capacity of 33.6MW.* ***Map ref. F3***

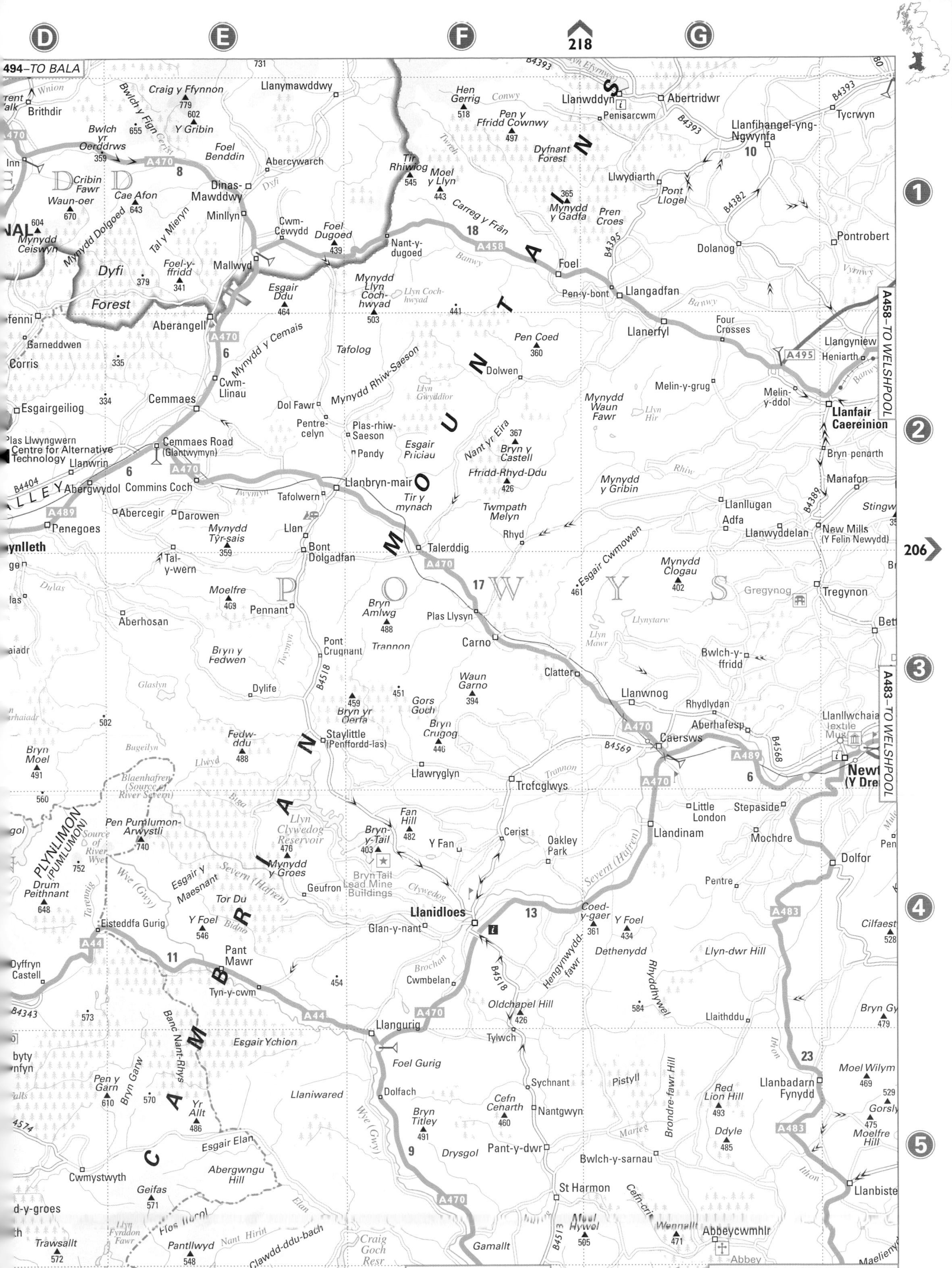
D
E
F
G
218
494–TO BALA
Wnion
Brithdir
Craig y Ffynnon
779
602
Y Gribin
Bwlch y Fign
655
Bwlch yr Oerddrws
359
A470
8
Foel Benddin
Llanymawddwy
731
Abercywarch
Dinas-Mawddwy
Minllyn
Cribin Fawr
Cae Afon
643
Waun-oer
670
604
Mynydd Ceiswyn
Mynydd Dolgoed
Tal y Mieryn
Dyfi
Dyfi Forest
379
Foel-y-ffridd
341
Mallwyd
Cwm-Cewydd
Foel Dugoed
439
Nant-y-dugoed
Esgair Ddu
464
Aberangell
A470
6
Mynydd y Cemais
Cwm-Llinau
Garneddwen
Corris
335
334
Cemmaes
Esgairgeiliog
Tafolog
Mynydd Rhiw-Saeson
Dol Fawr
Pentre-celyn
Plas-rhiw-Saeson
Pandy
Llyn Gwyddior
Mynydd Llyn Coch-hwyad
503
Llyn Coch-hwyad
441
Tir Rhiwiog
545
Moel y Llyn
443
Hen Gerrig
518
Conwy
Pen y Ffridd Cownwy
497
Twrch
Carreg y Frân
18
A458
Banwy
Dyfnant Forest
Mynydd y Gadfa
365
Pren Croes
Llanwddyn
Penisarcwm
Abertridwr
B4393
Llwydiarth
Pont Llogel
Foel
Pen-y-bont
Llangadfan
Llanerfyl
Pen Coed
360
Dolwen
B4395
Llanfihangel-yng-Ngwynfa
10
Tycrwyn
B4393
B4382
Pontrobert
Dolanog
Vyrnwy
Four Crosses
Llangyniew
Heniarth
A495
Melin-y-grug
Melin-y-ddol
Llanfair Caereinion
A458–TO WELSHPOOL
Mynydd Waun Fawr
Llyn Hir
Plas Llwyngwern
Centre for Alternative Technology
Llanwrin
Cemmaes Road (Glantwymyn)
A470
6
B4404
Abergwydol
Commins Coch
A489
Abercegir
Darowen
Penegoes
Mynydd Tŷr-sais
359
Tafolwern
Llanbryn-mair
Esgair Priciau
Nant yr Eira
367
Bryn y Castell
Ffridd-Rhyd-Ddu
426
Tir y mynach
Twmpath Melyn
Rhyd
Llan
Bont Dolgadfan
Talerddig
A470
Mynydd y Gribin
Rhiw
Bryn penarth
Manafon
Llanllugan
Adfa
Llanwyddelan
B4389
New Mills (Y Felin Newydd)
Stingw
206
Tal-y-wern
Moelfre
469
Pennant
Aberhosan
Dulas
POWYS
17
Esgair Cwmowen
461
Mynydd Clogau
402
Gregynog
Tregynon
Bryn Amlwg
488
Plas Llysyn
Llyn Mawr
Llynyrtarw
Bryn y Fedwen
Pont Crugnant
Trannon
Carno
Bwlch-y-ffridd
Glaslyn
Dylife
B4518
459
Bryn yr Oerfa
451
Gors Goch
Waun Garno
394
Clatter
Llanwnog
Rhydlydan
A483–TO WELSHPOOL
502
Bryn Moel
491
Fedw-ddu
488
Staylittle (Penffordd-las)
Bryn Crugog
446
A470
Caersws
B4569
Aberhafesp
B4568
A489
Llanllwchaiarn Textile Mus
Newt (Y Dre)
Bugeilyn
Llwyd
Blaenhafren (Source of River Severn)
Llawryglyn
Trefeglwys
Trannon
A470
6
560
Biga
Little London
Stepaside
PLYNLIMON (PUMLUMON)
Pen Pumlumon-Arwystli
740
Source of River Wye
752
Llyn Clywedog Reservoir
476
Mynydd y Groes
Fan Hill
482
Bryn-y-Tail
403
Y Fan
Cerist
Oakley Park
Llandinam
Mochdre
Dolfor
Bryn Tail Lead Mine Buildings
Geufron
Esgair y Maesnant
Severn (Hafren)
Wye (Gwy)
Drum Peithnant
648
Tor Du
Clywedog
Llanidloes
13
Severn (Hafren)
Coed-y-gaer
361
Y Foel
434
Pentre
A483
Cilfaest
528
Eisteddfa Gurig
A44
Y Foel
546
Glan-y-nant
Bidno
Tarenig
CAMBRIAN MOUNTAINS
11
Pant Mawr
Dyffryn Castell
Tyn-y-cwm
454
Brochan
Cwmbelan
B4518
Hengynwydd-fawr
Dethenydd
Rhydhywel
Llyn-dwr Hill
584
Oldchapel Hill
426
Llaithddu
Bryn Gy
479
B4343
573
Banc Nant-Rhys
A44
A470
Llangurig
Tylwch
Esgair Ychion
Foel Gurig
Ithon
23
Moel Wilym
469
Pen y Garn
610
Bryn Garw
570
Yr Allt
486
Llaniwared
Dolfach
Wye (Gwy)
Sychnant
Pistyll
Cefn Cenarth
460
Nantgwyn
Bryn Titley
491
Brondre-fawr Hill
Red Lion Hill
493
Llanbadarn Fynydd
529
Gorsly
475
Moelfre Hill
Ddyle
485
A483
Marteg
Esgair Elan
Cwmystwyth
Abergwngu Hill
9
Drysgol
Pant-y-dwr
Bwlch-y-sarnau
Ithon
Llanbister
Geifas
571
Elan
A470
St Harmon
Cefn-crin
Llyn Fyrddon Fawr
Pantllwyd
548
Nant Hirin
Clawdd-ddu-bach
Craig Goch Resr
Gamallt
B4513
Moel Hywel
505
Wennallt
471
Abbeycwmhir
Abbey
Maelienydd
Trawsallt
572
A470–TO BUILTH WELLS
A483–TO LLANDRINDOD WELLS
1
2
3
4
5

Llanfihangel yng Ngwynfa: *Anne Griffiths, the famous Welsh Methodist hymn writer was born here in 1776. Anne wrote 70 hymns in her short life. She died, aged 29 on the 12th August 1805 and is buried in the village.* ***Map ref. G1***

193

Llyn Clywedog: *The Dam, at the southern end of Llyn Clywedog Reservoir is the highest dam in Britain. It was constructed 1965–67 to regulate the flow of water into the River Severn. The dam is 236 feet (72m) high, 750 feet (229m) long and holds back 11,000,000 gallons (50,000 cubic metres) of water. The lake has a surface area of 615 acres (249ha), is 216 feet (66m) deep and 6 miles (9.5km) long.* ***Map ref. F4***

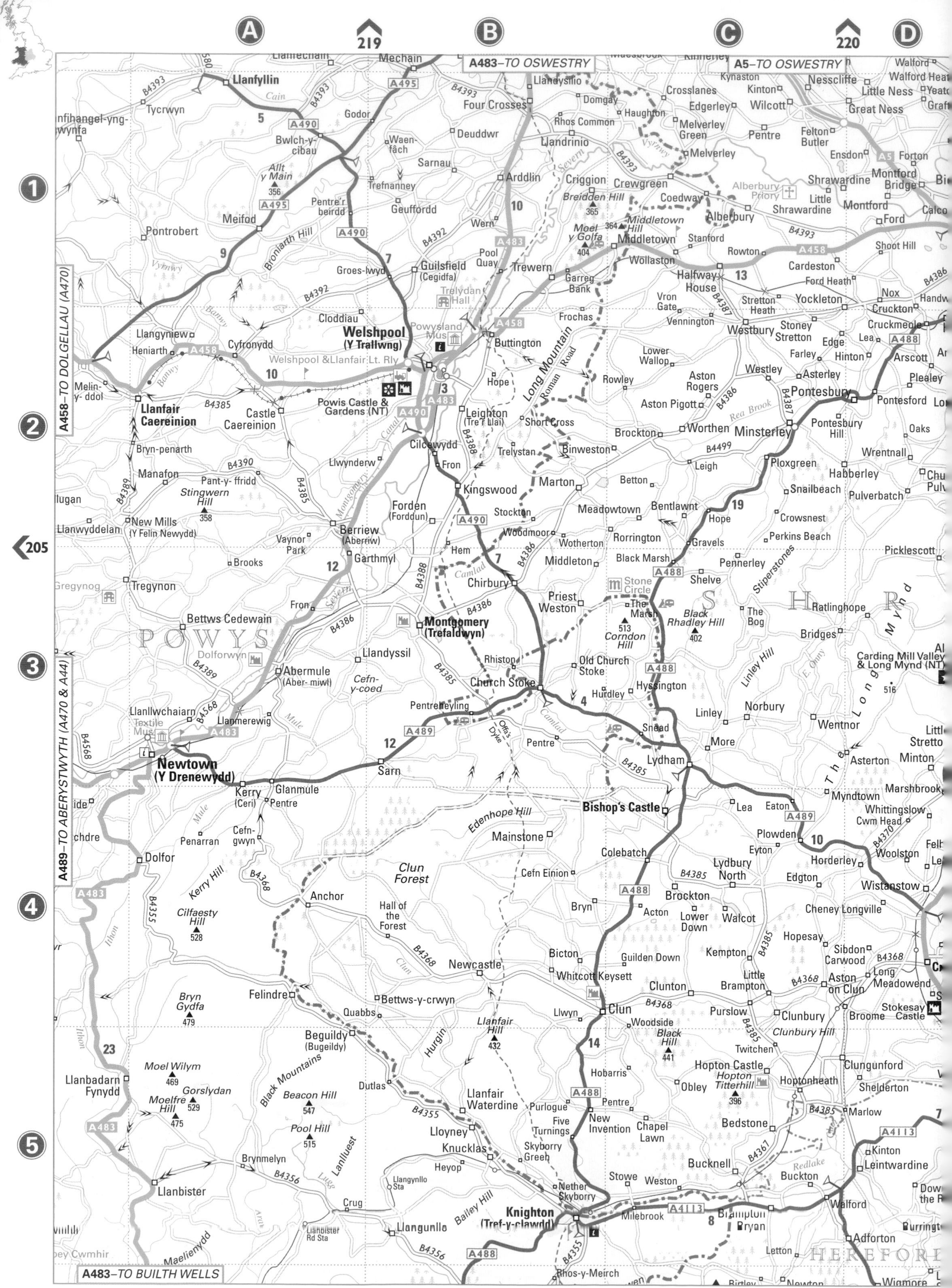

A
219
B
C
220
D
1
2
3
4
5
205
A483–TO OSWESTRY
A5–TO OSWESTRY
A458–TO DOLGELLAU (A470)
A489–TO ABERYSTWYTH (A470 & A44)
A483–TO BUILTH WELLS
Mechain
Llanfyllin
Tycrwyn
Godor
Bwlch-y-cibau
Waen-fâch
Deuddwr
Four Crosses
Llandysilio
Domgay
Haughton
Rhos Common
Llandrinio
Crosslanes
Edgerley
Kinton
Kynaston
Nesscliffe
Wilcott
Little Ness
Great Ness
Walford Heath
Melverley Green
Melverley
Pentre
Felton Butler
Ensdon
Forton
Sarnau
Arddlin
Criggion
Crewgreen
Breidden Hill
365
Coedway
Alberbury Priory
Alberbury
Shrawardine
Little Shrawardine
Montford Bridge
Montford
Ford
Allt y Main
356
Pentre'r beirdd
Trefnanney
Geuffordd
Meifod
Pontrobert
Broniarth Hill
Wern
Moel y Golfa
404
Middletown Hill
364
Middletown
Stanford
Rowton
Shoot Hill
Pool Quay
Trewern
Guilsfield (Cegidfa)
Groes-lwyd
Wollaston
Garreg Bank
Halfway House
Cardeston
Ford Heath
Trelydan Hall
Nox
Vron Gate
Stretton Heath
Yockleton
Cruckton
Cloddiau
Frochas
Vennington
Westbury
Stoney Stretton
Edge
Cruckmeole
Llangyniew
Welshpool (Y Trallwng)
Powysland Mus
Buttington
Lea
Arscott
Heniarth
Cyfronydd
Welshpool & Llanfair Lt. Rly
Long Mountain
Roman Road
Lower Wallop
Farley
Hinton
Plealey
Melin-y-ddol
Llanfair Caereinion
Castle Caereinion
Powis Castle & Gardens (NT)
Hope
Rowley
Aston Rogers
Westley
Asterley
Pontesbury
Pontesford
Aston Pigott
Leighton (Tre'r Llai)
Short Cross
Rea Brook
Pontesbury Hill
Brockton
Worthen
Minsterley
Oaks
Bryn-penarth
Cilcewydd
Trelystan
Binweston
Fron
Wrentnall
Manafon
Pant-y-ffridd
Llwynderw
Leigh
Ploxgreen
Habberley
Kingswood
Marton
Betton
Snailbeach
Pulverbatch
Stingwern Hill
358
Forden (Forddun)
Stockton
Meadowtown
Bentlawnt
Hope
Crowsnest
New Mills (Y Felin Newydd)
Llanwyddelan
Berriew (Aberriw)
Woodmoor
Wotherton
Rorrington
Gravels
Perkins Beach
Vaynor Park
Garthmyl
Hem
Black Marsh
Pennerley
Picklescott
Brooks
Middleton
Shelve
Stiperstones
Gregynog
Tregynon
Chirbury
Camlad
Stone Circle
Priest Weston
The Marsh
Black Rhadley Hill
402
The Bog
Ratlinghope
Fron
Montgomery (Trefaldwyn)
513
Corndon Hill
Bridges
Bettws Cedewain
POWYS
SHROPSHIRE
Dolforwyn
Llandyssil
Rhiston
Old Church Stoke
Carding Mill Valley & Long Mynd (NT)
Abermule (Aber-miwl)
Cefn-y-coed
Church Stoke
Hyssington
Linley Hill
516
Hurdley
Llanllwchaiarn
Textile Mus
Llanmerewig
Pentreheyling
Offa's Dyke
Linley
Norbury
Wentnor
The Long Mynd
Little Stretton
Newtown (Y Drenewydd)
Sarn
Pentre
Snead
More
Asterton
Minton
Kerry (Ceri)
Glanmule
Pentre
Lydham
Myndtown
Marshbrook
Bishop's Castle
Lea
Eaton
Whittingslow
Cwm Head
Edenhope Hill
Penarran
Cefn-gwyn
Mainstone
Plowden
Eyton
Woolston
Dolfor
Clun Forest
Colebatch
Horderley
Lydbury North
Cefn Einion
Edgton
Wistanstow
Kerry Hill
Anchor
Brockton
Bryn
Acton
Lower Down
Walcot
Cheney Longville
Cilfaesty Hill
528
Hall of the Forest
Hopesay
Kempton
Sibdon Carwood
Bicton
Guilden Down
Newcastle
Whitcott Keysett
Clunton
Little Brampton
Aston on Clun
Long Meadowend
Bryn Gydfa
479
Felindre
Bettws-y-crwyn
Quabbs
Llwyn
Clun
Purslow
Clunbury
Broome
Stokesay Castle
Llanfair Hill
432
Woodside
Black Hill
441
Clunbury Hill
Beguildy (Bugeildy)
Twitchen
Moel Wilym
469
Hurgin
Hobarris
Hopton Castle
Hopton Titterhill
396
Clungunford
Llanbadarn Fynydd
Gorslydan
529
Black Mountains
Beacon Hill
547
Dutlas
Llanfair Waterdine
Purlogue
Pentre
Obley
Hoptonheath
Shelderton
Moelfre Hill
475
Five Turnings
New Invention
Chapel Lawn
Marlow
Pool Hill
515
Lloyney
Bedstone
Knucklas
Skyborry Green
Lanlluest
Brynmelyn
Heyop
Bucknell
Kinton
Leintwardine
Llanbister
Llangynllo Sta
Stowe
Weston
Buckton
Redlake
Nether Skyborry
Downton on the Rock
Crug
Bailey Hill
Knighton (Tref-y-clawdd)
Milebrook
Brampton Bryan
Walford
Burrington
Llanbister Rd Sta
Llangunllo
Adforton
Maelienydd
Rhos-y-Meirch
Letton
HEREFORDSHIRE
Wigmore
Newton
A483
A458
A490
A495
A488
A489
A4113
A5
A458
B4393
B4392
B4385
B4390
B4389
B4388
B4386
B4387
B4368
B4355
B4356
B4367
B4370
B4499
B4568

194

Welshpool: *The Welshpool and Llanfair Light Railway starts from here. The railway was opened in 1903 with an unusual gauge of 2 feet 6 inches to allow it to negotiate the tight curves and steep gradients. It officially closed in 1956 but was re-opened by a group of enthusiasts in 1963. It is remarkable for the miscellany of rolling stock which they have sourced from different countries around the world. These include a Taiwan Sugar Corporation Locomotive, Romanian ballast hopper wagons and other locomotives that have seen service in Antigua, Sierra Leone, Austria and Finland.* ***Map ref. B2***

221

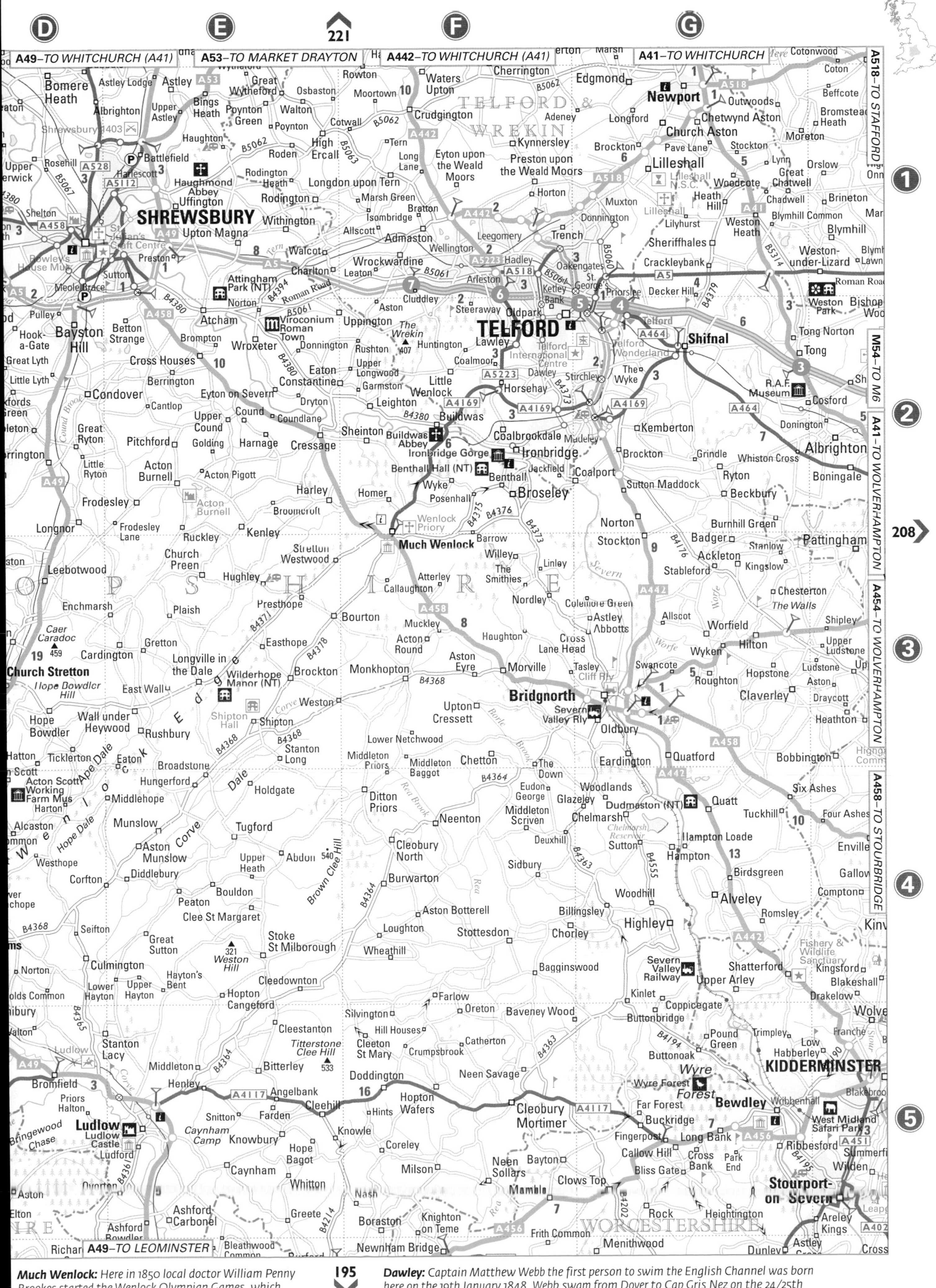

A49–TO WHITCHURCH (A41)
A53–TO MARKET DRAYTON
A442–TO WHITCHURCH (A41)
A41–TO WHITCHURCH
A518–TO STAFFORD
M54–TO M6
A41–TO WOLVERHAMPTON
A454–TO WOLVERHAMPTON
A458–TO STOURBRIDGE
A49–TO LEOMINSTER
SHREWSBURY
TELFORD
Newport
Shifnal
Much Wenlock
Bridgnorth
Church Stretton
Ludlow
Cleobury Mortimer
Bewdley
KIDDERMINSTER
Stourport-on-Severn

208

Much Wenlock: *Here in 1850 local doctor William Penny Brookes started the Wenlock Olympian Games, which inspired the modern revival of the Olympic Games. The games are still held annually.* ***Map ref. F2***

195

Dawley: *Captain Matthew Webb the first person to swim the English Channel was born here on the 19th January 1848. Webb swam from Dover to Cap Gris Nez on the 24/25th August 1875 in 21 hours 45 minutes. In total he swam 38 miles (61km) to cover the 20 mile (32km) straight line distance. Webb died on the 24th July 1883 in an attempt to swim across the bottom of Niagara Falls.* ***Map ref. F2***

222

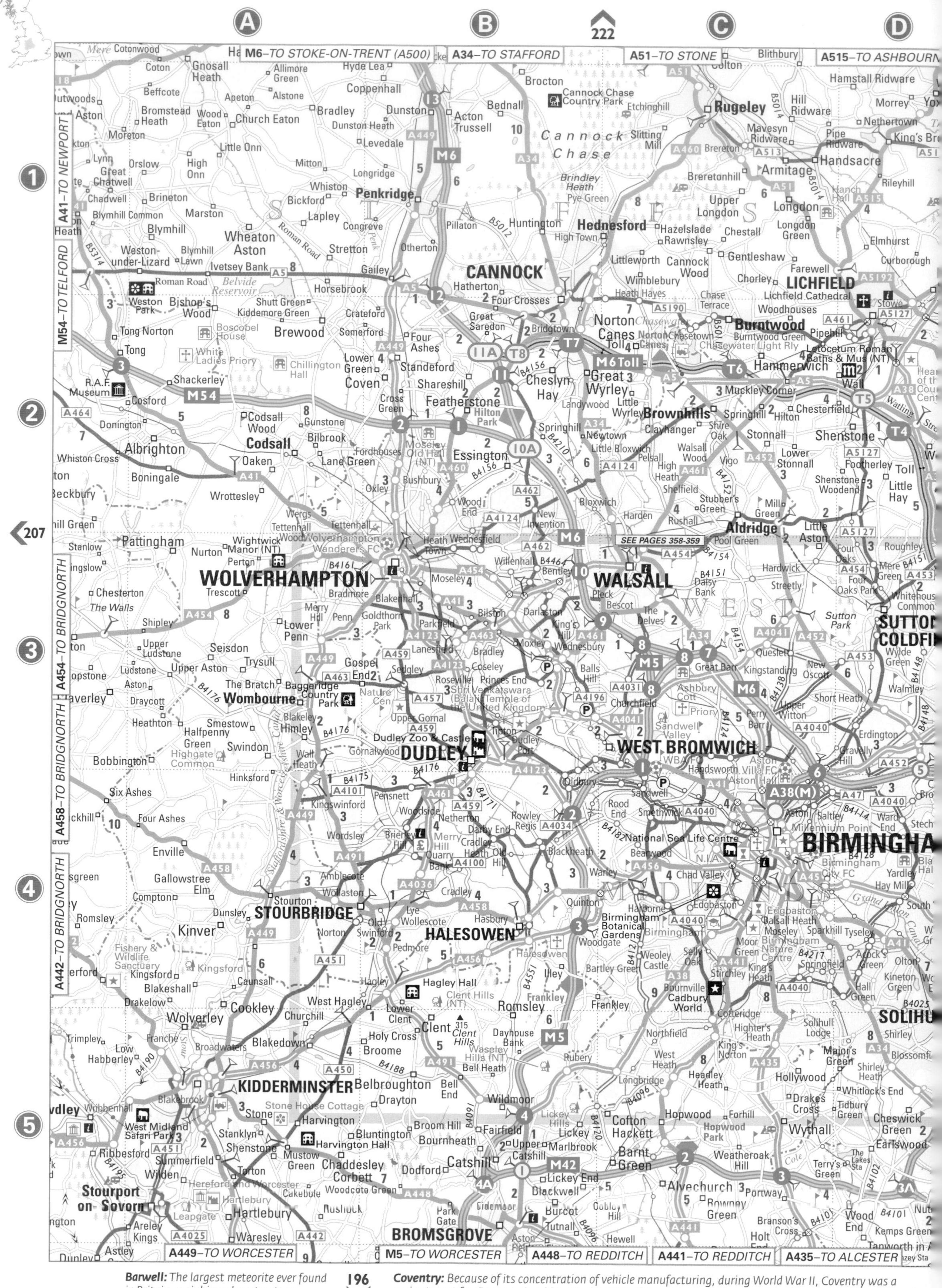
A
B
C
D
1
2
3
4
5
M6–TO STOKE-ON-TRENT (A500)
A34–TO STAFFORD
A51–TO STONE
A515–TO ASHBOURN
A41–TO NEWPORT
M54–TO TELFORD
A454–TO BRIDGNORTH
A458–TO BRIDGNORTH
A442–TO BRIDGNORTH
A449–TO WORCESTER
M5–TO WORCESTER
A448–TO REDDITCH
A441–TO REDDITCH
A435–TO ALCESTER
SEE PAGES 358-359
Penkridge
Rugeley
Cannock Chase
Hednesford
CANNOCK
LICHFIELD
Lichfield Cathedral
Burntwood
Brewood
Codsall
Brownhills
Aldridge
WOLVERHAMPTON
WALSALL
Wombourne
DUDLEY
Dudley Zoo & Castle
WEST BROMWICH
SUTTON COLDFIELD
BIRMINGHAM
STOURBRIDGE
HALESOWEN
Kinver
KIDDERMINSTER
Stourport on Sovern
Hartlebury
BROMSGROVE
Alvechurch
Romsley
Cadbury World
Hagley Hall
Harvington Hall
West Midland Safari Park
Clent Hills
National Sea Life Centre
Birmingham Botanical Gardens

207

196

Barwell: *The largest meteorite ever found in Britain, weighing almost 7 stone (44Kg), landed here on the 24th December 1965.* ***Map ref. G3***

Coventry: *Because of its concentration of vehicle manufacturing, during World War II, Coventry was a major target for German air raids. On the night of the 14th November 1940 500 German bombers dropped 500 tons of explosives and 900 incendiary bombs on the city in less than 10 hours. The city, including the Cathedral was almost totally destroyed and many people were killed. In 1948 during major rebuilding work, Coventry opened Europe's first ever traffic-free shopping precinct and in 1962 a new Cathedral was consecrated alongside the ruins of the old one.* ***Map ref. F5 Also on page 64***

223

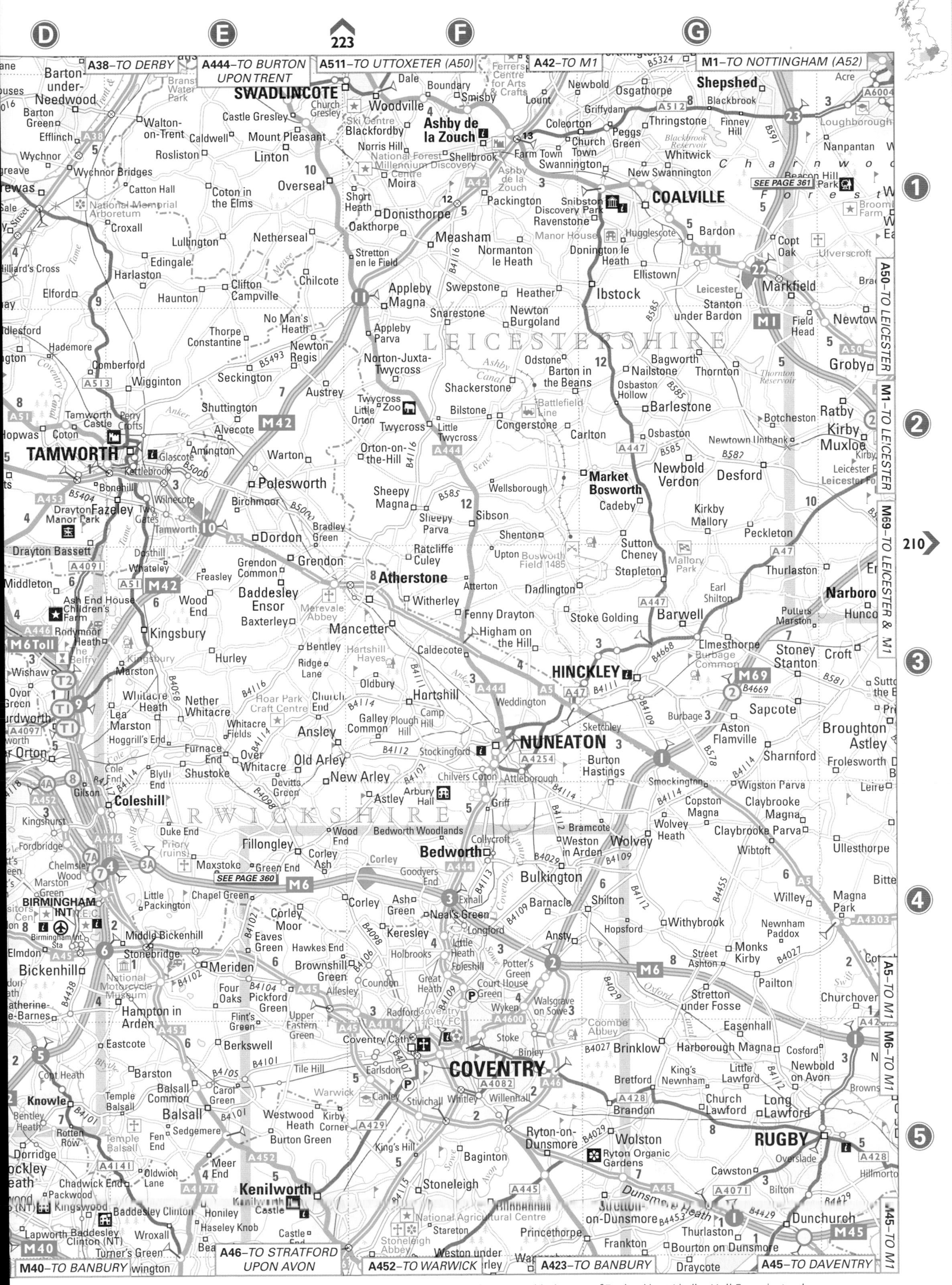
D
E
F
G
1
2
3
4
5
A38–TO DERBY
A444–TO BURTON UPON TRENT
A511–TO UTTOXETER (A50)
A42–TO M1
M1–TO NOTTINGHAM (A52)
A50–TO LEICESTER
M1–TO LEICESTER
M69–TO LEICESTER & M1
A5–TO M1
M6–TO M1
A45–TO M1
M40–TO BANBURY
A46–TO STRATFORD UPON AVON
A452–TO WARWICK
A423–TO BANBURY
A45–TO DAVENTRY
SEE PAGE 361
SEE PAGE 360
LEICESTERSHIRE
WARWICKSHIRE
SWADLINCOTE
Ashby de la Zouch
COALVILLE
Shepshed
Loughborough
TAMWORTH
Atherstone
HINCKLEY
NUNEATON
Bedworth
COVENTRY
Kenilworth
RUGBY
Market Bosworth
Ibstock
Coleshill
BIRMINGHAM INT.
Polesworth
Wolvey
Bulkington
Balsall
Knowle

Earlsdon: *Sir Frank Whittle, inventor of the jet engine was born here in 1907. The first jet aircraft to fly in Britain, a Gloster E28/39, made its maiden flight on the 15th May 1941 piloted by Gerry Sayer the Gloster test pilot. Frank Whittle moved to the USA in 1976 and died at his home in Maryland on the 8th August 1996.* ***Map ref. F5***

197

Fenny Drayton: *The geographical centre of England is at Lindley Hall Farm, just 1.5km east of Fenny Drayton, OS Grid Reference SP 36373.66 96143.05. Traditionally however, the village of Meriden near Coventry (square E4) has always been considered the centre and an historic monument there marks the spot. The point furthest from the sea in the whole of Britain is actually near Coton in the Elms (square E1).* ***Map ref. F3***

210

224

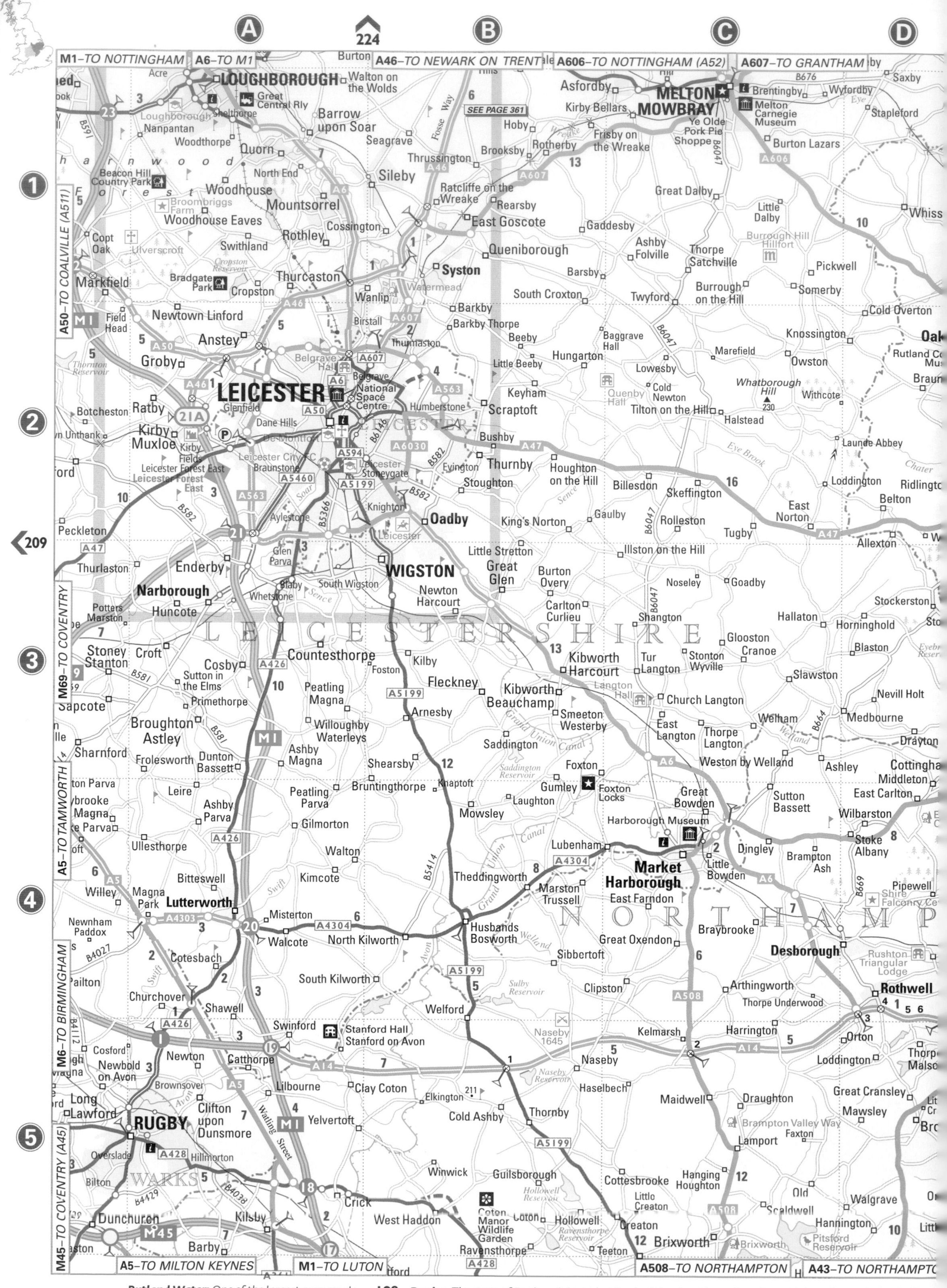
A
B
C
D
1
2
3
4
5
M1–TO NOTTINGHAM
A6–TO M1
A46–TO NEWARK ON TRENT
A606–TO NOTTINGHAM (A52)
A607–TO GRANTHAM
A50–TO COALVILLE (A511)
M69–TO COVENTRY
A5–TO TAMWORTH
M6–TO BIRMINGHAM
M45–TO COVENTRY (A45)
A5–TO MILTON KEYNES
M1–TO LUTON
A508–TO NORTHAMPTON
A43–TO NORTHAMPTON
LOUGHBOROUGH
Great Central Rly
Walton on the Wolds
Barrow upon Soar
Seagrave
SEE PAGE 361
Hoby
Asfordby
Kirby Bellars
MELTON MOWBRAY
Ye Olde Pork Pie Shoppe
Brentingby
Wyfordby
Melton Carnegie Museum
Saxby
Stapleford
Burton Lazars
Frisby on the Wreake
Rotherby
Brooksby
Thrussington
Nanpantan
Woodthorpe
Quorn
Sileby
Beacon Hill Country Park
Woodhouse
Broombriggs Farm
Woodhouse Eaves
Mountsorrel
Ratcliffe on the Wreake
Rearsby
East Goscote
Gaddesby
Great Dalby
Little Dalby
Whissendine
Cossington
Rothley
Queniborough
Ashby Folville
Thorpe Satchville
Burrough Hill Hillfort
Copt Oak
Ulverscroft
Swithland
Cropston Reservoir
Syston
Barsby
Pickwell
Markfield
Bradgate Park
Cropston
Thurcaston
Wanlip
Watermead
South Croxton
Twyford
Burrough on the Hill
Somerby
Field Head
Newtown Linford
Birstall
Barkby
Barkby Thorpe
Cold Overton
Anstey
Thurmaston
Beeby
Baggrave Hall
Marefield
Knossington
Owston
Groby
Thornton Reservoir
Belgrave Hall
Belgrave
Little Beeby
Hungarton
Lowesby
Whatborough Hill
Withcote
Rutland County Museum
Braunston
LEICESTER
National Space Centre
Keyham
Quenby Hall
Cold Newton
Tilton on the Hill
Halstead
Botcheston
Ratby
Glenfield
Humberstone
Scraptoft
Kirby Muxloe
Kirby Fields
Dane Hills
De Montfort
Bushby
Launde Abbey
Leicester City FC
Braunstone
Leicester Forest East
Stoneygate
Evington
Thurnby
Houghton on the Hill
Billesdon
Skeffington
Eye Brook
Chater
Loddington
Ridlington
Belton
Stoughton
Knighton
Oadby
King's Norton
Gaulby
Rolleston
East Norton
Tugby
Allexton
Peckleton
Aylestone
Glen Parva
Little Stretton
Great Glen
Illston on the Hill
Thurlaston
Enderby
WIGSTON
Burton Overy
Noseley
Goadby
Narborough
Blaby
South Wigston
Whetstone
Newton Harcourt
Carlton Curlieu
Stockerston
Potters Marston
Huncote
Shangton
Hallaton
Horninghold
LEICESTERSHIRE
Glooston
Cranoe
Blaston
Stoney Stanton
Croft
Countesthorpe
Foston
Kilby
Kibworth Harcourt
Tur Langton
Stonton Wyville
Cosby
Sutton in the Elms
Primethorpe
Fleckney
Kibworth Beauchamp
Langton Hall
Church Langton
Slawston
Nevill Holt
Sapcote
Peatling Magna
Arnesby
Smeeton Westerby
East Langton
Thorpe Langton
Welham
Medbourne
Broughton Astley
Willoughby Waterleys
Saddington
Grand Union Canal
Drayton
Sharnford
Frolesworth
Dunton Bassett
Ashby Magna
Shearsby
Saddington Reservoir
Foxton
Weston by Welland
Ashley
Cottingham
Middleton
Leire
Peatling Parva
Bruntingthorpe
Knaptoft
Gumley
Foxton Locks
Great Bowden
Sutton Bassett
East Carlton
Ashby Parva
Gilmorton
Mowsley
Laughton
Harborough Museum
Wilbarston
Ullesthorpe
Walton
Lubenham
Market Harborough
Little Bowden
Dingley
Brampton Ash
Stoke Albany
Bitteswell
Kimcote
Theddingworth
Marston Trussell
East Farndon
Pipewell
Shire Falconry Centre
Willey
Magna Park
Lutterworth
Misterton
Husbands Bosworth
NORTHAMPTONSHIRE
Newnham Paddox
Walcote
North Kilworth
Great Oxendon
Braybrooke
Desborough
Rushton Triangular Lodge
Cotesbach
South Kilworth
Sibbertoft
Sulby Reservoir
Clipston
Arthingworth
Thorpe Underwood
Rothwell
Churchover
Shawell
Welford
Swinford
Stanford Hall
Stanford on Avon
Naseby 1645
Kelmarsh
Harrington
Orton
Cosford
Newton
Catthorpe
Naseby
Newbold on Avon
Brownsover
Lilbourne
Clay Coton
Naseby Reservoir
Haselbech
Loddington
Long Lawford
Clifton upon Dunsmore
Elkington
Maidwell
Draughton
Great Cransley
Mawsley
RUGBY
Yelvertoft
Cold Ashby
Thornby
Brampton Valley Way
Faxton
Watling Street
Lamport
Overslade
Hillmorton
Winwick
Guilsborough
Hollowell Reservoir
Cottesbrooke
Hanging Houghton
WARKS
Bilton
Crick
Little Creaton
Old
Walgrave
Scaldwell
Dunchurch
Kilsby
West Haddon
Coton Manor Wildlife Garden
Hollowell
Ravensthorpe Reservoir
Creaton
Hannington
Brixworth
Pitsford Reservoir
Barby
Ravensthorpe
Teeton

Rutland Water: *One of the largest man-made reservoirs in Europe covering 3,100 acre (1,225ha). Completed in 1977 to supply 65 million gallons (300,000 cubic metres) of water per day to cities in the east Midlands.* ***Map ref. D2***

Rugby: *The sport of Rugby originated at Rugby School in the 19th Century. It is reputed that during a football game in 1823, William Webb Ellis picked up the ball and ran with it. His name lives on through the Webb Ellis Trophy, that is presented to the winners of the Rugby World Cup.* ***Map ref. A5***

Essendine: *On 3rd July 1938, a train hauled by Class A4 locomotive 'Mallard' here achieved the world rail record speed for steam traction of 126 mph (201km/h).* ***Map ref. F1***

209

198

225

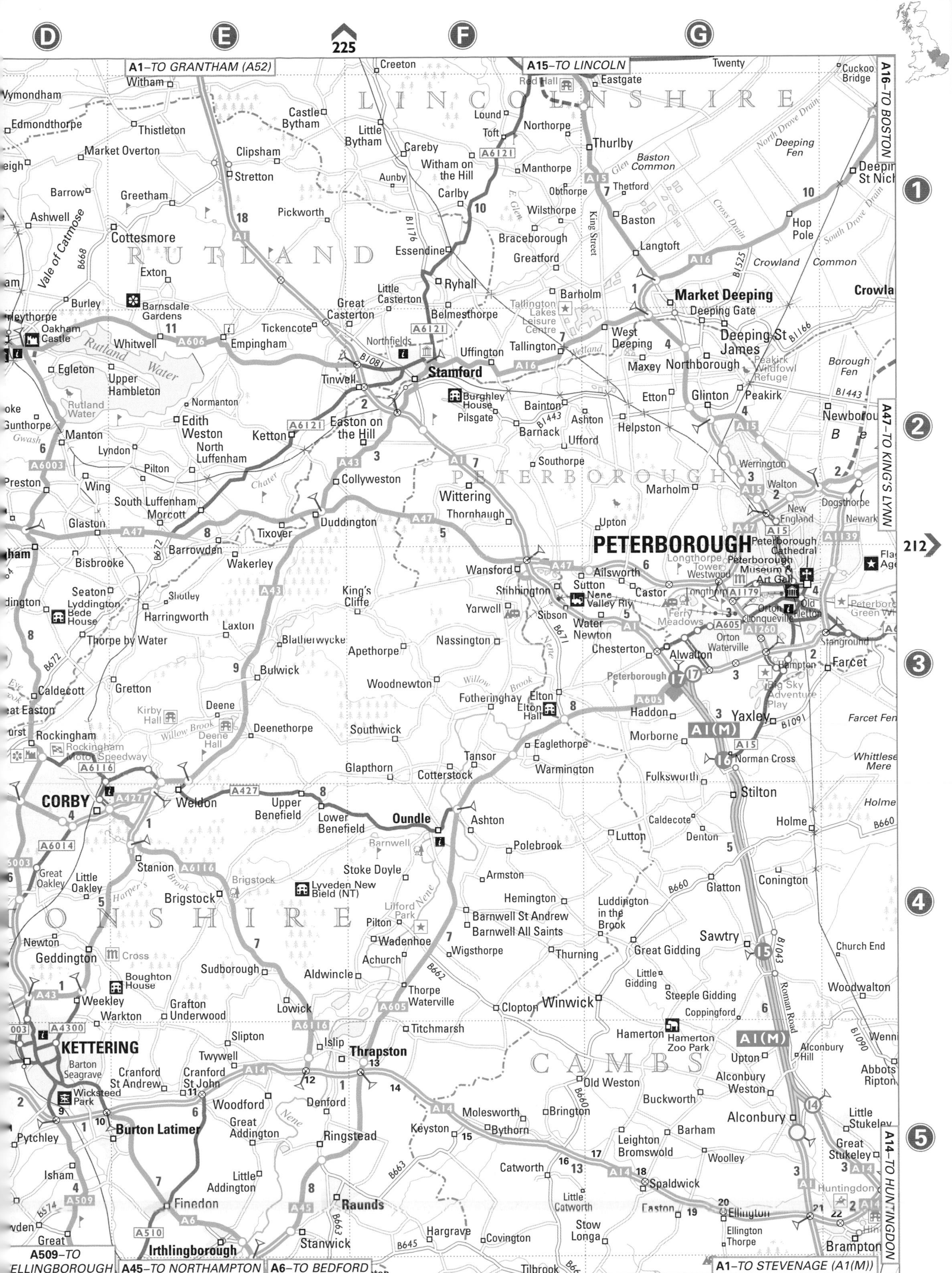

D
E
F
G
A1–TO GRANTHAM (A52)
A15–TO LINCOLN
A16–TO BOSTON
A47–TO KING'S LYNN
A14–TO HUNTINGDON
A1–TO STEVENAGE (A1(M))
A509–TO WELLINGBOROUGH
A45–TO NORTHAMPTON
A6–TO BEDFORD
LINCOLNSHIRE
RUTLAND
PETERBOROUGH
CAMBS
1
2
3
4
5
Creeton
Twenty
Cuckoo Bridge
Witham
Wymondham
Edmondthorpe
Thistleton
Castle Bytham
Little Bytham
Red Hall
Eastgate
Lound
Toft
Northorpe
Thurlby
Deeping Fen
Baston Common
Market Overton
Clipsham
Stretton
Careby
Witham on the Hill
Manthorpe
Aunby
Carlby
Obthorpe
Thetford
Deeping St Nicholas
Barrow
Greetham
Pickworth
Wilsthorpe
Baston
Hop Pole
Ashwell
Vale of Catmose
Cottesmore
Braceborough
Greatford
Langtoft
Crowland Common
Essendine
Exton
Ryhall
Barnsdale Gardens
Little Casterton
Barholm
Market Deeping
Crowland
Burley
Great Casterton
Tallington Lakes Leisure Centre
Deeping Gate
Oakham Castle
Tickencote
Belmesthorpe
West Deeping
Deeping St James
Whitwell
Empingham
Rutland Water
Northfields
Uffington
Tallington
Maxey
Northborough
Peakirk Wildfowl Refuge
Borough Fen
Egleton
Upper Hambleton
Tinwell
Stamford
Etton
Glinton
Peakirk
Normanton
Burghley House
Pilsgate
Bainton
Ashton
Helpston
Newborough
Edith Weston
Easton on the Hill
Barnack
Ufford
Gunthorpe
Manton
Ketton
Gwash
Lyndon
North Luffenham
Southorpe
Werrington
Preston
Pilton
Collyweston
Walton
Wing
Chater
Wittering
Marholm
Dogsthorpe
South Luffenham
Morcott
Thornhaugh
New England
Newark
Glaston
Tixover
Duddington
Upton
Barrowden
PETERBOROUGH
Peterborough Cathedral
Bisbrooke
Wakerley
Wansford
Longthorpe Tower
Peterborough Museum & Art Gallery
Ailsworth
Westwood
Seaton
Lyddington Bede House
Shotley
King's Cliffe
Stibbington
Sutton
Nene Valley Rly
Castor
Longthorpe
Yarwell
Sibson
Ferry Meadows
Orton Longueville
Harringworth
Laxton
Water Newton
Orton Waterville
Stanground
Thorpe by Water
Blatherwycke
Nassington
Apethorpe
Chesterton
Alwalton
Hampton
Farcet
Bulwick
Peterborough
Big Sky Adventure Play
Caldecott
Gretton
Woodnewton
Willow Brook
Fotheringhay
Elton
Elton Hall
Farcet Fen
Great Easton
Kirby Hall
Deene
Deene Hall
Deenethorpe
Haddon
Yaxley
Rockingham
Rockingham Motor Speedway
Southwick
Morborne
Norman Cross
Whittlesey Mere
Tansor
Eaglethorpe
Glapthorn
Cotterstock
Warmington
Folksworth
Stilton
CORBY
Weldon
Upper Benefield
Lower Benefield
Oundle
Ashton
Caldecote
Holme
Denton
Lutton
Barnwell
Polebrook
Stanion
Brigstock
Stoke Doyle
Armston
Great Oakley
Little Oakley
Lyveden New Bield (NT)
Glatton
Conington
Hemington
Luddington in the Brook
Lilford Park
Barnwell St Andrew
Barnwell All Saints
Pilton
Sawtry
Newton
Geddington
Cross
Wadenhoe
Wigsthorpe
Thurning
Great Gidding
Church End
Achurch
Sudborough
Boughton House
Aldwincle
Little Gidding
Steeple Gidding
Woodwalton
Weekley
Thorpe Waterville
Clopton
Winwick
Coppingford
Grafton Underwood
Warkton
Lowick
Roman Road
Titchmarsh
Hamerton
Hamerton Zoo Park
Alconbury Hill
KETTERING
Slipton
Islip
Thrapston
Upton
Barton Seagrave
Twywell
Cranford St Andrew
Cranford St John
Old Weston
Alconbury Weston
Abbots Ripton
Wicksteed Park
Woodford
Denford
Buckworth
Molesworth
Brington
Alconbury
Little Stukeley
Burton Latimer
Great Addington
Nene
Keyston
Bythorn
Barham
Pytchley
Ringstead
Leighton Bromswold
Woolley
Great Stukeley
Isham
Little Addington
Catworth
Spaldwick
Huntingdon
Finedon
Raunds
Little Catworth
Easton
Ellington
Stow Longa
Ellington Thorpe
Hargrave
Covington
Stanwick
Irthlingborough
Brampton
Tilbrook

212

Stamford: *The film of George Eliot's classic novel Middlemarch, released in 1994, was made on location around Stamford.* ***Map ref. F2***

199

Seaton and Harringworth: *The largest brick-built railway viaduct in Britain crosses the River Welland between these two villages. Built in 1875, of 20 million bricks, it stands 69 feet (21m) high, is 3,750 feet (1,143m) long and has 82 arches. The viaduct is no longer used by mainline passenger trains.* ***Map ref. E3***

226

211

Holme Fen *is the lowest land area of Britain. It is 9 feet (2.75m) below sea level.* ***Map ref. A4***

200

Huntingdon: *Oliver Cromwell was born here on the 25th April 1599. Despite modest beginnings, Cromwell became Lord Protector when Great Britain became a Commonwealth following the execution of Charles I in 1649. In 1657 he was offered the crown of England but refused it. He died on the 3rd September 1658 and was granted a state funeral. With the restoration of Charles II to the throne in 1660 Cromwell was discredited and on the 30th January 1661 his body was exhumed and he was symbolically executed and reburied at Tyburn.* ***Map ref. A5*** ***See page 78 for Cromwell Museum***

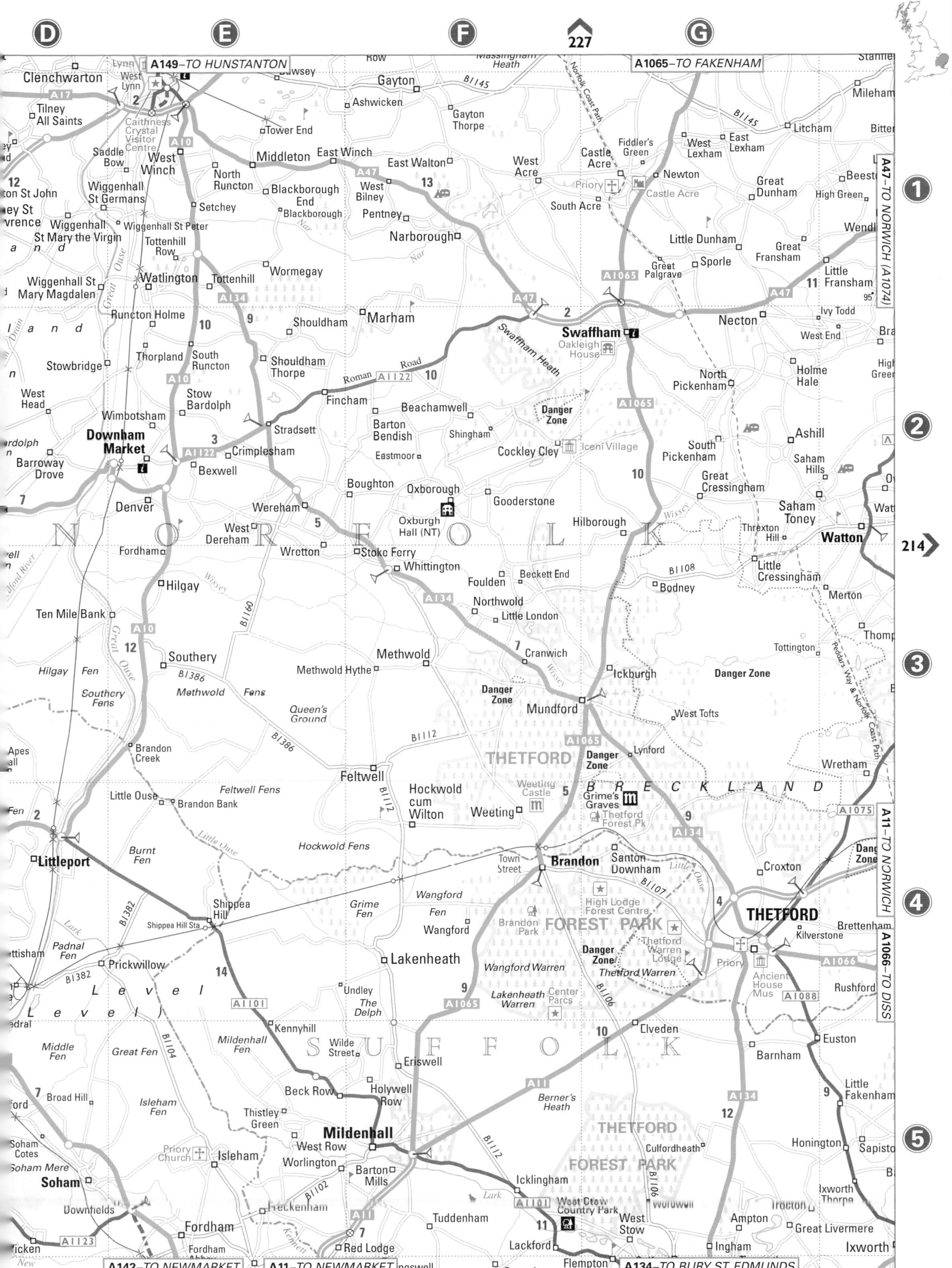
D
E
F
G
227
A149–TO HUNSTANTON
A1065–TO FAKENHAM
A47–TO NORWICH (A1074)
A11–TO NORWICH
A1066–TO DISS
214
A142–TO NEWMARKET
A11–TO NEWMARKET
A134–TO BURY ST. EDMUNDS
1
2
3
4
5
Clenchwarton
Tilney All Saints
West Lynn
Caithness Crystal Visitor Centre
Saddle Bow
West Winch
North Runcton
Middleton
East Winch
Gayton
Ashwicken
Tower End
Gayton Thorpe
East Walton
West Bilney
Pentney
Narborough
West Acre
Castle Acre
Fiddler's Green
Newton
South Acre
West Lexham
East Lexham
Litcham
Mileham
Great Dunham
High Green
Little Dunham
Great Fransham
Little Fransham
Sporle
Great Palgrave
Wiggenhall St Germans
Wiggenhall St Mary the Virgin
Wiggenhall St Peter
Wiggenhall St Mary Magdalen
Setchey
Blackborough End
Tottenhill Row
Tottenhill
Watlington
Wormegay
Runcton Holme
Shouldham
Marham
Swaffham
Oakleigh House
Swaffham Heath
Necton
Ivy Todd
West End
Stowbridge
Thorpland
South Runcton
Shouldham Thorpe
Roman Road
Fincham
Beachamwell
Danger Zone
North Pickenham
Holme Hale
West Head
Wimbotsham
Stow Bardolph
Stradsett
Barton Bendish
Shingham
Cockley Cley
Iceni Village
South Pickenham
Ashill
Saham Hills
Downham Market
Barroway Drove
Crimplesham
Bexwell
Eastmoor
Denver
Boughton
Oxborough
Oxburgh Hall (NT)
Gooderstone
Great Cressingham
Saham Toney
Watton
Wereham
West Dereham
Hilborough
Threxton Hill
NORFOLK
Fordham
Wretton
Stoke Ferry
Whittington
Foulden
Beckett End
Bodney
Little Cressingham
Merton
Hilgay
Ten Mile Bank
Northwold
Little London
Cranwich
Tottington
Southery
Methwold
Methwold Hythe
Ickburgh
Danger Zone
Hilgay Fen
Southery Fens
Methwold Fens
Queen's Ground
Mundford
West Tofts
Pedars Way & Norfolk Coast Path
Brandon Creek
THETFORD
Lynford
Wretham
Feltwell
Feltwell Fens
Little Ouse
Brandon Bank
Hockwold cum Wilton
Weeting
Weeting Castle
Grime's Graves
Thetford Forest Pk
BRECKLAND
Littleport
Burnt Fen
Hockwold Fens
Town Street
Brandon
Santon Downham
Croxton
Shippea Hill
Shippea Hill Sta
Grime Fen
Wangford Fen
Wangford
High Lodge Forest Centre
Brandon Park
FOREST PARK
THETFORD
Brettenham
Kilverstone
Padnal Fen
Prickwillow
Lakenheath
Wangford Warren
Thetford Warren Lodge
Thetford Warren
Priory
Ancient House Mus
Rushford
Level
Undley
The Delph
Lakenheath Warren
Center Parcs
Kennyhill
Elveden
Euston
Middle Fen
Great Fen
Mildenhall Fen
Wilde Street
SUFFOLK
Eriswell
Barnham
Broad Hill
Isleham Fen
Beck Row
Holywell Row
Berner's Heath
Little Fakenham
Thistley Green
Mildenhall
West Row
Culfordheath
Honington
Sapiston
Soham Cotes
Soham Mere
Priory Church
Isleham
Worlington
Barton Mills
FOREST PARK
Icklingham
Ixworth Thorpe
Soham
Downfields
Freckenham
West Stow Country Park
Troston
Fordham
Tuddenham
West Stow
Ampton
Great Livermere
Red Lodge
Lackford
Ingham
Ixworth
Fordham Abbey
Flempton
Cavenham
201

Mildenhall : *RAF Mildenhall officially opened in 1934 and just days later became the starting point for what is still known as the 'greatest air race in the world'. 20 aircraft from 7 different countries competed in the Royal Aero Club race to Melbourne, Australia. The winners, Charles Scott and Thomas Black, flying a De Havilland DH88 Comet, completed the flight in 2 days 23 hours.* ***Map ref. F5***

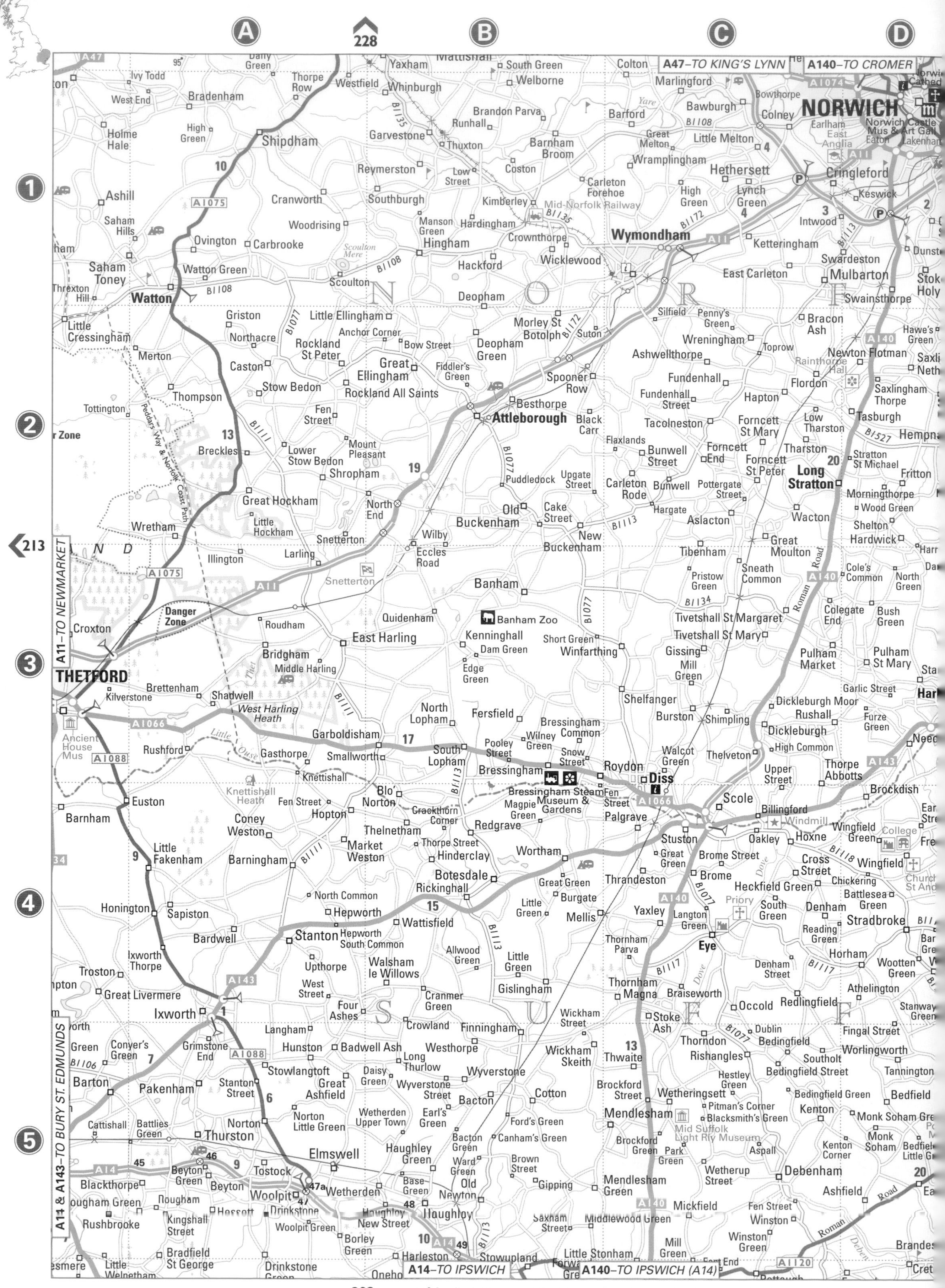

Norwich: *Elizabeth Fry, nee Gurney, was born here in 1780. She campaigned relentlessly for better conditions for prisoners, particularly women prisoners. In 1840 she founded the Institute of Nursing Sisters to train nurses to care for poor people in their own homes. Elizabeth Fry died in 1845.* ***Map ref. D1***

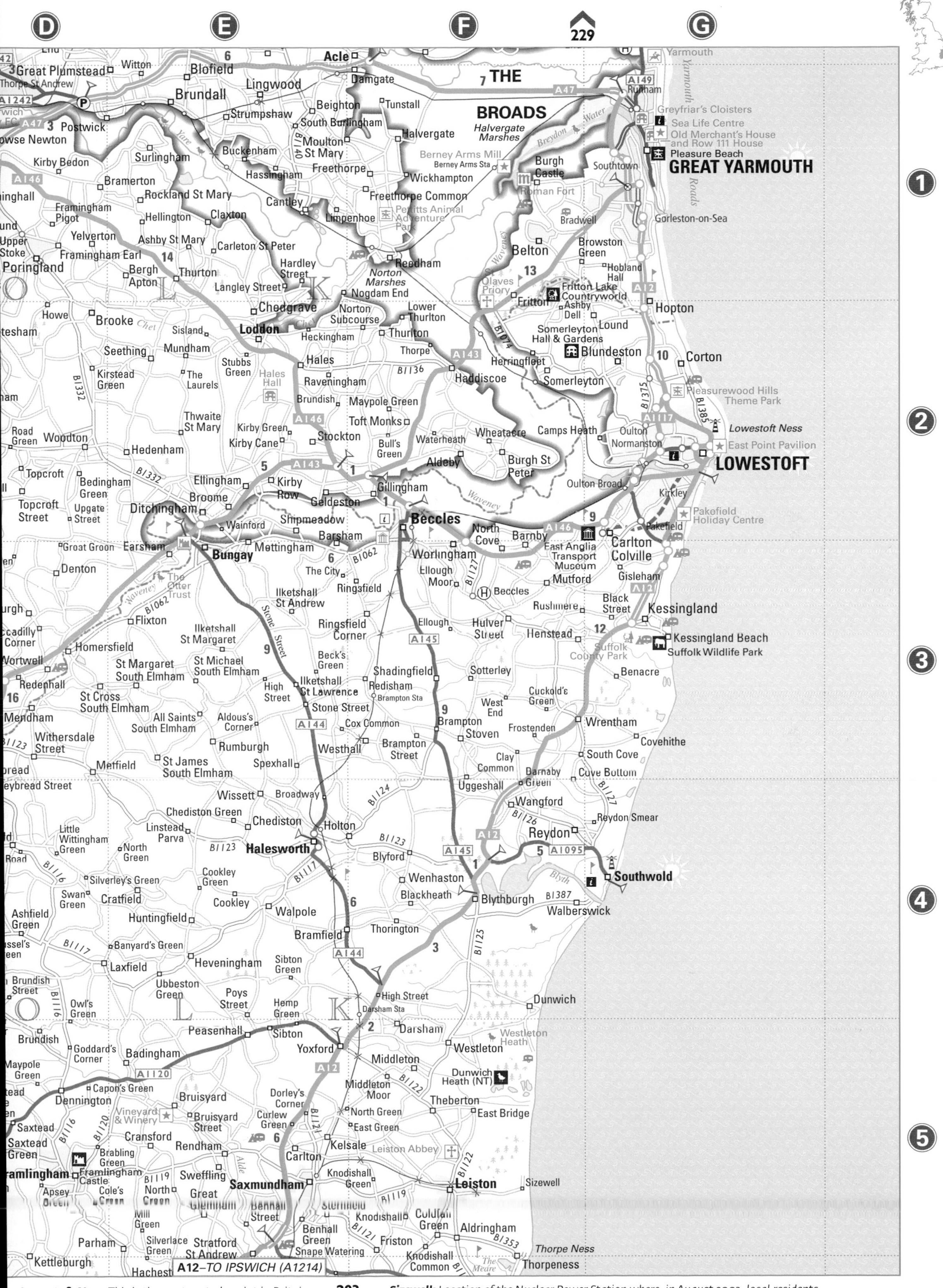
D
E
F
G
229
1
2
3
4
5
THE BROADS
GREAT YARMOUTH
LOWESTOFT
Acle
Blofield
Brundall
Lingwood
Great Plumstead
Witton
Thorpe St Andrew
Postwick
Strumpshaw
Damgate
Beighton
Tunstall
South Burlingham
Halvergate
Halvergate Marshes
Moulton St Mary
Freethorpe
Wickhampton
Freethorpe Common
Berney Arms Mill
Berney Arms Sta
Breydon Water
Burgh Castle
Roman Fort
Southtown
Yarmouth
Runham
Greyfriar's Cloisters
Sea Life Centre
Old Merchant's House and Row 111 House
Pleasure Beach
Gorleston-on-Sea
Bradwell
Kirby Bedon
Surlingham
Buckenham
Hassingham
Bramerton
Rockland St Mary
Cantley
Framingham Pigot
Hellington
Claxton
Limpenhoe
Pettitts Animal Adventure Park
Yelverton
Ashby St Mary
Carleton St Peter
Framingham Earl
Poringland
Bergh Apton
Thurton
Hardley Street
Langley Street
Reedham
Norton Marshes
Nogdam End
Belton
Browston Green
Hobland Hall
St Olaves Priory
Fritton
Fritton Lake Countryworld
Ashby Dell
Hopton
Lound
Somerleyton Hall & Gardens
Blundeston
Corton
Howe
Brooke
Sisland
Loddon
Chedgrave
Norton Subcourse
Heckingham
Lower Thurlton
Thurlton
Thorpe
Herringfleet
Haddiscoe
Somerleyton
Seething
Mundham
Kirstead Green
The Laurels
Stubbs Green
Hales Hall
Hales
Raveningham
Brundish
Maypole Green
Toft Monks
Pleasurewood Hills Theme Park
Lowestoft Ness
East Point Pavilion
Thwaite St Mary
Kirby Green
Kirby Cane
Stockton
Bull's Green
Waterheath
Wheatacre
Camps Heath
Oulton
Normanston
Woodton
Road Green
Hedenham
Aldeby
Burgh St Peter
Oulton Broad
Kirkley
Topcroft
Topcroft Street
Bedingham Green
Upgate Street
Ellingham
Kirby Row
Broome
Ditchingham
Geldeston
Gillingham
Beccles
Pakefield Holiday Centre
Pakefield
Wainford
Shipmeadow
Barsham
North Cove
Barnby
Carlton Colville
Groat Green
Earsham
Bungay
Mettingham
Worlingham
East Anglia Transport Museum
Denton
The City
Ellough Moor
Mutford
Gisleham
The Otter Trust
Ilketshall St Andrew
Ringsfield
Beccles
Rushmere
Black Street
Kessingland
Flixton
Ilketshall St Margaret
Ringsfield Corner
Ellough
Hulver Street
Henstead
Kessingland Beach
Suffolk Wildlife Park
Suffolk County Park
Scadilly Corner
Homersfield
St Margaret South Elmham
St Michael South Elmham
Stone Street
Beck's Green
Shadingfield
Sotterley
Benacre
Redenhall
St Cross South Elmham
High Street
Ilketshall St Lawrence
Redisham
Brampton Sta
Cuckold's Green
West End
Mendham
All Saints South Elmham
Aldous's Corner
Stone Street
Cox Common
Brampton
Stoven
Frostenden
Wrentham
Covehithe
Withersdale Street
Rumburgh
Westhall
Brampton Street
South Cove
Metfield
St James South Elmham
Spexhall
Clay Common
Barnaby Green
Cove Bottom
Weybread Street
Wissett
Broadway
Uggeshall
Wangford
Chediston Green
Chediston
Holton
Reydon Smear
Reydon
Little Wittingham Green
Linstead Parva
North Green
Halesworth
Blyford
Southwold
Silverley's Green
Cookley Green
Wenhaston
Swan Green
Cratfield
Cookley
Walpole
Blackheath
Blythburgh
Walberswick
Ashfield Green
Huntingfield
Bramfield
Thorington
Banyard's Green
Laxfield
Heveningham
Sibton Green
Brundish Street
Ubbeston Green
Owl's Green
Poys Street
Hemp Green
High Street
Darsham Sta
Dunwich
Brundish
Peasenhall
Sibton
Darsham
Westleton Heath
Goddard's Corner
Badingham
Yoxford
Westleton
Maypole Green
Middleton
Dunwich Heath (NT)
Capon's Green
Dennington
Bruisyard
Dorley's Corner
Middleton Moor
Theberton
Vineyard & Winery
Bruisyard Street
Curlew Green
North Green
East Bridge
Saxtead
East Green
Saxtead Green
Cransford
Rendham
Kelsale
Leiston Abbey
Brabling Green
Carlton
Framlingham
Framlingham Castle
Swefling
Knodishall Green
Leiston
Sizewell
Apsey Green
Cole's Green
North Green
Great Glemham
Saxmundham
Benhall Street
Sternfield
Knodishall
Coldfair Green
Aldringham
Benhall Green
Friston
Parham
Silverlace Green
Stratford St Andrew
Snape Watering
Knodishall Common
The Meare
Thorpe Ness
Thorpeness
Kettleburgh
Hachestn
A12–TO IPSWICH (A1214)
A47
A146
A143
A144
A145
A149
A12
A1117
A1095
A1120
A1242
B1140
B1332
B1136
B1074
B1062
B1127
B1375
B1385
B1123
B1124
B1117
B1116
B1387
B1125
B1122
B1121
B1119
B1353
B1126

Lowestoft Ness: *This is the most easterly point in Britain.* ***Map ref. G2***

Sizewell: *Location of the Nuclear Power Station where, in August 2003, local residents were given anti-radiation pills aimed at reducing the risk of cancer in the thyroid.* ***Map ref. F5***

203

A
B
230
C
D
1
2
3
4
5
Aberffraw
Llangadwaladr
Hermon
Malltraeth
Trefdraeth
Bodorgan
Aberffraw Bay
Malltraeth Sands
A4080
Newborough
(Niwbwrch)
Malltraeth Bay
Llanddwyn Island
Llanddwyn Bay
Newborough Warren
Abermenai Point
The Bar
C A E R N A R F O N
B A Y
Dinas Dinlle
Pontllyfni
Trwyn Maen Dylan
Aberdesach
Tai'n Lôn
Clynnog-fawr
Gyrn Goch
Bwlch Mawr
509
Gyrn Du
522
Trefor
Trwyn y Gorlech
Yr Eifl
564
Llanaelhaearn
A499
Pen-sarn
Llithfaen
Cefn-caer-Ferch
St Cybi's Well
Carreg Ddu
Pistyll
Porth Dinllaen
Pencaenewydd
Llwyndyrys
Morfa Nefyn
Nefyn
Llangybi
Groesffordd
Edern
Garn Boduan
Fron
B4354
Rhos-fawr
Y Ffôr
Porth Ysgaden
Rhos-y-llan
Ceidio Fawr
Tan-y-graig
Hendre
Bodfuan
Llannor
Tudweiliog
Dinas
Efailnewydd
Denio
Abererch
Carn Fadryn
Garnfadryn
371
A497
Rhyd-y-clafdy
Pwllheli
Penllech
Porth Colmon
Porth Colmon
Pen-y-Graig
Bryn-mawr
Llaniestyn
Penrhos
Carreg yr Imbill
Llangwnnadl
Sarn Meyllteyrn
Y Gamlas
Penrhyn Mawr
Rhedyn
Ty-hen
Bryncroes
Botwnnog
Nanhoron
Llanbedrog
Trwyn Llanbedrog
Methlem
Porth Oer
Llandegwning
Mynytho
Rhydlios
Mynydd Rhiw
Llangian
Capel Carmel
Rhoshirwaun
305
Plas-yn-Rhiw (NT)
Abersoch
Braich Anelog
Rhiw
Llawr-y-dref
Anelog
Rhydolion
Llanengan
St Tudwal's Road
Mynydd Anelog
191
Pwlldefaid
Aberdaron
Llanfaelrhys
Sarn Bach
Bwlchtocyn
Braich y Pwll
Aberdaron Bay
Porth Neigwl
(Hell's Mouth)
St Tudwal's Islands
Uwchmynydd
Ynys Gwylan-fawr
Porth Ceiriad
Trwyn yr Wylfa
Cilan Uchaf
Pen y Cil
Bardsey Sound (Swnt Enlli)
Trwyn Cilan
St Mary's Abbey
Bardsey Island
(Ynys Enlli)

Bardsey Island (Ynys Enlli): *A place of pilgrimage and centre of the Celtic church from the 6th century where according to legend 20,000 saints are buried. Particularly noted for its wildlife, it is home to a large breeding colony of up to 16,000 Manx Shearwater.* ***Map ref. A5***

Llanystumdwy: *Although born in Manchester where his father was a schoolteacher, David Lloyd George was brought up here in Llanystumdwy. He served as Prime Minister from 1916–22 and has been credited with the introduction of the Welfare State.* ***Map ref. D4***

D
E
F
231
G
A55–TO HOLYHEAD (CAERGYBI)
A55–TO COLWYN BAY
A470–TO LLANDUDNO
Llanddaniel Fab
Plas Newydd (NT)
Bodowyr Burial Chamber
Brynsiencyn
Y Felinheli
Capel-y-graig
Waen-wen
Glasinfryn
Llanllechid
Rachub
Moel Wnion
Aber Falls
Drum
Llanbedr-y-cennin
Eglwysbach
Castell
Tal-y-bont
Pentre'r Felin
Rhyd-y-groes
Tal-y-Cae
Tregarth
Bethesda
Gerlan
Braichmelyn
Pentir
Coed-y-parc
Rhiwlas
Mynydd Llandygai
Seion
Llanddeiniolen
Saron
Bethel
Penisa'r Waun
Anglesey Sea Zoo
Plas Menai National Watersports Centre
Menai Strait
Waterloo Port
Caernarfon
Welsh Highland Railway
Caernarfon Castle
Segontium Roman Mus (NT)
Caeathro
Ceunant
Pont-rug
Llanrug
Deiniolen
Brynrefail
Clwt-y-bont
Gallt-y-foel
Fachwen
Cwm-y-glo
Bryn Bras
Llyn Padarn
Dinorwig
Padarn
Electric Mountain
Llanberis Lake Railway
Welsh Slate Museum
Llanberis
Groeslon
Bontnewydd
Croesywaun
Waunfawr
Dinas
Snowdon Mountain Railway
Rhostryfan
Betws Garmon
Moel Eilio
Penyffridd
Rhosgadfan
Salem
Groeslon
Moel Tryfan
Bwlchyllyn
Mynydd Mawr
Carmel
Siop y Fron (Upper Llandwrog)
Llyn Cwellyn
Nantlle
Llyn Nantlle Uchaf
Y Garn
Rhyd-Ddu
Ffridd Uchaf
Talysarn
Llanllyfni
Trum y Ddysgl
Craig Cwm Silyn
Beddgelert Forest
Nebo
Nasareth
Garneddgoch
Pant Glas
Beddgelert
Moel Hebog
Pass of Aberglaslyn
Pont Aberglaslyn
Nantmor
Cae Ddafydd
Llanfihangel-y-pennant
Bryncir
Garndolbenmaen
Dolbenmaen
Llyn Cwmystradllyn
Moel-ddu
Golan
Rhoslan
Penmorfa
Tremadog
Prenteg
Pentrefelin
Wern
Gell
Llanystumdwy
Criccieth
Criccieth Castle
Lloyd George Museum
Moel-y-Gest
Porthmadog
Minffordd
Morfa Bychan
Black Rock Sands
Borth-y-Gest
Portmeirion
Portmeirion Village
Harlech Point
Traeth Bach
Penrhyndeudraeth
Toll
Bryn Bwbach
Talsarnau
Ynys
Glan-y-Wern
Eisingrug
Glyn-Cywarch
Morfa Harlech
TREMADOG BAY
Harlech
Harlech Castle
Llanfair
Llandanwg
Pen-sarn
Llanbedr
Pentre Gwynfryn
Morfa Dyffryn
Coed Ystumgwern
Llanenddwyn
Dyffryn Ardudwy
Dyffryn Burial Chamber
Tal-y-bont
Nant Ffrancon
Mynydd Perfedd
Elidyr Fawr
Foel Goch
Y Garn
Llyn Ogwen
Pont Pen-y-benglog
Glyder Fach
Glyder Fawr
Llyn Peris
Nant Peris
Gwastadnant
Pass of Llanberis
Pen-y-Pass
Glaslyn
Snowdon (Yr Wyddfa)
Llyn Llydaw
Llyn Gwynant
Yr Aran
Plas Gwynant
SNOWDONIA (ERYRI)
Llyn Dinas
Cnicht
Croesor
Moelwyn Mawr
Moelwyn Bach
Tan lan
Garreg
Rhyd
Llanfrothen
Vale of Ffestiniog
Drosgl
Llwytmor
Foel-Fras
Garnedd Uchaf
Foel Grach
Carnedd Llywelyn
Carnedd Dafydd
Dulyn Resr
Llyn Eigiau Resr
SNOWDONIA NATIONAL PARK
Pen Llithrig y-wrach
Llyn Crafnant
Llyn Cowlyd Resr
Llyn Geirionydd
Capel Curig
Pont Cyfyng
Pen-y-Gwryd Hotel
Llynnau Mymbyr
Carnedd Moel-siabod
Carnedd y Cribau
Llynau Diwaunedd
Nantygwryd
Blaenau Dolwyddelan
Yr Arddu
Bwlch y Gorddinan (Crimea Pass)
Moel Penamnen
Llechwedd Slate Caverns
Rhiwbryfdir
Blaenau Ffestiniog
Ffestiniog Rly
Tanygrisiau
Bethania
Rhyd-y-sarn
Ffestiniog (Llan Ffestiniog)
Rhaeadr Cynfal
Maentwrog
Gellilydan
Tomen-y-mur Roman Fort
Craig Gyfynys
Llyn Trawsfynydd
Trawsfynydd
Moel Ysgyfarnogod
Craig Ddrwg
Bronaber
Llyn Cwm Bychan
Roman Steps
Crawcwellt
Rhinog Fawr
Rhinog Fach
Llyn Hywel
Y Llethr
Moelfre
Llyn Bodlyn
Diffwys
Llawlech
Uwch-mynydd
Taicynhaeaf
Bontddu
A470,A494–TO DOLGELLAU
Dolgarrog
Pont Dolgarrog
Vale of Conwy
Trefriw
Trefriw Woollen Mill
Llanrwst
Gwydir
Gwydir Uchaf Chapel
Llanddoged
Pentre-tafarn
Melin-y-coed
Oaklands
Swallow Falls
Ty-Hyll
Glyn
Betws-y-coed
Conwy Valley Railway Museum
Mynydd Cribau
Capel Garmon
GWYDYR FOREST PARK
Pont-y-pant
Fairy Glen
Conwy Falls
Dolwyddelan
Pentre-bont
Roman Br. Sta
Ty'n-y-coed Uchaf
Penmachno
Y Ro Wen
Gwydyr Forest
Ysbyty Ifan
Cwm Penmachno
Carrog
Glanaber Terrace
Pen y Bedw
Llyn Conwy
Migneint
Arenig Fach
Carnedd Iago
Graig Wen
Cwm Prysor
SNOWDONIA NATIONAL PARK
Craig yr Hyrddod
Arenig Fawr
Moel Llyfnant
Ffridd Trawsgoed
Moel y Feidiog
Mynydd Bach
Mynydd Bryn-llech
COED Y BRENIN FOREST PARK
Visitor Centre
Moel Hafodowen
Cefndeuddwr
Dduallt
Rhobell Fawr
Ganllwyd
Craig-y-cae
Y Garn
Moel Cors-y-garnedd
Foel Ddu
Llanfachreth
Precipice Walk
Foel Offrwm
Nannau
Bont Newydd
Llanelltyd
Rhydymain
A5–TO LLANGOLLEN
A494–TO RUTHIN (RHUTHUN)
218
204

Snowdon: *At 3,560 feet (1085 metres) Snowdon is the highest mountain in England and Wales. It is possible to ascend the north-western side of Snowdon on the Snowdon Mountain Railway. This passenger railway opened on the 6th April 1896 but an accident on the first day led to its closure for the next year. The service reopened in April 1897 and has operated safely ever since.*
Map ref. F2 Also on page 14

231

217

A470–TO LLANDUDNO
A5–TO BETHESDA
A487–TO PORTHMADOG
A470–TO DOLGELLAU
A494–TO DOLGELLAU

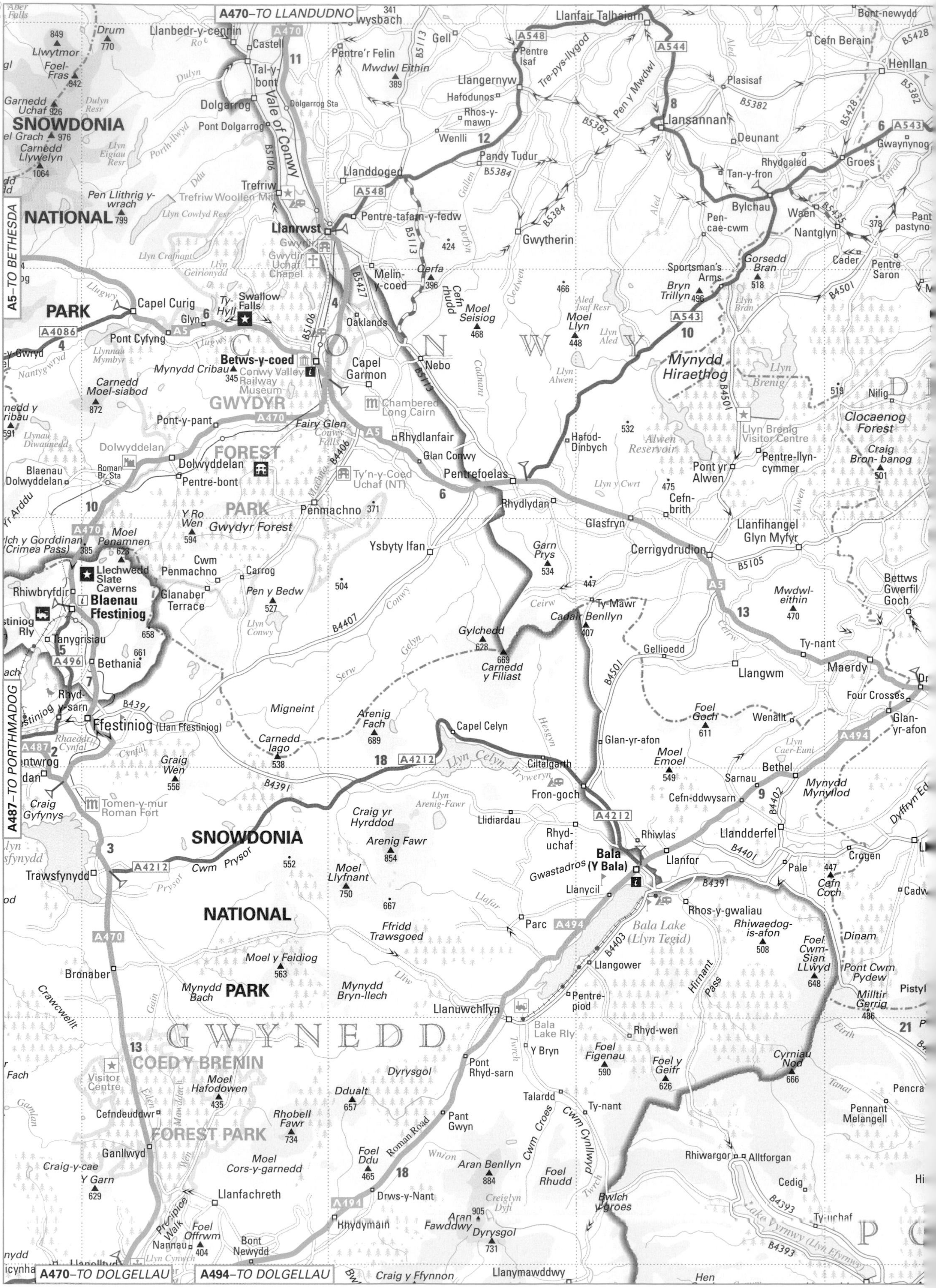

205

Bala: A centre for watersports near to both Bala Lake (Llyn Tegid), the largest natural lake in Wales, and the National White Water Centre. The Bala Lake Railway runs along the south-eastern shoreline of the lake. **Map ref. C4**

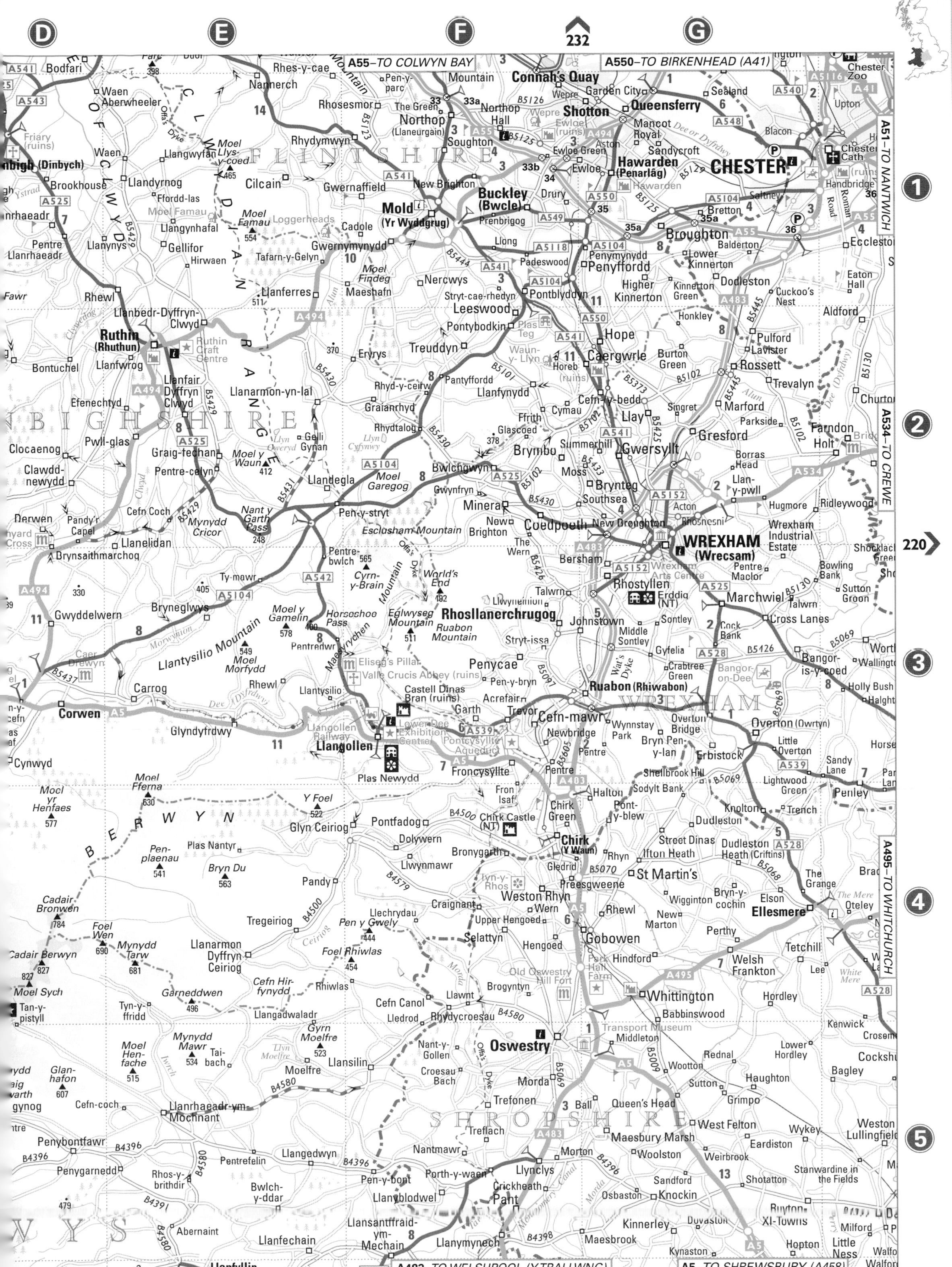

D
E
F
G
A55–TO COLWYN BAY
A550–TO BIRKENHEAD (A41)
A51–TO NANTWICH
A534–TO CREWE
A495–TO WHITCHURCH
A483–TO WELSHPOOL (Y TRALLWNG)
A5–TO SHREWSBURY (A458)
FLINTSHIRE
DENBIGHSHIRE
WREXHAM
SHROPSHIRE
CLWYDIAN RANGE
VALE OF CLWYD
BERWYN
CHESTER
Mold (Yr Wyddgrug)
Buckley (Bwcle)
Shotton
Queensferry
Connah's Quay
Hawarden (Penarlâg)
Broughton
Ruthin (Rhuthun)
Caergwrle
Hope
Gwersyllt
WREXHAM (Wrecsam)
Rhosllanerchrugog
Ruabon (Rhiwabon)
Cefn-mawr
Llangollen
Corwen
Chirk (Y Waun)
Gobowen
Whittington
Oswestry
Ellesmere
Overton (Owrtyn)
Llanfyllin
1
2
3
4
5

232
220

Llangollen: *Home every summer to the Eisteddfod Gerddorol Rygwladol Llangollen (International Musical Eisteddfod) a colourful festival of music, costume and dance famous the world over. The 14th century bridge here is one of the "Seven Wonders of Wales".* ***Map ref. F3***

206

233

A
B
C
D
A550–TO BIRKENHEAD (A41)
M53–TO BIRKENHEAD
A556–TO M56
A49–TO WARRINGTON
A55–TO COLWYN BAY
A5–TO LLANGOLLEN
A483–TO WELSHPOOL (YTRALLWNG)
A5–TO SHREWSBURY (A458)
A49, A53–TO SHREWSBURY
A442–TO TEL
Shotton
Queensferry
Sealand
Mancot Royal
Sandycroft
Hawarden (Penarlâg)
Ewloe
Broughton
Bretton
Saltney
CHESTER
Chester Cathedral
Hoole
Upton
Mickle Trafford
Guilden Sutton
Great Barrow
Ashton
Stamford Bridge
Tarvin Sands
Tarvin
Oscroft
Kelsall
Willington Corner
Delamere
FOREST PARK
Eddisbury Hill
Whitegate
Foxwist Green
Salterswall
Little Budworth Common
Cotebrook
Quarrybank
Little Budworth
Oulton Park
Rushton
Eaton
Clotton
Duddon
Burton
Tarporley
Birch Heath
Brassey Green
Huxley
Tiverton
Rhuddall Heath
Four Lane Ends
Tilstone Fearnall
Wettenhall Green
Littleton
Christleton
Brown Heath
Rowton
Rowton Heath 1645
Waverton
Milners Heath
Hargrave
Handbridge
Eccleston
Saighton
Balderton
Lower Kinnerton
Dodleston
Higher Kinnerton
Kinnerton Green
Penymynydd
Penyffordd
Padeswood
Pontblyddyn
FLINTSHIRE
Eaton Hall
Bruera
Cuckoo's Nest
Hatton Heath
Gatesheath
Cheshire Farm Ice Cream
Newton
Beeston Castle (ruins)
Beeston
Alpraham
Barrets Green
Calveley
Gosland Green
Bunbury
Bunbury Heath
Woodworth Green
Spurstow
Peckforton
Peckforton Hills
Wardle
Barbridge
Haughton
Radmore Green
Aldford
Pulford
Lavister
Rossett
Trevalyn
Honkley
Hope
Caergwrle
Burton Green
Horeb
Cefn-y-bedd
Llay
Singret
Marford
Gresford
Milton Green
Tattenhall
Newtown
Handley
Aldersey Green
Churton
Burwardsley
Cheshire Candle Workshops
Harthill
Chowley
Coddington
Farndon
Barton
Clutton
Broxton
Barnhill
Fuller's Moor
Bickerton Hill
Bickerton
Gallantry Bank
Bulkeley
Croxton Green
Egerton Green
Faddiley
Burland
Woodhey Green
Gradeley Green
Acton
Nantwich
Larden Green
Stoneley Green
Chorley
Ravensmoor
Ffrith
Cymau
Summerhill
Gwersyllt
Brymbo
Moss
Brynteg
Southsea
New Broughton
Coedpoeth
Borras Head
Llan-y-pwll
Acton
Rhosnesni
WREXHAM (Wrecsam)
Wrexham Industrial Estate
Hugmore
Holt
Crewe
Stretton
Ridleywood
Tilston
Duckington
Edge Green
Cholmondeley Castle Gardens
The Wern
Bersham
Rhostyllen
Pentre Maelor
Bowling Bank
Shocklach Green
Shocklach
Horton Green
Hampton Heath
Kidnal
Ebnal
Bickley Moss
Bickley Town
Norbury Common
Talwrn
Erddig (NT)
Middle Sontley
Sontley
Marchwiel
Talwrn
Sutton Green
Chorlton Lane
Malpas
No Man's Heath
Norbury
Wrenbury
Gauntons Bank
Sound
Broomhall Green
Johnstown
Cross Lanes
Cock Bank
Gyfelia
Worthenbury
Cuddington Heath
Swanwick Green
Quoisley
Marbury
Marley Green
Aston
Newhall
Wat's Dyke
Crabtree Green
Bangor-on-Dee
Bangor-is-y-coed
Wallington
Threapwood
Oldcastle Heath
Bell o' th' Hill
Ruabon (Rhiwabon)
Overton Bridge
Holly Bush
Halghton Mill
Tallarn Green
Higher Wych
Wirswall
Hollyhurst
Burleydam
Lightwood Green
Cefn-mawr
Newbridge
Wynnstay Park
Bryn Pen-y-lan
Erbistock
Overton (Owrtyn)
Little Overton
WREXHAM
Horseman's Green
Eglwys Cross
Whitewell
Redbrook
Grindley Brook
Brooklands
Whitchurch
Broughall
Wilkesley
Pentre
Shellbrook Hill
Lightwood Green
Sandy Lane
Penley
Hanmer
Little Green
The Chequer
Edgeley
Ash Magna
Ash Parva
Halton
Sodylt Bank
Chirk Green
Pont-y-blew
Dudleston
Knolton
Trench
Park Lane
Arowry
Gredington
Bronington
Alkington
Prees Heath
Ightfield
Calverhall
Chirk (Y Waun)
Street Dinas
Dudleston Heath (Criftins)
Fenn's Moss
Tilstock
Llangollen Canal
Roman Road
Gledrid
Rhyn
Ifton Heath
St Martin's
Preesgweene
Braden Heath
Platt Lane
Welsh End
Hollinwood
Prees Higher Heath
Willaston
Millenheath
Moreton Say
Upper Hengoed
Rhewl
Wigginton
Bryn-y-cochin
Elson
Ellesmere
The Grange
The Mere
Oteley
Welshampton
Balmer Heath
Bettisfield
Stanleygreen
Cotonwood
Newton
Sandford
New Marton
Hengoed
Gobowen
Perthy
Whixall
Quina Brook
Prees
Prees Sta
Prees Lower Heath
Darliston
Fauls
Bletchley
Tetchill
Wood Lane
Lyneal
Northwood
Colemere
Hindford
Welsh Frankton
Lee
White Mere
Old Oswestry Hill Fort
Park Hall Farm
Whittington
Paddolgreen
Newtown
Marchamley Wood
Ternhill
Hordley
Wolverley
Ryebank
Edstaston
Prees Green
Lowe
Creamore Bank
Babbinswood
Kenwick
Crose Mere
Transport Museum
Middleton
Oswestry
Crosemere
English Frankton
Brownheath
Horton
Wollerton
Marchamley
Hawkstone Park
Weston
Hodnet
Kenstone
Hodnet Hall Gardens
Hodnetheath
Rednal
Lower Hordley
Cockshutt
Loppington
Wem
Aston
Wixhill
Wootton
Stanwardine in the Wood
Tilley
Barkers Green
Bury Walls
Lee Brockhurst
Hopton
Ball
Queen's Head
Sutton
Haughton
Grimpo
Bagley
Noneley
Sleap
SHROPSHIRE
Maesbury
Maesbury Marsh
West Felton
Burlton
Petton
Moston
Booley
Weston Lullingfields
Preston Brockhurst
Besford
Stanton upon Hine Heath
Peplow
Woolston
Eardiston
Wykey
Weirbrook
Morton
Clive
High Hatton
Sandford
Stanwardine in the Fields
Marton
Myddlewood
Newton on the Hill
Yorton
Moreton Mill
Ellerdine Heath
Shotatton
Myddle
Grinshill
Moreton Corbet
Butlersbank
Osbaston
Knockin
Ruyton-XI-Towns
Baschurch
Harmer Hill
Yorton Heath
Shawbury
Edgebolton
Ellerdine
Cold Hatton
Dovaston
Milford
Prescott
Merrington
Muckleton
Maesbrook
Kinnerley
Hopton
Walford
Walford Heath
Old Woods
Preston Gubbals
Hadnall
Little Wytheford
Montgomery Canal
Shropshire Union Canal
Weaver
Dee (Dyfrdwy)
Perry
Roden
Gowy
Alun

219

Wem: *Home of the Sweet Pea, created by Henry Eckford and now famous throughout the world. Each July there is a Sweet Pea Festival in the town.* ***Map ref. C5***

206

Ruyton XI Towns: *A village created from eleven small hamlets under a charter of 1310. Believed to be the only village in Britain with Roman Numerals in its name.* ***Map ref. A5***

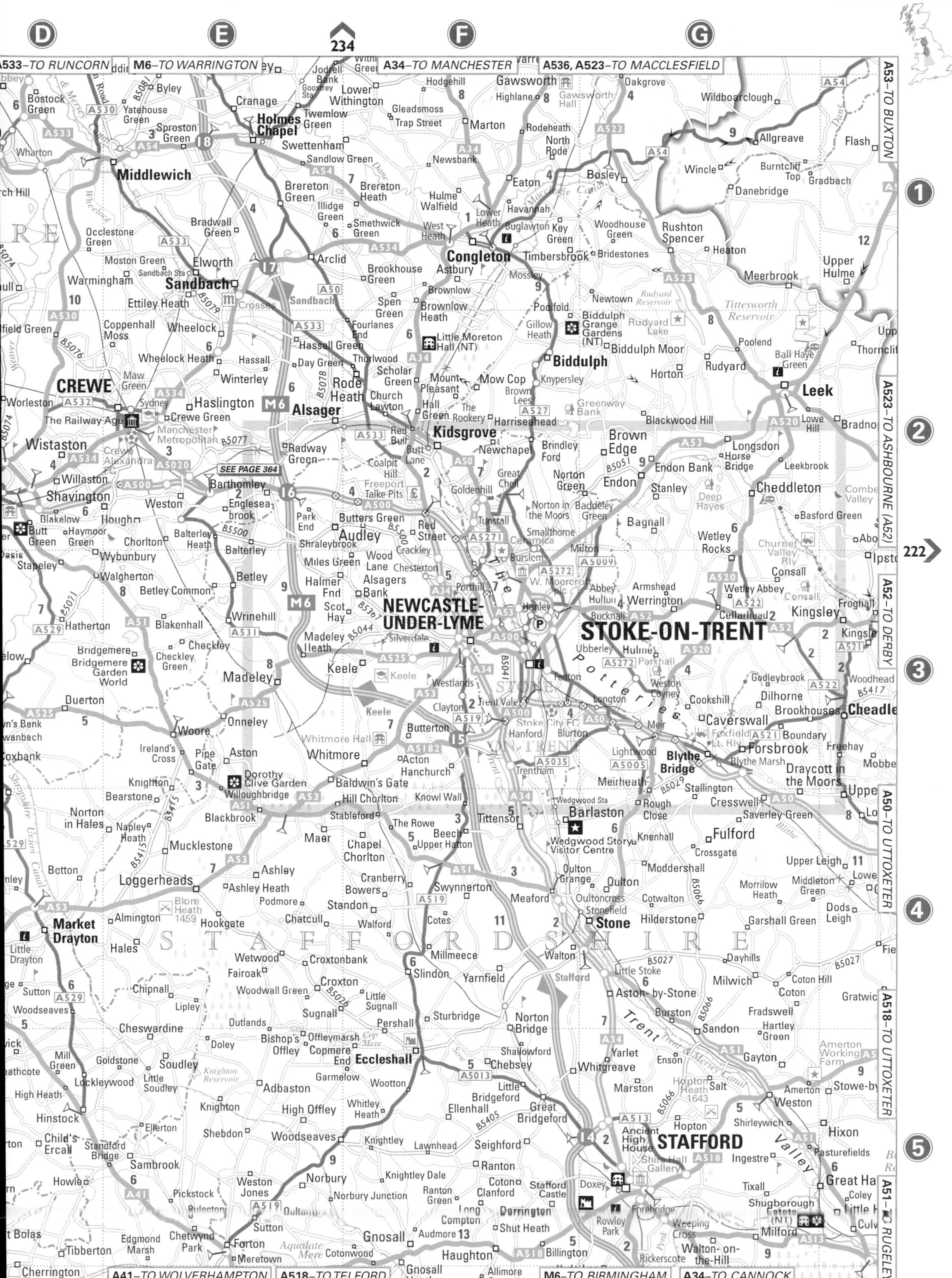
D
E
F
G
234
A533–TO RUNCORN
M6–TO WARRINGTON
A34–TO MANCHESTER
A536, A523–TO MACCLESFIELD
A53–TO BUXTON
A523–TO ASHBOURNE (A52)
A52–TO DERBY
A50–TO UTTOXETER
A518–TO UTTOXETER
A51–TO RUGELEY
A41–TO WOLVERHAMPTON
A518–TO TELFORD
M6–TO BIRMINGHAM
A34–TO CANNOCK
222
207
1
2
3
4
5
SEE PAGE 364
Middlewich
Holmes Chapel
Congleton
Sandbach
CREWE
Alsager
Kidsgrove
Biddulph
Leek
NEWCASTLE-UNDER-LYME
STOKE-ON-TRENT
Cheadle
Stone
Market Drayton
Eccleshall
STAFFORD
Loggerheads
Audley
Madeley
Keele
Barlaston
Gawsworth
Wincle
Rudyard
Cheddleton
Kingsley
Blythe Bridge
Fulford
Gnosall
Haughton
The Potteries
S T A F F O R D S H I R E
Tittesworth Reservoir
Rudyard Lake
The Railway Age
Little Moreton Hall (NT)
Biddulph Grange Gardens (NT)
Wedgwood Story Visitor Centre
Dorothy Clive Garden
Bridgemere Garden World
Stoke City FC
Shire Hall Gallery
Ancient High House
Shugborough Estate (NT)
Stafford Castle

Stoke-on-Trent: *The city of Stoke-on-Trent is unique in that it is made up of six separate towns; Tunstall, Burslem, Hanley, Stoke, Fenton and Longton. Together they are affectionately known as 'The Potteries' and are the home of Britain's ceramics industry. Some of the world's leading pottery manufacturers such as Wedgwood, Royal Doulton and Spode are based here.* ***Map ref. F3***

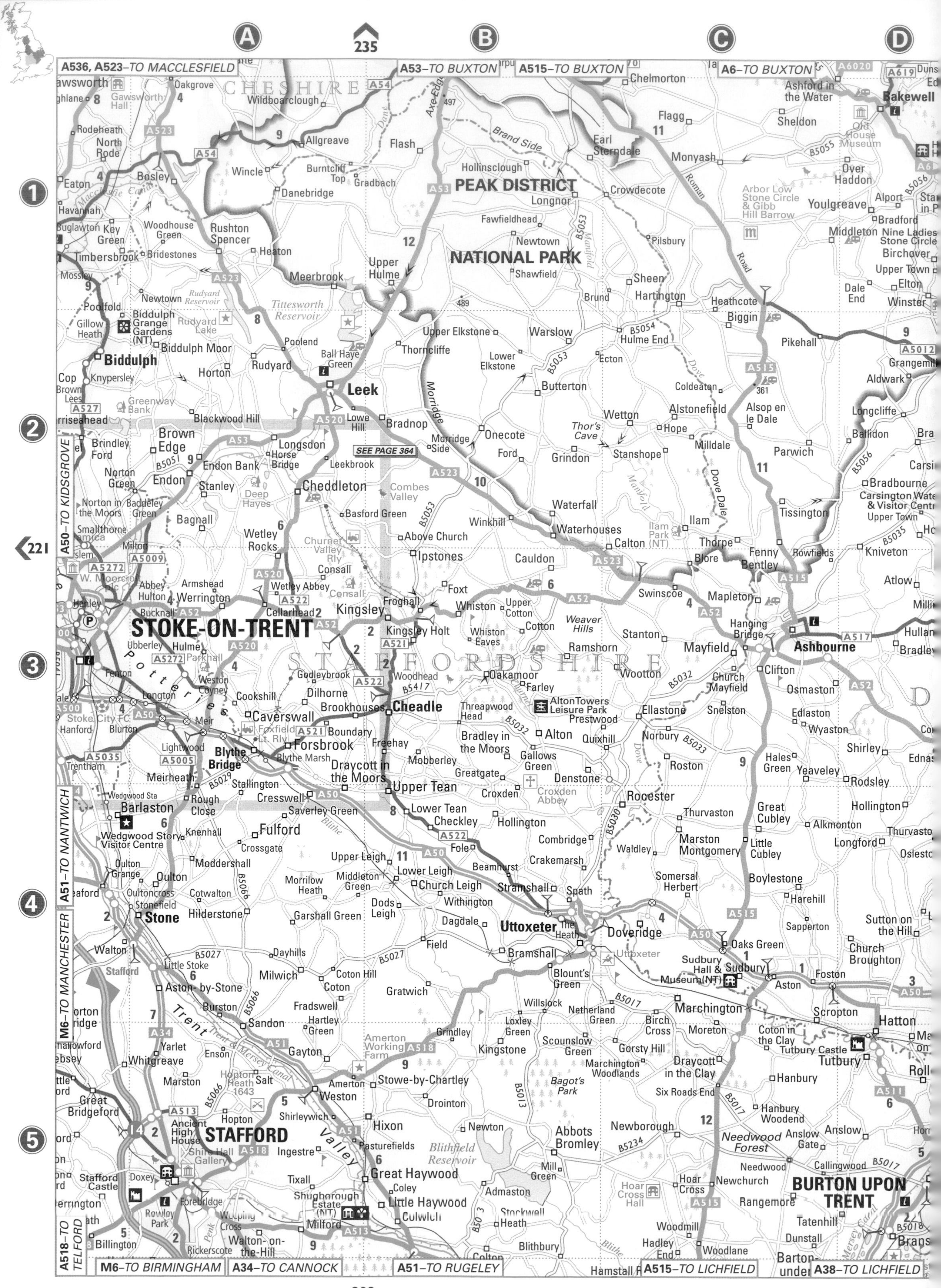

A
B
C
D
1
2
3
4
5
A536, A523–TO MACCLESFIELD
A53–TO BUXTON
A515–TO BUXTON
A6–TO BUXTON
A50–TO KIDSGROVE
A51–TO NANTWICH
M6–TO MANCHESTER
A518–TO TELFORD
M6–TO BIRMINGHAM
A34–TO CANNOCK
A51–TO RUGELEY
A515–TO LICHFIELD
A38–TO LICHFIELD
CHESHIRE
STAFFORDSHIRE
PEAK DISTRICT
NATIONAL PARK
SEE PAGE 364
STOKE-ON-TRENT
STAFFORD
BURTON UPON TRENT
Leek
Ashbourne
Bakewell
Uttoxeter
Cheadle
Stone
Biddulph
Tutbury
Flash
Longnor
Hartington
Ilam
Alton
Alton Towers Leisure Park
Rocester
Doveridge
Sudbury
Hatton
Great Haywood
Little Haywood
Hixon
Tittesworth Reservoir
Rudyard Lake
Blithfield Reservoir
Needwood Forest
Potteries
Trent
Dove Dale

235

221

208

Flash: *The highest village in Britain at 1,514 feet (461m) above sea level. It used to be known as a centre for outlawed activities, such as the production of counterfeit money, which became known as 'flash' because of its origin. Its position near the junction of three counties helped the locals to evade police forces by moving out of their jurisdiction into the next county.* ***Map ref. B1***

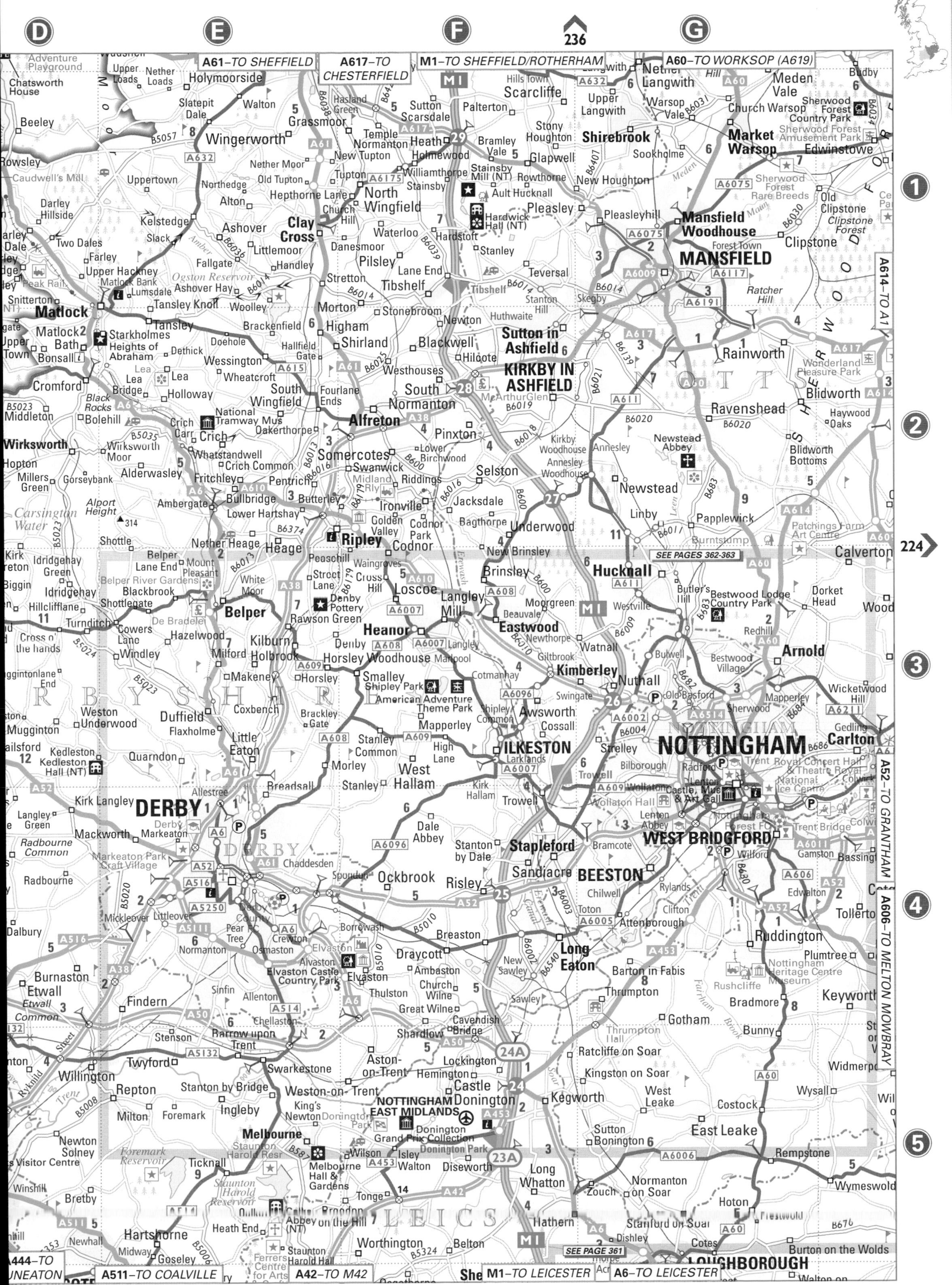
D
E
F
G
236
224
209
A61–TO SHEFFIELD
A617–TO CHESTERFIELD
M1–TO SHEFFIELD/ROTHERHAM
A60–TO WORKSOP (A619)
A614–TO A1
A52–TO GRANTHAM
A606–TO MELTON MOWBRAY
A444–TO NUNEATON
A511–TO COALVILLE
A42–TO M42
M1–TO LEICESTER
A6–TO LEICESTER
SEE PAGES 362-363
SEE PAGE 361
Matlock
Clay Cross
North Wingfield
Shirebrook
Market Warsop
Mansfield Woodhouse
MANSFIELD
Sutton in Ashfield
KIRKBY IN ASHFIELD
Alfreton
Somercotes
Ripley
Belper
Heanor
Eastwood
Hucknall
Kimberley
ILKESTON
NOTTINGHAM
Arnold
Carlton
DERBY
WEST BRIDGFORD
Stapleford
BEESTON
Long Eaton
Melbourne
Kegworth
LOUGHBOROUGH
NOTTINGHAM EAST MIDLANDS
Wirksworth
Cromford
Ruddington
Calverton
Ravenshead
Rainworth
Clipstone

Melbourne: *Thomas Cook (1820–1892) was born here. Cook pioneered packaged holiday travel through the rail excursions he organised in 1841.* ***Map ref. E5***

Eastwood: *D H Lawrence, famous as the writer of risqué novels detailing relationships between men and women, was born here on the 11th September 1885. Lawrence left England in 1918 and settled in Italy. He eventually moved to France where he died on the 2nd March 1930. He is buried at Venice overlooking the Adriatic.* ***Map ref. F3***

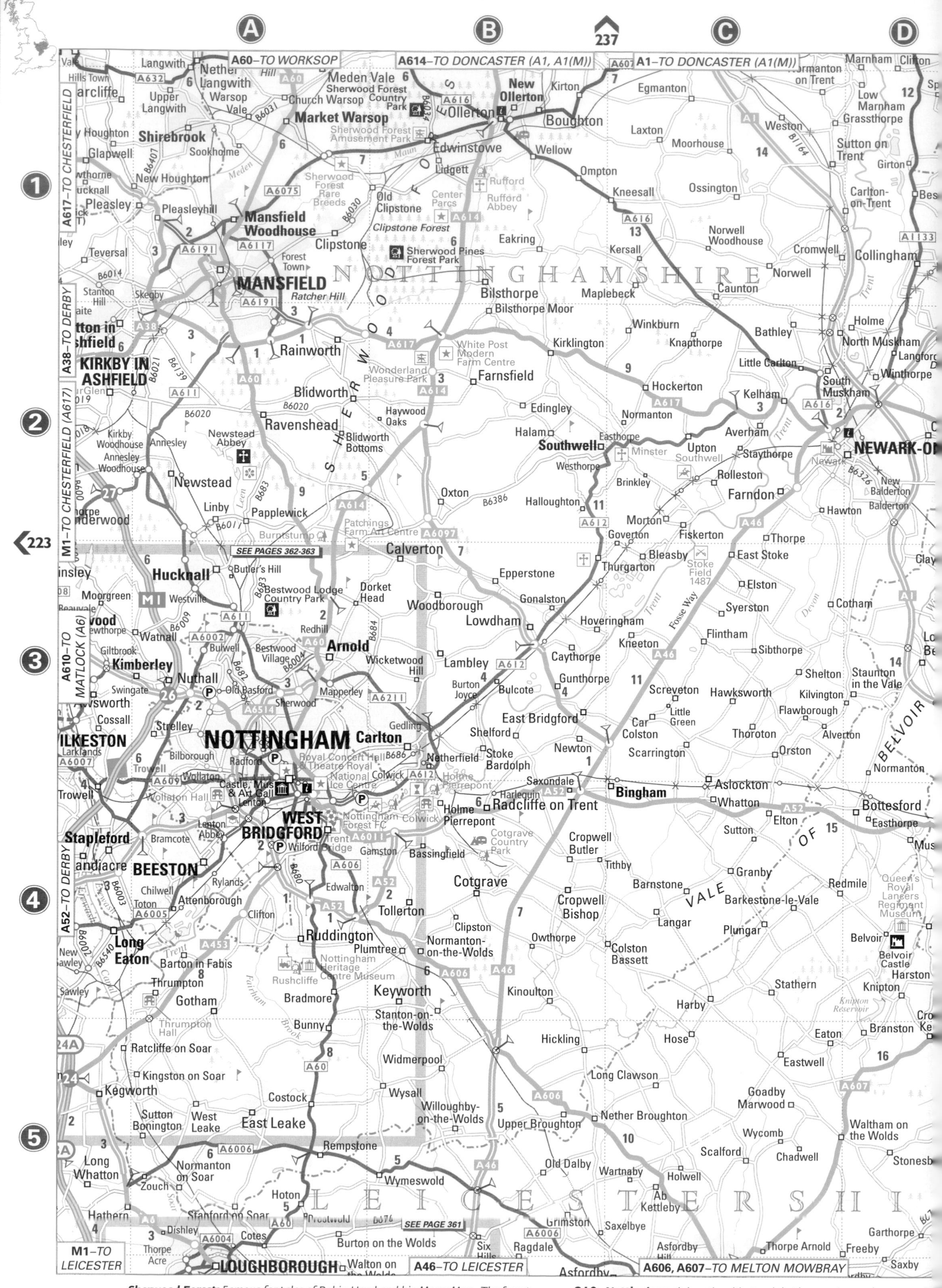

A
B
C
D
237
223
210
1
2
3
4
5
A60–TO WORKSOP
A614–TO DONCASTER (A1, A1(M))
A1–TO DONCASTER (A1(M))
A617–TO CHESTERFIELD
A38–TO DERBY
M1–TO CHESTERFIELD (A617)
A610–TO MATLOCK (A6)
A52–TO DERBY
M1–TO LEICESTER
A46–TO LEICESTER
A606, A607–TO MELTON MOWBRAY
SEE PAGES 362-363
SEE PAGE 361
N O T T I N G H A M S H I R E
L E I C E S T E R S H I
S H E R W O O D F O R E S T
VALE OF BELVOIR
NOTTINGHAM
MANSFIELD
NEWARK-ON
WEST BRIDGFORD
BEESTON
LOUGHBOROUGH
KIRKBY IN ASHFIELD
ILKESTON
Langwith
Nether Langwith
Meden Vale
Sherwood Forest Country Park
New Ollerton
Ollerton
Kirton
Egmanton
Marnham
Clifton
Upper Langwith
Warsop Vale
Church Warsop
Market Warsop
Boughton
Laxton
Moorhouse
Weston
Low Marnham
Grassthorpe
Shirebrook
Sookholme
Sherwood Forest Amusement Park
Edwinstowe
Wellow
Sutton on Trent
Glapwell
Ompton
Girton
New Houghton
Sherwood Forest Rare Breeds
Old Clipstone
Center Parcs
Lidgett
Rufford
Rufford Abbey
Kneesall
Ossington
Carlton-on-Trent
Pleasley
Pleasleyhill
Mansfield Woodhouse
Clipstone Forest
Norwell Woodhouse
Cromwell
Collingham
Teversal
Clipstone
Eakring
Kersall
Forest Town
Sherwood Pines Forest Park
Norwell
Stanton Hill
Skegby
Ratcher Hill
Bilsthorpe
Maplebeck
Caunton
Bilsthorpe Moor
Winkburn
Holme
Sutton in Ashfield
Rainworth
White Post Modern Farm Centre
Kirklington
Knapthorpe
Bathley
North Muskham
Langford
Wonderland Pleasure Park
Farnsfield
Little Carlton
Winthorpe
Blidworth
Hockerton
Kelham
South Muskham
Haywood Oaks
Edingley
Normanton
Ravenshead
Kirkby Woodhouse
Annesley
Newstead Abbey
Blidworth Bottoms
Halam
Averham
Annesley Woodhouse
Southwell
Minster
Easthorpe
Upton
Staythorpe
Newark
Westhorpe
Rolleston
New Balderton
Newstead
Brinkley
Farndon
Balderton
Oxton
Linby
Papplewick
Halloughton
Morton
Hawton
Patchings Farm Art Centre
Burntstump
Goverton
Fiskerton
Thorpe
Calverton
Bleasby
East Stoke
Hucknall
Butler's Hill
Epperstone
Thurgarton
Stoke Field 1487
Elston
Moorgreen
Westville
Bestwood Lodge Country Park
Dorket Head
Gonalston
Cotham
Woodborough
Syerston
Watnall
Lowdham
Hoveringham
Flintham
Giltbrook
Bulwell
Bestwood Village
Redhill
Arnold
Kneeton
Sibthorpe
Kimberley
Wicketwood Hill
Lambley
Caythorpe
Shelton
Staunton in the Vale
Nuthall
Gunthorpe
Swingate
Old Basford
Sherwood
Mapperley
Burton Joyce
Bulcote
Screveton
Hawksworth
Kilvington
Cossall
Little Green
Flawborough
East Bridgford
Strelley
Carlton
Gedling
Shelford
Car Colston
Thoroton
Alverton
Larklands
Bilborough
Radford
Royal Concert Hall & Theatre Royal
Netherfield
Stoke Bardolph
Newton
Scarrington
Orston
Normanton
Trowell
Wollaton
National Ice Centre
Colwick
Holme Pierrepont
Saxondale
Bingham
Aslockton
Castle, Mus & Art Gall
Lenton
Wollaton Hall
Harlequin
Whatton
Bottesford
Radcliffe on Trent
Elton
Nottingham Forest FC
Holme Pierrepont
Easthorpe
Stapleford
Bramcote
Lenton Abbey
Trent Bridge
Sutton
Wilford
Cotgrave Country Park
Cropwell Butler
Gamston
Bassingfield
Tithby
Sandiacre
Rylands
Edwalton
Cotgrave
Granby
Redmile
Barnstone
Queen's Royal Lancers Regiment Museum
Chilwell
Attenborough
Toton
Tollerton
Cropwell Bishop
Barkestone-le-Vale
Clifton
Clipston
Langar
Plungar
Belvoir
Ruddington
Normanton-on-the-Wolds
Owthorpe
Belvoir Castle
Long Eaton
Plumtree
Colston Bassett
Barton in Fabis
Nottingham Heritage Centre Museum
Harston
Rushcliffe
Keyworth
Thrumpton
Kinoulton
Stathern
Knipton
Gotham
Bradmore
Knipton Reservoir
Stanton-on-the-Wolds
Harby
Branston
Thrumpton Hall
Bunny
Hickling
Hose
Eaton
Ratcliffe on Soar
Widmerpool
Eastwell
Kingston on Soar
Long Clawson
Kegworth
Costock
Wysall
Goadby Marwood
Willoughby-on-the-Wolds
Sutton Bonington
West Leake
East Leake
Upper Broughton
Nether Broughton
Waltham on the Wolds
Wycomb
Rempstone
Scalford
Chadwell
Long Whatton
Normanton on Soar
Old Dalby
Wartnaby
Holwell
Zouch
Wymeswold
Hoton
Ab Kettleby
Hathern
Stanford on Soar
Prestwold
Grimston
Saxelbye
Dishley
Cotes
Garthorpe
Burton on the Wolds
Six Hills
Ragdale
Asfordby
Thorpe Arnold
Freeby
Thorpe Acre
Walton on the Wolds
Saxby
Asfordby Hill

Sherwood Forest: *Famous for tales of Robin Hood and his Merry Men. The forest contains the 'Major Oak', a tree reputed to be well over 800 years old. Its vital statistics are: spread over 90 feet (27.5m), girth 33 feet (10m) and weight estimated to be 23 tons (23.4 tonnes). It is so big that Robin is reputed to have hidden from his enemies inside its hollow trunk. In 1972 it was fenced off from the public after the 200,000 plus visitors it attracts every year were judged to be causing it damage.* ***Map ref. B1 Also on page 75***

Nottingham *claims the oldest pub in the country, perhaps even in the World. Ye Olde Trip to Jerusalem claims to date back to 1189 which was when King Richard I ascended the throne. It is said that the pub was a favourite resting place for soldiers on their way to the Crusades and in old English the word trip actually means rest or stop rather than journey as it does now.* ***Map ref. A3***

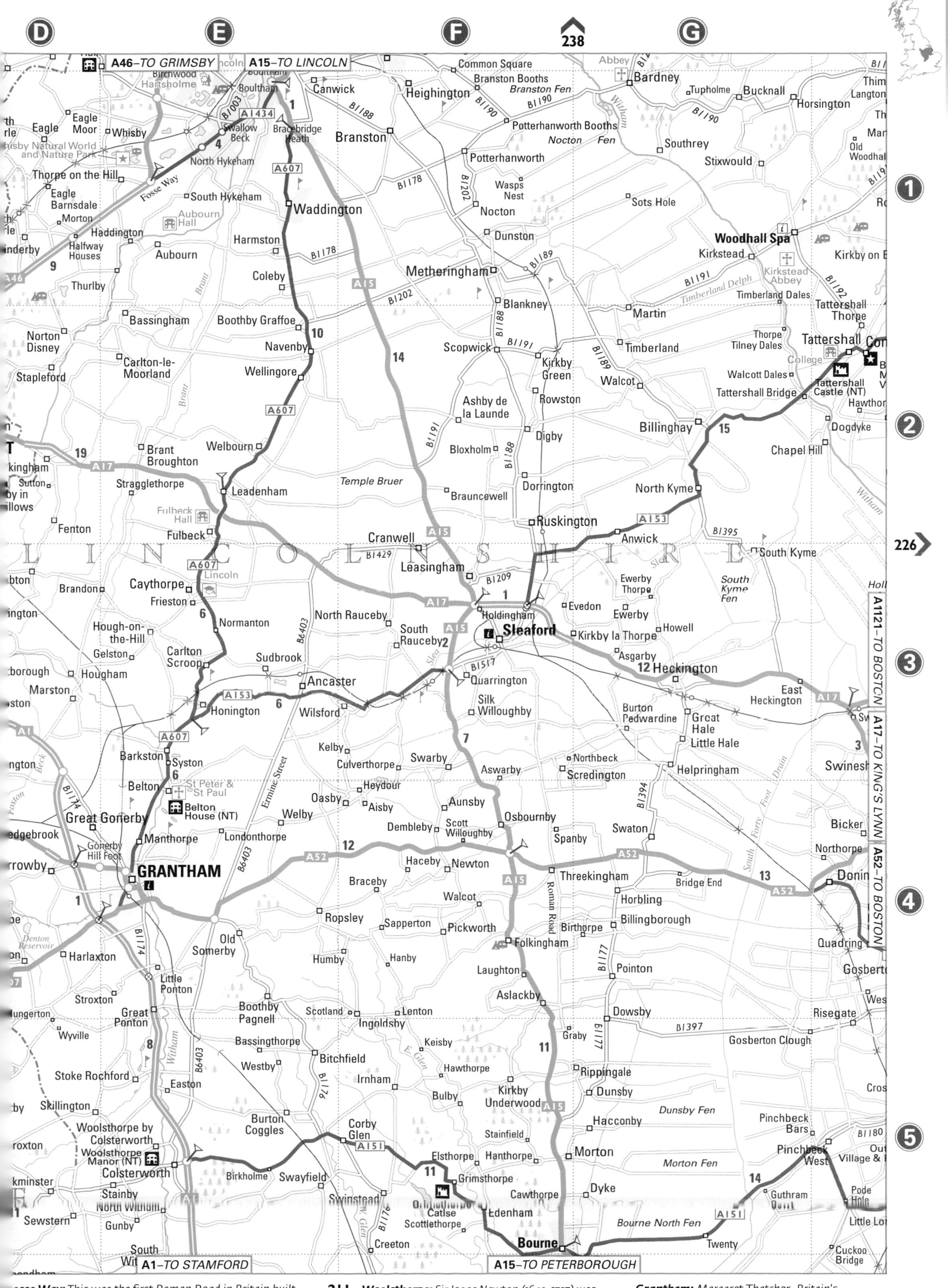
D
E
F
238
G
1
2
3
4
5
226
A46–TO GRIMSBY
A15–TO LINCOLN
Common Square
Abbey
Bardney
Birchwood
Hartsholme
Boultham
Canwick
Heighington
Branston Booths
Branston Fen
Tupholme
Bucknall
Horsington
Thimbleby
Langton
Eagle
Eagle Moor
Whisby
Swallow Beck
Bracebridge Heath
Branston
Potterhanworth Booths
Nocton Fen
Southrey
Whisby Natural World and Nature Park
North Hykeham
Potterhanworth
Stixwould
Old Woodhall
Thorpe on the Hill
Fosse Way
South Hykeham
Wasps Nest
Eagle Barnsdale
Morton
Aubourn Hall
Waddington
Nocton
Sots Hole
Haddington
Dunston
Woodhall Spa
Halfway Houses
Harmston
Aubourn
Kirkstead
Kirkby on Bain
Coleby
Metheringham
Kirkstead Abbey
Thurlby
Timberland Delph
Timberland Dales
Blankney
Tattershall Thorpe
Bassingham
Boothby Graffoe
Martin
Norton Disney
Navenby
Scopwick
Timberland
Thorpe Tilney Dales
Tattershall
Carlton-le-Moorland
Wellingore
Kirkby Green
Walcot
College
Stapleford
Walcott Dales
Tattershall Castle (NT)
Ashby de la Launde
Rowston
Tattershall Bridge
Hawthorn
Billinghay
Dogdyke
Digby
Brant Broughton
Welbourn
Bloxholm
Chapel Hill
Sutton
Stragglethorpe
Temple Bruer
Dorrington
North Kyme
Leadenham
Brauncewell
Fulbeck Hall
Ruskington
Fenton
Fulbeck
Cranwell
Anwick
South Kyme
L I N C O L N S H I R E
Leasingham
Brandon
Caythorpe
Lincoln
Ewerby Thorpe
South Kyme Fen
Frieston
Evedon
Ewerby
Hough-on-the-Hill
Normanton
North Rauceby
Holdingham
South Rauceby
Sleaford
Howell
Kirkby la Thorpe
Gelston
Carlton Scroop
Sudbrook
Asgarby
Heckington
A1121–TO BOSTON
Hougham
Ancaster
Quarrington
East Heckington
Marston
Silk Willoughby
Honington
Wilsford
Burton Pedwardine
Great Hale
A17–TO KING'S LYNN
Little Hale
Kelby
Barkston
Syston
Culverthorpe
Swarby
Northbeck
Aswarby
Scredington
Helpringham
Swineshead
St Peter & St Paul
Belton
Heydour
Oasby
Aisby
Aunsby
Belton House (NT)
Great Gonerby
Welby
Osbournby
Bicker
Dembleby
Scott Willoughby
Spanby
Swaton
Manthorpe
Londonthorpe
Gonerby Hill Foot
Northorpe
Haceby
Newton
A52–TO BOSTON
GRANTHAM
Threekingham
Donington
Bridge End
Braceby
Walcot
Horbling
Ropsley
Sapperton
Pickworth
Billingborough
Birthorpe
Quadring
Old Somerby
Folkingham
Denton Reservoir
Harlaxton
Humby
Hanby
Laughton
Pointon
Gosberton
Little Ponton
Aslackby
Stroxton
Boothby Pagnell
Scotland
Lenton
Dowsby
Risegate
Great Ponton
Ingoldsby
Graby
Wyville
Bassingthorpe
Keisby
Gosberton Clough
Bitchfield
Stoke Rochford
Westby
Irnham
Hawthorpe
Rippingale
Easton
Bulby
Kirkby Underwood
Dunsby
Skillington
Dunsby Fen
Burton Coggles
Corby Glen
Hacconby
Pinchbeck Bars
Woolsthorpe by Colsterworth
Stainfield
Woolsthorpe Manor (NT)
Elsthorpe
Hanthorpe
Morton
Pinchbeck West
Colsterworth
Morton Fen
Birkholme
Swayfield
Grimsthorpe
Stainby
Swinstead
Cawthorpe
Dyke
Guthram Gowt
Pode Hole
Sewstern
Gunby
Catsle
Scottlethorpe
Edenham
Bourne North Fen
Little London
Creeton
South Witham
Bourne
Twenty
Cuckoo Bridge
A1–TO STAMFORD
A15–TO PETERBOROUGH

Fosse Way: *This was the first Roman Road in Britain built around AD47. It extended from Exeter to Lincoln, running through Bath, Cirencester and Leicester. Much of its alignment is followed by present-day roads such as the A46.* ***Map ref. C3***

211

Woolsthorpe: *Sir Isaac Newton (1642–1727) was born at nearby Woolsthorpe Manor. Newton devoted his life to science, researching and developing theories on colour, light and the laws of motion, but is best remembered for his theory of universal gravitation.* ***Map ref. A4 Also on page 75***

Grantham: *Margaret Thatcher, Britain's first female Prime Minister, was born here on the 13th October 1925. She was elected as MP for Finchley in 1959 and went on to serve as PM from 1979 until her resignation in 1990.* ***Map ref. E4***

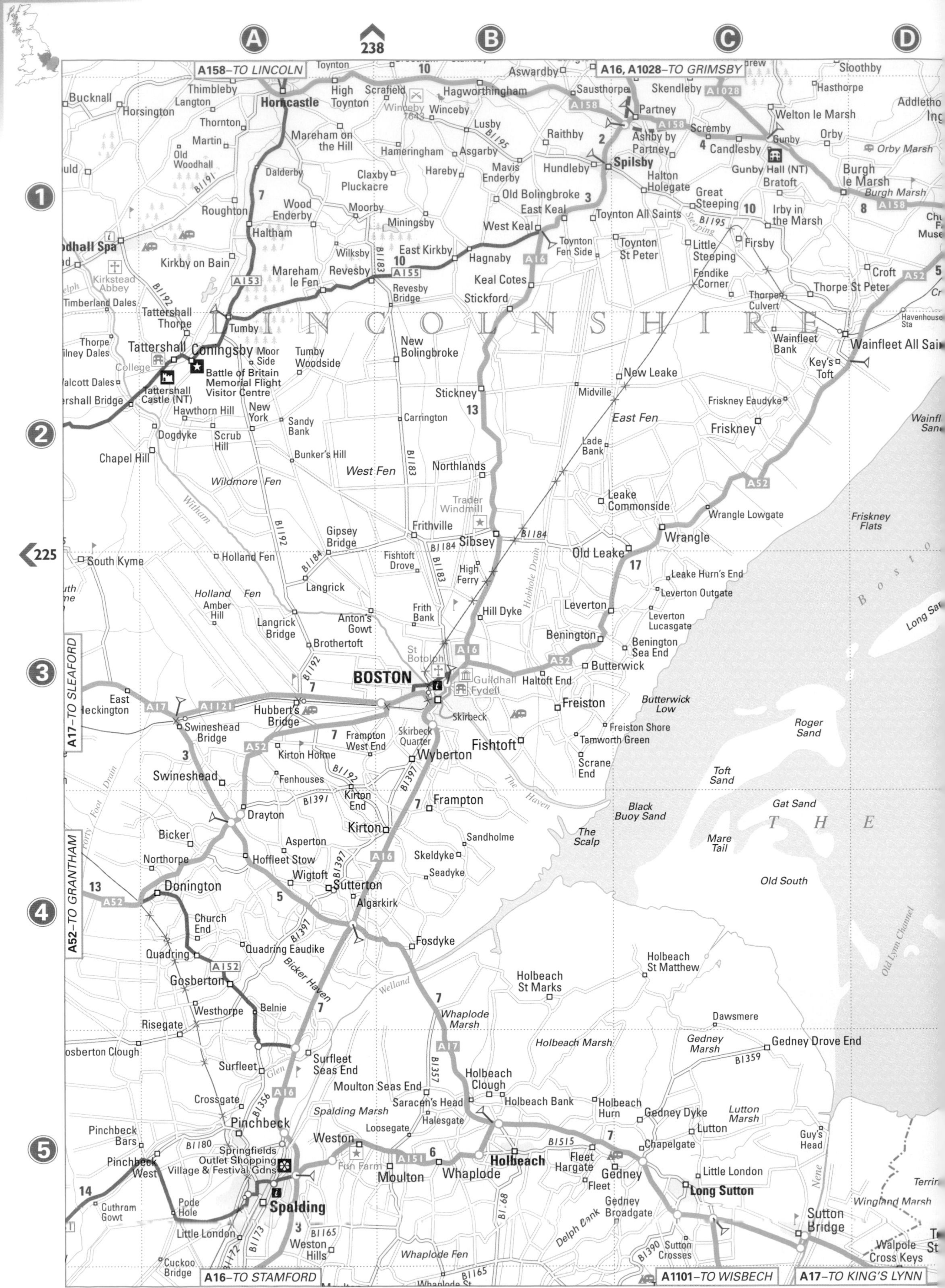

A
B
C
D
238
1
2
3
4
5
225
212
A158–TO LINCOLN
A16, A1028–TO GRIMSBY
A17–TO SLEAFORD
A52–TO GRANTHAM
A16–TO STAMFORD
A1101–TO WISBECH
A17–TO KING'S LYNN
LINCOLNSHIRE
Bucknall
Horsington
Thimbleby
Langton
Horncastle
High Toynton
Scrafield
Hagworthingham
Winceby
Aswardby
Sausthorpe
Skendleby
Slootbby
Hasthorpe
Welton le Marsh
Addletho
Thornton
Martin
Old Woodhall
Mareham on the Hill
Hameringham
Asgarby
Lusby
Raithby
Partney
Ashby by Partney
Scremby
Candlesby
Gunby
Orby
Orby Marsh
Gunby Hall (NT)
Burgh le Marsh
Burgh Marsh
Dalderby
Claxby
Pluckacre
Hareby
Mavis Enderby
Hundleby
Spilsby
Halton Holegate
Bratoft
Great Steeping
Irby in the Marsh
Old Bolingbroke
East Keal
Toynton All Saints
Roughton
Wood Enderby
Moorby
Miningsby
West Keal
Haltham
Woodhall Spa
Wilksby
East Kirkby
Hagnaby
Toynton Fen Side
Toynton St Peter
Little Steeping
Firsby
Kirkby on Bain
Kirkstead Abbey
Mareham le Fen
Revesby
Revesby Bridge
Keal Cotes
Stickford
Fendike Corner
Croft
Thorpe St Peter
Thorpe Culvert
Timberland Dales
Tattershall Thorpe
Tumby
Havenhouse Sta
Wainfleet Bank
Wainfleet All Saints
Thorpe
Tattershall
Coningsby
Moor Side
Tumby Woodside
New Bolingbroke
College
Battle of Britain Memorial Flight Visitor Centre
Tattershall Castle (NT)
Key's Toft
New Leake
Midville
Stickney
Friskney Eaudyke
Hawthorn Hill
New York
Sandy Bank
Carrington
East Fen
Friskney
Dogdyke
Scrub Hill
Lade Bank
Chapel Hill
Bunker's Hill
West Fen
Northlands
Wildmore Fen
Witham
Leake Commonside
Trader Windmill
Wrangle Lowgate
Friskney Flats
Frithville
Sibsey
Gipsey Bridge
Fishtoft Drove
High Ferry
Old Leake
Wrangle
South Kyme
Holland Fen
Langrick
Leake Hurn's End
Leverton Outgate
Holland Fen
Amber Hill
Frith Bank
Hill Dyke
Leverton
Leverton Lucasgate
Langrick Bridge
Anton's Gowt
Benington
Benington Sea End
Brothertoft
St Botolph
Butterwick
BOSTON
Guildhall
Fydell
Haltoft End
East Heckington
Hubbert's Bridge
Freiston
Butterwick Low
Swineshead Bridge
Skirbeck
Freiston Shore
Roger Sand
Frampton West End
Skirbeck Quarter
Tamworth Green
Kirton Holme
Wyberton
Fishtoft
Scrane End
Swineshead
Fenhouses
Toft Sand
Kirton End
Frampton
The Haven
Black Buoy Sand
Gat Sand
Drayton
Kirton
The Scalp
Mare Tail
Bicker
Asperton
Sandholme
Northorpe
Hoffleet Stow
Skeldyke
Seadyke
Wigtoft
Sutterton
Old South
Donington
Algarkirk
Church End
Quadring Eaudike
Fosdyke
Quadring
Holbeach St Matthew
Gosberton
Bicker Haven
Holbeach St Marks
Welland
Westhorpe
Belnie
Whaplode Marsh
Dawsmere
Risegate
Gedney Marsh
Gedney Drove End
Holbeach Marsh
Gosberton Clough
Surfleet Seas End
Surfleet
Glen
Moulton Seas End
Holbeach Clough
Crossgate
Spalding Marsh
Saracen's Head
Holbeach Bank
Holbeach Hurn
Gedney Dyke
Lutton Marsh
Pinchbeck Bars
Pinchbeck
Halesgate
Loosegate
Lutton
Guy's Head
Weston
Springfields Outlet Shopping Village & Festival Gdns
Chapelgate
Pinchbeck West
Fun Farm
Moulton
Whaplode
Holbeach
Fleet Hargate
Gedney
Fleet
Little London
Nene
Long Sutton
Cuthram Gowt
Pode Hole
Spalding
Gedney Broadgate
Wingland Marsh
Delph Bank
Sutton Bridge
Little London
Weston Hills
Whaplode Fen
Sutton Crosses
Walpole Cross Keys
Cuckoo Bridge
Whaplode St

Sutton Bridge: *King John, travelling from Spalding to King's Lynn is reputed to have lost his crown jewels here in the 12th Century. The coastal track running by The Wash was swamped by the incoming tide and the King's baggage train was swept away, never to be seen again.* ***Map ref. C5***

Boston: *St. Botolph's Church, better known as Boston Stump, is the largest parish church in England. It measures 282 feet (86m) long stands 272 feet (83m) high and covers 20,070 square feet (1865 sq m) in area. The main church was begun in 1309 and the tower was completed in 1520. From the tower, on a clear day, it is possible to see Lincoln Cathedral 32 miles (50km) away.* ***Map ref. B3***

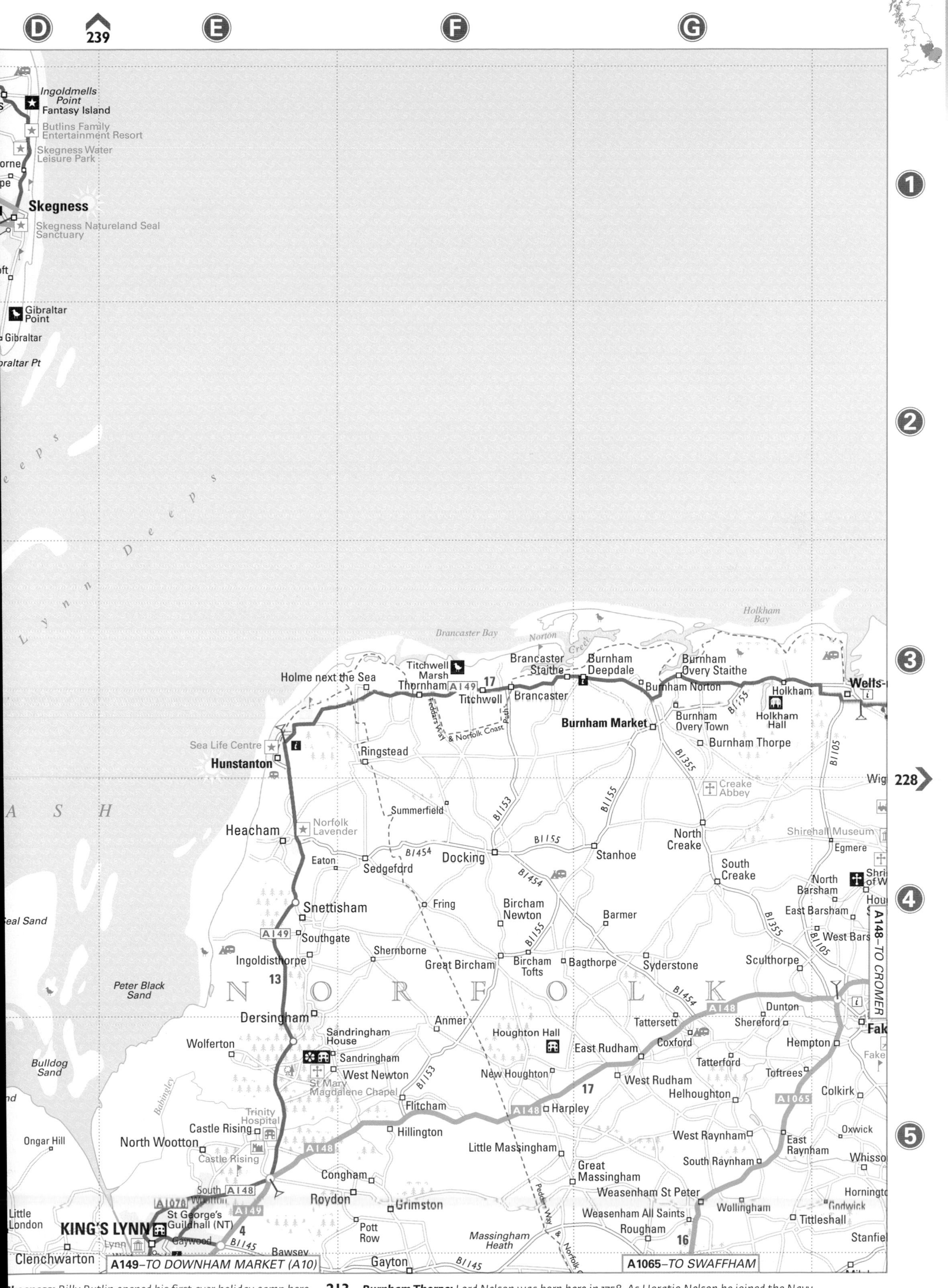

D
239
E
F
G
Ingoldmells Point
Fantasy Island
Butlins Family Entertainment Resort
Skegness Water Leisure Park
Skegness
Skegness Natureland Seal Sanctuary
Gibraltar Point
Lynn Deeps
Holkham Bay
Brancaster Bay
Titchwell Marsh
Holme next the Sea
Thornham
Titchwell
Brancaster Staithe
Brancaster
Burnham Deepdale
Burnham Overy Staithe
Burnham Norton
Burnham Market
Burnham Overy Town
Burnham Thorpe
Holkham
Holkham Hall
Wells
Sea Life Centre
Hunstanton
Ringstead
Creake Abbey
228
Summerfield
Heacham
Norfolk Lavender
North Creake
Docking
Stanhoe
Shirehall Museum
Egmere
Eaton
Sedgeford
South Creake
North Barsham
Snettisham
Fring
Bircham Newton
Barmer
East Barsham
Southgate
West Barsham
Ingoldisthorpe
Shernborne
Great Bircham
Bircham Tofts
Bagthorpe
Syderstone
Sculthorpe
Peter Black Sand
NORFOLK
A148–TO CROMER
Dunton
Dersingham
Anmer
Tattersett
Shereford
Sandringham House
Houghton Hall
Coxford
Hempton
Wolferton
Sandringham
East Rudham
Tatterford
Bulldog Sand
West Newton
New Houghton
West Rudham
Toftrees
St Mary Magdalene Chapel
Helhoughton
Colkirk
Flitcham
Harpley
Trinity Hospital
Castle Rising
Hillington
Oxwick
West Raynham
Ongar Hill
North Wootton
Little Massingham
East Raynham
Castle Rising
South Raynham
Great Massingham
Congham
Weasenham St Peter
South Wootton
Roydon
Wollingham
Little London
St George's Guildhall (NT)
Grimston
Weasenham All Saints
Tittleshall
KING'S LYNN
Pott Row
Rougham
Gaywood
Massingham Heath
Clenchwarton
Bawsey
A149–TO DOWNHAM MARKET (A10)
Gayton
A1065–TO SWAFFHAM
213

Skegness: *Billy Butlin opened his first ever holiday camp here in 1935. The camp was taken over by the Royal Navy for the duration of World War II and named HMS Royal Arthur. It was then returned to Butlins in 1946 and continued as Butlin's Holiday Camp until it was bought by the Rank Organisation in 1972.* ***Map ref. D1***

Burnham Thorpe: *Lord Nelson was born here in 1758. As Horatio Nelson he joined the Navy at the age of twelve and from then on spent almost his entire life at sea. He was dogged by ill health but from 1793 was almost always involved in a battle. He lost an eye at Calvi in Corsica, an arm at Santa Cruz in Tenerife and finally his life at the Battle of Trafalgar. As a monument to this inspirational leader Nelson's column was built in Trafalgar Square in London in 1840 and stands 170 feet (52m) high.* ***Map ref. G3***

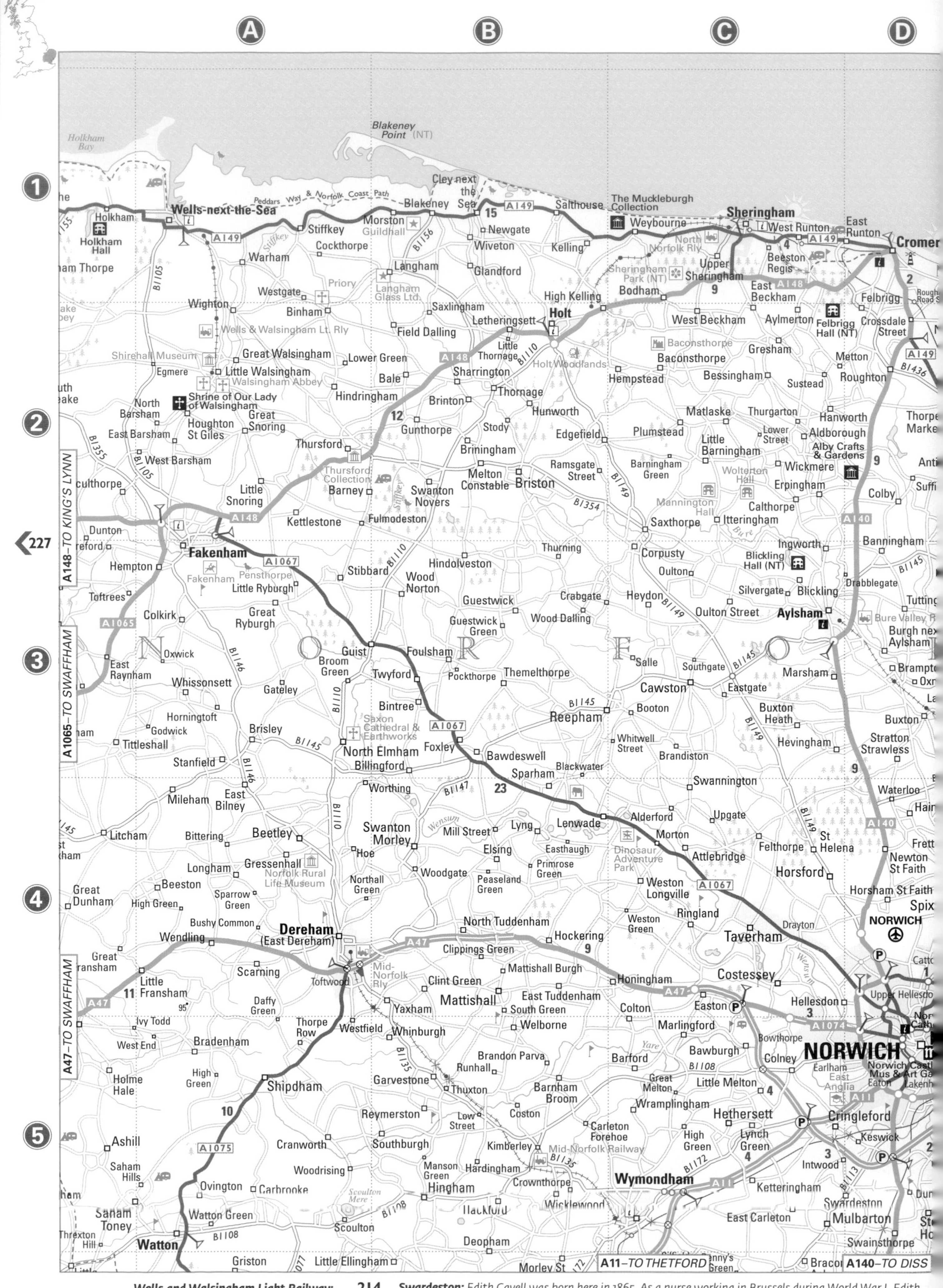
A
B
C
D
1
2
3
4
5
Holkham Bay
Blakeney Point (NT)
Cley next the Sea
Peddars Way & Norfolk Coast Path
Wells-next-the-Sea
Holkham
Holkham Hall
Blakeney
Salthouse
The Muckleburgh Collection
Sheringham
West Runton
East Runton
Cromer
Weybourne
North Norfolk Rly
Stiffkey
Morston
Guildhall
Newgate
Wiveton
Kelling
Cockthorpe
Warham
Langham
Langham Glass Ltd.
Glandford
Upper Sheringham
Beeston Regis
Sheringham Park (NT)
Bodham
East Beckham
Felbrigg
Priory
Westgate
Wighton
Binham
Saxlingham
High Kelling
Holt
Letheringsett
West Beckham
Aylmerton
Felbrigg Hall (NT)
Crossdale Street
Wells & Walsingham Lt. Rly
Field Dalling
Baconsthorpe
Gresham
Shirehall Museum
Great Walsingham
Lower Green
Little Thornage
Holt Woodlands
Metton
Egmere
Little Walsingham
Walsingham Abbey
Bale
Sharrington
Hempstead
Bessingham
Sustead
Roughton
North Barsham
Shrine of Our Lady of Walsingham
Hindringham
Thornage
Brinton
Hunworth
Matlaske
Thurgarton
Hanworth
Great Snoring
Houghton St Giles
East Barsham
Gunthorpe
Stody
Edgefield
Plumstead
Lower Street
Aldborough
Little Barningham
Alby Crafts & Gardens
Thursford
Briningham
West Barsham
Thursford Collection
Melton Constable
Briston
Ramsgate Street
Barningham Green
Wolterton Hall
Wickmere
Barney
Swanton Novers
Little Snoring
Erpingham
Colby
Sculthorpe
Mannington Hall
Calthorpe
Kettlestone
Fulmodeston
Saxthorpe
Itteringham
Dunton
Fakenham
Thurning
Ingworth
Banningham
227
A148–TO KING'S LYNN
Hempton
Pensthorpe
Stibbard
Hindolveston
Corpusty
Blickling Hall (NT)
Oulton
Little Ryburgh
Wood Norton
Drabblegate
Toftrees
Silvergate
Blickling
Colkirk
Great Ryburgh
Guestwick
Crabgate
Heydon
Oulton Street
Aylsham
Guestwick Green
Wood Dalling
Bure Valley Rly
Burgh next Aylsham
Oxwick
Guist
Foulsham
Salle
Southgate
Marsham
East Raynham
Broom Green
Twyford
Pockthorpe
Themelthorpe
Cawston
Eastgate
Whissonsett
Gateley
Bintree
Booton
Buxton Heath
Buxton
Reepham
Horningtoft
Saxon Cathedral & Earthworks
Godwick
Brisley
Whitwell Street
Stratton Strawless
Tittleshall
North Elmham
Foxley
Brandiston
Hevingham
Billingford
Bawdeswell
Stanfield
Blackwater
Sparham
A1065–TO SWAFFHAM
Worthing
Swannington
Mileham
East Bilney
Waterloo
Alderford
Upgate
Swanton Morley
Mill Street
Lyng
Lenwade
Litcham
Bittering
Beetley
Morton
St Helena
Felthorpe
Elsing
Easthaugh
Dinosaur Adventure Park
Attlebridge
Hoe
Newton St Faith
Longham
Gressenhall
Norfolk Rural Life Museum
Woodgate
Primrose Green
Horsford
Peaseland Green
Weston Longville
Great Dunham
Beeston
Northall Green
Horsham St Faith
Sparrow Green
High Green
Ringland
Weston Green
Bushy Common
North Tuddenham
Drayton
NORWICH
Dereham (East Dereham)
Hockering
Wendling
Taverham
Clippings Green
Great Fransham
Scarning
Mid-Norfolk Rly
Mattishall Burgh
Costessey
Toftwood
Clint Green
Honingham
Little Fransham
Daffy Green
Yaxham
Mattishall
East Tuddenham
Hellesdon
South Green
Colton
Easton
Ivy Todd
Thorpe Row
Westfield
Whinburgh
Welborne
Marlingford
Bowthorpe
West End
Bradenham
A47–TO SWAFFHAM
Brandon Parva
Bawburgh
Colney
High Green
Runhall
Barford
Earlham
Norwich Castle Mus & Art Gal
Holme Hale
Shipdham
Garvestone
Thuxton
Great Melton
Barnham Broom
Little Melton
East Anglia
Eaton
Lakenham
Wramplingham
Reymerston
Low Street
Coston
Hethersett
Cringleford
Ashill
Cranworth
Southburgh
Carleton Forehoe
High Green
Lynch Green
Keswick
Kimberley
Mid-Norfolk Railway
Intwood
Saham Hills
Woodrising
Manson Green
Hardingham
Hingham
Crownthorpe
Wymondham
Ketteringham
Ovington
Carbrooke
Scoulton Mere
Swardeston
Saham Toney
Watton Green
Hackford
Wicklewood
East Carleton
Mulbarton
Threxton Hill
Scoulton
Watton
Deopham
Swainsthorpe
Griston
Little Ellingham
Morley St
A11–TO THETFORD
A140–TO DISS

Wells and Walsingham Light Railway: *With a line gauge of 10.25 inches (260mm), this is the narrowest public railway in the world.* ***Map ref. A2***

214

Swardeston: *Edith Cavell was born here in 1865. As a nurse working in Brussels during World War I, Edith helped over 200 French, Belgian and British soldiers to escape from the Germans. She was eventually arreste[d,] convicted of treason and executed by firing squad on the 12th October 1915. After the war her body was exhumed and reburied in Norwich Cathedral.* ***Map ref. D5***

D
E
F
G
1
2
3
4
5
Sidestrand
Trimingham
Gimingham
Mundesley
Lower Street
Trunch
Knapton
Paston Street
Paston
Bacton
Keswick
Walcott
Bradfield
Old Hall Street
Edingthorpe
Swafield
Edingthorpe Green
North Walsham
Witton Bridge
Ridlington
Happisburgh
Whimpwell Green
Spa Common
Crostwight
Eccles-on-Sea
Tungate
Mooting House Hill
Happisburgh Common
Hempstead
Lessingham
Honing
Bengate
Lyngate
Briggate
East Ruston
Ingham Corner
Sea Palling
Waxham
Worstead
Ingham
Dilham
Stalham
Stalham Green
Frankfort
Sloley
Smallburgh
Sutton
Hickling
Hickling Green
Hickling Heath
Hill Common
Horsey Corner
Horsey
Horsey Windpump (NT)
Hickling Broad
Horsey Mere
Scottow
Market Street
Beeston St Lawrence
Pennygate
Clearwater 2000
Barton Turf
Wood Street
Catfield
Sco Ruston
Wroxham Barns
Tunstead
Ashmanhaugh
Neatishead
Barton Broad
Irstead
Potter Heigham
West Somerton
Winterton-on-Sea
Coltishall
Hoveton Hall Gardens
Butcher's Common
Threehammer Common
Sharp Street
Mustard Hyrn
Martham Broad
East Somerton
Hoveton
NORFOLK
Johnson Street
Ludham
Bastwick
Martham
Hemsby Holiday Centre
Hemsby Hole
Belaugh
Wroxham
Upper Street
Horning
BROADS
Hemsby
Newport
Repps
Thurne
Ormesby St Margaret
Scratby
California
Crostwick
Woodbastwick
St Helen
Rollesby
Clippesby
Bygone Village
Ormesby St Michael
Rackheath
Salhouse
Salhouse Sta
Ranworth
Fairhaven Gardens
Pilson Green
Cargate Green
Fleggburgh (Burgh St Margaret)
Billockby
Filby
Filby Broad
Roman Site
Caister-on-Sea
New Rackheath
Panxworth
South Walsham
Upton
Fishley
Thrigby
Caister Castle
Mauthy
Thrigby Hall Wildlife Gdns
Runham
West Caister
West End
Pedham
Town Green
Little Plumstead
Thorpe End
North Burlingham
Stokesby
Yarmouth
Blofield Heath
Acle
Great Plumstead
Witton
Blofield
Damgate
THE BROADS
Runham
Brundall
Lingwood
Beighton
Tunstall
Greyfriar's Cloisters
Sea Life Centre
Old Merchant's House and Row 111 House
Pleasure Beach
GREAT YARMOUTH
Postwick
Strumpshaw
South Burlingham
Halvergate Marshes
Breydon Water
Moulton St Mary
Halvergate
Berney Arms Mill
Berney Arms Sta
Burgh Castle
Southtown
Surlingham
Buckenham
Hassingham
Freethorpe
Wickhampton
Roman Fort
Kirby Bedon
Bramerton
Rockland St Mary
Cantley
Freethorpe Common
Pettitts Animal Adventure Park
Framingham Pigot
Hellington
Claxton
Limpenhoe
Bradwell
Gorleston-on-Sea
Yelverton
Ashby St Mary
Framingham Earl
Carleton St Peter
Reedham
Browston Green
Dalton
Poringland
Bergh Apton
Thurton
Hardley Street
Norton Marshes
Hobland Hall
Langley Street
Nogdam End
St Olaves Priory
Fritton Lake Countryworld
Ashby Dell
Howe
Brooke
Chedgrave
Norton Subcourse
Lower Thurlton
A146–TO BECCLES
A143–TO DISS
A12–TO LOWESTOFT
A149
A1151
A1062
A1064
A47
A12
B1145
B1150
B1354
B1140
B1152
B1140
Yarmouth Roads

Sheringham: *Norfolk is best known for its flat fenland and Broads. The highest point in the entire county is Roman Camp near Sheringham at just 336 feet (103 metres) above sea level.* ***Map ref. C1***

215

Great Yarmouth: *Anna Sewell, writer of the children's classic Black Beauty was born here on the 30th March 1820. Anna was crippled at an early age but constantly championed the better treatment and understanding of horses through her writing. She died on the 25th April 1878 and is buried at Lammas, near Buxton.* ***Map ref. G5***

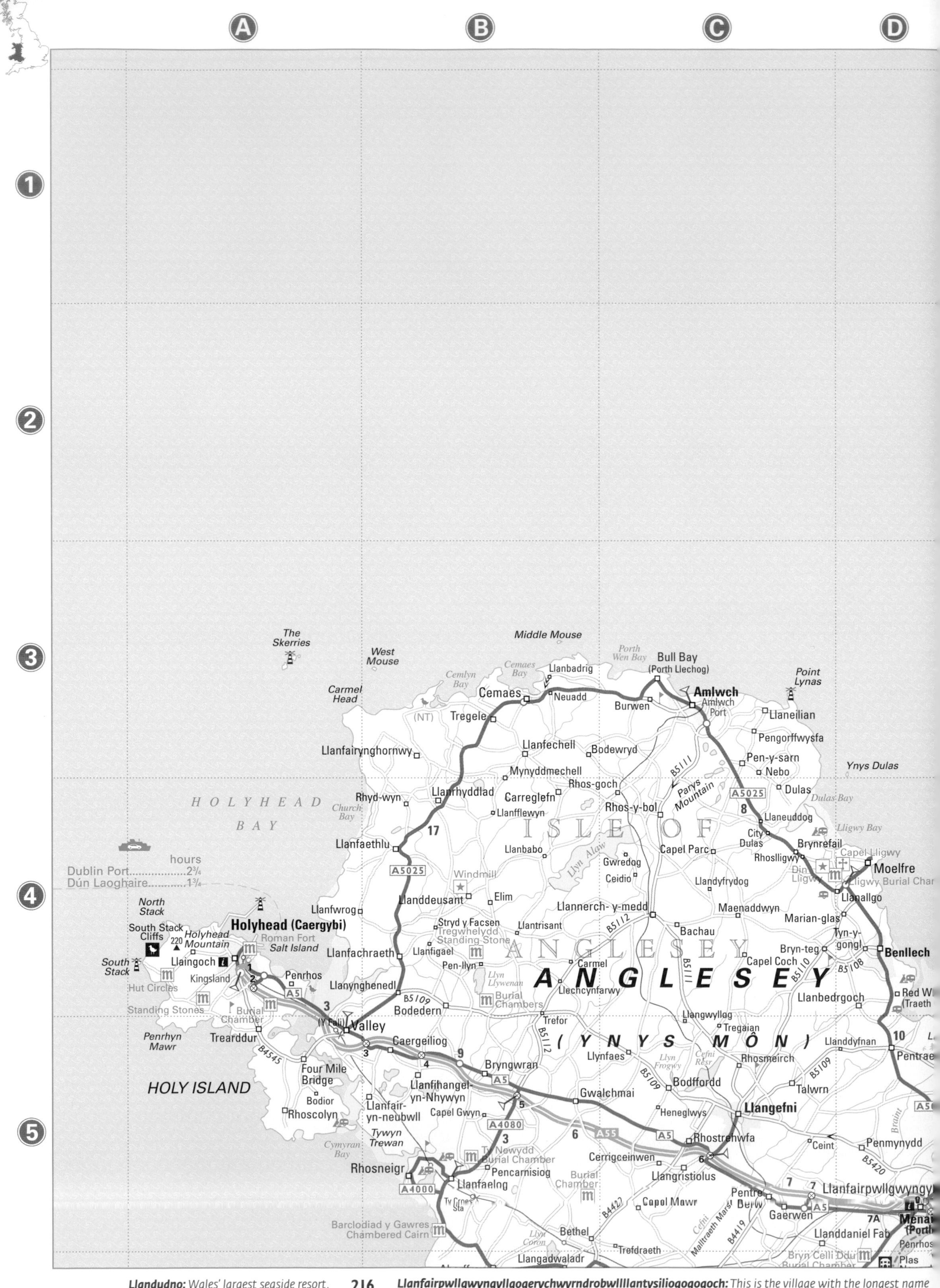

A
B
C
D
1
2
3
4
5
The Skerries
West Mouse
Middle Mouse
Carmel Head
Cemlyn Bay
Cemaes Bay
Porth Wen Bay
Bull Bay (Porth Llechog)
Point Lynas
Llanbadrig
Cemaes
Neuadd
Burwen
Amlwch
Amlwch Port
Llaneilian
Tregele
(NT)
Llanfairynghornwy
Llanfechell
Bodewryd
Pengorffwysfa
Pen-y-sarn
Nebo
Ynys Dulas
Mynyddmechell
Rhos-goch
B5111
Parys Mountain
A5025
Dulas
Dulas Bay
HOLYHEAD BAY
Church Bay
Rhyd-wyn
Llanrhyddlad
Carreglefn
Llanfflewyn
Rhos-y-bol
8
Llaneuddog
Lligwy Bay
ISLE OF
City Dulas
Brynrefail
Capel Lligwy
Moelfre
Llanfaethlu
17
Llanbabo
Llyn Alaw
Gwredog
Capel Parc
Rhosllligwy
Din Lligwy
Lligwy Burial Chamber
hours
Dublin Port 2¾
Dún Laoghaire 1¾
Windmill
Ceidio
Llandyfrydog
Llanallgo
North Stack
Llanddeusant
Elim
Llannerch-y-medd
Maenaddwyn
Marian-glas
Llanfwrog
South Stack Cliffs
Holyhead (Caergybi)
Roman Fort
Holyhead Mountain
220
Salt Island
Stryd y Facsen
Tregwhelydd Standing Stone
Llantrisant
B5112
Bachau
Tyn-y-gongl
Benllech
South Stack
Llaingoch
Llanfachraeth
Llanfigael
Carmel
Capel Coch
Bryn-teg
B5108
Kingsland
Hut Circles
Penrhos
Pen-llyn
Llyn Llywenan
ANGLESEY
Llanynghenedl
Llechcynfarwy
Red Wharf (Traeth...)
Standing Stones
Burial Chamber
A5
B5109
Bodedern
Burial Chambers
Llanbedrgoch
(Y Fali)
Valley
3
Trefor
Llangwyllog
Tregaian
Penrhyn Mawr
Trearddur
B4545
Caergeiliog
B5112
(YNYS MÔN)
Llanddyfnan
10
Pentraeth
HOLY ISLAND
Four Mile Bridge
4
Bryngwran
Llynfaes
Llyn Frogwy
Cefni Resr
Rhosmeirch
B5109
Talwrn
Bodior
Rhoscolyn
Llanfihangel-yn-Nhywyn
Llanfair-yn-neubwll
Gwalchmai
Bodffordd
Llangefni
Heneglwys
Capel Gwyn
5
A4080
Cymyran Bay
Tywyn Trewan
6
A55
Rhostrehwfa
Ceint
Penmynydd
B5420
Rhosneigr
Ty Newydd Burial Chamber
Pencarnisiog
Cerrigceinwen
Llangristiolus
7
Llanfairpwllgwyngyll
A4000
Llanfaelog
Ty Croes Sta
Burial Chamber
B4422
Capel Mawr
Pentre Berw
Gaerwen
7A
Menai (Porth...)
Malltraeth Marsh
Barclodiad y Gawres Chambered Cairn
Llyn Coron
Bethel
B4419
Llanddaniel Fab
Penrhos
Trefdraeth
Bryn Celli Ddu Burial Chamber
Llangadwaladr
Plas

Llandudno: *Wales' largest seaside resort. The town has numerous attractions and is the only place in Britain to feature a redundant lighthouse as a B&B.* ***Map ref. F4***

216

Llanfairpwllgwyngyllgogerychwyrndrobwllllantysiliogogogoch: *This is the village with the longest name in Britain. The final 38 characters of the name were added on in the 19th Century to attract tourists. The name actually means 'The Church of St Mary in a hollow of white hazel near a rapid whirlpool and near St Tysilio's Church by the red cave.…but now it's generally called Llanfair PG. Add the .com, and since 1999 it's also been the world's longest single-word internet domain name.* ***Map ref. D5***

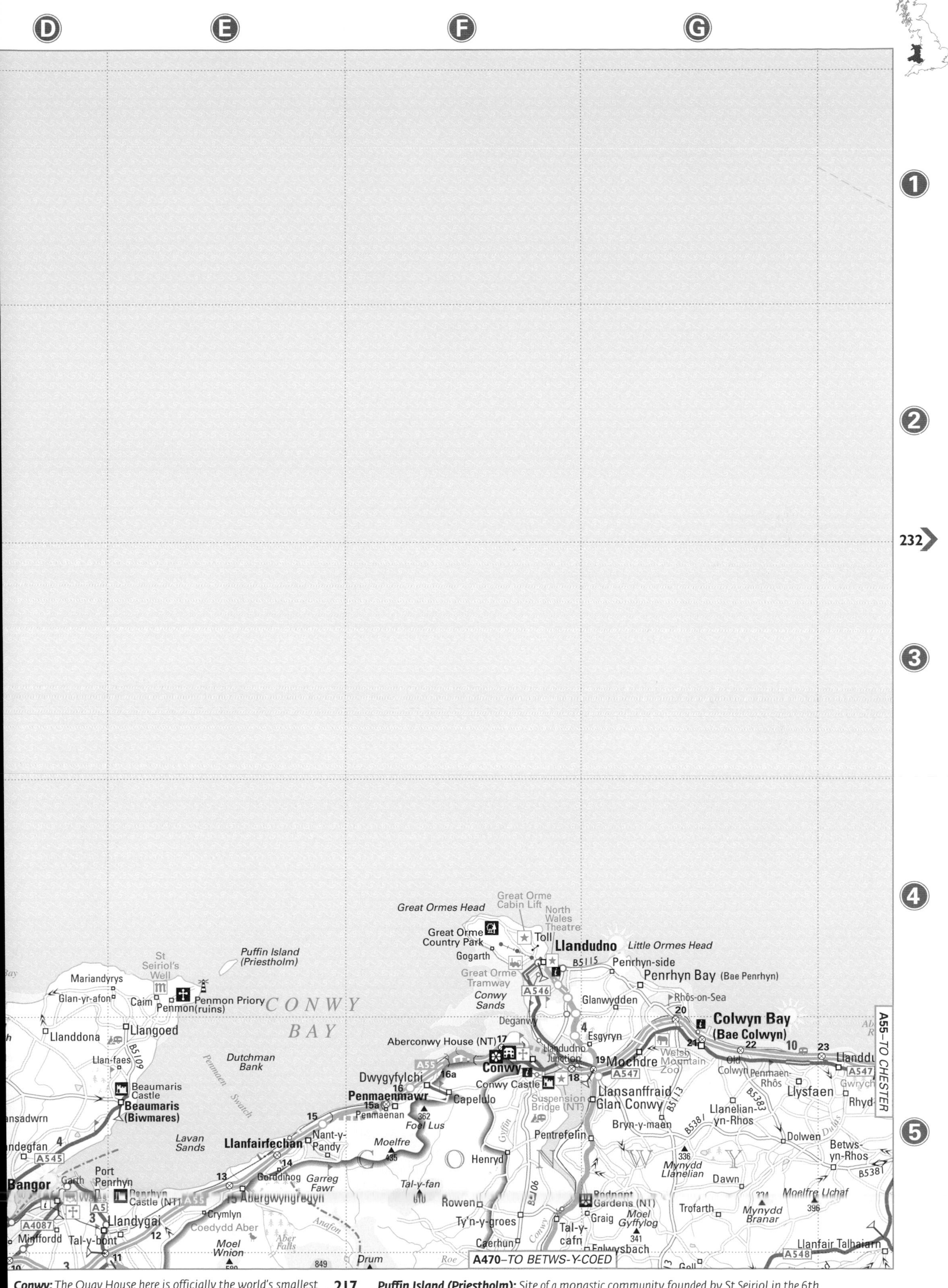
D
E
F
G
1
2
3
4
5
232
Great Ormes Head
Great Orme Cabin Lift
North Wales Theatre
Great Orme Country Park
Toll
Llandudno
Little Ormes Head
Gogarth
Penrhyn-side
Penrhyn Bay (Bae Penrhyn)
Great Orme Tramway
Conwy Sands
Glanwydden
Rhôs-on-Sea
Colwyn Bay (Bae Colwyn)
Puffin Island (Priestholm)
St Seiriol's Well
Mariandyrys
Glan-yr-afon
Caim
Penmon Priory (ruins)
CONWY BAY
Llanddona
Llangoed
Llan-faes
Dutchman Bank
Beaumaris Castle
Beaumaris (Biwmares)
Lavan Sands
Llanfairfechan
Nant-y-Pandy
Penmaenmawr
Penmaenan
Dwygyfylchi
Capelulo
Foel Lus
Moelfre
Aberconwy House (NT)
Conwy
Conwy Castle
Deganwy
Llandudno Junction
Esgyryn
Mochdre
Welsh Mountain Zoo
Llansanffraid Glan Conwy
Suspension Bridge (NT)
Pentrefelin
Henryd
Tal-y-fan
Rowen
Ty'n-y-groes
Caerhun
Tal-y-cafn
Bodnant Gardens (NT)
Graig
Moel Gyffylog
Eglwysbach
Bryn-y-maen
Mynydd Llanelian
Llanelian-yn-Rhos
Old Colwyn
Penmaen-Rhôs
Llysfaen
Dolwen
Betws-yn-Rhos
Dawn
Trofarth
Mynydd Branar
Moelfre Uchaf
Llanfair Talhaiarn
Rhyd-
Gwrych
Llanddu
Bangor
Garth
Port Penrhyn
Penrhyn Castle (NT)
Llandygai
Tal-y-bont
Minffordd
Abergwyngregyn
Crymlyn
Coedydd Aber
Aber Falls
Moel Wnion
Gorddinog
Garreg Fawr
Drum
ndegfan
nsadwrn
A55–TO CHESTER
A470–TO BETWS-Y-COED
A55
A546
A547
A545
A548
A5
A4087
B5115
B5109
B5113
B5106
B5381
B5383
362
435
336
341
396
849

Conwy: *The Quay House here is officially the world's smallest house.* ***Map ref. F5***

217

Puffin Island (Priestholm): *Site of a monastic community founded by St Seiriol in the 6th Century. By 2000, the Puffin population had been so severely decimated by rats that the Royal Air Force were called in to airlift in 2.5 tons of poisoned wheat onto the island in an attempt to wipe out the rat population.* ***Map ref. E4***

A
B
C
D
1
2
3
4
5
Port Sunlight: Village created by William Hesketh Lever who owned a soap factory making Sunlight Soap. This later became Lever Bros. The village was built to house his workforce. Work started on the 3rd March 1888 and by 1909 the village had 700 dwellings with all the facilities: school, theatre, library etc. Map ref. E4
hours
Belfast 7½
Dublin 4-8
Douglas, Isle of Man 2½-4
Formby
LIVERPOOL BAY
East Hoyle Bank
Hoylake
Manor Road Sta
Hoylake Sta
Meols Sta
West Hoyle Bank
Hilbre Island
West Kirby Sta
West Kirby
Grange
Caldy
Thurstaston
The Wirral (NT)
Dawpool Bank
Welsh Channel
Point of Ayr
Talacre
Llawndy
Prestatyn Sands Holiday Centre
Prestatyn
Mostyn Bank
Ffynnongroyw
Gronant
Gwespyr
Llanasa
Pen-y-ffordd
Mostyn Quay
Rhyl
Sky Tower
Sea Life Centre
Ocean Beach Amusement Park
Kinmel Bay (Bae Cinmel)
Meliden (Gallt Melyd)
Gwaenysgor
Gop Hill
Trelogan
Mostyn
Glan-y-don
Llannerch-y-Môr
Axton
Whitford (Chwitffordd)
Maen Achwyfaen
Holywell Bank
Greenfield Valley
Greenfield (Maes-Glas)
Basingwerk Abbey
Penrhyn
Abergele Roads
Towyn
Pensarn
Plas
Morfa Rhuddlan
Llwyd
Rhuddlan
Dyserth
Bodrhyddan Hall
Rhuddlan Castle & Twt Hill
Tan-yr-allt
Trelawnyd
Ochr-y-foel
Cwm
Marian Cwm
Llyn Helyg
Lloc
Carmel
Gorsedd
Pantasaph
St Winefride's Holy Well & Chapel
Walwen
Whelston
Holywell (Treffynnon)
Bagillt
Bagillt Bank
231
A55–TO CONWY
Bay
Llanddulas
Abergele
Gwrych
Llysfaen
Rhyd-y-foel
Penmaen-Rhôs
Dolwen
Betws-yn-Rhos
Moelfre Isaf
Moelfre Uchaf
Mynydd Bodrochwyn
Mynydd Branar
Llannefydd
Llanfair Talhaiarn
CONWY
DENBIGHSHIRE
Pengwern
Bodelwyddan
St George
St Asaph (Llanelwy)
Groesffordd Marli
Cefn Meiriadog
Plas-yn-Cefn
Bont-newydd
Cefn
Trefnant
Tremeirchion
Graig
Llannerch Hall
Bodfari
Rhuallt
Pen-y-cefn
Roman Road
Offa's Dyke
CLWYD
VALE
Caerwys
Sodom
Afon-wen
Afonwen Craft and Antique Centre
Moel y Parc
Ddôl
Ysceifiog
Calcoed
Brynford
Babell
Dolphin
Pentre Halkyn
Lixwm
Walwen
Rhes-y-cae
Nannerch
Halkyn
Halkyn Mountain
Bedol
Flint (Y Fflint)
Mount Pleasant
A55–TO CHESTER
FLINTSHIRE

Prestatyn: *Offa's Dyke was built by Offa, King of Mercia AD 757–796, to mark the boundary between England and Wales. It runs from Prestatyn in the north, to Sedbury, near Chepstow in the south, a distance of 182 miles (293km).* ***Map ref. B4***

219

Rhyl: *Ruth Ellis was born here in 1926. She was hanged on the 13th July 1955 at Holloway Prison for the murder of her lover. The execution so enraged the population that it opened the whole debate on capital punishment and she became the last woman in Britain to be hanged for murder. All executions were subsequently suspended from 1965 and capital punishment was abolished altogether in 1970.* ***Map ref. B4***

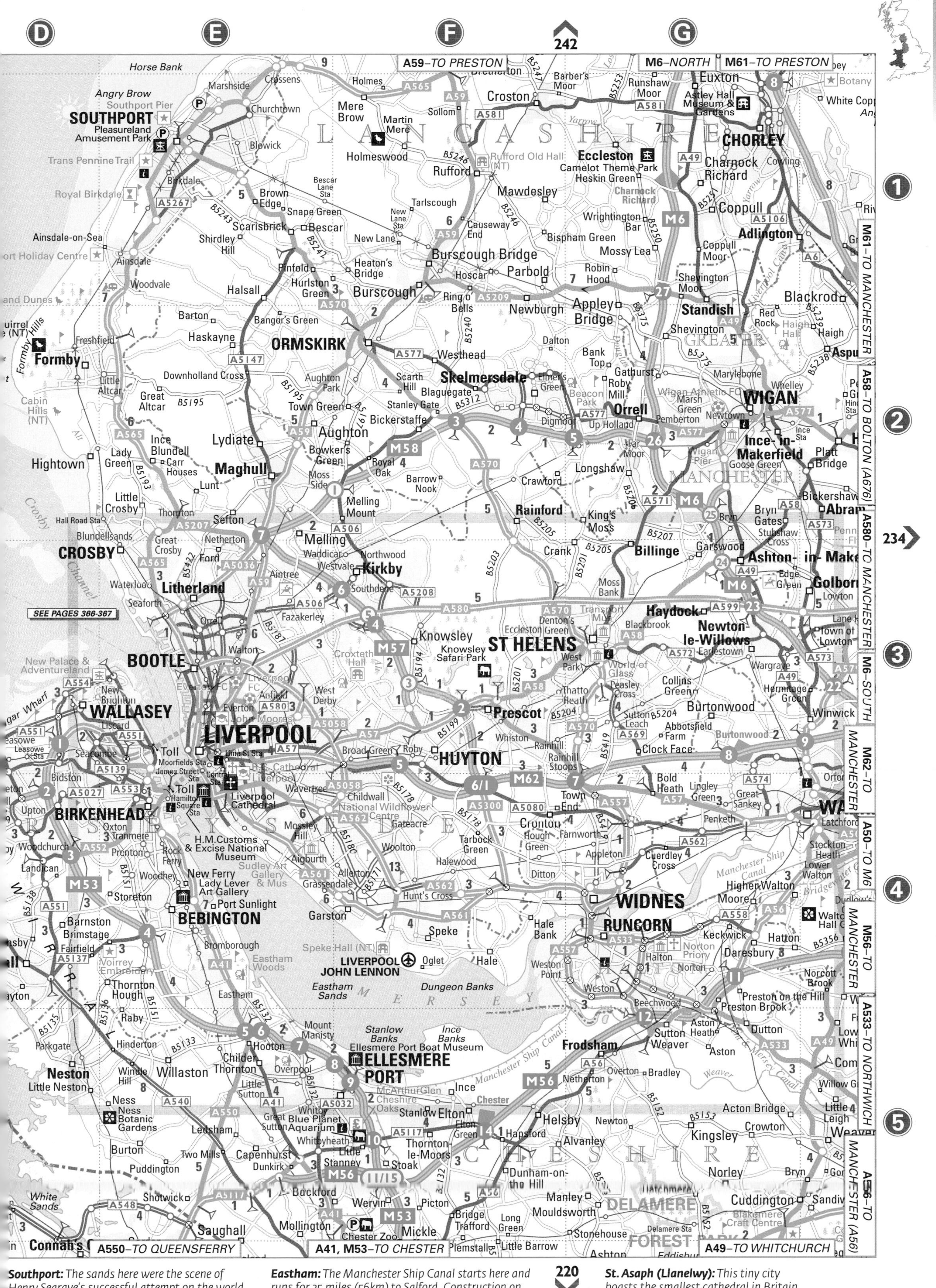
D
E
F
G
242
A59–TO PRESTON
M6–NORTH
M61–TO PRESTON
M61–TO MANCHESTER
A58–TO BOLTON (A676)
A580–TO MANCHESTER
M6–SOUTH
M62–TO MANCHESTER
A50–TO M6
M56–TO MANCHESTER
A533–TO NORTHWICH
A556–TO MANCHESTER (A56)
A550–TO QUEENSFERRY
A41, M53–TO CHESTER
A49–TO WHITCHURCH
234
220
1
2
3
4
5
SEE PAGES 366-367
LANCASHIRE
GREATER MANCHESTER
MERSEY
CHESHIRE
SOUTHPORT
Southport Pier
Pleasureland Amusement Park
Trans Pennine Trail
Royal Birkdale
Ainsdale-on-Sea
Ainsdale
Woodvale
Formby
Freshfield
Little Altcar
Great Altcar
Hightown
Crosby
Little Crosby
CROSBY
Blundellsands
Waterloo
Seaforth
Litherland
BOOTLE
WALLASEY
New Brighton
LIVERPOOL
BIRKENHEAD
Oxton
Tranmere
Bebington
BEBINGTON
Port Sunlight
Bromborough
Eastham
Eastham Woods
Neston
Little Neston
Parkgate
Willaston
Ness Botanic Gardens
Ledsham
Burton
Puddington
Two Mills
Capenhurst
Shotwick
Saughall
ELLESMERE PORT
Ellesmere Port Boat Museum
Hooton
Childer Thornton
Great Sutton
Little Sutton
Whitby
Blue Planet Aquarium
Stanney
Mollington
Chester Zoo
Mickle Trafford
Bridge Trafford
Picton
Wervin
Backford
Elton
Thornton-le-Moors
Ince
Stanlow
Helsby
Alvanley
Frodsham
Netherton
Overton
Bradley
Dunham-on-the Hill
Manley
Mouldsworth
DELAMERE FOREST PARK
Delamere Sta
Stonehouse
Little Barrow
Long Green
Kingsley
Crowton
Acton Bridge
Norley
Cuddington
Sandiway
Blakemere Craft Centre
Little Leigh
Weaverham
Willow Green
Sutton Weaver
Aston
Dutton
Preston on the Hill
Preston Brook
Norcott Brook
Daresbury
Keckwick
Hatton
Walton Hall
Higher Walton
Moore
Stockton Heath
Lower Walton
Latchford
RUNCORN
WIDNES
Halton
Norton Priory
Weston
Weston Point
Beechwood
Hale
Hale Bank
Oglet
Speke
Speke Hall (NT)
LIVERPOOL JOHN LENNON
Eastham Sands
Dungeon Banks
Stanlow Banks
Ince Banks
Garston
Grassendale
Allerton
Aigburth
Woolton
Halewood
Hunt's Cross
Gateacre
Childwall
National Wildflower Centre
Mossley Hill
Wavertree
Broad Green
Roby
HUYTON
Tarbock Green
Cronton
Farnworth
Appleton
Cuerdley Cross
Penketh
Great Sankey
Bold Heath
Lingley Green
Burtonwood
Collins Green
Clock Face
Abbotsfield Farm
Sutton Leach
Rainhill
Rainhill Stoops
Whiston
Prescot
Knowsley
Knowsley Safari Park
ST HELENS
Eccleston Green
West Park
World of Glass
Thatto Heath
Peasley Cross
Haydock
Blackbrook
Newton le-Willows
Earlestown
Wargrave
Hermitage Green
Winwick
Golborne
Lowton
Town of Lowton
Lane Head
Ashton-in-Makerfield
Garswood
Stubshaw Cross
Bryn Gates
Billinge
Crank
Moss Bank
King's Moss
Rainford
Crawford
Longshaw
Orrell
Up Holland
Far Moor
Pemberton
Marsh Green
Newtown
WIGAN
Ince-in-Makerfield
Goose Green
Platt Bridge
Bickershaw
Abram
Marylebone
Whelley
Haigh
Red Rock
Haigh Hall
Aspull
Standish
Shevington
Shevington Moor
Blackrod
Adlington
Coppull
Coppull Moor
CHORLEY
Charnock Richard
Cowling
Eccleston
Camelot Theme Park
Heskin Green
Wrightington Bar
Bispham Green
Mossy Lea
Robin Hood
Appley Bridge
Dalton
Bank Top
Gathurst
Roby Mill
Skelmersdale
Elmer's Green
Beacon Park
Dignmoor
Newburgh
Parbold
Hoscar
Burscough Bridge
Burscough
Ring o' Bells
Westhead
Scarth Hill
Blaguegate
Stanley Gate
Bickerstaffe
ORMSKIRK
Aughton Park
Town Green
Aughton
Bowker's Green
Royal Oak
Barrow Nook
Moss Side
Melling Mount
Melling
Waddicar
Westvale
Northwood
Kirkby
Southdene
Aintree
Fazakerley
Netherton
Ford
Sefton
Thornton
Lunt
Maghull
Lydiate
Ince Blundell
Carr Houses
Lady Green
Downholland Cross
Haskayne
Barton
Halsall
Bangor's Green
Hurlston Green
Pinfold
Scarisbrick
Bescar
Snape Green
Brown Edge
Shirdley Hill
Birkdale
Blowick
Churchtown
Crossens
Marshside
Horse Bank
Angry Brow
Mere Brow
Holmes
Martin Mere
Holmeswood
Rufford
Rufford Old Hall (NT)
Mawdesley
Tarlscough
Causeway End
New Lane
Croston
Sollom
Barber's Moor
Runshaw Moor
Euxton
Astley Hall Museum & Gardens
Botany
White Coppice
Walton
Everton
Orrell
Toll
Seacombe
Liscard
Leasowe
Bidston
Upton
Woodchurch
Landican
Prenton
Rock Ferry
New Ferry
Lady Lever Art Gallery
H.M.Customs & Excise National Museum
Sudley Art Gallery & Mus
Liverpool Cathedral
Woodhey
Storeton
Barnston
Brimstage
Fairfield
Thornton Hough
Raby
Hinderton
Mount Manisty
Overpool
Whitbyheath
Dunkirk
Stoak
Croxteth Hall
West Derby
Anfield
Hapsford
Bryn
Gorstage
Cabin Hills (NT)
Horse Bank

Southport: *The sands here were the scene of Henry Segrave's successful attempt on the world land speed record. On 16th March 1926, he took his Sunbeam to 152.3 mph (245km/h) to beat Malcolm Campbell's record.* ***Map ref. E1***

Eastham: *The Manchester Ship Canal starts here and runs for 35 miles (56km) to Salford. Construction on the canal started in 1887 and it was opened to the first ships on the 1st January 1894.* ***Map ref. E4***

St. Asaph (Llanelwy): *This tiny city boasts the smallest cathedral in Britain.* ***Map ref. B5***

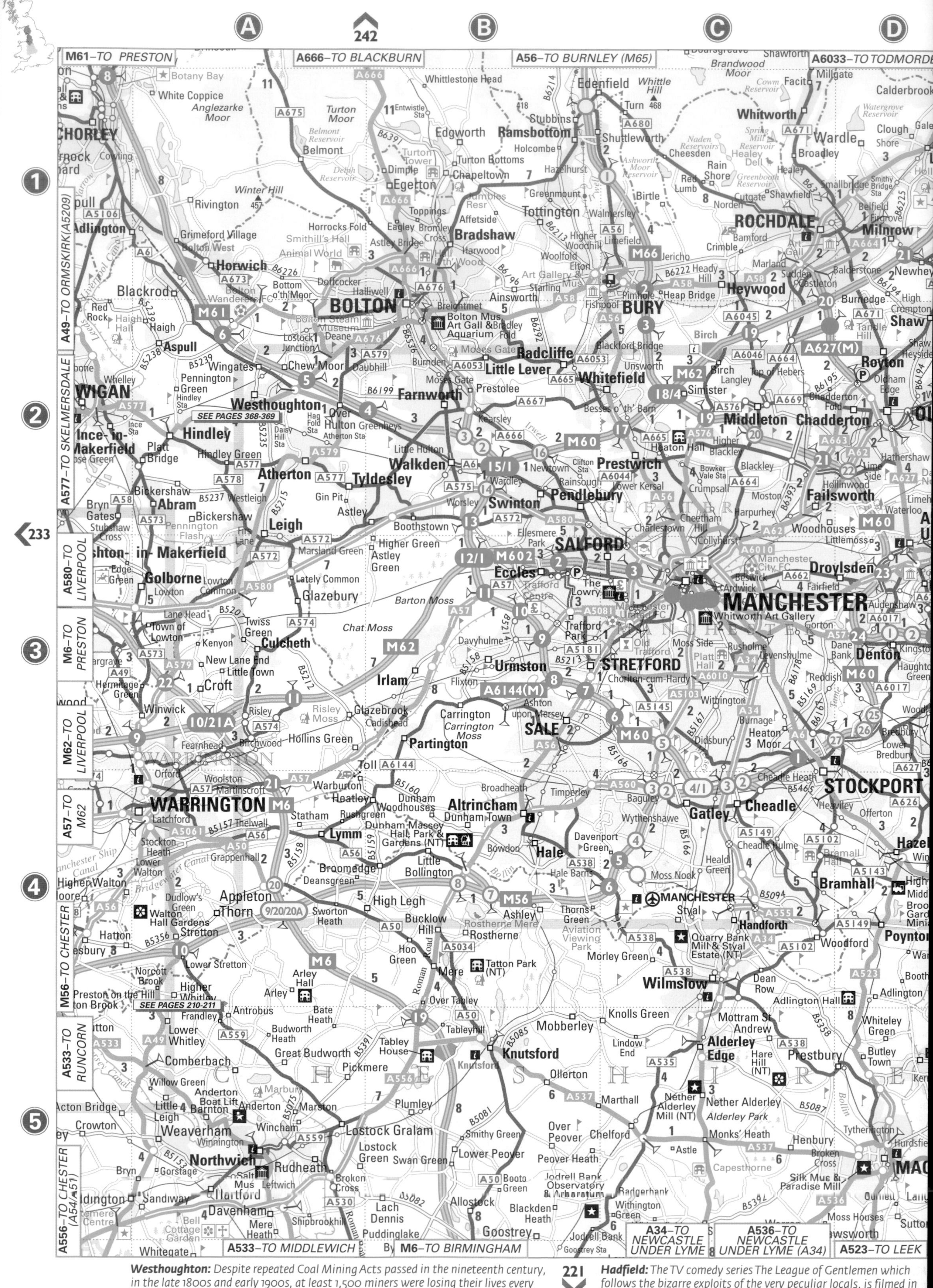

M61–TO PRESTON
A666–TO BLACKBURN
A56–TO BURNLEY (M65)
A6033–TO TODMORDEN
A49–TO ORMSKIRK (A5209)
A577–TO SKELMERSDALE
A580–TO LIVERPOOL
M6–TO PRESTON
M62–TO LIVERPOOL
A57–TO M62
M56–TO CHESTER
A533–TO RUNCORN
A556–TO CHESTER (A54, A51)
A533–TO MIDDLEWICH
M6–TO BIRMINGHAM
A34–TO NEWCASTLE UNDER LYME
A536–TO NEWCASTLE UNDER LYME (A34)
A523–TO LEEK
CHORLEY
BOLTON
BURY
ROCHDALE
WIGAN
SALFORD
MANCHESTER
WARRINGTON
STOCKPORT
STRETFORD
SALE
Altrincham
Knutsford
Northwich
Wilmslow
Leigh
Westhoughton
Horwich
Radcliffe
Heywood
Middleton
Prestwich
Eccles
Urmston
Irlam
Lymm
Hale
Cheadle
Gatley
Denton
Droylsden
Failsworth
Chadderton
Royton
Shaw
Milnrow
Whitworth
Ramsbottom
Edenfield
Tottington
Farnworth
Walkden
Atherton
Tyldesley
Hindley
Golborne
Culcheth
Weaverham
Alderley Edge
Prestbury
Bramhall
Poynton
MANCHESTER
SEE PAGES 368-369
SEE PAGES 210-211

242

233

221

Westhoughton: *Despite repeated Coal Mining Acts passed in the nineteenth century, in the late 1800s and early 1900s, at least 1,500 miners were losing their lives every year down the pits. England's worst pit disaster occurred here, between Atherton and Westhoughton, on the 21st December 1910. An underground explosion at Hulton Colliery's Pretoria Pit, Number 3 Bank, killed 344 mine workers. It was later proved that over 300 of these had died from Carbon Monoxide poisoning.* ***Map ref. A2***

Hadfield: *The TV comedy series The League of Gentlemen which follows the bizarre exploits of the very peculiar locals, is filmed in Hadfield. In the programme the village is known as Royston Vasey.* ***Map ref. E3***

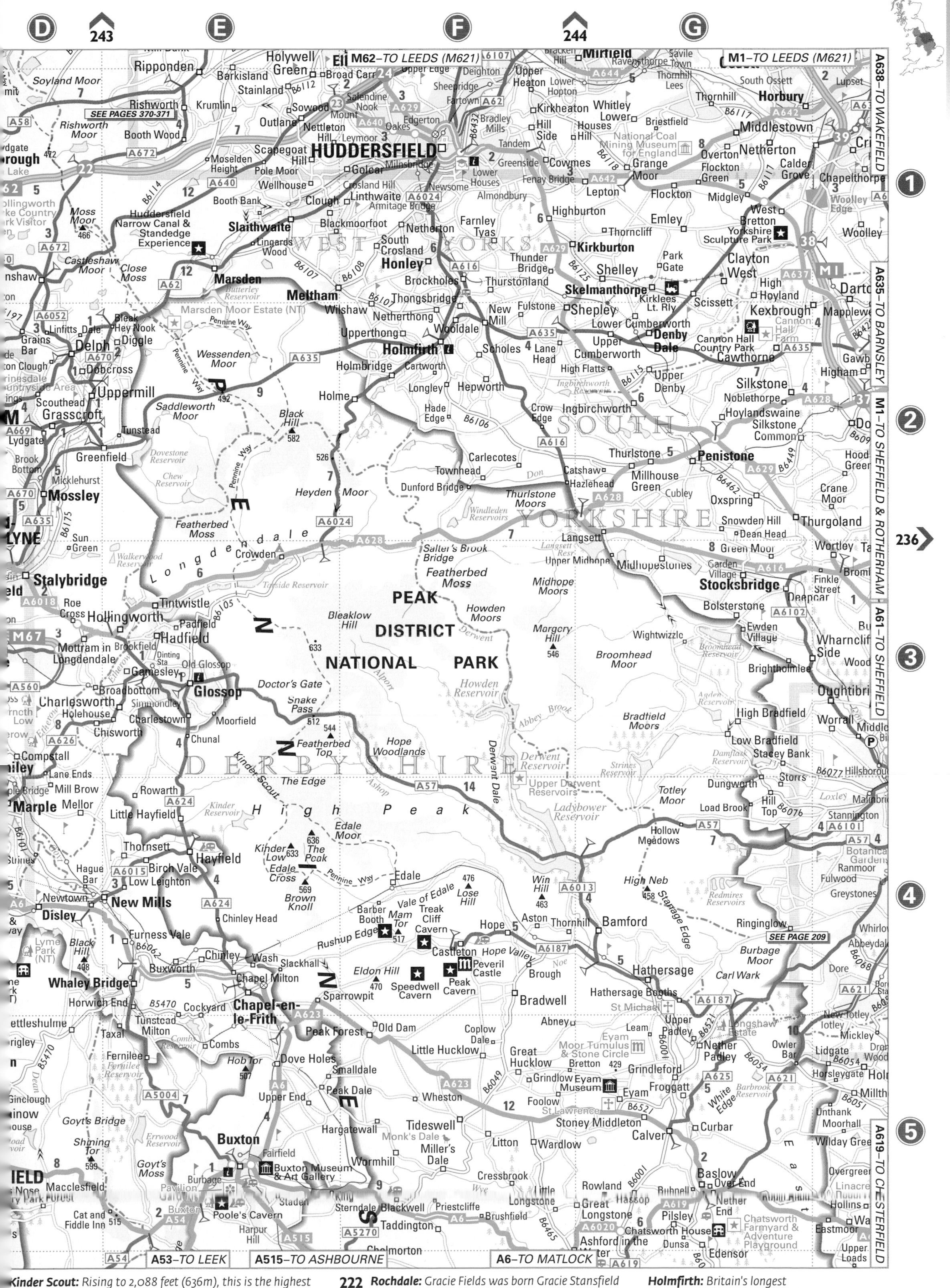

D
243
E
F
244
G
M62–TO LEEDS (M621)
M1–TO LEEDS (M621)
A638–TO WAKEFIELD
A635–TO BARNSLEY
M1–TO SHEFFIELD & ROTHERHAM
A61–TO SHEFFIELD
A619–TO CHESTERFIELD
A53–TO LEEK
A515–TO ASHBOURNE
A6–TO MATLOCK
236
SEE PAGES 370-371
SEE PAGE 209
HUDDERSFIELD
Ripponden
Barkisland
Stainland
Holywell Green
Rishworth
Krumlin
Outlane
Soyland Moor
Rishworth Moor
Booth Wood
Scapegoat Hill
Moselden Height
Pole Moor
Wellhouse
Golcar
Milnsbridge
Crosland Hill
Linthwaite
Armitage Bridge
Almondbury
Newsome
Lower Houses
Lepton
Flockton
Emley
Highburton
Kirkburton
Thorncliff
Shelley
Skelmanthorpe
Kirklees Lt. Rly
Scissett
Clayton West
High Hoyland
Kexbrough
Cannon Hall Country Park
Cawthorne
Silkstone
Noblethorpe
Hoylandswaine
Silkstone Common
Penistone
Thurlstone
Millhouse Green
Oxspring
Thurgoland
Langsett
Midhopestones
Stocksbridge
Deepcar
Bolsterstone
Ewden Village
Wharncliffe Side
Oughtibridge
High Bradfield
Low Bradfield
Dungworth
Hill Top
Stannington
Horbury
Middlestown
Netherton
Flockton Green
Calder Grove
Chapelthorpe
Woolley
West Bretton
Yorkshire Sculpture Park
National Coal Mining Museum for England
Grange Moor
Whitley Lower
Briestfield
Kirkheaton
Upper Heaton
Lower Hopton
Mirfield
Ravensthorpe
Thornhill Lees
South Ossett
Thornhill
Slaithwaite
Huddersfield Narrow Canal & Standedge Experience
Marsden
Marsden Moor Estate (NT)
Meltham
Wilshaw
Honley
Brockholes
Thongsbridge
Netherthong
Upperthong
Holmfirth
Wooldale
Scholes
New Mill
Fulstone
Shepley
Lower Cumberworth
Upper Cumberworth
Denby Dale
Upper Denby
Ingbirchworth
Hepworth
Cartworth
Holmbridge
Holme
Longley
Hade Edge
Farnley Tyas
Netherton
South Crosland
Thurstonland
Thunder Bridge
WEST YORKS
SOUTH YORKSHIRE
Delph
Diggle
Dobcross
Uppermill
Grasscroft
Greenfield
Mossley
Stalybridge
Hollingworth
Hadfield
Tintwistle
Mottram in Longdendale
Glossop
Gamesley
Charlesworth
Chisworth
Broadbottom
Simmondley
Charlestown
Chunal
Marple
Mellor
Rowarth
Little Hayfield
Hayfield
Birch Vale
New Mills
Disley
Whaley Bridge
Chinley
Chapel Milton
Chapel-en-le-Frith
Buxton
Buxton Museum & Art Gallery
Poole's Cavern
Wessenden Moor
Saddleworth Moor
Black Hill
Featherbed Moss
Longdendale
Crowden
PEAK DISTRICT NATIONAL PARK
Bleaklow Hill
Howden Moors
Howden Reservoir
Derwent Reservoir
Ladybower Reservoir
Doctor's Gate
Snake Pass
Kinder Scout
High Peak
DERBYSHIRE
Edale
Kinder Low
The Peak
Brown Knoll
Vale of Edale
Lose Hill
Win Hill
Castleton
Peveril Castle
Speedwell Cavern
Peak Cavern
Treak Cliff Cavern
Mam Tor
Rushup Edge
Hope
Bamford
Hathersage
Brough
Bradwell
Eyam
Eyam Museum
Grindleford
Froggatt
Calver
Stoney Middleton
Tideswell
Miller's Dale
Litton
Wardlow
Great Hucklow
Little Hucklow
Peak Forest
Dove Holes
Baslow
Chatsworth House
Pilsley
Edensor
Great Longstone
Hassop
Taddington
Blackwell
Stanage Edge
Curbar

Kinder Scout: *Rising to 2,088 feet (636m), this is the highest point in the Peak District National Park. On the 24th April 1932 over 450 Ramblers set off from Bowden Bridge near Hayfield on an organised 'mass trespass' in order to gain access to Kinder Scout for members of the public. They eventually succeeded when, in 1951, it was designated as Britain's first National Park.* **Map ref. E4**

222

Rochdale: *Gracie Fields was born Gracie Stansfield here in 1898. She went on to become a famous music hall star and recording artist. She eventually retired to the Isle of Capri and was created Dame of the British Empire in 1979. She died later the same year.* **Map ref. C1**

Holmfirth: *Britain's longest running comedy series, Last of the Summer Wine has been filmed on location here since 1973.* **Map ref. F2**

A
244
B
C
245
D
M1–TO LEEDS (M621)
A638–TO WAKEFIELD
A628–TO PONTEFRACT
A1–TO WETHERBY
A19–TO SELBY
A637, A642–TO HUDDERSFIELD
A628–TO MANCHESTER (M67)
A629–TO HUDDERSFIELD
A616–TO MANCHESTER (A628)
A619–TO BAKEWELL
A61–TO DERBY (A38)
A617–TO MANSFIELD
M1–TO NOTTINGHAM
A60–TO MANSFIELD
235
223
1
2
3
4
5
NORTH YORKS
SOUTH YORKSHIRE
DERBYSHIRE
SEE PAGES 370-371
SEE PAGE 365
Horbury
Netherton
Crigglestone
Sandal Magna
Walton
Sharlston
Crofton
Ackworth Moor Top
Fitzwilliam
Hemsworth
Ryhill
Royston
South Hiendley
Shafton
Brierley
Cudworth
Darton
Staincross
Mapplewell
BARNSLEY
Dodworth
Worsbrough
Darfield
Wombwell
Hoyland
Chapeltown
Thorpe Hesley
Rawmarsh
ROTHERHAM
SHEFFIELD
Dronfield
Eckington
Killamarsh
Staveley
Brimington
CHESTERFIELD
Bolsover
Clowne
Creswell
Barlborough
Whitwell
WORKSOP
Dinnington
Maltby
Tickhill
Conisbrough
Mexborough
Swinton
Wath upon Dearne
Goldthorpe
Thurnscoe
South Kirkby
South Elmsall
Upton
Askern
Campsall
Carcroft
Adwick le Street
Brodsworth
Barnby Dun
DONCASTER
Sprotbrough
Rossington
New Rossington
Harworth
Langold
Carlton in Lindrick
Thurcroft
Aughton
Aston
Wales
Kiveton Park
South Anston
North Anston
Shireoaks
The Dukeries
Clumber Country Park
Welbeck Abbey
Meden Vale
Cuckney

Doncaster: The legendary Flying Scotsman was built here in 1923 for just under £8000. As a passenger express train on the East Coast main line between London and Edinburgh it regularly reached a speed of 100 mph (160km/h). During its working life, up to 1963, it covered 2.4 million miles (3.86 million km). The Flying Scotsman is now in the National Railway Museum, York. **Map ref. C2**

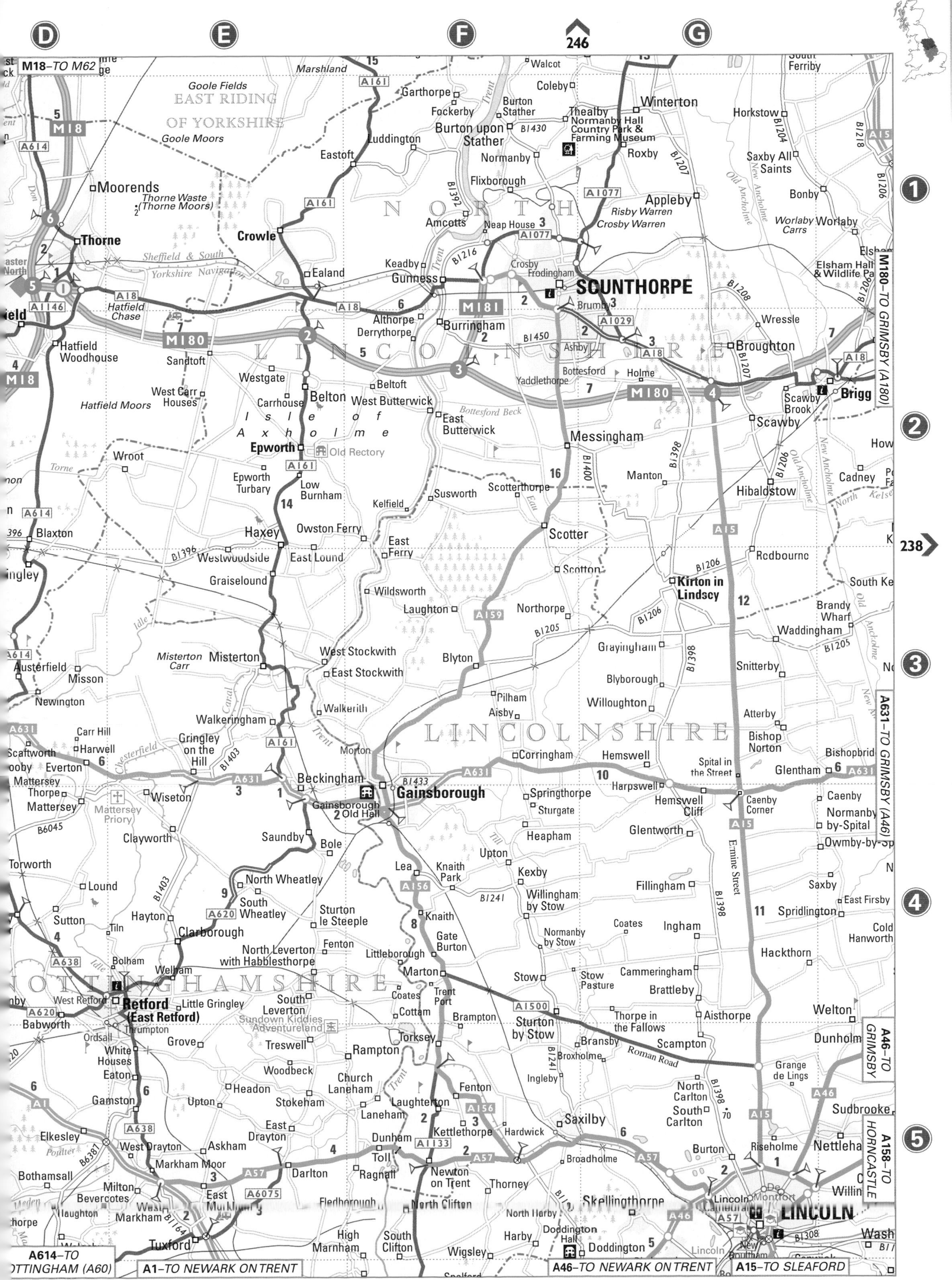
D
E
F
G
246
M18–TO M62
Marshland
Goole Fields
EAST RIDING
OF YORKSHIRE
Goole Moors
Garthorpe
Fockerby
Luddington
Eastoft
Walcot
Burton Stather
Burton upon Stather
Coleby
Thealby
Normanby Hall Country Park & Farming Museum
Winterton
Roxby
Normanby
Flixborough
Appleby
Risby Warren
Crosby Warren
Horkstow
Saxby All Saints
Bonby
Worlaby Carrs
Worlaby
South Ferriby
Moorends
Thorne Waste (Thorne Moors)
Thorne
Crowle
Amcotts
Neap House
NORTH
Sheffield & South Yorkshire Navigation
Ealand
Keadby
Gunness
Crosby
Frodingham
SCUNTHORPE
Brumby
Elsham Hall & Wildlife Park
M180–TO GRIMSBY (A180)
Hatfield Chase
Althorpe
Derrythorpe
Burringham
Wressle
Broughton
Hatfield Woodhouse
Sandtoft
LINCOLNSHIRE
Ashby
Bottesford
Yaddlethorpe
Holme
Scawby Brook
Brigg
Scawby
Westgate
West Carr Houses
Carrhouse
Belton
Beltoft
West Butterwick
East Butterwick
Bottesford Beck
Hatfield Moors
Isle of Axholme
Epworth
Old Rectory
Messingham
Wroot
Torne
Epworth Turbary
Low Burnham
Kelfield
Susworth
Scotterthorpe
Manton
Hibaldstow
Cadney
Blaxton
Haxey
Owston Ferry
East Ferry
Scotter
Westwoodside
East Lound
Scotton
Redbourne
238
Graiseloude
Wildsworth
Kirton in Lindsey
South Kelsey
Laughton
Northorpe
Brandy Wharf
Waddingham
Misterton Carr
Misterton
West Stockwith
East Stockwith
Blyton
Grayingham
Snitterby
Austerfield
Misson
Newington
Blyborough
Willoughton
Pilham
Aisby
Walkerith
Atterby
Bishop Norton
Walkeringham
Carr Hill
Harwell
Gringley on the Hill
Morton
Corringham
Hemswell
Spital in the Street
Glentham
Bishopbridge
Scaftworth
Everton
Mattersey
Mattersey Thorpe
Mattersey Priory
Wiseton
Beckingham
Gainsborough
Gainsborough Old Hall
Springthorpe
Sturgate
Harpswell
Hemswell Cliff
Caenby Corner
Caenby
Normanby by-Spital
Owmby-by-Spital
A631–TO GRIMSBY (A46)
Clayworth
Saundby
Bole
Heapham
Glentworth
Upton
Torworth
Lound
North Wheatley
South Wheatley
Lea
Knaith Park
Kexby
Willingham by Stow
Fillingham
Ermine Street
Saxby
East Firsby
Sutton
Hayton
Sturton le Steeple
Knaith
Gate Burton
Normanby by Stow
Coates
Ingham
Spridlington
Cold Hanworth
Tiln
Clarborough
Fenton
North Leverton with Habblesthorpe
Littleborough
Hackthorn
Bolham
Welham
NOTTINGHAMSHIRE
Marton
Trent Port
Stow
Stow Pasture
Cammeringham
Brattleby
West Retford
Retford (East Retford)
Little Gringley
Coates
South Leverton
Cottam
Sundown Kiddies Adventureland
Brampton
Sturton by Stow
Thorpe in the Fallows
Aisthorpe
Welton
Babworth
Ordsall
Thrumpton
Grove
Torksey
Bransby
Broxholme
Roman Road
Scampton
Dunholme
A46–TO GRIMSBY
White Houses
Eaton
Treswell
Rampton
Woodbeck
Church Laneham
Ingleby
Grange de Lings
North Carlton
South Carlton
Headon
Gamston
Upton
Stokeham
Laneham
Laughterton
Fenton
Sudbrooke
Elkesley
East Drayton
Kettlethorpe
Hardwick
Saxilby
Burton
Riseholme
Nettleham
A158–TO HORNCASTLE
West Drayton
Askham
Dunham
Toll
Broadholme
Bothamsall
Markham Moor
Darlton
Ragnall
Newton on Trent
Thorney
Milton
Beverootes
East Markham
West Markham
Fledborough
North Clifton
Skellingthorpe
Lincoln
LINCOLN
Montfort
Haughton
Tuxford
High Marnham
South Clifton
Wigsley
North Harby
Harby
Doddington Hall
Doddington
Boultham
Washingborough
A614–TO NOTTINGHAM (A60)
A1–TO NEWARK ON TRENT
A46–TO NEWARK ON TRENT
A15–TO SLEAFORD
224

Lincoln: *The world's first military tank was built here in 1915. The tank was built by Fosters and, to protect its secrecy, it was designated as a water carrier, hence it became shortened to 'tank'.* ***Map ref. G5***

Scampton: *On the night of the 16/17th May 1943, 65 Squadron's Lancaster Bombers took off from their base at RAF Scampton to attack dams in the Ruhr area of Germany. This was the famous Dam Busters raid. Although the operation was hailed as a great success, it cost the lives of 53 airmen and over 1300 mainly Ukrainian prisoners of war who were being held at a camp close to one of the dams.* ***Map ref. G5***

246

A
B
C
D
1
2
3
4
5
A15–TO KINGSTON UPON HULL
A180–TO SCUNTHORPE (A18)
A631–TO GAINSBOROUGH
A15–TO SLEAFORD
A158–TO SKEGNESS
NORTH LINCOLNSHIRE
LINCOLNSHIRE
NORTH EAST LINCOLNSHIRE
EAST RIDING OF YORKSHIRE
LINCOLNSHIRE
THE WOLDS
MOUTH OF THE HUMBER
Foulholme Sands
Sunk Island Sands
South End
East Halton
Thornton Abbey Sta
Thornton Abbey
Thornton Curtis
North Killingholme
South Killingholme
Immingham
Immingham Dock
Habrough
Stallingborough
Healing
Great Coates
West Marsh
Little Coates
GRIMSBY
Cleethorpes
Wellholme Galleries
National Fishing
Humberston
Pleasure Island Theme Park
Grange
Haven
Sunk Island
Old Hall
Burnham
Wootton
Ulceby
Ulceby Skitter
Croxton
Kirmington
Brocklesby
Keelby
Melton Ross
Coskills
HUMBERSIDE INTERNATIONAL
Great Limber
Riby
Aylesby
Laceby
Bradley
Scartho
Nunsthorpe
Irby upon Humber
New Waltham
Waltham
Holton le Clay
Barnoldby le Beck
Brigsley
Ashby Hill
Ashby cum Fenby
Tetney
North Cotes
Beelsby
Hatcliffe
East Ravendale
Grainsby
North Thoresby
Fulstow
Lincolnshire Wolds Railway
Wold Newton
Beesby
Thorganby
Swinhope
Croxby
Ludborough
Covenham St Bartholomew
Utterby
North Ormsby
Fotherby
Little Grimsby
North Elkington
South Elkington
Louth
Welton le Wold
Kelstern
Great Tows
Binbrook
Kirmond le Mire
Stainton le Vale
Thoresway
Rothwell
Cuxwold
Swallow
Cabourne
Cabourne Parva
Caistor
Roman Road
Nettleton
Clixby
Grasby
Owmby
Searby
Somerby
Bigby
Barnetby le Wold
Wrawby
Brigg
Scawby
Scawby Brook
Elsham
Elsham Hall Country & Wildlife Park
Worlaby
Worlaby Carrs
Bonby
Saxby All Saints
Horkstow
Wressle
Broughton
Howsham
Cadney
Poolthorne Farm
North Kelsey
North Kelsey Beck
Hibaldstow
Redbourne
Moortown
South Kelsey
Holton le Moor
Thornton le Moor
Brandy Wharf
Waddingham
Old Ancholme
New Ancholme
Snitterby
North Owersby
South Owersby
Usselby
Normanby le Wold
Claxby
Walesby
Osgodby
Osgodby Moor
Kingerby
Kirkby
Bishopbridge
Glentham
Caenby
Normanby-by-Spital
Owmby-by-Spital
Toft next Newton
Newton by Toft
Newtoft
West Rasen
Middle Rasen
Market Rasen
Tealby
North Willingham
Ludford
Burgh on Bain
Sixhills
Little London
Linwood
Legsby
Buslingthorpe
Saxby
East Firsby
Spridlington
Faldingworth
Cold Hanworth
Hackthorn
Snarford
Friesthorpe
Lissington
Bleasby
Bleasby Moor
East Torrington
West Torrington
Wickenby
Holton cum Beckering
Snelland
Beckering
Hainton
South Willingham
East Barkwith
West Barkwith
Gayton le Wold
Biscathorpe
Donington on Bain
Withcall
Raithby
Hallington
Maltby
Tathwell
Dovendale
Haugham
Stenigot
Cawkwell
Cadwell Park
Asterby
Scamblesby
Maidenwell
Farforth
Oxcombe
Worlaby
Flint Hill
Benniworth
Market Stainton
Sotby
Goulceby
Ranby
Panton
Welton
Dunholme
Grange de Lings
Stainton by Langworth
Fulnetby
Rand
Bullington
Wragby
Strubby
Langton by Wragby
Low Langton
Hatton
Great Sturton
Scothern
Sudbrooke
Newball
Langworth
Riseholme
Nettleham
Kingthorpe
Apley
Barlings
Low Barlings
Cherry Willingham
Reepham
Fiskerton
Stainfield
Minting
Baumber
Hemingby
Belchford
Tetford
Salmonby
Farthorpe
Midthorpe
Fulletby
West Ashby
Low Toynton
Achby Puerorum
Greetham
Wispington
Edlington
Gautby
Waddingworth
Horsington
Thimbleby
Bardney
Abbey
Branston Booths
Common Square
Washingborough
LINCOLN
Montfort
A15
A18
A46
A157
A158
A160
A180
A631
A1031
A1077
A1084
A1103
A1136
A1173
A1243
A16
B1202
B1203
B1204
B1205
B1206
B1210
B1211
B1218
B1219
B1225
B1308
B1399
B1434
B1190
B1201
168
150

Louth is a small market town which sits astride the Greenwich Meridian and is famous for its magnificent 15th Century church. The spire of St James at 295 feet (91 metres) high is the tallest parish church spire in England. **Map ref. D4**

Somersby: The great poet Alfred Lord Tennyson was born here on the 5th August 1809. He was the fourth son of the Rev. George Tennyson, Rector of Somersby and Bag Enderby. **Map ref. D5**

Grimsby: The game of darts was invented in the 1800s by the landlord of the Docker Arms Pub which stood in Freeman Street. The Spider's Web Pub, in Carr Lane, is so called because of the design of a dartboard **Map ref. C2**

237

226

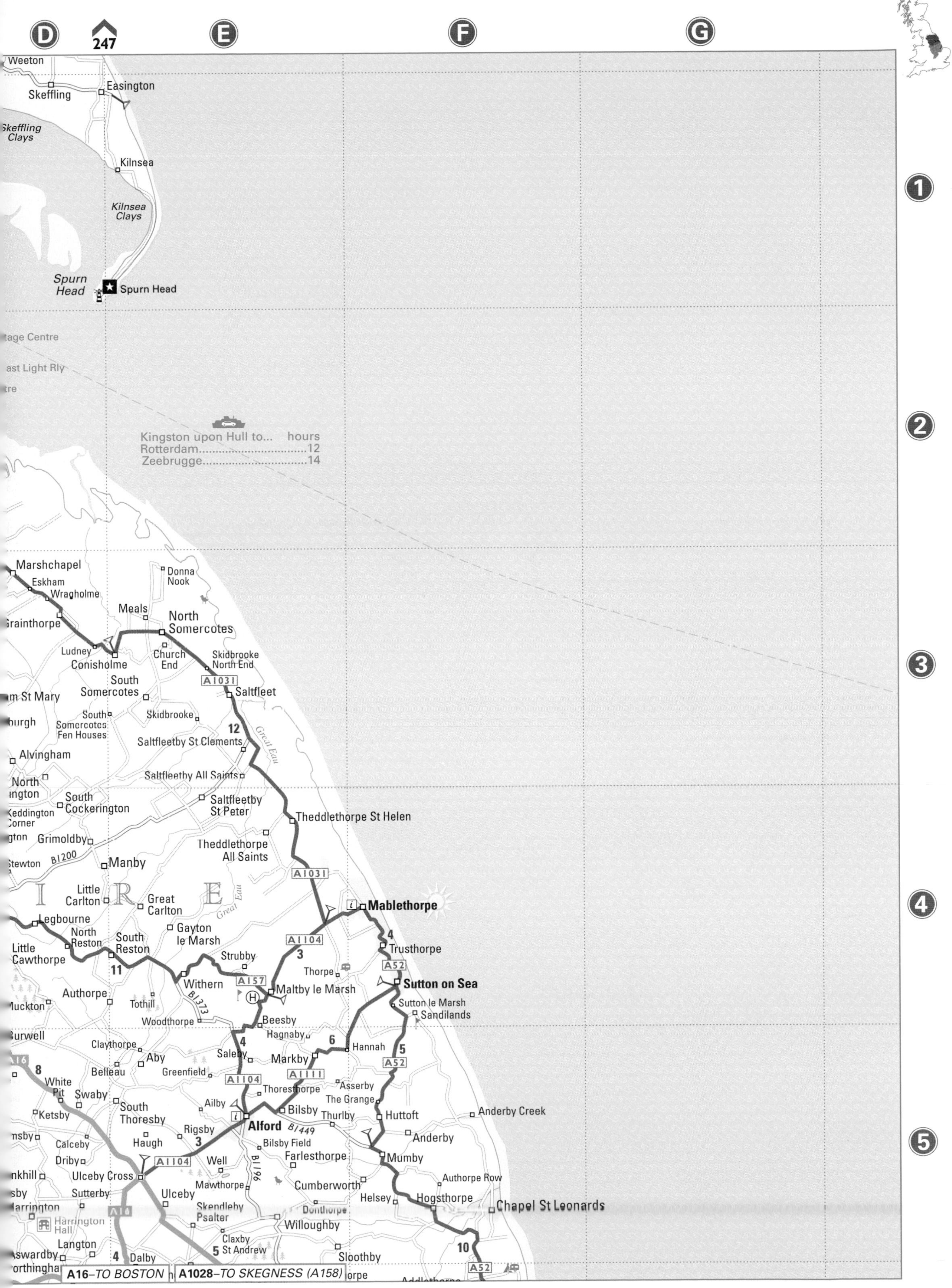

D
247
E
F
G
1
2
3
4
5
Weeton
Skeffling
Easington
Skeffling Clays
Kilnsea
Kilnsea Clays
Spurn Head
Spurn Head
Kingston upon Hull to... hours
Rotterdam.....12
Zeebrugge.....14
Marshchapel
Eskham
Wragholme
Donna Nook
Meals
North Somercotes
Ludney
Conisholme
Church End
Skidbrooke North End
South Somercotes
A1031
Saltfleet
Skidbrooke
South Somercotes Fen Houses
Saltfleetby St Clements
Great Eau
Alvingham
Saltfleetby All Saints
South Cockerington
Saltfleetby St Peter
Theddlethorpe St Helen
Keddington Corner
Grimoldby
Theddlethorpe All Saints
B1200
Manby
A1031
Little Carlton
Great Carlton
Mablethorpe
Legbourne
Gayton le Marsh
North Reston
South Reston
Strubby
A1104
Trusthorpe
Little Cawthorpe
Thorpe
A52
Sutton on Sea
Withern
A157
Maltby le Marsh
Authorpe
Tothill
B1373
Sutton le Marsh
Sandilands
Woodthorpe
Beesby
Hagnaby
Claythorpe
Aby
Saleby
Markby
Hannah
A52
Belleau
Greenfield
A1104
A1111
Asserby
White Pit
Swaby
Thoresthorpe
The Grange
Ailby
Bilsby
Thurlby
Huttoft
Anderby Creek
Ketsby
South Thoresby
Alford
B1449
Rigsby
Anderby
Calceby
Haugh
Bilsby Field
Farlesthorpe
Driby
A1104
Well
Mumby
Ulceby Cross
B1196
Authorpe Row
Sutterby
Ulceby
Mawthorpe
Cumberworth
Helsey
Hogsthorpe
Chapel St Leonards
A16
Harrington Hall
Skendleby Psalter
Willoughby
Langton
Claxby St Andrew
Sloothby
Dalby
A52
A16–TO BOSTON
A1028–TO SKEGNESS (A158)

Spurn Head: *Because of the rapid coastal erosion in this area, the road to the head is frequently eroded away and has to be relaid.* ***Map ref.*** ***E1***

227

Donna Nook: *An RAF Bombing Range which on the 18th July 2002 became the first national nature reserve to be established on MOD land. The reserve, which stretches for over 6 miles (10km) along the coast, is home to a range of flora and fauna including a colony of grey seals.* ***Map ref.*** ***E3***

A
B
C
D
1
2
3
4
5
ISLE OF MAN
Point of Ayre
The Ayres
A16
Ayres Visitor Centre
Rue Point
The Lhen
Glentruan
Cranstal
A10
13
A19
Dhowin
A17
Bride
Sartfield
B3
Andreas
Shellag Point
Jurby Head
Jurby West
Jurby
Jurby East
A9
Ballasalla
Sandygate
6
B7
Regaby
A13
Ballachurry Fort
A14
St Judes
Dhoor
Ramsey Bay
Crawyn
The Cronk
The Curraghs
Kella
Curraghs Wildlife Park
Sulby
Churchtown
Ramsey
Ballaugh
Orrisdale
Orrisdale Head
Glen Auldyn
Port e Vullen
Maughold Head & Brooghs
A15
Maughold Head
Maughold
Ravensdale
A18
Dreemskerry
Kirk Michael
T.T. Course
Slieau Curn
351
Slieau Managh
383
North Barrule
565
Ballajora
Port Mooar
I S L E
Slieau Dhoo
424
Corrany
Glen Auldyn
Clagh Ouyr
551
Glen Mona
Manx Electric Rly
Ballacarnane Beg
Slieau Freoaghane
488
Snaefell
621
469
Slieau Lhean
Barregarrow
A4
Gob y Deigan
Sartfell
454
Sulby Reservoir
Dhoon
Port Cornaa
Knocksharry
B10
Laxey Wheel
St German's Cath
Cronk-y-Voddy
Little London
O F
546
Beinn-y-Phott
Snaefell Mountain Rly
Bulgham Bay
St Patrick's Isle
Peel
Peel Castle & Round Tower
Ballagyr
Lambfell Moar
Injebreck
Injebreck Reservoir
Laxey Glen
Colden
487
B22
A2
Laxey
House of Manannan
A20
Ballaheannagh
Laxey Head
Contrary Head
A1
Tynwald
Ballig
Slieau Ruy
478
Ballacannell
B12
Laxey Bay
Knockaloe Moar
Patrick
A30
St John's
Greeba Mountain
422
Baldwin
M A N
Baldrine
Heysham 3½hrs
A27
B21
Sulby
B20
Garwick Bay
Clay Head
Glenmaye
333
Hillberry
A11
Dalby Point
Lower Foxdale
Crosby
A23
Dalby Mountain
280
Dalby
Foxdale
Eairy
Garth
Glen Vine
Strang
A22
Onchan
Port Groudle
Niarbyl Island
A36
B36
A24
B35
A26
Union Mills
Onchan Head
Niarbyl Bay
483
South Barrule
Stuggadhoo
Braaid
Cooil
A16
Manx Mus
DOUGLAS
Douglas Bay
Stroin Vuigh
341
Close Clark
Quine's Hill
A37
Douglas Head
Ballamodha
B30
St Mark's
Newtown
Ronague
Grenaby
B23
Ballaveare
Little Ness
Lingague
Liverpool 2½-4hrs
Fleshwick Bay
Ballakilpheric
A25
Isle of Man Steam Rly
Rushen
10
B2
Bradda
Ballafesson
Ballabeg
Santon Head
Bradda Head
Colby
A7
Ballasalla
B53
Port Grenaugh
Port Erin
Croit e Caley
A5
Balladoole
ISLE OF MAN
Nautical Mus
Derbyhaven
Meayl Circle
Bay ny Carrickey
Castle Rushen
1275
Derby Fort
Calf of Man
Cregneash
The Howe
Port St Mary
A31
Castletown
St Michael's Island
Perwick Bay
Langness
Spanish Head
Castletown Bay
Dreswick Point
Chicken Rock
hours
Belfast (summer only).......2¾
Dublin (summer only)..2¾-4¾

Laxey: *The Lady Isabella water wheel, built in 1854 to pump water from local mine workings, is allegedly the world's largest water wheel, with a diameter of over 72 feet (22 metres). It still turns, but no longer pumps.* ***Map ref. C3***

Isle of Man: *The Isle of Man is a self-governing Island. Although a Crown Dependency it doesn't belong to either the UK or the European Union. The Island is 33 miles (53km) long, 13 miles (21km) wide and covers 227 square miles (588 sq km). Over 40% of the island is uninhabited. Its strange three legged symbol means 'Quocunque Jeceris Stabit' (whichever way you throw me I stand).* ***Map ref. B3***

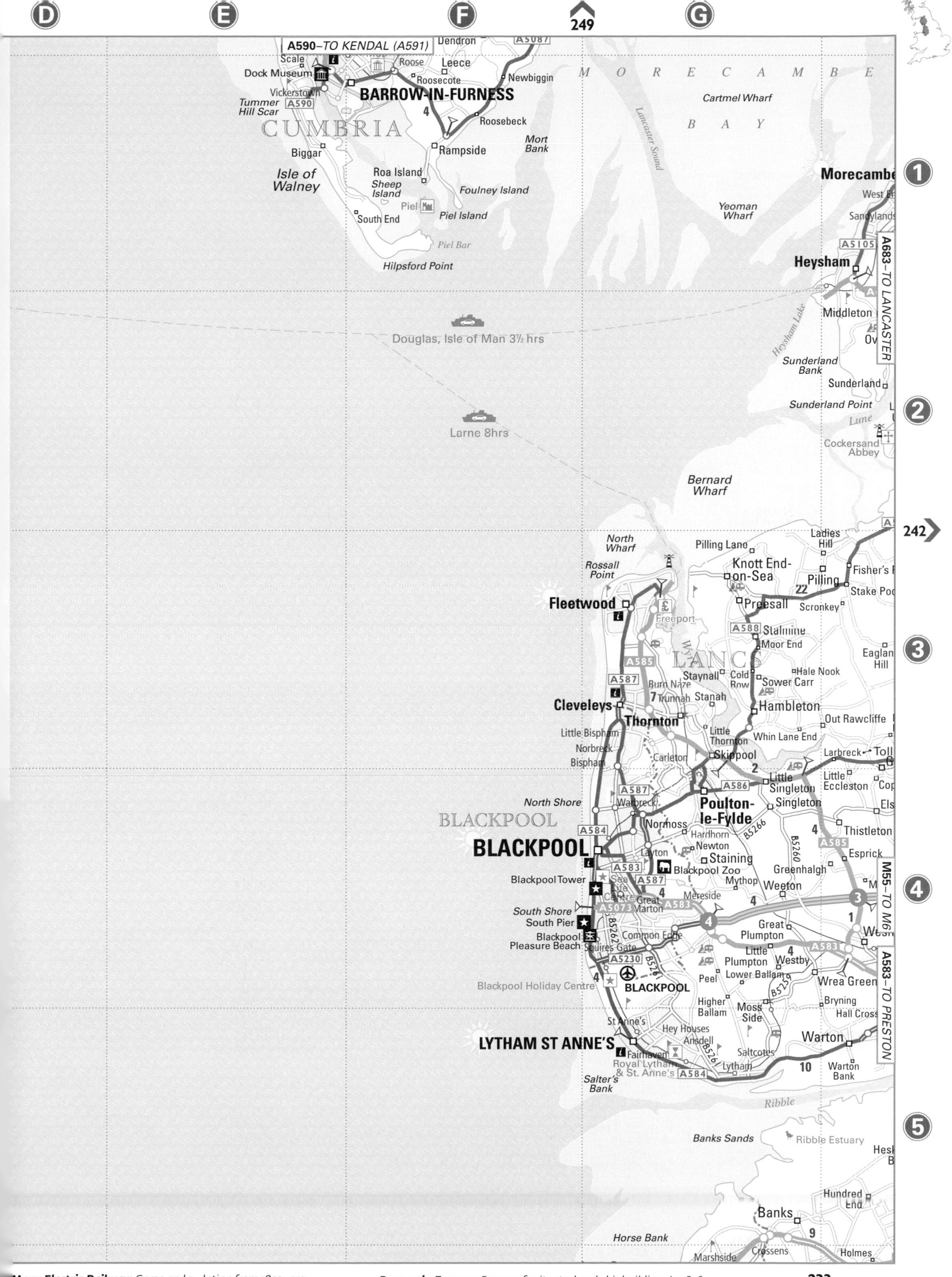
A590–TO KENDAL (A591)
Dendron
A5087
Scale
Dock Museum
Roose
Leece
Roosecote
Newbiggin
Vickerstown
BARROW-IN-FURNESS
Tummer Hill Scar
A590
Roosebeck
CUMBRIA
Rampside
Mort Bank
Biggar
Isle of Walney
Roa Island
Sheep Island
Foulney Island
Piel
South End
Piel Island
Piel Bar
Hilpsford Point
M O R E C A M B E
B A Y
Cartmel Wharf
Lancaster Sound
Morecambe
West End
Sandylands
Yeoman Wharf
A5105
Heysham
A683–TO LANCASTER
Middleton
Heysham Lake
Sunderland Bank
Sunderland
Sunderland Point
Lune
Cockersand Abbey
Douglas, Isle of Man 3½ hrs
Larne 8hrs
Bernard Wharf
North Wharf
Rossall Point
Pilling Lane
Ladies Hill
Knott End-on-Sea
Pilling
Fisher's
Stake Pool
Fleetwood
Preesall
Scronkey
Freeport
A588
Stalmine
Moor End
Eagland Hill
A585
LANCS
Staynall
Cold Row
Hale Nook
A587
Burn Naze
Sower Carr
Trunnah
Stanah
Cleveleys
Hambleton
Thornton
Little Thornton
Out Rawcliffe
Little Bispham
Whin Lane End
Norbreck
Larbreck
Bispham
Carleton
Skippool
A586
Little Singleton
Little Eccleston
A587
North Shore
Warbreck
Poulton-le-Fylde
Singleton
BLACKPOOL
Normoss
Thistleton
A584
Hardhorn
B5266
B5260
A585
BLACKPOOL
Newton
Layton
Staining
Esprick
A583
Blackpool Zoo
Greenhalgh
Blackpool Tower
Sea Life Centre
A587
Mythop
Weeton
M55–TO M6
Great Marton
Mereside
A583
South Shore
A5073
South Pier
B5262
Great Plumpton
Blackpool Pleasure Beach
Common Edge
Squires Gate
Little Plumpton
Westby
A583
A5230
B5261
A583–TO PRESTON
Blackpool Holiday Centre
BLACKPOOL
Peel
Lower Ballam
Wrea Green
B5259
Bryning
Higher Ballam
Moss Side
Hall Cross
St Anne's
Hey Houses
LYTHAM ST ANNE'S
Ansdell
Warton
Fairhaven
B5261
Saltcotes
Royal Lytham & St. Anne's
Lytham
Warton Bank
A584
Salter's Bank
Ribble
Banks Sands
Ribble Estuary
Hundred End
Banks
Horse Bank
Marshside
Crossens
Holmes

1 2 242 3 4 5 233

Manx Electric Railway: *Cars 1 and 2, dating from 1893, are the oldest trams still in service in the world, regularly running the 18 miles (29km) between Douglas and Ramsey.* ***Map ref. C3***

Barrow in Furness: *Famous for its steel and shipbuilding. In 1876 Barrow in Furness had the largest steelworks in the world. Today, it is England's busiest shipyard with the largest covered ship building hall in Europe.* ***Map ref. F1***

250

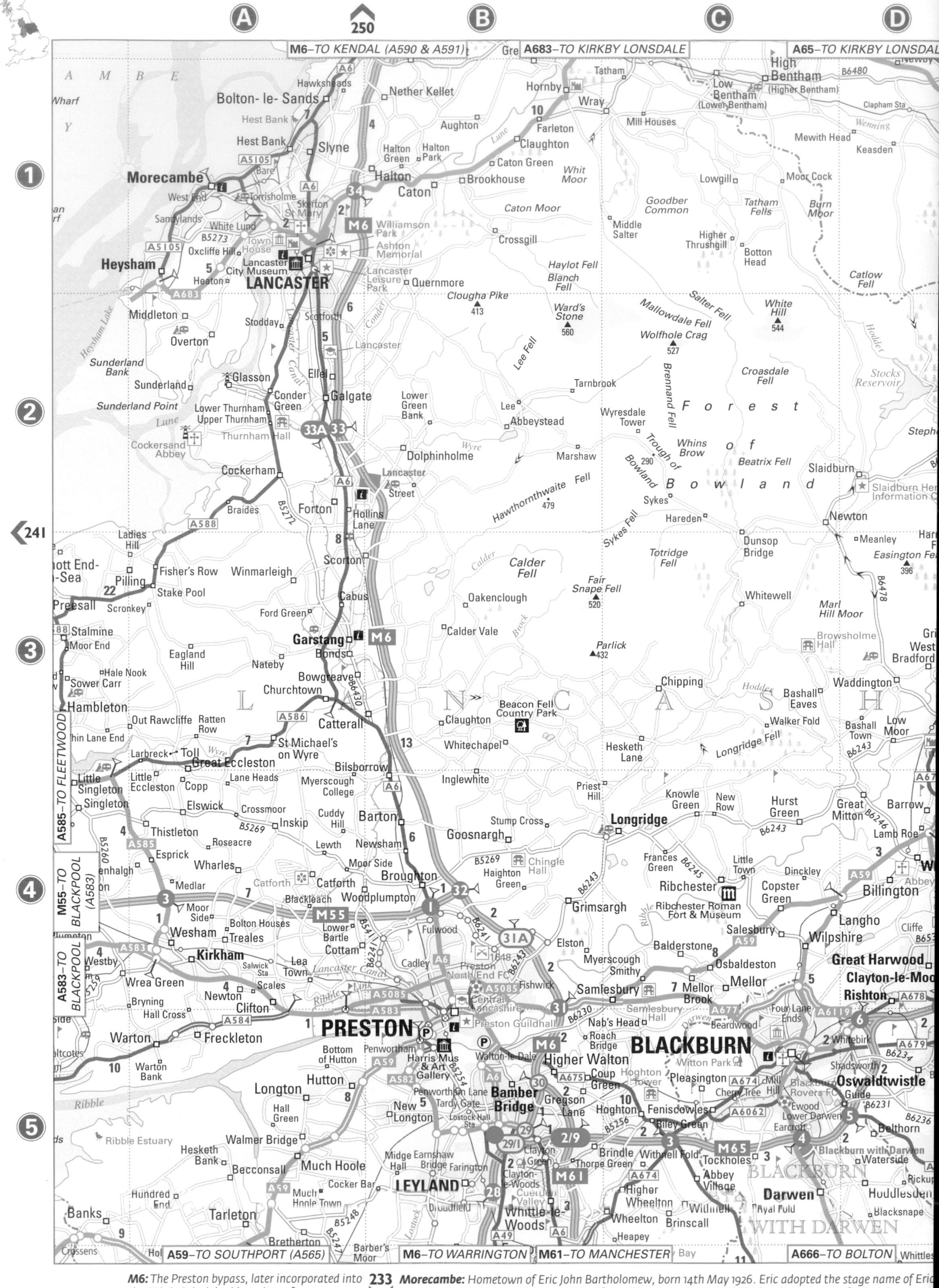
A
B
C
D
1
2
3
4
5
241
M6–TO KENDAL (A590 & A591)
A683–TO KIRKBY LONSDALE
A65–TO KIRKBY LONSDALE
A585–TO FLEETWOOD
M55–TO BLACKPOOL (A583)
A583–TO BLACKPOOL
A59–TO SOUTHPORT (A565)
M6–TO WARRINGTON
M61–TO MANCHESTER
A666–TO BOLTON
Hawksheads
Bolton- le- Sands
Nether Kellet
Hest Bank
Slyne
Aughton
Halton Green
Halton Park
Halton
Caton
Brookhouse
Caton Green
Caton Moor
Hornby
Tatham
Wray
Farleton
Claughton
Mill Houses
Low Bentham (Lower Bentham)
High Bentham (Higher Bentham)
Clapham Sta
Mewith Head
Keasden
Wenning
Lowgill
Moor Cock
Tatham Fells
Burn Moor
Goodber Common
Middle Salter
Higher Thrushgill
Botton Head
Whit Moor
Crossgill
Morecambe
West End
Torrisholme
Bare
Skerton
St Mary
Sandylands
White Lund
Oxcliffe Hill
Town House
Heysham
Heaton
Lancaster City Museum
LANCASTER
Williamson Park
Ashton Memorial
Lancaster Leisure Park
Quernmore
Clougha Pike
413
Haylot Fell
Blanch Fell
Ward's Stone
560
Mallowdale Fell
Salter Fell
Wolfhole Crag
527
White Hill
544
Catlow Fell
Middleton
Overton
Heysham Lake
Stodday
Scotforth
Lancaster
Lancaster Canal
Conder
Sunderland Bank
Sunderland
Glasson
Ellel
Galgate
Conder Green
Sunderland Point
Lower Thurnham
Upper Thurnham
Thurnham Hall
Lune
Cockersand Abbey
Cockerham
Lower Green Bank
Lee Fell
Tarnbrook
Lee
Abbeystead
Wyresdale Tower
Brennand Fell
Forest of Bowland
Croasdale Fell
Stocks Reservoir
Whins Brow
Trough of Bowland
Beatrix Fell
Slaidburn
Slaidburn Heritage Information Centre
Dolphinholme
Wyre
Marshaw
Lancaster Street
Hollins Lane
Forton
Braides
Hawthornthwaite Fell
479
Sykes
Hareden
Newton
Dunsop Bridge
Meanley
Easington Fell
396
Ladies Hill
Pilling
Fisher's Row
Stake Pool
Winmarleigh
Scorton
Sykes Fell
Calder
Calder Fell
Totridge Fell
Fair Snape Fell
520
Whitewell
Marl Hill Moor
Preesall
Scronkey
Cabus
Ford Green
Oakenclough
Stalmine
Moor End
Garstang
Bonds
Calder Vale
Brock
Parlick
432
Browsholme Hall
West Bradford
Eagland Hill
Nateby
Hale Nook
Sowerby Carr
Bowgreave
Churchtown
Chipping
Hodder
Bashall Eaves
Waddington
Hambleton
Catterall
Beacon Fell Country Park
Claughton
Whitechapel
Hesketh Lane
Longridge Fell
Walker Fold
Bashall Town
Low Moor
Out Rawcliffe
Ratten Row
Shin Lane End
Larbreck
Toll
Great Eccleston
St Michael's on Wyre
Bilsborrow
Little Singleton
Singleton
Little Eccleston
Copp
Lane Heads
Myerscough College
Inglewhite
Priest Hill
Knowle Green
New Row
Hurst Green
Great Mitton
Barrow
Elswick
Crossmoor
Inskip
Cuddy Hill
Barton
Stump Cross
Goosnargh
Longridge
Lamb Roe
Thistleton
Roseacre
Esprick
Wharles
Lewth
Newsham
Chingle Hall
Haighton Green
Frances Green
Little Town
Dinckley
Medlar
Catforth
Moor Side
Broughton
Ribchester
Ribchester Roman Fort & Museum
Copster Green
Billington
Blackleach
Woodplumpton
Grimsargh
Langho
Moor Side
Wesham
Bolton Houses
Treales
Lower Bartle
Cottam
Fulwood
Elston
Salesbury
Wilpshire
Balderstone
Osbaldeston
Kirkham
Westby
Salwick Sta
Lea Town
Cadley
Preston North End FC
Fishwick
Myerscough Smithy
Mellor
Mellor Brook
Great Harwood
Clayton-le-Moors
Rishton
Wrea Green
Scales
Newton
Clifton
Central Lancashire
Samlesbury
Samlesbury Hall
Four Lane Ends
Bryning
Hall Cross
Preston Guildhall
Nab's Head
Roach Bridge
BLACKBURN
Whitebirk
Warton
Freckleton
PRESTON
Bottom of Hutton
Penwortham
Harris Mus & Art Gallery
Walton-le-Dale
Higher Walton
Witton Park
Shadsworth
Oswaldtwistle
Warton Bank
Ribble
Hutton
Longton
Penwortham Lane
Tardy Gate
Bamber Bridge
Gregson Lane
Coup Green
Hoghton Tower
Pleasington
Cherry Tree
Mill Hill
Blackburn Rovers FC
Guide
Ewood
Lower Darwen
Belthorn
Hall Green
New Longton
Lostock Hall Sta
Hoghton
Feniscowles
Riley Green
Earcroft
Ribble Estuary
Walmer Bridge
Midge Hall
Earnshaw Bridge
Farington
Clayton Green
Brindle
Withnell Fold
Tockholes
Blackburn with Darwen
Waterside
Hesketh Bank
Becconsall
Much Hoole
Cocker Bar
LEYLAND
Clayton-le-Woods
Cuerden Valley
Thorpe Green
Higher Wheelton
Abbey Village
Darwen
Rickup
Huddlesden
Banks
Hundred End
Much Hoole Town
Tarleton
Whittle-le-Woods
Wheelton
Withnell
Royal Fold
Brinscall
Blacksnape
Crossens
Bretherton
Barber's Moor
Heapey
WITH DARWEN

M6: *The Preston bypass, later incorporated into the M6, is Britain's oldest piece of motorway and was opened on 5th December 1958.* ***Map ref. B4***

233

Morecambe: *Hometown of Eric John Bartholomew, born 14th May 1926. Eric adopted the stage name of Eric Morecambe and, along with Ernie Wise, formed 'Morecambe and Wise'. They became one of Britain's most successful comedy double-acts. Eric died on the 28th May 1984.* ***Map ref. A1***

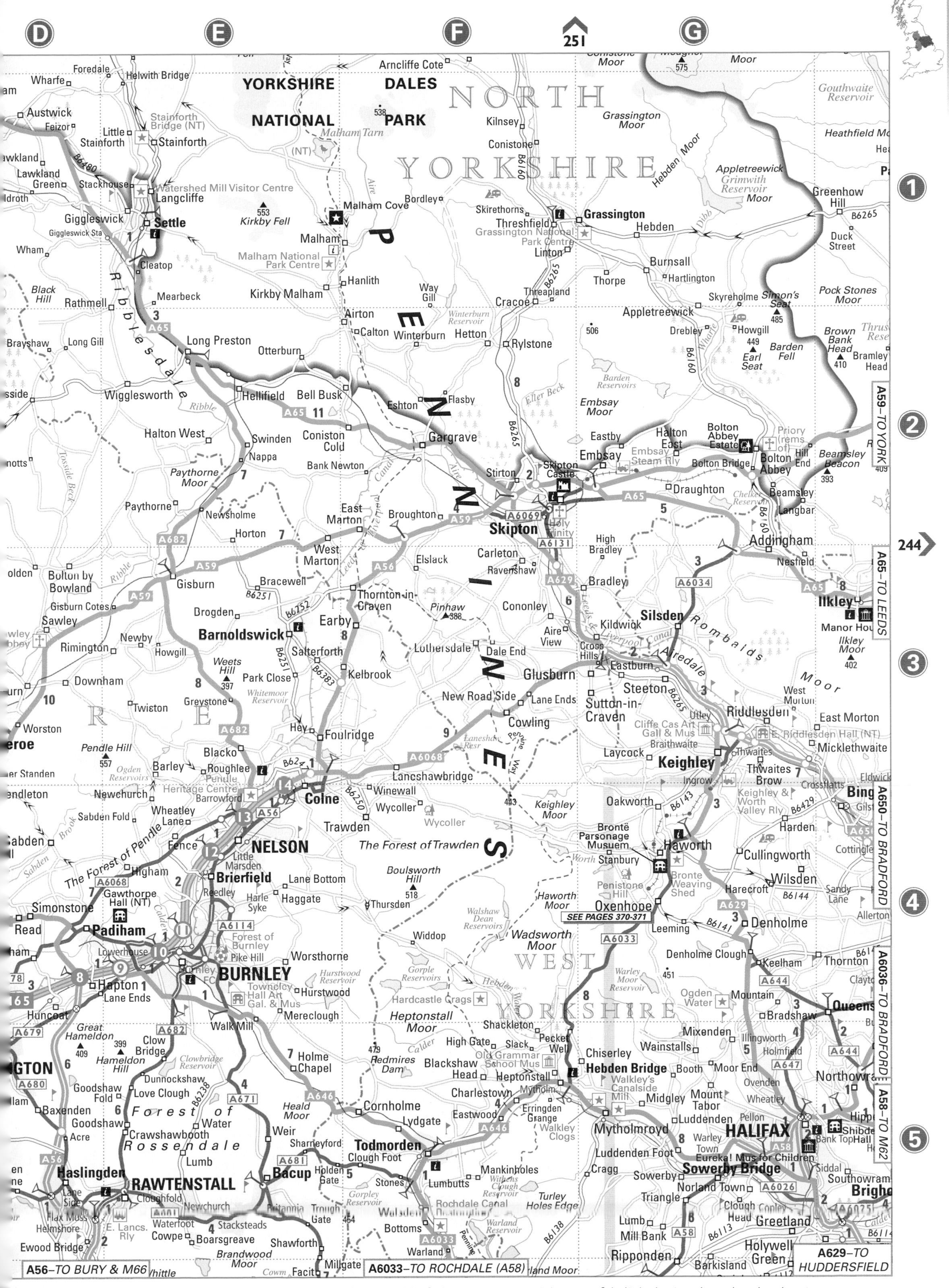

D
E
F
G
251
YORKSHIRE DALES NATIONAL PARK
NORTH YORKSHIRE
PENNINE
WEST YORKSHIRE
FOREST OF BOWLAND
Forest of Rossendale
The Forest of Pendle
The Forest of Trawden
Ribblesdale
Rombalds Moor
Aire
Ribble
Calder
Arncliffe Cote
Moor
575
Goulthwaite Reservoir
Heathfield Moor
Foredale
Helwith Bridge
Wharfe
Austwick
Feizor
Little Stainforth
Stainforth Bridge (NT)
Stainforth
Lawkland
Lawkland Green
Stackhouse
Watershed Mill Visitor Centre
Langcliffe
Giggleswick
Giggleswick Sta
Settle
Wham
Cleatop
Black Hill
Rathmell
Mearbeck
Brayshaw
Long Gill
Long Preston
Otterburn
Wigglesworth
Hellifield
Bell Busk
Halton West
Swinden
Nappa
Coniston Cold
Bank Newton
Paythorne Moor
Paythorne
Newsholme
Horton
East Marton
West Marton
Broughton
Gisburn
Bolton by Bowland
Gisburn Cotes
Sawley
Rimington
Newby
Howgill
Downham
Twiston
Worston
Pendle Hill
557
Barley
Roughlee
Blacko
Newchurch
Sabden Fold
Sabden
Wheatley Lane
Fence
Higham
Padiham
Simonstone
Read
Hapton
Lane Ends
Huncoat
Great Hameldon
Hameldon Hill
Clow Bridge
Clowbridge Reservoir
Dunnockshaw
Love Clough
Goodshaw Fold
Goodshaw
Crawshawbooth
Baxenden
Acre
Haslingden
RAWTENSTALL
Cloughfold
Newchurch
Waterfoot
Stacksteads
Cowpe
Boarsgreave
Helmshore
Ewood Bridge
E. Lancs. Rly
Brandwood Moor
Shawforth
Facit
Millgate
Bacup
Britannia
Weir
Heald Moor
Cornholme
Lydgate
Todmorden
Sharneyford
Clough Foot
Holden Gate
Stones
Lumbutts
Walsden
Bottoms
Warland
Warland Reservoir
Gorpley Reservoir
Trough Gate
Mankinholes
Withens Clough Reservoir
Turley Holes Edge
Rochdale Canal
Kirkby Fell
553
Malham Tarn
Malham Cove
Malham
Malham National Park Centre
Kirkby Malham
Hanlith
Airton
Calton
Winterburn
Winterburn Reservoir
Hetton
Way Gill
Bordley
Kilnsey
Conistone
Grassington Moor
Hebden Moor
Skirethorns
Threshfield
Grassington
Grassington National Park Centre
Linton
Hebden
Burnsall
Hartlington
Thorpe
Threapland
Cracoe
Rylstone
Appletreewick
Appletreewick Moor
Grimwith Reservoir
Skyreholme
Simon's Seat
485
Drebley
Howgill
Earl Seat
449
Barden Fell
Barden Reservoirs
Embsay Moor
Greenhow Hill
Duck Street
Pock Stones Moor
Brown Bank Head
410
Bramley Head
Eshton
Flasby
Gargrave
Stirton
Skipton
Skipton Castle
Holy Trinity
Embsay
Embsay Steam Rly
Eastby
Halton East
Bolton Abbey Estate
Priory (rems of)
Bolton Abbey
Bolton Bridge
Draughton
Chelker Reservoir
Beamsley
Beamsley Beacon
393
Langbar
Addingham
Nesfield
Ilkley
Ilkley Moor
402
Manor House
High Bradley
Carleton
Ravenshaw
Bradley
Elslack
Thornton-in-Craven
Earby
Pinhaw
388
Cononley
Kildwick
Silsden
Salterforth
Barnoldswick
Bracewell
Brogden
Weets Hill
397
Park Close
Whitemoor Reservoir
Kelbrook
Lothersdale
Dale End
Aire View
Cross Hills
Eastburn
Glusburn
Steeton
Leeds & Liverpool Canal
Greystone
New Road Side
Lane Ends
Sutton-in-Craven
Cowling
Utley
Riddlesden
East Riddlesden Hall (NT)
Cliffe Castle Art Gall & Mus
West Morton
East Morton
Micklethwaite
Braithwaite
Laycock
Keighley
Thwaites
Thwaites Brow
Ingrow
Crossflatts
Bingley
Foulridge
Lancshaw Resr
Lancshawbridge
Colne
Winewall
Wycoller
Trawden
Keighley Moor
Oakworth
Keighley & Worth Valley Rly
Harden
Cottingley
Haworth
Brontë Parsonage Museum
Stanbury
Cullingworth
Wilsden
Penistone Hill
Brontë Weaving Shed
Harecroft
Sandy Lane
Allerton
Haworth Moor
Oxenhope
SEE PAGES 370-371
Leeming
Denholme
Wadsworth Moor
Denholme Clough
Keelham
Thornton
Heritage Centre
Barrowford
NELSON
Little Marsden
Brierfield
Reedley
Lane Bottom
Harle Syke
Haggate
Boulsworth Hill
518
Thursden
Walshaw Dean Reservoirs
Widdop
Forest of Burnley
Pike Hill
Lowerhouse
Worsthorne
BURNLEY
Towneley Hall Art Gal. & Mus
Hurstwood
Hurstwood Reservoir
Gorple Reservoirs
Mereclough
Hardcastle Crags
Heptonstall Moor
Walk Mill
Holme Chapel
Shackleton
Warley Moor Reservoir
451
Ogden Water
Mountain
Queensbury
Bradshaw
Mixenden
Illingworth
Holmfield
Wainstalls
High Gate
Slack
Pecket Well
Chiserley
Old Grammar School Mus
Blackshaw Head
Heptonstall
Hebden Bridge
Walkley's Canalside Mill
Booth
Moor End
Ovenden
Northowram
Mytholm
Charlestown
Eastwood
Erringden Grange
Walkley Clogs
Midgley
Mount Tabor
Wheatley
Mytholmroyd
Luddenden
Pellon
HALIFAX
Hipperholme
Shibden Hall
Bank Top
Luddenden Foot
Warley Town
Eureka! Mus for Children
Cragg
Sowerby
Sowerby Bridge
Siddal
Southowram
Brighouse
Norland Town
Triangle
Clough Head
Greetland
Lumb
Mill Bank
Ripponden
Barkisland
Holywell Green
Redmires Dam
479
399
409
244
A59–TO YORK
A65–TO LEEDS
A650–TO BRADFORD
A6036–TO BRADFORD
A58–TO M62
A56–TO BURY & M66
A6033–TO ROCHDALE (A58)
A629–TO HUDDERSFIELD
234
1
2
3
4
5

Whalley: *A point to the west of the village, near Calderstones Hospital, can be calculated to be the 'centre of gravity' of mainland Britain.* ***Map ref. D4***

Oswaldtwistle: *James Hargreaves, inventor of the 'Spinning Jenny', was born here in 1720. The Spinning Jenny was the first machine to improve on the traditional spinning wheel and was capable of doing the work of 8 traditional spinners. The invention put Britain at the forefront of the textile industry.* ***Map ref. D5***

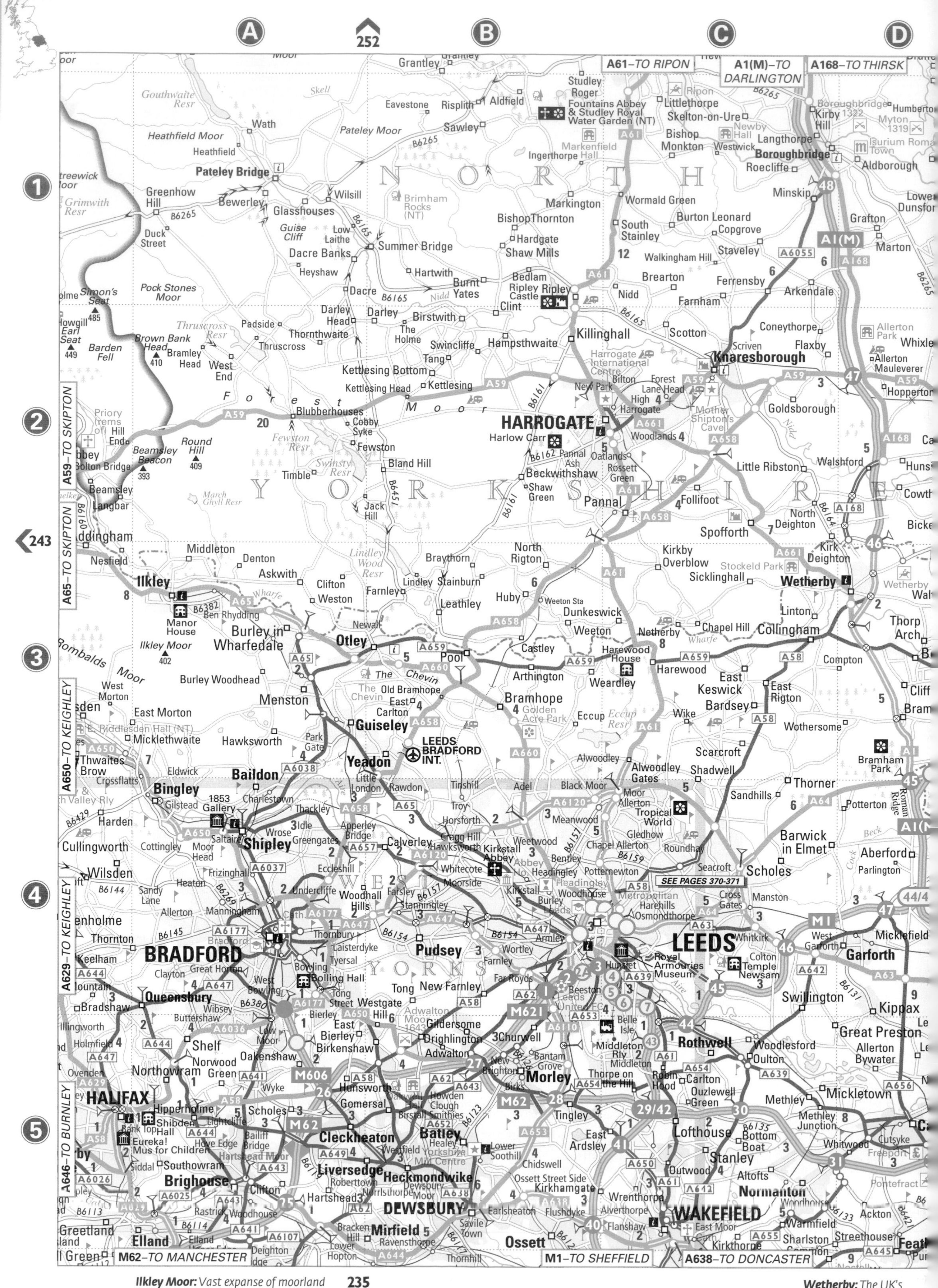
A
252
B
C
D
1
2
3
4
5
243
A61–TO RIPON
A1(M)–TO DARLINGTON
A168–TO THIRSK
A59–TO SKIPTON
A65–TO SKIPTON
A650–TO KEIGHLEY
A629–TO KEIGHLEY
A646–TO BURNLEY
M62–TO MANCHESTER
M1–TO SHEFFIELD
A638–TO DONCASTER
N O R T H
Y O R K S H I R E
W E S T
Y O R K S
Forest Moor
Grantley
Gouthwaite Resr
Wath
Heathfield Moor
Heathfield
Pateley Bridge
Pateley Moor
Eavestone
Risplith
Aldfield
Sawley
Studley Roger
Fountains Abbey & Studley Royal Water Garden (NT)
Ripon
Littlethorpe
Skelton-on-Ure
Bishop Monkton
Westwick
Newby Hall
Langthorpe
Boroughbridge
Kirby Hill
Aldborough
Roecliffe
Markenfield Hall
Ingerthorpe
Greenhow Hill
Bewerley
Glasshouses
Wilsill
Brimham Rocks (NT)
Markington
Wormald Green
Minskip
Grimwith Resr
Duck Street
Guise Cliff
Low Laithe
Summer Bridge
Dacre Banks
Bishop Thornton
Hardgate
Shaw Mills
South Stainley
Burton Leonard
Copgrove
Staveley
Grafton
Marton
Heyshaw
Hartwith
Burnt Yates
Bedlam
Ripley Castle
Ripley
Clint
Nidd
Brearton
Ferrensby
Farnham
Arkendale
Pock Stones Moor
Simon's Seat
Dacre
Darley Head
Darley
Birstwith
Thruscross Resr
Padside
Thornthwaite
Thruscross
Brown Bank Head
Bramley Head
West End
The Holme
Swincliffe
Tang
Hampsthwaite
Killinghall
Scotton
Coneythorpe
Scriven
Flaxby
Knaresborough
Allerton Park
Whixley
Allerton Mauleverer
Kettlesing Bottom
Kettlesing Head
Kettlesing
Harrogate International Centre
Bilton
New Park
Forest Lane Head
High Harrogate
Mother Shipton's Cave
Goldsborough
Hopperton
Blubberhouses
Cobby Syke
Fewston
Fewston Resr
HARROGATE
Harlow Carr
Woodlands
Priory (rems of)
Hill End
Bolton Abbey
Bolton Bridge
Beamsley Beacon
Round Hill
Swinsty Resr
Timble
Bland Hill
Pannal Ash
Oatlands
Rossett Green
Beckwithshaw
Shaw Green
Little Ribston
Walshford
Beamsley
Langbar
March Ghyll Resr
Jack Hill
Pannal
Follifoot
North Deighton
Spofforth
Kirk Deighton
Addingham
Nesfield
Middleton
Denton
Askwith
Lindley Wood Resr
Braythorn
North Rigton
Kirkby Overblow
Stockeld Park
Sicklinghall
Wetherby
Ilkley
Clifton
Weston
Farnley
Lindley
Stainburn
Leathley
Huby
Weeton Sta
Dunkeswick
Manor House
Ben Rhydding
Burley in Wharfedale
Newall
Otley
Weeton
Netherby
Chapel Hill
Linton
Collingham
Thorp Arch
Ilkley Moor
Rombalds Moor
Pool
Castley
Harewood House
Harewood
East Keswick
Compton
The Chevin
Arthington
Weardley
Burley Woodhead
West Morton
Old Bramhope
East Morton
Menston
East Carlton
Bramhope
Golden Acre Park
Eccup
Eccup Resr
Wike
East Rigton
Bardsey
Clifford
Bramham
East Riddlesden Hall (NT)
Micklethwaite
Hawksworth
Park Gate
Guiseley
Wothersome
Thwaites Brow
Eldwick
Baildon
Yeadon
LEEDS BRADFORD INT.
Alwoodley
Alwoodley Gates
Scarcroft
Shadwell
Bramham Park
Crossflatts
Bingley
Gilstead
1853 Gallery
Charlestown
Little London
Rawdon
Tinshill
Adel
Black Moor
Moor Allerton
Thorner
Sandhills
Potterton
Harden
Saltaire
Shipley
Thackley
Idle
Apperley Bridge
Wrose
Greengates
Calverley
Horsforth
Cragg Hill
Meanwood
Tropical World
Gledhow
Barwick in Elmet
Aberford
Parlington
Cullingworth
Cottingley
Moor Head
Hawksworth
Kirkstall Abbey
Weetwood
Chapel Allerton
Roundhay
Scholes
Wilsden
Frizinghall
Eccleshill
Whitecote
Bentley
Headingley
Potternewton
Seacroft
SEE PAGES 370-371
Sandy Lane
Heaton
Undercliffe
Woodhall Hills
Farsley
Moorside
Kirkstall
Woodhouse
Burley
Harehills
Cross Gates
Manston
Allerton
Manningham
Stanningley
Osmondthorpe
Denholme
Thornton
Bradford
Thornbury
Laisterdyke
Pudsey
Wortley
Armley
LEEDS
Whitkirk
Colton
Temple Newsam
West Garforth
Micklefield
Garforth
BRADFORD
Keelham
Clayton
Great Horton
Tyersal
Bowling
Farnley
Far Royds
Royal Armouries Museum
Hunslet
Mountain
West Bowling
Bolling Hall
Tong
New Farnley
Beeston
Leeds United FC
Swillington
Kippax
Queensbury
Bradshaw
Wibsey
Tong Street
Westgate Hill
Bierley
Adwalton Moor 1643
Gildersome
Belle Isle
Great Preston
Allerton Bywater
Buttershaw
East Bierley
Birkenshaw
Drighlington
Churwell
Middleton Rly
Middleton
Rothwell
Woodlesford
Oulton
Illingworth
Holmfield
Shelf
Low Moor
Adwalton
Bantam Grove
New Brighton
Morley
Thorpe on the Hill
Robin Hood
Carlton
Ovenden
Norwood Green
Northowram
Oakenshaw
Wyke
Hunsworth
Howden Clough
Birks
Ouzlewell Green
Methley
Mickletown
HALIFAX
Hipperholme
Shibden Hall
Lightcliffe
Scholes
Gomersal
Birstall Smithies
Tingley
Lofthouse
Methley Junction
Bank Top
Eureka! Mus for Children
Hove Edge
Bailiff Bridge
Hartshead Moor
Cleckheaton
Batley
Healey
Yorkshire Mill Centre
Lower Soothill
East Ardsley
Bottom Boat
Whitwood
Cutsyke
Siddal
Southowram
Westfield
Chidswell
Stanley
Outwood
Altofts
Freeport
Brighouse
Liversedge
Heckmondwike
Robertown
Ossett Street Side
Kirkhamgate
Wrenthorpe
Normanton
Pontefract
Clifton
Hartshead
Norristhorpe
Dewsbury Moor
Rastrick
Woodhouse
DEWSBURY
Earlsheaton
Flushdyke
Alverthorpe
WAKEFIELD
Woodhouse
Ackton
Greetland
Elland
Bracken Hill
Mirfield
Savile Town
Flanshaw
East Moor
Warmfield
Sharlston
Streethouse
Featherstone
Lower Hopton
Ravensthorpe
Ossett
Kirkthorpe
Sharlston Common
Deighton
Thornhill
Greetland
Elland

Ilkley Moor: *Vast expanse of moorland famous as the setting of the unofficial Yorkshire anthem recognised throughout the world 'On Ilkley Moor Bah t 'at'.* ***Map ref.*** ***A3***

235

York: *Guy Fawkes was born in York in 1570. Along with a group of conspirators he tried to blow up the Houses of Parliament on the 5th November 1605 but was arrested in the cellars before he could ignite the explosives. He is remembered every 5th November when we celebrate Bonfire Night.* ***Map ref. F2***

Wetherby: *The UK's longest lasting rainbow (6 hours) was recorded here on 14th March 1994.* ***Map ref. D3***

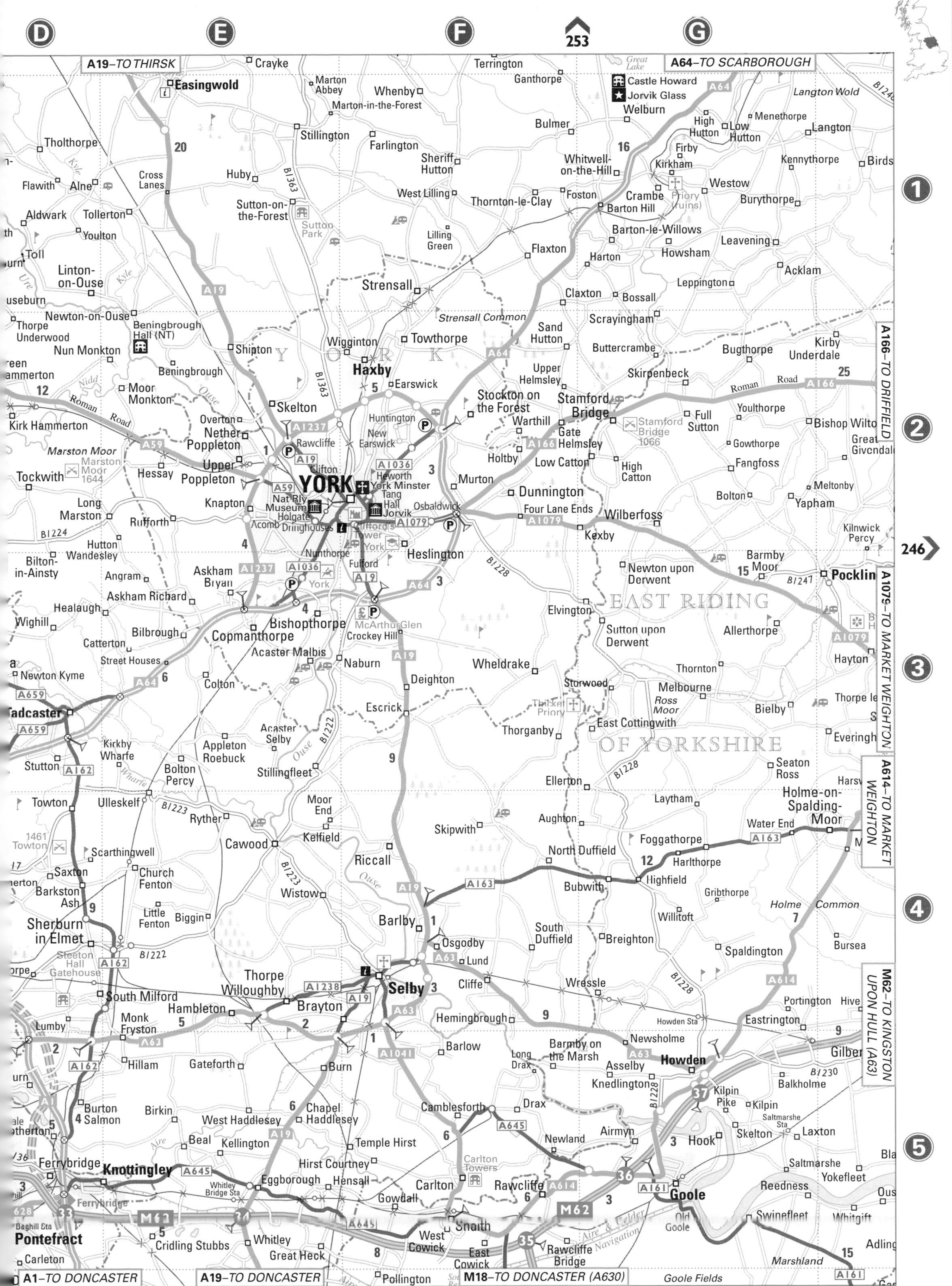
D
E
F
G
253
A19–TO THIRSK
A64–TO SCARBOROUGH
Crayke
Terrington
Easingwold
Marton Abbey
Whenby
Ganthorpe
Castle Howard
Jorvik Glass
Welburn
Marton-in-the-Forest
Langton Wold
Menethorpe
Stillington
Farlington
Bulmer
High Hutton
Low Hutton
Langton
Tholthorpe
Firby
Kirkham
Kennythorpe
Birds
Sheriff Hutton
Whitwell-on-the-Hill
Cross Lanes
Huby
Flawith
Alne
Westow
Sutton-on-the-Forest
West Lilling
Thornton-le-Clay
Foston
Crambe
Priory (ruins)
Barton Hill
Burythorpe
Aldwark
Tollerton
Sutton Park
Youlton
Lilling Green
Barton-le-Willows
Leavening
Flaxton
Harton
Howsham
Toll
Linton-on-Ouse
Acklam
Strensall
Leppington
Claxton
Bossall
Newton-on-Ouse
Beningbrough Hall (NT)
Strensall Common
Sand Hutton
Scrayingham
Thorpe Underwood
Wigginton
Towthorpe
Nun Monkton
Shipton
Buttercrambe
Bugthorpe
Kirby Underdale
Haxby
Beningbrough
Skirpenbeck
Moor Monkton
Earswick
Upper Helmsley
Roman Road
A166
Skelton
Stockton on the Forest
Stamford Bridge
Full Sutton
Youlthorpe
Kirk Hammerton
Overton
Huntington
Warthill
Stamford Bridge 1066
Bishop Wilton
Nether Poppleton
New Earswick
Gate Helmsley
Gowthorpe
Great Givendale
Marston Moor
Rawcliffe
Holtby
Low Catton
Fangfoss
Upper Poppleton
Clifton
Heworth
High Catton
Tockwith
Marston Moor 1644
Hessay
YORK
York Minster
Murton
Meltonby
Knapton
Nat Rly Museum
Tang Hall
Dunnington
Bolton
Yapham
Long Marston
Holgate
Jorvik
Osbaldwick
Four Lane Ends
Wilberfoss
Rufforth
Acomb
Dringhouses
Clifford's Tower
Kexby
Kilnwick Percy
Hutton Wandesley
Nunthorpe
York
Heslington
246
Bilton-in-Ainsty
Fulford
Barmby Moor
Angram
Askham Bryan
Newton upon Derwent
Pocklington
Askham Richard
York
EAST RIDING
A1079–TO MARKET WEIGHTON
Healaugh
Elvington
Wighill
Bishopthorpe
McArthurGlen
Sutton upon Derwent
Allerthorpe
Bilbrough
Copmanthorpe
Crockey Hill
Catterton
Acaster Malbis
Hayton
Street Houses
Naburn
Thornton
Wheldrake
Newton Kyme
Deighton
Colton
Storwood
Melbourne
Tadcaster
Thorpe le Street
Escrick
Thicket Priory
Ross Moor
Bielby
East Cottingwith
Acaster Selby
Thorganby
Kirkby Wharfe
Appleton Roebuck
Everingham
OF YORKSHIRE
Stutton
Bolton Percy
Seaton Ross
Stillingfleet
A614–TO MARKET WEIGHTON
Ellerton
Towton
Ulleskelf
Moor End
Laytham
Holme-on-Spalding-Moor
Ryther
Aughton
Water End
Kelfield
Skipwith
1461 Towton
Foggathorpe
Cawood
Scarthingwell
North Duffield
Riccall
Harlthorpe
Saxton
Church Fenton
Bubwith
Highfield
Barkston Ash
Wistow
Gribthorpe
Holme Common
Willitoft
Little Fenton
Biggin
Barlby
Sherburn in Elmet
South Duffield
Osgodby
Breighton
Bursea
Spaldington
Steeton Hall Gatehouse
Lund
Thorpe Willoughby
Cliffe
Wressle
M62–TO KINGSTON UPON HULL (A63)
Selby
South Milford
Brayton
Portington
Hambleton
Hemingbrough
Howden Sta
Eastrington
Monk Fryston
Lumby
Newsholme
Barmby on the Marsh
Barlow
Long Drax
Howden
Gilberdyke
Hillam
Gateforth
Burn
Asselby
Knedlington
Balkholme
Kilpin Pike
Kilpin
Burton Salmon
Birkin
Chapel Haddlesey
Camblesforth
Drax
Saltmarshe Sta
Laxton
West Haddlesey
Airmyn
Hook
Skelton
Beal
Kellington
Temple Hirst
Newland
Carlton Towers
Saltmarshe
Yokefleet
Ferrybridge
Knottingley
Hirst Courtney
Eggborough
Hensall
Carlton
Rawcliffe
Goole
Reedness
Whitley Bridge Sta
Gowdall
Swinefleet
Whitgift
Old Goole
Snaith
Baghill Sta
Pontefract
Cridling Stubbs
Whitley
West Cowick
Rawcliffe Bridge
Aire & Calder Navigation
Adlingfleet
Great Heck
East Cowick
Marshland
Carleton
A1–TO DONCASTER
A19–TO DONCASTER
Pollington
M18–TO DONCASTER (A630)
Goole Fields
1
2
3
4
5

Knaresborough: *Haunt of Mother Shipton, England's most famous prophetess and witch. Although born in 1488 she allegedly foretold of the Civil War, the Black Death and the Great Fire of London and one of her best known rhymes is uncannily accurate: Carriages without horses shall go, and accidents fill the world with woe. Around the world thoughts shall fly, in the twinkling of an eye. Under water men shall walk, shall ride, shall sleep, shall talk. In the air men shall be seen, in white, in black and in green. Iron on the water shall float, as easy as a wooden boat.* ***Map ref.*** ***C2***

236

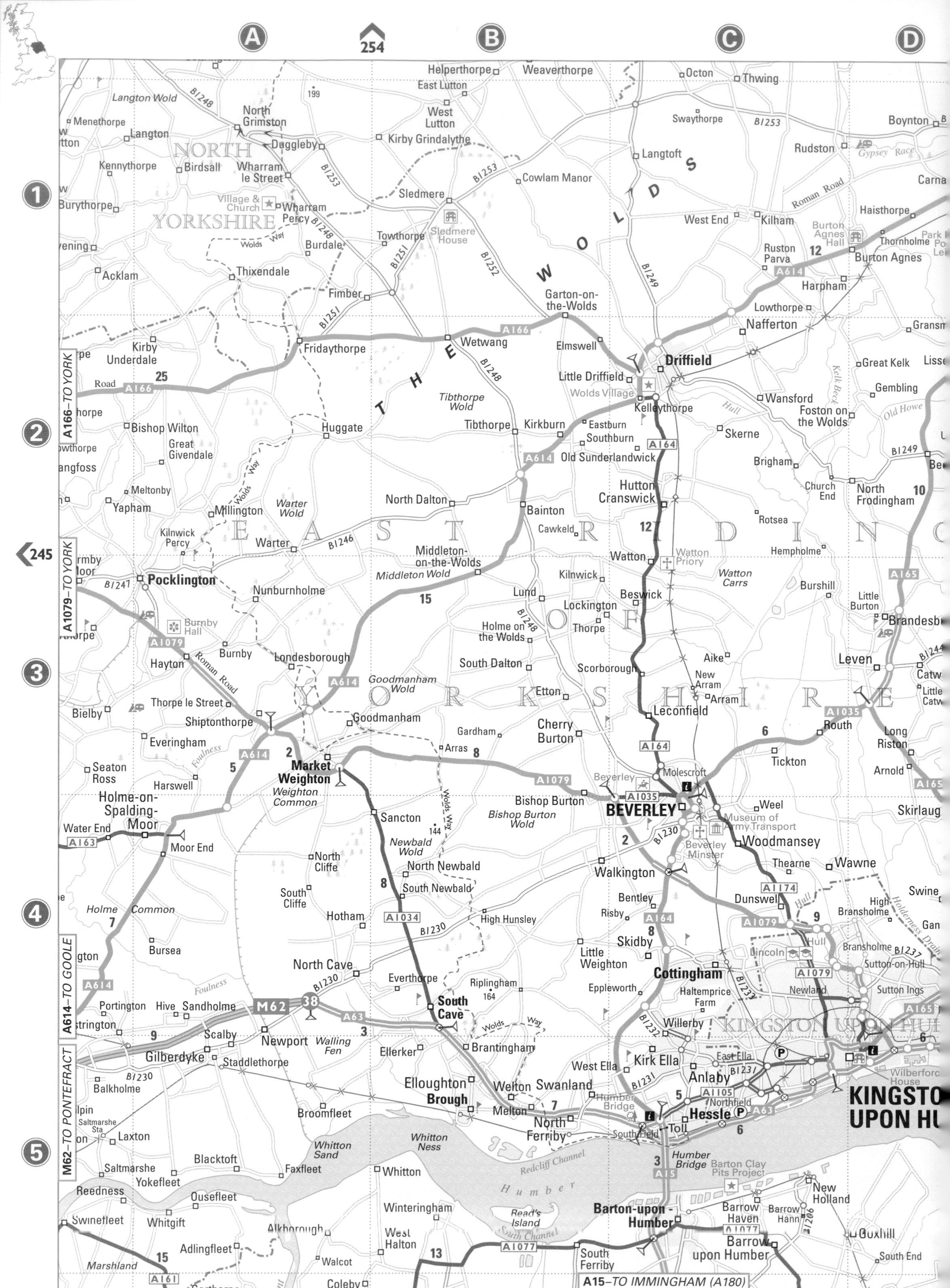

A
B
C
D
254
245
237
1
2
3
4
5
Helperthorpe
Weaverthorpe
Octon
Thwing
East Lutton
West Lutton
Langton Wold
B1248
199
North Grimston
Menethorpe
Langton
Duggleby
Kirby Grindalythe
Swaythorpe
B1253
Boynton
Rudston
Gypsey Race
NORTH
Kennythorpe
Birdsall
Wharram le Street
B1253
Langtoft
Cowlam Manor
Roman Road
Carna
Burythorpe
Village & Church
Wharram Percy
Sledmere
YORKSHIRE
Sledmere House
West End
Kilham
Haisthorpe
Towthorpe
Burton Agnes Hall
Thornholme
Burdale
Wolds Way
Ruston Parva
12
Burton Agnes
B1251
B1252
B1249
A614
Acklam
Thixendale
Harpham
Fimber
Garton-on-the-Wolds
Lowthorpe
B1251
Nafferton
Gransm
A166
Kirby Underdale
Fridaythorpe
Wetwang
Elmswell
Driffield
Great Kelk
Road
A166
25
B1248
Little Driffield
Kelk Beck
Gembling
Wolds Village
Wansford
A166–TO YORK
Tibthorpe Wold
Kelleythorpe
Foston on the Wolds
Old Howe
Bishop Wilton
Huggate
Tibthorpe
Kirkburn
Eastburn
Skerne
Great Givendale
Southburn
A164
B1249
A614
Old Sunderlandwick
Brigham
Meltonby
Hutton Cranswick
Church End
North Frodingham
Yapham
Millington
Warter Wold
North Dalton
Bainton
10
Kilnwick Percy
Cawkeld
12
Rotsea
Warter
B1246
Middleton-on-the-Wolds
Hempholme
Watton
Watton Priory
Kilnwick
Watton Carrs
B1247
Pocklington
Nunburnholme
Middleton Wold
Burshill
A165
A1079–TO YORK
15
Lund
Beswick
Little Burton
Burnby Hall
Lockington
Brandesb
B1248
Holme on the Wolds
Thorpe
A1079
Burnby
Londesborough
South Dalton
Scorborough
Aike
Leven
Hayton
Roman Road
New Arram
Arram
Goodmanham Wold
A614
Etton
Thorpe le Street
Bielby
Shiptonthorpe
Goodmanham
Leconfield
A1035
Little Catw
Cherry Burton
Routh
Everingham
Gardham
6
Long Riston
Arras
8
A164
Tickton
Foulness
Seaton Ross
2
Market Weighton
5
A614
Arnold
Harswell
A1079
Molescroft
Weighton Common
Beverley
A165
Holme-on-Spalding-Moor
Sancton
Bishop Burton
A1035
Weel
BEVERLEY
Skirlaug
Water End
Bishop Burton Wold
Museum of Army Transport
A163
Moor End
144
Wolds Way
B1230
Beverley Minster
Woodmansey
Newbald Wold
2
North Cliffe
North Newbald
Thearne
Wawne
Walkington
8
South Newbald
A1174
South Cliffe
Swine
Holme
Common
Bentley
Dunswell
Hull
7
Hotham
A1034
Risby
High Bransholme
A1079
9
High Hunsley
A164
B1230
Gan
Bursea
8
Skidby
Bransholme
Hull
B1237
Little Weighton
Lincoln
Sutton-on-Hull
North Cave
A1079
Everthorpe
Ripplingham
Cottingham
A614–TO GOOLE
Foulness
Eppleworth
Haltemprice Farm
B1233
Newland
Sutton Ings
B1230
164
South Cave
A614
Portington
Hive
Sandholme
M62
38
A63
A165
B1232
Willerby
KINGSTON UPON HULL
Scalby
Wolds Way
9
3
Newport
Walling Fen
Brantingham
6
Gilberdyke
Staddlethorpe
Ellerker
Kirk Ella
East Ella
B1230
West Ella
B1231
Anlaby
Wilberforce House
Balkholme
Elloughton
Welton
Swanland
B1231
5
A1105
Brough
Humber Bridge
Northfield
KINGSTON UPON HU
Melton
7
Hessle
A63
M62–TO PONTEFRACT
Saltmarshe Sta
Laxton
Broomfleet
North Ferriby
Toll
6
Whitton Sand
Whitton Ness
South Field
Humber Bridge
Blacktoft
Redcliff Channel
3
Barton Clay Pits Project
Saltmarshe
Faxfleet
Whitton
A15
Yokefleet
Humber
New Holland
Reedness
Ousefleet
Winteringham
Read's Island
Barton-upon-Humber
Barrow Haven
Barrow Haven
B1206
Swinefleet
Whitgift
Alkborough
South Channel
A1077
West Halton
A1077
Barrow upon Humber
Goxhill
Adlingfleet
15
13
South Ferriby
South End
Marshland
A161
Walcot
Garthorpe
Coleby
A15–TO IMMINGHAM (A180)

Humber Bridge: *Despite plans for a tunnel scheme in 1872 and numerous plans for a bridge, the first traffic didn't finally cross the river until the 24th June 1981. Work on the present suspension bridge began in 1973 with, at times, over 1000 workers being employed on the construction. The bridge was finally opened by HM The Queen on the 17th July 1981. At this time it had the longest bridge span in the world of 4626 feet (1410m).* ***Map ref. C5***

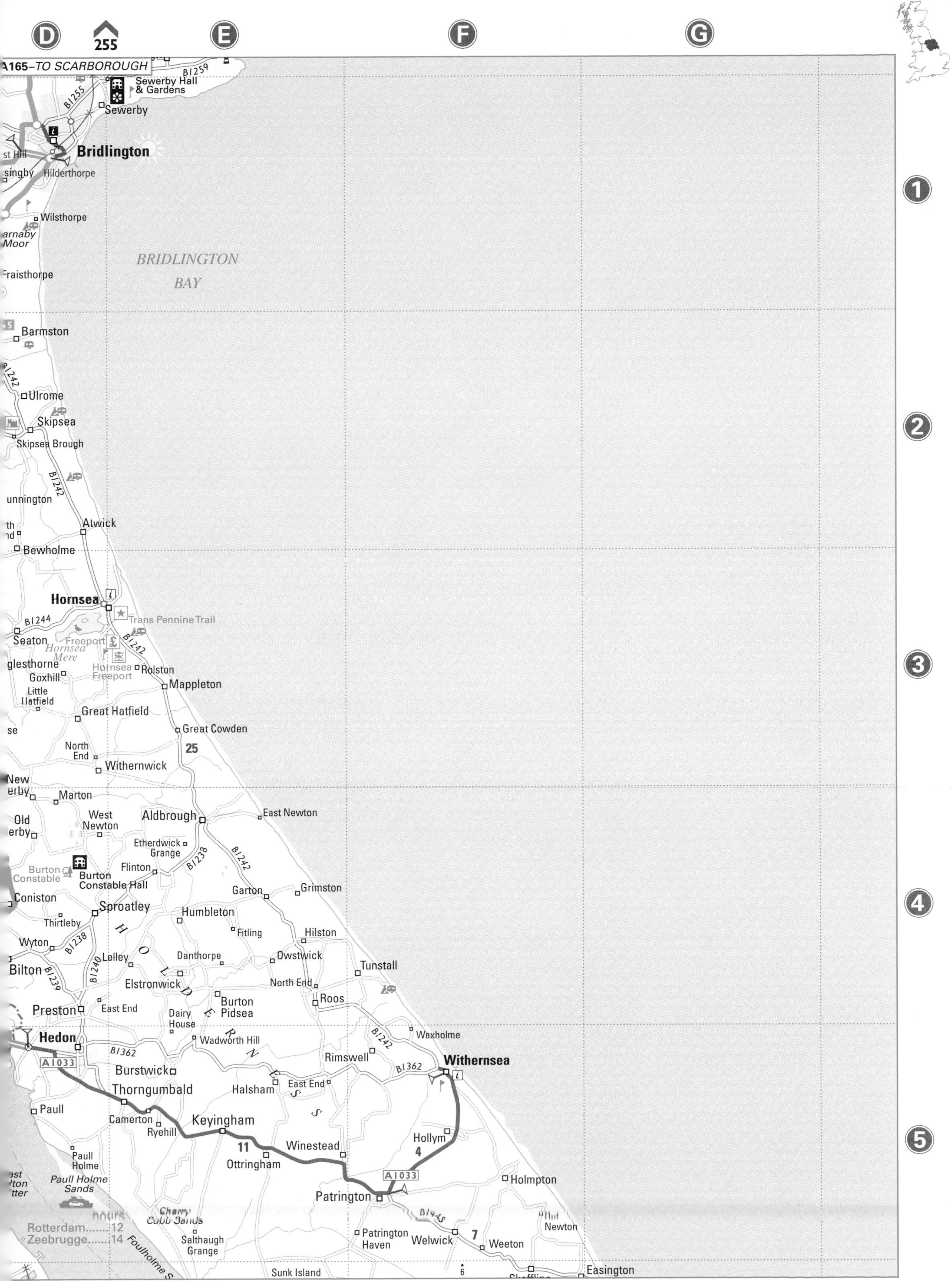
D
E
F
G
255
A165–TO SCARBOROUGH
Sewerby Hall & Gardens
Sewerby
Bridlington
Hilderthorpe
Wilsthorpe
BRIDLINGTON BAY
Barmston
Ulrome
Skipsea
Skipsea Brough
Atwick
Bewholme
Hornsea
Trans Pennine Trail
Seaton
Hornsea Mere
Hornsea Freeport
Rolston
Mappleton
Goxhill
Little Hatfield
Great Hatfield
Great Cowden
North End
Withernwick
Marton
West Newton
Aldbrough
East Newton
Etherdwick Grange
Burton Constable
Burton Constable Hall
Flinton
Garton
Grimston
Coniston
Sproatley
Humbleton
Fitling
Thirtleby
Hilston
Wyton
Lelley
Danthorpe
Owstwick
Tunstall
Bilton
Elstronwick
North End
Roos
Preston
East End
Burton Pidsea
Dairy House
Waxholme
Hedon
Wadworth Hill
Rimswell
Withernsea
Burstwick
HOLDERNESS
Thorngumbald
Halsham
East End
Paull
Camerton
Keyingham
Ryehill
Hollym
Winestead
Ottringham
Paull Holme
Paull Holme Sands
Holmpton
Patrington
Rotterdam.......12
Zeebrugge.......14
Salthaugh Grange
Patrington Haven
Welwick
Weeton
Newton
Sunk Island
Easington
A1033
B1242
B1362
B1238
B1240
B1239
B1244
B1259
B1255
1
2
3
4
5

Kingston Upon Hull: *William Wilberforce, the most important figure in the abolition of slavery, was born here in 1759. After years of campaigning, Wilberforce died on the 29th July 1833 and just one month later Parliament passed the Slavery Abolition Act which gave all slaves in the British Empire their freedom.* ***Map ref. D5***

239

Holderness Coast: *The coastline here is reputed to have the fastest rate of coastal erosion in the world. The Boulder Clay cliffs along this shoreline offer little resistance to the full force of the sea and are constantly 'slumping' (sliding slowly into the sea). This part of the coast from Spurn Head to Bridlington has lost a mile of shore in the last hundred years and is currently losing a further 6.5 feet (2m) every year.* ***Map ref. E4***

259

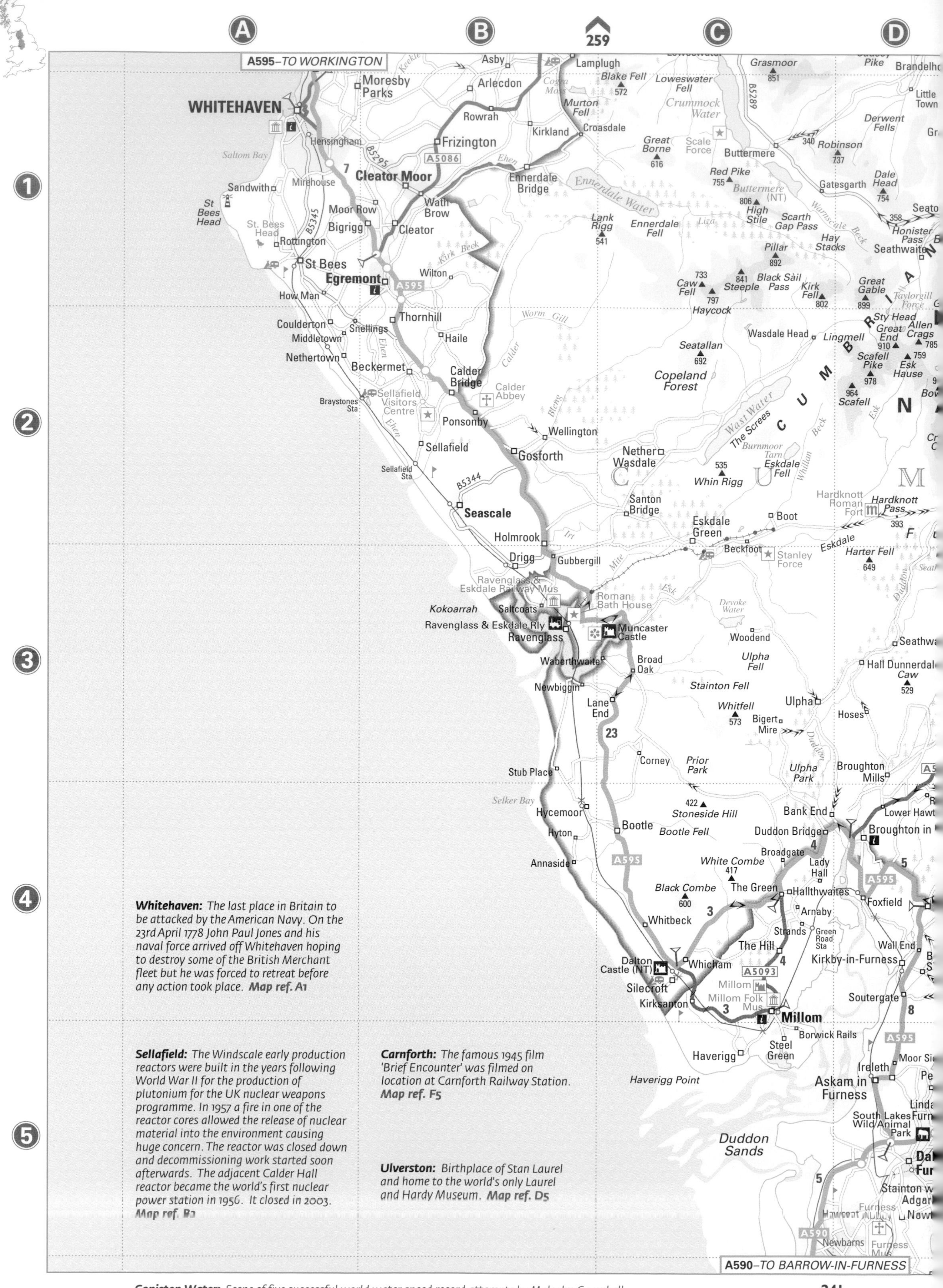

A
B
C
D
1
2
3
4
5
A595–TO WORKINGTON
WHITEHAVEN
Moresby Parks
Asby
Arlecdon
Lamplugh
Blake Fell
572
Loweswater Fell
Grasmoor
851
Rowrah
Murton Fell
Crummock Water
B5289
Little Town
Derwent Fells
Kirkland
Croasdale
Frizington
Hensingham
Saltom Bay
B5295
A5086
Great Borne
616
Scale Force
Buttermere
340
Robinson
737
Cleator Moor
Ennerdale Bridge
Ennerdale Water
Red Pike
755
Buttermere (NT)
Gatesgarth
Dale Head
754
Sandwith
Mirehouse
St Bees Head
St. Bees Head
B5345
Moor Row
Bigrigg
Wath Brow
Cleator
Rottington
Lank Rigg
541
Ennerdale Fell
806
High Stile
Scarth Gap Pass
Hay Stacks
358
Honister Pass
Seatoller
Seathwaite
Pillar
892
St Bees
Egremont
A595
Wilton
Kirk Beck
733
Caw Fell
841
Steeple
Black Sail Pass
Kirk Fell
802
797
Haycock
Great Gable
899
How Man
Thornhill
Worm Gill
Coulderton
Snellings
Middletown
Haile
Nethertown
Beckermet
Calder Bridge
Calder Abbey
Seatallan
692
Wasdale Head
Lingmell
Sty Head
Great End
910
Allen Crags
785
Scafell Pike
978
Esk Hause
759
964
Scafell
Copeland Forest
Braystones Sta
Sellafield Visitors Centre
Ponsonby
Wellington
Wast Water
The Screes
Sellafield
Gosforth
Nether Wasdale
Burnmoor Tarn
535
Whin Rigg
Eskdale Fell
Sellafield Sta
B5344
Seascale
Santon Bridge
Hardknott Roman Fort
Hardknott Pass
393
Holmrook
Eskdale Green
Boot
Eskdale
Drigg
Gubbergill
Beckfoot
Stanley Force
Harter Fell
649
Ravenglass & Eskdale Railway Mus
Roman Bath House
Kokoarrah
Saltcoats
Ravenglass & Eskdale Rly
Ravenglass
Muncaster Castle
Devoke Water
Woodend
Seathwaite
Waberthwaite
Broad Oak
Ulpha Fell
Hall Dunnerdale
Caw
529
Newbiggin
Stainton Fell
Lane End
Whitfell
573
Ulpha
Hoses
Bigert Mire
23
Corney
Prior Park
Stub Place
Ulpha Park
Broughton Mills
Selker Bay
422
Stoneside Hill
Bank End
Lower Hawthwaite
Hycemoor
Bootle
Bootle Fell
Duddon Bridge
Broughton in Furness
Hyton
A595
Broadgate
Annaside
White Combe
417
Lady Hall
Black Combe
600
The Green
Hallthwaites
Foxfield
Whitbeck
Arnaby
Strands
Green Road Sta
The Hill
Wall End
Dalton Castle (NT)
Whicham
A5093
Kirkby-in-Furness
Silecroft
Millom
Millom Folk Mus
Soutergate
Kirksanton
Millom
Borwick Rails
Haverigg
Steel Green
Haverigg Point
Moor Side
Ireleth
Askam in Furness
South Lakes Wild Animal Park
Duddon Sands
Stainton with Adgarley
Furness Abbey
Newbarns
Furness Mus
A590
A590–TO BARROW-IN-FURNESS

Whitehaven: *The last place in Britain to be attacked by the American Navy. On the 23rd April 1778 John Paul Jones and his naval force arrived off Whitehaven hoping to destroy some of the British Merchant fleet but he was forced to retreat before any action took place.* ***Map ref. A1***

Sellafield: *The Windscale early production reactors were built in the years following World War II for the production of plutonium for the UK nuclear weapons programme. In 1957 a fire in one of the reactor cores allowed the release of nuclear material into the environment causing huge concern. The reactor was closed down and decommissioning work started soon afterwards. The adjacent Calder Hall reactor became the world's first nuclear power station in 1956. It closed in 2003.* ***Map ref. B2***

Carnforth: *The famous 1945 film 'Brief Encounter' was filmed on location at Carnforth Railway Station.* ***Map ref. F5***

Ulverston: *Birthplace of Stan Laurel and home to the world's only Laurel and Hardy Museum.* ***Map ref. D5***

Coniston Water: *Scene of five successful world water speed record attempts by Malcolm Campbell and Donald Campbell between 1939 and 1959. Donald Campbell was killed here on the 4th January 1967 whilst trying to break his own record, when his boat Bluebird K7 bounced off the surface of the lake at about 300 mph (483 km/h), somersaulted several times and then sank. The wreck of Bluebird and Campbell's remains were eventually recovered from the lake in March 2001.* ***Map ref. E3***

241

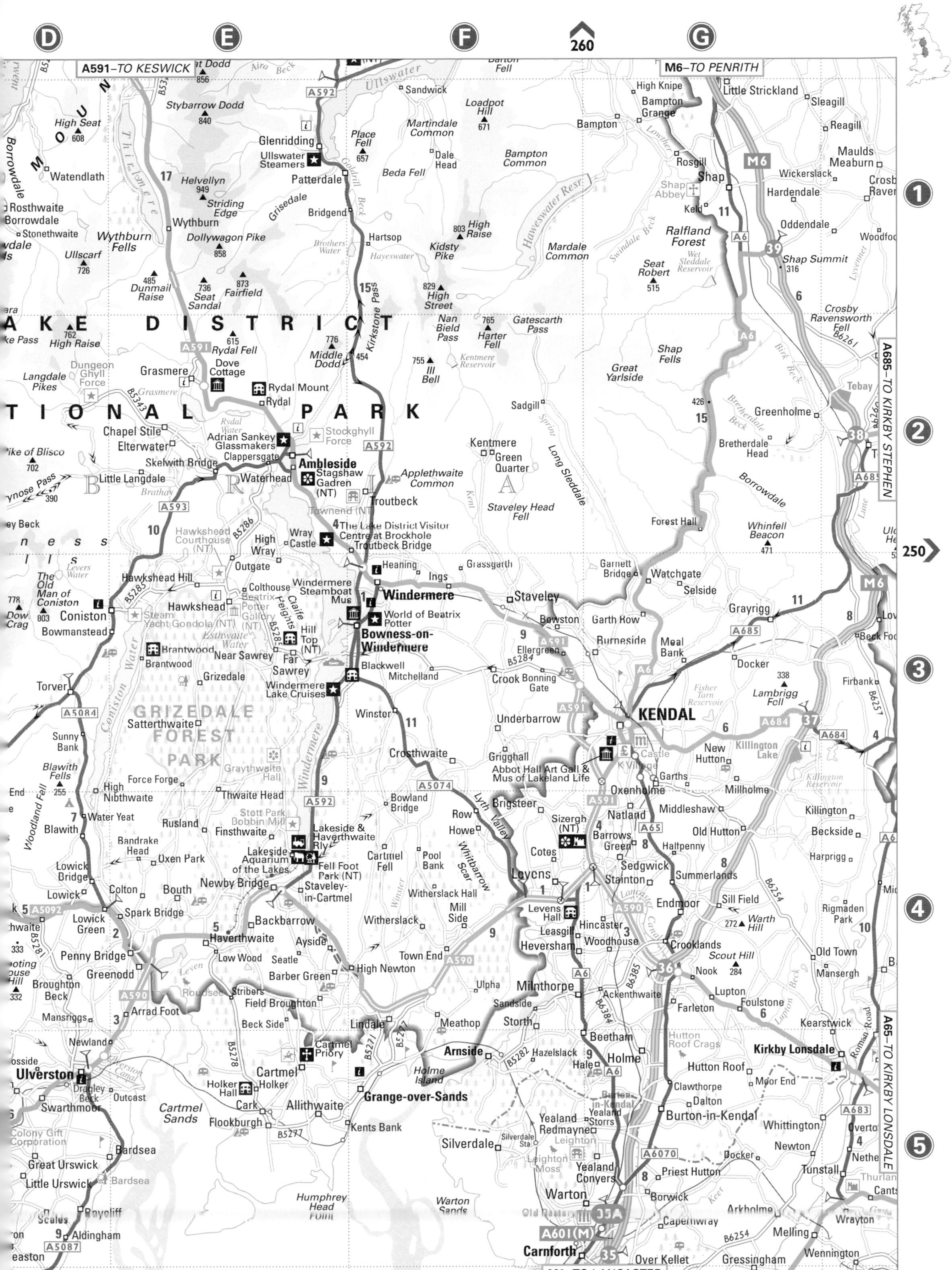

D
E
F
G
260
A591–TO KESWICK
M6–TO PENRITH
A685–TO KIRKBY STEPHEN
A65–TO KIRKBY LONSDALE
M6–TO LANCASTER
250
1
2
3
4
5
LAKE DISTRICT NATIONAL PARK
High Seat 608
Watendlath
Rosthwaite
Borrowdale
Stonethwaite
Wythburn Fells
Ullscarf 726
Stybarrow Dodd 840
Helvellyn 949
Striding Edge
Wythburn
Dollywagon Pike 858
Thirlmere
Dunmail Raise
Seat Sandal
Fairfield
High Raise
Langdale Pikes
Dungeon Ghyll Force
Grasmere
Dove Cottage
Rydal Mount
Rydal
Rydal Fell
Glenridding
Ullswater Steamers
Patterdale
Bridgend
Grisedale
Ullswater
Sandwick
Place Fell 657
Martindale Common
Loadpot Hill 671
Dale Head
Beda Fell
Bampton Common
Bampton
Hartsop
Brothers Water
Hayeswater
Kidsty Pike
High Raise
Haweswater Resr.
Mardale Common
High Street
Nan Bield Pass
Harter Fell
Gatescarth Pass
Kentmere Reservoir
Ill Bell
Kirkstone Pass
Middle Dodd
Little Strickland
Sleagill
Reagill
High Knipe
Bampton Grange
Maulds Meaburn
Rosgill
Shap
Shap Abbey
Wickerslack
Hardendale
Keld
Oddendale
Ralfland Forest
Wet Sleddale Reservoir
Seat Robert 515
Shap Summit 316
Crosby Ravensworth Fell
Shap Fells
Great Yarlside
Tebay
Greenholme
Bretherdale Head
Borrowdale
Whinfell Beacon 471
Sadgill
Long Sleddale
Kentmere
Green Quarter
Staveley Head Fell
Applethwaite Common
Chapel Stile
Elterwater
Adrian Sankey Glassmakers
Clappersgate
Skelwith Bridge
Little Langdale
Ambleside
Stagshaw Gadren (NT)
Stockghyll Force
Waterhead
Troutbeck
Townend (NT)
The Lake District Visitor Centre at Brockhole
Troutbeck Bridge
Wray Castle
High Wray
Hawkshead Courthouse (NT)
Outgate
Hawkshead Hill
Colthouse
Hawkshead
Beatrix Potter Gallery (NT)
Steam Yacht Gondola (NT)
Coniston
Bowmanstead
Esthwaite Water
Brantwood
Near Sawrey
Far Sawrey
Hill Top (NT)
Windermere Steamboat Mus
Windermere
World of Beatrix Potter
Bowness-on-Windermere
Blackwell
Windermere Lake Cruises
Heaning
Ings
Grassgarth
Staveley
Garnett Bridge
Watchgate
Selside
Bowston
Garth Row
Burneside
Meal Bank
Grayrigg
Forest Hall
Ellergreen
Crook
Bonning Gate
Mitchelland
Docker
Lambrigg Fell
Firbank
KENDAL
Castle
Abbot Hall Art Gall & Mus of Lakeland Life
Oxenholme
New Hutton
Killington Lake
Killington Reservoir
Millholme
Middleshaw
Killington
Beckside
Underbarrow
Grigghall
Brigsteer
Winster
Crosthwaite
Bowland Bridge
Row
Howe
Lyth Valley
Whitbarrow Scar
Pool Bank
Witherslack Hall
Witherslack
Mill Side
Sizergh (NT)
Natland
Barrows Green
Old Hutton
Haltpenny
Cotes
Levens
Levens Hall
Sedgwick
Stainton
Summerlands
Endmoor
Sill Field
Warth Hill
Rigmaden Park
Hincaster
Leasgill
Heversham
Woodhouse
Crooklands
Scout Hill 284
Old Town
Mansergh
Nook
Milnthorpe
Ackenthwaite
Lupton
Farleton
Foulstone
Kearstwick
Sandside
Storth
Beetham
Hutton Roof Crags
Kirkby Lonsdale
Arnside
Hazelslack
Hale
Holme
Hutton Roof
Moor End
Clawthorpe
Dalton
Burton-in-Kendal
Whittington
Yealand Redmayne
Yealand Storrs
Silverdale
Silverdale Sta
Leighton
Leighton Moss
Yealand Conyers
Priest Hutton
Docker
Newton
Tunstall
Warton
Borwick
Arkholme
Capernwray
Warton Sands
Melling
Wrayton
Carnforth
Over Kellet
Gressingham
Wennington
Tatham
Grizedale
Satterthwaite
GRIZEDALE FOREST PARK
Graythwaite Hall
Thwaite Head
Stott Park Bobbin Mill
Rusland
Finsthwaite
Lakeside & Haverthwaite Rly
Lakeside Aquarium of the Lakes
Fell Foot Park (NT)
Cartmel Fell
Newby Bridge
Staveley-in-Cartmel
Torver
Sunny Bank
Blawith Fells
Coniston Water
High Nibthwaite
Force Forge
Water Yeat
Blawith
Bandrake Head
Oxen Park
Lowick Bridge
Lowick
Colton
Bouth
Spark Bridge
Lowick Green
Backbarrow
Haverthwaite
Ayside
Low Wood
Seatle
Penny Bridge
Greenodd
Barber Green
High Newton
Town End
Ulpha
Broughton Beck
Mansriggs
Arrad Foot
Field Broughton
Beck Side
Lindale
Meathop
Newland
Ulverston
Dragley Beck
Outcast
Swarthmoor
Cartmel Priory
Cartmel
Holker Hall
Holker
Cark
Allithwaite
Grange-over-Sands
Cartmel Sands
Flookburgh
Kents Bank
Holme Island
Bardsea
Great Urswick
Little Urswick
Humphrey Head Point
Scales
Aldingham
A591
A592
A593
A5084
A5092
A590
A5087
A5074
A685
A684
A6
A65
A6070
A683
A601(M)
M6
B5286
B5285
B5343
B5284
B5277
B5271
B5278
B5282
B6254
B6257
B6385
B6384
B6261

Grasmere: *William Wordsworth lived for a number of years at nearby Dove Cottage. He died in 1850 and is buried in the churchyard of St Oswald's Church. His simple tombstone has since become one of the most visited literary shrines in the world.* **Map ref. E2**

242

Windermere: *Lake Windermere is the largest natural lake in England. It is 12 miles (19.3km) long, 1 mile (1.6km) wide and 220 feet (67m) deep. The lake is a major centre for water sports and there are over 10,000 boats registered on the lake. Henry Segrave was killed here in breaking the world water speed record in 1930.* **Map ref. E3**

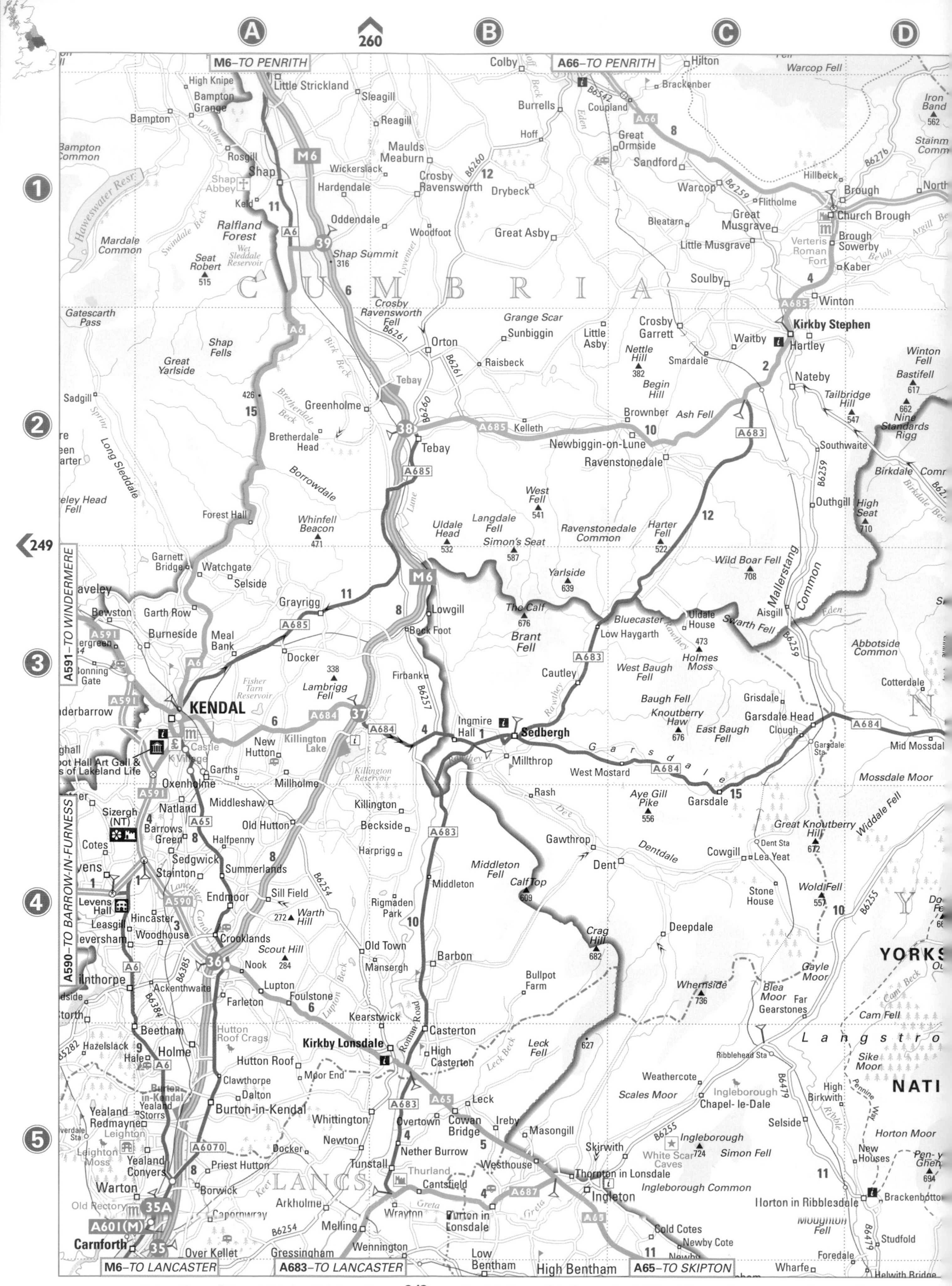

A
B
C
D
260
249
242
1
2
3
4
5
M6–TO PENRITH
A66–TO PENRITH
A591–TO WINDERMERE
A590–TO BARROW-IN-FURNESS
M6–TO LANCASTER
A683–TO LANCASTER
A65–TO SKIPTON
C U M B R I A
LANCS
YORKS
Warcop Fell
Hilton
Brackenber
Colby
Coupland
Burrells
Great Ormside
Sandford
Iron Band
562
High Knipe
Bampton Grange
Bampton
Bampton Common
Little Strickland
Sleagill
Reagill
Maulds Meaburn
Rosgill
Shap
Shap Abbey
Haweswater Resr.
Wickerslack
Hardendale
Crosby Ravensworth
Drybeck
Warcop
Flitholme
Hillbeck
Brough
Church Brough
North
Keld
Ralfland Forest
Mardale Common
Oddendale
Woodfoot
Great Asby
Bleatarn
Great Musgrave
Little Musgrave
Verteris Roman Fort
Brough Sowerby
Kaber
Seat Robert
515
Wet Sleddale Reservoir
Shap Summit
316
Soulby
Winton
Gatescarth Pass
Crosby Ravensworth Fell
Grange Scar
Sunbiggin
Crosby Garrett
Little Asby
Kirkby Stephen
Hartley
Waitby
Smardale
Nettle Hill
382
Begin Hill
Orton
Raisbeck
Shap Fells
Great Yarlside
Tebay
Nateby
Winton Fell
Bastifell
617
Tailbridge Hill
547
Nine Standards Rigg
662
Sadgill
426
Greenholme
Bretherdale Beck
Bretherdale Head
Brownber
Ash Fell
Kelleth
Newbiggin-on-Lune
Ravenstonedale
Southwaite
Long Sleddale
Borrowdale
Birkdale Common
Outhgill
High Seat
710
West Fell
541
Forest Hall
Whinfell Beacon
471
Uldale Head
532
Langdale Fell
Simon's Seat
587
Ravenstonedale Common
Harter Fell
522
Wild Boar Fell
708
Mallerstang Common
Garnett Bridge
Watchgate
Selside
Yarlside
639
Grayrigg
Bowston
Garth Row
Burneside
Meal Bank
Lowgill
The Calf
676
Brant Fell
Bluecaster
Uldale House
Low Haygarth
Swarth Fell
Aisgill
473
Holmes Moss
Abbotside Common
Docker
Beck Foot
Fisher Tarn Reservoir
338
Lambrigg Fell
Firbank
Cautley
West Baugh Fell
Cotterdale
Bonning Gate
KENDAL
Baugh Fell
Grisdale
Knoutberry Haw
676
East Baugh Fell
Garsdale Head
Clough
Garsdale Sta
Mid Mossdale
Ingmire Hall
Sedbergh
New Hutton
Killington Lake
Castle
K Village
Abbot Hall Art Gall & Mus of Lakeland Life
Garths
Millthrop
West Mostard
G a r s d a l e
Mossdale Moor
Oxenholme
Millholme
Killington Reservoir
Rash
Aye Gill Pike
556
Garsdale
Sizergh (NT)
Natland
Middleshaw
Killington
Dee
Great Knoutberry Hill
672
Widdale Fell
Barrows Green
Old Hutton
Beckside
Halfpenny
Cotes
Gawthrop
Dentdale
Dent
Cowgill
Lea Yeat
Dent Sta
Sedgwick
Harprigg
Stainton
Summerlands
Middleton Fell
Levens
Middleton
Calf Top
609
Levens Hall
Endmoor
Sill Field
Rigmaden Park
Stone House
Wold Fell
557
Hincaster
272
Warth Hill
Leasgill
Woodhouse
Heversham
Crooklands
Old Town
Deepdale
Crag Hill
682
Scout Hill
284
Nook
Manserg
Barbon
Bullpot Farm
Gayle Moor
Milnthorpe
Ackenthwaite
Lupton
Foulstone
Whernside
736
Blea Moor
Far Gearstones
Farleton
Cam Fell
Beetham
Hutton Roof Crags
Kearstwick
Roman Road
Casterton
Hazelslack
Holme
Hale
Kirkby Lonsdale
High Casterton
Leck Fell
Leck Beck
627
L a n g s t r o
Hutton Roof
Moor End
Ribblehead Sta
Sike Moor
Clawthorpe
Weathercote
Burton-in-Kendal
Dalton
Scales Moor
Ingleborough Caves
Chapel-le-Dale
High Birkwith
Pennine Way
NATI
Yealand Redmayne
Yealand Storrs
Whittington
Overtown
Leck
Cowan Bridge
Ireby
Masongill
Selside
Leighton
Newton
Nether Burrow
Horton Moor
Yealand Conyers
Leighton Moss
Docker
Priest Hutton
Tunstall
Westhouse
Skirwith
Ingleborough
724
White Scar Caves
Simon Fell
New Houses
Pen-y-Ghent
694
Warton
Thurland
Borwick
Cantsfield
Thornton in Lonsdale
Ingleborough Common
Old Rectory
Arkholme
Wrayton
Burton in Lonsdale
Ingleton
Horton in Ribblesdale
Brackenbottom
Capernwray
Greta
Melling
Moughton Fell
Carnforth
Over Kellet
Gressingham
Wennington
Cold Cotes
Newby Cote
Studfold
Foredale
Low Bentham
High Bentham
Wharfe
Helwith Bridge
Hale

Orton: *Home of George Whitehead (1636–1723) one of the founders of the Quaker Movement. Like many Quakers at the time Whitehead was imprisoned for his beliefs.* ***Map ref. B2***

Kendal: *Home of the famous Kendal Mint Cake, popular as an energy boosting food and eaten by Shackleton on his 1914–1917 Transarctic Expedition and by the 1953 Everest Expedition. Reputedly made by accident when a local confectioner Joseph Wiper, at his tiny Ferney Green factory, was intending to make glacier mints. It is now famous the world over.* ***Map ref. A3***

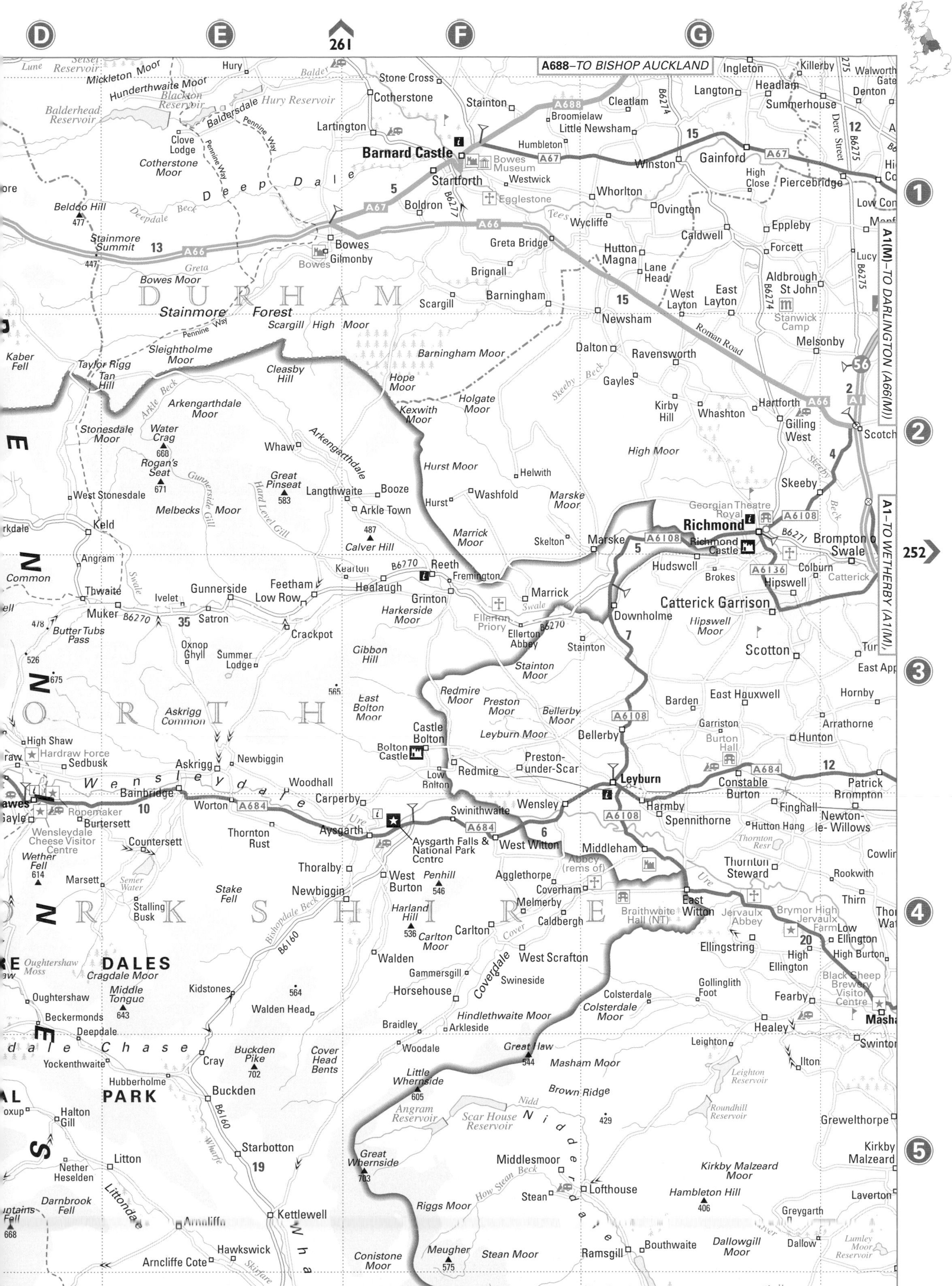
D
E
F
G
261
A688–TO BISHOP AUCKLAND
Mickleton Moor
Hunderthwaite Moor
Blackton Reservoir
Balderhead Reservoir
Hury
Hury Reservoir
Baldersdale
Pennine Way
Clove Lodge
Cotherstone Moor
Deep Dale
Deepdale
Stone Cross
Cotherstone
Lartington
Barnard Castle
Startforth
Boldron
Bowes Museum
Westwick
Egglestone
Stainton
Broomielaw
Little Newsham
Cleatlam
Humbleton
Winston
Whorlton
Ingleton
Langton
Headlam
Killerby
Summerhouse
Walworth Gate
Denton
Gainford
High Close
Piercebridge
Dere Street
Beldoo Hill
477
Stainmore Summit
447
A66
A67
Bowes
Gilmonby
Bowes Moor
Greta
Greta Bridge
Brignall
Barningham
Scargill
Wycliffe
Ovington
Hutton Magna
Lane Head
Caldwell
Eppleby
Forcett
Aldbrough St John
West Layton
East Layton
Stanwick Camp
Melsonby
Lucy
Low Coniscliffe
DURHAM
Stainmore Forest
Scargill High Moor
Barningham Moor
Newsham
Dalton
Ravensworth
Roman Road
Gayles
Kirby Hill
Washton
Hartforth
Gilling West
Scotch Corner
A1(M)–TO DARLINGTON (A66(M))
Kaber Fell
Taylor Rigg
Tan Hill
Sleightholme Moor
Cleasby Hill
Hope Moor
Holgate Moor
Kexwith Moor
Arkengarthdale Moor
Arkengarthdale
Stonesdale Moor
Water Crag
660
Whaw
Rogan's Seat
671
Great Pinseat
583
Langthwaite
Booze
Arkle Town
Hurst Moor
Hurst
Washfold
Helwith
Marske Moor
High Moor
Skeeby
West Stonesdale
Melbecks Moor
Keld
487
Calver Hill
Marrick Moor
Skelton
Marske
Richmond
Georgian Theatre Royal
Richmond Castle
Brompton on Swale
A1–TO WETHERBY (A1(M))
252
Angram
Common
Thwaite
Muker
Ivelet
Gunnerside
Feetham
Low Row
Kearton
Healaugh
Reeth
Fremington
Grinton
Harkerside Moor
Marrick
Ellerton Priory
Ellerton Abbey
Hudswell
Brokes
Colburn
Catterick
Hipswell
Catterick Garrison
Downholme
Hipswell Moor
Butter Tubs Pass
Satron
Crackpot
Oxnop Ghyll
Summer Lodge
Gibbon Hill
Stainton
Stainton Moor
Scotton
East Appleton
526
675
565
East Bolton Moor
Redmire Moor
Preston Moor
Bellerby Moor
Barden
East Hauxwell
Hornby
NORTH
Askrigg Common
Castle Bolton
Leyburn Moor
Bellerby
Garriston
Burton Hall
Arrathorne
Hunton
High Shaw
Hardraw Force
Sedbusk
Askrigg
Newbiggin
Bolton Castle
Redmire
Preston-under-Scar
Leyburn
Constable Burton
Patrick Brompton
Wensleydale
Woodhall
Low Bolton
Bainbridge
Carperby
Harmby
Spennithorne
Finghall
Newton-le-Willows
Hutton Hang
Hawes
Gayle
Ropemaker
Burtersett
Worton
A684
Aysgarth
Swinithwaite
Wensley
West Witton
Middleham
Thornton Rust
Aysgarth Falls & National Park Centre
Wensleydale Cheese Visitor Centre
Countersett
Widdale Fell
614
Marsett
Semer Water
Thoralby
West Burton
Penhill
546
Agglethorpe
Coverham
Abbey (rems of)
Thornton Steward
Rookwith
Stake Fell
Newbiggin
Harland Hill
536
Carlton Moor
Carlton
Melmerby
Caldbergh
Braithwaite Hall (NT)
East Witton
Jervaulx Abbey
Brymor High Jervaulx Farm
Thirn
Low Ellington
High Ellington
High Burton
YORKSHIRE
Stalling Busk
Bishopdale Beck
B6160
Cover
Coverdale
West Scrafton
Ellingstring
DALES
Oughtershaw Moss
Cragdale Moor
Walden
Gammersgill
Swineside
Gollinglith Foot
Black Sheep Brewery Visitor Centre
Oughtershaw
Middle Tongue
643
Kidstones
564
Horsehouse
Colsterdale
Colsterdale Moor
Fearby
Beckermonds
Walden Head
Hindlethwaite Moor
Healey
Masham
Deepdale
Braidley
Arkleside
Leighton
Swinton
Langstrothdale Chase
Yockenthwaite
Cray
Buckden Pike
702
Cover Head Bents
Woodale
Great Haw
544
Masham Moor
Ilton
Leighton Reservoir
Hubberholme
PARK
Buckden
Little Whernside
605
Brown Ridge
Nidd
Angram Reservoir
Scar House Reservoir
Roundhill Reservoir
Grewelthorpe
Halton Gill
B6160
Wharfe
429
Nidderdale
Starbotton
Great Whernside
703
Middlesmoor
Kirkby Malzeard Moor
Kirkby Malzeard
Litton
Nether Heselden
Littondale
How Stean Beck
Stean
Lofthouse
Hambleton Hill
406
Laverton
Darnbrook Fell
Fountains Fell
668
Arncliffe
Kettlewell
Riggs Moor
Greygarth
Hawkswick
Arncliffe Cote
Skirfare
Wharfedale
Conistone Moor
Meugher
575
Stean Moor
Ramsgill
Bouthwaite
Dallowgill Moor
Dallow
Lumley Moor Reservoir
1
2
3
4
5

Askrigg: *The village scenes for 'All Creatures Great and Small' were filmed here. The TV series, based on books by James Herriot was about country vets located in the Yorkshire Dales. The series ran from 1978 to 1990.* ***Map ref. E3***

243

Tan Hill: *The highest pub in Britain is the Tan Hill Inn, which stands 1732 feet (528m) above sea level.* ***Map ref. E2***

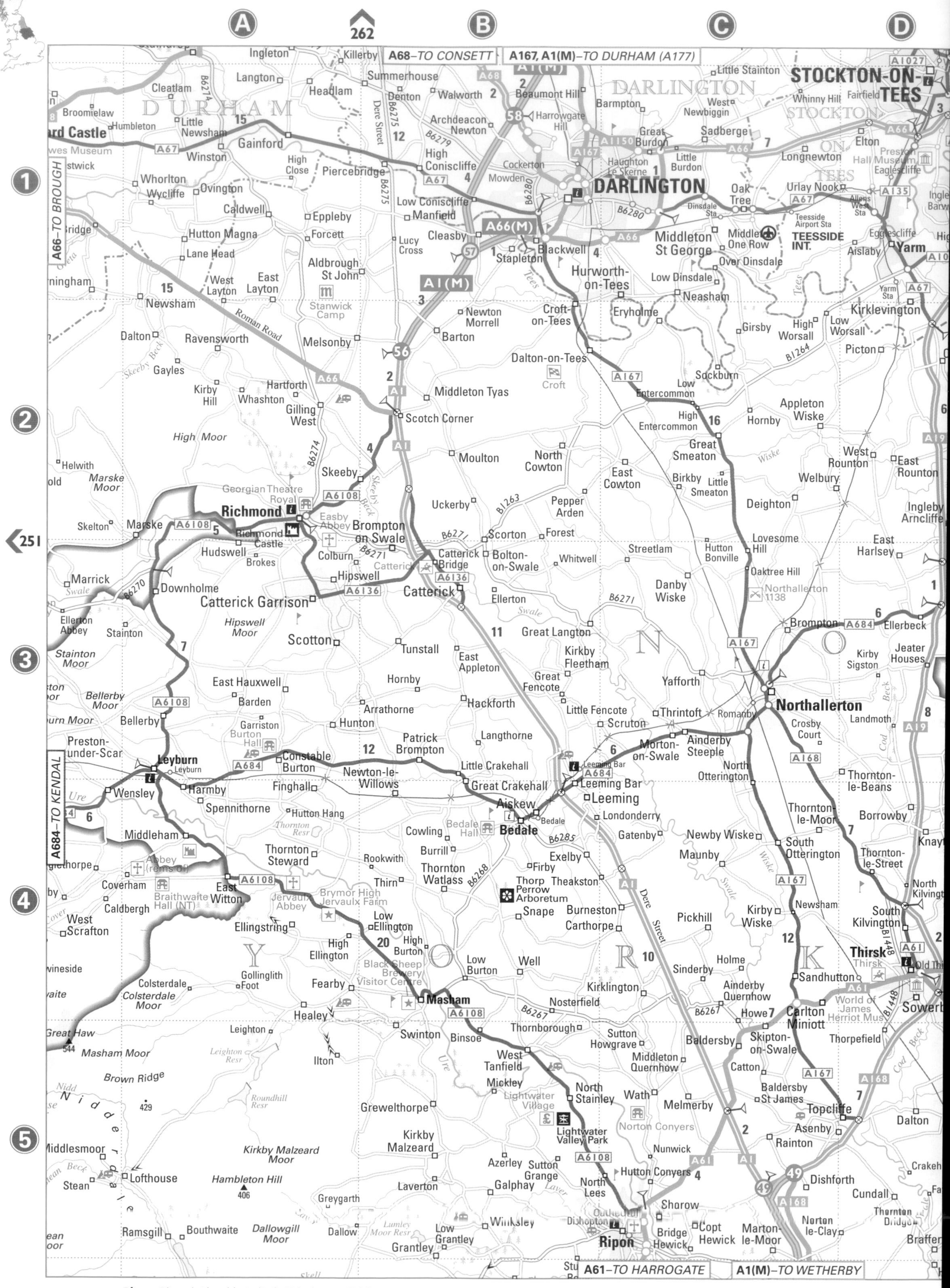
A
B
C
D
262
1
2
3
4
5
251
244
A68–TO CONSETT
A167, A1(M)–TO DURHAM (A177)
A66–TO BROUGH
A684–TO KENDAL
A61–TO HARROGATE
A1(M)–TO WETHERBY
DURHAM
DARLINGTON
STOCKTON-ON-TEES
STOCKTON-ON-TEES
NORTH YORKSHIRE
Ingleton
Killerby
Langton
Headlam
Summerhouse
Denton
Walworth
Beaumont Hill
Harrowgate Hill
Barmpton
Little Stainton
West Newbiggin
Whinny Hill
Fairfield
Cleatlam
Broomielaw
Humbleton
Little Newsham
Barnard Castle
Bowes Museum
Gainford
Winston
Archdeacon Newton
Great Burdon
Sadberge
Elton
Preston Hall Museum
Egglescliffe
Little Burdon
Longnewton
High Close
Piercebridge
High Coniscliffe
Cockerton
Mowden
Haughton Le Skerne
DARLINGTON
Oak Tree
Urlay Nook
Allens West Sta
Whorlton
Wycliffe
Ovington
Low Coniscliffe
Manfield
Dinsdale Sta
Teesside Airport Sta
Caldwell
Eppleby
Forcett
Hutton Magna
Lucy Cross
Cleasby
Blackwell
Middleton St George
Middleton One Row
TEESSIDE INT.
Aislaby
Yarm
Lane Head
Aldbrough St John
Stapleton
Hurworth-on-Tees
Over Dinsdale
Low Dinsdale
West Layton
East Layton
Newsham
Stanwick Camp
Neasham
Yarm Sta
Kirklevington
Newton Morrell
Croft-on-Tees
Eryholme
Barton
Girsby
High Worsall
Low Worsall
Dalton
Ravensworth
Roman Road
Melsonby
Picton
Gayles
Dalton-on-Tees
Croft
Sockburn
Kirby Hill
Hartforth
Whashton
Gilling West
Middleton Tyas
Scotch Corner
Low Entercommon
High Entercommon
Appleton Wiske
Hornby
High Moor
Moulton
North Cowton
Great Smeaton
Helwith
Marske Moor
Georgian Theatre Royal
Skeeby
East Cowton
Birkby
Little Smeaton
West Rounton
East Rounton
Welbury
Richmond
Easby Abbey
Brompton on Swale
Uckerby
Pepper Arden
Deighton
Ingleby Arncliffe
Skelton
Marske
Richmond Castle
Scorton
Forest
Lovesome Hill
East Harlsey
Hudswell
Brokes
Colburn
Catterick Bridge
Bolton-on-Swale
Whitwell
Streetlam
Hutton Bonville
Oaktree Hill
Marrick
Hipswell
Catterick
Downholme
Catterick Garrison
Ellerton
Danby Wiske
Northallerton 1138
Ellerton Abbey
Stainton
Brompton
Ellerbeck
Stainton Moor
Scotton
Hipswell Moor
Tunstall
East Appleton
Great Langton
Kirby Fleetham
Kirby Sigston
Jeater Houses
Bellerby Moor
East Hauxwell
Hornby
Great Fencote
Yafforth
Barden
Arrathorne
Hackforth
Little Fencote
Thrintoft
Romanby
Northallerton
Landmoth
Bellerby
Garriston
Burton Hall
Hunton
Scruton
Crosby Court
Preston-under-Scar
Patrick Brompton
Langthorne
Morton-on-Swale
Ainderby Steeple
Leyburn
Constable Burton
Little Crakehall
Leeming Bar
North Otterington
Thornton-le-Beans
Wensley
Harmby
Finghall
Newton-le-Willows
Great Crakehall
Leeming
Spennithorne
Hutton Hang
Aiskew
Bedale
Londonderry
Thornton-le-Moor
Borrowby
Middleham
Thornton Resr
Cowling
Bedale Hall
Gatenby
Newby Wiske
South Otterington
Thornton Steward
Burrill
Exelby
Maunby
Thornton-le-Street
Coverham
Rookwith
Thornton Watlass
Firby
Jervaulx Abbey
Thirn
Thorp Perrow Arboretum
Theakston
Newsham
North Kilvington
Caldbergh
Braithwaite Hall (NT)
East Witton
Brymor High Jervaulx Farm
Snape
Burneston
Pickhill
Kirby Wiske
South Kilvington
West Scrafton
Ellingstring
Low Ellington
Carthorpe
High Ellington
High Burton
Well
Holme
Thirsk
Sinderby
Sandhutton
Colsterdale
Colsterdale Moor
Gollinglith Foot
Black Sheep Brewery Visitor Centre
Fearby
Low Burton
Kirklington
Ainderby Quernhow
World of James Herriot Mus
Sowerby
Masham
Nosterfield
Howe
Carlton Miniott
Great Haw
Healey
Swinton
Binsoe
Thornborough
Sutton Howgrave
Baldersby
Skipton-on-Swale
Thorpefield
Masham Moor
Leighton
Leighton Resr
Ilton
West Tanfield
Middleton Quernhow
Catton
Brown Ridge
Mickley
Lightwater Village
North Stainley
Wath
Melmerby
Baldersby St James
Topcliffe
Dalton
Roundhill Resr
Grewelthorpe
Norton Conyers
Asenby
Nidderdale
Lightwater Valley Park
Rainton
Middlesmoor
Kirkby Malzeard
Kirkby Malzeard Moor
Nunwick
Azerley
Sutton Grange
Hutton Conyers
Dishforth
Stean
Lofthouse
Hambleton Hill
Laverton
Galphay
North Lees
Cundall
Greygarth
Sharow
Norton-le-Clay
Ramsgill
Bouthwaite
Dallowgill Moor
Dallow
Lumley Moor Resr
Low Grantley
Winksley
Bishopton
Cathedral
Ripon
Bridge Hewick
Copt Hewick
Marton-le-Moor
Grantley

Ripon: *Ripon is the oldest city in Britain with a charter dating back to AD886.* ***Map ref. C5***

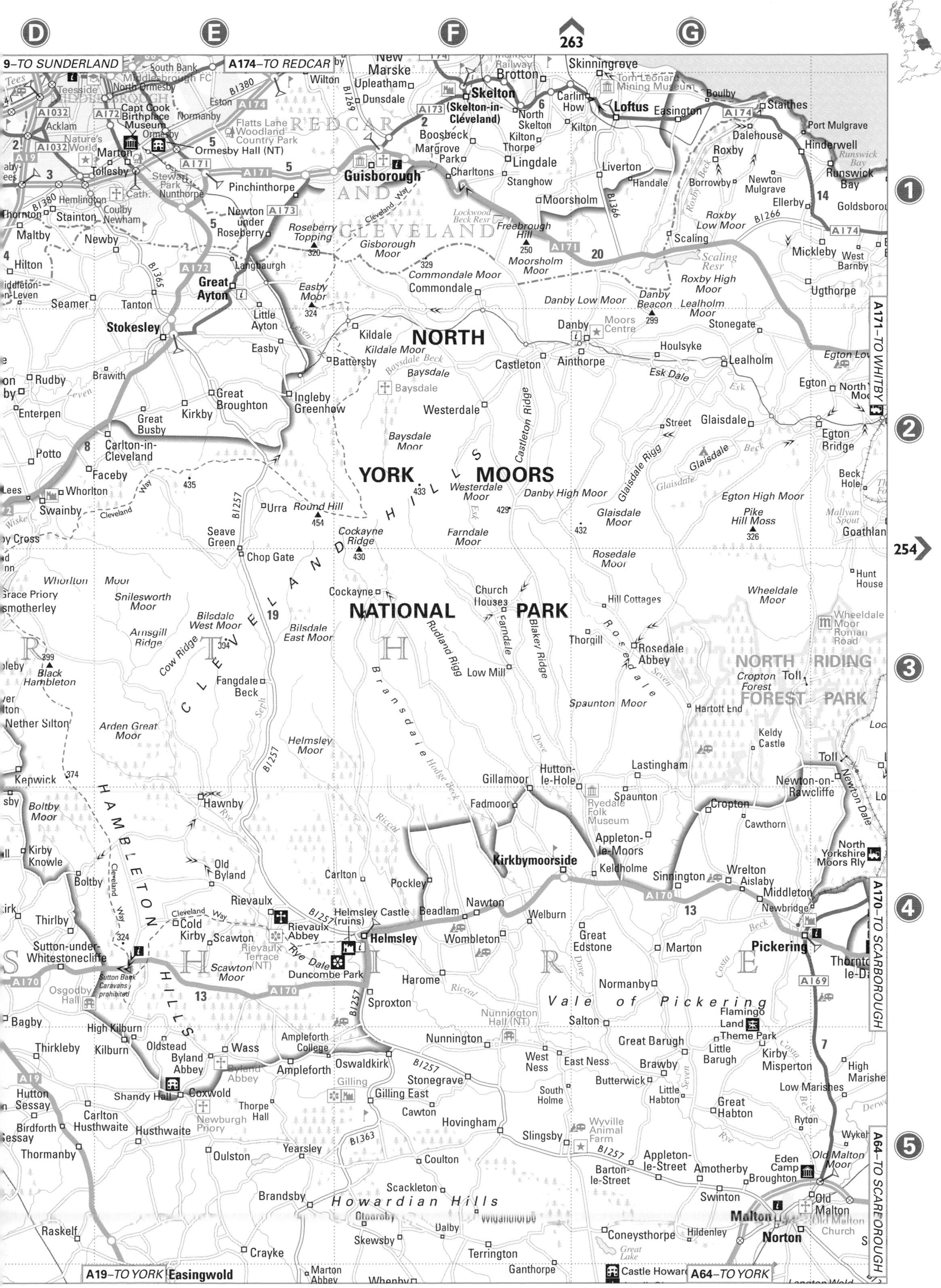

Boulby: *Boulby Cliff is the highest sea cliff on the east coast of Britain at 666 feet (203m).* ***Map ref. G1***

245

Marton: *Captain James Cook was born here on 27th October 1728. Cook enlisted in the Royal Navy and in 1768 began the first of three voyages to the Pacific where he spent over eight years charting previously unknown islands. He was stabbed to death by natives on the island of Hawaii in February 1779.* ***Map ref. G4***

263

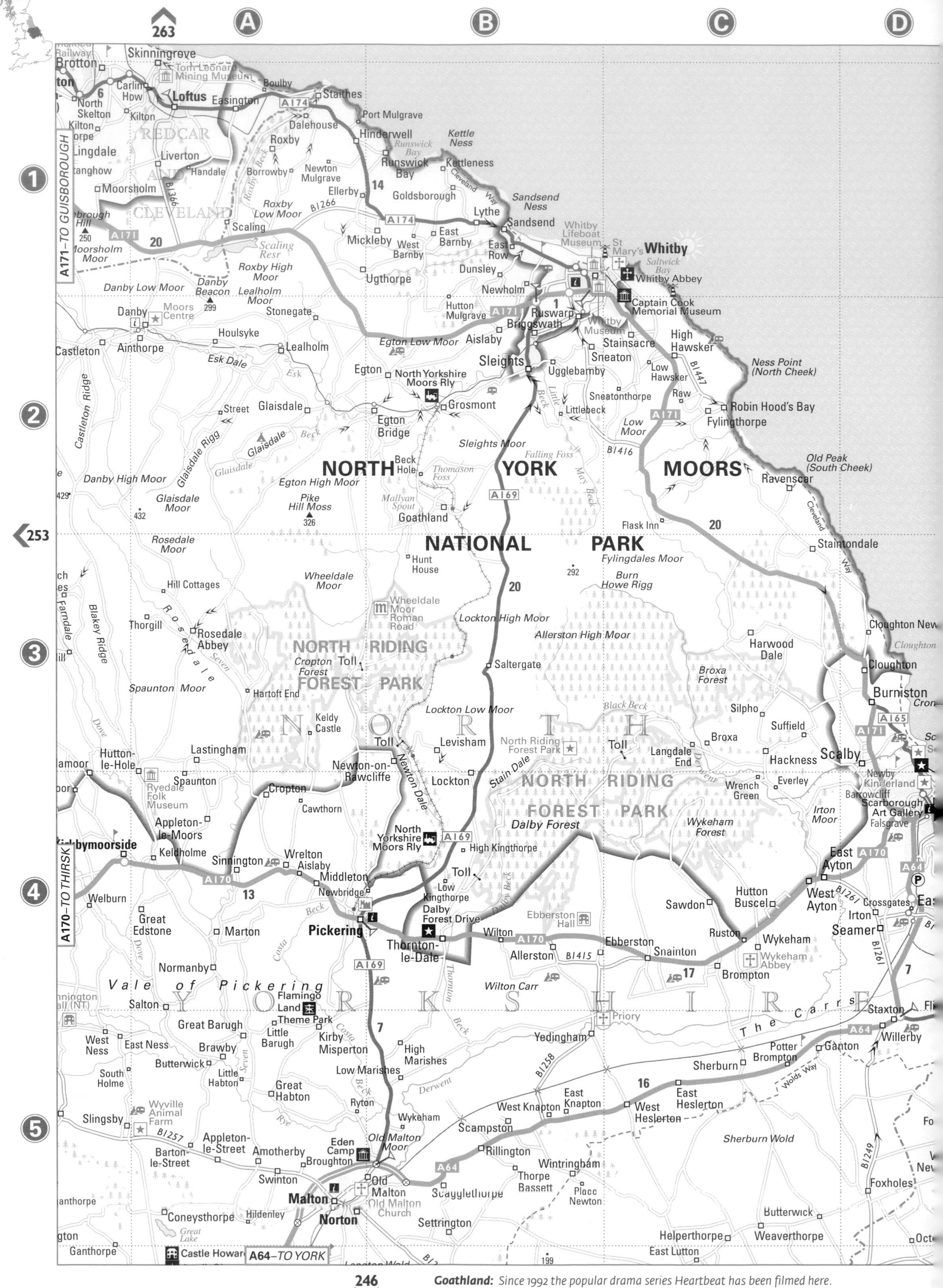
A
B
C
D
1
2
3
4
5
Skinningrove
Brotton
Tom Leonard Mining Museum
Boulby
Staithes
Carlin How
Loftus
Easington
A174
North Skelton
Kilton
Port Mulgrave
Dalehouse
REDCAR
AND
CLEVELAND
Lingdale
Liverton
Roxby
Hinderwell
Runswick Bay
Kettle Ness
Kettleness
Handale
Borrowby
Newton Mulgrave
Moorsholm
Ellerby
14
Goldsborough
Roxby Low Moor
B1266
Lythe
Sandsend Ness
Sandsend
Scaling
Scaling Resr
A171
20
A174
Mickleby
West Barnby
East Barnby
East Row
Whitby Lifeboat Museum
St Mary's
Whitby
Saltwick Bay
Whitby Abbey
A171–TO GUISBOROUGH
250
Moorsholm Moor
Roxby High Moor
Danby Beacon
Ugthorpe
Dunsley
Newholm
Captain Cook Memorial Museum
Danby Low Moor
299
Lealholm Moor
Hutton Mulgrave
1
Ruswarp
Briggswath
Whitby Museum
Stonegate
Danby
Moors Centre
Houlsyke
Lealholm
Egton Low Moor
Aislaby
Stainsacre
High Hawsker
Ainthorpe
Castleton
Esk Dale
Esk
Sleights
Sneaton
Egton
North Yorkshire Moors Rly
Ugglebarnby
Low Hawsker
B1447
Ness Point (North Cheek)
Castleton Ridge
Street
Glaisdale
Grosmont
Raw
Sneatonthorpe
Littlebeck
Robin Hood's Bay
Fylingthorpe
A171
Egton Bridge
Beck
Glaisdale Rigg
Glaisdale
Sleights Moor
Low Moor
Falling Foss
B1416
Old Peak (South Cheek)
Danby High Moor
Glaisdale
Egton High Moor
NORTH
Beck Hole
Thomason Foss
YORK
MOORS
Ravenscar
429
Glaisdale Moor
Pike Hill Moss
Mallyan Spout
A169
432
326
Goathland
Flask Inn
20
253
Rosedale Moor
NATIONAL
PARK
Staintondale
Fylingdales Moor
Hunt House
292
Burn Howe Rigg
Wheeldale Moor
Hill Cottages
20
Wheeldale Moor Roman Road
Farndale
Blakey Ridge
Thorgill
Rosedale
Rosedale Abbey
Lockton High Moor
Allerston High Moor
Cloughton Newlands
Cloughton
NORTH RIDING
FOREST PARK
Crompton Forest
Toll
Seven
Saltergate
Harwood Dale
Broxa Forest
Spaunton Moor
Hartoft End
Lockton Low Moor
Black Beck
Silpho
Burniston
A165
A171
Dove
Keldy Castle
N
O
R
T
H
Suffield
Broxa
Toll
Levisham
North Riding Forest Park
Hutton-le-Hole
Lastingham
Toll
Langdale End
Derwent
Hackness
Scalby
Newton-on-Rawcliffe
Stain Dale
Spaunton
Lockton
Newton Dale
Everley
Newby
Kinderland
Ryedale Folk Museum
Crompton
Wrench Green
Barrowcliff
Scarborough Art Gallery
Cawthorn
Irton Moor
Appleton-le-Moors
Dalby Forest
Wykeham Forest
Falsgrave
Kirkbymoorside
North Yorkshire Moors Rly
A169
High Kingthorpe
Keldholme
Sinnington
Wrelton
East Ayton
A170
Aislaby
A170
A170–TO THIRSK
A170
Middleton
Toll
Low Kingthorpe
A64
Welburn
13
Newbridge
Dalby Beck
Hutton Buscel
West Ayton
B1261
Crossgates
Great Edstone
Marton
Pickering
Dalby Forest Drive
Ebberston Hall
Sawdon
Irton
Seamer
Dove
Costa
Thornton-le-Dale
Wilton
A170
Ebberston
Ruston
Wykeham
A169
Allerston
B1415
Snainton
Wykeham Abbey
B1261
Normanby
Thornton
Wilton Carr
17
Brompton
7
Vale of Pickering
Flamingo Land
Y
O
R
K
S
H
I
R
E
The Carrs
Salton
Theme Park
Priory
Staxton
Great Barugh
Little Barugh
Kirby Misperton
7
Yedingham
A64
Willerby
Costa
Ganton
West Ness
East Ness
Brawby
High Marishes
Potter Brompton
South Holme
Butterwick
Little Habton
Low Marishes
B1258
Sherburn
Great Habton
Derwent
16
East Heslerton
Wolds Way
Slingsby
Wyville Animal Farm
Ryton
West Knapton
East Knapton
West Heslerton
Rye
Wykeham
B1257
Appleton-le-Street
Eden Camp
Old Malton
Moor
Scampston
Sherburn Wold
Barton-le-Street
Amotherby
Broughton
Rillington
B1249
A64
Wintringham
Swinton
Old Malton
Thorpe Bassett
Place Newton
Foxholes
Malton
Old Malton Church
Scagglethorpe
Coneysthorpe
Hildenley
Norton
Settrington
Butterwick
Great Lake
Helperthorpe
Weaverthorpe
Ganthorpe
Castle Howard
A64–TO YORK
East Lutton
199

246

Goathland: *Since 1992 the popular drama series Heartbeat has been filmed here. In the series the village is called Aidensfield and frequent references are made to nearby Whitby* ***Map ref. B2.***
The spin-off hospital series 'The Royal' is located in Scarborough. ***Map ref. D4***

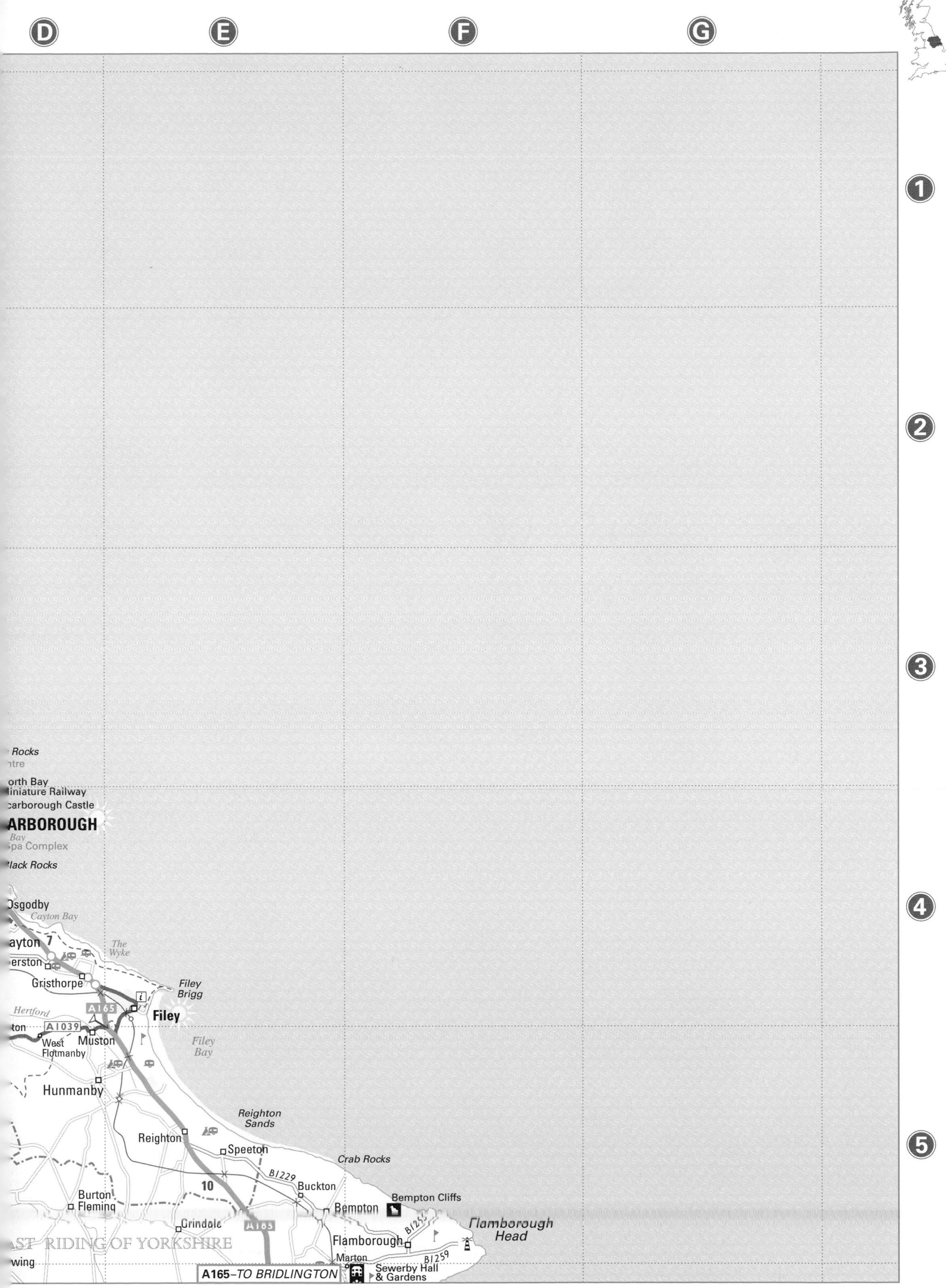

D
E
F
G
1
2
3
4
5
Rocks
ntre
orth Bay
iniature Railway
carborough Castle
ARBOROUGH
Bay
pa Complex
lack Rocks
sgodby
Cayton Bay
ayton
7
The Wyke
erston
Gristhorpe
Filey Brigg
Hertford
A165
Filey
ton
A1039
West Flotmanby
Muston
Filey Bay
Hunmanby
Reighton Sands
Reighton
Speeton
Crab Rocks
B1229
Buckton
10
Burton Fleming
Bempton
Bempton Cliffs
B1255
Flamborough Head
Grindale
A165
AST RIDING OF YORKSHIRE
Flamborough
Marton
B1259
wing
A165–TO BRIDLINGTON
Sewerby Hall & Gardens

Filey: *The Royal Crescent, built by John Wilkes Unett in 1850, was for 100 years the most fashionable address in the whole of the north of England.* ***Map ref. E4***

247

Flamborough Head: *This rocky chalk headland juts out 6 miles into the North Sea and features picturesque coves and sea caves. Because of its chalk-loving flora it is designated a Special Area of Conservation (SAC).* ***Map ref. F5***

A
B
264
C
D
1
2
3
4
5
Stranraer
A75–TO CAIRNRYAN (A751 & A77)
A75–TO NEWTON STEWART
Portslogan
Southern Upland Way
Loch Magillie
Soulseat Loch
Castle Kennedy
Dunragit Moor
Dunragit
Glenluce Abbey
Whitecairn
Glenluce
A75
A77
Whiteleys
Lochans
Cairn Pat
182
Kildrochet House
Head
Dinvin
Colfin
Portpatrick
A77
Awhirk
Dunskey
Piltanton Burn
Genoch
B7077
Genoch Square
B7084
Whitecrook
10
Castle of Park
A747
Knock Moss
Dernaglar Loch
Whitefield Loch
175
Knock Fell
Fell Loch
Old Place of Mochrum
Milton
8
Castle Loch
Sands of Luce
Crow's Nest
Stoneykirk
A716
B7042
Port of Spittal Bay
Auchenmalg
Auchenmalg Bay
Mochrum Loch
Culshabbin
B7005
Balgreggan
Sandhead
A747
Alticry
Elrig Loch
Kirkmadrine Stones
Chapel Finian
Loch Head
Cairngarroch Bay
Money Head
A716
Elrig
6
Clachanmore
Ardwell House
L U C E   B A Y
Ardwell Bay
Ardwell
Barr Point
14
Chapel Rossan
A747
Drumbreddan Bay
Logan
Balgowan
Port William
Logan Botanic Garden
New England Bay
Mull of Logan
Barsalloch Point
Danger Zone
Port Logan
Terally
B7065
A716
Kilstay
Clanyard Bay
Drummore
Laggantalluch Head
Kirkmaiden
Cailiness Point
Damnaglaur
B7041
Maryport
Crammag Head
Dunman
160
Portankill
Nick of Kindram
East Tarbet
West Tarbet
Mull of Galloway
R H I N N S   O F   G A L L O W A Y
D U M F R I E S

Port Logan: *Now famous as the setting for the BBC Television Series '2000 Acres of Sky', which starred Michelle Collins.*
Map ref. *A2*

Mull of Galloway: *A Mull is a high point of land on a rocky coast that juts out into the sea. Here, the Mull of Galloway is the most southerly point in Scotland.*
Map ref. *B3*

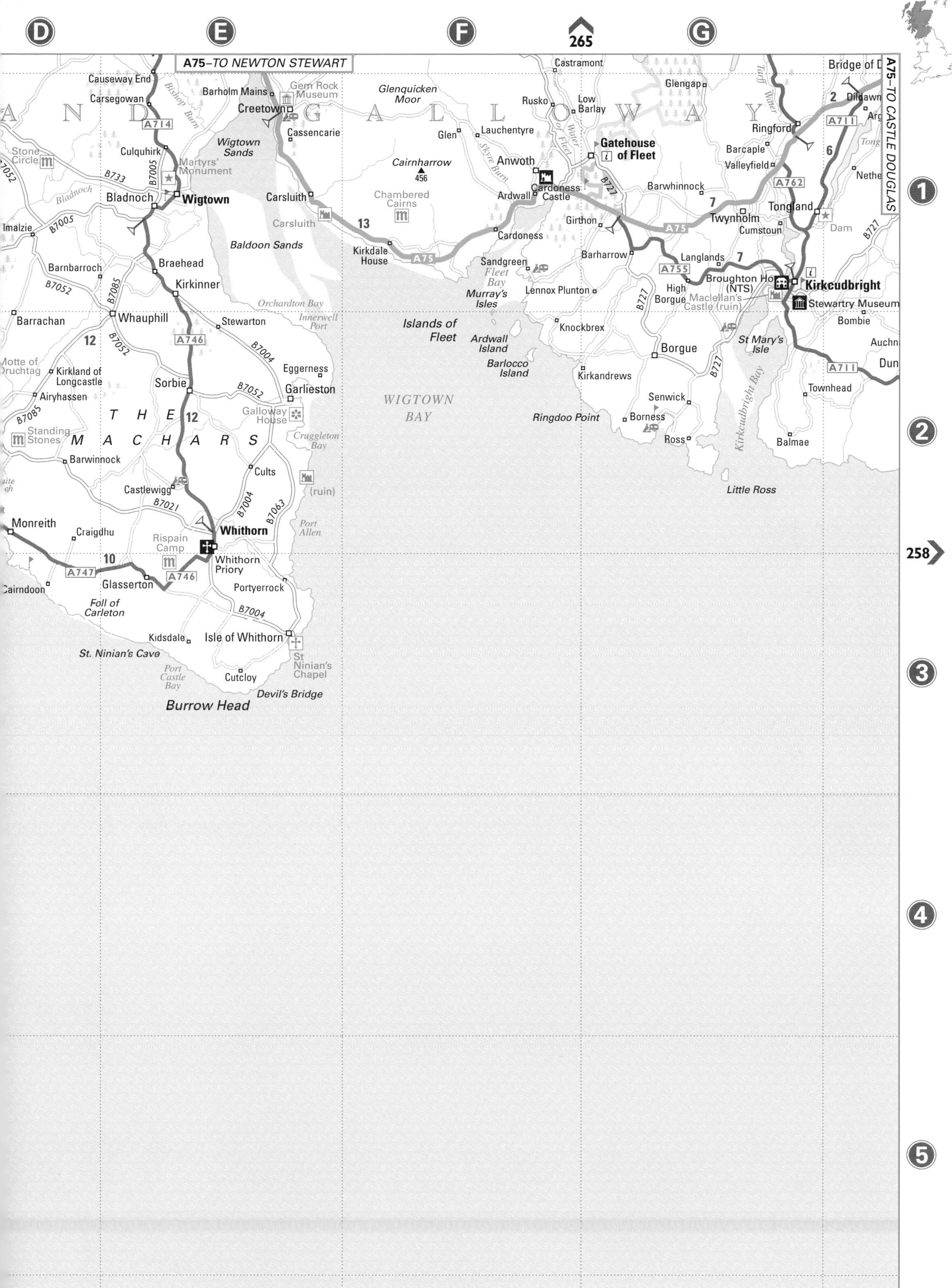

D
E
F
265
G
A75–TO NEWTON STEWART
A75–TO CASTLE DOUGLAS
1
2
3
4
5
258
Wigtown
Whithorn
Kirkcudbright
Gatehouse of Fleet
Creetown
Garlieston
Isle of Whithorn
Burrow Head
WIGTOWN BAY
Islands of Fleet
THE MACHARS

Wigtown: *The Martyrs Stake here marks the location of the execution by drowning of the 'Covenanters' Margaret Wilson and Margaret McLachlane in 1685. Their gravestones are in Wigtown churchyard.* ***Map ref. E1***

266
267
257

A B C D

1 2 3 4 5

A75–TO DUMFRIES
A75–TO STRANRAER
A595–TO BARROW-IN-FURNE

Rhonehouse (Kelton Hill)
Dildawn
Argrennan House
Breoch
Gelston
Palnackie
Airieland
Tongland Loch
Screel Hill
Bengairn
Netherthird
Tongland
Dam
Kirkcudbright
Stewartry Museum
Bombie
Bankhead
Auchnabony
Hazlefield
Dundrennan
Abbey
Rascarrel
Orroland
Townhead
Balmae
Abbey Head
Ross
Mary's Isle
Port Mary
Barlocco Bay
Rascarrel Bay
Auchencairn
Auchencairn Bay
Hestan Island
Balcary Point
Almorness Point
Castlehill Point
Orchardton Tower
Kippford (Scaur)
Mote of Mark (NTS)
Rough Firth
Rockcliffe
Colvend
White Loch
Sandyhills
Port o' Warren
Barnbarroch
Dalbeattie Forest
Fairgirth
Caulkerbush
Southwick
Mainsriddle
Kirkbean
Carsethorn
Cavens
Borron Point
Arbigland
Preston Merse
Gillfoot Bay
Southerness
Southerness Point
Mersehead Sands
Barnhourie Sands
DUMFRIES & GALLOWAY
SOLWAY FIRTH

Maryport
Flimby
Seaton
Stainburn
WORKINGTON
Schoose
Westfield
Salterbeck
High Harrington
Harrington
Distington
Pica
Howgate
Low Moresby
Parton
Moresby Parks
WHITEHAVEN
Hensingham
Saltom Bay
Cleator Moor
Sandwith
Mirehouse
St Bees Head
Moor Row
Wath Brow
Bigrigg
Cleator
St. Bees Head
Rottington
St Bees
Egremont
Wilton
How Man

A75 A711 A710 A762 A596 A597 A595 A66 A5086 B727 B736 B793 B5295 B5345

Cockermouth: *Fletcher Christian, ringleader of the Mutiny on the Bounty was born here in 1789. Following the mutiny Christian and eight other mutineers took refuge on Pitcairn Island where they founded a settlement.* ***Map ref. E3***

St Bees: *The nearby RSPB Nature Reserve is home to England's only colony of Black Guillemots.* ***Map ref. C5***

248

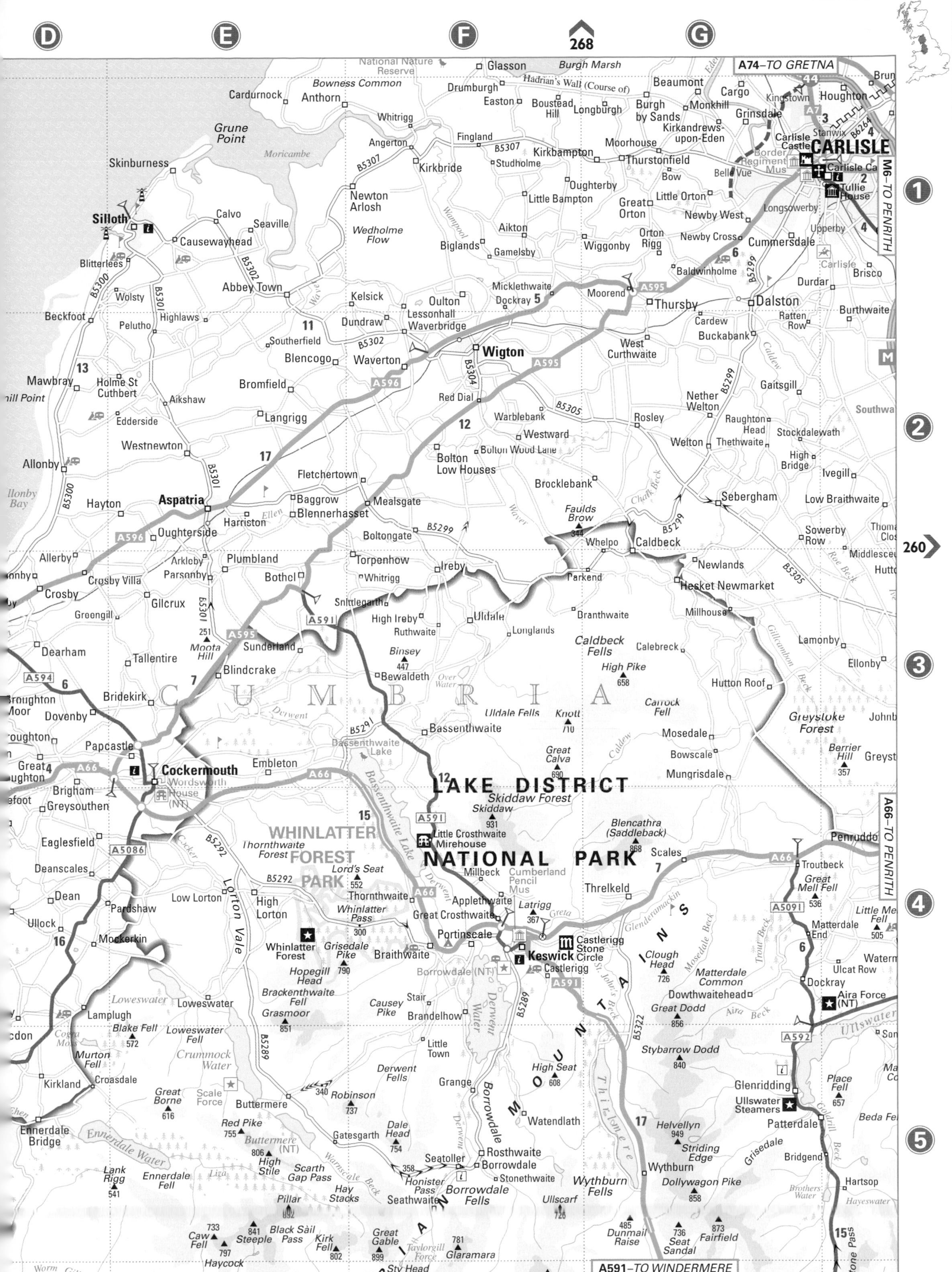
D
E
F
G
268
A74–TO GRETNA
M6–TO PENRITH
A66–TO PENRITH
A591–TO WINDERMERE
260
249
1
2
3
4
5
CARLISLE
Carlisle Castle
Tullie House
Border Regiment Mus
Glasson
Burgh Marsh
Hadrian's Wall (Course of)
Drumburgh
Bowness Common
National Nature Reserve
Cardurnock
Anthorn
Grune Point
Skinburness
Silloth
Calvo
Seaville
Causewayhead
Blitterlees
Abbey Town
Wolsty
Beckfoot
Highlaws
Pelutho
Mawbray
Holme St Cuthbert
Edderside
Aikshaw
Westnewton
Allonby
Allonby Bay
Hayton
Aspatria
Oughterside
Allerby
Crosby Villa
Crosby
Dearham
Tallentire
Bridekirk
Dovenby
Papcastle
Cockermouth
Wordsworth House (NT)
Brigham
Greysouthen
Eaglesfield
Deanscales
Dean
Pardshaw
Ullock
Mockerkin
Lamplugh
Loweswater
Kirkland
Croasdale
Ennerdale Bridge
Ennerdale Water
Whitrigg
Angerton
Kirkbride
Newton Arlosh
Wedholme Flow
Fingland
Kirkbampton
Studholme
Oughterby
Little Bampton
Aikton
Biglands
Gamelsby
Wiggonby
Easton
Boustead Hill
Longburgh
Burgh by Sands
Beaumont
Monkhill
Kirkandrews-upon-Eden
Moorhouse
Thurstonfield
Great Orton
Little Orton
Newby West
Orton Rigg
Newby Cross
Cummersdale
Baldwinholme
Cargo
Kingstown
Houghton
Grinsdale
Stanwix
Belle Vue
Longsowerby
Upperby
Carlisle
Brisco
Durdar
Moorend
Thursby
Dalston
Cardew
Buckabank
Ratten Row
Burthwaite
Micklethwaite
Dockray
Kelsick
Oulton
Lessonhall
Dundraw
Waverbridge
Southerfield
Blencogo
Waverton
Wigton
Bromfield
Langrigg
Red Dial
Warblebank
Westward
Bolton Wood Lane
Bolton Low Houses
Fletchertown
Baggrow
Blennerhasset
Mealsgate
Harriston
Boltongate
Torpenhow
Whitrigg
Ireby
Plumbland
Arkleby
Parsonby
Bothel
Gilcrux
Snittlegarth
High Ireby
Ruthwaite
Uldale
Longlands
Binsey
447
Bewaldeth
Over Water
Moota Hill
251
Sunderland
Blindcrake
Embleton
Bassenthwaite
Bassenthwaite Lake
Uldale Fells
Knott
710
Great Calva
690
Skiddaw Forest
Skiddaw
931
LAKE DISTRICT NATIONAL PARK
CUMBRIA
CUMBRIAN MOUNTAINS
West Curthwaite
Rosley
Nether Welton
Welton
Raughton Head
Thethwaite
Gaitsgill
Stockdalewath
High Bridge
Ivegill
Brocklebank
Faulds Brow
344
Whelpo
Caldbeck
Sebergham
Low Braithwaite
Sowerby Row
Newlands
Hesket Newmarket
Parkend
Branthwaite
Millhouse
Caldbeck Fells
Calebreck
High Pike
658
Carrock Fell
Lamonby
Ellonby
Hutton Roof
Greystoke Forest
Mosedale
Bowscale
Mungrisdale
Berrier Hill
357
Blencathra (Saddleback)
868
Scales
Threlkeld
Penruddock
Troutbeck
Great Mell Fell
536
Little Mell Fell
505
Matterdale End
Ulcat Row
Dockray
Aira Force (NT)
Ullswater
Glenridding
Ullswater Steamers
Place Fell
657
Patterdale
Bridgend
Hartsop
Brothers Water
Whinlatter Forest Park
Thornthwaite Forest
Lord's Seat
552
Thornthwaite
Little Crosthwaite
Mirehouse
Millbeck
Cumberland Pencil Mus
Applethwaite
Latrigg
367
Great Crosthwaite
Portinscale
Keswick
Castlerigg Stone Circle
Castlerigg
Whinlatter Pass
300
High Lorton
Low Lorton
Lorton Vale
Whinlatter Forest
Grisedale Pike
790
Braithwaite
Hopegill Head
Brackenthwaite Fell
Grasmoor
851
Causey Pike
Stair
Brandelhow
Borrowdale (NT)
Derwent Water
Little Town
Derwent Fells
Grange
Loweswater Fell
Blake Fell
572
Murton Fell
Crummock Water
Great Borne
616
Scale Force
Buttermere
Robinson
737
Red Pike
755
Buttermere (NT)
High Stile
806
Dale Head
754
Gatesgarth
Scarth Gap Pass
Honister Pass
358
Seatoller
Rosthwaite
Borrowdale
Stonethwaite
Watendlath
High Seat
608
Clough Head
726
Great Dodd
856
Matterdale Common
Dowthwaitehead
Stybarrow Dodd
840
Thirlmere
Helvellyn
949
Striding Edge
Wythburn
Dollywagon Pike
858
Wythburn Fells
Ullscarf
726
Borrowdale Fells
Seathwaite
Hay Stacks
Pillar
892
Lank Rigg
541
Ennerdale Fell
Caw Fell
733
Steeple
841
Haycock
797
Black Sail Pass
Kirk Fell
802
Great Gable
899
Glaramara
781
Taylorgill Force
Sty Head
Dunmail Raise
485
Seat Sandal
736
Fairfield
873
Kirkstone Pass
15

Seathwaite: *The small village of Seathwaite is northeast of Scafell Pike, at 3,210 feet (978m) the highest mountain in England. Seathwaite is thought to be the wettest settlement in Britain with about 130 inches (330 cm) average rainfall per year.* ***Map ref. F5***

268

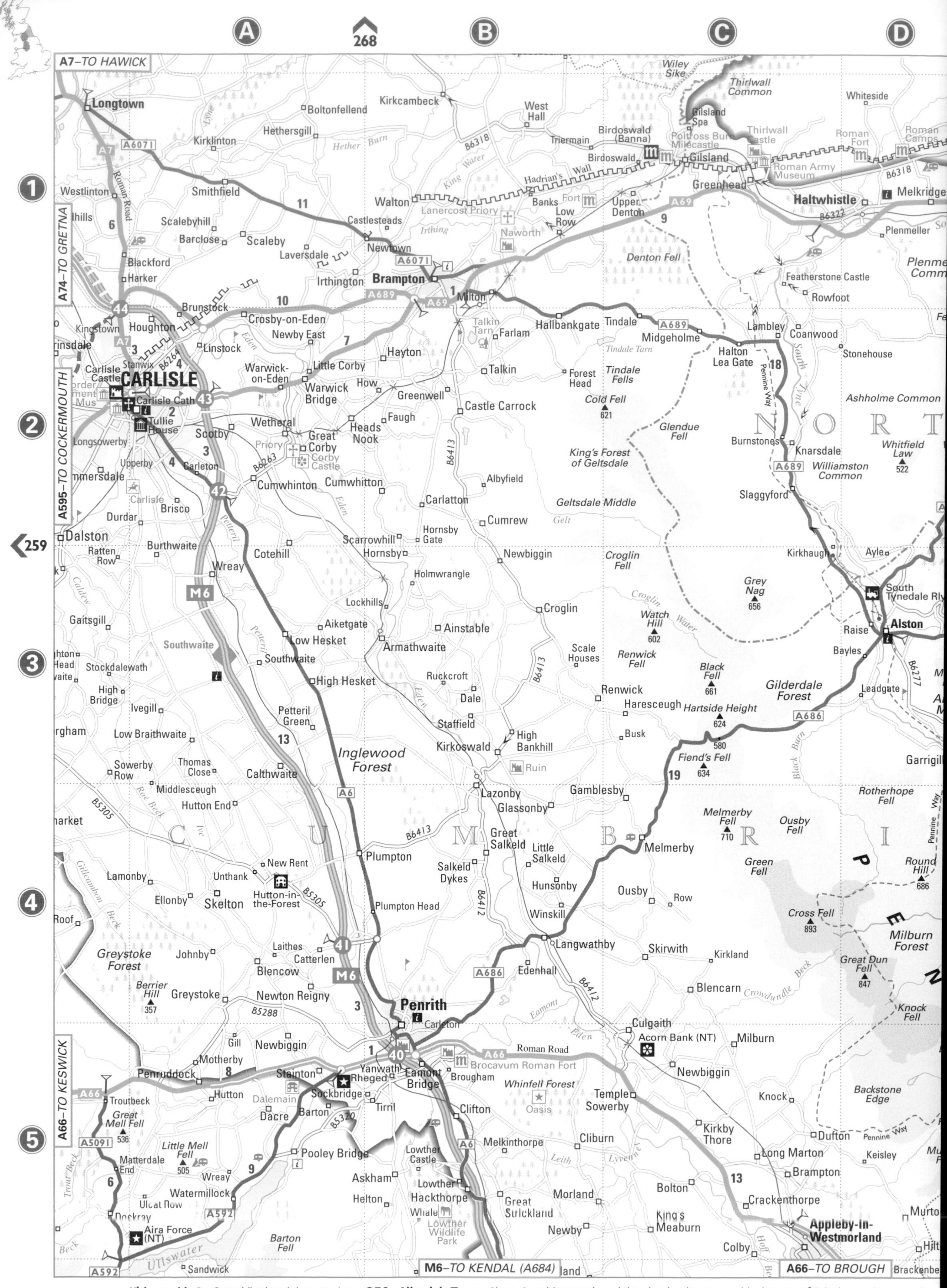
A
B
C
D
1
2
3
4
5
259
A7–TO HAWICK
A74–TO GRETNA
A595–TO COCKERMOUTH
A66–TO KESWICK
M6–TO KENDAL (A684)
A66–TO BROUGH
Longtown
Boltonfellend
Kirkcambeck
West Hall
Wiley Sike
Thirlwall Common
Whiteside
Gilsland Spa
Birdoswald (Banna)
Birdoswald
Poltross Burn Milecastle
Gilsland
Thirlwall Castle
Roman Fort
Roman Camps
Roman Army Museum
Greenhead
Melkridge
Haltwhistle
Plenmeller
Kirklinton
Hethersgill
Hether Burn
Triermain
Hadrian's Wall
Westlinton
Smithfield
Walton
Lanercost Priory
Banks
Upper Denton
Low Row
Naworth
Scalebyhill
Barclose
Scaleby
Castlesteads
Laversdale
Newtown
Irthing
Denton Fell
Blackford
Harker
Irthington
Brampton
Featherstone Castle
Rowfoot
Brunstock
Crosby-on-Eden
Milton
Kingstown
Houghton
Newby East
Talkin Tarn
Farlam
Hallbankgate
Tindale
Midgeholme
Lambley
Coanwood
Linstock
Hayton
Halton Lea Gate
Stonehouse
Tindale Tarn
Carlisle Castle
CARLISLE
Warwick-on-Eden
Little Corby
Talkin
Forest Head
Tindale Fells
Carlisle Cath
Warwick Bridge
Greenwell
Castle Carrock
Cold Fell
621
Ashholme Common
Tullie House
Wetheral
Faugh
Heads Nook
Great Corby
Glendue Fell
Burnstones
Knarsdale
Whitfield Law
522
Longsowerby
Scotby
Priory
Corby Castle
King's Forest of Geltsdale
Williamston Common
Upperby
Carleton
Cumwhinton
Cumwhitton
Albyfield
Slaggyford
Carlisle
Brisco
Carlatton
Geltsdale Middle
Durdar
Cumrew
Gelt
Dalston
Burthwaite
Scarrowhill
Hornsby Gate
Hornsby
Cotehill
Newbiggin
Croglin Fell
Kirkhaugh
Ayle
Ratten Row
Wreay
Holmwrangle
Grey Nag
656
South Tynedale Rly
Lockhills
Croglin
Croglin Water
Watch Hill
602
Alston
Gaitsgill
Aiketgate
Low Hesket
Ainstable
Raise
Southwaite
Armathwaite
Scale Houses
Renwick Fell
Bayles
Stockdalewath
Black Fell
661
Ruckcroft
High Hesket
High Bridge
Ivegill
Renwick
Gilderdale Forest
Leadgate
Dale
Haresceugh
Hartside Height
624
Petteril Green
Staffield
Busk
Low Braithwaite
13
Kirkoswald
High Bankhill
580
Inglewood Forest
Fiend's Fell
634
Sowerby Row
Thomas Close
Calthwaite
Ruin
Garrigill
Middlesceugh
Lazonby
Gamblesby
Rotherhope Fell
Hutton End
Glassonby
Melmerby Fell
710
Ousby Fell
Great Salkeld
Little Salkeld
Melmerby
Plumpton
New Rent
Green Fell
Round Hill
686
Lamonby
Unthank
Salkeld Dykes
Hunsonby
Ousby
Row
Ellonby
Skelton
Hutton-in-the-Forest
Plumpton Head
Winskill
Cross Fell
893
Milburn Forest
Greystoke Forest
Johnby
Laithes
Catterlen
Langwathby
Skirwith
Kirkland
Blencow
Edenhall
Great Dun Fell
847
Berrier Hill
357
Greystoke
Newton Reigny
Blencarn
Penrith
Carleton
Culgaith
Knock Fell
Gill
Newbiggin
Acorn Bank (NT)
Milburn
Motherby
Penruddock
Stainton
Yanwath
Rheged
Eamont Bridge
Brougham
Brocavum Roman Fort
Roman Road
Whinfell Forest
Newbiggin
Hutton
Dalemain
Sockbridge
Oasis
Temple Sowerby
Knock
Backstone Edge
Troutbeck
Great Mell Fell
536
Dacre
Barton
Tirril
Clifton
Kirkby Thore
Dufton
Pennine Way
Little Mell Fell
505
Pooley Bridge
Lowther Castle
Melkinthorpe
Cliburn
Long Marton
Keisley
Matterdale End
Wreay
Askham
Lowther
Brampton
Watermillock
Helton
Hackthorpe
Great Strickland
Morland
Bolton
Crackenthorpe
Ulcat Row
Whale
Lowther Wildlife Park
King's Meaburn
Dockray
Aira Force (NT)
Newby
Appleby-in-Westmorland
Barton Fell
Colby
Ullswater
Sandwick
Brackenber

Kirkoswald: St. Oswald's church has a unique feature in that the church bell tower is perched on a hill top 200 yards (180m) away from the actual church building. **Map ref. B3**

250

Allendale Town: Since 1842 this town has claimed to be the geographical centre of Britain, on the grounds that it is halfway between Cape Wrath and Beachy Head. Latitude and longitude figures are displayed on the sundial on the church tower. However, nearby Haltwhistle (**Map ref. D1**) also makes this claim, as the mid-point of Britain's longest line of longitude which stretches from the Orkney Islands to Dorset. **Map ref. E2**

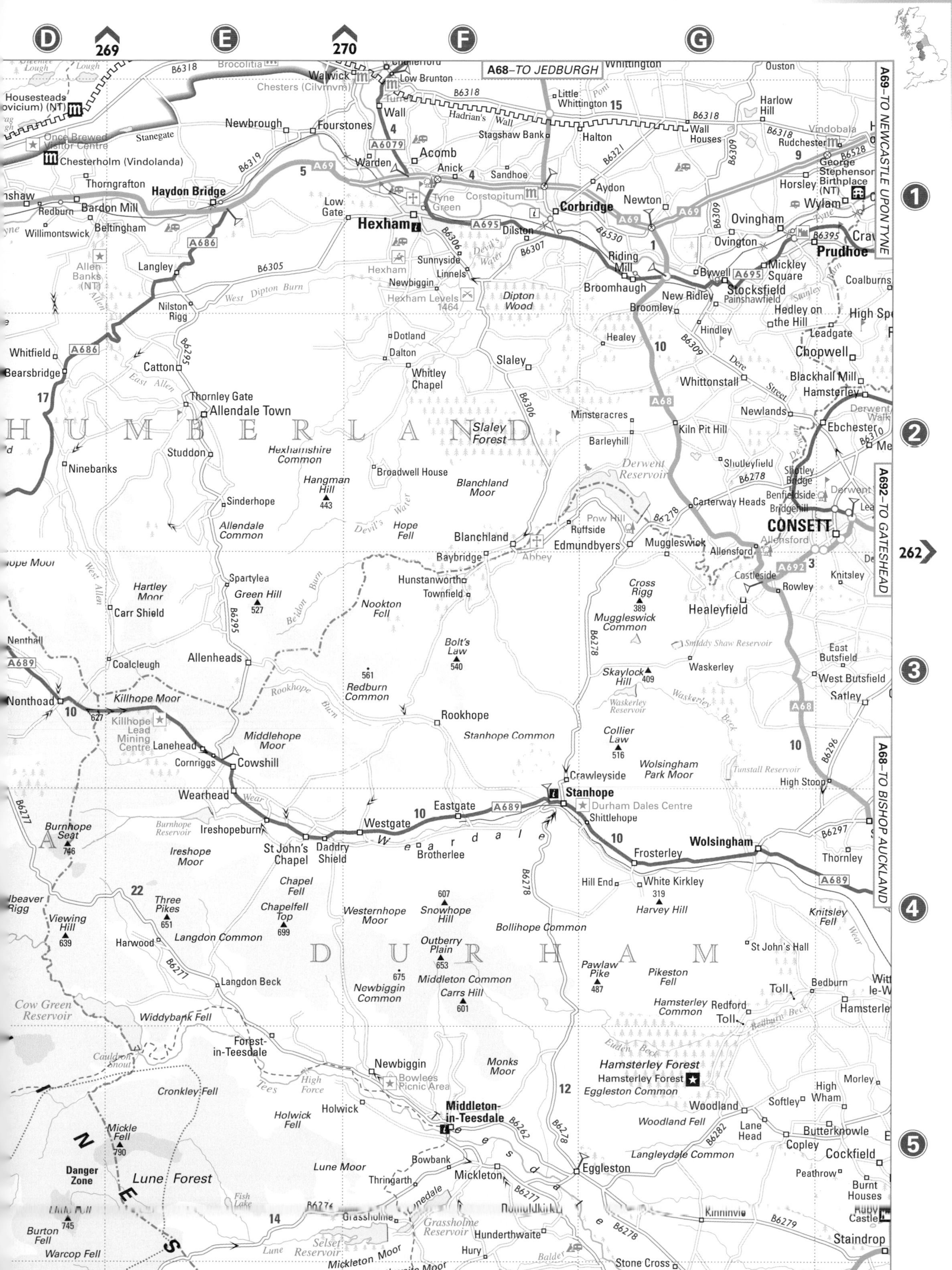

D
E
F
G
269
270
A68–TO JEDBURGH
A69–TO NEWCASTLE UPON TYNE
A692–TO GATESHEAD
A68–TO BISHOP AUCKLAND
262
1
2
3
4
5
Housesteads
Chesterholm (Vindolanda)
Newbrough
Fourstones
Haydon Bridge
Hexham
Corbridge
Acomb
Wall
Warden
Anick
Sandhoe
Stagshaw Bank
Halton
Aydon
Newton
Ovingham
Ovington
Prudhoe
Wylam
Horsley
Harlow Hill
Little Whittington
Wall Houses
Rudchester
George Stephenson Birthplace (NT)
Riding Mill
Broomhaugh
Bywell
Stocksfield
Mickley Square
New Ridley
Broomley
Hedley on the Hill
High Spen
Leadgate
Chopwell
Blackhall Mill
Hamsterley
Ebchester
Newlands
Whittonstall
Kiln Pit Hill
Healey
Slaley
Dipton Wood
Hexham Levels
Linnels
Sunnyside
Newbiggin
Dilston
Tyne Green
Low Gate
Corstopitum
Langley
Nilston Rigg
Beltingham
Bardon Mill
Redburn
Willimontswick
Thorngrafton
Allen Banks (NT)
Whitfield
Bearsbridge
Catton
Thornley Gate
Allendale Town
Dotland
Dalton
Whitley Chapel
Slaley Forest
Minsteracres
Barleyhill
Derwent Reservoir
Shotleyfield
Shotley Bridge
Benfieldside
Bridgehill
Carterway Heads
CONSETT
Allensford
Castleside
Rowley
Knitsley
Healeyfield
Muggleswick
Muggleswick Common
Cross Rigg
Edmundbyers
Ruffside
Pow Hill
Blanchland
Blanchland Moor
Baybridge
Hunstanworth
Townfield
Nookton Fell
Hope Fell
Broadwell House
Hangman Hill
Hexhamshire Common
Studdon
Ninebanks
Sinderhope
Allendale Common
Spartylea
Green Hill
Hartley Moor
Carr Shield
Nenthall
Coalcleugh
Allenheads
Nenthead
Killhope Moor
Killhope Lead Mining Centre
Lanehead
Cornriggs
Cowshill
Middlehope Moor
Wearhead
Redburn Common
Bolt's Law
Rookhope
Stanhope Common
Skaylock Hill
Waskerley
Smiddy Shaw Reservoir
East Butsfield
West Butsfield
Satley
Collier Law
Wolsingham Park Moor
Crawleyside
Stanhope
Durham Dales Centre
Shittlehope
Eastgate
Westgate
Ireshopeburn
St John's Chapel
Daddry Shield
Brotherlee
Weardale
Frosterley
Wolsingham
Thornley
High Stoop
Tunstall Reservoir
Burnhope Seat
Burnhope Reservoir
Ireshope Moor
Chapel Fell
Chapelfell Top
Westernhope Moor
Snowhope Hill
Hill End
White Kirkley
Harvey Hill
Knitsley Fell
Bollihope Common
St John's Hall
Three Pikes
Viewing Hill
Harwood
Langdon Common
Outberry Plain
DURHAM
Pawlaw Pike
Pikeston Fell
Langdon Beck
Newbiggin Common
Middleton Common
Carrs Hill
Hamsterley Common
Redford
Toll
Bedburn
Hamsterley
Cow Green Reservoir
Widdybank Fell
Forest-in-Teesdale
Cauldron Snout
Cronkley Fell
High Force
Newbiggin
Bowlees Picnic Area
Monks Moor
Hamsterley Forest
Eggleston Common
High Wham
Morley
Softley
Holwick
Holwick Fell
Middleton-in-Teesdale
Woodland
Woodland Fell
Lane Head
Butterknowle
Copley
Cockfield
Langleydale Common
Mickle Fell
Danger Zone
Lune Forest
Lune Moor
Bowbank
Mickleton
Thringarth
Eggleston
Peathrow
Burnt Houses
Grassholme
Grassholme Reservoir
Kinninvie
Raby Castle
Hunderthwaite
Burton Fell
Warcop Fell
Selset Reservoir
Mickleton Moor
Hury
Stone Cross
Staindrop

Hexham: *This is the administrative centre for Tynedale, the largest local authority district in England. With a land area of 856 square miles (2217 sq km) and only 57,400 residents, the authority has a population density of just 67 people per square mile (26 per sq km).* ***Map ref. F1***

251

Cauldron Snout: *This is now commonly cited as England's highest waterfall at 200 feet (61m), although it is more a cascade than a single unbroken fall.* ***Map ref. E5***

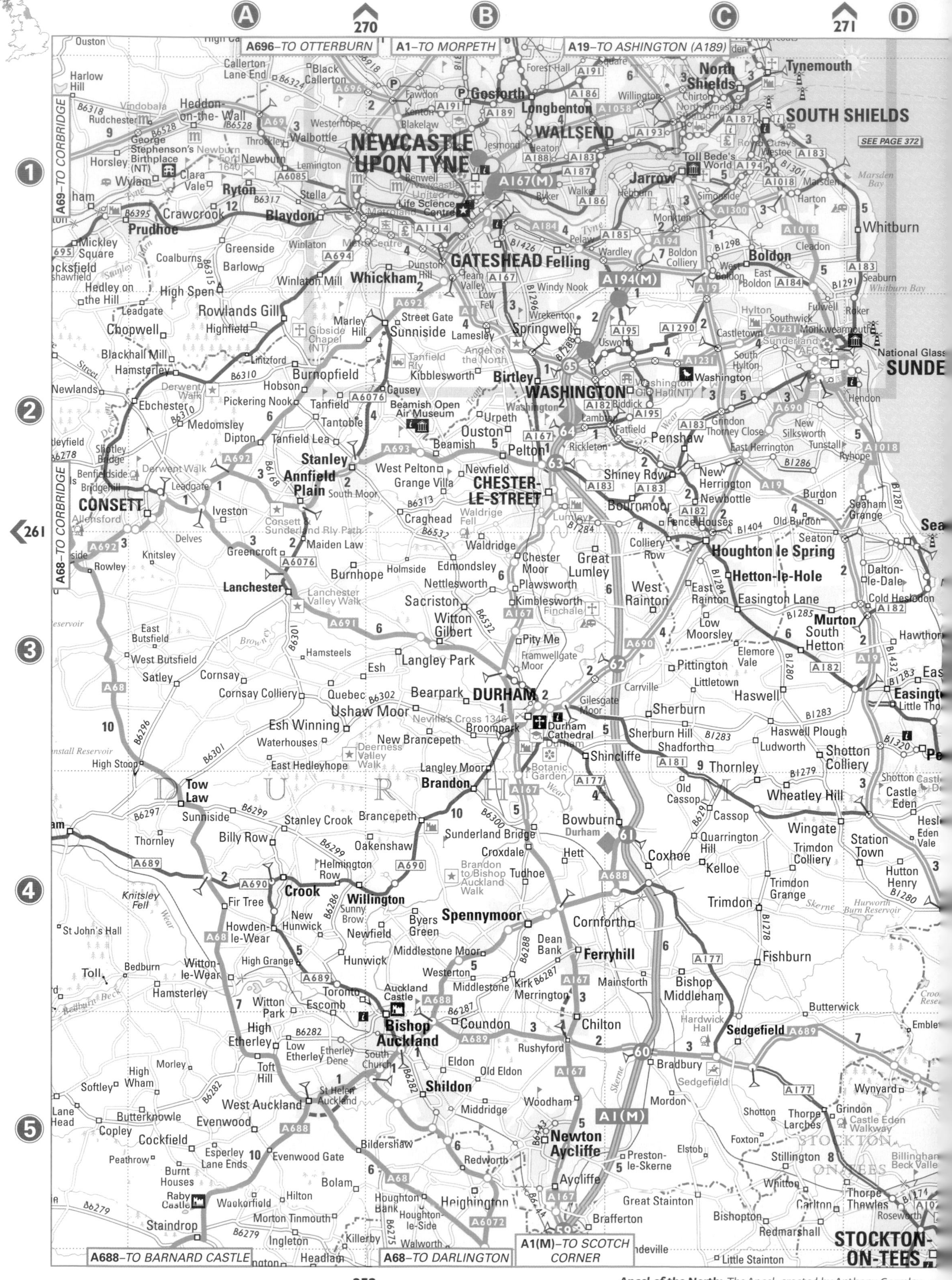

A
B
C
D
270
271
A696–TO OTTERBURN
A1–TO MORPETH
A19–TO ASHINGTON (A189)
Ouston
Harlow Hill
Callerton Lane End
Black Callerton
Forest Hall
North Shields
Tynemouth
Vindobala
Heddon-on-the-Wall
Rudchester
Fawdon
Gosforth
Longbenton
Willington
Chirton
SOUTH SHIELDS
A69–TO CORBRIDGE
George Stephenson's Birthplace (NT)
Westerhope
Walbottle
Throckley
Newburn
Kenton
Blakelaw
NEWCASTLE UPON TYNE
Jesmond
Heaton
WALLSEND
SEE PAGE 372
Horsley
Wylam
Clara Vale
Ryton
Lemington
Benwell
Toll
Bede's World
Westoe
Jarrow
Marsden
Marsden Bay
Stella
Blaydon
Crawcrook
Prudhoe
Life Science Centre
Metrocentre
Byker
Walker
Hebburn
Simonside
Harton
Whitburn
Mickley Square
Coalburns
Greenside
Barlow
Winlaton
Winlaton Mill
Whickham
Dunston Hill
GATESHEAD
Felling
Pelaw
Wardley
Boldon Colliery
Monkton
Boldon
West Boldon
East Boldon
Cleadon
Seaburn
Whitburn Bay
Hedley on the Hill
High Spen
Team Valley
Low Fell
Windy Nook
Leadgate
Rowlands Gill
Chopwell
Highfield
Marley Hill
Street Gate
Sunniside
Gibside Chapel (NT)
Lamesley
Wrekenton
Springwell
Usworth
Hylton
Southwick
Castletown
Fulwell
Roker
Monkwearmouth
Sunderland AFC
South Hylton
National Glass
SUNDE
Blackhall Mill
Hamsterley
Lintzford
Tanfield Rly
Angel of the North
Kibblesworth
Birtley
Washington
Newlands
Derwent Walk
Ebchester
Medomsley
Burnopfield
Hobson
Pickering Nook
Tanfield
Tantobie
Causey
Beamish Open Air Museum
Urpeth
WASHINGTON
Washington Old Hall (NT)
Biddick
Lambton
Fatfield
Penshaw
Grindon
Thorney Close
New Silksworth
Hendon
Tunstall
Ryhope
Slaley Bridge
Dipton
Tanfield Lea
Stanley
Beamish
Ouston
Pelton
Rickleton
East Herrington
Benfieldside
Bridgehill
CONSETT
Allensford
Leadgate
Iveston
Annfield Plain
South Moor
West Pelton
Grange Villa
Newfield
CHESTER-LE-STREET
Craghead
Waldridge Fell
Shiney Row
New Herrington
Newbottle
Bournmoor
Burdon
Seaham Grange
Old Burdon
Fence Houses
Consett & Sunderland Rly Path
Lumley
Knitsley
Delves
Greencroft
Maiden Law
Waldridge
Chester Moor
Great Lumley
Colliery Row
Houghton le Spring
Seaton
Dalton-le-Dale
Rowley
Burnhope
Holmside
Edmondsley
Nettlesworth
Plawsworth
Hetton-le-Hole
Lanchester
Lanchester Valley Walk
Sacriston
Kimblesworth
Finchale
West Rainton
East Rainton
Easington Lane
Cold Hesledon
Witton Gilbert
Low Moorsley
Murton
South Hetton
East Butsfield
West Butsfield
Hamsteels
Pity Me
Framwellgate Moor
Elemore Vale
Hawthorn
Esh
Langley Park
Pittington
Littletown
Satley
Cornsay
Cornsay Colliery
Quebec
Bearpark
DURHAM
Carrville
Haswell
Easington
Little Thorpe
Ushaw Moor
Neville's Cross 1346
Gilesgate Moor
Sherburn
Esh Winning
Broompark
Durham Cathedral
Sherburn Hill
Haswell Plough
Waterhouses
New Brancepeth
Shadforth
Ludworth
Shotton Colliery
High Stoop
Deerness Valley Walk
East Hedleyhope
Durham
Shincliffe
Thornley
Langley Moor
Botanic Garden
Brandon
Old Cassop
Wheatley Hill
Shotton
Castle Eden
Tow Law
Cassop
Sunniside
Stanley Crook
Brancepeth
Bowburn
Wingate
Thornley
Billy Row
Sunderland Bridge
Croxdale
Oakenshaw
Quarrington Hill
Station Town
Hett
Coxhoe
Trimdon Colliery
Kelloe
Helmington Row
Brandon to Bishop Auckland Walk
Tudhoe
Hutton Henry
Knitsley Fell
Fir Tree
Crook
Willington
Trimdon Grange
Trimdon
Hurworth Burn Reservoir
Sunny Brow
New Hunwick
Byers Green
Spennymoor
Cornforth
St John's Hall
Howden-le-Wear
Newfield
Dean Bank
Middlestone Moor
Ferryhill
Fishburn
High Grange
Hunwick
Toll
Bedburn
Witton-le-Wear
Westerton
Mainsforth
Bishop Middleham
Hamsterley
Toronto
Middlestone
Kirk Merrington
Witton Park
Escomb
Auckland Castle
Butterwick
Bishop Auckland
Coundon
Chilton
Hardwick Hall
Sedgefield
High Etherley
Low Etherley
Etherley Dene
South Church
Rushyford
Morley
Toft Hill
Eldon
Old Eldon
Bradbury
High Wham
Softley
St Helen Auckland
Shildon
Sedgefield
Wynyard
West Auckland
Woodham
Mordon
Lane Head
Butterknowle
Evenwood
Middridge
Shotton
Thorpe Larches
Grindon
Castle Eden Walkway
Copley
Cockfield
Newton Aycliffe
Esperley Lane Ends
Evenwood Gate
Bildershaw
Redworth
Preston-le-Skerne
Elstob
Foxton
Stillington
STOCKTON-ON-TEES
Billingham Beck Valley
Peathrow
Burnt Houses
Bolam
Aycliffe
Raby Castle
Wackerfield
Hilton
Houghton Bank
Heighington
Great Stainton
Whitton
Thorpe Thewles
Carlton
Roseworth
Staindrop
Morton Tinmouth
Houghton-le-Side
Brafferton
Bishopton
Redmarshall
Ingleton
Killerby
Walworth
Little Stainton
A688–TO BARNARD CASTLE
Headlam
A68–TO DARLINGTON
A1(M)–TO SCOTCH CORNER
STOCKTON-ON-TEES
A68–TO CORBRIDGE
261
252
DURHAM

Angel of the North: *The Angel, created by Anthony Gormley, was Britain's largest sculpture when opened in 1998, standing 65 feet (20m) high, a wingspan of 175 feet (54m) and weighing 197 tons (200 tonnes). The sculpture is made of weather resistant steel, can withstand 100 mph (160km/h) winds and has an estimated lifespan of 100 years.* ***Map ref. B2***

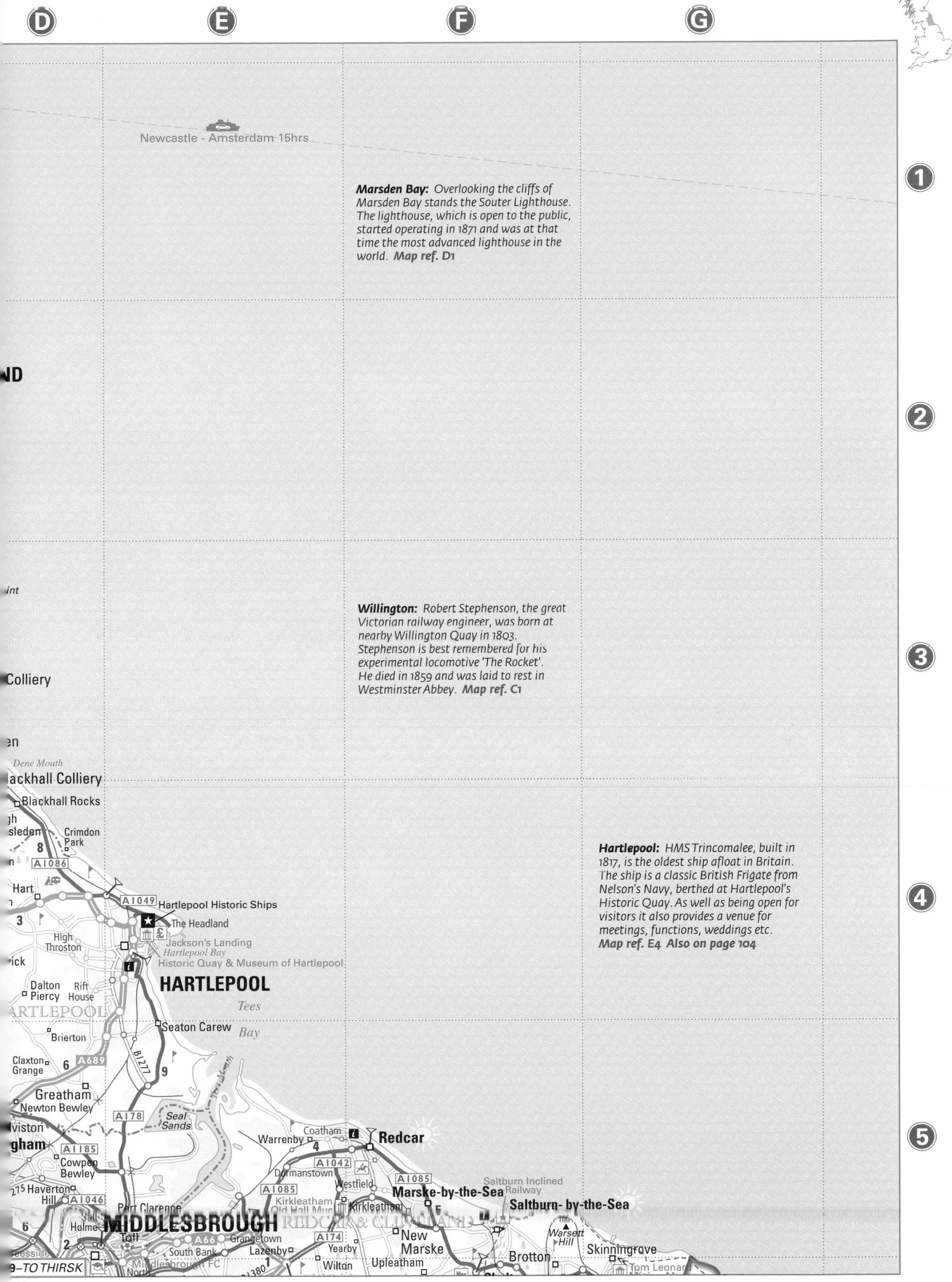
D
E
F
G
1
2
3
4
5
Newcastle - Amsterdam 15hrs
Colliery
Dene Mouth
Blackhall Colliery
Blackhall Rocks
Crimdon Park
A1086
Hart
A1049
Hartlepool Historic Ships
The Headland
High Throston
Jackson's Landing
Hartlepool Bay
Historic Quay & Museum of Hartlepool
Dalton Piercy
Rift House
HARTLEPOOL
Tees
Bay
Seaton Carew
Brierton
Claxton Grange
A689
B1277
Greatham
Newton Bewley
A178
Seal Sands
Cowpen Bewley
A1185
Haverton Hill
A1046
Port Clarence
MIDDLESBROUGH
REDCAR & CLEVELAND
Holme
Toll
A66
Grangetown
South Bank
Lazenby
Middlesbrough FC
9-TO THIRSK
Warrenby
Coatham
Redcar
A1042
Dormanstown
Westfield
A1085
Kirkleatham
Marske-by-the-Sea
Saltburn Inclined Railway
Saltburn- by-the-Sea
A174
Yearby
Wilton
New Marske
Upleatham
Brotton
Warsett Hill
Skinningrove
Tom Leonard

Marsden Bay: *Overlooking the cliffs of Marsden Bay stands the Souter Lighthouse. The lighthouse, which is open to the public, started operating in 1871 and was at that time the most advanced lighthouse in the world.* ***Map ref. D1***

Willington: *Robert Stephenson, the great Victorian railway engineer, was born at nearby Willington Quay in 1803. Stephenson is best remembered for his experimental locomotive 'The Rocket'. He died in 1859 and was laid to rest in Westminster Abbey.* ***Map ref. C1***

Hartlepool: HMS Trincomalee, built in 1817, is the oldest ship afloat in Britain. The ship is a classic British Frigate from Nelson's Navy, berthed at Hartlepool's Historic Quay. As well as being open for visitors it also provides a venue for meetings, functions, weddings etc. ***Map ref. E4 Also on page 104***

253

Middlesbrough: *The Middlesbrough Transporter Bridge, which featured prominently in a series of TV's 'Auf Wiedersehen Pet', is the only Transporter Bridge in Britain still running a daily service. It was built in 1911 and is over 850 feet (260m) long, 220 feet (67m) high and crosses the River Tees.* ***Map ref. D5***

A
273
B
C
D
1
2
3
4
5
A77–TO AYR
Ailsa Craig
Ailsa Craig: Unpopulated Island but features a lighthouse on Foreland Point built by Thomas and David Stevenson in 1886. Until 1935 all contact between the lighthouse and the mainland was by carrier pigeon. It is now unmanned and powered by solar panels. Map ref.B1
Girvan
Houdston
Saugh Hill
296
Glendoune
Glendrissaig
Black Neuk
A714
Pinminnoch
Ardwell
Kennedy's Pass
Grey Hill
297
Water of Lendal
12
Pinmore
Lendalfoot
Motte
Aldons
Daljarrock
Carleton Fishery
A77
Poundland
Pinwherry
B734
Bennane Head
Colmonell
Dalreoch
Glenduisk
Knockdolian
265
Stinchar
Craigneil
A714
Ballochmorrie
B7044
Mains of Tig
Ballantrae Bay
Water of Tig
Ballantrae
Auchairne
Balkissock
Shiel Hill
230
Barrhill
Glenapp Castle
Downan Point
Smyrton
Kilantringan Loch
Craigie Fell
Beneraird
439
Cross Water
Carlock Hill
323
Milljoan Hill
403
Altimeg Hill
Main Water of Luce
Chirmorrie
hours
Cairnryan-Larne........ 1-1¾
Stranraer-Belfast.... 1½-3¾
Finnarts Point
Glen App
Milleur Point
Markdhu
Standing Stones
Corsewall Point
A77
Miltonise
Cross Water of Luce
Glenwhilly
Barnhills
Dalnigap
17
North Cairn
DUMFRIES
South Cairn
B738
Cairnryan
Kirkcolm
Corsewall
Cairn Point
Dounan Bay
Airies
Ervie
Loch Connell
A718
Artfield Fell
B738
B798
A77
Portobello
St Mary's Croft
235
Braid Fell
Beoch Burn
7
Sole Burn
Knocknain
Soleburn
New Luce
Tarf
Leswalt
B7043
Innermessan
Lochnaw
Auchmantle
A77
Lochinch Castle
Galdenoch
Black Loch
164
B738
Piltanton Burn
B737
A751
Castle Kennedy
Craig Fell
Stranraer
White Loch
Broadsea Bay
Castle Kennedy
Southern Upland Way
Loch Magillie
A75
Dunragit Moor
Glenluce Abbey
Whitecairn
Portslogan
A77
Soulseat Loch
2
Whiteleys
Dunragit
Glenluce
Piltanton Burn
10
Lochans
Whitecrook
Black Head
Cairn Pat
182
Genoch
Castle of Park
B7077
A747
Kildrochet House
Dinvin
Genoch Square
B7084
6
Colfin
A77
B7084
Sands of Luce
Milton
Portpatrick
A716
8
Awhirk
Stoneykirk
Crow's Nest
Dunskey
B7042
Port of Spittal Bay
Auchenmalg Bay
Balgreggan
Sandhead
Kirkmadrine
256

Stranraer: *The world's first high-speed ferry operates from Stranraer to Belfast and is known as Stena HSS. This is one of the largest ferries in the world, capable of carrying 1500 passengers plus their cars and coaches. It is powered by four jet engines which provide the same thrust as that required for a jumbo jet and give it a cruising speed of 40 knots.* ***Map ref. B4***

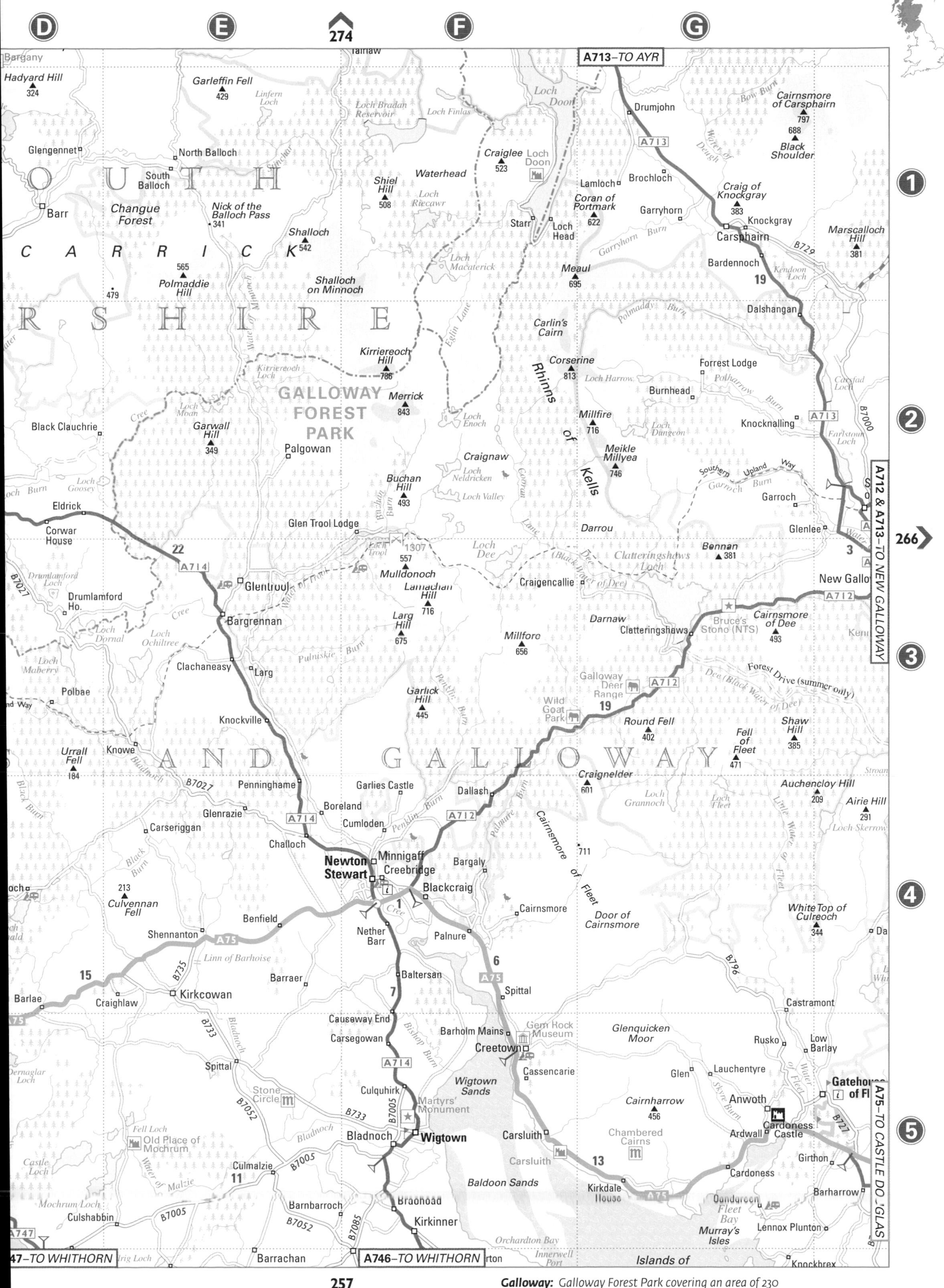
D
E
274
F
G
1
2
3
4
5
266
257
A713–TO AYR
A712 & A713–TO NEW GALLOWAY
A75–TO CASTLE DOUGLAS
A747–TO WHITHORN
A746–TO WHITHORN
SOUTH
CARRICK
AYRSHIRE
DUMFRIES AND GALLOWAY
GALLOWAY FOREST PARK
Bargany
Hadyard Hill
324
Garleffin Fell
429
Linfern Loch
Loch Bradan Reservoir
Loch Finlas
Loch Doon
Drumjohn
Cairnsmore of Carsphairn
797
688
Black Shoulder
Glengennet
North Balloch
South Balloch
Craiglee
523
Loch Doon
Shiel Hill
508
Waterhead
Loch Riecawr
Lamloch
Brochloch
Craig of Knockgray
383
Barr
Changue Forest
Nick of the Balloch Pass
341
Coran of Portmark
622
Garryhorn
Starr
Loch Head
Knockgray
Carsphairn
Marscalloch Hill
381
Shalloch
542
Loch Macaterick
Meaul
695
Bardennoch
19
Kendoon Loch
565
Polmaddie Hill
479
Shalloch on Minnoch
Dalshangan
Carlin's Cairn
Kirriereoch Hill
786
Corserine
813
Loch Harrow
Forrest Lodge
Kirriereoch Loch
Burnhead
Rhinns of Kells
Merrick
843
Loch Enoch
Millfire
716
Knocknalling
Carsfad Loch
Earlstoun Loch
Black Clauchrie
Loch Moan
Garwall Hill
349
Palgowan
Loch Dungeon
Meikle Millyea
746
Craignaw
Loch Neldricken
Loch Valley
Buchan Hill
493
Southern Upland Way
Garroch
Loch Goosey
Eldrick
Corwar House
Glen Trool Lodge
Darrou
Glenlee
Loch Trool
1307
557
Mulldonoch
Loch Dee
Bennan
381
22
Clatteringshaws Loch
Craigencallie
New Galloway
Drumlamford Loch
Glentrool
Lamachan Hill
716
Drumlamford Ho.
Bargrennan
Loch Dornal
Loch Ochiltree
Larg Hill
675
Darnaw
Clatteringshaws
Bruce's Stone (NTS)
Cairnsmore of Dee
493
Millfore
656
Loch Maberry
Clachaneasy
Larg
Forest Drive (summer only)
Galloway Deer Range
Polbae
Garlick Hill
445
Wild Goat Park
Round Fell
402
Shaw Hill
385
Knockville
Fell of Fleet
471
Urrall Fell
184
Knowe
Craignelder
601
Penninghame
Garlies Castle
Dallash
Loch Grannoch
Loch Fleet
Auchencloy Hill
209
Airie Hill
291
Glenrazie
Boreland
Cumloden
Cairnsmore of Fleet
Loch Skerrow
Carseriggan
Challoch
Minnigaff
Creebridge
Bargaly
711
Newton Stewart
Blackcraig
213
Culvennan Fell
Cairnsmore
White Top of Culreoch
344
Benfield
1
Nether Barr
Palnure
Door of Cairnsmore
Shennanton
Linn of Barhoise
6
15
Baltersan
Barraer
Kirkcowan
Spittal
Barlae
Craighlaw
7
Castramont
Causeway End
Carsegowan
Barholm Mains
Gem Rock Museum
Glenquicken Moor
Rusko
Low Barlay
Creetown
Spittal
Cassencarie
Glen
Lauchentyre
Culquhirk
Wigtown Sands
Stone Circle
Martyrs' Monument
Cairnharrow
456
Anwoth
Gatehouse of Fleet
Fell Loch
Old Place of Mochrum
Bladnoch
Wigtown
Carsluith
Chambered Cairns
Ardwall
Cardoness Castle
Castle Loch
Culmalzie
11
Carsluith
13
Girthon
Cardoness
Baldoon Sands
Kirkdale House
Mochrum Loch
Barnbarroch
Braehead
Dunduroon
Fleet Bay
Barharrow
Culshabbin
Kirkinner
Murray's Isles
Lennox Plunton
Orchardton Bay
Innerwell Port
Barrachan
Islands of Fleet
Knockbrex

Galloway: *Galloway Forest Park covering an area of 230 square miles (596 sq km) is generally regarded as the largest forest in Britain. The park contains over 200 miles (320km) of cycle routes.* ***Map ref. E2***

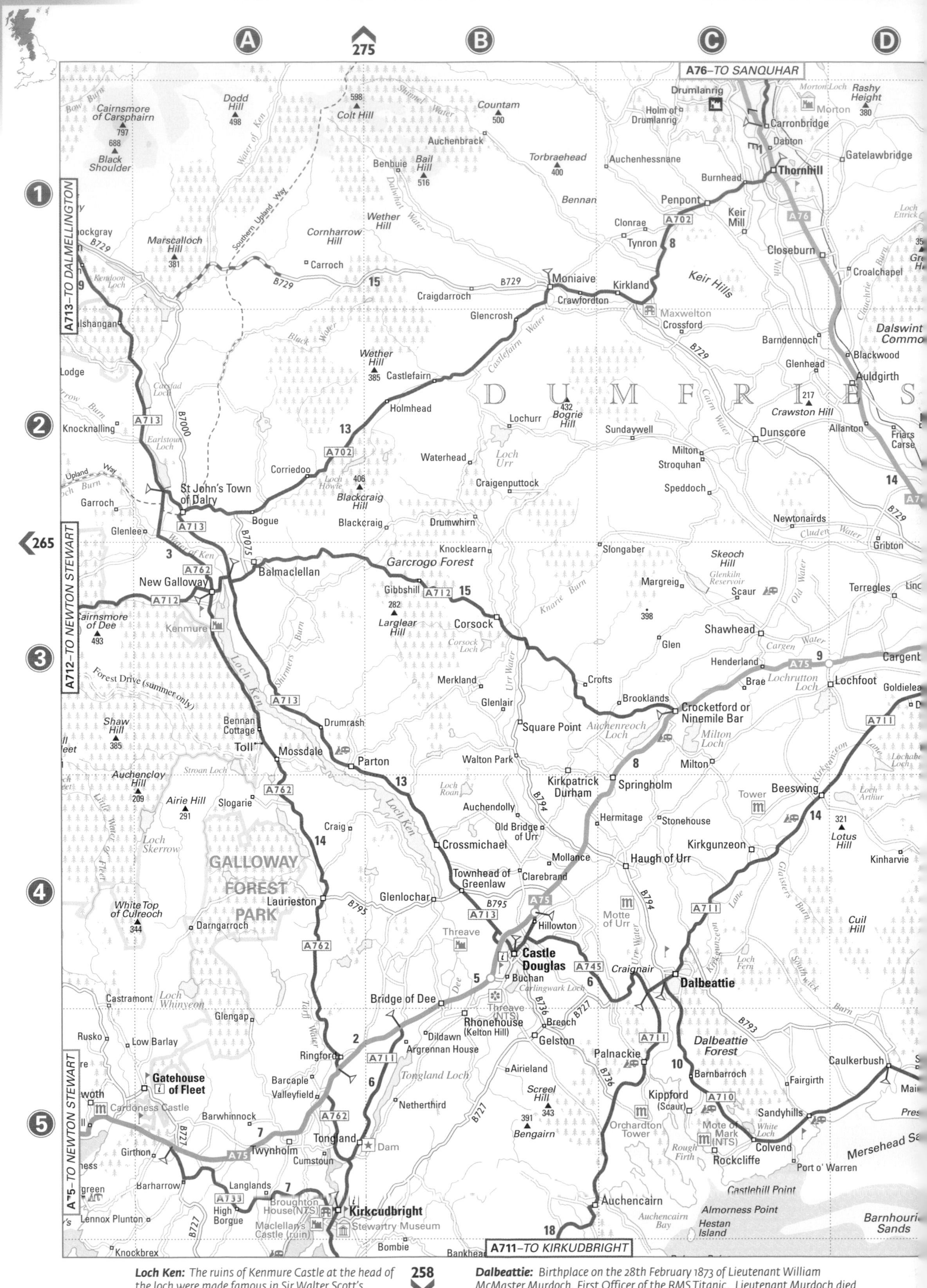

275

A B C D

1 2 3 4 5

A76–TO SANQUHAR

A713–TO DALMELLINGTON

265

A712–TO NEWTON STEWART

A75–TO NEWTON STEWART

A711–TO KIRKCUDBRIGHT

DUMFRIES

GALLOWAY FOREST PARK

Drumlanrig
Thornhill
Penpont
Moniaive
St John's Town of Dalry
New Galloway
Balmaclellan
Corsock
Crocketford or Ninemile Bar
Parton
Crossmichael
Castle Douglas
Dalbeattie
Gatehouse of Fleet
Kirkcudbright
Auchencairn

258

Loch Ken: *The ruins of Kenmure Castle at the head of the loch were made famous in Sir Walter Scott's ballad 'Young Lochinvar' and also in Robert Burns Jacobite song 'Kenmure's up and awa', Willie'*
Map ref. A3

Dalbeattie: *Birthplace on the 28th February 1873 of Lieutenant William McMaster Murdoch, First Officer of the RMS Titanic. Lieutenant Murdoch died aboard ship when the Titanic struck an iceberg and sank on the 15th April 1912.*
Map ref. C4

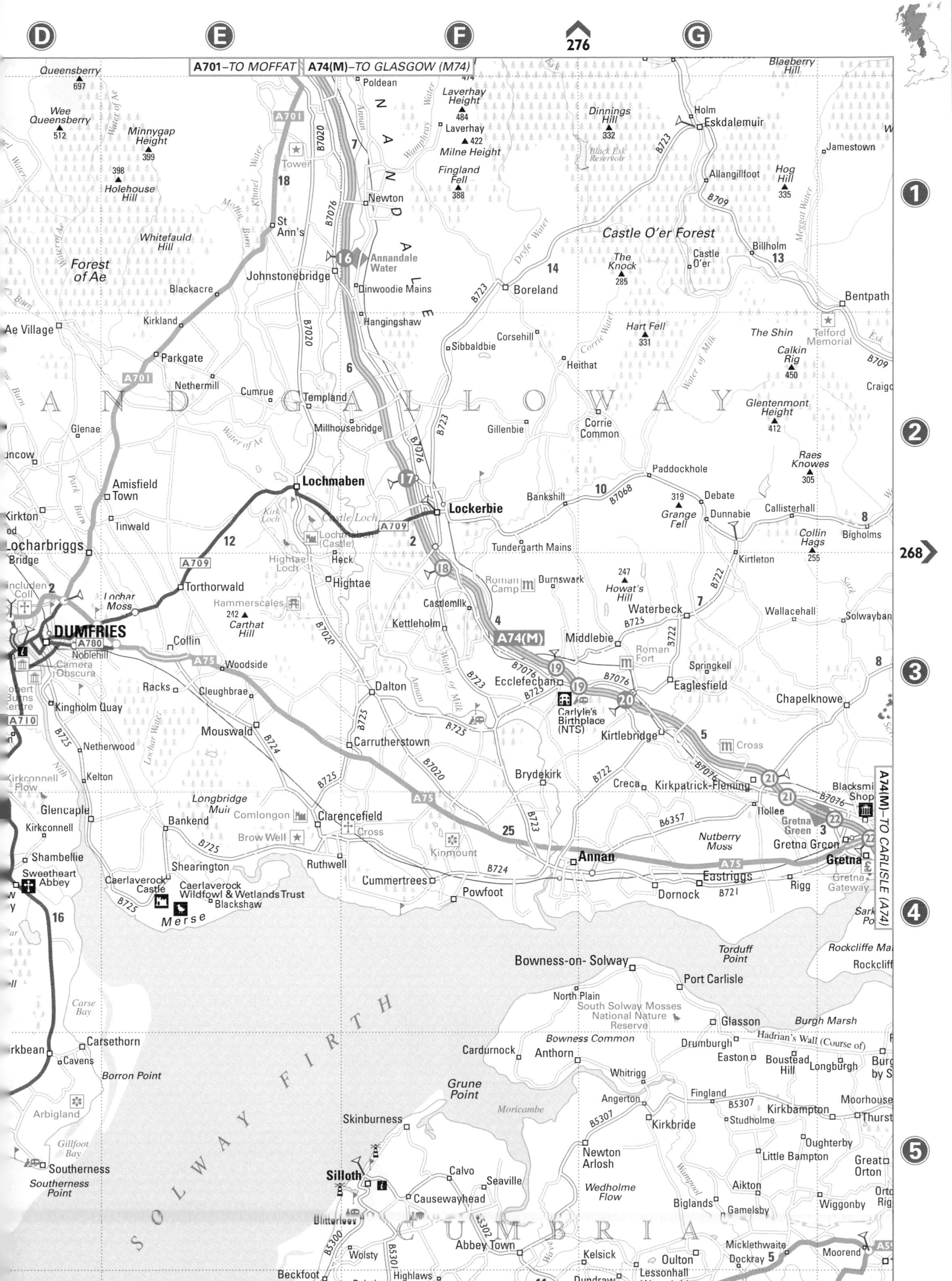

D
E
F
G
276
A701–TO MOFFAT
A74(M)–TO GLASGOW (M74)
Queensberry
697
Wee Queensberry
512
Minnygap Height
399
398
Holehouse Hill
Whitefauld Hill
Forest of Ae
Blackacre
Kirkland
Ae Village
Parkgate
Nethermill
Cumrue
Glenae
Amisfield Town
Tinwald
Locharbriggs
Torthorwald
Lochar Moss
DUMFRIES
Noblehill
Camera Obscura
Kingholm Quay
Netherwood
Kelton
Glencaple
Kirkconnell
Shambellie
Sweetheart Abbey
Carsethorn
Cavens
Borron Point
Arbigland
Gillfoot Bay
Carse Bay
Southerness
Southerness Point
Tower
St Ann's
Johnstonebridge
Poldean
Newton
Annandale Water
Dinwoodie Mains
Hangingshaw
Templand
Millhousebridge
Lochmaben
Castle Loch
Lochmaben (Castle)
Hightae Loch
Heck
Hightae
Hammerscales
Carthat Hill
212
Collin
Woodside
Racks
Cleughbrae
Mouswald
Carrutherstown
Dalton
Kettleholm
Castlemilk
Longbridge Muir
Bankend
Comlongon
Brow Well
Clarencefield
Cross
Ruthwell
Shearington
Caerlaverock Castle
Caerlaverock Wildfowl & Wetlands Trust
Blackshaw
Merse
Cummertrees
Powfoot
Kinmount
Laverhay Height
484
Laverhay
422
Milne Height
Fingland Fell
388
ANNANDALE
Boreland
Sibbaldbie
Corsehill
Heithat
Gillenbie
Lockerbie
Tundergarth Mains
Bankshill
Roman Camp
Burnswark
Middlebie
Roman Fort
Ecclefechan
Carlyle's Birthplace (NTS)
Kirtlebridge
Brydekirk
Creca
Kirkpatrick-Fleming
Annan
A74(M)
Dinnings Hill
332
Black Esk Reservoir
Holm
Eskdalemuir
Jamestown
Allangillfoot
Hog Hill
335
Castle O'er Forest
The Knock
285
Castle O'er
Billholm
Bentpath
Hart Fell
331
Telford Memorial
The Shin
Calkin Rig
450
Craig
Glentenmont Height
412
Corrie Common
Paddockhole
Raes Knowes
305
Debate
319
Grange Fell
Dunnabie
Callisterhall
Collin Hags
255
Bigholms
Kirtleton
Howat's Hill
247
Waterbeck
Wallacehall
Solwaybank
Springkell
Eaglesfield
Chapelknowe
Cross
Blacksmith Shop
Hollee
Gretna Green
Gretna
Gretna Gateway
Nutberry Moss
Eastriggs
Rigg
Dornock
Sark
A74(M)–TO CARLISLE (A74)
DUMFRIES AND GALLOWAY
268
Torduff Point
Rockcliffe Marsh
Rockcliffe
Bowness-on-Solway
Port Carlisle
North Plain
South Solway Mosses National Nature Reserve
Glasson
Burgh Marsh
Bowness Common
Drumburgh
Hadrian's Wall (Course of)
Cardurnock
Anthorn
Easton
Boustead Hill
Longburgh
Burgh by Sands
Whitrigg
Grune Point
Moricambe
Angerton
Fingland
Studholme
Kirkbampton
Moorhouse
Thurstonfield
Kirkbride
Oughterby
Little Bampton
Great Orton
Skinburness
Newton Arlosh
SOLWAY FIRTH
Silloth
Calvo
Seaville
Causewayhead
Wedholme Flow
Aikton
Biglands
Gamelsby
Wiggonby
Blitterlees
CUMBRIA
Abbey Town
Kelsick
Oulton
Micklethwaite
Dockray
Moorend
Wolsty
Beckfoot
Pelutho
Highlaws
Dundraw
Lessonhall
Waverbridge
1
2
3
4
5

Ruthwell: *Dr Henry Duncan (1774–1846) opened the worlds first bank here when he was the minister of this parish. He is regarded as the founder of savings banks and is remembered in Henry Duncan House, the Edinburgh headquarters of a national banking group.* ***Map ref. E4***

259

Lockerbie: *On the evening of the 21st December 1988 terrorists placed a bomb on board Pan Am flight 103. The plane exploded 6 miles (9.65km) above this small Scottish town. All 259 people on board, plus 11 people on the ground lost their lives in what proved to be the biggest mass murder in British history.* ***Map ref. F2***

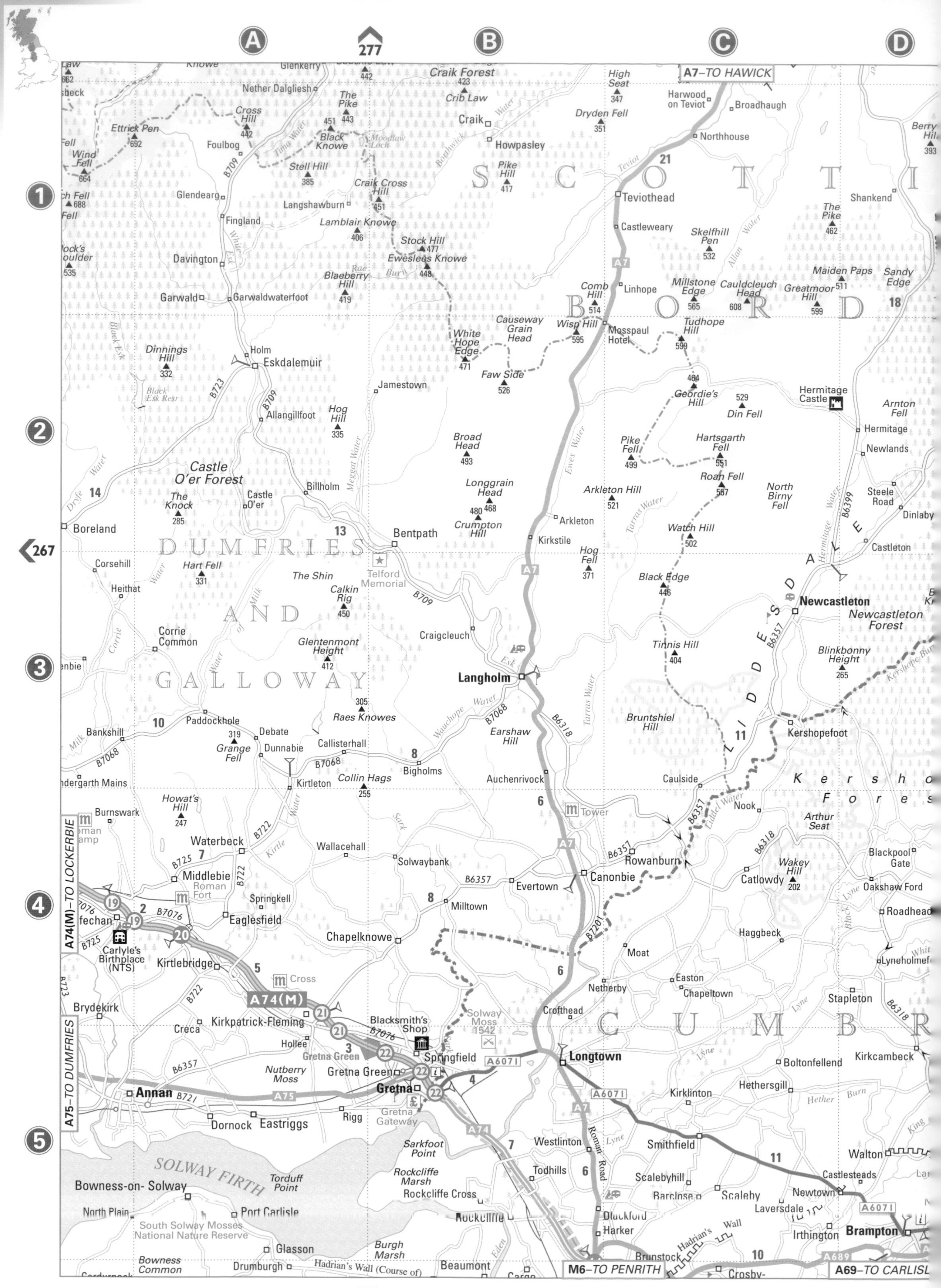

A 277 B C D

1 2 3 4 5

267

Newcastleton: *This village was planned and built specifically as a handloom weaving centre, in 1793, by the Duke of Buccleuch for his employees.* ***Map ref. C3***

259

Gretna: *Britain's worst ever rail disaster happened at Quintinshill, just north-east of Gretna on the 22nd May 1915. A troop train, towing wooden carriages, collided with a stationary passenger train and was then itself hit by an oncoming express train. 227 people, most of them soldiers, were killed in the crashes and subsequent fire.* ***Map ref. B5***

278

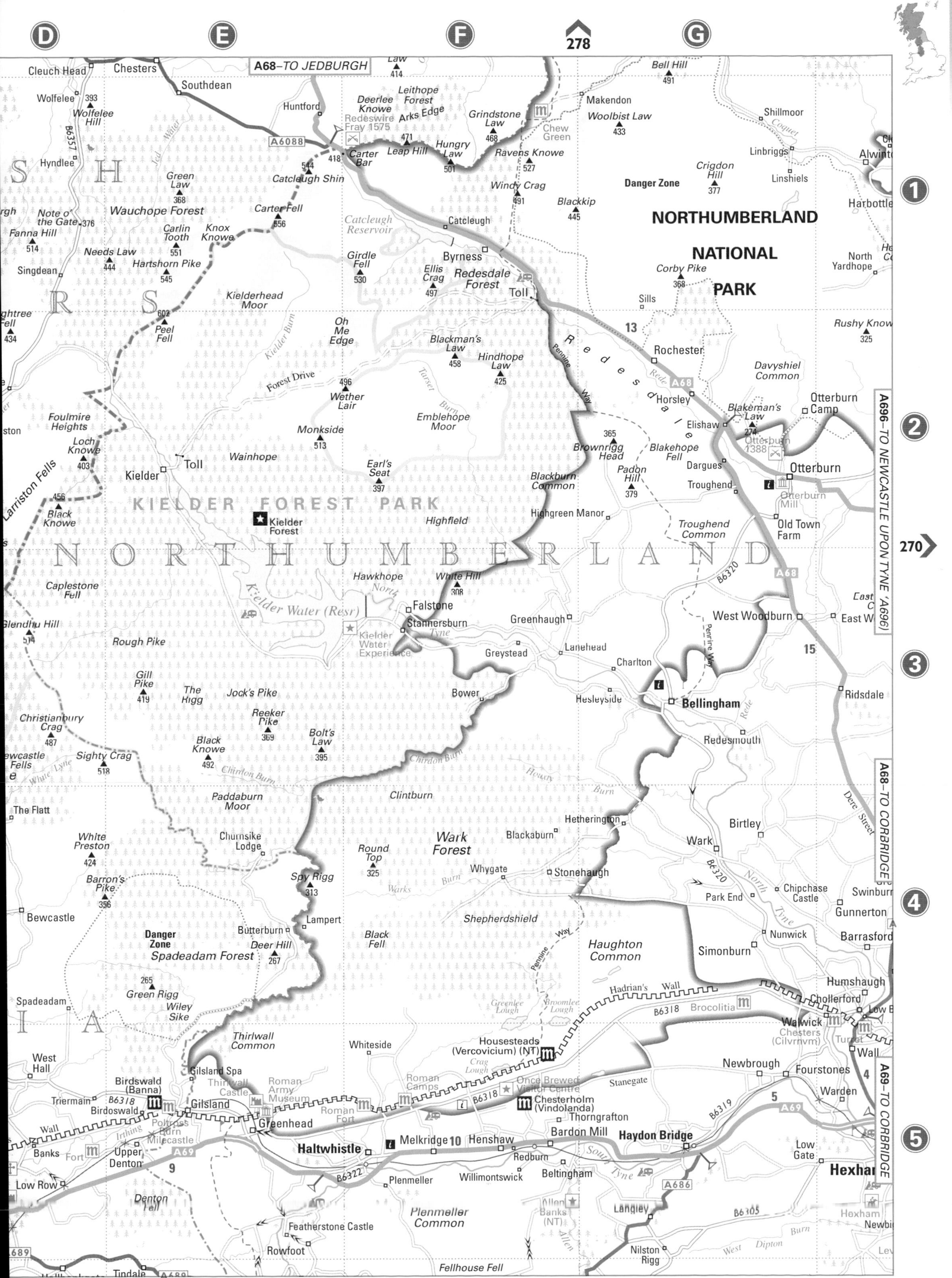
D
E
F
G
A68–TO JEDBURGH
Cleuch Head
Chesters
Southdean
Wolfelee 393
Wolfelee Hill
B6357
Hyndlee
Huntford
A6088
Law 414
Leithope Forest
Deerlee Knowe
Redeswire Fray 1575
Arks Edge
471
Carter Bar
Leap Hill
418
544
Grindstone Law 468
Hungry Law 501
Chew Green
Makendon
Woolbist Law 433
Bell Hill 491
Shillmoor
Linbriggs
Linshiels
Alwinton
Harbottle
Ravens Knowe 527
Windy Crag 491
Crigdon Hill 377
Danger Zone
Blackkip 445
NORTHUMBERLAND NATIONAL PARK
Green Law 368
Catcleugh Shin
Carter Fell 556
Wauchope Forest
Note o' the Gate 376
Fanna Hill 514
Carlin Tooth 551
Knox Knowe
Catcleugh Reservoir
Catcleugh
Needs Law 444
Hartshorn Pike 545
Singdean
Girdle Fell 530
Byrness
Ellis Crag 497
Redesdale Forest
Toll
North Yardhope
Corby Pike 368
Sills
Kielderhead Moor
602
Peel Fell
434
Oh Me Edge
Blackman's Law 458
Hindhope Law 425
Rochester
Rushy Knowe 325
Davyshiel Common
13
Redesdale
Pennine Way
Forest Drive
496
Wether Lair
Emblehope Moor
A68
Horsley
Blakeman's Law 274
Otterburn Camp
Otterburn 1388
Elishaw
Foulmire Heights
Monkside 513
365
Brownrigg Head
Blakehope Fell
Dargues
Otterburn
Loch Knowe 403
Larriston Fells
Toll
Kielder
Wainhope
Earl's Seat 397
Blackburn Common
Padon Hill 379
Troughend
Otterburn Mill
456
Black Knowe
KIELDER FOREST PARK
Kielder Forest
Highfield
Highgreen Manor
Troughend Common
Old Town Farm
NORTHUMBERLAND
A696–TO NEWCASTLE UPON TYNE 'A696'
Caplestone Fell
Hawkhope
White Hill 308
B6320
A68
Kielder Water (Resr)
Falstone
Stannersburn
Greenhaugh
West Woodburn
East Woodburn
Glendhu Hill 514
Kielder Water Experience
Rough Pike
Greystead
Lanehead
Charlton
15
Gill Pike 419
The Rigg
Jock's Pike
Bower
Hesleyside
Bellingham
Ridsdale
Reeker Pike 369
Christianbury Crag 487
Black Knowe 492
Bolt's Law 395
Redesmouth
Bewcastle Fells
Sighty Crag 518
Chirdon Burn
A68–TO CORBRIDGE
Paddaburn Moor
Clintburn
The Flatt
Hetherington
Birtley
White Preston 424
Churnsike Lodge
Round Top 325
Wark Forest
Blackaburn
Wark
Barron's Pike 356
Spy Rigg 313
Whygate
Stonehaugh
Park End
Chipchase Castle
Swinburn
Gunnerton
Bewcastle
Lampert
Shepherdshield
Butterburn
Danger Zone
Deer Hill 267
Black Fell
Nunwick
Simonburn
Barrasford
Spadeadam Forest
Haughton Common
265
Green Rigg
Spadeadam
Wiley Sike
Hadrian's Wall
B6318
Brocolitia
Humshaugh
Chollerford
Greenlee Lough
Broomlee Lough
Walwick
Chesters (Cilurnum)
Thirlwall Common
Whiteside
Housesteads (Vercovicium) (NT)
Crag Lough
Newbrough
Fourstones
West Hall
Gilsland Spa
Thirlwall Castle
Roman Army Museum
Roman Camps
Once Brewed Visitor Centre
Stanegate
Birdswald (Banna)
Chesterholm (Vindolanda)
Warden
Triermain
B6318
Birdoswald
Gilsland
Roman Fort
Thorngrafton
B6319
5
A69
Greenhead
Poltross Burn Milecastle
Bardon Mill
Haydon Bridge
A69–TO CORBRIDGE
Wall
Banks
Upper Denton
Haltwhistle
Melkridge 10
Henshaw
Low Gate
A69
Redburn
9
B6322
Plenmeller
Willimontswick
Beltingham
Hexham
Low Row
South Tyne
A686
Denton Fell
Plenmeller Common
Allen Banks (NT)
Langley
B6305
Featherstone Castle
Hexham
Rowfoot
Nilston Rigg
West Dipton Burn
Fellhouse Fell
A689
Tindale

Kielder Forest: *This is the largest forest in England covering an area of 200 square miles (518 sq km) and planted with over 150 million trees. The forest is man-made and the first tree was planted at Smales Farm in 1926.* ***Map ref. E2***

260

Kielder Water: *With a shoreline of over 27 miles (44km), Kielder Water is the largest artificial lake in Northern Europe.* ***Map ref. E3***

270

278

A
B
C
D
1
2
3
4
5
A68–TO JEDBURGH
A697–TO COLDSTREAM
A69–TO HALTWHISTLE
A68–TO CONSETT(A692)
Bell Hill
491
416
Alnham
Scrainwood
Yetlington
Callaly
Thrunton Wood
Edlingham
Makendon
Woolbist Law
433
Chew Green
Shillmoor
Coquet
Biddlestone
Elilaw
Netherton Northside
Netherton
Netherton Burnfoot
Lorbottle Hall
Long Crag
Bigges' Pillar
Ravens Knowe
527
Linbriggs
Clennell
Alwinton
Newton
Lorbottle
Crigdon Hill
377
Danger Zone
Linshiels
Burradon
High Trewhitt
B6341
Newton
Blackkip
445
NORTHUMBERLAND
NATIONAL
PARK
Harbottle
Sharperton
Cartington
Shirlaw Pike
308
Forest
Lady's Well
Plainfield
Warton
Snitter
Cragside (NT)
Nelly's Moss Lakes
A697
North Yardhope
Holystone Common
Holystone
Flotterton
Thropton
Rothbury
Caistron
North
Corby Pike
368
Hepple
B6341
Little Tosson
Sills
Bickerton
Great Tosson
Newtown
Whitton
Longframlington
13
Rushy Knowe
325
Pauperhaugh
B6344
Tosson Hill
440
Simonside
429
Rothbury
B6342
Brinkburn Priory
Redesdale
Pennine Way
Rochester
Low Hesleyhurst
Davyshiel Common
Rede
A68
Billsmoor Park
Horsley
Otterburn Camp
Dough Crag
386
B6341
Forestburn Gate
Blakeman's Law
274
Wingates
Elishaw
Coldrife
365
Brownrigg Head
Blakehope Fell
Otterburn 1388
Burn
Padon Hill
379
Dargues
Otterburn
Elsdon
Harwood Forest
Fallowlees
Fontburn Resr
Blackburn Common
Troughend
Font
Nunnykirk
Otterburn Mill
Highgreen Manor
Raylees
Ewesley Burn
Troughend Common
Old Town Farm
14
A696
Harwood
Rothley Lakes
269
Stanton
Ottercops Moss
B6342
Netherwitton
B6320
A68
Raylees Common
Hartington Hall
Longwitton
Font
East Woodburn Common
Raechester
Rothley
Hart Burn
Greenhaugh
West Woodburn
East Woodburn
Scots' Gap
Pennine Way
B6343
Hartburn
Throphill
Lanehead
15
Ray Fell
303
Knowesgate
Cambo
Middleton
B6343
Charlton
B6342
High Angerton
Kirkwhelpington
Wallington (NT)
Wansbeck
Meldon
Hesleyside
Bellingham
Rede
Ridsdale
Wansbeck
Low Angerton
Middleton Bank Top
Bolam Lake
Bolam
Sweethope Loughs
Kirkharle
Redesmouth
NORTHUMBERLAND
A696
Houxty Burn
Capheaton
Great Bavington
Bradford
Thockrington
Little Bavington
9
Blyth
Belsay
Hetherington
Colt Crag Resr
B6342
Belsay Hall, Castle & Gardens
Blackaburn
Birtley
Dere Street
Little Swinburne
Kirkheaton
16
Wark
Kearsley Fell
244
Black Heddon
Stonehaugh
B6320
North Tyne
Hallington
Blackheddon
Chipchase Castle
Great Swinburne
Colwell
Hallington Reservoir
Milbourne
Park End
Gunnerton
Ryal
Ingoe
Burn
Pennine Way
Nunwick
A6079
Barrasford
B6309
Grindstonelaw
223
Fenwick
Heugh
Haughton Common
Simonburn
4
A68
Chollerton
Bingfield
Stamfordham
Humshaugh
Cocklaw
Matfen
Hawkwell
Dalton
Hadrian's Wall
Chollerford
6
Pont
Eachwick
Broomlee Lough
B6318
Brocolitia
Low Brunton
Great Whittington
Ouston
Walwick
Little Whittington
Chesters (Cilurnum)
B6318
Harlow Hill
Housesteads (NT)
Turret
Wall
15
Wall Houses
Vindobala
Heddon-on-the-Wall
Newbrough
Hadrian's Wall
Fourstones
B6318
Halton
Once Brewed Visitor Centre
Stanegate
Stagshaw Bank
B6321
B6309
Rudchester
B6528
Chesterholm (Vindolanda)
Warden
5
4
Sandhoe
9
George Stephenson's Birthplace (NT)
Thorngrafton
B6319
A69
Acomb
Anick
Bardon Mill
Haydon Bridge
Aydon
Horsley
Wylam
Tyne Green
Corstopitum
A69
Low Gate
Corbridge
Newton
Clara Vale
South Tyne
A695
B6309
Ovingham
Hexham
Beltingham
A686
B6306
Dilston
A69
Ovington
B6395
Crawcrook
Sunnyside
B6307
B6530
Riding Mill
1
Mickley Square
Prudhoe
Allen Banks (NT)
Langley
Linnels
A695
Stocksfield
Bywell
B6305
Hexham
Newbiggin
Coalburns
Broomhaugh
Painshawfield
Burn
Allen
Hexham Levels 1464
Dipton Wood
Stanley Burn
Nilston Rigg
West Dipton Burn
New Ridley
Leadgate
High

261

Kirkharle: *Lancelot 'Capability' Brown, one of Britain's greatest landscape gardeners, was born here in 1715. He designed gardens for many stately homes and became head gardener at Hampton Court Palace in 1761. 'Capability' Brown died on the 6th February 1783.* ***Map ref. C3***

D
E
279
F
G
BERWICK-UPON-TWEED
A1068–TO ALNWICK
1
2
3
4
5
Alnmouth Bay
High Buston
Shilbottle
Low Buston
A1068
Birling
Eastfield Hall
Warkworth
Warkworth Castle
Coquet Island
Gloster Hill
Hazon
Amble
Guyzance
Morwick Hall
B6345
High Hauxley
North Togston
Hauxley Haven
Acklington
Togston
Radcliffe
B6345
Felton
West Thirston
Broomhill
B1330
Hadston Carrs
Thirston New Houses
East Thirston
South Broomhill
Chevington Drift
Red Row
Druridge Bay Country Pk
Eshott
Druridge Bay
15
West Chevington
A1068
A1
Causey Park
Widdrington
Druridge
Widdrington Station
17
Widdrington Sta
Earsdon Moor
Cresswell
The Scars
Fenrother
Tritlington
Snab Point
Ulgham
Ellington
Espley Hall
Cockle Park
B1337
Lynemouth
Beacon Point
Hebron
A189
Longhirst
Queen Elizabeth II
Woodhorn
A1068
Pegswood
ASHINGTON
B1334
Newbiggin-by-the-Sea
1
A197
Hirst
Northumbria Craft Centre
A1068
Bothal
A196
North Seaton
Mitford
Morpeth Chantry
Wansbeck
Sheepwash
Stakeford
Morpeth
Shadfen
A196
Guide Post
A1147
Cambois
A192
Choppington
6
A197
Tranwell
Clifton
Hepscott
East Sleekburn
Nedderton
A1068
B1331
Bebside
A193
Bedlington
Cowpen
BLYTH
A1068
B1505
A1
Saltwick
Plessey Woods
East Hartford
Newsham
Stannington
6
Blyth
A192
A1061
A193
Shotton
Nelson Village
Shankhouse
Seaton Delaval Hall
New Hartley
Cramlington
A189
A192
Seaton Sluice
A190
Seaton
Hartley
Berwick Hill
A1068
A1171
East Cramlington
Seaton Delaval
St Mary's Island (Bait Island)
Horton Grange
Brenkley
Seghill
Holywell
A193
B1325
Seaton Burn
Dudley
Spanish City
Dinnington
A192
Brunswick Village
Wide Open
Burradon
Earsdon
A1148
Whitley Bay
Camperdown
Prestwick
A1056
Backworth
A186
Monkseaton
Hazlerigg
Killingworth
Shiremoor
New York
Cullercoats
NEWCASTLE INTERNATIONAL
Newcastle
B1505
Benton
Marden
Tynemouth
Black Callerton
B6918
A191
A1
B1318
Forest Hall
Benton Square
A191
A1058
SEE PAGE 372
A696
Fawdon
A189
North Shields
B6324
Kenton
A186
Willington
Chirton
Gosforth
Longbenton
North Tyneside
SOUTH SHIELDS
A188
Westerhope
Blakelaw
WALLSEND
A193
A187
Newcastle United FC
Royal Quays
Jesmond
A183
NEWCASTLE UPON TYNE
Heaton
A183
Westoe
B1301
Newburn
Lemington
B1297
Toll
Bede's World
A194
Marsden Bay
A6085
Stella
Benwell
A167(M)
Walker
Jarrow
Hebburn
A1018
Marsden
Harton
Simonside
Blaydon
Life Science Centre
Byker
Tyne
A186
A185
Monkton
A1300
Whitburn
MetroCentre
A184
A1018
Amsterdam 15hrs
Winlaton
A1114
Pelaw
B1426
A194
B1298
Cleadon
Whickham
A694
GATESHEAD
Felling
Wardley
Boldon Colliery
Boldon
Winlaton Mill
Dunston Hill
A167
A184
East Boldon
A183
Team Valley
Whitburn Bay
West Boldon
B1291
Seaburn
A1–TO A1(M)
A194(M)–TO WASHINGTON
A1018–TO SUNDERLAND
hours
Bergen....................22-26
Göteborg....................25
Haugesund..............21½
Kristiansand...............17
Stavanger...................19

262

Jarrow: *Starting point on the 1st November 1936 of the protest march from Jarrow to London a distance of 300 miles (480km). 200 men marched in protest at the miseries of unemployment and the injustice of 'means testing'. The last surviving marcher Cornelius Whalen died in September 2003 aged 93.* ***Map ref. F5***

263

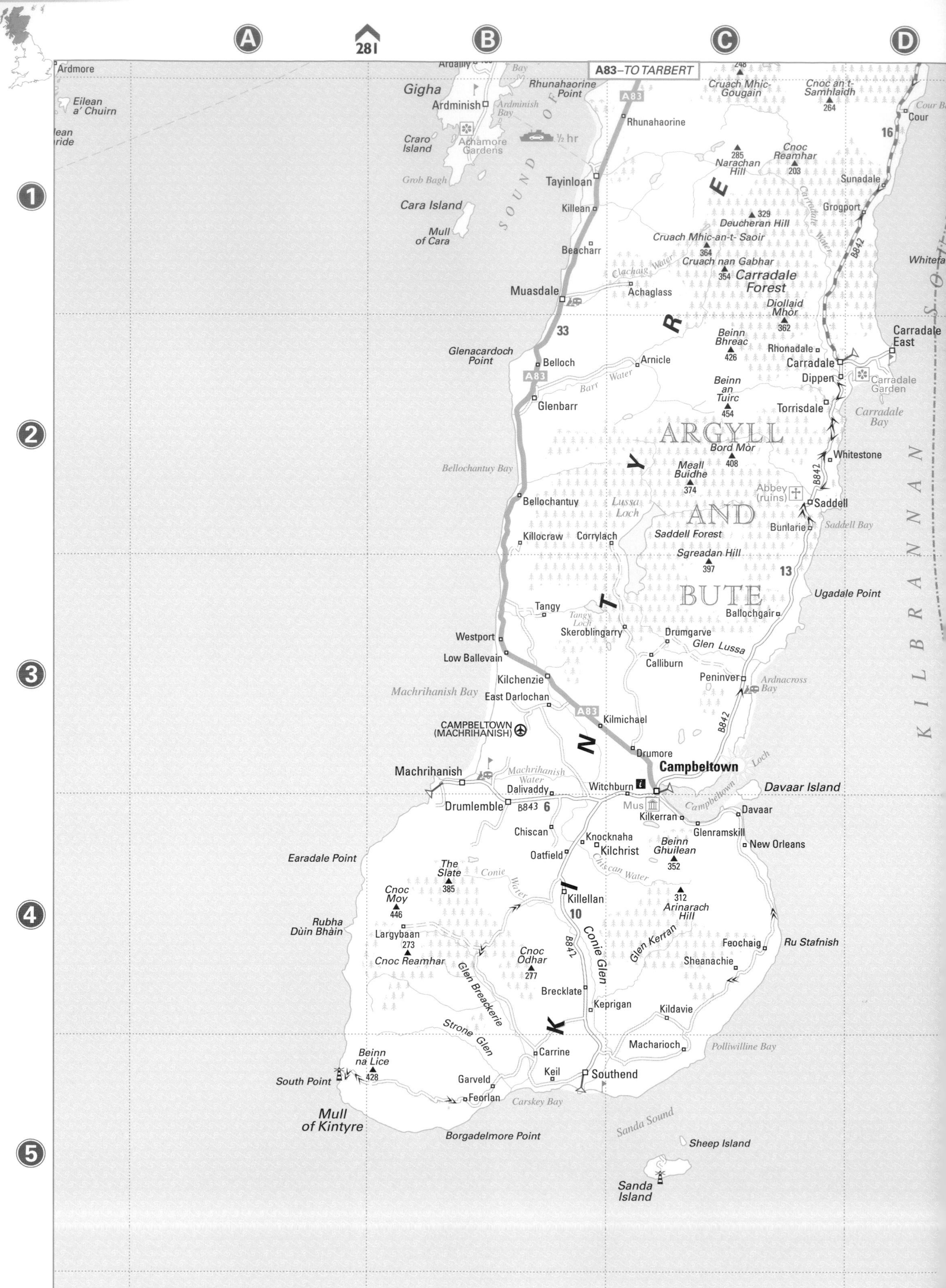

A
281
B
C
D
A83–TO TARBERT
Gigha
Ardminish
Craro Island
Achamore Gardens
Rhunahaorine Point
Rhunahaorine
Tayinloan
Cara Island
Mull of Cara
Killean
Beacharr
Muasdale
Achaglass
Cruach Mhic-Gougain
Cnoc an t-Samhlaidh
264
Cour
Narachan Hill
285
Cnoc Reamhar
203
Sunadale
Grogport
Deucheran Hill
329
Cruach Mhic-an-t- Saoir
364
Cruach nan Gabhar
354
Carradale Forest
Diollaid Mhòr
362
Beinn Bhreac
426
Rhonadale
Carradale
Carradale East
Dippen
Carradale Garden
Carradale Bay
Beinn an Tuirc
454
Torrisdale
Whitestone
Glenacardoch Point
Belloch
Arnicle
Glenbarr
ARGYLL
AND
BUTE
Bord Mòr
408
Meall Buidhe
374
Abbey (ruins)
Saddell
Bunlarie
Saddell Bay
Saddell Forest
Bellochantuy Bay
Bellochantuy
Lussa Loch
Killocraw
Corrylach
Sgreadan Hill
397
Ugadale Point
Tangy
Skeroblingarry
Ballochgair
Westport
Low Ballevain
Drumgarve
Glen Lussa
Calliburn
Peninver
Ardnacross Bay
Kilchenzie
Machrihanish Bay
East Darlochan
Kilmichael
CAMPBELTOWN (MACHRIHANISH)
Drumore
Campbeltown
Machrihanish
Davaar Island
Dalivaddy
Witchburn
Drumlemble
B843
Mus
Kilkerran
Davaar
Glenramskill
New Orleans
Chiscan
Knocknaha
Kilchrist
Beinn Ghuilean
352
Oatfield
Earadale Point
The Slate
385
Cnoc Moy
446
Killellan
Arinarach Hill
312
Rubha Dùin Bhàin
Largybaan
273
Cnoc Reamhar
Cnoc Odhar
277
Conie Glen
Glen Kerran
Feochaig
Ru Stafnish
Sheanachie
Glen Breackerie
Brecklate
Keprigan
Kildavie
Strone Glen
Macharioch
Polliwilline Bay
Carrine
Beinn na Lice
428
South Point
Garveld
Keil
Southend
Feorlan
Carskey Bay
Mull of Kintyre
Borgadelmore Point
Sanda Sound
Sheep Island
Sanda Island
KINTYRE
KILBRANNAN SOUND
Whitefa
Ardmore
Eilean a' Chuirn
1
2
3
4
5

Mull of Kintyre: *Made famous in the song 'Mull of Kintyre' by Paul McCartney and Wings in 1977.* ***Map ref. A5***

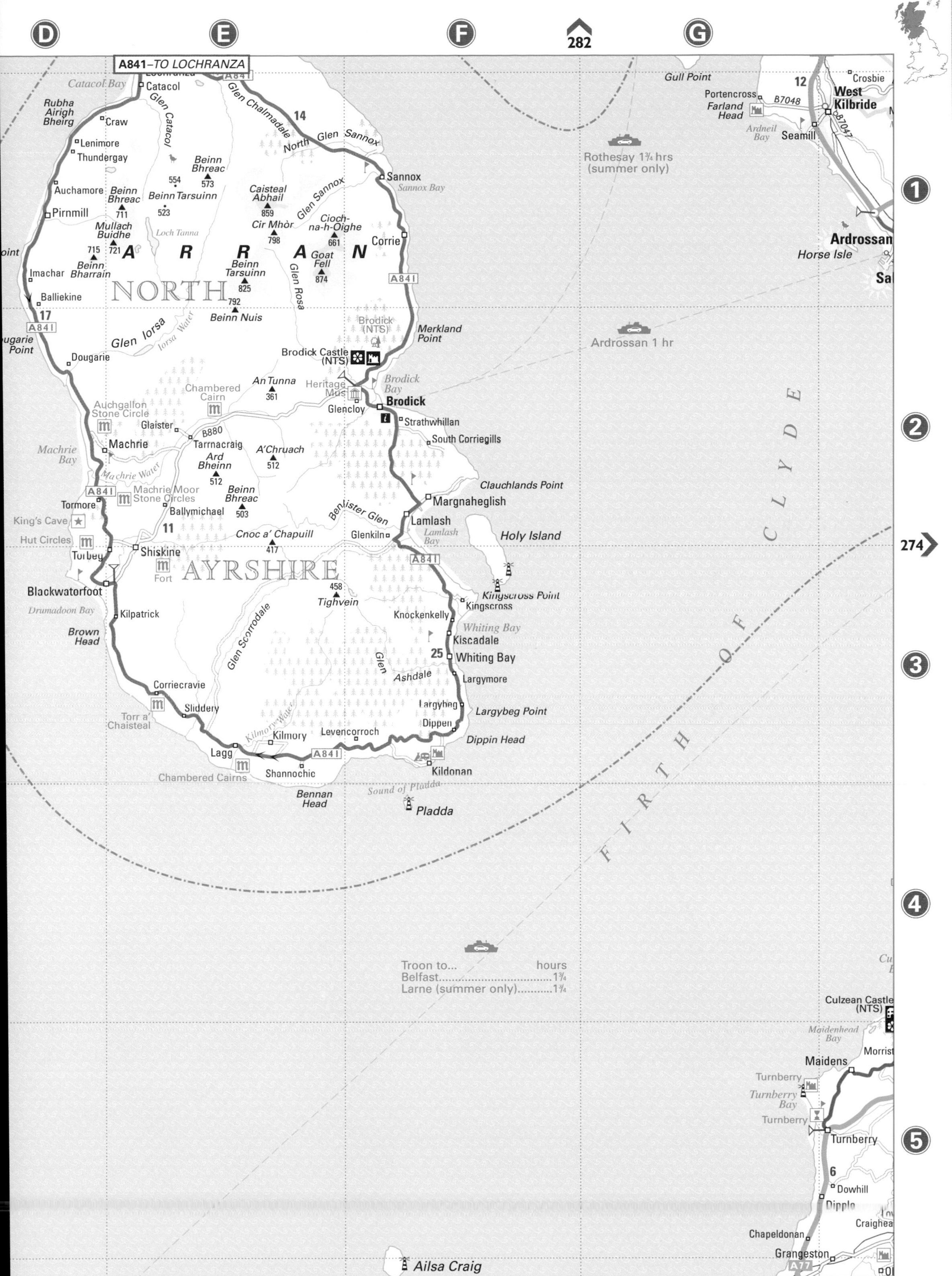
D
E
F
G
282
A841–TO LOCHRANZA
Catacol Bay
Catacol
Rubha Airigh Bheirg
Craw
Lenimore
Thundergay
Glen Catacol
Glen Chalmadale
14
North Glen Sannox
Beinn Bhreac
573
554
Auchamore
Beinn Bhreac
711
Beinn Tarsuinn
523
Caisteal Abhail
859
Glen Sannox
Sannox
Sannox Bay
Pirnmill
Mullach Buidhe
721
715
Loch Tanna
Cir Mhòr
798
Cioch-na-h-Oighe
661
Corrie
ARRAN
Goat Fell
874
Beinn Bharrain
Imachar
Beinn Tarsuinn
825
Glen Rosa
A841
NORTH
Balliekine
17
A841
792
Beinn Nuis
Brodick (NTS)
Merkland Point
Glen Iorsa
Iorsa Water
Dougarie Point
Dougarie
Brodick Castle (NTS)
Chambered Cairn
An Tunna
361
Heritage Mus
Brodick Bay
Brodick
Glencloy
Auchgalfon Stone Circle
Glaister
Strathwhillan
B880
South Corriegills
Machrie Bay
Machrie
Tarrnacraig
A'Chruach
512
Ard Bheinn
512
Machrie Water
Clauchlands Point
A841
Machrie Moor Stone Circles
Beinn Bhreac
503
Benlister Glen
Margnaheglish
Tormore
Ballymichael
Lamlash
King's Cave
11
Cnoc a' Chapuill
417
Glenkiln
Lamlash Bay
Holy Island
Hut Circles
Torbeg
Shiskine
A841
Fort
AYRSHIRE
Blackwaterfoot
458
Tighvein
Kingscross Point
Kingscross
Drumadoon Bay
Kilpatrick
Glen Scorrodale
Knockenkelly
Whiting Bay
Brown Head
Kiscadale
25
Whiting Bay
Glen Ashdale
Largymore
Corriecravie
Largybeg
Largybeg Point
Sliddery
Torr a' Chaisteal
Kilmory Water
Dippen
Kilmory
Levencorroch
Dippin Head
Lagg
A841
Kildonan
Chambered Cairns
Shannochie
Sound of Pladda
Bennan Head
Pladda
Gull Point
12
Crosbie
Portencross
West Kilbride
Farland Head
B7048
B7047
Ardneil Bay
Seamill
Rothesay 1¾ hrs (summer only)
Ardrossan
Horse Isle
Ardrossan 1 hr
FIRTH OF CLYDE
1
2
3
4
5
274
Troon to... hours
Belfast..........1¾
Larne (summer only)..........1¾
Culzean Castle (NTS)
Maidenhead Bay
Maidens
Turnberry
Turnberry Bay
Turnberry
Turnberry
6
Dowhill
Dipple
Craighead
Chapeldonan
Grangeston
A77
Ailsa Craig
264

Lamlash Bay *is where King Haakon of Norway sheltered his fleet on the way to the Battle of Largs in 1263. A cave on nearby Holy Island contains Viking inscriptions thought to have been made by his fighters.*
Map ref. F2

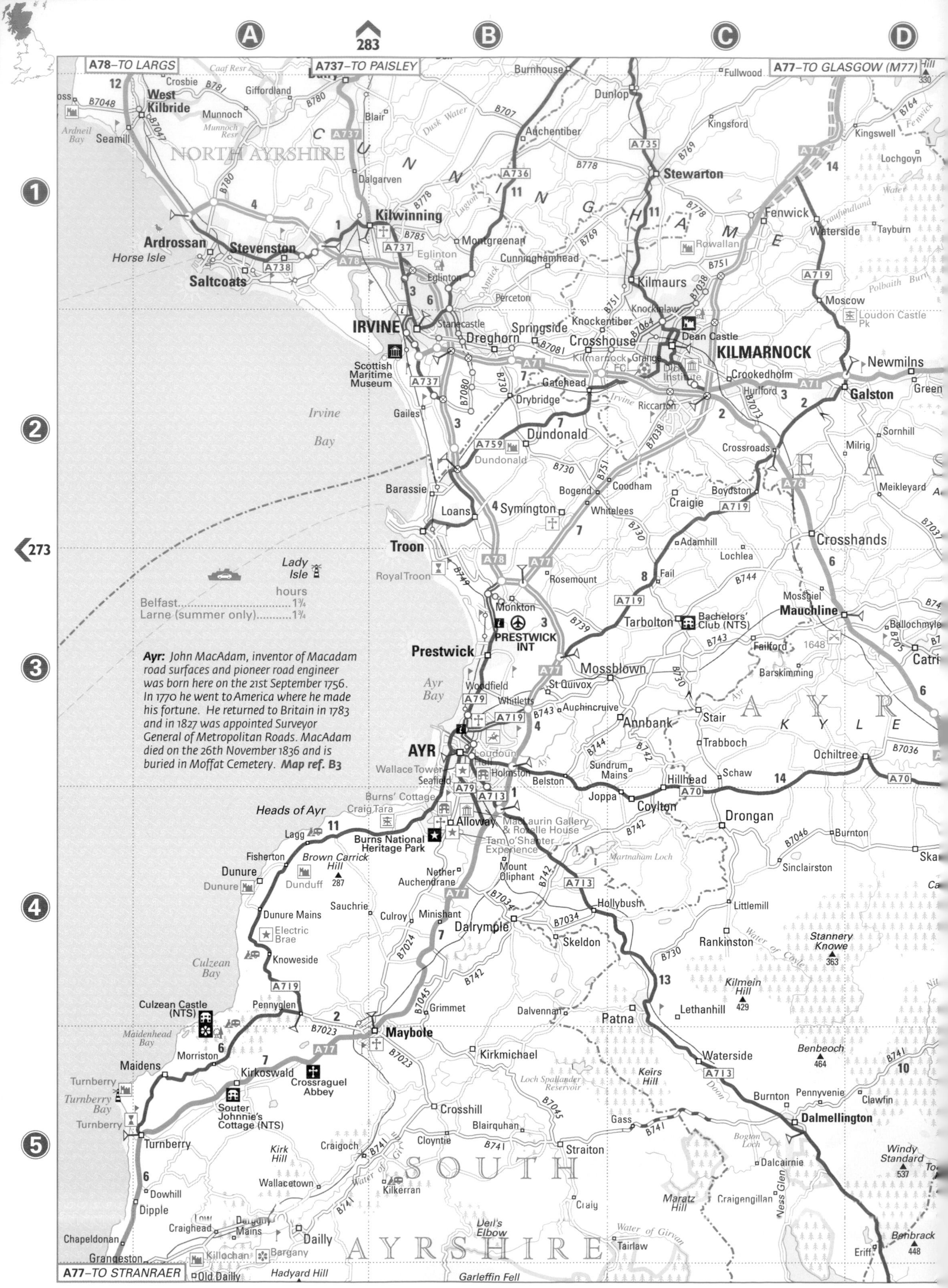

A
B
C
D
283
A78–TO LARGS
A737–TO PAISLEY
A77–TO GLASGOW (M77)
273
A77–TO STRANRAER
NORTH AYRSHIRE
CUNNINGHAME
KYLE
EAST AYRSHIRE
SOUTH AYRSHIRE
West Kilbride
Seamill
Ardrossan
Horse Isle
Saltcoats
Stevenston
Kilwinning
Dalgarven
Irvine
IRVINE
Scottish Maritime Museum
Irvine Bay
Dunlop
Stewarton
Kilmaurs
Fenwick
Waterside
Moscow
Loudon Castle Pk
Dean Castle
KILMARNOCK
Crookedholm
Newmilns
Galston
Dreghorn
Springside
Crosshouse
Knockentiber
Kilmarnock FC
Dick Institute
Gatehead
Drybridge
Riccarton
Hurlford
Dundonald
Barassie
Loans
Symington
Troon
Royal Troon
Lady Isle
hours
Belfast......................................1¾
Larne (summer only)...........1¾
Monkton
PRESTWICK INT
Prestwick
Ayr Bay
Tarbolton
Bachelors' Club (NTS)
Mauchline
Mossblown
Annbank
Stair
Trabboch
AYR
Wallace Tower
Seafield
Burns' Cottage
Heads of Ayr
Craig Tara
Alloway
MacLaurin Gallery & Rozelle House
Tam o'Shanter Experience
Burns National Heritage Park
Mount Oliphant
Coylton
Drongan
Ochiltree
Dunure
Brown Carrick Hill
Dalrymple
Electric Brae
Culzean Bay
Culzean Castle (NTS)
Maybole
Crossraguel Abbey
Kirkoswald
Souter Johnnie's Cottage (NTS)
Turnberry
Turnberry Bay
Maidens
Kirkmichael
Patna
Waterside
Dalmellington
Straiton
Dailly
Girvan

Ayr: *John MacAdam, inventor of Macadam road surfaces and pioneer road engineer was born here on the 21st September 1756. In 1770 he went to America where he made his fortune. He returned to Britain in 1783 and in 1827 was appointed Surveyor General of Metropolitan Roads. MacAdam died on the 26th November 1836 and is buried in Moffat Cemetery.* ***Map ref. B3***

Turnberry: *Robert Bruce (1274–1329) was born here. Bruce was proclaimed King of Scotland following the execution of William Wallace in 1306 and went on to defeat the English in several battles culminating at the Battle of Bannockburn on the 23–24th June 1314.* ***Map ref. A5***

265

Alloway: *Scotland's most famous poet, Robert Burns, was born here on the 25th January 1759. He died on the 21st July 1796 of heart disease at the age of 37, on the same day as his wife Jean gave birth to his last son. It is said that 10,000 people turned out for his funeral and, in his honour, Burns Nights are celebrated all around the world on his birthday. See Burns National Heritage Park.* ***Map ref. B4 Also on page 118***

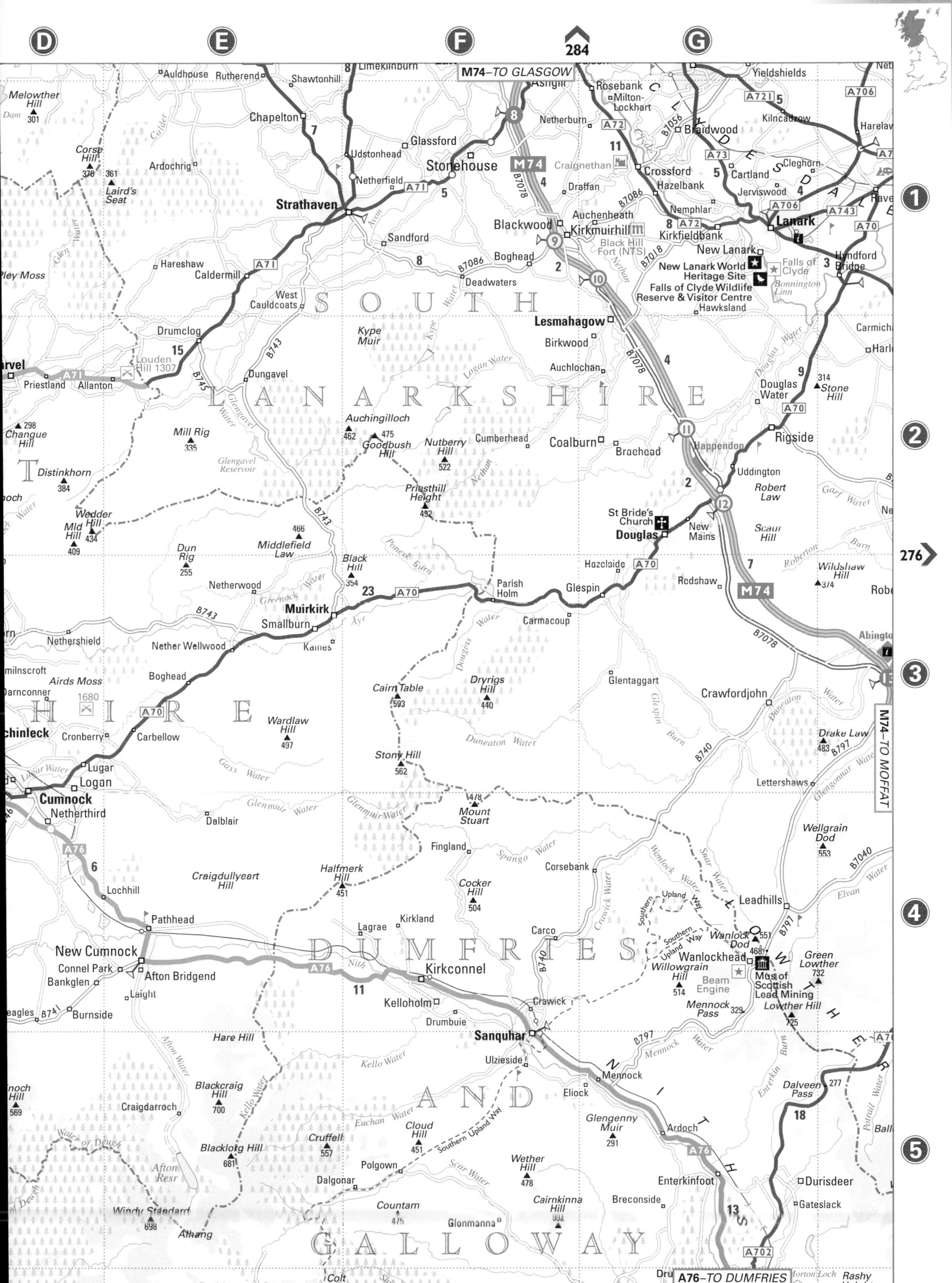

D
E
F
G
284
1
2
3
4
5
276
266
M74–TO GLASGOW
M74–TO MOFFAT
A76–TO DUMFRIES
SOUTH
LANARKSHIRE
DUMFRIES
AND
GALLOWAY
LOWTHER
NITH
CLYDESDALE
Auldhouse
Rutherend
Shawtonhill
Limekilnburn
Melowther Hill
301
Chapelton
Glassford
Udstonhead
Stonehouse
Corse Hill
370
361
Laird's Seat
Ardochrig
Netherfield
Strathaven
Sandford
Hareshaw
Caldermill
West Cauldcoats
Boghead
Deadwaters
Drumclog
Louden Hill 1307
Priestland
Allanton
Dungavel
Kype Muir
Auchingilloch
462
475
Goodbush Hill
Nutberry Hill
522
Cumberhead
Mill Rig
335
298
Changue Hill
Glengavel Reservoir
Distinkhorn
384
Wedder Hill
434
Mid Hill
409
Priesthill Height
492
Dun Rig
255
Middlefield Law
466
Black Hill
354
Netherwood
Muirkirk
Smallburn
Kames
Nethershield
Nether Wellwood
Parish Holm
Glespin
Carmacoup
Airds Moss
Boghead
1680
Cronberry
Carbellow
Lugar
Logan
Cumnock
Netherthird
Wardlaw Hill
497
Cairn Table
593
Dryrigs Hill
440
Stony Hill
562
Mount Stuart
478
Dalblair
Fingland
Craigdullyeart Hill
Halfmerk Hill
451
Cocker Hill
504
Corsebank
Lochhill
Pathhead
New Cumnock
Connel Park
Bankglen
Afton Bridgend
Laight
Burnside
Lagrae
Kirkland
Carco
Kirkconnel
Kelloholm
Drumbuie
Crawick
Sanquhar
Hare Hill
Blackcraig Hill
700
Craigdarroch
569
Blacklorg Hill
681
Afton Resr
Windy Standard
698
Athang
Cruffell
557
Cloud Hill
451
Polgown
Dalgonar
Countam
475
Glenmanna
Ulzieside
Mennock
Eliock
Glengenny Muir
291
Ardoch
Wether Hill
478
Cairnkinna Hill
Enterkinfoot
Breconside
Durisdeer
Gateslack
Dalveen Pass
277
Lowther Hill
725
Mennock Pass
329
Green Lowther
732
Wanlockhead
468
Wanlock Dod
551
Mus of Scottish Lead Mining
Beam Engine
Willowgrain Hill
514
Leadhills
Wellgrain Dod
553
Lettershaws
Drake Law
483
Crawfordjohn
Glentaggart
Redshaw
Hazelside
Douglas
St Bride's Church
New Mains
Coalburn
Brocloud
Happendon
Rigside
Uddington
Robert Law
Scaur Hill
Wildshaw Hill
374
Douglas Water
Stone Hill
314
Lesmahagow
Birkwood
Auchlochan
Blackwood
Kirkmuirhill
Auchenheath
Black Hill Fort (NTS)
Boghead
Netherburn
Craignethan
Draffan
Crossford
Hazelbank
Nemphlar
Kirkfieldbank
Rosebank
Milton-Lockhart
Braidwood
Yieldshields
Kilncadzow
Cartland
Cleghorn
Jerviswood
Lanark
New Lanark
New Lanark World Heritage Site
Falls of Clyde
Falls of Clyde Wildlife Reserve & Visitor Centre
Bonnington Linn
Hawksland
Hyndford Bridge
Carmichael
Abington
Southern Upland Way
M74
A71
A70
A76
A72
A73
A721
A706
A743
A702
B7078
B7086
B743
B745
B740
B797
B7040
B741
B7056
B7018

Darvel: *Sir Alexander Fleming, medical scientist and discoverer of the world's first antibiotic drug Penicillin was born at nearby Lochfield Farm in 1881. He made his discovery in 1928 and was widely honoured with a knighthood in 1944 and the Nobel Prize for Medicine in 1945. Fleming died in 1955 and is buried in St Paul's Cathedral, London.* ***Map ref. D2***

Sanquhar *Home to the oldest post office in the world, established in 1712.* ***Map ref. F5***

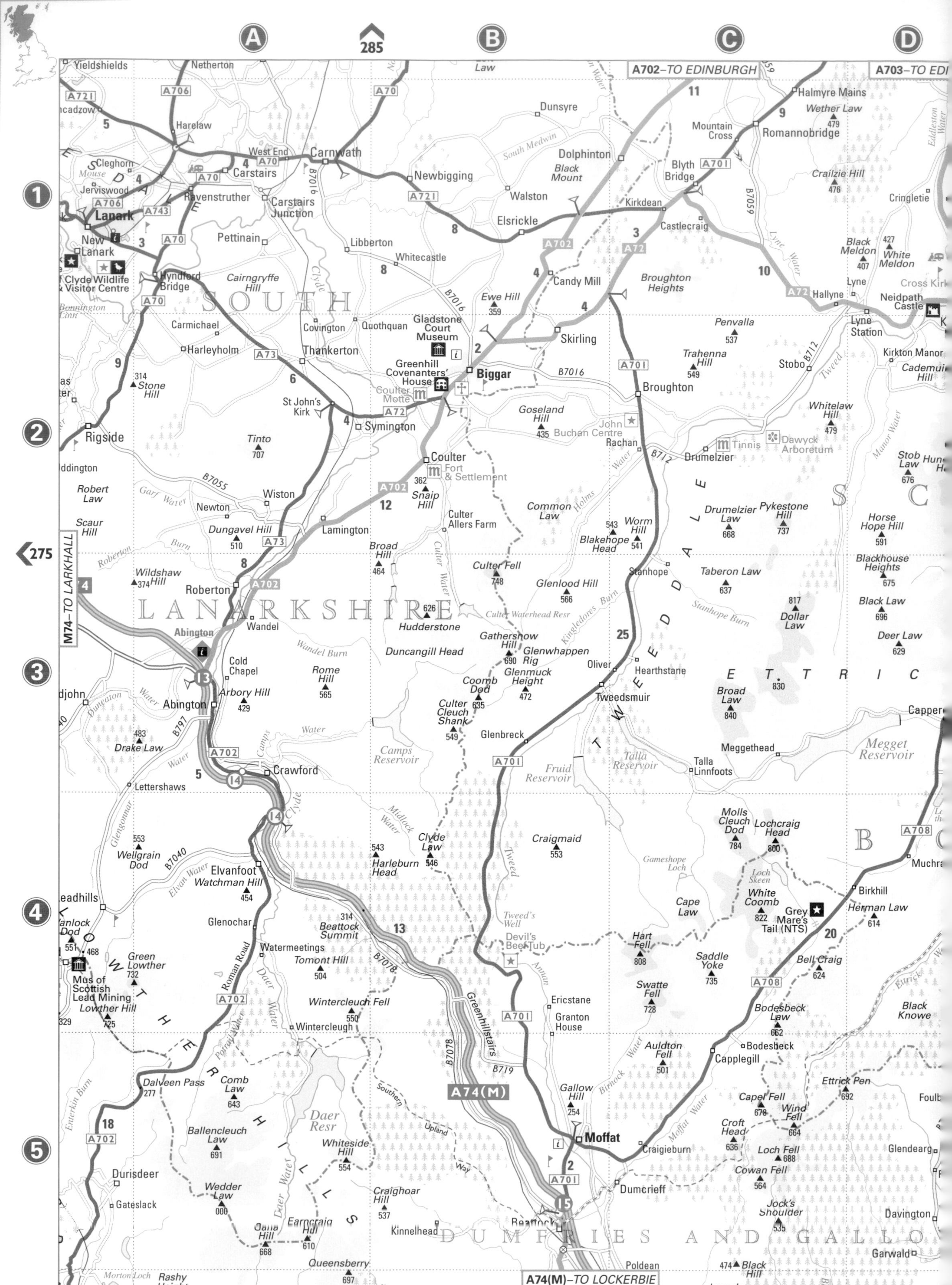
A
B
C
D
285
1
2
3
4
5
275
A702–TO EDINBURGH
A703–TO EDI
M74–TO LARKHALL
A74(M)–TO LOCKERBIE
Yieldshields
Netherton
Law
A721
A706
A70
Harelaw
Dunsyre
Halmyre Mains
Wether Law
479
Mountain Cross
Romannobridge
South Medwin
Dolphinton
Black Mount
Blyth Bridge
A701
B7059
Crailzie Hill
476
Cringletie
Cleghorn
Mouse
Jerviswood
Lanark
New Lanark
Clyde Wildlife Visitor Centre
West End
Carnwath
Carstairs
Carstairs Junction
Ravenstruther
Newbigging
Walston
Kirkdean
Castlecraig
Elsrickle
A743
Pettinain
Libberton
Whitecastle
Black Meldon
407
427
White Meldon
Lyne
Cross Kirk
Neidpath Castle
Hyndford Bridge
Cairngryffe Hill
SOUTH
Candy Mill
Broughton Heights
Hallyne
Lyne Station
Bonnington Linn
Carmichael
Covington
Quothquan
Gladstone Court Museum
Ewe Hill
359
B7016
Skirling
Penvalla
537
Stobo
B712
Kirkton Manor
Cademuir Hill
Harleyholm
A73
Thankerton
Greenhill Covenanters' House
Biggar
Trahenna Hill
549
Tweed
314
Stone Hill
Coulter Motte
St John's Kirk
Symington
A72
Goseland Hill
435
John Buchan Centre
Broughton
Whitelaw Hill
479
Manor Water
Rigside
Tinto
707
Rachan
Tinnis
Dawyck Arboretum
Drumelzier
Stob Law
676
Coulter
Fort & Settlement
Robert Law
B7055
Garf Water
Wiston
362
Snaip Hill
Newton
A702
12
Culter Allers Farm
Common Law
Holms Water
543
Worm Hill
541
Blakehope Head
Drumelzier Law
668
Pykestone Hill
737
Horse Hope Hill
591
Scaur Hill
Dungavel Hill
510
Lamington
Broad Hill
464
Culter Water
Culter Fell
748
Stanhope
Taberon Law
637
Blackhouse Heights
675
Robertson Burn
Wildshaw Hill
374
Roberton
Glenlood Hill
566
Stanhope Burn
817
Dollar Law
Black Law
696
LANARKSHIRE
626
Hudderstone
Culter Waterhead Resr
Kingledores Burn
TWEEDDALE
Abington
Wandel
Wandel Burn
Gathersnow Hill
690
Duncangill Head
Glenwhappen Rig
25
Deer Law
629
Cold Chapel
Rome Hill
565
Glenmuck Height
472
Coomb Dod
635
Oliver
Hearthstane
ETTRICK
830
Arbory Hill
429
Culter Cleuch Shank
549
Tweedsmuir
Broad Law
840
Capper
Duneaton Water
Glenbreck
B797
483
Drake Law
Camps Reservoir
A701
Fruid Reservoir
Talla Reservoir
Meggethead
Talla Linnfoots
Megget Reservoir
Crawford
Lettershaws
Clyde
Midlock Water
Molls Cleuch Dod
784
Lochcraig Head
800
A708
Glengonnar Water
553
Wellgrain Dod
B7040
543
Harleburn Head
Clyde Law
546
Craigmaid
553
Gameshope Loch
Loch Skeen
Elvanfoot
Elvan Water
Watchman Hill
454
Birkhill
Leadhills
Wanlock Dod
Glenochar
314
Beattock Summit
13
Tweed's Well
Cape Law
White Coomb
822
Grey Mare's Tail (NTS)
Herman Law
614
Watermeetings
Devil's Beef Tub
Hart Fell
808
Saddle Yoke
735
Bell Craig
624
468
551
Mus of Scottish Lead Mining
Green Lowther
732
Tomont Hill
504
B7078
Annan
Swatte Fell
728
Black Knowe
LOWTHER HILLS
Roman Road
Daer Water
Wintercleuch Fell
550
Greenhillstairs
Ericstane
Granton House
Bodesbeck Law
662
Lowther Hill
725
329
Potrail Water
Wintercleugh
Auldton Fell
501
Bodesbeck
Capplegill
B719
Ettrick Pen
692
Enterkin Burn
Dalveen Pass
277
Comb Law
643
Southern Upland Way
A74(M)
Gallow Hill
254
Birnock Water
Moffat Water
Capel Fell
678
Wind Fell
664
Foulb
18
Ballencleuch Law
691
Daer Resr
Moffat
Craigieburn
Croft Head
636
Loch Fell
688
Glendearg
Whiteside Hill
554
Cowan Fell
564
Durisdeer
Wedder Law
000
Craighoar Hill
537
Dumcrieff
Jock's Shoulder
535
Davington
Gateslack
Earncraig Hill
610
Kinnelhead
Beattock
DUMFRIES AND GALLOWAY
668
Garwald
Queensberry
697
Poldean
474
Black Hill
Morton Loch
Rashy Height

Tweeddale: *The area was the setting for some of the novels of John Buchan (1875–1940) – most famously The Thirty-Nine Steps.* **Map ref. C3**

267

Biggar: *Biggar Gasworks was first opened in 1839. In 1973, when natural gas from the North Sea, came to the town, the gasworks closed. However, unlike most other towns, Biggar didn't demolish its gasworks, instead it made it into a Gasworks Museum. It is now preserved for future generations by Historic Building and Monuments and the Museums of Scotland.* **Map ref. B2**

286

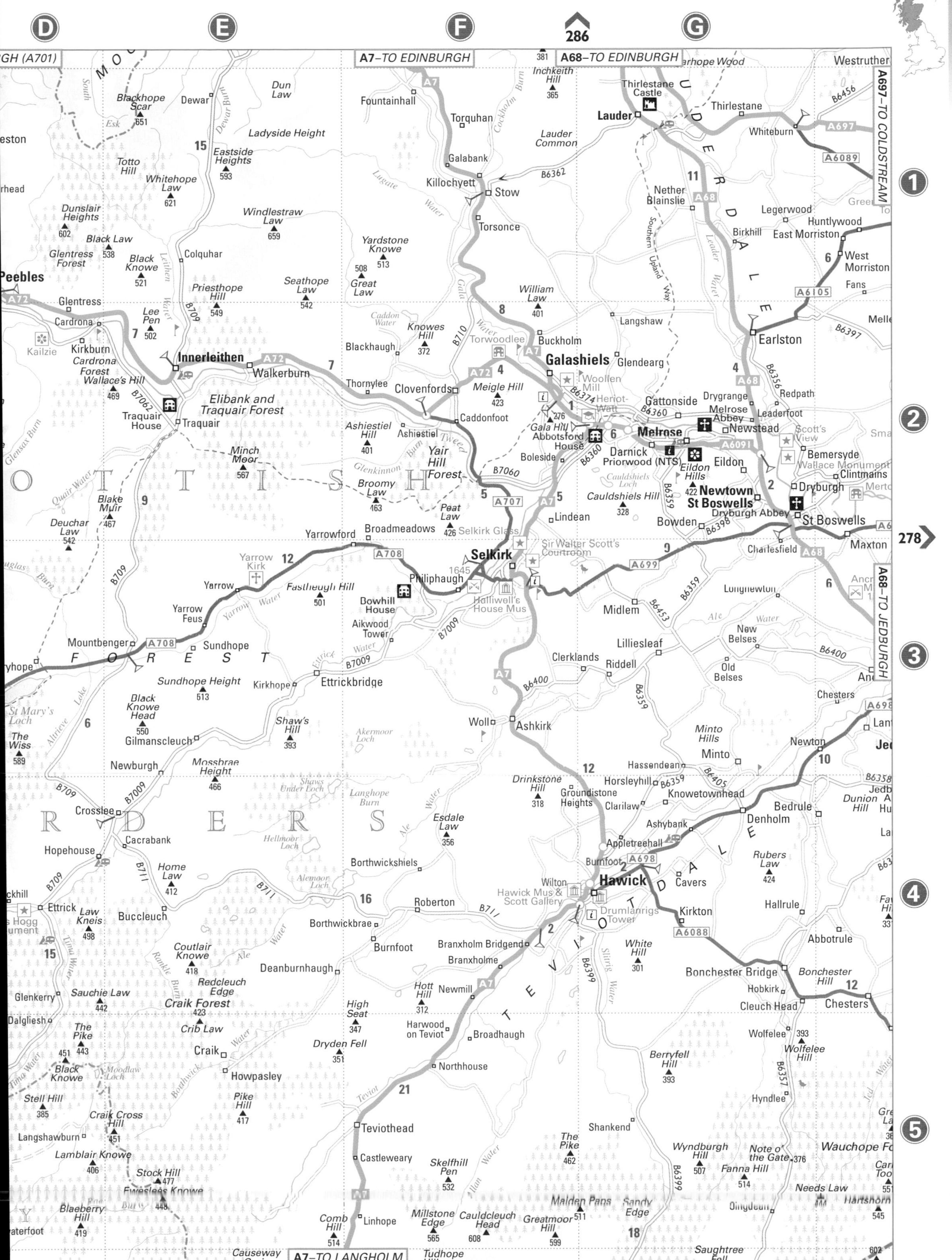
D
E
F
G
A7–TO EDINBURGH
A68–TO EDINBURGH
A697–TO COLDSTREAM
A68–TO JEDBURGH
A7–TO LANGHOLM
1
2
3
4
5
Westruther
Inchkeith Hill 365
Thirlestane Castle
Lauder
Thirlestane
Whiteburn
A697
A6089
Dun Law
Blackhope Scar 651
Dewar
Fountainhall
Torquhan
Lauder Common
Ladyside Height
Eastside Heights 593
Totto Hill
Whitehope Law 621
Galabank
Killochyett
Stow
B6362
Nether Blainslie
Legerwood
Huntlywood
East Morriston
Birkhill
West Morriston
Dunslair Heights 602
Windlestraw Law 659
Torsonce
Black Law
Glentress Forest 538
Black Knowe 521
Colquhar
Yardstone Knowe 513
Great Law 508
Peebles
Priesthope Hill 549
Seathope Law 542
William Law 401
Fans
A6105
Glentress
Cardrona
Lee Pen 502
Knowes Hill 372
Langshaw
Mellerstain
Earlston
Kailzie
Kirkburn
Cardrona Forest
Innerleithen
A72
Walkerburn
Blackhaugh
Torwoodlee
Buckholm
Galashiels
Glendearg
Wallace's Hill 469
Elibank and Traquair Forest
Thornylee
Clovenfords
Meigle Hill 423
Woollen Mill
Gattonside
Drygrange
Redpath
Traquair House
Traquair
Caddonfoot
Heriot-Watt
Melrose Abbey
Leaderfoot
Ashiestiel Hill 401
Ashiestiel
Gala Hill
Abbotsford House
Melrose
Newstead
Scott's View
Bemersyde
Minch Moor 567
Yair Hill Forest
Boleside
Darnick
Priorwood (NTS)
Eildon Hills 422
Eildon
Wallace Monument
Clintmains
Broomy Law 463
B7060
Cauldshiels Loch
Newtown St Boswells
Dryburgh
Blake Muir 467
Peat Law 426
A707
Cauldshiels Hill 328
Dryburgh Abbey
St Boswells
Deuchar Law 542
Yarrowford
Broadmeadows
Lindean
Bowden
Selkirk Glass
Sir Walter Scott's Courtroom
Charlesfield
Maxton
Yarrow Kirk
A708
Selkirk
1645
A699
Yarrow
Fastheugh Hill 501
Philiphaugh
Longnewton
Dowhill House
Halliwell's House Mus
Midlem
Yarrow Feus
Aikwood Tower
New Belses
Mountbenger
Sundhope
Lilliesleaf
Old Belses
FOREST
Clerklands
Riddell
B6400
Sundhope Height 513
Kirkhope
Ettrickbridge
B7009
Black Knowe Head 550
Shaw's Hill 393
Chesters
St Mary's Loch
The Wiss 589
Gilmanscleuch
Akermoor Loch
Woll
Ashkirk
Minto Hills
Minto
Newton
Newburgh
Mossbrae Height 466
Hassendean
Drinkstone Hill 318
Groundistone Heights
Horsleyhill
Knowetownhead
Crosslee
Shaws Under Loch
Langhope Burn
Clarilaw
Bedrule
Denholm
Dunion Hill
Cacrabank
Esdale Law 356
Ashybank
Hopehouse
Hellmoor Loch
Appletreehall
Rubers Law 424
Home Law 412
Borthwickshiels
Burnfoot
A698
Ettrick
Law Kneis 498
Buccleuch
Alemoor Loch
Robertson
Wilton
Hawick
Hawick Mus & Scott Gallery
Cavers
Drumlanrigs Tower
Kirkton
Hallrule
Borthwickbrae
Branxholm Bridgend
A6088
Abbotrule
Coutlair Knowe 418
Burnfoot
Branxholme
White Hill 301
Deanburnhaugh
Bonchester Bridge
Bonchester Hill
Glenkerry
Sauchie Law 442
Redcleuch Edge
Craik Forest 423
Hott Hill 312
Newmill
Hobkirk
Cleuch Head
Chesters
Dalgliesh
Crib Law
High Seat 347
The Pike 443
Harwood on Teviot
Broadhaugh
Wolfelee 393
Craik
Dryden Fell 351
Berryfell Hill 393
Wolfelee Hill
Black Knowe 451
Howpasley
Northhouse
Stell Hill 385
Pike Hill 417
Hyndlee
Craik Cross Hill 451
Teviothead
Shankend
Langshawburn
The Pike 462
Wyndburgh Hill 507
Note o' the Gate 376
Wauchope Forest
Lamblair Knowe 406
Castleweary
Skelfhill Pen 532
Fanna Hill 514
Stock Hill 477
Ewesless Knowe 448
Needs Law
Hartshorn 545
Maiden Paps
Sandy Edge
Blaeberry Hill 419
Millstone Edge 565
Cauldcleuch Head 608
Greatmoor Hill 599
Comb Hill 514
Linhope
Causeway Grain
Tudhope Hill
Saughtree Fell
TEVIOTDALE
LAUDERDALE
SCOTTISH BORDERS

278

268

Selkirk:** Stomping ground of William Wallace 'Braveheart' who was declared 'Guardian of Scotland' here in the 13th Century. For much of his life Wallace lived like an outlaw attacking anything English. He was finally caught and executed in 1305.* ***Map ref. F3

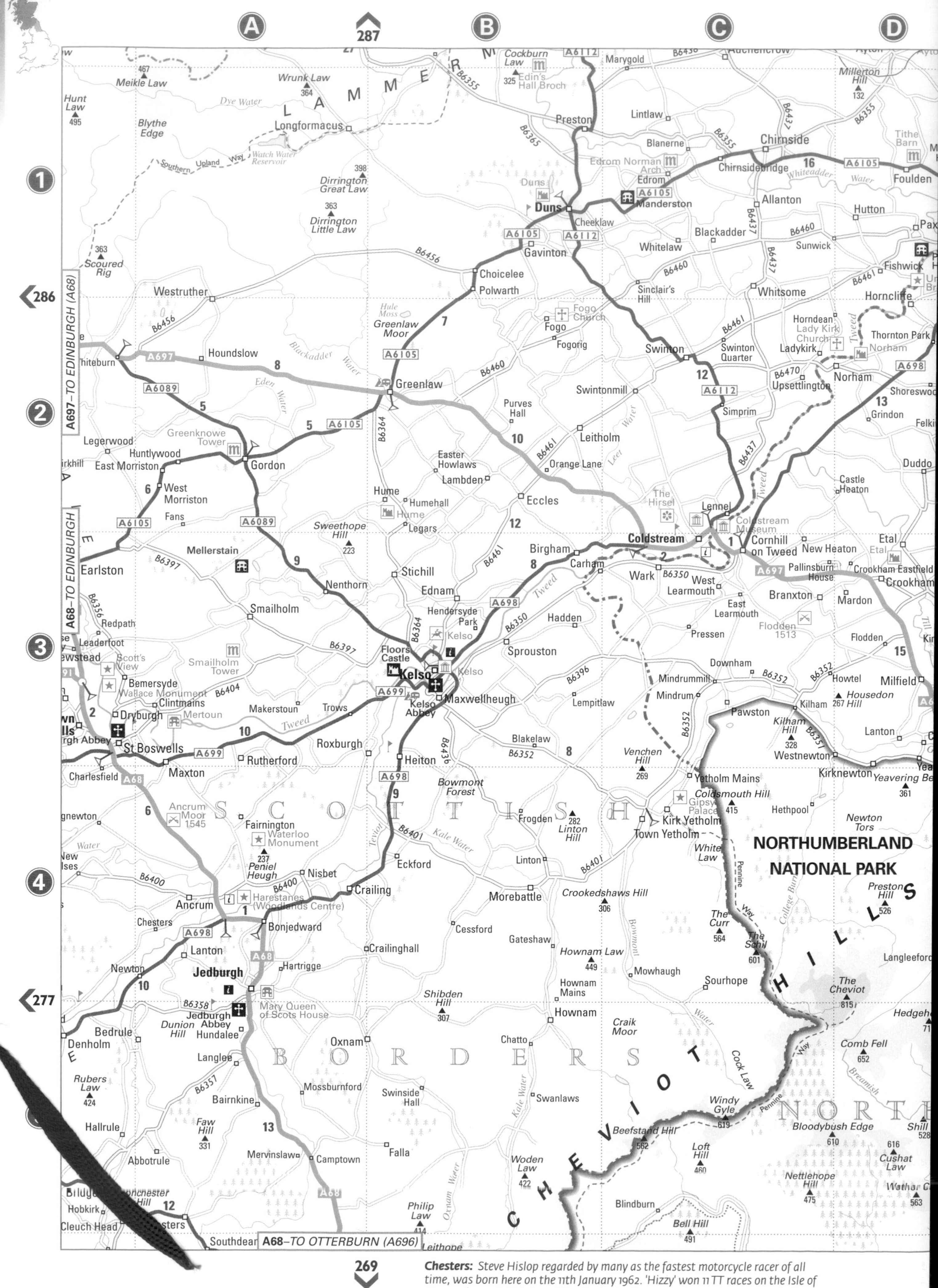

A
B
C
D
1
2
3
4
LAMMERMUIR
Cockburn Law 325
Edin's Hall Broch
Marygold
Millerton Hill 132
Meikle Law 467
Wrunk Law 364
Hunt Law 495
Dye Water
Blythe Edge
Longformacus
Preston
Lintlaw
Blanerne
Chirnside
Tithe Barn
Southern Upland Way
Watch Water Reservoir
398 Dirrington Great Law
363 Dirrington Little Law
Edrom Norman Arch
Edrom
Chirnsidebridge
Whiteadder Water
Foulden
Duns
Manderston
Allanton
Hutton
Cheeklaw
Blackadder
Sunwick
Whitelaw
Gavinton
Choicelee
Polwarth
Fishwick
Sinclair's Hill
Whitsome
Horncliffe
363 Scoured Rig
Westruther
Hule Moss
Greenlaw Moor
Fogo Church
Fogo
Fogorig
Horndean
Lady Kirk Church
Ladykirk
Thornton Park
Norham
Swinton
Swinton Quarter
Upsettlington
A697 – TO EDINBURGH (A68)
Whiteburn
Houndslow
Blackadder Water
Eden Water
Greenlaw
Swintonmill
Simprim
Shoreswood
Grindon
Purves Hall
Leitholm
Legerwood
Greenknowe Tower
Huntlywood
East Morriston
Gordon
West Morriston
Fans
Easter Howlaws
Lambden
Orange Lane
Leet Water
Duddo
Castle Heaton
Hume
Humehall
Hume
Legars
Eccles
The Hirsel
Lennel
Coldstream Museum
Coldstream
Cornhill on Tweed
New Heaton
Etal
A68 – TO EDINBURGH
Mellerstain
Sweethope Hill 223
Earlston
Stichill
Birgham
Carham
Wark
West Learmouth
Pallinsburn House
Crookham Eastfield
Crookham
Nenthorn
Ednam
Branxton
Mardon
East Learmouth
Redpath
Smailholm
Hendersyde Park
Hadden
Flodden 1513
Leaderfoot
Smailholm Tower
Floors Castle
Kelso
Sprouston
Pressen
Flodden
Scott's View
Bemersyde
Wallace Monument
Clintmains
Dryburgh
Mertoun
Dryburgh Abbey
St Boswells
Makerstoun
Trows
Tweed
Roxburgh
Rutherford
Kelso Abbey
Maxwellheugh
Lempitlaw
Downham
Mindrummill
Mindrum
Howtel
Milfield
Housedon Hill 267
Kilham
Pawston
Kilham Hill 328
Lanton
Charlesfield
Maxton
Heiton
Blakelaw
Venchen Hill 269
Westnewton
Kirknewton
Yeavering Bell 361
Yetholm Mains
Coldsmouth Hill 415
Hethpool
Bowmont Forest
Ancrum Moor 1545
Fairnington
Waterloo Monument
237 Peniel Heugh
Nisbet
Frogden
282 Linton Hill
Gipsy Palace
Kirk Yetholm
Town Yetholm
White Law
Kale Water
Eckford
Linton
NORTHUMBERLAND NATIONAL PARK
Newton Tors
SCOTTISH
Ancrum
Harestanes (Woodlands Centre)
Crailing
Morebattle
Crookedshaws Hill 306
Preston Hill 526
Chesters
Bonjedward
Cessford
Gateshaw
The Curr 564
The Schil 601
Lanton
Hartrigge
Crailinghall
Hownam Law 449
Mowhaugh
Sourhope
Langleeford
Newton
Jedburgh
Mary Queen of Scots House
Shibden Hill 307
Hownam Mains
The Cheviot 815
Jedburgh Abbey
Dunion Hill
Hundalee
Hownam
Craik Moor
Hedgehope
Bedrule
Denholm
Oxnam
Chatto
Comb Fell 652
BORDERS
Langlee
Rubers Law 424
Mossburnford
Swinside Hall
Kale Water
Swanlaws
Cock Law
Bairnkine
Windy Gyle 619
CHEVIOT HILLS
NORTH
Hallrule
Faw Hill 331
Beefstand Hill 562
Bloodybush Edge 610
Shill 528
Loft Hill 460
616 Cushat Law
Abbotrule
Mervinslaw
Camptown
Falla
Woden Law 422
Nettlehope Hill 475
Wether Cairn 563
Bonchester Bridge
Hobkirk
Cleuch Head
Southdean
Philip Law 414
Oxnam Water
Blindburn
Bell Hill 491
A68 – TO OTTERBURN (A696)
Leithope

287

286

277

269

Chesters: *Steve Hislop regarded by many as the fastest motorcycle racer of all time, was born here on the 11th January 1962. 'Hizzy' won 11 TT races on the Isle of Man and was British Superbike Champion in 1995 and 2002. He was tragically killed in a helicopter crash near Teviothead on the 30th July 2003.* ***Map ref. A4***

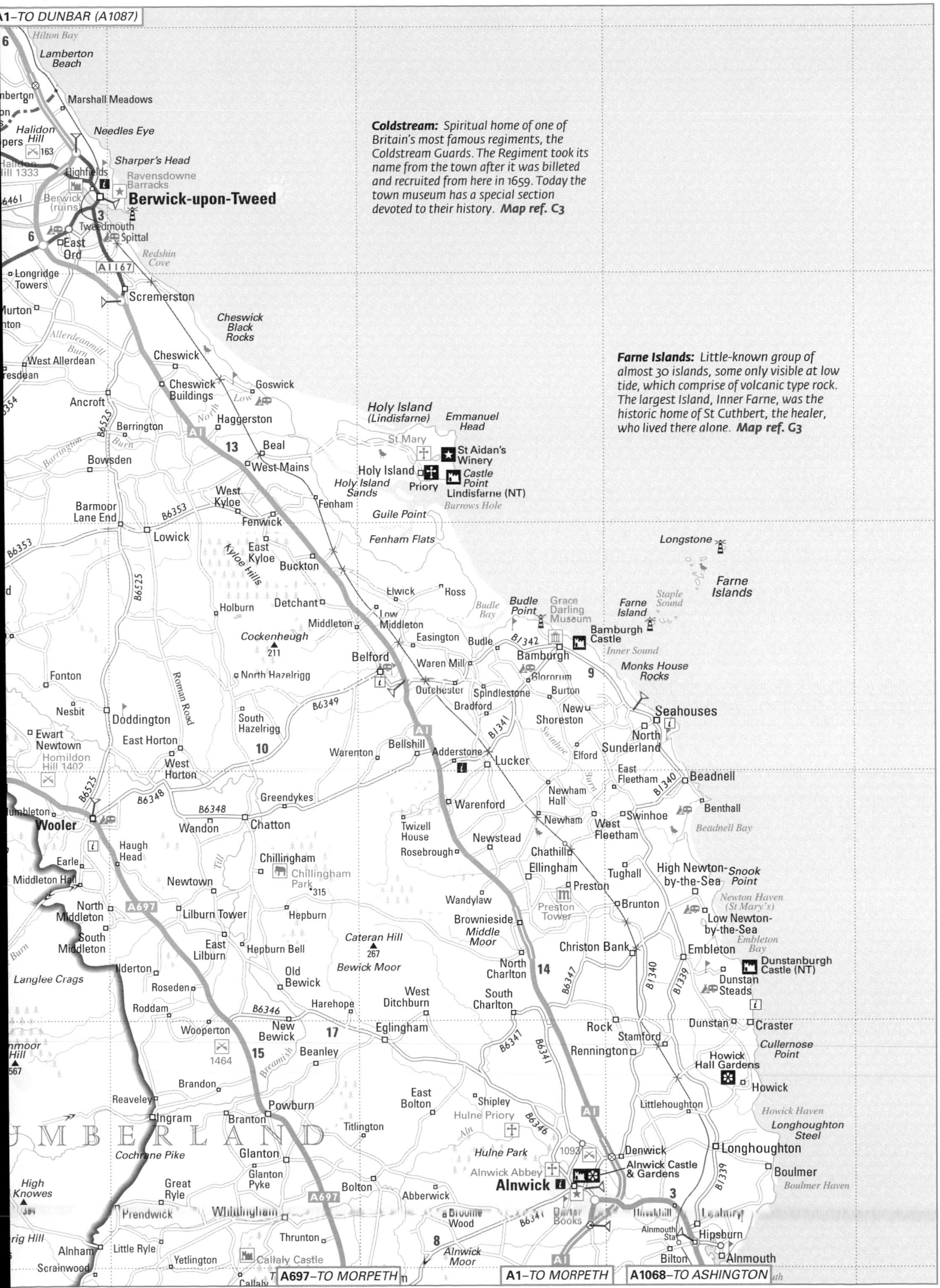

Coldstream: *Spiritual home of one of Britain's most famous regiments, the Coldstream Guards. The Regiment took its name from the town after it was billeted and recruited from here in 1659. Today the town museum has a special section devoted to their history.* ***Map ref. C3***

Farne Islands: *Little-known group of almost 30 islands, some only visible at low tide, which comprise of volcanic type rock. The largest Island, Inner Farne, was the historic home of St Cuthbert, the healer, who lived there alone.* ***Map ref. G3***

Bamburgh: *The great sandstone castle here was the first castle in Britain to be attacked by cannon fire when it was besieged by the artillery of Edward IV in 1464.*
Map ref. F3 Also on page 102

270

Bamburgh: *Grace Darling lived here with her father, a lighthouse keeper. She is famous for spotting a shipwreck during a dreadful storm and then assisting her father in the rescue of 5 survivors she had seen clinging to Big Harcar Rock. Grace died of flu in October 1842.* ***Map ref. F3***

A
288
B
C
D
1
2
3
4
5
Eilean Mhucaig
Rubha Bàn
Priory
Dubh Eilean
Oronsay
Eilean nan Ron
Caolas Mòr
Eilean Ghaoideamal
Shian Bay
Sgeir Mhòr a' Bhrein- phuirt
Rubh' an t- Sàilein
Colonsay 1¼ hrs (summer only)
Loch Tarbert
Rubh' a' Chrois-aoinidh
Glenbatrick
Rubh' a' Mhàil
Rubha Bholsa
Sgarbh Breac
364
Scrinadle
506
Jura Forest
Beinn an Oir
785
Beinn Shiantaidh
755
Na Peileirean
Nave Island
Ardnave Point
283
Margadale Hill
Gortantaoid Point
Bunnahabhain Bay
Giur-bheinn
316
Bunnahabhain
Beinn a' Chaolais
734
Paps of Jura
Loch a' Chnuic Bhric
Loch an t-Siob
Ardnave
Killinallan Point
Carraig Bhàn
Tayovullin
Killinallan
Beinn Bhreac
286
Ardnahoe
Loch Staoisha
Gleann Asdale
Leargybreck
Ton Mhòr
Kilnave
Ardnave Loch
Loch Gruinart
Sanaigmore
Glas Bheinn
561
Eilean Mòr
Braigo
A R G Y L L
Balulive
Feolin
Leckgruinart
Keills
Port Askaig
Feolin Ferry
Dubh Bheinn
530
Keils
Rubha Lamanais
Smaull
Loch Finlaggan
Aoradh
Ballinaby
Carnduncan
B8017
Craigens
Craighouse
Saligo Bay
Grainel
Loch Cam
Ballygrant
Loch Ballygrant
342
Brat Bheinn
I S L A Y
8
A846
Kilmeny
Loch Lossit
A846
SOUND OF ISLAY
Coul Point
Machrie
Loch Gorm
Aruadh
B8018
Lyrabus
Foreland
Moin'a'choire
Esknish
Beinn Dubh
267
Cabrach
Sannaig
Rockside
Kilchoman
A847
Blackrock
Islay Ho.
Redhouses
Ardfin
Jura Ho.
Rubha na Tràille
Machir Bay
Conisby
Bridgend
Cachlaidh Mhòr
Laggan
Am Fraoch Eilean
Brosdale Island
Bruichladdich
LOCH INDAAL
Sgorr nam Faoileann
429
Kilchiaran
RINNS OF ISLAY
Gartnatra
A846
Bowmore
Neriby
Barr
Cattadale
Beinn na Caillich
337
McArthur's Head
Kilchiaran Bay
15
Port Charlotte
Ronnachmore
Cruach
Glas Bheinn
471
Tormisdale
Gearach
Cluanach
Gartbreck
Proaig
Carn
Kilennan
Beinn Tart a' Mhill
232
Beinn Bhan
471
Beinn Bheigeir
491
Lossit
Laggan
Laggan
Kelsay
Nerabus
Lossit Bay
Duich
Rubha Liath
Beinn Uraraidh
454
Ardtalla
Rubha na Faing
Easter Ellister
A847
13
B8016
Loch Uraraidh
Claggain Bay
Portnahaven
A846
Kintour
Trudernish
Port Wemyss
Laggan Bay
ISLAY
Glenegedale
Sgorr Bhogachain
Loch Uigeadail
Kintour
Ardmore Point
Orsay
Rinns Point
Machrie
Beinn Sholum
347
Kildalton Church & Crosses
Ardmore
Leorin
Leorin Lochs
Eilean a' Chuirn
2¼ hrs
Rubha Mòr
Kintra
Machrie
Eilean Bhride
Ardbeg
Maol Buidhe
165
Cornabus
Port Ellen
Lagavulin
Rubha na Gainmhich
3
A846
Carnmore
Laphroaig
The Ard
Caolas an Eilein
THE OA
Lower Killeyan
Risabus
Texa
Port Chubaird
Inerval
Mull of Oa
Loch Kinnabus
Rubha nan Leacan

Islay: *Known as the 'Jewel of the Hebrides' this beautiful island is a major bird watching destination and is home to 8 different whisky distilleries. Islay enjoys a sort of micro-climate, warmed by the Gulf Stream: it has more hours of sunshine than most of mainland Britain and relatively mild winters as well.* ***Map ref. A3***

289

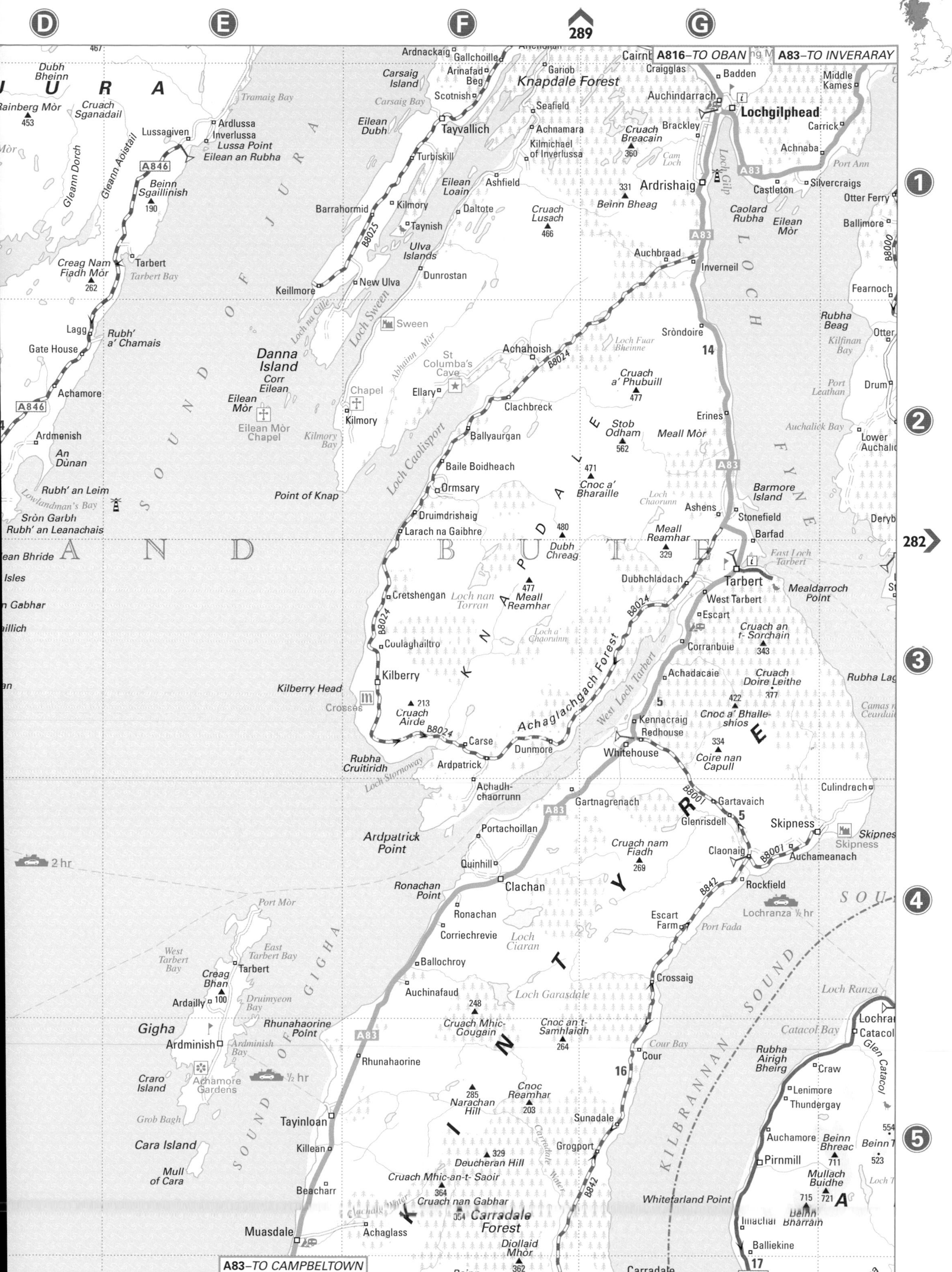
D
E
F
G
1
2
3
4
5
A816–TO OBAN
A83–TO INVERARAY
A83–TO CAMPBELTOWN
J U R A
Dubh Bheinn
Rainberg Mòr
453
Cruach Sganadail
Tramaig Bay
Lussagiven
Ardlussa
Inverlussa
Lussa Point
Eilean an Rubha
Gleann Dorch
Gleann Aoistail
A846
Beinn Sgaillinish
190
Creag Nam Fiadh Mòr
262
Tarbert
Tarbert Bay
Lagg
Rubh' a' Chamais
Gate House
Achamore
Ardmenish
An Dùnan
Rubh' an Leim
Lowlandman's Bay
Sròn Garbh
Rubh' an Leanachais
SOUND OF JURA
Danna Island
Corr Eilean
Eilean Mòr
Eilean Mòr Chapel
Kilmory Bay
Point of Knap
ARGYLL AND BUTE
Ardnackaig
Gallchoille
Carsaig Island
Carsaig Bay
Arinafad Beg
Scotnish
Eilean Dubh
Tayvallich
Turbiskill
Barrahormid
Kilmory
Taynish
B8025
Ulva Islands
Keillmore
New Ulva
Dunrostan
Loch na Cille
Loch Sween
Sween
Abhainn Mòr
St Columba's Cave
Chapel
Kilmory
Ellary
Knapdale Forest
Gariob
Seafield
Achnamara
Kilmichael of Inverlussa
Eilean Loain
Ashfield
Daltote
Cruach Lusach
466
Cairnbaan
Craigglas
Badden
Middle Kames
Auchindarroch
Lochgilphead
Carrick
Cruach Breacain
360
Brackley
Cam Loch
Achnaba
Port Ann
Loch Gilp
331
Ardrishaig
Beinn Bheag
Castleton
Silvercraigs
Otter Ferry
Caolard Rubha
Eilean Mòr
Ballimore
B8000
Auchbraad
Inverneil
Fearnoch
LOCH FYNE
Achahoish
B8024
Loch Fuar Bheinne
Srondoire
14
Rubha Beag
Kilfinan Bay
Otter
Cruach a' Phubuill
477
Clachbreck
Ballyaurgan
Loch Caolisport
Port Leathan
Drum
Stob Odham
562
Meall Mòr
Erines
Auchalick Bay
Lower Auchalick
Baile Boidheach
471
Cnoc a' Bharaille
Ormsary
Loch Chaorunn
Barmore Island
Ashens
Stonefield
Derybruich
Druimdrishaig
Larach na Gaibhre
480
Dubh Chreag
Meall Reamhar
329
Barfad
East Loch Tarbert
Tarbert
282
Dubhchladach
Mealdarroch Point
Cretshengan
Loch nan Torran
477
Meall Reamhar
West Tarbert
Escart
Cruach an t-Sorchain
343
KNAPDALE
Coulaghailtro
Loch a' Chaoruinn
Corranbuie
Kilberry
Kilberry Head
Crosses
Achaglachgach Forest
West Loch Tarbert
Achadacaie
Cruach Doire Leithe
377
Rubha Lag
213
Cruach Airde
5
422
Cnoc a' Bhaile-shios
Camas nan Ceardaich
Kennacraig
Redhouse
Carse
Dunmore
Whitehouse
334
Coire nan Capull
Rubha Cruitiridh
Ardpatrick
Loch Stornoway
Achadh-chaorrunn
Gartnagrenach
B8001
Gartavaich
Culindrach
Glenrisdell
Skipness
Skipness
Ardpatrick Point
Portachoillan
A83
Cruach nam Fiadh
269
Claonaig
Auchameanach
2 hr
Quinhill
Ronachan Point
Clachan
Rockfield
B842
Ronachan
Lochranza ½ hr
Escart Farm
Port Fada
Port Mòr
Corriechrevie
Loch Ciaran
West Tarbert Bay
East Tarbert Bay
Ballochroy
Creag Bhan
Tarbert
Crossaig
Ardailly
100
Druimyeon Bay
Auchinafaud
Loch Garasdale
Loch Ranza
SOUND OF GIGHA
248
Cruach Mhic-Gougain
Cnoc an t-Samhlaidh
264
Gigha
Rhunahaorine Point
Catacol Bay
Lochranza
Catacol
Ardminish
Ardminish Bay
Rhunahaorine
Cour Bay
Cour
Rubha Airigh Bheirg
Glen Catacol
Achamore Gardens
½ hr
16
Craw
Craro Island
285
Narachan Hill
Cnoc Reamhar
203
Lenimore
Thundergay
Grob Bagh
Tayinloan
Sunadale
KINTYRE
KILBRANNAN SOUND
554
Auchamore
Beinn Bhreac
Beinn Tarsuinn
Cara Island
Killean
329
Deucheran Hill
Grogport
Carradale Water
Pirnmill
711
523
Mull of Cara
Cruach Mhic-an-t-Saoir
364
Beacharr
B842
Mullach Buidhe
Loch Tanna
Cruach nan Gabhar
354
Carradale Forest
Whitefarland Point
715
721
Beinn Bharrain
Imachar
Muasdale
Achaglass
Diollaid Mhòr
362
Balliekine
Carradale
17

272

Ardrishaig: *The 9 mile (14.5km) long Crinan Canal was started here in 1794 by John Ronnie. The canal links Loch Fyne with the Atlantic Ocean and cuts out a 120 mile (193km) voyage around the Mull of Kintyre.* ***Map ref. G1***

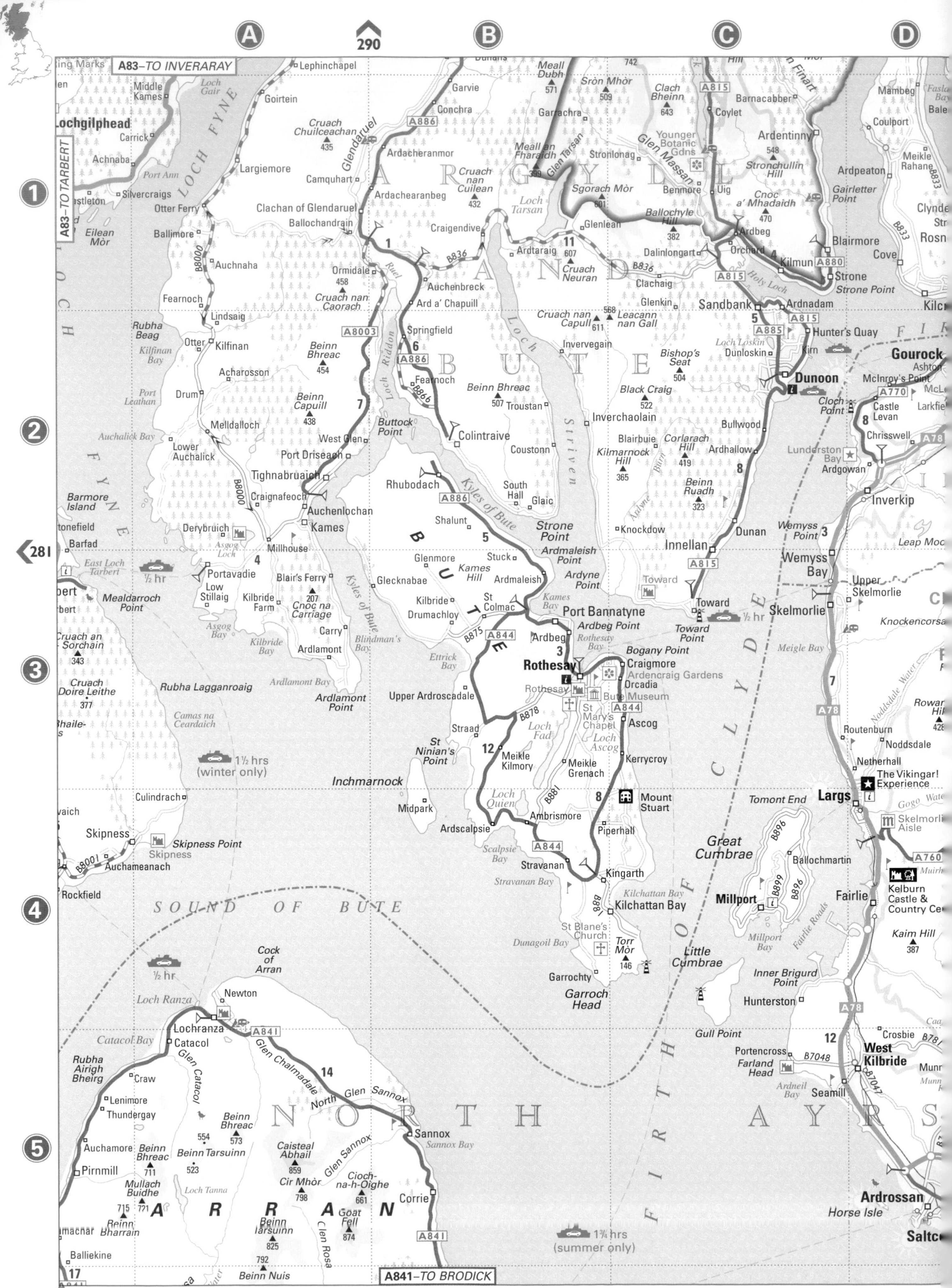

A
B
C
D
290
A83–TO INVERARAY
A83–TO TARBERT
281
273
A841–TO BRODICK
1
2
3
4
5
Lephinchapel
Middle Kames
Lochgilphead
Loch Gair
LOCH FYNE
Goirtein
Carrick
Achnaba
Largiemore
Port Ann
Silvercraigs
Otter Ferry
Eilean Mòr
Ballimore
Auchnaha
Fearnoch
Lindsaig
Rubha Beag
Kilfinan Bay
Otter
Kilfinan
Acharosson
Port Leathan
Drum
Melldalloch
Auchalick Bay
Lower Auchalick
Tighnabruaich
Craignafeoch
Barmore Island
Derybruich
Auchenlochan
Kames
Millhouse
Asgog Loch
East Loch Tarbert
Portavadie
Low Stillaig
Kilbride Farm
Blair's Ferry
Cnoc na Carriage
Mealdarroch Point
Asgog Bay
Kilbride Bay
Carry
Ardlamont
Ardlamont Bay
Ardlamont Point
Cruach an Sorchain
Cruach Doire Leithe
Rubha Lagganroaig
Camas na Ceardaich
1½ hrs (winter only)
Culindrach
Skipness
Skipness Point
Auchameanach
Rockfield
SOUND OF BUTE
Cock of Arran
½ hr
Loch Ranza
Newton
Lochranza
Catacol Bay
Catacol
Rubha Airigh Bheirg
Craw
Glen Catacol
Lenimore
Thundergay
Auchamore
Beinn Bhreac
Beinn Tarsuinn
Pirnmill
Mullach Buidhe
Loch Tanna
Caisteal Abhail
Cir Mhòr
Cioch-na-h-Oighe
Goat Fell
Beinn Iarsuinn
Beinn Nuis
Glen Rosa
ARRAN
Balliekine
Glen Chalmadale
North Glen Sannox
Sannox
Sannox Bay
Corrie
A841
Garvie
Conchra
Cruach Chuilceachan
Glendaruel
A886
Ardacheranmor
Camquhart
Ardachearanbeg
Clachan of Glendaruel
Ballochandrain
Craigendive
Cruach nan Cuilean
ARGYLL AND BUTE
Ormidale
Ruel
Auchenbreck
Ard a' Chapuill
Cruach nan Caorach
A8003
Springfield
Loch Riddon
Fearnoch
B866
B836
Beinn Bhreac
Beinn Capuill
Buttock Point
West Glen
Port Driseach
Colintraive
Rhubodach
Kyles of Bute
Shalunt
Glenmore
Kames Hill
Stuck
Gleenabae
Kilbride
Drumachloy
St Colmac
Ardmaleish
Ettrick Bay
Blindman's Bay
Upper Ardroscadale
BUTE
Port Bannatyne
Ardbeg Point
Ardbeg
Rothesay Bay
Rothesay
Bogany Point
Craigmore
Ardencraig Gardens
Orcadia
Bute Museum
St Mary's Chapel
A844
Ascog
Loch Ascog
Loch Fad
Straad
St Ninian's Point
Inchmarnock
Meikle Kilmory
Meikle Grenach
Kerrycroy
Midpark
Loch Quien
Mount Stuart
Ambrismore
Ardscalpsie
Piperhall
Scalpsie Bay
Stravanan
Stravanan Bay
Kingarth
Kilchattan Bay
Dunagoil Bay
St Blane's Church
Torr Mòr
Garrochty
Garroch Head
Meall Dubh
Sròn Mhòr
Clach Bheinn
Garrachra
Meall an Fharaidh
Glen Tarsan
Stronlonag
Glen Massan
Younger Botanic Gdns
Benmore
Sgorach Mòr
Loch Tarsan
Glenlean
Ballochyle Hill
Ardtaraig
Cruach Neuran
Dalinlongart
Clachaig
Glenkin
Cruach nan Capull
Leacann nan Gall
Invervegain
Loch Striven
Beinn Bhreac
Troustan
Inverchaolain
Blairbuie
Corlarach Hill
Kilmarnock Hill
Coustonn
South Hall
Glaic
Strone Point
Ardmaleish Point
Ardyne Point
Knockdow
Beinn Ruadh
Toward
Toward Point
Bishop's Seat
Black Craig
Coylet
Barnacabber
Ardentinny
Stronchullin Hill
Uig
Cnoc a' Mhadaidh
Ardbeg
Orchard
Holy Loch
Kilmun
A880
Strone
Strone Point
A815
Sandbank
Ardnadam
A885
Hunter's Quay
Loch Loskin
Dunloskin
Kirn
Dunoon
Bullwood
Ardhallow
Innellan
Dunan
FIRTH OF CLYDE
Mambeg
Coulport
Meikle Rahane
Ardpeaton
Gairletter Point
Blairmore
Cove
Clynder
Rosneath
B833
Kilcreggan
Gourock
Ashton
McInroy's Point
A770
Cloch Point
Castle Levan
Chrisswell
A78
Lunderston Bay
Ardgowan
Inverkip
Wemyss Point
Wemyss Bay
Leap Moor
Upper Skelmorlie
Skelmorlie
Knockencorsan
Meigle Bay
Routenburn
Noddsdale
Netherhall
The Vikingar! Experience
Largs
Tomont End
Gogo Water
Skelmorlie Aisle
A760
Great Cumbrae
Ballochmartin
Millport
Millport Bay
Fairlie
Fairlie Roads
Kelburn Castle & Country Centre
Kaim Hill
Little Cumbrae
Inner Brigurd Point
Hunterston
Gull Point
Crosbie
Portencross
B7048
Farland Head
West Kilbride
Ardneil Bay
Seamill
NORTH AYRSHIRE
Ardrossan
Horse Isle
Saltcoats
1¾ hrs (summer only)

Holy Loch: *During the Cold War of the 1960s this was a controversial US Navy nuclear submarine base housing Polaris Missiles. Over 700 Americans lived in the area and when it closed in 1992 many feared that the local economy would collapse. However the Government allocated £12 million to recreate employment in the area and a crisis was averted.* ***Map ref. C1***

Largs: *Scene of a great Scottish victory over the Vikings in 1263. The Viking fleet, under Kir Haakon left their base in the Western Isles to sail down the Clyde to subdue the Scottish resistance to Viking rule. But the Scots army, under Alexander III, helped by bad weather, managed to repulse the assault and end the Viking threat to mainland Scotland. The batt is commemorated by a monument just south of the town.* ***Map ref. D4***

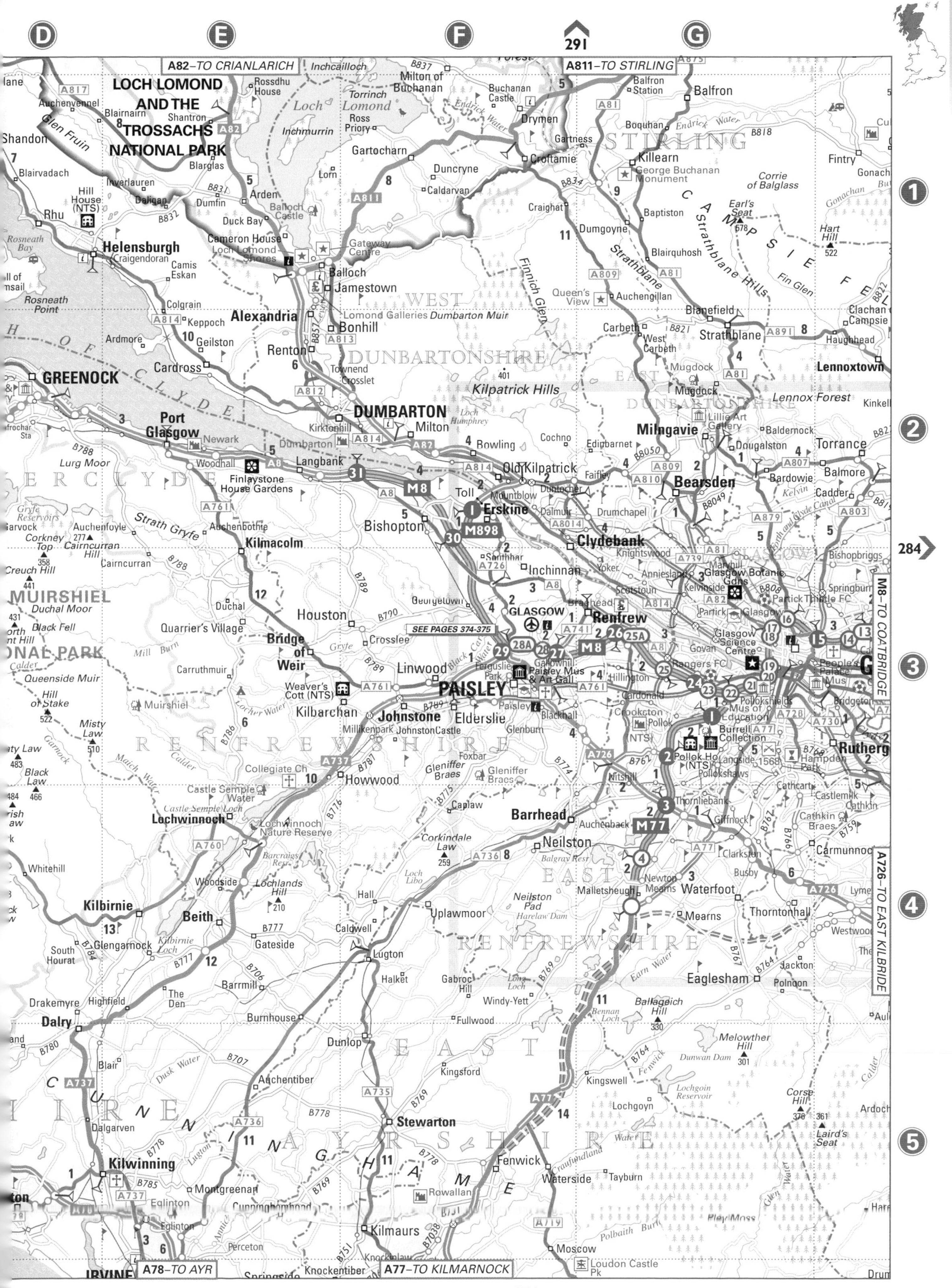

Helensburgh: *John Logie Baird, inventor of the television was born here on the 13th August 1888. He created the first televised pictures of an object in motion in 1925. He died on the 14th June 1946 at Bexhill, East Sussex.* **Map ref. D1**

Clydebank: *The liner Queen Mary (81,235 tons/82,539 tonnes) was built here at the John Brown Shipyard. It is said that over one million people turned out to watch her leaving the Clyde on the 24th March 1936.* **Map ref. F3**

Glasgow: *On the 17th April 1937 150,000 soccer supporters crammed into Hampden Park to watch Scotland play England. This is the European attendance record and stood as a world record until 1950.* **Map ref. G3**

274

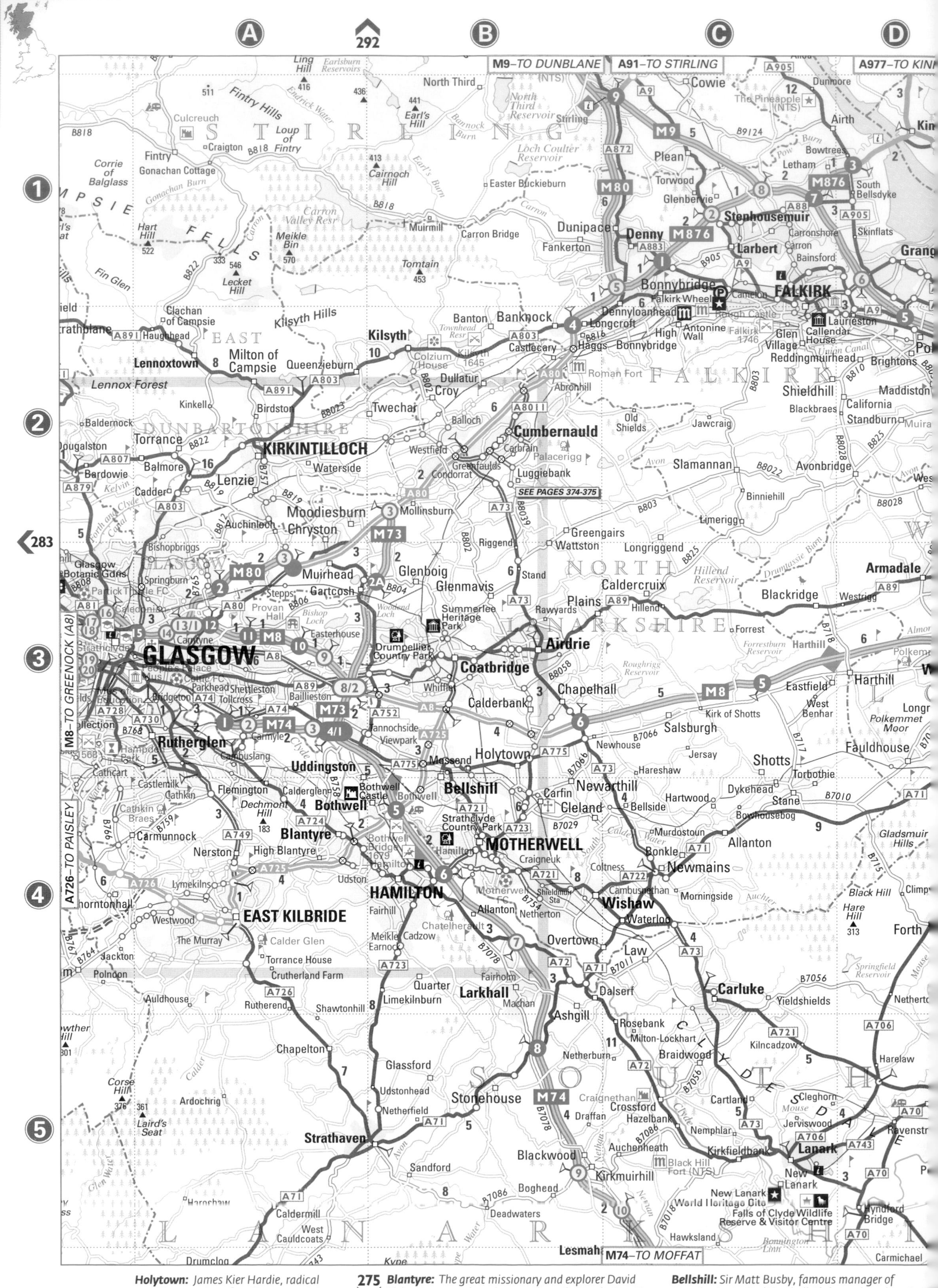
A
B
C
D
M9–TO DUNBLANE
A91–TO STIRLING
A977–TO KIN
S T I R L I N G
Ling Hill
Earlsburn Reservoirs
North Third
Cowie
Fintry Hills
Endrick Water
Earl's Hill
North Third Reservoir
Stirling
Culcreuch
Loup of Fintry
Craigton
Fintry
Corrie of Balglass
Gonachan Cottage
Cairnoch Hill
Loch Coulter Reservoir
Plean
Airth
Bowtrees
Letham
South Bellsdyke
Easter Buckieburn
Torwood
Glenbervie
Stenhousemuir
Carron Valley Resr
Muirmill
Carron Bridge
Dunipace
Denny
Larbert
Carronshore
Skinflats
Meikle Bin
Hart Hill
Fankerton
Bainsford
Tomtain
Lecket Hill
Fin Glen
Bonnybridge
Falkirk Wheel
Camelon
FALKIRK
Kilsyth Hills
Clachan of Campsie
Banton
Banknock
Dennyloanhead
Longcroft
Rough Castle
Antonine Wall
Laurieston
Callendar House
Haughhead
EAST
Kilsyth
Townhead Resr
Castlecary
High Bonnybridge
Haggs
Glen Village
Lennoxtown
Milton of Campsie
Queenzieburn
Colzium House
Kilsyth 1645
Reddingmuirhead
Brightons
Roman Fort
F A L K I R K
Lennox Forest
Dullatur
Croy
Abronhill
Shieldhill
Maddiston
Kinkell
Birdston
Twechar
Blackbraes
California
Standburn
Baldernock
DUNBARTONSHIRE
Balloch
Cumbernauld
Old Shields
Jawcraig
Torrance
KIRKINTILLOCH
Westfield
Carbrain
Palacerigg
Milngavie
Bardowie
Balmore
Waterside
Condorrat
Greenfaulds
Luggiebank
Slamannan
Avonbridge
Lenzie
SEE PAGES 374-375
Cadder
Binniehill
Moodiesburn
Mollinsburn
Auchinloch
Chryston
Limerigg
Bishopbriggs
Greengairs
Riggend
Wattston
Longriggend
GLASGOW
Glasgow Botanic Gdns
Springburn
Muirhead
Glenboig
NORTH
Armadale
Partick Thistle FC
Stepps
Gartcosh
Glenmavis
Stand
Calderchuix
Hillend Reservoir
Blackridge
Westrigg
Provan Hall
Bishop Loch
Woodend Loch
Summerlee Heritage Park
Plains
Rawyards
Hillend
LANARKSHIRE
Forrest
Carntyne
Easterhouse
Drumpellier Country Park
Airdrie
Forrestburn Reservoir
Harthill
Polkemmet
GLASGOW
People's Palace
Celtic FC
Coatbridge
Roughrigg Reservoir
Parkhead
Shettleston
Bridgeton
Tollcross
Baillieston
Whifflet
Chapelhall
Eastfield
West Benhar
Calderbank
Kirk of Shotts
Salsburgh
Polkemmet Moor
Rutherglen
Carmyle
Tannochside
Viewpark
Newhouse
Fauldhouse
Hampden Park
Cambuslang
Uddingston
Mossend
Holytown
Jersay
Shotts
Cathcart
Castlemilk
Cathkin
Flemington
Calderglen
Bothwell Castle
Bothwell
Bellshill
Hareshaw
Newarthill
Carfin
Torbothie
Dykehead
Cathkin Braes
Dechmont Hill
Bothwell
Strathclyde Country Park
Cleland
Bellside
Hartwood
Stane
Bowhousebog
Carmunnock
Blantyre
Bothwell Bridge 1679
Hamilton
MOTHERWELL
Craigneuk
Murdostoun
Allanton
Gladsmuir Hills
Nerston
High Blantyre
Bonkle
Newmains
Coltness
Lymekilns
Udston
HAMILTON
Motherwell FC
Shieldmuir Sta
Cambusnethan
Morningside
Black Hill
Thorntonhall
EAST KILBRIDE
Fairhill
Allanton
Netherton
Wishaw
Waterloo
Hare Hill
Westwood
Chatelherault
Forth
The Murray
Calder Glen
Meikle Earnock
Cadzow
Overtown
Jackton
Torrance House
Law
Springfield Reservoir
Polnoon
Crutherland Farm
Fairholm
Carluke
Quarter
Dalserf
Auldhouse
Limekilnburn
Larkhall
Machan
Yieldshields
Rutherend
Shawtonhill
Ashgill
Rosebank
Milton-Lockhart
Chapelton
Netherburn
Braidwood
Kilncadzow
Corse Hill
Glassford
Ardochrig
Laird's Seat
Udstonhead
Stonehouse
Craignethan
Crossford
Hazelbank
Cartland
Cleghorn
Netherfield
Draffan
Nemphlar
Jerviswood
Strathaven
Auchenheath
Kirkfieldbank
Lanark
Sandford
Blackwood
Black Hill Fort (NTS)
Kirkmuirhill
New Lanark
Boghead
New Lanark World Heritage Site
Falls of Clyde Wildlife Reserve & Visitor Centre
Hyndford Bridge
Deadwaters
Caldermill
West Cauldcoats
Hawksland
Lesmahagow
M74–TO MOFFAT
Drumclog
Carmichael
M8–TO GREENOCK (A8)
A726–TO PAISLEY

292

283

275

Holytown: *James Kier Hardie, radical socialist, member of parliament and the person central to the formation of the British Independent Labour Party was born at nearby Legbranock in 1856. Hardie died in Glasgow in 1915.* ***Map ref. B3***

Blantyre: *The great missionary and explorer David Livingstone was born here on the 19th March 1813. He first went to Africa in 1841 and whilst mapping the Zambezi River discovered and named the Victoria Falls. Livingstone died of fever in Africa in 1873 and his embalmed body was brought back to England and buried in Westminster Abbey.* ***Map ref. A4***

Bellshill: *Sir Matt Busby, famous manager of Manchester United Football Club was born here in 1... He is credited with re-building the team following th... Munich Air Disaster of 1958. He was knighted for his services to football in 1967, retired as manager in 197... and died in 1994.* ***Map ref. B4***

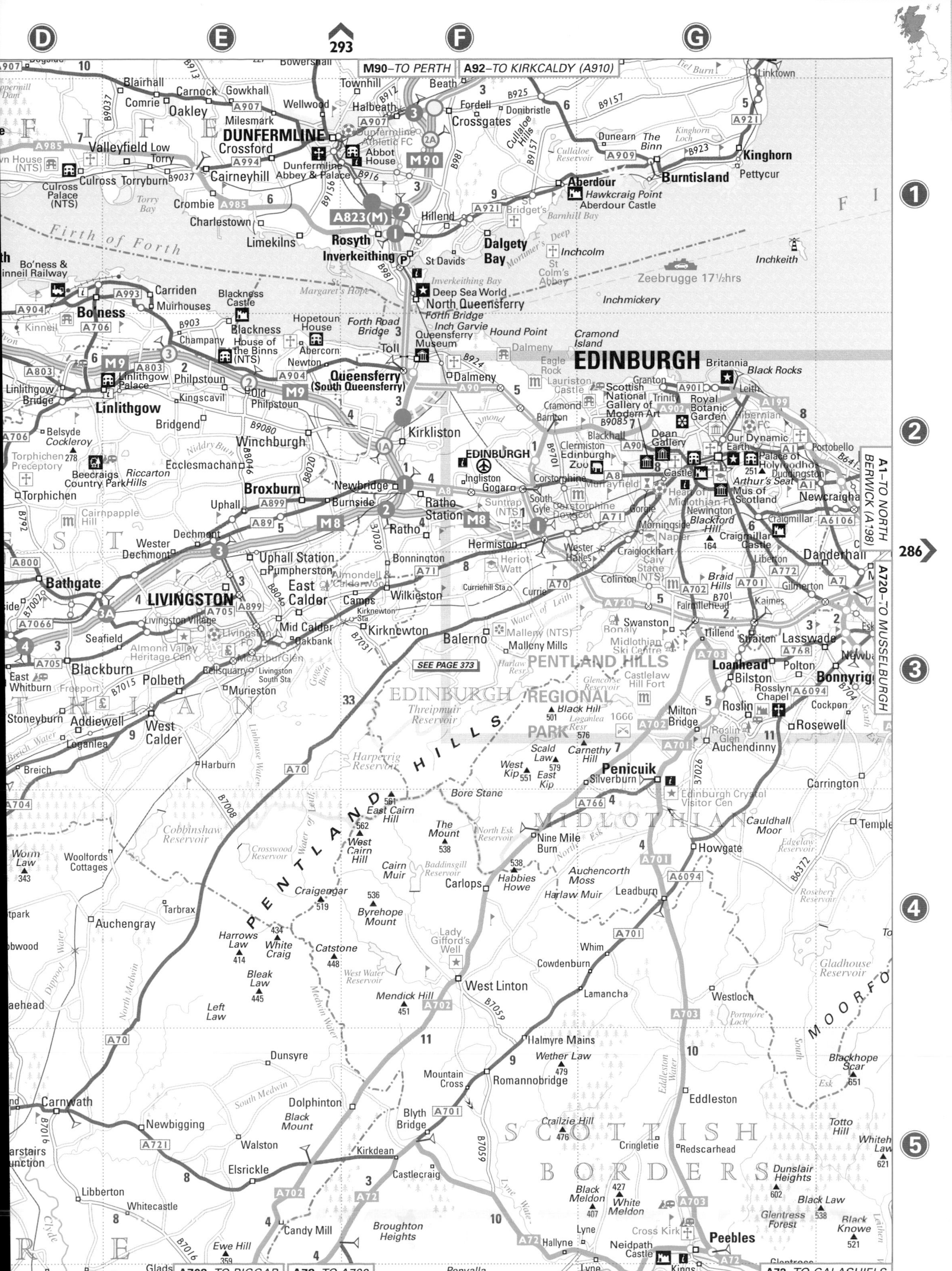

D
E
F
G
293
M90–TO PERTH
A92–TO KIRKCALDY (A910)
Blairhall
Carnock
Gowkhall
Comrie
Oakley
Wellwood
Townhill
Halbeath
Beath
Fordell
Crossgates
Donibristle
Cullaloe Hills
Linktown
Kinghorn
Pettycur
Dunearn
The Binn
Burntisland
Aberdour
Hawkcraig Point
Aberdour Castle
Milesmark
DUNFERMLINE
Dunfermline Athletic FC
Abbot House
Dunfermline Abbey & Palace
Crossford
Valleyfield
Low Torry
Torryburn
Cairneyhill
Culross
Culross Palace (NTS)
Crombie
Charlestown
Limekilns
Rosyth
Inverkeithing
Hillend
St Bridget's
Dalgety Bay
Inchcolm
St Colm's Abbey
St Davids
Firth of Forth
Inverkeithing Bay
Deep Sea World
North Queensferry
Forth Bridge
Inch Garvie
Queensferry Museum
Hound Point
Cramond Island
Inchmickery
Zeebrugge 17½hrs
Inchkeith
Bo'ness & Kinneil Railway
Carriden
Muirhouses
Bo'ness
Kinneil
Blackness Castle
Blackness
Champany
House of the Binns (NTS)
Hopetoun House
Abercorn
Forth Road Bridge
Newton
Toll
Queensferry (South Queensferry)
Dalmeny
Eagle Rock
EDINBURGH
Britannia
Black Rocks
Leith
Granton
Trinity
Royal Botanic Garden
Lauriston Castle
Scottish National Gallery of Modern Art
Cramond
Barnton
Blackhall
Dean Gallery
Our Dynamic Earth
Palace of Holyroodhouse
Portobello
Duddingston
Arthur's Seat
Newcraighall
Linlithgow
Linlithgow Palace
Philpstoun
Old Philpstoun
Kingscavil
Linlithgow Bridge
Bridgend
Winchburgh
Kirkliston
EDINBURGH
Ingliston
Gogar
Clermiston
Edinburgh Zoo
Corstorphine
Murrayfield
Castle
Heart of Midlothian FC
Mus of Scotland
Newington
Blackford Hill
Craigmillar
Craigmillar Castle
Belsyde
Cockleroy
Torphichen Preceptory
Beecraigs Country Park
Riccarton Hills
Ecclesmachan
Torphichen
Broxburn
Newbridge
Burnside
Ratho
Ratho Station
Suntrap (NTS)
South Gyle
Corstorphine Dovecot
Gorgie
Morningside
Napier
Craiglockhart
Liberton
Danderhall
Uphall
Cairnpapple Hill
Dechmont
Wester Dechmont
Bathgate
LIVINGSTON
Uphall Station
Pumpherston
East Calder
Almondell & Calderwood
Bonnington
Wilkieston
Hermiston
Heriot-Watt
Currie
Wester Hailes
Colinton
Caiy Stane (NTS)
Braid Hills
Fairmilehead
Gilmerton
Kaimes
Livingston Village
Seafield
Almond Valley Heritage Cen
Livingston FC
McArthurGlen
Mid Calder
Oakbank
Camps
Kirknewton
Balerno
Malleny (NTS)
Malleny Mills
Swanston
Bonaly
Midlothian Ski Centre
Hillend
Straiton
Lasswade
Loanhead
Polton
Bonnyrigg
Blackburn
East Whitburn
Polbeth
Bellsquarry
Livingston South Sta
Murieston
SEE PAGE 373
PENTLAND HILLS
EDINBURGH REGIONAL PARK
Threipmuir Reservoir
Glencorse Reservoir
Castlelaw Hill Fort
Bilston
Rosslyn Chapel
Roslin
Cockpen
Rosewell
Stoneyburn
Addiewell
Loganlea
West Calder
Breich
Black Hill
Loganlea Resr
Carnethy Hill
Scald Law
West Kip
East Kip
Penicuik
Silverburn
Milton Bridge
Roslin Glen
Auchendinny
Harburn
Harperrig Reservoir
PENTLAND HILLS
East Cairn Hill
West Cairn Hill
Bore Stane
Edinburgh Crystal Visitor Cen
Carrington
Cobbinshaw Reservoir
Crosswood Reservoir
The Mount
North Esk Reservoir
Nine Mile Burn
MIDLOTHIAN
Cauldhall Moor
Temple
Howgate
Edgelaw Reservoir
Worm Law
Woolfords Cottages
Cairn Muir
Baddinsgill Reservoir
Carlops
Habbies Howe
Auchencorth Moss
Harlaw Muir
Leadburn
Rosebery Reservoir
Craigengar
Byrehope Mount
Tarbrax
Auchengray
Harrows Law
White Craig
Catstone
Lady Gifford's Well
Whim
Cowdenburn
Bleak Law
West Water Reservoir
Mendick Hill
West Linton
Lamancha
Westloch
Gladhouse Reservoir
Portmore Loch
Left Law
Halmyre Mains
Wether Law
Romannobridge
Dunsyre
Mountain Cross
Blackhope Scar
Carnwath
Dolphinton
Black Mount
Blyth Bridge
Eddleston
Totto Hill
Newbigging
Walston
Kirkdean
Crailzie Hill
SCOTTISH BORDERS
Cringletie
Redscarhead
Elsrickle
Castlecraig
Dunslair Heights
Libberton
Whitecastle
Black Meldon
White Meldon
Black Law
Glentress Forest
Candy Mill
Broughton Heights
Lyne
Cross Kirk
Peebles
Black Knowe
Ewe Hill
Hallyne
Neidpath Castle
Covington
Quothquan
A702–TO BIGGAR
A72–TO A702
Penvalla
Lyne Station
Kings Muir
A72–TO GALASHIELS
A1–TO NORTH BERWICK (A198)
A720–TO MUSSELBURGH
286
276
1
2
3
4
5

Forth Rail Bridge: *At 1.5 miles (2.4km) long and 150 feet (46m) high, this remarkable cantilever structure is universally recognised as an engineering marvel. Its span of 1,710 feet (521m) is the largest of any railway bridge in Britain. Construction began under Sir William Arrol in 1883 and it was opened by the Prince of Wales in 1890. In all it cost £3.2 million and used 54,000 tons (54,900 tonnes) of steel, 640,000 cubic feet (18,123 cubic metres) of granite and 6.5 million rivets. It also cost the lives of 57 construction workers. And, yes, for over 100 years it was continuously being painted.* ***Map ref. F2***

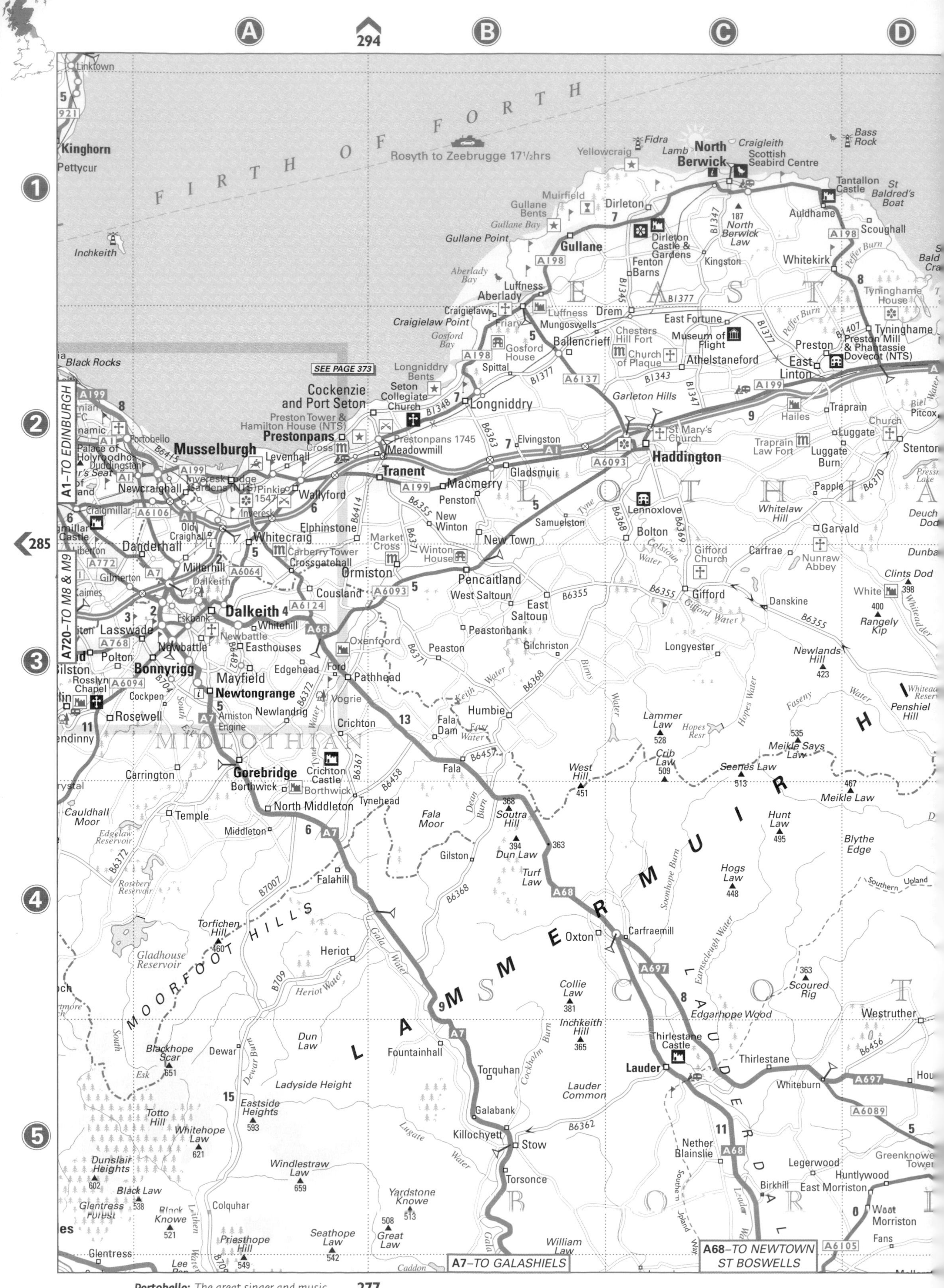

A
B
C
D
294
1
2
3
4
5
285
277
FIRTH OF FORTH
Rosyth to Zeebrugge 17½hrs
Linktown
Kinghorn
Pettycur
Inchkeith
Black Rocks
SEE PAGE 373
Fidra
Yellowcraig
Lamb
North Berwick
Craigleith
Scottish Seabird Centre
Bass Rock
Tantallon Castle
St Baldred's Boat
Auldhame
Scoughall
Muirfield
Gullane Bents
Gullane Bay
Dirleton
Dirleton Castle & Gardens
North Berwick Law
Gullane Point
Gullane
Fenton Barns
Kingston
Whitekirk
Tyninghame House
Aberlady Bay
Luffness
Aberlady
Craigielaw
Craigielaw Point
Luffness Friary
Mungoswells
Drem
East Fortune
Museum of Flight
Chesters Hill Fort
Church of Plaque
Athelstaneford
Ballencrieff
Gosford Bay
Gosford House
Spittal
Tyninghame
Preston Mill & Phantassie Dovecot (NTS)
Preston
East Linton
Longniddry Bents
Seton Collegiate Church
Cockenzie and Port Seton
Preston Tower & Hamilton House (NTS)
Prestonpans
Mercat Cross
Prestonpans 1745
Meadowmill
Longniddry
Garleton Hills
Elvington
St Mary's Church
Haddington
Hailes
Traprain
Traprain Law Fort
Luggate
Luggate Burn
Stenton
Pitcox
Musselburgh
Portobello
Palace of Holyroodhouse
Duddingston
Levenhall
Inveresk Lodge Gardens (NTS)
Pinkie 1547
Inveresk
Newcraighall
Tranent
Macmerry
Penston
Gladsmuir
New Winton
Samuelston
Lennoxlove
Bolton
Papple
Whitelaw Hill
Garvald
Wallyford
Elphinstone
Whitecraig
Craigmillar Castle
Danderhall
Old Craighall
Millerhill
Carberry Tower
Crossgatehall
Market Cross
Winton House
New Town
Gifford Church
Carfrae
Nunraw Abbey
Dunbar
Gilmerton
Dalkeith
Ormiston
Pencaitland
West Saltoun
East Saltoun
Cousland
Gifford
Danskine
Clints Dod
White
Rangely Kip
Eskbank
Lasswade
Whitehill
Newbattle
Easthouses
Peastonbank
Oxenfoord
Peaston
Gilchriston
Longyester
Newlands Hill
Polton
Bonnyrigg
Mayfield
Edgehead
Ford
Pathhead
Rosslyn Chapel
Cockpen
Newtongrange
Vogrie
Rosewell
Arniston Engine
Newlandrig
Crichton
Humbie
Fala Dam
Lammer Law
Hopes Resr
Faseny
Penshiel Hill
Meikle Says Law
MIDLOTHIAN
Carrington
Gorebridge
Crichton Castle
Borthwick
Fala
West Hill
Crib Law
Seenes Law
Meikle Law
North Middleton
Tynehead
Temple
Cauldhall Moor
Edgelaw Reservoir
Middleton
Fala Moor
Soutra Hill
Hunt Law
Blythe Edge
Gilston
Dun Law
Turf Law
Rosebery Reservoir
Falahill
Hogs Law
Southern Upland
Torfichen Hill
MOORFOOT HILLS
Oxton
Carfraemill
Gladhouse Reservoir
Heriot
Heriot Water
LAMMERMUIR
Collie Law
Scoured Rig
LAUDERDALE
Edgarhope Wood
Westruther
Blackhope Scar
Dewar
Dun Law
Fountainhall
Inchkeith Hill
Thirlestane Castle
Thirlestane
Lauder
Torquhan
Ladyside Height
Lauder Common
Whiteburn
Eastside Heights
Totto Hill
Whitehope Law
Galabank
Killochyett
Stow
Nether Blainslie
Greenknowe Tower
Legerwood
Huntlywood
Dunslair Heights
Windlestraw Law
Torsonce
Birkhill
East Morriston
Black Law
Glentress Forest
Colquhar
Black Knowe
Yardstone Knowe
Great Law
Wester Morriston
Priesthope Hill
Seathope Law
William Law
Fans
Glentress
Lee Pen
Caddon
A7–TO GALASHIELS
A68–TO NEWTOWN ST BOSWELLS
A1–TO EDINBURGH
A720–TO M8 & M9

Portobello: *The great singer and music hall entertainer Sir Harry Lauder was born here in 1870. Lauder died in 1950 and is buried in Bent Cemetery, Hamilton.*
Map ref. A2

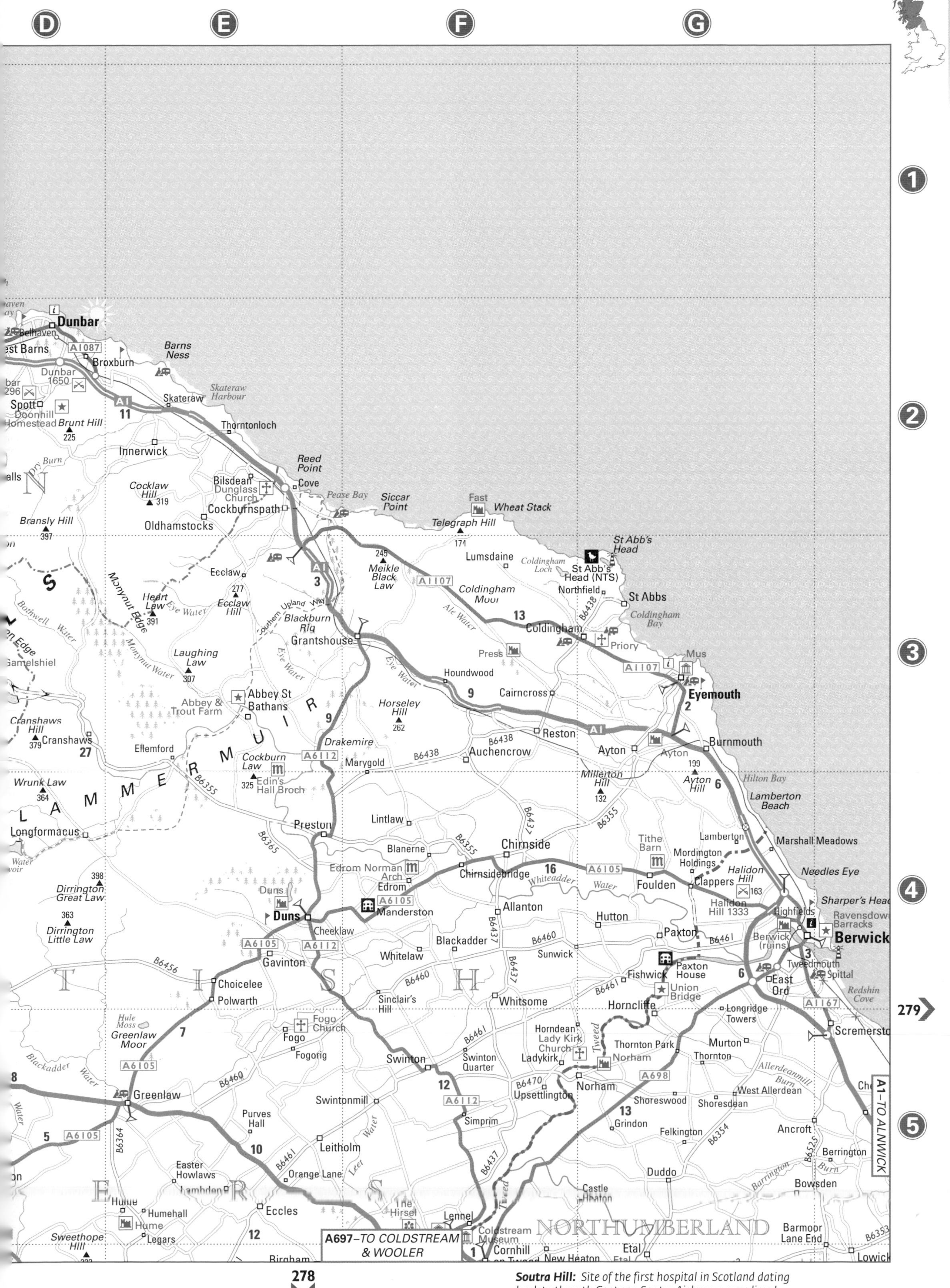
D
E
F
G
1
2
3
4
5
Dunbar
Belhaven
West Barns
Broxburn
Barns Ness
Dunbar 1650
Skateraw Harbour
Skateraw
Spott
Doonhill Homestead
Brunt Hill
225
A1087
A1
11
Thorntonloch
Innerwick
Reed Point
Cove
Bilsdean
Dunglass Church
Cocklaw Hill
319
Cockburnspath
Pease Bay
Siccar Point
Fast
Wheat Stack
Telegraph Hill
171
Bransly Hill
397
Oldhamstocks
St Abb's Head
Lumsdaine
Coldingham Loch
St Abb's Head (NTS)
Northfield
St Abbs
Coldingham Bay
245
Meikle Black Law
A1107
Coldingham Moor
13
Coldingham
Priory
Ecclaw
277
Ecclaw Hill
Heart Law
391
Monynut Edge
Eye Water
Southern Upland Way
Blackburn Rig
Grantshouse
Bothwell Water
Monynut Water
Laughing Law
307
Gamelshiel
Press
Mus
Houndwood
Eye Water
Ale Water
9
Cairncross
Eyemouth
2
Abbey St Bathans
Abbey & Trout Farm
Horseley Hill
262
Cranshaws Hill
379
Cranshaws
27
Ellemford
Drakemire
A6112
Marygold
B6438
Auchencrow
Reston
Ayton
Burnmouth
Cockburn Law
325
Edin's Hall Broch
LAMMERMUIR
Wrunk Law
364
Longformacus
B6355
Millerton Hill
132
Ayton Hill
199
6
Hilton Bay
Lamberton Beach
Preston
Lintlaw
B6365
B6437
Blanerne
Chirnside
Tithe Barn
Lamberton
Marshall Meadows
398
Dirrington Great Law
Edrom Norman Arch
Edrom
Chirnsidebridge
16
Whiteadder Water
A6105
Foulden
Mordington Holdings
Clappers
Halidon Hill
163
Halidon Hill 1333
Needles Eye
Sharper's Head
Duns
Manderston
Allanton
Hutton
Highfields
Ravensdowne Barracks
363
Dirrington Little Law
Cheeklaw
Blackadder
B6460
Paxton
B6461
Berwick (ruins)
Berwick
Gavinton
Whitelaw
Sunwick
Tweedmouth
Paxton House
Spittal
B6456
Choicelee
Fishwick
Union Bridge
East Ord
Redshin Cove
Polwarth
Sinclair's Hill
Whitsome
Horncliffe
Longridge Towers
A1167
279
Hule Moss
Greenlaw Moor
7
Fogo Church
Fogo
Fogorig
Horndean
Lady Kirk Church
Tweed
Thornton Park
Norham
Murton
Thornton
Scremerston
Blackadder Water
A6105
Swinton
Swinton Quarter
Ladykirk
12
A698
Allerdean Mill Burn
Greenlaw
B6470
Upsettlington
Norham
Shoreswood
Shoresdean
West Allerdean
A1–TO ALNWICK
Swintonmill
A6112
Purves Hall
13
Simprim
Grindon
Felkington
Ancroft
5
A6105
10
B6364
B6461
Leitholm
B6437
B6354
Berrington
B6525
Leet Water
Easter Howlaws
Orange Lane
Duddo
Barrington Burn
Bowsden
Lambden
Hume
Humehall
Eccles
The Hirsel
Lennel
Castle Heaton
NORTHUMBERLAND
Sweethope Hill
Legars
12
Birgham
A697–TO COLDSTREAM & WOOLER
Coldstream Museum
Cornhill on Tweed
New Heaton
Etal
Barmoor Lane End
Lowick
B6353
278

Soutra Hill: *Site of the first hospital in Scotland dating back to the 12th Century. Soutra Aisle was a medieval hospital and refuge for travellers on the 'Royal Road'; the main England to Scotland route. Now an archaeological site.* ***Map ref. B4***

296

Ulva: *The entire population of this island was 'cleared' between 1846–51 to allow for sheep grazing. Many Scottish Islands have a history of Viking invasion and occupation and often have Viking names. Ulva is Norse for 'Wolf Island'.* ***Map ref. D1***

Erraid: *Small, tidal Island immortalised in Robert Louis Stevenson's 'Kidnapped'. In the book the hero David Balfour was shipwrecked on this island and began his adventures.* ***Map ref. B3***

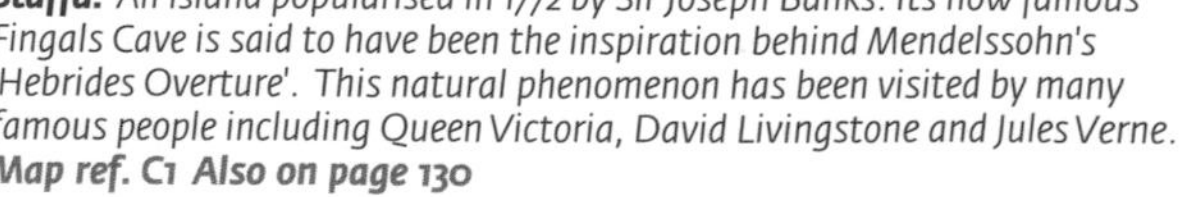

Staffa: *An island popularised in 1772 by Sir Joseph Banks. Its now famous Fingals Cave is said to have been the inspiration behind Mendelssohn's 'Hebrides Overture'. This natural phenomenon has been visited by many famous people including Queen Victoria, David Livingstone and Jules Verne.* ***Map ref. C1 Also on page 130***

280

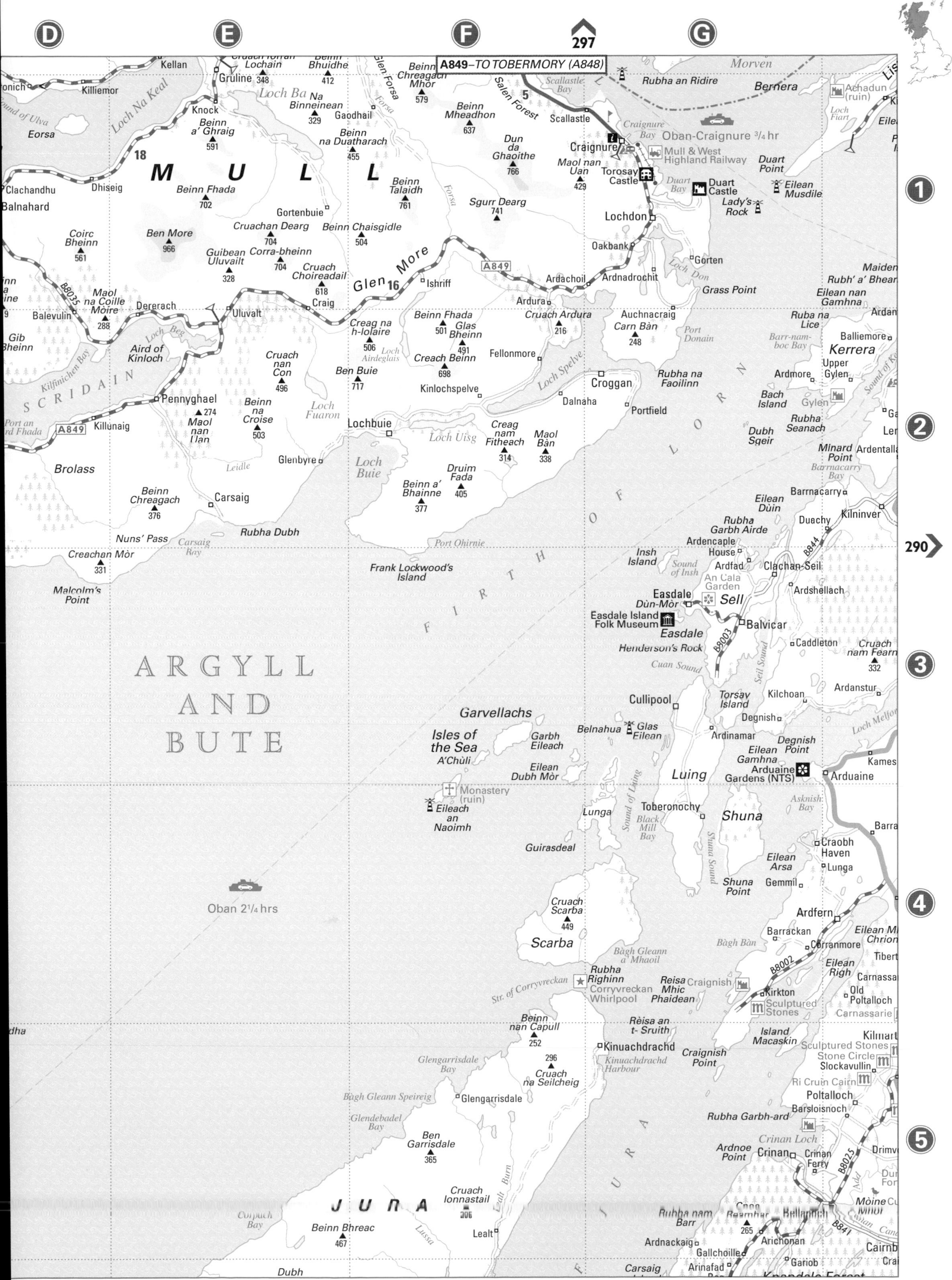

D
E
F
G
297
A849–TO TOBERMORY (A848)
Kellan
Gruline
Lochain
348
Bhuidhe
412
Beinn Chreagach Mhor
579
Morven
Rubha an Ridire
Bernera
Achadun (ruin)
Killiemor
Loch Ba
Na Binneinean
329
Gaodhail
Forsa
Glen Forsa
Salen Forest
Scallastle Bay
5
Scallastle
Beinn Mheadhon
637
Loch Fiart
Sound of Ulva
Eorsa
Loch Na Keal
Knock
Beinn a' Ghraig
591
Beinn na Duatharach
455
Dun da Ghaoithe
766
Craignure Bay
Craignure
Oban-Craignure 3/4 hr
Mull & West Highland Railway
Duart Point
18
MULL
Maol nan Uan
429
Torosay Castle
Clachandhu
Dhiseig
Beinn Fhada
702
Beinn Talaidh
761
Sgurr Dearg
741
Duart Bay
Duart Castle
Eilean Musdile
Lady's Rock
1
Balnahard
Gortenbuie
Lochdon
Coirc Bheinn
561
Ben More
966
Cruachan Dearg
704
Beinn Chaisgidle
504
Oakbank
Guibean Uluvailt
328
Corra-bheinn
704
Cruach Choireadail
618
Glen More
16
Ishriff
A849
Gorten
Loch Don
Maiden
Rubh' a' Bhear
Craig
Ardachoil
Ardnadrochit
Grass Point
Eilean nan Gamhna
B8035
Maol na Coille Moire
288
Dererach
Uluvalt
Ardura
Cruach Ardura
216
Auchnacraig
Ruba na Lice
Ardan
Balevulin
Beinn Fhada
501
Glas Bheinn
491
Carn Bàn
248
Port Donain
Barr-nam-boc Bay
Balliemore
Kerrera
Gib Bheinn
Loch Beg
Aird of Kinloch
Creag na h-Iolaire
506
Loch Airdeglais
Creach Beinn
698
Fellonmore
Loch Spelve
Upper Gylen
Kilfinichen Bay
Cruach nan Con
496
Ben Buie
717
Kinlochspelve
Croggan
Rubha na Faoilinn
Ardmore
Sound of Kerrera
SCRIDAIN
Pennyghael
274
Maol nan Ilan
Beinn na Croise
503
Loch Fuaron
Dalnaha
Portfield
Bach Island
Gylen
Port an Fhada
A849
Killunaig
Lochbuie
Loch Uisg
Creag nam Fitheach
314
Maol Bàn
338
Dubh Sgeir
Rubha Seanach
2
Minard Point
Ardentallan
Barnacarry Bay
Brolass
Leidle
Glenbyre
Loch Buie
Druim Fada
405
Beinn a' Bhainne
377
Barnacarry
Beinn Chreagach
376
Carsaig
Eilean Dùin
Rubha Garbh Airde
Duachy
Kilninver
Nuns' Pass
Carsaig Bay
Rubha Dubh
Port Ohirnie
Ardencaple House
B844
Creachan Mòr
331
Frank Lockwood's Island
Insh Island
Sound of Insh
Ardfad
Clachan-Seil
290
An Cala Garden
Ardshellach
Malcolm's Point
Easdale
Dùn-Mòr
Sell
Easdale Island Folk Museum
Balvicar
Easdale
B8003
Caddleton
Cruach nam Fearn
332
Henderson's Rock
Cuan Sound
Seil Sound
3
ARGYLL AND BUTE
FIRTH OF LORN
Cullipool
Torsay Island
Kilchoan
Ardanstur
Loch Melfort
Garvellachs
Belnahua
Glas Eilean
Degnish
Ardinamar
Degnish Point
Isles of the Sea
A'Chùli
Garbh Eileach
Eilean Gamhna
Kames
Eilean Dubh Mòr
Luing
Arduaine Gardens (NTS)
Arduaine
Monastery (ruin)
Eileach an Naoimh
Lunga
Sound of Luing
Toberonochy
Shuna
Asknish Bay
Black Mill Bay
Barra
Craobh Haven
Guirasdeal
Shuna Sound
Eilean Arsa
Lunga
Oban 2¼ hrs
Shuna Point
Gemmil
4
Cruach Scarba
449
Ardfern
Scarba
Barrackan
Eilean Mhic Chrion
Bàgh Gleann a' Mhaoil
Bàgh Bàn
Corranmore
Tibert
Str. of Corryvreckan
Rubha Righinn
Corryvreckan Whirlpool
Reisa Mhic Phaidean
Craignish
B8002
Eilean Righ
Carnassarie
Kirkton
Old Poltalloch
Sculptured Stones
Carnassarie
Beinn nan Capull
252
Rèisa an t- Sruith
Island Macaskin
Kilmartin
Sculptured Stones
Stone Circle
Slockavullin
Kinuachdrachd
Kinuachdrachd Harbour
Craignish Point
296
Cruach na Seilcheig
Glengarrisdale Bay
Ri Cruin Cairn
Poltalloch
Bàgh Gleann Speireig
Glengarrisdale
Barsloisnoch
Glendebadel Bay
Rubha Garbh-ard
JURA
Ben Garrisdale
365
Crinan Loch
Ardnoe Point
Crinan
Crinan Ferry
B8025
5
Cruach Ionnastail
Corpach Bay
Moine Mhor
JURA
Beinn Bhreac
467
Lussa
Lealt
Rubha nam Barr
265
Arichonan
B841
Ardnackaig
Gallchoille
Cairnbaan
Dubh
Carsaig
Arinafad
Gariob
281

Clachan-Seil: *A hump-backed stone bridge here links Seil Island to the mainland. It is known as 'The Bridge over the Atlantic' and was designed by Thomas Telford in 1792.* ***Map ref. G3***

Corryvreckan: *The swirling whirlpool here is one of the largest in the world and makes the Straits of Corryvreckan the most dangerous stretch of water around the British Isles. The sound of the raging water can often be heard 10 miles (16km) away.* ***Map ref. F4***

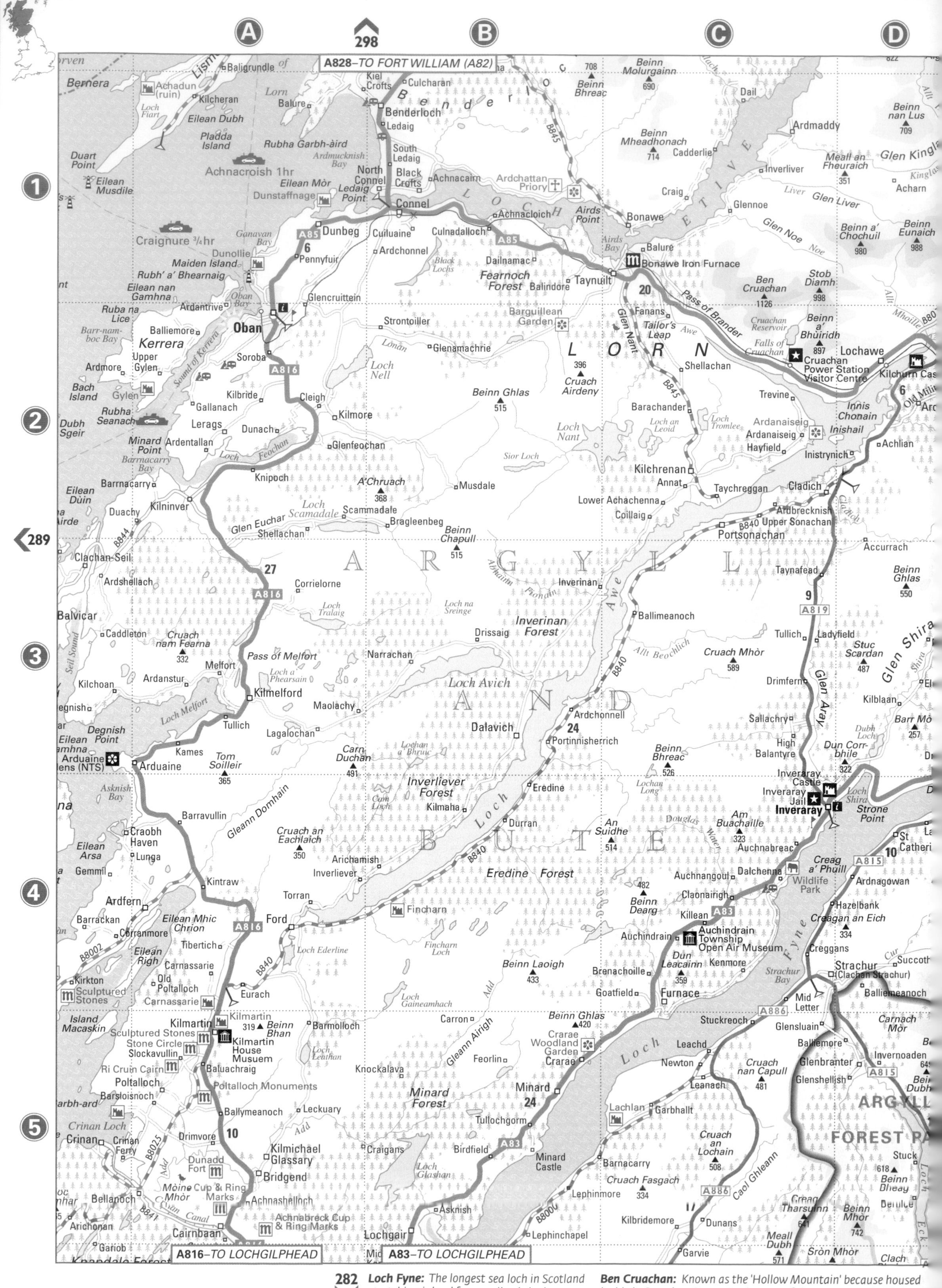
A
B
C
D
298
1
2
3
4
5
289
A828–TO FORT WILLIAM (A82)
Bernera
Lismore
Baligrundle
Achadun (ruin)
Kilcheran
Loch Fiart
Eilean Dubh
Pladda Island
Lorn
Balure
Rubha Garbh-àird
Ardmucknish Bay
Kiel Crofts
Culcharan
Benderloch
Ledaig
South Ledaig
Black Crofts
North Connel
Ledaig Point
Achnacairn
Ardchattan Priory
Beinn Bhreac
708
Beinn Molurgainn
690
B845
Dail
Beinn Mheadhonach
714
Cadderlie
Beinn nan Lus
709
Ardmaddy
Meall an Fheuraich
351
Glen Kinglass
Acharn
Inverliver
Glen Liver
Glennoe
Glen Noe
Craig
Bonawe
Airds Point
Airds Bay
Loch Etive
Duart Point
Eilean Musdile
Achnacroish 1hr
Eilean Mòr
Dunstaffnage
Connel
Achnacloich
Loch
Dunbeg
Cuiluaine
Culnadalloch
A85
Craignure ¾hr
Ganavan Bay
Dunollie
Maiden Island
Rubh' a' Bhearnaig
Eilean nan Gamhna
Pennyfuir
Ardchonnel
Black Lochs
Dailnamac
Fearnoch Forest
Balindore
Taynuilt
Balure
Bonawe Iron Furnace
Ben Cruachan
1126
Stob Diamh
998
Beinn a' Chochuil
980
Beinn Eunaich
988
Ruba na Lice
Ardantrive
Oban Bay
Oban
Glencruittein
Barr-nam-boc Bay
Balliemore
Kerrera
Upper Gylen
Ardmore
Soroba
Sound of Kerrera
A816
Strontoiller
Lonan
Glenamachrie
Barguillean Garden
Fanans
Glen Nant
Tailor's Leap
Awe
Pass of Brander
Cruachan Reservoir
Falls of Cruachan
Beinn a' Bhùiridh
897
Cruachan Power Station Visitor Centre
Lochawe
Kilchurn Castle
L O R N
396
Cruach Airdeny
Loch Nell
Shellachan
Bach Island
Gylen
Rubha Seanach
Kilbride
Gallanach
Cleigh
Kilmore
Beinn Ghlas
515
B845
Barachander
Trevine
Innis Chonain
Inishail
Dubh Sgeir
Lerags
Dunach
Minard Point
Ardentallan
Barnacarry Bay
Loch Feochan
Glenfeochan
Loch Nant
Loch an Leoid
Loch Tromlee
Ardanaiseig
Hayfield
Achlian
Sior Loch
Eilean Dùin
Barnacarry
Knipoch
A'Chruach
368
Musdale
Kilchrenan
Annat
Taychreggan
Inistrynich
Cladich
Lower Achachenna
Coillaig
Ardbrecknish
Upper Sonachan
B840
Portsonachan
Accurrach
Duachy
Kilninver
Loch Scamadale
Scammadale
Bragleenbeg
Glen Euchar
Shellachan
Beinn Chapull
515
B844
Clachan-Seil
A R G Y L L
Abhainn Fionain
Inverinan
Taynafead
Beinn Ghlas
550
Ardshellach
27
Corrielorne
A816
9
A819
Balvicar
Loch Tralaig
Loch na Sreinge
Ballimeanoch
Caddleton
Cruach nam Fearna
332
Seil Sound
Inverinan Forest
Drissaig
Tullich
Ladyfield
Stuc Scardan
487
Glen Shira
Pass of Melfort
Narrachan
Allt Beochlich
Cruach Mhòr
589
Kilchoan
Ardanstur
Melfort
Loch a' Phearsain
Loch Avich
Drimfern
Glen Aray
Kilmelford
A N D
Kilblaan
Degnish
Loch Melfort
Tullich
Maolachy
Ardchonnell
Sallachry
Barr Mòr
257
Degnish Point
Arduaine Gardens (NTS)
Arduaine
Kames
Lagalochan
Dalavich
24
Portinnisherrich
Dubh Loch
High Balantyre
Dun Corr-bhile
322
Tom Soilleir
365
Carn Duchan
491
Lochan a' Bhruic
Inverliever Forest
Beinn Bhreac
526
Inveraray Castle
Inveraray Jail
Inveraray
Loch Shira
Strone Point
Asknish Bay
Gleann Domhain
Cam Loch
Kilmaha
Eredine
Lochan Long
Barravullin
Craobh Haven
Lunga
Eilean Arsa
Cruach an Eachlaich
350
Durran
Loch Awe
An Suidhe
514
Douglas Water
Am Buachaille
323
Auchnabreac
St Catherines
10
B U T E
Gemmil
Arichamish
Inverliever
B840
Eredine Forest
Auchnangoul
Dalchenna
Creag a' Phuill
Wildlife Park
A815
Ardnagowan
Kintraw
482
Beinn Dearg
Claonairigh
Ardfern
Torran
Fincharn
Killean
A83
Hazelbank
Barrackan
Corranmore
Eilean Mhic Chrion
A816
Ford
Auchindrain
Auchindrain Township Open Air Museum
Creagan an Eich
334
Tibertich
Loch Ederline
Fincharn Loch
Creggans
B8002
Eilean Righ
Carnassarie
Beinn Laoigh
433
Dun Leacainn
359
Kenmore
Strachur Bay
Strachur (Clachan Strachur)
Succoth
Cur
Kirkton
Sculptured Stones
Old Poltalloch
Carnassarie
B840
Eurach
Brenachoille
Loch Fyne
Goatfield
Furnace
Mid Letter
Balliemeanoch
Loch Gaineamhach
Add
A886
Island Macaskin
Kilmartin
Kilmartin House Museum
319
Beinn Bhan
Barmolloch
Carron
Gleann Airigh
Beinn Ghlas
420
Crarae Woodland Garden
Crarae
Stuckreoch
Glensluain
Carnach Mòr
Sculptured Stones
Stone Circle
Slockavullin
Ri Cruin Cairn
Baluachraig
Loch Leathan
Knockalava
Feorlin
Loch
Leachd
Newton
Leanach
Cruach nan Capull
481
Balliemore
Glenbranter
Invernoaden
Glenshellish
A815
Poltalloch
Poltalloch Monuments
Minard Forest
Minard
24
Lachlan
Garbhallt
Barsloisnoch
Ballymeanoch
Leckuary
ARGYLL
FOREST PARK
Crinan Loch
Crinan
Crinan Ferry
Drimvore
10
Add
Tullochgorm
Kilmichael Glassary
Craigans
Birdfield
A83
Minard Castle
Cruach an Lochain
508
Stuck
618
Beinn Bheag
B8025
Dunadd Fort
Bridgend
Loch Glashan
Barnacarry
Cruach Fasgach
334
Caol Ghleann
Creag Tharsuinn
641
Beinn Mhòr
742
Bellanoch
Mòine Mhòr
Cup & Ring Marks
Achnashellach
Asknish
Lephinmore
A886
B8000
Kilbridemore
Dunans
Meall Dubh
571
B841
Crinan Canal
Achnabreck Cup & Ring Marks
Arichonan
Cairnbaan
Lochgair
Lephinchapel
Garvie
Sròn Mhòr
Clach
Gariob
A816–TO LOCHGILPHEAD
A83–TO LOCHGILPHEAD
282

Loch Fyne: *The longest sea loch in Scotland stretching inland for 44 miles (71km).* ***Map ref. B5***

Ben Cruachan: *Known as the 'Hollow Mountain' because housed inside is Cruachan Power Station one of the most remarkable feats of engineering in Scotland. Deep in the mountain a huge man-made cavern houses the world's first 'high head reversible pumped storage hydro scheme'.* ***Map ref. C2 Also on page 119***

299

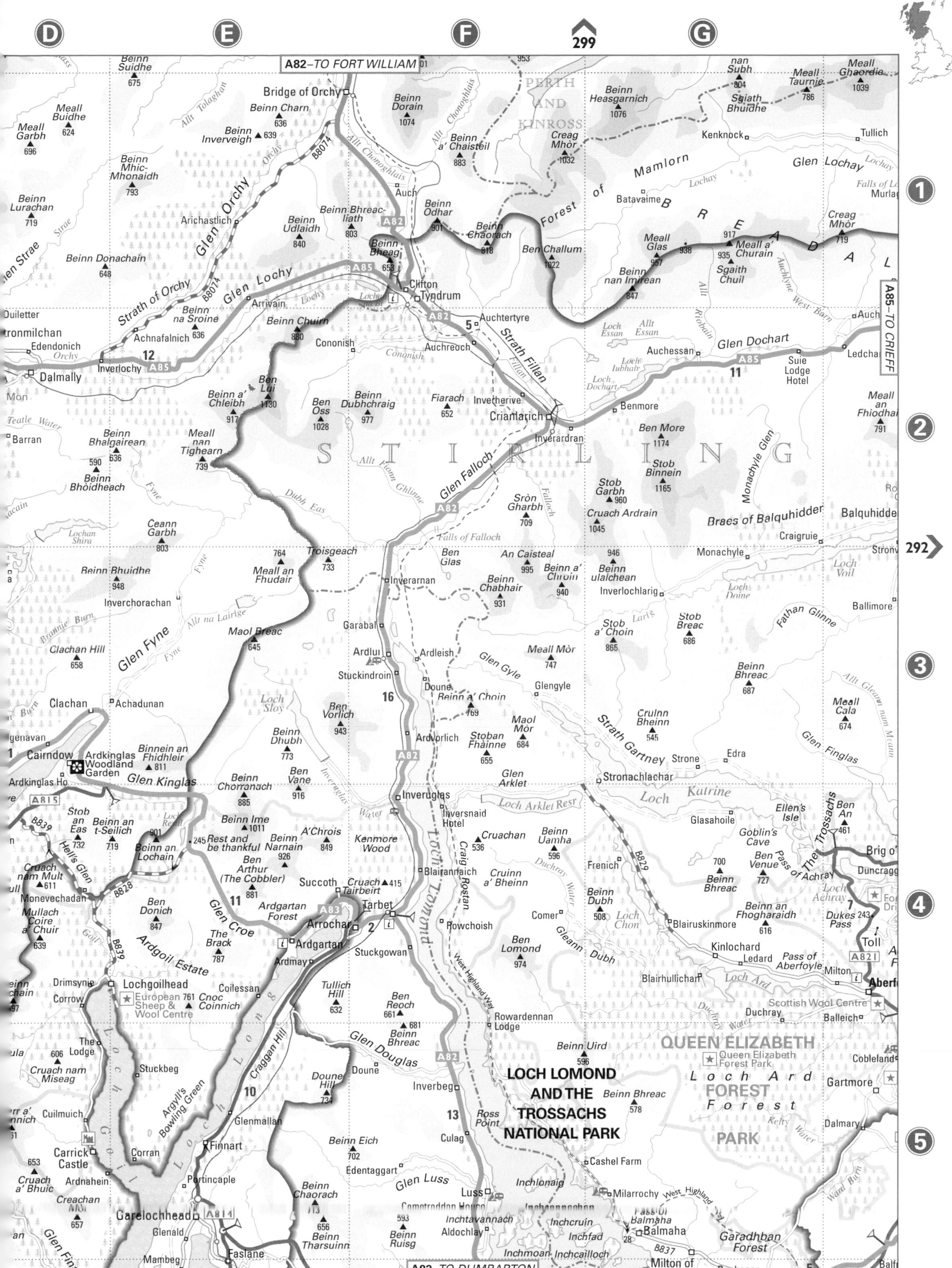

D
E
F
G
1
2
3
4
5
A82–TO FORT WILLIAM
A82–TO DUMBARTON
A85–TO CRIEFF
PERTH AND KINROSS
STIRLING
BREADALBANE
Forest of Mamlorn
Bridge of Orchy
Beinn Dorain 1074
Beinn a' Chaisteil 883
Creag Mhòr 1032
Beinn Heasgarnich 1076
Kenknock
Tullich
Glen Lochay
Meall Taurnie 786
Meall Ghaordie 1039
Sgiath Bhuidhe
Batavaime
Meall Glas 957
Meall a' Churain
Sgaith Chuil
Beinn nan Imirean 847
Creag Mhòr 719
Beinn Odhar 901
Beinn Chaorach 818
Ben Challum 1022
Beinn Udlaidh 840
Beinn Bhreac-liath 803
Beinn Bheag 653
Auch
Clifton
Tyndrum
Glen Orchy
Glen Lochy
Strath of Orchy
Arichastlich
Beinn Donachain 648
Beinn Mhic-Mhonaidh 793
Beinn Lurachan 719
Meall Garbh 696
Meall Buidhe 624
Beinn Suidhe 675
Beinn Charn 636
Beinn Inverveigh 639
Arrivain
Beinn na Sroine 636
Achnafalnich
Inverlochy
Dalmally
Edendonich
Beinn Chuirn 880
Cononish
Auchtertyre
Auchreoch
Strath Fillan
Auchessan
Glen Dochart
Suie Lodge Hotel
Ledcharrie
Loch Iubhair
Loch Dochart
Benmore
Crianlarich
Inverardran
Ben More 1174
Stob Binnein 1165
Stob Garbh 960
Cruach Ardrain 1045
Braes of Balquhidder
Balquhidder
Monachyle Glen
Meall an Fhiodhain 791
Beinn a' Chleibh 917
Ben Lui 1130
Ben Oss 1028
Beinn Dubhchraig 977
Fiarach 652
Invetherive
Glen Falloch
Sròn Gharbh 709
Falls of Falloch
Beinn Bhalgairean 636
Meall nan Tighearn 739
Beinn Bhòidheach
Barran
Lochan Shira
Ceann Garbh 803
Beinn Bhuidhe 948
Inverchorachan
Meall an Fhudair
Troisgeach 733
Inverarnan
Ben Glas
An Caisteal 995
Beinn a' Chroin 940
Beinn Chabhair 931
Beinn Tulaichean
Inverlochlarig
Monachyle
Craigruie
Loch Voil
Loch Doine
Ballimore
Stob a' Choin 865
Stob Breac 686
Glen Fyne
Maol Breac 645
Clachan Hill 658
Clachan
Achadunan
Garabal
Ardlui
Ardleish
Stuckindroin
Glen Gyle
Meall Mòr 747
Glengyle
Doune
Beinn a' Choin 769
Loch Sloy
Ben Vorlich 943
Beinn Dubh 773
Ardvorlich
Stoban Fhàinne 655
Maol Mòr 684
Strath Gartney
Crulnn Bheinn 545
Beinn Bhreac 687
Meall Cala 674
Glen Finglas
Strone
Edra
Stronachlachar
Glen Arklet
Loch Arklet Resr
Loch Katrine
Cairndow
Ardkinglas Woodland Garden
Binnein an Fhidhleir 811
Glen Kinglas
Ardkinglas Ho.
Beinn Chorranach 885
Ben Vane 916
Inveruglas
Inversnaid Hotel
Glasahoile
Ellen's Isle
Ben An 461
The Trossachs
Beinn an Lochain 901
Rest and be thankful
Beinn Ime 1011
Beinn Narnain 926
A'Chrois 849
Kenmore Wood
Cruachan 536
Beinn Uamha 596
Goblin's Cave
Ben Venue 727
Pass of Achray
Loch Achray
Brig o' Turk
Duncraggan
Stob an Eas 732
Beinn an t-Seilich 719
Hell's Glen
Ben Arthur (The Cobbler) 881
Succoth
Cruach 415
Tairbeirt
Blairannaich
Cruinn a' Bheinn
Frenich
Beinn Bhreac
Beinn Dubh 508
Loch Chon
Beinn an Fhogharaidh 616
Dukes Pass
Monevechadan
Cruach nam Mult 611
Mullach Coire a' Chuir 639
Ben Donich 847
Glen Croe
Ardgartan Forest
Arrochar
Tarbet
Craig Rostan
Rowchoish
Comer
Blairuskinmore
Kinlochard
Ledard
Pass of Aberfoyle
Milton
Aberfoyle
The Brack 787
Ardgoil Estate
Ardgartan
Ardmay
Stuckgowan
Ben Lomond 974
Gleann Dubh
Loch Ard
Blairhullichan
Toll
Lochgoilhead
Drimsynie
Corrow
European Sheep & Wool Centre
Cnoc Coinnich 761
Coilessan
Tullich Hill 632
Ben Reoch 661
Beinn Bhreac 681
Rowardennan Lodge
West Highland Way
Scottish Wool Centre
Duchray
Balleich
The Lodge
Cruach nam Miseag 606
Stuckbeg
Loch Long
Loch Goil
Craggan Hill
Argyll's Bowling Green
Glen Douglas
Doune Hill 734
Doune
Inverbeg
Beinn Uird 596
QUEEN ELIZABETH FOREST PARK
Queen Elizabeth Forest Park
Loch Ard Forest
Cobleland
Gartmore
LOCH LOMOND AND THE TROSSACHS NATIONAL PARK
Loch Lomond
Beinn Bhreac 578
Cuilmuich
Glenmallan
Ross Point
Culag
Dalmary
Carrick Castle
Corran
Finnart
Beinn Eich 702
Edentaggart
Cashel Farm
Ardnahein
Cruach a' Bhuic 653
Portincaple
Glen Luss
Luss
Inchlonaig
Milarrochy
Creachan Mòr 657
Garelochhead
Beinn Chaorach 713
Beinn Tharsuinn 656
Beinn Ruisg 593
Inchtavannach
Aldochlay
Inchcruin
Inchfad
Balmaha
Garadhban Forest
Glenald
Faslane
Mambeg
Glen Finart
Inchmoan
Inchcailloch
Milton of Buchanan
Buchanan
Balfron Station

Loch Lomond: *In Scotland the word 'loch' refers to an inland body of water. Loch Lomond is the largest such feature in Scotland. It has an area of 27.5 square miles (71 sq km) and is 617 feet (190m) deep. Here on 16th July 1932 Kaye Don in Miss England 3 raised the world water speed record to 119.81 mph (193km/h).* ***Map ref. F4***
See Loch Lomond & The Trossachs National Park ***on page 126***

283

An area known as ***The Trossachs*** *which was immortalised in Sir Walter Scott's ballads 'The Lady of the Lake' (1810) and 'Rob Roy' (1817).*
So wondrous wild the whole might seem
The scenery of a fairy dream. ***Map ref. G4***
See Loch Lomond & The Trossachs National Park ***on page 126***

292

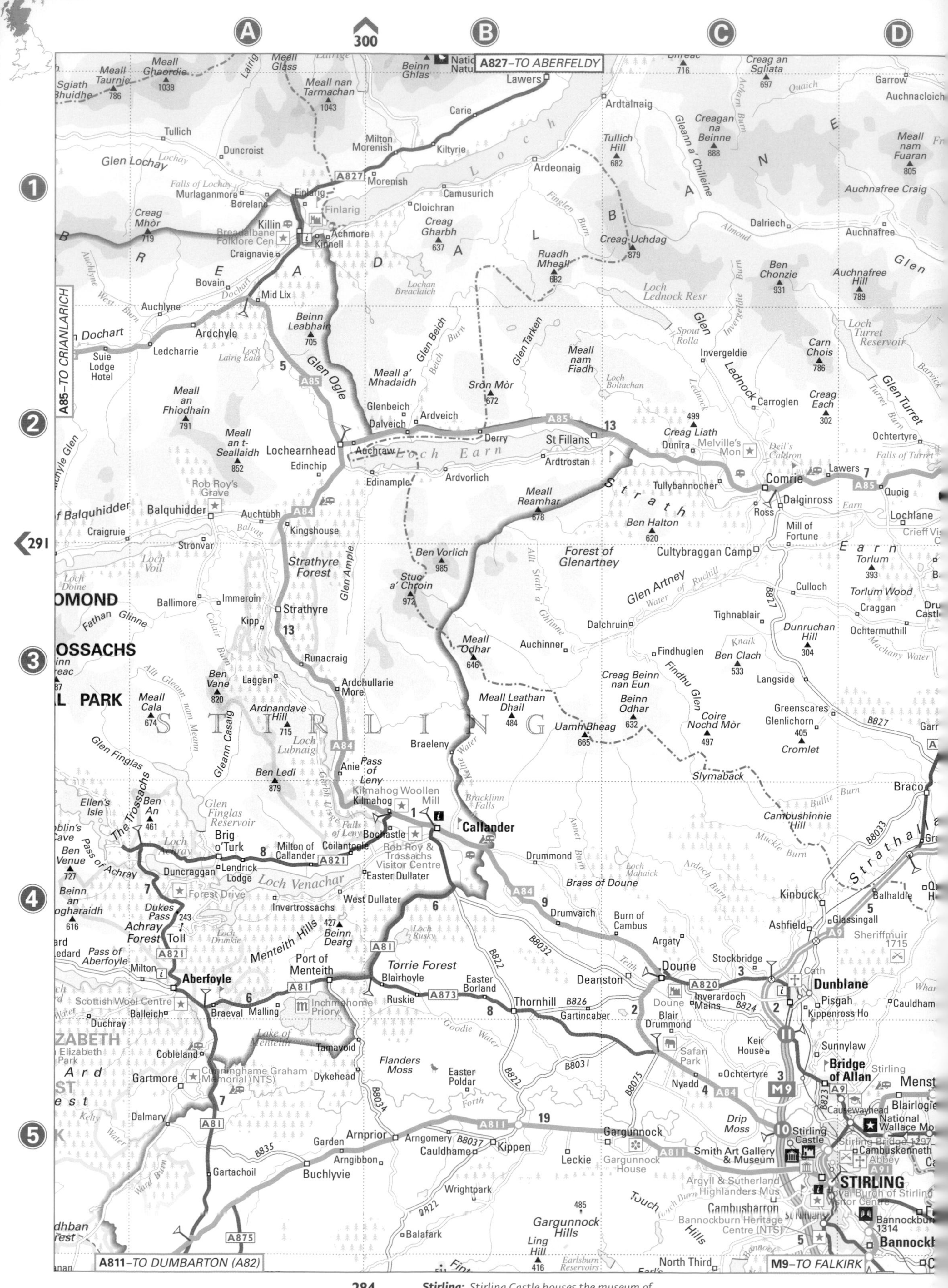

A
B
C
D
300
1
2
3
4
5
291
284
A827–TO ABERFELDY
A85–TO CRIANLARICH
A811–TO DUMBARTON (A82)
M9–TO FALKIRK
Meall Ghaordie 1039
Meall Taurnie 786
Meall Glass
Meall nan Tarmachan 1043
Beinn Ghlas
Lawers
Creag an Sgliata 697
Garrow
Auchnacloich
Carie
Ardtalnaig
Creagan na Beinne 888
Tullich
Duncroist
Milton Morenish
Kiltyrie
Tullich Hill 682
Glen Lochay
A827
Morenish
Ardeonaig
Meall nam Fuaran 805
Murlaganmore
Boreland
Finlarig
Camusurich
Cloichran
Auchnafree Craig
Creag Mhòr 719
Killin
Breadalbane Folklore Cen
Achmore
Kinnell
Creag Gharbh 637
Dalriech
Auchnafree
Craignavie
Ruadh Mheall 682
Creag Uchdag 879
Bovain
Mid Lix
Lochan Breaclaich
Loch Lednock Resr
Ben Chonzie 931
Auchnafree Hill 789
Auchlyne
Ardchyle
Dochart
Ledcharrie
Suie Lodge Hotel
Beinn Leabhain 705
Loch Lairig Eala
Glen Ogle
A85
Glen Beich
Glen Tarken
Spout Rolla
Invergeldie
Loch Turret Reservoir
Carn Chois 786
Meall nam Fiadh
Glen Lednock
Carroglen
Creag Each 302
Glen Turret
Meall an Fhiodhain 791
Meall a' Mhadaidh
Sròn Mòr 672
Loch Boltachan
Glenbeich
Ardveich
Dalveich
Creag Liath 499
Meall an t-Seallaidh 852
Lochearnhead
Aochraw
Loch Earn
Derry
St Fillans
13
Dunira
Melville's Mon
Ochtertyre
Edinchip
Edinample
Ardvorlich
Ardtrostan
Falls of Turret
Comrie
Lawers
Quoig
Rob Roy's Grave
Balquhidder
Auchtubh
A84
Meall Reamhar 678
Strath Earn
Tullybannocher
Dalginross
Ross
Lochlane
Kingshouse
Ben Halton 620
Mill of Fortune
Craigruie
Stronvar
Loch Voil
Loch Doine
Ben Vorlich 985
Forest of Glenartney
Cultybraggan Camp
Torlum 393
Strathyre Forest
Stuc a' Chroin 972
Glen Ample
Glen Artney
Culloch
Torlum Wood
Craggan
Ballimore
Immeroin
Kipp
Strathyre
Tighnablair
B827
Dalchruin
Dunruchan Hill 304
Ochtermuthill
Runacraig
Meall Odhar 646
Auchinner
Findhuglen
Ben Clach 533
Machany Water
Ben Vane 820
Laggan
Ardchullarie More
Creag Beinn nan Eun
Langside
Findhu Glen
Meall Cala 674
Ardnandave Hill 715
Meall Leathan Dhail 484
Beinn Odhar 632
Greenscares
Glenlichorn
Uamh Bheag 665
Coire Nochd Mòr 497
Cromlet 405
STIRLING
Loch Lubnaig
Braeleny
Glen Finglas
Ben Ledi 879
Anie
Pass of Leny
Slymaback
Braco
Ellen's Isle
Ben An 461
Kilmahog Woollen Mill
Kilmahog
Bracklinn Falls
Glen Finglas Reservoir
The Trossachs
Falls of Leny
Bochastle
Callander
Cambushinnie Hill
Brig o'Turk
Milton of Callander
Coilantogle
Rob Roy & Trossachs Visitor Centre
Drummond
Loch Mahaick
Strathallan
Ben Venue 727
Pass of Achray
Loch Achray
Duncraggan
Lendrick Lodge
A821
Easter Dullater
Braes of Doune
Kinbuck
Balhaldie
Beinn an Fhogharaidh 616
Forest Drive
Loch Venachar
West Dullater
A84
Drumvaich
Burn of Cambus
Glassingall
Dukes Pass 243
Invertrossachs
Beinn Dearg 427
Loch Rusky
Ashfield
Sheriffmuir 1715
Achray Forest
Toll
Loch Drunkie
Menteith Hills
Argaty
A9
Pass of Aberfoyle
Torrie Forest
B8032
Milton
Aberfoyle
Port of Menteith
A81
Blairhoyle
Easter Borland
Deanston
Doune
Stockbridge
Dunblane
Scottish Wool Centre
Inchmahome Priory
Ruskie
A873
Thornhill
B826
A820
Inverardoch Mains
Pisgah
Cauldham
Balleich
Braeval
Malling
Gartincaber
Doune
Blair Drummond
B824
Kippenross Ho
Duchray
Lake of Menteith
Goodie Water
Keir House
Sunnylaw
Cobleland
Tamavoid
Safari Park
Bridge of Allan
Flanders Moss
Easter Poldar
B8031
Ochtertyre
Menstrie
Gartmore
Cunninghame Graham Memorial (NTS)
Dykehead
Nyadd
M9
Blairlogie
National Wallace Mon
Dalmary
B8034
B8075
B822
Drip Moss
A811
A81
Forth
Gargunnock
Stirling Castle
Stirling Bridge 1297
Cambuskenneth Abbey
Arnprior
Arngomery
B8037
Kippen
Garden
Cauldhame
Smith Art Gallery & Museum
B835
Arngibbon
Leckie
Gargunnock House
STIRLING
A91
Gartachoil
Buchlyvie
Argyll & Sutherland Highlanders Mus
Royal Burgh of Stirling Visitor Centre
Wrightpark
Touch Hills
Cambusbarron
Bannockburn Heritage Centre (NTS)
Bannockburn 1314
Gargunnock Hills
485
B822
Balafark
Bannockburn
A875
Ling Hill 416
Earlsburn Reservoirs
North Third

Stirling: *Stirling Castle houses the museum of The Argyll and Sutherland Highlanders. This famous regiment won 6 Victoria Crosses in a single day's action at the Battle of Lucknow (India) in 1857.* ***Map ref. C5 Also on page 130***

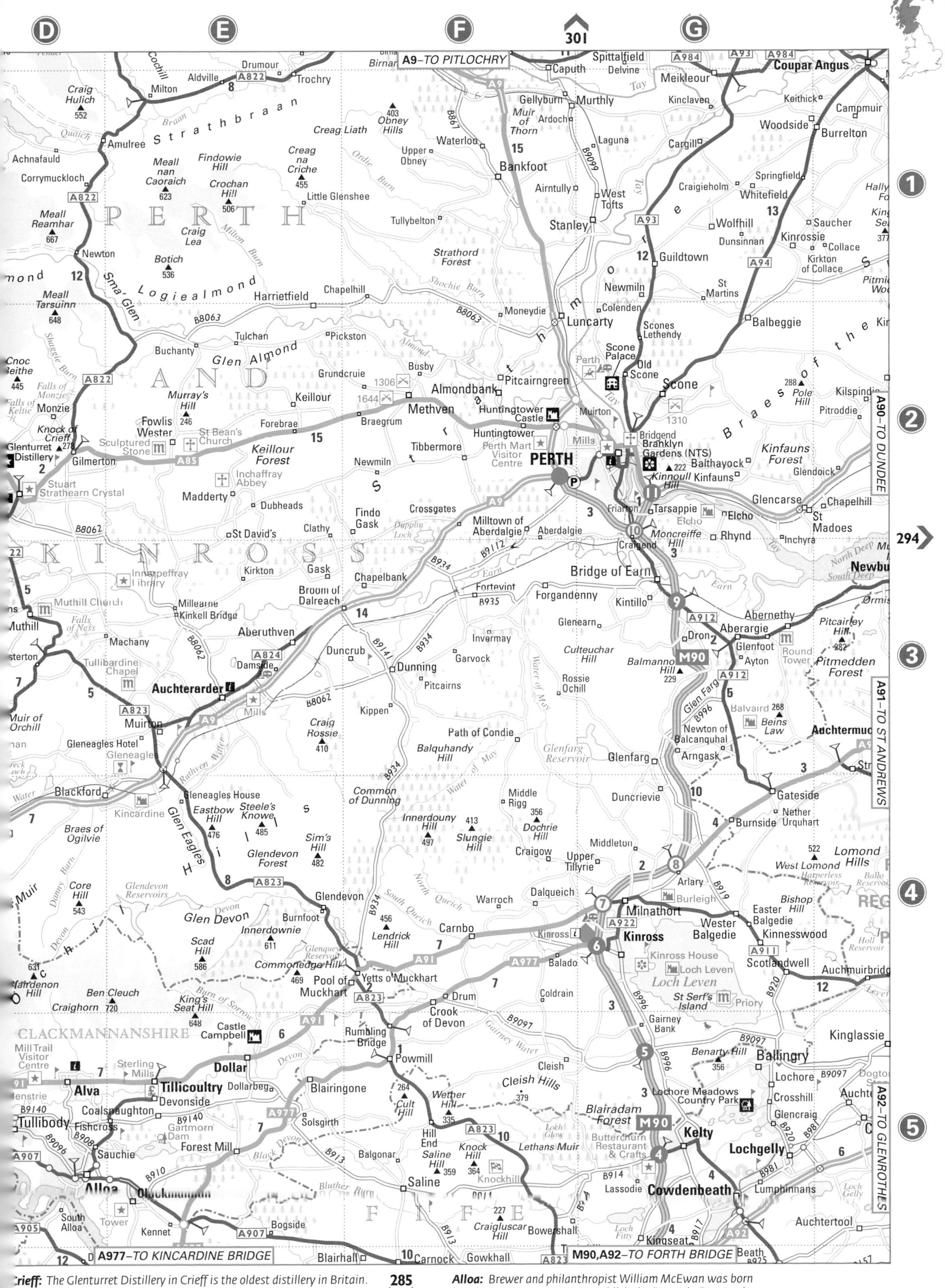

D
E
F
G
301
A9–TO PITLOCHRY
294
A90–TO DUNDEE
A91–TO ST ANDREWS
A92–TO GLENROTHES
A977–TO KINCARDINE BRIDGE
M90,A92–TO FORTH BRIDGE
PERTH
AND
KINROSS
CLACKMANNANSHIRE
FIFE
Strathbraan
Logiealmond
Glen Almond
Strathallan
Strathmore
Braes of the Carse
Ochil Hills
Coupar Angus
Meikleour
Caputh
Spittalfield
Murthly
Bankfoot
Stanley
Luncarty
Scone
Scone Palace
Almondbank
Methven
Huntingtower Castle
Bridgend
Branklyn Gardens (NTS)
Kinnoull Hill
Kinfauns
Balthayock
Glencarse
Bridge of Earn
Abernethy
Aberargie
Forgandenny
Dunning
Auchterarder
Gleneagles Hotel
Blackford
Kinross
Milnathort
Loch Leven
Kinross House
Loch Leven Castle
St Serf's Island
Kelty
Cowdenbeath
Lochgelly
Lumphinnans
Ballingry
Lochore Meadows Country Park
Dollar
Castle Campbell
Tillicoultry
Alva
Alloa
Tullibody
Sauchie
Clackmannan
Saline
Powmill
Rumbling Bridge
Crook of Devon
Glendevon
Yetts o'Muckhart
Pool of Muckhart
Gleneagles House
Glen Eagles
Glen Devon
Cleish Hills
Blairadam Forest
Gilmerton
Amulree
Milton
Aldville
Trochry
Drumour
Newton
Sma' Glen
Harrietfield
Tulchan
Buchanty
Fowlis Wester
Madderty
Inchaffray Abbey
Innerpeffray Library
Kinkell Bridge
Aberuthven
Muthill
Tibbermore
Perth Mart Visitor Centre
Moncreiffe Hill
Rhynd
Elcho
Glenfarg
Glenfarg Reservoir
Gateside
Burnside
Strathmiglo
Scotlandwell
Kinnesswood
Lomond Hills
West Lomond
Kinglassie
Crosshill
Glencraig
Lochore
Auchtertool
Kingseat
Lassodie
Knockhill

Crieff: *The Glenturret Distillery in Crieff is the oldest distillery in Britain. In the 18th century illegal stills were rife in this area and one operated here from 1717. It was legalised in 1775 and was a working still up to 1921 when it ceased production. It was re-born in 1957 and today is one of the Highland's established malts.* ***Map ref. D2***

285

Alloa: *Brewer and philanthropist William McEwan was born here in 1827. He went on to establish the Fountain Brewery in Edinburgh and to brew McEwans Export. He died in 1913 but both the brewery and beer survive.* ***Map ref. D5***

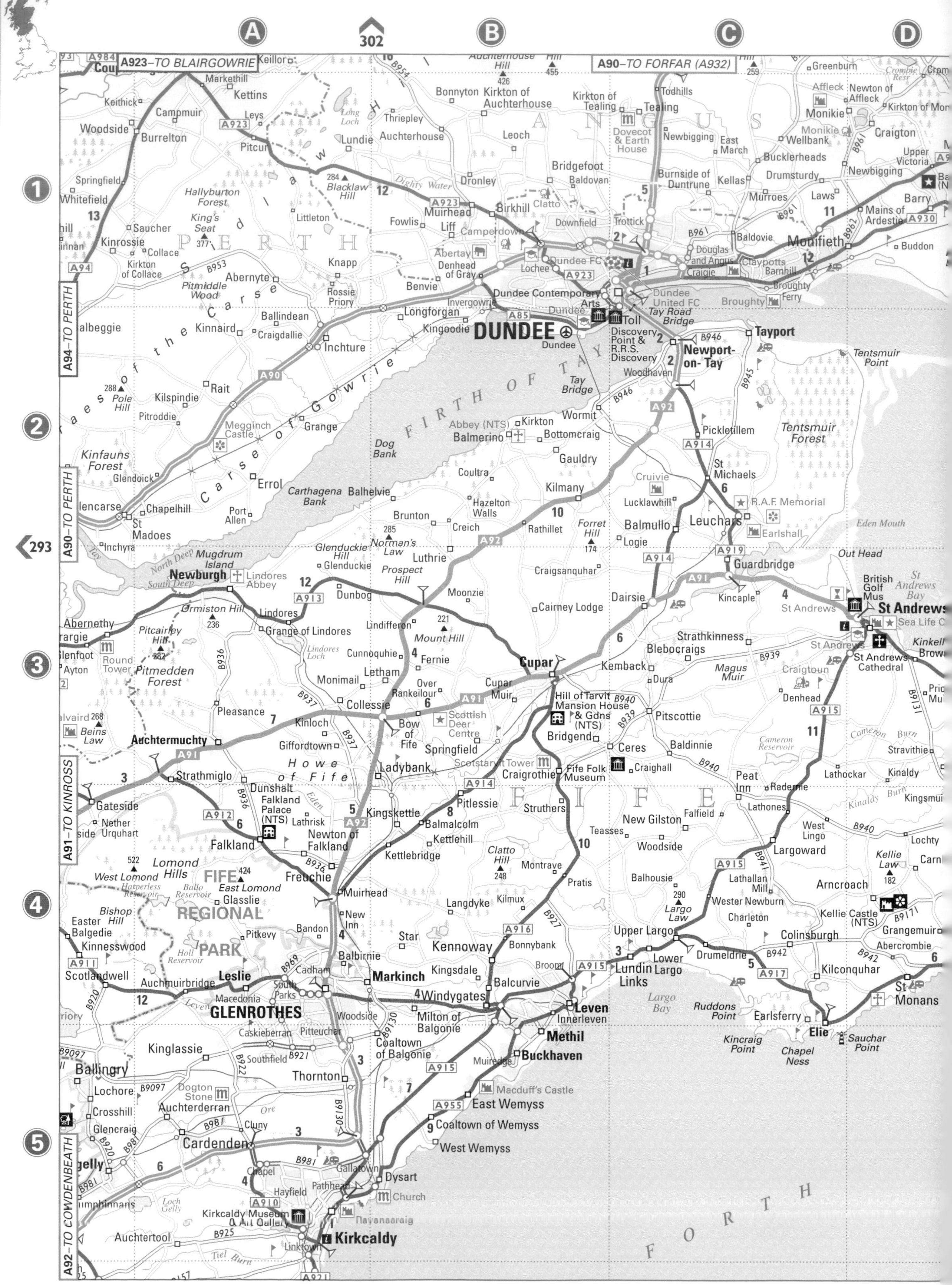
A
B
C
D
302
A923–TO BLAIRGOWRIE
A90–TO FORFAR (A932)
A94–TO PERTH
A90–TO PERTH
A91–TO KINROSS
A92–TO COWDENBEATH
293
286
Kettins
Campmuir
Woodside
Burrelton
Pitcur
Lundie
Auchterhouse
Bonnyton
Kirkton of Auchterhouse
Leoch
Kirkton of Tealing
Tealing
Dovecot & Earth House
Newbigging
East March
Monikie
Craigton
Wellbank
Bucklerheads
Drumsturdy
Newbigging
Barry
Laws
Mains of Ardestie
Monifieth
Buddon
Murroes
Kellas
Burnside of Duntrune
Bridgefoot
Baldovan
Dronley
Birkhill
Muirhead
Fowlis
Liff
Camperdown
Littleton
Blacklaw Hill
Hallyburton Forest
King's Seat
Saucher
Kinrossie
Collace
Kirkton of Collace
Abernyte
Pitmiddle Wood
Knapp
Rossie Priory
Benvie
Denhead of Gray
Abertay
Lochee
Dundee FC
Downfield
Trottick
Douglas and Angus
Craigie
Claypotts
Barnhill
Broughty Ferry
Dundee Contemporary Arts
Dundee United FC
Tay Road Bridge
DUNDEE
Dundee
Invergowrie
Longforgan
Kingoodie
Inchture
Ballindean
Kinnaird
Craigdallie
Discovery Point & R.R.S. Discovery
Tayport
Newport-on-Tay
Woodhaven
Tentsmuir Point
Tentsmuir Forest
Tay Bridge
FIRTH OF TAY
Carse of Gowrie
Rait
Kilspindie
Pitroddie
Megginch Castle
Grange
Pole Hill
Kinfauns Forest
Glendoick
Errol
Dog Bank
Abbey (NTS)
Balmerino
Kirkton
Bottomcraig
Wormit
Pickletillem
Gauldry
St Michaels
Coultra
Cruivie
Kilmany
Lucklawhill
R.A.F. Memorial
Carthagena Bank
Balhelvie
Hazelton Walls
Brunton
Creich
Rathillet
Forret Hill
Balmullo
Logie
Leuchars
Earlshall
Eden Mouth
Glencarse
Chapelhill
Port Allen
St Madoes
Inchyra
Mugdrum Island
North Deep
South Deep
Newburgh
Lindores Abbey
Glenduckie Hill
Glenduckie
Norman's Law
Luthrie
Prospect Hill
Craigsanquhar
Guardbridge
Out Head
Kincaple
British Golf Mus
St Andrews Bay
St Andrews
Sea Life C
Dunbog
Moonzie
Cairney Lodge
Dairsie
Abernethy
Ormiston Hill
Lindores
Grange of Lindores
Lindifferon
Mount Hill
Strathkinness
Blebocraigs
St Andrews Cathedral
Pitcairley Hill
Round Tower
Pitmedden Forest
Cunnoquhie
Fernie
Cupar
Kemback
Dura
Magus Muir
Craigtoun
Denhead
Letham
Monimail
Over Rankeilour
Cupar Muir
Hill of Tarvit Mansion House & Gdns (NTS)
Bridgend
Pitscottie
Pleasance
Collessie
Kinloch
Bow of Fife
Scottish Deer Centre
Beins Law
Auchtermuchty
Giffordtown
Howe of Fife
Springfield
Scotstarvit Tower
Ceres
Baldinnie
Craighall
Cameron Reservoir
Stravithie
Strathmiglo
Ladybank
Craigrothie
Fife Folk Museum
Peat Inn
Radernie
Lathockar
Kinaldy
Kingsmuir
Gateside
Nether Urquhart
Dunshalt
Falkland Palace (NTS)
Lathrisk
Kingskettle
Pitlessie
Struthers
FIFE
New Gilston
Falfield
Lathones
West Lingo
Falkland
Newton of Falkland
Balmalcolm
Kettlehill
Kettlebridge
Teasses
Woodside
Largoward
Lochty
Lomond Hills
West Lomond
East Lomond
Freuchie
Clatto Hill
Montrave
Pratis
Balhousie
Kellie Law
Lathallan Mill
Arncroach
FIFE REGIONAL PARK
Glasslie
Muirhead
New Inn
Langdyke
Kilmux
Largo Law
Wester Newburn
Charleton
Kellie Castle (NTS)
Grangemuir
Bishop Hill
Easter Balgedie
Kinnesswood
Pitkevy
Bandon
Star
Kennoway
Bonnybank
Upper Largo
Colinsburgh
Abercrombie
Balbirnie
Lower Largo
Drumeldrie
Kilconquhar
Scotlandwell
Auchmuirbridge
Leslie
Cadham
Markinch
Kingsdale
Balcurvie
Broom
Lundin Links
St Monans
Macedonia
South Parks
Windygates
Leven
Largo Bay
Ruddons Point
Earlsferry
Elie
GLENROTHES
Woodside
Milton of Balgonie
Innerleven
Methil
Kincraig Point
Chapel Ness
Sauchar Point
Caskieberran
Pitteuchar
Coaltown of Balgonie
Buckhaven
Kinglassie
Southfield
Muiredge
Ballingry
Thornton
Lochore
Dogton Stone
Macduff's Castle
Crosshill
Auchterderran
East Wemyss
Glencraig
Cluny
Coaltown of Wemyss
Cardenden
West Wemyss
Chapel
Gallatown
Dysart
Hayfield
Pathhead
Church
Ravenscraig
Kirkcaldy Museum & Art Gallery
Auchtertool
Kirkcaldy
Linktown
FORTH

Lower Largo: *Alexander Selkirk, the sailor, was born here in 1676. He was marooned on the uninhabited Island of Juan Fenandez for 4 years and became the model for the book Robinson Crusoe written by Daniel Defoe.* ***Map ref. C4***

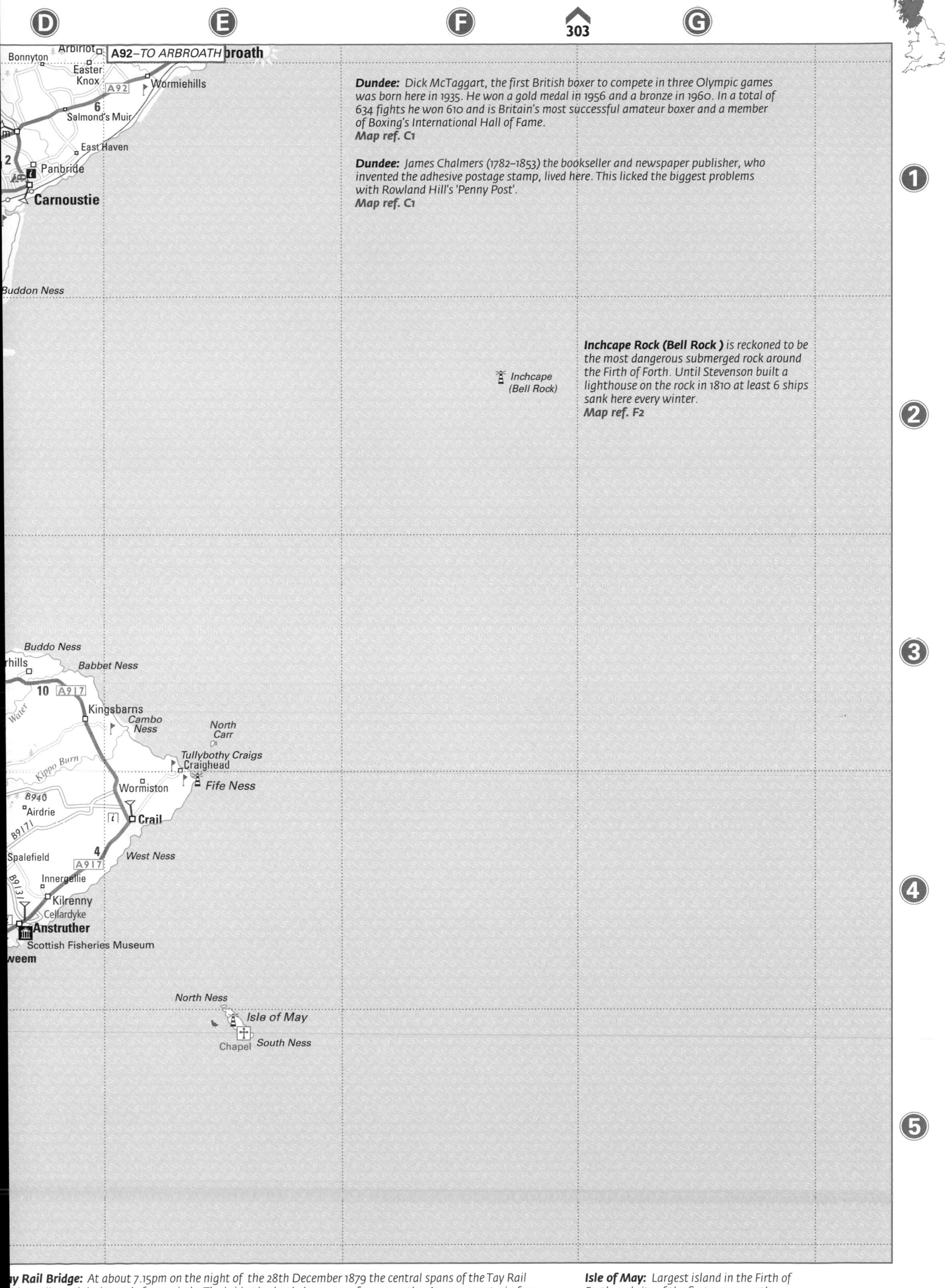
D
E
F
303
G
1
2
3
4
5
Bonnyton
Arbirlot
A92–TO ARBROATH
broath
Easter Knox
A92
Wormiehills
6
Salmond's Muir
East Haven
2
Panbride
Carnoustie
Buddon Ness
Dundee: Dick McTaggart, the first British boxer to compete in three Olympic games was born here in 1935. He won a gold medal in 1956 and a bronze in 1960. In a total of 634 fights he won 610 and is Britain's most successful amateur boxer and a member of Boxing's International Hall of Fame.
Map ref. C1
Dundee: James Chalmers (1782–1853) the bookseller and newspaper publisher, who invented the adhesive postage stamp, lived here. This licked the biggest problems with Rowland Hill's 'Penny Post'.
Map ref. C1
Inchcape (Bell Rock)
Inchcape Rock (Bell Rock) is reckoned to be the most dangerous submerged rock around the Firth of Forth. Until Stevenson built a lighthouse on the rock in 1810 at least 6 ships sank here every winter.
Map ref. F2
Buddo Ness
hills
Babbet Ness
10
A917
Kingsbarns
Water
Cambo Ness
North Carr
Kippo Burn
Tullybothy Craigs
Craighead
Fife Ness
Wormiston
B940
Airdrie
Crail
B9171
Spalefield
4
A917
West Ness
B9131
Innergellie
Kilrenny
Cellardyke
Anstruther
Scottish Fisheries Museum
weem
North Ness
Isle of May
Chapel
South Ness

ay Rail Bridge: At about 7.15pm on the night of the 28th December 1879 the central spans of the Tay Rail idge collapsed during gale force winds. The bridge had only been open for 19 months. A passenger train from inburgh, which was crossing the bridge at the time, plunged into the water below. In all 75 people lost their es in the disaster, there were no survivors and only 46 bodies were ever found. The engine itself, however, was covered from the river bed and put back into service where it continued to haul carriages until 1908. en today the supporting masonry piers of the old bridge in the river are still visible. **Map ref. B2**

Isle of May: Largest island in the Firth of Forth and site of the first permanently manned lighthouse beacon in Scotland built by Alexander Cunningham in 1636.
Map ref. E5

305

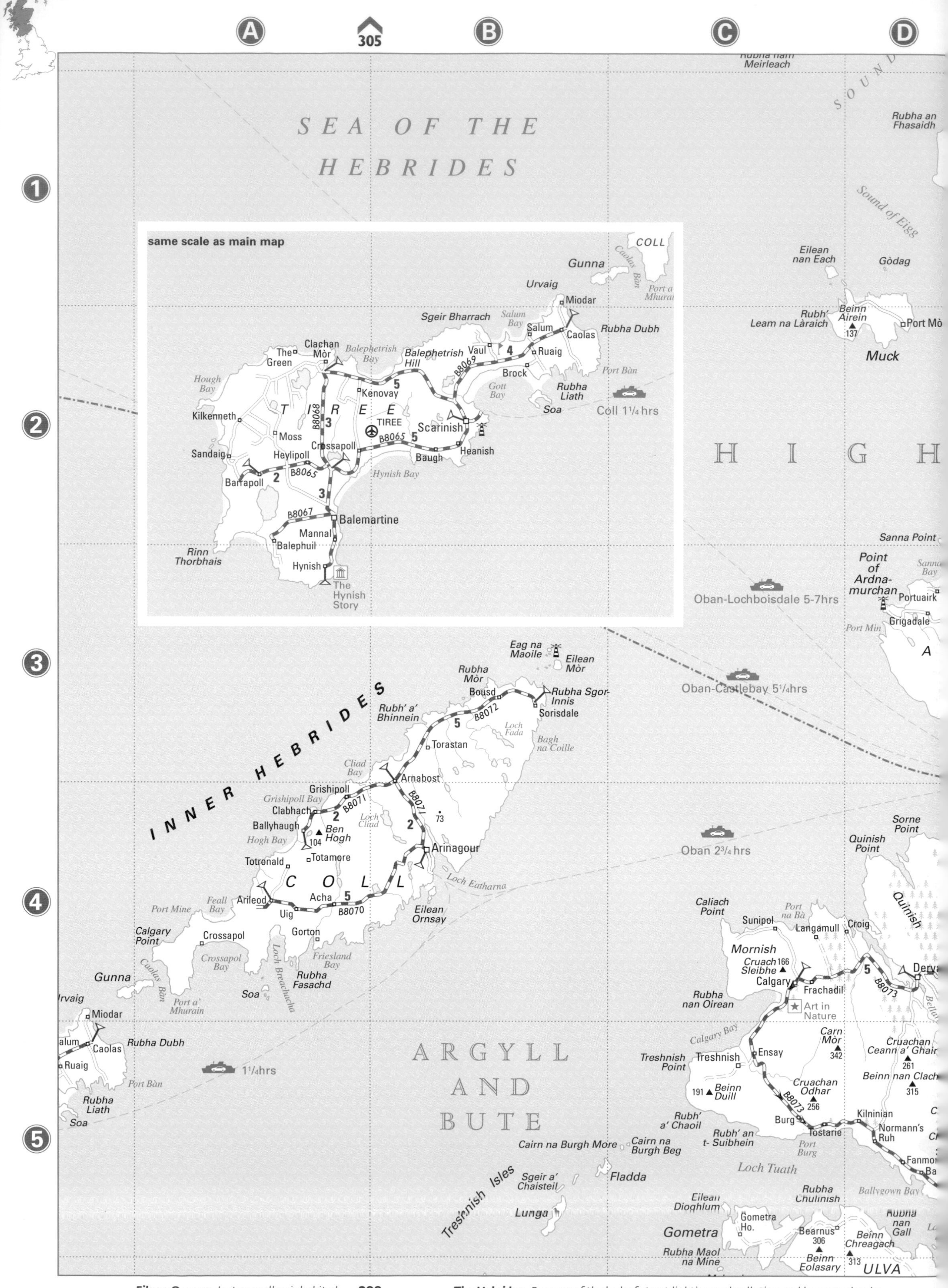
A
B
C
D
1
2
3
4
5
SEA OF THE HEBRIDES
Rubha nam Meirleach
SOUND
Rubha an Fhasaidh
Sound of Eigg
Eilean nan Each
Gòdag
Rubh' Airein
Beinn Airein
137
Leam na Làraich
Port Mò
Muck
same scale as main map
COLL
Gunna
Caolas Bàn
Port a' Mhurain
Urvaig
Miodar
Sgeir Bharrach
Salum Bay
Salum
Caolas
Rubha Dubh
Clachan Mòr
The Green
Balephetrish Bay
Balephetrish Hill
Vaul
Ruaig
B8069
Brock
Port Bàn
Hough Bay
Kenovay
Gott Bay
Rubha Liath
Soa
Coll 1¼hrs
TIREE
Kilkenneth
B8068
Scarinish
Moss
Crossapoll
B8065
Heanish
Sandaig
Heylipoll
Baugh
Barrapoll
Hynish Bay
B8067
Balemartine
Mannal
Balephuil
Rinn Thorbhais
Hynish
The Hynish Story
HIGHLAND
Sanna Point
Point of Ardnamurchan
Sanna Bay
Portuairk
Oban-Lochboisdale 5-7hrs
Grigadale
Port Min
Eag na Maoile
Eilean Mòr
Rubha Mòr
Bousd
Rubha Sgor-Innis
Sorisdale
Oban-Castlebay 5¼hrs
INNER HEBRIDES
Rubh' a' Bhinnein
B8072
Loch Fada
Bagh na Coille
Torastan
Cliad Bay
Arnabost
Grishipoll
Grishipoll Bay
Clabhach
B8071
Loch Cliad
Ballyhaugh
Ben Hogh
104
73
Hogh Bay
Arinagour
Oban 2¾hrs
Sorne Point
Quinish Point
Totronald
Totamore
COLL
Loch Eatharna
Quinish
Feall Bay
Arileod
Acha
Port Mine
Uig
B8070
Eilean Ornsay
Caliach Point
Port na Bà
Sunipol
Langamull
Croig
Calgary Point
Crossapol
Gorton
Mornish
Cruach Sleibhe 166
Crossapol Bay
Loch Breachacha
Friesland Bay
Calgary
Frachadil
Dervaig
B8073
Gunna
Caolas Bàn
Rubha Fasachd
Rubha nan Oirean
Art in Nature
Urvaig
Soa
Port a' Mhurain
Miodar
Calgary Bay
Carn Mòr 342
Salum
Caolas
Rubha Dubh
Cruachan Ceann a' Ghair 261
Ruaig
1¼hrs
ARGYLL AND BUTE
Treshnish Point
Treshnish
Ensay
Beinn nan Clach 315
Port Bàn
Cruachan Odhar 256
191 Beinn Duill
Rubha Liath
Soa
Rubh' a' Chaoil
Burg
Kilninian
Normann's Ruh
Tostarie
Cairn na Burgh More
Cairn na Burgh Beg
Rubh' an t-Suibhein
Port Burg
Fanmore
Treshnish Isles
Sgeir a' Chaisteil
Fladda
Loch Tuath
Rubha Chulinish
Ballygown Bay
Lunga
Eilean Dioghlum
Gometra Ho.
Rubha nan Gall
Gometra
Bearnus 306
Beinn Chreagach
Rubha Maol na Mine
Beinn Eolasary
313
ULVA

Eilean Ornsay: *Just a small uninhabited island. There are dozens like it called Eilean something or other. In this case Eilean simply means Island.* ***Map ref. B4***

288

The Hebrides: *Because of the lack of street lighting and pollution and because the sky is unusually clear, the Hebridean Islands are the best place in the UK for seeing the Aurora Borealis (The Northern Lights). This fantastic lightshow occurs naturally every autumn in the Arctic regions.*

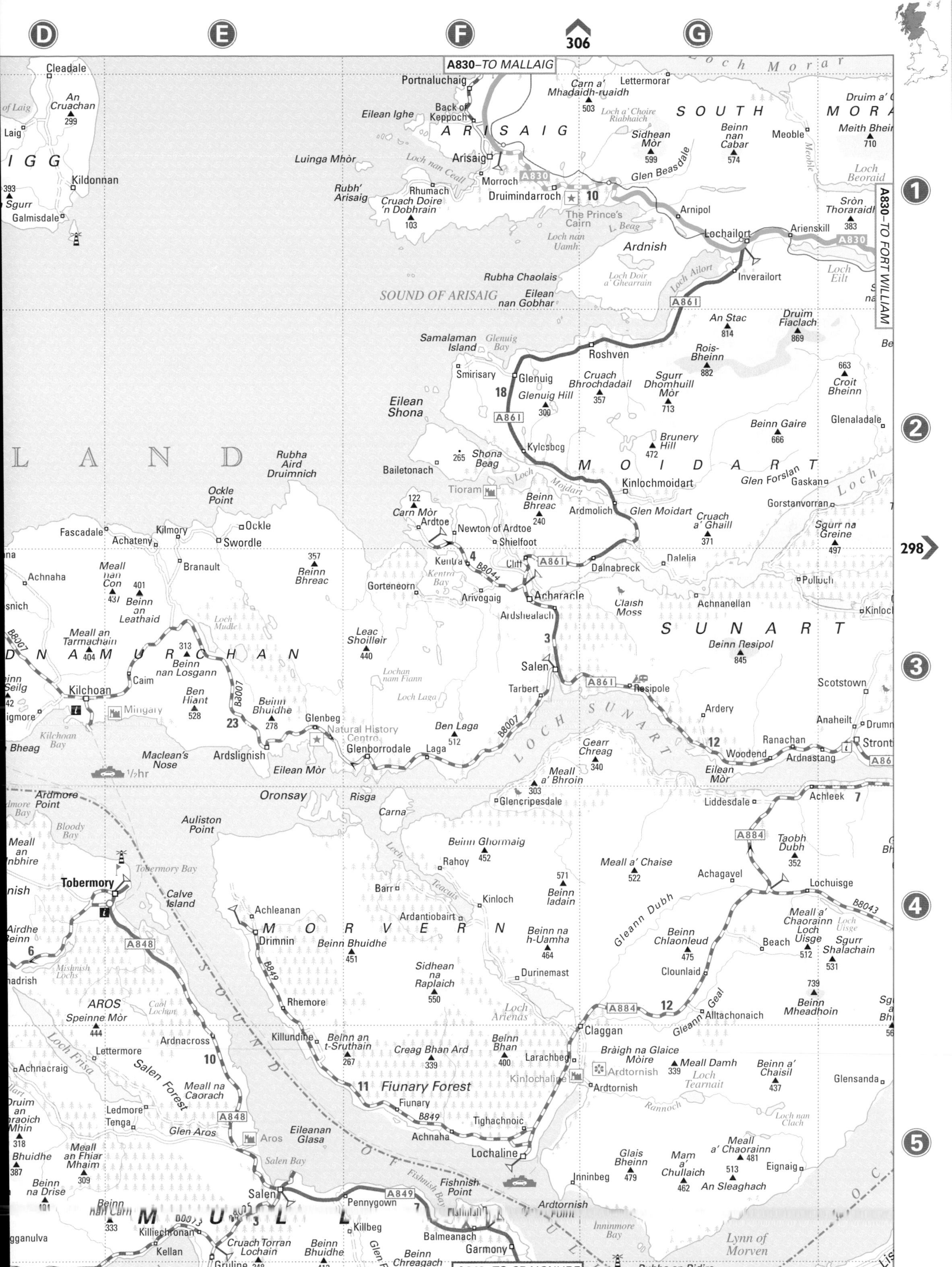
D
E
F
306
G
A830–TO MALLAIG
Loch Morar
Cleadale
An Cruachan
299
Laig
EIGG
Kildonnan
393
Sgurr
Galmisdale
Portnaluchaig
Carn a' Mhadaidh-ruaidh
503
Lettermorar
Loch a' Choire Riabhaich
SOUTH MORAR
Druim a' C
Eilean Ighe
Back of Keppoch
ARISAIG
Sidhean Mòr
599
Beinn nan Cabar
574
Meoble
Meith Bheir
710
Luinga Mhòr
Arisaig
Loch nan Ceall
Glen Beasdale
Loch Beoraid
Rubh' Arisaig
Rhumach
Morroch
A830
Druimindarroch
10
Cruach Doire 'n Dobhrain
103
Arnipol
Sròn Thoraraidh
383
The Prince's Cairn
L. Beag
Loch nan Uamh
Ardnish
Lochailort
Arienskill
A830
A830–TO FORT WILLIAM
1
Loch Eilt
Rubha Chaolais
Loch Doir a' Ghearrain
Loch Ailort
Inverailort
SOUND OF ARISAIG
Eilean nan Gobhar
A861
An Stac
814
Druim Fiaclach
869
Samalaman Island
Glenuig Bay
Roshven
Rois-Bheinn
882
663
Croit Bheinn
Smirisary
Glenuig
18
Cruach Bhrochdadail
357
Sgurr Dhomhuill Mòr
713
Glenuig Hill
300
Eilean Shona
A861
Beinn Gaire
666
Glenaladale
2
Kylesbeg
Brunery Hill
472
LAND
Rubha Aird Druimnich
265
Shona Beag
Baileatonach
MOIDART
Glen Forslan
Gaskan
Loch Moidart
Tioram
Kinlochmoidart
Ockle Point
122
Carn Mòr
Beinn Bhreac
240
Ardmolich
Glen Moidart
Gorstanvorran
Ardtoe
Cruach a' Ghaill
371
Sgurr na Greine
497
298
Fascadale
Kilmory
Ockle
Newton of Ardtoe
Achateny
Swordle
Shielfoot
357
Beinn Bhreac
Kentra
4
B8044
Clift
A861
Dalnabreck
Dalelia
Achnaha
Meall nan Con
437
401
Beinn an Leathaid
Branault
Kentra Bay
Gorteneorn
Arivegaig
Acharacle
Pulloch
Claish Moss
Achnanellan
Kinloch
Ardshealach
Loch Mudle
Meall an Tarmachain
404
313
Beinn nan Losgann
Leac Shoilleir
440
SUNART
B8007
ARDNAMURCHAN
3
Beinn Resipol
845
Salen
Lochan nam Fiann
Kilchoan
Caim
Mingary
Ben Hiant
528
B8007
Beinn Bhuidhe
278
Loch Laga
Tarbert
A861
Resipole
3
Scotstown
Ardery
Kilchoan Bay
23
Glenbeg
Natural History Centre
Ben Laga
512
B8007
LOCH SUNART
Anaheilt
Drumn
Bheag
Maclean's Nose
Ardslignish
Glenborrodale
Laga
Gearr Chreag
340
12
Ranachan
Woodend
Ardnastang
Strontian
A86
½hr
Eilean Mòr
Meall a' Bhroin
303
Eilean Mòr
Glencripesdale
Achleek
7
Ardmore Point
Oronsay
Risga
Carna
Liddesdale
Bloody Bay
Auliston Point
A884
Taobh Dubh
352
Meall an Inbhire
Beinn Ghormaig
452
Rahoy
Loch Teacuis
Meall a' Chaise
522
571
Achagavel
Tobermory Bay
Tobermory
Calve Island
Barr
Kinloch
Beinn Iadain
Lochuisge
Achleanan
Ardantiobairt
Gleann Dubh
B8043
4
Meall a' Chaorainn
Loch Uisge
Airdhe
MORVERN
Drimnin
Beinn Bhuidhe
451
Beinn na h-Uamha
464
Beinn Chlaonleud
475
Beach
Loch Uisge
512
Sgurr Shalachain
531
A848
B849
Sidhean na Raplaich
550
Durinemast
Clounlaid
Mishnish Lochs
739
Beinn Mheadhoin
Rhemore
Loch Arienas
A884
12
Gleann Geal
Alltachonaich
AROS
Caol Lochan
Speinne Mòr
444
Ardnacross
Killundine
Beinn an t-Sruthain
267
Creag Bhan Ard
339
Beinn Bhan
400
Claggan
Bràigh na Glaice Mòire
Loch Frisa
Lettermore
Larachbeg
Ardtornish
Meall Damh
339
Beinn a' Chaisil
437
Achnacraig
10
Salen Forest
Meall na Caorach
11
Funary Forest
Kinlochaline
Ardtornish
Loch Tearnait
Glensanda
SOUND OF MULL
Funary
Rannoch
Ledmore
Tenga
A848
B849
Tighachnoic
Loch nan Clach
318
Glen Aros
Aros
Eileanan Glasa
Achnaha
Meall a' Chaorainn
481
Meall an Fhiar Mhaim
309
Bhuidhe
387
Salen Bay
Lochaline
Glais Bheinn
479
Mam a' Chullaich
462
513
Eignaig
5
Beinn na Drise
Inninbeg
An Sleaghach
Salen
A849
Fishnish Bay
Fishnish Point
Pennygown
7
Beinn nan Lurn
333
MULL
Killiechronan
Killbeg
Ardtornish Point
Innimore Bay
Cruach Torran Lochain
Beinn Bhuidhe
412
Glen Forsa
Balmeanach
Lynn of Morven
Kellan
Garmony
Gruline
348
Beinn Chreagach Mhòr
A849–TO CRAIGNURE
Rubha an Ridire
Bernera
Killiemor
Achadun

289

Eigg: Feuding and fighting amongst the Scottish clans is legendary. Massacre Cave on the south side of Eigg is where 395 MacDonalds died in 1577. They were hiding in the cave when the MacLeods caught up with them. The MacLeods blocked the cave entrance and started a fire which suffocated the MacDonalds. After being owned by a succession of absentee landlords, the 60 islanders set up a trust which succeeded in buying Eigg for £1.5 million in 1997 and is dedicated to conserving the island and developing a sustainable economy.

Map ref. *D1*

307

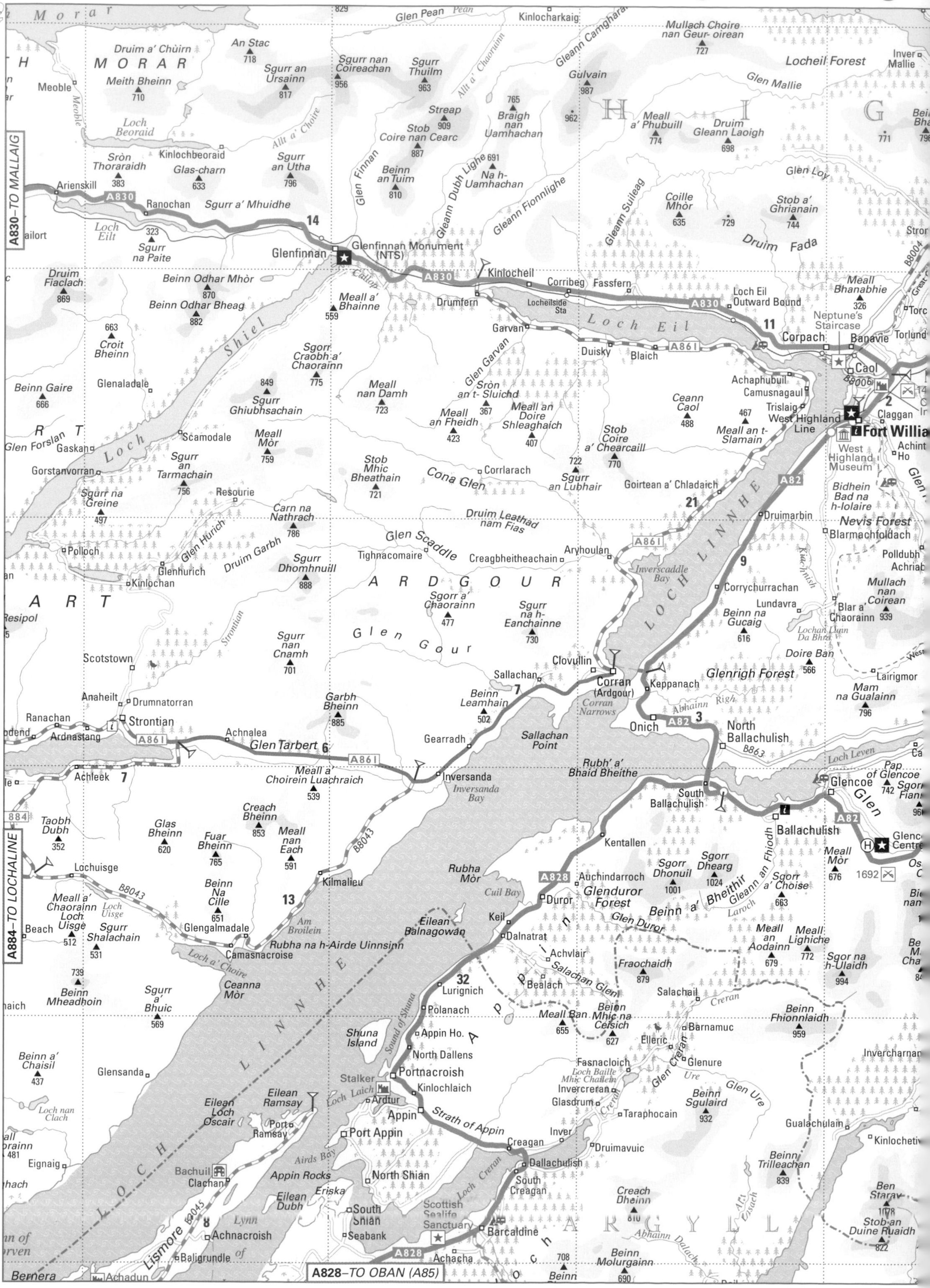

297

290

Corpach: *Starting point of the Caledonian Canal which is the longest canal in Scotland and connects Corpach, near Fort William to Clachnacarry, near Inverness, a distance of 60 miles (96.5km). Much of its length is made up of the lochs it passes through.* ***Map ref. D2***

Ballachulish: *James Stewart was hanged here in 1752 for the 'Appin' murder of the King's Factor, Colin Campbell of Glenure, as he rode through the woods of Lettermoor. Stewart's body was left on the gibbet for years afterwards with his bones wired.* ***Map ref. C4***

308

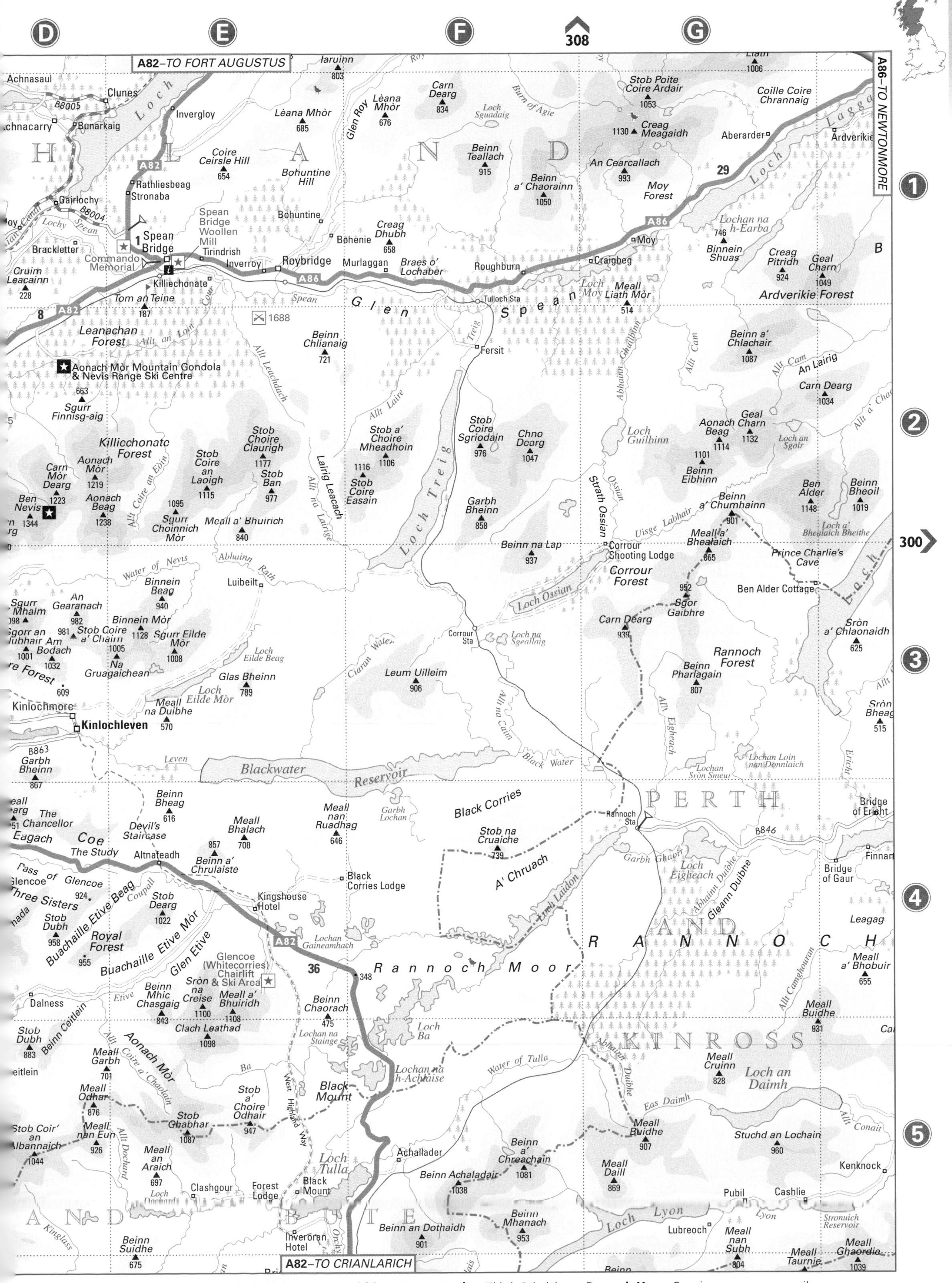
D
E
F
G
1
2
3
4
5
A82–TO FORT AUGUSTUS
A86–TO NEWTONMORE
A82–TO CRIANLARICH
Achnasaul
Clunes
B8005
Invergloy
Bunarkaig
Lèana Mhòr
685
Lèana Mhòr
676
Glen Roy
Carn Dearg
834
Loch Sguadaig
Burn of Agie
Stob Poite Coire Ardair
1053
Creag Meagaidh
1130
Coille Coire Chrannaig
Aberarder
Ardverikie
Loch Laggan
Coire Ceirsle Hill
654
Bohuntine Hill
Beinn Teallach
915
Beinn a' Chaorainn
1050
An Cearcallach
993
Moy Forest
29
Rathliesbeag
Stronaba
Gairlochy
B8004
Spean Bridge
Woollen Mill
Bohuntine
Creag Dhubh
658
Bohenie
A86
Moy
Lochan na h-Earba
746
Binnein Shuas
Creag Pitridh
924
Geal Charn
1049
Ardverikie Forest
Bracklettér
Commando Memorial
Tirindrish
Inverroy
Roybridge
Murlaggan
Braes o' Lochaber
Roughburn
Craigbeg
Loch Moy
Meall Liath Mòr
514
Cruim Leacainn
228
Killiechonate
Tom an Teine
187
Glen Spean
Tulloch Sta
8
A82
1688
Leanachan Forest
Beinn Chlianaig
721
Fersit
Beinn a' Chlachair
1087
An Lairig
Carn Dearg
1034
Aonach Mòr Mountain Gondola & Nevis Range Ski Centre
663
Sgurr Finnisg-aig
Allt Leachdach
Allt Laire
Stob a' Choire Mheadhoin
1106
1116
Stob Coire Easain
Stob Coire Sgriodain
976
Chno Dearg
1047
Loch Guilbinn
Aonach Beag
1114
Geal Charn
1132
Loch an Sgoir
Killiechonate Forest
Stob Choire Claurigh
1177
Stob Coire an Laoigh
1115
Stob Ban
977
Lairig Leacach
Loch Treig
Strath Ossian
1101
Beinn Eibhinn
Ben Alder
1148
Beinn Bheoil
1019
Carn Mòr Dearg
1219
Aonach Mòr
Ben Nevis
1344
1223
Aonach Beag
1238
1095
Sgurr Choinnich Mòr
Meall a' Bhuirich
840
Garbh Bheinn
858
Beinn a' Chumhainn
901
Uisge Labhair
Meall a' Bhealaich
865
Loch a' Bhealaich Bheithe
300
Water of Nevis
Abhainn Rath
Binnein Beag
940
Luibeilt
Beinn na Lap
937
Corrour Shooting Lodge
Corrour Forest
Prince Charlie's Cave
Ben Alder Cottage
Loch Ossian
952
Sgor Gaibhre
Loch Ericht
Sgurr a' Mhaim
An Gearanach
982
Binnein Mòr
1128
Stob Coire a' Chairn
981
Sgurr Eilde Mòr
1008
Am Bodach
1032
1001
1005
Na Gruagaichean
Corrour Sta
Loch na Sgeallaig
Carn Dearg
939
Sròn a' Chlaonaidh
625
Rannoch Forest
Loch Eilde Beag
Ciaran Water
Leum Uilleim
906
Beinn Pharlagain
807
Glas Bheinn
789
Loch Eilde Mòr
609
Kinlochmore
Meall na Duibhe
570
Kinlochleven
Allt na Caim
Allt Eigheach
Sròn Bheag
515
B863
Garbh Bheinn
867
Leven
Blackwater Reservoir
Black Water
Lochan Sròn Smeur
Lochan Loin nan Donnlaich
PERTH
Beinn Bheag
616
The Chancellor
Devil's Staircase
Meall Bhalach
708
Meall nan Ruadhag
646
Garbh Lochan
Black Corries
Stob na Cruaiche
739
Rannoch Sta
Bridge of Ericht
B846
Coe
The Study
Altnafeadh
857
Beinn a' Chrulaiste
Black Corries Lodge
A' Chruach
Garbh Ghaoir
Loch Eigheach
Gleann Duibhe
Bridge of Gaur
Finnart
Pass of Glencoe
Three Sisters
924
Buachaille Etive Beag
Stob Dearg
1022
Kingshouse Hotel
Loch Laidon
Leagag
Stob Dubh
958
Royal Forest
Buachaille Etive Mòr
A82
Lochan Gaineamhach
RANNOCH
Meall a' Bhobuir
655
955
Glen Etive
Glencoe (Whitecorries) Chairlift & Ski Area
Sròn na Creise
Meall a' Bhuiridh
1108
1100
36
348
Rannoch Moor
Dalness
Beinn Mhic Chasgaig
843
Clach Leathad
1098
Beinn Chaorach
475
Loch Ba
Lochan na Stainge
Allt Camghouran
Meall Buidhe
931
KINROSS
Stob Dubh
883
Beinn Ceitlein
Meall Garbh
701
Aonach Mòr
Ba
Water of Tulla
Lochan na h-Achlaise
Meall Cruinn
828
Loch an Daimh
Meall Odhar
876
Stob Ghabhar
1087
Stob a' Choire Odhair
947
West Highland Way
Black Mount
Eas Daimh
Meall Buidhe
907
Allt Conait
Stob Coir' an Albannaich
1044
Meall nan Eun
926
Allt Dochard
Meall an Araich
697
Achallader
Beinn a' Chreachain
1081
Stuchd an Lochain
960
Meall Daill
869
Kenknock
Loch Tulla
Black Mount
Clashgour
Forest Lodge
Beinn Achaladair
1038
Pubil
Cashlie
Stronuich Reservoir
Beinn Mhanach
953
Loch Lyon
ARGYLL AND BUTE
Kinglass
Beinn Suidhe
675
Inveroran Hotel
Beinn an Dothaidh
901
Lubreoch
Meall nan Subh
804
Meall Taurnie
Meall Ghaordie
1039

Ben Nevis: *At 4406 feet (1344m) Ben Nevis is the highest mountain in Britain. Scotland has 284 distinct mountains over 3000 feet (914.4m) which are collectively known as Munros, after Sir Hugh Munro who was the first man to catalogue them.* ***Map ref. D2***

291

Corrour Station: *This is Britain's most isolated railway station – there isn't even a road to it.* ***Map ref. F3***

Rannoch Moor: *Covering over 50 square miles and stretching from Bridge of Orchy to Loch Rannoch, this area is thought to be the largest uninhabited wilderness in Britain.* ***Map ref. F4 Also on page 129***

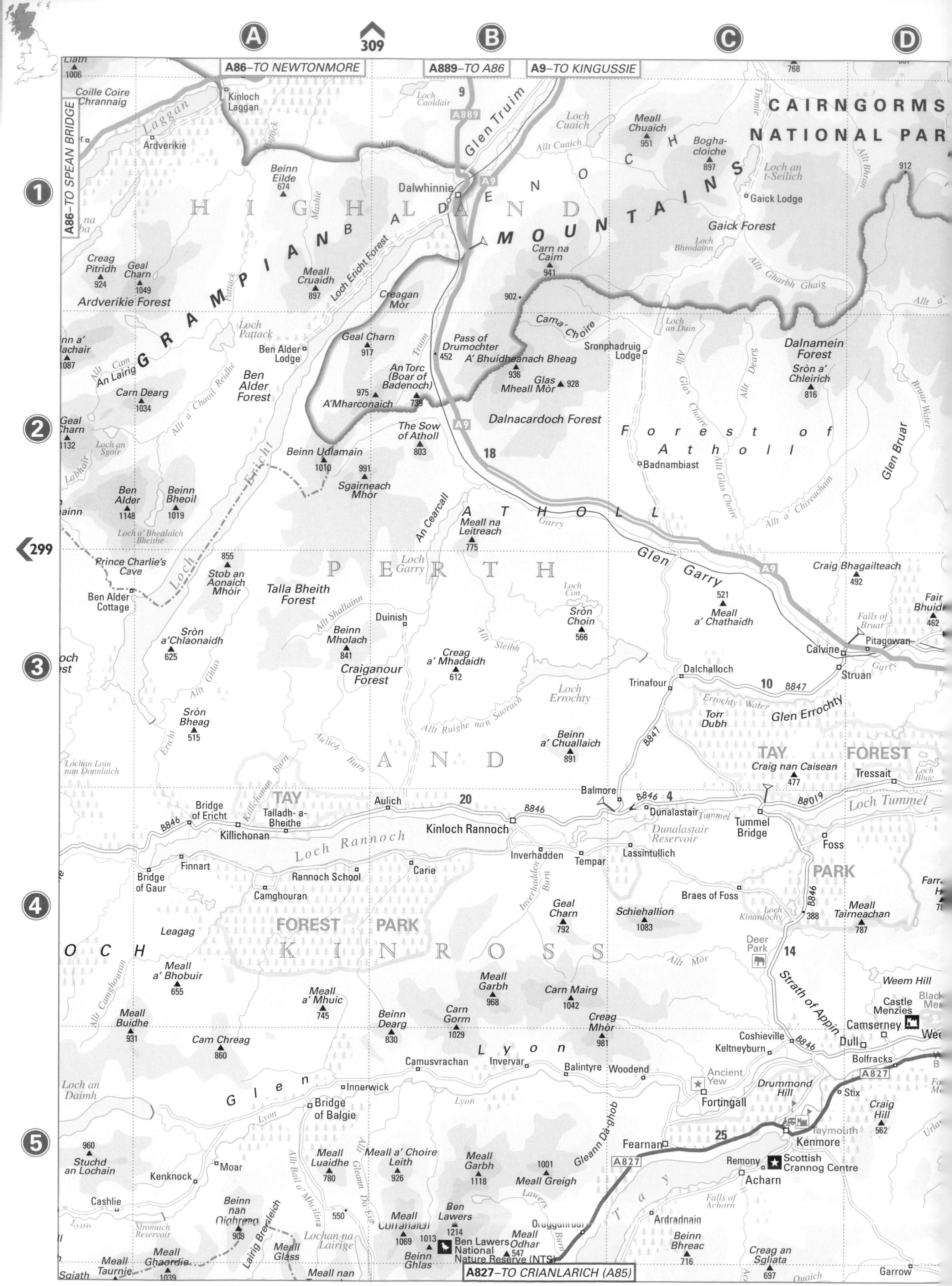
A
309
B
C
D
A86–TO NEWTONMORE
A889–TO A86
A9–TO KINGUSSIE
A86–TO SPEAN BRIDGE
Coille Coire Chrannaig
1006
768
Kinloch Laggan
Laggan
Ardverikie
Loch Caoldair
9
A889
Glen Truim
Loch Cuaich
Allt Cuaich
Meall Chuaich
951
Bogha-cloiche
897
CAIRNGORMS NATIONAL PAR
Loch an t-Seilich
Gaick Lodge
Gaick Forest
912
Beinn Eilde
674
Dalwhinnie
A9
HIGHLAND
BADENOCH
GRAMPIAN MOUNTAINS
Loch Ericht Forest
Creag Pitridh
924
Geal Charn
1049
Ardverikie Forest
Meall Cruaidh
897
Creagan Mòr
Carn na Caim
941
Loch Bhrodainn
Allt Gharbh Ghaig
902
Loch Pattack
Ben Alder Lodge
Ben Alder Forest
Geal Charn
917
Pass of Drumochter
452
Cama' Choire
A' Bhuidheanach Bheag
936
Sronphadruig Lodge
Loch an Duin
Dalnamein Forest
Sròn a' Chleirich
816
An Lairig
Carn Dearg
1034
An Torc (Boar of Badenoch)
739
975
A'Mharconaich
Glas Mheall Mòr
928
Dalnacardoch Forest
Forest of Atholl
Geal Charn
1132
Loch an Sgoir
The Sow of Atholl
803
Beinn Udlamain
1010
991
Sgairneach Mhòr
18
Badnambiast
Glen Bruar
Bruar Water
Ben Alder
1148
Beinn Bheoil
1019
Loch a' Bhealaich Bheithe
An Cearcall
Meall na Leitreach
775
ATHOLL
Glen Garry
299
Prince Charlie's Cave
855
Stob an Aonaich Mhòir
Ben Alder Cottage
Loch Ericht
Talla Bheith Forest
Loch Garry
PERTH
Loch Con
521
Meall a' Chathaidh
Craig Bhagailteach
492
Falls of Bruar
Pitagowan
Calvine
Struan
Sròn a'Chlaonaidh
625
Duinish
Beinn Mholach
841
Creag a' Mhadaidh
612
Sròn Choin
566
Craiganour Forest
Loch Errochty
Dalchalloch
Trinafour
10
B847
Torr Dubh
Glen Errochty
Sròn Bheag
515
Allt Ruighe nan Saorach
Beinn a' Chuallaich
891
TAY FOREST
Craig nan Caisean
477
Tressait
Lochan Loin nan Donnlaich
AND
Balmore
B846
4
Dunalastair
Tummel Bridge
B8019
Loch Tummel
TAY
Bridge of Ericht
Talladh-a-Bheithe
Killichonan
Aulich
20
B846
Kinloch Rannoch
Dunalastair Reservoir
Foss
Loch Rannoch
Inverhadden
Tempar
Lassintullich
Finnart
Bridge of Gaur
Rannoch School
Carie
Camghouran
PARK
Braes of Foss
Geal Charn
792
Schiehallion
1083
Loch Kinardochy
388
Meall Tairneachan
787
FOREST PARK
Leagag
KINROSS
Deer Park
14
Meall a' Bhobuir
655
Meall a' Mhuic
745
Meall Garbh
968
Carn Mairg
1042
Allt Mòr
Strath of Appin
Weem Hill
Castle Menzies
Camserney
Meall Buidhe
931
Beinn Dearg
830
Carn Gorm
1029
Creag Mhòr
981
Cam Chreag
860
Coshieville
B846
Keltneyburn
Dull
Camusvrachan
Invervar
Balintyre
Woodend
Bolfracks
Glen Lyon
Loch an Daimh
Innerwick
Ancient Yew
Fortingall
Drummond Hill
A827
Stix
Craig Hill
562
Bridge of Balgie
Gleann Dà-ghob
25
Taymouth
Kenmore
960
Stuchd an Lochain
Meall Luaidhe
780
Meall a' Choire Leith
926
Meall Garbh
1118
1001
Meall Greigh
Fearnan
A827
Remony
Scottish Crannog Centre
Acharn
Moar
Kenknock
Cashlie
Beinn nan Oighreag
909
550
Meall Corranaich
1069
Ben Lawers
1214
1013
Ben Lawers National Nature Reserve (NTS)
Meall Odhar
547
Falls of Acharn
Ardradnaig
Beinn Bhreac
716
Creag an Sgliata
697
Stronuich Reservoir
Lairig Breisleich
Lochan na Lairige
Meall Glas
Beinn Ghlas
Meall Taurnie
Meall Ghaordie
1039
A827–TO CRIANLARICH (A85)
Garrow
292

Pass of Drumochter: At 1484 feet (452m) this is the highest point on the British railway network. Allegedly, trains used to be so slow coming up to the summit, that passengers used to get off and walk instead. Nearby Dalwhinnie (***Map ref. B1***) claims to be the highest village in the Scottish Highlands at 1160 feet (358 metres). ***Map ref. B2***

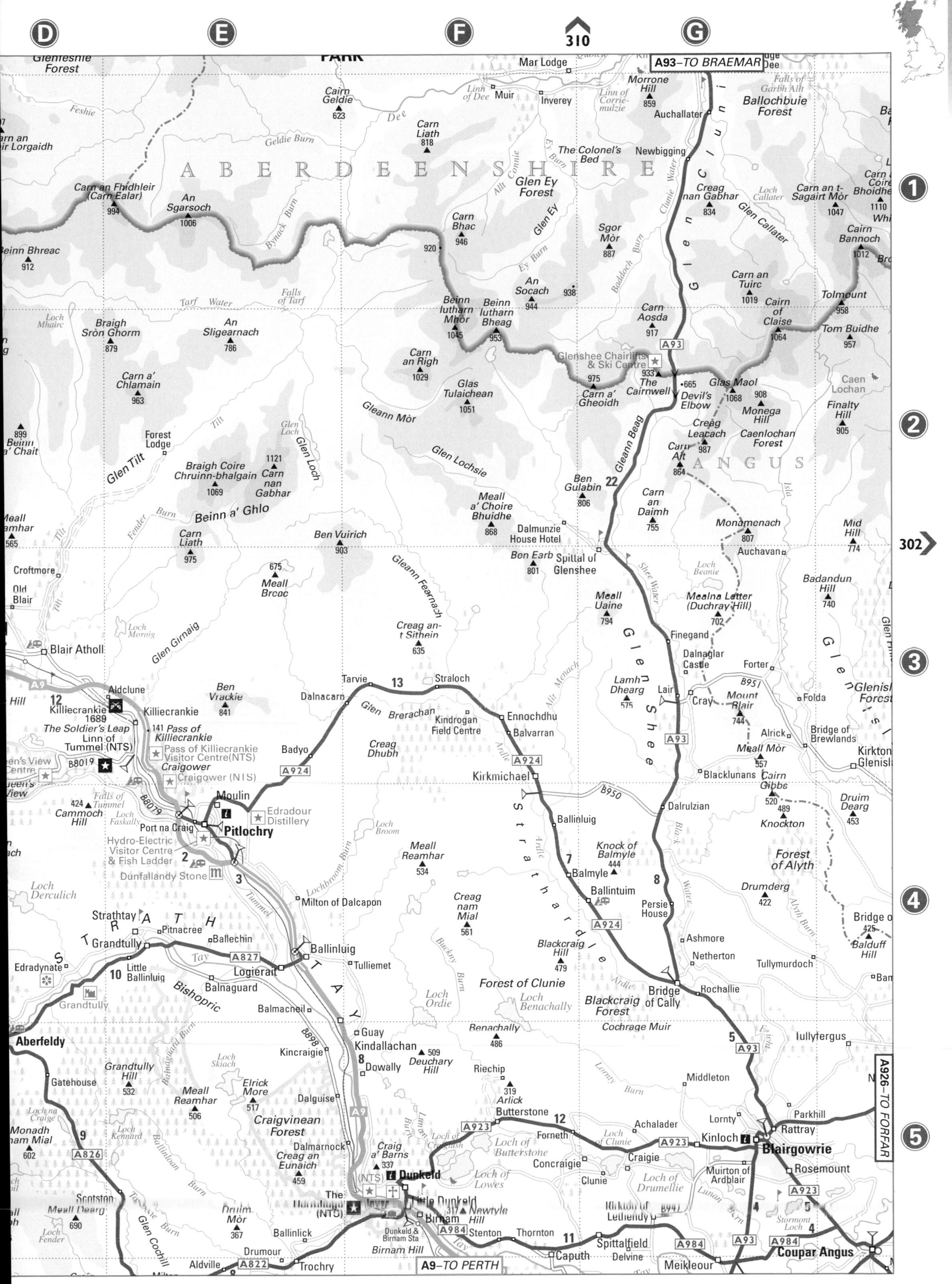

D
E
F
G
310
A93–TO BRAEMAR
Mar Lodge
Glenfeshie Forest
Cairn Geldie 623
Linn of Dee
Muir
Inverey
Linn of Corrie-mulzie
Morrone Hill 859
Falls of Garbh Allt
Ballochbuie Forest
Auchallater
Feshie
Dee
Carn Liath 818
Geldie Burn
The Colonel's Bed
Newbigging
ABERDEENSHIRE
Glen Ey Forest
Carn an Fhidhleir (Carn Ealar) 994
An Sgarsoch 1006
Creag nan Gabhar 834
Loch Callater
Carn an t-Sagairt Mòr 1047
Glen Callater
Bynack Burn
Carn Bhac 946
Glen Ey
Sgor Mòr 887
Cairn Bannoch 1012
Beinn Bhreac 912
920
Ey Burn
Baddoch Burn
Clunie Water
Glen Clunie
An Socach 944
938
Carn an Tuirc 1019
Tolmount 958
Tarf Water
Falls of Tarf
Beinn Iutharn Mhòr 1045
Beinn Iutharn Bheag 953
Carn Aosda 917
Cairn of Claise 1064
Tom Buidhe 957
Loch Mhairc
Braigh Sròn Ghorm 879
An Sligearnach 786
A93
Carn an Righ 1029
Glenshee Chairlifts & Ski Centre
975
933 The Cairnwell
665 Devil's Elbow
Glas Maol 1068
908
Caen Lochan
Carn a' Chlamain 963
Glas Tulaichean 1051
Carn a' Gheoidh
Monega Hill
Finalty Hill 905
Gleann Mòr
Creag Leacach 987
Caenlochan Forest
899 Beinn a' Chait
Forest Lodge
Tilt
Glen Loch
Glen Lochsie
Carn Aft 864
ANGUS
Gleann Beag
Glen Tilt
Braigh Coire Chruinn-bhalgain 1069
1121 Carn nan Gabhar
Ben Gulabin 806
22
Carn an Daimh 755
Isla
Meall a' Choire Bhuidhe 868
Beinn a' Ghlo
Fender Burn
Dalmunzie House Hotel
Monamenach 807
Mid Hill 774
Carn Liath 975
Ben Vuirich 903
Auchavan
302
Croftmore
Ben Earb 801
Spittal of Glenshee
Loch Beanie
Badandun Hill 740
Old Blair
675 Meall Breac
Gleann Fearnach
Shee Water
Mealna Letter (Duchray Hill) 702
Meall Uaine 794
Loch Moraig
Glen Girnaig
Creag an-t Sithein 635
Finegand
Blair Atholl
Dalnaglar Castle
Forter
Glen Isla
A9
Aldclune
Ben Vrackie 841
Tarvie
13
Straloch
Lamh Dhearg 575
Lair
B951
Glenisla Forest
12
Killiecrankie 1689
Killiecrankie
Dalnacarn
Glen Brerachan
Kindrogan Field Centre
Enochdhu
Cray
Mount Blair 744
Folda
The Soldier's Leap
141 Pass of Killiecrankie
Balvarran
Glen Shee
A93
Alrick
Bridge of Brewlands
Linn of Tummel (NTS)
Pass of Killiecrankie Visitor Centre (NTS)
Badyo
Creag Dhubh
A924
Meall Mòr 557
Kirkton of Glenisla
B8019
Queen's View Centre
Craigower
Craigower (NTS)
A924
Kirkmichael
Blacklunans
Cairn Gibbs 520
489
Moulin
B950
Dalrulzian
Druim Dearg 453
Falls of Tummel
424 Cammoch Hill
Loch Faskally
B8079
Edradour Distillery
Ballinluig
Knockton
Port na Craig
Pitlochry
Loch Broom
Strathardle
Hydro-Electric Visitor Centre & Fish Ladder
2
Meall Reamhar 534
Knock of Balmyle 444
Forest of Alyth
7
Balmyle
Dunfallandy Stone
3
Black Water
8
Loch Derculich
Lochbroom Burn
Ballintuim
Drumderg 422
Tummel
Milton of Dalcapon
Creag nam Mial 561
Persie House
Alyth Burn
Strathtay
A924
Bridge of ... 425
Pitnacree
Ballechin
Ashmore
Balduff Hill
STRATH TAY
Grandtully
Ballinluig
Blackcraig Hill 479
Netherton
Tay
A827
Edradynate
Tulliemet
Tullymurdoch
Little Ballinluig
10
Logierait
Bridge of Cally
Rochallie
Balnaguard
Bishopric
Loch Ordie
Forest of Clunie
Loch Benachally
Blackcraig Forest
Grandtully
Balmacneil
Buckny Burn
Ardle
Cochrage Muir
Aberfeldy
Guay
Benachally 486
5
A93
Iullyfergus
Kindallachan
509 Deuchary Hill
Loch Skiach
B898
Kincraigie
8 Dowally
Riechip
Grandtully Hill 532
Balnaguard Burn
Middleton
A926–TO FORFAR
Gatehouse
Elrick More 517
Meall Reamhar 506
Dalguise
319 Arlick
Lornty Burn
Loch na Craige
Craigvinean Forest
A9
Butterstone
12
Parkhill
Monadh Nam Mial 602
9
Loch Kennard
A923
Forneth
Achalader
Lornty
Rattray
Dalmarnock
Craig a' Barns 337
Loch of Craiglush
Loch of Butterstone
Loch of Clunie
A923
Kinloch
Blairgowrie
A826
Creag an Eunaich 459
Concraigie
Craigie
Rosemount
Dunkeld
Loch of Lowes
Clunie
Loch of Drumellie
Muirton of Ardblair
Lunan Burn
The Hermitage (NTS)
Inver
Little Dunkeld
A923
Scotston
Meall Dearg 690
Druim Mòr 367
317 Newtyle Hill
Birnam
Kinloch of Lethendy
B947
4
Stormont Loch
Loch Fender
Glen Cochill
Ballinlick
Dunkeld & Birnam Sta
A984
Stenton
Thornton
11
Spittalfield
A984
A93
A984
Coupar Angus
Drumour
Birnam Hill
Caputh
Delvine
Meikleour
Aldville
A822
Trochry
A9–TO PERTH
1
2
3
4
5

Fortingall: Britain's oldest tree is thought to be the Fortingall Yew (Taxus baccata) in the churchyard, which is estimated to be 3000 years old and consequently the oldest living thing in Europe. There is a long oral tradition that Pontius Pilate was born in the village. **Map ref. C5**

293

Blair Atholl: Queen Victoria loved the Highlands and was a keen 'rambler'. A cairn, close to here, marks the spot where she had a picnic in October 1861. **Map ref. D3**

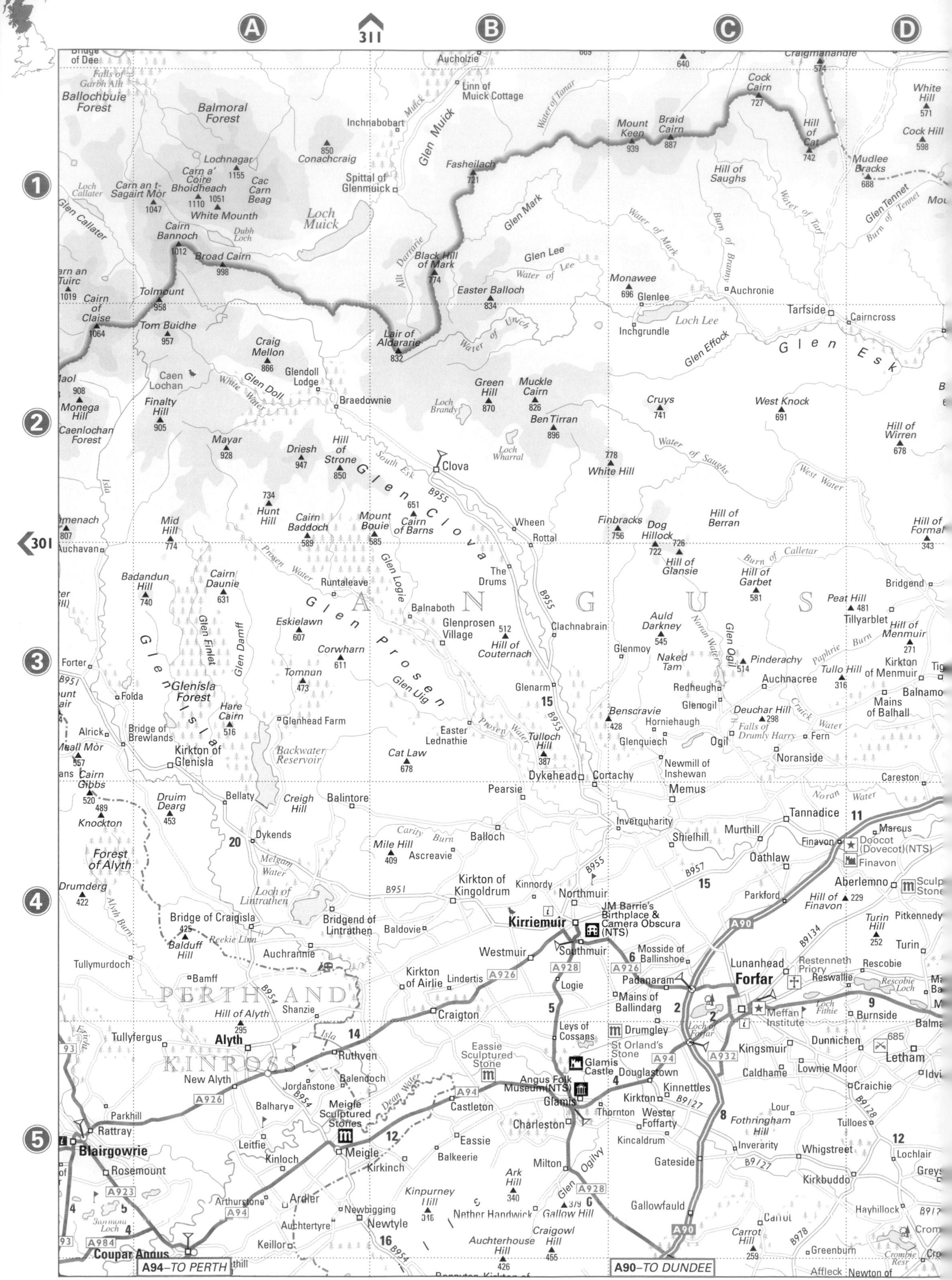

A
B
C
D
311
1
2
3
4
5
301
Ballochbuie Forest
Balmoral Forest
Inchnabobart
850 Conachcraig
Glen Muick
Linn of Muick Cottage
Lochnagar 1155
Carn a' Coire Bhoidheach 1110
Carn an t-Sagairt Mòr 1047
Cac Carn Beag 1051
White Mounth
Spittal of Glenmuick
Loch Muick
Cairn Bannoch 1012
Broad Cairn 998
Glen Callater
Tolmount 958
Cairn of Claise 1064
Tom Buidhe 957
Fasheilach 721
Glen Mark
Black Hill of Mark 774
Easter Balloch 834
Glen Lee
Water of Lee
Lair of Aldararie 832
Water of Unich
Mount Keen 939
Braid Cairn 887
Cock Cairn 727
Hill of Cat 742
Hill of Saughs
Water of Mark
Water of Tarf
Monawee 696
Glenlee
Auchronie
Loch Lee
Inchgrundle
Tarfside
Cairncross
Glen Effock
Glen Esk
White Hill 571
Cock Hill 598
Mudlee Bracks 688
Glen Tennet
Craig Mellon 866
Glendoll Lodge
Caen Lochan
Glen Doll
White Water
Braedownie
Monega Hill 908
Finalty Hill 905
Caenlochan Forest
Mayar 928
Driesh 947
Hill of Strone 850
Green Hill 870
Muckle Cairn 826
Ben Tirran 896
Loch Brandy
Loch Wharral
Cruys 741
West Knock 691
Hill of Wirren 678
Water of Saughs
West Water
Clova
South Esk
Glen Clova
B955
White Hill 778
734 Hunt Hill
Mid Hill 774
Cairn Baddoch 589
Mount Bouie 585
Cairn of Barns 651
Wheen
Rottal
Finbracks 756
Dog Hillock 722
726
Hill of Glansie
Hill of Berran
Hill of Formal 343
Auchavan
Prosen Water
Glen Logie
The Drums
Badandun Hill 740
Cairn Daunie 631
Runtaleave
A N G U S
Burn of Calletar
Hill of Garbet 581
Bridgend
Peat Hill 481
Tillyarblet
Hill of Menmuir 271
Glen Isla
Glen Finlet
Glen Damff
Eskielawn 607
Balnaboth
Glenprosen Village
Glen Prosen
512 Hill of Couternach
Clachnabrain
Auld Darkney 545
Noran Water
Glen Ogil
Glenmoy
Naked Tam
Pinderachy 514
Paphrie Burn
Kirkton of Menmuir
Tullo Hill 316
Forter
Corwharn 611
Tomnun 473
Glen Uig
Glenarm
Redheugh
Auchnacree
Glenisla Forest
Folda
B951
15
Glenogil
Mains of Balhall
Balnamoon
Hare Cairn 516
Glenhead Farm
Benscravie 428
Horniehaugh
Deuchar Hill 298
Falls of Drumly Harry
Cruick Water
Alrick
Bridge of Brewlands
Easter Lednathie
Tulloch Hill 387
Glenquiech
Ogil
Fern
Kirkton of Glenisla
Backwater Reservoir
Cat Law 678
Noranside
Cairn Gibbs
Dykehead
Cortachy
Newmill of Inshewan
Memus
Careston
Druim Dearg 453
Bellaty
Creigh Hill
Balintore
Pearsie
Knockton 520 489
Noran Water
Tannadice
Inverquharity
11
Forest of Alyth
Dykends
20
Melgam Water
Carity Burn
Mile Hill 409
Balloch
Ascreavie
Shielhill
Murthill
Finavon
Oathlaw
Doocot (Dovecot)(NTS)
Finavon
Marcus
B955
B957
Drumderg 422
Loch of Lintrathen
Kirkton of Kingoldrum
Kinnordy
Northmuir
15
Parkford
Hill of Finavon 229
Aberlemno
Sculptured Stones
Alyth Burn
Bridge of Craigisla
Balduff Hill 425
Reekie Linn
Bridgend of Lintrathen
Baldovie
Kirriemuir
JM Barrie's Birthplace & Camera Obscura (NTS)
A90
Turin Hill 252
Pitkennedy
Turin
B9134
Tullymurdoch
Auchrannie
Westmuir
Southmuir
6
Mosside of Ballinshoe
Lunanhead
Restenneth Priory
Rescobie
Bamff
A926
A928
Kirkton of Airlie
Lindertis
Logie
Padanaram
Forfar
Reswallie
Rescobie Loch
PERTH AND KINROSS
B954
Shanzie
Hill of Alyth 295
Craigton
5
Mains of Ballindarg
2
Meffan Institute
Loch Fithie
9
Burnside
Tullyfergus
Alyth
Isla
14
Ruthven
Leys of Cossans
Drumgley
Loch of Forfar
Dunnichen
685
Letham
Eassie Sculptured Stone
Glamis Castle
St Orland's Stone
A94
A932
Kingsmuir
New Alyth
Jordanstone
Balendoch
Dean Water
Angus Folk Museum (NTS)
Douglastown
Caldhame
Lownie Moor
Craichie
Parkhill
Balharry
Meigle Sculptured Stones
Castleton
Glamis
4
Kinnettles
Kirkton
B9127
Rattray
Blairgowrie
Leitfie
12
Charleston
Thornton
Wester Foffarty
Lour
8
Fothringham Hill
Tulloes
B9128
Eassie
Kincaldrum
Inverarity
Whigstreet
12
Lochlair
Rosemount
Kinloch
Meigle
Kirkinch
Balkeerie
Gateside
B9127
Kirkbuddo
A923
Ardler
Arthurstone
Newbigging
Kinpurney Hill 316
Ark Hill 340
Milton
Glen Ogilvy
A928
Gallow Hill 379
Gallowfauld
Hayhillock
Auchtertyre
Newtyle
Nether Handwick
Craigowl Hill 455
Auchterhouse Hill 426
Carrot Hill 259
B978
Greenburn
A90
A984
Coupar Angus
Keillor
16
B954
A94–TO PERTH
A90–TO DUNDEE
Affleck
Newton of

294

Kirriemuir: *James Barrie, creator of Peter Pan, 'the boy who wouldn't grow up', was born here in 1860. The book was published in 1904. Barrie died on the 19th June 1937 and is buried next to his mother in Kirriemuir.* ***Map ref. B4***

Kirriemuir: *The famous Hollywood actor David Niven was born here in 1909. He starred in over 100 films including 'Separate Tables', for which he won an Academy Award in 1958. Although Scottish, David Niven was invariably cast as the archetypal Englishman.* ***Map ref. B4***

312

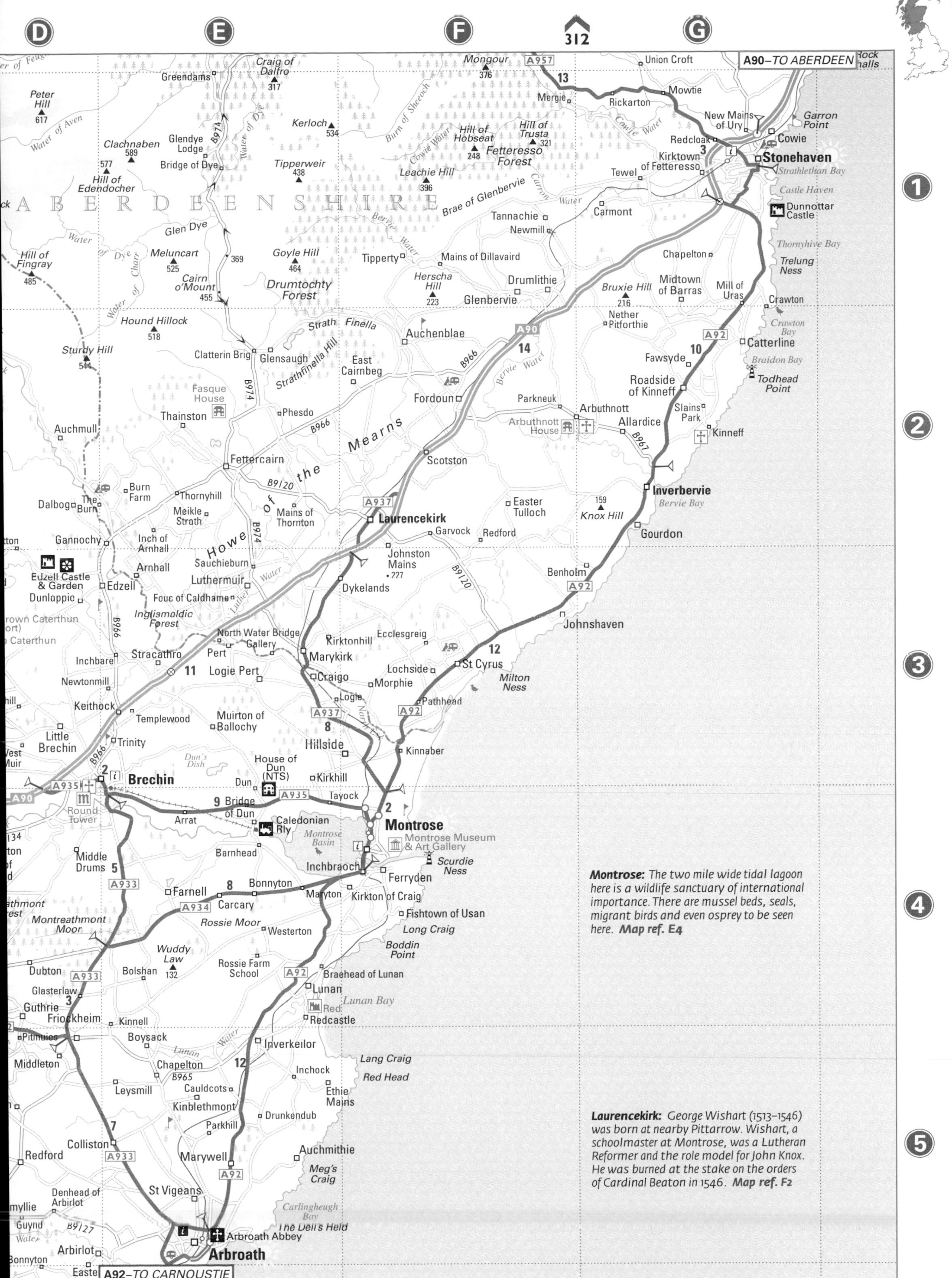
D
E
F
G
1
2
3
4
5
A90–TO ABERDEEN
A92–TO CARNOUSTIE
A B E R D E E N S H I R E
Craig of Dalfro 317
Mongour 376
A957
13
Union Croft
Greendams
Peter Hill 617
Water of Aven
Clachnaben 589
Glendye Lodge
B974
Water of Dye
Kerloch 534
Burn of Sheeoch
Cowie Water
Hill of Hobseat 248
Hill of Trusta 321
Fetteresso Forest
Mergie
Rickarton
Mowtie
New Mains of Ury
Garron Point
Cowie
Redcloak
Kirktown of Fetteresso
Stonehaven
Strathlethan Bay
Castle Haven
Dunnottar Castle
577
Hill of Edendocher
Bridge of Dye
Tipperweir 438
Leachie Hill 396
Brae of Glenbervie
Carron Water
Tewel
Carmont
Tannachie
Newmill
Glen Dye
Hill of Fingray 485
Meluncart 525
369
Goyle Hill 464
Tipperty
Mains of Dillavaird
Chapelton
Thornyhive Bay
Trelung Ness
Cairn o'Mount 455
Water of Charr
Drumtochty Forest
Herscha Hill 223
Drumlithie
Glenbervie
Bruxie Hill 216
Midtown of Barras
Mill of Uras
Crawton
Crawton Bay
Nether Pitforthie
Hound Hillock 518
Strath Finella
Auchenblae
A90
14
A92
10
Catterline
Braidon Bay
Sturdy Hill 544
Clatterin Brig
Glensaugh
Strathfinella Hill
East Cairnbeg
B966
Bervie Water
Fawsyde
Todhead Point
Fasque House
Roadside of Kinneff
Fordoun
Parkneuk
Arbuthnott
Slains Park
Thainston
Phesdo
Arbuthnott House
Allardice
B967
Kinneff
Auchmull
Mearns
Scotston
Fettercairn
the
of
Howe
B9120
Burn Farm
Thornyhill
Inverbervie
Bervie Bay
Dalbog
The Burn
Meikle Strath
Mains of Thornton
A937
Laurencekirk
Easter Tulloch
159 Knox Hill
Gourdon
Garvock
Redford
Gannochy
Inch of Arnhall
Johnston Mains 227
Arnhall
Sauchieburn
Edzell Castle & Garden
Edzell
Luthermuir
Luther Water
Dykelands
Benholm
Dunlappie
Fouc of Caldhame
Inglismaldic Forest
B966
Johnshaven
Brown Caterthun
Caterthun
North Water Bridge
Gallery
Ecclesgreig
Kirktonhill
12
Inchbare
Stracathro
Pert
Marykirk
St Cyrus
Newtonmill
11
Logie Pert
Lochside
Craigo
Morphie
Milton Ness
Keithock
Logie
North Esk
Pathhead
Templewood
Muirton of Ballochy
Little Brechin
Trinity
Hillside
Kinnaber
Duns Dish
House of Dun (NTS)
Brechin
A935
Dun
Kirkhill
Tayock
Round Tower
9 Bridge of Dun
Arrat
Caledonian Rly
Montrose
Montrose Basin
Montrose Museum & Art Gallery
Scurdie Ness
Barnhead
Middle Drums
5
Inchbraoch
Ferryden
A933
Farnell
8
Bonnyton
Maryton
Kirkton of Craig
A934
Carcary
Montreathmont Moor
Rossie Moor
Westerton
Fishtown of Usan
Long Craig
Boddin Point
Wuddy Law 132
Bolshan
Rossie Farm School
Dubton
Braehead of Lunan
Glasterlaw
Lunan
Lunan Bay
Guthrie
Friockheim
Kinnell
Red Castle
Redcastle
Pitmuies
Boysack
Lunan Water
Inverkeilor
Middleton
Chapelton
B965
Lang Craig
Inchock
Red Head
Leysmill
Cauldcots
Ethie Mains
Kinblethmont
Drunkendub
Parkhill
7
Colliston
Redford
Marywell
Auchmithie
Meg's Craig
Denhead of Arbirlot
St Vigeans
Carlingheugh Bay
Guynd
B9127
The Deil's Heid
Arbroath Abbey
Arbirlot
Arbroath
Bonnyton
Easter

Montrose: *The two mile wide tidal lagoon here is a wildlife sanctuary of international importance. There are mussel beds, seals, migrant birds and even osprey to be seen here.* ***Map ref. E4***

Laurencekirk: *George Wishart (1513–1546) was born at nearby Pittarrow. Wishart, a schoolmaster at Montrose, was a Lutheran Reformer and the role model for John Knox. He was burned at the stake on the orders of Cardinal Beaton in 1546.* ***Map ref. F2***

295

Arbroath: *Home of the legendary Arbroath Smokie, pairs of haddock tied by their tails and smoked over hardwood chips. Arbroath Smokies are afforded the same protection under EU law as Champagne and Parma Ham if they don't come from Arbroath then they cannot be called Arbroath Smokies.* ***Map ref. E5***

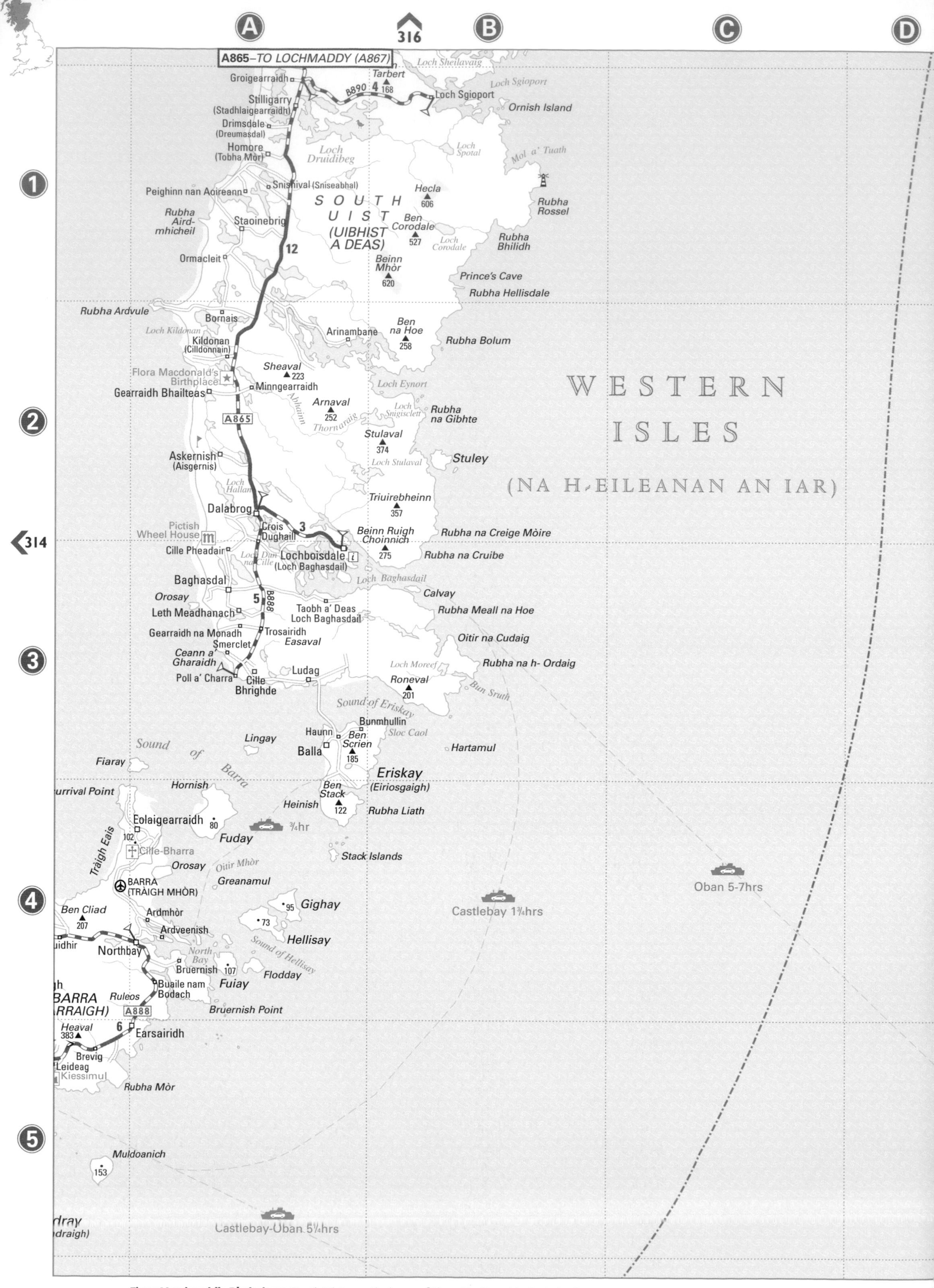
A
316
B
C
D
A865–TO LOCHMADDY (A867)
Tarbert
Loch Sheilavaig
Loch Sgioport
Ornish Island
Groigearraidh
Stilligarry (Stadhlaigearraidh)
Drimsdale (Dreumasdal)
Homore (Tobha Mòr)
Loch Druidibeg
Loch Spotal
Mol a' Tuath
Snishival (Sniseabhal)
Peighinn nan Aoireann
SOUTH UIST (UIBHIST A DEAS)
Hecla 606
Rubha Rossel
Rubha Aird-mhicheil
Staoinebrig
Ben Corodale 527
Loch Corodale
Rubha Bhilidh
Ormacleit
Beinn Mhòr 620
Prince's Cave
Rubha Hellisdale
Rubha Ardvule
Bornais
Loch Kildonan
Kildonan (Cilldonnain)
Arinambane
Ben na Hoe 258
Rubha Bolum
Sheaval 223
Flora Macdonald's Birthplace
Minngearraidh
Gearraidh Bhailteas
Loch Eynort
A865
Arnaval 252
Abhainn Thornaraig
Loch Snigisclett
Rubha na Gibhte
Stulaval 374
WESTERN ISLES
(NA H-EILEANAN AN IAR)
Askernish (Aisgernis)
Loch Stulaval
Stuley
Loch Hallan
Triuirebheinn 357
Dalabrog
Pictish Wheel House
Crois Dughaill
Beinn Ruigh Choinnich 275
Rubha na Creige Mòire
Cille Pheadair
Loch Dun na Cille
Lochboisdale (Loch Baghasdail)
Rubha na Cruibe
314
Baghasdal
Loch Baghasdail
Calvay
Orosay
B888
Taobh a' Deas Loch Baghasdail
Rubha Meall na Hoe
Leth Meadhanach
Gearraidh na Monadh
Trosairidh
Easaval
Oitir na Cudaig
Smerclet
Ceann a' Gharaidh
Loch Moreef
Rubha na h- Ordaig
Ludag
Poll a' Charra
Cille Bhrighde
Roneval 201
Bun Sruth
Sound of Eriskay
Bunmhullin
Haunn
Ben Scrien 185
Sloc Caol
Lingay
Sound of Barra
Balla
Hartamul
Fiaray
Eriskay (Eiriosgaigh)
Hornish
Ben Stack 122
Heinish
Rubha Liath
Eolaigearraidh
80
Fuday
¾hr
102
Cille-Bharra
Traigh Eais
Stack Islands
Orosay
Oitir Mhòr
Greanamul
BARRA (TRAIGH MHÒR)
Oban 5-7hrs
Ben Cliad 207
Ardmhòr
95
Gighay
Castlebay 1¾hrs
Ardveenish
73
Hellisay
Northbay
North Bay
Sound of Hellisay
Bruernish
107
Flodday
Buaile nam Bodach
Fuiay
Ruleos
A888
Bruernish Point
Heaval 383
Earsairidh
Brevig
Leideag
Kiessimul
Rubha Mòr
1
2
3
4
5
Muldoanich
153
Castlebay-Oban 5¼hrs

Flora Macdonald's Birthplace: *South Uist was the home of Flora MacDonald who helped Bonnie Prince Charlie escape from the English army after the defeat of his army at the battle of Culloden in April 1746. After narrowly evading the enemy several times she eventually got him to the Isle of Skye and then on to safety. Her home is now a ruin but a nearby memorial marks the site.* ***Map ref. A2***

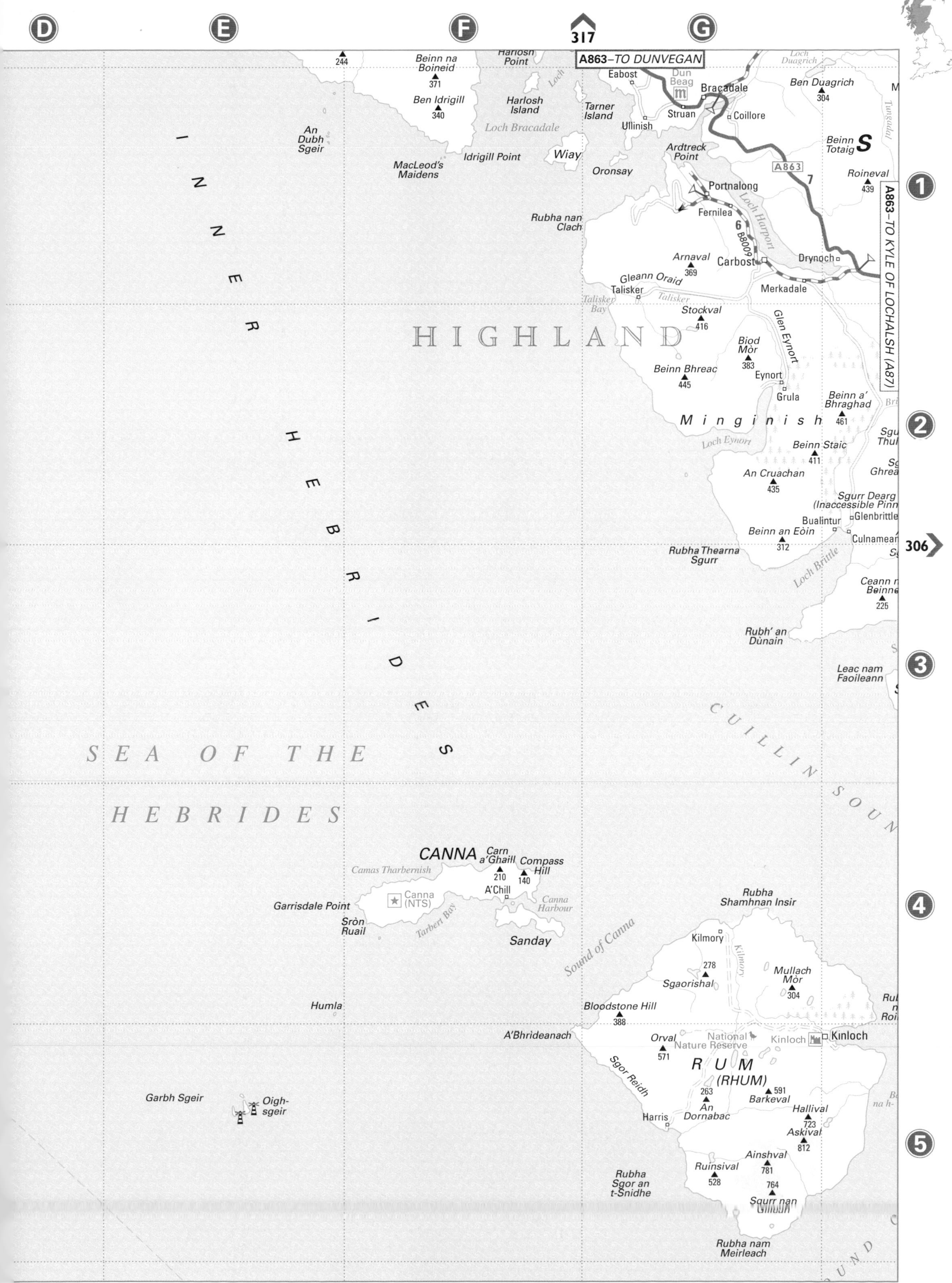
D
E
F
G
317
A863–TO DUNVEGAN
Harlosh Point
Beinn na Boineid 371
Ben Idrigill 340
Harlosh Island
Loch Bracadale
Tarner Island
Eabost
Dun Beag
Bracadale
Struan
Coillore
Ullinish
Ben Duagrich 304
Beinn Totaig
An Dubh Sgeir
Idrigill Point
MacLeod's Maidens
Wiay
Oronsay
Ardtreck Point
A863
Roineval 439
Portnalong
Fernilea
Loch Harport
Rubha nan Clach
B8009
Arnaval 369
Carbost
Drynoch
Gleann Oraid
Talisker
Talisker Bay
Merkadale
Stockval 416
A863–TO KYLE OF LOCHALSH (A87)
INNER HEBRIDES
HIGHLAND
Glen Eynort
Biod Mòr 383
Beinn Bhreac 445
Eynort
Grula
Beinn a' Bhraghad 461
Minginish
Loch Eynort
Beinn Staic 411
An Cruachan 435
Sgurr Dearg (Inaccessible Pinn
Glenbrittle
Bualintur
Beinn an Eòin 312
Culnamean
Rubha Thearna Sgurr
Loch Brittle
306
Rubh' an Dùnain
Leac nam Faoileann
CUILLIN SOUND
SEA OF THE HEBRIDES
CANNA
Carn a'Ghaill 210
Compass Hill 140
Camas Tharbernish
A'Chill
Canna (NTS)
Canna Harbour
Garrisdale Point
Tarbert Bay
Sròn Ruail
Sanday
Sound of Canna
Rubha Shamhnan Insir
Kilmory
Mullach Mòr 304
Sgaorishal 278
Humla
Bloodstone Hill 388
A'Bhrideanach
Orval 571
National Nature Reserve
Kinloch
RUM (RHUM)
Sgor Reidh
263
591 Barkeval
An Dornabac
Harris
Hallival 723
Askival 812
Garbh Sgeir
Oigh-sgeir
Ainshval 781
Ruinsival 528
764
Rubha Sgor an t-Snidhe
Sgurr nan Gillean
Rubha nam Meirleach
1
2
3
4
5
296

Rum: *Semi precious stones and rocks on this island are similar to those found on the moon. In the 19th Century the island was 'cleared' for sheep farming and the residents shipped off to Nova Scotia. It is now owned by the Nature Conservancy Council.* **Map ref. G5**

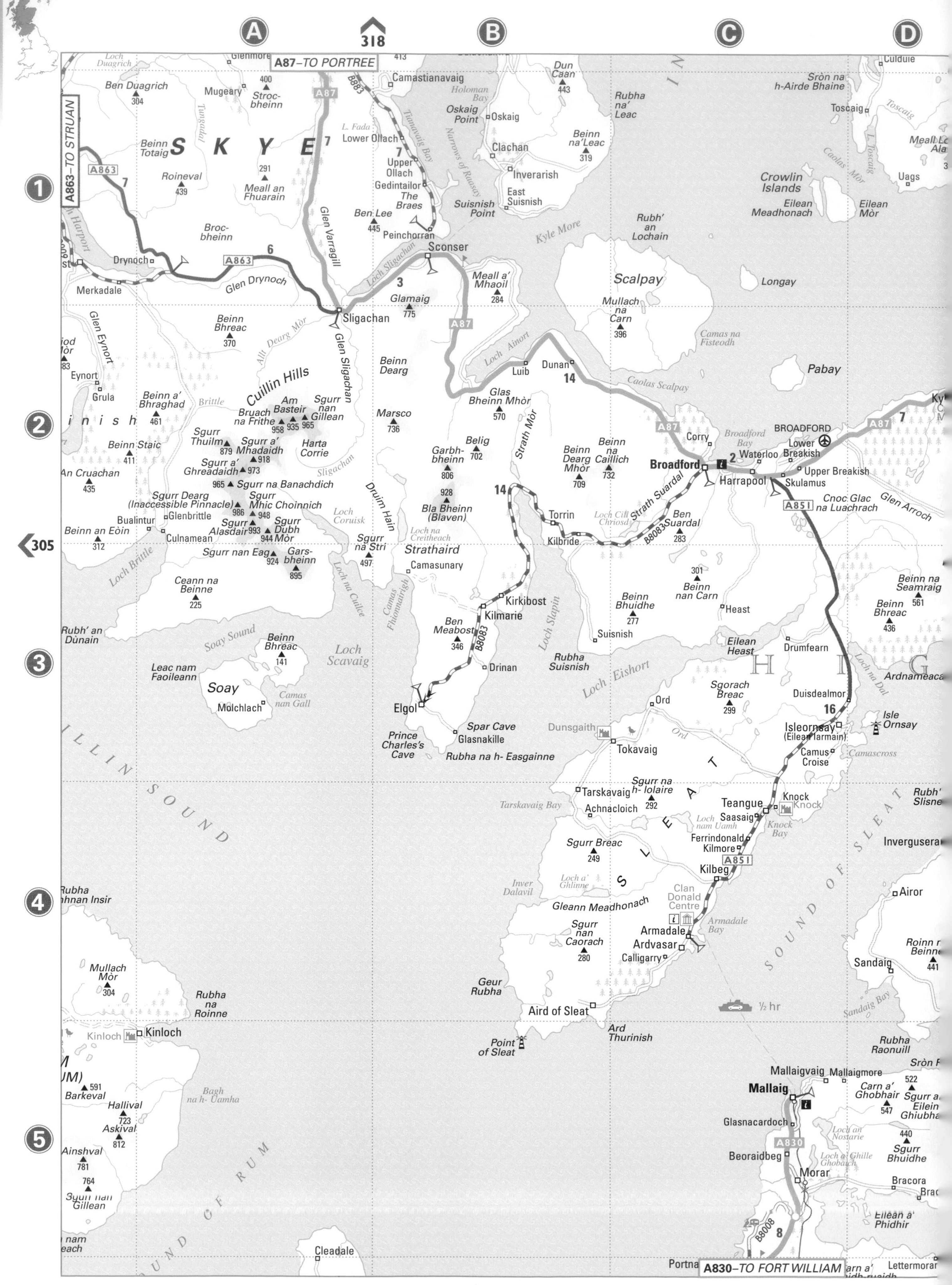

A
B
C
D
318
A87–TO PORTREE
A863–TO STRUAN
305
297
A830–TO FORT WILLIAM
1
2
3
4
5
SKYE
Ben Duagrich
304
Mugeary
400
Stroc-bheinn
Camastianavaig
Holoman Bay
Oskaig Point
Oskaig
Dun Caan
443
Rubha na' Leac
Beinn na'Leac
319
Sròn na h-Airde Bhaine
Toscaig
Beinn Totaig
Roineval
439
291
Meall an Fhuarain
Glen Varragill
L. Fada
Lower Ollach
Upper Ollach
Gedintailor
The Braes
Ben Lee
445
Peinchorran
Narrows of Raasay
Clachan
Inverarish
East Suisnish
Suisnish Point
Kyle More
Crowlin Islands
Eilean Meadhonach
Eilean Mòr
Uags
Rubh' an Lochain
Broc-bheinn
Drynoch
A863
Glen Drynoch
Merkadale
Sconser
Loch Sligachan
Glamaig
775
Meall a' Mhaoil
284
Scalpay
Mullach na Carn
396
Longay
Camas na Fisteodh
Pabay
Beinn Bhreac
370
Sligachan
Glen Sligachan
Glen Eynort
Eynort
Grula
Allt Dearg Mòr
Beinn Dearg
Loch Ainort
Luib
Dunan
Caolas Scalpay
Beinn a' Bhraghad
461
Brittle
Cuillin Hills
Bruach na Frithe
Am Basteir
Sgurr nan Gillean
958
935
965
Marsco
736
Glas Bheinn Mhòr
570
Strath Mòr
Corry
Broadford Bay
BROADFORD
Lower Breakish
Sgurr Thuilm
879
Sgurr a' Mhadaidh
918
Harta Corrie
Beinn Staic
411
Sgurr a' Ghreadaidh
973
Belig
702
Garbh-bheinn
806
Beinn Dearg Mhòr
709
Beinn na Caillich
732
Broadford
Waterloo
Upper Breakish
Harrapool
Skulamus
An Cruachan
435
965
Sgurr na Banachdich
Druim Hain
928
Bla Bheinn (Blaven)
Sgurr Dearg (Inaccessible Pinnacle)
986
Sgurr Mhic Choinnich
948
Bualintur
Glenbrittle
Sgurr Alasdair
993
Sgurr Dubh Mòr
944
Loch Coruisk
Torrin
Loch Cill Chriosd
Strath Suardal
Ben Suardal
283
Cnoc Glac na Luachrach
Glen Arroch
A851
Beinn an Eòin
312
Culnamean
Sgurr nan Eag
924
Gars-bheinn
895
Sgurr na Stri
497
Loch na Creitheach
Strathaird
Camasunary
Kilbride
B8083
301
Beinn nan Carn
Heast
Beinn na Seamraig
561
Beinn Bhreac
436
Loch Brittle
Ceann na Beinne
225
Loch na Cuilce
Camas Fhionnairigh
Kirkibost
Kilmarie
Loch Slapin
Beinn Bhuidhe
277
Suisnish
Rubh' an Dùnain
Soay Sound
Beinn Bhreac
141
Loch Scavaig
Ben Meabost
346
Drinan
Rubha Suisnish
Eilean Heast
Drumfearn
Leac nam Faoileann
Soay
Molchlach
Camas nan Gall
Elgol
Loch Eishort
Sgorach Breac
299
Duisdealmor
Ardnameacan
Ord
Isle Ornsay
Prince Charles's Cave
Spar Cave
Glasnakille
Rubha na h- Easgainne
Dunsgaith
Tokavaig
Isleornsay (Eilean Iarmain)
Camus Croise
Camascross
CUILLIN SOUND
SLEAT
Tarskavaig
Sgurr na h- Iolaire
292
Tarskavaig Bay
Achnacloich
Teangue
Knock
Saasaig
Loch nam Uamh
Knock Bay
Rubh' Slisne
Sgurr Breac
249
Ferrindonald
Kilmore
Inverguseran
Kilbeg
Inver Dalavil
Loch a' Ghlinne
Clan Donald Centre
Rubha Ghhnan Insir
Airor
Glean Meadhonach
Armadale
Sgurr nan Caorach
280
Ardvasar
Armadale Bay
Calligarry
SOUND OF SLEAT
Mullach Mòr
304
Geur Rubha
Sandaig
441
Sandaig Bay
Rubha na Roinne
½ hr
Aird of Sleat
Kinloch
Ard Thurinish
Point of Sleat
Rubha Raonuill
Mallaigvaig
Mallaigmore
591
Barkeval
Bagh na h- Uamha
Mallaig
Carn a' Ghobhair
547
522
Hallival
723
Askival
812
Glasnacardoch
A830
Loch an Nostarie
440
Sgurr Bhuidhe
Ainshval
781
Beoraidbeg
Loch a' Ghille Ghobaich
Morar
Bracora
764
Sgurr nan Gillean
SOUND OF RUM
B8008
8
Cleadale
Portnaluchaig
Lettermorar

Loch Morar: Known as the 'Loch without a bottom'. Loch Morar covers an area of over 10 square miles (28.6 sq km) and at 1077 feet (328m) is the deepest lake in Britain. **Map ref. D5**

The Cuillin Hills Considered by many to be the most dramatic mountain range in Britain. Comprises the tall, jagged peaks of the main Cuillin Ridge, known as the Black Cuillin and the more rounded hills of the Red Cuillin. There are over 20 Munros in the Cuillin Hills which have a fascinating geological composition dating back 500 million years. **Map ref. A2 Also on page 119**

Elgol: Just south of the village i[s] a cave called Suidhe Biorach where Bonnie Prince Charlie is said to have hidden before maki[ng] his escape to Europe in 1746. **Map ref. B3**

319

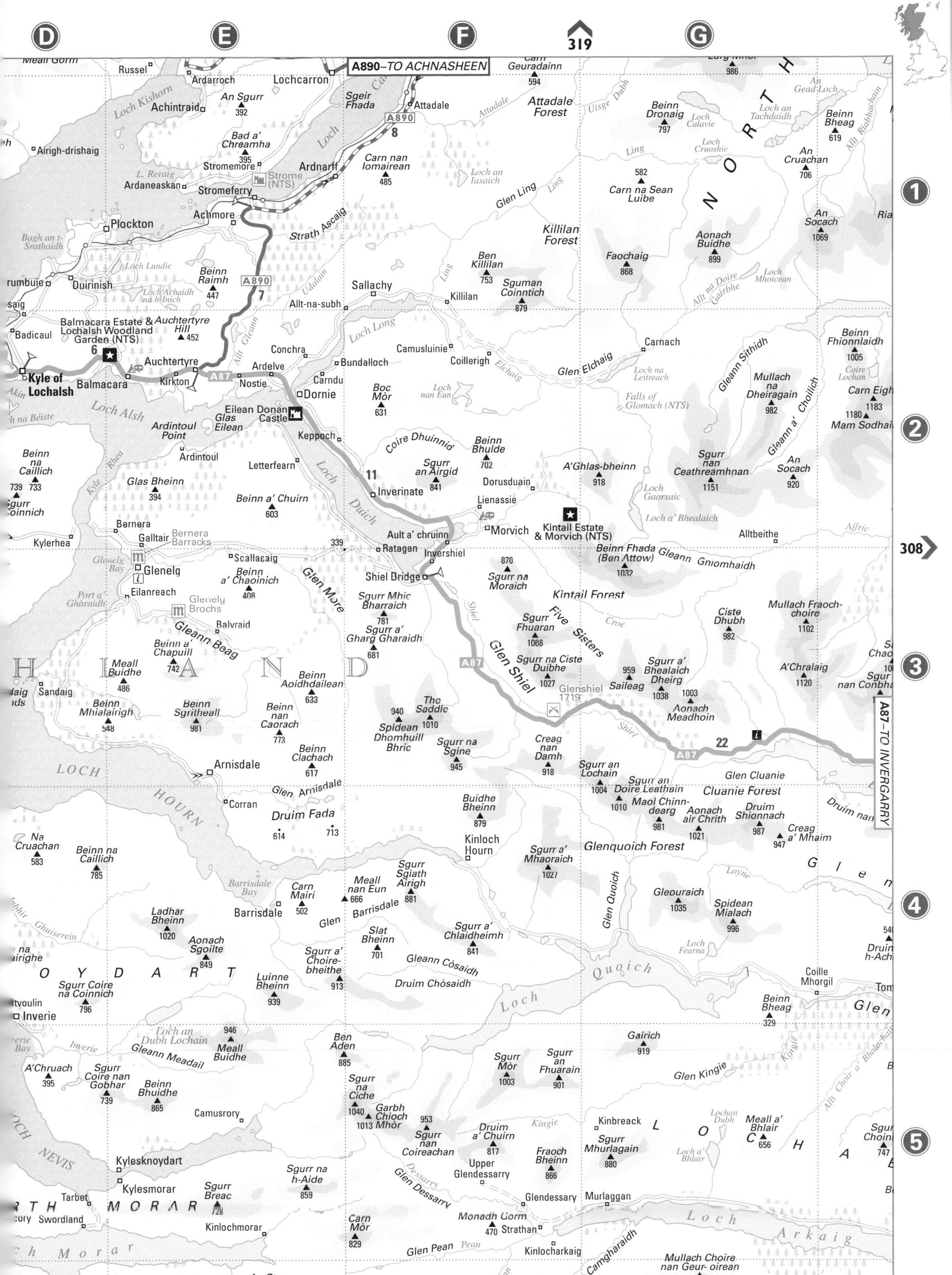

D
E
F
G
1
2
3
4
5
A890–TO ACHNASHEEN
A87–TO INVERGARRY
Russel
Ardarroch
Lochcarron
An Sgurr
392
Achintraid
Loch Kishorn
Airigh-drishaig
Bad a' Chreamha
395
Stromemore
L. Reraig
Ardaneaskan
Stromeferry
Strome (NTS)
Ardnarff
Achmore
Plockton
Bagh an t-Srathaidh
Loch Lundie
Beinn Raimh
447
Duirinish
Loch Achaidh na h-Inich
Balmacara Estate & Lochalsh Woodland Garden (NTS)
Auchtertyre Hill
452
Badicaul
Kyle of Lochalsh
Balmacara
Auchtertyre
Kirkton
Loch Alsh
Ardintoul Point
Ardintoul
Glas Eilean
Eilean Donan Castle
Ardelve
Nostie
Conchra
Dornie
Carndu
Bundalloch
Keppoch
Letterfearn
Loch Duich
Inverinate
Glas Bheinn
394
Beinn a' Chuirn
603
Bernera
Galltair
Bernera Barracks
Kylerhea
Glenelg Bay
Glenelg
Eilanreach
Scallasaig
Beinn a' Chaoinich
408
Glenelg Brochs
Balvraid
Gleann Beag
Beinn a' Chapuill
742
Meall Buidhe
486
Sandaig
Beinn na Mhialairigh
548
Beinn Sgritheall
981
Beinn nan Caorach
773
Beinn Aoidhdailean
633
Arnisdale
Beinn Clachach
617
Loch Hourn
Corran
Glen Arnisdale
Druim Fada
614
713
Na Cruachan
583
Beinn na Caillich
785
Barrisdale Bay
Barrisdale
Carn Mairi
502
Ladhar Bheinn
1020
Aonach Sgoilte
849
Knoydart
Sgurr Coire na Coinnich
796
Luinne Bheinn
939
Inverie
Loch an Dubh Lochain
946
Meall Buidhe
Gleann Meadail
A'Chruach
395
Sgurr Coire nan Gobhar
739
Beinn Bhuidhe
865
Camusrory
Kylesknoydart
Kylesmorar
Tarbet
Swordland
Sgurr Breac
728
Kinlochmorar
Loch Morar
Loch Nevis
A890
Sgeir Fhada
Attadale
Loch Carron
Carn nan Iomairean
485
Strath Ascaig
Sallachy
Allt-na-subh
Loch Long
Camusluinie
Coillerigh
Killilan
Ben Killilan
753
Sguman Coinntich
879
Glen Ling
Loch an Iasaich
Carn Geuradainn
594
Attadale Forest
Killilan Forest
Boc Mòr
631
Loch nan Eun
Coire Dhuinnid
Beinn Bhulde
702
Sgurr an Airgid
841
Dorusduain
Lienassie
Morvich
Kintail Estate & Morvich (NTS)
Ault a' chruinn
Ratagan
Invershiel
Shiel Dridge
339
Glen More
Sgurr Mhic Bharraich
781
Sgurr a' Gharg Gharaidh
681
870
Sgurr na Moraich
Kintail Forest
Five Sisters
Sgurr Fhuaran
1068
Sgurr na Ciste Duibhe
1027
Glen Shiel
Glenshiel 1719
A87
940
The Saddle
1010
Spidean Dhomhuill Bhric
Sgurr na Sgine
945
Creag nan Damh
918
Buidhe Bheinn
879
Kinloch Hourn
Sgurr a' Mhaoraich
1027
Glenquoich Forest
Sgurr Sgiath Airigh
881
Meall nan Eun
666
Glen Barrisdale
Slat Bheinn
701
Sgurr a' Chlaidheimh
841
Gleann Còsaidh
Druim Chòsaidh
Sgurr a' Choire-bheithe
913
Loch Quoich
Ben Aden
885
Sgurr na Ciche
1040
Garbh Chioch Mhòr
1013
953
Sgurr nan Coireachan
Sgurr Mòr
1003
Sgurr an Fhuarain
901
Druim a' Chuirn
817
Fraoch Bheinn
866
Upper Glendessarry
Glen Dessarry
Glendessary
Sgurr na h-Aide
859
Carn Mòr
829
Glen Pean
Monadh Gorm
470
Strathan
Kinlocharkaig
Beinn Dronaig
797
Loch Calavie
Loch Cruoshie
582
Carn na Sean Luibhe
North
Faochaig
868
Aonach Buidhe
899
Loch Mhoicean
Carnach
Glen Elchaig
Loch na Leitreach
Falls of Glomach (NTS)
A'Ghlas-bheinn
918
Loch Gaorsaic
Loch a' Bhealaich
Sgurr nan Ceathreamhnan
1151
Gleann Sithidh
Mullach na Dheiragain
982
Beinn Fhada (Ben Attow)
1032
Gleann Gniomhaidh
Alltbeithe
Ciste Dhubh
982
959
Saileag
Sgurr a' Bhealaich Dheirg
1038
1003
Aonach Meadhoin
Sgurr an Lochain
1004
Sgurr an Doire Leathain
1010
Maol Chinn-dearg
981
Aonach air Chrith
1021
Druim Shionnach
987
Glen Cluanie
Cluanie Forest
Glen Quoich
Gleouraich
1035
Spidean Mialach
996
Loch Fearna
Gairich
919
Glen Kingie
Kinbreack
Sgurr Mhurlagain
880
Murlaggan
Loch Arkaig
Mullach Choire nan Geur-oirean
Loch an Tachdaidh
Beinn Bheag
619
An Cruachan
706
An Socach
1069
Beinn Fhionnlaidh
1005
Coire Lochan
Carn Eigh
1183
1180
Mam Sodhai
An Socach
920
Mullach Fraoch-choire
1102
A'Chralaig
1120
Creag a' Mhaim
947
Coille Mhorgil
Beinn Bheag
329
Meall a' Bhlair
656
Loch Arkaig

308

Sandaig: *Former home of the enigmatic writer Gavin Maxwell (1914-1969) which he described as Camusfearna in his autobiographical 'Ring of Bright Water'. His grave is on the site of his house which burned down in 1968.* ***Map ref. D3***

298

Eilean Donan Castle *is used as a location for several famous films, including 'Highlander', 'Entrapment' and 'The World is not Enough'. It was originally built in the 13th century as a defence against the Vikings and was destroyed by three English warships during the 1715 Jacobite uprising. It was rebuilt in the 1930s and is today one of Scotland's most picturesque castles.* ***Map ref. E2*** ***Also on page 122***

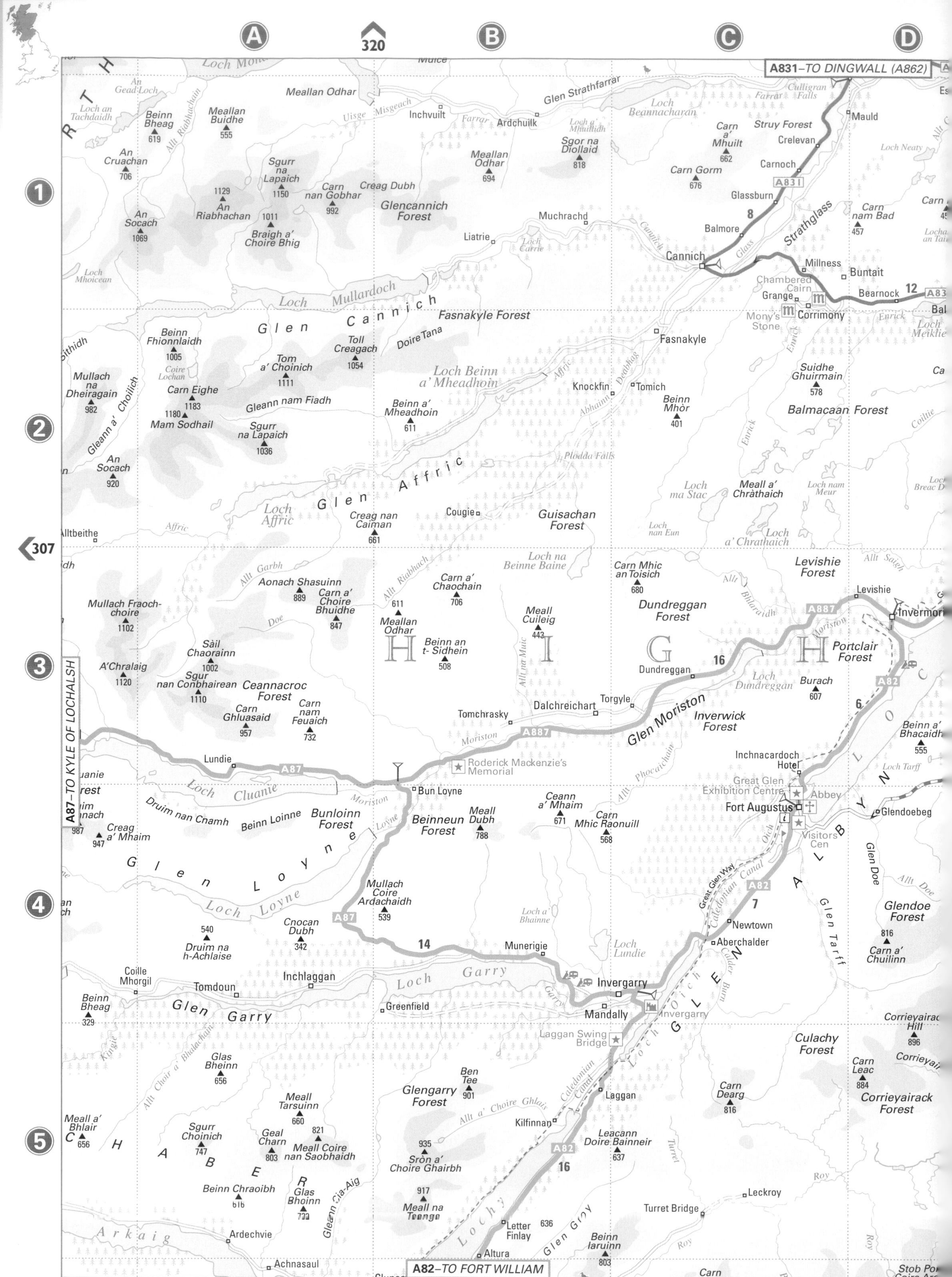

A
B
C
D
320
307
299
1
2
3
4
5
A831–TO DINGWALL (A862)
A87–TO KYLE OF LOCHALSH
A82–TO FORT WILLIAM
Loch Monar
An Gead Loch
Loch an Tachdaidh
Beinn Bheag
619
Meallan Buidhe
555
Meallan Odhar
Allt Riabhachain
Uisge Misgeach
Inchvuilt
Farrar
Ardchuilk
Glen Strathfarrar
Loch Beannacharan
Loch a' Mhuillidh
Sgor na Diollaid
818
Carn a' Mhuilt
662
Struy Forest
Crelevan
Culligran Falls
Mauld
Loch Neaty
Carnoch
Carn Gorm
676
A831
Glassburn
An Cruachan
706
Sgurr na Lapaich
1150
1129
An Riabhachan
1011
Braigh a' Choire Bhig
Carn nan Gobhar
992
Creag Dubh
Glencannich Forest
Meallan Odhar
694
An Socach
1069
Loch Mhoicean
Muchrachd
Liatrie
Loch Carrie
Cannich
Balmore
Strathglass
Glass
8
Carn nam Bad
457
Carn
Millness
Buntait
Chambered Cairn
Grange
Corrimony
Mony's Stone
Bearnock
12
A831
Enrick
Loch Meiklie
Loch Mullardoch
Glen Cannich
Fasnakyle Forest
Beinn Fhionnlaidh
1005
Coire Lochan
Tom a' Choinich
1111
Toll Creagach
1054
Doire Tana
Fasnakyle
Mullach na Dheiragain
982
Carn Eighe
1183
1180
Mam Sodhail
Gleann a' Choilich
Gleann nam Fiadh
Sgurr na Lapaich
1036
Loch Beinn a' Mheadhoin
Beinn a' Mheadhoin
611
Knockfin
Tomich
Abhainn Deabhag
Beinn Mhòr
401
Suidhe Ghuirmain
578
Balmacaan Forest
Plodda Falls
An Socach
920
Glen Affric
Loch Affric
Affric
Alltbeithe
Creag nan Caiman
661
Cougie
Guisachan Forest
Loch ma Stac
Meall a' Chràthaich
Loch nam Meur
Loch nan Eun
Loch a' Chrathaich
Loch na Beinne Baine
Carn Mhic an Toisich
680
Levishie Forest
Levishie
Invermoriston
A887
Allt Garbh
Aonach Shasuinn
889
Carn a' Choire Bhuidhe
847
Allt Riabhach
611
Meallan Odhar
Carn a' Chaochain
706
Meall Cuileig
443
Dundreggan Forest
Mullach Fraoch-choire
1102
Doe
H I G H
Beinn an t- Sidhein
508
Allt na Muic
Sàil Chaorainn
1002
A'Chralaig
1120
Sgurr nan Conbhairean
1110
Ceannacroc Forest
Dundreggan
16
Loch Dundreggan
Burach
607
Portclair Forest
A82
6
Carn Ghluasaid
957
Carn nam Feuaich
732
Tomchrasky
Dalchreichart
Torgyle
Glen Moriston
Inverwick Forest
Beinn a' Bhacaidh
555
Lundie
A87
Moriston
Roderick Mackenzie's Memorial
Inchnacardoch Hotel
Loch Tarff
Loch Cluanie
Bun Loyne
Great Glen Exhibition Centre
Abbey
Fort Augustus
Glendoebeg
Druim nan Cnamh
Beinn Loinne
Bunloinn Forest
Beinneun Forest
Meall Dubh
788
Ceann a' Mhaim
671
Carn Mhic Raonuill
568
Visitors Cen
Creag a' Mhaim
947
Glen Loyne
Loch Loyne
Mullach Coire Ardachaidh
539
Great Glen Way
Caledonian Canal
A82
7
Glen Doe
Glen Tarff
Glendoe Forest
816
Carn a' Chuilinn
540
Druim na h-Achlaise
Cnocan Dubh
342
A87
14
Munerigie
Loch a' Bhainne
Loch Lundie
Newtown
Aberchalder
Coille Mhorgil
Inchlaggan
Tomdoun
Loch Garry
Invergarry
Beinn Bheag
329
Glen Garry
Greenfield
Mandally
Invergarry
Laggan Swing Bridge
Loch Oich
Corrieyairack Hill
896
Culachy Forest
Glas Bheinn
656
Ben Tee
901
Glengarry Forest
Laggan
Carn Dearg
816
Carn Leac
884
Corrieyairack Forest
Meall Tarsuinn
660
Allt a' Choire Ghlais
Kilfinnan
Leacann Doire Bainneir
637
Meall a' Bhlair
656
Sgurr Choinich
747
Geal Charn
803
821
Meall Coire nan Saobhaidh
935
Sròn a' Choire Ghairbh
A82
16
Turret
Roy
Beinn Chraoibh
Glas Bhoinn
Gleann Cia-Aig
917
Meall na Teanga
Leckroy
Turret Bridge
Arkaig
Ardechvie
Letter Finlay
636
Glen Gloy
Beinn Iaruinn
803
Loch Lochy
Altura
Achnasaul
Carn
Stob Coire

Invergarry: Historic home of the MacDonells of Glen Garry whose nearby castle was repeatedly attacked and finally razed in 1746 by the Duke of Cumberland. It remains today as a ruin. **Map ref. C4**

Loch Ness: John Cobb, the 'record breakers' record breaker', died here whilst attempting to beat the world water speed record on 29th September 1952. Cobb had dedicated his life to speed records as a racing driver at Brooklands, then as holder of the world land speed record. He was recovered from the water following the accident and carried up the hill to Achnahannet where he died. Fifty years later his speedboat Crusader was located in 650 feet (200m) of water on the bed of Loch Ness. **Map ref. E2**

321

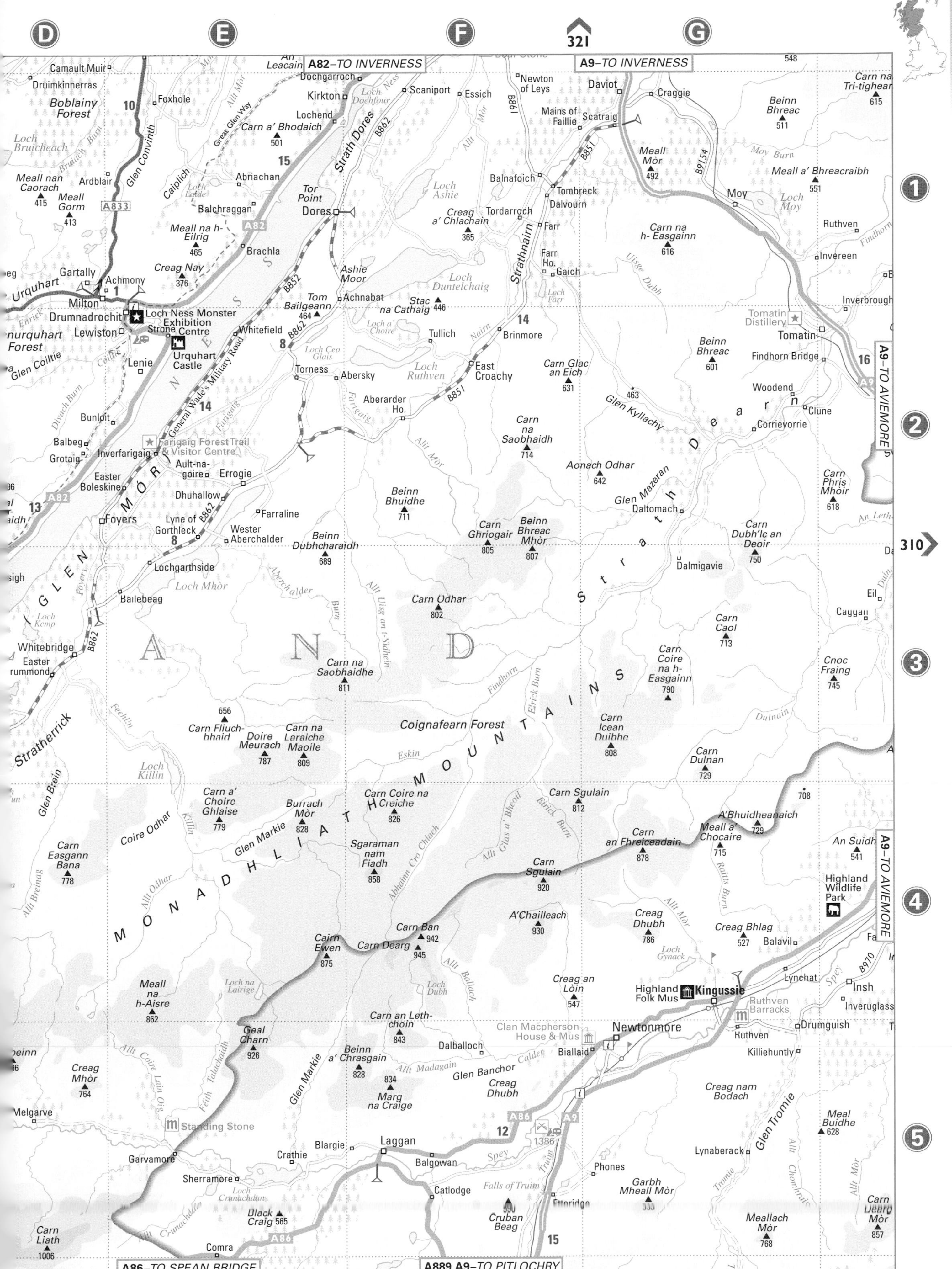
D
E
F
G
A82–TO INVERNESS
A9–TO INVERNESS
Camault Muir
Druimkinnerras
Boblainy Forest
Foxhole
Glen Convinth
Loch Bruicheach
Meall nan Caorach 415
Ardblair
Meall Gorm 413
A833
Caiplich
Great Glen Way
Carn a' Bhodaich 501
Abriachan
Balchraggan
Meall na h-Eilrig 465
Brachla
Creag Nay 376
Gartally
Achmony
Urquhart
Milton
Drumnadrochit
Loch Ness Monster Exhibition Centre
Lewiston
Strone
Urquhart Castle
Glen Coiltie
Lenie
Bunloit
Balbeg
Grotaig
Inverfarigaig
Farigaig Forest Trail & Visitor Centre
Ault-na-goire
Errogie
Easter Boleskine
Dhuhallow
Foyers
Lyne of Gorthleck
Farraline
Wester Aberchalder
Lochgarthside
Loch Mhòr
Bailebeag
Loch Kemp
Whitebridge
Easter Drummond
Stratherrick
Glen Brein
Loch Killin
General Wade's Military Road
Dochgarroch
Kirkton
Loch Dochfour
Lochend
Strath Dores
Tor Point
Dores
Ashie Moor
Tom Bailgeann 464
Achnabat
Whitefield
Torness
Abersky
Scaniport
Essich
Loch Ashie
Creag a' Chlachain 365
Loch Duntelchaig
Stac na Cathaig 446
Tullich
Loch Ruthven
East Croachy
Aberarder Ho.
Newton of Leys
Daviot
Craggie
Mains of Faillie
Scatraig
Balnafoich
Tombreck
Dalvourn
Tordarroch
Farr
Farr Ho.
Gaich
Strathnairn
Brinmore
Meall Mòr 492
Carn na h-Easgainn 616
Beinn Bhreac 511
Carn na Tri-tighearnan 615
Meall a' Bhreacraibh 551
Moy
Loch Moy
Ruthven
Invereen
Inverbrough
Tomatin Distillery
Tomatin
Findhorn Bridge
Beinn Bhreac 601
Woodend
Clune
Corrievorrie
Glen Kyllachy
Carn Glac an Eich 631
Carn na Saobhaidh 714
Aonach Odhar 642
Glen Mazeran
Daltomach
Carn Phris Mhòir 618
Beinn Bhuidhe 711
Carn Ghriogair 805
Beinn Bhreac Mhòr 807
Beinn Dubhcharaidh 689
Carn Dubh'Ic an Deoir 750
Dalmigavie
Strath Dearn
Carn Odhar 802
Carn Caol 713
Eil
Caggan
Carn na Saobhaidhe 811
Carn Coire na h-Easgainn 790
Cnoc Fraing 745
A N D
Coignafearn Forest
Carn Fliuch-bhaid 656
Doire Meurach 787
Carn na Laraiche Maoile 809
Carn Icean Duibhe 808
Carn Dulnan 729
MONADHLIATH MOUNTAINS
Carn a' Choire Ghlaise 779
Burrach Mòr 828
Carn Coire na h-Creiche 826
Carn Sgulain 812
708
A'Bhuidheanaich 729
Meall a' Chocaire 715
Carn an Fhreiceadain 878
An Suidh 541
Coire Odhar
Glen Markie
Sgaraman nam Fiadh 858
Carn Easgann Bana 778
Carn Sgulain 920
Highland Wildlife Park
A9–TO AVIEMORE
A'Chailleach 930
Creag Dhubh 786
Creag Bhlag 527
Balavil
Carn Ban 942
Carn Dearg 945
Cairn Ewen 875
Loch Gynack
Lynchat
Insh
Inveruglass
Meall na h-Aisre 862
Creag an Loin 547
Highland Folk Mus
Kingussie
Ruthven Barracks
Ruthven
Drumguish
Carn an Leth-choin 843
Clan Macpherson House & Mus
Newtonmore
Geal Charn 926
Beinn a' Chrasgain 828
Dalballoch
Biallaid
Killiehuntly
Creag Mhòr 764
834
Marg na Craige
Glen Banchor
Creag Dhubh
Creag nam Bodach
Glen Tromie
Meal Buidhe 628
Melgarve
Standing Stone
1386
Garvamore
Crathie
Blargie
Laggan
Balgowan
Lynaberack
Sherramore
Catlodge
Falls of Truim
Phones
Garbh Mheall Mòr
Etteridge
Cruban Beag 590
Black Craig 565
Carn Liath 1006
Comra
Meallach Mòr 768
Carn Dearg Mòr 857
Coille Coire
A86–TO SPEAN BRIDGE
A889,A9–TO PITLOCHRY
1
2
3
4
5

310

300

Newtonmore: *The Spey valley is the heartland of the sport of Shinty. The advantages of being double-handed in the sport have led to the area having allegedly the highest proportion of left-handed golfers in the country: about half of the members of Newtonmore Golf Club play left-handed, and it regularly hosts the Scottish left-handed golf championships.* ***Map ref. G5***

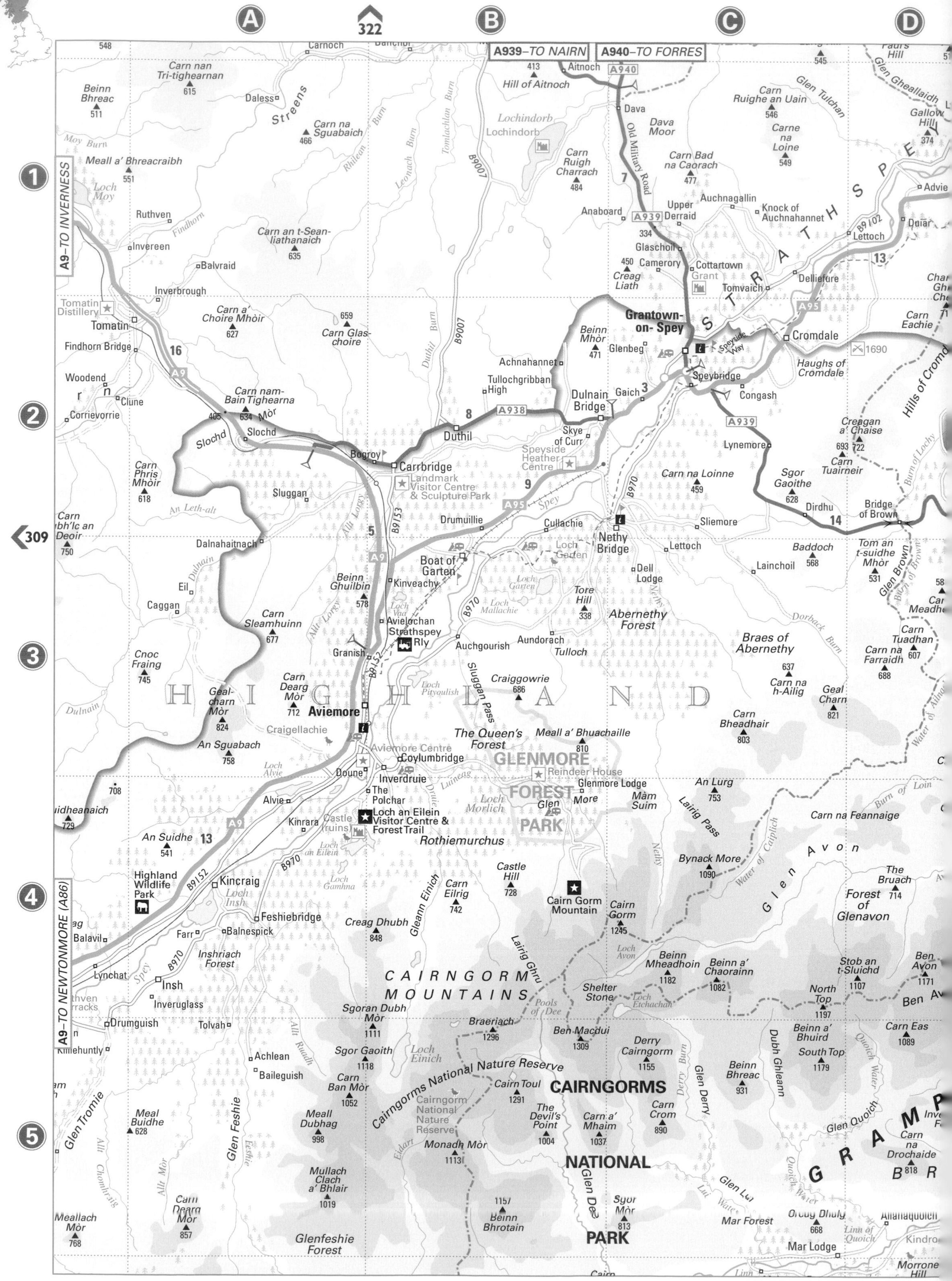

322

A B C D

1 2 3 4 5

A939–TO NAIRN
A940–TO FORRES
A9–TO INVERNESS
A9–TO NEWTONMORE (A86)

Carnoch
Carn nan Tri-tighearnan 615
Beinn Bhreac 511
Daless
Streens
Carn na Sguabaich 466
Moy Burn
Meall a' Bhreacraibh 551
Loch Moy
Ruthven
Findhorn
Invereen
Balvraid
Carn an t-Sean-liathanaich 635
Inverbrough
Tomatin Distillery
Tomatin
Findhorn Bridge
Carn a' Choire Mhòir 627
Carn Glas-choire 659
16
Woodend
Clune
Corrievorrie
Carn nam-Bain Tighearna 634
Slochd 405
Slochd Mòr
Carn Phris Mhòir 618
Sluggan
An Leth-allt
Carn Dubh'Ic an Deoir 750
Dalnahaitnach
Dulnain
Eil
Caggan
Carn Sleamhuinn 677
Cnoc Fraing 745
Geal-charn Mòr 824
An Sguabach 758
Craigellachie
708
Alvie
Uidheanaich 729
An Suidhe 541
13
Highland Wildlife Park
Kincraig
Loch Insh
Feshiebridge
Balavil
Farr
Balnespick
Inshriach Forest
Lynchat
Insh
Inveruglass
Ruthven Barracks
Drumguish
Tolvah
Kingussie
Achlean
Baileguish
Glen Tromie
Meal Buidhe 628
Glen Feshie
Allt Mòr
Carn Dearg Mòr 857
Meallach Mòr 768
Glenfeshie Forest

Hill of Aitnoch 413
Aitnoch
Lochindorb
Carn Ruigh Charrach 484
B9007
Tomlachlan Burn
Leonach Burn
Rhilean Burn
Duthil Burn
Achnahannet
Tullochgribban High
A938
8
Duthil
Bogroy
Carrbridge
Landmark Visitor Centre & Sculpture Park
Drumuillie
Boat of Garten
Beinn Ghuilbin 578
Kinveachy
Avielochan
Strathspey Rly
Granish
Loch Vaa
B9153
5
A9
B9152
Carn Dearg Mòr 712
Aviemore
Aviemore Centre
Coylumbridge
Doune
Inverdruie
The Polchar
Loch an Eilein Visitor Centre & Forest Trail
Kinrara
Castle (ruins)
Rothiemurchus
B970
Loch Gamhna
Creag Dhubh 848
Gleann Einich
Carn Eilrig 742
Sgoran Dubh Mòr 1111
Sgor Gaoith 1118
Loch Einich
Carn Ban Mòr 1052
Meall Dubhag 998
Mullach Clach a' Bhlair 1019
Cairngorms National Nature Reserve
Monadh Mòr 1113
Eidart
Beinn Bhrotain 1157

H I G H L A N D

Old Military Road
7
Dava
Dava Moor
Carn Bad na Caorach 477
Anaboard
A939
Upper Derraid
Auchnagallin
Knock of Auchnahannet
334
Glaschoil
450 Creag Liath
Camerory
Cottartown
Castle Grant
Tomvaich
Grantown-on-Spey
Beinn Mhòr 471
Glenbeg
Speyside Way
Speybridge
Congash
Dulnain Bridge
Gaich
3
Skye of Curr
Speyside Heather Centre
9
A95
Spey
Cullachie
Nethy Bridge
Loch Garten
Loch Mallachie
Dell Lodge
Tore Hill 338
Abernethy Forest
Auchgourish
Aundorach
Tulloch
Sluggan Pass
Craiggowrie 686
Loch Pityoulish
The Queen's Forest
Meall a' Bhuachaille 810
GLENMORE FOREST PARK
Reindeer House
Glenmore Lodge
Glen More
Loch Morlich
Luineag
Druie
Castle Hill 728
Cairn Gorm Mountain
Cairn Gorm 1245
Loch Avon
Lairig Ghru
C A I R N G O R M
M O U N T A I N S
Pools of Dee
Braeriach 1296
Ben Macdui 1309
Shelter Stone
Loch Etchachan
Derry Cairngorm 1155
Cairn Toul 1291
The Devil's Point 1004
Carn a' Mhaim 1037
CAIRNGORMS NATIONAL PARK
Glen Dee
Sgor Mòr 813
Mâm Suim
Lairig Pass
Nethy
Bynack More 1090
Beinn Mheadhoin 1182
Beinn a' Chaorainn 1082
Derry Burn
Glen Derry
Carn Crom 890
Glen Lui
Mar Forest
Lui Water

Carn Ruighe an Uain 546
545
Glen Tulchan
Carne na Loine 549
Strathspey
Advie
B9102
Lettoch
13
Dellefure
Cromdale
A95
1690
Haughs of Cromdale
Hills of Cromdale
A939
Lynemore
Carn na Loinne 459
Creagan a' Chaise 722 693
Sgor Gaoithe 628
Carn Tuairneir
Dirdhu
14
Bridge of Brown
Sliemore
Lettoch
Baddoch 568
Lainchoil
Tom an t-suidhe Mhòr 531
Glen Brown
Burn of Brown
Dorback Burn
Braes of Abernethy
637
Carn na h-Ailig
Carn Tuadhan
Carn na Farraidh 688 607
Geal Charn 821
Carn Bheadhair 803
Water of Ailnack
An Lurg 753
Burn of Loin
Carn na Feannaige
Water of Caiplich
Glen Avon
The Bruach 714
Forest of Glenavon
Stob an t-Sluichd 1107
Ben Avon 1171
North Top 1197
Carn Eas 1089
Beinn a' Bhuird
South Top 1179
Dubh Ghleann
Quoich Water
Beinn Bhreac 931
Glen Quoich
Carn na Drochaide 818
G R A M P
Creag Bhalg 668
Linn of Quoich
Allanaquoich
Mar Lodge
Morrone Hill
Kindrochit

309

Findhorn: *One of the best fishing rivers in Scotland, famous for its salmon and trout. It is said that 360 salmon were caught here in one day from a single pool.* **Map ref. A1**

301

Cairngorms: *Home of Britain's biggest Ski Centre with 28 runs and over 22 miles (35km) of pist…* **Map ref. B4**

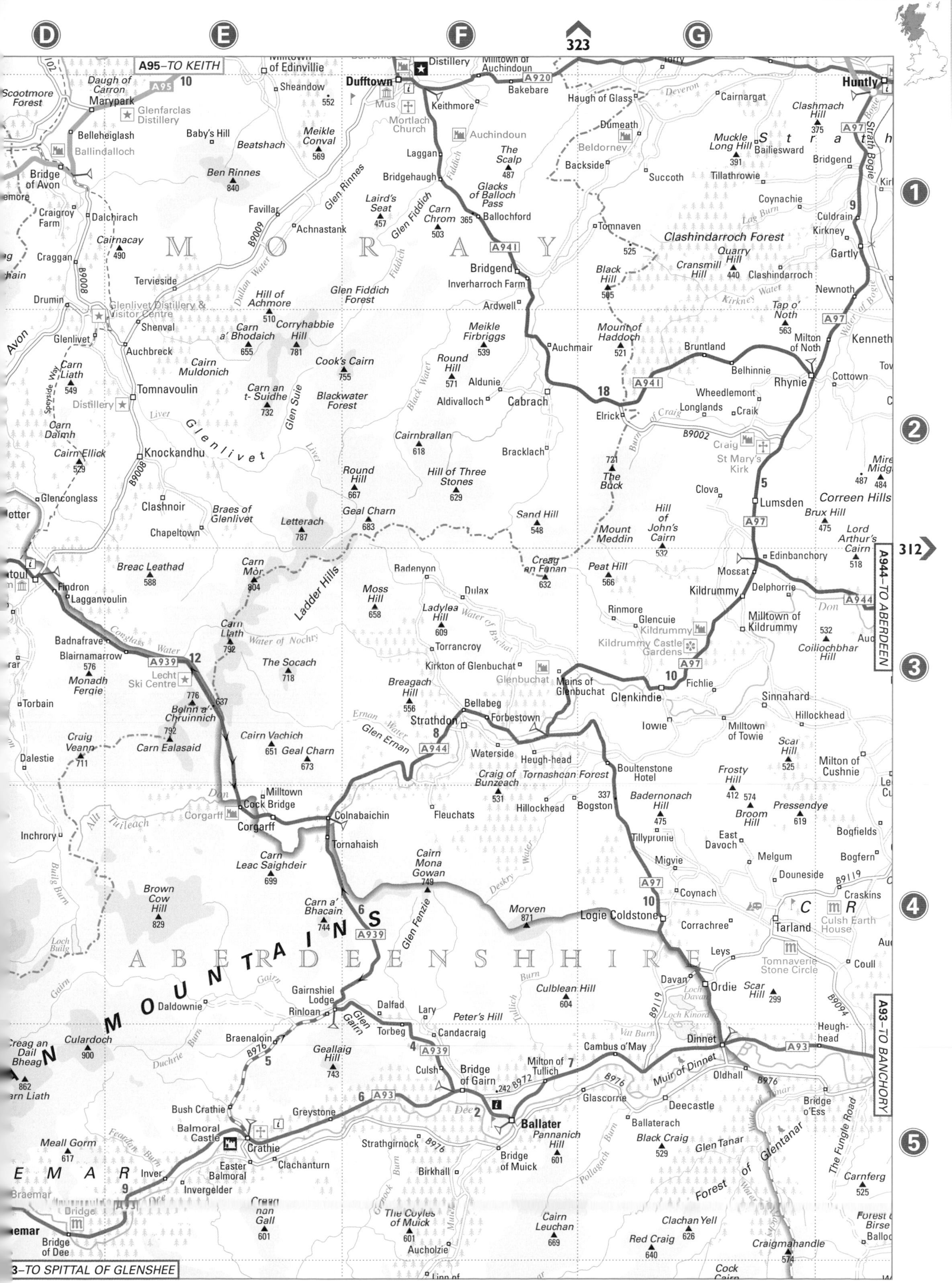

Tomintoul: *At a height of 1160 feet (354m) this claims to be the highest village in the Scottish Highlands. The A939 from here across the Lecht pass to Cock Bridge (**Map ref. E4**) is frequently closed in winter.* ***Map ref. D3***

302

Braemar: *Location of the most famous of the Highland Games. The Braemar Gathering has a history going back almost 1,000 years and is always held on the first Saturday in September.* ***Map ref. D5***

Dufftown: *With seven separate whisky distilleries, the earliest of which dates back to 1823, Dufftown is described as the Malt Whisky Capital of Scotland.* ***Map ref. F1***

A
B
C
D
324
A96–TO ELGIN
A947–TO BANFF
Huntly
Drumblade
Corse
Auchterless
Backhill
Fyvie Castle (NTS)
Fyvie
Woodhead
Strathbogie
Clashmach Hill
Mosshead
Brideswell
Slioch
Beggshill
Ythanwells
Logie Newton
Badenscoth
Gordonstown
Rothiebrisbane
Thomastown
Denend
Millburn
Redhill
Blackford
Rothienorman
Petty
Greenmyre
Bailiesward
Bridgend
Kirkstile
Winds Eye
Bainshole
Hill of Tillymorgan
Fisherford
Coynachie
Culdrain
Kirkney
Gartly
Backburn
Wishach Hill
Glens of Foudland
Hill of Foudland
Skares
Kirkton of Culsalmond
Colpy
Cairnhill
Newseat
Folla Rule
Springleys
St Katherines
Cromblet
Barthol Chapel
South Flobbets
Core Hill
The Banking
Silvermoss
Cross of Jackston
Balgove
South Blackbog
Jackstown
Tulloch
Tocher
Meikle Wartle
Pitinnan
Clashindarroch
Knockandy Hill
Cults
Largie
Wrangham
Bonnyton
Kirkton of Rayne
Newnoth
Leith Hall (NTS)
Slack
Wardhouse
Tap o' Noth
Picardy Stone
Upper Boddam
Loanhead Stone Circle
Mounie Castle
Glengarioch Distillery
Forman
Milton of Noth
Kennethmont
B9002
Glanderston
Aulton
Greenhall
Old Rayne
Mains of Glack
Daviot
Whitefield
Fingask
Oldmeldrum
Rhynie
Cottown
Towie
Ardlair
Duncanston
Hill of Christ's Kirk
Christskirk
Rothney
Insch
Ardoyne
Westhall
Durno
Whiteford
Pitcaple
Milton of Inveramsay
Hill of Barra
Mill of Kingoodie
Clatt
New Leslie
Old Leslie
Leslie
Kirkton
Ryehill
Oyne
Auchleven
Garioch
Archaeolink Prehistory Park
Pittodrie Ho.
Maiden Stone
Chapel of Garioch
Balhalgardy
Kirkton of Bourtie
Hillbrae
Mire of Midgates
Whitehaugh Forest
Suie Hill
Knock Saul
Millburn
Muckletown
Black Hill
Bennachie
Mither Tap
Newmill
Inverurie
Lumsden
Correen Hills
Brux Hill
Lord Arthur's Cairn
Tepersie Castle
Old Military Road
Redhouse
Glenton
Millstone Hill
Easter Aquorthies Stone Circle
ABERDEENSHIRE
311
Edinbanchory
Tullynessle
Keig
Woodend
Bograxie
Kemnay Forest
Burnhervie
Port Elphinstone
Balbithan
Kinkell Church
Kinmuck
Delphorrie
Grampian Transport Mus
Montgarrie
Rorandle
Overton
Thainstone
Tavelty
Milltown of Kildrummy
Bridge of Alford
Haughton House
Bankhead
Cairn William
Pitfichie
Grantlodge
Dalmadilly
Clovenstone
Fetternear Ho.
Balbithan
Wester Fintray
Coiliochbhar Hill
Auchintoul
Alford
Howe of Alford
Gateside
Pitfichie Forest
Pitmunie
Monymusk
Kemnay
Cottown
Kintore
Asloun
Dorsell
Kingsford
Whitehouse
Todlachie
Craigearn
Leschangie
Denhead
Sinnahard
Hillockhead
Bridgeton
Kirkton
Lauchintilly
Castle Fraser (NTS)
Leylodge
Kinellar
Ley
Muir of Fowlis
Tillyfourie
Black Hill
Tillycairn Castle
Burnside
Blackburn
Scar Hill
Milton of Cushnie
Muirhead
Ardgowse
Little Ley
Sauchen
Achath
Lyne of Skene
Blackchambers
Leochel-Cushnie
Craigievar Castle (NTS)
Tillyfour
Corrennie Forest
Ordhead
Mains of Linton
Dunecht
Clinterty
Pressendye
Corrennie Moor
Benaquhallie
Shiels
Old Kinnernie
Auchronie
Kintocher
Corsindae
Lyne
Bogfields
Barmekin Hill
Loch of Skene
Kirkton of Skene
Elrick
Melgum
Bogfern
Oldmill
Tullochvenus
Bankhead
Comers
Tillybirloch
Douneside
Collmuir
Craiglich
Glenshalg
Perkhill
Drumlasie
Echt
Garlogie
Cairnie
Craskins
Tornaveen
Auchorrie
Midmar Forest
South Kirkton
Lapidary Workshops
Wester Ord
Tarland
CROMAR
Wartle
Lumphanan
East Learney
Redhill
Cullerlie Stone Circle
Cairnbeathie
Cullerlie Stone Circle
Culsh Earth House
Milton of Auchinhove
Peel Ring
Hill of Fare
Landerberry
Benthoul
Tomnaverie Stone Circle
Coull
The Birks
Milton of Cullerlie
Torphins
Craigmyle Ho.
Hardgate
Craigton
Mortlich
Kincardine O'Neil
Mid Beltie
Milton of Campfield
Raemoir Ho.
Hirn
Glashmore
Drum Castle (NTS)
Peterculter
A93–TO BALLATER
Heugh-head
Rosehill
Aboyne
Glassel
Kennerty
Brathens
Drumoak
Mains of Drum
Tillydrine
Myrebird
Cordach
Backhill of Trustach
East Mains
Upper Lochton
Crathes Castle (NTS)
The Neuk
West Park
Craiglug
Birsemore
Birse
Potarch
Allancreich
Bridge of Canny
Inchmarlo
Banchory
Crathes
Upper Muirskie
Bridge o'Ess
Kirkton of Durris
Denside
Balfour
Ballogie
Marywell
Tom's Cairn
Blackhall Forest
Hill of Goauch
Bridge of Dee
Auchattie
Bridge of Feugh
Glen Tanar
The Fungle Road
Carnferg
Glencat
Finzean
Baulds
Scolty
Invery Ho.
Crossroads
Durris Forest
Borrowfield
Lamahip
Drumhead
Whitestone
Blackness
Strachan
Blairydryne
Darnford
Cairn-mon-earn
Meikle Carewe Hill
Forest of Birse
Ballochan
Percie
Water of Feugh
Bridge of Bogendreip
Westerton
Craigmahandle
Greendams
Craig of Dalfro
Mongour
A957–TO STONEHAVEN
Union
303

Huntly: *George MacDonald, novelist, poet and preacher was born here in 1824. His works of fantasy and fairy tales are said to have influenced the work of J R R Tolkien and C S Lewis. He died in Italy in 1905.* ***Map ref.*** ***A1***

Tillyfour: *In the 1820s William McCombie and others in this area perfected the breeding of the 'Aberdeen Angus' which is acknowledged as one of the best cattle breeds in the world.* ***Map ref. A3***

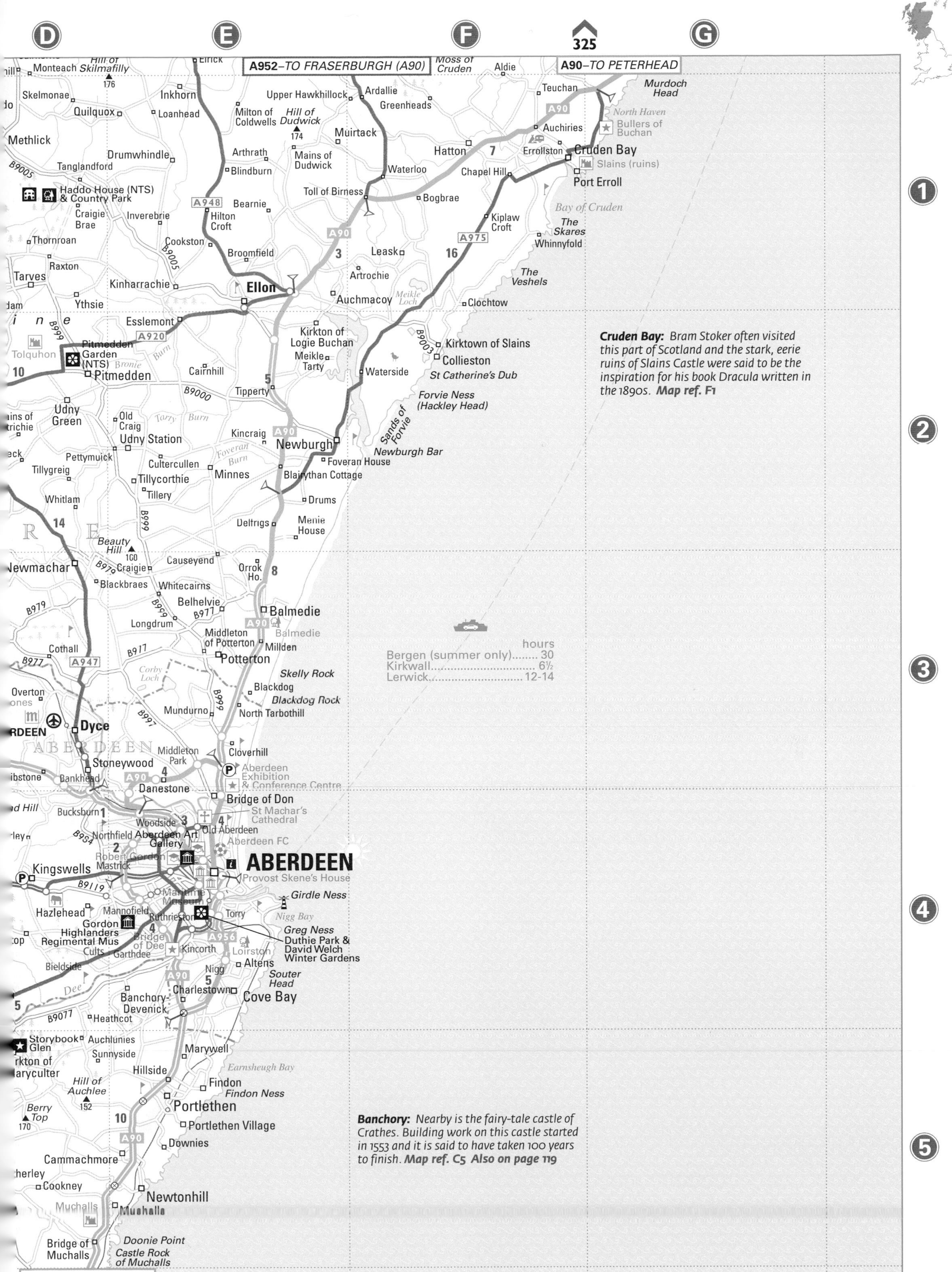
D
E
F
G
325
1
2
3
4
5
A952–TO FRASERBURGH (A90)
A90–TO PETERHEAD
A90–TO STONEHAVEN
Monteach
Skelmonae
Quilquox
Inkhorn
Loanhead
Methlick
Tanglandford
Drumwhindle
Haddo House (NTS) & Country Park
Craigie Brae
Inverebrie
Thornroan
Raxton
Tarves
Kinharrachie
Ythsie
Esslemont
Tolquhon
Pitmedden Garden (NTS)
Pitmedden
Udny Green
Old Craig
Udny Station
Pettymuick
Tillygreig
Whitlam
Newmachar
Upper Hawkhillock
Ardallie
Greenheads
Moss of Cruden
Aldie
Teuchan
Murdoch Head
Milton of Coldwells
Hill of Dudwick
Muirtack
North Haven
Bullers of Buchan
Auchiries
Arthrath
Mains of Dudwick
Hatton
Errollston
Cruden Bay
Slains (ruins)
Port Erroll
Blindburn
Waterloo
Chapel Hill
Toll of Birness
Bogbrae
Bearnie
Hilton Croft
Cookston
Broomfield
Leask
Kiplaw Croft
Bay of Cruden
The Skares
Whinnyfold
Artrochie
Ellon
Auchmacoy
Meikle Loch
The Veshels
Clochtow
Kirkton of Logie Buchan
Meikle Tarty
Kirktown of Slains
Collieston
St Catherine's Dub
Waterside
Forvie Ness (Hackley Head)
Sands of Forvie
Newburgh Bar
Cairnhill
Tipperty
Kincraig
Newburgh
Foveran House
Blairythan Cottage
Cultercullen
Tillycorthie
Tillery
Minnes
Drums
Delfrigs
Menie House
Cruden Bay: Bram Stoker often visited this part of Scotland and the stark, eerie ruins of Slains Castle were said to be the inspiration for his book Dracula written in the 1890s. Map ref. F1
Beauty Hill
Craigie
Causeyend
Orrok Ho.
Blackbraes
Whitecairns
Belhelvie
Balmedie
Longdrum
Cothall
Middleton of Potterton
Milden
Potterton
Skelly Rock
Blackdog
Blackdog Rock
North Tarbothill
Mundurno
Overton
Dyce
Corby Loch
hours
Bergen (summer only)........ 30
Kirkwall.............................. 6½
Lerwick.............................. 12-14
ABERDEEN
Stoneywood
Middleton Park
Cloverhill
Aberdeen Exhibition & Conference Centre
Bankhead
Danestone
Bridge of Don
St Machar's Cathedral
Bucksburn
Woodside
Old Aberdeen
Aberdeen FC
Northfield
Aberdeen Art Gallery
Robert Gordon
Mastrick
Kingswells
ABERDEEN
Provost Skene's House
Girdle Ness
Hazlehead
Mannofield
Torry
Nigg Bay
Gordon Highlanders Regimental Mus
Ruthrieston
Greg Ness
Duthie Park & David Welch Winter Gardens
Bridge of Dee
Kincorth
Loirston
Altens
Cults
Garthdee
Bieldside
Nigg
Souter Head
Charlestown
Cove Bay
Banchory-Devenick
Heathcot
Storybook Glen
Auchlunies
Sunnyside
Maryculter
Marywell
Earnsheugh Bay
Hillside
Findon
Findon Ness
Hill of Auchlee
Portlethen
Berry Top
Portlethen Village
Downies
Banchory: Nearby is the fairy-tale castle of Crathes. Building work on this castle started in 1553 and it is said to have taken 100 years to finish. Map ref. C5 Also on page 119
Cammachmore
Cookney
Newtonhill
Muchalls
Bridge of Muchalls
Doonie Point
Castle Rock of Muchalls

Kemnay: Famous for its magnificent silver-grey granite which was quarried here for generations before the main quarry closed in 1960. Kemnay granite was used in building many of the bridges over the River Thames. *Map ref. C3*

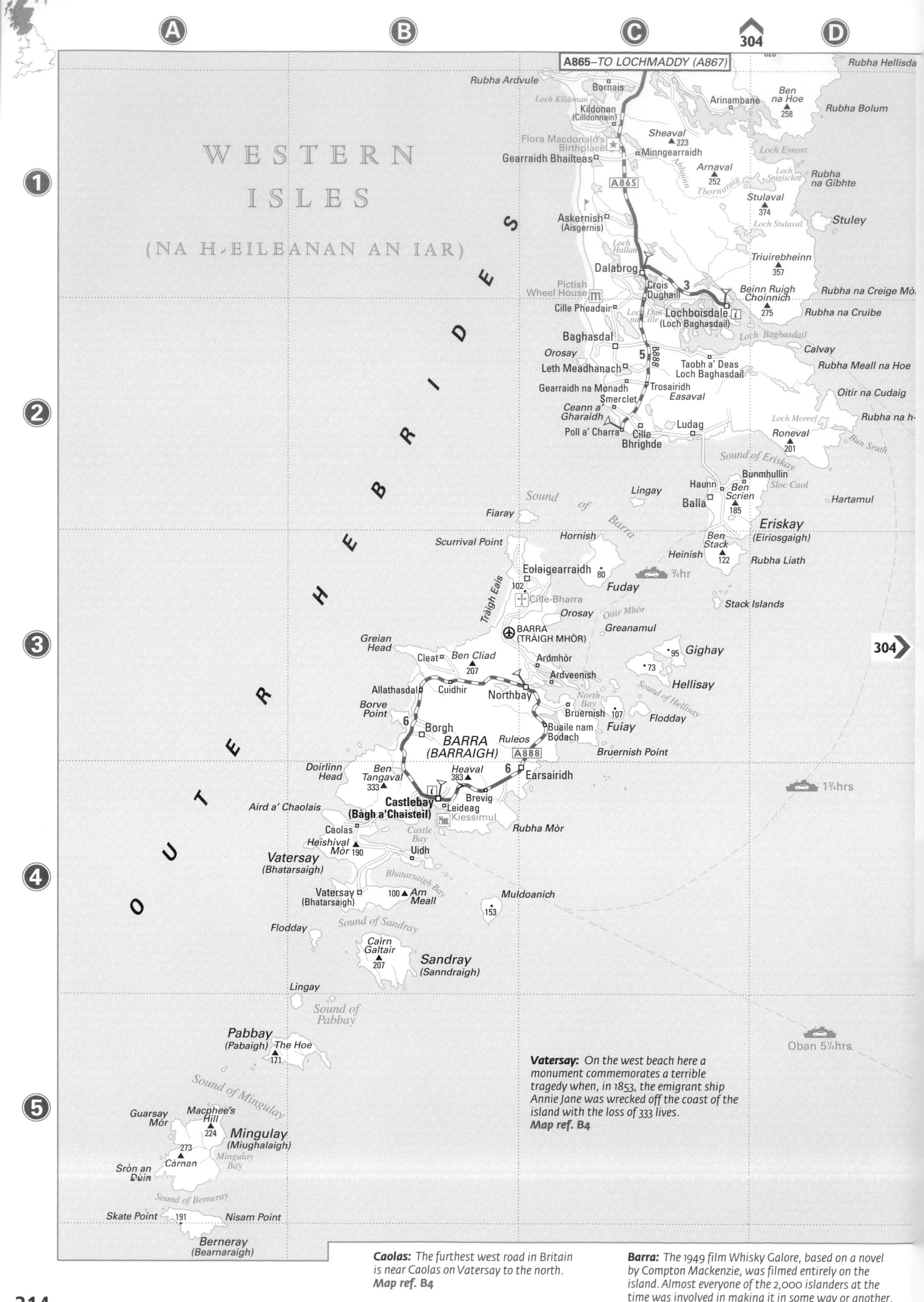

A
B
C
304
D
1
2
3
4
5
A865–TO LOCHMADDY (A867)
WESTERN ISLES
(NA H-EILEANAN AN IAR)
OUTER HEBRIDES
Rubha Ardvule
Bornais
Loch Kildonan
Kildonan (Cilldonnain)
Arinambane
Ben na Hoe 258
Rubha Hellisda
Rubha Bolum
Flora Macdonald's Birthplace
Sheaval 223
Gearraidh Bhailteas
Minngearraidh
Loch Eynort
Arnaval 252
Abhainn Thornaraig
Loch Snigisclett
Rubha na Gibhte
A865
Stulaval 374
Loch Stulaval
Askernish (Aisgernis)
Stuley
Loch Hallan
Triuirebheinn 357
Dalabrog
Pictish Wheel House
Crois Dughaill
3
Beinn Ruigh Choinnich 275
Rubha na Creige Mò
Cille Pheadair
Loch Dun na Cille
Lochboisdale (Loch Baghasdail)
Rubha na Cruibe
Baghasdal
Loch Baghasdail
Orosay
5
B888
Calvay
Leth Meadhanach
Taobh a' Deas Loch Baghasdail
Rubha Meall na Hoe
Gearraidh na Monadh
Trosairidh
Smerclet
Easaval
Oitir na Cudaig
Ceann a' Gharaidh
Loch Moreef
Rubha na h-
Poll a' Charra
Cille Bhrighde
Ludag
Roneval 201
Bun Sruth
Sound of Eriskay
Bunmhullin
Sloc Caol
Haunn
Ben Scrien 185
Lingay
Balla
Hartamul
Sound of Barra
Fiaray
Eriskay (Eiriosgaigh)
Hornish
Ben Stack 122
Scurrival Point
Heinish
Rubha Liath
Eolaigearraidh
80
¾hr
Fuday
102
Cille-Bharra
Tràigh Eais
Stack Islands
Orosay
Oitir Mhòr
BARRA (TRÀIGH MHÒR)
Greanamul
Greian Head
Gighay 95
304
Cleat
Ben Cliad 207
Ardmhòr
73
Hellisay
Ardveenish
Allathasdal
Cuidhir
Northbay
North Bay
Sound of Hellisay
Borve Point
Bruernish
107
Flodday
6
Borgh
Buaile nam Bodach
Fuiay
BARRA (BARRAIGH)
Ruleos
A888
Bruernish Point
Doirlinn Head
Ben Tangaval 333
Heaval 383
6
Earsairidh
1¾hrs
Brevig
Castlebay (Bàgh a'Chaisteil)
Leideag
Aird a' Chaolais
Kiessimul
Rubha Mòr
Caolas
Castle Bay
Heishival Mòr 190
Uidh
Vatersay (Bhatarsaigh)
Bhatarsaigh Bay
Vatersay (Bhatarsaigh)
100 Am Meall
Muldoanich
153
Sound of Sandray
Flodday
Cairn Galtair 207
Sandray (Sanndraigh)
Lingay
Sound of Pabbay
Oban 5¼hrs
Pabbay (Pabaigh)
The Hoe 171
Sound of Mingulay
Guarsay Mòr
Macphee's Hill 224
Mingulay (Miughalaigh)
273 Càrnan
Mingulay Bay
Sròn an Dùin
Sound of Berneray
Skate Point
191
Nisam Point
Berneray (Bearnaraigh)

Vatersay: *On the west beach here a monument commemorates a terrible tragedy when, in 1853, the emigrant ship Annie Jane was wrecked off the coast of the island with the loss of 333 lives.*
Map ref. B4

Caolas: *The furthest west road in Britain is near Caolas on Vatersay to the north.*
Map ref. B4

Barra: *The 1949 film Whisky Galore, based on a novel by Compton Mackenzie, was filmed entirely on the island. Almost everyone of the 2,000 islanders at the time was involved in making it in some way or another.*
Map ref. B3

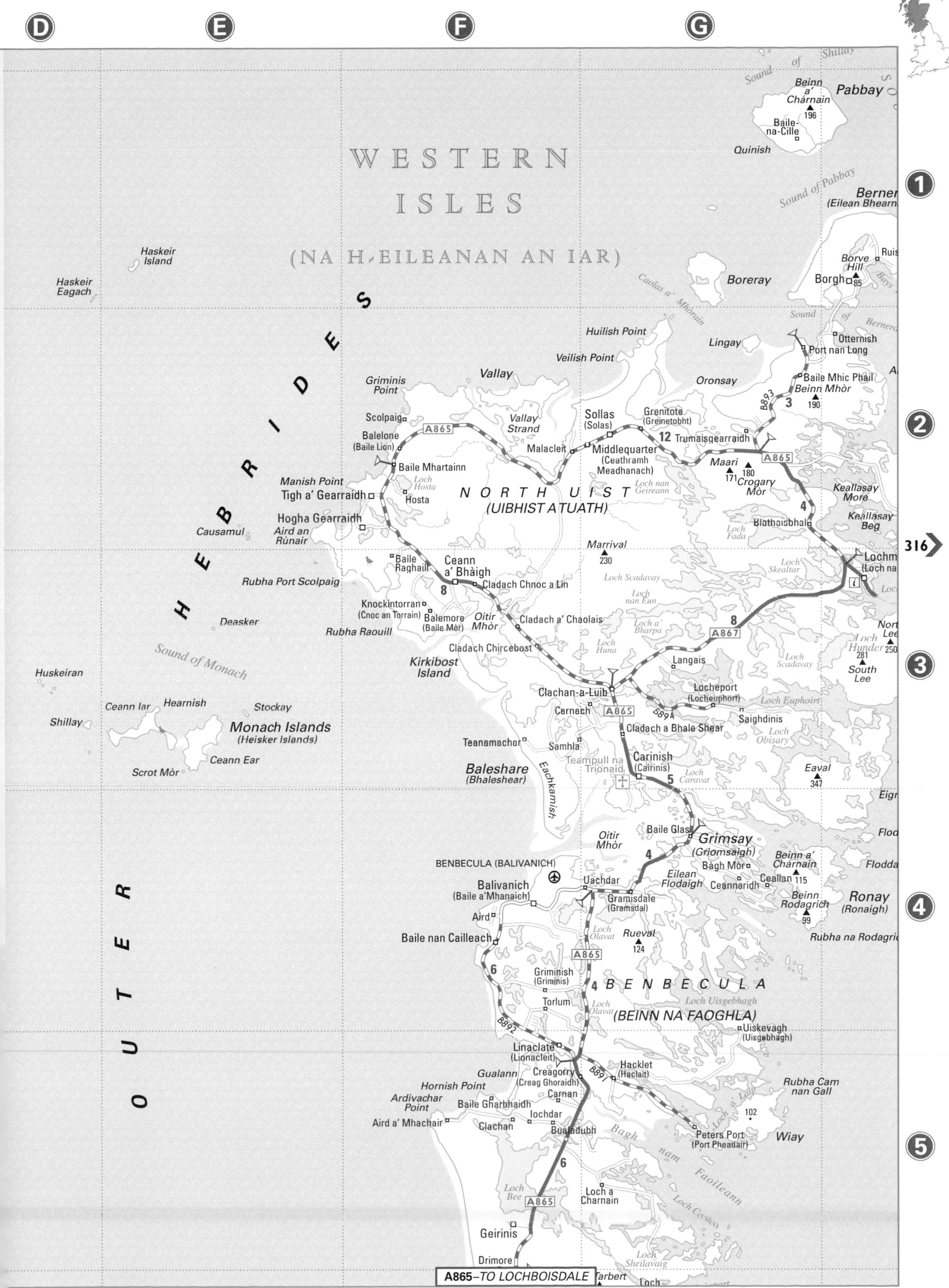

WESTERN ISLES
(NA H-EILEANAN AN IAR)
OUTER HEBRIDES
NORTH UIST
(UIBHIST A TUATH)
BENBECULA
(BEINN NA FAOGHLA)
Monach Islands
(Heisker Islands)
Pabbay
Boreray
Grimsay
(Griomsaigh)
Ronay
(Ronaigh)
Baleshare
(Bhaleshear)
Kirkibost Island
Sound of Monach
Sound of Pabbay
Lochmaddy
Clachan-a-Luib
Balivanich
(Baile a'Mhanaich)
BENBECULA (BALIVANICH)
Sollas
(Solas)
Carinish
(Cairinis)
Creagorry
(Creag Ghoraidh)
Eaval
347
Marrival
230
Rueval
124
A865
A867
A865–TO LOCHBOISDALE
316

Monach Islands: Over 9,000 grey seal pups are born on these islands every year. *Map ref. E3*

304

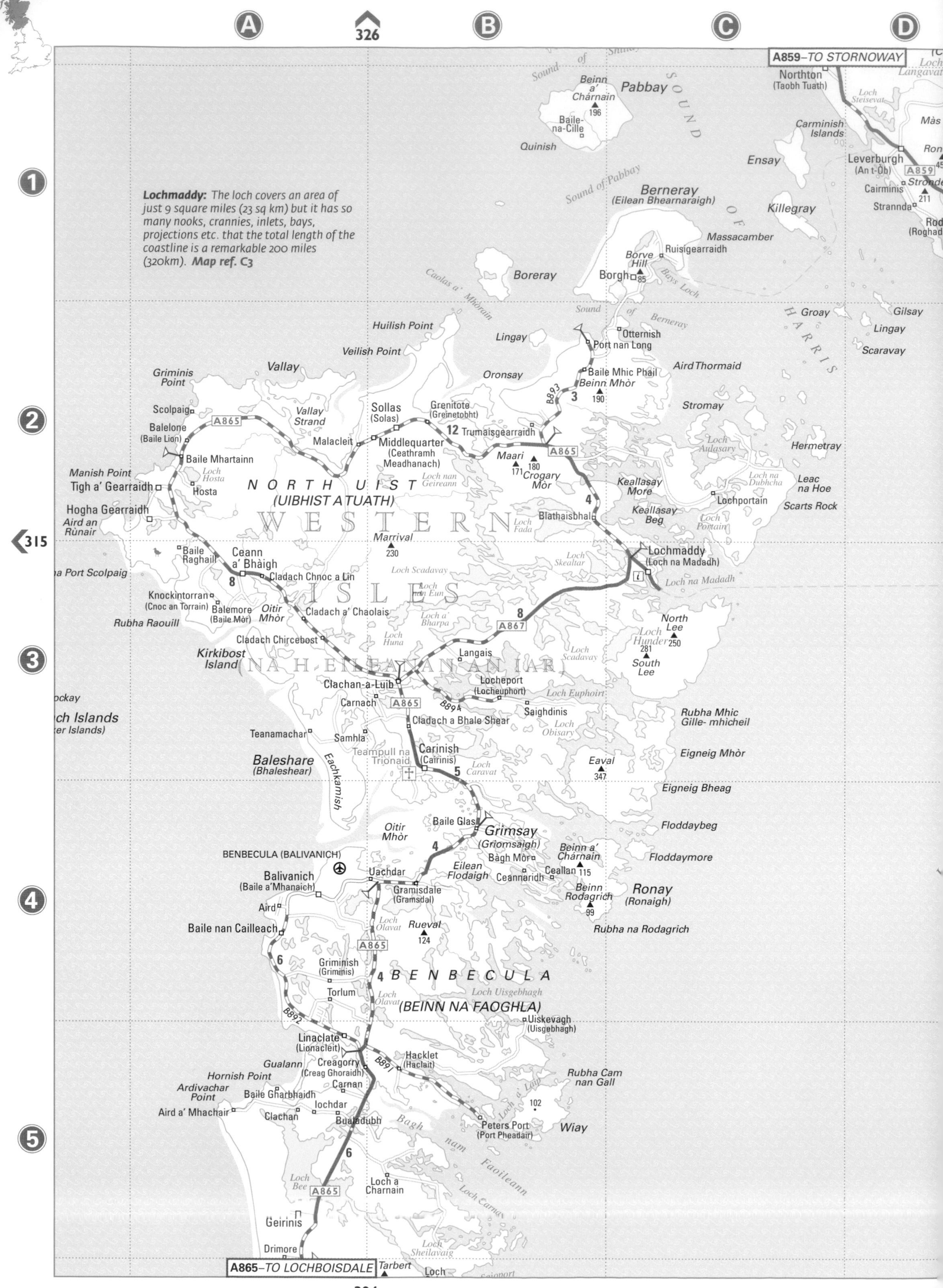
A
B
C
D
326
1
2
3
4
5
315
304
A859–TO STORNOWAY
A865–TO LOCHBOISDALE
Lochmaddy: The loch covers an area of just 9 square miles (23 sq km) but it has so many nooks, crannies, inlets, bays, projections etc. that the total length of the coastline is a remarkable 200 miles (320km). Map ref. C3
Sound of Shillay
Pabbay
Beinn a' Chàrnain
196
Baile-na-Cille
Quinish
SOUND OF HARRIS
Northton
(Taobh Tuath)
Loch Langavat
Loch Steisevat
Màs
Carminish Islands
Ensay
Leverburgh
(An t-Òb)
A859
Rone
Strond
Cairminis
211
Strannda
Rod
(Roghadal)
Sound of Pabbay
Berneray
(Eilean Bhearnaraigh)
Killegray
Massacamber
Ruisigearraidh
Borve Hill
85
Borgh
Bays Loch
Boreray
Caolas a' Mhòrain
Sound of Berneray
Groay
Gilsay
Lingay
Scaravay
Otternish
Port nan Long
Huilish Point
Veilish Point
Lingay
Oronsay
Aird Thormaid
Baile Mhic Phail
Beinn Mhòr
190
B893
3
Griminis Point
Vallay
Vallay Strand
Sollas
(Solas)
Grenitote
(Greinetobht)
12
Trumaisgearraidh
Stromay
Scolpaig
A865
Balelone
(Baile Lion)
Malacleit
Middlequarter
(Ceathramh Meadhanach)
Maari
171
180
Crogary Mòr
A865
Loch Aulasary
Hermetray
Baile Mhartainn
Loch Hosta
Hosta
Manish Point
Tigh a' Gearraidh
NORTH UIST
(UIBHIST A TUATH)
Loch nan Geireann
4
Keallasay More
Keallasay Beg
Loch na Dubhcha
Lochportain
Leac na Hoe
Scarts Rock
Hogha Gearraidh
Aird an Rùnair
WESTERN
Loch Fada
Blathaisbhal
Loch Portain
Marrival
230
Baile Raghaill
Ceann a' Bhàigh
8
Cladach Chnoc a Lin
Loch Scadavay
Loch Skealtar
Lochmaddy
(Loch na Madadh)
Loch na Madadh
na Port Scolpaig
Knockintorran
(Cnoc an Torrain)
Balemore
(Baile Mòr)
Oitir Mhòr
Cladach a' Chaolais
ISLES
Loch an Eun
Loch a' Bharpa
8
A867
North Lee
Loch Hunder
281
250
South Lee
Rubha Raouill
Cladach Chircebost
Loch Huna
Langais
Loch Scadavay
Kirkibost Island
(NA H-EILEANAN AN IAR)
Clachan-a-Luib
Locheport
(Locheuphort)
Loch Euphoirt
ockay
ch Islands
er Islands)
Carnach
A865
B894
Saighdinis
Cladach a Bhale Shear
Rubha Mhic Gille-mhicheil
Teanamachar
Samhla
Loch Obisary
Baleshare
(Bhaleshear)
Teampull na Trionaid
Carinish
(Cairinis)
5
Loch Caravat
Eaval
347
Eigneig Mhòr
Eachkamish
Eigneig Bheag
Baile Glas
Oitir Mhòr
Grimsay
(Griomsaigh)
Floddaybeg
BENBECULA (BALIVANICH)
4
Bàgh Mòr
Beinn a' Chàrnain
115
Floddaymore
Balivanich
(Baile a'Mhanaich)
Uachdar
Eilean Flodaigh
Ceannaridh
Ceallan
Ronay
(Ronaigh)
Gramisdale
(Gramsdal)
Beinn Rodagrich
99
Aird
Loch Olavat
Rueval
124
Rubha na Rodagrich
Baile nan Cailleach
A865
6
Griminish
(Griminis)
4
BENBECULA
Torlum
Loch Uisgebhagh
Loch Olavat
(BEINN NA FAOGHLA)
B892
Uiskevagh
(Uisgebhagh)
Linaclate
(Lionacleit)
Hacklet
(Haclait)
Gualann
Creagorry
(Creag Ghoraidh)
B891
Rubha Cam nan Gall
Hornish Point
Ardivachar Point
Carnan
Loch a' Laip
Baile Gharbhaidh
102
Iochdar
Aird a' Mhachair
Clachan
Bualadubh
Bagh nam Faoileann
Peters Port
(Port Pheadair)
Wiay
6
Loch Bee
A865
Loch a Charnain
Loch Carnan
Geirinis
Drimore
Loch Sheilavaig
Tarbert
Loch

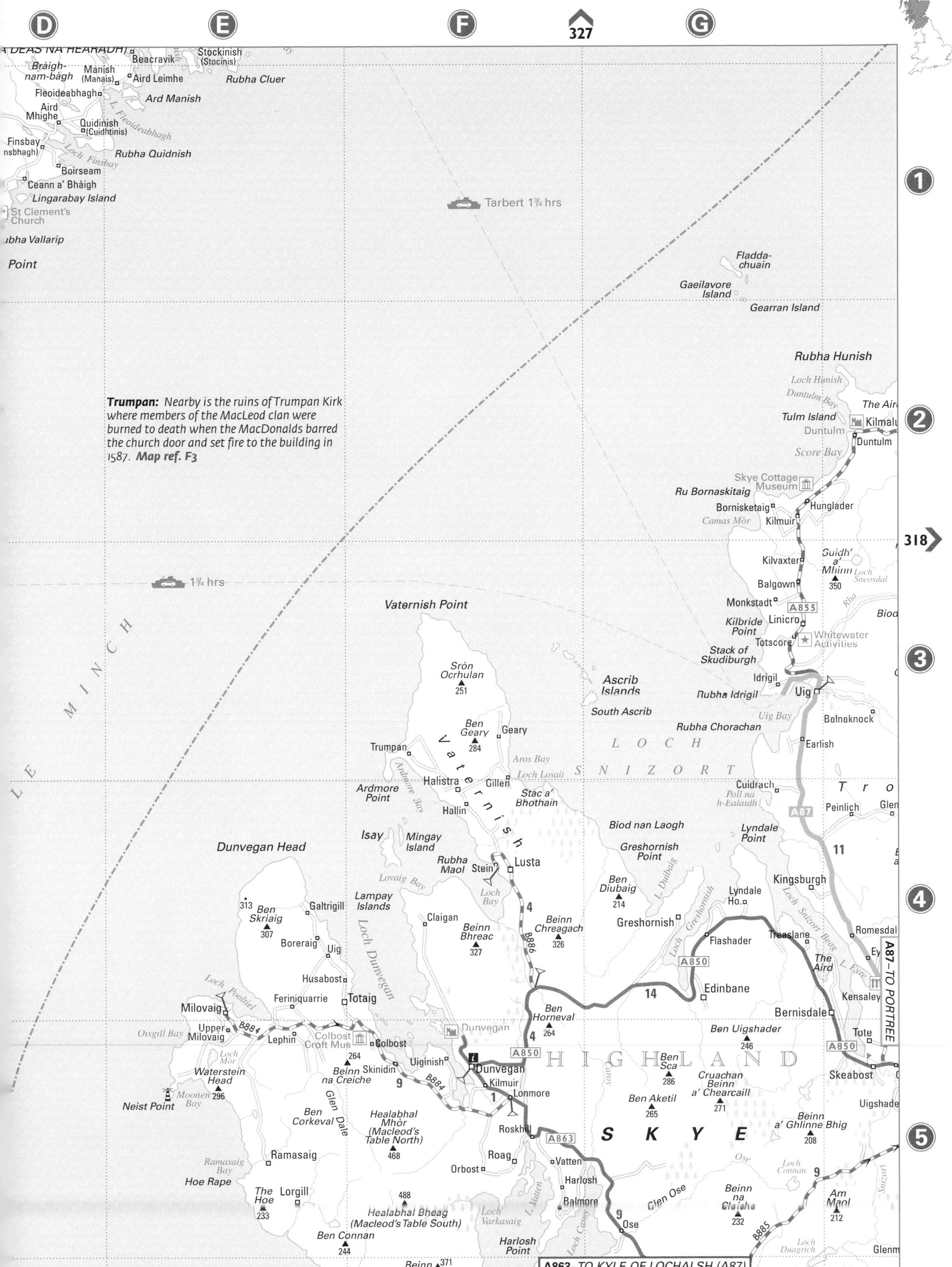

D
E
F
G
327
1
2
3
4
5
318
305
Stockinish (Stocinis)
Beacravik
Bràigh-nam-bàgh
Manish (Manais)
Aird Leimhe
Rubha Cluer
Fleoideabhagh
Ard Manish
Aird Mhighe
Quidinish (Cuidhtinis)
L. Fleoideabhagh
Finsbay
Loch Finsbay
Rubha Quidnish
Boirseam
Ceann a' Bhàigh
Lingarabay Island
St Clement's Church
Point
Tarbert 1¾ hrs
Fladda-chuain
Gaeilavore Island
Gearran Island
Rubha Hunish
Loch Hunish
Duntulm Bay
The Air
Tulm Island
Kilmalu
Duntulm
Score Bay
Trumpan: Nearby is the ruins of Trumpan Kirk where members of the MacLeod clan were burned to death when the MacDonalds barred the church door and set fire to the building in 1587. Map ref. F3
Skye Cottage Museum
Ru Bornaskitaig
Borniskitaig
Hunglader
Camas Mòr
Kilmuir
Guidh' a' Mhinn
Loch Sneosdal
Kilvaxter
Balgown
350
1¾ hrs
Monkstadt
A855
Vaternish Point
Kilbride Point
Linicro
Whitewater Activities
Totscore
Stack of Skudiburgh
Sròn Ocrhulan
251
Ascrib Islands
Idrigil
Rubha Idrigil
Uig
South Ascrib
Uig Bay
Balnaknock
Ben Geary
284
Geary
Rubha Chorachan
Earlish
Trumpan
Aros Bay
LOCH SNIZORT
Vaternish
Loch Losait
Halistra
Gillen
Ardmore Point
Ardmore Bay
Stac a' Bhothain
Cuidrach
Poll na h-Ealaidh
Peinlich
A87
Glen
Hallin
Biod nan Laogh
Lyndale Point
Isay
Mingay Island
Dunvegan Head
Greshornish Point
11
Rubha Maol
Stein
Lusta
Ben Diubaig
Kingsburgh
Lovaig Bay
L. Diubaig
Loch Bay
Lyndale Ho.
Lampay Islands
214
313
Ben Skriaig
Galtrigill
4
Loch Greshornish
Loch Snizort Beag
Claigan
Beinn Chreagach
Greshornish
Romesdal
307
Beinn Bhreac
326
Flashader
Treaslane
Boreraig
Uig
327
B886
The Aird
A87–TO PORTREE
Loch Dunvegan
A850
Edinbane
Husabost
Loch Pooltiel
Kensaley
Feriniquarrie
Totaig
14
Ben Horneval
Bernisdale
Milovaig
B884
264
Dunvegan
Ben Uigshader
Oisgill Bay
Upper Milovaig
Lephin
Colbost Croft Mus
Colbost
A850
246
Tote
Loch Mòr
264
Uiginish
HIGHLAND
Ben Sca
286
Waterstein Head
Beinn na Creiche
Skinidin
Dunvegan
Kilmuir
Cruachan Beinn a' Chearcaill
Skeabost
Moonen Bay
296
9
Lonmore
Neist Point
Glen Dale
1
Ben Aketil
265
271
Uigshade
Ben Corkeval
Healabhal Mhòr (Macleod's Table North)
Roskhill
SKYE
Beinn a' Ghlinne Bhig
468
A863
208
Ramasaig Bay
Ramasaig
Roag
Vatten
Ose
Loch Connan
Orbost
Harlosh
Hoe Rape
The Hoe
Lorgill
488
L. Vatten
Glen Ose
Beinn na Cloiche
Am Maol
233
Healabhal Bheag (Macleod's Table South)
Loch Varkasaig
Balmore
232
212
9
Loch Caroy
Ose
Ben Connan
244
Harlosh Point
B885
Loch Duagrich
Glenm
Beinn na Boineid
371
A863–TO KYLE OF LOCHALSH (A87)
Ben Duagrich

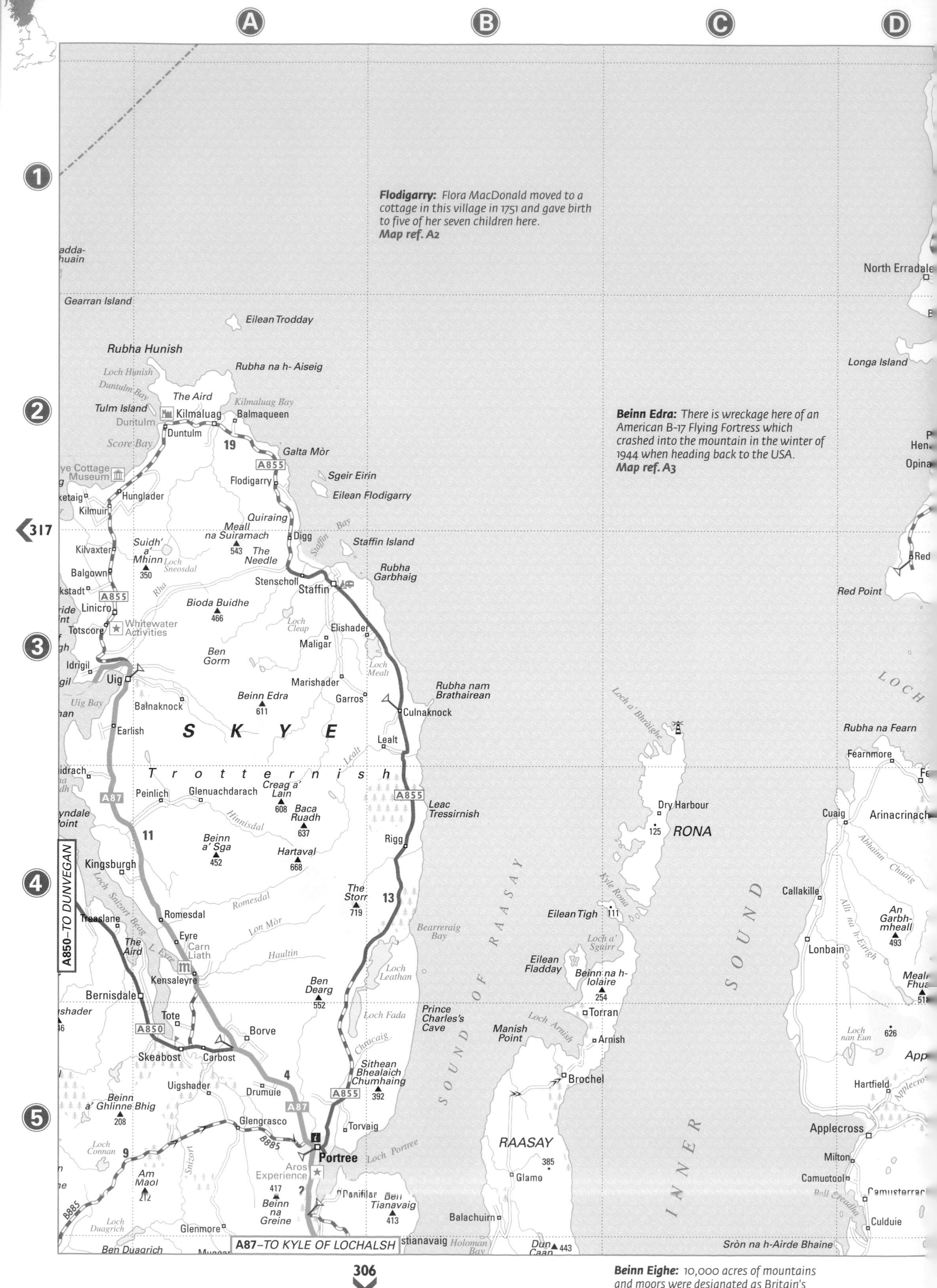
A
B
C
D
1
2
3
4
5
317
306
Flodigarry: Flora MacDonald moved to a cottage in this village in 1751 and gave birth to five of her seven children here.
Map ref. A2
Beinn Edra: There is wreckage here of an American B-17 Flying Fortress which crashed into the mountain in the winter of 1944 when heading back to the USA.
Map ref. A3
North Erradale
Gearran Island
Eilean Trodday
Rubha Hunish
Loch Hunish
Duntulm Bay
Rubha na h- Aiseig
Longa Island
Tulm Island
The Aird
Kilmaluag Bay
Kilmaluag
Balmaqueen
Duntulm
Score Bay
19
Galta Mòr
A855
Flodigarry
Sgeir Eirin
Eilean Flodigarry
Hunglader
Kilmuir
Quiraing
Meall na Suiramach
543
Digg
Staffin Bay
Staffin Island
Suidh' a' Mhinn
350
Loch Sneosdal
The Needle
Kilvaxter
Balgown
Rubha Garbhaig
Red Point
Stenscholl
Staffin
A855
Linicro
Bioda Buidhe
466
Rha
Whitewater Activities
Totscore
Loch Cleap
Elishader
Maligar
Ben Gorm
Idrigil
Uig
Loch Mealt
Marishader
Rubha nam Brathairean
Uig Bay
Balnaknock
Beinn Edra
611
Garros
Culnaknock
Loch a' Bhràighe
LOCH
Earlish
SKYE
Lealt
Rubha na Fearn
Fearnmore
Trotternish
Lealt
Creag a' Lain
608
A87
Peinlich
Glenuachdarach
A855
Leac Tressirnish
Dry Harbour
Cuaig
Arinacrinach
Baca Ruadh
637
Hinnisdal
125
RONA
11
Beinn a' Sga
452
Rigg
Abhainn Chuaig
Hartaval
668
A850–TO DUNVEGAN
Kingsburgh
Loch Snizort Beag
The Storr
719
13
Kyle Rona
Callakille
SOUND OF RAASAY
INNER SOUND
Eilean Tigh
111
An Garbh-mheall
493
Treaslane
Romesdal
Romesdal
Bearreraig Bay
Lon Mòr
Eyre
Carn Liath
Loch a' Sgàirr
Lonbain
The Aird
L. Eyre
Haultin
Allt na h-Eirigh
Eilean Fladday
Beinn na h-Iolaire
254
Kensaleyre
Loch Leathan
Bernisdale
Ben Dearg
552
Meall Fhua
Torran
Tote
Prince Charles's Cave
Loch Fada
Manish Point
Loch Arnish
Arnish
A850
Borve
Loch nan Eun
626
Skeabost
Carbost
Chracaig
Sithean Bhealaich Chumhaing
392
Brochel
4
Uigshader
Hartfield
Applecross
Beinn a' Ghlinne Bhig
208
Drumuie
A87
A855
Torvaig
Glengrasco
Applecross
B885
Loch Conan
9
Snizort
Portree
Loch Portree
RAASAY
Milton
Aros Experience
385
Am Maol
Glamo
Camusteel
Camusterrach
417
Beinn na Greine
Ben Tianavaig
413
Allt Creadha
B885
Loch Duagrich
Glenmore
Balachuirn
Culduie
A87–TO KYLE OF LOCHALSH
Holoman Bay
Dun Caan
443
Sròn na h-Airde Bhaine
Ben Duagrich

Beinn Eighe: 10,000 acres of mountains and moors were designated as Britain's first national nature reserve in 1951.
Map ref. F3

330

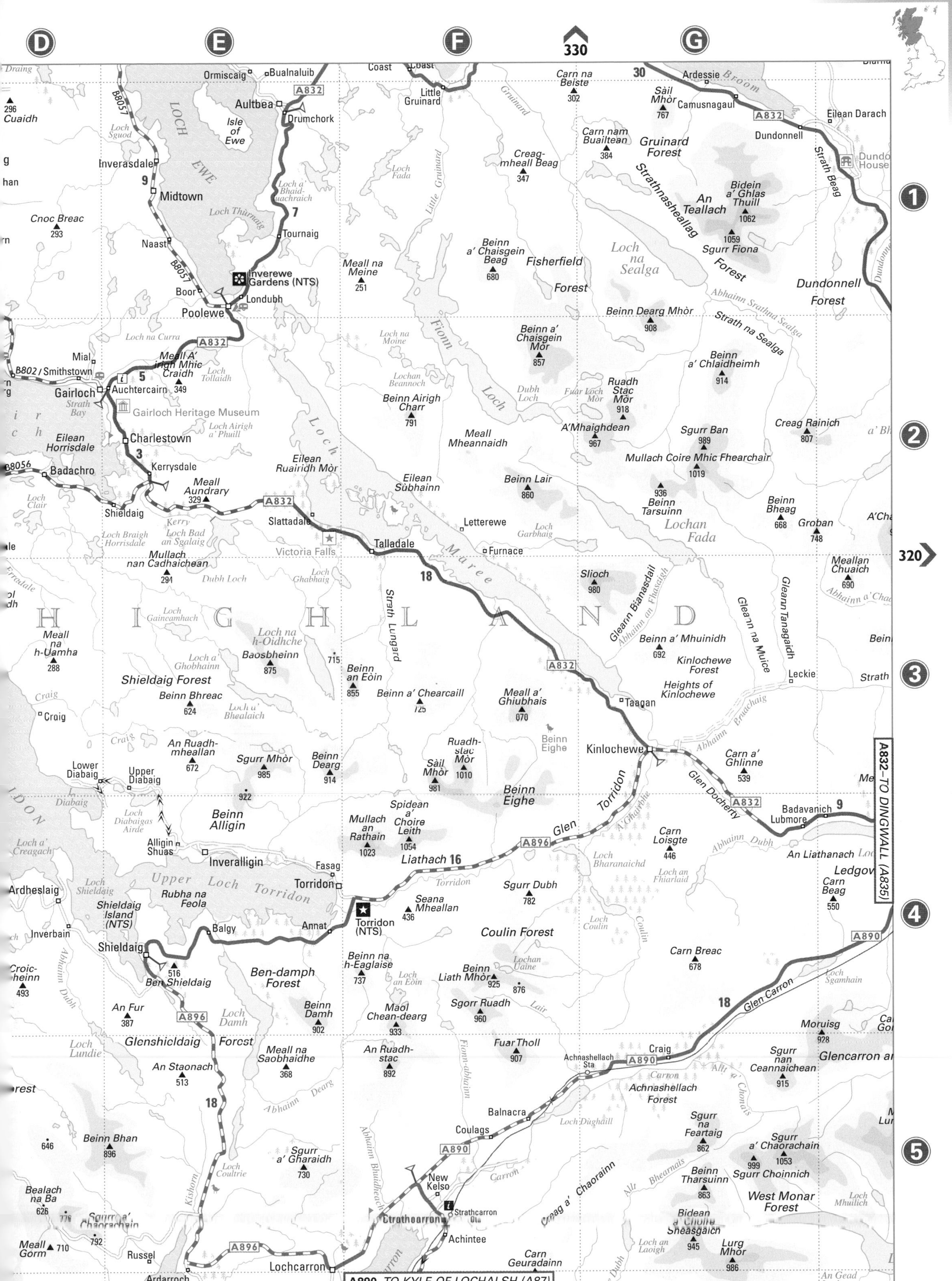
D
E
F
G
1
2
3
4
5
Ormiscaig
Bualnaluib
Coast
Carn na Beiste
302
30
Ardessie
Broom
296
Cuaidh
B8057
LOCH
Aultbea
A832
Drumchork
Little Gruinard
Gruinard
Sàil Mhòr
767
Camusnagaul
A832
Eilean Darach
Isle of Ewe
Loch Sguod
Carn nam Buailtean
384
Gruinard Forest
Dundonnell
Inverasdale
EWE
Loch Fada
Little Gruinard
Creag-mheall Beag
347
Strathnasheallag
Dundonnell House
Strath Beag
9
Midtown
Loch a' Bhaid-luachraich
An Teallach
Bidein a' Ghlas Thuill
1062
Loch Thùrnaig
7
Cnoc Breac
293
Tournaig
Naast
Beinn a' Chaisgein Beag
680
Fisherfield
Loch na Sealga
1059
Sgurr Fiona
Forest
Meall na Meine
251
B8057
Inverewe Gardens (NTS)
Forest
Dundonnell Forest
Boor
Londubh
Abhainn Srathnd Sealga
Poolewe
Fionn
Beinn Dearg Mhòr
908
Strath na Sealga
Loch na Curra
A832
Loch na Moine
Beinn a' Chaisgein Mòr
857
Mial
Meall A' irigh Mhic Craidh
349
Loch Tollaidh
Lochan Beannoch
Beinn a' Chlaidheimh
914
B8802 / Smithstown
5
Loch
Dubh Loch
Fuar Loch Mòr
Ruadh Stac Mòr
918
Gairloch
Auchtercairn
Strath Bay
Beinn Airigh Charr
791
Gairloch Heritage Museum
Loch Airigh a' Phuill
A'Mhaighdean
967
Creag Rainich
807
Eilean Horrisdale
Charlestown
Loch
Meall Mheannaidh
Sgurr Ban
989
3
Mullach Coire Mhic Fhearchair
1019
B8056
Badachro
Kerrysdale
Eilean Ruairidh Mòr
Meall Aundrary
329
Eilean Sùbhainn
Beinn Lair
860
936
Beinn Tarsuinn
Beinn Bheag
668
Groban
748
Loch Clair
Shieldaig
A832
Kerry
Slattadale
Letterewe
Lochan Fada
Loch Braigh Horrisdale
Loch Bad an Sgalaig
Loch Garbhaig
Talladale
Victoria Falls
Furnace
Maree
320
Mullach nan Cadhaichean
291
Dubh Loch
Loch Ghabhaig
18
Slioch
980
Meallan Chuaich
690
Abhainn a' Chad
Gleann Bianasdail
Abhainn an Fhasaigh
Gleann na Muice
Gleann Tanagaidh
Loch Gaineamhach
Loch na h-Oidhche
Strath Lungard
H I G H L A N D
Meall na h-Uamha
288
Baosbheinn
875
715
Beinn a' Mhuinidh
692
Loch a' Ghobhainn
A832
Kinlochewe Forest
Beinn an Eòin
855
Beinn a' Chearcaill
725
Meall a' Ghiubhais
070
Heights of Kinlochewe
Leckie
Shieldaig Forest
Strath
Beinn Bhreac
624
Loch a' Bhealaich
Taagan
Craig
Bruachaig
Craig
Beinn Eighe
Abhainn
An Ruadh-mheallan
672
Sgurr Mhòr
985
Beinn Dearg
914
Ruadh-stac Mòr
1010
Sàil Mhòr
981
Kinlochewe
Carn a' Ghlinne
539
Lower Diabaig
Upper Diabaig
A832–TO DINGWALL (A835)
922
Glen Docherty
Diabaig
Beinn Eighe
Torridon
Loch Diabaigas Airde
Beinn Alligin
Spidean a' Choire Leith
1054
Mullach an Rathain
1023
A832
Badavanich
9
Lubmore
Glen
Carn Loisgte
446
Abhainn Dubh
Loch a' Creagach
Alligin Shuas
A896
A' Ghairbhe
Inveralligin
Fasag
Liathach
16
Loch Bharanaichd
Loch an Fhiarlaid
An Liathanach
Ledgow
Carn Beag
550
Upper Loch Torridon
Torridon
Torridon
Ardheslaig
Loch Shieldaig
Rubha na Feola
Seana Mheallan
436
Sgurr Dubh
782
Shieldaig Island (NTS)
Torridon (NTS)
Loch Coulin
Coulin
Inverbain
Balgy
Annat
Coulin Forest
A890
Shieldaig
Croic-bheinn
493
516
Ben Shieldaig
Beinn na h-Eaglaise
737
Loch an Eòin
Beinn Liath Mhòr
925
Lochan Uaine
876
Carn Breac
678
Ben-damph Forest
Loch Sgamhain
Abhainn Dubh
An Fur
387
A896
Loch Damh
Beinn Damh
902
Sgorr Ruadh
960
Lair
18
Glen Carron
Moruisg
928
Loch Lundie
Glenshieldaig
Forest
Maol Chean-dearg
933
Fuar Tholl
907
Meall na Saobhaidhe
368
An Ruadh-stac
892
Achnashellach Sta
Craig
A890
Sgurr nan Ceannaichean
915
Glencarron
An Staonach
513
Fionn-abhainn
Carron
Allt a' Chonais
Achnashellach Forest
18
Abhainn Dearg
Balnacra
Loch Dùghaill
Sgurr na Feartaig
862
Coulags
Beinn Bhan
896
646
Sgurr a' Gharaidh
730
A890
Abhainn Bhuidheach
Sgurr a' Chaorachain
1053
999
Sgurr Choinnich
Loch Coultrie
New Kelso
Carron
Creag a' Chaorainn
Allt Bhearnais
Beinn Tharsuinn
863
West Monar Forest
Loch Mhuilich
Bealach na Ba
626
776
Sgurr a' Chaorachain
792
Kishorn
Strathcarron
Strathcarron Sta
Bidean a' Choire Sheasgaich
945
Meall Gorm
710
Russel
A896
Achintee
Loch an Laoigh
Lurg Mhòr
986
Carn Geuradainn
Ardarroch
Lochcarron
A890–TO KYLE OF LOCHALSH (A87)
An Gead Loch

Victoria Falls: *Victoria Falls were named after a visit to Loch Maree by Queen Victoria in 1877.* ***Map ref. E2***

307

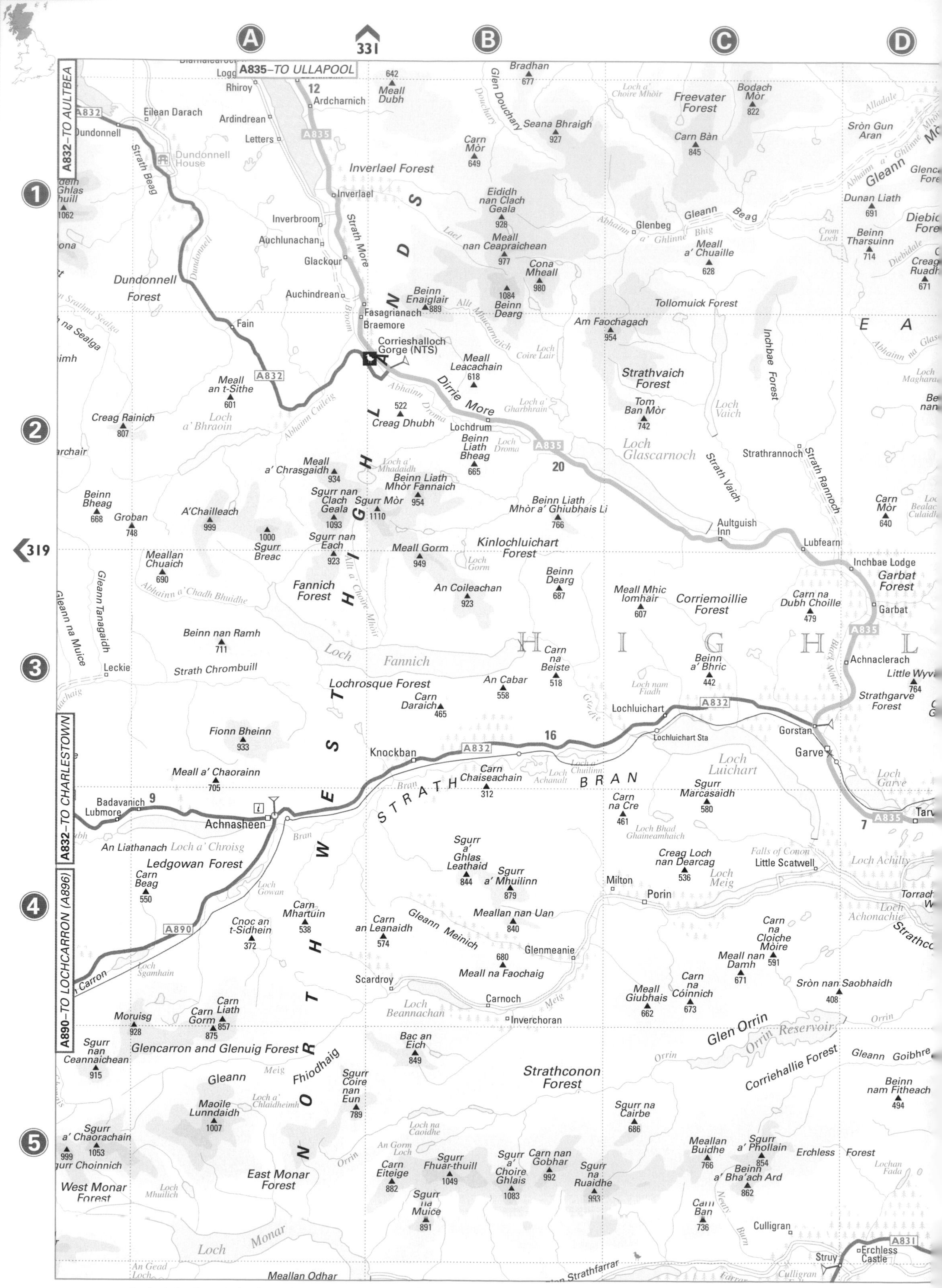
A
331
B
C
D
1
2
3
4
5
319
A835–TO ULLAPOOL
A832–TO AULTBEA
A832–TO CHARLESTOWN
A890–TO LOCHCARRON (A896)
Logg
Rhiroy
Eilean Darach
Dundonnell
Ardindrean
Letters
Dundonnell House
Strath Beag
12
Ardcharnich
642
Meall Dubh
A835
Inverlael Forest
Inverlael
Inverbroom
Auchlunachan
Glackour
Strath More
Auchindrean
Dundonnell Forest
Fain
Fasagrianach
Braemore
Corrieshalloch Gorge (NTS)
Beinn Enaiglair 889
Glen Douchary
Bradhan 677
Loch a' Choire Mhòir
Seana Bhraigh 927
Carn Mòr 649
Eididh nan Clach Geala 928
Meall nan Ceapraichean 977
Cona Mheall 980
1084 Beinn Dearg
Freevater Forest
Bodach Mòr 822
Carn Bàn 845
Gleann Beag
Glenbeg
Meall a' Chuaille 628
Tollomuick Forest
Am Faochagach 954
Strathvaich Forest
Tom Ban Mòr 742
Loch Vaich
Inchbae Forest
Sròn Gun Aran
Dunan Liath 691
Beinn Tharsuinn 714
E A
Meall an t-Sithe 601
A832
Creag Rainich 807
Loch a' Bhraoin
522 Creag Dhubh
Meall Leacachain 618
Dirrie More
Lochdrum
Beinn Liath Bheag 665
Loch Droma
A835
20
Loch Glascarnoch
Strath Vaich
Strathrannoch
Strath Rannoch
Meall a' Chrasgaidh 934
Beinn Liath Mhòr Fannaich 954
Sgurr nan Clach Geala 1093
Sgurr Mòr 1110
Beinn Liath Mhòr a' Ghiubhais Li 766
Aultguish Inn
Lubfearn
Beinn Bheag 668
Groban 748
A'Chailleach 999
1000 Sgurr Breac
Sgurr nan Each 923
Meall Gorm 949
Kinlochluichart Forest
Meallan Chuaich 690
Fannich Forest
An Coileachan 923
Beinn Dearg 687
Meall Mhic Iomhair 607
Corriemoillie Forest
Inchbae Lodge
Garbat Forest
Carn na Dubh Choille 479
Garbat
Gleann Tanagaidh
Gleann na Muice
Beinn nan Ramh 711
Loch Fannich
Carn na Beiste 518
Beinn a' Bhric 442
Achnaclerach
Little Wyvis 764
Strathgarve Forest
Leckie
Strath Chrombuill
Lochrosque Forest
Carn Daraich 465
An Cabar 558
Lochluichart
Lochluichart Sta
Gorstan
Garve
Fionn Bheinn 933
16
Knockban
A832
Meall a' Chaorainn 705
Carn Chaiseachain 312
STRATH BRAN
Loch Luichart
Sgurr Marcasaidh 580
Carn na Cre 461
Badavanich 9
Lubmore
Achnasheen
A835
7
An Liathanach
Loch a' Chroisg
Ledgowan Forest
Carn Beag 550
Sgurr a' Ghlas Leathaid 844
Sgurr a' Mhuilinn 879
Creag Loch nan Dearcag 536
Falls of Conon
Little Scatwell
Loch Achilty
Milton
Porin
Loch Meig
A890
Cnoc an t-Sidhein 372
Carn Mhartuin 538
Carn an Leanaidh 574
Gleann Meinich
Meallan nan Uan 840
Carn na Cloiche Mòire 591
Meall nan Damh 671
Glenmeanie
680
Meall na Faochaig
Scardroy
Carnoch
Loch Beannachan
Inverchoran
Meall Giubhais 662
Carn na Còinnich 673
Sròn nan Saobhaidh 408
Moruisg 928
Carn Gorm 875
Carn Liath 857
Sgurr nan Ceannaichean 915
Glencarron and Glenuig Forest
Bac an Eich 849
Glen Orrin
Orrin Reservoir
Gleann Goibhre
Gleann Fhiodhaig
Sgurr Coire nan Eun 789
Strathconon Forest
Corriehallie Forest
Beinn nam Fitheach 494
Maoile Lunndaidh 1007
Sgurr na Cairbe 686
Sgurr a' Chaorachain 1053
999
East Monar Forest
Carn Eiteige 882
Sgurr Fhuar-thuill 1049
Sgurr a' Choire Ghlais 1083
Carn nan Gobhar 992
Sgurr na Ruaidhe 993
Meallan Buidhe 766
Sgurr a' Phollain 854
Beinn a' Bha'ach Ard 862
Erchless Forest
West Monar Forest
Sgurr na Muice 891
Carn Ban 736
Culligran
Loch Monar
Struy
Erchless Castle
A831
Meallan Odhar
WEST HIGHLANDS
NORTH WEST HIGHLANDS
HIGHLAND

Loch a' Chroisg: *The landscape here features some spectacular reminders of the ice-age. Here the moving glaciers have left unusual flat-topped terraces on the south side of the Loch.* ***Map ref. A4***

308

Culloden: *The last battle to be fought on British soil took place here on the 16th April 1746 between the supporters of Bonnie Prince Charlie, known as Jacobites and the Government troops, known as Hanoverians. The engagement itself was over in less than an hour and resulted in a resounding defeat for the Jacobites, who lost over 1,200 men on the battlefield.* ***Map ref. G5 Also on page 119***

332

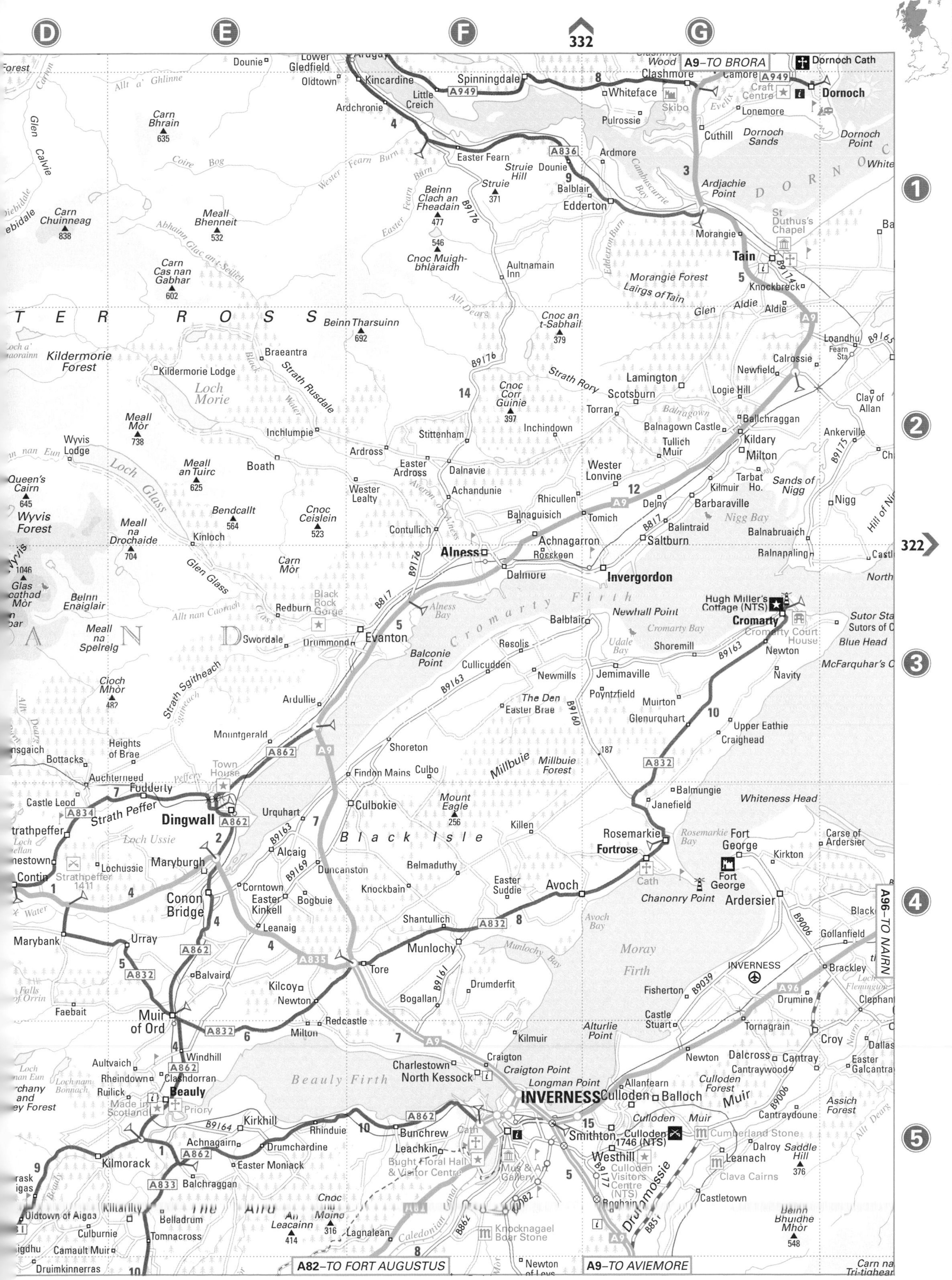
D
E
F
G
1
2
3
4
5
Dornoch Cath
Dornoch
A9–TO BRORA
Wood
Clashmore
Camore
A949
Craft Centre
Lonemore
Skibo
Evelix
Whiteface
Dounie
Lower Gledfield
Oldtown
Kincardine
Spinningdale
Little Creich
A949
Ardchronie
Pulrossie
Cuthill
Dornoch Sands
Dornoch Point
Ardmore
A836
Easter Fearn
Struie Hill
Dounie
Struie
371
Balblair
Edderton
Ardjachie Point
Cambuscurrie Bay
St Duthus's Chapel
Morangie
Tain
Knockbreck
Morangie Forest
Lairgs of Tain
Glen Aldie
Aldie
A9
Loandhu
B9165
Fearn Sta
Calrossie
Newfield
Logie Hill
Clay of Allan
Ballchraggan
Balnagown Castle
Balnagown
Kildary
Milton
Ankerville
B9175
Tullich Muir
Tarbat Ho.
Kilmuir
Sands of Nigg
Nigg
Hill of Nigg
Barbaraville
Nigg Bay
Balintraid
Balnabruaich
Balnapaling
Saltburn
B817
Delny
Wester Lonvine
Rhicullen
Tomich
Achnagarron
Rosskeen
Invergordon
Alness
Dalmore
Forest
Carn Chuinneag
838
Glen Calvie
Carn Bhrain
635
Allt a' Ghlinne
Coire Bog
Wester Fearn Burn
Beinn Clach an Fheadain
477
546
Cnoc Muigh-bhlaraidh
B9176
Meall Bhenneit
532
Abhainn Glac an t-Seilich
Carn Cas nan Gabhar
602
Aultnamain Inn
Allt Dearg
Cnoc an t-Sabhail
379
E R R O S S
Beinn Tharsuinn
692
Kildermorie Forest
Kildermorie Lodge
Braeantra
Strath Rusdale
Black Water
Loch Morie
Strath Rory
Lamington
Scotsburn
Torran
Cnoc Corr Guinie
397
14
Inchindown
Stittenham
Meall Mòr
738
Inchlumpie
Ardross
Easter Ardross
Dalnavie
Achandunie
Wyvis Lodge
Loch Glass
Meall an Tuirc
625
Boath
Queen's Cairn
645
Wyvis Forest
Bendcallt
564
Meall na Drochaide
704
Kinloch
Cnoc Ceislein
523
Wester Lealty
Contullich
Balnaguisich
12
Glen Glass
Carn Mòr
1046
Glas Leathad Mòr
Beinn Enaiglair
Allt nan Caorach
Redburn
Black Rock Gorge
Meall na Speireig
Swordale
Drummond
Evanton
B817
5
Alness Bay
Cromarty Firth
Balblair
Newhall Point
Hugh Miller's Cottage (NTS)
Cromarty
Cromarty Bay
Cromarty Court House
Sutors of Cromarty
Blue Head
McFarquhar's Cave
Udale Bay
Shoremill
B9163
Newton
Navity
Resolis
Balconie Point
Cullicudden
Newmills
Jemimaville
Poyntzfield
Muirton
B9163
The Den
Easter Brae
B9160
Glenurquhart
10
Upper Eathie
Craighead
Cioch Mhòr
482
Strath Sgitheach
Ardullie
Heights of Brae
Mountgerald
Shoreton
A862
A9
Millbuie
Millbuie Forest
187
A832
Bottacks
Auchterneed
Town House
Fodderty
Findon Mains
Culbo
7
Castle Leod
Strath Peffer
Dingwall
A834
A862
Urquhart
Culbokie
Mount Eagle
256
Balmungie
Janefield
Whiteness Head
Strathpeffer
Loch Ussie
Killen
Black Isle
Rosemarkie
Rosemarkie Bay
Fortrose
Fort George
Carse of Ardersier
Kirkton
Maryburgh
B9163
Alcaig
B9169
Lochussie
Duncanston
Belmaduthy
Contin
Strathpeffer
1411
Corntown
Conon Bridge
Easter Kinkell
Bogbuie
Knockbain
Easter Suddie
Avoch
Cath
Chanonry Point
Ardersier
A96–TO NAIRN
Avoch Bay
Blackness
B9006
Gollanfield
Marybank
Urray
Leanaig
Shantullich
A832
8
Munlochy
Munlochy Bay
Moray Firth
A862
A835
Tore
INVERNESS
Brackley
Loch Flemington
A832
Balvaird
Kilcoy
Newton
B9161
Bogallan
Drumderfit
Fisherton
B9039
A96
Drumine
Clephanton
Falls of Orrin
Faebait
Muir of Ord
A832
6
Redcastle
Milton
7
Kilmuir
Alturlie Point
Castle Stuart
Tornagrain
Croy
Nairn
Dallas
Aultvaich
A862
Windhill
Charlestown
Craigton
Craigton Point
Newton
Dalcross
Cantray
Cantraywood
Easter Galcantray
Rheindown
Clashdorran
Beauly Firth
North Kessock
Longman Point
Allanfearn
Culloden Forest
Ruilick
Beauly
Made in Scotland
Priory
INVERNESS
Culloden
Balloch
Culloden Muir
B9006
Assich Forest
Cantraydoune
Kirkhill
B9164
Rhinduie
10
A862
Bunchrew
Smithton
15
Culloden 1746 (NTS)
Cumberland Stone
Dalroy
Saddle Hill
376
Allt Dearg
Achnagairn
Drumchardine
Leachkin
Bught Floral Hall & Visitor Centre
Westhill
Culloden Visitors Centre (NTS)
Leanach
Clava Cairns
Kilmorack
A862
Easter Moniack
Mus & Art Gallery
5
B9177
Drummossie
Balchraggan
A833
B9006
Cnoc Moine
316
B8082
Kiltarlity
The Aird
Belladrum
Culburnie
Tomnacross
Camault Muir
Druimkinnerras
Oldtown of Aigas
Leacainn
414
Lagnalean
Caledonian Canal
B862
Knocknagael Boar Stone
Rogham
B851
Castletown
Beinn Bhuidhe Mhòr
548
A82
A9
Newton of Leys
A82–TO FORT AUGUSTUS
A9–TO AVIEMORE
Carn na Tri-tighearnan
8
10
9

322

309

Cromarty Firth: *The navy cruiser Natal accidentally ploded here on the 30th December 1915. Although over 280 rvivors were plucked from the water, over 370 officers and en lost their lives including many preparing to celebrate ogmanay on board ship.* ***Map ref. F3***

Fort George: *This is the largest fort in the world, enclosing an area of 42 acres (17ha) and almost a mile (1.6km) around. The fort was built during the reign of George II as a defence against any further unrest by the Jacobite Army. Despite taking 21 years to build, Fort George never saw any military action.* ***Map ref. G4 Also on page 123***

A
B
C
D
333
1
2
3
4
5
321
310
Dornoch Cath
A949
Craft Centre
Dornoch
Lonemore
Dornoch Sands
Dornoch Point
DORNOCH FIRTH
Whiteness Sands
Innis Mhòr
Tarbat Ness
Port Mòr
Wilkhaven
Hilton
Innis Bheag
Portmahomack
Bindal
St Duthus's Chapel
Balcherry
Inver Bay
Inver
Rockfield
Tarrel
Balnagall
Knockbreck
Lochslin
Aldie
A9
Balaldie
B9165
Rhynie
Loandhu
Fearn Sta
Hill of Fearn
Geanies Ho.
Calrossie
Cadboll
Fearn
Tullich
Fearn Abbey
Clay of Allan
B9166
Hilton of Cadboll
Ballchraggan
Balintore
Shandwick
Kildary
Ankerville
Milton
B9175
Chapelhill
Sands of Nigg
Nigg
Hill of Nigg
Balnabruaich
Balnapaling
Castlecraig
North Sutor
MORAY FIRTH
Sutor Stacks
Sutors of Cromarty
Cromarty Court House
Newton
Blue Head
McFarquhar's Caves
Navity
Hopeman
Burghead Well
Burghead
Roseisle Forest
Burghead Bay
Buthill
Findhorn
Hempriggs
B9089
Muirhead
Coltfield
Miltonhill
Findhorn Bay
B9011
Culbin Forest
Kinloss
Alves
Wellhill
Kintessack
Inverene
Grange Hall
Toreduff
Moy House
Muirtown
Springfield
The Bar
Forres
Sueno's Stone
Mains of Burgie
Monaughty Forest
Whiteness Head
Brodie Castle (NTS)
Dyke
Falconer Mus
Heldon Hill
234
Carse of Ardersier
Macbeth's Hillock
49
Kingsteps
Newton of Dalvey
A96
Kirkton
Nairn
Boath Dovecot (NTS)
10
A940
Rafford
Dallas Dhu Distillery
B9010
Blervie Castle
Califer
Hilton of Delnies
Tradespark
B9092
Househill
Auldearn
Auldearn 1645
Boghole Fm
Darnaway
Loch of Blairs
Tulloch
Blackcastle
15
B9091
B9090
B9006
Whitemire
Old Military Road
Altyre Woods
Briach
Edinvale
Hill of Wangie
319
Gollanfield
Muir of the Clans
Moss-side
Laiken Forest
Milton
Conicavel
Newtyle Forest
Branchill
Dallas
Brackley
B9101
Mains of Sluie
Phorp
Ardoch
Loch Flemington
Torrich
A939
Darnaway Forest
Presley
Romach Hill
313
Mill Buie
371
Drumine
Clephanton
Regoul
Fornighty
Drumine Forest
Tomnamoon
Craigroy
A96–TO INVERNESS
Cawdor
Piperhill
Culcharry
Littlemill
Lethen Bar
258
Logie
Randolph's Leap
Hill of Tomechole
344
Croy
Cawdor Castle
Dallaschyle
Urchany
Cantray
Easter Galcantray
Relugas
Loch Dallas
Carnachie
359
Cantraywood
Achindown
Redburn
Kirkton of Barevan
Clunas
Bruachmary
B9007
Carn Ghiubhais
430
Cantraydoune
Assich Forest
Findhorn
Ardclach Bell Tower
Mount
Dalroy
Saddle Hill
376
Balmore
Ferness
HIGHLAND
MORAY
Tomdow
Carn a' Chrasgie
401
Daltra
B9007
Carn Kitty
521
Carn Shalag
470
Cairns
Cairn Duhie
6
Knock of Braemoray
456
Sliabh Bainneach
483
Reinn Bhuidhe Mhòr
548
Carn Sgumain
417
Dulsie
Milltown
Larig Hill
545
Paul's Hill
Carnoch
Banchor
A939, A940–TO GRANTOWN-ON-SPEY
Carn nan Tri-tighearnan

Burghead: *Site of the biggest 'Iron Age' fort in Britain built on the end of a promontory by the Picts between the 4th and 7th centuries AD. The Picts lived in northern Britain and though very little is known about them they are thought to be the original inhabitants of Scotland. From the 9th century however they seem to have vanished, perhaps swallowed up in battles with the Vikings, Romans and between their own tribes.* ***Map ref. D3.***

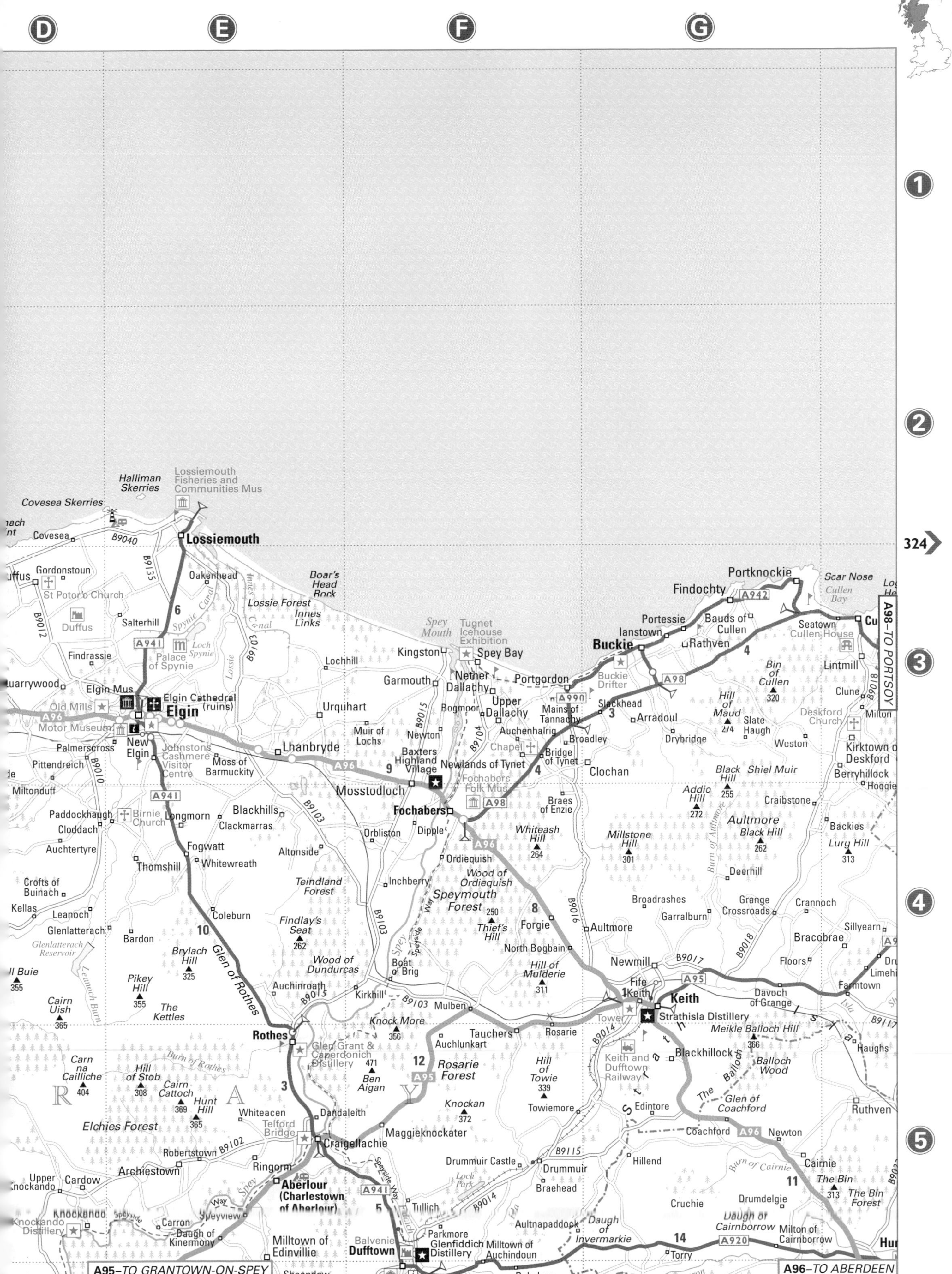
D
E
F
G
1
2
3
4
5
324
A98–TO PORTSOY
A95–TO GRANTOWN-ON-SPEY
A96–TO ABERDEEN
Halliman Skerries
Lossiemouth Fisheries and Communities Mus
Covesea Skerries
Covesea
B9040
Lossiemouth
Gordonstoun
St Peter's Church
Duffus
Oakenhead
Doar's Head Rock
Lossie Forest
Innes Links
B9012
B9135
Salterhill
Spynie Canal
Findrassie
Palace of Spynie
Loch Spynie
B9103
A941
Quarrywood
Elgin Mus
Elgin Cathedral (ruins)
Old Mills
Elgin
A96
Motor Museum
Lochhill
Urquhart
Kingston
Spey Mouth
Tugnet Icehouse Exhibition
Spey Bay
Garmouth
Nether Dallachy
Portgordon
Upper Dallachy
Bogmoor
Muir of Lochs
Newton
B9015
New Elgin
Palmerscross
Pittendreich
Johnstons Cashmere Visitor Centre
Moss of Barmuckity
Lhanbryde
Baxters Highland Village
Newlands of Tynet
Auchenhalrig
Chapel
Bridge of Tynet
Clochan
Mosstodloch
Fochabers
Fochabers Folk Mus
A98
Miltonduff
Paddockhaugh
Birnie Church
Longmorn
Blackhills
Clackmarras
Cloddach
Auchtertyre
Fogwatt
Whitewreath
Thomshill
Altonside
Orbliston
Dipple
Braes of Enzie
Whiteash Hill
264
Ordiequish
Wood of Ordiequish
Inchberry
Speymouth Forest
250
Teindland Forest
Crofts of Buinach
Kellas
Leanoch
Glenlatterach
Glenlatterach Reservoir
Bardon
Coleburn
Findlay's Seat
262
Thief's Hill
Forgie
North Bogbain
Hill of Mulderie
311
Brylach Hill
325
Glen of Rothes
Wood of Dundurcas
Boat o' Brig
Pikey Hill
355
The Kettles
Cairn Uish
365
Auchinroath
B9015
Kirkhill
B9103
Mulben
Knock More
356
Rothes
Glen Grant & Caperdonich Distillery
471
Ben Aigan
Tauchers
Auchlunkart
Rosarie
Rosarie Forest
A95
Carn na Cailliche
404
Hill of Stob
308
Cairn Catloch
369
Hunt Hill
365
Burn of Rothes
Elchies Forest
Whiteacen
Telford Bridge
Dandaleith
Knockan
372
Hill of Towie
339
Towiemore
Maggieknockater
Craigellachie
Robertstown
B9102
Archiestown
Ringorm
Drummuir Castle
Drummuir
Braehead
Loch Park
Upper Knockando
Cardow
Aberlour (Charlestown of Aberlour)
A941
Tullich
B9014
Speyside Way
Knockando
Knockando Distillery
Carron
Speyview
Daugh of Kinermony
Milltown of Edinvillie
Balvenie
Dufftown
Parkmore
Glenfiddich Distillery
Milltown of Auchindoun
Aultnapaddock
Daugh of Invermarkie
Sheandow
Bakebare
Portknockie
Scar Nose
Cullen Bay
Findochty
A942
Portessie
Ianstown
Bauds of Cullen
Rathven
Seatown
Cullen House
Buckie
Buckie Drifter
A98
Bin of Cullen
320
Lintmill
A990
Slackhead
Arradoul
Mains of Tannachy
Broadley
Hill of Maud
274
Slate Haugh
Drybridge
Weston
Clune
Deskford Church
Milton
Kirktown of Deskford
Berryhillock
Hoggie
Black Hill
Shiel Muir
255
Addie Hill
272
Craibstone
Aultmore
Black Hill
262
Backies
Lurg Hill
313
Millstone Hill
301
Deerhill
Burn of Aultmore
Broadrashes
Garralburn
Grange Crossroads
Crannoch
Sillyearn
Bracobrae
B9016
Aultmore
B9018
Newmill
B9017
Floors
Fife Keith
Keith
A95
Davoch of Grange
Farmtown
Tower
Strathisla Distillery
Meikle Balloch Hill
366
B9014
Keith and Dufftown Railway
Blackhillock
Balloch Wood
Haughs
Isla
Strath Isla
The Balloch
Glen of Coachford
Edintore
Coachford
A96
Newton
Ruthven
B9115
Hillend
Burn of Cairnie
Cairnie
The Bin
313
The Bin Forest
Cruchie
Drumdelgie
Daugh of Cairnborrow
Milton of Cairnborrow
A920
Torry
Deveron

311

Lossiemouth: *Birthplace in 1866 of James Ramsay MacDonald, Britain's first Labour Prime Minister. After a successful first term in 1924 he was re-elected in 1929 to form a 'National Government' during the Depression. He died at sea, en-route to South America, in 1937 and is buried near Lossiemouth in Old Spynie churchyard.* ***Map ref. E2.***

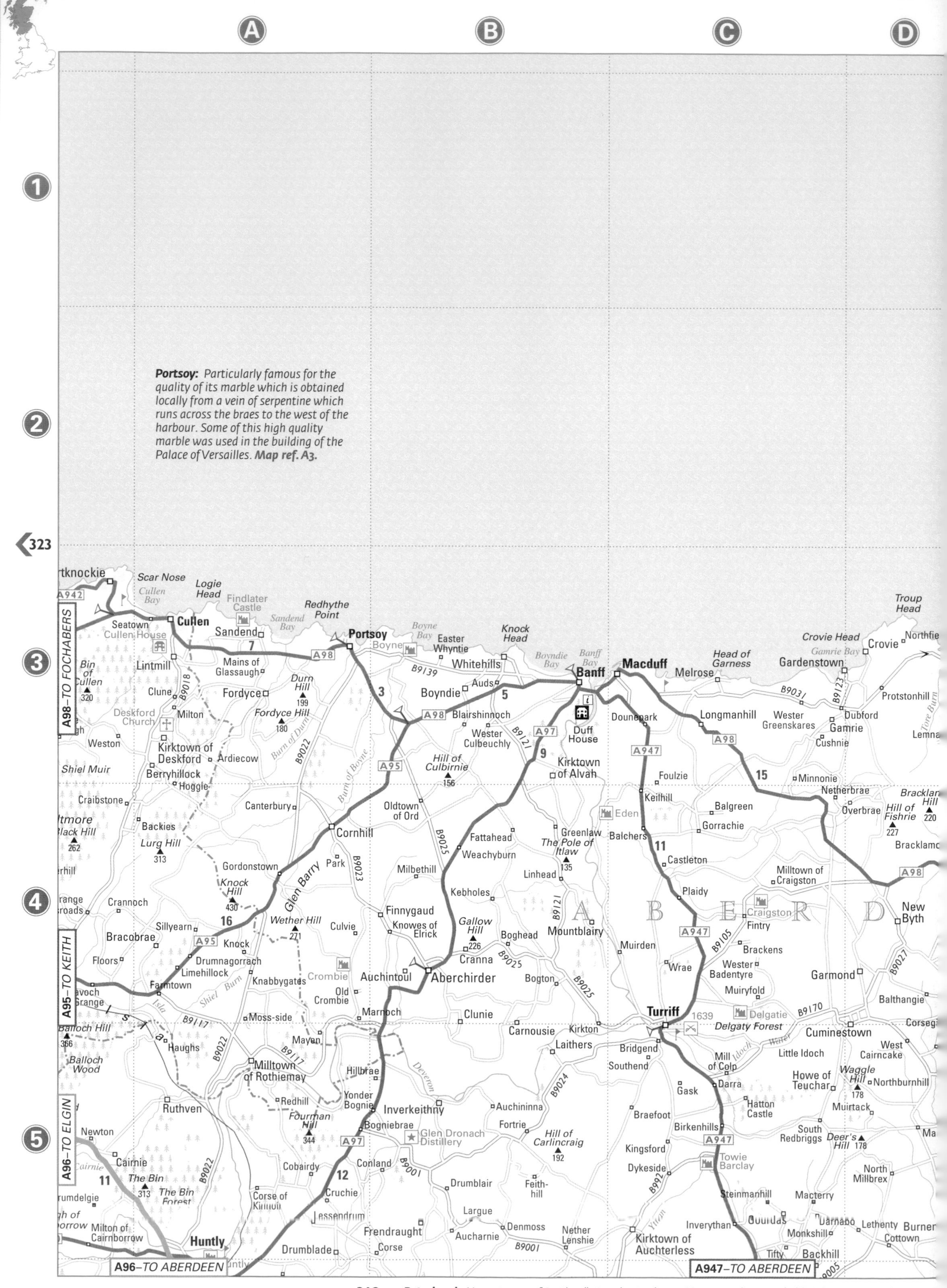
A
B
C
D
1
2
3
4
5
323
Portsoy: *Particularly famous for the quality of its marble which is obtained locally from a vein of serpentine which runs across the braes to the west of the harbour. Some of this high quality marble was used in the building of the Palace of Versailles.* ***Map ref. A3.***
A98–TO FOCHABERS
A95–TO KEITH
A96–TO ELGIN
A96–TO ABERDEEN
A947–TO ABERDEEN
Scar Nose
Cullen Bay
Logie Head
Findlater Castle
Sandend Bay
Redhythe Point
Boyne Bay
Knock Head
Boyndie Bay
Banff Bay
Head of Garness
Crovie Head
Gamrie Bay
Troup Head
Seatown
Cullen House
Cullen
Sandend
Portsoy
Boyne
Easter Whyntie
Whitehills
Banff
Macduff
Melrose
Gardenstown
Crovie
Lintmill
Mains of Glassaugh
Durn Hill
Bin of Cullen
Clune
Fordyce
Fordyce Hill
Boyndie
Auds
Duff House
Dounepark
Longmanhill
Wester Greenskares
Dubford
Gamrie
Cushnie
Protstonhill
Deskford Church
Milton
Weston
Kirktown of Deskford
Ardiecow
Blairshinnoch
Wester Culbeuchly
Hill of Culbirnie
Kirktown of Alvah
Foulzie
Minnonie
Netherbrae
Overbrae
Hill of Fishrie
Shiel Muir
Berryhillock
Hoggie
Craibstone
Canterbury
Oldtown of Ord
Keilhill
Balgreen
Gorrachie
Eden
Backies
Lurg Hill
Cornhill
Fattahead
Weachyburn
Greenlaw
The Pole of Itlaw
Balchers
Castleton
Gordonstown
Park
Milbethill
Linhead
Milltown of Craigston
Knock Hill
Glen Barry
Kebholes
Plaidy
Crannoch
Sillyearn
Bracobrae
Wether Hill
Culvie
Finnygaud
Knowes of Elrick
Gallow Hill
Boghead
Mountblairy
Craigston
Fintry
New Byth
Floors
Knock
Drumnagorrach
Limehillock
Farmtown
Knabbygates
Crombie
Old Crombie
Auchintoul
Aberchirder
Cranna
Bogton
Muirden
Wrae
Brackens
Wester Badentyre
Muiryfold
Garmond
Balthangie
Balloch Hill
Balloch Wood
Haughs
Moss-side
Marnoch
Mayen
Milltown of Rothiemay
Clunie
Carnousie
Kirkton
Laithers
Turriff
Delgatie
Delgaty Forest
Cuminestown
Bridgend
Southend
Mill of Colp
Little Idoch
West Cairncake
Hillbrae
Redhill
Yonder Bognie
Inverkeithny
Auchininna
Gask
Darra
Howe of Teuchar
Waggle Hill
Northburnhill
Ruthven
Fourman Hill
Bogniebrae
Glen Dronach Distillery
Fortrie
Hill of Carlincraig
Braefoot
Hatton Castle
Muirtack
Birkenhills
South Redbriggs
Deer's Hill
Newton
Cairnie
The Bin
The Bin Forest
Cobairdy
Conland
Kingsford
Dykeside
Towie Barclay
North Millbrex
Corse of Kinnoir
Cruchie
Drumblair
Feith-hill
Steinmanhill
Macterry
Milton of Cairnborrow
Huntly
Drumblade
Frendraught
Corse
Largue
Aucharnie
Denmoss
Nether Lenshie
Kirktown of Auchterless
Inverythan
Monkshill
Lethenty
Cottown
Tifty
Backhill
A B E R D

312

Peterhead: *Home to one of Scotland's toughest prisons. However, the remarkable Johnny Ramensky escaped from it five times (three times in a single year in 1958). Ramensky was a career burglar who was released from prison in 1942 and joined a crack commando unit which operated behind German lines. Using his explosives and burglary skills he stole important documents. His wartime exploits became legendary and he was awarded the Military Medal and granted a free pardon. Unfortunately he returned to a life of crime and died while serving time in Perth Prison, in 1972 at the age of 67.* ***Map ref. G5.***

Fraserburgh: *Both the oldest, and the newest lighthouses in Scotland are situated here. The old Kinnaird Head Lighthouse was built in 1787 into the 16th Century Fraser Castle. This was replaced by a new unmanned lighthouse in 1991. The old Lighthouse is now the Museum of Scottish Lighthouses.* ***Map ref. E3.***

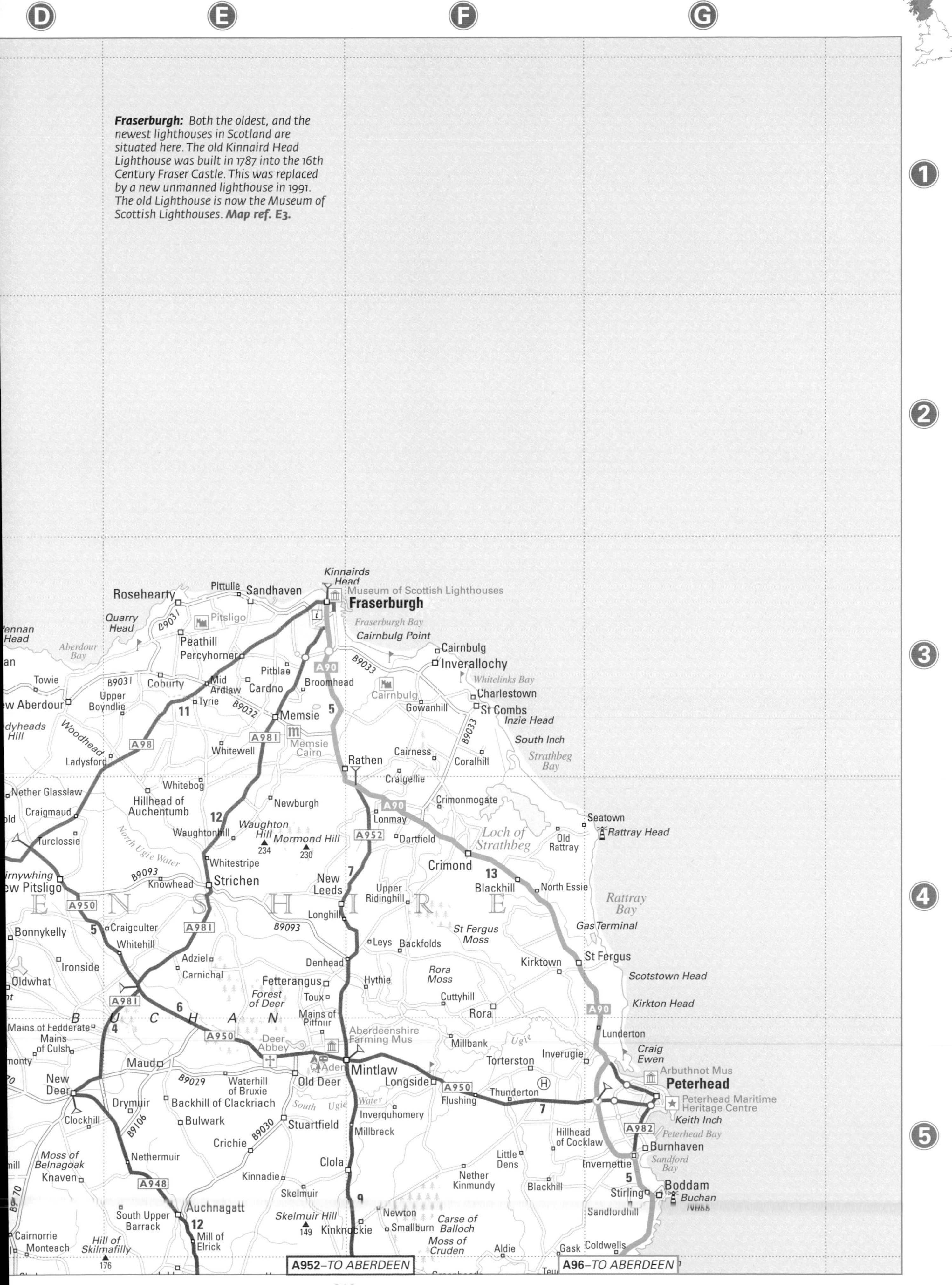

D
E
F
G
1
2
3
4
5
Kinnairds Head
Museum of Scottish Lighthouses
Fraserburgh
Fraserburgh Bay
Cairnbulg Point
Rosehearty
Pittulle
Sandhaven
Pitsligo
Quarry Head
Peathill
Percyhorner
Aberdour Bay
Towie
New Aberdour
Upper Boyndlie
Coburty
Mid Ardlaw
Cardno
Pitblae
Broomhead
Iyrie
Memsie
Memsie Cairn
Cairnbulg
Inverallochy
Whitelinks Bay
Charlestown
St Combs
Gowanhill
Inzie Head
South Inch
Strathbeg Bay
Coralhill
Cairness
Rathen
Craigellie
Crimonmogate
Lonmay
Dartfield
Loch of Strathbeg
Old Rattray
Seatown
Rattray Head
Rattray Bay
Crimond
Blackhill
North Essie
Gas Terminal
St Fergus
Kirktown
Scotstown Head
Kirkton Head
Lunderton
Craig Ewen
Arbuthnot Mus
Peterhead
Peterhead Maritime Heritage Centre
Keith Inch
Peterhead Bay
Burnhaven
Sandford Bay
Invernettie
Boddam
Buchan Ness
Stirling
Sandfordhill
Coldwells
Gask
Aldie
Moss of Cruden
Carse of Balloch
Smallburn
Newton
Kinknockie
Skelmuir Hill
Skelmuir
Kinnadie
Clola
Millbreck
Inverquhomery
Flushing
Longside
Thunderton
Torterston
Inverugie
Millbank
Hillhead of Cocklaw
Little Dens
Nether Kinmundy
Blackhill
Mintlaw
Old Deer
Aden
Aberdeenshire Farming Mus
Deer Abbey
Mains of Pitfour
Toux
Fetterangus
Forest of Deer
Hythie
Rora Moss
Cuttyhill
Rora
Leys
Backfolds
St Fergus Moss
Denhead
Longhill
New Leeds
Upper Ridinghill
Newburgh
Waughton Hill
Mormond Hill
Waughton
Whitestripe
Strichen
Knowhead
Whitebog
Whitewell
Hillhead of Auchentumb
North Ugie Water
Woodhead
Ladysford
Nether Glasslaw
Craigmaud
Turclossie
New Pitsligo
Craigculter
Whitehill
Bonnykelly
Ironside
Oldwhat
Adziel
Carnichal
B U C H A N
E N S H I R E
Mains of Fedderate
Mains of Culsh
Maud
New Deer
Clockhill
Drymuir
Waterhill of Bruxie
Backhill of Clackriach
Bulwark
Stuartfield
South Ugie Water
Crichie
Nethermuir
Moss of Belnagoak
Knaven
Auchnagatt
South Upper Barrack
Mill of Elrick
Cairnorrie
Monteach
Hill of Skilmafilly
A90
A98
A981
A950
A952
A948
A982
B9031
B9032
B9033
B9093
B9029
B9106
B9030
A952–TO ABERDEEN
A96–TO ABERDEEN

313

328

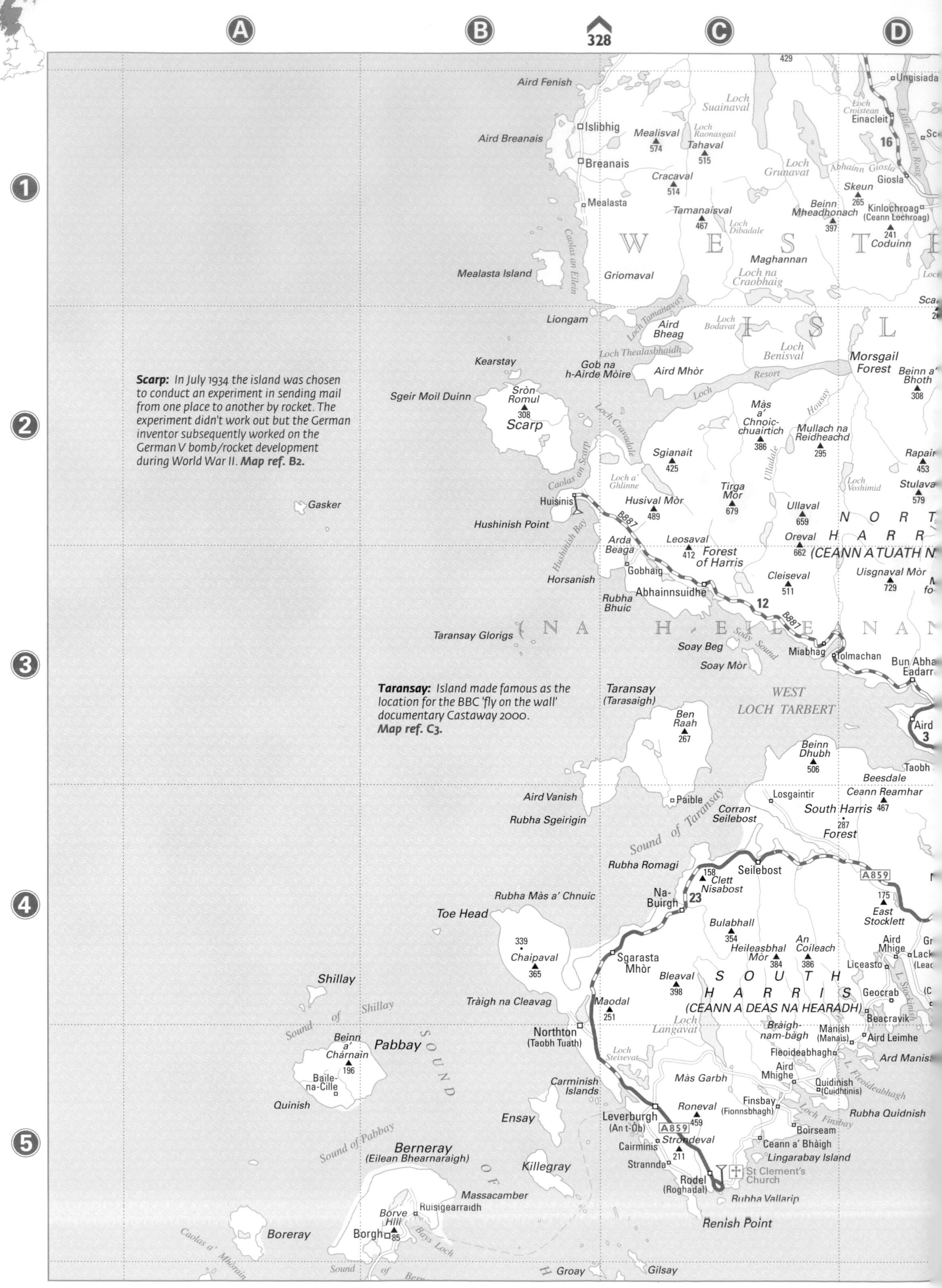
A
B
C
D
1
2
3
4
5
Scarp: In July 1934 the island was chosen to conduct an experiment in sending mail from one place to another by rocket. The experiment didn't work out but the German inventor subsequently worked on the German V bomb/rocket development during World War II. ***Map ref. B2.***
Taransay: Island made famous as the location for the BBC 'fly on the wall' documentary Castaway 2000. ***Map ref. C3.***
Aird Fenish
Aird Breanais
Islibhig
Breanais
Mealasta
Mealasta Island
Caolas an Eilein
Mealisval 574
Tahaval 515
Cracaval 514
Tamanaisval 467
Loch Suainaval
Loch Raonasgail
Loch Grunavat
Loch Dibadale
Griomaval
Maghannan
Loch na Craobhaig
Ungisiadar
Loch Croistean
Einacleit
Little Loch Roag
16
Abhainn Giosla
Giosla
Skeun 265
Beinn Mheadhonach 397
Kinlochroag (Ceann Lochroag)
241 Coduinn
W E S T
Liongam
Loch Tamanavay
Aird Bheag
Loch Bodavat
I S L
Loch Thealasbhaidh
Kearstay
Gob na h-Airde Mòire
Aird Mhòr
Loch Benisval
Loch Resort
Morsgail Forest
Beinn a' Bhoth 308
Sgeir Moil Duinn
Sròn Romul 308
Scarp
Loch Cravadale
Caolas an Scarp
Màs a' Chnoic-chuairtich 386
Housay
Mullach na Reidheachd 295
Sgianait 425
Loch a' Ghlinne
Ulladale
Tirga Mòr 679
Loch Voshimid
Rapaire 453
Stulaval 579
Gasker
Huisinis
Hushinish Point
Hushinish Bay
Husival Mòr 489
B887
Ullaval 659
Oreval 662
N O R T H
H A R R
(CEANN A TUATH N
Arda Beaga
Leosaval 412
Forest of Harris
Gobhaig
Horsanish
Cleiseval 511
Uisgnaval Mòr 729
Abhainnsuidhe
12
Rubha Bhuic
Taransay Glorigs
(N A H - E I L E A N A N
Soay Beg
Soay Mòr
Soay Sound
Miabhag
Tolmachan
Bun Abhainn Eadarra
Taransay (Tarasaigh)
Ben Raah 267
WEST LOCH TARBERT
Aird
3
Beinn Dhubh 506
Taobh
Beesdale
Aird Vanish
Rubha Sgeirigin
Paible
Losgaintir
Corran Seilebost
Ceann Reamhar 467
South Harris Forest
287
Sound of Taransay
Rubha Romagi
Seilebost
A859
158 Clett Nisabost
Rubha Màs a' Chnuic
Na-Buirgh
23
175 East Stocklett
Toe Head
339
Chaipaval 365
Bulabhall 354
Heileasbhal Mòr 384
An Coileach 386
Aird Mhige
Lackle
Liceasto
Sgarasta Mhòr
Bleaval 398
S O U T H
H A R R I S
(CEANN A DEAS NA HEARADH)
Geocrab
Shillay
Tràigh na Cleavag
Maodal 251
Loch Langavat
Loch Stockinish
Beacravik
Sound of Shillay
Northton (Taobh Tuath)
Bràigh-nam-bàgh
Manish (Manais)
Aird Leimhe
Beinn a' Chàrnain 196
Pabbay
Loch Steisevat
Fioideabhagh
Ard Manish
Baile-na-Cille
SOUND OF H
Carminish Islands
Màs Garbh
Aird Mhighe
Quidinish (Cuidhtinis)
Loch Fleoideabhagh
Quinish
Finsbay (Fionnsbhagh)
Loch Finsbay
Rubha Quidnish
Ensay
Leverburgh (An t-Ob)
Roneval 459
Boirseam
Sound of Pabbay
Berneray (Eilean Bhearnaraigh)
Cairminis
Strondeval 211
Ceann a' Bhàigh
Lingarabay Island
Killegray
Strannda
St Clement's Church
Rodel (Roghadal)
Rubha Vallarip
Massacamber
Ruisigearraidh
Borve Hill
Borgh 85
Bays Loch
Boreray
Renish Point
Caolas a' Mhòrain
Groay
Gilsay
Sound of Berneray

316

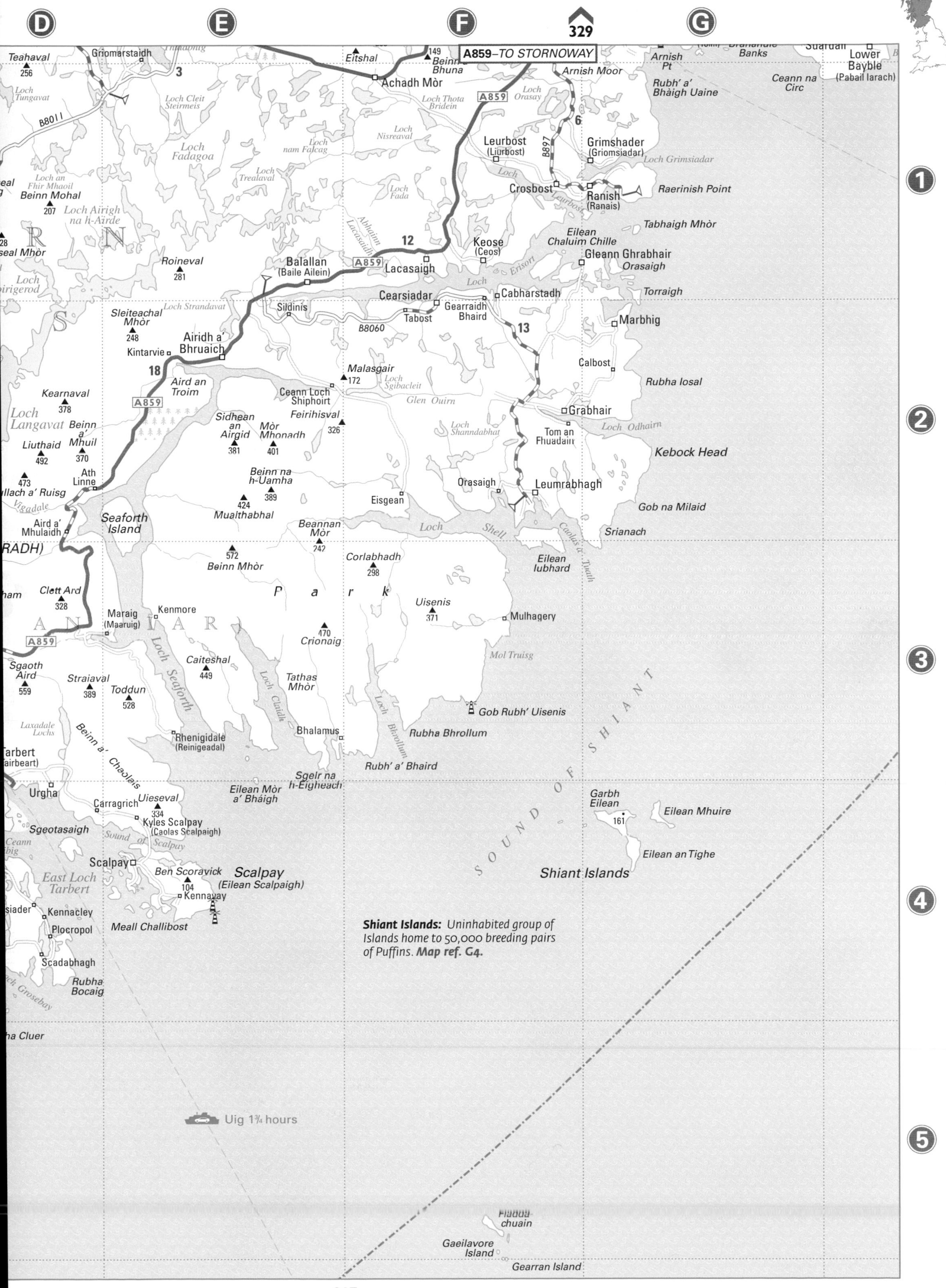

D
E
F
329
G
A859–TO STORNOWAY
Teahaval
256
Griomarstaidh
3
Loch Tungavat
B8011
Loch Cleit Steirmeis
Eitshal
149
Beinn Bhuna
Achadh Mòr
Loch Thota Bridein
A859
Loch Orasay
Arnish Moor
Arnish Pt
Rubh' a' Bhàigh Uaine
Ceann na Circ
Lower Bayble
(Pabail Iarach)
Banks
Loch Nisreaval
Loch nam Falcag
Loch Fadagoa
Loch Trealaval
Leurbost
(Liurbost)
B897
6
Grimshader
(Griomsiadar)
Loch Grimsiadar
Loch an Fhir Mhaoil
Beinn Mohal
207
Loch Airigh na h-Airde
Loch Fada
Abhainn Lacasaidh
Crosbost
Loch Leurbost
Ranish
(Ranais)
Raerinish Point
Tabhaigh Mhòr
Eilean Chaluim Chille
12
Keose
(Ceos)
Gleann Ghrabhair
Orasaigh
Roineval
281
Balallan
(Baile Ailein)
A859
Lacasaigh
Loch Erisort
Loch
Torraigh
Loch Strandavat
Sildinis
Cearsiadar
Cabharstadh
Gearraidh Bhaird
Tabost
B8060
13
Marbhig
Sleiteachal Mhòr
248
Airidh a' Bhruaich
Kintarvie
18
Aird an Troim
Malasgair
172
Loch Sgibacleit
Calbost
Rubha Iosal
Kearnaval
378
Ceann Loch Shiphoirt
Glen Ouirn
Grabhair
Loch Langavat
A859
Beinn a' Mhuil
370
Sidhean an Airgid
381
Mòr Mhonadh
401
Feirihisval
326
Loch Shanndabhat
Tom an Fhuadain
Loch Odhairn
Kebock Head
Liuthaid
492
473
Ath Linne
Beinn na h-Uamha
389
424
Mualthabhal
Orasaigh
Eisgean
Leumrabhagh
Gob na Milaid
Aird a' Mhulaidh
Seaforth Island
Beannan Mòr
242
Loch Shell
Caolas a' Tuath
Srianach
572
Beinn Mhòr
Corlabhadh
298
Eilean Iubhard
Clett Ard
328
Park
Uisenis
371
Mulhagery
Maraig
(Maaruig)
Kenmore
A859
470
Crionaig
Mol Truisg
Sgaoth Aird
559
Straiaval
389
Toddun
528
Caiteshal
449
Loch Seaforth
Loch Claidh
Tathas Mhòr
Laxadale Lochs
Beinn a' Chaolais
Rhenigidale
(Reinigeadal)
Bhalamus
Loch Bhrollum
Gob Rubh' Uisenis
Rubha Bhrollum
Rubh' a' Bhaird
Sgeir na h-Eigheach
Eilean Mòr a' Bhàigh
Urgha
Carragrich
Uieseval
334
Kyles Scalpay
(Caolas Scalpaigh)
Sound of Scalpay
Sgeotasaigh
Sound of Shiant
Garbh Eilean
161
Eilean Mhuire
Eilean an Tighe
Shiant Islands
Scalpay
Ben Scoravick
104
Scalpay
(Eilean Scalpaigh)
Kennavay
East Loch Tarbert
Kennacley
Plocropol
Meall Challibost
Scadabhagh
Rubha Bocaig
Loch Grosebay
Shiant Islands: Uninhabited group of Islands home to 50,000 breeding pairs of Puffins. ***Map ref. G4.***
Uig 1¾ hours
Gaeilavore Island
Gearran Island
317
1
2
3
4
5

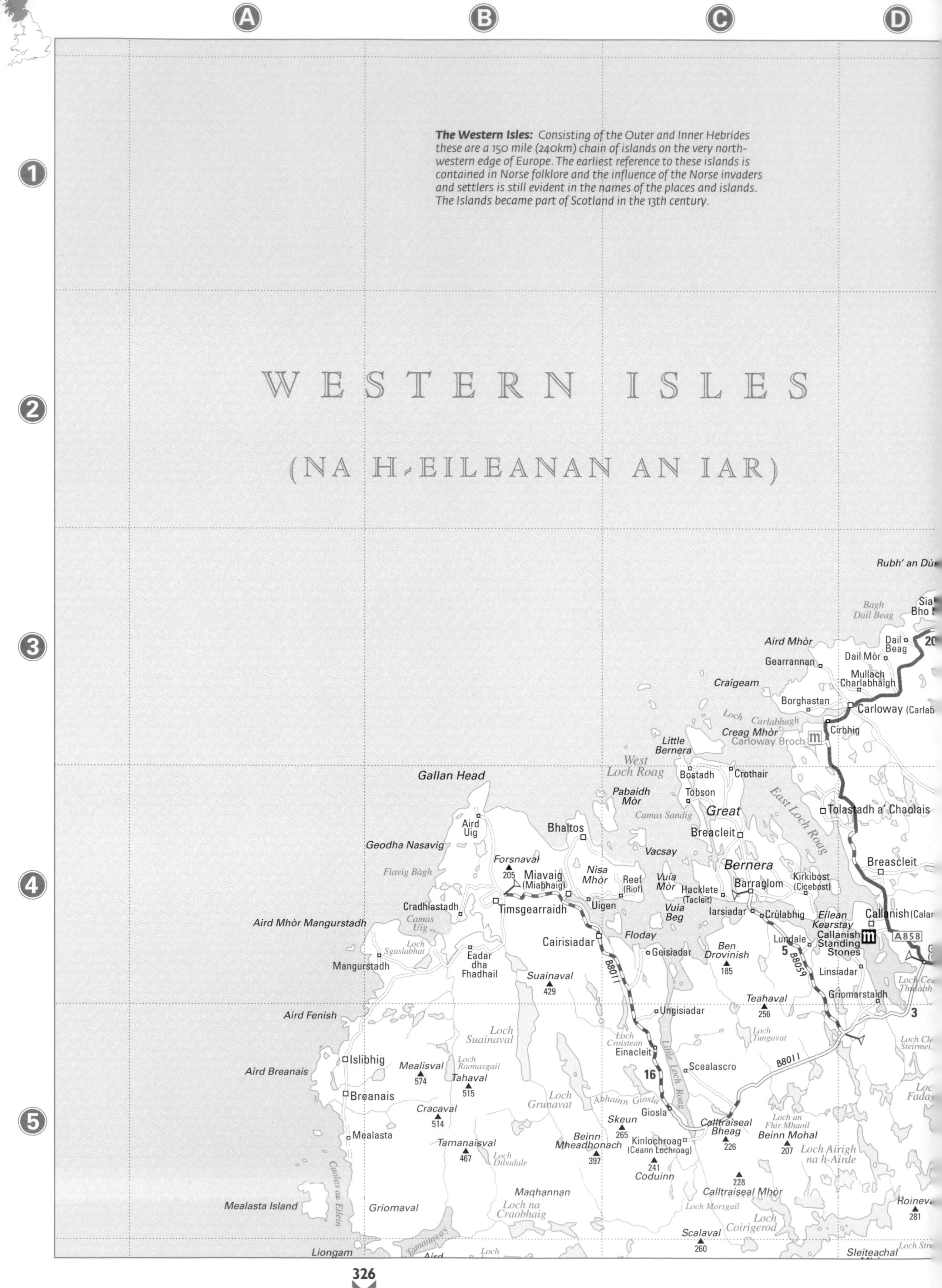
A
B
C
D
1
2
3
4
5
The Western Isles: *Consisting of the Outer and Inner Hebrides these are a 150 mile (240km) chain of islands on the very north-western edge of Europe. The earliest reference to these islands is contained in Norse folklore and the influence of the Norse invaders and settlers is still evident in the names of the places and islands. The Islands became part of Scotland in the 13th century.*
WESTERN ISLES
(NA H-EILEANAN AN IAR)
Rubh' an Dù
Bagh Dail Beag
Aird Mhòr
Dail Beag
Dail Mòr
Gearrannan
Craigeam
Mullach Charlabhaigh
Borghastan
Carloway (Carlab
Loch Carlabhagh
Creag Mhòr
Carloway Broch
Cirbhig
Little Bernera
West Loch Roag
Bostadh
Crothair
Gallan Head
Pabaidh Mòr
Tobson
East Loch Roag
Camas Sandig
Great
Tolastadh a' Chaolais
Aird Uig
Bhaltos
Breacleit
Geodha Nasavig
Vacsay
Breascleit
Forsnaval
205
Fiavig Bàgh
Miavaig (Miabhaig)
Nisa Mhòr
Reef (Riof)
Vuia Mòr
Bernera
Kirkibost (Cicebost)
Hacklete (Tacleit)
Barraglom
Cradhlastadh
Timsgearraidh
Uigen
Vuia Beg
Iarsiadar
Crùlabhig
Eilean Kearstay
Callanish (Calar
Aird Mhòr Mangurstadh
Camas Uig
Cairisiadar
Floday
Lundale
Callanish Standing Stones
A858
Loch Sgaslabhat
Eadar dha Fhadhail
Geisiadar
Ben Drovinish
185
5
B8059
Mangurstadh
B8011
Suainaval
429
Linsiadar
Teahaval
256
Griomarstaidh
Aird Fenish
Ungisiadar
3
Loch Suainaval
Loch Croistean
Loch Tungavat
Islibhig
Loch Raonasgail
Einacleit
Little Loch Roag
Scealascro
Aird Breanais
Mealisval
574
Tahaval
515
16
B8011
Breanais
Loch Grunavat
Abhainn Giosla
Cracaval
514
Giosla
Skeun
265
Calltraiseal Bheag
226
Loch an Fhir Mhaoil
Mealasta
Beinn Mheadhonach
397
Beinn Mohal
207
Tamanaisval
467
Loch Dibadale
Kinlochroag (Ceann Lochroag)
241
Coduinn
Loch Airigh na h-Àirde
228
Maqhannan
Calltraiseal Mhòr
Mealasta Island
Caolas an Eilein
Griomaval
Loch na Craobhaig
Loch Morsgail
Hoinev
281
Loch Coirigerod
Scalaval
260
Liongam
Sleiteachal

326

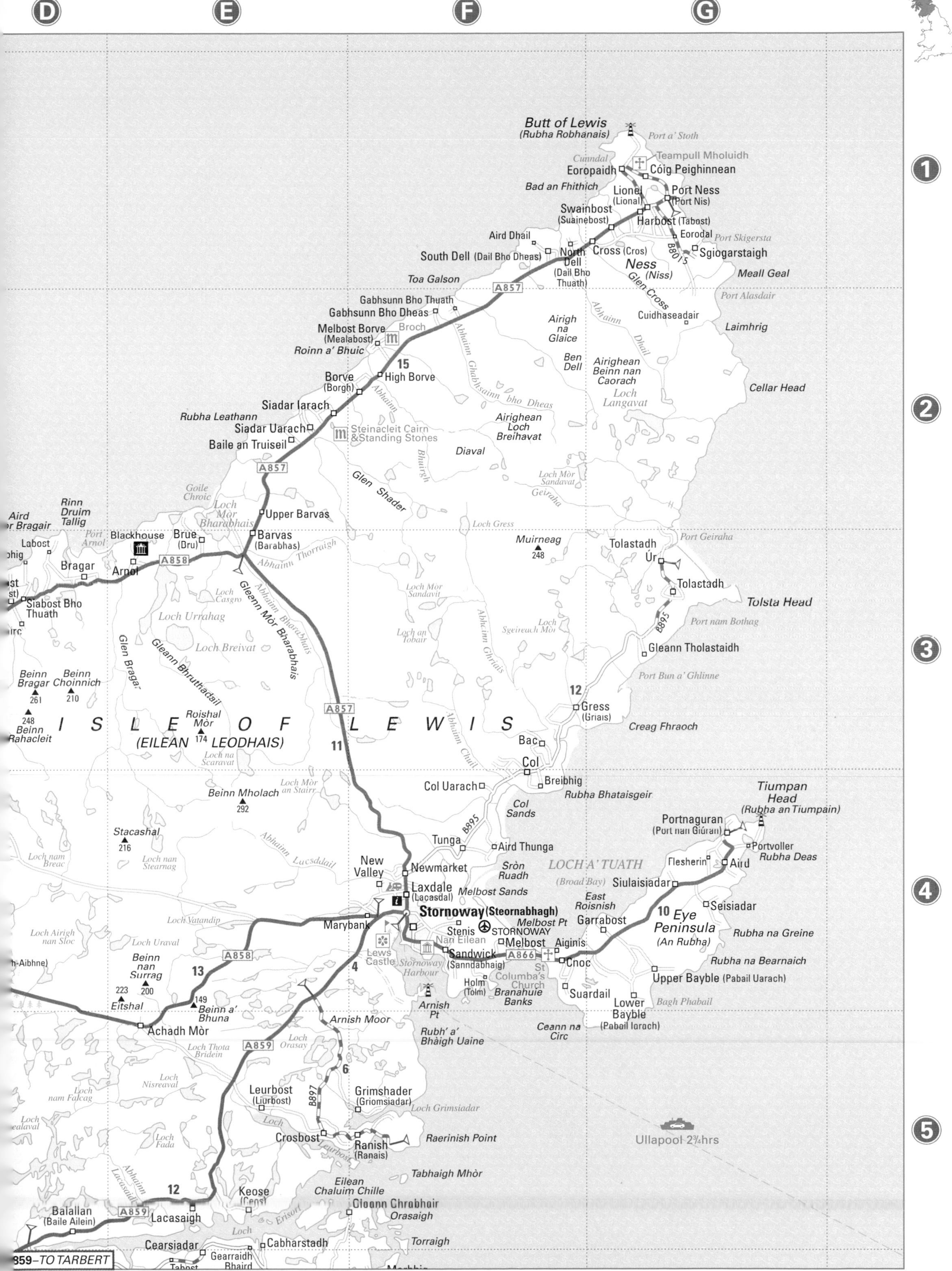
D
E
F
G
1
2
3
4
5
Butt of Lewis
(Rubha Robhanais)
Port a' Stoth
Teampull Mholuidh
Eoropaidh
Còig Peighinnean
Bad an Fhithich
Lionel
(Lional)
Port Ness
(Port Nis)
Swainbost
(Suainebost)
Harbost (Tabost)
Eorodal
Port Skigersta
Aird Dhail
South Dell (Dail Bho Dheas)
North Dell
(Dail Bho Thuath)
Cross (Cros)
Sgiogarstaigh
Ness
(Niss)
Meall Geal
Toa Galson
Glen Cross
Port Alasdair
Gabhsunn Bho Thuath
Gabhsunn Bho Dheas
Cuidhaseadair
Melbost Borve
(Mealabost)
Broch
Roinn a' Bhuic
Airigh na Glaice
Laimhrig
Ben Dell
Airighean Beinn nan Caorach
Loch Langavat
Borve
(Borgh)
High Borve
Cellar Head
Siadar Iarach
Rubha Leathann
Siadar Uarach
Airighean Loch Breihavat
Steinacleit Cairn & Standing Stones
Baile an Truiseil
Diaval
Glen Shader
Upper Barvas
Rinn Druim Tallig
Blackhouse
Brue
(Dru)
Barvas
(Barabhas)
Loch Gress
Muirneag
248
Tolastadh Úr
Port Geiraha
Bragar
Arnol
Tolastadh
Tolsta Head
Siabost Bho Thuath
Loch Urrahag
Gleann Mòr Barabhais
Port nam Bothag
Loch Breivat
Gleann Tholastaidh
Glen Bragar
Gleann Bhruthadail
Port Bun a' Ghlinne
Beinn Bragar
261
Beinn Choinnich
210
Gress
(Griais)
Creag Fhraoch
Roishal Mòr
174
ISLE OF LEWIS
(EILEAN LEODHAIS)
Beinn Rahacleit
248
Bac
Col
Breibhig
Col Uarach
Rubha Bhataisgeir
Beinn Mholach
292
Tiumpan Head
(Rubha an Tiumpain)
Col Sands
Portnaguran
(Port nan Giùran)
Stacashal
216
Tunga
Aird Thunga
Portvoller
Rubha Deas
New Valley
Newmarket
Sròn Ruadh
LOCH A' TUATH
(Broad Bay)
Flesherin
Aird
Laxdale
(Lacasdal)
Melbost Sands
Siulaisiadar
East Roisnish
Seisiadar
Stornoway (Steornabhagh)
STORNOWAY
Melbost Pt
Garrabost
Eye Peninsula
(An Rubha)
Marybank
Stenis
Nan Eilean
Melbost
Aiginis
Rubha na Greine
Lewis Castle
Sandwick
(Sanndabhaig)
St Columba's Church
Cnoc
Rubha na Bearnaich
Beinn nan Surrag
223
200
Eitshal
Holm
(Tolm)
Branahuie Banks
Suardail
Upper Bayble (Pabail Uarach)
Arnish Pt
Lower Bayble
(Pabail Iarach)
Bagh Phabail
Beinn a' Bhuna
149
Achadh Mòr
Arnish Moor
Ceann na Circ
Rubh' a' Bhàigh Uaine
Leurbost
(Liurbost)
Grimshader
(Griomsiadar)
Loch Grimsiadar
Crosbost
Ranish
(Ranais)
Raerinish Point
Ullapool 2¾hrs
Tabhaigh Mhòr
Eilean Chaluim Chille
Keose
Cloann Chrabhair
Orasaigh
Balallan
(Baile Ailein)
Lacasaigh
Cearsiadar
Cabharstadh
Torraigh
Gearraidh Bhaird
A857
A858
A859
A866
B895
B8015
B897
A859–TO TARBERT
327

Stornoway: *One of Stornoway's most famous sons is Sir Alexander Mackenzie who, in 1793, became the first European to cross the North American continent as far as the Arctic Ocean. The river that he followed was subsequently called the Mackenzie River.* ***Map ref. F4.***

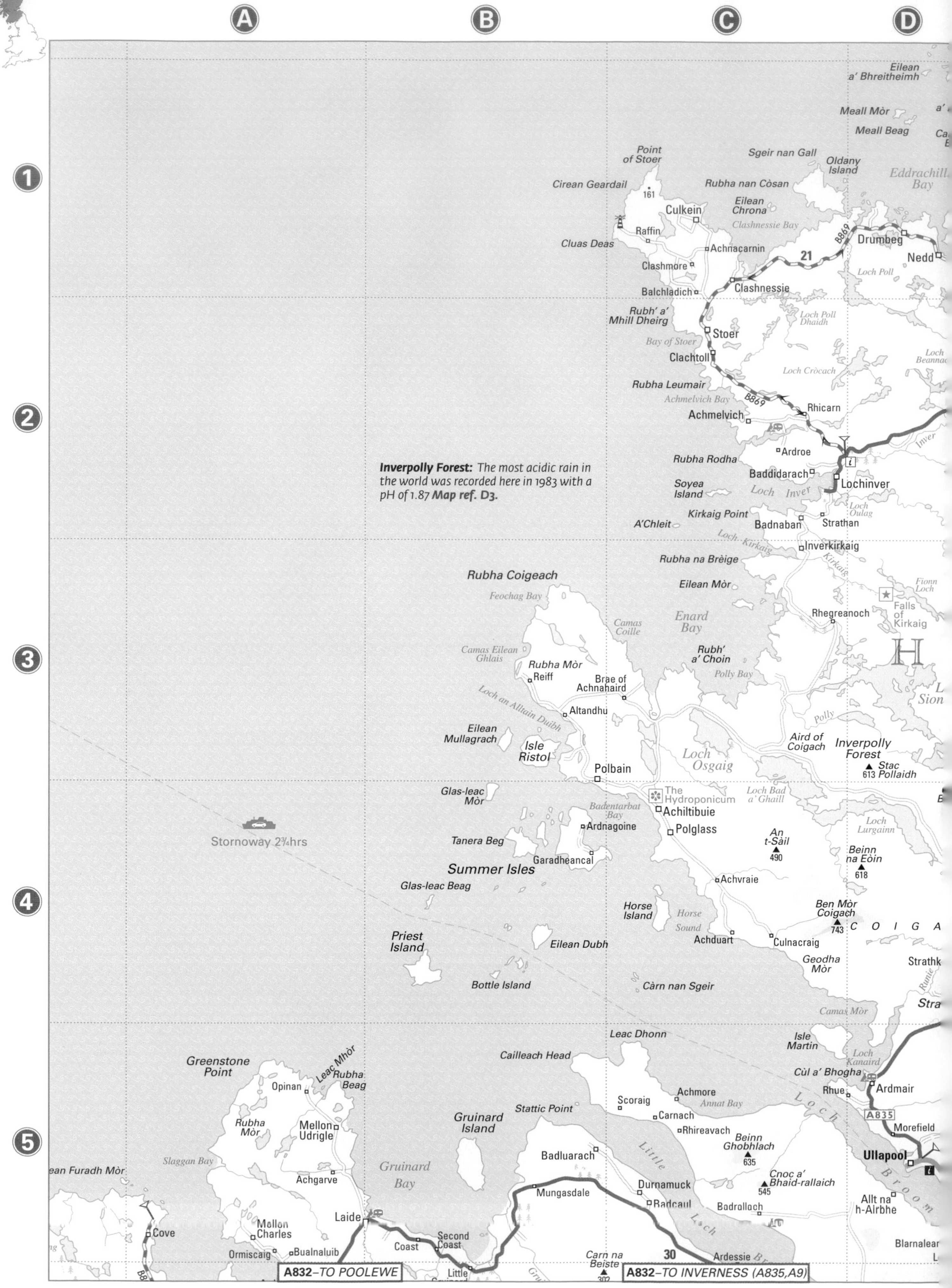
A
B
C
D
1
2
3
4
5
Eilean
a' Bhreitheimh
Meall Mòr
Meall Beag
Point
of Stoer
Sgeir nan Gall
Oldany
Island
Eddrachill
Bay
Cirean Geardail
161
Rubha nan Còsan
Culkein
Eilean
Chrona
Clashnessie Bay
Raffin
Cluas Deas
Achnacarnin
B869
Drumbeg
Nedd
21
Clashmore
Loch Poll
Balchladich
Clashnessie
Rubh' a'
Mhill Dheirg
Loch Poll
Dhaidh
Stoer
Bay of Stoer
Clachtoll
Loch
Beannac
Loch Cròcach
Rubha Leumair
Achmelvich Bay
B869
Rhicarn
Achmelvich
Inver
Ardroe
Rubha Rodha
Inverpolly Forest: The most acidic rain in the world was recorded here in 1983 with a pH of 1.87 Map ref. D3.
Baddidarach
Lochinver
Soyea
Island
Loch Inver
Kirkaig Point
Loch
Oulag
A'Chleit
Badnaban
Strathan
Loch Kirkaig
Inverkirkaig
Rubha na Brèige
Kirkaig
Rubha Coigeach
Eilean Mòr
Fionn
Loch
Feochag Bay
Falls
of
Kirkaig
Enard
Bay
Rhegreanoch
Camas
Coille
Camas Eilean
Ghlais
Rubh'
a' Choin
Rubha Mòr
Reiff
Polly Bay
Brae of
Achnahaird
Sion
Loch an Alltain Duibh
Altandhu
Polly
Eilean
Mullagrach
Isle
Ristol
Loch
Osgaig
Aird of
Coigach
Inverpolly
Forest
Stac
613 Pollaidh
Polbain
Glas-leac
Mòr
The
Hydroponicum
Loch Bad
a' Ghaill
Badentarbat
Bay
Achiltibuie
Ardnagoine
Loch
Lurgainn
Stornoway 2¾hrs
Polglass
An
t-Sàil
490
Tanera Beg
Beinn
na Eòin
618
Garadheancal
Summer Isles
Achvraie
Glas-leac Beag
Ben Mòr
Coigach
743
C O I G A
Horse
Island
Horse
Sound
Priest
Island
Eilean Dubh
Achduart
Culnacraig
Geodha
Mòr
Strathk
Runie
Bottle Island
Càrn nan Sgeir
Stra
Camas Mòr
Leac Dhonn
Isle
Martin
Greenstone
Point
Leac Mhòr
Cailleach Head
Loch
Kanaird
Rubha
Beag
Opinan
Cùl a' Bhogha
Ardmair
Rhue
Scoraig
Achmore
Annat Bay
Stattic Point
Loch
A835
Rubha
Mòr
Mellon
Udrigle
Carnach
Morefield
Gruinard
Island
Rhireavach
Beinn
Ghobhlach
635
Slaggan Bay
Little
Ullapool
Badluarach
ean Furadh Mòr
Gruinard
Bay
Cnoc a'
Bhaid-rallaich
545
Broom
Achgarve
Durnamuck
Mungasdale
Badcaul
Loch
Allt na
h-Airbhe
Badrolloch
Laide
Mellon
Charles
Cove
Second
Coast
Coast
Blarnalear
Ormiscaig
Bualnaluib
Carn na
Beiste
302
30
Ardessie
A832–TO POOLEWE
Little
A832–TO INVERNESS (A835,A9)
B8

319

Gruinard Island: Known as 'Anthrax Island' because of 1942 biological warfare experiments. Anthrax spores were released this 520 acre (210ha), uninhabited island to test its killing power on a flock of sheep. The island was so contaminated that remained out of bounds for 50 years. In 1986 a company was paid £500,000 to decontaminate it by soaking the ground in 276 tons (280 tonnes) of formaldehyde diluted in 1,968 tons (2,000 tonnes) of sea water. Also much of the topsoil was rem in sealed containers. A flock of sheep have since grazed there without harm…still not the place to go for a picnic! **Map re**

334

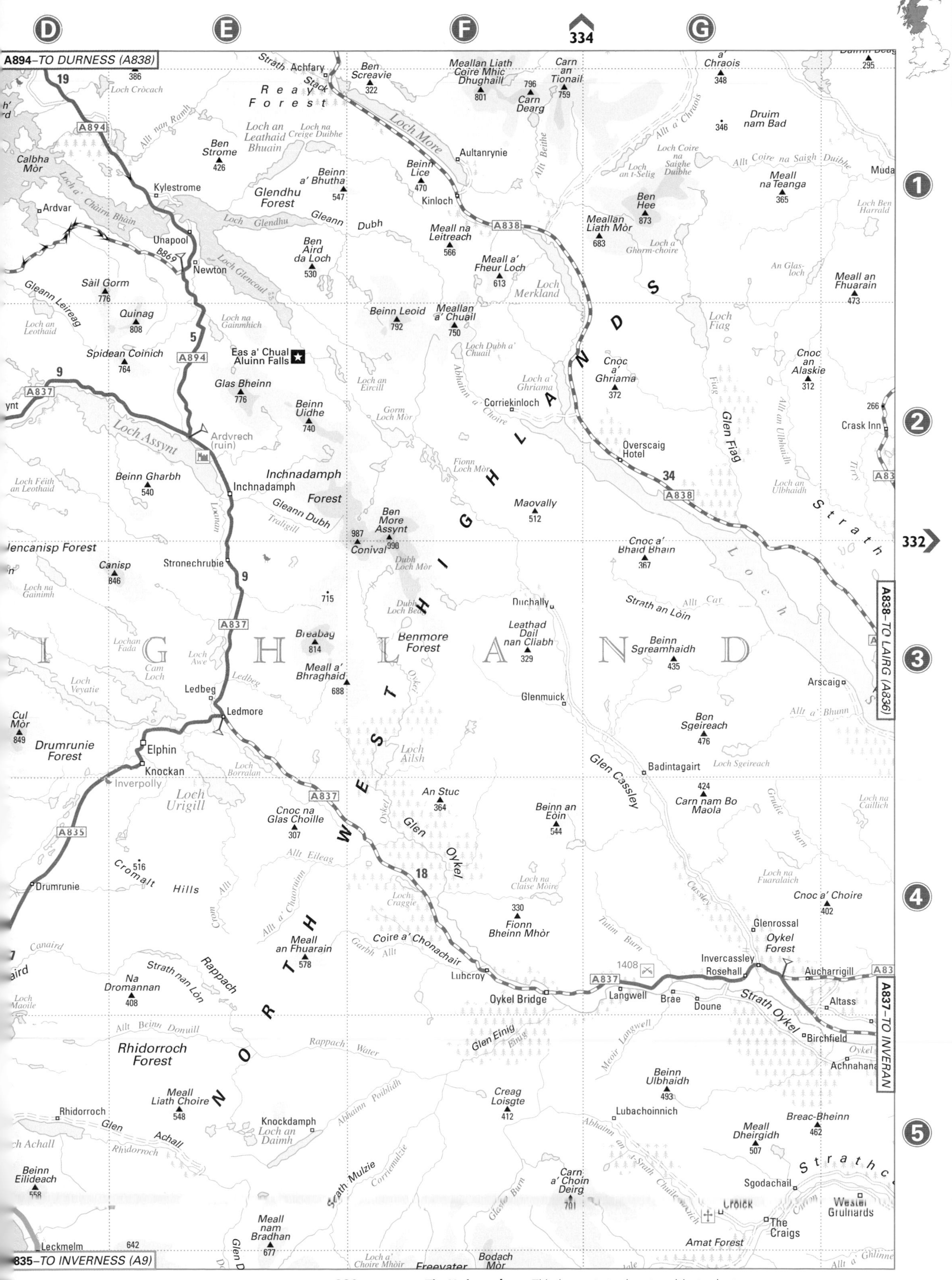
D
E
F
G
A894–TO DURNESS (A838)
Strath
Achfary
Stack
Ben Screavie
322
Meallan Liath Coire Mhic Dhughaill
801
796
Carn Dearg
Carn an Tionail
759
a' Chraois
348
295
386
Loch Cròcach
Reay Forest
Loch More
Loch an Leathaid Bhuain
Loch na Creige Duibhe
Allt nan Ramh
A894
Ben Strome
426
Druim nam Bad
346
Allt a' Chraois
Loch Coire na Saighe Duibhe
Allt Coire na Saigh Duibhe
Muda
Calbha Mòr
Kylestrome
Glendhu Forest
Beinn a' Bhutha
547
Beinn Lice
470
Aultanrynie
Allt Beithe
Loch an t-Selig
Meall na Teanga
365
Ardvar
Loch a' Chàirn Bhàin
Loch Glendhu
Gleann Dubh
Kinloch
Ben Hee
873
Loch Ben Harrald
Meallan Liath Mòr
683
Unapool
B869
Newton
Loch Glencoul
Ben Aird da Loch
530
Meall na Leitreach
566
A838
Meall a' Fheur Loch
613
Loch Merkland
Loch a' Ghorm-choire
An Glas-loch
Meall an Fhuarain
473
Gleann Leireag
Sàil Gorm
776
Quinag
808
Loch an Leothaid
Loch na Gainmhich
Beinn Leoid
792
Meallan a' Chuail
750
Loch Dubh a' Chuail
Loch Fiag
5
Spidean Coinich
764
A894
Eas a' Chual Aluinn Falls
Cnoc a' Ghriama
372
Cnoc an Alaskie
312
9
A837
Glas Bheinn
776
Loch an Eircill
Loch a' Ghriama
Fiag
Glen Fiag
266
Crask Inn
Beinn Uidhe
740
Gorm Loch Mòr
Corriekinloch
Abhainn a' Choire
Allt an Ulbhaidh
Loch Assynt
Ardvrech (ruin)
Overscaig Hotel
Loch Fèith an Leothaid
Beinn Gharbh
540
Inchnadamph
Inchnadamph Forest
Fionn Loch Mòr
34
A838
Loch an Ulbhaidh
Loanan
Gleann Dubh
Traligill
Ben More Assynt
987
Conival
998
Maovally
512
Strath
Glencanisp Forest
Canisp
846
Stronechrubie
Dubh Loch Mòr
Cnoc a' Bhaid Bhain
367
332
Loch na Gainimh
9
715
Duchally
Strath an Lòin
Allt Car
Loch
A838–TO LAIRG (A836)
Dubh Loch Beag
A837
Breabag
814
Benmore Forest
Leathad Dail nan Cliabh
329
Beinn Sgreamhaidh
435
Lochan Fada
Loch Awe
Cam Loch
HIGHLAND
Meall a' Bhraghaid
688
Loch Veyatie
Ledbeg
Ledbeg
Oykel
Glenmuick
Arscaig
Ledmore
Allt a' Bhunn
Ben Sgeireach
476
Cul Mòr
849
Drumrunie Forest
Elphin
Knockan
Loch Ailsh
Glen Cassley
Badintagairt
Loch Sgeireach
Inverpolly
Loch Borralan
Loch Urigill
A837
An Stuc
364
424
Carn nam Bo Maola
Loch na Caillich
Cnoc na Glas Choille
307
Glen Oykel
Beinn an Eòin
544
Grudie Burn
A835
Allt Eileag
516
Cromalt Hills
18
Loch na Claise Mòire
Loch na Fuaralaich
Drumrunie
Loch Craggie
Cassley
330
Fionn Bheinn Mhòr
Cnoc a' Choire
402
Allt a' Chaorainn
Glenrossal
Oykel Forest
Canaird
Meall an Fhuarain
578
Coire a' Chonachair
Garbh Allt
Tutim Burn
1408
Invercassley
Rosehall
Aucharrigill
Strath nan Lòn
Rappach
Lubcroy
A837
Langwell
Brae
Doune
Strath Oykel
A837–TO INVERAN
Na Dromannan
408
Oykel Bridge
Altass
Loch Maoile
Allt Beinn Donuill
Meoir Langwell
Birchfield
Rhidorroch Forest
Rappach Water
Glen Einig
Einig
Oykel
Achnahanat
NORTH WEST HIGHLANDS
Beinn Ulbhaidh
493
Meall Liath Choire
548
Abhainn Poiblidh
Creag Loisgte
412
Rhidorroch
Glen Achall
Knockdamph
Loch an Daimh
Lubachoinnich
Breac-Bheinn
462
Loch Achall
Rhidorroch
Abhainn an t-Srath Chuileannaich
Meall Dheirgidh
507
Beinn Eilideach
558
Strath Mulzie
Corriemulzie
Glasha Burn
Carn a' Choin Deirg
701
Strathcarron
Sgodachail
Croick
Wester Gruinards
Meall nam Bradhan
677
Glen Douchary
The Craigs
Leckmelm
642
Amat Forest
A835–TO INVERNESS (A9)
Loch a' Choire Mhòir
Freevater
Bodach Mòr
Allt a' Ghlinne
1
2
3
4
5

Achmelvich: *Could almost be in the tropics, a stunning little bay with fantastic white sand and clear turquoise water. Go on, check it out.* ***Map ref. C2.***

320

The Hydroponicum: *This demonstrates how to cultivate plants by growing them in gravel or similar material and pumping water containing dissolved nutrient salts through them.* ***Map ref. C4.***

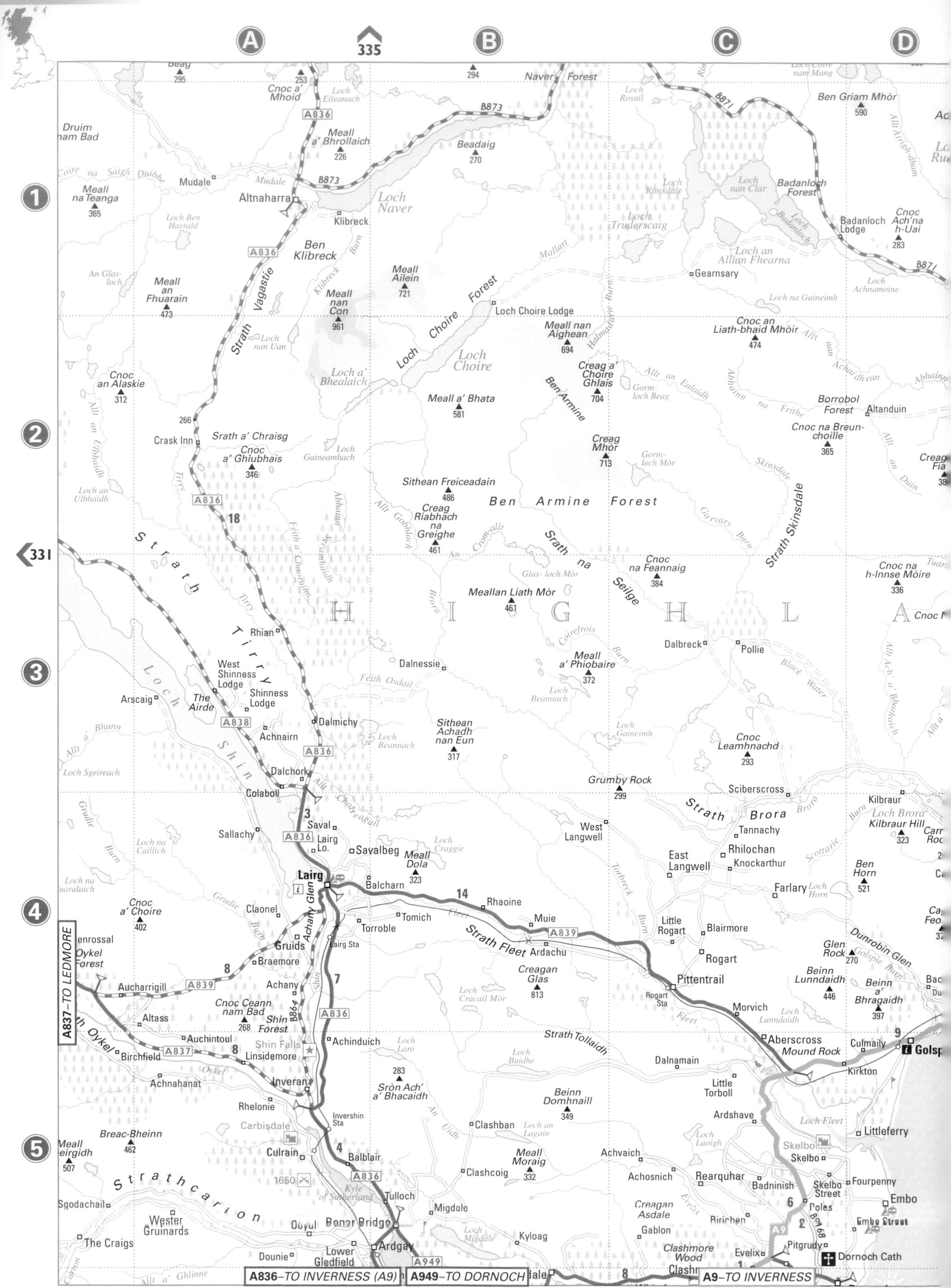

A
B
C
D
1
2
3
4
5
335
331
321
A836–TO INVERNESS (A9)
A949–TO DORNOCH
A9–TO INVERNESS
A837–TO LEDMORE
Altnaharra
Loch Naver
Ben Klibreck
Loch Choire
Ben Armine Forest
Strath Vagastie
Crask Inn
Loch Shin
Lairg
Strath Fleet
Strath Brora
Golspie
Bonar Bridge
Ardgay
Dornoch Cath
Embo
Skelbo
Pittentrail
Rogart
Shin Falls
Inveran
Culrain
Strathcarron
HIGHLAND

Loch Shin: The largest freshwater lake in Sutherland. The Lairg Dam, at the southern end of the loch is 1,400 feet (427m) long and 40 feet (12m) high. It raised the water level of the loch by 36 feet (11m) and is used to create hydro-electricity. It is the most northern hydro-electric scheme in mainland Britain. **Map ref. A3.**

D
E
F
336
G
A9–TO THURSO
A99–TO WICK
337
322
1
2
3
4
5
Forest
Cnoc Cromuillt
365
337
Dalganachan
Ben Alisky
349
na Beinne
226
Sheppardstown
Crofts of Benachielt
Ben-a-chielt
287
Rumster Forest
Cnocan Conachreag
269
Cnoc na Saobhaidhe
290
Lochside
Knockfin Heights
438
Burn of Houstry
Houstry
Nottingham
Gillivoan
Landhallow
Latheron
Achnaclyth
Smerral
Achentoul
Féith Gaineimh Mhòr
Glutt Water
Dunbeath Water
Badnagie
Latheronwheel
Kinbrace
Cnoc Coire na Fearna
437
Gobernuisgeach
Berriedale Water
Maiden Pap
484
Braemore
Achorn
Dunbeath
Laidhay Croft Museum
Heritage Centre
Toremore
Inver
Burnfoot
Morven
706
Cnoc an Eireannaich
517
Knockally
Dunbeath
Dunbeath Bay
A897
Meall na Caorach
396
Ramscraigs
Scaraben
626
Suisgill Burn
Wag
Borgue
Langwell Forest
20
17
Strath of Kildonan
Loch Scalabsdale
Creag Scalabsdale
555
Garvery Hill
333
Cnoc Sallslade
483
Aultibea
Newport
Ceann Leathad nam Bo
Mid Hill
312
330
Blar a' Ghille Dhomhnaich
Langwell House
Berriedale
Braigh na h-Eaglaise
422
Kildonan Burn
Kildonan Lodge
Torrish Burn
Beinn Dubhain
Duible 414
Ousdale
Craggie
Craggie Water
Creag Thoraraidh
404
Badbea
Kilphedir
Torrish
Caen
A9
Ord of Caithness
Eldrable Hill
416
The Craggan
482
Ben Uarie
623
Beinn Dhorain
628
Marrel
Navidale
East Helmsdale
Helmsdale
West Helmsdale
Gartymore
Meallan Liath Beag
479
Beinn Mhealaich
592
Glen Sletdale
Glen Loth
Allt Smeorail
Portgower
Culgower
Lothmore
Creag a' Chrionaich
394
Kilmote
Col-bheinn
538
Lothbeg
11
Lothbeg Point
Kintradwell
Killin
Killin Rock
215
West Clyne
East Clyne
Greenhill
Dalchalm
Clynelish
East Brora
Brora
Doll
nrobin Castle

Helmsdale: The practise of deer stalking in the Highlands dates back to the 19th Century and was made popular by Queen Victoria and Prince Albert who took out a lease on Balmoral in 1848. Deer stalking is regarded as a skilful way of hunting deer by getting within 100 yards (91m) of the quarry before making the kill. There are now over 300,000 Red Deer in the Highlands and deer stalking remains a popular sport with hunters and photographers from both Britain and abroad. The area around Helmsdale is regarded as particularly good 'deer stalking' country. **Map ref. F3.**

322

Dunbeath: Purpose built village created in the early 1800s to take advantage of the Herring boom. Dunbeath is also the birthplace of Neil Miller Gunn the celebrated Scottish novelist (1891–1973). **Map ref. G1.**

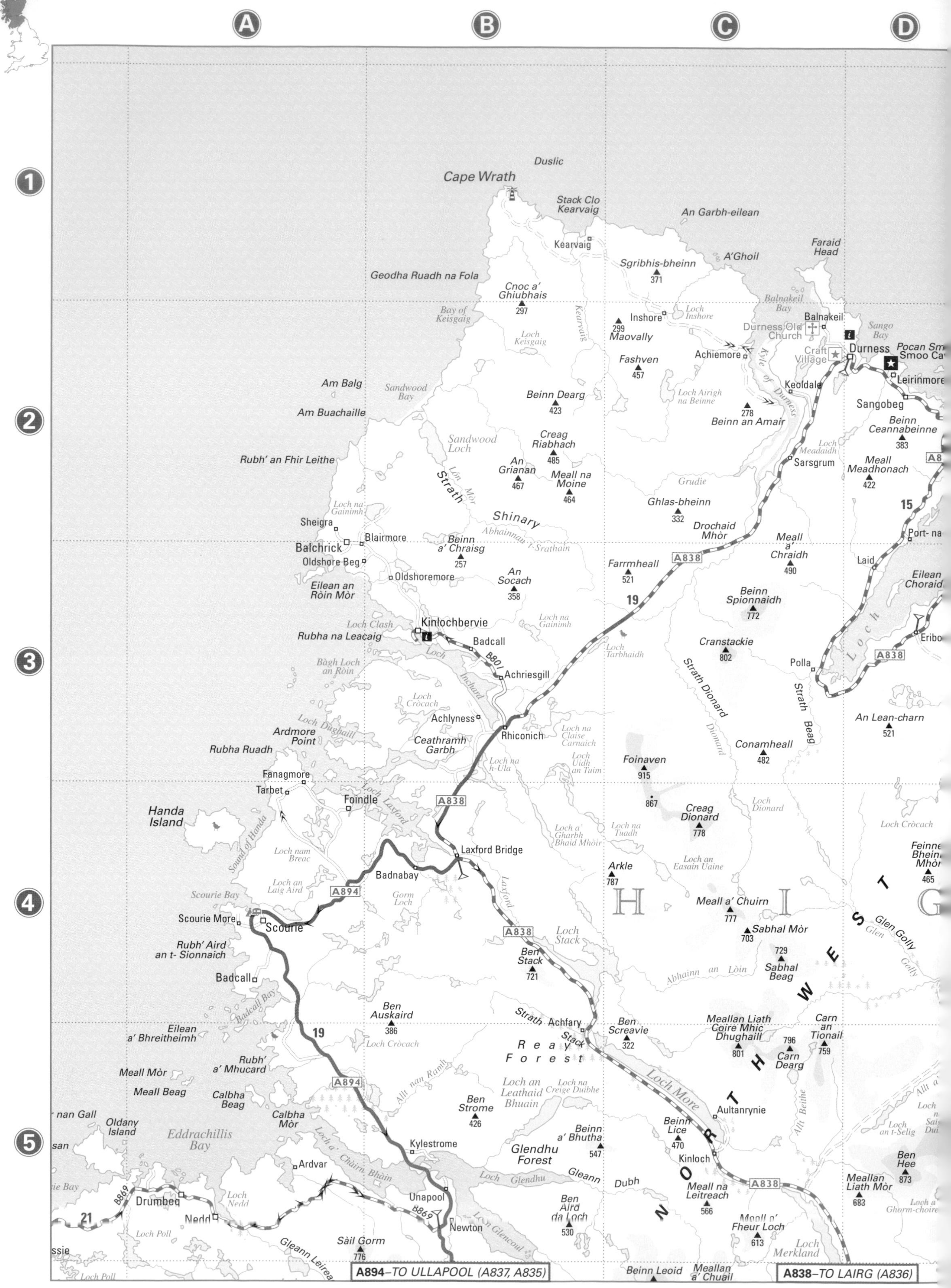
A
B
C
D
1
2
3
4
5
Cape Wrath
Duslic
Stack Clo Kearvaig
An Garbh-eilean
Kearvaig
Faraid Head
A'Ghoil
Sgribhis-bheinn
371
Geodha Ruadh na Fola
Cnoc a' Ghiubhais
297
Bay of Keisgaig
Loch Keisgaig
Inshore
Loch Inshore
299
Maovally
Balnakeil Bay
Balnakeil
Durness Old Church
Sango Bay
Durness
Pocan Smoo
Craft Village
Achiemore
Kyle of Durness
Fashven
457
Keoldale
Leirinmore
Am Balg
Sandwood Bay
Beinn Dearg
423
Loch Airigh na Beinne
Sangobeg
Am Buachaille
278
Beinn an Amair
Beinn Ceannabeinne
383
Sandwood Loch
Creag Riabhach
485
Loch Meadaidh
Sarsgrum
Meall Meadhonach
422
Rubh' an Fhir Leithe
An Grianan
467
Meall na Moine
464
Strath
Lòn Mòr
Grudie
Ghlas-bheinn
332
15
Loch na Gainimh
Shinary
Sheigra
Abhainnan t-Srathain
Drochaid Mhòr
Port-na
Balchrick
Blairmore
Beinn a' Chraisg
257
Meall a' Chraidh
490
Oldshore Beg
Farrmheall
521
A838
Laid
Oldshoremore
An Socach
358
Eilean Choraid
Eilean an Ròin Mòr
19
Beinn Spionnaidh
772
Loch Clash
Kinlochbervie
Loch na Gainimh
Rubha na Leacaig
Badcall
Loch Tarbhaidh
Cranstackie
802
Eriboll
Bàgh Loch an Ròin
Loch
B801
Achriesgill
Inchard
Strath Dionard
Polla
A838
Loch Cròcach
Strath Beag
Loch Dùghaill
Achlyness
An Lean-charn
521
Ardmore Point
Rhiconich
Loch na Claise Carnaich
Dionard
Ceathramh Garbh
Rubha Ruadh
Loch na h-Ula
Loch Uidh an Tuim
Conamheall
482
Foinaven
915
Fanagmore
Tarbet
Loch Laxford
A838
Foindle
867
Creag Dionard
778
Loch Dionard
Handa Island
Loch Cròcach
Sound of Handa
Loch a' Gharbh Bhaid Mhòir
Loch na Tuadh
Feinne Bheinn Mhòr
465
Loch nam Breac
Laxford Bridge
Badnabay
Laxford
Loch an Easain Uaine
Arkle
787
Loch an Laig Aird
Scourie Bay
A894
Gorm Loch
Meall a' Chuirn
777
Scourie More
Scourie
A838
Sabhal Mòr
703
Glen Golly
Loch Stack
729
Rubh' Aird an t-Sionnaich
Ben Stack
721
Sabhal Beag
Abhainn an Lòin
Badcall
Badcall Bay
Ben Auskaird
386
Strath
Achfary
Meallan Liath Coire Mhic Dhughaill
801
Carn an Tionail
759
Eilean a' Bhreitheimh
19
Loch Cròcach
Stack
Ben Screavie
322
796
Carn Dearg
Reay Forest
Rubh' a' Mhucard
Loch More
Meall Mòr
Allt nan Ramh
Meall Beag
A894
Loch an Leathaid Bhuain
Loch na Creige Duibhe
Calbha Beag
Ben Strome
426
Allt Beithe
Calbha Mòr
Aultanrynie
nan Gall
Oldany Island
Eddrachillis Bay
Beinn Lice
470
Loch an t-Selig
san
Kylestrome
Beinn a' Bhutha
547
Glendhu Forest
Ben Hee
873
Ardvar
Loch a' Chàirn Bhàin
Kinloch
ie Bay
Loch Glendhu
Gleann Dubh
A838
Meallan Liath Mòr
683
Unapool
Drumbeg
B869
Loch Nedd
B869
Ben Aird da Loch
530
Meall na Leitreach
566
21
Nedd
Newton
Loch Glencoul
Meall a' Fheur Loch
613
Loch Poll
Loch Merkland
Sàil Gorm
776
ssie
Gleann Leireag
Loch Poll
A894–TO ULLAPOOL (A837, A835)
Beinn Leoid
Meallan a' Chuail
A838–TO LAIRG (A836)
NORTH WEST HIGHLANDS

331

Laid: Between 1785 and 1850 the Highlands and Islands were subjected to 'The Clearances'. Under this system tens of thousands of clansmen were removed from their homes and holdings to make way for large-scale sheep farming by the wealthy landowners. Though generally acrimonious, some resettlement took place often involving re-location to poorer land along the coast where fishing and kelping were supposed to compensate for their previous existence. Some however were more fortunate and new villages were built to house them. Such a place is Laid which was created in 1832 to house those cleared from Eriboll on the other side of the loch. ***Map ref. D3.***

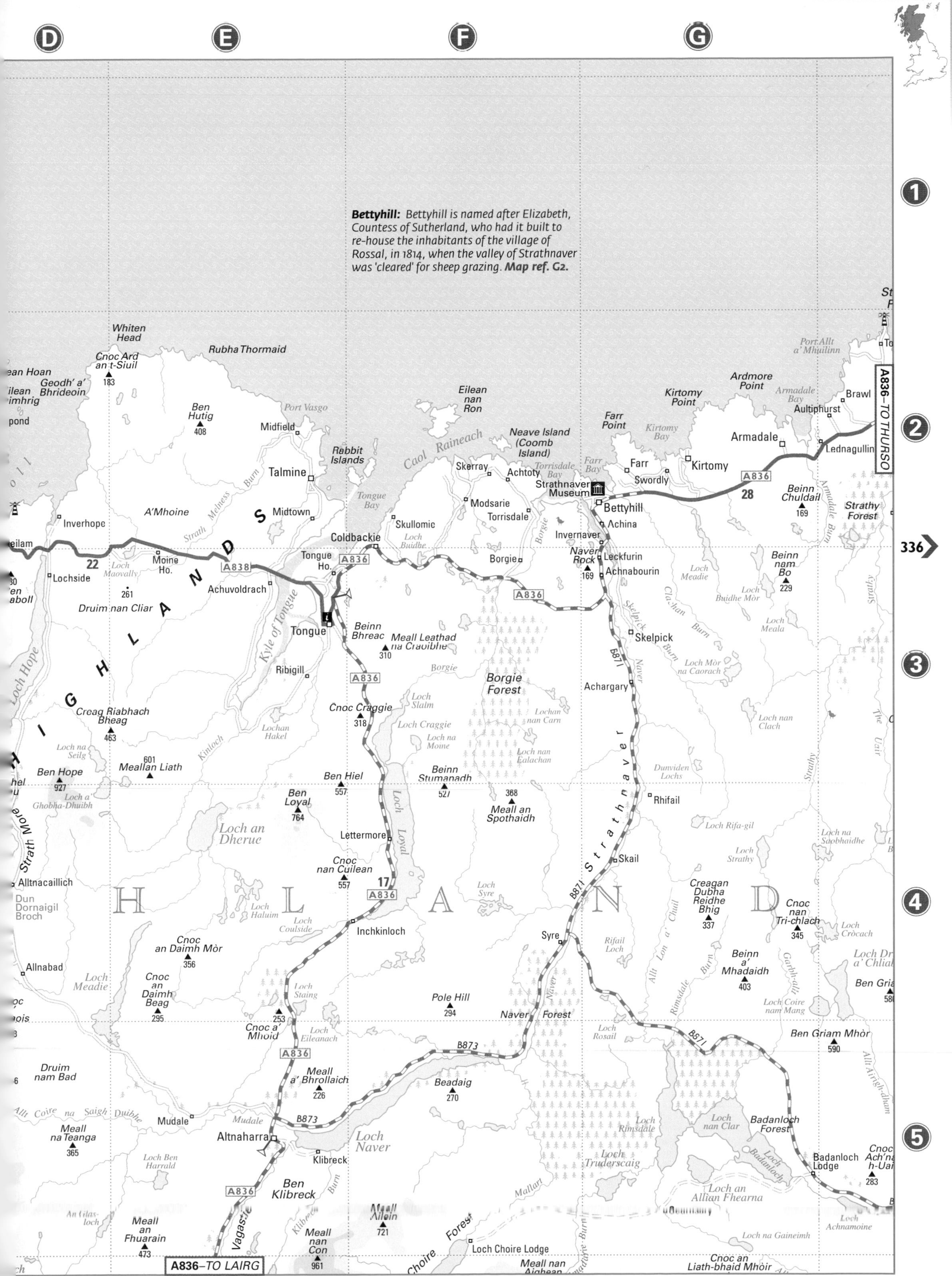

D
E
F
G
1
2
3
4
5
336
Bettyhill: Bettyhill is named after Elizabeth, Countess of Sutherland, who had it built to re-house the inhabitants of the village of Rossal, in 1814, when the valley of Strathnaver was 'cleared' for sheep grazing. Map ref. G2.
Whiten Head
Cnoc Ard an t-Siuil
183
Rubha Thormaid
Geodh' a' Bhrideoin
Ben Hutig
408
Port Vasgo
Midfield
Eilean nan Ron
Rabbit Islands
Caol Raineach
Neave Island (Coomb Island)
Farr Point
Kirtomy Bay
Kirtomy Point
Ardmore Point
Armadale Bay
Port Allt a' Mhuilinn
Brawl
Aultiphurst
Armadale
Kirtomy
Lednagullin
A836–TO THURSO
Talmine
Skerray
Achtoty
Torrisdale Bay
Farr Bay
Farr
Swordly
Strathnaver Museum
Bettyhill
A836
28
Beinn Chuldail
169
Strathy Forest
Inverhope
A'Mhoine
Strath Melness
Burn
Midtown
Tongue Bay
Modsarie
Torrisdale
Skullomic
Achina
Coldbackie
Loch Buidhe
Invernaver
Naver Rock
169
Leckfurin
Achnabourin
Borgie
Beinn nam Bo
229
Loch Meadie
Loch Buidhe Mòr
22
Moine Ho.
Loch Maovally
A838
Lochside
Tongue Ho.
A836
Achuvoldrach
261
Druim nan Cliar
Kyle of Tongue
Tongue
Beinn Bhreac
Meall Leathad na Craoibhe
310
Skelpick
B871
Loch Meala
Loch Mòr na Caorach
Ribigill
Borgie
Borgie Forest
Achargary
Naver
Loch Slaim
Cnoc Craggie
318
Loch Craggie
Lochan nan Carn
Loch nan Clach
Creag Riabhach Bheag
463
Lochan Hakel
Loch na Moine
Loch nan Ealachan
Loch na Seilg
601
Meallan Liath
Kinloch
Ben Hope
927
Loch a' Ghobha-Dhuibh
Ben Hiel
557
Beinn Stumanadh
527
368
Meall an Spothaidh
Dunviden Lochs
Rhifail
Strathnaver
Ben Loyal
764
Loch an Dherue
Loch Loyal
Lettermore
Loch Rifa-gil
Loch Strathy
Loch na Saobhaidhe
Strath More
Loch Hope
Cnoc nan Cuilean
557
17
A836
Skail
Alltnacaillich
Dun Dornaigil Broch
HIGHLAND
Loch Haluim
Loch Coulside
Loch Syre
B871
Creagan Dubha Reidhe Bhig
337
Cnoc nan Tri-chlach
345
Loch Cròcach
Inchkinloch
Syre
Rifail Loch
Cnoc an Daimh Mòr
356
Beinn a' Mhadaidh
403
Allnabad
Loch Meadie
Cnoc an Daimh Beag
295
Loch Staing
Pole Hill
294
Naver Forest
Loch Coire nam Mang
Ben Griam Mhòr
590
253
Cnoc a' Mhoid
Loch Eileanach
A836
B873
Loch Rosail
B871
Druim nam Bad
Meall a' Bhrollaich
226
Beadaig
270
Allt Coire na Saigh Duibhe
Mudale
Mudale
B873
Loch Rimsdale
Loch nan Clar
Badanloch Forest
Meall na Teanga
365
Altnaharra
Loch Naver
Loch Truderscaig
Loch Badanloch
Badanloch Lodge
Loch Ben Harrald
Klibreck
Ben Klibreck
Loch an Allan Fhearna
283
A836
Mallart
An Glas-loch
Meall an Fhuarain
473
Meall Ailein
721
Meall nan Con
961
Vagastie
Choire Forest
Loch Choire Lodge
Meall nan Aighean
Loch na Gaineimh
Loch Achnamoine
Cnoc an Liath-bhaid Mhòir
A836–TO LAIRG

332

Altnaharra: Altnaharra recorded the lowest ever temperature in Britain (-27.2°C) on the 30th December 1955. **Map ref. E5.**

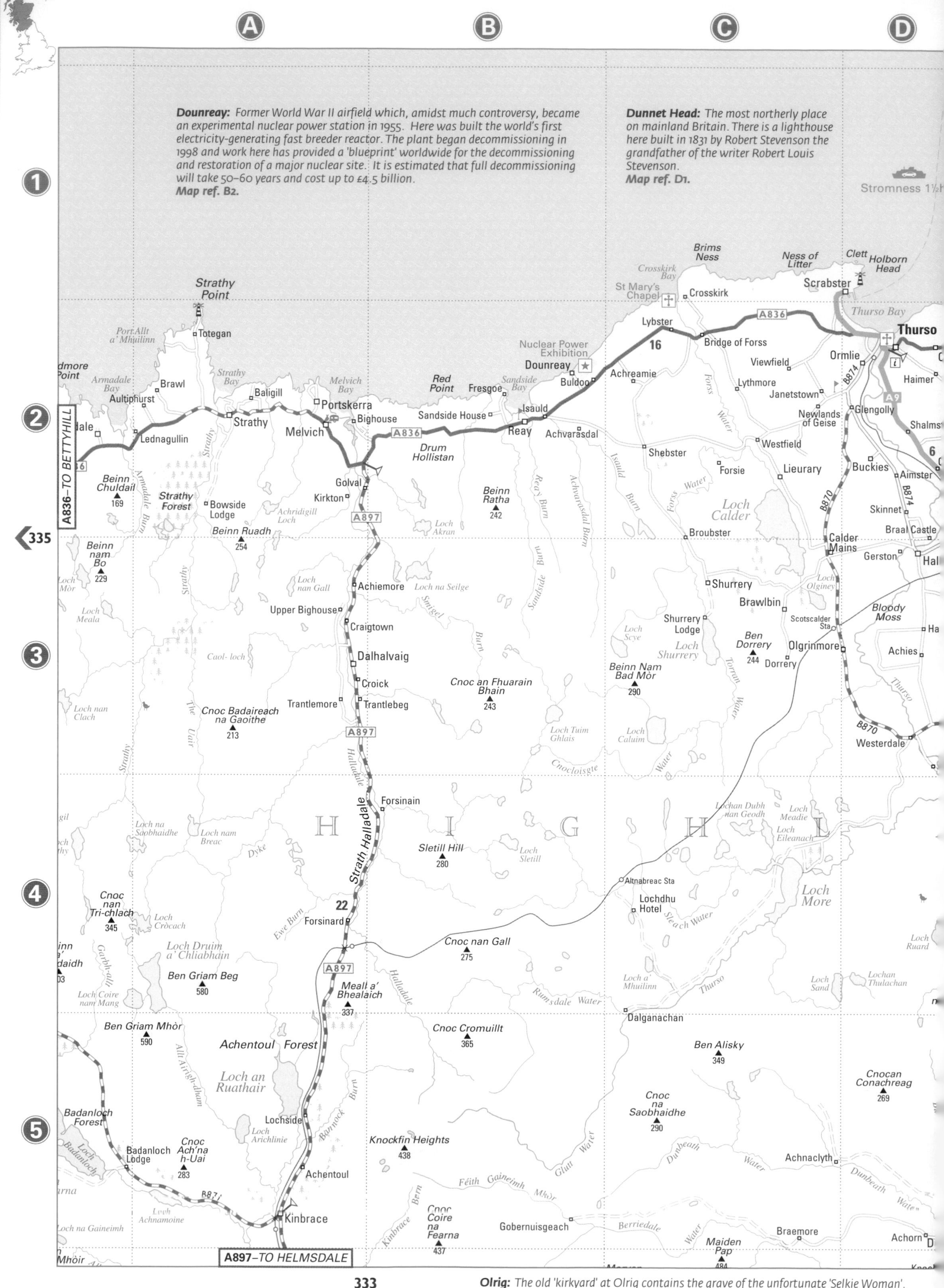
A
B
C
D
1
2
3
4
5
335
333
Dounreay: Former World War II airfield which, amidst much controversy, became an experimental nuclear power station in 1955. Here was built the world's first electricity-generating fast breeder reactor. The plant began decommissioning in 1998 and work here has provided a 'blueprint' worldwide for the decommissioning and restoration of a major nuclear site. It is estimated that full decommissioning will take 50–60 years and cost up to £4.5 billion. Map ref. B2.
Dunnet Head: The most northerly place on mainland Britain. There is a lighthouse here built in 1831 by Robert Stevenson the grandfather of the writer Robert Louis Stevenson. Map ref. D1.
Stromness
Brims Ness
Ness of Litter
Clett
Holborn Head
Crosskirk Bay
St Mary's Chapel
Crosskirk
Scrabster
Thurso Bay
Thurso
Strathy Point
Totegan
Port Allt a' Mhuilinn
Lybster
16
Bridge of Forss
Nuclear Power Exhibition
Dounreay
Buldoo
Achreamie
Viewfield
Ormlie
Haimer
Lythmore
Janetstown
Newlands of Geise
Glengolly
Shalmsi
A836
A9
B874
Strathy Bay
Melvich Bay
Red Point
Fresgoe
Sandside Bay
Armadale Bay
Brawl
Aultiphurst
Baligill
Portskerra
Bighouse
Sandside House
Isauld
Strathy
Melvich
Reay
Achvarasdal
Lednagullin
A836–TO BETTYHILL
Drum Hollistan
Shebster
Westfield
Forsie
Lieurary
Buckies
Aimster
6
Beinn Chuldail
169
Strathy Forest
Bowside Lodge
Golval
Kirkton
Achridigill Loch
Beinn Ratha
242
Loch Calder
Broubster
Skinnet
Braal Castle
A897
Loch Akran
Beinn Ruadh
254
Calder Mains
Gerston
Beinn nam Bo
229
Achiemore
Loch nan Gall
Loch na Seilge
Shurrery
Brawlbin
Loch Olginey
Bloody Moss
Upper Bighouse
Craigtown
Shurrery Lodge
Scotscalder Sta
Loch Scye
Loch Shurrery
Ben Dorrery
244
Olgrinmore
Dorrery
Achies
Loch Meala
Caol-loch
Dalhalvaig
Croick
Trantlemore
Trantlebeg
Cnoc an Fhuarain Bhain
243
Beinn Nam Bad Mòr
290
Loch nan Clach
Cnoc Badaireach na Gaoithe
213
Loch Tuim Ghlais
Loch Caluim
B870
Westerdale
Forsinain
Lochan Dubh nan Geodh
Loch Meadie
Loch Eileanach
H I G H L
Loch na Saobhaidhe
Loch nam Breac
Strath Halladale
Sletill Hill
280
Loch Sletill
Altnabreac Sta
Lochdhu Hotel
Loch More
Cnoc nan Tri-chlach
345
Loch Cròcach
22
Forsinard
Loch Druim a' Chliabhain
Cnoc nan Gall
275
Loch Ruard
Ben Griam Beg
580
Loch Coire nam Mang
Meall a' Bhealaich
337
Loch a' Mhuilinn
Loch Sand
Lochan Thulachan
Dalganachan
Ben Griam Mhòr
590
Achentoul Forest
Cnoc Cromuillt
365
Ben Alisky
349
Loch an Ruathair
Cnocan Conachreag
269
Cnoc na Saobhaidhe
290
Badanloch Forest
Lochside
Loch Arichlinie
Knockfin Heights
438
Badanloch Lodge
Cnoc Ach'na h-Uai
283
Achentoul
Achnaclyth
B871
Loch Achnamoine
Kinbrace
Cnoc Coire na Fearna
437
Gobernuisgeach
Braemore
Maiden Pap
484
Achorn
Loch na Gaineimh
A897–TO HELMSDALE

Olrig: The old 'kirkyard' at Olrig contains the grave of the unfortunate 'Selkie Woman'. She was found as a baby wrapped in a sealskin and grew up around the settlement. She was later accused of Devil Worship and banished from the kirk and later died in childbirth. It is said that the stone which covers her grave fills with tears and never dries out. ***Map ref. D2.***

D
E
F
338
G
1
2
3
4
5
St. Margaret's Hope 1hr (summer only)
Langaton Point
Island of Stroma
Nethertown
Red Head
Uppertown
Mell Head
Inner Sound
Boars of Duncansby
Muckle Skerry
Pentland Skerries
Dunnet Head
Easter Head
Men of Mey
St John's Point
Tang Head
Castle of Mey
Skarfskerry Point
Scarfskerry
Harrow
Head of Crees
Ness of Duncansby
Bay of Sannick
Dunnet Hill
121
B855
Brough
Ham
Loch of Mey
East Mey
A836
Gills Bay
Huna
Duncansby Head
The Thirl
Hunspow
St John's Loch
Rattar
20
Mey
Gills
Kirkstyle
John o' Groats
Stacks of Duncansby
West Dunnet
Whitebridge
Rigifa
Canisbay
Dwarwick Head
Barrock
Upper Gills
Dunnet
The Spur
Dunnet Bay
Inkstack
Warth Hill
124
Wife Geo
Murkle Bay
Links of Dunnet
Brabster
Everley
Murkle
Tofts
Skirza
Skirza Head
Castletown
Greenland
Loch Heilen
Lochend
Gill Burn
Freswick Bay
Thurdistoft
Slickly
Freswick
Olrig House
Hayfield
Tain
A99
Ness Head
Lochside
Reaster
Burn of Lyth
Alterwall
Auckengill
Kirk Burn
Hilliclay
dale
Durran
Hoy
B876
Bowermadden
Ruthers of Howe
Nybster
Lyth
Sortat
Achingills
17
Brough Head
Stemster
Tister
Bowertower
Howe
Keiss
Knockdee
Stemster House
Halcro
Burn of Lyth
Mireland
Tang Head
Corsback
Hastigrow
Stain
Roadside
B874
Clayock
Gillock
Loch Scarmclate
Kirk
Loch of Wester
Georgemas Junc. Sta
A882
North Watten
B870
Westerloch
Sinclair's Bay
Lynegar
Quoys of Reiss
Spittal Hill
176
Dunn
Oldhall
Loch Watten
Mains of Watten
Killimster
A99
B876
A9
B874
Loch of Winless
Ackergill Tower
Girnigoe
Noss Head
Houstry of Dunn
Reiss
Spital
Newton
Watten
Wick
Winless
Sinclair
15
Whitefield
Ackergill
Backlass
WICK
Staxigoe
Mybster
Bilbster
Sibster
A882
Caithness Glass
Loch of Toftingall
Burn of Acharole
Strath
Thuster
Haster
Milton
Broadhaven
Burn of Strath
North Head
Janetstown
Wick
Stirkoke House
Newton
South Head
17
Badlipster
Achairn Burn
Whiterow
Puldagon
Northfield
Castle of Old Wick
Camster Burn
Loch Hempriggs
Tannach
Hempriggs House
Tacher
17
Toftcarl
Ires Geo
Lower Camster
Thrumster
Stemster
Ballharn Hill
Grey Cairns of Camster
145
Corbiegoe
Sarclet
Loch Stemster
Hill of Yarrows
Loch of Yarrows
Sarclet Head
213
Whiteleen
havanich
Stemster Hill
Cnoc an Earrannaiche
A99
Stack of Ulbster
248
211
Upper Camster
Cairn of Get
Ulbster
Loch Rangag
Whaligoe
Sheppardstown
Roster
East Clyth
A9
Prehistoric Stones
Bruan
Crofts of Benachielt
Ben-a-chielt
287
Upper Lybster
Mid Clyth
Rumster Forest
Reisgill Burn
Blackness
Reisgill
Occumster
Swiney
Lybster
Houstry
Nottingham
Inwershore
Gillivoan
Landhallow
A99
Forse
Smerral
Latheron
Dunbeath
Latheronwheel
Heritage Centre
Toremore
TO BRORA

John O' Groats: *Though Dunnet Head is slightly further north and Duncansby Head further east, John O' Groats is generally regarded as the most north-easterly settlement of mainland Britain. It therefore features as the start or finish point for all sorts of games and charity events. From here a sign says it is 874 miles to Land's End.* ***Map ref. F1.***

Island of Stroma: *This is the only island in Caithness and has been uninhabited since 1962. Once the home of the notorious Sweyn the Pirate who raided and plundered along the northern coast of Scotland in the 12th Century.* ***Map ref. F1.***

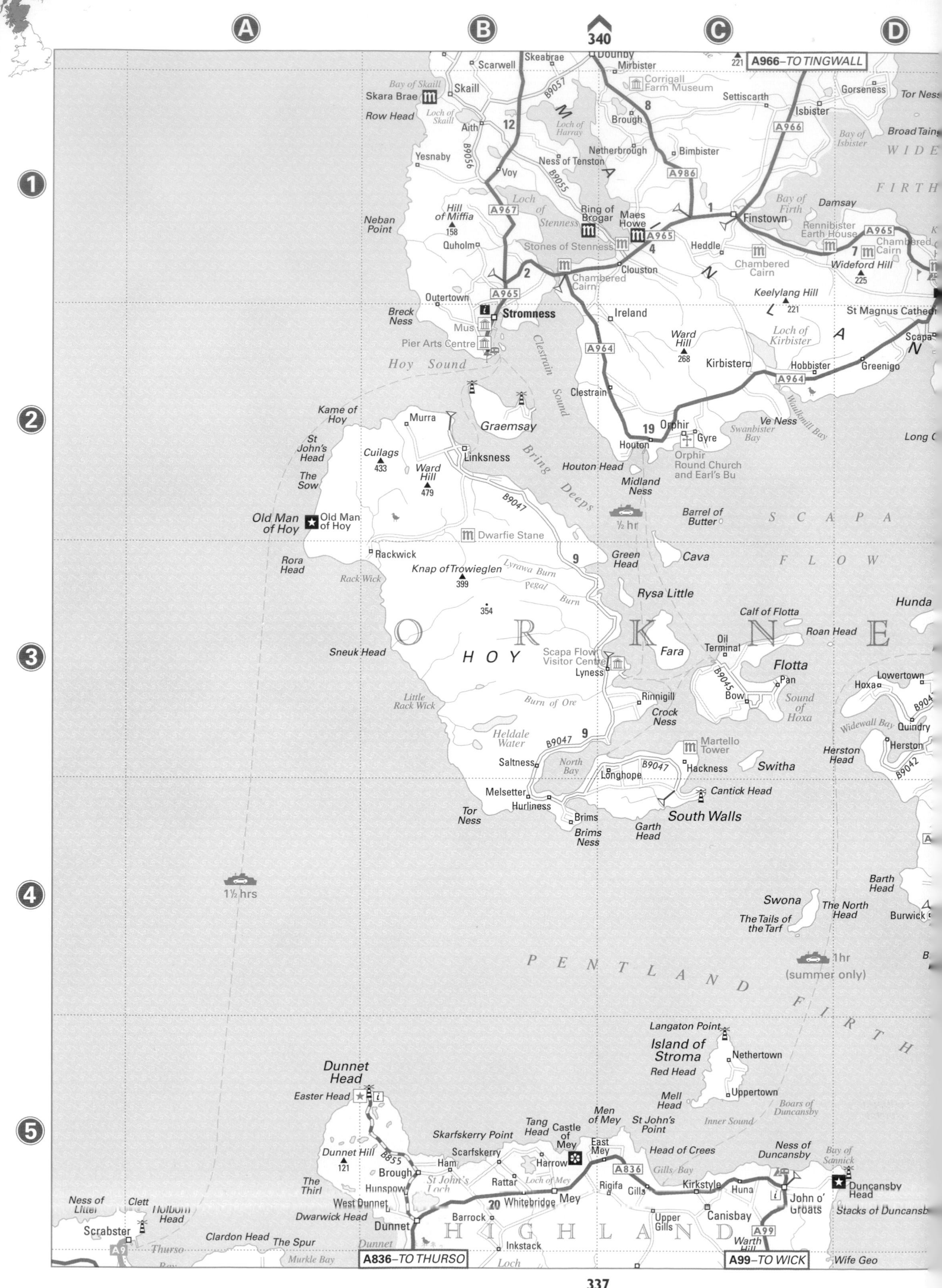
340
A966–TO TINGWALL
Skara Brae
Skaill
Stromness
Hoy Sound
Graemsay
Old Man of Hoy
HOY
ORKNEY
Scapa Flow Visitor Centre
Lyness
Flotta
South Walls
Longhope
Finstown
Ring of Brogar
Maes Howe
Stones of Stenness
Orphir
SCAPA FLOW
PENTLAND FIRTH
Swona
Island of Stroma
Dunnet Head
Dunnet
Castle of Mey
Mey
John o' Groats
Duncansby Head
Scrabster
HIGHLAND
A836–TO THURSO
A99–TO WICK
337

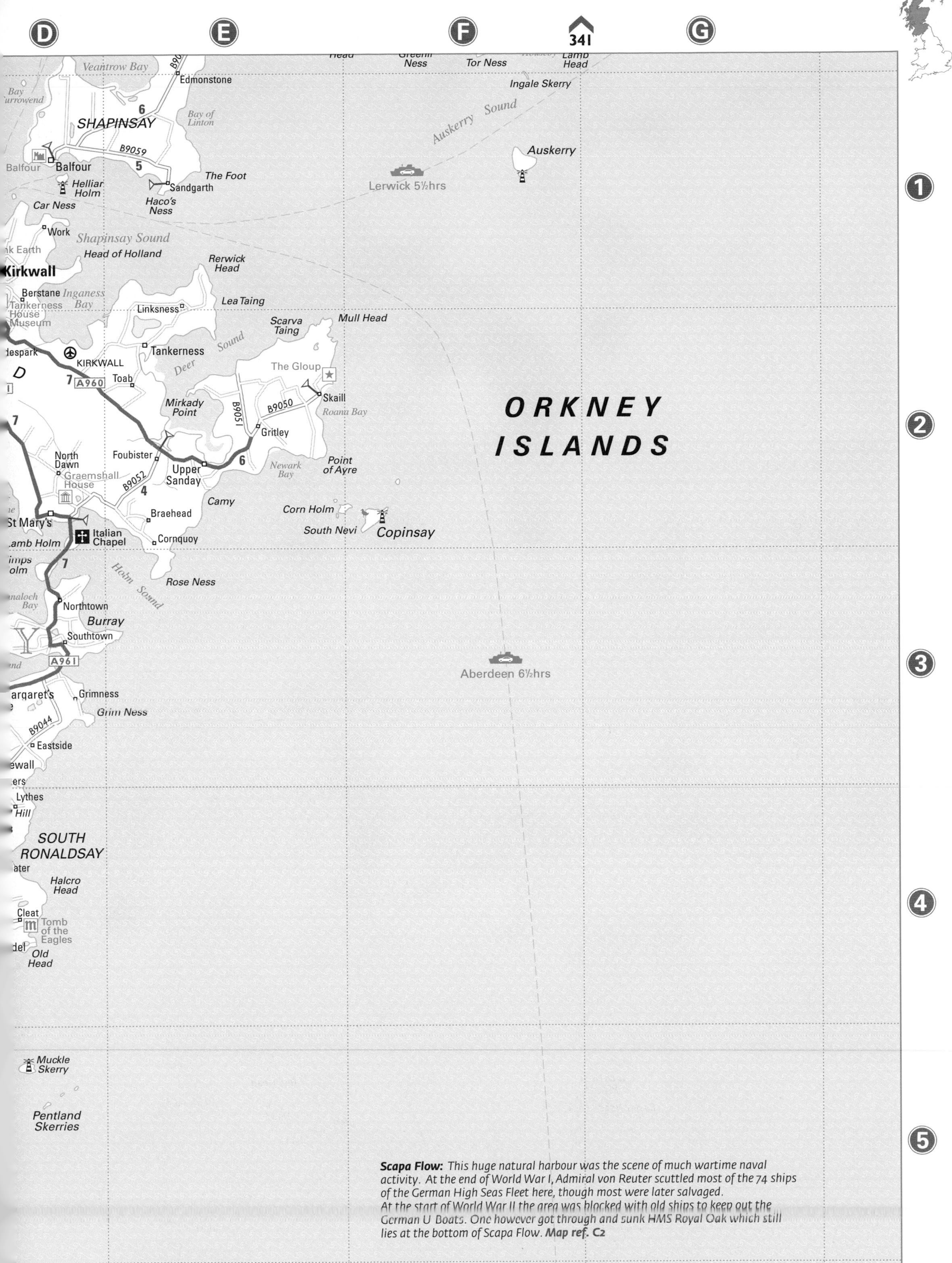
D
E
F
G
341
1
2
3
4
5
Veantrow Bay
Edmonstone
SHAPINSAY
Bay of Linton
B9059
Balfour
Helliar Holm
Sandgarth
The Foot
Haco's Ness
Car Ness
Work
Shapinsay Sound
Head of Holland
Kirkwall
Berstane
Inganess Bay
Tankerness House Museum
Linksness
Rerwick Head
Lea Taing
Scarva Taing
Mull Head
Tankerness
Deer Sound
The Gloup
KIRKWALL
A960
Toab
Mirkady Point
B9051
B9050
Skaill
Roana Bay
Gritley
North Dawn
Foubister
Graemshall House
B9052
Upper Sanday
Newark Bay
Point of Ayre
Camy
Braehead
Corn Holm
South Nevi
Copinsay
St Mary's
Italian Chapel
Cornquoy
Lamb Holm
Holm Sound
Rose Ness
Northtown
Burray
Southtown
A961
Grimness
Grim Ness
B9044
Eastside
Lythes
Hill
SOUTH RONALDSAY
Halcro Head
Cleat
Tomb of the Eagles
Old Head
Muckle Skerry
Pentland Skerries
Ness
Tor Ness
Lamb Head
Ingale Skerry
Auskerry Sound
Auskerry
Lerwick 5½hrs
ORKNEY ISLANDS
Aberdeen 6½hrs

Scapa Flow: This huge natural harbour was the scene of much wartime naval activity. At the end of World War I, Admiral von Reuter scuttled most of the 74 ships of the German High Seas Fleet here, though most were later salvaged. At the start of World War II the area was blocked with old ships to keep out the German U Boats. One however got through and sunk HMS Royal Oak which still lies at the bottom of Scapa Flow. **Map ref. C2**

Lamb Holm: *After the sinking of HMS Royal Oak in World War II Churchill ordered the entrance to Scapa Flow to be filled in. This work was carried out by Italian Prisoners of War and became known as the Churchill Barrier. During their stay the Italians converted two Nissen huts into a Roman Catholic Chapel which still stands today.* ***Also on page 125****. The barrier now forms part of the A961 road.*
Map ref. D2

Papa Westray Airport: *The world's shortest scheduled flight, from here to Westray, takes less than two minutes.* ***Map ref. C1***

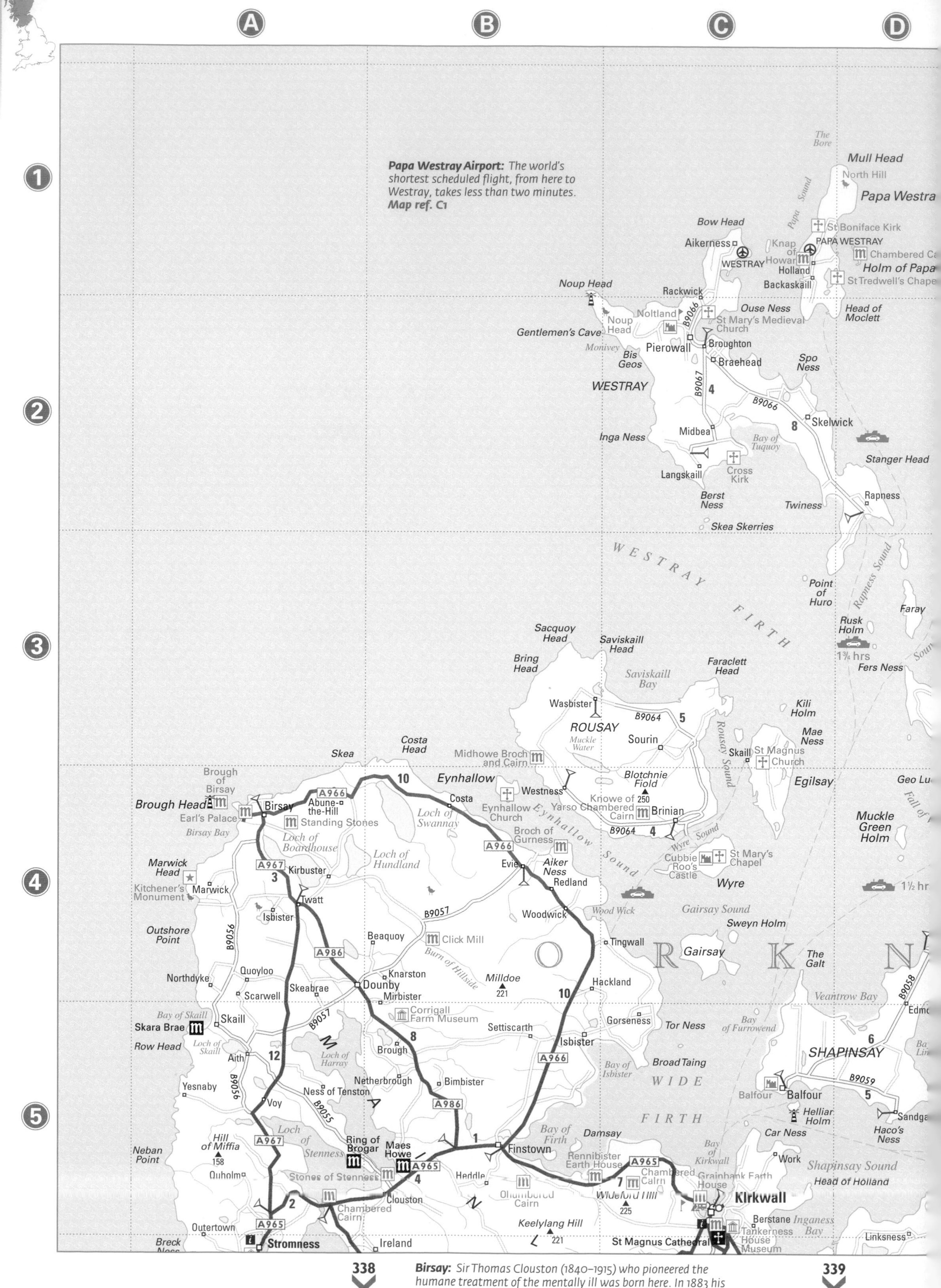

A
B
C
D
1
2
3
4
5
Mull Head
North Hill
Papa Westray
St Boniface Kirk
PAPA WESTRAY
Chambered Cairn
Holm of Papay
St Tredwell's Chapel
Head of Moclett
Bow Head
Aikerness
WESTRAY
Knap of Howar
Holland
Backaskaill
Noup Head
Rackwick
Noltland
St Mary's Medieval Church
Ouse Ness
Noup Head
Gentlemen's Cave
Pierowall
Broughton
Braehead
Bis Geos
WESTRAY
B9066
B9067
Spo Ness
Skelwick
Inga Ness
Midbea
Bay of Tuquoy
Stanger Head
Langskaill
Cross Kirk
Rapness
Berst Ness
Twiness
Skea Skerries
WESTRAY FIRTH
Point of Huro
Rapness Sound
Faray
Rusk Holm
1¾ hrs
Fers Ness
Sacquoy Head
Saviskaill Head
Bring Head
Faraclett Head
Saviskaill Bay
Wasbister
B9064
ROUSAY
Muckle Water
Sourin
Kili Holm
Mae Ness
Skaill
St Magnus Church
Rousay Sound
Costa Head
Skea
Midhowe Broch and Cairn
Brough of Birsay
Eynhallow
Westness
Blotchnie Fiold
Egilsay
Geo Lu
Knowe of Yarso Chambered Cairn
Brinian
Muckle Green Holm
Brough Head
Birsay
A966
Abune-the-Hill
Costa
Loch of Swannay
Eynhallow Church
Eynhallow Sound
Earl's Palace
Standing Stones
Birsay Bay
Loch of Boardhouse
Broch of Gurness
Wyre Sound
Cubbie Roo's Castle
St Mary's Chapel
Marwick Head
Loch of Hundland
A967
Kirbuster
Evie
Aiker Ness
Redland
Wyre
1½ hrs
Kitchener's Monument
Marwick
Twatt
Woodwick
Wood Wick
Gairsay Sound
Outshore Point
Isbister
B9057
Sweyn Holm
Beaquoy
Click Mill
Tingwall
B9056
A986
Gairsay
The Galt
ORKNEY
Burn of Hillside
Northdyke
Quoyloo
Knarston
Milldoe
221
Hackland
B9058
Scarwell
Skeabrae
Dounby
Mirbister
Veantrow Bay
Bay of Skaill
Skaill
Corrigall Farm Museum
Gorseness
Tor Ness
Bay of Furrowend
Skara Brae
Loch of Skaill
Settiscarth
Row Head
Aith
Loch of Harray
Brough
Isbister
SHAPINSAY
Bay of Isbister
Broad Taing
WIDE FIRTH
Yesnaby
Netherbrough
Bimbister
Balfour
B9059
Ness of Tenston
Voy
B9055
Helliar Holm
Sandgarth
Haco's Ness
Loch of Stenness
Bay of Firth
Damsay
Car Ness
Hill of Miffia
158
Ring of Brogar
Maes Howe
Finstown
Neban Point
Rennibister Earth House
Bay of Kirkwall
Work
Shapinsay Sound
Quholm
Stones of Stenness
A965
Heddle
Chambered Cairn
Grainbank Earth House
Head of Holland
Wideford Hill
225
Kirkwall
Clouston
Chambered Cairn
Outertown
Keelylang Hill
221
Berstane
Inganess Bay
Tankerness House Museum
Breck Ness
Stromness
Ireland
St Magnus Cathedral
Linksness
338
339

Birsay: *Sir Thomas Clouston (1840–1915) who pioneered the humane treatment of the mentally ill was born here. In 1883 his book on mental diseases established his international reputation as a leading figure in the diagnosis and treatment of such illnesses.* ***Map ref. A4***

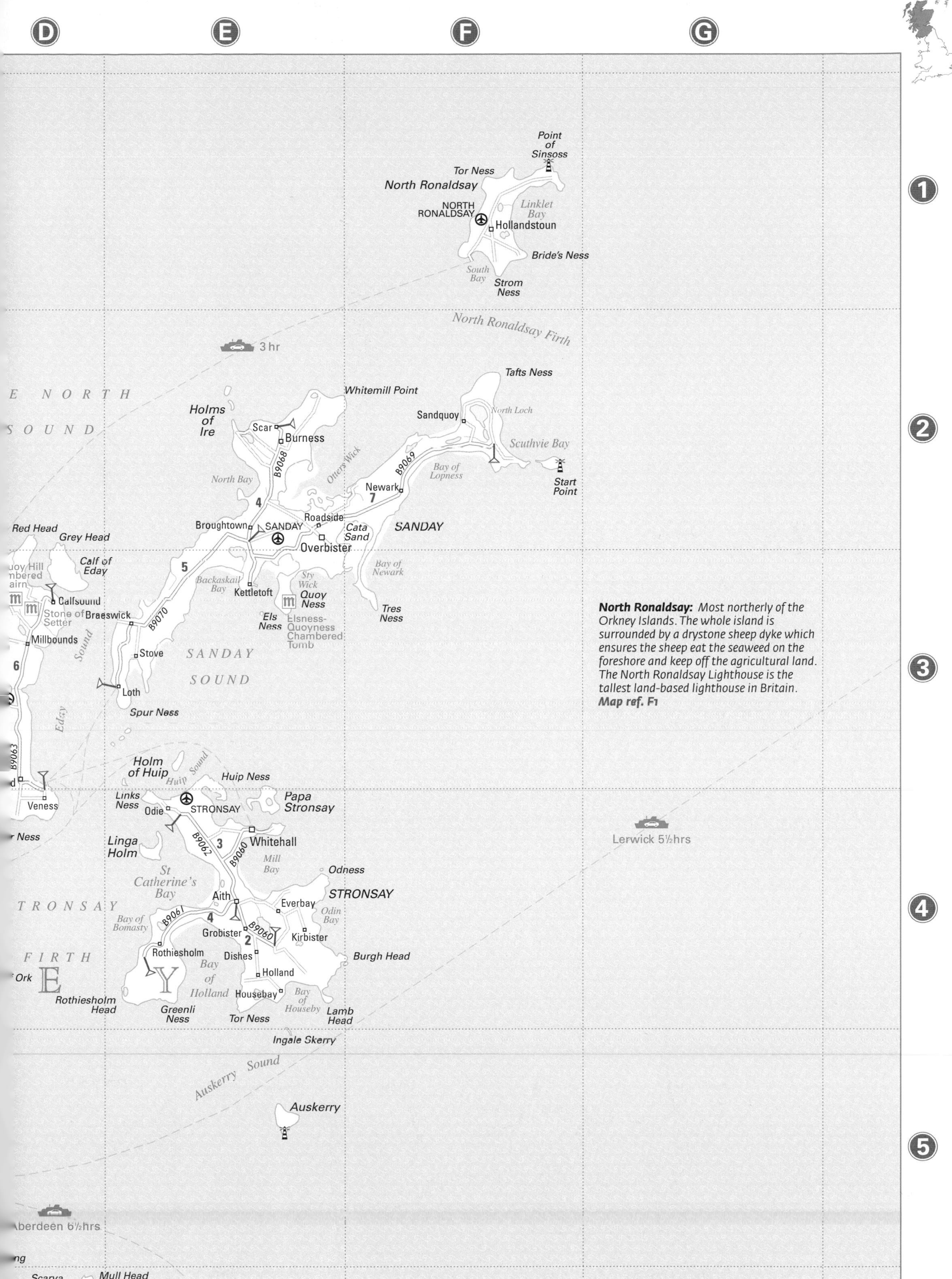
D
E
F
G
1
2
3
4
5
Point of Sinsoss
Tor Ness
North Ronaldsay
NORTH RONALDSAY
Linklet Bay
Hollandstoun
Bride's Ness
South Bay
Strom Ness
North Ronaldsay Firth
3 hr
Tafts Ness
Whitemill Point
Holms of Ire
Scar
Burness
Sandquoy
North Loch
Scuthvie Bay
B9068
Otters Wick
B9069
Bay of Lopness
North Bay
Newark
Start Point
Roadside
Broughtown
SANDAY
Cata Sand
SANDAY
Overbister
Red Head
Grey Head
Calf of Eday
Bay of Newark
Backaskail Bay
Sty Wick
Kettletoft
Quoy Ness
Calfsound
Stone of Setter
Braeswick
B9070
Els Ness
Elsness-Quoyness Chambered Tomb
Tres Ness
Millbounds
Stove
SANDAY
SOUND
Loth
Spur Ness
Eday Sound
B9063
Holm of Huip
Huip Sound
Huip Ness
Links Ness
Odie
STRONSAY
Papa Stronsay
Veness
Lerwick 5½hrs
Linga Holm
B9062
Whitehall
B9060
Mill Bay
St Catherine's Bay
Odness
Aith
STRONSAY
Bay of Bomasty
B9061
Everbay
Odin Bay
Grobister
Kirbister
Rothiesholm
Dishes
Burgh Head
Bay of Holland
Holland
Rothiesholm Head
Housebay
Bay of Houseby
Greenli Ness
Tor Ness
Lamb Head
Ingale Skerry
Auskerry Sound
Auskerry
Aberdeen 6½hrs
Scarva
Mull Head

North Ronaldsay: *Most northerly of the Orkney Islands. The whole island is surrounded by a drystone sheep dyke which ensures the sheep eat the seaweed on the foreshore and keep off the agricultural land. The North Ronaldsay Lighthouse is the tallest land-based lighthouse in Britain.* ***Map ref. F1***

Orkney Islands: *There are more than 70 islands in the Orkneys but only 17 are inhabited. Orkney summers feature almost continual daylight with the sun above the horizon for over 18 hours a day....by contrast, in winter, the sun rises after 9am and sets around 3.30pm so there are barely 7 hours of daylight.*

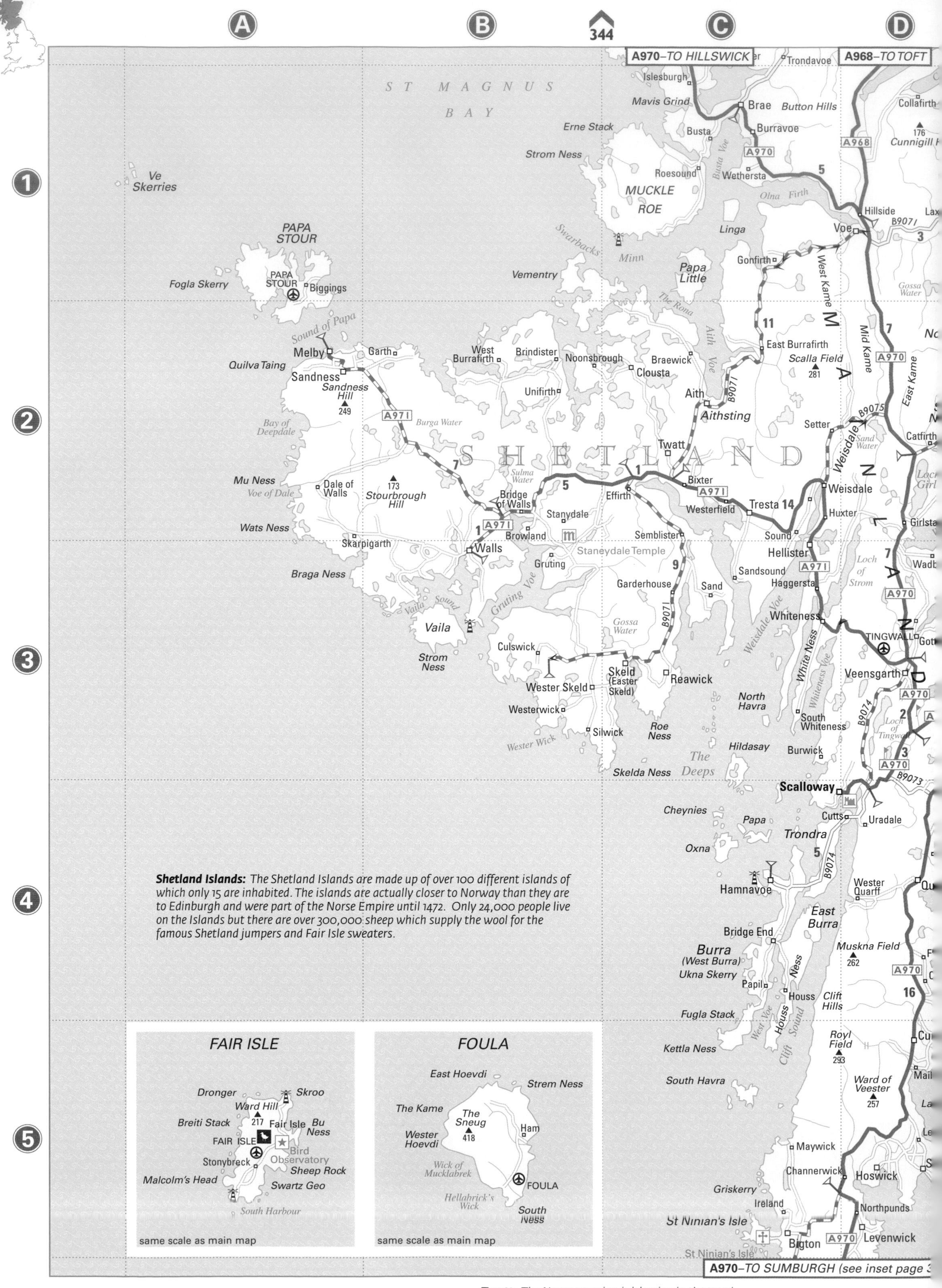
A
B
C
D
344
1
2
3
4
5
A970–TO HILLSWICK
A968–TO TOFT
A970–TO SUMBURGH (see inset page 3
ST MAGNUS BAY
Trondavoe
Islesburgh
Mavis Grind
Brae
Button Hills
Collafirth
Busta
Burravoe
Erne Stack
Strom Ness
A968
176
Cunnigill
A970
Roesound
Busta Voe
Wethersta
MUCKLE ROE
Olna Firth
Hillside
Voe
B9071
Linga
Swarbacks
Minn
Ve Skerries
PAPA STOUR
Fogla Skerry
PAPA STOUR
Biggings
Vementry
Papa Little
Gonfirth
West Kame
Gossa Water
The Rona
Aith Voe
Sound of Papa
Melby
Garth
Quilva Taing
Sandness
Sandness Hill
249
West Burrafirth
Brindister
Noonsbrough
Braewick
Clousta
East Burrafirth
Scalla Field
281
Mid Kame
A970
East Kame
Unifirth
Aith
Aithsting
B9071
Bay of Deepdale
A971
Burga Water
SHETLAND
MAINLAND
Setter
Weisdale
Sand Water
B9075
Catfirth
Twatt
Sulma Water
Bixter
Mu Ness
Voe of Dale
Dale of Walls
173
Stourbrough Hill
Bridge of Walls
Effirth
A971
Weisdale
Westerfield
Tresta
Huxter
Wats Ness
Stanydale
A971
Browland
Sound
Girlsta
Skarpigarth
Walls
Semblister
Staneydale Temple
Hellister
Gruting
Sandsound
A971
Loch of Strom
Wadb
Braga Ness
Gruting Voe
Garderhouse
Sand
Haggersta
A970
Vaila Sound
Vaila
B9071
Gossa Water
Weisdale Voe
Whiteness
Strom Ness
Culswick
Skeld (Easter Skeld)
Reawick
TINGWALL
White Ness
Whiteness Voe
Veensgarth
Wester Skeld
North Havra
A970
Westerwick
South Whiteness
B9074
Loch of Tingwall
Silwick
Roe Ness
Wester Wick
The Deeps
Hildasay
Burwick
A970
Skelda Ness
B9073
Scalloway
Cheynies
Papa
Cutts
Uradale
Trondra
Oxna
B9074
Hamnavoe
Wester Quarff
East Burra
Bridge End
Muskna Field
262
Burra (West Burra)
Ukna Skerry
Papil
A970
Houss
Ness
Clift Hills
16
Fugla Stack
West Voe
Houss Ness
Clift Sound
Kettla Ness
Royl Field
293
South Havra
Ward of Veester
257
Maywick
Channerwick
Hoswick
Griskerry
Ireland
Northpunds
St Ninian's Isle
Bigton
A970
Levenwick
St Ninian's Isle
FAIR ISLE
Dronger
Skroo
Ward Hill
217
Breiti Stack
Fair Isle
Bu Ness
FAIR ISLE
Bird Observatory
Stonybreck
Sheep Rock
Malcolm's Head
Swartz Geo
South Harbour
same scale as main map
FOULA
East Hoevdi
Strem Ness
The Kame
The Sneug
418
Ham
Wester Hoevdi
Wick of Mucklabrek
FOULA
Hellabrick's Wick
South Ness
same scale as main map

Shetland Islands: *The Shetland Islands are made up of over 100 different islands of which only 15 are inhabited. The islands are actually closer to Norway than they are to Edinburgh and were part of the Norse Empire until 1472. Only 24,000 people live on the Islands but there are over 300,000 sheep which supply the wool for the famous Shetland jumpers and Fair Isle sweaters.*

Twatt: *The Norse meaning is 'clearing in the trees', proving that at some time there must have been trees growing here.*
Map ref. C2

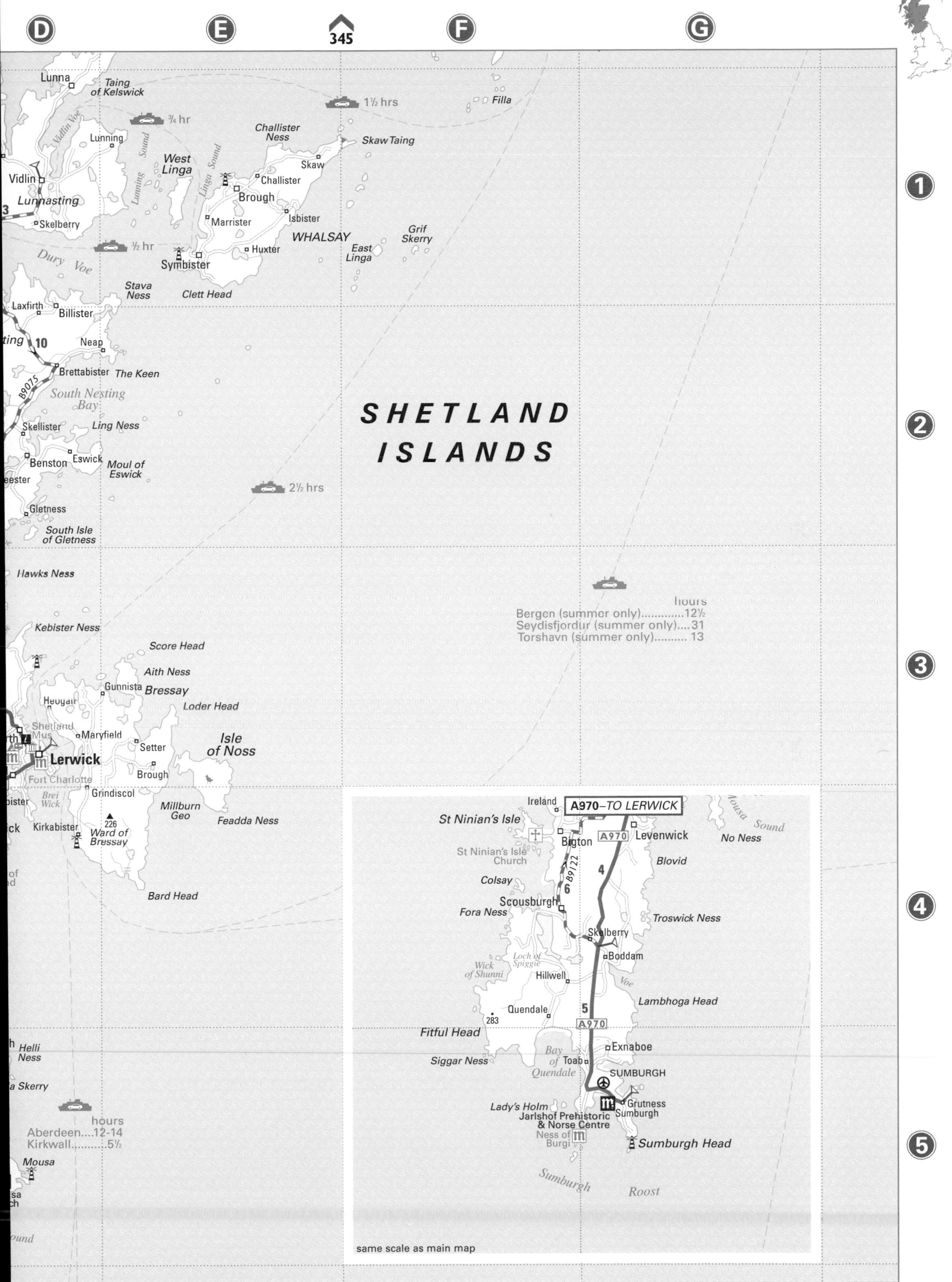

D
E
345
F
G
1
2
3
4
5
SHETLAND ISLANDS
Lunna
Taing of Kelswick
Lunning
West Linga
Challister Ness
Skaw Taing
Skaw
Challister
Brough
Vidlin
Lunnasting
Skelberry
Marrister
Isbister
WHALSAY
Grif Skerry
East Linga
Huxter
Symbister
Filla
1½ hrs
¾ hr
½ hr
Dury Voe
Stava Ness
Clett Head
Laxfirth
Billister
Neap
Brettabister
The Keen
South Nesting Bay
Skellister
Ling Ness
Benston
Eswick
Moul of Eswick
Gletness
South Isle of Gletness
2½ hrs
Hawks Ness
Kebister Ness
Score Head
Aith Ness
Gunnista
Bressay
Loder Head
Shetland Mus
Maryfield
Setter
Isle of Noss
Lerwick
Brough
Fort Charlotte
Grindiscol
Brei Wick
Kirkabister
226
Ward of Bressay
Millburn Geo
Feadda Ness
Bard Head
hours
Bergen (summer only).............12½
Seydisfjordur (summer only)....31
Torshavn (summer only)......... 13
Helli Ness
Skerry
hours
Aberdeen....12-14
Kirkwall..........5½
Mousa
Ireland
A970–TO LERWICK
St Ninian's Isle
Bigton
A970
Levenwick
No Ness
Mousa Sound
St Ninian's Isle Church
B9122
Blovid
Colsay
4
Scousburgh
6
Fora Ness
Troswick Ness
Skelberry
Boddam
Loch of Spiggie
Wick of Shunni
Hillwell
Voe
Lambhoga Head
Quendale
5
283
A970
Fitful Head
Exnaboe
Bay of Quendale
Toab
Siggar Ness
SUMBURGH
Lady's Holm
Grutness
Jarlshof Prehistoric & Norse Centre
Sumburgh
Ness of Burgi
Sumburgh Head
Sumburgh Roost
same scale as main map

Lerwick: *Arthur Anderson (1792–1868) was born here. Anderson formed the Union Steam Ship Company in 1853 which later became the great Union-Castle Line.* ***Map ref. D3***

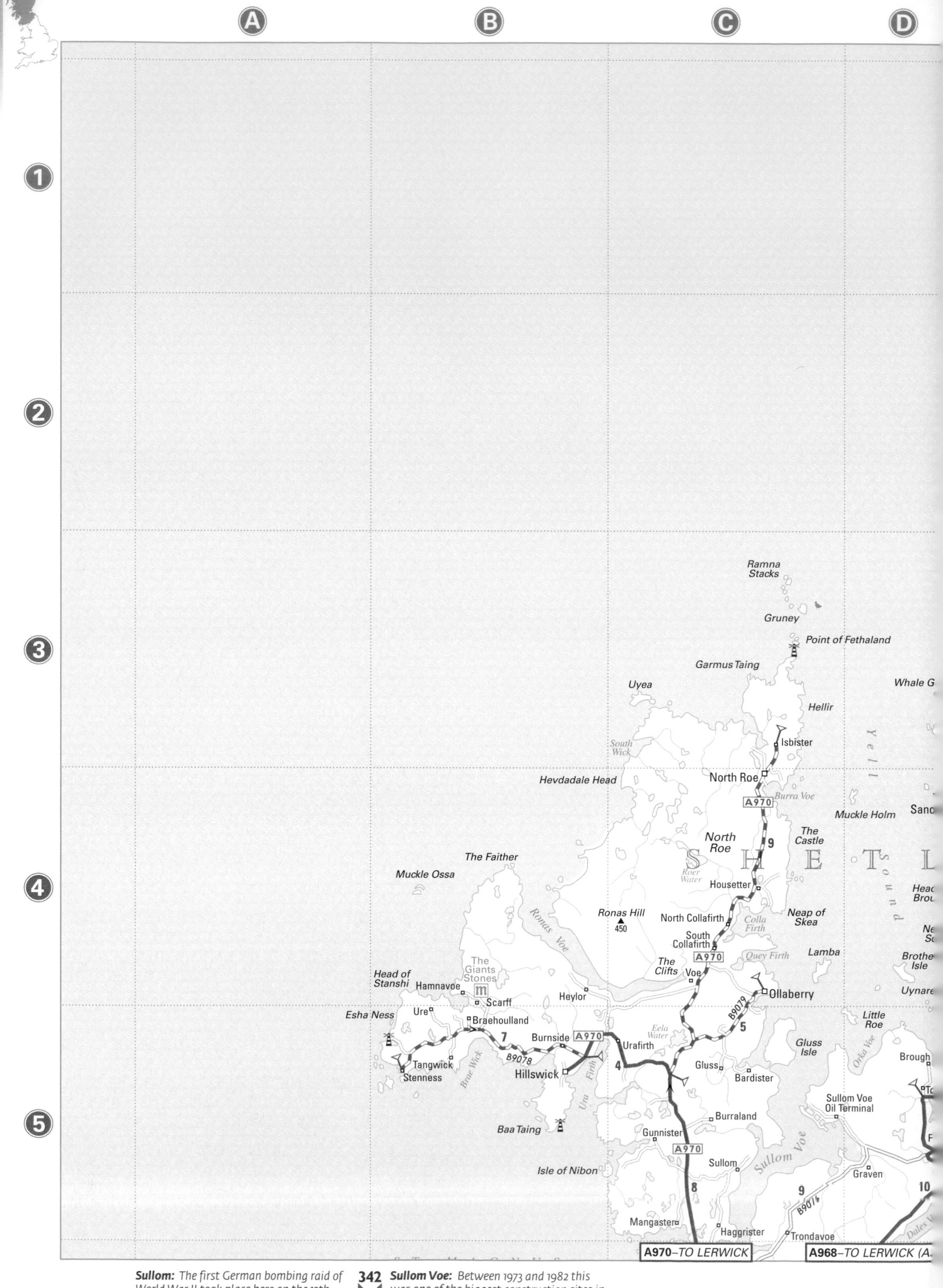

A
B
C
D
1
2
3
4
5
Ramna Stacks
Gruney
Point of Fethaland
Garmus Taing
Uyea
Whale G
Hellir
Isbister
South Wick
Hevdadale Head
North Roe
Burra Voe
A970
Muckle Holm
The Castle
North Roe
9
The Faither
Muckle Ossa
Roer Water
Housetter
Ronas Voe
Ronas Hill
450
North Collafirth
Colla Firth
Neap of Skea
South Collafirth
A970
Quey Firth
Lamba
The Giants Stones
Head of Stanshi
Hamnavoe
The Clifts
Voe
Ollaberry
Heylor
Scarff
B9079
Esha Ness
Ure
Braehoulland
Eela Water
Little Roe
7
Burnside
A970
5
Urafirth
Gluss Isle
Brough
Tangwick
B9078
4
Gluss
Stenness
Brae Wick
Hillswick
Ura Firth
Bardister
Sullom Voe Oil Terminal
Burraland
Baa Taing
Gunnister
A970
Sullom
Sullom Voe
Isle of Nibon
Graven
8
9
10
B9076
Mangaster
Haggrister
Trondavoe
A970–TO LERWICK
A968–TO LERWICK

Sullom: *The first German bombing raid of World War II took place here on the 13th November 1939 and the first casualty of a German bomb on British soil was a rabbit.* ***Map ref. C5***

342

Sullom Voe: *Between 1973 and 1982 this was one of the biggest construction sites in Europe with over 6,000 people employed building the oil terminal.* ***Map ref. C5***

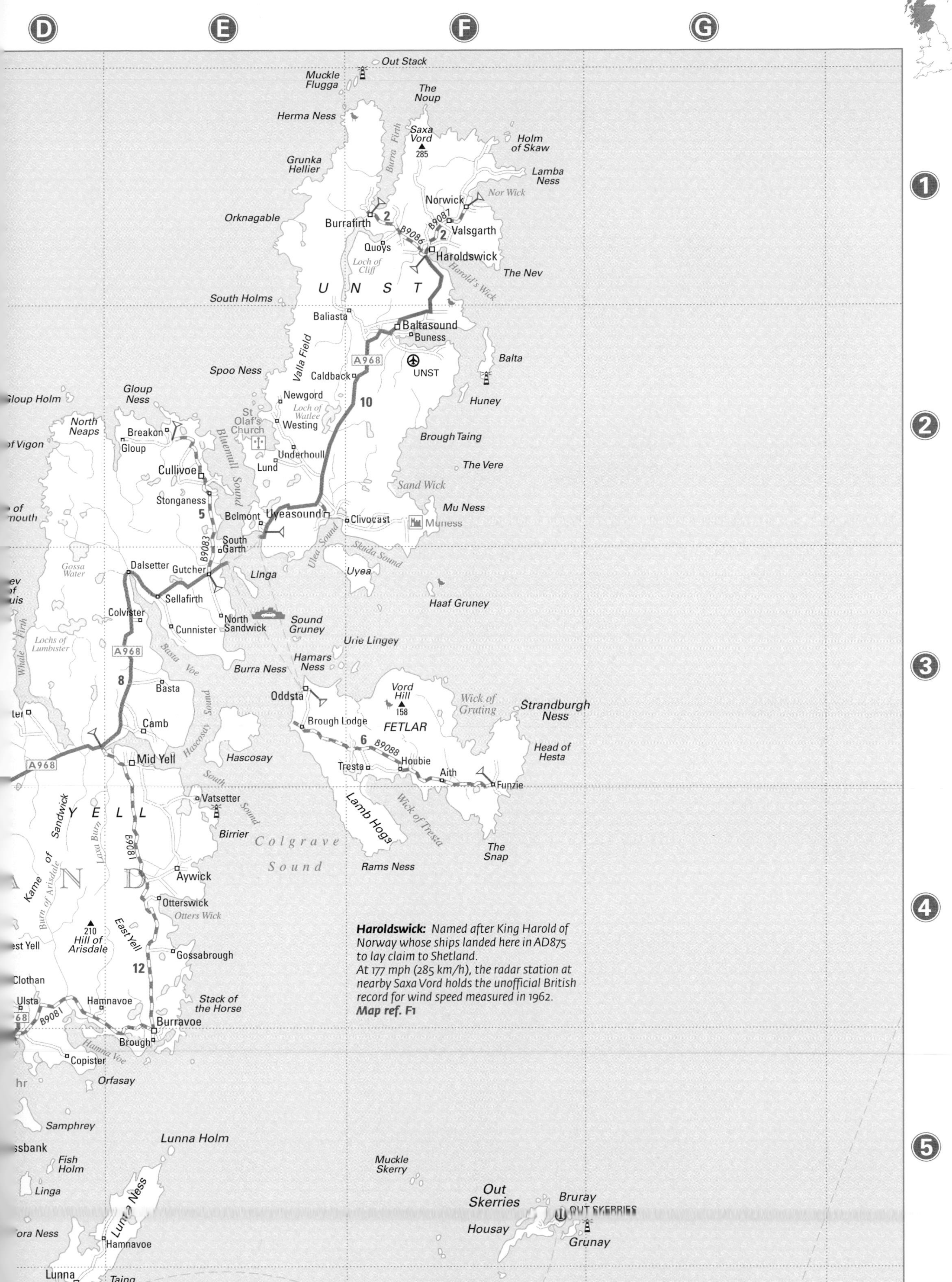
D
E
F
G
1
2
3
4
5
Out Stack
Muckle Flugga
The Noup
Herma Ness
Saxa Vord
285
Holm of Skaw
Burra Firth
Grunka Hellier
Lamba Ness
Nor Wick
Norwick
Orknagable
Burrafirth
B9087
B9086
Valsgarth
Quoys
Haroldswick
Loch of Cliff
Harold's Wick
The Nev
U N S T
South Holms
Baliasta
Baltasound
Buness
Balta
A968
Valla Field
Spoo Ness
Caldback
UNST
Huney
Gloup Holm
Gloup Ness
Newgord
Loch of Watlee
10
St Olaf's Church
Westing
North Neaps
Breakon
Gloup
of Vigon
Brough Taing
Bluemull Sound
Underhoull
Lund
The Vere
Cullivoe
Sand Wick
Stonganess
Mu Ness
5
Belmont
Uyeasound
Clivocast
Muness
B9083
South Garth
Ulea Sound
Skuda Sound
Dalsetter
Gutcher
Gossa Water
Linga
Uyea
Sellafirth
Haaf Gruney
Colvister
North Sandwick
Sound Gruney
Cunnister
Lochs of Lumbister
Urie Lingey
Whale Firth
A968
Basta Voe
Hamars Ness
Burra Ness
8
Basta
Oddsta
Vord Hill
158
Wick of Gruting
Strandburgh Ness
Brough Lodge
FETLAR
Camb
Hascosay Sound
Head of Hesta
6
B9088
A968
Mid Yell
Hascosay
Houbie
Tresta
Aith
Funzie
South Sound
Vatsetter
Y E L L
Sandwick
Lamb Hoga
Wick of Tresta
Birrier
B9081
Colgrave Sound
The Snap
Laxa Burn
Rams Ness
Aywick
Kame of
Burn of Arisdale
Otterswick
Otters Wick
East Yell
210
Hill of Arisdale
Gossabrough
12
Clothan
Ulsta
Hamnavoe
Stack of the Horse
B9081
Burravoe
Brough
Hamna Voe
Copister
Orfasay
Samphrey
Lunna Holm
Fish Holm
Muckle Skerry
Out Skerries
Bruray
OUT SKERRIES
Housay
Linga
Grunay
Lunna Ness
Hamnavoe
Lunna
Taing

Haroldswick: Named after King Harold of Norway whose ships landed here in AD875 to lay claim to Shetland.
At 177 mph (285 km/h), the radar station at nearby Saxa Vord holds the unofficial British record for wind speed measured in 1962.
Map ref. F1

Graven: *During the war this was an air base from which the RAF flying boats patrolled the North Atlantic in search of German U Boats.* ***Map ref. D5***

343

Muckle Flugga: *When the lighthouse keeper was at home this was once the most northerly inhabited island in Britain. The next rock along, the uninhabited 'Out Stack' is the most northern bit of the whole of Britain.* ***Map ref. F1***

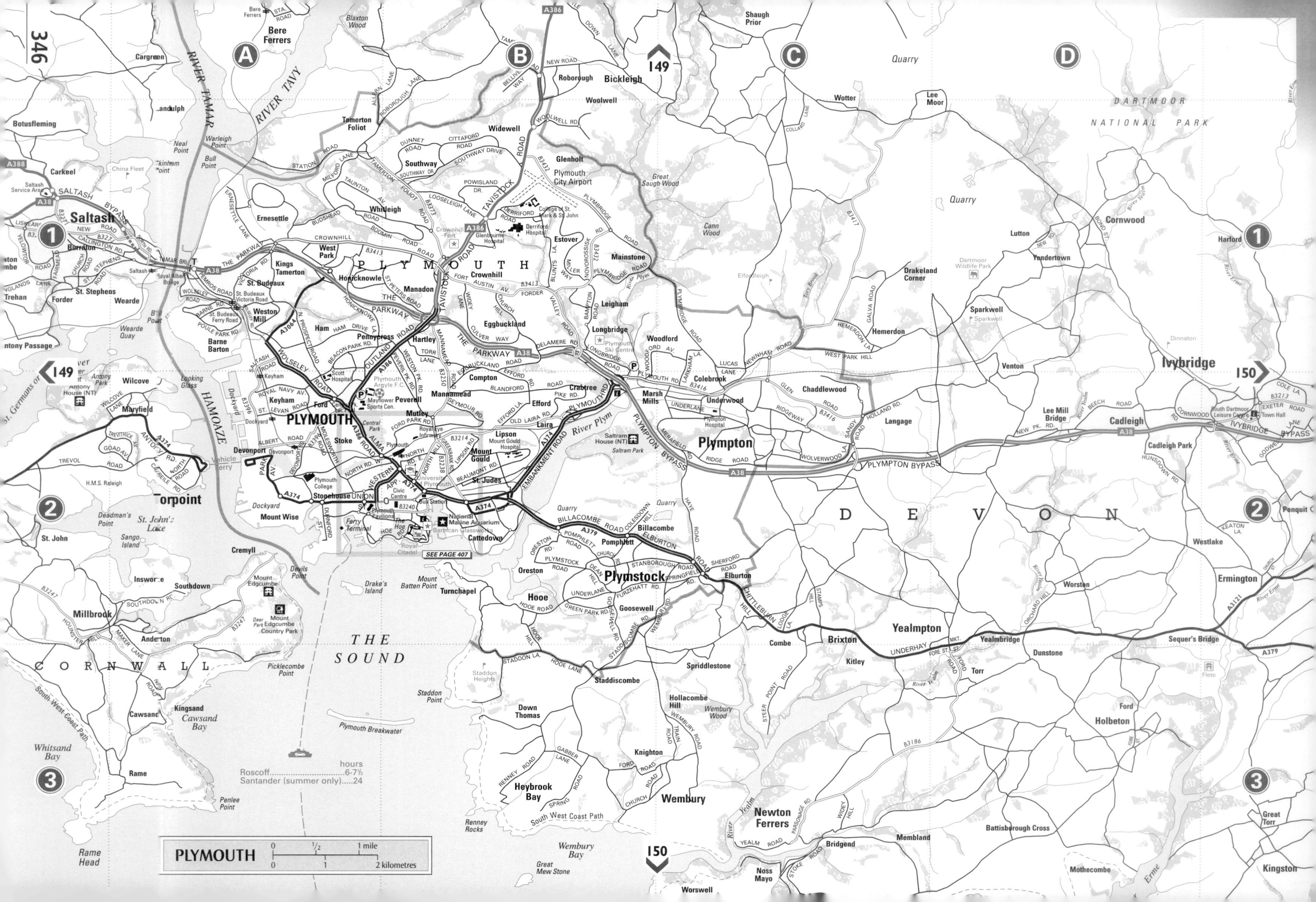
PLYMOUTH
0 ½ 1 mile
0 1 2 kilometres
Roscoff..........6-7½
Santander (summer only).....24
hours
SEE PAGE 407
149
150
DARTMOOR
NATIONAL PARK
DEVON
CORNWALL
THE SOUND
HAMOAZE
RIVER TAMAR
RIVER TAVY
Plymouth Breakwater
Drake's Island
Ivybridge
Plympton
Plymstock
Saltash
Torpoint
Yealmpton
Wembury
Newton Ferrers
Noss Mayo
Cornwood
Cadleigh
Lee Mill Bridge
Sparkwell
Hemerdon
Lee Moor
Shaugh Prior
Wotter
Bickleigh
Roborough
Woolwell
Glenholt
Plymouth City Airport
Estover
Mainstone
Leigham
Widewell
Southway
Tamerton Foliot
Whitleigh
Crownhill
Eggbuckland
Manadon
Hartley
Mannamead
Compton
Efford
Crabtree
Marsh Mills
Colebrook
Underwood
Chaddlewood
Woodford
Honicknowle
Pennycross
Peverell
Mutley
Stoke
Ham
West Park
Kings Tamerton
St. Budeaux
Ernesettle
Weston Mill
Keyham
Ford
Devonport
Stonehouse
Mount Wise
Lipson
Mount Gould
St. Judes
Cattedown
Laira
Billacombe
Pomphlett
Elburton
Goosewell
Oreston
Hoe
Turnchapel
Staddiscombe
Down Thomas
Heybrook Bay
Knighton
Hollacombe Hill
Spriddlestone
Brixton
Combe
Kitley
Torr
Yealmbridge
Dunstone
Worston
Holbeton
Ford
Membland
Bridgend
Mothecombe
Battisborough Cross
Sequer's Bridge
Ermington
Westlake
Great Torr
Kingston
Harford
Lutton
Venton
Langage
Drakeland Corner
Cremyll
Mount Edgcumbe
Kingsand
Cawsand
Cawsand Bay
Rame
Rame Head
Whitsand Bay
Millbrook
Anderton
Southdown
St. John
Wilcove
Mayfield
Antony House (NT)
Wearde
St. Stephens
Carkeel
Botusfleming
Burraton
Forder
Trehan
Antony Passage
Bere Ferrers
Barne Barton
Saltram House (NT)
Mount Batten Point
Staddon Point
Renney Rocks
Wembury Bay
Great Mew Stone
Picklecombe Point
Penlee Point
Saltash Service Area
South West Coast Path
A38
A386
A374
A379
A3064
B3416
B3432
B3413
B3417
B3186

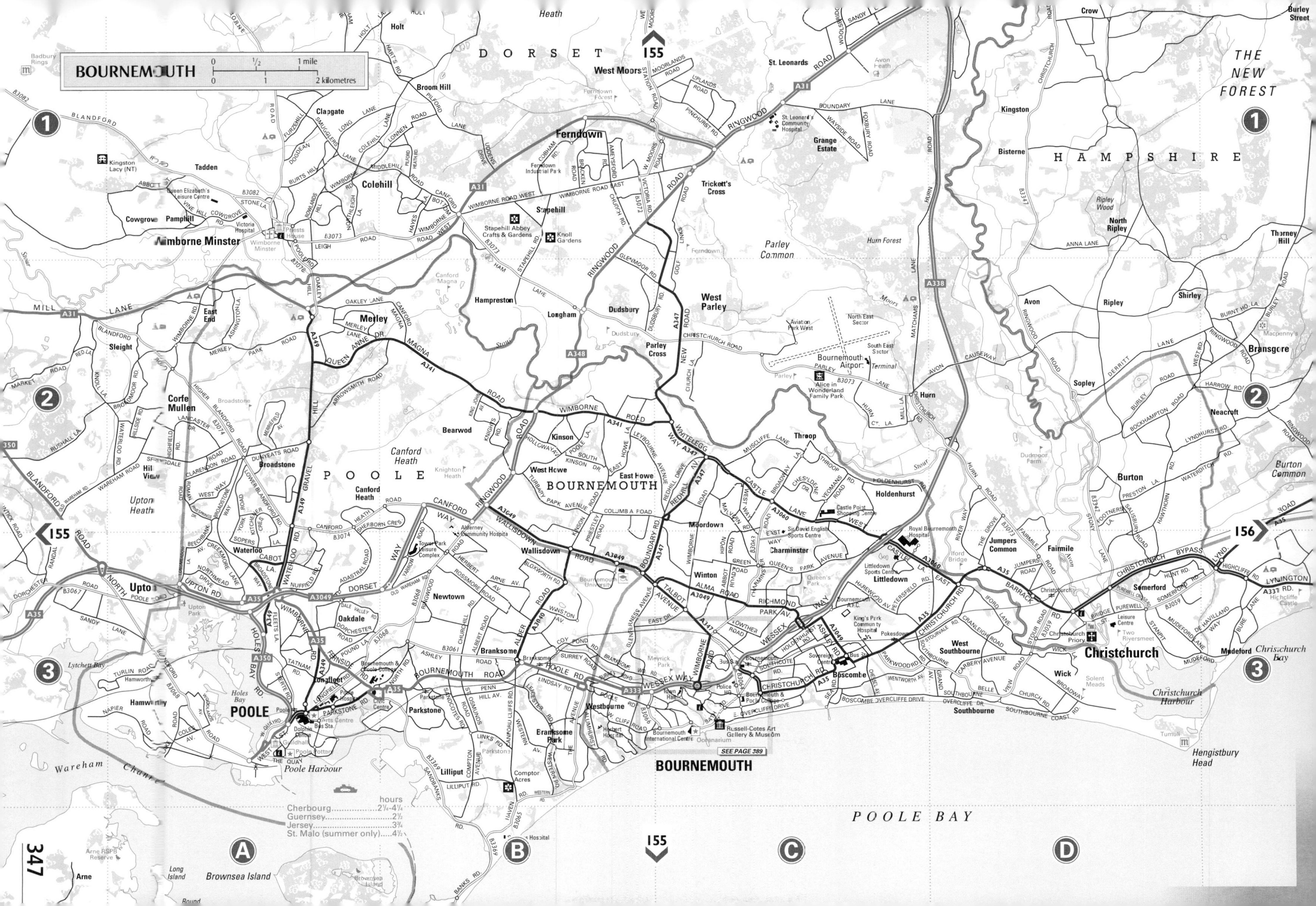
BOURNEMOUTH
0 1/2 1 mile
0 1 2 kilometres
DORSET
HAMPSHIRE
THE NEW FOREST
155
156
POOLE
BOURNEMOUTH
POOLE BAY
Christchurch Bay
Poole Harbour
Christchurch Harbour
Hengistbury Head
Brownsea Island
Christchurch
Wimborne Minster
Ferndown
West Moors
St. Leonards
West Parley
Bournemouth Airport
Canford Heath
Broadstone
Corfe Mullen
Upton
Hamworthy
Parkstone
Branksome
Westbourne
Boscombe
Southbourne
Kinson
Wallisdown
Winton
Moordown
Charminster
Littledown
Holdenhurst
Throop
Hurn
Burton
Sopley
Ripley
Bransgore
Neacroft
Mudeford
SEE PAGE 389
hours
Cherbourg 2¼-4¼
Guernsey 2½
Jersey 3¾
St. Malo (summer only) 4½

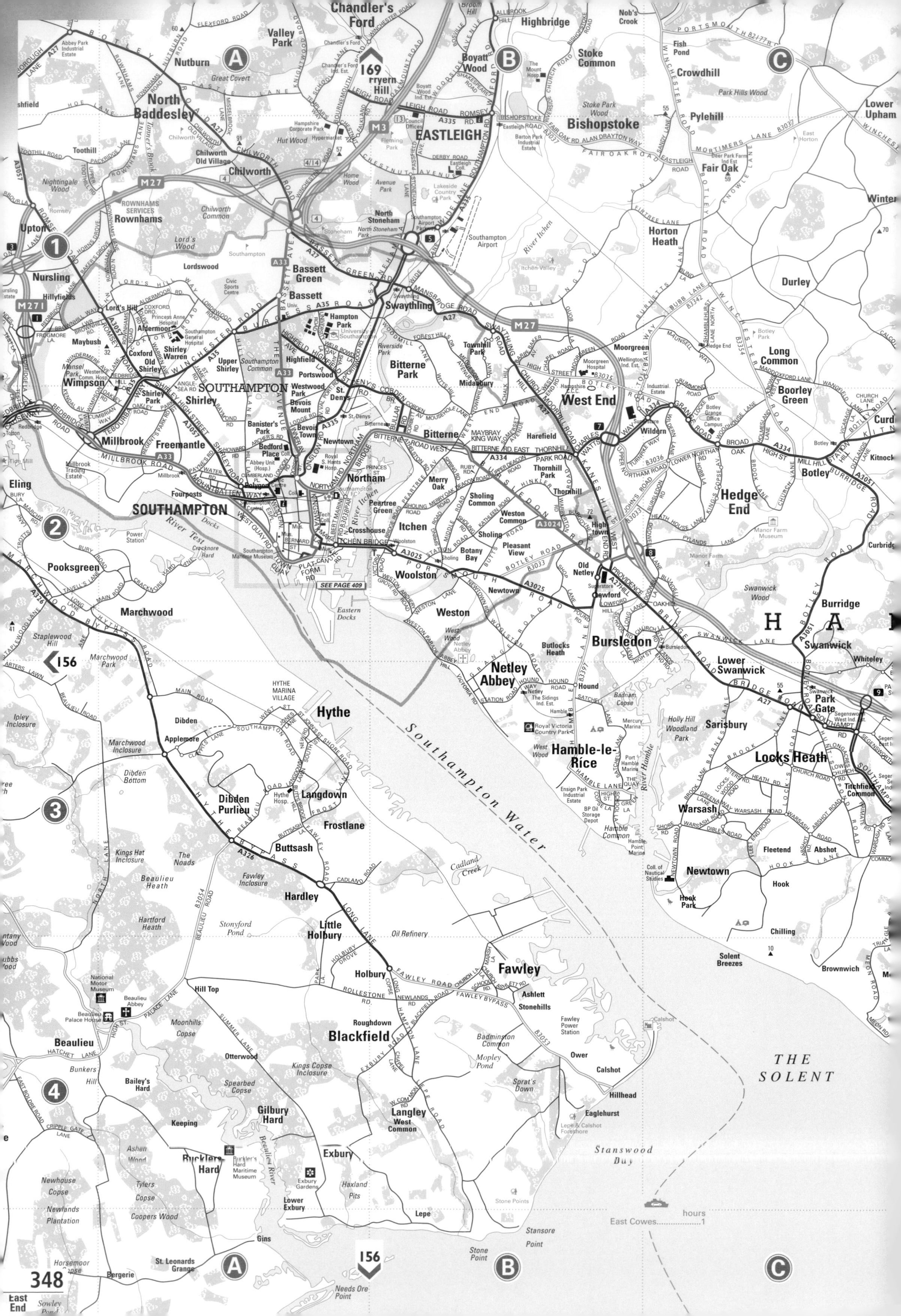

Chandler's Ford
Valley Park
Nutburn
Highbridge
Nob's Crook
Fish Pond
Boyatt Wood
Fryern Hill
169
Stoke Common
Crowdhill
Park Hills Wood
North Baddesley
Great Covert
Chilworth
Chilworth Old Village
Hut Wood
EASTLEIGH
Bishopstoke
Stoke Park Wood
Pylehill
Lower Upham
Fair Oak
Toothill
Nightingale Wood
Home Wood
Avenue Park
Lakeside Country Park
Rownhams
Chilworth Common
North Stoneham
Southampton Airport
Horton Heath
Upton
Lord's Wood
Lordswood
Nursling
Hillyfields
Bassett Green
Bassett
Swaythling
Durley
Civic Sports Centre
River Itchen
Itchen Valley
Lord's Hill
Aldermoor
Maybush
Hampton Park
Coxford
Shirley Warren
Highfield
Townhill Park
Moorgreen
Long Common
Mansel Park
Wimpson
Old Shirley
Upper Shirley
Southampton Common
Portswood
Bitterne Park
Midanbury
Boorley Green
SOUTHAMPTON
Shirley Park
Shirley
Westwood Park
Bevois Mount
St. Denys
West End
Wildern
Curdridge
Millbrook
Freemantle
Banister's Park
Bevois Town
Newtown
Bitterne
Harefield
Botley
Kitnocks
Millbrook Trading Estate
Bedford Place
Northam
Merry Oak
Thornhill Park
Thornhill
Eling
Fourposts
Polygon
Sholing Common
Hedge End
SOUTHAMPTON
River Test
Docks
Peartree Green
Itchen
Weston Common
Sholing
High Town
Manor Farm Museum
Power Station
Crosshouse
Pleasant View
Botany Bay
Curbridge
Cracknore Hard
Pooksgreen
Woolston
Old Netley
Manor Farm
Town Quay
Platform Rd
SEE PAGE 409
Newtown
Swanwick Wood
Burridge
Marchwood
Eastern Docks
Weston
Bursledon
H A
Staplewood Hill
Butlocks Heath
Swanwick
Marchwood Park
156
West Wood
Netley Abbey
Lower Swanwick
Whiteley
Hythe Marina Village
Hythe
Hound
Badnam Copse
Park Gate
Ipley Inclosure
Dibden
Southampton Water
Royal Victoria Country Park
Holly Hill Woodland Park
Sarisbury
Marchwood Inclosure
Applemore
West Wood
Hamble-le-Rice
Locks Heath
Dibden Bottom
Port Hamble Marina
Titchfield Common
Dibden Purlieu
Langdown
Warsash
Frostlane
Hamble Common
Kings Hat Inclosure
The Noads
Buttsash
Fleetend
Abshot
Beaulieu Heath
Fawley Inclosure
Cadland Creek
Newtown
Hook
Hardley
Coll. of Nautical Studies
Hook Park
Hartford Heath
Stonyford Pond
Little Holbury
Oil Refinery
Chilling
Solent Breezes
Brownwich
National Motor Museum
Holbury
Fawley
Beaulieu Abbey
Hill Top
Ashlett
Beaulieu Palace House
Stonehills
Moonhills Copse
Roughdown
Fawley Power Station
Beaulieu
Blackfield
Badminston Common
Calshot
Otterwood
Mopley Pond
Ower
THE SOLENT
Bunkers Hill
Kings Copse Inclosure
Calshot
Bailey's Hard
Sprat's Down
Spearbed Copse
Hillhead
Gilbury Hard
Langley
West Common
Eaglehurst
Keeping
Lepe & Calshot Foreshore
Ashen Wood
Bucklers Hard
Buckler's Hard Maritime Museum
Beaulieu River
Exbury
Stanswood Bay
Newhouse Copse
Exbury Gardens
Haxland Pits
Tylers Copse
Newlands Plantation
Lower Exbury
Stone Points
Coopers Wood
Lepe
hours
East Cowes.......................1
Gins
Stansore Point
Horsemoor Copse
St. Leonards Grange
Stone Point
156
Bergerie
Needs Ore Point
East End
Sowley Pond
M27
M3
M271
A27
A33
A35
A335
A334
A3024
A3025
A326
A3051
A3057

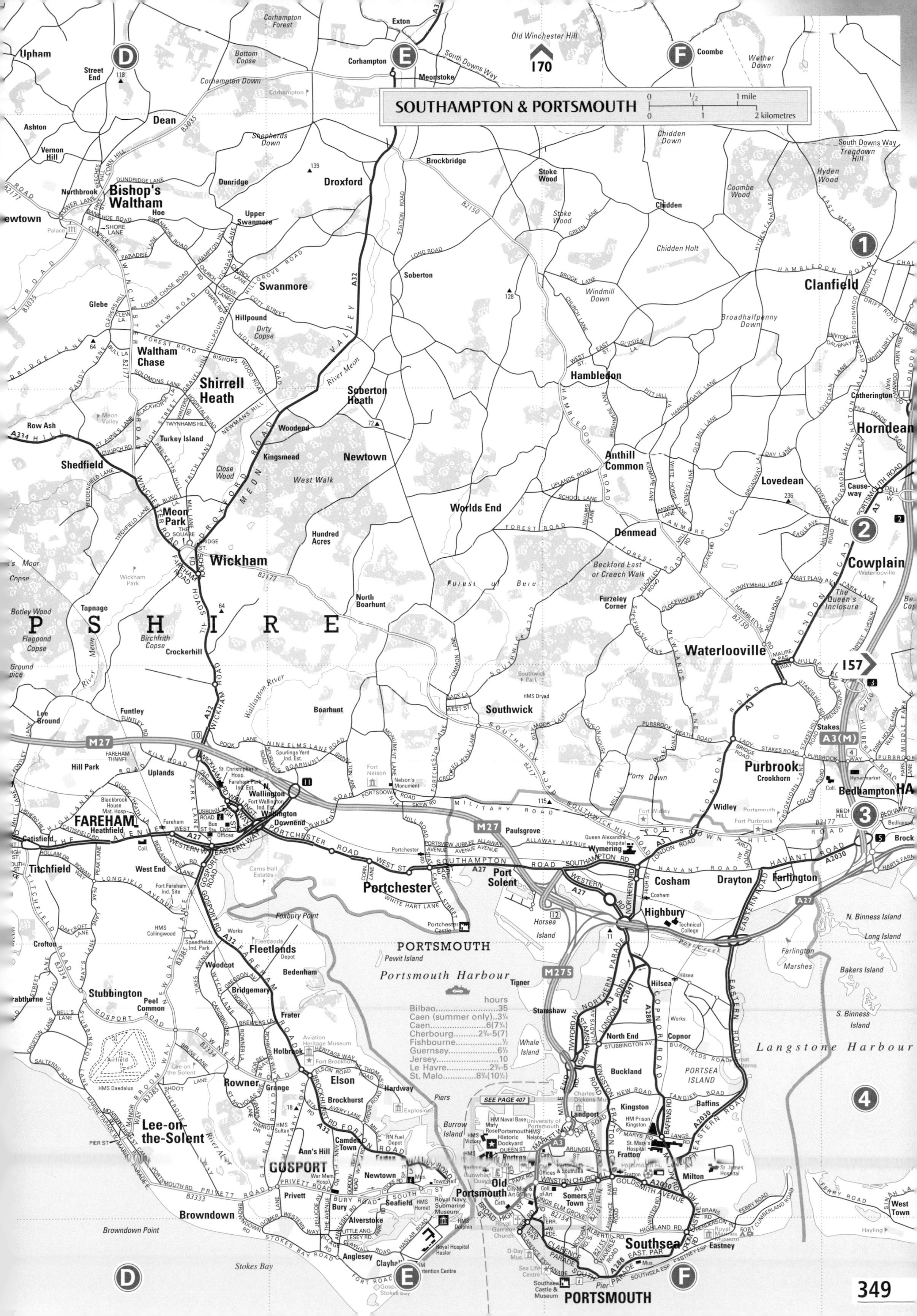

SOUTHAMPTON & PORTSMOUTH
0 1/2 1 mile
0 1 2 kilometres
170
157
SEE PAGE 407
hours
Bilbao........................35
Caen (summer only)..3¼
Caen.....................6(7¼)
Cherbourg..........2¾-5(7)
Fishbourne....................½
Guernsey......................6½
Jersey..........................10
Le Havre.................2¾-5
St. Malo............8¾(10½)
Upham
Street End
Corhampton Forest
Exton
Old Winchester Hill
Coombe
Wether Down
Bottom Copse
Corhampton
Meonstoke
South Downs Way
Corhampton Down
Dean
Ashton
Vernon Hill
Shepherds Down
Brockbridge
Droxford
Dunridge
Northbrook
Bishop's Waltham
Hoe
Upper Swanmore
Stoke Wood
Chidden Down
Chidden
Coombe Wood
Hyden Wood
Tregdown Hill
Chidden Holt
Soberton
Swanmore
Windmill Down
Clanfield
Broadhalfpenny Down
Hillpound
Dirty Copse
Glebe
Waltham Chase
Shirrell Heath
Hambledon
Catherington
Horndean
Soberton Heath
Row Ash
Woodend
Turkey Island
Shedfield
Kingsmead
Newtown
West Walk
Close Wood
Anthill Common
Lovedean
Causeway
Meon Park
Worlds End
Denmead
Hundred Acres
Wickham
Beckford East or Creech Walk
Cowplain
Forest of Bere
North Boarhunt
Tapnage
Furzeley Corner
Botley Wood
Flagpond Copse
Birchfrith Copse
Crockerhill
PSHIRE
Waterlooville
Ground
Funtley
Lee Ground
Boarhunt
Southwick
HMS Dryad
Stakes
Hill Park
Uplands
Fort Nelson
Nelson's Monument
Purbrook
Crookhorn
Bedhampton
Wallington
Downend
Widley
FAREHAM
Heathfield
Catisfield
Paulsgrove
Wymering
Titchfield
West End
Portchester
Port Solent
Cosham
Drayton
Farlington
Portchester Castle
Highbury
Foxbury Point
N. Binness Island
Long Island
Crofton
Fleetlands
PORTSMOUTH
Pewit Island
Horsea Island
Farlington Marshes
Woodcot
Bedenham
Portsmouth Harbour
Tipner
Bakers Island
Stubbington
Peel Common
Bridgemary
Stamshaw
Hilsea
Frater
S. Binness Island
Whale Island
North End
Copnor
Langstone Harbour
Holbrook
Buckland
PORTSEA ISLAND
Rowner
Grange
Elson
Hardway
Lee-on-the-Solent
Brockhurst
Piers
Burrow Island
Kingston
Baffins
HMS Daedalus
Landport
Camden Town
Ann's Hill
Fratton
GOSPORT
Newtown
Old Portsmouth
Milton
Privett
Somers Town
Browndown
Bury
Seafield
West Town
Browndown Point
Alverstoke
Southsea
Eastney
Anglesey
Clayhall
Stokes Bay
Hayling
Southsea Castle & Museum
PORTSMOUTH

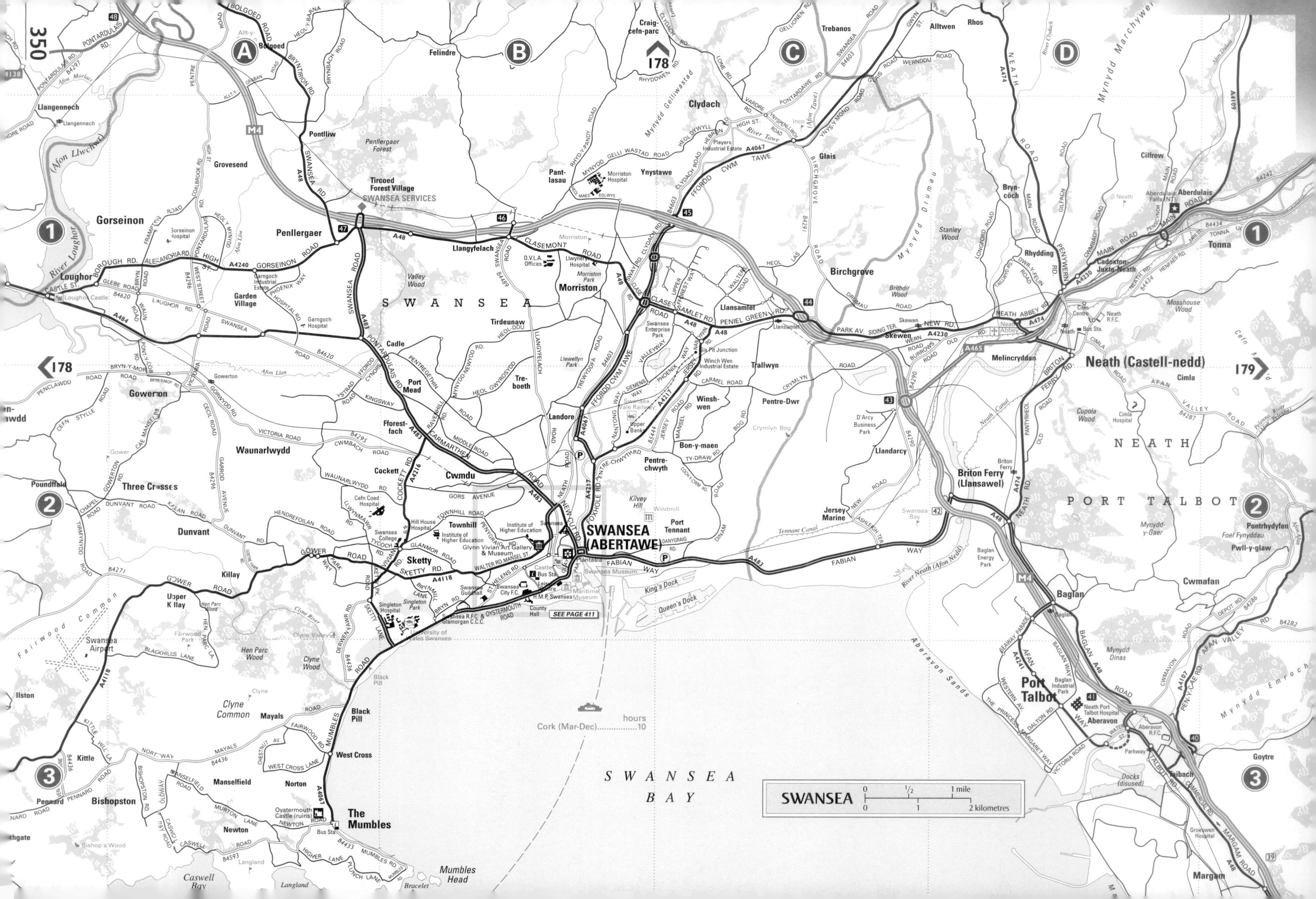
SWANSEA
SWANSEA BAY
SWANSEA (ABERTAWE)
Neath (Castell-nedd)
NEATH
PORT TALBOT
Port Talbot
Briton Ferry (Llansawel)
Aberavon
Baglan
Margam
Taibach
Tonna
Aberdulais
Cilfrew
Cadoxton Juxta-Neath
Melincryddan
Skewen
Llandarcy
Jersey Marine
Birchgrove
Glais
Trebanos
Clydach
Ynystawe
Morriston
Llansamlet
Trallwyn
Pentre-Dwr
Winch-wen
Bon-y-maen
Pentre-chwyth
Port Tennant
Landore
Tre-boeth
Tirdeunaw
Llangyfelach
Pant-lasau
Felindre
Tircoed Forest Village
SWANSEA SERVICES
Penllergaer
Pontlliw
Bolgoed
Grovesend
Garden Village
Gorseinon
Loughor
Llangennech
Gowerton
Waunarlwydd
Three Crosses
Dunvant
Poundffald
Killay
Upper Killay
Cockett
Fforest-fach
Cadle
Port Mead
Cwmdu
Townhill
Sketty
Black Pill
West Cross
The Mumbles
Norton
Mayals
Manselfield
Newton
Mumbles Head
Bishopston
Kittle
Pennard
Ilston
Swansea Airport
Fairwood Common
Clyne Common
Craig-cefn-parc
Rhos
Alltwen
Bryn-côch
Rhydding
Cwmafan
Pontrhydyfen
Pwll-y-glaw
Goytre
Cimla
Mynydd Marchywel
Mynydd Drumau
Mynydd Gelliwastad
Aberavon Sands
King's Dock
Queen's Dock
M4
A48
A483
A4067
A4118
A474
A465
178
179
SEE PAGE 411
Cork (Mar-Dec) hours 10
SWANSEA 0 1/2 1 mile
0 1 2 kilometres

CARDIFF & NEWPORT
0 1/2 1 mile
0 1 2 kilometres
BRISTOL CHANNEL
CAERPHILLY
RHONDDA CYNON TAFF
VALE OF GLAMORGAN
CARDIFF
NEWPORT
Caerphilly
Bedwas
Machen
Rogerstone
Bassaleg
Duffryn
Castleton
Marshfield
St. Brides Wentlooge
Peterstone Wentlooge
Llanrumney
St. Mellons
Trowbridge
Rumney
Newton
Wentloog
Lisvane
Llanishen
Cyncoed
Pentwyn
Llanedeyrn
Whitchurch
Llandaff
Cathays
Roath
Splott
Tremorfa
Butetown
Grangetown
Riverside
Canton
Ely
Fairwater
St. Fagans
Pentrebane
Radyr
Coryton
Tongwynlais
Nantgarw
Thornhill
Rhiwbina
Birchgrove
Heath
Gabalfa
Maendy
Blackweir
Pontcanna
Caerau
Michaelston-super-Ely
Cyntwell
Llanmaes
Pentre-poeth
Rhiwderin
Michaelston-y-Fedw
Blacktown
Coedkernew
Pye Corner
Broadstreet Common
Nash
Uskmouth
Lliswerry
Somerton
Alway
Ringland
Bishpool
Beechwood
Maindee
Summerhill
St. Julians
Christchurch
Crindau
Barrack Hill
Brynglas
Bettws
Pontymister
Gaer
Stelvio
Mendalgief
Maes-glas
Pillgwenlly
Glasllwch
Ridgeway
High Cross
Cefn
Garth
Waterloo
Draethen
Rudry
Trethomas
Pwllypant
Penyrheol
Caledfryn
Abertridwr
Glan-y-llyn
Ty Rhiw
M4
A48(M)
180
179
SEE PAGE 392

BRISTOL
0 1/2 1 mile
0 1 2 kilometres
180
181
182
166
SEE PAGE 391
Avonmouth
Shirehampton
Lawrence Weston
Henbury
Coombe Dingle
Sea Mills
Westbury-on-Trym
Stoke Bishop
Sneyd Park
Almondsbury
Patchway
Bradley Stoke
Little Stoke
Stoke Gifford
Great Stoke
Filton
Filton Airfield
Cribbs Causeway
Catbrain
Brentry
Southmead
Henleaze
Horfield
Lockleaze
Eastfield
Golden Hill
Bishopston
Ashley Down
Redland
Cotham
Montpelier
Westbury Park
Clifton
Hotwells
Bedminster
Ashton Gate
Windmill Hill
Knowle
Lower Knowle
Bedminster Down
Novers Park
Filwood Park
Hengrove
Hengrove Park
Headley Park
Bishopsworth
Highridge
Brislington
Arno's Vale
St. Anne's Park
Broom Hill
Conham
Barton Hill
Netham
St. George
Crew's Hole
Easton
Whitehall
Eastville
Stapleton
Ridgeway
Fishponds
Hillfields
Speedwell
Two Mile Hill
Clay Hill
Broomhill
Frenchay
Harry Stoke
Stapleton
Kingswood
Mount Hill
Hanham
Hanham Green
Longwell Green
Oldland
Cadbury Heath
Barr's Court
Stone Hill
New Cheltenham
Soundwell
Staple Hill
Rodway Hill
Mangotsfield
Downend
Bromley Heath
Blackhorse
Emersons Green
Vinny Green
Lyde Green
Pucklechurch
Parkfield
Warmley
Goose Green
Webb's Heath
Siston
Abson
Holbrook Common
Doynton
Wick
Bridgeyate
North Common
Oldland Common
Bitton
Swineford
North Stoke
Upton Cheyney
Beach
Tadwick
Langridge
Lansdown
Keynsham
Somerdale
Keynsham Hams
Stockwood
Stockwood Vale
Hicks Gate
BATH & NORTH
Winterbourne
Winterbourne Down
Whiteshill
Hambrook
Moorend
Frampton Cotterell
Frampton End
Coalpit Heath
Watley's End
Hick's Common
Kendleshire
Henfield
Ram Hill
Westerleigh
Westerleigh Hill
Wapley
Codrington
Iron Acton
Yate
Mayshill
Rodford
Stover
Nibley
Goose Green
Chipping Sodbury
Kingrove Common
Engine Common
Brins Park
The Rocks
Mead Riding
Stub Riding
Frogland Cross
North Woods
Gaunt's Earthcott
North Corner
Easter Compton
Over
Marsh Common
Compton Greenfield
Berwick
Hallen
Haw Wood
Dyer's Common
Chemical Works
Beach
BRISTOL
Lodway
Pill
Easton-in-Gordano
Ham Green
Abbots Leigh
Leigh Woods
Bower Ashton
Ashton Vale
Long Ashton
Yanley
Failand
Lower Failand
Cambridge Batch
Flax Bourton
Barrow Gurney
Barrow Wood
NORTH SOMERSET
SOUTH GLOUCESTERSHIRE
A
B
C
D
1
2
3

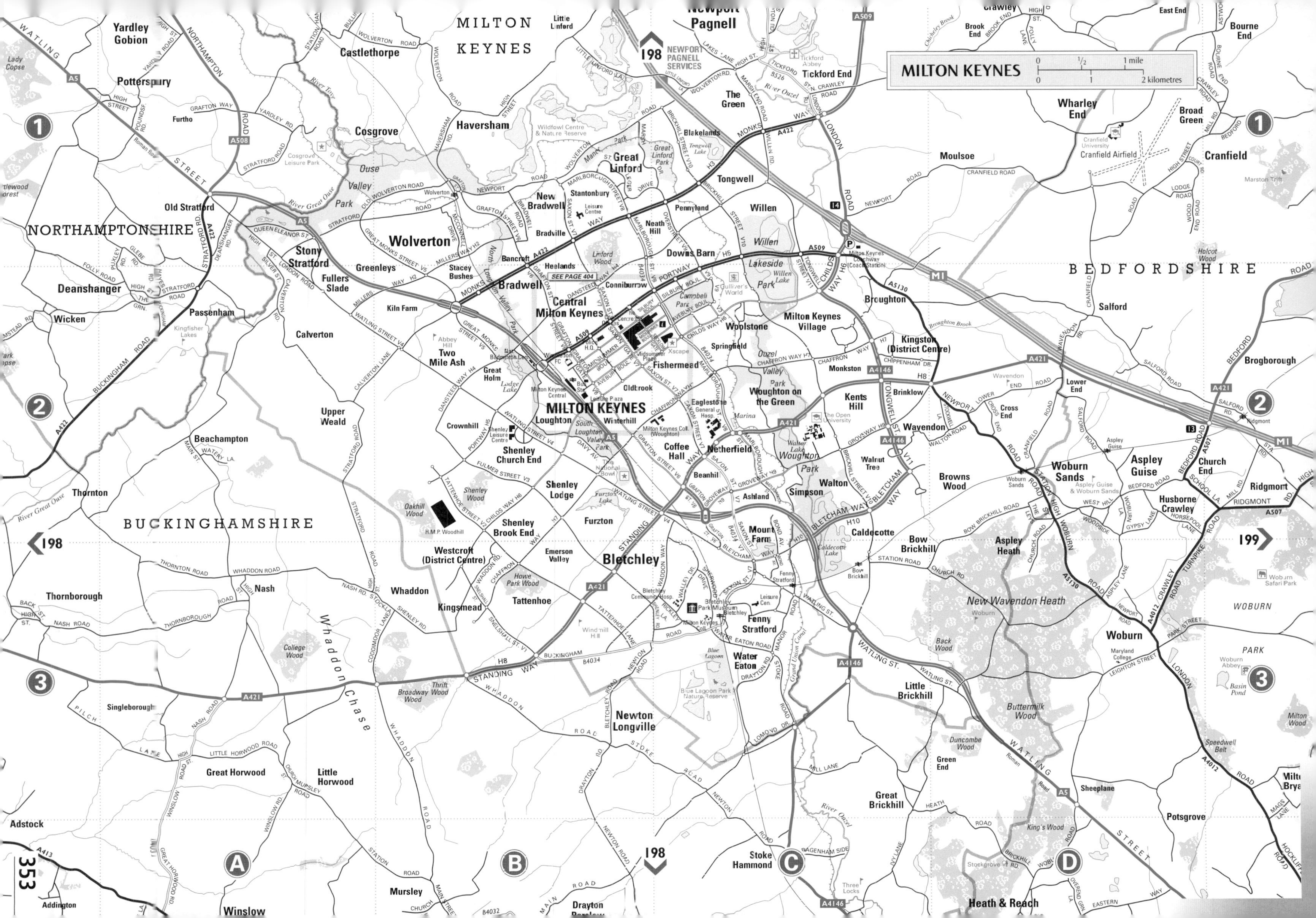

MILTON KEYNES
0
1/2
1 mile
1
2 kilometres
BEDFORDSHIRE
BUCKINGHAMSHIRE
NORTHAMPTONSHIRE
MILTON KEYNES
198
199
Newport Pagnell
NEWPORT PAGNELL SERVICES
Tickford End
Moulsoe
Wharley End
Cranfield
Cranfield Airfield
Cranfield University
Broad Green
Bourne End
Brook End
East End
Salford
Brogborough
Ridgmont
Church End
Husborne Crawley
Aspley Guise
Woburn Sands
Woburn
Woburn Abbey
Woburn Safari Park
WOBURN
PARK
Potsgrove
Lower End
Cross End
Wavendon
Browns Wood
Aspley Heath
New Wavendon Heath
Buttermilk Wood
Heath & Reach
Sheeplane
Broughton
Kingston (District Centre)
Brinklow
Kents Hill
Monkston
Walnut Tree
Caldecotte
Bow Brickhill
Little Brickhill
Great Brickhill
Green End
Duncombe Wood
Milton Keynes Village
Walton
Woughton Park
Simpson
Woughton on the Green
Woolstone
Springfield
Fishermead
Oldbrook
Eaglestone
Netherfield
Beanhill
Coffee Hall
Ashland
Mount Farm
Fenny Stratford
Water Eaton
Stoke Hammond
Willen
Willen Lake
Lakeside
Tongwell
The Green
Pennyland
Downs Barn
Conniburrow
Neath Hill
Blakelands
Great Linford
Stantonbury
Bradville
Heelands
New Bradwell
Bradwell
Bancroft
Central Milton Keynes
MILTON KEYNES
SEE PAGE 404
Winterhill
Loughton
Furzton
Bletchley
Newton Longville
Drayton Parslow
Shenley Lodge
Emerson Valley
Tattenhoe
Shenley Brook End
Shenley Church End
Crownhill
Great Holm
Two Mile Ash
Westcroft (District Centre)
Kingsmead
Whaddon
H.M.P. Woodhill
Oakhill Wood
Thrift Wood
Broadway Wood
Stacey Bushes
Wolverton
Greenleys
Kiln Farm
Fullers Slade
Stony Stratford
Calverton
Upper Weald
Haversham
Little Linford
Castlethorpe
Cosgrove
Cosgrove Leisure Park
Ouse Valley Park
Old Stratford
Passenham
Beachampton
Nash
Whaddon Chase
College Wood
Little Horwood
Great Horwood
Winslow
Mursley
Singleborough
Thornborough
Thornton
Deanshanger
Wicken
Potterspury
Furtho
Yardley Gobion
Adstock
Addington
Lady Copse
WATLING STREET

354
LONDON - WEST
0
1/2
1 mile
0
1
2 kilometres
SEE PAGES 376-377
FRIERN BARNET
HORNSEY
HAMPSTEAD
CAMDEN
MARYLEBONE
WESTMINSTER
FINCHLEY
MILL HILL
EDGWARE
HENDON
Dollis Hill
Willesden
Kilburn
PADDINGTON
Bayswater
Mayfair
Queensbury
Kingsbury
Neasden
WEMBLEY
BRENT
Harlesden
Stonebridge
ACTON
HARROW
Stanmore
Wealdstone
Kenton
Harrow on the Hill
North Wembley
Sudbury
Perivale
EALING
Greenford
Northolt
Rayners Lane
Pinner
Hatch End
South Ruislip
Ruislip Manor
Eastcote Village
Dormer's Wells

North Hyde
Norwood Green
HESTON SERVICES
Osterley Park
Osterley
HESTON
HOUNSLOW
Lampton
Hounslow West
HOUNSLOW
Spring Grove
Woodlands
ISLEWORTH
Brentford
Little Ealing
Gunnersbury Park
Gunnersbury
Acton
Bedford Park
HAMMERSMITH
Kew
Royal Botanic Gardens Kew
North Sheen
CHISWICK
Grove Park
Castelnau
BARNES
Mortlake
East Sheen
Putney
Roehampton
Putney Heath
FULHAM
HAMMERSMITH & FULHAM
Walham Green
Parsons Green
Sands End
BATTERSEA
Battersea Park
KENSINGTON & CHELSEA
CHELSEA
Brompton
Pimlico
WANDSWORTH
Clapham Common
Hounslow Heath
Whitton
TWICKENHAM
St. Margarets
RICHMOND
RICHMOND UPON THAMES
Old Deer Park
Petersham
Richmond Park
Ham
Strawberry Hill
Hanworth
Hampton Hill
Teddington
Bushy Park
Hampton
Hampton Wick
KINGSTON upon THAMES
Hampton Court
East Molesey
West Molesey
Thames Ditton
Queen Elizabeth II Reservoir
Putney Vale
Kingston Vale
Wimbledon Common
Coombe
Norbiton
KINGSTON UPON THAMES
Berrylands
New Malden
Raynes Park
West Barnes
Motspur Park
Bushey Mead
Southfields
Earlsfield
Balham
Wimbledon Park
Summerstown
Upper Tooting
WIMBLEDON
MERTON
MORDEN
Morden Park
Tooting Graveney
Collier's Wood
MITCHAM
St. Helier
Streatham Park
Furzedown
171
357

LONDON - EAST
0 1/2 1 mile
0 1 2 kilometres
186
354
SEE PAGES 376-377
FRIERN BARNET
TOTTENHAM
WOOD GREEN
Upper Edmonton
South Chingford
Chingford Hatch
Woodford Green
Highams Park
Hale End
WALTHAMSTOW
Tottenham Hale
Higham Hill
South Woodford
Snaresbrook
Fullwell Cross
Clayhall
Gants Hill
REDBRIDGE
Wanstead
Leytonstone
LEYTON
HARINGEY
HARRINGAY
HORNSEY
Muswell Hill
Crouch End
Stroud Green
West Green
Noel Park
South Tottenham
STOKE NEWINGTON
Stamford Hill
Upper Clapton
Lea Bridge
Lower Clapton
Clapton Park
HACKNEY
Hackney Wick
Homerton
Stratford
Forest Gate
WEST HAM
Upton
Upton Park
EAST HAM
BARKING
ILFORD
Little Ilford
Manor Park
Aldersbrook
Cranbrook
Loxford
NEWHAM
Plaistow
Canning Town
Custom House
Beckton
Highgate
Finsbury Park
Holloway
Upper Holloway
Tufnell Park
Kentish Town
Camden Town
CAMDEN
ISLINGTON
Highbury
Barnsbury
Dalston
Shacklewell
King's Cross
ST PANCRAS
FINSBURY
St. Luke's
Hoxton
Haggerston
SHOREDITCH
Bethnal Green
Old Ford
Bow
Mile End
TOWER HAMLETS
Bromley
Poplar
Limehouse
Stepney
Whitechapel
Shadwell
Wapping
CITY
HOLBORN
Bloomsbury
MARYLEBONE
Soho
Mayfair
WESTMINSTER
Regents Park
HAMPSTEAD
Dartmouth Park
Belsize Park
Victoria Park
Hackney Marsh
Lee Valley Park
Walthamstow Marshes
Wanstead Flats
Epping Forest
Royal Victoria Dock
Royal Albert Dock
Royal George V Dock
River Thames
NORTH CIRCULAR ROAD

Woolwich
Thamesmead West
Plumstead
WOOLWICH
New Charlton
Charlton
GREENWICH
Cubitt Town
Millwall
Deptford
BERMONDSEY
Brompton
Pimlico
LAMBETH
Walworth
Kennington
Vauxhall
SOUTHWARK
CAMBERWELL
Peckham
Nunhead
New Cross Gate
New Cross
St. John's
Blackheath
Kidbrooke
Shooters Hill
Falcon
Eltham
Avery Hill
Lewisham
LEWISHAM
Blackheath Park
Lee
Hither Green
Ladywell
Brockley
Honor Oak Park
Honor Oak
East Dulwich
DULWICH
Herne Hill
Brixton
Stockwell
South Lambeth
BATTERSEA
Clapham
Clapham Park
LAMBETH
Streatham Hill
Tulse Hill
West Dulwich
West Norwood
Balham
STREATHAM
Streatham Park
Furzedown
Tooting Graveney
Collier's Wood
Streatham Vale
Norbury
MITCHAM
Thornton Heath
Selhurst
Norwood New Town
Norwood
Upper Norwood
South Norwood
Anerley
Penge
Upper Sydenham
SYDENHAM
Forest Hill
Lower Sydenham
Bell Green
Bellingham
Catford
Southend
New Beckenham
BECKENHAM
Elmers End
Upper Elmers End
Monks Orchard
Park Langley
Shortlands
Downham
Grove Park
Mottingham
New Eltham
Elmstead
Chislehurst West
CHISLEHURST
Sundridge
Plaistow
BROMLEY
Widmore
Bickley
Southborough
Petts Wood
172
355

WOLVERHAMPTON
208
WILLENHALL
WALSALL
Bentley
Birchills
Pleck
Caldmore
Palfrey
The Chuckery
Castlecroft
Bradmore
Merry Hill
Blakenhall
Goldthorn Park
Penn
Colton Hills
Spring Hill
Lower Penn
Orton
Monmore Green
Moseley
Portobello
Stow Lawn
Priestfield
Parkfield
Ettingshall
Bilston
Lanesfield
Ettingshall Park
Spring Vale
Darlaston Green
Darlaston
Fallings Heath
Kings Hill
Wednesbury
Wood Green
Woods Bank
Moxley
Bescot
Church Hill
Mesty Croft
The Woods
The Delves
Yew Tree
Friar Park
Stone Cross
Bradley
Lower Bradley
Cinder Hill
Coseley
Wednesbury Oak
Princes End
Ocker Hill
Balls Hill
Hateley Heath
Golds Green
Hill Top
Charlemont
STAFFORDSHIRE
Gospel End
Sedgley
Hurst Hill
Roseville
Wallbrook
Bramford
Bloomfield
Summer Hill
Toll End
Black Lake
Churchfield
Wombourne
Baggeridge Country Park
Upper Gornal
Ruiton
Woodsetton
Tipton Green
Tipton
Horseley Heath
Harvils Hawthorn
Swan Village
Guns Village
West Bromwich
Lyndon
Himley
Lower Gornal
Redhall
Gornalwood
London Fields
Eve Hill
Dudley Port
New Town
Burnt Tree
Tividale
Brades Village
Wall Heath
Russell's Hall
DUDLEY
Kate's Hill
Dixon's Green
Oakham
Darby's Hill
Rounds Green
SANDWELL
Pensnett
Woodside
Oldbury
Langley
Rood End
Kingswinford
Summer Hill
Baptist End
Netherton
Portway
Mount Pleasant
Bromley
Brockmoor
Primrose Hill
Darby End
The Knowle
Langley Green
Smethwick
208
Wordsley
Buckpool
Hawbush
Brierley Hill
Bowling Green
Rowley Regis
Causeway Green
Bristnall Fields
Bearwood
Dudley Wood
Ross
Old Hill
Blackheath
Audnam
Withymoor Village
Quarry Bank
Cradley Heath
Warley
Amblecote
Amblecote Bank
Dunn's Bank
Netherend
Haden Cross
Cockshot
Hurst Green
Coombeswood
STOURBRIDGE
Wollaston
Holloway End
Lye
The Hayes
Stambermill
Cradley
Overend
Belle Vale
Hawne
Quinton
Ridgacre
Harborne
High Park
Wollescote
HALESOWEN
Gigmill
Lapal
Hasbury
Spring Hill
Moor Street
California
Woodgate
Bartley Green
Weoley Castle
Shenley Fields
Hunnington
Illey
Hagley
West Hagley
Romsley
Clent
Churchill
Blakedown
Broome
Holy Cross
Romsley Hill
Frankley
Dayhouse Bank
WORCESTERSHIRE
Rubery
Rednal
Longbridge
Bell End
Belbroughton
Drayton
M5
M6
WEST MIDLANDS
0 1/2 1 mile
0 1 2 kilometres

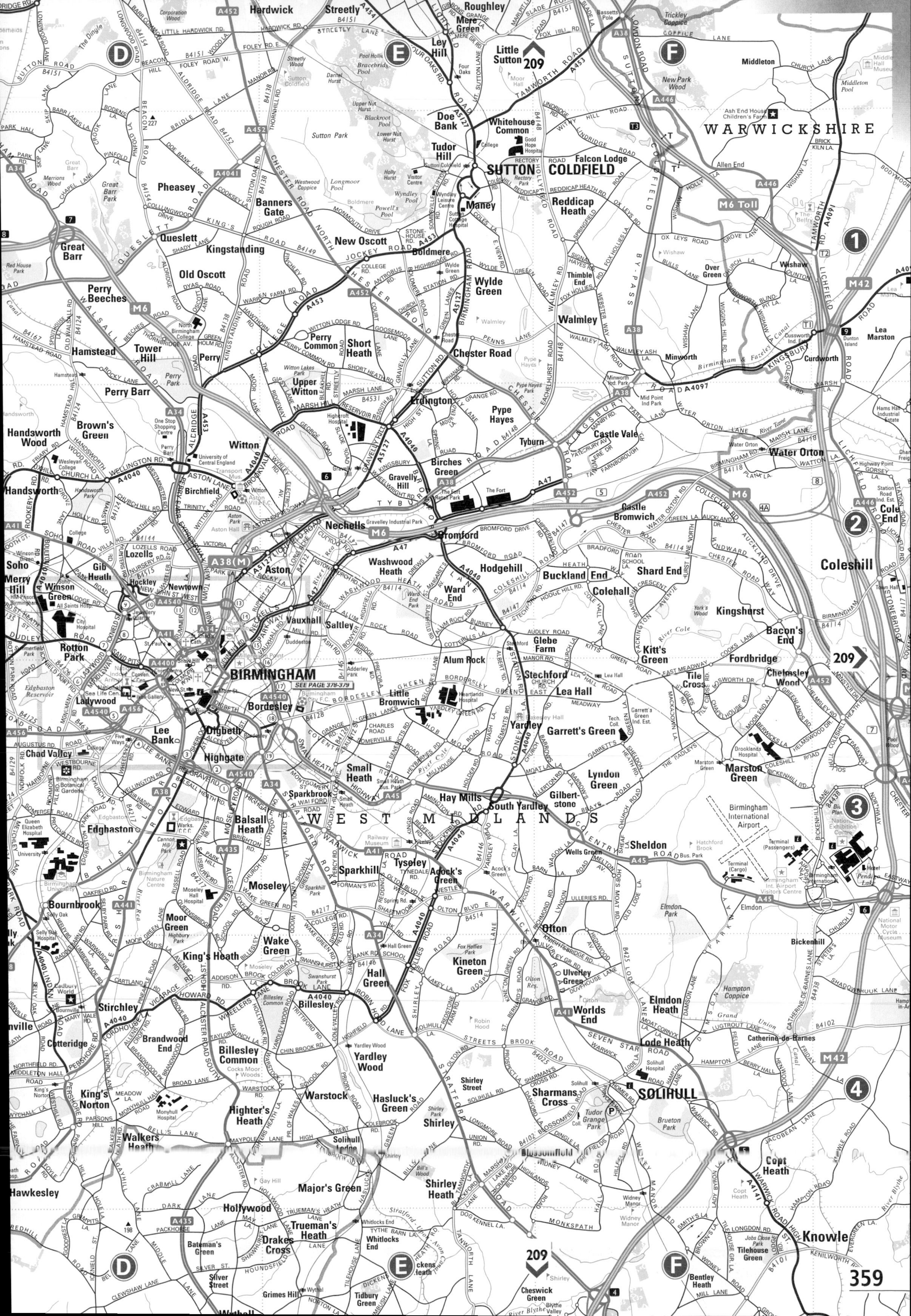

WARWICKSHIRE
WEST MIDLANDS
SUTTON COLDFIELD
BIRMINGHAM
SOLIHULL
SEE PAGE 378-379
Coleshill
Knowle
Hardwick
Streetly
Roughley
Mere Green
Little Sutton
Ley Hill
Doe Bank
Whitehouse Common
Tudor Hill
Falcon Lodge
Pheasey
Banners Gate
Maney
Reddicap Heath
Queslett
Kingstanding
New Oscott
Boldmere
Great Barr
Old Oscott
Perry Beeches
Wylde Green
Walmley
Hamstead
Tower Hill
Perry
Perry Common
Short Heath
Chester Road
Minworth
Perry Barr
Upper Witton
Erdington
Pype Hayes
Handsworth Wood
Brown's Green
Witton
Castle Vale
Tyburn
Birches Green
Gravelly Hill
Water Orton
Handsworth
Birchfield
Nechells
Castle Bromwich
Bromford
Soho
Lozells
Aston
Washwood Heath
Hodgehill
Buckland End
Shard End
Merry Hill
Gib Heath
Winson Green
Hockley
Newtown
Ward End
Colehall
Kingshurst
Vauxhall
Saltley
Bacon's End
Rotton Park
Alum Rock
Glebe Farm
Kitt's Green
Fordbridge
Stechford
Tile Cross
Chelmsley Wood
Ladywood
Bordesley
Little Bromwich
Lea Hall
Lee Bank
Digbeth
Yardley
Garrett's Green
Chad Valley
Highgate
Small Heath
Lyndon Green
Marston Green
Sparkbrook
Hay Mills
South Yardley
Gilbertstone
Balsall Heath
Edgbaston
Tyseley
Acock's Green
Sheldon
Sparkhill
Moseley
Bournbrook
Olton
Moor Green
Wake Green
King's Heath
Kineton Green
Ulverley Green
Hall Green
Stirchley
Billesley
Worlds End
Elmdon Heath
Brandwood End
Billesley Common
Yardley Wood
Lode Heath
Catherine-de-Barnes
Cotteridge
King's Norton
Warstock
Hasluck's Green
Shirley Street
Sharmans Cross
Highter's Heath
Shirley
Walkers Heath
Copt Heath
Major's Green
Shirley Heath
Hawkesley
Hollywood
Trueman's Heath
Drakes Cross
Whitlocks End
Bateman's Green
Silver Street
Grimes Hill
Tidbury Green
Cheswick Green
Bentley Heath
Tilehouse Green
Middleton
Over Green
Wishaw
Curdworth
Lea Marston
Birmingham International Airport
National Exhibition Centre
Elmdon
Bickenhill
Sutton Park
Edgbaston Reservoir
D
E
F
1
2
3
4
M6
M6 Toll
M42
A38(M)
209

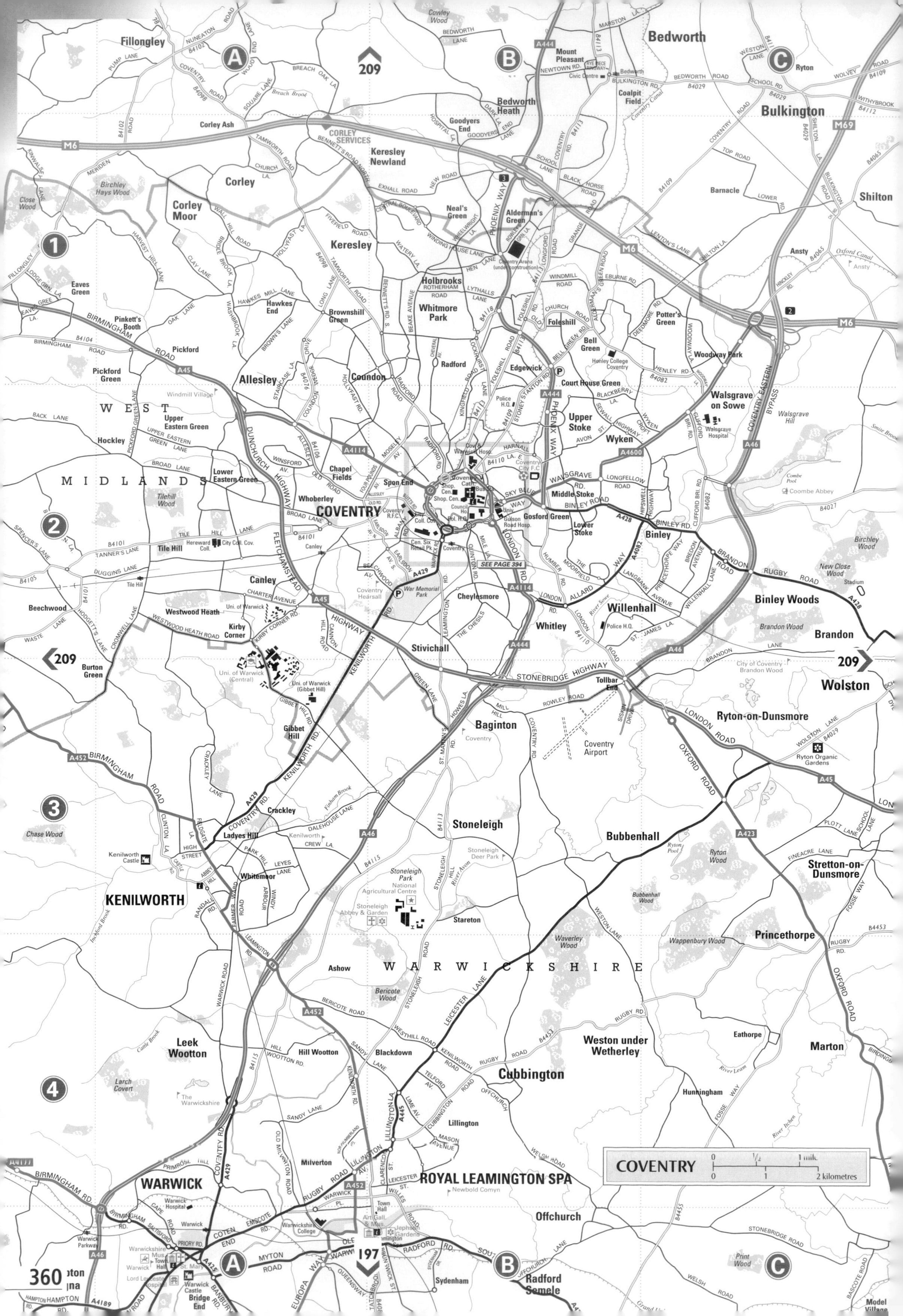
COVENTRY
0 1/2 1 mile
0 1 2 kilometres
209
209
209
197
SEE PAGE 394
A
B
C
A
B
C
1
2
3
4
Fillongley
Bedworth
Ryton
Bulkington
Mount Pleasant
Bedworth Heath
Coalpit Field
Goodyers End
Corley Ash
CORLEY SERVICES
Keresley Newland
Corley
Corley Moor
Birchley Hays Wood
Close Wood
Shilton
Barnacle
Ansty
Neal's Green
Alderman's Green
Keresley
Holbrooks
Whitmore Park
Eaves Green
Hawkes End
Brownshill Green
Pinkett's Booth
Pickford
Pickford Green
Radford
Foleshill
Potter's Green
Bell Green
Woodway Park
Edgewick
Court House Green
Walsgrave on Sowe
Walsgrave Hospital
Allesley
Coundon
Upper Stoke
Wyken
Windmill Village
WEST
MIDLANDS
WARWICKSHIRE
Upper Eastern Green
Hockley
Lower Eastern Green
Chapel Fields
Spon End
Whoberley
COVENTRY
Middle Stoke
Gosford Green
Lower Stoke
Binley
Coombe Abbey
Tilehill Wood
Tile Hill
Canley
Birchley Wood
New Close Wood
Binley Woods
Brandon Wood
Brandon
Beechwood
Westwood Heath
Kirby Corner
Cheylesmore
Whitley
Willenhall
Stivichall
Burton Green
Uni. of Warwick (Central)
Uni. of Warwick (Gibbet Hill)
Gibbet Hill
Tollbar End
City of Coventry Brandon Wood
Wolston
Baginton
Coventry Airport
Ryton-on-Dunsmore
Ryton Organic Gardens
Chase Wood
Crackley
Ladyes Hill
Kenilworth Castle
Stoneleigh
Bubbenhall
Ryton Pool
Ryton Wood
Stretton-on-Dunsmore
Stoneleigh Deer Park
Whitemoor
KENILWORTH
Stoneleigh Park National Agricultural Centre
Stoneleigh Abbey & Garden
Stareton
Bubbenhall Wood
Waverley Wood
Wappenbury Wood
Princethorpe
Ashow
Bericote Wood
Leek Wootton
Hill Wootton
Blackdown
Weston under Wetherley
Eathorpe
Marton
Larch Covert
The Warwickshire
Cubbington
Hunningham
Lillington
Milverton
WARWICK
ROYAL LEAMINGTON SPA
Newbold Comyn
Offchurch
Warwick Hospital
Warwickshire College
Warwick Parkway
Print Wood
Sydenham
Radford Semele
Bridge End
Warwick Castle
Model Village
M6
M69
A45
A46
A444
A4114
A4600
A428
A4082
A429
A423
A452
A445
A425
A4189
A4177
B4102
B4098
B4104
B4101
B4105
B4113
B4109
B4029
B4065
B4112
B4115
B4110
B4082
B4027
B4453
B4455
B4118
B4076
B4106
BIRMINGHAM ROAD
KENILWORTH ROAD
LONDON ROAD
STONEBRIDGE HIGHWAY
FLETCHAMSTEAD HIGHWAY
COVENTRY EASTERN BYPASS
PHOENIX WAY
LEICESTER LANE
OXFORD ROAD
FOSSE WAY

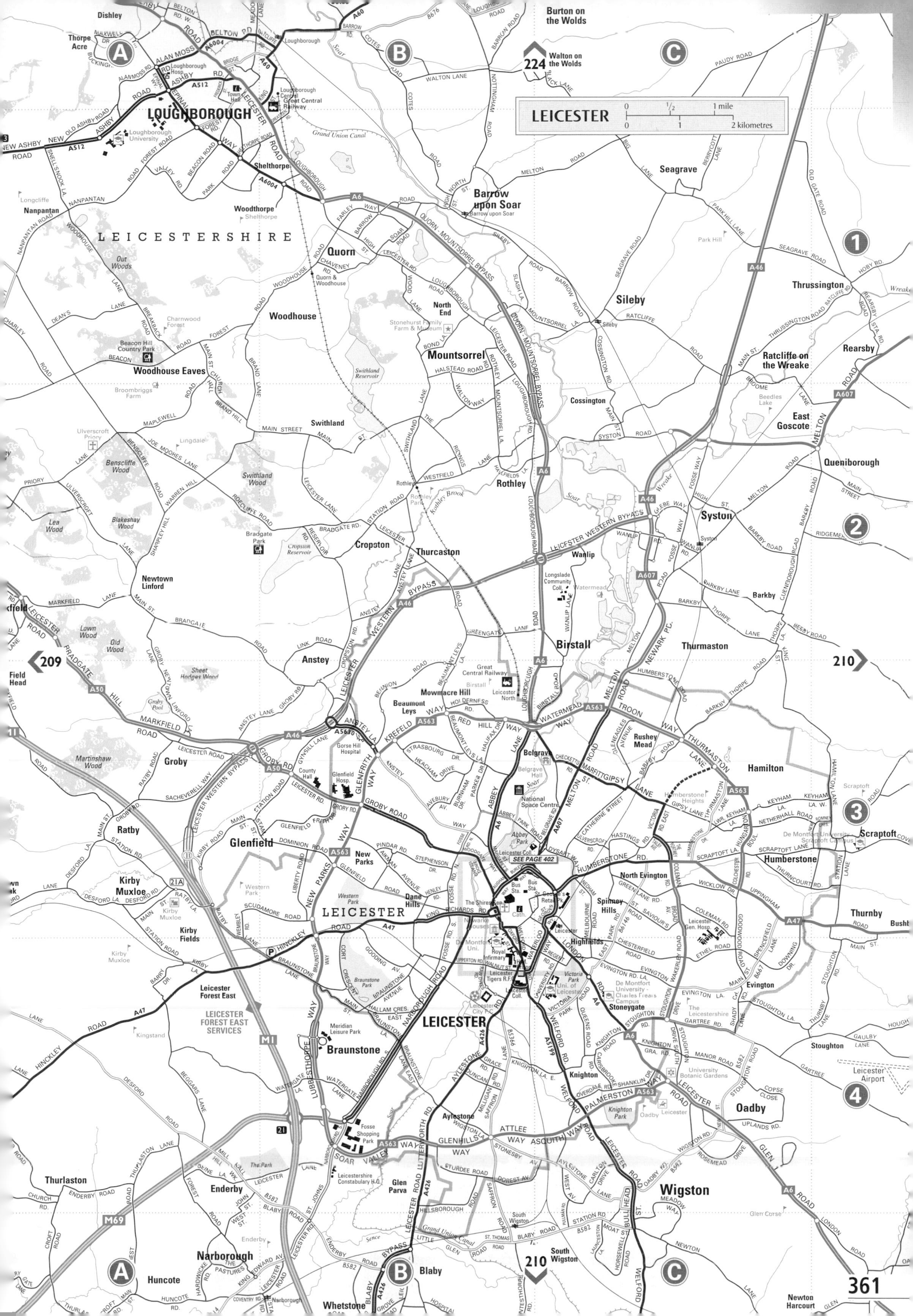
LEICESTER
0 1/2 1 mile
0 1 2 kilometres
LEICESTERSHIRE
Dishley
Thorpe Acre
LOUGHBOROUGH
Loughborough University
Loughborough Central Great Central Railway
Town Hall
Loughborough Hosp.
Shelthorpe
Woodthorpe
Nanpantan
Longcliffe
Burton on the Wolds
224 Walton on the Wolds
Seagrave
Barrow upon Soar
Quorn
Quorn & Woodhouse
Woodhouse
Out Woods
Charnwood Forest
Beacon Hill Country Park
Woodhouse Eaves
Broombriggs Farm
North End
Stonehurst Family Farm & Museum
Mountsorrel
Swithland Reservoir
Swithland
Ulverscroft Priory
Lingdale
Bensclliffe Wood
Swithland Wood
Rothley
Rothley Park
Rothley Brook
Cossington
Sileby
Thrussington
Rearsby
Ratcliffe on the Wreake
Beedles Lake
East Goscote
Queniborough
Park Hill
Syston
Lea Wood
Blakeshay Wood
Bradgate Park
Cropston Reservoir
Cropston
Thurcaston
Wanlip
Longslade Community Coll.
Watermead
Barkby
Newtown Linford
Lawn Wood
Old Wood
Sheet Hedges Wood
Groby Pool
Anstey
Birstall
Great Central Railway
Leicester North
Thurmaston
209
210
Field Head
Mowmacre Hill
Beaumont Leys
Martinshaw Wood
Groby
Gorse Hill Hospital
County Hall
Glenfield Hosp.
Rushey Mead
Belgrave
Belgrave Hall
National Space Centre
Abbey Park
Hamilton
Humberstone Heights
Scraptoft
De Montfort University Scraptoft Campus
Humberstone
Ratby
Glenfield
New Parks
Leicester Coll.
SEE PAGE 402
North Evington
Kirby Muxloe
Western Park
Dane Hills
Spinney Hills
Thurnby
LEICESTER
Bus Sta.
The Shires
Cath.
Newarke Houses
De Montfort Uni.
Royal Infirmary
Leicester Tigers R.F.C.
Highfields
Victoria Park
Uni. of Leicester
Leicester Gen. Hosp.
Kirby Fields
Leicester Forest East
LEICESTER FOREST EAST SERVICES
Braunstone Park
Meridian Leisure Park
Braunstone
Leicester City F.C.
Stoneygate
Evington
De Montfort University - Charles Frears Campus
The Leicestershire Hosp.
Stoughton
Leicester Airport
Kingstand
University Botanic Gardens
Knighton
Knighton Park
Oadby
Aylestone
Fosse Shopping Park
The Park
Leicestershire Constabulary H.Q.
Glen Parva
Wigston
Glen Corse
Thurlaston
Enderby
Narborough
South Wigston
Grand Union Canal
Huncote
Blaby
Whetstone
Newton Harcourt
M1
M69
A6
A46
A47
A50
A512
A563
A607
A6004
A426
A5199
1
2
3
4
A
B
C

A
B
C
1
2
3
4
223
DERBYSHIRE
DERBY
LEICESTERS
SEE PAGE 395
Belper
Heanor
Duffield
Quarndon
Little Eaton
Allestree
Mackworth
Mickleover
Littleover
Normanton
Spondon
Ockbrook
Borrowash
Draycott
Chellaston
Shardlow
Melbourne
Repton
Willington
Castle Donington
Smalley
Horsley
Kilburn
Milford
Holbrook
Denby
Morley
Breadsall
Chaddesden
Oakwood
Alvaston
Elvaston
Allenton
Sinfin
Findern
Stenson
Twyford
Swarkestone
Barrow upon Trent
Stanton by Bridge
Ingleby
Foremark
Milton
King's Newton
Weston Underwood
Kedlestone
Kedleston Park
Kedleston Hall
Windley
Hazelwood
Turnditch
Shottlegate
Blackbrook
Mount Pleasant
Farnah Green
Makeney
Duffieldbank
Flaxholme
Coxbench
Brackley Gate
Woodside
Horsley Woodhouse
Lower Kilburn
Rawson Green
Denby Bottles
Smithy Houses
Open Woodgate
Bargate
Holbrook Moor
Loscoe
Cross Hill
Aldercar
Langley Mill
Newlands
Langley
Marlpool
Heanor Gate
Stanley Common
West Hallam
Stanley
Mapperley
Shipley Common
High Lane
Dale Moor
Dale Abbey
Locko Park
Chaddesden Common
Breadsall Hilltop
Darley Abbey
Little Chester
Markeaton
New Zealand
Rose Hill
Pear Tree
Osmaston
Crewton
Sunny Hill
Cherrytree Hill
Pride Park
Shacklecross
Ambaston
Thulston
Aston-on-Trent
Cavendish Bridge
Great Wilne
Church Wilne
Wootton on Trent
Shelton Lock
Micklemeadow
Donington Grand Prix Collection
Nottingham East Mid
River Derwent
River Trent
Trent and Mersey Canal
A6
A38
A52
A50
A61
A608
A609
A6005
A5111
A514
A516
A5132
A453
A6096
A517
A610

DERBY & NOTTINGHAM
0 1/2 1 mile
0 1 2 kilometres
224
SEE PAGE 405
NOTTINGHAMSHIRE
NOTTINGHAM
Beauvale
Ruffs
Hucknall
Hazelgrove
Westville
Broomhill
Bestwood Village
Calverton
Moorgreen
Greasley
Eastwood
Newthorpe
Watnall
Giltbrook
Newthorpe Common
Kimberley
Nuthall
Awsworth
Swingate
Rise Park
Top Valley
Bestwood
Bulwell
Hempshill Vale
Highbury Vale
Cinderhill
Old Basford
Redhill
Arnold
Lambley
Daybrook
Woodthorpe
Mapperley
Gedling
Sherwood
Porchester
Carrington
Mapperley Park
New Basford
Whitemoor
Broxtowe
Aspley
Strelley
Cossall Marsh
Cossall
Carlton
Thorneywood
Bilborough
St. Ann's
Radford
Wollaton
Lenton
Sneinton
Colwick
Trowell
Bramcote Hills
Lenton Abbey
Dunkirk
Meadows
Adbolton
Holme Pierrepont
Stanton Gate
Bramcote
Gamston
Sandiacre
Stapleford
Wilford
West Bridgford
BEESTON
Rylands
Chilwell
Edwalton
Toton
Attenborough
Clifton
Mickleborough Hill
Tollerton
Brook Hill
Wilsthorpe
Long Eaton
Barton in Fabis
Manor Park
Ruddington
Plumtree
New Sawley
Sawley
Plumtree Park
Thrumpton
Trentlock
Ruddington Moor
Bradmore
Gotham
Keyworth
Bunny
Ratcliffe on Soar
Kingston on Soar
Bunny Hill
Wysall
West Leake
Sharpley Hill
Kegworth
Costock
East Leake
Sutton Bonington
TROWELL SERVICES
Normanton-on-the-Wolds

STOKE-ON-TRENT
0
1/2
1 mile
0
1
2 kilometres
222
221
221
221
STAFFORDSHIRE
STAFFORDSHIRE
CHESHIRE
STOKE-ON-TRENT
STOKE-ON-TRENT
Newcastle-under-Lyme
Hanley
Burslem
Stoke
Longton
Fenton
Tunstall
Kidsgrove
Cheadle
Cheddleton
Endon
Werrington
Meir
Trentham
Madeley
Keele
Audley
Wetley Rocks
Cellarhead
Milton
Bucknall
Norton-in-the-Moors
Brown Edge
Stockton Brook
Bagnall
Caverswall
Blythe Bridge
Forsbrook
Dilhorne
Consall
Basford Green
Longsdon
Denford
Dunwood
Endon Bank
Blackwood Hill
Birchall
Barnfields
Horse Bridge
Brindley Ford
Whitfield
Ball Green
Fegg Hayes
Oxford
Turnhurst
Newchapel
Packmoor
Harriseahead
The Rookery
Whitehill
Acres Nook
Clough Hall
Talke
Talke Pits
Red Street
Chesterton
Crackley
Wood Lane
Apedale
Miles Green
Butters Green
Halmer End
Alsagers Bank
Scott Hay
Silverdale
Knutton
Shraleybrook
Park End
Radway Green
Madeley Heath
Mid Madeley
Church Lawton
Hardings Wood
Butt Lane
Walstanton
Port Hill
Dimsdale
May Bank
Basford
Etruria
Cobridge
Sneyd Green
Smallthorne
Northwood
Abbey Hulton
Carmountside
Light Oaks
Baddeley Edge
Baddeley Green
Stanley Moor
Stanley
Ash Bank
Hulme
Weston Coyney
Adderley Green
Ubberley
Berry Hill
Mount Pleasant
Hollybush
Blurton
Dresden
Normacot
Lightwood
Meir Heath
Newstead
Wedgwood
Hanford
Oak Hill
Trent Vale
Boothen
Springfields
Clayton
Westlands
Seabridge
Westbury Park
Butterton
Hanchurch
Acton
Whitmore
Baldwin's Gate
Swynnerton Old Park
KEELE SERVICES
Sandyford
Newfield
Pits Hill
Little Chell
Great Chell
Chell Heath
Bank Top
Bradeley
Stanfield
Middleport
Longport
Bradwell
Cross Heath
Westcliffe
Goldenhill
Lane Ends
Boon Hill
Broad Meadow
High Carr
Cookshill
Godleybrook
Brookhouses
Boundary
Commonside
Stonehouses
Draycott in the Moors
Blythe Marsh
Washerwall
Withysakes
Townsend
The Folly
Lowe Hill
Caldon Canal
Trent & Mersey Canal
River Trent
M6
A500
A50
A52
A53
A34
A520
A522
A521
A5009
A5272
A5035
A519
A527
A5011
A525
SEE PAGE 410

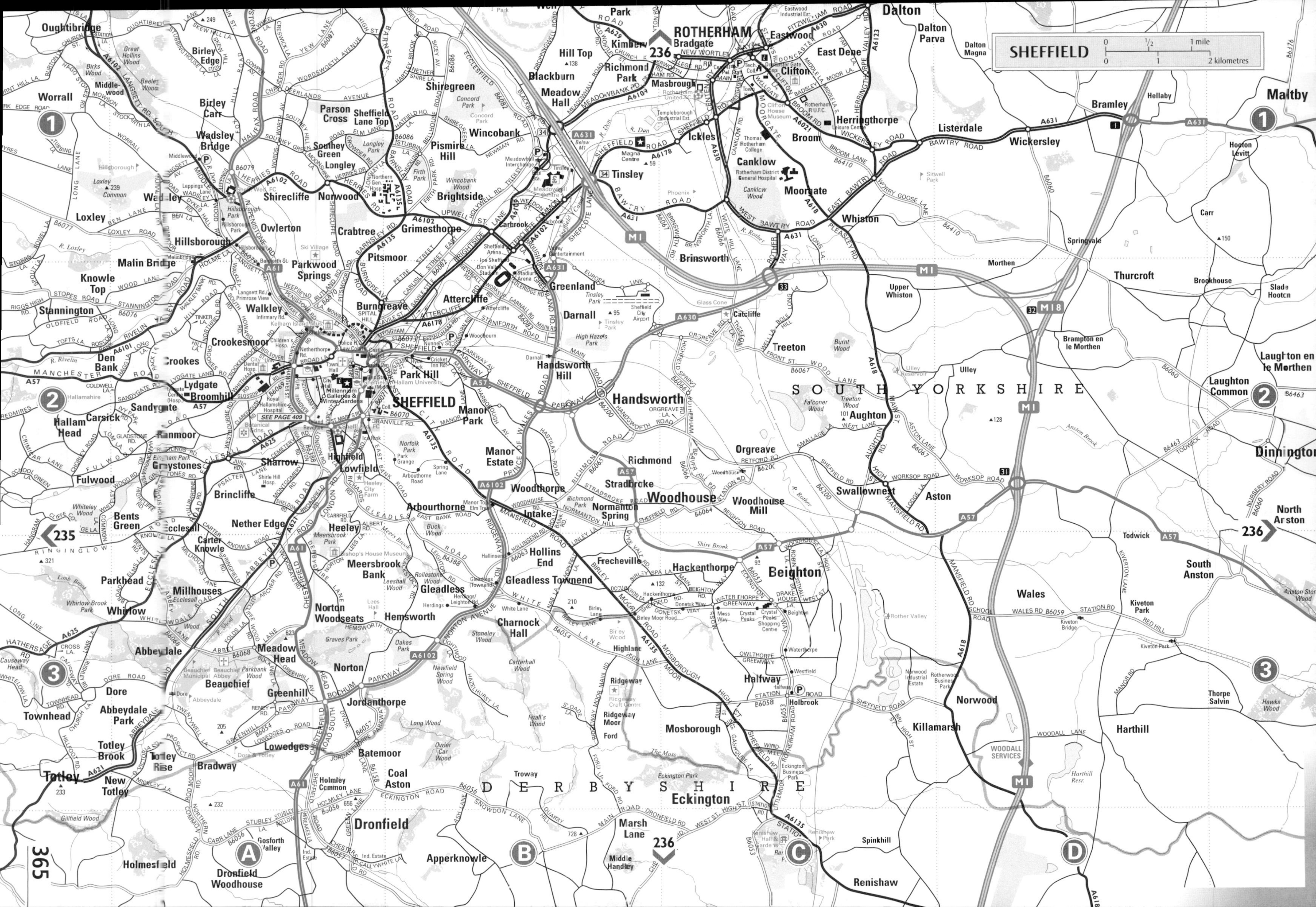
SHEFFIELD
0 1/2 1 mile
0 1 2 kilometres
ROTHERHAM
SHEFFIELD
SOUTH YORKSHIRE
DERBYSHIRE
Maltby
Dinnington
North Anston
South Anston
Laughton en le Morthen
Laughton Common
Thurcroft
Bramley
Wickersley
Hellaby
Brookhouse
Carr
Slade Hooton
Hooton Levitt
Listerdale
Dalton
Dalton Parva
Dalton Magna
Brampton en le Morthen
Morthen
Ulley
Upper Whiston
Whiston
Herringthorpe
East Dene
Clifton
Broom
Moorgate
Eastwood
Canklow
Ickles
Masbrough
Bradgate
Kimberworth
Tinsley
Brinsworth
Treeton
Aughton
Swallownest
Aston
Todwick
Kiveton Park
Harthill
Wales
Thorpe Salvin
Norwood
Killamarsh
Renishaw
Spinkhill
Beighton
Halfway
Holbrook
Eckington
Mosborough
Orgreave
Woodhouse Mill
Woodhouse
Handsworth
Hackenthorpe
Frecheville
Richmond
Stradbroke
Normanton Spring
Darnall
Handsworth Hill
Greenland
Attercliffe
Brightside
Wincobank
Blackburn
Meadow Hall
Hill Top
Richmond Park
Park Hill
Manor Park
Manor Estate
Woodthorpe
Intake
Hollins End
Gleadless Townend
Charnock Hall
Gleadless
Arbourthorne
Heeley
Highfield
Lowfield
Meersbrook Bank
Hemsworth
Norton Woodseats
Norton
Jordanthorpe
Batemoor
Coal Aston
Dronfield
Dronfield Woodhouse
Apperknowle
Marsh Lane
Middle Handley
Ridgeway
Ridgeway Moor
Ford
Highlane
Troway
Holmley Common
Lowedges
Greenhill
Meadow Head
Bradway
Beauchief
Abbeydale
Totley Rise
Totley
New Totley
Totley Brook
Abbeydale Park
Dore
Townhead
Holmesfield
Gosforth Valley
Millhouses
Nether Edge
Sharrow
Brincliffe
Ecclesall
Carter Knowle
Whirlow
Parkhead
Bents Green
Greystones
Ranmoor
Fulwood
Broomhill
Crookesmoor
Walkley
Crookes
Lydgate
Sandygate
Carsick
Hallam Head
Den Bank
Stannington
Knowle Top
Malin Bridge
Hillsborough
Wadsley
Wadsley Bridge
Owlerton
Shirecliffe
Parkwood Springs
Norwood
Crabtree
Pitsmoor
Burngreave
Grimesthorpe
Pismire Hill
Shiregreen
Parson Cross
Sheffield Lane Top
Longley
Southey Green
Birley Carr
Birley Edge
Middlewood
Worrall
Oughtibridge
Loxley
SEE PAGE 409
M1
M18
A57
A618
A630
A631
A61
A621
A625
A6102
A6135
236
235

MERSEYSIDE
0 1/2 1 mile
0 1 2 kilometres
LIVERPOOL BAY
hours
Belfast.......7½
Douglas.......2½-4
Dublin.......4-8
Crosby Channel
River Mersey
MERSEYSIDE
SEE PAGE 380-381
233
232
CROSBY
Great Crosby
Waterloo
Waterloo Park
Seaforth
Litherland
Orrell
Aintree
Buckley Hill
Northwood
Westvale
Kirkby
Southdene
Fazakerley
Gillmoss
Croxteth
Knowsley
BOOTLE
Walton
Dog and Gun
Norris Green
Kirkdale
Anfield
Clubmoor
Tuebrook
Stoneycroft
Fairfield
Everton
LIVERPOOL
Old Swan
Knotty Ash
Dovecot
Swanside
Page Moss
Roby
Huyton with Roby
Huyton Park
Fincham
Woolfall Heath
Court Hey
Bowring Park
Childwall
Edge Hill
Princes Park
Toxteth
Dingle
St Michael's Hamlet
Mossley Hill
Calderstones
Aigburth
Otterspool
Grassendale
Allerton
Garston
Gateacre
Belle Vale
Netherley
Woolton
Halewood
Hunts Cross
Speke
Liverpool John Lennon Airport
New Brighton
WALLASEY
Liscard
Egremont
Poulton
Seacombe
Bidston
BIRKENHEAD
Claughton
Oxton
Tranmere
Prenton
Rock Ferry
Higher Bebington
Woodhey
New Ferry
BEBINGTON
Lower Bebington
Port Sunlight
Bromborough Pool
Barnston
Brimstage
Poulton
Bromborough
Thornton Hough
Brookhurst
Raby
Eastham
Willaston
Hooton
Childer Thornton
Overpool
ELLESMERE PORT
Stanlow
Little Neston
Ness
Greater Sutton
Little Sutton
Whitby
M53
M57
M62
A41
A59
A580
A5058
A562
A561

Rainford
Billinge
Chadwick
Garswood
Ashton in Makerfield
233
Golborne
GREATER MANCHESTER
Lowton
Town of Lowton
Moss Bank
Blackbrook
Haydock
Haydock Park Race Course
Denton's Green
Newtown
Eccleston
ST. HELENS
Parr
Broad Oak
Derbyshire Hill
Newton-le-Willows
Wargrave
Vulcan Village
Collins Green
West Park
Ravenhead
Toll Bar
Grange Park
Portico
Thatto Heath
Peasley Cross
Sutton Oak
Sutton Heath
Eccleston Park
Prescot
Nutgrove
Marshall's Cross
Sutton Leach
Burtonwood
Winwick
Holt
Rainhill
Whiston Cross
Whiston
Clock Face
Sutton Manor
Rainhill Stoops
Windy Arbor
Hulme
Cinnamon Brow
Longford
Orford
Callands
Dallam
Bewsey
Old Hall
Lingley Green
WARRINGTON
Great Sankey
Penketh
Sankey Bridges
Howley
Latchford
Bold Heath
Town End
Cronton
Lunts Heath
Farnworth
Crow Wood
Cuerdley Cross
Tarbock Green
Hough Green
Appleton
Halton
Kingsway
Ball o' Ditton
Ditton
Moss Bank
Lugs Dale
Woodend
WIDNES
Stockton Heath
Lower Walton
Hillcliffe
Cobbs
Higher Walton
Moore
Appleton Park
West Bank
Hale Bank
HALTON
Astmoor
Keckwick
Castlefields
Norton
Halton Brook
Halton
RUNCORN
Grange
Halton Lea
Weston Point
Weston
Beechwood
Hale
Daresbury
Hatton
Stretton
Preston on the Hill
Preston Brook
Higher Whitley
Sutton Weaver
Dutton
Lower Whitley
Aston
Frodsham Bridge
Marsh Green
Frodsham
Bradley
Overton
Netherton
Acton Bridge
Ince Marshes
M6
M62
M56
368

GREATER MANCHESTER
0 1/2 1 mile
0 1 2 kilometres
Deane
Furnhill
Darcy Lever
Burnden
Little Lever
Radcliffe
Blackford Bridge
Chew Moor
Hunger Hill
Lever Edge
Great Lever
Wingates
Water's Nook
Moses Gate
Harper Green
Nob End
Farnworth
Highfield
Prestolee
Cinder Hill
Ringley
Outwood
Chapel Field
Stand
Stoneclough
Kearsley
New Bury
Park Lane
Daisy Hill
Hill Top
Greenheys
Little Hulton
Atherton
Kearsley Moss
Clifton
Philips Park
Dangerous Corner
Shakerley
Linnyshaw
Walkden
Clifton Junction
Clifton Green
Howe Bridge
Hindsford
Tyldesley
Wardley
Newtown
Pendlebury
Westleigh
Parr Brow
Mosley Common
Roe Green
Swinton
Moorside
Hazelhurst
Gin Pit
Worsley
Swinton Park
Irlams o' th' Height
Higher Folds
Blackmoor
Astley
Boothstown
Dales Brow
LEIGH
Firs Lane
Bedford
Lark Hill
Town Lane
Higher Green
Alder Forest
Pennington
Astley Green
Ellesmere Park
Monton
Moss Side
Winton
Little Bolton
Patricroft
ECCLES
Lately Common
Pocket Nook
Botany Bay Wood
Worsley Moss
Peel Green
Barton upon Irwell
Astley Moss
Barton Moss
Dumplington
Glazebury
Trafford Park
Fowley Common
Chat Moss
Twiss Green
Crofts Bank
Davyhulme
Culcheth
Larkhill
Higher Irlam
Irlam Moss
URMSTON
Little Woolden Moss
STRETFORD
WARRINGTON
Little Town
Irlam
Flixton
Cadishead Moss
Lower Irlam
Holcroft Moss
Ashton upon Mersey
Carrington
Glazebrook
Risley
Risley Moss
Cadishead
Chemical Works
Carrington Moss
SALE
Partington
Birchwood
Hollins Green
Woolston Moss
Brooklands
Woodhouses
Sinderland Green
Pixton Moss
Warburton
Broadheath
Mossbrow
Timperley
Oldfield Brow
Carr Green
Heatley
Dunham Woodhouses
Dunham Town
ALTRINCHAM
Statham
Rushgreen
Dunham Massey Hall, Park & Gardens (NT)
Lymm
Little Bollington
Bowdon
Hale
Well Green
Rosehill
Bowgreen
Ashley Heath
CHESHIRE
Broomedge
Arthill
Booth Bank
Halebarns
Warburton Green
Sworton Heath
Ashley
Manchester Ship Canal
Bridgewater Canal
Leeds & Liverpool Canal
River Mersey
M61
M60
M62
M6
M56
A6144(M)
367
234
368

MANCHESTER
Whitefield
Middleton
Chadderton
Rhodes
Alkrington
Higher Blackley
Nimble Nook
Werneth
Coppice
OLDHAM
Mumps
Oldham Edge
Derker
Higginshaw
Moorside
Watersheddings
Springhead
Lees
Grotton
Glodwick
Hathershaw
Holts
Quick Edge
Brook Bottom
Hollinwood
Failsworth
Woodhouses
Daisy Nook
Limehurst
Waterloo
Smallshaw
Hurst
Hazelhurst
Heyrod
Taunton
Crowhill
ASHTON-UNDER-LYNE
Stalybridge
Copley
Dukinfield
Yew Tree
Newton
Godley
Hyde
Godley Hill
Backbower
Gee Cross
Kingston
Flowery Field
Denton
Dane Bank
Audenshaw
Guide Bridge
Fairfield
Droylsden
Clayton
Clayton Bridge
Openshaw
Beswick
Ardwick
Abbey Hey
Gorton
Debdale
West Gorton
Longsight
Levenshulme
North Reddish
Reddish
Heaton Chapel
Houldsworth
Brinnington
South Reddish
Portwood
STOCKPORT
Bredbury
Lower Bredbury
Romiley
Compstall
Cherry Tree
Woodley
Greave
Haughton Green
Castle Hill
Werneth Low
Marple
Marple Bridge
Ley Hey Park
Bunkers Hill
Bredbury Green
Foggbrook
Offerton Green
Offerton Fold
Marpleridge
Windlehurst
Strines
High Lane
Disley
Hazel Grove
Torkington
Norbury Moor
Stepping Hill
Great Moor
Woods Moor
Davenport
Heaviley
Shaw Heath
Cale Green
Edgeley
Cheadle Heath
Adswood
Cheadle
Cheadle Hulme
Bramhall
Bramhall Park
Smithy Green
Stanley Green
Kitt's Moss
Heaton Norris
Heaton Mersey
Heaton Moor
Norris Bank
Lane End
Green End
Burnage
Withington
Didsbury
East Didsbury
West Didsbury
Ladybarn
Fallowfield
Rusholme
Moss Side
Whalley Range
Chorlton-cum-Hardy
Barlow Moor
Northenden
Gatley
Sharston
Benchill
Wythenshawe
Newall Green
Peel Hall
Woodhouse Park
Heald Green
Moss Nook
Heyhead
Baguley
Manchester Airport
Hulme
Old Trafford
St. George's
Ordsall
Pendleton
Brunswick
Ancoats
Bradford
Miles Platting
Collyhurst
Newton Heath
Cheetwood
Strangeways
Cheetham
Cheetham Hill
Higher Broughton
Lower Broughton
Broughton Park
Crumpsall
Harpurhey
Blackley
Moston
New Moston
Charlestown
Chain Bar
Moor Close
Langley
Top of Hebers
Hollins
Higher Boarshaw
Birch
Whittle Hill
Bowlee
Simister
Unsworth
Sedgley Park
Hilton Park
Kersal
Lower Kersal
The Cliff
Wallness
Royton
Thorp
Luzley Brook
Heyside
Sholver
Busk
Werneth
Austerlands
Southead
Greenacres
Moorhey
Alt
Bardsley
Copster Hill
Lime Side
Knott Lanes
Smallshaw
Mossley Brow
Hartshead Pike
White Gate
SEE PAGE 382-383
234
235
CHESHIRE
M60
M62
M66
M67
M56
A627(M)
A57(M)
369

LEEDS & BRADFORD
0 1/2 1 mile
0 1 2 kilometres
244
243
235
370
A
B
C
1
2
3
4
Bogthorn
Oakworth
Harewood Hill
Lane End
Whins Wood
Hainworth
Harden Moor
Harden
Bingley
Baildon
Baildon Green
Myrtle Park
Heather Park
Stanbury
Haworth
Upper Marsh
Marsh
Cullingworth Moor
Cullingworth
Wilsden
Cottingley Park
Cottingley
Saltaire
Nab Wood
Moorhead
Shipley
West Royd
Windhill
Idle Moor
Swain House
Gaisby
Frizinghall
Heaton
Heaton Shay
Heaton Royds
Daisy Hill
Noon Nick
Sandy Lane
Shay Gate
Norr
Oxenhope
Leeming
Denholme
Stake Hill
Sun Hill
Oxenhope Moor
Thornton Moor
Thornton Moor Resr.
Stubden Resr.
Denholme Clough
Hill Top
Thornton
School Green
Chat Hill
Allerton
Lower Grange
Four Lane Ends
Crossley Hall
Lidget Green
Girlington
Manningham
Dean Lane Head
Scholemoor
Clayton
Great Horton
Little Horton
West Bowling
Warley Moor Resr.
Warley Moor
Dean Head Reservoirs
Ovenden Moor
Ogden
Rocking Stone
Cold Edge Dams
West Scholes
Mountain
Old Dolphin
Littlemoor Park
Wibsey
Wibsey Park
Buttershaw
Odsal
Bradshaw
Queensbury
Ambler Thorn
Brookhouse
Upper Brockholes
Holdsworth
Shibden Head
Catherine Slack
Pepper Hill
Shelf
Harold Park
Low Moor
Moor Side
Oakenshaw
Midgley Moor
Luddenden Dean
Wainstalls
Moor End
Mixenden
Illingworth
Holmfield
Mount Tabor
Booth
Jagger Park Wood
Old Hanna Wood
Stone Chair
WEST
Coley
Wyke
Wyke Common
Norwood Green
Priestley Green
Low Wood
Midgley
Mytholmroyd
Brearley
Hall Bank
Luddenden
Luddenden Foot
Highroad Well Moor
Ovenden
Pule Hill
Boothtown
Akroydon
Lee Mount
Stump Cross
Northowram
Mt Pellon
Warley Town
HALIFAX
Piece Hall
Shibden Park
Shibden Hall
Hipperholme
Lightcliffe
Lower Wyke
Bailiff Bridge
Birkhouse
Hartshead Moor Top
Blackwood Common
Hove Edge
Thornhills
Bank Top
Southowram
Siddal
Long Edge Moor
Crow Hill
Sowerby
Sowerby Bridge
Brookfoot
Brighouse
Clifton
Triangle
Cromwell Bottom
Elland Park Wood
Norland
Norland Moor
Lindwell
Greetland
Elland
Lower Edge
Rastrick
Toothill
Woodhouse
Bradley Wood
Mill Bank
Soyland Town
Ripponden
Barkisland
Holywell Green
Stainland
Broad Carr
Blackley
Bradley
Brackenhall
Deighton
Sheepridge
Netheroyd Hill
Fartown
Prince Royd
Birchencliffe
Birkby
Edgerton
Lindley
Salendine Nook
Rishworth
Sowood
Mount
Snow Lee
Oakes
Bradley Mills
HUDDERSFIELD
Dalton
Booth Wood
Longwood
Quarmby
Paddock
Moselden Height
Milnsbridge
Golcar
Town End
Pole Moor
Worts
Moldgreen
M62
A629
A644
A646
A58
A641
A643
A650
A6036
A647
A640

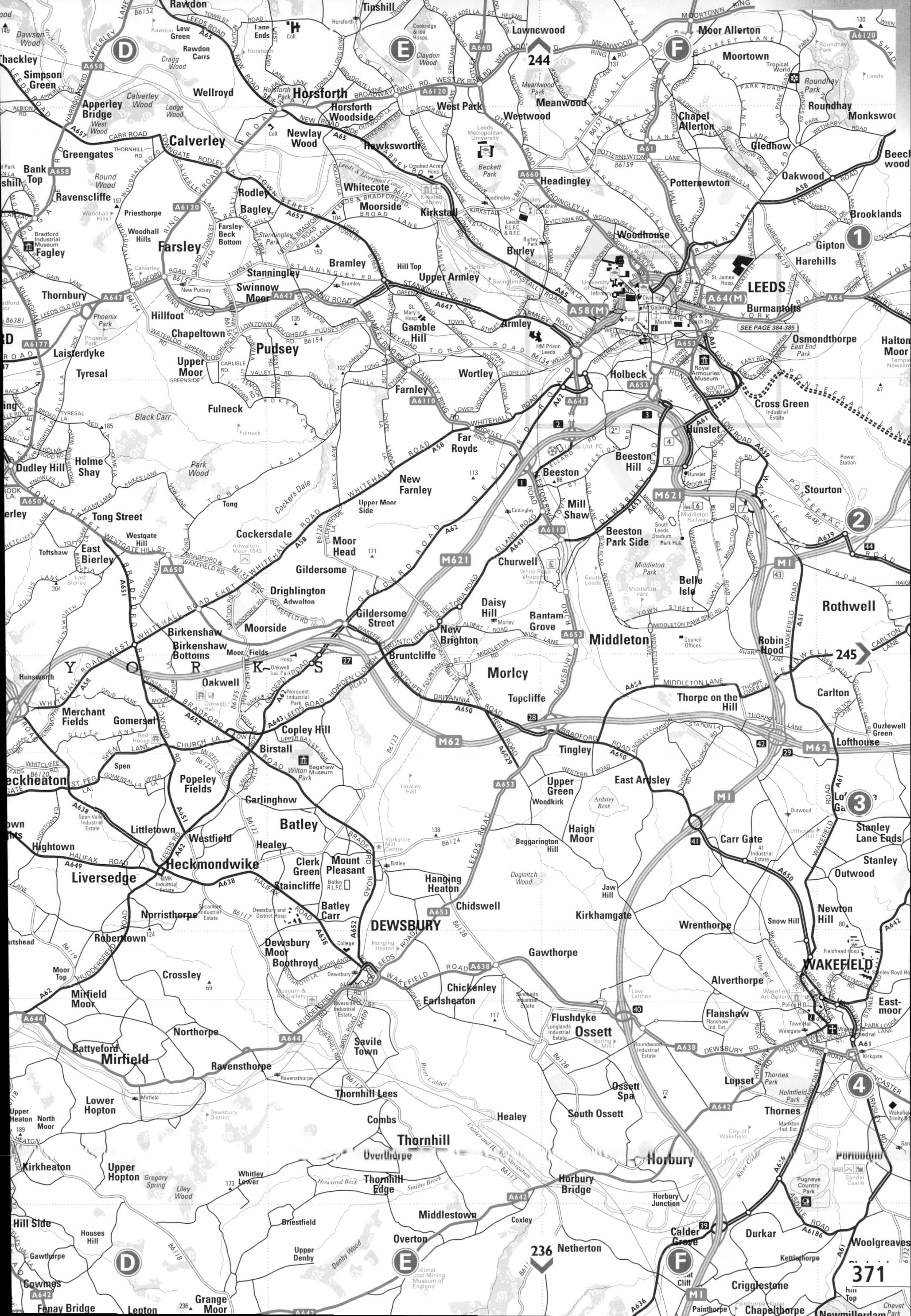
Rawdon
Tinshill
Lawnswood
Moor Allerton
Dawson Wood
Low Green
Rawdon Carrs
Lane Ends
Cookridge
Claydon Wood
244
Moortown
Thackley
Simpson Green
Cragg Wood
Horsforth
West Park
Meanwood Park
Meanwood
Roundhay Park
Tropical World
Roundhay
Calverley Wood
Wellroyd
Horsforth Woodside
Weetwood
Chapel Allerton
Monkswood
Apperley Bridge
West Wood
Lodge Wood
Newlay Wood
Hawksworth
Leeds Metropolitan University
Gledhow
Calverley
Greengates
Beckett Park
Headingley
Potternewton
Oakwood
Bank Top
Round Wood
Whitecote
Kirkstall Abbey
Rodley
Moorside
Kirkstall
Ravenscliffe
Bagley
Brooklands
Priesthorpe
Woodhall Hills
Farsley-Beck Bottom
Stanningley Park
Woodhouse
Bradford Industrial Museum
Fagley
Farsley
Burley
Gipton
Harehills
Bramley
Hill Top
Upper Armley
Stanningley
St. James Hosp.
LEEDS
Thornbury
Swinnow Moor
New Pudsey
Burmantofts
Phoenix Park
Hillfoot
Gamble Hill
Armley
HM Prison Leeds
Chapeltown
Osmondthorpe
East End Park
Halton Moor
Laisterdyke
Pudsey
Upper Moor
Wortley
Holbeck
Royal Armouries Museum
Tyresal
Farnley
Cross Green
Fulneck
Black Carr
Hunslet
Far Royds
Beeston Hill
Holme Shay
Dudley Hill
Park Wood
New Farnley
Beeston
Stourton
Tong
Cockers Dale
Upper Moor Side
Mill Shaw
Tong Street
Middleton Railway
Westgate Hill
Cockersdale
Adwalton Moor 1643
Moor Head
Beeston Park Side
South Leeds Stadium
Toftshaw
East Bierley
Gildersome
Churwell
White Rose Shopping Centre
Middleton Park
Belle Isle
Drighlington
Adwalton
Daisy Hill
Rothwell
Gildersome Street
New Brighton
Bantam Grove
Birkenshaw
Moorside
Birkenshaw Bottoms
Bruntcliffe
Middleton
Robin Hood
245
Hunsworth
Oakwell
Oakwell Hall
Morley
Norquest Industrial Park
Merchant Fields
Gomersal
Topcliffe
Thorpe on the Hill
Carlton
Copley Hill
Oulzewell Green
Lofthouse
Birstall
Bagshaw Museum
Wilton Park
Tingley
Spen
Cleckheaton
Popeley Fields
Upper Green
East Ardsley
Woodkirk
Ardsley Resr.
Carlinghow
Howley Hall
Lofthouse Gate
Haigh Moor
Batley
Spen Valley Industrial Estate
Littletown
Westfield
Healey
Yorkshire Mill Centre
Beggarington Hill
Carr Gate
Stanley Lane Ends
Hightown
Heckmondwike
Clerk Green
Mount Pleasant
Hanging Heaton
Stanley
Liversedge
Staincliffe
Dogloitch Wood
Jaw Hill
Outwood
Batley Carr
Chidswell
Norristhorpe
Newton Hill
Kirkhamgate
Snow Hill
Wrenthorpe
DEWSBURY
Robertown
Dewsbury Moor
Boothroyd
Gawthorpe
WAKEFIELD
Moor Top
Crossley
Mirfield Moor
Chickenley
Alverthorpe
Earlsheaton
East-moor
Flanshaw
Flushdyke
Ossett
Northorpe
Savile Town
Battyeford
Mirfield
Ravensthorpe
Lupset
Thornhill Lees
Ossett Spa
Thornes Park
Lower Hopton
Holmfield Park
Combs
Healey
South Ossett
Thornes
Upper Heaton
North Moor
Thornhill
Overthorpe
Horbury
Kirkheaton
Upper Hopton
Gregory Spring
Whitley Lower
Thornhill Edge
Liley Wood
Horbury Bridge
Pugneys Country Park
Sandal Castle
Horbury Junction
Hill Side
Houses Hill
Briestfield
Middlestown
Coxley
Calder Grove
Durkar
Woolgreaves
Gawthorpe
Overton
236
Netherton
Kettlethorpe
Upper Denby
National Coal Mining Museum of England
Cowmes
Crigglestone
Fenay Bridge
Lepton
Grange Moor
Painthorpe
Chapelthorpe
Newmillerdam

NEWCASTLE UPON TYNE
0 ½ 1 mile
0 1 2 kilometres
Tyne and Wear Metro
Course of Hadrian's Wall
hours
Amsterdam 15
Bergen 22-26
Göteborg 25
Haugesund 21½
Kristiansand 17
Stavanger 19
Whitley Bay
Cullercoats
Tynemouth
North Shields
South Shields
Westoe
Marsden
Harton
Cleadon Park
Cleadon
Whitburn
Seaburn
Fulwell
Roker
Monkwearmouth
SUNDERLAND
Millfield
Pallion
Southwick
Witherwack
Carley Hill
Hylton Red House
Hylton Castle
Castletown
South Hylton
Town End Farm
Downhill
East Boldon
West Boldon
Boldon
Boldon Colliery
Whiteleas
Simonside
Jarrow
Hebburn
Monkton
Hedworth
Fellgate
Primrose
Wardley
Felling
Heworth
Pelaw
Bill Quay
Windy Nook
High Felling
Wrekenton
Eighton Banks
Springwell
Washington
Usworth
Sulgrave
Stephenson
Donwell
Blackfell
Birtley
Gateshead
Low Fell
Deckham
Carr Hill
Harlow Green
Chowdene
Kibblesworth
Team Valley
Lobley Hill
Dunston
Dunston Hill
Swalwell
Whickham
Sunniside
Blaydon
Scotswood
Benwell
Elswick
Arthur's Hill
Spital Tongues
Fenham
Cowgate
Blakelaw
Kenton
Newbiggin Hall Estate
Fawdon
Gosforth
South Gosforth
Jesmond
Heaton
High Heaton
Sandyford
Byker
Walker
Wallsend
Howdon
Willington Quay
Rosehill
Battle Hill
Holy Cross
Longbenton
Forest Hall
Benton
Killingworth
Camperdown
Palmersville
Holystone
Backworth
Shiremoor
Earsdon
Monkseaton
New York
Preston
Preston Grange
Marden
Chirton
West Chirton
Percy Main
Royal Quays
East Brunton
Brunswick Village
Hazlerigg
Wide Open
Burradon
West Moor
Nuns Moor
Town Moor
West Denton
East Denton
Woolsington
Newcastle International Airport
River Tyne
River Wear
TYNE & WEAR
SEE PAGE 404
SEE PAGE 411
271
262

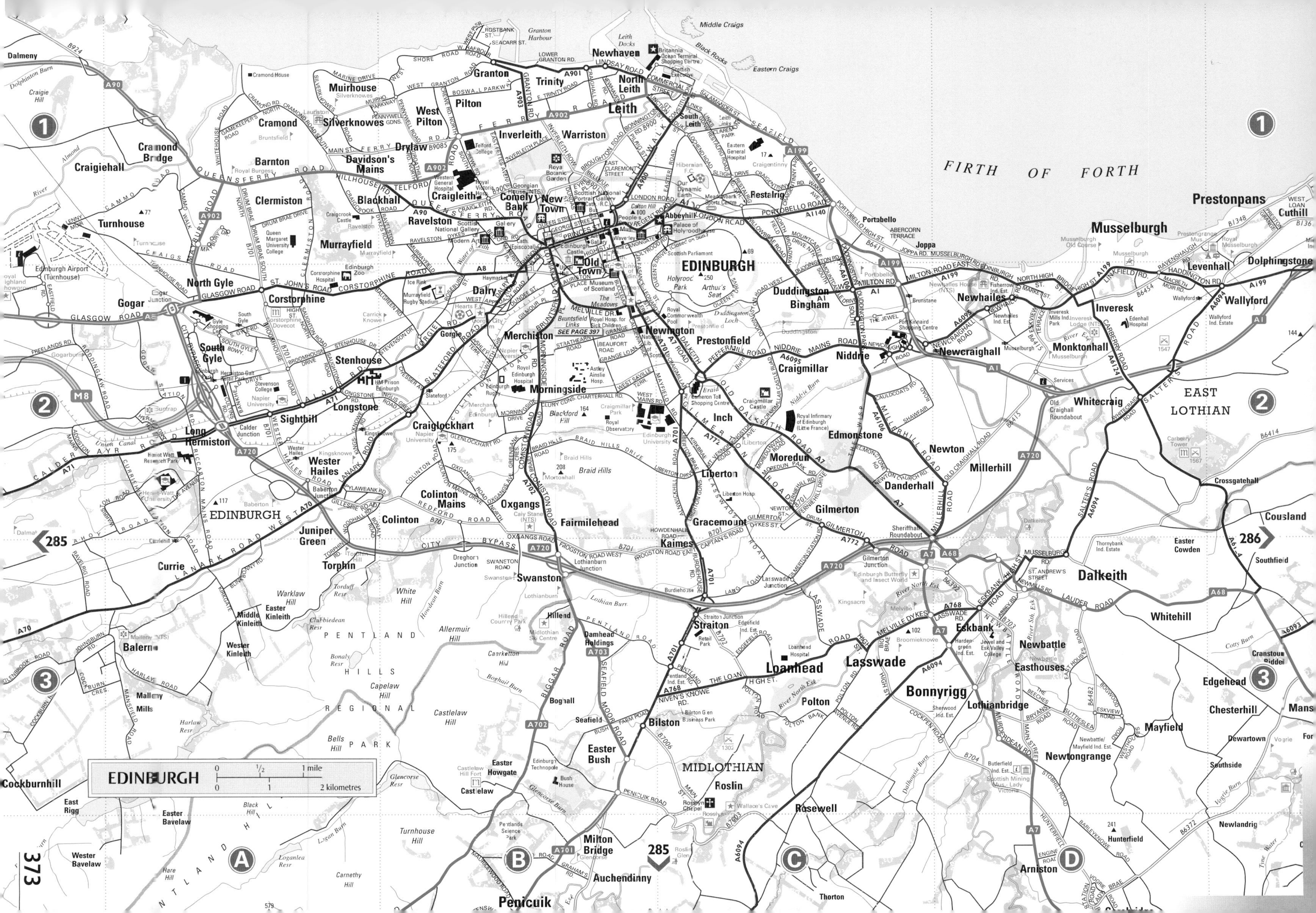
EDINBURGH
FIRTH OF FORTH
EAST LOTHIAN
MIDLOTHIAN
PENTLAND HILLS REGIONAL PARK
Dalmeny
Craigiehall
Cramond Bridge
Turnhouse
Edinburgh Airport (Turnhouse)
Gogar
Cramond
Barnton
Clermiston
Muirhouse
Silverknowes
Granton
Pilton
West Pilton
Davidson's Mains
Drylaw
Trinity
Newhaven
North Leith
Leith
Inverleith
Warriston
Craigleith
Blackhall
Ravelston
Murrayfield
Corstorphine
North Gyle
South Gyle
Comely Bank
New Town
Old Town
Abbeyhill
Restalrig
Portobello
Joppa
Musselburgh
Prestonpans
Levenhall
Dolphingstone
Wallyford
Inveresk
Newhailes
Monktonhall
Newcraighall
Whitecraig
Duddingston
Bingham
Niddrie
Craigmillar
Prestonfield
Newington
Dalry
Gorgie
Stenhouse
Merchiston
Morningside
Sighthill
Longstone
Craiglockhart
Long Hermiston
Wester Hailes
Colinton
Colinton Mains
Oxgangs
Fairmilehead
Inch
Liberton
Moredun
Edmonstone
Newton
Millerhill
Danderhall
Gilmerton
Gracemount
Kaimes
Juniper Green
Currie
Torphin
Swanston
Balerno
Middle Kinleith
Easter Kinleith
Wester Kinleith
Hillend
Damhead Holdings
Straiton
Loanhead
Lasswade
Bilston
Seafield
Easter Bush
Roslin
Rosewell
Bonnyrigg
Lothianbridge
Eskbank
Newbattle
Easthouses
Dalkeith
Whitehill
Newtongrange
Mayfield
Edgehead
Chesterhill
Arniston
Milton Bridge
Auchendinny
Penicuik
Cockburnhill
Easter Bavelaw
Wester Bavelaw
Castlelaw
Easter Howgate
Crossgatehall
Cousland
Southfield
Cranstoun Riddel
Dewartown
Southside
Newlandrig
Hunterfield
Thorton
285
286
SEE PAGE 397
EDINBURGH 0 ½ 1 mile 0 1 2 kilometres

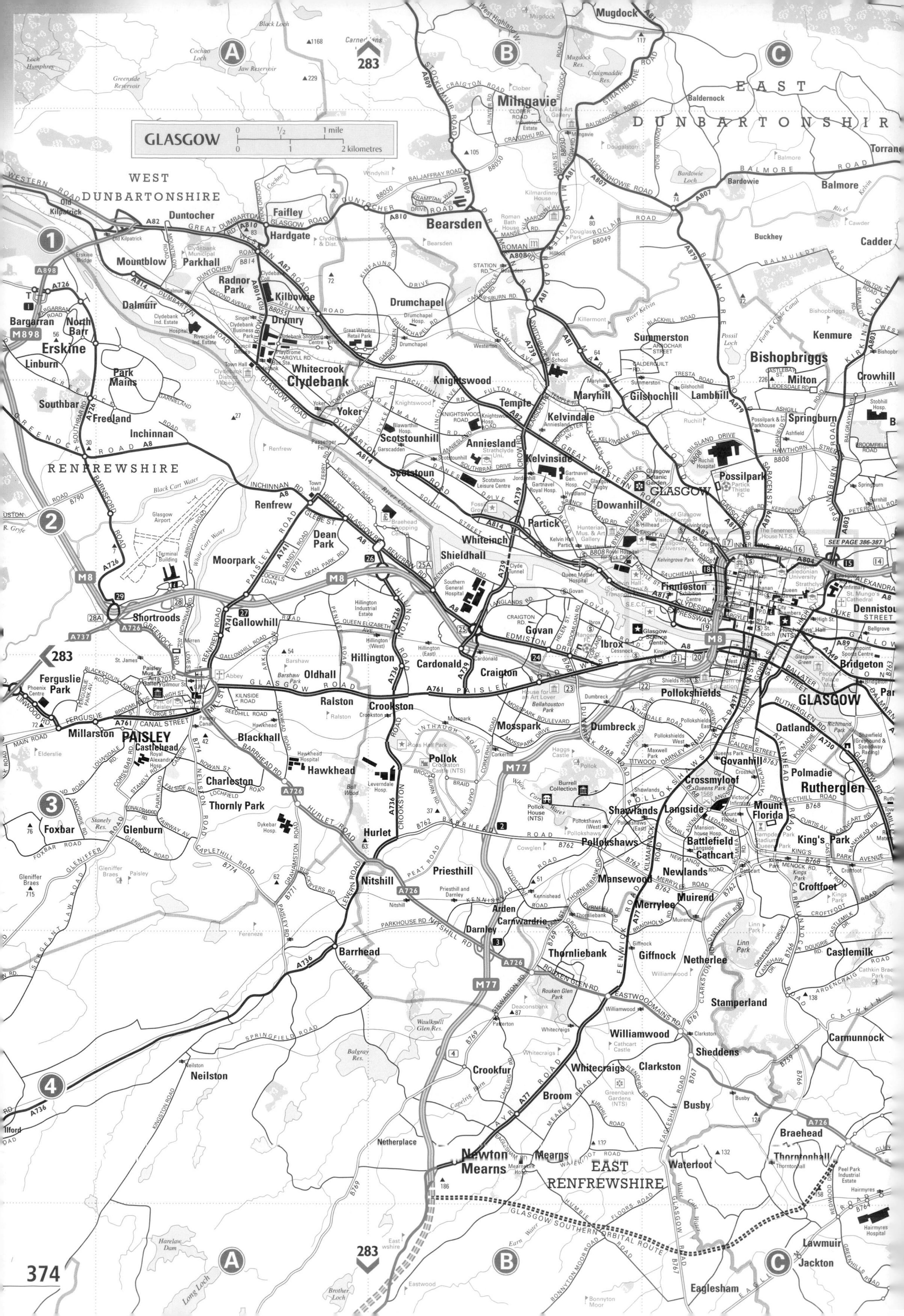
GLASGOW
1 mile
2 kilometres
A
B
C
1
2
3
4
283
Mugdock
Milngavie
Bearsden
EAST DUNBARTONSHIRE
WEST DUNBARTONSHIRE
RENFREWSHIRE
EAST RENFREWSHIRE
Old Kilpatrick
Duntocher
Faifley
Hardgate
Mountblow
Parkhall
Radnor Park
Kilbowie
Dalmuir
Drumry
Drumchapel
Whitecrook
Clydebank
Bargarran
North Barr
Erskine
Linburn
Park Mains
Southbar
Freeland
Inchinnan
Yoker
Knightswood
Scotstounhill
Scotstoun
Anniesland
Temple
Kelvindale
Kelvinside
Maryhill
Gilshochill
Summerston
Lambhill
Possilpark
Bishopbriggs
Kenmure
Milton
Crowhill
Springburn
Baldernock
Bardowie
Balmore
Torrance
Buckhey
Cadder
Renfrew
Dean Park
Moorpark
Shortroods
Gallowhill
Whiteinch
Partick
Shieldhall
Dowanhill
Finnieston
GLASGOW
Govan
Ibrox
Cardonald
Craigton
Hillington
Oldhall
Ralston
Crookston
Ferguslie Park
Millarston
PAISLEY
Castlehead
Blackhall
Charleston
Thornly Park
Hawkhead
Foxbar
Glenburn
Pollok
Mosspark
Dumbreck
Pollokshields
Govanhill
Crossmyloof
Shawlands
Langside
Mount Florida
Battlefield
Cathcart
Pollokshaws
Hurlet
Priesthill
Nitshill
Mansewood
Newlands
Croftfoot
Muirend
Merrylee
Arden
Carnwadric
Darnley
Thornliebank
Giffnock
Netherlee
Barrhead
Castlemilk
Stamperland
Carmunnock
Williamwood
Sheddens
Clarkston
Whitecraigs
Crookfur
Broom
Busby
Neilston
Newton Mearns
Mearns
Waterfoot
Thorntonhall
Braehead
Lawmuir
Jackton
Eaglesham
Dennistoun
Bridgeton
Oatlands
Polmadie
Rutherglen
King's Park
M8
M77
M898
A726
A736
A77
GLASGOW SOUTHERN ORBITAL ROUTE
SEE PAGE 386-387

Milton of Campsie
Croy
Twechar
Carrickstone
Craigmarloch
Eastfield
Seafar
Kildrum
Cumbernauld
Balloch
Carbrain
Kirkintilloch
Harestanes
Broadwood
Westfield
Greenfaulds
Condorrat
Lenziemill
Gallowhill
Oxgang
Waterside
Blairlinn
Lenzie
Mollinsburn
Greengairs
Auchinloch
Moodiesburn
Bridgend
Riggend
Wattston
Woodhill
Chryston
NORTH LANARKSHIRE
Marnock
Muirhead
Stepps
Glenboig
Craigendmuir
Gartcosh
Glenmavis
Millerston
Provanmill
Gartgill
Townhead
Holehills
Rawyards
Thrashbush
Riddrie
Ruchazie
Garthamlock
Lochwood
Gartsherrie
Easterhouse
Airdrie
Craigneuk
Carntyne
Springboig
Coatbridge
Coatdyke
Gartlea
Barlanark
Swinton
Whifflet
Greenend
Gartness
Barrachnie
Baillieston
Garrowhill
Crosshill
Shettleston
Kirkwood
Rosehall
Woodlands
Old Monkland
Kirkshaws
Shawhead
Carnbroe
Muirhead
Calderbank
Mount Vernon
Braidfauld
Chapelhall
Broomhouse
Carmyle
Birkenshaw
Thorniewood
Newhouse West
Tannochside
Viewpark
Eastfield
Kylepark
Newton
Fallside
Mossend
Holytown
Uddingston
Hallside
New Stevenston
Bellshill
Yett
Cambuslang
Flemington
Kirkfield
Forgewood
Carfin
Low Blantyre
Bothwell
North Motherwell
SOUTH LANARKSHIRE
Cleekhimin
Motherwell
Blantyre
Springwells
Craigneuk
Nerston
Whitehill
Rogerton
Burnbank
High Blantyre
Hamilton
Sheildmuir
Stewartfield
Calderwood
Hillhouse
Muirhouse
Mains
EAST KILBRIDE
West Mains
Auchentibber
Earnock
Laighstonehall
Low Waters
Ferniegair
Allanton
Gowkthrapple
Westwood
St. Leonards
The Murray
Woodhead
Fairhill
Silvertonhill
Cadzow
Birniehill
Meikle Earnock
Greenhills
284

CENTRAL LONDON
0
1/4 mile
0
0.25
0.5 kilometres
A
B
C
D
E
F
G
H
J
1
2
3
4
5
6
7
8
9
10
11
12
13
356
357
MAYFAIR
SOHO
WESTMINSTER
BELGRAVIA
GREEN PARK
ST. JAMES'S PARK
BUCKINGHAM PALACE GARDENS
BUCKINGHAM PALACE
THE BRITISH MUSEUM
NATIONAL GALLERY
ROYAL ACAD. OF ARTS
MADAME TUSSAUD'S
PLANETARIUM
REGENT'S PARK
MARBLE ARCH
OXFORD CIRCUS
PICCADILLY CIRCUS
HYDE PARK CORNER
TRAFALGAR SQ
VICTORIA
WESTMINSTER ABBEY
OXFORD ST
PICCADILLY
REGENT ST
PARK LANE
WIGMORE ST
TOTTENHAM COURT RD
GOWER ST
SHAFTESBURY AV
CHARING CROSS RD
HAYMARKET
PALL MALL
THE MALL
WHITEHALL
KNIGHTSBRIDGE
GROSVENOR PL
VICTORIA ST
BUCKINGHAM GATE
CONSTITUTION HILL
BIRDCAGE WALK
BAKER ST
PORTLAND PL
EUSTON RD
MARYLEBONE RD

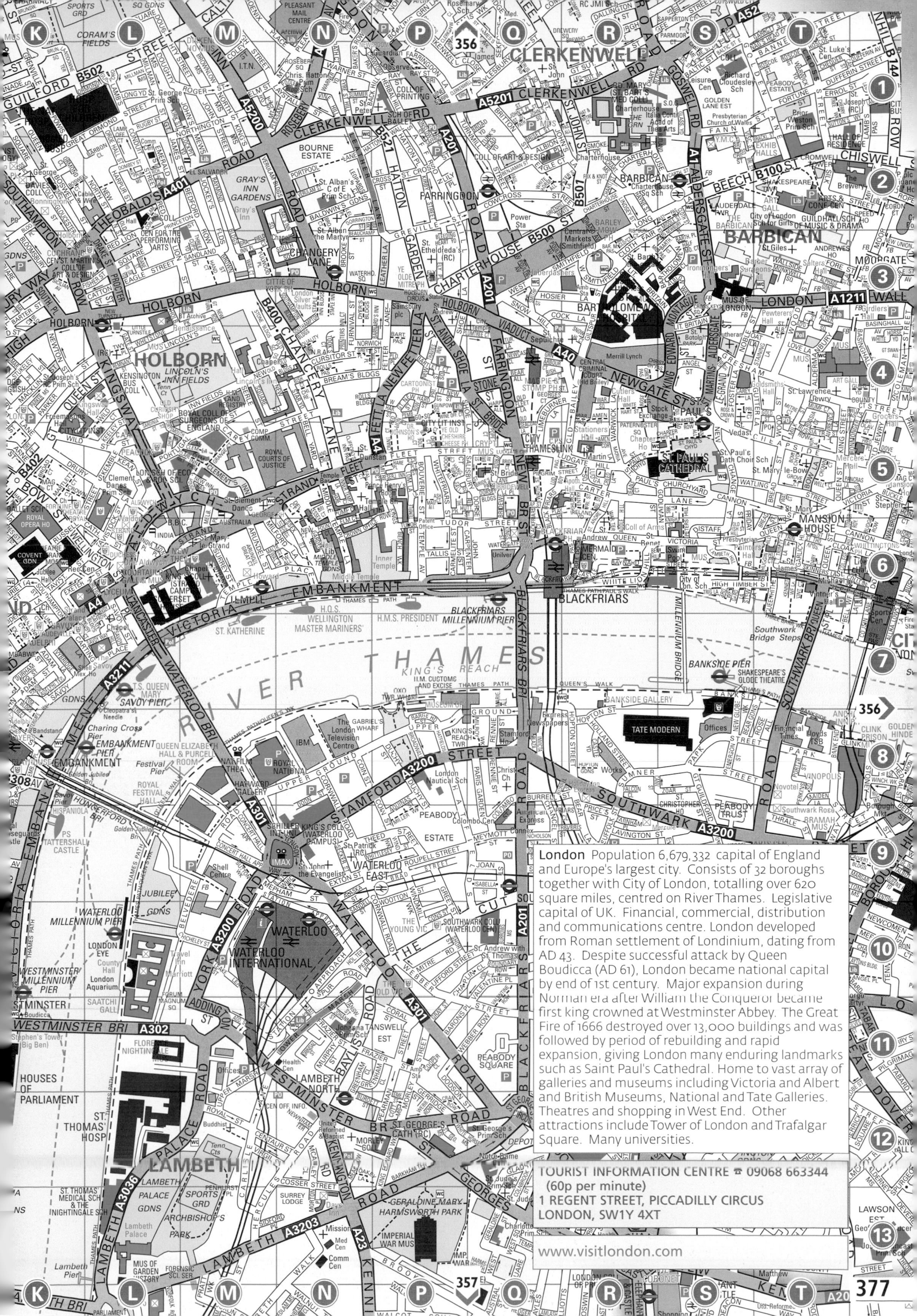
CLERKENWELL
BARBICAN
HOLBORN
LAMBETH
RIVER THAMES
KING'S REACH
WATERLOO
WATERLOO INTERNATIONAL
BLACKFRIARS
TATE MODERN
ST. PAUL'S CATHEDRAL
HOUSES OF PARLIAMENT
MANSION HOUSE
CHANCERY LANE
FARRINGDON
TEMPLE
EMBANKMENT
LAMBETH NORTH
VICTORIA EMBANKMENT
ALBERT EMBANKMENT
WESTMINSTER BRI
WATERLOO BRI
BLACKFRIARS BRI
SOUTHWARK BRI
MILLENNIUM BRIDGE
SOUTHWARK STREET
STAMFORD STREET
WESTMINSTER BRIDGE ROAD
HOLBORN
CLERKENWELL RD
THEOBALD'S ROAD
KINGSWAY
ALDWYCH
STRAND
FLEET STREET
NEWGATE ST
LONDON WALL
CHEAPSIDE
FARRINGDON ROAD
CHANCERY LANE
GRAY'S INN GARDENS
LINCOLN'S INN FIELDS
GERALDINE MARY HARMSWORTH PARK
IMPERIAL WAR MUS
LONDON EYE
ST. THOMAS' HOSP
LAMBETH PALACE
356
357
K
L
M
N
P
Q
R
S
T
1
2
3
4
5
6
7
8
9
10
11
12
13

London Population 6,679,332 capital of England and Europe's largest city. Consists of 32 boroughs together with City of London, totalling over 620 square miles, centred on River Thames. Legislative capital of UK. Financial, commercial, distribution and communications centre. London developed from Roman settlement of Londinium, dating from AD 43. Despite successful attack by Queen Boudicca (AD 61), London became national capital by end of 1st century. Major expansion during Norman era after William the Conqueror became first king crowned at Westminster Abbey. The Great Fire of 1666 destroyed over 13,000 buildings and was followed by period of rebuilding and rapid expansion, giving London many enduring landmarks such as Saint Paul's Cathedral. Home to vast array of galleries and museums including Victoria and Albert and British Museums, National and Tate Galleries. Theatres and shopping in West End. Other attractions include Tower of London and Trafalgar Square. Many universities.

TOURIST INFORMATION CENTRE ☎ 09068 663344
(60p per minute)
1 REGENT STREET, PICCADILLY CIRCUS
LONDON, SW1Y 4XT

www.visitlondon.com

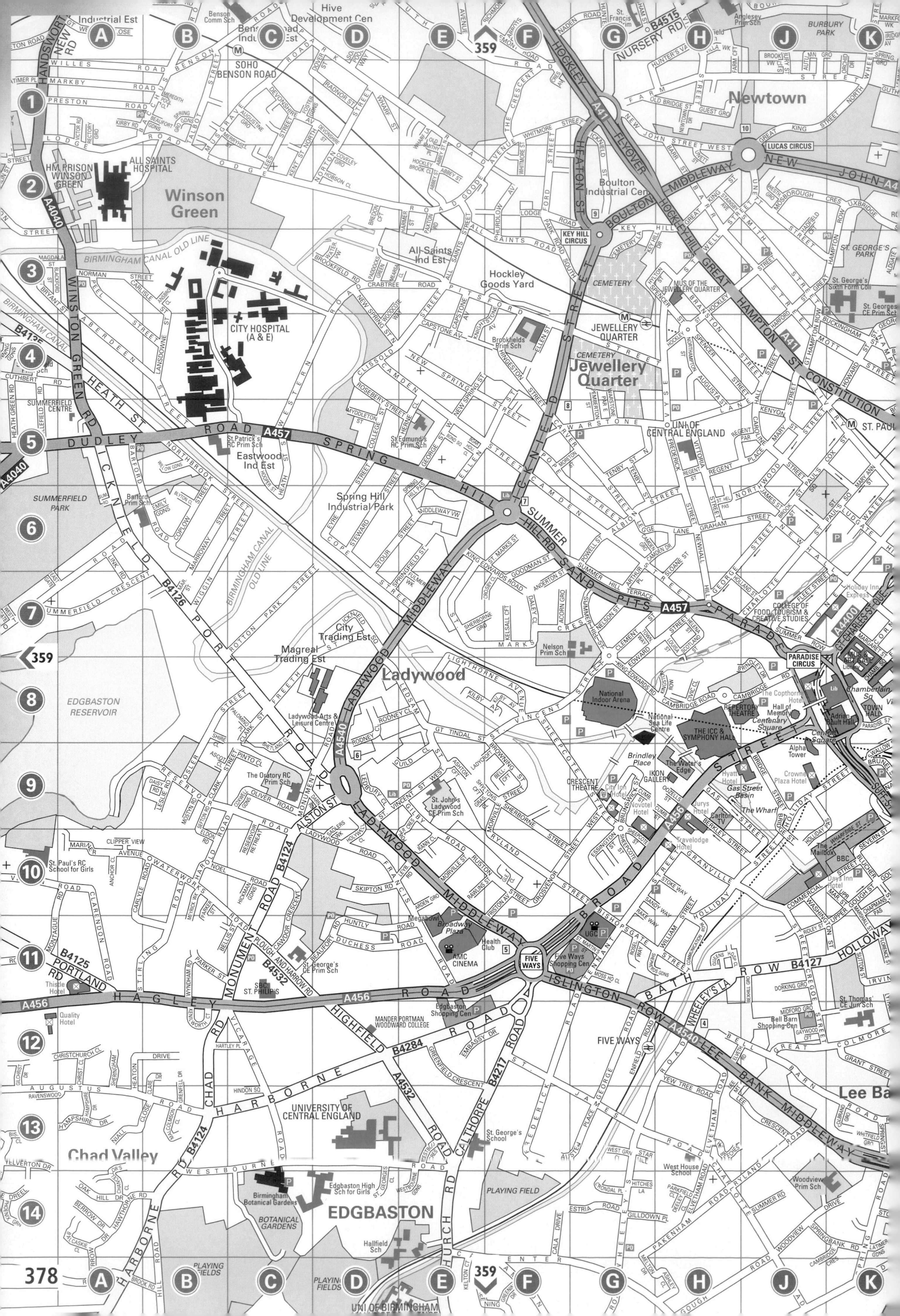

359
Winson Green
HM PRISON WINSON GREEN
ALL SAINTS HOSPITAL
CITY HOSPITAL (A & E)
SOHO BENSON ROAD
Hive Development Cen
Newtown
LUCAS CIRCUS
Boulton Industrial Cen
KEY HILL CIRCUS
All Saints Ind Est
Hockley Goods Yard
CEMETERY
MUS OF THE JEWELLERY QUARTER
JEWELLERY QUARTER
Jewellery Quarter
UNI OF CENTRAL ENGLAND
ST. PAULS
ST. GEORGE'S PARK
BURBURY PARK
Eastwood Ind Est
SUMMERFIELD PARK
SUMMERFIELD CENTRE
Spring Hill Industrial Park
City Trading Est
Magreal Trading Est
Ladywood
Ladywood Arts & Leisure Centre
EDGBASTON RESERVOIR
National Indoor Arena
National Sea Life Centre
THE ICC & SYMPHONY HALL
REPERTORY THEATRE
Centenary Square
PARADISE CIRCUS
COLLEGE OF FOOD, TOURISM & CREATIVE STUDIES
TOWN HALL
Brindley Place
IKON GALLERY
CRESCENT THEATRE
Gas Street Basin
The Wharf
The Mailbox
BBC
Broadway Plaza
AMC CINEMA
FIVE WAYS
Five Ways Shopping Cen
Edgbaston Shopping Cen
MANDER PORTMAN WOODWARD COLLEGE
UNIVERSITY OF CENTRAL ENGLAND
Chad Valley
EDGBASTON
Birmingham Botanical Gardens
BOTANICAL GARDENS
Edgbaston High Sch for Girls
PLAYING FIELD
Lee Bank
UNI OF BIRMINGHAM
HAGLEY ROAD
A456
A457
A4540
A41
A4040

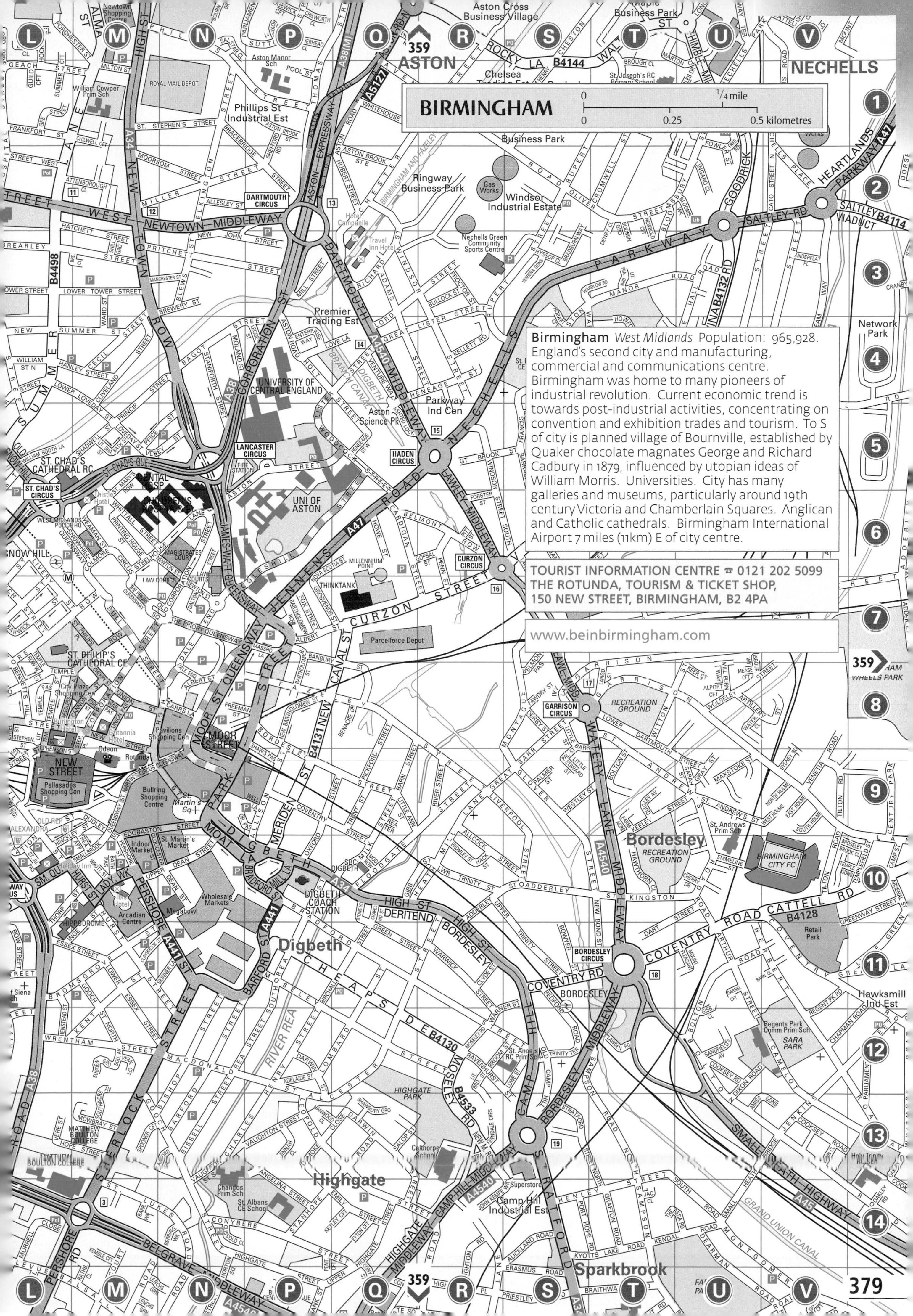
BIRMINGHAM
0 1/4 mile
0 0.25 0.5 kilometres
Birmingham West Midlands Population: 965,928. England's second city and manufacturing, commercial and communications centre. Birmingham was home to many pioneers of industrial revolution. Current economic trend is towards post-industrial activities, concentrating on convention and exhibition trades and tourism. To S of city is planned village of Bournville, established by Quaker chocolate magnates George and Richard Cadbury in 1879, influenced by utopian ideas of William Morris. Universities. City has many galleries and museums, particularly around 19th century Victoria and Chamberlain Squares. Anglican and Catholic cathedrals. Birmingham International Airport 7 miles (11km) E of city centre.
TOURIST INFORMATION CENTRE ☎ 0121 202 5099
THE ROTUNDA, TOURISM & TICKET SHOP,
150 NEW STREET, BIRMINGHAM, B2 4PA
www.beinbirmingham.com
ASTON
NECHELLS
Bordesley
Digbeth
Highgate
Sparkbrook
Aston Cross Business Village
Phillips St Industrial Est
Ringway Business Park
Windsor Industrial Estate
Premier Trading Est
UNIVERSITY OF CENTRAL ENGLAND
UNI OF ASTON
Aston Science Pk
Parkway Ind Cen
LANCASTER CIRCUS
DARTMOUTH CIRCUS
ST. CHAD'S CIRCUS
CURZON CIRCUS
GARRISON CIRCUS
BORDESLEY CIRCUS
ST. CHAD'S CATHEDRAL RC
ST. PHILIP'S CATHEDRAL CE
NEW STREET
Bullring Shopping Centre
Pallasades Shopping Cen
Pavilions Shopping Cen
MOOR STREET
DIGBETH COACH STATION
Wholesale Markets
Parcelforce Depot
MILLENNIUM POINT
THINKTANK
BIRMINGHAM CITY FC
RECREATION GROUND
Network Park
Hawksmill Ind Est
SARA PARK
Camp Hill Industrial Est
Matthew Boulton College
GRAND UNION CANAL
RIVER REA

359 ASTON
359 HAM WHEELS PARK
359

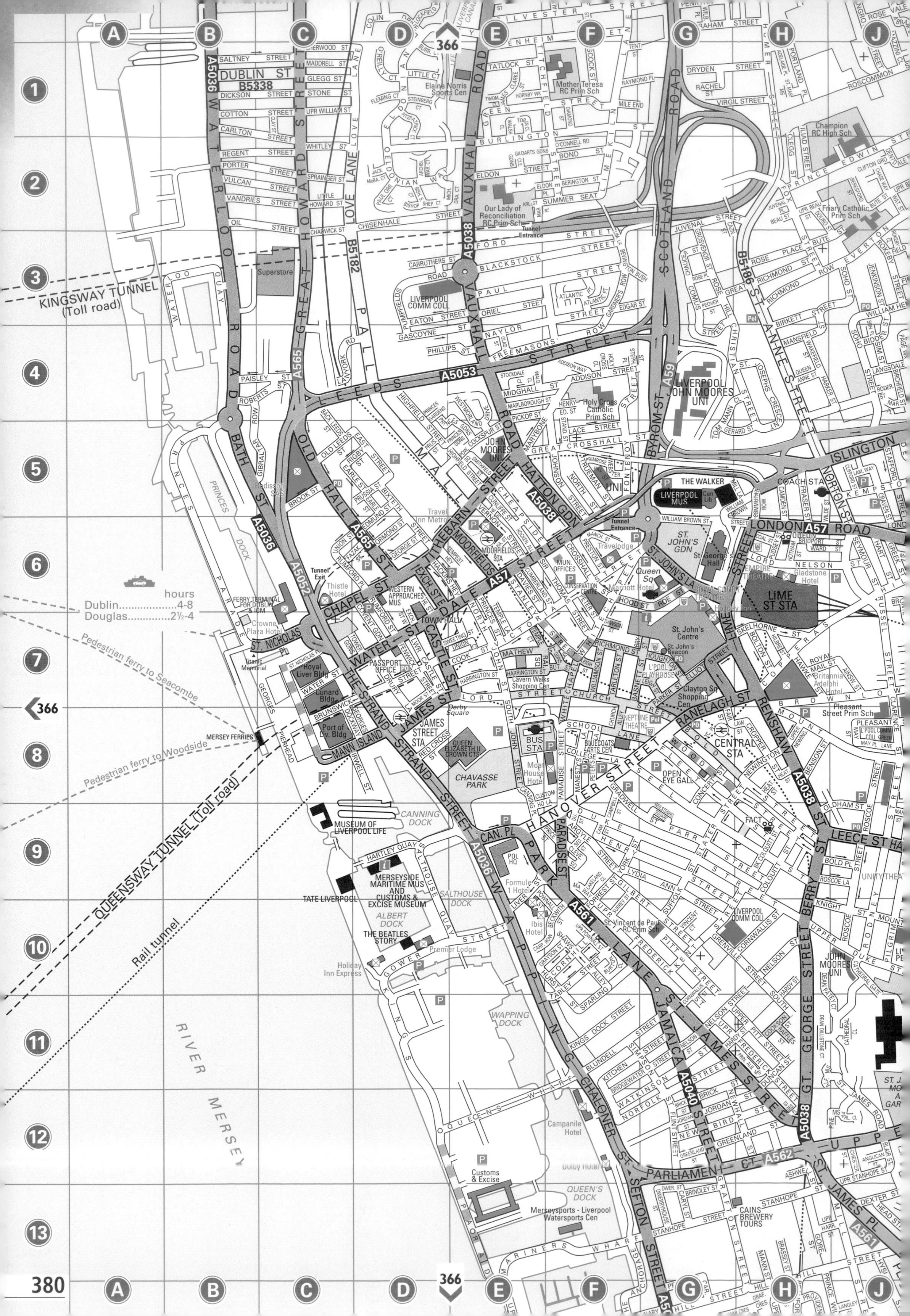

A
B
C
D
E
F
G
H
J
1
2
3
4
5
6
7
8
9
10
11
12
13
366
KINGSWAY TUNNEL
(Toll road)
QUEENSWAY TUNNEL (Toll road)
Rail tunnel
RIVER MERSEY
Pedestrian ferry to Seacombe
Pedestrian ferry to Woodside
hours
Dublin..................4-8
Douglas.............2½-4
FERRY TERMINAL FOR DUBLIN & IOM
MERSEY FERRIES
Superstore
WATERLOO QUAY
PRINCES DOCK
PRINCES PARADE
Crowne Plaza Hotel
Titanic Memorial
Royal Liver Bldg
Cunard Bldg
Port of Liv. Bldg
MANN ISLAND
MUSEUM OF LIVERPOOL LIFE
CANNING DOCK
HARTLEY QUAY
MERSEYSIDE MARITIME MUS AND CUSTOMS & EXCISE MUSEUM
TATE LIVERPOOL
ALBERT DOCK
THE BEATLES STORY
SALTHOUSE DOCK
Premier Lodge
Holiday Inn Express
WAPPING DOCK
QUEENS WHARF
Campanile Hotel
Customs & Excise
QUEEN'S DOCK
Merseysports - Liverpool Watersports Cen
MARINERS WHARF
Dolby Hotel
CAINS BREWERY TOURS
SALTNEY STREET
DUBLIN ST
B5338
DICKSON STREET
COTTON STREET
CARLTON STREET
REGENT STREET
PORTER STREET
VULCAN STREET
VANDRIES STREET
OIL STREET
CHISENHALE STREET
WATERLOO ROAD
A5036
GREAT HOWARD STREET
A565
LOVE LANE
B5182
PALL MALL
LEEDS STREET
A5053
PAISLEY ST
ROBERTS ST
BATH ST
A5052
ST. NICHOLAS PL
CHAPEL ST
WATER ST
JAMES ST
JAMES STREET STA
THE STRAND
STRAND STREET
Radisson SAS
BROOK ST
OLD HALL ST
Thistle Hotel
Tunnel Exit
WESTERN APPROACHES MUS
TOWN HALL
PASSPORT OFFICE
DALE ST
A57
MOORFIELDS
MOORFIELDS STA
TITHEBARN ST
Travel Inn Metro
VAUXHALL ROAD
A5038
Elaine Norris Sports Cen
Our Lady of Reconciliation RC Prim Sch
Tunnel Entrance
LIVERPOOL COMM COLL
BLACKSTOCK STREET
FREEMASONS ROW
JOHN MOORES UNI
HATTON GDN
Holy Cross Catholic Prim Sch
MUN. OFFICES
Travelodge
Queen Sq
Marriott Hotel
ST. JOHN'S GDN
St George's Hall
THE WALKER
LIVERPOOL MUS
Cen Lib
WILLIAM BROWN ST
St. John's Centre
St. John's Beacon
L'POOL PLAYHOUSE
Clayton Sq Shopping Cen
ROYAL COURT THEATRE
Holiday Inn
LIME ST STA
EMPIRE THEATRE
Gladstone Hotel
LONDON ROAD
ROYAL MAIL ST
Britannia Adelphi Hotel
Pleasant Street Prim Sch
LORD ST
Derby Square
QUEEN ELIZABETH II CROWN CTS
CHAVASSE PARK
BUS STA
Moat House Hotel
Cavern Walks Shopping Cen
BLUECOATS ARTS CEN
NEPTUNE THEATRE
CENTRAL STA
RANELAGH ST
HANOVER STREET
OPEN EYE GALL
FACT
RENSHAW ST
BERRY ST
LEECE ST
UNITY THEATRE
POL HQ
Formule 1 Hotel
Ibis Hotel
St. Vincent de Paul RC Prim Sch
WAPPING
PARK LANE
A561
PARADISE ST
LIVERPOOL COMM COLL
JAMAICA STREET
A5040
ST. JAMES STREET
GT. GEORGE STREET
JOHN MOORES UNI
CHALONER ST
SEFTON STREET
PARLIAMENT ST
A562
UPPER PARLIAMENT ST
LIVERPOOL JOHN MOORES UNI
BYROM ST
A59
SCOTLAND ROAD
ISLINGTON
ST ANNE STREET
B5186
Mother Teresa RC Prim Sch
Champion RC High Sch
Friary Catholic Prim Sch
PRINCE EDWIN ST
ROSCOMMON
COACH STA
KIRKDALE
MOUNT PLEASANT
HOPE ST

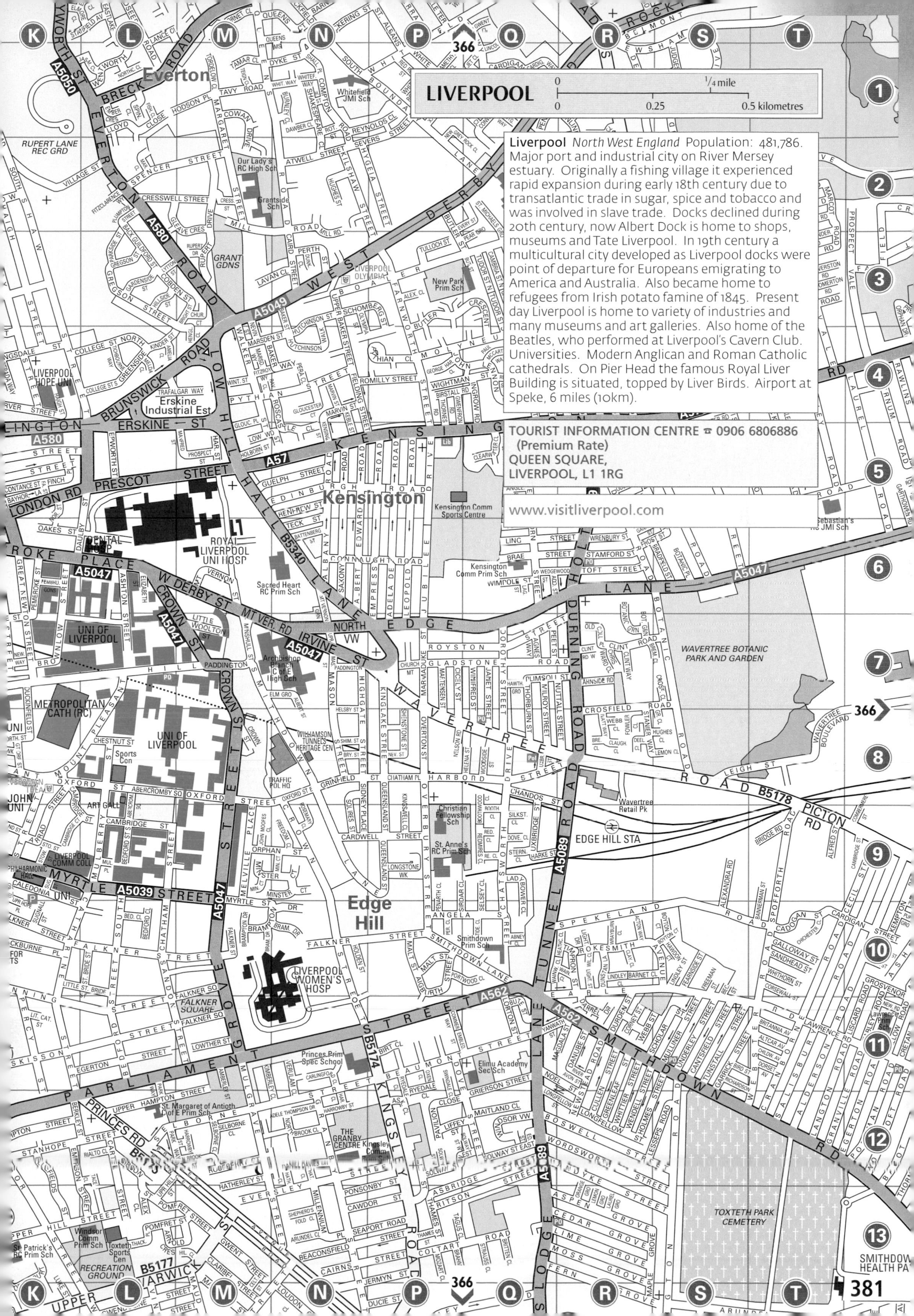
LIVERPOOL
0 1/4 mile
0 0.25 0.5 kilometres
Liverpool North West England Population: 481,786. Major port and industrial city on River Mersey estuary. Originally a fishing village it experienced rapid expansion during early 18th century due to transatlantic trade in sugar, spice and tobacco and was involved in slave trade. Docks declined during 20th century, now Albert Dock is home to shops, museums and Tate Liverpool. In 19th century a multicultural city developed as Liverpool docks were point of departure for Europeans emigrating to America and Australia. Also became home to refugees from Irish potato famine of 1845. Present day Liverpool is home to variety of industries and many museums and art galleries. Also home of the Beatles, who performed at Liverpool's Cavern Club. Universities. Modern Anglican and Roman Catholic cathedrals. On Pier Head the famous Royal Liver Building is situated, topped by Liver Birds. Airport at Speke, 6 miles (10km).
TOURIST INFORMATION CENTRE ☎ 0906 6806886
(Premium Rate)
QUEEN SQUARE,
LIVERPOOL, L1 1RG
www.visitliverpool.com
Everton
Kensington
Edge Hill
WAVERTREE BOTANIC PARK AND GARDEN
TOXTETH PARK CEMETERY
ROYAL LIVERPOOL UNI HOSP
UNI OF LIVERPOOL
METROPOLITAN CATH (RC)
LIVERPOOL WOMEN'S HOSP
EDGE HILL STA
366
366
366

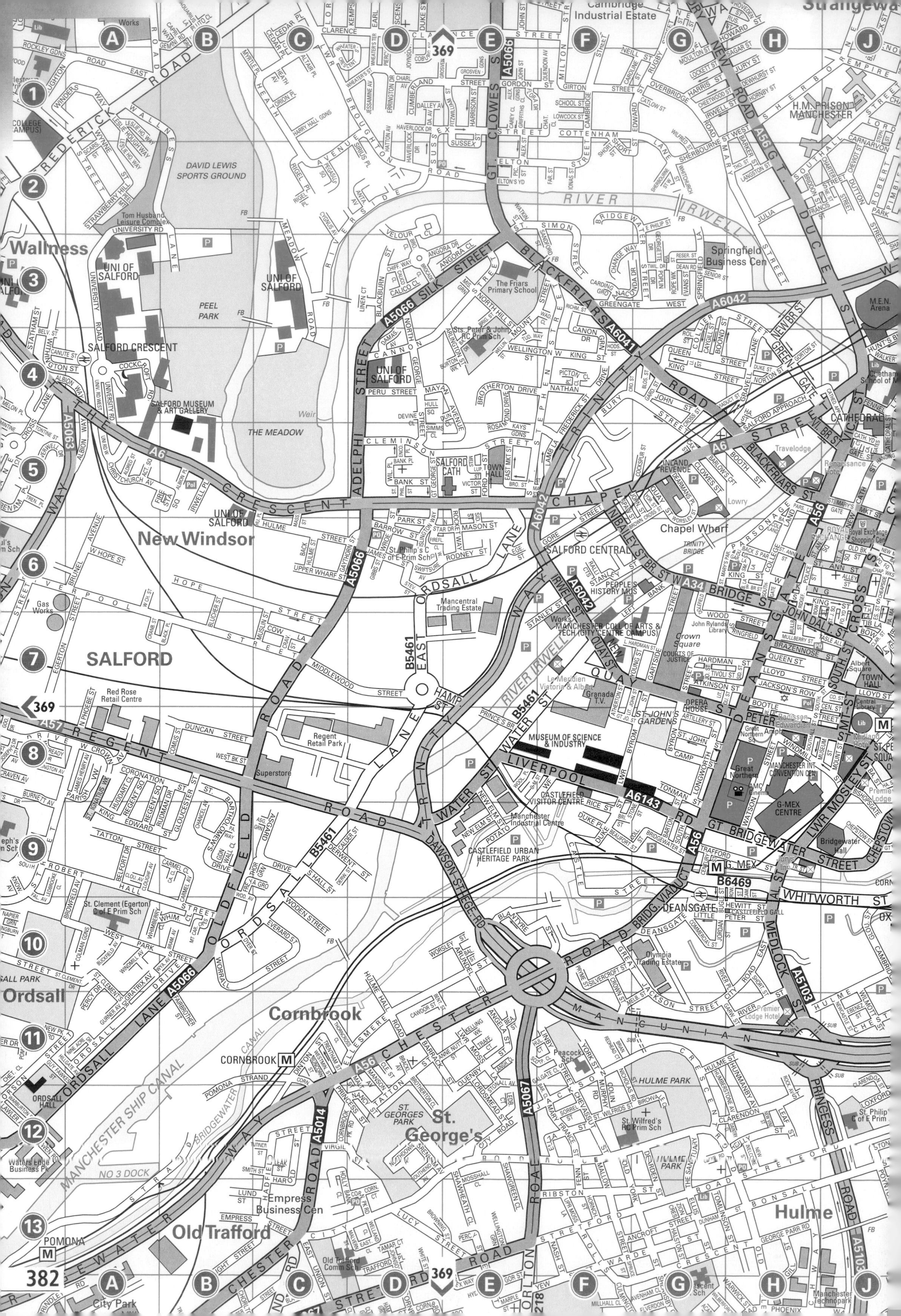

369
Cambridge Industrial Estate
Wallness
UNI OF SALFORD
DAVID LEWIS SPORTS GROUND
Tom Husband Leisure Complex
PEEL PARK
SALFORD CRESCENT
SALFORD MUSEUM & ART GALLERY
THE MEADOW
Weir
RIVER IRWELL
H.M. PRISON MANCHESTER
Springfield Business Cen
The Friars Primary School
Sts. Peter & John RC Prim Sch
M.E.N. Arena
Chetham's School of Music
CATHEDRAL
SALFORD CATH
TOWN HALL
INLAND REVENUE
Lowry
Chapel Wharf
Travelodge
Renaissance Hotel
Royal Exchange Shopping Cen
New Windsor
SALFORD CENTRAL
St. Philip's C of E Prim Sch
PEOPLE'S HISTORY MUS
MANCHESTER COLL OF ARTS & TECH (CITY CENTRE CAMPUS)
Mancentral Trading Estate
Gas Works
SALFORD
John Rylands Library
Crown Square
COURTS OF JUSTICE
Albert Square
TOWN HALL
Central Library
Le Meridien Victoria & Albert
Granada T.V.
OPERA HOUSE
ST. JOHN'S GARDENS
Radisson Edwardian
Red Rose Retail Centre
Regent Retail Park
MUSEUM OF SCIENCE & INDUSTRY
Superstore
Great Northern
MANCHESTER INT CONVENTION CEN
G-MEX CENTRE
Midland Hotel
Premier Lodge
CASTLEFIELD VISITOR CENTRE
Manchester Industrial Centre
CASTLEFIELD URBAN HERITAGE PARK
Bridgewater Hall
G-MEX
DEANSGATE
St. Clement (Egerton) C of E Prim Sch
Olympia Trading Estate
Ordsall
Cornbrook
CORNBROOK
Premier Lodge Hotel
MANCUNIAN WAY
Peacock Sch
HULME PARK
St. Wilfred's RC Prim Sch
St. Philip C of E Prim
ORDSALL HALL
MANCHESTER SHIP CANAL
BRIDGEWATER CANAL
NO 3 DOCK
Waters Edge Business Pk
ST. GEORGES PARK
St. George's
Empress Business Cen
Old Trafford
Old Trafford Comm Sch
POMONA
Hulme
Manchester Technopark
City Park
A6
A34
A56
A57
A5066
A6041
A6042
A6143
A5063
A5014
A5067
A5103
B5461
B6469

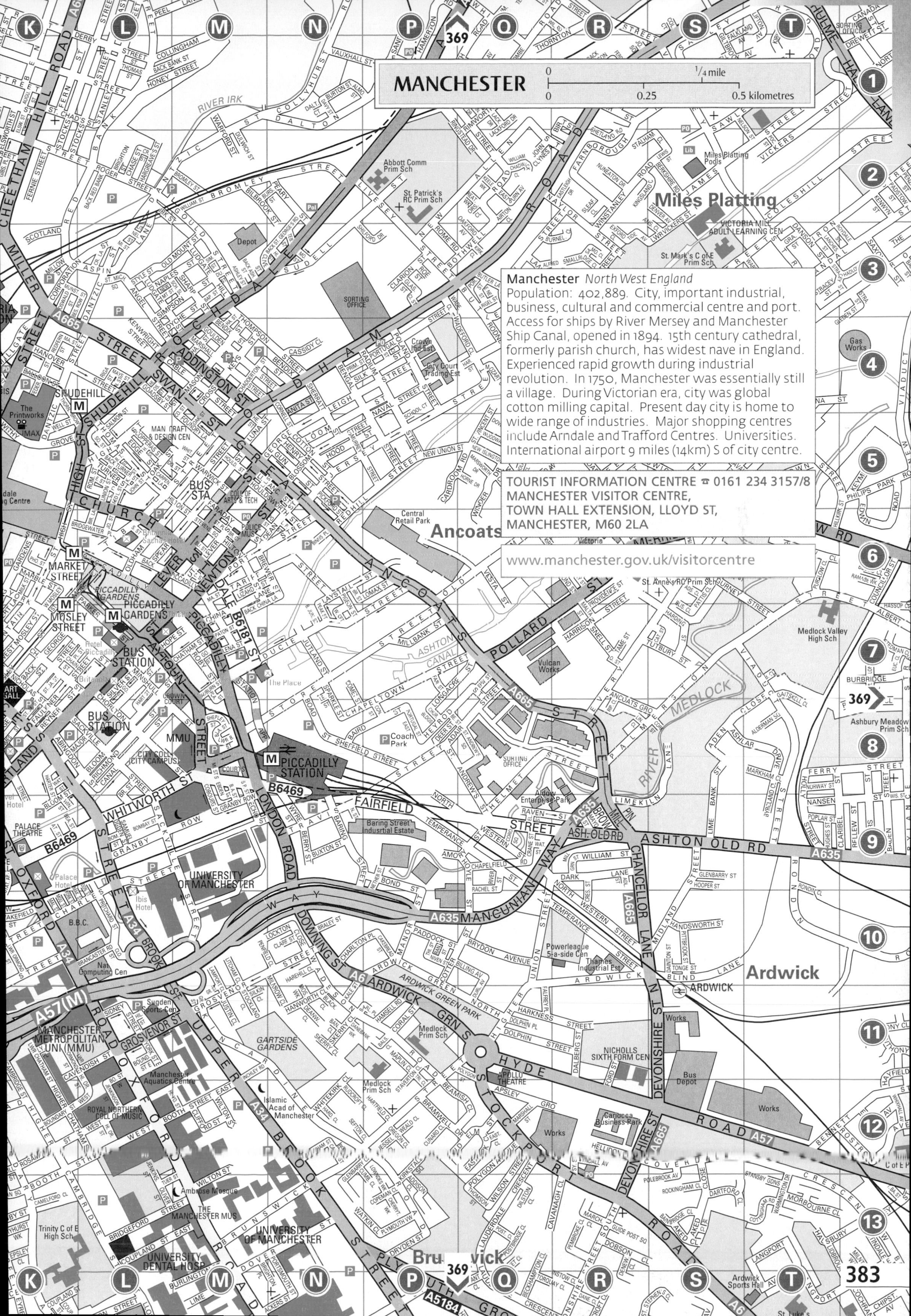
MANCHESTER
0 1/4 mile
0 0.25 0.5 kilometres
Manchester North West England
Population: 402,889. City, important industrial, business, cultural and commercial centre and port. Access for ships by River Mersey and Manchester Ship Canal, opened in 1894. 15th century cathedral, formerly parish church, has widest nave in England. Experienced rapid growth during industrial revolution. In 1750, Manchester was essentially still a village. During Victorian era, city was global cotton milling capital. Present day city is home to wide range of industries. Major shopping centres include Arndale and Trafford Centres. Universities. International airport 9 miles (14km) S of city centre.
TOURIST INFORMATION CENTRE ☎ 0161 234 3157/8
MANCHESTER VISITOR CENTRE,
TOWN HALL EXTENSION, LLOYD ST,
MANCHESTER, M60 2LA
www.manchester.gov.uk/visitorcentre
Miles Platting
Ancoats
Ardwick
PICCADILLY STATION
UNIVERSITY OF MANCHESTER
369

LEEDS
0 ¼ mile
0 0.25 0.5 kilometres
371
371
371
Woodhouse Moor
St. Georges Park
University of Leeds
Leeds Dental Institute
Leeds General Infirmary
Leeds Met Uni
Studio Theatre
BBC TV Studios
Leeds College of Art & Design
Notre Dame Coll
Civic Hall
Millennium Square
Town Hall
Crown Court
Nuffield Hosp
Leeds City Art Gall & Museum
St. Michael's Catholic Coll
Rosebank Prim Sch
Yorkshire TV Studios
Radio Aire
Kirkstall Industrial Park
Bowl Alley
Richard Oastler Spec Sch
Burley St. Matthias C of E Prim Sch
Rec Grd
Scotch Park Trading Est
Holiday Inn Express Hotel
Wellington Road Industrial Est
Crowne Plaza Hotel
Novotel Hotel
Metropole Hotel
Airside Centre
Int Pool
Leeds Station
River Aire
Leeds & Liverpool Canal
H.M. Prison Leeds
New Wortley Cemetery
Castleton Prim Sch
N.E.G.B. College
Armley
Wortley
Holbeck
Corus
Wortley Recreation Ground
Gelderd Trading Estate
Ingram Road Prim Sch
Matthew Murray High Sch
Sports Ground
South Leeds Sports Centre
St. Lukes C of E Prim Sch
Bowling Alley
Hillside Prim Sch
Latchmore
Junction 2
Junction
Kirkstall Road
Armley Road
Canal Street
Wellington Road
Whitehall Road
Gelderd Road
Domestic Road
Domestic Street
Holbeck Lane
Water Lane
Globe Road
Nineveh Road
Meadow Lane
Victoria Road
Woodhouse Lane
Blenheim Walk
Clarendon Road
Burley Road
Park Lane
Westgate
The Headrow
Wellington Street
West Street
Great George Street
Whitehall Road
Kirkstall
A65
A660
A58(M)
A58
A647
A62
A643
A653
B6154
M621

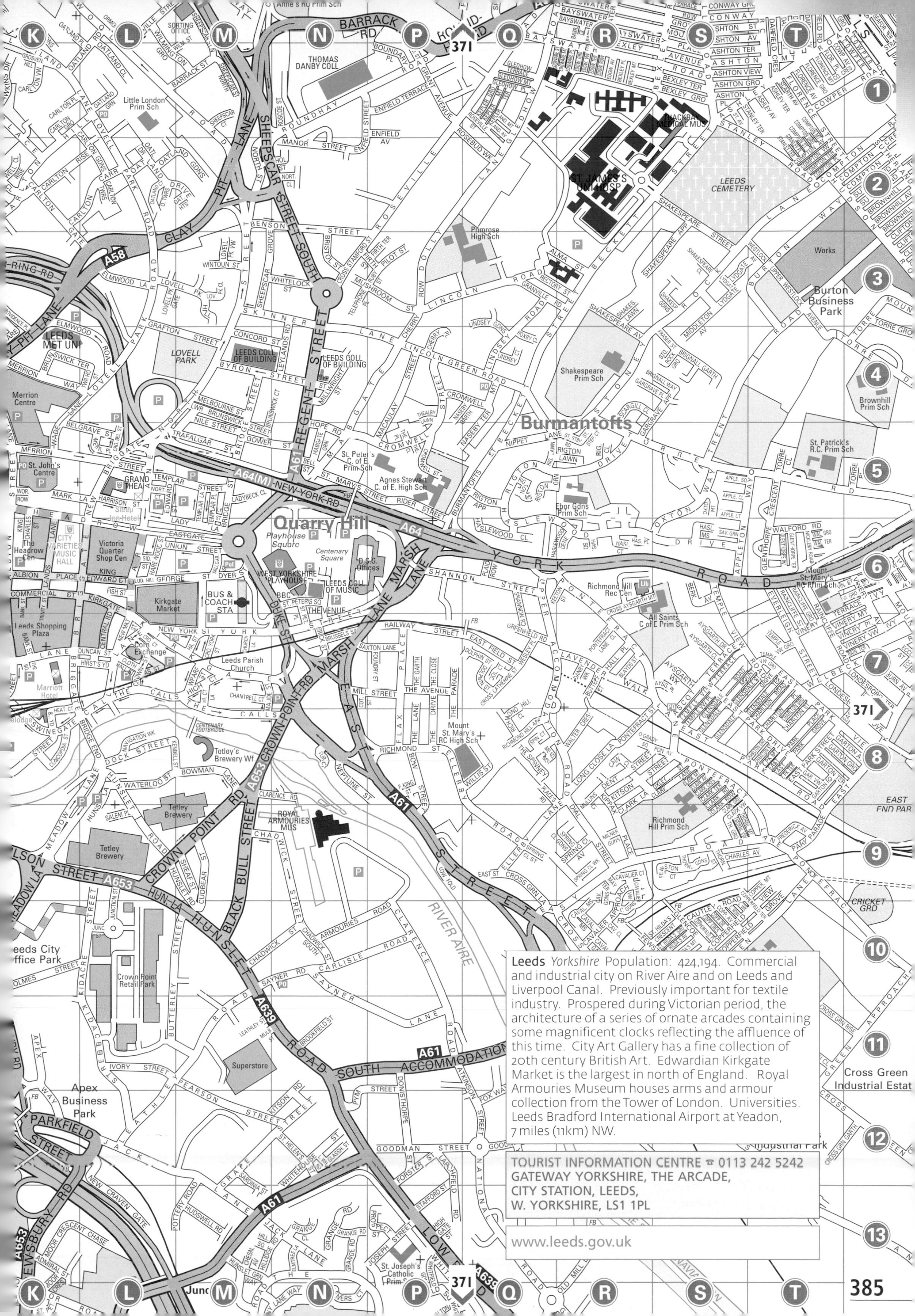
Quarry Hill
Burmantofts
St. James's Univ Hosp
Leeds Cemetery
Thackray Medical Mus
Little London Prim Sch
Thomas Danby Coll
Primrose High Sch
Shakespeare Prim Sch
Burton Business Park
Brownhill Prim Sch
St. Patrick's R.C. Prim Sch
Works
Leeds Met Uni
Lovell Park
Leeds Coll of Building
Merrion Centre
St. John's Centre
Grand Theatre
City Varieties Music Hall
Victoria Quarter Shop Cen
The Headrow Cen
Leeds Shopping Plaza
Kirkgate Market
Bus & Coach Sta
West Yorkshire Playhouse
Playhouse Square
Centenary Square
D.S.S. Offices
Leeds Coll of Music
The Venue
Corn Exchange
Leeds Parish Church
Marriott Hotel
St. Peter's C. of E. Prim Sch
Agnes Stewart C. of E. High Sch
Ebor Gdns Prim Sch
Richmond Hill Rec Cen
All Saints C. of E. Prim Sch
Mount St. Mary's RC Prim Sch
Mount St. Mary's RC High Sch
Richmond Hill Prim Sch
Tetley's Brewery Wf
Tetley Brewery
Royal Armouries Mus
River Aire
Crown Point Retail Park
Superstore
Apex Business Park
Leeds City Office Park
Cross Green Industrial Estate
Cricket Grd
East End Park
St. Joseph's Catholic Prim Sch
Ring Rd
A58
A64(M) New York Rd
A64
A61
A653
A639
York Road
Regent Street
Sheepscar Street South
Crown Point Rd
Black Bull Street
South Accommodation Rd
Hunslet Rd
Kirkstall Rd
Barrack Rd
Roseville Rd
Beckett Street
Lincoln Green Road
Burmantofts St
Marsh Lane
East St
Low Rd
Pontefract Lane
Clay Pit Lane
Meadow La
Dewsbury Rd
Parkfield Street
Jack La
Richmond Hill
371

Leeds *Yorkshire* Population: 424,194. Commercial and industrial city on River Aire and on Leeds and Liverpool Canal. Previously important for textile industry. Prospered during Victorian period, the architecture of a series of ornate arcades containing some magnificent clocks reflecting the affluence of this time. City Art Gallery has a fine collection of 20th century British Art. Edwardian Kirkgate Market is the largest in north of England. Royal Armouries Museum houses arms and armour collection from the Tower of London. Universities. Leeds Bradford International Airport at Yeadon, 7 miles (11km) NW.

TOURIST INFORMATION CENTRE ☎ 0113 242 5242
GATEWAY YORKSHIRE, THE ARCADE,
CITY STATION, LEEDS,
W. YORKSHIRE, LS1 1PL

www.leeds.gov.uk

Hillhead
Glasgow Academy
374
KELVINBRIDGE
Hutchesons' Gram Sch
Hillhead High Sch
UNI LIB
HUNTERIAN ART GALLERY
VISITOR CENTRE
HUNTERIAN MUS
UNI OF GLASGOW
WESTERN INFIRMARY
Dowanhill Prim Sch
UNIVERSITY PLACE
ST. MARY'S CATH
Willowbank Cres Prim Sch
GLASGOW CALEDONIAN UNI PARK CAMPUS
ST. GEORGES CROSS
Glasgow Gaelic Sch (Prim)
Kelvingrove
RIVER KELVIN
TRANSPORT MUS
KELVIN HALL
KELVINGROVE ART GALL & MUS (RE-OPENS MARCH 2006)
KELVINGROVE PARK
BOWL GRNS
QUEEN MOTHER'S MATERNITY HOSP
ROYAL HOSP FOR SICK CHILDREN
Yorkhill
Kelvin Sch (Spec)
Glasgow Steiner Sch
Kelvinhaugh
Kelvinhaugh Prim Sch
Junction 18
Garnethill
SCH OF ART
ROYAL HIGHLAND FUSILIERS REGIMENTAL MUS
DENTAL HOSP
CHARING CROSS STA
KING'S THEATRE
MITCHELL THEA
Mitchell Lib
DISUSED SCHOOL
Blythswood
Finnieston
Cranston Hill
EXHIBITION CENTRE STA
CLYDESIDE EXPRESSWAY
Anderston Prim Sch
St. Patrick's Prim Sch
Bowling
Hilton Hotel
Holiday Inn
Junction 19
Anderston
ANDERSTON STA
Marriott Hotel
Pumphouse Visitor Cen
Heliport
RIVER CLYDE
SCOTTISH EXHIB & CONFERENCE CEN
The Moat House Hotel
CLYDE AUDITORIUM
Campanile Hotel
Glasgow Tower
FOOTBRIDGE
BELLS BRIDGE
GLASGOW SCIENCE CEN
PRINCE'S DOCK
IMAX CINEMA
PACIFIC QUAY
FINNIESTON CRANE
City Inn Hotel
STOBCROSS ST A814
LANCEFIELD QUAY A814
ANDERSTON QUAY
STRATHCLYDE ARTS CEN
KENTIGERN HO
Broomielaw
P.S. WAVERLEY (PADDLE STEAMER)
KINGSTON BRIDGE
FESTIVAL PARK
Cessnock
Lorne Street Prim Sch
Odeon Cinema
Bingo
THE BOMBAY CINEMA
CESSNOCK
PAISLEY ROAD WEST A8
Junction 20
PAISLEY RD A8
MORRISON ST A8
Kinning Park
Bellahouston Prim Sch
KINNING PARK
Junction 21
M8
SHIELDS ROAD
Kingston
Tradeston
WEST STREET
Junction 22
SCOTLAND STREET SCHOOL: MUS OF EDUCATION
Parcelforce Depot
St. Albert's Prim Sch
Port Eglington
Glendale Prim Sch
A B C D E F G H J
1 2 3 4 5 6 7 8 9 10 11 12 13

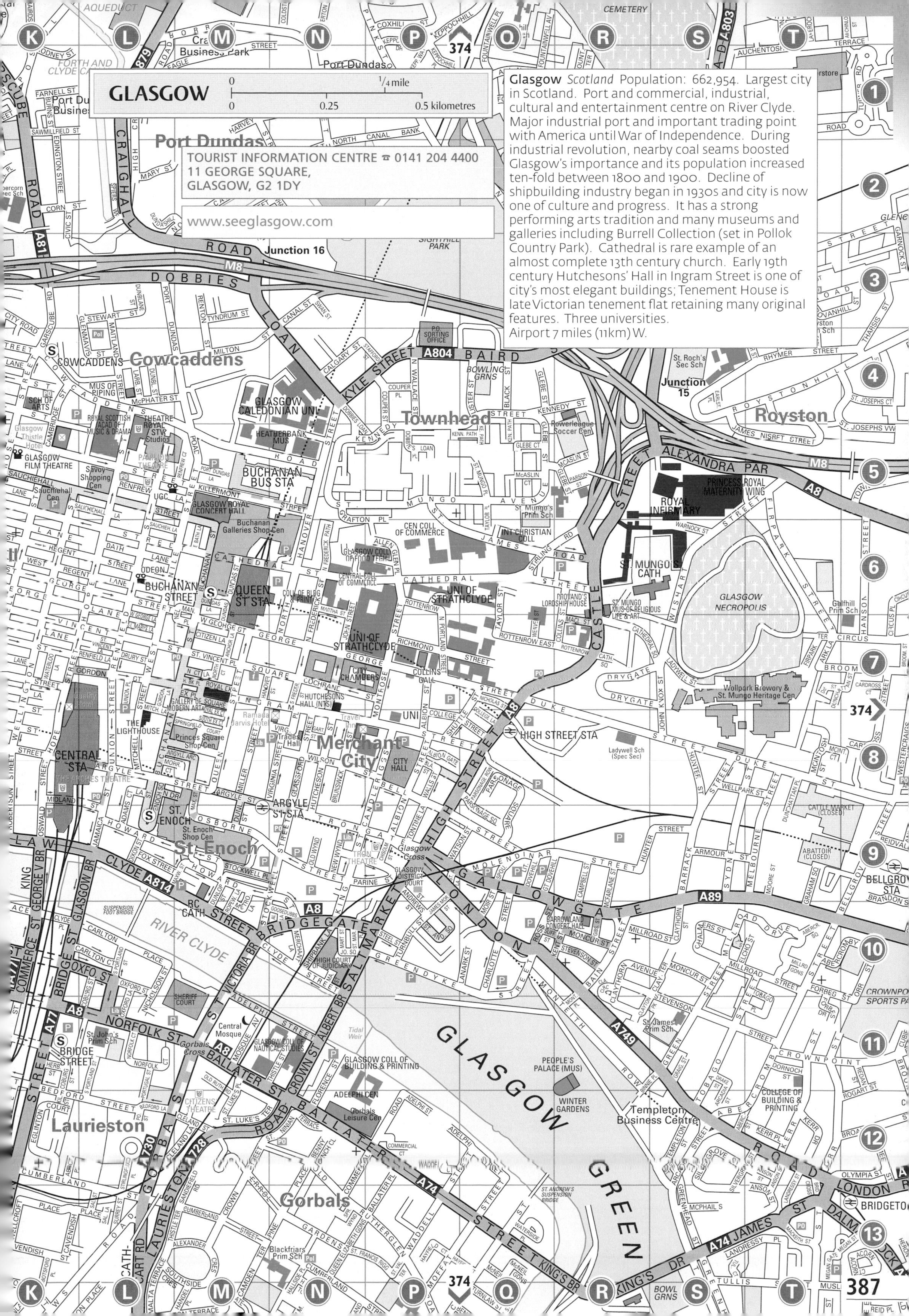
GLASGOW
0 ¼ mile
0 0.25 0.5 kilometres
TOURIST INFORMATION CENTRE ☎ 0141 204 4400
11 GEORGE SQUARE,
GLASGOW, G2 1DY
www.seeglasgow.com
Glasgow *Scotland* Population: 662,954. Largest city in Scotland. Port and commercial, industrial, cultural and entertainment centre on River Clyde. Major industrial port and important trading point with America until War of Independence. During industrial revolution, nearby coal seams boosted Glasgow's importance and its population increased ten-fold between 1800 and 1900. Decline of shipbuilding industry began in 1930s and city is now one of culture and progress. It has a strong performing arts tradition and many museums and galleries including Burrell Collection (set in Pollok Country Park). Cathedral is rare example of an almost complete 13th century church. Early 19th century Hutchesons' Hall in Ingram Street is one of city's most elegant buildings; Tenement House is late Victorian tenement flat retaining many original features. Three universities.
Airport 7 miles (11km) W.
Port Dundas
Cowcaddens
Townhead
Royston
Merchant City
St. Enoch
Laurieston
Gorbals
GLASGOW GREEN
RIVER CLYDE
GLASGOW NECROPOLIS
CENTRAL STA
QUEEN ST STA
HIGH STREET STA
374

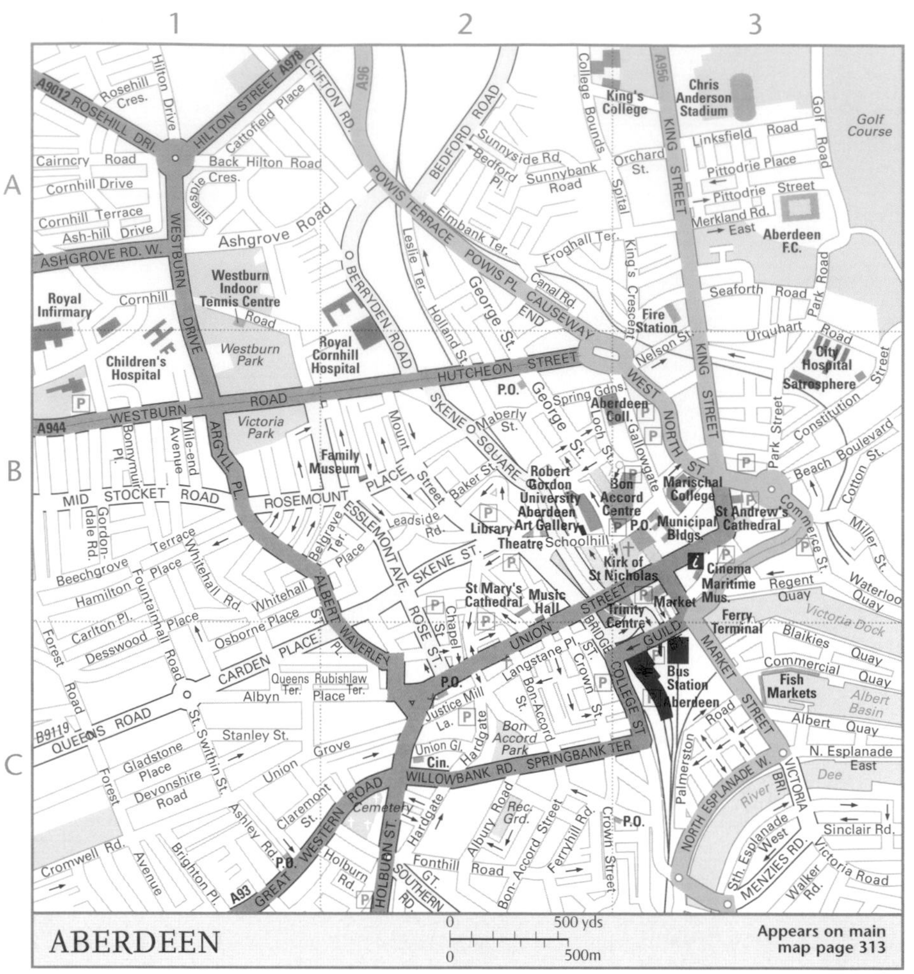

King's College
Chris Anderson Stadium
Golf Course
Aberdeen F.C.
Royal Infirmary
Westburn Indoor Tennis Centre
Children's Hospital
Westburn Park
Royal Cornhill Hospital
Victoria Park
Family Museum
Fire Station
City Hospital
Satrosphere
Aberdeen Coll.
Robert Gordon University
Aberdeen Art Gallery
Library
Theatre
Bon Accord Centre
Marischal College
Municipal Bldgs.
St Andrew's Cathedral
Kirk of St Nicholas
Cinema
Maritime Mus.
St Mary's Cathedral
Music Hall
Trinity Centre
Market
Ferry Terminal
Bus Station
Aberdeen
Fish Markets
Victoria Dock
Albert Basin
River Dee
Cemetery
HILTON STREET
WESTBURN DRIVE
ASHGROVE RD. W.
WESTBURN ROAD
HUTCHEON STREET
POWIS TERRACE
KING STREET
UNION STREET
ROSEMOUNT
MID STOCKET ROAD
ALBERT STREET
QUEENS ROAD
GREAT WESTERN ROAD
HOLBURN ST.
WILLOWBANK RD.
SPRINGBANK TER.
COLLEGE ST.
MARKET STREET
NORTH ESPLANADE W.
MENZIES RD.
A9012
A978
A96
A956
A944
B9119
A93

ABERDEEN

0 500 yds
0 500m

Appears on main map page 313

TOURIST INFORMATION CENTRE ☎ 01224 288828
23 UNION STREET,
ABERDEEN, AB11 5BP

HOSPITAL A & E ☎ 01224 681818
ABERDEEN ROYAL INFIRMARY,
FORESTERHILL, ABERDEEN, AB25 2ZN

COUNCIL OFFICE ☎ 01224 522000
ST. NICHOLAS HOUSE, BROAD STREET,
ABERDEEN, AB10 1AR

Aberdeen *Scotland* Population: 189,707. Cathedral and university city and commercial centre on E coast. Known as 'The Granite City', local stone having been used in many of its buildings. By 13th century, Aberdeen had become an important centre for trade and fishing and remains a major port and commercial base. In 19th century shipbuilding brought great prosperity to the city. These industries had receded by mid 20th century but the city's prospects were transformed when North Sea oil was discovered in 1970, turning it into a city of great wealth. St. Machar's Cathedral at Old Aberdeen. Many museums and art galleries. Extensive flower gardens. Airport at Dyce, 6 miles (9km) NW of Aberdeen.

LOCAL RADIO:
BBC RADIO SCOTLAND 585, 810, 990 AM / 92.6-94.7 FM;
NORTHSOUND ONE 96.9, 97.6, 103 FM;
NORTHSOUND TWO 1035 AM

www.agtb.org

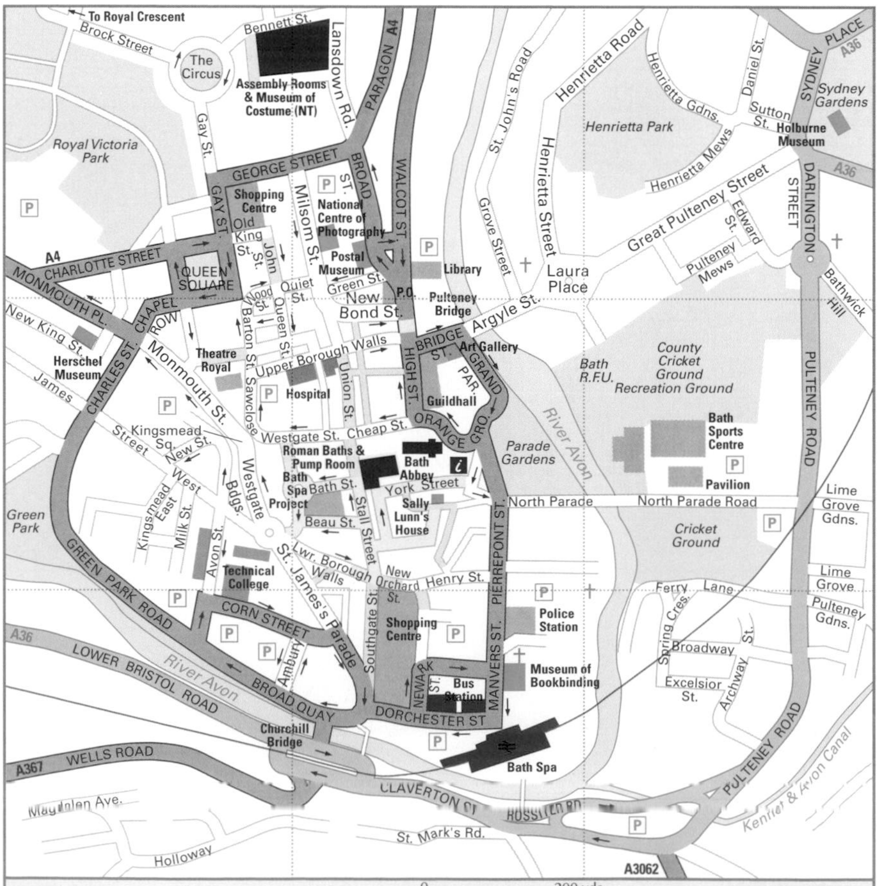

BATH

0 200 yds
0 200m

Appears on main map page 167

TOURIST INFORMATION CENTRE ☎ 0906 7112000
(Premium Rate)
ABBEY CHAMBERS, ABBEY CHURCHYARD,
BATH, BA1 1LY

HOSPITAL A & E ☎ 01225 428331
ROYAL UNITED HOSPITAL, COMBE PARK,
BATH, BA1 3NG

COUNCIL OFFICE ☎ 01225 477000
THE GUILDHALL, HIGH STREET,
BATH, BA1 5AW

Bath *South West England* Population: 85,202. City, spa on River Avon. Abbey church rebuilt 1501. Natural hot springs unique in Britain drew Romans to Bath, which they named 'Aquae Sulis'. Roman baths and 18th century Pump Room are open to visitors. In 18th century, it was most fashionable resort in country. Many Georgian buildings and elegant crescents remain, including The Circus and Royal Crescent. Museum of Costume in restored Assembly Rooms. Holds annual summer music festival. University 3 miles (4km) SE.

LOCAL RADIO:
BBC RADIO BRISTOL 1548 AM / 104.6 FM; BATH FM 107.9 FM;
CLASSIC GOLD 1260 AM; GWR (BATH) FM 103 FM

www.visitbath.co.uk

TOURIST INFORMATION CENTRE ☎ 01253 478222
1 CLIFTON STREET,
BLACKPOOL, FY1 1LY

HOSPITAL A & E ☎ 01253 300000
VICTORIA HOSPITAL, WHINNEY HEYS ROAD,
BLACKPOOL, FY3 8NR

COUNCIL OFFICE ☎ 01253 477477
TOWN HALL, TALBOT SQUARE,
BLACKPOOL, FY1 1AD

Blackpool *North West England* Population: 146,262. Town, large coastal resort and conference centre on Irish Sea. 19th century fashionable resort, still very popular today. 7 miles (11km) long 'Golden Mile' of tram route, beach, piers and amusement arcades. Blackpool Pleasure Beach, 518 ft (158m) high Tower entertainment complex, annual autumn Illuminations along 5 miles (8km) of Promenade, Zoo, Sea Life Centre, The Sandcastle indoor pool complex and Winter Gardens. Airport 3 miles (5km) S.

LOCAL RADIO:
BBC RADIO LANCASHIRE 104.5 FM
MAGIC 999 AM; WAVE 96.5 FM; ROCK FM 97.4 FM

www.visitblackpool.com

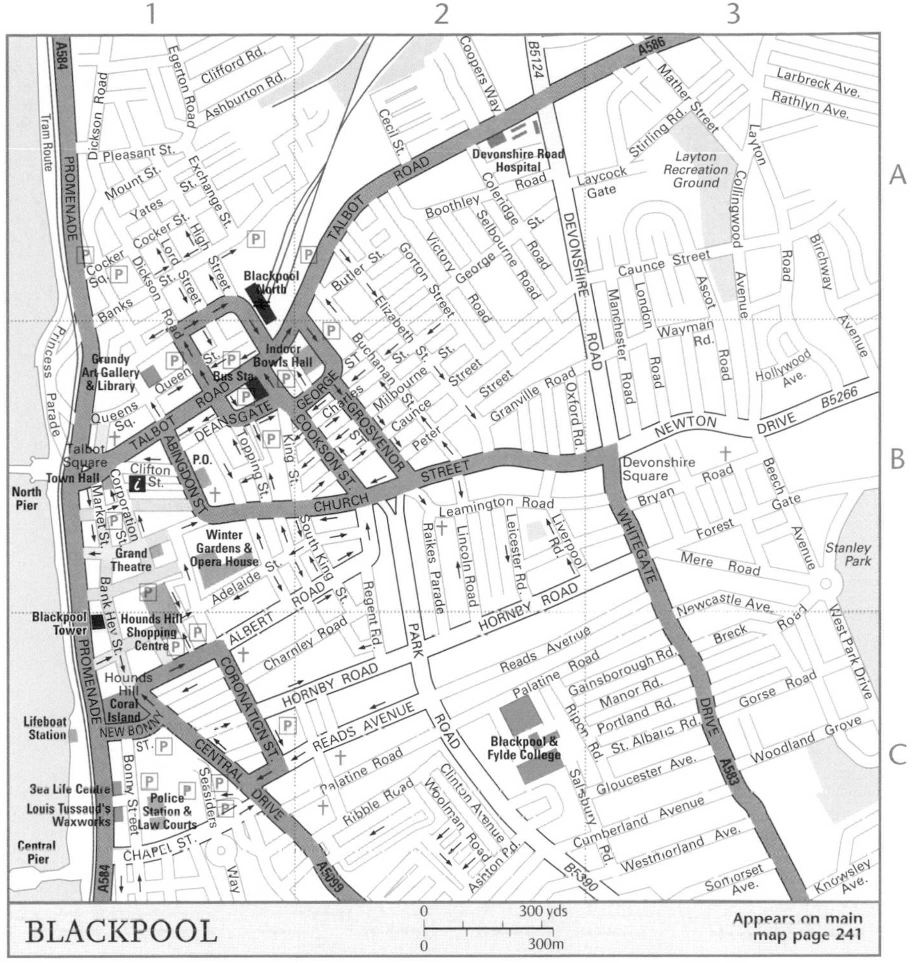
1
2
3
A
B
C
BLACKPOOL
Appears on main map page 241
0 300 yds
0 300m
PROMENADE
TALBOT ROAD
CHURCH STREET
DEVONSHIRE ROAD
WHITEGATE DRIVE
CENTRAL DRIVE
HORNBY ROAD
Blackpool North
Blackpool Tower
North Pier
Central Pier
Winter Gardens & Opera House
Grand Theatre
Hounds Hill Shopping Centre
Devonshire Road Hospital
Layton Recreation Ground
Stanley Park
Blackpool & Fylde College
Sea Life Centre
Louis Tussaud's Waxworks
Police Station & Law Courts
Lifeboat Station
Indoor Bowls Hall
Grundy Art Gallery & Library
Talbot Square
Town Hall
Devonshire Square

TOURIST INFORMATION CENTRE ☎ 0906 802 0234
(Premium Rate)
WESTOVER ROAD, BOURNEMOUTH, BH1 2BU

HOSPITAL A & E ☎ 01202 303626
ROYAL BOURNEMOUTH HOSPITAL,
CASTLE LANE EAST, BOURNEMOUTH, BH7 7DW

COUNCIL OFFICE ☎ 01202 451451
TOWN HALL, BOURNE AVENUE,
BOURNEMOUTH, BH2 6DY

Bournemouth *South West* Population: 155,488. Town, large seaside resort with mild climate. Town developed from a few cottages in 1810 to present conurbation. Sandy beach and pier. Extensive parks and gardens including Compton Acres, a display of international garden styles. Russell-Cotes Art Gallery and Museum houses Victorian and oriental collection. University. Conference, business and shopping centre. Bournemouth International Airport, 5 miles (8km) NE of town centre.

LOCAL RADIO:
BBC RADIO SOLENT (DORSET) 1359 AM / 103.8 FM;
2CR FM 102.3 FM; CLASSIC GOLD 828 AM; FIRE 107.6 FM;
WAVE 105 105.2 FM

www.bournemouth.co.uk

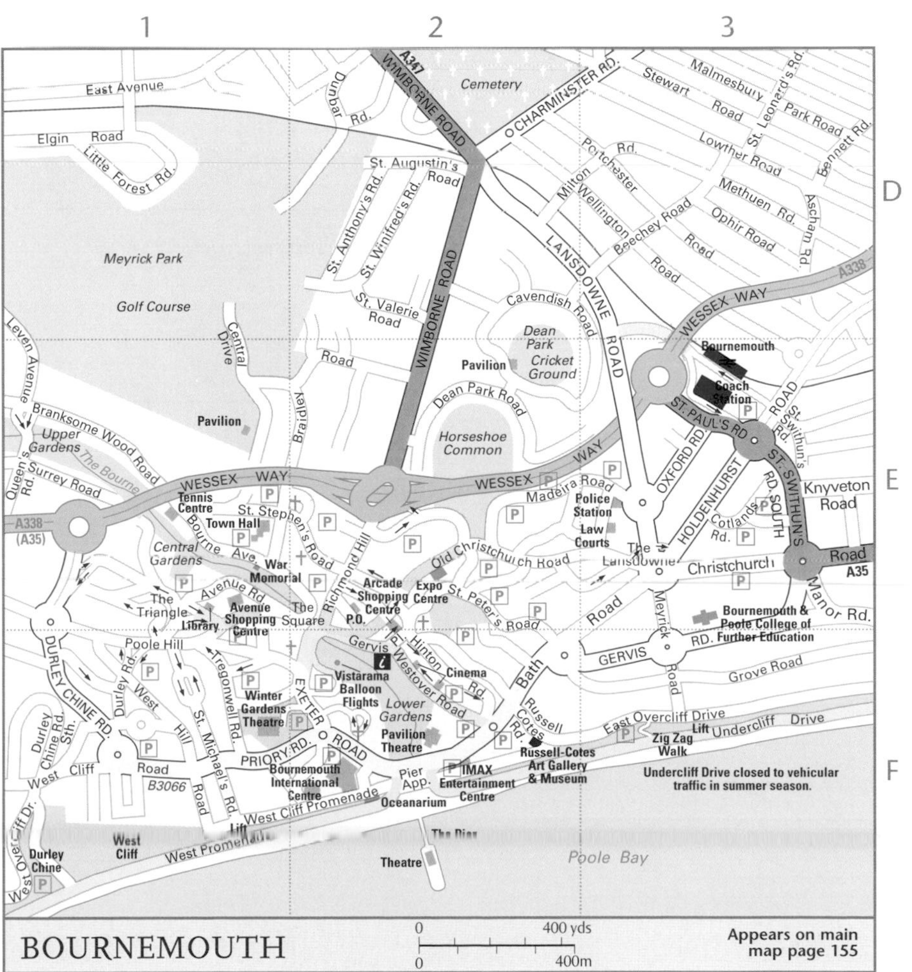
1
2
3
D
E
F
BOURNEMOUTH
Appears on main map page 155
0 400 yds
0 400m
WIMBORNE ROAD
WESSEX WAY
LANSDOWNE ROAD
Cemetery
Meyrick Park
Golf Course
Dean Park Cricket Ground
Horseshoe Common
Bournemouth Coach Station
Town Hall
Central Gardens
Upper Gardens
War Memorial
Library
Arcade Shopping Centre
Expo Centre
Winter Gardens Theatre
Vistarama Balloon Flights
Lower Gardens
Pavilion Theatre
Bournemouth International Centre
Oceanarium
IMAX Entertainment Centre
Russell-Cotes Art Gallery & Museum
Bournemouth & Poole College of Further Education
Zig Zag Walk
Undercliff Drive closed to vehicular traffic in summer season.
Poole Bay
West Cliff
Durley Chine
Police Station
Law Courts
The Lansdowne
Christchurch Road

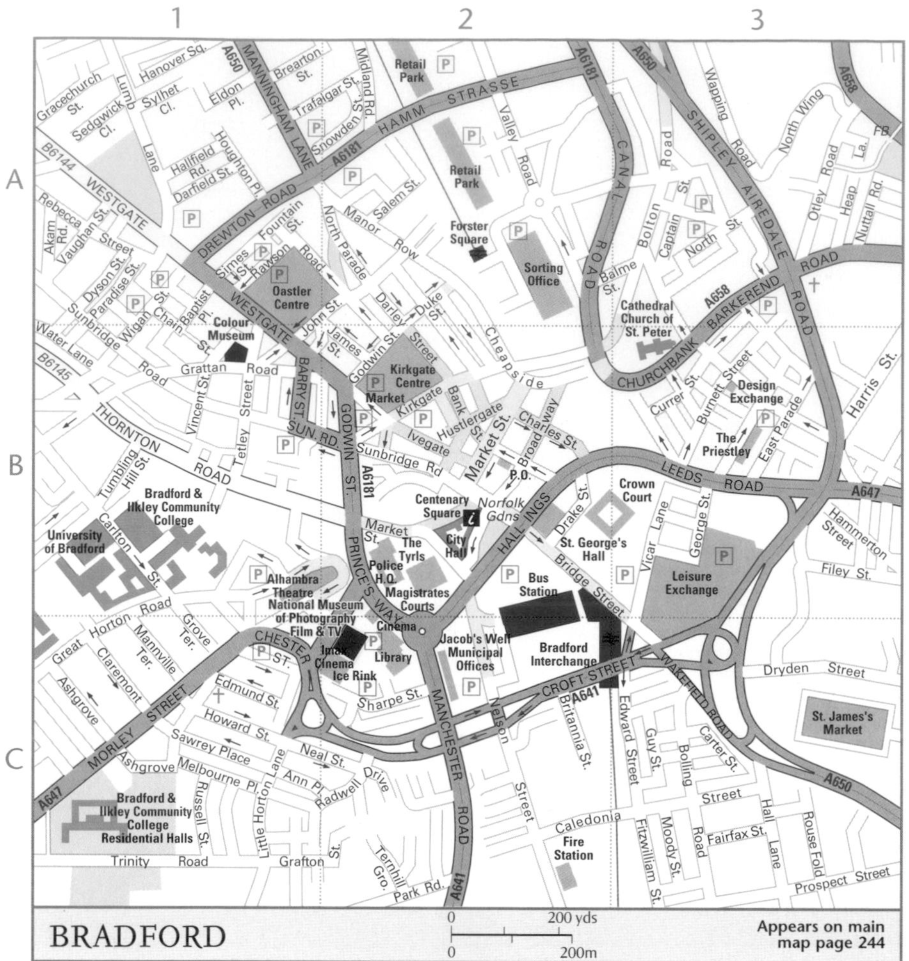
1
2
3
A
B
C
Manningham Lane
Hamm Strasse
Drewton Road
Westgate
Canal Road
Shipley Airedale Road
Barkerend Road
Churchbank
Leeds Road
Thornton Road
Godwin St.
Sun Rd
Barry St.
Princes Way
Chester St.
Morley Street
Manchester Road
Croft Street
Hall Ings
Bridge Street
Wakefield Road
Retail Park
Forster Square
Sorting Office
Oastler Centre
Colour Museum
Kirkgate Centre
Market
Cathedral Church of St. Peter
Design Exchange
The Priestley
Crown Court
Centenary Square
City Hall
Norfolk Gdns
P.O.
St. George's Hall
The Tyrls
Police H.Q.
Magistrates Courts
Bus Station
Leisure Exchange
Bradford & Ilkley Community College
University of Bradford
Alhambra Theatre
National Museum of Photography Film & TV
Imax Cinema
Ice Rink
Library
Cinema
Jacob's Well Municipal Offices
Bradford Interchange
St. James's Market
Bradford & Ilkley Community College Residential Halls
Fire Station
Caledonia
Dryden Street
A650
A6181
A658
A647
A641
BRADFORD
0 200 yds
0 200m
Appears on main map page 244

TOURIST INFORMATION CENTRE ☎ 01274 753678
CITY HALL, CENTENARY SQUARE,
BRADFORD, BD1 1HY

HOSPITAL A & E ☎ 01274 542200
BRADFORD ROYAL INFIRMARY, DUCKWORTH LANE, BRADFORD, BD9 6RJ

COUNCIL OFFICE ☎ 01274 752111
CITY HALL, CENTENARY SQUARE,
BRADFORD, BD1 1HY

Bradford *Yorkshire* Population: 289,376. Industrial city. Cathedral is former parish church. Previously known as wool capital of the world, Bradford is now less dependent upon the textile industry. Colour Museum documents history of dyeing and textile printing. University. Home to National Museum of Photography, Film and Television with IMAX cinema screen. Titus Salt built Saltaire 3 miles (5km) N, which is now considered a model industrial village. Salt's Mill, originally for textiles, now houses David Hockney art in the 1853 gallery. Leeds Bradford International Airport at Yeadon, 6 miles (10km) NE.

LOCAL RADIO:
BBC RADIO LEEDS 774 AM / 92.4, 95.3 FM;
WEST YORKS CLASSIC GOLD 1278 AM; THE PULSE 97.5 FM;
SUNRISE RADIO 103.2 FM

www.visitbradford.com

BRIGHTON

0 200 yds
0 200m

Appears on main map page 159

TOURIST INFORMATION CENTRE ☎ 0906 711 2255
(Premium Rate)
10 BARTHOLOMEW SQUARE, BRIGHTON, BN1 1JS

HOSPITAL A & E ☎ 01273 696955
ROYAL SUSSEX COUNTY HOSPITAL, EASTERN ROAD, BRIGHTON, BN2 5BE

COUNCIL OFFICE ☎ 01273 290000
TOWN HALL, BARTHOLOMEW SQUARE
BRIGHTON, BN1 1JA

Brighton *South East England* Population: 124,851. Town, seaside resort, sailing and conference centre. Previously a fishing village known as Brighthelmstone, centred on current Lanes area. Brighton became fashionable as a sea-bathing resort in the 18th century. Patronized by the Prince Regent in 1780s who built the Royal Pavilion in Oriental style as a summer palace. Regency squares at Kemp Town. Amusement arcades on 1899 Palace Pier. Annual festivals. Language schools. Universities.

LOCAL RADIO:
BBC SOUTHERN COUNTIES RADIO 1485 AM / 95.3 FM;
CAPITAL GOLD 1323 AM; SOUTHERN FM 103.5; JUICE 107.2 FM

www.visitbrighton.com

TOURIST INFORMATION CENTRE ☎ 0906 711 2191 (Premium Rate)
THE ANNEXE, WILDSCREEN WALK, HARBOURSIDE, BRISTOL, BS1 5DB

HOSPITAL A & E ☎ 0117 923 0000
BRISTOL ROYAL INFIRMARY, MARLBOROUGH STREET, BRISTOL, BS2 8HW

COUNCIL OFFICE ☎ 0117 922 2000
THE COUNCIL HOUSE, COLLEGE GREEN, BRISTOL, BS1 5TR

Bristol *South West England* Population: 407,992. City. Port on River Avon dates from medieval times. Bristol grew from transatlantic trade in rum, tobacco and slaves. In Georgian times, Bristol's population was second only to London and many Georgian buildings still stand, including the Theatre Royal, the oldest working theatre in the country. Bristol is now a commercial and industrial centre. Cathedral dates from 12th century and was originally an abbey. 15th century Temple Church tower and walls (English Heritage). Restored iron ship SS Great Britain and Industrial Museum in city docks area. Universities. 245 ft (75m) high Clifton Suspension Bridge completed in 1864 across the Avon Gorge NW of the city. Bristol International Airport at Lulsgate 7 miles (11km) SW.

LOCAL RADIO:
BBC RADIO BRISTOL 1548 AM / 94.9 FM; CLASSIC GOLD 1260 AM; GWR FM 96.3 FM; VIBE 101 97.2 FM; STAR 107.2 FM

www.visitbristol.co.uk

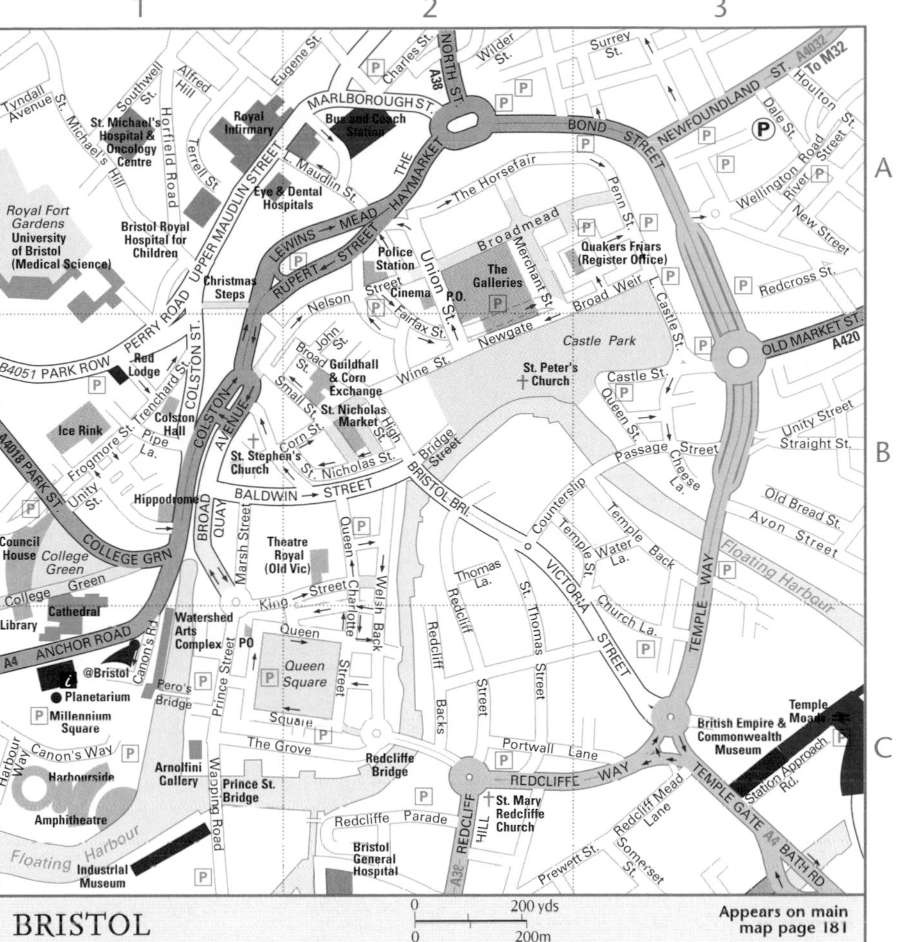
1
2
3
A
B
C
Royal Infirmary
Bus and Coach Station
St. Michael's Hospital & Oncology Centre
Eye & Dental Hospitals
Bristol Royal Hospital for Children
Royal Fort Gardens
University of Bristol (Medical Science)
Christmas Steps
Police Station
Cinema
P.O.
Broadmead
The Galleries
Quakers Friars (Register Office)
Castle Park
St. Peter's Church
Red Lodge
Guildhall & Corn Exchange
St. Nicholas Market
Ice Rink
Colston Hall
St. Stephen's Church
Hippodrome
Theatre Royal (Old Vic)
Council House
College Green
Cathedral
Library
Watershed Arts Complex
@Bristol
Planetarium
Millennium Square
Queen Square
The Grove
Harbourside
Amphitheatre
Arnolfini Gallery
Prince St. Bridge
Redcliffe Bridge
St. Mary Redcliffe Church
Bristol General Hospital
Industrial Museum
Floating Harbour
British Empire & Commonwealth Museum
Temple Meads
Temple Way
Victoria Street
Redcliffe Way
Temple Gate
Bond Street
Newfoundland St.
Old Market St.
Marlborough St.
Upper Maudlin Street
Lewins Mead
Rupert Street
Perry Road
Park Row
Colston Avenue
Baldwin Street
King Street
Anchor Road
Welsh Back
Redcliff Hill
Portwall Lane
BRISTOL
0 200 yds
0 200m
Appears on main map page 181

TOURIST INFORMATION CENTRE ☎ 0870 225 4900
WHEELER STREET, CAMBRIDGE, CAMBRIDGESHIRE, CB2 3QB

HOSPITAL A & E ☎ 01223 245151
ADDENBROOKE'S HOSPITAL, HILLS ROAD, CAMBRIDGE, CB2 2QQ

COUNCIL OFFICE ☎ 01223 457000
THE GUILDHALL, MARKET SQUARE, CAMBRIDGE, CB2 3QJ

Cambridge *East of England* Population: 95,682. University city on River Cam. First college founded here in 1284. Historic tensions existed between students and townspeople since 14th century, and came to a head during Peasants' Revolt of 1381 in which five townsfolk were hanged. Oliver Cromwell was a graduate of Sidney Sussex College and local MP at a time when the University was chiefly Royalist. 1870's saw foundation of first women's colleges, but women were not awarded degrees until after 1947. University's notable graduates include prime ministers, foreign heads of state, literary giants, philosophers and spies. Cambridge Footlights regularly provide a platform for future stars of stage, screen and television. Cambridge boasts many fine museums, art galleries and buildings of interest, including King's College Chapel and Fitzwilliam Museum. Airport at Teversham 3 miles (4km) E.

LOCAL RADIO:
BBC RADIO CAMBRIDGESHIRE 96 FM; Q 103 FM; STAR 107.9 FM

www.visitcambridge.org

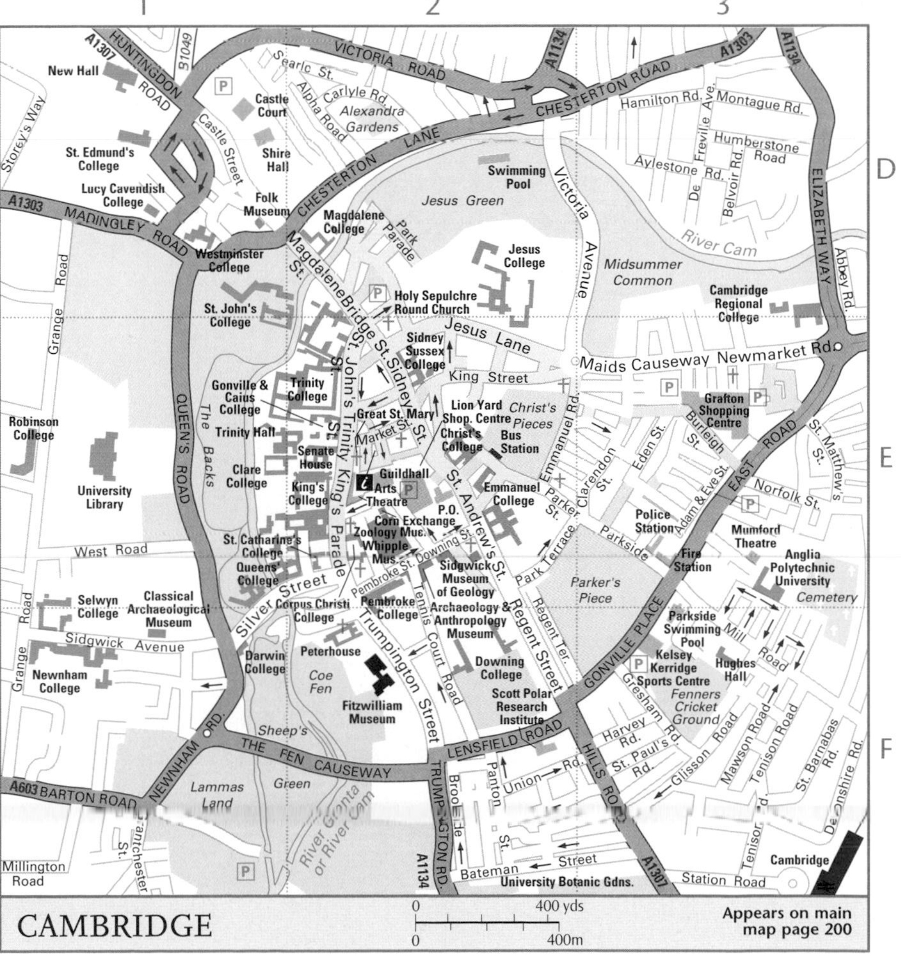
1
2
3
D
E
F
New Hall
Castle Court
Shire Hall
St. Edmund's College
Lucy Cavendish College
Folk Museum
Magdalene College
Westminster College
St. John's College
Jesus Green
Swimming Pool
Jesus College
Midsummer Common
River Cam
Cambridge Regional College
Holy Sepulchre Round Church
Sidney Sussex College
Jesus Lane
Maids Causeway
Newmarket Rd.
Grafton Shopping Centre
Trinity College
Gonville & Caius College
Great St. Mary's
Lion Yard Shop. Centre
Christ's College
Christ's Pieces
Bus Station
Robinson College
Trinity Hall
Senate House
Clare College
King's College
Guildhall
Arts Theatre
University Library
Emmanuel College
P.O.
Corn Exchange
Zoology Muc.
Whipple Mus.
Sedgwick Museum of Geology
Archaeology & Anthropology Museum
Police Station
Fire Station
Mumford Theatre
Anglia Polytechnic University
Parker's Piece
St. Catharine's College
Queens' College
Corpus Christi College
Pembroke College
Selwyn College
Classical Archaeological Museum
Sidgwick Avenue
Newnham College
Darwin College
Peterhouse
Coe Fen
Fitzwilliam Museum
Downing College
Scott Polar Research Institute
Parkside Swimming Pool
Kelsey Kerridge Sports Centre
Fenners Cricket Ground
Hughes Hall
Sheep's Green
Lammas Land
The Fen Causeway
Lensfield Road
Trumpington Street
Hills Road
Gonville Place
East Road
Queen's Road
Victoria Road
Chesterton Road
Chesterton Lane
Huntingdon Road
Madingley Road
Barton Road
Newnham Rd.
Elizabeth Way
Silver Street
King's Parade
Trinity St.
St. John's St.
Sidney St.
St. Andrew's St.
Regent Street
Station Road
University Botanic Gdns.
Cambridge
CAMBRIDGE
0 400 yds
0 400m
Appears on main map page 200

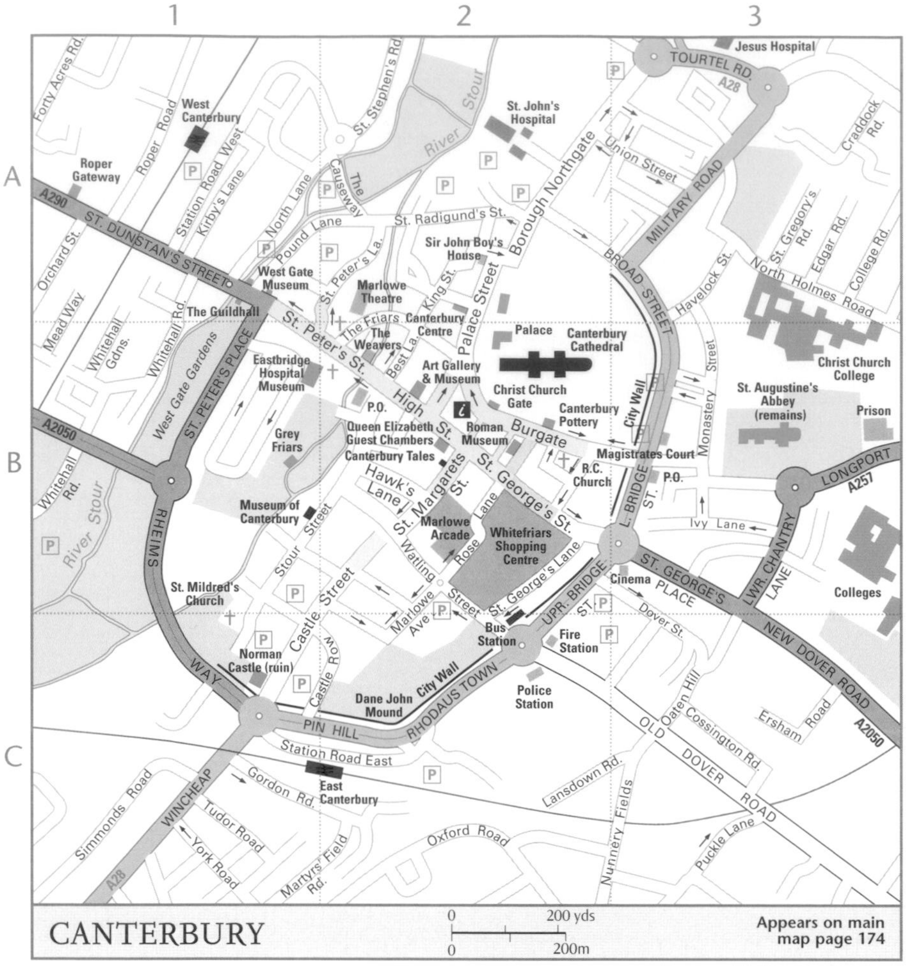

CANTERBURY

TOURIST INFORMATION CENTRE ☎ 01227 378100
12/13 SUN STREET, THE BUTTERMARKET,
CANTERBURY, CT1 2HX

HOSPITAL A & E ☎ 01227 766877
KENT & CANTERBURY HOSPITAL,
ETHELBERT ROAD, CANTERBURY, CT1 3NG

COUNCIL OFFICE ☎ 01227 862000
COUNCIL OFFICES, MILITARY ROAD,
CANTERBURY, CT1 1YW

Canterbury *South East England* Population: 36,464. Premier cathedral city and seat of Primate of Church of England on Great Stour River. Site of Roman settlement Durovernum. After Romans left, Saxons renamed town Cantwarabyrig. First cathedral in England built on site of current Christ Church Cathedral in AD 602. Thomas à Becket assassinated in Canterbury in 1170, turning Cathedral into great Christian shrine and destination of many pilgrimages, such as those detailed in Geoffrey Chaucer's Canterbury Tales. Becket's tomb destroyed on orders of Henry VIII. Cathedral was backdrop for premiere of T.S. Eliot's play 'Murder in the Cathedral' in 1935. City suffered extensive damage during World War II. Many museums and galleries explaining city's rich heritage. Roman and medieval remains, including city walls. Modern shopping centre; industrial development on outskirts. University of Kent on hill to N.

LOCAL RADIO:
BBC RADIO KENT 774 AM / 97.6 FM;
INVICTA FM 103.1 FM; KM-fm 106 FM

www.canterbury.co.uk

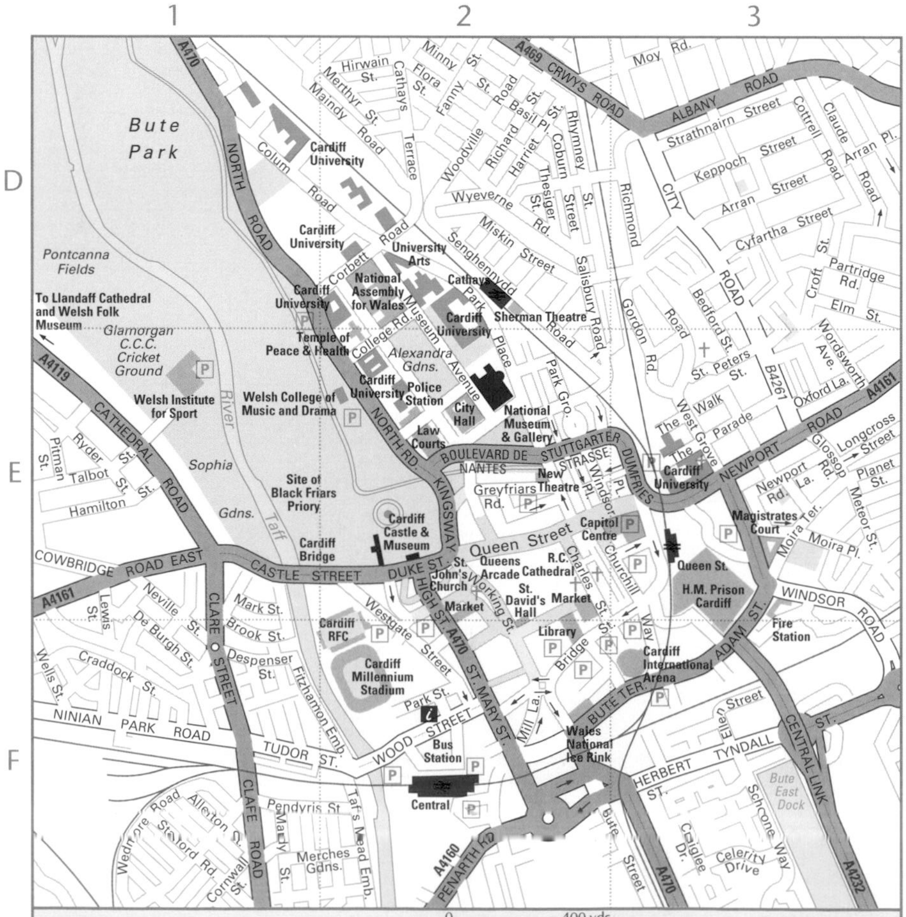

CANTERBURY

0 200 yds / 0 200m

Appears on main map page 174

CARDIFF

TOURIST INFORMATION CENTRE ☎ 029 2022 7281
CARDIFF VISITOR CENTRE, 16 WOOD STREET,
CARDIFF, CF10 1ES

HOSPITAL A & E ☎ 029 2074 7747
UNIVERSITY HOSPITAL OF WALES, HEATH PARK,
CARDIFF, CF14 4XW

COUNCIL OFFICE ☎ 029 2087 2087
THE HELP CENTRE, MARLAND HOUSE,
CENTRAL SQUARE, CARDIFF, CF10 1EP

Cardiff (Caerdydd) *Wales* Population: 272,129. City, capital of Wales since 1955, since when, many governmental, administrative and media organisations have moved to city. Romans founded military fort and small settlement on site of present day Cardiff. Uninhabited between departure of Romans and Norman conquest centuries later. Fishing village until development of coal mining in 19th century. Population rose from 1000 in 1801 to 170,000 a century later, becoming one of busiest ports in the world. Dock trade collapsed in 1930's. Major development programme still under way. Cardiff Bay area now major tourist centre and includes Techniquest, a science discovery centre, and the location of the new Welsh Assembly building. Millennium Stadium Cardiff Arms Park is the home of the Welsh Rugby Union and also hosts other sporting and entertainment events. Many museums including National Museum of Wales. Universities.

LOCAL RADIO:
BBC RADIO WALES 657, 882 AM / 103.9 FM; CAPITAL GOLD 1305, 1359 AM; RED DRAGON FM 103.2 FM; REAL 105-106 FM

www.visitcardiff.info

CARDIFF

0 400 yds / 0 400m

Appears on main map page 180

TOURIST INFORMATION CENTRE ☎ 01228 625600
CARDIFF VISITOR CENTRE, OLD TOWN HALL, GREEN MARKET, CARLISLE, CA3 8JH

HOSPITAL A & E ☎ 01228 523444
CUMBERLAND INFIRMARY, NEWTOWN ROAD, CARLISLE, CA2 7HY

COUNCIL OFFICE ☎ 01228 817000
CARLISLE CITY COUNCIL, THE CIVIC CENTRE, CARLISLE, CA3 8QG

Carlisle *North West England* Population: 72,439. Cathedral city at confluence of River Eden and River Caldew. Once a Roman military base and later fought over by Scots and English, line of Hadrian's wall runs through the northern suburbs. Castle above the River Eden, completed in 12th century, houses a military museum. Cathedral partially destroyed by fire in 17th century has two surviving bays of 12th century and a magnificent East window. Tullie House Museum imaginatively tells of the city's turbulent past. University of Northumbria. Racecourse . Airport 6 miles (9km) NE.

LOCAL RADIO:
BBC RADIO CUMBRIA 95.6, 96.1 & 104.1 FM;
CFM RADIO 96.4 FM

www.historic-carlisle.org.uk

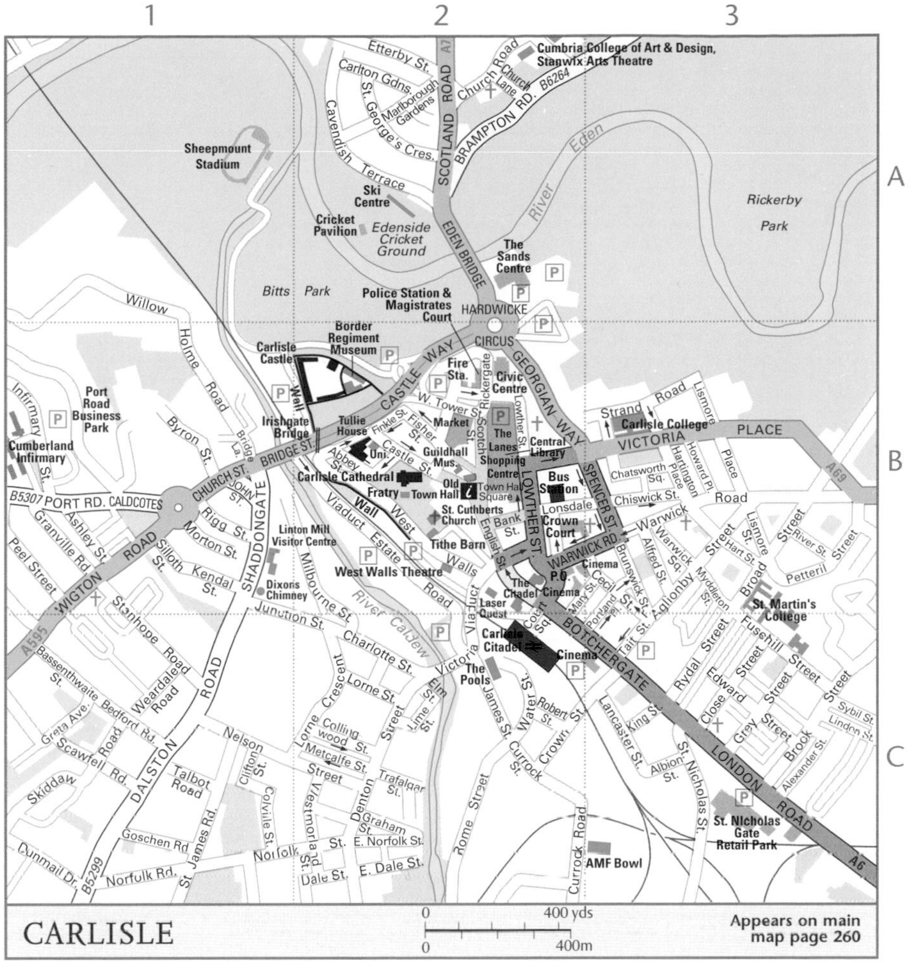
1
2
3
A
B
C
Cumbria College of Art & Design, Stanwix Arts Theatre
Sheepmount Stadium
Rickerby Park
River Eden
Ski Centre
Cricket Pavilion
Edenside Cricket Ground
The Sands Centre
Bitts Park
Police Station & Magistrates Court
HARDWICKE CIRCUS
Border Regiment Museum
Carlisle Castle
Fire Sta.
Civic Centre
Port Road Business Park
Cumberland Infirmary
Irishgate Bridge
Tullie House
Uni.
Carlisle Cathedral
Market
Guildhall Mus.
The Lanes Shopping Centre
Central Library
Bus Station
Carlisle College
Fratry
Town Hall
St. Cuthberts Church
Crown Court
Tithe Barn
Linton Mill Visitor Centre
West Walls Theatre
Dixons Chimney
Cinema
The Citadel
Laser Quest
Carlisle Citadel
The Pools
St. Martin's College
St. Nicholas Gate Retail Park
AMF Bowl
SCOTLAND ROAD
EDEN BRIDGE
CASTLE WAY
GEORGIAN WAY
VICTORIA PLACE
WIGTON ROAD
PORT RD. CALDCOTES
CHURCH ST.
BRIDGE ST.
SHADDONGATE
DALSTON ROAD
BOTCHERGATE
LONDON ROAD
WARWICK RD.
LOWTHER ST.
SPENCER ST.
BRAMPTON RD.
CARLISLE
0 400 yds
0 400m
Appears on main map page 260

TOURIST INFORMATION CENTRE ☎ 01242 522878
77 THE PROMENADE, CHELTENHAM, GLOUCESTERSHIRE, GL50 1PJ

HOSPITAL A & E ☎ 08454 222222
CHELTENHAM GENERAL HOSPITAL, SANDFORD ROAD, CHELTENHAM, GL53 7AN

COUNCIL OFFICE ☎ 01242 262626
MUNICIPAL OFFICES, THE PROMENADE, CHELTENHAM, GL50 1PP

Cheltenham *South West England* Population: 91,301. Largest town in The Cotswolds. Shopping and tourist centre, with some light industry. Mainly residential, with many Regency and Victorian buildings and public gardens. Formerly a spa town, Pittville Pump Room built between 1825 and 1830 overlooks Pittville Park and is now used for concerts. Art Gallery and Museum. Ladies' College founded 1853. Racecourse to the N hosts Cheltenham Gold Cup race meeting, Cheltenham International Music Festival and Festival of Literature, among other events. Birthplace of composer Gustav Holst. University of Gloucestershire.

LOCAL RADIO:
BBC RADIO GLOUCESTERSHIRE 1413 AM / 104.7 FM;
CLASSIC GOLD 774 AM; SEVERN SOUND FM 102.4 FM;
STAR 107.5 FM

www.visitcheltenham.info

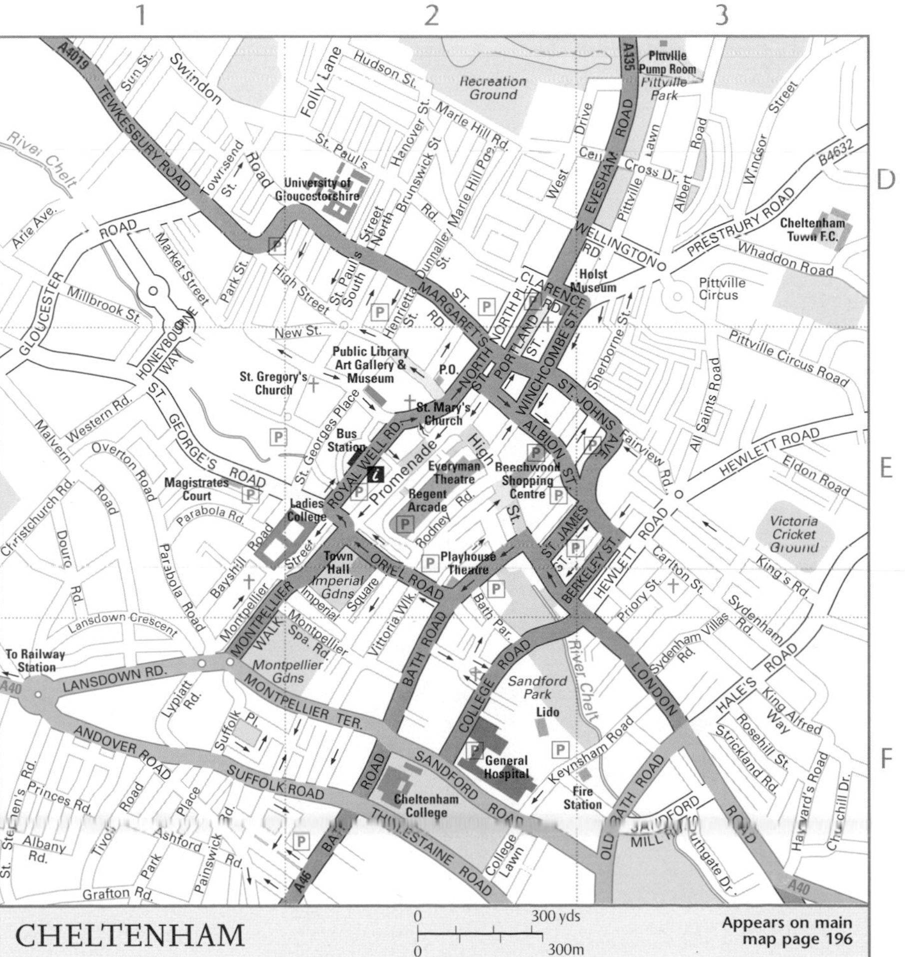
1
2
3
D
E
F
Pittville Pump Room
Pittville Park
Recreation Ground
River Chelt
University of Gloucestershire
Cheltenham Town F.C.
Holst Museum
Pittville Circus
Public Library Art Gallery & Museum
P.O.
St. Gregory's Church
St. Mary's Church
Bus Station
Everyman Theatre
Regent Arcade
Beechwood Shopping Centre
Magistrates Court
Ladies College
Town Hall
Imperial Gdns
Playhouse Theatre
Victoria Cricket Ground
Montpellier Gdns
Sandford Park
Lido
General Hospital
Cheltenham College
Fire Station
To Railway Station
TEWKESBURY ROAD
GLOUCESTER ROAD
EVESHAM ROAD
PRESTBURY ROAD
WELLINGTON RD.
ST. MARGARET'S RD.
NORTH PL.
PORTLAND ST.
WINCHCOMBE ST.
ALBION ST.
ST. JOHNS AVE.
HEWLETT ROAD
ST. GEORGE'S ROAD
ROYAL WELL RD.
Promenade
HIGH STREET
ORIEL ROAD
BATH ROAD
COLLEGE ROAD
LONDON ROAD
LANSDOWN RD.
MONTPELLIER TER.
ANDOVER ROAD
SUFFOLK ROAD
SANDFORD ROAD
THIRLESTAINE ROAD
OLD BATH ROAD
HALE'S ROAD
CHELTENHAM
0 300 yds
0 300m
Appears on main map page 196

CHESTER COVENTRY

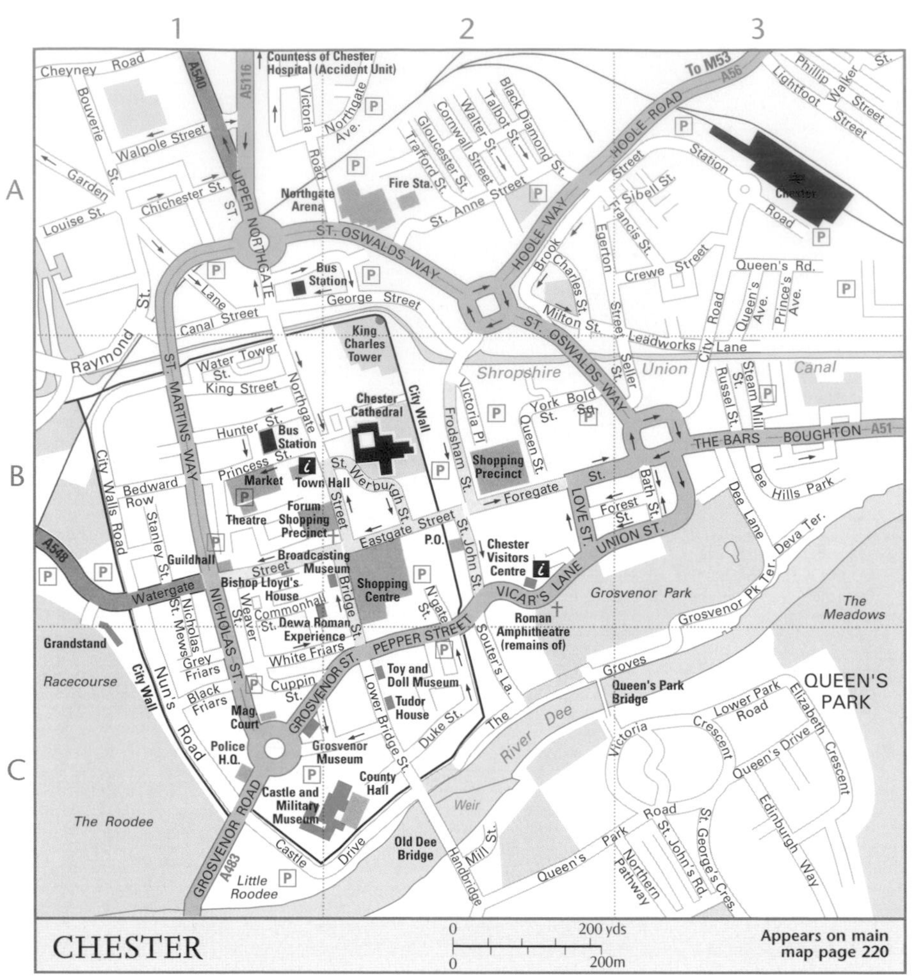

1
2
3
A
B
C
Cheyney Road
Bouverie St.
Walpole Street
Garden
Louise St.
Chichester St.
Countess of Chester Hospital (Accident Unit)
A540
A5116
Victoria Road
Northgate Ave.
UPPER NORTHGATE ST.
Northgate Arena
Fire Sta.
Trafford St.
Gloucester St.
Cornwall Street
Walter St.
Talbot St.
Black Diamond St.
St. Anne Street
To M53
A56
HOOLE ROAD
HOOLE WAY
Phillip St.
Walker St.
Lightfoot Street
Station Road
Chester
Sibell St.
Francis St.
Egerton Street
Brook St.
Charles St.
Crewe Street
Queen's Rd.
Queen's Ave.
Prince's Ave.
ST. OSWALDS WAY
Bus Station
George Street
Lane
Canal Street
Raymond St.
King Charles Tower
Milton St.
Leadworks Lane
City Road
Shropshire
Union
Canal
Seller Street
Russel St.
Steam Mill St.
Water Tower St.
King Street
Northgate Street
Chester Cathedral
City Wall
Victoria Pl.
York St.
Bold Sq.
Queen St.
Hunter St.
Bus Station
Princess St.
St. Werburgh St.
Market
Town Hall
Shopping Precinct
Frodsham St.
Foregate
THE BARS
BOUGHTON
A51
Dee Hills Park
Dee Lane
City Walls Road
Bedward Row
Stanley St.
ST. MARTINS WAY
Theatre
Forum Shopping Precinct
Eastgate Street
Forest St.
Bath St.
LOVE ST.
UNION ST.
Chester Visitors Centre
A548
Guildhall
Broadcasting Museum
Bishop Lloyd's House
Watergate Street
Shopping Centre
St. John St.
VICAR'S LANE
Deva Ter.
Grosvenor Park
Grosvenor Pk Ter.
The Meadows
Nicholas St. Mews
NICHOLAS ST.
Weaver St.
Commonhall St.
Bridge St.
Dewa Roman Experience
Newgate St.
Roman Amphitheatre (remains of)
PEPPER STREET
Grandstand
Racecourse
City Wall
Grey Friars
White Friars
Toy and Doll Museum
Souter's La.
Groves
Queen's Park Bridge
Lower Park Road
QUEEN'S PARK
Elizabeth Crescent
Black Friars
Cuppin St.
Nun's Road
Mag Court
GROSVENOR ST.
Lower Bridge St.
Tudor House
Duke St.
The
River Dee
Victoria Crescent
Queen's Drive
Police H.Q.
Grosvenor Museum
County Hall
Castle and Military Museum
GROSVENOR ROAD
A483
The Roodee
Castle Drive
Weir
Old Dee Bridge
Handbridge
Mill St.
Queen's Park Road
Northern Pathway
St. John's Rd.
St. George's Cres.
Edinburgh Way
Little Roodee
0
200 yds
200m

CHESTER

Appears on main map page 220

TOURIST INFORMATION CENTRE ☎ 01244 402111
TOWN HALL, NORTHGATE STREET,
CHESTER, CHESHIRE, CH1 2HJ

HOSPITAL A & E ☎ 01244 365000
COUNTESS OF CHESTER HOSPITAL, HEALTH PK,
LIVERPOOL ROAD, CHESTER, CH2 1UL

COUNCIL OFFICE ☎ 01244 324324
THE FORUM,
CHESTER, CH1 2HS

Chester *North West England* Population: 80110. County town and cathedral city on River Dee. Commercial, financial and tourist centre built on Roman town of Deva. Includes biggest Roman amphitheatre in Britain and well preserved medieval walls. Castle, now county hall, includes 12th century Agricola Tower. Cathedral with remains of original Norman abbey. Famed for Tudor timber-framed buildings which include Chester Rows, two-tier galleried shops and Bishop Lloyd's House, with ornate 16th century carved façade. Eastgate clock built to commemorate Queen Victoria's diamond jubilee in 1897. Racecourse and zoo.

LOCAL RADIO:
BBC RADIO MERSEYSIDE 95.8 FM;
MAGIC 1548 AM; MFM 103.4 FM; RADIO CITY 96.7 FM

www.chestercc.gov.uk/tourism

COVENTRY

0 500 yds
0 500m

Appears on main map page 209

TOURIST INFORMATION CENTRE ☎ 024 7622 7264
BAYLEY LANE, COVENTRY,
WEST MIDLANDS, CV1 5RN

HOSPITAL A & E ☎ 024 7622 4055
COVENTRY & WARWICKSHIRE HOSPITAL,
STONEY STANTON ROAD, COVENTRY, CV1 4FH

COUNCIL OFFICE ☎ 024 7683 3333
COUNCIL HOUSE, EARL STREET,
COVENTRY, CV1 5RR

Coventry *West Midlands* Population: 299,316. City. St. Michael's cathedral built 1954-62 beside ruins of medieval cathedral destroyed in air raid in 1940. The centre of the city was rebuilt in the 1950s and 1960s following WW II bombing, but some old buildings remain, including Bonds Hospital and the medieval Guildhall. A town rich from textile industry in middle ages, Coventry is now known for its motor car industry; other important industries are manufacturing and engineering. Coventry Transport Museum. Herbert Art Gallery and Museum. Universities. Civil airport at Baginton to S. Coventry Canal runs N to Trent and Mersey Canal at Fradley Junction near Lichfield.

LOCAL RADIO:
BBC RADIO WM 103.7 FM; CLASSIC GOLD 1359 AM; KIX 96.2 FM;
MERCIA FM 97 FM; HEART FM 100.7 FM

www.visitcoventry.co.uk

TOURIST INFORMATION CENTRE ☎ 01332 255802
ASSEMBLY ROOMS, MARKET PLACE,
DERBY, DE1 3AH

HOSPITAL A & E ☎ 01332 347141
DERBYSHIRE ROYAL INFIRMARY,
LONDON ROAD, DERBY, DE1 2QY

COUNCIL OFFICE ☎ 01332 293111
THE COUNCIL HOUSE, CORPORATION STREET,
DERBY, DE1 2FS

Derby *East Midlands* Population: 223,836. Industrial city and county town on River Derwent. Shopping and entertainment centre. Cathedral mainly by James Gibbs, 1725. Both manufacturing and engineering are important to local economy. Derby Industrial Museum charts city's industrial history with emphasis on Rolls Royce aircraft engineering. Tours at Royal Crown Derby porcelain factory. University.

LOCAL RADIO:
BBC RADIO DERBY 1116 AM / 104.5 FM;
CLASSIC GOLD GEM 945 AM; RAM FM 102.8 FM;
96 TRENT FM 96.2 FM

www.visitderby.co.uk

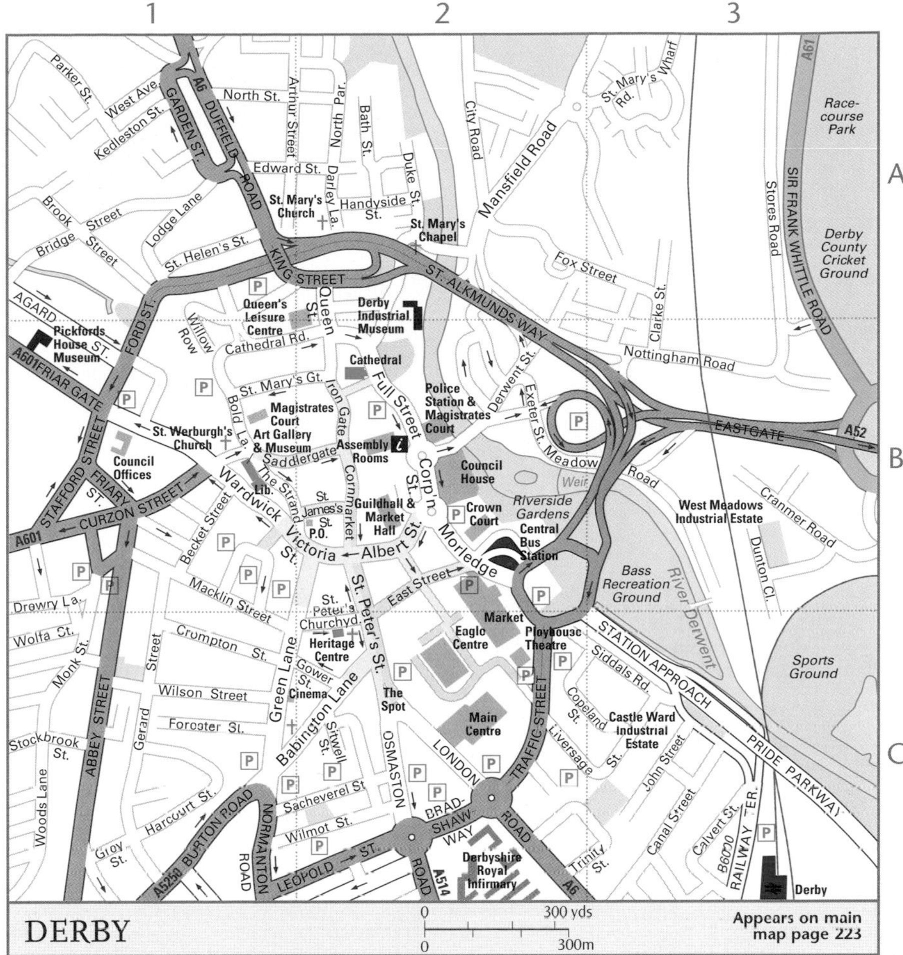

1
2
3
A
B
C
North St.
Edward St.
St. Mary's Church
St. Mary's Chapel
Mansfield Road
City Road
Race-course Park
Derby County Cricket Ground
SIR FRANK WHITTLE ROAD
Stores Road
Fox Street
Clarke St.
Nottingham Road
KING STREET
ST. ALKMUNDS WAY
Queen's Leisure Centre
Derby Industrial Museum
Cathedral
Cathedral Rd.
Pickfords House Museum
AGARD ST.
A601 FRIAR GATE
FORD ST.
St. Mary's Gt.
Magistrates Court
Art Gallery & Museum
St. Werburgh's Church
Council Offices
Assembly Rooms
Police Station & Magistrates Court
Council House
Crown Court
Riverside Gardens
Central Bus Station
EASTGATE
A52
Meadow Rd.
West Meadows Industrial Estate
Cranmer Road
Dunton Cl.
Bass Recreation Ground
River Derwent
Sports Ground
Guildhall & Market Hall
Victoria St.
Albert St.
Morledge
East Street
Market
Eagle Centre
Playhouse Theatre
Heritage Centre
Cinema
STATION APPROACH
Siddals Rd.
Castle Ward Industrial Estate
PRIDE PARKWAY
Main Centre
The Spot
TRAFFIC STREET
LONDON ROAD
Derbyshire Royal Infirmary
Derby
Green Lane
Babington Lane
St. Peter's St.
Wilson Street
Crompton St.
Macklin Street
ABBEY STREET
STAFFORD STREET
CURZON STREET
Wardwick
Sacheverel St.
Wilmot St.
LEOPOLD ST.
NORMANTON ROAD
BURTON ROAD
OSMASTON ROAD
DERBY
300 yds
300m
Appears on main map page 223

TOURIST INFORMATION CENTRE ☎ 01304 205108
THE OLD TOWN GAOL, BIGGIN STREET,
DOVER, CT16 1DL

HOSPITAL A & E ☎ 01227 766877
KENT & CANTERBURY HOSPITAL,
ETHELBERT ROAD, CANTERBURY, CT1 3NG

COUNCIL OFFICE ☎ 01304 821199
WHITE CLIFFS BUSINESS PARK,
DOVER, CT16 3PJ

Dover *South East England* Population: 34,179. Town, cinque port, resort and Channel port on Strait of Dover, with large modern docks for freight and passengers. Dominated by high white cliffs and medieval castle enclosing the Pharos, AD50 remains of Roman lighthouse. Remains of 12th century Knights Templar Church across valley from castle. Sections of moat of 19th century fort at Western Heights, above town on W side of harbour.

LOCAL RADIO:
BBC RADIO KENT 774 AM / 104.2 FM;
KM-fm 106.8 FM; INVICTA FM 97 FM

www.whitecliffscountry.org.uk

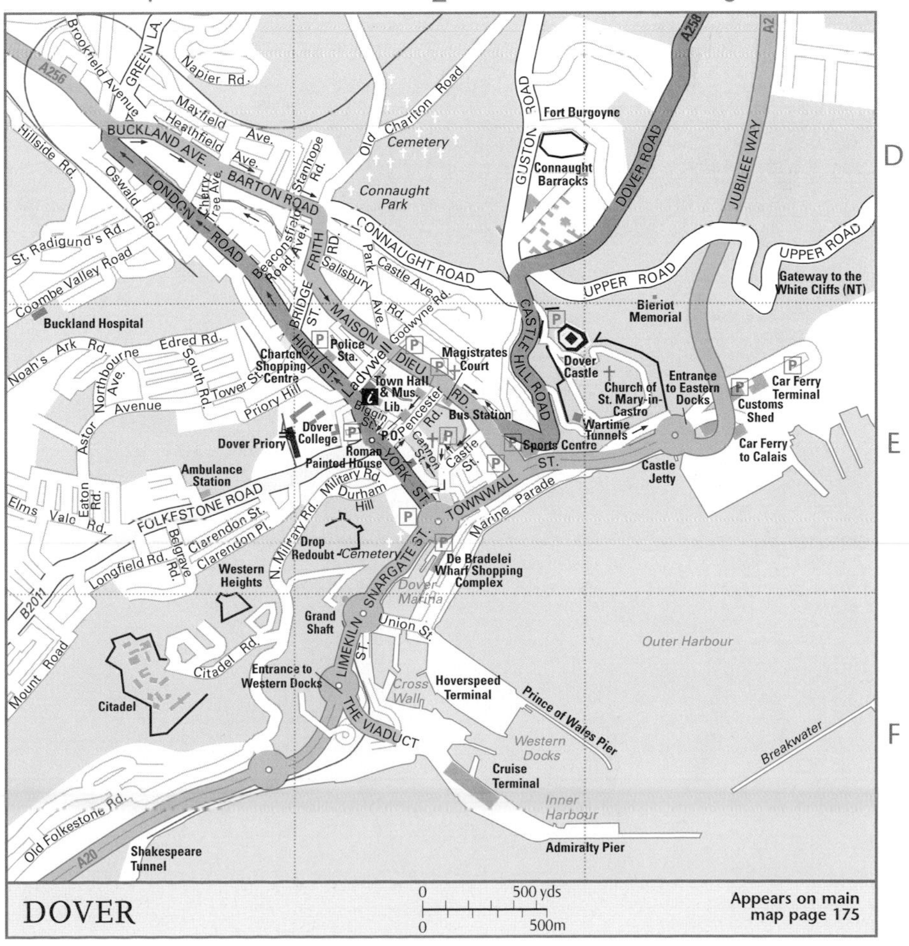

1
2
3
D
E
F
A256
Brookfield Avenue
BUCKLAND AVE.
BARTON ROAD
Cemetery
Connaught Park
Fort Burgoyne
Connaught Barracks
GUSTON ROAD
DOVER ROAD
JUBILEE WAY
A258
A2
CONNAUGHT ROAD
UPPER ROAD
Gateway to the White Cliffs (NT)
Bleriot Memorial
Buckland Hospital
LONDON ROAD
Coombe Valley Road
St. Radigund's Rd.
CASTLE HILL ROAD
Dover Castle
Church of St. Mary-in-Castro
Wartime Tunnels
Entrance to Eastern Docks
Car Ferry Terminal
Customs Shed
Car Ferry to Calais
Castle Jetty
Magistrates Court
Police Sta.
Charlton Shopping Centre
Town Hall & Mus.
Bus Station
Sports Centre
Dover Priory
Dover College
Roman Painted House
Ambulance Station
FOLKESTONE ROAD
TOWNWALL ST.
Marine Parade
YORK ST.
Drop Redoubt
Western Heights
De Bradelei Wharf Shopping Complex
Dover Marina
Grand Shaft
Citadel
Entrance to Western Docks
Hoverspeed Terminal
Prince of Wales Pier
Outer Harbour
Western Docks
Cruise Terminal
Inner Harbour
Admiralty Pier
Breakwater
THE VIADUCT
Shakespeare Tunnel
Old Folkestone Rd.
A20
Mount Road
B2011
DOVER
500 yds
500m
Appears on main map page 175

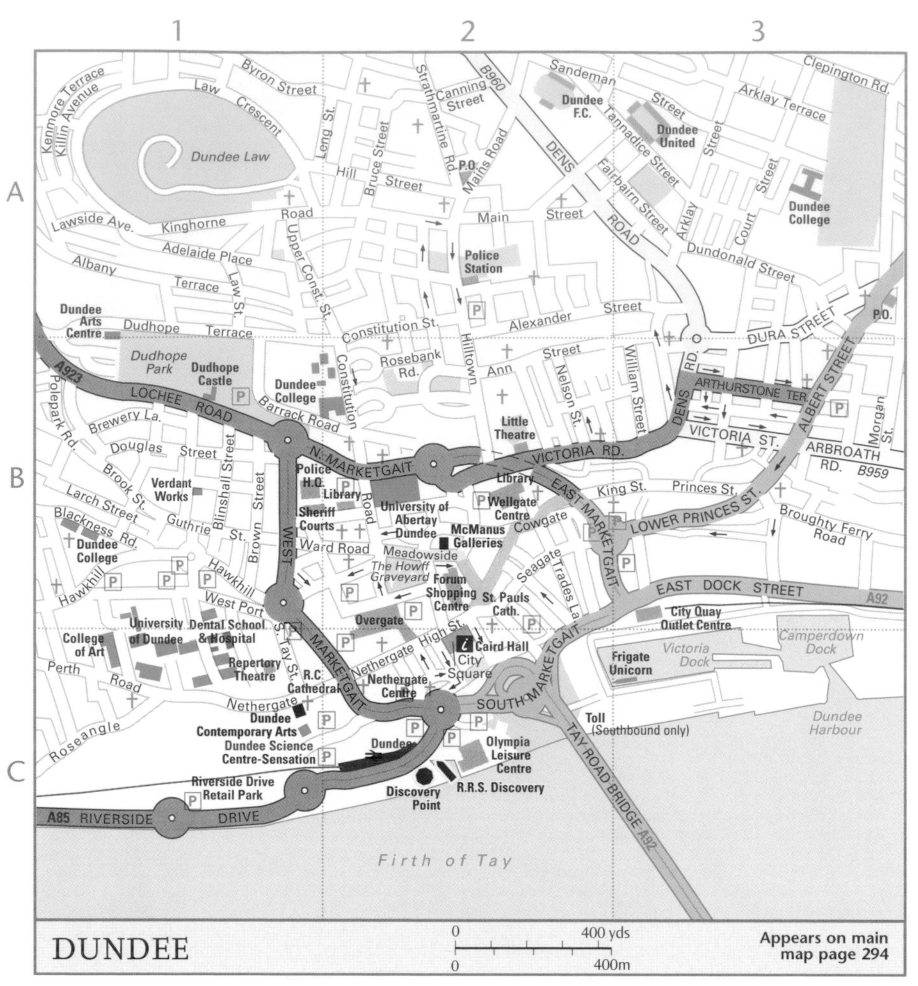
1
2
3
A
B
C
Dundee Law
Byron Street
Law Crescent
Kenmore Terrace
Killin Avenue
Lawside Ave.
Kinghorne Road
Adelaide Place
Albany Terrace
Dundee Arts Centre
Dudhope Terrace
Dudhope Park
Dudhope Castle
Lochee Road
A923
Brewery La.
Douglas Street
Polepark Rd.
Brook St.
Larch Street
Blackness Rd.
Dundee College
Hawkhill
College of Art
Perth Road
Roseangle
University of Dundee
Dental School & Hospital
Repertory Theatre
Verdant Works
Guthrie St.
Blinshall Street
Brown Street
West Port
Police H.Q.
Library
Sheriff Courts
Ward Road
R.C. Cathedral
Nethergate
Dundee Contemporary Arts
Dundee Science Centre-Sensation
Riverside Drive Retail Park
A85 Riverside Drive
Discovery Point
R.R.S. Discovery
Firth of Tay
Strathmartine Rd.
Canning Street
Hill Street
Bruce Street
Long St.
Upper Const. St.
Constitution St.
Constitution Road
Dundee College
Barrack Road
P.O.
Mains Road
Main Street
Police Station
Alexander Street
Rosebank Rd.
Hilltown
Ann Street
Little Theatre
Nelson St.
William Street
N. Marketgait
West Marketgait
University of Abertay Dundee
McManus Galleries
Meadowside
The Howff Graveyard
Forum Shopping Centre
Overgate
St. Pauls Cath.
High St.
Caird Hall
City Square
Nethergate Centre
South Marketgait
Olympia Leisure Centre
Wellgate Centre
Cowgate
Seagate
Trades La.
East Marketgait
Victoria Rd.
King St.
Princes St.
Lower Princes St.
East Dock Street
A92
City Quay Outlet Centre
Frigate Unicorn
Victoria Dock
Camperdown Dock
Dundee Harbour
Toll (Southbound only)
Tay Road Bridge A92
Sandeman Street
Dundee F.C.
Dundee United
Tannadice Street
Dens Road
Fairbairn Street
Arklay Street
Court Street
Dundonald Street
Dura Street
Dens Rd.
Arthurstone Ter.
Victoria St.
Arbroath Rd. B959
Albert Street
Morgan St.
Broughty Ferry Road
Clepington Rd.
Arklay Terrace
Dundee College
P.O.
B960

DUNDEE

0 400 yds
0 400m

Appears on main map page 294

TOURIST INFORMATION CENTRE ☎ 01382 527527
21 CASTLE STREET,
DUNDEE, DD1 3AA

HOSPITAL A & E ☎ 01382 660111
NINEWELLS HOSPITAL, NINEWELLS ROAD,
DUNDEE, DD1 9SY

COUNCIL OFFICE ☎ 01382 434000
CITY CHAMBERS, 21 CITY SQUARE,
DUNDEE, DD1 3BY

Dundee *Scotland* Population: 158,981. Scotland's fourth largest city, commercial and industrial centre and port. Robert the Bruce declared King of the Scots in Dundee in 1309. Sustained severe damage during Civil War and again prior to Jacobite uprising. City recovered in early 19th century and became Britain's main processor of jute. One of largest employers in Dundee today is D.C. Thomson, publisher of The Beano and The Dandy. Many museums and art galleries. Cultural centre, occasionally playing host to overflow from Edinburgh Festival. Episcopal cathedral on site of former castle. Universities. Ship 'Discovery' in which Captain Scott travelled to Antarctic has returned to Victoria dock, where she was built.

LOCAL RADIO:
BBC RADIO SCOTLAND 585, 810, 990 AM / 92.6-94.7 FM;
TAY AM 1161 AM; TAY FM 102.8 FM; WAVE 102 FM

www.angusanddundee.co.uk

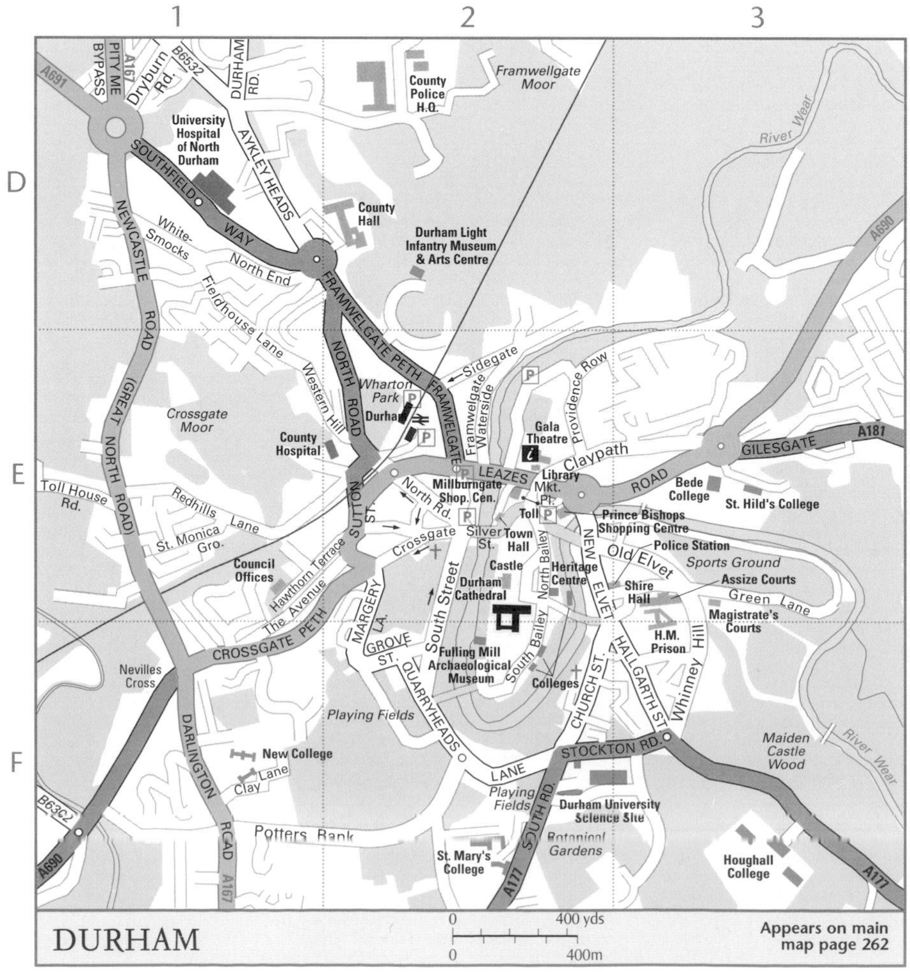

DURHAM

0 400 yds
0 400m

Appears on main map page 262

TOURIST INFORMATION CENTRE ☎ 0191 384 3720
2 MILLENNIUM PLACE, DURHAM,
COUNTY DURHAM, DH1 1WA

HOSPITAL A & E ☎ 0191 333 2333
UNIVERSITY HOSPITAL OF NORTH DURHAM,
NORTH ROAD, DURHAM, DH1 5TW

COUNCIL OFFICE ☎ 0191 386 4411
COUNTY HALL,
DURHAM, DH1 5UB

Durham *North East England* Population: 36,937. Cathedral city on narrow bend in River Wear. Norman-Romanesque cathedral founded in 1093 on site of shrine of St. Cuthbert is World Heritage Site. England's third oldest University founded in 1832. Motte-and-bailey castle dating from 1072 now part of the University. Collection in Fulling Mill Museum of Archaelogy illustrates history of city. Museum of Oriental Art. Light Infantry Museum. Art Gallery. University Botanic Garden S of city.

LOCAL RADIO:
BBC RADIO NEWCASTLE 95.4 FM;
SUN FM 103.4 FM; GALAXY 105-106 105.3, 105.6, 105.8 & 106.4 FM

www.durhamtourism.co.uk

TOURIST INFORMATION CENTRE ☎ 01323 411400
3 CORNFIELD ROAD,
EASTBOURNE, BN21 4QL

HOSPITAL A & E ☎ 01323 417400
EASTBOURNE DISTRICT GENERAL HOSPITAL,
KING'S DRIVE, EASTBOURNE, BN21 2UD

COUNCIL OFFICE ☎ 01323 410000
EASTBOURNE BOROUGH COUNCIL, TOWN HALL,
GROVE ROAD, EASTBOURNE BN21 4UG,

Eastbourne *South East England* Population: 94,793. Town, coastal resort and conference centre. Towner Art Gallery in 18th century manor house shows a contemporary collection of work. South Downs Way begins at Beachy Head, the 536 ft (163m) chalk cliff on the outskirts of the town. Eastbourne hosts an International Folk Festival and international tennis at Devonshire Park.

LOCAL RADIO:
BBC SOUTHERN COUNTIES RADIO 1161 AM / 104.5 FM;
SOVEREIGN RADIO 107.5 FM

www.eastbourne.org

EASTBOURNE

0 200 yds
0 200m

Appears on main map page 160

TOURIST INFORMATION CENTRE ☎ 0131 473 3800
EDINBURGH & SCOTLAND INFORMATION CENTRE,
3 PRINCES STREET, EDINBURGH, EH2 2QP

HOSPITAL A & E ☎ 0131 536 1000
ROYAL INFIRMARY OF EDINBURGH
(LITTLE FRANCE), 51 LITTLE FRANCE CRESCENT,
EDINBURGH, EH16 4SA

COUNCIL OFFICE ☎ 0131 200 2000
COUNCIL HEADQUARTERS, 10 WATERLOO PLACE,
EDINBURGH, EH1 3EG

Edinburgh *Scotland* Population: 401,910. City, capital of Scotland, built on a range of rocky crags and extinct volcanoes, on S side of Firth of Forth. Administrative, financial and legal centre of Scotland. Medieval castle overlooks centre and was one of main seats of Royal court, while Arthur's Seat (largest of the volcanoes) guards eastern approaches. Three universities. Royal Yacht Britannia docked at Leith and is open to public. Important industries include brewing, distilling, food and electronics. Palace of Holyroodhouse is chief royal residence of Scotland. Old Town typified by Gladstone's Land, 17th century six-storey tenement with arcaded front, outside stair and stepped gables. Birthplace of Sir Arthur Conan Doyle. Many galleries and museums including National Gallery of Scotland. Largest arts festival in the world attracting over a million visitors each year.

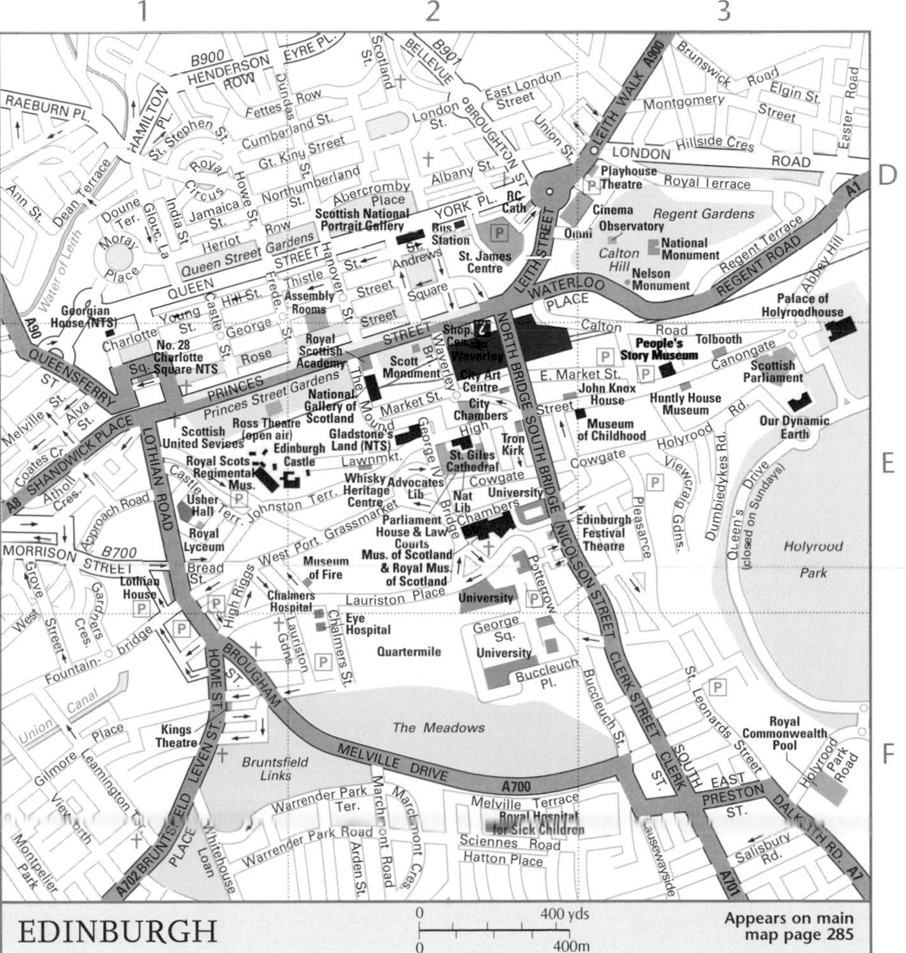

EDINBURGH
0 400 yds
0 400m
Appears on main map page 285
Palace of Holyroodhouse
Scottish Parliament
Our Dynamic Earth
Holyrood Park
Regent Gardens
Calton Hill
Nelson Monument
National Monument
Playhouse Theatre
Scottish National Portrait Gallery
St. James Centre
Scott Monument
National Gallery of Scotland
Edinburgh Castle
Royal Scottish Academy
Princes Street Gardens
Queen Street Gardens
Georgian House (NTS)
No. 28 Charlotte Square NTS
Gladstone's Land (NTS)
St. Giles Cathedral
People's Story Museum
Museum of Childhood
John Knox House
Huntly House Museum
Edinburgh Festival Theatre
Royal Lyceum
Usher Hall
Museum of Fire
Chalmers Hospital
Eye Hospital
Quartermile
University
George Sq. University
The Meadows
Bruntsfield Links
Kings Theatre
Royal Commonwealth Pool
Royal Hospital for Sick Children

LOCAL RADIO:
BBC RADIO SCOTLAND 585, 810, 990 AM / 92.6-94.7 FM;
BEAT 106 105.7 FM; FORTH ONE 97.3, 97.6, 102.2 FM;
FORTH 2 1548 AM; REAL RADIO 101.1, 100.3 FM

www.edinburgh.org

EXETER

0 400 yds
0 400m

Appears on main map page 152

TOURIST INFORMATION CENTRE ☎ 01392 265700
CIVIC CENTRE, PARIS STREET, EXETER,
DEVON, EX1 1JJ

HOSPITAL A & E ☎ 01392 411611
ROYAL DEVON & EXETER HOSPITAL (WONFORD),
BARRACK ROAD, EXETER, EX2 5DW

COUNCIL OFFICE ☎ 01392 277888
CIVIC CENTRE, PARIS STREET,
EXETER, EX1 1JN

Exeter *South West England* Population: 94,717. City, county capital on River Exe. Major administrative, business and financial centre on site of Roman town Isca Dumnoniorum. Cathedral is decorated, with Norman towers and façade with hundreds of stone statues. 15th century guildhall. Modern buildings in centre built after extensive damage from World War II. Beneath the city lie remains of medieval water-supply system built in 14th century to supply fresh water to city centre. Royal Albert Memorial Museum and Art Gallery. Early 16th century mansion of Bowhill, with preserved Great Hall, 2 miles (3km) SW. University. Airport 5 miles (8km) E at Clyst Honiton.

LOCAL RADIO:
BBC RADIO DEVON 990 AM / 95.8 FM;
CLASSIC GOLD 666 AM; GEMINI FM 97 & 103 FM

www.exeter.gov.uk/visiting

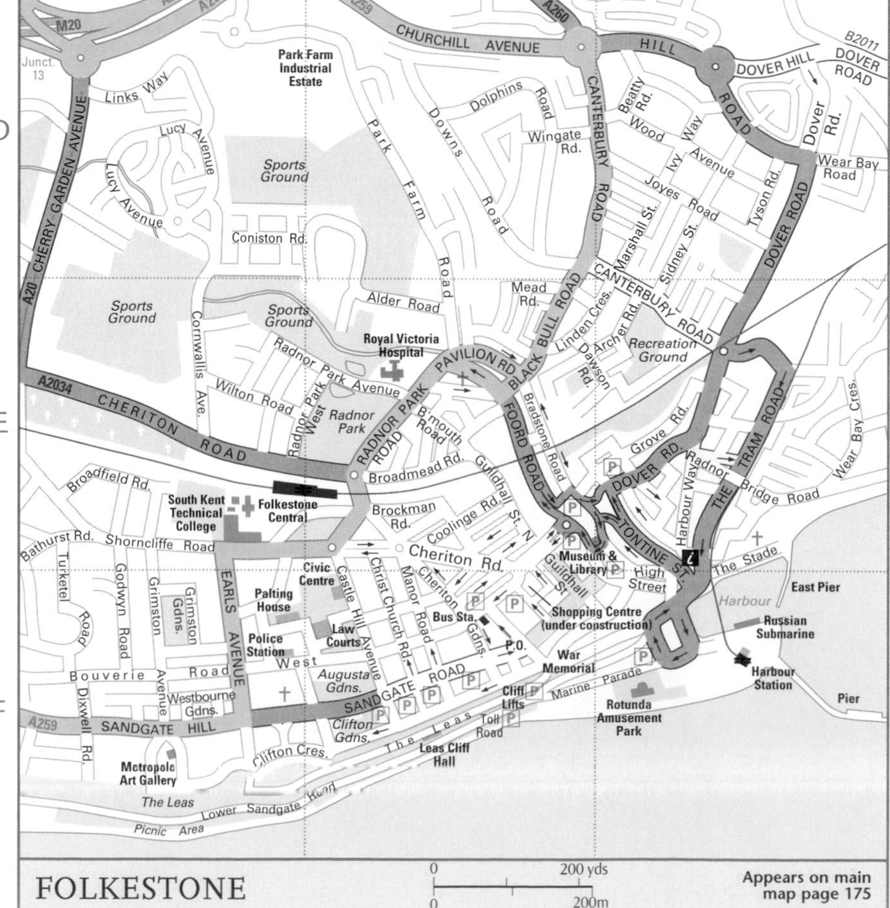
FOLKESTONE
0 200 yds
0 200m
Appears on main map page 175
Churchill Avenue
Cherry Garden Avenue
Park Farm Industrial Estate
Sports Ground
Royal Victoria Hospital
Cheriton Road
Canterbury Road
Dover Road
Folkestone Central
South Kent Technical College
Civic Centre
Sandgate Road
Sandgate Hill
Metropole Art Gallery
The Leas
Leas Cliff Hall
Rotunda Amusement Park
Harbour
East Pier
Russian Submarine
Harbour Station
Pier
Recreation Ground

TOURIST INFORMATION CENTRE ☎ 01303 258594
HARBOUR STREET, FOLKESTONE,
KENT, CT20 1QN

HOSPITAL A & E ☎ 01233 633331
WILLIAM HARVEY HOSPITAL, KENNINGTON RD,
WILLESBOROUGH, ASHFORD, TN24 OLZ

COUNCIL OFFICE ☎ 01303 850388
CIVIC CENTRE, CASTLE HILL AVENUE,
FOLKESTONE, CT20 2QY

Folkestone *South East England* Population: 45,587. Town, Channel port and resort. Russian submarine docked in harbour is open to the public. The Lear marine promenade accessed by Victorian cliff lift. Ornate Victorian hotels. Martello tower on East Cliff. Kent Battle of Britain Museum at Hawkinge airfield 3 miles (5km) N. Channel Tunnel terminal on N side.

LOCAL RADIO:
BBC RADIO KENT 97.6 FM;
INVICTA FM 97 FM

www.discoverfolkestone.co.uk

TOURIST INFORMATION CENTRE ☎ 01452 421188
28 SOUTHGATE STREET, GLOUCESTER,
GLOUCESTERSHIRE, GL1 2DP

HOSPITAL A & E ☎ 08454 222222
GLOUCESTERSHIRE ROYAL HOSPITAL
GREAT WESTERN RD, GLOUCESTER, GL1 3NN

COUNCIL OFFICE ☎ 01452 522232
COUNCIL OFFICES, NORTH WAREHOUSE,
THE DOCKS, GLOUCESTER, GL1 2EP

Gloucester *South West England* Population: 114,003. Industrial city on River Severn, on site of Roman town of Glevum. Norman era saw Gloucester grow in political importance, from here William the Conqueror ordered survey of his Kingdom which resulted in Domesday Book of 1086. City became a religious centre during middle ages. Cathedral built in mixture of Norman and Perpendicular styles, has cloisters and England's largest stained glass window, dating from 14th century. Remains of 15th century - 16th century Franciscan friary, Greyfriars. Historic docks, now largely redeveloped, on Gloucester and Sharpness Canal. Three Choirs Festival held every third year.

LOCAL RADIO:
BBC RADIO GLOUCESTERSHIRE 1413 AM / 104.7 FM;
CLASSIC GOLD 774 AM, SEVERN SOUND FM 102.4 & 103 FM

www.gloucester.gov.uk/tourism

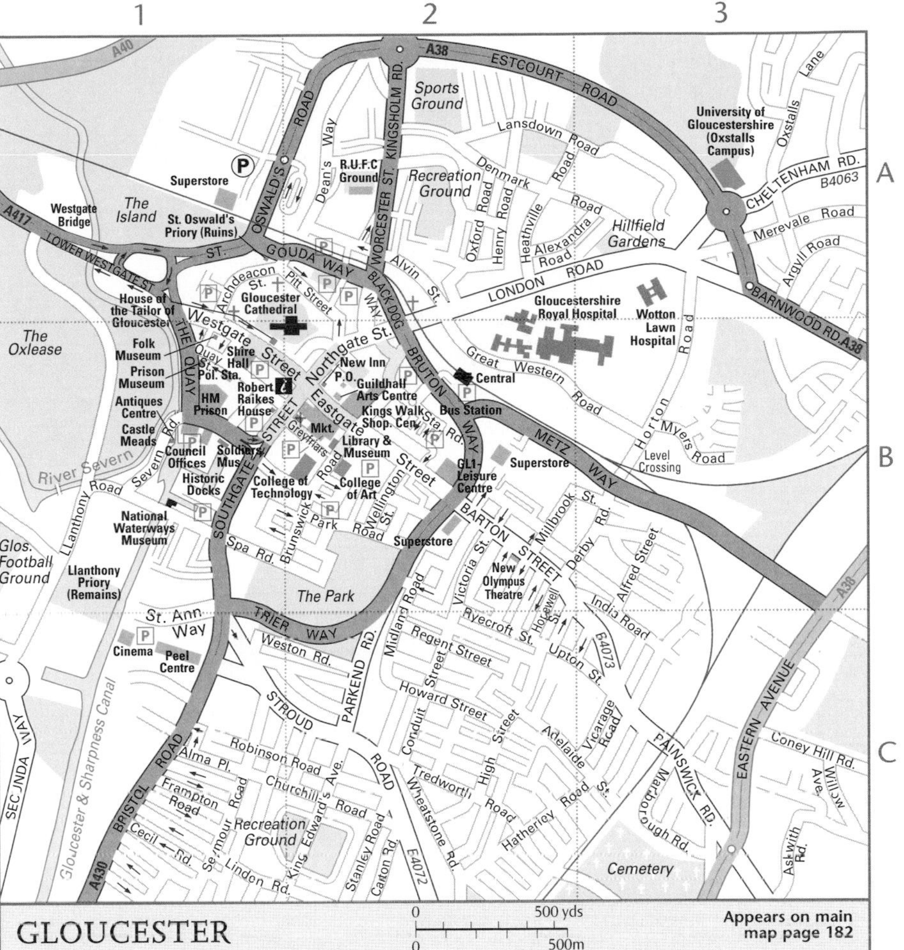
1
2
3
A
B
C
A40
A38
Estcourt Road
Sports Ground
Kingsholm Rd.
Lansdown Road
University of Gloucestershire (Oxstalls Campus)
Oxstalls Lane
Cheltenham Rd.
B4063
Merevale Road
Argyll Road
Barnwood Rd. A38
Superstore
Oswald's Road
Dean's Way
R.U.F.C. Ground
Recreation Ground
Denmark Road
Oxford Road
Henry Road
Heathville Road
Alexandra Road
Hillfield Gardens
London Road
Westgate Bridge
The Island
St. Oswald's Priory (Ruins)
A417
Lower Westgate St.
Gouda Way
Worcester St.
Black Dog Way
Alvin St.
Gloucestershire Royal Hospital
Wotton Lawn Hospital
House of the Tailor of Gloucester
Archdeacon St.
Pitt Street
Gloucester Cathedral
The Oxlease
Folk Museum
Prison Museum
Antiques Centre
Castle Meads
The Quay
Westgate Street
Shire Hall
Pol. Sta.
HM Prison
Robert Raikes House
Northgate St.
New Inn
P.O.
Guildhall Arts Centre
Bruton Way
Central
Great Western Road
Kings Walk Shop. Cen.
Bus Station
Eastgate
Mkt.
Library & Museum
Metz Way
Horton Road
Myers Road
Level Crossing
River Severn
Llanthony Road
Severn Rd.
Council Offices
Historic Docks
Soldiers Mus.
Southgate Street
Greyfriars
College of Technology
College of Art
Street
GL1 Leisure Centre
Superstore
Millbrook St.
Barton Street
Derby Rd.
Alfred Street
National Waterways Museum
Glos. Football Ground
Llanthony Priory (Remains)
Spa Rd.
Brunswick Rd.
Park Road
Wellington St.
Superstore
Victoria St.
New Olympus Theatre
India Road
The Park
St. Ann Way
Trier Way
Cinema
Peel Centre
Weston Rd.
Parkend Rd.
Midland Road
Regent Street
Ryecroft St.
Upton St.
B4073
A38
Eastern Avenue
Stroud Road
Howard Street
Conduit Street
Vicarage Road
Adelaide St.
Painswick Rd.
Coney Hill Rd.
Willow Ave.
Sec Jnda Way
Gloucester & Sharpness Canal
Bristol Road
Alma Pl.
Robinson Road
Churchill Road
Frampton Road
Seymour Road
King Edward's Ave.
Recreation Ground
Stanley Road
Tredworth Road
Wheatstone Rd.
High Street
Hatherley Road
Marlborough Rd.
Cemetery
Askwith Rd.
Cecil Rd.
Linden Rd.
Calton Rd
E4072
A430
0
500 yds
500m
GLOUCESTER
Appears on main map page 182

TOURIST INFORMATION CENTRE ☎ 01483 444333
14 TUNSGATE,
GUILDFORD, GU1 3QT

HOSPITAL A & E ☎ 01483 571122
ROYAL SURREY COUNTY HOSPITAL,
EGERTON ROAD, GUILDFORD, GU2 5XX

COUNCIL OFFICE ☎ 01483 505050
GUILDFORD BOROUGH COUNCIL,
MILLMEAD HOUSE, MILLMEAD,
GUILDFORD, GU2 4BB

Guildford *South East England* Population: 65,998. County town and former weaving centre on River Wey. High Street lined with Tudor buildings, the Guildhall the most impressive. Remains of Norman castle keep built c.1173, on an 11th century motte, used as county gaol for 400 years. Cathedral consecrated in 1961 and built of red brick, the interior is designed in a modern gothic style. University of Surrey. Royal Grammar School noted for its chained library

LOCAL RADIO:
BBC SOUTHERN COUNTIES RADIO 104.6 FM;
THE EAGLE 96.4 FM; COUNTY SOUND 1566 AM

www.guildfordborough.co.uk

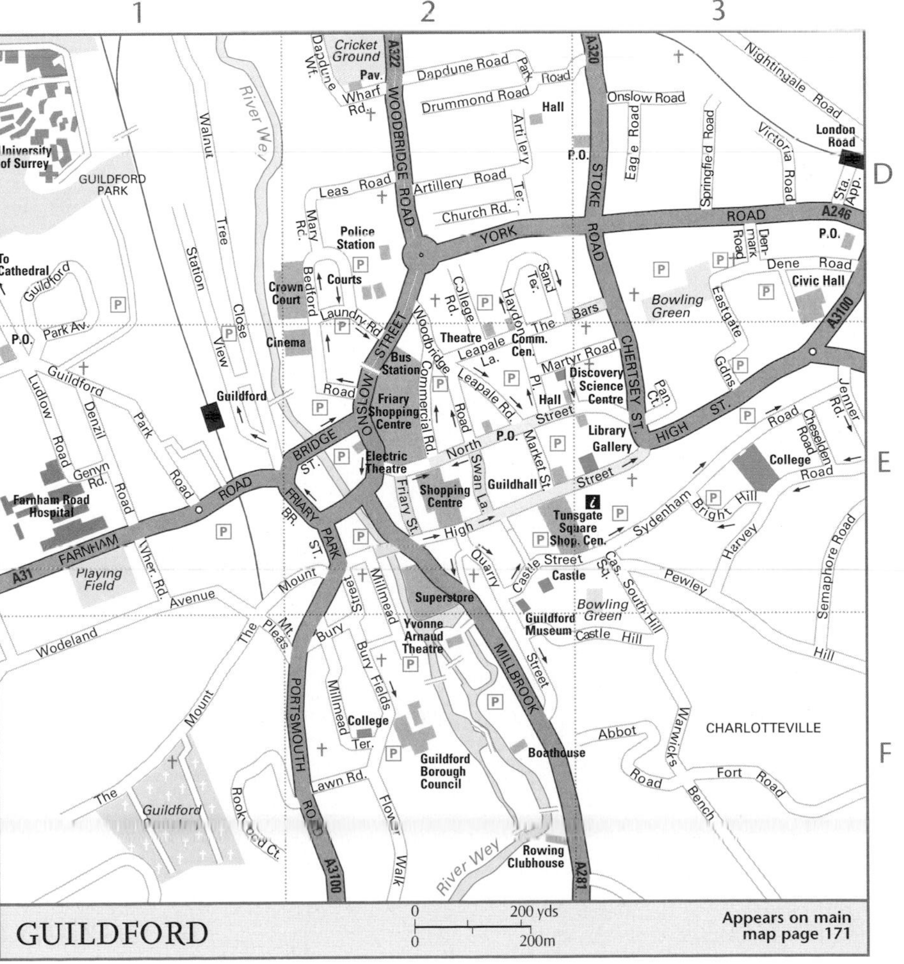
1
2
3
D
E
F
Cricket Ground
Dapdune Wf.
Pav.
Wharf Rd.
A322
A320
Dapdune Road
Park Road
Nightingale Road
Drummond Road
Hall
Onslow Road
University of Surrey
Guildford Park
Walnut Tree Close
River Wey
Artillery Ter.
Eagle Road
Springfield Road
Victoria Road
London Road
P.O.
Station Approach
Leas Road
Artillery Road
Woodbridge Road
Stoke Road
Church Rd.
York Road
A246
Mary Rd.
Police Station
To Cathedral
Guildford Park Av.
Bedford Rd.
Crown Court
Courts
College Rd.
Haydon Pl.
Sand Ter.
Denmark Road
Dene Road
Civic Hall
Bowling Green
Eastgate Gdns
A3100
Station View
Laundry Rd.
Cinema
Theatre
Leapale La.
The Bars
Comm. Cen.
Martyr Road
Discovery Science Centre
Chertsey St.
Pan. Ct.
Jenner Rd.
Ludlow Road
Denzil Road
Guildford
Onslow Street
Bus Station
Commercial Rd.
Leapale Rd.
Friary Shopping Centre
Hall
Street
Library Gallery
High St.
Cheselden Road
College
Bridge St.
Electric Theatre
North Street
P.O.
Market St.
Swan La.
Guildhall
Farnham Road Hospital
Genyn Rd.
Farnham Road
A31
Friary Br.
Friary St.
Shopping Centre
Tunsgate Square Shop. Cen.
Sydenham Road
Bright Hill
Harvey Road
Semaphore Road
Playing Field
Vhler. Rd.
Avenue
Park St.
Mount
High Street
Quarry St.
Castle Street
Castle
South Hill
Pewley
Wodeland Avenue
The Mount
Mt. Pleas.
Bury Street
Millmead
Superstore
Yvonne Arnaud Theatre
Millbrook
Guildford Museum
Bowling Green
Castle Hill
Hill
Bury Fields
Millmead Ter.
College
Guildford Borough Council
Boathouse
Abbot Road
Warwicks Bench
Charlotteville
Fort Road
Portsmouth Road
Lawn Rd.
Guildford Cemetery
Rookwood Ct.
Flower Walk
River Wey
Rowing Clubhouse
A3100
A281
0
200 yds
200m
GUILDFORD
Appears on main map page 171

HARROGATE HASTINGS

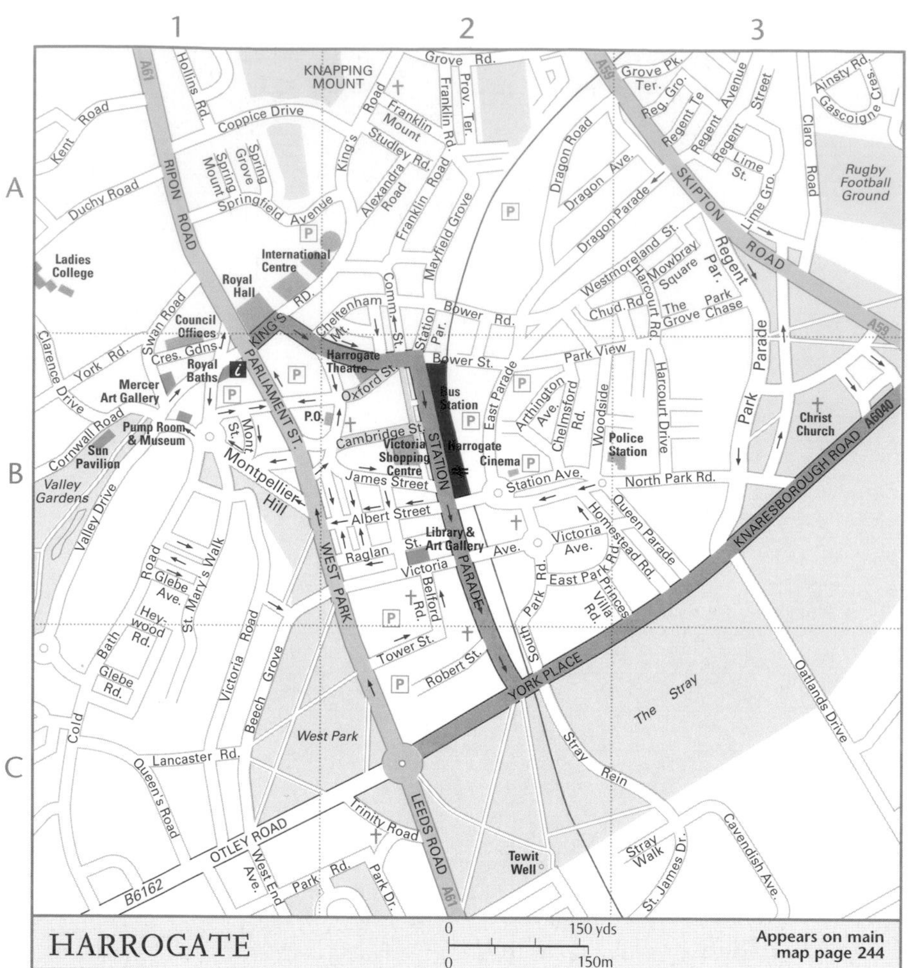

1
2
3
A
B
C
KNAPPING MOUNT
Grove Rd.
Hollins Rd.
Coppice Drive
Kent Road
Duchy Road
RIPON ROAD
Spring Grove
Spring Mount
Springfield Avenue
King's Road
Franklin Mount
Studley Rd.
Alexandra Road
Franklin Road
Franklin Rd.
Prov. Ter.
Mayfield Grove
Dragon Road
Dragon Ave.
Dragon Parade
Grove Pk. Ter.
Reg. Gro.
Regent Te.
Regent Avenue
Regent St.
Lime St.
Lime Gro.
Ainsty Rd.
Gascoigne Cres.
Claro Road
Rugby Football Ground
SKIPTON ROAD
Ladies College
International Centre
Royal Hall
Council Offices
Swan Road
Cres. Gdns.
Royal Baths
Cheltenham Mt.
Comm. St.
Station Par.
Bower Rd.
Bower St.
Westmoreland St.
Mowbray Square
Chud. Rd.
Harcourt Rd.
The Grove
Park Chase
Regent Par.
Park Parade
Park View
Harcourt Drive
A59
Clarence Drive
York Rd.
Mercer Art Gallery
Harrogate Theatre
Oxford St.
Bus Station
East Parade
Arthington Ave.
Chelmsford Rd.
Woodside
Christ Church
Cornwall Road
Pump Room & Museum
Sun Pavilion
Valley Gardens
Valley Drive
PARLIAMENT ST.
Mont. St.
Montpellier Hill
P.O.
Cambridge St.
Victoria Shopping Centre
James Street
STATION PARADE
Harrogate
Cinema
Police Station
Station Ave.
North Park Rd.
KNARESBOROUGH ROAD
A6040
Albert Street
Library & Art Gallery
Raglan St.
Victoria Ave.
Victoria Ave.
Homestead Rd.
Queen Parade
East Park Rd.
Princes Villa Rd.
South Park Rd.
Glebe Road
Glebe Ave.
St. Mary's Walk
Heywood Rd.
Bath Rd.
Glebe Rd.
Victoria Road
Belford Rd.
Tower St.
Robert St.
WEST PARK
YORK PLACE
The Stray
Oatlands Drive
Beech Grove
West Park
Cold Bath Rd.
Lancaster Rd.
Queen's Road
Stray Rein
OTLEY ROAD
B6162
Trinity Road
West End Ave.
Park Rd.
Park Dr.
LEEDS ROAD
A61
Tewit Well
Stray Walk
St. James Dr.
Cavendish Ave.
HARROGATE
0 150 yds
0 150m
Appears on main map page 244

TOURIST INFORMATION CENTRE ☎ 01423 537300
ROYAL BATHS ASSEMBLY ROOMS, CRESCENT RD, HARROGATE, NORTH YORKSHIRE, HG1 2RR

HOSPITAL A & E ☎ 01423 885959
HARROGATE DISTRICT HOSPITAL, LANCASTER PARK ROAD, HARROGATE, HG2 7SX

COUNCIL OFFICE ☎ 01423 500600
COUNCIL OFFICES, CRESCENT GARDENS HARROGATE, HG1 2SG

Harrogate *Yorkshire* Population: 66,178. Spa town and conference centre. Fashionable spa town of 19th century with many distinguished Victorian buildings, extensive gardens and pleasant tree-lined streets. Royal Baths Assembly Rooms (1897) open for Turkish baths. Royal Pump Room (1842) now a museum. The Stray park and gardens are S of town centre. The Valley Gardens to the SW are the venue for band concerts and flower shows. Harlow Carr Botanical Gardens and Museum of Gardening 2 miles (3km) SW. Mother Shipton's cave, reputed home to the 16th century prophetess, near Knaresborough, 4 miles (6km) NW.

LOCAL RADIO:
BBC RADIO YORK 103.7 FM;
STRAY FM 97.2 FM

www.harrogate.gov.uk/tourism

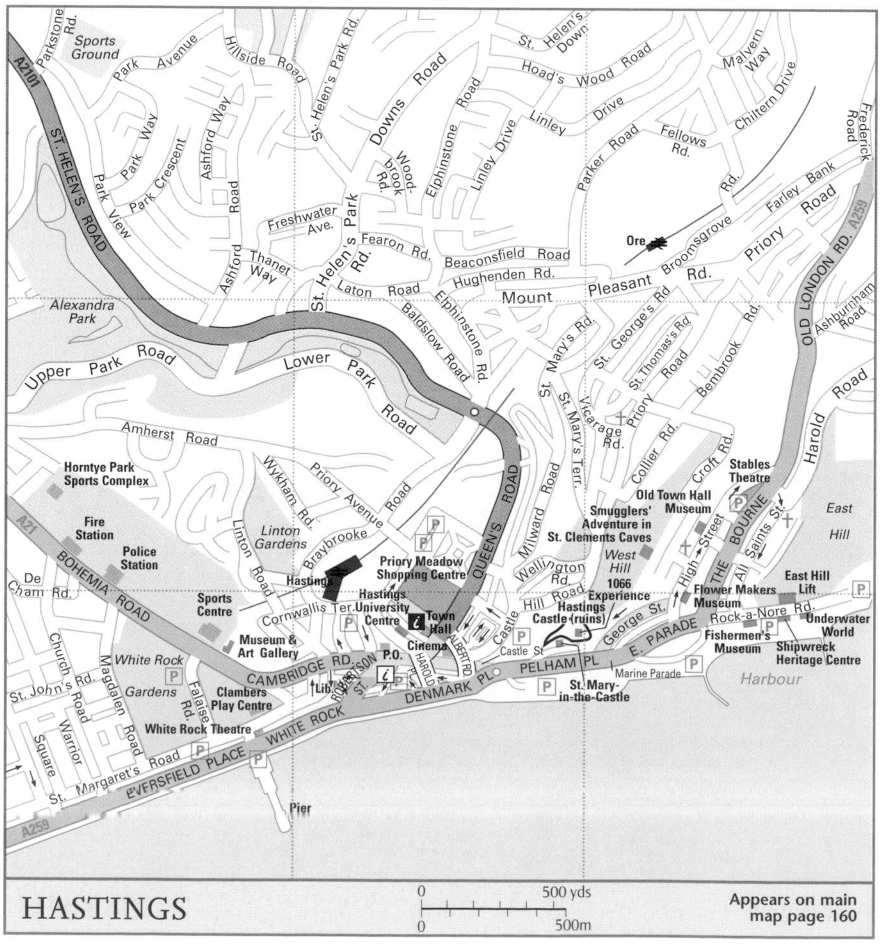

1 2 3

D E F

HASTINGS

0 500 yds
0 500m

Appears on main map page 160

TOURIST INFORMATION CENTRE ☎ 01424 781111
QUEENS SQUARE, PRIORY MEADOW, HASTINGS, TN34 1TL

HOSPITAL A & E ☎ 01424 755255
CONQUEST HOSPITAL, THE RIDGE, ST. LEONARDS-ON-SEA, TN37 7RD

COUNCIL OFFICE ☎ 01424 781066
HASTINGS BOROUGH COUNCIL, TOWN HALL, QUEENS ROAD, HASTINGS, TN34 1QR

Hastings *South East England* Population: 84,139. Town, Cinque port and seaside resort. Remains of Norman castle built 1068-1080 on hill in town centre, houses the 1066 exhibition which relates the history of castle and Norman invasion. Battle of 1066 fought at Battle, 6 miles (9km) NW. Former smugglers caves have a display on smuggling, once a vital part of the towns economy.

LOCAL RADIO:
BBC SOUTHERN COUNTIES RADIO 1161 AM / 104.5 FM;
ARROW FM 107.8 FM

www.visithastings.com

TOURIST INFORMATION CENTRE ☎ 01432 268430
1 KING STREET,
HEREFORD, HR4 9BW

HOSPITAL A & E ☎ 01432 355444
COUNTY HOSPITAL,
STONEBOW ROAD, HEREFORD, HR1 2ER

COUNCIL OFFICE ☎ 01432 260456
COUNCIL OFFICES, THE TOWN HALL,
ST. OWEN STREET, HEREFORD, HR1 2PJ

Hereford *West Midlands* Population: 54,326. County town and cathedral city on River Wye. Many old buildings and museums, including Waterworks museum and City Museum and Art Gallery. 1621 Old House is a museum of local history. Medieval Wye Bridge. Cathedral includes richly ornamented Early English style Lady chapel. New building houses Chained Library of 1500 volumes and 1289 Mappa Mundi Map of the world. Three Choirs Festival every third year. Cider Museum and King Offa Distillery W of city centre depicts history of cider making.

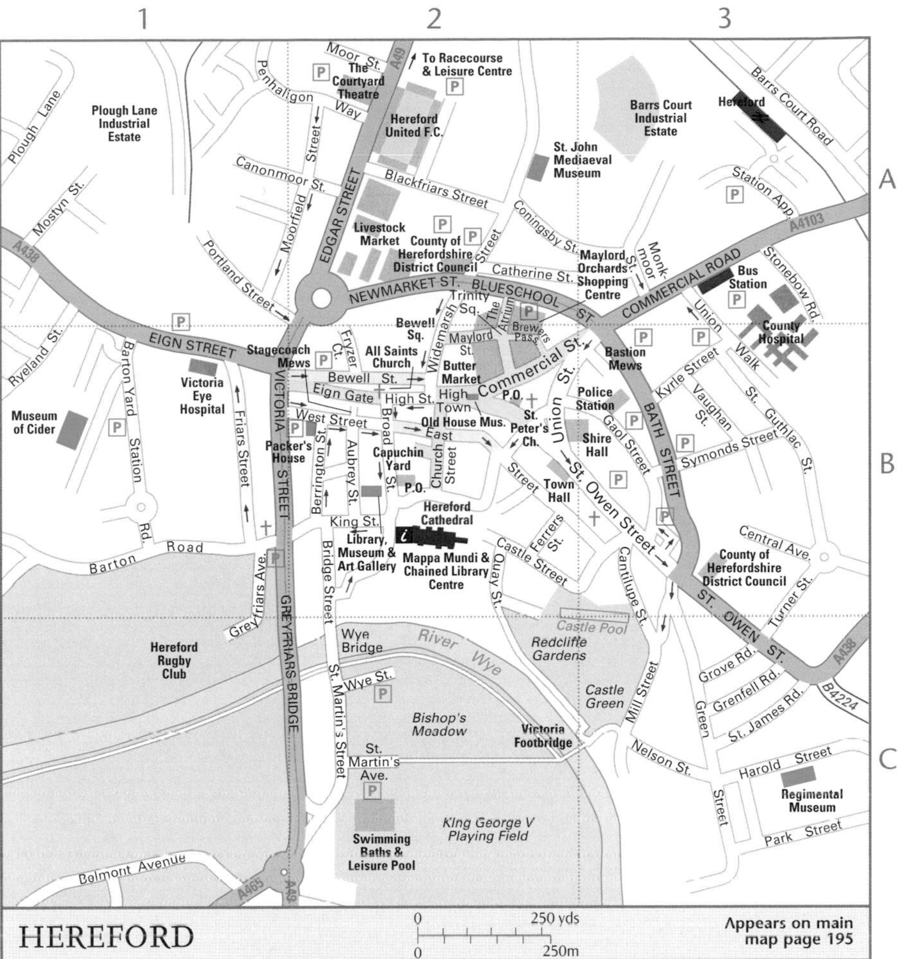
1
2
3
A
B
C
To Racecourse & Leisure Centre
Moor St.
The Courtyard Theatre
Plough Lane Industrial Estate
Barrs Court Industrial Estate
Hereford
Barrs Court Road
Hereford United F.C.
St. John Mediaeval Museum
Blackfriars Street
Canonmoor St.
Station App.
Livestock Market
County of Herefordshire District Council
Maylord Orchards Shopping Centre
Bus Station
COMMERCIAL ROAD
Catherine St.
NEWMARKET ST.
BLUESCHOOL ST.
EDGAR STREET
County Hospital
Stonebow Rd.
EIGN STREET
Stagecoach Mews
All Saints Church
Butter Market
Bastion Mews
Victoria Eye Hospital
Museum of Cider
Eign Gate
High Town
Commercial St.
Police Station
Old House Mus.
St. Peter's Ch.
Shire Hall
Packer's House
Capuchin Yard
Town Hall
Hereford Cathedral
Library, Museum & Art Gallery
Mappa Mundi & Chained Library Centre
St. Owen Street
BATH STREET
County of Herefordshire District Council
Barton Road
GREYFRIARS BRIDGE
VICTORIA STREET
Wye Bridge
River Wye
Castle Pool
Redcliffe Gardens
Castle Green
Hereford Rugby Club
Bishop's Meadow
Victoria Footbridge
St. Martin's Ave.
Harold Street
Regimental Museum
Park Street
King George V Playing Field
Swimming Baths & Leisure Pool
Belmont Avenue
HEREFORD
0
250 yds
250m
Appears on main map page 195

LOCAL RADIO:
BBC RADIO HEREFORD & WORCESTER 1584 AM / 94.7 FM
WYVERN FM 97.6 FM; CLASSIC HITS 954 AM

www.visitherefordshire.co.uk

TOURIST INFORMATION CENTRE ☎ 0845 2255121
CASTLE WYND,
INVERNESS, HIGHLAND, IV2 3BJ

HOSPITAL A & E ☎ 01463 704000
RAIGMORE HOSPITAL, OLD PERTH ROAD,
INVERNESS, IV2 3UJ

COUNCIL OFFICE ☎ 01463 702000
COUNCIL OFFICES, GLENURQUHART ROAD,
INVERNESS, IV3 5NX

Inverness *Scotland* Population: 41,234. Town, at mouth of River Ness at entrance to Beauly Firth. Administrative, commercial and tourist centre. Caledonian Canal passes to W of town. Victorian castle in town centre used as law courts. Inverness Museum and Art Gallery depicts history of Highlands. Balnain House is a museum of Highland music and musical instruments. University of the Highlands and Islands. 1746 Culloden battle site 5 miles (8km) E. Airport at locality of Dalcross, 7 miles (11km) NE of town.

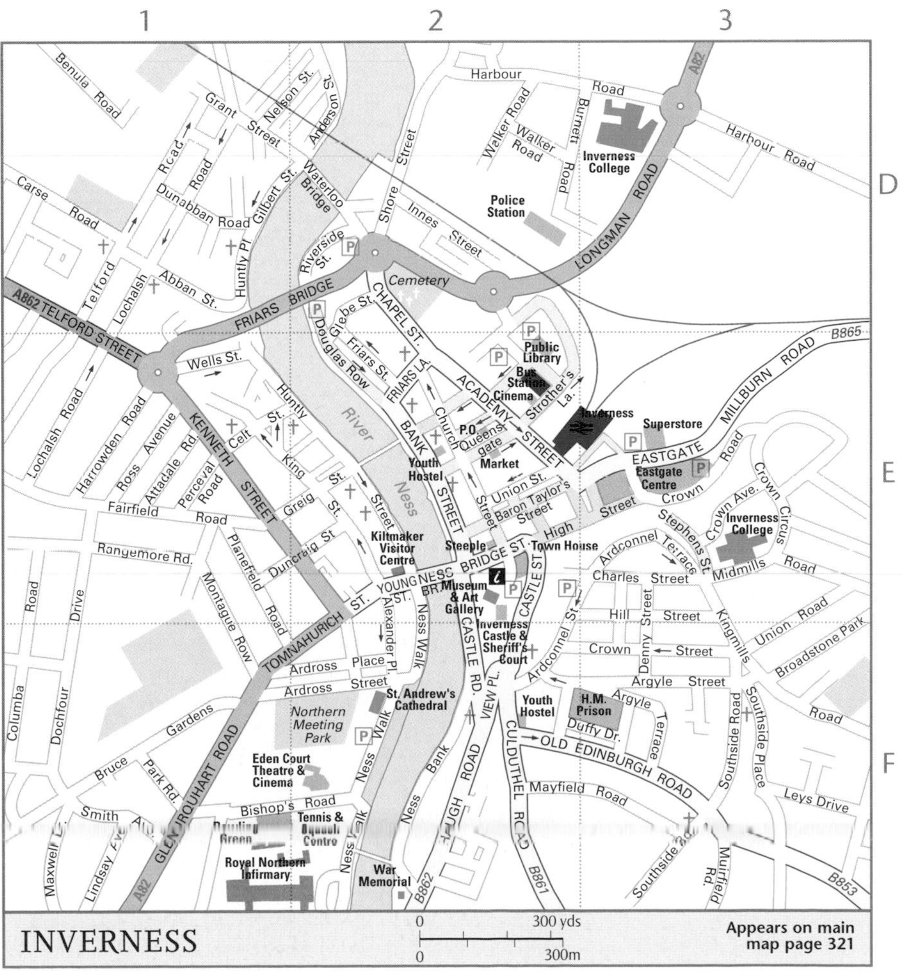
1
2
3
D
E
F
Harbour Road
Inverness College
Police Station
LONGMAN ROAD
Harbour Road
FRIARS BRIDGE
Cemetery
TELFORD STREET
Public Library
Bus Station
Cinema
Inverness
Superstore
MILLBURN ROAD
EASTGATE
Eastgate Centre
ACADEMY STREET
KENNETH STREET
River Ness
Youth Hostel
Market
Inverness College
Kiltmaker Visitor Centre
Steeple
Town House
NESS BRIDGE
Museum & Art Gallery
Inverness Castle & Sheriff's Court
CASTLE ST.
TOMNAHURICH ST.
St. Andrew's Cathedral
Northern Meeting Park
Youth Hostel
H.M. Prison
OLD EDINBURGH ROAD
GLENURQUHART ROAD
Eden Court Theatre & Cinema
Tennis & Squash Centre
Royal Northern Infirmary
War Memorial
CULDUTHEL ROAD
INVERNESS
0
300 yds
300m
Appears on main map page 321

LOCAL RADIO:
BBC RADIO SCOTLAND 585, 810, 990 AM / 92.6-94.7 FM
MORAY FIRTH RADIO (MFR) 1107 AM / 96.6, 96.7, 97.4, 102.5, 102.8 FM

www.visithighlands.com/inverness-loch-ness

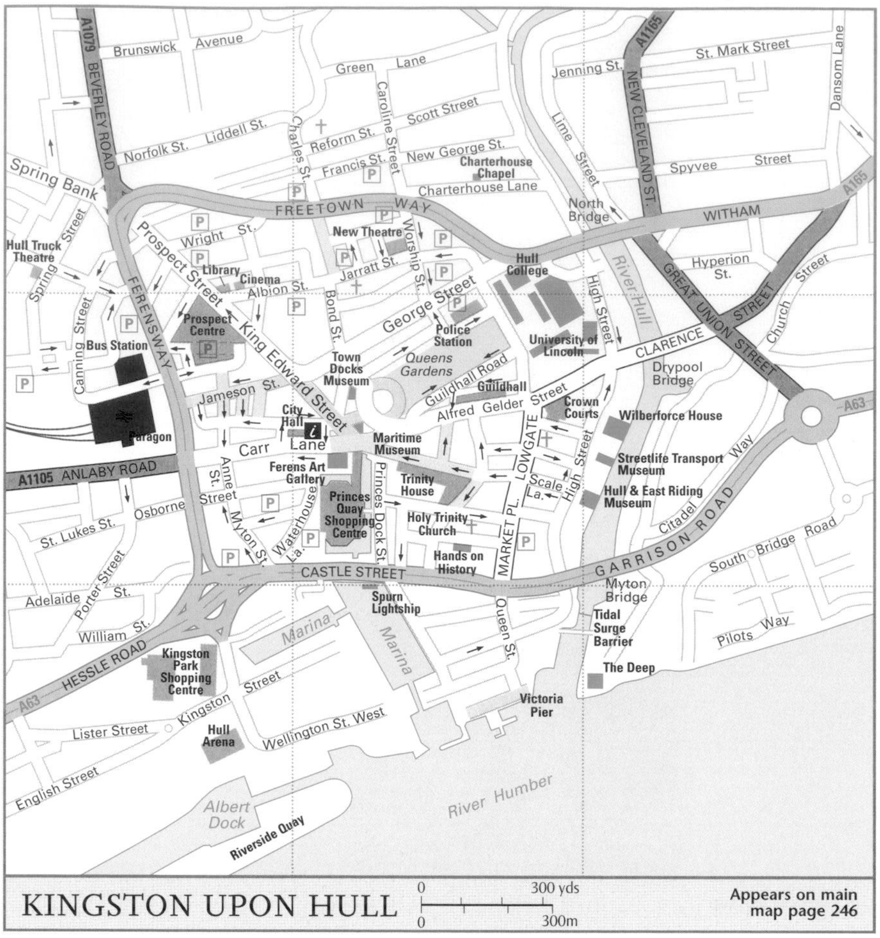

KINGSTON UPON HULL

TOURIST INFORMATION CENTRE ☎ 01482 223559
1 PARAGON STREET,
KINGSTON UPON HULL, HU1 3NA

HOSPITAL A & E ☎ 01482 328541
HULL ROYAL INFIRMARY, ANLABY ROAD,
KINGSTON UPON HULL, HU3 2JZ

COUNCIL OFFICE ☎ 01482 300300
GUILDHALL, ALFRED GELDER STREET,
KINGSTON UPON HULL, HU1 2AA

Kingston upon Hull (Commonly known as Hull.) *Yorkshire* Population: 310,636. City, port at confluence of Rivers Humber and Hull. Much of town destroyed during bombing of World War II; town centre has been rebuilt. Formerly had a thriving fishing industry. Major industry nowadays is frozen food processing. Restored docks, cobble streeted Old Town and modern marina. Universities. Birthplace of William Wilberforce, slavery abolitionist, 1759. Wilberforce Museum covers history of slavery. Streetlife Transport Museum. Town Docks Museum explores city's maritime history. Famous for associations with poets Andrew Marvell, Stevie Smith and Philip Larkin.

KINGSTON UPON HULL — 0–300 yds; 0–300m

Appears on main map page 246

LOCAL RADIO:
BBC RADIO HUMBERSIDE 1485 AM / 95.9 FM;
MAGIC 1161 AM; VIKING FM 96.9 FM

www.hullcc.gov.uk/visithull

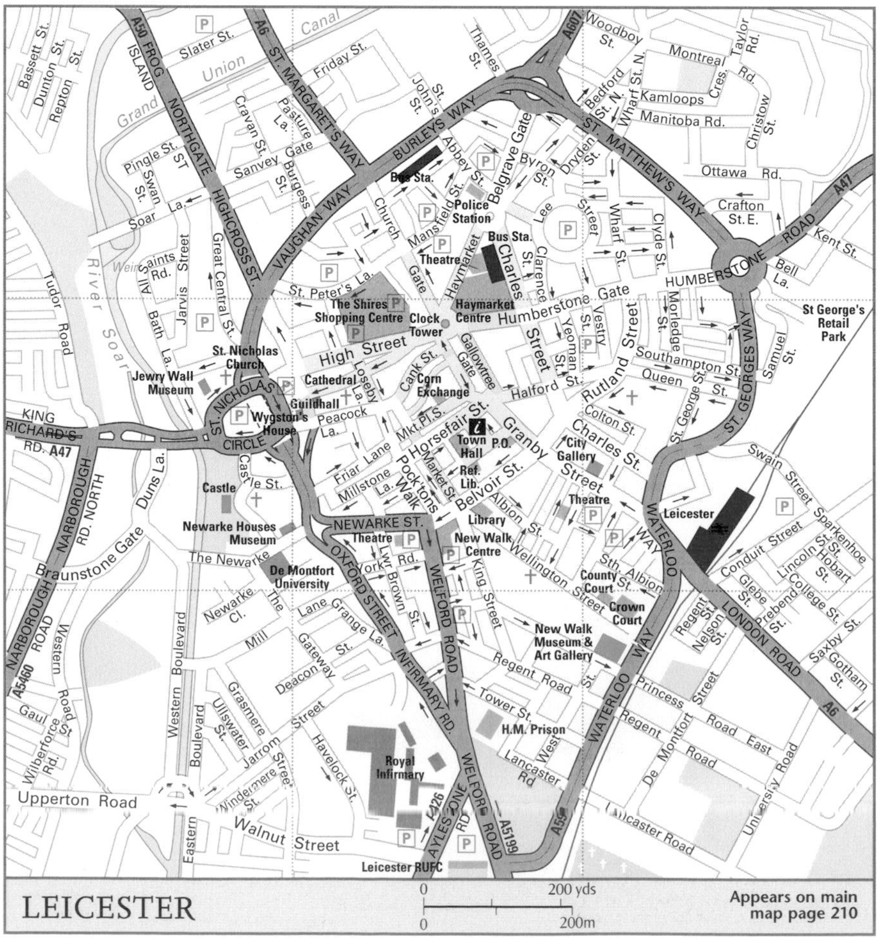

LEICESTER

TOURIST INFORMATION CENTRE ☎ 0906 294 1113
(Premium Rate)
7-9 EVERY STREET, TOWN HALL SQUARE,
LEICESTER, LE1 6AG

HOSPITAL A & E ☎ 0116 254 1414
LEICESTER ROYAL INFIRMARY,
INFIRMARY SQUARE, LEICESTER, LE1 5WW

COUNCIL OFFICE ☎ 0116 252 6480
COUNCIL OFFICES, NEW WALK CENTRE,
WELFORD PLACE, LEICESTER, LE1 6ZG

Leicester *East Midlands* Population: 318,518. City, county town and commercial and industrial centre on River Soar, on site of Roman town of Ratae Coritanorum. Industries include hosiery and footwear, alongside more modern industries. Universities. Many historic remains including Jewry Wall, one of largest surviving sections of Roman wall in the country, Roman baths and a medieval guildhall. Saxon Church of St. Nicholas. 11th century St. Martin's Cathedral. Victorian clock tower. Newarke Houses Museum explores the city's social history. Home to England's second biggest street festival after Notting Hill Carnival. Joseph Merrick, the 'Elephant Man' born and lived here.

LEICESTER — 0–200 yds; 0–200m

Appears on main map page 210

LOCAL RADIO:
BBC RADIO LEICESTER 104.9 FM
SABRAS 1260 AM; LEICESTER SOUND 105.4 FM

www.discoverleicester.co.uk

TOURIST INFORMATION CENTRE ☎ 01522 873213
9 CASTLE HILL, LINCOLN,
LINCOLNSHIRE, LN1 3AA

HOSPITAL A & E ☎ 01522 512512
LINCOLN COUNTY HOSPITAL,
GREETWELL ROAD, LINCOLN, LN2 5QY

COUNCIL OFFICE ☎ 01522 881188
CITY HALL, BEAUMONT FEE,
LINCOLN, LN1 1DD

Lincoln *East Midlands* Population: 80,281. County town and cathedral city on River Witham, on site of Roman town of Lindum. City grew as a result of strategic importance in the wool trade. Many ancient monuments and archaeological features. Castle built by William I. 13th century cathedral, is the third largest in Britain with its three towers on hilltop dominating the skyline. Carvings in the Angel Choir include the stone figure of the Lincoln Imp which is the city's emblem. Lincoln Bishop's Old Palace is medieval building on S side of cathedral. 12th century Jew's House. Museum of Lincolnshire Life. Universities.

LOCAL RADIO:
BBC RADIO LINCOLNSHIRE 1368 AM / 94.9 FM;
LINCS FM 102.2 FM

www.lincoln.gov.uk

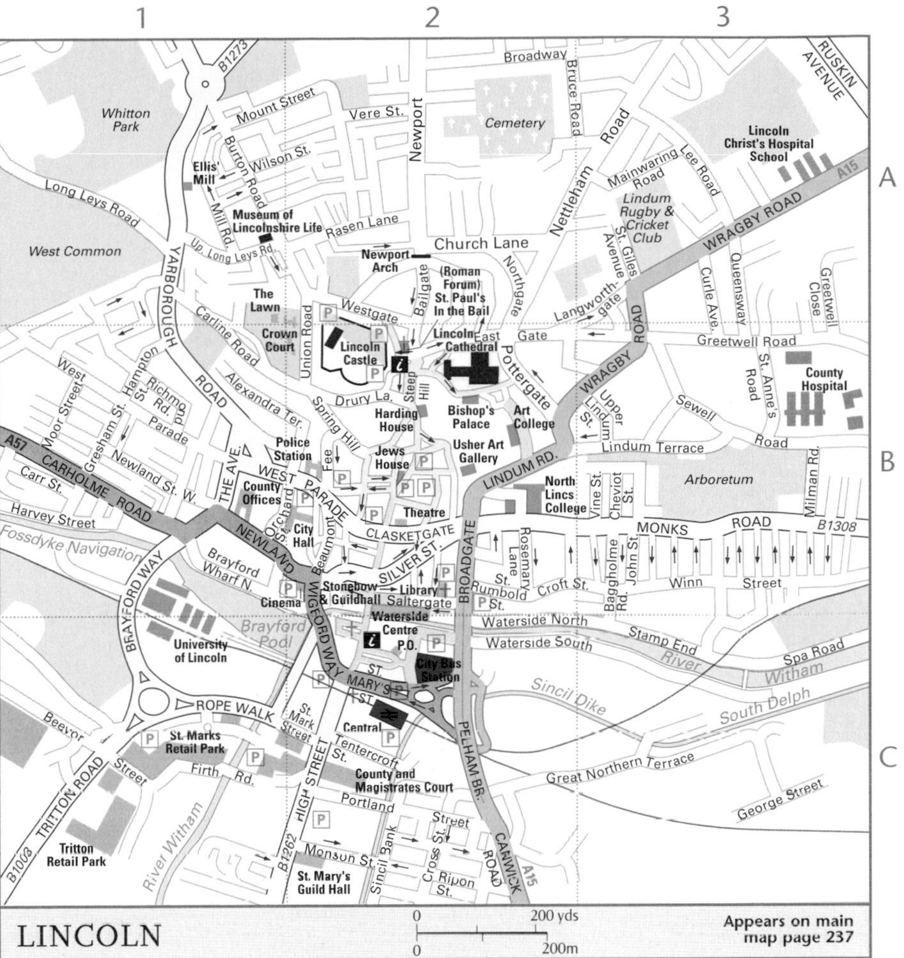

1
2
3
A
B
C
Whitton Park
Mount Street
Vere St.
Broadway
Bruce Road
Cemetery
Ruskin Avenue
Lincoln Christ's Hospital School
Ellis' Mill
Wilson St.
Burton Road
Newport
Long Leys Road
Museum of Lincolnshire Life
Rasen Lane
Church Lane
Nettleham Road
Lindum Rugby & Cricket Club
Wragby Road
West Common
Yarborough Road
Newport Arch
(Roman Forum) St. Paul's In the Bail
Northgate
The Lawn
Westgate
Bailgate
Crown Court
Lincoln Castle
Lincoln Cathedral
East Gate
Langworth-gate
Greetwell Road
County Hospital
Union Road
Carline Road
Alexandra Ter.
Drury La.
Steep Hill
Harding House
Bishop's Palace
Art College
Pottergate
Sewell Road
Lindum Terrace
Arboretum
Jews House
Usher Art Gallery
Police Station
Spring Hill
Lindum Rd.
North Lincs College
Monks Road
B1308
Carholme Road
A57
Carr St.
Harvey Street
Newland
The Ave.
County Offices
West Parade
City Hall
Theatre
Clasketgate
Silver St.
Broadgate
Fossdyke Navigation
Brayford Way
Brayford Wharf N.
Cinema
Stonebow & Guildhall
Library
Saltergate
St. Rumbold St.
Croft St.
Winn Street
Brayford Pool
Wigford Way
Waterside Centre
P.O.
Waterside North
Waterside South
Stamp End
University of Lincoln
City Bus Station
St. Mary's St.
Sincil Dike
River Witham
Spa Road
South Delph
Rope Walk
St. Marks Retail Park
Central
Tentercroft St.
Pelham Br.
Beevor Street
Tritton Road
Firth Rd.
High Street
County and Magistrates Court
Great Northern Terrace
George Street
Portland Street
B1003
Tritton Retail Park
B1262
Monson St.
Cross St.
Ripon St.
Canwick Road
A15
Sincil Bank
St. Mary's Guild Hall
LINCOLN
0 200 yds
0 200m
Appears on main map page 237

TOURIST INFORMATION CENTRE ☎ 01642 358086
99-101 ALBERT ROAD,
MIDDLESBROUGH, TS1 2PA

HOSPITAL A & E ☎ 01642 850850
JAMES COOK UNIVERSITY HOSPITAL,
MARTON ROAD, MIDDLESBROUGH, TS4 3BW

COUNCIL OFFICE ☎ 01642 245432
MUNICIPAL BUILDINGS, PO BOX 99A,
RUSSELL STREET, MIDDLESBROUGH, TS1 2QQ

Middlesbrough *North East England* Population: 147,430. Town, port, with extensive dock area, on S bank of River Tees, forming part of Teesside urban complex. A former iron and steel town, its chief industries now involve oil and petrochemicals. Unusual 1911 transporter bridge over River Tees. University of Teesside. Captian Cook Birthplace Museum in Stewart Park at Marton.

LOCAL RADIO:
BBC RADIO CLEVELAND 95 FM;
MAGIC 1170 AM; TFM 96.6 FM; CENTURY FM 100.7 FM

www.destinationteesvalley.co.uk

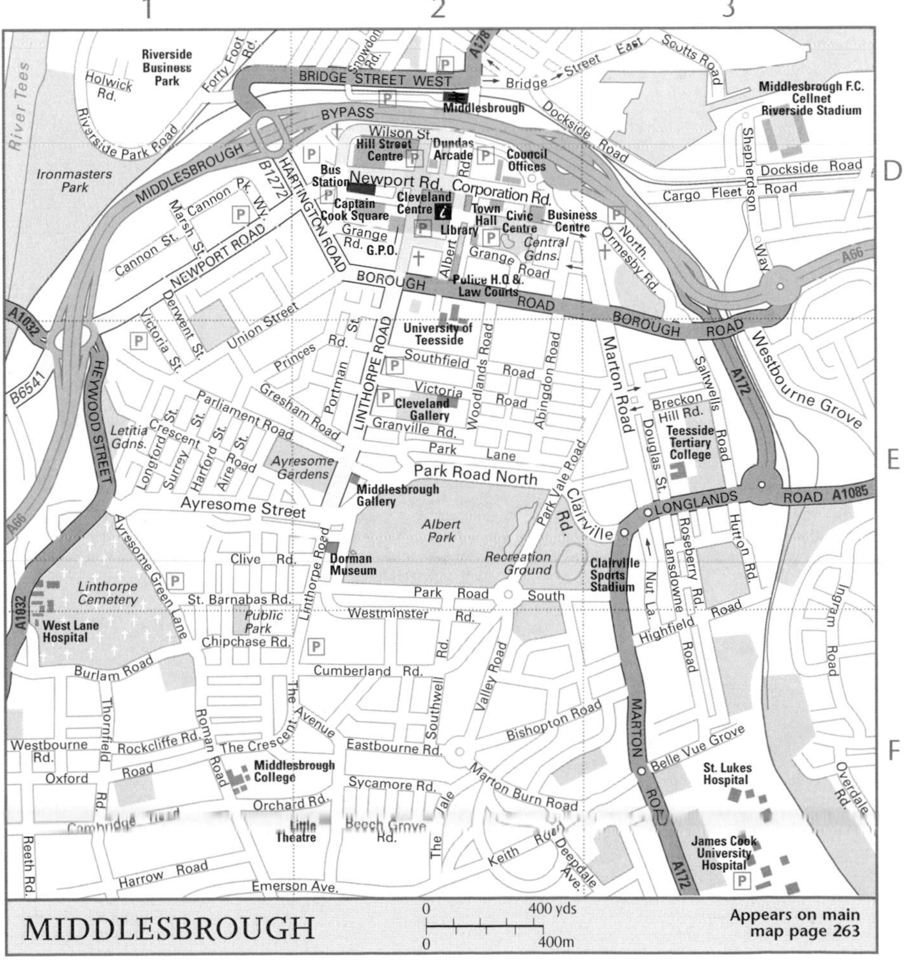

1
2
3
D
E
F
River Tees
Riverside Business Park
Holwick Rd.
Bridge Street West
Bridge Street East
A178
Middlesbrough
Scotts Road
Middlesbrough F.C. Cellnet Riverside Stadium
Riverside Park Road
Bypass
Wilson St.
Hill Street Centre
Dundas Arcade
Council Offices
Dockside Road
Shepherdson Way
Ironmasters Park
Middlesbrough
Bus Station
Newport Rd.
Corporation Rd.
Cargo Fleet Road
Captain Cook Square
Cleveland Centre
Town Hall
Civic Centre
Business Centre
Cannon St.
Newport Road
Marsh St.
Hartington Road
Grange Rd.
G.P.O.
Library
Albert Rd.
Central Gdns.
Grange Road
North Ormesby Rd.
A66
Borough Road
Police H.Q & Law Courts
A1032
Union Street
Victoria St.
Derwent St.
University of Teesside
Southfield Road
Westbourne Grove
B6541
Princes Rd.
Linthorpe Road
Woodlands Road
Abingdon Road
Marton Road
Saltwells Road
A172
Heywood Street
Parliament Road
Victoria Road
Cleveland Gallery
Gresham Road
Portman St.
Granville Rd.
Breckon Hill Rd.
Teesside Tertiary College
Letitia Gdns.
Crescent Road
Park Lane
Aire St.
Ayresome Gardens
Park Road North
Park Vale Road
Middlesbrough Gallery
Ayresome Street
Clairville Rd.
Longlands Road
A1085
Albert Park
A66
Ayresome Green Lane
Clive Rd.
Dorman Museum
Recreation Ground
Clairville Sports Stadium
Linthorpe Cemetery
St. Barnabas Rd.
Park Road South
Roseberry Rd.
Hutton Rd.
West Lane Hospital
Public Park
Westminster Rd.
Highfield Road
Ingram Road
Chipchase Rd.
Burlam Road
Cumberland Rd.
Southwell Rd.
Valley Road
Bishopton Road
Thornfield Rd.
The Avenue
Westbourne Rd.
Rockcliffe Rd.
The Crescent
Eastbourne Rd.
Marton Road
Belle Vue Grove
Oxford Road
Roman Road
Middlesbrough College
Sycamore Rd.
Marton Burn Road
St. Lukes Hospital
Overdale Rd.
Orchard Rd.
Little Theatre
Beech Grove Rd.
The Vale
Keith Rd.
Deepdale Ave.
Reeth Rd.
James Cook University Hospital
Harrow Road
Emerson Ave.
MIDDLESBROUGH
0 400 yds
0 400m
Appears on main map page 263

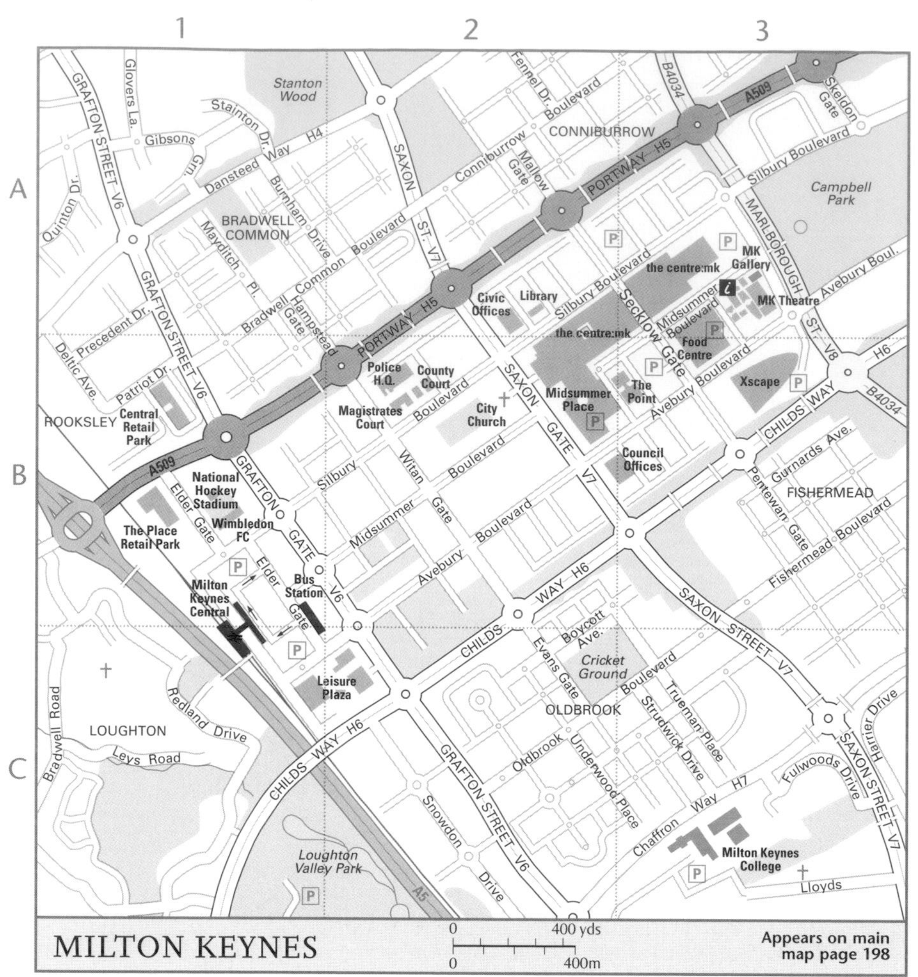
1
2
3
A
B
C
Stanton Wood
CONNIBURROW
Campbell Park
BRADWELL COMMON
PORTWAY H5
Civic Offices
Library
the centre:mk
MK Gallery
MK Theatre
Food Centre
The Point
Xscape
Police H.Q.
County Court
Magistrates Court
City Church
Midsummer Place
Council Offices
ROOKSLEY
Central Retail Park
National Hockey Stadium
Wimbledon FC
The Place Retail Park
FISHERMEAD
Milton Keynes Central
Bus Station
Leisure Plaza
Cricket Ground
OLDBROOK
LOUGHTON
Leys Road
Loughton Valley Park
Milton Keynes College
Lloyds
SAXON STREET V7
GRAFTON STREET V6
CHILDS WAY H6
A509
A5
MILTON KEYNES
0 400 yds
0 400m
Appears on main map page 198

TOURIST INFORMATION CENTRE ☎ 01908 558300
MARGARET POWELL SQUARE,
890 MIDSUMMER BOULEVARD,
MILTON KEYNES, MK9 3QA

HOSPITAL A & E ☎ 01908 660033
MILTON KEYNES GENERAL HOSPITAL,
STANDING WAY, EAGLESTONE,
MILTON KEYNES, MK6 5LD

COUNCIL OFFICE ☎ 01908 691691
CIVIC OFFICES, 1 SAXON GATE EAST,
MILTON KEYNES, MK9 3HQ

Milton Keynes *South East England*
Population: 156,148. New town designated in 1967. Includes Bletchley, Stony Stratford, Wolverton and original village of Milton Keynes. Regional commercial centre and location for many international companies. The centre:mk is one of the longest under-cover shopping areas in Europe. Major open-air concert venue at the National Bowl. MK Theatre and art gallery. Cinema, bowling, climbing wall and Europe's largest indoor snow ski slope at Xscape. The Open University at Walton Hall. Woburn Safari Park 8 miles (13km) SE.

LOCAL RADIO:
BBC THREE COUNTIES RADIO 1161 AM / 104.5 FM;
FM 103 HORIZON 103.3 FM

www.mkweb.co.uk/visitorinfo

NEWCASTLE

0 400 yds
0 400m

Appears on main map page 262

TOURIST INFORMATION CENTRE ☎ 0191 277 8000
132 GRAINGER STREET, NEWCASTLE
UPON TYNE, TYNE & WEAR, NE1 5AF

HOSPITAL A & E ☎ 0191 273 8811
NEWCASTLE GENERAL HOSPITAL, WESTGATE
ROAD, NEWCASTLE UPON TYNE, NE4 6BE

COUNCIL OFFICE ☎ 0191 232 8520
CIVIC CENTRE, BARRAS BRIDGE,
NEWCASTLE UPON TYNE, NE99 1RD

Newcastle upon Tyne *North East England*
Population: 189,150. City, port on River Tyne about 11 miles (17km) upstream from river mouth. The 'new castle' of city's name started in 1080 by Robert Curthose, eldest son of William the Conqueror. 13th century castle gatehouse known as 'Black Gate'. Commercial and industrial centre, previously dependent upon coalmining and shipbuilding. In its heyday, 25 percent of world's shipping built here. Cathedral dates from 14th to 15th century. Bessie Surtees House comprises 16th and 17th century merchants' houses. Tyne Bridge, opened in 1928 and longest of its type at the time. Venerable Bede (AD 672-735) born near Jarrow. Catherine Cookson, writer, also born in Jarrow, Universities. Newcastle International Airport 5m/8km NW.

LOCAL RADIO:
BBC RADIO NEWCASTLE 95.4 FM;
MAGIC 1152 AM; METRO RADIO 97.1 FM; CENTURY FM 101.8 FM

www.visitnewcastlegateshead.com

TOURIST INFORMATION CENTRE ☎ 0870 225 4830
THE FORUM, MILLENNIUM PLAIN,
NORWICH, NR2 1TF

HOSPITAL A & E ☎ 01603 286286
NORFOLK & NORWICH UNIVERSITY HOSPITAL,
COLNEY LANE, NORWICH, NR4 7UZ

COUNCIL OFFICE ☎ 01603 622233
CITY HALL, ST. PETER'S STREET,
NORWICH, NR2 1NH

Norwich *East of England* Population: 171,304. County town and cathedral city at confluence of River Wensum and River Yare. Middle ages saw Norwich become second richest city in country through exporting textiles. Medieval streets and buildings are well preserved. Sections of 14th century flint city wall defences still exist, including Cow Tower. Current chief industries are high technology and computer based. Notable buildings include partly Norman cathedral with second highest spire in Britain, Norman castle with keep (now museum and art gallery), 15th century guildhall, modern city hall, numerous medieval churches. University of East Anglia. Airport 3 miles (5km) N.

LOCAL RADIO:
BBC RADIO NORFOLK 95.1, 104.4 FM;
CLASSIC GOLD AMBER 1152 AM; BROADLAND 102 102.4 FM

www.visitnorwich.co.uk

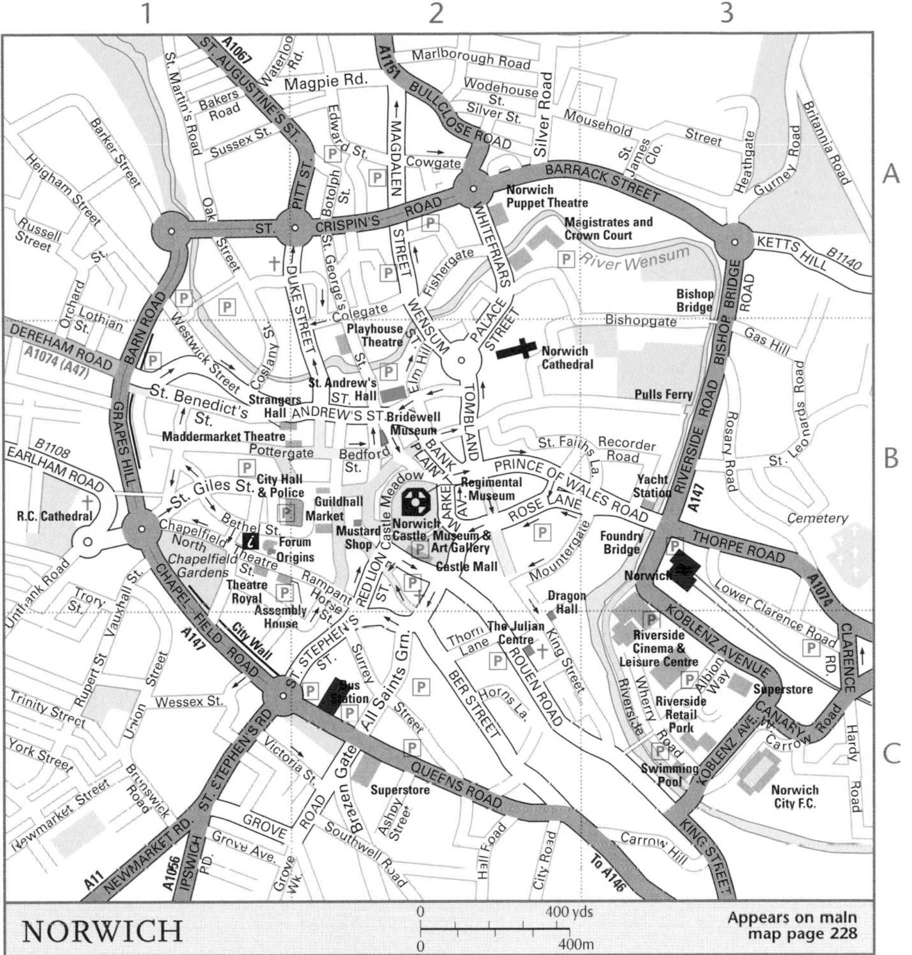

1
2
3
A
B
C
Magpie Rd.
Marlborough Road
BULLCLOSE ROAD
MAGDALEN STREET
Silver Road
Mousehold Street
BARRACK STREET
Norwich Puppet Theatre
Magistrates and Crown Court
River Wensum
KETTS HILL
Bishop Bridge
Bishopgate
Gas Hill
ST. CRISPIN'S ROAD
WHITEFRIARS
PALACE STREET
Norwich Cathedral
Pulls Ferry
BARN ROAD
DEREHAM ROAD
GRAPES HILL
EARLHAM ROAD
R.C. Cathedral
St. Benedict's St.
Maddermarket Theatre
Playhouse Theatre
St. Andrew's Hall
Bridewell Museum
TOMBLAND
PRINCE OF WALES ROAD
Regimental Museum
ROSE LANE
Yacht Station
RIVERSIDE ROAD
St. Giles St.
City Hall & Police
Guildhall
Market
Forum
Origins
Norwich Castle, Museum & Art Gallery
Castle Mall
Theatre Royal
Assembly House
Foundry Bridge
Norwich
THORPE ROAD
Cemetery
Dragon Hall
The Julian Centre
Riverside Cinema & Leisure Centre
Riverside Retail Park
Superstore
KOBLENZ AVENUE
CHAPEL FIELD ROAD
City Wall
Bus Station
ST. STEPHEN'S ROAD
All Saints Grn.
BER STREET
ROUEN ROAD
QUEENS ROAD
Superstore
Swimming Pool
Norwich City F.C.
Carrow Road
KING STREET
NEWMARKET RD.
IPSWICH RD.
Unthank Road
Trinity Street
York Street
Wessex St.
Carrow Hill
To A146
NORWICH
0 400 yds
0 400m
Appears on main map page 228

TOURIST INFORMATION CENTRE ☎ 0115 915 5330
1-4 SMITHY ROW,
NOTTINGHAM, NG1 2BY

HOSPITAL A & E ☎ 0115 924 9924
QUEENS MEDICAL CENTRE, UNIVERSITY HOSP,
DERBY ROAD, NOTTINGHAM, NG7 2UH

COUNCIL OFFICE ☎ 0115 915 5555
THE GUILDHALL, SOUTH SHERWOOD STREET,
NOTTINGHAM, NG1 4BT

Nottingham *East Midlands* Population: 270,222. City, on River Trent. Originally Saxon town built on one of a pair of hills. In 1068, Normans built castle on other hill and both communities traded in valley between. Important commercial, industrial, entertainment and sports centre. Key industries include manufacture of lace, mechanical products, tobacco and pharmaceuticals. 17th century castle, restored 19th century, houses museum and art gallery. Two universities. Repertory theatre.

LOCAL RADIO:
BBC RADIO NOTTINGHAM 103.8 FM; CENTURY FM 106 FM;
CLASSIC GOLD GEM 999 AM; SAGA 101.4, 106.6 FM;
TRENT FM 96.2 FM

www.nottinghamcity.gov.uk/visitors

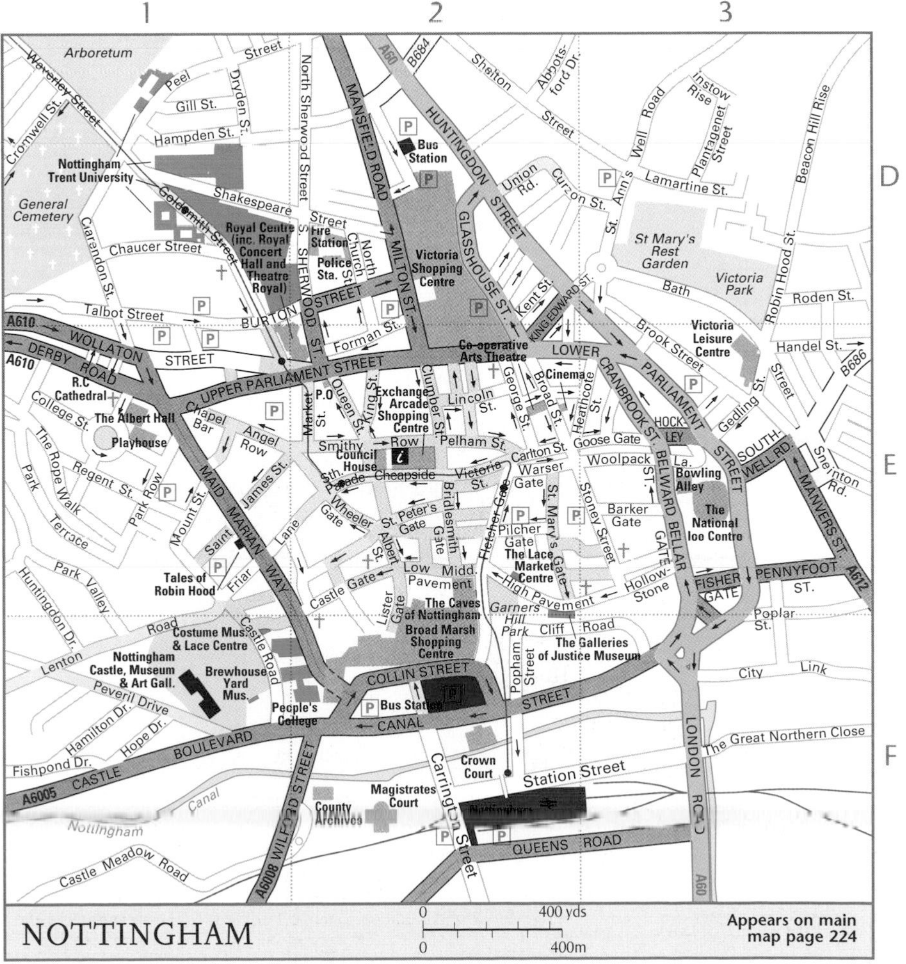

1
2
3
D
E
F
Arboretum
Nottingham Trent University
General Cemetery
Shakespeare Street
Royal Centre (inc. Royal Concert Hall and Theatre Royal)
Fire Station
Police Sta.
MANSFIELD ROAD
HUNTINGDON STREET
Bus Station
Victoria Shopping Centre
St Mary's Rest Garden
Victoria Park
Victoria Leisure Centre
WOLLATON STREET
DERBY ROAD
UPPER PARLIAMENT STREET
Co-operative Arts Theatre
LOWER PARLIAMENT STREET
Cinema
R.C. Cathedral
The Albert Hall
Playhouse
Exchange Arcade Shopping Centre
Council House
Goose Gate
Bowling Alley
The National Ice Centre
MAID MARIAN WAY
Tales of Robin Hood
Lace Market Centre
The Caves of Nottingham
Broad Marsh Shopping Centre
The Galleries of Justice Museum
Costume Mus. & Lace Centre
Nottingham Castle, Museum & Art Gall.
Brewhouse Yard Mus.
People's College
COLLIN STREET
Bus Station
CANAL STREET
Crown Court
Station Street
Magistrates Court
County Archives
QUEENS ROAD
LONDON ROAD
The Great Northern Close
CASTLE BOULEVARD
Castle Meadow Road
Canal
FISHER GATE
PENNYFOOT ST.
MANVERS ST.
NOTTINGHAM
0 400 yds
0 400m
Appears on main map page 224

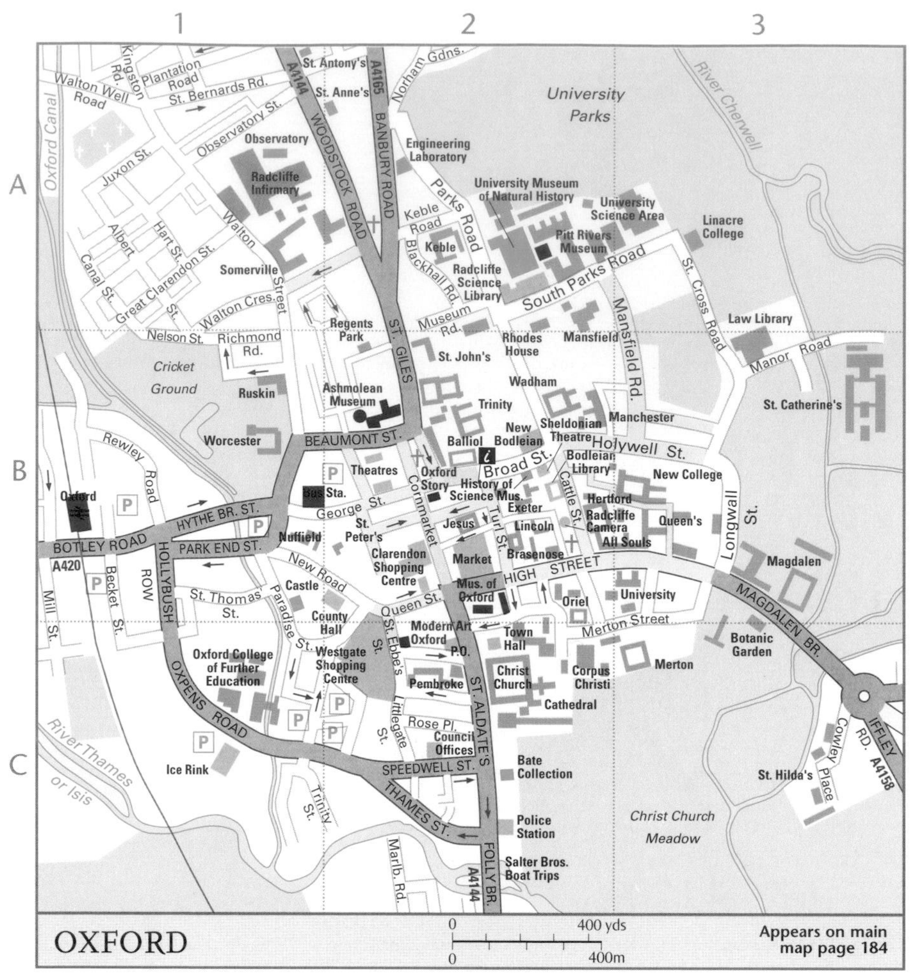
University Parks
River Cherwell
Oxford Canal
Walton Well Road
Kingston Rd
Plantation Road
St. Bernards Rd.
St. Antony's
St. Anne's
Observatory St.
Observatory
Radcliffe Infirmary
Juxon St.
Engineering Laboratory
University Museum of Natural History
University Science Area
Linacre College
Keble Road
Parks Road
Keble
Pitt Rivers Museum
South Parks Road
Radcliffe Science Library
Somerville
Walton Cres.
Great Clarendon St.
Walton St.
Nelson St.
Richmond Rd.
Regents Park
Museum Rd.
Rhodes House
Mansfield
Mansfield Rd.
St. Cross Road
Law Library
Manor Road
St. John's
Cricket Ground
Ruskin
Wadham
Ashmolean Museum
Trinity
St. Catherine's
Manchester
Worcester
BEAUMONT ST.
Balliol
New Bodleian
Sheldonian Theatre
Holywell St.
Bodleian Library
Broad St.
New College
Theatres
Oxford Story
History of Science Mus.
Rewley Road
Bus Sta.
George St.
Exeter
Hertford
Radcliffe Camera
Queen's
Longwall St.
HYTHE BR. ST.
BOTLEY ROAD
PARK END ST.
Nuffield
St. Peter's
Jesus
Lincoln
All Souls
A420
Clarendon Shopping Centre
Market
Brasenose
HIGH STREET
Magdalen
New Road
Castle
Mus. of Oxford
Oriel
University
MAGDALEN BR.
Mill St.
Becket St.
ROW
HOLLYBUSH
St. Thomas St.
Queen St.
Modern Art Oxford
Town Hall
Merton Street
Botanic Garden
County Hall
Paradise St.
Westgate Shopping Centre
P.O.
Oxford College of Further Education
St. Ebbe's
Pembroke
Christ Church
Corpus Christi
Merton
OXPENS ROAD
Cathedral
Rose Pl.
Council Offices
Cowley Place
IFFLEY RD.
A4158
River Thames or Isis
Ice Rink
SPEEDWELL ST.
Bate Collection
St. Hilda's
Trinity St.
THAMES ST.
Police Station
Christ Church Meadow
Marlb. Rd.
FOLLY BR.
A4144
Salter Bros. Boat Trips
ST. ALDATE'S
WOODSTOCK ROAD
BANBURY ROAD
A4165
ST. GILES
Cornmarket
OXFORD
0 400 yds
0 400m
Appears on main map page 184

TOURIST INFORMATION CENTRE ☎ 01865 726871
15-16 BROAD STREET,
OXFORD, OX1 3AS

HOSPITAL A & E ☎ 01865 741166
JOHN RADCLIFFE HOSPITAL, HEADLEY WAY,
HEADINGTON, OXFORD, OX3 9DU

COUNCIL OFFICE ☎ 01865 249811
PO BOX 10,
OXFORD, OX1 1EN

Oxford *South East England* Population: 118,795. City, at confluence of Rivers Thames and Cherwell. Began as Saxon settlement, flourished under Normans when it was chosen as royal residence. University dating from 13th century, recognised as being among best in the world. Many notable buildings create spectacular skyline. Cathedral. Bodleian Library, second largest in UK. Ashmolean museum, oldest public museum in country. Tourist and commercial centre. Ancient St. Giles Fair held every September. Oxford Brookes University at Headington. Airport at Kidlington.

LOCAL RADIO:
BBC RADIO OXFORD 95.2 FM;
FOX FM 102.6 FM; FUSION 107.3 FM

www.visitoxford.org

PERTH

0 300 yds
0 300m

Appears on main map page 293

TOURIST INFORMATION CENTRE ☎ 01738 450600
LOWER CITY MILLS, WEST MILL STREET,
PERTH, PH1 5QP

HOSPITAL A & E ☎ 01738 623311
PERTH ROYAL INFIRMARY,
TAYMOUNT TERRACE, PERTH, PH1 1NX

COUNCIL OFFICE ☎ 01738 475000
PERTH & KINROSS COUNCIL,
2 HIGH STREET, PERTH, PH1 5PH

Perth *Scotland* Population: 41,453. Ancient cathedral city (Royal Charter granted 1210) on River Tay. Once capital of Medieval Scotland. Centre of livestock trade. Previously cotton manufacturing centre; now important industries include whisky distilling. St. John's Kirk founded 1126. 15th century Balhousie Castle houses regimental headquarters and Museum of the Black Watch. Art Gallery and Museum. 16th century Fair Maid's House. Gothic mansion Scone Palace 2 miles (3km) N contains collections of furniture, needlework and porcelain with site of Coronation Stone of Destiny in its grounds. Airfield (Scone) to NE.

LOCAL RADIO:
BBC RADIO SCOTLAND 810 AM / 92.4-94.7 FM;
TAY AM1584, TAY FM 96.4 FM

www.perthshire.co.uk

TOURIST INFORMATION CENTRE ☎ 01752 264849
ISLAND HOUSE, 9 THE BARBICAN,
PLYMOUTH, DEVON, PL1 2LS

HOSPITAL A & E ☎ 01752 777111
DERRIFORD HOSPITAL, DERRIFORD ROAD,
CROWNHILL, PLYMOUTH, PL6 8DH

COUNCIL OFFICE ☎ 01752 668000
CIVIC CENTRE, ARMADA WAY,
PLYMOUTH, PL1 2EW

Plymouth *South West England* Population: 245,295. Largest city in SW England. Port and naval base. Regional shopping centre. City centre rebuilt after bombing in World War II. Has strong commercial and naval tradition. In 1588 Sir Francis Drake sailed from Plymouth to defeat Spanish Armada. Captain Cook's voyages to Australia, South Seas and Antarctica all departed from here. University. Plymouth City Airport to N of city.

LOCAL RADIO:
BBC RADIO DEVON 103.4 FM;
CLASSIC GOLD 1152 AM; PLYMOUTH SOUND 97 FM

www.visitplymouth.co.uk

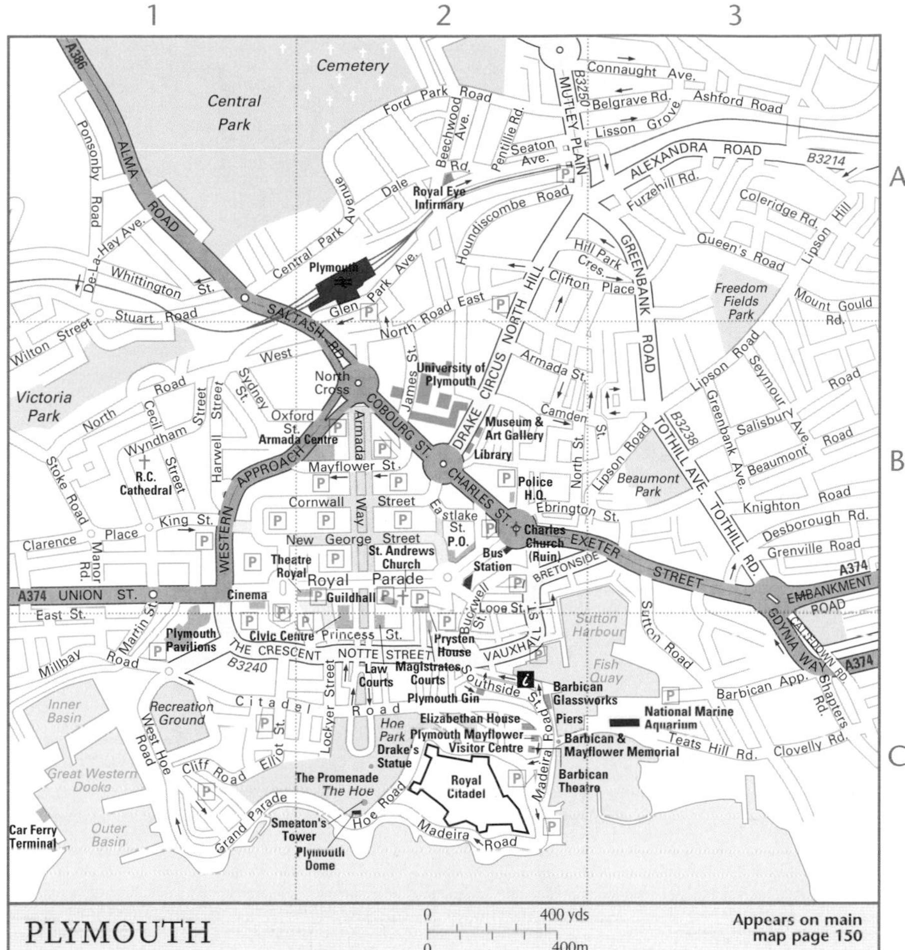
PLYMOUTH
Appears on main map page 150
400 yds
400m
Cemetery
Central Park
Victoria Park
Freedom Fields Park
Beaumont Park
Sutton Harbour
Royal Citadel
The Promenade
The Hoe
Smeaton's Tower
Plymouth Dome
Car Ferry Terminal
Great Western Docks
Outer Basin
Inner Basin
Millbay
Recreation Ground
National Marine Aquarium
Barbican Theatre
Theatre Royal
Civic Centre
Guildhall
Museum & Art Gallery
University of Plymouth
Royal Eye Infirmary
R.C. Cathedral
Charles Church (Ruin)
Bus Station
Police H.Q.
Armada Centre
Plymouth Pavilions
Law Courts
Magistrates Courts
Plymouth Gin
Elizabethan House
Plymouth Mayflower Visitor Centre
Barbican Glassworks
Barbican & Mayflower Memorial
Drake's Statue
Prysten House
St. Andrews Church
Library
Cinema

TOURIST INFORMATION CENTRE ☎ 023 9282 6722
THE HARD,
PORTSMOUTH, PO1 3QJ

HOSPITAL A & E ☎ 023 9228 6000
QUEEN ALEXANDRA HOSPITAL, SOUTHWICK
HILL ROAD, COSHAM, PORTSMOUTH, PO6 3LY

COUNCIL OFFICE ☎ 023 9283 4092
CIVIC OFFICES, GUILDHALL SQUARE,
PORTSMOUTH, PO1 2AL

Portsmouth *South East England* Population: 174,690. City, port and naval base (Portsmouth Harbour, on W side of city), extending from S end of Portsea Island to S slopes of Ports Down. Various industries, including tourism, financial services and manufacturing. Partly bombed in World War II and now rebuilt; however, some 18th century buildings remain. Boat and hovercraft ferries to Isle of Wight. University. Two cathedrals. Nelson's ship, HMS Victory, in harbour, alongside which are remains of Henry VIII's flagship, Mary Rose, which sank in 1545. King James's Gate and Landport Gate were part of 17th century defences, and Fort Cumberland is 18th century coastal defence at Eastney. Royal Garrison Church was 16th century chapel prior to Dissolution. Museums, many with nautical theme.

LOCAL RADIO:
BBC RADIO SOLENT 96.1 FM;
CAPITAL GOLD 1170 AM; OCEAN FM 97.5 FM; THE QUAY 107.4 FM;
WAVE 105.2 FM

www.visitportsmouth.co.uk

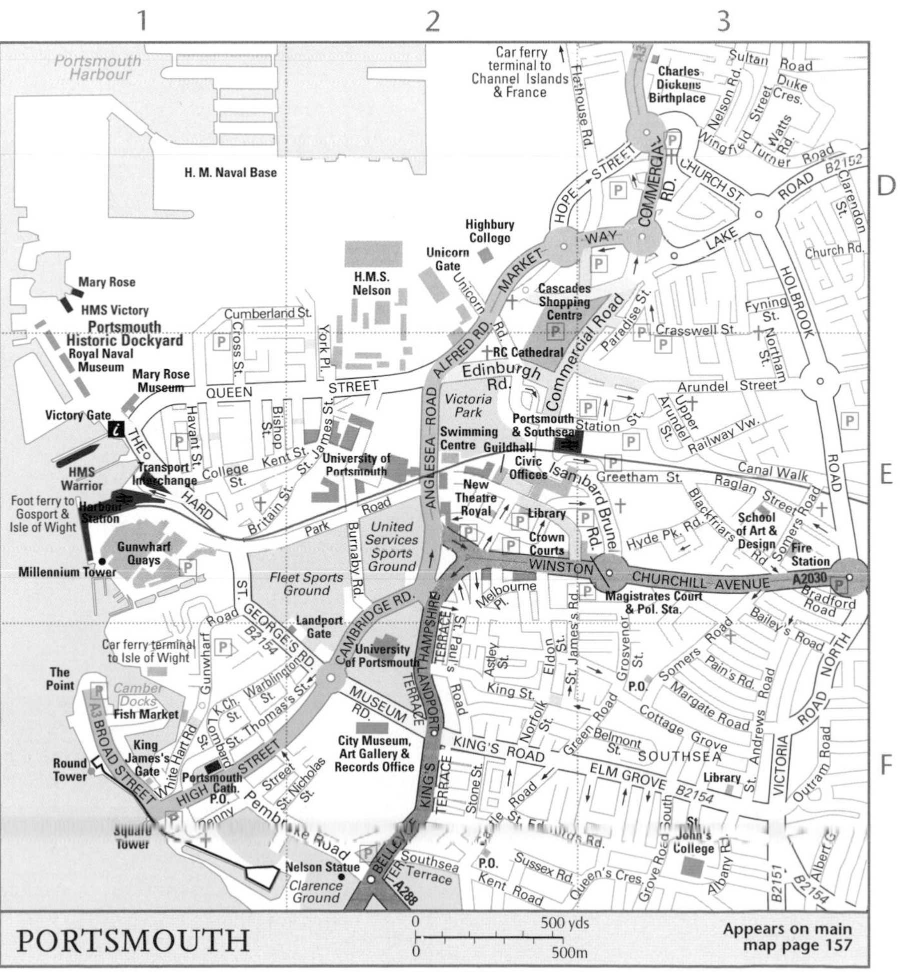
PORTSMOUTH
Appears on main map page 157
500 yds
500m
Portsmouth Harbour
H. M. Naval Base
Car ferry terminal to Channel Islands & France
Charles Dickens Birthplace
Highbury College
Unicorn Gate
H.M.S. Nelson
Mary Rose
HMS Victory
Portsmouth Historic Dockyard
Royal Naval Museum
Mary Rose Museum
Victory Gate
HMS Warrior
Foot ferry to Gosport & Isle of Wight
Harbour Station
Transport Interchange
Gunwharf Quays
Millennium Tower
Cascades Shopping Centre
RC Cathedral
Victoria Park
Swimming Centre
Portsmouth & Southsea Station
Guildhall
Civic Offices
University of Portsmouth
New Theatre Royal
Library
Crown Courts
United Services Sports Ground
Fleet Sports Ground
Landport Gate
Magistrates Court & Pol. Sta.
School of Art & Design
Fire Station
Car ferry terminal to Isle of Wight
The Point
Camber Docks
Fish Market
King James's Gate
Round Tower
Portsmouth Cath.
Square Tower
City Museum, Art Gallery & Records Office
Nelson Statue
Clarence Ground
St. John's College
Library
SOUTHSEA

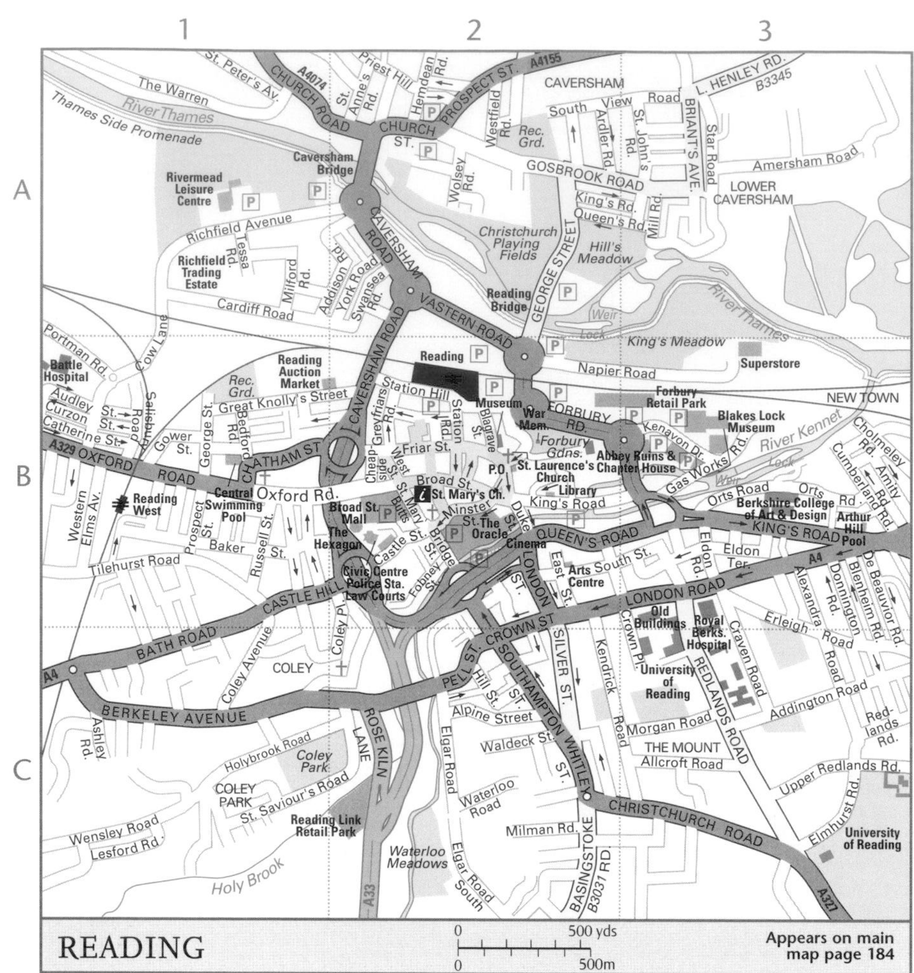

CAVERSHAM
LOWER CAVERSHAM
Caversham Bridge
Reading Bridge
River Thames
Thames Side Promenade
Rivermead Leisure Centre
Richfield Trading Estate
Christchurch Playing Fields
Hill's Meadow
King's Meadow
Superstore
Forbury Retail Park
Blakes Lock Museum
Battle Hospital
Reading Auction Market
Museum
Forbury Gdns.
Abbey Ruins & Chapter House
St. Laurence's Church
Library
St. Mary's Ch.
The Oracle
Cinema
Broad St. Mall
The Hexagon
Civic Centre
Police Sta.
Law Courts
Central Swimming Pool
Reading West
Berkshire College of Art & Design
Arthur Hill Pool
Arts Centre
Old Buildings
Royal Berks. Hospital
University of Reading
COLEY
Coley Park
COLEY PARK
Reading Link Retail Park
Waterloo Meadows
Holy Brook
THE MOUNT
NEW TOWN
OXFORD ROAD
CASTLE HILL
BATH ROAD
BERKELEY AVENUE
LONDON ROAD
KING'S ROAD
QUEEN'S ROAD
CHRISTCHURCH ROAD
REDLANDS ROAD
ROSE KILN LANE
BASINGSTOKE RD.
VASTERN ROAD
CAVERSHAM ROAD

READING

0 500 yds 0 500m

Appears on main map page 184

TOURIST INFORMATION CENTRE ☎ 0118 956 6226
CHURCH HOUSE, CHAIN STREET,
READING, RG1 2HX

HOSPITAL A & E ☎ 0118 987 5111
ROYAL BERKSHIRE HOSPITAL, LONDON ROAD,
READING, RG1 5AN

COUNCIL OFFICE ☎ 0118 939 0900
CIVIC CENTRE,
READING, RG1 7TD

Reading *South East England* Population: 213,474. County and industrial town and railway centre on River Thames. During Victorian times Reading was an important manufacturing town, particularly for biscuit-making and brewing. University. Remains of Norman abbey, founded by Henry I who lies buried there. Currently major centre for information technology.

LOCAL RADIO:
BBC RADIO BERKSHIRE 104.4 FM;
CLASSIC GOLD 1431/1485 AM; 2-TEN FM 97 FM; READING 107 FM

www.readingtourism.org.uk

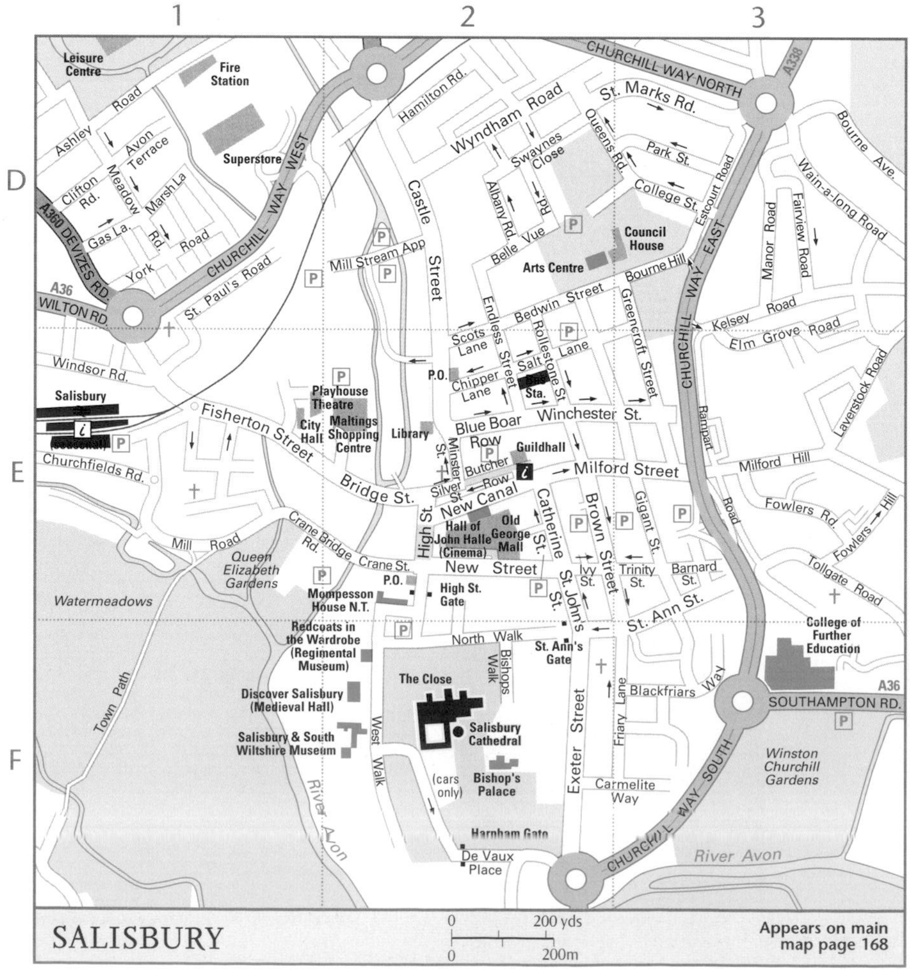

SALISBURY

0 200 yds 0 200m

Appears on main map page 168

TOURIST INFORMATION CENTRE ☎ 01722 334956
FISH ROW,
SALISBURY, SP1 1EJ

HOSPITAL A & E ☎ 01722 336262
SALISBURY DISTRICT HOSPITAL, ODSTOCK ROAD,
SALISBURY, SP2 8BJ

COUNCIL OFFICE ☎ 01722 336272
THE COUNCIL HOUSE, BOURNE HILL,
SALISBURY, SP1 3UZ

Salisbury (Former and official name New Sarum) *South East England* Population: 39,268. Cathedral city at confluence of Rivers Avon and Nadder. Shopping centre and market town, with buildings ranging from medieval to Victorian; several medieval churches. Cathedral, in Early English style, built between 1220 and 1260, has the tallest spire in England at 123 metres (404ft).

LOCAL RADIO:
BBC WILTSHIRE SOUND 1368 AM / 103.5 FM;
SPIRE FM 102 FM

www.visitsalisbury.com

TOURIST INFORMATION CENTRE ☎ 0114 221 1900
1 TUDOR SQUARE,
SHEFFIELD, S1 2LH

HOSPITAL A & E ☎ 0114 243 4343
NORTHERN GENERAL HOSPITAL, HERRIES ROAD,
SHEFFIELD, S5 7AU

COUNCIL OFFICE ☎ 0114 272 6444
FIRST POINT, 1 UNION STREET,
SHEFFIELD, S1 2SH

Sheffield *Yorkshire* Population: 431,607. City, on River Don. Former centre of heavy steel industry, now largely precision steel and cutlery industries. University of Sheffield and Sheffield Hallam University. Various museums dedicated to Sheffield's industrial past. Meadowhall shopping centre and Sheffield City Airport, 3 miles (5km) NE of city centre.

LOCAL RADIO:
BBC RADIO SHEFFIELD 88.6 FM; GALAXY 105 105.6 FM; HALLAM FM 97.4 FM; MAGIC AM 1548 AM; REAL RADIO 107.7 FM

www.sheffield.gov.uk/out--about

SHEFFIELD

0 300 yds
0 300m

Appears on main map page 236

TOURIST INFORMATION CENTRE ☎ 023 8083 3333
9 CIVIC CENTRE ROAD,
SOUTHAMPTON, SO14 7FJ

HOSPITAL A & E ☎ 023 8077 7222
SOUTHAMPTON GENERAL HOSP, TREMONA RD,
SHIRLEY, SOUTHAMPTON, SO16 6YD

COUNCIL OFFICE ☎ 023 8083 3333
CIVIC CENTRE, CIVIC CENTRE ROAD,
SOUTHAMPTON, SO14 7LY

Southampton *South East England* Population: 210,138. City, at confluence of Rivers Itchen and Test at head of Southampton Water. Southern centre for business, culture and recreation. Container and transatlantic passenger port, dealing with 7 percent of UK's seaborne trade. Site of many famous departures: Henry V's army bound for Agincourt; the Pilgrim Fathers sailed to America on the Mayflower in 1620; maiden voyage of Queen Mary and only voyage of Titanic. Remains of medieval town walls. Medieval Merchant's House has authentically recreated furnishings. Boat and helicopter ferries to Isle of Wight. Host to many international boating events including Southampton International Boat Show, Whitbread Round the World, and BT Global Challenge. University. Southampton International Airport 1 mile (2km) S of Eastleigh.

LOCAL RADIO:
BBC RADIO SOLENT 999 AM / 96.1 FM, CAPITAL GOLD 1557 AM; POWER FM 103.2 FM; SOUTHCITY 107.8 FM; WAVE 105.2 FM

www.southampton.co.uk/leisure/tourism

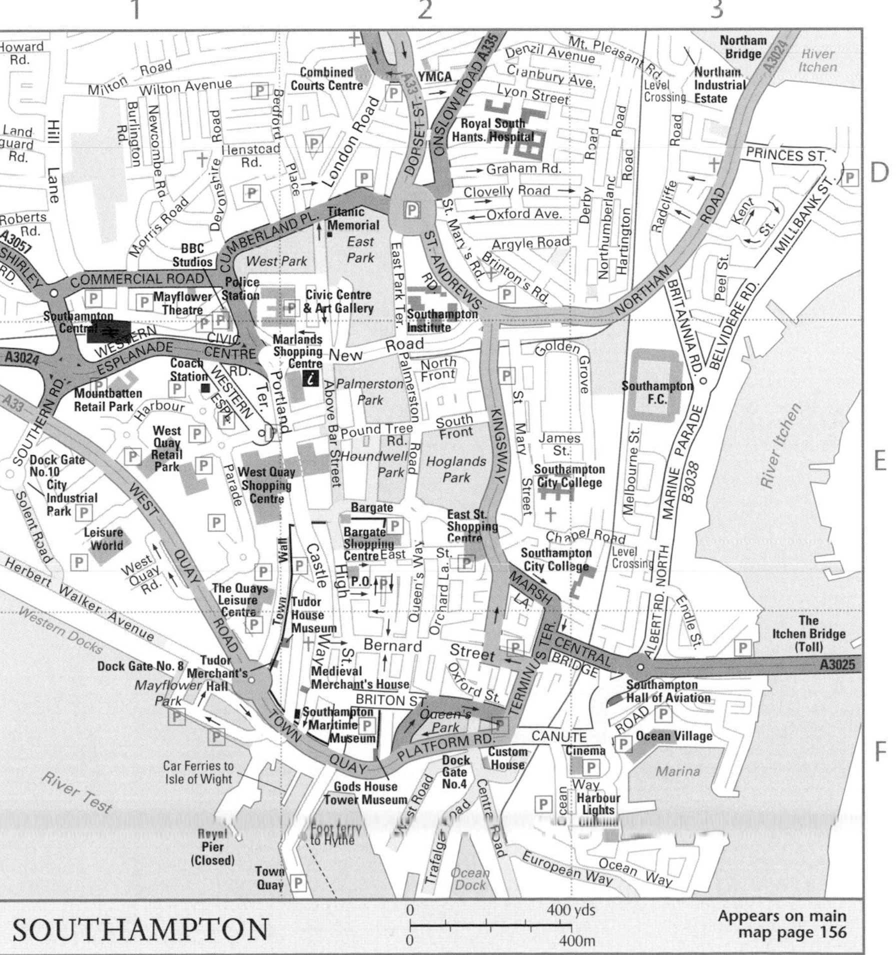
SOUTHAMPTON
Royal South Hants. Hospital
Combined Courts Centre
YMCA
Titanic Memorial
East Park
West Park
BBC Studios
Mayflower Theatre
Police Station
Civic Centre & Art Gallery
Southampton Institute
Southampton Central
Marlands Shopping Centre
Coach Station
Mountbatten Retail Park
West Quay Retail Park
West Quay Shopping Centre
Palmerston Park
Houndwell Park
Hoglands Park
Southampton F.C.
Southampton City College
Bargate
Bargate Shopping Centre
East St. Shopping Centre
Leisure World
The Quays Leisure Centre
Tudor House Museum
Tudor Merchant's Hall
Medieval Merchant's House
Southampton Maritime Museum
Mayflower Park
Queen's Park
Custom House
Gods House Tower Museum
Southampton Hall of Aviation
Ocean Village
Itchen Bridge (Toll)
Royal Pier (Closed)
Town Quay
Car Ferries to Isle of Wight
Foot ferry to Hythe
River Test
River Itchen
Marina
Ocean Dock
Northam Bridge
Northam Industrial Estate
Dock Gate No.4
Dock Gate No.8
Dock Gate No.10
City Industrial Park
Western Docks
Harbour Lights
0 400 yds
0 400m

Appears on main map page 156

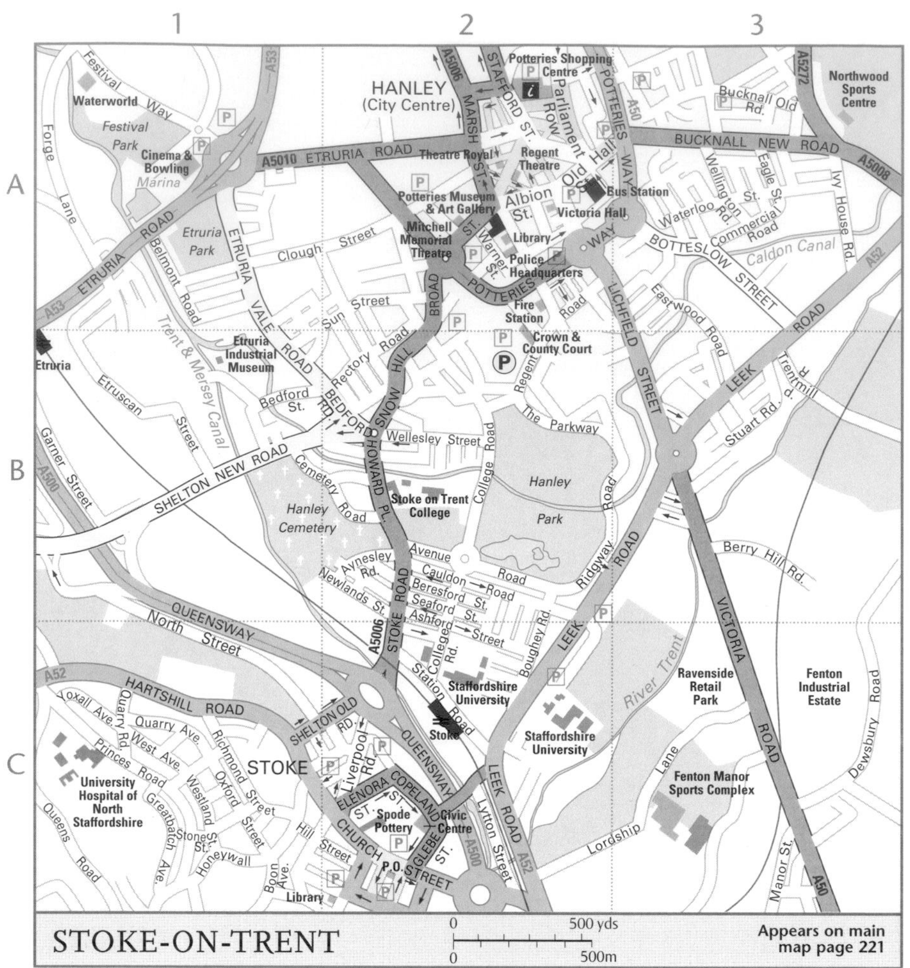
1
2
3
A
B
C
HANLEY
(City Centre)
Potteries Shopping Centre
Waterworld
Festival Park
Cinema & Bowling
Marina
Etruria Park
ETRURIA ROAD
A5010 ETRURIA ROAD
Theatre Royal
Regent Theatre
Potteries Museum & Art Gallery
Mitchell Memorial Theatre
Albion St.
Bus Station
Victoria Hall
Library
Police Headquarters
Fire Station
Crown & County Court
BUCKNALL NEW ROAD
Northwood Sports Centre
Caldon Canal
BOTTESLOW STREET
LICHFIELD STREET
LEEK ROAD
Etruria
Etruria Industrial Museum
Trent & Mersey Canal
SHELTON NEW ROAD
Hanley Cemetery
Stoke on Trent College
Hanley Park
The Parkway
QUEENSWAY
North Street
HARTSHILL ROAD
Staffordshire University
Stoke
STOKE
University Hospital of North Staffordshire
Spode Pottery
Civic Centre
P.O.
Library
Ravenside Retail Park
River Trent
Fenton Industrial Estate
Fenton Manor Sports Complex
VICTORIA ROAD
STOKE-ON-TRENT
0 500 yds
0 500m
Appears on main map page 221

TOURIST INFORMATION CENTRE ☎ 01782 236000
POTTERIES SHOPPING CENTRE, QUADRANT ROAD, HANLEY, STOKE-ON-TRENT, ST1 1RZ

HOSPITAL A & E ☎ 01782 715444
UNIVERSITY HOSP. OF NORTH STAFFORDSHIRE, PRINCE'S ROAD, STOKE-ON-TRENT, ST4 7LN

COUNCIL OFFICE ☎ 01782 234567
TOWN HALL, CIVIC CENTRE, GLEBE STREET, STOKE-ON-TRENT, ST4 1RN

Stoke-on-Trent *West Midlands* Population: 266,543. City, on River Trent. Centre for employment, shopping and leisure. Created by an amalgamation of former Stoke-upon-Trent and the towns of Burslem, Fenton, Hanley, Longton and Tunstall in 1910. Capital of The Potteries (largest claywear producer in the world), now largely a finishing centre for imported pottery. Many pottery factories open to public including Wedgwood, Royal Doulton and Spode. Potteries Museum in Hanley charts history of the potteries. Gladstone Pottery Museum in Longton is centred around large bottle-kiln and demonstrates traditional skills of pottery production. Staffordshire University.

LOCAL RADIO:
BBC RADIO STOKE 94.6 FM
SIGNAL TWO 1170 AM; SIGNAL 1 102.6 FM

www.visitstoke.co.uk

STRATFORD-UPON-AVON

0 500 yds
0 500m

Appears on main map page 197

TOURIST INFORMATION CENTRE ☎ 0870 160 7930
BRIDGEFOOT, STRATFORD-UPON-AVON, WARWICKSHIRE, CV37 6GW

HOSPITAL A & E ☎ 01926 495321
WARWICK HOSPITAL, LAKIN ROAD, WARWICK, CV34 5BW

COUNCIL OFFICE ☎ 01789 267575
COUNCIL OFFICES, ELIZABETH HOUSE, CHURCH ST, STRATFORD-UPON-AVON, CV37 6HX

Stratford-upon-Avon (Also called Stratford-on-Avon.) *West Midlands* Population: 22,231. Town, on River Avon. Tourist centre. Many attractive 16th century buildings. Reconstructed Shakespeare's Birthplace. Elizabethan garden at New Place. Hall's Croft Elizabethan town house and doctor's dispensary. Royal Shakespeare Theatre. Shakespeare's grave at Holy Trinity Church. Anne Hathaway's Cottage to W, at Shottery.

LOCAL RADIO:
BBC RADIO COVENTRY & WARWICKSHIRE 94.8 & 103.7 FM
FM 102 - THE BEAR 102 FM

www.shakespeare-country.co.uk

TOURIST INFORMATION CENTRE ☎ 0191 553 2000
50 FAWCETT STREET,
SUNDERLAND, SR1 1RF

HOSPITAL A & E ☎ 0191 565 6256
SUNDERLAND ROYAL HOSPITAL,
KAYLL ROAD, SUNDERLAND, SR4 7TP

COUNCIL OFFICE ☎ 0191 553 1000
SUNDERLAND CITY COUNCIL, CIVIC CENTRE,
BURDON ROAD, SUNDERLAND, SR2 7DN

Sunderland *North East England* Population 183,310. Industrial city and seaport at mouth of River Wear. Previously largest ship-building town in the world; coal mining was also important. Several museums celebrate city's industrial past. Service sector and manufacturing account for largest contribution to local economy. National Glass Centre commemorates importance of stained glass to area. University.

LOCAL RADIO:
BBC RADIO NEWCASTLE 1458 AM / 95.4 FM;
CENTURY RADIO 100.7 FM; GALAXY 105.3 FM;
METRO RADIO 97.1, 103 FM; SUN FM 103.4 FM

www.sunderland.gov.uk/visitors

SUNDERLAND

0 400 yds
0 400m

Appears on main map page 262

TOURIST INFORMATION CENTRE ☎ 01792 468321
WESTWAY,
SWANSEA, SA1 3QG

HOSPITAL A & E ☎ 01792 702222
MORRISTON HOSPITAL, MORRISTON,
SWANSEA, SA6 6NL

COUNCIL OFFICE ☎ 01792 636000
COUNTY HALL, OYSTERMOUTH ROAD,
SWANSEA, SA1 3SN

Swansea (Abertawe) *Wales* Population: 171,038. City, port on Swansea Bay at mouth of River Tawe, and Wales' second city. Settlement developed next to Norman castle built in 1099, but claims made that a Viking settlement existed before this date. Previously a port for local metal smelting industries. Bombed in World War II, and city centre rebuilt. Birthplace of Dylan Thomas, who described it as 'an ugly, lovely town'. Remains of 14th century castle or fortified manor house. University of Wales. Tropical plant and wildlife leisure centre, Plantasia. Airport 5 miles (9km) W at Fairwood Common.

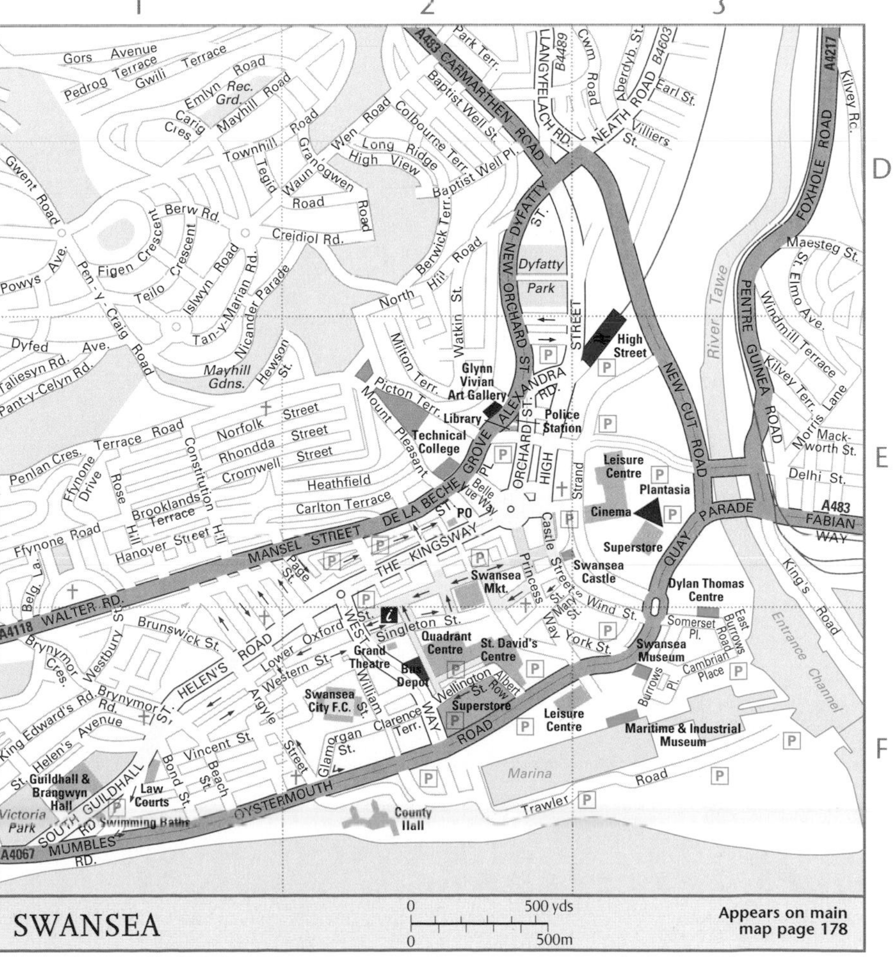

Dyfatty Park
High Street
Glynn Vivian Art Gallery
Library
Police Station
Technical College
Leisure Centre
Plantasia
Cinema
Superstore
Swansea Castle
Swansea Mkt.
Dylan Thomas Centre
Quadrant Centre
St. David's Centre
Grand Theatre
Bus Depot
Swansea City F.C.
Swansea Museum
Maritime & Industrial Museum
Marina
Guildhall & Brangwyn Hall
Law Courts
County Hall
Swimming Baths
Victoria Park
MANSEL STREET
THE KINGSWAY
OYSTERMOUTH ROAD
NEW CUT ROAD
QUAY PARADE
FABIAN WAY
CARMARTHEN ROAD
WALTER RD.
MUMBLES RD.

LOCAL RADIO:
BBC RADIO WALES 657, 882 AM / 93.9 FM;
REAL RADIO 106 FM; SWANSEA SOUND 1170 AM

www1.swansea.gov.uk/tourism

SWANSEA

0 500 yds
0 500m

Appears on main map page 178

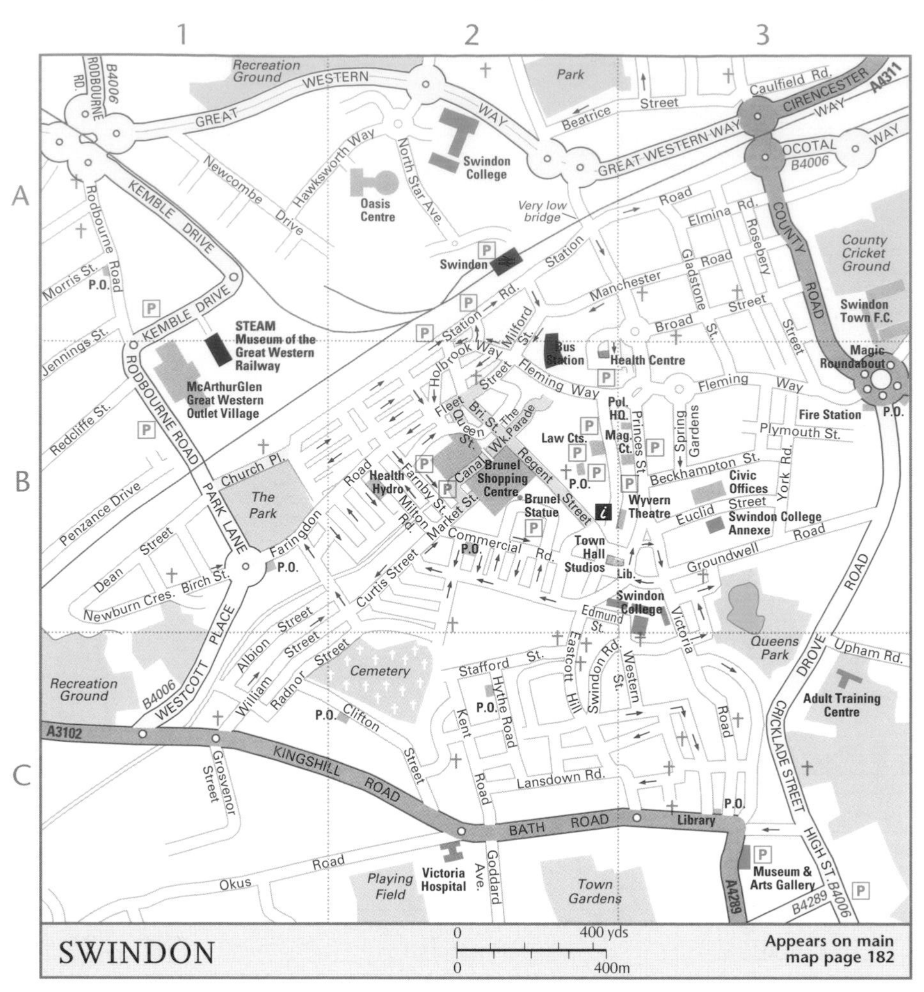
Recreation Ground
GREAT WESTERN WAY
Park
Beatrice Street
Caulfield Rd.
CIRENCESTER WAY
A4311
OCOTAL B4006
RODBOURNE RD. B4006
KEMBLE DRIVE
Newcombe Drive
Hawksworth Way
North Star Ave.
Swindon College
Oasis Centre
Very low bridge
Swindon
Station Rd.
Manchester Road
Elmina Rd.
Rosebery Street
COUNTY ROAD
County Cricket Ground
Swindon Town F.C.
Magic Roundabout
Morris St.
Rodbourne Road
Jennings St.
STEAM Museum of the Great Western Railway
McArthurGlen Great Western Outlet Village
RODBOURNE ROAD
Redcliffe St.
Holbrook Way
Milford St.
Bus Station
Health Centre
Fleming Way
Gladstone St.
Broad Street
Fire Station
Plymouth St.
Pol. HQ.
Law Cts.
Mag. Ct.
Princes St.
Spring Gardens
Beckhampton St.
Civic Offices
Euclid Street
Swindon College Annexe
York Rd.
Penzance Drive
Church Pl.
The Park
PARK LANE
Health Hydro
Farnsby St.
Milton Rd.
Canal Wk.
Brunel Shopping Centre
Regent Street
Brunel Statue
Wyvern Theatre
Commercial Rd.
Town Hall Studios
Lib.
Groundwell Road
Dean Street
Birch St.
Newburn Cres.
Faringdon Road
Curtis Street
Swindon College
Edmund St.
Victoria Rd.
Queens Park
DROVE ROAD
Upham Rd.
Adult Training Centre
Recreation Ground
WESTCOTT PLACE
Albion Street
William St.
Radnor Street
Cemetery
Stafford St.
Hythe Road
Eastcott Hill
Swindon Rd.
Western St.
Kent Road
Clifton Street
A3102
KINGSHILL ROAD
Grosvenor Street
Lansdown Rd.
CRICKLADE STREET
HIGH ST. B4006
BATH ROAD
Library
Okus Road
Playing Field
Victoria Hospital
Goddard Ave.
Town Gardens
A4289
Museum & Arts Gallery
B4289
P.O.
SWINDON
0 400 yds
0 400m
Appears on main map page 182

TOURIST INFORMATION CENTRE ☎ 01793 530328
37 REGENT STREET,
SWINDON, SN1 1JL

HOSPITAL A & E ☎ 01793 604020
GREAT WESTERN HOSPITAL, MARLBOROUGH RD,
SWINDON, SN3 6BB

COUNCIL OFFICE ☎ 01793 463000
CIVIC OFFICES, EUCLID STREET,
SWINDON, SN1 2JH

Swindon *South West England* Population: 145,236. Town, industrial and commercial centre. Large, modern shopping centre. Town expanded considerably in 19th century with arrival of the railway. The Museum of the Great Western Railway exhibits Swindon built locomotives and documents the history of the railway works.

LOCAL RADIO:
BBC WILTSHIRE SOUND 103.6 FM / 1368 MW;
CLASSIC GOLD 1161 AM; GWR FM 97.2 FM

www.swindon.gov.uk/tourism

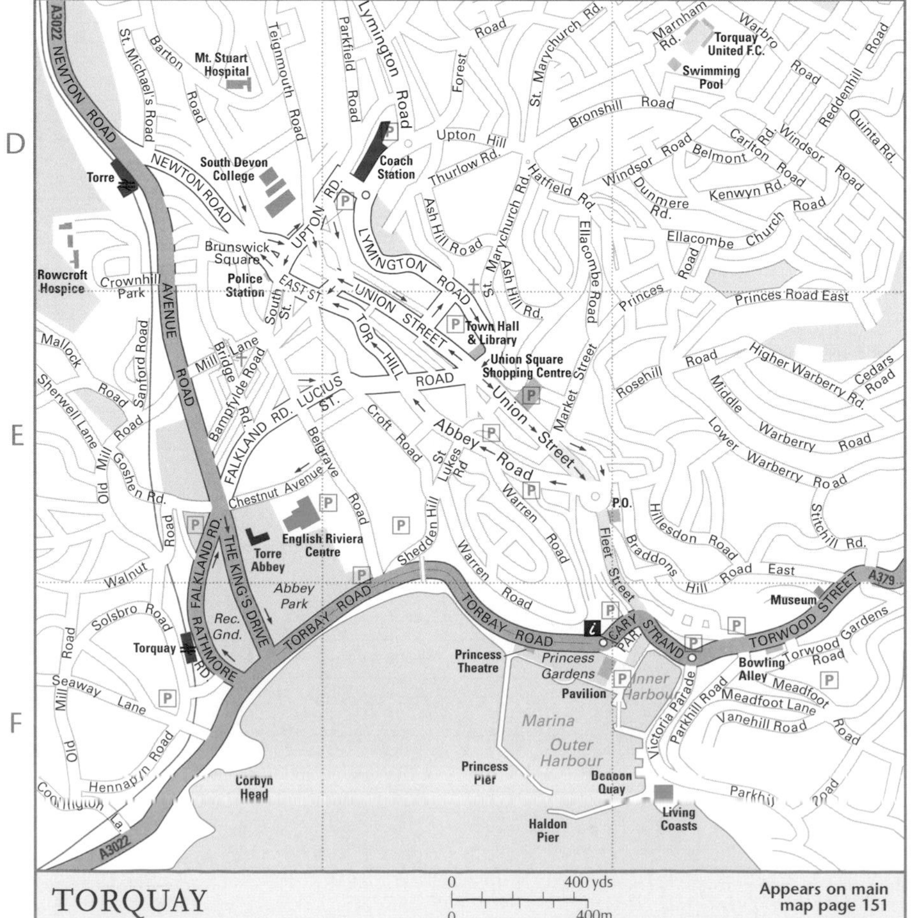
A3022 NEWTON ROAD
St. Michael's Road
Barton Road
Mt. Stuart Hospital
Teignmouth Road
Parkfield Road
Lymington Road
Forest Road
St. Marychurch Rd.
Marnham Rd.
Torquay United F.C.
Swimming Pool
Warbro Road
Reddenhill Road
Quinta Rd.
Bronshill Road
Upton Hill
Coach Station
Thurlow Rd.
Windsor Road
Belmont Road
Carlton Rd.
Torre
South Devon College
NEWTON ROAD
UPTON RD.
Hatfield Rd.
Dunmere Rd.
Kenwyn Rd.
Ash Hill Road
Ellacombe Church Road
Brunswick Square
Police Station
Rowcroft Hospice
Crownhill Park
AVENUE ROAD
LYMINGTON ROAD
UNION STREET
TOR HILL ROAD
EAST ST.
South St.
Town Hall & Library
Union Square Shopping Centre
Ellacombe Road
Princes Road
Princes Road East
Mallock Road
Sanford Road
Mill Lane
Bridge Road
Market Street
Rosehill Road
Higher Warberry Rd.
Cedars Road
Sherwell Lane
Old Mill Road
Goshen Rd.
Bampfylde Rd.
FALKLAND RD.
LUCIUS ST.
Croft Road
Belgrave Road
Abbey Road
Union Street
Middle Warberry Road
Lower Warberry Road
Chestnut Avenue
St. Lukes Rd.
Warren Road
P.O.
Hillesdon Road
Stitchill Rd.
Torre Abbey
English Riviera Centre
Abbey Park
Shedden Hill
Braddons Hill Road East
A379
Walnut Road
Solsbro Road
Rec. Gnd.
THE KING'S DRIVE
RATHMORE RD.
TORBAY ROAD
Fleet Street
Museum
TORWOOD STREET
Torwood Gardens Road
Torquay
Princess Theatre
Princess Gardens
CARY PAR.
STRAND
Bowling Alley
Pavilion
Inner Harbour
Victoria Parade
Parkhill Road
Meadfoot Lane
Meadfoot Road
Vanehill Road
Seaway Lane
Old Mill Road
Marina
Outer Harbour
Princess Pier
Beacon Quay
Living Coasts
Parkhill Road
Hennapyn Road
Corbyn Head
Haldon Pier
A3022
TORQUAY
0 400 yds
0 400m
Appears on main map page 151

TOURIST INFORMATION CENTRE ☎ 01803 297428
VAUGHAN PARADE,
TORQUAY, TQ2 5JG

HOSPITAL A & E ☎ 01803 614567
TORBAY DISTRICT GENERAL HOSPITAL,
NEWTON ROAD, TORQUAY, TQ2 7AA

COUNCIL OFFICE ☎ 01803 201201
TOWN HALL, CASTLE CIRCUS,
TORQUAY, TQ1 3DR

Torquay *South West England* Population: 59,587. Chief town and resort of Torbay English Riviera district, with harbour and several beaches. Noted for mild climate. Torre Abbey with 15th century gatehouse, is a converted monastery housing a collecion of furniture and glassware. Torquay Museum has display on crimewriter Agatha Christie born in Torquay. Kent's Cavern showcaves are an important prehistoric site. Babbacombe Model village 2 miles (3km) N.

LOCAL RADIO:
BBC RADIO DEVON 104.3 FM;
CLASSIC GOLD 954 AM; GEMINI FM 96.4 FM;
SOUTH HAMS RADIO 100.8 FM

www.theenglishriviera.co.uk

TOURIST INFORMATION CENTRE ☎ 01727 864511
TOWN HALL, MARKET PLACE,
ST ALBANS, AL3 5DJ

HOSPITAL A & E ☎ 01923 244366
WATFORD GENERAL HOSPITAL, VICARAGE ROAD,
WATFORD, WD1 8HB

COUNCIL OFFICE ☎ 01923 226400
WATFORD COUNCIL, TOWN HALL,
WATFORD, WD17 3EX

Watford *East of England* Population: 113,080. Old market town on River Colne. Printing and brewing developed as the main industries; now the industrial base is more diverse. Shopping and leisure centre with modern sculptures in redeveloped central area. Parish church of Saint Mary's has 16th century chapel. Local history museum housed in Georgian house. Edwardian Palace Theatre originally opened as a music hall in 1908.

LOCAL RADIO:
BBC THREE COUNTIES RADIO 1161 AM / 103.8 FM;
MERCURY 96.6 FM

www.watford.gov.uk/tourism

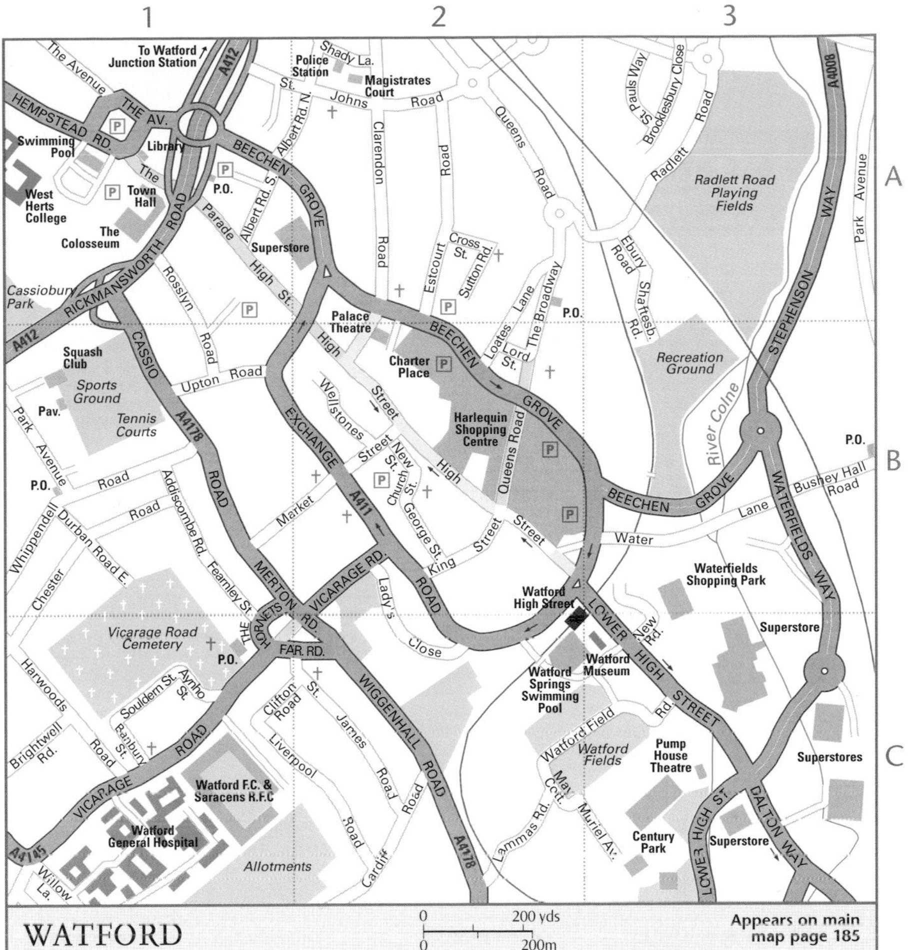

1
2
3
A
B
C
To Watford Junction Station
Police Station
Magistrates Court
Swimming Pool
Library
West Herts College
Town Hall
The Colosseum
Superstore
Cassiobury Park
Palace Theatre
Charter Place
Harlequin Shopping Centre
Squash Club
Sports Ground
Tennis Courts
Radlett Road Playing Fields
Recreation Ground
River Colne
Waterfields Shopping Park
Superstore
Vicarage Road Cemetery
Watford High Street
Watford Museum
Watford Springs Swimming Pool
Watford Fields
Pump House Theatre
Superstores
Watford F.C. & Saracens R.F.C.
Watford General Hospital
Allotments
Century Park
Superstore
P.O.
WATFORD
0 200 yds
0 200m
Appears on main map page 185

TOURIST INFORMATION CENTRE ☎ 01934 888800
BEACH LAWNS,
WESTON-SUPER-MARE, BS23 1AT

HOSPITAL A & E ☎ 01934 636363
WESTON GENERAL HOSPITAL, GRANGE ROAD,
UPHILL, WESTON-SUPER-MARE, BS23 3NT

COUNCIL OFFICE ☎ 01934 888888
NORTH SOMERSET COUNCIL, TOWN HALL,
WESTON-SUPER-MARE, BS23 1UJ

Weston-super-Mare *South West England* Population: 69,372. Town and popular resort on the Bristol Channel, situated on Weston Bay and first developed in the 19th century. Over 1 mile (2km) of sands with traditional beach donkeys; promenade, marine lake, miniature steam railway and Winter Gardens. Amusement park located on the central Grand Pier, built in 1904. The Aquarium houses ocean and coastal waters display tanks. Local history and heritage museums give an insight into the town as a Victorian seaside resort. Annual motorbike beach race, Enduro, is held in October. International Helicopter Museum at Locking 2 miles (3km) E.

LOCAL RADIO:
BBC SOMERSET SOUND 94.9, 104.6 FM
STAR 107.7 FM

www.somersetcoast.com

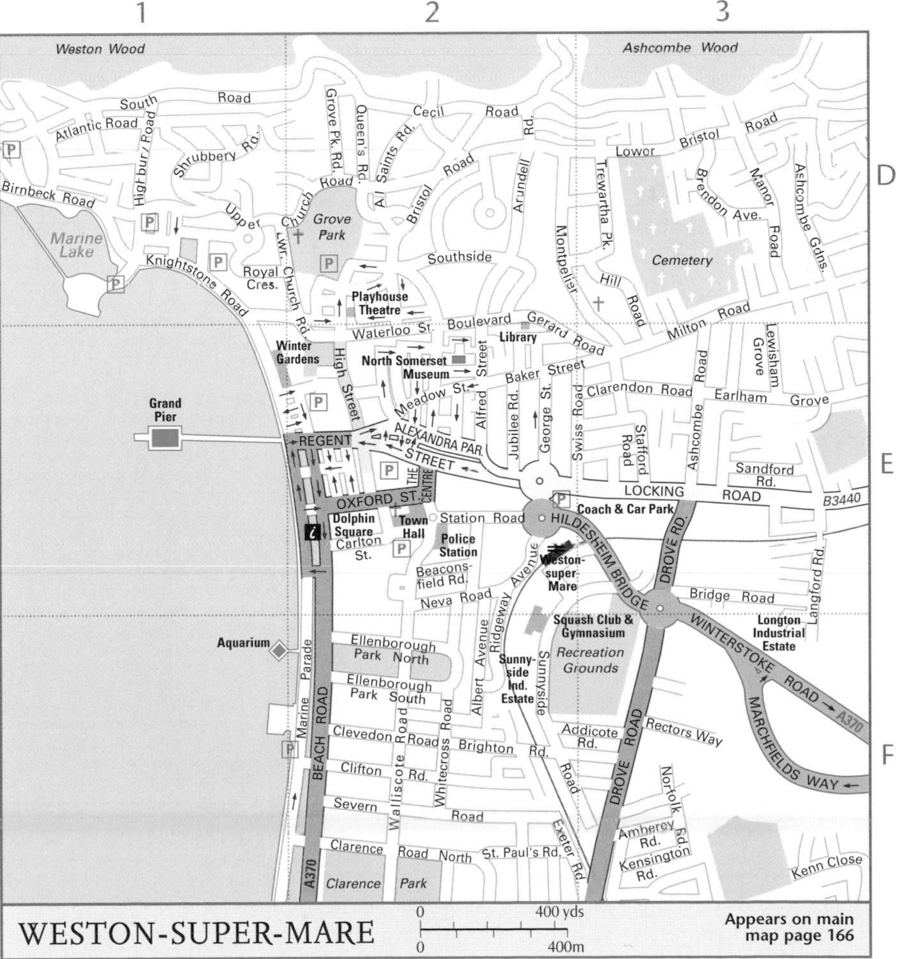

1
2
3
D
E
F
Weston Wood
Ashcombe Wood
Marine Lake
Grove Park
Playhouse Theatre
Library
Cemetery
Winter Gardens
North Somerset Museum
Grand Pier
Dolphin Square
Town Hall
Police Station
Weston-super-Mare
Coach & Car Park
Squash Club & Gymnasium
Recreation Grounds
Sunnyside Ind. Estate
Longton Industrial Estate
Aquarium
WESTON-SUPER-MARE
0 400 yds
0 400m
Appears on main map page 166

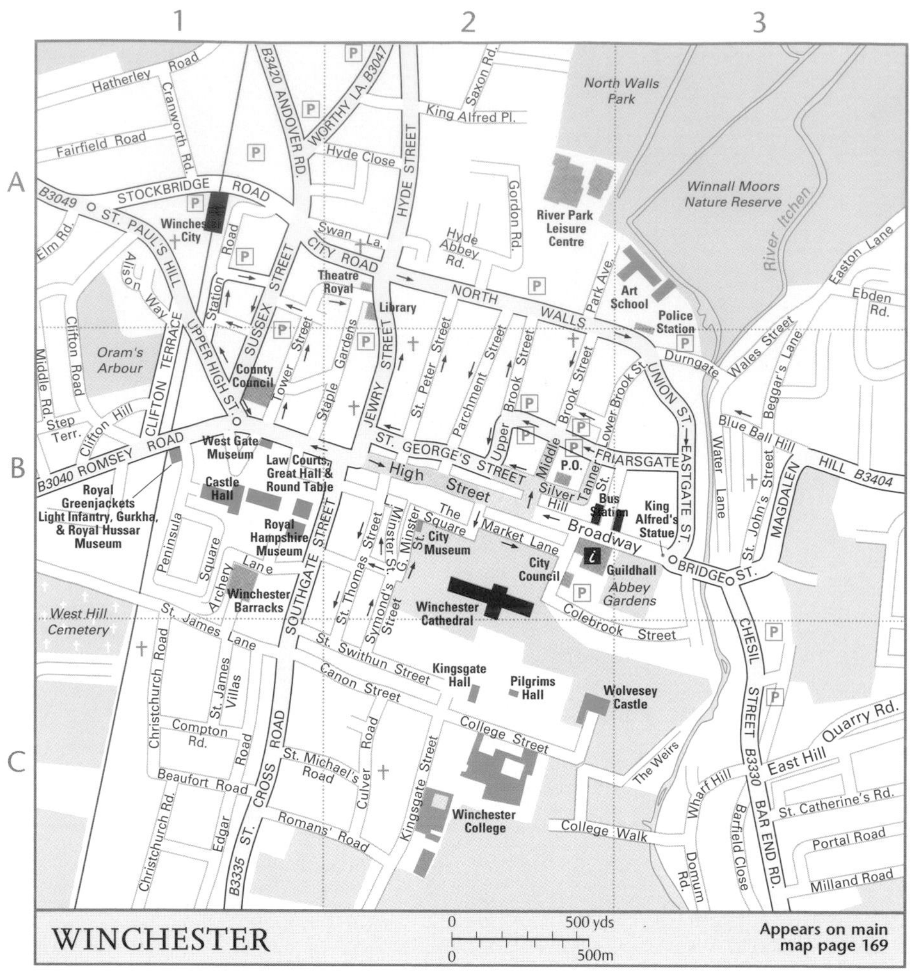
1
2
3
A
B
C
Hatherley Road
Cranworth Rd.
Fairfield Road
B3420 ANDOVER RD.
WORTHY LA B3047
Hyde Close
HYDE STREET
Saxon Rd.
King Alfred Pl.
North Walls Park
Winnall Moors Nature Reserve
River Itchen
B3049 STOCKBRIDGE ROAD
ST. PAUL'S HILL
Elm Rd.
Alison Way
Winchester City
Station Road
Swan La.
CITY ROAD
Hyde Abbey Rd.
Gordon Rd.
River Park Leisure Centre
Art School
Easton Lane
Ebden Rd.
NORTH WALLS
Police Station
Theatre Royal
Library
SUSSEX STREET
Clifton Road
Oram's Arbour
Middle Rd.
Step Terr.
Clifton Hill
CLIFTON TERRACE
UPPER HIGH ST.
County Council
Tower Street
Staple Gardens
JEWRY STREET
St. Peter Street
Parchment Street
Upper Brook Street
Middle Brook Street
Lower Brook St.
UNION ST.
Durngate
Wales Street
Beggar's Lane
B3040 ROMSEY ROAD
West Gate Museum
Law Courts, Great Hall & Round Table
ST. GEORGE'S STREET
FRIARSGATE
EASTGATE ST.
Water Lane
Blue Ball Hill
St. John's Street
MAGDALEN HILL B3404
Royal Greenjackets Light Infantry, Gurkha, & Royal Hussar Museum
Castle Hall
High Street
P.O.
Silver Hill
Tanner St.
Bus Station
King Alfred's Statue
Royal Hampshire Museum
Peninsula Square
Archery Lane
SOUTHGATE STREET
St. Thomas Street
Minster St.
St. Square
The Square
City Museum
Market Lane
Broadway
City Council
Guildhall
Abbey Gardens
BRIDGE ST.
Winchester Barracks
West Hill Cemetery
St. James Lane
Symonds Street
Winchester Cathedral
Colebrook Street
CHESIL STREET B3330
St. Swithun Street
Kingsgate Hall
Pilgrims Hall
Wolvesey Castle
Christchurch Road
St. James Villas
Canon Street
Compton Rd.
Quarry Rd.
College Street
CROSS ROAD
St. Michael's Road
Culver Road
Kingsgate Street
The Weirs
Wharf Hill
East Hill
Beaufort Road
St. Catherine's Rd.
Winchester College
Christchurch Rd.
Edgar Road
B3335 ST.
Romans' Road
College Walk
Barfield Close
BAR END RD.
Portal Road
Domum Rd.
Milland Road
WINCHESTER
0 500 yds
0 500m
Appears on main map page 169

TOURIST INFORMATION CENTRE ☎ 01962 840500
GUILDHALL, THE BROADWAY, WINCHESTER
HAMPSHIRE, SO23 9LJ

HOSPITAL A & E ☎ 01962 863535
ROYAL HAMPSHIRE COUNTY HOSPITAL,
ROMSEY ROAD, WINCHESTER, SO22 5DG

COUNCIL OFFICE ☎ 01962 840222
CITY OFFICES, COLEBROOK STREET,
WINCHESTER, SO23 9LJ

Winchester *South East England* Population: 36,121. City, county town on River Itchen on site of Roman town of Venta Belgarum. Ancient capital of Wessex and of Anglo-Saxon England. 11th century cathedral, longest in Europe with carved Norman font and England's oldest complete choir-stalls. Winchester College, boys' public school founded 1382. 13th century Great Hall is only remaining part of Winchester Castle. Westgate Museum is in 12th century gatehouse in medieval city wall, once a debtors' prison. 12th century hospital of St. Cross. City Mill, built over river in 18th century. To S across river, St. Catherine's Hill, Iron Age fort. Extensive ruins of medieval Wolvesey Castle, also known as Old Bishop's Palace, 1 mile (2km) SE.

LOCAL RADIO:
BBC RADIO SOLENT 999 AM / 96.1 FM;
OCEAN FM 96.7 FM; WIN 107.2 FM

www.visitwinchester.co.uk

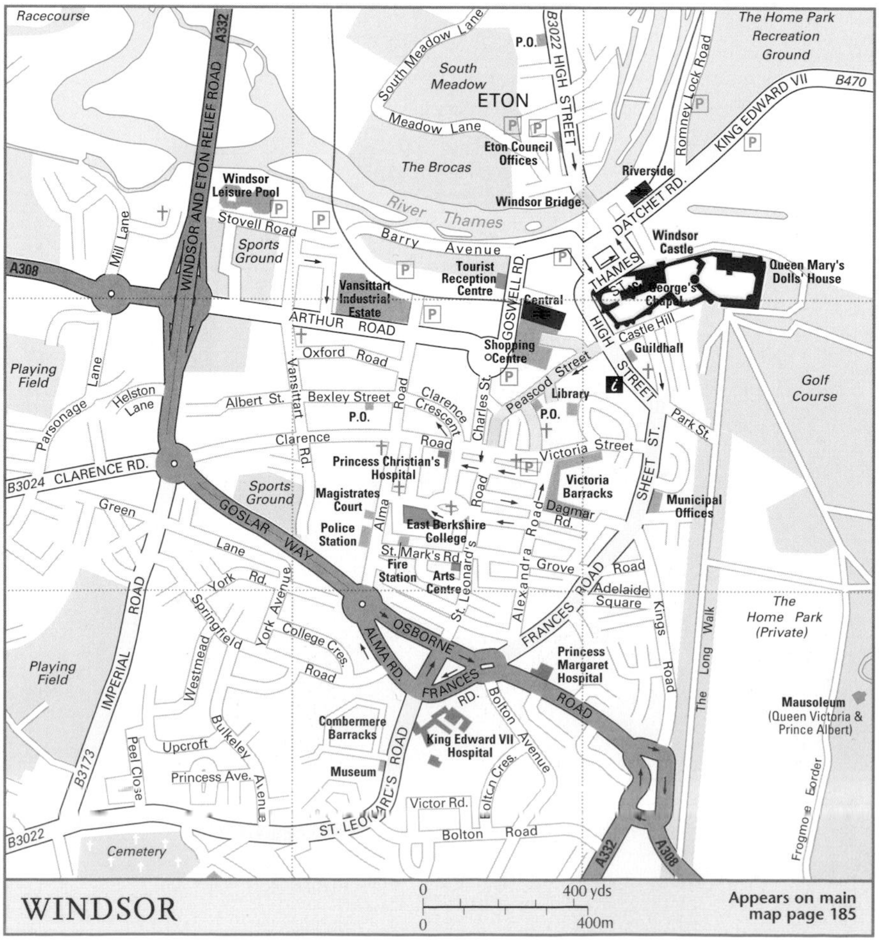

WINDSOR
0 400 yds
0 400m
Appears on main map page 185

TOURIST INFORMATION CENTRE ☎ 01753 743900
24 HIGH STREET,
WINDSOR, SL4 1LH

HOSPITAL A & E ☎ 01753 633000
WEXHAM PARK HOSPITAL, WEXHAM STREET,
SLOUGH, SL2 4HL

COUNCIL OFFICE ☎ 01753 810525
COUNCIL OFFICES, YORK HOUSE, SHEET STREET,
WINDSOR, SL4 1DD

Windsor *South East England* Population: 26,369. Town, attractive market town on S bank of River Thames. Castle is royal residence. Great Park to S of town is open to public; Home Park bordering river is private. St. George's Chapel is impressive. Many Georgian houses, and guildhall designed by Sir Christopher Wren.

LOCAL RADIO:
BBC RADIO BERKSHIRE 95.4 FM;
STAR FM 106.6 FM

www.windsor.gov.uk

TOURIST INFORMATION CENTRE ☎ 01905 726311
THE GUILDHALL, HIGH STREET,
WORCESTER, WR1 2EY

HOSPITAL A & E ☎ 01905 763333
WORCESTERSHIRE ROYAL HOSPITAL,
CHARLES HASTINGS WAY,
WORCESTER, WR5 1DD

COUNCIL OFFICE ☎ 01905 723471
THE GUILDHALL, HIGH STREET,
WORCESTER, WR1 2EY

Worcester *West Midlands* Population: 82,661. City, on River Severn. Shopping, cultural, sports and industrial centre; industries include porcelain and sauces and condiments. 18th century Guildhall. Cathedral mainly Early English includes England's largest Norman crypt, 13th century choir and Lady Chapel and tomb of King John. Three Choirs Festival held here every third year. Civil War Centre at the Commandery, headquarters for Charles II during Battle of Worcester. Factory tours and museum at Royal Worcester Porcelain. Elgar's Birthplace, home of composer Sir Edward Elgar, in Broadheath, 3 miles (5km) W.

LOCAL RADIO:
BBC RADIO HEREFORD & WORCESTER 738 AM / 104 FM;
CLASSIC HITS 1530 AM; WYVERN FM 102.8 FM

www.visitworcester.com

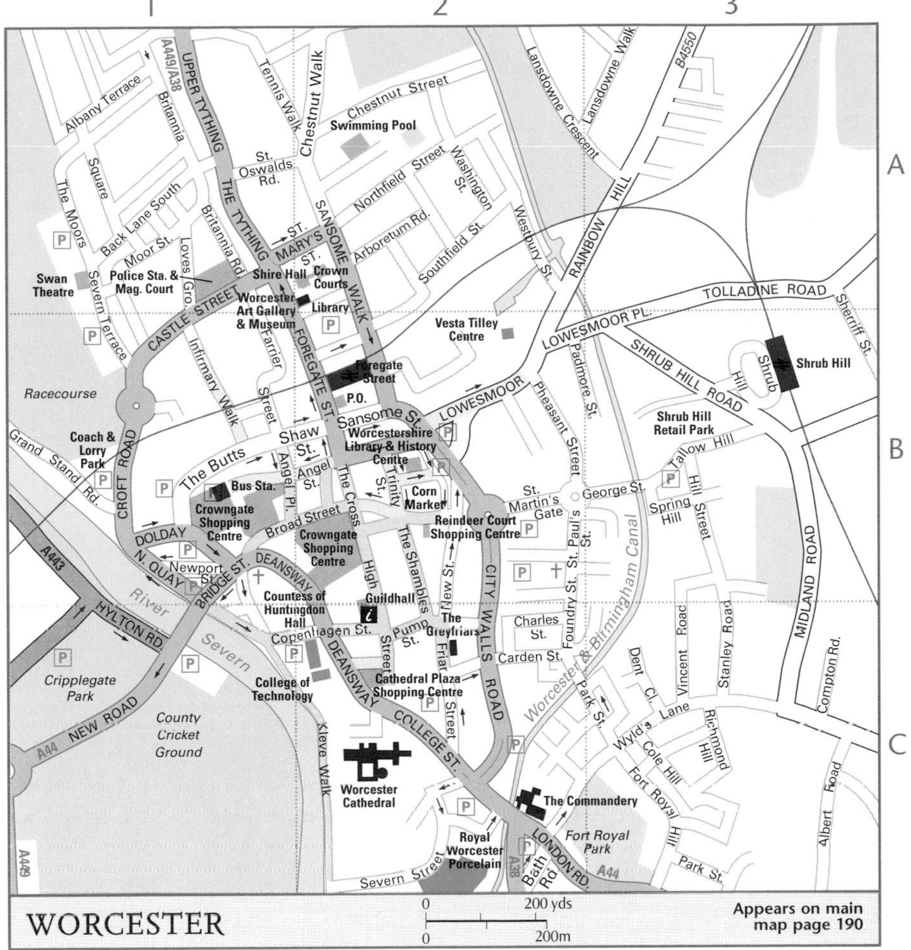
1
2
3
A
B
C
WORCESTER
0
200 yds
200m
Appears on main map page 190
Upper Tything
The Tything
Foregate St.
Sansome Walk
Chestnut Walk
Chestnut Street
Swimming Pool
Tennis Walk
Albany Terrace
Britannia
The Moors
Square
Back Lane South
Moor St.
Swan Theatre
Police Sta. & Mag. Court
Shire Hall
Crown Courts
Worcester Art Gallery & Museum
Library
Castle Street
Severn Terrace
Infirmary Walk
Racecourse
Coach & Lorry Park
Grand Stand Rd.
Croft Road
The Butts
Bus Sta.
Crowngate Shopping Centre
Dolday
Newport St.
Deansway
Bridge St.
Hylton Rd.
New Road
River Severn
Cripplegate Park
County Cricket Ground
College of Technology
Countess of Huntingdon Hall
Copenhagen St.
Guildhall
High Street
The Shambles
Worcester Cathedral
Kleve Walk
Severn Street
Royal Worcester Porcelain
The Commandery
Fort Royal Park
London Rd.
College St.
Cathedral Plaza Shopping Centre
Friar Street
City Walls Road
Reindeer Court Shopping Centre
Corn Market
Lowesmoor
Lowesmoor Pl.
Sansome St.
Worcestershire Library & History Centre
Vesta Tilley Centre
Rainbow Hill
Tolladine Road
Shrub Hill Road
Shrub Hill
Shrub Hill Retail Park
Midland Road
Worcester & Birmingham Canal
Sidbury
Carden St.
Charles St.
St. Martin's Gate
George St.
Spring Hill
Hill Street
Vincent Road
Stanley Road
Compton Rd.
Richmond Hill
Fort Royal Hill
Park St.
Albert Road
Lansdowne Crescent
Lansdowne Walk
Northfield Street
Arboretum Rd.
Southfield St.
Washington St.
Westbury St.
Pheasant Street
Padmore St.
Tallow Hill
Sheriff St.
Bath Rd.

TOURIST INFORMATION CENTRE ☎ 01904 621756
DE GREY ROOMS, EXHIBITION SQUARE,
YORK, YO1 2HB

HOSPITAL A & E ☎ 01904 631313
YORK DISTRICT HOSPITAL, WIGGINTON ROAD,
YORK, YO31 8HE

COUNCIL OFFICE ☎ 01904 613161
THE GUILDHALL,
YORK, YO1 9QN

York *Yorkshire* Population: 124,609. Ancient city and archiepiscopal see on River Ouse. On site of Roman Eboracum. Constantine the Great proclaimed Roman Emperor in York in AD 306; only emperor to be enthroned in Britain. City fell to Danes in AD 867 and became known as Jorvik. Medieval wall largely intact, other fortifications including Clifford's Tower. York Minster has largest Medieval stained glass window in country. Previously a wool trading, craft and railway centre. Museum. Jorvik Viking Centre in Coppergate. Merchant Adventurers' Hall in Fossgate is finest remaining guildhall in Europe. University of York at Heslington. Racecourse at Knavesmire.

LOCAL RADIO:
BBC RADIO YORK 666, 1260 AM / 103.7 FM;
MINSTER FM 104.7 FM; GALAXY 105 105.1 FM

www.visityork.org

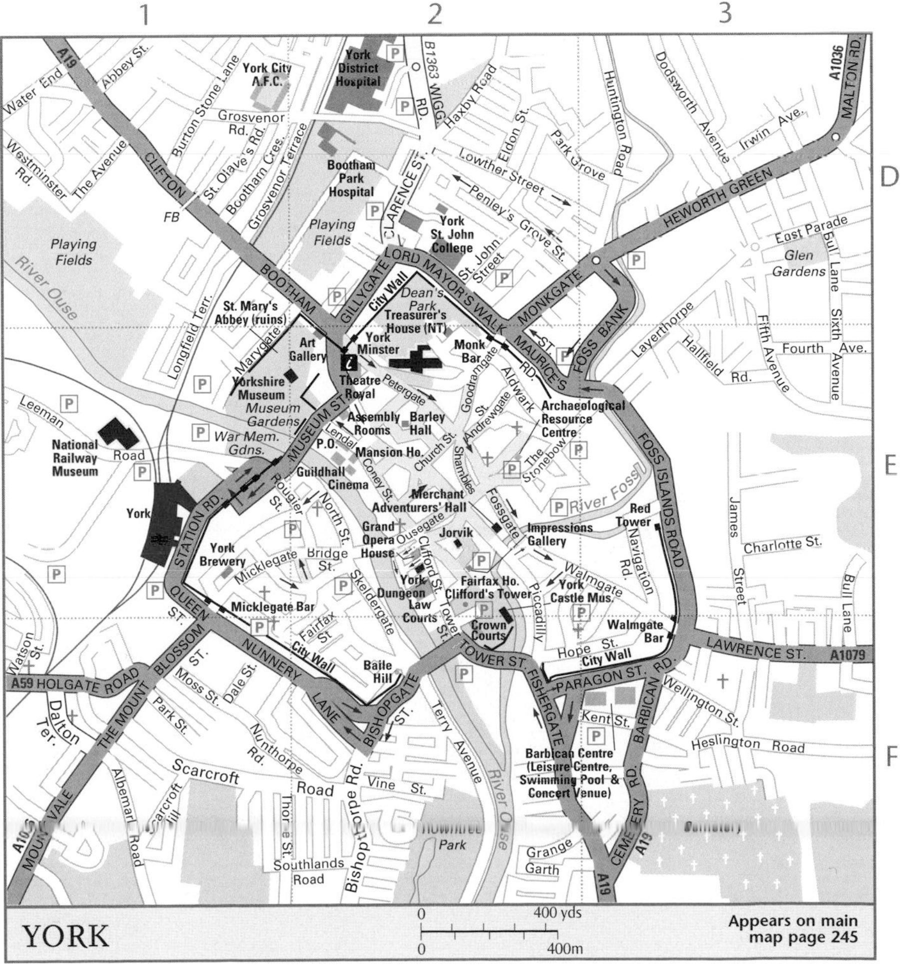
1
2
3
D
E
F
YORK
0
400 yds
400m
Appears on main map page 245
York City A.F.C.
York District Hospital
Bootham Park Hospital
Clifton
Bootham
Gillygate
Lord Mayor's Walk
Monkgate
Heworth Green
Malton Rd.
Huntington Road
Haxby Road
Wigginton Rd.
Clarence St.
York St. John College
St. Mary's Abbey (ruins)
Yorkshire Museum
Museum Gardens
Art Gallery
York Minster
Treasurer's House (NT)
Theatre Royal
Assembly Rooms
Barley Hall
Mansion Ho.
Guildhall
Cinema
Merchant Adventurers' Hall
Jorvik
Grand Opera House
York Dungeon
Fairfax Ho.
Clifford's Tower
Law Courts
Crown Courts
York Castle Mus.
Archaeological Resource Centre
Impressions Gallery
Red Tower
Walmgate Bar
Foss Islands Road
Lawrence St.
National Railway Museum
Leeman Road
York
Station Rd.
York Brewery
Micklegate
Micklegate Bar
Queen St.
Blossom St.
Nunnery Lane
Bishopgate St.
Baile Hill
Tower St.
Paragon St.
Barbican Rd.
Barbican Centre (Leisure Centre, Swimming Pool & Concert Venue)
Fishergate
Piccadilly
River Ouse
River Foss
Playing Fields
War Mem. Gdns.
Museum St.
Holgate Road
The Mount
Mount Vale
Scarcroft Road
Southlands Road
Bishopthorpe Rd.
Terry Avenue
Cemetery Rd.
Grange Garth
Heslington Road
Wellington St.
Hope St.
City Wall
Water End
Westminster Rd.
The Avenue
Grosvenor Rd.
Burton Stone Lane
Lowther Street
Penley's Grove St.
Eldon St.
Park Grove
Dodsworth Avenue
Irwin Ave.
East Parade
Glen Gardens
Fourth Ave.
Laverthorpe
Hallfield Rd.
James Street
Charlotte St.
Bull Lane
Dalton Ter.
Albemarle Road
Nunthorpe Rd.
Vine St.
Skeldergate
Coney St.
Stonegate
Goodramgate
Aldwark
Fossgate
Walmgate
Navigation Rd.
Kent St.

INDEX

Abbreviations

Aber.	Aberdeenshire	E.Ayr.	East Ayrshire	Lancs.	Lancashire	P. & K.	Perth & Kinross	Surr.	Surrey
Arg. & B.	Argyll & Bute	E.Dun.	East Dunbartonshire	Leic.	Leicester	Pembs.	Pembrokeshire	Swan.	Swansea
B'burn.	Blackburn with Darwen	E.Loth.	East Lothian	Leics.	Leicestershire	Peter.	Peterborough	Swin.	Swindon
B'pool	Blackpool	E.Renf.	East Renfrewshire	Lincs.	Lincolnshire	Plym.	Plymouth	T. & W.	Tyne & Wear
B. & H.	Brighton & Hove	E.Riding	East Riding of Yorkshire	M.K.	Milton Keynes	Ports.	Portsmouth	Tel. & W.	Telford & Wrekin
B. & N.E.Som.	Bath & North East Somerset	E.Suss.	East Sussex	M.Tyd.	Merthyr Tydfil	R. & C.	Redcar & Cleveland	Thur.	Thurrock
B.Gwent	Blaenau Gwent	Edin.	Edinburgh	Med.	Medway	R.C.T.	Rhondda Cynon Taff	V. of Glam.	Vale of Glamorgan
Beds.	Bedfordshire	Falk.	Falkirk	Mersey.	Merseyside	Read.	Reading	W'ham	Wokingham
Bourne.	Bournemouth	Flints.	Flintshire	Middbro.	Middlesbrough	Renf.	Renfrewshire	W. & M.	Windsor & Maidenhead
Brack.F.	Bracknell Forest	Glas.	Glasgow	Midloth.	Midlothian	Rut.	Rutland	W.Berks.	West Berkshire
Bucks.	Buckinghamshire	Glos.	Gloucestershire	Mon.	Monmouthshire	S'end	Southend	W.Dun.	West Dunbartonshire
Caerp.	Caerphilly	Gt.Lon.	Greater London	N.Ayr.	North Ayrshire	S'ham.	Southampton	W.Isles	Western Isles (Na h-Eileanan an Iar)
Cambs.	Cambridgeshire	Gt.Man.	Greater Manchester	N.E.Lincs.	North East Lincolnshire	S.Ayr.	South Ayrshire	W.Loth.	West Lothian
Carmar.	Carmarthenshire	Gwyn.	Gwynedd	N.Lan.	North Lanarkshire	S.Glos.	South Gloucestershire	W.Mid.	West Midlands
Cere.	Ceredigion	Hants.	Hampshire	N.Lincs.	North Lincolnshire	S.Lan.	South Lanarkshire	W.Suss.	West Sussex
Chan.I.	Channel Islands	Hart.	Hartlepool	N.P.T.	Neath Port Talbot	S.Yorks.	South Yorkshire	W.Yorks.	West Yorkshire
Ches.	Cheshire	Here.	Herefordshire	N.Som.	North Somerset	Sc.Bord.	Scottish Borders	Warks.	Warwickshire
Cornw.	Cornwall	Herts.	Hertfordshire	N.Yorks.	North Yorkshire	Shet.	Shetland	Warr.	Warrington
Cumb.	Cumbria	High.	Highland	Norf.	Norfolk	Shrop.	Shropshire	Wilts.	Wiltshire
D. & G.	Dumfries & Galloway	Hull	Kingston upon Hull	Northants.	Northamptonshire	Slo.	Slough	Worcs.	Worcestershire
Darl.	Darlington	I.o.A.	Isle of Anglesey	Northumb.	Northumberland	Som.	Somerset	Wrex.	Wrexham
Denb.	Denbighshire	I.o.M.	Isle of Man	Nott.	Nottingham	Staffs.	Staffordshire		
Derbys.	Derbyshire	I.o.S.	Isles of Scilly	Notts.	Nottinghamshire	Stir.	Stirling		
Dur.	Durham	I.o.W.	Isle of Wight	Ork.	Orkney	Stock.	Stockton-on-Tees		
		Inclyde	Inverclyde	Oxon.	Oxfordshire	Stoke	Stoke-on-Trent		
						Suff.	Suffolk		

Places of interest are shown in the index in **purple** type.

1853 Gallery 86

A

A La Ronde 24 C5
Ab Kettleby 224 C5
Ab Lench 196 C2
Abbas Combe 167 E5
Abberley 195 G1
Abberley Common 195 G1
Abberton *Essex* 188 D1
Abberton *Worcs.* 196 B2
Abberwick 279 F5
Abbess Roding 187 E1
Abbey Dore 194 C4
Abbey Hulton 221 G3
Abbey St. Bathans 287 E3
Abbey Town 259 E1
Abbey Village 242 C5
Abbey Wood 187 D5
Abbeycwmhir 205 G5
Abbeydale 236 A4
Abbeystead 242 B2
Abbot Hall Art Gallery & Museum of Lakeland Life 93
Abbot House 116
Abbotrule 278 A5
Abbots Bickington 163 D4
Abbots Bromley 222 B5
Abbots Langley 185 F2
Abbots Leigh 181 E5
Abbots Morton 196 C2
Abbots Ripton 212 A5
Abbot's Salford 196 C2
Abbots Worthy 169 F4
Abbotsbury 154 B4
Abbotsbury Swannery & Sub-Tropical Gardens 24
Abbotsfield Farm 233 G3
Abbotsford House 116
Abbotsham 163 E3
Abbotskerswell 151 E1
Abbotsley 200 A2
Abbotstone 169 G4
Abbotts Ann 169 E3
Abbott's Barton 169 F4
Abbottswood 169 E5
Abdon 207 E4
Abdy 236 B3
Abenhall 181 F1
Aber 192 A3
Aber Village 194 A5
Aberaeron 192 A1
Aberaman 179 G2
Aberangell 205 E2
Aber-Arad 191 G3
Aberarder 299 G1
Aberarder House 309 F2
Aberargie 293 G3
Aberarth 192 A1
Aberavon 178 D4
Aber-banc 191 G3
Aberbargoed 180 A2
Aberbeeg 180 B2
Aberbowlan 192 C4
Aberbran 193 F5
Abercanaid 179 G2
Abercarn 180 B3
Abercastle 190 B4
Abercegir 205 E2
Aberchalder 308 C4
Aberchirder 324 B4
Aberconwy House 107
Abercorn 285 E2
Abercraf 179 E1
Abercregan 179 E3
Abercrombie 294 D4
Abercrychan 193 D4
Abercwmboi 179 G2
Abercych 191 F3
Abercynafon 179 G1
Abercynon 179 G3
Abercywarch 205 E1
Aberdalgie 293 F2
Aberdare 179 F2
Aberdaron 216 A5
Aberdaugleddau (Milford Haven) 176 B2
Aberdeen 313 E4
Aberdeen Airport 313 D3
Aberdeen Art Gallery 116
Aberdesach 216 D2
Aberdour 285 F1
Aberdour Castle 116
Aberdovey (Aberdyfi) 204 C3
Aberduhonw 193 G2
Aberdulais 179 D3
Aberdulais Falls 107
Aberdyfi (Aberdovey) 204 C3
Aberedw 193 G3
Abereiddy 190 A4
Abererch 216 C4
Aberfan 179 G2
Aberfeldy 301 D5
Aberffraw 216 C1
Aberffrwd 204 C5
Aberford 244 D4
Aberfoyle 292 A4
Abergavenny (Y Fenni) 180 B1
Abergele 232 A5
Aber-Giâr 192 B3
Aberglasney Gardens 107
Abergorlech 192 B4
Abergwaun (Fishguard) 190 C4
Abergwesyn 193 E2
Abergwesyn Pass 107
Abergwili 192 A5
Abergwydol 205 D2
Abergwynant 204 C1
Abergwynfi 179 E3
Abergwyngregyn 231 E5
Abergynolwyn 204 C2
Aberhafesp 205 G3
Aberhonddu (Brecon) 193 G5
Aberhosan 205 E3
Aberkenfig 179 E4
Aberlady 286 B1
Aberlemno 302 D4
Aberllefenni 205 D2
Aber-llia 179 F1
Aberllynfi (Three Cocks) 194 A4
Aberlour (Charlestown of Aberlour) 323 E5
Abermad 204 B5
Abermaw (Barmouth) 204 C1
Abermeurig 192 B2
Abermule 206 A3
Abernaint 219 E5
Abernant *Carmar.* 191 G5
Aber-nant *R.C.T.* 179 G2
Abernethy 293 G3
Abernyte 294 A1
Aberpennar (Mountain Ash) 179 G3
Aberporth 191 F2
Aberriw (Berriew) 206 A2
Aberscross 332 C5
Abersky 309 E2
Abersoch 216 C5
Abersychan 180 B2
Abertawe (Swansea) 178 C3
Aberteifi (Cardigan) 191 E3
Aberthin 179 G5
Abertillery 180 B2
Abertridwr *Caerp.* 180 A4
Abertridwr *Powys* 205 G1
Abertysswg 180 A2
Aberuthven 293 E3
Aberyscir 193 F5
Aberystwyth 204 B4
Abhainnsuidhe 326 C3
Abingdon 183 G3
Abinger Common 171 G3
Abinger Hammer 171 F3
Abington 276 A3
Abington Pigotts 200 B3
Abingworth 158 D2
Ablington *Glos.* 182 D2
Ablington *Wilts.* 168 C3
Abney 235 F5
Above Church 222 B2
Aboyne 312 A5
Abram 234 A2
Abriachan 309 E1
Abridge 187 D3
Abronhill 284 B2
Abson 181 G5
Abthorpe 198 B3
Abune-the-Hill 340 A4
Aby 239 E5
Acaster Malbis 245 E3
Acaster Selby 245 E3
Accrington 243 D5
Accurrach 290 D2
Acha 296 A4
Achacha 298 B5
Achadacaie 281 G3
Achadh Mòr 329 E5
Achadh-chaorrunn 281 F4
Achadunan 291 E3
Achagavel 297 G4
Achaglass 281 F5
Achahoish 281 F2
Achalader 301 G5
Achallader 299 F5
Achamore 281 D2
Achandunie 321 F2
Achany 332 A4
Achaphubuil 298 C2
Acharacle 297 F3
Achargary 335 G3
Acharn *Arg. & B.* 290 D1
Acharn *P. & K.* 300 C5
Acharonich 289 D1
Acharosson 282 A2
Achateny 297 E2
Achath 312 C3
Achavanich 337 D4
Achddu 178 A2
Achduart 330 C4
Achentoul 336 A5
Achfary 334 B5
Achgarve 330 A5
Achiemore *High.* 334 C2
Achiemore *High.* 336 A3
Achies 336 D3
A'Chill 305 F4
Achiltibuie 330 C4
Achina 335 G2
Achindown 322 A5
Achinduich 332 A5
Achingills 337 D2
Achintee 319 F5
Achintee House 298 D2
Achintraid 307 E1
Achlean 310 A5
Achleanan 297 E4
Achleek 297 G4
Achlian 290 D2
Achlyness 334 B3
Achmelvich 330 C2
Achmony 309 E1
Achmore *High.* 307 E1
Achmore *High.* 330 C5
Achmore *Stir.* 292 A1
Achnaba 282 A1
Achnabat 309 E1
Achnabourin 335 G3
Achnacairn 290 B1
Achnacarnin 330 C1
Achnacarry 299 D1
Achnaclerach 320 D3
Achnacloich *Arg. & B.* 290 B1
Achnacloich *High.* 306 B4
Achnaclyth 336 C5
Achnacraig 297 D5
Achnacroish 298 A5
Achnadrish 296 D4
Achnafalnich 291 E2
Achnafauld 293 D1
Achnagairn 321 E5
Achnagarron 321 F2
Achnaha *High.* 297 F5
Achnaha *High.* 297 D3
Achnahanat 332 A5
Achnahannet 310 B2
Achnairn 332 A3
Achnalea 298 A3
Achnamara 281 F1
Achnanellan 297 G3
Achnasaul 299 D1
Achnasheen 320 A4
Achnashelloch 290 A5
Achnastank 311 E1
Achorn 336 D5
Achosnich *High.* 332 C5
Achosnich *High.* 296 D3
Achreamie 336 C2
Achriabhach 298 D3
Achriesgill 334 B3
Achtoty 335 F2
Achurch 211 F4
Achuvoldrach 335 E3
Achvaich 332 C5
Achvarasdal 336 B2
Achvlair 298 B4
Achvraie 330 C4
Ackenthwaite 249 G4
Ackergill 337 F3
Acklam *Middbro.* 253 D1
Acklam *N.Yorks.* 245 G1
Ackleton 207 G3
Acklington 271 E1
Ackton 244 D5
Ackworth Moor Top 236 B1
Acle 229 F4
Acock's Green 208 D4
Acol 175 F2
Acomb *Northumb.* 261 F1
Acomb *York* 245 E2
Aconbury 195 E4
Acorn Bank 93
Acre 243 D5
Acrefair 219 F3
Acrise Place 175 D4
Acton *Ches.* 220 D2
Acton *Dorset* 155 F5
Acton *Gt.Lon.* 186 A4
Acton *Shrop.* 206 C4
Acton *Staffs.* 221 F3
Acton *Suff.* 201 G3
Acton *Worcs.* 196 A1
Acton *Wrex.* 220 A2
Acton Beauchamp 195 F2
Acton Bridge 233 G5
Acton Burnell 207 E2
Acton Green 195 F2
Acton Pigott 207 E2
Acton Round 207 F3
Acton Scott 207 D4
Acton Scott Working Farm Museum 93
Acton Trussell 208 B1
Acton Turville 182 A4
Adamhill 274 C2
Adbaston 221 E5
Adber 166 C5
Adderbury 197 G4
Adderley 221 D4
Adderstone 279 F3
Addiewell 285 D3
Addingham 243 G3
Addington *Bucks.* 198 C5
Addington *Gt.Lon.* 172 C2
Addington *Kent* 173 F3
Addiscombe 172 C2
Addlestone 171 F1
Addlethorpe 226 D1
Adel 244 B4
Adeney 207 G1
Adeyfield 185 F2
Adfa 205 G2
Adforton 206 D5
Adisham 175 E3
Adlestrop 197 E5
Adlingfleet 246 A5
Adlington *Ches.* 234 D4
Adlington *Lancs.* 233 G1
Adlington Hall 93
Admaston *Staffs.* 222 B5
Admaston *Tel. & W.* 207 F1
Admington 197 E3
Adrian Sankey Glass Makers 93
Adsborough 165 F5
Adscombe 165 E4
Adstock 198 C4
Adstone 198 A2
Adversane 171 F5
Advie 310 D1
Adwalton 244 B5
Adwell 184 B3
Adwick le Street 236 C2
Adwick upon Dearne 236 B2
Adziel 325 E4
Ae Village 267 D2
Afan Argoed Country Park 107
Affetside 234 B1
Affleck 313 D2
Affpuddle 155 E3
Afon Wen 216 D4
Afon-wen 232 C5
Afton 156 C4
Afton Bridgend 275 E4
Agglethorpe 251 F4
Aigburth 233 F4
Aiginis 329 F4
Aike 246 C3
Aikerness 340 C1
Aikers 339 D3
Aiketgate 260 A3
Aikshaw 259 E2
Aikton 259 F1
Aikwood Tower 277 F3
Ailby 239 E5
Ailey 194 C3
Ailsworth 211 G3
Aimes Green 186 D2
Aimster 336 D2
Ainderby Quernhow 252 C4
Ainderby Steeple 252 C3
Aingers Green 202 C5
Ainsdale 233 E1
Ainsdale-on-Sea 233 E1
Ainstable 260 B3
Ainsworth 234 B1
Ainthorpe 253 G2
Aintree 233 E3
Aira Force 93
Aird *W.Isles* 315 F4
Aird *W.Isles* 329 G4
Aird a' Mhachair 315 F5
Aird a' Mhulaidh 327 D2
Aird Asaig 326 D3
Aird Dhail 329 F1
Aird Leimhe 326 D5
Aird Mhige 326 D4
Aird Mhighe 326 C5
Aird of Sleat 306 B4
Aird Thunga 329 F4
Aird Uig 328 B4
Airdrie *Fife* 295 D4
Airdrie *N.Lan.* 284 B3
Aire View 243 F3
Airidh a' Bhruaich 327 E2
Airieland 266 B5
Airies 264 A4
Airigh-drishaig 307 D1
Airmyn 245 G5
Airntully 293 F1
Airor 306 D4
Airth 284 C1
Airton 243 F2
Airyhassen 257 D2
Aisby *Lincs.* 237 F3
Aisby *Lincs.* 225 F4
Aisgernis (Askernish) 314 C1
Aisgill 250 C3
Aish *Devon* 150 C1
Aish *Devon* 151 E2
Aisholt 165 E4
Aiskew 252 B4
Aislaby *N.Yorks.* 254 B2
Aislaby *N.Yorks.* 253 G4
Aislaby *Stock.* 252 D1
Aisthorpe 237 G4
Aith *Ork.* 340 A5
Aith *Ork.* 341 E4
Aith *Shet.* 342 C2
Aith *Shet.* 345 F3
Aithsetter 342 D4
Aitnoch 310 B1
Akeld 279 D4
Akeley 198 C4
Akenham 202 C3
Albaston 149 E3
Albecq 151 E5
Alberbury 206 C1
Albert Town 176 C1
Albourne 159 E2
Albourne Green 159 E2
Albrighton *Shrop.* 208 A2
Albrighton *Shrop.* 207 D1
Alburgh 215 D3
Albury *Herts.* 200 C5
Albury *Oxon.* 184 B2
Albury *Surr.* 171 F3
Albury End 200 C5
Albury Heath 171 F3
Alby Crafts & Gardens 77
Albyfield 260 B2
Alcaig 321 E4
Alcaston 207 D4
Alcester 196 C2
Alciston 160 A3
Alcombe 164 C3
Alconbury 211 G5
Alconbury Hill 211 G5
Alconbury Weston 211 G5
Aldborough *N.Yorks.* 244 D1
Aldborough *Norf.* 228 C2
Aldbourne 183 E5
Aldbrough 247 E4
Aldbrough St. John 252 B1
Aldbury 185 E1
Aldclune 301 E3
Aldeburgh 203 F2
Aldeby 215 F2
Aldenham 186 A3
Aldenham Reservoir Country Park 77
Alderbury 168 C5
Alderford 228 C4
Alderholt 156 A1
Alderley 181 G3
Alderley Edge 234 C5
Aldermaston 169 G1
Aldermaston Wharf 170 B1
Alderminster 197 E3
Alderney 151 G4
Alderney Airport 151 F4
Alder's End 195 F4
Aldersey Green 220 B2
Aldershot 171 D2
Alderton *Glos.* 196 B4
Alderton *Northants.* 198 C3
Alderton *Suff.* 203 E3
Alderton *Wilts.* 182 A4
Alderwasley 223 E2
Aldfield 244 B1
Aldford 220 B2
Aldham *Essex* 202 A5
Aldham *Suff.* 202 B3
Aldie *Aber.* 325 F5
Aldie *High.* 321 G1
Aldingbourne 158 B3
Aldingham 249 D5
Aldington *Kent* 174 C5
Aldington *Worcs.* 196 C3
Aldivalloch 311 F2
Aldochlay 291 F5
Aldons 264 C2
Aldous's Corner 215 E3
Aldreth 212 C5
Aldridge 208 C2
Aldringham 203 F1
Aldsworth *Glos.* 183 D2
Aldsworth *W.Suss.* 157 G2
Aldunie 311 F2
Aldville 293 E1
Aldwark *Derbys.* 222 D2
Aldwark *N.Yorks.* 245 D1
Aldwick 158 B4
Aldwincle 211 F4
Aldworth 184 A5
Alexander Keiller Museum (see Avebury Ring) 24
Alexandria 283 E2
Aley 165 E4
Aley Green 185 F1
Alfardisworthy 162 C4
Alfington 153 F3
Alfold 171 F4
Alfold Crossways 171 F4
Alford *Aber.* 312 A3
Alford *Lincs.* 239 E5
Alford *Som.* 166 D4
Alfreton 223 F2
Alfrick 195 G2
Alfrick Pound 195 G2
Alfriston 160 A3
Alfriston Clergy House 40
Algarkirk 226 A4
Alhampton 166 D4
Alice in Wonderland Family Park 24
Alkborough 246 A5
Alkerton 197 F3
Alkham 175 E4
Alkington 220 C4
Alkmonton 222 C4
All Cannings 168 B1
All Saints South Elmham 215 E3
All Stretton 207 D3
Allaleigh 151 E2
Allanaquoich 310 D5
Allancreich 312 A5
Allanfearn 321 G5
Allangillfoot 268 A2
Allanton *D. & G.* 266 D2
Allanton *E.Ayr.* 275 E2
Allanton *N.Lan.* 284 C4
Allanton *S.Lan.* 284 B4
Allanton *Sc.Bord.* 287 F4
Allardice 303 G2
Allathasdal 314 B3
Allbrook 169 F5
Allendale Town 261 E2
Allenheads 261 E3
Allen's Green 187 D1
Allensford 261 G2
Allensmore 195 D4
Allenton 223 E4
Aller 166 B5
Allerby 259 D3
Allercombe 152 D3
Allerford *Devon* 149 E2
Allerford *Som.* 164 C3
Allerston 254 B4
Allerthorpe 245 G3
Allerton *Mersey.* 233 F4
Allerton *W.Yorks.* 244 A4
Allerton Bywater 244 D5
Allerton Mauleverer 244 D2
Allesley 209 E4
Allestree 223 E4
Allet Common 146 B5
Allexton 210 D2
Allgreave 221 G1
Allhallows 174 A1
Allhallows-on-Sea 174 A1
Alligin Shuas 319 E4
Allimore Green 208 A1
Allington *Dorset* 154 A3
Allington *Lincs.* 225 D3
Allington *Wilts.* 168 D4
Allington *Wilts.* 168 B1
Allington *Wilts.* 182 A5
Allithwaite 249 E5
Allnabad 335 D4
Alloa 293 D5
Allonby 259 D2
Allostock 234 B5
Alloway 274 B4
Allowenshay 153 G1
Allscot 207 G3
Allscott 207 F1
Allt na h-Airbhe 330 D5
Alltachonaich 297 G4
Alltbeithe 307 G2
Alltforgan 218 C5
Alltmawr 193 G3
Alltnacaillich 335 D4
Allt-na-subh 307 F1
Alltsigh 309 D3
Alltwalis 192 A4
Alltwen 178 D2
Alltyblaca 192 B3
Allwood Green 214 B4
Almeley 194 C2
Almeley Wootton 194 C2
Almer 155 F3
Almington 221 E4
Almiston Cross 163 D3
Almondbank 293 F2
Almondbury 235 F1
Almondsbury 181 F4
Alne 245 D1
Alness 321 F3
Alnham 279 D5
Alnmouth 279 G5
Alnwick 279 F5
Alnwick Castle & Garden 102

Alperton 186 A4
Alphamstone 201 G4
Alpheton 201 G2
Alphington 152 C3
Alport 222 D1
Alpraham 220 C2
Alresford 202 B5
Alrewas 209 D1
Alrick 301 G3
Alsager 221 E2
Alsagers Bank 221 F3
Alsop en le Dale 222 C2
Alston *Cumb.* 260 D3
Alston *Devon* 153 G2
Alston Sutton 166 B2
Alstone *Glos.* 196 B4
Alstone *Som.* 166 A3
Alstone *Staffs.* 208 A1
Alstonefield 222 C2
Alswear 164 A5
Alt 234 D2
Altandhu 330 B3
Altanduin 332 D2
Altarnun 147 G1
Altass 332 A4
Altens 313 E4
Alterwall 337 E2
Altham 243 D4
Althorne 188 C3
Althorp House 70
Althorpe 237 F2
Alticry 265 D5
Altnafeadh 299 E4
Altnaharra 335 E5
Altofts 244 C5
Alton *Derbys.* 223 E1
Alton *Hants.* 170 C4
Alton *Staffs.* 222 B3
Alton Barnes 168 C1
Alton Pancras 154 D2
Alton Priors 168 C1
Alton Towers Leisure Park 63
Altonside 323 E4
Altrincham 234 B4
Altura 308 B5
Alva 293 D5
Alvanley 233 F5
Alvaston 223 E4
Alvechurch 208 C5
Alvecote 209 E2
Alvediston 168 A5
Alveley 207 G4
Alverdiscott 163 F3
Alverstoke 157 F3
Alverstone 157 E4
Alverthorpe 244 C5
Alverton 224 C3
Alves 322 D3
Alvescot 183 E2
Alveston *S.Glos.* 181 F4
Alveston *Warks.* 197 E2
Alvie 310 A4
Alvingham 239 D3
Alvington 181 F2
Alwalton 211 G3
Alweston 154 C1
Alwington 163 E3
Alwinton 270 B1
Alwoodley 244 C3
Alwoodley Gates 244 C3
Alyth 302 A5
Amalebra 144 B3
Ambaston 223 F4
Amber Hill 226 A3
Ambergate 223 E2
Amberley *Glos.* 182 A2
Amberley *W.Suss.* 158 C2
Amberley Museum 40
Amble 271 E1
Amblecote 208 A4
Ambleside 249 E2
Ambleston 190 D5
Ambrismore 282 B4
Ambrosden 184 B1
Amcotts 237 F1
American Adventure Theme Park 70
American Museum 24
Amersham 185 E3
Amerton 221 G5
Amesbury 168 C3
Ameysford 155 G2
Amington 209 E2
Amisfield Town 267 E2
Amlwch 230 C3
Amlwch Port 230 C3
Ammanford (Rhydaman) 178 C1
Amotherby 253 G5
Ampfield 169 E5
Ampleforth 253 E5
Ampleforth College 253 E5
Ampney Crucis 182 C2
Ampney St. Mary 182 C2
Ampney St. Peter 182 C2
Amport 169 E3
Ampthill 199 F4
Ampton 213 G5
Amroth 177 E2
Amulree 293 D1
An Tairbeart (Tarbert) 327 D3
An T-òb (Leverburgh) 326 C5
Anaboard 310 C1
[illegible]
Ancaster 225 E3
Anchor 206 A4
Anchor Corner 214 B2
Ancient High House 63
Ancroft 279 G5
Ancrum 278 A4
Ancton 158 B3
Anderby 239 F5
Anderby Creek 239 F5
Andersea 166 A4
Andersfield 165 F4
Anderson 155 E3
Anderton 234 A5
Anderton Boat Lift 93
Andover 169 E3
Andover Down 169 E3
Andoversford 182 C1
Andreas 240 C2
Anelog 216 A5
Anfield 233 E3
Angarrack 144 C3
Angarrick 145 E3
Angelbank 207 E5
Angerton 259 F1
Angle 176 B2
Angler's Retreat 204 D3
Anglesey (Ynys Môn) 230 B4
Anglesey Abbey 77
Anglesey Sea Zoo 107
Angmering 158 C3
Angmering-on-Sea 158 C3
Angram *N.Yorks.* 245 E3
Angram *N.Yorks.* 251 D3
Angus Folk Museum 116
Anick 261 F1
Anie 292 A3
Ankerville 322 A2
Anlaby 246 C5
Anmer 227 F5
Anmore 157 F1
Anna Valley 169 E3
Annan 267 F4
Annaside 248 B4
Annat *Arg. & B.* 290 C2
Annat *High.* 319 E4
Annbank 274 C3
Anne Hathaway's Cottage 63
Annesley 223 G2
Annesley Woodhouse 223 F2
Annfield Plain 262 A2
Anniesland 283 G3
Annscroft 207 D2
Ansdell 241 G5
Ansford 166 D4
Ansley 209 E3
Anslow 222 D5
Anslow Gate 222 C5
Ansteadbrook 171 E4
Anstey *Herts.* 200 C4
Anstey *Leics.* 210 A2
Anstruther 295 D4
Ansty *W.Suss.* 159 E1
Ansty *Warks.* 209 F4
Ansty *Wilts.* 168 A5
Ansty Coombe 168 A5
Ansty Cross 155 D2
Anthill Common 157 F1
Anthorn 259 E1
Antingham 229 D2
Antonine Wall 116
Anton's Gowt 226 A3
Antony 149 D5
Antony House 24
Antrobus 234 A5
Anvil Corner 163 D5
Anvil Green 174 D4
Anwick 225 G2
Anwoth 265 G5
Aonach Mòr Mountain Gondola & Nevis Range Ski Centre 116
Aoradh 280 A3
Apes Hall, The 213 D3
Apethorpe 211 F3
Apeton 208 A1
Apley 238 B5
Apperknowle 236 A5
Apperley 196 A5
Apperley Bridge 244 A4
Appersett 251 D3
Appin 298 B5
Appin House 298 B5
Appleby 237 G1
Appleby Magna 209 F1
Appleby Parva 209 F2
Appleby-in-Westmorland 260 C5
Applecross 318 D5
Appledore *Devon* 163 E2
Appledore *Devon* 153 D1
Appledore *Kent* 161 E1
Appledore Heath 174 B5
Appleford 184 A3
Appleshaw 169 E3
Applethwaite 259 F4
Appleton *Halton* 233 G4
Appleton *Oxon.* 183 G2
Appleton Roebuck 245 E3
Appleton Thorn 234 A4
Appleton Wiske 252 C2
Appleton-le-Moors 253 G4
Appleton-le-Street 253 G5
Appletreehall 277 G4
Appletreewick 243 G1
Appley 165 D5
Appley Bridge 233 G2
Apse Heath 157 E4
Apsey Green 203 D1
Apsley 185 F2
Apsley End 199 G4
Apuldram 158 A3
Aquarium of the Lakes 93
Arbeia Roman Fort & Museum 102
Arberth (Narberth) 177 E1
[illegible]
Arborfield 170 C1
Arborfield Cross 170 C1
Arborfield Garrison 170 C1
Arbourthorne 236 A4
Arbroath 303 E5
Arbroath Abbey 116
Arbury Hall 63
Arbuthnott 303 F2
Archdeacon Newton 252 B1
Archiestown 323 E5
Arclid 221 E1
Ard a' Chapuill 282 B1
Ardachearanbeg 282 B1
Ardacheranmor 282 B1
Ardachoil 289 G1
Ardachu 332 B4
Ardailly 281 E4
Ardalanish 288 C3
Ardallie 313 F1
Ardanaiseig 290 C2
Ardaneaskan 307 E1
Ardanstur 290 A3
Ardantiobairt 297 F4
Ardantrive 290 A2
Ardarroch 319 E5
Ardbeg *Arg. & B.* 282 B3
Ardbeg *Arg. & B.* 280 C5
Ardbeg *Arg. & B.* 282 C1
Ardblair 309 E1
Ardbrecknish 290 C2
Ardcharnich 320 A1
Ardchiavaig 288 C3
Ardchonnel 290 B1
Ardchonnell 290 B3
Ardchrishnish 288 D2
Ardchronie 321 F1
Ardchuilk 308 B1
Ardchullarie More 292 A3
Ardchyle 292 A2
Arddlin 206 B1
Ardechvie 308 A5
Ardeley 200 B5
Ardelve 307 E2
Arden 283 E1
Ardencaple House 289 G3
Ardens Grafton 196 D2
Ardentallan 290 A2
Ardentinny 282 C1
Ardeonaig 292 B1
Ardersier 321 G4
Ardery 297 G3
Ardessie 319 G1
Ardfad 289 G3
Ardfern 290 A4
Ardfin 280 C3
Ardgartan 291 E4
Ardgay 332 B5
Ardgenavan 291 D3
Ardgowan 282 D2
Ardgowse 312 B3
Ardgye 322 D3
Ardhallow 282 C2
Ardheslaig 319 D4
Ardiecow 324 A3
Ardinamar 289 G3
Ardindrean 320 A1
Ardingly 159 F1
Ardington 183 G4
Ardington Wick 183 G4
Ardintoul 307 E2
Ardkinglas House 291 D3
Ardkinglas Woodland Garden 116
Ardlair 312 A2
Ardlamont 282 A3
Ardleigh 202 B5
Ardleigh Green 187 E4
Ardleigh Heath 202 B4
Ardleish 291 F3
Ardler 302 A5
Ardley 198 A5
Ardley End 187 E1
Ardlui 291 F3
Ardlussa 281 E1
Ardmaddy 290 C1
Ardmair 330 D5
Ardmaleish 282 B3
Ardmay 291 F4
Ardmenish 281 D2
Ardmhór 314 C3
Ardminish 281 C5
Ardmolich 297 G2
Ardmore *Arg. & B.* 280 C4
Ardmore *Arg. & B.* 289 G2
Ardmore *Arg. & B.* 283 E2
Ardmore *High.* 321 G1
Ardnackaig 289 G5
Ardnacross 297 E5
Ardnadam 282 C1
Ardnadrochit 289 G1
Ardnagoine 330 B4
Ardnagowan 290 D4
Ardnahein 291 D5
Ardnahoe 280 C2
Ardnarff 307 E1
Ardnastang 298 A3
Ardnave 280 A2
Ardno 291 D4
Ardo 313 D1
Ardoch *D. & G.* 275 G5
Ardoch *Moray* 322 D4
Ardoch *P. & K.* 293 F1
Ardochrig 284 A5
Ardoyne 312 B2
Ardpatrick 281 F3
Ardpeaton 282 D1
Ardradnaig 300 C5
Ardrishaig 281 G1
Ardroe 330 C2
Ardross 321 F2
Ardrossan 282 D5
Ardscalpsie 282 B4
Ardshave 332 C5
Ardshealach 297 F3
Ardshellach 289 G3
Ardsley 236 A2
Ardslignish 297 E3
Ardtalla 280 C4
Ardtalnaig 292 C1
[illegible]
Ardteatle 290 D2
Ardtoe 297 F2
Ardtornish 297 G5
Ardtrostan 292 B2
Ardtur 298 B5
Arduaine 290 A3
Arduaine Gardens 116
Ardullie 321 E3
Ardura 289 F1
Ardvar 334 A5
Ardvasar 306 C4
Ardveenish 314 C3
Ardveich 292 B2
Ardverikie 300 A1
Ardvorlich 291 F3
Ardvorlich *Arg. & B.* 292 B2
Ardvorlich *P. & K.* 265 G5
Ardwall 256 B2
Ardwell *D. & G.* 311 F1
Ardwell *Moray* 264 C1
Ardwell *S.Ayr.* 234 C3
Ardwick 208 A5
Areley Kings 170 D4
Arford 292 C4
Argaty 180 A3
Argoed 193 F1
Argoed Mill 160 A1
Argos Hill 266 B5
Argrennan House 290 B4
Arichamish 291 E1
Arichastlich 289 G5
Arichonan 288 C2
Aridhglas 297 G1
Arienskill 296 A4
Arileod 318 D4
Arinacrinachd 281 F1
Arinafad Beg 296 B4
Arinagour 314 C1
Arinambane 297 F1
Arisaig 297 F3
Arivegaig 244 C1
Arkendale 200 C4
Arkesden 249 G5
Arkholme 251 F2
Arkle Town 259 E3
Arkleby 251 F4
Arkleside 268 B2
Arkleton 186 B3
Arkley 236 C2
Arksey 236 B5
Arkwright Town 293 G4
Arlary 196 B5
Arle 258 D5
Arlecdon 199 G4
Arlesey 207 F1
Arleston 234 A4
Arley
Arley Hall 93
Arlingham 181 G1
Arlington *Devon* 163 G1
Arlington *E.Suss.* 160 A3
Arlington *Glos.* 182 D2
Arlington Beccott 163 G1
Arlington Court 24
Armadale *High.* 335 G2
Armadale *High.* 306 C4
Armadale *W.Loth.* 284 D3
Armathwaite 260 B3
Arminghall 229 D5
Armitage 208 C1
Armitage Bridge 235 F1
Armley 244 B4
Armscote 197 E3
Armshead 221 G3
Armston 211 F4
Armthorpe 236 D2
Arnabost 296 B3
Arnaby 248 C4
Arncliffe 251 E5
Arncliffe Cote 251 E5
Arncroach 294 D4
Arne 155 F4
Arnesby 210 B3
Arngask 293 G3
Arngibbon 292 B5
Arngomery 292 B5
Arnhall 303 E3
Arnicle 272 C2
Arnipol 297 G1
Arnisdale 307 E3
Arnish 318 B5
Arniston Engine 286 A3
Arnol 329 E3
Arnold *E.Riding* 246 D3
Arnold *Notts.* 223 G3
Arnprior 292 B5
Arnside 249 F5
Arowry 220 B4
Arrad Foot 249 E4
Arradoul 323 G3
Arram 246 C3
Arran 273 E2
Arras 246 B3
Arrat 303 E4
Arrathorne 252 B3
Arreton 157 E4
Arrington 200 B2
Arrivain 291 E1
Arrochar 291 F4
Arrow 196 C2
Arscaig 332 A3
Arscott 206 D2
Arthington 244 B3
Arthingworth 210 C4
Arthog 204 C1
Arthrath 313 E1
Arthurstone 302 A5
Artrochie 313 F1
Aruadh 280 A3
Arundel 158 C3
Arundel Castle 40
Aryhoulan 298 C3
Asby 259 D4
Ascog 282 C3
Ascot 171 E1
Ascott *Bucks.* 40
Ascott *Warks.* 197 F4
Ascott d'Oyley 183 F1
Ascott Earl 183 E1
Ascott-under-Wychwood 183 F1
Ascreavie 302 B4
Asenby 252 D5
Asfordby 210 C1
Asfordby Hill 210 C1
Asgarby *Lincs.* 226 B1
Asgarby *Lincs.* 225 G3
Ash *Dorset* 155 E1
Ash *Kent* 175 E3
Ash *Kent* 173 F2
Ash *Som.* 166 B5
Ash *Surr.* 171 D2
Ash Barton 163 F5
Ash Bullayne 152 A2
Ash End House Children's Farm 63
Ash Green *Surr.* 171 E3
Ash Green *Warks.* 209 F4
Ash Magna 220 C4
Ash Mill 164 A5
Ash Parva 220 C4
Ash Priors 165 E5
Ash Street 202 B3
Ash Thomas 152 D1
Ash Vale 171 D2
Ashampstead 184 A5
Ashbocking 202 C2
Ashbourne 222 C3
Ashbrittle 165 D5
Ashburnham Place 160 B2
Ashburton 151 D1
Ashbury *Devon* 149 F1
Ashbury *Oxon.* 183 E4
Ashby 237 F2
Ashby by Partney 226 C1
Ashby cum Fenby 238 C2
Ashby de la Launde 225 F2
Ashby de la Zouch 209 F1
Ashby Dell 215 F2
Ashby Folville 210 C1
Ashby Hill 238 C2
Ashby Magna 210 A3
Ashby Parva 210 A4
Ashby Puerorum 238 D5
Ashby St. Ledgers 198 A1
Ashby St. Mary 229 E5
Ashchurch 196 B4
Ashcombe *Devon* 152 C5
Ashcombe *N.Som.* 166 A1
Ashcott 166 B4
Ashdon 201 D3
Ashdown House 40
Ashe 169 G3
Asheldham 188 C2
Ashen 201 F3
Ashenden 174 A5
Ashendon 184 C1
Ashens 281 G2
Ashfield *Arg. & B.* 281 F1
Ashfield *Here.* 195 E5
Ashfield *Stir.* 292 C4
Ashfield *Suff.* 202 D1
Ashfield Green *Suff.* 215 D4
Ashfield Green *Suff.* 201 F2
Ashfold Crossways 159 E1
Ashford *Devon* 150 C3
Ashford *Devon* 163 F2
Ashford *Hants.* 156 A1
Ashford *Kent* 174 C4
Ashford *Surr.* 185 F5
Ashford Bowdler 207 E5
Ashford Carbonel 207 E5
Ashford Hill 169 G1
Ashford in the Water 235 F5
Ashgill 284 B4
Ashiestiel 277 F2
Ashill *Devon* 153 D1
Ashill *Norf.* 213 G2
Ashill *Som.* 153 G1
Ashingdon 188 B3
Ashington *Northumb.* 271 E3
Ashington *Som.* 166 C5
Ashington *W.Suss.* 158 D2
Ashkirk 277 F3
Ashlett 157 D2
Ashleworth 196 A5
Ashleworth Quay 196 A5
Ashley *Cambs.* 201 E1
Ashley *Ches.* 234 B4
Ashley *Devon* 163 G4
Ashley *Glos.* 182 B3
Ashley *Hants.* 169 E4
Ashley *Hants.* 156 B3
Ashley *Kent* 175 F4
Ashley *Northants.* 210 C3
Ashley *Staffs.* 221 E4
Ashley *Wilts.* 167 F1
Ashley Down 181 E5
Ashley Green 185 E2
Ashley Heath *Dorset* 156 A2
Ashley Heath *Staffs.* 221 E4
Ashmanhaugh 229 E3
Ashmansworth 169 F2
Ashmansworthy 162 D4
Ashmolean Museum 40
Ashmore *Dorset* 155 F1
Ashmore *P. & K.* 301 G4
Ashmore Green 169 G1
Ashorne 197 F2
Ashover 223 E1
Ashover Hay 223 E1
Ashow 209 F5
Ashperton 195 F3
Ashprington 151 E2
Ashreigney 163 G4
Ashtead 171 G2
Ashton *Ches.* 220 C1
Ashton *Cornw.* 144 D4
Ashton *Cornw.* 149 D4
Ashton *Hants.* 157 E1
Ashton *Here.* 195 E1
Ashton *Inclyde* 282 D2
Ashton *Northants.* 211 F4
Ashton *Northants.* 198 C3
Ashton *Peter.* 211 G2
Ashton Common 167 F2
Ashton Court Estate 24
Ashton Keynes 182 C3
Ashton under Hill 196 B4
Ashton upon Mersey 234 B3
Ashton-in-Makerfield 233 G3
Ashton-under-Lyne 234 D3
Ashurst *Hants.* 156 C1
Ashurst *Kent* 173 E5
Ashurst *W.Suss.* 159 D2
Ashurst Bridge 156 C1
Ashurstwood 172 D5
Ashwater 149 D1
Ashwell *Herts.* 200 A4
Ashwell *Rut.* 211 D1
Ashwell End 200 A3
Ashwellthorpe 214 C2
Ashwick 166 D3
Ashwicken 213 F1
Ashybank 277 G4
Askam in Furness 248 D5
Askern 236 C1
Askernish (Aisgernis) 314 C1
Askerswell 154 B3
Askett 184 D2
Askham *Cumb.* 260 B5
Askham *Notts.* 237 E5
Askham Bryan 245 E3
Askham Richard 245 E3
Asknish 290 B5
Askrigg 251 E3
Askwith 244 A3
Aslackby 225 F4
Aslacton 214 C2
Aslockton 224 C3
Asloun 312 A3
Aspall 202 C1
Aspatria 259 E2
Aspenden 200 B5
Asperton 226 A4
Aspley Guise 199 E4
Aspley Heath 199 E4
Aspull 234 A2
Asselby 245 G5
Asserby 239 E5
Assington 202 A4
Assington Green 201 F2
Astbury 221 F1
Astcote 198 B2
Asterby 238 C5
Asterley 206 C2
Asterton 206 D3
Asthall 183 E1
Asthall Leigh 183 F1
Astle 234 C5
Astley *Gt.Man.* 234 B2
Astley *Shrop.* 207 E1
Astley *Warks.* 209 F4
Astley *Worcs.* 195 G1
Astley Abbotts 207 G3
Astley Bridge 234 B1
Astley Cross 196 A1
Astley Green 234 B3
Astley Hall Museum & Gardens 93
Astley Lodge 207 E1
Aston *Ches.* 220 D3
Aston *Ches.* 233 G5
Aston *Derbys.* 235 F4
Aston *Derbys.* 222 C4
Aston *Flints.* 220 A1
Aston *Here.* 207 D5
Aston *Here.* 195 D1
Aston *Herts.* 200 A5
Aston *Oxon.* 183 F2
Aston *S.Yorks.* 236 B4
Aston *Shrop.* 220 C5
Aston *Shrop.* 208 A3
Aston *Staffs.* 221 E3
Aston *Tel. & W.* 207 F2
Aston *W'ham* 184 C4
Aston *W.Mid.* 208 C4
Aston Abbotts 198 D5
Aston Botterell 207 F4
Aston Cantlow 196 D2
Aston Clinton 185 D1
Aston Crews 195 F5
Aston Cross 196 B4
Aston End 200 A5
Aston Eyre 207 F3
Aston Fields 196 B1
Aston Flamville 209 G3
Aston Heath 233 G5
Aston Ingham 195 F5
Aston juxta Mondrum 221 D2
Aston le Walls 197 G2
Aston Magna 197 D4
Aston Munslow 207 E4
Aston on Carrant 196 B4
Aston on Clun 206 C4
Aston Pigott 206 C2
Aston Rogers 206 C2
Aston Rowant 184 C3
Aston Sandford 184 C2
Aston Somerville 196 C4
Aston Subedge 196 D3
Aston Tirrold 184 A4
Aston Upthorpe 184 A4
Aston-by-Stone 221 G4
Aston-on-Trent 223 F5
Astwick 200 A4
Astwood 199 E3
Astwood Bank 196 C1
Aswarby 225 F3
Aswardby 239 D5
Aswick Grange 212 B1
At-Bristol 24
Atch Lench 196 C2
Atcham 207 E2
Ath Linne 327 D2
Athelhampton *Dorset* 155 D3
Athelhampton *Dorset* 24
Athelington 214 D4
Athelney 166 A5
Athelstaneford 286 C2
Atherington *Devon* 163 F3
Atherington *W.Suss.* 158 C3
Athersley North 236 A2
Atherstone 209 F3
Atherstone on Stour 197 E2
Atherton 234 A2
Atlow 222 D3
Attadale 307 F1
Attenborough 223 G4
Atterby 237 G3
Attercliffe 236 A4
Atterley 207 F3
Atterton 209 F3
Attingham Park 63
Attleborough *Norf.* 214 B2
Attleborough *Warks.* 209 F3
Attlebridge 228 C4
Attleton Green 201 F2
Atwick 247 D2
Atworth 167 F1
Auberrow 195 D3
Aubourn 225 E1
Auch 291 F1
Auchairne 264 C2
Auchallater 301 G1
Auchameanach 281 G4
Auchamore 281 G5
Aucharnie 324 B5
Aucharrigill 331 G4
Auchattie 312 B5
Auchavan 301 G3
Auchbraad 281 G1
Auchbreck 311 E2
Auchenback 283 G4
Auchenblae 303 F2
Auchenbothie 283 E2
Auchenbrack 266 B1
Auchenbreck 282 B1
Auchencairn 266 B5
Auchencrow 287 F3
Auchendinny 285 G3
Auchendolly 266 B4
Auchenfoyle 283 E2
Auchengillan 283 G1
Auchengray 285 D4
Auchenhalrig 323 F3
Auchenheath 284 C5
Auchenhessnane 266 C1
Auchenlochan 282 A2
Auchenmalg 264 D5
Auchenrivock 268 B3
Auchentiber 283 E5
Auchenvennel 283 D1
Auchessan 291 G2
Auchgourish 310 B3
Auchinafaud 281 F4
Auchincruive 274 B3
Auchindarrach 281 G1
Auchindarroch 298 C4
Auchindrain 290 C4
Auchindrain Township Open Air Museum 116
Auchindrean 320 A1
Auchininna 324 B5
Auchinleck 274 D3
Auchinloch 284 A2
Auchinner 292 B3
Auchinroath 323 E4
Auchintoul *Aber.* 312 A3
Auchintoul *Aber.* 324 B4
Auchintoul *High.* 332 A5
Auchiries 313 F1
Auchleven 312 B2
Auchlochan 275 G2
Auchlunachan 320 A1
Auchlunies 313 D5
Auchlunkart 323 F5
Auchlyne 292 A2
Auchmacoy 313 E1
Auchmair 311 F2
Auchmantle 264 C4
Auchmithie 303 E5
Auchmuirbridge 294 A4
Auchmull 303 D2
Auchnabony 258 A2
Auchnabreac 290 C4
Auchnacloich 292 D1
Auchnacraig 289 G1
Auchnacree 302 C3
Auchnafree 292 D1
Auchnagallin 310 C1
Auchnagatt 325 E5
Auchnaha 282 A1
Auchnangoul 290 C4
Aucholzie 311 F5
Auchorrie 312 B4
Auchrannie 302 A4
Auchraw 292 A2
Auchreoch 291 F2
Auchronie 302 C1
Auchterarder 293 E3
Auchtercairn 319 E2
Auchterderran 294 A5
Auchterhouse 294 B1
Auchtermuchty 294 A3
Auchterneed 321 D4
Auchtertool 294 A5
Auchtertyre *Angus* 302 A5
Auchtertyre *High.* 307 E2
Auchtertyre *Moray* 323 D4
Auchtertyre *Stir.* 291 F2
Auchtubh 292 A2
Auckengill 337 F2
Auckland Castle 102
Auckley 236 D2
Audenshaw 234 D3
Audlem 221 D3
Audley 221 E2
Audley End *Essex* 200 D4
Audley End *Essex* 201 G4
Audley End *Essex* 77
Audley End *Suff.* 201 G2
Audmore 221 F5
Auds 324 B3
Aughton *E.Riding* 245 G4
Aughton *Lancs.* 233 E2
Aughton *Lancs.* 242 B1
Aughton *S.Yorks.* 236 B4
Aughton *Wilts.* 168 D2
Aughton Park 233 F2
Auk Walk 24
Auldearn 322 B4
Aulden 195 D2
Auldgirth 266 D2
Auldhame 286 C1
Auldhouse 284 A4
Aulich 300 B4

Ault a' chruinn 307 F2
Ault Hucknall 223 F1
Aultanrynie 334 C5
Aultbea 319 E1
Aultgrishan 318 D1
Aultguish Inn 320 C2
Aultibea 333 F2
Aultiphurst 336 A2
Aultmore 323 G4
Ault-na-goire 309 E2
Aultnamain Inn 321 F1
Aultnapaddock 323 F5
Aulton 312 B2
Aultvaich 321 E5
Aultvoulin 307 D4
Aunby 211 F1
Aundorach 310 B3
Aunk 152 D2
Aunsby 225 F4
Auquhorthies 312 D2
Aust 181 E4
Austerfield 237 D3
Austrey 209 E2
Austwick 243 D1
Authorpe 239 E4
Authorpe Row 239 F5
Avebury 182 D5
Avebury Ring & Alexander Keiller Museum 24
Avebury Trusloe 168 B1
Aveley 187 E4
Avening 182 A3
Averham 224 C2
Avery Hill 186 D5
Aveton Gifford 150 C3
Avielochan 310 B3
Aviemore 310 A3
Avington *Hants.* 169 G4
Avington *W.Berks.* 169 E1
Avoch 321 F4
Avon 156 A3
Avon Dassett 197 G2
Avonbridge 284 D2
Avoncliff 167 F2
Avoncroft Museum of Historic Buildings 63
Avonmouth 181 E5
Avonwick 150 D2
Awbridge 169 E5
Awhirk 264 B5
Awkley 181 E4
Awliscombe 153 E2
Awre 181 G2
Awsworth 223 F3
Axbridge 166 B2
Axford *Hants.* 170 B3
Axford *Wilts.* 183 E5
Axminster 153 F3
Axmouth 153 F3
Axton 232 C4
Axtown 150 B1
Aycliffe 262 B5
Aydon 261 G1
Aylburton 181 F2
Ayle 260 D3
Aylesbeare 152 D3
Aylesbury 184 D1
Aylesby 238 C2
Aylesford 173 G3
Aylesham 175 E3
Aylestone 210 A2
Aylmerton 228 C2
Aylsham 228 C3
Aylton 195 F4
Aymestrey 194 D1
Aynho 198 A4
Ayot Green 186 B1
Ayot St. Lawrence 186 A1
Ayot St. Peter 186 B1
Ayr 274 B3
Aysgarth 251 F4
Aysgarth Falls & National Park Centre 86
Ayshford 152 D1
Ayside 249 E4
Ayston 211 D2
Aythorpe Roding 187 E1
Ayton *P. & K.* 293 G3
Ayton *Sc.Bord.* 287 G3
Aywick 345 E4
Azerley 252 B5

B

Babbacombe 151 F1
Babbacombe Model Village 24
Babbinswood 220 A4
Babb's Green 186 C1
Babcary 166 C5
Babel 193 E4
Babell 232 C5
Babeny 149 G3
Bablock Hythe 183 G2
Babraham 200 D2
Babworth 237 D4
Baby's Hill 311 E1
Bac 329 F3
Bachau 230 C4
Bachelors' Club 116
Back of Keppoch 297 F1
Back Street 201 F2
Backaland 341 D3
Backaskaill 340 C1
Backbarrow 249 E4
Backburn 312 A1
Backe 177 F1
Backfolds 325 F4
Backford 233 F5
Backhill 312 C1
Backhill of Clackriach 325 E5
Backhill of Trustach 312 B5
Backies *High.* 332 D4
Backies *Moray* 324 A4
Backlass 337 E3
Backside 311 G1
Backwell 166 B1
Backworth 271 E4
Bacon End 187 E1
Baconend Green 187 E1
Baconsthorpe 228 C2
Bacton *Here.* 194 C4
Bacton *Norf.* 229 E2
Bacton *Suff.* 202 B1
Bacton Green 202 B1
Bacup 243 E5
Badachro 319 D2
Badanloch Lodge 335 G5
Badavanich 320 A4
Badbea 333 F3
Badbury 183 D4
Badbury Wick 183 D4
Badby 198 A2
Badcall *High.* 334 A4
Badcall *High.* 334 B3
Badcaul 330 C5
Baddeley Green 221 G2
Badden 281 G1
Baddesley Clinton *Warks.* 209 D5
Baddesley Clinton *Warks.* 63
Baddesley Ensor 209 E3
Baddidarach 330 C2
Badenscoth 312 C1
Badenyon 311 F3
Badgall 147 G1
Badger 207 G3
Badgerbank 234 C5
Badgers Mount 173 D2
Badgeworth 182 B1
Badgworth 166 A2
Badicaul 307 D2
Badingham 203 E1
Badintagairt 331 G3
Badlesmere 174 C3
Badley 202 B2
Badlipster 337 E4
Badluarach 330 B5
Badminton 182 A4
Badnaban 330 C2
Badnabay 334 B4
Badnafrave 311 E3
Badnagie 337 D5
Badnambiast 300 C2
Badninish 332 C5
Badrallach 330 C5
Badsey 196 C3
Badshot Lea 171 D3
Badsworth 236 B1
Badwell Ash 202 A1
Badworthy 150 C1
Badyo 301 E3
Bae Cinmel (Kinmel Bay) 232 A4
Bae Colwyn (Colwyn Bay) 231 G5
Bae Penrhyn (Penrhyn Bay) 231 G4
Bag Enderby 239 D5
Bagber 155 D1
Bagby 253 D4
Bage, The 194 B3
Bagendon 182 C2
Baggeridge Country Park 63
Bagginswood 207 F4
Baggrave Hall 210 B2
Baggrow 259 E2
Bàgh a' Chaisteil (Castlebay) 314 B4
Bàgh Mòr 315 G4
Baghasdal 314 C2
Bagillt 232 D5
Baginton 209 F5
Baglan 178 D3
Bagley *Shrop.* 220 B5
Bagley *Som.* 166 B3
Bagmore 170 B3
Bagnall 221 G2
Bagnor 169 F1
Bagpath 182 A3
Bagshaw Museum 86
Bagshot *Surr.* 171 E1
Bagshot *Wilts.* 169 E1
Bagstone 181 F4
Bagthorpe *Norf.* 227 F4
Bagthorpe *Notts.* 223 F2
Baguley 234 C4
Bagworth 209 G2
Bagwyllydiart 194 D5
Baildon 244 A4
Baile a' Mhanaich (Balivanich) 315 F4
Baile Ailein (Balallan) 329 D5
Baile an Truiseil 329 E2
Baile Boidheach 281 F2
Baile Gharbhaidh 315 F5
Baile Glas 315 G4
Baile Mhartainn 315 F2
Baile Mhic Phail 315 G2
Baile Mòr *Arg. & B.* 288 B2
Baile Mòr (Balemore) *W.Isles* 315 F3
Baile nan Cailleach 315 F4
Baile Raghaill 315 F3
Bailebeag 309 E3
Baileguish 310 A5
Baile-na-Cille 315 G1
Bailetonach 297 F2
Bailiesward 311 G1
Bailiff Bridge 244 A5
Baillieston 284 A3
Bainbridge 251 E3
Bainsford 284 C1
Bainshole 312 B1
Bainton *E.Riding* 246 B2
Bainton *Oxon.* 198 A5
Bainton *Peter.* 211 F2
Bairnkine 278 A5
Bakebare 311 F1
Baker Street 187 F4
Baker's End 186 C1
Bakewell 222 D1
Bala 218 C4
Balachuirn 318 B5
Balado 293 F4
Balafark 292 B5
Baladie 322 A2
Balallan (Baile Ailein) 329 D5
Balavil 309 G4
Balbeg *High.* 309 D1
Balbeg *High.* 309 D2
Balbeggie 293 G2
Balbirnie 294 A4
Balbithan 312 C3
Balblair *High.* 321 G3
Balblair *High.* 332 A5
Balblair *High.* 321 G1
Balby 236 C2
Balcharn 332 A4
Balcherry 322 A1
Balchers 324 C4
Balchladich 330 C1
Balchraggan *High.* 321 E5
Balchraggan *High.* 309 E1
Balchrick 334 A3
Balcombe 172 C5
Balcurvie 294 B4
Baldernock 283 G2
Baldersby 252 C5
Baldersby St. James 252 C5
Balderstone *Gt.Man.* 234 D1
Balderstone *Lancs.* 242 C4
Balderton *Ches.* 220 A1
Balderton *Notts.* 224 D2
Baldhu 146 B5
Baldinnie 294 C3
Baldock 200 A4
Baldon Row 184 A2
Baldovan 294 B1
Baldovie *Angus* 302 B4
Baldovie *Dundee* 294 C1
Baldrine 240 C3
Baldslow 160 C2
Baldwin 240 B3
Baldwinholme 259 G1
Baldwin's Gate 221 E3
Baldwins Hill 172 C5
Bale 228 B2
Balelone 315 F2
Balemartine 296 A2
Balemore (Baile Mòr) 315 F3
Balendoch 302 A5
Balephuil 296 A2
Balerno 285 F3
Balernock 283 D1
Baleromindubh 288 C5
Baleromínmore 288 C5
Baleshare (Bhaleshear) 315 F3
Balevulin 289 D2
Balfield 302 D3
Balfour *Aber.* 312 A5
Balfour *Ork.* 340 C5
Balfron 283 G1
Balfron Station 283 G1
Balgonar 293 F5
Balgove 312 D1
Balgowan *D. & G.* 256 B2
Balgowan *High.* 309 F5
Balgown 317 G3
Balgreen 324 C4
Balgreggan 264 B5
Balgy 319 E4
Balhaldie 292 D4
Balhalgardy 312 C2
Balham 186 B5
Balhary 302 A5
Balhelvie 294 B2
Balhousie 294 C4
Baliasta 345 F2
Baligill 336 A2
Baligrundle 298 A5
Balindore 290 B1
Balintore *Angus* 302 A4
Balintore *High.* 322 A2
Balintraid 321 G2
Balintyre 300 B5
Balivanich (Baile a' Mhanaich) 315 F4
Balkeerie 302 B5
Balkholme 245 G5
Balkissock 264 C2
Ball 220 A5
Ball Haye Green 221 G2
Ball Hill 169 F1
Balla 314 C2
Ballabeg 240 A4
Ballacannell 240 C3
Ballacarnane Beg 240 A3
Ballachulish 298 C4
Balladoole 240 A5
Ballafesson 240 A4
Ballagyr 240 A3
Ballajora 240 C2
Ballakilpheric 240 A4
Ballamodha 240 A4
Ballantrae 264 B2
Ballards Gore 188 C3
Ballasalla *I.o.M.* 240 A4
Ballasalla *I.o.M.* 240 B2
Ballater 311 F5
Ballaterach 311 G5
Ballaugh 240 B2
Ballaveare 240 B4
Ballchraggan 321 G2
Ballechin 301 E4
Balleich 292 A4
Ballencrieff 286 B2
Ballidon 222 D2
Balliekine 281 G5
Balliemeanoch 290 D4
Balliemore *Arg. & B.* 290 D5
Balliemore *Arg. & B.* 290 A2
Ballig 240 A3
Ballimeanoch 290 C3
Ballimore *Arg. & B.* 282 A1
Ballimore *Stir.* 292 A3
Ballinaby 280 A3
Ballindean 294 A2
Ballingdon 201 G3
Ballinger Common 185 E2
Ballingham 195 E4
Ballingry 293 G5
Ballinlick 301 E5
Ballinluig *P. & K.* 301 E4
Ballinluig *P. & K.* 301 F4
Ballintuim 301 G4
Balloch *Angus* 302 B4
Balloch *High.* 321 G5
Balloch *N.Lan.* 284 B2
Balloch *W.Dun.* 283 E1
Ballochan 292 D3
Ballochandrain 312 A5
Ballochford 282 A1
Ballochgair 311 F1
Ballochmartin 272 C3
Ballochmorrie 282 C4
Ballochmyle 264 D2
Ballochroy 274 D3
Ballogie 281 F4
Balls Cross 312 A5
Balls Green *Essex* 171 E5
Ball's Green *Glos.* 202 B5
Balls Hill 182 A3
Ballyaurgan 208 B3
Ballygown 281 F2
Ballygrant 296 D5
Ballyhaugh 280 B3
Ballymeanoch 296 A4
Ballymichael 290 A5
Balmacara 273 E2
Balmacara Estate & Lochalsh Woodland Garden 116
Balmaclellan 266 A3
Balmacneil 301 E4
Balmadies 303 D5
Balmae 257 G2
Balmaha 291 G5
Balmalcolm 294 B4
Balmaqueen 318 A2
Balmeanach *Arg. & B.* 297 F5
Balmeanach *Arg. & B.* 288 D1
Balmedie 313 E3
Balmer Heath 220 B4
Balmerino 294 B2
Balmerlawn 156 C2
Balminnoch 265 D4
Balmoral Castle 116
Balmore *E.Dun.* 284 A2
Balmore *High.* 322 A5
Balmore *High.* 308 C1
Balmore *High.* 317 F5
Balmore *P. & K.* 300 C4
Balmullo 294 C2
Balmungie 321 G4
Balmyle 301 F4
Balnaboth 302 B3
Balnabruaich 321 G2
Balnacra 319 F5
Balnafoich 309 F1
Balnagall 322 A1
Balnagown Castle 321 G2
Balnaguard 301 E4
Balnaguisich 321 F2
Balnahard *Arg. & B.* 288 D5
Balnahard *Arg. & B.* 289 D1
Balnain 309 D1
Balnakeil 334 C2
Balnaknock 318 A3
Balnamoon 302 D3
Balnapaling 321 G3
Balnespick 310 A4
Balquhidder 292 A2
Balsall 209 E5
Balsall Common 209 E5
Balsall Heath 208 C4
Balscote 197 F3
Balsham 201 D2
Baltasound 345 F2
Balterley 221 E2
Balterley Heath 221 E2
Baltersan 265 F4
Balthangie 324 D4
Balthayock 293 G2
BALTIC The Centre for Contemporary Art 102
Baltonsborough 166 C4
Baluachraig 290 A5
Balulive 280 C3
Balure *Arg. & B.* 290 C1
Balure *Arg. & B.* 290 A1
Balvaird 321 E4
Balvarran 301 F3
Balvicar 289 G3
Balvraid *High.* 307 E3
Balvraid *High.* 310 A1
Bamber Bridge 242 B5
Bamber's Green 201 D5
Bamburgh 279 F3
Bamburgh Castle 102
Bamff 302 A4
Bamford *Derbys.* 235 G4
Bamford *Gt.Man.* 234 C1
Bampton *Cumb.* 249 G1
Bampton *Devon* 164 C5
Bampton *Oxon.* 183 F2
Bampton Grange 249 G1
Banavie 298 D2
Banbury 197 G3
Bancffosfelen 178 A1
Banchor 322 B5
Banchory 312 C5
Banchory-Devenick 313 E4
Bancycapel 178 A1
Bancyfelin 177 G1
Bancyffordd 192 A4
Bandon 294 A4
Bandrake Head 249 E4
Banff 324 B3
Bangor 231 D5
Bangor-is-y-coed 220 A3
Bangor's Green 233 E2
Banham 214 B3
Banham Zoo 77
Bank 156 B2
Bank End 248 C4
Bank Newton 243 F2
Bank of England Museum 55
Bank Street 195 F1
Bank Top *Lancs.* 233 G2
Bank Top *W.Yorks.* 244 A5
Bankend 267 E4
Bankfoot 293 F1
Bankglen 275 D4
Bankhead *Aber.* 312 B3
Bankhead *Aber.* 312 B4
Bankhead *Aberdeen* 313 D3
Bankhead *D. & G.* 258 A2
Banking 312 C1
Bankland 166 A5
Banknock 284 B2
Banks *Cumb.* 260 B1
Banks *Lancs.* 241 G5
Bankshill 267 F2
Banningham 228 D3
Bannister Green 201 E5
Bannockburn 292 D5
Bannockburn 1314 116
Banstead 172 B3
Bantam Grove 244 B5
Bantham 150 C3
Banton 284 B2
Banwell 166 A2
Banwen Pyrddin 179 E2
Banyard's Green 215 E4
Bapchild 174 B2
Baptiston 283 G1
Bapton 168 A4
Bar End 169 F5
Bar Hill 200 B1
Bar, The 171 G5
Barabhas (Barvas) 329 E3
Barachander 290 C2
Barassie 274 B2
Barbaraville 321 G2
Barber Booth 235 F4
Barber Green 249 E4
Barber's Moor 233 F1
Barbon 250 B4
Barbridge 220 D2
Barbrook 164 A3
Barby 210 A5
Barcaldine 298 B5
Barcaple 266 A5
Barcheston 197 E4
Barclose 260 A1
Barcombe 159 G2
Barcombe Cross 159 G2
Barden 252 A3
Barden Park 173 E4
Bardennoch 265 G1
Bardfield End Green 201 E4
Bardfield Saling 201 E5
Bardister 344 C5
Bardney 225 G1
Bardon *Leics.* 209 G1
Bardon *Moray* 323 E4
Bardon Mill 261 D1
Bardowie 283 G2
Bardsea 249 D5
Bardsey 244 C3
Bardsey Island (Ynys Enlli) 216 A5
Bardwell 214 A4
Bare 242 A1
Barewood 194 C2
Barfad 281 G3
Barford *Norf.* 228 C5
Barford *Warks.* 197 E1
Barford St. John 197 G4
Barford St. Martin 168 B4
Barford St. Michael 197 G4
Barfrestone 175 E3
Bargaly 265 F4
Bargany Mains 274 A5
Bargoed 180 A3
Bargrennan 265 E3
Barham *Cambs.* 211 G5
Barham *Kent* 175 E3
Barham *Suff.* 202 C2
Barharrow 266 A5
Barholm 211 F1
Barholm Mains 265 F5
Barkby 210 B2
Barkby Thorpe 210 B2
Barkers Green 220 C5
Barkestone-le-Vale 224 C4
Barkham 170 C1
Barking *Gt.Lon.* 186 D4
Barking *Suff.* 202 B2
Barking Tye 202 B2
Barkisland 243 G5
Barkston 225 E3
Barkston Ash 245 D4
Barkway 200 B4
Barlae 265 D4
Barland 194 B1
Barlaston 221 F4
Barlavington 158 B2
Barlborough 236 B5
Barlby 245 F4
Barlestone 209 G2
Barley *Herts.* 200 B4
Barley *Lancs.* 243 E3
Barley Green 214 D4
Barleycroft End 200 C5
Barleyhill 261 G2
Barleythorpe 210 D2
Barling 188 C4
Barlings 238 A5
Barlow *Derbys.* 236 A5
Barlow *N.Yorks.* 245 F5
Barlow *T. & W.* 262 A1
Barmby Moor 245 G3
Barmby on the Marsh 245 F5
Barmer 227 G4
Barmolloch 290 A5
Barmoor Lane End 279 E3
Barmouth (Abermaw) 204 C1
Barmpton 252 C1
Barmston 247 D2
Barnaby Green 215 F4
Barnacabber 282 C1
Barnacarry 290 B5
Barnack 211 F2
Barnacle 209 F4
Barnamuc 298 C5
Barnard Castle 251 F1
Barnard Gate 183 G1
Barnardiston 201 F3
Barnard's Green 195 G3
Barnbarroch *D. & G.* 265 E5
Barnbarroch *D. & G.* 266 C5
Barnburgh 236 B2
Barnby 215 F3
Barnby Dun 236 D2
Barnby in the Willows 225 D2
Barnby Moor 237 D4
Barndennoch 266 C2
Barne Barton 150 A2
Barnehurst 187 E5
Barnes 186 B5
Barnes Street 173 F4
Barnet 186 B3
Barnet Gate 186 B3
Barnetby le Wold 238 A2
Barney 228 A2
Barnham *Suff.* 213 G5
Barnham *W.Suss.* 158 B3
Barnham Broom 228 B5
Barnhead 303 E4
Barnhill *Ches.* 220 B2
Barnhill *Dundee* 294 C1
Barnhill *Moray* 322 D4
Barnhills 264 A3
Barningham *Dur.* 251 F1
Barningham *Suff.* 214 A4
Barningham Green 228 C2
Barnoldby le Beck 238 C2
Barnoldswick 243 E3
Barns Green 171 G5
Barnsdale Bar 236 C1
Barnsdale Gardens 70
Barnsley *Glos.* 182 C2
Barnsley *S.Yorks.* 236 A2
Barnsole 175 E3
Barnstaple 163 F2
Barnston *Essex* 187 F1
Barnston *Mersey.* 233 D4
Barnstone 224 C4
Barnt Green 208 C5
Barnton *Ches.* 234 A5
Barnton *Edin.* 285 F2
Barnwell All Saints 211 F4
Barnwell St. Andrew 211 F4
Barnwood 182 A1
Barons' Cross 195 D2
Barr *Arg. & B.* 280 B3
Barr *High.* 297 F4
Barr *S.Ayr.* 265 D1
Barr *Som.* 165 E5
Barr Hall 201 F4
Barra (Barraigh) 314 B3
Barra (Tràigh Mhòr) Airport 314 B3
Barrachan 257 D2
Barrackan 289 G4
Barraer 265 E4
Barraglom 328 C4
Barrahormid 281 F1
Barraigh (Barra) 314 B3
Barran 291 D2
Barrapoll 296 A2
Barrasford 270 B4
Barravullin 290 A4
Barregarrow 240 B3
Barrets Green 220 C2
Barrhead 283 F4
Barrhill 264 D2
Barrington *Cambs.* 200 B3
Barrington *Som.* 153 G1
Barrington Court 24
Barripper 144 D3
Barrisdale 307 E4
Barrmill 283 E4
Barrnacarry 290 A2
Barrock 337 E1
Barrow *Glos.* 196 A5
Barrow *Lancs.* 242 D4
Barrow *Rut.* 211 D1
Barrow *Shrop.* 207 F2
Barrow *Som.* 167 E4
Barrow *Som.* 166 C3
Barrow *Suff.* 201 F1
Barrow Gurney 166 C1
Barrow Hann 246 C5
Barrow Haven 246 C5
Barrow Hill 236 B5
Barrow Nook 233 F2
Barrow Street 167 F4
Barrow upon Humber 246 C5
Barrow upon Soar 210 A1
Barrow upon Trent 223 E5
Barroway Drove 213 D2
Barrowby 225 D4
Barrowcliff 254 D4
Barrowden 211 E2
Barrowford 243 E4
Barrow-in-Furness 241 F1
Barrows Green 249 G4
Barry *Angus* 294 D1
Barry *V. of Glam.* 165 E1
Barry Island Pleasure Park 107
Barry Mill 116
Barsby 210 B1
Barsham 215 E3
Barskimming 274 C3
Barsloisnoch 290 A5
Barston 209 E5
Bartestree 195 E3
Barthol Chapel 312 D1
Bartholomew Green 201 F5
Barthomley 221 E2
Bartley 156 C1
Bartley Green 208 C4
Bartlow 201 D3
Barton *Cambs.* 200 C2
Barton *Ches.* 220 B2
Barton *Cumb.* 260 A5
Barton *Glos.* 196 C5
Barton *Lancs.* 242 B4
Barton *Lancs.* 233 E2
Barton *N.Yorks.* 252 B2
Barton *Oxon.* 184 A2
Barton *Torbay* 151 F1
Barton *Warks.* 196 D2
Barton Bendish 213 F2
Barton End 182 A3
Barton Green 209 D1
Barton Hartshorn 198 B4
Barton Hill 245 G1
Barton in Fabis 223 G4
Barton in the Beans 209 F2
Barton Mills 213 F5
Barton on Sea 156 B3
Barton St. David 166 C4
Barton Seagrave 211 D5
Barton Stacey 169 F3
Barton Town 163 G1
Barton Turf 229 E3
Bartongate 197 G5
Barton-le-Clay 199 F4
Barton-le-Street 253 G5
Barton-le-Willows 245 G1
Barton-on-the-Heath 197 E4
Barton-under-Needwood 209 D1
Barton-upon-Humber 246 C5
Barvas (Barabhas) 329 E3
Barway 212 D5
Barwell 209 G3
Barwhinnock 266 A5
Barwick *Herts.* 186 C1
Barwick *Som.* 154 B1
Barwick in Elmet 244 C4
Barwinnock 257 D2
Baschurch 220 B5
Bascote 197 G1
Base Green 202 B1
Basford Green 221 G2
Bashall Eaves 242 C3
Bashall Town 242 D3
Bashley 156 B3
Basildon *Essex* 187 G4
Basildon *W.Berks.* 184 B5
Basildon Park 40
Basingstoke 170 B2
Baslow 235 G5
Bason Bridge 166 A3
Bassaleg 180 B4
Bassenthwaite 259 F3
Basset's Cross 163 F5
Bassett 156 D1
Bassingbourn 200 B3
Bassingfield 224 B4
Bassingham 225 E2
Bassingthorpe 225 E5
Basta 345 E3
Baston 211 G1
Bastonford 196 A2
Bastwick 229 F4
Batavaime 291 G1
Batch 166 A2
Batchley 196 C1
Batchworth 185 F3
Batchworth Heath 185 F3
Batcombe *Dorset* 154 C2
Batcombe *Som.* 167 D4
Bate Heath 234 A5
Bateman's 40
Bath 25
Bath Abbey 25
Bathampton 167 E1
Bathealton 165 D5
Batheaston 167 E1
Bathford 167 E1
Bathgate 285 D3
Bathley 224 C2
Bathpool *Cornw.* 147 G2
Bathpool *Som.* 165 F5
Bathway 166 C2
Batley 244 B5
Batsford 197 D4
Batsford Arboretum 25
Batson 150 D4
Battersby 253 E2
Battersea 186 B5
Battisborough Cross 150 C3
Battisford 202 B2
Battisford Tye 202 B2
Battle *E.Suss.* 160 C2
Battle *Powys* 193 G4
Battle Abbey 40
Battle of Britain Memorial Flight Visitor Centre 70
Battledown 196 B5
Battlefield 207 E1
Battlesbridge 187 G3
Battlesden 199 E5
Battlesea Green 214 D4
Battleton 164 C5
Battlies Green 202 A1
Battramsley 156 C3
Batt's Corner 170 D3
Bauds of Cullen 323 G3
Baugh 296 B2
Baughton 196 A3
Baughurst 169 G1
Baulds 312 D5
Baulking 183 F3
Baumber 238 C5
Baunton 182 C2
Baveney Wood 207 F5
Baverstock 168 B4
Bawburgh 228 C5
Bawdeswell 228 B3
Bawdrip 166 A4
Bawdsey 203 E3
Bawdsey Manor 203 E4
Bawsey 213 E1
Bawtry 237 D3

Baxenden 243 D5
Baxterley 209 E3
Baxter's Green 201 F2
Baxters Highland Village 116
Bay 167 F5
Baybridge 261 F3
Baycliff 249 D5
Baydon 183 E5
Bayford *Herts.* 186 C2
Bayford *Som.* 167 E5
Bayfordbury 186 C1
Bayham Abbey *E.Suss.* 40
Bayham Abbey *Kent* 173 F5
Bayles 260 D3
Baylham 202 C2
Baynards Green 198 A5
Baysham 195 E5
Bayston Hill 207 D2
Bayswater 186 B4
Baythorn End 201 F3
Bayton 207 F5
Bayworth 184 A2
Beach *High.* 297 G4
Beach *S.Glos.* 181 G5
Beachampton 198 C4
Beachamwell 213 F2
Beacharr 281 E5
Beachley 181 E3
Beachy Head 40
Beacon *Devon* 153 E2
Beacon *Devon* 153 F2
Beacon Fell Country Park 93
Beacon Hill *Dorset* 155 F3
Beacon Hill *Essex* 188 B1
Beacon Hill *Surr.* 171 D4
Beacon Hill Country Park 70
Beacon's Bottom 184 C3
Beaconsfield 185 E3
Beacravik 326 D4
Beadlam 253 F4
Beadlow 199 G4
Beadnell 279 G4
Beaford 163 F4
Beal *N.Yorks.* 245 E5
Beal *Northumb.* 279 E2
Bealach 298 B4
Bealach na Ba 116
Beale Park 40
Bealsmill 149 D3
Beambridge 220 D2
Beamhurst 222 B4
Beaminster 154 A2
Beamish 262 B2
Beamish, North of England Open Air Museum 102
Beamsley 243 G2
Bean 187 E5
Beanacre 168 A1
Beanley 279 E5
Beaquoy 340 B4
Beardon 149 F2
Beardwood 242 C5
Beare 152 C2
Beare Green 171 G3
Bearley 197 D1
Bearnie 313 E1
Bearnock 308 D1
Bearnus 296 C5
Bearpark 262 B3
Bearsbridge 261 D2
Bearsden 283 G2
Bearsted 173 G3
Bearstone 221 E4
Bearwood *Poole* 155 G3
Bearwood *W.Mid.* 208 C4
Beatles Story 93
Beattock 276 B5
Beauchamp Roding 187 E1
Beauchief 236 A4
Beaudesert 197 D1
Beaufort 180 A1
Beaulieu 156 C2
Beaulieu Abbey 40
Beaulieu Palace House 40
Beauly 321 E5
Beaumaris (Biwmaris) 231 E5
Beaumaris Castle 107
Beaumont *Chan.I.* 150 C5
Beaumont *Cumb.* 259 G1
Beaumont *Essex* 202 C5
Beaumont Hill 252 B1
Beausale 209 E5
Beauvale 223 F3
Beauworth 169 G5
Beaver Green 174 B4
Beaworthy 149 E1
Beazley End 201 F5
Bebington 233 E4
Bebside 271 E3
Beccles 215 F2
Becconsall 242 A5
Beck Foot 250 B3
Beck Hole 254 B2
Beck Row 213 E5
Beck Side *Cumb.* 248 D4
Beck Side *Cumb.* 249 E4
Beckbury 207 G2
Beckenham 172 C2
Beckering 238 B4
Beckermet 248 B2
Beckermonds 251 D1
Beckett End 213 F3
Beckfoot *Cumb.* 248 C2
Beckfoot *Cumb.* 259 D2
Beckford 196 B4
Beckhampton 168 B1
Beckingham *Lincs.* 225 D2
Beckingham *Notts.* 237 E4
Beckington 167 F2
Beckley *E.Suss.* 161 D1
Beckley *Oxon.* 184 A1
Beck's Green 215 E3
Beckside 250 B4
Beckton 186 D4
Beckwithshaw 244 B2
Becontree 187 D4
Bedale 252 B4
Bedburn 261 G4
Bedchester 155 E1
Beddau 179 G4
Beddgelert 217 E3
Beddingham 159 G3
Beddington 172 B2
Beddington Corner 172 B2
Bede's World 102
Bedfield 202 D1
Bedfield Little Green 202 D1
Bedford 199 F3
Bedford Museum 77
Bedgebury Cross 173 G5
Bedgebury National Pinetum 40
Bedgrove 184 D1
Bedham 171 F5
Bedhampton 157 G2
Bedingfield 202 C1
Bedingfield Green 202 C1
Bedingfield Street 202 C1
Bedingham Green 215 D2
Bedlam *Lancs.* 243 D5
Bedlam *N.Yorks.* 244 B1
Bedlar's Green 200 D5
Bedlington 271 E3
Bedlinog 179 G2
Bedminster 181 E5
Bedmond 185 F2
Bednall 208 B1
Bedol 232 D5
Bedrule 278 A5
Bedstone 206 C5
Bedwas 180 A4
Bedwell 200 A5
Bedwellty 180 A2
Bedworth 209 F4
Bedworth Woodlands 209 F4
Beeby 210 B2
Beech *Hants.* 170 B4
Beech *Staffs.* 221 F4
Beech Hill 170 B1
Beechingstoke 168 B2
Beechwood 233 G4
Beecraigs Country Park 117
Beedon 183 G5
Beeford 246 D2
Beeley 223 D1
Beelsby 238 C2
Beenham 169 G1
Beeny 148 B1
Beer 153 F4
Beer Hackett 154 C1
Beercrocombe 166 A5
Beesands 151 E3
Beesby *Lincs.* 239 E4
Beesby *N.E.Lincs.* 238 C3
Beeson 151 E3
Beeston *Beds.* 199 G3
Beeston *Ches.* 220 C2
Beeston *Norf.* 228 A4
Beeston *Notts.* 223 G4
Beeston *W.Yorks.* 244 B4
Beeston Castle 93
Beeston Regis 228 C1
Beeston St. Lawrence 229 E3
Beeswing 266 C4
Beetham *Cumb.* 249 F5
Beetham *Som.* 153 F1
Beetley 228 A4
Beffcote 208 A1
Began 180 B4
Begbroke 183 G1
Begdale 212 C2
Begelly 177 E2
Beggar's Bush 194 B1
Beggearn Huish 164 D4
Beggshill 312 A1
Beguildy (Bugeildy) 206 A5
Beighton *Norf.* 229 E5
Beighton *S.Yorks.* 236 B4
Beili-glas 180 C2
Beinn na Faoghla (Benbecula) 315 G4
Beith 283 E4
Bekesbourne 175 D3
Bekonscot Model Village 40
Belaugh 229 D4
Belbroughton 208 B5
Belchalwell 155 D2
Belchalwell Street 155 D2
Belchamp Otten 201 G3
Belchamp St. Paul 201 F3
Belchamp Walter 201 G3
Belchford 238 C5
Belfield 234 D1
Belford 279 F3
Belgrave 210 A2
Belhaven 287 D2
Belhelvie 313 E3
Belhinnie 311 G2
Bell Bar 186 B2
Bell Busk 243 F2
Bell End 208 B5
Bell Heath 208 B5
Bell Hill 170 C5
Bell o' th' Hill 220 C3
Bellabeg 311 F3
Belladrum 321 E5
Bellanoch 290 A5
Bellaty 302 A4
Belle Isle 244 C5
Belle Vue 259 G1
Belleau 239 E5
Belleheiglash 311 D1
Bellerby 252 A3
Bellever 149 G3
Bellfields 171 E2
Belliehill 303 D3
Bellingdon 185 E2
Bellingham *Gt.Lon.* 186 C5
Bellingham *Northumb.* 270 A3
Belloch 272 B2
Bellochantuy 272 B2
Bell's Cross 202 C2
Bells Yew Green 173 F5
Bellshill *N.Lan.* 284 B3
Bellshill *Northumb.* 279 F3
Bellside 284 C4
Bellsquarry 285 E3
Belluton 166 D1
Belmaduthy 321 F4
Belmesthorpe 211 F1
Belmont *B'burn.* 234 A1
Belmont *Gt.Lon.* 172 B2
Belmont *Gt.Lon.* 186 A3
Belmont *Shet.* 345 E2
Belnie 226 A4
Belowda 147 D3
Belper 223 E3
Belper Lane End 223 E3
Belsay 270 D4
Belsay Hall, Castle & Gardens 102
Belsford 151 D2
Belsize 185 F2
Belstead 202 C3
Belston 274 B3
Belstone 149 G1
Belstone Corner 149 G1
Belsyde 285 D2
Belthorn 242 D5
Beltinge 175 D2
Beltingham 261 D1
Beltoft 237 F2
Belton *Leics.* 223 F5
Belton *Lincs.* 225 E4
Belton *N.Lincs.* 237 E2
Belton *Norf.* 229 F5
Belton *Rut.* 210 D2
Belton House 70
Beltring 173 F4
Belvedere 187 D5
Belvoir 224 D4
Belvoir Castle 70
Bembridge 157 F4
Bembridge Windmill 41
Bemersyde 277 G2
Bemerton 168 C4
Bempton 255 E5
Bempton Cliffs 86
Ben Alder Cottage 299 G3
Ben Alder Lodge 300 A2
Ben Lawers National Nature Reserve 117
Ben Nevis 117
Ben Rhydding 244 A3
Benacre 215 G3
Benbecula (Beinn na Faoghla) 315 G4
Benbecula (Balivanich) Airport 315 F4
Benbuie 266 B1
Benderloch 290 B1
Bendish 199 G5
Benenden 174 A5
Benfield 265 E4
Benfieldside 261 G2
Bengate 229 E3
Bengeo 186 C1
Bengeworth 196 C3
Benhall 196 B5
Benhall Green 203 F1
Benhall Street 203 E1
Benholm 303 G3
Beningbrough 245 E2
Beningbrough Hall 86
Benington *Herts.* 200 A5
Benington *Lincs.* 226 B3
Benington Sea End 226 C3
Benllech 230 D4
Benmore *Arg. & B.* 282 C1
Benmore *Stir.* 291 G2
Bennacott 148 C1
Bennan Cottage 266 A3
Bennett End 184 C3
Bennetts End 185 F2
Bennetts Water Garden 25
Benniworth 238 C4
Benover 173 G4
Benson 184 B3
Benston 343 D2
Benthall *Northumb.* 279 G4
Benthall *Shrop.* 207 F2
Benthall Hall 63
Bentham 182 B1
Benthoul 312 D4
Bentlawnt 206 C2
Bentley *E.Riding* 246 C4
Bentley *Essex* 187 E3
Bentley *Hants.* 170 C3
Bentley *S.Yorks.* 236 C2
Bentley *Suff.* 202 C4
Bentley *W.Mid.* 208 B3
Bentley *W.Yorks.* 244 B4
Bentley *Warks.* 209 E3
Bentley Heath *Herts.* 186 B3
Bentley Heath *W.Mid.* 209 D5
Bentley Rise 236 C2
Bentley Wildfowl & Motor Museum 41
Benton 163 G2
Benton Square 271 E4
Bentpath 268 B2
Bentworth 170 B3
Benvie 294 B1
Benville Lane 154 B2
Benwell 262 B1
Benwick 212 B3
Beoley 196 C1
Beoraidbeg 306 C5
Bepton 158 A2
Berden 200 C5
Bere Alston 150 A1
Bere Ferrers 150 A1
Bere Regis 155 E3
Berea 190 A4
Berepper 145 D4
Bergh Apton 229 E5
Berinsfield 184 A3
Berkeley 181 F3
Berkeley Castle & Gardens 25
Berkhamsted 185 E2
Berkley 167 F3
Berkswell 209 E5
Bermondsey 186 C5
Bernera 307 E2
Berneray (Eilean Bhearnaraigh) 326 B5
Berners Roding 187 F2
Bernice 290 D5
Bernisdale 318 A4
Berrick Prior 184 B3
Berrick Salome 184 B3
Berriedale 333 G2
Berriew (Aberriw) 206 A2
Berrington *Northumb.* 279 E2
Berrington *Shrop.* 207 E2
Berrington *Worcs.* 195 E1
Berrington Green 195 E1
Berrington Hall 63
Berriowbridge 147 G2
Berrow *Som.* 165 F2
Berrow *Worcs.* 195 G4
Berrow Green 195 G2
Berry Cross 163 E4
Berry Down Cross 163 F1
Berry Hill *Glos.* 181 E1
Berry Hill *Pembs.* 191 D3
Berry Pomeroy 151 E1
Berry Pomeroy Castle 25
Berryhillock 324 A3
Berrynarbor 163 F1
Berry's Green 172 D3
Bersham 220 A3
Berstane 340 C5
Berthlŵyd 178 B3
Berwick 160 A3
Berwick Bassett 182 D5
Berwick Hill 271 D4
Berwick St. James 168 B4
Berwick St. John 168 A5
Berwick St. Leonard 168 A4
Berwick-upon-Tweed 287 G4
Bescar 233 E1
Bescot 208 C3
Besford *Shrop.* 220 C5
Besford *Worcs.* 196 B3
Bessacarr 236 D2
Bessels Leigh 183 G2
Besses o' th' Barn 234 C2
Bessingby 247 D1
Bessingham 228 C2
Best Beech Hill 173 F5
Besthorpe *Norf.* 214 B2
Besthorpe *Notts.* 224 D1
Bestwood Lodge Country Park 70
Bestwood Village 223 G3
Beswick *E.Riding* 246 C3
Beswick *Gt.Man.* 234 C3
Betchworth 172 B3
Beth Chatto Gardens, The 77
Bethania *Cere.* 192 B1
Bethania *Gwyn.* 218 A3
Bethel *Gwyn.* 217 E1
Bethel *Gwyn.* 218 C4
Bethel *I.o.A.* 230 B5
Bethersden 174 B5
Bethesda *Gwyn.* 217 F1
Bethesda *Pembs.* 177 D1
Bethlehem 192 C5
Bethnal Green 186 C4
Betley 221 E3
Betley Common 221 E3
Betsham 187 F5
Betteshanger 175 F3
Bettiscombe 153 G3
Bettisfield 220 B4
Betton *Shrop.* 206 C2
Betton *Shrop.* 221 D4
Betton Strange 207 E2
Bettws 180 B3
Bettws Bledrws 192 B2
Bettws Cedewain 206 A3
Bettws Gwerfil Goch 218 D3
Bettws Newydd 180 C2
Bettws-y-crwyn 206 B4
Bettyhill 335 G2
Betws *Bridgend* 179 F4
Betws *Carmar.* 178 C1
Betws Disserth 194 A2
Betws Garmon 217 E2
Betws Ifan 191 G3
Betws-y-coed 218 A2
Betws-yn-Rhos 232 A5
Beulah *Cere.* 191 F3
Beulah *Powys* 193 F2
Bevendean 159 F3
Bevercotes 237 D5
Beverley 246 C4
Beverstone 182 A3
Bevington 181 F3
Bewaldeth 259 F3
Bewcastle 269 D4
Bewdley 207 G5
Bewerley 244 A1
Bewholme 247 D2
Bewley Common 168 A1
Bexhill 160 C3
Bexley 187 D5
Bexleyheath 187 D5
Bexwell 213 E2
Beyton 202 A1
Beyton Green 202 A1
Bhalamus 327 E3
Bhaleshear (Baleshare) 315 F3
Bhaltos 328 B4
Bhatarsaigh (Vatersay) 314 B4
Biallaid 309 G5
Bibury 182 D2
Bicester 198 A5
Bickenhall 153 F1
Bickenhill 209 D4
Bicker 226 A4
Bickershaw *Gt.Man.* 234 A2
Bickershaw *Gt.Man.* 234 A2
Bickerstaffe 233 F2
Bickerton *Ches.* 220 C2
Bickerton *Devon* 151 E4
Bickerton *N.Yorks.* 245 D2
Bickerton *Northumb.* 270 B1
Bickford 208 A1
Bickham 164 C3
Bickham Bridge 150 D2
Bickham House 152 C4
Bickington *Devon* 163 F2
Bickington *Devon* 152 A5
Bickleigh *Devon* 150 B1
Bickleigh *Devon* 152 C2
Bickleton 163 F2
Bickley 172 D2
Bickley Moss 220 C3
Bickley Town 220 C3
Bicknacre 187 G2
Bicknoller 165 E4
Bicknor 174 A3
Bickton 156 A1
Bicton *Here.* 195 D1
Bicton *Shrop.* 206 D1
Bicton *Shrop.* 206 B4
Bicton Heath 207 D1
Bicton Park Gardens 25
Bidborough 173 E4
Biddenden 174 A5
Biddenden Green 174 A4
Biddenham 199 F3
Biddestone 182 A5
Biddick 262 C2
Biddisham 166 A2
Biddlesden 198 B3
Biddlestone 270 B1
Biddulph 221 F2
Biddulph Grange Garden 63
Biddulph Moor 221 G2
Bideford 163 E3
Bidford-on-Avon 196 D2
Bidlake 149 E2
Bidston 233 D3
Bidwell 199 F5
Bielby 245 G3
Bieldside 313 D4
Bierley *I.o.W.* 157 E5
Bierley *W.Yorks.* 244 A4
Bierton 184 D1
Big Pit Mining Museum 107
Big Sand 319 D2
Big Sheep, The 25
Bigbury 150 C3
Bigbury-on-Sea 150 C3
Bigby 238 A2
Bigert Mire 248 C3
Biggar *Cumb.* 241 E1
Biggar *S.Lan.* 276 B2
Biggin *Derbys.* 223 D3
Biggin *Derbys.* 222 C2
Biggin *N.Yorks.* 245 E4
Biggin Hill 172 D3
Biggings 342 A1
Biggleswade 199 G3
Bigholms 268 B3
Bighouse 336 A2
Bighton 170 B4
Biglands 259 F1
Bignor 158 B2
Bigrigg 258 D5
Bigton 342 C5
Bilberry 147 E4
Bilborough 223 G3
Bilbrook *Som.* 164 D3
Bilbrook *Staffs.* 208 A2
Bilbrough 245 E3
Bilbster 337 E3
Bilby 236 D4
Bildershaw 262 A5
Bildeston 202 A3
Billericay 187 F3
Billesdon 210 C2
Billesley 196 D2
Billholm 268 A2
Billingborough 225 G4
Billinge 233 G3
Billingford *Norf.* 214 C4
Billingford *Norf.* 228 B3
Billingham 263 D5
Billinghay 225 G2
Billingley 236 B2
Billingshurst 171 F5
Billingsley 207 G4
Billington *Beds.* 199 E5
Billington *Lancs.* 242 D4
Billington *Staffs.* 221 F5
Billister 343 D1
Billockby 229 F4
Billy Row 262 A4
Bilsborrow 242 B4
Bilsby 239 E5
Bilsby Field 239 E5
Bilsdean 287 E2
Bilsham 158 B3
Bilsington 174 C5
Bilson Green 181 F1
Bilsthorpe 224 B1
Bilsthorpe Moor 224 B2
Bilston *Midloth.* 285 G3
Bilston *W.Mid.* 208 B3
Bilstone 209 F2
Bilting 174 C4
Bilton *E.Riding* 247 D4
Bilton *N.Yorks.* 244 C2
Bilton *Northumb.* 279 G5
Bilton *Warks.* 209 G5
Bilton-in-Ainsty 245 D3
Bimbister 340 B5
Binbrook 238 C3
Bincombe 154 C4
Bindal 322 B1
Bindon 165 E5
Binegar 166 D3
Bines Green 159 D2
Binfield 184 D5
Binfield Heath 184 C5
Bingfield 270 B4
Bingham 224 C4
Bingham's Melcombe 155 D2
Bingley 244 A4
Bings Heath 207 E1
Binham 228 A2
Binley *Hants.* 169 F2
Binley *W.Mid.* 209 F5
Binniehill 284 C2
Binsoe 252 B5
Binstead 157 E3
Binsted *Hants.* 170 C3
Binsted *W.Suss.* 158 B3
Binton 196 D2
Bintree 228 B3
Binweston 206 C2
Birch *Essex* 202 A5
Birch *Gt.Man.* 234 C2
Birch Cross 222 C4
Birch Green *Essex* 188 C1
Birch Green *Herts.* 186 B1
Birch Grove 159 G1
Birch Heath 220 C1
Birch Vale 235 E4
Birch Wood 153 F1
Bircham Newton 227 F4
Bircham Tofts 227 F4
Birchanger 200 D5
Bircher 195 D1
Bircher Common 195 D1
Birchfield 331 G5
Birchgrove *Cardiff* 180 A4
Birchgrove *Swan.* 178 D3
Birchington 175 F2
Birchmoor 209 E2
Birchover 222 D1
Birchwood *Lincs.* 225 E1
Birchwood *Warr.* 234 A3
Bircotes 236 D3
Bird Street 202 B2
Birdbrook 201 F3
Birdbush 168 A5
Birdfield 290 B5
Birdforth 253 D5
Birdham 158 A3
Birdingbury 197 G1
Birdland 25
Birdlip 182 B1
Birdoswald 260 C1
Birdoswald (Banna) 93
Birds Green 187 E2
Birdsall 246 A1
Birdsgreen 207 G4
Birdsmoor Gate 153 G2
Birdston 284 A2
Birdwell 236 A2
Birdwood 181 G1
Birdworld 41
Birgham 278 B3
Birichen 332 C5
Birkby *Cumb.* 259 D3
Birkby *N.Yorks.* 252 C2
Birkdale *Mersey.* 233 E1
Birkdale *N.Yorks.* 251 D2
Birkenhead 233 F4
Birkenhills 324 C5
Birkenshaw 244 B5
Birkhall 311 F5
Birkhill *Angus* 294 B1
Birkhill *Sc.Bord.* 286 C5
Birkhill *Sc.Bord.* 276 D4
Birkholme 225 E5
Birkin 245 E5
Birks 244 B5
Birks, The 312 C4
Birkwood 275 G2
Birley 195 D2
Birley Carr 236 A3
Birling *Kent* 173 F2
Birling *Northumb.* 271 E1
Birling Gap 160 A4
Birlingham 196 B3
Birmingham 208 C4
Birmingham Botanical Gardens 63
Birmingham International Airport 209 D4
Birnam 301 F5
Birsay 340 A4
Birse 312 A5
Birsemore 312 A5
Birstall 210 A2
Birstall Smithies 244 B5
Birstwith 244 B2
Birthorpe 225 G4
Birtle 234 C1
Birtley *Here.* 194 C1
Birtley *Northumb.* 270 A4
Birtley *T. & W.* 262 B2
Birts Street 195 G4
Birtsmorton 196 A4
Bisbrooke 211 D3
Biscathorpe 238 C4
Bish Mill 164 A5
Bisham 185 D4
Bishampton 196 B2
Bishop Auckland 262 B5
Bishop Burton 246 B3
Bishop Middleham 262 C4
Bishop Monkton 244 C1
Bishop Norton 237 G3
Bishop Sutton 166 C2
Bishop Thornton 244 B1
Bishop Wilton 245 G2
Bishopbridge 238 A3
Bishopbriggs 284 A2
Bishopmill 323 E3
Bishops Cannings 168 B1
Bishop's Castle 206 C4
Bishop's Caundle 154 C1
Bishop's Cleeve 196 B5
Bishop's Frome 195 F3
Bishops Gate 185 E5
Bishop's Green *Essex* 187 F1
Bishop's Green *Hants.* 169 G1
Bishop's Hull 165 F5
Bishop's Itchington 197 F2
Bishop's Lydeard 165 E5
Bishop's Norton 196 A5
Bishops Nympton 164 A5
Bishop's Offley 221 E5
Bishop's Palace 41
Bishop's Stortford 200 C5
Bishop's Sutton 170 B4
Bishop's Tachbrook 197 F1
Bishop's Tawton 163 F2
Bishop's Waltham 157 E1
Bishop's Wood 208 A2
Bishopsbourne 175 D3
Bishopsteignton 152 C5
Bishopstoke 157 D1
Bishopston *Bristol* 181 E5
Bishopston *Swan.* 178 B4
Bishopstone *Bucks.* 184 D1
Bishopstone *E.Suss.* 159 G3
Bishopstone *Here.* 194 D3
Bishopstone *Swin.* 183 E4
Bishopstone *Wilts.* 168 B5
Bishopstrow 167 F3
Bishopswood 153 F1
Bishopsworth 166 C1
Bishopthorpe 245 E3
Bishopton *Darl.* 262 C5
Bishopton *N.Yorks.* 252 B5
Bishopton *Renf.* 283 F2
Bishopton *Warks.* 197 D2
Bishton 180 C4
Bisley *Glos.* 182 B2
Bisley *Surr.* 171 E2
Bispham 241 G4
Bispham Green 233 F1
Bissoe 146 B5
Bisterne 156 A2
Bisterne Close 156 B2
Bitchet Green 173 E3
Bitchfield 225 E5
Bittadon 163 F1
Bittaford 150 C2
Bittering 228 A4
Bitterley 207 E5
Bitterne 156 D1
Bitteswell 210 A4
Bitton 167 D1
Bix 184 C4
Bixter 342 C2
Blaby 210 A3
Black Bourton 183 E2
Black Bridge 176 C2
Black Callerton 262 A1
Black Carr 214 B2
Black Clauchrie 265 D2
Black Corries Lodge 299 E4
Black Country Living Museum 64
Black Crofts 290 B1
Black Cross 146 D3
Black Dog 152 B2
Black Heddon 270 C4
Black Hill 197 E2
Black Marsh 206 C3
Black Moor 244 B3
Black Mount 299 E5
Black Notley 201 F5
Black Pill 178 C3
Black Street 215 G3
Black Torrington 163 E5
Blackaburn 269 F4
Blackacre 267 E1
Blackadder 287 F4
Blackawton 151 E2
Blackborough *Devon* 153 D2
Blackborough *Norf.* 213 E1
Blackborough End 213 E1
Blackboys 160 A1
Blackbraes *Aber.* 313 D3
Blackbraes *Falk.* 284 D2
Blackbrook *Derbys.* 223 E3
Blackbrook *Leics.* 209 G1
Blackbrook *Mersey.* 233 G3
Blackbrook *Staffs.* 221 E4
Blackburn *Aber.* 312 D3
Blackburn *B'burn.* 242 C5
Blackburn *W.Loth.* 285 D3
Blackbushe 170 C2
Blackcastle 322 A4
Blackchambers 312 C3
Blackcraig *D. & G.* 265 F4
Blackcraig *D. & G.* 266 B2
Blackden Heath 234 B5
Blackdog 313 E3
Blackdown *Devon* 149 F3
Blackdown *Dorset* 153 G2
Blackdown *Warks.* 197 F1
Blacker Hill 236 A2
Blackfen 187 D5
Blackfield 156 D2
Blackford *Aber.* 312 C1
Blackford *Cumb.* 268 B5
Blackford *P. & K.* 293 D4
Blackford *Som.* 167 D5
Blackford *Som.* 166 B3
Blackford Bridge 234 C2
Blackfordby 209 F1
Blackgang 157 D5
Blackgang Chine 41
Blackhall *Edin.* 285 G2
Blackhall *Renf.* 283 F3
Blackhall Colliery 263 D4
Blackhall Mill 262 A2
Blackhall Rocks 263 D4
Blackham 173 E5
Blackhaugh 277 F2

Blackheath *Essex* 202 B5
Blackheath *Gt.Lon.* 186 C5
Blackheath *Suff.* 215 F4
Blackheath *Surr.* 171 F3
Blackheath *W.Mid.* 208 B4
Blackhill *Aber.* 325 F4
Blackhill *Aber.* 325 F5
Blackhillock 323 G5
Blackhills 323 E4
Blackhouse 117
Blackland 168 B1
Blacklands 164 B4
Blackleach 242 A4
Blackley 234 C2
Blacklunans 301 G3
Blackmill 179 F4
Blackmoor *Hants.* 170 C4
Blackmoor *Som.* 153 E1
Blackmoor Gate 163 G1
Blackmoorfoot 235 E1
Blackmore 187 F2
Blackmore End *Essex* 201 F4
Blackmore End *Herts.* 186 A1
Blackness *Aber.* 312 B5
Blackness *Falk.* 285 E2
Blackness *High.* 337 E5
Blackness Castle 117
Blacknest 170 C3
Blackney 154 A3
Blacko 243 E3
Blackpole 196 A2
Blackpool *B'pool* 241 G4
Blackpool *Devon* 151 E3
Blackpool Airport 241 G4
Blackpool Bridge 177 D1
Blackpool Gate 268 D4
Blackpool Piers 93
Blackpool Pleasure Beach 93
Blackpool Tower 93
Blackpool Zoo 94
Blackridge 284 C3
Blackrock *Arg. & B.* 280 B3
Blackrock *Mon.* 180 B1
Blackrod 234 A1
Blackshaw 267 E4
Blackshaw Head 243 F5
Blacksmith's Green 202 C1
Blacksmith's Shop 117
Blacksnape 242 D5
Blackstone 159 E2
Blackthorn 184 B1
Blackthorpe 202 A1
Blacktoft 246 A5
Blacktop 313 D4
Blacktown 180 B4
Blackwater *Cornw.* 146 B5
Blackwater *Hants.* 170 D2
Blackwater *I.o.W.* 157 E4
Blackwater *Norf.* 228 B3
Blackwater *Som.* 153 F1
Blackwaterfoot 273 E3
Blackwell *Darl.* 252 B1
Blackwell *Derbys.* 235 F5
Blackwell *Derbys.* 223 F2
Blackwell *W.Suss.* 172 C5
Blackwell *Warks.* 197 E3
Blackwell *Worcs.* 208 B5
Blackwell The Arts & Crafts House 94
Blackwells End 195 G5
Blackwood (Coed-duon) *Caerp.* 180 A3
Blackwood *D. & G.* 266 D2
Blackwood *S.Lan.* 284 B5
Blackwood Hill 221 G2
Blacon 220 A1
Bladbean 175 D4
Bladnoch 265 F5
Bladon 183 G1
Blaen Clydach 179 F3
Blaenannerch 191 F3
Blaenau Dolwyddelan 217 F2
Blaenau Ffestiniog 217 F3
Blaenavon 180 B2
Blaenawey 180 B1
Blaencelyn 191 G2
Blaencwm 179 F2
Blaendyryn 193 F4
Blaenffos 191 E4
Blaengarw 179 F3
Blaengeuffordd 204 C4
Blaengweche 178 C1
Blaengwrach 179 E2
Blaengwynfi 179 E3
Blaenllechau 179 G3
Blaenos 193 D4
Blaenpennal 192 C1
Blaenplwyf 204 B5
Blaenporth 191 F3
Blaenrhondda 179 F2
Blaenwaun 191 F5
Blaen-y-coed 191 G5
Blagdon *N.Som.* 166 B2
Blagdon *Torbay* 151 E1
Blagdon Hill 153 F1
Blaguegate 233 F2
Blaich 298 C2
Blaina 180 A2
Blair 283 E5
Blair Atholl 301 D3
Blair Castle 117
Blair Drummond 292 C3
Blairannaich 291 F4
Blairbuie 282 C2
Blairgowrie 301 G5
Blairhall 285 E1
Blairhoyle 292 B4
Blairhullichan 291 G4
Blairingone 293 E5
Blairkip 274 D2
Blairlogie 292 D5
Blairmore *Arg. & B.* 282 C1
Blairmore *High.* 332 C4
Blairmore *High.* 334 A3
Blairnairn 283 D1
Blairnamarrow 311 E3
Blairpark 282 D4
Blairquhan 274 B5
Blairquhosh 283 G1
Blair's Ferry 282 A3
Blairshinnoch 324 B3
Blairuskinmore 291 G4
Blairvadach 283 D1
Blairydryne 312 C5
Blairythan Cottage 313 E2
Blaisdon 181 G1
Blaise Castle House Museum 25
Blake End 201 F5
Blakebrook 208 A5
Blakedown 208 A5
Blakelaw *Sc.Bord.* 278 B3
Blakelaw *T. & W.* 262 B1
Blakeley 208 A3
Blakelow 221 D2
Blakemere 194 C3
Blakeney *Glos.* 181 F2
Blakeney *Norf.* 228 B1
Blakenhall *Ches.* 221 E3
Blakenhall *W.Mid.* 208 B3
Blakeshall 208 A4
Blakesley 198 B2
Blanchland 261 F2
Bland Hill 244 B2
Blandford Camp 155 F2
Blandford Forum 155 E2
Blandford St. Mary 155 E2
Blanefield 283 G2
Blanerne 287 F4
Blankney 225 F1
Blantyre 284 A4
Blar a' Chaorainn 298 D3
Blargie 309 F5
Blarglas 283 E1
Blarmachfoldach 298 C3
Blarnalearoch 330 D5
Blashford 156 A2
Blaston 210 D3
Blathaisbhal 315 G2
Blatherwycke 211 E3
Blawith 249 D4
Blaxhall 203 E2
Blaxton 237 D2
Blaydon 262 A1
Bleadney 166 B3
Bleadon 166 A2
Bleak Hey Nook 235 E2
Blean 174 D2
Bleasby *Lincs.* 238 B4
Bleasby *Notts.* 224 C3
Bleasby Moor 238 B4
Bleatarn 250 C1
Bleathwood Common 195 E1
Blebocraigs 294 C3
Bleddfa 194 B1
Bledington 197 E5
Bledlow 184 C2
Bledlow Ridge 184 C3
Blencarn 260 C4
Blencogo 259 E2
Blencow 260 A4
Blendworth 157 G1
Blenheim Palace 41
Blennerhasset 259 E2
Blervie Castle 322 C4
Bletchingdon 184 A1
Bletchingley 172 C3
Bletchley *M.K.* 199 D4
Bletchley *Shrop.* 220 D4
Bletchley Park Museum 41
Bletherston 191 D5
Bletsoe 199 F2
Blewbury 184 A4
Blickling 228 C3
Blickling Hall 77
Blidworth 223 G2
Blidworth Bottoms 223 G2
Blindburn *Aber.* 313 E1
Blindburn *Northumb.* 278 C5
Blindcrake 259 E3
Blindley Heath 172 C4
Blisland 147 E2
Bliss Gate 207 G5
Blissford 156 A1
Blisworth 198 C2
Blithbury 222 B5
Blitterlees 259 E1
Blo' Norton 214 B4
Blockley 197 D4
Blofield 229 E5
Blofield Heath 229 E4
Blore 222 C3
Blossomfield 208 D5
Blount's Green 222 B4
Blowick 233 E1
Bloxham 197 G4
Bloxholm 225 F2
Bloxwich 208 B2
Bloxworth 155 E3
Blubberhouses 244 A2
Blue Anchor *Cornw.* 146 D4
Blue Anchor *Som.* 164 D3
Blue Bell Hill 173 G2
Blue Planet Aquarium 94
Bluebell Railway 41
Bluewater 187 E5
Blundellsands 233 E3
Blundeston 215 G2
Blunham 199 G2
Blunsdon St. Andrew 182 D4
Bluntington 208 A5
Bluntisham 212 B5
Blunts 148 D4
Blurton 221 F3
Blyborough 237 G3
Blyford 215 F4
Blymhill 208 A1
Blymhill Common 207 G1
Blymhill Lawn 208 A1
Blyth *Northumb.* 271 F3
Blyth *Notts.* 236 D4
Blyth Bridge 285 F5
Blyth End 209 E3
Blythburgh 215 F4
Blythe Bridge 221 G3
Blythe Marsh 221 G3
Blyton 237 F3
Boarhills 295 D3
Boarhunt 157 F2
Boars Hill 183 G2
Boarsgreave 243 E5
Boarshead 173 E5
Boarstall 184 B1
Boarzell 160 C1
Boasley Cross 149 F1
Boat o' Brig 323 F4
Boat of Garten 310 B3
Boath 321 E2
Bobbing 174 A2
Bobbington 208 A3
Bobbingworth 187 E2
Bocaddon 147 F4
Bochastle 292 B4
Bocketts Farm Park 41
Bockhampton 183 F5
Bocking 201 F5
Bocking Churchstreet 201 F5
Bockleton 195 E1
Boconnoc 147 F3
Boddam *Aber.* 325 G5
Boddam *Shet.* 343 G4
Bodden 166 D3
Boddington 196 A5
Bodedern 230 B4
Bodelwyddan 232 B5
Bodenham *Here.* 195 E2
Bodenham *Wilts.* 168 C5
Bodenham Moor 195 E2
Bodesbeck 276 C5
Bodewryd 230 B3
Bodfari 232 B5
Bodffordd 230 C5
Bodfuan 216 C4
Bodham 228 C1
Bodiam 160 C1
Bodiam Castle 41
Bodicote 197 G4
Bodieve 147 D2
Bodinnick 147 F4
Bodior 230 A5
Bodle Street Green 160 B2
Bodmin 147 E3
Bodmin & Wenford Railway 25
Bodmin Moor 25
Bodnant Gardens 107
Bodney 213 G3
Bodorgan 216 C1
Bodrane 147 G3
Bodsham Green 174 D4
Bodwen 147 E3
Bodymoor Heath 209 D3
Bog, The 206 C3
Bogallan 321 F4
Bogbain 321 G5
Bogbrae 313 F1
Bogbuie 321 E4
Bogend 274 B2
Bogfern 312 A4
Bogfields 312 A4
Bogfold 324 D4
Boghead *Aber.* 324 B4
Boghead *E.Ayr.* 275 E3
Boghead *S.Lan.* 284 B5
Boghole Farm 322 B4
Bogmoor 323 F3
Bogniebrae 324 A5
Bognor Regis 158 B4
Bograxie 312 C3
Bogroy 310 B2
Bogside 293 E5
Bogston 311 F4
Bogton 324 B4
Bogue 266 A2
Bohemia 156 B1
Bohenie 299 E1
Bohetherick 150 A1
Bohortha 145 F3
Bohuntine 299 E1
Boirseam 326 C5
Bojewyan 144 A3
Bokiddick 147 E3
Bolam *Dur.* 262 A5
Bolam *Northumb.* 270 C3
Bolberry 150 C4
Bold Heath 233 G4
Bolderwood 156 B2
Boldon 262 C1
Boldon Colliery 262 C1
Boldre 156 C3
Boldron 251 F1
Bole 237 E4
Bolehill 223 D2
Boleigh 144 B4
Bolenowe 145 D3
Boleside 277 F2
Bolfracks 300 D5
Bolgoed 178 C2
Bolham *Devon* 152 C1
Bolham *Notts.* 237 E4
Bolham Water 153 E1
Bolingey 146 B4
Bolling Hall 86
Bollington 234 D5
Bolney 159 E1
Bolnhurst 199 F2
Bolshan 303 E4
Bolsover 236 B5
Bolsover Castle 70
Bolsterstone 235 G3
Bolstone 195 E4
Boltby 253 D4
Bolter End 184 C3
Bolton *Cumb.* 260 C5
Bolton *E.Loth.* 286 C2
Bolton *E.Riding* 245 G2
Bolton *Gt.Man.* 234 B2
Bolton *Northumb.* 279 F5
Bolton Abbey 243 G2
Bolton Abbey Estate 86
Bolton Bridge 243 G2
Bolton by Bowland 243 D3
Bolton Castle 86
Bolton Houses 242 A4
Bolton Low Houses 259 F2
Bolton Museum, Art Gallery & Aquarium 94
Bolton Percy 245 E3
Bolton upon Dearne 236 B2
Bolton Wood Lane 259 F2
Boltonfellend 260 A1
Boltongate 259 F2
Bolton-le-Sands 242 A1
Bolton-on-Swale 252 B3
Bolventor 147 F2
Bombie 258 A2
Bomere Heath 207 D1
Bonar Bridge 332 B5
Bonawe 290 C1
Bonawe Iron Furnace 117
Bonby 238 A1
Boncath 191 F4
Bonchester Bridge 277 G4
Bonchurch 157 E5
Bondleigh 163 G5
Bonds 242 A3
Bonehill 209 D2
Bo'ness 285 D1
Bo'ness & Kinneil Railway 117
Bonhill 283 E2
Boningale 208 A2
Bonjedward 278 A4
Bonkle 284 C4
Bonning Gate 249 F3
Bonnington *Edin.* 285 F3
Bonnington *Kent* 174 C5
Bonnybank 294 B4
Bonnybridge 284 C1
Bonnykelly 325 D4
Bonnyrigg 286 A3
Bonnyton *Aber.* 312 B1
Bonnyton *Angus* 295 D1
Bonnyton *Angus* 303 E4
Bonnyton *Angus* 294 B1
Bonsall 223 D2
Bont 180 C1
Bont Dolgadfan 205 E2
Bont Newydd 218 A5
Bontddu 204 C1
Bont-goch (Elerch) 204 C4
Bonthorpe 239 E5
Bont-newydd *Conwy* 232 B5
Bontnewydd *Gwyn.* 217 D1
Bontuchel 219 D2
Bonvilston 179 G5
Bon-y-maen 178 C3
Boode 163 F2
Boohay 151 F2
Booker 184 D3
Booley 220 C5
Boor 319 E1
Boosbeck 253 F1
Boose's Green 201 G4
Boot 248 C2
Boot Street 202 D3
Booth 243 G5
Booth Bank 235 E1
Booth Green 234 D4
Booth Wood 235 E1
Boothby Graffoe 225 E2
Boothby Pagnell 225 E4
Boothstown 234 B2
Boothville 198 C1
Bootle *Cumb.* 248 C4
Bootle *Mersey.* 233 E3
Booton 228 C3
Boots Green 234 B5
Booze 251 F2
Boquhan 283 G1
Boraston 207 F5
Borde Hill 41
Bordeaux 151 F4
Borden *Kent* 174 A2
Borden *W.Suss.* 170 D5
Bordley 243 F1
Bordon 170 C4
Boreham *Essex* 187 G2
Boreham *Wilts.* 167 F3
Boreham Street 160 B2
Borehamwood 186 A3
Boreland *D. & G.* 267 F1
Boreland *D. & G.* 265 E4
Boreland *Stir.* 292 A1
Boreley 196 A1
Boreraig 317 E4
Borgh *W.Isles* 326 B5
Borgh *W.Isles* 314 B3
Borgh (Borve) *W.Isles* 329 F2
Borghastan 328 C3
Borgie 335 F3
Borgue *D. & G.* 257 G2
Borgue *High.* 333 G2
Borley 201 G3
Borley Green *Essex* 201 G3
Borley Green *Suff.* 202 A1
Bornais 314 C1
Borness 257 G2
Bornisketaig 317 G2
Borough Green 173 F3
Boroughbridge 244 C1
Borras Head 220 A2
Borrowash 223 F4
Borrowby *N.Yorks.* 253 G1
Borrowby *N.Yorks.* 252 D4
Borrowdale 259 F5
Borrowfield 312 D5
Borstal 173 G2
Borth 204 C4
Borthwick 286 A4
Borthwickbrae 277 F4
Borthwickshiels 277 F4
Borth-y-Gest 217 E4
Borve *High.* 318 A5
Borve (Borgh) *W.Isles* 329 F2
Borwick 249 G5
Borwick Rails 248 C5
Bosavern 144 A3
Bosbury 195 F3
Boscarne 147 E3
Boscastle 148 A1
Boscombe *Bourne.* 156 A3
Boscombe *Wilts.* 168 D4
Bosham 158 A3
Bosham Hoe 158 A3
Bosherston 176 C3
Bosley 221 G1
Bossall 245 G1
Bossiney 147 E1
Bossingham 175 D4
Bossington *Hants.* 169 E4
Bossington *Som.* 164 B3
Bostadh 328 C4
Bostock Green 221 D1
Boston 226 B3
Boston Spa 244 D3
Boswarthan 144 B3
Boswinger 147 D5
Botallack 144 A3
Botany Bay 186 C3
Botcheston 209 G2
Botesdale 214 B4
Bothal 271 E3
Bothamsall 237 D5
Bothel 259 E3
Bothenhampton 154 A3
Bothwell 284 B4
Bothwell Castle 117
Botley *Bucks.* 185 E2
Botley *Hants.* 157 E1
Botley *Oxon.* 183 G2
Botloe's Green 195 G5
Botolph Claydon 198 C5
Botolphs 159 D3
Botolph's Bridge 174 D5
Bottacks 321 D3
Bottesford *Leics.* 224 D4
Bottesford *N.Lincs.* 237 F2
Bottisham 200 D1
Bottlesford 168 C2
Bottom Boat 244 C5
Bottom of Hutton 242 A5
Bottom o'th'Moor 234 A1
Bottomcraig 294 B2
Bottoms 243 F5
Botton Head 242 C1
Botusfleming 150 A1
Botwnnog 216 B4
Bough Beech 173 D4
Boughrood 194 A4
Boughspring 181 E3
Boughton *Norf.* 213 F2
Boughton *Northants.* 198 C1
Boughton *Notts.* 224 B1
Boughton Aluph 174 C4
Boughton Green 173 G3
Boughton House 70
Boughton Lees 174 C4
Boughton Malherbe 174 A4
Boughton Street 174 C3
Boulby 253 G1
Bouldnor 156 C4
Bouldon 207 E4
Boulge 203 D2
Boulmer 279 G5
Boulston 176 C1
Boultenstone Hotel 311 G3
Boultham 225 E1
Boundary *Derbys.* 209 F1
Boundary *Staffs.* 221 G3
Bourn 200 B2
Bourne 225 F5
Bourne End *Beds.* 199 E3
Bourne End *Bucks.* 185 D4
Bourne End *Herts.* 185 F2
Bourne Mill 77
Bourne, The 170 D3
Bournebridge 187 E3
Bournemouth 155 G3
Bournemouth Airport 156 A3
Bournheath 208 B5
Bournmoor 262 C2
Bournville 208 C4
Bourton *Bucks.* 198 C4
Bourton *Dorset* 167 E4
Bourton *N.Som.* 166 A1
Bourton *Oxon.* 183 E4
Bourton *Shrop.* 207 E3
Bourton *Wilts.* 168 B1
Bourton on Dunsmore 209 G5
Bourton-on-the-Hill 197 D4
Bourton-on-the-Water 197 D5
Bousd 296 B3
Boustead Hill 259 F1
Bouth 249 E4
Bouthwaite 252 A5
Bovain 292 A1
Boveney 185 E5
Boveridge 155 G1
Boverton 164 C1
Bovey Tracey 152 B5
Bovingdon 185 F2
Bovinger 187 E2
Bovington Camp 155 E4
Bow *Cumb.* 259 G1
Bow *Devon* 152 A2
Bow *Devon* 151 E2
Bow *Ork.* 338 C3
Bow Brickhill 199 E4
Bow of Fife 294 B3
Bow Street *Cere.* 204 C4
Bow Street *Norf.* 214 B2
Bowbank 261 F5
Bowburn 262 C4
Bowcombe 157 D4
Bowd 153 E3
Bowden *Devon* 151 E3
Bowden *Sc.Bord.* 277 G2
Bowden Hill 168 A1
Bowdon 234 B4
Bower 269 F3
Bower Hinton 154 A1
Bower House Tye 202 A3
Bowerchalke 168 B5
Bowerhill 168 A1
Bowermadden 337 E2
Bowers 221 F4
Bowers Gifford 187 G4
Bowershall 293 F5
Bowertower 337 E2
Bowes 251 E1
Bowgreave 242 A3
Bowhill House 117
Bowhousebog 284 C4
Bowithick 147 F1
Bowker's Green 233 F2
Bowland Bridge 249 F4
Bowley 195 E2
Bowley Town 195 E2
Bowlhead Green 171 E4
Bowling *W.Dun.* 283 F2
Bowling *W.Yorks.* 244 A4
Bowling Bank 220 A3
Bowlish 166 D3
Bowmanstead 249 E3
Bowmore 280 B3
Bowness-on-Solway 268 A5
Bowness-on-Windermere 249 F3
Bowood House & Gardens 25
Bowscale 259 G3
Bowsden 287 G5
Bowside Lodge 336 A2
Bowston 249 F3
Bowthorpe 228 C5
Bowtrees 284 D1
Box *Glos.* 182 A2
Box *Wilts.* 167 F1
Box End 199 F3
Box Hill Country Park 42
Boxbush *Glos.* 181 G1
Boxbush *Glos.* 195 F5
Boxford *Suff.* 202 A3
Boxford *W.Berks.* 183 G5
Boxgrove 158 B3
Boxley 173 G3
Boxmoor 185 F2
Box's Shop 162 C5
Boxted *Essex* 202 A4
Boxted *Suff.* 201 G2
Boxted Cross 202 A4
Boxwell 182 A3
Boxworth 200 B1
Boxworth End 200 B1
Boyden Gate 175 E2
Boydston 274 C2
Boylestone 222 C4
Boyndie 324 B3
Boynton 246 D1
Boys Hill 154 C2
Boysack 303 E5
Boyton *Cornw.* 148 D1
Boyton *Suff.* 203 E3
Boyton *Wilts.* 168 A4
Boyton Cross 187 F2
Boyton End 201 F3
Bozeat 199 E2
Braaid 240 B4
Braal Castle 336 D2
Brabling Green 203 D1
Brabourne 174 C4
Brabourne Lees 174 C4
Brabster 337 F2
Bracadale 305 G1
Braceborough 211 F1
Bracebridge Heath 225 E1
Braceby 225 F4
Bracewell 243 E3
Brachla 309 E1
Bracken Hill 244 A5
Brackenber 250 C1
Brackenbottom 250 D5
Brackenfield 223 E2
Brackens 324 C4
Bracklach 311 F2
Bracklamore 324 D4
Bracklesham 158 A4
Brackletter 299 D1
Brackley *Arg. & B.* 281 G1
Brackley *High.* 322 A4
Brackley *Northants.* 198 A4
Brackley Gate 223 E3
Brackley Hatch 198 B3
Bracknell 171 D1
Braco 292 D4
Bracobrae 324 A4
Bracon Ash 214 C2
Bracora 306 D5
Bracorina 306 D5
Bradbourne 222 D2
Bradbury 262 C5
Bradda 240 A4
Bradden 198 B3
Braddock 147 F3
Braden Heath 220 B4
Bradenham *Bucks.* 184 D3
Bradenham *Norf.* 228 A5
Bradenstoke 182 C5
Bradfield *Devon* 153 D2
Bradfield *Essex* 202 C4
Bradfield *Norf.* 229 D2
Bradfield *W.Berks.* 184 B5
Bradfield Combust 201 G2
Bradfield Green 221 D2
Bradfield Heath 202 C5
Bradfield St. Clare 202 A2
Bradfield St. George 202 A1
Bradford *Cornw.* 147 F2
Bradford *Derbys.* 222 D1
Bradford *Devon* 163 E5
Bradford *Northumb.* 279 F3
Bradford *Northumb.* 270 C4
Bradford *W.Yorks.* 244 A4
Bradford Abbas 154 B1
Bradford Industrial Museum 86
Bradford Leigh 167 F1
Bradford Peverell 154 C3
Bradford-on-Avon 167 F1
Bradford-on-Tone 165 E5
Bradgate Park 70
Bradiford 163 F2
Brading 157 F4
Bradley *Ches.* 233 G5
Bradley *Derbys.* 222 D3
Bradley *Hants.* 170 B3
Bradley *N.E.Lincs.* 238 C2
Bradley (Low Bradley) *N.Yorks.* 243 G3
Bradley *Staffs.* 208 A1
Bradley *W.Mid.* 208 B3
Bradley Fold 234 B2
Bradley Green *Warks.* 209 E2
Bradley Green *Worcs.* 196 B1
Bradley in the Moors 222 B3
Bradley Manor 25
Bradley Mills 235 F1
Bradley Stoke 181 F4
Bradmore *Notts.* 223 G4
Bradmore *W.Mid.* 208 A3
Bradney 166 A4
Bradninch 152 D2
Bradnop 222 B2
Bradnor Green 194 B2
Bradpole 154 A3
Bradshaw *Gt.Man.* 234 B1
Bradshaw *W.Yorks.* 243 G4
Bradstone 149 D2
Bradwall Green 221 E1
Bradwell *Derbys.* 235 F4
Bradwell *Devon* 163 E1
Bradwell *Essex* 201 G5
Bradwell *M.K.* 198 D4
Bradwell *Norf.* 229 G5
Bradwell Grove 183 E2
Bradwell Waterside 188 C2
Bradwell-on-Sea 188 D2
Bradworthy 162 D4
Brae *D. & G.* 266 C3
Brae *High.* 331 G4
Brae *Shet.* 342 C1
Brae of Achnahaird 330 C3
Braeantra 321 E2
Braedownie 302 A2
Braefoot 324 C5
Braegrum 293 F2
Braehead *D. & G.* 265 F5
Braehead *Glas.* 283 G3
Braehead *Moray* 323 F5
Braehead *Ork.* 339 E2
Braehead *Ork.* 340 C2
Braehead *S.Lan.* 275 G2
Braehead *S.Lan.* 285 D4
Braehead of Lunan 303 E4
Braehoulland 344 B5
Braeleny 292 B3
Braemar 311 D5
Braemore *High.* 332 A4
Braemore *High.* 336 C5
Braemore *High.* 320 A2
Braenaloin 311 E5
Braes of Enzie 323 F4
Braes of Foss 300 C4
Braes of Ullapool 330 D5
Braeswick 341 E3
Braeval 292 A4
Braewick 342 C2
Brafferton *Darl.* 262 B5
Brafferton *N.Yorks.* 252 D5
Brafield-on-the-Green 198 D2
Bragar 329 D3
Bragbury End 200 A5
Bragenham 199 E5
Bragleenbeg 290 B2
Braichmelyn 217 F1
Braides 242 A2
Braidley 251 F4
Braidwood 284 C5
Braigo 280 A3
Brailsford 223 D3
Brain's Green 181 F2
Braintree 201 F5
Braiseworth 214 C4
Braishfield 169 E5
Braithwaite *Cumb.* 259 F4
Braithwaite *S.Yorks.* 236 D1
Braithwaite *W.Yorks.* 243 G3
Braithwell 236 C3
Bramber 159 D2
Brambletye 172 D5
Brambridge 169 F5
Bramcote *Notts.* 223 G4
Bramcote *Warks.* 209 G4
Bramdean 170 B5
Bramerton 229 D5
Bramfield *Herts.* 186 B1
Bramfield *Suff.* 215 E4
Bramford 202 C3
Bramhall 234 C4
Bramham 244 D3
Bramham Park 86
Bramhope 244 B3
Bramley *Hants.* 170 B2
Bramley *S.Yorks.* 236 B3
Bramley *Surr.* 171 F3
Bramley Corner 170 B2
Bramley Head 244 A2
Bramley Vale 223 F1
Bramling 175 E3
Brampford Speke 152 C3
Brampton *Cambs.* 212 A5
Brampton *Cumb.* 260 B1
Brampton *Cumb.* 260 C5
Brampton *Derbys.* 236 A5
Brampton *Lincs.* 237 F5
Brampton *Norf.* 228 D3
Brampton *S.Yorks.* 236 B2

Brampton *Suff.* 215 F3
Brampton Abbotts 195 F5
Brampton Ash 210 C4
Brampton Bryan 206 C5
Brampton en le Morthen 236 B4
Brampton Street 215 F3
Bramshall 222 B4
Bramshaw 156 B1
Bramshill 170 C1
Bramshott 170 D4
Bramwell 166 B5
Bran End 201 E5
Branault 297 E3
Brancaster 227 F3
Brancaster Staithe 227 F3
Brancepeth 262 B4
Branchill 322 C4
Brand Green 195 G5
Brandelhow 259 F4
Branderburgh 323 E2
Brandesburton 246 D3
Brandeston 202 D1
Brandis Corner 163 E5
Brandiston 228 C3
Brandon *Dur.* 262 B4
Brandon *Lincs.* 225 E3
Brandon *Northumb.* 279 E5
Brandon *Suff.* 213 F4
Brandon *Warks.* 209 G5
Brandon Bank 213 E4
Brandon Creek 213 E3
Brandon Parva 228 B5
Brandsby 253 E5
Brandy Wharf 238 A3
Brane 144 B4
Branklyn Gardens 117
Branksome 155 G3
Branksome Park 155 G3
Bransbury 169 F3
Bransby 237 F5
Branscombe 153 E4
Bransford 195 G2
Bransford Bridge 196 A2
Bransgore 156 A3
Bransholme 246 D4
Branson's Cross 208 C5
Branston *Leics.* 224 D5
Branston *Lincs.* 225 F1
Branston *Staffs.* 222 D5
Branston Booths 225 F1
Brant Broughton 225 E2
Brantham 202 C4
Branthwaite *Cumb.* 259 F3
Branthwaite *Cumb.* 259 D4
Brantingham 246 B5
Branton *Northumb.* 279 E5
Branton *S.Yorks.* 236 D2
Brantwood *Cumb.* 249 E3
Brantwood *Cumb.* 94
Branxholm Bridgend 277 F4
Branxholme 277 F4
Branxton 278 C3
Brassey Green 220 C1
Brassington 222 D2
Brasted 173 D3
Brasted Chart 173 D3
Bratch, The 208 A3
Brathens 312 B5
Bratoft 226 C1
Brattleby 237 G4
Bratton *Som.* 164 C3
Bratton *Tel. & W.* 207 F1
Bratton *Wilts.* 168 A2
Bratton Clovelly 149 E1
Bratton Fleming 163 G2
Bratton Seymour 167 D5
Braughing 200 B5
Brauncewell 225 F2
Braunston *Northants.* 198 A1
Braunston *Rut.* 210 D2
Braunstone 210 A2
Braunton 163 E2
Brawby 253 G5
Brawdy 190 B5
Brawith 253 E2
Brawl 336 A2
Brawlbin 336 C3
Bray 185 E5
Bray Shop 148 D3
Bray Wick 185 D5
Braybrooke 210 C4
Braydon Side 182 C4
Brayford 163 G2
Brayshaw 243 D2
Braythorn 244 B3
Brayton 245 F4
Braywoodside 185 D5
Brazacott 148 C1
Brea 146 A5
Breach *Kent* 175 D4
Breach *Kent* 174 A2
Breachwood Green 199 G5
Breacleit 328 C4
Breadsall 223 E4
Breadstone 181 G2
Breage 144 D4
Breakon 345 E2
Bream 181 F2
Breamore *Hants.* 156 A1
Breamore *Hants.* 42
Brean 165 F2
Breanais 328 A5
Brearton 244 C1
Breascleit 328 D4
Breaston 223 F4
Brechfa 192 B4
Brechin 303 E3
Brecklate 272 B4
Breckles 214 A2
Brecon (Aberhonddu) 193 G5
Brecon Beacons 107
Brecon Beacons Visitor Centre 108
Brecon Mountain Railway 108
Breconside 275 G5
Bredbury 234 D3
Brede 160 D2
Bredenbury 195 F2
Bredfield 203 D2
Bredgar 174 A2
Bredhurst 173 G2
Bredon 196 B4
Bredon Tithe Barn 64
Bredon's Hardwick 196 B4
Bredon's Norton 196 B4
Bredwardine 194 C3
Breedon on the Hill 223 F5
Breibhig 329 F4
Breich 285 D3
Breightmet 234 B2
Breighton 245 G4
Breinton 195 D4
Breinton Common 195 D4
Bremhill 182 B5
Bremhill Wick 182 B5
Brenachoille 290 C4
Brenchley 173 F4
Brendon *Devon* 164 A3
Brendon *Devon* 163 D4
Brendon *Devon* 163 D5
Brenkley 271 E4
Brent Eleigh 202 A3
Brent Knoll 166 A2
Brent Pelham 200 C4
Brentford 186 A5
Brentingby 210 C1
Brentwood 187 E3
Brenzett 161 F1
Brenzett Green 161 F1
Breoch 266 B5
Brereton 208 C1
Brereton Green 221 E1
Brereton Heath 221 F1
Breretonhill 208 C1
Bressay 343 E3
Bressingham 214 B3
Bressingham Common 214 B3
Bressingham Steam Museum & Gardens 77
Bretby 223 D5
Bretford 209 G5
Bretforton 196 C3
Bretherdale Head 249 G2
Bretherton 242 A5
Brettabister 343 D2
Brettenham *Norf.* 214 A3
Brettenham *Suff.* 202 A2
Bretton *Derbys.* 235 F5
Bretton *Flints.* 220 A1
Brevig 314 B4
Brewers Quay 25
Brewood 208 A2
Briach 322 C4
Briantspuddle 155 E3
Brick End 201 D5
Bricket Wood 186 A2
Brickkiln Green 201 F4
Bricklehampton 196 B3
Bride 240 C1
Bridekirk 259 E3
Bridell 191 E3
Bridestones 221 G1
Bridestowe 149 F2
Brideswell 312 A1
Bridford 152 B4
Bridge *Cornw.* 146 A5
Bridge *Kent* 175 D3
Bridge End *Cumb.* 248 D4
Bridge End *Devon* 150 C3
Bridge End *Essex* 201 E4
Bridge End *Lincs.* 225 G4
Bridge End *Shet.* 342 C4
Bridge Hewick 252 C5
Bridge o' Ess 312 A5
Bridge of Alford 312 A3
Bridge of Allan 292 C5
Bridge of Avon 311 D1
Bridge of Balgie 300 A5
Bridge of Bogendreip 312 B5
Bridge of Brewlands 301 G3
Bridge of Brown 310 D2
Bridge of Cally 301 G4
Bridge of Canny 312 B5
Bridge of Craigisla 302 A4
Bridge of Dee *Aber.* 311 D5
Bridge of Dee *Aber.* 312 B5
Bridge of Dee *D. & G.* 266 B4
Bridge of Don 313 E4
Bridge of Dun 303 E4
Bridge of Dye 303 E1
Bridge of Earn 293 G3
Bridge of Ericht 300 A4
Bridge of Feugh 312 B5
Bridge of Forss 336 C2
Bridge of Gairn 311 F5
Bridge of Gaur 300 A4
Bridge of Muchalls 313 D5
Bridge of Muick 311 F5
Bridge of Orchy 291 E1
Bridge of Tynet 323 F3
Bridge of Walls 342 B2
Bridge of Weir 283 F3
Bridge Reeve 163 G4
Bridge Sollers 194 D3
Bridge Street 201 G3
Bridge Trafford 233 F5
Bridgefoot *Angus* 294 B1
Bridgefoot *Cambs.* 200 C3
Bridgefoot *Cumb.* 259 D4
Bridgehampton 166 C5
Bridgehaugh 311 F1
Bridgehill 261 G2
Bridgemary 157 E2
Bridgemere 221 E3
Bridgemere Garden World 94
Bridgend *Aber.* 312 A1
Bridgend *Aber.* 324 C5
Bridgend *Angus* 302 D3
Bridgend *Arg. & B.* 280 B3
Bridgend *Arg. & B.* 290 A5
Bridgend (Pen-y-bont ar Ogwr) *Bridgend* 179 F5
Bridgend *Cornw.* 147 F4
Bridgend *Cumb.* 249 F1
Bridgend *Fife* 294 B3
Bridgend *Moray* 311 F1
Bridgend *P. & K.* 293 G2
Bridgend *W.Loth.* 285 E2
Bridgend of Lintrathen 302 A4
Bridgerule 162 C5
Bridges 206 C3
Bridgeton *Aber.* 312 A3
Bridgeton *Glas.* 284 A3
Bridgetown *Cornw.* 148 D2
Bridgetown *Som.* 164 C4
Bridgeyate 181 F5
Bridgham 214 A3
Bridgnorth 207 G3
Bridgtown 208 B2
Bridgwater 165 F4
Bridlington 247 D1
Bridport 154 A3
Bridstow 195 E5
Brierfield 243 E4
Brierley *Glos.* 181 F1
Brierley *Here.* 195 D2
Brierley *S.Yorks.* 236 B1
Brierley Hill 208 B4
Brierton 263 D5
Briestfield 235 G1
Brig o'Turk 292 A4
Brigg 238 A2
Briggate 229 E3
Briggswath 254 B2
Brigham *Cumb.* 259 D3
Brigham *E.Riding* 246 C2
Brighouse 244 A5
Brighstone 156 D4
Brightgate 223 D2
Brighthampton 183 F2
Brightholmlee 235 G3
Brightling 160 B1
Brightlingsea 189 D1
Brighton *B. & H.* 159 F3
Brighton *Cornw.* 146 D4
Brighton Pavilion (see Royal Pavilion) 50
Brightons 284 D2
Brightwalton 183 G5
Brightwalton Green 183 G5
Brightwell 202 D3
Brightwell Baldwin 184 B3
Brightwell Upperton 184 B3
Brightwell-cum-Sotwell 184 A3
Brignall 251 F1
Brigsley 238 C2
Brigsteer 249 F4
Brigstock 211 E4
Brill *Bucks.* 184 B1
Brill *Cornw.* 145 E4
Brilley 194 B3
Brilley Mountain 194 B2
Brimaston 190 C5
Brimfield 195 E1
Brimington 236 B5
Brimington Common 236 B5
Brimley 152 B5
Brimpsfield 182 B1
Brimpton 169 G1
Brims 338 B4
Brimscombe 182 A2
Brimstage 233 E4
Brinacory 307 D5
Brindham 166 C3
Brindister *Shet.* 342 D4
Brindister *Shet.* 342 B2
Brindle 242 B5
Brindley Ford 221 F2
Brineton 208 A1
Bringhurst 210 D3
Brington 211 F5
Brinian 340 C4
Briningham 228 B2
Brinkburn Priory 103
Brinkhill 239 D5
Brinkley *Cambs.* 201 E2
Brinkley *Notts.* 224 C2
Brinklow 209 G5
Brinkworth 182 C4
Brinmore 309 F2
Brinscall 242 C5
Brinsea 166 B1
Brinsley 223 F3
Brinsop 194 D3
Brinsworth 236 B3
Brinton 228 B2
Brisco 260 A2
Brisley 228 A3
Brislington 181 F5
Brissenden Green 174 B5
Bristol 181 E5
Bristol City Museum & Art Gallery 25
Bristol Industrial Museum 25
Bristol International Airport 166 C1
Bristol Zoo 26
Briston 228 B2
Britain At War 55
Britannia *Edin.* 117
Britannia *Lancs.* 243 E5
Britford 168 C5
Brithdir *Caerp.* 180 A2
Brithdir *Gwyn.* 205 D1
Brithem Bottom 152 D1
British Empire & Commonwealth Museum 26
British Golf Museum 117
British Museum 55
Briton Ferry (Llansawel) 178 D3
Britwell 185 E4
Britwell Salome 184 B3
Brixham 151 F2
Brixton *Devon* 150 B2
Brixton *Gt.Lon.* 186 C5
Brixton Deverill 167 F4
Brixworth 210 C5
Brize Norton 183 E2
Broad Alley 196 A1
Broad Blunsdon 183 D3
Broad Campden 197 D4
Broad Carr 235 E1
Broad Chalke 168 B5
Broad Ford 173 G5
Broad Green *Beds.* 199 E3
Broad Green *Cambs.* 201 E2
Broad Green *Essex* 201 G5
Broad Green *Essex* 200 C4
Broad Green *Mersey.* 233 F3
Broad Green *Suff.* 202 B2
Broad Green *Worcs.* 195 G2
Broad Haven 176 B1
Broad Hill 213 D5
Broad Hinton 182 D5
Broad Laying 169 F1
Broad Marston 196 D3
Broad Oak *Carmar.* 192 B5
Broad Oak *Cumb.* 248 C3
Broad Oak *E.Suss.* 160 D2
Broad Oak *E.Suss.* 160 B1
Broad Oak *Here.* 195 D5
Broad Road 215 D4
Broad Street *E.Suss.* 161 D2
Broad Street *Kent* 174 A3
Broad Street *Kent* 174 D5
Broad Street *Wilts.* 168 C2
Broad Street Green 188 B2
Broad, The 195 D1
Broad Town 182 C5
Broadbottom 235 D3
Broadbridge 158 A3
Broadbridge Heath 171 G4
Broadclyst 152 C3
Broadfield *Lancs.* 242 D5
Broadfield *Lancs.* 242 B5
Broadford 306 C2
Broadford Bridge 171 F5
Broadgate 248 C4
Broadhaugh 277 F5
Broadhaven 337 F3
Broadheath *Gt.Man.* 234 B4
Broadheath *Worcs.* 195 F1
Broadhembury 153 E2
Broadhempston 151 E1
Broadholme 237 F5
Broadland Row 160 D2
Broadlands 42
Broadlay 177 G2
Broadley *Lancs.* 234 C1
Broadley *Moray* 323 F3
Broadley Common 186 D2
Broadmayne 154 D4
Broadmeadows 277 F2
Broadmere 170 B3
Broadmoor 177 D2
Broadnymett 152 A2
Broadoak *Dorset* 154 A3
Broadoak *Glos.* 181 F1
Broadoak *Kent* 175 D2
Broadoak End 186 C1
Broadrashes 323 G4
Broad's Green 187 F1
Broadsea 325 E3
Broadstairs 175 F2
Broadstone *Poole* 155 G3
Broadstone *Shrop.* 207 E4
Broadstreet Common 180 C4
Broadwas 195 G2
Broadwater *Herts.* 200 A5
Broadwater *W.Suss.* 158 D3
Broadwater Down 173 E5
Broadwaters 208 A5
Broadway *Carmar.* 177 G2
Broadway *Carmar.* 177 F1
Broadway *Pembs.* 176 B1
Broadway *Som.* 153 G1
Broadway *Suff.* 215 E4
Broadway *Worcs.* 196 D4
Broadwell *Glos.* 197 E5
Broadwell *Oxon.* 183 E2
Broadwell *Warks.* 197 G1
Broadwell House 261 F2
Broadwey 154 C4
Broadwindsor 154 A2
Broadwood Kelly 163 G5
Broadwoodwidger 149 E2
Brobury 194 C3
Brocastle 179 F5
Brochel 318 B5
Brochloch 265 G1
Brock 296 B2
Brockamin 195 G2
Brockbridge 157 F1
Brockdish 214 D4
Brockenhurst 156 B2
Brockford Green 202 C1
Brockford Street 202 C1
Brockhall 198 B1
Brockham 171 G3
Brockhampton *Glos.* 196 C5
Brockhampton *Glos.* 196 B5
Brockhampton *Here.* 195 E4
Brockhampton *Here.* 195 F2
Brockhampton Green 154 D2
Brockholes 235 F1
Brockhurst *Hants.* 157 E2
Brockhurst *W.Suss.* 172 D5
Brocklebank 259 G2
Brocklesby 238 B1
Brockley *N.Som.* 166 B1
Brockley *Suff.* 201 G2
Brockley Green 201 F3
Brock's Green 169 F1
Brockton *Shrop.* 207 E3
Brockton *Shrop.* 207 G2
Brockton *Shrop.* 206 C2
Brockton *Shrop.* 206 C4
Brockton *Tel. & W.* 207 G1
Brockweir 181 E2
Brockwood Park 170 B5
Brockworth 182 A1
Brocton 208 B1
Brodick 273 F2
Brodick Castle 117
Brodie Castle 117
Brodsworth 236 C2
Brogborough 199 E4
Brogden 243 E3
Brogyntyn 219 F4
Broken Cross *Ches.* 234 C5
Broken Cross *Ches.* 234 A5
Brokenborough 182 B4
Brokes 252 A3
Bromborough 233 E4
Brome 214 C4
Brome Street 214 C4
Bromeswell 203 E2
Bromfield *Cumb.* 259 E2
Bromfield *Shrop.* 207 D5
Bromham *Beds.* 199 F2
Bromham *Wilts.* 168 A1
Bromley *Gt.Lon.* 172 D2
Bromley *S.Yorks.* 236 A3
Bromley Cross 234 B1
Bromley Green 174 B5
Brompton *Med.* 173 G2
Brompton *N.Yorks.* 252 C3
Brompton *N.Yorks.* 254 C4
Brompton *Shrop.* 207 E2
Brompton on Swale 252 B3
Brompton Ralph 165 D4
Brompton Regis 164 C4
Bromsash 195 F5
Bromsberrow 195 G4
Bromsberrow Heath 195 G4
Bromsgrove 208 B5
Bromstead Heath 208 A1
Bromyard 195 F2
Bromyard Downs 195 F2
Bronaber 218 A4
Brondesbury 186 B4
Brongest 191 G3
Bronington 220 B4
Bronllys 194 A4
Bronnant 192 C1
Brontë Parsonage Museum 86
Bronwydd Arms 192 A5
Bronydd 194 B3
Bron-y-gaer 177 G1
Bronygarth 219 F4
Brook *Carmar.* 177 F2
Brook *Hants.* 156 B1
Brook *Hants.* 169 E5
Brook *I.o.W.* 156 C4
Brook *Kent* 174 C4
Brook *Surr.* 171 E4
Brook *Surr.* 171 F3
Brook Bottom 235 D2
Brook End *Beds.* 199 F1
Brook End *Herts.* 200 B5
Brook End *M.K.* 199 E3
Brook End *Worcs.* 196 A3
Brook Hill 156 B1
Brook Street *Essex* 187 E3
Brook Street *Kent* 174 B5
Brook Street *Suff.* 201 G3
Brook Street *W.Suss.* 159 F1
Brooke *Norf.* 215 D2
Brooke *Rut.* 210 D2
Brookend *Glos.* 181 E3
Brookend *Glos.* 181 F2
Brookfield 235 E3
Brookhampton 184 B3
Brookhouse *Ches.* 234 D5
Brookhouse *Denb.* 219 D1
Brookhouse *Lancs.* 242 B1
Brookhouse *S.Yorks.* 236 C4
Brookhouse Green 221 F1
Brookhouses 221 G3
Brookland 161 E1
Brooklands *D. & G.* 266 C3
Brooklands *Shrop.* 220 C3
Brooklands Museum 42
Brookmans Park 186 B2
Brooks 206 A3
Brooks Green 171 G5
Brooksby 210 B1
Brookside Garden Centre & Miniature Railway 94
Brookthorpe 182 A1
Brookwood 171 E2
Broom *Beds.* 199 G3
Broom *Fife* 294 B4
Broom *Warks.* 196 C2
Broom Green 228 A3
Broom Hill *Dorset* 155 G2
Broom Hill *Worcs.* 208 B5
Broom of Dalreach 293 F3
Broomcroft 207 E2
Broome *Norf.* 215 E2
Broome *Shrop.* 206 D4
Broome *Worcs.* 208 B5
Broome Wood 279 F5
Broomedge 234 B4
Broomer's Corner 171 G5
Broomfield *Aber.* 313 E1
Broomfield *Essex* 187 G1
Broomfield *Kent* 175 D2
Broomfield *Kent* 174 A3
Broomfield *Som.* 165 F4
Broomfleet 246 A5
Broomhall Green 220 D3
Broomhaugh 261 G1
Broomhead 325 E3
Broomhill *Bristol* 181 F5
Broomhill *Northumb.* 271 E1
Broomielaw 251 F1
Broomley 261 G1
Broompark 262 B3
Broom's Green 195 G4
Brora 333 E4
Broseley 207 F2
Brotherlee 261 F4
Brothertoft 226 A3
Brotherton 245 D5
Brotton 253 F1
Broubster 336 C2
Brough *Cumb.* 250 C1
Brough *Derbys.* 235 F4
Brough *E.Riding* 246 B5
Brough *High.* 337 E1
Brough *Notts.* 224 D2
Brough *Ork.* 340 B5
Brough *Shet.* 343 E3
Brough *Shet.* 344 D5
Brough *Shet.* 343 E1
Brough *Shet.* 345 E5
Brough Lodge 345 E3
Brough Sowerby 250 C1
Broughall 220 C3
Brougham 260 B5
Broughton *Bucks.* 184 D1
Broughton *Cambs.* 212 A5
Broughton *Flints.* 220 A1
Broughton *Hants.* 169 E4
Broughton *Lancs.* 242 B4
Broughton *M.K.* 199 D3
Broughton *N.Lincs.* 237 G2
Broughton *N.Yorks.* 253 G5
Broughton *N.Yorks.* 243 F2
Broughton *Northants.* 210 D5
Broughton *Ork.* 340 C2
Broughton *Oxon.* 197 G4
Broughton *Sc.Bord.* 276 C2
Broughton *V. of Glam.* 179 F5
Broughton Astley 210 A3
Broughton Beck 249 D4
Broughton Castle 42
Broughton Gifford 167 F1
Broughton Green 196 B1
Broughton Hackett 196 B2
Broughton House 118
Broughton in Furness 248 D4
Broughton Mills 248 D3
Broughton Moor 259 D3
Broughton Poggs 183 E2
Broughtown 341 E2
Broughty Ferry 294 C1
Browland 342 B2
Brown Candover 169 G4
Brown Edge *Lancs.* 233 E1
Brown Edge *Staffs.* 221 G2
Brown Heath 220 B1
Brown Lees 221 F2
Brown Street 202 B1
Brownber 250 C2
Brownheath 220 B5
Brownhill 325 D5
Brownhills *Fife* 294 D3
Brownhills *W.Mid.* 208 C2
Brownieside 279 F4
Brownlow 221 F1
Brownlow Heath 221 F1
Brown's Bank 220 D3
Brownsea Island 26
Brownshill 182 A2
Brownshill Green 209 F4
Brownsover 210 A5
Brownston 150 C2
Browston Green 229 F5
Broxa 254 C3
Broxbourne 186 C2
Broxburn *E.Loth.* 287 D2
Broxburn *W.Loth.* 285 E2
Broxholme 237 G5
Broxted 201 D5
Broxton 220 B2
Broxwood 194 C2
Broyle Side 159 G2
Bru (Brue) 329 E3
Bruachmary 322 A5
Bruan 337 F5
Brue (Bru) 329 E3
Bruera 220 B1
Bruern 197 E5
Bruernish 314 C3
Bruichladdich 280 A3
Bruisyard 203 E1
Bruisyard Street 203 E1
Brumby 237 G1
Brund 222 C1
Brundall 229 E5
Brundish *Norf.* 215 E2
Brundish *Suff.* 203 D1
Brundish Street 215 D4
Brunstock 260 A2
Brunswick Village 271 E4
Bruntingthorpe 210 B3
Bruntland 311 G2
Brunton *Fife* 294 B2
Brunton *Northumb.* 279 G4
Brunton *Wilts.* 168 D2
Brushfield 235 F5
Brushford *Devon* 163 G5
Brushford *Som.* 164 C5
Bruton 167 D4
Bryanston 155 E2
Bryant's Bottom 185 D3
Brydekirk 267 F3
Brymbo 219 F2
Brympton 154 B1
Bryn *Caerp.* 180 A3
Bryn *Carmar.* 178 B2
Bryn *Ches.* 234 A5
Bryn *Gt.Man.* 233 G2
Bryn *N.P.T.* 179 E3
Bryn *Shrop.* 206 B4
Bryn Bwbach 217 F4
Bryn Gates 233 G2
Bryn Pen-y-lan 220 A3
Bryn, The 180 C2
Brynamman 178 D1
Brynberian 191 E4
Bryncae 179 F4
Bryncethin 179 F4
Bryncir 217 D3
Bryncoch *Bridgend* 179 F4
Bryn-côch *N.P.T.* 178 D3
Bryncroes 216 B4
Bryncrug 204 C2
Bryneglwys 219 E3
Brynford 232 C5
Bryngwran 230 B5
Bryngwyn *Mon.* 180 C2
Bryngwyn *Powys* 194 A3
Bryn-henllan 190 D4
Brynhoffnant 191 G2
Bryning 242 A4
Brynithel 180 B2
Brynmawr *B.Gwent* 180 A1
Bryn-mawr *Gwyn.* 216 B4
Brynmelyn 206 A5
Brynmenyn 179 F4
Brynna 179 F4
Brynnau Gwynion 179 F4
Brynog 192 B2
Bryn-penarth 206 A2
Brynrefail *Gwyn.* 217 E1
Brynrefail *I.o.A.* 230 C4
Brynsadler 179 G4
Brynsaithmarchog 219 D2
Brynsiencyn 217 D1
Bryn-teg *I.o.A.* 230 C4
Brynteg *Wrex.* 220 A2
Bryn-y-cochin 220 A4
Brynygwenin 180 C1
Bryn-y-maen 231 G5
Buaile nam Bodach 314 C3
Bualadubh 315 F5
Bualintur 306 A2
Bualnaluib 330 A5
Bubbenhall 209 F5
Bubnell 235 G5
Bubwith 245 G4
Buccleuch 277 E4
Buchan 266 B4
Buchanan Castle 283 F1
Buchanhaven 325 G5
Buchanty 293 E2
Buchlyvie 292 A5
Buckabank 259 G2
Buckby Wharf 198 B1
Buckden *Cambs.* 199 G1
Buckden *N.Yorks.* 251 E5
Buckenham 229 E5
Buckerell 153 E2
Buckfast 150 D1
Buckfast Abbey 26
Buckfastleigh 150 D1
Buckhaven 294 B5
Buckholm 277 F2
Buckholt 181 E1
Buckhorn Weston 167 E5
Buckhurst Hill 186 D3
Buckie 323 G3
Buckies 336 D2
Buckingham 198 B4
Buckingham Palace 55
Buckinghamshire County Museum 42
Buckinghamshire Railway Centre 42
Buckland *Bucks.* 185 D1
Buckland *Devon* 150 C3
Buckland *Glos.* 196 C4
Buckland *Hants.* 156 C3
Buckland *Here.* 195 E2
Buckland *Herts.* 200 B4
Buckland *Kent* 175 F4
Buckland *Oxon.* 183 F3
Buckland *Surr.* 172 B3
Buckland Abbey 26
Buckland Brewer 163 E3
Buckland Common 185 E2
Buckland Dinham 167 E2
Buckland Filleigh 163 E5
Buckland in the Moor 152 A5
Buckland Monachorum 150 A1
Buckland Newton 154 C2
Buckland Ripers 154 C4
Buckland St. Mary 153 F1
Buckland-tout-Saints 151 D3
Bucklebury 184 A5
Bucklerheads 294 C1
Bucklers Hard 156 D3
Buckler's Hard Maritime Museum 42
Bucklesham 202 D3
Buckley (Bwcle) 219 F1
Buckley Green 197 D1
Bucklow Hill 234 B4
Buckman Corner 171 G5
Buckminster 225 D5
Bucknall *Lincs.* 225 G1
Bucknall *Stoke* 221 G3
Bucknell *Oxon.* 198 A5
Bucknell *Shrop.* 206 C5
Buckridge 207 G5
Buck's Cross 162 D3
Bucks Green 171 F4
Bucks Hill 185 F2
Bucks Horn Oak 170 D3
Buck's Mills 163 D3
Bucksburn 313 D4

Buc - Car

Buckspool 176 C3
Buckton *E.Riding* 255 E5
Buckton *Here.* 206 C5
Buckton *Northumb.* 279 E3
Buckworth 211 G5
Budbrooke 197 E1
Budby 236 D5
Buddon 294 D1
Bude 162 C5
Budge's Shop 148 D5
Budlake 152 C2
Budle 279 F3
Budleigh Salterton 153 D4
Budock Water 145 E3
Budworth Heath 234 A5
Buerton 221 D3
Bugbrooke 198 B2
Bugeildy (Beguildy) 206 A5
Buglawton 221 F1
Bugle 147 E4
Bugthorpe 245 G2
Building End 200 C4
Buildwas 207 F2
Buildwas Abbey 64
Builth Road 193 G2
Builth Wells 193 G2
Bulby 225 F5
Bulcote 224 B3
Buldoo 336 B2
Bulford 168 C3
Bulford Camp 168 C3
Bulkeley 220 C2
Bulkington *Warks.* 209 F4
Bulkington *Wilts.* 168 A2
Bulkworthy 163 D4
Bull Bay 230 C3
Bull Green 174 B5
Bullbridge 223 E2
Bullbrook 171 D1
Bullen's Green 186 B2
Bulley 181 G1
Bullington 238 A5
Bullpot Farm 250 B4
Bulls Cross 186 C3
Bull's Green *Herts.* 186 B1
Bull's Green *Norf.* 215 F2
Bullwood 282 C2
Bulmer *Essex* 201 G3
Bulmer *N.Yorks.* 245 F1
Bulmer Tye 201 G4
Bulphan 187 F4
Bulstone 153 E4
Bulverhythe 160 C3
Bulwark 325 E5
Bulwell 223 G3
Bulwick 211 E3
Bumble's Green 186 D2
Bun Abhainn Eadarra 326 D3
Bun Loyne 308 B4
Bunarkaig 299 D1
Bunbury 220 C2
Bunbury Heath 220 C2
Bunchrew 321 F5
Bundalloch 307 E2
Buness 345 F2
Bunessan 288 C2
Bungay 215 E3
Bunker's Hill 226 A2
Bunlarie 272 C2
Bunloit 309 E2
Bunmhullin 314 C2
Bunnahabhain 280 C2
Bunny 223 G5
Buntait 308 C1
Buntingford 200 B5
Bunwell 214 C2
Bunwell Street 214 C2
Burbage *Derbys.* 235 E5
Burbage *Leics.* 209 G3
Burbage *Wilts.* 168 D1
Burchett's Green 184 D4
Burcombe 168 B4
Burcot *Oxon.* 184 A3
Burcot *Worcs.* 208 B5
Burcott 199 D5
Burdale 246 A1
Burdocks 171 F5
Burdon 262 C2
Burdrop 197 F4
Bures 202 A4
Bures Green 202 A4
Burf, The 196 A1
Burfa 194 B1
Burford *Oxon.* 183 E1
Burford *Shrop.* 195 E1
Burford House Gardens 64
Burg *Arg. & B.* 296 C5
Burg 118
Burgate 214 B4
Burgates 170 C5
Burge End 199 G4
Burgess Hill 159 F2
Burgh 202 D2
Burgh by Sands 259 G1
Burgh Castle 229 F5
Burgh Heath 172 B3
Burgh le Marsh 226 C1
Burgh next Aylsham 228 D3
Burgh on Bain 238 C4
Burgh St. Margaret (Fleggburgh) 229 F4
Burgh St. Peter 215 F2
Burghclere 169 F1
Burghead 322 D3
Burghfield 170 B1
Burghfield Common 170 B1
Burghfield Hill 170 B1
Burghill 195 D3
Burghley House 77
Burghwallis 236 C1
Burham 173 G2
Buriton 170 C5
Burland 220 D2
Burlawn 147 D3
Burleigh 171 E1
Burlescombe 153 D1
Burleston 155 D3
Burley *Hants.* 156 B2
Burley *Rut.* 211 D1
Burley *W.Yorks.* 244 B4
Burley Gate 195 E3
Burley in Wharfedale 244 A3
Burley Street 156 B2
Burley Woodhead 244 A3
Burleydam 220 D3
Burlingjobb 194 B2
Burlow 160 A2
Burlton 220 B5
Burmarsh 174 D5
Burmington 197 E4
Burn 245 E5
Burn Farm 303 E2
Burn Naze 241 G3
Burn of Cambus 292 C4
Burn, The 303 D2
Burnage 234 C3
Burnaston 223 D4
Burnby 246 A3
Burncross 236 A3
Burndell 158 B3
Burnden 234 B2
Burnedge 234 D1
Burnend 324 D5
Burneside 249 G3
Burness 341 E2
Burneston 252 C4
Burnett 167 D1
Burnfoot *High.* 333 D2
Burnfoot *P. & K.* 293 E4
Burnfoot *Sc.Bord.* 277 G4
Burnfoot *Sc.Bord.* 277 F4
Burnham *Bucks.* 185 E4
Burnham *N.Lincs.* 238 A1
Burnham Beeches 42
Burnham Deepdale 227 G3
Burnham Green 186 B1
Burnham Market 227 G3
Burnham Norton 227 G3
Burnham Overy Staithe 227 G3
Burnham Overy Town 227 G3
Burnham Thorpe 227 G3
Burnham-on-Crouch 188 C3
Burnham-on-Sea 166 A3
Burnhaven 325 G5
Burnhead *D. & G.* 265 G2
Burnhead *D. & G.* 266 C1
Burnhervie 312 C3
Burnhill Green 207 G2
Burnhope 262 A3
Burnhouse 283 E4
Burniston 254 D3
Burnley 243 E4
Burnmouth 287 G3
Burnopfield 262 A2
Burn's Green 200 B5
Burns National Heritage Park 118
Burnsall 243 G1
Burnside *Aber.* 312 C3
Burnside *Angus* 302 D4
Burnside *E.Ayr.* 275 D4
Burnside *Fife* 293 G4
Burnside *Shet.* 344 B5
Burnside *W.Loth.* 285 E2
Burnside of Duntrune 294 C1
Burnstones 260 C2
Burnswark 267 F3
Burnt Hill 184 A5
Burnt Houses 262 A5
Burnt Oak 186 B3
Burnt Yates 244 B1
Burntcliff Top 221 G1
Burntisland 285 G1
Burnton *E.Ayr.* 274 C4
Burnton *E.Ayr.* 274 C5
Burntwood 208 C2
Burntwood Green 208 C2
Burnworthy 153 E1
Burpham *Surr.* 171 F2
Burpham *W.Suss.* 158 C3
Burra 342 C4
Burradon *Northumb.* 270 B1
Burradon *T. & W.* 271 E4
Burrafirth 345 F1
Burraland 344 C5
Burras 145 D3
Burraton *Cornw.* 150 A1
Burraton *Cornw.* 150 A2
Burravoe *Shet.* 345 E5
Burravoe *Shet.* 342 C1
Burray 339 D3
Burrell Collection 118
Burrells 250 B1
Burrelton 294 A1
Burridge *Devon* 153 G2
Burridge *Hants.* 157 E1
Burrill 252 B4
Burringham 237 F2
Burrington *Devon* 163 G4
Burrington *Here.* 206 D5
Burrington *N.Som.* 166 B2
Burrough Green 201 E2
Burrough on the Hill 210 C1
Burrow *Som.* 164 C3
Burrow *Som.* 154 A1
Burrow Bridge 166 A4
Burrowhill 171 E1
Burrows Cross 171 F3
Burry 178 A3
Burry Green 178 A3
Burry Port 178 A2
Burscough 233 F1
Burscough Bridge 233 F1
Bursea 246 A4
Burshill 246 C3
Bursledon 157 D2
Burslem 221 F3
Burstall 202 C3
Burstock 154 A2
Burston *Norf.* 214 C3
Burston *Staffs.* 221 G4
Burstow 172 C4
Burstwick 247 E5
Burtersett 251 D4
Burthorpe 201 F1
Burthwaite 260 A3
Burtle 166 B3
Burtle Hill 166 A3
Burton *Ches.* 233 E5
Burton *Ches.* 220 C1
Burton *Dorset* 156 A3
Burton *Lincs.* 237 G5
Burton *Northumb.* 279 F3
Burton *Pembs.* 176 C2
Burton *Som.* 165 E3
Burton *Wilts.* 182 A5
Burton *Wilts.* 167 F4
Burton Agnes 246 D1
Burton Bradstock 154 A4
Burton Coggles 225 E5
Burton Constable Hall 86
Burton End 200 D5
Burton Ferry 176 C2
Burton Fleming 255 D5
Burton Green *Warks.* 209 E5
Burton Green *Wrex.* 220 A2
Burton Hastings 209 G4
Burton in Lonsdale 250 B5
Burton Joyce 224 B3
Burton Latimer 211 E5
Burton Lazars 210 C1
Burton Leonard 244 C1
Burton on the Wolds 223 G5
Burton Overy 210 B3
Burton Pedwardine 225 G3
Burton Pidsea 247 E4
Burton Salmon 245 D5
Burton Stather 237 F1
Burton upon Stather 237 F1
Burton upon Trent 222 D5
Burton-in-Kendal 249 G5
Burton's Green 201 G5
Burtonwood 233 G3
Burwardsley 220 C2
Burwarton 207 F4
Burwash 160 B1
Burwash Common 160 B1
Burwash Weald 160 B1
Burwell *Cambs.* 201 D1
Burwell *Lincs.* 239 D5
Burwen 230 C3
Burwick *Ork.* 338 D4
Burwick *Shet.* 342 C3
Bury *Cambs.* 212 A4
Bury *Gt.Man.* 234 C1
Bury *Som.* 164 C5
Bury *W.Suss.* 158 C2
Bury End 196 C4
Bury Green 200 C5
Bury St. Edmunds 201 G1
Buryas Bridge 144 B4
Burythorpe 245 G1
Busbridge 171 E3
Busby *E.Renf.* 283 G4
Busby *P. & K.* 293 F2
Buscot 183 E3
Buscot Park 42
Bush 162 C5
Bush Bank 195 D2
Bush Crathie 311 E5
Bush Green 214 D3
Bushbury 208 B2
Bushby 210 B2
Bushey 186 A3
Bushey Heath 186 A3
Bushley 196 A4
Bushley Green 196 A4
Bushton 182 C5
Bushy Common 228 A4
Busk 260 C3
Buslingthorpe 238 A4
Bussage 182 A2
Busta 342 C1
Butcher's Common 229 E3
Butcher's Cross 160 A1
Butcher's Pasture 201 E5
Butcombe 166 C1
Bute 282 B3
Bute Town 180 A2
Buthill 322 D3
Butleigh 166 C4
Butleigh Wootton 166 C4
Butler's Cross 184 D2
Butler's Hill 223 G3
Butlers Marston 197 F3
Butlersbank 220 C5
Butley 203 E2
Butley Abbey 203 E3
Butley Low Corner 203 E3
Butley Mills 203 E2
Butley Town 234 D5
Butt Green 221 D2
Butt Lane 221 F2
Butterburn 269 E4
Buttercrambe 245 G2
Butterknowle 262 A5
Butterleigh 152 C2
Butterley 223 F2
Buttermere *Cumb.* 259 E5
Buttermere *Wilts.* 169 E1
Butters Green 221 F2
Buttershaw 244 A4
Butterstone 301 F5
Butterton *Staffs.* 222 B2
Butterton *Staffs.* 221 F3
Butterwick *Dur.* 262 C5
Butterwick *Lincs.* 226 B3
Butterwick *N.Yorks.* 254 C5
Butterwick *N.Yorks.* 253 G5
Buttington 206 B2
Buttonbridge 207 G5
Buttonoak 207 G5
Buttons' Green 202 A2
Butts 152 B4
Butt's Green *Essex* 187 G2
Butt's Green *Hants.* 169 D5
Butts, The 167 E3
Buttsash 156 D2
Buxhall 202 B2
Buxted 159 G1
Buxton *Derbys.* 235 E5
Buxton *Norf.* 228 D3
Buxton Heath 228 C3
Buxton Museum & Art Gallery 70
Buxworth 235 E4
Bwcle (Buckley) 219 F1
Bwlch 194 A5
Bwlch-clawdd 191 G4
Bwlch-derwin 217 D3
Bwlchgwyn 219 F2
Bwlch-llan 192 B2
Bwlchnewydd 191 G5
Bwlchtocyn 216 C5
Bwlch-y-cibau 206 A1
Bwlch-y-ddar 219 E5
Bwlchyfadfa 192 A3
Bwlch-y-ffridd 205 G3
Bwlch-y-groes 191 F4
Bwlchyllyn 217 E2
Bwlchymynydd 178 B3
Bwlch-y-sarnau 205 G5
Byers Green 262 B4
Byfield 198 A2
Byfleet 171 F1
Byford 194 C3
Bygrave 200 A4
Byker 262 B1
Byland Abbey 253 E5
Bylane End 147 G4
Bylchau 218 C1
Byley 221 E1
Bynea 178 B3
Byrness 269 F1
Bystock 152 D4
Bythorn 211 F5
Byton 194 C1
Bywell 261 G1
Byworth 171 E5

C

Cabharstadh 329 E5
Cabinet War Rooms 55
Cabourne 238 B2
Cabourne Parva 238 B2
Cabrach *Arg. & B.* 280 C3
Cabrach *Moray* 311 F2
Cabus 242 A3
Cackle Street *E.Suss.* 160 D2
Cackle Street *E.Suss.* 159 G1
Cacrabank 277 E4
Cadair Idris 108
Cadboll 322 A2
Cadbury 152 C2
Cadbury Barton 163 G4
Cadbury Heath 181 F5
Cadbury World 64
Cadder 284 A2
Cadderlie 290 C1
Caddington 185 F1
Caddleton 289 G3
Caddonfoot 277 F2
Cade Street 160 B1
Cadeby *Leics.* 209 G2
Cadeby *S.Yorks.* 236 C2
Cadeleigh 152 C2
Cader 218 D1
Cadgwith 145 E5
Cadham 294 A4
Cadhay 26
Cadishead 234 B3
Cadle 178 C3
Cadley *Lancs.* 242 B4
Cadley *Wilts.* 168 D1
Cadmore End 184 C3
Cadnam 156 B1
Cadney 238 A2
Cadole 219 F1
Cadover Bridge 150 B1
Cadoxton 165 E1
Cadoxton-Juxta-Neath 179 D3
Cadwell 199 G4
Cadwst 218 D4
Cadzow 284 B4
Cae Ddafydd 217 F3
Caeathro 217 E1
Caehopkin 179 E1
Caen 333 F3
Caen Hill Locks 26
Caenby 238 A4
Caenby Corner 237 G4
Caer Llan 181 D2
Caerau *Bridgend* 179 E3
Caerau *Cardiff* 180 A5
Caerdeon 204 C1
Caerdydd (Cardiff) 180 A5
Caerfarchell 190 A5
Caerfyrddin (Carmarthen) 192 A5
Caergeiliog 230 B5
Caergwrle 220 A2
Caergybi (Holyhead) 230 A4
Caerhun 231 F5
Caer-Lan 179 E1
Caerlaverock Castle 118
Caerlaverock Wildfowl & Wetlands Trust 118
Caerleon 180 C3
Caerleon Roman Fortress, Baths & Amphitheatre 108
Caernarfon 217 D1
Caernarfon Castle 108
Caerphilly 180 A4
Caerphilly Castle 108
Caersws 205 G3
Caerwedros 191 G2
Caerwent 181 D3
Caerwys 232 C5
Caethle Farm 204 C3
Caggan 310 A3
Caggle Street 180 C1
Caim *High.* 297 E3
Caim *I.o.A.* 231 E4
Caio 192 C4
Cairinis (Carinish) 315 G3
Cairisiadar 328 B4
Cairminis 326 C5
Cairn Gorm Mountain 118
Cairnargat 311 G1
Cairnbaan 290 A5
Cairnbeathie 312 A4
Cairnbrogie 313 D2
Cairnbulg 325 F3
Cairncross *Angus* 302 D2
Cairncross *Sc.Bord.* 287 F3
Cairncurran 283 E3
Cairndoon 257 D3
Cairndow 291 D3
Cairness 325 F3
Cairney Lodge 294 B3
Cairneyhill 285 E1
Cairngorms National Park 118
Cairnhill *Aber.* 313 E2
Cairnhill *Aber.* 312 B1
Cairnie *Aber.* 312 D4
Cairnie *Aber.* 323 G5
Cairnorrie 325 D5
Cairnryan 264 B4
Cairnsmore 265 F4
Caister-on-Sea 229 G4
Caistor 238 B2
Caistor St. Edmund 228 D5
Caistron 270 B1
Cake Street 214 B2
Cakebole 208 A5
Calanais (Callanish) 328 D4
Calbost 327 G2
Calbourne 156 D4
Calceby 239 D5
Calcoed 232 C5
Calcot 184 B5
Calcott *Kent* 175 D2
Calcott *Shrop.* 206 D1
Calcotts Green 181 G1
Calcutt 182 D3
Caldarvan 283 F1
Caldback 345 F2
Caldbeck 259 G3
Caldbergh 251 F4
Caldecote *Cambs.* 200 B2
Caldecote *Cambs.* 211 G4
Caldecote *Herts.* 200 A4
Caldecote *Northants.* 198 B2
Caldecote *Warks.* 209 F3
Caldecott *Northants.* 199 E1
Caldecott *Oxon.* 183 G3
Caldecott *Rut.* 211 D3
Calder Bridge 248 B2
Calder Grove 236 A1
Calder Mains 336 C3
Calder Vale 242 B3
Calderbank 284 B3
Calderbrook 234 D1
Caldercruix 284 C3
Calderglen 284 A4
Calderglen Country Park 118
Caldermill 284 A5
Caldey Island 177 E3
Caldhame 302 C5
Caldicot 181 D4
Caldwell *Derbys.* 209 E1
Caldwell *E.Renf.* 283 F4
Caldwell *N.Yorks.* 252 A1
Caldy 232 D4
Calebreck 259 G3
Caledonian Railway 118
Caledrhydiau 192 A2
Calford Green 201 E3
Calfsound 341 D3
Calgary 296 C4
Califer 322 C4
California *Falk.* 284 D2
California *Norf.* 229 G4
California *Suff.* 202 D3
Calke 223 E5
Calke Abbey 70
Callakille 318 C4
Callaly 270 C1
Callander 292 B4
Callanish (Calanais) 328 D4
Callanish Standing Stones 118
Callaughton 207 F3
Callendar House 118
Callerton Lane End 262 A1
Calliburn 272 C3
Calligarry 306 C4
Callington 149 D4
Callingwood 222 C5
Callisterhall 268 A3
Callow 195 D4
Callow End 196 A3
Callow Hill *Wilts.* 182 C4
Callow Hill *Worcs.* 207 G5
Callow Hill *Worcs.* 196 C1
Callows Grave 195 E1
Calmore 156 C1
Calmsden 182 C2
Calne 182 B5
Calow 236 B5
Calrossie 321 G2
Calshot 157 D2
Calstock 150 A1
Calstone Wellington 168 B1
Calthorpe 228 C2
Calthwaite 260 A3
Calton *N.Yorks.* 243 F2
Calton *Staffs.* 222 C2
Calveley 220 C2
Calver 235 G5
Calver Hill 194 C3
Calverhall 220 D4
Calverleigh 152 C1
Calverley 244 B4
Calvert 198 B5
Calverton *M.K.* 198 C4
Calverton *Notts.* 224 B3
Calvine 300 C3
Calvo 259 E1
Cam 181 G3
Camasnacroise 298 A4
Camastianavaig 306 B1
Camasunary 306 B3
Camault Muir 321 E5
Camb 345 E3
Camber 161 E2
Camberley 171 D1
Camberwell 186 C5
Camblesforth 245 F5
Cambo 270 C3
Cambois 271 F3
Camborne 145 D3
Cambridge *Cambs.* 77
Cambridge *Glos.* 181 G2
Cambridge Airport 200 C2
Cambridge American Military Cemetery & Memorial 78
Cambridge University Botanic Gardens 78
Cambus 293 D5
Cambus o'May 311 G5
Cambusbarron 292 C5
Cambuskenneth 292 D5
Cambuslang 284 A3
Cambusnethan 284 C4
Camden Town 186 B4
Camel Hill 166 C5
Cameley 166 D2
Camelford 147 F1
Camelon 284 C1
Camelot Theme Park 94
Camelsdale 171 D4
Camer 173 F2
Cameron House 283 E1
Camerory 310 C1
Camer's Green 195 G4
Camerton *B. & N.E.Som.* 167 D2
Camerton *Cumb.* 258 D3
Camerton *E.Riding* 247 E5
Camghouran 300 A4
Camis Eskan 283 E1
Cammachmore 313 E5
Cammeringham 237 G4
Camore 332 C5
Camp Hill *Pembs.* 177 E1
Camp Hill *Warks.* 209 F3
Camp, The 182 B2
Campbeltown 272 C3
Campbeltown (Machrihanish) Airport 272 B3
Camperdown 271 E4
Campmuir 294 A1
Camps 285 F3
Camps End 201 E3
Camps Heath 215 G2
Campsall 236 C1
Campsea Ashe 203 E2
Campton 199 G4
Camptown 278 A5
Camquhart 282 A1
Camrose 190 C5
Camserney 300 D5
Camstraddan House 291 F5
Camus Croise 306 C3
Camus-luinie 307 F2
Camusnagaul *High.* 298 C2
Camusnagaul *High.* 319 G1
Camusrory 307 E5
Camusteel 318 D5
Camusterrach 318 D5
Camusurich 292 B1
Camusvrachan 300 B5
Canada 156 B1
Canaston Bridge 177 D1
Candacraig 311 F5
Candlesby 226 C1
Candy Mill 285 E5
Cane End 184 B5
Canewdon 188 B3
Canfield End 201 D5
Canford Bottom 155 G2
Canford Cliffs 155 G4
Canford Magna 155 G3
Canham's Green 202 B1
Canisbay 337 F1
Canley 209 F5
Cann 167 F5
Cann Common 167 F5
Canna 305 F4
Cannard's Grave 166 D3
Cannich 308 C1
Canning Town 186 D4
Cannington 165 F4
Cannock 208 B2
Cannock Chase Country Park 64
Cannock Wood 208 C1
Cannon Hall Country Park 86
Cannon Hill Park 64
Cannop 181 F1
Canon Bridge 194 D3
Canon Frome 195 F3
Canon Pyon 195 D3
Canonbie 268 B4
Canons Ashby *Northants.* 198 A2
Canons Ashby ***Northants.*** 70
Canon's Town 144 C3
Canonteign Falls 26
Canterbury *Aber.* 324 A4
Canterbury *Kent* 174 D3
Canterbury Cathedral 42
Canterbury Tales, The 42
Cantley *Norf.* 229 E5
Cantley *S.Yorks.* 236 D2
Cantlop 207 E2
Canton 180 A5
Cantray 321 G5
Cantraydoune 321 G5
Cantraywood 321 G5
Cantsfield 250 B5
Canvey Island 187 G4
Canwell Hall 208 D2
Canwick 225 E1
Canworthy Water 148 C1
Caol 298 D2
Caolas *Arg. & B.* 296 B2
Caolas *W.Isles* 314 B4
Caolas Scalpaigh (Kyles Scalpay) 327 E4
Caolasnacon 298 D3
Capel *Kent* 173 F4
Capel *Surr.* 171 G3
Capel Bangor 204 C4
Capel Betws Lleucu 192 C2
Capel Carmel 216 A5
Capel Celyn 218 B3
Capel Coch 230 C4
Capel Curig 218 A2
Capel Cynon 191 G3
Capel Dewi *Carmar.* 192 A5
Capel Dewi *Cere.* 204 C4
Capel Dewi *Cere.* 192 A3
Capel Garmon 218 B2
Capel Gwyn *Carmar.* 192 A5
Capel Gwyn *I.o.A.* 230 B5
Capel Gwynfe 192 D5
Capel Hendre 178 B1
Capel Isaac 192 B5
Capel Iwan 191 F4
Capel le Ferne 175 E5
Capel Llanilltern 179 G4
Capel Mawr 230 C5
Capel Parc 230 C4
Capel St. Andrew 203 E3
Capel St. Mary 202 B4
Capel St. Silin 192 B2
Capel Seion 204 C5
Capel Tygwydd 191 F3
Capeluchaf 216 D3
Capelulo 231 F5
Capel-y-ffin 194 B4
Capel-y-graig 217 E1
Capenhurst 233 E5
Capernwray 249 G5
Capheaton 270 C3
Caplaw 283 F4
Capon's Green 203 D1
Cappercleuch 276 D3
Capplegill 276 C5
Capstone 173 G2
Captain Cook Birthplace Museum 103
Captain Cook Memorial Museum 86
Capton *Devon* 151 E2
Capton *Som.* 165 D4
Caputh 301 F5
Car Colston 224 C3
Caradon Town 147 G2
Carbellow 275 E3
Carbeth 283 G2
Carbis Bay 144 C3
Carbost *High.* 318 A5
Carbost *High.* 305 G1
Carbrain 284 B2
Carbrooke 228 A5
Carburton 236 D5
Carcary 303 E4
Carco 275 F4
Carcroft 236 C1
Cardenden 294 A5
Cardeston 206 C1
Cardew 259 G2
Cardiff (Caerdydd) 180 A5
Cardiff Castle & Museum 108
Cardiff International Airport 165 D1
Cardigan (Aberteifi) 191 E3
Cardinal's Green 201 E3
Carding Mill Valley and Long Mynd 64
Cardington *Beds.* 199 F3
Cardington *Shrop.* 207 E3
Cardinham 147 F3
Cardno 325 E3
Cardonald 283 G3
Cardoness 265 G5
Cardoness Castle 118
Cardow 323 D5
Cardrona 277 D2
Cardross 283 E2
Cardurnock 259 E1
Careby 211 F1
Careston 302 D4
Carew 176 D2
Carew Castle 109
Carew Cheriton 176 D2
Carew Newton 176 D2
Carey 195 E4
Carfin 284 B4
Carfrae 286 C3
Carfraemill 286 C4
Cargate Green 229 E4
Cargen 267 D3
Cargenbridge 267 D3
Cargill 293 G1
Cargo 259 G1
Cargreen 150 A1
Carham 278 B3
Carhampton 164 D3
Carharrack 146 B5
Carie *P. & K.* 300 B4
Carie *P. & K.* 292 B1
Carines 146 B4
Carinish (Cairinis) 315 G3
Carisbrooke 157 D4
Carisbrooke Castle & Museum 42
Cark 249 E5
Carkeel 150 A1
Carlabhagh (Carloway) 328 D3
Carland Cross 146 C4

Carlatton 260 B2
Carlby 211 F1
Carlecotes 235 F2
Carleen 144 D4
Carleton *Cumb.* 260 A2
Carleton *Cumb.* 260 B5
Carleton *Lancs.* 241 G3
Carleton *N.Yorks.* 243 F3
Carleton *W.Yorks.* 245 D5
Carleton Fishery 264 C2
Carleton Forehoe 228 B5
Carleton Rode 214 C2
Carleton St. Peter 229 E5
Carlin How 253 G1
Carlisle 260 A2
Carlisle Castle 94
Carlisle Cathedral 94
Carloggas 146 C3
Carlops 285 F4
Carloway (Carlabhagh) 328 D3
Carlton *Beds.* 199 E2
Carlton *Cambs.* 201 E2
Carlton *Leics.* 209 F2
Carlton *N.Yorks.* 245 F5
Carlton *N.Yorks.* 251 F4
Carlton *N.Yorks.* 253 F4
Carlton *Notts.* 224 B3
Carlton *S.Yorks.* 236 A1
Carlton *Stock.* 262 C5
Carlton *Suff.* 203 E1
Carlton *W.Yorks.* 244 C5
Carlton Colville 215 G2
Carlton Curlieu 210 B3
Carlton Green 201 E2
Carlton Husthwaite 253 D5
Carlton in Lindrick 236 C4
Carlton Miniott 252 C4
Carlton Scroop 225 E3
Carlton-in-Cleveland 253 E2
Carlton-le-Moorland 225 E2
Carlton-on-Trent 224 D1
Carluke 284 C4
Carlyle's Birthplace 119
Carlyon Bay 147 E4
Carmacoup 275 F3
Carmarthen (Caerfyrddin) 192 A5
Carmel *Carmar.* 178 B1
Carmel *Flints.* 232 C5
Carmel *Gwyn.* 217 D2
Carmel *I.o.A.* 230 B4
Carmichael 276 A2
Carmont 303 G1
Carmunnock 283 G4
Carmyle 284 A3
Carmyllie 303 D5
Carn 280 A4
Carn Brea Village 146 A5
Carn Dearg 319 D2
Carnaby 246 D1
Carnach *High.* 307 G2
Carnach *High.* 330 C5
Carnach *W.Isles* 315 G3
Carnan 315 F5
Carnassarie 290 A4
Carnbee 294 D4
Carnbo 293 F4
Carndu 307 E2
Carnduncan 280 A3
Carnewas & Bedruthan Steps 26
Carnforth 249 F5
Carnhedryn 190 B5
Carnhell Green 144 D3
Carnichal 325 E4
Carnkie *Cornw.* 145 D3
Carnkie *Cornw.* 145 E3
Carnmore 280 B5
Carno 205 F3
Carnoch *High.* 308 C1
Carnoch *High.* 320 B4
Carnoch *High.* 322 A5
Carnock 285 E1
Carnon Downs 146 C5
Carnousie 324 B4
Carnoustie 295 D1
Carntyne 284 A3
Carnwath 285 D5
Carnyorth 144 A3
Carol Green 209 E5
Carperby 251 F4
Carr 236 C3
Carr Hill 237 D3
Carr Houses 233 E2
Carr Shield 261 E3
Carr Vale 236 B5
Carradale 272 C2
Carradale East 272 D2
Carragrich 327 D4
Carrbridge 310 B2
Carrefour Selous 150 C5
Carreg Cennen Castle 109
Carreg-lefn 230 B4
Carreg-wen 191 F3
Carrhouse 237 E2
Carrick 282 A1
Carrick Castle 291 D5
Carriden 285 E1
Carrine 272 B5
Carrington *Gt.Man.* 234 B3
Carrington *Lincs.* 226 B2
Carrington *Midloth.* 286 A3
Carroch 266 A1
Carrog *Conwy* 218 A3
Carrog *Denb.* 219 E3
Carroglen 292 C2
Carrol 332 D4
Carron *Arg. & B.* 290 B5
Carron *Falk.* 284 C1
Carron *Moray* 323 E5
Carron Bridge 284 B1
Carronbridge 266 C1
Carronshore 284 C1
Carrot 302 C5
Carrow Hill 180 D3
Carrutherstown 267 F3
Carruthmuir 283 E3
Carrville 262 C3
Carry 282 A3
Carsaig 289 E2
Carscreugh 264 D4
Carse 281 F3
Carse of Ardersier 322 A4
Carsegowan 265 F5
Carseriggan 265 E4
Carsethorn 267 D5
Carsgoe 336 D2
Carshalton 172 B2
Carshalton Beeches 172 B2
Carsington 223 D2
Carsington Water 71
Carsluith 265 F5
Carsphairn 265 G1
Carstairs 284 D5
Carstairs Junction 285 D5
Carswell Marsh 183 F3
Carter's Clay 169 E5
Carterton 183 E2
Carterway Heads 261 G2
Carthew 147 E4
Carthorpe 252 C4
Cartington 270 C1
Cartland 284 C5
Cartmel 249 E5
Cartmel Fell 249 F4
Cartmel Priory 94
Cartworth 235 F2
Carway 178 A2
Cascob 194 B1
Cas-gwent (Chepstow) 181 E3
Cashel Farm 291 G5
Cashes Green 182 A2
Cashlie 299 G5
Cashmoor 155 F1
Caskieberran 294 A4
Casnewydd (Newport) 180 C4
Cassencarie 265 F5
Cassington 183 G1
Cassop 262 C4
Castell 218 A1
Castell Dinas Bran 109
Castell Gorfod 191 F5
Castell Howell 192 A3
Castell Newydd Emlyn (Newcastle Emlyn) 191 G3
Castellau 179 G4
Castell-Nedd (Neath) 179 D3
Castell-y-bwch 180 B3
Casterton 250 B5
Castle Acre 213 G1
Castle Ashby 199 D2
Castle Bolton 251 F3
Castle Bromwich 208 D4
Castle Bytham 211 E1
Castle Caereinion 206 A2
Castle Campbell 119
Castle Camps 201 E3
Castle Carrock 260 B2
Castle Cary 166 D4
Castle Combe 182 A5
Castle Donington 223 F5
Castle Douglas 266 B4
Castle Drogo 26
Castle Eaton 182 D3
Castle Eden 262 D4
Castle End 209 E5
Castle Fraser 119
Castle Frome 195 F3
Castle Gate 144 B3
Castle Goring 158 D3
Castle Green 171 E1
Castle Gresley 209 E1
Castle Heaton 287 G5
Castle Hedingham 201 F4
Castle Hill *Kent* 173 F4
Castle Hill *Suff.* 202 C3
Castle House (Sir Alfred Munnings Art Museum) 78
Castle Howard 86
Castle Kennedy 264 C5
Castle Leod 321 D4
Castle Levan 282 D2
Castle Madoc 193 G4
Castle Menzies 119
Castle Morris 190 C4
Castle O'er 268 A2
Castle of Mey 119
Castle Rising 227 E5
Castle Stuart 321 G5
Castlebay (Bàgh a' Chaisteil) 314 B4
Castlebythe 190 D5
Castlecary 284 B2
Castlecraig *High.* 322 A3
Castlecraig *Sc.Bord.* 285 F5
Castlefairn 266 B2
Castleford 244 D5
Castlemartin 176 C3
Castlemilk *D. & G.* 267 F3
Castlemilk *Glas.* 284 A4
Castlemorton 195 G4
Castlerigg 259 F4
Castlerigg Stone Circle 94
Castleside 261 G3
Castlesteads 260 B1
Castlethorpe 198 D3
Castleton *Aber.* 324 C4
Castleton *Angus* 302 B5
Castleton *Arg. & B.* 281 G1
Castleton *Derbys.* 235 F4
Castleton *Gt.Man.* 234 C1
Castleton *N.Yorks.* 253 F2
Castleton *Newport* 180 B4
Castleton *Sc.Bord.* 268 D2
Castletown *Dorset* 154 C5
Castletown *High.* 337 D2
Castletown *High.* 321 G5
Castletown *I.o.M.* 240 A5
Castletown *T. & W.* 262 C2
Castleweary 277 F5
Castlewigg 257 E2
Castley 244 B3
Caston 214 A2
Castor 211 G3
Castramont 265 G4
Caswell 178 B4
Cat and Fiddle Inn 235 E5
Catacol 282 A5
Catbrain 181 E4
Catbrook 181 E2
Catchall 144 B4
Catcleugh 269 F1
Catcliffe 236 B4
Catcott 166 A4
Caterham 172 C3
Catfield 229 E3
Catfirth 342 D2
Catford 186 C5
Catforth 242 A4
Cathays 180 A5
Cathcart 283 G3
Cathedine 194 A5
Catherine-de-Barnes 209 D4
Catherington 157 F1
Catherston Leweston 153 G3
Catherton 207 F5
Cathkin 284 A4
Catisfield 157 E2
Catlodge 309 F5
Catlowdy 268 C4
Catmere End 200 C4
Catmore 183 G4
Caton *Devon* 152 A5
Caton *Lancs.* 242 B1
Caton Green 242 B1
Cator Court 149 G3
Catrine 274 D3
Catsfield 160 C2
Catsfield Stream 160 C2
Catshaw 235 G2
Catshill 208 B5
Cattadale 280 B3
Cattal 244 D2
Cattawade 202 B4
Catterall 242 B3
Catterick 252 B3
Catterick Bridge 252 B3
Catterick Garrison 252 A3
Catterlen 260 A4
Catterline 303 G2
Catterton 245 E3
Catteshall 171 E3
Catthorpe 210 A5
Cattishall 201 G1
Cattistock 154 B2
Catton *N.Yorks.* 252 C5
Catton *Norf.* 228 D4
Catton *Northumb.* 261 E2
Catton Hall 209 E1
Catwick 246 D3
Catworth 211 F5
Caudle Green 182 B1
Caulcott *Beds.* 199 F3
Caulcott *Oxon.* 198 A5
Cauldcots 303 E5
Cauldhame *Stir.* 292 B5
Cauldhame *Stir.* 292 D4
Cauldon 222 B3
Caulkerbush 266 D5
Caulside 268 C3
Caundle Marsh 154 C1
Caunsall 208 A4
Caunton 224 C1
Causeway End *D. & G.* 265 F4
Causeway End *Essex* 187 F1
Causeway End *Lancs.* 233 F1
Causewayhead *Cumb.* 259 E1
Causewayhead *Stir.* 292 D5
Causey 262 B2
Causey Park 271 D2
Causeyend 313 E3
Cautley 250 B3
Cavendish 201 G3
Cavendish Bridge 223 F5
Cavenham 201 F1
Cavens 267 D5
Cavers 277 G4
Caversfield 198 A5
Caversham 184 C5
Caverswall 221 G3
Cawdor 322 A4
Cawdor Castle 119
Cawkeld 246 B2
Cawkwell 238 C4
Cawood 245 E4
Cawsand 150 A3
Cawston *Norf.* 228 C3
Cawston *Warks.* 209 G5
Cawthorn 253 G4
Cawthorne 235 G2
Cawthorpe 225 F5
Cawton 253 F5
Caxton 200 B2
Caxton Gibbet 200 A1
Caynham 207 E5
Caythorpe *Lincs.* 225 E3
Caythorpe *Notts.* 224 B3
Cayton 255 D4
Ceallan 315 G4
Ceann a' Bhàigh *W.Isles* 315 F3
Ceann a' Bhàigh *W.Isles* 326 C5
Ceann Loch Shiphoirt 327 E2
Ceann Lochroag (Kinlochroag) 328 C5
Ceannaridh 315 G4
Cearsiadar 327 F2
Ceathramh Meadhanach (Middlequarter) 315 G2
Cecil Higgins Art Gallery 78
Cedig 218 C5
Cefn Berain 218 C1
Cefn Bycharn (Newbridge) 180 B3
Cefn Canol 219 F4
Cefn Cantref 193 G5
Cefn Coch 219 E2
Cefn Cribwr 179 E4
Cefn Cross 179 E4
Cefn Einion 206 B4
Cefn Hengoed 180 A3
Cefn Llwyd 204 C4
Cefn Rhigos 179 F2
Cefn-brith 218 C2
Cefn-caer-Ferch 216 D3
Cefn-coch 219 E5
Cefn-coed-y-cymmer 179 G2
Cefn-ddwysarn 218 C4
Cefndeuddwr 218 A5
Cefneithin 178 B1
Cefn-gorwydd 193 F3
Cefn-gwyn 206 A4
Cefn-mawr 219 F3
Cefnpennar 179 G2
Cefn-y-bedd 220 A2
Cefn-y-pant 191 E5
Cegidfa (Guilsfield) 206 B1
Ceidio 230 C4
Ceidio Fawr 216 B4
Ceinewydd (New Quay) 191 G1
Ceint 230 C5
Cellan 192 C3
Cellardyke 295 D4
Cellarhead 221 G3
Celtica 109
Cemaes 230 B3
Cemmaes 205 E2
Cemmaes Road (Glantwymyn) 205 E2
Cenarth 191 F3
Cennin 217 D3
Centre For Alternative Technology 109
Ceos (Keose) 329 E5
Ceredigion Museum 109
Ceres 294 C3
Cerist 205 F4
Cerne Abbas 154 C2
Cerney Wick 182 C3
Cerrigceinwen 230 C5
Cerrigydrudion 218 C3
Cessford 278 B4
Ceunant 217 E1
Chaceley 196 A4
Chacewater 146 B5
Chackmore 198 B4
Chacombe 197 G3
Chad Valley 208 C4
Chadderton 234 D2
Chadderton Fold 234 C2
Chaddesden 223 E4
Chaddesley Corbett 208 A5
Chaddleworth 183 G5
Chadlington 197 F5
Chadshunt 197 F2
Chadstone 199 D2
Chadwell *Leics.* 224 C5
Chadwell *Shrop.* 207 G1
Chadwell St. Mary 187 F5
Chadwick End 209 E5
Chaffcombe 153 G1
Chafford Hundred 187 F5
Chagford 152 A4
Chailey 159 F2
Chainhurst 173 G4
Chalbury 155 G2
Chalbury Common 155 G2
Chaldon 172 C3
Chaldon Herring (East Chaldon) 155 D4
Chale 157 D5
Chale Green 157 D4
Chalfont Common 185 F3
Chalfont St. Giles 185 E3
Chalfont St. Peter 185 F3
Chalford *Glos.* 182 A2
Chalford *Wilts.* 167 F3
Chalgrove 184 B3
Chalk 187 F5
Chalk End 187 F1
Challacombe 163 G1
Challister 343 E1
Challoch 265 E4
Challock 174 C3
Chalmington 154 B2
Chalton *Beds.* 199 F5
Chalton *Hants.* 157 G1
Chalvey 185 E5
Chalvington 160 A3
Chambercombe Manor 26
Champany 285 E2
Chancery 204 B5
Chandler's Cross 185 F3
Chandler's Ford 169 F5
Channel Islands 150 A5
Channel's End 199 G2
Channerwick 342 D5
Chantry *Som.* 167 E3
Chantry *Suff.* 202 C3
Chapel 294 A5
Chapel Allerton *Som.* 166 B2
Chapel Allerton *W.Yorks.* 244 C4
Chapel Amble 147 D2
Chapel Brampton 198 C1
Chapel Chorlton 221 F4
Chapel Cleeve 164 D3
Chapel Cross 160 B1
Chapel End 199 F3
Chapel Green *Warks.* 209 E4
Chapel Green *Warks.* 197 G1
Chapel Haddlesey 245 E5
Chapel Hill *Aber.* 313 F1
Chapel Hill *Lincs.* 226 A2
Chapel Hill *Mon.* 181 E2
Chapel Hill *N.Yorks.* 244 C3
Chapel Knapp 167 F1
Chapel Lawn 206 C5
Chapel Leigh 165 E5
Chapel Milton 235 E4
Chapel of Garioch 312 C2
Chapel Rossan 256 B2
Chapel Row *Essex* 187 G2
Chapel Row *W.Berks.* 169 G1
Chapel St. Leonards 239 F5
Chapel Stile 249 E2
Chapel Town 146 C4
Chapelbank 293 F3
Chapeldonan 273 G5
Chapelend Way 201 F4
Chapel-en-le-Frith 235 E4
Chapelgate 226 C5
Chapelhall 284 B3
Chapelhill *High.* 322 A2
Chapelhill *P. & K.* 294 A2
Chapelhill *P. & K.* 293 F1
Chapelknowe 268 B4
Chapel-le-Dale 250 C5
Chapelthorpe 236 A1
Chapelton *Aber.* 303 G1
Chapelton *Angus* 303 E5
Chapelton *Devon* 163 F3
Chapelton *S.Lan.* 284 A5
Chapeltown *B'burn.* 234 B1
Chapeltown *Cumb.* 268 C4
Chapeltown *Moray* 311 E2
Chapeltown *S.Yorks.* 236 A3
Chapmans Well 149 D1
Chapmanslade 167 F3
Chapmore End 186 C1
Chappel 201 G5
Charaton 148 D4
Chard 153 G2
Chard Junction 153 G2
Chardleigh Green 153 G1
Chardstock 153 G2
Charfield 181 G3
Charing 174 B4
Charing Cross 156 A1
Charing Heath 174 B4
Charingworth 197 D4
Charlbury 183 F1
Charlcombe 167 E1
Charlecote 197 E2
Charlecote Park 64
Charles 163 G2
Charles Tye 202 B2
Charlesfield 277 G3
Charleshill 171 D3
Charleston 302 B5
Charlestown *Aber.* 325 F3
Charlestown *Aberdeen* 313 E4
Charlestown *Cornw.* 147 E4
Charlestown *Derbys.* 235 E3
Charlestown *Dorset* 154 C5
Charlestown *Fife* 285 E1
Charlestown *Gt.Man.* 234 C2
Charlestown *High.* 319 E2
Charlestown *High.* 321 F5
Charlestown *W.Yorks.* 244 A4
Charlestown *W.Yorks.* 243 F5
Charlestown of Aberlour (Aberlour) 323 E5
Charlesworth 235 E3
Charleton 294 C4
Charlinch 165 F4
Charlotteville 171 F3
Charlton *Gt.Lon.* 186 D5
Charlton *Hants.* 169 E3
Charlton *Herts.* 199 G5
Charlton *Northants.* 198 A4
Charlton *Northumb.* 270 A3
Charlton *Oxon.* 183 G4
Charlton *Som.* 167 D2
Charlton *Som.* 166 D3
Charlton *Som.* 165 F5
Charlton *Tel. & W.* 207 E1
Charlton *W.Suss.* 158 A2
Charlton *Wilts.* 168 A5
Charlton *Wilts.* 182 B4
Charlton *Wilts.* 168 C2
Charlton *Worcs.* 196 C3
Charlton Abbots 196 C5
Charlton Adam 166 C5
Charlton Horethorne 167 D5
Charlton Kings 196 B5
Charlton Mackrell 166 C5
Charlton Marshall 155 E2
Charlton Musgrove 167 E5
Charlton on the Hill 155 E2
Charlton-All-Saints 168 C5
Charlton-on-Otmoor 184 A1
Charltons 253 F1
Charlwood 172 B4
Charminster 154 C3
Charmouth 153 G3
Charndon 198 B5
Charney Bassett 183 F3
Charnock Richard 233 G1
Charsfield 203 D2
Chart Corner 173 G4
Chart Sutton 174 A4
Charter Alley 169 G2
Charterhouse 166 B2
Charterville Allotments 183 F2
Chartham 174 D3
Chartham Hatch 174 D3
Chartridge 185 E2
Chartwell 42
Charvil 184 C5
Charwelton 198 A2
Chase End Street 195 G4
Chase Terrace 208 C2
Chasetown 208 C2
Chastleton 197 E5
Chastleton House 43
Chasty 162 D5
Chatburn 243 D3
Chatcull 221 E4
Chatham 173 G2
Chatham Green 187 G1
Chatham Historic Dockyard & World Naval Base 43
Chathill 279 F4
Chatsworth House 71
Chattenden 187 G5
Chatteris 212 B4
Chattisham 202 B3
Chatto 278 B5
Chatton 279 E4
Chaul End 199 F5
Chavey Down 171 D1
Chawleigh 152 A1
Chawley 183 G2
Chawston 199 G2
Chawton 170 C4
Chazey Heath 184 B5
Cheadle *Gt.Man.* 234 C4
Cheadle *Staffs.* 222 B3
Cheadle Heath 234 C4
Cheadle Hulme 234 C4
Cheam 172 B2
Cheapside 171 E1
Chearsley 184 C1
Chebsey 221 F5
Checkendon 184 B4
Checkley *Ches.* 221 E3
Checkley *Here.* 195 E4
Checkley *Staffs.* 222 B4
Checkley Green 221 E3
Chedburgh 201 F2
Cheddar 166 B2
Cheddar Gorge & Caves 26
Cheddington 185 E1
Cheddleton 221 G2
Cheddon Fitzpaine 165 F5
Chedglow 182 B3
Chedgrave 215 E2
Chedington 154 A2
Chediston 215 E4
Chediston Green 215 E4
Chedworth 182 C1
Chedworth Roman Villa 26
Chedzoy 166 A4
Cheeklaw 287 E4
Cheesden 234 C1
Cheeseman's Green 174 C5
Cheetham Hill 234 C2
Cheglinch 163 F1
Cheldon 152 A1
Chelford 234 C5
Chellaston 223 E4
Chells 200 A5
Chelmarsh 207 G4
Chelmondiston 202 D4
Chelmorton 222 C1
Chelmsford 187 G2
Chelmsley Wood 209 D4
Chelsea 186 B5
Chelsfield 173 D2
Chelsham 172 C3
Chelston Heath 165 E5
Chelsworth 202 A3
Cheltenham 196 B5
Chelveston 199 E1
Chelvey 166 B1
Chelwood 166 D1
Chelwood Common 159 G1
Chelwood Gate 159 G1
Chelworth 182 B3
Cheney Longville 206 D4
Chenies 185 F3
Chenies Manor House 43
Chepstow (Cas-gwent) 181 E3
Chepstow Castle 109
Chepstow Museum 109
Chequer, The 220 B3
Cherhill 182 C5
Cherington *Glos.* 182 B3
Cherington *Warks.* 197 E4
Cheriton *Devon* 164 A3
Cheriton *Hants.* 169 G5
Cheriton *Kent* 175 D5
Cheriton *Pembs.* 176 C3
Cheriton *Swan.* 178 A3
Cheriton Bishop 152 A3
Cheriton Cross 152 A3
Cheriton Fitzpaine 152 B2
Cherrington 221 D5
Cherry Burton 246 B3
Cherry Green 201 D5
Cherry Hinton 200 C2
Cherry Tree 242 C5
Cherry Willingham 238 A5
Chertsey 171 F1
Cheselbourne 155 D3
Chesham 185 E2
Chesham Bois 185 E2
Cheshunt 186 C2
Chesil Beach 26
Cheslyn Hay 208 B2
Chessington 171 G1
Chessington World of Adventures 55
Chestall 208 C1
Chester 94
Chester Cathedral 95
Chester Moor 262 B3
Chester Zoo 95
Chesterblade 167 D3
Chesterfield *Derbys.* 236 A5
Chesterfield *Staffs.* 208 D2
Chesterholm Roman Fort (see Vindolanda Roman Fort) 105
Chester-le-Street 262 B2
Chesters *Sc.Bord.* 278 A5
Chesters *Sc.Bord.* 278 A4
Chesterton *Cambs.* 200 C1
Chesterton *Cambs.* 211 G3
Chesterton *Oxon.* 198 A5
Chesterton *Shrop.* 207 G3
Chesterton *Staffs.* 221 F3
Chesterton *Warks.* 197 F2
Chesterton Green 197 F2
Chestfield 174 D2
Cheston 150 C2
Cheswardine 221 E5
Cheswick 279 E2
Cheswick Buildings 279 E2
Cheswick Green 208 D5
Chetnole 154 C2
Chettiscombe 152 C1
Chettisham 212 D4
Chettle 155 F1
Chettle House 26
Chetton 207 F3
Chetwode 198 B5
Chetwynd Aston 207 G1
Chetwynd Park 221 E5
Cheveley 201 E1
Chevening 173 D3
Cheverell's Green 185 F1
Chevington 201 F2
Chevington Drift 271 E2
Chevithorne 152 C1
Chew Magna 166 C1
Chew Moor 234 A2
Chew Stoke 166 C1
Chewton Keynsham 166 D1
Chewton Mendip 166 C2
Chichacott 149 G1
Chicheley 199 E3
Chichester 158 A3
Chichester District Museum 43
Chickerell 154 C4
Chickering 214 D4
Chicklade 168 A4
Chickney 201 D5
Chicksands 199 G4
Chidden 157 F1
Chidden Holt 157 F1
Chiddingfold 171 E4
Chiddingly 160 A2
Chiddingstone 173 D4
Chiddingstone Causeway 173 E4
Chiddingstone Hoath 173 D4
Chideock 154 A3
Chidham 157 G2
Chidswell 244 B5
Chieveley 183 G5
Chignall St. James 187 F2
Chignall Smealy 187 F1
Chigwell 186 D3
Chigwell Row 187 D3
Chilbolton 169 E3
Chilcomb 169 G5
Chilcombe 154 B3
Chilcompton 167 D2
Chilcote 209 E1
Child Okeford 155 E1
Childer Thornton 233 E5
Childerditch 187 F4
Childrey 183 F4
Child's Ercall 221 D5
Child's Hill 186 B4
Childswickham 196 C4
Childwall 233 F4
Childwick Green 186 A1
Chilfrome 154 B3
Chilgrove 158 A2
Chilham 174 C3
Chilhampton 168 B4
Chilla 163 E5
Chillaton 149 E2
Chillenden 175 E3
Chillerton 157 D4
Chillesford 203 E2
Chilley 151 D2
Chillingham 279 E4
Chillington *Devon* 151 D3
Chillington *Som.* 153 G1
Chilmark 168 A4
Chilson *Oxon.* 183 F1
Chilson *Som.* 153 G2
Chilsworthy *Cornw.* 149 E3
Chilsworthy *Devon* 162 D5
Chiltern Open Air Museum 43
Chilterns 43
Chilthorne Domer 154 B1
Chilton *Bucks.* 184 B1
Chilton *Devon* 152 B2
Chilton *Dur.* 262 B5
Chilton *Oxon.* 183 G4
Chilton *Suff.* 201 G3
Chilton Candover 169 G4
Chilton Cantelo 166 C5
Chilton Foliat 183 F5
Chilton Polden 166 A4
Chilton Street 201 F3
Chilton Trinity 165 F4
Chilvers Coton 209 F3
Chilwell 223 G4
Chilworth *Hants.* 156 D1
Chilworth *Surr.* 171 F3
Chimney 183 F2
Chimney Street 201 F3
Chineham 170 B2
Chingford 186 C3
Chinley 235 E4
Chinley Head 235 E4
Chinnor 184 C2
Chipchase Castle 270 A4

Chipley 165 E5
Chipnall 221 E4
Chippenham Cambs. 201 E1
Chippenham Wilts. 182 B5
Chipperfield 185 F2
Chipping Herts. 200 B4
Chipping Lancs. 242 C3
Chipping Campden 197 D4
Chipping Hill 188 B1
Chipping Norton 197 F5
Chipping Ongar 187 E2
Chipping Sodbury 181 G4
Chipping Warden 197 G3
Chipstable 164 D5
Chipstead Kent 173 D3
Chipstead Surr. 172 B3
Chirbury 206 B3
Chirk (Y Waun) 219 F4
Chirk Castle 109
Chirk Green 219 F4
Chirmorrie 264 D3
Chirnside 287 F4
Chirnsidebridge 287 F4
Chirton T. & W. 262 C1
Chirton Wilts. 168 B2
Chisbury 169 D1
Chiscan 272 B4
Chiselborough 154 A1
Chiseldon 183 D5
Chiserley 243 G5
Chislehampton 184 A3
Chislehurst 186 D5
Chislet 175 E2
Chiswell Green 186 A2
Chiswick 186 B5
Chiswick End 200 B3
Chiswick House 55
Chisworth 235 D3
Chithurst 170 D5
Chittering 212 C5
Chitterne 168 A3
Chittlehamholt 163 G3
Chittlehampton 163 G3
Chittoe 168 A1
Chivelstone 151 D4
Chivenor 163 F2
Chobham 171 E1
Choicelee 287 E4
Cholderton 168 D3
Cholesbury 185 E2
Chollerford 270 B4
Chollerton 270 B4
Cholmondeley Castle Gardens 95
Cholsey 184 A4
Cholstrey 195 D2
Cholwell B. & N.E.Som. 166 D2
Cholwell Devon 149 E3
Chop Gate 253 E3
Choppington 271 E3
Chopwell 262 A2
Chorley Ches. 220 C2
Chorley Lancs. 233 G1
Chorley Shrop. 207 F4
Chorley Staffs. 208 C1
Chorleywood 185 F3
Chorlton 221 E2
Chorlton Lane 220 B3
Chorlton-cum-Hardy 234 C3
Chowley 220 B2
Chrishall 200 C4
Chrishall Grange 200 C3
Chrisswell 282 D2
Christchurch Cambs. 212 C3
Christchurch Dorset 156 A3
Christchurch Glos. 181 E1
Christchurch Newport 180 C4
Christchurch Priory 26
Christian Malford 182 B5
Christleton 220 B1
Christmas Common 184 C3
Christon 166 A2
Christon Bank 279 G4
Christow 152 B4
Christskirk 312 B2
Chryston 284 A2
Chudleigh 152 B5
Chudleigh Knighton 152 B5
Chulmleigh 163 G4
Chunal 235 E3
Church 242 D5
Church Aston 207 G1
Church Brampton 198 C1
Church Brough 250 C1
Church Broughton 222 D4
Church Charwelton 198 A2
Church Common 203 E2
Church Crookham 170 D2
Church Eaton 208 A1
Church End Beds. 199 G4
Church End Beds. 199 E5
Church End Beds. 199 G2
Church End Beds. 199 E4
Church End Beds. 199 E4
Church End Cambs. 212 B2
Church End Cambs. 212 B5
Church End Cambs. 212 A4
Church End E.Riding 246 C2
Church End Essex 201 D3
Church End Essex 201 F5
Church End Glos. 196 A4
Church End Hants. 170 B2
Church End Herts. 186 A1
Church End Herts. 200 C5
Church End Lincs. 226 A4
Church End Lincs. 239 E3
Church End Warks. 209 E3
Church End Wilts. 182 C5
Church Enstone 197 F5
Church Farm Museum 71
Church Fenton 245 E4
Church Green 153 E3
Church Gresley 209 E1
Church Hanborough 183 G1
Church Hill Ches. 220 D1
Church Hill Derbys. 223 F1
Church Houses 253 F3
Church Knowle 155 F4
Church Laneham 237 F5
Church Langley 187 D2
Church Langton 210 C3
Church Lawford 209 G5
Church Lawton 221 F2
Church Leigh 222 B4
Church Lench 196 C2
Church Mayfield 222 C3
Church Minshull 221 D1
Church Norton 158 A4
Church Preen 207 E3
Church Pulverbatch 206 D2
Church Stoke 206 B3
Church Stowe 198 B2
Church Street Essex 201 F3
Church Street Kent 187 G5
Church Stretton 207 D3
Church Town Leics. 209 F1
Church Town Surr. 172 C3
Church Village 179 G4
Church Warsop 223 G1
Church Westcote 197 E5
Church Wilne 223 F4
Churcham 181 G1
Churchdown 182 A1
Churchend Essex 188 D3
Churchend Essex 201 E5
Churchend S.Glos. 181 G3
Churchfield 208 C3
Churchgate 186 C2
Churchgate Street 187 D1
Churchill Devon 163 F1
Churchill Devon 153 F2
Churchill N.Som. 166 B2
Churchill Oxon. 197 E5
Churchill Worcs. 196 B2
Churchill Worcs. 208 A5
Churchingford 153 F1
Churchover 210 A4
Churchstanton 153 E1
Churchstow 150 D3
Churchtown Devon 163 G1
Churchtown I.o.M. 240 C2
Churchtown Lancs. 242 A3
Churchtown Mersey. 233 E1
Churnsike Lodge 269 E4
Churston Ferrers 151 F2
Churt 171 D4
Churton 220 B2
Churwell 244 B5
Chute Cadley 169 E2
Chute Standen 169 E2
Chwilog 216 D4
Chwitffordd (Whitford) 232 C5
Chyandour 144 B3
Chysauster 144 B3
Chysauster Ancient Village 26
Cilan Uchaf 216 B5
Cilcain 219 E1
Cilcennin 192 B1
Cilcewydd 206 B2
Cilfrew 179 D2
Cilfynydd 179 G3
Cilgerran 191 E3
Cilgwyn Carmar. 192 D4
Cilgwyn Pembs. 191 D4
Ciliau Aeron 192 B2
Cilldonnain (Kildonan) 314 C1
Cille Bhrighde 314 C2
Cille Pheadair 314 C2
Cilmaengwyn 178 D2
Cilmery 193 G2
Cilrhedyn 191 F4
Cilrhedyn Bridge 190 D4
Cilsan 192 B5
Ciltalgarth 218 B3
Cilwendeg 191 F4
Cilybebyll 178 D2
Cilycwm 193 D3
Cimla 179 D3
Cinderford 181 F1
Cippenham 185 E4
Cippyn 191 E3
Cirbhig 328 C3
Cirencester 182 C2
City Gt.Lon. 186 C4
City V. of Glam. 179 F5
City Airport 186 D4
City Dulas 230 C4
City, The Bucks. 184 C3
City, The Suff. 215 E3
Clabhach 296 A4
Clachaig 282 C1
Clachan Arg. & B. 291 D3
Clachan Arg. & B. 298 A5
Clachan Arg. & B. 281 F4
Clachan High. 306 B1
Clachan W.Isles 315 F5
Clachan Mòr 296 A2
Clachan of Campsie 284 A2
Clachan of Glendaruel 282 A1
Clachan Strachur (Strachur) 290 C4
Clachan-a-Luib 315 G3
Clachandhu 289 D1
Clachaneasy 265 E3
Clachanmore 256 A2
Clachan-Seil 289 G3
Clachanturn 311 E5
Clachbreck 281 F2
Clachnabrain 302 B3
Clachnaharry 321 F5
Clachtoll 330 C2
Clackmannan 293 E5
Clackmarras 323 E4
Clacton Pier 78
Clacton-on-Sea 189 E1
Cladach a Bhale Shear 315 G3
Cladach a' Chaolais 315 F3
Cladach Chircebost 315 F3
Cladach Chnoc a Lin 315 F3
Cladich 290 C2
Cladswell 196 C2
Claggan High. 298 D2
Claggan High. 297 G5
Claigan 317 F4
Claines 196 A2
Clandon Park 43
Clandown 167 D2
Clanfield Hants. 157 G1
Clanfield Oxon. 183 E2
Clannaborough Barton 152 A2
Clanville 169 E3
Claonaig 281 G4
Claonairigh 290 C4
Claonel 332 A4
Clapgate 200 C5
Clapham Beds. 199 F2
Clapham Devon 152 B4
Clapham Gt.Lon. 186 B5
Clapham N.Yorks. 242 D1
Clapham W.Suss. 158 C3
Clapham Green 199 F2
Clapham Hill 174 D2
Clappers 287 G4
Clappersgate 249 E2
Clapton Som. 154 A2
Clapton Som. 166 D2
Clapton-in-Gordano 181 D5
Clapton-on-the-Hill 183 D1
Clapworthy 163 G3
Clara Vale 262 A1
Clarach 204 C4
Clarbeston 191 D5
Clarbeston Road 190 D5
Clarborough 237 E4
Clardon 336 D2
Clare 201 F3
Clarebrand 266 B4
Claremont Landscape Garden 43
Clarencefield 267 E4
Clarilaw 277 G4
Clark's Green 171 G4
Clarkston 283 G4
Clashban 332 B5
Clashcoig 332 B5
Clashdorran 321 E5
Clashgour 299 E5
Clashindarroch 311 G1
Clashmore High. 321 G1
Clashmore High. 330 C1
Clashnessie 330 C1
Clashnoir 311 E2
Clatford 168 C1
Clathy 293 E2
Clatt 312 A2
Clatter 205 F3
Clattercote 197 G3
Clatterford 157 D4
Clatterford End 187 E2
Clatterin Brig 303 E2
Clatteringshaws 265 G3
Clatworthy 165 D4
Claughton Lancs. 242 B1
Claughton Lancs. 242 B3
Clavelshay 165 F4
Claverdon 197 D1
Claverham 166 B1
Clavering 200 C4
Claverley 207 G3
Claverton 167 E1
Claverton Down 167 E1
Clawdd-côch 179 G5
Clawdd-newydd 219 D2
Clawfin 274 D5
Clawthorpe 249 G5
Clawton 149 D1
Claxby 238 B3
Claxby Pluckacre 226 B1
Claxby St. Andrew 239 E5
Claxton N.Yorks. 245 F1
Claxton Norf. 229 E5
Claxton Grange 263 D5
Clay Common 215 F3
Clay Coton 210 A5
Clay Cross 223 E1
Clay End 200 B5
Clay Hill 181 F5
Clay of Allan 322 A2
Claybrooke Magna 209 G4
Claybrooke Parva 209 G4
Claydene 173 D4
Claydon Bucks. 43
Claydon Oxon. 197 G2
Claydon Suff. 202 C3
Claygate Kent 173 G4
Claygate Surr. 171 G1
Claygate Cross 173 F3
Clayhanger Devon 164 D5
Clayhanger W.Mid. 208 C2
Clayhidon 153 E1
Clayhill E.Suss. 160 D1
Clayhill Hants. 156 C2
Clayhithe 200 D1
Claylock 337 D3
Claypit Hill 200 B2
Claypits 181 G2
Claypole 224 D3
Claythorpe 239 E5
Clayton S.Yorks. 236 B2
Clayton Staffs. 221 F3
Clayton W.Suss. 159 E2
Clayton W.Yorks. 244 A4
Clayton Green 242 B5
Clayton West 235 G1
Clayton-le-Moors 242 D4
Clayton-le-Woods 242 B5
Clayworth 237 E4
Cleadale 297 D1
Cleadon 262 C1
Clearbrook 150 B1
Clearwell 181 E2
Cleasby 252 B1
Cleat Ork. 339 D4
Cleat W.Isles 314 B3
Cleatlam 252 A1
Cleatop 243 E1
Cleator 258 D5
Cleator Moor 258 D5
Cleckheaton 244 A5
Clee St. Margaret 207 E4
Cleedownton 207 E4
Cleehill 207 E5
Cleestanton 207 E5
Cleethorpes 238 D2
Cleeton St. Mary 207 F5
Cleeve N.Som. 166 B1
Cleeve Oxon. 184 B4
Cleeve Abbey 26
Cleeve Common 27
Cleeve Hill 196 B5
Cleeve Prior 196 C3
Cleghorn 284 C5
Clehonger 195 D4
Cleigh 290 A2
Cleish 293 F5
Cleland 284 B4
Clement's End 185 F1
Clench Common 168 C1
Clenchwarton 227 D5
Clennell 270 B1
Clent 208 B5
Cleobury Mortimer 207 F5
Cleobury North 207 F4
Clephanton 322 A4
Clerklands 277 G3
Clermiston 285 F2
Clestrain 338 C2
Cleuch Head 277 G4
Cleughbrae 267 E3
Clevancy 182 C5
Clevedon 180 D5
Clevedon Court 27
Cleveland Tontine Inn 252 D3
Cleveley 197 F5
Cleveleys 241 G3
Clevelode 196 A3
Cleverton 182 B4
Clewer 166 B2
Clewer Green 185 E5
Clewer Village 185 E5
Cley next the Sea 228 B1
Cliburn 260 B5
Cliddesden 170 B3
Cliff Carmar. 177 G2
Cliff High. 297 F3
Cliff End 161 D2
Cliff Grange 220 D4
Cliffe Lancs. 242 D4
Cliffe Med. 187 G5
Cliffe N.Yorks. 245 F4
Cliffe Woods 187 G5
Clifford Here. 194 B3
Clifford W.Yorks. 244 D3
Clifford Chambers 197 D2
Clifford's Mesne 195 F5
Cliffs End 175 F2
Clifton Beds. 199 G4
Clifton Bristol 181 E5
Clifton Cumb. 260 B5
Clifton Derbys. 222 C3
Clifton Devon 163 F1
Clifton Lancs. 242 A4
Clifton N.Yorks. 244 A3
Clifton Northumb. 271 E3
Clifton Nott. 223 G4
Clifton Oxon. 197 G4
Clifton S.Yorks. 236 C3
Clifton Stir. 291 F1
Clifton W.Yorks. 244 A5
Clifton Worcs. 196 A3
Clifton York 245 E2
Clifton Campville 209 E1
Clifton Hampden 184 A3
Clifton Maybank 154 B1
Clifton Reynes 199 E2
Clifton upon Dunsmore 210 A5
Clifton upon Teme 195 G1
Cliftonville 175 F1
Climping 158 C3
Climpy 284 D4
Clink 167 E3
Clint 244 B2
Clint Green 228 B4
Clinterty 312 D3
Clintmains 278 A3
Clippesby 229 F4
Clippings Green 228 B4
Clipsham 211 E1
Clipston Northants. 210 C4
Clipston Notts. 224 B4
Clipstone 223 G1
Clitheroe 242 D3
Clive 220 C5
Cliveden 43
Clivocast 345 F2
Clixby 238 B2
Clocaenog 219 D2
Clochan 323 G3
Clochtow 313 F1
Clock Face 233 G3
Clockhill 325 D5
Cloddach 323 D4
Cloddiau 206 A2
Clodock 194 C5
Cloford 167 E3
Cloichran 292 B1
Clola 325 F5
Clonrae 266 C1
Clophill 199 F4
Clopton 211 F4
Clopton Corner 202 D2
Clopton Green Suff. 201 F2
Clopton Green Suff. 202 D2
Close Clark 240 A4
Closeburn 266 C1
Closworth 154 B1
Clothall 200 A4
Clothan 345 D4
Clotton 220 C1
Clouds Hill 27
Clough Cumb. 250 C3
Clough Gt.Man. 234 D1
Clough Gt.Man. 234 D2
Clough W.Yorks. 235 E1
Clough Foot 243 F5
Clough Head 243 G5
Cloughfold 243 E5
Cloughton 254 D3
Cloughton Newlands 254 D3
Clounlaid 297 G4
Clousta 342 C2
Clouston 340 B5
Clova Aber. 311 G2
Clova Angus 302 B2
Clove Lodge 251 E1
Clovelly 27
Clovelly Cross 162 D3
Clovenfords 277 F2
Clovenstone 312 C3
Cloverhill 313 E3
Cloves 322 D3
Clovullin 298 C3
Clow Bridge 243 E5
Clowne 236 B5
Clows Top 207 G5
Cloyntie 274 B5
Cluanach 280 B4
Clubworthy 148 C1
Cluddley 207 F1
Cluer 326 D4
Clumber Country Park 71
Clun 206 B4
Clunas 322 A5
Clunbury 206 C4
Clune High. 309 G2
Clune Moray 324 A3
Clunes 299 E1
Clungunford 206 C5
Clunie Aber. 324 B4
Clunie P. & K. 301 G5
Clunton 206 C4
Cluny 294 A5
Clutton B. & N.E.Som. 166 D2
Clutton Ches. 220 B2
Clwt-y-bont 217 E1
Clwydyfagwyr 179 G2
Clydach Mon. 180 B1
Clydach Swan. 178 C2
Clydach Terrace 180 A1
Clydach Vale 179 F3
Clydebank 283 F2
Clydey 191 F4
Clyffe Pypard 182 C5
Clynder 282 D1
Clynderwen 177 E1
Clyne 179 E2
Clynelish 333 D4
Clynfyw 191 F4
Clynnog-fawr 216 D3
Clyro 194 B3
Clyst Honiton 152 C3
Clyst Hydon 152 D2
Clyst St. George 152 C4
Clyst St. Lawrence 152 D2
Clyst St. Mary 152 C3
Clyst William 153 D2
Cnewr 193 E5
Cnoc 329 F4
Cnoc an Torrain (Knockintorran) 315 F3
Cnwch Coch 204 C5
Coachford 323 G5
Coad's Green 147 G2
Coal Aston 236 A5
Coalbrookdale 207 F2
Coalbrookvale 180 A2
Coalburn 275 G2
Coalburns 262 A1
Coalcleugh 261 E3
Coaley 181 G2
Coalmoor 207 F2
Coalpit Heath 181 F4
Coalpit Hill 221 F2
Coalport 207 G2
Coalsnaughton 293 E5
Coaltown of Balgonie 294 B5
Coaltown of Wemyss 294 B5
Coalville 209 G1
Coalway 181 E1
Coanwood 260 C2
Coast 330 B5
Coat 166 B5
Coatbridge 284 B3
Coate Swin. 183 D4
Coate Wilts. 168 B1
Coates Cambs. 212 B3
Coates Glos. 182 B2
Coates Lincs. 237 G4
Coates Notts. 237 F4
Coates W.Suss. 158 B2
Coatham 263 E5
Coatham Mundeville 262 B5
Cobairdy 324 A5
Cobbaton 163 G3
Cobbler's Plain 181 D2
Cobby Syke 244 A2
Cobden 152 D3
Coberley 182 B1
Cobhall Common 195 D4
Cobham Kent 173 F2
Cobham Surr. 171 G1
Cobham Hall 43
Cobleland 292 A5
Cobley Hill 208 C5
Cobnash 195 D1
Coburty 325 E3
Cochno 283 F2
Cock Alley 223 F1
Cock Bank 220 A3
Cock Bevington 196 C2
Cock Bridge 311 E4
Cock Clarks 188 B2
Cock Green 187 G1
Cockayne 253 F3
Cockayne Hatley 200 A3
Cockburnspath 287 E2
Cockenzie and Port Seton 286 B2
Cocker Bar 242 B5
Cockerham 242 A2
Cockermouth 259 E3
Cockernhoe 199 G5
Cockerton 252 B1
Cockett 178 C3
Cockfield Dur. 262 A5
Cockfield Suff. 202 A2
Cockfosters 186 B3
Cocking 158 A2
Cockington 151 E1
Cocklake 166 B3
Cocklaw 270 B4
Cockle Park 271 E2
Cockleford 182 B1
Cockley Beck 248 D2
Cockley Cley 213 F2
Cockpen 286 A3
Cockpole Green 184 C4
Cockshutt 220 B5
Cockthorpe 228 A1
Cockwood Devon 152 C4
Cockwood Som. 165 F3
Cockyard 235 E4
Codda 147 F2
Coddenham 202 C2
Coddington Ches. 220 B2
Coddington Here. 195 G3
Coddington Notts. 224 D2
Codford St. Mary 168 A4
Codford St. Peter 168 A4
Codicote 186 B1
Codmore Hill 158 C2
Codnor 223 F3
Codnor Park 223 F2
Codrington 181 G5
Codsall 208 A2
Codsall Wood 208 A2
Coed Morgan 180 C1
Coed Ystumgwern 217 E5
Coedcae 180 B2
Coed-duon (Blackwood) 180 A3
Coedely 179 G4
Coedkernew 180 B4
Coedpoeth 219 F2
Coedway 206 C1
Coed-y-bryn 191 G3
Coed-y-caerau 180 C3
Coed-y-paen 180 C3
Coed-y-parc 217 F1
Coed-yr-ynys 194 A5
Coelbren 179 E1
Coffinswell 151 E1
Cofton 152 C4
Cofton Hackett 208 C5
Cogan 180 A5
Cogenhoe 198 D1
Cogges 183 F2
Coggeshall 201 G5
Coggeshall Hamlet 201 G5
Coggins Mill 160 A1
Cóig Peighinnean 329 G1
Coilantogle 292 A4
Coileitir 298 D5
Coilessan 291 E4
Coillaig 290 C2
Coille Mhorgil 307 G4
Coille-righ 307 F2
Coillore 305 G1
Coity 179 F4
Col 329 F4
Col Uarach 329 F4
Colaboll 332 A3
Colan 146 C3
Colaton Raleigh 153 D4
Colbost 317 F5
Colburn 252 A3
Colbury 156 C1
Colby Cumb. 260 C5
Colby I.o.M. 240 A4
Colby Norf. 228 D2
Colby Woodland Garden 109
Colchester 202 A5
Colchester Castle Museum 78
Colchester Green 202 A2
Colchester Zoo 78
Colcot 165 E1
Cold Ash 169 G1
Cold Ashby 210 B5
Cold Ashton 181 G5
Cold Aston 182 D1
Cold Blow 177 E1
Cold Brayfield 199 E2
Cold Chapel 276 A3
Cold Cotes 250 C5
Cold Hanworth 238 A4
Cold Harbour 184 B4
Cold Hatton 220 D5
Cold Hatton Heath 220 D5
Cold Hesledon 262 D3
Cold Higham 198 B2
Cold Inn 177 E2
Cold Kirby 253 E4
Cold Newton 210 C2
Cold Northcott 147 G1
Cold Norton 188 B2
Cold Overton 210 D2
Cold Row 241 G3
Coldbackie 335 F2
Coldblow 187 E5
Coldean 159 F3
Coldeast 152 B5
Coldeaton 222 C2
Colden Common 169 F5
Coldfair Green 203 F1
Coldham 212 C2
Coldharbour Glos. 181 E2
Coldharbour Surr. 171 G3
Coldingham 287 G3
Coldrain 293 F4
Coldred 175 E4
Coldrey 170 C3
Coldridge 163 G5
Coldrife 270 C2
Coldstream 278 C3
Coldvreath 147 D4
Coldwaltham 158 C2
Coldwells 325 G5
Cole 167 D4
Cole End 209 D4
Cole Green 186 B1
Cole Henley 169 F2
Colebatch 206 C4
Colebrook 152 D2
Colebrooke 152 A2
Coleburn 323 E4
Coleby Lincs. 225 E1
Coleby N.Lincs. 237 F1
Coleford Devon 152 A2
Coleford Glos. 181 E1
Coleford Som. 167 D3
Colegate End 214 C3
Colehill 155 G2
Coleman Green 186 A1
Coleman's Hatch 172 D5
Colemere 220 B4
Colemore 170 C4
Colemore Green 207 G3
Colenden 293 G2
Coleorton 209 G1
Coleridge Cottage 27
Colerne 182 A5
Cole's Common 214 D3
Cole's Cross 151 D3
Cole's Green 203 D1
Colesbourne 182 C1
Colesden 199 G2
Coleshill Bucks. 185 E3
Coleshill Oxon. 183 E3
Coleshill Warks. 209 E4
Colestocks 153 D2
Coleton Fishacre 27
Coley B. & N.E.Som. 166 C2
Coley Staffs. 222 B5
Colfin 264 B5
Colgate 172 B5
Colgrain 283 E2
Colindale 186 B4
Colinsburgh 294 C4
Colinton 285 G3
Colintraive 282 B2
Colkirk 228 A3
Coll 296 A4
Collace 294 A1
Collafirth 342 D1
Collamoor Head 148 B1
Collaton St. Mary 151 E1
Collessie 294 A3
Colleton Mills 163 G4
Collett's Green 196 A2
Collier Row 187 E3
Collier Street 173 G4
Collier's End 200 B5
Collier's Wood 186 B5
Colliery Row 262 C3
Collieston 313 F2
Collin 267 E3
Collingbourne Ducis 168 D2
Collingbourne Kingston 168 D2
Collingham Notts. 224 D1
Collingham W.Yorks. 244 C3
Collington 195 F1
Collingtree 198 C2
Collins End 184 B5
Collins Green Warr. 233 G3
Collins Green Worcs. 195 G2
Colliston 303 E5
Colliton 153 D2
Collmuir 312 A4
Collycroft 209 F4
Collyhurst 234 C2
Collynie 312 D1
Collyweston 211 E2
Colmonell 264 C2
Colmworth 199 G2
Coln Rogers 182 C2
Coln St. Aldwyns 182 D2
Coln St. Dennis 182 C1
Colnabaichin 311 E4
Colnbrook 185 F5
Colne Cambs. 212 B5
Colne Lancs. 243 E4
Colne Engaine 201 G4
Colney 228 C5
Colney Heath 186 B2
Colney Street 186 A2
Colonsay 288 C5
Colonsay House 288 C5
Colour Museum 87
Colpy 312 B1
Colquhar 286 A5
Colsterdale 252 A4
Colsterworth 225 E5
Colston Bassett 224 C4
Coltfield 322 D3
Colthouse 249 E3
Coltishall 229 D4
Coltness 284 C4
Colton Cumb. 249 E4
Colton N.Yorks. 245 E3
Colton Norf. 228 C5
Colton Staffs. 222 B5
Colton W.Yorks. 244 C4
Colva 194 B2
Colvend 266 C5
Colvister 345 E3
Colwall 195 G3
Colwall Green 195 G3
Colwall Stone 195 G3
Colwell 270 B4
Colwich 222 B5
Colwick 224 B4
Colwinston 179 F5
Colworth 158 B3
Colwyn Bay (Bae Colwyn) 231 G5
Colyford 153 F3
Colyton 153 F3

Combe *Here.* 194 C1
Combe *Oxon.* 183 G1
Combe *Som.* 166 B5
Combe *W.Berks.* 169 E1
Combe Common 171 E4
Combe Cross 152 A5
Combe Down 167 E1
Combe Florey 165 E4
Combe Hay 167 E2
Combe Martin 163 F1
Combe Martin Wildlife & Dinosaur Park 27
Combe Pafford 151 F1
Combe Raleigh 153 E2
Combe St. Nicholas 153 G1
Combeinteignhead 152 B5
Comberbach 234 A5
Comberford 209 D2
Comberton *Cambs.* 200 B2
Comberton *Here.* 195 D1
Combpyne 153 F3
Combridge 222 B4
Combrook 197 F2
Combs *Derbys.* 235 E5
Combs *Suff.* 202 B2
Combs Ford 202 B2
Combwich 165 F3
Comer 291 F4
Comers 312 B4
Comhampton 196 A1
Comins Coch 204 C4
Commandery, The 64
Commercial End 201 D1
Commins Coch 205 E2
Common Edge 241 G4
Common Moor 147 G2
Common Platt 182 D4
Common Side 236 A5
Common Square 238 A5
Common, The *Wilts.* 168 D4
Common, The *Wilts.* 182 C4
Commondale 253 F1
Commonside 222 D3
Compstall 235 D3
Compton *Devon* 151 E1
Compton *Hants.* 169 F5
Compton *Plym.* 150 A2
Compton *Staffs.* 208 A4
Compton *Surr.* 171 E3
Compton *W.Berks* 184 A5
Compton *W.Suss.* 157 G1
Compton *W.Yorks.* 244 D3
Compton *Wilts.* 168 C2
Compton Abbas 155 E1
Compton Abdale 182 C1
Compton Acres 27
Compton Bassett 182 C5
Compton Beauchamp 183 E4
Compton Bishop 166 A2
Compton Castle 27
Compton Chamberlayne 168 B5
Compton Dando 166 D1
Compton Dundon 166 B4
Compton Martin 166 C2
Compton Pauncefoot 166 D5
Compton Valence 154 B3
Compton Verney 197 F2
Comra 309 E5
Comrie *Fife* 285 E1
Comrie *P. & K.* 292 C2
Conchra *Arg. & B.* 282 B1
Conchra *High.* 307 E2
Concraigie 301 G5
Conder Green 242 A2
Conderton 196 B4
Condicote 196 D5
Condorrat 284 B2
Condover 207 D2
Coney Weston 214 A4
Coneyhurst 171 G5
Coneysthorpe 253 G5
Coneythorpe 244 C2
Conford 170 D4
Congash 310 C2
Congdon's Shop 147 G2
Congerstone 209 F2
Congham 227 F5
Congleton 221 F1
Congresbury 166 B1
Congreve 208 B1
Conicavel 322 B4
Coningsby 226 A2
Conington *Cambs.* 211 G4
Conington *Cambs.* 200 B1
Conisbrough 236 C3
Conisby 280 A3
Conisholme 239 E3
Coniston *Cumb.* 249 E3
Coniston *E.Riding* 247 D4
Coniston Cold 243 F2
Conistone 243 F1
Conland 324 B5
Connah's Quay 219 F1
Connel 290 B1
Connel Park 275 E4
Connor Downs 144 C3
Conock 168 B2
Conon Bridge 321 E4
Cononish 291 F2
Cononley 243 F3
Cononsyth 303 D5
[illegible]
Consett 262 A2
Constable Burton 252 A3
Constantine 145 E4
Constantine Bay 146 C2
Contin 321 D4
Contlaw 312 D4
Contullich 321 F2
Conwy 231 F5
Conwy Castle 109
Conyer 174 B2
Conyer's Green 201 G1
Cooden 160 C3
Coodham 274 C2
Cooil 240 B4
Cookbury 163 E5
Cookbury Wick 163 D5
Cookham 185 D4
Cookham Dean 185 D4
Cookham Rise 185 D4
Cookhill 196 C2
Cookley *Suff.* 215 E4
Cookley *Worcs.* 208 A4
Cookley Green *Oxon.* 184 B3
Cookley Green *Suff.* 215 E4
Cookney 313 D5
Cook's Green 202 A2
Cooksbridge 159 F2
Cooksey Green 196 B1
Cookshill 221 G3
Cooksmill Green 187 F2
Cookston 313 E1
Cookworthy Museum 27
Coolham 171 G5
Cooling 187 G5
Cooling Street 187 G5
Coombe *Cornw.* 147 D4
Coombe *Cornw.* 162 C4
Coombe *Cornw.* 146 A5
Coombe *Cornw.* 146 C5
Coombe *Devon* 151 D3
Coombe *Devon* 152 B4
Coombe *Devon* 153 E3
Coombe *Som.* 165 F5
Coombe *Som.* 154 A2
Coombe *Wilts.* 168 C2
Coombe Bissett 168 C5
Coombe End 164 D5
Coombe Hill *Bucks.* 43
Coombe Hill *Glos.* 196 A5
Coombe Keynes 155 E4
Coombes 159 D3
Coombes Moor 194 C1
Cooper's Corner *E.Suss.* 160 C1
Cooper's Corner *Kent* 173 D4
Cooper's Green 186 A2
Coopersale Common 187 D2
Coopersale Street 187 D2
Coors Visitor Centre 64
Cootham 158 C2
Cop Street 175 F3
Copdock 202 C3
Copford Green 202 A5
Copgrove 244 C1
Copister 345 D5
Cople 199 G3
Copley *Dur.* 261 G5
Copley *W.Yorks.* 243 G5
Coplow Dale 235 F5
Copmanthorpe 245 E3
Copmere End 221 F5
Copp 242 A4
Coppathorne 162 C5
Coppenhall 208 B1
Coppenhall Moss 221 E2
Copperhouse 144 C3
Coppicegate 207 G4
Coppingford 211 G4
Coppleridge 167 F5
Copplestone 152 A2
Coppull 233 G1
Coppull Moor 233 G1
Copsale 171 G5
Copse Hill 172 B2
Copster Green 242 C4
Copston Magna 209 G4
Copt Heath 209 D5
Copt Hewick 252 C5
Copt Oak 209 G1
Copthall Green 186 D2
Copthorne 172 C5
Copy Lake 163 G4
Copythorne 156 C1
Coralhill 325 F3
Corbets Tey 187 E4
Corbiegoe 337 F4
Corbridge 261 F1
Corby 211 D4
Corby Glen 225 F5
Cordach 312 B5
Coreley 207 F5
Corfcott Green 148 D1
Corfe 153 F1
Corfe Castle *Dorset* 155 F4
Corfe Castle *Dorset* 27
Corfe Mullen 155 F3
Corfton 207 D4
Corgarff 311 E4
Corhampton 170 B5
Corley 209 E4
Corley Ash 209 E4
Corley Moor 209 E4
Cornabus 280 B5
Cornard Tye 202 A3
Corndon 149 G2
Corney 248 C3
Cornforth 262 C4
Cornhill 324 A4
Cornhill on Tweed 278 C3
Cornholme 243 F5
Cornish Cyder Farm, The 27
Cornish Engines 27
[illegible]
Cornish Seal Sanctuary 27
Cornquoy 339 E2
Cornriggs 261 E3
Cornsay 262 A3
Cornsay Colliery 262 A3
Corntown *High.* 321 E4
Corntown *V. of Glam.* 179 F5
Cornwell 197 E5
Cornwood 150 C2
Cornworthy 151 E2
Corpach 298 D2
Corpusty 228 C3
Corrachree 311 G4
Corran *Arg. & B.* 291 E5
Corran *High.* 307 E4
Corran *High.* 298 C3
Corranbuie 281 G3
Corranmore 289 G4
Corrany 240 C3
Corribeg 298 B2
Corrie 282 B5
Corrie Common 268 A3
Corriechrevie 281 F4
Corriecravie 273 E3
Corriedoo 266 A2
Corriekinloch 331 F2
Corrielorne 290 A3
Corrieshalloch Gorge 119
Corrievorrie 309 G2
Corrimony 308 C1
Corringham *Lincs.* 237 F3
Corringham *Thur.* 187 G4
Corris 205 D2
Corris Uchaf 204 D2
Corrlarach 298 B2
Corrour Shooting Lodge 299 G3
Corrow 291 D4
Corry 306 C2
Corrychurrachan 298 C3
Corrylach 272 C2
Corrymuckloch 293 D1
Corsback 337 E2
Corscombe 154 B2
Corse *Aber.* 324 B5
Corse *Glos.* 195 G5
Corse Lawn 196 A4
Corse of Kinnoir 324 A5
Corsebank 275 G4
Corsegight 324 D4
Corsehill 267 F2
Corsewall 264 B4
Corsham 182 A5
Corsindae 312 B4
Corsley 167 F3
Corsley Heath 167 F3
Corsock 266 B3
Corston *B. & N.E.Som.* 167 D1
Corston *Wilts.* 182 B4
Corstorphine 285 F2
Cortachy 302 B4
Corton *Suff.* 215 G2
Corton *Wilts.* 168 A3
Corton Denham 166 D5
Corwar House 265 D2
Corwen 219 D3
Coryton *Devon* 149 E2
Coryton *Thur.* 187 G4
Cosby 210 A3
Coscote 184 A4
Coseley 208 B3
Cosford *Shrop.* 207 G2
Cosford *Warks.* 210 A5
Cosgrove 198 C3
Cosham 157 F2
Cosheston 176 D2
Coshieville 300 C5
Coskills 238 A2
Cosmeston 165 E1
Cosmeston Country Park 109
Cossall 223 F3
Cossington *Leics.* 210 B1
Cossington *Som.* 166 A3
Costa 340 B4
Costessey 228 C4
Costock 223 G5
Coston *Leics.* 224 D5
Coston *Norf.* 228 B5
Cote *Oxon.* 183 F2
Cote *Som.* 166 A3
Cotebrook 220 C1
Cotehele 27
Cotehill 260 A2
Cotes *Cumb.* 249 F4
Cotes *Leics.* 223 G5
Cotes *Staffs.* 221 F4
Cotesbach 210 A4
Cotgrave 224 B4
Cothall 313 D3
Cotham 224 C3
Cothelstone 165 E4
Cotheridge 195 G2
Cotherstone 251 F1
Cothill 183 G3
Cotleigh 153 F2
Cotmanhay 223 F3
Coton *Cambs.* 200 C2
Coton *Northants.* 210 B5
Coton *Staffs.* 221 G4
Coton *Staffs.* 209 D2
Coton *Staffs.* 221 F5
Coton Clanford 221 F5
Coton Hill 221 G4
Coton in the Clay 222 C5
Coton in the Elms 209 E1
Coton Manor Wildlife Garden 71
Cotonwood *Shrop.* 220 C4
Cotonwood *Staffs.* 221 F5
Cotswold Farm Park 27
Cotswold Hills 28
Cotswold Water Park 28
Cotswold Wildlife Park [illegible]
Cott 151 D1
Cottam *Lancs.* 242 A4
Cottam *Notts.* 237 F4
Cottartown 310 C1
Cottenham 200 C1
Cotterdale 250 D3
Cottered 200 B5
Cotteridge 208 C5
Cotterstock 211 F3
Cottesbrooke 210 C5
Cottesmore 211 E1
Cottingham *E.Riding* 246 C4
Cottingham *Northants.* 210 D3
Cottingley 244 A4
Cottisford 198 A4
Cotton *Staffs.* 222 B3
Cotton *Suff.* 202 B1
Cotton End 199 F3
Cottonworth 169 E4
Cottown *Aber.* 312 A2
Cottown *Aber.* 324 D5
Cottown *Aber.* 312 C3
Cotts 150 A1
Cottwood 163 G4
Cotwall 207 F1
Cotwalton 221 G4
Couch's Mill 147 F4
Coughton *Here.* 195 E5
Coughton *Warks.* 196 C1
Coughton Court 64
Cougie 308 B2
Coulaghailtro 281 F3
Coulags 319 F5
Coulby Newham 253 E1
Coulderton 248 A2
Coull 312 A4
Coulport 282 D1
Coulsdon 172 B3
Coulston 168 A2
Coulter 276 B2
Coultershaw Bridge 158 B2
Coultings 165 F3
Coulton 253 F5
Coultra 294 B2
Cound 207 E2
Coundlane 207 E2
Coundon *Dur.* 262 B5
Coundon *W.Mid.* 209 F4
Countersett 251 E4
Countess Wear 152 C3
Countesthorpe 210 A3
Countisbury 164 A3
Coup Green 242 B5
Coupar Angus 302 A5
Coupland *Cumb.* 250 C1
Coupland *Northumb.* 278 D3
Cour 281 G5
Court Colman 179 E4
Court Henry 192 B5
Court House Green 209 F4
Court-at-Street 174 C5
Courteenhall 198 C2
Courtsend 188 D3
Courtway 165 F4
Cousland 286 A3
Cousley Wood 173 F5
Coustonn 282 B2
Cove *Arg. & B.* 282 D1
Cove *Devon* 152 C1
Cove *Hants.* 170 D2
Cove *High.* 330 A5
Cove *Sc.Bord.* 287 E2
Cove Bay 313 E4
Cove Bottom 215 F3
Covehithe 215 G3
Coven 208 B2
Coveney 212 C4
Covenham St. Bartholomew 238 D3
Covenham St. Mary 238 D3
Covent Garden 55
Coventry 209 F5
Coventry Cathedral 64
Coventry Transport Museum 64
Coverack 145 E5
Coverham 252 A4
Covesea 323 D2
Covingham 183 D4
Covington *Cambs.* 211 F5
Covington *S.Lan.* 276 A2
Cowan Bridge 250 B5
Cowbeech 160 B2
Cowbit 212 A1
Cowbridge *Som.* 164 C3
Cowbridge *V. of Glam.* 179 F5
Cowden 173 D4
Cowden Pound 173 D4
Cowdenbeath 293 G5
Cowdenburn 285 G4
Cowers Lane 223 E3
Cowes 157 D3
Cowesby 253 D4
Cowesfield Green 169 D5
Cowey Green 202 B5
Cowfold 159 E1
Cowgill 250 C4
Cowie *Aber.* 303 G1
Cowie *Stir.* 284 C1
Cowlam Manor 246 B1
Cowley *Devon* 152 C3
Cowley *Glos.* 182 B1
Cowley *Gt.Lon.* 185 F4
Cowley *Oxon.* 184 A2
Cowling *Lancs.* 233 G1
Cowling *N.Yorks.* 243 F3
Cowling *N.Yorks.* 252 B4
Cowlinge 201 F2
Cowmes 235 F1
Cowpe 243 E5
Cowpen 271 E3
Cowpen Bewley 263 D5
Cowper & Newton Museum 43
Cowplain 157 F1
Cowsden 196 B2
[illegible]
Cowthorpe 244 D2
Cox Common 215 E3
Coxbank 221 D3
Coxbench 223 E3
Coxbridge 166 C4
Coxford 227 G5
Coxheath 173 G3
Coxhoe 262 C4
Coxley 166 C3
Coxley Wick 166 C3
Coxpark 149 E3
Coxtie Green 187 E3
Coxwold 253 E5
Coychurch 179 F5
Coylet 282 C1
Coylton 274 C4
Coylumbridge 310 B3
Coynach 311 G4
Coynachie 311 G1
Coytrahen 179 E4
Crabbet Park 172 C5
Crabgate 228 B3
Crabtree *Plym.* 150 B2
Crabtree *S.Yorks.* 236 A4
Crabtree *W.Suss.* 159 E1
Crabtree Green 220 A3
Crackaig 280 D3
Crackenthorpe 260 C5
Crackington 148 B1
Crackington Haven 148 B1
Crackley 221 F3
Crackleybank 207 G1
Crackpot 251 E3
Crackthorn Corner 214 B4
Cracoe 243 F1
Craddock 153 D1
Cradhlastadh 328 B4
Cradley *Here.* 195 G3
Cradley *W.Mid.* 208 B4
Cradley Heath 208 B4
Crafthole 149 D5
Crafton 185 D1
Cragg 243 G5
Cragg Hill 244 B4
Craggan *Moray* 311 D1
Craggan *P. & K.* 292 D3
Cragganruar 300 B5
Craggie *High.* 309 G1
Craggie *High.* 333 D3
Craghead 262 B2
Cragside 103
Craibstone *Aberdeen* 313 D3
Craibstone *Moray* 323 G4
Craichie 302 D5
Craig *Arg. & B.* 290 C1
Craig *Arg. & B.* 289 E1
Craig *D. & G.* 266 A4
Craig *High.* 319 D3
Craig *High.* 319 G5
Craig *S.Ayr.* 274 B5
Craig Berthlŵyd 179 G3
Craigans 290 A5
Craigbeg 299 G1
Craig-cefn-parc 178 C2
Craigcleuch 268 B3
Craigculter 325 E4
Craigdallie 294 A2
Craigdam 312 D1
Craigdarroch *D. & G.* 266 B1
Craigdarroch *E.Ayr.* 275 E5
Craigdhu *D. & G.* 257 D2
Craigdhu *High.* 321 D5
Craigearn 312 C3
Craigellachie 323 E5
Craigellie 325 F3
Craigencallie 265 G3
Craigend *Moray* 322 D4
Craigend *P. & K.* 293 G2
Craigendive 282 B1
Craigendoran 283 E1
Craigengillan 274 C5
Craigenputtock 266 B2
Craigens 280 A3
Craigglas 290 A5
Craighall 294 C3
Craighat 283 F1
Craighead *Fife* 295 F3
Craighead *High.* 321 G3
Craighlaw 265 E4
Craighouse 280 D3
Craigie *Aber.* 313 E3
Craigie *Dundee* 294 C1
Craigie *P. & K.* 301 G5
Craigie *S.Ayr.* 274 C2
Craigie Brae 313 D1
Craigieburn 276 C5
Craigieholm 293 G1
Craigielaw 286 B2
Craigievar Castle 119
Craiglockhart 285 G2
Craiglug 312 D5
Craigmaud 325 D4
Craigmillar 285 G2
Craigmillar Castle 119
Craigmore 282 C3
Craigmyle House 312 B4
Craignafeoch 282 A2
Craignant 219 F4
Craignavie 292 A1
Craigneil 264 C2
Craigneuk 284 B4
Craignure 289 G1
Craigo 303 E3
Craigoch 274 A5
Craigow 293 F4
Craigrothie 294 B3
Craigroy 322 D4
Craigroy Farm 311 D1
Craigruie 291 G2
Craigs, The 331 G5
Craigsanquhar 294 B3
Craigton *Aberdeen* 312 D4
Craigton *Angus* 294 D1
Craigton *Angus* 302 B4
Craigton *High.* 321 F5
Craigton *Stir.* 284 A1
Craigtown 336 A3
Craig-y-nos 179 E1
[illegible]
Craik *Sc.Bord.* 277 E5
Crail 295 E4
Crailing 278 A4
Crailinghall 278 A4
Crakehill 252 D5
Crakemarsh 222 B4
Crambe 245 G1
Cramlington 271 E4
Cramond 285 F2
Cranage 221 E1
Cranberry 221 F4
Cranborne 155 G1
Cranbourne 185 E5
Cranbrook *Gt.Lon.* 186 D4
Cranbrook *Kent* 173 G5
Cranbrook Common 173 G5
Crane Moor 236 A2
Cranfield 199 E3
Cranford *Devon* 162 D3
Cranford *Gt.Lon.* 186 A5
Cranford St. Andrew 211 E5
Cranford St. John 211 E5
Cranham *Glos.* 182 A1
Cranham *Gt.Lon.* 187 E4
Crank 233 G3
Cranleigh 171 F4
Cranmer Green 214 B4
Cranmore *I.o.W.* 156 C4
Cranmore *Som.* 167 D3
Cranna 324 B4
Crannoch 323 G4
Cranoe 210 C3
Cransford 203 E1
Cranshaws 287 D3
Cranstal 240 C1
Crantock 146 B3
Cranwell 225 F3
Cranwich 213 F3
Cranworth 228 A5
Craobh Haven 289 G4
Crapstone 150 B1
Crarae 290 B5
Crask Inn 332 A2
Crask of Aigas 321 D5
Craskins 312 A4
Craster 279 G5
Craswall 194 B4
Crateford 208 B2
Cratfield 215 E4
Crathes 312 C5
Crathes Castle 119
Crathie *Aber.* 311 E5
Crathie *High.* 309 E5
Crathorne 252 D2
Craven Arms 206 D4
Craw 281 G5
Crawcrook 262 A1
Crawford *Lancs.* 233 F2
Crawford *S.Lan.* 276 A3
Crawfordjohn 275 G3
Crawfordton 266 B1
Crawick 275 F4
Crawley *Devon* 153 F2
Crawley *Hants.* 169 F4
Crawley *Oxon.* 183 F1
Crawley *W.Suss.* 172 B5
Crawley Down 172 C5
Crawleyside 261 F3
Crawshawbooth 243 E5
Crawton 303 G2
Crawyn 240 B2
Cray *N.Yorks.* 251 E5
Cray *P. & K.* 301 G3
Cray *Powys* 193 E5
Crayford 187 E5
Crayke 253 E5
Crays Hill 187 G3
Cray's Pond 184 B4
Crazies Hill 184 C4
Creacombe 152 B1
Creag Ghoraidh (Creagorry) 315 F5
Creagan 298 B5
Creagbheitheachain 298 B3
Creagorry (Creag Ghoraidh) 315 F5
Crealy Adventure Park 28
Creamore Bank 220 C4
Creaton 210 C5
Creca 268 A4
Credenhill 195 D3
Crediton 152 B2
Creebridge 265 F4
Creech Heathfield 165 F5
Creech St. Michael 165 F5
Creed 146 D5
Creedy Park 152 B2
Creekmouth 187 D4
Creeting St. Mary 202 B2
Creeton 225 F5
Creetown 265 F5
Creggans 290 C4
Cregneash 240 A5
Cregrina 194 A2
Creich 294 B2
Creigau 181 D3
Creigiau 179 G4
Crelevan 308 C1
Crelly 145 D3
Cremyll 150 A2
Crendell 155 G1
Cressage 207 E2
Cressbrook 235 F5
Cresselly 177 D2
Cressing 201 F5
Cressing Temple Barns 78
Cresswell *Northumb.* 271 E2
Cresswell *Staffs.* 221 G4
Cresswell Quay 177 D2
Creswell 236 C5
Cretingham 202 D2
Cretshengan 281 F3
Crewe *Ches.* 221 E2
Crewe *Ches.* 220 B2
Crewe Green 221 E2
[illegible]
Crewkerne 154 A2
Crew's Hole 181 F5
Crewton 223 E4
Crianlarich 291 F2
Cribbs Causeway 181 E4
Cribyn 192 B2
Criccieth 217 D4
Criccieth Castle 110
Crich 223 E2
Crich Carr 223 E2
Crich Common 223 E2
Crichie 325 E5
Crichton 286 A3
Crichton Castle 119
Crick *Mon.* 181 D3
Crick *Northants.* 210 A5
Crickadarn 193 G3
Cricket Hill 170 D1
Cricket St. Thomas 153 G2
Crickham 166 B3
Crickheath 219 F5
Crickhowell 180 B1
Cricklade 182 D3
Cricklewood 186 B4
Crick's Green 195 F2
Criddlestyle 156 A1
Cridling Stubbs 245 E5
Crieff 293 D2
Criggan 147 E3
Criggion 206 B1
Crigglestone 236 A1
Crimble 234 C1
Crimchard 153 G2
Crimdon Park 263 D4
Crimond 325 F4
Crimonmogate 325 F4
Crimplesham 213 E2
Crinan 289 G5
Crinan Ferry 289 G5
Cringleford 228 C5
Cringletie 285 G5
Crinow 177 E1
Cripplestyle 155 G1
Cripp's Corner 160 C1
Crix 187 G1
Crizeley 194 D4
Croalchapel 266 D1
Croasdale 259 D5
Crock Street 153 G1
Crockenhill 173 E2
Crocker End 184 C4
Crockerhill 157 E2
Crockernwell 152 A3
Crockerton 167 F3
Crockerton Green 167 F3
Crocketford (Ninemile Bar) 266 C3
Crockey Hill 245 F3
Crockham Hill 172 D3
Crockhurst Street 173 F4
Crockleford Heath 202 B5
Croes Hywel 180 C1
Croes y pant 180 C2
Croesau Bach 219 F5
Croeserw 179 E3
Croesgoch 190 B4
Croes-lan 191 G3
Croesor 217 F3
Croespenmaen 180 A3
Croesyceiliog *Carmar.* 178 A1
Croesyceiliog *Torfaen* 180 C3
Croes-y-mwyalch 180 C3
Croesywaun 217 E2
Croford 165 E5
Croft *Here.* 195 D1
Croft *Leics.* 210 A3
Croft *Lincs.* 226 D1
Croft *Warr.* 234 A3
Croft Castle 64
Croftamie 283 F1
Crofthead 268 B4
Croftmore 301 D3
Crofton *W.Yorks.* 236 A1
Crofton *Wilts.* 169 D1
Croft-on-Tees 252 B2
Crofts 266 B3
Crofts of Benachielt 337 D5
Crofts of Buinach 323 D4
Crofts of Haddo 312 D1
Crofty 178 B3
Crogen 218 D4
Croggan 289 G2
Croglin 260 B3
Croick *High.* 331 G5
Croick *High.* 336 A3
Croig 296 D4
Crois Dughaill 314 C2
Croit e Caley 240 A5
Cromarty 321 G3
Crombie 285 E1
Crombie Mill 294 D1
Cromblet 312 C1
Cromdale 310 C2
Cromer *Herts.* 200 A5
Cromer *Norf.* 228 D1
Cromford 223 D2
Cromhall 181 F3
Cromhall Common 181 F4
Crompton Fold 235 D1
Cromwell 224 C1
Cromwell Museum 78
Cronberry 275 E3
Crondall 170 C3
Cronk, The 240 B2
Cronk-y-Voddy 240 B3
Cronton 233 F4
Crook *Cumb.* 249 F3
Crook *Dur.* 262 A4
Crook of Devon 293 F4
Crooked Soley 183 F5
Crookedholm 274 C2
Crookham *Northumb.* 278 D3
Crookham *W.Berks.* 169 G1
[illegible]
Crookham Village 170 C2
Crooklands 249 G4
Cropredy 197 G3
Cropston 210 A1
Cropthorne 196 B3
Cropton 253 G4
Cropwell Bishop 224 B4
Cropwell Butler 224 B4
Cros (Cross) 329 G1
Crosbie 282 D5
Crosbost 329 E5
Crosby *Cumb.* 259 D3
Crosby *I.o.M.* 240 B4

Crosby *Mersey.* 233 E3
Crosby *N.Lincs.* 237 F1
Crosby Court 252 C3
Crosby Garrett 250 C2
Crosby
Ravensworth 250 B1
Crosby Villa 259 D3
Crosby-on-Eden 260 A2
Croscombe 166 C3
Crosemere 220 B5
Crosland Hill 235 F1
Cross *Som.* 166 B2
Cross (Cros) *W.Isles* 329 G1
Cross Ash 180 D1
Cross Bank 207 G5
Cross End *Beds.* 199 F2
Cross End *Essex* 201 G4
Cross Foxes Inn 205 D1
Cross Gates 244 C4
Cross Green *Devon* 149 D2
Cross Green *Staffs.* 208 B2
Cross Green *Suff.* 202 A2
Cross Green *Suff.* 201 G2
Cross Green *Suff.* 201 G2
Cross Hands
Carmar. 178 B1
Cross Hands *Pembs.* 177 D1
Cross Hill 223 F3
Cross Hills 243 G3
Cross Houses 207 E2
Cross in Hand 160 A1
Cross Inn *Cere.* 191 G2
Cross Inn *Cere.* 192 B1
Cross Inn *R.C.T.* 179 G4
Cross Keys 182 A5
Cross Lane 157 E4
Cross Lane Head 207 G3
Cross Lanes *Cornw.* 146 B5
Cross Lanes *Cornw.* 145 D4
Cross Lanes
N.Yorks. 245 E1
Cross Lanes *Wrex.* 220 A3
Cross of Jackston 312 C1
Cross o'th'hands 223 D3
Cross Street 214 C4
Crossaig 281 G4
Crossapol 296 A4
Crossapoll 296 A2
Cross-at-Hand 173 G4
Crossbush 158 C3
Crosscanonby 259 D3
Crossdale Street 228 D2
Crossens 233 E1
Crossflatts 244 A3
Crossford *D. & G.* 266 C2
Crossford *Fife* 285 E1
Crossford *S.Lan.* 284 C5
Crossgate *Lincs.* 226 A5
Crossgate *Staffs.* 221 G4
Crossgatehall 286 A3
Crossgates *Fife* 285 F1
Crossgates
N.Yorks. 254 D4
Crossgates *P. & K.* 293 F2
Crossgates *Powys* 193 G1
Crossgill 242 B1
Crosshands 274 C2
Crosshill *Fife* 293 G5
Crosshill *S.Ayr.* 274 B5
Crosshouse 274 B2
Crosskeys 180 B3
Crosskirk 336 C1
Crosslanes 206 C1
Crosslee *Renf.* 283 F3
Crosslee *Sc.Bord.* 277 E4
Crosslet 283 F2
Crossmichael 266 B4
Crossmoor 242 A4
Crossraguel Abbey 119
Crossroads *Aber.* 312 C5
Crossroads *E.Ayr.* 274 C2
Crossway *Mon.* 180 D1
Crossway *Powys* 193 G2
Crossway Green
Mon. 181 E3
Crossway Green
Worcs. 196 A1
Crossways *Dorset* 155 D4
Crossways *Glos.* 181 E1
Crosswell 191 E4
Crosswood 204 C5
Crosthwaite 249 F3
Croston 233 F1
Crostwick 229 D4
Crostwight 229 E3
Crothair 328 C4
Crouch 173 F3
Crouch End 186 B4
Crouch Hill 154 D1
Croucheston 168 B5
Croughton 198 A4
Crovie 324 D3
Crow 156 A2
Crow Edge 235 F2
Crow Green 187 E3
Crow Hill 195 F5
Crowan 144 D3
Crowborough 173 E5
Crowborough
Warren 173 E5
Crowcombe 165 E4
Crowdecote 222 C1
Crowden 235 E3
Crowdhill 169 F5
Crowell 184 C3
Crowfield
Northants. 198 B3
Crowfield *Suff.* 202 C2
Crowhurst *E.Suss.* 160 C2
Crowhurst *Surr.* 172 C4
Crowhurst
Lane End 172 C4
Crowland *Lincs.* 212 A1
Crowland *Suff.* 214 B4
Crowlas 144 C3
Crowle *N.Lincs.* 237 E1
Crowle *Worcs.* 196 B2
Crowle Green 196 B2
Crowmarsh Gifford 184 B4
Crown Corner 215 D4
Crownhill 150 A2
Crownthorpe 228 B5
Crowntown 144 D3
Crow's Nest 147 G3
Crows-an-wra 144 A4
Crowsnest 206 C2
Crowthorne 170 D1
Crowton 233 G5
Croxall 209 E1
Croxby 238 B3
Croxdale 262 B4
Croxden 222 B4
Croxley Green 185 F3
Croxton *Cambs.* 200 A2
Croxton *N.Lincs.* 238 A1
Croxton *Norf.* 213 G4
Croxton *Staffs.* 221 E4
Croxton Green 220 C2
Croxton Kerrial 224 D5
Croxtonbank 221 E4
Croy *High.* 321 G5
Croy *N.Lan.* 284 B2
Croyde 163 E2
Croyde Bay 163 E2
Croydon *Cambs.* 200 B3
Croydon *Gt.Lon.* 172 C2
Cruach 280 B4
Cruachan Power Station Visitor Centre 119
Cruchie 324 A5
Cruckmeole 206 D2
Cruckton 206 D1
Cruden Bay 313 F1
Crudgington 207 F1
Crudwell 182 B3
Crug 206 A5
Crugmeer 146 D2
Crugybar 192 C4
Crùlabhig 328 C4
Crumlin 180 B3
Crumpsall 234 C2
Crumpsbrook 207 F5
Crundale *Kent* 174 C4
Crundale *Pembs.* 176 C1
Crunwere Farm 177 E1
Crutherland Farm 284 A4
Cruwys Morchard 152 B1
Crux Easton 169 F2
Crwbin 178 A1
Cryers Hill 185 D3
Crymlyn 231 E5
Crymych 191 E4
Crynant 179 D2
Crystal Palace 186 C5
Cuaig 318 D4
Cubbington 197 F1
Cubert 146 B4
Cubley 235 G2
Cublington *Bucks.* 198 D5
Cublington *Here.* 194 D4
Cuckfield 159 F1
Cucklington 167 E5
Cuckney 236 C5
Cuckold's Green 215 F3
Cuckoo Bridge 226 A5
Cuckoo's Corner 170 C3
Cuckoo's Nest 220 A1
Cuddesdon 184 A2
Cuddington *Bucks.* 184 C1
Cuddington *Ches.* 233 G5
Cuddington Heath 220 B3
Cuddy Hill 242 A4
Cudham 172 D3
Cudlipptown 149 F3
Cudworth *S.Yorks.* 236 A2
Cudworth *Som.* 153 G1
Cuerdley Cross 233 G4
Cuffley 186 C2
Cuidhaseadair 329 G2
Cuidhir 314 B3
Cuidhtinis
(Quidinish) 326 C5
Cuidrach 317 G4
Cuillin Hills 119
Cuilmuich 291 D5
Cuil-uaine 290 B1
Culag 291 F5
Culbo 321 F3
Culbokie 321 F4
Culbone 164 B3
Culburnie 321 D5
Culcabock 321 F5
Culcharan 290 B1
Culcharry 322 A4
Culcheth 234 A3
Culdrain 312 A1
Culduie 318 D5
Culford 201 G1
Culfordheath 213 G5
Culgaith 260 C5
Culgower 333 E3
Culham 184 A3
Culindrach 282 A4
Culkein 330 C1
Culkerton 182 B3
Cullachie 310 B2
Cullen 324 A3
Cullercoats 271 F4
Cullicudden 321 F3
Culligran 320 C5
Cullingworth 243 G4
Cullipool 289 G3
Cullivoe 345 E2
Culloch 292 C3
Culloden 321 G5
Culloden 119
Cullompton 152 D2
Culmaily 332 D5
Culmalzie 265 E5
Culmington 207 D4
Culmstock 153 E1
Culnacraig 330 C4
Culnadalloch 290 B1
Culnaknock 318 B3
Culnamean 306 A2
Culpho 202 D3
Culquhirk 265 F5
Culrain 332 A5
Culross 285 D1
Culross Palace 119
Culroy 274 B4
Culsh 311 F5
Culshabbin 265 E5
Culswick 342 B3
Culter Allers Farm 276 B2
Cultercullen 313 E2
Cults *Aber.* 312 A1
Cults *Aberdeen* 313 D4
Cults *D. & G.* 257 E2
Cultybraggan Camp 292 C3
Culverhouse Cross 180 A5
Culverstone Green 173 F2
Culverthorpe 225 F3
Culvie 324 A4
Culworth 198 A3
Culzean Castle 119
Cumberhead 275 F2
Cumberlow Green 200 B4
Cumbernauld 284 B2
Cumberworth 239 F5
Cuminestown 324 D5
Cumloden 265 F4
Cummersdale 259 G1
Cummertrees 267 F4
Cummingstown 322 D3
Cumnock 275 D3
Cumnor 183 G2
Cumrew 260 B2
Cumrue 267 E2
Cumstoun 266 A5
Cumwhinton 260 A2
Cumwhitton 260 B2
Cundall 252 D5
Cunninghamhead 283 E5
Cunningsburgh 342 D5
Cunnister 345 E3
Cunnoquhie 294 B3
Cupar 294 B3
Cupar Muir 294 B3
Curbar 235 G5
Curborough 208 D1
Curbridge *Hants.* 157 E1
Curbridge *Oxon.* 183 F2
Curdridge 157 E1
Curdworth 209 D3
Curland 153 F1
Curlew Green 203 E1
Curling Tye Green 188 B2
Curload 166 A5
Curridge 183 G5
Currie 285 F3
Curry Mallet 166 A5
Curry Rivel 166 A5
Curteis' Corner 174 A5
Curtisden Green 173 G4
Curtisknowle 150 D2
Cury 145 D4
Cusgarne 146 B5
Cushnie 324 C3
Cushuish 165 E4
Cusop 194 B3
Cusworth 236 C2
Cutcloy 257 E3
Cutcombe 164 C4
Cutgate 234 C1
Cuthill 321 G1
Cutiau 204 C1
Cutlers Green 201 D4
Cutnall Green 196 A1
Cutsdean 196 C4
Cutsyke 244 D5
Cutthorpe 236 A5
Cutts 342 D4
Cutty Sark 55
Cuttyhill 325 F4
Cuxham 184 B3
Cuxton 173 G2
Cuxwold 238 B2
Cwm *B.Gwent* 180 A2
Cwm *Denb.* 232 B5
Cwm Ffrwd-oer 180 B2
Cwm Gwaun 190 D4
Cwm Head 206 D4
Cwm Irfon 193 E3
Cwm Penmachno 218 A3
Cwm Plysgog 191 E3
Cwmafan 179 D3
Cwmaman 179 G3
Cwmann 192 B3
Cwmbach *Carmar.* 191 F5
Cwmbach *Carmar.* 178 A2
Cwmbach *Powys* 194 A4
Cwmbach *Powys* 193 G2
Cwmbach *R.C.T.* 179 G2
Cwmbelan 205 F4
Cwmbrân 180 B3
Cwmbrwyno 204 D4
Cwmcarn 180 B3
Cwmcarvan 181 D2
Cwm-Cewydd 205 E1
Cwm-cou 191 F3
Cwmcrawnon 180 A1
Cwmdare 179 F2
Cwmdu *Carmar.* 192 C4
Cwmdu *Powys* 194 A5
Cwmduad 191 G4
Cwmerfyn 204 D4
Cwmfelin 179 G2
Cwmfelin Boeth 177 E1
Cwmfelin Mynach 191 F5
Cwmfelinfach 180 A3
Cwmffrwd 178 A1
Cwmgiedd 179 D1
Cwmgors 178 D1
Cwmgwili 178 B1
Cwmgwrach 179 E2
Cwmgwyn 179 G2
Cwmhiraeth 191 G4
Cwmifor 192 C5
Cwmisfael 178 A1
Cwm-Llinau 205 E2
Cwmllyfri 177 G1
Cwmllynfell 178 D1
Cwm-mawr 178 B1
Cwm-miles 191 E5
Cwm-Morgan 191 F4
Cwm-parc 179 F3
Cwmpengraig 191 G4
Cwmpennar 179 G2
Cwmsychbant 192 A3
Cwmsymlog 204 C4
Cwmtillery 180 B2
Cwm-twrch Isaf 179 D1
Cwm-twrch Uchaf 179 D1
Cwm-y-glo 217 E1
Cwmyoy 194 C5
Cwm-yr-Eglwys 190 D3
Cwmyrhaiadr 205 D3
Cwmystwyth 205 D5
Cwrt 204 C2
Cwrt-newydd 192 A3
Cwrt-y-cadno 192 C3
Cwrt-y-gollen 180 B1
Cydwelli (Kidwelly) 178 A2
Cyffylliog 219 D2
Cyfronydd 206 A2
Cymau 219 F2
Cymmer *N.P.T.* 179 E3
Cymmer *R.C.T.* 179 G3
Cyncoed 180 A4
Cynghordy 193 E4
Cynheidre 178 A2
Cynwyd 219 D3
Cynwyl Elfed 191 G5

D

Dabton 266 C1
Daccombe 151 F1
Dacre *Cumb.* 260 A5
Dacre *N.Yorks.* 244 A1
Dacre Banks 244 A1
Daddry Shield 261 E4
Dadford 198 B4
Dadlington 209 G3
Dafen 178 B2
Daffy Green 228 A5
Dagdale 222 B4
Dagenham 187 D4
Daggons 156 A1
Daglingworth 182 B2
Dagnall 185 E1
Dail 290 C1
Dail Beag 328 D3
Dail Bho Dheas
(South Dell) 329 F1
Dail Bho Thuath
(North Dell) 329 F1
Dail Mòr 328 D3
Dailly 274 A5
Dailnamac 290 B1
Dainton 151 E1
Dairsie
(Osnaburgh) 294 C3
Dairy House 247 E5
Daisy Bank 208 C3
Daisy Green 202 B1
Dalabrog 314 C1
Dalavich 290 B3
Dalballoch 309 F5
Dalbeattie 266 C4
Dalblair 275 E4
Dalbog 303 D2
Dalbreck 332 C3
Dalbury 223 D4
Dalby *I.o.M.* 240 A4
Dalby *Lincs.* 226 C1
Dalby *N.Yorks.* 253 F5
Dalby Forest Drive 87
Dalcairnie 274 C5
Dalchalloch 300 C3
Dalchalm 333 E4
Dalchenna 290 C4
Dalchirach 311 D1
Dalchork 332 A3
Dalchreichart 308 B3
Dalchruin 292 C3
Dalcross 321 G5
Dalderby 226 A1
Dalditch 152 D4
Daldownie 311 E4
Dale *Cumb.* 260 B3
Dale *Gt.Man.* 235 D2
Dale *Pembs.* 176 B2
Dale Abbey 223 F4
Dale End *Derbys.* 222 D1
Dale End *N.Yorks.* 243 F3
Dale Head 249 F1
Dale of Walls 342 A2
Dale Park 158 B2
Dalehouse 253 G1
Dalelia 297 G3
Daless 310 A1
Dalestie 311 D3
Dalfad 311 F4
Dalganachan 336 C4
Dalgarven 283 D5
Dalgety Bay 285 F1
Dalgig 275 D4
Dalginross 292 C2
Dalgonar 275 F5
Dalguise 301 E5
Dalhalvaig 336 A3
Dalham 201 F1
Daligan 283 E1
Dalinlongart 282 C1
Dalivaddy 272 B3
Daljarrock 264 C2
Dalkeith 286 A3
Dallachulish 298 B5
Dallas 322 D4
Dallas Dhu Distillery 120
Dallaschyle 322 A5
Dallash 265 F4
Dalleagles 275 D4
Dallinghoo 203 D2
Dallington *E.Suss.* 160 B2
Dallington
Northants. 198 C1
Dallow 252 A5
Dalmadilly 312 C3
Dalmally 291 D2
Dalmarnock 301 F5
Dalmary 292 A5
Dalmellington 274 C5
Dalmeny 285 F2
Dalmichy 332 A3
Dalmigavie 309 G3
Dalmore 321 F3
Dalmuir 283 F2
Dalmunzie House
Hotel 301 F2
Dalnabreck 297 G3
Dalnacarn 301 F3
Dalnaglar Castle 301 G3
Dalnaha 289 F2
Dalnahaitnach 310 A3
Dalnamain 332 C5
Dalnatrat 298 B4
Dalnavie 321 F2
Dalness 299 D4
Dalnessie 332 B3
Dalnigap 264 C3
Dalqueich 293 F4
Dalreoch 264 C2
Dalriech 292 C1
Dalroy 321 G5
Dalrulzian 301 G4
Dalry 283 D5
Dalrymple 274 B4
Dalscote 198 B2
Dalserf 284 B4
Dalsetter 345 E3
Dalshangan 265 G2
Dalskairth 266 D3
Dalston 259 G1
Dalswinton 266 D2
Daltomach 309 G2
Dalton *Cumb.* 249 G5
Dalton *D. & G.* 267 F3
Dalton *Lancs.* 233 F2
Dalton *N.Yorks.* 252 D5
Dalton *N.Yorks.* 252 A2
Dalton *Northumb.* 270 D4
Dalton *Northumb.* 261 F2
Dalton *S.Yorks.* 236 B3
Dalton Castle 95
Dalton Magna 236 B3
Dalton Piercy 263 D4
Dalton-in-Furness 248 D5
Dalton-le-Dale 262 D3
Dalton-on-Tees 252 B2
Daltote 281 F1
Daltra 322 B5
Dalveich 292 B2
Dalvennan 274 B4
Dalvourn 309 F1
Dalwhinnie 300 B1
Dalwood 153 F2
Dam Green 214 B3
Damask Green 200 A5
Damerham 156 A1
Damgate 229 F5
Damnaglaur 256 B3
Damside 293 E3
Danaway 174 A2
Danbury 187 G2
Danby 253 G2
Danby Wiske 252 C3
Dancers Hill 186 B3
Dandaleith 323 E5
Danderhall 286 A3
Dane Bank 234 D3
Dane End 200 B5
Dane Hills 210 A2
Danebridge 221 G1
Danebury Ring 43
Danehill 159 G1
Danesmoor 223 F1
Danestone 313 E3
Daniel's Water 174 B4
Danskine 286 C3
Danthorpe 247 E4
Danzey Green 196 D1
Darby End 208 B4
Darby Green 170 D1
Darenth 187 E5
Daresbury 233 G4
Darfield 236 B2
Dargate 174 C2
Dargues 270 A2
Darite 147 G3
Darland 173 G2
Darlaston 208 B3
Darley 244 B2
Darley Bridge 223 D1
Darley Dale 223 D1
Darley Head 244 A2
Darley Hillside 223 D1
Darlingscott 197 E3
Darlington 252 B1
Darliston 220 C4
Darlton 237 E5
Darnabo 324 C5
Darnall 236 A4
Darnconner 275 D3
Darnford 312 C5
Darngarroch 266 A4
Darnick 277 G2
Darowen 205 E2
Darra 324 C5
Darracott 162 C4
Darras Hall 271 D4
Darrington 236 B1
Darrow Green 215 D3
Darsham 203 F1
Dartfield 325 F4
Dartford 187 E5
Dartington 151 D1
Dartington Crystal 28
Dartmeet 149 G3
Dartmoor 28
Dartmouth 151 E2
Dartmouth Castle 28
Darton 236 A1
Darvel 275 D2
Darvell 160 C1
Darwell Hole 160 B2
Darwen 242 C5
Datchet 185 E5
Datchworth 186 B1
Datchworth Green 186 B1
Daubhill 234 A2
Daugh of
Kinermony 323 E5
Dauntsey 182 B4
Dauntsey Green 182 B4
Dauntsey Lock 182 B4
Dava 310 C1
Davaar 272 C4
Davan 311 G4
Davenham 234 A5
Davenport Green 234 C4
Daventry 198 A1
David Livingstone Centre 120
Davidstow 147 F1
Davington 276 D5
Daviot *Aber.* 312 C2
Daviot *High.* 309 G1
Davoch of Grange 323 G4
Davyhulme 234 B3
Dawley 207 F2
Dawlish 152 C5
Dawn 231 G5
Daws Heath 188 B4
Daw's House 148 D2
Dawsmere 226 C4
Day Green 221 E2
Dayhills 221 G4
Dayhouse Bank 208 B5
Daylesford 197 E5
Ddôl 232 C5
Deadman's Cross 199 G3
Deadwaters 284 B5
Deal 175 F3
Deal Castle 43
Deal Hall 188 D3
Dean *Cumb.* 259 D4
Dean *Devon* 150 D1
Dean *Dorset* 155 F1
Dean *Hants.* 157 E1
Dean *Oxon.* 197 F5
Dean *Som.* 167 D3
Dean Bank 262 B4
Dean Castle 120
Dean Cross 163 F1
Dean Gallery 120
Dean Head 235 G2
Dean Heritage Centre 28
Dean Prior 150 D1
Dean Row 234 C4
Dean Street 173 G3
Deanburnhaugh 277 E4
Deane *Gt.Man.* 234 A2
Deane *Hants.* 169 G2
Deanland 155 F1
Deanlane End 157 G1
Deans Bottom 174 A2
Deanscales 259 D4
Deansgreen 234 A4
Deanshanger 198 C4
Deanston 292 C4
Dearham 259 D3
Debach 202 D2
Debate 268 A3
Debden 201 D4
Debden Cross 201 D4
Debden Green
Essex 201 D4
Debden Green
Essex 186 D3
Debenham 202 C1
Deblin's Green 196 A3
Dechmont 285 E2
Decker Hill 207 G1
Deddington 197 G4
Dedham 202 B4
Dedham Heath 202 B4
Dedworth 185 E5
Deecastle 311 G5
Deene 211 E3
Deenethorpe 211 E3
Deep Sea World 120
Deepcar 235 G3
Deepcut 171 E2
Deepdale *Cumb.* 250 C4
Deepdale *N.Yorks.* 251 D5
Deeping Gate 211 G2
Deeping St. James 211 G2
Deeping
St. Nicholas 212 A1
Deepweir 181 D4
Deerhill 323 G4
Deerhurst 196 A5
Deerhurst Walton 196 A5
Deerton Street 174 B2
Defford 196 B3
Defynnog 193 F5
Deganwy 231 F5
Degnish 289 G3
Deighton *N.Yorks.* 252 C2
Deighton *W.Yorks.* 235 F1
Deighton *York* 245 F3
Deiniolen 217 E1
Delabole 147 E1
Delamere 220 C1
Delavorar 311 D3
Delfrigs 313 E2
Dell Lodge 310 C3
Dell Quay 158 A3
Delliefure 310 C1
Delly End 183 F1
Delnabo 311 D3
Delny 321 G2
Delph 235 D2
Delphorrie 311 G3
Delves 262 A3
Delves, The 208 C3
Delvine 301 G5
Dembleby 225 F4
Den, The 283 E4
Denaby 236 B3
Denaby Main 236 B3
Denbies Wine Estate 43
Denbigh (Dinbych) 218 D1
Denbigh Castle 118
Denbury 151 E1
Denby 223 E3
Denby Dale 235 G2
Denby Pottery 71
Denchworth 183 F3
Dendron 248 D5
Denend 312 B1
Denford 211 E5
Dengie 188 C2
Denham *Bucks.* 185 F4
Denham *Suff.* 214 C4
Denham *Suff.* 201 F1
Denham Green 185 F4
Denham Street 214 C4
Denhead *Aber.* 312 C3
Denhead *Aber.* 325 F4
Denhead *Fife* 294 C3
Denhead of
Arbirlot 303 D5
Denhead of Gray 294 B1
Denholm 277 G4
Denholme 243 G4
Denholme Clough 243 G4
Denio 216 C4
Denmans 44
Denmead 157 F1
Denmill 312 D3
Denmoss 324 B5
Dennington 203 D1
Denny 284 C1
Denny Abbey & Farmland Museum 78
Dennyloanhead 284 C1
Denshaw 235 D1
Denside 312 D5
Densole 175 E4
Denston 201 F2
Denstone 222 B3
Dent 250 C4
Denton *Cambs.* 211 G4
Denton *Darl.* 252 B1
Denton *E.Suss.* 159 G3
Denton *Gt.Man.* 234 D3
Denton *Kent* 175 E4
Denton *Kent* 187 F5
Denton *Lincs.* 225 D4
Denton *N.Yorks.* 244 A3
Denton *Norf.* 215 D3
Denton *Northants.* 198 D2
Denton *Oxon.* 184 A2
Denton's Green 233 F3
Denver 213 E2
Denvilles 157 G2
Denwick 279 G5
Deopham 228 B5
Deopham Green 214 B2
Depden 201 F2
Depden Green 201 F2
Deptford *Gt.Lon.* 186 C5
Deptford *Wilts.* 168 B4
Derby 223 E4
Derby Industrial Museum 71
Derbyhaven 240 A5
Dereham
(East Dereham) 228 A4
Dererach 289 E2
Deri 180 A2
Derril 162 D5
Derringstone 175 E4
Derrington 221 F5
Derriton 162 D5
Derry 292 B2
Derry Hill 182 B5
Derrythorpe 237 F2
Dersingham 227 E4
Dervaig 296 D4
Derwen 219 D2
Derwenlas 204 D3
Derwydd 178 C1
Derybruich 282 A2
Desborough 210 D4
Desford 209 G2
Detchant 279 E3
Dethick 223 E2
Detling 173 G3
Deuddwr 206 B1
Deunant 218 C1
Deuxhill 207 F4
Devauden 181 D3
Devil's Bridge
(Pontarfynach) 204 D5
Devitts Green 209 E3
Devizes 168 B1
Devonport 150 A2
Devonside 293 E5
Devoran 145 E3
Dewar 286 A5
Dewlish 155 D3
Dewsall Court 195 D4
Dewsbury 244 B5
Dewsbury Moor 244 B5
Dhiseig 289 D1
Dhoon 240 C3
Dhoor 240 C2
Dhowin 240 C1
Dhuhallow 309 E2
Dial Green 171 E5
Dial Post 159 D2
Dibden 156 D2
Dibden Hill 185 E3
Dibden Purlieu 156 D2
Dickens House Museum 44
Dicker, The 160 A3
Dickleburgh 214 C3
Dickleburgh Moor 214 C3
Didbrook 196 C4
Didcot 184 A3
Diddington 199 G1
Diddlebury 207 E4
Didley 195 D4
Didling 158 A2
Didmarton 182 A4
Didsbury 234 C3
Didworthy 150 C1
Digby 225 F2
Digg 318 A3
Diggle 235 F2
Digmoor 233 F2
Digswell 186 B1
Dihewyd 192 A2
Dildawn 266 B5
Dilham 229 E3
Dilhorne 221 G3
Dillington 199 G1
Dilston 261 F1
Dilton Marsh 167 F3
Dilwyn 194 D2
Dilwyn Common 194 D2
Dimple 234 B1
Dinas *Carmar.* 191 F4
Dinas *Gwyn.* 217 D2

Dinas *Gwyn.* 216 B4
Dinas Cross 190 D4
Dinas Dinlle 216 D2
Dinas Powys 180 A5
Dinas-Mawddwy 205 E1
Dinbych (Denbigh) 218 D1
Dinbych-y-Pysgod (Tenby) 177 E2
Dinckley 242 C4
Dinder 166 C3
Dinedor 195 E4
Dinefwr Park 110
Dingestow 181 D1
Dingley 210 C4
Dingwall 321 E4
Dinlabyre 268 D2
Dinnet 311 G5
Dinnington *S.Yorks.* 236 C4
Dinnington *Som.* 154 A1
Dinnington *T. & W.* 271 E4
Dinorwig 217 E1
Dinosaur Museum 28
Dinton *Bucks.* 184 C1
Dinton *Wilts.* 168 B4
Dinvin 264 B5
Dinwoodie Mains 267 F1
Dinworthy 162 D4
Dipford 165 F5
Dippen *Arg. & B.* 272 C2
Dippen *N.Ayr.* 273 F3
Dippenhall 170 D3
Dipple *Moray* 323 F4
Dipple *S.Ayr.* 274 A5
Diptford 150 D2
Dipton 262 A2
Dirdhu 310 C2
Dirleton 286 C1
Dirleton Castle & Gardens 120
Discoed 194 B1
Discovery Point & R.R.S Discovery 120
Diseworth 223 F5
Dishes 341 E4
Dishforth 252 C5
Dishley 223 G5
Disley 235 D4
Diss 214 C3
Disserth 193 G2
Distington 258 D4
Ditcheat 166 D4
Ditchingham 215 E2
Ditchley 197 F5
Ditchling 159 F2
Ditteridge 167 F1
Dittisham 151 E2
Ditton *Halton* 233 F4
Ditton *Kent* 173 G3
Ditton Green 201 E2
Ditton Priors 207 F4
Dixton *Glos.* 196 B4
Dixton *Mon.* 181 E1
Dobcross 235 D2
Dobwalls 147 G3
Dobwalls Family Adventure Park 28
Doc Penfro (Pembroke Dock) 176 C2
Doccombe 152 A4
Dochgarroch 309 F1
Dock Museum 95
Dockenfield 170 D3
Docker *Cumb.* 249 G3
Docker *Lancs.* 249 G5
Docking 227 F4
Docklow 195 E2
Dockray *Cumb.* 259 G4
Dockray *Cumb.* 259 F1
Docwra's Manor Gardens 78
Dodbrooke 150 D3
Doddenham 195 G2
Doddinghurst 187 E3
Doddington *Cambs.* 212 C3
Doddington *Kent* 174 B3
Doddington *Lincs.* 237 G5
Doddington *Northumb.* 279 D3
Doddington *Shrop.* 207 F5
Doddington Hall 71
Doddiscombsleigh 152 B4
Doddycross 148 D4
Dodford *Northants.* 198 B1
Dodford *Worcs.* 208 B5
Dodington *S.Glos.* 181 G4
Dodington *Som.* 165 E3
Dodington Ash 181 G5
Dodleston 220 A1
Dods Leigh 222 B4
Dodscott 163 F4
Dodworth 236 A2
Doehole 223 E2
Doffcocker 234 A1
Dog Village 152 C3
Dogdyke 226 A2
Dogmersfield 170 C2
Dogsthorpe 212 A2
Dol Fawr 205 E2
Dolanog 205 G1
Dolau *Powys* 194 A1
Dolau *R.C.T.* 179 G4
Dolaucothi Gold Mine 110
Dolbenmaen 217 E3
Doley 221 E5
Dolfach 205 F5
Dolfor 206 A4
Dolgarreg 192 D4
Dolgarrog 218 A1
Dolgellau 204 D1
Dolgoch 204 C2
Dolgran 192 A4
Doll 333 D4
Dollar 293 E5
Dollarbeg 293 E5
Dolphin 232 C5
Dolphinholme 242 B2
Dolphinton 285 F5
Dolton 163 F4
Dolwen *Conwy* 231 G5
Dolwen *Powys* 205 F2
Dolwyddelan 218 A2
Dôl-y-bont 204 C4
Dol-y-cannau 194 A3
Dolyhir 194 B2
Dolywern 219 F4
Domgay 206 B1
Doncaster 236 C2
Donhead St. Andrew 168 A5
Donhead St. Mary 168 A5
Donibristle 285 F1
Doniford 165 D3
Donington *Lincs.* 226 A4
Donington *Shrop.* 208 A2
Donington Grand Prix Collection 71
Donington le Heath 209 G1
Donington on Bain 238 C4
Donisthorpe 209 F1
Donna Nook 239 E3
Donnington *Glos.* 197 D5
Donnington *Here.* 195 G4
Donnington *Shrop.* 207 E2
Donnington *Tel. & W.* 207 G1
Donnington *W.Berks.* 169 F1
Donnington *W.Suss.* 158 A3
Donyatt 153 G1
Dorchester *Dorset* 154 C3
Dorchester *Oxon.* 184 A3
Dordon 209 E2
Dore 236 A4
Dores 309 E1
Dorket Head 223 G3
Dorking 171 G3
Dorley's Corner 203 E1
Dormans Park 172 C4
Dormansland 172 D4
Dormanstown 263 E5
Dormer's Wells 186 A4
Dormington 195 E3
Dormston 196 B2
Dorn 197 E4
Dorney 185 E5
Dorney Court 44
Dorney Reach 185 E5
Dornie 307 E2
Dornoch 321 G1
Dornoch Cathedral 120
Dornock 268 A5
Dorothy Clive Garden, The 65
Dorrery 336 C3
Dorridge 209 D5
Dorrington *Lincs.* 225 F2
Dorrington *Shrop.* 207 D2
Dorsell 312 A3
Dorsington 196 D3
Dorstone 194 C3
Dorton 184 B1
Dorusduain 307 F2
Dosthill 209 E3
Dotland 261 F2
Dottery 154 A3
Doublebois 147 F3
Dougalston 283 G2
Dougarie 273 D2
Doughton 182 A3
Douglas *I.o.M.* 240 B4
Douglas *S.Lan.* 275 G2
Douglas and Angus 294 C1
Douglas Water 275 G2
Douglastown 302 C5
Doulting 166 D3
Dounby 340 A4
Doune *Arg. & B.* 291 F5
Doune *Arg. & B.* 291 F3
Doune *High.* 310 A3
Doune *High.* 331 G4
Doune *Stir.* 292 C4
Dounepark 324 C3
Douneside 311 G4
Dounie *High.* 321 F1
Dounie *High.* 332 A5
Dounreay 336 B2
Dousland 150 B1
Dovaston 220 A5
Dove Cottage 95
Dove Dale 71
Dove Holes 235 E5
Dovenby 259 D3
Dovendale 238 D4
Dover 175 F4
Dover Castle 44
Dovercourt 202 D4
Doverdale 196 A1
Doveridge 222 C4
Doversgreen 172 B4
Dowally 301 F5
Dowdeswell 196 C5
Dowhill 274 A5
Dowlais 179 G2
Dowland 163 F4
Dowlands 153 F3
Dowlish Ford 153 G1
Dowlish Wake 153 G1
Down Ampney 182 D3
Down End 166 A3
Down Hatherley 196 A5
Down St. Mary 152 A2
Down, The 207 F3
Down Thomas 150 B3
Downderry 148 D5
Downe 172 D2
Downend *I.o.W.* 157 E4
Downend *S.Glos.* 181 F5
Downend *W.Berks.* 183 G5
Downfield 294 B1
Downfields 213 E5
Downgate 149 D3
Downham *Essex* 187 G3
Downham *Lancs.* 243 D3
Downham *Northumb.* 278 C3
Downham Market 213 E2
Downhead *Cornw.* 147 G1
Downhead *Som.* 167 D3
Downhead *Som.* 166 C5
Downholland Cross 233 E2
Downholme 252 A3
Downies 313 E5
Downley 185 D3
Downs 180 A5
Downside *N.Som.* 166 B1
Downside *Som.* 166 D3
Downside *Som.* 166 D2
Downside *Surr.* 171 G2
Downton *Devon* 149 F2
Downton *Devon* 151 E2
Downton *Hants.* 156 B3
Downton *Wilts.* 168 C5
Downton on the Rock 206 D5
Dowsby 225 G5
Dowthwaitehead 259 G4
Doxey 221 G5
Doynton 181 G5
Drabblegate 228 D3
Draethen 180 B4
Draffan 284 B5
Dragley Beck 249 D5
Drakeland Corner 150 B2
Drakelow 208 A4
Drakemyre 283 D4
Drakes Broughton 196 B3
Drakes Cross 208 C5
Draughton *N.Yorks.* 243 G2
Draughton *Northants.* 210 C5
Drax 245 F5
Draycot Foliat 183 D5
Draycote 197 G1
Draycott *Derbys.* 223 F4
Draycott *Glos.* 197 D4
Draycott *Shrop.* 208 A3
Draycott *Som.* 166 B2
Draycott *Worcs.* 196 A3
Draycott in the Clay 222 C5
Draycott in the Moors 221 G4
Drayford 152 A1
Draynes 147 G3
Drayton *Leics.* 210 D3
Drayton *Lincs.* 226 A4
Drayton *Norf.* 228 C4
Drayton *Oxon.* 197 G3
Drayton *Oxon.* 183 G3
Drayton *Ports.* 157 F2
Drayton *Som.* 166 B5
Drayton *Warks.* 197 D2
Drayton *Worcs.* 208 B5
Drayton Bassett 209 D2
Drayton Beauchamp 185 E1
Drayton Manor Park 65
Drayton Parslow 198 D5
Drayton St. Leonard 184 A3
Drebley 243 G2
Dreemskerry 240 C2
Dreenhill 176 C1
Drefach *Carmar.* 191 G4
Drefach *Carmar.* 178 B1
Dre-fach *Cere.* 192 B3
Drefelin 191 G4
Dreghorn 274 B2
Drem 286 C2
Dreumasdal (Drimsdale) 304 A1
Drewsteignton 152 A3
Driby 239 D5
Driffield *E.Riding* 246 C2
Driffield *Glos.* 182 C3
Drigg 248 B3
Drighlington 244 B5
Drimfern 290 C3
Drimlee 290 D3
Drimnin 297 E4
Drimore 315 F5
Drimpton 154 A2
Drimsdale (Dreumasdal) 304 A1
Drimsynie 291 D4
Drimvore 290 A5
Drinan 306 B3
Dringhouses 245 E2
Drinisiader 327 D4
Drinkstone 202 A1
Drinkstone Green 202 A1
Drishaig 291 D3
Drissaig 290 B3
Drointon 222 B5
Droitwich Spa 196 A1
Dron 293 G3
Dronfield 236 A5
Dronfield Woodhouse 236 A5
Drongan 274 C4
Dronley 294 B1
Droop 155 D2
Dropmore 185 E4
Droxford 157 F1
Droylsden 234 D3
Druid 218 D3
Druidston 176 B1
Druidstone Park 44
Druimarbin 298 C2
Druimavuic 298 C5
Druimdrishaig 281 F2
Druimindarroch 297 F1
Druimkinnerras 309 D1
Drum *Arg. & B.* 282 A2
Drum *P. & K.* 293 F4
Drum Castle 120
Drumachloy 282 B3
Drumbeg 334 A5
Drumblade 324 A5
Drumblair 324 B5
Drumbuie *D. & G.* 275 F4
Drumbuie *High.* 307 D1
Drumburgh 259 F1
Drumchapel 283 G2
Drumchardine 321 E5
Drumchork 319 E1
Drumclog 275 E2
Drumdelgie 323 G5
Drumderfit 321 F4
Drumeldrie 294 C4
Drumelzier 276 C2
Drumfearn 306 C3
Drumfern 298 B2
Drumgarve 272 C3
Drumgley 302 C4
Drumguish 309 G5
Drumhead 312 B5
Drumin 311 D1
Drumine 321 G4
Drumjohn 265 G1
Drumlamford House 265 D3
Drumlanrig Castle 120
Drumlasie 312 B4
Drumlemble 272 B4
Drumlithie 303 F1
Drummond *High.* 321 F3
Drummond *Stir.* 292 B4
Drummond Castle Gardens 120
Drummore 256 B3
Drummuir 323 F5
Drummuir Castle 323 F5
Drumnadrochit 309 E2
Drumnagorrach 324 A4
Drumnatorran 298 A3
Drumoak 312 C5
Drumore 272 C3
Drumour 293 E1
Drumpellier Country Park 120
Drumrash 266 A3
Drumrunie 331 D4
Drums 313 E2
Drums, The 302 B3
Drumsturdy 294 C1
Drumuie 318 A5
Drumuillie 310 B2
Drumvaich 292 B4
Drumwhindle 313 E1
Drumwhirn 266 B2
Drunkendub 303 E5
Druridge 271 E2
Drury 219 F1
Drusillas Park 44
Drws-y-nant 218 B5
Dry Doddington 224 D3
Dry Drayton 200 B1
Dry Harbour 318 C4
Dry Sandford 183 G2
Dry Street 187 F4
Drybeck 250 B1
Drybridge *Moray* 323 G3
Drybridge *N.Ayr.* 274 B2
Drybrook 181 F1
Dryburgh 277 G2
Dryburgh Abbey 120
Drygrange 277 G2
Dryhope 277 D3
Drymen 283 F1
Drymuir 325 E5
Drynoch 306 A1
Dryslwyn 192 B5
Dryton 207 E2
Duachy 290 A2
Duart Castle 120
Dubford 324 C3
Dubhchladach 281 G3
Dubheads 293 E2
Dublin 202 C1
Dubton 303 D4
Duchal 283 E3
Duchally 331 F3
Duchray 291 G4
Duck Bay 283 E1
Duck End *Beds.* 199 F3
Duck End *Cambs.* 200 A1
Duck End *Essex* 201 E5
Duck Street 244 A1
Duckington 220 B2
Ducklington 183 F2
Duckmanton 236 B5
Duck's Cross 199 G2
Ducks Island 186 B3
Duddenhoe End 200 C4
Duddingston 285 G2
Duddington 211 E2
Duddlestone 165 F5
Duddleswell 159 G1
Duddo 287 G5
Duddon 220 C1
Duddon Bridge 248 C4
Dudleston 220 A4
Dudleston Heath 220 A4
Dudley *T. & W.* 271 E4
Dudley *W.Mid.* 208 B3
Dudley Port 208 B3
Dudley Zoo & Castle 65
Dudlow's Green 234 A4
Dudmaston 65
Dudsbury 155 G3
Duff House 120
Duffield 223 E3
Duffryn 179 E3
Dufftown 311 F1
Duffus 323 D3
Dufton 260 C5
Duggleby 246 A1
Duiar 310 D1
Duible 333 E2
Duiletter 291 D2
Duinish 300 B3
Duirinish 307 D1
Duisdealmor 306 D3
Duisky 298 C2
Duke End 209 E4
Dukestown 180 A1
Dukinfield 234 D3
Dulas 230 C4
Dulax 311 F3
Dulcote 166 C3
Dulford 153 D2
Dull 300 D5
Dullatur 284 B2
Dullingham 201 E2
Dullingham Ley 201 E2
Dulnain Bridge 310 B2
Duloe *Beds.* 199 G1
Duloe *Cornw.* 147 G4
Dulsie 322 B5
Dulverton 164 C5
Dulwich 186 C5
Dulwich Picture Gallery 55
Dumbarton 283 E2
Dumbleton 196 C4
Dumcrieff 276 C5
Dumeath 311 G1
Dumfin 283 E1
Dumfries 267 D3
Dumgoyne 283 G1
Dummer 169 G3
Dun 303 E4
Dunach 290 A2
Dunalastair 300 C4
Dunan *Arg. & B.* 282 C2
Dunan *High.* 306 B2
Dunans 290 C5
Dunball 166 A3
Dunbar 287 D2
Dunbeath 337 D5
Dunbeg 290 A1
Dunblane 292 C4
Dunbog 294 A3
Dunbridge 169 E5
Duncansby Head 120
Duncanston *Aber.* 312 A2
Duncanston *High.* 321 E4
Dunchideock 152 B4
Dunchurch 209 G5
Duncombe Park 87
Duncote 198 B2
Duncow 267 D2
Duncraggan 292 A4
Duncrievie 293 G4
Duncroist 292 A1
Duncrub 293 F3
Duncryne 283 F1
Duncton 158 B2
Dundee 294 C1
Dundee Airport 294 B2
Dundee Contemporary Arts 121
Dundon 166 B4
Dundon Hayes 166 B4
Dundonald 274 B2
Dundonnell 319 G1
Dundraw 259 F2
Dundreggan 308 C3
Dundrennan 258 A2
Dundridge 157 E1
Dundry 166 C1
Dunearn 285 G1
Dunecht 312 C4
Dunfermline 285 E1
Dunfermline Abbey & Palace 121
Dunfield 182 D3
Dunford Bridge 235 F2
Dungate 174 B3
Dungavel 275 E2
Dungworth 235 G3
Dunham 237 F5
Dunham Massey Hall, Park & Gardens 95
Dunham Town 234 B4
Dunham Woodhouses 234 B4
Dunham-on-the-Hill 233 F5
Dunhampton 196 A1
Dunholme 238 A5
Dunino 294 D3
Dunipace 284 C1
Dunira 292 C2
Dunkeld 301 F5
Dunkerton 167 E2
Dunkeswell 153 E2
Dunkeswick 244 C3
Dunkirk *Ches.* 233 E5
Dunkirk *Kent* 174 C3
Dunk's Green 173 F3
Dunlappie 303 D3
Dunley *Hants.* 169 F2
Dunley *Worcs.* 195 G1
Dunlop 283 F5
Dunloskin 282 C2
Dunmere 147 E3
Dunmore *Arg. & B.* 281 F3
Dunmore *Falk.* 284 C1
Dunn 337 D3
Dunn Street 173 G2
Dunnabie 268 A3
Dunnet 337 E1
Dunnichen 302 D5
Dunning 293 F3
Dunnington *E.Riding* 247 D2
Dunnington *Warks.* 196 C2
Dunnington *York* 245 F2
Dunnockshaw 243 E5
Dunnottar Castle 121
Dunoon 282 C2
Dunragit 264 C5
Dunrobin Castle 121
Dunrostan 281 F1
Duns 287 E4
Duns Tew 197 G5
Dunsa 235 G5
Dunsby 225 G5
Dunscore 266 C2
Dunscroft 237 D2
Dunsdale 253 F1
Dunsden Green 184 C5
Dunsfold 171 F4
Dunsford 152 B4
Dunshalt 294 A3
Dunshill 196 A4
Dunsinnan 293 G1
Dunsland Cross 163 E5
Dunsley *N.Yorks.* 254 B1
Dunsley *Staffs.* 208 A4
Dunsmore 185 D2
Dunsop Bridge 242 C2
Dunstable 199 F5
Dunstable Downs 78
Dunstall 222 C5
Dunstall Green 201 F1
Dunstan 279 G5
Dunstan Steads 279 G4
Dunstanburgh Castle 103
Dunster 164 C3
Dunster Castle & Gardens 28
Dunster Watermill 28
Dunston *Lincs.* 225 F1
Dunston *Norf.* 228 D5
Dunston *Staffs.* 208 B1
Dunston Heath 208 B1
Dunston Hill 262 B1
Dunstone *Devon* 152 A5
Dunstone *Devon* 150 B2
Dunsville 237 D2
Dunswell 246 C4
Dunsyre 285 E5
Dunterton 149 D3
Duntisbourne Abbots 182 B2
Duntisbourne Leer 182 B2
Duntisbourne Rouse 182 B2
Duntish 154 C2
Duntocher 283 F2
Dunton *Beds.* 200 A3
Dunton *Bucks.* 198 D5
Dunton *Norf.* 227 G4
Dunton Bassett 210 A3
Dunton Green 173 E3
Dunton Wayletts 187 F3
Duntulm 318 A2
Dunure 274 A4
Dunure Mains 274 A4
Dunvant 178 B3
Dunvegan 317 F5
Dunwich 215 F4
Dunwich Heath 78
Dura 294 C3
Durdar 260 A2
Durdle Door 28
Durgan 145 F4
Durgates 173 F5
Durham 262 B3
Durham Cathedral 103
Durinemast 297 F4
Durisdeer 275 G5
Durleigh 165 F4
Durley *Hants.* 157 E1
Durley *Wilts.* 168 D1
Durley Street 157 E1
Durlow Common 195 F4
Durnamuck 330 C5
Durness 334 D2
Durno 312 C2
Duror 298 B4
Durran *Arg. & B.* 290 B4
Durran *High.* 337 D2
Durrants 157 G2
Durrington *W.Suss.* 158 D3
Durrington *Wilts.* 168 C3
Dursley 181 G3
Dursley Cross 181 F1
Durston 165 F5
Durweston 155 E2
Dury 343 D1
Duston 198 C1
Duthie Park & David Welch Winter Gardens 121
Duthil 310 B2
Dutlas 206 B5
Duton Hill 201 E5
Dutson 148 D2
Dutton 233 G5
Duxford 200 C3
Dwygyfylchi 231 F5
Dwyran 216 D1
Dyce 313 D3
Dyfatty 178 A2
Dyffryn *Bridgend* 179 E3
Dyffryn (Valley) *I.o.A.* 230 A5
Dyffryn *Pembs.* 190 C4
Dyffryn *V. of Glam.* 179 G5
Dyffryn Ardudwy 217 E5
Dyffryn Castell 205 D4
Dyffryn Ceidrych 192 D5
Dyffryn Cellwen 179 E1
Dyke *Devon* 162 D3
Dyke *Lincs.* 225 G5
Dyke *Moray* 322 B4
Dykehead *Angus* 302 B3
Dykehead *N.Lan.* 284 C4
Dykehead *Stir.* 292 A5
Dykelands 303 F3
Dykends 302 A4
Dykeside 324 C5
Dylife 205 E3
Dymchurch 161 G1
Dymock 195 G4
Dyrham 181 G5
Dyrham Park 28
Dysart 294 B5
Dyserth 232 B5

E

Eabost 305 G1
Eachwick 270 D4
Eadar dha Fhadhail 328 B4
Eagland Hill 242 A3
Eagle 225 D1
Eagle Barnsdale 225 D1
Eagle Moor 225 D1
Eaglescliffe 252 D1
Eaglesfield *Cumb.* 259 D4
Eaglesfield *D. & G.* 268 A4
Eaglesham 283 G4
Eaglethorpe 211 F3
Eagley 234 B1
Eairy 240 A4
Eakley 198 D2
Eakring 224 B1
Ealand 237 E1
Ealing 186 A4
Eamont Bridge 260 B5
Earby 243 F3
Earcroft 242 C5
Eardington 207 G3
Eardisland 194 D2
Eardisley 194 C3
Eardiston *Shrop.* 220 A5
Eardiston *Worcs.* 195 F1
Earith 212 B5
Earl Shilton 209 G3
Earl Soham 202 D1
Earl Sterndale 222 B1
Earl Stonham 202 C2
Earle 279 D4
Earlestown 233 G3
Earley 184 C5
Earlham 228 C5
Earlish 317 G3
Earls Barton 199 D1
Earls Colne 201 G5
Earl's Common 196 B2
Earl's Court 186 B5
Earl's Croome 196 A3
Earl's Green 202 B1
Earlsdon 209 F5
Earlsferry 294 C4
Earlsford 312 D1
Earlsheaton 244 B5
Earlston 277 G2
Earlswood *Mon.* 181 D3
Earlswood *Surr.* 172 B4
Earlswood *Warks.* 208 D5
Earnley 158 A4
Earnshaw Bridge 242 B5
Earsairidh 314 C4
Earsdon 271 F4
Earsdon Moor 271 D2
Earsham 215 E3
Earsham Street 214 D4
Earswick 245 F2
Eartham 158 B3
Earthcott Green 181 F4
Eas a' Chual Aluinn 121
Easby 253 E2
Easdale *Arg. & B.* 289 G3
Easdale *Arg. & B.* 289 G3
Easdale Island Folk Museum 121
Easebourne 171 D5
Easenhall 209 G5
Eashing 171 E3
Easington *Bucks.* 184 B1
Easington *Dur.* 262 D3
Easington *E.Riding* 239 D1
Easington *Northumb.* 279 F3
Easington *Oxon.* 184 B3
Easington *R. & C.* 253 G1
Easington Colliery 262 D3
Easington Lane 262 C3
Easingwold 245 E1
Easole Street 175 E3
Eassie 302 B5
East Aberthaw 164 D1
East Acton 186 B4
East Allington 151 D3
East Anglia Transport Museum 70
East Anstey 164 B5
East Anton 169 E3
East Appleton 252 B3
East Ardsley 244 C5
East Ashey 157 E4
East Ashling 158 A3
East Auchronie 312 D4
East Ayton 254 C4
East Barkwith 238 B4
East Barming 173 G3
East Barnby 254 B1
East Barnet 186 B3
East Barsham 228 A2
East Beckham 228 C2
East Bedfont 185 F5
East Bergholt 202 B4
East Bierley 244 A5
East Bilney 228 A4
East Blatchington 159 G4
East Boldon 262 C1
East Boldre 156 C2
East Bolton 279 F5
East Bower 166 A4
East Brent 166 A2
East Bridge 203 F1
East Bridgford 224 B3
East Brora 333 E4
East Buckland 163 G2
East Budleigh 153 D4
East Burnham 185 E4
East Burra 342 C4
East Burrafirth 342 C2
East Burton 155 E4
East Butsfield 262 A3
East Butterleigh 152 C2
East Butterwick 237 F2
East Cairnbeg 303 F2
East Calder 285 E3
East Carleton 228 C5
East Carlton *Northants.* 210 D4
East Carlton *W.Yorks.* 244 B3
East Chaldon (Chaldon Herring) 155 D4
East Challow 183 F4
East Charleton 151 D3
East Chelborough 154 B2
East Chiltington 159 F2
East Chinnock 154 A1
East Chisenbury 168 C2
East Clandon 171 F2
East Claydon 198 C5
East Clyne 333 E4
East Clyth 337 E5
East Coker 154 B1
East Compton *Dorset* 155 E1
East Compton *Som.* 166 D3
East Coombe 152 B2
East Cornworthy 151 E2
East Cottingwith 245 G3
East Cowes 157 E3

East Cowick 245 F5
East Cowton 252 C2
East Cramlington 271 E4
East Cranmore 167 D3
East Creech 155 F4
East Croachy 309 F2
East Darlochan 272 B3
East Davoch 311 G4
East Dean *E.Suss.* 160 A4
East Dean *Hants.* 169 D5
East Dean *W.Suss.* 158 B2
East Dereham (Dereham) 228 A4
East Down 163 F1
East Drayton 237 E5
East Dundry 166 C1
East Ella 246 C5
East End *E.Riding* 247 D4
East End *E.Riding* 247 E5
East End *Essex* 188 D2
East End *Hants.* 169 F1
East End *Hants.* 156 C3
East End *Herts.* 200 C5
East End *Kent* 174 A5
East End *Kent* 174 B1
East End *M.K.* 199 E3
East End *N.Som.* 181 D5
East End *Oxon.* 183 F1
East End *Poole* 155 F3
East End *Som.* 166 C2
East End *Suff.* 202 C4
East End *Suff.* 202 C2
East Farleigh 173 G3
East Farndon 210 C4
East Ferry 237 F3
East Firsby 238 A4
East Fleetham 279 G4
East Fortune 286 C2
East Garston 183 F5
East Ginge 183 G4
East Goscote 210 B1
East Grafton 169 D1
East Green *Suff.* 203 F1
East Green *Suff.* 201 E2
East Grimstead 168 D5
East Grinstead 172 C5
East Guldeford 161 E1
East Haddon 198 B1
East Hagbourne 184 A4
East Halton 238 B1
East Ham 186 D4
East Hanney 183 G3
East Hanningfield 187 G2
East Hardwick 236 B1
East Harling 214 A3
East Harlsey 252 D3
East Harnham 168 C5
East Harptree 166 C2
East Hartford 271 E4
East Harting 157 G1
East Hatch 168 A5
East Hatley 200 A2
East Hauxwell 252 A3
East Haven 295 D1
East Heckington 225 G3
East Hedleyhope 262 A3
East Helmsdale 333 F3
East Hendred 183 G4
East Herrington 262 C2
East Heslerton 254 C5
East Hewish 166 B1
East Hoathly 160 A2
East Holme 155 E4
East Horndon 187 F4
East Horrington 166 C3
East Horsley 171 F2
East Horton 279 E3
East Howe 155 G3
East Huntspill 166 A3
East Hyde 186 A1
East Ilsley 183 G4
East Keal 226 B1
East Kennett 168 C1
East Keswick 244 C3
East Kilbride 284 A4
East Kimber 149 E1
East Kirkby 226 B1
East Knapton 254 B5
East Knighton 155 E4
East Knowstone 164 B5
East Knoyle 167 F4
East Kyloe 279 E3
East Lambrook 154 A1
East Lambrook Manor 28
East Langdon 175 F4
East Langton 210 C3
East Langwell 332 C4
East Lavant 158 A3
East Lavington 158 B2
East Layton 252 A1
East Leake 223 G5
East Learmouth 278 C3
East Learney 312 B4
East Leigh *Devon* 152 A2
East Leigh *Devon* 152 A1
East Leigh *Devon* 151 D2
East Leigh *Devon* 150 C2
East Lexham 213 G1
East Lilburn 279 E4
East Linton 286 C2
East Liss 170 C5
East Lockinge 183 G4
East Looe 147 G4
East Lound 237 E2
East Lulworth 155 E4
East Lutton 246 B1
East Lydford 166 C4
East Lyn 164 A3
East Lyng 166 A5
East Mains 312 B5
East Malling 173 G3
East Malling Heath 173 F3
East March 294 C1
East Marden 158 A2
East Markham 237 E5
East Martin 155 G1
East Marton 243 F2
East Meon 170 B5
East Mere 152 C1
East Mersea 189 D1
East Mey 337 F1
East Molesey 171 G1
East Moor 244 C5
East Morden 155 F3
East Morriston 286 D5
East Morton 244 A3
East Ness 253 F5
East Newton 247 E4
East Norton 210 C2
East Oakley 169 G2
East Ogwell 152 B5
East Orchard 155 E1
East Ord 287 G4
East Panson 149 D1
East Parley 156 A3
East Peckham 173 F4
East Pennard 166 C4
East Portlemouth 150 D4
East Prawle 151 D4
East Preston 158 C3
East Pulham 154 D2
East Putford 163 D4
East Quantoxhead 165 E3
East Rainton 262 C3
East Ravendale 238 C3
East Raynham 227 G5
East Rigton 244 C3
East Rolstone 166 A1
East Rounton 252 D2
East Row 254 B1
East Rudham 227 G5
East Runton 228 D1
East Ruston 229 E3
East Saltoun 286 B3
East Shefford 183 F5
East Sleekburn 271 E3
East Somerset Railway 29
East Somerton 229 F4
East Stockwith 237 E3
East Stoke *Dorset* 155 E4
East Stoke *Notts.* 224 C3
East Stour 167 F5
East Stourmouth 175 E2
East Stratton 169 G3
East Street 166 C4
East Studdal 175 F4
East Suisnish 306 B1
East Taphouse 147 F3
East Thirston 271 D2
East Tilbury 187 F5
East Tisted 170 C4
East Torrington 238 B4
East Town 166 D3
East Tuddenham 228 B4
East Tytherley 169 D5
East Tytherton 182 B5
East Village 152 B2
East Wall 207 E3
East Walton 213 F1
East Wellow 169 E5
East Wemyss 294 B5
East Whitburn 285 D3
East Wickham 187 D5
East Williamston 177 D2
East Winch 213 E1
East Winterslow 168 D4
East Wittering 157 G3
East Witton 252 A4
East Woodburn 270 B3
East Woodhay 169 F1
East Woodlands 167 E3
East Worldham 170 C4
East Worlington 152 A1
East Youlstone 162 C4
Eastacott 163 G3
Eastbourne 160 B4
Eastbourne Pier 44
Eastbrook 180 A5
Eastburn *E.Riding* 246 B2
Eastburn *W.Yorks.* 243 G3
Eastbury *Herts.* 186 A3
Eastbury *W.Berks.* 183 F5
Eastby 243 G2
Eastchurch 174 B1
Eastcombe *Glos.* 182 A2
Eastcombe *Som.* 165 E4
Eastcote *Gt.Lon.* 186 A4
Eastcote *Northants.* 198 B2
Eastcote *W.Mid.* 209 D5
Eastcott *Cornw.* 162 C4
Eastcott *Wilts.* 168 B2
Eastcourt 182 B3
Eastdown 151 E3
Eastend 197 F5
Easter Ardross 321 F2
Easter Balgedie 293 G4
Easter Balmoral 311 E5
Easter Boleskine 309 E2
Easter Borland 292 B4
Easter Brae 321 F3
Easter Buckieburn 284 B1
Easter Compton 181 E4
Easter Drummond 309 D3
Easter Dullater 292 A4
Easter Ellister 280 A4
Easter Fearn 321 F1
Easter Galcantray 322 A5
Easter Howlaws 287 E5
Easter Kinkell 321 E4
Easter Knox 303 D5
Easter Lednathie 302 B3
Easter Moniack 321 E5
Easter Ord 312 D4
Easter Poldar 292 B5
Easter Skeld (Skeld) 342 C3
Easter Suddie 321 F4
Easter Tulloch 303 F2
Easter Whyntie 324 B3
Eastergate 158 B3
Easterhouse 284 A3
Easterton 168 B2
Easterton Sands 168 B2
Eastertown 166 A2
Eastfield *Bristol* 181 E5
Eastfield *N.Lan.* 284 C3
Eastfield *N.Yorks.* 254 D4
Eastfield Hall 271 E1
Eastgate *Dur.* 261 F4
Eastgate *Lincs.* 211 G1
Eastgate *Norf.* 228 C3
Easthall 200 A5
Eastham *Mersey.* 233 E4
Eastham *Worcs.* 195 F1
Easthampstead 171 D1
Easthampton 194 D1
Easthaugh 228 B4
Eastheath 170 D1
Easthope 207 E3
Easthorpe *Essex* 202 A5
Easthorpe *Leics.* 224 D4
Easthorpe *Notts.* 224 C2
Easthouses 286 A3
Eastington *Devon* 152 A2
Eastington *Glos.* 182 D1
Eastington *Glos.* 181 G2
Eastleach Martin 183 E2
Eastleach Turville 183 E2
Eastleigh *Devon* 163 E3
Eastleigh *Hants.* 156 D1
Eastling 174 B3
Eastmoor *Derbys.* 236 A5
Eastmoor *Norf.* 213 F2
Eastnor 195 G4
Eastnor Castle 65
Eastoft 237 F1
Eastoke 157 G3
Easton *Cambs.* 211 G5
Easton *Cumb.* 268 C4
Easton *Cumb.* 259 F1
Easton *Devon* 152 A4
Easton *Dorset* 154 C5
Easton *Hants.* 169 G4
Easton *I.o.W.* 156 C4
Easton *Lincs.* 225 E5
Easton *Norf.* 228 C4
Easton *Som.* 166 C3
Easton *Suff.* 203 D2
Easton *Wilts.* 182 A5
Easton Farm Park 79
Easton Grey 182 A4
Easton Maudit 199 D2
Easton on the Hill 211 F2
Easton Royal 168 D1
Easton-in-Gordano 181 E5
Eastrea 212 A3
Eastriggs 268 A5
Eastrington 245 G4
Eastry 175 F3
Eastside 339 D3
East-the-Water 163 E3
Eastville 181 F5
Eastwell 224 C5
Eastwick 186 D1
Eastwood *Notts.* 223 F3
Eastwood *S'end* 188 B4
Eastwood *S.Yorks.* 236 B3
Eastwood *W.Yorks.* 243 F5
Eastwood End 212 C3
Eathorpe 197 F1
Eaton *Ches.* 221 F1
Eaton *Ches.* 220 C1
Eaton *Leics.* 224 C5
Eaton *Norf.* 228 D5
Eaton *Norf.* 227 E4
Eaton *Notts.* 237 E5
Eaton *Oxon.* 183 G2
Eaton *Shrop.* 207 E3
Eaton *Shrop.* 206 C4
Eaton Bishop 194 D4
Eaton Bray 199 E5
Eaton Constantine 207 F2
Eaton Ford 199 G2
Eaton Hall 220 B1
Eaton Hastings 183 E3
Eaton Socon 199 G2
Eaton upon Tern 221 D5
Eaves Green 209 E4
Eaves, The 181 F2
Eavestone 244 B1
Ebberston 254 B4
Ebbesborne Wake 168 A5
Ebbw Vale 180 A2
Ebchester 262 A2
Ebdon 166 A1
Ebford 152 C4
Ebley 182 A2
Ebnal 220 B3
Ebrington 197 D3
Ebsworthy Town 149 F1
Ecchinswell 169 F2
Ecclaw 287 E3
Ecclefechan 267 F3
Eccles *Gt.Man.* 234 B3
Eccles *Kent* 173 G2
Eccles *Sc.Bord.* 287 E5
Eccles Green 194 C3
Eccles Road 214 B2
Ecclesfield 236 A3
Ecclesgreig 303 F3
Eccleshall 221 F5
Eccleshill 244 A4
Ecclesmachan 285 E2
Eccles-on-Sea 229 F3
Eccleston *Ches.* 220 B1
Eccleston *Lancs.* 233 G1
Eccleston *Mersey.* 233 F3
Eccup 244 B3
Echt 312 C4
Eckford 278 B4
Eckington *Derbys.* 236 B5
Eckington *Worcs.* 196 B3
Ecton *Northants.* 198 D1
Ecton *Staffs.* 222 B2
Edale 235 F4
Eday 340 D3
Edburton 159 E2
Edderside 259 E2
Edderton 321 G1
Eddington 169 E1
Eddleston 285 G5
Eden Camp 87
Eden Park 172 C2
Eden Project 29
Eden Vale 262 D4
Edenbridge 172 D4
Edendonich 291 D2
Edenfield 234 B1
Edenhall 260 B4
Edenham 225 F5
Edensor 235 G5
Edentaggart 291 F5
Edenthorpe 236 D2
Edern 216 B4
Edgarley 166 C4
Edgbaston 208 C4
Edgcote 198 A3
Edgcott *Bucks.* 198 B5
Edgcott *Som.* 164 B4
Edgcumbe 145 E3
Edge *Glos.* 182 A2
Edge *Shrop.* 206 C2
Edge End 181 E1
Edge Green *Ches.* 220 B2
Edge Green *Gt.Man.* 233 G3
Edge Green *Norf.* 214 B3
Edgebolton 220 C5
Edgefield 228 B2
Edgehead 286 A3
Edgeley 220 C3
Edgerley 206 C1
Edgerton 235 F1
Edgeworth 182 B2
Edginswell 151 E1
Edgmond 207 G1
Edgmond Marsh 221 E5
Edgton 206 C4
Edgware 186 B3
Edgworth 234 B1
Edinample 292 B2
Edinbanchory 311 G3
Edinbane 317 G4
Edinbarnet 283 G2
Edinburgh 121
Edinburgh Airport 285 F2
Edinburgh Castle 122
Edinburgh Zoo 122
Edinchip 292 A2
Edingale 209 E1
Edingley 224 B2
Edingthorpe 229 E2
Edingthorpe Green 229 E2
Edington *Som.* 166 A4
Edington *Wilts.* 168 A2
Edintore 323 G5
Edinvale 322 D4
Edistone 162 C3
Edith Weston 211 E2
Edithmead 166 A3
Edlaston 222 C3
Edlesborough 185 E1
Edlingham 270 D1
Edlington 238 C5
Edmondsham 155 G1
Edmondsham House 29
Edmondsley 262 B3
Edmondstown 179 G3
Edmondthorpe 211 D1
Edmonstone 340 D4
Edmonton *Cornw.* 147 D2
Edmonton *Gt.Lon.* 186 C3
Edmundbyers 261 G2
Ednam 278 B3
Ednaston 222 D3
Edney Common 187 F2
Edra 291 G3
Edradynate 301 D4
Edrom 287 F4
Edstaston 220 C4
Edstone 197 D1
Edvin Loach 195 F2
Edwalton 223 G4
Edwardstone 202 A3
Edwardsville 179 G3
Edwinsford 192 C4
Edwinstowe 224 B1
Edworth 200 A3
Edwyn Ralph 195 F2
Edzell 303 E3
Edzell Castle & Garden 122
Efail Isaf 179 G4
Efail-fâch 179 D3
Efailnewydd 216 C4
Efailwen 191 E5
Efenechtyd 219 E2
Effingham 171 G2
Effirth 342 C2
Efflinch 209 D1
Efford 152 B2
Egbury 169 F2
Egdean 171 E5
Egdon 196 B2
Egerton *Gt.Man.* 234 B1
Egerton *Kent* 174 B4
Egerton Forstal 174 A4
Egerton Green 220 C2
Egg Buckland 150 A2
Eggborough 245 E5
Eggerness 257 E2
Eggesford Barton 163 G4
Eggington 199 E5
Egginton 223 D5
Egglescliffe 252 D1
Eggleston 261 F5
Egham 185 F5
Egham Wick 185 E5
Egilsay 340 C4
Egleton 211 D2
Eglingham 279 F5
Eglinton 283 E5
Egloshayle 147 E2
Egloskerry 147 G1
Eglwys Cross 220 B3
Eglwys Fach 204 C3
Eglwys Nunydd 179 D4
Eglwysbach 231 G5
Eglwys-Brewis 164 D1
Eglwyswrw 191 E4
Egmanton 224 C1
Egmere 228 A2
Egremont 258 D5
Egton 254 B2
Egton Bridge 254 B2
Egypt 169 F3
Eigg 297 D1
Eight Ash Green 202 A5
Eignaig 297 G5
Eil 310 A3
Eilanreach 307 E3
Eildon 277 G2
Eilean Bhearnaraigh (Berneray) 326 B5
Eilean Darach 320 A1
Eilean Donan Castle 122
Eilean Iarmain (Isleornsay) 306 C3
Eilean Leodhais (Isle of Lewis) 329 E3
Eilean Scalpaigh (Scalpay) 327 E4
Eilean Shona 297 F2
Einacleit 328 C5
Eiriosgaigh (Eriskay) 314 C2
Eisgean 327 F2
Eisingrug 217 F4
Eisteddfa Gurig 205 D4
Elan Valley Visitor Centre 110
Elan Village 193 F1
Elberton 181 F4
Elburton 150 B2
Elcho 293 G2
Elcombe 182 D4
Elder Street 201 D4
Eldernell 212 B3
Eldersfield 195 G4
Elderslie 283 F3
Eldon 262 B5
Eldrick 265 D2
Eldroth 243 D1
Eldwick 244 A3
Electric Mountain 110
Elemore Vale 262 C3
Elerch (Bont-goch) 204 C4
Elford *Northumb.* 279 F3
Elford *Staffs.* 209 D1
Elford Closes 212 D5
Elgin 323 E3
Elgin Cathedral 122
Elgin Museum 122
Elgol 306 B3
Elham 175 D4
Elie 294 C4
Elilaw 270 B1
Elim 230 B4
Eling *Hants.* 156 C1
Eling *W.Berks.* 184 A5
Eliock 275 G5
Elishader 318 A3
Elishaw 270 A2
Elkesley 237 D5
Elkington 210 B5
Elkstone 182 B1
Elland 244 A5
Elland Upper Edge 244 A5
Ellary 281 F2
Ellastone 222 C3
Ellbridge 150 A1
Ellel 242 A2
Ellemford 287 E3
Ellenborough 258 D3
Ellenhall 221 F5
Ellen's Green 171 F4
Ellerbeck 252 D3
Ellerby 253 G1
Ellerdine 220 D5
Ellerdine Heath 220 D5
Ellergreen 249 F3
Elleric 298 C5
Ellerker 246 B5
Ellerton *E.Riding* 245 G3
Ellerton *N.Yorks.* 252 B3
Ellerton *Shrop.* 221 E5
Ellerton Abbey 251 F3
Ellesborough 184 D2
Ellesmere 220 A4
Ellesmere Park 234 B3
Ellesmere Port 233 F5
Ellesmere Port Boat Museum 95
Ellingham *Hants.* 156 A2
Ellingham *Norf.* 215 E2
Ellingham *Northumb.* 279 F4
Ellingstring 252 A4
Ellington *Cambs.* 211 G5
Ellington *Northumb.* 271 E2
Ellington Thorpe 211 G5
Elliot's Green 167 E3
Ellisfield 170 B3
Ellistown 209 G1
Ellon 313 E1
Ellonby 260 A4
Ellough 215 F3
Ellough Moor 215 F3
Elloughton 246 B5
Ellwood 181 E2
Elm 212 C2
Elm Park 187 E4
Elmbridge 196 B1
Elmdon *Essex* 200 C4
Elmdon *W.Mid.* 209 D4
Elmdon Heath 209 D4
Elmers End 172 C2
Elmer's Green 233 F2
Elmesthorpe 209 G3
Elmhurst 208 D1
Elmley Castle 196 B3
Elmley Lovett 196 A1
Elmore 181 G1
Elmore Back 181 G1
Elmscott 162 C3
Elmsett 202 B3
Elmstead *Essex* 202 B5
Elmstead *Gt.Lon.* 186 D5
Elmstead Market 202 B5
Elmstone 175 E2
Elmstone Hardwicke 196 B5
Elmswell *E.Riding* 246 B2
Elmswell *Suff.* 202 A1
Elmton 236 C5
Elphin 331 E3
Elphinstone 286 A2
Elrick *Aber.* 312 D4
Elrick *Moray* 311 G2
Elrig 256 D2
Elrigbeag 290 D3
Elsdon 270 B2
Elsecar 236 A2
Elsenham 200 D5
Elsfield 184 A1
Elsham 238 A1
Elsham Hall Country & Wildlife Park 87
Elsing 228 B4
Elslack 243 F3
Elson *Hants.* 157 F2
Elson *Shrop.* 220 A4
Elsrickle 285 E5
Elstead 171 E3
Elsted 158 A2
Elsthorpe 225 F5
Elstob 262 C5
Elston *Lancs.* 242 B4
Elston *Notts.* 224 C3
Elstone 163 G4
Elstow 199 F3
Elstree 186 A3
Elstronwick 247 E4
Elswick 242 A4
Elsworth 200 B1
Elterwater 249 E2
Eltham 186 D5
Eltham Palace 55
Eltisley 200 A2
Elton *Cambs.* 211 F3
Elton *Ches.* 233 F5
Elton *Derbys.* 222 D1
Elton *Glos.* 181 G1
Elton *Gt.Man.* 234 B1
Elton *Here.* 207 D5
Elton *Notts.* 224 C4
Elton *Stock.* 252 D1
Elton Green 233 F5
Elton Hall 79
Elvanfoot 276 A4
Elvaston 223 F4
Elvaston Castle Country Park 72
Elveden 213 G5
Elvingston 286 B2
Elvington *Kent* 175 E3
Elvington *York* 245 G3
Elwick *Hart.* 263 D4
Elwick *Northumb.* 279 F3
Elworth 221 E1
Elworthy 165 D4
Ely *Cambs.* 212 D5
Ely *Cardiff* 180 A5
Ely Cathedral 79
Emberton 199 D3
Embleton *Cumb.* 259 E3
Embleton *Hart.* 262 D5
Embleton *Northumb.* 279 G4
Embo 332 D5
Embo Street 332 D5
Emborough 166 D2
Embsay 243 G2
Emerson Park 187 E4
Emery Down 156 B2
Emley 235 G1
Emmetts 44
Emmington 184 C2
Emneth 212 C2
Emneth Hungate 212 D2
Empingham 211 E2
Empshott 170 C4
Empshott Green 170 C4
Emsworth 157 G2
Enborne 169 F1
Enborne Row 169 F1
Enchmarsh 207 E3
Enderby 210 A3
Endmoor 249 G4
Endon 221 G2
Endon Bank 221 G2
Enfield 186 C3
Enfield Wash 186 C3
Enford 168 C2
Engine Common 181 F4
Englefield 184 B5
Englefield Green 185 E5
Englesea-brook 221 E2
English Bicknor 181 E1
English Frankton 220 B5
Englishcombe 167 E1
Enham Alamein 169 E3
Enmore 165 F4
Ennerdale Bridge 259 D5
Enniscaven 147 D4
Ennochdhu 301 F3
Ensay 296 C5
Ensdon 206 D1
Ensis 163 F3
Enson 221 G5
Enstone 197 F5
Enterkinfoot 275 G5
Enterpen 253 D2
Enton Green 171 E3
Enville 208 A4
Eolaigearraidh 314 C3
Eorabus 288 C2
Eorodal 329 G1
Eoropaidh 329 G1
Epney 181 G1
Epperstone 224 B3
Epping 187 D2
Epping Forest 79
Epping Green *Essex* 186 D2
Epping Green *Herts.* 186 B2
Epping Upland 186 D2
Eppleby 252 A1
Eppleworth 246 C4
Epsom 172 B2
Epwell 197 F3
Epworth 237 E2
Epworth Turbary 237 E2
Erbistock 220 A3
Erbusaig 307 D2
Erchless Castle 320 D5
Erddig 110
Erdington 208 D3
Eredine 290 B4
Eriboll 334 D3
Ericstane 276 B4
Eridge Green 173 E5
Eriff 274 D5
Erines 281 G2
Erisey Barton 145 E5
Eriskay (Eiriosgaigh) 314 C2
Eriswell 213 F5
Erith 187 E5
Erlestoke 168 A2
Ermington 150 C2
Ernesettle 150 A1
Erpingham 228 C2
Erringden Grange 243 F5
Errogie 309 E2
Errol 294 A2
Errollston 313 F1
Erskine 283 F2
Ervie 264 A4
Erwarton 202 D4
Erwood 193 G3
Eryholme 252 C2
Eryrys 219 F2
Escart 281 G3
Escart Farm 281 G4
Escomb 262 A5
Escot 29
Escrick 245 F3
Esgair 191 G5
Esgairgeiliog 205 D2
Esgyryn 231 G5
Esh 262 A3
Esh Winning 262 A3
Esher 171 G1
Eshott 271 E2
Eshton 243 F2
Eskadale 309 D1
Eskbank 286 A3
Eskdale Green 248 C2
Eskdalemuir 268 A2
Eskham 239 D3
Esknish 280 B3
Esperley Lane Ends 262 A5
Espley Hall 271 D2
Esprick 242 A4
Essendine 211 F1
Essendon 186 B2
Essich 309 F1
Essington 208 B2
Esslemont 313 E2
Eston 253 E1
Eswick 343 D2
Etal 278 D3
Etchilhampton 168 B1
Etchingham 160 C1
Etchinghill *Kent* 175 D5
Etchinghill *Staffs.* 208 C1
Etherdwick Grange 247 E4
Etherley Dene 262 A5
Ethie Mains 303 E5
Eton 185 E5
Eton Wick 185 E5
Etteridge 309 F5
Ettiley Heath 221 E1
Ettington 197 E3
Etton *E.Riding* 246 B3
Etton *Peter.* 211 G2
Ettrick 277 D4
Ettrickbridge 277 E3
Ettrickhill 277 D4
Etwall 223 D4
Eudon George 207 F4
Eurach 290 A4
Eureka! Museum for Children 87
Euston 213 G5
Euxton 233 G1
Evanstown 179 F4
Evanton 321 F3
Evedon 225 F3
Evelix 332 C5
Evenjobb 194 B1
Evenley 198 A4
Evenlode 197 E5
Evenwood 262 A5
Evenwood Gate 262 A5
Everbay 341 E4
Evercreech 166 D4
Everdon 198 A2
Everingham 246 A3
Everleigh 168 D2
Everley *High.* 337 F2
Everley *N.Yorks.* 254 C4
Eversholt 199 E4
Evershot 154 B2
Eversley 170 C1
Eversley Cross 170 C1
Everthorpe 246 B4
Everton *Beds.* 200 A2
Everton *Hants.* 156 B3
Everton *Mersey.* 233 E3
Everton *Notts.* 237 D3
Evertown 268 B4
Eves Corner 188 C3
Evesbatch 195 F3
Evesham 196 C3
Evie 340 B4
Evington 210 B2
Ewart Newtown 279 D3
Ewden Village 235 G3
Ewell 172 B2
Ewell Minnis 175 E4
Ewelme 184 B3
Ewen 182 C3
Ewenny 179 F5
Ewerby 225 G3
Ewerby Thorpe 225 G3
Ewhurst *E.Suss.* 160 C1
Ewhurst *Surr.* 171 F3
Ewhurst Green 171 F4
Ewloe 220 A1
Ewloe Green 219 F1
Ewood 242 C5
Ewood Bridge 243 D5
Eworthy 149 E1
Ewshot 170 D3
Ewyas Harold 194 C5
Exbourne 163 G5
Exbury 156 D2
Exbury Gardens 44
Exceat 160 A4

Exebridge 164 C5
Exelby 252 B4
Exeter 152 C3
Exeter Airport 152 C3
Exeter Cathedral 29
Exford 164 B4
Exfords Green 207 D2
Exhall *Warks.* 196 D2
Exhall *Warks.* 209 F4
Exlade Street 184 B4
Exminster 152 C4
Exmoor 29
Exmouth 152 D4
Exnaboe 343 G5
Exning 201 E1
Exton *Devon* 152 C4
Exton *Hants.* 170 B5
Exton *Rut.* 211 E1
Exton *Som.* 164 C4
Exwick 152 C3
Eyam 235 G5
Eyam Museum 72
Eydon 198 A3
Eye *Here.* 195 D1
Eye *Peter.* 212 A2
Eye *Suff.* 214 C4
Eye Green 212 A2
Eyemouth 287 G3
Eyeworth 200 A3
Eyhorne Street 174 A3
Eyke 203 E2
Eynesbury 199 G2
Eynort 305 G2
Eynsford 173 E2
Eynsham 183 G2
Eype 154 A3
Eyre 318 A4
Eythorne 175 E4
Eyton *Here.* 195 D1
Eyton *Shrop.* 206 C4
Eyton on Severn 207 E2
Eyton upon the Weald Moors 207 F1
Eywood 194 C2

F

Faccombe 169 E2
Faceby 253 D2
Fachwen 217 E1
Facit 234 C1
Faddiley 220 C2
Fadmoor 253 F4
Faebait 321 D4
Faifley 283 G2
Fail 274 C3
Failand 181 E5
Failford 274 C3
Failsworth 234 C2
Fain 320 A2
Fair Isle 122
Fair Oak *Devon* 152 D1
Fair Oak *Hants.* 157 D1
Fair Oak *Hants.* 169 G1
Fair Oak Green 170 B1
Fairbourne 204 C1
Fairburn 245 D5
Fairfield *Derbys.* 235 E5
Fairfield *Gt.Man.* 234 D3
Fairfield *Kent* 161 E1
Fairfield *Mersey.* 233 D4
Fairfield *Stock.* 252 D1
Fairfield *Worcs.* 208 B5
Fairford 182 D2
Fairgirth 266 C5
Fairhaven 241 G5
Fairhaven Gardens 79
Fairhill 284 B4
Fairholm 284 B4
Fairlands Valley Park 79
Fairley 313 D4
Fairlie 282 D4
Fairlight 161 D2
Fairlight Cove 161 D2
Fairmile *Devon* 153 D3
Fairmile *Surr.* 171 G1
Fairmilehead 285 G3
Fairnington 278 A4
Fairoak 221 E4
Fairseat 173 F2
Fairstead 187 G1
Fairwarp 159 G1
Fairwater 180 A5
Fairy Cross 163 E3
Fairyhill 178 A3
Fakenham 228 A3
Fala 286 B3
Fala Dam 286 B3
Falahill 286 A4
Faldingworth 238 A4
Falfield *Fife* 294 C4
Falfield *S.Glos.* 181 F3
Falin-Wnda 191 G3
Falkenham 203 D4
Falkirk 284 C2
Falkirk Wheel 122
Falkland 294 A4
Falkland Palace 122
Falla 278 B5
Fallgate 223 E1
Fallin 292 D5
Falls of Clyde Wildlife Reserve & Visitor Centre 122
Falmer 159 F3
Falmouth 145 F3
Falsgrave 254 D4
Falstone 269 F3
Fanagmore 334 A4
Fanans 290 C2
Fancott 199 F5
Fangdale Beck 253 E3
Fangfoss 245 G2
Fankerton 284 B1
Fanmore 296 D5
Fanner's Green 187 F1
Fans 286 D5
Fantasy Island 72
Far Cotton 198 C2
Far Forest 207 G5
Far Gearstones 250 C4
Far Green 181 G2
Far Moor 233 G2
Far Oakridge 182 B2
Far Royds 244 B4
Far Sawrey 249 E3
Farcet 212 A3
Farden 207 E5
Fareham 157 E2
Farewell 208 C1
Farforth 238 D5
Faringdon 183 E3
Farington 242 B5
Farlam 260 B2
Farlary 332 C4
Farleigh *N.Som.* 166 C1
Farleigh *Surr.* 172 C2
Farleigh Hungerford 167 F2
Farleigh Hungerford Castle 29
Farleigh Wallop 170 B3
Farlesthorpe 239 E5
Farleton *Cumb.* 249 G4
Farleton *Lancs.* 242 B1
Farley *Derbys.* 223 D1
Farley *Shrop.* 206 C2
Farley *Staffs.* 222 B3
Farley *Wilts.* 168 D5
Farley Green *Suff.* 201 F2
Farley Green *Surr.* 171 F3
Farley Hill 170 C1
Farleys End 181 G1
Farlington 245 F1
Farlow 207 F4
Farm Town 209 F1
Farmborough 167 D1
Farmcote 196 C5
Farmington 182 D1
Farmoor 183 G2
Farmtown 324 A4
Farnborough *Gt.Lon.* 172 D2
Farnborough *Hants.* 171 D2
Farnborough *W.Berks.* 183 G4
Farnborough *Warks.* 197 G3
Farnborough Street 171 D2
Farncombe 171 E3
Farndish 199 E1
Farndon *Ches.* 220 B2
Farndon *Notts.* 224 C2
Farne Islands 279 G3
Farnell 303 E4
Farnham *Dorset* 155 F1
Farnham *Essex* 200 C5
Farnham *N.Yorks.* 244 C1
Farnham *Suff.* 203 E1
Farnham *Surr.* 170 D3
Farnham Common 185 E4
Farnham Green 200 C5
Farnham Royal 185 E4
Farningham 173 E2
Farnley *N.Yorks.* 244 B3
Farnley *W.Yorks.* 244 B4
Farnley Tyas 235 F1
Farnsfield 224 B2
Farnworth *Gt.Man.* 234 B2
Farnworth *Halton* 233 G4
Farr *High.* 335 G2
Farr *High.* 309 F1
Farr *High.* 310 A4
Farr House 309 F1
Farraline 309 E2
Farringdon 152 D3
Farrington Gurney 166 D2
Farsley 244 B4
Farthing Corner 174 A2
Farthing Green 174 A4
Farthinghoe 198 A4
Farthingstone 198 B2
Farthorpe 238 C5
Fartown 235 F1
Farway 153 E3
Fasag 319 E4
Fasagrianach 320 A1
Fascadale 297 E2
Faslane 282 D1
Fasnacloich 298 C5
Fasnakyle 308 C2
Fassfern 298 C2
Fatfield 262 C2
Fattahead 324 B4
Faugh 260 B2
Fauldhouse 284 D3
Faulkbourne 187 G1
Faulkland 167 E2
Fauls 220 C4
Faulston 168 B5
Faversham 174 C2
Favillar 311 E1
Fawdington 252 D5
Fawdon 262 B1
Fawfieldhead 222 B1
Fawkham Green 173 E2
Fawler 183 F1
Fawley *Bucks.* 184 C4
Fawley *Hants.* 157 D2
Fawley *W.Berks.* 183 F4
Fawley Chapel 195 E5
Fawsyde 303 G2
Faxfleet 246 A5
Faxton 210 C5
Faygate 172 B5
Fazakerley 233 E3
Fazeley 209 F2
Fearby 252 A4
Fearn 322 A2
Fearnan 300 C5
Fearnbeg 318 D4
Fearnhead 234 A3
Fearnmore 318 D3
Fearnoch *Arg. & B.* 282 B2
Fearnoch *Arg. & B.* 282 A1
Featherstone *Staffs.* 208 B2
Featherstone *W.Yorks.* 244 D5
Featherstone Castle 260 C1
Feckenham 196 C1
Feering 201 G5
Feetham 251 E3
Feith-hill 324 B5
Feizor 243 D1
Felbridge 172 C5
Felbrigg 228 D2
Felbrigg Hall 79
Felcourt 172 C4
Felden 185 F2
Felhampton 206 D4
Felindre *Carmar.* 192 D5
Felindre *Carmar.* 192 B5
Felindre *Carmar.* 191 G4
Felindre *Carmar.* 192 C4
Felindre *Cere.* 192 B2
Felindre *Powys* 206 A4
Felindre *Powys* 194 A5
Felindre *Swan.* 178 C2
Felinfach *Cere.* 192 B2
Felinfach *Powys* 193 G4
Felinfoel 178 B2
Felingwmisaf 192 B5
Felingwmuchaf 192 B5
Felixkirk 253 D4
Felixstowe 203 E4
Felixstowe Ferry 203 E4
Felkington 287 G5
Fell Foot Park 95
Felldownhead 149 D2
Felling 262 B1
Fellonmore 289 F2
Felmersham 199 E2
Felmingham 229 D3
Felpham 158 B4
Felsham 202 A2
Felsted 201 E5
Feltham 186 A5
Felthamhill 186 A5
Felthorpe 228 C4
Felton *Here.* 195 E3
Felton *N.Som.* 166 C1
Felton *Northumb.* 271 D1
Felton Butler 206 C1
Feltwell 213 F3
Fen Ditton 200 C1
Fen Drayton 200 B1
Fen End 209 E5
Fen Street *Norf.* 214 A2
Fen Street *Norf.* 214 B3
Fen Street *Suff.* 214 A4
Fen Street *Suff.* 202 C1
Fenay Bridge 235 F1
Fence 243 E4
Fence Houses 262 C2
Fencott 184 A1
Fendike Corner 226 C1
Fenham 279 E2
Fenhouses 226 A3
Feniscowles 242 C5
Feniton 153 E3
Fenn Street 187 G5
Fenni-fach 193 G5
Fenny Bentley 222 C2
Fenny Bridges 153 E3
Fenny Compton 197 G2
Fenny Drayton 209 F3
Fenny Stratford 199 D4
Fenrother 271 D2
Fenstanton 200 B1
Fenton *Cambs.* 212 B5
Fenton *Lincs.* 237 F5
Fenton *Lincs.* 225 D2
Fenton *Northumb.* 279 D3
Fenton *Notts.* 237 E4
Fenton *Stoke* 221 F3
Fenton Barns 286 C1
Fenton House 56
Fenwick *E.Ayr.* 283 F5
Fenwick *Northumb.* 270 C4
Fenwick *Northumb.* 279 E2
Fenwick *S.Yorks.* 236 C1
Feochaig 272 C4
Feock 145 F3
Feolin 280 D3
Feolin Ferry 280 C3
Feorlan 272 B5
Feorlin 290 B5
Ferguslie Park 283 F3
Feriniquarrie 317 E4
Fern 302 C3
Ferndale 179 F3
Ferndown 155 G2
Ferness 322 B5
Fernham 183 E3
Fernhill Heath 196 A2
Fernhurst 171 D5
Fernie 294 B3
Fernilea 305 G1
Fernilee 235 E5
Fernybank 302 D2
Ferrensby 244 C1
Ferrindonald 306 C4
Ferring 158 C3
Ferry Hill 212 B4
Ferrybridge 245 D5
Ferryden 303 F4
Ferryhill 262 B4
Ferryside (Glanyferi) 177 G1
Fersfield 214 B3
Fersit 299 F2
Ferwig 191 E3
Feshiebridge 310 A4
Fetcham 171 G2
Fetlar 345 F3
Fetterangus 325 E4
Fettercairn 303 E2
Fetternear House 312 C3
Feus of Caldhame 303 E3
Fewcott 198 A5
Fewston 244 A2
Ffairfach 192 C5
Ffair-Rhos 192 D1
Ffaldybrenin 192 C3
Ffarmers 192 C3
Ffawyddog 180 B1
Ffestiniog (Llan Ffestiniog) 218 A3
Ffestiniog Railway 110
Ffordd-las *Denb.* 219 E1
Ffordd-las *Powys* 194 B4
Fforest 178 B2
Fforest-fach 178 C3
Ffostrasol 191 G3
Ffos-y-ffin 192 A1
Ffridd Uchaf 217 E2
Ffrith *Denb.* 232 B4
Ffrith *Flints.* 219 F2
Ffrwdgrech 193 G5
Ffynnon 177 G1
Ffynnon Taf (Taff's Well) 180 A4
Ffynnongroyw 232 C4
Fibhig 329 D3
Fichlie 311 G3
Fidden 288 C2
Fiddington *Glos.* 196 B4
Fiddington *Som.* 165 F3
Fiddleford 155 E1
Fiddler's Green *Glos.* 196 B5
Fiddler's Green *Here.* 195 E4
Fiddler's Green *Norf.* 213 G1
Fiddler's Green *Norf.* 214 B2
Fiddlers Hamlet 187 D2
Field 222 B4
Field Broughton 249 E4
Field Dalling 228 B2
Field Head 209 G2
Fife Folk Museum 122
Fife Keith 323 G4
Fifehead Magdalen 167 E5
Fifehead Neville 155 D1
Fifehead St. Quintin 155 D1
Fifield *Oxon.* 183 E1
Fifield *W. & M.* 185 E5
Fifield Bavant 168 B5
Figheldean 168 C3
Filby 229 F4
Filey 255 E4
Filgrave 199 D3
Filham 150 C2
Filkins 183 E2
Filleigh *Devon* 163 G3
Filleigh *Devon* 152 A1
Fillingham 237 G4
Fillongley 209 F4
Filmore Hill 170 B5
Filton 181 F5
Fimber 246 A1
Finavon 302 C4
Finch Foundry 29
Fincham 213 E2
Finchampstead 170 C1
Finchdean 157 G1
Finchingfield 201 E4
Finchley 186 B3
Findern 223 E4
Findhorn 322 C3
Findhorn Bridge 310 A2
Findhuglen 292 C3
Findo Gask 293 F2
Findochty 323 G3
Findon *Aber.* 313 E5
Findon *W.Suss.* 158 D3
Findon Mains 321 F3
Findon Valley 158 D3
Findrassie 323 D3
Findron 311 D3
Finedon 211 E5
Finegand 301 G3
Fingal Street 214 D4
Fingal's Cave (see Staffa) 130
Fingask 312 C2
Fingerpost 207 G5
Fingest 184 C3
Finghall 252 A4
Fingland *Cumb.* 259 F1
Fingland *D. & G.* 276 D5
Fingland *D. & G.* 275 F4
Finglesham 175 F3
Fingringhoe 202 B5
Finkle Street 236 A3
Finkley Down Farm Park 44
Finlarig 292 A1
Finlaystone House Gardens 122
Finmere 198 B4
Finnart *Arg. & B.* 291 E5
Finnart *P. & K.* 300 A4
Finney Hill 209 G1
Finningham 202 B1
Finningley 237 D3
Finnygaud 324 B4
Finsbay (Fionnsbhagh) 326 C5
Finsbury 186 C4
Finstall 208 B5
Finsthwaite 249 E4
Finstock 183 F1
Finstown 340 B5
Fintry *Aber.* 324 C4
Fintry *Stir.* 284 A1
Finwood 197 D1
Finzean 312 A5
Fionnphort 288 B2
Fionnsbhagh (Finsbay) 326 C5
Fir Tree 262 A4
Firbank 250 B3
Firbeck 236 C4
Firby *N.Yorks.* 252 B4
Firby *N.Yorks.* 245 G1
Firgrove 234 D1
Firle Place 44
Firs Lane 234 A2
Firsby 226 C1
Firsdown 168 D4
Firth 344 D5
Fishbourne *I.o.W.* 157 E3
Fishbourne *W.Suss.* 158 A3
Fishbourne Roman Palace 44
Fishburn 262 C4
Fishcross 293 E5
Fisherford 312 B1
Fisher's Farm Park 44
Fisher's Pond 169 F5
Fisher's Row 242 A3
Fishersgate 159 E3
Fisherstreet 171 E4
Fisherton *High.* 321 G4
Fisherton *S.Ayr.* 274 A4
Fisherton de la Mere 168 A4
Fishguard (Abergwaun) 190 C4
Fishlake 237 D1
Fishleigh Barton 163 F3
Fishley 229 F4
Fishnish 297 F5
Fishpond Bottom 153 G3
Fishponds 181 F5
Fishpool 234 C2
Fishtoft 226 B3
Fishtoft Drove 226 B3
Fishtown of Usan 303 F4
Fishwick *Lancs.* 242 B4
Fishwick *Sc.Bord.* 287 G4
Fiskerton *Lincs.* 238 A5
Fiskerton *Notts.* 224 C2
Fitling 247 E4
Fittleton 168 C3
Fittleworth 158 C2
Fitton End 212 C1
Fitz 206 D1
Fitzhead 165 E5
Fitzroy 165 E5
Fitzwilliam 236 B1
Fitzwilliam Museum 79
Fiunary 297 F5
Five Acres 181 E1
Five Ash Down 159 G1
Five Ashes 160 A1
Five Bridges 195 F3
Five Houses 156 D4
Five Lanes 180 D3
Five Oak Green 173 F4
Five Oaks *Chan.I.* 150 C5
Five Oaks *W.Suss.* 171 F5
Five Roads 178 A2
Five Turnings 206 B5
Five Wents 174 A3
Fivehead 166 A5
Fivelanes 147 G1
Flack's Green 187 G1
Flackwell Heath 185 D4
Fladbury 196 B3
Fladdabister 342 D4
Flag Fen Bronze Age Centre 79
Flagg 222 C1
Flambards Village Theme Park 29
Flamborough 255 F5
Flamingo Land Theme Park 87
Flamstead 185 F1
Flamstead End 186 C2
Flansham 158 B3
Flanshaw 244 C5
Flasby 243 F2
Flash 222 B1
Flashader 317 G4
Flask Inn 254 C2
Flatford Mill & Bridge Cottage 79
Flatt, The 269 D4
Flaunden 185 F2
Flawborough 224 C3
Flawith 245 D1
Flax Bourton 166 C1
Flax Moss 243 D5
Flaxby 244 C2
Flaxholme 223 E3
Flaxlands 214 C2
Flaxley 181 F1
Flaxpool 165 E4
Flaxton 245 F1
Fleckney 210 B3
Flecknoe 198 A1
Fledborough 237 F5
Fleece Inn, The 65
Fleet *Hants.* 170 D2
Fleet *Hants.* 157 G2
Fleet *Lincs.* 226 B5
Fleet Air Arm Museum 29
Fleet Hargate 226 B5
Fleetville 186 A2
Fleetwood 241 G3
Fleggburgh (Burgh Saint Margaret) 229 F4
Flemingston 179 G5
Flemington 284 A4
Flempton 201 G1
Fleoideabhagh 326 C5
Flesherin 329 G4
Fletchersbridge 147 F3
Fletchertown 259 F2
Fletching 159 G1
Flete 150 C2
Fleuchats 311 F4
Fleur-de-lis 180 A3
Flexbury 162 C5
Flexford 171 E2
Flimby 258 D3
Flimwell 173 G5
Flint (Y Fflint) 232 D5
Flint Cross 200 C3
Flint Mountain 232 D5
Flintham 224 C3
Flinton 247 E4
Flint's Green 209 E5
Flishinghurst 173 G5
Flitcham 227 F5
Flitholme 250 C1
Flitton 199 F4
Flitwick 199 F4
Flixborough 237 F1
Flixton *Gt.Man.* 234 B3
Flixton *N.Yorks.* 254 D5
Flixton *Suff.* 215 E3
Flockton 235 G1
Flockton Green 235 G1
Flodden 278 D3
Flodigarry 318 A2
Flood's Ferry 212 B3
Flookburgh 249 E5
Floors 323 G4
Floors Castle 122
Flordon 214 C2
Flore 198 B1
Flotta 338 C3
Flotterton 270 C1
Flowton 202 B3
Flushdyke 244 B5
Flushing *Aber.* 325 F5
Flushing *Cornw.* 145 F3
Flushing *Cornw.* 145 E4
Fluxton 153 D3
Flyford Flavell 196 B2
Foals Green 215 D4
Fobbing 187 G4
Fochabers 323 F4
Fochriw 180 A2
Fockerby 237 F1
Fodderletter 310 D2
Fodderty 321 E4
Foddington 166 C5
Foel 205 F1
Foelgastell 178 B1
Foggathorpe 245 G4
Fogo 287 E5
Fogorig 287 E5
Fogwatt 323 E4
Foindle 334 A4
Folda 301 G3
Fole 222 B4
Foleshill 209 F4
Folke 154 C1
Folkestone 175 E5
Folkingham 225 F4
Folkington 160 A3
Folksworth 211 G4
Folkton 255 D5
Folla Rule 312 C1
Follifoot 244 C2
Folly *Dorset* 154 D2
Folly *Pembs.* 190 C5
Folly Gate 149 F1
Folly, The 186 A1
Fonmon 165 D1
Fonthill Bishop 168 A4
Fonthill Gifford 168 A4
Fontmell Magna 155 E1
Fontmell Parva 155 E1
Fontwell 158 B3
Font-y-gary 165 D1
Foolow 235 F5
Footherley 208 D2
Foots Cray 187 D5
Forbestown 311 F3
Force Forge 249 E3
Force Green 172 D3
Forcett 252 A1
Forches Cross 152 A2
Ford *Arg. & B.* 290 A4
Ford *Bucks.* 184 C2
Ford *Devon* 150 C2
Ford *Devon* 163 E3
Ford *Devon* 151 D3
Ford *Glos.* 196 C5
Ford *Mersey.* 233 E3
Ford *Midloth.* 286 A3
Ford *Northumb.* 279 D3
Ford *Pembs.* 190 C5
Ford *Plym.* 150 A2
Ford *Shrop.* 206 D1
Ford *Som.* 165 D5
Ford *Staffs.* 222 B2
Ford *W.Suss.* 158 B3
Ford *Wilts.* 182 A5
Ford End 187 F1
Ford Green 242 A3
Ford Heath 206 D1
Ford Street 153 E1
Forda 149 F1
Fordbridge 209 D4
Fordcombe 173 E4
Forde Abbey 29
Fordell 285 F1
Forden 206 B2
Forder Green 151 D1
Fordgate 166 A4
Fordham *Cambs.* 213 E5
Fordham *Essex* 202 A5
Fordham *Norf.* 213 E3
Fordham Abbey 201 E1
Fordham Heath 202 A5
Fordhouses 208 B2
Fordingbridge 156 A1
Fordon 255 D5
Fordoun 303 F2
Ford's Green 202 B1
Fordstreet 202 A5
Fordwells 183 F1
Fordwich 175 D3
Fordyce 324 A3
Forebrae 293 E2
Forebridge 221 G5
Foredale 243 E1
Foreland 280 A3
Foremark 223 E5
Forest 252 B2
Forest Coal Pit 194 B5
Forest Gate 186 D4
Forest Green 171 G3
Forest Hall *Cumb.* 249 G2
Forest Hall *T. & W.* 262 B1
Forest Head 260 B2
Forest Hill *Gt.Lon.* 186 C5
Forest Hill *Oxon.* 184 A2
Forest Lane Head 244 C2
Forest Lodge *Arg. & B.* 299 E5
Forest Lodge *P. & K.* 301 E2
Forest Mill 293 E5
Forest of Dean 29
Forest Row 172 D5
Forest Side 157 D4
Forest Town 223 G1
Forestburn Gate 270 C2
Forest-in-Teesdale 261 E5
Forestside 157 G1
Forfar 302 C4
Forgandenny 293 F3
Forge 205 D3
Forge, The 194 C2
Forgie 323 F4
Forhill 208 C5
Formby 233 D2
Formby Red Squirrel Reserve 95
Forncett End 214 C2
Forncett St. Mary 214 C2
Forncett St. Peter 214 C2
Forneth 301 F5
Fornham All Saints 201 G1
Fornham St. Martin 201 G1
Fornighty 322 B4
Forres 322 C4
Forrest 284 C3
Forrest Lodge 265 G2
Forsbrook 221 G3
Forse 337 E5
Forsie 336 C2
Forsinain 336 B4
Forsinard 336 A4
Forstal, The *E.Suss.* 173 E5
Forstal, The *Kent* 174 C5
Forston 154 C3
Fort Augustus 308 C4
Fort Brockhurst 44
Fort George *High.* 321 G4
Fort George *High.* 123
Fort Victoria Country Park 44
Fort William 298 D2
Forter 301 G3
Forteviot 293 F3
Forth 284 D4
Forthampton 196 A4
Fortingall 300 C5
Fortis Green 186 B4
Forton *Hants.* 169 F3
Forton *Lancs.* 242 A2
Forton *Shrop.* 206 D1
Forton *Som.* 153 G2
Forton *Staffs.* 221 E5
Fortrie 324 B5
Fortrose 321 G4
Fortuneswell 154 C5
Forty Green 185 E3
Forty Hill 186 C3
Forward Green 202 B2
Fosbury 169 E2
Foscot 197 E5
Fosdyke 226 B4
Foss 300 C4
Foss Cross 182 C2
Fossdale 251 D3
Fossebridge 182 C1
Foster Street 187 D2
Fosterhouses 236 D1
Foster's Booth 198 B2
Foston *Derbys.* 222 C4
Foston *Leics.* 210 B3
Foston *Lincs.* 223 D3
Foston *N.Yorks.* 245 F1
Foston on the Wolds 246 D2
Fotherby 238 D3
Fotheringhay 211 F3
Foubister 339 E2
Foul Mile 160 B2
Foula 342 B5
Foulbog 276 D5
Foulden *Norf.* 213 F3
Foulden *Sc.Bord.* 287 G4
Foulness Island 188 D3
Foulridge 243 E3
Foulsham 228 B3
Foulstone 249 G4
Foulzie 324 C3
Fountainhall 286 B5
Fountains Abbey & Studley Royal Water Garden 87
Four Ashes *Staffs.* 208 B2
Four Ashes *Staffs.* 208 A4
Four Ashes *Suff.* 214 A4
Four Crosses *Denb.* 218 D3
Four Crosses *Powys* 206 B1
Four Crosses *Powys* 205 G2
Four Crosses *Staffs.* 208 B2
Four Elms 173 D4
Four Forks 165 F4
Four Gotes 212 C1
Four Lane Ends *B'burn.* 242 C5
Four Lane Ends *Ches.* 220 C1
Four Lane Ends *York* 245 F2
Four Lanes 145 D3
Four Marks 170 B4
Four Mile Bridge 230 A5
Four Oaks *E.Suss.* 161 D1
Four Oaks *Glos.* 195 F5
Four Oaks *W.Mid.* 209 E4
Four Oaks *W.Mid.* 208 D3
Four Oaks Park 208 D3
Four Roads 178 A2
Four Throws 160 C1
Fourlane Ends 223 E2
Fourlanes End 221 F2
Fourpenny 332 D5
Fourstones 261 E1
Fovant 168 B5
Foveran House 313 E2
Fowey 147 F4
Fowlis 294 B1
Fowlis Wester 293 E2
Fowlmere 200 C3
Fownhope 195 E4
Fox Hatch 187 E3
Fox Lane 171 D2
Fox Street 202 B5
Foxbar 283 F3

Foxcombe Hill 183 G2
Foxcote *Glos.* 182 C1
Foxcote *Som.* 167 E2
Foxdale 240 A4
Foxearth 201 G3
Foxfield 248 D4
Foxham 182 B5
Foxhole *Cornw.* 147 D4
Foxhole *High.* 309 E1
Foxholes 254 D5
Foxhunt Green 160 A2
Foxley *Here.* 194 D3
Foxley *Norf.* 228 B3
Foxley *Northants.* 198 B2
Foxley *Wilts.* 182 A4
Foxt 222 B3
Foxton *Cambs.* 200 C3
Foxton *Dur.* 262 C5
Foxton *Leics.* 210 B3
Foxton Locks 72
Foxup 251 D5
Foxwist Green 220 D1
Foy 195 E5
Foyers 309 D2
Frachadil 296 C4
Fraddam 144 C3
Fraddon 146 D4
Fradley 209 D1
Fradswell 221 G4
Fraisthorpe 247 D1
Framfield 159 G1
Framingham Earl 229 D5
Framingham Pigot 229 D5
Framlingham 203 D1
Framlingham Castle 79
Frampton *Dorset* 154 C3
Frampton *Lincs.* 226 B4
Frampton Cotterell 181 F4
Frampton Mansell 182 B2
Frampton on Severn 181 G2
Frampton West End 226 A3
Framsden 202 D2
Framwellgate Moor 262 B3
France Lynch 182 B2
Frances Green 242 C4
Franche 208 A5
Frandley 234 A5
Frankby 232 D4
Frankfort 229 E3
Frankley 208 C4
Franksbridge 194 A2
Frankton 209 G5
Frant 173 E5
Fraserburgh 325 E3
Frating 202 B5
Fratton 157 F2
Freasley 209 E3
Freathy 149 D5
Freckenham 213 E5
Freckleton 242 A5
Freeby 224 D5
Freefolk 169 F3
Freehay 222 B3
Freeland 183 G1
Freester 343 D2
Freethorpe 229 F5
Freethorpe Common 229 F5
Freiston 226 B3
Freiston Shore 226 B3
Fremington *Devon* 163 F2
Fremington *N.Yorks.* 251 F3
Frenchay 181 F5
Frenchbeer 149 G2
Frendraught 324 B5
Frenich 291 G4
Frensham 170 D3
Fresgoe 336 B2
Freshbrook 182 D4
Freshfield 233 D2
Freshford 167 E2
Freshwater 156 C4
Freshwater Bay 156 C4
Freshwater East 176 D3
Fressingfield 215 D4
Freston 202 C4
Freswick 337 F2
Fretherne 181 G2
Frettenham 228 D4
Freuchie 294 A4
Freystrop Cross 176 C1
Friars Carse 266 D2
Friar's Gate 173 D5
Friarton 293 G2
Friday Bridge 212 C2
Friday Street *E.Suss.* 160 B3
Friday Street *Suff.* 202 D2
Friday Street *Suff.* 203 E2
Friday Street *Surr.* 171 G3
Fridaythorpe 246 A2
Friern Barnet 186 B3
Friesthorpe 238 A4
Frieston 225 E3
Frieth 184 C3
Frilford 183 G3
Frilsham 184 A5
Frimley 171 D2
Frimley Green 171 D2
Frindsbury 173 G2
Fring 227 F4
Fringford 198 B5
Friningham 174 A3
Frinsted 174 A3
Frinton-on-Sea 189 F1
Friockheim 303 D4
Friog 204 C1
Frisby on the Wreake 210 B1
Friskney 226 C2
Friskney Eaudyke 226 C2
Friston *E.Suss.* 160 A4
Friston *Suff.* 203 F1
Fritchley 223 E2
Frith 174 B3
Frith Bank 226 B3
Frith Common 195 F1
Fritham 156 B1
Frithelstock 163 E4
Frithelstock Stone 163 E4
Frithville 226 B2
Frittenden 174 A4
Frittiscombe 151 E3
Fritton *Norf.* 214 D2
Fritton *Norf.* 229 F5
Fritton Lake Countryworld 79
Fritwell 198 A5
Frizinghall 244 A4
Frizington 258 D5
Frocester 181 G2
Frochas 206 B2
Frodesley 207 E2
Frodesley Lane 207 E2
Frodingham 237 F1
Frodsham 233 G5
Frog End 200 C2
Frog Pool 195 G1
Frogden 278 B4
Froggatt 235 G5
Froghall 222 B3
Frogham 156 A1
Frogland Cross 181 F4
Frogmore *Devon* 151 D3
Frogmore *Hants.* 170 D2
Frogmore *Herts.* 186 A2
Frogwell 148 D4
Frolesworth 210 A3
Frome 167 E3
Frome Market 167 F2
Frome St. Quintin 154 B2
Frome Whitfield 154 C3
Fromes Hill 195 F3
Fron *Gwyn.* 216 C4
Fron *Powys* 206 B2
Fron *Powys* 193 G1
Fron *Powys* 206 A3
Fron Isaf 219 F4
Froncysyllte 219 F3
Fron-goch 218 C4
Frostenden 215 F3
Frosterley 261 G4
Froxfield 169 E1
Froxfield Green 170 C5
Fryerning 187 F2
Fugglestone St. Peter 168 C4
Fulbeck 225 E2
Fulbourn 200 D2
Fulbrook 183 E1
Fulflood 169 F5
Fulford *Som.* 165 F5
Fulford *Staffs.* 221 G4
Fulford *York* 245 F3
Fulham 186 B5
Fulking 159 E2
Full Sutton 245 G2
Fullaford 163 G2
Fuller Street 187 G1
Fuller's Moor 220 B2
Fullerton 169 E4
Fulletby 238 C5
Fullwood 283 F4
Fulmer 185 F4
Fulmodeston 228 A2
Fulnetby 238 B5
Fulready 197 E3
Fulstone 235 F2
Fulstow 238 D3
Fulwell *Oxon.* 197 F5
Fulwell *T. & W.* 262 C2
Fulwood *Lancs.* 242 B4
Fulwood *S.Yorks.* 236 A4
Fundenhall 214 C2
Fundenhall Street 214 C2
Funtington 158 A3
Funtley 157 E2
Funzie 345 F3
Furley 153 F2
Furnace *Arg. & B.* 290 C4
Furnace *Carmar.* 178 B2
Furnace *Cere.* 204 C3
Furnace *High.* 319 F2
Furnace End 209 E3
Furner's Green 159 G1
Furness Abbey 95
Furness Vale 235 E4
Furneux Pelham 200 C5
Furnham 153 G2
Further Quarter 174 A5
Furtho 198 C3
Furze Green 214 D3
Furze Platt 185 D4
Furzehill *Devon* 164 A3
Furzehill *Dorset* 155 G2
Furzeley Corner 157 F1
Furzey Lodge 156 C2
Furzley 156 B1
Fyfett 153 F1
Fyfield *Essex* 187 E2
Fyfield *Glos.* 183 E2
Fyfield *Hants.* 169 D3
Fyfield *Oxon.* 183 G3
Fyfield *Wilts.* 168 C1
Fyfield *Wilts.* 168 C1
Fylingthorpe 254 C2
Fyning 170 D5
Fyvie 312 C1
Fyvie Castle 123

G

Gabalfa 180 A5
Gabhsunn Bho Dheas 329 F2
Gabhsunn Bho Thuath 329 F2
Gablon 332 C5
Gabroc Hill 283 F4
Gaddesby 210 B1
Gaddesden Row 185 F1
Gadebridge 185 F2
Gadshill 187 G5
Gaer *Newport* 180 B4
Gaer *Powys* 194 A5
Gaer-fawr 180 D3
Gaerllwyd 180 D3
Gaerwen 230 C5
Gagingwell 197 G5
Gaich *High.* 310 C2
Gaich *High.* 309 F1
Gaick Lodge 300 C1
Gailes 274 B2
Gailey 208 B1
Gainford 252 A1
Gainsborough 237 F3
Gainsborough Old Hall 72
Gainsborough's House 79
Gainsford End 201 F4
Gairloch 319 D2
Gairlochy 299 D1
Gairney Bank 293 G5
Gairnshiel Lodge 311 E4
Gaitsgill 259 G2
Galabank 286 B5
Galashiels 277 F2
Galdenoch 264 C4
Gale 234 D1
Galgate 242 A2
Galhampton 166 D5
Gallanach 290 A2
Gallantry Bank 220 C2
Gallatown 294 A5
Gallchoille 289 G5
Gallery 303 E3
Gallery of Modern Art 123
Galley Common 209 F3
Galleyend 187 G2
Galleywood 187 G2
Gallowfauld 302 C5
Gallowhill 283 F3
Gallows Green 222 B3
Gallowstree Common 184 B4
Gallowstree Elm 208 A4
Gallt Melyd (Meliden) 232 B4
Galltair 307 E2
Gallt-y-foel 217 E1
Gallypot Street 173 D5
Galmington 165 F5
Galmisdale 297 D1
Galmpton *Devon* 150 C3
Galmpton *Torbay* 151 E2
Galmpton Warborough 151 E2
Galphay 252 B5
Galston 274 C2
Galtrigill 317 E4
Gamble's Green 187 G1
Gamblesby 260 C4
Gamelsby 259 F1
Gamesley 235 E3
Gamlingay 200 A2
Gamlingay Cinques 200 A2
Gamlingay Great Heath 200 A2
Gammaton 163 E3
Gammaton Moor 163 E3
Gammersgill 251 F4
Gamrie 324 C3
Gamston *Notts.* 237 E5
Gamston *Notts.* 224 B4
Ganarew 181 E1
Gang 148 D4
Ganllwyd 218 A5
Gannochy 303 E2
Ganstead 247 D4
Ganthorpe 253 F5
Ganton 254 C5
Ganwick Corner 186 B3
Gaodhail 289 F1
Gappah 152 B5
Gara Bridge 150 D2
Garabal 291 F3
Garadheancal 330 B4
Garbat 320 D3
Garbhallt 290 C5
Garboldisham 214 B3
Garden 292 A5
Garden City 220 A1
Garden Village 235 G3
Gardeners Green 170 D1
Gardenstown 324 C3
Garderhouse 342 C3
Gardham 246 B3
Gare Hill 167 E3
Garelochhead 291 E5
Garford 183 G3
Garforth 244 D4
Gargrave 243 F2
Gargunnock 292 C5
Gariob 281 F1
Garlic Street 214 D3
Garlies Castle 265 F4
Garlieston 257 E2
Garlinge Green 174 D3
Garlogie 312 C4
Garmelow 221 F5
Garmond 324 D4
Garmony 297 F5
Garmouth 323 F3
Garmston 207 F2
Garnant 178 C1
Garndolbenmaen 217 D3
Garneddwen 205 D2
Garnett Bridge 249 G3
Garnfadryn 216 B4
Garnswllt 178 C2
Garrabost 329 G4
Garrachra 282 B1
Garralburn 323 G4
Garras 145 E4
Garreg 217 F3
Garreg Bank 206 B1
Garrett's Green 209 D4
Garrick 292 D3
Garrigill 260 D3
Garriston 252 A3
Garroch 265 G2
Garrochty 282 B4
Garros 318 A3
Garrow 292 D1
Garryhorn 265 G1
Garrynahine (Gearraidh na h-Aibhne) 328 D4
Garsdale 250 C4
Garsdale Head 250 C3
Garsdon 182 B4
Garshall Green 221 G4
Garsington 184 A2
Garstang 242 A3
Garston 233 F4
Garswood 233 G3
Gartachoil 292 A5
Gartally 309 D1
Gartavaich 281 G4
Gartbreck 280 A4
Gartcosh 284 A3
Garth *Bridgend* 179 E3
Garth *Cere.* 204 C4
Garth *Gwyn.* 231 D5
Garth *I.o.M.* 240 B4
Garth *Powys* 193 F3
Garth *Shet.* 342 B2
Garth *Wrex.* 219 F3
Garth Row 249 G3
Garthbrengy 193 G4
Garthdee 313 E4
Gartheli 192 B2
Garthmyl 206 A3
Garthorpe *Leics.* 224 D5
Garthorpe *N.Lincs.* 237 F1
Garths 249 G3
Garthynty 192 D3
Gartincaber 292 B4
Gartly 312 A1
Gartmore 292 A5
Gartnagrenach 281 F4
Gartnatra 280 B3
Gartness 283 G1
Gartocharn 283 F1
Garton 247 E4
Garton-on-the-Wolds 246 B1
Gartymore 333 F3
Garvald 286 C2
Garvamore 309 E5
Garvan 298 B2
Garvard 288 C5
Garve 320 C3
Garveld 272 B5
Garvestone 228 B5
Garvie 282 B1
Garvock *Aber.* 303 F2
Garvock *Inclyde* 283 D2
Garvock *P. & K.* 293 F3
Garwald 276 D5
Garwaldwaterfoot 276 D5
Garway 195 D5
Garway Hill 194 D5
Gask *Aber.* 325 F5
Gask *Aber.* 324 C5
Gask *P. & K.* 293 E3
Gaskan 298 A2
Gass 274 C5
Gastard 167 F1
Gasthorpe 214 A3
Gaston Green 187 E1
Gatcombe 157 D4
Gate Burton 237 F4
Gate Helmsley 245 F2
Gate House 281 D2
Gateacre 233 F4
Gateford 236 C4
Gateforth 245 E5
Gatehead 274 B2
Gatehouse 301 D5
Gatehouse of Fleet 266 A5
Gatelawbridge 266 D1
Gateley 228 A3
Gatenby 252 C4
Gatesgarth 259 E5
Gateshaw 278 B4
Gateshead 262 B1
Gatesheath 220 B1
Gateside *Aber.* 312 B3
Gateside *Angus* 302 C5
Gateside *Fife* 293 G4
Gateside *N.Ayr.* 283 E4
Gateslack 275 G5
Gathurst 233 G2
Gatley 234 C4
Gattonside 277 G2
Gatwick Airport (London Gatwick Airport) 172 B4
Gaufron 193 F1
Gaulby 210 B2
Gauldry 294 B2
Gauntons Bank 220 C3
Gaunt's Common 155 G2
Gaunt's Earthcott 181 F4
Gautby 238 B5
Gavinton 287 E4
Gawber 236 A2
Gawcott 198 B4
Gawsworth 234 C5
Gawthorpe Hall 95
Gawthrop 250 B4
Gawthwaite 249 D4
Gay Bowers 187 G2
Gay Street 171 F5
Gaydon 197 F2
Gayhurst 198 D3
Gayle 251 D4
Gayles 252 A2
Gayton *Mersey.* 233 D4
Gayton *Norf.* 213 F1
Gayton *Northants.* 198 C2
Gayton *Staffs.* 221 G5
Gayton le Marsh 239 E4
Gayton le Wold 238 C4
Gayton Thorpe 213 F1
Gaywood 227 E5
Gazeley 201 F1
Geanies House 322 A2
Gearach 280 A4
Gearnsary 335 G5
Gearradh 298 B3
Gearraidh Bhailteas 314 C1
Gearraidh Bhaird 329 E5
Gearraidh na h-Aibhne (Garrynahine) 328 D4
Gearraidh na Monadh 314 C2
Gearrannan 328 C3
Geary 317 F3
Gedding 202 A2
Geddington 211 D4
Gedgrave Hall 203 F3
Gedintailor 306 B1
Gedling 224 B3
Gedney 226 C5
Gedney Broadgate 226 C5
Gedney Drove End 226 C5
Gedney Dyke 226 C5
Gedney Hill 212 B1
Gee Cross 235 D3
Geevor Tin Mine 30
Geffrye Museum 56
Geilston 283 E2
Geirinis 315 F5
Geisiadar 328 C4
Geldeston 215 E2
Gell *Conwy* 218 B1
Gell *Gwyn.* 217 D4
Gelli 179 F3
Gelli Gynan 219 E2
Gellideg 179 G2
Gellifor 219 E1
Gelligaer 180 A3
Gellilydan 217 F4
Gellioedd 218 C3
Gelly 177 D1
Gellyburn 293 F1
Gellywen 191 F5
Gelston *D. & G.* 266 B5
Gelston *Lincs.* 225 E3
Gembling 246 D2
Gemmil 289 G4
Genoch 264 C5
Genoch Square 264 C5
Gentleshaw 208 C1
Geocrab 326 D4
George Green 185 F4
George Nympton 164 A5
George Stephenson's Birthplace 103
Georgeham 163 E2
Georgetown 283 F3
Georgian House 123
Gerlan 217 F1
Germansweek 149 E1
Germoe 144 C4
Gerrans 145 F3
Gerrards Cross 185 F4
Gerston 336 D3
Gestingthorpe 201 G4
Geuffordd 206 B1
Geufron 205 E4
Gibbet Hill 167 E3
Gibbshill 266 B3
Gibraltar *Lincs.* 227 D2
Gibraltar *Suff.* 202 C2
Gibraltar Point 72
Giddeahall 182 A5
Giddy Green 155 E4
Gidea Park 187 E4
Gidleigh 149 G2
Giffnock 283 G4
Gifford 286 C3
Giffordland 283 D5
Giffordtown 294 A3
Giggleswick 243 E1
Gigha 281 E5
Gilberdyke 246 A5
Gilbert's End 196 A3
Gilchriston 286 B3
Gilcrux 259 E3
Gildersome 244 B5
Gildingwells 236 C4
Gilesgate Moor 262 B3
Gileston 164 D1
Gilfach 180 A3
Gilfach Goch 179 F4
Gilfachrheda 192 A2
Gilgarran 258 D4
Gill 260 A5
Gillamoor 253 F4
Gillen 317 F3
Gillenbie 267 F2
Gillfoot 267 D3
Gilling East 253 F5
Gilling West 252 A2
Gillingham *Dorset* 167 F5
Gillingham *Med.* 173 G2
Gillingham *Norf.* 215 F2
Gillivoan 337 D5
Gillock 337 E3
Gillow Heath 221 F2
Gills 337 F1
Gill's Green 173 G5
Gilmanscleuch 277 E3
Gilmerton *Edin.* 285 G3
Gilmerton *P. & K.* 293 D2
Gilmilnscroft 275 D3
Gilmonby 251 E1
Gilmorton 210 A4
Gilsland 260 C1
Gilsland Spa 260 C1
Gilson 209 D4
Gilstead 244 A4
Gilston 286 B4
Gilston Park 186 D1
Gilthrook 223 F3
Gilwern 180 B1
Gimingham 229 D2
Gin Pit 234 A2
Ginclough 235 D5
Ginger's Green 160 B2
Giosla 328 C5
Gipping 202 B1
Gipsey Bridge 226 A3
Girlsta 342 D2
Girsby 252 C2
Girtford 199 G3
Girthon 266 A5
Girton *Cambs.* 200 C1
Girton *Notts.* 224 D1
Girvan 264 C1
Gisburn 243 E3
Gisburn Cotes 243 E3
Gisleham 215 G3
Gislingham 214 B4
Gissing 214 C3
Gittisham 153 E3
Givons Grove 171 G2
Glackour 320 A1
Gladestry 194 B2
Gladsmuir 286 B2
Gladstone Court Museum 123
Gladstones Land 123
Glaic 282 B2
Glais 178 D2
Glaisdale 253 G2
Glaister 273 E2
Glame 318 B5
Glamis 302 B5
Glamis Castle 123
Glan Conwy 218 B2
Glanaber Terrace 218 A3
Glanaman 178 C1
Glanbran 193 E4
Glan-Denys 192 B2
Glanderston 312 A2
Glandford 228 B1
Glan-Duar 192 B3
Glandwr 191 E5
Glan-Dwyfach 217 D3
Glangrwyney 180 B1
Glanllynfi 179 E3
Glanmule 206 A3
Glan-rhyd *N.P.T.* 179 D2
Glanrhyd *Pembs.* 191 E3
Glanton 279 E5
Glanton Pyke 279 E5
Glantwymyn (Cemmaes Road) 205 E2
Glanvilles Wootton 154 C2
Glendurgan 30
Glanwern 204 C4
Glanwydden 231 G4
Glan-y-don 232 C5
Glanyferi (Ferryside) 177 G1
Glan-y-llyn 180 A4
Glan-y-nant 205 F4
Glan-yr-afon *Gwyn.* 218 C3
Glan-yr-afon *Gwyn.* 218 D3
Glan-yr-afon *I.o.A.* 231 E4
Glan-y-Wern 217 F4
Glapthorn 211 F3
Glapwell 223 F1
Glasahoile 291 G4
Glasbury 194 A4
Glaschoil 310 C1
Glascoed *Mon.* 180 C2
Glascoed *Wrex.* 219 F2
Glascorrie 311 G5
Glascote 209 E2
Glascwm 194 A2
Glasdrum 298 C5
Glasfryn 218 C2
Glasgow 283 G3
Glasgow Airport 283 F3
Glasgow Botanic Garden 123
Glasgow Prestwick International Airport (Prestwick International Airport) 274 B3
Glasgow School of Art 123
Glasgow Science Centre 123
Glashmore 312 C4
Glasinfryn 217 E1
Glasnacardoch 306 C5
Glasnakille 306 B3
Glaspant 191 F4
Glaspwll 204 D3
Glassburn 308 C1
Glassel 312 B5
Glassenbury 173 G5
Glasserton 257 E3
Glassford 284 B5
Glasshouse 195 G5
Glasshouse Hill 195 G5
Glasshouses 244 A1
Glassingall 292 C4
Glasslie 294 A4
Glasson *Cumb.* 268 A5
Glasson *Lancs.* 242 A2
Glassonby 260 B4
Glasterlaw 303 D4
Glaston 211 D2
Glastonbury 166 B4
Glastonbury Abbey 30
Glastonbury Tor 30
Glatton 211 G4
Glazebrook 234 A3
Glazebury 234 A3
Glazeley 207 G4
Gleadless 236 A4
Gleadsmoss 221 F1
Gleann Ghrabhair 329 F5
Gleann Tholastaidh 329 G3
Gleaston 249 D5
Glecknabae 282 B3
Gledhow 244 C4
Gledrid 219 F4
Glemsford 201 G3
Glen *D. & G.* 266 C3
Glen *D. & G.* 265 F5
Glen Auldyn 240 C2
Glen Mona 240 C3
Glen Parva 210 A3
Glen Trool Lodge 265 F2
Glen Village 284 C2
Glen Vine 240 B4
Glenae 267 D2
Glenaladale 298 A2
Glenald 291 E5
Glenamachrie 290 B2
Glenapp Castle 264 B2
Glenarm 302 B3
Glenbarr 272 B2
Glenbatrick 280 D2
Glenbeg *High.* 320 C1
Glenbeg *High.* 310 C2
Glenbeg *High.* 297 E3
Glenbeich 292 B2
Glenbervie *Aber.* 303 F1
Glenbervie *Falk.* 284 C1
Glenboig 284 B3
Glenborrodale 297 F3
Glenbranter 290 D5
Glenbreck 276 B3
Glenbrittle 306 A2
Glenbuck 275 F3
Glenburn 283 F3
Glenbyre 289 E2
Glencaple 267 D4
Glencarse 293 G2
Glencat 312 A5
Glenceitlein 298 D5
Glencloy 273 F2
Glencoe *High.* 298 D4
Glencoe *High.* 123
Glencoe Visitor Centre 123
Glenconglass 311 D2
Glencraig 293 G5
Glencripesdale 297 F4
Glencrosh 266 B2
Glencruittein 290 A2
Glencuie 311 G3
Glendearg *D. & G.* 276 D5
Glendearg *Sc.Bord.* 277 G2
Glendessary 307 F5
Glendevon 293 E4
Glendoebeg 308 D4
Glendoick 294 A2
Glendoll Lodge 302 A2
Glendoune 264 C1
Glendrissaig 264 C1
Glenduckie 294 A3
Glenduisk 264 D2
Glendye Lodge 303 E1
Gleneagles Hotel 293 E3
Gleneagles House 293 E4
Glenearn 293 G3
Glenegedale 280 B4
Glenelg 307 E3
Glenfarg 293 G3
Glenfeochan 290 A2
Glenfiddich Distillery 123
Glenfield 210 A2
Glenfinnan 298 B1
Glenfinnan Monument 123
Glenfoot 293 G3
Glengalmadale 298 A4
Glengap 266 A5
Glengarnock 283 E4
Glengarrisdale 289 F5
Glengennet 265 D1
Glengolly 336 D2
Glengrasco 318 A5
Glengyle 291 F3
Glenhead 266 C2
Glenhead Farm 302 A3
Glenhurich 298 A3
Glenkerry 277 D4
Glenkiln 273 F2
Glenkin 282 C1
Glenkindie 311 G3
Glenlair 266 B3
Glenlatterach 323 E4
Glenlean 282 B1
Glenlee *Angus* 302 C2
Glenlee *D. & G.* 266 A2
Glenlichorn 292 C3
Glenlivet 311 D2
Glenlochar 266 B4
Glenluce 264 C5
Glenluce Abbey 123
Glenmallan 291 E5
Glenmanna 275 F5
Glenmavis 284 B3
Glenmaye 240 A4
Glenmeanie 320 B4
Glenmore *Arg. & B.* 282 B3
Glenmore *High.* 318 A5
Glenmore Lodge 310 B4
Glenmoy 302 C3
Glenmuick 331 F3
Glennoe 290 C1
Glenochar 276 A4
Glenogil 302 C3
Glenprosen Village 302 B3
Glenquiech 302 C3
Glenramskill 272 C4
Glenrazie 265 E4
Glenridding 259 G5
Glenrisdell 281 G4
Glenrossal 331 G4
Glenrothes 294 A4
Glensanda 298 A5
Glensaugh 303 E2
Glensgaich 321 D3
Glenshalg 312 A4
Glenshellish 290 D5
Glensluain 290 C5
Glentaggart 275 G3
Glentham 238 A3
Glenton 312 B2
Glentress 277 D2
Glentrool 265 E3
Glentruan 240 C1
Glenturret Distillery 123
Glentworth 237 G4
Glenuachdarach 310 A4
Glenuig 297 F2
Glenure 298 C5
Glenurquhart 321 G3
Glenwhilly 264 C3
Glespin 275 G3
Gletness 343 D2
Glewstone 195 E5
Glinton 211 G2
Globe Theatre (see Shakespeare's Globe Theatre) 60
Glooston 210 C3

Glororum 279 F3
Glossop 235 E3
Gloster Hill 271 E1
Gloucester 182 A1
Gloucester Cathedral 30
Gloucestershire & Warwickshire Railway 30
Gloup 345 E2
Gloweth 146 B5
Glusburn 243 G3
Gluss 344 C5
Glympton 197 G5
Glyn 218 A2
Glyn Ceiriog 219 F4
Glynarthen 191 G3
Glyncoch 179 G3
Glyncorrwg 179 E3
Glyn-Cywarch 217 F4
Glynde 159 G3
Glyndebourne 159 G2
Glyndyfrdwy 219 E3
Glynn Vivian Art Gallery & Museum 110
Glynneath 179 E2
Glynogwr 179 F4
Glyntaff 179 G4
Gnosall 221 F5
Gnosall Heath 221 F5
Goadby 210 C3
Goadby Marwood 224 C5
Goatacre 182 C5
Goatfield 290 C4
Goathill 154 C1
Goathland 254 B2
Goathurst 165 F4
Gobernuisgeach 336 B5
Gobhaig 326 C3
Gobowen 220 A4
Godalming 171 E3
Goddard's Corner 203 D1
Goddards Green 159 E1
Godden Green 173 E3
Goddington 173 D2
Godford Cross 153 E2
Godington 198 B5
Godleybrook 221 G3
Godmanchester 212 A5
Godmanstone 154 C3
Godmersham 174 C3
Godney 166 B3
Godolphin Cross 144 D3
Godolphin House 30
Godor 206 B1
Godre'r-graig 179 D2
Godshill *Hants.* 156 A1
Godshill *I.o.W.* 157 E4
Godstone 172 C3
Godstone Farm 44
Godwick 228 A3
Goetre 180 C2
Goff's Oak 186 C2
Gogar 285 F2
Gogarth 231 F4
Goginan 204 C4
Goirtean a' Chladaich 298 C2
Goirtein 282 A1
Golan 217 E3
Golant 147 F4
Golberdon 148 D3
Golborne 234 A3
Golcar 235 F1
Gold Hill *Cambs.* 212 D3
Gold Hill *Dorset* 155 E1
Goldcliff 180 C4
Golden Cap 30
Golden Cross 160 A2
Golden Green 173 F4
Golden Grove 178 B1
Golden Pot 170 C3
Golden Valley *Derbys.* 223 F2
Golden Valley *Glos.* 196 B5
Goldenhill 221 F2
Golders Green 186 B4
Goldhanger 188 C2
Goldielea 266 D3
Golding 207 E2
Goldington 199 F2
Goldsborough *N.Yorks.* 254 B1
Goldsborough *N.Yorks.* 244 C2
Goldsithney 144 C3
Goldstone 221 E5
Goldthorn Park 208 B3
Goldthorpe 236 B2
Goldworthy 163 D3
Golford 173 G5
Gollanfield 322 A4
Gollinglith Foot 252 A4
Golspie 332 D5
Golval 336 A2
Gomeldon 168 C4
Gomersal 244 B5
Gometra 296 C5
Gometra House 296 C5
Gomshall 171 F3
Gonachan Cottage 284 A1
Gonalston 224 B3
Gonerby Hill Foot 225 E4
Gonfirth 342 C1
Good Easter 187 F1
Gooderstone 213 F2
Goodleigh 163 G2
Goodmanham 246 A3
Goodmayes 187 D4
Goodnestone *Kent* 175 E3
Goodnestone *Kent* 174 C2
Goodrich 181 E1
Goodrich Castle 65
Goodrington 151 E2
Goodshaw 243 E5
Goodshaw Fold 243 E5
Goodwick (Wdig) 190 C4
Goodworth Clatford 169 E3
Goodyers End 209 F4
Goole 245 G5
Goom's Hill 196 C2
Goonbell 146 B5
Goonhavern 146 B4
Goonhilly Satellite Earth Station 30
Goonvrea 146 B5
Goose Green *Essex* 202 C5
Goose Green *Essex* 202 C5
Goose Green *Gt.Man.* 233 G2
Goose Green *Kent* 173 F3
Goose Green *S.Glos.* 181 F5
Goose Pool 195 D4
Gooseham 162 C4
Goosehill Green 196 B1
Goosewell 150 B2
Goosey 183 F3
Goosnargh 242 B4
Goostrey 234 B5
Gorcott Hill 196 C1
Gorddinog 231 E5
Gordon 286 D5
Gordon Highlanders Regimental Museum 124
Gordonbush 332 D4
Gordonstoun 323 D3
Gordonstown *Aber.* 324 A4
Gordonstown *Aber.* 312 C1
Gore Cross 168 B2
Gore End 169 F1
Gore Pit 188 B1
Gore Street 175 E2
Gorebridge 286 A3
Gorefield 212 C1
Gorey 150 D5
Gorgie 285 G2
Goring 184 B4
Goring Heath 184 B5
Goring-by-Sea 158 D3
Gorleston-on-Sea 229 G5
Gorllwyn 191 G4
Gornalwood 208 B3
Gorrachie 324 C4
Gorran Churchtown 147 D5
Gorran Haven 147 E5
Gors 204 C5
Gorsedd 232 C5
Gorseinon 178 B3
Gorseness 340 C5
Gorseybank 223 D2
Gorsgoch 192 A2
Gorslas 178 B1
Gorsley 195 F5
Gorsley Common 195 F5
Gorstage 234 A5
Gorstan 320 C3
Gorstanvorran 298 A2
Gorsty Hill 222 C5
Gorten 289 G1
Gortenbuie 289 E1
Gorteneorn 297 F3
Gorton *Arg. & B.* 296 A4
Gorton *Gt.Man.* 234 C3
Gosbeck 202 C2
Gosberton 226 A4
Gosberton Clough 225 G5
Goseley Dale 223 E5
Gosfield 201 F5
Gosford *Here.* 195 E1
Gosford *Oxon.* 184 A1
Gosforth *Cumb.* 248 B2
Gosforth *T. & W.* 262 B1
Gosland Green 220 C2
Gosmore 199 G5
Gospel End 208 B3
Gosport 157 F3
Gossabrough 345 F4
Gossington 181 G2
Gossops Green 172 B5
Goswick 279 E2
Gotham 223 G4
Gotherington 196 B5
Gothers 147 D4
Gott 342 D3
Gotton 165 F5
Goudhurst 173 G5
Goulceby 238 C5
Gourdas 324 C5
Gourdon 303 G2
Gourock 282 D2
Govan 283 G3
Goverton 224 C2
Goveton 151 D3
Govilon 180 B1
Gowanhill 325 F3
Gowdall 245 F5
Gower 110
Gowerton 178 B3
Gowkhall 285 E1
Gowthorpe 245 G2
Goxhill *E.Riding* 247 D3
Goxhill *N.Lincs.* 246 D5
Goytre 179 D4
Gozzard's Ford 183 G3
Grabhair 327 F2
Graby 225 F5
Gradbach 221 G1
Grade 145 E5
Gradeley Green 220 C2
Graffham 158 B2
Grafham *Cambs.* 199 G1
Grafham *Surr.* 171 F3
Grafham Water 79
Grafton *Here.* 195 D4
Grafton *N.Yorks.* 244 D1
Grafton *Oxon.* 183 E2
Grafton *Shrop.* 206 D1
Grafton *Worcs.* 195 E1
Grafton *Worcs.* 196 B4
Grafton Flyford 196 B2
Grafton Regis 198 C3
Grafton Underwood 211 E4
Grafty Green 174 A4
Graianrhyd 219 F2
Graig *Carmar.* 178 A2
Graig *Conwy* 231 G5
Graig *Denb.* 232 B5
Graig-fechan 219 E2
Grain 174 A1
Grainel 280 A3
Grainhow 325 D5
Grains Bar 235 D2
Grainsby 238 C3
Grainthorpe 239 D3
Graiselound 237 E3
Gramisdale (Gramsdal) 315 G4
Grampian Transport Museum 124
Grampound 146 D5
Grampound Road 146 D4
Gramsdal (Gramisdale) 315 G4
Granborough 198 C5
Granby 224 C4
Grandborough 197 G1
Grandes Rocques 151 F4
Grandtully 301 E4
Grange *Cumb.* 259 F5
Grange *E.Ayr.* 274 C2
Grange *High.* 308 C1
Grange *Med.* 173 G2
Grange *Mersey.* 232 D4
Grange *P. & K.* 294 A2
Grange Crossroads 323 G4
Grange de Lings 237 G5
Grange Hall 322 C3
Grange Hill 186 D3
Grange Moor 235 G1
Grange of Lindores 294 A3
Grange, The *Lincs.* 239 F5
Grange, The *Shrop.* 220 A4
Grange, The *Surr.* 172 C4
Grange Villa 262 B2
Grangemill 222 D2
Grangemouth 284 D1
Grangemuir 294 D4
Grange-over-Sands 249 F5
Grangeston 264 D1
Grangetown *Cardiff* 180 A5
Grangetown *R. & C.* 263 E5
Granish 310 B3
Gransmoor 246 D2
Granston 190 B4
Grantchester 200 C2
Grantham 225 E4
Grantley 252 B5
Grantlodge 312 C3
Granton 285 G2
Granton House 276 B5
Grantown-on-Spey 310 C2
Grantsfield 195 E1
Grantshouse 287 F3
Grappenhall 234 A4
Grasby 238 A2
Grasmere 249 E2
Grass Green 201 F4
Grasscroft 235 D2
Grassendale 233 E4
Grassgarth 249 F3
Grassholme 261 F5
Grassington 243 G1
Grassmoor 223 F1
Grassthorpe 224 C1
Grateley 169 D3
Gratwich 222 B4
Gravel Hill 185 F3
Graveley *Cambs.* 200 A1
Graveley *Herts.* 200 A5
Gravelly Hill 208 D3
Gravels 206 C2
Graven 344 D5
Graveney 174 C2
Gravesend 187 F5
Grayingham 237 G3
Grayrigg 249 G3
Grays 187 F5
Grayshott 171 D4
Grayswood 171 E4
Grazeley 170 B1
Greasbrough 236 B3
Greasby 233 D4
Great Aberystwyth Camera Obscura 110
Great Abington 200 D3
Great Addington 211 E5
Great Alne 196 D2
Great Altcar 233 E2
Great Amwell 186 C1
Great Asby 250 B1
Great Ashfield 202 A1
Great Ayton 253 E1
Great Baddow 187 G2
Great Bardfield 201 E4
Great Barford 199 G2
Great Barr 208 C3
Great Barrington 183 E1
Great Barrow 220 B1
Great Barton 201 G1
Great Barugh 253 G5
Great Bavington 270 B3
Great Bealings 202 D3
Great Bedwyn 169 D1
Great Bentley 202 C5
Great Bernera 328 C4
Great Billing 198 D1
Great Bircham 227 F4
Great Blakenham 202 C2
Great Bolas 220 D5
Great Bookham 171 G2
Great Bourton 197 G3
Great Bowden 210 C4
Great Bradley 201 E2
Great Braxted 188 B1
Great Bricett 202 B2
Great Brickhill 199 E4
Great Bridgeford 221 F5
Great Brington 198 B1
Great Bromley 202 B5
Great Broughton *Cumb.* 259 D3
Great Broughton *N.Yorks.* 253 E2
Great Buckland 173 F2
Great Budworth 234 A5
Great Burdon 252 C1
Great Burstead 187 F3
Great Busby 253 E2
Great Cambourne 200 B2
Great Canfield 187 E1
Great Canney 188 B2
Great Carlton 239 E4
Great Casterton 211 F2
Great Central Railway 72
Great Chalfield 167 F1
Great Chalfield Manor 30
Great Chart 174 B4
Great Chatwell 207 G1
Great Chell 221 F2
Great Chesterford 200 D3
Great Cheverell 168 A2
Great Chishill 200 C4
Great Clacton 189 E1
Great Clifton 258 D4
Great Coates 238 C2
Great Comberton 196 B3
Great Corby 260 A2
Great Cornard 201 G3
Great Cowden 247 E3
Great Coxwell 183 E3
Great Coxwell Barn 44
Great Crakehall 252 B4
Great Cransley 210 D5
Great Cressingham 213 G2
Great Crosby 233 E2
Great Crosthwaite 259 F4
Great Cubley 222 C4
Great Cumbrae 282 C4
Great Dalby 210 C1
Great Dixter 44
Great Doddington 199 D1
Great Doward 181 E1
Great Dunham 213 G1
Great Dunmow 201 E5
Great Durnford 168 C4
Great Easton *Essex* 201 E5
Great Easton *Leics.* 210 D3
Great Eccleston 242 A3
Great Edstone 253 G4
Great Ellingham 214 B2
Great Elm 167 E3
Great Eversden 200 B2
Great Fencote 252 B3
Great Finborough 202 B2
Great Fransham 213 G1
Great Gaddesden 185 F1
Great Gidding 211 G4
Great Givendale 246 A2
Great Glemham 203 E1
Great Glen 210 B3
Great Gonerby 225 D4
Great Gransden 200 A2
Great Green *Cambs.* 200 A3
Great Green *Norf.* 215 D3
Great Green *Suff.* 202 A2
Great Green *Suff.* 214 C4
Great Green *Suff.* 214 B4
Great Habton 253 G5
Great Hale 225 G3
Great Hallingbury 187 E1
Great Hampden 184 D2
Great Harrowden 211 D5
Great Harwood 242 D4
Great Haseley 184 B2
Great Hatfield 247 D3
Great Haywood 222 B5
Great Heath 209 F4
Great Heck 245 E5
Great Henny 201 G4
Great Hinton 168 A2
Great Hockham 214 A2
Great Holland 189 F1
Great Horkesley 202 A4
Great Hormead 200 C4
Great Horton 244 A4
Great Horwood 198 C4
Great Houghton *Northants.* 198 C2
Great Houghton *S.Yorks.* 236 B2
Great Hucklow 235 F5
Great Kelk 246 D2
Great Kimble 184 D2
Great Kingshill 185 D3
Great Langton 252 B3
Great Leighs 187 G1
Great Limber 238 B2
Great Linford 198 D3
Great Livermere 213 G5
Great Longstone 235 G5
Great Lumley 262 B3
Great Lyth 207 D2
Great Malvern 195 G3
Great Maplestead 201 G4
Great Marton 241 G4
Great Massingham 227 F5
Great Melton 228 C5
Great Milton 184 B2
Great Missenden 185 D2
Great Mitton 242 D4
Great Mongeham 175 F3
Great Moulton 214 C2
Great Munden 200 B5
Great Musgrave 250 C1
Great Ness 206 D1
Great Notley 201 F5
Great Nurcot 164 C4
Great Oak 180 C2
Great Oakley *Essex* 202 C5
Great Oakley *Northants.* 211 D4
Great Offley 199 G5
Great Orme Country Park 110
Great Ormside 250 C1
Great Orton 259 G1
Great Ouseburn 244 D1
Great Oxendon 210 C4
Great Oxney Green 187 F2
Great Palgrave 213 G1
Great Parndon 186 D2
Great Paxton 200 A1
Great Plumpton 241 G4
Great Plumstead 229 E5
Great Ponton 225 E4
Great Potheridge 163 F4
Great Preston 244 C5
Great Purston 198 A4
Great Raveley 212 A4
Great Rissington 183 D1
Great Rollright 197 F4
Great Ryburgh 228 A3
Great Ryle 279 E5
Great Ryton 207 D2
Great Saling 201 F5
Great Salkeld 260 B4
Great Sampford 201 E4
Great Sankey 233 G4
Great Saredon 208 B2
Great Saxham 201 F1
Great Shefford 183 F5
Great Shelford 200 C2
Great Smeaton 252 C2
Great Snoring 228 A2
Great Somerford 182 B4
Great Stainton 262 C5
Great Stambridge 188 C3
Great Staughton 199 G1
Great Steeping 226 C1
Great Stonar 175 F3
Great Strickland 260 B5
Great Stukeley 212 A5
Great Sturton 238 C5
Great Sutton *Ches.* 233 E5
Great Sutton *Shrop.* 207 E4
Great Swinburne 270 B4
Great Tew 44
Great Tey 201 G5
Great Thorness 157 D3
Great Thurlow 201 E3
Great Torr 150 C3
Great Torrington 163 E4
Great Tosson 270 C1
Great Totham *Essex* 188 B1
Great Totham *Essex* 188 B1
Great Tows 238 C3
Great Urswick 249 D5
Great Wakering 188 C4
Great Waldingfield 202 A3
Great Walsingham 228 A2
Great Waltham 187 F1
Great Warley 187 E3
Great Washbourne 196 B4
Great Weeke 152 A4
Great Welnetham 201 G2
Great Wenham 202 B4
Great Whittington 270 C4
Great Wigborough 188 C1
Great Wigsell 160 C1
Great Wilbraham 200 D2
Great Wilne 223 F4
Great Wishford 168 B4
Great Witcombe 182 B1
Great Witley 195 G1
Great Wolford 197 E4
Great Wratting 201 E3
Great Wymondley 200 A5
Great Wyrley 208 B2
Great Wytheford 207 E1
Great Yarmouth 229 G5
Great Yeldham 201 F4
Greatford 211 F1
Greatgate 222 B3
Greatham *Hants.* 170 C4
Greatham *Hart.* 263 D5
Greatham *W.Suss.* 158 C2
Greatness 173 E3
Greatstone-on-Sea 161 F1
Greatworth 198 A3
Green 219 D1
Green Cross 171 D4
Green End *Beds.* 199 G2
Green End *Bucks.* 199 E4
Green End *Cambs.* 212 A5
Green End *Cambs.* 212 B5
Green End *Herts.* 200 B5
Green End *Herts.* 200 B4
Green End *Warks.* 209 E4
Green Hammerton 245 D2
Green Hill 182 C4
Green Lane 196 C1
Green Moor 235 G3
Green Ore 166 C2
Green Quarter 249 F2
Green Street *E.Suss.* 160 C2
Green Street *Herts.* 186 A3
Green Street *Herts.* 200 C5
Green Street *W.Suss.* 171 G5
Green Street *Worcs.* 196 A3
Green Street Green *Gt.Lon.* 173 D2
Green Street Green *Kent* 187 E5
Green, The *Arg. & B.* 296 A2
Green, The *Cumb.* 248 C4
Green, The *Essex* 187 G1
Green, The *Flints.* 219 F1
Green, The *Wilts.* 167 F4
Green Tye 186 D1
Greenburn 302 C5
Greencroft 262 A3
Greendams 303 E1
Greendykes 279 E4
Greenend 197 F5
Greenfaulds 284 B2
Greenfield *Beds.* 199 F4
Greenfield (Maes-Glas) *Flints.* 232 C5
Greenfield *Gt.Man.* 235 E2
Greenfield *High.* 308 B4
Greenfield *Lincs.* 239 E5
Greenfield *Oxon.* 184 C3
Greenford 186 A4
Greengairs 284 B2
Greengates 244 A4
Greengill 259 E3
Greenhalgh 242 A4
Greenhall 312 B2
Greenham 169 F1
Greenhaugh 269 F3
Greenhead 260 C1
Greenheads 313 F1
Greenheys 234 B2
Greenhill *Gt.Lon.* 186 A4
Greenhill *High.* 333 E4
Greenhill *S.Yorks.* 236 A4
Greenhill Covenanters' House 124
Greenhithe 187 E5
Greenholm 274 D2
Greenholme 249 G2
Greenhow Hill 244 A1
Greenigo 338 D2
Greenland 337 E2
Greenlands 184 C4
Greenlaw *Aber.* 324 B4
Greenlaw *Sc.Bord.* 287 E5
Greenloaning 292 D4
Greenmeadow 180 B3
Greenmoor Hill 184 B4
Greenmount 234 B1
Greenmyre 312 D1
Greenock 283 D2
Greenodd 249 E4
Greens Norton 198 B3
Greenscares 292 C3
Greenside *T. & W.* 262 A1
Greenside *W.Yorks.* 235 F1
Greenstead 202 B5
Greenstead Green 201 G5
Greensted 187 E2
Greensted Green 187 E2
Greenway *Pembs.* 191 D4
Greenway *Som.* 166 A5
Greenwell 260 B2
Greenwich 56
Greet 196 C4
Greete 207 E5
Greetham *Lincs.* 238 D5
Greetham *Rut.* 211 E1
Greetland 243 G5
Gregson Lane 242 B5
Greinetobht (Grenitote) 315 G2
Greinton 166 B4
Grenaby 240 A4
Grendon *Northants.* 199 D1
Grendon *Warks.* 209 E3
Grendon Common 209 E3
Grendon Green 195 E2
Grendon Underwood 198 B5
Grenitote (Greinetobht) 315 G2
Grenofen 149 E3
Grenoside 236 A3
Greosabhagh 327 D4
Gresford 220 A2
Gresham 228 C2
Greshornish 317 G4
Gress (Griais) 329 F3
Gressenhall 228 A4
Gressingham 242 B1
Greta Bridge 251 F1
Gretna 268 B5
Gretna Green 268 B5
Gretton *Glos.* 196 C4
Gretton *Northants.* 211 E3
Gretton *Shrop.* 207 E3
Grewelthorpe 252 B5
Grey Mare's Tail 124
Greyfriars, The 65
Greygarth 252 A5
Greylake 166 A4
Grey's Court 45
Greys Green 184 C4
Greysouthen 259 D4
Greystead 269 F3
Greystoke 260 A4
Greystone *Aber.* 311 E5
Greystone *Angus* 302 D5
Greystone *Lancs.* 243 E3
Greystones 236 A4
Greywell 170 C2
Griais (Gress) 329 F3
Gribthorpe 245 G4
Gribton 266 D2
Griff 209 F4
Griffithstown 180 B3
Grigadale 296 D3
Grigghall 249 F3
Grimeford Village 234 A1
Grime's Graves 79
Grimesthorpe 236 A3
Grimethorpe 236 B2
Griminis (Griminish) 315 F4
Griminish (Griminis) 315 F4
Grimister 345 D3
Grimley 196 A1
Grimmet 274 B4
Grimness 339 D3
Grimoldby 239 D4
Grimpo 220 A5
Grimsargh 242 B4
Grimsay (Griomsaigh) 315 G4
Grimsbury 197 G3
Grimsby 238 C2
Grimscote 198 B2
Grimscott 162 C5
Grimshader (Griomsiadar) 329 F5
Grimsthorpe 225 F5
Grimsthorpe Castle 72
Grimston *E.Riding* 247 E4
Grimston *Leics.* 224 B5
Grimston *Norf.* 227 F5
Grimstone 154 C3
Grimstone End 202 A1
Grindale 255 E5
Grindiscol 343 D4
Grindle 207 G2
Grindleford 235 G5
Grindleton 243 D3
Grindley 222 B5
Grindley Brook 220 C3
Grindlow 235 F5
Grindon *Northumb.* 287 G5
Grindon *Staffs.* 222 B2
Grindon *Stock.* 262 C5
Grindon *T. & W.* 262 C2
Gringley on the Hill 237 E3
Grinsdale 259 G1
Grinshill 220 C5
Grinton 251 F3
Griomarstaidh 328 D4
Griomsaigh (Grimsay) 315 G4
Griomsiadar (Grimshader) 329 F5
Grisdale 250 C3
Grishipoll 296 A4
Gristhorpe 255 D4
Griston 214 A2
Gritley 339 E2
Grittenham 182 C4
Grittleton 182 A5
Grizebeck 248 D4
Grizedale 249 E3
Grizedale Forest Park 96
Grobister 341 E4
Groby 210 A2
Groes 218 D1
Groes-faen 179 G4
Groesffordd 216 B4
Groesffordd Marli 232 B5
Groeslon *Gwyn.* 217 D2
Groeslon *Gwyn.* 217 E1
Groes-lwyd 206 B1
Groes-wen 180 A4
Grogport 281 G5
Groigearraidh 304 A1
Gromford 203 E2
Gronant 232 B4
Groombridge 173 E5
Groombridge Place Gardens 45
Grosmont *Mon.* 194 D5
Grosmont *N.Yorks.* 254 B2
Grotaig 309 D2
Groton 202 A3
Groundistone Heights 277 F4
Grouville 150 C5
Grove *Bucks.* 199 E5
Grove *Dorset* 154 C5
Grove *Kent* 175 E2
Grove *Notts.* 237 E5
Grove *Oxon.* 183 G3
Grove End 174 A2
Grove Green 173 G3
Grove Park 186 D5
Grove, The 196 A3
Grove Town 245 D5
Grovehill 185 F2
Grovesend *S.Glos.* 181 F4
Grovesend *Swan.* 178 B2
Gruids 332 A4
Grula 305 G2
Gruline 297 E5
Grumbla 144 B4
Grundcruie 293 F2
Grundisburgh 202 D2
Gruting 342 B3
Grutness 343 G5
Gualachulain 298 D5
Guardbridge 294 C3
Guarlford 196 A3
Guay 301 F5
Gubbergill 248 B3
Gubblecote 185 E1
Guernsey 151 F5
Guernsey Airport 151 E5
Guestling Green 161 D2
Guestling Thorn 161 D2
Guestwick 228 B3
Guestwick Green 228 B3
Guide 242 D5
Guide Post 271 E3
Guilden Down 206 C4
Guilden Morden 200 A3
Guilden Sutton 220 B1
Guildford 171 E3
Guildtown 293 G1
Guilsborough 210 B5
Guilsfield (Cegidfa) 206 B1
Guilthwaite 236 B4
Guisborough 253 F1
Guiseley 244 A3
Guist 228 B3
Guith 341 D3
Guiting Power 196 C5
Gulberwick 342 D4
Gullane 286 B1
Gulval 144 B3
Gulworthy 149 E3
Gumfreston 177 E2
Gumley 210 B3
Gunby *Lincs.* 225 E5
Gunby *Lincs.* 226 C1
Gunby Hall 72
Gundleton 170 B4
Gunn 163 G2
Gunnersbury 186 A5
Gunnerside 251 E3
Gunnerton 270 B4
Gunness 237 F1
Gunnislake 149 E3
Gunnista 343 E3
Gunnister 344 C5
Gunstone 208 A2
Gunter's Bridge 171 E5
Gunthorpe *Norf.* 228 B2
Gunthorpe *Notts.* 224 B3
Gunthorpe *Rut.* 211 D2
Gunville 157 D4
Gunwalloe 145 D4
Gupworthy 164 C4

Gurnard 157 D3
Gurnett 234 D5
Gurney Slade 166 D3
Gurnos *M.Tyd.* 179 G2
Gurnos *Powys* 179 D2
Gushmere 174 C3
Gussage All Saints 155 G1
Gussage St. Andrew 155 F1
Gussage St. Michael 155 F1
Guston 175 F4
Gutcher 345 E3
Guthram Gowt 225 G5
Guthrie 303 D4
Guyhirn 212 B2
Guynd 303 D5
Guy's Head 226 C5
Guy's Marsh 167 F5
Guyzance 271 E1
Gwaelod-y-garth 180 A4
Gwaenysgor 232 B4
Gwaithla 194 B2
Gwalchmai 230 B5
Gwastad 190 D5
Gwastadnant 217 F2
Gwaun-Cae-Gurwen 178 D1
Gwaynynog 218 D1
Gwbert 191 E3
Gweek 145 E4
Gwehelog 180 C2
Gwenddwr 193 G3
Gwendreath 145 E5
Gwennap 146 B5
Gwenter 145 E5
Gwernaffield 219 F1
Gwernesney 180 D2
Gwernogle 192 B4
Gwernymynydd 219 F1
Gwern-y-Steeple 179 G5
Gwersyllt 220 A2
Gwespyr 232 C4
Gwinear 144 C3
Gwithian 144 C2
Gwredog 230 C4
Gwrhay 180 A3
Gwyddelwern 219 D3
Gwyddgrug 192 A4
Gwynfryn 219 F2
Gwystre 193 G1
Gwytherin 218 B1
Gyfelia 220 A3
Gyre 338 C2
Gyrn Goch 216 C3

H

Habberley 206 C2
Habin 170 D5
Habrough 238 B1
Haccombe 152 B5
Hacconby 225 G5
Haceby 225 F4
Hacheston 203 E2
Hackbridge 172 B2
Hackenthorpe 236 B4
Hackford 228 B5
Hackforth 252 B3
Hackland 340 B4
Hacklet (Haclait) 315 G5
Hacklete (Tacleit) 328 C4
Hackleton 198 D2
Hacklinge 175 F3
Hackness *N.Yorks.* 254 C3
Hackness *Ork.* 338 C3
Hackney 186 C4
Hackthorn 237 G4
Hackthorpe 260 B5
Haclait (Hacklet) 315 G5
Hacton 187 E4
Hadden 278 B3
Haddenham *Bucks.* 184 C2
Haddenham *Cambs.* 212 C5
Haddington *E.Loth.* 286 C2
Haddington *Lincs.* 225 E1
Haddiscoe 215 F2
Haddo House & Country Park 124
Haddon 211 G3
Haddon Hall 72
Hade Edge 235 F2
Hademore 209 D2
Hadfield 235 E3
Hadham Cross 186 D1
Hadham Ford 200 C5
Hadleigh *Essex* 188 B4
Hadleigh *Suff.* 202 B3
Hadleigh Heath 202 A3
Hadley *Tel. & W.* 207 F1
Hadley *Worcs.* 196 A1
Hadley End 222 C5
Hadley Wood 186 B3
Hadlow 173 F4
Hadlow Down 160 A1
Hadnall 220 C5
Hadrian's Wall 104
Hadspen 167 D4
Hadstock 201 D3
Hadzor 196 B1
Haffenden Quarter 174 A4
Hafod Bridge 192 C4
Hafod-Dinbych 218 B2
Hafodunos [illegible] D1
Hafodyrynys 180 B3
Haggate 243 E4
Haggbeck 268 C4
Haggersta 342 C3
Haggerston *Gt.Lon.* 186 C4
Haggerston *Northumb.* 279 E2
Haggrister 344 C5
Haggs 284 B2
Hagley *Here.* 195 E3
Hagley *Worcs.* 208 B4

Hagley Hall 65
Hagnaby *Lincs.* 226 B1
Hagnaby *Lincs.* 239 E5
Hague Bar 235 D4
Hagworthingham 226 B1
Haigh 234 A2
Haighton Green 242 B4
Hail Weston 199 G1
Haile 248 B2
Hailes 196 C4
Hailes Abbey 30
Hailey *Herts.* 186 C1
Hailey *Oxon.* 184 B4
Hailey *Oxon.* 183 F1
Hailsham 160 A3
Haimer 336 D2
Hainault 187 D3
Haine 175 F2
Hainford 228 D4
Hainton 238 B4
Haisthorpe 246 D1
Hakin 176 B2
Halam 224 B2
Halbeath 285 F1
Halberton 152 D1
Halcro 337 E2
Hale *Cumb.* 249 G5
Hale *Gt.Man.* 234 B4
Hale *Halton* 233 F4
Hale *Hants.* 156 A1
Hale *Surr.* 170 D3
Hale Bank 233 F4
Hale Barns 234 B4
Hale Nook 241 G3
Hale Street 173 F4
Hales *Norf.* 215 E2
Hales *Staffs.* 221 E4
Hales Green 222 C3
Hales Place 174 D3
Halesgate 226 B5
Halesowen 208 B4
Halesworth 215 E4
Halewood 233 F4
Half Way Inn 152 D4
Halford *Devon* 152 B5
Halford *Shrop.* 206 D4
Halford *Warks.* 197 E3
Halfpenny 249 G4
Halfpenny Green 208 A3
Halfway *Carmar.* 192 C4
Halfway *Carmar.* 178 B2
Halfway *Powys* 193 E4
Halfway *S.Yorks.* 236 B4
Halfway *W.Berks.* 169 F1
Halfway Bridge 171 E5
Halfway House 206 C1
Halfway Houses *Kent* 174 B1
Halfway Houses *Lincs.* 225 D1
Halghton Mill 220 B3
Halifax 243 G5
Halistra 317 F4
Halket 283 F4
Halkirk 336 D3
Halkyn 232 D5
Hall 283 F4
Hall Cross 242 A5
Hall Dunnerdale 248 D3
Hall Green *Ches.* 221 F2
Hall Green *Lancs.* 242 A5
Hall Green *W.Mid.* 208 D4
Hall Grove 186 B1
Hall of the Forest 206 B4
Halland 160 A2
Hallaton 210 C3
Hallatrow 166 D2
Hallbankgate 260 B2
Hallen 181 E4
Hallfield Gate 223 E2
Hallin 317 F4
Halling 173 G2
Hallington *Lincs.* 238 D4
Hallington *Northumb.* 270 B4
Halliwell 234 A1
Halloughton 224 B2
Hallow 196 A2
Hallow Heath 196 A2
Hallrule 277 G4
Halls 287 D2
Hall's Croft 65
Halls Green *Essex* 186 D2
Hall's Green *Herts.* 200 A5
Hallsands 151 E4
Hallthwaites 248 C4
Hallwood Green 195 F4
Hallworthy 147 F1
Hallyne 285 F5
Halmer End 221 E3
Halmond's Frome 195 F3
Halmore 181 F2
Halmyre Mains 285 F5
Halnaker 158 B3
Halsall 233 E1
Halse *Northants.* 198 A3
Halse *Som.* 165 E5
Halsetown 144 C3
Halsham 247 E5
Halsinger 163 F2
Halstead *Essex* 201 G4
Halstead *Kent* 173 D2
Halstead *Leics.* 210 C2
Halstock 154 B2
Halsway 165 E4
Haltemprice Farm 246 C4
Haltham 226 A1
Haltoft End 226 B3
Halton *Bucks.* [illegible] D1
Halton *Halton* 233 G4
Halton *Lancs.* 242 B1
Halton *Northumb.* 261 F1
Halton *Wrex.* 220 A4
Halton East 243 G2
Halton Gill 251 D5
Halton Green 242 B1
Halton Holegate 226 C1
Halton Lea Gate 260 C2
Halton Park 242 B1
Halton West 243 E2
Haltwhistle 260 D1

Halvergate 229 F5
Halwell 151 D2
Halwill 149 E1
Halwill Junction 149 E1
Ham *Devon* 153 F2
Ham *Glos.* 181 F3
Ham *Glos.* 196 B5
Ham *Gt.Lon.* 186 A5
Ham *High.* 337 E1
Ham *Kent* 175 F3
Ham *Plym.* 150 A2
Ham *Shet.* 342 B5
Ham *Som.* 165 F5
Ham *Som.* 153 F1
Ham *Wilts.* 169 E1
Ham Common 167 F5
Ham Green *Here.* 195 G3
Ham Green *Kent* 174 A2
Ham Green *Kent* 161 D1
Ham Green *N.Som.* 181 E5
Ham Green *Worcs.* 196 C1
Ham Hill 173 F2
Ham House 56
Ham Street 166 C4
Hambleden 184 C4
Hambledon *Hants.* 157 F1
Hambledon *Surr.* 171 E4
Hamble-le-Rice 157 D2
Hambleton *Lancs.* 241 G3
Hambleton *N.Yorks.* 245 E4
Hambridge 166 A5
Hambrook *S.Glos.* 181 F5
Hambrook *W.Suss.* 157 G2
Hameringham 226 B1
Hamerton 211 G5
Hamerton Zoo Park 79
Hamilton 284 B4
Hamlet *Devon* 153 E3
Hamlet *Dorset* 154 B2
Hammer 171 D4
Hammerpot 158 C3
Hammersmith 186 B5
Hammerwich 208 C2
Hammerwood 172 D5
Hammerwood Park 45
Hammond Street 186 C2
Hammoon 155 E1
Hamnavoe *Shet.* 342 C4
Hamnavoe *Shet.* 345 D4
Hamnavoe *Shet.* 344 B4
Hamnavoe *Shet.* 345 D5
Hamnish Clifford 195 E2
Hamp 165 F4
Hampden Park 160 B3
Hamperden End 201 D4
Hampnett 182 D1
Hampole 236 C2
Hampreston 155 G3
Hampstead 186 B4
Hampstead Norreys 184 A5
Hampsthwaite 244 B2
Hampton *Devon* 153 F3
Hampton *Gt.Lon.* 171 G1
Hampton *Kent* 175 D2
Hampton *Peter.* 211 G3
Hampton *Shrop.* 207 G4
Hampton *Swin.* 183 D3
Hampton *Worcs.* 196 C3
Hampton Bishop 195 E4
Hampton Court Palace and Garden 56
Hampton Fields 182 A3
Hampton Heath 220 B3
Hampton in Arden 209 E4
Hampton Loade 207 G4
Hampton Lovett 196 A1
Hampton Lucy 197 E2
Hampton on the Hill 197 E1
Hampton Poyle 184 A1
Hampton Wick 171 G1
Hamptworth 156 B1
Hamsey 159 G2
Hamstall Ridware 208 D1
Hamstead 156 C3
Hamstead Marshall 169 F1
Hamsteels 262 A3
Hamsterley *Dur.* 262 A4
Hamsterley *Dur.* 262 A2
Hamsterley Forest 104
Hamstreet 174 C5
Hamworthy 155 F3
Hanbury *Staffs.* 222 C5
Hanbury *Worcs.* 196 B1
Hanbury Hall 65
Hanbury Woodend 222 C5
Hanby 225 F4
Hanchurch 221 F3
Hancock Museum 104
Handa Island 334 A4
Handale 253 G1
Handbridge 220 B1
Handcross 172 B5
Handforth 234 C4
Handley *Ches.* 220 B2
Handley *Derbys.* 223 E1
Handley Green 187 F2
Handsacre 208 C1
Handside 186 B1
Handsworth *S.Yorks.* 236 B4
Handsworth *W.Mid.* 208 C3
Handwoodbank 206 D1
Handy Cross 185 D3
Hanford *Dorset* 155 E1
Hanford *Stoke* 221 F3
Hanging Bridge [illegible]
Hanging Houghton 210 C5
Hanging Langford 168 B4
Hangingshaw 267 F2
Hanham 181 F5
Hankelow 221 D3
Hankerton 182 B3
Hankham 160 B3
Hanley 221 F3
Hanley Castle 196 A3
Hanley Child 195 F1
Hanley Swan 196 A3
Hanley William 195 F1

Hanlith 243 F1
Hanmer 220 B4
Hannah 239 E5
Hannington *Hants.* 169 G2
Hannington *Northants.* 210 D5
Hannington *Swin.* 183 D3
Hannington Wick 183 D3
Hanslope 198 D3
Hanthorpe 225 F5
Hanwell *Gt.Lon.* 186 A4
Hanwell *Oxon.* 197 G3
Hanwood 206 D2
Hanworth *Gt.Lon.* 186 A5
Hanworth *Norf.* 228 C2
Happisburgh 229 E2
Happisburgh Common 229 E3
Hapsford 233 F5
Hapton *Lancs.* 243 D4
Hapton *Norf.* 214 C2
Harberton 151 D2
Harbertonford 151 D2
Harbledown 174 D3
Harborne 208 C4
Harborough Magna 209 G5
Harborough Museum 72
Harbost (Tarbost) 329 G1
Harbottle 270 B1
Harbourneford 150 D1
Harbridge 156 A1
Harbridge Green 156 A1
Harburn 285 E3
Harbury 197 F2
Harby *Leics.* 224 C4
Harby *Notts.* 237 F5
Harcombe 153 E3
Harcombe Bottom 153 G3
Harden *W.Mid.* 208 C2
Harden *W.Yorks.* 243 G4
Hardendale 249 G1
Hardenhuish 182 B5
Hardgate *Aber.* 312 C4
Hardgate *N.Yorks.* 244 B1
Hardham 158 C2
Hardhorn 241 G4
Hardingham 228 B5
Hardingstone 198 C2
Hardington 167 E2
Hardington Mandeville 154 B1
Hardington Marsh 154 B2
Hardington Moor 154 B1
Hardley 156 D2
Hardley Street 229 E5
Hardmead 199 E3
Hardraw 251 D3
Hardstoft 223 F1
Hardway *Hants.* 157 F2
Hardway *Som.* 167 E4
Hardwick *Bucks.* 184 D1
Hardwick *Cambs.* 200 B2
Hardwick *Lincs.* 237 F5
Hardwick *Norf.* 214 D2
Hardwick *Northants.* 199 D1
Hardwick *Oxon.* 183 F2
Hardwick *Oxon.* 198 A5
Hardwick *S.Yorks.* 236 B4
Hardwick *W.Mid.* 208 C3
Hardwick Hall 72
Hardwick Village 236 D5
Hardwicke *Glos.* 196 B5
Hardwicke *Glos.* 181 G1
Hardwicke *Here.* 194 B3
Hardy Monument 30
Hardy's Cottage 30
Hardy's Green 202 A5
Hare Green 202 B5
Hare Hatch 184 D5
Hare Hill 96
Hare Street *Herts.* 200 B5
Hare Street *Herts.* 200 B5
Hareby 226 B1
Harecroft 243 G4
Hareden 242 C2
Harefield 185 F3
Harehill 222 C4
Harehills 244 C4
Harehope 279 E4
Harelaw 284 D5
Hareplain 174 A5
Haresceugh 260 C3
Harescombe 182 A1
Haresfield 182 A1
Hareshaw *N.Lan.* 284 C3
Hareshaw *S.Lan.* 284 A5
Harestock 169 F4
Harewood 244 C3
Harewood End 195 E5
Harewood House 87
Harford *Devon* 150 C2
Harford *Devon* 152 B3
Hargate 214 C2
Hargatewall 235 F5
Hargrave *Ches.* 220 B1
Hargrave *Northants.* 211 F5
Hargrave *Suff.* 201 F2
Hargrave Green 201 F2
Harker 268 B5
Harkstead 202 C4
Harlaston 209 E1
Harlaxton 225 D4
Harle Syke 243 E4
Harlech 217 E4
Harlech Castle 110
Harlequin 224 B4
Harlescott 207 E1
Harlesden 186 B4
Harleston *Devon* 151 D3
Harleston *Norf.* 214 D3
Harleston *Suff.* 202 B1
Harlestone 198 C1
Harley *S.Yorks.* 236 A3
Harley *Shrop.* 207 E2
Harleyholm 276 A2
Harlington *Beds.* 199 F4
Harlington *Gt.Lon.* 185 F5

Harlosh 317 F5
Harlow 186 D1
Harlow Carr 87
Harlow Hill 261 G1
Harlthorpe 245 G4
Harlton 200 B2
Harlyn 146 C2
Harman's Cross 155 F4
Harmby 252 A4
Harmer Green 186 B1
Harmer Hill 220 B5
Harmondsworth 185 F5
Harmston 225 E1
Harnage 207 E2
Harnham 168 C5
Harnhill 182 C2
Harold Hill 187 E3
Harold Park 187 E3
Harold Wood 187 E3
Haroldston West 176 B1
Haroldswick 345 F1
Harome 253 F4
Harpenden 186 A1
Harpford 153 D3
Harpham 246 C1
Harpley *Norf.* 227 F5
Harpley *Worcs.* 195 F1
Harpole 198 B1
Harprigg 250 B4
Harpsdale 336 D3
Harpsden 184 C4
Harpswell 237 G4
Harpur Hill 235 E5
Harpurhey 234 C2
Harracott 163 F3
Harrapool 306 C2
Harrietfield 293 E1
Harrietsham 174 A3
Harringay 186 C4
Harrington *Cumb.* 258 C4
Harrington *Lincs.* 239 D5
Harrington *Northants.* 210 C5
Harringworth 211 E3
Harris 305 G5
Harris Green 214 D2
Harris Museum & Art Gallery 96
Harriseahead 221 F2
Harriston 259 E2
Harrogate 244 C2
Harrold 199 E2
Harrold-Odell Country Park 79
Harrop Fold 242 D3
Harrow *Gt.Lon.* 186 A4
Harrow *High.* 337 E1
Harrow Green 201 G2
Harrow on the Hill 186 A4
Harrow Weald 186 A3
Harrowbarrow 149 E3
Harrowden 199 F3
Harrowgate Hill 252 B1
Harry Stoke 181 F5
Harston *Cambs.* 200 C2
Harston *Leics.* 224 D4
Harswell 246 A3
Hart 263 D4
Hartburn 270 C3
Hartest 201 G2
Hartfield *E.Suss.* 173 D5
Hartfield *High.* 318 D5
Hartford *Cambs.* 212 A5
Hartford *Ches.* 234 A5
Hartford *Som.* 164 C5
Hartford End 187 F1
Hartfordbridge 170 C2
Hartforth 252 A2
Hartgrove 155 E1
Harthill *Ches.* 220 C2
Harthill *N.Lan.* 284 D3
Harthill *S.Yorks.* 236 B4
Hartington 222 C1
Hartington Hall 270 C3
Hartland 162 C3
Hartland Quay 30
Hartlebury 208 A5
Hartlepool 263 E4
Hartlepool Historic Ships 104
Hartley *Cumb.* 250 C2
Hartley *Kent* 173 F2
Hartley *Kent* 173 G5
Hartley *Northumb.* 271 F4
Hartley Green 221 G5
Hartley Mauditt 170 C4
Hartley Wespall 170 B2
Hartley Wintney 170 C2
Hartlington 243 G1
Hartlip 174 A2
Hartoft End 253 G3
Harton *N.Yorks.* 245 G1
Harton *Shrop.* 207 D4
Harton *T. & W.* 262 C1
Hartpury 196 A5
Hartrigge 278 A4
Hartshead 244 A5
Hartshill 209 F3
Hartshorne 223 E5
Hartsop 249 F1
Hartwell *Bucks.* 184 C1
Hartwell *E.Suss.* 173 D5
Hartwell *Northants.* 198 C2
Hartwith 244 B1
Hartwood 284 C4
Harvard House 65
Harvel 173 F2
Harvington *Worcs.* [illegible]
Harvington *Worcs.* 208 A5
Harvington Hall 66
Harwell *Notts.* 237 D3
Harwell *Oxon.* 183 G4
Harwich 202 D4
Harwood *Dur.* 261 E4
Harwood *Gt.Man.* 234 B1
Harwood *Northumb.* 270 C2
Harwood Dale 254 C3
Harwood on Teviot 277 F5
Harworth 236 D3

Hasbury 208 B4
Hascombe 171 F3
Haselbech 210 C5
Haselbury Plucknett 154 A1
Haseley 197 E1
Haseley Knob 209 E5
Haselor 196 D2
Hasfield 196 A5
Hasguard 176 B2
Haskayne 233 E2
Hasketon 203 D2
Hasland 223 E1
Hasland Green 223 E1
Haslemere 171 E4
Haslemere Educational Museum 45
Haslingden 243 D5
Haslingden Grane 243 D5
Haslingfield 200 C2
Haslington 221 E2
Hassall 221 E2
Hassall Green 221 E2
Hassell Street 174 C4
Hassendean 277 G3
Hassingham 229 E5
Hassocks 159 F2
Hassop 235 G5
Haster 337 F3
Hasthorpe 226 C1
Hastigrow 337 E2
Hastingleigh 174 C4
Hastings *E.Suss.* 160 D3
Hastings *Som.* 153 G1
Hastings Castle 45
Hastingwood 187 D2
Hastoe 185 E2
Haswell 262 C3
Haswell Plough 262 C3
Hatch *Beds.* 199 G3
Hatch *Hants.* 170 B2
Hatch Beauchamp 166 A5
Hatch End 186 A3
Hatch Green 153 G1
Hatching Green 186 A1
Hatchlands 45
Hatchmere 233 G5
Hatcliffe 238 C2
Hatfield *Here.* 195 E2
Hatfield *Herts.* 186 B2
Hatfield *S.Yorks.* 237 D2
Hatfield Broad Oak 187 E1
Hatfield Forest 79
Hatfield Heath 187 E1
Hatfield House 79
Hatfield Peverel 187 G1
Hatfield Woodhouse 237 D2
Hatford 183 F3
Hatherden 169 E2
Hatherleigh 163 F5
Hathern 223 F5
Hatherop 183 D2
Hathersage 235 G4
Hathersage Booths 235 G4
Hathershaw 234 D2
Hatherton *Ches.* 221 D3
Hatherton *Staffs.* 208 B1
Hatley St. George 200 A2
Hatt 149 D4
Hattingley 170 B4
Hatton *Aber.* 313 F1
Hatton *Derbys.* 222 D5
Hatton *Gt.Lon.* 186 A5
Hatton *Lincs.* 238 B5
Hatton *Shrop.* 207 D3
Hatton *Warks.* 197 E1
Hatton *Warr.* 233 G4
Hatton Castle 324 C5
Hatton Country World 66
Hatton Heath 220 B1
Hatton of Fintray 312 D3
Hattoncrook 312 D2
Haugh 239 E5
Haugh Head 279 E4
Haugh of Glass 311 G1
Haugh of Urr 266 C4
Haugham 238 D4
Haughhead 284 A2
Haughley 202 B1
Haughley Green 202 B1
Haughley New Street 202 B1
Haughmond Abbey 66
Haughs 324 A5
Haughton *Ches.* 220 C2
Haughton *Notts.* 237 D5
Haughton *Powys* 206 C1
Haughton *Shrop.* 207 F3
Haughton *Shrop.* 207 E1
Haughton *Shrop.* 220 A5
Haughton *Staffs.* 221 F5
Haughton Green 234 D3
Haughton Le Skerne 252 C1
Haultwick 200 B5
Haunn 314 C2
Haunton 209 E1
Hauxton 200 C2
Havannah 221 F1
Havant 157 G2
Haven 194 D2
Haven, The 171 F4
Havenstreet 157 E3
Havercroft 236 A1
Haverfordwest (Hwllffordd) 176 C1
Haverhill 201 E3
Haverigg [illegible]
Havering Park 187 D3
Havering-atte-Bower 187 E3
Haversham 198 D3
Haverthwaite 249 E4
Haverton Hill 263 D5
Haviker Street 173 G4
Havyat 166 C4
Hawarden 220 A1
Hawbridge 196 B3
Hawbush Green 201 F5
Hawcoat 248 D5

Hawes 251 D4
Hawe's Green 214 D2
Hawick 277 G4
Hawkchurch 153 G2
Hawkedon 201 F2
Hawkenbury *Kent* 173 E5
Hawkenbury *Kent* 174 A4
Hawkeridge 167 F2
Hawkerland 153 D4
Hawkes End 209 E4
Hawkesbury 181 G4
Hawkesbury Upton 181 G4
Hawkhill 279 G5
Hawkhurst 173 G5
Hawkinge 175 E4
Hawkley 170 C5
Hawkridge 164 B4
Hawkshead 249 E3
Hawkshead Hill 249 E3
Hawksheads 242 A1
Hawksland 284 C5
Hawkstone Park 66
Hawkswick 251 E5
Hawksworth *Notts.* 224 C3
Hawksworth *W.Yorks.* 244 A3
Hawksworth *W.Yorks.* 244 B4
Hawkwell *Essex* 188 B3
Hawkwell *Northumb.* 270 C4
Hawley *Hants.* 171 D2
Hawley *Kent* 187 E5
Hawley's Corner 172 D3
Hawling 196 C5
Hawnby 253 E4
Haworth 243 G4
Hawstead 201 G2
Hawstead Green 201 G2
Hawthorn *Dur.* 262 D3
Hawthorn *Hants.* 170 B4
Hawthorn *R.C.T.* 179 G4
Hawthorn *Wilts.* 167 F1
Hawthorn Hill *Brack.F.* 185 D5
Hawthorn Hill *Lincs.* 226 A2
Hawthorpe 225 F5
Hawton 224 C2
Haxby 245 F2
Haxey 237 E2
Haxted 172 D4
Haxton 168 C3
Hay Green 212 D1
Hay Mills 208 D4
Hay Street 200 B5
Hay Tor Granite Tramway 30
Haydock 233 G3
Haydon *Dorset* 154 C1
Haydon *Swin.* 182 D4
Haydon Bridge 261 E1
Haydon Wick 182 D4
Hayes *Gt.Lon.* 185 F4
Hayes *Gt.Lon.* 172 D2
Hayes End 185 F4
Hayfield *Arg. & B.* 290 C2
Hayfield *Derbys.* 235 E4
Hayfield *Fife* 294 A5
Hayfield *High.* 337 D2
Haygrove 165 F4
Hayhillock 302 D5
Hayle 144 C3
Hayling Island 157 G2
Haymoor Green 221 D2
Hayne 152 C1
Haynes 199 G3
Haynes Church End 199 F3
Haynes West End 199 F3
Hay-on-Wye 194 B3
Hayscastle 190 B5
Hayscastle Cross 190 C5
Hayton *Cumb.* 260 B2
Hayton *Cumb.* 259 E2
Hayton *E.Riding* 246 A3
Hayton *Notts.* 237 E4
Hayton's Bent 207 E4
Haytor Vale 152 A5
Haytown 163 D4
Haywards Heath 159 F1
Haywood Oaks 224 B2
Hazel End 200 C5
Hazel Grove 234 D4
Hazel Street 173 F5
Hazelbank *Arg. & B.* 290 C4
Hazelbank *S.Lan.* 284 C5
Hazelbury Bryan 154 D2
Hazeleigh 188 B2
Hazeley 170 C2
Hazelhurst 234 B1
Hazelside 275 G3
Hazelslack 249 F5
Hazelslade 208 C1
Hazelton Walls 294 B2
Hazelwood *Derbys.* 223 E3
Hazelwood *Gt.Lon.* 172 D2
Hazlefield 258 A2
Hazlehead *Aberdeen* 313 D4
Hazlehead *S.Yorks.* 235 F2
Hazlemere 185 D3
Hazlerigg 271 E4
Hazleton 182 C1
Hazon 271 D1
Heacham 227 E4
Head Bridge 163 G4
Headbourne Worthy [illegible] F4
Headcorn 174 A4
Headingley 244 B4
Headington 184 A2
Headlam 252 A1
Headland, The 263 E4
Headless Cross 196 C1
Headley *Hants.* 170 D4
Headley *Hants.* 169 G1
Headley *Surr.* 172 B3
Headley Down 170 D4
Headley Heath 208 C5
Headon 237 E5

Heads Nook 260 A2
Heady Hill 234 C1
Heage 223 E2
Healaugh *N.Yorks.* 251 F3
Healaugh *N.Yorks.* 245 E3
Heald Green 234 C4
Heale *Devon* 163 G1
Heale *Som.* 166 A5
Healey *Lancs.* 234 C1
Healey *N.Yorks.* 252 A4
Healey *Northumb.* 261 G2
Healey *W.Yorks.* 244 B5
Healeyfield 261 G3
Healing 238 C1
Heamoor 144 B3
Heaning 249 F3
Heanish 296 B2
Heanor 223 F3
Heanton Punchardon 163 F2
Heanton Satchville 163 F4
Heap Bridge 234 C1
Heapey 242 C5
Heapham 237 F4
Hearn 170 D4
Hearthstane 276 C3
Heasley Mill 164 A4
Heast 306 C3
Heath *Cardiff* 180 A4
Heath *Derbys.* 223 F1
Heath *W.Yorks.* 236 A1
Heath and Reach 199 E5
Heath End *Derbys.* 223 E5
Heath End *Hants.* 169 G1
Heath End *Hants.* 169 F1
Heath End *Surr.* 170 D3
Heath Hayes 208 C1
Heath Hill 207 G1
Heath House 166 B3
Heath, The 222 B4
Heath Town 208 B3
Heathbrook 220 D5
Heathcot 313 D4
Heathcote *Derbys.* 222 C1
Heathcote *Shrop.* 221 D5
Heathencote 198 C3
Heather 209 F1
Heathfield *Devon* 152 B5
Heathfield *E.Suss.* 160 A1
Heathfield *N.Yorks.* 244 A1
Heathfield *Som.* 165 E5
Heathrow Airport 185 F5
Heathton 208 A3
Heatley 234 B4
Heaton *Lancs.* 242 A1
Heaton *Staffs.* 221 G1
Heaton *T. & W.* 262 B1
Heaton *W.Yorks.* 244 A4
Heaton Hall 96
Heaton Moor 234 C3
Heaton's Bridge 233 F1
Heaverham 173 E3
Heaviley 234 D4
Heavitree 152 C3
Hebburn 262 C1
Hebden 243 G1
Hebden Bridge 243 F5
Hebden Green 220 D1
Hebing End 200 B5
Hebron *Carmar.* 191 E5
Hebron *Northumb.* 271 D3
Heck 267 E2
Heckfield 170 C1
Heckfield Green 214 C4
Heckfordbridge 202 A5
Heckingham 215 E2
Heckington 225 G3
Heckmondwike 244 B5
Heddington 168 A1
Heddle 340 B5
Heddon-on-the-Wall 262 A1
Hedenham 215 E2
Hedge End 157 D1
Hedgerley 185 E4
Hedging 166 A5
Hedley on the Hill 261 G2
Hednesford 208 C1
Hedon 247 D5
Hedsor 185 E4
Heeley 236 A4
Heglibister 342 C2
Heighington *Darl.* 262 B5
Heighington *Lincs.* 225 F1
Heightington 207 G5
Heights of Abraham 73
Heights of Brae 321 E3
Heilam 335 D3
Heisker Islands (Monach Islands) 315 E3
Heithat 267 F2
Heiton 278 B3
Hele *Devon* 163 F1
Hele *Devon* 152 C2
Hele *Devon* 148 D1
Hele *Devon* 152 A5
Hele *Som.* 165 E5
Hele *Torbay* 151 F1
Hele Bridge 163 F5
Hele Lane 152 A1
Helebridge 162 C5
Helensburgh 283 D1
Helford 145 E4
Helhoughton 227 G5
Helions Bumpstead 201 E3
Hell Corner 169 E1
Hellaby 236 C3
Helland *Cornw.* 147 F2
Helland *Som.* 166 A5
Hellandbridge 147 E2
Hellesdon 228 D4
Hellidon 198 A2
Hellifield 243 E2
Hellingly 160 A2
Hellington 229 E5
Hellister 342 C3
Helmdon 198 A3
Helmingham 202 C2
Helmington Row 262 A4
Helmsdale 333 F3
Helmshore 243 D5
Helmsley 253 F4
Helmsley Castle 88
Helperby 244 D1
Helperthorpe 254 C5
Helpringham 225 G3
Helpston 211 G2
Helsby 233 F5
Helsey 239 F5
Helston 145 D4
Helstone 147 E1
Helton 260 B5
Helwith 251 F2
Helwith Bridge 243 E1
Hem 206 B2
Hemborough Post 151 E2
Hemel Hempstead 185 F2
Hemerdon 150 B2
Hemingbrough 245 F4
Hemingby 238 C5
Hemingfield 236 A2
Hemingford Abbots 212 A5
Hemingford Grey 212 A5
Hemingstone 202 C2
Hemington *Leics.* 223 F5
Hemington *Northants.* 211 F4
Hemington *Som.* 167 E2
Hemley 203 D3
Hemlington 253 D1
Hemp Green 203 E1
Hempholme 246 C2
Hempnall 214 D2
Hempnall Green 214 D2
Hempriggs 322 D3
Hempriggs House 337 F4
Hempstead *Essex* 201 E4
Hempstead *Med.* 173 G2
Hempstead *Norf.* 229 F3
Hempstead *Norf.* 228 C2
Hempsted 182 A1
Hempton *Norf.* 228 A3
Hempton *Oxon.* 197 G4
Hemsby 229 F4
Hemswell 237 G3
Hemswell Cliff 237 G4
Hemsworth 236 B1
Hemyock 153 E1
Henbury *Bristol* 181 E5
Henbury *Ches.* 234 C5
Henderland 266 C3
Hendersyde Park 278 B3
Hendham 150 D2
Hendon *Gt.Lon.* 186 B4
Hendon *T. & W.* 262 C2
Hendraburnick 147 F1
Hendre *Bridgend* 179 F4
Hendre *Gwyn.* 216 C4
Hendreforgan 179 F4
Hendy 178 B2
Heneglwys 230 C5
Henfield *S.Glos.* 181 F5
Henfield *W.Suss.* 159 E2
Henford 149 D1
Hengherst 174 B5
Hengoed *Caerp.* 180 A3
Hengoed *Powys* 194 B2
Hengoed *Shrop.* 219 F4
Hengrave 201 G1
Henham 200 D5
Heniarth 206 A2
Henlade 165 F5
Henley *Dorset* 154 C2
Henley *Shrop.* 207 E5
Henley *Som.* 166 B4
Henley *Som.* 154 A2
Henley *Suff.* 202 C2
Henley *W.Suss.* 171 D5
Henley Corner 166 B4
Henley Park 171 E2
Henley-in-Arden 197 D1
Henley-on-Thames 184 C4
Henley's Down 160 C2
Henllan *Carmar.* 191 G3
Henllan *Denb.* 218 D1
Henllan Amgoed 191 E5
Henllys 180 B3
Henlow 199 G4
Hennock 152 B4
Henny Street 201 G4
Henry Moore Foundation 80
Henryd 231 F5
Henry's Moat 190 D5
Hensall 245 E5
Henshaw 261 D1
Hensingham 258 C5
Henstead 215 F3
Hensting 169 F5
Henstridge 154 D1
Henstridge Ash 154 D1
Henstridge Bowden 167 D5
Henstridge Marsh 167 E5
Henton *Oxon.* 184 C2
Henton *Som.* 166 B3
Henwood 147 G2
Heogan 343 D3
Heol Senni 193 F5
Heolgerrig 179 G2
Heol-y-Cyw 179 F4
Hepburn 279 E4
Hepburn Bell 279 E4
Hepple 270 B1
Hepscott 271 E3
Hepthorne Lane 223 F1
Heptonstall 243 F5
Hepworth *Suff.* 214 A4
Hepworth *W.Yorks.* 235 F2
Hepworth South Common 214 A4
Herberts, The 179 F5
Herbrandston 176 B2
Hereford 195 E3
Hereford Cathedral 66
Hergest Croft Gardens 66
Heriot 286 A4
Herm 151 F5
Hermiston 285 F2
Hermitage *D. & G.* 266 B4
Hermitage *Dorset* 154 C2
Hermitage *Sc.Bord.* 268 D2
Hermitage *W.Berks.* 104 A5
Hermitage *W.Suss.* 157 G2
Hermitage Castle 124
Hermitage Green 234 A3
Hermitage, The NTS) 124
Hermitage, The 172 B3
Hermon *Carmar.* 191 G4
Hermon *I.o.A.* 216 C1
Hermon *Pembs.* 191 F4
Herne 175 D2
Herne Bay 175 D2
Herne Common 175 D2
Herne Pound 173 F3
Herner 163 F3
Hernhill 174 C2
Herodsfoot 147 G3
Herongate 187 F3
Heron's Ghyll 159 G1
Heronsgate 185 F3
Herriard 170 B3
Herringfleet 215 F2
Herring's Green 199 F3
Herringswell 201 F1
Herringthorpe 236 B3
Hersden 175 D2
Hersham *Cornw.* 162 C5
Hersham *Surr.* 171 G1
Herstmonceux 160 B2
Herstmonceux Castle 45
Herston 338 D3
Hertford 186 C1
Hertford Heath 186 C1
Hertingfordbury 186 C1
Hesket Newmarket 259 G3
Hesketh Bank 242 A5
Hesketh Lane 242 C3
Heskin Green 233 G1
Hesleden 262 D4
Hesleyside 270 A3
Heslington 245 F2
Hessay 245 E2
Hessenford 148 D5
Hessett 202 A1
Hessle 246 C5
Hest Bank 242 A1
Hestercombe 30
Hester's Way 196 B5
Hestley Green 202 C1
Heston 186 A5
Heswall 233 D4
Hethe 198 A5
Hethelpit Cross 195 G5
Hetherington 270 A4
Hethersett 228 C5
Hethersgill 260 A1
Hethpool 278 C4
Hett 262 B4
Hetton 243 F2
Hetton-le-Hole 262 C3
Heugh 270 C4
Heugh-head *Aber.* 311 F3
Heugh-head *Aber.* 312 A5
Heveningham 215 E4
Hever 173 D4
Hever Castle 45
Heversham 249 F4
Hevingham 228 C3
Hewas Water 147 D5
Hewell Grange 196 C1
Hewell Lane 196 C1
Hewelsfield 181 E2
Hewelsfield Common 181 F2
Hewish *N.Som.* 166 B1
Hewish *Som.* 154 A2
Hewood 153 G2
Heworth 245 F2
Hewton 149 F1
Hexham 261 F1
Hextable 187 E5
Hexthorpe 236 C2
Hexton 199 G4
Hexworthy 149 G3
Hey 243 E3
Hey Houses 241 G5
Heybridge *Essex* 187 F3
Heybridge *Essex* 188 B2
Heybridge Basin 188 B2
Heybrook Bay 150 A3
Heydon *Cambs.* 200 C3
Heydon *Norf.* 228 C3
Heydour 225 F4
Heylipoll 296 A2
Heylor 344 B4
Heyop 206 B5
Heysham 242 A1
Heyshaw 244 A1
Heyshott 158 A2
Heyside 234 D2
Heytesbury 168 A3
Heythrop 197 F5
Heywood *Gt.Man.* 234 C1
Heywood *Wilts.* 167 F2
Hibaldstow 237 G2
Hibb's Green 201 G2
Hickleton 236 B2
Hickling *Norf.* 229 F3
Hickling *Notts.* 224 B5
Hickling Green 229 F3
Hickling Heath 229 F3
Hickstead 159 E1
Hidcote Bartrim 197 D3
Hidcote Boyce 197 D3
Hidcote Manor Gardens 30
High Ackworth 236 B1
High Angerton 270 C3
High Balantyre 290 C3
High Bankhill 260 B3
High Beach 186 D3
High Beeches 45
High Bentham 242 C1
High Bickington 163 F3
High Birkwith 250 C5
High Blantyre 284 A4
High Bonnybridge 284 C2
High Borgue 266 A5
High Borve 329 F2
High Bradfield 235 G3
High Bradley 243 G3
High Bransholme 246 D4
High Bray 163 G2
High Bridge 259 G2
High Brooms 173 E4
High Bullen 163 F3
High Burton 252 B4
High Buston 271 E1
High Callerton 271 D4
High Casterton 250 B5
High Catton 245 G2
High Close 252 A1
High Cogges 183 F2
High Common 214 C3
High Coniscliffe 252 B1
High Crompton 234 D2
High Cross *Hants.* 170 C5
High Cross *Herts.* 186 C1
High Cross *W.Suss.* 159 E2
High Cup Nick 96
High Easter 187 F1
High Ellington 252 A4
High Entercommon 252 C2
High Ercall 207 E1
High Etherley 262 A5
High Ferry 226 B3
High Flatts 235 G2
High Force 104
High Garrett 201 F5
High Gate 243 F5
High Grange 262 A4
High Green *Norf.* 228 C5
High Green *Norf.* 228 A4
High Green *Norf.* 228 A5
High Green *S.Yorks.* 236 A3
High Green *Suff.* 201 G1
High Green *Worcs.* 196 A3
High Halden 174 A5
High Halstow 187 G5
High Ham 166 B4
High Harrington 258 D4
High Harrogate 244 C2
High Hatton 220 D5
High Hauxley 271 E1
High Hawsker 254 C2
High Heath *Shrop.* 221 D5
High Heath *W.Mid.* 208 C2
High Hesket 260 A3
High Hesleden 263 D4
High Hoyland 235 G1
High Hunsley 246 B4
High Hurstwood 159 G1
High Hutton 245 G1
High Ireby 259 F3
High Kelling 228 B2
High Kilburn 253 E5
High Kingthorpe 254 B4
High Knipe 249 G1
High Lane *Derbys.* 223 F3
High Lane *Gt.Man.* 235 D4
High Lane *Worcs.* 195 F1
High Laver 187 E2
High Legh 234 B4
High Leven 252 D1
High Littleton 166 D2
High Lorton 259 E4
High Marishes 254 B5
High Marnham 237 F5
High Melton 236 C2
High Moor 236 B4
High Newton 249 F4
High Newton-by-the-Sea 279 G4
High Nibthwaite 249 D3
High Offley 221 E5
High Ongar 187 E2
High Onn 208 A1
High Park Corner 202 B5
High Roding 187 F1
High Shaw 251 D3
High Spen 262 A1
High Stoop 262 A3
High Street *Cornw.* 147 D4
High Street *Kent* 173 G5
High Street *Suff.* 203 F2
High Street *Suff.* 215 E3
High Street *Suff.* 215 F4
High Street *Suff.* 201 G3
High Street Green 202 B2
High Throston 263 D4
High Town 208 B1
High Toynton 226 A1
High Trewhitt 270 C1
High Wham 262 A5
High Wigsell 160 C1
High Woolaston 181 E3
High Worsall 252 C2
High Wray 249 E3
High Wych 187 D1
High Wycombe 185 D3
Higham *Derbys.* 223 E2
Higham *Kent* 187 G5
Higham *Lancs.* 243 E4
Higham *S.Yorks.* 236 A2
Higham *Suff.* 201 F1
Higham *Suff.* 202 B4
Higham Dykes 270 D4
Higham Ferrers 199 E1
Higham Gobion 199 G4
Higham on the Hill 209 F3
Higham Wood 173 F4
Highampton 163 E5
Highams Park 186 C3
Highbridge *Hants.* 169 F5
Highbridge *Som.* 166 A3
Highbrook 172 C5
Highburton 235 F1
Highbury 167 D3
Highclere 169 F1
Highclere Castle 45
Highcliffe 156 B3
Higher Alham 167 D3
Higher Ansty 155 D2
Higher Ashton 152 B4
Higher Ballam 241 G4
Higher Blackley 234 C2
Higher Brixham 151 F2
Higher Cheriton 153 E2
Higher Combe 164 C4
Higher Gabwell 151 F1
Higher Green 234 B3
Higher Halstock Leigh 154 B2
Higher Kingcombe 154 B3
Higher Kinnerton 220 A1
Higher Muddiford 163 F2
Higher Nyland 167 E5
Higher Prestacott 149 D1
Higher Standen 243 D3
Higher Tale 153 D2
Higher Thrushgill 242 C1
Higher Town *Cornw.* 147 E3
Higher Town *I.o.S.* 146 B1
Higher Walreddon 149 E3
Higher Walton *Lancs.* 242 B5
Higher Walton *Warr.* 233 G4
Higher Wambrook 153 F2
Higher Whatcombe 155 E2
Higher Wheelton 242 C5
Higher Whiteleigh 148 C1
Higher Whitley 234 A4
Higher Woodhill 234 B1
Higher Woodsford 155 D4
Higher Wraxall 154 B2
Higher Wych 220 B3
Highfield *E.Riding* 245 G4
Highfield *N.Ayr.* 283 E4
Highfield *Oxon.* 198 A5
Highfield *S.Yorks.* 236 A4
Highfield *T. & W.* 262 A2
Highfields *Cambs.* 200 B2
Highfields *Northumb.* 287 G4
Highgate *E.Suss.* 172 D5
Highgate *Gt.Lon.* 186 B4
Highgreen Manor 270 A2
Highland Folk Museum 124
Highland Wildlife Park 124
Highlane *Ches.* 221 F1
Highlane *Derbys.* 236 B4
Highlaws 259 E2
Highleadon 195 G5
Highleigh *Devon* 164 C5
Highleigh *W.Suss.* 158 A4
Highley 207 G4
Highmead 192 B3
Highmoor Cross 184 B4
Highmoor Hill 181 D4
Highnam 181 G1
Highstead 175 E2
Highsted 174 B2
Highstreet 174 C2
Highstreet Green *Essex* 201 F4
Highstreet Green *Surr.* 171 E4
Hightae 267 E3
Highter's Heath 208 C5
Hightown *Hants.* 156 A2
Hightown *Mersey.* 233 D2
Hightown Green 202 A2
Highway 182 C5
Highweek 152 B5
Highwood 195 F1
Highwood Hill 186 B3
Highworth 183 E3
Hilborough 213 G2
Hilcote 223 F2
Hilcott 168 C2
Hilden Park 173 E4
Hildenborough 173 E4
Hildenley 253 G5
Hildersham 200 D3
Hilderstone 221 G4
Hilderthorpe 247 D1
Hilfield 154 C2
Hilgay 213 E3
Hill *S.Glos.* 181 F3
Hill *Warks.* 197 G1
Hill *Worcs.* 196 B3
Hill Brow 170 C5
Hill Chorlton 221 E4
Hill Common 229 F3
Hill Cottages 253 G3
Hill Croome 196 A3
Hill Deverill 167 F3
Hill Dyke 226 B3
Hill End *Dur.* 261 G4
Hill End *Fife* 293 F5
Hill End *Glos.* 196 A4
Hill End *Gt.Lon.* 185 F3
Hill End *N.Yorks.* 243 G2
Hill Green 200 C4
Hill Head 157 E2
Hill House 124
Hill Houses 207 F5
Hill Mountain 176 C2
Hill of Beath 285 F1
Hill of Fearn 322 A2
Hill of Tarvit Mansion House & Garden 124
Hill Ridware 208 C1
Hill Row 212 C5
Hill Side 235 F1
Hill Street 156 C1
Hill, The 248 C4
Hill Top *Cumb.* 96
Hill Top *Hants.* 156 D2
Hill Top *S.Yorks.* 236 B3
Hill Top *S.Yorks.* 235 G4
Hill View 155 F3
Hill Wootton 197 F1
Hillam 245 E5
Hillbeck 250 C1
Hillberry 240 B4
Hillborough 175 E2
Hillbrae *Aber.* 324 B5
Hillbrae *Aber.* 312 C2
Hillbrae *Aber.* 312 D1
Hillbutts 155 F2
Hillcliffane 223 D3
Hillend *Aber.* 323 G5
Hillend *Fife* 285 F1
Hillend *Midloth.* 285 G3
Hillend *N.Lan.* 284 C3
Hillend *Swan.* 178 A3
Hillend Green 195 G5
Hillersland 181 E1
Hillesden 198 B5
Hillesley 181 G4
Hillfarrance 165 E5
Hillfoot End 199 G4
Hillhead *Devon* 151 F2
Hillhead *S.Ayr.* 274 C3
Hillhead of Auchentumb 325 E4
Hillhead of Cocklaw 325 F5
Hilliard's Cross 209 D1
Hilliclay 337 D2
Hillingdon 185 F4
Hillington *Glas.* 283 G3
Hillington *Norf.* 227 F5
Hillmorton 210 A5
Hillockhead *Aber.* 311 F4
Hillockhead *Aber.* 311 G3
Hillowton 266 B4
Hillpound 157 E1
Hill's End 199 E4
Hills Town 223 F1
Hillsborough 236 A3
Hillsford Bridge 164 A3
Hillside *Aber.* 313 E5
Hillside *Angus* 303 F3
Hillside *Moray* 323 D3
Hillside *Shet.* 342 D1
Hillside *Worcs.* 195 G1
Hillswick 344 B5
Hillway 157 F4
Hillwell 343 F4
Hillyfields 156 C1
Hilmarton 182 C5
Hilperton 167 F2
Hilsea 157 F2
Hilston 247 E4
Hilton *Cambs.* 200 A1
Hilton *Cumb.* 260 D5
Hilton *Derbys.* 222 D4
Hilton *Dorset* 155 D2
Hilton *Dur.* 262 A5
Hilton *High.* 322 B1
Hilton *Shrop.* 207 G3
Hilton *Staffs.* 208 C2
Hilton *Stock.* 253 D1
Hilton Croft 313 E1
Hilton of Cadboll 322 A2
Hilton of Delnies 322 A4
Himbleton 196 B2
Himley 208 A3
Hincaster 249 G4
Hinchley Wood 171 G1
Hinckley 209 G3
Hinderclay 214 B4
Hinderton 233 E5
Hinderwell 253 G1
Hindford 220 A4
Hindhead 171 D4
Hindley *Gt.Man.* 234 A2
Hindley *Northumb.* 261 G2
Hindley Green 234 A2
Hindlip 196 A2
Hindolveston 228 B3
Hindon *Som.* 164 C3
Hindon *Wilts.* 168 A4
Hindringham 228 A2
Hingham 228 B5
Hinksford 208 A4
Hinstock 221 D5
Hintlesham 202 B3
Hinton *Glos.* 181 F2
Hinton *Hants.* 156 B3
Hinton *Here.* 194 C4
Hinton *Northants.* 198 A2
Hinton *S.Glos.* 181 G5
Hinton *Shrop.* 206 D2
Hinton Admiral 156 B3
Hinton Ampner *Hants.* 169 G5
Hinton Ampner *Hants.* 45
Hinton Blewett 166 C2
Hinton Charterhouse 167 E2
Hinton Martell 155 G2
Hinton on the Green 196 C3
Hinton Parva *Dorset* 155 F2
Hinton Parva *Swin.* 183 E4
Hinton St. George 154 A1
Hinton St. Mary 155 D1
Hinton Waldrist 183 F3
Hinton-in-the-Hedges 198 A4
Hints *Shrop.* 207 F5
Hints *Staffs.* 209 D2
Hinwick 199 E1
Hinxhill 174 C4
Hinxton 200 C3
Hinxworth 200 A3
Hipperholme 244 A5
Hipsburn 279 G5
Hipswell 252 A3
Hirn 312 C4
Hirnant 219 D5
Hirst 271 E3
Hirst Courtney 245 F5
Hirwaen 219 E1
Hirwaun 179 F2
Hiscott 163 F3
Histon 200 C1
Hitcham *Bucks.* 185 E4
Hitcham *Suff.* 202 A2
Hitchin 199 G5
Hither Green 186 C5
Hittisleigh 152 A3
Hittisleigh Barton 152 A3
Hive 246 A4
Hixon 222 B5
H.M. Customs and Excise National Museum 96
H.M.S. Belfast 56
H.M.S. Victory 45
H.M.S. Warrior 45
Hoaden 175 E3
Hoaldalbert 194 C5
Hoar Cross 222 C5
Hoarwithy 195 E5
Hoath 175 E2
Hobarris 206 C5
Hobbister 338 C2
Hobbles Green 201 F2
Hobbs Cross 187 D3
Hobbs Lots Bridge 212 B2
Hobkirk 277 G4
Hobland Hall 229 G5
Hobson 262 A2
Hoby 210 B1
Hockerill 200 C5
Hockering 228 B4
Hockerton 224 C2
Hockley 188 B3
Hockley Heath 209 D5
Hockliffe 199 E5
Hockwold cum Wilton 213 F4
Hockworthy 152 D1
Hoddesdon 186 C2
Hoddlesden 242 D5
Hodgehill 221 F1
Hodgeston 176 D3
Hodnet 220 D5
Hodnet Hall Gardens 66
Hodnetheath 220 D5
Hodsoll Street 173 F2
Hodson 183 D4
Hodthorpe 236 C5
Hoe 228 A4
Hoe Gate 157 F1
Hoff 250 B1
Hoffleet Stow 226 A4
Hoggard's Green 201 G2
Hoggeston 198 D5
Hoggie 324 A4
Hoggrill's End 209 E3
Hogha Gearraidh 315 F2
Hoghton 242 C5
Hognaston 222 D2
Hogsthorpe 239 F5
Holbeach 226 B5
Holbeach Bank 226 B5
Holbeach Clough 226 B5
Holbeach Drove 212 B1
Holbeach Hurn 226 B5
Holbeach St. Johns 212 B1
Holbeach St. Marks 226 B4
Holbeach St Matthew 226 C4
Holbeck 236 C5
Holbeck Woodhouse 236 C5
Holberrow Green 196 C2
Holbeton 150 C2
Holborough 173 G2
Holbrook *Derbys.* 223 E3
Holbrook *Suff.* 202 C4
Holbrooks 209 F4
Holburn 279 E3
Holbury 156 D2
Holcombe *Devon* 152 C5
Holcombe *Gt.Man.* 234 B1
Holcombe *Som.* 167 D3
Holcombe Burnell Barton 152 B3
Holcombe Rogus 153 D1
Holcot 198 C1
Holden 243 D3
Holden Gate 243 E5
Holdenby 198 B1
Holdenhurst 156 A3
Holder's Green 201 E5
Holders Hill 186 B4
Holdgate 207 E4
Holdingham 225 F3
Holditch 153 G2
Hole 153 E1
Hole Park 174 A5
Hole Street 158 D2
Holehouse 235 E3
Hole-in-the-Wall 195 F5
Holford 165 E3
Holgate 245 E2
Holker 249 E5
Holker Hall 96
Holkham 227 G3
Holkham Hall 80
Hollacombe *Devon* 163 D5
Hollacombe *Devon* 152 B2
Hollacombe Town 163 G4
Holland *Ork.* 340 C1
Holland *Ork.* 341 E4
Holland *Surr.* 172 D3
Holland Fen 226 A3
Holland-on-Sea 189 E1
Hollandstoun 341 F1
Hollee 268 A5
Hollesley 203 E3
Hollicombe 151 F1
Hollingbourne 174 A3
Hollingbury 159 F3
Hollingrove 160 B1
Hollington *Derbys.* 222 D4
Hollington *E.Suss.* 160 C2
Hollington *Staffs.* 222 B4
Hollingworth 235 E3
Hollins 236 A5
Hollins Green 234 A3
Hollins Lane 242 A2
Hollinsclough 222 B1
Hollinwood *Gt.Man.* 234 D2
Hollinwood *Shrop.* 220 C4
Hollocombe 163 G4
Hollow Meadows 235 G4
Holloway 223 E2
Hollowell 210 B5
Holly Bush 220 B3
Holly End 212 C2
Holly Green 184 C2
Hollybush *Caerp.* 180 A2
Hollybush *E.Ayr.* 274 B4
Hollybush *Worcs.* 195 G4

Hollyhurst 220 C3
Hollym 247 F5
Hollywater 170 D4
Hollywood 208 C5
Holm *D. & G.* 268 A2
Holm (Tolm) *W.Isles* 329 F4
Holm of Drumlanrig 266 C1
Holmbridge 235 F2
Holmbury St. Mary 171 G3
Holmbush 172 B5
Holme *Cambs.* 211 G4
Holme *Cumb.* 249 G5
Holme *N.Lincs.* 237 G2
Holme *N.Yorks.* 252 C4
Holme *Notts.* 224 D2
Holme *W.Yorks.* 235 F2
Holme Chapel 243 E5
Holme Hale 213 G2
Holme Lacy 195 E4
Holme Marsh 194 C2
Holme next the Sea 227 F3
Holme on the Wolds 246 B3
Holme Pierrepont 224 B4
Holme St. Cuthbert 259 E2
Holme, The 244 B2
Holme-on-Spalding-Moor 246 A4
Holmer 195 E3
Holmer Green 185 E3
Holmes 233 F1
Holmes Chapel 221 E1
Holme's Hill 160 A2
Holmesfield 236 A5
Holmeswood 233 F1
Holmewood 223 F1
Holmfield 243 G5
Holmfirth 235 F2
Holmhead *D. & G.* 266 B2
Holmhead *E.Ayr.* 275 D3
Holmpton 247 F5
Holmrook 248 B2
Holmsgarth 343 D3
Holmside 262 B3
Holmsleigh Green 153 F2
Holmston 274 B3
Holmwrangle 260 B3
Holne 150 D1
Holnest 154 C2
Holnicote 164 C3
Holnicote Estate 31
Holsworthy 162 D5
Holsworthy Beacon 163 D5
Holt *Dorset* 155 G2
Holt *Norf.* 228 B2
Holt *Wilts.* 167 F1
Holt *Worcs.* 196 A1
Holt *Wrex.* 220 B2
Holt End *Hants.* 170 B4
Holt End *Worcs.* 196 C1
Holt Fleet 196 A1
Holt Heath *Dorset* 155 G2
Holt Heath *Worcs.* 196 A1
Holt Wood 155 G2
Holtby 245 F2
Holton *Oxon.* 184 B2
Holton *Som.* 167 D5
Holton *Suff.* 215 F4
Holton cum Beckering 238 B4
Holton Heath 155 F3
Holton le Clay 238 C2
Holton le Moor 238 A3
Holton St. Mary 202 B4
Holtspur 185 E4
Holtye 173 D5
Holtye Common 173 D5
Holway 165 F5
Holwell *Dorset* 154 C1
Holwell *Herts.* 199 G4
Holwell *Leics.* 224 C5
Holwell *Oxon.* 183 E2
Holwell *Som.* 167 E3
Holwick 261 F5
Holworth 155 D4
Holy Cross 208 B5
Holy Island *I.o.A.* 230 A5
Holy Island (Lindisfarne) **Northumb.** 104
Holybourne 170 C3
Holyfield 186 C2
Holyhead (Caergybi) 230 A4
Holymoorside 223 E1
Holyport 185 D5
Holystone 270 B1
Holytown 284 B3
Holywell *Cambs.* 212 B5
Holywell *Cornw.* 146 B4
Holywell *Dorset* 154 B2
Holywell *E.Suss.* 160 B4
Holywell (Treffynnon) *Flints.* 232 C5
Holywell *Northumb.* 271 F4
Holywell Green 235 E1
Holywell Lake 165 E5
Holywell Row 213 F5
Holywood 266 D2
Hom Green 195 E5
Homer 207 F2
Homersfield 215 D3
Homington 168 C5
Homore (Tobha Mòr) 304 A1
Honey Hill 174 D2
Honey Street 168 C1
Honey Tye 202 A4
Honeyborough 176 C2
Honeybourne 196 D3
Honeychurch 163 G5
Honicknowle 150 A2
Honiley 209 E5
Honing 229 E3
Honingham 228 C4
Honington *Lincs.* 225 E3
Honington *Suff.* 214 A4
Honington *Warks.* 197 E3
Honiton 153 E2
Honkley 220 A2
Honley 235 F1
Hoo *Med.* 187 G5
Hoo *Suff.* 203 D2
Hoo Green 234 B4
Hoo Meavy 150 B1
Hood Green 236 A2
Hood Hill 236 A3
Hooe *E.Suss.* 160 B3
Hooe *Plym.* 150 B2
Hooe Common 160 B2
Hook *Cambs.* 212 C3
Hook *E.Riding* 245 G5
Hook *Gt.Lon.* 171 G1
Hook *Hants.* 170 C2
Hook *Hants.* 157 E2
Hook *Pembs.* 176 C1
Hook *Wilts.* 182 C4
Hook Green *Kent* 173 F5
Hook Green *Kent* 173 F2
Hook Green *Kent* 187 F5
Hook Green *Kent* 187 E5
Hook Norton 197 F4
Hook-a-Gate 207 D2
Hooke 154 B2
Hookgate 221 E4
Hookway 152 B3
Hookwood 172 B4
Hoole 220 B1
Hooley 172 B3
Hoop 181 E2
Hooton 233 E5
Hooton Levitt 236 C3
Hooton Pagnell 236 B2
Hooton Roberts 236 B3
Hop Farm Country Park 45
Hop Pole 211 G1
Hopcrofts Holt 197 G5
Hope *Derbys.* 235 F4
Hope *Devon* 150 C4
Hope *Flints.* 220 A2
Hope *Powys* 206 B2
Hope *Shrop.* 206 C2
Hope *Staffs.* 222 C2
Hope Bagot 207 E5
Hope Bowdler 207 D3
Hope End Green 201 D5
Hope Mansell 181 F1
Hope under Dinmore 195 E2
Hopehouse 277 D4
Hopeman 322 D3
Hope's Green 187 G4
Hopesay 206 C4
Hopetoun House 124
Hopkinstown 179 G3
Hopley's Green 194 C2
Hopperton 244 D2
Hopsford 209 G4
Hopstone 207 G3
Hopton *Derbys.* 223 D2
Hopton *Norf.* 215 G2
Hopton *Shrop.* 220 C5
Hopton *Shrop.* 220 A5
Hopton *Staffs.* 221 G5
Hopton *Suff.* 214 A4
Hopton Cangeford 207 E4
Hopton Castle 206 C5
Hopton Wafers 207 F5
Hoptonheath 206 C5
Hopwas 209 D2
Hopwood 208 C5
Horam 160 A2
Horbling 225 G4
Horbury 235 G1
Horden 262 D3
Horderley 206 D4
Hordle 156 B3
Hordley 220 A4
Horeb *Carmar.* 178 A2
Horeb *Cere.* 191 G3
Horeb *Flints.* 219 F2
Horfield 181 E5
Horham 214 D4
Horkesley Heath 202 A5
Horkstow 237 G1
Horley *Oxon.* 197 G3
Horley *Surr.* 172 B4
Horn Hill 185 F3
Hornblotton 166 C4
Hornblotton Green 166 C4
Hornby *Lancs.* 242 B1
Hornby *N.Yorks.* 252 B3
Hornby *N.Yorks.* 252 C2
Horncastle 226 A1
Hornchurch 187 E4
Horncliffe 287 G5
Horndean *Hants.* 157 G1
Horndean *Sc.Bord.* 287 G5
Horndon 149 F2
Horndon on the Hill 187 F4
Horne 172 C4
Horne Row 187 G2
Horner 164 B3
Horniehaugh 302 C3
Horniman Museum 56
Horning 229 E4
Horninghold 210 D3
Horninglow 222 D5
Horningsea 200 C1
Horningsham 167 F3
Horningtoft 228 A3
Horningtops 147 G3
Horns Cross *Devon* 163 D3
Horns Cross *E.Suss.* 160 D1
Horns Green 173 D3
Hornsbury 153 G1
Hornsby 260 B3
Hornsby Gate 260 B2
Hornsea 247 E3
Hornsey 186 C4
Hornton 197 F3
Horrabridge 150 B1
Horridge 152 A5
Horringer 201 G1
Horrocks Fold 234 B1
Horse Bridge 221 G2
Horsebridge *Devon* 149 E3
Horsebridge *Hants.* 169 E4
Horsebrook 208 A1
Horsecastle 166 B1
Horsehay 207 F2
Horseheath 201 E3
Horsehouse 251 F4
Horsell 171 E2
Horseman's Green 220 B3
Horsenden 184 C2
Horseshoe Green 173 D4
Horseway 212 C4
Horsey 229 F3
Horsey Corner 229 F3
Horsey Windpump 80
Horsford 228 C4
Horsforth 244 B4
Horsham *W.Suss.* 171 G4
Horsham *Worcs.* 195 G2
Horsham St. Faith 228 D4
Horsington *Lincs.* 225 G1
Horsington *Som.* 167 E5
Horsington Marsh 167 E5
Horsley *Derbys.* 223 E3
Horsley *Glos.* 182 A3
Horsley *Northumb.* 261 G1
Horsley *Northumb.* 270 A2
Horsley Cross 202 C5
Horsley Woodhouse 223 E3
Horsleycross Street 202 C5
Horsleygate 236 A5
Horsleyhill 277 G4
Horsmonden 173 F4
Horspath 184 A2
Horstead 229 D4
Horsted Keynes 159 F1
Horton *Bucks.* 185 E1
Horton *Dorset* 155 G2
Horton *Lancs.* 243 E2
Horton *Northants.* 198 D2
Horton *S.Glos.* 181 G4
Horton *Shrop.* 220 B5
Horton *Som.* 153 G1
Horton *Staffs.* 221 G2
Horton *Swan.* 178 A4
Horton *Tel. & W.* 207 F1
Horton *W. & M.* 185 F5
Horton *Wilts.* 168 B1
Horton Court 31
Horton Cross 153 G1
Horton Grange 271 E4
Horton Green 220 B3
Horton Heath 157 D1
Horton in Ribblesdale 250 D5
Horton Inn 155 G2
Horton Kirby 173 E2
Horton Park Farm 45
Horton-cum-Studley 184 B1
Horwich 234 A1
Horwich End 235 E4
Horwood 163 F3
Hoscar 233 F1
Hose 224 C5
Hoses 248 D3
Hosh 293 D2
Hosta 315 F2
Hoswick 342 D5
Hotham 246 A4
Hothfield 174 B4
Hoton 223 G5
Houbie 345 F3
Houdston 264 C1
Hough 221 E2
Hough Green 233 F4
Hougham 225 D3
Hough-on-the-Hill 225 E3
Houghton *Cambs.* 212 A5
Houghton *Cumb.* 260 A2
Houghton *Devon* 150 C3
Houghton *Hants.* 169 E4
Houghton *Pembs.* 176 C2
Houghton *W.Suss.* 158 C2
Houghton Bank 262 B5
Houghton Conquest 199 F3
Houghton Hall 80
Houghton le Spring 262 C3
Houghton Mill 80
Houghton on the Hill 210 B2
Houghton Regis 199 F5
Houghton St. Giles 228 A2
Houghton-le-Side 262 B5
Houlsyke 253 G2
Hound 157 D2
Hound Green 170 C2
Houndslow 286 D5
Houndsmoor 165 E5
Houndwood 287 F3
Hounsdown 156 C1
Hounslow 186 A5
House of Dun 124
House of the Binns 124
Housebay 341 E4
Househill 322 A4
Houses Hill 235 F1
Houses of Parliament 56
Housesteads (Vercovicium) 104
Housetter 344 C4
Housham Tye 187 E1
Houss 342 C4
Houston 283 F3
Houstry 337 D5
Houstry of Dunn 337 F3
Houton 338 C2
Hove 159 E3
Hove Edge 244 A5
Hoveringham 224 B3
Hoveton 229 E4
Hovingham 253 F5
How 260 B2
How Caple 195 F4
How End 199 F3
How Green 173 D4
How Man 258 C5
Howbrook 236 A3
Howden 245 G5
Howden Clough 244 B5
Howden-le-Wear 262 A4
Howe *Cumb.* 249 F4
Howe *High.* 337 F2
Howe *N.Yorks.* 252 C4
Howe *Norf.* 215 D2
Howe Green 187 G2
Howe of Teuchar 324 C5
Howe Street *Essex* 187 F1
Howe Street *Essex* 201 E4
Howe, The 240 A5
Howegreen 188 B2
Howell 225 G3
Howey 193 G2
Howgate *Cumb.* 258 C4
Howgate *Midloth.* 285 G4
Howgill *Lancs.* 243 E3
Howgill *N.Yorks.* 243 G2
Howick 279 G5
Howick Hall Gardens 104
Howle 221 D5
Howle Hill 195 F5
Howlett End 201 D4
Howletts Wild Animal Park 45
Howley 153 F2
Hownam 278 B5
Hownam Mains 278 B4
Howpasley 277 E5
Howsham *N.Lincs.* 238 A2
Howsham *N.Yorks.* 245 G1
Howt Green 174 A2
Howtel 278 C3
Howton 194 D5
Howwood 283 F3
Hoxa 338 D3
Hoxne 214 C4
Hoy *High.* 337 E2
Hoy *Ork.* 338 B3
Hoylake 232 D4
Hoyland 236 A2
Hoylandswaine 235 G2
Hoyle 158 B2
Hubberholme 251 E5
Hubberston 176 B2
Hubbert's Bridge 226 A3
Huby *N.Yorks.* 245 E1
Huby *N.Yorks.* 244 B3
Hucclecote 182 A1
Hucking 174 A3
Hucknall 223 G3
Huddersfield 235 F1
Huddersfield Narrow Canal & Standedge Experience 88
Huddington 196 B2
Huddlesford 208 D2
Hudnall 185 F1
Hudscott 163 G3
Hudswell 252 A3
Huggate 246 A2
Hugglescote 209 G1
Hugh Miller's Cottage 124
Hugh Town 146 B1
Hughenden Manor 45
Hughenden Valley 185 D3
Hughley 207 E3
Hugmore 220 A2
Hugus 146 B5
Huish *Devon* 163 F4
Huish *Wilts.* 168 C1
Huish Champflower 164 D5
Huish Episcopi 166 B5
Huisinis 326 B2
Hulcote 199 E4
Hulcott 185 D1
Hull 246 D5
Hulland 222 D3
Hulland Ward 223 D3
Hullavington 182 A4
Hullbridge 188 B3
Hulme 221 G3
Hulme End 222 C2
Hulme Walfield 221 F1
Hulver Street 215 F3
Hulverstone 156 C4
Humber *Devon* 152 B5
Humber *Here.* 195 E2
Humberside International Airport 238 A1
Humberston 238 D2
Humberstone 210 B2
Humberton 244 D1
Humbie 286 B3
Humbleton *Dur.* 251 F1
Humbleton *E.Riding* 247 E4
Humbleton *Northumb.* 279 D4
Humby 225 F4
Hume 287 E5
Humehall 287 E5
Hummer 154 B1
Humshaugh 270 B4
Huna 337 F1
Huncoat 243 D4
Huncote 210 A3
Hundalee 278 A5
Hundall 236 A5
Hunderthwaite 261 F5
Hundleby 226 B1
Hundleton 176 C2
Hundon 201 F3
Hundred Acres 157 E1
Hundred End 242 A5
Hundred House 194 A2
Hungarton 210 B2
Hungate End 198 C3
Hungerford *Hants.* 156 A1
Hungerford *Shrop.* 207 E4
Hungerford *W.Berks.* 169 E1
Hungerford Newtown 183 F5
Hungerton 225 D5
Hunglader 317 G2
Hunmanby 255 D5
Hunningham 197 F1
Hunningham Hill 197 F1
Hunny Hill 157 D4
Hunsdon 186 D1
Hunsingore 244 D2
Hunslet 244 C4
Hunsonby 260 B4
Hunspow 337 E1
Hunstanton 227 E3
Hunstanworth 261 F3
Hunston *Suff.* 202 A1
Hunston *W.Suss.* 158 A3
Hunsworth 244 A5
Hunt End 196 C1
Hunt House 254 B3
Huntercombe End 184 B4
Hunters Forstal 175 D2
Hunter's Inn 163 G1
Hunter's Quay 282 C2
Hunterston 282 C4
Huntford 269 E1
Huntham 166 A5
Huntingdon 212 A5
Huntingfield 215 E4
Huntingford 167 F4
Huntington *Here.* 194 B2
Huntington *Here.* 195 D3
Huntington *Staffs.* 208 B1
Huntington *Tel. & W.* 207 F2
Huntington *York* 245 F2
Huntingtower 293 F2
Huntingtower Castle 124
Huntley 181 G1
Huntly 312 A1
Huntlywood 286 D5
Hunton *Hants.* 169 F3
Hunton *Kent* 173 G4
Hunton *N.Yorks.* 252 A3
Hunton Bridge 185 F2
Hunt's Cross 233 F4
Huntscott 164 C3
Huntsham 164 D5
Huntshaw 163 F3
Huntshaw Cross 163 F3
Huntshaw Water 163 F3
Huntspill 166 A3
Huntworth 166 A4
Hunwick 262 A4
Hunworth 228 B2
Hurcott *Som.* 166 C5
Hurcott *Som.* 153 G1
Hurdley 206 B3
Hurdsfield 234 D5
Hurley *W. & M.* 184 D4
Hurley *Warks.* 209 E3
Hurley Bottom 184 D4
Hurlford 274 C2
Hurliness 338 B4
Hurlston Green 233 E1
Hurn 156 A3
Hursley 169 F5
Hurst *N.Yorks.* 251 F2
Hurst *W'ham* 184 C5
Hurst Green *E.Suss.* 160 C1
Hurst Green *Essex* 189 D1
Hurst Green *Lancs.* 242 C4
Hurst Green *Surr.* 172 C3
Hurst Wickham 159 E2
Hurstbourne Priors 169 F3
Hurstbourne Tarrant 169 E2
Hurstpierpoint 159 E2
Hurstwood 243 E4
Hurtmore 171 E3
Hurworth-on-Tees 252 C1
Hury 261 F5
Husabost 317 F4
Husbands Bosworth 210 B4
Husborne Crawley 199 E4
Husthwaite 253 E5
Hutcherleigh 151 D2
Hutchesons' Hall 124
Huthwaite 223 F2
Huttoft 239 F5
Hutton *Cumb.* 260 A5
Hutton *Essex* 187 F3
Hutton *Lancs.* 242 A5
Hutton *N.Som.* 166 A2
Hutton *Sc.Bord.* 287 G4
Hutton Bonville 252 C2
Hutton Buscel 254 C4
Hutton Conyers 252 C5
Hutton Cranswick 246 C2
Hutton End 260 A4
Hutton Hang 252 A4
Hutton Henry 262 D4
Hutton Magna 252 A1
Hutton Mount 187 F3
Hutton Mulgrave 254 B2
Hutton Roof *Cumb.* 249 G5
Hutton Roof *Cumb.* 259 G3
Hutton Rudby 253 D2
Hutton Sessay 253 D5
Hutton Wandesley 245 E2
Hutton-in-the-Forest 96
Hutton-le-Hole 253 G3
Huxham 152 C3
Huxham Green 166 C4
Huxley 220 C1
Huxter *Shet.* 342 C2
Huxter *Shet.* 343 E1
Huyton 233 F3
Hwllffordd (Haverfordwest) 176 C1
Hycemoor 240 D1
Hyde *Glos.* 182 A2
Hyde *Gt.Man.* 234 D3
Hyde End *W'ham* 170 C1
Hyde End *W.Berks.* 169 G1
Hyde Hall 80
Hyde Heath 185 E2
Hyde Lea 208 B1
Hydestile 171 E3
Hyndford Bridge 284 D5
Hyndlee 277 G5
Hynish 296 A3
Hyssington 206 C3
Hythe *Hants.* 156 D2
Hythe *Kent* 175 D5
Hythe End 185 F5
Hythie 325 F4
Hyton 248 B4

I

Ianstown 323 G3
Iarsiadar 328 C4
Ibberton 155 D2
Ible 222 D2
Ibsley 156 A2
Ibstock 209 G1
Ibstone 184 C3
Ibthorpe 169 E2
Ibworth 169 G2
Icelton 166 A1
Ickburgh 213 G3
Ickenham 185 F4
Ickford 184 B2
Ickham 175 E3
Ickleford 199 G4
Icklesham 161 D2
Ickleton 200 C3
Icklingham 213 F5
Ickwell Green 199 G3
Ickworth 80
Icomb 197 E5
Idbury 197 E5
Iddesleigh 163 F5
Ide 152 C3
Ide Hill 173 D3
Ideford 152 B5
Iden 161 E1
Iden Green *Kent* 173 G5
Iden Green *Kent* 174 A5
Idle 244 A4
Idless 146 C5
Idlicote 197 E3
Idmiston 168 C4
Idridgehay 223 D3
Idridgehay Green 223 D3
Idrigil 317 G3
Idstone 183 E4
Idvies 302 D5
Iffley 184 A2
Ifield (Singlewell) *Kent* 187 F5
Ifield *W.Suss.* 172 B5
Ifieldwood 172 B5
Ifold 171 F4
Iford *Bourne.* 156 A3
Iford *E.Suss.* 159 G3
Iford Manor 31
Ifton 181 D4
Ifton Heath 220 A4
Ightfield 220 C4
Ightham 173 E3
Ightham Mote 45
Iken 203 F2
Ilam 222 C2
Ilchester 166 C5
Ilderton 279 E4
Ilford 186 D4
Ilfracombe 163 F1
Ilkeston 223 F3
Ilketshall St. Andrew 215 E3
Ilketshall St. Lawrence 215 E3
Ilketshall St. Margaret 215 E3
Ilkley 244 A3
Illey 208 B4
Illidge Green 221 E1
Illington 214 A3
Illingworth 243 G5
Illogan 146 A5
Illston on the Hill 210 C3
Ilmer 184 C2
Ilmington 197 E3
Ilminster 153 G1
Ilsington *Devon* 152 A5
Ilsington *Dorset* 155 D3
Ilston 178 B3
Ilton *N.Yorks.* 252 A5
Ilton *Som.* 153 G1
Imachar 281 G5
Imber 168 A3
Immeroin 292 A3
Immingham 238 B1
Immingham Dock 238 C1
Imperial War Museum 56
Imperial War Museum (Duxford) 80
Impington 200 C1
Ince 233 F5
Ince Blundell 233 E2
Ince-in-Makerfield 233 G2
Inch Kenneth 288 D1
Inch of Arnhall 303 E2
Inchbae Lodge 320 D3
Inchbare 303 E3
Inchberry 323 F4
Inchbraoch 303 F4
Inchgrundle 302 C2
Inchindown 321 F2
Inchinnan 283 F3
Inchkinloch 335 F4
Inchlaggan 308 A4
Inchlumpie 321 E2
Inchmarlo 312 B5
Inchmarnock 282 B4
Inchnabobart 302 B1
Inchnacardoch Hotel 308 C3
Inchnadamph 331 E2
Inchock 303 E5
Inchrory 311 D4
Inchture 294 A2
Inchvuilt 308 B1
Inchyra 293 G2
Indian Queens 146 D4
Inerval 280 B5
Ingatestone 187 F3
Ingbirchworth 235 G2
Ingerthorpe 244 B1
Ingestre 221 G5
Ingham *Lincs.* 237 G4
Ingham *Norf.* 229 E3
Ingham *Suff.* 213 G5
Ingham Corner 229 E3
Ingleborough 212 C1
Ingleby *Derbys.* 223 E5
Ingleby *Lincs.* 237 F5
Ingleby Arncliffe 252 D2
Ingleby Barwick 252 D1
Ingleby Cross 252 D2
Ingleby Greenhow 253 E2
Ingleigh Green 163 G5
Inglesbatch 167 E1
Inglesham 183 E3
Ingleton *Dur.* 262 A5
Ingleton *N.Yorks.* 250 B5
Inglewhite 242 B4
Ingliston 285 F2
Ingmire Hall 250 B3
Ingoe 270 C4
Ingoldisthorpe 227 E4
Ingoldmells 227 D1
Ingoldsby 225 F4
Ingon 197 E2
Ingram 279 E5
Ingrave 187 F3
Ingrow 243 G4
Ings 249 F3
Ingst 181 E4
Ingworth 228 C3
Inhurst 169 G1
Inistrynich 290 D2
Injebreck 240 B3
Inkberrow 196 C2
Inkersall 236 B5
Inkersall Green 236 B5
Inkhorn 313 E1
Inkpen 169 E1
Inkstack 337 E1
Inmarsh 168 A1
Innellan 282 C3
Innergellie 295 D4
Innerleithen 277 E2
Innerleven 294 B4
Innermessan 264 B4
Innerwick *E.Loth.* 287 E2
Innerwick *P. & K.* 300 A5
Inninbeg 297 F5
Innsworth 196 A5
Insch 312 B2
Insh 310 A4
Inshore 334 C2
Inskip 242 A4
Instow 163 E2
Intake 236 C2
Intwood 228 C5
Inver *Aber.* 311 E5
Inver *Arg. & B.* 298 B5
Inver *High.* 322 A1
Inver *High.* 337 D5
Inver *P. & K.* 301 F5
Inver Mallie 298 D1
Inverailort 297 G1
Inveralligin 319 E4
Inverallochy 325 F3
Inveran 332 A5
Inveraray 290 C4
Inveraray Castle 124
Inveraray Jail 124
Inverardoch Mains 292 C4
Inverardran 291 F2
Inverarish 306 B1
Inverarity 302 C5
Inverarnan 291 F3
Inverasdale 319 E1
Inverbain 319 D4
Inverbeg 291 F5
Inverbervie 303 G2
Inverbroom 320 A1
Inverbrough 310 A2
Invercassley 331 G4
Inverchaolain 282 B2
Invercharnan 298 D5
Inverchorachan 291 E3
Inverchoran 320 B4
Invercreran 298 C5
Inverdruie 310 B3
Inverebrie 313 E1
Invereen 309 G1
Inverernie 322 C3
Inveresk 286 A2
Inverewe Gardens 125
Inverey 301 F1
Inverfarigaig 309 E2
Invergarry 308 C4
Invergelder 311 E5
Invergeldie 292 C2
Invergloy 299 E1
Invergordon 321 G3
Invergowrie 294 B1
Inverguseran 306 D4
Inverhadden 300 B4
Inverharroch Farm 311 F1
Inverherive 291 F2
Inverhope 335 D2
Inverie 307 D4
Inverinan 290 B3
Inverinate 307 F2
Inverkeilor 303 E5
Inverkeithing 285 F1
Inverkeithny 324 B5
Inverkip 282 D2
Inverkirkaig 330 C3
Inverlael 320 A1
Inverlauren 283 E1
Inverliever 290 A4
Inverliver 290 C1
Inverlochlarig 291 G3
Inverlochy 291 D2
Inverlussa 281 E1
Invermay 293 F3
Invermoriston 308 D3
Invernaver 335 G2
Inverneil 281 G1
Inverness 321 F5
Inverness Airport 321 G4
Invernettie 325 G5
Invernoaden 290 D5
Inveroran Hotel 299 E5
Inverquharity 302 C4
Inverquhomery 325 F5
Inverroy 299 E1

Inversanda 298 B4
Invershiel 307 F3
Invershore 337 E5
Inversnaid Hotel 291 F4
Invertrossachs 292 A4
Inverugie 325 G5
Inveruglas 291 F4
Inveruglass 310 A4
Inverurie 312 C2
Invervar 300 B5
Invervegain 282 B2
Invery House 312 B5
Inverythan 324 C5
Inwardleigh 149 F1
Inworth 188 B1
Iochdar 315 F5
Iona 288 B2
Iping 171 D5
Ipplepen 151 E1
Ipsden 184 B4
Ipstones 222 B3
Ipswich 202 C3
Irby 233 D4
Irby Hill 233 D4
Irby in the Marsh 226 C1
Irby upon Humber 238 B2
Irchester 199 E1
Ireby *Cumb.* 259 F3
Ireby *Lancs.* 250 B5
Ireland *Ork.* 338 C2
Ireland *Shet.* 342 C5
Ireland's Cross 221 E3
Ireleth 248 D5
Ireshopeburn 261 E4
Irlam 234 B3
Irnham 225 F5
Iron Acton 181 F4
Iron Cross 196 C2
Ironbridge 207 F2
Ironbridge Gorge 66
Irons Bottom 172 B4
Ironside 325 D4
Ironville 223 F2
Irstead 229 E3
Irthington 260 A1
Irthlingborough 211 E5
Irton 254 D4
Irvine 274 B2
Isauld 336 B2
Isbister *Ork.* 340 B5
Isbister *Ork.* 340 A4
Isbister *Shet.* 343 E1
Isbister *Shet.* 344 C3
Isfield 159 G2
Isham 211 D5
Ishriff 289 F1
Islington 170 C3
Island of Stroma 337 F1
Islay 280 A3
Islay Airport 280 B4
Islay House 280 B3
Isle Abbotts 166 A5
Isle Brewers 166 A5
Isle of Lewis (Eilean Leodhais) 329 E3
Isle of Man 240 B3
Isle of Man Airport 240 A5
Isle of May 295 E5
Isle of Noss 343 E3
Isle of Sheppey 174 B1
Isle of Walney 241 E1
Isle of Whithorn 257 E3
Isle of Wight 157 D4
Isle of Wight Pearl 45
Isle of Wight Zoo 45
Isle, The 207 D1
Isleham 213 E5
Isleornsay (Eilean Iarmain) 306 C3
Isles of Scilly (Scilly Isles) 146 B1
Islesburgh 342 C1
Isleworth 186 A5
Isley Walton 223 F5
Islibhig 328 A5
Islip *Northants.* 211 E5
Islip *Oxon.* 184 A1
Isombridge 207 F1
Istead Rise 173 F2
Italian Chapel 125
Itchen 156 D1
Itchen Abbas 169 G4
Itchen Stoke 169 G4
Itchingfield 171 G5
Itchington 181 F4
Itteringham 228 C2
Itton *Devon* 149 G1
Itton *Mon.* 181 D3
Itton Common 181 D3
Ivegill 260 A3
Ivelet 251 E3
Iver 185 F4
Iver Heath 185 F4
Iveston 262 A2
Ivetsey Bank 208 A1
Ivinghoe 185 E1
Ivinghoe Aston 185 E1
Ivington 195 D2
Ivington Green 195 D2
Ivy Hatch 173 E3
Ivy Todd 213 G2
Ivybridge 150 C2
Ivychurch 161 F1
Iwade 174 B2
Iwerne Courtney (Shroton) 155 E1
Iwerne Minster 155 E1
Ixworth 214 A4
Ixworth Thorpe 214 A4

J

Jack Hill 244 A2
Jackfield 207 F2
Jacksdale 223 F2
Jackstown 312 C1
Jackton 283 G4
Jacobstow 148 B1
Jacobstowe 163 F5
Jacobswell 171 E2
Jameston 177 D3
Jamestown *D. & G.* 268 B2
Jamestown *High.* 321 D4
Jamestown *W.Dun.* 283 E1
Jane Austen's House 46
Janefield 321 G4
Janetstown *High.* 336 C2
Janetstown *High.* 337 F3
Jarlshof Prehistoric & Norse Settlement 125
Jarrow 262 C1
Jarvis Brook 173 E5
Jasper's Green 201 F5
Jawcraig 284 C2
Jayes Park 171 G3
Jaywick 189 E1
Jealott's Hill 185 D5
Jeater Houses 252 D3
Jedburgh 278 A4
Jedburgh Abbey 125
Jeffreyston 177 D2
Jemimaville 321 G3
Jericho 234 C1
Jersay 284 C3
Jersey 150 C5
Jersey Airport 150 B5
Jersey Marine 178 D3
Jerviswood 284 C5
Jesmond 262 B1
Jevington 160 A3
J.M. Barrie's Birthplace & Camera Obscura 125
Jockey End 185 F1
Jodrell Bank 234 B5
Jodrell Bank Observatory & Arboretum 96
John o' Groats 337 F1
Johnby 260 A4
John's Cross 160 C1
Johnshaven 303 F3
Johnson Street 229 E4
Johnston 176 C1
Johnston Mains 303 F2
Johnstone 283 F3
Johnstone Castle 283 F3
Johnstonebridge 267 E1
Johnstown *Carmar.* 177 G1
Johnstown *Wrex.* 220 A3
Joppa 274 C4
Jordans 185 E3
Jordanston 190 C4
Jordanstone 302 A5
Jorvik 88
Jorvik Glass 88
Joy's Green 181 F1
Jumpers Common 156 A3
Juniper Hill 198 A4
Jura 281 D1
Jura House 280 C3
Jurassic Coast 31
Jurby East 240 B2
Jurby West 240 B2

K

Kaber 250 C1
Kaimes 285 G3
Kames *Arg. & B.* 282 A2
Kames *Arg. & B.* 290 A3
Kames *E.Ayr.* 275 E3
Kea 146 C5
Keadby 237 F1
Keal Cotes 226 B1
Kearsley 234 B2
Kearstwick 250 B5
Kearton 251 F3
Kearvaig 334 B1
Keasden 242 D1
Kebholes 324 B4
Keckwick 233 G4
Keddington 238 D4
Keddington Corner 239 D4
Kedington 201 F3
Kedleston 223 D3
Kedleston Hall 73
Keelby 238 B1
Keele 221 F3
Keeley Green 199 F3
Keelham 243 G4
Keeres Green 187 E1
Keeston 176 B1
Keevil 168 A2
Kegworth 223 F5
Kehelland 146 A5
Keig 312 B3
Keighley 243 G3
Keil *Arg. & B.* 272 B5
Keil *High.* 298 B4
Keilhill 324 C4
Keillmore 281 E1
Keillor 302 A5
Keillour 293 E2
Keills 280 C3
Keils 280 D3
Keinton Mandeville 166 C4
Keir House 292 C5
Keir Mill 266 C1
Keisby 225 F5
Keisley 260 D5
Keiss 337 F2
Keith 323 G4
Keithick 294 A1
Keithmore 311 F1
Keithock 303 E3
Kelbrook 243 F3
Kelburn Castle & Country Centre 125
Kelby 225 F3
Keld *Cumb.* 249 G1
Keld *N.Yorks.* 251 D2
Keldholme 253 G4
Keldy Castle 253 G3
Kelfield *N.Lincs.* 237 F2
Kelfield *N.Yorks.* 245 E4
Kelham 224 C2
Kella 240 B2
Kellacott 149 E2
Kellan 297 E5
Kellas *Angus* 294 C1
Kellas *Moray* 323 D4
Kellaton 151 D4
Kellaways 182 B5
Kelleth 250 B2
Kelleythorpe 246 C2
Kellie Castle 125
Kelling 228 B1
Kellington 245 E5
Kelloe 262 C4
Kelloholm 275 F4
Kelly *Cornw.* 147 E2
Kelly *Devon* 149 D2
Kelly Bray 149 D3
Kelmarsh 210 C5
Kelmscott 183 E3
Kelsale 203 E1
Kelsall 220 C1
Kelsay 280 A4
Kelshall 200 B4
Kelsick 259 F1
Kelso 278 B3
Kelso Abbey 125
Kelstedge 223 E1
Kelstern 238 C3
Kelston 167 E1
Keltneyburn 300 C5
Kelton 267 D3
Kelton Hill (Rhonehouse) 266 B5
Kelty 293 G5
Kelvedon 188 B1
Kelvedon Hatch 187 E3
Kelvinside 283 G3
Kelynack 144 A4
Kemacott 163 G1
Kemback 294 C3
Kemberton 207 G2
Kemble 182 B3
Kemerton 196 B4
Kemeys Commander 180 C2
Kemeys Inferior 180 C3
Kemnay 312 C3
Kemp Town 159 F3
Kempe's Corner 174 C4
Kempley 195 F5
Kempley Green 195 F5
Kemps Green 208 D5
Kempsey 196 A3
Kempsford 183 D3
Kempshott 169 G3
Kempston 199 F3
Kempston Hardwick 199 F3
Kempston West End 199 F3
Kempton 206 C4
Kemsing 173 E3
Kemsley 174 B2
Kenardington 174 B5
Kenchester 194 D3
Kencott 183 E2
Kendal 249 G3
Kenderchurch 194 D5
Kendleshire 181 F5
Kenfig 179 D4
Kenfig Hill 179 E4
Kenidjack 144 A3
Kenilworth 209 E5
Kenilworth Castle 66
Kenknock *P. & K.* 300 A5
Kenknock *Stir.* 291 G1
Kenley *Gt.Lon.* 172 C2
Kenley *Shrop.* 207 E2
Kenmore *Arg. & B.* 290 C4
Kenmore *High.* 319 D4
Kenmore *P. & K.* 300 C5
Kenmore *W.Isles* 327 E3
Kenn *Devon* 152 C4
Kenn *N.Som.* 166 B1
Kennack Sands 31
Kennacley 327 D4
Kennacraig 281 G3
Kennards House 147 G1
Kennavay 327 E4
Kenneggy Downs 144 C4
Kennerleigh 152 B2
Kennerty 312 B5
Kennet 293 E5
Kennethmont 312 A2
Kennett 201 E1
Kennford 152 C4
Kenninghall 214 B3
Kennington *Kent* 174 C4
Kennington *Oxon.* 184 A2
Kennoway 294 B4
Kenny 153 G1
Kennyhill 213 E5
Kennythorpe 245 G1
Kenovay 296 A2
Kensaleyre 318 A4
Kensington 186 B4
Kensington Palace 57
Kenstone 220 C5
Kensworth 185 F1
Kent & East Sussex Railway 46
Kent Street *E.Suss.* 160 C2
Kent Street *Kent* 173 F3
Kentallen 298 C4
Kentchurch 194 D5
Kentford 201 F1
Kentisbeare 153 D2
Kentisbury 163 G1
Kentisbury Ford 163 G1
Kentish Town 186 B4
Kentmere 249 F2
Kenton *Devon* 152 C4
Kenton *Suff.* 202 C1
Kenton *T. & W.* 262 B1
Kenton Corner 202 D1
Kentra 297 F3
Kents Bank 249 E5
Kent's Green 195 G5
Kent's Oak 169 E5
Kentwell Hall 81
Kenwick 220 B4
Kenwood House 57
Kenwyn 146 C5
Kenyon 234 A3
Keoldale 334 C2
Keose (Ceos) 329 E5
Keppanach 298 C3
Keppoch *Arg. & B.* 283 E2
Keppoch *High.* 307 E2
Keprigan 272 B4
Kepwick 253 D3
Keresley 209 F4
Kernborough 151 D3
Kerrera 290 A2
Kerridge 234 D5
Kerris 144 B4
Kerry 206 A3
Kerrycroy 282 C3
Kerry's Gate 194 C4
Kerrysdale 319 E2
Kersall 224 C1
Kersey 202 B3
Kersey Vale 202 B3
Kershopefoot 268 C3
Kerswell 153 D2
Kerswell Green 196 A3
Kerthen Wood 144 C3
Kesgrave 202 D3
Kessingland 215 G3
Kessingland Beach 215 G3
Kestle 147 D5
Kestle Mill 146 C4
Keston 172 D2
Keswick *Cumb.* 259 F4
Keswick *Norf.* 228 D5
Keswick *Norf.* 229 E2
Ketley Bank 207 F1
Ketsby 239 D5
Kettering 211 D5
Ketteringham 228 C5
Kettins 294 A1
Kettle Corner 173 G3
Kettlebaston 202 A2
Kettlebridge 294 B4
Kettlebrook 209 E2
Kettleburgh 203 D1
Kettlehill 294 B4
Kettleholm 267 F3
Kettleness 254 B1
Kettleshulme 235 D5
Kettlesing 244 B2
Kettlesing Bottom 244 B2
Kettlesing Head 244 B2
Kettlestone 228 A2
Kettlethorpe 237 F5
Kettletoft 341 E3
Kettlewell 251 E5
Ketton 211 E2
Kevingtown 173 D2
Kew 186 A5
Kew Gardens (see Royal Botanic Gardens, Kew) 59
Kewstoke 166 A1
Kexbrough 236 A2
Kexby *Lincs.* 237 F4
Kexby *York* 245 G2
Key Green 221 F1
Keyham 210 B2
Keyhaven 156 C3
Keyingham 247 E5
Keymer 159 F2
Keynsham 167 D1
Key's Toft 226 C2
Keysoe 199 F1
Keysoe Row 199 F1
Keyston 211 F5
Keyworth 224 B4
Kibblesworth 262 B2
Kibworth Beauchamp 210 B3
Kibworth Harcourt 210 B3
Kidbrooke 186 D5
Kiddemore Green 208 A2
Kidderminster 208 A5
Kiddington 197 G5
Kidlington 183 G1
Kidmore End 184 B5
Kidnal 220 B3
Kidsdale 257 E3
Kidsgrove 221 F2
Kidstones 251 E4
Kidwelly (Cydweli) 178 A2
Kidwelly Castle 111
Kiel Crofts 290 A1
Kielder 269 E2
Kielder Forest 105
Kilbarchan 283 F3
Kilbeg 306 C4
Kilberry 281 F3
Kilbirnie 283 E4
Kilblaan 290 D3
Kilbraur 332 D3
Kilbrennan 296 D5
Kilbride *Arg. & B.* 290 A2
Kilbride *Arg. & B.* 282 B3
Kilbride *High.* 306 B2
Kilbride Farm 282 A3
Kilbridemore 290 C5
Kilburn *Derbys.* 223 E3
Kilburn *Gt.Lon.* 186 B4
Kilburn *N.Yorks.* 253 E5
Kilby 210 B3
Kilchattan Bay 282 C4
Kilchenzie 272 B3
Kilcheran 290 A1
Kilchiaran 280 A3
Kilchoan *Arg. & B.* 289 G3
Kilchoan *High.* 297 D3
Kilchoman 280 A3
Kilchrenan 290 C2
Kilchrist 272 B4
Kilchurn Castle 125
Kilconquhar 294 C4
Kilcot 195 F5
Kilcoy 321 E4
Kilcreggan 282 D1
Kildale 253 F2
Kildalton Church & Crosses 125
Kildary 321 G2
Kildavie 272 C4
Kildermorie Lodge 321 E2
Kildonan *N.Ayr.* 273 F3
Kildonan (Cilldonnain) *W.Isles* 314 C1
Kildonan Lodge 333 E2
Kildonnan 297 D1
Kildrochet House 264 B5
Kildrummy 311 G3
Kildwick 243 G3
Kilfinan 282 A2
Kilfinnan 308 B5
Kilgetty 177 E2
Kilgwrrwg Common 181 D3
Kilham *E.Riding* 246 C1
Kilham *Northumb.* 278 C3
Kilkenneth 296 A2
Kilkenny 182 C1
Kilkerran *Arg. & B.* 272 C4
Kilkerran *S.Ayr.* 274 B5
Kilkhampton 162 C4
Killamarsh 236 B4
Killay 178 C3
Killbeg 297 F5
Killean *Arg. & B.* 281 E5
Killean *Arg. & B.* 290 C4
Killearn 283 G1
Killellan 272 B4
Killen 321 F4
Killerby 262 A5
Killerton *Devon* 152 C2
Killerton ***Devon*** 31
Killichonan 300 A4
Killiechonate 299 E1
Killiechronan 297 E5
Killiecrankie 301 E3
Killiecrankie 125
Killiehuntly 309 G5
Killiemor 289 D1
Killilan 307 F1
Killimster 337 F3
Killin *High.* 333 D4
Killin *Stir.* 292 A1
Killinallan 280 B2
Killinghall 244 B2
Killington *Cumb.* 250 B4
Killington *Devon* 163 G1
Killingworth 271 E4
Killochyett 286 B5
Killocraw 272 B2
Killunaig 289 D2
Killundine 297 E5
Kilmacolm 283 E3
Kilmaha 290 B4
Kilmahog 292 B4
Kilmalieu 298 A4
Kilmaluag 318 A2
Kilmany 294 B2
Kilmarie 306 B3
Kilmarnock 274 C2
Kilmartin 290 A5
Kilmartin House Museum 125
Kilmaurs 283 F5
Kilmelford 290 A3
Kilmeny 280 B3
Kilmersdon 167 D2
Kilmeston 169 G5
Kilmichael 272 B3
Kilmichael Glassary 290 A5
Kilmichael of Inverlussa 281 F1
Kilmington *Devon* 153 F3
Kilmington *Wilts.* 167 E4
Kilmington Common 167 E4
Kilmorack 321 D5
Kilmore *Arg. & B.* 290 A2
Kilmore *High.* 306 C4
Kilmory *Arg. & B.* 281 F1
Kilmory *Arg. & B.* 281 F2
Kilmory *High.* 305 G4
Kilmory *High.* 297 E2
Kilmory *N.Ayr.* 273 E3
Kilmote 333 E3
Kilmuir *High.* 317 F5
Kilmuir *High.* 321 F5
Kilmuir *High.* 321 G2
Kilmuir *High.* 317 G2
Kilmun 282 C1
Kilmux 294 B4
Kiln Green *Here.* 181 F1
Kiln Green *W'ham* 184 D5
Kiln Pit Hill 261 G2
Kilnave 280 A2
Kilncadzow 284 C5
Kilndown 173 G5
Kilnhurst 236 B3
Kilninian 296 D5
Kilninver 290 A2
Kilnsea 239 E1
Kilnsey 243 F1
Kilnwick 246 B3
Kilnwick Percy 246 A2
Kiloran 288 C5
Kilpatrick 273 E3
Kilpeck 194 D4
Kilphedir 333 E3
Kilpin 245 G5
Kilpin Pike 245 G5
Kilrenny 295 D4
Kilsby 210 A5
Kilspindie 294 A2
Kilstay 256 B3
Kilsyth 284 B2
Kiltarlity 321 E5
Kilton *Notts.* 236 C5
Kilton *R. & C.* 253 F1
Kilton *Som.* 165 E3
Kilton Thorpe 253 F1
Kiltyrie 292 B1
Kilvaxter 317 G3
Kilve 165 E3
Kilverstone 213 G4
Kilvington 224 D3
Kilwinning 283 E5
Kimberley *Norf.* 228 B5
Kimberley *Notts.* 223 G3
Kimberworth 236 B3
Kimble Wick 184 D2
Kimblesworth 262 B3
Kimbolton *Cambs.* 199 F1
Kimbolton *Here.* 195 E1
Kimbridge 169 E5
Kimcote 210 A4
Kimmeridge 155 F5
Kimmerston 279 D3
Kimpton *Hants.* 169 D3
Kimpton *Herts.* 186 A1
Kinaldy 294 D3
Kinblethmont 303 E5
Kinbrace 336 A5
Kinbreack 307 G5
Kinbuck 292 C4
Kincaldrum 302 C5
Kincaple 294 C3
Kincardine *Fife* 284 D1
Kincardine *High.* 321 F1
Kincardine O'Neil 312 A5
Kinclaven 293 G1
Kincorth 313 E4
Kincraig *Aber.* 313 E2
Kincraig *High.* 310 A4
Kincraigie 301 E5
Kindallachan 301 E4
Kindrogan Field Centre 301 F3
Kinellar 312 D3
Kineton *Glos.* 196 C5
Kineton *Warks.* 197 F2
Kineton Green 208 D4
Kinfauns 293 G2
King Sterndale 235 E5
Kingarth 282 B4
Kingcoed 180 D2
Kingerby 238 A3
Kingham 197 E5
Kingholm Quay 267 D3
Kinghorn 285 G1
Kinglassie 294 A5
Kingoodie 294 B2
King's Acre 195 D3
King's Bank 161 D1
King's Bromley 208 D1
Kings Caple 195 E5
King's Cliffe 211 F3
King's Coughton 196 C2
King's Green 195 G4
King's Heath 208 C4
Kings Hill *Kent* 173 F3
King's Hill *W.Mid.* 208 B3
King's Hill *Warks.* 209 F5
Kings Langley 185 F2
King's Lynn 227 E5
King's Meaburn 260 C5
Kings Mills 151 E5
King's Moss 233 G2
Kings Muir 277 D2
King's Newnham 209 G5
King's Newton 223 E5
King's Norton *Leics.* 210 B2
King's Norton *W.Mid.* 208 C5
Kings Nympton 163 G4
King's Pyon 194 D2
Kings Ripton 212 A5
King's Somborne 169 E4
King's Stag 154 D1
King's Stanley 182 A2
King's Sutton 197 G4
King's Tamerton 150 A2
King's Walden 199 G5
Kings Worthy 169 F4
Kingsand 150 A2
Kingsbarns 295 D3
Kingsbridge *Devon* 150 D3
Kingsbridge *Som.* 164 C4
Kingsburgh 317 G4
Kingsbury *Gt.Lon.* 186 A4
Kingsbury *Warks.* 209 E3
Kingsbury Episcopi 166 B5
Kingscavil 285 E2
Kingsclere 169 G2
Kingscote 182 A3
Kingscott 163 F4
Kingscross 273 F3
Kingsdale 294 B4
Kingsdon 166 C5
Kingsdown *Kent* 175 F4
Kingsdown *Swin.* 183 D4
Kingsdown *Wilts.* 167 F1
Kingseat 293 G5
Kingsey 184 C2
Kingsfold *Pembs.* 176 C3
Kingsfold *W.Suss.* 171 G4
Kingsford *Aber.* 324 C5
Kingsford *Aber.* 312 A3
Kingsford *Aberdeen* 313 D4
Kingsford *E.Ayr.* 283 F5
Kingsford *Worcs.* 208 A4
Kingsgate 175 F1
Kingshall Street 202 A1
Kingsheanton 163 F2
Kingshouse 292 A2
Kingshouse Hotel 299 E4
Kingshurst 209 D4
Kingskerswell 151 E1
Kingskettle 294 B4
Kingsland *Here.* 194 D1
Kingsland *I.o.A.* 230 A4
Kingsley *Ches.* 233 G5
Kingsley *Hants.* 170 C4
Kingsley *Staffs.* 222 B3
Kingsley Green 171 D4
Kingsley Holt 222 B3
Kingslow 207 G3
Kingsmoor 186 D2
Kingsmuir *Angus* 302 C5
Kingsmuir *Fife* 294 D4
Kingsnorth 174 C5
Kingsnorth Power Station 174 A1
Kingstanding 208 C3
Kingsteignton 152 B5
Kingsteps 322 B4
Kingsthorne 195 D4
Kingsthorpe 198 C1
Kingston *Cambs.* 200 B2
Kingston *Cornw.* 149 D3
Kingston *Devon* 150 C3
Kingston *Devon* 153 D4
Kingston *Dorset* 154 D2
Kingston *Dorset* 155 F5
Kingston *E.Loth.* 286 C1
Kingston *Gt.Man.* 234 D3
Kingston *Hants.* 156 A2
Kingston *I.o.W.* 157 D4
Kingston *Kent* 175 D3
Kingston *Moray* 323 F3
Kingston *W.Suss.* 158 C3
Kingston Bagpuize 183 F3
Kingston Blount 184 C3
Kingston by Sea 159 E3
Kingston Deverill 167 F4
Kingston Gorse 158 C3
Kingston Lacy 31
Kingston Lisle 183 F4
Kingston Maurward 154 D3
Kingston Maurward Park 31
Kingston near Lewes 159 F3
Kingston on Soar 223 G5
Kingston Russell 154 B3
Kingston St. Mary 165 F5
Kingston Seymour 166 B1
Kingston Stert 184 C2
Kingston Upon Hull 246 D5
Kingston upon Thames 171 G1
Kingston Warren 183 F4
Kingstone *Here.* 194 D4
Kingstone *Here.* 195 F5
Kingstone *Som.* 153 G1
Kingstone *Staffs.* 222 B5
Kingstone Winslow 183 E4
Kingstown 259 G1
Kingswear 151 E2
Kingswell 283 G5
Kingswells 313 D4
Kingswinford 208 A4
Kingswood *Bucks.* 184 B1
Kingswood *Glos.* 181 G3
Kingswood *Here.* 194 B2
Kingswood *Kent* 174 A3
Kingswood *Powys* 206 B2
Kingswood *S.Glos.* 181 F5
Kingswood *Som.* 165 E4
Kingswood *Surr.* 172 B3
Kingswood *Warks.* 209 D5
Kingthorpe 238 B5
Kington *Here.* 194 B2
Kington *Worcs.* 196 B2
Kington Langley 182 B5
Kington Magna 167 E5
Kington St. Michael 182 B5
Kingussie 309 G4
Kingweston 166 C4
Kinharrachie 313 E1
Kinharvie 266 D4
Kinkell 284 A2
Kinkell Bridge 293 E3
Kinknockie 325 F5
Kinlet 207 G4
Kinloch *Fife* 294 A3
Kinloch *High.* 334 C5
Kinloch *High.* 297 F4
Kinloch *High.* 306 A5
Kinloch *High.* 321 E2
Kinloch *P. & K.* 302 A5
Kinloch *P. & K.* 301 G5
Kinloch Hourn 307 F4
Kinloch Laggan 300 A1
Kinloch Rannoch 300 B4
Kinlochan 298 A3
Kinlochard 291 G4
Kinlocharkaig 307 F5
Kinlochbeoraid 298 A1
Kinlochbervie 334 B3
Kinlocheil 298 B2
Kinlochetive 298 D5
Kinlochewe 319 G3
Kinlochlaich 298 B5
Kinlochleven 299 D3
Kinlochmoidart 297 G2
Kinlochmorar 307 E5
Kinlochmore 299 D3
Kinlochroag (Ceann Lochroag) 328 C5
Kinlochspelve 289 F2
Kinloss 322 C3
Kinmel Bay (Bae Cinmel) 232 A4
Kinmuck 312 D3
Kinnaber 303 F3
Kinnadie 325 E5
Kinnaird 294 A2
Kinneff 303 G2
Kinnelhead 276 B5
Kinnell *Angus* 303 E4
Kinnell *Stir.* 292 A1
Kinnerley 220 A5
Kinnersley *Here.* 194 C3
Kinnersley *Worcs.* 196 A3
Kinnerton 194 B1
Kinnerton Green 220 A1
Kinnesswood 293 G4
Kinnettles 302 C5
Kinninvie 261 G5
Kinnordy 302 B4
Kinoulton 224 B4
Kinrara 310 A4
Kinross 293 G4
Kinrossie 293 G1
Kinsbourne Green 186 A1
Kinsham *Here.* 194 C1
Kinsham *Worcs.* 196 B4
Kinsley 236 B1
Kinson 155 G3
Kintail Estate & Morvich 125
Kintarvie 327 E2
Kintbury 169 E1
Kintessack 322 B3
Kintillo 293 G3
Kintocher 312 A4
Kinton *Here.* 206 D5
Kinton *Shrop.* 206 C1
Kintore 312 C3
Kintour 280 C4
Kintra *Arg. & B.* 280 B5
Kintra *Arg. & B.* 288 C2

Kintradwell 333 E4
Kintraw 290 A4
Kinuachdrachd 289 G5
Kinveachy 310 B3
Kinver 208 A4
Kinwarton 196 D2
Kiplaw Croft 313 F1
Kipp 292 A3
Kippax 244 D4
Kippen *P. & K.* 293 F3
Kippen *Stir.* 292 B5
Kippenross House 292 C4
Kippford (Scaur) 266 C5
Kipping's Cross 173 F4
Kippington 173 E3
Kirbister *Ork.* 338 C2
Kirbister *Ork.* 341 E4
Kirbuster 340 A4
Kirby Bedon 229 D5
Kirby Bellars 210 C1
Kirby Cane 215 E2
Kirby Corner 209 E5
Kirby Cross 202 D5
Kirby Fields 210 A2
Kirby Green 215 E2
Kirby Grindalythe 246 B1
Kirby Hill *N.Yorks.* 252 A2
Kirby Hill *N.Yorks.* 244 C1
Kirby Knowle 253 D4
Kirby le Soken 202 D5
Kirby Misperton 253 G5
Kirby Muxloe 210 A2
Kirby Row 215 E2
Kirby Sigston 252 D3
Kirby Underdale 246 A2
Kirby Wiske 252 C4
Kirdford 171 F5
Kirk 337 E3
Kirk Bramwith 236 D1
Kirk Deighton 244 C2
Kirk Ella 246 C5
Kirk Hallam 223 F3
Kirk Hammerton 245 D2
Kirk Ireton 223 D2
Kirk Langley 223 D4
Kirk Merrington 262 B4
Kirk Michael 240 B2
Kirk of Shotts 284 C3
Kirk Sandall 236 D2
Kirk Smeaton 236 C1
Kirk Yetholm 278 C4
Kirkabister 343 D4
Kirkandrews 257 G2
Kirkandrews-upon-Eden 259 G1
Kirkbampton 259 G1
Kirkbean 267 D5
Kirkbride 259 F1
Kirkbuddo 302 D5
Kirkburn *E.Riding* 246 B2
Kirkburn *Sc.Bord.* 277 D2
Kirkburton 235 F1
Kirkby *Lincs.* 238 A3
Kirkby *Mersey.* 233 F3
Kirkby *N.Yorks.* 253 E2
Kirkby Fleetham 252 B3
Kirkby Green 225 F2
Kirkby in Ashfield 223 F2
Kirkby la Thorpe 225 F3
Kirkby Lonsdale 250 B5
Kirkby Malham 243 E1
Kirkby Mallory 209 G2
Kirkby Malzeard 252 B5
Kirkby on Bain 226 A1
Kirkby Overblow 244 C3
Kirkby Stephen 250 C2
Kirkby Thore 260 C5
Kirkby Underwood 225 F5
Kirkby Wharfe 245 E3
Kirkby Woodhouse 223 F2
Kirkby-in-Furness 248 D4
Kirkbymoorside 253 F4
Kirkcaldy 294 A5
Kirkcaldy Museum & Art Gallery 125
Kirkcambeck 260 B1
Kirkcolm 264 B4
Kirkconnel 275 F4
Kirkconnell 267 D4
Kirkcowan 265 E4
Kirkcudbright 266 A5
Kirkdale House 265 G5
Kirkdean 285 F5
Kirkfieldbank 284 C5
Kirkgunzeon 266 C4
Kirkham *Lancs.* 242 A4
Kirkham *N.Yorks.* 245 G1
Kirkhamgate 244 C5
Kirkharle 270 C3
Kirkhaugh 260 C3
Kirkheaton *Northumb.* 270 C4
Kirkheaton *W.Yorks.* 235 F1
Kirkhill *Angus* 303 E3
Kirkhill *High.* 321 E5
Kirkhill *Moray* 323 F4
Kirkhope 277 E3
Kirkibost *High.* 306 B3
Kirkibost *W.Isles* 328 C4
Kirkinch 302 B5
Kirkinner 265 F5
Kirkintilloch 284 A2
Kirkland *Cumb.* 260 C4
Kirkland *Cumb.* 259 D5
Kirkland *D. & G.* 266 C1
Kirkland *D. & G.* 275 F4
Kirkland *D. & G.* 267 E2
Kirkland of Longcastle 257 D2
Kirkleatham 263 E5
Kirklees Light Railway 88
Kirklevington 252 D1
Kirkley 215 G2
Kirklington *N.Yorks.* 252 C4
Kirklington *Notts.* 224 B2
Kirklinton 260 A1
Kirkliston 285 F2
Kirkmaiden 256 B3
Kirkmichael *P. & K.* 301 F3
Kirkmichael *S.Ayr.* 274 B5
Kirkmuirhill 284 B5
Kirknewton *Northumb.* 278 D3
Kirknewton *W.Loth.* 285 F3
Kirkney 312 A1
Kirkoswald *Cumb.* 260 B3
Kirkoswald *S.Ayr.* 274 A5
Kirkpatrick Durham 266 B3
Kirkpatrick-Fleming 268 A4
Kirksanton 248 C4
Kirkstall 244 B4
Kirkstall Abbey 88
Kirkstead 225 G1
Kirkstile *Aber.* 312 A1
Kirkstile *D. & G.* 268 B2
Kirkstyle 337 F1
Kirkthorpe 244 C5
Kirkton *Aber.* 312 B2
Kirkton *Aber.* 324 B4
Kirkton *Aber.* 312 B3
Kirkton *Angus* 302 C5
Kirkton *Arg. & B.* 289 G4
Kirkton *D. & G.* 267 D2
Kirkton *Fife* 294 B2
Kirkton *High.* 309 F1
Kirkton *High.* 332 C5
Kirkton *High.* 321 G4
Kirkton *High.* 336 A2
Kirkton *High.* 307 E2
Kirkton *P. & K.* 293 E3
Kirkton *Sc.Bord.* 277 G4
Kirkton Manor 276 D2
Kirkton of Airlie 302 B4
Kirkton of Auchterhouse 294 B1
Kirkton of Barevan 322 A5
Kirkton of Bourtie 312 D2
Kirkton of Collace 293 G1
Kirkton of Craig 303 F4
Kirkton of Culsalmond 312 B1
Kirkton of Durris 312 C5
Kirkton of Glenbuchat 311 F3
Kirkton of Glenisla 302 A3
Kirkton of Kingoldrum 302 B4
Kirkton of Lethendy 301 G5
Kirkton of Logie Buchan 313 E2
Kirkton of Maryculter 313 D5
Kirkton of Menmuir 302 D3
Kirkton of Monikie 294 D1
Kirkton of Rayne 312 B1
Kirkton of Skene 312 D4
Kirkton of Tealing 294 C1
Kirktonhill *Aber.* 303 E3
Kirktonhill *W.Dun.* 283 E2
Kirktown 325 F4
Kirktown of Alvah 324 B3
Kirktown of Auchterless 324 C5
Kirktown of Deskford 324 A3
Kirktown of Fetteresso 303 G1
Kirktown of Slains 313 F2
Kirkwall 340 C5
Kirkwall Airport 339 D2
Kirkwhelpington 270 B3
Kirmington 238 B1
Kirmond le Mire 238 B3
Kirn 282 C2
Kirriemuir 302 B4
Kirstead Green 215 D2
Kirtlebridge 268 A4
Kirtleton 268 A3
Kirtling 201 E2
Kirtling Green 201 E2
Kirtlington 184 A1
Kirtomy 335 G2
Kirton *Lincs.* 226 B4
Kirton *Notts.* 224 B1
Kirton *Suff.* 203 D4
Kirton End 226 A3
Kirton Holme 226 A3
Kirton in Lindsey 237 G3
Kiscadale 273 F3
Kislingbury 198 B2
Kismeldon Bridge 163 D4
Kites Hardwick 197 G1
Kitley 150 B2
Kittisford 165 D5
Kittisford Barton 165 D5
Kittle 178 B4
Kitts End 186 B3
Kitt's Green 209 D4
Kitwood 170 B4
Kivernoll 195 D4
Kiveton Park 236 B4
Klibreck 335 E5
Knabbygates 324 A4
Knaith 237 F4
Knaith Park 237 F4
Knap Corner 167 F5
Knaphill 171 E2
Knaplock 164 B4
Knapp *P. & K.* 294 A1
Knapp *Som.* 166 A5
Knapthorpe 224 C2
Knaptoft 210 B4
Knapton *Norf.* 229 E2
Knapton *York* 245 E2
Knapton Green 194 D2
Knapwell 200 B1
Knaresborough 244 C2
Knarsdale 260 C2
Knarston 340 B4
Knaven 325 D5
Knayton 252 D4
Knebworth 200 A5
Knebworth House 81
Knedlington 245 G5
Kneesall 224 C1
Kneesworth 200 B3
Kneeton 224 C3
Knelston 178 A4
Knenhall 221 G4
Knettishall 214 A3
Knightacott 163 G2
Knightcote 197 G2
Knightley 221 F5
Knightley Dale 221 F5
Knighton *Devon* 150 B3
Knighton *Dorset* 154 C1
Knighton *Leic.* 210 B2
Knighton *Poole* 155 G3
Knighton (Tref-y-clawdd) *Powys* 206 B5
Knighton *Som.* 165 E3
Knighton *Staffs.* 221 E5
Knighton *Staffs.* 221 E3
Knighton *Wilts.* 183 E5
Knighton on Teme 207 F5
Knightshayes Court 31
Knightswood 283 G3
Knightwick 195 G2
Knill 194 B1
Knipoch 290 A2
Knipton 224 D4
Knitsley 262 A3
Kniveton 222 D2
Knock *Arg. & B.* 289 E1
Knock *Cumb.* 260 C5
Knock *High.* 306 C4
Knock *Moray* 324 A4
Knock of Auchnahannet 310 C1
Knockalava 290 B5
Knockally 333 G2
Knockaloe Moar 240 A3
Knockan 331 E3
Knockandhu 311 E2
Knockando 323 D5
Knockarthur 332 C4
Knockbain 321 F4
Knockban 320 B3
Knockbreck 321 G1
Knockbrex 257 F2
Knockdamph 331 E5
Knockdee 337 D2
Knockdow 282 C2
Knockdown 182 A4
Knockenkelly 273 F3
Knockentiber 274 B2
Knockfin 308 C2
Knockgray 265 G1
Knockholt 173 D3
Knockholt Pound 173 D3
Knockin 220 A5
Knockinlaw 274 C2
Knockintorran (Cnoc an Torrain) 315 F3
Knocklearn 266 B3
Knockmill 173 E2
Knocknaha 272 B4
Knocknain 264 A4
Knocknalling 265 G2
Knockrome 281 D2
Knocksharry 240 A3
Knockville 265 E3
Knockvologan 288 C3
Knodishall 203 F1
Knodishall Common 203 F1
Knodishall Green 203 F1
Knole *Kent* 46
Knole *Som.* 166 B5
Knoll Gardens 31
Knolls Green 234 C5
Knolton 220 A4
Knook 168 A3
Knossington 210 D2
Knott End-on-Sea 241 G3
Knotting 199 F1
Knotting Green 199 F1
Knottingley 245 E5
Knotts 243 D2
Knotty Green 185 E3
Knowbury 207 E5
Knowe 265 E3
Knowes of Elrick 324 B4
Knowesgate 270 B3
Knoweside 274 A4
Knowetownhead 277 G4
Knowhead 325 E4
Knowl Green 201 F3
Knowl Hill 184 D5
Knowl Wall 221 F4
Knowle *Bristol* 181 F5
Knowle *Devon* 152 A2
Knowle *Devon* 163 E2
Knowle *Devon* 153 D4
Knowle *Shrop.* 207 E5
Knowle *Som.* 164 C3
Knowle *W.Mid.* 209 D5
Knowle Cross 152 D3
Knowle Green 242 C4
Knowle Hall 166 A3
Knowle St. Giles 153 G1
Knowlton *Dorset* 155 G1
Knowlton *Kent* 175 E3
Knowsley 233 F3
Knowsley Safari Park 96
Knowstone 164 B5
Knox Bridge 173 G4
Knucklas 208 B5
Knutsford 234 B5
Knypersley 221 F2
Krumlin 235 E1
Kuggar 145 E5
Kyle of Lochalsh 307 D2
Kyleakin 307 D2
Kylerhea 307 D2
Kyles Scalpay (Caolas Scalpaigh) 327 E4
Kylesbeg 297 F2
Kylesknoydart 307 E5
Kylesmorar 307 E5
Kylestrome 334 B5
Kyloag 332 B5
Kynaston 220 A5
Kynnersley 207 F1
Kyre Park 195 F1

L

Labost 329 D3
Lacasaigh 329 E5
Lacasdal (Laxdale) 329 F4
Laceby 238 C2
Lacey Green 184 D2
Lach Dennis 234 B5
Lacharn (Laugharne) 177 G1
Lackford 213 F5
Lacklee (Leac a' Li) 326 D4
Lacock 168 A1
Lacock Abbey 31
Ladbroke 197 G2
Laddingford 173 F4
Lade Bank 226 B2
Ladies Hill 242 A3
Ladock 146 C4
Lady Hall 248 C4
Lady Lever Art Gallery 96
Ladybank 294 B3
Ladycross 148 D2
Ladyfield 290 C3
Ladykirk 287 F5
Ladysford 325 E3
Ladywood 196 A1
Laga 297 F3
Lagalochan 290 A3
Lagavulin 280 C5
Lagg *Arg. & B.* 281 D2
Lagg *N.Ayr.* 273 E3
Lagg *S.Ayr.* 274 A4
Laggan *Arg. & B.* 280 A4
Laggan *High.* 308 B5
Laggan *High.* 309 F5
Laggan *Moray* 311 F1
Laggan *Stir.* 292 A3
Lagganulva 297 D5
Lagganvoulin 311 D3
Laglingarten 290 D4
Lagnalean 321 F5
Lagrae 275 F4
Laguna 293 G1
Laid 334 D3
Laide 330 B5
Laig 297 D1
Laight 275 E4
Lainchoil 310 C3
Laindon 187 F4
Laing Art Gallery 105
Lair 301 G3
Lairg 332 A4
Lairg Lodge 332 A4
Lairigmor 298 D3
Laisterdyke 244 A4
Laithers 324 B5
Laithes 260 A4
Lake *Devon* 163 F2
Lake *Devon* 150 B1
Lake *I.o.W.* 157 E4
Lake *Wilts.* 168 C4
Lake District 96
Lake District Visitor Centre at Brockhole 96
Lakenham 228 D5
Lakenheath 213 F4
Lakesend 212 D3
Lakeside *Cumb.* 249 E4
Lakeside *Thur.* 187 E5
Lakeside & Haverthwaite Railway 97
Laleham 171 F1
Laleston 179 E5
Lamancha 285 G4
Lamarsh 201 G4
Lamas 228 D3
Lamb Corner 202 B4
Lamb House 46
Lamb Roe 242 D4
Lambden 287 E5
Lamberhurst 173 F5
Lamberhurst Quarter 173 F5
Lamberton 287 G4
Lambfell Moar 240 A3
Lambley *Northumb.* 260 C2
Lambley *Notts.* 224 B3
Lambourn 183 F5
Lambourn Woodlands 183 F5
Lambourne End 187 D3
Lambs Green 172 B5
Lambston 176 C1
Lambton 262 B2
Lamellion 147 G3
Lamerton 149 E3
Lamesley 262 B2
Lamington *High.* 321 G2
Lamington *S.Lan.* 276 A2
Lamlash 273 F2
Lamloch 265 G1
Lamonby 260 A4
Lamorna 144 B4
Lamorran 146 C5
Lampert 269 E4
Lampeter 192 B3
Lampeter Velfrey 177 E1
Lamphey 176 D2
Lamphey Palace 111
Lamplugh 259 D4
Lamport 210 C5
Lamyatt 167 D4
Lana *Devon* 148 D1
Lana *Devon* 162 D5
Lanark 284 C5
Lanarth 145 E4
Lancaster 242 A1
Lancaster City Museum 97
Lanchester 262 A3
Lancing 159 D3
Landbeach 200 C1
Landcross 163 E3
Landerberry 312 C4
Landewednack 145 E5
Landford 156 B1
Landhallow 337 D5
Landican 233 D4
Landimore 178 A3
Landkey 163 F2
Landmoth 252 D3
Landore 178 C3
Landrake 149 D4
Land's End 31
Landscove 151 D1
Landshipping 176 D1
Landulph 150 A1
Landwade 201 E1
Landywood 208 B2
Lane Bottom 243 E4
Lane End *Bucks.* 184 D3
Lane End *Cumb.* 248 C3
Lane End *Derbys.* 223 F1
Lane End *Dorset* 155 E3
Lane End *Hants.* 169 G5
Lane End *Here.* 181 F1
Lane End *Kent* 187 E5
Lane End *Wilts.* 167 F3
Lane Ends *Derbys.* 222 D4
Lane Ends *Gt.Man.* 235 D3
Lane Ends *Lancs.* 243 D4
Lane Ends *N.Yorks.* 243 F3
Lane Green 208 A2
Lane Head *Dur.* 252 A1
Lane Head *Dur.* 261 G5
Lane Head *Gt.Man.* 234 A3
Lane Head *W.Yorks.* 235 F2
Lane Heads 242 A4
Lane Side 243 D5
Laneast 147 G1
Lane-end 147 E3
Laneham 237 F5
Lanehead *Dur.* 261 E3
Lanehead *Northumb.* 269 F3
Lanesend 177 D2
Lanesfield 208 B3
Laneshawbridge 243 F3
Langais 315 G3
Langamull 296 C4
Langar 224 C4
Langbank 283 E2
Langbar 243 G2
Langbaurgh 253 E1
Langcliffe 243 E1
Langdale End 254 C3
Langdon *Cornw.* 148 C1
Langdon *Cornw.* 148 D2
Langdon Beck 261 E4
Langdon Hills 187 F4
Langdon House 152 C5
Langdyke 294 B4
Langford *Beds.* 199 G3
Langford *Essex* 188 B2
Langford *Notts.* 224 D2
Langford *Oxon.* 183 E2
Langford Budville 165 E5
Langham *Essex* 202 B4
Langham *Norf.* 228 B1
Langham *Rut.* 210 D1
Langham *Suff.* 202 A1
Langham Moor 202 B4
Langho 242 C4
Langholm 268 B3
Langland 178 C4
Langlands 266 A5
Langlee 278 A5
Langleeford 278 D4
Langley *Ches.* 234 D5
Langley *Derbys.* 223 F3
Langley *Essex* 200 C4
Langley *Glos.* 196 C5
Langley *Gt.Man.* 234 C2
Langley *Hants.* 156 D2
Langley *Herts.* 200 A5
Langley *Kent* 173 G3
Langley *Northumb.* 261 E1
Langley *Oxon.* 183 F1
Langley *Slo.* 185 F5
Langley *Som.* 165 D5
Langley *W.Suss.* 170 D5
Langley *Warks.* 197 D1
Langley Burrell 182 B5
Langley Corner 185 F4
Langley Green *Derbys.* 223 D4
Langley Green *W.Suss.* 172 B5
Langley Green *Warks.* 197 E1
Langley Heath 174 A3
Langley Marsh 165 D5
Langley Mill 223 F3
Langley Moor 262 B3
Langley Park 262 B3
Langley Street 229 E5
Langney 160 B3
Langold 236 C4
Langore 147 G1
Langport 166 B5
Langrick 226 A3
Langrick Bridge 226 A3
Langridge *B. & N.E.Som.* 167 E1
Langridge *Devon* 163 F3
Langridgeford 163 F3
Langrigg 259 E2
Langrish 170 C5
Langsett 235 G2
Langshaw 277 G2
Langshawburn 277 D5
Langside *Glas.* 283 G3
Langside *P. & K.* 292 C3
Langskaill 340 C2
Langstone *Hants.* 157 G2
Langstone *Newport* 180 C3
Langthorne 252 B3
Langthorpe 244 C1
Langthwaite 251 F2
Langtoft *E.Riding* 246 C1
Langtoft *Lincs.* 211 G1
Langton *Dur.* 252 A1
Langton *Lincs.* 239 D5
Langton *Lincs.* 226 A1
Langton *N.Yorks.* 245 G1
Langton by Wragby 238 B5
Langton Green *Kent* 173 E5
Langton Green *Suff.* 214 C4
Langton Herring 154 C4
Langton Long Blandford 155 E2
Langton Matravers 155 F5
Langtree 163 E4
Langtree Week 163 E4
Langwathby 260 B4
Langwell 331 G4
Langwell House 333 G2
Langwith 236 C5
Langworth 238 A5
Lanhydrock 31
Lanivet 147 E3
Lank 147 E2
Lanlivery 147 E4
Lanner 146 B5
Lanoy 148 C3
Lanreath 147 F4
Lansallos 147 F4
Lansdown 167 E1
Lanteglos 147 E1
Lanteglos Highway 147 F4
Lanton *Northumb.* 278 D3
Lanton *Sc.Bord.* 278 A4
Lanvean 146 C3
Lapford 152 A2
Laphroaig 280 B5
Lapley 208 A1
Lappa Valley Railway 31
Lapworth 209 D5
Larach na Gaibhre 281 F2
Larachbeg 297 F5
Larbert 284 C1
Larbreck 242 A3
Larden Green 220 C2
Larg 265 E3
Largie 312 B1
Largiemore 282 A1
Largoward 294 C4
Largs 282 D4
Largue 324 B5
Largybaan 272 B4
Largybeg 273 F3
Largymore 273 F3
Lark Hall 201 D2
Larkfield 282 D2
Larkhall 284 B4
Larkhill 168 C3
Larklands 223 F3
Larling 214 A3
Larriston 268 D2
Lartington 251 F1
Lary 311 F4
Lasborough 182 A3
Lasham 170 B3
Lashbrook 163 E5
Lashenden 174 A4
Lassington 195 G5
Lassintullich 300 C4
Lassodie 293 G5
Lasswade 286 A3
Lastingham 253 G3
Latchford 234 A4
Latchingdon 188 B2
Latchley 149 E3
Lately Common 234 A3
Lathallan Mill 294 C4
Lathbury 199 D3
Latheron 337 D5
Latheronwheel 337 D5
Lathockar 294 C3
Lathones 294 C4
Lathrisk 294 A4
Latimer 185 F3
Latteridge 181 F4
Lattiford 167 D5
Latton 182 C3
Lauchentyre 265 G5
Lauchintilly 312 C3
Lauder 286 C5
Laugharne (Lacharn) 177 G1
Laughterton 237 F5
Laughton *E.Suss.* 160 A2
Laughton *Leics.* 210 B4
Laughton *Lincs.* 225 F4
Laughton *Lincs.* 237 F3
Laughton en le Morthen 236 C4
Launcells 162 C5
Launcells Cross 162 C5
Launceston 148 D2
Launceston Castle 31
Launceston Steam Railway 31
Launde Abbey 210 C2
Launton 198 B5
Laurels, The 215 E2
Laurencekirk 303 F2
Laurieston *D. & G.* 266 A4
Laurieston *Falk.* 284 D2
Lavendon 199 E2
Lavenham 202 A3
Lavenham Guildhall 81
Laverhay 267 F1
Lavernock 165 F1
Laversdale 260 A1
Laverstock 168 C4
Laverstoke 169 F3
Laverton *Glos.* 196 C4
Laverton *N.Yorks.* 252 B5
Laverton *Som.* 167 E2
Lavister 220 A2
Law 284 C4
Lawers *P. & K.* 292 C2
Lawers *P. & K.* 292 B1
Lawford *Essex* 202 B4
Lawford *Som.* 165 E4
Lawhitton 149 D2
Lawkland 243 D1
Lawkland Green 243 D1
Lawley 207 F2
Lawnhead 221 F5
Lawrence Weston 181 E5
Lawrenny 176 D2
Laws 294 C1
Lawshall 201 G2
Lawshall Green 201 G2
Lawton 194 D2
Laxdale (Lacasdal) 329 F4
Laxey 240 C3
Laxfield 215 D4
Laxfirth *Shet.* 343 D2
Laxfirth *Shet.* 342 D3
Laxford Bridge 334 B4
Laxo 342 D1
Laxton *E.Riding* 245 G5
Laxton *Northants.* 211 E3
Laxton *Notts.* 224 C1
Laycock 243 G3
Layer Breton 188 C1
Layer de la Haye 188 C1
Layer Marney 188 C1
Layer Marney Tower 81
Layham 202 B3
Laymore 153 G2
Layter's Green 185 E3
Laytham 245 G4
Layton 241 G4
Lazenby 263 E5
Lazonby 260 B4
Lea *Derbys.* 223 E2
Lea *Here.* 195 F5
Lea *Lincs.* 237 F4
Lea *Shrop.* 206 C4
Lea *Shrop.* 206 D2
Lea *Wilts.* 182 B4
Lea Bridge 223 E2
Lea Green 195 F1
Lea Marston 209 E3
Lea Town 242 A4
Lea Yeat 250 C4
Leac a' Li (Lacklee) 326 D4
Leachd 290 C5
Leachkin 321 F5
Leacon, The 174 B5
Leadburn 285 G4
Leaden Roding 187 E1
Leadenham 225 E2
Leaderfoot 277 G2
Leadgate *Cumb.* 260 D3
Leadgate *Dur.* 262 A2
Leadgate *Northumb.* 262 A2
Leadhills 275 G4
Leadingcross Green 174 A3
Leafield 183 F1
Leagrave 199 F5
Leake Commonside 226 B2
Leake Hurn's End 226 C3
Lealands 160 A2
Lealholm 253 G2
Lealt *Arg. & B.* 289 F5
Lealt *High.* 318 B3
Leam 235 G5
Leamington Hastings 197 G1
Leamington Spa 197 F1
Leamoor Common 206 D4
Leanach *Arg. & B.* 290 C5
Leanach *High.* 321 G5
Leanaig 321 E4
Leanoch 323 D4
Leargybreck 280 D2
Leasgill 249 F4
Leasingham 225 F3
Leask 313 F1
Leason 178 A3
Leasowe 233 D3
Leat 148 D2
Leatherhead 171 G2
Leathley 244 B3
Leaton *Shrop.* 207 D1
Leaton *Tel. & W.* 207 F1
Leaveland 174 C3
Leavenheath 202 A4
Leavening 245 G1
Leaves Green 172 D2
Leavesden Green 186 A2
Lebberston 255 D4
Lechlade 183 E3
Leck 250 B5
Leckford 169 E4
Leckfurin 335 G3
Leckgruinart 280 A3
Leckhampstead *Bucks.* 198 C4
Leckhampstead *W.Berks.* 183 G5
Leckhampstead Thicket 183 G5
Leckhampton 182 B1
Leckie *High.* 319 G3
Leckie *Stir.* 292 B5
Leckmelm 320 A1
Leckroy 308 C5
Leckuary 290 A5
Leckwith 180 A5
Leconfield 246 C3
Ledaig 290 B1
Ledard 291 G4
Ledbeg 331 E3
Ledburn 199 D5
Ledbury 195 G4
Ledcharrie 292 A2
Ledgemoor 194 D2
Ledicot 194 D1
Ledmore *Arg. & B.* 297 E5
Ledmore *High.* 331 E3
Lednagullin 336 A2
Ledsham *Ches.* 233 E5
Ledsham *W.Yorks.* 245 D5
Ledston 244 D5
Ledstone 150 D3
Ledwell 197 G5
Lee *Arg. & B.* 288 D2
Lee *Devon* 163 E1
Lee *Hants.* 156 C1
Lee *Lancs.* 242 B2

Lee *Shrop.* 220 B4
Lee Brockhurst 220 C5
Lee Chapel 187 F4
Lee Clump 185 E2
Lee Mill Bridge 150 B2
Lee Moor 150 B1
Lee, The 185 D2
Leebotten 342 D5
Leebotwood 207 D3
Leece 241 F1
Leeds *Kent* 174 A3
Leeds *W.Yorks.* 244 B4
Leeds Bradford International Airport 244 B3
Leeds Castle & Gardens 46
Leeds City Art Gallery & Museum 88
Leedstown 144 D3
Leegomery 207 F1
Leek 221 G2
Leek Wootton 197 E1
Leekbrook 221 G2
Leeming *N.Yorks.* 252 B4
Leeming *W.Yorks.* 243 G4
Leeming Bar 252 B4
Lee-on-the-Solent 157 E2
Lees *Derbys.* 223 D4
Lees *Gt.Man.* 235 D2
Leeswood 219 F2
Leftwich 234 A5
Legars 287 E5
Legbourne 239 D4
Legerwood 286 C5
Legoland 46
Legsby 238 B4
Leicester 210 A2
Leicester Forest East 210 A2
Leideag 314 B4
Leigh *Dorset* 154 C2
Leigh *Dorset* 155 G3
Leigh *Gt.Man.* 234 A2
Leigh *Kent* 173 E4
Leigh *Shrop.* 206 C2
Leigh *Surr.* 172 B4
Leigh *Wilts.* 182 C3
Leigh *Worcs.* 195 G2
Leigh Beck 188 B4
Leigh Common 167 E5
Leigh Delamere 182 A5
Leigh Green 174 B5
Leigh Park 157 G2
Leigh Sinton 195 G2
Leigh, The 196 A5
Leigh upon Mendip 167 D3
Leigh Woods 181 E5
Leigham 150 B2
Leighland Chapel 164 D4
Leigh-on-Sea 188 B4
Leighterton 182 A3
Leighton *N.Yorks.* 252 A5
Leighton *Powys* 206 B2
Leighton *Shrop.* 207 F2
Leighton *Som.* 167 E3
Leighton Bromswold 211 G5
Leighton Buzzard 199 F5
Leighton Buzzard Light Railway 81
Leighton Hall 97
Leinthall Earls 194 D1
Leinthall Starkes 194 D1
Leintwardine 206 D5
Leire 210 A4
Leirinmore 334 D2
Leiston 203 F1
Leitfie 302 A5
Leith 285 G2
Leitholm 287 E5
Lelant 144 C3
Lelley 247 E4
Lemington 262 A1
Lemnas 324 D3
Lempitlaw 278 B3
Lemsford 186 B1
Lenchwick 196 C3
Lendalfoot 264 C1
Lendrick Lodge 292 A4
Lenham 174 A3
Lenham Heath 174 B4
Lenie 309 E2
Lenimore 281 G5
Lennel 287 F5
Lennox Plunton 266 A5
Lennoxlove 126
Lennoxtown 284 A2
Lent Rise 185 E4
Lenton *Lincs.* 225 F4
Lenton *Nott.* 223 G4
Lenton Abbey 223 G4
Lenwade 228 B4
Lenzie 284 A2
Leoch 294 B1
Leochel-Cushnie 312 A3
Leominster 195 D2
Leonard Stanley 182 A2
Leonardslee Gardens 46
Leorin 280 B5
Lepe 156 D3
Lephin 317 E5
Lephinchapel 290 B5
Lephinmore 290 B5
Leppington 245 G1
Lepton 235 G1
Lerags 290 A2
Lerryn 147 F4
Lerwick 343 D3
Lesbury 279 G5
Leschangie 312 C3
Lescrow 147 F4
Leslie *Aber.* 312 A2
Leslie *Fife* 294 A4
Lesmahagow 275 G2
Lesnewth 148 B1
Lessendrum 324 A5
Lessingham 229 E3
Lessness Heath 187 D5
Lessonhall 259 F1
Leswalt 264 B4
Letchmore Heath 186 A3
Letchworth Garden City 200 A4
Letcombe Bassett 183 F4
Letcombe Regis 183 F4
Leth Meadhanach 314 C2
Letham *Angus* 302 D5
Letham *Falk.* 284 C1
Letham *Fife* 294 B3
Lethanhill 274 C4
Lethenty 324 D5
Letheringham 203 D2
Letheringsett 228 B2
Letocetum Roman Baths & Museum 66
Lettaford 152 A4
Letter Finlay 308 B5
Letterewe 319 F2
Letterfearn 307 E2
Lettermorar 297 G1
Lettermore *Arg. & B.* 297 D5
Lettermore *High.* 335 F4
Letters 320 A1
Lettershaws 275 G3
Letterston 190 C5
Lettoch *High.* 310 C3
Lettoch *High.* 310 D1
Letton *Here.* 206 C5
Letton *Here.* 194 C3
Letty Green 186 B1
Letwell 236 C4
Leuchars 294 C2
Leumrabhagh 327 F2
Leurbost (Liurbost) 329 E5
Leusdon 152 A5
Levedale 208 A1
Level's Green 200 C5
Leven *E.Riding* 246 D3
Leven *Fife* 294 B4
Levencorroch 273 F3
Levenhall 286 A2
Levens 249 F4
Levens Green 200 B5
Levens Hall 97
Levenshulme 234 C3
Levenwick 342 D5
Leverburgh (An T-òb) 326 C5
Leverington 212 C1
Leverstock Green 185 F2
Leverton 226 B3
Leverton Lucasgate 226 C3
Leverton Outgate 226 C3
Levington 202 D4
Levisham 254 B3
Levishie 308 D3
Lew 183 F2
Lewannick 147 G1
Lewcombe 154 B2
Lewdown 149 E2
Lewes 159 G2
Lewes Castle 46
Leweston 190 C5
Lewisham 186 C5
Lewiston 309 E2
Lewistown 179 F4
Lewknor 184 C3
Leworthy 163 G2
Lewson Street 174 B2
Lewth 242 A4
Lewtrenchard 149 E2
Ley *Aber.* 312 A3
Ley *Cornw.* 147 F3
Ley Green 199 G5
Leybourne 173 F3
Leyburn 252 A3
Leyland 242 B5
Leylodge 312 C3
Leymoor 235 F1
Leys *Aber.* 325 F4
Leys *Aber.* 311 G4
Leys *P. & K.* 294 A1
Leys of Cossans 302 B5
Leysdown-on-Sea 174 C1
Leysmill 303 E5
Leysters 195 E1
Leyton 186 C4
Leytonstone 186 C4
Lezant 148 D3
Lezerea 145 D3
Lhanbryde 323 E3
Lhen, The 240 B1
Liatrie 308 B1
Libanus 193 F5
Libberton 285 D5
Libbery 196 B2
Liberton 285 G3
Liceasto 326 D4
Lichfield 208 D2
Lichfield Cathedral 66
Lickey 208 B5
Lickey End 208 B5
Lickfold 171 E5
Liddaton Green 149 E2
Liddel 339 D4
Liddesdale 297 G4
Liddington 183 E4
Lidgate *Derbys.* 236 A5
Lidgate *Suff.* 201 F2
Lidgett 224 B1
Lidlington 199 E4
Lidsey 158 B3
Lidsing 173 G2
Lidstone 197 F5
Lienassie 307 F2
Lieurary 336 C2
Life Science Centre 105
Liff 294 B1
Lifton 149 D2
Liftondown 149 D2
Lightcliffe 244 A5
Lighthorne 197 F2
Lighthorne Heath 197 F2
Lighthouse, The 126
Lightwater 171 E1
Lightwater Valley Park 88
Lightwood 221 G3
Lightwood Green *Ches.* 220 D3
Lightwood Green *Wrex.* 220 A3
Lilbourne 210 A5
Lilburn Tower 279 E4
Lillesdon 166 A5
Lilleshall 207 G1
Lilley *Herts.* 199 G5
Lilley *W.Berks.* 183 G5
Lilliesleaf 277 G3
Lilling Green 245 F1
Lillingstone Dayrell 198 C4
Lillingstone Lovell 198 C3
Lillington *Dorset* 154 C1
Lillington *Warks.* 197 F1
Lilliput 155 G4
Lilly 163 F2
Lilstock 165 E3
Lilyhurst 207 G1
Limbury 199 F5
Lime Side 234 D2
Limefield 234 C1
Limehillock 324 A4
Limehurst 234 D2
Limekilnburn 284 B4
Limekilns 285 E1
Limerigg 284 C2
Limerstone 156 D4
Limington 166 C5
Limpenhoe 229 E5
Limpley Stoke 167 E1
Limpsfield 172 D3
Limpsfield Chart 172 D3
Linaclate (Lionacleit) 315 F5
Linbriggs 270 A1
Linby 223 G2
Linchmere 171 D4
Lincluden 267 D3
Lincoln 237 G5
Lincoln Castle 73
Lincoln Cathedral 73
Lincomb 196 A1
Lincombe *Devon* 150 D2
Lincombe *Devon* 150 D3
Lindal in Furness 249 D5
Lindale 249 F4
Lindean 277 F2
Lindertis 302 B4
Lindfield 159 F1
Lindford 170 D4
Lindifferon 294 B3
Lindisfarne (see Holy Island) 104
Lindley 244 B3
Lindores 294 A3
Lindow End 234 C5
Lindridge 195 F1
Lindsaig 282 A2
Lindsell 201 E5
Lindsey 202 A3
Lindsey Tye 202 A3
Linfitts 235 D2
Linford *Hants.* 156 A2
Linford *Thur.* 187 F5
Linford Wood 198 D3
Lingague 240 A4
Lingards Wood 235 E1
Lingdale 253 F1
Lingen 194 C1
Lingfield 172 C4
Lingley Green 233 G4
Lingwood 229 E5
Linhead 324 B4
Linhope 277 F5
Linicro 317 G3
Linkend 196 A4
Linkenholt 169 E2
Linkhill 160 D1
Linkinhorne 148 D3
Linklater 339 D4
Linksness *Ork.* 338 B2
Linksness *Ork.* 340 D5
Linktown 294 A5
Linley *Shrop.* 206 C3
Linley *Shrop.* 207 F3
Linley Green 195 F2
Linlithgow 285 E2
Linlithgow Bridge 285 D2
Linlithgow Palace 126
Linn of Muick Cottage 302 B1
Linn of Tummel 126
Linnels 261 F1
Linney 176 B3
Linshiels 270 A1
Linsiadar 328 D4
Linsidemore 332 A5
Linslade 199 E5
Linstead Parva 215 E4
Linstock 260 A2
Linthwaite 235 F1
Lintlaw 287 F4
Lintmill 324 A3
Linton *Cambs.* 201 D3
Linton *Derbys.* 209 E1
Linton *Here.* 195 F5
Linton *Kent* 173 G3
Linton *N.Yorks.* 243 F1
Linton *Sc.Bord.* 278 B4
Linton *W.Yorks.* 244 C3
Linton Zoo 81
Linton-on-Ouse 245 D1
Lintzford 262 A2
Linwood *Hants.* 156 A2
Linwood *Lincs.* 238 B4
Linwood *Renf.* 283 F3
Lionacleit (Linaclate) 315 F5
Lional (Lionel) 329 G1
Lionel (Lional) 329 G1
Liphook 170 D4
Lipley 221 E4
Liscard 233 E3
Liscombe 164 B4
Liskeard 147 G3
L'Islet 151 F4
Lismore 290 A1
Liss 170 C5
Liss Forest 170 C5
Lissett 246 D2
Lissington 238 B4
Liston 201 G3
Lisvane 180 A4
Liswerry 180 C4
Litcham 213 G1
Litchborough 198 B2
Litchfield 169 F2
Litherland 233 E3
Litlington *Cambs.* 200 B3
Litlington *E.Suss.* 160 A3
Little Abington 200 D3
Little Addington 211 E5
Little Alne 196 D1
Little Altcar 233 E2
Little Amwell 186 C1
Little Ann 169 E3
Little Asby 250 B2
Little Assynt 330 D2
Little Aston 208 C3
Little Atherfield 157 D5
Little Ayton 253 E1
Little Baddow 187 G2
Little Badminton 182 A4
Little Ballinluig 301 E4
Little Bampton 259 F1
Little Bardfield 201 E4
Little Barford 199 G2
Little Barningham 228 C2
Little Barrington 183 E1
Little Barrow 220 B1
Little Barugh 253 G5
Little Bavington 270 B4
Little Bealings 202 D3
Little Bedwyn 169 D1
Little Beeby 210 B2
Little Bentley 202 C5
Little Berkhamsted 186 B2
Little Billing 198 D1
Little Birch 195 E4
Little Bispham 241 G3
Little Blakenham 202 C3
Little Bloxwich 208 C2
Little Bollington 234 B4
Little Bookham 171 G2
Little Bourton 197 G3
Little Bowden 210 C4
Little Bradley 201 E2
Little Brampton 206 C4
Little Braxted 188 B1
Little Brechin 303 D3
Little Brickhill 199 E4
Little Bridgeford 221 F5
Little Brington 198 B1
Little Bromley 202 B5
Little Broughton 259 D3
Little Budworth 220 C1
Little Burdon 252 C1
Little Burstead 187 F3
Little Burton 246 D3
Little Bytham 211 F1
Little Canford 155 G3
Little Carlton *Lincs.* 239 D4
Little Carlton *Notts.* 224 C2
Little Casterton 211 F2
Little Catwick 246 D3
Little Catworth 211 F5
Little Cawthorpe 239 D4
Little Chalfield 167 F1
Little Chalfont 185 E3
Little Chart 174 B4
Little Chesterford 200 D3
Little Chesterton 198 A5
Little Cheverell 168 A2
Little Clacton 189 E1
Little Clanfield 183 E2
Little Clifton 259 D4
Little Coates 238 C2
Little Comberton 196 B3
Little Common 160 C3
Little Compton 197 E4
Little Corby 260 A2
Little Cornard 201 G4
Little Cowarne 195 F2
Little Coxwell 183 E3
Little Crakehall 252 B3
Little Cransley 210 D5
Little Crawley 199 E3
Little Creaton 210 C5
Little Creich 321 F1
Little Cressingham 213 G3
Little Crosby 233 E2
Little Crosthwaite 259 F4
Little Cubley 222 C4
Little Dalby 210 C1
Little Dens 325 F5
Little Dewchurch 195 E4
Little Ditton 201 E2
Little Doward 181 E1
Little Down 169 E2
Little Downham 212 D4
Little Drayton 221 D4
Little Driffield 246 C2
Little Dunham 213 G1
Little Dunkeld 301 F5
Little Dunmow 201 E5
Little Durnford 168 C4
Little Easton 201 E5
Little Eaton 223 E3
Little Eccleston 242 A4
Little Ellingham 214 B2
Little End 187 E2
Little Everdon 198 A2
Little Eversden 200 B2
Little Fakenham 214 A4
Little Faringdon 183 E2
Little Fencote 252 B3
Little Fenton 245 E4
Little Finborough 202 B2
Little Fransham 228 A4
Little Gaddesden 185 E1
Little Garway 194 D5
Little Gidding 211 G4
Little Glemham 203 E2
Little Glenshee 293 E1
Little Gorsley 195 F5
Little Gransden 200 A2
Little Green *Cambs.* 200 A3
Little Green *Notts.* 224 C3
Little Green *Suff.* 214 B4
Little Green *Suff.* 214 B4
Little Green *Wrex.* 220 B3
Little Grimsby 238 D3
Little Gringley 237 E4
Little Gruinard 319 F1
Little Habton 253 G5
Little Hadham 200 C5
Little Hale 225 G3
Little Hallingbury 187 D1
Little Hampden 185 D2
Little Haresfield 182 A2
Little Harrowden 211 D5
Little Haseley 184 B2
Little Hatfield 247 D3
Little Hautbois 229 D3
Little Haven *Pembs.* 176 B1
Little Haven *W.Suss.* 171 G4
Little Hay 208 D2
Little Hayfield 235 E4
Little Haywood 222 B5
Little Heath 209 F4
Little Hereford 195 E1
Little Hockham 214 A2
Little Horkesley 202 A4
Little Hormead 200 C5
Little Horsted 159 G2
Little Horton 168 B1
Little Horwood 198 C4
Little Houghton 198 D2
Little Hucklow 235 F5
Little Hulton 234 B2
Little Hungerford 184 A5
Little Hutton 253 D5
Little Idoch 324 C5
Little Irchester 199 E1
Little Keyford 167 E3
Little Kimble 184 D2
Little Kineton 197 F2
Little Kingshill 185 D3
Little Langdale 249 E2
Little Langford 168 B4
Little Laver 187 E2
Little Lawford 209 G5
Little Leigh 234 A5
Little Leighs 187 G1
Little Lever 234 B2
Little Ley 312 B3
Little Linford 198 D3
Little Linton 201 D3
Little London *Bucks.* 184 B1
Little London *E.Suss.* 160 A2
Little London *Essex* 200 C5
Little London *Hants.* 169 E3
Little London *Hants.* 170 B2
Little London *I.o.M.* 240 B3
Little London *Lincs.* 226 C5
Little London *Lincs.* 226 A5
Little London *Lincs.* 238 D5
Little London *Lincs.* 238 B4
Little London *Norf.* 227 D5
Little London *Norf.* 213 F3
Little London *Oxon.* 184 A2
Little London *Powys* 205 G4
Little London *Suff.* 202 B2
Little London *W.Yorks.* 244 B4
Little Longstone 235 F5
Little Lyth 207 D2
Little Malvern 195 G3
Little Malvern Court 66
Little Maplestead 201 G4
Little Marcle 195 F4
Little Marland 163 F4
Little Marlow 185 D4
Little Marsden 243 E4
Little Massingham 227 F5
Little Melton 228 C5
Little Milford 176 C1
Little Mill 180 C2
Little Milton 184 B2
Little Missenden 185 E3
Little Moreton Hall 97
Little Musgrave 250 C1
Little Ness 206 D1
Little Neston 233 D5
Little Newcastle 190 C5
Little Newsham 252 A1
Little Oakley *Essex* 202 D5
Little Oakley *Northants.* 211 D4
Little Odell 199 E2
Little Offley 199 G5
Little Onn 208 A1
Little Orton *Cumb.* 259 G1
Little Orton *Leics.* 209 F2
Little Ouse 213 E4
Little Ouseburn 244 D1
Little Overton 220 A3
Little Packington 209 E4
Little Parndon 186 D1
Little Paxton 199 G1
Little Petherick 146 D2
Little Plumpton 241 G4
Little Plumstead 229 E4
Little Ponton 225 E4
Little Posbrook 157 E2
Little Potheridge 163 F4
Little Preston 198 A2
Little Raveley 212 A4
Little Ribston 244 C2
Little Rissington 183 D1
Little Rogart 332 C4
Little Rollright 197 E4
Little Ryburgh 228 A3
Little Ryle 279 E5
Little Ryton 207 D2
Little Salkeld 260 B4
Little Sampford 201 E4
Little Saxham 201 G1
Little Scatwell 320 C4
Little Shelford 200 C2
Little Shrawardine 206 C1
Little Silver 152 C2
Little Singleton 241 G4
Little Smeaton *N.Yorks.* 236 C1
Little Smeaton *N.Yorks.* 252 C2
Little Snoring 228 A2
Little Sodbury 181 G4
Little Sodbury End 181 G4
Little Somborne 169 E4
Little Somerford 182 B4
Little Soudley 221 E5
Little Stainforth 243 E1
Little Stainton 252 C1
Little Stanney 233 F5
Little Staughton 199 G1
Little Steeping 226 C1
Little Stoke 221 G4
Little Stonham 202 C2
Little Street 212 D4
Little Stretton *Leics.* 210 B3
Little Stretton *Shrop.* 206 D3
Little Strickland 249 G1
Little Stukeley 212 A5
Little Sugnall 221 F4
Little Sutton 233 E5
Little Swinburne 270 B4
Little Tarrington 195 F3
Little Tew 197 F5
Little Tey 201 G5
Little Thetford 212 D5
Little Thornage 228 B2
Little Thornton 241 G3
Little Thorpe 262 D3
Little Thurlow 201 E2
Little Thurlow Green 201 E2
Little Thurrock 187 F5
Little Torboll 332 C5
Little Torrington 163 E4
Little Tosson 270 C1
Little Totham 188 B1
Little Town *Cumb.* 259 F5
Little Town *Lancs.* 242 C4
Little Town *Warr.* 234 A3
Little Twycross 209 F2
Little Urswick 249 D5
Little Wakering 188 C4
Little Walden 200 D3
Little Waldingfield 202 A3
Little Walsingham 228 A2
Little Waltham 187 G1
Little Warley 187 F3
Little Washbourne 196 B4
Little Weighton 246 B4
Little Welland 196 A4
Little Welnetham 201 G1
Little Wenham 202 B4
Little Wenlock 207 F2
Little Whittington 261 F1
Little Wilbraham 200 D2
Little Wishford 168 B4
Little Witcombe 182 B1
Little Witley 195 G1
Little Wittenham 184 A3
Little Wittingham Green 215 D4
Little Wolford 197 E4
Little Woodcote 172 B2
Little Wratting 201 E3
Little Wymington 199 E1
Little Wymondley 200 A5
Little Wyrley 208 C2
Little Wytheford 207 E1
Little Yeldham 201 F4
Littlebeck 254 B2
Littleborough *Devon* 152 B1
Littleborough *Gt.Man.* 234 D1
Littleborough *Notts.* 237 F4
Littlebourne 175 E3
Littlebredy 154 B4
Littlebury 200 D4
Littlebury Green 200 C4
Littledean 181 F1
Littleferry 332 D5
Littleham *Devon* 163 E3
Littleham *Devon* 152 D4
Littlehampton 158 C3
Littlehempston 151 E1
Littlehoughton 279 G5
Littlemill *E.Ayr.* 274 C4
Littlemill *High.* 322 B4
Littlemoor *Derbys.* 223 E1
Littlemoor *Dorset* 154 C4
Littlemore 184 A2
Littlemoss 234 D3
Littleover 223 E4
Littleport 213 D4
Littlestead Green 184 C5
Littlestone-on-Sea 161 F1
Littlethorpe 244 C1
Littleton *Ches.* 220 B1
Littleton *Hants.* 169 F4
Littleton *P. & K.* 294 A1
Littleton *Som.* 166 B4
Littleton *Surr.* 171 F1
Littleton Drew 182 A4
Littleton Panell 168 B2
Littleton-on-Severn 181 E3
Littletown *Dur.* 262 C3
Littletown *I.o.W.* 157 E3
Littlewick Green 184 D5
Littlewindsor 154 A2
Littleworth *Glos.* 196 D4
Littleworth *Oxon.* 183 F3
Littleworth *S.Yorks.* 236 D3
Littleworth *Staffs.* 208 C1
Littleworth *Worcs.* 196 A3
Littley Green 187 F1
Litton *Derbys.* 235 F5
Litton *N.Yorks.* 251 E5
Litton *Som.* 166 C2
Litton Cheney 154 B3
Liurbost (Leurbost) 329 E5
Liverpool 233 E3
Liverpool Cathedral 97
Liverpool John Lennon Airport 233 F4
Liverpool Museum 97
Liversedge 244 B5
Liverton *Devon* 152 B5
Liverton *R. & C.* 253 G1
Liverton Street 174 A4
Living Rainforest 46
Livingston 285 E3
Livingston Village 285 E3
Lixwm 232 C5
Lizard 145 E5
Lizard Peninsula 31
Llaingarreglwyd 192 A2
Llaingoch 230 A4
Llaithddu 205 G4
Llampha 179 F5
Llan 205 E2
Llan Ffestiniog (Ffestiniog) 218 A3
Llanaber 204 C1
Llanaelhaearn 216 C3
Llanaeron 192 A1
Llanafan 204 C5
Llanafan-fawr 193 F2
Llanafan-fechan 193 F2
Llanallgo 230 D4
Llanarmon 216 D4
Llanarmon Dyffryn Ceiriog 219 E4
Llanarmon-yn-Ial 219 E2
Llanarth *Cere.* 192 A2
Llanarth *Mon.* 180 C1
Llanarthney 192 B5
Llanasa 232 C4
Llanbabo 230 B4
Llanbadarn Fawr 204 B4
Llanbadarn Fynydd 205 G5
Llanbadarn-y-garreg 194 A3
Llanbadoc 180 C2
Llanbadrig 230 B3
Llanbeder 180 C3
Llanbedr *Gwyn.* 217 E5
Llanbedr *Powys* 194 B5
Llanbedr *Powys* 194 A3
Llanbedr-Dyffryn-Clwyd 219 F2
Llanbedrgoch 230 D4
Llanbedrog 216 C4
Llanbedr-y-cennin 218 A1
Llanberis 217 E2
Llanberis Lake Railway 111
Llanbethery 164 D1
Llanbister 206 A5
Llanblethian 179 F5
Llanboidy 191 F5
Llanbradach 180 A3
Llanbryn-mair 205 E2
Llancadle 164 D1
Llancarfan 179 G5
Llancayo 180 C2
Llancynfelyn 204 C3
Llandafal 180 A2
Llandaff 180 A5
Llandaff North 180 A5
Llandanwg 217 E5
Llandawke 177 F1
Llanddaniel Fab 230 C5
Llanddarog 178 A1
Llanddeiniol 204 B5
Llanddeiniolen 217 E1
Llandderfel 218 C4
Llanddeusant *Carmar.* 193 D5
Llanddeusant *I.o.A.* 230 B4
Llanddew 193 G4
Llanddewi 178 A4
Llanddewi Rhydderch 180 C1
Llanddewi Skirrid 180 C1
Llanddewi Velfrey 177 E1
Llanddewi Ystradenni 194 A1
Llanddewi-Brefi 192 C2
Llanddewi'r Cwm 193 G3
Llanddoged 218 B1
Llanddona 231 D5
Llanddowror 177 F1
Llanddulas 232 A5
Llanddwywe 217 E5
Llanddyfnan 230 D5
Llandefaelog Fach 193 G4
Llandefaelog-tre'r-graig 194 A5
Llandefalle 194 A4
Llandegfan 231 D5
Llandegla 219 E2
Llandegley 194 A1
Llandegveth 180 C3
Llandegwning 216 B4
Llandeilo 192 C5
Llandeilo Abercywyn 177 G1
Llandeilo Graban 193 G3
Llandeilo'r-Fan 193 E4
Llandeloy 190 B5
Llandenny 180 D2
Llandevaud 180 D3
Llandevenny 180 D4
Llandinabo 195 E5
Llandinam 205 G4
Llandissilio 191 E5
Llandogo 181 E2
Llandough *V. of Glam.* 180 A5
Llandough *V. of Glam.* 179 F5

Llandovery (Llanymddyfri) 193 D4
Llandow 179 F5
Llandre *Carmar.* 192 C3
Llandre *Carmar.* 191 E5
Llandre *Cere.* 204 C4
Llandrillo 218 D4
Llandrindod Wells 193 G1
Llandrinio 206 B1
Llandudno 231 F4
Llandudno Junction 231 F5
Llandudoch (Saint Dogmaels) 191 E3
Llandwrog 217 D2
Llandybie 178 C1
Llandyfaelog 178 A1
Llandyfan 178 C1
Llandyfriog 191 G3
Llandyfrydog 230 C4
Llandygai 231 D5
Llandygwydd 191 F3
Llandyrnog 219 E1
Llandyry 178 A2
Llandysilio 206 B1
Llandyssil 206 A3
Llandysul 192 A3
Llanedeyrn 180 B4
Llanedy 178 B2
Llaneglwys 193 G4
Llanegryn 204 C2
Llanegwad 192 B5
Llaneilian 230 C3
Llanelian-yn-Rhos 231 G5
Llanelidan 219 E2
Llanelieu 194 A4
Llanellen 180 C1
Llanelli 178 B2
Llanelltyd 204 D1
Llanelly 180 B1
Llanelly Hill 180 B1
Llanelwedd 193 G2
Llanelwy (Saint Asaph) 232 B5
Llanenddwyn 217 E5
Llanengan 216 B5
Llanerchaeron 111
Llanerfyl 205 G2
Llaneuddog 230 C4
Llanfachraeth 230 B4
Llanfachreth 218 C5
Llanfaelog 230 B5
Llanfaelrhys 216 B5
Llanfaenor 180 D1
Llan-faes *I.o.A.* 231 E5
Llanfaes *Powys* 193 G5
Llanfaethlu 230 B4
Llanfaglan 217 D1
Llanfair 217 E5
Llanfair Caereinion 206 A2
Llanfair Clydogau 192 C2
Llanfair Dyffryn Clwyd 219 E2
Llanfair Talhaiarn 232 A5
Llanfair Waterdine 206 B5
Llanfairfechan 231 E5
Llanfair-Nant-Gwyn 191 E4
Llanfair-Orllwyn 191 G3
Llanfair-pwllgwyngyll 230 D5
Llanfairynghornwy 230 B3
Llanfair-yn-neubwll 230 B5
Llanfallteg 177 E1
Llanfaredd 193 G2
Llanfarian 204 B5
Llanfechain 219 E5
Llanfechell 230 B3
Llanfendigaid 204 B2
Llanferres 219 E1
Llanfflewyn 230 B4
Llanfigael 230 B4
Llanfihangel Crucornau (Llanvihangel Crucorney) 194 C5
Llanfihangel Glyn Myfyr 218 C3
Llanfihangel Nant Bran 193 F4
Llanfihangel Rhydithon 194 A1
Llanfihangel Rogiet 180 D4
Llanfihangel Tal-y-llyn 194 A5
Llanfihangel-ar-arth 192 A3
Llanfihangel-nant-Melan 194 A2
Llanfihangel-uwch-Gwili 192 A5
Llanfihangel-y-Creuddyn 204 C5
Llanfihangel-yng-Ngwynfa 205 G1
Llanfihangel-yn-Nhywyn 230 B5
Llanfihangel-y-pennant *Gwyn.* 217 E3
Llanfihangel-y-pennant *Gwyn.* 204 C2
Llanfilo 194 A4
Llanfoist 180 B1
Llanfor 218 C4
Llanfrechfa 180 C3
Llanfrothen 217 F3
Llanfrynach 193 G5
Llanfwrog *Denb.* 219 E2
Llanfwrog *I.o.A.* 230 A4
Llanfyllin 206 A1
Llanfynydd *Carmar.* 192 B5
Llanfynydd *Flints.* 219 F2
Llanfyrnach 191 F4
Llangadfan 205 G1
Llangadog 192 D5
Llangadwaladr *I.o.A.* 216 C1
Llangadwaladr *Powys* 219 E4
Llangaffo 216 D1
Llangain 177 G1
Llangammarch Wells 193 F3
Llangan 179 F5
Llangarron 195 E5
Llangasty-Talyllyn 194 A5
Llangathen 192 B5
Llangattock 180 B1
Llangattock Lingoed 180 C1
Llangattock-Vibon-Avel 181 D1
Llangedwyn 219 E5
Llangefni 230 C5
Llangeinor 179 F4
Llangeitho 192 C2
Llangeler 191 G4
Llangelynin 204 B2
Llangendeirne 178 A1
Llangennech 178 B2
Llangennith 178 A3
Llangenny 180 B1
Llangernyw 218 B1
Llangian 216 B5
Llangiwg 178 D2
Llangloffan 190 C4
Llanglydwen 191 E5
Llangoed 231 E5
Llangoedmor 191 E3
Llangollen 219 F3
Llangolman 191 E5
Llangorse 194 A5
Llangorwen 204 C4
Llangovan 181 D2
Llangower 218 C4
Llangrannog 191 G2
Llangristiolus 230 C5
Llangrove 181 E1
Llangua 194 C5
Llangunllo 206 B5
Llangunnor 192 A5
Llangurig 205 F5
Llangwm *Conwy* 218 C3
Llangwm *Mon.* 180 D2
Llangwm *Pembs.* 176 C2
Llangwnnadl 216 B4
Llangwyfan 219 E1
Llangwyllog 230 C5
Llangwyryfon 204 C5
Llangybi *Cere.* 192 C2
Llangybi *Gwyn.* 216 D3
Llangybi *Mon.* 180 C3
Llangyfelach 178 C3
Llangynhafal 219 E1
Llangynidr 180 A1
Llangyniew 206 A2
Llangynin 177 F1
Llangynllo 191 G3
Llangynog *Carmar.* 177 G1
Llangynog *Powys* 219 D5
Llangynwyd 179 E4
Llanhamlach 193 G5
Llanharan 179 G4
Llanharry 179 G4
Llanhennock 180 C3
Llanhilleth 180 B2
Llanidloes 205 F4
Llaniestyn 216 B4
Llanigon 194 B4
Llanilar 204 C5
Llanilid 179 F4
Llanishen *Cardiff* 180 A4
Llanishen *Mon.* 181 D2
Llanllawddog 192 A5
Llanllechid 217 F1
Llanlleonfel 193 F2
Llanllugan 205 G2
Llanllwch 177 G1
Llanllwchaiarn 206 A3
Llanllwni 192 A3
Llanllyfni 217 D2
Llanllywel 180 C3
Llanmadoc 178 A3
Llanmaes 164 C1
Llanmartin 180 C4
Llanmerewig 206 A3
Llanmihangel 179 F5
Llan-mill 177 E1
Llanmiloe 177 F2
Llanmorlais 178 B3
Llannefydd 232 A5
Llannerch Hall 232 B5
Llannerch-y-medd 230 C4
Llannerch-y-Môr 232 C5
Llannon *Carmar.* 178 B2
Llan-non *Cere.* 192 B1
Llannor 216 C4
Llanover 180 C2
Llanpumsaint 192 A5
Llanreithan 190 B5
Llanrhaeadr 219 D1
Llanrhaeadr-ym-Mochnant 219 E5
Llanrhian 190 B4
Llanrhidian 178 A3
Llanrhyddlad 230 B4
Llanrhystud 192 B1
Llanrothal 181 D1
Llanrug 217 E1
Llanrumney 180 B4
Llanrwst 218 A1
Llansadurnen 177 F1
Llansadwrn *Carmar.* 192 C4
Llansadwrn *I.o.A.* 231 D5
Llansaint 177 G2
Llansamlet 178 C3
Llansanffraid 192 B1
Llansanffraid Glan Conwy 231 G5
Llansannan 218 C1
Llansannor 179 F5
Llansantffraed 194 A5
Llansantffraed-Cwmdeuddwr 193 F1
Llansantffraed-in-Elwel 193 G2
Llansantffraid-ym-Mechain 219 F5
Llansawel *Carmar.* 192 C4
Llansawel (Briton Ferry) *N.P.T.* 178 D3
Llansilin 219 F5
Llansoy 180 D2
Llanspyddid 193 G5
Llanstadwell 176 C2
Llansteffan 177 G1
Llansteffan Castle 111
Llanstephan 194 A3
Llantarnam 180 C3
Llanteg 177 E1
Llanthony 194 B5
Llanthony Priory 111
Llantilio Crossenny 180 C1
Llantilio Pertholey 180 C1
Llantood 191 E3
Llantrisant *I.o.A.* 230 B4
Llantrisant *Mon.* 180 C3
Llantrisant *R.C.T.* 179 G4
Llantrithyd 179 G5
Llantwit Fardre 179 G4
Llantwit Major 164 C1
Llantysilio 219 E3
Llanuwchllyn 218 B5
Llanvaches 180 D3
Llanvair-Discoed 180 D3
Llanvapley 180 C1
Llanvetherine 180 C1
Llanveynoe 194 C4
Llanvihangel Crucorney (Llanfihangel Crucornau) 194 C5
Llanvihangel Gobion 180 C2
Llanvihangel-Ystern-Llewern 180 D1
Llanvithyn 179 G5
Llanwarne 195 E5
Llanwddyn 205 G1
Llanwenog 192 A3
Llanwern 180 C4
Llanwinio 191 F5
Llanwnda *Gwyn.* 217 D2
Llanwnda *Pembs.* 190 C4
Llanwnnen 192 B3
Llanwnog 205 G3
Llanwonno 179 G3
Llanwrda 192 D4
Llanwrin 205 D2
Llanwrthwl 193 F1
Llanwrtyd 193 E3
Llanwrtyd Wells 193 E3
Llanwyddelan 205 G2
Llanyblodwel 219 F5
Llanybri 177 G1
Llanybydder 192 B3
Llanycefn 191 E5
Llanychaer Bridge 190 C4
Llanycil 218 C4
Llanycrwys 192 C3
Llanymawddwy 205 E1
Llanymddyfri (Llandovery) 193 D4
Llanymynech 219 F5
Llanynghenedl 230 B4
Llanynys 219 E1
Llan-y-pwll 220 A2
Llanyre 193 G1
Llanystumdwy 217 D4
Llanywern 194 A5
Llawhaden 177 D1
Llawndy 232 C4
Llawnt 219 F4
Llawr-y-dref 216 B5
Llawryglyn 205 F3
Llay 220 A2
Llechcynfarwy 230 B4
Llecheiddior 217 D3
Llechfaen 193 G5
Llechryd *Caerp.* 180 A2
Llechryd *Cere.* 191 F3
Llechrydau 219 F4
Llechwedd Slate Caverns 111
Lledrod *Cere.* 204 C5
Lledrod *Powys* 219 F5
Llethrid 178 B3
Llidiad-Nenog 192 B4
Llidiardau 218 B4
Llithfaen 216 C3
Lloc 232 C5
Llong 219 F1
Llowes 194 A3
Lloyney 206 B5
Llundain-fach 192 B2
Llwydcoed 179 F2
Llwydiarth 205 G1
Llwyn *M.Tyd.* 179 G1
Llwyn *Shrop.* 206 B4
Llwyncelyn 192 A2
Llwyn-croes 192 A5
Llwyndafydd 191 G2
Llwynderw 206 B2
Llwyndyrys 216 C3
Llwyneinion 219 F3
Llwyngwril 204 B2
Llwynhendy 178 B3
Llwyn-Madoc 193 F2
Llwynmawr 219 F4
Llwyn-onn 192 A2
Llwyn-y-brain *Carmar.* 177 E1
Llwyn-y-brain *Carmar.* 192 D4
Llwyn-y-groes 192 B2
Llwynypia 179 F3
Llynclys 219 F5
Llynfaes 230 C5
Llysfaen 231 G5
Llyswen 194 A4
Llysworney 179 F5
Llys-y-frân 190 D5
Llywel 193 E4
Load Brook 235 G4
Loandhu 322 A2
Loanhead *Aber.* 313 E1
Loanhead *Midloth.* 285 G3
Loans 274 B2
Lobb 163 E2
Lobhillcross 149 E2
Loch a Charnain 315 G5
Loch an Eilein Visitor Centre & Forest Trail 126
Loch Baghasdail (Lochboisdale) 314 C2
Loch Choire Lodge 335 F5
Loch Eil Outward Bound 298 C2
Loch Head *D. & G.* 256 D2
Loch Head *D. & G.* 265 F1
Loch Lomond & The Trossachs National Park 126
Loch na Madadh (Lochmaddy) 316 C3
Loch Ness Monster Exhibition Centre 126
Loch Sgioport 304 B1
Lochailort 297 G1
Lochaline 297 F5
Lochans 264 B5
Locharbriggs 267 D2
Lochawe 290 D2
Lochboisdale (Loch Baghasdail) 314 C2
Lochbuie 289 F2
Lochcarron 319 E5
Lochdhu Hotel 336 C4
Lochdon 289 G1
Lochdrum 320 B2
Lochearnhead 292 A2
Lochee 294 B1
Lochend *High.* 337 E2
Lochend *High.* 309 E1
Locheport (Locheuphort) 315 G3
Locheuphort (Locheport) 315 G3
Lochfoot 266 D3
Lochgair 290 B5
Lochgarthside 309 E3
Lochgelly 293 G5
Lochgilphead 281 G1
Lochgoilhead 291 E4
Lochgoyn 283 G5
Lochhill *E.Ayr.* 275 D4
Lochhill *Moray* 323 E3
Lochinch Castle 264 C4
Lochinver 330 C2
Lochlair 302 D5
Lochlane 292 D2
Lochlea 274 C2
Lochluichart 320 C3
Lochmaben 267 E2
Lochmaddy (Loch na Madadh) 316 C3
Lochore 293 G5
Lochore Meadows Country Park 126
Lochportain 316 C2
Lochranza 282 A4
Lochside *Aber.* 303 F3
Lochside *High.* 335 D3
Lochside *High.* 336 A5
Lochside *High.* 337 E2
Lochslin 322 A1
Lochton 265 D2
Lochty 294 D4
Lochuisge 297 G4
Lochurr 266 B2
Lochussie 321 D4
Lochwinnoch 283 E4
Lockengate 147 E3
Lockerbie 267 F2
Lockeridge 168 C1
Lockerley 169 D5
Lockhills 260 B3
Locking 166 A2
Lockington *E.Riding* 246 B3
Lockington *Leics.* 223 F5
Lockleywood 221 D5
Locks Heath 157 E2
Locksbottom 172 D2
Locksgreen 156 D3
Lockton 254 B4
Loddington *Leics.* 210 C2
Loddington *Northants.* 210 D5
Loddiswell 150 D3
Loddon 215 E2
Lode 200 D1
Loders 154 A3
Lodge RSPB Nature Reserve, The 81
Lodge, The 291 D5
Lodsworth 171 E5
Lofthouse *N.Yorks.* 252 A5
Lofthouse *W.Yorks.* 244 C5
Loftus 253 G1
Logan *D. & G.* 256 A2
Logan *E.Ayr.* 275 D3
Logan Botanic Garden 126
Loganlea 285 D3
Loggerheads 221 E4
Loggie 330 D5
Logie *Angus* 303 E3
Logie *Angus* 302 B4
Logie *Fife* 294 C2
Logie *Moray* 322 C4
Logie Coldstone 311 G4
Logie Hill 321 G2
Logie Newton 312 B1
Logie Pert 303 E3
Logieralt 301 E4
Login 191 F5
Lolworth 200 B1
Lonbain 318 C4
Londesborough 246 A3
London 186 C4
London Apprentice 147 E5
London Aquarium 57
London Beach 174 A5
London City Airport 186 D4
London Colney 186 A2
London Dungeon 57
London Eye 57
London Gatwick Airport (Gatwick Airport) 172 B4
London Heathrow Airport 185 F5
London Luton Airport (Luton Airport) 199 G5
London Minstead 156 B1
London Stansted Airport (Stansted Airport) 200 D5
London Zoo 57
Londonderry 252 B4
London's Transport Museum 57
Londonthorpe 225 E4
Londubh 319 E1
Lonemore 321 G1
Long Ashton 181 E5
Long Bank 207 G5
Long Bennington 224 D3
Long Bredy 154 B3
Long Buckby 198 B1
Long Clawson 224 C5
Long Common 157 E1
Long Compton *Staffs.* 221 F5
Long Compton *Warks.* 197 E4
Long Crendon 184 B2
Long Crichel 155 F1
Long Dean 182 A5
Long Downs 145 E3
Long Drax 245 F5
Long Duckmanton 236 B5
Long Eaton 223 F4
Long Gill 243 D2
Long Green *Ches.* 233 F5
Long Green *Essex* 202 A5
Long Green *Worcs.* 196 A4
Long Hanborough 183 G1
Long Itchington 197 G1
Long Lane 207 F1
Long Lawford 209 G5
Long Load 166 B5
Long Marston *Herts.* 185 D1
Long Marston *N.Yorks.* 245 E2
Long Marston *Warks.* 197 D3
Long Marton 260 C5
Long Meadowend 206 D4
Long Melford 201 G3
Long Newnton 182 B3
Long Preston 243 E2
Long Riston 246 D3
Long Stratton 214 C2
Long Street 198 C3
Long Sutton *Hants.* 170 C3
Long Sutton *Lincs.* 226 C5
Long Sutton *Som.* 166 B5
Long Thurlow 202 B1
Long Whatton 223 F5
Long Wittenham 184 A3
Longbenton 262 B1
Longborough 197 D5
Longbridge *Plym.* 150 B2
Longbridge *W.Mid.* 208 C5
Longbridge *Warks.* 197 E1
Longbridge Deverill 167 F3
Longburgh 259 G1
Longburton 154 C1
Longcliffe 222 D2
Longcombe 151 E2
Longcot 183 E3
Longcroft 284 B2
Longcross *Devon* 149 E3
Longcross *Surr.* 171 E1
Longden 206 D2
Longdon *Staffs.* 208 C1
Longdon *Worcs.* 196 A4
Longdon Green 208 C1
Longdon upon Tern 207 F1
Longdown 152 B3
Longdrum 313 E3
Longfield 173 F2
Longfield Hill 173 F2
Longfleet 155 G3
Longford *Derbys.* 222 D4
Longford *Glos.* 196 A5
Longford *Gt.Lon.* 185 F5
Longford *Shrop.* 220 D4
Longford *Tel. & W.* 207 G1
Longford *W.Mid.* 209 F4
Longforgan 294 B2
Longformacus 287 D4
Longframlington 270 D1
Longham *Dorset* 155 G3
Longham *Norf.* 228 A4
Longhill 325 E4
Longhirst 271 E3
Longhope *Glos.* 181 F1
Longhope *Ork.* 338 C3
Longhorsley 270 D2
Longhoughton 279 G5
Longlands *Aber.* 311 G2
Longlands *Cumb.* 259 F3
Longlands *Gt.Lon.* 186 D5
Longlane *Derbys.* 223 D4
Longlane *W.Berks.* 183 G5
Longleat House 32
Longleat Safari Park 32
Longlevens 182 A1
Longley 235 F2
Longley Green 195 G2
Longmanhill 324 C3
Longmoor Camp 170 C4
Longmorn 323 E4
Longnewton *Sc.Bord.* 277 G3
Longnewton *Stock.* 252 C1
Longney 181 G1
Longniddry 286 B2
Longnor *Shrop.* 207 D2
Longnor *Staffs.* 222 B1
Longparish 169 F3
Longridge *Lancs.* 242 C4
Longridge *Staffs.* 208 B1
Longridge *W.Loth.* 285 D3
Longridge End 196 A5
Longridge Towers 287 G4
Longriggend 284 C2
Longrock 144 C3
Longsdon 221 G2
Longshaw 233 G2
Longside 325 F5
Longslow 221 D4
Longsowerby 259 G1
Longstanton 200 C1
Longstock 169 E4
Longstone 144 C3
Longstowe 200 B2
Longstreet 168 C2
Longthorpe 211 G3
Longton *Lancs.* 242 A5
Longton *Stoke* 221 G3
Longtown *Cumb.* 268 B5
Longtown *Here.* 194 C5
Longville in the Dale 207 E3
Longwell Green 181 F5
Longwick 184 C2
Longwitton 270 C3
Longworth 183 F3
Longyester 286 C3
Lonmay 325 F4
Lonmore 317 F5
Looe 147 G4
Look Out Discovery Park 46
Loose 173 G3
Loosebeare 152 A2
Loosegate 226 B5
Loosley Row 184 D2
Lopcombe Corner 169 D4
Lopen 154 A1
Loppington 220 B5
Lorbottle 270 C1
Lorbottle Hall 270 C1
Lordington 157 G2
Lord's Cricket Ground & Museum 57
Lord's Hill 156 C1
Lorgill 317 E5
Lorn 283 E1
Lornty 301 G5
Loscoe 223 F3
Loscombe 154 A3
Loseley House 46
Losgaintir 326 C4
Lossiemouth 323 E2
Lossit 280 A4
Lost Gardens of Heligan 32
Lostock Gralam 234 A5
Lostock Green 234 A5
Lostock Junction 234 A2
Lostwithiel 147 F4
Loth 341 E3
Lothbeg 333 E3
Lothersdale 243 F3
Lotherton Hall 88
Lothmore 333 E3
Loudwater 185 E3
Loughborough 210 A1
Loughor 178 B3
Loughton *Essex* 186 D3
Loughton *M.K.* 198 D4
Loughton *Shrop.* 207 F4
Lound *Lincs.* 211 F1
Lound *Notts.* 237 D4
Lound *Suff.* 215 G2
Lount 209 F1
Lour 302 C5
Louth 238 D4
Love Clough 243 E5
Lovedean 157 F1
Lover 156 B1
Loversall 236 C3
Loves Green 187 F2
Lovesome Hill 252 C3
Loveston 177 D2
Lovington 166 C4
Low Ackworth 236 B1
Low Angerton 270 C3
Low Ballevain 272 B3
Low Barlay 265 G5
Low Barlings 238 A5
Low Bentham 242 C1
Low Bolton 251 F3
Low Bradfield 235 G3
Low Bradley (Bradley) 243 G3
Low Braithwaite 260 A3
Low Brunton 270 B4
Low Burnham 237 E2
Low Burton 252 B4
Low Buston 271 E1
Low Catton 245 G2
Low Coniscliffe 252 B1
Low Craighead 274 A5
Low Dinsdale 252 C1
Low Ellington 252 B4
Low Entercommon 252 C2
Low Etherley 262 A5
Low Fell 262 B2
Low Gate 261 F1
Low Grantley 252 B5
Low Green 201 G1
Low Habberley 208 A5
Low Ham 166 B5
Low Hawsker 254 C2
Low Haygarth 250 B3
Low Hesket 260 A3
Low Hesleyhurst 270 C2
Low Hutton 245 G1
Low Kingthorne 254 B4
Low Laithe 244 A1
Low Langton 238 B5
Low Leighton 235 E4
Low Lorton 259 E4
Low Marishes 254 B5
Low Marnham 224 D1
Low Middleton 279 F3
Low Mill 253 F3
Low Moor *Lancs.* 242 D3
Low Moor *W.Yorks.* 244 A5
Low Moorsley 262 C3
Low Moresby 258 C4
Low Newton-by-the-Sea 279 G4
Low Row *Cumb.* 260 B1
Low Row *N.Yorks.* 251 E3
Low Stillaig 282 A3
Low Street 228 B5
Low Tharston 214 C2
Low Torry 285 E1
Low Town 270 D1
Low Toynton 238 C5
Low Wood 249 E4
Low Worsall 252 C2
Lowbands 195 G4
Lowdham 224 B3
Lowe 220 C4
Lowe Hill 221 G2
Lower Achachenna 290 C2
Lower Aisholt 165 F4
Lower Apperley 196 A5
Lower Arncott 184 B1
Lower Ashtead 171 G2
Lower Ashton 152 B4
Lower Assendon 184 C4
Lower Auchalick 282 A2
Lower Ballam 241 G4
Lower Barewood 194 C2
Lower Bartle 242 A4
Lower Bayble (Pabail Iarach) 329 G4
Lower Beeding 159 E1
Lower Benefield 211 E4
Lower Bentley 196 B1
Lower Berry Hill 181 E1
Lower Birchwood 223 F2
Lower Boddington 197 G2
Lower Boscaswell 144 A3
Lower Bourne 170 D3
Lower Brailes 197 F4
Lower Breakish 306 C2
Lower Bredbury 234 D3
Lower Broadheath 196 A2
Lower Brynamman 178 D1
Lower Bullingham 195 E4
Lower Bullington 169 F3
Lower Burgate 156 A1
Lower Burrow 166 B5
Lower Burton 194 D2
Lower Caldecote 199 G3
Lower Cam 181 G2
Lower Camster 337 E4
Lower Canada 166 A2
Lower Chapel 193 G4
Lower Cheriton 153 E2
Lower Chicksgrove 168 A4
Lower Chute 169 E2
Lower Clent 208 B4
Lower Creedy 152 B2
Lower Cumberworth 235 G2
Lower Darwen 242 C5
Lower Dean 199 F1
Lower Diabaig 319 D3
Lower Dicker 160 A2
Lower Dinchope 207 D4
Lower Down 206 C4
Lower Drift 144 B4
Lower Dunsforth 244 D1
Lower Earley 184 C5
Lower Edmonton 186 C3
Lower Elkstone 222 B2
Lower End *Bucks.* 184 B2
Lower End *M.K.* 199 E4
Lower End *Northants.* 199 D1
Lower Everleigh 168 C2
Lower Eythorne 175 E4
Lower Failand 181 E5
Lower Farringdon 170 C4
Lower Fittleworth 158 C2
Lower Foxdale 240 A4
Lower Freystrop 176 C1
Lower Froyle 170 C3
Lower Gabwell 151 F1
Lower Gledfield 332 A5
Lower Godney 166 B3
Lower Gravenhurst 199 G4
Lower Green *Essex* 200 C4
Lower Green *Herts.* 199 G4
Lower Green *Kent* 173 F4
Lower Green *Norf.* 228 A2
Lower Green *Staffs.* 208 B2
Lower Green Bank 242 B2
Lower Halstock Leigh 154 B2
Lower Halstow 174 A2
Lower Hardres 174 D3
Lower Harpton 194 B1
Lower Hartshay 223 E2
Lower Hartwell 184 C1
Lower Hawthwaite 248 D4
Lower Haysden 173 E4
Lower Hayton 207 E4
Lower Heath 221 F1
Lower Hergest 194 B2
Lower Heyford 197 G5
Lower Higham 187 G5
Lower Holbrook 202 C4
Lower Hopton 235 F1
Lower Hordley 220 A5
Lower Horncroft 158 C2
Lower Horsebridge 160 A2
Lower Houses 235 F1
Lower Howsell 195 G3
Lower Kersal 234 C2
Lower Kilchattan 288 C5
Lower Kilcott 181 G4
Lower Killeyan 280 A5
Lower Kingcombe 154 B3
Lower Kingswood 172 B3
Lower Kinnerton 220 A1
Lower Langford 166 B1
Lower Largo 294 C4
Lower Leigh 222 B4
Lower Lemington 197 E4
Lower Lovacott 163 F3
Lower Loxhore 163 G2
Lower Lydbrook 181 E1
Lower Lye 194 D1

Lower Machen 180 B4
Lower Maes-coed 194 C4
Lower Mannington 155 G2
Lower Middleton Cheney 198 A3
Lower Milton 166 C3
Lower Moor 196 B3
Lower Morton 181 F3
Lower Nash 176 D2
Lower Nazeing 186 C2
Lower Netchwood 207 F3
Lower Nyland 167 E5
Lower Oddington 197 E5
Lower Ollach 306 B1
Lower Penarth 180 A5
Lower Penn 208 A3
Lower Pennington 156 C3
Lower Peover 234 B5
Lower Pollicott 184 C1
Lower Quinton 197 D3
Lower Race 180 B2
Lower Rainham 174 A2
Lower Roadwater 164 D4
Lower Sapey 195 F1
Lower Seagry 182 B4
Lower Shelton 199 E3
Lower Shiplake 184 C5
Lower Shuckburgh 197 G1
Lower Slaughter 197 D5
Lower Soothill 244 B5
Lower Stanton St. Quintin 182 B4
Lower Stoke 174 A1
Lower Stondon 199 G4
Lower Stone 181 F3
Lower Stonnall 208 C2
Lower Stow Bedon 214 A2
Lower Street *Dorset* 155 E3
Lower Street *E.Suss.* 160 C2
Lower Street *Norf.* 229 D2
Lower Street *Norf.* 228 C2
Lower Street *Suff.* 202 C2
Lower Stretton 234 A4
Lower Sundon 199 F5
Lower Swanwick 157 D2
Lower Swell 197 D5
Lower Tadmarton 197 G4
Lower Tale 153 D2
Lower Tean 222 B4
Lower Thurlton 215 F2
Lower Thurnham 242 A2
Lower Town *Cornw.* 145 D4
Lower Town *Devon* 152 A5
Lower Town *I.o.S.* 146 B1
Lower Town *Pembs.* 190 C4
Lower Trebullett 148 D3
Lower Tysoe 197 F3
Lower Upcott 152 B4
Lower Upham 157 F1
Lower Upnor 187 G5
Lower Vexford 165 E4
Lower Wallop 206 C2
Lower Walton 234 A4
Lower Waterhay 182 C3
Lower Weald 198 C4
Lower Wear 152 C4
Lower Weare 166 B2
Lower Welson 194 B2
Lower Whatley 167 E3
Lower Whitley 234 A5
Lower Wick 196 A2
Lower Wield 170 B3
Lower Winchendon (Nether Winchendon) 184 C1
Lower Withington 221 F1
Lower Woodend 184 D4
Lower Woodford 168 C4
Lower Wyche 195 G3
Lowerhouse 243 E4
Lowertown 338 D3
Lowesby 210 C2
Lowestoft 215 G2
Loweswater 259 E4
Lowfield Heath 172 B4
Lowgill *Cumb.* 250 B3
Lowgill *Lancs.* 242 C1
Lowick *Cumb.* 249 D4
Lowick *Northants.* 211 E4
Lowick *Northumb.* 279 E3
Lowick Bridge 249 D4
Lowick Green 249 D4
Lownie Moor 302 C5
Lowry, The 97
Lowsonford 197 D1
Lowther 260 B5
Lowther Castle 260 B5
Lowthorpe 246 C1
Lowton *Devon* 163 G5
Lowton *Gt.Man.* 234 A3
Lowton *Som.* 153 E1
Lowton Common 234 A3
Loxbeare 152 C1
Loxhill 171 F4
Loxhore 163 G2
Loxley 197 E2
Loxley Green 222 B4
Loxton 166 A2
Loxwood 171 F4
Lubachoinnich 331 G5
Lubcroy 331 F4
Lubenham 210 C4
Lubfearn 320 C2
Lubmore 319 G4
Lubreoch 299 G5
Luccombe 164 C3
Luccombe Village 157 E4
Lucker 279 F3
Luckett 149 D3
Luckington 182 A4
Lucklawhill 294 C2
Luckwell Bridge 164 C4
Lucton 194 D1
Lucy Cross 252 B1
Ludag 314 C2
Ludborough 238 C3
Ludbrook 150 C2
Ludchurch 177 E1
Luddenden 243 G5
Luddenden Foot 243 G5
Luddenham Court 174 B2
Luddesdown 173 F2
Luddington *N.Lincs.* 237 F1
Luddington *Warks.* 197 D2
Luddington in the Brook 211 G4
Ludford *Lincs.* 238 B4
Ludford *Shrop.* 207 E5
Ludgershall *Bucks.* 184 B1
Ludgershall *Wilts.* 169 D2
Ludgvan 144 C3
Ludham 229 E4
Ludlow 66
Ludlow Castle 66
Ludney 239 D3
Ludstock 195 F4
Ludstone 208 A3
Ludwell 168 A5
Ludworth 262 C3
Luffincott 148 D1
Luffness 286 B1
Lufton 154 B1
Lugar 275 D3
Luggate 286 C2
Luggate Burn 286 D2
Luggiebank 284 B2
Lugton 283 F4
Lugwardine 195 E3
Luib 306 B2
Luibeilt 299 E3
Luing 289 G3
Lulham 194 D3
Lullingstone Castle 46
Lullingstone Roman Villa 47
Lullington *Derbys.* 209 E1
Lullington *Som.* 167 E2
Lulsgate Bottom 166 C1
Lulsley 195 G2
Lulworth Camp 155 E4
Lulworth Castle 32
Lulworth Cove & Heritage Centre 32
Lumb *Lancs.* 243 E5
Lumb *W.Yorks.* 243 G5
Lumbutts 243 F5
Lumby 245 D4
Lumphanan 312 A4
Lumphinnans 293 G5
Lumsdaine 287 F3
Lumsdale 223 E1
Lumsden 311 G2
Lunan 303 E4
Lunanhead 302 C4
Luncarty 293 F2
Lund *E.Riding* 246 B3
Lund *N.Yorks.* 245 F4
Lund *Shet.* 345 E2
Lundale 328 C4
Lundavra 298 C3
Lunderton 325 G5
Lundie *Angus* 294 A1
Lundie *High.* 308 A3
Lundin Links 294 C4
Lundwood 236 A2
Lundy 162 B1
Lundy Island 32
Lunga 290 A4
Lunna 343 D1
Lunning 343 E1
Lunnon 178 B4
Lunsford's Cross 160 C2
Lunt 233 E2
Luntley 194 C2
Luppitt 153 E2
Lupset 236 A1
Lupton 249 G4
Lurgashall 171 E5
Lurignich 298 B4
Lusby 226 B1
Luss 291 F5
Lussagiven 281 E1
Lusta 317 F4
Lustleigh 152 A4
Luston 195 D1
Luthermuir 303 E3
Luthrie 294 B3
Luton *Devon* 153 D2
Luton *Devon* 152 B5
Luton *Luton* 199 F5
Luton *Med.* 173 G2
Luton Airport (London Luton Airport) 199 G5
Lutterworth 210 A4
Lutton *Devon* 150 B2
Lutton *Dorset* 155 F4
Lutton *Lincs.* 226 C5
Lutton *Northants.* 211 G4
Luxborough 164 C4
Luxulyan 147 E4
Lybster *High.* 336 C2
Lybster *High.* 337 E5
Lydacott 163 E5
Lydbury North 206 C4
Lydcott 163 G2
Lydd 161 F1
Lydd Airport 161 F1
Lydden 175 E4
Lyddington 211 D3
Lyddington Bede House 73
Lydd-on-Sea 161 F1
Lyde Green 181 F5
Lydeard St. Lawrence 165 E4
Lydford 149 F2
Lydford Gorge 32
Lydford-on-Fosse 166 C4
Lydgate *Gt.Man.* 235 D1
Lydgate *Gt.Man.* 235 D2
Lydgate *W.Yorks.* 243 F5
Lydham 206 C3
Lydiard Mansion 32
Lydiard Millicent 182 C4
Lydiard Tregoze 182 D4
Lydiate 233 E2
Lydlinch 154 D1
Lydney 181 F2
Lydstep 177 D3
Lye 208 B4
Lye Cross 166 B1
Lye Green *Bucks.* 185 E2
Lye Green *E.Suss.* 173 E5
Lye Green *Warks.* 197 D1
Lye's Green 167 F3
Lyford 183 F3
Lymbridge Green 174 D4
Lyme Park 97
Lyme Regis 153 G3
Lymekilns 284 A4
Lyminge 175 D4
Lymington 156 C3
Lyminster 158 C3
Lymm 234 A4
Lymore 156 B3
Lympne 174 D5
Lympsham 166 A2
Lympstone 152 C4
Lynaberack 309 G5
Lynch 164 B3
Lynch Green 228 C5
Lynchat 309 G4
Lyndhurst 156 B2
Lyndon 211 E2
Lyne *Aber.* 312 C4
Lyne *Sc.Bord.* 285 G5
Lyne *Surr.* 171 F1
Lyne Down 195 F4
Lyne of Gorthleck 309 E2
Lyne of Skene 312 C3
Lyne Station 285 G5
Lyneal 220 B4
Lynedale House 317 G4
Lynegar 337 E3
Lyneham *Oxon.* 197 E5
Lyneham *Wilts.* 182 C5
Lyneholmeford 268 D4
Lynemore *High.* 310 C2
Lynemore *Moray* 310 D1
Lynemouth 271 F2
Lyness 338 C3
Lynford 213 G3
Lyng *Norf.* 228 B4
Lyng *Som.* 166 A5
Lyngate 229 E3
Lynmouth 164 A3
Lynn 207 G1
Lynsted 174 B2
Lynstone 162 C5
Lynton 164 A3
Lynton & Lynmouth Cliff Railway 32
Lyon's Gate 154 C2
Lyonshall 194 C2
Lyrabus 280 A3
Lytchett Matravers 155 F3
Lytchett Minster 155 F3
Lytes Cary Manor 32
Lyth 337 E2
Lytham 241 G5
Lytham St. Anne's 241 G5
Lythe 254 B1
Lythe Hill 171 E4
Lythes 339 D4
Lythmore 336 C2
Lyveden New Bield 73

M

Maaruig (Maraig) 327 E3
Mabe Burnthouse 145 E3
Mabie 267 D3
Mablethorpe 239 F4
Macclesfield 234 D5
Macclesfield Forest 235 D5
Macduff 324 C3
Macedonia 294 A4
Machan 284 B4
Machany 293 D3
Macharioch 272 C5
Machen 180 B4
Machrie *Arg. & B.* 280 A3
Machrie *Arg. & B.* 280 B5
Machrie *N.Ayr.* 273 D2
Machrihanish 272 B3
Machrins 288 C5
Machynlleth 204 D2
McInroy's Point 282 D2
Mackerye End 186 A1
Mackworth 223 E4
McManus Galleries 126
Macmerry 286 B2
Macterry 324 C5
Madame Tussaud's & The Planetarium 57
Madderty 293 E2
Maddiston 284 D2
Madehurst 158 B2
Madeley *Staffs.* 221 E3
Madeley *Tel. & W.* 207 G2
Madeley Heath 221 E3
Maders 148 D3
Madford 153 E1
Madingley 200 B1
Madjeston 167 F5
Madley 194 D4
Madresfield 196 A3
Madron 144 B3
Maenaddwyn 230 C4
Maenclochog 191 D5
Maendy *Cardiff* 180 A5
Maendy *V. of Glam.* 179 G5
Maenporth 145 E4
Maentwrog 217 F3
Maen-y-groes 191 G2
Maer *Cornw.* 162 C5
Maer *Staffs.* 221 E4
Maerdy *Carmar.* 192 C5
Maerdy *Carmar.* 192 C5
Maerdy *Conwy* 218 D3
Maerdy *R.C.T.* 179 F3
Maes Howe 126
Maesbrook 219 F5
Maesbury Marsh 220 A5
Maes-Glas (Greenfield) *Flints.* 232 C5
Maes-glas *Newport* 180 C4
Maesgwynne 191 F5
Maeshafn 219 F1
Maesllyn 191 G3
Maesmynis 193 G3
Maesteg 179 E3
Maes-Treylow 194 B1
Maesybont 178 B1
Maesycrugiau 192 A3
Maesycwmmer 180 A3
Maesyfed (New Radnor) 194 B1
Magdalen Laver 187 E2
Maggieknockater 323 F5
Maggots End 200 C5
Magham Down 160 B2
Maghull 233 E2
Magna Centre 88
Magna Park 210 A4
Magor 180 D4
Magpie Green 214 B4
Maiden Bradley 167 E4
Maiden Castle 33
Maiden Head 166 C1
Maiden Law 262 A3
Maiden Newton 154 B3
Maiden Wells 176 C3
Maidencombe 151 F1
Maidenhayne 153 F3
Maidenhead 185 D4
Maidens 274 A5
Maiden's Green 185 D5
Maidensgrove 184 C4
Maidenwell *Cornw.* 147 F2
Maidenwell *Lincs.* 238 D5
Maidford 198 B2
Maids' Moreton 198 C4
Maidstone 173 G3
Maidwell 210 C5
Mail 342 D5
Maindee 180 C4
Mainland *Ork.* 340 A5
Mainland *Shet.* 342 C2
Mains of Ardestie 294 D1
Mains of Balgavies 302 D4
Mains of Balhall 302 D3
Mains of Ballindarg 302 C4
Mains of Burgie 322 C4
Mains of Culsh 325 D5
Mains of Dillavaird 303 F1
Mains of Drum 312 D4
Mains of Dudwick 313 E1
Mains of Faillie 309 G1
Mains of Fedderate 325 D5
Mains of Glack 312 C2
Mains of Glassaugh 324 A3
Mains of Glenbuchat 311 F3
Mains of Linton 312 C3
Mains of Melgund 302 D4
Mains of Pitfour 325 E5
Mains of Pittrichie 313 D2
Mains of Sluie 322 C4
Mains of Tannachy 323 F3
Mains of Thornton 303 E2
Mains of Tig 264 C2
Mains of Watten 337 E3
Mainsforth 262 C4
Mainsriddle 266 D5
Mainstone 206 B4
Maisemore 196 A5
Major's Green 208 D5
Makendon 270 A1
Makeney 223 E3
Makerstoun 278 A3
Malacleit 315 F2
Malborough 150 D4
Malden Rushett 171 G1
Maldon 188 B2
Malham 243 F1
Malham Cove 88
Maligar 318 A3
Malinbridge 236 A4
Mallaig 306 C5
Mallaigmore 306 C5
Mallaigvaig 306 C5
Malleny Mills 285 F3
Malletsheugh 283 G4
Malling 292 A4
Mallows Green 200 C5
Malltraeth 216 D1
Mallwyd 205 E1
Malmesbury 182 B4
Malmsmead 164 A3
Malpas *Ches.* 220 B3
Malpas *Cornw.* 146 C5
Malpas *Newport* 180 C3
Maltby *Lincs.* 238 D4
Maltby *S.Yorks.* 236 C3
Maltby *Stock.* 253 D1
Maltby le Marsh 239 E4
Malting End 201 F2
Malting Green 188 C1
Maltman's Hill 174 A4
Malton 253 G5
Malvern Hills 67
Malvern Link 195 G3
Malvern Wells 195 G3
Mam Tor 73
Mambeg 282 D1
Mamble 207 F5
Mamhead 152 C4
Mamhilad 180 C2
Manaccan 145 E4
Manadon 150 A2
Manafon 206 A2
Manais (Manish) 326 D5
Manaton 152 A4
Manby 239 D4
Mancetter 209 F3
Manchester 234 C3
Manchester Airport 234 C4
Manchester Art Gallery 97
Mancot Royal 220 A1
Mandally 308 B4
Manderston 126
Manea 212 C4
Maneight 274 D5
Manfield 252 B1
Mangapps Railway Museum 81
Mangaster 344 C5
Mangerton 154 A3
Mangotsfield 181 F5
Mangrove Green 199 G5
Mangurstadh 328 B4
Manish (Manais) 326 D5
Mankinholes 243 F5
Manley 233 G5
Manmoel 180 A2
Mannal 296 A2
Manningford Abbots 168 C2
Manningford Bohune 168 C2
Manningford Bruce 168 C2
Manningham 244 A4
Mannings Heath 159 E1
Mannington 155 G2
Manningtree 202 C4
Mannofield 313 E4
Manor House 88
Manor Park 185 E4
Manorbier 177 D3
Manorbier Castle 111
Manorbier Newton 176 D2
Manordeifi 191 F3
Manordeilo 192 C5
Manorowen 190 C4
Mansell Gamage 194 C3
Mansell Lacy 194 D3
Mansergh 250 B4
Mansfield 223 G1
Mansfield Woodhouse 223 G1
Manson Green 228 B5
Mansriggs 249 D4
Manston *Dorset* 155 E1
Manston *Kent* 175 F2
Manston *W.Yorks.* 244 C4
Manswood 155 F2
Manthorpe *Lincs.* 211 F1
Manthorpe *Lincs.* 225 E4
Manton *N.Lincs.* 237 G2
Manton *Notts.* 236 C5
Manton *Rut.* 211 D2
Manton *Wilts.* 168 C1
Manuden 200 C5
Manwood Green 187 E1
Maolachy 290 A3
Maperton 167 D5
Maple Cross 185 F3
Maplebeck 224 C1
Mapledurham 184 B5
Mapledurham House & Mill 47
Mapledurwell 170 B2
Maplehurst 171 G5
Maplescombe 173 E2
Mapleton 222 C3
Mapperley *Derbys.* 223 F3
Mapperley *Notts.* 223 G3
Mapperton *Dorset* 154 B3
Mapperton *Dorset* 155 F3
Mapperton *Dorset* 33
Mappleborough Green 196 C1
Mappleton 247 E3
Mapplewell 236 A2
Mappowder 154 D2
Mar Lodge 310 C5
Maraig (Maaruig) 327 E3
Marazion 144 C3
Marbhig 327 G2
Marbury 220 C3
March 212 C3
Marcham 183 G3
Marchamley 220 C5
Marchamley Wood 220 C4
Marchington 222 C4
Marchington Woodlands 222 C5
Marchwiel 220 A3
Marchwood 156 C1
Marcross 164 C1
Marcus 302 D4
Marden *Here.* 195 E3
Marden *Kent* 173 G4
Marden *T. & W.* 271 F4
Marden *Wilts.* 168 B2
Marden Ash 187 E2
Marden Beech 173 G4
Marden Thorn 173 G4
Marden's Hill 173 D5
Mardon 278 D3
Mardy 180 C1
Mare Green 166 A5
Marefield 210 C2
Mareham le Fen 226 A1
Mareham on the Hill 226 A1
Maresfield 159 G1
Marfleet 246 D4
Marford 220 A2
Margam 179 D4
Margaret Marsh 155 E1
Margaret Roding 187 E1
Margaretting 187 F2
Margaretting Tye 187 F2
Margate 175 F1
Margnaheglish 273 F2
Margreig 266 C3
Margrove Park 253 F1
Marham 213 F2
Marhamchurch 162 C5
Marholm 211 G2
Marian Cwm 232 B5
Mariandyrys 231 C4
Marian-Glas 230 D4
Mariansleigh 164 A5
Marine Town 174 B1
Marishader 318 A3
Maristow House 150 A1
Mark 166 A3
Mark Causeway 166 A3
Mark Cross 173 E5
Markbeech 173 D4
Markby 239 E5
Markdhu 264 C3
Markeaton 223 E4
Market Bosworth 209 G2
Market Deeping 211 G1
Market Drayton 221 D4
Market Harborough 210 C4
Market Lavington 168 B2
Market Overton 211 D1
Market Rasen 238 B4
Market Stainton 238 C5
Market Street 229 D3
Market Warsop 223 G1
Market Weighton 246 A3
Market Weston 214 A4
Markethill 294 A1
Markfield 209 G1
Markham 180 A2
Markham Moor 237 E5
Markinch 294 A4
Markington 244 B1
Marks Gate 187 D3
Marks Tey 202 A5
Marksbury 167 D1
Markwell 149 D5
Markyate 185 F1
Marl Bank 195 G3
Marland 234 C1
Marlborough 168 C1
Marlbrook 208 B5
Marlcliff 196 C2
Marldon 151 E1
Marle Green 160 A2
Marlesford 203 E2
Marley Green 220 C3
Marley Hill 262 B2
Marlingford 228 C5
Marloes 176 A2
Marlow *Bucks.* 185 D4
Marlow *Here.* 206 D5
Marlpit Hill 172 D4
Marlpool 223 F3
Marnhull 155 D1
Marnoch 324 A4
Marple 235 D4
Marple Bridge 235 D4
Marr 236 C2
Marrel 333 F3
Marrick 251 F3
Marrister 343 E1
Marros 177 F2
Marsden *T. & W.* 262 C1
Marsden *W.Yorks.* 235 E1
Marsett 251 E4
Marsh 153 F1
Marsh Baldon 184 A3
Marsh Benham 169 F1
Marsh Gibbon 198 B5
Marsh Green *Devon* 152 D3
Marsh Green *Gt.Man.* 233 G2
Marsh Green *Kent* 172 D4
Marsh Green *Tel. & W.* 207 F1
Marsh Lane 236 B5
Marsh Street 164 C3
Marsh, The 206 C3
Marshall Meadows 287 G4
Marshalsea 153 G2
Marshalswick 186 A2
Marsham 228 C3
Marshaw 242 B2
Marshborough 175 F3
Marshbrook 206 D4
Marshchapel 239 D3
Marshfield *Newport* 180 B4
Marshfield *S.Glos.* 181 G5
Marshgate 148 B1
Marshland St. James 212 D2
Marshside 233 E1
Marshwood 153 G3
Marske 252 A2
Marske-by-the-Sea 263 F5
Marsland Green 234 A3
Marston *Ches.* 234 A5
Marston *Here.* 194 C2
Marston *Lincs.* 225 D3
Marston *Oxon.* 184 A2
Marston *Staffs.* 221 G5
Marston *Staffs.* 208 A1
Marston *Warks.* 209 E3
Marston *Wilts.* 168 A2
Marston Doles 197 G2
Marston Green 209 D4
Marston Magna 166 C5
Marston Meysey 182 D3
Marston Montgomery 222 C4
Marston Moretaine 199 E3
Marston on Dove 222 D5
Marston St. Lawrence 198 A3
Marston Stannett 195 E2
Marston Trussell 210 B4
Marstow 181 E1
Marsworth 185 E1
Marten 169 D1
Marthall 234 B5
Martham 229 F4
Martin *Hants.* 155 G1
Martin *Lincs.* 225 G2
Martin *Lincs.* 226 A1
Martin Drove End 168 B5
Martin Hussingtree 196 A1
Martin Mere 98
Martinhoe 163 G1
Martinscroft 234 A4
Martinstown 154 C4
Martlesham 202 D3
Martlesham Heath 202 D3
Martletwy 176 D1
Martley 195 G1
Martock 154 A1
Marton *Ches.* 221 F1
Marton *Cumb.* 248 D5
Marton *E.Riding* 247 D4
Marton *E.Riding* 247 E1
Marton *Lincs.* 237 F4
Marton *Middbro.* 253 E1
Marton *N.Yorks.* 244 D1
Marton *N.Yorks.* 253 G4
Marton *Shrop.* 206 B2
Marton *Shrop.* 220 B5
Marton *Warks.* 197 G1
Marton Abbey 245 E1
Marton-in-the-Forest 245 E1
Marton-le-Moor 252 C5
Martyr Worthy 169 G4
Martyr's Green 171 F2
Marwell Zoo 47
Marwick 340 A4
Marwood 163 F2
Marwood Hill 33
Mary Arden's House 67
Mary Rose 47
Mary Tavy 149 F3
Marybank *High.* 321 D4
Marybank *W.Isles* 329 F4
Maryburgh 321 E4
Maryfield *Cornw.* 150 A2
Maryfield *Shet.* 343 D3
Marygold 287 F4
Maryhill *Aber.* 324 D5
Maryhill *Glas.* 283 G3
Marykirk 303 E3
Marylebone *Gt.Lon.* 186 B4
Marylebone *Gt.Man.* 233 G2
Marypark 311 D1
Maryport *Cumb.* 258 D3
Maryport *D. & G.* 256 B3
Marystow 149 E2
Maryton 303 E4
Marywell *Aber.* 313 E5
Marywell *Aber.* 312 A5
Marywell *Angus* 303 E5
Masham 252 B4
Mashbury 187 F1
Masongill 250 B5
Mastin Moor 236 B5
Mastrick 313 E4
Matchborough 196 C1
Matching 187 E1
Matching Green 187 E1
Matching Tye 187 E1
Matfen 270 C4
Matfield 173 F4
Mathern 181 E3
Mathon 195 G3
Mathry 190 B4
Matlaske 228 C2
Matlock 223 E1
Matlock Bank 223 E1
Matlock Bath 223 D2
Matson 182 A1
Matterdale End 259 G4
Mattersey 237 D4
Mattersey Thorpe 237 D4
Mattingley 170 C2
Mattishall 228 B4
Mattishall Burgh 228 B4
Mauchline 274 C3
Maud 325 E5
Maufant 150 C5
Maugersbury 197 D5
Maughold 240 C2
Mauld 308 C1
Maulden 199 F4
Maulds Meaburn 250 B1
Maunby 252 C4
Maund Bryan 195 E2
Maundown 165 D5
Mautby 229 F4
Mavesyn Ridware 208 C1
Mavis Enderby 226 B1
Maw Green 221 E2
Mawbray 259 D2
Mawdesley 233 F1
Mawdlam 179 E4
Mawgan 145 E4
Mawgan Porth 146 C3
Mawla 146 A5
Mawnan 145 E4
Mawnan Smith 145 E4
Mawsley 210 D5
Mawthorpe 239 E5
Maxey 211 G2
Maxstoke 209 E4
Maxted Street 174 D4
Maxton *Kent* 175 F4
Maxton *Sc.Bord.* 278 A3
Maxwellheugh 278 B3
Maxwelltown 267 D3
Maxworthy 148 C1
Mayals 178 C3
Maybole 274 B5
Maybury 171 F2
Mayen 324 A5
Mayfair 186 B4
Mayfield *E.Suss.* 160 A1
Mayfield *Midloth.* 286 A3
Mayfield *Staffs.* 222 C3
Mayford 171 E2
Mayland 188 C2
Maylandsea 188 C2
Maynard's Green 160 A2
Maypole *I.o.S.* 146 B1
Maypole *Kent* 175 D2
Maypole *Mon.* 181 D1
Maypole Green *Essex* 202 A5
Maypole Green *Norf.* 215 F2
Maypole Green *Suff.* 203 D1
Maypole Green *Suff.* 202 A2
May's Green *N.Som.* 166 A1
Mays Green *Oxon.* 184 C4
Maywick 342 C5
Mead 162 C4
Mead End 168 B5
Meadgate 167 D2
Meadle 184 D2
Meadow Green 195 G2

Meadowhall 236 A3
Meadowmill 286 B2
Meadowtown 206 C2
Meadwell 149 E2
Meaford 221 F4
Meal Bank 249 G3
Mealabost (Melbost Borve) 329 F2
Mealasta 328 A5
Meals 239 E3
Mealsgate 259 F2
Meanley 242 D3
Meanwood 244 B4
Mearbeck 243 E1
Meare 166 B3
Meare Green 165 F5
Mearns 283 G4
Mears Ashby 198 D1
Measham 209 F1
Meathop 249 F4
Meavy 150 B1
Medbourne 210 D3
Meddon 162 C4
Meden Vale 223 G1
Medlar 242 A4
Medmenham 184 D4
Medomsley 262 A2
Medstead 170 B4
Meer Common 194 C2
Meer End 209 E5
Meerbrook 221 G1
Meesden 200 C4
Meeson 221 D5
Meeth 163 F5
Meeting House Hill 229 E3
Meggethead 276 C3
Meidrim 191 F5
Meifod *Denb.* 218 D2
Meifod *Powys* 206 A1
Meigle 302 A5
Meigle Sculptured Stones 126
Meikle Earnock 284 B4
Meikle Grenach 282 B3
Meikle Kilmory 282 B3
Meikle Rahane 282 D1
Meikle Strath 303 E2
Meikle Tarty 313 E2
Meikle Wartle 312 C1
Meikleour 293 G1
Meikleyard 274 D2
Meinciau 178 A1
Meir 221 G3
Meirheath 221 G4
Melbost 329 F4
Melbost Borve (Mealabost) 329 F2
Melbourn 200 B3
Melbourne *Derbys.* 223 E5
Melbourne *E.Riding* 245 G3
Melbourne Hall & Gardens 73
Melbury 163 D4
Melbury Abbas 155 E1
Melbury Bubb 154 B2
Melbury Osmond 154 B2
Melbury Sampford 154 B2
Melby 342 A2
Melchbourne 199 F1
Melcombe Bingham 155 D2
Melcombe Regis 154 C4
Meldon *Devon* 149 F1
Meldon *Northumb.* 270 D3
Meldreth 200 B3
Meledor 146 D4
Melford Hall 81
Melfort 290 A3
Melgarve 309 D5
Melgum 311 G4
Meliden (Gallt Melyd) 232 B4
Melincourt 179 E2
Melin-y-coed 218 B1
Melin-y-ddol 205 G2
Melin-y-grug 205 G2
Melin-y-Wig 218 D3
Melkinthorpe 260 B5
Melkridge 260 D1
Melksham 168 A1
Melksham Forest 168 A1
Melldalloch 282 A2
Mellerstain 127
Melling *Lancs.* 249 G5
Melling *Mersey.* 233 E2
Melling Mount 233 F2
Mellis 214 B4
Mellon Charles 330 A5
Mellon Udrigle 330 A5
Mellor *Gt.Man.* 235 D4
Mellor *Lancs.* 242 C4
Mellor Brook 242 C4
Mells 167 E3
Melmerby *Cumb.* 260 C4
Melmerby *N.Yorks.* 251 F4
Melmerby *N.Yorks.* 252 C5
Melplash 154 A3
Melrose *Aber.* 324 C3
Melrose *Sc.Bord.* 277 G2
Melrose Abbey 127
Melsetter 338 B4
Melsonby 252 A2
Meltham 235 E1
Melton *E.Riding* 246 B5
Melton *Suff.* 203 D2
Melton Carnegie Museum 73
Melton Constable 228 B2
Melton Mowbray 210 C1
Melton Ross 238 A1
Meltonby 245 G2
Melvaig 318 D1
Melverley 206 C1
Melverley Green 206 C1
Melvich 336 A2
Membury 153 F2
Memsie 325 E3
Memus 302 C4
Menabilly 147 E4
Menai Bridge (Porthaethwy) 231 D5
Mendham 215 D3
Mendips 33
Mendlesham 202 C1
Mendlesham Green 202 B1
Menethorpe 245 G1
Menheniot 147 G3
Menie House 313 E2
Menithwood 195 G1
Mennock 275 G5
Menston 244 A3
Menstrie 292 D5
Mentmore 185 E1
Meoble 297 G1
Meole Brace 207 D1
Meon 157 E2
Meonstoke 157 F1
Meopham 173 F2
Meopham Green 173 F2
Mepal 212 C4
Meppershall 199 G4
Merbach 194 C3
Mercaston 223 D3
Merchant Adventurers Hall 88
Mere *Ches.* 234 B4
Mere *Wilts.* 167 F4
Mere Brow 233 F1
Mere Green 208 D3
Mere Heath 234 A5
Mereclough 243 E4
Mereside 241 G4
Meretown 221 E5
Mereworth 173 F3
Mergie 303 F1
Meriden 209 E4
Merkadale 305 G1
Merkinch 321 F5
Merkland 266 B3
Merley 155 G3
Merlin's Bridge 176 C1
Merridge 165 F4
Merrifield 151 E3
Merrington 220 B5
Merrion 176 C3
Merriott 154 A1
Merrivale 149 F3
Merrow 171 F2
Merry Hill *Herts.* 186 A3
Merry Hill *W.Mid.* 208 B4
Merry Hill *W.Mid.* 208 A3
Merrymeet 147 G3
Mersea Island 188 D1
Mersey Ferries 98
Merseyside Maritime Museum 98
Mersham 174 C5
Merstham 172 B3
Merston 158 A3
Merstone 157 E4
Merther 146 C5
Merthyr 191 G5
Merthyr Cynog 193 F4
Merthyr Dyfan 165 E1
Merthyr Mawr 179 E5
Merthyr Tydfil 179 G2
Merthyr Vale 179 G3
Merton *Devon* 163 F4
Merton *Norf.* 214 A2
Merton *Oxon.* 184 A1
Mervinslaw 278 A5
Meshaw 152 A1
Messing 188 C1
Messingham 237 F2
Metcombe 153 D3
Metfield 215 D3
Metheringham 225 F1
Metherwell 150 A1
Methil 294 B5
Methlem 216 A4
Methley 244 C5
Methley Junction 244 C5
Methlick 313 D1
Methven 293 F2
Methwold 213 F3
Methwold Hythe 213 F3
MetroCentre 262 B1
Mettingham 215 E3
Metton 228 C2
Mevagissey 147 E5
Mewith Head 242 D1
Mexborough 236 B3
Mey 337 E1
Meysey Hampton 182 D2
Miabhag *W.Isles* 327 D4
Miabhag *W.Isles* 326 C3
Miabhaig (Miavaig) 328 B4
Mial 319 D2
Miavaig (Miabhaig) 328 B4
Michaelchurch 195 E5
Michaelchurch Escley 194 C4
Michaelchurch-on-Arrow 194 B2
Michaelston-le-Pit 180 A5
Michaelston-super-Ely 180 A5
Michaelston-y-Fedw 180 B4
Michaelstow 147 E2
Michelcombe 150 C1
Micheldever 169 G4
Michelham Priory 47
Michelmersh 169 E5
Mickfield 202 C1
Mickle Trafford 220 B1
Micklebring 236 C3
Mickleby 254 B1
Micklefield 244 D4
Micklefield Green 185 F3
Mickleham 171 G2
Micklehurst 235 D2
Mickleover 223 E4
Micklethwaite *Cumb.* 259 F1
Micklethwaite *W.Yorks.* 243 G3
Mickleton *Dur.* 261 F5
Mickleton *Glos.* 197 D3
Mickletown 244 C5
Mickley *Derbys.* 236 A5
Mickley *N.Yorks.* 252 B5
Mickley Green 201 G2
Mickley Square 261 G1
Mid Ardlaw 325 E3
Mid Beltie 312 B4
Mid Calder 285 E3
Mid Clyth 337 E5
Mid Hants Railway 47
Mid Lambrook 154 A1
Mid Lavant 158 A3
Mid Letter 290 C4
Mid Lix 292 A1
Mid Mossdale 250 D3
Mid Yell 345 E3
Midbea 340 C2
Middle Assendon 184 C4
Middle Aston 197 G5
Middle Barton 197 G5
Middle Bickenhill 209 E4
Middle Bockhampton 156 A3
Middle Claydon 198 C5
Middle Drift 147 F3
Middle Drums 303 D4
Middle Duntisbourne 182 B2
Middle Handley 236 B5
Middle Harling 214 A3
Middle Kames 282 A1
Middle Littleton 196 C3
Middle Maes-coed 194 C4
Middle Marwood 163 F2
Middle Mill 190 B5
Middle Quarter 174 A5
Middle Rasen 238 A4
Middle Rigg 293 F4
Middle Salter 242 C1
Middle Sontley 220 A3
Middle Stoford 165 E5
Middle Taphouse 147 F3
Middle Town 146 B1
Middle Tysoe 197 F3
Middle Wallop 169 D4
Middle Winterslow 168 D4
Middle Woodford 168 C4
Middlebie 268 A4
Middlecliff 236 B2
Middlecott 163 E5
Middleham 252 A4
Middlehill *Aber.* 324 D5
Middlehill *Cornw.* 147 G3
Middlehope 207 E4
Middlemarsh 154 C2
Middlemoor 149 E3
Middlequarter (Ceathramh Meadhanach) 315 G2
Middlesbrough 263 D5
Middlesceugh 260 A3
Middleshaw 249 G4
Middlesmoor 251 F5
Middlestone 262 B4
Middlestone Moor 262 B4
Middlestown 235 G1
Middleton *Aber.* 312 D3
Middleton *Angus* 303 D5
Middleton *Cumb.* 250 B4
Middleton *Derbys.* 223 D2
Middleton *Derbys.* 222 C1
Middleton *Essex* 201 G3
Middleton *Gt.Man.* 234 C2
Middleton *Hants.* 169 F3
Middleton *Here.* 195 E1
Middleton *Lancs.* 242 A2
Middleton *Midloth.* 286 A4
Middleton *N.Yorks.* 253 G4
Middleton *Norf.* 213 E1
Middleton *Northants.* 210 D4
Middleton *Northumb.* 270 C3
Middleton *Northumb.* 279 E3
Middleton *P. & K.* 293 G4
Middleton *P. & K.* 301 G5
Middleton *Shrop.* 206 B3
Middleton *Shrop.* 207 E5
Middleton *Shrop.* 220 A5
Middleton *Suff.* 203 F1
Middleton *Swan.* 178 A4
Middleton *W.Yorks.* 244 A3
Middleton *W.Yorks.* 244 C5
Middleton *Warks.* 209 D3
Middleton Baggot 207 F3
Middleton Bank Top 270 C3
Middleton Cheney 197 G3
Middleton Green 221 G4
Middleton Hall 279 D4
Middleton Moor 203 F1
Middleton of Potterton 313 E3
Middleton on the Hill 195 E1
Middleton One Row 252 C1
Middleton Park 313 E3
Middleton Priors 207 F4
Middleton Quernhow 252 C5
Middleton Railway 88
Middleton St. George 252 C1
Middleton Scriven 207 F4
Middleton Stoney 198 A5
Middleton Tyas 252 B2
Middleton-in-Teesdale 261 F5
Middleton-on-Leven 253 D1
Middleton-on-Sea 158 B3
Middleton-on-the-Wolds 246 B3
Middletown *Cumb.* 248 A2
Middletown *Powys* 206 C1
Middlewich 221 E1
Middlewood *Ches.* 234 D4
Middlewood *S.Yorks.* 236 A3
Middlewood Green 202 B1
Middlezoy 166 A4
Middridge 262 B5
Midfield 335 E2
Midford 167 E1
Midge Hall 242 B5
Midgeholme 260 C2
Midgham 169 G1
Midgley *W.Yorks.* 235 G1
Midgley *W.Yorks.* 243 G5
Midhopestones 235 G3
Midhurst 171 D5
Midlem 277 G3
Midloe Grange 199 G1
Midpark 282 B4
Midsomer Norton 167 D2
Midthorpe 238 C5
Midtown *High.* 335 E2
Midtown *High.* 319 E1
Midtown of Barras 303 G1
Midville 226 B2
Midway 223 E5
Migdale 332 B5
Migvie 311 G4
Milarrochy 291 G5
Milber 152 B5
Milbethill 324 B4
Milborne Port 154 C1
Milborne St. Andrew 155 D3
Milborne Wick 167 D5
Milbourne *Northumb.* 270 D4
Milbourne *Wilts.* 182 B4
Milburn 260 C5
Milbury Heath 181 F3
Milcombe 197 G4
Milden 202 A3
Mildenhall *Suff.* 213 F5
Mildenhall *Wilts.* 168 D1
Mile Elm 168 A1
Mile End *Essex* 202 A5
Mile End *Glos.* 181 E1
Mile Oak 173 F4
Mile Town 174 B1
Milebrook 206 C5
Milebush 173 G4
Mileham 228 A4
Miles Green 221 F3
Miles Hope 195 E1
Milesmark 285 E1
Miles's Green 169 G1
Milfield 278 D3
Milford *Derbys.* 223 E3
Milford *Devon* 162 C3
Milford *Shrop.* 220 B5
Milford *Staffs.* 221 G5
Milford *Surr.* 171 E3
Milford Haven (Aberdaugleddau) 176 B2
Milford on Sea 156 B3
Milkwall 181 E2
Mill Bank 243 G5
Mill Brow 235 D4
Mill End *Bucks.* 184 C4
Mill End *Cambs.* 201 E2
Mill End *Herts.* 200 B4
Mill End Green 201 E5
Mill Green *Cambs.* 201 E3
Mill Green *Essex* 187 F2
Mill Green *Herts.* 186 B2
Mill Green *Norf.* 214 C3
Mill Green *Shrop.* 221 D5
Mill Green *Staffs.* 222 B5
Mill Green *Suff.* 203 E1
Mill Green *Suff.* 202 C2
Mill Green *Suff.* 202 A2
Mill Green *W.Mid.* 208 C2
Mill Hill *B'burn.* 242 C5
Mill Hill *Cambs.* 200 A2
Mill Hill *Gt.Lon.* 186 B3
Mill Houses 242 C1
Mill Lane 170 C2
Mill of Camsail 283 D1
Mill of Colp 324 C5
Mill of Elrick 325 E5
Mill of Fortune 292 C2
Mill of Kingoodie 312 D2
Mill of Monquich 313 D5
Mill of Uras 303 G1
Mill Side 249 F4
Mill Street *Kent* 173 F3
Mill Street *Norf.* 228 B4
Milland 170 D5
Millbank 325 F5
Millbeck 259 F4
Millbounds 341 D3
Millbreck 325 F5
Millbridge 170 D3
Millbrook *Beds.* 199 F4
Millbrook *Cornw.* 150 A2
Millbrook *Devon* 153 G3
Millbrook *S'ham.* 156 C1
Millburn *Aber.* 312 A2
Millburn *Aber.* 312 B1
Millcombe 151 E3
Millcorner 160 D1
Milldale 222 C2
Millden 313 E3
Milldens 302 D4
Millearne 293 E3
Millend 197 F5
Millenheath 220 [illegible]
Millennium Galleries & Winter Gardens 89
Millerhill 286 A3
Miller's Dale 235 F5
Millers Green *Derbys.* 223 D2
Miller's Green *Essex* 187 E2
Millgate 243 E5
Millhalf 194 B3
Millhayes *Devon* 153 E1
Millhayes *Devon* 153 F2
Millholme 249 G3
Millhouse *Arg. & B.* 282 A2
Millhouse *Cumb.* 259 G3
Millhouse Green 235 G2
Millhousebridge 267 F2
Millikenpark 283 F3
Millin Cross 176 C1
Millington 246 A2
Millington Green 223 D3
Millmeece 221 F4
Millness 308 C1
Millom 248 C4
Millow 200 A3
Millpool 147 F2
Millport 282 C4
Millthorpe 236 A5
Millthrop 250 B3
Milltimber 313 D4
Milltown *Aber.* 311 E4
Milltown *Cornw.* 147 F4
Milltown *D. & G.* 268 B4
Milltown *Devon* 163 F2
Milltown *High.* 322 B5
Milltown of Aberdalgie 293 F2
Milltown of Auchindoun 311 F1
Milltown of Craigston 324 C4
Milltown of Edinvillie 323 E5
Milltown of Kildrummy 311 G3
Milltown of Rothiemay 324 A5
Milltown of Towie 311 G3
Milnathort 293 G4
Milners Heath 220 B1
Milngavie 283 G2
Milnrow 234 D1
Milnsbridge 235 F1
Milnthorpe 249 F4
Milovaig 317 E4
Milrig 274 D2
Milson 207 F5
Milstead 174 B3
Milston 168 C3
Milton *Angus* 302 B5
Milton *Cambs.* 200 C1
Milton *Cumb.* 260 B1
Milton *D. & G.* 266 C2
Milton *D. & G.* 266 C3
Milton *D. & G.* 264 D5
Milton *Derbys.* 223 E5
Milton *High.* 320 C4
Milton *High.* 321 G2
Milton *High.* 322 B4
Milton *High.* 318 D5
Milton *High.* 321 E5
Milton *High.* 337 F3
Milton *High.* 309 D1
Milton *Moray* 324 A3
Milton *N.Som.* 166 A1
Milton *Newport* 180 C4
Milton *Notts.* 237 E5
Milton *Oxon.* 197 G4
Milton *Oxon.* 183 G3
Milton *P. & K.* 293 E1
Milton *Pembs.* 176 D2
Milton *Ports.* 157 F3
Milton *Som.* 166 B5
Milton *Stir.* 292 A4
Milton *Stoke* 221 G2
Milton *W.Dun.* 283 F2
Milton Abbas 155 E2
Milton Abbot 149 E3
Milton Bridge 285 G3
Milton Bryan 199 E4
Milton Clevedon 167 D4
Milton Combe 150 A1
Milton Damerel 163 D4
Milton End 181 G1
Milton Ernest 199 F2
Milton Green 220 B2
Milton Hill 183 G3
Milton Keynes 199 D4
Milton Keynes Village 199 D4
Milton Lilbourne 168 C1
Milton Lodge 33
Milton Malsor 198 C2
Milton Morenish 292 B1
Milton of Auchinhove 312 A4
Milton of Balgonie 294 B4
Milton of Buchanan 291 G5
Milton of Cairnborrow 323 G5
Milton of Callander 292 A4
Milton of Campfield 312 B4
Milton of Campsie 284 A2
Milton of Coldwells 313 E1
Milton of Cullerlie 312 C4
Milton of Cushnie 312 A3
Milton of Dalcapon 301 E4
Milton of Inveramsay 312 C2
Milton of Noth 312 A2
Milton of Tullich 311 F5
Milton on Stour 167 E5
Milton Regis 174 A2
Milton Street 160 A3
Miltonduff 323 D3
Miltonhill 322 C3
Miltonise 264 C3
Milton-Lockhart 284 C5
Milton's Cottage 47
Milton-under-Wychwood 183 E1
Milverton *Som.* 165 E5
Milverton *Warks.* 197 F1
Milwich 221 G4
Mimbridge 171 E1
Minack Theatre 33
Minard 290 B5
Minard Castle 290 B5
Minchington 155 F1
Minchinhampton 182 A2
Mindrum 278 C3
Mindrummill 278 C3
Minehead 164 C3
Minera 219 F2
Minety 182 C3
Minety Lower Moor 182 C3
Minffordd *Gwyn.* 204 D1
Minffordd *Gwyn.* 217 E4
Minffordd *Gwyn.* 231 D5
Miningsby 226 B1
Minions 147 G2
Minishant 274 B4
Minley Manor 170 D2
Minllyn 205 E1
Minnes 313 E2
Minngearraidh 314 C1
Minnigaff 265 F4
Minnonie 324 C3
Minskip 244 C1
Minstead 156 B1
Minsted 171 D5
Minster *Kent* 174 B1
Minster *Kent* 175 F2
Minster Lovell 183 F1
Minsteracres 261 G2
Minsterley 206 C2
Minsterworth 181 G1
Minterne 33
Minterne Magna 154 C2
Minterne Parva 154 C2
Minting 238 B5
Mintlaw 325 F5
Minto 277 G3
Minton 206 D3
Minwear 176 D1
Minworth 209 D3
Miodar 296 B1
Mirbister 340 B5
Mirehouse *Cumb.* 258 C5
Mirehouse *Cumb.* 98
Mireland 337 F2
Mirfield 244 B5
Miserden 182 B2
Miskin *R.C.T.* 179 G4
Miskin *R.C.T.* 179 G3
Misselfore 168 B5
Misson 237 D3
Misterton *Leics.* 210 A4
Misterton *Notts.* 237 E3
Misterton *Som.* 154 A2
Mistley 202 C4
Mitcham 172 B2
Mitchel Troy 181 D1
Mitcheldean 181 F1
Mitchell 146 C4
Mitchelland 249 F3
Mitcheltroy Common 181 D2
Mitford 271 D3
Mithian 146 B4
Mitton 208 A1
Mixbury 198 B4
Mixenden 243 G5
Moar 300 A5
Moat 268 C4
Moats Tye 202 B2
Mobberley *Ches.* 234 B5
Mobberley *Staffs.* 222 B3
Moccas 194 C3
Mochdre *Conwy* 231 G5
Mochdre *Powys* 205 G4
Mochrum 256 D2
Mockbeggar *Hants.* 156 A2
Mockbeggar *Kent* 173 G4
Mockerkin 259 D4
Modbury 150 C2
Moddershall 221 G4
Modern Art Oxford 47
Modsarie 335 F2
Moelfre *I.o.A.* 230 D4
Moelfre *Powys* 219 E5
Moffat 276 B5
Mogerhanger 199 G3
Moin'a'choire 280 B3
Moine House 335 E3
Moira 209 F1
Molash 174 C3
Mol-chlach 306 A3
Mold (Yr Wyddgrug) 219 F1
Mole Hall Wildlife Park 81
Molehill Green *Essex* 201 D5
Molehill Green *Essex* 201 F5
Molescroft 246 C3
Molesden 270 D3
Molesworth 211 F5
Mollance 266 B4
Molland 164 B5
Mollington *Ches.* 233 E5
Mollington *Oxon.* 197 G3
Mollinsburn 284 B2
Monach Islands (Heisker Islands) 315 E3
Monachty 192 B1
Monachyle 291 G3
Monevechadan 291 D4
Monewden 202 D2
Moneydie 293 F2
Moneyrow Green 185 D5
Moniaive 266 B1
Monifieth 294 D1
Monikie 294 D1
Monimail 294 A3
Monington 191 E3
Monk Bretton 236 A2
Monk Fryston 245 E5
Monk Hesleden 263 D4
Monk Sherborne 170 B2
Monk Soham 202 D1
Monk Soham Green 202 D1
Monk Street 201 E5
Monken Hadley 186 B3
Monkerton 152 C3
Monkey World 33
Monkhide 195 F3
Monkhill 259 G1
Monkhopton 207 F3
Monkland 195 D2
Monkleigh 163 E3
Monknash 179 F5
Monkokehampton 163 F5
Monks Eleigh 202 A3
Monks Eleigh Tye 202 A3
Monk's Gate 159 E1
Monks' Heath 234 C5
Monk's Hill 174 A4
Monk's House 47
Monks Kirby 209 G4
Monks Risborough 184 D2
Monkscross 149 D3
Monkseaton 271 F4
Monkshill 324 C5
Monksilver 165 D4
Monkstadt 317 G3
Monkswood 180 C2
Monkton *Devon* 153 E2
Monkton *Kent* 175 E2
Monkton *Pembs.* 176 C2
Monkton *S.Ayr.* 274 B3
Monkton *T. & W.* 262 C1
Monkton *V. of Glam.* 179 F5
Monkton Combe 167 E1
Monkton Deverill 167 F4
Monkton Farleigh 167 F1
Monkton Heathfield 165 F5
Monkton Up Wimborne 155 G1
Monkton Wyld 153 G3
Monkwearmouth 262 C2
Monkwood 170 B4
Monmouth (Trefynwy) 181 E1
Monnington Court 194 C4
Monnington on Wye 194 C3
Monreith 257 D2
Montacute 154 B1
Monteach 325 D5
Montford 206 D1
Montford Bridge 206 D1
Montgarrie 312 A3
Montgomery (Trefaldwyn) 206 B3
Montgreenan 283 E5
Montrave 294 B4
Montrose 303 F4
Monument, The 58
Monxton 169 E3
Monyash 222 C1
Monymusk 312 B3
Monzie 293 D2
Moodiesburn 284 A2
Moons Moat North 196 C1
Moonzie 294 B3
Moor Allerton 244 C4
Moor Cock 242 C1
Moor Crichel 155 F2
Moor End *Beds.* 199 F2
Moor End *Beds.* 199 E5
Moor End *Cumb.* 249 G5
Moor End *E.Riding* 246 A4
Moor End *Lancs.* 241 G3
Moor End *N.Yorks.* 245 E4
Moor End *W.Yorks.* 243 G5
Moor Green *W.Mid.* 208 C4
Moor Green *Wilts.* 167 F1
Moor Head 244 A4
Moor Monkton 245 E2
Moor Row 258 D5
Moor Side *Cumb.* 248 D5
Moor Side *Lancs.* 242 A4
Moor Side *Lancs.* 242 A4
Moor Side *Lincs.* 226 A2
Moor Street 174 A2
Moor, The *E.Suss.* 160 D2
Moor, The *Kent* 160 C1
Moorby 226 A1
Moorcot 194 C2
Moordown 155 G3
Moore 233 G4
Moorend 259 G1
Moorends 237 D1
Moorfield 235 E3
Moorgreen *Hants.* 157 D1
Moorgreen *Notts.* 223 F3
Moorhall 236 A5
Moorhampton 194 C3
Moorhouse *Cumb.* 259 G1
Moorhouse *Notts.* 224 C1
Moorland (Northmoor Green) 166 A4
Moorlinch 166 A4
Moors Valley Country Park 33
Moorsholm 253 F1
Moorside *Dorset* 155 D1
Moorside *Gt.Man.* 235 D2
Moorside *W.Yorks.* 244 B4
Moorthorpe 236 B1
Moortown *I.o.W.* 156 D4
Moortown *Lincs.* 238 A3
Moortown *Tel. & W.* 207 F1
Morangie 321 G1
Morar 306 C5
Morborne 211 G3
Morchard Bishop 152 A2
Morcombelake 154 A3
Morcott 211 E2
Morda 219 F5
Morden *Dorset* 155 F3
Morden *Gt.Lon.* 172 B2
Morden Hall Park 58
Morden Park 172 B2
Mordiford 195 E4
Mordington Holdings 287 G4
Mordon 262 C5
More 206 C3
Morebath 164 C5
Morebattle 278 B4
Morecambe 242 A1

Morefield 330 D5
Moreleigh 151 D2
Morenish 292 B1
Moresby Parks 258 C5
Morestead 169 G5
Moreton *Dorset* 155 E4
Moreton *Essex* 187 E2
Moreton *Here.* 195 E1
Moreton *Mersey.* 233 D4
Moreton *Oxon.* 184 B2
Moreton *Staffs.* 222 C4
Moreton *Staffs.* 207 G1
Moreton Corbet 220 C5
Moreton Jeffries 195 F3
Moreton Mill 220 C5
Moreton Morrell 197 F2
Moreton on Lugg 195 E3
Moreton Paddox 197 F2
Moreton Pinkney 198 A3
Moreton Say 220 D4
Moreton Valence 181 G2
Moretonhampstead 152 A4
Moreton-in-Marsh 197 E4
Morfa *Carmar.* 178 B1
Morfa *Cere.* 191 G2
Morfa Bychan 217 E4
Morfa Glas 179 E2
Morfa Nefyn 216 B3
Morgan's Vale 168 C5
Morganstown 180 A4
Mork 181 E2
Morland 260 B5
Morley *Derbys.* 223 E3
Morley *Dur.* 262 A5
Morley *W.Yorks.* 244 B5
Morley Green 234 C4
Morley St. Botolph 214 B2
Mornick 148 D3
Morningside *Edin.* 285 G2
Morningside *N.Lan.* 284 C4
Morningthorpe 214 D2
Morpeth 271 E3
Morphie 303 F3
Morrey 208 D1
Morridge Side 222 B2
Morrilow Heath 221 G4
Morriston *S.Ayr.* 274 A5
Morriston *Swan.* 178 C3
Morristown 180 A5
Morroch 297 F1
Morston 228 B1
Mortehoe 163 E1
Morthen 236 B4
Mortimer 170 B1
Mortimer West End 170 B1
Mortimer's Cross 194 D1
Mortlake 186 B5
Morton *Derbys.* 223 F1
Morton *Lincs.* 225 F5
Morton *Lincs.* 237 F3
Morton *Lincs.* 225 D1
Morton *Notts.* 224 C2
Morton *S.Glos.* 181 F3
Morton *Shrop.* 219 F5
Morton Bagot 196 D1
Morton on the Hill 228 C4
Morton Tinmouth 262 A5
Morton-on-Swale 252 C3
Morvah 144 B3
Morval 147 G4
Morvich *High.* 307 F2
Morvich *High.* 332 C4
Morvil 190 D4
Morville 207 F3
Morwellham 150 A1
Morwellham Quay Museum 33
Morwenstow 162 C4
Morwick Hall 271 E1
Mosborough 236 B4
Moscow 283 F5
Mosedale 259 G3
Moselden Height 235 E1
Moseley *W.Mid.* 208 C4
Moseley *W.Mid.* 208 B3
Moseley *Worcs.* 196 A2
Moses Gate 234 B2
Moss *Arg. & B.* 296 A2
Moss *S.Yorks.* 236 C1
Moss *Wrex.* 220 A2
Moss Bank 233 G3
Moss Houses 234 C5
Moss Nook 234 C4
Moss of Barmuckity 323 E3
Moss Side *Gt.Man.* 234 C3
Moss Side *Lancs.* 241 G4
Moss Side *Mersey.* 233 E2
Mossat 311 G3
Mossbank 345 D5
Mossblown 274 C3
Mossburnford 278 A5
Mossdale 266 A3
Mossend 284 B3
Mossgiel 274 C3
Mosshead 312 A1
Mosside of Ballinshoe 302 C4
Mossley *Ches.* 221 F1
Mossley *Gt.Man.* 235 D2
Mossley Hill 233 E4
Mosspaul Hotel 268 B2
Moss-side *High.* 322 A4
Moss-side *Moray* 324 A4
Mosstodloch 323 F3
Mosston 302 D5
Mossy Lea 233 G1
Mosterton 154 A2
Moston *Gt.Man.* 234 C3
Moston *Shrop.* 220 C5
Moston Green 221 E1
Mostyn 232 C4
Motcombe 167 F5
Mothecombe 150 C3
Motherby 260 A5
Motherwell 284 B4
Mottingham 186 D5
Mottisfont 169 E5
Mottisfont Abbey Gardens 47
Mottistone 156 D4
Mottram in Longdendale 235 D3
Mottram St. Andrew 234 C5
Mouldsworth 233 G5
Moulin 301 E4
Moulsecoomb 159 F3
Moulsford 184 A4
Moulsham 187 G2
Moulsoe 199 E3
Moulton *Ches.* 221 D1
Moulton *Lincs.* 226 B5
Moulton *N.Yorks.* 252 B2
Moulton *Northants.* 198 C1
Moulton *Suff.* 201 E1
Moulton *V. of Glam.* 179 G5
Moulton Chapel 212 A1
Moulton St. Mary 229 F5
Moulton Seas End 226 B5
Mounie Castle 312 C2
Mount *Cornw.* 146 B4
Mount *Cornw.* 147 F3
Mount *High.* 322 B5
Mount *Kent* 175 D4
Mount *W.Yorks.* 235 F1
Mount Ambrose 146 B5
Mount Bures 202 A4
Mount Charles 147 E4
Mount Edgcumbe 33
Mount Edgcumbe Country Park 33
Mount Grace Priory 89
Mount Hawke 146 B5
Mount Manisty 233 E5
Mount Oliphant 274 B4
Mount Pleasant *Ches.* 221 F2
Mount Pleasant *Derbys.* 223 F3
Mount Pleasant *Derbys.* 209 E1
Mount Pleasant *E.Suss.* 159 G2
Mount Pleasant *Flints.* 232 D5
Mount Pleasant *Gt.Lon.* 185 F3
Mount Pleasant *Hants.* 156 C3
Mount Pleasant *Norf.* 214 A2
Mount Pleasant *Suff.* 201 F3
Mount Sorrel 168 B5
Mount Stuart 127
Mount Tabor 243 G5
Mountain 243 G4
Mountain Ash (Aberpennar) 179 G3
Mountain Cross 285 F5
Mountain Water 190 C5
Mountbenger 277 E3
Mountblairy 324 B4
Mountblow 283 F2
Mountfield 160 C1
Mountfitchet Castle 81
Mountgerald 321 E3
Mountjoy 146 C3
Mountnessing 187 F3
Mounton 181 E3
Mountsorrel 210 A1
Mousa 343 D5
Mousa Broch 127
Mousehole 144 B4
Mouswald 267 E3
Mow Cop 221 F2
Mowden 252 B1
Mowhaugh 278 C4
Mowsley 210 B4
Mowtie 303 G1
Moxley 208 B3
Moy *High.* 299 D1
Moy *High.* 299 G1
Moy *High.* 309 G1
Moy House 322 C4
Moylgrove 191 E3
Muasdale 281 E5
Much Birch 195 E4
Much Cowarne 195 F3
Much Dewchurch 195 D4
Much Hadham 186 D1
Much Hoole 242 A5
Much Hoole Town 242 A5
Much Marcle 195 F4
Much Wenlock 207 F2
Muchalls 313 E5
Muchelney 166 B5
Muchelney Ham 166 B5
Muchlarnick 147 G4
Muchra 276 D4
Muchrachd 308 B1
Muck 296 D2
Mucking 187 F4
Muckle Roe 342 C1
Muckleburgh Collection, The 81
Muckleford 154 C3
Mucklestone 221 E4
Muckleton 220 C5
Muckletown 312 A2
Muckley 207 F3
Muckley Corner 208 C2
Muckton 239 D4
Mudale 335 E5
Muddiford 163 F2
Muddles Green 160 A3
Muddleswood 159 E2
Mudeford 156 A3
Mudford 154 B1
Mudgley 166 B3
Mugdock 283 G2
Mugeary 306 A1
Mugginton 223 D3
Muggintonlane End 223 D3
Muggleswick 261 G3
Mugswell 172 B3
Muie 332 B4
Muir 301 F1
Muir of Fowlis 312 A3
Muir of Lochs 323 F3
Muir of Ord 321 E4
Muirden 324 C4
Muirdrum 295 D1
Muiredge 294 B5
Muirhead *Aber.* 312 A3
Muirhead *Angus* 294 B1
Muirhead *Fife* 294 A4
Muirhead *Moray* 322 C3
Muirhead *N.Lan.* 284 A3
Muirhouses 285 E1
Muirkirk 275 E3
Muirmill 284 B1
Muirtack *Aber.* 313 E1
Muirtack *Aber.* 324 D5
Muirton *High.* 321 G3
Muirton *P. & K.* 293 E3
Muirton *P. & K.* 293 G2
Muirton of Ardblair 301 G5
Muirton of Ballochy 303 E3
Muirtown 322 B4
Muiryfold 324 C4
Muker 251 E3
Mulbarton 228 C5
Mulben 323 F4
Mulhagery 327 F3
Mull 289 E1
Mullach Charlabhaigh 328 D3
Mullacott Cross 163 F1
Mullion 145 D5
Mumbles, The 178 C4
Mumby 239 F5
Muncaster Castle 98
Munderfield Row 195 F2
Munderfield Stocks 195 F2
Mundesley 229 E2
Mundford 213 G3
Mundham 215 E2
Mundon 188 B2
Mundurno 313 E3
Munerigie 308 B4
Mungasdale 330 B5
Mungoswells 286 B2
Mungrisdale 259 G3
Munlochy 321 F4
Munnoch 282 D5
Munsley 195 F3
Munslow 207 E4
Murchington 149 G2
Murcott *Oxon.* 184 A1
Murcott *Wilts.* 182 B3
Murdostoun 284 C4
Murieston 285 E3
Murkle 337 D2
Murlaganmore 292 A1
Murlaggan *High.* 307 G5
Murlaggan *High.* 299 F1
Murra 338 B2
Murray, The 284 A4
Murrell Green 170 C2
Murroes 294 C1
Murrow 212 B2
Mursley 198 D5
Murston 174 B2
Murthill 302 C4
Murthly 293 F1
Murton *Cumb.* 260 D5
Murton *Dur.* 262 C3
Murton *Northumb.* 287 G5
Murton *Swan.* 178 B4
Murton *York* 245 F2
Musbury 153 F3
Muscliff 155 G3
Musdale 290 B2
Museum in Docklands 58
Museum of Canterbury 47
Museum of Childhood *Edin.* 127
Museum of Childhood *Gt.Lon.* 58
Museum of Costume 33
Museum of East Anglian Life 81
Museum of Flight 127
Museum of Garden History 58
Museum of Lakeland Life (see Abbot Hall Art Gallery) 93
Museum of Lincolnshire Life 73
Museum of Liverpool Life 98
Museum of London 58
Museum of Oxford 47
Museum of Science & Industry 98
Museum of Scotland 127
Museum of Scottish Lead Mining 127
Museum of Welsh Life 111
Musselburgh 286 A2
Mustard Hyrn 229 F4
Muston *Leics.* 224 D4
Muston *N.Yorks.* 255 D5
Mustow Green 208 A5
Mutford 215 F3
Muthill 293 D3
Mutley 150 A2
Mutterton 152 D2
Muxton 207 G1
Mybster 337 D3
Myddfai 193 D4
Myddle 220 B5
Myddlewood 220 B5
Mydroilyn 192 A2
Myerscough College 242 A4
Myerscough Smithy 242 C4
Mylor 145 F3
Mylor Bridge 145 F3
Mynachdy 180 A5
Mynachlog-ddu 191 E4
Myndtown 206 C4
Mynydd Fechell 230 B3
Mynydd Llandygai 217 F1
Mynydd-bach *Mon.* 181 D3
Mynydd-bach *Swan.* 178 C3
Mynyddygarreg 178 A2
Mynytho 216 C4
Myrebird 312 C5
Mytchett 171 D2
Mythe, The 196 A4
Mytholm 243 F5
Mytholmroyd 243 G5
Mythop 241 G4
Myton-on-Swale 244 D1
Mytton 206 D1

N

Naast 319 E1
Nab's Head 242 C5
Na-Buirgh 326 C4
Naburn 245 E3
Nackington 175 D3
Nacton 202 D3
Nadderwater 152 B3
Nafferton 246 C2
Nailbridge 181 F1
Nailsbourne 165 F5
Nailsea 181 D5
Nailstone 209 G2
Nailsworth 182 A3
Nairn 322 A4
Nancegollan 144 D3
Nancekuke 146 A5
Nancledra 144 B3
Nanhoron 216 B4
Nannau 218 A5
Nannerch 219 E1
Nanpantan 210 A1
Nanpean 147 D4
Nanstallon 147 E3
Nant Peris 217 F2
Nant-ddu 179 G1
Nanternis 191 G2
Nantgaredig 192 A5
Nantgarw 180 A4
Nant-glas 193 F1
Nantglyn 218 D1
Nantgwyn 205 F5
Nantlle 217 E2
Nantmawr 219 F5
Nantmel 193 G1
Nantmor 217 F3
Nantwich 221 D2
Nantycaws 178 A1
Nant-y-derry 180 C2
Nant-y-dugoed 205 F1
Nantyffyllon 179 E3
Nantyglo 180 A1
Nant-y-Gollen 219 F5
Nant-y-groes 193 G1
Nant-y-moel 179 F3
Nant-y-Pandy 231 E5
Naphill 185 D3
Napley Heath 221 E4
Nappa 243 E2
Napton on the Hill 197 G1
Narberth (Arberth) 177 E1
Narborough *Leics.* 210 A3
Narborough *Norf.* 213 F1
Narkurs 148 D5
Narrachan 290 B3
Narth, The 181 E2
Nasareth 217 D3
Naseby 210 B5
Nash *Bucks.* 198 C4
Nash *Here.* 194 C1
Nash *Newport* 180 C4
Nash *Shrop.* 207 F5
Nash *V. of Glam.* 179 F5
Nash Street 173 F2
Nassington 211 F3
Nasty 200 B5
Nateby *Cumb.* 250 C2
Nateby *Lancs.* 242 A3
Nately Scures 170 C2
National Army Museum 58
National Botanic Garden of Wales 111
National Gallery 58
National Gallery of Scotland 127
National Glass Centre 105
National Horseracing Museum 82
National Marine Aquarium 33
National Maritime Museum 58
National Maritime Museum Cornwall 34
National Motor Museum 47
National Museum & Gallery, Cardiff 111
National Museum of Photography, Film & TV 89
National Portrait Gallery 58
National Railway Museum 89
National Sea Life Centre 67
National Showcaves Centre for Wales 111
National Space Centre 73
National Tramway Museum 73
National Wallace Monument 127
National Waterways Museum 34
National Woollen Museum 112
Natland 249 G4
Natural History Museum 59
Naughton 202 B3
Naunton *Glos.* 196 D5
Naunton *Worcs.* 196 A4
Naunton Beauchamp 196 B2
Navenby 225 E2
Navestock 187 E3
Navestock Side 187 E3
Navidale 333 F3
Navity 321 G3
Nawton 253 F4
Nayland 202 A4
Nazeing 186 D2
Neacroft 156 A3
Neal's Green 209 F4
Neap 343 E2
Neap House 237 F1
Near Sawrey 249 E3
Nearton End 198 D5
Neasden 186 B4
Neasham 252 C1
Neat Enstone 197 F5
Neath (Castell-Nedd) 179 D3
Neatham 170 C3
Neatishead 229 E3
Nebo *Cere.* 192 B1
Nebo *Conwy* 218 B2
Nebo *Gwyn.* 217 D2
Nebo *I.o.A.* 230 C3
Necton 213 G2
Nedd 334 A5
Nedderton 271 E3
Nedging 202 A3
Nedging Tye 202 B3
Needham 214 D3
Needham Market 202 B2
Needham Street 201 F1
Needingworth 212 B5
Needles Pleasure Park 47
Needwood 222 C5
Neen Savage 207 F5
Neen Sollars 207 F5
Neenton 207 F4
Nefyn 216 C3
Neidpath Castle 127
Neighbourne 166 D3
Neilston 283 F4
Neithrop 197 G3
Nelson *Caerp.* 180 A3
Nelson *Lancs.* 243 E4
Nelson Village 271 E4
Nemphlar 284 C5
Nempnett Thrubwell 166 C1
Nene Valley Railway 82
Nenthall 261 D3
Nenthead 261 D3
Nenthorn 278 A3
Neopardy 152 A3
Nerabus 280 A4
Nercwys 219 F1
Neriby 280 B3
Nerston 284 A4
Nesbit 279 D3
Nesfield 243 G3
Ness 233 E5
Ness Botanic Gardens 98
Ness of Tenston 340 A5
Nesscliffe 206 C1
Neston *Ches.* 233 D5
Neston *Wilts.* 167 F1
Nether Alderley 234 C5
Nether Alderley Mill 98
Nether Auchendrane 274 B4
Nether Barr 265 F4
Nether Blainslie 286 C5
Nether Broughton 224 B5
Nether Burrow 250 B5
Nether Cerne 154 C3
Nether Compton 154 B1
Nether Crimond 312 D2
Nether Dalgliesh 277 D5
Nether Dallachy 323 F3
Nether Edge 236 A4
Nether End 235 G5
Nether Exe 152 C3
Nether Glasslaw 325 D4
Nether Handwick 302 B5
Nether Haugh 236 B3
Nether Heage 223 E2
Nether Heselden 251 D5
Nether Heyford 198 B2
Nether Kellet 242 B1
Nether Kinmundy 325 F5
Nether Langwith 236 C5
Nether Lenshie 324 B5
Nether Loads 223 E1
Nether Moor 223 E1
Nether Padley 235 G5
Nether Pitforthie 303 G2
Nether Poppleton 245 E2
Nether Silton 253 D3
Nether Skyborry 206 B5
Nether Stowey 165 E4
Nether Urquhart 293 G4
Nether Wallop 169 E4
Nether Wasdale 248 C2
Nether Wellwood 275 E3
Nether Welton 259 G2
Nether Westcote 197 F5
Nether Whitacre 209 E3
Nether Winchendon (Lower Winchendon) 184 C1
Nether Worton 197 G5
Netheravon 168 C3
Netherbrae 324 C4
Netherbrough 340 B5
Netherburn 284 C5
Netherbury 154 A3
Netherby *Cumb.* 268 B4
Netherby *N.Yorks.* 244 C3
Nethercott 197 G5
Netherend 181 E2
Netherfield *E.Suss.* 160 C2
Netherfield *Notts.* 224 B3
Netherfield *S.Lan.* 284 B5
Netherhall 282 D3
Netherhampton 168 C5
Netherhay 154 A2
Netherland Green 222 C4
Netherley 313 D5
Nethermill 267 E2
Nethermuir 325 E5
Netherseal 209 E1
Nethershield 275 D3
Netherstreet 168 A1
Netherthird *D. & G.* 266 B5
Netherthird *E.Ayr.* 275 D4
Netherthong 235 F2
Netherthorpe 236 C4
Netherton *Angus* 302 D4
Netherton *Ches.* 233 G5
Netherton *Devon* 152 B5
Netherton *Hants.* 169 E2
Netherton *Mersey.* 233 E2
Netherton *N.Lan.* 284 B4
Netherton *Northumb.* 270 B1
Netherton *Oxon.* 183 G2
Netherton *P. & K.* 301 G4
Netherton *S.Lan.* 284 D4
Netherton *W.Mid.* 208 B4
Netherton *W.Yorks.* 235 G1
Netherton *W.Yorks.* 235 F1
Netherton *Worcs.* 196 B3
Netherton Burnfoot 270 B1
Netherton Northside 270 B1
Nethertown *Cumb.* 248 A2
Nethertown *Ork.* 337 F1
Nethertown *Staffs.* 208 D1
Netherwitton 270 D2
Netherwood *D. & G.* 267 D3
Netherwood *E.Ayr.* 275 E3
Nethy Bridge 310 C2
Netley Abbey 157 D2
Netley Marsh 156 C1
Nettlebed 184 B4
Nettlebridge 166 D3
Nettlecombe *Dorset* 154 B3
Nettlecombe *I.o.W.* 157 E5
Nettlecombe *Som.* 165 D4
Nettleden 185 F1
Nettleham 238 A5
Nettlestead *Kent* 173 F3
Nettlestead *Suff.* 202 B3
Nettlestead Green 173 F3
Nettlestone 157 F3
Nettlesworth 262 B3
Nettleton *Lincs.* 238 B2
Nettleton *Wilts.* 182 A5
Nettleton Hill 235 E1
Netton *Devon* 150 B3
Netton *Wilts.* 168 C4
Neuadd *Cere.* 192 A2
Neuadd *I.o.A.* 230 B3
Neuadd *Powys* 193 F3
Neuk, The 312 C5
Nevendon 187 G3
Nevern 191 D4
Nevill Holt 210 D3
Nevis Range Ski Centre (see Aonach Mòr Mountain Gondola) 116
New Abbey 267 D4
New Aberdour 325 D3
New Addington 172 C2
New Alresford 169 G4
New Alyth 302 A5
New Arley 209 E3
New Arram 246 C3
New Ash Green 173 F2
New Balderton 224 D2
New Barn 173 F2
New Belses 277 G3
New Bewick 279 E4
New Bolingbroke 226 B2
New Boultham 237 G5
New Bradwell 198 D3
New Brancepeth 262 B3
New Bridge *D. & G.* 266 D3
New Bridge *Devon* 152 A5
New Brighton *Flints.* 219 F1
New Brighton *Hants.* 157 G2
New Brighton *Mersey.* 233 E3
New Brighton *W.Yorks.* 244 B5
New Brighton *Wrex.* 219 F2
New Brinsley 223 F2
New Broughton 220 A2
New Buckenham 214 B2
New Byth 324 D4
New Cheriton 169 G5
New Cross *Cere.* 204 C5
New Cross *Gt.Lon.* 186 C5
New Cumnock 275 E4
New Deer 325 D5
New Duston 198 C1
New Earswick 245 F2
New Edlington 236 C3
New Elgin 323 E3
New Ellerby 247 D4
New Eltham 186 D5
New End 196 C1
New England 211 G2
New Farnley 244 B4
New Ferry 233 E4
New Forest 47
New Forest Museum & Information Centre 48
New Galloway 266 A3
New Gilston 294 C4
New Greens 186 A2
New Grimsby 146 A1
New Hartley 271 F4
New Haw 171 F1
New Heaton 278 C3
New Hedges 177 E2
New Herrington 262 C2
New Hinksey 184 A2
New Holland 246 C5
New Houghton *Derbys.* 223 G1
New Houghton *Norf.* 227 F5
New Houses 250 D5
New Hunwick 262 A4
New Hutton 249 G3
New Hythe 173 G3
New Inn *Carmar.* 192 A4
New Inn *Fife* 294 A4
New Inn *Mon.* 181 D2
New Inn *Torfaen* 180 B3
New Invention *Shrop.* 206 B5
New Invention *W.Mid.* 208 B2
New Kelso 319 F5
New Lanark 284 C5
New Lanark World Heritage Site 127
New Lane 233 F1
New Lane End 234 A3
New Leake 226 C2
New Leeds 325 E4
New Leslie 312 A2
New Lodge 236 A2
New Longton 242 B5
New Luce 264 C4
New Mains 275 G2
New Mains of Ury 303 G1
New Malden 172 B2
New Marske 263 F5
New Marton 220 A4
New Mill *Cornw.* 144 B3
New Mill *Herts.* 185 E1
New Mill *W.Yorks.* 235 F2
New Mill End 186 A1
New Mills *Cornw.* 146 C4
New Mills *Derbys.* 235 E4
New Mills *Glos.* 181 F2
New Mills *Mon.* 181 E2
New Mills *Powys* 205 G2
New Milton 156 B3
New Mistley 202 C4
New Moat 191 D5
New Ollerton 224 B1
New Orleans 272 C4
New Oscott 208 C3
New Park *Cornw.* 147 F1
New Park *N.Yorks.* 244 B2
New Pitsligo 325 D4
New Polzeath 146 D2
New Quay (Ceinewydd) 191 G1
New Rackheath 229 D4
New Radnor (Maesyfed) 194 B1
New Rent 260 A4
New Ridley 261 G1
New Road Side 243 F3
New Romney 161 F1
New Rossington 236 D3
New Row *Cere.* 204 D5
New Row *Lancs.* 242 C4
New Sawley 223 F4
New Shoreston 279 F3
New Silksworth 262 C2
New Swannington 209 G1
New Totley 236 A5
New Town *Beds.* 199 G3
New Town *Cere.* 191 E3
New Town *Dorset* 155 F1
New Town *Dorset* 155 F2
New Town *E.Loth.* 286 B2
New Town *E.Suss.* 159 G1
New Town *Glos.* 196 C4
New Tredegar 180 A2
New Tupton 223 E1
New Ulva 281 F1
New Valley 329 F4
New Village 236 C2
New Walsoken 212 C2
New Waltham 238 C2
New Winton 286 B2
New World 212 B3
New Yatt 183 F1
New York *Lincs.* 226 A2
New York *T. & W.* 271 F4
Newall 244 B3
Newark *Ork.* 341 F2
Newark *Peter.* 212 A2
Newark Park 34
Newark-on-Trent 224 D2
Newarthill 284 B4
Newball 238 A5
Newbarn 175 D5
Newbarns 248 D5
Newbattle 286 A3
Newbiggin *Cumb.* 260 A5
Newbiggin *Cumb.* 260 C5
Newbiggin *Cumb.* 260 B3
Newbiggin *Cumb.* 241 F1
Newbiggin *Cumb.* 248 B3
Newbiggin *Dur.* 261 F5
Newbiggin *N.Yorks.* 251 F4
Newbiggin *N.Yorks.* 251 E3
Newbiggin *Northumb.* 261 F1
Newbiggin-by-the-Sea 271 F3
Newbigging *Aber.* 313 D5
Newbigging *Aber.* 301 G1
Newbigging *Angus* 294 C1

Newbigging *Angus* 294 C1
Newbigging *Angus* 302 A5
Newbigging *S.Lan.* 285 E5
Newbiggin-on-Lune 250 C2
Newbold *Derbys.* 236 A5
Newbold *Leics.* 209 G1
Newbold on Avon 209 G5
Newbold on Stour 197 E3
Newbold Pacey 197 E2
Newbold Verdon 209 G2
Newborough *I.o.A.* 216 D1
Newborough *Peter.* 212 A2
Newborough *Staffs.* 222 C5
Newborough Warren 112
Newbottle *Northants.* 198 A4
Newbottle *T. & W.* 262 C2
Newbourne 203 D3
Newbridge (Cefn Bychan) *Caerp.* 180 B3
Newbridge *Cornw.* 144 B3
Newbridge *Cornw.* 148 D4
Newbridge *E.Suss.* 173 D5
Newbridge *Edin.* 285 F2
Newbridge *Hants.* 156 B1
Newbridge *I.o.W.* 156 D4
Newbridge *N.Yorks.* 254 B4
Newbridge *Oxon.* 183 G2
Newbridge *Pembs.* 190 C4
Newbridge *Wrex.* 219 F3
Newbridge Green 196 A4
Newbridge on Wye 193 G2
Newbridge-on-Usk 180 C3
Newbrough 261 E1
Newbuildings 152 A2
Newburgh *Aber.* 325 E4
Newburgh *Aber.* 313 E2
Newburgh *Fife* 294 A3
Newburgh *Lancs.* 233 F1
Newburgh *Sc.Bord.* 277 E3
Newburn 262 A1
Newbury *Som.* 167 D2
Newbury *W.Berks.* 169 F1
Newbury *Wilts.* 167 F3
Newbury Park 186 D4
Newby *Cumb.* 260 B5
Newby *Lancs.* 243 E3
Newby *N.Yorks.* 253 E1
Newby *N.Yorks.* 242 D1
Newby *N.Yorks.* 254 D4
Newby Bridge 249 E4
Newby Cote 250 C5
Newby Cross 259 G1
Newby East 260 A2
Newby West 259 G1
Newby Wiske 252 C4
Newcastle *Bridgend* 179 E5
Newcastle *Mon.* 180 D1
Newcastle *Shrop.* 206 B4
Newcastle Emlyn (Castell Newydd Emlyn) 191 G3
Newcastle International Airport 271 D4
Newcastle upon Tyne 262 B1
Newcastleton 268 C3
Newcastle-under-Lyme 221 F3
Newchapel *Pembs.* 191 F4
Newchapel *Stoke* 221 F2
Newchapel *Surr.* 172 C4
Newchurch *Carmar.* 191 G5
Newchurch *I.o.W.* 157 E4
Newchurch *Kent* 174 C5
Newchurch *Lancs.* 243 E5
Newchurch *Lancs.* 243 E4
Newchurch *Mon.* 181 D3
Newchurch *Powys* 194 B2
Newchurch *Staffs.* 222 C5
Newcott 153 F2
Newcraighall 286 A2
Newdigate 171 G3
Newell Green 185 D5
Newenden 160 D1
Newent 195 G5
Newerne 181 F2
Newfield *Dur.* 262 B4
Newfield *Dur.* 262 B2
Newfield *High.* 321 G2
Newfound 169 G2
Newgale 190 B5
Newgate 228 B1
Newgate Street 186 C2
Newgord 345 E2
Newhall *Ches.* 220 D3
Newhall *Derbys.* 223 D5
Newham 279 F4
Newham Hall 279 F4
Newhaven 159 G3
Newhey 234 D1
Newholm 254 B1
Newhouse 284 B3
Newick 159 G1
Newingreen 174 D5
Newington *Edin.* 285 G2
Newington *Kent* 175 D5
Newington *Kent* 171 A2
Newington *Notts.* 237 D3
Newington *Oxon.* 184 B3
Newington Bagpath 182 A3
Newland *Cumb.* 249 E5
Newland *Glos.* 181 E2
Newland *Hull* 246 C4
Newland *N.Yorks.* 245 F5
Newland *Oxon.* 183 F1
Newland *Worcs.* 195 G3
Newlandrig 286 A3
Newlands *Cumb.* 259 G3
Newlands *Essex* 188 B4
Newlands *Northumb.* 261 G2
Newlands *Sc.Bord.* 268 D2
Newland's Corner 171 F3
Newlands of Geise 336 C2
Newlands of Tynet 323 F3
Newlyn 144 B4
Newlyn East 146 C4
Newmachar 313 D3
Newmains 284 C4
Newman's End 187 E1
Newman's Green 201 G3
Newmarket *Suff.* 201 E1
Newmarket *W.Isles* 329 F4
Newmill *Aber.* 303 F1
Newmill *Aber.* 324 D5
Newmill *Aber.* 312 D2
Newmill *Moray* 323 G4
Newmill *Sc.Bord.* 277 F4
Newmill of Inshewan 302 C3
Newmillerdam 236 A1
Newmills 321 F3
Newmiln *P. & K.* 293 G1
Newmiln *P. & K.* 293 F2
Newmilns 274 D2
Newney Green 187 F2
Newnham *Glos.* 181 F1
Newnham *Hants.* 170 C2
Newnham *Herts.* 200 A4
Newnham *Kent* 174 B3
Newnham *Northants.* 198 A2
Newnham Bridge 195 F1
Newnham Paddox 209 G4
Newnoth 312 A1
Newport *Cornw.* 148 D2
Newport *Devon* 163 F2
Newport *E.Riding* 246 A4
Newport *Essex* 200 D4
Newport *Glos.* 181 F3
Newport *High.* 333 G2
Newport *I.o.W.* 157 E4
Newport (Casnewydd) *Newport* 180 C4
Newport *Norf.* 229 G4
Newport (Trefdraeth) *Pembs.* 191 D4
Newport *Som.* 166 A5
Newport *Tel. & W.* 207 G1
Newport Pagnell 199 D3
Newport-on-Tay 294 C2
Newpound Common 171 F5
Newquay 146 C3
Newquay Cornwall Airport 146 C3
Newquay Zoo 34
Newsbank 221 F1
Newseat 312 C1
Newsells 200 B4
Newsham *Lancs.* 242 B4
Newsham *N.Yorks.* 252 A1
Newsham *N.Yorks.* 252 C4
Newsham *Northumb.* 271 E4
Newsholme *E.Riding* 245 G5
Newsholme *Lancs.* 243 E2
Newsome 235 F1
Newstead *Northumb.* 279 F4
Newstead *Notts.* 223 G2
Newstead *Sc.Bord.* 277 G2
Newstead Abbey 74
Newthorpe *N.Yorks.* 245 D4
Newthorpe *Notts.* 223 F3
Newtoft 238 A4
Newton *Aber.* 323 G5
Newton *Aber.* 325 F5
Newton *Arg. & B.* 290 C5
Newton *Bridgend* 179 E5
Newton *Cambs.* 212 C1
Newton *Cambs.* 200 C3
Newton *Cardiff* 180 B5
Newton *Ches.* 220 C2
Newton *Ches.* 233 G5
Newton *Cumb.* 248 D5
Newton *D. & G.* 267 F1
Newton *Derbys.* 223 F2
Newton *Gt.Man.* 235 D3
Newton *Here.* 194 C1
Newton *Here.* 195 E2
Newton *Here.* 194 C4
Newton *High.* 337 F3
Newton *High.* 321 G5
Newton *High.* 337 E3
Newton *High.* 334 B5
Newton *High.* 321 E4
Newton *High.* 321 G3
Newton *Lancs.* 242 C2
Newton *Lancs.* 249 G5
Newton *Lancs.* 241 G4
Newton *Lancs.* 242 A4
Newton *Lincs.* 225 F4
Newton *Moray* 323 F3
Newton *N.Ayr.* 282 A4
Newton *Norf.* 213 G1
Newton *Northants.* 211 D4
Newton *Northumb.* 261 G1
Newton *Northumb.* 270 B1
Newton *Notts.* 224 B3
Newton *P. & K.* 302 D1
Newton *Pembs.* 190 B5
Newton *Pembs.* 176 C2
Newton *S.Glos.* 181 F3
Newton *S.Lan.* 276 A2
Newton *Sc.Bord.* 278 A4
Newton *Shrop.* 220 B4
Newton *Som.* 165 E4
Newton *Staffs.* 222 B5
Newton *Suff.* 202 A3
Newton *Swan.* 178 C4
Newton *W.Loth.* 285 E2
Newton *W.Yorks.* 244 D5
Newton *Warks.* 210 A5
Newton *Wilts.* 168 D5
Newton Abbot 152 B5
Newton Arlosh 259 F1
Newton Aycliffe 262 B5
Newton Bewley 263 D5
Newton Blossomville 199 E2
Newton Bromswold 199 E1
Newton Burgoland 209 F2
Newton by Toft 238 A4
Newton Ferrers 150 B3
Newton Flotman 214 D2
Newton Green 181 E3
Newton Harcourt 210 B3
Newton Kyme 245 D3
Newton Longville 198 D4
Newton Mearns 283 G4
Newton Morrell *N.Yorks.* 252 B2
Newton Morrell *Oxon.* 198 B5
Newton Mountain 176 C2
Newton Mulgrave 253 G1
Newton of Affleck 294 C1
Newton of Ardtoe 297 F2
Newton of Balcanquhal 293 G3
Newton of Dalvey 322 C4
Newton of Falkland 294 A4
Newton of Leys 309 F1
Newton on the Hill 220 B5
Newton on Trent 237 F5
Newton Poppleford 153 D4
Newton Purcell 198 B4
Newton Regis 209 E2
Newton Reigny 260 A4
Newton St. Cyres 152 B3
Newton St. Faith 228 D4
Newton St. Loe 167 E1
Newton St. Petrock 163 E4
Newton Solney 223 D5
Newton Stacey 169 F3
Newton Stewart 265 F4
Newton Tony 168 D3
Newton Tracey 163 F3
Newton under Roseberry 253 E1
Newton Underwood 271 D3
Newton upon Derwent 245 G3
Newton Valence 170 C4
Newtonairds 266 C2
Newtongrange 286 A3
Newtonhill 313 E5
Newton-le-Willows *Mersey.* 233 G3
Newton-le-Willows *N.Yorks.* 252 B4
Newtonmill 303 E3
Newtonmore 309 G5
Newton-on-Ouse 245 E2
Newton-on-Rawcliffe 254 B3
Newton-on-the-Moor 271 D1
Newtown *Bucks.* 185 E2
Newtown *Ches.* 220 C2
Newtown *Cornw.* 147 G2
Newtown *Cornw.* 144 C4
Newtown *Cumb.* 260 B1
Newtown *Derbys.* 235 D4
Newtown *Devon* 164 A5
Newtown *Devon* 153 D3
Newtown *Dorset* 154 A2
Newtown *Glos.* 181 F2
Newtown *Gt.Man.* 233 G2
Newtown *Gt.Man.* 234 B2
Newtown *Hants.* 157 F1
Newtown *Hants.* 169 F1
Newtown *Hants.* 156 B1
Newtown *Hants.* 169 E5
Newtown *Hants.* 157 E1
Newtown *Here.* 195 F3
Newtown *Here.* 195 D2
Newtown *High.* 308 C4
Newtown *I.o.M.* 240 B4
Newtown *I.o.W.* 156 D3
Newtown *Northumb.* 270 C1
Newtown *Northumb.* 279 E4
Newtown *Oxon.* 184 C4
Newtown (Y Drenewydd) *Powys* 206 A3
Newtown *R.C.T.* 179 G3
Newtown *Shrop.* 220 B4
Newtown *Som.* 165 F4
Newtown *Som.* 153 F1
Newtown *Staffs.* 221 G1
Newtown *Staffs.* 222 B1
Newtown *Staffs.* 208 B2
Newtown *Wilts.* 168 A5
Newtown *Wilts.* 169 E1
Newtown Linford 210 A2
Newtown St. Boswells 277 G2
Newtown Unthank 209 G2
Newtown-in-Saint-Martin 145 E4
Newtyle 302 A5
Newyears Green 185 F4
Neyland 176 C2
Nibley *Glos.* 181 F2
Nibley *S.Glos.* 181 F4
Nibley Green 181 G3
Nicholashayne 152 E1
Nicholaston 178 B4
Nidd 244 C1
Nigg *Aberdeen* 313 E4
Nigg *High.* 322 A2
Nightcott 164 B5
Nilig 218 D2
Nilston Rigg 261 E1
Nimlet 181 G5
Nine Ashes 187 E2
Nine Elms 182 D4
Nine Ladies Stone Circle 74
Nine Mile Burn 285 F4
Ninebanks 261 D2
Ninemile Bar (Crocketford) 266 C3
Nineveh 195 F1
Ninfield 160 C2
Ningwood 156 D4
Nisbet 278 A4
Niton 157 E5
Nitshill 283 G3
Nizels 173 E3
No. 1 Royal Crescent 34
No Man's Heath *Ches.* 220 C3
No Man's Heath *Warks.* 209 E2
No Man's Land 147 G4
Noah's Ark 173 E3
Noak Hill 187 E3
Noblehill 267 D3
Noblethorpe 235 G2
Nobottle 198 B1
Nocton 225 F1
Noddsdale 282 D3
Node, The 186 B1
Nogdam End 229 E5
Noke 184 A1
Nolton 176 B1
Nolton Haven 176 B1
Nomansland *Devon* 152 B1
Nomansland *Wilts.* 156 B1
Noneley 220 B5
Nonington 175 E3
Nook *Cumb.* 268 C4
Nook *Cumb.* 249 G4
Noonsbrough 342 B2
Noranside 302 C3
Norbreck 241 G3
Norbury *Ches.* 220 C3
Norbury *Derbys.* 222 C3
Norbury *Gt.Lon.* 186 C5
Norbury *Shrop.* 206 C3
Norbury *Staffs.* 221 E5
Norbury Common 220 C3
Norbury Junction 221 E5
Norchard 177 D3
Norcott Brook 234 A4
Nordelph 213 D2
Norden *Dorset* 155 F4
Norden *Gt.Man.* 234 C1
Nordley 207 F3
Norfolk Broads 82
Norham 287 G5
Norland Town 243 G5
Norley 233 G5
Norleywood 156 C3
Norlington 159 G2
Norman Cross 211 G3
Normanby *N.Lincs.* 237 F1
Normanby *N.Yorks.* 253 G4
Normanby *R. & C.* 253 E1
Normanby by Stow 237 F4
Normanby Hall Country Park & Farming Museum 89
Normanby le Wold 238 B3
Normanby-by-Spital 238 A4
Normandy 171 E2
Normann's Ruh 296 D5
Norman's Bay 160 B3
Norman's Green 153 D2
Normanston 215 G2
Normanton *Derby* 223 E4
Normanton *Leics.* 224 D3
Normanton *Lincs.* 225 E3
Normanton *Notts.* 224 C2
Normanton *Rut.* 211 E2
Normanton *W.Yorks.* 244 C5
Normanton le Heath 209 F1
Normanton on Soar 223 G5
Normanton on Trent 224 C1
Normanton-on-the-Wolds 224 B4
Normoss 241 G4
Norrington Common 167 F1
Norris Green 150 A1
Norris Hill 209 F1
Norristhorpe 244 B5
North Acton 186 B4
North Anston 236 C4
North Ascot 171 E1
North Aston 197 G5
North Baddesley 156 C1
North Ballachulish 298 C3
North Balloch 265 E1
North Barrow 166 D5
North Barsham 228 A2
North Bay Miniature Railway 89
North Benfleet 187 G4
North Bersted 158 B3
North Berwick 286 C1
North Boarhunt 157 F1
North Bogbain 323 F4
North Bovey 152 A4
North Bradley 167 F2
North Brentor 149 E2
North Brewham 167 E4
North Bridge 171 E4
North Buckland 163 E1
North Burlingham 229 E4
North Cadbury 166 D5
North Cairn 264 A3
North Camp 171 D2
North Carlton *Lincs.* 237 G5
North Carlton *Notts.* 236 C4
North Cave 246 A4
North Cerney 182 C2
North Chailey 159 F1
North Charford 156 A1
North Charlton 279 F4
North Cheriton 167 D5
North Chideock 154 A3
North Cliffe 246 A4
North Clifton 237 F5
North Cockerington 239 D3
North Coker 154 B1
North Collafirth 344 C4
North Common *S.Glos.* 181 F5
North Common *Suff.* 214 A4
North Commonty 325 D5
North Connel 290 B1
North Coombe 152 B2
North Cornelly 179 E4
North Corner 181 F4
North Cotes 238 D2
North Cove 215 F3
North Cowton 252 B2
North Crawley 199 E3
North Cray 187 D5
North Creake 227 G4
North Curry 166 A5
North Dallens 298 B5
North Dalton 246 B2
North Dawn 339 D2
North Deighton 244 C2
North Dell (Dail Bho Thuath) 329 F1
North Duffield 245 F4
North Elkington 238 C3
North Elmham 228 A3
North Elmsall 236 B1
North End *Bucks.* 198 D5
North End *Dorset* 167 F5
North End *E.Riding* 247 D2
North End *E.Riding* 247 D3
North End *E.Riding* 247 E4
North End *Essex* 187 F1
North End *Hants.* 169 G5
North End *Hants.* 156 A1
North End *Leics.* 210 A1
North End *N.Som.* 166 B1
North End *Norf.* 214 B2
North End *Northumb.* 270 D1
North End *Ports.* 157 F2
North End *W.Suss.* 158 D2
North End *W.Suss.* 158 B3
North Erradale 318 D1
North Essie 325 F4
North Fambridge 188 B3
North Ferriby 246 B5
North Frodingham 246 D2
North Gorley 156 A1
North Green *Norf.* 214 D3
North Green *Suff.* 215 E4
North Green *Suff.* 203 E1
North Green *Suff.* 203 E1
North Grimston 246 A1
North Halling 173 G2
North Harby 237 F5
North Hayling 157 G2
North Hazelrigg 279 E3
North Heasley 164 A4
North Heath *W.Berks.* 183 G5
North Heath *W.Suss.* 171 F5
North Hill 147 G2
North Hillingdon 185 F4
North Hinksey 183 G2
North Holmwood 171 G3
North Houghton 169 E4
North Huish 150 D2
North Hykeham 225 E1
North Johnston 176 C1
North Kelsey 238 A2
North Kessock 321 F5
North Killingholme 238 B1
North Kilvington 252 D4
North Kilworth 210 B4
North Kingston 156 A2
North Kyme 225 G2
North Lancing 159 D3
North Lee 184 D2
North Lees 252 C5
North Leigh 183 F1
North Leverton with Habblesthorpe 237 E4
North Littleton 196 C3
North Lopham 214 B3
North Luffenham 211 E2
North Marden 158 A2
North Marston 198 C5
North Middleton *Midloth.* 286 A4
North Middleton *Northumb.* 279 E4
North Millbrex 324 D5
North Molton 164 A5
North Moreton 184 A4
North Mundham 158 A3
North Muskham 224 C2
North Newbald 246 B4
North Newington 197 G4
North Newnton 168 C2
North Newton 165 F4
North Nibley 181 G3
North Oakley 169 G2
North Ockendon 187 E4
North Ormesby 253 E1
North Ormsby 238 C3
North Otterington 252 C4
North Owersby 238 A3
North Perrott 161 A2
North Petherton 165 F4
North Petherwin 147 G1
North Pickenham 213 G2
North Piddle 196 B2
North Plain 267 F4
North Pool 151 D3
North Poorton 154 B3
North Quarme 164 C4
North Queensferry 285 F1
North Radworthy 164 A4
North Rauceby 225 F3
North Reston 239 D4
North Rigton 244 B3
North Rode 221 F1
North Roe 344 C4
North Ronaldsay 341 F1
North Runcton 213 E1
North Sandwick 345 E3
North Scale 241 E1
North Scarle 225 D1
North Seaton 271 E3
North Shian 298 B5
North Shields 262 C1
North Shoebury 188 C4
North Side 212 A3
North Skelton 253 F1
North Somercotes 239 E3
North Stainley 252 B5
North Stainmore 250 D1
North Stifford 187 F4
North Stoke *B. & N.E.Som.* 167 E1
North Stoke *Oxon.* 184 B4
North Stoke *W.Suss.* 158 C2
North Stoneham 156 D1
North Street *Hants.* 170 B4
North Street *Kent* 174 C3
North Street *Med.* 174 A1
North Street *W.Berks.* 184 B5
North Sunderland 279 G3
North Tamerton 148 D1
North Tarbothill 313 E3
North Tawton 163 G5
North Third 284 B1
North Thoresby 238 C3
North Tidworth 168 D3
North Togston 271 E1
North Town *Devon* 163 F5
North Town *Hants.* 171 D2
North Town *W. & M.* 185 D4
North Tuddenham 228 B4
North Uist (Uibhist a Tuath) 315 G2
North Walsham 229 D2
North Waltham 169 G3
North Warnborough 170 C2
North Water Bridge 303 E3
North Watten 337 E3
North Weald Bassett 187 D2
North Wembley 186 A4
North West Highlands 128
North Wheatley 237 E4
North Whilborough 151 E1
North Wick 166 C1
North Widcombe 166 C2
North Willingham 238 B4
North Wingfield 223 F1
North Witham 225 E5
North Wootton *Dorset* 154 C1
North Wootton *Norf.* 227 E5
North Wootton *Som.* 166 C3
North Wraxall 182 A5
North Wroughton 182 D4
North Yardhope 270 B1
North York Moors 89
North Yorkshire Moors Railway 89
Northacre 214 A2
Northall 199 E5
Northall Green 228 A4
Northallerton 252 C3
Northam *Devon* 163 E3
Northam *S'ham.* 156 D1
Northampton 198 C1
Northampton Central Museum 74
Northaw 186 B2
Northay *Devon* 153 G2
Northay *Som.* 153 F1
Northbay 314 C3
Northbeck 225 F3
Northborough 211 G2
Northbourne *Kent* 175 F3
Northbourne *Oxon.* 184 A4
Northbridge Street 160 C1
Northbrook *Hants.* 169 G4
Northbrook *Oxon.* 197 G5
Northburnhill 324 D5
Northchapel 171 E5
Northchurch 185 E2
Northcote Manor 163 G4
Northcott 148 D1
Northcourt 184 A3
Northdyke 340 A4
Northedge 223 E1
Northend *B. & N.E.Som.* 167 E1
Northend *Bucks.* 184 C3
Northend *Warks.* 197 F2
Northfield *Aber.* 324 D3
Northfield *Aberdeen* 313 E4
Northfield *High.* 337 F4
Northfield *Hull* 246 C5
Northfield *Sc.Bord.* 287 G3
Northfield *Som.* 165 F4
Northfield *W.Mid.* 208 C5
Northfields 211 F2
Northfleet 187 F5
Northhouse 277 F5
Northiam 160 D1
Northill 199 G3
Northington *Glos.* 181 G2
Northington *Hants.* 169 G4
Northlands 226 B2
Northleach 182 D1
Northleigh *Devon* 153 E3
Northleigh *Devon* 163 G2
Northlew 149 F1
Northmoor 183 G2
Northmoor Green (Moorland) 166 A4
Northmuir 302 B4
Northney 157 G2
Northolt 186 A4
Northop 219 F1
Northop Hall 219 F1
Northorpe *Lincs.* 226 A4
Northorpe *Lincs.* 237 F3
Northorpe *Lincs.* 211 F1
Northover *Som.* 166 C5
Northover *Som.* 166 B4
Northowram 244 A5
Northport 155 F4
Northpunds 342 D5
Northrepps 228 D2
Northton (Taobh Tuath) 326 B5
Northtown 339 D3
Northway *Glos.* 196 B4
Northway *Som.* 165 E5
Northwich 234 A5
Northwick *S.Glos.* 181 E4
Northwick *Som.* 166 A3
Northwick *Worcs.* 196 A2
Northwold 213 F3
Northwood *Gt.Lon.* 185 F3
Northwood *I.o.W.* 157 D3
Northwood *Kent* 175 F2
Northwood *Mersey.* 233 F3
Northwood *Shrop.* 220 B4
Northwood Green 181 G1
Northwood Hills 186 A3
Norton *Glos.* 196 A5
Norton *Halton* 233 G4
Norton *Herts.* 200 A4
Norton *I.o.W.* 156 C4
Norton *Mon.* 194 D5
Norton *N.Som.* 166 A1
Norton *N.Yorks.* 253 G5
Norton *Northants.* 198 B1
Norton *Notts.* 236 C5
Norton *Powys* 194 C1
Norton *S.Yorks.* 236 C1
Norton *S.Yorks.* 236 A4
Norton *Shrop.* 207 E2
Norton *Shrop.* 207 G2
Norton *Shrop.* 207 D4
Norton *Stock.* 262 D5
Norton *Suff.* 202 A1
Norton *Swan.* 178 C4
Norton *V. of Glam.* 179 E5
Norton *W.Mid.* 208 A4
Norton *W.Suss.* 158 B3
Norton *W.Suss.* 158 A4
Norton *Wilts.* 182 A4
Norton *Worcs.* 196 A2
Norton *Worcs.* 196 C3
Norton Bavant 168 A3
Norton Bridge 221 F4
Norton Canes 208 C2
Norton Canon 194 C3
Norton Disney 225 D2
Norton Ferris 167 E4
Norton Fitzwarren 165 E5
Norton Green *Herts.* 200 A5
Norton Green *I.o.W.* 156 C4
Norton Green *Stoke* 221 G2
Norton Hawkfield 166 C1
Norton Heath 187 F2
Norton in Hales 221 E4
Norton in the Moors 221 F2
Norton Lindsey 197 E1
Norton Little Green 202 A1
Norton Malreward 166 D1
Norton Mandeville 187 E2
Norton St. Philip 167 E2
Norton Subcourse 215 F2
Norton Wood 194 C3
Norton Woodseats 236 A4
Norton-Juxta-Twycross 209 F2
Norton-le-Clay 252 D5
Norton-sub-Hamdon 154 A1
Norwell 224 C1
Norwell Woodhouse 224 C1
Norwich 228 D5
Norwich Airport 228 D4
Norwich Castle Museum & Art Gallery 82
Norwich Cathedral 82
Norwick 345 F1
Norwood End 187 E2
Norwood Green *Gt.Lon.* 186 A5
Norwood Green *W.Yorks.* 244 A5
Norwood Hill 172 B4
Norwood Park 166 C4
Noseley 210 C3
Noss Mayo 150 B3
Nosterfield 252 B4
Nosterfield End 201 E3
Nostie 307 E2
Notgrove 196 D5
Nottage 179 E5
Notting Hill 186 B4
Nottingham *High.* 337 E5
Nottingham *Nott.* 223 G3
Nottingham Castle Museum & Art Gallery 74
Nottingham East Midlands Airport 223 F5
Nottington 154 C4
Notton *W.Yorks.* 236 A1
Notton *Wilts.* 168 A1
Nottswood Hill 181 G1
Nounsley 187 G1
Noutard's Green 195 G1
Nowton 201 G1
Nox 206 D1
Noyadd Trefawr 191 F3
Nuffield 184 B4
Nun Monkton 245 E2
Nunburnholme 246 A3

Nuneaton 209 F3
Nuneham Courtenay 184 A3
Nunney 167 E3
Nunnington *Here.* 195 E3
Nunnington *N.Yorks.* 253 F5
Nunnington Park 165 D5
Nunnykirk 270 C2
Nunsthorpe 238 C2
Nunthorpe *Middbro.* 253 E1
Nunthorpe *York* 245 E2
Nunton 168 C5
Nunwick *N.Yorks.* 252 C5
Nunwick *Northumb.* 270 A4
Nup End 186 B1
Nupend 181 G2
Nursling 156 C1
Nursted 170 C5
Nurton 208 A3
Nutbourne *W.Suss.* 158 C2
Nutbourne *W.Suss.* 157 G2
Nutfield 172 C3
Nuthall 223 G3
Nuthampstead 200 C4
Nuthurst *W.Suss.* 171 G5
Nuthurst *Warks.* 209 D5
Nutley *E.Suss.* 159 G1
Nutley *Hants.* 170 B3
Nutwell 236 D2
Nyadd 292 C5
Nybster 337 F2
Nyetimber 158 A4
Nyewood 170 C5
Nymans 48
Nymet Rowland 152 A2
Nymet Tracey 152 A2
Nympsfield 182 A2
Nynehead 165 E5
Nythe 166 B4
Nyton 158 B3

O

Oad Street 174 A2
Oadby 210 B2
Oak Cross 149 F1
Oak Tree 252 C1
Oakamoor 222 B3
Oakbank *Arg. & B.* 289 G1
Oakbank *W.Loth.* 285 E3
Oakdale *Caerp.* 180 A3
Oakdale *Poole* 155 G3
Oake 165 E5
Oaken 208 A2
Oakenclough 242 B3
Oakengates 207 G1
Oakenhead 323 E3
Oakenholt 233 D5
Oakenshaw *Dur.* 262 B4
Oakenshaw *W.Yorks.* 244 A5
Oakerthorpe 223 E2
Oakes 235 F1
Oakfield *I.o.W.* 157 E3
Oakfield *Torfaen* 180 B3
Oakford *Cere.* 192 A2
Oakford *Devon* 164 C5
Oakfordbridge 164 C5
Oakgrove 221 G1
Oakham 211 D2
Oakham Castle 74
Oakhanger 170 C4
Oakhill 166 D3
Oakington 200 C1
Oaklands *Conwy* 218 B2
Oaklands *Herts.* 186 B1
Oakle Street 181 G1
Oakley *Beds.* 199 F2
Oakley *Bucks.* 184 B1
Oakley *Fife* 285 E1
Oakley *Hants.* 169 G2
Oakley *Oxon.* 184 C2
Oakley *Poole* 155 G3
Oakley *Suff.* 214 C4
Oakley Green 185 E5
Oakley Park 205 F4
Oakridge Lynch 182 B2
Oaks 206 D2
Oaks Green 222 C4
Oaksey 182 B3
Oakshaw Ford 268 D4
Oakshott 170 C5
Oakthorpe 209 F1
Oaktree Hill 252 C3
Oakwood Leisure Park 112
Oakwoodhill 171 G4
Oakworth 243 G4
Oare *Kent* 174 C2
Oare *Som.* 164 B3
Oare *Wilts.* 168 C1
Oasby 225 F4
Oatfield 272 B4
Oath 166 A5
Oathlaw 302 C4
Oatlands 244 C2
Oban 290 A2
Obley 206 C5
Oborne 154 C1
Obthorpe 211 F1
Occlestone Green 221 D1
Occold 214 C4
Occumster 337 E5
Ochiltree 274 D3
Ochr-y-foel 232 B5
Ochtermuthill 292 D3
Ochtertyre *P. & K.* 292 D2
Ochtertyre *Stir.* 292 C5
Ockbrook 223 F4
Ockeridge 195 G1
Ockham 171 F2
Ockle 297 E2
Ockley 171 G4
Ocle Pychard 195 E3
Octon 254 D5
Odcombe 154 B1
Odd Down 167 E1
Oddendale 250 B1
Oddingley 196 B2
Oddington 184 A1
Oddsta 345 E3
Odell 199 E2
Odham 163 E5
Odie 341 E4
Odiham 170 C2
Odsey 200 A4
Odstock 168 C5
Odstone 209 F2
Offchurch 197 F1
Offenham 196 C3
Offerton 234 D4
Offham *E.Suss.* 159 F2
Offham *Kent* 173 F3
Offham *W.Suss.* 158 C3
Offley Hoo 199 G5
Offleymarsh 221 E5
Offord Cluny 200 A1
Offord D'Arcy 200 A1
Offton 202 B3
Offwell 153 E3
Ogbourne Maizey 183 D5
Ogbourne St. Andrew 183 D5
Ogbourne St. George 183 D5
Ogil 302 C3
Ogle 270 D4
Oglet 233 F4
Ogmore 179 E5
Ogmore Vale 179 F3
Ogmore-by-Sea 179 E5
Oil Terminal 338 C3
Okeford Fitzpaine 155 E1
Okehampton 149 F1
Okehampton Camp 149 F1
Okraquoy 342 D4
Olchard 152 B5
Olchfa 178 C3
Old 210 C5
Old Aberdeen 313 E4
Old Alresford 169 G4
Old Arley 209 E3
Old Basford 223 G3
Old Basing 170 B2
Old Belses 277 G3
Old Bewick 279 E4
Old Blair 301 D3
Old Bolingbroke 226 B1
Old Bramhope 244 B3
Old Brampton 236 A5
Old Bridge of Urr 266 B4
Old Buckenham 214 B2
Old Burdon 262 C2
Old Burghclere 169 F2
Old Byland 253 E4
Old Cassop 262 C4
Old Church Stoke 206 B3
Old Cleeve 164 D3
Old Clipstone 224 B1
Old Colwyn 231 G5
Old Craig 313 E2
Old Craighall 286 A2
Old Crombie 324 A4
Old Dailly 264 D1
Old Dalby 224 B5
Old Dam 235 F5
Old Deer 325 E5
Old Dilton 167 F3
Old Down *S.Glos.* 181 F4
Old Down *Som.* 166 D2
Old Edlington 236 C3
Old Eldon 262 B5
Old Ellerby 247 D4
Old Felixstowe 203 E4
Old Fletton 211 G3
Old Ford 186 C4
Old Glossop 235 E3
Old Goginan 204 C4
Old Goole 245 G5
Old Gore 195 F5
Old Grimsby 146 A1
Old Hall 238 C1
Old Hall Green 200 B5
Old Hall Street 229 E2
Old Harlow 187 D1
Old Heath 202 B5
Old Heathfield 160 A1
Old Hill 208 B4
Old Hurst 212 B5
Old Hutton 249 G4
Old Kea 146 C5
Old Kilpatrick 283 F2
Old Kinnernie 312 C4
Old Knebworth 200 A5
Old Leake 226 C2
Old Leslie 312 A2
Old Malton 254 B5
Old Man of Hoy 128
Old Milton 156 B3
Old Milverton 197 E1
Old Montsale 188 D3
Old Netley 157 D1
Old Newton 202 B1
Old Philpstoun 285 E2
Old Poltalloch 290 A4
Old Radnor (Pencraig) 194 B2
Old Rattray 325 F4
Old Rayne 312 B2
Old Romney 161 F1
Old Scone 293 G2
Old Shields 284 C2
Old Sodbury 181 G4
Old Somerby 225 E4
Old Stratford 198 C3
Old Sunderlandwick 246 C2
Old Swarland 271 D1
Old Swinford 208 B4
Old Thirsk 252 D4
Old Town *Cumb.* 249 G4
Old Town *I.o.S.* 146 B1
Old Town Farm 270 A2
Old Tupton 223 E1
Old Warden 199 G3
Old Weston 211 F5
Old Windsor 185 E5
Old Wives Lees 174 C3
Old Woking 171 F2
Old Woodhall 226 A1
Old Woods 220 B5
Oldberrow 196 D1
Oldborough 152 A2
Oldbury *Kent* 173 E3
Oldbury *Shrop.* 207 G3
Oldbury *W.Mid.* 208 B4
Oldbury *Warks.* 209 F3
Oldbury Naite 181 F3
Oldbury on the Hill 182 A4
Oldbury-on-Severn 181 F3
Oldcastle *Bridgend* 179 F5
Oldcastle *Mon.* 194 C5
Oldcastle Heath 220 B3
Oldcotes 236 C4
Oldcroft 181 F2
Oldeamere 212 B3
Oldfield 196 A1
Oldford 167 E2
Oldhall *Aber.* 311 G5
Oldhall *High.* 337 E3
Oldham 234 D2
Oldham Edge 234 D2
Oldhamstocks 287 E2
Oldland 181 F5
Oldmeldrum 312 D2
Oldmill 312 A4
Oldpark 207 F2
Oldridge 152 B3
Oldshore Beg 334 A3
Oldshoremore 334 B3
Oldstead 253 E5
Oldtown 321 E1
Oldtown of Aigas 321 D5
Oldtown of Ord 324 B4
Oldwalls 178 A3
Oldways End 164 B5
Oldwhat 325 D4
Oldwich Lane 209 E5
Olgrinmore 336 D3
Oliver 276 C3
Oliver's Battery 169 F5
Ollaberry 344 C4
Ollerton *Ches.* 234 B5
Ollerton *Notts.* 224 B1
Ollerton *Shrop.* 220 D5
Olmstead Green 201 E3
Olney 199 D2
Olrig House 337 D2
Olton 208 D4
Olveston 181 F4
Ombersley 196 A1
Ompton 224 B1
Onchan 240 B4
Onecote 222 B2
Onehouse 202 B2
Ongar Hill 227 D5
Ongar Street 194 C1
Onibury 207 D5
Onich 298 C3
Onllwyn 179 E1
Onneley 221 E3
Onslow Green 187 F1
Onslow Village 171 E3
Opinan *High.* 330 A5
Opinan *High.* 318 D2
Orange Lane 287 E5
Orasaigh 327 F2
Orbliston 323 F4
Orbost 317 F5
Orby 226 C1
Orcadia 282 C3
Orchard 282 C1
Orchard Portman 165 F5
Orcheston 168 B3
Orcop 195 D5
Orcop Hill 195 D5
Ord 306 C3
Ordhead 312 B3
Ordie 311 G4
Ordiequish 323 F4
Ordsall 237 D5
Ordsall Hall 98
Ore 160 D2
Oreham Common 159 E2
Oreston 150 B2
Oreton 207 F5
Orford *Suff.* 203 F3
Orford *Warr.* 234 A3
Orford Castle 82
Orford Ness 82
Organford 155 F3
Orgreave 208 D1
Orlestone 174 B5
Orleton *Here.* 195 D1
Orleton *Worcs.* 195 F1
Orleton Common 195 D1
Orlingbury 211 D5
Ormacleit 304 A1
Ormesby 253 E1
Ormesby Hall 105
Ormesby St. Margaret 229 F4
Ormesby St. Michael 229 F4
Ormidale 282 B1
Ormiscaig 330 A5
Ormiston 286 B3
Ormlie 336 D2
Ormsaigmore 297 D3
Ormsary 281 F2
Ormskirk 233 F2
Oronsay 280 B1
Orphir 338 C2
Orpington 173 D2
Orrell *Gt.Man.* 233 G2
Orrell *Mersey.* 233 E3
Orrisdale 240 B2
Orrok House 313 E3
Orroland 258 A2
Orsett 187 F4
Orsett Heath 187 F4
Orslow 208 A1
Orston 224 C3
Orton *Cumb.* 250 B2
Orton *Northants.* 210 D5
Orton Longueville 211 G3
Orton Rigg 259 G1
Orton Waterville 211 G3
Orton-on-the-Hill 209 F2
Orwell 200 B2
Osbaldeston 242 C4
Osbaldwick 245 F2
Osbaston *Leics.* 209 G2
Osbaston *Shrop.* 220 A5
Osbaston *Tel. & W.* 207 E1
Osbaston Hollow 209 G2
Osborne 157 E3
Osborne House 48
Osbournby 225 F4
Oscroft 220 C1
Ose 317 G5
Osgathorpe 209 G1
Osgodby *Lincs.* 238 A3
Osgodby *N.Yorks.* 245 F4
Osgodby *N.Yorks.* 255 D4
Oskaig 306 B1
Osleston 222 D4
Osmaston *Derby* 223 E4
Osmaston *Derbys.* 222 C3
Osmington 154 D4
Osmington Mills 154 D4
Osmondthorpe 244 C4
Osmotherley 253 D3
Osnaburgh (Dairsie) 294 C3
Ospringe 174 C2
Ossett 244 B5
Ossett Street Side 244 B5
Ossington 224 C1
Ostend 188 C3
Osterley 186 A5
Osterley Park & House 59
Oswaldkirk 253 F5
Oswaldtwistle 242 D5
Oswestry 219 F5
Oteley 220 B4
Otford 173 E3
Otham 173 G3
Otherton 208 B1
Othery 166 A4
Otley *Suff.* 202 D2
Otley *W.Yorks.* 244 B3
Otter 282 A2
Otter Ferry 282 A1
Otterbourne 169 F5
Otterburn *N.Yorks.* 243 E2
Otterburn *Northumb.* 270 A2
Otterburn Camp 270 A2
Otterden Place 174 B3
Otterham 148 B1
Otterham Quay 174 A2
Otterhampton 165 F3
Otternish 316 C2
Ottershaw 171 F1
Otterswick 345 E4
Otterton 153 D4
Otterwood 156 D2
Ottery St. Mary 153 D3
Ottinge 175 D4
Ottringham 247 E5
Oughterby 259 F1
Oughtershaw 251 D4
Oughterside 259 E2
Oughtibridge 236 A3
Oulston 253 E5
Oulton *Cumb.* 259 F1
Oulton *Norf.* 228 C3
Oulton *Staffs.* 221 G4
Oulton *Staffs.* 221 E5
Oulton *Suff.* 215 G2
Oulton *W.Yorks.* 244 C5
Oulton Broad 215 G2
Oulton Grange 221 G4
Oulton Street 228 C3
Oultoncross 221 G4
Oundle 211 F4
Our Dynamic Earth 128
Ousby 260 C4
Ousdale 333 F2
Ousden 201 F2
Ousefleet 246 A5
Ouston *Dur.* 262 B2
Ouston *Northumb.* 270 C4
Out Newton 247 F5
Out Rawcliffe 242 A3
Outcast 249 E5
Outchester 279 F3
Outertown 340 A5
Outgate 249 E3
Outhgill 250 C2
Outlands 221 E5
Outlane 235 E1
Outwell 212 D2
Outwood *Surr.* 172 C4
Outwood *W.Yorks.* 244 C5
Outwoods 207 G1
Ouzlewell Green 244 C5
Oval, The 167 E1
Ovenden 243 G5
Over *Cambs.* 212 B5
Over *Ches.* 220 D1
Over *Glos.* 182 A1
Over *S.Glos.* 181 E4
Over Burrows 223 D4
Over Compton 154 B1
Over Dinsdale 252 C1
Over End 235 G5
Over Green 209 D3
Over Haddon 222 D1
Over Hulton 234 A2
Over Kellet 242 B1
Over Kiddington 197 G5
Over Monnow 181 D1
Over Norton 197 F5
Over Peover 234 B5
Over Rankeilour 294 B3
Over Silton 253 D3
Over Stowey 165 E4
Over Stratton 154 A1
Over Tabley 234 B4
Over Wallop 169 D4
Over Whitacre 209 E3
Over Winchendon (Upper Winchendon) 184 C1
Over Worton 197 G5
Overbister 341 E2
Overbrae 324 D4
Overbury 196 B4
Overcombe 154 C4
Overgreen 236 A5
Overleigh 166 B4
Overpool 233 E5
Overscaig Hotel 331 G2
Overseal 209 E1
Overslade 209 G5
Oversland 174 C3
Oversley Green 196 C2
Overstone 198 D1
Overstrand 228 D1
Overthorpe 197 G3
Overton *Aber.* 312 C3
Overton *Aberdeen* 313 D3
Overton *Ches.* 233 G5
Overton *Hants.* 169 G3
Overton *Lancs.* 242 A2
Overton *N.Yorks.* 245 E2
Overton *Shrop.* 207 E5
Overton *Swan.* 178 A4
Overton *W.Yorks.* 235 G1
Overton *Wrex.* 220 A3
Overton Bridge 220 A3
Overtown *Lancs.* 250 B5
Overtown *N.Lan.* 284 C4
Overtown *Swin.* 183 D5
Overy 184 A3
Oving *Bucks.* 198 C5
Oving *W.Suss.* 158 B3
Ovingdean 159 F3
Ovingham 261 G1
Ovington *Dur.* 252 A1
Ovington *Essex* 201 F3
Ovington *Hants.* 169 G4
Ovington *Norf.* 228 A5
Ovington *Northumb.* 261 G1
Ower *Hants.* 156 C1
Ower *Hants.* 157 D2
Owermoigne 155 D4
Owl House, The 48
Owler Bar 235 G5
Owlpen 181 G3
Owlpen Manor 34
Owl's Green 203 D1
Owlswick 184 C2
Owmby 238 A2
Owmby-by-Spital 238 A4
Owslebury 169 G5
Owston 210 C2
Owston Ferry 237 F2
Owstwick 247 E4
Owthorpe 224 B4
Oxborough 213 F2
Oxburgh Hall 82
Oxcliffe Hill 242 A1
Oxcombe 238 D5
Oxen End 201 E5
Oxen Park 249 E4
Oxencombe 152 B4
Oxenhall 195 G5
Oxenholme 249 G3
Oxenhope 243 G4
Oxenpill 166 B3
Oxenton 196 B4
Oxenwood 169 E2
Oxford 48
Oxford Story 48
Oxfordshire Museum, The 48
Oxhey 186 A3
Oxhill 197 F3
Oxley 208 B2
Oxley Green 188 C1
Oxley's Green 160 B1
Oxnam 278 B5
Oxnead 228 D3
Oxnop Ghyll 251 E3
Oxshott 171 G1
Oxspring 235 G2
Oxted 172 C3
Oxton *Mersey.* 233 E4
Oxton *Notts.* 224 B2
Oxton *Sc.Bord.* 286 B4
Oxwich 178 A4
Oxwich Green 178 A4
Oxwick 228 A3
Oykel Bridge 331 F4
Oyne 312 B2
Oystermouth Castle 112
Ozleworth 181 G3

P

Pabail Iarach (Lower Bayble) 329 G4
Pabail Uarach (Upper Bayble) 329 G4
Pabbay 326 B5
Packington 209 F1
Packwood 209 D5
Packwood House 67
Padanaram 302 C4
Padbury 198 C4
Paddington 186 B4
Paddlesworth 175 D4
Paddock 174 B3
Paddock Wood 173 F4
Paddockhaugh 323 E4
Paddockhole 268 A3
Paddolgreen 220 C4
Padeswood 219 F1
Padfield 235 E3
Padiham 243 D4
Padside 244 A2
Padstow 146 D2
Padworth 170 B1
Paganhill 182 A2
Pagham 158 A4
Paglesham Churchend 188 C3
Paglesham Eastend 188 C3
Paible 326 C4
Paignton 151 E1
Paignton & Dartmouth Steam Railway 34
Paignton Zoo 34
Pailton 209 G4
Paine's Corner 160 B1
Painscastle 194 A3
Painshawfield 261 G1
Painswick 182 A2
Painswick Rococo Garden 34
Pairc 329 D3
Paisley 283 F3
Paisley Museum & Art Galleries 128
Pakefield 215 G2
Pakenham 202 A1
Palace of Holyroodhouse 128
Palace Pier 48
Pale 218 C4
Palehouse Common 159 G2
Palestine 169 D3
Paley Street 185 D5
Palgowan 265 E2
Palgrave 214 C4
Pallinsburn House 278 C3
Palmarsh 174 D5
Palmers Cross 171 F3
Palmers Green 186 C3
Palmerscross 323 E3
Palmerstown 180 A5
Palms Tropical Oasis (see Stapeley Water Gardens) 99
Palnackie 266 C5
Palnure 265 F4
Palterton 223 F1
Pamber End 170 B2
Pamber Green 170 B2
Pamber Heath 170 B1
Pamington 196 B4
Pamphill 155 F3
Pampisford 200 C3
Pan 338 C3
Panborough 166 B3
Panbride 295 D1
Pancrasweek 162 C5
Pancross 164 D1
Pandy *Gwyn.* 204 C2
Pandy *Mon.* 194 C5
Pandy *Powys* 205 F2
Pandy *Wrex.* 219 E4
Pandy Tudur 218 B1
Pandy'r Capel 219 D2
Panfield 201 F5
Pangbourne 184 B5
Pannal 244 C2
Pannal Ash 244 B2
Panshanger 186 B1
Pant 219 F5
Pant Glas 217 D3
Pant Gwyn 218 B5
Pant Mawr 205 E4
Pantasaph 232 C5
Panteg 180 C3
Pantglas 205 D3
Pantgwyn *Carmar.* 192 B5
Pantgwyn *Cere.* 191 F3
Pant-lasau 178 C2
Panton 238 B5
Pant-pastynog 218 D1
Pantperthog 204 D2
Pant-y-dwr 205 F5
Pantyffordd 219 F2
Pant-y-ffridd 206 A2
Pantyffynnon 178 C1
Pantygasseg 180 B3
Pantygelli 180 C1
Panxworth 229 E4
Papa Stour 342 A1
Papa Westray 340 C1
Papcastle 259 E3
Papil 342 C4
Papple 286 C2
Papplewick 223 G2
Papworth Everard 200 A1
Papworth St. Agnes 200 A1
Par 147 E4
Paradise Mill (see Silk Museum) 99
Paradise Park 48
Paradise Wildlife Park 82
Parbold 233 F1
Parbrook *Som.* 166 C4
Parbrook *W.Suss.* 171 F5
Parc 218 B4
Parcllyn 191 F2
Parcrhydderch 192 C2
Parc-Seymour 180 D3
Parc-y-rhôs 192 B3
Pardshaw 259 D4
Parham 203 E1
Parham House 48
Parish Holm 275 F3
Park 324 A4
Park Close 243 E3
Park Corner *E.Suss.* 173 E5
Park Corner *Oxon.* 184 B4
Park End *Northumb.* 270 A4
Park End *Staffs.* 221 E2
Park End *Worcs.* 207 G5
Park Gate *Hants.* 157 E2
Park Gate *W.Yorks.* 244 A3
Park Gate *W.Yorks.* 235 G1
Park Gate *Worcs.* 208 B5
Park Green 202 C1
Park Hill 236 A4
Park Lane 220 B4
Park Langley 172 C2
Park Street 186 A2
Parkend *Cumb.* 259 G3
Parkend *Glos.* 181 F2
Parker's Green 173 F4
Parkeston 202 D4
Parkfield *Cornw.* 148 D4
Parkfield *S.Glos.* 181 F5
Parkfield *W.Mid.* 208 B3
Parkford 302 C4
Parkgate *Ches.* 233 D5
Parkgate *D. & G.* 267 E2
Parkgate *Kent* 174 A5
Parkgate *S.Yorks.* 236 B3
Parkgate *Surr.* 172 B4
Parkham 163 D3
Parkham Ash 163 D3
Parkhead 284 A3
Parkhill *Angus* 303 E5
Parkhill *P. & K.* 301 G5
Parkhouse 181 D2
Parkhurst 157 D3
Parkmill 178 B4
Parkmore 323 F5
Parkneuk 303 F2
Parkside 220 A2
Parkstone 155 G3
Parkway 166 C5
Parley Cross 155 G3
Parley Green 156 A3
Parlington 244 D4
Parracombe 163 G1
Parrog 190 D4
Parson Cross 236 A3
Parson Drove 212 B2
Parsonage Green 187 F1
Parsonby 259 E3
Partick 283 G3
Partington 234 B3
Partney 226 C1
Parton *Cumb.* 258 C4
Parton *D. & G.* 266 A3
Partridge Green 159 D2
Parwich 222 C2
Paslow Wood Common 187 E2
Passenham 198 C4
Passfield 170 D4
Passingford Bridge 187 E3
Paston 229 E2
Paston Street 229 E2
Pasturefields 221 G5
Patchacott 149 E1
Patcham 159 F3
Patchetts Green 186 A3
Patching 158 C3
Patchole 163 G1
Patchway 181 F4
Pateley Bridge 244 A1
Path of Condie 293 F3
Pathe 166 A4
Pathfinder Village 152 B3
Pathhead *Aber.* 303 F3
Pathhead *E.Ayr.* 275 E4
Pathhead *Fife* 294 A5
Pathhead *Midloth.* 286 A3
Pathlow 197 D2
Patmore Heath 200 C5
Patna 274 C4
Patney 168 B2
Patrick 240 A3
Patrick Brompton 252 B3
Patrington 247 F5
Patrington Haven 247 F5
Patrishow 194 B5
Patrixbourne 175 D3
Patterdale 249 G5
Pattingham 208 A3
Pattishall 198 B2
Pattiswick 201 G5
Paul 144 B4
Paulerspury 198 C3
Paull 247 D5
Paull Holme 247 D5
Paul's Green 144 D3
Paulton 167 D2
Paulton's Park 48
Pauperhaugh 270 C2
Pave Lane 207 G1
Pavenham 199 E2
Pawlett 166 A3
Pawston 278 C3
Paxford 197 D4
Paxhill Park 159 F1
Paxton 287 G4
Paxton House 128
Paycocke's 82
Payden Street 174 B3
Payhembury 153 D2
Paythorne 243 E2
Peacehaven 159 G3
Peacemarsh 167 F5
Peachley 196 A2
Peak Cavern 74
Peak Dale 235 E5
Peak District 74
Peak Forest 235 F5
Peakirk 211 G2
Pean Hill 174 D2
Pear Tree 223 E4
Pearsie 302 B4
Pearson's Green 173 F4
Peartree 186 B1
Peartree Green *Essex* 187 E3
Peartree Green *Here.* 195 F4
Pease Pottage 172 B5
Peasedown St. John 167 E2
Peasehill 223 F3
Peaseland Green 228 B4
Peasemore 183 G5
Peasenhall 203 E1
Peaslake 171 F3
Peasley Cross 233 G3
Peasmarsh *E.Suss.* 161 D1
Peasmarsh *Surr.* 171 E3
Peaston 286 B3
Peastonbank 286 B3
Peat Inn 294 C4
Peathill 325 E3
Peathrow 262 A5
Peatling Magna 210 A3
Peatling Parva 210 A4
Peaton 207 E4
Pebble Coombe 172 B3
Pebmarsh 201 G4
Pebworth 196 D3
Pecket Well 243 F5
Peckforton 220 C2
Peckham 186 C5
Peckleton 209 G2

Peckover House & Garden 82
Pedham 229 E4
Pedmore 208 B4
Pedwell 166 B4
Peebles 285 G5
Peel *I.o.M.* 240 A3
Peel *Lancs.* 241 G4
Peening Quarter 161 D1
Peggs Green 209 G1
Pegsdon 199 G4
Pegswood 271 E3
Pegwell 175 F2
Peighinn nan Aoireann 304 A1
Peinchorran 306 B1
Peinlich 318 A4
Pelaw 262 B1
Pelcomb 176 C1
Pelcomb Bridge 176 C1
Pelcomb Cross 176 C1
Peldon 188 C1
Pellon 243 G5
Pelsall 208 C2
Pelton 262 B2
Pelutho 259 E2
Pelynt 147 G4
Pemberton 233 G2
Pembrey (Pen-bre) 178 A2
Pembrey Country Park 112
Pembridge 194 C2
Pembroke (Penfro) 176 C2
Pembroke Castle 112
Pembroke Dock (Doc Penfro) 176 C2
Pembrokeshire Coast National Park 112
Pembury 173 F4
Penallt 181 E1
Penally 177 E3
Penalt 195 E5
Penare 147 D5
Penarran 206 A4
Penarth 180 A5
Pen-bont Rhydybeddau 204 C4
Penboyr 191 G4
Pen-bre (Pembrey) 178 A2
Penbryn 191 F2
Pencader 192 A4
Pen-cae 192 A2
Pen-cae-cwm 218 C1
Pencaenewydd 216 D3
Pencaitland 286 B3
Pencarnisiog 230 B5
Pencarreg 192 B3
Pencarrow *Cornw.* 147 F1
Pencarrow *Cornw.* 34
Pencelli 193 G5
Pen-clawdd 178 B3
Pencoed 179 F4
Pencombe 195 E2
Pencoyd 195 E5
Pencraig *Here.* 195 E5
Pencraig *Powys* 218 D5
Pencraig (Old Radnor) *Powys* 194 B2
Pendeen 144 A3
Pendennis Castle 34
Penderyn 179 F2
Pendine (Pentywyn) 177 F2
Pendlebury 234 B2
Pendleton 243 D4
Pendock 195 G4
Pendoggett 147 E2
Pendomer 154 B1
Pendoylan 179 G5
Penegoes 205 D2
Penelewey 146 C5
Pen-ffordd 191 D5
Penffordd-las (Staylittle) 205 E3
Penfro (Pembroke) 176 C2
Pengam 180 A3
Penge 186 C5
Pengenffordd 194 A5
Pengorffwysfa 230 C3
Pengover Green 147 G3
Pen-groes-oped 180 C2
Pengwern 232 B5
Penhale 145 D5
Penhallow 146 B4
Penhalvean 145 E3
Penhelig 204 C3
Penhill 183 D4
Penhow 180 D3
Penhow Castle 112
Penhurst 160 B2
Peniarth 204 C2
Penicuik 285 G3
Peniel 192 A5
Penifiler 318 A5
Peninver 272 C3
Penisa'r Waun 217 E1
Penisarcwn 205 G1
Penishawain 193 G4
Penistone 235 G2
Penjerrick 145 E3
Penketh 233 G4
Penkill 264 D1
Penkridge 208 B1
Penlean 148 C1
Penley 220 B4
Penllech 216 B4
Penllergaer 178 C3
Pen-llyn *I.o.A.* 230 B4
Penllyn *V. of Glam.* 179 F5
Pen-lôn 216 D1
Penmachno 218 A2
Penmaen 178 B4
Penmaenan 231 F5
Penmaenmawr 231 F5
Penmaenpool 204 C1
Penmaen-Rhôs 231 G5
Penmark 165 D1
Penmon 231 E4
Penmon Priory 112
Penmorfa 217 E3
Penmynydd 230 D5
Penn *Bucks.* 185 E3
Penn *W.Mid.* 208 A3
Penn Street 185 E3
Pennal 204 C2
Pennal-isaf 204 D2
Pennan 324 D3
Pennance 146 B5
Pennant *Cere.* 192 B1
Pennant *Powys* 205 E3
Pennant Melangell 218 D5
Pennar 176 C2
Pennard 178 B4
Pennerley 206 C3
Penninghame 265 E4
Pennington *Cumb.* 249 D5
Pennington *Hants.* 156 C3
Pennington Green 234 A2
Pennorth 194 A5
Pennsylvania 181 G5
Penny Bridge 249 E4
Pennycross 150 A2
Pennyfuir 290 A1
Pennygate 229 E3
Pennyghael 289 E2
Pennyglen 274 A4
Pennygown 297 F5
Pennymoor 152 B1
Penny's Green 214 C2
Pennyvenie 274 C5
Penparc *Cere.* 191 F3
Penparc *Pembs.* 190 B4
Penparcau 204 B4
Penpedairheol 180 C2
Penpethy 147 E1
Penpillick 147 E4
Penpol 145 F3
Penpoll 147 F4
Penponds 144 D3
Penpont *D. & G.* 266 C1
Penpont *Powys* 193 F5
Penprysg 179 F4
Penquit 150 C2
Penrherber 191 F4
Penrhiw 191 F3
Penrhiwceiber 179 G3
Penrhiwgoch 178 B1
Penrhiw-llan 191 G3
Penrhiw-pâl 191 G3
Penrhiwtyn 178 D3
Penrhos *Gwyn.* 216 C4
Penrhos *I.o.A.* 230 A4
Penrhos *Mon.* 180 D1
Penrhos *Powys* 179 E1
Penrhos-garnedd 231 D5
Penrhyn Bay (Bae Penrhyn) 231 G4
Penrhyn Castle 112
Penrhyn-coch 204 C4
Penrhyndeudraeth 217 F4
Penrhyn-side 231 G4
Penrhys 179 G3
Penrice 178 A4
Penrith 260 B5
Penrose *Cornw.* 146 C2
Penrose *Cornw.* 147 G1
Penruddock 260 A5
Penryn 145 E3
Pensarn *Carmar.* 178 A1
Pensarn *Conwy* 232 A5
Pen-sarn *Gwyn.* 217 E5
Pen-sarn *Gwyn.* 216 D3
Pensax 195 G1
Pensby 233 D4
Penselwood 167 E4
Pensford 166 D1
Pensham 196 B3
Penshaw 262 C2
Penshurst 173 E4
Penshurst Place 49
Pensilva 147 G3
Pensnett 208 B4
Penston 286 B2
Pentewan 147 E5
Pentir 217 E1
Pentire 146 B3
Pentireglaze 146 D2
Pentlepoir 177 E2
Pentlow 201 G3
Pentlow Street 201 G3
Pentney 213 F1
Penton Mewsey 169 E3
Pentonville 186 C4
Pentraeth 230 D5
Pentre *Powys* 219 D5
Pentre *Powys* 205 G4
Pentre *Powys* 194 B1
Pentre *Powys* 206 B3
Pentre *Powys* 206 A4
Pentre *R.C.T.* 179 F3
Pentre *Shrop.* 206 C1
Pentre *Shrop.* 206 C5
Pentre *Wrex.* 219 F5
Pentre *Wrex.* 220 A3
Pentre Berw 230 C5
Pentre Ffwrndan 233 D5
Pentre Galar 191 E4
Pentre Gwenlais 178 C1
Pentre Gwynfryn 217 E5
Pentre Halkyn 232 D5
Pentre Isaf 218 B1
Pentre Llanrhaeadr 219 D1
Pentre Maelor 220 A3
Pentre Meyrick 179 F5
Pentre Poeth 178 C3
Pentre Saron 218 D1
Pentre-bach *Cere.* 192 B3
Pentrebach *M.Tyd.* 179 G2
Pentre-bach *Powys* 193 F4
Pentrebach *R.C.T.* 179 G4
Pentrebach *Swan.* 178 B2
Pentre-bont 218 A2
Pentre-bwlch 219 E3
Pentrecagal 191 G3
Pentre-celyn *Denb.* 219 E2
Pentre-celyn *Powys* 205 E2
Pentre-chwyth 178 C3
Pentreclwydau 179 E2
Pentre-cwrt 191 G4
Pentre-Dolau-Honddu 193 F3
Pentredwr *Denb.* 219 E3
Pentre-dwr *Swan.* 178 C3
Pentrefelin *Carmar.* 192 C5
Pentrefelin *Cere.* 192 C3
Pentrefelin *Conwy* 231 G5
Pentrefelin *Gwyn.* 217 E4
Pentrefelin *Powys* 219 E5
Pentrefoelas 218 B2
Pentregat 191 G2
Pentreheyling 206 B3
Pentre-llwyn-llŵyd 193 F2
Pentre-llyn 204 C5
Pentre-llyn-cymmer 218 C2
Pentre-piod 218 B4
Pentre-poeth 180 B4
Pentre'r beirdd 206 A1
Pentre'r Felin 218 B1
Pentre'r-felin 193 F4
Pentre-tafarn-y-fedw 218 B1
Pentre-ty-gwyn 193 E4
Pentrich 223 E2
Pentridge 155 G1
Pentwyn *Caerp.* 180 A2
Pen-twyn *Caerp.* 180 B2
Pentwyn *Cardiff* 180 B4
Pen-twyn *Mon.* 181 E2
Pentwyn-mawr 180 A3
Pentyrch 180 A4
Pentywyn (Pendine) 177 F2
Penuwch 192 B1
Penwithick 147 E4
Penwood 169 F1
Penwortham 242 B5
Penwortham Lane 242 B5
Penwyllt 179 E1
Pen-y-banc 192 C5
Pen-y-bont *Carmar.* 193 D4
Pen-y-bont *Carmar.* 191 G5
Pen-y-bont *Powys* 205 G1
Pen-y-bont *Powys* 219 F5
Penybont *Powys* 194 A1
Pen-y-bont ar Ogwr (Bridgend) 179 F5
Penybontfawr 219 D5
Penybryn *Caerp.* 180 A3
Pen-y-bryn *Gwyn.* 204 C1
Pen-y-bryn *Pembs.* 191 E3
Pen-y-bryn *Wrex.* 219 F3
Pen-y-cae *Powys* 179 E1
Penycae *Wrex.* 219 F3
Pen-y-cae-mawr 180 D3
Pen-y-cefn 232 C5
Pen-y-clawdd 180 D2
Pen-y-coedcae 179 G4
Penycwm 190 B5
Pen-y-Darren 179 G2
Pen-y-fai 179 E4
Penyffordd *Flints.* 220 A1
Pen-y-ffordd *Flints.* 232 C4
Penyffridd 217 E2
Pen-y-gaer 194 A5
Pen-y-garn *Carmar.* 192 B4
Pen-y-garn *Cere.* 204 C4
Penygarn *Torfaen* 180 B2
Penygarnedd 219 E5
Pen-y-garreg 193 G3
Pen-y-Graig *Gwyn.* 216 B4
Penygraig *R.C.T.* 179 G3
Penygroes *Carmar.* 178 B1
Penygroes *Gwyn.* 217 D2
Pen-y-Gwryd Hotel 217 F2
Pen-y-lan 180 A5
Penymynydd 220 A1
Pen-y-parc 219 F1
Pen-y-Park 194 B3
Pen-yr-englyn 179 F3
Pen-yr-heol *Mon.* 180 D1
Penyrheol *Swan.* 178 B3
Pen-y-sarn 230 C3
Pen-y-stryt 219 E2
Penywaun 179 F2
Penzance 144 B3
Penzance Heliport 144 B3
People's Story Museum 128
Peopleton 196 B2
Peover Heath 234 B5
Peper Harow 171 E3
Peplow 220 D5
Pepper Arden 252 B2
Pepper's Green 187 F1
Perceton 283 E5
Percie 312 A5
Percyhorner 325 E3
Perham Down 169 D3
Periton 164 C3
Perivale 186 A4
Perkhill 312 A4
Perkins Beach 206 C2
Perkin's Village 152 D3
Perlethorpe 236 D5
Perran Downs 144 C3
Perranarworthal 145 E3
Perranporth 146 B4
Perranuthnoe 144 C4
Perranzabuloe 146 B4
Perrott's Brook 182 C2
Perry Barr 208 C3
Perry Crofts 209 E2
Perry Green *Essex* 201 G5
Perry Green *Herts.* 186 D1
Perry Green *Wilts.* 182 B4
Perry Street 187 F5
Perrymead 167 E1
Pershall 221 F5
Pershore 196 B3
Persie House 301 G4
Pert 303 E3
Pertenhall 199 F1
Perth 293 G2
Perthcelyn 179 G3
Perthy 220 A4
Perton 208 A3
Pestalozzi Children's Village 160 C2
Peter Tavy 149 F3
Peterborough 211 G3
Peterborough Cathedral 82
Peterborough Museum & Art Gallery 82
Peterburn 318 D1
Peterchurch 194 C4
Peterculter 312 D4
Peterhead 325 G5
Peterlee 262 D3
Peter's Green 186 A1
Peters Marland 163 E4
Peters Port (Port Pheadair) 315 G5
Petersfield 170 C5
Petersfinger 168 C5
Peterstone Wentlooge 180 B4
Peterston-super-Ely 179 G5
Peterstow 195 E5
Petham 174 D3
Petrockstowe 163 F5
Pett 161 D2
Pettaugh 202 C2
Petteril Green 260 A3
Pettinain 285 D5
Pettistree 203 D2
Petton *Devon* 164 D5
Petton *Shrop.* 220 B5
Petts Wood 172 D2
Petty 312 C1
Pettycur 285 G1
Pettymuick 313 E2
Petworth 171 E5
Petworth House 49
Pevensey 160 B3
Pevensey Bay 160 B3
Pevensey Castle 49
Peverell 150 A2
Peveril Castle 74
Pewsey 168 C1
Pheasant's Hill 184 C4
Phesdo 303 E2
Philham 162 C3
Philiphaugh 277 F3
Phillack 144 C3
Philleigh 145 F3
Philpstoun 285 E2
Phocle Green 195 F5
Phoenix Green 170 C2
Phones 309 G5
Phorp 322 C4
Pibsbury 166 B5
Pica 258 D4
Piccadilly Corner 215 D3
Pickerells 187 E2
Pickering 253 G4
Pickering Nook 262 A2
Picket Piece 169 E3
Picket Post 156 A2
Pickford Green 209 E4
Pickfords House Museum 74
Pickhill 252 C4
Picklescott 206 D3
Pickletillem 294 C2
Pickmere 234 A5
Pickney 165 E5
Pickstock 221 E5
Pickston 293 E2
Pickup Bank 242 D5
Pickwell *Devon* 163 E1
Pickwell *Leics.* 210 C1
Pickworth *Lincs.* 225 F4
Pickworth *Rut.* 211 E1
Picton *Ches.* 233 F5
Picton *N.Yorks.* 252 D2
Piddinghoe 159 G3
Piddington *Bucks.* 184 D3
Piddington *Northants.* 198 D2
Piddington *Oxon.* 184 B1
Piddlehinton 154 D3
Piddletrenthide 154 D3
Pidley 212 B5
Piercebridge 252 B1
Pierowall 340 C2
Pigdon 271 D3
Pike Hill 243 E4
Pikehall 222 C2
Pikeshill 156 B2
Pilgrims Hatch 187 E3
Pilham 237 F3
Pill 181 E5
Pillaton *Cornw.* 149 D4
Pillaton *Staffs.* 208 B1
Pillerton Hersey 197 E3
Pillerton Priors 197 E3
Pilleth 194 B1
Pilley *Hants.* 156 C3
Pilley *S.Yorks.* 236 A2
Pilling 242 A3
Pilling Lane 241 G3
Pillowell 181 F2
Pilning 181 E4
Pilsbury 222 C1
Pilsdon 154 A3
Pilsgate 211 F2
Pilsley *Derbys.* 223 F1
Pilsley *Derbys.* 235 G5
Pilson Green 229 E4
Piltdown 159 G1
Pilton *Devon* 163 F2
Pilton *Northants.* 211 F4
Pilton *Rut.* 211 E2
Pilton *Som.* 166 C3
Pilton *Swan.* 178 A4
Pilton Green 178 A4
Pimhole 234 C1
Pimlico 185 F2
Pimperne 155 F2
Pin Mill 202 D4
Pinchbeck 226 A5
Pinchbeck Bars 226 A5
Pinchbeck West 226 A5
Pincheon Green 237 D1
Pinchinthorpe 253 E1
Pindon End 198 C3
Pinehurst 182 D4
Pinfold 233 E1
Pinged 178 A2
Pinhay 153 G3
Pinhoe 152 C3
Pinkneys Green 185 D4
Pinley Green 197 E1
Pinminnoch 264 C1
Pinmore 264 D1
Pinn 153 E4
Pinner 186 A4
Pinner Green 186 A3
Pinvin 196 B3
Pinwherry 264 C2
Pinxton 223 F2
Pipe and Lyde 195 E3
Pipe Gate 221 E3
Pipe Ridware 208 C1
Pipehill 208 C2
Piperhall 282 B4
Piperhill 322 A4
Pipers Pool 147 G1
Pipewell 210 D4
Pippacott 163 F2
Pipton 194 A4
Pirbright 171 E2
Pirnmill 281 G5
Pirton *Herts.* 199 G4
Pirton *Worcs.* 196 A3
Pisgah 292 C4
Pishill 184 C4
Pistyll 216 C3
Pistyll Rhaeadr 112
Pitagowan 300 D3
Pitblae 325 E3
Pitcairngreen 293 F2
Pitcairns 293 F3
Pitcaple 312 C2
Pitch Green 184 C2
Pitch Place *Surr.* 171 E2
Pitch Place *Surr.* 171 D4
Pitchcombe 182 A2
Pitchcott 198 C5
Pitchford 207 E2
Pitcombe 167 D4
Pitcot 179 E5
Pitcox 286 D2
Pitcur 294 A1
Pitfichie 312 B3
Pitgrudy 332 C5
Pitinnan 312 C1
Pitkennedy 302 D4
Pitkevy 294 A4
Pitlessie 294 B4
Pitlochry 301 E4
Pitman's Corner 202 C1
Pitmedden 313 D2
Pitmedden Garden 128
Pitminster 153 F1
Pitmuies 303 D5
Pitmunie 312 B3
Pitnacree 301 E4
Pitney 166 B5
Pitroddie 294 A2
Pitscottie 294 C3
Pitsea 187 G4
Pitsford 198 C1
Pitsford Hill 165 D4
Pitstone 185 E1
Pitstone Green 185 E1
Pitt *Devon* 152 D1
Pitt *Hants.* 169 F5
Pitt Rivers Museum 49
Pittendreich 323 D3
Pittentrail 332 C4
Pittenweem 294 D4
Pitteuchar 294 A5
Pittington 262 C3
Pittodrie House 312 B2
Pitton *Swan.* 178 A4
Pitton *Wilts.* 168 D4
Pittulie 325 E3
Pittville 196 B5
Pity Me 262 B3
Pityme 146 D2
Pixey Green 214 D4
Pixley 195 F4
Place Newton 254 B5
Plaidy 324 C4
Plain Dealings 177 D1
Plainfield 270 B1
Plains 284 B3
Plainsfield 165 E4
Plaish 207 E3
Plaistow *Gt.Lon.* 186 C4
Plaistow *W.Suss.* 171 F4
Plaitford 156 B1
Plaitford Green 169 D5
Planetarium, The (see Madame Tussaud's) 57
Plantasia 112
Plas 192 A5
Plas Gwynant 217 F2
Plas Isaf 219 D3
Plas Llwyd 232 A5
Plas Llwyngwern 205 D2
Plas Llysyn 205 F3
Plas Nantyr 219 E4
Plas Newydd, Llangollen 112
Plas Newydd, Anglesey 112
Plashett 177 F2
Plasisaf 218 C1
Plas-rhiw-Saeson 205 F2
Plastow Green 169 G1
Plas-yn-Cefn 232 B5
Plas-yn-Rhiw 113
Platt 173 F3
Platt Bridge 234 A2
Platt Lane 220 C4
Platt's Heath 174 A3
Plawsworth 262 B3
Plaxtol 173 F3
Play Hatch 184 C5
Playden 161 E1
Playford 202 D3
Playing Place 146 C5
Playley Green 195 G4
Plealey 206 D2
Plean 284 C1
Pleasance 294 A3
Pleasant Valley 200 D4
Pleasington 242 C5
Pleasley 223 G1
Pleasleyhill 223 G1
Pleasure Beach 82
Pleasure Island Theme Park 89
Pleasureland Amusement Park 98
Pleck *Dorset* 154 D1
Pleck *W.Mid.* 208 B3
Pledgdon Green 201 D5
Pledwick 236 A1
Plemstall 233 F5
Plenmeller 260 D1
Pleshey 187 F1
Plockton 307 E1
Plocropol 327 D4
Plomer's Hill 185 D3
Plot Gate 166 C4
Plough Hill 209 F3
Plowden 206 C4
Ploxgreen 206 C2
Pluckley 174 B4
Pluckley Thorne 174 B4
Plucks Gutter 175 E2
Plumbland 259 E3
Plumbley 236 B4
Plumley 234 B5
Plumpton *Cumb.* 260 A4
Plumpton *E.Suss.* 159 F2
Plumpton *Northants.* 198 B3
Plumpton Green 159 F2
Plumpton Head 260 B4
Plumstead *Gt.Lon.* 187 D5
Plumstead *Norf.* 228 C2
Plumtree 224 B4
Plungar 224 C4
Plush 154 D2
Plusha 147 G1
Plushabridge 148 D3
Plwmp 191 G2
Plym Bridge 150 B2
Plymouth 150 A2
Plymouth City Airport 150 B1
Plymouth Dome 34
Plympton 150 B2
Plymstock 150 B2
Plymtree 153 D2
Pockley 253 F4
Pocklington 246 A3
Pockthorpe 228 B3
Pocombe Bridge 152 B3
Pode Hole 226 A5
Podimore 166 C5
Podington 199 E1
Podmore 221 E4
Podsmead 182 A1
Poffley End 183 F1
Point Clear 189 D1
Pointon 225 G4
Polanach 298 B4
Polapit Tamar 148 D2
Polbae 265 D3
Polbain 330 B3
Polbathic 148 D5
Polbeth 285 E3
Polchar, The 310 B4
Poldean 267 F1
Pole Moor 235 E1
Polebrook 211 F4
Polegate 160 A3
Poles 332 C5
Polesden Lacey 49
Polesworth 209 E2
Polglass 330 C4
Polgooth 147 D4
Polgown 275 F5
Poling 158 C3
Poling Corner 158 C3
Polkerris 147 E4
Poll a' Charra 314 C2
Polla 334 C3
Pollardras 144 D3
Polldubh 298 D3
Pollie 332 C3
Pollington 236 D1
Polloch 297 G3
Pollok 283 G3
Pollok House 128
Pollokshaws 283 G3
Pollokshields 283 G3
Polmassick 147 D5
Polmont 284 D2
Polnoon 283 G4
Polperro 147 G4
Polruan 147 F4
Polsham 166 C3
Polstead 202 A4
Polstead Heath 202 A3
Poltalloch 290 A5
Poltimore 152 C3
Polton 285 G3
Polwarth 287 E4
Polyphant 147 G1
Polzeath 146 D2
Pomphlett 150 B2
Pond Street 200 C4
Ponders End 186 C3
Pondersbridge 212 A3
Ponsanooth 145 E3
Ponsonby 248 B2
Ponsongath 145 E5
Ponsworthy 152 A5
Pont Aber 192 D5
Pont Aberglaslyn 217 E3
Pont ar Hydfer 193 E5
Pont Crugnant 205 E3
Pont Cyfyng 218 A2
Pont Dolgarrog 218 A1
Pont Pen-y-benglog 217 F1
Pont Rhyd-sarn 218 B5
Pont Rhyd-y-cyff 179 E4
Pont Walby 179 E2
Pont yr Alwen 218 C2
Pontamman 178 C1
Pontantwn 178 A1
Pontardawe 178 D2
Pontarddulais 178 B2
Pontarfynach (Devil's Bridge) 204 D5
Pontargothi 192 B5
Pont-ar-llechau 192 D5
Pontarsais 192 A5
Pontblyddyn 219 F1
Pontbren Llwyd 179 F2
Pontefract 245 D5
Ponteland 271 D4
Ponterwyd 204 D4
Pontesbury 206 D2
Pontesbury Hill 206 C2
Pontesford 206 D2
Pontfadog 219 F4
Pontfaen *Pembs.* 190 D4
Pont-faen *Powys* 193 F4
Pontgarreg 191 G2
Pont-Henri 178 A2
Ponthir 180 C3
Ponthirwaun 191 F3
Pont-iets (Pontyates) 178 A2
Pontllanfraith 180 A3
Pontlliw 178 C2
Pontllyfni 216 D2
Pontlottyn 180 A2
Pontneddfechan 179 F2
Pontrhydfendigaid 192 D1
Pontrhydyfen 179 D3
Pont-rhyd-y-groes 204 D5
Pontrhydyrun 180 B3
Pontrilas 194 C5
Pontrobert 206 A1
Pont-rug 217 E1
Ponts Green 160 B2
Pontshill 195 F5
Pont-siân 192 A3
Pontsticill 179 G1
Pontwelly 192 A4
Pontyates (Pont-iets) 178 A2
Pontyberem 178 B1
Pont-y-blew 220 A4
Pontybodkin 219 F2
Pontyclun 179 G4
Pontycymer 179 F3
Pontygwaith 179 G3
Pontymister 180 B3
Pontymoel 180 B2
Pont-y-pant 218 A2
Pontypool 180 B2
Pontypridd 179 G3
Pont-y-rhyl 179 F4
Pontywaun 180 B3
Pooksgreen 156 C1
Pool *Cornw.* 146 A5
Pool *W.Yorks.* 244 B3
Pool Bank 249 F4
Pool Green 208 C2
Pool Head 195 E2
Pool of Muckhart 293 F4
Pool Quay 206 B1
Pool Street 201 F4
Poole 155 G3
Poole Keynes 182 B3
Poolend 221 G2
Poole's Cavern 74
Poolewe 319 E1
Pooley Bridge 260 A5
Pooley Street 214 B3
Poolfold 221 F2
Poolhill 195 G5
Poolsbrook 236 B5
Poolthorne Farm 238 A2
Pope Hill 176 C1
Popeswood 170 D1
Popham 169 G3
Poplar 186 C4
Porchfield 156 D3
Porin 320 C4
Poringland 229 D5
Porkellis 145 D3
Porlock 164 B3
Porlock Weir 164 B3
Port Allen 294 A2
Port Appin 298 B5
Port Askaig 280 C3
Port Bannatyne 282 B3
Port Carlisle 268 A5
Port Charlotte 280 A4
Port Clarence 263 E5
Port Driseach 282 A2
Port e Vullen 240 C2
Port Ellen 280 B5
Port Elphinstone 312 C3
Port Erin 240 A5
Port Erroll 313 F1
Port Eynon 178 A4
Port Gaverne 147 E1
Port Glasgow 283 E2
Port Henderson 319 D2
Port Isaac 147 D1
Port Logan 256 A2
Port Lympne Wild Animal Park 49
Port Mòr 296 D2
Port Mulgrave 253 G1
Port na Craig 301 E4
Port nan Giùran (Portnaguran) 329 G4
Port nan Long 315 G2
Port Ness (Port Nis) 329 G1
Port Nis (Port Ness) 329 G1
Port o' Warren 266 C5
Port of Menteith 292 A4
Port Penrhyn 231 D5
Port Pheadair (Peters Port) 315 G5
Port Quin 147 D1
Port Ramsay 298 A5
Port St. Mary 240 A5
Port Solent 157 F2
Port Sunlight 233 E4
Port Talbot 179 D3
Port Tennant 178 C3
Port Wemyss 280 A4
Port William 256 D2
Portachoillan 281 F4
Portavadie 282 A3
Portbury 181 E5

Portchester 157 F2
Portchester Castle 49
Portencross 282 C5
Portesham 154 C4
Portessie 323 G3
Portfield *Arg. & B.* 289 G2
Portfield *W.Suss.* 158 A3
Portfield Gate 176 C1
Portgate 149 E2
Portgordon 323 F3
Portgower 333 F3
Porth *Cornw.* 146 C3
Porth *R.C.T.* 179 G3
Porth Colmon 216 A4
Porth Mellin 145 D5
Porth Navas 145 E4
Porthaethwy
(Menai Bridge) 231 D5
Porthallow *Cornw.* 145 E4
Porthallow *Cornw.* 147 G4
Porthcawl 179 E5
Porthcothan 146 C2
Porthcurno 144 A4
Porthcurno Sands 34
Porthgain 190 B4
Porthill 221 F3
Porthkerry 165 D1
Porthleven 144 D4
Porthmadog 217 E4
Porthmeor 144 B3
Portholland 147 D5
Porthoustock 145 F4
Porthpean 147 E4
Porthtowan 146 A5
Porthyrhyd *Carmar.* 192 D4
Porthyrhyd *Carmar.* 178 B1
Porth-y-waen 219 F5
Portincaple 291 E5
Portington 245 G4
Portinnisherrich 290 B3
Portinscale 259 F4
Portishead 181 D5
Portknockie 323 G3
Portland Castle 34
Portlethen 313 E5
Portlethen Village 313 E5
Portloe 145 G3
Portlooe 147 G4
Portmahomack 322 B1
Portmeirion 217 E4
Portmeirion Village 113
Portmellon 147 E5
Portmore 156 C3
Port-na-Con 334 D2
Portnacroish 298 B5
Portnaguran
(Port nan Giùran) 329 G4
Portnahaven 280 A4
Portnalong 305 G1
Portnaluchaig 297 F1
Portobello 286 A2
Porton 168 C4
Portpatrick 264 B5
Portreath 146 A5
Portree 318 A5
Portscatho 145 F3
Portsea 157 F2
Portskerra 336 A2
Portskewett 181 E4
Portslade 159 E3
Portslade-by-Sea 159 E3
Portslogan 264 A5
Portsmouth 157 F3
Portsmouth Cathedral 49
Portsmouth Historic Dockyard 49
Portsonachan 290 C2
Portsoy 324 A3
Portuairk 296 D3
Portvoller 329 G4
Portway *Here.* 194 C3
Portway *Here.* 195 D3
Portway *Here.* 195 D4
Portway *Worcs.* 208 C5
Portwrinkle 149 D5
Portyerrock 257 E3
Posenhall 207 F2
Poslingford 201 F3
Postbridge 149 G3
Postcombe 184 C3
Postling 174 D5
Post-mawr
(Synod Inn) 192 A2
Postwick 229 D5
Potarch 312 B5
Potsgrove 199 E5
Pott Row 227 F5
Pott Shrigley 234 D5
Potten End 185 F2
Potter Brompton 254 C5
Potter Heigham 229 F4
Potter Street 187 D2
Pottergate Street 214 C2
Potterhanworth 225 F1
Potterhanworth Booths 225 F1
Potteries Museum & Art Gallery 67
Potterne 168 A2
Potterne Wick 168 B2
Potternewton 244 C4
Potters Bar 186 B2
Potters Crouch 186 A2
Potter's Green 209 F4
Potters Marston 209 G3
Potterspury 198 C3
Potterton *Aber.* 313 F3
Potterton *W.Yorks.* 244 D4
Pottle Street 167 F3
Potto 253 D2
Potton 200 A3
Pott's Green 202 A5
Poughill *Cornw.* 162 C5
Poughill *Devon* 152 B2
Poulshot 168 A2
Poulton 182 D2
Poulton-le-Fylde 241 G4
Pound Bank 195 G3
Pound Green
E.Suss. 160 A1
Pound Green *Suff.* 201 F2
Pound Green
Worcs. 207 G5
Pound Hill 172 B5
Pound Street 169 F1
Poundbury 154 C3
Poundffald 178 B3
Poundfield 173 E5
Poundgate 159 G1
Poundland 264 C2
Poundon 198 B5
Poundsbridge 173 E4
Poundsgate 152 A5
Poundstock 148 C1
Povey Cross 172 B4
Pow Green 195 G3
Powburn 279 E5
Powderham 152 C4
Powderham Castle 34
Powerstock 154 B3
Powfoot 267 F4
Powick 196 A2
Powis Castle & Garden 113
Powler's Piece 163 D4
Powmill 293 F5
Poxwell 154 D4
Poyle 185 F5
Poynings 159 E2
Poyntington 167 D5
Poynton *Ches.* 234 D4
Poynton *Tel. & W.* 207 E1
Poynton Green 207 E1
Poyntzfield 321 G3
Poys Street 215 E4
Poyston 176 C1
Poyston Cross 176 C1
Poystreet Green 202 A2
Praa Sands 144 C4
Pratis 294 B4
Pratt's Bottom 173 D2
Praze-an-Beeble 144 D3
Predannack Wollas 145 D5
Prees 220 C4
Prees Green 220 C4
Prees Heath 220 C4
Prees Higher Heath 220 C4
Prees Lower Heath 220 C4
Preesall 241 G3
Preesgweene 219 F4
Prenbrigog 219 F1
Prendergast 176 C1
Prendwick 279 E5
Pren-gwyn 192 A3
Prenteg 217 E3
Prenton 233 E4
Prescot 233 F3
Prescott *Devon* 153 D1
Prescott *Shrop.* 220 B5
Presley 322 C4
Pressen 278 C3
Prestatyn 232 B4
Prestbury *Ches.* 234 D5
Prestbury *Glos.* 196 B5
Presteigne 194 C1
Presthope 207 E3
Prestleigh 166 D3
Prestolee 234 B2
Preston *B. & H.* 159 F3
Preston *Devon* 152 B5
Preston *Dorset* 154 D4
Preston *E.Loth.* 286 C2
Preston *E.Riding* 247 D4
Preston *Glos.* 195 F4
Preston *Glos.* 182 C2
Preston *Herts.* 199 G5
Preston *Kent* 174 C2
Preston *Kent* 175 E2
Preston *Lancs.* 242 B5
Preston *Northumb.* 279 F4
Preston *Rut.* 211 D2
Preston *Sc.Bord.* 287 E4
Preston *Shrop.* 207 E1
Preston *Som.* 165 D4
Preston *Suff.* 202 A2
Preston *Torbay* 151 E1
Preston *Wilts.* 182 C5
Preston Bagot 197 D1
Preston Bissett 198 B4
Preston Bowyer 165 E5
Preston Brockhurst 220 C5
Preston Brook 233 G4
Preston Candover 170 B3
Preston Capes 198 A2
Preston Deanery 198 C2
Preston Gubbals 207 D1
Preston Mill & Phantassie Dovecot 128
Preston on Stour 197 E3
Preston on the Hill 233 G4
Preston on Wye 194 C3
Preston Plucknett 154 B1
Preston upon the
Weald Moors 207 F1
Preston Wynne 195 E3
Preston-le-Skerne 262 C5
Prestonpans 286 A2
Preston-under-Scar 251 F3
Prestwich 234 C2
Prestwick
Northumb. 271 D4
Prestwick *S.Ayr.* 274 B3
Prestwick International
Airport (Glasgow
Prestwick
International
Airport) 274 D3
Prestwold 223 G5
Prestwood *Bucks.* 185 D2
Prestwood *Staffs.* 222 C3
Price Town 179 F3
Prickwillow 213 D4
Priddy 166 C2
Priest Hill 242 C4
Priest Hutton 249 G5
Priest Weston 206 B3
Priestcliffe 235 F5
Priestland 275 D2
Priestwood 173 F2
Primethorpe 210 A3
Primrose Green 228 B4
Primrose Hill 186 B4
Princes End 208 B3
Princes Gate 177 E1
Princes Risborough 184 D2
Princethorpe 209 G5
Princetown *Caerp.* 180 A1
Princetown *Devon* 149 F3
Prinknash Abbey & Park 34
Prior Muir 294 D3
Prior Park 34
Prior's Frome 195 E4
Priors Halton 207 D5
Priors Hardwick 197 G2
Priors Marston 197 G2
Prior's Norton 196 A5
Priors Park 196 A4
Priorslee 207 G1
Priorwood 128
Priory Wood 194 B3
Priston 167 D1
Priston Green 214 C3
Prittlewell 188 B4
Privett 170 B5
Prixford 163 F2
Proaig 280 C4
Probus 146 C5
Protstonhill 324 D3
Prudhoe 261 G1
Prussia Cove 144 C4
Pubil 299 G5
Publow 166 D1
Puckeridge 200 B5
Puckington 153 G1
Pucklechurch 181 F5
Pucknall 169 E5
Puckrup 196 A4
Puddinglake 221 E1
Puddington *Ches.* 233 E5
Puddington *Devon* 152 B1
Puddlebrook 181 F1
Puddledock 214 B2
Puddletown 155 D3
Pudleston 195 E2
Pudsey 244 B4
Pugneys Country Park 90
Pulborough 158 C2
Pulborough Brooks R.S.P.B. Nature Reserve 49
Puldagon 337 F4
Puleston 221 E5
Pulford 220 A2
Pulham 154 D2
Pulham Market 214 C3
Pulham St. Mary 214 D3
Pulley 207 D2
Pulloxhill 199 F4
Pulrossie 321 G1
Pulverbatch 206 D2
Pumpherston 285 E3
Pumsaint 192 C3
Puncheston 190 D5
Puncknowle 154 B4
Punnett's Town 160 B1
Purbrook 157 F2
Purewell 156 A3
Purfleet 187 E5
Puriton 166 A3
Purleigh 188 B2
Purley 172 C2
Purley on Thames 184 B5
Purlogue 206 B5
Purlpit 167 F1
Purls Bridge 212 C4
Purse Caundle 154 C1
Purslow 206 C4
Purston Jaglin 236 B1
Purtington 153 G2
Purton *Glos.* 181 F2
Purton *Glos.* 181 F2
Purton *Wilts.* 182 C4
Purton Stoke 182 C3
Purves Hall 287 E5
Pury End 198 C3
Pusey 183 F3
Putlake Adventure Farm 34
Putley 195 F4
Putley Green 195 F4
Putney 186 B5
Putsborough 163 E1
Puttenham *Herts.* 185 D1
Puttenham *Surr.* 171 E3
Puttock End 201 G3
Putts Corner 153 E3
Puxton 166 B1
Pwll 178 A2
Pwllcrochan 176 C2
Pwlldefaid 216 A5
Pwll-glas 219 E2
Pwllgloyw 193 G4
Pwllheli 216 C4
Pwll-Mawr 180 B5
Pwllmeyric 181 E3
Pwll-trap 177 F1
Pwll-y-glaw 179 D3
Pye Corner *Herts.* 187 D1
Pye Corner *Kent* 174 A4
Pye Corner
Newport 180 C4
Pye Green 208 B1
Pyecombe 159 E2
Pyle *Bridgend* 179 E4
Pyle *I.o.W.* 157 D5
Pyleigh 165 E4
Pylle 166 D4
Pymore *Cambs.* 212 C4
Pymore *Dorset* 154 A3
Pyrford 171 F2
Pyrford Green 171 F2
Pyrton 184 B3
Pytchley 211 D5
Pyworthy 162 D5

Q

Quabbs 206 B4
Quadring 226 A4
Quadring Eaudike 226 A4
Quainton 198 C5
Quarff 342 D4
Quarley 169 D3
Quarndon 223 E3
Quarr Hill 157 E3
Quarrier's Village 283 E3
Quarrington 225 F3
Quarrington Hill 262 C4
Quarry Bank 208 B4
Quarry Bank Mill & Styal Estate 98
Quarrybank 220 C1
Quarrywood 323 D3
Quarter 284 B4
Quarter, The 174 A4
Quatford 207 G3
Quatt 207 G4
Quebec 262 A3
Quebec House 49
Quedgeley 182 A1
Queen Adelaide 213 D4
Queen Camel 166 C5
Queen Charlton 166 D1
Queen Dart 152 B1
Queen Elizabeth II Country Park 105
Queen Oak 167 E4
Queen Street 173 F4
Queenborough 174 B1
Queen's Bower 157 E4
Queen's Head 220 A5
Queensbury
Gt.Lon. 186 A4
Queensbury
W.Yorks. 244 A4
Queensferry
(South Queensferry)
Edin. 285 F2
Queensferry *Flints.* 220 A1
Queensferry Museum 129
Queenzieburn 284 A2
Quemerford 168 B1
Quendale 343 F4
Quendon 200 D4
Queniborough 210 B1
Quenington 182 D2
Quernmore 242 B1
Queslett 208 C3
Quethiock 148 D4
Quholm 340 A5
Quick's Green 184 A5
Quidenham 214 B3
Quidhampton 169 G2
Quidinish
(Cuidhtinis) 326 C5
Quilquox 313 E1
Quina Brook 220 C4
Quince Honey Farm 34
Quindry 338 D3
Quine's Hill 240 B4
Quinhill 281 F4
Quinton
Northants. 198 C2
Quinton *W.Mid.* 208 B4
Quinton Green 198 C2
Quintrell Downs 146 C3
Quixhill 222 C3
Quoditch 149 E1
Quoig 292 D2
Quoiggs House 292 D4
Quoisley 220 C3
Quorn 210 A1
Quothquan 276 A2
Quoyloo 340 A4
Quoys 345 F1
Quoys of Reiss 337 F3

R

Raasay 318 B5
Raby 233 E5
Raby Castle 105
Rachan 276 C2
Rachub 217 F1
Rackenford 152 B1
Rackham 158 C2
Rackheath 229 D4
Racks 267 E3
Rackwick *Ork.* 338 B3
Rackwick *Ork.* 340 C2
Radbourne 223 D4
Radcliffe *Gt.Man.* 234 B2
Radcliffe
Northumb. 271 E1
Radcliffe on Trent 224 B4
Radclive 198 B4
Radcot 183 E3
Raddington 164 D5
Radernie 294 C4
Radford
B. & N.E.Som. 167 D2
Radford *Nott.* 223 G3
Radford *Oxon.* 197 G5
Radford *W.Mid.* 209 F4
Radford Semele 197 F1
Radipole 154 C4
Radlett 186 A2
Radley 184 A3
Radley Green 187 F2
Radmore Green 220 C2
Radnage 184 C3
Radstock 167 D2
Radstone 198 A3
Radway 197 F3
Radway Green 221 E2
Radwell *Beds.* 199 F2
Radwell *Herts.* 200 A4
Radwinter 201 E4
Radyr 180 A4
Raechester 270 B3
Raemoir House 312 B5
RAF Museum 67
Raffin 330 C1
Rafford 322 C4
Ragdale 224 B5
Ragged Appleshaw 169 E3
Raglan 180 D2
Raglan Castle 113
Ragley Hall 67
Ragnall 237 F5
Rahoy 297 F4
Railway Age, The 99
Rain Shore 234 C1
Rainford 233 F2
Rainham *Gt.Lon.* 187 E4
Rainham *Med.* 174 A2
Rainhill 233 F3
Rainhill Stoops 233 G3
Rainow 235 D5
Rainsough 234 B2
Rainton 252 C5
Rainworth 223 G2
Raisbeck 250 B2
Raise 260 D3
Rait 294 A2
Raithby *Lincs.* 226 B1
Raithby *Lincs.* 238 D4
Rake 170 D5
Raleigh's Cross 164 D4
Ram 192 B3
Ram Alley 168 D1
Ram Lane 174 B4
Ramasaig 317 E5
Rame *Cornw.* 145 E3
Rame *Cornw.* 150 A3
Rampisham 154 B2
Rampside 241 F1
Rampton *Cambs.* 200 C1
Rampton *Notts.* 237 F5
Ramsbottom 234 B1
Ramsbury 183 E5
Ramscraigs 333 G2
Ramsdean 170 C5
Ramsdell 169 G2
Ramsden 183 F1
Ramsden Bellhouse 187 G3
Ramsden Heath 187 G3
Ramsey *Cambs.* 212 A4
Ramsey *Essex* 202 D4
Ramsey *I.o.M.* 240 C2
Ramsey Forty Foot 212 B4
Ramsey Heights 212 A4
Ramsey Island
Essex 188 C2
Ramsey Island
Pembs. 190 A5
Ramsey Mereside 212 A4
Ramsey St. Mary's 212 A4
Ramsgate 175 F2
Ramsgate Street 228 B2
Ramsgill 252 A5
Ramsholt 203 E3
Ramshorn 222 B3
Ramsnest Common 171 E4
Ranachan 297 G3
Ranais (Ranish) 329 F5
Ranby *Lincs.* 238 C5
Ranby *Notts.* 237 D4
Rand 238 B5
Randwick 182 A2
Rangemore 222 C5
Rangeworthy 181 F4
Ranish (Ranais) 329 F5
Rankinston 274 C4
Rank's Green 187 G1
Ranmoor 236 A4
Rannoch Moor 129
Rannoch School 300 A4
Ranochan 298 A1
Ranscombe 164 C3
Ranskill 237 D4
Ranton 221 F5
Ranton Green 221 F5
Ranworth 229 E4
Rapness 340 D2
Rapps 153 G1
Rascarrel 258 A2
Rash 250 B4
Rashwood 196 B1
Raskelf 253 D5
Rassau 180 A1
Rastrick 244 A5
Ratagan 307 F3
Ratby 210 A2
Ratcliffe Culey 209 F3
Ratcliffe on Soar 223 F5
Ratcliffe on the
Wreake 210 B1
Ratford Bridge 176 B1
Ratfyn 168 C3
Rathen 325 E3
Rathillet 294 B2
Rathliesbeag 299 E1
Rathmell 243 E1
Ratho 285 F2
Ratho Station 285 F2
Rathven 323 G3
Ratley 197 F3
Ratling 175 E3
Ratlinghope 206 D3
Ratsloe 152 C3
Rattar 337 E1
Ratten Row *Cumb.* 259 G2
Ratten Row *Lancs.* 242 A3
Rattery 150 D1
Rattlesden 202 A2
Rattray 301 G5
Raughton Head 259 G2
Raunds 211 E5
Ravenfield 236 B3
Ravenglass 248 B3
Ravenglass & Eskdale Railway 99
Raveningham 215 E2
Raven's Green 202 C5
Ravenscar 254 C2
Ravensdale 240 B2
Ravensden 199 F2
Ravenshaw 243 F3
Ravenshayes 152 C2
Ravenshead 223 G2
Ravensmoor 220 D2
Ravensthorpe
Northants. 210 B5
Ravensthorpe
W.Yorks. 244 B5
Ravenstone *Leics.* 209 G1
Ravenstone *M.K.* 199 D2
Ravenstonedale 250 C2
Ravenstruther 284 D5
Ravensworth 252 A2
Raw 254 C2
Rawcliffe *E.Riding* 245 F5
Rawcliffe *York* 245 E2
Rawcliffe Bridge 245 F5
Rawdon 244 B4
Rawmarsh 236 B3
Rawnsley 208 C1
Rawreth 187 G3
Rawridge 153 F2
Rawson Green 223 E3
Rawtenstall 243 E5
Rawyards 284 B3
Raxton 313 D1
Raydon 202 B4
Raylees 270 B2
Rayleigh 188 B3
Raymond's Hill 153 G3
Rayne 201 F5
Rayners Lane 186 A4
Raynes Park 172 B2
Reach 201 D1
Read 243 D4
Reading 184 C5
Reading Green 214 C4
Reading Street 174 B5
Reagill 250 B1
Rearquhar 332 C5
Rearsby 210 B1
Rease Heath 220 D2
Reaster 337 E2
Reaveley 279 E5
Reawick 342 C3
Reay 336 B2
Reculver 175 E2
Red Ball 153 D1
Red Bull 221 F2
Red Dial 259 F2
Red Hill *Hants.* 157 G1
Red Hill *Warks.* 196 D2
Red Lodge *Bristol* 34
Red Lodge *Suff.* 213 E5
Red Lumb 234 C1
Red Oaks Hill 201 D4
Red Point 318 D3
Red Post *Cornw.* 162 C5
Red Post *Devon* 151 E1
Red Rail 195 E5
Red Rock 233 G2
Red Roses 177 F1
Red Row 271 E2
Red Street 221 F2
Red Wharf Bay
(Traeth Coch) 230 D4
Redberth 177 D2
Redbourn 186 A1
Redbourne 237 G3
Redbrook *Glos.* 181 E1
Redbrook *Wrex.* 220 C3
Redbrook Street 174 B5
Redburn *High.* 321 E3
Redburn *High.* 322 B5
Redburn
Northumb. 261 D1
Redcar 263 F5
Redcastle *Angus* 303 E4
Redcastle *High.* 321 E5
Redcliff Bay 180 D5
Redcloak 303 G1
Reddingmuirhead 284 D2
Reddings, The 196 B5
Reddish 234 C3
Redditch 196 C1
Rede 201 G2
Redenhall 215 D3
Redesmouth 270 A3
Redford *Aber.* 303 F2
Redford *Angus* 303 D5
Redford *Dur.* 261 G4
Redford *W.Suss.* 171 D5
Redgrave 214 B4
Redheugh 302 C3
Redhill *Aber.* 312 B1
Redhill *Aber.* 312 C4
Redhill *Moray* 324 A5
Redhill *N.Som.* 166 B1
Redhill *Notts.* 223 G3
Redhill *Surr.* 172 B3
Redhill Aerodrome
& Heliport 172 B4
Redhouse *Aber.* 312 A2
Redhouse
Arg. & B. 281 G3
Redhouses 280 B3
Redisham 215 F3
Redland *Bristol* 181 E5
Redland *Ork.* 340 B4
Redlingfield 214 C4
Redlynch *Som.* 167 E4
Redlynch *Wilts.* 168 D5
Redmarley D'Abitot 195 G4
Redmarshall 262 C5
Redmile 224 C4
Redmire 251 F3
Redmoor 147 E3
Rednal 220 A5
Redpath 277 G2
Redruth 146 A5
Redscarhead 285 G5
Redshaw 275 G3
Redstone Bank 177 E1
Redwick *Newport* 180 D4
Redwick *S.Glos.* 181 E4
Redworth 262 B5
Reed 200 B4
Reed End 200 B4
Reedham 229 F5
Reedley 243 E4
Reedness 245 G5
Reef (Riof) 328 C4
Reepham *Lincs.* 238 A5
Reepham *Norf.* 228 B3
Reeth 251 F3
Regaby 240 C2
Regil 166 C1
Regoul 322 A4
Reiff 330 B3
Reigate 172 B3
Reighton 255 E5
Reinigeadal
(Rhenigidale) 327 E3
Reisgill 337 E5
Reiss 337 F3
Rejerrah 146 B4
Releath 145 D3
Relubbus 144 C3
Relugas 322 B5
Remenham 184 C4
Remenham Hill 184 C4
Remony 300 C5
Rempstone 223 G5
Rendcomb 182 C1
Rendham 203 E1
Rendlesham 203 E2
Renfrew 283 G3
Renhold 199 F2
Renishaw 236 B5
Renishaw Hall & Gardens 74
Rennington 279 G5
Renton 283 E2
Renwick 260 B3
Repps 229 F4
Repton 223 E5
Rescobie 302 D4
Rescorla 147 E4
Resipole 297 G3
Resolis 321 F3
Resolven 179 E2
Resourie 298 A2
Respryn 147 F3
Reston 287 F3
Restormel 147 F3
Reswallie 302 D4
Reterth 146 D3
Retew 146 D4
Retford 237 E4
Rettendon 187 G3
Rettendon Place 187 G3
Retyn 146 C4
Revesby 226 A1
Revesby Bridge 226 B1
Rew 152 A5
Rew Street 157 D3
Rewe *Devon* 152 C3
Rewe *Devon* 152 B3
Reybridge 168 A1
Reydon 215 F4
Reydon Smear 215 G4
Reymerston 228 B5
Reynalton 177 D2
Reynoldston 178 A4
Rezare 149 D3
Rhadyr 180 C2
Rhandirmwyn 193 D3
Rhaoine 332 B4
Rhayader 193 F1
Rhedyn 216 B4
Rheged-the Village in the Hill 99
Rhegreanoch 330 C3
Rheindown 321 E5
Rhelonie 332 A5
Rhemore 297 E4
Rhenigidale
(Reinigeadal) 327 E3
Rheola 179 E2
Rhes-y-cae 219 E1
Rhewl *Denb.* 219 E3
Rhewl *Denb.* 219 E1
Rhewl *Shrop.* 220 A4
Rhian 332 A3
Rhicarn 330 C2
Rhiconich 334 B3
Rhicullen 321 F2
Rhidorroch 331 D5
Rhifail 335 G4
Rhigos 179 F2
Rhilochan 332 C4
Rhinduie 321 E5
Rhireavach 330 C5
Rhiroy 320 A1
Rhiston 206 B3
Rhiw 216 B5
Rhiwargor 218 C5
Rhiwbina 180 A4
Rhiwbryfdir 217 F3
Rhiwderin 180 B4
Rhiwinder 179 G4
Rhiwlas *Gwyn.* 217 E1
Rhiwlas *Gwyn.* 218 C4
Rhiwlas *Powys* 219 F4
Rhode 165 F4
Rhodes Minnis 174 D4
Rhodesia 236 C5
Rhodiad-y-brenin 190 A5
Rhodmad 204 B5
Rhonadale 272 C2
Rhonehouse
(Kelton Hill) 266 B5
Rhoose 165 D1
Rhos *Carmar.* 191 G4
Rhos *N.P.T.* 178 D2
Rhos Common 206 B1
Rhôs Lligwy 230 C4
Rhos, The 176 D1
Rhosaman 178 D1
Rhoscolyn 230 A5
Rhoscrowther 176 C2
Rhosesmor 219 F1
Rhos-fawr 216 C4
Rhosgadfan 217 E2
Rhos-goch *I.o.A.* 230 C4
Rhosgoch *Powys* 194 A3
Rhos-hill 191 E3
Rhoshirwaun 216 A5
Rhoslan 217 D3
Rhoslefain 204 B2
Rhosllanerchrugog 219 F3
Rhosmaen 192 C5
Rhosmeirch 230 C5
Rhosneigr 230 B5
Rhosnesni 220 A2
Rhôs-on-Sea 231 G4
Rhossili 178 A4
Rhosson 190 A5
Rhostrehwfa 230 C5
Rhostryfan 217 D2
Rhostyllen 220 A3

Rhos-y-bol 230 C4
Rhos-y-brithdir 219 E5
Rhosycaerau 190 C4
Rhos-y-garth 204 C5
Rhos-y-gwaliau 218 C4
Rhos-y-llan 216 B4
Rhos-y-mawn 218 B1
Rhos-y-Meirch 194 B1
Rhu 283 D1
Rhualt 232 B5
Rhubodach 282 B2
Rhuddall Heath 220 C1
Rhuddlan 232 B5
Rhuddlan Castle & Twt Hill 113
Rhue 330 D5
Rhulen 194 A3
Rhumach 297 F1
Rhunahaorine 281 F5
Rhuthun (Ruthin) 219 E2
Rhyd *Gwyn.* 217 F3
Rhyd *Powys* 205 F2
Rhydaman (Ammanford) 178 C1
Rhydargaeau 192 A5
Rhydcymerau 192 B4
Rhyd-Ddu 217 E2
Rhydding 178 D3
Rhydgaled 218 C1
Rhydlanfair 218 B2
Rhydlewis 191 G3
Rhydlios 216 A4
Rhydlydan *Conwy* 218 B2
Rhydlydan *Powys* 205 G3
Rhydolion 216 B5
Rhydowen 192 A3
Rhyd-Rosser 192 B1
Rhydspence 194 B3
Rhydtalog 219 F2
Rhyd-uchaf 218 B4
Rhyd-wen 218 C5
Rhyd-wyn 230 B4
Rhyd-y-ceirw 219 F2
Rhyd-y-clafdy 216 C4
Rhydycroesau 219 F4
Rhydyfelin *Cere.* 204 B5
Rhydyfelin *R.C.T.* 179 G4
Rhyd-y-foel 232 A5
Rhyd-y-fro 178 D2
Rhyd-y-groes 217 E1
Rhydymain 218 B5
Rhydymwyn 219 F1
Rhyd-yr-onnen 204 C2
Rhyd-y-sarn 217 F3
Rhydywrach 177 E1
Rhyl 232 B4
Rhymney 180 A2
Rhyn 220 A4
Rhynd 293 G2
Rhynie *Aber.* 311 G2
Rhynie *High.* 322 A2
Ribbesford 207 G5
Ribchester 242 C4
Ribchester Roman Fort & Museum 99
Ribigill 335 E3
Riby 238 B2
Riccall 245 F4
Riccarton 274 C2
Richards Castle 195 D1
Richborough Castle 50
Richings Park 185 F5
Richmond *Gt.Lon.* 186 A5
Richmond *N.Yorks.* 252 A2
Richmond *S.Yorks.* 236 B4
Richmond Castle 90
Rich's Holford 165 E4
Rickarton 303 G1
Rickerscote 221 G5
Rickford 166 B2
Rickinghall 214 B4
Rickleton 262 B2
Rickling 200 C4
Rickling Green 200 D5
Rickmansworth 185 F3
Riddell 277 G3
Riddings 223 F2
Riddlecombe 163 G4
Riddlesden 243 G3
Ridge *Dorset* 155 F4
Ridge *Herts.* 186 B2
Ridge *Wilts.* 168 A4
Ridge Green 172 C4
Ridge Lane 209 E3
Ridgebourne 193 G1
Ridgeway 236 B4
Ridgeway Cross 195 G3
Ridgeway Moor 236 B4
Ridgeway 34
Ridgewell 201 F3
Ridgewood 159 G1
Ridgmont 199 E4
Riding Gate 167 E5
Riding Mill 261 G1
Ridley 173 F2
Ridleywood 220 A2
Ridlington *Norf.* 229 E2
Ridlington *Rut.* 210 D2
Ridsdale 270 B3
Riechip 301 F5
Rievaulx 253 E4
Rievaulx Abbey 90
Rift House 263 D4
Rigg *D. & G.* 268 A5
Rigg *High.* 318 B4
Riggend 284 B3
Rigifa 337 F1
Rigmaden Park 250 B4
Rigsby 239 E5
Rigside 275 G2
Riley Green 242 C5
Rileyhill 208 D1
Rilla Mill 147 G2
Rillaton 147 G2
Rillington 254 B5
Rimington 243 E3
Rimpton 166 D5
Rimswell 247 F5
Rinaston 190 C5
Ring o' Bells 233 F1
Ring of Brogar 129
Ringford 266 A5
Ringinglow 235 G4
Ringland 228 C4
Ringles Cross 159 G1
Ringmer 159 G2
Ringmore *Devon* 150 C3
Ringmore *Devon* 152 C5
Ringorm 323 E5
Ring's End 212 C2
Ringsfield 215 F3
Ringsfield Corner 215 F3
Ringshall *Herts.* 185 E1
Ringshall *Suff.* 202 B2
Ringshall Stocks 202 B2
Ringstead *Norf.* 227 F3
Ringstead *Northants.* 211 E5
Ringwood 156 A2
Ringwould 175 F4
Rinloan 311 E4
Rinmore 311 G3
Rinnigill 338 C3
Rinsey 144 C4
Riof (Reef) 328 C4
Ripe 160 A3
Ripley *Derbys.* 223 E2
Ripley *Hants.* 156 A3
Ripley *N.Yorks.* 244 B1
Ripley *Surr.* 171 F2
Ripley Castle 90
Riplingham 246 B4
Ripon 252 C5
Rippingale 225 G5
Ripple *Kent* 175 F4
Ripple *Worcs.* 196 A4
Ripponden 235 E1
Risabus 280 B5
Risbury 195 E2
Risby *E.Riding* 246 C4
Risby *Suff.* 201 F1
Risca 180 B3
Rise 247 D3
Riseden 173 G5
Risegate 226 A5
Riseholme 237 G5
Riseley *Beds.* 199 F1
Riseley *W'ham* 170 C1
Rishangles 202 C1
Rishton 242 D4
Rishworth 235 E1
Risinghurst 184 A2
Risley *Derbys.* 223 F4
Risley *Warr.* 234 A3
Risplith 244 B1
Rispond 335 D2
Rivar 169 E1
Rivenhall 188 B1
Rivenhall End 188 B1
River *Kent* 175 E4
River *W.Suss.* 171 E5
River & Rowing Museum 50
River Bank 200 D1
River Bridge 166 A3
Riverford Bridge 151 D1
Riverhead 173 E3
Riverside 180 A5
Riverton 163 G2
Riverview Park 187 F5
Rivington 234 A1
Roa Island 241 F1
Roach Bridge 242 B5
Road Green 215 D2
Road Weedon 198 B2
Roade 198 C2
Roadhead 268 D4
Roadside *High.* 337 D2
Roadside *Ork.* 341 E2
Roadside of Kinneff 303 G2
Roadwater 164 D4
Roag 317 F5
Roast Green 200 C4
Roath 180 A5
Roberton *S.Lan.* 276 A3
Roberton *Sc.Bord.* 277 F4
Robertsbridge 160 C1
Robertstown *Moray* 323 E5
Robertstown *R.C.T.* 179 G2
Roberttown 244 A5
Robeston Cross 176 B2
Robeston Wathen 177 D1
Robeston West 176 B2
Robin Hill Country Park 50
Robin Hood *Derbys.* 235 G5
Robin Hood *Lancs.* 233 G1
Robin Hood *W.Yorks.* 244 C5
Robin Hood's Bay 254 C2
Robinhood End 201 F4
Robins 170 D5
Roborough *Devon* 163 F4
Roborough *Plym.* 150 B1
Roby 233 F3
Roby Mill 233 G2
Rocester 222 C4
Roch 190 B5
Roch Bridge 190 B5
Roch Gate 190 B5
Rochallie 301 G4
Rochdale 234 C1
Roche 147 D3
Roche Chapel 35
Rochester *Med.* 173 G2
Rochester *Northumb.* 270 A2
Rochford *Essex* 188 B3
Rochford *Worcs.* 195 F1
Rock *Cornw.* 146 D2
Rock *Northumb.* 279 G5
Rock *Worcs.* 207 G5
Rock Ferry 233 E4
Rockbeare 152 D3
Rockbourne 156 A1
Rockbourne Roman Villa 50
Rockcliffe *Cumb.* 268 B5
Rockcliffe *D. & G.* 266 C5
Rockcliffe Cross 268 B5
Rockfield *Arg. & B.* 281 G4
Rockfield *High.* 322 B1
Rockfield *Mon.* 181 D1
Rockford 156 A2
Rockhampton 181 F3
Rockhead 147 E1
Rockingham 211 D3
Rockland All Saints 214 A2
Rockland St. Mary 229 E5
Rockland St. Peter 214 A2
Rockley 183 D5
Rockside 280 A3
Rockwell End 184 C4
Rockwell Green 153 E1
Rodborough 182 A2
Rodbourne 182 B4
Rodbridge Corner 201 G3
Rodd 194 C1
Roddam 279 E4
Rodden 154 C4
Rode 167 F2
Rode Heath 221 F2
Rodeheath 221 F1
Rodel (Roghadal) 326 C5
Roden 207 E1
Rodhuish 164 D4
Rodington 207 E1
Rodington Heath 207 E1
Rodley 181 G1
Rodmarton 182 B3
Rodmell 159 G3
Rodmersham 174 B2
Rodmersham Green 174 B2
Rodney Stoke 166 B2
Rodsley 222 D3
Rodway 165 F3
Roe Cross 235 D3
Roe Green 200 B4
Roecliffe 244 C1
Roehampton 186 B5
Roesound 342 C1
Roffey 171 G4
Rogart 332 C4
Rogate 170 D5
Rogerstone 180 B4
Roghadal (Rodel) 326 C5
Rogiet 181 D4
Rokemarsh 184 B3
Roker 262 D2
Rollesby 229 F4
Rolleston *Leics.* 210 C2
Rolleston *Notts.* 224 C2
Rolleston *Staffs.* 222 D5
Rollestone 168 B3
Rolston 247 E3
Rolstone 166 A1
Rolvenden 174 A5
Rolvenden Layne 174 A5
Romaldkirk 261 F5
Roman Baths & Pump Room 35
Romanby 252 C3
Romannobridge 285 F5
Romansleigh 164 A5
Romesdal 318 A4
Romford *Dorset* 155 G2
Romford *Gt.Lon.* 187 E4
Romiley 234 D3
Romney, Hythe & Dymchurch Railway 50
Romney Marsh 50
Romney Street 173 E2
Romsey 169 E5
Romsley *Shrop.* 207 G4
Romsley *Worcs.* 208 B5
Rona 318 C4
Ronachan 281 F4
Ronague 240 A4
Ronnachmore 280 B4
Rood End 208 C4
Rookery, The 221 F2
Rookhope 261 F3
Rookley 157 E4
Rookley Green 157 E4
Rooks Bridge 166 A2
Rook's Nest 165 D4
Rookwith 252 B4
Roos 247 E4
Roose 241 F1
Roosebeck 241 F1
Roosecote 241 F1
Rootham's Green 199 F2
Rootpark 285 D4
Ropley 170 B4
Ropley Dean 170 B4
Ropley Soke 170 B4
Ropsley 225 E4
Rora 325 F4
Rorandle 312 B3
Rorrington 206 C2
Rosarie 323 F5
Rose 146 B4
Rose Ash 164 A5
Rose Green *Essex* 202 A5
Rose Green *W.Suss.* 158 B4
Rose Hill 159 G2
Roseacre *Kent* 173 G3
Roseacre *Lancs.* 242 A4
Rosebank 284 C5
Rosebrough 279 F4
Rosebush 191 D5
Rosecare 148 B1
Rosecliston 146 C4
Rosedale Abbey 253 G3
Roseden 279 E4
Rosehall 331 G4
Rosehearty 325 E3
Rosehill *Aber.* 312 A5
Rosehill *Shrop.* 207 D1
Roseisle 322 D3
Roselands 160 B3
Rosemarket 176 C2
Rosemarkie 321 G4
Rosemary Lane 153 E1
Rosemoor 35
Rosemount *P. & K.* 301 G5
Rosemount *S.Ayr.* 274 B3
Rosenannon 147 D3
Rosenithon 145 F4
Rosepool 176 B1
Rosevean 147 E4
Roseville 208 B3
Rosewell 285 G3
Roseworth 262 D5
Rosgill 249 G1
Roshven 297 G2
Roskhill 317 F5
Roskorwell 145 E4
Rosley 259 G2
Roslin 285 G3
Rosliston 209 E1
Rosneath 283 D1
Ross *D. & G.* 257 G2
Ross *Northumb.* 279 F3
Ross *P. & K.* 292 C2
Ross Priory 283 F1
Rossdhu House 283 E1
Rossett 220 A2
Rossett Green 244 C2
Rosside 249 D5
Rossie Farm School 303 E4
Rossie Ochill 293 F3
Rossie Priory 294 A1
Rossington 236 D3
Rosskeen 321 F3
Rosslyn Chapel 129
Rossmore 155 G3
Ross-on-Wye 195 F5
Roster 337 E5
Rostherne 234 B4
Rosthwaite *Cumb.* 259 F5
Rosthwaite *Cumb.* 248 D4
Roston 222 C3
Rosudgeon 144 C4
Rosyth 285 F1
Rothbury 270 C1
Rotherby 210 B1
Rotherfield 173 E5
Rotherfield Greys 184 C4
Rotherfield Peppard 184 C4
Rotherham 236 B3
Rothersthorpe 198 C2
Rotherwick 170 C2
Rothes 323 E5
Rothesay 282 B3
Rothiebrisbane 312 C1
Rothienorman 312 C1
Rothiesholm 341 E4
Rothley *Leics.* 210 A1
Rothley *Northumb.* 270 C3
Rothney 312 B2
Rothwell *Lincs.* 238 B3
Rothwell *Northants.* 210 D4
Rothwell *W.Yorks.* 244 C5
Rotsea 246 C2
Rottal 302 B3
Rotten Row *Bucks.* 184 C4
Rotten Row *W.Mid.* 209 D5
Rottingdean 159 F3
Rottington 258 C5
Roud 157 E4
Roudham 214 A3
Rough Close 221 G4
Rough Common 174 D3
Rougham *Norf.* 227 G5
Rougham *Suff.* 202 A1
Rougham Green 202 A1
Roughburn 299 F1
Roughlee 243 E3
Roughley 208 D3
Roughton *Lincs.* 226 A1
Roughton *Norf.* 228 D2
Roughton *Shrop.* 207 G3
Round Bush 186 A3
Roundbush Green 187 E1
Roundham 154 A2
Roundhay 244 C4
Roundstreet Common 171 F5
Roundway 168 B1
Rous Lench 196 C2
Rousay 340 B3
Rousdon 153 F3
Rousham 197 G5
Rousham Gap 197 G5
Rousham House 50
Routenburn 282 C3
Routh 246 C3
Rout's Green 184 C3
Row *Cornw.* 147 E2
Row *Cumb.* 249 F4
Row *Cumb.* 260 C4
Row Heath 189 E1
Row Town 171 F1
Rowanburn 268 C4
Rowardennan Lodge 291 F5
Rowarth 235 E4
Rowbarton 165 F5
Rowberrow 166 B2
Rowchoish 291 F4
Rowde 168 A1
Rowden 149 G1
Rowe, The 221 F4
Rowen 231 F5
Rowfields 222 C3
Rowfoot 260 C1
Rowhedge 202 B5
Rowhook 171 G4
Rowington 197 E1
Rowland 235 G5
Rowland's Castle 157 G1
Rowlands Gill 262 A2
Rowledge 170 D3
Rowlestone 194 C5
Rowley *Devon* 152 A1
Rowley *Dur.* 261 G3
Rowley *Shrop.* 206 C2
Rowley Park 221 G5
Rowley Regis 208 B4
Rowly 171 F3
Rowner 157 E2
Rowney Green 208 C5
Rownhams 156 C1
Rowrah 259 D5
Rowsham 185 D1
Rowsley 223 D1
Rowstock 183 G4
Rowston 225 F2
Rowthorne 223 F1
Rowton *Ches.* 220 B1
Rowton *Shrop.* 206 C1
Rowton *Tel. & W.* 207 F1
Roxburgh 278 B3
Roxby *N.Lincs.* 237 G1
Roxby *N.Yorks.* 253 G1
Roxton 199 G2
Roxwell 187 F2
Royal Academy of Arts 59
Royal Air Force Museum 59
Royal Armouries Museum 90
Royal Botanic Garden 129
Royal Botanic Gardens, Kew 59
Royal British Legion Village 173 G3
Royal Leamington Spa 197 F1
Royal Mews, Buckingham Palace 59
Royal Museum of Scotland 129
Royal Navy Submarine Museum 50
Royal Oak 233 F2
Royal Pavilion 50
Royal Scots Regimental Museum, The 129
Royal Tunbridge Wells 173 E5
Royal Victoria Country Park 50
Roybridge 299 E1
Roydon *Essex* 186 D1
Roydon *Norf.* 214 B3
Roydon *Norf.* 227 F5
Roydon Hamlet 186 D2
Royston *Herts.* 200 B3
Royston *S.Yorks.* 236 A1
Royton 234 D2
Rozel 150 D5
R.R.S Discovery (see Discovery Point) 120
Ruabon 220 A3
Ruaig 296 B2
Ruan Lanihorne 146 C5
Ruan Major 145 D5
Ruan Minor 145 E5
Ruanaich 288 B2
Ruardean 181 F1
Ruardean Hill 181 F1
Ruardean Woodside 181 F1
Rubery 208 B5
Ruckcroft 260 B3
Ruckinge 174 C5
Ruckland 238 D5
Rucklers Lane 185 F2
Ruckley 207 E2
Rudbaxton 190 C5
Rudby 253 D2
Rudchester 262 A1
Ruddington 223 G4
Ruddlemoor 147 E4
Rudford 195 G5
Rudge 167 F2
Rudgeway 181 F4
Rudgwick 171 F4
Rudhall 195 F5
Rudheath 234 A5
Rudley Green 188 B2
Rudloe 167 F1
Rudry 180 A4
Rudston 246 C1
Rudyard 221 G2
Rufford 233 F1
Rufforth 245 E2
Ruffside 261 F2
Rugby 210 A5
Rugeley 208 C1
Ruilick 321 E5
Ruishton 165 F5
Ruisigearraidh 326 B5
Ruislip 185 F4
Ruislip Gardens 185 F4
Ruislip Manor 186 A4
Rum 305 G5
Rumbling Bridge 293 F5
Rumburgh 215 E3
Rumford 146 C3
Rumleigh 150 A1
Rumney 180 B5
Rumwell 165 E5
Runacraig 292 A3
Runcorn 233 G4
Runcton 158 A3
Runcton Holme 213 E2
Rundlestone 149 F3
Runfold 171 D3
Runhall 228 B5
Runham *Norf.* 229 F4
Runham *Norf.* 229 G5
Runnington 165 E5
Runsell Green 187 G2
Runshaw Moor 233 G1
Runswick Bay 254 B1
Runtaleave 302 A3
Runwell 187 G3
Ruscombe *Glos.* 182 A2
Ruscombe *W'ham* 184 C5
Rush Green *Gt.Lon.* 187 E4
Rush Green *Herts.* 200 A5
Rushall *Here.* 195 F4
Rushall *Norf.* 214 C3
Rushall *W.Mid.* 208 C2
Rushall *Wilts.* 168 C2
Rushbrooke 201 G1
Rushbury 207 E3
Rushden *Herts.* 200 B4
Rushden *Northants.* 199 E1
Rushford *Devon* 149 E3
Rushford *Norf.* 214 A3
Rushgreen 234 A4
Rushlake Green 160 B2
Rushmere 215 F3
Rushmere St. Andrew 202 D3
Rushmoor 171 D3
Rushock 208 A5
Rusholme 234 C3
Rushton *Ches.* 220 C1
Rushton *Northants.* 210 D4
Rushton *Shrop.* 207 F2
Rushton Spencer 221 G1
Rushwick 196 A2
Rushy Green 159 G2
Rushyford 262 B5
Ruskie 292 B4
Ruskington 225 F2
Rusko 265 G5
Rusland 249 E4
Rusper 172 B5
Ruspidge 181 F1
Russ Hill 172 B4
Russel 319 E5
Russell Green 187 G1
Russell-Cotes Art Gallery & Museum 35
Russell's Green 160 C2
Russell's Water 184 C3
Russel's Green 215 D4
Rusthall 173 E5
Rustington 158 C3
Ruston 254 C4
Ruston Parva 246 C1
Ruswarp 254 B2
Rutherend 284 A4
Rutherford 278 A3
Rutherglen 284 A3
Ruthernbridge 147 E3
Ruthers of Howe 337 F2
Ruthin *Denb.* 219 E2
Ruthin *V. of Glam.* 179 F5
Ruthrieston 313 E4
Ruthven *Aber.* 324 A5
Ruthven *Angus* 302 A5
Ruthven *High.* 310 A1
Ruthven *High.* 309 G5
Ruthvoes 146 D3
Ruthwaite 259 F3
Ruthwell 267 E4
Rutland County Museum 74
Ruyton-XI-Towns 220 A5
Ryal 270 C4
Ryal Fold 242 C5
Ryall *Dorset* 154 A3
Ryall *Worcs.* 196 A3
Ryarsh 173 F3
Rycote Chapel 50
Rydal 249 E2
Rydal Mount 99
Ryde 157 E3
Rydon 162 D5
Rye 161 E1
Rye Foreign 161 D1
Rye Harbour 161 E2
Rye Park 186 C2
Rye Street 195 G4
Ryebank 220 C4
Ryeford 195 F5
Ryehill *Aber.* 312 B2
Ryehill *E.Riding* 247 E5
Ryhall 211 F1
Ryhill 236 A1
Ryhope 262 D2
Rylands 223 G4
Rylstone 243 F2
Ryme Intrinseca 154 B1
Ryther 245 E4
Ryton *Glos.* 195 G4
Ryton *N.Yorks.* 253 G5
Ryton *Shrop.* 207 G2
Ryton *T. & W.* 262 A1
Ryton Organic Gardens 67
Ryton-on-Dunsmore 209 F5

S

Saasaig 306 C4
Sabden 243 D4
Sabden Fold 243 E4
Sackers Green 202 A4
Sacombe 186 C1
Sacombe Green 186 C1
Sacriston 262 B3
Sadberge 252 C1
Saddell 272 C2
Saddington 210 B3
Saddle Bow 213 E1
Sadgill 249 F2
Saffron Walden 200 D4
Sageston 177 D2
Saham Hills 228 A5
Saham Toney 213 G2
Saighdinis 315 G3
Saighton 220 B1
St. Abbs 287 G3
St. Abb's Head 129
St. Agnes 146 B4
St. Albans 186 A2
St. Albans Cathedral 83
St. Allen 146 C4
St. Andrews 294 D3
St. Andrews Cathedral 129
St. Andrews Major 180 A5
St. Anne 151 G4
St. Anne's 241 G5
St. Ann's 267 E1
St. Ann's Chapel *Cornw.* 149 E3
St. Ann's Chapel *Devon* 150 C3
St. Anthony 145 F3
St. Anthony-in-Meneage 145 E4
St. Anthony's Hill 160 B3
St. Arvans 181 E3
St. Asaph (Llanelwy) 232 B5
St. Athan 164 D1
St. Aubin 150 C5
St. Audries 165 E3
St. Austell 147 E4
St. Bees 258 C5
St. Blazey 147 E4
St. Blazey Gate 147 E4
St. Boswells 277 G2
St. Brelade 150 B5
St. Breock 147 D2
St. Breward 147 E2
St. Briavels 181 E2
St. Brides 176 B1
St. Bride's Church 129
St. Brides Major 179 E5
St. Bride's Netherwent 180 D4
St. Brides Wentlooge 180 B4
St. Bride's-super-Ely 179 G5
St. Budeaux 150 A2
St. Buryan 144 B4
St. Catherine 167 E1
St. Catherines 290 D4
St. Clears 177 F1
St. Cleer 147 G3
St. Clement *Chan.I.* 150 C5
St. Clement *Cornw.* 146 C5
St. Clether 147 G1
St. Colmac 282 B3
St. Columb Major 146 D3
St. Columb Minor 146 C3
St. Columb Road 146 D4
St. Combs 325 F3
St. Cross South Elmham 215 D3
St. Cyrus 303 F3
St. Davids *Fife* 285 F1
St. David's *P. & K.* 293 E2
St. David's (Tyddewi) *Pembs.* 190 A5
St. David's Cathedral & Bishop's Palace 113
St. David's Head 114
St. Day 146 B5
St. Decumans 165 D3
St. Dennis 147 D4
St. Denys 156 D1
St. Dogmaels (Llandudoch) 191 E3
St. Dogwells 190 C5
St. Dominick 150 A1
St. Donats 164 C1
St. Edith's Marsh 168 A1
St. Endellion 147 D2
St. Enoder 146 C4
St. Erme 146 C5
St. Erney 149 D5
St. Erth 144 C3
St. Erth Praze 144 C3
St. Ervan 146 C2
St. Eval 146 C3
St. Ewe 147 D5
St. Fagans 180 A5
St. Fergus 325 F4
St. Fillans 292 B2
St. Florence 177 D2
St. Gennys 148 B1
St. George *Bristol* 181 F5
St. George *Conwy* 232 A5
St. Georges *N.Som.* 166 A1
St. George's *Tel. & W.* 207 G1
St. George's *V. of Glam.* 179 G5
St. George's Guildhall 82
St. Germans 149 D5
St. Giles Cathedral 129
St. Giles in the Wood 163 F4
St. Giles on the Heath 149 D1
St. Harmon 205 F5
St. Helen Auckland 262 A5
St. Helena 228 C4
St. Helen's *E.Suss.* 160 D2
St. Helens *I.o.W.* 157 F4
St. Helens *Mersey.* 233 G3
St. Helier *Chan.I.* 150 C5
St. Helier *Gt.Lon.* 172 B2
St. Hilary *Cornw.* 144 C3
St. Hilary *V. of Glam.* 179 G5
St. Hill 172 C5
St. Ibbs 199 G5
St. Illtyd 180 B2
St. Ippollitts 199 G5
St. Ishmael 177 G2
St. Ishmael's 176 B2
St. Issey 146 D2
St. Ive 148 D4
St. Ives *Cambs.* 212 B5
St. Ives *Cornw.* 144 C2
St. Ives *Dorset* 156 A2
St. James South Elmham 215 E3
St. John *Chan.I.* 150 C4
St. John *Cornw.* 150 A2
St. John's *Gt.Lon.* 186 C5
St. John's *I.o.M.* 240 A3
St. John's *Surr.* 171 E2
St. John's *Worcs.* 196 A2
St. John's Chapel *Devon* 163 F3
St. John's Chapel *Dur.* 261 E4
St. John's Fen End 212 D1
St. John's Hall 261 G4
St. John's Highway 212 D1
St. John's Kirk 276 A2
St. John's Town of Dalry 266 A2

St. Judes 240 B2
St. Just 144 A3
St. Just in Roseland
Cornw. 145 F3
St. Just in Roseland
Cornw. **35**
St. Katherines 312 C1
St. Keverne 145 E4
St. Kew 147 E2
St. Kew Highway 147 E2
St. Keyne 147 G3
St. Lawrence
Cornw. 147 E3
St. Lawrence *Essex* 188 C2
St. Lawrence *I.o.W.* 157 E5
St. Leonards *Bucks.* 185 E2
St. Leonards
Dorset 156 A4
St. Leonards *E.Suss.* 160 D3
St. Leonards
Grange 156 D3
St. Leonard's Street 173 F3
St. Levan 144 A4
St. Lythans 180 A5
St. Mabyn 147 E2
St. Madoes 293 G2
St. Magnus
Cathedral **129**
St. Margaret
South Elmham 215 E3
St. Margarets *Here.* 194 C4
St. Margarets
Herts. 186 C1
St. Margarets
Wilts. 168 D1
St. Margaret's
at Cliffe 175 F4
St. Margaret's Hope 338 D3
St. Mark's 240 A4
St. Martin *Chan.I.* 151 F5
St. Martin *Chan.I.* 150 C5
St. Martin *Cornw.* 147 G4
St. Martin *Cornw.* 145 E4
St. Martin-in-the-Fields
Church **59**
St. Martin's *I.o.S.* 146 B1
St. Martins *P. & K.* 293 G1
St. Martin's *Shrop.* 220 A4
St. Mary 150 C5
St. Mary Bourne 169 F2
St. Mary Church 179 G5
St. Mary Cray 173 D2
St. Mary Hill 179 F5
St. Mary Hoo 187 G5
St. Mary in the
Marsh 161 F1
St. Marychurch 151 F1
St. Mary's *I.o.S.* 146 B1
St. Mary's *Ork.* 339 D2
St. Mary's Airport 146 B1
St. Mary's Bay 161 F1
St. Mary's Croft 264 B4
St. Mary's Grove 166 B1
St. Mary's House **50**
St. Maughans
Green 181 D1
St. Mawes 145 F3
St. Mawes Castle **35**
St. Mawgan 146 C3
St. Mellion 149 D4
St. Mellons 180 B4
St. Merryn 146 C2
St. Mewan 147 D4
St. Michael
Caerhays 147 D5
St. Michael Church 166 A4
St. Michael Penkevil 146 C5
St. Michael South
Elmham 215 E3
St. Michaels *Fife* 294 C2
St. Michaels *Kent* 174 A5
St. Michaels *Worcs.* 195 E1
St. Michael's
Mount **35**
St. Michael's
on Wyre 242 A3
St. Minver 147 D2
St. Monans 294 D4
St. Neot 147 F3
St. Neots 199 G1
St. Nicholas *Pembs.* 190 C4
St. Nicholas
V. of Glam. 179 G5
St. Nicholas
at Wade 175 E2
St. Ninians 292 C5
St. Osyth 189 E1
St. Ouen 150 B5
St. Owen's Cross 195 E5
St. Paul's Cathedral **59**
St. Paul's Cray 173 D2
St. Paul's Walden 199 G5
St. Peter 150 C5
St. Peter Port 151 F5
St. Peter's 175 F2
St. Petrox 176 C3
St. Pinnock 147 G3
St. Quivox 274 B3
St. Ruan 145 E5
St. Sampson 151 F5
St. Saviour *Chan.I.* 151 E5
St. Saviour *Chan.I.* 150 C5
St. Stephen 146 D4
St. Stephens
Cornw. 150 A2
St. Stephens
Cornw. 148 D2
St. Stephens *Herts.* 186 A2
St. Teath 147 E1
St. Thomas 152 C3
St. Tudy 147 E2
St. Twynnells 176 C3
St. Veep 147 F4
St. Vigeans 303 E5
St. Wenn 147 D3
St. Weonards 195 D5
St. Winnow 147 F4
St. y Nyll 179 G5
Saintbury 196 D4
Salachail 298 C4
Salcombe 150 D4
Salcombe Regis 153 E4
Salcott 188 C1
Sale 234 B3
Sale Green 196 B2
Sale, The 209 D1
Saleby 239 E5
Salehurst 160 C1
Salem *Carmar.* 192 C5
Salem *Cere.* 204 C4
Salem *Gwyn.* 217 E2
Salen *Arg. & B.* 297 E5
Salen *High.* 297 F3
Salendine Nook 235 F1
Salesbury 242 C4
Saleway 196 B2
Salford *Beds.* 199 E4
Salford *Gt.Man.* 234 C3
Salford *Oxon.* 197 E5
Salford Museum &
Art Gallery **99**
Salford Priors 196 C2
Salfords 172 B4
Salhouse 229 E4
Saline 293 F5
Salisbury 168 C5
Salisbury Cathedral **35**
Salkeld Dykes 260 B4
Sallachan 298 B3
Sallachry 290 C3
Sallachy *High.* 332 A4
Sallachy *High.* 307 F1
Salle 228 C3
Salmonby 238 D5
Salmond's Muir 295 D1
Salperton 196 C5
Salph End 199 F2
Salsburgh 284 C3
Salt 221 G5
Salt Hill 185 E4
Salt Holme 263 D5
Salt Museum **99**
Saltaire 244 A4
Saltash 150 A2
Saltburn 321 G2
Saltburn-by-the-Sea 263 F5
Saltby 225 D5
Saltcoats *Cumb.* 248 B3
Saltcoats *N.Ayr.* 282 D5
Saltcotes 241 G5
Saltdean 159 F3
Salterbeck 258 C4
Salterforth 243 E3
Saltergate 254 B3
Salterhill 323 E3
Salterswall 220 D1
Saltfleet 239 E3
Saltfleetby
All Saints 239 E3
Saltfleetby
St. Clements 239 E3
Saltfleetby
St. Peter 239 E4
Saltford 167 D1
Salthaugh Grange 247 E5
Salthouse 228 B1
Saltley 208 C4
Saltmarshe 245 G5
Saltness 338 B3
Saltney 220 A1
Salton 253 G4
Saltram House **35**
Saltrens 163 E3
Saltwick 271 D4
Saltwood 175 D5
Salum 296 B2
Salvington 158 D3
Salwarpe 196 A1
Salwayash 154 A3
Sambourne 196 C1
Sambrook 221 E5
Samhla 315 F3
Samlesbury 242 C4
Sampford Arundel 153 E1
Sampford Brett 165 D3
Sampford
Courtenay 163 G5
Sampford Moor 153 E1
Sampford Peverell 152 D1
Sampford Spiney 149 F3
Samuelston 286 B2
Sanaigmore 280 A2
Sancreed 144 B4
Sancton 246 B4
Sand *Shet.* 342 C3
Sand *Som.* 166 B3
Sand Hutton 245 F2
Sandaig *Arg. & B.* 296 A2
Sandaig *High.* 306 D4
Sandaig *High.* 307 D3
Sandal Magna 236 A1
Sanday 341 F2
Sandbach 221 E1
Sandbank 282 C1
Sandbanks 155 G4
Sandend 324 A3
Sanderstead 172 C2
Sandford *Cumb.* 250 C1
Sandford *Devon* 152 B2
Sandford *Dorset* 155 F4
Sandford *I.o.W.* 157 E4
Sandford *N.Som.* 166 B2
Sandford *S.Lan.* 284 B5
Sandford *Shrop.* 220 C4
Sandford *Shrop.* 220 A5
Sandford Orcas 166 D5
Sandford St. Martin 197 G5
Sandfordhill 325 G5
Sandford-on-
Thames 184 A2
Sandgarth 340 D5
Sandgate 175 E5
Sandgreen 265 G5
Sandham Memorial
Chapel **50**
Sandhaven 325 E3
Sandhead 264 B5
Sandhills *Dorset* 154 C1
Sandhills *Dorset* 154 B2
Sandhills *Surr.* 171 E4
Sandhills *W.Yorks.* 244 C4
Sandhoe 261 F1
Sandholme
E.Riding 246 A4
Sandholme *Lincs.* 226 B4
Sandhurst *Brack.F.* 170 D1
Sandhurst *Glos.* 196 A5
Sandhurst *Kent* 160 C1
Sandhurst Cross 160 C1
Sandhutton 252 C4
Sandiacre 223 F4
Sandilands 239 F4
Sandiway 234 A5
Sandleheath 156 A1
Sandleigh 183 G2
Sandling 173 G3
Sandlow Green 221 E1
Sandness 342 A2
Sandon *Essex* 187 G2
Sandon *Herts.* 200 B4
Sandon *Staffs.* 221 G5
Sandown 157 F4
Sandplace 147 G4
Sandquoy 341 F2
Sandridge *Devon* 151 E2
Sandridge *Herts.* 186 A1
Sandridge *Wilts.* 168 A1
Sandringham 227 E5
Sandringham House **83**
Sandrocks 159 F1
Sands, The 171 D3
Sandsend 254 B1
Sandside 249 F4
Sandside House 336 B2
Sandsound 342 C3
Sandtoft 237 E2
Sanduck 152 A4
Sandway 174 A3
Sandwell 208 C4
Sandwich 175 F3
Sandwick *Cumb.* 249 F1
Sandwick *Shet.* 342 D5
Sandwick
(Sanndabhaig)
W.Isles 329 F4
Sandwith 258 C5
Sandy *Beds.* 199 G3
Sandy *Carmar.* 178 A2
Sandy Bank 226 A2
Sandy Haven 176 B2
Sandy Lane
W.Yorks. 244 A4
Sandy Lane *Wilts.* 168 A1
Sandy Lane *Wrex.* 220 B3
Sandy Way 157 D4
Sandycroft 220 A1
Sandygate *Devon* 152 B5
Sandygate *I.o.M.* 240 B2
Sandyhills 266 C5
Sandylands 242 A1
Sandypark 152 A4
Sandyway 195 D5
Sangobeg 334 D2
Sankyn's Green 195 G1
Sanna 297 D3
Sannaig 280 D3
Sanndabhaig
(Sandwick) 329 F4
Sannox 282 B5
Sanquhar 275 F5
Santon Bridge 248 C2
Santon Downham 213 G4
Sapcote 209 G3
Sapey Common 195 G1
Sapiston 214 A4
Sapperton *Derbys.* 222 C4
Sapperton *Glos.* 182 B2
Sapperton *Lincs.* 225 F4
Saracen's Head 226 B5
Sarclet 337 F4
Sardis 176 C2
Sarisbury 157 E2
Sark 151 G5
Sarn *Bridgend* 179 F4
Sarn *Powys* 206 B3
Sarn Bach 216 C5
Sarn Meyllteyrn 216 B4
Sarnau *Carmar.* 177 G1
Sarnau *Cere.* 191 G2
Sarnau *Gwyn.* 218 C4
Sarnau *Powys* 206 B1
Sarnau *Powys* 193 G4
Sarnesfield 194 C2
Saron *Carmar.* 178 C1
Saron *Carmar.* 191 G4
Saron *Gwyn.* 217 E1
Saron *Gwyn.* 217 D2
Sarratt 185 F3
Sarre 175 E2
Sarsden 197 E5
Sarsgrum 334 C2
Sartfield 240 B2
Satley 262 A3
Satron 251 E3
Satterleigh 163 G3
Satterthwaite 249 E3
Sauchen 312 B3
Saucher 293 G1
Sauchie 293 D5
Sauchieburn 303 E3
Sauchrie 274 B4
Saughall 233 E5
Saughall Massie 233 D4
Saughtree 269 D2
Saul 181 G2
Saundby 237 E4
Saundersfoot 177 E2
Saunderton 184 C2
Saunton 163 E2
Sausthorpe 226 D1
Saval 332 A1
Savalbeg 332 A4
Saverley Green 221 G4
Savile Town 244 B5
Savill Garden **50**
Sawbridge 198 A1
Sawbridgeworth 187 D1
Sawdon 254 C4
Sawley *Derbys.* 223 F4
Sawley *Lancs.* 243 D3
Sawley *N.Yorks.* 244 B1
Sawston 200 C3
Sawtry 211 G4
Saxby *Leics.* 210 D1
Saxby *Lincs.* 238 A4
Saxby All Saints 237 G1
Saxelbye 224 B5
Saxham Street 202 B1
Saxilby 237 F5
Saxlingham 228 B2
Saxlingham Green 214 D2
Saxlingham
Nethergate 214 D2
Saxlingham Thorpe 214 D2
Saxmundham 203 E1
Saxon Street 201 E2
Saxondale 224 B4
Saxtead 203 D1
Saxtead Green 203 D1
Saxtead
Little Green 203 D1
Saxthorpe 228 C2
Saxton 245 D4
Sayers Common 159 E2
Scackleton 253 F5
Scadabhagh 327 D4
Scaftworth 237 D3
Scagglethorpe 254 B5
Scaitcliffe 243 D5
Scalasaig 288 C5
Scalby *E.Riding* 246 A5
Scalby *N.Yorks.* 254 D3
Scaldwell 210 C5
Scale Houses 260 B3
Scaleby 260 A1
Scalebyhill 260 A1
Scales *Cumb.* 259 G4
Scales *Cumb.* 249 D5
Scales *Lancs.* 242 A4
Scalford 224 C5
Scaling 253 G1
Scallasaig 307 E3
Scallastle 289 G1
Scalloway 342 C4
Scalpay 327 E4
Scamblesby 238 C5
Scammadale 290 A2
Scamodale 298 A2
Scampston 254 B5
Scampton 237 G5
Scaniport 309 F1
Scapa 338 D2
Scapegoat Hill 235 E1
Scar 341 E2
Scarborough 254 D4
Scarborough Art
Gallery **90**
Scarborough Castle **90**
Scarcewater 146 D4
Scarcliffe 223 F1
Scarcroft 244 C3
Scardroy 320 B4
Scarff 344 B4
Scarfskerry 337 E1
Scargill 251 F1
Scarinish 296 B2
Scarisbrick 233 E1
Scarning 228 A4
Scarrington 224 C3
Scarrowhill 260 B3
Scarth Hill 233 F2
Scarthingwell 245 D4
Scartho 238 C2
Scarwell 340 A4
Scatraig 309 G1
Scaur *D. & G.* 266 C3
Scaur (Kippford)
D. & G. 266 C5
Scawby 237 G2
Scawby Brook 237 G2
Scawton 253 E4
Scayne's Hill 159 F1
Scealascro 328 C5
Scethrog 194 A5
Schaw 274 C3
Scholar Green 221 F2
Scholes *S.Yorks.* 236 A3
Scholes *W.Yorks.* 244 C4
Scholes *W.Yorks.* 235 F2
Scholes *W.Yorks.* 244 A5
School Green 220 D1
School House 153 G2
Schoose 258 D4
Sciberscross 332 C4
Science Museum **60**
Scilly Isles
(Isles of Scilly) 146 B1
Scissett 235 G1
Scleddau 190 C4
Sco Ruston 229 D3
Scofton 236 D4
Scole 214 C4
Scolpaig 315 F2
Scone 293 G2
Scone Palace **130**
Scones Lethendy 293 G2
Sconser 306 B1
Scoor 288 D3
Scopwick 225 F2
Scoraig 330 C5
Scorborough 246 C3
Scorrier 146 B5
Scorriton 150 D1
Scorton *Lancs.* 242 B3
Scorton *N.Yorks.* 252 B2
Scot Hay 221 F3
Scotby 260 A2
Scotch Corner 252 B2
Scotforth 242 A2
Scothern 238 A5
Scotland 225 F1
Scotland End 197 F1
Scotland Street 202 A4
Scotlandwell 293 G4
Scotney Castle
Garden **50**
Scotnish 281 F1
Scots' Gap 270 C3
Scotsburn 321 G2
Scotston *Aber.* 303 F2
Scotston *P. & K.* 301 E5
Scotstoun 283 G3
Scotstown 298 A3
Scott Willoughby 225 F4
Scotter 237 F2
Scotterthorpe 237 F2
Scottish Crannog
Centre **130**
Scottish Fisheries
Museum **130**
Scottish Maritime
Museum **130**
Scottish National
Gallery of
Modern Art **130**
Scottish National
Portrait Gallery **130**
Scottish Seabird
Centre **130**
Scottlethorpe 225 F5
Scotton *Lincs.* 237 F3
Scotton *N.Yorks.* 252 A3
Scotton *N.Yorks.* 244 C2
Scottow 229 D3
Scoughall 286 D1
Scoulton 228 A5
Scounslow Green 222 B5
Scourie 334 A4
Scourie More 334 A4
Scousburgh 343 F4
Scouthead 235 D2
Scrabster 336 D1
Scrafield 226 B1
Scrainwood 270 B1
Scrane End 226 B3
Scraptoft 210 B2
Scratby 229 G4
Scrayingham 245 G2
Scredington 225 F3
Scremby 226 C1
Scremerston 279 E2
Screveton 224 C3
Scriven 244 C2
Scronkey 242 A3
Scrooby 237 D3
Scropton 222 C4
Scrub Hill 226 A2
Scruton 252 C3
Sculthorpe 227 G4
Scunthorpe 237 F1
Scurlage 178 A4
Sea 153 G1
Sea Life Centre **50**
Sea Mills 181 E5
Sea Palling 229 F3
Seabank 298 B5
Seaborough 154 A2
Seaburn 262 D1
Seacombe 233 D3
Seacroft *Lincs.* 227 D1
Seacroft *W.Yorks.* 244 C4
Seadyke 226 B4
Seafield *Arg. & B.* 281 F1
Seafield *S.Ayr.* 274 B3
Seafield *W.Loth.* 285 E3
Seaford 159 G4
Seaforth 233 E3
Seagrave 210 B1
Seagry Heath 182 B4
Seaham 262 D3
Seaham Grange 262 D2
Seahouses 279 G3
Seal 173 E3
Sealand 220 A1
Seale 171 D3
Sealyham 190 C5
Seamer *N.Yorks.* 253 D1
Seamer *N.Yorks.* 254 D4
Seamill 282 C5
Searby 238 A2
Seasalter 174 C2
Seascale 248 B2
Seathorne 227 D1
Seathwaite *Cumb.* 259 F5
Seathwaite *Cumb.* 248 D3
Seatle 249 E4
Seatoller 259 F5
Seaton *Cornw.* 148 D5
Seaton *Cumb.* 258 D3
Seaton *Devon* 153 F3
Seaton *Dur.* 262 C2
Seaton *E.Riding* 247 D3
Seaton *Northumb.* 271 F4
Seaton *Rut.* 211 E3
Seaton Burn 271 E4
Seaton Carew 263 E5
Seaton Delaval 271 F4
Seaton Delaval
Hall **105**
Seaton Junction 153 F3
Seaton Ross 245 G3
Seaton Sluice 271 F4
Seatown *Aber.* 325 F4
Seatown *Dorset* 154 A3
Seatown *Moray* 324 A3
Seave Green 253 E2
Seaview 157 F3
Seaville 259 E1
Seavington
St. Mary 154 A1
Seavington
St. Michael 154 A1
Seawick 189 E1
Sebastopol 180 B3
Sebergham 259 G2
Seckington 209 E2
Second Coast 330 B5
Sedbergh 250 B3
Sedbury 181 E3
Sedbusk 251 D3
Seddington 199 G3
Sedgeberrow 196 C1
Sedgebrook 225 D4
Sedgefield 262 C5
Sedgeford 227 F4
Sedgehill 167 F5
Sedgemere 209 E5
Sedgley 208 B3
Sedgwick 249 G4
Sedlescombe 160 C2
Sedlescombe Street 160 C2
Seend 168 A1
Seend Cleeve 168 A1
Seer Green 185 E3
Seething 215 E2
Sefton 233 E2
Seghill 271 E4
Segontium Roman
Museum **114**
Seifton 207 D4
Seighford 221 F5
Seil 289 G3
Seilebost 326 C4
Seion 217 E1
Seisdon 208 A3
Seisiadar 329 G4
Selattyn 219 F4
Selborne 170 C4
Selby 245 F4
Selham 171 E5
Selhurst 172 C2
Selkirk 277 F3
Sellack 195 E5
Sellafield 248 B2
Sellafirth 345 E3
Sellindge 174 C5
Selling 174 C3
Sells Green 168 A1
Selly Oak 208 C4
Selmeston 160 A3
Selsdon 172 C2
Selsey 158 A4
Selsfield Common 172 C5
Selside *Cumb.* 249 G3
Selside *N.Yorks.* 250 C5
Selsley 182 A2
Selstead 175 E4
Selston 223 F2
Selworthy 164 C3
Semblister 342 C2
Semer 202 A3
Semington 167 F1
Semley 167 F5
Send 171 F2
Send Marsh 171 F2
Senghenydd 180 A3
Sennen 144 A4
Sennen Cove 144 A4
Sennybridge 193 F5
Senwick 257 G2
Sequer's Bridge 150 C2
Serlby 236 D4
Serrington 168 B4
Sessay 253 D5
Setchey 213 E1
Setley 156 C2
Seton Collegiate
Church **130**
Setter *Shet.* 343 E3
Setter *Shet.* 342 C2
Settiscarth 340 B5
Settle 243 E1
Settrington 254 B5
Seven Ash 165 E4
Seven Bridges 182 D3
Seven Kings 187 D4
Seven Sisters 179 E2
Seven Sisters
Country Park **51**
Seven Springs 182 B1
Sevenhampton
Glos. 196 C5
Sevenhampton
Swin. 183 E3
Sevenoaks 173 E3
Sevenoaks Weald 173 E3
Severn Beach 181 E4
Severn Stoke 196 A3
Severn Valley
Railway **67**
Sevick End 199 F2
Sevington 174 C4
Sewards End 201 D4
Sewardstone 186 C3
Sewerby 247 D1
Sewerby Hall
& Gardens **90**
Seworgan 145 E3
Sewstern 225 D5
Seymour Villas 163 E1
Sezincote 197 D4
Sgarasta Mhòr 326 C4
Sgiogarstaigh 329 G1
Sgodachail 331 G5
Shabbington 184 B2
Shackerley 208 A2
Shackerstone 209 F2
Shackleford 171 E3
Shadfen 271 E3
Shadforth 262 C3
Shadingfield 215 F3
Shadoxhurst 174 B5
Shadsworth 242 D5
Shadwell *Norf.* 214 A3
Shadwell
W.Yorks. 244 C3
Shaftenhoe End 200 C4
Shaftesbury 167 F5
Shafton 236 A1
Shakespeare's
Birthplace **67**
Shakespeare's Globe
Theatre **60**
Shalbourne 169 E1
Shalcombe 156 C4
Shalden 170 B3
Shalden Green 170 C3
Shaldon 152 C5
Shalfleet 156 D4
Shalford *Essex* 201 F5
Shalford *Surr.* 171 F3
Shalford Green 201 F5
Shallowford
Devon 164 A3
Shallowford *Staffs.* 221 F5
Shalmsford Street 174 C3
Shalmstry 336 D2
Shalstone 198 B4
Shalunt 282 B2
Shambellie 267 D4
Shamley Green 171 F3
Shandon 283 D1
Shandwick 322 A2
Shandy Hall **90**
Shangton 210 C3
Shankend 277 G5
Shankhouse 271 E4
Shanklin 157 E4
Shannochie 273 E3
Shantron 283 E1
Shantullich 321 F4
Shanzie 302 A4
Shap 249 G1
Shapinsay 340 D5
Shapwick *Dorset* 155 F2
Shapwick *Som.* 166 B4
Sharcott 168 C2
Shard End 209 D4
Shardlow 223 F4
Shareshill 208 B2
Sharlston 236 A1
Sharlston Common 236 A1
Sharnal Street 187 G5
Sharnbrook 199 E2
Sharneyford 243 E5
Sharnford 209 G3
Sharnhill Green 154 D2
Sharow 252 C5
Sharp Street 229 E3
Sharpenhoe 199 F4
Sharperton 270 B1
Sharpham House 151 E2
Sharpness 181 F2
Sharpthorne 172 C5
Sharrington 228 B2
Shatterford 207 G4
Shatterling 175 E3
Shaugh Prior 150 B1
Shave Cross 154 A3
Shavington 221 E2
Shaw *Gt.Man.* 234 D2
Shaw *Swin.* 182 D4
Shaw *W.Berks.* 169 F1
Shaw *Wilts.* 167 F1
Shaw Green *Herts.* 200 A4
Shaw Green
N.Yorks. 244 B2
Shaw Mills 244 B1
Shaw Side 234 D2
Shawbost (Siabost) 329 D3
Shawbury 220 C5
Shawell 210 A4
Shawfield *Gt.Man.* 234 C1
Shawfield *Staffs.* 222 B1
Shawford 169 F5
Shawforth 243 E5
Shawhead 266 C3
Shaw's Corner **83**
Shawtonhill 284 A5
Sheanachie 272 C4
Sheandow 311 E1
Shearington 267 E4
Shearsby 210 B3
Shebbear 163 E5
Shebdon 221 E5
Shebster 336 C2
Shedfield 157 E1
Sheen 222 C1
Sheepridge 235 F1
Sheepscombe 182 A1
Sheepstor 150 B1
Sheepwash *Devon* 163 E5
Sheepwash
Northumb. 271 E3
Sheepway 181 D5
Sheepy Magna 209 F2
Sheepy Parva 209 F2
Sheering 187 E1
Sheerness 174 B1
Sheet 170 C5
Sheffield 236 A4
Sheffield Bottom 170 B1
Sheffield City
Airport 236 B4
Sheffield Green 159 G1
Sheffield Park **51**
Shefford 199 G4
Shefford
Woodlands 183 F5
Sheigra 334 A2
Sheinton 207 F2
Shelderton 206 D5
Sheldon *Derbys.* 222 C1
Sheldon *Devon* 153 E2
Sheldon *W.Mid.* 208 D4
Sheldwich 174 C3
Sheldwich Lees 174 C3
Shelf *Bridgend* 179 F4
Shelf *W.Yorks.* 244 A5
Shelfanger 214 C3
Shelfield *W.Mid.* 208 C2
Shelfield *Warks.* 196 D1
Shelfield Green 196 D1
Shelford 224 B3
Shellachan
Arg. & B. 290 A2
Shellachan
Arg. & B. 290 C2
Shellbrook 209 F1
Shellbrook Hill 220 A3
Shelley *Essex* 187 E2
Shelley *Suff.* 202 B4
Shelley *W.Yorks.* 235 G1
Shellingford 183 F3
Shellow Bowells 187 F2
Shelsley Beauchamp 195 G1
Shelsley Walsh 195 G1
Shelswell 198 B4
Shelthorpe 210 A1
Shelton *Beds.* 199 F1
Shelton *Norf.* 211 D2
Shelton *Notts.* 224 C3
Shelton *Shrop.* 207 D1
Shelve 206 C3
Shelwick 195 E3
Shelwick Green 195 E3
Shenfield 187 F3
Shenington 197 F3
Shenley 186 A2
Shenley Brook End 198 D4
Shenley
Church End 198 D4
Shenleybury 186 A2
Shenmore 194 C4

She - Sou

Shennanton 265 E4
Shenstone *Staffs.* 208 D2
Shenstone *Worcs.* 208 A5
Shenstone Woodend 208 D2
Shenton 209 F2
Shenval 311 E2
Shepeau Stow 212 B1
Shephall 200 A5
Shepherd's Bush 186 B5
Shepherd's Green 184 C4
Shepherd's Patch 181 G2
Shepherdswell (Sibertswold) 175 E4
Shepley 235 F2
Sheppardstown 337 E5
Shepperdine 181 F3
Shepperton 171 F1
Shepreth 200 B3
Shepreth Wildlife Park 83
Shepshed 209 G1
Shepton Beauchamp 154 A1
Shepton Mallet 166 D3
Shepton Montague 167 D4
Shepway 173 G3
Sheraton 262 D4
Sherborne *Dorset* 154 C1
Sherborne *Glos.* 183 D1
Sherborne Castle 35
Sherborne St. John 170 B2
Sherbourne 197 E1
Sherbourne Street 202 A3
Sherburn *Dur.* 262 C3
Sherburn *N.Yorks.* 254 C5
Sherburn Hill 262 C3
Sherburn in Elmet 245 D4
Shere 171 F3
Shereford 227 G5
Sherfield English 169 D5
Sherfield on Loddon 170 B2
Sherford *Devon* 151 D3
Sherford *Som.* 165 F5
Sheriff Hutton 245 F1
Sheriffhales 207 G1
Sheringham 228 C1
Sherington 199 D3
Shernal Green 196 B1
Shernborne 227 F4
Sherramore 309 E5
Sherrington 168 A4
Sherston 182 A4
Sherwood 223 G3
Sherwood Forest Country Park 75
Sherwood Green 163 F3
Sherwood Pines Forest Park 75
Shettleston 284 A3
Shevington 233 G2
Shevington Moor 233 G1
Sheviock 149 D5
Shibden Hall 90
Shide 157 E4
Shiel Bridge 307 F3
Shieldaig *High.* 319 E4
Shieldaig *High.* 319 E2
Shieldhill 284 C2
Shielfoot 297 F2
Shielhill 302 C4
Shiels 312 B4
Shifford 183 F2
Shifnal 207 G2
Shilbottle 271 D1
Shildon 262 B5
Shillingford *Devon* 164 C5
Shillingford *Oxon.* 184 A3
Shillingford Abbot 152 C4
Shillingford St. George 152 C4
Shillingstone 155 E1
Shillington 199 G4
Shillmoor 270 A1
Shilstone 163 F5
Shilton *Oxon.* 183 E2
Shilton *Warks.* 209 G4
Shimpling *Norf.* 214 C3
Shimpling *Suff.* 201 G2
Shimpling Street 201 G2
Shincliffe 262 B3
Shiney Row 262 C2
Shinfield 170 C1
Shingay 200 B3
Shingham 213 F2
Shingle Street 203 E3
Shinness Lodge 332 A3
Shipbourne 173 E3
Shipbrookhill 234 A5
Shipdham 228 A5
Shipham 166 B2
Shiphay 151 E1
Shiplake 184 C5
Shiplake Row 184 C5
Shipley *Northumb.* 279 F5
Shipley *Shrop.* 208 A3
Shipley *W.Suss.* 171 G5
Shipley *W.Yorks.* 244 A4
Shipley Art Gallery 105
Shipley Bridge *Devon* 150 C1
Shipley Bridge *Surr.* 172 C1
Shipley Common 223 F3
Shipley Country Park 75
Shipmeadow 215 E2
Shippea Hill 213 E4
Shippon 183 G3
Shipston on Stour 197 E3
Shipton *Glos.* 182 C1
Shipton *N.Yorks.* 245 E2
Shipton *Shrop.* 207 E3
Shipton Bellinger 168 D3
Shipton Gorge 154 A3
Shipton Green 158 A3
Shipton Moyne 182 A4
Shipton Oliffe 182 C1
Shipton Solers 182 C1
Shipton-on-Cherwell 183 G1
Shiptonthorpe 246 A3
Shipton-under-Wychwood 183 E1
Shira 291 D3
Shirburn 184 B3
Shirdley Hill 233 E1
Shire Oak 208 C2
Shirebrook 223 G1
Shirecliffe 236 A3
Shiregreen 236 A3
Shirehampton 181 E5
Shiremoor 271 F4
Shirenewton 181 D3
Shireoaks 236 C4
Shirl Heath 194 D2
Shirland 223 E2
Shirley *Derbys.* 222 D3
Shirley *Gt.Lon.* 172 C2
Shirley *Hants.* 156 A3
Shirley *S'ham.* 156 D1
Shirley *W.Mid.* 208 D5
Shirley Heath 208 D5
Shirley Warren 156 C1
Shirleywich 221 G5
Shirrell Heath 157 E1
Shirwell 163 F2
Shirwell Cross 163 F2
Shiskine 273 E3
Shittlehope 261 G4
Shobdon 194 C1
Shobley 156 A2
Shobrooke 152 B2
Shocklach 220 B3
Shocklach Green 220 B3
Shoe, The 182 A5
Shoeburyness 188 C4
Sholden 175 F3
Sholing 157 D1
Shoot Hill 206 D1
Shooter's Hill 186 D5
Shop *Cornw.* 146 C2
Shop *Cornw.* 162 C4
Shop Corner 202 D4
Shopnoller 165 E4
Shore 234 D1
Shoreditch 186 C4
Shoreham 173 E2
Shoreham-by-Sea 159 E3
Shoremill 321 G3
Shoresdean 287 G5
Shoreswood 287 G5
Shoreton 321 F3
Shorley 169 G5
Shorncote 182 C3
Shorne 187 F5
Shorne Ridgeway 187 F5
Short Cross 206 B2
Short Green 214 B3
Short Heath *Derbys.* 209 F1
Short Heath *W.Mid.* 208 C3
Shortacombe 149 F2
Shortbridge 159 G1
Shortfield Common 170 D3
Shortgate 159 G2
Shortgrove 200 D4
Shorthampton 197 F5
Shortlands 172 C2
Shortlanesend 146 C5
Shorton 151 E1
Shorwell 157 D4
Shoscombe 167 E2
Shotatton 220 A5
Shotesham 214 D2
Shotgate 187 G3
Shotley *Northants.* 211 E3
Shotley *Suff.* 202 D4
Shotley Bridge 261 G2
Shotley Gate 202 D4
Shotleyfield 261 G2
Shottenden 174 C3
Shottermill 171 D4
Shottery 197 D2
Shotteswell 197 G3
Shottisham 203 E3
Shottle 223 E3
Shottlegate 223 E3
Shotton *Dur.* 262 D4
Shotton *Dur.* 262 C5
Shotton *Flints.* 220 A1
Shotton *Northumb.* 271 E4
Shotton Colliery 262 C3
Shotts 284 C3
Shotwick 233 E5
Shouldham 213 E2
Shouldham Thorpe 213 E2
Shoulton 196 A2
Shover's Green 173 F5
Shrawardine 206 C1
Shrawley 196 A1
Shreding Green 185 F4
Shrewley 197 E1
Shrewsbury 207 D1
Shrewton 168 B3
Shrine of Our Lady of Walsingham 83
Shripney 158 B3
Shrivenham 183 E4
Shropham 214 A2
Shroton (Iwerne Courtney) 155 E1
Shrub End 202 A5
Shucknall 195 E3
Shudy Camps 201 E3
Shugborough Estate 67
Shurdington 182 B1
Shurlock Row 184 D5
Shurnock 196 C1
Shurrery 336 C3
Shurrery Lodge 336 C3
Shurton 165 F3
Shustoke 209 E3
Shut Heath 221 F5
Shute *Devon* 153 F3
Shute *Devon* 152 B2
Shutford 197 F3
Shuthonger 196 A4
Shutlanger 198 C3
Shutt Green 208 A2
Shuttington 209 E2
Shuttlewood 236 B5
Shuttleworth 234 B1
Siabost (Shawbost) 329 D3
Siabost Bho Dheas 329 D3
Siabost Bho Thuath 329 D3
Siadar Iarach 329 E2
Siadar Uarach 329 E2
Sibbaldbie 267 F2
Sibbertoft 210 B4
Sibdon Carwood 206 D4
Sibertswold (Shepherdswell) 175 E4
Sibford Ferris 197 F4
Sibford Gower 197 F4
Sible Hedingham 201 F4
Sibley's Green 201 E5
Sibsey 226 B2
Sibson *Cambs.* 211 F3
Sibson *Leics.* 209 F2
Sibster 337 F3
Sibthorpe 224 C3
Sibton 203 E1
Sibton Green 215 E4
Sicklesmere 201 G1
Sicklinghall 244 C3
Sidbury *Devon* 153 E3
Sidbury *Shrop.* 207 F4
Sidcot 166 B2
Sidcup 187 D5
Siddal 244 A5
Siddington *Ches.* 234 C5
Siddington *Glos.* 182 C3
Sidemoor 208 B5
Sidestrand 229 D2
Sidford 153 E3
Sidlesham 158 A4
Sidley 160 C3
Sidlow 172 B4
Sidmouth 153 E4
Sigford 152 A5
Sigglesthorne 247 D3
Sigingstone 179 F5
Signet 183 E1
Silbury Hill 36
Silchester 170 B1
Sildinis 327 E2
Sileby 210 B1
Silecroft 248 C4
Silfield 214 C2
Silian 192 B2
Silk Museum & Paradise Mill 99
Silk Willoughby 225 F3
Silkstead 169 F5
Silkstone 235 G2
Silkstone Common 235 G2
Sill Field 249 G4
Silloth 259 E1
Sills 270 A1
Sillyearn 324 A4
Silpho 254 C3
Silsden 243 G3
Silsoe 199 F4
Silver End *Beds.* 199 G3
Silver End *Essex* 201 G5
Silver Green 215 D2
Silver Street *Kent* 174 A2
Silver Street *Som.* 166 C4
Silverburn 285 G3
Silvercraigs 281 G1
Silverdale *Lancs.* 249 F5
Silverdale *Staffs.* 221 F3
Silvergate 228 C3
Silverhill 160 C2
Silverlace Green 203 E2
Silverley's Green 215 D4
Silvermoss 312 D1
Silverstone 198 B3
Silverton 152 C2
Silvington 207 F5
Silwick 342 B3
Simister 234 C2
Simmondley 235 E3
Simonburn 270 A4
Simonsbath 164 A4
Simonside 262 C1
Simonstone *Bridgend* 179 F4
Simonstone *Lancs.* 243 D4
Simprim 287 F5
Simpson 199 D4
Sinclair's Hill 287 F4
Sinclairston 274 C4
Sinderby 252 C4
Sinderhope 261 E2
Sindlesham 170 C1
Sinfin 223 E4
Singdean 277 G5
Singleton *Lancs.* 241 G4
Singleton *W.Suss.* 158 A2
Singlewell (Ifield) 187 F5
Singret 220 A2
Sinkhurst Green 174 A4
Sinnahard 311 G3
Sinnington 253 G4
Sinton Green 196 A1
Siop y Fron (Upper Llandwrog) 217 E2
Sipson 185 F5
Sir Alfred Munnings Art Museum (see **Castle House**) 70
Sir Harold Hillier Gardens & Arboretum 51
Sirhowy 180 A1
Sisland 215 E2
Sissinghurst 173 G5
Sissinghurst Castle 51
Siston 181 F5
Sithney 144 D4
Sittingbourne 174 B2
Siulaisiadar 329 G4
Six Ashes 207 G4
Six Hills 224 B5
Six Mile Bottom 201 D2
Six Roads End 222 C5
Sixhills 238 B4
Sixmile 174 D4
Sixpenny Handley 155 G1
Sizergh Castle & Gardens 99
Sizewell 203 F1
Skail 335 G4
Skaill *Ork.* 340 A5
Skaill *Ork.* 339 E2
Skaill *Ork.* 340 C3
Skara Brae 130
Skares *Aber.* 312 B1
Skares *E.Ayr.* 274 D4
Skarpigarth 342 A2
Skateraw 287 E2
Skaw 343 E1
Skeabost 318 A5
Skeabrae 340 A4
Skeeby 252 B2
Skeffington 210 C2
Skeffling 239 D1
Skegby 223 G1
Skegness 227 D1
Skelberry *Shet.* 343 G4
Skelberry *Shet.* 343 D1
Skelbo 332 C5
Skelbo Street 332 C5
Skelbrooke 236 C1
Skeld (Easter Skeld) 342 C3
Skeldon 274 B4
Skeldyke 226 B4
Skellingthorpe 237 G5
Skellister 343 D2
Skellow 236 C1
Skelmanthorpe 235 G1
Skelmersdale 233 F2
Skelmonae 313 D1
Skelmorlie 282 C3
Skelmuir 325 E5
Skelpick 335 G3
Skelton *Cumb.* 260 A4
Skelton *E.Riding* 245 G5
Skelton *N.Yorks.* 251 F2
Skelton *R. & C.* 253 F1
Skelton *York* 245 E2
Skelton-on-Ure 244 C1
Skelwick 340 C2
Skelwith Bridge 249 E2
Skendleby 226 C1
Skendleby Psalter 239 E5
Skenfrith 195 D5
Skerne 246 C2
Skeroblingarry 272 C3
Skerray 335 F2
Skerton 242 A1
Sketchley 209 G3
Sketty 178 C3
Skewen 178 D3
Skewsby 253 F5
Skeyton 228 D3
Skeyton Corner 229 D3
Skidbrooke 239 E3
Skidbrooke North End 239 E3
Skidby 246 C4
Skilgate 164 C5
Skillington 225 D5
Skinburness 259 E1
Skinflats 284 D1
Skinidin 317 F5
Skinnet 336 D2
Skinningrove 253 G1
Skipness 281 G4
Skippool 241 G3
Skipsea 247 D2
Skipsea Brough 247 D2
Skipton 243 F2
Skipton Castle 90
Skipton-on-Swale 252 C5
Skipwith 245 F4
Skirbeck 226 B3
Skirbeck Quarter 226 B3
Skirethorns 243 F1
Skirlaugh 246 D4
Skirling 276 B2
Skirmett 184 C4
Skirpenbeck 245 G2
Skirwith *Cumb.* 260 C4
Skirwith *N.Yorks.* 250 C5
Skirza 337 F2
Skittle Green 184 C2
Skomer Island 176 A2
Skulamus 306 C2
Skullomie 335 F2
Skyborry Green 206 B5
Skye 306 A1
Skye Green 201 G5
Skye of Curr 310 B2
Skyreholme 243 G1
Slack *Aber.* 312 A1
Slack *Derbys.* 223 E1
Slack *W.Yorks.* 243 F5
Slackhall 235 E4
Slackhead 323 G3
Slad 182 A2
Slade *Devon* 163 F1
Slade *Devon* 153 E2
Slade *Pembs.* 176 C1
Slade *Swan.* 178 A4
Slade Green 187 E5
Slade Hooton 236 C4
Slade, The 184 A5
Sladesbridge 147 E2
Slaggyford 260 C2
Slaidburn 242 D2
Slains Park 303 G2
Slaithwaite 235 E1
Slaley 261 F2
Slamannan 284 C2
Slapton *Bucks.* 199 E5
Slapton *Devon* 151 E3
Slapton *Northants.* 198 B3
Slate Haugh 323 G3
Slatepit Dale 223 E1
Slattadale 319 E2
Slaugham 159 E1
Slaughden 203 F2
Slaughterford 182 A5
Slawston 210 C3
Sleaford *Hants.* 170 D4
Sleaford *Lincs.* 225 F3
Sleagill 249 G1
Sleap 220 B5
Sledge Green 196 A4
Sledmere 246 B1
Sleights 254 B2
Slepe 155 F3
Slerra 162 D3
Slickly 337 E2
Sliddery 273 E3
Sliemore 310 C2
Sligachan 306 A2
Slimbridge 181 G2
Slimbridge Wildfowl & Wetlands Trust 36
Slindon *Staffs.* 221 F4
Slindon *W.Suss.* 158 B3
Slinfold 171 G4
Sling 181 E2
Slingsby 253 F5
Slioch 312 A1
Slip End *Beds.* 185 F1
Slip End *Herts.* 200 A4
Slipton 211 E5
Slitting Mill 208 C1
Slochd 310 A2
Slockavullin 290 A5
Slogarie 266 A4
Sloley 229 D3
Slongaber 266 C3
Sloothby 239 E5
Slough 185 E4
Slough Green *Som.* 165 F5
Slough Green *W.Suss.* 159 E1
Sluggan 310 A2
Slyne 242 A1
Smailholm 278 A3
Small Dole 159 E2
Small Hythe 174 A5
Smallbridge 234 D1
Smallbrook 152 B3
Smallburgh 229 E3
Smallburn *Aber.* 325 F5
Smallburn *E.Ayr.* 275 E3
Smalldale 235 E5
Smalley 223 F3
Smallfield 172 C4
Smallford 186 A2
Smallhythe Place 51
Smallridge 153 F2
Smallthorne 221 F2
Smallworth 214 B3
Smannell 169 E3
Smardale 250 C2
Smarden 174 A4
Smaull 280 A3
Smeatharpe 153 E1
Smeeth 174 C5
Smeeton Westerby 210 B3
Smerclet 314 C2
Smerral 337 D5
Smestow 208 A3
Smethwick 208 C4
Smethwick Green 221 F1
Smirisary 297 F2
Smisby 209 F1
Smith Art Gallery & Museum 130
Smith End Green 195 G2
Smithfield 260 A1
Smithies 236 A2
Smithies, The 207 F3
Smithincott 153 D1
Smith's End 200 B4
Smith's Green *Essex* 201 D5
Smith's Green *Essex* 201 E3
Smithstown 319 D2
Smithton 321 G5
Smithy Green 234 B5
Smockington 209 G4
Smoo Cave 130
Smyrton 264 C2
Smythe's Green 188 C1
Snailbeach 206 C2
Snailwell 201 E1
Snainton 254 C4
Snaith 245 F5
Snape *N.Yorks.* 252 B4
Snape *Suff.* 203 E2
Snape Green 233 E1
Snape Watering 203 E2
Snarestone 209 F2
Snarford 238 A4
Snargate 161 E1
Snave 161 F1
Sneachill 196 B2
Snead 206 C3
Snead's Green 196 A1
Sneath Common 214 C3
Sneaton 254 B2
Sneatonthorpe 254 C2
Snelland 238 A4
Snellings 248 A2
Snelston 222 C3
Snetterton 214 A2
Snettisham 227 E4
Snibston Discovery Park 75
Snipeshill 174 B2
Snishival 304 A1
Snitter 270 C1
Snitterby 237 G3
Snitterfield 197 E2
Snitterton 223 D1
Snittlegarth 259 F3
Snitton 207 E5
Snodhill 194 C3
Snodland 173 G2
Snow End 200 C4
Snow Street 214 B3
Snowden Hill 235 G2
Snowdon Mountain Railway 114
Snowdonia National Park 114
Snowshill 196 C4
Snowshill Manor 36
Soar *Cardiff* 179 G4
Soar *Carmar.* 192 C5
Soar *Devon* 150 D4
Soay 306 A3
Soberton 157 F1
Soberton Heath 157 F1
Sockbridge 260 B5
Sockburn 252 C2
Sodom 232 B5
Sodylt Bank 220 A4
Softley 261 G5
Soham 213 D5
Soham Cotes 213 D5
Solas (Sollas) 315 G2
Soldon 162 D4
Soldon Cross 162 D4
Soldridge 170 B4
Sole Street *Kent* 174 C4
Sole Street *Kent* 173 F2
Soleburn 264 B4
Solihull 209 D5
Solihull Lodge 208 C5
Sollas (Solas) 315 G2
Sollers Dilwyn 194 D2
Sollers Hope 195 F4
Sollom 233 F1
Solomon's Tump 181 G1
Solsgirth 293 E5
Solva 190 A5
Solwaybank 268 B4
Somerby *Leics.* 210 C1
Somerby *Lincs.* 238 A2
Somercotes 223 F2
Somerford 208 B2
Somerford Keynes 182 C3
Somerley 158 A4
Somerleyton 215 F2
Somerleyton Hall & Gardens 83
Somersal Herbert 222 C4
Somersby 238 D5
Somerset House 60
Somersham *Cambs.* 212 B5
Somersham *Suff.* 202 B3
Somerton *Newport* 180 C4
Somerton *Oxon.* 197 G5
Somerton *Som.* 166 B5
Somerton *Suff.* 201 G2
Sompting 159 D3
Sompting Abbotts 159 D3
Sonning 184 C5
Sonning Common 184 C4
Sonning Eye 184 C5
Sontley 220 A3
Sookholme 223 G1
Sopley 156 A3
Sopworth 182 A4
Sorbie 257 E2
Sordale 336 D2
Sorisdale 296 B3
Sorn 275 D3
Sornhill 274 D2
Soroba 290 A2
Sortat 337 E2
Sotby 238 C5
Sots Hole 225 G1
Sotterley 215 F3
Soudley 221 E5
Soughton 219 F1
Soulbury 199 D5
Soulby 250 C1
Souldern 198 A4
Souldrop 199 E1
Sound *Ches.* 220 D3
Sound *Shet.* 343 D3
Sound *Shet.* 342 C2
Sourhope 278 C4
Sourin 340 C3
Sourton 149 F1
Souter Johnnie's Cottage 130
Soutergate 248 D4
South Acre 213 G1
South Acton 186 A5
South Alkham 175 E4
South Allington 151 D4
South Alloa 293 D5
South Ambersham 171 E5
South Anston 236 C4
South Ascot 171 E1
South Baddesley 156 C3
South Ballachulish 298 C4
South Balloch 265 E1
South Bank 263 E5
South Barrow 166 D5
South Bellsdyke 284 D1
South Benfleet 187 G4
South Bersted 158 B3
South Blackbog 312 C1
South Bockhampton 156 A3
South Bowood 154 A3
South Brent 150 C1
South Brentor 149 E2
South Brewham 167 E4
South Broomhill 271 E2
South Burlingham 229 E5
South Cadbury 166 D5
South Cairn 264 A4
South Carlton 237 G5
South Cave 246 B4
South Cerney 182 C3
South Chard 153 G2
South Charlton 279 F4
South Cheriton 167 D5
South Church 262 B5
South Cliffe 246 A4
South Clifton 237 F5
South Cockerington 239 D4
South Collafirth 344 C4
South Common 159 F2
South Cornelly 179 E4
South Corriegills 273 F2
South Cove 215 F3
South Creagan 298 B5
South Creake 227 G4
South Crosland 235 F1
South Croxton 210 B1
South Dalton 246 B3
South Darenth 187 E5
South Dell (Dail Bho Dheas) 329 F1
South Devon Railway 36
South Duffield 245 F4
South Elkington 238 C4
South Elmsall 236 B1
South End *Bucks.* 199 D5
South End *Cumb.* 241 F1
South End *Hants.* 156 A1
South End *N.Lincs.* 246 D5
South Erradale 318 D2
South Fambridge 188 B3
South Fawley 183 F4
South Ferriby 246 B5
South Field 246 C5
South Flobbets 312 C1
South Garth 345 E3
South Godstone 172 C4
South Gorley 156 A1
South Green *Essex* 187 F3
South Green *Essex* 188 D1
South Green *Norf.* 228 B4
South Green *Suff.* 214 C4
South Gyle 285 F2
South Hall 282 B2
South Hanningfield 187 G3
South Harefield 185 F4
South Harting 157 G1
South Hayling 157 G3
South Hazelrigg 279 E3
South Heath 185 E2
South Heighton 159 G3
South Hetton 262 C3
South Hiendley 236 A1
South Hill 148 D3
South Hinksey 184 A2
South Hole 162 C4
South Holme 253 F5
South Holmwood 171 G3
South Hornchurch 187 E4
South Hourat 283 D4
South Huish 150 C3
South Hykeham 225 E1
South Hylton 262 C2
South Kelsey 238 A3
South Kessock 321 F5
South Killingholme 238 B1
South Kilvington 252 D4
South Kilworth 210 B4
South Kirkby 236 B1
South Kirkton 312 C4
South Knighton 152 B5
South Kyme 225 G3
South Lakes Wild Animal Park 99
South Lancing 159 D3
South Ledaig 290 B1
South Leigh 183 F2
South Leverton 237 E4
South Littleton 196 C3
South Lopham 214 B3
South Luffenham 211 E2
South Malling 159 G2
South Marston 183 D4
South Middleton 279 D4
South Milford 245 D4
South Milton 150 C3
South Mimms 186 B2
South Molton 164 A5
South Moor 262 A2
South Moreton 184 A4
South Mundham 158 A3
South Muskham 224 C2
South Newbald 246 B4
South Newington 197 G4
South Newton 168 B4
South Normanton 223 F2
South Norwood 172 C2
South Nutfield 172 C4
South Ockendon 187 E4
South Ormsby 239 D5
South Ossett 235 G1
South Otterington 252 C4
South Owersby 238 A3
South Oxhey 186 A3
South Park 172 B4
South Parks 294 A4
South Perrott 154 A2
South Petherton 154 A1
South Petherwin 148 D2
South Pickenham 213 G2
South Pool 151 D3
South Queensferry (Queensferry) 285 F2
South Radworthy 164 A4
South Rauceby 225 F3
South Raynham 227 G5
South Redbriggs 324 C5
South Reston 239 E4
South Ronaldsay 339 D4
South Ruislip 186 A4
South Runcton 213 E2
South Scarle 224 D1
South Shian 298 B5
South Shields 262 C1
South Shields Museum & Art Gallery 105
South Somercotes 239 E3
South Somercotes Fen Houses 239 E3
South Stack Cliffs 114
South Stainley 244 C1
South Stoke *Oxon.* 184 B4
South Stoke *W.Suss.* 158 C3
South Street *E.Suss.* 159 F2
South Street *Gt.Lon.* 172 D3
South Street *Kent* 173 F2
South Street *Kent* 174 D2
South Street *Kent* 174 A2
South Tawton 149 G1
South Thoresby 239 E5
South Tidworth 168 D3
South Tottenham 186 C4
South Town *Devon* 152 C4
South Town *Hants.* 170 B4
South Tynedale Railway 99

South Uist (Uibhist a Deas) 304 A1
South Upper Barrack 325 E5
South View 170 B2
South Walsham 229 E4
South Warnborough 170 C3
South Weald 187 E3
South Weston 184 C3
South Wheatley *Cornw.* 148 C1
South Wheatley *Notts.* 237 E4
South Whiteness 342 C3
South Wigston 210 A3
South Willingham 238 B4
South Wingfield 223 E2
South Witham 211 E1
South Wonston 169 F4
South Woodham Ferrers 188 B3
South Wootton 227 E5
South Wraxall 167 F1
South Yardley 208 D4
South Zeal 149 G1
Southall 186 A4
Southam *Glos.* 196 B5
Southam *Warks.* 197 G1
Southampton 156 D1
Southampton Airport 157 D1
Southampton Maritime Museum 51
Southbar 283 F3
Southborough *Gt.Lon.* 172 D2
Southborough *Kent* 173 E4
Southbourne *Bourne.* 156 A3
Southbourne *W.Suss.* 157 G2
Southbrook 152 D3
Southburgh 228 B5
Southburn 246 B2
Southchurch 188 C4
Southcott *Devon* 149 F1
Southcott *Wilts.* 168 C2
Southcourt 184 D1
Southdean 269 E1
Southdene 233 F3
Southease 159 G3
Southend *Aber.* 324 C5
Southend *Arg. & B.* 272 B5
Southend *Bucks* 184 C4
Southend *W.Berks.* 184 A5
Southend *Wilts.* 183 D5
Southend Pier 83
Southend-on-Sea 188 B4
Southerfield 259 E2
Southerly 149 F2
Southern Green 200 B4
Southerndown 179 E5
Southerness 267 D5
Southery 213 E3
Southfield 294 A5
Southfields 186 B5
Southfleet 187 F5
Southgate *Cere.* 204 B4
Southgate *Gt.Lon.* 186 C3
Southgate *Norf.* 228 C3
Southgate *Norf.* 227 E4
Southgate *Swan.* 178 B4
Southill 199 G3
Southington 169 G3
Southleigh 153 F3
Southmarsh 167 E4
Southminster 188 C3
Southmuir 302 B4
Southoe 199 G1
Southolt 202 C1
Southorpe 211 F2
Southowram 244 A5
Southport 233 E1
Southrepps 229 D2
Southrey 225 G1
Southrop 183 D2
Southrope 170 B3
Southsea *Ports.* 157 F3
Southsea *Wrex.* 219 F2
Southsea Castle & Museum 51
Southstoke 167 E1
Southtown *Norf.* 229 G5
Southtown *Ork.* 339 D3
Southwaite *Cumb.* 250 C2
Southwaite *Cumb.* 260 A3
Southwater 171 G5
Southwater Street 171 G5
Southway 166 C3
Southwell *Dorset* 154 C5
Southwell *Notts.* 224 B2
Southwick *D. & G.* 266 D5
Southwick *Hants.* 157 F2
Southwick *Northants.* 211 F3
Southwick *Som.* 166 A3
Southwick *T. & W.* 262 C2
Southwick *W.Suss.* 159 E3
Southwick *Wilts.* 167 F2
Southwold 215 G4
Southwood 166 C4
Sowden 152 C4
Sower Carr 241 G3
Sowerby *N.Yorks.* 253 D4
Sowerby *W.Yorks.* 243 G5
Sowerby Bridge 243 G5
Sowerby Row 259 G2
Sowerhill 164 B5
Sowley Green 201 F2
Sowood 235 E1
Sowton 152 C3
Soyal 332 A5
Spa Common 229 D2
Spadeadam 269 D4
Spalding 226 A5
Spaldington 245 G4
Spaldwick 211 G5
Spalefield 295 D4
Spalford 224 D1
Spanby 225 F4
Sparham 228 B4
Spark Bridge 249 E4
Sparkford 166 D5
Sparkhill 208 C4
Sparkwell 150 B2
Sparrow Green 228 A4
Sparrowpit 235 E4
Sparrow's Green 173 F5
Sparsholt *Hants.* 169 F4
Sparsholt *Oxon.* 183 F4
Spartylea 261 E3
Spath 222 B4
Spaunton 253 G4
Spaxton 165 F4
Spean Bridge 299 E1
Spear Hill 158 D2
Speddoch 266 C2
Speedwell 181 F5
Speedwell Cavern 75
Speen *Bucks.* 184 D2
Speen *W.Berks.* 169 F1
Speeton 255 E5
Speke 233 F4
Speldhurst 173 E4
Spellbrook 187 D1
Spelsbury 197 F5
Spen Green 221 F1
Spencers Wood 170 C1
Spennithorne 252 A4
Spennymoor 262 B4
Spernall 196 C1
Spetchley 196 A2
Spetchley Park 67
Spetisbury 155 F2
Spexhall 215 E3
Spey Bay 323 F3
Speybridge 310 C2
Speyview 323 E5
Spilsby 226 B1
Spindlestone 279 F3
Spinkhill 236 B5
Spinningdale 321 F1
Spirthill 182 B5
Spital *High.* 337 D3
Spital *W. & M.* 185 E5
Spital in the Street 237 G3
Spitalbrook 186 C2
Spitfire & Hurricane Memorial, R.A.F. Manston 51
Spithurst 159 G2
Spittal *D. & G.* 265 F4
Spittal *D. & G.* 265 E5
Spittal *E.Loth.* 286 B2
Spittal *Northumb.* 279 E1
Spittal *Pembs.* 190 C5
Spittal of Glenmuick 302 B1
Spittal of Glenshee 301 G3
Spittalfield 301 G5
Spixworth 228 D4
Splayne's Green 159 G1
Splott 180 B5
Spofforth 244 C2
Spondon 223 F4
Spooner Row 214 B2
Spoonley 221 D4
Sporle 213 G1
Sportsman's Arms 218 C2
Spott 287 D2
Spratton 210 C5
Spreakley 170 D3
Spreyton 149 G1
Spriddlestone 150 B2
Spridlington 238 A4
Spring Grove 186 A5
Spring Vale 157 F3
Springburn 284 A3
Springfield *Arg. & B.* 282 B2
Springfield *D. & G.* 268 B5
Springfield *Fife* 294 B3
Springfield *Moray* 322 C4
Springfield *P. & K.* 293 G1
Springfield *W.Mid.* 208 C4
Springfields Outlet Shopping Village & Festival Gardens 75
Springfields Outlet Village 226 A5
Springhill *Staffs.* 208 C2
Springhill *Staffs.* 208 B2
Springholm 266 C4
Springkell 268 A4
Springleys 312 C1
Springside 274 B2
Springthorpe 237 F4
Springwell 262 B2
Sproatley 247 D4
Sproston Green 221 E1
Sprotbrough 236 C2
Sproughton 202 C3
Sprouston 278 B3
Sprowston 228 D4
Sproxton *Leics.* 225 D5
Sproxton *N.Yorks.* 253 F4
Sprytown 149 E2
Spurlands End 185 D3
Spurn Head 90
Spurstow 220 C2
Spyway 154 B3
Square Point 266 B3
Squerryes Court 51
Squires Gate 241 G4
Sròndoire 281 G2
Sronphadruig Lodge 300 C2
S.S. Great Britain 35
Stableford *Shrop.* 207 G3
Stableford *Staffs.* 221 F4
Stacey Bank 235 G3
Stackhouse 243 E1
Stackpole 176 C3
Stacksteads 243 E5
Staddiscombe 150 B2
Staddlethorpe 246 A5
Staden 235 E5
Stadhampton 184 B3
Stadhlaigearraidh (Stilligarry) 304 A1
Staffa (Fingal's Cave) 130
Staffield 260 B3
Staffin 318 A3
Stafford 221 G5
Stafford Castle 67
Stagden Cross 187 F1
Stagsden 199 E3
Stagshaw Bank 261 F1
Stagshaw Garden 99
Stain 337 F2
Stainburn *Cumb.* 258 D4
Stainburn *N.Yorks.* 244 B3
Stainby 225 E5
Staincross 236 A1
Staindrop 262 A5
Staines 185 F5
Stainfield *Lincs.* 225 F5
Stainfield *Lincs.* 238 B5
Stainforth *N.Yorks.* 243 E1
Stainforth *S.Yorks.* 236 D1
Staining 241 G4
Stainland 235 E1
Stainsacre 254 C2
Stainsby *Derbys.* 223 F1
Stainsby *Lincs.* 238 D5
Stainsby Mill 75
Stainton *Cumb.* 249 G4
Stainton *Cumb.* 260 A5
Stainton *Dur.* 251 F1
Stainton *Middbro.* 253 D1
Stainton *N.Yorks.* 252 A3
Stainton *S.Yorks.* 236 C3
Stainton by Langworth 238 A5
Stainton le Vale 238 B3
Stainton with Adgarley 248 D5
Staintondale 254 C3
Stair *Cumb.* 259 F4
Stair *E.Ayr.* 274 C3
Stairfoot 236 A2
Staithes 253 G1
Stake Pool 242 A3
Stakeford 271 E3
Stakes 157 F2
Stalbridge 154 D1
Stalbridge Weston 154 D1
Stalham 229 E3
Stalham Green 229 E3
Stalisfield Green 174 B3
Stalling Busk 251 E4
Stallingborough 238 B1
Stallington 221 G4
Stalmine 241 G3
Stalybridge 235 D3
Stambourne 201 F4
Stamford *Lincs.* 211 F2
Stamford *Northumb.* 279 G5
Stamford Bridge *Ches.* 220 B1
Stamford Bridge *E.Riding* 245 G2
Stamfordham 270 C4
Stanah 241 G3
Stanborough 186 B1
Stanbridge *Beds.* 199 E5
Stanbridge *Dorset* 155 G2
Stanbridge Earls 169 E5
Stanbury 243 G4
Stand 284 B3
Standalone Farm 83
Standburn 284 D2
Standedge Experience (see Huddersfield Narrow Canal) 88
Standeford 208 B2
Standen *Kent* 174 A5
Standen *W.Suss.* 51
Standen Street 174 A5
Standerwick 167 F2
Standford 170 D4
Standford Bridge 221 E5
Standish *Glos.* 182 A2
Standish *Gt.Man.* 233 G1
Standlake 183 F2
Standon *Hants.* 169 F5
Standon *Herts.* 200 B5
Standon *Staffs.* 221 F4
Standon Green End 186 C1
Stane 284 C4
Stanecastle 274 B2
Stanfield 228 A3
Stanford *Beds.* 199 G3
Stanford *Kent* 174 D5
Stanford *Shrop.* 206 C1
Stanford Bishop 195 F2
Stanford Bridge 195 G1
Stanford Dingley 184 A5
Stanford End 170 C1
Stanford Hall 75
Stanford in the Vale 183 F3
Stanford on Avon 210 A5
Stanford on Soar 223 G5
Stanford on Teme 195 G1
Stanford Rivers 187 E2
Stanford-le-Hope 187 F4
Stanfree 236 B5
Stanghow 253 F1
Stanground 212 A3
Stanhoe 227 G4
Stanhope *Dur.* 261 F4
Stanhope *Sc.Bord.* 276 C3
Stanion 211 E4
Stanklyn 208 A5
Stanley *Derbys.* 223 F3
Stanley *Dur.* 262 A2
Stanley *Notts.* 223 F1
Stanley *P. & K.* 293 G1
Stanley *Staffs.* 221 G2
Stanley *W.Yorks.* 244 C5
Stanley *Wilts.* 182 B5
Stanley Common 223 F3
Stanley Crook 262 A4
Stanley Gate 233 F2
Stanley Green 155 G3
Stanley Hill 195 F3
Stanleygreen 220 C4
Stanlow *Ches.* 233 F5
Stanlow *Shrop.* 207 G3
Stanmer 159 F2
Stanmore *Gt.Lon.* 186 A3
Stanmore *W.Berks.* 183 G5
Stannersburn 269 F3
Stanningfield 201 G2
Stanningley 244 B4
Stannington *Northumb.* 271 E4
Stannington *S.Yorks.* 236 A4
Stansbatch 194 C1
Stansfield 201 F2
Stanshope 222 C2
Stanstead 201 G3
Stanstead Abbotts 186 C1
Stansted 173 F2
Stansted Airport (London Stansted Airport) 200 D5
Stansted Mountfitchet 200 D5
Stanton *Derbys.* 209 E1
Stanton *Glos.* 196 C4
Stanton *Northumb.* 270 D2
Stanton *Staffs.* 222 C3
Stanton *Suff.* 214 A4
Stanton by Bridge 223 E5
Stanton by Dale 223 F4
Stanton Drew 166 C1
Stanton Fitzwarren 183 D3
Stanton Harcourt 183 G2
Stanton Hill 223 F1
Stanton in Peak 222 D1
Stanton Lacy 207 D5
Stanton Lees 223 D1
Stanton Long 207 E3
Stanton Prior 167 D1
Stanton St. Bernard 168 B1
Stanton St. John 184 A2
Stanton St. Quintin 182 B5
Stanton Street 202 A1
Stanton under Bardon 209 G1
Stanton upon Hine Heath 220 C5
Stanton Wick 166 D1
Stanton-on-the-Wolds 224 B4
Stanwardine in the Fields 220 B5
Stanwardine in the Wood 220 B5
Stanway *Essex* 202 A5
Stanway *Glos.* 196 C4
Stanway Green *Essex* 202 A5
Stanway Green *Suff.* 214 D4
Stanwell 185 F5
Stanwell Moor 185 F5
Stanwick 211 E5
Stanwix 260 A2
Stanydale 342 B2
Staoinebrig 304 A1
Stapehill Abbey Crafts & Garden 36
Stapeley 221 D3
Stapeley Water Gardens & Palms Tropical Oasis 99
Stapenhill 223 D5
Staple *Kent* 175 E3
Staple *Som.* 165 E3
Staple Cross 164 D5
Staple Fitzpaine 153 F1
Staplecross 160 C1
Staplefield 159 E1
Stapleford *Cambs.* 200 C2
Stapleford *Herts.* 186 C1
Stapleford *Leics.* 210 D1
Stapleford *Lincs.* 225 D2
Stapleford *Notts.* 223 F4
Stapleford *Wilts.* 168 B4
Stapleford Abbotts 187 D3
Stapleford Tawney 187 E3
Staplegrove 165 F5
Staplehay 165 F5
Staplehurst 173 G4
Staplers 157 E4
Staplestreet 174 C2
Stapleton *Cumb.* 268 D4
Stapleton *Here.* 194 C1
Stapleton *Leics.* 209 G3
Stapleton *N.Yorks.* 252 B1
Stapleton *Shrop.* 207 D2
Stapleton *Som.* 166 B5
Stapley 153 E1
Staploe 199 G1
Staplow 195 F3
Star *Fife* 294 B4
Star *Pembs.* 191 F4
Star *Som.* 166 B2
Starbotton 251 E5
Starcross 152 C4
Stareton 209 F5
Starkholmes 223 E2
Starling 234 B1
Starling's Green 200 C4
Starr 265 F1
Starston 214 D3
Startforth 251 F1
Startley 182 B4
Statham 234 A4
Stathe 166 A5
Stathern 224 C4
Station Town 262 D4
Staughton Green 199 G1
Staughton Highway 199 G1
Staunton *Glos.* 181 E1
Staunton *Glos.* 195 G5
Staunton Country Park 51
Staunton Harold Hall 223 E5
Staunton in the Vale 224 D3
Staunton on Arrow 194 C1
Staunton on Wye 194 C3
Staveley *Cumb.* 249 F3
Staveley *Derbys.* 236 B5
Staveley *N.Yorks.* 244 C1
Staveley-in-Cartmel 249 E4
Staverton *Devon* 151 D1
Staverton *Glos.* 196 A5
Staverton *Northants.* 198 A1
Staverton *Wilts.* 167 F1
Staverton Bridge 196 A5
Stawell 166 A4
Stawley 165 D5
Staxigoe 337 F3
Staxton 254 D5
Staylittle (Penffordd-las) 205 E3
Staynall 241 G3
Staythorpe 224 C2
STEAM Museum of the Great Western Railway 36
Stean 251 F5
Steane 198 A4
Stearsby 253 F5
Steart 165 F3
Stebbing 201 E5
Stebbing Green 201 E5
Stechford 208 D4
Stedham 171 D5
Steel Cross 173 E5
Steel Green 248 C5
Steele Road 268 D2
Steen's Bridge 195 E2
Steep 170 C5
Steep Marsh 170 C5
Steeple *Dorset* 155 F4
Steeple *Essex* 188 C2
Steeple Ashton 168 A2
Steeple Aston 197 G5
Steeple Barton 197 G5
Steeple Bumpstead 201 E3
Steeple Claydon 198 B5
Steeple Gidding 211 G4
Steeple Langford 168 B4
Steeple Morden 200 A3
Steeraway 207 F2
Steeton 243 G3
Stein 317 F4
Steinmanhill 324 C5
Stella 262 A1
Stelling Minnis 174 D4
Stembridge 166 B5
Stembridge Tower Mill 36
Stemster *High.* 337 D2
Stemster *High.* 337 D4
Stemster House 337 D2
Stenalees 147 E4
Stenhill 153 D1
Stenhousemuir 284 C1
Stenigot 238 C4
Stenis 329 F4
Stenness 344 B5
Stenscholl 318 A3
Stenson 223 E5
Stenton *E.Loth.* 286 D2
Stenton *P. & K.* 301 F5
Steornabhagh (Stornoway) 329 F4
Stepaside *Pembs.* 177 E2
Stepaside *Powys* 205 G4
Stepney 186 C4
Steppingley 199 F4
Stepps 284 A3
Sternfield 203 E1
Sterridge 163 F1
Stert 168 B2
Stetchworth 201 E2
Stevenage 200 A5
Stevenston 283 D5
Steventon *Hants.* 169 G3
Steventon *Oxon.* 183 G3
Steventon End 201 E3
Stevington 199 E2
Stewartby 199 F3
Stewarton *D. & G.* 257 E2
Stewarton *E.Ayr.* 283 F5
Stewartry Museum 130
Stewkley 199 D5
Stewley 153 G1
Stewton 239 D4
Steyning 159 D2
Steynton 176 C2
Stibb 162 C4
Stibb Cross 163 E4
Stibb Green 168 D1
Stibbard 228 A3
Stibbington 211 F3
Stichill 278 B3
Sticker 147 D4
Stickford 226 B1
Sticklepath *Devon* 149 G1
Sticklepath *Som.* 153 G1
Stickling Green 200 C4
Stickney 226 B2
Stiff Street 174 A2
Stiffkey 228 A1
Stifford's Bridge 195 G3
Stileway 166 B3
Stilligarry (Stad-hlaigearraidh) 304 A1
Stillingfleet 245 E3
Stillington *N.Yorks.* 245 E1
Stillington *Stock.* 262 C5
Stilton 211 G4
Stinchcombe 181 G3
Stinsford 154 D3
Stirchley *Tel. & W.* 207 G2
Stirchley *W.Mid.* 208 C4
Stirkoke House 337 F3
Stirling *Aber.* 325 G5
Stirling *Stir.* 292 C5
Stirling Castle 130
Stirton 243 F2
Stisted 201 G5
Stitchcombe 183 E5
Stithians 145 E3
Stittenham 321 F2
Stivichall 209 F5
Stix 300 C5
Stixwould 225 G1
Stoak 233 F5
Stobo 276 C2
Stoborough 155 F4
Stoborough Green 155 F4
Stobwood 285 D4
Stocinis (Stockinish) 326 D4
Stock 187 F3
Stock Green 196 B2
Stock Lane 183 E5
Stock Wood 196 C2
Stockbridge *Hants.* 169 E4
Stockbridge *Stir.* 292 C4
Stockbridge *W.Suss.* 158 A3
Stockbury 174 A2
Stockcross 169 F1
Stockdale 145 E3
Stockdalewath 259 G2
Stockerston 210 D3
Stocking Green *Essex* 201 D4
Stocking Green *M.K.* 198 D3
Stocking Pelham 200 C5
Stockingford 209 F3
Stockinish (Stocinis) 326 D4
Stockland *Cardiff* 180 A5
Stockland *Devon* 153 F2
Stockland Bristol 165 F3
Stockleigh English 152 B2
Stockleigh Pomeroy 152 B2
Stockley 168 B1
Stocklinch 153 G1
Stockport 234 C3
Stocks, The 161 E1
Stocksbridge 235 G3
Stocksfield 261 G1
Stockton *Here.* 195 E1
Stockton *Norf.* 215 E2
Stockton *Shrop.* 207 G3
Stockton *Shrop.* 206 B2
Stockton *Tel. & W.* 207 G1
Stockton *Warks.* 197 G1
Stockton *Wilts.* 168 A4
Stockton Heath 234 A4
Stockton on Teme 195 G1
Stockton on the Forest 245 F2
Stockton-on-Tees 252 D1
Stockwell 182 B1
Stockwell Heath 222 B5
Stockwood *Bristol* 166 D1
Stockwood *Dorset* 154 B2
Stodday 242 A2
Stodmarsh 175 E2
Stody 228 B2
Stoer 330 C2
Stoford *Som.* 154 B1
Stoford *Wilts.* 168 B4
Stogumber 165 D4
Stogursey 165 F3
Stoke *Devon* 162 C3
Stoke *Hants.* 169 F2
Stoke *Hants.* 157 G2
Stoke *Med.* 174 A1
Stoke *Plym.* 150 A2
Stoke *W.Mid.* 209 F5
Stoke Abbott 154 A2
Stoke Albany 210 D4
Stoke Ash 214 C4
Stoke Bardolph 224 B3
Stoke Bishop 181 E5
Stoke Bliss 195 F1
Stoke Bruerne 198 C2
Stoke Bruerne Waterways Museum 75
Stoke by Clare 201 F3
Stoke Canon 152 C3
Stoke Charity 169 F4
Stoke Climsland 149 D3
Stoke D'Abernon 171 G2
Stoke Doyle 211 F4
Stoke Dry 211 D3
Stoke Edith 195 F3
Stoke Farthing 168 B5
Stoke Ferry 213 F3
Stoke Fleming 151 E3
Stoke Gabriel 151 E2
Stoke Gifford 181 F5
Stoke Golding 209 F3
Stoke Goldington 198 D3
Stoke Green 185 E4
Stoke Hammond 199 D5
Stoke Heath *Shrop.* 221 D5
Stoke Heath *Worcs.* 196 B1
Stoke Holy Cross 228 D5
Stoke Lacy 195 F3
Stoke Lyne 198 A5
Stoke Mandeville 184 D1
Stoke Newington 186 C4
Stoke on Tern 220 D5
Stoke Orchard 196 B5
Stoke Pero 164 B3
Stoke Poges 185 E4
Stoke Pound 196 B1
Stoke Prior *Here.* 195 E2
Stoke Prior *Worcs.* 196 B1
Stoke Rivers 163 G2
Stoke Rochford 225 E5
Stoke Row 184 B4
Stoke St. Gregory 166 A5
Stoke St. Mary 165 F5
Stoke St. Michael 167 D3
Stoke St. Milborough 207 E4
Stoke sub Hamdon 154 A1
Stoke sub Hamdon Priory 36
Stoke Talmage 184 B3
Stoke Trister 167 E5
Stoke Villice 166 C1
Stoke Wake 155 D2
Stoke-by-Nayland 202 A4
Stokeford 155 E4
Stokeham 237 E5
Stokeinteignhead 152 C5
Stokenchurch 184 C3
Stokenham 151 E3
Stoke-on-Trent 221 F3
Stokesay 206 D4
Stokesay Castle 67
Stokesby 229 F4
Stokesley 253 E2
Stolford 165 F3
Ston Easton 166 D2
Stonar Cut 175 F2
Stondon Massey 187 E2
Stone *Bucks.* 184 C1
Stone *Glos.* 181 F3
Stone *Kent* 187 E5
Stone *Kent* 161 E1
Stone *S.Yorks.* 236 C4
Stone *Som.* 166 C4
Stone *Staffs.* 221 G4
Stone *Worcs.* 208 A5
Stone Allerton 166 B2
Stone Cross *Dur.* 251 F1
Stone Cross *E.Suss.* 160 B3
Stone Cross *E.Suss.* 160 A1
Stone Cross *Kent* 174 C5
Stone Cross *Kent* 173 E5
Stone House 250 C4
Stone Street *Kent* 173 E3
Stone Street *Suff.* 215 E3
Stone Street *Suff.* 202 A4
Stonea 212 C3
Stoneacre 51
Stonebridge *E.Suss.* 160 A1
Stonebridge *N.Som.* 166 A2
Stonebridge *Warks.* 209 E4
Stonebroom 223 F2
Stonecross Green 201 G2
Stonefield *Arg. & B.* 281 G2
Stonefield *Staffs.* 221 G4
Stonegate *E.Suss.* 160 B1
Stonegate *N.Yorks.* 253 G2
Stonegrave 253 F5
Stonehaugh 269 F4
Stonehaven 303 G1
Stonehenge 36
Stonehill 171 E1
Stonehouse *Ches.* 233 G5
Stonehouse *D. & G.* 266 C4
Stonehouse *Glos.* 182 A2
Stonehouse *Northumb.* 260 C2
Stonehouse *Plym.* 150 A2
Stonehouse *S.Lan.* 284 B5
Stoneleigh *Surr.* 172 B2
Stoneleigh *Warks.* 209 F5
Stoneley Green 220 D2
Stonely 199 G1
Stoner Hill 170 C5
Stones 243 F5
Stones Green 202 C5
Stonesby 224 D5
Stonesfield 183 F1
Stonestreet Green 174 C5
Stonethwaite 259 F5
Stoney Cross 156 B1
Stoney Middleton 235 G5
Stoney Stanton 209 G3
Stoney Stoke 167 E4
Stoney Stratton 167 D4
Stoney Stretton 206 C2
Stoneyburn 285 D3
Stoneyford 153 D4
Stoneygate 210 B2
Stoneyhills 188 C3
Stoneykirk 264 B5
Stoneywood 313 D3
Stonganess 345 E2
Stonham Aspal 202 C2
Stonnall 208 C2
Stonor 184 C4
Stonor Park 51
Stonton Wyville 210 C3
Stony Houghton 223 F1
Stony Stratford 198 C3
Stonybreck 342 A5
Stoodleigh *Devon* 152 C1
Stoodleigh *Devon* 163 G2
Stopham 158 C2
Stopsley 199 G5
Stoptide 146 D2
Storeton 233 E4
Stornoway (Steornabhagh) 329 F4
Stornoway Airport 329 F4
Storridge 195 G3
Storrington 158 C2
Storrs 235 G4
Storth 249 F4
Storwood 245 G3
Storybook Glen 130
Stotfield 323 E2
Stotfold 200 A4
Stottesdon 207 F4
Stoughton *Leics.* 210 B2
Stoughton *Surr.* 171 E2
Stoughton *W.Suss.* 157 G1
Stoughton Cross 166 B3
Stoul 307 D5
Stoulton 196 B3
Stour Provost 167 E5
Stour Row 167 F5
Stourbridge 208 A4
Stourhead 36
Stourpaine 155 E2
Stourport-on-Severn 208 A5
Stourton *Staffs.* 208 A4
Stourton *Warks.* 197 E4
Stourton *Wilts.* 167 E4
Stourton Caundle 154 D1
Stove 341 E3
Stoven 215 F3
Stow *Lincs.* 237 F4
Stow *Sc.Bord.* 286 B5

Stow Bardolph 213 E2
Stow Bedon 214 A2
Stow cum Quy 200 D1
Stow Longa 211 G5
Stow Maries 188 B3
Stow Pasture 237 F4
Stowbridge 213 D2
Stowe *Glos.* 181 E2
Stowe *Shrop.* 206 C5
Stowe *Staffs.* 208 D1
Stowe School 51
Stowe-by-Chartley 222 B5
Stowehill 198 B2
Stowell *Glos.* 182 C1
Stowell *Som.* 167 D5
Stowey 166 C2
Stowford *Devon* 149 E2
Stowford *Devon* 163 G3
Stowford *Devon* 153 E4
Stowlangtoft 202 A1
Stowmarket 202 B2
Stow-on-the-Wold 197 D5
Stowting 174 D4
Stowupland 202 B2
Straad 282 B3
Stracathro 303 E3
Strachan 312 B5
Strachur (Clachan Strachur) 290 C4
Stradbroke 214 D4
Stradishall 201 F2
Stradsett 213 E2
Stragglethorpe 225 E2
Straight Soley 183 F5
Straiton *Edin.* 285 G3
Straiton *S.Ayr.* 274 B5
Straloch *Aber.* 313 D2
Straloch *P. & K.* 301 F3
Stramshall 222 B4
Strands 248 C4
Strang 240 B4
Strangford 195 E5
Strannda 326 C5
Stranraer 264 B4
Strata Florida 192 D1
Strata Florida Abbey 114
Stratfield Mortimer 170 B1
Stratfield Saye 170 B1
Stratfield Turgis 170 B2
Stratford *Beds.* 199 G3
Stratford *Glos.* 196 A4
Stratford *Gt.Lon.* 186 C4
Stratford St. Andrew 203 E2
Stratford St. Mary 202 B4
Stratford sub Castle 168 C4
Stratford Tony 168 B5
Stratford-upon-Avon 197 D2
Strath 337 E3
Strathan *High.* 330 C2
Strathan *High.* 307 F5
Strathaven 284 B5
Strathblane 283 G2
Strathcarron 319 F5
Strathclyde Country Park 130
Strathdon 311 F3
Strathgirnock 311 F5
Strathisla Distillery 131
Strathkanaird 331 D4
Strathkinness 294 C3
Strathmiglo 294 A3
Strathnaver Museum 131
Strathpeffer 321 D4
Strathrannoch 320 C2
Strathspey Railway 131
Strathtay 301 E4
Strathwhillan 273 F2
Strathy 336 A2
Strathyre 292 A3
Stratton *Cornw.* 162 C5
Stratton *Dorset* 154 C3
Stratton *Glos.* 182 C2
Stratton Audley 198 B5
Stratton Hall 202 D4
Stratton St. Margaret 183 D4
Stratton St. Michael 214 D2
Stratton Strawless 228 D3
Stratton-on-the-Fosse 167 D2
Stravanan 282 B4
Stravithie 294 D3
Strawberry Hill 186 A5
Stream 165 D4
Streat 159 F2
Streatham 186 B5
Streatham Vale 186 B5
Streatley *Beds.* 199 F5
Streatley *W.Berks.* 184 A4
Street *Devon* 153 E4
Street *Lancs.* 242 B2
Street *N.Yorks.* 253 G2
Street *Som.* 166 B4
Street *Som.* 153 G2
Street Ashton 209 G4
Street Dinas 220 A4
Street End 158 A4
Street Gate 262 B2
Street Houses 245 E3
Street Lane 223 E3
Street on the Fosse 166 D4
Streethay 208 D1
Streethouse 244 C5
Streetlam 252 C3
Streetly 208 C3
Streetly End 201 E3
Strefford 206 D4
Strelley 223 G3
Strensall 245 F1
Strensham 196 B3
Stretcholt 165 F3
Strete 151 E3
Stretford *Gt.Man.* 234 B3
Stretford *Here.* 194 D2
Stretford *Here.* 195 E2
Strethall 200 C4
Stretham 212 D5
Strettington 158 A3
Stretton *Ches.* 220 B2
Stretton *Derbys.* 223 E1
Stretton *Rut.* 211 E1
Stretton *Staffs.* 208 A1
Stretton *Staffs.* 223 D5
Stretton *Warr.* 234 A4
Stretton en le Field 209 F1
Stretton Grandison 195 F3
Stretton Heath 206 C1
Stretton Sugwas 195 D3
Stretton under Fosse 209 G4
Stretton Westwood 207 E3
Stretton-on-Dunsmore 209 G5
Stretton-on-Fosse 197 E4
Stribers 249 E4
Strichen 325 E4
Strines 235 D4
Stringston 165 E3
Strixton 199 E1
Stroat 181 E3
Stromeferry 307 E1
Stromemore 307 E1
Stromness 338 B2
Stronaba 299 E1
Stronachlachar 291 G3
Strone *Arg. & B.* 282 C1
Strone *High.* 309 E2
Strone *High.* 298 D1
Strone *Stir.* 291 G3
Stronechrubie 331 E3
Stronlonag 282 C1
Stronmilchan 291 D2
Stronsay 341 E4
Strontian 298 A3
Strontoiller 290 B2
Stronvar 292 A2
Strood 173 G2
Strood Green *Surr.* 172 B4
Strood Green *W.Suss.* 171 F5
Strood Green *W.Suss.* 171 G4
Stroquhan 266 C2
Stroud *Glos.* 182 A2
Stroud *Hants.* 170 C5
Stroud Common 171 F3
Stroud Green *Essex* 188 B3
Stroud Green *Glos.* 182 A2
Stroude 171 F1
Stroul 282 D1
Stroxton 225 E4
Struan *High.* 305 G1
Struan *P. & K.* 300 C3
Strubby *Lincs.* 239 E4
Strubby *Lincs.* 238 B5
Strumpshaw 229 E5
Struthers 294 B4
Struy 308 D1
Stryd y Facsen 230 B4
Stryt-cae-rhedyn 219 F1
Stryt-issa 219 F3
Stuart Line Cruises 36
Stuartfield 325 E5
Stub Place 248 B3
Stubber's Green 208 C2
Stubbington 157 E2
Stubbins 234 B1
Stubbs Green 215 E2
Stubhampton 155 F1
Stubley 236 A5
Stubshaw Cross 233 G2
Stubton 225 D3
Stuck *Arg. & B.* 282 B3
Stuck *Arg. & B.* 290 D5
Stuckbeg 291 E5
Stuckgowan 291 F4
Stuckindroin 291 F3
Stuckreoch 290 C5
Stuckton 156 A1
Stud Green 185 D5
Studdon 261 E2
Studfold 250 D5
Studham 185 F1
Studholme 259 F1
Studland 155 G4
Studland Heath 36
Studley *Warks.* 196 C1
Studley *Wilts.* 182 B5
Studley Common 196 C1
Studley Green 184 C3
Studley Roger 252 B5
Studley Royal Water Garden (see Fountains Abbey) 87
Stuggadhoo 240 B4
Stump Cross *Essex* 200 D3
Stump Cross *Lancs.* 242 B4
Stuntney 213 D5
Stunts Green 160 B2
Sturbridge 221 F4
Sturgate 237 F4
Sturmer 201 E3
Sturminster Common 155 D1
Sturminster Marshall 155 F2
Sturminster Newton 155 D1
Sturry 175 D2
Sturton by Stow 237 F4
Sturton le Steeple 237 E4
Stuston 214 C4
Stutton *N.Yorks.* 245 D3
Stutton *Suff.* 202 C4
Styal 234 C4
Styal Estate (see Quarry Bank Mill) 98
Styrrup 236 D3
Suainebost (Swainbost) 329 G1
Suardail 329 F4
Succoth *Aber.* 311 G1
Succoth *Arg. & B.* 291 E4
Succothmore 290 D4
Suckley 195 G2
Suckley Green 195 G2
Suckley Knowl 195 G2
Sudborough 211 E4
Sudbourne 203 F2
Sudbrook *Lincs.* 225 E3
Sudbrook *Mon.* 181 E4
Sudbrooke 238 A5
Sudbury *Derbys.* 222 C4
Sudbury *Gt.Lon.* 186 A4
Sudbury *Suff.* 201 G3
Sudbury Hall 75
Sudbury Hall Museum 75
Sudden 234 C1
Sudeley Castle 36
Sudgrove 182 B2
Suffield *N.Yorks.* 254 C3
Suffield *Norf.* 228 D2
Suffolk Wildlife Park 83
Sugarloaf 174 B5
Sugnall 221 E4
Sugwas Pool 195 D3
Suie Lodge Hotel 291 G2
Suisnish 306 B3
Sulby *I.o.M.* 240 B2
Sulby *I.o.M.* 240 B3
Sulgrave 198 A3
Sulgrave Manor 75
Sulham 184 B5
Sulhamstead 170 B1
Sullington 158 C2
Sullom 344 C5
Sullom Voe Oil Terminal 344 C5
Sully 165 E1
Sumburgh 343 G5
Sumburgh Airport 343 G5
Summer Bridge 244 B1
Summer Isles 330 B4
Summer Lodge 251 E3
Summercourt 146 C4
Summerfield *Norf.* 227 F4
Summerfield *Worcs.* 208 A5
Summerhill 220 A2
Summerhouse 252 B1
Summerlands 249 G4
Summerleaze 180 D4
Summerlee Heritage Park 131
Summertown 184 A2
Summit 234 D1
Sun Green 235 D3
Sunadale 281 G5
Sunbiggin 250 B2
Sunbury 171 G1
Sundaywell 266 C2
Sunderland *Cumb.* 259 E3
Sunderland *Lancs.* 242 A2
Sunderland *T. & W.* 262 C2
Sunderland Bridge 262 B4
Sundhope 277 E3
Sundon Park 199 F5
Sundridge 173 D3
Sundrum Mains 274 C3
Sunhill 182 D2
Sunipol 296 C4
Sunk Island 238 C1
Sunningdale 171 E1
Sunninghill 171 E1
Sunningwell 183 G2
Sunniside *Dur.* 262 A4
Sunniside *T. & W.* 262 B2
Sunny Bank 249 D3
Sunny Brow 262 A4
Sunnylaw 292 C5
Sunnyside *Aber.* 313 D5
Sunnyside *Northumb.* 261 F1
Sunnyside *S.Yorks.* 236 B3
Sunnyside *W.Suss.* 172 C5
Sunton 168 D2
Sunwick 287 F4
Surbiton 171 G1
Surfleet 226 A5
Surfleet Seas End 226 A5
Surlingham 229 E5
Sustead 228 C2
Susworth 237 F2
Sutcombe 162 D4
Sutcombemill 162 D4
Suton 214 B2
Sutors of Cromarty 322 A3
Sutterby 239 D5
Sutterton 226 A4
Sutton *Beds.* 200 A3
Sutton *Cambs.* 212 C5
Sutton *Devon* 152 A2
Sutton *Devon* 150 D3
Sutton *Gt.Lon.* 172 B2
Sutton *Kent* 175 F4
Sutton *Lincs.* 225 D2
Sutton *Norf.* 229 E3
Sutton *Notts.* 224 C4
Sutton *Notts.* 237 D4
Sutton *Oxon.* 183 G2
Sutton *Pembs.* 176 C1
Sutton *Peter.* 211 F3
Sutton *S.Yorks.* 236 C1
Sutton *Shrop.* 207 G4
Sutton *Shrop.* 221 D4
Sutton *Shrop.* 207 E1
Sutton *Shrop.* 220 A5
Sutton *Staffs.* 221 E5
Sutton *Suff.* 203 E3
Sutton *W.Suss.* 158 B2
Sutton Abinger 171 G3
Sutton at Hone 187 E5
Sutton Bassett 210 C4
Sutton Benger 182 B5
Sutton Bingham 154 B1
Sutton Bonington 223 G5
Sutton Bridge 226 C5
Sutton Cheney 209 G2
Sutton Coldfield 208 D3
Sutton Courtenay 184 A3
Sutton Crosses 226 C5
Sutton Grange 252 B5
Sutton Green *Oxon.* 183 G2
Sutton Green *Surr.* 171 F2
Sutton Green *Wrex.* 220 B3
Sutton Holms 155 G2
Sutton Howgrave 252 C5
Sutton in Ashfield 223 F2
Sutton in the Elms 210 A3
Sutton Ings 246 D4
Sutton Lane Ends 234 D5
Sutton le Marsh 239 F4
Sutton Leach 233 G3
Sutton Maddock 207 G2
Sutton Mallet 166 A4
Sutton Mandeville 168 A5
Sutton Montis 166 D5
Sutton on Sea 239 F4
Sutton on the Hill 222 D4
Sutton on Trent 224 C1
Sutton Poyntz 154 D4
Sutton St. Edmund 212 B1
Sutton St. James 212 C1
Sutton St. Nicholas 195 E3
Sutton Scarsdale 223 F1
Sutton Scotney 169 F4
Sutton upon Derwent 245 G3
Sutton Valence 174 A4
Sutton Veny 167 F3
Sutton Waldron 155 E1
Sutton Weaver 233 G5
Sutton Wick *B. & N.E.Som.* 166 C2
Sutton Wick *Oxon.* 183 G3
Sutton-in-Craven 243 G3
Sutton-on-Hull 246 D4
Sutton-on-the-Forest 245 E1
Sutton-under-Brailes 197 F4
Sutton-under-Whitestonecliffe 253 D4
Swaby 239 D5
Swadlincote 209 F1
Swaffham 213 G2
Swaffham Bulbeck 201 D1
Swaffham Prior 201 D1
Swafield 229 D2
Swainbost (Suainebost) 329 G1
Swainby 253 D2
Swainsthorpe 228 D5
Swainswick 167 E1
Swalcliffe 197 F4
Swalecliffe 174 D2
Swallow 238 B2
Swallow Beck 225 E1
Swallow Falls 114
Swallowcliffe 168 A5
Swallowfield 170 C1
Swallows Cross 187 F3
Swampton 169 F2
Swan Green *Ches.* 234 B5
Swan Green *Suff.* 215 D4
Swan Street 201 G5
Swanage 155 G5
Swanage Railway 37
Swanbach 221 D3
Swanbourne 198 D5
Swanbridge 165 E1
Swancote 207 G3
Swanland 246 B5
Swanlaws 278 B5
Swanley 173 E2
Swanley Village 173 E2
Swanmore *Hants.* 157 E1
Swanmore *I.o.W.* 157 E3
Swannington *Leics.* 209 G1
Swannington *Norf.* 228 C4
Swanscombe 187 F5
Swansea (Abertawe) 178 C3
Swanston 285 G3
Swanton Abbot 229 D3
Swanton Morley 228 B4
Swanton Novers 228 B2
Swanton Street 174 A3
Swanwick *Derbys.* 223 F2
Swanwick *Hants.* 157 E2
Swanwick Green 220 C3
Swarby 225 F3
Swardeston 228 D5
Swarkestone 223 E5
Swarland 271 D1
Swarraton 169 G4
Swarthmoor 249 D5
Swaton 225 G4
Swavesey 200 B1
Sway 156 B3
Swayfield 225 E5
Swaythling 156 D1
Swaythorpe 246 C1
Sweetham 152 B3
Sweethay 165 F5
Sweetheart Abbey 131
Sweetshouse 147 E3
Sweffling 203 E1
Swell 166 A5
Swepstone 209 F1
Swerford 197 F4
Swettenham 221 F1
Swffryd 180 B3
Swift's Green 174 A1
Swiftsden 160 C1
Swilland 202 C2
Swillett, The 185 F3
Swillington 244 C4
Swimbridge 163 G3
Swimbridge Newland 163 F2
Swinbrook 183 E1
Swincliffe 244 B2
Swincombe 163 G1
Swinden 243 E2
Swinderby 225 D1
Swindon *Staffs.* 208 A3
Swindon *Swin.* 183 D4
Swindon Village 196 B5
Swine 246 D4
Swinefleet 245 G5
Swineford 167 D1
Swineshead *Beds.* 199 F1
Swineshead *Lincs.* 226 A3
Swineshead Bridge 226 A3
Swineside 251 F4
Swiney 337 E5
Swinford *Leics.* 210 A5
Swinford *Oxon.* 183 G2
Swingate 223 G3
Swingfield Minnis 175 E4
Swingleton Green 202 A3
Swinhoe 279 G4
Swinhope 238 C3
Swining 343 D1
Swinithwaite 251 F4
Swinscoe 222 C3
Swinside Hall 278 B5
Swinstead 225 F5
Swinton *Gt.Man.* 234 B2
Swinton *N.Yorks.* 253 G5
Swinton *N.Yorks.* 252 B5
Swinton *S.Yorks.* 236 B3
Swinton *Sc.Bord.* 287 F5
Swinton Quarter 287 F5
Swintonmill 287 F5
Swiss Garden 83
Swithland 210 A1
Swordale 321 E3
Swordland 307 D5
Swordle 297 E2
Swordly 335 G2
Sworton Heath 234 A4
Swyddffynnon 192 C1
Swyncombe 184 B3
Swynnerton 221 F4
Swyre 154 B4
Sychnant 205 F5
Syde 182 B1
Sydenham *Gt.Lon.* 186 C5
Sydenham *Oxon.* 184 C2
Sydenham Damerel 149 E3
Syderstone 227 G4
Sydling St. Nicholas 154 C3
Sydmonton 169 F2
Sydney 221 E2
Syerston 224 C3
Sykehouse 236 D1
Sykes 242 C2
Sylen 178 B2
Symbister 343 E1
Symington *S.Ayr.* 274 B2
Symington *S.Lan.* 276 A2
Symonds Yat 67
Symondsbury 154 A3
Synod Inn (Post-mawr) 192 A2
Syon House 60
Syre 335 F4
Syreford 196 C5
Syresham 198 B3
Syston *Leics.* 210 B1
Syston *Lincs.* 225 E3
Sytchampton 196 A1
Sywell 198 D1

T

Taagan 319 G3
Tabley House 100
Tableyhill 234 B5
Tabost *W.Isles* 327 F2
Tabost (Harbost) *W.Isles* 329 G1
Tachbrook Mallory 197 F1
Tacher 337 D4
Tackley 197 G5
Tacleit (Hacklete) 328 C4
Tacolneston 214 C2
Tadcaster 245 D3
Tadden 155 F2
Taddington *Derbys.* 235 F5
Taddington *Glos.* 196 C4
Taddiport 163 E4
Tadley 170 B1
Tadlow 200 A3
Tadmarton 197 F4
Tadpole Bridge 183 F2
Tadworth 172 B3
Tafarnaubach 180 A1
Tafarn-y-bwlch 191 D4
Tafarn-y-Gelyn 219 E1
Taff Merthyr Garden Village 180 A3
Taff's Well (Ffynnon Taf) 180 A4
Tafolwern 205 E2
Taibach *N.P.T.* 179 D4
Tai-bach *Powys* 219 E5
Taicynhaeaf 204 C1
Tain *High.* 337 E2
Tain *High.* 321 G1
Tai'n Lôn 216 D2
Tai'r Bull 193 F5
Tairgwaith 178 D1
Tai'r-heol 180 A3
Tairlaw 274 C5
Tai'r-ysgol 178 C3
Takeley 201 D5
Takeley Street 200 D5
Talachddu 193 G4
Talacre 232 C4
Talardd 218 B5
Talaton 153 D2
Talbenny 176 B1
Talbot Green 179 G4
Talbot Village 155 G3
Talerddig 205 F2
Tales of Robin Hood 75
Talgarreg 192 A2
Talgarth 194 A4
Taliesin 204 C3
Talisker 305 G1
Talke Pits 221 F2
Talkin 260 B2
Talla Linnfoots 276 C3
Talladale 319 F2
Talladh-a-Bheithe 300 A4
Talland 147 G4
Tallarn Green 220 B3
Tallentire 259 E3
Talley (Talyllychau) 192 C4
Tallington 211 F2
Talmine 335 E2
Talog 191 G5
Tal-sarn 192 B2
Talsarnau 217 F4
Talskiddy 146 D3
Talwrn *I.o.A.* 230 C5
Talwrn *Wrex.* 219 F3
Talwrn *Wrex.* 220 A3
Talybont *Cere.* 204 C4
Tal-y-bont *Conwy* 218 A1
Tal-y-bont *Gwyn.* 217 E5
Tal-y-bont *Gwyn.* 231 E5
Talybont-on-Usk 194 A5
Tal-y-Cae 217 F1
Tal-y-cafn 231 F5
Tal-y-coed 180 D1
Talygarn 179 G4
Talyllychau (Talley) 192 C4
Tal-y-llyn *Gwyn.* 204 D2
Talyllyn *Powys* 194 A5
Talyllyn Railway 114
Talysarn 217 D2
Tal-y-wern 205 E2
Tamavoid 292 A5
Tamerton Foliot 150 A1
Tamworth 209 E2
Tamworth Castle 67
Tamworth Green 226 B3
Tan Office Green 201 F2
Tandem 235 F1
Tandridge 172 C3
Tanerdy 192 A5
Tanfield 262 A2
Tanfield Lea 262 A2
Tang 244 B2
Tang Hall 245 F2
Tangiers 176 C1
Tanglandford 313 D1
Tangley 169 E2
Tangmere 158 B3
Tangmere Military Aviation Museum 52
Tangwick 344 B5
Tangy 272 B3
Tank Museum 37
Tankerness 339 E2
Tankersley 236 A2
Tankerton 174 D2
Tan-lan 217 F3
Tannach 337 F4
Tannachie 303 F1
Tannachy 332 C4
Tannadice 302 C4
Tannington 202 D1
Tannochside 284 A3
Tansley 223 E2
Tansley Knoll 223 E2
Tansor 211 F3
Tantallon Castle 131
Tantobie 262 A2
Tanton 253 E1
Tanworth in Arden 208 D5
Tan-y-fron 218 C1
Tan-y-graig 216 C4
Tanygrisiau 217 F3
Tan-y-groes 191 F3
Tan-y-pistyll 219 D5
Tan-yr-allt 232 B4
Taobh a' Deas Loch Baghasdail 314 C2
Taobh Siar 326 D3
Taobh Tuath (Northton) 326 B5
Tapeley 163 E3
Taplow 185 E4
Tapton Grove 236 B5
Taransay (Tarasaigh) 326 C3
Taraphocain 298 C5
Tarasaigh (Taransay) 326 C3
Tarbat House 321 G2
Tarbert *Arg. & B.* 281 G3
Tarbert *Arg. & B.* 281 E4
Tarbert *Arg. & B.* 281 F1
Tarbert *High.* 297 F3
Tarbert (An Tairbeart) *W.Isles* 327 D3
Tarbet *Arg. & B.* 291 F4
Tarbet *High.* 307 D5
Tarbet *High.* 334 A4
Tarbock Green 233 F4
Tarbolton 274 C3
Tarbrax 285 E4
Tardebigge 196 B1
Tardy Gate 242 B5
Tarfside 302 C2
Tarland 311 G4
Tarleton 242 A5
Tarlscough 233 F1
Tarlton 182 B3
Tarnbrook 242 B2
Tarnock 166 A2
Tarporley 220 C1
Tarr 165 E4
Tarrant Crawford 155 F2
Tarrant Gunville 155 F1
Tarrant Hinton 155 F1
Tarrant Keyneston 155 F2
Tarrant Launceston 155 F2
Tarrant Monkton 155 F2
Tarrant Rawston 155 F2
Tarrant Rushton 155 F2
Tarrel 322 A1
Tarring Neville 159 G3
Tarrington 195 F3
Tarrnacraig 273 E2
Tarsappie 293 G2
Tarskavaig 306 B4
Tarves 313 D1
Tarvie *High.* 320 D4
Tarvie *P. & K.* 301 F3
Tarvin 220 B1
Tarvin Sands 220 B1
Tasburgh 214 D2
Tasley 207 F3
Taston 197 F5
Tate Britain 60
Tate Liverpool 100
Tate Modern 60
Tate St. Ives 37
Tatenhill 222 D5
Tathall End 198 D3
Tatham 242 C1
Tathwell 238 D4
Tatsfield 172 D3
Tattenhall 220 B2
Tattenhoe 198 D4
Tatterford 227 G5
Tattersett 227 G4
Tattershall 226 A2
Tattershall Bridge 225 G2
Tattershall Castle 75
Tattershall Thorpe 226 A2
Tattingstone 202 C4
Tatton Park 100
Tatworth 153 G2
Tauchers 323 F5
Taunton 165 F5
Tavelty 312 C3
Taverham 228 C4
Tavernspite 177 E1
Tavistock 149 E3
Taw Bridge 163 G5
Taw Green 149 G1
Tawstock 163 F3
Taxal 235 E5
Tayburn 283 G5
Taychreggan 290 C2
Tayinloan 281 E5
Taylors Cross 162 C4
Taynafead 290 C3
Taynish 281 F1
Taynton *Glos.* 195 G5
Taynton *Oxon.* 183 E1
Taynuilt 290 C1
Tayock 303 E4
Tayovullin 280 A2
Tayport 294 C2
Tayvallich 281 F1
Tea Green 199 G5
Tealby 238 B3
Tealing 294 C1
Team Valley 262 B1
Teanamachar 315 F3
Teangue 306 C4
Teasses 294 C4
Tebay 250 B2
Tebworth 199 E5
Techniquest 114
Tedburn St. Mary 152 B3
Teddington *Glos.* 196 B4
Teddington *Gt.Lon.* 186 A5
Tedstone Delamere 195 F2
Tedstone Wafre 195 F2
Teesdale Hay Meadows 105
Teesside International Airport 252 C1
Teeton 210 B5
Teffont Evias 168 A4
Teffont Magna 168 A4
Tegg's Nose Country Park 100
Tegryn 191 F4
Teigh 211 D1
Teign Village 152 B4
Teigngrace 152 B5
Teignmouth 152 C5
Telford 207 F2
Telham 160 C2
Tellisford 167 F2
Telscombe 159 G3
Telscombe Cliffs 159 G3
Tempar 300 B4
Templand 267 E2
Temple *Cornw.* 147 F2
Temple *Midloth.* 286 A4
Temple Balsall 209 E5
Temple Bar 192 B2
Temple Cloud 166 D2
Temple End 201 E2
Temple Ewell 175 E4
Temple Grafton 196 D2
Temple Guiting 196 C5
Temple Herdewyke 197 F2
Temple Hirst 245 F5
Temple Newsam 90
Temple Normanton 223 F1
Temple Sowerby 260 C5
Templecombe 167 E5
Templeton *Devon* 152 B1
Templeton *Pembs.* 177 E1
Templeton Bridge 152 B1
Templewood 303 E3
Tempsford 199 G2
Ten Mile Bank 213 E3
Tenbury Wells 195 E1
Tenby (Dinbych-y-Pysgod) 177 E2
Tendring 202 C5
Tendring Green 202 C5
Tenga 297 E5
Tenterden 174 A5
Tepersie Castle 312 A2
Terally 256 B2
Terling 187 G1
Tern 207 F1
Ternhill 220 D4
Terregles 266 D3
Terriers 185 D3
Tarrington 253 F5
Terrington St. Clement 227 D5
Terrington St. John 212 D1
Terry's Green 208 D5
Tervieside 311 E1
Teston 173 G3
Testwood 156 C1
Tetbury 182 A3
Tetbury Upton 182 A3
Tetchill 220 A4
Tetcott 148 D1
Tetford 238 D5

Tetney 238 D2
Tetney Lock 238 D2
Tetsworth 184 B2
Tettenhall 208 A2
Tettenhall Wood 208 A3
Tetworth 200 A2
Teuchan 313 F1
Teversal 223 F1
Teversham 200 C2
Teviothead 277 F5
Tewel 303 G1
Tewin 186 B1
Tewkesbury 196 A4
Teynham 174 B2
Thackley 244 A4
Thainston 303 E2
Thainstone 312 C3
Thakeham 158 D2
Thame 184 C2
Thames Barrier Visitor Centre 61
Thames Ditton 171 G1
Thames Haven 187 G4
Thamesmead 187 D4
Thanington 174 D3
Thankerton 276 A2
Tharston 214 C2
Thatcham 169 G1
Thatto Heath 233 G3
Thaxted 201 E4
Theakston 252 C4
Thealby 237 F1
Theale *Som.* 166 B3
Theale *W.Berks.* 184 B5
Thearne 246 C4
Theatre Museum 61
Theberton 203 F1
Thedden Grange 170 B4
Theddingworth 210 B4
Theddlethorpe All Saints 239 E4
Theddlethorpe St. Helen 239 E4
Thelbridge Barton 152 A1
Thelbridge Cross 152 A1
Thelnetham 214 B4
Thelveton 214 C3
Thelwall 234 A4
Themelthorpe 228 B3
Thenford 198 A3
Therfield 200 B4
Thetford *Lincs.* 211 G1
Thetford *Norf.* 213 G4
Thetford Forest Park 83
Thethwaite 259 G2
Theydon Bois 186 D3
Theydon Garnon 187 D3
Theydon Mount 187 D3
Thickwood 182 A5
Thimbleby *Lincs.* 226 A1
Thimbleby *N.Yorks.* 252 D3
Thingley 167 F1
Thinktank 67
Thirkleby 253 D5
Thirlby 253 D4
Thirlestane 286 C5
Thirlestane Castle 131
Thirn 252 B4
Thirsk 252 D4
Thirston New Houses 271 D2
Thirtleby 247 D4
Thistleton *Lancs.* 242 A4
Thistleton *Rut.* 211 E1
Thistley Green 213 E5
Thixendale 246 A3
Thockrington 270 B4
Tholomas Drove 212 B2
Tholthorpe 245 D1
Thomas Chapel 177 E2
Thomas Close 260 A3
Thomastown 312 A1
Thompson 214 A2
Thomshill 323 E4
Thong 187 F5
Thongsbridge 235 F2
Thoralby 251 F4
Thoresby 236 D5
Thoresthorpe 239 E5
Thoresway 238 B3
Thorganby *Lincs.* 238 C3
Thorganby *N.Yorks.* 245 F3
Thorgill 253 G3
Thorington 215 F4
Thorington Street 202 B4
Thorley 187 D1
Thorley Houses 200 C5
Thorley Street *Herts.* 187 D1
Thorley Street *I.o.W.* 156 C4
Thormanby 253 D5
Thornaby-on-Tees 253 D1
Thornage 228 B2
Thornborough *Bucks.* 198 C4
Thornborough *N.Yorks.* 252 B5
Thornbury *Devon* 163 D5
Thornbury *Here.* 195 F2
Thornbury *S.Glos.* 181 F3
Thornbury *W.Yorks.* 244 A4
Thornby 210 B5
Thorncliff 235 G1
Thorncliffe 222 B2
Thorncombe 153 G2
Thorncombe Street 171 F3
Thorncote Green 199 G3
Thorncross 156 D4
Thorndon 202 C1
Thorndon Cross 149 F1
Thorne 237 D1
Thorne St. Margaret 165 D5
Thorner 244 C4
Thorney *Bucks.* 185 F5
Thorney *Notts.* 237 F5
Thorney *Peter.* 212 A2
Thorney *Som.* 166 B5
Thorney Close 262 C2
Thorney Hill 156 B3
Thornfalcon 165 F5
Thornford 154 C1
Thorngrafton 261 D1
Thorngrove 166 A4
Thorngumbald 247 E5
Thornham 227 F3
Thornham Magna 214 C4
Thornham Parva 214 C4
Thornhaugh 211 F2
Thornhill *Cardiff* 180 A4
Thornhill *Cumb.* 248 B2
Thornhill *D. & G.* 266 C1
Thornhill *Derbys.* 235 F4
Thornhill *S'ham.* 157 D1
Thornhill *Stir.* 292 B4
Thornhill *W.Yorks.* 235 G1
Thornhill Lees 235 G1
Thornholme 246 D1
Thornicombe 155 E2
Thornley *Dur.* 262 C4
Thornley *Dur.* 262 A4
Thornley Gate 261 E2
Thornliebank 283 G4
Thornroan 313 D1
Thorns 201 F2
Thorns Green 234 B4
Thornsett 235 E4
Thornthwaite *Cumb.* 259 F4
Thornthwaite *N.Yorks.* 244 A2
Thornton *Angus* 302 B5
Thornton *Bucks.* 198 C4
Thornton *E.Riding* 245 G3
Thornton *Fife* 294 A5
Thornton *Lancs.* 241 G3
Thornton *Leics.* 209 G2
Thornton *Lincs.* 226 A1
Thornton *Mersey.* 233 E2
Thornton *Middbro.* 253 D1
Thornton *Northumb.* 287 G5
Thornton *P. & K.* 301 F5
Thornton *Pembs.* 176 C2
Thornton *W.Yorks.* 244 A4
Thornton Bridge 252 D5
Thornton Curtis 238 A1
Thornton Heath 172 C2
Thornton Hough 233 E4
Thornton in Lonsdale 250 B5
Thornton le Moor 238 A3
Thornton Park 287 G5
Thornton Rust 251 E4
Thornton Steward 252 A4
Thornton Watlass 252 B4
Thorntonhall 283 G4
Thornton-In-Craven 243 F3
Thornton-le-Beans 252 D3
Thornton-le-Clay 245 F1
Thornton-le-Dale 254 B4
Thornton-le-Moor 252 C4
Thornton-le-Moors 233 F5
Thornton-le-Street 252 D4
Thorntonloch 287 E2
Thornwood Common 187 D2
Thornyhill 303 E2
Thornylee 277 F2
Thoroton 224 C3
Thorp Arch 244 D3
Thorp Perrow Arboretum 90
Thorpe *Derbys.* 222 C2
Thorpe *E.Riding* 246 B3
Thorpe *Lincs.* 239 E4
Thorpe *N.Yorks.* 243 G1
Thorpe *Norf.* 215 F2
Thorpe *Notts.* 224 C2
Thorpe *Surr.* 171 F1
Thorpe Abbotts 214 C3
Thorpe Acre 210 A1
Thorpe Arnold 224 C5
Thorpe Audlin 236 B1
Thorpe Bassett 254 B5
Thorpe Bay 188 C4
Thorpe by Water 211 D3
Thorpe Constantine 209 E2
Thorpe Culvert 226 C1
Thorpe End 229 D4
Thorpe Green *Essex* 202 C5
Thorpe Green *Lancs.* 242 B5
Thorpe Green *Suff.* 202 A2
Thorpe Hall 253 E5
Thorpe Hesley 236 A3
Thorpe in Balne 236 C1
Thorpe in the Fallows 237 G4
Thorpe Langton 210 C3
Thorpe Larches 262 C5
Thorpe le Street 246 A3
Thorpe Malsor 210 D5
Thorpe Mandeville 198 A3
Thorpe Market 228 D2
Thorpe Morieux 202 A2
Thorpe on the Hill *Lincs.* 225 E1
Thorpe on the Hill *W.Yorks.* 244 C5
Thorpe Park 52
Thorpe Row 228 A5
Thorpe St. Andrew 229 D5
Thorpe St. Peter 226 C1
Thorpe Salvin 236 C4
Thorpe Satchville 210 C1
Thorpe Street 214 B4
Thorpe Thewles 262 D5
Thorpe Tilney Dales 225 G2
Thorpe Underwood *N.Yorks.* 245 D2
Thorpe Underwood *Northants.* 210 C4
Thorpe Waterville 211 F4
Thorpe Willoughby 245 E4
Thorpefield 252 D5
Thorpe-le-Soken 202 C5
Thorpeness 203 F1
Thorpland 213 E2
Thorrington 202 B5
Thorverton 152 C2
Thrandeston 214 C4
Thrapston 211 E5
Threapland 243 F1
Threapwood 220 B3
Threapwood Head 222 B3
Threave Castle 131
Threave Gardens 131
Three Ashes 167 D3
Three Bridges 172 B5
Three Burrows 146 B5
Three Chimneys 174 A5
Three Cocks (Aberllynfi) 194 A4
Three Crosses 178 B3
Three Cups Corner 160 B1
Three Hammers 147 G1
Three Holes 212 D2
Three Leg Cross 173 F5
Three Legged Cross 155 G2
Three Mile Cross 170 C1
Three Oaks 160 D2
Threehammer Common 229 E4
Threekingham 225 F4
Threemilestone 146 B5
Threlkeld 259 G4
Threshfield 243 F1
Threxton Hill 213 G2
Thriepley 294 B1
Thrift, The 200 B4
Thrigby 229 F4
Thringarth 261 F5
Thringstone 209 G1
Thrintoft 252 C3
Thriplow 200 C3
Throapham 236 C4
Throckenholt 212 B2
Throcking 200 D4
Throckley 262 A1
Throckmorton 196 B3
Throop 155 E3
Throphill 270 D3
Thropton 270 C1
Througham 182 B2
Throwleigh 149 G1
Throwley 174 B3
Throws 201 E5
Thrumpton *Notts.* 223 G4
Thrumpton *Notts.* 237 E5
Thrumster 337 F4
Thrunton 279 E5
Thrupp *Glos.* 182 A2
Thrupp *Oxon.* 183 G1
Thrupp *Oxon.* 183 E3
Thruscross 244 A2
Thrushelton 149 E2
Thrussington 210 B1
Thruxton *Hants.* 169 D3
Thruxton *Here.* 194 D4
Thrybergh 236 B3
Thulston 223 F4
Thunder Bridge 235 F1
Thundergay 281 G5
Thundersley 188 B4
Thunderton 325 F5
Thundridge 186 C1
Thurcaston 210 A1
Thurcroft 236 B4
Thurdistoft 337 E2
Thurdon 162 C4
Thurgarton *Norf.* 228 C2
Thurgarton *Notts.* 224 B3
Thurgoland 235 G2
Thurlaston *Leics.* 210 A3
Thurlaston *Warks.* 209 G5
Thurlbear 165 F5
Thurlby *Lincs.* 211 G1
Thurlby *Lincs.* 225 E1
Thurlby *Lincs.* 239 E5
Thurleigh 199 F2
Thurlestone 150 C3
Thurloxton 165 F4
Thurlstone 235 G2
Thurlton 215 F2
Thurlwood 221 F2
Thurmaston 210 B2
Thurnby 210 B2
Thurne 229 F4
Thurnham 174 A3
Thurning *Norf.* 228 B3
Thurning *Northants.* 211 F4
Thurnscoe 236 B2
Thursby 259 G1
Thursden 243 F4
Thursford 228 A2
Thursley 171 E4
Thurso 336 D2
Thurstaston 232 D4
Thurston 202 A1
Thurston Clough 235 D2
Thurstonfield 259 G1
Thurstonland 235 F1
Thurton 229 E5
Thurvaston *Derbys.* 222 D4
Thurvaston *Derbys.* 222 C4
Thuster 337 E3
Thuxton 228 B5
Thwaite *N.Yorks.* 251 D3
Thwaite *Suff.* 202 C1
Thwaite Head 249 E3
Thwaite St. Mary 215 E2
Thwaites 243 G3
Thwaites Brow 243 G3
Thwing 255 D5
Tibbermore 293 F2
Tibberton *Glos.* 195 G5
Tibberton *Tel. & W.* 221 D5
Tibberton *Worcs.* 196 B2
Tibbie Shiels Inn 276 D3
Tibenham 214 C2
Tibertich 290 A4
Tibshelf 223 F1
Tibthorpe 246 B2
Ticehurst 173 F5
Tichborne 169 G4
Tickencote 211 E2
Tickenham 181 D5
Tickford End 199 D3
Tickhill 236 C3
Ticklerton 207 D3
Ticknall 223 E5
Tickton 246 C3
Tidbury Green 208 D5
Tidcombe 169 D2
Tiddington *Oxon.* 184 B2
Tiddington *Warks.* 197 E2
Tiddleywink 182 A5
Tidebrook 160 B1
Tideford 148 D5
Tideford Cross 148 D4
Tidenham 181 E3
Tidenham Chase 181 E3
Tideswell 235 F5
Tidmarsh 184 B5
Tidmington 197 E4
Tidpit 155 G1
Tidworth 168 D3
Tiers Cross 176 C1
Tiffield 198 B2
Tifty 324 C5
Tigerton 302 D3
Tigh a' Gearraidh 315 F2
Tighachnoic 297 F5
Tighnablair 292 C3
Tighnabruaich 282 A2
Tighnacomaire 298 B3
Tigley 151 D1
Tilbrook 199 F1
Tilbury 187 F5
Tilbury Fort 83
Tilbury Green 201 F3
Tile Hill 209 E5
Tilehurst 184 B5
Tilford 171 D3
Tilgate 172 B5
Tilgate Forest Row 172 B5
Tillathrowie 311 G1
Tillers' Green 195 F4
Tillery 313 E2
Tilley 220 C5
Tillicoultry 293 E5
Tillingham 188 C2
Tillington *Here.* 195 D3
Tillington *W.Suss.* 171 E5
Tillington Common 195 D3
Tillyarblet 302 D3
Tillybirloch 312 B4
Tillycairn Castle 312 B3
Tillycorthie 313 E2
Tillydrine 312 B5
Tillyfar 325 D5
Tillyfour 312 A3
Tillyfourie 312 B3
Tillygreig 313 D2
Tillypronie 311 G4
Tilmanstone 175 F3
Tiln 237 E4
Tilney All Saints 213 D1
Tilney Fen End 212 D1
Tilney High End 213 D1
Tilney St. Lawrence 212 D1
Tilshead 168 B3
Tilstock 220 C4
Tilston 220 B2
Tilstone Fearnall 220 C1
Tilsworth 199 E5
Tilton on the Hill 210 C2
Tiltups End 182 A3
Timberland 225 G2
Timberland Dales 225 G1
Timbersbrook 221 F1
Timberscombe 164 C3
Timble 244 A2
Timewell 164 C5
Timperley 234 B4
Timsbury *B. & N.E.Som.* 167 D2
Timsbury *Hants.* 169 E5
Timsgearraidh 328 B4
Timworth 201 G1
Timworth Green 201 G1
Tincleton 155 D3
Tindale 260 C2
Tindon End 201 E4
Tingewick 198 B4
Tingley 244 B5
Tingrith 199 F4
Tingwall 340 C4
Tinhay 149 D2
Tinney 148 C1
Tinshill 244 B4
Tinsley 236 B3
Tinsley Green 172 B5
Tintagel 147 E1
Tintagel Castle 37
Tintagel Old Post Office 37
Tintern Abbey 114
Tintern Parva 181 E2
Tintinhull 154 A1
Tintinhull House 37
Tintwistle 235 E3
Tinwald 267 E2
Tinwell 211 F2
Tippacott 164 A3
Tipperty *Aber.* 303 F1
Tipperty *Aber.* 313 E2
Tips End 212 C3
Tiptoe 156 B3
Tipton 208 B3
Tipton St. John 153 D3
Tiptree 188 B1
Tiptree Heath 188 B1
Tirabad 193 E3
Tiree 296 A2
Tiree Airport 296 B2
Tirindrish 299 E1
Tirley 196 A5
Tirphil 180 A2
Tirril 260 B5
Tir-y-dail 178 C1
Tisbury 168 A5
Tisman's Common 171 F4
Tissington 222 C2
Tister 337 D2
Titchberry 162 C3
Titchfield 157 E2
Titchmarsh 211 F5
Titchwell 227 F3
Titchwell Marsh 83
Tithby 224 B4
Titley 194 C1
Titlington 279 F5
Titmore Green 200 A5
Titsey 172 D3
Titson 162 C5
Tittensor 221 F4
Tittleshall 227 G5
Tiverton *Ches.* 220 C1
Tiverton *Devon* 152 C1
Tiverton Castle 37
Tiverton Museum 37
Tivetshall St. Margaret 214 C3
Tivetshall St. Mary 214 C3
Tivington 164 C3
Tixall 221 G5
Tixover 211 E2
Toab *Ork.* 339 E2
Toab *Shet.* 343 G5
Tobermory 297 E4
Toberonochy 289 G4
Tobha Mòr (Homore) 304 A1
Tobson 328 C4
Tocher 312 B1
Tockenham 182 C5
Tockenham Wick 182 C4
Tockholes 242 C5
Tockington 181 F4
Tockwith 245 D2
Todber 167 E5
Toddington *Beds.* 199 F5
Toddington *Glos.* 196 C4
Todenham 197 E4
Todhills *Angus* 294 C1
Todhills *Cumb.* 268 B5
Todlachie 312 B3
Todmorden 243 F5
Todwick 236 B4
Toft *Cambs.* 200 B2
Toft *Lincs.* 211 F1
Toft *Shet.* 344 D5
Toft Hill 262 A5
Toft Monks 215 F2
Toft next Newton 238 A4
Toftcarl 337 F4
Toftrees 227 G5
Tofts 337 F2
Toftwood 228 A4
Togston 271 E1
Tokavaig 306 C3
Tokers Green 184 B5
Tolastadh 329 G3
Tolastadh a' Chaolais 328 C4
Tolastadh Ùr 329 G3
Toll Bar 236 C2
Toll of Birness 313 F1
Tolland 165 E4
Tollard Farnham 155 F1
Tollard Royal 155 F1
Tollcross 284 A3
Toller Down Gate 154 B2
Toller Fratrum 154 B3
Toller Porcorum 154 B3
Toller Whelme 154 B2
Tollerton *N.Yorks.* 245 E1
Tollerton *Notts.* 224 B4
Tollesbury 188 C1
Tollesby 253 E1
Tolleshunt D'Arcy 188 C1
Tolleshunt Knights 188 C1
Tolleshunt Major 188 B1
Tolm (Holm) 329 F4
Tolmachan 326 C3
Tolpuddle 155 D3
Tolvah 310 A5
Tolworth 171 G1
Tom an Fhuadain 327 F2
Tomatin 310 A2
Tombreck 309 F1
Tomchrasky 308 B3
Tomdoun 308 A4
Tomdow 322 C5
Tomich *High.* 308 C2
Tomich *High.* 321 G2
Tomich *High.* 332 B4
Tomintoul 311 D3
Tomnacross 321 E5
Tomnamoon 322 C4
Tomnaven 311 G1
Tomnavoulin 311 E2
Tomvaich 310 C1
Ton Pentre 179 F3
Tonbridge 173 E4
Tonbridge Castle 52
Tondu 179 E4
Tonedale 165 E5
Tonfanau 204 B2
Tong *Kent* 174 A4
Tong *Shrop.* 207 G2
Tong *W.Yorks.* 244 B4
Tong Norton 207 G2
Tong Street 244 A4
Tonge 223 F5
Tongham 171 D3
Tongland 266 A5
Tongue 335 E3
Tongue House 335 E3
Tongwynlais 180 A4
Tonmawr 179 E3
Tonna 179 D3
Tonwell 186 C1
Tonypandy 179 F3
Tonyrefail 179 G4
Toot Baldon 184 A2
Toot Hill 187 E2
Toothill *Hants.* 156 C1
Toothill *Swin.* 182 D4
Tooting Graveney 186 B5
Top End 199 F1
Top of Hebers 234 C2
Topcliffe 252 D5
Topcroft 215 D2
Topcroft Street 215 D2
Toppesfield 201 F4
Toppings 234 B1
Toprow 214 C2
Topsham 152 C4
Topsham Bridge 150 D2
Torastan 296 B3
Torbain 311 D3
Torbeg *Aber.* 311 F5
Torbeg *N.Ayr.* 273 E3
Torbothie 284 C4
Torbryan 151 E1
Torcastle 298 D2
Torcross 151 E3
Tordarroch 309 F1
Tore 321 F4
Toreduff 322 D3
Toremore *High.* 311 D1
Toremore *High.* 337 D5
Torfrey 147 F4
Torgyle 308 C3
Torksey 237 F5
Torlum 315 F4
Torlundy 298 D2
Tormarton 181 G5
Tormisdale 280 A4
Tormore 273 D2
Tormsdale 336 D3
Tornagrain 321 G4
Tornahaish 311 E4
Tornaveen 312 B4
Torness 309 E2
Toronto 262 A4
Torosay Castle 131
Torpenhow 259 F3
Torphichen 285 D2
Torphins 312 B4
Torpoint 150 A2
Torquay 151 F1
Torquhan 286 B5
Torr 150 B2
Torran *Arg. & B.* 290 A4
Torran *High.* 321 G2
Torran *High.* 318 B5
Torrance 284 A2
Torrance House 284 A4
Torrancroy 311 F3
Torre *Som.* 164 D3
Torre *Torbay* 151 F1
Torre Abbey 37
Torrich 322 A4
Torridon *High.* 319 E4
Torridon *High.* 131
Torrin 306 B2
Torrisdale *Arg. & B.* 272 C2
Torrisdale *High.* 335 F2
Torrish 333 E3
Torrisholme 242 A1
Torroble 332 A4
Torry *Aber.* 323 G5
Torry *Aberdeen* 313 E4
Torryburn 285 E1
Torsonce 286 B5
Torterston 325 F5
Torthorwald 267 E3
Tortington 158 B3
Tortworth 181 G3
Torvaig 318 A5
Torver 249 D3
Torwood 284 C1
Torworth 237 D4
Tosberry 162 C3
Toscaig 306 D1
Toseland 200 A1
Tosside 243 D2
Tostarie 296 C5
Tostock 202 A1
Totaig 317 E4
Totamore 296 A4
Tote 318 A5
Tote Hill 171 D5
Totegan 336 A2
Totford 169 G4
Totham Hill 188 B1
Tothill 239 E4
Totland 156 C4
Totley 236 A5
Totnes 151 E1
Toton 223 G4
Totronald 296 A4
Totscore 317 G3
Tottenham 186 C3
Tottenhill 213 E1
Tottenhill Row 213 E1
Totteridge *Bucks.* 185 D3
Totteridge *Gt.Lon.* 186 B3
Totternhoe 199 E5
Tottington *Gt.Man.* 234 B1
Tottington *Norf.* 213 G3
Totton 156 C1
Toulton 165 E4
Tournaig 319 E1
Toux 325 E4
Tovil 173 G3
Tow Law 262 A4
Towan Cross 146 B5
Toward 282 C3
Towcester 198 B3
Towednack 144 B3
Tower Bridge Experience 61
Tower End 213 E1
Tower of London 61
Towersey 184 C2
Towie *Aber.* 325 D3
Towie *Aber.* 312 A2
Towie *Aber.* 311 G3
Towiemore 323 F5
Town End *Cambs.* 212 C3
Town End *Cumb.* 249 F4
Town End *Mersey.* 233 F4
Town Green *Lancs.* 233 F2
Town Green *Norf.* 229 E4
Town of Lowton 234 A3
Town Row 173 E5
Town Street 213 F4
Town Yetholm 278 C4
Townend 283 F2
Townfield 261 F3
Townhead *D. & G.* 257 G2
Townhead *S.Yorks.* 235 F2
Townhead of Greenlaw 266 B4
Townhill *Fife* 285 F1
Townhill *Swan.* 178 C3
Towns End 169 G2
Towns Green 220 D1
Townshend 144 C3
Towthorpe *E.Riding* 246 B1
Towthorpe *York* 245 F2
Towton 245 D4
Towyn 232 A5
Toynton All Saints 226 B1
Toynton Fen Side 226 B1
Toynton St. Peter 226 C1
Toy's Hill 173 D3
Trabboch 274 C3
Traboe 145 E4
Tradespark *High.* 322 A4
Tradespark *Ork.* 339 D2
Traeth Coch (Red Wharf Bay) 230 D4
Trafford Centre 234 B3
Trafford Park 234 B3
Trallong 193 F5
Trallwn 178 C3
Tranent 286 B2
Tranmere 233 E4
Trantlebeg 336 A3
Trantlemore 336 A3
Tranwell 271 D3
Trap 178 C1
Trap Street 221 F1
Traprain 286 C2
Trap's Green 196 D1
Traquair 277 E2
Traquair House 131
Trawden 243 F4
Trawsfynydd 218 A4
Treak Cliff Cavern 75
Trealaw 179 G3
Treales 242 A4
Trearddur 230 A5
Treaslane 317 G4
Tre-Aubrey 179 G5
Trebah Garden 37
Trebanog 179 G3
Trebanos 178 D2
Trebarrow 148 C1
Trebartha 147 G2
Trebarvah 145 E3
Trebarwith 147 E1
Trebeath 147 G1
Trebetherick 146 D2
Trebister 343 D4
Tre-boeth 178 C3
Treborough 164 D4
Trebudannon 146 C3
Trebullett 148 D3
Treburley 148 D3
Treburrick 146 C2
Trebyan 147 E3
Trecastle 193 E5
Trecott 163 G5
Trecrogo 148 D2
Trecwn 190 C4
Trecynon 179 F2
Tredaule 147 G1
Tredavoe 144 B4
Treddiog 190 B5
Tredegar 180 A2
Tredegar House 114
Tredington *Glos.* 196 B5
Tredington *Warks.* 197 E3
Tredinnick *Cornw.* 146 D3
Tredinnick *Cornw.* 147 G4
Tredogan 165 D1
Tredomen 194 A4
Tredrissi 191 D3
Tredunnock 180 C3
Tredustan 194 A4
Tredworth 182 A1
Treen *Cornw.* 144 A4
Treen *Cornw.* 144 B3
Treesmill 147 E4
Treeton 236 B4
Trefaldwyn (Montgomery) 206 B3
Trefasser 190 B4
Trefdraeth *I.o.A.* 230 C5
Trefdraeth (Newport) *Pembs.* 191 D4
Trefecca 194 A4
Trefechan 179 G2
Trefeglwys 205 F3
Trefenter 192 C1
Treffgarne 190 C5
Treffynnon (Holywell) *Flints.* 232 C5
Treffynnon *Pembs.* 190 B5
Trefgarn Owen 190 B5
Trefil 180 A1
Trefilan 192 B2
Treflach 219 F5
Trefnanney 206 B1
Trefnant 232 B5
Trefonen 219 F5
Trefor *Gwyn.* 216 C3
Trefor *I.o.A.* 230 B4
Treforest 179 G4
Treforest Industrial Estate 180 A4
Trefriw 218 A1
Tref-y-clawdd (Knighton) 206 B5
Trefynwy (Monmouth) 181 E1
Tregadillett 147 G1
Tregaian 230 C5
Tregare 180 D1
Tregarland 147 G4
Tregarne 145 E4
Tregaron 192 C2

Tre - Uss

Tregarth 217 F1
Tregaswith 146 C3
Tregavethan 146 B5
Tregear 146 C4
Tregeare 147 G1
Tregeiriog 219 E4
Tregele 230 B3
Tregidden 145 E4
Tregiskey 147 E5
Treglemais 190 B5
Tregolds 146 C2
Tregole 148 B1
Tregonetha 147 D3
Tregony 146 D5
Tregoodwell 147 F1
Tregoss 147 D3
Tregowris 145 E4
Tregoyd 194 A4
Tregrehan Mills 147 E4
Tre-groes 192 A3
Treguff 179 G5
Tregullon 147 E3
Tregunnon 147 G1
Tregurrian 146 C3
Tregynon 205 G3
Trehafod 179 G3
Trehan 150 A2
Treharris 179 G3
Treherbert 179 F3
Tre-hill 179 G5
Trekenner 148 D3
Treknow 147 E1
Trelan 145 E5
Trelash 148 B1
Trelassick 146 C4
Trelawnyd 232 B5
Trelech 191 F4
Treleddyd-fawr 190 A5
Trelewis 180 A3
Treligga 147 E1
Trelights 147 D2
Trelill 147 E2
Trelissick *Cornw.* 145 F3
Trelissick *Cornw.* 37
Trelleck 181 E2
Trelleck Grange 181 D2
Trelogan 232 C4
Trelowla 147 G4
Trelystan 206 B2
Tremadog 217 E3
Tremail 147 F1
Tremain 191 F3
Tremaine 147 G1
Tremar 147 G3
Trematon 149 D5
Tremeirchion 232 B5
Tremethick Cross 144 B3
Tremore 147 E3
Trenance *Cornw.* 146 C3
Trenance *Cornw.* 146 D2
Trenarren 147 E5
Trench *Tel. & W.* 207 F1
Trench *Wrex.* 220 A4
Trencreek 146 C3
Trenear 145 D3
Treneglos 147 G1
Trenewan 147 F4
Trengune 148 B1
Trengwainton 37
Trent 154 B1
Trent Port 237 F4
Trent Vale 221 F3
Trentham 221 F3
Trentishoe 163 G1
Trenwheal 144 D3
Treoes 179 F5
Treorchy 179 F3
Treowen 180 B3
Trequite 147 E2
Tre'r-ddol 204 C3
Trerhyngyll 179 G5
Tre-Rhys 191 E3
Trerice 37
Trerulefoot 148 D5
Tresaith 191 F2
Tresco 146 A1
Tresco Abbey Gardens 37
Trescott 208 A3
Trescowe 144 C3
Tresean 146 B4
Tresham 181 G3
Treshnish 296 C5
Tresillian 146 C5
Tresinney 147 F1
Tresinwen 190 B3
Treskinnick Cross 148 C1
Treslea 147 F3
Tresmeer 147 G1
Tresowes Green 144 D4
Tresparrett 148 B1
Tresparrett Posts 148 B1
Tressait 300 D3
Tresta *Shet.* 345 F3
Tresta *Shet.* 342 C2
Treswell 237 E5
Trethewey 144 A4
Trethomas 180 A4
Trethurgy 147 E4
Tretio 190 A5
Tretire 195 E5
Tretower 194 A5
Tretower Castle & Court 114
Treuddyn 219 F2
Trevadlock 147 G2
Trevalga 148 A1
Trevalyn 220 A2
Trevanson 147 D2
Trevarnon 144 C3
Trevarrack 144 B3
Trevarren 146 D3
Trevarrian 146 C3
Trevarrick 147 D5
Tre-vaughan *Carmar.* 191 G5
Trevaughan *Carmar.* 177 E1
Treveighan 147 E2
Trevellas 146 B4
Trevelmond 147 G3
Trevenen 145 D4
Treverva 145 E3
Trevescan 144 A4
Trevethin 180 B2
Trevigro 148 D4
Trevine *Arg. & B.* 290 C2
Trevine *Pembs.* 190 B4
Treviscoe 146 D4
Trevivian 147 F1
Trevone 146 C2
Trevor 219 F3
Trewalder 147 E1
Trewarmett 147 E1
Trewarthenick 146 D5
Trewassa 147 F1
Trewellard 144 A3
Trewen *Cornw.* 147 G1
Trewen *Here.* 181 E1
Trewennack 145 D4
Trewent 176 D3
Trewern 206 B1
Trewethern 147 E2
Trewidland 147 G4
Trewilym 191 E3
Trewint *Cornw.* 148 B1
Trewint *Cornw.* 147 G1
Trewithen 37
Trewithian 145 F3
Trewoon 147 D4
Treworga 146 C5
Treworlas 145 F3
Trewornan 147 D2
Treworthal 145 F3
Tre-wyn 194 C5
Treyarnon 146 C2
Treyford 158 A2
Trezaise 147 D4
Triangle 243 G5
Trickett's Cross 155 G2
Triermain 260 B1
Trimdon 262 C4
Trimdon Colliery 262 C4
Trimdon Grange 262 C4
Trimingham 229 D2
Trimley Lower Street 203 D4
Trimley St. Martin 203 D4
Trimley St. Mary 203 D4
Trimpley 207 G5
Trimsaran 178 A2
Trimstone 163 E1
Trinafour 300 C3
Trinant 180 B3
Tring 185 E1
Trinity *Angus* 303 E3
Trinity *Chan.I.* 150 C5
Trinity *Edin.* 285 G2
Trisant 204 D5
Triscombe *Som.* 164 C4
Triscombe *Som.* 165 E4
Trislaig 298 C2
Trispen 146 C4
Tritlington 271 E2
Trochry 293 E1
Troedyraur 191 G3
Troedyrhiw 179 G2
Trofarth 231 G5
Trondavoe 344 C5
Troon *Cornw.* 145 D3
Troon *S.Ayr.* 274 B2
Tropical World 91
Trosairidh 314 C2
Troston 213 G5
Troswell 148 C1
Trottick 294 C1
Trottiscliffe 173 F2
Trotton 170 D5
Trough Gate 243 E5
Troughend 270 A2
Troustan 282 B2
Troutbeck *Cumb.* 249 F2
Troutbeck *Cumb.* 259 G4
Troutbeck Bridge 249 F2
Trow Green 181 E2
Troway 236 A5
Trowbridge *Cardiff* 180 B4
Trowbridge *Wilts.* 167 F2
Trowell 223 F4
Trowle Common 167 F2
Trowley Bottom 185 F1
Trows 278 A3
Trowse Newton 228 D5
Troy 244 B4
Trudernish 280 C4
Trudoxhill 167 E3
Trull 165 F5
Trumaisgearraidh 315 G2
Trumpan 317 F3
Trumpet 195 F4
Trumpington 200 C2
Trumps Green 171 E1
Trunch 229 D2
Trunnah 241 G3
Truro 146 C5
Truro Cathedral 37
Truscott 148 D2
Trusham 152 B4
Trusley 223 D4
Trusthorpe 239 F4
Truthan 146 C4
Trysull 208 A3
Tubney 183 G3
Tuckenhay 151 E2
Tuckhill 207 G4
Tuckingmill 146 A5
Tuddenham *Suff.* 202 C3
Tuddenham *Suff.* 213 F5
Tudeley 173 F4
Tudeley Hale 173 F4
Tudhoe 262 B4
Tudor Merchant's House 114
Tudweiliog 216 B4
Tuesley 171 E3
Tuffley 182 A1
Tufton *Hants.* 169 F3
Tufton *Pembs.* 190 D5
Tugby 210 C2
Tugford 207 E4
Tughall 279 G4
Tulchan 293 E2
Tullibody 293 D5
Tullich *Arg. & B.* 290 C3
Tullich *Arg. & B.* 290 A3
Tullich *High.* 322 A2
Tullich *High.* 309 F2
Tullich *Moray* 323 F5
Tullich *Stir.* 292 A1
Tullich Muir 321 G2
Tullie House 100
Tulliemet 301 F4
Tulloch *Aber.* 312 D1
Tulloch *High.* 332 B5
Tulloch *Moray* 322 C4
Tullochgorm 290 B5
Tullochgribban High 310 B2
Tullochvenus 312 A4
Tulloes 302 D5
Tullybannocher 292 C2
Tullybelton 293 F1
Tullyfergus 302 A5
Tullymurdoch 301 G4
Tullynessle 312 A3
Tulse Hill 186 C5
Tumble (Y Tymbl) 178 B1
Tumby 226 A2
Tumby Woodside 226 A2
Tummel Bridge 300 C4
Tunbridge Wells 173 E5
Tunbridge Wells Museum & Art Gallery 52
Tundergarth Mains 267 F2
Tunga 329 F4
Tungate 229 D3
Tunley 167 D2
Tunstall *E.Riding* 247 F4
Tunstall *Kent* 174 A2
Tunstall *Lancs.* 250 B5
Tunstall *N.Yorks.* 252 B3
Tunstall *Norf.* 229 F5
Tunstall *Stoke* 221 F2
Tunstall *Suff.* 203 E2
Tunstall *T. & W.* 262 C2
Tunstead *Gt.Man.* 235 E2
Tunstead *Norf.* 229 E3
Tunstead Milton 235 E4
Tunworth 170 B3
Tupholme 225 G1
Tupsley 195 E4
Tupton 223 E1
Tur Langton 210 C3
Turbiskill 281 F1
Turclossie 325 D4
Turgis Green 170 B2
Turin 302 D4
Turkdean 182 D1
Turleigh 167 F1
Turn 234 C1
Turnastone 194 C4
Turnberry 274 A5
Turnchapel 150 A2
Turnditch 223 D3
Turner's Green 197 D1
Turners Hill 172 C5
Turners Puddle 155 E3
Turnford 186 C2
Turnworth 155 E2
Turret Bridge 308 C5
Turriff 324 C5
Turton Bottoms 234 B1
Turvey 199 E2
Turville 184 C3
Turville Heath 184 C3
Turweston 198 B4
Tutbury 222 D5
Tutbury Castle 68
Tutnall 208 B5
Tutshill 181 E3
Tuttington 228 D3
Tutts Clump 184 A5
Tutwell 149 D3
Tuxford 237 E5
Twatt *Ork.* 340 A4
Twatt *Shet.* 342 C2
Twechar 284 B2
Tweedmouth 287 G4
Tweedsmuir 276 B3
Twelve Oaks 160 B1
Twelveheads 146 B5
Twemlow Green 221 E1
Twenty 225 G5
Twickenham 186 A5
Twigworth 196 A5
Twineham 159 E1
Twineham Green 159 E1
Twinhoe 167 E2
Twinstead 201 G4
Twiss Green 234 A3
Twiston 243 E3
Twitchen *Devon* 164 A4
Twitchen *Shrop.* 206 C5
Twitton 173 E3
Twizell House 279 F4
Two Bridges *Devon* 149 G3
Two Bridges *Glos.* 181 F2
Two Dales 223 D1
Two Gates 209 E2
Two Mills 233 E5
Twycross 209 F2
Twycross Zoo 75
Twyford *Bucks.* 198 B5
Twyford *Derbys.* 223 F5
Twyford *Dorset* 155 E1
Twyford *Hants.* 169 F5
Twyford *Leics.* 210 C1
Twyford *Norf.* 228 B3
Twyford *Oxon.* 197 G4
Twyford *W'ham* 184 C5
Twyford Common 195 E4
Twyn Shôn-Ifan 180 A3
Twynholm 266 A5
Twyning 196 A4
Twynllanan 193 D5
Twyn-yr-odyn 180 A5
Twyn-y-Sheriff 180 D2
Twywell 211 E5
T[y] Mawr Wybrnant 114
Tyberton 194 C4
Tycroes 178 C1
Tycrwyn 206 A1
Tydd Gote 212 C1
Tydd St. Giles 212 C1
Tydd St. Mary 212 C1
Tyddewi (Saint David's) 190 A5
Tye Common 187 F3
Tye Green *Essex* 201 F5
Tye Green *Essex* 200 D5
Tye Green *Essex* 187 F1
Tye Green *Essex* 186 D2
Tyersal 244 A4
Ty-hen 216 A4
Tyldesley 234 A2
Tyle-garw 179 G4
Tyler Hill 174 D2
Tylers Green *Bucks.* 185 E3
Tyler's Green *Essex* 187 E2
Tylorstown 179 G3
Tylwch 205 F5
Ty-Mawr *Conwy* 218 C3
Ty-mawr *Denb.* 219 E3
Ty-nant *Conwy* 218 C3
Ty-nant *Gwyn.* 218 C5
Tyndrum 291 F1
Tyneham 155 E4
Tynehead 286 A4
Tynemouth 262 C1
Tynewydd 179 F3
Tyninghame 286 D2
Tynron 266 C1
Tyntesfield *N.Som.* 181 E5
Tyntesfield *N.Som.* 37
Ty-nyn-y-cefn 219 D3
Ty'n-y-coedcae 180 A4
Tyn-y-cwm 205 E4
Tyn-y-ffridd 219 E4
Ty'n-y-garn 179 E4
Tyn-y-Gongl 230 D4
Tynygraig *Cere.* 192 C1
Tyn-y-graig *Powys* 193 G3
Ty'n-y-groes 231 F5
Tyrie 325 E3
Tyringham 199 D3
Tyseley 208 D4
Tythegston 179 E5
Tytherington *Ches.* 234 D5
Tytherington *S.Glos.* 181 F4
Tytherington *Som.* 167 E3
Tytherington *Wilts.* 168 A3
Tytherton Lucas 182 B5
Tyttenhanger 186 A2
Ty-uchaf 218 C5
Tywardreath 147 E4
Tywardreath Highway 147 E4
Tywyn 204 B2

U

Uachdar 315 G4
Uags 306 D1
Ubberley 221 G3
Ubbeston Green 215 E4
Ubley 166 C2
Uckerby 252 B2
Uckfield 159 G1
Uckinghall 196 A4
Uckington 196 B5
Uddingston 284 A3
Uddington 275 G2
Udimore 161 D2
Udley 166 B1
Udny Green 313 D2
Udny Station 313 E2
Udston 284 B4
Udstonhead 284 B5
Uffcott 182 D5
Uffculme 153 D1
Uffington *Lincs.* 211 F2
Uffington *Oxon.* 183 F4
Uffington *Shrop.* 207 E1
Uffington Castle & White Horse 52
Ufford *Peter.* 211 F2
Ufford *Suff.* 203 D2
Ufton 197 F1
Ufton Green 170 B1
Ufton Nervet 170 B1
Ugborough 150 C2
Ugbrooke 37
Ugford 168 B4
Uggeshall 215 F3
Ugglebarnby 254 B2
Ugley 200 D5
Ugley Green 200 D5
Ugthorpe 253 G1
Uibhist a Deas (South Uist) 304 A1
Uibhist a Tuath (North Uist) 315 G2
Uidh 314 B4
Uig *Arg. & B.* 296 A4
Uig *Arg. & B.* 282 C1
Uig *High.* 317 G3
Uig *High.* 317 E4
Uigen 328 B4
Uiginish 317 F5
Uigshader 318 A5
Uisgebhagh (Uiskevagh) 315 G4
Uisken 288 C3
Uiskevagh (Uisgebhagh) 315 G4
Ulbster 337 F4
Ulcat Row 260 A5
Ulceby *Lincs.* 239 E5
Ulceby *N.Lincs.* 238 B1
Ulceby Skitter 238 B1
Ulcombe 174 A4
Uldale 259 F3
Uldale House 250 C3
Uley 181 G3
Ulgham 271 E2
Ullapool 330 D5
Ullenhall 196 D1
Ullenwood 182 B1
Ulleskelf 245 E4
Ullesthorpe 210 A4
Ulley 236 B4
Ullingswick 195 E3
Ullinish 305 G1
Ullock 259 D4
Ullswater Steamers 100
Ulpha *Cumb.* 248 C3
Ulpha *Cumb.* 249 F4
Ulrome 247 D2
Ulsta 345 D4
Ulting 188 B2
Uluvalt 289 E1
Ulva 288 D1
Ulverston 249 D5
Ulwell 155 G4
Ulzieside 275 F5
Umberleigh 163 G3
Unapool 334 B5
Underbarrow 249 F3
Undercliffe 244 A4
Underhill 186 B3
Underhoull 345 E2
Underling Green 173 G4
Underriver 173 E3
Underwood *Newport* 180 C4
Underwood *Notts.* 223 F2
Underwood *Plym.* 150 B2
Undley 213 E4
Undy 180 D4
Ungisiadar 328 C5
Unifirth 342 B2
Union Croft 312 D5
Union Mills 240 B4
Union Street 173 G5
Unst 345 F1
Unstone 236 A5
Unstone Green 236 A5
Unsworth 234 C2
Unthank *Cumb.* 260 A4
Unthank *Derbys.* 236 A5
Up Cerne 154 C2
Up Exe 152 C2
Up Hatherley 196 B5
Up Holland 233 G2
Up Marden 157 G1
Up Mudford 154 B1
Up Nately 170 B2
Up Somborne 169 E4
Up Sydling 154 C2
Upavon 168 C2
Upchurch 174 A2
Upcott *Devon* 149 E1
Upcott *Devon* 163 F2
Upcott *Here.* 194 C2
Upcott *Som.* 164 C5
Upend 201 E2
Upgate 228 C4
Upgate Street *Norf.* 214 B2
Upgate Street *Norf.* 215 D2
Uphall *Dorset* 154 B2
Uphall *W.Loth.* 285 E2
Uphall Station 285 E3
Upham *Devon* 152 B2
Upham *Hants.* 169 G5
Uphampton *Here.* 194 C1
Uphampton *Worcs.* 196 A1
Uphempston 151 E1
Uphill 166 A2
Uplands *Glos.* 182 A2
Uplands *Swan.* 178 C3
Uplawmoor 283 F4
Upleadon 195 G5
Upleatham 253 F1
Uplees 174 C2
Uploders 154 B3
Uplowman 152 D1
Uplyme 153 G3
Upminster 187 E4
Upottery 153 F2
Uppark 52
Upper Affcot 206 D4
Upper Ardroscadale 282 B3
Upper Arley 207 G4
Upper Arncott 184 B1
Upper Astley 207 E1
Upper Aston 208 A3
Upper Astrop 198 A4
Upper Barvas 329 E2
Upper Basildon 184 B5
Upper Bayble (Pabail Uarach) 329 G4
Upper Beeding 159 D2
Upper Benefield 211 E4
Upper Bentley 196 B1
Upper Berwick 207 D1
Upper Bighouse 336 A3
Upper Boat 180 A4
Upper Boddam 312 B1
Upper Boddington 197 G2
Upper Borth 204 C4
Upper Boyndlie 325 E3
Upper Brailes 197 F4
Upper Breakish 306 C2
Upper Breinton 195 D3
Upper Broadheath 196 A2
Upper Broughton 224 B5
Upper Brynamman 178 D1
Upper Bucklebury 169 G1
Upper Burgate 156 A1
Upper Burnhaugh 312 D5
Upper Caldecote 199 G3
Upper Camster 337 E4
Upper Canada 166 A2
Upper Catesby 198 A2
Upper Catshill 208 B5
Upper Chapel 193 G3
Upper Cheddon 165 F5
Upper Chicksgrove 168 A4
Upper Chute 169 D2
Upper Clatford 169 E3
Upper Coberley 182 B1
Upper Colwall 195 G3
Upper Cotton 222 B3
Upper Cound 207 E2
Upper Cumberworth 235 G2
Upper Cwmbran 180 B3
Upper Dallachy 323 F3
Upper Dean 199 F1
Upper Denby 235 G2
Upper Denton 260 C1
Upper Derraid 310 C1
Upper Diabaig 319 E3
Upper Dicker 160 A2
Upper Dovercourt 202 D4
Upper Dunsforth 244 D1
Upper Dunsley 185 E1
Upper Eastern Green 209 E4
Upper Eathie 321 G3
Upper Egleton 195 F3
Upper Elkstone 222 B2
Upper End 235 E5
Upper Enham 169 E3
Upper Farringdon 170 C4
Upper Framilode 181 G1
Upper Froyle 170 C3
Upper Gills 337 F1
Upper Glendessarry 307 F5
Upper Godney 166 B3
Upper Gornal 208 B3
Upper Gravenhurst 199 G4
Upper Green *Essex* 200 C4
Upper Green *Essex* 201 D4
Upper Green *Mon.* 180 C1
Upper Green *W.Berks.* 169 E1
Upper Grove Common 195 E5
Upper Gylen 290 A2
Upper Hackney 223 D1
Upper Halliford 171 F1
Upper Halling 173 F2
Upper Hambleton 211 E2
Upper Harbledown 174 D3
Upper Hardres Court 175 D3
Upper Hartfield 173 D5
Upper Hatton 221 F4
Upper Hawkhillock 313 F1
Upper Hayesden 173 E4
Upper Hayton 207 E4
Upper Heath 207 E4
Upper Heaton 235 F1
Upper Hellesdon 228 D4
Upper Helmsley 245 F2
Upper Hengoed 219 F4
Upper Hergest 194 B2
Upper Heyford *Northants.* 198 B2
Upper Heyford *Oxon.* 197 G5
Upper Hill *Here.* 195 D2
Upper Hill *S.Glos.* 181 F3
Upper Horsebridge 160 A2
Upper Howsell 195 G3
Upper Hulme 222 B1
Upper Inglesham 183 E3
Upper Kilchattan 288 C5
Upper Killay 178 B3
Upper Knockando 323 D5
Upper Lambourn 183 F4
Upper Langford 166 B2
Upper Langwith 223 G1
Upper Largo 294 C4
Upper Leigh 222 B4
Upper Ley 181 G1
Upper Llandwrog (Siop y Fron) 217 E2
Upper Loads 223 E1
Upper Lochton 312 B5
Upper Longdon 208 C1
Upper Longwood 207 F2
Upper Ludstone 208 A3
Upper Lybster 337 E5
Upper Lydbrook 181 F1
Upper Lyde 195 D3
Upper Lye 194 C1
Upper Maes-coed 194 C4
Upper Midhope 235 G3
Upper Milovaig 317 E5
Upper Milton 183 E1
Upper Minety 182 C3
Upper Moor 196 B3
Upper Morton 181 F3
Upper Muirskie 312 D5
Upper Nash 176 D2
Upper Newbold 236 A5
Upper North Dean 185 D3
Upper Norwood 186 C5
Upper Obney 293 F1
Upper Oddington 197 E5
Upper Ollach 306 B1
Upper Padley 235 G5
Upper Pennington 156 B3
Upper Pollicott 184 C1
Upper Poppleton 245 E2
Upper Quinton 197 D3
Upper Ratley 169 E5
Upper Ridinghill 325 F4
Upper Rissington 197 E5
Upper Rochford 195 F1
Upper Sanday 339 E2
Upper Sapey 195 F1
Upper Scolton 190 C5
Upper Seagry 182 B4
Upper Shelton 199 E3
Upper Sheringham 228 C1
Upper Shuckburgh 197 G1
Upper Siddington 182 C3
Upper Skelmorlie 282 D3
Upper Slaughter 197 D5
Upper Sonachan 290 C2
Upper Soudley 181 F1
Upper Staploe 199 G2
Upper Stoke 229 D5
Upper Stondon 199 G4
Upper Stowe 198 B2
Upper Street *Hants.* 156 A1
Upper Street *Norf.* 229 E4
Upper Street *Norf.* 214 C4
Upper Street *Suff.* 202 C4
Upper Street *Suff.* 202 C2
Upper Strensham 196 B4
Upper Sundon 199 F5
Upper Swanmore 157 E1
Upper Swell 197 D5
Upper Tean 222 B4
Upper Thurnham 242 A2
Upper Tillyrie 293 G4
Upper Tooting 186 B5
Upper Town *Derbys.* 222 D1
Upper Town *Derbys.* 223 D2
Upper Town *Derbys.* 222 D2
Upper Town *Here.* 195 E3
Upper Town *N.Som.* 166 C1
Upper Tysoe 197 F3
Upper Upham 183 E5
Upper Upnor 187 G5
Upper Victoria 294 D1
Upper Vobster 167 E3
Upper Wardington 197 G3
Upper Waterhay 182 C3
Upper Weald 198 D4
Upper Weedon 198 B2
Upper Welson 194 B2
Upper Weston 167 E1
Upper Whiston 236 B4
Upper Wick 196 A2
Upper Wield 170 B4
Upper Winchendon (Over Winchendon) 184 C1
Upper Witton 208 C3
Upper Woodford 168 C4
Upper Woolhampton 169 G1
Upper Wootton 169 G2
Upper Wraxall 182 A5
Upper Wyche 195 G3
Upperby 260 A2
Uppermill 235 D2
Upperthong 235 F2
Upperton 171 E5
Uppertown *Derbys.* 223 E1
Uppertown *Ork.* 337 F1
Uppingham 211 D2
Uppington 207 E2
Upsall 253 D4
Upsettlington 287 F5
Upshire 186 D2
Upstreet 175 E2
Upthorpe 214 A4
Upton *Bucks.* 184 C1
Upton *Cambs.* 211 G5
Upton *Ches.* 220 B1
Upton *Cornw.* 147 G2
Upton *Cornw.* 162 C5
Upton *Devon* 153 D2
Upton *Devon* 150 D3
Upton *Dorset* 155 F3
Upton *Dorset* 154 D4
Upton *E.Riding* 246 D2
Upton *Hants.* 169 E2
Upton *Hants.* 156 C1
Upton *Leics.* 209 F3
Upton *Lincs.* 237 F4
Upton *Mersey.* 233 D4
Upton *Norf.* 229 E4
Upton *Northants.* 198 C1
Upton *Notts.* 237 E5
Upton *Notts.* 224 C2
Upton *Oxon.* 184 A4
Upton *Oxon.* 183 E1
Upton *Pembs.* 176 D2
Upton *Peter.* 211 G2
Upton *Slo.* 185 E5
Upton *Som.* 164 C5
Upton *Som.* 166 B5
Upton *W.Yorks.* 236 B1
Upton *Wilts.* 167 F4
Upton Bishop 195 F5
Upton Cheyney 167 D1
Upton Cressett 207 F3
Upton Crews 195 F5
Upton Cross 147 G2
Upton End 199 G4
Upton Gardens 114
Upton Grey 170 B3
Upton Hellions 152 B2
Upton House 68
Upton Lovell 168 A3
Upton Magna 207 E1
Upton Noble 167 E4
Upton Park 186 D4
Upton Pyne 152 C3
Upton St. Leonards 182 A1
Upton Scudamore 167 F3
Upton Snodsbury 196 B2
Upton upon Severn 196 A3
Upton Warren 196 B1
Upwaltham 158 B2
Upware 212 D5
Upwell 212 D2
Upwey 154 C4
Upwick Green 200 C5
Upwood 212 A4
Uradale 342 D4
Urafirth 344 C5
Urchany 322 A5
Urchfont 168 B2
Urdimarsh 195 E3
Ure 344 B5
Urgha 327 D4
Urlay Nook 252 D1
Urmston 234 B3
Urpeth 262 B2
Urquhart *High.* 321 E4
Urquhart *Moray* 323 E3
Urquhart Castle 131
Urra 253 E2
Urray 321 E4
Ushaw Moor 262 B3
Usk 180 C2
Usselby 238 A3

Usworth 262 C2
Utley 243 G3
Uton 152 B3
Utterby 238 D3
Uttoxeter 222 B4
Uwchmynydd 216 A5
Uxbridge 185 F4
Uyeasound 345 E2
Uzmaston 176 C1

V

Vale of Rheidol Railway 114
Valley (Dyffryn) 230 A5
Valley Gardens 52
Valley Truckle 147 F1
Valleyfield *D. & G.* 266 A5
Valleyfield *Fife* 285 E1
Valsgarth 345 F1
Vange 187 G4
Vardre 178 C2
Varteg 180 B2
Vatersay (Bhatarsaigh) 314 B4
Vatsetter 345 E4
Vatten 317 F5
Vaul 296 B2
Vauld, The 195 E3
Vaynor 179 G1
Vaynor Park 206 A2
Veaullt 194 A2
Veensgarth 342 D3
Velindre *Pembs.* 191 D4
Velindre *Powys* 194 A4
Vellow 165 D4
Veness 341 D4
Venn 150 D3
Venn Ottery 153 D3
Venngreen 163 D4
Vennington 206 C2
Venny Tedburn 152 B3
Venterdon 149 D3
Ventnor 157 E5
Ventnor Botanic Gardens 52
Venton 150 B2
Vernham Dean 169 E2
Vernham Street 169 E2
Vernolds Common 207 D4
Verulamium Museum 83
Verulamium Roman Town 84
Verwood 155 G2
Veryan 145 G3
Veryan Green 146 D5
Vickerstown 241 E1
Victoria 147 D3
Victoria & Albert Museum 61
Vidlin 343 D1
Viewfield 336 C2
Viewpark 284 B3
Vigo 208 C2
Vigo Village 173 F2
Vikingar! Experience, The 131
Villavin 163 F4
Vindolanda (Chesterholm) Roman Fort 105
Vinehall Street 160 C1
Vine's Cross 160 A2
Viney Hill 181 F2
Virginia Water 171 E1
Virginstow 149 D1
Virley 188 C1
Viroconium Roman Town 68
Vobster 167 E3
Voe *Shet.* 342 D1
Voe *Shet.* 344 C4
Vowchurch 194 C4
Voy 340 A5
Vron Gate 206 C2
Vyne, The 52

W

Waberthwaite 248 C3
Wackerfield 262 A5
Wacton 214 C2
Wadbister 342 D3
Wadborough 196 B3
Waddesdon 184 C1
Waddesdon Manor 52
Waddeton 151 E2
Waddicar 233 E3
Waddingham 237 G3
Waddington *Lancs.* 242 D3
Waddington *Lincs.* 225 E1
Waddingworth 238 B5
Waddon *Devon* 152 B5
Waddon *Gt.Lon.* 172 C2
Wadebridge 147 D2
Wadeford 153 G1
Wadenhoe 211 F4
Wadesmill 186 C1
Wadhurst 173 F5
Wadshelf 236 A5
Wadsley Bridge 236 A3
Wadworth 236 C3
Wadworth Hill 247 E5
Waen *Denb.* 219 E1
Waen *Denb.* 218 C1
Waen Aberwheeler 219 D1
Waen-fâch 206 B1
Waen-wen 217 E1
Wag 333 F2
Wainfleet All Saints 226 C2
Wainfleet Bank 226 C2
Wainford 215 E2
Waingroves 223 F3
Wainhouse Corner 148 B1
Wainscott 187 G5
Wainstalls 243 G5
Waitby 250 C2
Wakefield 244 C5
Wakefield Cathedral 91
Wakehurst Place 52
Wakerley 211 E3
Wakes Colne 201 G5
Walberswick 215 F4
Walberton 158 B3
Walbottle 262 A1
Walcot *Lincs.* 225 F4
Walcot *Lincs.* 225 G2
Walcot *N.Lincs.* 246 A5
Walcot *Shrop.* 206 C4
Walcot *Tel. & W.* 207 E1
Walcot Green 214 C3
Walcote *Leics.* 210 A4
Walcote *Warks.* 196 D2
Walcott 229 E2
Walcott Dales 225 G2
Walden 251 F4
Walden Head 251 E4
Walden Stubbs 236 C1
Walderslade 173 G2
Walderton 157 G1
Walditch 154 A3
Waldley 222 C4
Waldridge 262 B3
Waldringfield 203 D3
Waldron 160 A2
Wales 236 B4
Walesby *Lincs.* 238 B3
Walesby *Notts.* 237 D5
Waleswood 236 B4
Walford *Here.* 206 C5
Walford *Here.* 195 E5
Walford *Shrop.* 220 B5
Walford *Staffs.* 221 F4
Walford Heath 206 D1
Walgherton 221 D3
Walgrave 210 D5
Walhampton 156 C3
Walk Mill 243 E4
Walkden 234 B2
Walker 262 B1
Walker Fold 242 C3
Walker, The 100
Walkerburn 277 E2
Walkeringham 237 E3
Walkerith 237 E3
Walkern 200 A5
Walker's Green 195 E3
Walkford 156 B3
Walkhampton 150 B1
Walkingham Hill 244 C1
Walkington 246 B4
Walkwood 196 C1
Wall *Cornw.* 144 D3
Wall *Northumb.* 261 F1
Wall *Staffs.* 208 D2
Wall End 248 D4
Wall Heath 208 A4
Wall Houses 261 G1
Wall under Heywood 207 E3
Wallacehall 268 A4
Wallacetown 274 A5
Wallasey 233 D3
Wallaston Green 176 C2
Wallend 174 A1
Waller's Green 195 F4
Wallingford 184 B4
Wallington *Gt.Lon.* 172 B2
Wallington *Hants.* 157 E2
Wallington *Herts.* 200 A4
Wallington *Northumb.* 105
Wallington *Wrex.* 220 B3
Wallingwells 236 C4
Wallis 190 D5
Wallisdown 155 G3
Walliswood 171 G4
Walls 342 B3
Wallsend 262 C1
Wallyford 286 A2
Walmer 175 F3
Walmer Bridge 242 A5
Walmer Castle & Garden 52
Walmersley 234 C1
Walmley 208 D3
Walmsgate 239 D5
Walpole 215 E4
Walpole Cross Keys 212 D1
Walpole Highway 212 D1
Walpole Marsh 212 C1
Walpole St. Andrew 212 D1
Walpole St. Peter 212 D1
Walrond's Park 166 A5
Walrow 166 A3
Walsall 208 C3
Walsall Wood 208 C2
Walsden 243 F5
Walsgrave on Sowe 209 F4
Walsham le Willows 214 B4
Walshford 244 D2
Walsoken 212 C1
Walston 285 E5
Walsworth 199 G4
Walterston 179 G5
Walterstone 194 C5
Waltham *Kent* 174 D4
Waltham *N.E.Lincs.* 238 C2
Waltham Abbey *Essex* 186 C2
Waltham Abbey *Essex* 84
Waltham Chase 157 E1
Waltham Cross 186 C2
Waltham on the Wolds 224 C5
Waltham St. Lawrence 184 D5
Walthamstow 186 C4
Walton *Bucks.* 184 D1
Walton *Cumb.* 260 B1
Walton *Derbys.* 223 E1
Walton *Leics.* 210 A4
Walton *M.K.* 199 D4
Walton *Mersey.* 233 E3
Walton *Peter.* 211 G2
Walton *Powys* 194 B2
Walton *Shrop.* 207 D5
Walton *Som.* 166 B4
Walton *Staffs.* 221 F4
Walton *Suff.* 203 E4
Walton *Tel. & W.* 207 E1
Walton *W.Yorks.* 236 A1
Walton *W.Yorks.* 244 D3
Walton *Warks.* 197 E2
Walton Cardiff 196 B4
Walton East 190 D5
Walton Elm 155 D1
Walton Hall Gardens 100
Walton Highway 212 C1
Walton Lower Street 203 D4
Walton on the Hill 172 B3
Walton on the Naze 203 D5
Walton on the Wolds 210 A1
Walton Park *D. & G.* 266 B3
Walton Park *N.Som.* 180 D5
Walton West 176 B1
Walton-in-Gordano 180 D5
Walton-le-Dale 242 B5
Walton-on-Thames 171 G1
Walton-on-the-Hill 221 G5
Walton-on-Trent 209 E1
Walwen *Flints.* 232 C5
Walwen *Flints.* 232 D5
Walwick 270 B4
Walworth 252 B1
Walworth Gate 262 B5
Walwyn's Castle 176 B1
Wambrook 153 F2
Wanborough *Surr.* 171 E3
Wanborough *Swin.* 183 E4
Wandel 276 A3
Wandon 279 E4
Wandon End 199 G5
Wandsworth 186 B5
Wandylaw 279 F4
Wangford *Suff.* 215 F4
Wangford *Suff.* 213 F4
Wanlip 210 B1
Wanlockhead 275 G4
Wannock 160 A3
Wansford *E.Riding* 246 C2
Wansford *Peter.* 211 F3
Wanshurst Green 173 G4
Wanstrow 167 E3
Wanswell 181 F2
Wantage 183 F4
Wapley 181 G5
Wappenbury 197 F1
Wappenham 198 B3
Warblebank 259 F2
Warbleton 160 B2
Warblington 157 G2
Warborough 184 A3
Warboys 212 B4
Warbreck 241 G4
Warbstow 148 C1
Warburton 234 A4
Warcop 250 C1
Ward End 208 D4
Ward Green 202 B1
Warden *Kent* 174 C1
Warden *Northumb.* 261 F1
Warden Hill 196 B5
Warden Street 199 G3
Wardhouse 312 A1
Wardington 197 G3
Wardle *Ches.* 220 D2
Wardle *Gt.Man.* 234 D1
Wardley *Gt.Man.* 234 B2
Wardley *Rut.* 210 D2
Wardley *T. & W.* 262 C1
Wardlow 235 F5
Wardsend 234 D4
Wardy Hill 212 C4
Ware *Herts.* 186 C1
Ware *Kent* 175 E2
Wareham 155 F4
Warehorne 174 B5
Waren Mill 279 F3
Warenford 279 F4
Warenton 279 F3
Wareside 186 C1
Waresley *Cambs.* 200 A2
Waresley *Worcs.* 208 A5
Warfield 185 D5
Wargrave *Mersey.* 233 G3
Wargrave *W'ham* 184 C5
Warham *Here.* 195 D4
Warham *Norf.* 228 A1
Wark *Northumb.* 270 A4
Wark *Northumb.* 278 C3
Warkleigh 163 G3
Warkton 211 D5
Warkworth *Northants.* 197 G3
Warkworth *Northumb.* 271 E1
Warkworth Castle 105
Warland 243 F5
Warleggan 147 F3
Warley *Essex* 187 E3
Warley *W.Mid.* 208 C4
Warley Town 243 G5
Warlingham 172 C3
Warmfield 244 C5
Warmingham 221 E1
Warminghurst 158 D2
Warmington *Northants.* 211 F3
Warmington *Warks.* 197 G3
Warminster 167 F3
Warmlake 174 A4
Warmley 181 F5
Warmley Hill 181 F5
Warmsworth 236 C2
Warmwell 155 D4
Warndon 196 A2
Warners End 185 F2
Warnford 170 B5
Warnham 171 G4
Warningcamp 158 C3
Warninglid 159 E1
Warren *Ches.* 234 C5
Warren *Pembs.* 176 C3
Warren House 149 G2
Warren Row 184 D4
Warren Street 174 B3
Warrenby 263 E5
Warren's Green 200 A5
Warrington *M.K.* 199 D2
Warrington *Warr.* 234 A4
Warroch 293 F4
Warsash 157 D2
Warslow 222 B2
Warsop Vale 223 G1
Warter 246 A2
Warthill 245 F2
Wartle 312 A4
Wartling 160 B3
Wartnaby 224 C5
Warton *Lancs.* 249 G5
Warton *Lancs.* 242 A5
Warton *Northumb.* 270 C1
Warton *Warks.* 209 E2
Warton Bank 242 A5
Warwick 197 E1
Warwick Bridge 260 A2
Warwick Castle 68
Warwick Wold 172 C3
Warwick-on-Eden 260 A2
Wasbister 340 B3
Wasdale Head 248 C2
Wash 235 E4
Wash Common 169 F1
Washall Green 200 C4
Washaway 147 E3
Washbourne 151 D2
Washbrook 166 B3
Washfield 152 C1
Washfold 251 F2
Washford *Som.* 164 D3
Washford *Warks.* 196 C1
Washford Pyne 152 B1
Washingborough 238 A5
Washington *T. & W.* 262 C2
Washington *W.Suss.* 158 D2
Washmere Green 202 A3
Wasing 169 G1
Waskerley 261 G3
Wasperton 197 E2
Wasps Nest 225 F1
Wass 253 E5
Watchet 165 D3
Watchfield *Oxon.* 183 E3
Watchfield *Som.* 166 A3
Watchgate 249 G3
Watcombe 151 F1
Watendlath 259 F5
Water 243 E5
Water Eaton *M.K.* 199 D4
Water Eaton *Oxon.* 184 A1
Water End *Beds.* 199 G3
Water End *Beds.* 199 F4
Water End *E.Riding* 245 G4
Water End *Essex* 201 D3
Water End *Herts.* 186 B2
Water End *Herts.* 185 F1
Water Newton 211 G3
Water Orton 209 D3
Water Stratford 198 B4
Water Yeat 249 D4
Waterbeach 200 C1
Waterbeck 268 A4
Watercombe 155 D4
Waterend 184 C3
Waterfall 222 B2
Waterfoot *E.Renf.* 283 G4
Waterfoot *Lancs.* 243 E5
Waterford 186 C1
Watergate 147 F1
Waterhead *Cumb.* 249 E2
Waterhead *D. & G.* 266 B2
Waterheath 215 F2
Waterhill of Bruxie 325 E5
Waterhouses *Dur.* 262 A3
Waterhouses *Staffs.* 222 B2
Wateringbury 173 F3
Waterlane 182 B2
Waterloo *Aber.* 313 F1
Waterloo *Derbys.* 223 F1
Waterloo *Gt.Man.* 234 D2
Waterloo *High.* 306 C2
Waterloo *Mersey.* 233 E3
Waterloo *N.Lan.* 284 C4
Waterloo *Norf.* 228 D4
Waterloo *P. & K.* 293 F1
Waterloo *Pembs.* 176 C2
Waterloo *Poole* 155 G3
Waterloo Cross 153 D1
Waterloo Port 217 D1
Waterlooville 157 F1
Watermeetings 276 A4
Watermillock 260 A5
Watermouth Castle 37
Waterperry *Oxon.* 184 B2
Waterperry *Oxon.* 52
Waterrow 165 D5
Waters Upton 207 F1
Watersfield 158 C2
Watersheddings 234 D2
Waterside *Aber.* 311 F3
Waterside *Aber.* 313 F2
Waterside *B'burn.* 242 D5
Waterside *Bucks.* 185 E2
Waterside *E.Ayr.* 274 C5
Waterside *E.Ayr.* 283 F5
Waterside *E.Dun.* 284 A2
Watersmeet House 37
Waterstock 184 B2
Waterston 176 C2
Waterthorpe 236 B4
Watford *Herts.* 186 A3
Watford *Northants.* 198 B1
Watford Park 180 A4
Wath *N.Yorks.* 252 C5
Wath *N.Yorks.* 244 A1
Wath Brow 258 D5
Wath upon Dearne 236 B2
Watley's End 181 F4
Watlington *Norf.* 213 E1
Watlington *Oxon.* 184 B3
Watnall 223 G3
Watten 337 E3
Wattisfield 214 B4
Wattisham 202 B2
Watton *Dorset* 154 A3
Watton *E.Riding* 246 C3
Watton *Norf.* 228 A5
Watton at Stone 186 C1
Watton Green 228 A5
Watton's Green 187 E3
Wattston 284 B3
Wattstown 179 G3
Wattsville 180 B3
Waughtonhill 325 E4
Waun Fawr 204 C4
Waun y Clyn 178 A2
Waunarlwydd 178 C3
Waunclunda 192 C4
Waunfawr 217 E2
Waun-Lwyd 180 A2
Wavendon 199 E4
Waverbridge 259 F2
Waverton *Ches.* 220 B1
Waverton *Cumb.* 259 F2
Wavertree 233 E4
Wawne 246 C4
Waxham 229 F3
Waxholme 247 F5
Way Gill 243 F1
Way Village 152 B1
Way Wick 166 A1
Wayford 154 A2
Waytown 154 A3
Wdig (Goodwick) 190 C4
Weachyburn 324 B4
Weacombe 165 E3
Weald 183 F2
Weald & Downland Open Air Museum 52
Wealdstone 186 A3
Weardley 244 B3
Weare 166 B2
Weare Giffard 163 E3
Wearhead 261 E4
Wearne 166 B5
Weasenham All Saints 227 G5
Weasenham St. Peter 227 G5
Weathercote 250 C5
Weatheroak Hill 208 C5
Weaverham 234 A5
Weaver's Cottage 131
Weaverthorpe 254 C5
Webheath 196 C1
Webton 194 D4
Wedderlairs 313 D1
Weddington 209 F3
Wedgwood Story Visitor Centre 68
Wedhampton 168 B2
Wedmore 166 B3
Wednesbury 208 B3
Wednesfield 208 B3
Weedon 184 D1
Weedon Bec 198 B2
Weedon Lois 198 B3
Weeford 208 D2
Week *Devon* 152 A1
Week *Devon* 151 D1
Week *Som.* 164 C4
Week Orchard 162 C5
Week St. Mary 148 C1
Weeke 169 F4
Weekley 211 D4
Weel 246 C4
Weeley 202 C5
Weeley Heath 202 C5
Weem 300 D4
Weeping Cross 221 G5
Weethley 196 C2
Weeting 213 F4
Weeton *E.Riding* 247 F5
Weeton *Lancs.* 241 G4
Weeton *N.Yorks.* 244 B3
Weetwood 244 B4
Weir *Essex* 188 B4
Weir *Lancs.* 243 E5
Weir Quay 150 A1
Weirbrook 220 A5
Weisdale 342 C2
Welbeck Abbey 236 C5
Welborne 228 B5
Welbourn 225 E2
Welburn *N.Yorks.* 245 G1
Welburn *N.Yorks.* 253 F4
Welbury 252 C2
Welby 225 E4
Welches Dam 212 C4
Welcombe 162 C4
Weldon 211 E4
Welford *Northants.* 210 B4
Welford *W.Berks.* 183 G5
Welford-on-Avon 196 D2
Welham *Leics.* 210 C3
Welham *Notts.* 237 E4
Welham Green 186 B2
Well *Hants.* 170 C3
Well *Lincs.* 239 E5
Well *N.Yorks.* 252 B4
Well End *Bucks.* 185 D4
Well End *Herts.* 186 B3
Well Hill 173 D2
Well Street 173 F3
Well Town 152 C2
Welland 195 G3
Wellbank 294 C1
Wellesbourne 197 E2
Wellhill 322 B3
Wellhouse *W.Berks.* 184 A5
Wellhouse *W.Yorks.* 235 E1
Welling 187 D5
Wellingborough 199 D1
Wellingham 227 G5
Wellingore 225 E2
Wellington *Cumb.* 248 B2
Wellington *Here.* 195 D3
Wellington *Som.* 165 E5
Wellington *Tel. & W.* 207 F1
Wellington Country Park 52
Wellington Heath 195 G3
Wellington Marsh 195 D3
Wellow *B. & N.E.Som.* 167 E2
Wellow *I.o.W.* 156 C4
Wellow *Notts.* 224 B1
Wells 166 C3
Wells Cathedral 38
Wells Green 208 D4
Wellsborough 209 F2
Wells-next-the-Sea 228 A1
Wellstyle Green 187 F1
Wellwood 285 E1
Welney 212 D3
Welsh Bicknor 181 E1
Welsh End 220 C4
Welsh Frankton 220 A4
Welsh Hook 190 C5
Welsh Newton 181 D1
Welsh St. Donats 179 G5
Welsh Slate Museum 114
Welshampton 220 B4
Welshpool (Y Trallwng) 206 B2
Welton *B. & N.E.Som.* 167 D2
Welton *Cumb.* 259 G2
Welton *E.Riding* 246 B5
Welton *Lincs.* 238 A4
Welton *Northants.* 198 A1
Welton le Marsh 226 C1
Welton le Wold 238 C4
Welwick 247 F5
Welwyn 186 B1
Welwyn Garden City 186 B1
Wem 220 C5
Wembdon 165 F4
Wembley 186 A4
Wembley Park 186 A4
Wembury 150 B3
Wembworthy 163 G4
Wemyss Bay 282 C3
Wenallt *Cere.* 204 C5
Wenallt *Gwyn.* 218 C3
Wendens Ambo 200 D4
Wendlebury 184 A1
Wendling 228 A4
Wendover 185 D2
Wendover Dean 185 D2
Wendron 145 D3
Wendy 200 B3
Wenfordbridge 147 E2
Wenhaston 215 F4
Wenlli 218 B1
Wennington *Cambs.* 212 A5
Wennington *Gt.Lon.* 187 E4
Wennington *Lancs.* 250 B5
Wensley *Derbys.* 223 D1
Wensley *N.Yorks.* 251 F4
Wentbridge 236 B1
Wentnor 206 C3
Wentworth *Cambs.* 212 C5
Wentworth *S.Yorks.* 236 A3
Wenvoe 180 A5
Weobley 194 C2
Weobley Marsh 194 D2
Weoley Castle 208 C4
Wepham 158 C3
Wepre 219 F1
Wereham 213 E2
Wergs 208 A2
Wern *Gwyn.* 217 E4
Wern *Powys* 206 B1
Wern *Powys* 180 A1
Wern *Shrop.* 219 F4
Wern, The 219 F2
Wernffrwd 178 B3
Wern-olau 178 B3
Wernrheolydd 180 C1
Wern-y-cwrt 180 C2
Werrington *Cornw.* 148 D2
Werrington *Peter.* 211 G2
Werrington *Staffs.* 221 G3
Wervil Grange 191 G2
Wervin 233 F5
Wesham 242 A4
Wessington 223 E2
West Aberthaw 164 D1
West Acre 213 F1
West Acton 186 A4
West Allerdean 287 G5
West Alvington 150 D3
West Amesbury 168 C3
West Anstey 164 B5
West Ashby 238 C5
West Ashford 163 F2
West Ashling 158 A3
West Ashton 167 F2
West Auckland 262 A5
West Ayton 254 C4
West Bagborough 165 E4
West Barkwith 238 B4
West Barnby 254 B1
West Barns 287 D2
West Barsham 228 A2
West Bay 154 A3
West Beckham 228 C2
West Benhar 284 C3
West Bergholt 202 A5
West Berkshire Museum 53
West Bexington 154 B4
West Bilney 213 F1
West Blatchington 159 E3
West Boldon 262 C1
West Bourton 167 E5
West Bowling 244 A4
West Brabourne 174 C4
West Bradford 242 D3
West Bradley 166 C4
West Bretton 235 G1
West Bridgford 223 G4
West Bromwich 208 C3
West Buckland *Devon* 163 G2
West Buckland *Som.* 165 E5
West Burrafirth 342 B2
West Burton *N.Yorks.* 251 F4
West Burton *W.Suss.* 158 B2
West Butsfield 261 G3
West Butterwick 237 F2
West Byfleet 171 F1
West Cairncake 324 D5
West Caister 229 G4
West Calder 285 E3
West Camel 166 C5
West Carbeth 283 G2
West Carr Houses 237 E2
West Cauldcoats 284 A5
West Chaldon 155 D4
West Challow 183 F4
West Charleton 151 D3
West Chevington 271 E2
West Chiltington 158 C2
West Chiltington Common 158 C2
West Chinnock 154 A1
West Chisenbury 168 C2
West Clandon 171 F2
West Cliffe 175 F4
West Clyne 333 D4
West Coker 154 B1
West Compton *Dorset* 154 B3
West Compton *Som.* 166 C3
West Cowick 245 F5
West Cross 178 C4
West Crudwell 182 B3
West Curry 148 C1
West Curthwaite 259 G2
West Dean *W.Suss.* 158 A2
West Dean *Wilts.* 169 D5
West Dean Gardens 53
West Deeping 211 G2
West Derby 233 E3
West Dereham 213 E2
West Ditchburn 279 F4
West Down 163 F1
West Drayton *Gt.Lon.* 185 F5
West Drayton *Notts.* 237 E5
West Dullater 292 A4
West Dunnet 337 E1
West Edington 271 D3
West Ella 246 C5
West End *Beds.* 199 E2
West End *Brack.F.* 185 D5
West End *Caerp.* 180 B3
West End *Cambs.* 212 C3
West End *E.Riding* 246 C1
West End *Hants.* 157 D1
West End *Herts.* 186 C2
West End *Kent* 175 D2
West End *Lancs.* 242 A1
West End *Lincs.* 239 D3
West End *N.Som.* 166 B1
West End *N.Yorks.* 244 A2
West End *Norf.* 229 F4
West End *Norf.* 228 A5
West End *Oxon.* 183 G2
West End *Oxon.* 184 A4
West End *S.Lan.* 285 D5
West End *Suff.* 215 F3
West End *Surr.* 171 G1
West End *Surr.* 171 E1
West End *Wilts.* 182 B5
West End *Wilts.* 168 A5
West End *Wilts.* 168 A5
West End Green 170 B1
West Farleigh 173 G3
West Farndon 198 A2
West Felton 220 A5
West Firle 159 G3
West Fleetham 279 F4
West Flotmanby 255 D5
West Garforth 244 C4
West Ginge 183 G4
West Glen 282 A2
West Grafton 168 D1
West Green *Gt.Lon.* 186 C4
West Green *Hants.* 170 C2
West Grimstead 168 D5
West Grinstead 171 G5
West Haddlesey 245 E5
West Haddon 210 B5
West Hagbourne 184 A4
West Hagley 208 B4
West Hall 260 B1
West Hallam 223 F3
West Halton 246 B5
West Ham 186 C4
West Handley 236 A5
West Hanney 183 G3
West Hanningfield 187 G3
West Hardwick 236 B1
West Harnham 168 C5
West Harptree 166 C2
West Harrow 186 A4

West Harting 170 C5
West Hatch *Som.* 165 F5
West Hatch *Wilts.* 168 A5
West Head 213 D2
West Heath *Ches.* 221 F1
West Heath *Gt.Lon.* 187 D5
West Heath *Hants.* 171 D2
West Heath *Hants.* 169 G2
West Heath *W.Mid.* 208 C5
West Helmsdale 333 F3
West Hendon 186 B4
West Hendred 183 G4
West Heslerton 254 C5
West Hewish 166 A1
West Highland Line 131
West Hill *Devon* 153 D3
West Hill *E.Riding* 247 D1
West Hill *N.Som.* 181 D5
West Hoathly 172 C5
West Holme 155 E4
West Horndon 187 F4
West Horrington 166 C3
West Horsley 171 F2
West Horton 279 E3
West Hougham 175 E5
West Howe 155 G3
West Howetown 164 C4
West Huntspill 166 A3
West Hyde 185 F3
West Hythe 174 D5
West Ilsley 183 G4
West Itchenor 157 G2
West Keal 226 B1
West Kennet Long Barrow 38
West Kennett 168 C1
West Kilbride 282 D5
West Kingsdown 173 E2
West Kington 182 A5
West Kington Wick 182 A5
West Kirby 232 D4
West Knapton 254 B5
West Knighton 154 D4
West Knoyle 167 F4
West Kyloe 279 E2
West Lambrook 154 A1
West Langdon 175 F4
West Langwell 332 B4
West Lavington *W.Suss.* 171 D5
West Lavington *Wilts.* 168 B2
West Layton 252 A2
West Leake 223 G5
West Learmouth 278 C3
West Lees 253 D2
West Leigh *Devon* 163 G5
West Leigh *Devon* 151 D2
West Leigh *Som.* 165 E4
West Leith 185 E1
West Lexham 213 G1
West Lilling 245 F1
West Lingo 294 C4
West Linton 285 F4
West Liss 170 C5
West Littleton 181 G5
West Lockinge 183 G4
West Looe 147 G4
West Lulworth 155 E4
West Lutton 246 B1
West Lydford 166 C4
West Lyn 164 A3
West Lyng 166 A5
West Lynn 213 E1
West Mains 279 E2
West Malling 173 F3
West Malvern 195 G3
West Marden 157 G1
West Markham 237 E5
West Marsh 238 C2
West Marton 243 E2
West Melbury 167 F5
West Melton 236 B2
West Meon 170 B5
West Meon Hut 170 B5
West Mersea 188 D1
West Midland Safari Park 68
West Milton 154 A3
West Minster 174 B1
West Molesey 171 G1
West Monkton 165 F5
West Moors 155 G2
West Morden 155 F3
West Morriston 286 D5
West Morton 243 G3
West Mostard 250 C3
West Mudford 166 C5
West Muir 303 D3
West Ness 253 F5
West Newbiggin 252 C1
West Newton *E.Riding* 247 D4
West Newton *Norf.* 227 E5
West Norwood 186 C5
West Ogwell 151 E1
West Orchard 155 E1
West Overton 168 C1
West Panson 148 D1
West Park *Aber.* 312 C5
West Park *Mersey.* 233 G3
West Parley 155 G3
West Peckham 173 F3
West Pelton 262 B2
West Pennard 166 C4
West Pentire 146 B3
West Perry 199 G1
West Porlock 164 B3
West Prawle 151 D4
West Preston 158 C3
West Pulham 154 D2
West Putford 163 D4
West Quantoxhead 165 E3
West Raddon 152 B2
West Rainton 262 C3
West Rasen 238 A4
West Raynham 227 G5
West Retford 237 D4
West Rounton 252 D2
West Row 213 E5
West Rudham 227 G5
West Runton 228 C1
West Saltoun 286 B3
West Sandford 152 B2
West Sandwick 345 D4
West Scrafton 251 F4
West Shepton 166 D3
West Shinness Lodge 332 A3
West Somerset Railway 38
West Somerton 229 F4
West Stafford 154 D4
West Stockwith 237 E3
West Stoke 158 A3
West Stonesdale 251 D2
West Stoughton 166 B3
West Stour 167 E5
West Stourmouth 175 E2
West Stow 213 G5
West Stow Country Park 84
West Stowell 168 C1
West Stratton 169 G3
West Street *Kent* 174 B3
West Street *Med.* 187 G5
West Street *Suff.* 214 A4
West Tanfield 252 B5
West Taphouse 147 F3
West Tarbert 281 G3
West Tarring 158 D3
West Thirston 271 D1
West Thorney 157 G2
West Thurrock 187 E5
West Tilbury 187 F5
West Tisted 170 B5
West Tofts *Norf.* 213 G3
West Tofts *P. & K.* 293 G1
West Torrington 238 B4
West Town *B. & N.E.Som.* 166 C1
West Town *Hants.* 157 G3
West Town *N.Som.* 166 B1
West Town *Som.* 166 C4
West Tytherley 169 D5
West Walton 212 C1
West Wellow 156 B1
West Wembury 150 B3
West Wemyss 294 B5
West Wick 166 A1
West Wickham *Cambs.* 201 E3
West Wickham *Gt.Lon.* 172 C2
West Williamston 176 D2
West Winch 213 E1
West Winterslow 168 D4
West Wittering 157 G3
West Witton 251 F4
West Woodburn 270 A3
West Woodhay 169 E1
West Woodlands 167 E3
West Worldham 170 C4
West Worlington 152 A1
West Worthing 158 D3
West Wratting 201 E2
West Wycombe 184 D3
West Wycombe Park 53
West Yatton 182 A5
West Yell 345 D4
West Youlstone 162 C4
Westbere 175 D2
Westborough 224 D3
Westbourne *Bourne.* 155 G3
Westbourne *W.Suss.* 157 G2
Westbourne Green 186 B4
Westbrook *Kent* 175 F1
Westbrook *W.Berks.* 183 G5
Westbrook *Wilts.* 168 A1
Westbury *Bucks.* 198 B4
Westbury *Shrop.* 206 C2
Westbury *Wilts.* 167 F2
Westbury Court 38
Westbury Leigh 167 F2
Westbury on Trym 181 E5
Westbury White Horse 38
Westbury-on-Severn 181 G1
Westbury-sub-Mendip 166 C3
Westby *Lancs.* 241 G4
Westby *Lincs.* 225 E5
Westcliff-on-Sea 188 B4
Westcombe 167 D4
Westcot 183 F4
Westcott *Bucks.* 184 C1
Westcott *Devon* 152 D2
Westcott *Surr.* 171 G3
Westcott Barton 197 G5
Westcourt 168 D1
Westdean 160 A4
Westdowns 147 E1
Westend Town 181 G5
Wester Aberchalder 309 E2
Wester Badentyre 324 C4
Wester Balgedie 293 G4
Wester Culbeuchly 324 B3
Wester Dechmont 285 E2
Wester Fintray 312 D3
Wester Foffarty 302 C5
Wester Greenskares 324 C3
Wester Gruinards 332 A5
Wester Hailes 285 G3
Wester Lealty 321 F2
Wester Lonvine 321 G2
Wester Newburn 294 C4
Wester Ord 312 D4
Wester Quarff 342 D4
Wester Skeld 342 B3
Westerdale *High.* 336 D3
Westerdale *N.Yorks.* 253 F2
Westerfield *Shet.* 342 C2
Westerfield *Suff.* 202 C3
Westergate 158 B3
Westerham 172 D3
Westerhope 262 A1
Westerleigh 181 F5
Westerloch 337 F3
Westerton *Aber.* 312 C5
Westerton *Angus* 303 E4
Westerton *Dur.* 262 B4
Westerton *P. & K.* 293 D3
Westerwick 342 B3
Westfield *Cumb.* 258 C4
Westfield *E.Suss.* 160 D2
Westfield *High.* 336 C2
Westfield *N.Lan.* 284 B2
Westfield *Norf.* 228 A5
Westfield *R. & C.* 263 E5
Westfield *W.Loth.* 284 D2
Westfield *W.Yorks.* 244 B5
Westfield Sole 173 G2
Westgate *Dur.* 261 F4
Westgate *N.Lincs.* 237 E2
Westgate *Norf.* 228 A1
Westgate *Northumb.* 270 D4
Westgate Hill 244 B5
Westgate on Sea 175 F1
Westhall *Aber.* 312 B2
Westhall *Suff.* 215 F3
Westham *Dorset* 154 C5
Westham *E.Suss.* 160 B3
Westham *Som.* 166 B3
Westhampnett 158 A3
Westhay *Devon* 153 G2
Westhay *Som.* 166 B3
Westhead 233 F2
Westhide 195 E3
Westhill *Aber.* 312 D4
Westhill *High.* 321 G5
Westhope *Here.* 195 D2
Westhope *Shrop.* 207 D4
Westhorp 198 A2
Westhorpe *Lincs.* 226 A4
Westhorpe *Notts.* 224 B2
Westhorpe *Suff.* 202 B1
Westhoughton 234 A2
Westhouse 250 B5
Westhouses 223 F2
Westhumble 171 G2
Westing 345 E2
Westlake 150 C2
Westlands 221 F3
Westlea 182 D4
Westleigh *Devon* 163 E3
Westleigh *Devon* 153 D1
Westleigh *Gt.Man.* 234 A2
Westleton 203 F1
Westley *Shrop.* 206 C2
Westley *Suff.* 201 G1
Westley Heights 187 F4
Westley Waterless 201 E2
Westlington 184 C1
Westlinton 268 B5
Westloch 285 G4
Westmancote 196 B4
Westmarsh 175 E2
Westmeston 159 F2
Westmill 200 B5
Westminster 186 B5
Westminster Abbey 61
Westminster Cathedral 61
Westmuir 302 B4
Westness 340 B4
Westnewton *Cumb.* 259 E2
Westnewton *Northumb.* 278 D3
Westoe 262 C1
Weston *B. & N.E.Som.* 167 E1
Weston *Ches.* 221 E2
Weston *Devon* 153 E4
Weston *Devon* 153 E2
Weston *Dorset* 154 C5
Weston *Halton* 233 G4
Weston *Hants.* 170 C5
Weston *Here.* 194 C2
Weston *Herts.* 200 A4
Weston *Lincs.* 226 A5
Weston *Moray* 323 G3
Weston *N.Yorks.* 244 A3
Weston *Northants.* 198 A3
Weston *Notts.* 224 C1
Weston *S'ham.* 157 D1
Weston *Shrop.* 220 C5
Weston *Shrop.* 207 E3
Weston *Shrop.* 206 C5
Weston *Staffs.* 221 G5
Weston *W.Berks.* 183 G5
Weston Bampfylde 166 D5
Weston Beggard 195 E3
Weston by Welland 210 C3
Weston Colville 201 E2
Weston Corbett 170 B3
Weston Coyney 221 G3
Weston Favell 198 C1
Weston Green *Cambs.* 201 E2
Weston Green *Norf.* 228 C4
Weston Heath 207 G1
Weston Hills 226 A5
Weston in Arden 209 F4
Weston Jones 221 E5
Weston Longville 228 C4
Weston Lullingfields 220 B5
Weston Park 68
Weston Patrick 170 B3
Weston Point 233 F4
Weston Rhyn 219 F4
Weston Subedge 196 D3
Weston Town 167 E3
Weston Turville 185 D1
Weston under Penyard 195 F5
Weston under Wetherley 197 F1
Weston Underwood *Derbys.* 223 D3
Weston Underwood *M.K.* 199 D2
Westonbirt 182 A4
Westonbirt - The National Arboretum 38
Westoning 199 F4
Weston-in-Gordano 181 D5
Weston-on-Avon 197 D2
Weston-on-the-Green 184 A1
Weston-on-Trent 223 F5
Weston-super-Mare 166 A1
Weston-under-Lizard 208 A1
Westonzoyland 166 A4
Westow 245 G1
Westport *Arg. & B.* 272 B3
Westport *Som.* 166 A5
Westra 180 A5
Westray 340 C2
Westridge Green 184 A5
Westrigg 284 D3
Westruther 286 D5
Westry 212 B3
Westside 313 D5
Westvale 233 F3
Westville 223 G3
Westward 259 F2
Westward Ho! 163 E3
Westwell *Kent* 174 B4
Westwell *Oxon.* 183 E2
Westwell Leacon 174 B4
Westwick *Cambs.* 200 C1
Westwick *Dur.* 251 F1
Westwick *N.Yorks.* 244 C1
Westwick *Norf.* 229 D3
Westwood *Devon* 152 D3
Westwood *Peter.* 211 G3
Westwood *S.Lan.* 284 A4
Westwood *Wilts.* 167 F2
Westwood Heath 209 E5
Westwoodside 237 E3
Wetham Green 174 A2
Wetheral 260 A2
Wetherby 244 D3
Wetherden 202 B1
Wetherden Upper Town 202 B1
Wetheringsett 202 C1
Wethersfield 201 F4
Wethersta 342 C1
Wetherup Street 202 C1
Wetley Abbey 221 G3
Wetley Rocks 221 G3
Wettenhall 220 D1
Wettenhall Green 220 D1
Wetton 222 C2
Wetwang 246 B2
Wetwood 221 E4
Wexcombe 169 D2
Wexham Street 185 E4
Weybourne *Norf.* 228 C1
Weybourne *Surr.* 171 D3
Weybread 214 D3
Weybread Street 215 D4
Weybridge 171 F1
Weycroft 153 G2
Weydale 336 D2
Weyhill 169 E3
Weymouth 154 C5
Whaddon *Bucks.* 198 D4
Whaddon *Cambs.* 200 B3
Whaddon *Glos.* 182 A1
Whaddon *Glos.* 196 B5
Whaddon *Wilts.* 168 C5
Whaddon *Wilts.* 167 F1
Whaddon Gap 200 B3
Whale 260 B5
Whaley 236 C5
Whaley Bridge 235 E4
Whaley Thorns 236 C5
Whaligoe 337 F4
Whalley 242 D4
Whalsay 343 E1
Whalton 270 D3
Wham 243 D1
Whaplode 226 B5
Whaplode Drove 212 B1
Whaplode St. Catherine 212 B1
Wharfe 243 D1
Wharles 242 A4
Wharley End 199 E3
Wharncliffe Side 235 G3
Wharram le Street 246 A1
Wharram Percy 246 A1
Wharton *Ches.* 221 D1
Wharton *Here.* 195 E2
Whashton 252 A2
Whatcote 197 F3
Whateley 209 E3
Whatfield 202 B3
Whatley 167 E3
Whatlington 160 C2
Whatsole Street 174 D4
Whatstandwell 223 E2
Whatton 224 C4
Whauphill 257 E2
Whaw 251 E2
Wheal Martyn 38
Wheatacre 215 F2
Wheatcroft 223 E2
Wheatenhurst 181 G2
Wheatfield 184 B3
Wheathampstead 186 A1
Wheathill *Shrop.* 207 F4
Wheathill *Som.* 166 C4
Wheatley *Hants.* 170 C4
Wheatley *Oxon.* 184 B2
Wheatley *W.Yorks.* 243 G5
Wheatley Hill 262 C4
Wheatley Lane 243 E4
Wheatley Park 236 C2
Wheaton Aston 208 A1
Wheddon Cross 164 C4
Wheedlemont 311 G2
Wheelerstreet 171 E3
Wheelock 221 E2
Wheelock Heath 221 E2
Wheelton 242 C5
Wheen 302 B2
Wheldale 245 D5
Wheldrake 245 F3
Whelford 183 D3
Whelley 233 G2
Whelpley Hill 185 E2
Whelpo 259 G3
Whelston 232 D5
Whenby 245 F1
Whepstead 201 G2
Wherstead 202 C3
Wherwell 169 E3
Wheston 235 F5
Whetley Cross 154 A2
Whetsted 173 F4
Whetstone *Gt.Lon.* 186 B3
Whetstone *Leics.* 210 A3
Whicham 248 C4
Whichford 197 F4
Whickham 262 B1
Whiddon 163 E5
Whiddon Down 149 G1
Whifflet 284 B3
Whigstreet 302 C5
Whilton 198 B1
Whim 285 G4
Whimble 162 D5
Whimple 152 D3
Whimpwell Green 229 E3
Whin Lane End 241 G3
Whinburgh 228 B5
Whinlatter Forest 100
Whinny Hill 252 C1
Whinnyfold 313 F1
Whippingham 157 E3
Whipsnade 185 F1
Whipsnade Wild Animal Park 84
Whipton 152 C3
Whirlow 236 A4
Whisby 225 E1
Whissendine 210 D1
Whissonsett 228 A3
Whisterfield 234 C5
Whistley Green 184 C5
Whiston *Mersey.* 233 F3
Whiston *Northants.* 198 D1
Whiston *S.Yorks.* 236 B3
Whiston *Staffs.* 222 B3
Whiston *Staffs.* 208 A1
Whiston Cross 207 G2
Whiston Eaves 222 B3
Whitacre Fields 209 E3
Whitacre Heath 209 E3
Whitbeck 248 C4
Whitbourne 195 G2
Whitburn *T. & W.* 262 D1
Whitburn *W.Loth.* 284 D3
Whitby *Ches.* 233 E5
Whitby *N.Yorks.* 254 B1
Whitby Abbey 91
Whitbyheath 233 E5
Whitchurch *B. & N.E.Som.* 166 D1
Whitchurch *Bucks.* 198 D5
Whitchurch *Cardiff* 180 A4
Whitchurch *Devon* 149 E3
Whitchurch *Hants.* 169 F3
Whitchurch *Here.* 181 E1
Whitchurch *Pembs.* 190 A5
Whitchurch *Shrop.* 220 C3
Whitchurch *Warks.* 197 E3
Whitchurch Canonicorum 153 G3
Whitchurch Hill 184 B5
Whitchurch-on-Thames 184 B5
Whitcombe 154 D4
Whitcott Keysett 206 B4
White Ball 153 D1
White Colne 201 G5
White Coppice 234 A1
White Cross *Cornw.* 146 C4
White Cross *Devon* 152 D3
White Cross *Here.* 195 D3
White Cross *Wilts.* 167 E4
White End 196 A5
White Hill 167 F4
White Houses 237 E5
White Kirkley 261 G4
White Lackington 154 D3
White Ladies Aston 196 B2
White Lund 242 A1
White Mill 192 A5
White Moor 223 E3
White Notley 187 G1
White Ox Mead 167 E2
White Pit 239 D5
White Rocks 194 D5
White Roding 187 E1
White Scar Cave 91
White Waltham 184 D5
Whiteacen 323 E5
Whiteash Green 201 F4
Whitebirk 242 D5
Whitebog 325 E4
Whitebridge *High.* 337 E1
Whitebridge *High.* 309 D3
Whitebrook 181 E2
Whiteburn 286 C5
Whitecairn 264 D5
Whitecairns 313 E3
Whitecastle 285 E5
Whitechapel 242 B3
Whitechurch 191 E4
Whitecote 244 B4
Whitecraig 286 A2
Whitecroft 181 F2
Whitecrook 264 C5
Whitecross *Cornw.* 144 C3
Whitecross *Cornw.* 147 D2
Whitecross *Dorset* 154 A3
Whiteface 321 G1
Whitefield *Aber.* 312 C2
Whitefield *Devon* 164 A4
Whitefield *Dorset* 155 F3
Whitefield *Gt.Man.* 234 C2
Whitefield *High.* 309 E2
Whitefield *High.* 337 E3
Whitefield *P. & K.* 293 G1
Whiteford 312 C2
Whitegate 220 D1
Whitehall *Devon* 153 E1
Whitehall *Hants.* 170 C2
Whitehall *Ork.* 341 E4
Whitehall *W.Suss.* 171 G5
Whitehall Street 228 C3
Whitehaven 258 C5
Whitehill *Aber.* 325 E4
Whitehill *Hants.* 170 C4
Whitehill *Kent* 174 B3
Whitehill *Midloth.* 286 A3
Whitehill *N.Ayr.* 283 D4
Whitehills 324 B3
Whitehouse *Aber.* 312 B3
Whitehouse *Arg. & B.* 281 G3
Whitehouse Common 208 D3
Whitekirk 286 C1
Whitelackington 153 G1
Whitelaw 287 F4
Whiteleen 337 F4
Whitelees 274 B2
Whiteley 157 E2
Whiteley Bank 157 E4
Whiteley Green 234 D5
Whiteley Village 171 F1
Whiteleys 264 B5
Whitemans Green 159 F1
Whitemire 322 B4
Whitemoor 147 D4
Whiteness 342 C3
Whiteoak Green 183 F1
Whiteparish 168 D5
Whiterashes 313 D2
Whiterow 337 F4
Whiteshill 182 A2
Whiteside *Northumb.* 260 D1
Whiteside *W.Loth.* 285 D3
Whitesmith 160 A2
Whitestaunton 153 F1
Whitestone *Aber.* 312 B5
Whitestone *Arg. & B.* 272 C2
Whitestone *Devon* 152 B3
Whitestreet Green 202 A4
Whitestripe 325 E4
Whiteway 182 B1
Whitewell *Aber.* 325 E3
Whitewell *Lancs.* 242 C3
Whitewell *Wrex.* 220 B3
Whiteworks 149 G3
Whitewreath 323 E4
Whitfield *Here.* 194 D4
Whitfield *Kent* 175 F4
Whitfield *Northants.* 198 B4
Whitfield *Northumb.* 261 D2
Whitfield *S.Glos.* 181 F3
Whitford *Devon* 153 F3
Whitford (Chwitffordd) *Flints.* 232 C5
Whitgift 246 A5
Whitgreave 221 F5
Whithorn 257 E2
Whithorn Priory 131
Whiting Bay 273 F3
Whitkirk 244 C4
Whitlam 313 D2
Whitland 177 F1
Whitland Abbey 177 F1
Whitleigh 150 A1
Whitletts 274 B3
Whitley *N.Yorks.* 245 E5
Whitley *Read.* 170 C1
Whitley *W.Mid.* 209 F5
Whitley *Wilts.* 167 F1
Whitley Bay 271 F4
Whitley Chapel 261 F2
Whitley Heath 221 F5
Whitley Lower 235 G1
Whitley Row 173 D3
Whitlock's End 208 D5
Whitminster 181 G2
Whitmore *Dorset* 155 G2
Whitmore *Staffs.* 221 F3
Whitnage 152 D1
Whitnash 197 F1
Whitnell 165 F3
Whitney-on-Wye 194 B3
Whitrigg *Cumb.* 259 F1
Whitrigg *Cumb.* 259 F3
Whitsbury 156 A1
Whitsome 287 F4
Whitson 180 C4
Whitstable 174 D2
Whitstone 148 C1
Whittingham 279 E5
Whittingslow 206 D4
Whittington *Derbys.* 236 A5
Whittington *Glos.* 196 C5
Whittington *Lancs.* 250 B5
Whittington *Norf.* 213 F3
Whittington *Shrop.* 220 A4
Whittington *Staffs.* 209 D2
Whittington *Staffs.* 208 A4
Whittington *Worcs.* 196 A2
Whittlebury 198 B3
Whittle-le-Woods 242 B5
Whittlesey 212 A3
Whittlesford 200 C3
Whittlestone Head 234 B1
Whitton *Gt.Lon.* 186 A5
Whitton *N.Lincs.* 246 B5
Whitton *Northumb.* 270 C1
Whitton *Powys* 194 B1
Whitton *Shrop.* 207 E5
Whitton *Stock.* 262 C5
Whitton *Suff.* 202 C3
Whittonditch 183 E5
Whittonstall 261 G2
Whitway 169 F2
Whitwell *Derbys.* 236 C5
Whitwell *Herts.* 199 G5
Whitwell *I.o.W.* 157 E5
Whitwell *N.Yorks.* 252 B3
Whitwell *Rut.* 211 E2
Whitwell Street 228 C3
Whitwell-on-the-Hill 245 G1
Whitwick 209 G1
Whitwood 244 D5
Whitworth 234 C1
Whitworth Art Gallery 100
Whixall 220 C4
Whixley 244 D2
Whorlton *Dur.* 252 A1
Whorlton *N.Yorks.* 253 D2
Whygate 269 F4
Whyle 195 E1
Whyteleafe 172 C3
Wibdon 181 E3
Wibsey 244 A4
Wibtoft 209 G4
Wichenford 195 G1
Wichling 174 B3
Wick *Bourne.* 156 A3
Wick *Devon* 153 E2
Wick *High.* 337 F3
Wick *S.Glos.* 181 G5
Wick *Som.* 165 F3
Wick *Som.* 166 C4
Wick *V. of Glam.* 179 F5
Wick *W.Suss.* 158 C3
Wick *Wilts.* 168 C5
Wick *Worcs.* 196 B3
Wick Airport 337 F3
Wick Hill *Kent* 174 A4
Wick Hill *W'ham* 170 C1
Wick St. Lawrence 166 A1
Wicken *Cambs.* 213 D5
Wicken *Northants.* 198 C4
Wicken Bonhunt 200 C4
Wicken Fen National Nature Reserve 84
Wickenby 238 A4
Wicker Street Green 202 A3
Wickersiack 250 B1
Wickersley 236 B3
Wicketwood Hill 224 B3
Wickford 187 G3
Wickham *Hants.* 157 E1
Wickham *W.Berks.* 183 F5
Wickham Bishops 188 B1
Wickham Heath 169 F1
Wickham Market 203 E2
Wickham St. Paul 201 G4
Wickham Skeith 202 B1
Wickham Street *Suff.* 201 F2
Wickham Street *Suff.* 202 B1
Wickhambreaux 175 E3
Wickhambrook 201 F2
Wickhamford 196 C3
Wickhampton 229 F5
Wicklewood 228 B5
Wickmere 228 C2
Wicksteed Park 75
Wickstreet 160 A3
Wickwar 181 G4
Widcombe 167 E1
Widdington 200 D4
Widdop 243 F4
Widdrington 271 E2
Widdrington Station 271 E2
Wide Open 271 E4
Widecombe in the Moor 152 A5
Widegates 147 G4
Widemouth Bay 162 C5
Widewall 338 D3
Widford *Essex* 187 F2
Widford *Herts.* 186 D1
Widford *Oxon.* 183 E1
Widgham Green 201 E2
Widmer End 185 D3
Widmerpool 224 B5
Widnes 233 G4
Widworthy 153 F3
Wigan 233 G2
Wiganthorpe 253 F5
Wigborough 154 A1
Wiggaton 153 E3
Wiggenhall St. Germans 213 D1
Wiggenhall St. Mary Magdalen 213 D1
Wiggenhall St. Mary the Virgin 213 D1
Wiggenhall St. Peter 213 E1
Wiggens Green 201 E3
Wigginton *Herts.* 185 E1
Wigginton *Oxon* 197 F4
Wigginton *Shrop.* 220 A4
Wigginton *Staffs.* 209 E2
Wigginton *York* 245 E2
Wigglesworth 243 E2
Wiggonby 259 G1
Wiggonholt 158 C2
Wighill 245 D3
Wighton 228 A2
Wightwick Manor 68
Wightwizzle 235 G3
Wigley 156 C1
Wigmore *Here.* 194 D1
Wigmore *Med.* 174 A2
Wigsley 237 F5
Wigsthorpe 211 F4

Wigston 210 B3
Wigston Parva 209 G4
Wigthorpe 236 C4
Wigtoft 226 A4
Wigton 259 F2
Wigtown 265 F5
Wike 244 C3
Wilbarston 210 D4
Wilberfoss 245 G2
Wilburton 212 C5
Wilby *Norf.* 214 B2
Wilby *Northants.* 199 D1
Wilby *Suff.* 214 D4
Wilcot 168 C1
Wilcott 206 C1
Wilcrick 180 D4
Wilday Green 236 A5
Wildboarclough 221 D2
Wilde Street 213 F5
Wilden *Beds.* 199 F2
Wilden *Worcs.* 208 A5
Wilderhope Manor 68
Wildfowl & Wetlands Trust Washington 105
Wildhern 169 E2
Wildhill 186 B2
Wildmoor 208 B5
Wildsworth 237 F3
Wilford 223 G4
Wilkesley 220 D3
Wilkhaven 322 B1
Wilkieston 285 F3
Wilksby 226 A1
Willand *Devon* 152 D1
Willand *Som.* 153 E1
Willaston *Ches.* 233 E5
Willaston *Ches.* 221 D2
Willaston *Shrop.* 220 C4
Willen 199 D3
Willenhall *W.Mid.* 208 B3
Willenhall *W.Mid.* 209 F5
Willerby *E.Riding* 246 C4
Willerby *N.Yorks.* 254 D5
Willersey 196 D4
Willersley 194 C3
Willesborough 174 C4
Willesborough Lees 174 C4
Willesden 186 B4
Willesleigh 163 F2
Willesley 182 A4
Willett 165 E4
Willey *Shrop.* 207 F3
Willey *Warks.* 209 G4
Willey Green 171 E2
William's Green 202 A3
Williamscot 197 G3
Williamthorpe 223 F1
Willian 200 A4
Willimontswick 261 D1
Willingale 187 E2
Willingdon 160 A3
Willingham 212 C5
Willingham by Stow 237 F4
Willingham Green 201 E2
Willington *Beds.* 199 G2
Willington *Derbys.* 223 D5
Willington *Dur.* 262 A4
Willington *Kent* 173 G3
Willington *T. & W.* 262 C1
Willington *Warks.* 197 E4
Willington Corner 220 C1
Willisham 202 B2
Willitoft 245 G4
Williton 165 D3
Willoughbridge 221 E3
Willoughby *Lincs.* 239 E5
Willoughby *Warks.* 198 A1
Willoughby Waterleys 210 A3
Willoughby-on-the-Wolds 224 B5
Willoughton 237 G3
Willow Green 234 A5
Willows Green 187 G1
Willsbridge 181 F5
Willslock 222 B4
Willsworthy 149 F2
Willtown 166 A5
Wilmcote 197 D2
Wilmington *B. & N.E.Som.* 167 D1
Wilmington *Devon* 153 F2
Wilmington *E.Suss.* 160 A3
Wilmington *Kent* 187 E5
Wilmslow 234 C4
Wilnecote 209 E2
Wilney Green 214 B3
Wilpshire 242 C4
Wilsden 243 G4
Wilsford *Lincs.* 225 F3
Wilsford *Wilts.* 168 C4
Wilsford *Wilts.* 168 C2
Wilsham 164 A3
Wilshaw 235 F2
Wilsill 244 A1
Wilsley Green 173 G5
Wilsley Pound 173 G5
Wilson 223 F5
Wilstead 199 F3
Wilsthorpe *E.Riding* 247 D1
Wilsthorpe *Lincs.* 211 F1
Wilstone 185 E1
Wilton *Cumb.* 258 D5
Wilton *Here.* 195 E5
Wilton *N.Yorks.* 254 B4
Wilton *R. & C.* 263 E5
Wilton *Sc.Bord.* 277 F4
Wilton *Wilts.* 169 D1
Wilton *Wilts.* 168 B4
Wilton House 38
Wiltown 153 E1
Wimbish 201 D4
Wimbish Green 201 E4
Wimblebury 208 C1
Wimbledon 186 B5
Wimblington 212 C3
Wimborne Minster 155 G2
Wimborne St. Giles 155 G1
Wimbotsham 213 E2
Wimpole 200 B2
Wimpole Hall 84
Wimpole Home Farm 84
Wimpole Lodge 200 B3
Wimpstone 197 E3
Wincanton 167 E5
Winceby 226 B1
Wincham 234 A5
Winchburgh 285 E2
Winchcombe 196 C5
Winchelsea 161 E2
Winchelsea Beach 161 E2
Winchester 169 F5
Winchester Cathedral 53
Winchet Hill 173 G4
Winchfield 170 C2
Winchmore Hill *Bucks.* 185 E3
Winchmore Hill *Gt.Lon.* 186 C3
Wincle 221 G1
Wincobank 236 A3
Windermere 249 F3
Windermere Lake Cruises 100
Windermere Steamboat Museum 100
Winderton 197 F3
Windhill 321 E5
Windle Hill 233 E5
Windlehurst 235 D4
Windlesham 171 E1
Windley 223 E3
Windmill Hill *E.Suss.* 160 B2
Windmill Hill *Som.* 153 G1
Windmill Hill *Worcs.* 196 B3
Windrush 183 D1
Windsor 185 E5
Windsor Castle 53
Windsor Green 201 G2
Windy Nook 262 B1
Windygates 294 B4
Windy-Yett 283 F4
Wineham 159 E1
Winestead 247 E5
Winewall 243 F4
Winfarthing 214 C3
Winford *I.o.W.* 157 E4
Winford *N.Som.* 166 C1
Winforton 194 B3
Winfrith Newburgh 155 E4
Wing *Bucks.* 199 D5
Wing *Rut.* 211 D2
Wingate 262 C4
Wingates *Gt.Man.* 234 A2
Wingates *Northumb.* 270 C2
Wingerworth 223 E1
Wingfield *Beds.* 199 F5
Wingfield *Suff.* 214 D4
Wingfield *Wilts.* 167 F2
Wingfield Green 214 D4
Wingham 175 E3
Wingham Well 175 E3
Wingmore 175 D4
Wingrave 185 D1
Winkburn 224 C2
Winkfield 185 E5
Winkfield Row 185 D5
Winkhill 222 B2
Winkleigh 163 G5
Winksley 252 B5
Winkton 156 A3
Winlaton 262 A1
Winlaton Mill 262 A1
Winless 337 F3
Winmarleigh 242 A3
Winnard's Perch 146 D3
Winnersh 184 C5
Winnington 234 A5
Winscombe 166 B2
Winsford *Ches.* 221 D1
Winsford *Som.* 164 C4
Winsham *Devon* 163 E2
Winsham *Som.* 153 G2
Winshill 223 D5
Winsh-wen 178 C3
Winskill 260 B4
Winslade 170 B3
Winsley 167 F1
Winslow 198 C5
Winson 182 C2
Winsor 156 C1
Winster *Cumb.* 249 F3
Winster *Derbys.* 222 D1
Winston *Dur.* 252 A1
Winston *Suff.* 202 C1
Winston Green 202 C1
Winstone 182 B2
Winswell 163 E4
Winterborne Came 154 D4
Winterborne Clenston 155 E2
Winterborne Herringston 154 C4
Winterborne Houghton 155 E2
Winterborne Kingston 155 E3
Winterborne Monkton 154 C4
Winterborne Stickland 155 E2
Winterborne Whitechurch 155 E2
Winterborne Zelston 155 E3
Winterbourne *S.Glos.* 181 F4
Winterbourne *W.Berks.* 183 G5
Winterbourne Abbas 154 C3
Winterbourne Bassett 182 D5
Winterbourne Dauntsey 168 C4
Winterbourne Earls 168 C4
Winterbourne Gunner 168 C4
Winterbourne Monkton 182 D5
Winterbourne Steepleton 154 C4
Winterbourne Stoke 168 B3
Winterbrook 184 B4
Winterburn 243 F2
Wintercleugh 276 A4
Winteringham 246 B5
Winterley 221 E2
Wintersett 236 A1
Wintershill 157 E1
Winterslow 168 D4
Winterton 237 G1
Winterton-on-Sea 229 F4
Winthorpe *Lincs.* 227 D1
Winthorpe *Notts.* 224 D2
Winton *Bourne.* 155 G3
Winton *Cumb.* 250 C1
Wintringham 254 B5
Winwick *Cambs.* 211 G4
Winwick *Northants.* 210 B5
Winwick *Warr.* 234 A3
Wirksworth 223 D2
Wirksworth Moor 223 E2
Wirswall 220 C3
Wisbech 212 C2
Wisbech St. Mary 212 C2
Wisborough Green 171 F5
Wiseton 237 E4
Wishaw *N.Lan.* 284 B4
Wishaw *Warks.* 209 D3
Wisley 171 F2
Wisley R.H.S. Gardens 53
Wispington 238 C5
Wissett 215 E4
Wissington 202 A4
Wistanstow 206 D4
Wistanswick 221 D5
Wistaston 221 D2
Wiston *Pembs.* 176 D1
Wiston *S.Lan.* 276 A2
Wistow *Cambs.* 212 A4
Wistow *N.Yorks.* 245 E4
Wiswell 242 D4
Witcham 212 C5
Witchampton 155 F2
Witchburn 272 C3
Witchford 212 D5
Witcombe 166 B5
Witham 188 B1
Witham Friary 167 E3
Witham on the Hill 211 F1
Withcall 238 C4
Withcote 210 C2
Withdean 159 F3
Witherenden Hill 160 B1
Witherhurst 160 B1
Witheridge 152 B1
Witherley 209 F3
Withern 239 E4
Withernsea 247 F5
Withernwick 247 D3
Withersdale Street 215 D3
Withersfield 201 E3
Witherslack 249 F4
Witherslack Hall 249 F4
Withiel 147 D3
Withiel Florey 164 C4
Withielgoose 147 E3
Withington *Glos.* 182 C1
Withington *Gt.Man.* 234 C3
Withington *Here.* 195 E3
Withington *Shrop.* 207 E1
Withington *Staffs.* 222 B4
Withington Green 234 C5
Withington Marsh 195 E3
Withleigh 152 C1
Withnell 242 C5
Withnell Fold 242 C5
Withybrook *Som.* 167 D3
Withybrook *Warks.* 209 G4
Withycombe 164 D3
Withycombe Raleigh 152 D4
Withyham 173 D5
Withypool 164 B4
Witley 171 E4
Witley Common Information Centre 53
Witnesham 202 C2
Witney 183 F2
Wittering 211 F2
Wittersham 161 D1
Witton *Angus* 303 D2
Witton *Norf.* 229 E5
Witton *Worcs.* 196 A1
Witton Bridge 229 E2
Witton Gilbert 262 B3
Witton Park 262 A4
Witton-le-Wear 262 A4
Wiveliscombe 165 D5
Wivelsfield 159 F1
Wivelsfield Green 159 F2
Wivenhoe 202 B5
Wiveton 228 B1
Wix 202 C5
Wixford 196 C2
Wixhill 220 C5
Wixoe 201 F3
Woburn 199 E4
Woburn Abbey 84
Woburn Sands 199 E4
Wokefield Park 170 B1
Woking 171 F2
Wokingham 170 D1
Wolborough 152 B5
Wold Newton *E.Riding* 254 D5
Wold Newton *N.E.Lincs.* 238 C3
Woldingham 172 C3
Wolfelee 277 G5
Wolferlow 195 F1
Wolferton 227 E5
Wolfhampcote 198 A1
Wolfhill 293 G1
Wolfpits 194 B2
Wolf's Castle 190 C5
Wolfsdale 190 C5
Woll 277 F3
Wollaston *Northants.* 199 E1
Wollaston *Shrop.* 206 C1
Wollaston *W.Mid.* 208 A4
Wollaton 223 G4
Wollerton 220 D5
Wollescote 208 B4
Wolsingham 261 G4
Wolston 209 G5
Wolsty 259 E1
Wolvercote 184 A2
Wolverhampton 208 B3
Wolverley *Shrop.* 220 B4
Wolverley *Worcs.* 208 A5
Wolverton *Hants.* 169 G2
Wolverton *M.K.* 198 D3
Wolverton *Warks.* 197 E1
Wolverton *Wilts.* 167 E4
Wolverton Common 169 G2
Wolvesnewton 181 D3
Wolvey 209 G4
Wolvey Heath 209 G4
Wolviston 263 D5
Womaston 194 B1
Wombleton 253 F4
Wombourne 208 A3
Wombwell 236 A2
Womenswold 175 E3
Womersley 236 C1
Wonastow 181 D1
Wonersh 171 F3
Wonford 152 C3
Wonson 149 G2
Wonston 169 F4
Wooburn 185 E4
Wooburn Green 185 E4
Wood Bevington 196 C2
Wood Burcote 198 B3
Wood Dalling 228 B3
Wood Eaton 208 A1
Wood End *Beds.* 199 F3
Wood End *Beds.* 199 F1
Wood End *Bucks.* 198 C4
Wood End *Herts.* 200 B5
Wood End *W.Mid.* 208 B2
Wood End *Warks.* 209 E3
Wood End *Warks.* 208 D5
Wood End *Warks.* 209 E4
Wood Enderby 226 A1
Wood Green *Essex* 186 D2
Wood Green *Gt.Lon.* 186 C3
Wood Green *Norf.* 214 D2
Wood Green Animal Shelter 84
Wood Lane 220 B4
Wood Norton 228 B3
Wood Seats 236 A3
Wood Stanway 196 C4
Wood Street 229 E3
Wood Street Village 171 E2
Woodacott 163 D5
Woodale 251 F5
Woodall 236 B4
Woodbastwick 229 E4
Woodbeck 237 E5
Woodborough *Notts.* 224 B3
Woodborough *Wilts.* 168 C2
Woodbridge *Devon* 153 E3
Woodbridge *Dorset* 154 D1
Woodbridge *Suff.* 203 D3
Woodbridge Tide Mill 84
Woodbury *Devon* 152 D4
Woodbury *Som.* 166 C3
Woodbury Salterton 152 D4
Woodchester 182 A2
Woodchester Mansion 38
Woodchurch *Kent* 174 B5
Woodchurch *Mersey.* 233 D4
Woodcombe 164 C3
Woodcote *Oxon.* 184 B4
Woodcote *Tel. & W.* 207 G1
Woodcote Green 208 B5
Woodcott 169 F2
Woodcroft 181 E3
Woodcutts 155 F1
Woodditton 201 E2
Woodeaton 184 A1
Woodend *Aber.* 312 B3
Woodend *Cumb.* 248 C3
Woodend *High.* 309 G2
Woodend *High.* 297 G3
Woodend *Northants.* 198 B3
Woodend *P. & K.* 300 C5
Woodend *W.Suss.* 158 A3
Woodend Green 201 D5
Woodfalls 168 C5
Woodfield *Oxon.* 198 A5
Woodfield *S.Ayr.* 274 B3
Woodfoot 250 B1
Woodford *Cornw.* 162 C4
Woodford *Devon* 151 D2
Woodford *Glos.* 181 F3
Woodford *Gt.Lon.* 186 D3
Woodford *Gt.Man.* 234 C4
Woodford *Northants.* 211 E5
Woodford *Som.* 165 D4
Woodford Bridge 186 D3
Woodford Green 186 D3
Woodford Halse 198 A2
Woodgate *Devon* 153 E1
Woodgate *Norf.* 228 B4
Woodgate *W.Mid.* 208 B4
Woodgate *W.Suss.* 158 B3
Woodgate *Worcs.* 196 B1
Woodgreen 156 A1
Woodhall *Inclyde* 283 E2
Woodhall *N.Yorks.* 251 E3
Woodhall Hills 244 A4
Woodhall Spa 225 G1
Woodham *Bucks.* 184 B1
Woodham *Dur.* 262 B5
Woodham *Surr.* 171 F1
Woodham Ferrers 187 G3
Woodham Mortimer 188 B2
Woodham Walter 188 B2
Woodhaven 294 C2
Woodhead *Aber.* 312 C1
Woodhead *Staffs.* 222 B3
Woodhey 233 E4
Woodhey Green 220 C2
Woodhill *Shrop.* 207 G4
Woodhill *Som.* 166 A5
Woodhorn 271 E3
Woodhouse *Cumb.* 249 G4
Woodhouse *Leics.* 210 A1
Woodhouse *S.Yorks.* 236 B4
Woodhouse *W.Yorks.* 244 B4
Woodhouse *W.Yorks.* 244 C5
Woodhouse *W.Yorks.* 244 A5
Woodhouse Down 181 F4
Woodhouse Eaves 210 A1
Woodhouse Green 221 G1
Woodhouses *Gt.Man.* 234 C2
Woodhouses *Staffs.* 209 D1
Woodhouses *Staffs.* 208 C2
Woodhuish 151 F2
Woodhurst 212 B5
Woodingdean 159 F3
Woodington 169 E5
Woodland *Devon* 151 D1
Woodland *Dur.* 261 G5
Woodland *Kent* 174 D4
Woodland Head 152 A3
Woodlands *Dorset* 155 G2
Woodlands *Hants.* 156 C1
Woodlands *N.Yorks.* 244 C2
Woodlands *Shrop.* 207 G4
Woodlands *Som.* 165 E3
Woodlands Leisure Park 38
Woodlands Park 185 D5
Woodlands St. Mary 183 F5
Woodlane 222 C5
Woodleigh 150 D3
Woodlesford 244 C5
Woodley *Gt.Man.* 234 D3
Woodley *W'ham* 184 C5
Woodmancote *Glos.* 182 C2
Woodmancote *Glos.* 196 B5
Woodmancote *Glos.* 181 G3
Woodmancote *W.Suss.* 159 E2
Woodmancote *W.Suss.* 157 G2
Woodmancott 169 G3
Woodmansey 246 C4
Woodmansterne 172 B3
Woodmanton 152 D4
Woodmill 222 C5
Woodminton 168 B5
Woodmoor 206 B2
Woodnesborough 175 F3
Woodnewton 211 F3
Woodperry 184 A1
Woodplumpton 242 B4
Woodrising 228 A5
Woodrow 155 D1
Wood's Corner 160 B2
Woods Eaves 194 B3
Wood's Green 173 F5
Woodseaves *Shrop.* 221 D4
Woodseaves *Staffs.* 221 E5
Woodsend 183 E5
Woodsetts 236 C4
Woodsford 155 D3
Woodside *Aberdeen* 313 E4
Woodside *Beds.* 185 F1
Woodside *Brack.F.* 185 E5
Woodside *Cumb.* 258 D3
Woodside *D. & G.* 267 E3
Woodside *Fife* 294 C4
Woodside *Fife* 294 A4
Woodside *Gt.Lon.* 172 C2
Woodside *Hants.* 156 C3
Woodside *Herts.* 186 B2
Woodside *N.Ayr.* 283 E4
Woodside *P. & K.* 293 G1
Woodside *Shrop.* 206 C4
Woodside *W.Mid.* 208 B4
Woodside Farm 84
Woodside Green 174 B3
Woodstock *Oxon.* 183 G1
Woodstock *Pembs.* 190 D5
Woodthorpe *Derbys.* 236 B5
Woodthorpe *Leics.* 210 A1
Woodthorpe *Lincs.* 239 E4
Woodthorpe *S.Yorks.* 236 A4
Woodton 215 D2
Woodtown 163 E3
Woodvale 233 E1
Woodville 209 F1
Woodwall Green 221 E4
Woodwalton 212 A4
Woodwick 340 B4
Woodworth Green 220 C2
Woodyates 155 G1
Woofferton 195 E1
Wookey 166 C3
Wookey Hole 166 C3
Wookey Hole Caves & Papermill 38
Wool 155 E4
Woolacombe 163 E1
Woolage Green 175 E4
Woolage Village 175 E3
Woolaston 181 E3
Woolaston Slade 181 E2
Woolavington 166 A3
Woolbeding 171 D5
Woolcotts 164 C4
Wooldale 235 F2
Wooler 279 D4
Woolfardisworthy *Devon* 152 B2
Woolfardisworthy *Devon* 162 D3
Woolfold 234 B1
Woolfords Cottages 285 E4
Woolgarston 155 F4
Woolgreaves 236 A1
Woolhampton 169 G1
Woolhope 195 F4
Woolland 155 D2
Woollard 166 D1
Woollaton 163 E4
Woollensbrook 186 C2
Woolley *B. & N.E.Som.* 167 E1
Woolley *Cambs.* 211 G5
Woolley *Cornw.* 162 C4
Woolley *Derbys.* 223 E1
Woolley *W.Yorks.* 236 A1
Woolley Green *W. & M.* 185 D5
Woolley Green *Wilts.* 167 F1
Woolmer Green 186 B1
Woolmere Green 196 B1
Woolmersdon 165 F4
Woolpit 202 A1
Woolpit Green 202 A1
Woolscott 197 G1
Woolsgrove 152 A2
Woolstaston 207 D3
Woolsthorpe 224 D4
Woolsthorpe by Colsterworth 225 E5
Woolsthorpe Manor 75
Woolston *Devon* 150 D3
Woolston *S'ham.* 156 D1
Woolston *Shrop.* 220 A5
Woolston *Shrop.* 206 D4
Woolston *Warr.* 234 A4
Woolston Green 151 D1
Woolstone *Glos.* 196 B4
Woolstone *M.K.* 199 D4
Woolstone *Oxon.* 183 E4
Woolton 233 F4
Woolton Hill 169 F1
Woolverstone 202 C4
Woolverton 167 E2
Woolwich 186 D5
Woonton 194 C2
Wooperton 279 E5
Woore 221 E3
Wootten Green 214 D4
Wootton *Beds.* 199 F3
Wootton *Hants.* 156 B3
Wootton *I.o.W.* 157 E3
Wootton *Kent* 175 E4
Wootton *N.Lincs.* 238 A1
Wootton *Northants.* 198 C2
Wootton *Oxon.* 183 G1
Wootton *Oxon.* 183 G2
Wootton *Shrop.* 207 D5
Wootton *Shrop.* 220 A5
Wootton *Staffs.* 221 F5
Wootton *Staffs.* 222 C3
Wootton Bassett 182 C4
Wootton Bridge 157 E3
Wootton Common 157 E3
Wootton Courtenay 164 C3
Wootton Fitzpaine 153 G3
Wootton Green 199 F3
Wootton Rivers 168 C1
Wootton St. Lawrence 169 G2
Wootton Wawen 197 D1
Worcester 196 A2
Worcester Art Gallery & Museum 68
Worcester Cathedral 68
Worcester Park 172 B2
Wordsley 208 A4
Wordwell 213 G5
Worfield 207 G3
Worgret 155 F4
Work 340 C5
Workhouse End 199 G2
Workington 258 D4
Worksop 236 C5
Worlaby *Lincs.* 238 D5
Worlaby *N.Lincs.* 238 A1
World of Beatrix Potter Attraction 100
World's End *Bucks.* 185 D2
Worlds End *Hants.* 157 F1
World's End *W.Berks.* 183 G5
Worlds End *W.Mid.* 208 D4
Worle 166 A1
Worleston 221 D2
Worlingham 215 F3
Worlington 213 E5
Worlingworth 202 D1
Wormald Green 244 C1
Wormbridge 194 D4
Wormegay 213 E1
Wormelow Tump 195 D4
Wormhill 235 F5
Wormiehills 295 E1
Wormingford 202 A4
Worminghall 184 B2
Wormington 196 C4
Worminster 166 C3
Wormiston 295 E4
Wormit 294 B2
Wormleighton 197 G2
Wormley *Herts.* 186 C2
Wormley *Surr.* 171 E4
Wormley West End 186 B2
Wormshill 174 A3
Wormsley 194 D3
Worplesdon 171 E2
Worrall 236 A3
Worsbrough 236 A2
Worsley 234 B2
Worstead 229 E3
Worsted Lodge 200 D2
Worsthorne 243 E4
Worston 243 D3
Worswell 150 B3
Worth *Kent* 175 F3
Worth *W.Suss.* 172 B5
Worth Matravers 155 F5
Wortham 214 B4
Worthen 206 C2
Worthenbury 220 B3
Worthing *Norf.* 228 A4
Worthing *W.Suss.* 158 D3
Worthing Museum & Art Gallery 53
Worthington 223 F5
Worting 170 B2
Wortley *Glos.* 181 G3
Wortley *S.Yorks.* 236 A3
Wortley *W.Yorks.* 244 B4
Worton *N.Yorks.* 251 E4
Worton *Wilts.* 168 A2
Wortwell 215 D3
Wothersome 244 D3
Wotherton 206 B2
Wotter 150 B1
Wotton 171 G3
Wotton Underwood 184 B1
Wotton-under-Edge 181 G3
Woughton on the Green 199 D4
Wouldham 173 G2
Wrabness 202 C4
Wrae 324 C4
Wrafton 163 E2
Wragby 238 B5
Wragholme 239 D3
Wramplingham 228 C5
Wrangaton 150 C2
Wrangham 312 B1
Wrangle 226 C2
Wrangle Lowgate 226 C2
Wrangway 153 E1
Wrantage 166 A5
Wrawby 238 A2
Wraxall *N.Som.* 181 D5
Wraxall *Som.* 166 D4
Wray 242 C1
Wray Castle 249 E2
Wrays 172 B4
Wraysbury 185 F5
Wrayton 250 B5
Wrea Green 241 G4
Wreay *Cumb.* 260 A5
Wreay *Cumb.* 260 A3
Wrecclesham 170 D3
Wrecsam (Wrexham) 220 A3
Wrekenton 262 B2
Wrelton 253 G4
Wrenbury 220 C3
Wrench Green 254 C4
Wreningham 214 C2
Wrentham 215 F3
Wrenthorpe 244 C5
Wrentnall 206 D2
Wressle *E.Riding* 245 G4
Wressle *N.Lincs.* 237 G2
Wrest Park 84
Wrestlingworth 200 A3
Wretham 214 A2
Wretton 213 E2
Wrexham (Wrecsam) 220 A3
Wrexham Industrial Estate 220 A3
Wribbenhall 207 G5
Wrightington Bar 233 G1
Wrightpark 292 B5
Wright's Green 187 E1
Wrinehill 221 E3
Wrington 166 B1
Writhlington 167 D2
Writtle 187 F2
Wrockwardine 207 F1
Wroot 237 E2
Wrose 244 A4
Wrotham 173 F3
Wrotham Heath 173 F3
Wrotham Hill Park 173 F2
Wrottesley 208 A2
Wroughton 182 D4
Wroxall *I.o.W.* 157 E5
Wroxall *Warks.* 209 E5
Wroxeter 207 E2
Wroxham 229 E4
Wroxham Barns 84
Wroxton 197 G3
Wstrws 191 G3
Wyaston 222 C3
Wyberton 226 B3
Wyboston 199 G2
Wybunbury 221 D3
Wych Cross 172 D5
Wychbold 196 B1
Wychnor 209 D1
Wychnor Bridges 209 D1

Wyc - Zou

Wyck **170** C4
Wyck Rissington **197** D5
Wycliffe **252** A1
Wycoller **243** F4
Wycomb **224** C5
Wycombe Marsh **185** D3
Wyddial **200** B4
Wye **174** C4
Wyesham **181** E1
Wyfordby **210** C1
Wyke *Devon* **152** B3
Wyke *Dorset* **167** E5
Wyke *Shrop.* **207** F2
Wyke *Surr.* **171** E2
Wyke *W.Yorks.* **244** A5
Wyke Champflower **167** D4
Wyke Regis **154** C5
Wyke, The **207** G2
Wykeham *N.Yorks.* **254** C4
Wykeham *N.Yorks.* **254** B5
Wyken *Shrop.* **207** G3
Wyken *W.Mid.* **209** F4
Wykey **220** A5
Wylam **262** A1
Wylde Green **208** D3
Wyllie **180** A3
Wylye **168** B4
Wymering **157** F2
Wymeswold **224** B5
Wymington **199** E1
Wymondham *Leics.* **211** D1
Wymondham *Norf.* **228** C5
Wyndham **179** F3
Wynford Eagle **154** B3
Wynnstay Park **220** A3
Wynyard **262** D5
Wyre Forest **68**
Wyre Piddle **196** B3
Wyresdale Tower **242** C2
Wysall **224** B5
Wyson **195** E1
Wythall **208** C5
Wytham **183** G2
Wythburn **259** G5
Wythenshawe **234** C4
Wyton *Cambs.* **212** A5
Wyton *E.Riding* **247** D4
Wyverstone **202** B1
Wyverstone Street **202** B1
Wyville **225** D5
Wyvis Lodge **321** D2

Y

Y Bryn **218** B5
Y Drenewydd (Newtown) **206** A3
Y Fan **205** F4
Y Felinheli **217** E1
Y Fenni (Abergavenny) **180** B1
Y Fflint (Flint) **232** D5
Y Ffôr **216** C4
Y Trallwng (Welshpool) **206** B2
Y Tymbl (Tumble) **178** B1
Y Waun (Chirk) **219** F4
Yaddlethorpe **237** F2
Yafford **156** D4
Yafforth **252** C3
Yalberton **151** E2
Yalding **173** F4
Yanley **166** C1
Yanwath **260** B5
Yanworth **182** C1
Yapham **245** G2
Yapton **158** B3
Yarburgh **238** D3
Yarcombe **153** F2
Yardley **208** D4
Yardley Gobion **198** C3
Yardley Hastings **199** D2
Yardro **194** B2
Yarford **165** F5
Yarkhill **195** F3
Yarlet **221** G5
Yarley **166** C3
Yarlington **167** D5
Yarm **252** D1
Yarmouth **156** C4
Yarmouth Castle **53**
Yarnacott **163** G2
Yarnbrook **167** F2
Yarnfield **221** F4
Yarnscombe **163** F3
Yarnton **183** G1
Yarpole **195** D1
Yarrow *Sc.Bord.* **277** E3
Yarrow *Som.* **166** A3
Yarrow Feus **277** E3
Yarrowford **277** F3
Yarsop **194** D3
Yarwell **211** F3
Yate **181** G4
Yatehouse Green **221** E1
Yateley **170** D1
Yatesbury **182** C5
Yattendon **184** A5
Yatton *Here.* **194** D1
Yatton *N.Som.* **166** B1
Yatton Keynell **182** A5
Yaverland **157** F4
Yawl **153** G3
Yaxham **228** B4
Yaxley *Cambs.* **211** G3
Yaxley *Suff.* **214** C4
Yazor **194** D3
Ye Olde Pork Pie Shoppe **75**
Yeabridge **154** A1
Yeading **186** A4
Yeadon **244** B3
Yealand Conyers **249** G5
Yealand Redmayne **249** G5
Yealand Storrs **249** G5
Yealmbridge **150** B2
Yealmpton **150** B2
Yearby **263** F5
Yearsley **253** E5
Yeaton **206** D1
Yeaveley **222** C3
Yeavering **278** D3
Yeavering Bell **105**
Yedingham **254** B5
Yelford **183** F2
Yell **345** D4
Yelland *Devon* **163** E2
Yelland *Devon* **149** F1
Yelling **200** A1
Yelvertoft **210** A5
Yelverton *Devon* **150** B1
Yelverton *Norf.* **229** D5
Yenston **167** E5
Yeo Mill **164** B5
Yeo Vale **163** E3
Yeoford **152** A3
Yeolmbridge **148** D2
Yeomadon **162** D5
Yeovil **154** B1
Yeovil Marsh **154** B1
Yeovilton **166** C5
Yerbeston **177** D2
Yesnaby **340** A5
Yetholm Mains **278** C4
Yetlington **279** E5
Yetminster **154** B1
Yettington **153** D4
Yetts o'Muckhart **293** F4
Yew Green **197** E1
Yielden **199** F1
Yieldshields **284** C4
Ynys **217** E4
Ynys Enlli (Bardsey Island) **216** A5
Ynys Môn (Anglesey) **230** B4
Ynys Tachwedd **204** C3
Ynysboeth **179** G3
Ynysddu **180** A3
Ynyshir **179** G3
Ynyslas **204** C3
Ynysmaerdy **179** G4
Ynysmeudwy **178** D2
Ynystawe **178** C2
Ynyswen **179** F3
Ynysybwl **179** G3
Yockenthwaite **251** E5
Yockleton **206** C1
Yokefleet **246** A5
Yoker **283** G3
Yonder Bognie **324** B5
York **91**
York Castle Museum **91**
York Dungeon **91**
York Minster **91**
Yorkletts **174** C2
Yorkley **181** F2
Yorkshire Dales **91**
Yorkshire Museum **91**
Yorkshire Sculpture Park **91**
Yorton **220** C5
Yorton Heath **220** C5
Youldon **162** D5
Youldonmoor Cross **162** D5
Youlgreave **222** D1
Youlthorpe **245** G2
Youlton **245** D1
Young's End **187** G1
Yoxall **208** D1
Yoxford **203** E1
Yr Wyddgrug (Mold) **219** F1
Ysbyty Cynfyn **205** D5
Ysbyty Ifan **218** B3
Ysbyty Ystwyth **204** D5
Ysceifiog **232** C5
Ysgubor-y-coed **204** C3
Ystalyfera **179** D2
Ystrad **179** F3
Ystrad Aeron **192** B2
Ystrad Meurig **192** D1
Ystrad Mynach **180** A3
Ystradfellte **179** F1
Ystradffin **193** D3
Ystradgynlais **179** D1
Ystradowen *N.P.T.* **178** D1
Ystradowen *V. of Glam.* **179** G5
Ystumtuen **204** D5
Ythanwells **312** B1
Ythsie **313** D1

Z

Zeal Monachorum **152** A2
Zeals **167** E4
Zelah **146** C4
Zennor **144** B3
Zouch **223** G5

Published by Collins
An imprint of HarperCollins*Publishers*
77-85 Fulham Palace Road, Hammersmith, London W6 8JB

www.collins.co.uk

Mapping generated from Collins Bartholomew digital databases

The grid used on the main mapping in this atlas is the National Grid taken from the Ordnance Survey map with the permission of the Controller of Her Majesty's Stationery Office.

Printed and bound in Slovenia

SG12037 BDB

e-mail: roadcheck@harpercollins.co.uk

CREDITS

Contributors

Published by Mike Cottingham. Pages 5 to 22 researched and written by Karen Lloyd. Consultant geologist Duncan Friend Ph.D. Regional introductions written by Ellen Webster and Mike Cottingham. Attraction descriptions written by Amanda Berry, Andy Slater, Ellen Webster, Gill Coombs, Karen Lloyd, Rebekah Hart, Richard Knight and Rosemary MacLeod. All regional descriptions were edited by Juliet Lawler and Graham Gill. Infosnips compiled by Graham Gill and Mike Cottingham.

Picture credits

Aberdeen & Grampian Tourist Board: Red deer p16; Bottle nosed dolphin p19; Balmoral Castle p116

Althorp House: Althorp House p70

Ben BARDEN, Cumbria Tourist Board: Jetty on Derwent Water p92; Levens Hall p97; Hadrian's Wall p101

Beamish: Beamish p103

Ted BENTON, Frank Lane Picture Agency: Holly blue p15; Mountain ringlet p16; Marsh fritillary p18

Amanda BERRY: Babbacombe Model Village p24; London Aquarium p57; National Portrait Gallery p58; National Botanic Garden of Wales p111

Black Country Living Museum: Black Country Living Museum p64

Blue Planet Aquarium: Blue Planet Aquarium p94

John BRAINE: Arundel Castle p40

Helen BROWN: Lincoln Cathedral p69; Lincoln Cathedral p73

Burrell Collection: Burrell Collection p118

Chatsworth House: Chatsworth House p71

Chiltern Open Air Museum: Chiltern Open Air Museum p43

Clogau Welsh Gold mine: Welsh Gold p6

Colchester Zoo: Colchester Zoo p78

Colin Raw/Stone/Getty Images: View of hillside p85

Huw DAVIES: Ebley Mill p21

Dave DAWKINS: Poole's Cavern p74

Sonia DAWKINS: Roof tiles p8; Veteran tree p10; Cambrian Mountains p12; Tawny owl p15; Butterfly bush p17; Sculpture Trail p21; Severn Bore p22; Dartmoor p28; Forest of Dean p29; Goonhilly Satellite Earth Station p30; Lydford Gorge p33; Blenheim Palace p41; Oxford p48; Natural History Museum p59; American Adventure Theme Park p70; Carsington Water p71; Haddon Hall p72; Heights of Abraham p73; Twycross Zoo p75; Brecon Beacons p108; Chepstow Castle p109; Raglan Castle p113; Edinburgh p121; Our Dynamic Earth p128; Endpapers

Drayton Manor Park: Drayton Manor Park p65

Drummond Castle: Drummond Castle Gardens p120

Edinburgh & Lothians Tourist Board: The Royal Mile p13

English Heritage Photo Library: Grimes Graves p8; Dover Castle p44; Osborne House p48; Hardwick Hall p72; Audley End p77

Neil FORREST: Blue John p6; River Teifi p12; Royal Pavilion p50; St. Paul's Cathedral p59

Graham GILL: Dove Dale p71; Peak District p74; Loch Lomond p126

Helen GORDON: Gairloch sunset p1; Wast Water p4; Holker Hall Great Lime p10; Caledonian pines p10; background pp10 & 11; Wast Water p11; background p17; Dunsfold church p22; Batsford Arboretum p25; Chesil Beach p26; Bodiam Castle p39; Bodiam Castle p41; Knole p46; Wisley R.H.S. Gardens p53; Tower of London p61; Warwick Castle p68; Cambridge p77; Holker Hall p96; Lake District p97

John GORDON: Suilven p13; Callanish Stones p22; Seven Sisters Country Park p51; North West Highlands p128

Grampian Tourist Board: Dunnottar Castle p121

Sylvia GRAY: Leeds Castle & Gardens p46; Legoland p46; Imperial War Museum p81; National Railway Museum p89

Greater Glasgow & the Clyde Valley Tourist Board: New Lanark World Heritage Site p127

H.M. The Queen: Sandringham House p83 (photograph by gracious permission of H.M. The Queen)

Geoff HASSALL: New Forest p48

Hatfield House: Hatfield House p80

Hestercombe: Hestercombe p30

Highlands of Scotland Tourist Board - www.visithighlands.com: Cairngorms & Loch Morlich p14; Red squirrel p17; Ben Nevis p117; Cuillin Hills p119; Dunrobin Castle p121; Glencoe p123

His Grace The Duke of Buccleuch K.T.: Boughton House p70 (photograph by kind permission of His Grace The Duke of Buccleuch K.T.)

Paul HOBSON: Stag beetle p10; Silver-washed fritillary p15; Glow worm p15; Orange tip p16; Swallowtail p18; Banded demoiselle p18; Common toad p18

Holkham Hall: Holkham Hall p80

Hopetoun House: Hopetoun House p124

Houghton Hall: Houghton Hall p80

David HUNT: Pollarded tree p10; Hatfield Forest p10

G.E. HYDE, Frank Lane Picture Agency: Clouded buff moth p16

Ed JAMES: Alnwick Castle & Garden p102; Bamburgh Castle p102

Ele JAMES: Llywernog wind farm p20

Ian JENKINS: Loch Ness p13

Lou JOHNSON - www.walkingbritain.co.uk: Norber Stones p11

Sarah KIRK: Staffa, Fingal's Cave p14

Dave KJAER: Common newt p18

Knebworth House: Knebworth House p81

Richard KNIGHT: London Zoo p57; Westminster Abbey p61

Lancashire Tourism: Blackpool Tower p93

Mike LANE: Common dormouse p15; Ptarmigan p15; Hobby p16; Stoat p16; Exmoor pony p16; Harvest mouse p17; Grey partridge p17; Capercaillie p17; Wild cat p17; Pine marten p17; House cricket p17; Marsh harrier p18; Daubenton's bat p18; Bittern p18; Common lizard p19

Andrew LAWSON: Rousham House p50

Lightwater Valley Park: Lightwater Valley Park p88

Karen LLOYD: Fields - ridge & furrow p9; Field margin p9; Maiden Castle p9; Coppiced woodland p10; Winchelsea beach p10; Charmouth p10; Malham Cove p11; Gwaun Valley p12; Rhossili Beach p12; background p15; Hazlenut p15; Adder p16; Raft spider p18; Brown hare p17; Giant wood wasp p17; Mason bee p17; Hedgehog p17; Pinewood mushroom p17; Otter spraint p18; Atlantic salmon p18; Green tiger beetle p19; Sea gooseberry p19; Gem anemone p19; Green shore crab p19; Puffin p19; Common brittlestar p19; Common seal p19; Thornback ray p19; Field of short rotation willow coppice p20; Open ride in modern woodland p21; Nevern churchyard p22; Cowslip p22

Stephen LLOYD: Glastonbury Tor p9; Mortehoe coastline p10; Sand dunes p10; Pembrokeshire coastal path p10; Pillow Lava p12; Brampton Valley Way p20; The Sockburn Worm p22; Foxton Locks p72; Pembrokeshire Coast p112

Loch Lomond & Trossachs Tourist Boards: Inveraray Jail p125

Lynton & Lynmouth Cliff Railway: Lynton & Lynmouth Cliff Railway p32

Alan McDONNELL: Isolated sea eroded arch p14

Jackie McGEOUGH: Westonbirt p38; Chester Zoo p95; The Lowry p97

Rosemary MacLEOD: Edinburgh Castle p13; Fox p17; Britannia p117; Edinburgh Castle p122; Edinburgh Zoo p122; Museum of Scotland p127; Royal Botanic Garden p129

Madame Tussaud's: Madame Tussaud's and the Planetarium p57

Mellerstain Trust: Mellerstain p127

Derek MIDDLETON: Common shrew p15

National Marine Aquarium: National Marine Aquarium p33

National Trust: Avebury standing stone p8; Avebury Ring p24; Corfe Castle p27; Hidcote Manor Gardens p31; Petworth House p49; Sissinghurst Castle p51; Biddulph Grange Garden p63; Quarry Bank Mill & Styal Estate p98; Plas Newydd p112; Powis Castle & Garden p113

Needles Pleasure Park: Needles Pleasure Park p47

Mark NEWTON: Tree creeper p15; Blue tit p15; Song thrush p15; Golden eagle p15; Stonechat p16; Common blue p16; Barn owl p17; Peacock butterfly p17; Curlew p19; Shelduck p19

Norfolk Tourism: Norfolk Broads p82

Mike PAGE: Norfolk Broads p8

Perthshire Tourist Board: R.R.S. Discovery p120

Portsmouth Historic Dockyard: H.M.S. Victory p49

Leigh PRESTON: Flint building detail p8; North Pennines p11; Blea Tarn p11; High Force p11; Holy Island p11; Brecon Beacons p12; Rannoch Moor p13; Regular basalt columns p14; Raised beach p14; Railway track p20; Weavers Triangle p20; Colliery p20; Derelict mill p21; Block conifer plantation p21; Cranes in disused docks p21; Wicken Fen National Nature Reserve p76; Rannoch Moor p129

RAC: Stonehenge p36; Harlech Castle p110

Ravenglass & Eskdale Railway Co. Ltd: Ravenglass & Eskdale Railway p99

Richard REVELS: Cinnabar moth p16; Common field grasshopper p16; Emperor dragonfly p18

Science Museum: Science Museum p60

Scottish Borders Tourist Board: Floors Castle p122

Sheena SHANKS: Dunvegan Castle p22

Andy SLATER: Rackwick Bay p14

Jenny SLATER: Inverewe Gardens p125

Slimbridge Wildfowl & Wetlands Trust: Slimbridge p36

South West Tourism: Bowerman's Nose p9; Cerne Abbas giant p22; Bath p25; Lanhydrock p31; Longleat House p32; Roman Baths & Pump Room p35; Salisbury Cathedral p35

Robert TALBOT: Mevagissey harbour p23; National Maritime Museum Cornwall p34

Thetford Forest Park: Thetford Forest Park p83

Thorpe Park: Thorpe Park p52

Tourism South East: Canterbury Cathedral p42; Wakehurst Place p53

Visit London: Houses of Parliament p54; British Museum p55; Buckingham Palace p55; Houses of Parliament p56; London Eye p57; National Gallery p58; Royal Botanic Gardens, Kew p59; Tate Britain p60; Tate Modern p60; Victoria & Albert Museum p61

Joe WAINWRIGHT, Cheshire County Council: Chester p94; Chester Cathedral p95; Ness Botanic Gardens p98; Tatton Park p100

Alex WALLACE: BALTIC p102; Durham Cathedral p103

Norma WALLACE: Whitby Jet p6

Bill WATT: Marlborough Downs p8; Cotswold Water Park p8; background p18; Bibury p28; New Place Garden p62; Burns National Heritage Park p118; Stirling Castle p130; Strathclyde Country Park p131

Ellen WEBSTER: Hadrian's Wall p11; Llanberis Pass p12; Snowdonia p12; Loch Lomond p13; Eden Project p29; Lost Gardens of Heligan p32; Wells Cathedral p38; Jorvik p88; Hadrian's Wall p104; Bodnant Gardens p107; Erddig p110; Ffestiniog Railway p110; Portmeirion Village p113; Snowdonia p114

Welsh Tourist Board: Cardiff Bay p21; Llynnau Mymbyr & Snowdon p106; Beaumaris Castle p107; Big Pit Mining Museum p107; Caernarfon Castle p108; Caerphilly Castle p108; Conwy Castle p109

West Midlands Tourist Board: Shropshire Union Canal p20; Alton Towers Leisure Park p63; Ironbridge Gorge p66

Roger WILMSHURST: Badger p15; Mountain hare p15; Otter p18; Water vole p18

Woburn Abbey: Woburn Safari Park p81

Yorkshire Tourist Board: Ingleborough p11; Limestone pavement p11; background p16; Castle Howard p86; Eden Camp p87; Flamingo Land Theme Park p87; Fountains Abbey & Studley Royal Water Garden p87; National Museum of Photography, Film & TV p88; North York Moors p89; North Yorkshire Moors Railway p89; Rievaulx Abbey p90; Whitby Abbey p91; Yorkshire Dales p91

All other pictures supplied by Collins